World Tables 1992

The software edition of **World Tables** provides in electronic form all the data from both sections of the book — the topical pages, covering 20 economic indicators, and the country pages, presenting up-to-date economic, demographic, and social data for 146 countries and territories. What is more, when you purchase **World Tables 1992 Data on Diskette** you will automatically receive the diskette edition of the semiannual supplement scheduled to be published in Fall 1992.

The data for each country and each topic are accessible through ★STARS★ – the World Bank's Socioeconomic Time-series Access and Retrieval System. This user-friendly system allows you to view and manipulate the data and to extract your data selection into other computer programs, including Lotus 1-2-3, Javelin Plus, Aremos, and word-processing programs that read ASCII characters.

The **World Tables** diskette set includes the complete ★STARS★ software and data on double-density diskettes in two sizes – 5 1/4" and 3 1/2" – for use on personal computers with a hard disk with at least 512K memory and MS-DOS version 2.1 or higher. A user's manual provides a complete guide to getting started, viewing and extracting data, and using extract files.

For details on how to order this – and other statistical data collections available in ★STARS★ – just turn the page.

"With your diskettes, I accomplished in three and a half hours more than I had accomplished in three months of manual data collection." – Emeka Akaezuwa, Rutgers University

How to Order
Data Collections on Diskette

__ **Yes, please send me World Tables 1992 on diskette as indicated below.**

__ In addition to World Tables, please send me the other data collections indicated.

__ Please send me a complimentary copy of "World Bank Statistics Including Data on Diskette". I understand that this booklet provides details on the six titles listed below.

Quantity	Title	Stock Number	Price	Total
	World Tables 1992			
_____	Print edition	#44447	$35.95	_____
_____	Print edition update (Fall 1992)	#44448	$15.95	_____
_____	Diskettes	#12141	$95.00	_____
	Social Indicators of Development 1991-92			
_____	Print edition	#44330	$24.95	_____
_____	Diskettes	#12140	$70.00	_____
	African Development Indicators			
_____	English print edition	#12044	$21.95	_____
_____	Diskettes	#12135	$70.00	_____
	World Debt Tables 1991-92			
_____	Print edition, vol. 1	#11971	$16.95	_____
_____	Print edition, 2 vol. set w/supplement	#11984	$125.00	_____
_____	Country Tables, 1970-79	#11172	$24.95	_____
_____	Diskettes	#11998	$95.00	_____
	World Development Report 1992			
_____	English paperback print edition	#60876	$16.95	_____
	World Development Indicators 1992			
_____	Diskettes	#12134	$70.00	_____

Subtotal US$		_____
Shipping and handling US$		$3.50
Airmail surcharge outside USA (US$6.00 per copy) US$		_____
Total US$		_____

Check your method of payment. Orders from individuls must be accompanied by payment or credit card information. Ask local distributors about forms of payment acceptable to them.

❑ Enclosed is my check payable to World Bank Publications

❑ Charge my ❑ VISA ❑ MasterCard ❑ American Express

These credit cards are accepted for orders addressed to Philadelphia. (Check with your local distributor about acceptance of credit cards in your country.)

_____   _____
Credit card account number   Expiration date

_____
Signature

❑ Enclosed is my purchase order; send invoice. (Institutional customers only.)

Please print clearly

Name _____

Firm _____

Address _____

City _____ State _____ Postal Code _____

Country _____ Telephone _____

CUSTOMERS IN THE U.S.

Complete this form and mail to:
World Bank Publications
Box 7247-8619
Philadelphia, PA 19170-8619
U.S.A.

Telephone orders:
 908/225-2165
Facsimile orders:
 908/417-0482
Telex orders:
 WUI 64145
Customer service:
 908/225-2165

CUSTOMERS OUTSIDE THE U.S.

Prices and payment terms vary by country. Contact your local distributor (listed at the back of this book) before placing an order. When requesting information about specific prices and payment terms, provide the complete title and stock number of the publications you wish to order. If no distributor is listed for your country, complete this order form and return it to the U.S. address. Orders received in the U.S. from countries with authorized distributors will be returned to the customer.

World Tables 1992

Published for the World Bank
The Johns Hopkins University Press
Baltimore and London

ISBN 0-8018-4447-9
ISSN   1043-5573

Library of Congress Catalog No.: 89-647121

Contents

Symbols and Conventions

..	data not available, or nonexistent
Scientific notation e.g. .63E-2	data with insignificant digits, using units appropriate for the latest year
0, 0.0, .0E-0	zero, or less than half the unit shown and not known more precisely
A, B, C, etc.	general issue of methodology; see Codes for General and Country Notes
f	country specific issue of methodology; see Country Notes
Billion	1,000,000,000

1987 is the base year for constant price series data.

The cutoff date for all data is April 30, 1992.

Introduction

This 1992 edition of the *World Tables* (WT) updates core socio-economic indicators given on country and topical pages in the 1991 edition. The data cover the period 1970 to 1990 and projections for 1991 for some of the series in the topical pages. The base year for constant prices is 1987; see Sources and Methods for details of the rebasing and "chain-linking" of the constant price series.

In addition to Czechoslovakia, Mongolia, Namibia, and Romania, which were covered in the *World Tables 1991 Update*, three new countries (Djibouti, Lao PDR, and Yemen) have been added to the country list. Germany, recently unified, does not yet have a fully merged statistical system. Data for Germany are footnoted to explain coverage; most economic data refer to the Federal Republic of Germany before unification; but demographic and social data refer to the unified Germany. The secession of Slovenia and Croatia from Yugoslavia occurred too near the publication time to permit separate pages; hence the former Yugoslavia is shown in this edition. Increased World Bank data collection and analysis in the former Soviet Union will result in coverage and reporting of these emerging economies in future editions. WT contains data for 146 economies.

The *World Tables* disseminates, with little delay, country estimates used by the Bank in analysis of economic and social trends in developing countries, which emphasizes Bank borrowers. To make the volume a more useful resource, other economies are covered to the extent that they provide internationally comparable measures in readily usable form; these are not subject to detailed scrutiny by Bank staff. Data for high-income OECD economies are based on reports of the Organization for Economic Cooperation and Development (OECD) and the International Monetary Fund (IMF). National publications are used for the remaining economies. Such sources, generally specified in the Country Notes, should be consulted by readers wishing to be assured of the most timely and complete reports.

Country time series are also used by the Bank to measure trends in groups of countries, notably for the Bank's *World Development Report* (WDR), including the World Development Indicators (WDI) section. The *World Tables* topical pages fill a gap between the country pages and measures for analytical groupings of countries given in the WDR and WDI; how group indicators are derived from country time series is more evident in the topical pages and is explained more fully below.

The *World Tables* is issued annually on diskette and magnetic tape as well as in book form, with a semi-annual update. The tables report annual time series. The book and the diskettes have the same time coverage (1970-90 for country pages and 1970-91 for topical pages); the tape contains data from 1950 for some countries and series. The diskettes contain the country pages and topical pages in ☆STARS☆ software. ☆STARS☆ software compresses WT data into diskettes and allows easy retrieval of data into Lotus, Javelin, Aremos, or ASCII format. To order the diskette version of *World Tables*, use the coupon at the front of this book. For information about WT on magnetic tape, contact the Office of the Publisher, World Bank, 1818 H Street, N.W., Washington, D.C. 20433, U.S.A.

Topical Pages

Topical pages cover two double-page spreads and report annual data for 1970-90 and projections for 1991. Topical pages recast some indicators from country pages as a global backdrop for analyzing how low- and middle-income economies have fared in recent decades. Economies are grouped first by geographic region and, in a sub-table, by income groups and other analytical groupings used in the WDI. The last few lines of each sub-table indicate trends for high-income economies.

Income groups

For operational and analytical purposes, the World Bank's main criterion for classifying economies is gross national product (GNP) per capita. Every economy is classified as low-, middle- or high-income. Additonal analytical groups are based on geographical regions. Following from the *World Tables 1991 Update*, in this edition two additional aggregates are shown in the topical pages: "high-income economies," and "world."

As the latest GNP per capita estimates are used to classify economies in each new edition, the country composition of each group may change from one edition to the next. Once the classification is fixed for any publication, all the historical data presented are based on the same grouping. The country groups used in this edition are defined as follows:

• *Low-income economies* are those with a GNP per capita of $610 or less in 1990.

• *Middle-income economies* are those with a GNP per capita of more than $610 but less than $7,620 in 1990.

• *High-income economies* are those with a GNP per capita of $7,620 or more in 1990.

• *World* comprises all economies, including those not listed in the topical pages.

Low- and middle-income economies are sometimes referred to as "developing economies." The use of the term is convenient; it is not intended to imply that all economies in the group are experiencing similar development or that other economies have reached a preferred or final stage of development. Similarly, the use of the term "country" does not imply political independence but may refer to any territory whose authorities present for it separate social or economic statistics.

Data aggregation

Simple addition is used when a variable is expressed in reasonably comparable units of account. Indicators that do not seem naturally additive, for instance, "value added in agriculture in local currency," are usually combined by a weighting scheme—real dollar values of agricultural output in 1987. Fixed (Laspeyres) weights are normally used for quantities, with moving (Paasche) weights for prices, to fulfill the expectation that [value = price x quantity]. The identity also means that one part of the identity can be derived from the other two; the one derived being described as implicit, for example, "implicit deflators in national accounts."

The weighting scheme has been incorporated into the indicator by scaling the volume indicator to match the 1987 weights. The ratio of the sums of agricultural output in current and constant dollars can then provide the implicit deflator for agricultural output. It should be emphasized, however, that use of single base year joined in a chain-linked series raises problems over a period encompassing profound structural changes and significant movements in relative prices, as certainly occurred during 1970-90. The problems exist in indicators for a single country and are simply more apparent when country indicators are agglomerated.

It is debatable whether an analytical ratio, say, "agricultural output to GDP," should be a weighted average of country ratios or a ratio of separately aggregated numerator and denominator. The results will be different, sometimes significantly so. *World Tables* first estimates the numerator and denominator for the group and then calculates the group ratio.

World Tables strives for group time series that retain the same country composition over time and across topics. It does so by permitting group measures to be compiled only if the country data available for a given year account for *at least two-thirds of the full group*, as defined by 1987 benchmarks. So long as that criterion is met, uncurrent reporters (and those not providing ample history) are assumed to behave like the portion of the group that does provide estimates.

The same technique applies to regional groupings in the main part of the topical pages; for these, however, South Africa is omitted from Sub-Saharan Africa.

The benchmarking procedure underlying group measures requires that some weight be assigned to each economy within the group. For an economy reporting inadequate data in every year, Bank staff must choose some arbitrary 1987 base value within a broad range of plausible estimates. Readers should keep in mind that the purpose is to maintain an appropriate relationship across topics, despite myriad country problems, and that nothing meaningful can be deduced about behavior at the country level by working back from group indicators. In addition, the weighting process may result in discrepancies between summed subgroup figures and overall totals.

Contributions to growth of GDP

Several topical pages express sources and uses of gross domestic production (or expenditure) as "contributions" to growth of GDP. The term "contribution" combines information about growth rates and percentage shares of GDP components. This form of presentation, sometimes referred to as "percentage points of GDP," shows by how much GDP would have changed if other GDP components were unchanged.

For example, if agriculture has a 9 percent growth rate and accounts for a third of GDP, it contributes 3 percentage points to GDP growth. If industry and services remained unchanged, GDP's growth rate would have been 3 percent. In practice, contributions are obtained by expressing the year-to-year change in a component, for instance, agriculture, as a percentage of GDP in the earlier year.

National accounts in constant 1987 prices are used.

Regional aggregation requires that country estimates be expressed in 1987 US dollars and then summed. Even so, regional aggregation raises an index number problem closely related to the partial rebasing issue arising at the country level (see Sources and Methods), which is resolved in a similar manner. Moreover, regional measures of the contribution to GDP of resource balance are actually the difference between separately compiled measures for exports and imports (of goods and nonfactor services); regional measures for private consumption are then derived as a residual (GDP less government consumption, investment, and the net export of goods and nonfactor services).

Coverage of Country Pages

Most time series selected for the country pages are concerned with national accounts and international transactions (foreign trade, balance of payments, and external debt). The Bank uses methodologies and historical data files developed by other international organizations, but adds information obtained by Bank staff directly from national sources, when it can be fitted to internationally agreed classification schemes.

For other data sets (manufacturing, monetary and fiscal, and social indicators), WT recasts a few of the time series made available to the Bank by other international agencies, but readers should refer to publications of the agencies concerned for fuller information. A more diverse selection of indicators, not in time series form, is given in the WDI.

WT provides limited time series on external debt, since the Bank's *World Debt Tables* is the authoritative source. Similarly, a wider range of social indicators is available in the Bank's *Social Indicators of Development*. Both of these publications are available in print and diskette form (see the order coupon at the front of this book).

The country pages are in alphabetical order. The country list on page 681 also notes the original base years for constant price national accounts prior to partial rebasing (see Sources and Methods).

Basic Concepts

As far as is practicable, the WT economic indicators conform to the UN System of National Accounts (SNA), and its social indicators conform to methodologies of UN specialized agencies. In some areas of economic statistics, additional guidelines have been developed that are broadly in line with the SNA but differ in some respects. For example, the IMF has played a leading role in helping national compilers elaborate balance of payments, monetary, and government finance statistics. While further revision of the SNA, already under study, may reduce definitional and classification differences, few are resolved in the WT amalgam of statistical sources.

Where possible, however, the Bank harmonizes related data sets drawn from diverse sources. This conceptual process, perhaps as much as national estimates obtained by Bank staff, imparts a unique quality to the national accounts and international transactions data reported in WT. The Bank has devised for its analytical purposes certain methods and concepts such as partial rebasing, gross domestic income (GDY), and gross national income (GNY).

The concepts and methods are described in Sources and Methods and in the Glossary of Terms. It should be emphasized, however, that the notes are selective rather than encyclopedic. Readers interested in more comprehensive and technically precise descriptions should consult the basic references noted in Sources and Methods.

Statistical Issues

A concerted effort has been made to standardize data and to note exceptions to standards. However, full comparability cannot be ensured, and care must be taken in interpreting the indicators. The data are drawn from sources thought to be most authoritative, but many of them are subject to considerable margins of error. This is particularly true for the most recent year or two, since conventional statistical reports take time to digest.

Moreover, intercountry and intertemporal comparisons always involve complex technical problems, which have no full and unequivocal solution.

The statistical systems in many developing economies are weak, and this affects the availability and reliability of the data. Readers are urged to take these limitations into account in interpreting the indicators, particularly when making comparisons across economies. WT addresses issues of data reliability partly by omitting questionable estimates but also by flagging methodological issues that can influence analysis.

Country pages for about ten Bank members have been omitted for lack of adequate data; some time series on other country pages are blank or uncertain.

Unless otherwise stated, data are reported for calendar years.

Sources and Methods

The **GNP per capita** figures are calculated according to the *World Bank Atlas* method of converting data in national currency to US dollars. In this method, the conversion factor for any year is the average exchange rate for that year and the two preceding years, adjusted for differences in rates of inflation between the country and the United States. This averaging smooths fluctuations in prices and exchange rates. The resulting estimate of GNP in US dollars is divided by the midyear population to obtain the per capita GNP in current US dollars.

The following formulas describe the procedures for computing the conversion factor for year t:

$$(e^*_{t-2,t}) = \frac{1}{3}\left[e_{t-2}\left(\frac{P_t}{P_{t-2}} \middle/ \frac{P^\$_t}{P^\$_{t-2}}\right) + e_{t-1}\left(\frac{P_t}{P_{t-1}} \middle/ \frac{P^\$_t}{P^\$_{t-1}}\right) + e_t\right]$$

and for calculating per capita GNP in US dollars for year t:

$$(Y^\$_t) = (Y_t / N_t + e^*_{t-2,t})$$

where

$Y^\$_t$ = per capita GNP in US$ for year t
Y_t = current GNP (local currency) for year t
P_t = GNP deflator for year t
e_t = annual average exchange rate (local currency/US dollars) for year t
N_t = midyear population for year t
$P^\$_t$ = US GNP deflator for year t

The **conversion factor** line on each country page reports the underlying annual observations used for this *Atlas* method. As a rule, it is the official exchange rate reported in the IMF's *International Financial Statistics* (IFS), line *rf*.

Exceptions arise where *World Tables* recasts IFS-style measures to report on a fiscal year basis or to average multiple exchange rates; in highly exceptional cases, further refinements are made by Bank staff (see Country Conversion Factors for a list of all three exceptions).

Where multiple exchange rate practices are officially maintained and the spread between rates is analytically significant a transactions-weighted average is given, if possible. However, no account of unofficial parallel market rates is taken in the calculations. When the official exchange rate, including any multiple rate, is judged to diverge by an exceptionally large margin from the rate effectively applied to international transactions, a different conversion factor is used by the Bank. Where national compilers used an official exchange rate to assign a national currency value to international transactions, however, that rate must be used to convert the same items to dollars, regardless of whether it was the rate actually applied to international transactions. In these cases, country pages report both the *conversion factor*, underlying the *Atlas* method of converting values of international transactions, and an *additional conversion factor* underlying the *Atlas* method of converting the remaining components of GNP.

Current **population** estimates and estimates of fertility and mortality are made by the World Bank from data provided by the UN Population Division, the UN Statistical Office, country statistical offices, and other sources. In many cases, the data take into account the results of recent population censuses. Refugees not permanently settled in the country of asylum are generally considered to be part of the population of their country of origin.

Statistical background for the estimates is available in the UN annual *Population and Vital Statistics Report* and the Bank's annual *World Population Projections*.

Use and Origin of Resources

The time series are based mainly on national sources as collected by World Bank regional country economists. They generally accord with the System of National Accounts (SNA). Most definitions of indicators given below are those in UN SNA, series F, no. 2, revision 3.

For most countries, GDP by industrial origin is the sum of value added measured at producer prices.

To provide long-term trend analysis, facilitate international comparisons and include the effects of changes in intersectoral relative prices, constant price data for most economies are partially rebased to three base years and linked together. The year 1970 is the base year for data from 1960 to 1975, 1980 for 1976 to 1982, and 1987 for 1983 and beyond. These three periods are "chain-linked" to obtain 1987 prices throughout all three periods.

Chain-linking is accomplished for each of the three subperiods by rescaling; this moves the year in which current and constant price versions of the same time series have the same value, without altering the trend of either. Components of GDP are individually rescaled and summed to provide GDP and its subaggregates. In this process, a rescaling deviation may occur between the constant price GDP by expenditure. Such rescaling deviations are absorbed under the heading *private consumption, etc.* on the assumption that GDP by industrial origin is a more reliable estimate than GDP by expenditure.

This approach takes into account the effects of changes in intersectoral relative prices between the original and new base period (original base periods are noted in the country list on page 681). Because private consumption is calculated as a residual, the national accounting identities are maintained. This method of accounting does, however, involve "burying" in private consumption whatever statistical discrepancies arise on the expenditures side in the rebasing and chain linking process. Large discrepancies are flagged in the General Notes.

Partial rebasing requires constant price estimates by industrial origin at the rather aggregated level shown in these tables. If sufficient data are not available for partially rebasing to 1987, then 1980 is used, or the original base year if 1980 data are not available. If only GDP or GNP is available, the original constant price estimates of GDP are directly rescaled to 1987 prices.

Domestic Prices/Deflators

These data are based on national accounts data, discussed above. **Overall (GDP)** and **domestic absorption** prices are implicit deflators, that is, they are ratios of current and constant price estimates of relevant aggregates. Domestic prices for **agriculture, industry,** and **manufacturing** are, in principle, price indexes of value added; the **consumer price index** reflects prices of goods and services used for private consumption of households. For most countries, price indexes are implicit deflators derived from volume and value estimates.

Manufacturing Activity

The primary source is the United Nations Industrial Development Organization (UNIDO) database. To improve cross-country comparability, UNIDO has standardized the coverage of establishments to those with five or more employees.

The concepts and definitions are in accordance with the *International Recommendations for Industrial Statistics*, published by the United Nations. The term *employees* refers to two categories defined by the UN: *employees* and *persons engaged*. The term *employees* excludes working proprietors, active business partners, and unpaid family workers, whereas the term *persons engaged* includes them. Most countries report data on *employees*, but some, as indicated in the *Notes* column, report data on *persons engaged*. Both terms exclude homeworkers. The number of employees or persons engaged usually refers to the average number employed throughout the year.

Real earnings per employee (wages and salaries) covers all payments in cash or kind made by the employer during the year, in connection with work done. The payments include (a) all regular and overtime cash payments, bonuses, and cost of living allowances, (b) wages and salaries paid during vacation and sick leave, (c) taxes and social insurance contributions and the like, payable by the employees and deducted by the employer, and (d) payments in kind.

The value of gross **real output per employee** is estimated on the basis of either production or shipments. On the production basis, it consists of (a) the value of all products of the establishment, (b) the value of industrial services rendered to others, (c) the value of goods shipped in the same condition as received, (d) the value of electricity sold, and (e) the net change between the value of work-in-progress at the beginning and the end of the reference period. In the case of estimates compiled on a shipment basis, the net change between the beginning and the end of the reference period in the value of stocks of finished goods is also included. **Value added** is defined as the current value of gross output less the current cost of (a) materials, fuels, and other supplies consumed, (b) contract and commission work done by others, (c) repair and maintenance work done by others, and (d) goods shipped in the same condition as received.

Monetary Holdings

The primary source is the IMF's *International Financial Statistics* (IFS) database. The concepts and definitions are from the Fund's *A Guide to Money and Banking Statistics in IFS*.

For most countries, the **money supply broadly defined** comprises money (IFS line 34) and quasi-money

(IFS line 35), the normal forms of financial liquidity that economic transactors hold in the monetary system. By definition, holdings of nonresidents and the central government are excluded.

In some countries, other (nonmonetary) financial institutions may also incur quasi-monetary liabilities, that is, they may issue financial instruments on terms similar to those for quasi-money. Where these are significant, **money supply broadly defined** is a measure of liquid liabilities comprising the monetary and quasi-monetary liabilities of both monetary and nonmonetary financial institutions.

Government Deficit or Surplus

The primary source is the IMF's *Government Finance Statistics Yearbook* (GFSY). GFSY data are reported by countries using the system of common definitions and classifications found in the IMF *Manual on Government Finance Statistics (1986)*.

The inadequate statistical coverage of state, provincial, and local governments has dictated the use of central government data only. This may seriously understate or distort the role of government, especially in large countries where lower levels of government are important. A *general note* (E) indicates instances where this is thought to be likely.

Grants, reported separately in GFSY, are here included in **current revenue**; government lending operations (GFSY lending minus repayments) are classified as **capital payments**.

Foreign Trade (Customs Basis)

Exports and imports cover movements of goods across customs borders; generally, exports are valued f.o.b. (free on board) and imports c.i.f. (cost, insurance, and freight).

The primary source is COMTRADE, the UN trade data system, made available through the UN Statistical Office (UNSO). The data are based on countries' customs returns. The data may differ from trade data reported by other agencies because of differences in the valuation, concepts and definitions, exchange rate conversion, coverage, estimation method, vintage, etc. A major effort is currently under way to rectify these differences; this effort may eventually reduce or eliminate these differences.

Data for the most recent years for many countries, particularly developing countries, are often obtained from other sources or estimated by World Bank Staff.

Export and import price indexes for developing countries are World Bank estimates; for industrial economies, the indexes are taken from other sources such as the UN's *Monthly Bulletin of Statis-*

tics and the *IFS*. The price indexes may differ from those reported by other agencies because of differences in the estimation technique, base year, and/or rebasing procedure, etc.

Balance of Payments

The primary sources are the files from the IMF's *Balance of Payments Statistics Yearbook*. The methodology is described in the Fund's *Balance of Payments Manual* (fourth edition). Supplementary data, usually most recent estimates, are obtained from national sources or estimated by World Bank staff.

For **long-term loans** (net disbursements, gross disbursements, and repayments), data are reported to the World Bank's Debtor Reporting System (DRS). Any difference between the IMF balance of payments long-term capital and those in the DRS is shown as **other long-term capital**.

It is not yet possible to reconcile related measures in the sections on balance of payments, foreign trade, and national accounts. This reflects differences in definitions used, timing, recording, and valuation of transactions as well as the nature of basic data sources. Both general and country notes indicate classification and coverage issues that produce discrepancies. The Country Pages report related time series on international transactions in each section in order to help readers make their own judgments about how such discrepancies may affect the analytical purpose at hand.

External Debt (Total)

External debt statistics are presented by type of borrower instead of by type of creditor.

The source of debt data is the DRS, supplemented by World Bank estimates. The DRS is concerned solely with low- and middle-income economies and does not collect data on external debt for other groups of borrowers, nor from economies that are not members of the World Bank. The figures on debt refer to amounts disbursed and outstanding, expressed in US dollars converted at official exchange rates. Total disbursements and total repayments are also reported as separate items of the balance of payments. Valuation adjustments explain differences between the change in debt outstanding and the net movements shown in the balance of payment items.

Data on **international reserves** and **gold holdings** are from the IFS data files.

Social Indicators

The primary sources of social indicators data are the data files and publications of specialized international agencies, such as Food and Agriculture Organization,

International Labour Organisation, United Nations Educational, Scientific, and Cultural Organization, the UN Statistical Office, and World Health Organization. Supplementary sources are the Population Council, UN Research Institute for Social Development, and World Bank data files. Some demographic and labor force indicators are estimated by interpolating census observations.

The index of **food production per capita** shows the average annual quantity of food produced per capita. For this index, food is defined as comprising nuts, fruits, pulses, cereals, vegetables, starchy roots, sugar beet, sugar cane, edible oils, livestock, and livestock products. Quantities of food are measured net of animal feed, seeds for use in agriculture, and food lost in processing and distribution.

The data on **primary school enrollment** are estimates of children of all ages enrolled in primary school. Figures are expressed as the ratio of pupils to the population of children in the country's school age group. While many countries consider primary school age to be 6 to 11 years, others do not. For some countries with universal primary education, the gross enrollment ratios may exceed 100 percent because some pupils are younger or older than the country's standard primary-school age.

The data on **secondary school enrollment** are calculated in the same manner, and the definition of secondary school age also differs among countries. It is most commonly considered to be 12 to 17 years.

Many indicators are based on census or household surveys, which occur infrequently. Thus some reported figures are interpolated or extrapolated estimates.

Glossary of Terms
in order of appearance on country pages

Current GNP per capita
GNP per capita estimates at current purchaser values (market prices), in US dollars, are calculated according to *World Bank Atlas* methodology.

Population
Total population – midyear estimates.

USE AND ORIGIN OF RESOURCES
(current and constant prices)

Gross national product (GNP)
Comprises gross domestic product (GDP) at purchaser values (market prices) plus net factor income from abroad.

Net factor income from abroad (current prices)
Includes the net compensation of employees (with less than one year of residence in the host country) and the net property and entrepreneurial income components of the System of National Accounts (SNA). The major components of the latter are investment income and interest on short- and long-term capital.

Gross domestic product (GDP)
Gross domestic product at purchaser values (market prices) is the sum of GDP at factor cost and indirect taxes, less subsidies.

Resource balance
Equals exports of goods and nonfactor services less imports of goods and nonfactor services.

Exports/imports of goods and nonfactor services
Consists of transactions of residents of a given country with the rest of the world, and covers insurance, merchandise, transportation, travel, and other nonfactor services such as government transactions and various fees but excludes dividends, interest, and other investment income receipts or payments, as well as labor income.

Domestic absorption
Equals private consumption, and general government consumption, plus gross domestic investment.

Private consumption
Equals the market value of all goods and services purchased or received as income in kind by individuals and nonprofit institutions. It excludes purchases of dwellings, but includes the imputed rent of owner-occupied dwellings. The line is called **Private consumption, etc.** because it includes any statistical discrepancy in the use of resources. At constant prices, it also includes the rescaling deviation from partial rebasing (see Sources and Methods).

General government consumption
Equals the sum of (i) purchases, less sales, of consumer goods and services, reduced by the value of the own-account production of fixed assets, (ii) compensation of employees, (iii) consumption of fixed assets, and (iv) any payments of indirect taxes.

Gross domestic investment
The sum of gross domestic fixed investment and the change in stocks.

Fixed investment
Made up of all outlays (purchases and own-account production) of industries, producers of government services, and producers of private nonprofit services on additions of new and imported durable goods to their stocks of fixed assets, reduced by the proceeds of net sales (sales less purchases) of similar second-hand and scrapped goods. Excluded is the outlay of producers of government services on durable goods primarily for military purposes, which is classified by the SNA as current consumption.

Indirect taxes, net
Equals total indirect taxes less subsidies.

GDP at factor cost (producer prices)
Derived as the sum of the value added in the agriculture, industry, and services sectors. If the value added of these sectors is calculated at purchaser values (mar-

ket prices), GDP at factor cost is derived by subtracting the net indirect taxes from the GDP at purchaser values (market prices).

Agriculture (value added)
Comprises agricultural and livestock production and services, fishing, hunting, logging, and forestry.

Industry (value added)
Comprises mining and quarrying; manufacturing; construction; and electricity, gas, and water.

Services (value added)
Includes all service activities, that is, transport, storage, and communications; wholesale and retail trade; banking, insurance, and real estate; ownership of dwellings; public administration and defense; and other services. The line is called **Services, etc.**, because it includes any statistical discrepancy in the origin of resources.

Gross domestic saving (at current prices)
Equals gross domestic product minus total consumption, etc. (or gross domestic investment plus the resource balance). *Gross Domestic Saving* (at constant prices) equals gross domestic income minus total consumption, etc. (or gross domestic investment plus the resource balance plus the terms of trade adjustment).

Gross national saving (at current prices)
Equals gross domestic saving plus net factor income and net current transfers from abroad.

Capacity to import
Value of exports of goods and nonfactor services deflated by the import price index.

Terms of trade adjustment
Equals capacity to import less exports of goods and nonfactor services in constant prices.

Gross domestic income (constant prices)
Derived as the sum of GDP and the terms of trade adjustment.

Gross national income
Derived as the sum of GNP and the terms of trade adjustment.

DOMESTIC PRICES/DEFLATORS

Overall (GDP)
The deflator is derived by dividing current price estimates of GDP at purchaser values (market prices) by constant price estimates; also called the implicit GDP deflator.

Domestic absorption
The deflator is derived by dividing current price domestic absorption estimates by constant price estimates.

Agriculture, industry, manufacturing
Price indexes are mostly implicit deflators derived from volume and value estimates.

Consumer price index
Comprises the price index of goods and services used for private final consumption of households.

MANUFACTURING ACTIVITY

Employment
The average number of employees or persons engaged during the year. For further information about these classifications, see Sources and Methods.

Real earnings per employee
Derived by deflating nominal earnings per employee data from UNIDO by the consumer price index.

Real output per employee
Presented as an index of overall labor productivity in manufacturing. To derive this indicator, UNIDO data on gross output per employee in current prices are adjusted using the implicit deflators for value added in manufacturing or in industry, taken from the World Bank's national account data files.

Earnings as % of value added
Derived by dividing total nominal earnings of employees by value added in current prices, to show labor's share in income generated in the manufacturing sector.

MONETARY HOLDINGS

Money supply, broadly defined
Comprises the monetary and quasi-monetary liabilities of a country's financial institutions to residents other than the central government.

Money
The sum of currency outside banks plus demand deposits held in the financial system by the rest of the domestic economy, other than central government.

Currency outside banks
Comprises bank notes and coin accepted as legal tender in the domestic economy, excluding amounts held by the monetary system, central government, and nonresidents.

Demand deposits
Deposits payable on demand. Typically comprises accounts transferable by checks and any alternative instruments, forms, and mechanisms for transferring money.

Quasi-money
Comprises time and savings deposits, and similar bank accounts that the issuer will readily exchange for money. Where nonmonetary financial institutions are important issuers of quasi-monetary liabilities, these are also included in the measure of monetary holdings.

GOVERNMENT DEFICIT OR SURPLUS

Government deficit or surplus
Defined as the sum of current and capital revenue and all grants received, less the sum of current and capital expenditure and government lending minus repayments.

Current revenue
Comprises tax revenue and nontax revenue. Capital receipts are excluded. Tax revenue covers tax on income, profits, social security contributions, taxes on property, domestic taxes on goods and services, etc. Nontax revenue consists of grants, property income and operating surpluses of departmental enterprises, receipts from public enterprises, administrative fees and charges, fines, etc.

Current expenditure
Expenditure for goods and services, interest payments, and subsidies and other current transfers. Excludes capital payments.

Current budget balance
The excess of current revenue over current expenditure.

Capital receipts
Proceeds from the sale of nonfinancial capital assets, including land, intangible assets, stocks, and fixed capital assets of buildings, construction, and equipment of more than a minimum value and usable for more than one year in the process of production, and receipts of unrequited transfers for capital purposes from nongovernmental sources.

Capital payments
Expenditure for acquisition of land, intangible assets, government stocks, and nonmilitary and nonfinancial assets; also for capital grants and lending minus repayments.

FOREIGN TRADE (CUSTOMS BASIS)

Value of exports, f.o.b./imports, c.i.f.
With some exceptions, covers international movements of goods only across customs borders. Exports are valued f.o.b. (free on board), imports c.i.f. (cost, insurance, and freight), unless otherwise specified.

Nonfuel primary products
Comprises commodities in SITC revision 1, Sections 0, 1, 2, 4, and Division 68 (food and live animals, beverages and tobacco, inedible crude materials, oils, fats, waxes, and nonferrous metals).

Fuels
Comprises commodities in SITC revision 1, Section 3 (mineral fuels and lubricants and related materials).

Manufactures
Comprises commodities in SITC revision 1, Sections 5 through 9 (chemicals and related products, basic manufactures, machinery and transport equipment, other manufactured articles and goods not elsewhere classified) excluding Division 68 (nonferrous metals).

Terms of trade
The relative level of export prices compared with import prices, calculated as the ratio of a country's index of average export price to the average import price index.

Export price, f.o.b./import price, c.i.f.
Price index measuring changes in the aggregate price level of a country's merchandise exports and imports over time.

BALANCE OF PAYMENTS

Exports/imports of goods and services
Comprises all transactions involving a change of ownership of goods and services between residents of a country and the rest of the world. It includes merchandise, nonfactor services, and factor services.

Merchandise, f.o.b.
Comprises the market value of movable goods, including nonmonetary gold. It also includes the market value of related distributive services up to the customs frontier of the exporting economy, that is, f.o.b. (free on board) value. The few types of goods that are not covered by the merchandise account include travelers' purchases abroad, which are included in travel, and purchases of goods by diplomatic and military personnel, which are classified under other official goods, services, and income.

Nonfactor services

Comprises shipment, passenger and other transport services, and travel, as well as current account transactions not separately reported (e.g., not classified as merchandise, nonfactor services, or transfers). These include transactions with nonresidents by government agencies and their personnel abroad, and also transactions by private residents with foreign governments and government personnel stationed in the reporting country.

Factor services

Comprises services of labor and capital, thus covering income from direct investment abroad, interest, dividends, and property and labor income.

Long-term interest

Comprises interest on the disbursed portion of outstanding public and private loans repayable in foreign currencies, goods, or services. It may include commitment charges on undisbursed loans.

Private current transfers, net

Comprises net transfer payments—between private persons and nonofficial organizations of the reporting country and the rest of the world—that carry no provisions for repayments. Included are workers' remittances; transfers by migrants; gifts, dowries, and inheritances; and alimony and other support remittances.

Workers' remittances

Comprises remittances of income by migrants who have come to an economy to stay for a year or more and who are employed by their new economy, where they are considered to be residents.

Current account balance before official transfers

Comprises the sum of the net exports of goods and nonfactor services, net factor service income, and net private transfers.

Net official transfers

Comprises net transfer payment between governments of the reporting country and the rest of the world.

Current account balance after official transfers

Comprises the sum of the net exports of goods and nonfactor services, net factor service income, and net transfers; official capital grants are always included.

Long-term capital, net

Comprises changes, apart from valuation adjustments in residents' long-term foreign liabilities less their long-term assets, excluding any long-term items classified as reserves.

Direct investment

Comprises all capital transactions that are made to acquire a lasting interest in an enterprise operating in an economy other than that of the investor, where the investor's purpose is to have an effective voice in the management of the enterprise. Direct investment includes items such as equity capital, reinvestment of earnings, and other long- and short-term capital.

Long-term loans

Comprises all public, publicly guaranteed, and private nonguaranteed loans that have an original or extended maturity of more than a year and that are repayable in foreign currencies, goods, or services. These data are as reported in the Bank's Debtor Reporting System and accord with the stock data on external debt, discussed below.

Disbursements

Comprises the total amounts drawn on public, publicly guaranteed, and private nonguaranteed loans, net of commitment cancellations.

Repayments

Comprises repayments (amortization) of the principal of public, publicly guaranteed, and private nonguaranteed loans.

Other long-term capital

Comprises the difference between long-term capital, as defined above, and the similar item reported in IMF balance of payments statistics.

Other capital, net

Comprises the sum of short-term capital, net errors and omissions, and capital transactions not included elsewhere.

Change in reserves

Comprises the net change in a country's holdings of international reserves resulting from transactions on the current and capital accounts. These include changes in holdings of monetary gold, SDRs, reserve position in the Fund, foreign exchange assets, and other claims on nonresidents that are available to the central authority. The measure is net of liabilities constituting foreign authorities' reserves, and counterpart items for valuation of monetary gold and SDRs, which are reported separately in IMF sources.

Conversion factor (annual average)

Is the annual average of market exchange rates for countries quoting rates in units of national currency per US dollar. (See Sources and Methods for details of additional conversion factors.)

EXTERNAL DEBT

Long-term debt (by debtor)
Is all external obligation of both public and private debtors with maturity of more than one year. It comprises both publicly guaranteed and nonguaranteed debt.

Central government
Is the borrower when the name of the republic, kingdom, etc., or any agencies and departments of central government, appears as the obligor in the contract.

Rest of general government
Is the borrower when the name of the state, province, city, etc., or any agencies and departments of local government, appears as the obligor in the contract.

Nonfinancial public enterprises
Are those described in the SNA definition of "nonfinancial public enterprises."

Private sector, including non-guaranteed
Private sector borrowers are other than those listed above.

Short-term debt
Is the sum of public and private external obligations with original or extended maturity of a year or less.

International reserves excluding gold
Comprises a country's monetary authorities' (central banks, currency boards, exchange stabilization funds, and treasuries) holdings of SDRs, reserve position in the Fund, and foreign exchange.

Gold holdings (at market price)
Are official holdings of gold (fine troy ounces) valued at year-end London market prices.

SOCIAL INDICATORS

Total fertility rate
Is the average number of children that would be born alive to a woman during her lifetime if she were to bear children at each age in accordance with prevailing age-specific fertility rates.

Infant mortality rate
Is the number of infants per thousand live births, in a given year, who die before reaching one year of age.

Life expectancy at birth
Is the number of years a newborn infant would live if prevailing patterns of mortality for all people at the time of his or her birth were to stay the same throughout his or her life.

Urban population, % of total
Is the urban population as a percentage of the total population

Food production per capita
Is the index of annual production of all food commodities adjusted for population growth. Production excludes animal feed and seed for agriculture.

Labor force, agriculture (%)
Is the labor force in farming, forestry, hunting, and fishing as a percentage of total labor force, which comprises so-called "economically active" persons, including armed forces and unemployed but excluding caregivers and students.

Labor force, female (%)
Female labor force as a percentage of total labor force.

Primary school enrollment ratio
Gross enrollment of all ages at primary level as a percentage of children in the country's primary school age group.

Primary school enrollment ratio, female
Gross enrollment of females of all ages at primary level as a percentage of children in the country's primary school age group.

Secondary school enrollment ratio
Computed in a similar manner to primary enrollment, but includes pupils enrolled in vocational or teacher-training secondary schools.

Topical Pages

Table 1. Gross national product per capita

US dollars, Atlas methodology	1970	1971	1972	1973	1974	1975	1976	1977	1978	1979	1980
SUB-SAHARAN AFRICA	*160*	*180*	*180*	*200*	*250*	*290*	*340*	*380*	*400*	*470*	*540*
Excluding Nigeria	*180*	*190*	*180*	*190*	*230*	*260*	*280*	*310*	*330*	*380*	*420*
Benin	130	130	140	160	180	200	220	240	260	320	390
Botswana	130	150	190	240	340	350	420	430	490	600	780
Burkina Faso	80	80	90	100	120	130	150	160	170	210	240
Burundi	70	90	80	80	90	100	120	140	150	170	200
Cameroon	180	180	180	210	270	310	360	410	500	600	760
Cape Verde	..	..	200	230	290	310	350	320	330	360	530
Central African Rep.	110	100	110	120	150	170	200	230	260	280	320
Chad	100	90	100	100	120	150	150	160	170	150	160
Comoros	100	110	110	140	150	170	190	200	220	260	340
Congo	240	260	290	340	430	530	520	490	530	650	850
Côte d'Ivoire	270	280	290	310	390	510	560	630	830	1,010	1,180
Equatorial Guinea	..		..		..		..		..		..
Ethiopia	60	70	70	70	80	90	90	90	100	110	120
Gabon	670	700	740	850	1,530	2,620	4,180	3,810	2,950	3,200	3,830
Gambia, The	100	120	130	140	200	210	230	250	260	350	350
Ghana	250	270	250	260	290	280	280	300	350	380	410
Guinea-Bissau	..	..	160	160	170	190	170	160	170	170	130
Kenya	130	160	180	180	210	230	240	270	310	370	420
Lesotho	100	110	110	150	200	230	250	290	330	360	410
Liberia	300	310	320	320	370	410	460	500	540	580	580
Madagascar	170	170	180	190	230	280	280	300	310	370	430
Malawi	60	80	80	90	110	120	120	130	160	170	180
Mali	70	70	80	80	90	120	140	170	170	210	240
Mauritania	180	170	180	200	260	300	340	360	360	390	440
Mauritius	280	300	340	430	590	710	860	930	1,020	1,200	1,180
Mozambique	..	..	..	..	..	..	..	..	..	..	..
Namibia	..		..		..		..		..		..
Niger	160	170	160	160	200	230	230	250	300	360	440
Nigeria	140	170	210	240	330	400	540	630	660	780	930
Rwanda	60	60	60	70	70	90	120	160	180	210	240
Senegal	220	220	230	240	280	350	400	400	380	460	510
Seychelles	350	410	470	580	700	800	870	950	1,120	1,610	2,010
Sierra Leone	160	160	160	170	190	220	210	220	220	270	320
Somalia	80	80	90	90	90	140	150	140	130	110	110
Sudan	140	150	160	150	200	260	330	390	410	400	430
Swaziland	270	320	330	370	460	590	580	590	600	720	820
Tanzania	100	100	110	130	140	170	180	200	230	260	290
Togo	140	140	150	170	210	250	270	300	340	350	410
Uganda	190	200	210	210	220	220	270	280	280	290	280
Zaire	250	260	270	320	380	400	400	440	480	560	590
Zambia	440	430	430	430	530	550	540	500	500	510	600
Zimbabwe	310	340	360	400	500	550	570	540	530	590	710
SOUTH ASIA	*110*	*120*	*110*	*120*	*140*	*160*	*160*	*170*	*190*	*200*	*230*
Bangladesh	100	100	80	80	100	130	130	120	110	130	150
Bhutan	..		..		..		..		..		..
India	110	110	110	130	140	170	160	170	190	200	240
Nepal	80	80	80	80	100	110	120	120	120	130	130
Pakistan	170	170	160	130	130	130	170	190	220	250	290
Sri Lanka	180	190	190	220	250	290	290	300	260	260	260
EAST ASIA AND PACIFIC	*130*	*130*	*140*	*160*	*180*	*210*	*220*	*240*	*290*	*340*	*390*
China	130	130	130	150	160	180	170	190	220	260	300
Fiji	400	450	520	660	840	1,030	1,190	1,290	1,350	1,580	1,750
Indonesia	80	90	90	110	150	210	270	320	370	400	470
Korea, Rep.	270	310	330	390	480	580	740	910	1,190	1,520	1,620
Malaysia	390	410	450	550	700	820	920	1,010	1,150	1,400	1,690
Mongolia	..		..		..		..		..		..
Papua New Guinea	260	280	300	370	450	530	520	540	650	710	760
Philippines	230	210	200	230	280	340	390	430	480	560	650
Solomon Islands	..	..	..		..	290	270	300	320	430	400
Thailand	210	210	220	250	300	360	410	460	530	590	670
Tonga	..	..	..	..	..	..	..	..	..	..	..
Vanuatu	..	..	..	..	..	..	..	..	..	..	..
Western Samoa	..	..	..	..	..	..	..	..	..	..	..

1981	1982	1983	1984	1985	1986	1987	1988	1989	1990	1991	
570	550	500	450	450	390	350	340	340	340	..	*SUB-SAHARAN AFRICA*
440	430	390	350	330	340	350	370	370	360	..	*Excluding Nigeria*
420	400	320	300	280	280	310	340	340	..	..	Benin
1,040	1,020	1,070	1,080	960	970	1,030	1,200	1,610	2,040	..	Botswana
250	250	220	190	190	210	240	300	310	330	..	Burkina Faso
250	250	240	230	250	250	240	240	220	210	..	Burundi
900	900	870	820	810	890	920	990	1,010	960	..	Cameroon
530	510	490	460	450	480	570	700	780	890		Cape Verde
330	340	280	280	270	290	310	370	380	390	..	Central African Rep.
160	150	140	130	150	150	140	180	190	190	..	Chad
380	350	330	310	300	320	370	440	460	480	..	Comoros
1,100	1,320	1,240	1,150	1,040	940	960	930	970	1,010	..	Congo
1,150	1,000	800	700	670	730	780	850	810	750	..	Côte d'Ivoire
..	..	..	..		..	270	310	310	330	..	Equatorial Guinea
120	120	120	120	110	120	120	120	120	120	..	Ethiopia
4,390	4,190	3,730	3,710	3,380	3,310	2,790	3,010	3,160	3,470	..	Gabon
360	360	290	250	210	170	190	210	240	260	..	Gambia, The
410	380	350	370	370	390	390	400	380	390	..	Ghana
170	190	200	190	180	160	170	170	180	180	..	Guinea-Bissau
430	400	350	320	310	330	340	370	370	370	..	Kenya
480	550	510	480	390	340	340	410	490	530	..	Lesotho
590	550	500	460	470	450	450	..	..	..	..	Liberia
410	400	380	340	310	290	260	240	220	230	..	Madagascar
180	190	180	180	170	160	150	160	170	200	..	Malawi
240	220	170	160	150	180	200	230	270	270	..	Mali
480	450	470	420	410	430	420	470	500	500	..	Mauritania
1,260	1,210	1,120	1,080	1,100	1,230	1,500	1,830	2,030	2,250	..	Mauritius
..	190	160	180	180	220	150	110	80	80	..	Mozambique
..	1,210	1,130	1,030	930	840	830	960	1,030	..	..	Namibia
440	380	310	240	230	240	260	300	290	310	..	Niger
970	960	850	790	850	580	360	300	270	290	..	Nigeria
260	260	270	260	270	300	310	330	320	310	..	Rwanda
490	510	440	380	380	430	520	650	660	710	..	Senegal
2,300	2,350	2,370	2,360	2,560	2,710	3,110	3,700	4,230	4,670	..	Seychelles
370	380	380	360	340	330	240	230	210	240	..	Sierra Leone
120	130	120	110	120	130	130	130	130	120	..	Somalia
460	450	400	350	320	..	..	..	..	..	..	Sudan
1,010	1,010	930	870	800	710	670	800	790	810	..	Swaziland
310	330	330	330	320	280	210	170	140	110	..	Tanzania
400	340	280	260	250	270	300	370	390	410	..	Togo
220	240	220	220	230	230	220	260	250	220	..	Uganda
540	490	430	340	260	240	230	240	230	220	..	Zaire
720	660	560	460	370	260	240	290	400	420	..	Zambia
860	900	850	730	630	570	560	620	670	640	..	Zimbabwe
260	270	270	270	280	280	300	320	330	330	..	*SOUTH ASIA*
170	170	160	150	160	160	170	180	190	210	..	Bangladesh
..	110	110	130	130	140	180	190	190	190	..	Bhutan
270	280	280	280	280	290	310	340	350	350	..	India
150	160	160	170	170	160	160	170	180	180	..	Nepal
330	350	350	350	340	340	340	350	370	380	..	Pakistan
290	330	340	350	390	410	410	420	430	470	..	Sri Lanka
430	440	440	450	440	430	440	480	540	590	..	*EAST ASIA AND PACIFIC*
320	320	320	330	320	300	300	330	350	370	..	China
2,000	1,870	1,700	1,770	1,640	1,760	1,620	1,580	1,700	1,780	..	Fiji
550	610	610	590	550	530	500	490	510	570	..	Indonesia
1,830	1,930	2,110	2,240	2,320	2,570	2,950	3,600	4,400	5,400	..	Korea, Rep.
1,880	1,900	1,900	2,040	1,970	1,840	1,830	1,930	2,120	2,320	..	Malaysia
..	..	..	..	..	..	..	..	..	..	..	Mongolia
820	780	760	750	740	740	760	850	890	860	..	Papua New Guinea
720	760	710	610	540	550	570	620	680	730	..	Philippines
490	560	540	620	520	580	560	550	590	590	..	Solomon Islands
750	780	810	840	800	800	860	1,030	1,220	1,420	..	Thailand
..	..	..	..	750	760	760	800	910	1,010	..	Tonga
..	..	..	..	960	930	820	890	1,010	1,100	..	Vanuatu
..	..	..	..	620	630	630	670	720	730	..	Western Samoa

Table 1. Gross national product per capita (cont'd.)

US dollars, Atlas methodology	1970	1971	1972	1973	1974	1975	1976	1977	1978	1979	1980
LATIN AMERICA AND CARIBBEAN	*600*	*630*	*670*	*780*	*960*	*1,120*	*1,260*	*1,350*	*1,460*	*1,670*	*1,920*
Argentina	1,020	1,070	1,050	1,240	1,630	1,810	1,680	1,610	1,570	1,800	1,970
Bahamas	2,700	2,900	2,900	3,260	2,950	2,730	3,000	3,330	3,670	5,100	5,830
Barbados	750	830	910	1,040	1,220	1,520	1,740	1,960	2,250	2,670	3,130
Belize	430	470	520	570	660	790	840	870	910	1,090	1,170
Bolivia	230	250	270	290	320	360	400	410	440	460	490
Brazil	450	500	570	710	880	1,070	1,300	1,470	1,640	1,870	2,060
Chile	840	990	1,080	1,090	1,140	860	880	1,030	1,330	1,690	2,100
Colombia	340	360	390	430	500	550	610	690	850	1,030	1,190
Costa Rica	560	610	660	750	860	950	1,070	1,320	1,560	1,790	1,960
Dominican Rep.	330	370	430	490	570	660	760	840	900	1,000	1,090
Ecuador	290	290	300	370	430	540	680	790	930	1,080	1,260
El Salvador	290	300	310	330	380	430	500	580	700	760	750
Grenada	..	..	..	..	..	..	..	..	..	..	..
Guatemala	360	380	390	430	500	570	660	790	900	1,030	1,120
Guyana	380	410	400	410	510	640	650	610	610	640	720
Haiti	90	100	100	110	130	150	170	180	200	220	250
Honduras	270	280	290	310	340	360	400	460	530	600	640
Jamaica	720	770	910	960	1,090	1,260	1,330	1,440	1,420	1,250	1,130
Mexico	820	800	820	940	1,120	1,360	1,500	1,490	1,580	1,810	2,320
Nicaragua	380	390	390	430	560	630	700	780	740	560	650
Panama	680	740	770	840	920	1,030	1,080	1,120	1,290	1,420	1,630
Paraguay	260	270	300	350	440	550	620	720	830	1,030	1,340
Peru	520	580	620	700	850	1,000	1,040	970	840	850	990
St. Vincent	220	230	300	300	320	350	380	390	440	500	570
Trinidad and Tobago	770	870	960	1,110	1,360	1,720	2,350	2,860	3,310	3,830	4,610
Uruguay	740	870	860	950	1,090	1,330	1,400	1,400	1,580	2,030	2,710
Venezuela	1,260	1,270	1,350	1,540	1,920	2,380	2,890	3,150	3,380	3,730	4,070
MIDDLE EAST AND NORTH AFRICA	*310*	*340*	*390*	*470*	*640*	*850*	*1,240*	*1,430*	*1,490*	*1,740*	*1,900*
Algeria	360	340	430	500	670	870	1,060	1,180	1,380	1,650	1,940
Egypt, Arab Rep.	230	250	260	280	280	320	360	410	410	440	500
Iran, Islamic Rep.	380	430	510	690	950	1,320	1,890	2,170	1,970	2,080	1,990
Jordan	..	..	..	..	..	..	..	..	..	..	..
Morocco	260	280	300	340	410	500	560	600	650	770	930
Oman	360	370	390	390	550	1,280	2,840	2,860	2,790	3,080	3,660
Saudi Arabia	560	760	980	1,140	2,070	3,290	5,410	7,120	7,720	8,790	10,400
Syrian Arab Rep.	360	400	480	460	630	860	1,030	1,020	1,130	1,220	1,450
Tunisia	280	320	390	430	560	710	800	850	930	1,080	1,280
EUROPE	*..*	*..*	*..*	*..*	*..*	*..*	*..*	*..*	*..*	*..*	*..*
Bulgaria	..	..	..	..	..	..	..	..	..	..	..
Czechoslovakia	..	..	..	..	..	..	..	..	..	..	..
Greece	1,170	1,300	1,460	1,720	1,940	2,370	2,650	2,850	3,270	3,860	4,370
Hungary	..	..	..	..	..	..	..	1,320	1,500	1,680	1,930
Malta	760	830	900	1,030	1,220	1,540	1,700	1,860	2,090	2,500	3,150
Poland	..	..	..	..	..	..	..	..	..	..	..
Portugal	700	820	940	1,200	1,430	1,540	1,700	1,830	1,890	2,090	2,370
Romania	..	..	..	..	..	..	..	..	..	..	..
Turkey	400	400	410	470	630	830	1,000	1,110	1,220	1,370	1,400
Yugoslavia	660	740	780	870	1,150	1,380	1,620	1,970	2,400	2,880	3,250
Low- and middle-income economies	**220**	**240**	**250**	**280**	**340**	**410**	**460**	**510**	**560**	**640**	**730**
Low-income economies	120	130	130	140	160	190	190	210	230	260	310
Low-income Africa	150	170	170	180	220	260	310	350	370	430	490
China and India	120	120	120	140	150	180	170	180	210	230	280
Other low-income	110	110	110	120	130	170	200	220	240	260	300
Middle-income economies	490	520	560	660	830	1,020	1,220	1,350	1,450	1,680	1,900
High-income economies	**3,040**	**3,310**	**3,690**	**4,320**	**4,930**	**5,550**	**6,180**	**6,810**	**7,730**	**8,990**	**10,170**
OECD members	3,110	3,380	3,780	4,420	5,040	5,680	6,310	6,960	7,900	9,190	10,400
Japan	1,950	2,140	2,540	3,230	3,860	4,530	4,990	5,650	7,000	8,630	9,830
United States	4,970	5,340	5,800	6,420	6,890	7,400	8,190	9,050	10,100	11,140	11,990
WORLD	**840**	**900**	**980**	**1,140**	**1,300**	**1,470**	**1,630**	**1,790**	**2,000**	**2,300**	**2,590**

1981	1982	1983	1984	1985	1986	1987	1988	1989	1990	1991	
2,140	*2,100*	*1,890*	*1,790*	*1,730*	*1,700*	*1,720*	*1,780*	*1,920*	*2,140*	..	*LATIN AMERICA AND CARIBBEAN*
1,960	1,880	1,970	2,150	2,130	2,380	2,400	2,560	2,160	2,400	..	Argentina
5,650	6,600	7,110	8,190	8,950	9,530	10,360	10,630	11,070	11,420	..	Bahamas
3,510	3,760	4,010	4,420	4,640	5,170	5,330	5,880	6,410	6,540	..	Barbados
1,220	1,140	1,090	1,120	1,140	1,200	1,370	1,560	1,780	1,990	..	Belize
560	530	490	460	430	450	530	620	640	630	..	Bolivia
2,030	2,050	1,820	1,700	1,630	1,780	1,910	2,040	2,400	2,680	..	Brazil
2,610	2,220	1,910	1,700	1,420	1,330	1,360	1,510	1,780	1,940	..	Chile
1,330	1,390	1,390	1,380	1,270	1,230	1,200	1,220	1,230	1,260	..	Colombia
1,530	1,150	1,060	1,250	1,400	1,550	1,650	1,680	1,760	1,900	..	Costa Rica
1,210	1,260	1,210	990	790	740	770	740	790	830	..	Dominican Rep.
1,490	1,500	1,320	1,170	1,180	1,160	1,090	1,080	1,010	980	..	Ecuador
750	740	760	820	840	830	860	970	1,070	1,110	..	El Salvador
..	..	..	..	..	1,350	1,560	1,770	1,970	2,190	..	Grenada
1,200	1,190	1,170	1,180	1,200	1,050	950	890	920	900	..	Guatemala
740	620	550	500	540	550	430	400	420	330	..	Guyana
270	270	280	290	320	340	360	360	360	370	..	Haiti
690	680	690	720	740	760	820	830	740	590	..	Honduras
1,250	1,320	1,340	1,140	910	850	950	1,140	1,390	1,500	..	Jamaica
3,000	2,770	2,290	2,120	2,180	1,890	1,780	1,770	2,080	2,490	..	Mexico
760	800	810	790	760	760	810	..	..	..	..	Nicaragua
1,820	1,950	1,950	1,990	2,060	2,170	2,210	1,800	1,750	1,850	..	Panama
1,680	1,740	1,660	1,500	2,440	100	100	990	1,020	1,110	..	Paraguay
1,240	1,380	1,150	1,120	980	1,090	1,190	1,070	1,050	1,160	..	Peru
680	790	880	960	1,050	1,140	1,330	1,450	1,570	1,720	..	St. Vincent
5,780	6,620	6,710	6,340	7,020	5,390	4,230	3,580	3,530	3,650	..	Trinidad and Tobago
3,500	3,340	2,300	1,920	1,580	1,740	2,020	2,270	2,450	2,560	..	Uruguay
4,730	4,920	4,790	4,250	3,830	3,580	3,180	3,120	2,470	2,560	..	Venezuela
2,170	*2,450*	*2,500*	*2,390*	*2,340*	*2,250*	*2,130*	*1,960*	*1,860*	*1,820*	..	*MIDDLE EAST AND NORTH AFRICA*
2,240	2,430	2,420	2,470	2,590	2,650	2,690	2,470	2,280	2,060	..	Algeria
550	600	620	640	660	670	690	660	640	610	..	Egypt, Arab Rep.
2,540	3,140	3,530	3,750	3,990	3,960	3,650	3,070	2,580	2,490	..	Iran, Islamic Rep.
..	..	..	..	1,880	2,010	2,080	2,050	1,630	1,240	..	Jordan
880	860	730	660	610	650	680	830	880	950	..	Morocco
5,830	7,110	7,220	7,280	7,550	6,680	5,820	4,990	5,220	..	..	Oman
13,010	14,310	12,810	10,140	8,630	7,820	6,690	6,470	6,430	7,060	..	Saudi Arabia
1,680	1,790	1,810	1,730	1,740	1,460	1,180	1,080	880	1,000	..	Syrian Arab Rep.
1,380	1,310	1,240	1,210	1,170	1,110	1,180	1,240	1,290	1,440	..	Tunisia
..	..	..	..	..	..	..	..	..	..		*EUROPE*
..	2,450	2,260	2,150	2,040	2,170	2,560	2,760	2,710	2,250	..	Bulgaria
..	2,980	3,000	2,860	2,740	2,790	3,030	3,350	3,450	3,140	..	Czechoslovakia
4,470	4,320	3,950	3,810	3,610	3,670	3,980	4,780	5,380	5,990	..	Greece
2,150	2,220	2,120	2,030	1,930	2,010	2,250	2,480	2,620	2,780	..	Hungary
3,590	3,790	3,510	3,440	3,390	3,580	4,160	5,170	6,010	6,610	..	Malta
..	1,520	1,790	2,070	2,080	2,030	1,860	1,850	1,890	1,690	..	Poland
2,490	2,500	2,250	1,990	1,970	2,270	2,830	3,650	4,250	4,900	..	Portugal
..	..	..	..	..	..	..	..	1,720	1,620	..	Romania
1,450	1,300	1,180	1,100	1,080	1,110	1,220	1,280	1,370	1,640	..	Turkey
3,450	3,230	2,640	2,270	2,040	2,290	2,510	2,710	2,940	3,060	..	Yugoslavia
820	**840**	**800**	**780**	**760**	**750**	**750**	**780**	**830**	**870**	..	**Low- and middle-income economies**
340	340	340	330	330	320	310	330	340	350	..	Low-income economies
500	490	440	400	410	340	280	270	260	260	..	Low-income Africa
300	300	300	310	310	300	310	330	350	360	..	China and India
350	380	380	370	360	360	350	350	360	380	..	Other low-income
2,150	2,200	2,080	2,000	1,930	1,920	1,940	2,020	2,140	2,310	..	Middle-income economies
10,940	**10,890**	**10,870**	**11,240**	**11,560**	**12,410**	**14,040**	**16,660**	**18,370**	**19,760**	..	**High-income economies**
11,180	11,130	11,110	11,480	11,830	12,710	14,390	17,100	18,840	20,250	..	OECD members
10,350	10,310	10,340	10,570	11,350	13,010	16,020	21,400	24,240	25,890	..	Japan
13,310	13,650	14,520	15,930	16,790	17,520	18,450	19,700	20,850	21,790	..	United States
2,800	**2,780**	**2,720**	**2,750**	**2,780**	**2,890**	**3,170**	**3,650**	**3,960**	**4,210**	..	**WORLD**

Table 2. Gross national income per capita

1987 US dollars	1970	1971	1972	1973	1974	1975	1976	1977	1978	1979	1980
SUB-SAHARAN AFRICA	*320*	*330*	*320*	*330*	*390*	*360*	*380*	*400*	*390*	*380*	*410*
Excluding Nigeria	*370*	*370*	*370*	*360*	*390*	*370*	*390*	*410*	*390*	*390*	*390*
Benin	380	370	370	390	370	340	330	350	340	350	360
Botswana	290	300	350	440	540	470	520	510	510	640	770
Burkina Faso	230	230	230	230	250	240	260	260	250	250	250
Burundi	140	190	170	190	180	170	200	230	200	210	200
Cameroon	670	650	610	630	700	660	650	740	780	820	910
Cape Verde	..	..	..	220	250	230	270	310	320	360	520
Central African Rep.	470	470	460	460	440	400	460	490	490	450	410
Chad	210	200	200	180	190	190	190	180	180	130	130
Comoros	..	..	..	..	..	..	..	..	..	..	..
Congo	710	740	720	840	1,000	860	840	730	710	770	960
Côte d'Ivoire	910	930	920	950	1,010	1,010	1,090	1,180	1,210	1,140	1,130
Equatorial Guinea	..	..	..	..	..	..	..	..	..	..	..
Ethiopia	..	..	..	..	..	..	..	..	..	..	..
Gabon	4,070	4,170	4,280	4,090	6,750	7,040	8,780	7,470	5,560	5,730	6,760
Gambia, The	310	300	330	310	350	360	340	390	320	360	330
Ghana	490	460	430	490	510	440	390	430	450	440	440
Guinea-Bissau	200	200	200	200	200	200	180	160	170	170	120
Kenya	320	350	390	380	370	350	350	410	390	390	380
Lesotho	200	210	230	290	320	350	380	430	460	440	420
Liberia	..	..	..	..	..	..	..	..	..	..	..
Madagascar	410	400	390	370	360	340	330	320	300	310	300
Malawi	150	170	170	170	180	180	180	180	200	180	170
Mali	180	180	190	180	170	190	210	220	210	230	220
Mauritania	550	540	510	480	570	540	580	520	480	480	490
Mauritius	750	780	880	920	1,320	1,370	1,300	1,320	1,340	1,370	1,160
Mozambique	..	..	..	..	..	..	..	..	..	..	130
Namibia	..	..	..	..	..	..	..	..	..	..	1,550
Niger	430	450	410	310	370	290	290	320	340	400	400
Nigeria	230	260	250	280	430	360	390	430	410	390	500
Rwanda	300	300	290	290	280	280	290	300	310	340	350
Senegal	710	700	710	650	670	690	720	700	640	670	630
Seychelles	..	..	..	..	..	..	..	..	..	..	..
Sierra Leone	150	150	140	150	150	140	130	140	150	150	150
Somalia	130	130	140	130	100	140	130	170	170	160	140
Sudan	690	720	680	600	650	720	820	920	880	770	750
Swaziland	..	..	..	..	..	..	..	..	..	..	..
Tanzania	190	190	190	190	190	180	200	190	180	180	170
Togo	450	360	360	370	520	380	440	460	480	430	450
Uganda	..	..	..	..	..	..	..	..	..	..	..
Zaire	320	300	290	310	310	270	250	250	220	220	..
Zambia	710	520	550	610	600	350	380	320	280	320	300
Zimbabwe	..	..	..	..	..	..	680	620	590	590	640
SOUTH ASIA	*230*	*230*	*220*	*230*	*220*	*230*	*230*	*250*	*250*	*240*	*250*
Bangladesh	170	160	130	120	140	130	130	130	140	150	150
Bhutan	..	..	..	..	..	..	..	..	..	..	..
India	240	240	240	240	230	250	250	270	270	250	260
Nepal	..	..	..	..	..	..	..	..	..	..	..
Pakistan	250	230	220	230	240	220	230	230	250	250	270
Sri Lanka	250	250	240	260	260	250	280	320	330	330	330
EAST ASIA AND PACIFIC	*180*	*180*	*190*	*200*	*210*	*210*	*220*	*230*	*250*	*270*	*280*
China	110	120	120	120	120	130	120	130	150	160	170
Fiji	1,250	1,290	1,360	1,490	1,690	1,770	1,750	1,820	1,810	1,940	1,890
Indonesia	160	170	170	180	210	220	220	240	260	290	340
Korea, Rep.	970	1,040	1,080	1,220	1,280	1,310	1,500	1,640	1,810	1,900	1,710
Malaysia	950	940	970	1,140	1,210	1,130	1,310	1,400	1,460	1,620	1,740
Mongolia	..	..	..	..	..	..	..	..	..	..	..
Papua New Guinea	910	920	970	1,120	1,070	950	980	990	1,010	1,060	950
Philippines	500	510	520	570	570	570	580	600	630	660	660
Solomon Islands	..	..	..	..	..	..	..	..	..	..	480
Thailand	510	500	510	570	560	560	590	630	670	690	700
Tonga	..	..	..	..	..	..	..	..	..	..	..
Vanuatu	..	..	..	..	..	..	..	..	..	..	..
Western Samoa	..	..	..	..	..	..	..	..	..	..	..

1981	1982	1983	1984	1985	1986	1987	1988	1989	1990	1991	
390	*380*	*360*	*350*	*360*	*330*	*310*	*310*	*320*	*320*	*..*	*SUB-SAHARAN AFRICA*
390	*390*	*380*	*380*	*370*	*370*	*360*	*350*	*350*	*340*	*..*	*Excluding Nigeria*
360	380	350	370	370	350	350	350	320	320	330	Benin
730	680	700	730	880	1,000	1,110	1,240	1,600	..	..	Botswana
260	280	280	270	290	300	300	310	300	300	..	Burkina Faso
210	200	210	200	220	230	220	230	220	220	..	Burundi
990	1,020	1,060	1,090	1,140	1,210	1,110	1,000	940	880	840	Cameroon
540	550	570	590	610	630	680	690	680	760	..	Cape Verde
390	410	370	400	400	390	370	370	370	360	..	Central African Rep.
130	130	150	140	170	160	150	170	170	160	..	Chad
..	..	..	510	490	490	490	460	..	..	..	Comoros
1,090	1,540	1,570	1,670	1,380	960	990	860	970	960	860	Congo
1,080	1,040	990	1,000	1,000	1,030	900	830	740	650	620	Côte d'Ivoire
..	..	..	..	310	290	300	300	280	290	..	Equatorial Guinea
..	..	..	..	..	..	..	..	..	..	..	Ethiopia
7,010	6,060	5,940	5,830	5,240	3,810	2,970	2,900	2,990	2,800	..	Gabon
270	290	210	240	220	220	200	240	230	240	..	Gambia, The
410	350	340	360	360	360	360	370	380	..	..	Ghana
160	170	160	170	170	170	170	180	190	180	..	Guinea-Bissau
370	350	340	340	330	350	350	360	370	380	..	Kenya
430	470	460	460	430	410	400	420	460	480	..	Lesotho
..	..	..	..	..	..	..	..	..	..	..	Liberia
260	250	250	250	240	240	230	230	220	230	..	Madagascar
160	160	160	170	160	150	150	140	150	160	..	Malawi
220	230	220	220	210	240	240	240	260	250	..	Mali
510	480	480	440	470	500	460	450	480	440	..	Mauritania
1,160	1,140	1,180	1,210	1,280	1,510	1,720	1,770	1,720	1,790	..	Mauritius
130	120	100	110	90	90	90	100	100	100	..	Mozambique
1,220	1,090	970	990	1,110	1,080	970	1,050	1,060	..	..	Namibia
400	390	380	300	300	320	300	300	270	270	..	Niger
450	380	340	330	350	250	230	240	260	290	..	Nigeria
360	360	370	350	350	360	330	330	300	270	..	Rwanda
600	650	640	610	620	640	640	650	620	640	..	Senegal
..	..	..	..	..	..	..	..	..	..	..	Seychelles
160	160	150	150	140	130	140	140	140	140	..	Sierra Leone
150	150	130	130	130	130	140	130	120	..	..	Somalia
730	800	790	730	660	670	680	640	690	630	..	Sudan
..	..	..	..	..	..	..	..	..	..	..	Swaziland
160	150	150	150	150	150	150	150	..	..	..	Tanzania
420	390	360	380	380	390	370	380	390	390	..	Togo
..	..	..	..	..	..	..	..	..	..	..	Uganda
..	..	..	..	..	..	..	..	..	..	..	Zaire
290	220	230	220	230	210	240	290	230	260	..	Zambia
680	670	650	620	640	630	600	660	690	670	690	Zimbabwe
260	*260*	*280*	*280*	*290*	*300*	*300*	*320*	*330*	*340*	*340*	*SOUTH ASIA*
160	160	160	170	170	170	170	180	170	180	..	Bangladesh
..	..	..	..	..	..	..	..	..	..	..	Bhutan
270	280	290	290	300	310	320	340	350	360	370	India
..	..	..	..	..	..	..	..	..	..	..	Nepal
270	280	280	290	300	310	320	330	340	340	350	Pakistan
330	350	380	400	400	410	410	410	410	420	..	Sri Lanka
290	*300*	*320*	*350*	*370*	*390*	*420*	*450*	*480*	*500*	*520*	*EAST ASIA AND PACIFIC*
170	180	200	220	240	250	280	300	310	320	340	China
1,870	1,700	1,590	1,690	1,600	1,730	1,560	1,740	1,960	2,050	..	Fiji
370	360	380	410	410	410	430	430	460	500	510	Indonesia
1,770	1,900	2,110	2,280	2,400	2,740	3,090	3,450	3,730	4,030	..	Korea, Rep.
1,730	1,750	1,800	1,950	1,830	1,660	1,790	1,950	2,060	2,230	2,350	Malaysia
..	..	..	..	..	..	..	..	..	..	..	Mongolia
840	790	810	820	820	810	820	850	760	690	..	Papua New Guinea
660	670	650	570	540	550	570	610	620	620	610	Philippines
440	460	450	680	480	430	500	560	..	..	..	Solomon Islands
710	710	760	790	790	830	890	990	1,090	1,200	..	Thailand
..	..	..	..	..	..	..	..	..	..	..	Tonga
..	..	890	1,040	1,030	880	830	860	890	..	..	Vanuatu
..	..	690	670	680	640	650	660	660	630	..	Western Samoa

Table 2. Gross national income per capita (cont'd.)

1987 US dollars	1970	1971	1972	1973	1974	1975	1976	1977	1978	1979	1980
LATIN AMERICA AND CARIBBEAN	*1,340*	*1,400*	*1,460*	*1,560*	*1,620*	*1,610*	*1,680*	*1,730*	*1,730*	*1,790*	*1,880*
Argentina	2,690	2,790	2,770	2,850	2,910	2,840	2,800	2,910	2,780	2,950	2,990
Bahamas	..	..	..	..	..	..	..	5,880	5,990	8,170	8,650
Barbados	..	..	..	..	..	..	..	..	..	..	..
Belize	..	..	..	..	..	..	..	..	..	..	..
Bolivia	780	790	810	840	910	870	910	910	890	880	850
Brazil	1,170	1,260	1,390	1,570	1,640	1,680	1,810	1,860	1,850	1,910	2,000
Chile	1,640	1,730	1,640	1,580	1,560	1,130	1,190	1,280	1,360	1,490	1,580
Colombia	770	790	850	900	920	910	960	1,010	1,060	1,080	1,110
Costa Rica	1,380	1,390	1,440	1,510	1,500	1,500	1,600	1,800	1,800	1,790	1,740
Dominican Rep.	490	530	620	670	690	700	690	720	710	720	730
Ecuador	710	720	750	850	1,010	1,020	1,100	1,180	1,180	1,270	1,310
El Salvador	1,080	1,080	1,120	1,160	1,150	1,170	1,320	1,490	1,380	1,350	1,170
Grenada	..	..	..	..	..	..	..	..	..	..	..
Guatemala	890	880	900	950	950	940	990	1,110	1,090	1,070	1,060
Guyana	750	780	700	620	850	1,060	800	730	690	610	660
Haiti	330	350	340	340	350	340	370	370	380	390	420
Honduras	770	760	790	830	800	780	860	950	980	980	950
Jamaica	1,490	1,460	1,620	1,610	1,610	1,640	1,430	1,430	1,400	1,240	1,100
Mexico	1,310	1,320	1,380	1,450	1,500	1,530	1,560	1,560	1,650	1,750	1,920
Nicaragua	1,440	1,430	1,370	1,380	1,590	1,520	1,580	1,720	1,470	960	1,080
Panama	1,750	1,890	1,940	1,960	1,940	1,940	1,870	1,810	1,990	1,990	2,030
Paraguay	580	610	630	690	720	710	780	890	930	860	1,100
Peru	1,230	1,230	1,220	1,270	1,340	1,300	1,280	1,250	1,190	1,280	1,310
St. Vincent	..	..	..	..	..	..	..	730	790	760	780
Trinidad and Tobago	2,680	3,130	3,060	3,240	3,500	3,450	3,820	4,090	4,460	4,840	5,120
Uruguay	2,090	2,100	2,070	2,150	2,040	2,110	2,180	2,170	2,280	2,430	2,550
Venezuela	..	..	..	..	3,020	3,020	3,210	3,320	3,170	3,180	3,270
MIDDLE EAST AND NORTH AFRICA	*1,130*	*1,190*	*1,290*	*1,480*	*1,640*	*1,650*	*1,860*	*1,920*	*1,720*	*1,700*	*1,540*
Algeria	1,750	1,650	1,900	1,940	2,290	2,240	2,360	2,400	2,490	2,670	2,780
Egypt, Arab Rep.	370	370	370	400	410	420	480	520	520	580	640
Iran, Islamic Rep.	2,410	2,630	2,900	3,640	4,110	4,070	4,740	4,920	3,900	3,670	2,850
Jordan	..	..	..	..	..	..	..	..	..	..	..
Morocco	540	560	560	560	600	640	660	670	670	690	730
Oman	..	..	..	..	..	..	..	..	..	..	..
Saudi Arabia	..	..	..	..	..	..	..	..	..	..	..
Syrian Arab Rep.	..	..	..	..	..	1,040	1,110	1,090	1,140	1,170	1,240
Tunisia	700	760	890	860	970	990	990	1,000	1,050	1,130	1,210
EUROPE	*..*	*..*	*..*	*..*	*..*	*..*	*..*	*..*	*..*	*..*	*2,140*
Bulgaria	..	..	..	..	..	..	..	..	..	..	..
Czechoslovakia	..	..	..	..	..	..	..	..	..	..	3,160
Greece	3,170	3,400	3,670	3,950	3,760	3,910	4,090	4,200	4,390	4,470	4,520
Hungary	..	..	..	1,800	1,850	1,920	2,010	2,050	2,140	2,150	2,160
Malta	2,110	2,170	2,260	2,320	2,430	2,860	3,210	3,370	3,550	3,690	4,010
Poland	..	..	..	..	..	..	..	..	..	..	1,610
Portugal	2,250	2,520	2,760	3,080	3,070	2,700	2,750	2,920	2,980	3,120	3,150
Romania	..	..	..	..	..	..	..	..	..	..	1,790
Turkey	820	870	920	930	960	1,010	1,080	1,100	1,110	1,070	1,020
Yugoslavia	1,780	1,920	1,980	2,020	2,250	2,250	2,350	2,520	2,750	2,840	2,880
Low- and middle-income economies	**460**	**480**	**490**	**530**	**550**	**560**	**590**	**630**	**620**	**630**	**640**
Low-income economies	180	180	180	190	190	200	200	210	220	220	240
Low-income Africa	260	270	260	270	320	290	300	330	310	300	330
China and India	160	170	160	170	170	180	170	190	200	190	210
Other low-income	190	190	180	190	210	200	220	230	240	260	280
Middle-income economies	1,360	1,420	1,500	1,640	1,710	1,720	1,850	1,950	1,880	1,910	1,900
High-income economies	**11,150**	**11,430**	**11,920**	**12,500**	**12,280**	**12,140**	**12,610**	**12,940**	**13,430**	**13,760**	**13,690**
OECD members	11,410	11,690	12,200	12,800	12,560	12,430	12,910	13,250	13,760	14,090	14,010
Japan	11,820	12,280	13,170	13,970	13,370	13,480	13,920	14,430	15,160	15,640	15,730
United States	14,000	14,280	14,800	15,460	15,050	14,730	15,310	15,810	16,420	16,590	16,200
WORLD	**2,830**	**2,880**	**2,970**	**3,090**	**3,040**	**2,990**	**3,080**	**3,150**	**3,220**	**3,270**	**3,240**

1981	1982	1983	1984	1985	1986	1987	1988	1989	1990	1991	
1,810	*1,710*	*1,610*	*1,650*	*1,870*	*1,670*	*1,700*	*1,680*	*1,660*	*1,630*	..	*LATIN AMERICA AND CARIBBEAN*
2,750	2,460	2,490	2,540	2,380	2,490	2,460	2,370	2,170	2,170	2,280	Argentina
7,860	8,340	8,540	9,480	10,190	10,410	10,630	..	..	..	..	Bahamas
											Barbados
..	..	..	..	..	..	..	..	..	..	..	Belize
840	760	710	690	650	610	610	600	610	600	..	Bolivia
1,830	1,780	1,670	1,730	1,830	1,980	2,000	1,960	1,950	1,820	..	Brazil
1,570	1,250	1,230	1,230	1,210	1,260	1,380	1,540	1,660	1,640	..	Chile
1,080	1,060	1,050	1,070	1,050	1,130	1,130	1,150	1,150	1,180	..	Colombia
1,550	1,370	1,430	1,530	1,540	1,690	1,630	1,630	1,640	1,660	1,670	Costa Rica
750	710	730	760	690	710	720	720	780	690	660	Dominican Rep.
1,290	1,230	1,170	1,160	1,180	1,070	1,020	1,040	1,040	1,080	1,000	Ecuador
1,000	920	900	910	930	970	920	960	940	900	910	El Salvador
..	..	..	1,090	1,140	1,390	1,640	1,730	1,720	1,720	..	Grenada
1,010	930	890	870	830	830	820	830	840	830	830	Guatemala
590	480	410	390	380	390	340	360	410	300	..	Guyana
400	370	370	360	360	360	350	340	330	320	..	Haiti
900	820	800	800	810	800	820	830	810	750	700	Honduras
1,130	1,140	1,120	1,070	960	1,010	1,070	1,170	1,230	1,180	1,220	Jamaica
2,040	1,930	1,760	1,800	1,800	1,590	1,630	1,630	1,680	1,750	1,780	Mexico
1,070	1,020	1,050	990	940	890	910	600	610	..	..	Nicaragua
2,100	2,070	2,070	2,120	2,150	2,230	2,170	1,740	1,640	1,670	1,750	Panama
1,140	1,080	1,020	1,000	23,660	900	930	980	1,020	1,010	..	Paraguay
1,320	1,290	1,090	1,100	1,090	1,190	1,290	1,160	1,000	950	950	Peru
850	930	1,000	1,040	1,160	1,250	1,320	..	..	..	..	St. Vincent
5,140	4,860	4,460	3,800	4,680	4,080	3,780	3,430	3,500	3,190	..	Trinidad and Tobago
2,590	2,290	1,930	1,960	1,870	2,100	2,310	2,300	2,280	2,260	..	Uruguay
3,240	2,940	2,700	2,880	2,750	2,450	2,550	2,550	2,430	2,580	..	Venezuela
1,580	*1,680*	*1,740*	*1,770*	*1,790*	*1,650*	*1,630*	*1,540*	*1,520*	..	..	*MIDDLE EAST AND NORTH AFRICA*
2,850	2,850	2,940	3,000	3,080	2,750	2,720	2,460	2,480	2,420	2,340	Algeria
640	660	690	710	710	680	660	670	670	650	660	Egypt, Arab Rep.
2,980	3,370	3,560	3,600	3,590	3,050	2,950	2,580	2,540	..	..	Iran, Islamic Rep.
..	..	2,070	1,970	1,960	2,220	2,160	2,100	1,940	1,800	1,790	Jordan
680	730	700	720	740	800	770	830	820	820	820	Morocco
..	..	..	..	..	..	..	..	..	..	..	Oman
..	..	..	..	..	..	..	..	..	..	..	Saudi Arabia
1,280	1,240	1,200	1,120	1,170	1,030	980	1,060	1,010	1,130	..	Syrian Arab Rep.
1,250	1,210	1,230	1,250	1,250	1,150	1,200	1,180	1,210	1,290	..	Tunisia
2,070	*2,050*	*2,030*	*2,070*	*2,090*	*2,160*	*2,200*	*2,270*	*2,300*	*2,160*	..	*EUROPE*
..	..	2,650	2,720	2,800	2,940	3,130	3,170	3,170	2,850	2,050	Bulgaria
3,110	3,110	3,150	3,180	3,240	3,290	3,330	3,440	3,500	3,430	2,690	Czechoslovakia
4,510	4,450	4,380	4,410	4,490	4,520	4,560	4,760	4,860	4,850	..	Greece
2,190	2,190	2,210	2,240	2,240	2,250	2,360	2,390	2,400	2,320	2,110	Hungary
4,190	4,400	4,220	4,390	4,570	4,640	4,860	5,340	5,770	..	..	Malta
1,400	1,320	1,390	1,450	1,530	1,590	1,620	1,680	1,740	1,470	1,370	Poland
3,070	3,080	3,040	2,890	3,010	3,300	3,490	3,680	3,900	..	..	Portugal
1,770	1,730	1,600	1,820	1,640	1,640	1,650	1,950	1,960	1,650	1,420	Romania
1,020	1,020	1,030	1,080	1,110	1,200	1,260	1,280	1,240	1,340	1,340	Turkey
2,870	2,860	2,790	2,770	2,720	2,890	2,780	2,700	2,710	2,510	..	Yugoslavia
640	**640**	**640**	**660**	**690**	**670**	**690**	**700**	**710**	**710**	..	**Low- and middle-income economies**
240	250	260	270	280	280	300	310	320	330	330	Low-income economies
310	290	280	270	270	240	240	240	250	250	..	Low-income Africa
210	220	240	250	270	280	300	320	330	340	350	China and India
300	300	310	320	330	320	330	330	340	350	360	Other low-income
1,890	1,870	1,830	1,870	1,980	1,880	1,910	1,910	1,920	1,890	..	Middle-income economies
13,760	**13,630**	**13,940**	**14,480**	**14,880**	**15,340**	**15,770**	**16,390**	**16,820**	**17,120**	..	**High-income economies**
14,090	13,970	14,300	14,860	15,290	15,800	16,230	16,880	17,320	17,640	..	OECD members
16,120	16,520	16,860	17,470	18,260	19,100	19,850	20,990	21,800	22,770	..	Japan
16,420	15,850	16,300	17,280	17,700	18,040	18,400	19,070	19,430	19,500	..	United States
3,230	**3,180**	**3,210**	**3,300**	**3,370**	**3,410**	**3,470**	**3,570**	**3,620**	**3,650**	..	**WORLD**

Table 3. Private consumption per capita

1987 US dollars	1970	1971	1972	1973	1974	1975	1976	1977	1978	1979	1980
SUB-SAHARAN AFRICA	*220*	*240*	*230*	*220*	*240*	*240*	*240*	*260*	*280*	*260*	*270*
Excluding Nigeria	*250*	*260*	*260*	*250*	*260*	*260*	*260*	*280*	*290*	*280*	*270*
Benin	320	320	320	320	310	300	290	320	320	330	330
Botswana	340	310	320	410	430	420	430	410	440	530	570
Burkina Faso	210	210	200	190	200	210	220	240	230	240	250
Burundi	110	170	160	160	150	160	170	180	160	170	170
Cameroon	530	560	540	520	560	550	560	610	600	690	750
Cape Verde	..	..	..	310	250	270	290	310	370	380	470
Central African Rep.	300	300	310	290	310	320	350	400	390	360	370
Chad	..	..	..	..	..	..	..	..	..	..	..
Comoros	..	..	..	..	..	..	..	..	..	..	..
Congo	590	560	530	500	470	470	570	470	510	440	520
Côte d'Ivoire	560	610	620	640	640	700	690	660	730	720	550
Equatorial Guinea	..	..	..	..	..	..	..	..	..	..	..
Ethiopia	..	..	..	..	..	..	..	..	..	..	..
Gabon	1,730	1,800	1,840	2,050	1,630	1,610	1,800	1,900	2,510	2,180	2,100
Gambia, The	280	350	340	340	330	290	400	410	510	380	390
Ghana	380	380	320	360	420	330	310	320	370	350	360
Guinea-Bissau	130	170	200	220	230	190	170	140	120	100	80
Kenya	140	210	240	210	230	230	210	210	230	240	230
Lesotho	170	180	220	260	300	330	360	360	390	380	320
Liberia	..	..	..	..	..	..	..	..	..	..	..
Madagascar	370	380	360	350	320	320	290	300	280	310	310
Malawi	110	140	130	130	130	130	130	130	130	130	130
Mali	140	130	150	140	160	170	190	180	190	200	190
Mauritania	430	420	400	360	400	360	400	360	330	340	340
Mauritius	510	530	520	480	690	790	820	890	920	930	860
Mozambique	..	..	..	..	..	..	..	..	..	..	110
Namibia	..	..	..	..	..	..	..	..	..	..	650
Niger	370	390	350	240	330	240	230	250	250	310	330
Nigeria	170	190	170	170	220	220	220	250	310	230	290
Rwanda	270	270	260	240	250	230	230	240	260	290	310
Senegal	540	540	530	500	490	520	550	530	520	540	530
Seychelles	..	..	..	..	..	..	..	..	..	..	..
Sierra Leone	..	..	..	..	..	..	..	..	130	150	150
Somalia	110	110	90	90	70	100	90	140	120	100	100
Sudan	450	490	500	420	450	520	560	690	690	600	550
Swaziland	..	..	..	..	..	..	..	..	..	..	..
Tanzania	..	..	..	..	..	..	140	140	160	140	150
Togo	290	190	200	210	230	170	230	220	210	200	240
Uganda	..	..	..	..	..	..	..	..	..	..	..
Zaire	230	240	240	250	250	230	220	200	190	170	160
Zambia	180	160	150	110	110	110	110	110	100	150	130
Zimbabwe	..	..	..	..	..	..	340	340	360	370	340
SOUTH ASIA	*170*	*170*	*160*	*160*	*160*	*170*	*160*	*180*	*180*	*170*	*180*
Bangladesh	150	140	140	110	140	130	140	120	140	140	140
Bhutan	..	..	..	..	..	..	..	..	..	..	..
India	170	170	170	170	160	170	170	180	180	170	180
Nepal	..	..	..	..	..	..	..	..	..	..	..
Pakistan	220	210	180	170	190	190	190	200	210	220	230
Sri Lanka	200	200	180	200	200	210	210	230	240	240	260
EAST ASIA AND PACIFIC	*120*	*120*	*130*	*130*	*140*	*140*	*140*	*150*	*160*	*170*	*180*
China	70	70	70	80	80	80	80	80	90	90	100
Fiji	890	950	1,000	1,160	1,250	1,240	1,260	1,290	1,270	1,290	1,200
Indonesia	150	150	140	140	160	170	170	170	180	200	210
Korea, Rep.	670	740	740	820	850	880	960	990	1,060	1,160	1,110
Malaysia	570	590	610	650	690	670	700	750	810	880	960
Mongolia	..	..	..	..	..	..	..	..	..	..	..
Papua New Guinea	460	470	500	520	520	520	520	560	590	570	590
Philippines	360	380	380	400	410	400	400	410	430	460	450
Solomon Islands	..	..	..	..	..	..	..	..	..	..	390
Thailand	360	340	350	380	380	390	410	420	430	480	480
Tonga	..	..	..	..	..	..	..	..	..	..	..
Vanuatu	..	..	..	..	..	..	..	..	..	..	..
Western Samoa	..	..	..	..	..	..	..	..	..	520	520

1981	1982	1983	1984	1985	1986	1987	1988	1989	1990	1991	
290	*280*	*260*	*250*	*260*	*250*	*240*	*240*	*240*	*230*	..	**SUB-SAHARAN AFRICA**
280	*280*	*280*	*270*	*270*	*270*	*270*	*270*	*270*	*250*	..	*Excluding Nigeria*
350	290	290	300	310	310	300	300	290	290	..	Benin
550	560	490	460	570	460	540	640	940		..	Botswana
250	250	250	230	240	250	250	250	250	240	..	Burkina Faso
170	180	160	160	180	190	180	190	180	180	..	Burundi
760	740	720	680	720	760	800	790	710	680	670	Cameroon
460	440	470	500	510	520	500	500	500	..	..	Cape Verde
320	350	300	320	320	340	330	330	330	320	..	Central African Rep.
..	..	150	130	180	170	150	170	160	150	..	Chad
..	..	330	380	380	360	390	..	..	..	..	Comoros
550	830	680	700	710	650	630	610	600	470	370	Congo
660	650	640	700	660	730	670	560	570	500	470	Côte d'Ivoire
..	..	..		220	200	230	220	200	210	..	Equatorial Guinea
..	..	..	..	..	..	..	..	..	..	..	Ethiopia
2,070	1,830	2,060	1,760	1,580	1,970	1,610	1,820	1,330	1,100	..	Gabon
280	260	180	220	210	200	170	210	190	200	..	Gambia, The
330	260	270	290	300	310	310	310	330	330	..	Ghana
130	140	130	140	150	140	150	160	150	160	..	Guinea-Bissau
210	220	210	210	190	220	230	240	240	250	..	Kenya
350	350	380	370	330	310	320	320	330	320	..	Lesotho
..	..	..	..	..	..	..	..	..	..	..	Liberia
260	250	240	230	230	220	210	200	190	200	..	Madagascar
130	120	110	120	120	120	100	110	120	120	..	Malawi
200	210	200	200	210	210	200	200	210	200	..	Mali
360	380	470	400	380	380	380	400	420	430	..	Mauritania
830	800	810	830	870	910	1,070	1,220	1,160	1,230	..	Mauritius
110	110	100	100	90	90	100	100	100	90	..	Mozambique
760	750	670	660	610	600	650	600	610	..	..	Namibia
330	350	320	290	270	280	260	250	230	..	..	Niger
370	320	260	240	260	220	180	190	190	190	200	Nigeria
310	310	330	300	290	280	270	260	240	230	..	Rwanda
560	560	550	510	550	530	530	530	510	510	..	Senegal
..	..	..	..	..	..	..	..	..	..	..	Seychelles
150	150	130	120	120	110	120	110	120	120	..	Sierra Leone
110	120	110	110	70	100	90	100	100	..	..	Somalia
560	600	660	620	620	550	560	550	580	520	..	Sudan
..	..	..	..	..	..	..	..	..	..	..	Swaziland
130	120	120	130	130	130	140	130	..	..	..	Tanzania
250	260	240	260	250	270	260	280	280	280	..	Togo
..	..	..	..	..	..	..	..	..	..	..	Uganda
170	170	170	170	160	170	180	170	160	..	..	Zaire
130	100	120	110	130	120	170	190	150	150	..	Zambia
330	360	400	310	310	310	330	300	340	340	370	Zimbabwe
180	*190*	*200*	*200*	*200*	*210*	*210*	*230*	*230*	*240*	*250*	**SOUTH ASIA**
150	150	150	150	150	150	160	160	160	170	..	Bangladesh
..	..	..	..	..	..	..	..	..	..	..	Bhutan
180	190	210	210	210	220	220	230	240	240	250	India
..	..	..	..	..	..	..	..	..	..	..	Nepal
220	220	230	230	240	240	240	260	250	260	260	Pakistan
270	300	320	300	320	330	320	330	330	..	..	Sri Lanka
180	*190*	*200*	*210*	*220*	*220*	*240*	*250*	*270*	*270*	*290*	**EAST ASIA AND PACIFIC**
110	110	120	130	140	140	150	160	170	160	170	China
1,320	1,180	1,090	1,160	1,100	1,110	1,050	1,330	1,490	1,530	..	Fiji
220	230	250	260	250	250	260	260	270	290	300	Indonesia
1,150	1,220	1,310	1,390	1,460	1,560	1,670	1,810	1,970	2,130	..	Korea, Rep.
980	990	1,000	1,040	1,020	900	900	1,020	1,140	1,260	1,350	Malaysia
..	..	..	880	840	710	1,010	1,080	1,010	1,140	..	Mongolia
580	550	550	530	570	540	540	530	510	480	..	Papua New Guinea
450	460	440	420	410	400	430	440	450	470	490	Philippines
390	300	330	370	350	340	380	490	..	..	..	Solomon Islands
470	460	510	510	510	530	580	620	690	740	..	Thailand
..	..	..	..	..	..	..	..	..	..	..	Tonga
..	..	480	530	560	460	530	540	540	..	..	Vanuatu
500	480	520	510	580	610	620	650	630	600	..	Western Samoa

Table 3. Private consumption per capita (cont'd.)

1987 US dollars	1970	1971	1972	1973	1974	1975	1976	1977	1978	1979	1980
LATIN AMERICA AND CARIBBEAN	*910*	*960*	*1,000*	*1,030*	*1,070*	*1,070*	*1,110*	*1,140*	*1,160*	*1,220*	*1,280*
Argentina	2,010	2,070	2,070	2,140	2,250	2,210	2,020	2,040	1,990	2,220	2,360
Bahamas	..	..	..	..	..	..	..	3,890	4,410	6,170	5,970
Barbados	..	..	..	..	..	..	..	..	..	..	..
Belize	..	..	..	..	..	..	..	..	..	..	..
Bolivia	420	420	370	420	420	370	430	440	460	480	490
Brazil	750	820	900	970	1,050	1,020	1,130	1,190	1,190	1,270	1,320
Chile	1,160	1,290	1,360	1,250	1,010	840	820	960	1,020	1,090	1,160
Colombia	550	570	610	630	640	650	680	690	730	740	750
Costa Rica	970	950	990	1,010	1,030	1,020	1,020	1,120	1,190	1,190	1,130
Dominican Rep.	410	440	490	510	540	500	560	560	550	530	620
Ecuador	500	510	530	560	590	630	680	710	720	750	780
El Salvador	860	860	880	920	920	930	1,000	1,090	1,100	1,010	900
Grenada	..	..	..	..	..	..	..	..	..	..	..
Guatemala	720	730	750	770	780	780	830	870	890	890	880
Guyana	410	390	450	490	480	450	560	520	420	350	410
Haiti	280	300	300	290	310	290	320	320	320	320	340
Honduras	590	570	590	630	590	590	650	710	700	700	710
Jamaica	770	820	1,020	790	930	940	930	940	850	820	770
Mexico	940	960	990	1,020	1,050	1,080	1,090	1,070	1,130	1,220	1,300
Nicaragua	1,230	1,220	1,190	1,200	1,320	1,310	1,330	1,390	1,280	890	940
Panama	1,070	1,100	1,060	1,060	1,160	1,090	1,060	1,120	1,220	1,260	1,310
Paraguay	450	470	480	490	540	530	570	630	640	560	800
Peru	910	910	920	890	900	910	920	910	860	880	850
St. Vincent	..	..	..	..	..	..	..	..	..	..	..
Trinidad and Tobago	1,790	1,980	2,000	2,010	2,040	2,280	2,550	2,750	2,960	2,980	2,980
Uruguay	1,580	1,570	1,590	1,610	1,570	1,600	1,520	1,480	1,500	1,530	1,660
Venezuela	..	..	..	..	1,240	1,480	1,640	1,750	1,800	1,760	1,850
MIDDLE EAST AND NORTH AFRICA	..	..	..	..	*930*	*900*	*1,020*	*1,150*	*1,060*	*1,010*	*880*
Algeria	1,150	1,050	1,180	1,130	1,150	1,160	1,220	1,220	1,180	1,300	1,260
Egypt, Arab Rep.	..	..	..	..	370	360	370	410	430	490	540
Iran, Islamic Rep.	1,790	1,790	1,830	2,140	1,960	1,820	2,190	2,690	2,230	1,910	1,340
Jordan	..	..	..	..	..	..	..	..	..	..	..
Morocco	420	420	430	440	450	460	490	500	520	540	560
Oman	..	..	..	..	..	..	..	..	..	..	..
Saudi Arabia	..	..	..	..	..	..	..	..	..	..	..
Syrian Arab Rep.	..	..	..	..	..	720	740	810	830	810	840
Tunisia	380	410	480	510	530	580	600	630	650	670	740
EUROPE	..	..	..	..	..	..	..	..	..	..	*1,210*
Bulgaria	..	..	..	..	..	..	..	..	..	..	..
Czechoslovakia	..	..	..	..	..	..	..	..	..	..	1,500
Greece	1,860	1,990	2,130	2,150	2,160	2,300	2,400	2,480	2,570	2,540	2,530
Hungary	990	1,050	1,090	1,140	1,290	1,260	1,280	1,290	1,330	1,350	1,360
Malta	1,770	1,760	1,790	1,790	1,900	1,910	2,060	2,300	2,250	2,250	2,380
Poland	..	..	..	..	..	..	..	..	..	..	1,000
Portugal	1,290	1,520	1,550	1,760	1,990	1,900	1,940	1,950	1,900	1,880	1,860
Romania	..	..	..	..	..	..	..	..	..	..	..
Turkey	580	640	690	660	700	720	770	790	800	770	720
Yugoslavia	870	1,010	940	960	1,290	1,200	1,100	1,300	1,490	1,550	1,480
Low- and middle-income economies	**320**	**330**	**330**	**340**	**360**	**360**	**370**	**390**	**400**	**400**	**410**
Low-income economies	130	130	130	130	130	140	130	140	150	150	160
Low-income Africa	180	200	190	180	200	200	200	220	240	210	230
China and India	110	110	110	110	110	120	110	120	130	120	130
Other low-income	..	..	..	..	160	160	170	170	180	200	210
Middle-income economies	910	950	980	1,030	1,070	1,060	1,120	1,170	1,170	1,200	1,190
High-income economies	**6,520**	**6,700**	**7,050**	**7,370**	**7,320**	**7,420**	**7,680**	**7,900**	**8,160**	**8,380**	**8,410**
OECD members	6,680	6,860	7,230	7,560	7,510	7,620	7,890	8,110	8,380	8,620	8,640
Japan	6,640	6,940	7,460	8,000	7,840	8,120	8,320	8,590	8,950	9,400	9,540
United States	8,640	8,820	9,290	9,630	9,420	9,480	9,880	10,210	10,540	10,660	10,530
WORLD	**1,690**	**1,720**	**1,790**	**1,850**	**1,830**	**1,840**	**1,890**	**1,930**	**1,980**	**2,010**	**2,010**

1981	1982	1983	1984	1985	1986	1987	1988	1989	1990	1991	
1,260	*1,200*	*1,160*	*1,180*	*1,170*	*1,190*	*1,180*	*1,160*	*1,160*	*1,140*	*1,170*	*LATIN AMERICA AND CARIBBEAN*
2,220	1,960	2,020	2,110	1,950	2,080	2,070	1,940	1,930	1,870	1,980	Argentina
5,520	5,410	5,380	6,810	7,020	7,120	7,200	..	..	..	..	Bahamas
											Barbados
											Belize
580	480	520	530	580	550	540	510	510	500	..	Bolivia
1,240	1,260	1,240	1,270	1,280	1,330	1,290	1,240	1,230	1,180	1,180	Brazil
1,290	1,050	980	990	950	980	1,020	1,110	1,190	1,180	..	Chile
750	750	740	750	760	770	780	800	810	810	..	Colombia
1,070	960	980	1,030	1,030	1,050	1,080	1,090	1,130	1,150	1,150	Costa Rica
590	590	600	550	540	560	570	520	580	480	430	Dominican Rep.
810	800	770	770	780	760	770	760	770	770	730	Ecuador
810	750	740	760	780	770	760	770	760	770	780	El Salvador
			820	840	1,020	1,210	1,260	1,360	1,390	..	Grenada
860	790	740	740	700	680	710	720	720	710	710	Guatemala
480	400	390	310	350	270	300	320	290	330	..	Guyana
330	300	310	290	290	300	300	290	280	..	..	Haiti
680	660	630	610	610	600	620	640	640	620	610	Honduras
750	770	750	780	750	700	730	700	840	..	..	Jamaica
1,380	1,260	1,150	1,180	1,200	1,150	1,120	1,150	1,210	1,270	1,340	Mexico
830	760	710	660	590	540	510	560	570	570	..	Nicaragua
1,260	1,280	1,340	1,450	1,450	1,370	1,340	1,090	1,260	1,340	1,240	Panama
790	780	650	720	730	720	760	750	650	670	..	Paraguay
860	840	780	800	810	870	910	830	730	680	720	Peru
											St. Vincent
3,200	3,270	3,040	2,110	2,440	2,760	2,300	2,150	2,090	2,100	..	Trinidad and Tobago
1,710	1,550	1,360	1,330	1,350	1,480	1,690	1,660	1,640	1,590	..	Uruguay
1,890	1,900	1,770	1,740	1,680	1,690	1,700	1,790	1,640	1,640	..	Venezuela
890	*1,060*	*1,030*	*1,150*	*1,170*	*1,080*	*1,080*	*1,040*	*1,030*	*..*	*..*	*MIDDLE EAST AND NORTH AFRICA*
1,310	1,360	1,380	1,440	1,520	1,460	1,380	1,270	1,290	1,190	1,140	Algeria
540	540	550	580	600	590	580	580	590	590	570	Egypt, Arab Rep.
1,400	2,100	1,960	2,370	2,360	1,930	1,910	1,730	1,700	..	..	Iran, Islamic Rep.
		1,570	1,440	1,530	1,770	1,650	1,620	1,360	1,570	1,440	Jordan
520	540	520	530	530	560	540	570	580	570	620	Morocco
										..	Oman
										..	Saudi Arabia
870	780	720	620	750	630	790	860	800	860	..	Syrian Arab Rep.
770	770	780	810	810	810	810	830	840	870	..	Tunisia
1,200	*1,170*	*1,190*	*1,200*	*1,220*	*1,280*	*1,320*	*1,320*	*1,350*	*1,400*	*..*	*EUROPE*
		1,310	1,290	1,400	1,440	1,620	1,550	1,580	1,590	1,440	Bulgaria
1,510	1,470	1,520	1,540	1,550	1,570	1,600	1,660	1,690	1,750	1,700	Czechoslovakia
2,720	2,890	2,880	2,890	3,030	3,110	3,240	3,210	3,420	3,530	..	Greece
1,420	1,420	1,420	1,440	1,480	1,490	1,560	1,500	1,530	1,460	1,370	Hungary
2,380	2,420	2,470	2,640	2,890	2,900	2,940	3,190	3,510	..	..	Malta
950	830	860	880	950	990	1,010	1,030	1,040	860	930	Poland
1,890	1,910	1,950	1,920	1,930	2,030	2,350	2,640	2,780	..	..	Portugal
											Romania
690	700	730	780	770	830	870	870	890	1,000	930	Turkey
1,450	1,400	1,370	1,330	1,260	1,380	1,220	1,160	1,130	1,430	..	Yugoslavia
410	**420**	**420**	**430**	**440**	**440**	**440**	**450**	**460**	**460**	**..**	**Low- and middle-income economies**
170	170	180	180	190	190	190	200	210	210	210	Low-income economies
240	230	220	210	210	200	190	190	190	190	..	Low-income Africa
140	140	160	160	170	170	180	190	200	200	210	China and India
210	220	230	230	240	240	240	240	240	250	260	Other low-income
1,190	1,200	1,180	1,220	1,220	1,220	1,220	1,220	1,230	1,240	..	Middle-income economies
8,470	**8,500**	**8,710**	**8,930**	**9,200**	**9,470**	**9,740**	**10,070**	**10,270**	**10,430**	**..**	**High-income economies**
8,700	8,740	8,960	9,200	9,480	9,770	10,050	10,390	10,600	10,770	..	OECD members
9,670	10,060	10,370	10,590	10,940	11,210	11,590	12,060	12,440	12,860	..	Japan
10,600	10,500	10,850	11,260	11,650	11,980	12,220	12,600	12,770	12,830	..	United States
2,010	**2,000**	**2,020**	**2,060**	**2,090**	**2,130**	**2,160**	**2,210**	**2,230**	**2,240**	**..**	**WORLD**

Table 4. Gross domestic investment per capita

1987 US dollars	1970	1971	1972	1973	1974	1975	1976	1977	1978	1979	1980
SUB-SAHARAN AFRICA	*70*	*80*	*80*	*80*	*100*	*110*	*120*	*130*	*100*	*90*	*100*
Excluding Nigeria	*70*	*80*	*70*	*80*	*100*	*100*	*100*	*100*	*90*	*80*	*90*
Benin	30	30	40	40	60	60	60	50	50	70	90
Botswana	90	130	160	200	190	160	150	110	140	170	210
Burkina Faso	20	30	40	50	50	50	50	40	40	40	40
Burundi	10	20	10	10	20	10	20	30	40	40	30
Cameroon	80	100	100	110	100	110	100	130	190	170	190
Cape Verde	..	..	..	80	80	70	110	150	130	170	210
Central African Rep.	90	90	90	90	50	40	50	50	40	40	20
Chad	..	..	..	..	..	..	..	..	..	..	..
Comoros	..	..	..	..	..	..	..	..	..	..	..
Congo	270	310	360	410	470	530	400	310	240	250	350
Côte d'Ivoire	220	210	190	230	220	220	260	360	410	370	420
Equatorial Guinea	..	..	..	..	..	..	..	..	..	..	..
Ethiopia	..	..	..	..	..	..	..	..	..	..	..
Gabon	990	1,090	1,240	1,360	3,640	4,290	5,850	4,370	1,590	1,880	1,850
Gambia, The	10	10	10	10	10	30	30	40	70	50	60
Ghana	80	80	40	50	80	60	50	70	50	50	40
Guinea-Bissau	190	150	130	100	80	70	70	80	100	110	80
Kenya	140	140	120	140	130	90	90	120	150	110	140
Lesotho	20	30	30	40	40	50	80	110	90	110	130
Liberia	..	..	..	..	..	..	..	..	..	..	..
Madagascar	40	50	40	40	40	40	30	30	30	40	40
Malawi	60	50	70	50	60	70	60	60	90	70	50
Mali	40	40	40	30	30	30	30	40	40	40	40
Mauritania	40	40	60	40	130	190	230	200	140	110	160
Mauritius	130	190	210	350	410	420	400	390	410	430	240
Mozambique	..	..	..	..	..	..	..	..	..	..	30
Namibia	..	..	..	..	..	..	..	..	..	..	490
Niger	60	40	60	80	70	60	60	60	80	90	80
Nigeria	70	90	90	100	100	150	190	210	150	120	140
Rwanda	10	20	20	20	20	30	30	30	30	20	30
Senegal	130	130	140	140	140	120	140	130	120	100	100
Seychelles	..	..	..	..	..	..	..	..	..	..	..
Sierra Leone	40	20	20	20	20	30	20	20	20	20	20
Somalia	20	20	20	20	20	20	30	40	50	40	70
Sudan	90	80	60	70	110	120	170	140	120	90	100
Swaziland	..	..	..	..	..	..	..	..	..	..	..
Tanzania	50	60	50	50	50	50	50	60	50	50	50
Togo	90	100	110	110	110	150	120	210	250	230	140
Uganda	..	..	..	..	..	..	..	..	..	..	..
Zaire	30	40	40	40	40	40	30	50	20	40	50
Zambia	250	270	280	250	310	260	130	120	110	60	100
Zimbabwe	260	300	310	330	440	390	270	220	130	140	220
SOUTH ASIA	*50*	*50*	*40*	*50*	*50*	*50*	*50*	*50*	*60*	*60*	*60*
Bangladesh	30	20	10	20	10	10	10	20	20	20	30
Bhutan	..	..	..	..	..	..	..	..	..	..	40
India	50	50	50	60	60	60	60	60	70	60	60
Nepal	..	..	..	..	..	..	..	..	..	..	..
Pakistan	50	50	40	40	40	40	40	40	40	50	50
Sri Lanka	40	40	40	30	50	40	50	50	70	100	110
EAST ASIA AND PACIFIC	*40*	*40*	*40*	*50*	*50*	*60*	*60*	*60*	*80*	*80*	*80*
China	30	30	30	30	30	40	30	40	50	50	50
Fiji	310	340	370	400	350	370	370	360	390	510	540
Indonesia	20	30	30	40	50	50	50	60	70	70	70
Korea, Rep.	220	240	220	270	340	330	370	460	590	670	520
Malaysia	230	230	240	300	380	290	320	380	400	450	520
Mongolia	..	..	..	..	..	..	..	..	..	..	..
Papua New Guinea	520	550	360	220	230	220	200	210	210	250	250
Philippines	100	90	90	90	110	130	150	150	160	170	180
Solomon Islands	..	..	..	..	..	..	..	..	..	..	160
Thailand	140	130	120	160	150	150	140	170	200	190	190
Tonga	..	..	..	..	..	..	..	..	..	..	..
Vanuatu	..	..	..	..	..	..	..	..	..	..	..
Western Samoa	..	..	..	..	..	..	..	..	..	430	290

1981	1982	1983	1984	1985	1986	1987	1988	1989	1990	1991	
100	*90*	*80*	*60*	*60*	*70*	*50*	*50*	*50*	*50*	*50*	*SUB-SAHARAN AFRICA*
90	*90*	*80*	*70*	*70*	*80*	*60*	*60*	*60*	*60*	*60*	*Excluding Nigeria*
100	130	80	50	70	60	50	60	40	60	70	Benin
210	190	130	120	190	140	80	130	260	..	..	Botswana
40	40	40	40	70	80	60	70	70	60	60	Burkina Faso
40	30	50	40	40	30	50	30	40	40	40	Burundi
260	250	260	240	250	390	280	160	120	100	90	Cameroon
230	270	260	250	250	290	300	310	300	310	..	Cape Verde
30	40	60	60	60	50	50	40	40	40	50	Central African Rep.
..	..	0	10	10	10	20	10	20	20	20	Chad
..	..	160	210	140	130	110	70	60	70	..	Comoros
620	820	670	570	530	330	220	180	150	150	100	Congo
320	270	230	110	150	140	120	140	80	70	60	Côte d'Ivoire
..	..	..	..	30	40	70	60	60	70	140	Equatorial Guinea
..	..	..	..	..	..	..	..	..	..	..	Ethiopia
2,570	2,290	2,090	2,100	2,210	1,800	820	800	1,230	880	890	Gabon
60	50	40	40	40	50	40	40	50	50	50	Gambia, The
40	30	30	30	40	30	40	40	50	50	60	Ghana
60	80	80	80	90	80	60	70	100	60	..	Guinea-Bissau
130	90	80	80	100	80	90	90	90	90	80	Kenya
130	140	80	100	120	100	100	120	160	200	190	Lesotho
..	..	..	..	..	..	..	..	..	..	..	Liberia
30	20	20	20	20	20	20	30	30	40	40	Madagascar
40	40	50	30	40	20	20	30	30	30	30	Malawi
40	40	30	30	40	50	60	60	60	70	70	Mali
190	230	90	120	120	120	110	100	90	80	110	Mauritania
290	240	230	280	300	360	450	470	500	510	530	Mauritius
30	30	20	20	10	20	20	30	30	30	30	Mozambique
410	270	190	190	160	140	160	240	170	..	..	Namibia
80	60	60	0	40	30	30	40	30	30	30	Niger
150	110	80	50	50	50	40	40	40	50	50	Nigeria
30	40	30	40	50	70	50	50	40	10	..	Rwanda
60	80	80	70	60	80	80	90	70	80	80	Senegal
..	..	..	720	830	830	700	800	890	920	..	Seychelles
30	20	20	20	20	20	20	20	20	20	..	Sierra Leone
50	50	40	50	60	40	50	30	40	..	..	Somalia
100	170	120	100	30	90	70	60	60	50	50	Sudan
..	..	..	..	..	..	..	..	..	..	..	Swaziland
40	50	30	40	40	40	30	40	..	..	..	Tanzania
140	110	80	80	110	90	80	80	80	80	80	Togo
..	..	..	..	..	..	..	..	..	..	..	Uganda
40	30	30	40	40	30	30	30	30	20	..	Zaire
80	60	40	50	50	70	40	40	40	50	30	Zambia
310	260	180	190	220	190	120	190	190	190	220	Zimbabwe
70	*60*	*60*	*60*	*70*	*60*	*70*	*70*	*70*	*70*	*70*	*SOUTH ASIA*
30	30	20	20	20	20	20	20	20	20	..	Bangladesh
60	60	70	60	80	70	60	90	..	..	..	Bhutan
70	70	60	60	70	70	70	80	80	80	80	India
..	..	..	..	..	..	..	..	..	..	..	Nepal
50	50	60	60	60	60	60	60	60	60	60	Pakistan
100	100	100	100	90	90	100	110	100	100	100	Sri Lanka
90	*90*	*100*	*110*	*130*	*130*	*140*	*150*	*170*	*180*	*190*	*EAST ASIA AND PACIFIC*
50	50	60	70	100	100	110	120	120	130	130	China
560	400	340	300	280	320	240	190	210	320	260	Fiji
130	120	120	120	140	140	140	130	150	170	180	Indonesia
530	560	630	710	730	810	920	1,030	1,310	1,540	1,700	Korea, Rep.
590	660	690	710	550	470	440	530	620	750	870	Malaysia
..	..	..	880	1,030	1,120	780	740	780	540	..	Mongolia
240	260	270	240	170	170	180	240	180	170	220	Papua New Guinea
180	190	200	130	90	90	100	110	140	140	100	Philippines
150	130	140	140	150	140	140	170	..	..	..	Solomon Islands
200	180	210	220	210	190	220	290	330	400	410	Thailand
..	..	..	..	..	..	..	..	..	..	..	Tonga
..	..	250	260	300	330	310	270	310	..	..	Vanuatu
300	200	190	210	190	190	230	190	190	230	..	Western Samoa

Table 4. Gross domestic investment per capita (cont'd.)

1987 US dollars	1970	1971	1972	1973	1974	1975	1976	1977	1978	1979	1980
LATIN AMERICA AND CARIBBEAN	*330*	*340*	*360*	*400*	*460*	*470*	*470*	*490*	*490*	*490*	*530*
Argentina	610	660	660	620	610	610	640	770	630	690	740
Bahamas	..	..	..	..	..	..	..	810	770	1,060	1,580
Barbados	..	..	..	..	..	..	..	..	..	..	..
Belize	..	..	..	..	..	..	..	..	..	..	..
Bolivia	300	320	380	330	320	450	390	400	390	330	240
Brazil	310	340	390	470	540	580	570	550	560	550	600
Chile	310	300	210	190	330	150	150	180	210	270	350
Colombia	180	190	180	190	220	180	190	220	230	220	240
Costa Rica	290	350	320	370	390	350	430	510	500	530	560
Dominican Rep.	90	110	120	150	170	180	160	170	170	180	190
Ecuador	210	250	210	230	310	350	320	380	410	390	410
El Salvador	120	150	130	170	210	180	200	280	280	210	140
Grenada	..	..	..	..	..	..	..	..	..	..	..
Guatemala	130	140	120	140	180	150	200	220	230	190	160
Guyana	350	290	240	350	310	530	450	310	210	290	290
Haiti	20	20	30	30	40	40	50	50	60	70	70
Honduras	160	120	120	140	190	140	150	190	230	230	210
Jamaica	710	700	610	810	590	650	450	300	340	320	240
Mexico	360	330	350	390	440	450	430	420	460	520	620
Nicaragua	190	190	130	250	340	190	190	310	130	-50	150
Panama	480	570	640	640	590	560	540	370	450	470	540
Paraguay	90	90	100	140	150	160	190	200	250	280	380
Peru	220	250	210	320	430	400	340	280	260	290	390
St. Vincent	..	..	..	..	..	..	..	210	250	300	320
Trinidad and Tobago	410	640	560	500	720	870	980	1,000	1,260	1,280	1,550
Uruguay	320	340	290	270	280	360	430	500	570	700	730
Venezuela	..	..	..	..	880	1,050	1,220	1,500	1,430	1,100	890
MIDDLE EAST AND NORTH AFRICA	*240*	*240*	*270*	*300*	*380*	*500*	*530*	*540*	*440*	*430*	*480*
Algeria	490	470	530	640	850	900	900	1,020	1,190	1,070	1,060
Egypt, Arab Rep.	50	40	40	50	80	120	120	130	140	150	150
Iran, Islamic Rep.	470	480	580	630	750	1,140	1,210	1,150	720	710	950
Jordan	..	..	..	..	..	..	..	..	..	..	..
Morocco	120	130	110	110	130	200	230	260	190	190	190
Oman	..	..	..	..	..	..	..	..	1,130	1,280	1,270
Saudi Arabia	..	..	..	..	..	..	..	..	..	..	..
Syrian Arab Rep.	..	..	..	..	..	240	310	340	290	280	330
Tunisia	260	260	320	290	330	340	360	360	380	400	390
EUROPE	*..*	*..*	*..*	*..*	*..*	*..*	*..*	*..*	*..*	*..*	*640*
Bulgaria	..	..	..	..	..	..	..	..	..	..	840
Czechoslovakia	..	..	..	..	..	..	..	..	..	..	1,090
Greece	1,040	1,100	1,220	1,540	1,180	1,150	1,160	1,160	1,230	1,340	1,270
Hungary	370	480	420	420	470	610	610	670	810	690	670
Malta	770	690	630	550	610	610	750	780	790	850	930
Poland	..	..	..	..	..	..	..	..	..	..	570
Portugal	880	960	1,090	1,260	1,140	790	860	1,030	1,090	1,170	1,290
Romania	..	..	..	..	..	440	530	540	620	600	590
Turkey	200	190	200	220	270	320	330	360	260	260	280
Yugoslavia	370	400	360	400	430	470	480	560	540	660	630
Low- and middle-income economies	**110**	**120**	**120**	**130**	**150**	**160**	**160**	**170**	**170**	**170**	**180**
Low-income economies	40	40	40	40	40	50	50	50	60	60	60
Low-income Africa	50	60	60	60	70	80	90	100	80	70	80
China and India	40	40	40	40	40	50	40	50	60	60	50
Other low-income	30	30	30	30	40	40	40	50	50	60	60
Middle-income economies	350	360	370	420	470	510	520	540	530	530	570
High-income economies	**2,580**	**2,620**	**2,740**	**2,990**	**2,860**	**2,500**	**2,720**	**2,810**	**2,910**	**3,020**	**2,930**
OECD members	2,630	2,670	2,790	3,050	2,920	2,550	2,770	2,860	2,970	3,090	2,990
Japan	3,950	3,910	4,210	4,690	4,330	4,000	4,110	4,210	4,440	4,740	4,660
United States	2,310	2,500	2,660	2,860	2,650	2,200	2,480	2,780	3,010	2,930	2,610
WORLD	**660**	**670**	**690**	**750**	**720**	**650**	**690**	**710**	**730**	**750**	**730**

1981	1982	1983	1984	1985	1986	1987	1988	1989	1990	1991	
510	*430*	*310*	*320*	*330*	*350*	*360*	*360*	*330*	*310*	*320*	*LATIN AMERICA AND CARIBBEAN*
560	440	390	340	270	310	360	330	220	200	310	Argentina
1,570	1,860	1,830	1,640	2,070	2,010	2,130	..	..	..	..	Bahamas
..	..	..	..	..	..	..	..	..	..	..	Barbados
..	..	..	..	..	..	..	..	..	..	..	Belize
230	170	100	70	80	50	70	70	70	60	..	Bolivia
510	450	340	350	400	480	460	430	430	390	360	Brazil
420	140	120	200	180	210	260	270	360	340	310	Chile
270	280	270	240	220	220	240	250	230	230	220	Colombia
340	250	320	350	370	470	470	430	450	460	390	Costa Rica
170	130	140	150	140	140	190	200	220	180	210	Dominican Rep.
350	380	260	250	260	260	250	230	240	230	240	Ecuador
130	120	110	110	100	120	120	140	170	120	120	El Salvador
..	..	..	350	390	560	570	560	550	520	..	Grenada
180	140	110	120	90	90	120	110	110	100	110	Guatemala
260	180	150	200	190	240	140	110	140	160	200	Guyana
70	60	60	60	50	40	50	40	40	40	40	Haiti
170	100	110	160	150	120	130	120	110	110	110	Honduras
300	310	310	280	270	230	290	330	390	370	330	Jamaica
700	520	370	380	420	320	330	370	380	410	420	Mexico
220	170	180	180	170	160	150	110	90	80	80	Nicaragua
600	560	420	370	380	410	410	150	60	140	290	Panama
420	330	240	230	230	230	240	240	260	250	260	Paraguay
460	410	250	220	190	250	310	270	180	190	200	Peru
300	290	270	310	350	380	420	..	..	..	..	St. Vincent
1,270	1,320	1,160	1,140	1,160	1,010	800	650	660	640	800	Trinidad and Tobago
670	540	340	280	250	290	340	320	280	270	270	Uruguay
860	900	430	560	570	580	650	730	340	300	490	Venezuela
520	*390*	*510*	*450*	*450*	*460*	*400*	*340*	*350*	*..*	*..*	*MIDDLE EAST AND NORTH AFRICA*
1,070	1,040	1,070	1,060	1,020	930	840	770	770	750	690	Algeria
150	170	170	180	190	160	130	140	130	130	130	Egypt, Arab Rep.
1,070	490	1,010	710	690	800	690	490	560	..	..	Iran, Islamic Rep.
..	..	640	550	460	500	490	450	310	270	270	Jordan
190	220	170	180	190	190	170	180	200	210	200	Morocco
1,510	1,960	2,030	2,930	3,010	2,200	1,080	..	..	..	..	Oman
..	..	..	..	..	..	..	..	..	..	..	Saudi Arabia
330	330	330	330	330	280	180	170	130	130	..	Syrian Arab Rep.
440	420	400	430	360	290	260	200	270	340	330	Tunisia
590	*580*	*550*	*550*	*560*	*580*	*580*	*570*	*580*	*500*	*..*	*EUROPE*
910	880	890	930	930	1,070	1,040	1,120	1,070	800	460	Bulgaria
1,000	970	920	890	910	970	980	940	990	1,040	550	Czechoslovakia
1,080	1,000	990	930	1,010	910	790	960	950	940	..	Greece
650	630	610	600	580	630	660	640	630	570	530	Hungary
1,120	1,510	1,300	1,270	1,270	1,170	1,270	1,550	1,590	..	..	Malta
440	420	440	460	470	490	490	530	560	410	310	Poland
1,310	1,380	1,080	870	870	990	990	990	1,080	..	..	Portugal
500	510	520	550	530	570	530	480	460	450	280	Romania
290	270	260	260	290	320	330	300	280	320	250	Turkey
630	610	600	610	590	580	600	570	620	280	..	Yugoslavia
190	**170**	**160**	**160**	**170**	**170**	**170**	**180**	**180**	**180**	**170**	**Low- and middle-income economies**
60	60	60	70	80	80	80	90	90	90	90	Low-income economies
80	70	50	40	40	40	40	40	40	40	40	Low-income Africa
60	60	60	70	90	90	90	100	110	110	110	China and India
80	80	80	80	80	80	80	80	80	90	90	Other low-income
560	490	460	450	440	460	450	450	450	440	430	Middle-income economies
2,870	**2,690**	**2,740**	**3,040**	**3,100**	**3,170**	**3,330**	**3,590**	**3,810**	**3,900**	**..**	**High-income economies**
2,930	2,740	2,790	3,100	3,180	3,260	3,420	3,690	3,920	4,010	..	OECD members
4,730	4,680	4,540	4,770	5,060	5,240	5,650	6,410	6,970	7,660	..	Japan
2,770	2,320	2,490	3,190	3,180	3,170	3,260	3,330	3,440	3,350	..	United States
720	**660**	**660**	**710**	**720**	**730**	**760**	**800**	**840**	**840**	**..**	**WORLD**

Table 5. Gross national income

Average annual growth (percent)	1970	1971	1972	1973	1974	1975	1976	1977	1978	1979	1980
SUB-SAHARAN AFRICA	*6.5*	*4.6*	*0.9*	*5.2*	*21.2*	*-4.7*	*9.0*	*8.2*	*-1.5*	*0.4*	*11.9*
Excluding Nigeria	*3.7*	*2.0*	*1.8*	*2.4*	*9.9*	*-1.2*	*8.3*	*7.1*	*-0.9*	*1.1*	*4.4*
Benin	4.9	-0.3	1.8	8.8	-3.0	-6.1	-0.5	8.2	1.8	5.1	4.6
Botswana	3.6	7.2	20.4	30.0	28.7	-8.6	12.8	2.9	2.2	31.7	24.0
Burkina Faso	-1.0	1.2	1.5	2.2	8.7	-0.1	11.6	1.3	-2.8	3.9	3.0
Burundi	38.9	36.6	-6.8	10.4	-2.5	-1.8	17.3	20.0	-11.0	4.0	-2.0
Cameroon	5.1	-0.8	-2.4	5.2	14.4	-2.8	2.1	16.4	9.7	7.4	14.6
Cape Verde	..	..	..	..	12.5	-4.3	15.0	13.9	4.4	15.5	47.2
Central African Rep.	4.4	-0.1	1.1	0.8	-2.6	-8.3	18.0	9.8	2.1	-4.5	-5.6
Chad	2.4	-2.4	3.4	-7.0	7.9	0.2	1.5	0.0	0.2	-25.1	-1.8
Comoros	..	..	..	..	..	..	..	..	..	..	..
Congo	4.0	7.2	0.2	19.1	22.1	-11.4	1.2	-10.4	0.8	12.4	28.1
Côte d'Ivoire	8.9	5.8	3.9	7.7	10.0	4.7	12.3	12.7	6.4	-1.9	2.4
Equatorial Guinea	..	..	..	..	..	..	..	..	..	..	..
Ethiopia	..	..	..	..	..	..	..	..	..	..	..
Gabon	19.7	6.7	7.5	0.6	73.2	9.5	30.7	-11.1	-22.4	7.6	23.6
Gambia, The	-5.0	1.7	12.8	-5.9	19.5	4.9	-2.0	17.0	-13.4	14.5	-3.7
Ghana	1.6	-2.8	-3.7	16.0	7.0	-11.6	-8.5	10.5	7.4	-1.6	3.3
Guinea-Bissau	..	0.8	4.4	1.9	4.0	3.8	-3.8	-5.9	14.2	4.3	-25.7
Kenya	0.4	13.6	16.2	1.5	1.4	-3.8	6.1	18.9	-1.0	4.2	3.1
Lesotho	14.3	10.0	9.5	29.9	14.2	11.0	12.0	15.5	10.0	-1.1	-1.3
Liberia	..	..	..	..	..	..	..	..	..	..	..
Madagascar	7.8	0.6	-0.8	-3.1	-0.9	-0.7	-2.4	1.9	-3.7	6.3	-1.1
Malawi	5.7	17.5	2.8	1.2	9.8	5.6	1.0	4.6	9.2	-6.0	-3.2
Mali	4.8	1.3	4.9	-3.5	-4.5	13.6	16.8	7.3	-2.8	9.0	-2.1
Mauritania	14.6	-1.3	-2.0	-3.5	20.6	-2.2	9.0	-7.4	-4.9	0.8	5.0
Mauritius	3.7	4.7	14.0	6.5	44.2	5.9	-3.8	3.1	3.9	3.8	-13.3
Mozambique	..	..	..	..	..	..	..	..	..	..	..
Namibia	..	..	..	..	..	..	..	..	..	..	..
Niger	1.8	6.3	-6.1	-22.0	22.5	-18.9	2.9	12.9	10.7	19.3	3.3
Nigeria	19.1	15.2	-2.2	15.5	58.2	-12.7	10.8	11.1	-3.2	-1.4	31.9
Rwanda	6.1	1.6	-0.2	3.8	-0.2	3.1	7.5	9.1	5.1	13.3	6.4
Senegal	12.6	1.5	4.5	-5.0	5.2	6.0	8.1	-0.5	-5.6	7.6	-3.3
Seychelles	..	..	..	..	..	..	..	..	..	..	..
Sierra Leone	13.1	-1.2	-4.5	12.8	2.3	-6.4	-5.3	13.4	6.3	6.8	2.2
Somalia	5.7	3.6	7.1	-1.3	-19.9	36.7	0.9	28.2	5.8	-5.4	-6.8
Sudan	4.5	7.0	-2.3	-9.4	11.7	13.0	17.6	16.6	-1.4	-10.3	-0.4
Swaziland	..	..	..	..	..	..	..	..	..	..	..
Tanzania	7.2	3.0	3.6	4.5	-0.2	-0.4	10.3	2.1	-4.0	1.6	-0.4
Togo	2.3	-17.1	2.6	3.9	45.3	-25.8	18.8	7.7	6.6	-7.7	6.4
Uganda	..	..	..	..	..	..	..	..	..	..	..
Zaire	2.0	-1.8	0.2	10.7	2.0	-8.6	-4.2	2.3	-8.4	2.7	..
Zambia	-21.1	-24.0	7.9	16.4	0.3	-39.0	9.7	-11.8	-9.5	16.7	-4.6
Zimbabwe	..	..	..	..	..	..	..	-6.6	-2.5	3.3	11.3
SOUTH ASIA	*5.9*	*1.3*	*-1.5*	*3.7*	*1.4*	*7.2*	*2.6*	*8.5*	*4.4*	*-3.1*	*6.6*
Bangladesh	6.0	-5.7	-12.3	-5.1	16.6	-2.6	4.2	1.2	7.3	6.5	1.9
Bhutan	..	..	..	..	..	..	..	..	..	..	..
India	5.5	2.3	-0.7	3.9	0.0	9.3	1.8	9.2	3.8	-5.2	6.6
Nepal	..	..	..	..	..	..	..	..	..	..	..
Pakistan	9.5	-2.0	-1.3	8.1	4.4	-2.1	5.4	6.0	7.9	4.9	10.1
Sri Lanka	5.9	1.3	-4.1	9.4	2.4	0.3	11.9	14.9	5.1	2.3	2.9
EAST ASIA AND PACIFIC	*14.8*	*6.3*	*4.6*	*11.3*	*4.9*	*4.5*	*3.7*	*9.3*	*11.3*	*8.5*	*5.3*
China	24.7	7.2	3.8	8.0	1.1	7.4	-4.6	8.8	14.2	8.1	8.1
Fiji	13.7	5.3	7.9	11.8	15.3	7.0	0.7	6.3	0.9	9.5	-0.5
Indonesia	7.2	6.9	3.7	9.4	22.5	2.8	5.7	11.2	8.7	14.6	20.0
Korea, Rep.	8.7	9.5	6.0	15.0	7.2	4.8	15.9	11.4	11.8	6.4	-8.5
Malaysia	3.9	1.6	5.0	20.8	8.8	-4.5	18.5	9.9	6.3	13.9	10.1
Mongolia	..	..	..	..	..	..	..	..	..	..	..
Papua New Guinea	8.4	3.6	7.9	17.6	-1.5	-9.6	6.3	3.4	3.7	7.7	-7.9
Philippines	6.1	4.8	4.3	12.9	3.4	2.2	4.6	6.1	6.2	7.8	2.8
Solomon Islands	..	..	..	..	..	..	..	..	..	..	..
Thailand	6.6	0.5	6.5	15.6	1.0	1.9	8.8	8.3	9.7	5.2	4.5
Tonga	..	..	..	..	..	..	..	..	..	..	..
Vanuatu	..	..	..	..	..	..	..	..	..	..	..
Western Samoa	..	..	..	..	..	..	..	..	..	..	..

1981	1982	1983	1984	1985	1986	1987	1988	1989	1990	1991	
-0.5	-2.0	-1.2	1.7	3.2	-4.3	-1.6	3.1	4.2	2.5	..	*SUB-SAHARAN AFRICA*
2.1	2.6	1.3	1.7	1.1	3.3	-0.5	1.9	2.2	-1.0	..	*Excluding Nigeria*
3.2	10.1	-5.6	9.3	2.8	-0.2	2.6	2.3	-6.5	5.4	4.0	Benin
-1.2	-4.6	7.6	7.9	23.8	17.3	15.5	15.3	32.6	..	..	Botswana
3.4	11.0	2.6	-0.6	9.3	8.5	1.3	7.4	-1.7	1.9	..	Burkina Faso
8.6	-1.3	5.2	1.5	10.1	6.3	0.7	6.8	-0.3	0.9	..	Burundi
12.9	5.7	7.9	5.6	7.7	9.4	-5.1	-7.4	-3.5	-3.0	-2.7	Cameroon
3.9	4.6	7.3	4.8	6.8	5.7	11.0	3.8	2.6	14.0		Cape Verde
-3.0	7.4	-7.9	10.4	3.0	2.4	-4.4	3.2	2.6	0.8	..	Central African Rep.
1.1	7.8	13.0	1.1	22.6	-4.5	-3.5	17.6	0.9	-2.4	..	Chad
..	..	..	-1.0	5.2	3.1	-2.0					Comoros
17.7	46.7	5.3	10.5	-14.6	-28.2	6.4	-10.4	16.8	2.3	-7.2	Congo
-1.4	0.3	-1.4	4.5	3.1	7.4	-9.3	-4.0	-6.5	-8.8	-1.9	Côte d'Ivoire
..	..	..	..	..	-1.8	3.0	4.8	-3.9	2.8	..	Equatorial Guinea
											Ethiopia
8.7	-9.3	2.5	2.5	-6.3	-25.4	-20.0	0.1	5.7	-3.8	..	Gabon
-16.6	13.3	-25.5	19.0	-5.1	3.0	-7.7	25.4	-2.3	6.6	..	Gambia, The
-4.7	-13.2	1.5	8.1	4.5	4.6	4.5	5.8	5.5	..	..	Ghana
36.5	3.8	-1.6	7.0	4.1	0.2	3.9	6.6	5.4	-3.6	..	Guinea-Bissau
0.0	-0.6	0.9	4.3	1.1	10.0	3.1	6.5	4.8	5.9	..	Kenya
5.0	12.2	-1.4	3.9	-3.5	-2.3	0.8	7.7	12.5	5.4	..	Lesotho
..										..	Liberia
-11.0	-0.5	1.5	1.0	0.7	2.6	-3.3	3.2	0.9	5.5	..	Madagascar
0.7	2.4	2.3	9.4	0.2	-5.1	1.0	1.8	8.2	6.7	..	Malawi
3.4	7.6	-4.2	4.3	-2.0	15.4	4.4	1.6	10.4	-0.1	..	Mali
7.5	-4.5	2.5	-5.7	8.7	7.6	-5.7	1.4	9.2	-4.9	..	Mauritania
1.2	0.1	4.0	3.6	6.2	19.3	15.1	3.8	-1.8	5.3	..	Mauritius
2.7	-9.2	-11.3	7.8	-9.8	2.1	-5.3	15.4	1.0	2.9	..	Mozambique
-19.2	-8.0	-8.4	5.6	15.9	-0.1	-6.6	11.8	3.9	..	..	Namibia
4.0	1.9	-0.1	-17.1	2.8	8.3	-2.6	2.9	-6.7	4.4	..	Niger
-6.3	-13.0	-8.3	1.6	9.9	-26.5	-6.3	8.1	12.1	13.8	..	Nigeria
7.5	2.9	6.1	-1.8	1.7	6.1	-4.0	1.2	-6.0	-4.7	..	Rwanda
-1.4	11.1	1.5	-2.0	4.3	6.5	3.3	4.7	-1.8	6.2	..	Senegal
											Seychelles
8.4	-1.8	-2.8	2.6	-3.2	-3.5	9.6	-0.5	6.7	2.7	..	Sierra Leone
10.2	5.4	-10.3	-3.3	8.6	2.9	5.2	-1.8	-0.9	..	..	Somalia
0.9	12.3	1.3	-5.2	-6.9	3.8	4.5	-3.0	10.9	-7.0	..	Sudan
											Swaziland
-4.6	0.8	0.2	5.5	0.0	5.5	-0.7	5.2	..	..	..	Tanzania
-2.9	-3.9	-5.6	9.3	2.9	6.4	-1.7	6.8	5.7	3.6	..	Togo
..	..	..	..	..	..	..	..	..	..	..	Uganda
..	..	..	..	..	..	..	..	..	..	..	Zaire
0.6	-21.0	8.9	-0.4	9.3	-6.7	19.4	24.6	-16.1	13.7	..	Zambia
11.0	1.4	1.4	-1.2	6.5	2.1	-2.0	13.9	7.3	0.3	5.9	Zimbabwe
6.5	3.5	7.4	3.9	5.4	4.2	4.4	8.3	4.6	4.6	3.7	*SOUTH ASIA*
8.6	2.2	5.3	6.2	5.4	2.2	5.2	2.6	1.8	6.7	..	Bangladesh
											Bhutan
6.8	3.3	7.7	3.5	5.5	4.6	4.5	9.7	4.8	4.3	3.6	India
											Nepal
4.2	5.0	6.2	6.0	7.0	4.6	7.3	7.8	4.6	5.1	4.8	Pakistan
1.9	7.7	10.0	5.4	2.1	3.4	1.6	2.7	0.8	4.8	..	Sri Lanka
5.2	5.7	8.3	9.4	6.6	6.9	10.8	9.9	6.5	7.3	5.5	*EAST ASIA AND PACIFIC*
4.7	8.3	8.8	13.6	10.8	7.0	11.8	9.8	4.5	5.3	6.1	China
0.5	-7.2	-4.3	8.4	-3.5	9.4	-8.4	12.7	14.0	5.6	..	Fiji
12.9	-0.7	6.8	7.0	4.8	1.3	6.0	2.9	7.9	10.4	4.6	Indonesia
5.2	8.8	12.6	9.5	6.4	15.3	13.7	12.8	9.3	9.0	..	Korea, Rep.
2.1	3.7	5.3	11.7	-3.8	-7.0	11.0	11.4	8.1	11.6	7.9	Malaysia
..	..	..	..	..	..	..	..	..	..	..	Mongolia
-10.1	-3.3	5.6	3.8	1.5	2.0	3.1	6.2	-8.7	-6.7	..	Papua New Guinea
2.8	2.8	-0.5	-9.4	-3.3	4.3	6.3	9.6	3.6	2.9	-0.5	Philippines
-4.7	6.8	2.5	53.1	-26.3	-7.5	17.3	15.3	..	..	..	Solomon Islands
2.5	2.3	10.1	6.1	1.4	7.0	9.4	12.7	11.7	11.3	..	Thailand
..	..	..	..	..	..	..	..	..	..	..	Tonga
..	..	..	20.8	1.2	-12.1	-3.7	6.8	8.0	..	..	Vanuatu
..	..	..	-2.4	0.1	-5.9	3.3	2.6	1.0	-3.0	..	Western Samoa

Table 5. Gross national income (cont'd.)

Average annual growth (percent)	1970	1971	1972	1973	1974	1975	1976	1977	1978	1979	1980
LATIN AMERICA AND CARIBBEAN	**12.7**	**6.8**	**7.1**	**9.6**	**6.2**	**2.1**	**6.8**	**5.5**	**2.3**	**6.1**	**7.0**
Argentina	3.6	5.3	0.9	4.7	4.0	-0.8	0.2	6.0	-3.2	7.9	2.9
Bahamas	..	..	..	..	..	..	..	..	4.0	39.7	8.0
Barbados	..	..	..	..	..	..	..	..	..	..	..
Belize	..	..	..	..	..	..	..	..	..	..	..
Bolivia	5.7	3.1	5.5	6.2	10.9	-1.4	7.1	2.6	0.1	1.7	-0.4
Brazil	10.7	11.0	12.6	15.5	7.3	4.5	10.5	5.5	1.5	5.6	7.3
Chile	-0.8	7.6	-3.4	-2.4	0.7	-26.4	6.9	8.8	7.9	11.6	7.2
Colombia	10.0	5.4	8.7	8.4	4.8	0.8	8.2	7.6	7.4	3.6	5.1
Costa Rica	9.3	3.6	5.9	8.1	1.6	2.8	9.4	14.7	2.4	1.9	-0.2
Dominican Rep.	11.7	11.0	19.9	10.9	6.8	4.2	1.1	6.9	0.0	3.7	4.1
Ecuador	9.6	3.6	7.1	17.2	23.2	3.4	10.8	11.2	2.7	10.9	6.1
El Salvador	9.5	3.0	6.9	6.3	1.8	3.5	15.9	15.6	-5.4	-0.6	-11.8
Grenada	..	..	..	..	..	..	..	..	..	..	..
Guatemala	9.3	2.0	4.9	8.1	3.5	1.0	8.5	15.6	0.6	1.4	1.5
Guyana	-3.6	5.5	-8.5	-8.8	38.7	26.5	-23.8	-6.9	-4.8	-11.3	8.4
Haiti	1.0	8.1	0.5	0.1	4.9	-1.3	11.0	2.5	4.2	4.8	7.8
Honduras	1.6	1.7	6.6	8.7	0.2	-0.2	14.4	14.8	6.3	3.7	0.9
Jamaica	13.6	-0.6	13.1	0.5	1.9	3.4	-11.7	1.0	-1.4	-10.2	-9.9
Mexico	41.8	4.1	8.1	8.2	6.7	5.2	4.5	2.7	8.6	9.0	12.3
Nicaragua	1.1	2.6	-0.8	3.9	19.0	-1.6	7.4	11.5	-12.0	-33.1	16.0
Panama	6.7	11.1	5.5	4.0	1.5	2.4	-1.0	-1.0	12.2	2.2	4.0
Paraguay	5.7	6.7	7.1	11.8	7.1	1.3	13.6	18.0	7.3	-4.0	31.9
Peru	4.9	2.7	1.7	7.6	8.2	-0.4	1.1	0.2	-1.7	10.2	5.1
St. Vincent	..	..	..	..	..	..	..	..	9.3	-2.5	3.6
Trinidad and Tobago	-4.7	17.9	-1.4	6.5	8.7	-0.6	11.9	8.8	10.4	10.1	7.3
Uruguay	3.1	0.7	-1.4	3.9	-5.1	3.5	4.0	0.3	5.7	7.1	5.4
Venezuela	..	..	..	..	..	3.6	10.1	7.2	-1.1	3.9	6.1
MIDDLE EAST AND NORTH AFRICA	**8.0**	**8.1**	**11.8**	**17.1**	**14.2**	**3.3**	**15.2**	**6.5**	**-8.4**	**1.5**	**-6.6**
Algeria	9.4	-2.6	18.6	4.9	21.7	0.9	8.6	5.2	6.6	10.6	7.7
Egypt, Arab Rep.	5.4	3.2	1.3	8.8	3.7	5.8	15.9	12.2	2.1	13.2	13.4
Iran, Islamic Rep.	9.9	12.3	14.0	29.5	16.4	2.1	20.4	7.3	-18.1	-2.9	-19.5
Jordan	..	..	..	..	..	..	..	..	..	..	..
Morocco	3.7	6.4	1.1	3.7	9.7	8.4	5.9	3.4	1.8	5.8	8.4
Oman	..	..	..	..	..	..	..	..	..	..	..
Saudi Arabia	..	..	..	..	..	..	..	..	..	..	..
Syrian Arab Rep.	..	..	..	..	..	..	9.5	2.0	7.3	6.1	9.4
Tunisia	8.7	10.9	18.7	-1.6	14.6	4.3	2.0	4.1	7.7	10.8	9.5
EUROPE	**..**	**..**	**..**	**..**	**..**	**..**	**..**	**..**	**..**	**..**	**..**
Bulgaria	..	..	..	..	..	..	..	..	..	..	..
Czechoslovakia	..	..	..	..	..	..	..	..	..	..	..
Greece	7.8	7.6	8.7	8.1	-4.4	4.8	6.1	4.1	6.1	3.0	2.1
Hungary	..	..	..	..	2.9	4.1	5.2	2.8	4.7	0.6	0.5
Malta	5.6	1.9	3.6	3.0	5.4	19.1	14.2	7.9	8.2	6.0	10.0
Poland	..	..	..	..	..	..	..	..	..	..	..
Portugal	7.1	7.2	9.3	11.7	0.9	-8.5	4.8	7.1	3.3	5.7	2.0
Romania	..	..	..	..	..	..	..	..	..	..	..
Turkey	4.7	9.5	7.9	4.2	6.3	7.3	8.9	4.1	2.8	-1.7	-2.8
Yugoslavia	3.8	9.2	4.0	2.8	12.5	1.1	5.6	8.2	9.9	4.2	2.0
Low- and middle-income economies	**9.8**	**6.0**	**5.6**	**9.8**	**6.6**	**3.4**	**7.5**	**8.4**	**0.4**	**3.7**	**3.8**
Low-income economies	10.1	3.9	0.7	5.7	6.0	4.2	2.3	9.2	6.0	2.3	9.4
Low-income Africa	5.8	5.0	0.3	5.3	21.2	-6.8	8.2	10.2	-1.8	-1.0	12.8
China and India	12.5	4.3	1.2	5.7	0.4	8.5	-1.0	9.0	8.1	0.7	7.3
Other low-income	6.5	1.6	-0.7	6.0	11.2	1.7	7.7	8.9	6.5	9.9	12.7
Middle-income economies	9.6	7.1	8.0	11.8	6.9	3.0	9.7	8.1	-1.8	4.2	1.5
High-income economies	**4.0**	**3.7**	**5.3**	**5.7**	**-0.8**	**-0.3**	**4.5**	**3.4**	**4.5**	**3.3**	**0.3**
OECD members	4.0	3.6	5.3	5.7	-1.0	-0.3	4.4	3.3	4.5	3.1	0.1
Japan	11.0	5.3	8.8	7.0	-2.5	2.5	4.0	4.7	6.0	4.1	1.4
United States	0.0	3.3	4.8	5.5	-1.8	-1.2	5.0	4.3	5.0	2.1	-1.2
WORLD	**4.6**	**3.9**	**5.3**	**6.2**	**0.1**	**0.2**	**4.9**	**4.1**	**3.9**	**3.3**	**0.8**

1981	1982	1983	1984	1985	1986	1987	1988	1989	1990	1991	
-1.1	*-3.7*	*-3.9*	*4.8*	*16.0*	*-8.8*	*3.6*	*0.5*	*0.8*	*0.2*	*..*	*LATIN AMERICA AND CARIBBEAN*
-6.5	-9.4	2.9	3.3	-5.1	6.1	0.0	-2.3	-7.2	1.3	6.1	Argentina
-7.4	8.5	4.8	13.5	8.9	3.9	3.8	..	..	..	..	Bahamas
..	..	..	..	..	..	..		..	..		Barbados
..	..	..	..	..	..	..	..		..		Belize
0.9	-7.6	-3.9	0.0	-3.1	-4.9	3.0	1.8	3.0	1.8	..	Bolivia
-6.4	-0.8	-4.0	6.2	7.8	10.7	3.3	0.2	1.4	-4.9	..	Brazil
1.4	-19.1	-0.3	2.3	-0.5	6.4	10.7	13.5	9.9	0.3	..	Chile
-0.4	0.3	1.3	3.4	0.1	10.6	1.5	4.2	1.7	3.9	..	Colombia
-9.1	-9.4	7.1	9.6	2.4	12.4	-1.3	2.7	3.5	3.5	2.4	Costa Rica
5.1	-2.6	4.9	7.0	-6.8	4.9	3.2	2.9	9.6	-10.5	-2.0	Dominican Rep.
1.0	-2.6	-2.2	1.5	4.0	-6.7	-2.9	4.5	2.3	5.9	-5.7	Ecuador
-13.6	-6.8	-1.4	2.1	2.9	6.9	-3.5	5.0	0.2	-2.5	3.8	El Salvador
				6.1	17.2	17.4	6.0	-0.4	0.2	..	Grenada
-2.0	-4.8	-2.2	0.6	-1.5	2.2	1.9	4.5	3.6	1.9	3.4	Guatemala
-9.3	-18.5	-12.7	-5.5	-2.7	5.1	-13.6	5.2	15.7	-27.2	..	Guyana
-3.2	-4.7	1.3	0.4	0.7	1.9	-0.6	-2.0	-0.4	-1.0	..	Haiti
-1.8	-5.9	1.6	3.5	4.3	2.5	5.6	4.4	0.7	-4.3	-3.8	Honduras
3.8	3.0	-0.5	-2.9	-9.2	7.0	6.6	10.8	5.6	-3.0	3.8	Jamaica
8.8	-3.2	-7.2	4.4	2.3	-9.8	4.5	1.7	4.9	6.2	3.5	Mexico
2.9	-1.4	6.5	-2.8	-1.9	-2.0	5.7	-32.4	5.1	..	..	Nicaragua
5.8	1.1	2.0	4.5	3.7	6.2	-0.7	-18.4	-3.5	3.9	6.5	Panama
7.1	-2.6	-2.7	2.0	..	6.6	8.6	7.0	2.2	..		Paraguay
2.8	0.0	-13.7	3.8	0.9	12.0	11.0	-8.6	-11.8	-2.2	1.2	Peru
9.9	11.1	7.5	5.1	12.4	8.8	6.6	..	..	..	..	St. Vincent
1.7	-4.1	-6.8	-13.7	24.7	11.6	-6.1	-8.1	3.3	12.8	..	Trinidad and Tobago
2.4	-10.9	-15.4	2.0	-3.7	13.0	10.5	0.2	-0.5	-0.2	..	Uruguay
2.1	-6.6	-5.6	9.8	-2.1	-8.4	7.1	2.7	-2.4	8.9	..	Venezuela
5.4	*9.4*	*6.7*	*4.8*	*4.3*	*-5.2*	*1.8*	*-3.1*	*1.5*	*..*	*..*	*MIDDLE EAST AND NORTH AFRICA*
5.8	3.1	6.2	5.4	6.0	-8.2	1.8	-7.2	3.4	0.4	-0.7	Algeria
3.5	5.5	7.9	5.0	2.8	-2.3	-0.9	4.1	1.9	0.1	2.3	Egypt, Arab Rep.
7.9	16.9	9.4	4.5	3.3	-11.9	0.2	-9.2	2.2	..	..	Iran, Islamic Rep.
..	..	..	-0.8	2.9	17.7	0.6	0.7	-4.5	-3.8	3.3	Jordan
-4.8	9.8	-0.5	4.5	5.4	12.1	-1.2	11.1	0.2	2.7	2.8	Morocco
											Oman
..	..	..	..	..	..	..	..	..	..	..	Saudi Arabia
6.3	0.9	-0.4	-3.3	8.1	-8.5	-0.9	12.0	-1.9	15.9	..	Syrian Arab Rep.
5.9	-0.4	4.8	3.9	2.8	-5.4	6.4	-0.1	4.4	8.5	..	Tunisia
-1.8	*-0.2*	*0.2*	*3.3*	*1.6*	*4.7*	*2.6*	*4.2*	*1.8*	*-4.9*	*..*	*EUROPE*
..	..	..	2.8	3.3	5.1	6.8	1.4	-0.1	-11.6	-28.3	Bulgaria
-1.4	0.6	1.4	1.3	2.3	1.7	1.5	3.5	2.0	-1.9	-21.3	Czechoslovakia
0.5	-0.6	-1.0	1.0	2.3	1.0	1.0	4.6	2.5	0.0	..	Greece
1.6	-0.2	0.8	1.2	-0.1	0.1	4.9	0.8	0.3	-3.3	-9.4	Hungary
4.5	4.4	-5.4	2.3	2.1	1.9	4.9	10.6	8.6	..	..	Malta
-12.1	-4.8	5.6	5.8	6.1	4.6	2.5	4.3	3.7	-15.0	-6.4	Poland
-1.6	1.2	-0.6	-4.2	5.0	10.0	6.3	5.8	6.5	..	..	Portugal
-0.4	-1.3	-7.1	13.8	-9.4	0.2	1.1	18.6	1.0	-15.7	-13.7	Romania
2.4	3.3	3.2	7.4	5.7	10.0	7.5	3.8	-0.8	10.1	1.9	Turkey
0.4	0.6	-1.7	0.0	-1.3	7.0	-3.3	-2.0	0.9	-7.0	..	Yugoslavia
2.4	**1.8**	**2.0**	**5.2**	**7.4**	**-1.1**	**4.5**	**4.1**	**3.1**	**2.2**	**..**	**Low- and middle-income economies**
4.8	3.3	6.2	6.8	6.7	3.2	6.4	7.8	4.8	5.1	3.0	Low-income economies
-2.4	-3.9	-2.8	0.8	3.3	-6.8	-0.2	4.6	5.7	4.3	..	Low-income Africa
5.8	5.7	8.2	8.4	8.2	5.8	8.4	9.8	4.6	4.8	5.0	China and India
7.5	2.1	6.5	6.0	4.4	1.2	3.8	3.1	5.1	6.3	4.0	Other low-income
1.5	1.2	0.3	4.5	7.7	-3.0	3.6	2.4	2.3	0.6	..	Middle-income economies
1.2	**-0.2**	**2.9**	**4.5**	**3.4**	**3.8**	**3.5**	**4.6**	**3.3**	**2.4**	**..**	**High-income economies**
1.2	-0.2	2.9	4.5	3.4	3.9	3.4	4.6	3.3	2.4	..	OECD members
3.2	3.2	2.8	4.3	5.2	5.3	4.4	6.2	4.3	4.8	..	Japan
2.4	-2.5	3.8	7.0	3.4	3.0	3.0	4.6	2.9	0.9	..	United States
1.4	**0.1**	**2.7**	**4.6**	**4.0**	**2.9**	**3.6**	**4.5**	**3.3**	**2.4**	**..**	**WORLD**

Table 6. Gross domestic product

Average annual growth (percent)	1970	1971	1972	1973	1974	1975	1976	1977	1978	1979	1980
SUB-SAHARAN AFRICA	*8.3*	*7.7*	*2.7*	*2.6*	*7.6*	*1.2*	*7.0*	*4.0*	*-0.2*	*2.4*	*3.2*
Excluding Nigeria	*5.6*	*6.6*	*3.2*	*1.2*	*6.5*	*2.6*	*6.3*	*3.4*	*1.5*	*1.1*	*3.0*
Benin	2.1	-1.5	6.3	4.0	2.7	-5.1	1.1	4.9	1.6	6.5	6.4
Botswana	4.2	18.7	32.3	21.9	19.9	-1.3	15.0	2.2	18.6	12.0	15.3
Burkina Faso	0.1	1.2	3.7	0.4	8.3	2.7	8.5	1.5	4.8	5.9	-0.1
Burundi	26.6	44.6	-7.0	7.9	-0.7	0.7	7.9	11.5	-0.9	1.7	1.0
Cameroon	2.9	3.8	2.3	5.5	10.7	-0.8	4.3	8.5	14.7	13.3	15.6
Cape Verde	..	-7.0	-4.6	-0.7	-2.8	3.2	0.0	0.7	10.6	11.0	37.7
Central African Rep.	3.1	0.9	2.4	2.2	5.9	0.3	4.7	3.6	2.5	-2.7	-4.6
Chad	2.0	-2.2	1.1	-8.1	5.0	9.0	3.0	2.2	-0.5	-21.4	-6.0
Comoros	..	..	..	..	..	..	..	..	..	..	..
Congo	6.3	7.9	8.7	8.3	9.9	10.3	2.3	-10.8	6.1	12.0	18.8
Côte d'Ivoire	9.6	11.6	6.4	4.3	6.2	10.2	5.8	-0.2	13.9	2.9	-0.8
Equatorial Guinea	..	..	..	..	..	..	..	..	..	..	..
Ethiopia	6.5	4.2	5.1	3.3	1.2	0.1	2.7	2.7	-1.1	6.4	4.4
Gabon	8.7	10.3	11.3	10.2	39.5	19.2	35.6	-12.6	-24.0	0.5	2.6
Gambia, The	-9.9	11.5	7.2	4.6	19.8	-2.1	9.9	3.0	-5.6	17.3	-9.8
Ghana	9.7	5.4	-3.0	2.9	7.3	-13.4	-3.5	1.8	9.8	-1.7	0.6
Guinea-Bissau	..	1.1	4.3	4.0	4.3	6.9	4.8	-7.7	13.6	0.5	-18.9
Kenya	-4.7	22.5	18.3	5.8	3.6	1.3	2.2	9.4	6.8	7.5	5.4
Lesotho	2.2	6.1	9.6	29.9	11.0	-13.5	11.0	21.8	18.3	2.9	-3.0
Liberia	6.6	4.9	4.2	-2.3	4.5	-2.3	5.9	2.6	5.1	3.2	-4.5
Madagascar	5.3	4.7	-1.5	-3.0	2.0	1.3	-3.1	2.4	-2.6	9.9	0.8
Malawi	0.4	16.4	6.1	2.4	7.1	6.2	4.8	5.0	10.0	4.5	0.5
Mali	6.2	3.4	5.2	-2.5	-2.4	13.9	13.6	6.8	-2.7	10.9	-1.3
Mauritania	10.2	1.0	1.3	-6.2	10.3	-6.4	8.0	-1.3	-0.4	4.6	4.0
Mauritius	-0.4	3.8	8.0	13.3	8.8	0.4	12.3	7.8	5.7	5.6	-10.4
Mozambique	..	..	..	..	..	..	..	..	..	..	..
Namibia	..	..	..	..	..	..	..	..	..	..	..
Niger	3.1	5.7	-5.2	-17.0	8.8	-2.8	0.7	7.8	13.5	7.1	4.8
Nigeria	19.3	11.5	1.0	7.6	11.2	-3.2	9.2	6.1	-5.5	6.8	3.7
Rwanda	6.0	1.2	0.3	3.4	0.8	2.7	7.0	5.0	9.2	10.0	10.2
Senegal	8.8	1.4	5.8	-5.3	4.1	7.6	8.7	-1.5	-5.9	8.6	-2.0
Seychelles	8.9	15.9	6.3	9.1	1.3	3.2	11.3	7.4	6.8	16.5	-2.5
Sierra Leone	10.5	3.0	-0.9	2.8	5.3	2.6	-4.3	0.6	-3.1	8.0	3.1
Somalia	4.6	2.6	10.1	-1.9	-20.4	34.6	-0.4	25.2	5.1	-3.6	-4.2
Sudan	4.9	6.9	-2.1	-8.1	10.1	12.7	18.4	15.2	-1.6	-10.4	1.0
Swaziland	2.5	13.6	4.4	11.3	3.3	2.9	-2.3	1.3	13.2	-0.3	-4.8
Tanzania	7.1	3.9	7.1	6.2	2.1	4.0	3.3	0.0	2.1	2.5	2.7
Togo	0.8	0.1	8.1	4.2	4.7	2.5	-2.0	6.5	11.1	-5.1	14.7
Uganda	1.3	6.4	-1.1	-3.0	1.6	-5.3	2.6	1.5	-6.6	-14.8	-4.8
Zaire	3.5	6.5	0.0	8.7	3.4	-5.0	-5.8	0.6	-5.6	-0.2	2.4
Zambia	2.7	0.5	10.3	-0.4	6.6	-2.3	6.0	-4.7	0.8	-3.1	3.0
Zimbabwe	22.6	8.9	8.3	2.6	6.4	-2.1	0.3	-7.1	-2.8	3.6	10.6
SOUTH ASIA	*5.7*	*1.2*	*-1.0*	*3.5*	*2.3*	*7.8*	*2.4*	*6.5*	*6.0*	*-3.3*	*6.6*
Bangladesh	6.2	-3.9	-11.1	-0.2	13.4	-1.3	4.5	1.0	7.3	5.9	1.4
Bhutan	..	..	..	..	..	..	..	..	..	..	..
India	5.2	1.6	-0.6	3.4	1.2	9.2	1.8	7.2	5.8	-5.2	6.6
Nepal	2.6	-1.2	3.1	-0.5	6.3	1.5	4.4	3.0	4.4	2.4	-2.3
Pakistan	11.3	0.5	0.8	7.1	3.4	4.1	5.3	4.0	8.1	3.7	10.4
Sri Lanka	3.1	2.3	-2.3	9.5	3.8	6.5	3.5	5.1	5.4	6.4	5.8
EAST ASIA AND PACIFIC	*15.1*	*7.3*	*4.8*	*9.9*	*4.2*	*6.6*	*3.2*	*8.5*	*10.2*	*6.9*	*5.0*
China	25.3	7.6	3.5	8.3	1.1	8.3	-5.4	7.9	12.5	7.2	7.9
Fiji	12.8	7.2	7.4	11.3	2.6	0.5	2.7	5.9	1.9	12.2	-1.6
Indonesia	7.4	7.0	6.3	8.7	7.7	5.0	6.9	9.0	7.7	6.2	7.9
Korea, Rep.	8.9	10.0	5.8	15.2	8.9	7.7	13.5	11.0	10.9	7.4	-3.3
Malaysia	6.0	5.5	9.7	11.9	8.2	0.8	11.7	7.8	6.8	9.5	7.4
Mongolia	..	..	..	..	..	..	..	..	..	..	..
Papua New Guinea	10.9	6.3	5.6	6.5	2.6	-0.9	-3.4	0.8	8.5	1.8	-2.3
Philippines	4.7	5.4	5.4	8.8	3.4	5.4	8.8	5.5	5.1	5.6	5.1
Solomon Islands	5.1	2.4	-28.3	11.6	26.3	-11.9	13.8	14.4	8.9	24.8	-6.0
Thailand	9.6	4.9	4.2	9.8	4.3	4.8	9.3	9.6	10.6	5.0	4.7
Tonga	..	..	..	..	..	..	..	..	..	..	..
Vanuatu	..	..	..	..	..	..	..	..	..	..	-11.4
Western Samoa	..	..	..	..	..	..	..	..	..	10.9	-6.2

1981	1982	1983	1984	1985	1986	1987	1988	1989	1990	1991	
0.7	*2.7*	*0.0*	*0.2*	*3.4*	*3.6*	*0.9*	*4.4*	*3.1*	*1.1*	*2.5*	***SUB-SAHARAN AFRICA***
3.7	*3.7*	*1.7*	*1.0*	*1.9*	*4.5*	*1.4*	*3.2*	*2.4*	*-0.1*	*1.6*	*Excluding Nigeria*
9.2	2.8	-4.1	8.1	7.5	2.5	-1.6	3.3	-1.9	3.9	3.0	Benin
7.4	-1.1	24.0	19.1	8.4	8.1	10.3	9.2	13.4	8.7	..	Botswana
4.2	10.4	1.0	-1.7	8.5	9.4	1.2	6.2	-0.4	1.3	4.0	Burkina Faso
12.2	-1.1	3.7	0.3	11.7	3.2	5.6	4.8	1.6	3.4	3.3	Burundi
12.9	2.6	7.8	5.8	7.6	8.0	-6.5	-7.7	-3.4	-2.5	-0.7	Cameroon
8.5	2.8	9.5	3.8	8.7	2.9	7.0	3.2	5.5	4.0	..	Cape Verde
-2.2	7.5	-6.7	9.3	3.9	1.3	-3.4	3.4	2.6	0.8	0.5	Central African Rep.
1.0	5.3	15.7	2.0	21.8	-4.1	-3.4	17.6	0.9	-3.2	6.0	Chad
..	..	..	4.3	2.8	2.1	1.9	0.7	0.2	1.5	..	Comoros
13.9	26.1	7.7	7.0	-1.2	-6.9	0.2	1.8	3.1	0.5	2.2	Congo
4.3	1.6	-1.2	-1.1	5.2	3.0	-1.2	-1.6	-1.0	-2.6	-2.2	Côte d'Ivoire
..	..	..	..	..	-0.4	4.4	5.3	-0.5	3.1	-1.0	Equatorial Guinea
2.1	1.6	5.1	-2.1	-6.8	6.7	9.1	3.8	2.3	-4.1	-3.3	Ethiopia
2.2	-1.3	3.5	7.3	-2.5	-0.9	-17.1	8.3	5.3	4.7	1.7	Gabon
10.2	12.7	-5.3	3.0	0.6	2.8	6.0	7.8	5.0	4.4	4.5	Gambia, The
-2.9	-6.5	-4.4	8.8	5.1	5.1	4.6	5.5	5.0	2.6	4.2	Ghana
18.9	4.4	-3.2	5.5	4.3	-1.0	6.0	6.8	5.0	3.0	..	Guinea-Bissau
4.1	1.9	1.5	1.7	4.3	7.1	5.9	6.0	4.6	5.0	4.3	Kenya
1.1	3.7	-5.7	7.6	3.2	-0.9	7.3	12.3	9.4	8.0	7.2	Lesotho
-1.2	-2.0	-1.6	-2.1	-0.8	-1.7	-1.0	..	..	..	..	Liberia
-9.8	-1.9	0.9	1.7	1.1	2.0	1.2	3.4	4.1	3.5	3.0	Madagascar
-5.3	2.5	3.8	5.6	4.6	-0.6	1.7	2.9	5.2	4.7	4.7	Malawi
4.6	6.7	-4.5	1.3	-0.4	17.9	1.4	2.4	10.8	0.7	3.9	Mali
3.8	-2.1	4.9	-7.2	2.9	5.6	3.1	3.7	3.4	-1.5	2.3	Mauritania
5.4	5.8	0.3	4.8	7.3	10.1	9.9	6.6	4.0	6.7	5.0	Mauritius
0.5	-3.4	-12.8	2.6	-8.8	1.3	5.7	5.4	5.5	1.9	4.5	Mozambique
2.0	-4.7	-3.1	-2.0	5.7	5.9	0.2	5.0	-2.5	..	..	Namibia
1.2	-1.2	-1.8	-16.9	3.1	6.4	-2.4	5.0	-3.5	3.1	1.5	Niger
-9.3	-0.8	-6.5	-3.3	10.2	-0.6	-1.8	9.9	6.0	5.7	5.2	Nigeria
8.8	1.7	6.3	-4.6	3.0	5.2	-0.4	0.1	-5.9	-1.7	..	Rwanda
-1.7	15.1	2.1	-4.2	4.0	4.6	4.0	5.1	-1.7	4.5	1.2	Senegal
-6.3	-2.3	-1.4	7.7	10.2	0.7	5.1	4.2	5.7	6.7	..	Seychelles
8.7	0.0	-3.1	2.3	-3.4	-1.9	5.4	3.3	4.2	3.0	..	Sierra Leone
8.0	3.6	-9.2	3.4	8.1	3.5	5.1	-0.7	-0.1	-1.6	..	Somalia
2.1	12.7	2.1	-5.0	-6.3	3.9	2.2	1.2	7.9	-8.0	-0.2	Sudan
6.7	1.2	-0.8	3.8	14.4	3.7	-1.3	8.9	4.1	2.1	..	Swaziland
-1.0	-0.3	-0.5	4.6	1.3	5.3	4.1	5.3	4.4	4.1	4.5	Tanzania
-3.4	-3.7	-5.2	5.9	3.2	3.4	1.5	5.0	3.9	-0.5	3.2	Togo
7.5	11.7	9.6	-8.5	-1.9	-1.5	5.7	6.1	6.6	4.5	4.0	Uganda
2.2	-0.7	1.6	5.5	0.5	4.7	2.7	0.6	-2.0	-1.9	..	Zaire
6.1	-2.7	-2.1	-1.0	1.8	0.2	3.1	5.6	-0.9	-1.4	-1.8	Zambia
12.5	2.6	1.6	-2.0	7.1	2.6	-0.9	9.0	6.4	2.1	4.2	Zimbabwe
6.8	*4.2*	*6.9*	*3.9*	*5.5*	*4.4*	*4.6*	*8.3*	*4.8*	*4.9*	*3.5*	***SOUTH ASIA***
9.5	3.8	4.6	4.8	3.9	4.4	4.1	2.8	2.5	6.6	3.3	Bangladesh
10.1	5.3	8.4	7.1	3.2	10.0	19.4	3.2	2.6	3.6	..	Bhutan
6.5	3.8	7.4	3.7	5.4	4.5	4.9	9.8	5.0	4.7	3.1	India
8.3	3.8	-3.0	9.7	6.1	4.3	3.9	7.3	3.9	3.6	4.0	Nepal
7.9	6.5	6.8	5.1	7.6	5.5	6.5	7.6	4.9	5.3	6.5	Pakistan
5.6	7.5	3.9	-0.3	9.8	4.4	0.7	2.7	2.1	6.3	3.4	Sri Lanka
5.6	*6.0*	*9.0*	*9.5*	*7.0*	*7.8*	*9.4*	*9.5*	*5.6*	*6.4*	*6.7*	***EAST ASIA AND PACIFIC***
4.5	8.7	10.1	14.4	12.3	8.3	10.9	9.7	3.4	4.5	6.1	China
6.3	-6.0	-4.2	8.5	-3.2	7.9	-6.5	0.9	12.7	4.9	2.3	Fiji
7.4	-0.4	8.8	6.8	2.6	5.8	4.9	5.8	7.5	7.2	6.2	Indonesia
6.9	7.4	12.1	9.2	6.9	12.3	11.6	11.3	6.4	9.3	8.7	Korea, Rep.
6.9	6.0	6.4	7.8	-1.1	1.2	5.4	8.9	8.7	9.8	8.6	Malaysia
8.4	8.4	5.7	7.8	4.7	8.3	4.5	5.1	4.2	-2.1	..	Mongolia
0.2	0.3	3.0	-0.5	4.3	3.3	3.5	3.0	-1.8	-1.5	7.8	Papua New Guinea
3.4	3.6	1.8	-7.3	-7.3	3.4	4.8	6.3	5.9	2.1	0.7	Philippines
13.4	2.9	13.9	1.2	0.8	19.8	1.7	4.3	5.7	3.4	..	Solomon Islands
6.3	4.0	7.2	7.2	3.4	5.1	9.6	13.4	12.2	10.3	8.2	Thailand
..	..	..	2.4	5.6	3.2	3.4	-2.2	3.6	2.5	..	Tonga
4.2	10.7	5.6	6.8	1.1	-2.0	0.3	0.5	4.4	..	..	Vanuatu
-9.0	-1.0	0.4	1.3	4.0	5.4	0.5	0.0	2.2	-4.5	..	Western Samoa

Table 6. Gross domestic product (cont'd.)

Average annual growth (percent)	1970	1971	1972	1973	1974	1975	1976	1977	1978	1979	1980
LATIN AMERICA AND CARIBBEAN	*6.6*	*6.5*	*6.9*	*8.6*	*6.5*	*3.3*	*5.9*	*4.8*	*3.6*	*6.2*	*5.9*
Argentina	4.6	4.4	2.1	3.7	5.5	-0.5	-0.2	6.5	-3.4	7.2	1.9
Bahamas	-5.6	1.6	-3.5	7.6	-16.8	-14.8	5.2	9.2	14.2	26.1	6.5
Barbados	9.7	4.5	1.9	1.3	-4.7	4.0	0.0	4.3	6.1	7.7	4.7
Belize	4.8	4.0	10.2	5.4	13.6	3.6	0.0	6.5	7.9	6.3	3.6
Bolivia	-0.3	4.9	5.4	5.3	5.1	6.6	6.1	4.2	3.4	0.0	-0.9
Brazil	8.7	11.3	12.3	14.4	9.0	5.2	9.8	4.6	3.2	6.8	9.1
Chile	2.0	9.1	-1.1	-5.5	0.8	-13.2	3.6	9.8	8.4	8.3	7.8
Colombia	7.1	6.0	7.6	6.7	5.7	2.1	4.8	4.1	8.4	5.4	4.1
Costa Rica	7.6	6.8	8.2	7.7	5.4	2.0	5.4	8.9	6.2	5.0	0.7
Dominican Rep.	18.2	10.9	10.4	12.9	5.8	4.8	6.7	4.9	2.3	4.3	6.1
Ecuador	6.5	6.6	16.6	28.4	5.8	5.3	9.7	6.4	7.0	5.4	4.6
El Salvador	3.1	4.8	5.4	4.9	6.5	5.3	3.7	5.8	6.7	-1.6	-8.5
Grenada	..	..	..	..	..	..	..	..	..	..	..
Guatemala	5.7	5.6	7.3	6.8	6.4	2.0	7.4	7.8	5.0	4.7	3.8
Guyana	4.6	3.0	-2.8	1.5	7.9	7.9	1.4	-2.7	-1.5	-2.1	1.8
Haiti	-0.3	8.4	1.4	1.2	6.3	-2.3	8.6	0.5	4.8	7.3	7.6
Honduras	3.8	3.9	5.9	7.9	-0.9	2.5	10.5	10.5	8.3	6.3	1.3
Jamaica	11.9	3.1	9.1	0.4	-3.3	-0.8	-7.1	-2.8	0.4	-2.1	-6.2
Mexico	7.3	4.2	8.5	8.2	6.1	5.7	4.2	3.2	8.2	9.3	8.4
Nicaragua	0.8	3.3	2.0	6.5	14.2	-0.2	4.8	8.8	-7.9	-26.5	4.6
Panama	7.0	9.6	4.6	5.4	2.6	1.7	1.6	1.1	9.8	4.6	15.4
Paraguay	4.8	5.4	6.4	7.2	8.3	6.4	6.8	10.7	10.9	11.1	14.5
Peru	5.5	4.2	2.6	5.2	9.3	3.5	1.9	0.4	0.2	5.8	4.5
St. Vincent	10.7	3.0	25.8	-11.1	-8.8	-7.6	5.5	5.1	10.7	3.1	2.1
Trinidad and Tobago	-2.8	8.3	4.6	2.1	5.4	1.9	9.6	6.4	11.7	4.6	8.0
Uruguay	2.5	-0.3	-1.6	0.4	2.9	6.1	3.9	1.5	4.9	6.0	6.2
Venezuela	7.7	1.5	1.3	7.1	2.1	2.9	7.7	6.3	2.4	0.8	-4.5
MIDDLE EAST AND NORTH AFRICA	*7.7*	*2.2*	*6.4*	*9.6*	*3.6*	*6.1*	*14.7*	*6.4*	*-3.3*	*6.3*	*-9.1*
Algeria	8.8	-7.6	19.8	3.0	7.4	5.1	8.4	5.3	9.2	7.4	0.9
Egypt, Arab Rep.	6.0	4.2	2.6	5.1	3.9	10.1	15.4	13.1	7.7	7.9	10.8
Iran, Islamic Rep.	12.2	2.2	12.9	15.0	3.8	2.4	17.5	6.7	-17.1	-9.2	-19.3
Jordan	..	..	..	..	..	..	..	..	..	..	..
Morocco	4.9	5.6	2.4	3.5	5.4	6.7	11.0	4.9	2.9	4.6	9.1
Oman	13.9	0.9	9.8	-14.3	11.5	24.4	20.5	1.0	-3.7	1.1	3.8
Saudi Arabia	9.4	14.4	15.4	19.7	15.6	-0.4	7.4	15.2	4.3	5.5	9.4
Syrian Arab Rep.	-2.6	10.1	23.0	-6.7	22.7	20.4	10.7	-0.8	7.9	4.5	10.6
Tunisia	6.8	11.0	18.7	-0.4	8.1	7.1	7.9	3.4	6.4	6.6	7.4
EUROPE	*..*	*..*	*..*	*..*	*..*	*..*	*..*	*..*	*..*	*..*	*..*
Bulgaria	..	..	..	..	..	..	..	..	..	..	..
Czechoslovakia	..	..	..	..	..	..	..	..	..	..	..
Greece	8.0	7.1	8.9	7.3	-3.2	6.0	6.0	3.0	6.8	3.4	2.1
Hungary	4.5	6.4	6.4	7.5	5.8	6.3	3.6	6.8	4.7	1.6	0.0
Malta	12.6	2.5	5.8	9.8	9.9	19.6	17.0	12.2	11.2	10.5	7.0
Poland	..	..	..	..	..	..	..	..	..	..	..
Portugal	9.1	6.6	8.0	11.2	1.2	-4.3	6.9	5.6	3.4	5.7	4.6
Romania	..	..	..	..	..	..	11.4	7.5	8.0	6.6	3.3
Turkey	4.8	9.2	6.6	4.2	8.6	8.9	8.8	4.7	3.3	-0.9	-0.7
Yugoslavia	4.8	8.8	3.5	2.6	14.8	0.7	5.3	8.3	9.2	5.3	2.6
Low- and middle-income economies	**8.0**	**5.1**	**4.9**	**7.6**	**5.0**	**4.6**	**6.9**	**5.8**	**3.4**	**4.8**	**2.1**
Low-income economies	10.4	4.5	1.3	4.9	3.3	6.1	1.9	7.2	6.5	1.6	6.5
Low-income Africa	8.1	7.7	1.6	2.1	6.7	-0.3	6.2	6.1	-1.1	1.2	2.4
China and India	12.5	4.0	1.1	5.5	1.1	8.8	-1.3	7.5	8.6	0.1	7.2
Other low-income	6.9	3.2	1.6	5.9	6.4	4.6	7.5	7.3	7.4	5.9	7.7
Middle-income economies	7.1	5.6	6.7	9.1	6.1	3.9	8.7	5.8	2.4	5.9	1.0
High-income economies	**3.8**	**3.4**	**5.2**	**5.7**	**0.6**	**-0.3**	**4.6**	**3.5**	**4.1**	**3.5**	**1.3**
OECD members	3.8	3.4	5.1	5.7	0.6	-0.3	4.5	3.5	4.1	3.3	1.3
Japan	10.7	4.3	8.3	7.8	-0.7	2.8	4.2	4.6	4.9	5.6	3.6
United States	-0.1	3.2	5.1	4.8	-0.9	-1.2	4.9	4.4	5.1	2.0	-0.2
WORLD	**4.4**	**3.7**	**5.2**	**6.0**	**1.3**	**0.4**	**5.0**	**4.0**	**4.0**	**3.7**	**1.5**

1981	1982	1983	1984	1985	1986	1987	1988	1989	1990	1991	
-0.2	*-1.4*	*-2.8*	*3.7*	*3.4*	*4.4*	*3.1*	*0.5*	*1.2*	*-0.4*	*2.4*	*LATIN AMERICA AND CARIBBEAN*
-6.9	-5.5	2.9	2.3	-4.8	6.0	2.4	-3.0	-4.1	-0.5	5.0	Argentina
-9.2	6.7	3.6	14.2	4.8	1.8	3.0	-1.2	0.2	0.2	..	Bahamas
-3.2	-5.0	0.2	3.3	0.3	10.4	0.6	6.9	3.6	-2.7	..	Barbados
1.4	-1.7	-0.6	5.3	2.1	3.4	16.1	9.6	13.4	12.2	..	Belize
0.9	-4.4	-4.5	1.0	-0.7	-3.2	2.6	3.8	2.8	3.1	3.5	Bolivia
-4.4	0.6	-3.4	5.4	7.9	8.0	3.3	-0.2	3.3	-4.2	0.0	Brazil
5.6	-14.2	-0.7	6.3	2.4	5.7	5.7	7.4	10.0	2.2	5.0	Chile
2.1	1.0	1.6	3.6	3.3	6.1	5.4	4.1	3.2	4.2	2.5	Colombia
-2.3	-7.0	2.8	7.9	0.8	5.5	4.8	3.5	5.7	3.8	0.9	Costa Rica
4.1	1.8	4.4	0.3	-2.5	3.0	7.5	0.7	4.0	-5.1	-0.8	Dominican Rep.
4.1	1.1	-2.1	4.1	4.2	3.0	-6.3	10.7	0.5	2.3	2.5	Ecuador
-8.2	-5.5	0.6	2.2	2.4	1.1	2.8	3.1	1.0	3.0	3.3	El Salvador
..	..	..	..	7.2	3.3	7.9	6.7	5.0	5.6	..	Grenada
0.6	-3.5	-2.6	0.5	-0.6	0.1	3.6	3.9	3.9	3.0	3.0	Guatemala
1.8	-13.6	-6.6	0.0	1.0	1.5	-3.9	-3.9	-0.2	-1.2	-2.5	Guyana
-2.7	-3.4	0.8	0.3	0.2	0.6	-0.4	-1.5	-0.6	-2.9	-3.0	Haiti
1.5	-2.0	-0.3	2.7	3.6	2.9	5.3	5.4	2.3	-1.1	1.5	Honduras
2.4	0.9	2.4	-1.4	-4.8	2.0	6.4	1.9	6.3	4.2	2.5	Jamaica
8.8	-0.6	-4.2	3.7	2.7	-3.9	1.9	1.5	3.2	4.0	4.0	Mexico
5.4	-0.8	4.6	-2.1	-4.2	-2.0	-0.8	-11.2	-4.4	0.6	-0.4	Nicaragua
4.2	5.6	0.4	-0.5	4.7	3.4	2.3	-15.7	-1.4	3.7	4.6	Panama
8.6	-1.5	-5.0	3.1	4.0	-0.1	4.4	6.5	5.8	3.1	3.0	Paraguay
4.5	0.2	-12.5	4.6	2.2	9.3	8.3	-8.4	-11.6	-4.8	5.5	Peru
8.1	9.4	5.6	5.9	6.1	4.0	12.3	9.2	6.4	5.8	..	St. Vincent
4.4	-5.9	-7.8	-13.8	-18.4	0.9	-5.1	-2.3	0.4	3.9	2.5	Trinidad and Tobago
1.7	-9.7	-9.9	-1.4	2.0	8.0	8.0	0.0	0.4	0.9	2.0	Uruguay
-0.3	-2.1	-3.8	1.4	0.2	6.5	3.6	5.8	-8.6	5.3	6.0	Venezuela
-6.9	*5.6*	*10.5*	*3.5*	*1.8*	*-3.8*	*0.5*	*-1.8*	*2.6*	*2.6*	*-0.9*	*MIDDLE EAST AND NORTH AFRICA*
3.0	6.4	5.4	5.8	5.6	1.1	-0.5	-2.6	3.9	-2.0	1.4	Algeria
4.0	10.7	7.7	6.1	6.6	2.6	2.5	3.9	3.0	2.5	2.3	Egypt, Arab Rep.
8.2	15.0	10.1	5.0	5.2	-7.9	-1.6	-6.5	2.9	10.1	4.2	Iran, Islamic Rep.
..	..	..	0.9	3.0	12.3	3.8	0.0	-7.7	1.1	0.8	Jordan
-2.8	9.6	-0.6	4.2	6.3	7.8	-2.3	10.2	1.4	2.9	4.4	Morocco
16.7	10.6	18.1	15.7	15.6	6.3	1.4	..	..	..	..	Oman
7.2	-4.9	-7.6	-8.2	-4.4	5.3	-1.8	7.4	0.0	8.7	..	Saudi Arabia
9.6	2.5	1.6	-4.4	6.1	-4.1	0.8	13.5	-5.6	14.0	..	Syrian Arab Rep.
5.5	-0.5	4.7	5.8	5.8	-1.5	6.1	1.0	3.7	7.1	3.0	Tunisia
-0.2	*1.0*	*2.2*	*3.3*	*2.4*	*3.7*	*2.2*	*2.2*	*0.7*	*-3.1*	*..*	*EUROPE*
4.9	1.9	4.0	3.3	2.5	4.2	6.0	2.6	-0.6	-11.6	-25.9	Bulgaria
0.1	0.7	2.4	2.1	2.1	1.8	0.7	2.6	1.3	-3.5	-14.7	Czechoslovakia
0.0	0.5	0.1	2.8	3.1	1.4	-0.6	4.1	2.8	0.3	..	Greece
3.9	1.9	0.7	2.6	-0.1	1.5	4.5	-0.5	0.1	-3.9	-7.7	Hungary
3.3	2.3	-0.6	0.9	2.6	3.9	4.1	8.4	8.2	5.5	..	Malta
-10.0	-4.8	5.6	5.6	5.1	4.2	2.1	4.0	0.3	-12.0	-8.0	Poland
1.0	3.1	-0.1	-1.6	3.3	4.3	4.3	4.5	5.0	4.4	..	Portugal
0.1	3.9	6.0	6.1	-0.1	2.1	0.5	-0.3	-5.8	-8.1	-9.0	Romania
4.2	4.9	3.8	5.9	5.1	8.3	7.5	3.7	1.3	9.1	2.4	Turkey
1.2	0.6	-1.1	1.7	-0.6	3.6	-2.0	-1.6	0.6	-7.6	..	Yugoslavia
0.5	**2.3**	**3.7**	**4.5**	**3.7**	**3.3**	**3.9**	**3.7**	**3.0**	**1.9**	**2.2**	**Low- and middle-income economies**
4.6	4.9	6.7	6.6	7.0	5.5	6.3	8.0	4.4	4.4	4.6	Low-income economies
-1.6	2.3	-1.2	-1.4	2.7	2.9	1.8	5.3	4.3	1.2	3.2	Low-income Africa
5.6	6.0	8.7	8.9	8.9	6.5	8.1	9.7	4.2	4.6	4.7	China and India
6.6	3.7	6.8	5.6	4.6	4.4	3.8	4.3	5.1	5.5	4.9	Other low-income
-0.6	1.0	2.0	3.2	2.1	2.4	2.6	2.0	2.3	0.9	0.9	Middle-income economies
1.7	**-0.2**	**2.7**	**4.6**	**3.5**	**2.8**	**3.4**	**4.5**	**3.4**	**2.6**	**..**	**High-income economies**
1.7	-0.2	2.7	4.6	3.5	2.9	3.3	4.5	3.3	2.6	..	OECD members
3.6	3.2	2.7	4.3	5.0	2.7	4.1	6.2	4.6	5.6	..	Japan
2.3	-2.6	3.7	7.1	3.8	3.2	3.5	4.5	2.8	0.9	..	United States
1.5	**0.2**	**2.8**	**4.5**	**3.5**	**2.9**	**3.4**	**4.4**	**3.3**	**2.5**	**..**	**WORLD**

Table 7. Agriculture: contribution to growth of gross domestic product

Percentage points	1970	1971	1972	1973	1974	1975	1976	1977	1978	1979	1980
SUB-SAHARAN AFRICA	*3.7*	*1.9*	*0.2*	*0.2*	*2.3*	*-1.1*	*0.8*	*1.5*	*-0.1*	*-0.6*	*0.6*
Excluding Nigeria	*2.2*	*1.6*	*1.3*	*-0.9*	*1.6*	*0.1*	*1.2*	*1.2*	*1.0*	*-0.4*	*0.2*
Benin	..	-1.3	1.2	4.8	-5.5	-1.7	3.6	-0.2	3.5	1.7	1.1
Botswana	-5.6	4.5	7.9	5.3	9.5	-3.1	0.3	1.0	-1.5	0.0	-0.6
Burkina Faso	..	0.6	-0.1	-2.5	6.4	-0.4	1.7	-2.5	2.2	-2.6	0.9
Burundi	23.3	31.4	-6.4	7.6	-2.6	2.9	2.4	2.6	-1.7	0.9	0.8
Cameroon	1.8	0.5	2.1	1.5	1.8	0.4	0.5	0.5	1.2	4.4	2.5
Cape Verde	..	..	..	..	..	..	..	..	..	..	..
Central African Rep.	0.7	1.3	0.2	0.3	1.7	0.9	1.3	0.7	1.2	-0.6	-0.6
Chad	-0.3	-1.1	1.5	-6.2	1.4	3.8	-0.5	0.5	0.6	-4.3	2.0
Comoros	..	..	..	..	..	..	..	..	..	..	..
Congo	1.8	0.7	0.8	0.7	0.7	0.6	-0.8	0.6	-0.1	1.1	1.2
Côte d'Ivoire	2.6	4.5	0.3	3.2	-5.6	4.1	2.5	-2.0	4.6	0.2	5.3
Equatorial Guinea	..	..	..	..	..	..	..	..	..	..	..
Ethiopia	1.4	1.1	2.0	0.4	-0.3	-1.0	1.4	-0.2	-0.7	1.2	2.4
Gabon	..	..	..	..	..	..	..	..	..	..	..
Gambia, The	-3.5	4.1	2.5	1.7	7.0	-2.2	0.5	-0.1	-4.6	1.6	-1.8
Ghana	6.0	2.6	2.1	-1.1	4.8	-11.1	-0.8	-2.8	9.2	2.0	1.2
Guinea-Bissau	..	-5.2	5.0	-0.5	2.1	0.8	4.4	-7.5	7.9	-4.4	-18.9
Kenya	-3.3	6.5	4.4	1.0	-0.9	2.6	0.7	3.6	1.4	1.0	0.4
Lesotho	..	2.2	-14.4	8.7	10.9	-12.9	-2.5	10.1	4.7	1.4	-15.2
Liberia	..	..	..	..	..	..	..	..	..	..	..
Madagascar	..	-0.6	0.6	0.3	2.9	-0.2	-2.9	1.0	-2.1	2.2	0.7
Malawi	-0.6	7.3	4.2	-2.8	0.8	0.4	4.4	4.4	1.2	1.2	-2.6
Mali	5.1	1.5	1.0	-6.9	-3.7	13.6	8.7	4.9	-4.7	9.4	-2.0
Mauritania	-1.8	-5.0	13.7	-8.6	-0.1	-6.0	0.9	1.8	-0.9	0.6	3.6
Mauritius	..	2.8	4.8	1.7	-0.5	-9.4	2.4	0.0	0.0	0.8	-6.7
Mozambique	..	..	..	..	..	..	..	..	..	..	..
Namibia	..	..	..	..	..	..	..	..	..	..	..
Niger	2.6	2.4	-4.4	-14.5	7.7	-7.9	-2.9	4.6	4.4	-1.9	1.5
Nigeria	9.4	2.7	-3.6	4.0	4.6	-4.5	-0.6	2.5	-3.2	-1.1	1.6
Rwanda	3.6	1.1	-2.2	1.9	7.3	-2.7	12.6	0.4	1.4	10.3	-0.8
Senegal	1.7	-4.7	5.5	-4.4	5.6	1.1	4.2	-2.0	-6.5	6.1	-4.8
Seychelles	..	..	..	..	..	..	..	-0.5	-0.5	0.9	0.0
Sierra Leone	0.0	0.6	-0.3	0.5	-0.2	1.1	1.4	1.5	9.6	3.7	-1.2
Somalia	..	-0.9	3.4	-2.3	-18.2	32.4	1.9	19.5	2.2	-3.6	2.5
Sudan	9.9	4.3	-0.7	-4.4	8.0	2.5	1.7	7.4	0.8	-6.9	-2.4
Swaziland	..	..	..	..	..	..	..	..	..	..	..
Tanzania	2.5	-0.8	5.1	0.6	-2.6	4.9	-3.1	0.6	-0.9	0.4	2.1
Togo	-2.3	-0.2	1.7	0.9	0.4	0.8	-1.4	-1.6	4.1	-1.2	4.2
Uganda	0.8	-1.6	2.3	3.3	-0.7	-0.2	0.5	1.9	-0.3	-10.5	-4.5
Zaire	-4.1	0.7	0.4	0.9	0.5	-0.3	1.3	-0.9	0.0	0.9	0.8
Zambia	0.4	0.2	0.4	-0.1	0.4	0.4	0.7	0.1	0.1	-0.6	-0.2
Zimbabwe	-1.5	4.1	2.3	-3.6	2.7	-1.0	1.7	-3.7	1.5	0.0	0.3
SOUTH ASIA	*3.0*	*-0.8*	*-1.9*	*2.2*	*0.0*	*4.0*	*-1.5*	*3.2*	*1.3*	*-3.7*	*4.0*
Bangladesh	2.9	-2.4	-5.6	0.1	3.9	-2.7	2.9	-1.8	4.9	0.5	0.4
Bhutan	..	..	..	..	..	..	..	..	..	..	..
India	3.1	-0.8	-2.2	3.0	-0.6	5.3	-2.5	4.0	0.9	-5.0	4.7
Nepal	..	..	..	..	..	..	..	..	..	..	..
Pakistan	3.6	-1.1	1.2	0.6	1.5	-0.7	1.4	0.8	0.9	0.9	1.9
Sri Lanka	1.4	-0.9	1.1	-0.3	1.9	-0.8	0.4	3.3	1.8	0.6	1.0
EAST ASIA AND PACIFIC	*2.7*	*1.2*	*0.0*	*2.9*	*1.3*	*0.7*	*1.2*	*0.0*	*1.0*	*1.6*	*-0.7*
China	5.4	1.0	-0.6	3.7	1.7	0.9	0.4	-0.9	2.2	2.4	-0.7
Fiji	2.5	-1.5	-0.2	1.5	-0.8	0.1	0.8	3.3	-0.3	3.8	-1.5
Indonesia	1.8	2.1	0.5	3.1	1.2	0.0	1.4	0.4	1.4	1.8	1.9
Korea, Rep.	-0.5	1.0	0.6	2.0	1.9	1.1	2.5	0.7	-2.2	1.3	-3.6
Malaysia	..	..	..	..	..	..	..	..	..	..	..
Mongolia	..	..	..	..	..	..	..	..	..	..	..
Papua New Guinea	1.1	0.8	0.9	0.5	1.2	1.1	0.4	0.2	1.2	0.5	1.3
Philippines	0.6	1.1	1.5	2.0	-0.9	0.4	2.4	1.1	0.9	0.8	0.9
Solomon Islands	..	..	..	..	..	..	..	..	..	..	..
Thailand	1.1	1.1	-0.5	2.3	0.7	1.0	1.4	0.5	2.6	-0.4	0.4
Tonga	..	..	..	..	..	..	..	..	..	..	..
Vanuatu	..	..	..	..	..	..	..	..	..	..	-4.1
Western Samoa	..	..	..	..	..	..	..	..	..	..	..

1981	1982	1983	1984	1985	1986	1987	1988	1989	1990	1991	
-0.8	**2.0**	**-0.8**	**-0.5**	**1.0**	**2.2**	**0.3**	**1.4**	**1.5**	**-0.3**	**..**	*SUB-SAHARAN AFRICA*
0.6	**2.3**	**-1.0**	**-0.2**	**0.0**	**1.9**	**0.7**	**0.8**	**1.4**	**-0.7**	**..**	*Excluding Nigeria*
-2.5	0.6	0.0	5.8	2.6	1.9	-1.9	4.1	2.3	0.5	1.7	Benin
-1.3	-0.5	-1.8	-1.1	-0.4	0.6	-0.2	0.7	0.0	..		Botswana
2.9	1.0	0.1	-0.4	2.4	3.6	-1.4	4.4	-1.0	-1.1	..	Burkina Faso
8.3	-4.5	2.4	-2.0	7.1	2.3	2.9	0.9	-1.2	2.8	..	Burundi
3.7	1.1	-2.1	2.1	-2.8	3.0	1.2	-0.8	-0.5	0.5	0.0	Cameroon
-1.1	-3.6	-0.1	0.2	3.2	1.0	1.7	0.6	0.6	0.0	..	Cape Verde
-0.7	0.6	-1.6	3.7	1.4	3.1	-1.0	2.3	0.5	0.0	..	Central African Rep.
-5.9	2.4	5.6	-6.6	14.5	-7.6	-1.3	11.4	-4.9	3.2	..	Chad
			1.2	1.7	1.1	3.1	1.1	0.9	..	..	Comoros
0.6	0.7	0.5	-0.2	0.1	0.1	1.1	0.8	0.7	0.5	0.3	Congo
1.0	-0.6	-4.8	1.1	3.9	-1.0	-0.9	2.3	2.8	2.0	-0.7	Côte d'Ivoire
					2.4	3.6	0.1	0.3	1.8	..	Equatorial Guinea
1.2	-0.6	2.3	-4.7	-7.3	3.7	5.9	-0.3	2.4	-1.5	..	Ethiopia
0.0	-0.2	0.4	0.3	0.4	-0.1	-0.2	0.8	-0.7	0.3	..	Gabon
11.3	7.2	-7.9	2.2	1.4	3.9	1.2	0.1	2.2	-2.9	..	Gambia, The
-1.5	-3.1	-4.0	5.4	0.4	1.8	0.0	1.8	2.1	-1.2	..	Ghana
11.0	2.4	-0.8	1.4	2.8	1.9	4.9	1.5	3.6	1.2	..	Guinea-Bissau
1.9	2.4	0.6	-1.2	1.3	1.6	1.3	1.5	1.2	1.1	..	Kenya
1.7	-5.6	7.4	-5.9	-1.0	-1.0	1.1	5.2	..	..	..	Lesotho
..	..	..	..	..	..	..	..	..	..	..	Liberia
-1.4	1.3	0.9	1.1	0.4	1.1	0.8	0.9	1.9	0.5	..	Madagascar
-3.0	2.3	1.7	2.2	0.2	0.2	0.3	0.7	0.9	0.0	..	Malawi
-1.0	4.4	-7.1	-4.2	-2.8	14.3	-0.9	0.5	9.8	-0.8	..	Mali
3.0	0.6	5.7	-7.6	0.9	3.3	1.1	-0.3	0.6	-5.1	..	Mauritania
3.2	3.3	-2.4	0.1	1.8	1.7	-0.5	-0.8	-1.0	1.0	..	Mauritius
0.0	0.0	-9.2	5.0	0.5	0.4	3.6	4.6	3.5	0.8	..	Mozambique
0.5	-1.4	-2.9	-1.2	0.8	0.0	2.8	0.2	0.5	..	..	Namibia
-0.2	-0.7	3.1	-3.1	5.0	2.9	-5.0	..	..	..	..	Niger
-5.5	0.8	-0.1	-1.6	5.5	3.2	-1.2	3.6	1.7	1.5	1.8	Nigeria
-2.9	5.8	2.2	-4.0	-2.4	1.1	-0.6	-0.9	-4.3	1.9	..	Rwanda
-1.3	5.2	1.1	-4.1	1.6	2.1	0.6	2.1	-1.9	2.2	..	Senegal
1.6	-1.7	1.5	-1.1	0.0	0.4	-0.3	-0.3	0.4	..	..	Seychelles
0.3	1.2	-0.3	0.1	3.8	-1.2	2.8	3.0	-1.9	0.7	..	Sierra Leone
8.5	1.8	-7.7	8.0	6.1	-0.9	5.2	2.2	-1.8	0.9	..	Somalia
-1.5	13.3	-3.5	-1.6	-4.2	5.4	1.1	-2.2	5.8	-7.4	..	Sudan
..	..	..	..	..	..	..	..	..	..	..	Swaziland
0.5	0.7	1.6	2.3	3.5	3.4	2.6	2.7	2.8	1.8	..	Tanzania
0.1	-2.3	0.2	8.0	1.3	1.6	0.5	2.1	2.5	-0.4	..	Togo
4.7	4.1	5.6	-7.5	1.7	0.4	3.8	4.0	3.9	1.9	..	Uganda
0.6	0.9	0.6	0.8	0.8	0.7	0.6	0.9	0.8		..	Zaire
0.8	-1.1	0.7	0.6	0.4	0.9	-0.3	2.1	-0.3	-0.9	..	Zambia
2.1	-1.1	-2.2	2.8	3.5	-1.0	-2.8	3.3	-0.1	-0.9	0.9	Zimbabwe
2.4	*0.1*	*3.4*	*0.1*	*0.5*	*-0.2*	*0.1*	*3.6*	*0.9*	*1.3*	*0.5*	*SOUTH ASIA*
1.4	2.9	1.9	2.2	0.4	1.4	0.2	-0.3	-0.4	3.8	0.5	Bangladesh
1.3	4.6	3.9	4.6	1.8	3.1	2.6	0.7	0.2	-0.1	..	Bhutan
2.2	-0.5	3.9	0.0	0.1	-0.6	0.1	4.8	0.8	1.1	0.3	India
..	..	..	..	..	..	..	..	..	..	..	Nepal
3.1	1.4	1.3	-1.4	2.9	1.6	0.9	0.7	1.7	0.7	1.3	Pakistan
2.1	0.8	1.5	-0.1	2.5	0.8	-1.7	0.6	-0.3	2.3	..	Sri Lanka
1.9	*2.1*	*1.7*	*2.3*	*0.6*	*0.9*	*0.7*	*1.0*	*0.6*	*1.0*	*0.6*	*EAST ASIA AND PACIFIC*
2.4	4.1	3.0	4.6	0.6	1.2	1.4	0.9	0.9	1.8	0.8	China
2.8	0.4	-4.4	5.3	-3.3	4.1	-1.7	-0.5	2.6	0.8	..	Fiji
1.3	0.3	0.6	1.0	1.0	0.6	0.5	1.1	0.9	0.6	0.5	Indonesia
2.1	1.2	1.2	-0.2	0.5	0.6	-0.9	0.9	-0.2	-0.1	..	Korea, Rep.
..	..	..	..	..	..	..	..	..	..	..	Malaysia
..	..	..	..	..	..	..	..	..	..	..	Mongolia
2.4	-0.5	0.3	0.9	-0.9	0.5	1.6	1.1	0.5	-0.2	..	Papua New Guinea
0.8	0.2	-0.8	-0.2	-0.4	0.9	0.8	0.8	0.6	0.4	0.2	Philippines
..	..	..	..	..	..	..	..	..	..	..	Solomon Islands
1.0	0.6	0.9	1.0	1.1	0.1	0.0	1.7	1.1	-0.3	..	Thailand
..	..	..	..	..	..	..	..	..	..	..	Tonga
4.6	-2.8	7.4	1.7	-0.5	-2.1	-1.4	-2.1	1.8	..	..	Vanuatu
..	..	..	..	..	..	..	..	..	..	..	Western Samoa

Table 7. Agriculture: contribution to growth of gross domestic product (cont'd.)

Percentage points	1970	1971	1972	1973	1974	1975	1976	1977	1978	1979	1980
LATIN AMERICA AND CARIBBEAN	*0.3*	*0.6*	*0.3*	*0.4*	*0.3*	*0.4*	*0.3*	*0.7*	*0.2*	*0.2*	*0.4*
Argentina	-1.2	0.2	0.2	1.2	0.3	-0.3	0.5	0.3	0.3	0.3	-0.6
Bahamas	..	..	..	..	..	..	..	..	..		
Barbados	0.9	-1.5	-2.1	0.5	-0.6	-0.4	0.8	0.2	0.0	0.8	0.6
Belize	..	..	..	..	1.9	0.8	-2.2	7.1	1.3	-0.4	0.2
Bolivia	0.9	1.6	1.6	1.2	1.0	2.0	1.3	-0.2	0.5	0.8	0.4
Brazil	0.1	1.3	0.5	0.0	0.1	0.7	0.2	1.1	-0.3	0.4	0.9
Chile	..	..	..	..	..	..	..	..	..	..	..
Colombia	0.8	0.2	1.6	0.5	1.1	1.1	0.7	0.6	1.6	0.9	0.4
Costa Rica	1.0	1.1	1.2	1.2	-0.4	0.6	0.1	0.4	1.2	0.1	-0.1
Dominican Rep.	8.9	1.5	1.0	2.1	0.0	-0.6	1.5	0.4	0.9	0.2	1.0
Ecuador	1.6	1.2	0.9	0.2	1.4	0.4	0.5	0.4	-0.6	0.4	0.7
El Salvador	1.0	0.6	0.2	0.3	1.5	0.9	-1.2	0.5	1.8	0.5	-0.8
Grenada	..	..	..	..	..	..	..	..	..		..
Guatemala	..	..	..	..	..	..	..	..	..		
Guyana	-0.1	1.5	-2.3	0.0	3.7	-0.9	0.8	-0.7	1.9	-1.7	0.1
Haiti	..	..	..	..	..	..	..	..	..		
Honduras	-1.3	2.4	0.5	1.5	-2.3	-1.6	2.5	1.3	1.5	1.7	-0.2
Jamaica	0.3	0.7	0.1	-0.7	0.2	0.1	0.0	0.2	0.6	-0.7	-0.2
Mexico	0.6	0.6	0.1	0.4	0.3	0.2	0.1	0.7	0.6	-0.2	0.6
Nicaragua	2.9	1.2	0.0	2.8	3.2	0.5	0.5	1.7	2.0	-5.2	-7.5
Panama	-0.1	1.1	-0.4	0.1	-0.7	0.8	0.6	0.6	1.0	-0.5	-0.5
Paraguay	2.0	0.5	1.2	2.0	3.1	2.6	1.2	2.1	1.5	1.9	2.3
Peru	1.4	-0.3	-0.8	-0.1	0.6	-0.1	0.2	-0.1	0.0	0.5	-0.7
St. Vincent	..	..	..	..	..	..	..	..	3.3	-3.2	-2.3
Trinidad and Tobago	0.9	-0.3	0.8	-0.6	-0.1	0.3	-0.2	0.1	-0.2	-0.2	-0.3
Uruguay	1.7	-1.1	-1.6	0.4	0.5	0.8	0.3	0.5	-1.0	-0.1	2.0
Venezuela	0.3	0.1	-0.1	0.3	0.3	0.3	-0.2	0.4	0.2	0.1	0.1
MIDDLE EAST AND NORTH AFRICA	*..*	*1.1*	*1.1*	*-0.5*	*1.3*	*1.2*	*0.9*	*-0.7*	*0.7*	*0.6*	*0.9*
Algeria	..	0.4	0.0	-0.7	2.3	3.1	-0.3	-0.9	1.2	1.0	1.3
Egypt, Arab Rep.	1.1	0.6	3.5	1.4	0.1	2.5	0.5	-1.0	1.7	1.2	1.0
Iran, Islamic Rep.	0.7	0.6	0.8	0.8	0.8	0.9	0.8	-0.5	0.2	1.0	0.2
Jordan	..	..	..	..	..	..	..	..	..		
Morocco	1.0	2.4	-0.6	-2.2	0.4	-1.3	2.7	-2.2	2.7	-0.3	2.3
Oman	..	..	..	..	..	..	..	..	..	0.8	0.7
Saudi Arabia	0.1	0.1	0.1	0.1	0.1	0.1	0.1	0.1	0.3	0.1	0.1
Syrian Arab Rep.	-7.1	3.0	20.0	-16.3	13.9	1.6	5.6	-4.0	6.2	-4.5	10.3
Tunisia	1.3	4.2	5.0	-2.3	3.0	1.0	1.4	-2.1	1.1	-0.9	1.7
EUROPE	*..*	*..*	*..*	*..*	*..*	*..*	*..*	*..*	*..*	*..*	*..*
Bulgaria	..	..	..	..	..	..	..	..	..		
Czechoslovakia	..	..	..	..	..	..	..	..	..		..
Greece	2.0	0.7	1.2	-0.1	0.9	1.1	-0.3	-1.4	1.7	-1.1	2.0
Hungary	-2.4	1.2	0.5	1.0	0.5	0.4	-0.6	1.8	0.1	-0.2	0.5
Malta	..	..	..	..	..	..	..	..	..		
Poland	..	..	..	..	..	..	..	..	..		
Portugal	..	..	..	..	..	..	..	..	..		
Romania	..	..	..	..	..	..	..	..	1.1	-2.1	-3.8
Turkey	0.6	3.3	-0.4	-2.5	2.2	2.3	1.6	-0.2	0.5	0.5	0.4
Yugoslavia	-1.1	1.1	0.7	1.5	1.0	-0.4	1.1	1.0	-0.9	0.5	0.0
Low- and middle-income economies	**1.3**	**0.7**	**0.1**	**0.9**	**0.9**	**0.9**	**0.3**	**0.6**	**0.5**	**-0.1**	**0.6**
Low-income economies	3.7	0.5	-0.9	2.3	1.1	1.6	-0.3	1.6	1.3	-0.9	1.7
Low-income Africa	4.5	2.1	-0.4	0.3	2.9	-1.7	0.5	2.4	-0.2	-1.4	0.4
China and India	4.0	0.0	-1.5	3.3	0.4	3.3	-1.1	1.8	1.5	-1.6	2.0
Other low-income	2.2	0.7	0.2	1.3	1.6	0.0	1.6	0.2	2.0	1.5	1.7
Middle-income economies	0.2	0.8	0.5	0.2	0.8	0.6	0.6	0.3	0.3	0.3	0.2
High-income economies	**..**	**0.1**	**0.2**	**0.2**	**0.0**	**0.0**	**-0.1**	**-0.4**	**0.1**	**0.1**	**-0.1**
OECD members	..	0.1	0.2	0.2	0.0	0.0	-0.1	-0.4	0.1	0.1	-0.1
Japan	-0.7	-0.3	0.6	0.2	0.0	0.0	-0.2	-0.1	0.0	0.1	-0.4
United States	0.1	0.1	0.0	0.0	0.0	0.1	-0.1	0.0	0.0	0.1	0.0
WORLD	**..**	**0.2**	**0.1**	**0.3**	**0.1**	**0.1**	**0.0**	**-0.3**	**0.2**	**0.1**	**0.0**

1981	1982	1983	1984	1985	1986	1987	1988	1989	1990	1991	
0.6	**0.1**	**0.0**	**0.4**	**0.5**	**-0.3**	**0.8**	**0.1**	**0.0**	**0.1**	**0.3**	***LATIN AMERICA AND CARIBBEAN***
0.2	0.8	0.2	0.4	-0.2	-0.4	0.2	0.1	-0.4	1.4	0.7	Argentina
										..	Bahamas
-1.8	-0.2	0.3	0.9	-0.1	0.4	-1.1	-0.5	-0.7	0.3	..	Barbados
-0.1	1.0	-1.4	0.5	-0.3	-0.9	3.7	-0.2	2.4	2.7	..	Belize
-0.2	1.8	-4.9	4.7	2.3	-1.1	1.1	0.8	-0.5	0.5	..	Bolivia
0.7	-0.1	-0.1	0.4	1.0	-0.8	1.3	0.1	0.3	-0.4	0.3	Brazil
										..	Chile
0.6	-0.4	0.5	0.3	0.3	0.6	1.1	0.5	0.8	1.2	..	Colombia
0.9	-0.9	0.8	1.9	-1.1	0.9	0.8	0.8	1.3	0.7	0.6	Costa Rica
1.1	0.9	0.7	0.0	-0.7	-0.2	0.6	-0.2	0.4	-1.1	0.2	Dominican Rep.
0.9	0.3	-1.8	1.2	1.2	1.3	0.4	1.2	0.5	0.6	0.7	Ecuador
-1.0	-0.7	-0.5	0.5	-0.2	-0.4	0.3	-0.1	0.1	1.0	0.0	El Salvador
1.6	-2.7	0.5	3.1	-1.6	-0.1	1.8	0.5	0.5	-0.2	..	Grenada
			0.4	0.1	-0.2	1.3	1.2	0.9	0.9	0.8	Guatemala
0.5	-0.3	-1.0	0.9	0.0	1.0	-0.8	-2.0	0.1	-4.5	..	Guyana
										0.3	Haiti
0.8	-0.1	-0.1	0.3	0.6	0.5	0.9	0.4	0.5	0.1	0.3	Honduras
0.1	-0.5	0.4	0.6	-0.2	-0.1	0.3	-0.3	-0.2	0.6	0.1	Jamaica
0.5	-0.2	0.2	0.2	0.3	-0.2	0.2	-0.3	-0.4	0.3	0.3	Mexico
2.9	0.9	1.9	-1.8	-1.5	-2.8	-1.0	-2.9	0.7	0.6	..	Nicaragua
0.8	-0.2	0.3	0.2	0.5	-0.2	0.7	-0.5	0.3	0.4	0.3	Panama
2.6	0.1	-0.7	1.6	1.3	-1.7	1.9	3.3	2.2	0.7	..	Paraguay
0.8	0.3	-1.1	1.2	0.4	0.7	0.5	0.8	-0.6	-1.1	-0.6	Peru
5.8	1.0	1.5	1.2	1.6	0.8	-0.9	4.2	0.3	2.9	..	St. Vincent
0.0	0.1	0.7	0.0	-2.2	-0.7	0.1	-0.1	0.5	0.5	..	Trinidad and Tobago
0.7	-1.0	0.3	-2.1	1.8	-0.4	0.6	-0.2	0.2	0.3	..	Uruguay
-0.1	0.2	0.0	0.0	0.5	0.5	0.2	0.3	-0.3	0.0	..	Venezuela
0.7	**1.1**	**0.2**	**0.8**	**1.4**	**1.0**	**0.1**	**-0.3**	**0.1**	**0.6**	..	***MIDDLE EAST AND NORTH AFRICA***
0.0	-0.9	-0.2	0.7	2.5	0.6	0.8	-0.6	1.5	-2.2	2.8	Algeria
0.4	1.0	0.7	0.5	0.7	0.4	0.4	0.5	0.4	0.3	0.4	Egypt, Arab Rep.
2.2	2.0	0.7	1.4	1.6	0.9	0.6	-2.5	1.3	1.0	..	Iran, Islamic Rep.
			-1.4	0.7	0.2	1.6	1.6	-1.3	1.2	-0.9	Jordan
-4.9	4.4	-1.6	0.5	2.6	5.7	-4.6	4.8	0.5	-1.3	0.7	Morocco
0.1	0.3	0.6	0.3	0.6	-0.4	-0.4	0.3	..		..	Oman
0.1	0.4	0.3	0.6	0.7	0.8	0.9	0.7	0.5	0.5	..	Saudi Arabia
1.0	-0.9	-0.1	-2.4	1.6	1.7	-4.1	8.4	-9.3	4.5	..	Syrian Arab Rep.
1.1	-1.8	0.4	1.9	2.8	-2.2	2.8	-4.2	0.8	3.6	..	Tunisia
0.0	**0.8**	**-0.5**	**0.7**	**-0.2**	**0.6**	**-0.4**	**0.4**	**-0.3**	**0.1**	..	***EUROPE***
0.8	1.0	-3.0	1.7	-3.3	2.8	-2.1	-0.2	-0.2	-0.7	-1.8	Bulgaria
-0.8	0.6	0.0	0.6	-0.5	0.1	-0.2	0.0	0.1	..	..	Czechoslovakia
-0.3	0.4	-1.5	1.1	0.3	0.4	-0.7	0.9	0.6	-0.8	..	Greece
0.6	1.7	0.0	0.8	-0.7	0.6	-0.5	1.2	0.0	-1.4	0.1	Hungary
											Malta
				0.8	0.7	-0.8	0.2				Poland
											Portugal
-0.1	0.5	-0.2	1.3	0.2	-1.0	-1.3	1.1	-0.8	1.7	0.3	Romania
0.0	1.3	0.0	0.7	0.5	1.5	0.4	1.5	-2.1	1.9	0.4	Turkey
0.4	1.0	-0.1	0.3	-1.0	0.9	0.2	-0.5	0.6	-1.1	..	Yugoslavia
0.8	**0.8**	**0.6**	**0.8**	**0.6**	**0.5**	**0.3**	**0.8**	**0.4**	**0.5**	..	**Low- and middle-income economies**
1.5	1.7	2.3	1.5	0.7	0.8	0.7	2.0	1.0	1.2	0.7	Low-income economies
-1.7	2.7	-0.4	-1.0	1.2	2.9	0.4	1.6	2.2	-0.7	..	Low-income Africa
2.3	1.7	3.5	2.3	2.3	0.4	0.9	2.6	0.8	1.5	0.6	China and India
1.8	1.1	1.0	0.8	1.3	0.9	0.3	0.4	0.9	1.1	0.7	Other low-income
0.6	0.4	-0.1	0.5	0.6	0.3	0.2	0.2	0.1	0.1	..	Middle-income economies
0.2	**0.1**	**-0.1**	**0.2**	**0.1**	**0.1**	**0.0**	..	..	..	..	**High-income economies**
0.2	0.1	-0.1	0.2	0.1	0.1	0.0	..	..	..	..	OECD members
0.0	0.2	0.1	0.1	0.0	-0.1	0.1	-0.1	0.1	..	..	Japan
0.3	0.0	-0.4	0.2	0.3	0.1	0.0	..	..	..	..	United States
0.3	**0.2**	**0.0**	**0.3**	**0.2**	**0.1**	**0.1**	..	..	..	..	**WORLD**

Table 8. Industry: contribution to growth of gross domestic product

Percentage points	1970	1971	1972	1973	1974	1975	1976	1977	1978	1979	1980
SUB-SAHARAN AFRICA	*4.1*	*3.4*	*2.3*	*0.6*	*2.5*	*-1.1*	*2.7*	*1.0*	*-0.3*	*2.6*	*1.1*
Excluding Nigeria	*1.6*	*1.4*	*0.9*	*1.0*	*1.1*	*0.5*	*0.7*	*0.6*	*0.2*	*0.9*	*2.0*
Benin	..	-0.8	1.5	-0.3	2.9	-1.8	-1.5	1.5	-0.7	0.8	-0.1
Botswana	26.2	4.6	10.3	7.0	5.8	0.6	7.9	-1.3	16.4	2.4	5.8
Burkina Faso	..	1.1	0.6	3.7	-3.8	5.5	3.3	-5.4	2.0	-0.8	1.0
Burundi	0.7	10.3	-0.3	0.2	0.4	0.1	1.2	2.8	1.6	0.1	1.5
Cameroon	-0.2	2.0	-0.6	0.7	0.9	0.6	1.3	3.1	1.9	7.7	7.5
Cape Verde	..	..	..	..	..	..	..	..	..	..	..
Central African Rep.	1.0	-0.1	1.6	0.5	1.3	-0.1	-0.7	1.2	1.8	-0.8	0.2
Chad	0.4	0.2	0.2	0.1	0.9	1.4	1.5	0.2	-0.7	-6.5	-2.8
Comoros	..	..	..	..	..	..	..	..	..	..	..
Congo	3.6	0.3	1.6	3.4	6.2	7.4	3.2	-6.9	1.4	7.5	8.4
Côte d'Ivoire	5.0	4.0	1.4	-0.7	-0.4	2.5	2.6	2.0	4.7	1.9	2.1
Equatorial Guinea	..	..	..	..	..	..	..	..	..	..	..
Ethiopia	1.6	1.4	0.7	0.4	-0.1	-0.2	-0.6	0.2	-0.5	2.0	1.4
Gabon	..	..	..	..	..	..	..	..	..	..	..
Gambia, The	-1.1	1.3	0.8	0.5	2.2	-0.7	0.1	0.3	3.2	-0.9	1.9
Ghana	1.5	0.3	-2.2	4.0	-0.1	-0.2	-0.7	1.0	-1.9	-3.1	0.1
Guinea-Bissau	..	-1.6	1.5	-0.6	0.2	3.2	-7.3	3.6	5.9	0.0	-2.5
Kenya	-0.8	3.9	7.1	1.5	0.2	0.1	-0.1	2.4	2.0	0.7	1.0
Lesotho	..	-2.4	5.4	4.7	2.4	-0.8	5.2	10.0	3.7	4.2	5.6
Liberia	..	..	..	..	..	..	..	..	..	..	..
Madagascar	..	-1.4	0.1	-0.3	1.0	0.0	-1.4	0.4	0.6	2.0	-0.4
Malawi	0.7	1.0	3.0	-0.2	1.4	3.2	-0.6	0.9	2.3	0.1	0.3
Mali	1.2	-2.7	1.3	0.2	0.0	1.0	0.6	1.2	-0.2	-1.7	-0.1
Mauritania	2.0	1.2	-2.1	-0.6	3.1	-2.1	2.4	-2.3	0.8	2.0	-1.3
Mauritius	..	1.2	2.5	3.7	5.7	-0.1	5.5	2.5	1.9	0.3	-2.6
Mozambique	..	..	..	..	..	..	..	..	..	..	..
Namibia	..	..	..	..	..	..	..	..	..	..	..
Niger	-1.9	1.8	0.1	1.9	-2.1	2.3	2.3	1.9	3.6	7.0	1.0
Nigeria	12.8	9.7	6.9	-0.5	6.5	-5.4	8.3	2.0	-1.5	7.6	-1.0
Rwanda	..	..	..	..	..	..	..	2.1	1.3	0.4	5.1
Senegal	1.4	2.1	0.4	-0.7	1.7	1.1	1.3	2.7	-1.4	0.0	1.2
Seychelles	..	..	..	..	..	..	..	0.1	1.3	3.6	-0.2
Sierra Leone	7.3	-1.1	-1.9	0.1	0.0	1.4	-3.7	-2.8	-4.4	1.5	3.8
Somalia	..	0.7	0.3	-3.3	0.3	-0.8	1.8	1.5	-5.4	1.9	0.5
Sudan	-0.6	-0.1	-0.7	-1.1	2.0	1.7	2.8	1.0	-1.3	-0.4	1.2
Swaziland	..	..	..	..	..	..	..	..	..	..	..
Tanzania	0.7	2.2	0.8	0.4	0.1	-0.2	1.5	-0.4	-0.2	0.9	-0.1
Togo	-1.3	0.4	3.0	2.0	1.7	0.5	1.8	3.5	0.1	-0.1	3.8
Uganda	-0.2	0.2	-0.6	-1.0	0.1	-1.6	-0.6	-0.2	-1.6	-2.0	-1.3
Zaire	4.8	2.1	0.1	2.7	1.9	-1.3	-2.7	-0.6	-2.3	-1.9	1.3
Zambia	-1.0	0.9	5.9	0.4	4.3	-1.4	1.3	-3.1	2.0	-2.4	1.0
Zimbabwe	5.2	2.5	4.2	4.3	1.0	-0.3	-1.9	-3.1	-1.7	2.2	3.8
SOUTH ASIA	*0.6*	*0.4*	*0.2*	*0.9*	*0.8*	*1.1*	*1.8*	*1.6*	*2.0*	*-0.2*	*1.0*
Bangladesh	0.1	-3.0	-6.0	5.4	4.5	-1.0	-0.6	1.8	0.3	3.0	-0.9
Bhutan	..	..	..	..	..	..	..	..	..	..	..
India	0.3	0.7	0.9	0.5	0.5	1.3	2.1	1.7	2.2	-0.8	0.9
Nepal	..	..	..	..	..	..	..	..	..	..	..
Pakistan	2.8	0.7	-1.0	2.3	2.0	0.5	1.0	1.5	2.1	1.7	2.5
Sri Lanka	2.5	0.1	-0.3	1.7	-1.0	0.5	2.0	-1.1	3.8	2.7	1.4
EAST ASIA AND PACIFIC	*6.1*	*3.0*	*2.5*	*4.1*	*1.5*	*3.1*	*1.9*	*4.5*	*4.6*	*2.6*	*2.4*
China	9.9	4.0	1.7	2.8	0.3	4.4	-1.3	4.7	5.8	3.0	4.1
Fiji	2.8	0.0	2.0	2.5	-1.1	-1.2	0.7	2.6	0.0	3.8	0.3
Indonesia	4.5	1.3	6.4	7.3	2.7	0.3	4.7	5.1	1.3	1.5	2.9
Korea, Rep.	3.3	2.7	2.1	6.2	3.8	3.3	5.8	5.2	7.0	2.9	-0.3
Malaysia	..	..	..	..	..	..	..	..	..	..	..
Mongolia	..	..	..	..	..	..	..	..	..	..	..
Papua New Guinea	..	..	..	..	..	..	..	..	..	..	..
Philippines	2.1	2.4	2.4	4.5	2.4	3.3	4.2	2.9	2.2	2.9	2.0
Solomon Islands	..	..	..	..	..	..	..	..	..	..	..
Thailand	2.7	2.4	2.5	3.1	1.3	1.4	4.9	5.0	3.8	2.2	1.2
Tonga	..	..	..	..	..	..	..	..	..	..	..
Vanuatu	..	..	..	..	..	..	..	..	..	..	..
Western Samoa	..	..	..	..	..	..	..	..	..	..	..

1981	1982	1983	1984	1985	1986	1987	1988	1989	1990	1991	
-0.4	*0.0*	*-0.2*	*0.9*	*0.5*	*0.7*	*-0.1*	*1.2*	*1.5*	*0.5*	*..*	*SUB-SAHARAN AFRICA*
0.8	*0.5*	*1.3*	*1.2*	*0.2*	*1.4*	*0.1*	*0.7*	*1.2*	*0.0*	*..*	*Excluding Nigeria*
1.9	3.6	-0.5	1.2	1.3	-1.0	0.0	-0.1	-0.5	0.9	0.3	Benin
7.2	-3.0	19.9	16.2	1.6	2.0	2.3	2.1	7.1	..	..	Botswana
-0.4	1.9	0.2	0.4	1.3	2.5	2.0	0.8	-0.6	1.0	..	Burkina Faso
1.5	1.4	0.6	0.3	1.6	0.2	1.2	0.1	0.1	1.0	..	Burundi
7.9	4.9	7.0	1.6	-2.7	3.3	-6.2	-2.3	5.6	-1.9	-0.8	Cameroon
1.8	0.0	2.7	-0.1	2.4	0.3	1.0	0.9	1.4	..	..	Cape Verde
-1.2	-0.1	1.2	0.4	0.5	-0.6	0.5	0.4	2.1	0.7	..	Central African Rep.
4.0	1.7	3.6	3.0	0.4	1.6	-1.2	1.8	2.9	-6.3	..	Chad
..	..	..	1.2	-0.6	0.1	-1.8	-1.6	-0.8	..	..	Comoros
-1.4	12.3	5.9	3.2	-1.8	-3.1	0.6	1.1	3.4	0.3	0.6	Congo
2.6	-4.1	0.7	0.7	0.8	1.5	1.9	-1.9	-1.2	-2.5	-0.4	Côte d'Ivoire
..	..	..	..	..	-1.5	1.0	1.6	0.3	0.4	..	Equatorial Guinea
0.5	0.5	0.8	0.8	0.1	0.7	0.8	0.2	0.3	-0.8	..	Ethiopia
-2.9	1.9	-1.3	5.4	0.1	0.8	-7.9	-1.8	5.7	7.3	..	Gabon
-2.9	-1.3	1.6	-0.3	0.0	1.4	0.8	-0.4	1.9	0.2	..	Gambia, The
-3.0	-2.8	-1.7	1.2	2.3	1.1	1.7	1.2	0.7	0.7	..	Ghana
-0.8	1.5	-0.3	5.4	1.1	-2.5	-3.3	1.5	0.6	0.5	..	Guinea-Bissau
0.8	0.3	0.1	0.4	1.1	0.7	1.0	1.0	1.1	1.0	..	Kenya
-4.7	8.7	-16.6	7.8	5.1	-1.7	3.7	5.1	..	..	..	Lesotho
..	..	..	..	..	..	..	..	..	..	..	Liberia
-3.5	-1.9	0.2	1.4	0.3	0.5	0.6	0.3	0.1	0.8	..	Madagascar
-0.6	0.0	0.6	-0.1	1.4	-0.3	0.3	1.3	1.5	1.9	..	Malawi
2.3	0.5	0.6	2.1	0.8	1.3	-0.7	0.6	-0.5	1.1	..	Mali
0.0	-0.7	-1.0	5.3	0.9	0.8	-0.2	1.0	2.6	-1.2	..	Mauritania
1.0	1.2	0.1	2.5	3.8	4.9	3.9	3.0	2.1	2.8	..	Mauritius
0.1	-2.2	-1.8	-2.7	-2.6	1.4	0.1	0.7	0.8	-0.5	..	Mozambique
-3.4	-2.8	-0.9	-1.2	-1.0	1.6	-0.5	0.4	-1.4	..	..	Namibia
1.1	-0.9	-2.6	-1.4	-0.7	0.2	1.0	..	..	..	..	Niger
-4.4	-1.7	-5.9	-0.2	2.0	-2.1	-1.0	3.3	2.6	2.2	3.4	Nigeria
0.6	-0.5	3.5	-0.7	-0.7	1.0	0.2	0.1	-0.2	-1.4	..	Rwanda
-1.9	2.6	0.4	-0.3	0.4	0.8	1.3	1.5	-0.3	0.7	..	Senegal
-1.3	-1.8	-1.5	5.0	2.7	0.6	-0.6	0.6	1.3	..	..	Seychelles
-2.3	-2.2	-2.9	2.1	-3.5	1.5	0.1	-0.1	2.2	1.3	..	Sierra Leone
-1.8	1.3	-1.6	0.3	0.2	2.4	0.5	-0.9	-1.1	-0.1	..	Somalia
1.2	1.6	1.8	-0.9	0.1	1.0	0.1	-0.2	0.7	-0.9	..	Sudan
..	..	..	..	..	..	..	..	..	..	..	Swaziland
-1.2	-0.1	-2.2	0.8	-0.5	0.3	0.5	0.4	0.7	0.9	..	Tanzania
-3.8	0.6	-1.5	-2.1	1.3	0.4	0.9	2.1	0.7	-1.4	..	Togo
-0.2	0.8	0.7	-0.2	-0.6	-0.5	1.1	1.4	1.0	0.5	..	Uganda
0.1	-0.9	1.0	3.3	0.1	1.4	0.3	-0.5	-1.4	..	..	Zaire
2.3	-0.3	-1.4	-1.3	0.8	-0.2	1.9	3.0	-0.3	-1.0	..	Zambia
2.8	-0.3	-0.9	-1.1	2.3	1.5	1.2	1.4	2.2	1.3	5.8	Zimbabwe
1.7	*1.2*	*1.9*	*1.6*	*1.2*	*1.7*	*1.7*	*2.0*	*1.7*	*1.7*	*0.7*	*SOUTH ASIA*
0.5	0.2	0.2	1.5	0.4	0.4	1.2	0.8	0.7	1.0	0.8	Bangladesh
6.7	2.7	2.6	-0.1	0.1	2.3	13.6	-0.1	1.4	3.2	..	Bhutan
2.0	1.2	2.3	1.6	1.2	1.9	1.8	2.3	1.9	1.8	0.6	India
..	..	..	..	..	..	..	..	..	..	..	Nepal
0.0	2.4	1.1	1.6	1.8	1.9	2.0	2.4	1.2	1.6	1.5	Pakistan
0.7	0.7	0.5	1.8	0.9	1.6	1.6	1.2	1.0	2.1	..	Sri Lanka
1.4	*1.3*	*3.9*	*3.9*	*3.5*	*3.7*	*4.9*	*6.2*	*3.3*	*4.0*	*5.3*	*EAST ASIA AND PACIFIC*
0.7	2.2	3.6	5.4	7.2	3.7	5.6	8.4	3.4	3.9	6.7	China
1.6	-1.5	-1.8	0.5	-1.5	2.5	-2.8	-1.0	3.1	1.0	..	Fiji
1.9	-2.9	5.4	3.5	-0.1	2.4	1.9	1.9	3.0	3.5	3.0	Indonesia
2.5	3.0	6.2	5.7	2.8	6.5	6.9	5.1	2.9	5.2	..	Korea, Rep.
..	..	..	..	..	..	..	..	..	..	..	Malaysia
..	..	..	..	..	..	..	..	..	..	..	Mongolia
-3.6	0.2	2.6	-1.8	4.0	3.6	-0.4	2.0	-3.6	0.8	..	Papua New Guinea
1.9	1.0	0.6	-4.6	-6.0	0.8	1.8	2.7	2.8	0.4	-0.2	Philippines
..	..	..	..	..	..	..	..	..	..	..	Solomon Islands
1.9	1.0	2.7	2.9	-0.1	2.6	4.3	6.1	5.8	5.8	..	Thailand
..	..	..	..	..	..	..	..	..	..	..	Tonga
..	..	..	1.2	0.3	0.7	2.3	1.7	1.3	..	..	Vanuatu
..	..	..	..	..	..	..	..	..	..	..	Western Samoa

Table 8. Industry: contribution to growth of gross domestic product (cont'd.)

Percentage points	1970	1971	1972	1973	1974	1975	1976	1977	1978	1979	1980
LATIN AMERICA AND CARIBBEAN	**2.8**	**2.5**	**3.4**	**4.4**	**2.4**	**0.9**	**2.9**	**1.6**	**2.6**	**3.0**	**2.4**
Argentina	-0.6	3.2	1.7	0.6	2.9	-0.4	0.2	4.1	-3.9	3.8	-0.6
Bahamas	..	..	..	..	..	..	..	..	..	..	..
Barbados	1.1	0.2	1.0	1.4	-1.1	-0.2	3.5	-1.2	1.3	3.0	1.0
Belize	..	..	..	..	2.8	1.2	0.5	2.5	2.0	0.9	2.4
Bolivia	-1.1	2.2	3.8	7.4	-0.2	0.4	1.9	1.1	-1.1	-2.7	0.1
Brazil	3.9	5.1	6.2	7.6	3.8	2.1	5.2	1.4	5.0	3.3	4.5
Chile	..	..	..	..	..	..	..	..	..	..	..
Colombia	1.7	2.3	3.3	3.2	1.8	0.0	1.5	0.5	2.5	1.7	1.2
Costa Rica	2.0	2.3	2.9	2.1	2.8	0.9	2.3	2.9	2.1	1.7	0.3
Dominican Rep.	4.3	4.2	4.3	5.5	1.5	2.3	2.2	1.4	-0.4	2.2	0.8
Ecuador	1.4	3.0	12.6	21.0	-0.9	-0.3	5.3	0.8	3.5	2.5	-0.2
El Salvador	0.8	1.6	1.7	1.0	1.3	2.3	1.3	2.4	0.8	-0.7	-2.7
Grenada	..	..	..	..	..	..	..	..	..	..	..
Guatemala	..	..	..	..	..	..	..	..	..	..	..
Guyana	2.0	1.5	-2.8	-1.1	3.6	3.9	-1.7	-1.4	-3.0	-0.7	1.3
Haiti	..	..	..	..	..	..	..	..	..	..	..
Honduras	0.9	0.6	1.6	3.0	1.2	0.1	1.2	3.0	3.1	3.9	-1.8
Jamaica	7.4	1.4	3.1	-0.2	-0.6	-2.1	-5.7	-2.8	-0.5	-1.4	-4.2
Mexico	3.2	0.6	3.4	3.8	2.5	1.9	1.9	0.8	3.8	4.2	3.5
Nicaragua	2.7	0.7	1.2	0.9	3.8	-0.2	1.1	3.0	-2.5	-7.4	3.3
Panama	2.0	2.8	0.9	2.5	-0.7	0.7	0.8	-1.8	2.7	1.6	2.3
Paraguay	1.7	1.6	1.5	2.2	1.8	0.6	1.9	4.2	3.7	3.7	7.8
Peru	2.9	1.2	1.4	2.2	3.3	0.3	1.2	0.4	1.1	2.9	2.0
St. Vincent	..	..	..	..	..	..	..	..	2.3	4.1	1.5
Trinidad and Tobago	1.5	1.6	3.3	1.0	3.3	-0.3	6.3	1.2	6.8	1.5	2.4
Uruguay	0.4	-0.7	0.6	-0.7	0.8	3.2	1.4	1.8	3.3	3.0	1.2
Venezuela	6.5	-0.7	-1.1	3.5	-2.0	-3.2	2.2	1.6	1.4	1.0	-2.1
MIDDLE EAST AND NORTH AFRICA	**..**	**-3.2**	**7.1**	**3.6**	**-0.6**	**-0.2**	**4.3**	**1.0**	**-3.3**	**-2.5**	**-4.5**
Algeria	..	-9.5	20.0	3.0	-10.9	-2.6	5.7	3.8	5.0	1.9	0.7
Egypt, Arab Rep.	2.0	1.2	0.4	-0.5	-1.1	4.2	3.9	5.7	4.6	2.7	4.3
Iran, Islamic Rep.	6.1	-3.5	5.4	3.9	0.8	-1.5	3.7	-0.7	-6.9	-5.1	-8.9
Jordan	..	..	..	..	..	..	..	..	..	..	..
Morocco	1.1	2.6	2.1	2.1	2.4	3.9	3.5	3.0	-0.4	2.9	-0.5
Oman	..	..	..	..	..	..	..	..	-3.4	-0.2	
Saudi Arabia	6.7	10.2	11.6	14.0	9.8	-0.7	3.4	9.1	1.3	2.1	4.8
Syrian Arab Rep.	3.1	3.0	2.1	0.3	3.8	4.2	2.9	-0.9	0.7	0.6	1.2
Tunisia	2.5	2.0	4.1	0.3	1.2	4.5	-0.3	2.3	2.9	3.6	3.1
EUROPE	**..**	**..**	**..**	**..**	**..**	**..**	**..**	**..**	**..**	**..**	**..**
Bulgaria	..	..	..	..	..	..	..	..	..	..	..
Czechoslovakia	..	..	..	..	..	..	..	..	..	..	..
Greece	2.4	3.6	3.8	3.9	-3.7	1.7	2.8	1.5	2.0	1.9	-0.8
Hungary	2.6	2.6	2.5	3.0	3.2	2.8	2.3	2.6	2.2	2.1	-0.7
Malta	..	..	..	..	..	..	..	..	..	..	..
Poland	..	..	..	..	..	..	..	..	..	..	..
Portugal	..	..	..	..	..	..	..	..	..	..	..
Romania	..	..	..	..	..	..	..	..	4.7	1.8	8.4
Turkey	1.3	1.6	1.9	3.3	2.5	2.9	3.2	2.9	2.1	-1.2	-1.5
Yugoslavia	2.9	3.0	8.5	1.7	4.6	3.4	1.9	4.6	4.5	3.3	1.6
Low- and middle-income economies	**3.5**	**1.5**	**3.3**	**3.3**	**1.4**	**1.1**	**2.7**	**2.0**	**1.8**	**1.6**	**1.1**
Low-income economies	3.7	2.0	1.5	1.8	1.1	1.5	1.4	2.7	1.8	1.6	1.1
Low-income Africa	4.1	3.4	2.4	0.4	2.6	-1.7	2.9	0.9	-0.8	2.2	2.0
China and India	4.0	2.1	1.2	1.5	0.4	2.7	0.5	3.0	3.8	0.9	2.5
Other low-income	2.5	0.4	1.5	3.9	1.7	0.7	2.7	3.4	1.9	1.8	2.2
Middle-income economies	3.5	1.6	4.5	4.5	2.0	0.8	3.3	2.1	1.4	1.7	0.9
High-income economies	**..**	**1.0**	**2.1**	**2.9**	**-1.2**	**-2.1**	**2.4**	**0.4**	**1.5**	**1.4**	**0.0**
OECD members	..	1.0	2.1	2.9	-1.2	-2.1	2.4	0.4	1.5	1.4	0.0
Japan	5.4	2.4	3.5	3.9	-1.6	0.4	2.3	0.9	2.1	2.9	1.4
United States	-1.5	0.2	2.0	2.5	-1.3	-2.0	2.1	1.7	1.7	0.4	-1.0
WORLD	**..**	**1.2**	**2.3**	**3.0**	**-0.8**	**-1.6**	**2.5**	**0.7**	**1.5**	**1.5**	**0.3**

1981	1982	1983	1984	1985	1986	1987	1988	1989	1990	1991	
-1.7	*-0.9*	*-2.0*	*1.9*	*1.5*	*2.7*	*0.8*	*-0.3*	*0.3*	*-0.8*	*-0.3*	*LATIN AMERICA AND CARIBBEAN*
-6.0	-3.0	2.5	0.4	-3.5	4.5	0.7	-2.1	-3.2	-1.9	2.0	Argentina
					..	..		..		..	Bahamas
-0.2	-1.6	0.7	0.6	-1.2	1.4	-0.3	1.5	1.2	-1.1	..	Barbados
0.8	-0.8	-0.7	-0.2	0.0	0.9	2.6	2.3	4.8	4.9	..	Belize
-0.9	-2.8	-1.3	-2.2	-3.1	-2.4	0.5	3.7	2.9	2.4	..	Bolivia
-4.3	0.0	-2.7	3.0	3.7	5.3	0.5	-1.2	1.3	-3.3	-1.7	Brazil
..					..		..		..		Chile
-0.3	-0.1	1.0	2.2	1.9	3.4	2.1	1.3	1.4	1.8	..	Colombia
-1.2	-3.8	1.1	3.0	0.4	1.8	1.4	0.5	1.4	0.6	0.4	Costa Rica
0.9	-1.3	2.5	0.1	-2.1	1.6	4.8	-0.6	1.2	-3.2	-2.4	Dominican Rep.
2.5	0.1	2.4	1.2	1.5	0.4	-7.6	8.2	-1.2	0.6	1.4	Ecuador
-2.3	-1.6	0.5	0.1	0.9	0.6	0.7	-2.7	0.6	0.1	0.0	El Salvador
3.3	1.4	-2.2	-0.7	1.6	1.6	2.3	2.2	2.5	1.8	..	Grenada
			-0.6	-0.2	0.5	0.4	0.8	0.8	0.2	0.4	Guatemala
-0.8	-7.3	-7.2	0.7	1.2	-1.0	0.3	-0.4	-2.6	2.1	..	Guyana
									..	..	Haiti
-2.1	1.1	0.5	1.4	-0.2	1.3	0.3	1.6	0.7	-1.3	0.4	Honduras
0.4	-0.7	1.2	-1.5	-2.2	1.5	3.1	1.4	6.3	2.8	0.2	Jamaica
3.4	-0.8	-3.3	1.7	1.7	-2.0	1.2	0.9	1.9	2.0	1.6	Mexico
0.6	-0.6	1.2	0.2	-0.6	0.8	-0.4	-7.1	-1.6	-0.7	..	Nicaragua
0.1	1.9	-2.5	-1.1	0.4	0.8	0.5	-6.2	-0.2	1.3	0.9	Panama
2.0	-1.3	-5.7	0.6	0.8	-0.1	0.7	1.1	1.1	0.4	..	Paraguay
0.4	0.1	-5.7	1.6	0.9	3.4	3.1	-3.8	-4.5	-1.3	-5.2	Peru
0.5	1.0	0.9	0.9	0.8	2.2	2.6	1.3	2.1	-0.3	..	St. Vincent
0.9	-5.4	-4.5	-3.1	-1.3	-3.1	-3.5	-0.7	-0.3	0.3	..	Trinidad and Tobago
-1.1	-4.9	-3.6	0.5	-1.5	3.5	3.9	0.6	-0.8	..		Uruguay
-0.8	-1.5	-2.1	2.9	-0.4	3.0	1.5	2.6	-3.9	3.6		Venezuela
1.9	*4.2*	*2.5*	*0.8*	*1.3*	*0.0*	*0.8*	*0.9*	*1.5*	*2.2*	*..*	*MIDDLE EAST AND NORTH AFRICA*
-0.3	4.6	3.6	1.7	1.8	1.0	-1.1	0.7	-0.1	0.6	-4.1	Algeria
1.1	0.7	2.0	2.6	2.3	0.5	0.7	1.3	-0.3	1.3	0.6	Egypt, Arab Rep.
2.4	5.8	1.9	-1.0	-0.1	-1.8	0.4	0.3	2.3	2.1	..	Iran, Islamic Rep.
			3.3	-3.2	1.3	0.3	-1.7	2.9	-0.4	0.4	Jordan
0.9	1.0	0.5	0.5	2.0	0.3	0.5	2.7	-0.9	2.3	1.6	Morocco
12.0	6.5	15.5	11.1	12.9	8.3	0.7	..	..	..		Oman
3.4	-7.2	-6.9	-8.4	-5.0	7.4	-2.0	5.5	-0.5	6.6	..	Saudi Arabia
0.2	1.2	0.9	-1.6	4.1	-2.2	1.1	3.6	4.5	6.6	..	Syrian Arab Rep.
2.4	0.0	2.3	1.3	0.6	-0.3	0.1	0.8	1.8	1.8	..	Tunisia
0.9	*0.5*	*1.4*	*1.8*	*0.9*	*1.7*	*1.4*	*0.6*	*0.3*	*..*	*..*	*EUROPE*
2.8	4.9	4.3	3.6	3.0	3.2	3.3	1.5	3.4	-10.6	-21.0	Bulgaria
0.8	-1.1	0.8	1.7	1.8	1.1	1.6	2.0	0.6	..	..	Czechoslovakia
-0.5	-0.7	0.1	0.4	1.1	0.0	-0.5	1.5	0.7	0.2	..	Greece
2.9	0.5	0.8	0.6	-1.1	-0.2	1.6	-3.0	-0.5	-3.2	-4.7	Hungary
..							..		..		Malta
				0.9	2.2	1.5	2.5	..	..	..	Poland
..								..			Portugal
-1.1	3.0	5.7	3.2	-0.9	3.2	0.4	-1.8	-4.0	-11.5	-8.8	Romania
1.8	1.3	2.1	2.8	1.9	3.0	3.2	0.8	1.1	2.1	1.1	Turkey
1.1	-0.9	-0.7	1.7	1.0	2.0	1.1	-0.3	0.4	-5.2	..	Yugoslavia
0.3	**0.7**	**0.9**	**2.1**	**1.6**	**2.0**	**1.9**	**2.0**	**1.5**	**1.0**	**..**	**Low- and middle-income economies**
0.8	0.8	2.2	2.8	3.0	2.2	2.9	4.3	2.3	2.5	3.4	Low-income economies
-1.4	-0.4	-1.5	0.2	0.8	0.0	0.2	1.3	1.0	0.6	..	Low-income Africa
1.4	1.7	2.9	3.5	4.4	2.9	3.9	5.8	2.7	3.0	4.1	China and India
1.0	-0.6	2.7	2.4	0.7	1.4	1.4	1.4	1.5	2.1	1.8	Other low-income
0.3	0.1	-0.2	1.2	0.7	2.2	1.2	1.1	1.0	0.4	..	Middle-income economies
0.3	**-0.7**	**0.8**	**2.1**	**1.1**	**0.1**	**1.2**	**..**	**..**	**..**	**..**	**High-income economies**
0.3	-0.6	0.8	2.1	1.2	0.1	1.2	..	..	..	..	OECD members
1.7	1.2	0.7	2.4	2.5	-0.5	3.0	3.7	2.4	..	..	Japan
0.3	-1.6	1.2	3.1	0.9	0.3	1.1	..	..	..	..	United States
0.3	**-0.5**	**0.7**	**2.0**	**1.2**	**0.5**	**1.3**	**..**	**..**	**..**	**..**	**WORLD**

Table 9. Services: contribution to growth of gross domestic product

Percentage points	1970	1971	1972	1973	1974	1975	1976	1977	1978	1979	1980
SUB-SAHARAN AFRICA	*0.5*	*2.4*	*0.2*	*1.8*	*2.8*	*3.4*	*3.6*	*1.5*	*0.2*	*0.4*	*1.5*
Excluding Nigeria	*1.9*	*3.5*	*1.1*	*1.0*	*3.9*	*2.0*	*4.5*	*1.6*	*0.4*	*0.6*	*0.8*
Benin	..	0.7	3.6	-0.6	5.3	-1.6	-1.0	3.5	-1.2	3.9	5.5
Botswana	-16.4	9.6	14.1	9.5	4.7	1.2	6.8	2.5	3.6	9.6	10.2
Burkina Faso	..	-0.4	3.2	-0.7	5.6	-2.4	3.4	9.3	0.6	9.3	-1.9
Burundi	2.6	2.9	-0.3	0.1	1.5	-2.3	4.4	6.0	-0.8	0.7	-1.3
Cameroon	1.3	1.3	0.8	3.3	8.1	-1.8	2.6	4.9	11.5	1.2	5.6
Cape Verde	..	..	..	..	..	..	..	..	..	..	..
Central African Rep.	1.3	-0.3	0.5	1.5	3.0	-0.6	4.1	1.7	-0.6	-1.3	-4.2
Chad	1.8	-1.3	-0.7	-2.0	2.7	3.8	2.0	1.6	-0.3	-10.7	-5.2
Comoros	..	..	..	..	..	..	..	..	..	..	..
Congo	0.9	6.9	6.3	4.2	3.1	2.2	-0.1	-4.5	4.8	3.4	9.1
Côte d'Ivoire	2.0	3.1	4.7	1.8	12.1	3.6	0.6	-0.2	4.6	0.9	-8.2
Equatorial Guinea	..	..	..	..	..	..	..	..	..	..	..
Ethiopia	3.5	1.7	2.5	2.4	1.6	1.4	1.9	2.7	0.0	3.2	0.6
Gabon	..	..	..	..	..	..	..	..	..	..	..
Gambia, The	-5.2	6.2	3.9	2.5	10.6	0.8	9.3	2.8	-4.1	16.6	-9.8
Ghana	2.1	2.6	-2.8	0.1	2.6	-2.1	-2.0	3.6	2.5	-0.6	-0.7
Guinea-Bissau	..	7.9	-2.1	5.2	2.0	2.9	7.7	-3.8	-0.2	4.9	2.5
Kenya	-0.6	12.1	6.8	3.3	4.4	-1.3	1.6	3.4	3.4	5.8	4.0
Lesotho	..	6.3	18.5	16.5	-2.2	0.2	8.4	1.7	9.9	-2.7	6.6
Liberia	..	..	..	..	..	..	..	..	..	..	..
Madagascar	..	6.7	-2.3	-3.0	-1.9	1.4	1.2	0.9	-1.1	5.7	0.5
Malawi	0.3	8.1	-1.1	5.5	4.9	2.6	1.0	-0.3	6.5	3.2	2.8
Mali	-0.1	4.6	2.9	4.2	1.3	-0.7	4.3	0.7	2.1	3.2	0.8
Mauritania	10.0	4.8	-10.4	2.9	7.4	1.7	4.8	-0.9	-0.3	2.0	1.7
Mauritius	..	-0.3	0.6	7.9	3.7	9.9	4.4	5.3	3.8	4.5	-1.0
Mozambique	..	..	..	..	..	..	..	..	..	..	..
Namibia	..	..	..	..	..	..	..	..	..	..	..
Niger	2.3	1.5	-0.8	-4.4	3.2	2.8	1.3	1.2	5.5	2.1	2.4
Nigeria	-2.9	-0.9	-2.3	4.2	0.0	6.7	1.5	1.6	-0.9	0.3	3.1
Rwanda	..	..	..	..	..	..	..	2.5	6.5	-0.7	5.9
Senegal	5.6	4.0	-0.2	-0.2	-3.2	5.5	3.3	-2.2	2.1	2.6	1.6
Seychelles	..	..	..	..	..	..	..	7.8	6.0	12.0	-2.3
Sierra Leone	3.2	3.6	1.2	2.2	5.5	0.1	-1.9	2.0	-8.3	2.9	0.6
Somalia	..	2.8	6.5	3.7	-2.5	3.0	-4.0	4.2	8.3	-1.8	-7.2
Sudan	-4.4	2.7	-0.8	-2.6	0.1	8.5	13.9	6.7	-1.1	-3.1	2.2
Swaziland	..	..	..	..	..	..	..	..	..	..	..
Tanzania	3.9	2.5	1.2	5.2	4.5	-0.7	4.9	-0.2	3.1	1.2	0.7
Togo	4.4	-0.1	3.4	1.3	2.6	1.1	-2.4	4.6	6.9	-3.7	6.7
Uganda	0.7	7.8	-2.8	-5.3	2.1	-3.4	2.7	-0.1	-4.7	-2.4	1.0
Zaire	2.8	3.7	-0.4	5.1	1.0	-3.3	-4.4	2.1	-3.4	0.9	0.3
Zambia	3.3	-0.6	4.0	-0.7	1.9	-1.3	4.0	-1.7	-1.2	-0.2	2.2
Zimbabwe	18.9	2.3	1.8	1.9	2.7	-0.8	0.5	-0.3	-2.6	1.4	6.5
SOUTH ASIA	*2.1*	*1.6*	*0.7*	*0.3*	*1.4*	*2.8*	*2.2*	*1.7*	*2.7*	*0.7*	*1.6*
Bangladesh	3.2	1.4	0.5	-5.7	5.0	2.4	2.2	1.0	2.1	2.4	1.8
Bhutan	..	..	..	..	..	..	..	..	..	..	..
India	1.8	1.8	0.7	0.0	1.4	2.6	2.2	1.5	2.6	0.6	1.0
Nepal	..	..	..	..	..	..	..	..	..	..	..
Pakistan	4.9	0.9	0.6	4.2	0.0	4.4	2.8	1.6	5.1	1.0	5.9
Sri Lanka	-0.7	3.1	-3.1	8.1	2.9	6.9	1.1	2.9	-0.2	3.1	3.4
EAST ASIA AND PACIFIC	*6.3*	*3.1*	*2.4*	*2.8*	*1.4*	*2.8*	*0.0*	*4.0*	*4.6*	*2.7*	*3.2*
China	10.0	2.5	2.4	1.9	-1.0	3.0	-4.5	4.1	4.5	1.8	4.5
Fiji	7.5	8.8	5.6	7.3	4.5	1.6	1.2	0.0	2.2	4.6	-0.4
Indonesia	1.0	3.6	-0.6	-1.7	3.8	4.7	0.8	3.5	5.0	2.9	3.2
Korea, Rep.	6.1	6.3	3.1	7.0	3.3	3.3	5.2	5.1	6.2	3.2	0.6
Malaysia	..	..	..	..	..	..	..	..	..	..	..
Mongolia	..	..	..	..	..	..	..	..	..	..	..
Papua New Guinea	..	..	..	..	..	..	..	..	..	..	..
Philippines	2.0	1.9	1.6	2.2	1.8	1.7	2.2	1.6	2.0	1.9	2.2
Solomon Islands	..	..	..	..	..	..	..	..	..	..	..
Thailand	5.8	1.4	2.2	4.5	2.3	2.4	3.1	4.2	4.1	3.3	3.1
Tonga	..	..	..	..	..	..	..	..	..	..	..
Vanuatu	..	..	..	..	..	..	..	..	..	..	..
Western Samoa	..	..	..	..	..	..	..	..	..	..	..

1981	1982	1983	1984	1985	1986	1987	1988	1989	1990	1991	
1.9	*0.7*	*1.1*	*-0.2*	*1.9*	*0.6*	*0.6*	*1.8*	*0.1*	*0.8*	*..*	*SUB-SAHARAN AFRICA*
2.4	*0.8*	*1.4*	*0.0*	*1.8*	*1.2*	*0.7*	*1.7*	*-0.2*	*0.7*	*..*	*Excluding Nigeria*
9.8	-1.4	-3.6	1.1	3.6	1.6	0.2	-0.7	-3.7	2.4	1.0	Benin
1.5	2.3	5.9	4.1	7.1	5.5	8.2	6.4	6.3	..	..	Botswana
1.7	7.5	0.7	-1.8	4.7	3.2	0.7	1.0	1.2	1.4	..	Burkina Faso
2.4	2.0	0.7	2.1	3.0	0.7	1.5	3.9	2.6	-0.3	..	Burundi
1.3	-3.3	2.8	2.1	13.1	1.8	-1.5	-4.7	-8.5	-1.1	0.1	Cameroon
7.8	6.4	6.9	3.7	3.0	1.6	4.4	1.7	3.5	..	..	Cape Verde
-0.4	6.9	-6.3	5.2	1.9	-1.3	-2.9	0.6	0.0	0.0	..	Central African Rep.
2.8	1.3	6.4	5.6	6.9	2.0	-0.9	4.4	3.0	0.0	..	Chad
..	..	..	1.8	1.7	0.9	0.6	1.2	0.1	..	..	Comoros
14.7	13.1	1.3	4.0	0.5	-3.8	-1.4	-0.1	-0.9	-0.3	1.2	Congo
0.7	6.3	2.9	-2.9	0.5	2.6	-2.3	-2.1	-2.6	-2.0	-1.1	Côte d'Ivoire
					-1.3	-0.2	3.7	-1.1	0.9	..	Equatorial Guinea
0.3	1.7	2.0	1.8	0.3	2.3	2.3	3.9	-0.3	-1.8	..	Ethiopia
5.1	-3.0	4.5	1.6	1.6	-2.9	-1.5	-9.1	9.3	0.4	-2.9	Gabon
1.8	6.7	1.0	1.1	-0.8	-2.6	4.1	8.1	1.0	7.1	..	Gambia, The
1.5	-0.6	1.3	2.1	2.4	2.2	2.9	2.5	2.2	3.1	..	Ghana
8.7	0.5	-2.1	-1.2	0.4	-0.5	4.4	3.8	0.8	1.4	..	Guinea-Bissau
1.3	-0.9	0.7	2.5	1.9	4.8	3.6	3.5	2.2	3.0	..	Kenya
4.1	0.5	3.5	5.7	-1.0	1.8	2.5	1.9	..	..	..	Lesotho
..	..	..	..	..	..	..	..	..	..	..	Liberia
-5.0	-1.3	-0.1	-0.8	0.3	0.4	-0.3	2.3	2.1	2.2	..	Madagascar
-1.7	0.1	1.5	3.5	3.1	-0.5	1.2	0.8	2.8	2.7	..	Malawi
3.3	1.8	2.0	3.4	1.6	2.2	2.9	1.4	1.5	0.4	..	Mali
0.8	-1.9	0.2	-5.0	1.0	1.5	2.2	3.1	0.2	4.8	..	Mauritania
1.2	1.3	2.6	2.2	1.7	3.5	6.5	4.4	2.8	2.9	..	Mauritius
0.4	-1.3	-1.8	0.3	-6.6	-0.5	2.0	0.1	1.1	1.6	..	Mozambique
4.9	-0.6	0.8	0.4	5.9	4.3	-2.1	4.4	-1.6	..	..	Namibia
0.4	0.4	-2.3	-12.5	-1.2	3.3	1.6	..	..	..	..	Niger
0.6	0.1	-0.5	-1.5	2.7	-1.8	0.4	2.9	1.7	2.1	0.0	Nigeria
11.1	-3.6	0.6	0.0	6.0	3.1	0.1	0.9	-1.4	-2.2	..	Rwanda
1.5	7.4	0.6	0.2	2.0	1.6	2.0	1.5	0.5	1.7	..	Senegal
-6.6	1.2	-1.4	3.8	7.6	-0.3	6.0	3.8	4.0	..	..	Seychelles
10.6	1.0	0.1	0.0	-3.7	-2.2	2.5	0.3	4.0	1.0	..	Sierra Leone
1.3	0.5	0.1	-4.8	1.8	2.0	-0.7	-2.0	2.7	-2.4	..	Somalia
2.4	-2.2	3.7	-2.5	-2.1	-2.4	1.0	3.6	1.4	0.2	..	Sudan
..	..	..	..	..	..	..	..	..	..	..	Swaziland
-0.3	-0.9	0.2	1.6	-1.7	1.6	0.9	2.1	0.9	1.5	..	Tanzania
0.3	-2.0	-3.9	-0.1	0.5	1.4	0.0	0.8	0.7	1.3	..	Togo
3.0	6.9	3.3	-0.8	-2.9	-1.4	0.7	0.6	1.7	2.0	..	Uganda
1.5	-0.8	-0.1	1.5	-0.4	2.7	1.8	0.2	-1.4	..	..	Zaire
3.1	-1.3	-1.4	-0.3	0.6	-0.6	1.5	0.4	-0.2	0.6	..	Zambia
7.6	4.0	4.7	-3.7	1.3	2.1	0.7	4.3	4.3	1.7	-2.5	Zimbabwe
2.8	*2.8*	*1.6*	*2.2*	*3.8*	*2.9*	*2.9*	*2.7*	*2.2*	*1.9*	*2.4*	*SOUTH ASIA*
7.6	0.7	2.5	1.0	3.0	2.6	2.8	2.4	2.2	1.9	2.0	Bangladesh
2.1	-2.1	1.9	2.6	1.3	4.6	3.1	2.6	1.0	0.5	..	Bhutan
2.3	3.0	1.2	2.1	4.1	3.2	3.0	2.6	2.3	1.8	2.2	India
..	..	..	..	..	..	..	..	..	..	..	Nepal
4.9	2.7	4.3	4.9	2.9	2.0	3.6	4.6	2.1	3.1	3.7	Pakistan
2.8	6.0	1.9	-2.0	6.4	2.1	0.8	1.0	1.5	1.9	..	Sri Lanka
2.3	*2.6*	*3.4*	*3.3*	*2.9*	*3.2*	*3.9*	*2.4*	*1.7*	*1.5*	*0.9*	*EAST ASIA AND PACIFIC*
1.5	2.4	3.5	4.5	4.5	3.4	3.8	0.4	-0.9	-1.2	-1.5	China
1.9	-4.9	1.9	2.7	1.6	1.3	-2.1	2.5	7.1	3.1	..	Fiji
4.2	2.2	2.8	2.2	1.8	2.8	2.5	2.8	3.7	3.1	2.7	Indonesia
2.3	3.2	4.6	3.7	3.6	5.2	5.6	5.2	3.7	4.2	..	Korea, Rep.
..	..	..	..	..	..	..	..	..	..	..	Malaysia
..	..	..	..	..	..	..	..	..	..	..	Mongolia
1.4	0.6	0.1	0.4	1.3	-0.8	2.3	0.0	1.3	-2.1	..	Papua New Guinea
0.7	2.4	2.0	-2.5	-0.8	1.7	2.2	2.9	2.5	1.3	0.6	Philippines
..	..	..	..	..	..	..	..	..	..	..	Solomon Islands
3.3	2.4	3.6	3.3	2.3	2.4	5.4	5.7	5.4	4.7	..	Thailand
..	..	..	..	..	..	..	..	..	..	..	Tonga
..	..	..	3.9	1.3	-0.7	-0.5	1.0	1.3	..	..	Vanuatu
..	..	..	..	..	..	..	..	..	..	..	Western Samoa

Table 9. Services: contribution to growth of gross domestic product (cont'd.)

Percentage points	1970	1971	1972	1973	1974	1975	1976	1977	1978	1979	1980
LATIN AMERICA AND CARIBBEAN	*3.6*	*3.3*	*3.3*	*3.8*	*3.8*	*2.0*	*2.8*	*2.4*	*0.8*	*3.0*	*3.2*
Argentina	6.4	1.0	0.1	1.9	2.3	0.2	-1.0	2.1	0.2	3.1	3.2
Bahamas	..	..	..	..	..	..	..	..	..	..	..
Barbados	7.7	5.9	2.9	-0.7	-3.0	4.6	-4.2	5.2	4.8	3.9	3.1
Belize	..	..	..	..	8.8	1.6	1.7	-3.1	4.6	5.9	0.9
Bolivia	-0.2	1.1	0.0	-3.4	4.4	4.2	2.9	3.3	3.9	1.8	-1.4
Brazil	4.7	4.9	5.5	6.8	5.2	2.4	4.3	2.1	-1.5	3.0	3.7
Chile	..	..	..	..	..	..	..	..	..	..	..
Colombia	4.7	3.5	2.8	3.0	2.8	1.0	2.6	2.9	4.4	2.7	2.5
Costa Rica	4.6	3.4	4.0	4.4	2.9	0.5	3.0	5.6	2.9	3.2	0.5
Dominican Rep.	4.9	5.2	5.1	5.3	4.3	3.1	3.0	3.1	1.8	1.8	4.3
Ecuador	3.4	2.5	3.0	7.2	5.3	5.2	3.9	5.2	4.0	2.6	4.1
El Salvador	1.4	2.6	3.5	3.7	3.8	2.1	3.5	3.0	4.1	-1.4	-5.0
Grenada	..	..	..	..	..	..	..	..	..	..	..
Guatemala	..	..	..	..	..	..	..	..	..	..	..
Guyana	2.7	0.0	2.3	2.6	0.6	4.9	2.3	-0.5	-0.5	0.4	0.4
Haiti	..	..	..	..	..	..	..	..	..	..	..
Honduras	4.2	0.8	3.8	3.4	0.3	4.0	6.9	6.1	3.7	0.7	3.3
Jamaica	4.2	0.9	5.9	1.3	-2.9	1.2	-1.4	-0.1	0.4	0.0	-1.7
Mexico	3.5	2.9	5.0	4.0	3.3	3.6	2.3	1.7	3.9	5.3	4.3
Nicaragua	-4.8	1.4	0.9	2.8	7.2	-0.5	3.2	4.1	-7.4	-13.9	8.8
Panama	5.1	5.8	4.2	2.7	4.0	0.2	0.1	2.3	6.2	3.5	13.6
Paraguay	1.0	3.3	3.7	3.0	3.5	3.3	3.7	4.4	5.7	5.5	4.3
Peru	1.2	3.3	2.0	3.1	5.4	3.3	0.5	0.0	-0.8	2.4	3.2
St. Vincent	..	..	..	..	..	..	..	..	..	5.0	2.1	2.9
Trinidad and Tobago	-5.3	7.0	0.6	1.8	2.2	2.0	3.4	5.1	5.1	3.3	5.9
Uruguay	0.5	1.5	-0.5	0.7	1.7	2.0	2.2	-0.8	2.6	3.1	3.0
Venezuela	1.0	2.1	2.5	3.3	3.9	5.7	5.7	4.3	0.9	-0.4	-2.5
MIDDLE EAST AND NORTH AFRICA	*..*	*4.4*	*-1.8*	*6.4*	*2.9*	*5.1*	*9.5*	*6.0*	*-0.7*	*8.2*	*-5.4*
Algeria	..	1.5	-0.3	0.7	16.0	4.6	3.0	2.4	2.9	4.6	-1.1
Egypt, Arab Rep.	2.9	2.4	-1.3	4.3	4.8	3.4	11.0	8.3	1.4	4.0	5.5
Iran, Islamic Rep.	5.4	5.1	6.7	10.3	2.3	3.0	13.0	7.9	-10.3	-5.1	-10.6
Jordan	..	..	..	..	..	..	..	..	..	..	..
Morocco	2.8	0.7	0.8	3.5	2.6	4.1	4.8	4.2	0.5	2.0	7.3
Oman	..	..	..	..	..	..	..	..	..	3.7	3.3
Saudi Arabia	2.6	4.1	3.7	5.7	5.7	0.2	3.9	6.0	2.7	3.2	4.5
Syrian Arab Rep.	1.5	4.1	1.0	9.3	4.9	14.6	2.2	4.1	1.0	8.4	-0.9
Tunisia	2.9	4.8	9.6	1.5	3.9	1.6	6.8	3.3	2.5	3.9	2.7
EUROPE	*..*	*..*	*..*	*..*	*..*	*..*	*..*	*..*	*..*	*..*	*..*
Bulgaria	..	..	..	..	..	..	..	..	..	..	..
Czechoslovakia	..	..	..	..	..	..	..	..	..	..	..
Greece	3.5	2.7	3.8	3.5	-0.5	3.1	3.5	2.9	3.1	2.5	0.9
Hungary	4.3	2.6	3.4	3.5	2.1	3.2	1.9	2.4	2.4	-0.3	0.2
Malta	..	..	..	..	..	..	..	..	..	..	..
Poland	..	..	..	..	..	..	..	..	..	..	..
Portugal	..	..	..	..	..	..	..	..	..	..	..
Romania	..	..	..	..	..	..	..	..	2.2	6.9	-1.3
Turkey	3.0	4.3	5.1	3.4	3.9	3.7	3.9	2.0	0.7	-0.3	0.4
Yugoslavia	3.0	4.7	-5.6	-0.6	9.2	-2.3	2.3	2.8	5.5	1.4	1.0
Low- and middle-income economies	**3.2**	**2.9**	**1.5**	**3.4**	**2.7**	**2.7**	**3.8**	**3.2**	**1.1**	**3.3**	**0.4**
Low-income economies	3.1	2.0	0.7	0.8	1.0	3.0	0.8	2.9	2.7	1.1	2.8
Low-income Africa	-0.6	2.2	-0.5	1.4	1.1	3.0	2.8	2.7	-0.1	0.4	1.8
China and India	4.5	1.9	1.3	0.7	0.3	2.8	-0.7	2.7	3.3	0.8	2.7
Other low-income	2.2	2.1	-0.1	0.7	3.0	3.8	3.2	3.7	3.6	2.6	3.7
Middle-income economies	3.4	3.2	1.7	4.4	3.3	2.5	4.8	3.4	0.7	4.0	-0.1
High-income economies	**..**	**2.3**	**2.9**	**2.6**	**1.8**	**1.8**	**2.3**	**3.6**	**2.6**	**1.9**	**1.4**
OECD members	..	2.3	2.9	2.6	1.8	1.8	2.3	3.6	2.6	1.9	1.3
Japan	6.1	2.2	4.1	3.7	1.0	2.4	2.1	3.8	2.7	2.7	2.5
United States	1.2	3.0	3.0	2.2	0.4	0.8	2.9	2.7	3.4	1.4	0.9
WORLD	**..**	**2.4**	**2.7**	**2.7**	**1.9**	**1.9**	**2.5**	**3.5**	**2.3**	**2.1**	**1.2**

1981	1982	1983	1984	1985	1986	1987	1988	1989	1990	1991	
0.9	*-0.6*	*-0.8*	*1.4*	*1.4*	*2.1*	*1.5*	*0.7*	*0.9*	*0.3*	*2.4*	*LATIN AMERICA AND CARIBBEAN*
-1.1	-3.3	0.2	1.4	-1.2	1.9	1.5	-1.0	-0.4	0.0	2.3	Argentina
..	..	..	..	..	..	..	..	..	..	..	Bahamas
-1.2	-3.2	-0.9	1.8	1.5	8.6	1.9	5.9	3.0	-2.0	..	Barbados
0.7	-1.9	1.5	5.0	2.3	3.5	9.8	7.4	6.2	4.6	..	Belize
2.1	-3.4	1.7	-1.5	0.1	0.4	1.1	-0.7	0.3	0.1	..	Bolivia
-0.8	0.6	-0.7	2.1	3.2	3.5	1.5	0.9	1.7	-0.5	1.4	Brazil
..	..	..	..	..	..	..	..	..	..	..	Chile
1.8	1.5	0.0	1.1	1.0	2.1	2.1	2.3	1.0	1.2	..	Colombia
-1.9	-2.4	1.0	3.0	1.5	2.9	2.6	2.1	3.0	2.5	0.0	Costa Rica
2.1	2.2	1.3	0.2	0.2	1.5	2.0	1.5	2.4	-0.8	1.4	Dominican Rep.
0.7	0.8	-2.6	1.7	1.6	1.2	0.9	1.3	1.3	1.2	0.4	Ecuador
-4.9	-3.2	0.6	1.6	1.6	0.9	1.7	5.9	0.4	2.0	3.3	El Salvador
..	..	..		7.2	1.8	3.7	4.0	2.0	4.0	..	Grenada
..	..	..	0.7	-0.5	-0.1	1.8	1.9	2.2	1.9	1.8	Guatemala
2.0	-5.9	1.6	-1.7	-0.2	1.4	-3.3	-1.5	2.2	1.3	..	Guyana
..	..	..	..	..	..	..	..	..	..	..	Haiti
2.8	-3.0	-0.6	1.0	3.2	1.1	4.1	3.4	1.2	0.1	0.8	Honduras
1.9	2.1	0.8	-0.5	-2.4	0.7	3.0	0.8	0.3	0.8	2.2	Jamaica
4.9	0.3	-1.0	1.8	0.7	-1.6	0.5	0.9	1.6	1.7	2.2	Mexico
1.8	-1.1	1.5	-0.5	-2.1	0.0	0.6	-1.2	-3.5	0.7	..	Nicaragua
3.3	3.8	2.6	0.5	3.8	2.9	1.1	-9.0	-1.5	2.0	3.4	Panama
4.0	-0.3	1.3	0.9	1.9	1.7	1.8	2.0	2.5	2.0	..	Paraguay
3.3	-0.2	-5.8	1.9	0.9	5.2	4.7	-5.3	-6.6	-2.4	11.3	Peru
1.8	7.4	3.2	3.8	3.7	1.1	10.5	3.6	4.1	3.2	..	St. Vincent
3.6	-0.5	-4.0	-8.4	-1.6	2.5	-1.6	-2.6	-0.3	-0.2	..	Trinidad and Tobago
2.0	-3.7	-6.6	0.1	1.8	4.9	3.4	-0.4	1.0	0.8	..	Uruguay
0.6	-0.7	-1.7	-1.5	0.2	3.0	1.8	2.9	-4.4	1.7	..	Venezuela
-9.5	*0.3*	*7.8*	*1.9*	*-0.9*	*-4.8*	*-0.4*	*-2.4*	*1.1*	*-0.2*	*..*	*MIDDLE EAST AND NORTH AFRICA*
3.3	2.8	2.0	3.5	1.3	-0.5	-0.1	-2.6	2.5	-0.5	2.6	Algeria
2.4	9.0	5.0	3.0	3.6	1.7	1.4	2.1	2.9	0.9	1.3	Egypt, Arab Rep.
3.5	7.2	7.6	4.6	3.7	-6.9	-2.6	-4.2	-0.7	6.9	..	Iran, Islamic Rep.
..	..	..	-1.0	5.5	10.8	1.9	0.1	-9.3	0.4	1.3	Jordan
1.3	4.2	0.6	3.2	1.7	1.8	1.8	2.7	1.8	1.8	2.1	Morocco
4.7	3.8	2.0	4.2	2.2	-1.6	1.1	..	..	..	..	Oman
3.6	2.0	-1.0	-0.4	-0.2	-2.8	-0.7	1.2	0.0	1.5	..	Saudi Arabia
8.4	2.2	0.8	-0.4	0.4	-3.6	3.9	1.5	-0.8	3.0	..	Syrian Arab Rep.
2.1	1.2	2.0	2.5	2.4	0.9	3.2	4.3	1.2	1.7	..	Tunisia
-1.1	*-0.3*	*1.3*	*0.7*	*1.7*	*1.4*	*1.3*	*1.2*	*0.8*	*..*	*..*	*EUROPE*
1.2	-4.0	2.7	-2.0	2.7	-1.7	4.8	1.3	-3.7	-0.2	-3.2	Bulgaria
0.1	1.2	1.5	-0.2	0.8	0.5	-0.7	0.5	0.7	..	..	Czechoslovakia
0.8	0.8	1.6	1.4	1.7	0.9	0.6	1.6	1.5	0.9	..	Greece
0.4	-0.4	-0.1	1.3	1.7	1.1	3.4	1.4	0.6	0.8	-3.0	Hungary
..	..	..	..	..	..	..	..	..	..	..	Malta
..	..	..	..	3.5	1.3	1.4	1.3	..	..	..	Poland
..	..	..	..	..	..	..	..	..	..	..	Portugal
1.3	0.3	0.4	1.6	0.6	-0.1	1.4	0.4	-1.1	1.7	-0.6	Romania
2.4	2.3	1.8	2.4	2.7	3.7	3.9	1.4	2.3	5.1	0.9	Turkey
-0.2	0.5	-0.3	-0.3	-0.6	0.7	-3.3	-0.8	-0.5	-1.4	..	Yugoslavia
-0.7	**0.8**	**2.2**	**1.7**	**1.5**	**0.8**	**1.7**	**0.9**	**1.1**	**0.4**	**..**	**Low- and middle-income economies**
2.3	2.3	2.2	2.3	3.3	2.6	2.8	1.7	1.1	0.7	0.5	Low-income economies
1.4	0.0	0.7	-0.6	0.7	0.1	1.2	2.3	1.0	1.3	..	Low-income Africa
1.9	2.6	2.3	3.0	4.1	3.2	3.3	1.4	0.6	0.1	0.1	China and India
3.8	3.2	3.1	2.4	2.6	2.1	2.2	2.5	2.7	2.2	2.4	Other low-income
-1.4	0.4	2.3	1.5	0.9	-0.1	1.2	0.7	1.2	0.4	..	Middle-income economies
1.3	**0.3**	**2.1**	**2.3**	**2.2**	**2.7**	**2.1**	**..**	**..**	**..**	**..**	**High-income economies**
1.2	0.3	2.0	2.3	2.2	2.7	2.1	..	..	..	..	OECD members
1.9	1.8	1.9	1.8	2.5	3.2	1.0	2.6	2.1	..	..	Japan
1.8	-1.1	2.9	3.7	2.5	2.8	2.5	..	..	..	..	United States
0.9	**0.4**	**2.1**	**2.2**	**2.1**	**2.3**	**2.0**	**..**	**..**	**..**	**..**	**WORLD**

Table 10. Total consumption: contribution to growth of gross domestic product

Percentage points	1970	1971	1972	1973	1974	1975	1976	1977	1978	1979	1980
SUB-SAHARAN AFRICA	*3.1*	*7.3*	*-0.7*	*0.5*	*7.4*	*3.9*	*3.0*	*8.4*	*8.9*	*-5.8*	*5.1*
Excluding Nigeria	*2.5*	*6.4*	*1.2*	*-0.4*	*4.2*	*2.3*	*3.3*	*6.1*	*4.8*	*1.1*	*0.8*
Benin	3.3	0.7	4.8	5.0	-1.9	-2.7	-1.5	8.9	2.9	5.0	6.4
Botswana	2.7	-4.5	9.1	24.6	19.2	2.9	6.4	4.9	10.2	14.2	13.4
Burkina Faso	-4.3	1.0	-1.8	-0.7	6.0	7.9	6.4	9.3	0.1	6.1	4.0
Burundi	37.1	42.8	-2.6	4.1	-3.5	7.5	3.9	12.2	-4.6	4.6	2.3
Cameroon	0.4	7.7	-0.2	0.7	9.2	0.7	5.2	9.0	2.9	13.6	10.8
Cape Verde	..	..	..	..	-12.3	8.0	9.8	11.4	16.2	3.4	28.2
Central African Rep.	3.2	-1.6	1.9	-0.6	-0.5	2.5	7.1	12.3	4.5	-3.8	2.3
Chad	..	..	..	..	..	..	..	..	..	..	..
Comoros	..	..	..	..	..	..	..	..	..	..	..
Congo	9.0	-1.0	-0.7	-1.6	-0.6	3.7	12.6	-10.1	9.8	-6.7	15.0
Côte d'Ivoire	7.5	10.3	4.1	6.0	4.0	10.1	4.4	1.0	12.9	3.3	-7.4
Equatorial Guinea	..	..	..	..	..	..	..	..	..	..	..
Ethiopia	..	..	..	..	..	..	..	..	..	..	..
Gabon	3.5	5.2	7.9	5.3	-5.4	6.7	6.1	3.5	6.4	-4.8	4.5
Gambia, The	-30.4	41.2	1.5	5.7	-2.1	-9.6	52.8	9.2	53.6	-49.5	12.2
Ghana	-1.6	0.7	-9.0	9.1	15.4	-15.2	-3.4	6.6	14.2	-5.6	6.5
Guinea-Bissau	..	16.7	21.7	12.1	11.7	-16.9	-1.5	-16.8	1.2	-10.4	-6.6
Kenya	-9.1	32.9	13.9	-5.5	11.5	3.3	-2.7	6.1	10.6	8.3	-1.8
Lesotho	11.0	16.9	33.0	36.2	27.3	21.7	26.1	6.7	21.7	3.5	-6.9
Liberia	..	..	..	..	..	..	..	..	..	..	..
Madagascar	6.0	7.2	-3.8	-3.5	-3.9	0.7	-5.9	4.4	-0.9	14.0	1.4
Malawi	-11.0	24.6	-1.8	0.7	1.4	5.8	3.6	1.1	4.4	6.2	5.0
Mali	4.6	0.5	9.4	-1.3	9.8	6.9	9.2	-0.7	8.3	10.0	-1.2
Mauritania	9.7	0.4	-1.2	-2.1	10.2	-2.3	24.4	-5.0	-5.2	0.7	-5.6
Mauritius	10.4	4.0	0.9	-3.5	22.0	11.3	8.0	7.3	4.2	2.5	-3.9
Mozambique	..	..	..	..	..	..	..	..	..	..	..
Namibia	..	..	..	..	..	..	..	..	..	..	..
Niger	-4.2	4.5	-5.7	-22.9	28.7	-20.0	0.5	7.1	3.0	15.0	7.0
Nigeria	5.7	10.1	-7.0	3.5	17.1	6.9	1.3	15.2	20.8	-27.2	17.5
Rwanda	3.8	1.9	0.8	-1.0	5.8	-0.3	4.3	6.5	10.6	9.8	10.5
Senegal	6.3	2.5	0.1	-1.5	1.4	7.7	5.7	1.9	1.1	7.5	0.2
Seychelles	..	..	..	..	..	..	..	..	..	..	..
Sierra Leone	5.9	3.9	-2.0	11.0	5.5	-4.6	-1.6	9.4	8.2	13.6	2.3
Somalia	3.9	5.6	1.1	2.5	-17.4	33.7	-2.9	37.6	-6.4	10.2	-25.6
Sudan	2.4	9.1	0.1	-10.5	4.4	13.8	8.4	18.9	1.7	-8.3	-0.1
Swaziland	..	..	..	..	..	..	..	..	..	..	..
Tanzania	2.5	3.2	9.1	8.8	7.5	0.2	-7.3	-0.1	19.9	-6.2	2.3
Togo	1.4	-20.3	5.5	3.4	5.2	-7.3	17.3	-0.1	-0.7	2.7	10.7
Uganda	..	..	..	..	..	..	..	..	..	..	..
Zaire	3.5	4.1	0.9	8.8	2.1	-4.3	-4.6	-3.8	-2.5	-3.8	-2.1
Zambia	-10.6	3.9	1.1	-8.6	0.6	3.5	1.0	-0.2	-4.6	12.3	0.1
Zimbabwe	..	..	..	..	..	..	..	1.7	9.1	5.0	-1.2
SOUTH ASIA	*5.9*	*0.2*	*-1.0*	*0.5*	*2.0*	*5.6*	*0.6*	*7.3*	*3.2*	*-1.8*	*8.1*
Bangladesh	8.7	-1.7	-3.0	-16.9	23.7	-1.7	6.4	-6.4	10.9	4.9	1.0
Bhutan	..	..	..	..	..	..	..	..	..	..	..
India	4.4	0.8	-0.2	1.2	-0.4	7.1	-0.5	8.4	2.1	-3.7	8.8
Nepal	..	..	..	..	..	..	..	..	..	..	..
Pakistan	22.1	-4.3	-8.6	2.6	10.0	-0.6	5.1	6.3	7.9	9.0	8.2
Sri Lanka	-3.6	0.2	-5.9	11.3	1.6	1.5	2.5	8.4	5.6	2.2	6.5
EAST ASIA AND PACIFIC	*8.1*	*3.8*	*3.6*	*5.9*	*4.6*	*3.7*	*1.6*	*4.8*	*6.7*	*5.9*	*5.3*
China	12.7	2.3	4.3	4.8	2.8	3.3	-2.6	5.4	7.0	4.7	8.2
Fiji	11.7	6.8	6.4	12.4	7.9	1.5	5.8	4.1	0.5	5.2	-3.7
Indonesia	1.0	3.0	-1.0	3.9	7.2	5.7	3.1	3.4	7.1	5.7	7.9
Korea, Rep.	9.0	9.8	3.0	8.6	6.4	5.3	7.0	4.0	7.0	6.6	-0.8
Malaysia	3.7	4.4	5.7	5.8	6.9	0.8	4.8	6.6	6.4	6.3	10.4
Mongolia	..	..	..	..	..	..	..	..	..	..	..
Papua New Guinea	2.2	3.3	5.6	2.2	2.1	1.7	-1.1	3.3	5.6	0.7	1.7
Philippines	1.4	7.1	3.7	5.7	6.2	1.3	2.0	3.2	5.2	5.3	1.5
Solomon Islands	..	..	..	..	..	..	..	..	..	..	..
Thailand	6.5	-1.4	6.3	8.5	2.2	4.5	7.3	6.4	4.7	10.2	2.5
Tonga	..	..	..	..	..	..	..	..	..	..	..
Vanuatu	..	..	..	..	..	..	..	..	..	..	..
Western Samoa	..	..	..	..	..	..	..	..	..	..	-6.3

1981	1982	1983	1984	1985	1986	1987	1988	1989	1990	1991	
8.9	*-0.4*	*-1.4*	*-1.4*	*2.3*	*1.5*	*0.2*	*3.6*	*1.7*	*0.6*	*2.7*	***SUB-SAHARAN AFRICA***
3.0	*1.8*	*2.9*	*0.3*	*1.5*	*4.3*	*3.7*	*2.8*	*1.9*	*-0.4*	*1.9*	*Excluding Nigeria*
8.9	-14.9	4.5	7.4	3.1	4.3	-0.3	1.7	-2.3	1.4	1.4	Benin
2.5	8.4	-3.8	0.5	16.3	-6.8	10.2	13.1	27.6	..	..	Botswana
4.8	7.7	0.9	-4.9	4.3	8.1	2.9	4.0	0.0	1.9	3.6	Burkina Faso
3.1	5.8	-4.1	2.4	12.5	9.6	-4.3	10.5	-3.7	3.6	2.1	Burundi
4.6	0.1	1.2	-1.0	5.9	5.8	6.6	0.0	-3.7	-1.1	1.0	Cameroon
0.4	3.9	10.0	8.3	7.9	7.7	-2.9	3.9	0.4	5.3	..	Cape Verde
-11.1	8.2	-12.8	9.1	3.8	7.2	-4.5	2.8	1.8	2.8	0.6	Central African Rep.
..	..	..	-3.0	41.9	-2.2	-8.3	15.6	1.1	-1.7	5.1	Chad
..	..	..	14.5	5.0	-2.5	9.1	..	..	..	..	Comoros
7.4	35.2	-7.9	6.6	3.9	-3.9	-3.0	-0.4	1.4	7.4	9.3	Congo
7.8	0.6	0.2	4.0	0.4	7.8	-3.6	-5.6	0.5	-7.1	-2.2	Côte d'Ivoire
..	..	..	..	..	-3.3	7.7	11.5	-7.8	5.7	-2.0	Equatorial Guinea
											Ethiopia
4.7	-2.3	12.0	-2.8	-3.1	9.1	-12.5	7.1	-15.0	-5.2	-0.3	Gabon
-40.1	-5.4	-28.1	17.6	-3.3	7.0	-13.6	18.7	-4.0	3.5	2.7	Gambia, The
-3.7	-15.0	3.9	7.1	5.2	5.3	3.0	2.9	9.0	2.1	2.9	Ghana
											Guinea-Bissau
31.4	10.5	-3.0	6.6	5.8	-3.2	8.9	4.3	2.0	5.0	..	Kenya
-3.0	3.8	0.4	4.4	-5.3	13.4	5.3	5.2	3.7	6.6	4.4	Lesotho
14.5	4.2	20.5	2.0	-13.5	-5.9	9.3	7.1	5.6	-1.8	3.3	Liberia
-14.7	-0.1	-1.3	-1.0	1.9	0.9	-3.0	0.4	-0.4	3.9	2.0	Madagascar
-2.3	-2.8	0.6	9.6	2.8	1.0	-2.8	3.9	12.4	0.9	4.7	Malawi
2.8	5.3	1.3	2.1	7.3	3.9	-1.7	0.6	6.2	-2.2	4.5	Mali
0.3	3.2	18.2	-14.2	-2.4	2.2	4.1	6.4	5.3	0.5	-6.9	Mauritania
-1.2	-1.4	1.3	3.0	2.9	3.9	11.4	9.6	-2.1	4.9	3.3	Mauritius
3.1	1.1	-1.6	0.6	-11.2	5.5	2.7	3.9	6.6	-0.6	4.2	Mozambique
17.0	1.8	-4.3	1.9	0.1	1.1	6.7	-1.2	1.7	..	..	Namibia
1.7	7.8	-3.2	-5.4	-2.8	5.8	-3.3	-0.2	-3.6	3.1	1.6	Niger
27.0	-8.5	-17.7	-8.8	6.1	-10.2	-14.1	7.6	1.1	4.3	5.1	Nigeria
8.8	1.3	6.5	-5.6	1.0	0.2	1.6	1.8	-3.3	2.1	..	Rwanda
6.8	4.2	0.7	-1.8	8.0	0.1	3.6	2.9	-0.5	1.8	1.1	Senegal
											Seychelles
1.4	1.0	-8.4	-3.5	-0.4	-5.5	8.8	-0.9	8.3	2.1	..	Sierra Leone
21.0	4.0	-1.4	-1.6	-27.5	34.6	-1.4	0.5	3.4	..	..	Somalia
3.7	3.4	8.0	-3.2	2.0	-4.2	4.4	1.1	8.1	-8.1	-0.8	Sudan
											Swaziland
-10.0	-1.8	5.2	7.3	2.2	10.3	4.1	1.9	..	..	..	Tanzania
0.3	3.1	-5.6	9.3	-0.5	14.2	-1.1	7.1	2.3	5.6	1.6	Togo
											Uganda
8.1	1.8	-1.2	1.5	-1.0	6.8	6.0	1.1	-4.9	2.1	..	Zaire
7.7	-13.9	2.3	0.8	7.6	-3.7	16.2	7.3	-5.4	-1.4	6.1	Zambia
2.2	8.7	8.4	-9.3	2.1	2.8	8.4	0.6	8.1	2.0	7.1	Zimbabwe
1.5	*4.8*	*8.2*	*3.4*	*3.3*	*4.8*	*2.9*	*6.1*	*3.6*	*4.1*	*3.8*	***SOUTH ASIA***
7.0	3.5	7.1	5.2	5.9	2.3	4.0	3.4	3.6	6.0	..	Bangladesh
											Bhutan
1.1	4.7	9.1	3.0	2.6	5.5	3.0	6.8	3.8	4.0	3.9	India
											Nepal
-0.5	4.0	5.0	6.1	7.1	3.4	4.0	8.1	2.8	4.7	3.7	Pakistan
3.0	10.9	6.6	-3.1	10.5	2.6	0.0	3.4	0.7	1.5	2.6	Sri Lanka
4.0	*3.4*	*5.8*	*5.0*	*3.1*	*2.3*	*5.2*	*5.9*	*4.7*	*2.4*	*5.9*	***EAST ASIA AND PACIFIC***
4.9	3.1	6.8	8.4	4.2	2.0	5.7	6.2	3.7	-1.3	6.3	China
7.5	-4.4	-2.4	6.1	-3.3	2.5	-3.3	14.5	14.4	3.5	3.5	Fiji
4.9	4.2	6.7	2.7	1.1	1.8	2.3	2.9	3.2	5.5	4.3	Indonesia
3.6	4.7	5.9	4.7	4.0	5.3	5.2	6.1	5.9	5.6	4.9	Korea, Rep.
4.9	3.6	2.9	2.7	0.1	-4.6	1.6	8.1	8.3	8.2	7.3	Malaysia
..	..	..	..	1.1	-2.9	19.9	6.4	-5.4	10.4	..	Mongolia
-0.5	-3.4	0.6	-0.1	6.6	-2.1	2.8	-0.4	0.3	-3.8	-0.4	Papua New Guinea
0.9	4.0	-1.6	-3.0	0.4	0.3	6.4	5.5	3.7	4.3	5.2	Philippines
5.2	-21.2	12.7	14.6	0.2	1.5	10.6	28.0	..	..	..	Solomon Islands
0.9	1.2	9.4	2.1	1.7	3.8	7.2	6.3	8.2	4.7	7.4	Thailand
											Tonga
..	..	..	9.8	6.7	-9.7	6.4	3.1	-1.9	..	..	Vanuatu
-3.9	-3.5	2.5	3.4	6.9	2.9	1.5	6.4	0.0	-4.8	..	Western Samoa

Table 10. Total consumption: contribution to growth of gross domestic product (cont'd.)

Percentage points	1970	1971	1972	1973	1974	1975	1976	1977	1978	1979	1980
LATIN AMERICA AND CARIBBEAN	**6.3**	**5.6**	**4.7**	**5.0**	**4.5**	**2.1**	**5.0**	**3.4**	**2.9**	**6.0**	**5.1**
Argentina	1.9	3.6	1.2	4.0	5.7	-0.2	-5.2	2.2	-0.4	9.8	5.8
Bahamas	..	..	..	..	..	..	..	..	10.1	24.3	-0.4
Barbados	..	..	..	..	..	..	..	..	..	..	..
Belize	..	..	..	..	..	..	..	..	..	..	..
Bolivia	2.9	2.1	-3.0	9.2	2.6	-4.3	9.0	3.0	4.5	5.5	3.2
Brazil	10.2	9.4	8.5	8.7	7.0	0.7	9.4	3.8	2.0	6.9	4.4
Chile	0.3	12.3	7.2	-6.0	-14.5	-13.4	-0.3	13.0	7.4	7.3	4.8
Colombia	6.1	6.6	5.5	4.7	2.1	3.1	4.9	2.7	6.5	4.4	3.7
Costa Rica	8.4	1.9	5.8	3.7	4.3	2.4	3.0	8.9	6.5	2.6	-1.4
Dominican Rep.	17.2	9.3	11.0	6.4	10.0	-6.2	8.7	3.1	1.5	0.5	16.5
Ecuador	5.4	3.7	5.2	7.1	9.8	8.5	7.9	7.4	3.4	5.2	5.8
El Salvador	5.5	3.0	5.1	7.3	2.1	3.1	9.4	10.7	3.8	-5.5	-7.8
Grenada	..	..	..	..	..	..	..	..	..	..	..
Guatemala	6.0	4.4	5.0	5.1	4.0	2.6	9.0	7.6	4.5	2.5	2.3
Guyana	3.4	-1.4	11.5	10.5	-0.1	2.0	24.1	-9.4	-19.0	-11.1	12.3
Haiti	-0.3	8.1	0.9	-1.4	5.8	-3.9	9.8	3.0	2.6	2.7	7.8
Honduras	4.8	0.2	4.9	6.9	-0.8	4.0	12.0	10.2	2.5	3.2	5.1
Jamaica	9.9	4.0	14.3	-10.5	9.7	1.6	1.8	1.2	-5.3	-1.5	-3.7
Mexico	4.4	4.4	5.7	5.3	4.5	5.2	3.6	0.2	6.8	7.8	7.1
Nicaragua	1.2	2.2	1.1	2.6	10.2	2.6	4.0	5.8	-3.0	-20.5	9.9
Panama	4.8	6.3	2.7	2.1	7.4	0.1	0.4	5.4	8.2	4.3	5.2
Paraguay	1.1	6.7	2.3	4.0	8.5	2.3	7.1	12.6	4.1	-6.8	28.7
Peru	13.8	2.5	3.8	0.0	3.7	4.4	3.0	2.8	-3.7	1.9	1.9
St. Vincent	..	..	..	..	..	..	..	..	-11.2	5.3	3.4
Trinidad and Tobago	-7.0	8.0	2.8	1.1	0.9	4.0	8.5	6.9	7.3	9.1	2.2
Uruguay	4.3	-0.6	0.0	2.7	-1.0	1.3	-2.4	-1.7	2.2	2.9	5.5
Venezuela	..	..	..	..	..	9.5	8.3	5.6	3.1	1.0	5.0
MIDDLE EAST AND NORTH AFRICA	..	..	..	..	..	..	..	..	..	..	..
Algeria	4.2	-2.2	10.5	-0.7	3.1	5.0	5.6	2.9	1.6	7.7	2.7
Egypt, Arab Rep.	9.5	5.7	3.3	4.9	13.7	6.2	5.2	10.3	6.5	13.8	12.0
Iran, Islamic Rep.	6.8	2.5	6.4	12.2	3.8	0.7	14.2	10.8	-7.8	-11.0	-16.6
Jordan	..	..	..	..	..	..	..	..	..	..	..
Morocco	3.7	2.7	2.8	3.8	4.2	7.0	11.7	2.6	5.8	5.3	4.4
Oman	..	..	..	..	..	..	..	..	..	..	..
Saudi Arabia	..	..	..	..	..	..	..	..	..	..	..
Syrian Arab Rep.	..	..	..	..	..	..	3.7	10.0	6.9	6.3	5.4
Tunisia	11.1	5.7	11.4	4.5	4.6	8.4	4.9	6.5	4.0	3.9	9.3
EUROPE	..	..	..	..	..	..	..	..	..	..	..
Bulgaria	..	..	..	..	..	..	..	..	..	..	..
Czechoslovakia	..	..	..	..	..	..	..	..	..	..	..
Greece	4.3	5.3	5.7	1.8	2.2	6.4	4.4	4.1	3.6	1.1	0.4
Hungary	..	5.1	3.0	4.4	9.2	-0.8	2.0	0.8	2.6	1.5	0.5
Malta	17.0	-1.0	0.8	0.6	7.2	4.2	11.1	11.4	2.0	3.2	4.8
Poland	..	..	..	..	..	..	..	..	..	..	..
Portugal	1.9	7.8	2.0	8.6	10.5	0.1	4.6	2.2	-0.5	1.0	0.9
Romania	..	..	..	..	..	..	..	..	..	..	..
Turkey	1.4	11.4	6.6	0.0	6.8	4.9	7.5	3.6	3.7	-1.2	-2.8
Yugoslavia	9.0	9.5	-1.0	2.7	19.8	-2.2	-2.1	11.1	9.5	4.4	-1.8
Low- and middle-income economies	**5.6**	**4.2**	**2.2**	**4.6**	**5.2**	**3.3**	**4.6**	**5.4**	**3.4**	**3.7**	**2.3**
Low-income economies	6.4	2.5	0.4	2.0	4.3	4.4	0.4	7.1	5.6	0.0	7.9
Low-income Africa	2.2	7.5	-1.4	0.0	9.0	2.8	1.5	9.8	9.1	-9.1	6.3
China and India	7.4	1.4	1.7	2.8	1.0	5.4	-1.4	7.1	4.2	-0.1	8.5
Other low-income	7.3	1.3	-1.5	1.5	9.6	3.2	4.9	4.5	6.8	6.9	7.7
Middle-income economies	..	..	..	..	..	..	..	..	..	..	..
High-income economies	**2.9**	**2.7**	**4.1**	**3.7**	**0.6**	**1.9**	**3.0**	**2.5**	**3.1**	**2.6**	**1.1**
OECD members	2.9	2.7	4.1	3.7	0.6	1.9	3.0	2.5	3.0	2.6	1.0
Japan	4.9	3.8	5.8	5.3	0.2	3.9	2.4	2.9	3.6	4.0	1.7
United States	1.3	2.0	3.9	3.0	-0.3	1.0	3.8	3.1	3.3	1.8	0.2
WORLD	**3.2**	**2.9**	**3.8**	**3.8**	**1.3**	**2.1**	**3.2**	**3.0**	**3.1**	**2.8**	**1.2**

1981	1982	1983	1984	1985	1986	1987	1988	1989	1990	1991	
0.6	*-1.2*	*-1.4*	*2.6*	*1.8*	*3.6*	*1.7*	*0.2*	*1.9*	*0.4*	*3.3*	*LATIN AMERICA AND CARIBBEAN*
-3.2	-8.9	3.5	4.6	-4.9	6.6	1.2	-5.5	-1.9	-2.3	5.7	Argentina
-2.7	0.2	2.2	17.2	3.4	2.0	2.0	..	..	..	..	Bahamas
..	..	..	..	..	..	..	..	..	..	..	Barbados
..	..	..	..	..	..	..	..	..	..	..	Belize
8.5	-6.7	5.4	1.8	5.4	-2.1	1.0	0.1	1.6	1.1	..	Bolivia
-3.0	3.2	-0.4	2.6	4.1	6.0	1.8	-0.5	3.0	-1.4	1.1	Brazil
9.2	-13.7	-3.8	2.1	-1.9	3.2	3.7	7.5	6.8	0.4	4.3	Chile
1.8	1.2	0.7	3.1	2.6	2.8	3.0	3.3	2.3	2.0	4.6	Colombia
-2.9	-5.3	1.7	5.3	2.0	2.7	3.7	2.8	4.5	3.0	1.2	Costa Rica
-0.2	2.9	2.6	-4.7	1.2	4.5	1.9	-4.5	8.5	-10.4	-7.0	Dominican Rep.
4.2	0.8	-1.0	1.0	1.5	0.0	2.5	1.0	1.3	1.6	-1.0	Ecuador
-7.5	-5.8	0.2	3.5	4.0	0.4	1.3	2.4	1.1	2.0	3.4	El Salvador
				4.4	10.6	13.5	2.8	7.4	0.4	..	Grenada
..	..	..	..	-1.3	0.0	6.5	4.0	2.8	1.5	2.3	Guatemala
0.5	-4.5	-2.6	1.7	-1.3	0.0	6.5	4.0	2.8	1.5	2.3	Guatemala
10.5	-18.2	-0.5	-24.5	8.9	-9.9	7.6	2.4	-8.3	6.6	1.8	Guyana
-0.8	-5.7	1.6	-1.6	2.5	2.7	0.4	-1.5	0.1	-0.7	-2.7	Haiti
0.2	-0.1	-0.8	1.2	3.2	4.0	4.9	5.7	2.1	-1.2	0.1	Honduras
0.0	3.0	-0.8	2.9	-2.7	-2.7	3.8	-0.4	10.9	-4.2	3.4	Jamaica
6.6	-4.2	-4.2	3.4	2.7	-1.6	-0.3	2.8	4.7	5.0	5.9	Mexico
-4.4	-0.9	4.2	1.5	-2.3	-1.5	0.0	-6.4	-1.7	2.7	-1.0	Nicaragua
2.2	4.0	2.9	6.3	1.8	-0.2	1.1	-14.2	7.3	6.4	-3.6	Panama
2.5	1.6	-10.5	9.0	3.3	1.4	6.8	1.6	-6.3	3.8	3.3	Paraguay
1.6	2.3	-4.9	2.9	2.6	7.5	5.4	-6.6	-8.5	-4.2	4.4	Peru
4.3	20.4	1.8	-4.7	1.5	11.5	14.8	..	..	..	..	St. Vincent
7.6	1.3	-6.1	-20.7	15.9	7.9	-10.0	-4.9	-0.3	1.6	5.2	Trinidad and Tobago
3.3	-5.9	-8.4	-0.9	1.9	7.5	10.6	-0.9	-0.3	-1.3	4.4	Uruguay
3.6	2.3	-3.1	0.7	-0.6	2.6	2.5	6.2	-3.8	2.3	4.7	Venezuela
..	..	..	..	..	..	..	..	..	..	..	*MIDDLE EAST AND NORTH AFRICA*
4.6	4.6	3.4	4.8	5.3	0.1	-1.4	-2.3	2.8	-2.8	2.3	Algeria
5.1	2.6	5.3	8.3	5.2	0.6	-0.1	2.3	2.6	2.2	0.0	Egypt, Arab Rep.
											Iran, Islamic Rep.
4.8	26.8	-2.4	13.5	3.1	-13.5	0.9	-3.4	-0.5	..	..	Jordan
			0.2	4.9	15.4	-1.3	1.9	-9.7	13.8	-6.1	Morocco
-2.3	5.4	-0.9	3.0	4.0	8.3	-0.5	6.0	3.3	0.3	5.8	Morocco
										..	Oman
..	..	..	..	..	..	..	..	..	..	..	Saudi Arabia
6.1	-3.9	-0.8	-4.5	12.3	-11.6	12.8	8.4	0.3	11.6	..	Syrian Arab Rep.
5.5	2.7	4.0	4.7	2.8	1.5	1.9	2.5	2.8	4.3	2.1	Tunisia
-0.3	*-1.0*	*0.7*	*2.4*	*1.1*	*3.3*	*2.4*	*2.0*	*2.0*	*3.4*	*..*	*EUROPE*
			-0.8	5.9	2.9	6.9	-2.3	1.5	-2.8	-15.0	Bulgaria
..	..	..									Czechoslovakia
0.5	0.1	3.1	1.4	0.6	1.3	1.0	2.8	1.9	1.0	-9.2	Czechoslovakia
5.9	4.8	0.6	1.2	4.0	1.9	3.2	0.6	5.7	2.5	..	Greece
3.4	0.3	-0.4	1.2	1.8	1.1	2.9	-2.0	0.5	-2.3	-2.7	Hungary
1.2	1.6	0.3	2.8	5.5	1.2	2.8	6.9	9.0	..	..	Malta
-3.1	-7.4	3.1	3.0	5.2	3.0	1.9	1.4	-1.0	-9.7	5.2	Poland
1.8	1.2	2.0	-0.1	1.0	3.6	9.7	9.0	4.4	..	..	Portugal
-3.3	-8.6	-7.2	9.3	-7.4	-1.5	2.0	11.1	5.5	5.9	-7.1	Romania
-1.1	2.9	4.4	6.8	1.3	7.5	5.2	1.5	2.7	11.2	4.0	Turkey
-2.3	-1.2	-1.6	-0.8	-1.6	6.1	-4.2	-2.5	-0.8	8.4	..	Yugoslavia
0.4	**1.8**	**2.2**	**3.4**	**1.7**	**1.3**	**2.3**	**2.4**	**2.7**	**1.7**	**2.9**	**Low- and middle-income economies**
4.3	3.0	5.7	4.1	3.3	2.7	3.1	5.4	3.4	1.8	4.5	Low-income economies
10.0	-1.8	-2.7	-2.5	1.8	-0.3	-1.3	4.3	2.5	1.1	3.0	Low-income Africa
2.9	4.0	8.0	5.5	3.4	3.7	4.5	6.5	3.7	1.1	5.2	China and India
3.9	3.8	5.6	4.6	3.8	2.0	2.0	3.0	2.9	4.3	3.1	Other low-income
..	..	..	..	..	..	..	..	..	..	..	Middle-income economies
1.2	**1.0**	**2.3**	**2.5**	**2.8**	**2.8**	**2.6**	**2.8**	**1.8**	**1.6**	**..**	**High-income economies**
1.2	1.0	2.3	2.5	2.8	2.9	2.5	2.8	1.8	1.6	..	OECD members
1.7	3.0	2.6	1.9	2.5	2.2	2.3	2.9	2.3	2.3	..	Japan
1.3	0.5	3.6	4.1	3.9	3.5	2.6	3.2	1.6	1.0	..	United States
1.1	**1.1**	**2.2**	**2.5**	**2.5**	**2.5**	**2.5**	**2.7**	**1.8**	**1.6**	**..**	**WORLD**

Table 11. Gross domestic investment: contribution to growth of gross domestic product

Percentage points	1970	1971	1972	1973	1974	1975	1976	1977	1978	1979	1980
SUB-SAHARAN AFRICA	**5.5**	**2.8**	**0.0**	**2.9**	**4.2**	**3.5**	**4.7**	**2.6**	**-5.6**	**-2.3**	**3.5**
Excluding Nigeria	*3.7*	*1.6*	*-0.5*	*2.2*	*5.4*	*-0.2*	*1.5*	*1.3*	*-2.5*	*-0.7*	*3.1*
Benin	-0.6	-0.3	3.9	0.2	5.4	0.0	0.3	-1.4	-0.9	6.1	7.0
Botswana	10.1	12.5	13.6	9.8	0.8	-4.2	-1.1	-6.7	6.9	4.8	6.8
Burkina Faso	0.4	4.3	4.1	3.1	2.3	-0.2	0.2	-1.7	0.6	-2.9	0.3
Burundi	-5.0	6.9	-7.4	3.7	4.6	-3.2	4.0	5.3	2.5	0.4	-0.8
Cameroon	3.3	2.9	1.1	1.1	-1.4	2.3	-1.2	5.3	8.6	-1.0	2.2
Cape Verde	..	..	..	..	1.4	-3.3	11.6	14.4	-6.0	11.8	10.5
Central African Rep.	1.8	0.7	0.0	0.9	-7.5	-2.0	0.7	0.1	-0.3	-1.4	-2.4
Chad	..	..	..	..	..	..	..	..	..	..	..
Comoros	..	..	..	..	..	..	..	..	..	..	..
Congo	-3.0	7.5	8.1	8.8	9.4	10.6	-14.7	-9.2	-8.8	2.3	15.0
Côte d'Ivoire	4.4	-0.1	-0.8	4.8	-0.5	0.6	5.1	10.1	5.4	-2.4	5.7
Equatorial Guinea	..	..	..	..	..	..	..	..	..	..	..
Ethiopia	..	..	..	..	..	..	..	..	..	..	..
Gabon	3.0	3.9	5.6	4.7	57.9	15.3	28.8	-15.5	-39.1	7.4	1.0
Gambia, The	-2.7	1.1	1.5	-0.5	0.4	7.3	0.5	4.0	15.5	-7.5	2.4
Ghana	4.0	0.8	-7.4	2.6	4.9	-2.2	-3.0	5.4	-5.5	0.4	-0.9
Guinea-Bissau	..	-14.3	-10.5	-11.4	-10.7	-1.8	3.2	5.3	13.8	11.8	-18.1
Kenya	15.1	0.8	-3.9	7.8	-2.3	-12.3	3.1	10.3	8.5	-10.2	10.1
Lesotho	0.7	4.6	3.3	10.1	-1.1	6.9	15.8	20.7	-6.0	7.4	9.8
Liberia	..	..	..	..	..	..	..	..	..	..	..
Madagascar	-1.0	2.0	-2.9	0.4	0.7	-0.5	-1.7	-0.6	0.1	6.4	-0.7
Malawi	17.9	-7.0	10.9	-14.5	9.4	11.6	-8.4	-0.5	24.0	-13.8	-5.1
Mali	-3.0	0.9	0.3	-1.0	-4.1	5.0	-0.4	4.0	-0.5	1.4	-0.7
Mauritania	0.9	0.4	2.9	-2.5	16.7	11.0	9.7	-4.6	-11.5	-3.9	8.3
Mauritius	-6.7	7.5	3.0	14.7	6.5	1.4	-1.3	-0.4	2.6	1.5	-12.6
Mozambique	..	..	..	..	..	..	..	..	..	..	..
Namibia	..	..	..	..	..	..	..	..	..	..	..
Niger	4.8	-2.8	2.9	5.5	-0.9	-3.3	0.4	2.0	4.3	3.5	-2.2
Nigeria	12.6	7.0	1.2	5.3	0.8	14.1	14.7	6.3	-14.9	-7.3	5.1
Rwanda	0.6	1.5	0.3	0.1	0.8	2.5	0.7	1.4	-0.3	-1.7	3.2
Senegal	3.4	0.5	1.8	0.4	1.7	-2.5	2.8	-0.8	-0.9	-2.3	0.1
Seychelles	..	..	..	..	..	..	..	..	..	..	..
Sierra Leone	5.2	-6.8	-3.9	0.7	4.2	0.4	-4.4	0.0	0.7	1.7	3.5
Somalia	-0.1	-0.1	4.1	-0.2	0.4	1.8	4.9	12.7	6.6	-6.3	20.5
Sudan	1.3	-0.9	-2.5	1.4	7.7	1.2	8.9	-3.2	-2.6	-2.2	1.2
Swaziland	..	..	..	..	..	..	..	..	..	..	..
Tanzania	11.0	6.0	-7.0	1.2	3.3	-2.4	3.0	4.7	-0.6	0.8	-2.1
Togo	2.3	2.4	2.5	1.3	0.6	11.7	-6.6	23.3	8.8	-2.9	-18.0
Uganda	..	..	..	..	..	..	..	..	..	..	..
Zaire	0.3	3.0	-0.1	1.0	0.9	-1.0	-2.6	8.9	-9.8	6.4	4.9
Zambia	20.7	7.1	2.2	-3.4	16.1	-10.0	-29.9	-3.3	-1.0	-12.9	11.1
Zimbabwe	8.3	7.1	4.1	4.0	17.1	-6.0	-15.3	-7.3	-13.1	2.3	14.9
SOUTH ASIA	**1.5**	**1.3**	**-1.6**	**2.5**	**0.4**	**1.1**	**1.2**	**1.1**	**3.1**	**-0.3**	**0.0**
Bangladesh	-1.3	-3.9	-7.1	6.2	-0.6	-1.2	0.5	1.9	3.1	0.6	5.3
Bhutan	..	..	..	..	..	..	..	..	..	..	..
India	1.5	2.0	-1.4	2.9	0.4	1.3	1.2	0.9	3.2	-0.8	-0.8
Nepal	..	..	..	..	..	..	..	..	..	..	..
Pakistan	3.5	0.0	-1.1	0.7	-0.9	2.0	0.3	2.2	0.8	0.9	1.5
Sri Lanka	1.9	-1.2	1.2	-3.2	6.3	-1.4	4.3	-0.6	8.1	7.5	6.5
EAST ASIA AND PACIFIC	**7.3**	**1.6**	**-0.5**	**4.1**	**2.5**	**1.8**	**0.1**	**3.9**	**6.4**	**3.1**	**-1.0**
China	14.6	2.7	-0.9	4.3	0.5	3.4	-2.6	3.3	9.0	3.4	-0.1
Fiji	0.1	2.9	3.0	1.9	-2.5	1.9	0.2	0.3	1.7	7.6	2.4
Indonesia	2.9	2.4	2.4	2.4	2.9	2.4	1.1	2.9	2.9	2.1	0.3
Korea, Rep.	-0.5	1.8	-1.4	5.4	6.9	-0.8	3.6	6.4	8.3	5.2	-7.2
Malaysia	6.5	0.3	1.8	5.9	8.0	-6.6	2.7	5.2	2.2	3.6	5.2
Mongolia	..	..	..	..	..	..	..	..	..	..	..
Papua New Guinea	24.7	4.5	-19.3	-14.1	1.3	-0.2	-2.3	1.7	0.7	5.1	1.1
Philippines	-0.8	-2.3	0.4	0.9	4.1	5.4	3.6	0.3	2.0	2.9	1.5
Solomon Islands	..	..	..	..	..	..	..	..	..	..	..
Thailand	2.0	-0.9	-1.9	9.0	-1.1	0.7	-0.1	6.4	5.3	-1.4	0.4
Tonga	..	..	..	..	..	..	..	..	..	..	..
Vanuatu	..	..	..	..	..	..	..	..	..	..	..
Western Samoa	..	..	..	..	..	..	..	..	..	..	-19.6

1981	1982	1983	1984	1985	1986	1987	1988	1989	1990	1991	
1.6	*-2.0*	*-4.3*	*-2.7*	*0.5*	*1.7*	*-3.3*	*0.5*	*0.4*	*0.0*	*0.4*	***SUB-SAHARAN AFRICA***
1.2	*0.4*	*-3.2*	*-1.3*	*1.1*	*1.5*	*-2.7*	*0.3*	*-0.1*	*-0.4*	*0.4*	*Excluding Nigeria*
3.4	11.0	-14.8	-5.7	4.2	-2.0	-1.4	3.5	-5.4	4.6	3.9	Benin
0.5	-0.8	-7.5	-0.3	6.6	-3.8	-4.7	4.0	10.7	..	..	Botswana
0.0	4.1	-1.2	0.2	11.4	3.8	-5.3	3.5	0.1	-1.2	1.1	Burkina Faso
3.7	-2.8	11.4	-4.4	-3.4	-3.0	11.0	-7.0	1.9	0.8	0.1	Burundi
7.8	0.5	1.6	-1.4	1.8	12.5	-8.3	-9.6	-4.2	-1.6	-0.1	Cameroon
3.5	8.3	-0.5	-0.8	0.9	7.9	3.1	1.4	1.0	1.7	..	Cape Verde
1.3	3.1	4.6	1.6	0.6	-1.7	-0.3	-1.8	-0.1	0.0	1.7	Central African Rep.
..	..	..	2.5	4.5	0.6	2.7	-3.1	1.2	1.0	0.3	Chad
..	..	..	12.0	-12.9	-1.2	-3.9	-7.2	-2.0	1.6	..	Comoros
31.1	22.4	-10.2	-5.7	-2.2	-14.7	-8.9	-2.9	-2.4	0.1	-3.7	Congo
-7.8	-3.8	-2.1	-11.3	4.2	-0.5	-1.5	2.8	-5.6	-1.1	-0.7	Côte d'Ivoire
..	..	..	..	..	3.4	12.3	-2.8	-0.3	4.7	23.1	Equatorial Guinea
..	..	..	..	..	..	..	..	..	..	..	Ethiopia
17.9	-3.8	-2.4	2.5	4.6	-8.7	-23.9	0.1	13.4	-9.4	0.9	Gabon
0.5	-1.2	-4.0	2.4	-3.4	5.5	-0.9	0.4	5.1	-0.6	0.9	Gambia, The
-0.9	-2.1	0.0	1.2	2.1	-0.7	2.1	0.7	3.8	0.8	2.0	Ghana
-8.7	10.5	-1.4	2.5	4.6	0.0	-13.5	6.8	14.3	-15.2	..	Guinea-Bissau
-1.2	-8.0	-3.5	1.0	6.4	-4.6	3.7	2.2	1.1	-1.6	0.0	Kenya
0.5	8.3	-25.0	9.0	12.5	-9.6	1.1	10.4	19.7	19.0	-1.8	Lesotho
..	..	..	..	..	..	..	..	..	..	..	Liberia
-3.9	-1.8	-0.1	0.4	0.1	0.5	1.5	3.4	0.6	3.4	-0.6	Madagascar
-9.4	5.7	3.1	-13.3	7.8	-10.9	3.4	4.2	3.6	-0.7	1.6	Malawi
1.6	0.8	-3.9	1.5	4.1	5.8	1.8	2.9	2.1	2.1	-0.2	Mali
6.7	8.9	-26.5	6.5	1.0	-0.6	-1.9	-1.2	-1.7	-0.5	5.4	Mauritania
4.4	-3.8	-0.3	3.5	1.4	4.3	5.8	1.7	1.8	0.9	1.2	Mauritius
1.0	-1.1	-12.3	2.5	-2.6	7.6	3.4	4.0	1.9	1.3	0.5	Mozambique
-5.2	-10.8	-7.0	0.7	-2.3	-1.7	2.7	7.8	-5.7	..	..	Namibia
0.6	-2.7	-0.9	-13.6	12.2	-4.5	1.0	2.5	-1.9	0.2	0.5	Niger
3.2	-10.8	-8.3	-8.2	-1.8	2.4	-6.2	1.5	2.2	1.6	0.6	Nigeria
-0.3	3.5	-1.8	3.1	3.5	4.9	-4.0	-0.4	-3.4	-8.0	..	Rwanda
-5.3	2.9	0.9	-0.8	-1.5	2.9	0.4	1.2	-1.9	2.4	0.1	Senegal
..	..	..	..	3.5	0.1	-3.5	2.9	2.6	0.9	..	Seychelles
3.3	-4.2	-0.6	0.3	-1.5	0.9	-1.9	3.4	0.2	0.5	..	Sierra Leone
-13.3	4.8	-6.3	4.2	11.9	-12.4	4.0	-10.6	4.9	..	..	Somalia
0.2	10.3	-5.8	-1.7	-9.5	8.4	-1.5	-1.0	-0.1	-0.8	-0.1	Sudan
..	..	..	..	..	..	..	..	..	..	..	Swaziland
-0.8	2.4	-9.5	3.5	2.0	0.5	-0.7	4.6	..	..	..	Tanzania
-0.9	-5.2	-5.3	0.4	8.5	-3.9	-3.5	0.9	1.2	1.8	0.5	Togo
..	..	..	..	..	..	..	..	..	..	..	Uganda
-3.2	-3.8	2.3	1.2	1.6	-0.9	-0.6	-0.3	-0.5	-3.1	..	Zaire
-3.0	-5.4	-4.4	1.0	1.2	7.6	-9.3	0.7	-0.9	4.3	-4.1	Zambia
16.3	-6.4	-10.0	2.8	4.6	-3.5	-10.5	12.2	1.4	1.7	4.7	Zimbabwe
4.8	*-0.9*	*-1.1*	*0.6*	*3.4*	*-0.5*	*1.1*	*2.9*	*0.3*	*0.6*	*-0.7*	***SOUTH ASIA***
0.6	-0.4	-3.2	0.6	1.6	-1.1	1.2	0.2	-1.0	0.2	..	Bangladesh
10.5	5.6	2.8	-3.5	12.7	-7.3	-0.7	12.1	..	..	..	Bhutan
5.9	-1.4	-1.3	0.7	4.0	-0.6	1.2	3.7	0.3	0.5	-1.0	India
..	..	..	..	..	..	..	..	..	..	..	Nepal
1.1	2.6	1.2	0.9	2.0	0.9	0.8	-0.2	1.3	0.2	0.8	Pakistan
-3.9	1.5	0.6	-0.6	-2.8	1.8	0.5	2.7	-1.7	0.4	1.2	Sri Lanka
2.4	*1.6*	*3.2*	*3.3*	*5.6*	*2.4*	*2.6*	*3.9*	*3.4*	*3.9*	*1.8*	***EAST ASIA AND PACIFIC***
-1.7	3.0	3.7	6.5	12.9	3.6	3.1	4.8	0.9	2.0	1.1	China
1.8	-8.4	-3.0	-2.1	-0.7	2.5	-4.1	-2.8	1.4	6.2	-2.9	Fiji
16.6	-1.8	1.0	0.7	4.5	1.9	-0.1	-1.5	3.9	5.3	1.7	Indonesia
0.5	2.1	3.7	4.2	1.1	3.4	4.3	3.8	8.2	6.7	4.4	Korea, Rep.
5.3	4.9	2.8	2.0	-7.1	-3.9	-0.7	5.5	5.1	6.8	6.2	Malaysia
..	..	..	..	11.4	7.0	-18.4	-1.4	3.5	-12.8	..	Mongolia
-1.2	3.6	1.4	-2.7	-8.1	0.8	1.4	8.3	-7.2	0.0	7.4	Papua New Guinea
0.8	2.2	1.6	-9.4	-6.5	1.3	2.8	2.1	4.5	0.6	-5.6	Philippines
-0.6	-3.8	4.3	-0.5	3.3	0.3	-0.4	6.6	..	..	..	Solomon Islands
2.7	-3.0	5.4	1.9	-1.2	-1.5	3.5	8.5	4.0	7.2	1.0	Thailand
..	..	..	..	..	..	..	..	..	..	..	Tonga
..	..	..	2.1	4.4	4.7	-1.5	-3.9	6.0	..	..	Vanuatu
2.3	-17.2	-2.0	3.7	-3.8	0.0	6.8	-5.9	0.5	7.6	..	Western Samoa

Table 11. Gross domestic investment: contribution to growth of gross domestic product (cont'd.)

Percentage points	1970	1971	1972	1973	1974	1975	1976	1977	1978	1979	1980
LATIN AMERICA AND CARIBBEAN	*1.1*	*1.9*	*1.6*	*3.9*	*4.2*	*1.6*	*0.7*	*1.8*	*0.6*	*0.7*	*3.1*
Argentina	0.5	2.5	0.2	-1.1	0.2	0.4	1.5	4.8	-4.1	2.3	2.1
Bahamas	..	..	..	..	..	..	..	..	-0.3	4.0	5.6
Barbados	..	..	..	..	..	..	..	..	..	..	..
Belize	..	..	..	..	..	..	..	..	..	..	..
Bolivia	-1.1	4.4	9.6	-5.7	-0.3	17.0	-5.1	1.4	0.4	-5.9	-9.0
Brazil	-0.1	3.8	4.5	7.0	5.1	3.3	0.2	0.0	1.0	0.1	3.5
Chile	1.7	-0.7	-5.4	-1.6	11.0	-12.8	0.0	2.2	3.2	4.5	5.8
Colombia	3.6	1.0	-0.6	1.9	4.2	-4.3	1.8	3.2	1.5	-0.1	2.3
Costa Rica	2.8	5.2	-1.8	4.0	2.0	-2.2	5.8	5.9	-0.1	2.6	2.0
Dominican Rep.	3.9	3.3	2.5	5.5	4.4	2.1	-1.7	1.9	0.7	2.0	2.2
Ecuador	1.8	8.2	-4.8	3.0	9.2	5.4	-1.8	6.4	4.1	-1.0	2.9
El Salvador	1.3	2.7	-0.9	3.8	4.2	-1.9	1.7	7.5	0.7	-5.2	-5.7
Grenada	..	..	..	..	..	..	..	..	..	..	..
Guatemala	3.0	2.5	-2.8	2.6	5.4	-3.2	6.3	2.4	2.2	-3.0	-2.7
Guyana	5.6	-8.9	-8.2	21.3	-6.3	38.0	-11.9	-21.2	-15.9	13.5	-0.7
Haiti	2.5	0.2	1.3	1.4	1.0	2.5	2.5	0.5	1.6	2.5	0.1
Honduras	1.0	-3.7	-0.3	3.9	5.7	-4.9	1.2	5.8	5.1	0.9	-1.1
Jamaica	0.6	0.2	-5.1	12.0	-11.7	3.9	-11.9	-10.3	3.3	-1.0	-5.4
Mexico	5.2	-1.3	2.6	3.9	4.7	1.5	-0.7	-0.1	3.2	4.9	6.6
Nicaragua	-0.1	0.4	-3.9	8.2	6.1	-7.6	0.3	7.1	-9.4	-10.8	16.8
Panama	4.7	6.5	4.7	1.3	-1.8	-1.1	-0.3	-9.1	5.1	1.8	4.1
Paraguay	-0.1	1.5	2.0	6.1	2.4	1.5	4.7	3.0	6.9	4.6	11.5
Peru	-11.1	2.9	-2.3	9.4	9.5	-1.7	-3.7	-3.6	-1.3	3.4	7.9
St. Vincent	..	..	..	..	..	..	..	..	4.8	5.8	2.8
Trinidad and Tobago	3.7	6.4	-1.9	-1.3	5.3	3.5	2.8	0.7	5.6	0.7	5.1
Uruguay	1.8	1.2	-2.8	-0.7	0.5	3.8	3.5	3.3	3.2	5.8	1.5
Venezuela	..	..	..	..	..	6.6	6.7	9.9	-0.6	-8.7	-5.4
MIDDLE EAST AND NORTH AFRICA	*1.9*	*0.4*	*2.4*	*2.3*	*4.8*	*7.9*	*2.1*	*1.5*	*-4.4*	*0.0*	*3.5*
Algeria	5.2	-0.4	4.2	6.0	11.1	3.3	1.2	6.5	8.3	-3.3	0.9
Egypt, Arab Rep.	0.7	-1.7	0.4	3.7	7.0	11.9	-0.1	3.3	2.9	3.1	-0.4
Iran, Islamic Rep.	0.9	0.8	3.3	1.7	3.5	10.1	2.6	-0.5	-8.1	0.3	7.7
Jordan	..	..	..	..	..	..	..	..	..	..	..
Morocco	3.7	2.3	-4.3	0.7	3.6	13.5	5.6	5.2	-9.6	0.4	1.2
Oman	..	..	..	..	..	..	..	..	..	5.5	1.4
Saudi Arabia	..	..	..	..	..	..	..	..	..	..	..
Syrian Arab Rep.	..	..	..	..	..	..	8.3	3.9	-4.5	0.3	5.6
Tunisia	-1.2	0.6	7.6	-2.6	5.7	2.2	2.3	0.7	3.7	2.2	0.3
EUROPE	..	..	..	..	..	..	..	..	..	..	..
Bulgaria	..	..	..	..	..	..	..	..	..	..	..
Czechoslovakia	..	..	..	..	..	..	..	..	..	..	..
Greece	3.7	2.1	3.8	9.4	-9.5	-0.4	0.6	0.3	2.3	2.8	-1.4
Hungary	4.7	7.8	-3.7	0.1	3.0	8.1	0.7	3.0	7.3	-5.6	-1.1
Malta	0.6	-6.0	-4.2	-4.3	3.6	0.2	6.3	2.0	0.9	2.4	2.7
Poland	..	..	..	..	..	..	..	..	..	..	..
Portugal	8.0	1.3	5.5	6.1	-3.3	-10.8	3.4	6.5	2.3	3.1	4.1
Romania	..	..	..	..	..	..	9.0	0.6	7.0	-0.8	-0.7
Turkey	4.8	0.2	1.9	3.0	6.2	6.2	1.4	3.2	-7.9	0.1	2.1
Yugoslavia	3.0	2.0	-1.6	2.1	1.7	1.9	0.8	3.6	-0.7	4.5	-1.0
Low- and middle-income economies	**3.1**	**1.7**	**0.5**	**3.5**	**3.0**	**2.7**	**1.1**	**2.0**	**0.7**	**0.9**	**2.0**
Low-income economies	5.2	1.8	-0.9	3.0	1.2	2.7	0.8	2.4	3.0	0.6	0.5
Low-income Africa	5.9	2.8	-0.7	2.6	2.4	4.0	5.3	3.7	-5.6	-3.2	3.1
China and India	6.3	2.3	-1.2	3.5	0.4	2.2	-0.4	1.9	5.6	1.0	-0.5
Other low-income	1.8	-0.2	-0.2	2.2	2.5	3.0	0.8	2.5	2.9	2.2	1.1
Middle-income economies	2.2	1.7	1.1	3.8	3.9	2.7	1.3	1.9	-0.2	1.0	2.6
High-income economies	**1.1**	**0.6**	**1.3**	**2.4**	**-0.9**	**-2.8**	**2.0**	**0.9**	**1.0**	**1.1**	**-0.5**
OECD members	1.1	0.6	1.3	2.4	-0.9	-2.8	1.9	0.8	1.0	1.0	-0.6
Japan	6.3	0.1	3.1	4.1	-2.0	-2.0	1.1	1.0	1.9	2.3	-0.3
United States	-1.6	1.6	1.3	1.6	-1.3	-2.9	2.2	2.2	1.7	-0.3	-1.8
WORLD	**1.4**	**0.8**	**1.2**	**2.6**	**-0.3**	**-2.0**	**1.9**	**1.1**	**0.9**	**1.0**	**-0.1**

1981	1982	1983	1984	1985	1986	1987	1988	1989	1990	1991	
-0.9	*-3.9*	*-5.9*	*0.7*	*1.2*	*1.4*	*1.0*	*0.1*	*-1.3*	*-0.4*	*1.0*	*LATIN AMERICA AND CARIBBEAN*
-5.8	-4.0	-1.8	-1.7	-2.6	2.0	1.8	-1.0	-4.3	-0.6	4.8	Argentina
0.1	3.6	0.1	-1.6	4.3	-0.2	1.4	..	..	..	..	Bahamas
..	..	..	..	..	..	..	..	..	..	..	Barbados
..	..	..	..	..	..	..	..	..	..	..	Belize
-0.4	-6.9	-9.1	-3.1	0.6	-3.7	3.7	0.5	-0.9	0.0	..	Bolivia
-3.8	-2.4	-5.4	0.7	3.2	4.7	-0.3	-1.1	0.3	-1.7	-0.9	Brazil
5.0	-17.0	-1.9	6.6	-1.0	1.9	3.7	1.4	5.6	-0.5	-1.5	Chile
2.9	1.3	-0.6	-1.5	-2.2	0.9	1.8	1.6	-1.2	-0.2	-0.1	Colombia
-11.5	-5.0	5.2	2.2	1.6	6.8	0.9	-1.7	1.7	1.4	-3.4	Costa Rica
-2.8	-4.0	1.5	0.9	-0.9	0.8	8.0	2.0	2.3	-3.7	3.6	Dominican Rep.
-4.6	3.6	-9.9	-0.3	1.7	0.7	-0.7	-0.8	1.2	-0.5	1.0	Ecuador
-0.5	-1.3	-1.2	0.4	-0.7	2.4	-0.6	2.3	3.7	-5.2	0.9	El Salvador
..	..	..	..	3.2	10.5	0.3	-0.2	-0.6	-1.7	..	Grenada
2.4	-3.4	-2.5	0.8	-2.6	0.0	3.5	-0.1	0.3	-1.3	1.3	Guatemala
-3.9	-14.0	-5.0	11.9	-3.3	11.5	-20.5	-7.4	6.0	6.0	9.4	Guyana
1.8	-2.8	0.8	0.7	-2.3	-2.1	0.6	-0.1	-0.1	0.2	-1.1	Haiti
-3.5	-7.2	2.3	5.5	-0.1	-2.7	1.1	-0.7	-0.7	0.7	0.7	Honduras
4.5	1.2	0.9	-2.2	-0.1	-3.8	5.2	3.9	4.9	-1.5	-2.8	Jamaica
5.0	-8.7	-7.3	1.3	2.2	-4.8	0.9	2.4	1.1	2.4	1.0	Mexico
6.2	-3.0	1.2	0.1	-0.1	-0.2	-0.2	-4.6	-1.8	-1.1	0.2	Nicaragua
3.1	-1.0	-5.6	-2.0	1.1	1.4	0.4	-11.1	-4.3	4.7	7.8	Panama
5.3	-6.8	-8.5	0.4	0.3	0.9	1.6	1.0	2.5	0.3	1.1	Paraguay
5.8	-2.4	-11.8	-2.1	-2.0	5.2	5.4	-2.1	-7.5	1.4	1.4	Peru
-1.9	-0.8	-1.9	4.5	3.2	3.5	3.2	..	..	..	..	St. Vincent
-4.2	1.1	-2.5	-0.2	0.9	-3.3	-4.7	-3.7	0.4	-0.2	4.6	Trinidad and Tobago
-2.5	-4.6	-8.4	-2.7	-1.4	2.1	2.4	-1.0	-1.6	-0.3	0.0	Uruguay
0.0	2.0	-16.3	5.7	0.9	1.0	3.1	3.7	-14.1	-1.2	8.0	Venezuela
2.8	*-7.0*	*7.6*	*-2.5*	*0.8*	*1.2*	*-2.4*	*-3.2*	*1.5*	*..*	*..*	*MIDDLE EAST AND NORTH AFRICA*
1.5	0.1	2.4	0.8	-0.2	-2.2	-2.3	-1.6	0.9	-0.3	-1.2	Algeria
2.0	3.2	1.0	2.6	2.0	-3.3	-4.0	1.1	0.0	-0.3	-0.1	Egypt, Arab Rep.
5.7	-19.5	17.3	-8.1	0.3	3.9	-2.5	-6.5	3.7	..	..	Iran, Islamic Rep.
..	..	..	-3.4	-3.2	2.8	0.4	-1.3	-5.9	-1.8	0.4	Jordan
0.1	4.2	-4.6	1.7	1.3	1.0	-1.9	1.8	2.7	1.9	0.1	Morocco
8.5	12.8	4.0	20.6	3.9	-11.5	-17.4	..	..	..	..	Oman
..	..	..	..	..	..	..	..	..	..	..	Saudi Arabia
0.7	0.8	1.6	0.4	1.5	-3.2	-8.8	-0.6	-3.2	0.3	..	Syrian Arab Rep.
5.0	-0.2	-0.8	2.9	-4.4	-5.4	-1.8	-4.2	5.6	6.0	-0.1	Tunisia
-2.0	*-0.6*	*-0.8*	*-0.1*	*0.7*	*1.6*	*-0.1*	*0.1*	*0.6*	*-3.3*	*..*	*EUROPE*
3.2	-1.2	0.5	1.4	-0.1	5.2	-1.0	2.4	-1.3	-7.3	-13.7	Bulgaria
-3.0	-0.8	-1.5	-0.6	0.6	1.9	0.2	-1.0	1.5	1.3	-14.7	Czechoslovakia
-4.1	-1.6	-0.2	-1.1	1.9	-2.1	-2.6	3.7	-0.1	-0.2	..	Greece
-0.7	-1.0	-1.0	-0.7	-0.9	2.4	0.9	-0.9	-0.1	-2.5	-2.1	Hungary
5.1	9.8	-5.6	-1.5	-0.6	-2.1	2.2	6.4	1.0	..	..	Malta
-7.5	-1.0	1.6	1.9	1.1	1.3	0.0	2.3	1.7	-7.8	-6.6	Poland
1.1	2.4	-8.7	-5.9	0.2	3.8	0.0	0.0	2.5	..	..	Portugal
-5.5	0.5	1.1	1.6	-0.6	2.1	-2.1	-2.9	-0.9	-0.7	-12.2	Romania
2.0	-1.3	-0.1	0.4	3.1	3.2	1.4	-1.6	-1.1	3.5	-4.9	Turkey
0.3	-0.7	-0.1	0.6	-0.4	-0.4	0.7	-0.9	2.0	-12.2	..	Yugoslavia
0.9	**-2.5**	**-0.5**	**0.4**	**2.0**	**1.2**	**0.5**	**1.1**	**0.9**	**0.5**	**-0.2**	**Low- and middle-income economies**
3.2	0.0	0.0	2.1	6.0	1.3	1.1	2.9	0.9	1.5	0.3	Low-income economies
0.5	-2.3	-4.9	-2.6	-0.4	1.7	-1.8	0.8	1.1	0.4	0.4	Low-income Africa
2.4	0.6	1.1	3.5	8.5	1.6	2.2	4.3	0.6	1.3	0.1	China and India
7.3	0.0	0.4	1.0	2.6	0.0	-0.6	-0.4	1.7	2.6	1.0	Other low-income
0.1	-3.5	-0.7	-0.3	0.2	1.2	0.2	0.3	0.9	-0.1	-0.5	Middle-income economies
-0.3	**-1.2**	**0.4**	**2.3**	**0.6**	**0.6**	**1.1**	**1.8**	**1.5**	**0.7**	**..**	**High-income economies**
-0.3	-1.2	0.4	2.3	0.6	0.6	1.2	1.8	1.5	0.6	..	OECD members
0.7	-0.1	-0.6	1.5	1.8	1.1	2.3	4.0	2.8	3.3	..	Japan
1.2	-2.7	1.3	4.5	0.2	0.1	0.7	0.5	0.8	-0.4	..	United States
-0.1	**-1.4**	**0.3**	**2.0**	**0.8**	**0.7**	**1.0**	**1.7**	**1.4**	**0.6**	**..**	**WORLD**

Table 12. Resource balance: contribution to growth of gross domestic product

Percentage points	1970	1971	1972	1973	1974	1975	1976	1977	1978	1979	1980
SUB-SAHARAN AFRICA	*-0.2*	*-2.5*	*3.5*	*-0.8*	*-4.0*	*-6.1*	*-0.7*	*-6.9*	*-3.5*	*10.6*	*-5.5*
Excluding Nigeria	*-0.5*	*-1.5*	*2.5*	*-0.7*	*-3.1*	*0.5*	*1.6*	*-4.0*	*-0.8*	*0.7*	*-0.8*
Benin	-0.5	-1.9	-2.4	-1.2	-0.7	-2.5	2.3	-2.7	-0.5	-4.7	-7.0
Botswana	-8.6	10.8	9.6	-12.6	-0.1	0.0	9.8	4.0	1.4	-7.0	-4.9
Burkina Faso	4.0	-4.1	1.4	-2.0	0.1	-5.0	1.8	-6.1	4.1	2.8	-4.3
Burundi	-5.5	-5.1	3.0	0.1	-1.9	-3.6	0.0	-6.0	1.1	-3.4	-0.5
Cameroon	-0.8	-6.8	1.4	3.7	2.9	-3.8	0.2	-5.9	3.2	0.6	2.6
Cape Verde	..	..	..	..	8.1	-1.6	-21.5	-25.1	0.4	-4.2	-0.9
Central African Rep.	-1.9	1.8	0.5	2.0	13.9	-0.2	-3.0	-8.7	-1.7	2.5	-4.5
Chad	-2.7	0.8	-2.4	-5.9	-1.2	2.7	2.4	-1.8	2.3	3.2	0.7
Comoros	..	..	..	..	..	..	..	..	..	..	..
Congo	0.3	1.3	1.3	1.2	1.2	-4.0	4.4	8.5	5.1	16.4	-11.2
Côte d'Ivoire	-2.3	1.4	3.2	-6.5	2.6	-0.5	-3.7	-11.3	-4.5	2.0	1.0
Equatorial Guinea	..	..	..	..	..	..	..	..	..	..	..
Ethiopia	..	..	..	..	..	..	..	..	..	..	..
Gabon	2.2	1.1	-2.1	0.2	-13.1	-2.8	0.7	-0.6	8.6	-2.2	-3.0
Gambia, The	23.2	-30.7	4.2	-0.6	21.6	0.1	-43.4	-10.2	-74.7	74.3	-24.3
Ghana	7.3	4.0	13.5	-8.8	-12.9	4.0	3.0	-10.1	1.1	3.6	-4.9
Guinea-Bissau	..	-1.3	-6.9	3.3	3.3	25.6	3.1	3.8	-1.4	-0.9	5.8
Kenya	-10.7	-11.3	8.3	3.5	-5.6	10.3	1.8	-7.0	-12.3	9.3	-2.9
Lesotho	-9.5	-15.3	-26.7	-16.4	-15.2	-42.1	-30.9	-5.5	2.6	-8.1	-5.9
Liberia	..	..	..	..	..	..	..	..	..	..	..
Madagascar	0.3	-4.6	5.1	0.1	5.3	1.0	4.5	-1.5	-1.8	-10.6	0.1
Malawi	-6.5	-1.2	-3.0	16.2	-3.7	-11.2	9.6	4.4	-18.4	12.2	0.6
Mali	4.5	2.0	-4.4	-0.3	-8.1	2.0	4.9	3.6	-10.5	-0.5	0.6
Mauritania	-0.4	0.1	-0.3	-1.6	-16.6	-15.2	-26.1	8.3	16.3	7.9	1.2
Mauritius	-4.0	-7.7	4.1	2.1	-19.7	-12.2	5.6	0.8	-1.1	1.6	6.2
Mozambique	..	..	..	..	..	..	..	..	..	..	..
Namibia	..	..	..	..	..	..	..	..	..	..	..
Niger	2.4	3.9	-2.4	0.4	-19.1	20.5	-0.2	-1.4	6.2	-11.3	0.0
Nigeria	1.0	-5.6	6.8	-1.1	-6.7	-24.2	-6.8	-15.4	-11.4	41.4	-18.9
Rwanda	1.7	-2.2	-0.8	4.3	-5.8	0.6	2.0	-2.9	-1.2	1.9	-3.5
Senegal	-0.9	-1.6	3.9	-4.2	0.9	2.4	0.2	-2.5	-6.1	3.4	-2.3
Seychelles	..	..	..	..	..	..	..	..	..	..	..
Sierra Leone	-0.6	5.9	4.9	-8.9	-4.5	6.7	1.7	-8.8	-12.0	-7.2	-2.7
Somalia	0.7	-2.9	5.0	-4.2	-3.4	-0.8	-2.4	-25.1	4.9	-7.5	0.9
Sudan	1.2	-1.2	0.3	1.0	-2.0	-2.3	1.1	-0.5	-0.6	0.1	-0.2
Swaziland	..	..	..	..	..	..	..	..	..	..	..
Tanzania	-6.4	-5.3	5.0	-3.8	-8.7	6.1	7.6	-4.5	-17.3	7.9	2.6
Togo	-3.0	18.0	0.0	-0.4	-1.1	-2.0	-12.7	-16.6	3.0	-4.8	22.0
Uganda	..	..	..	..	..	..	..	..	..	..	..
Zaire	-0.3	-0.7	-0.7	-1.1	0.4	0.3	1.4	-4.6	6.7	-2.7	-0.5
Zambia	-7.4	-10.6	7.0	11.7	-10.1	4.2	35.0	-1.2	6.4	-2.5	-8.1
Zimbabwe	..	..	..	..	..	..	..	-1.5	1.1	-3.6	-3.1
SOUTH ASIA	*-1.7*	*-0.3*	*1.6*	*0.5*	*-0.1*	*1.1*	*0.7*	*-1.9*	*-0.3*	*-1.2*	*-1.5*
Bangladesh	-1.1	1.7	-1.0	10.4	-9.7	1.6	-2.4	5.6	-6.6	0.4	-4.9
Bhutan	..	..	..	..	..	..	..	..	..	..	..
India	-0.7	-1.2	0.9	-0.7	1.2	0.7	1.1	-2.0	0.4	-0.7	-1.4
Nepal	..	..	..	..	..	..	..	..	..	..	..
Pakistan	-14.3	4.7	10.5	3.8	-5.7	2.7	-0.2	-4.5	-0.6	-6.3	0.7
Sri Lanka	4.8	3.3	2.4	1.5	-4.1	6.4	-3.4	-2.7	-8.4	-3.3	-7.2
EAST ASIA AND PACIFIC	*-0.2*	*1.8*	*1.8*	*-0.2*	*-2.9*	*1.0*	*1.5*	*-0.2*	*-2.9*	*-2.2*	*0.6*
China	-2.1	2.6	0.1	-0.8	-2.2	1.6	-0.2	-0.8	-3.4	-0.9	-0.1
Fiji	1.1	-2.5	-1.9	-2.9	-2.9	-2.8	-3.3	1.4	-0.3	-0.5	-0.3
Indonesia	3.4	1.6	5.0	2.4	-2.4	-3.1	2.7	2.7	-2.3	-1.6	-0.3
Korea, Rep.	0.4	-1.6	4.2	1.2	-4.4	3.2	2.9	0.6	-4.3	-4.3	4.7
Malaysia	-4.2	0.9	2.2	0.2	-6.7	6.7	4.2	-4.0	-1.7	-0.4	-8.2
Mongolia	..	..	..	..	..	..	..	..	..	..	..
Papua New Guinea	-16.0	-1.5	19.3	18.5	-0.8	-2.4	-0.1	-4.2	2.3	-3.9	-5.2
Philippines	4.1	0.6	1.3	2.2	-6.9	-1.3	3.2	2.0	-2.1	-2.6	2.1
Solomon Islands	..	..	..	..	..	..	..	..	..	..	..
Thailand	1.1	7.2	-0.3	-7.7	3.3	-0.4	2.1	-3.1	0.5	-3.8	1.7
Tonga	..	..	..	..	..	..	..	..	..	..	..
Vanuatu	..	..	..	..	..	..	..	..	..	..	..
Western Samoa	..	..	..	..	..	..	..	..	..	..	19.7

1981	1982	1983	1984	1985	1986	1987	1988	1989	1990	1991	
-9.9	*5.2*	*5.7*	*4.3*	*0.6*	*0.4*	*3.9*	*0.2*	*1.0*	*0.5*	*-0.7*	*SUB-SAHARAN AFRICA*
-0.4	*1.4*	*2.0*	*2.0*	*-0.6*	*-1.3*	*0.4*	*0.1*	*0.7*	*0.8*	*-0.7*	*Excluding Nigeria*
-3.1	6.7	6.1	6.3	0.2	0.2	0.1	-1.9	5.8	-2.2	-2.2	Benin
4.4	-8.7	35.3	18.9	-14.6	18.7	4.8	-7.9	-24.9	..	..	Botswana
-0.5	-1.3	1.2	2.9	-7.2	-2.6	3.6	-1.2	-0.5	0.6	-0.8	Burkina Faso
5.3	-4.0	-3.6	2.3	2.5	-3.4	-1.1	1.3	3.3	-1.0	1.1	Burundi
0.5	2.0	5.0	8.2	-0.1	-10.3	-4.9	1.9	4.5	0.2	-1.6	Cameroon
4.5	-9.4	0.0	-3.7	-0.1	-12.6	6.8	-2.2	4.1	-3.0	..	Cape Verde
7.6	-3.8	1.6	-1.3	-0.5	-4.2	1.5	2.3	0.9	-2.0	-1.9	Central African Rep.
6.6	-6.4	2.3	2.6	-24.6	-2.5	2.2	5.1	-1.4	-2.5	0.6	Chad
..	..	..	-22.1	10.7	5.8	-3.3	..	..	..	..	Comoros
-24.5	-31.5	25.8	6.1	-2.9	11.8	12.2	5.1	4.0	-7.0	-3.4	Congo
4.3	4.8	0.6	6.1	0.6	-4.3	3.9	1.2	4.1	5.6	0.6	Côte d'Ivoire
..	..	..	..	..	-0.6	-15.6	-3.4	7.6	-7.3	-22.1	Equatorial Guinea
..	..	..	..	..	..	..	..	..	..	..	Ethiopia
-20.5	4.7	-6.1	7.5	-3.9	-1.3	19.2	1.2	6.9	19.4	1.1	Gabon
49.8	19.4	26.9	-17.1	7.3	-9.7	20.5	-11.3	3.9	1.5	0.9	Gambia, The
1.6	10.7	-8.3	0.5	-2.2	0.5	-0.5	2.0	-7.8	-0.2	-0.8	Ghana
-3.8	-16.6	1.1	-3.7	-6.1	2.2	10.6	-4.3	-11.3	13.3	..	Guinea-Bissau
8.2	6.0	4.5	-3.7	3.2	-1.7	-3.1	-1.4	-0.3	0.0	-0.2	Kenya
-13.9	-8.8	-1.3	-3.4	4.2	14.6	-3.0	-5.3	-15.9	-9.3	5.8	Lesotho
..	..	..	..	..	..	..	..	..	..	..	Liberia
8.8	0.0	2.3	2.3	-0.8	0.6	2.8	-0.4	3.9	-3.8	1.6	Madagascar
6.4	-0.5	0.0	9.3	-6.0	9.3	1.1	-5.2	-10.7	4.5	-1.6	Malawi
0.2	0.6	-1.9	-2.3	-11.8	8.2	1.3	-1.1	2.4	0.8	-0.5	Mali
-3.2	-14.1	13.2	0.4	4.3	4.0	0.9	-1.5	-0.2	-1.5	3.8	Mauritania
2.2	10.9	-0.8	-1.8	3.0	1.9	-7.3	-4.8	4.3	0.9	0.5	Mauritius
-3.6	-3.4	1.2	-0.5	5.1	-11.8	-0.5	-2.4	-3.0	1.1	-0.2	Mozambique
-9.8	4.2	8.1	-4.7	8.0	6.4	-9.2	-1.5	1.5	..	..	Namibia
-1.2	-6.3	2.3	2.1	-6.3	5.1	-0.1	2.7	1.9	-0.2	-0.6	Niger
-39.4	18.4	19.5	13.7	5.9	7.2	18.5	0.8	2.7	-0.2	-0.5	Nigeria
0.4	-3.1	1.5	-2.1	-1.5	0.1	2.0	-1.4	0.7	4.3	..	Rwanda
-3.1	8.1	0.6	-1.6	-2.6	1.6	0.0	1.0	0.8	0.3	0.0	Senegal
..	..	..	..	..	..	..	..	..	..	..	Seychelles
4.0	3.2	6.0	5.5	-1.5	2.7	-1.5	0.8	-4.4	0.4	..	Sierra Leone
0.2	-5.3	-1.5	0.9	23.7	-18.7	2.5	9.5	-8.5	..	..	Somalia
-1.8	-1.0	-0.1	-0.2	1.2	-0.2	-0.7	1.2	-0.1	0.8	0.8	Sudan
..	..	..	..	..	..	..	..	..	..	..	Swaziland
9.8	-0.9	3.8	-6.2	-2.9	-5.5	0.7	-1.2	..	..	..	Tanzania
-2.8	-1.6	5.7	-3.9	-4.8	-6.9	6.1	-3.0	0.4	-8.0	1.0	Togo
..	..	..	..	..	..	..	..	..	..	..	Uganda
-2.7	1.3	0.5	2.9	-0.2	-1.2	-2.7	-0.3	3.4	-0.9	..	Zaire
1.4	16.6	-0.1	-2.8	-7.0	-3.7	-3.9	-2.4	5.4	-4.3	-3.8	Zambia
-6.0	0.3	3.2	4.4	0.4	3.3	1.2	-3.8	-3.1	-1.6	-7.6	Zimbabwe
0.5	*0.3*	*-0.1*	*-0.1*	*-1.2*	*0.1*	*0.6*	*-0.7*	*0.9*	*0.2*	*0.4*	*SOUTH ASIA*
1.9	0.6	0.7	-1.1	-3.5	3.2	-1.0	-0.7	-0.1	0.5	..	Bangladesh
..	..	..	..	..	..	..	..	..	..	..	Bhutan
-0.5	0.5	-0.4	0.1	-1.2	-0.4	0.7	-0.7	0.9	0.2	0.3	India
..	..	..	..	..	..	..	..	..	..	..	Nepal
7.3	-0.1	0.5	-1.9	-1.5	1.3	1.7	-0.2	0.9	0.4	2.0	Pakistan
6.5	-4.9	-3.3	3.4	2.0	0.1	0.2	-3.4	3.0	4.4	-0.3	Sri Lanka
-0.9	*0.9*	*0.0*	*1.2*	*-1.8*	*3.1*	*1.6*	*-0.3*	*-2.5*	*0.1*	*-1.0*	*EAST ASIA AND PACIFIC*
1.3	2.5	-0.4	-0.5	-4.8	2.6	2.1	-1.3	-1.2	3.8	-1.3	China
-3.0	6.8	1.1	4.5	0.8	2.9	0.9	-10.7	-3.0	-4.8	1.8	Fiji
-14.1	-2.8	1.2	3.4	-3.0	2.1	2.7	4.4	0.3	-3.6	0.1	Indonesia
2.8	0.5	2.4	0.4	1.8	3.6	2.2	1.3	-7.7	-3.0	-0.5	Korea, Rep.
-3.4	-2.5	0.7	3.1	5.9	9.6	4.5	-4.7	-4.7	-5.2	-4.9	Malaysia
-11.1	4.9	-5.6	5.6	-7.8	4.2	3.1	0.1	6.1	0.4	..	Mongolia
1.9	0.1	1.0	2.2	5.8	4.6	-0.7	-4.9	5.1	2.3	0.8	Papua New Guinea
1.8	-2.6	1.8	5.1	-1.2	1.9	-4.4	-1.2	-2.2	-2.8	1.1	Philippines
8.8	28.0	-3.2	-12.8	-2.7	18.0	-8.5	-30.3	..	..	..	Solomon Islands
2.7	5.8	-7.6	3.2	2.9	2.7	-1.1	-1.4	0.0	-1.6	-0.2	Thailand
..	..	..	..	..	..	..	..	..	..	..	Tonga
..	..	..	-5.1	-10.0	3.0	-4.5	1.3	0.3	..	..	Vanuatu
-7.4	19.7	-0.1	-5.8	0.9	2.5	-7.8	-0.5	1.7	-7.3	..	Western Samoa

Table 12. Resource balance: contribution to growth of gross domestic product (cont'd.)

Percentage points	1970	1971	1972	1973	1974	1975	1976	1977	1978	1979	1980
LATIN AMERICA AND CARIBBEAN	*-0.8*	*-1.1*	*0.7*	*-0.3*	*-2.2*	*-0.4*	*0.2*	*-0.4*	*0.1*	*-0.5*	*-2.4*
Argentina	2.2	-1.7	0.6	0.9	-0.4	-0.7	3.4	-0.5	1.2	-4.8	-6.0
Bahamas	..	..	..	..	..	..	..	..	4.4	-2.2	1.3
Barbados	..	..	..	..	..	..	..	..	..	..	..
Belize	..	..	..	..	..	..	..	..	..	..	..
Bolivia	-2.1	-1.7	-1.2	1.8	2.9	-6.1	2.2	-0.2	-1.6	0.4	4.9
Brazil	-1.5	-1.8	-0.7	-1.3	-3.0	1.2	0.1	0.8	0.2	-0.3	1.2
Chile	0.0	-2.5	-2.9	2.0	4.3	13.0	3.9	-5.4	-2.3	-3.5	-2.8
Colombia	-2.6	-1.6	2.7	0.2	-0.5	3.4	-1.9	-1.8	0.4	1.1	-1.9
Costa Rica	-3.7	-0.3	4.2	0.0	-1.0	1.8	-3.3	-6.0	-0.2	-0.2	0.1
Dominican Rep.	-2.9	-1.6	-3.1	1.0	-8.7	8.9	-0.2	-0.1	0.2	1.8	-12.6
Ecuador	-0.8	-5.3	16.1	18.3	-13.2	-8.6	3.6	-7.5	-0.5	1.2	-4.1
El Salvador	-3.7	-0.9	1.2	-6.2	0.3	4.1	-7.4	-12.4	2.2	9.0	5.0
Grenada	..	..	..	..	..	..	..	..	..	..	..
Guatemala	-3.3	-1.3	5.2	-0.9	-3.0	2.5	-8.0	-2.1	-1.7	5.2	4.2
Guyana	-4.5	13.2	-6.1	-30.2	14.4	-32.1	-10.7	27.9	33.4	-4.4	-9.9
Haiti	-2.5	0.2	-0.8	1.2	-0.5	-0.9	-3.7	-3.0	0.6	2.1	-0.3
Honduras	-2.0	7.4	1.3	-2.8	-5.8	3.4	-2.8	-5.6	0.6	2.2	-2.6
Jamaica	1.4	-1.1	-0.1	-1.1	-1.2	-6.3	3.1	6.3	2.4	0.5	2.9
Mexico	-2.3	1.1	0.2	-1.0	-3.2	-1.0	1.3	3.2	-1.8	-3.4	-5.4
Nicaragua	-0.3	0.7	4.8	-4.3	-2.1	4.8	0.6	-4.1	4.6	4.9	-22.0
Panama	-2.5	-3.3	-2.8	2.0	-3.0	2.7	1.5	4.7	-3.5	-1.5	6.2
Paraguay	3.8	-2.8	2.1	-3.0	-2.6	2.6	-5.1	-4.9	0.0	13.2	-25.8
Peru	2.8	-1.1	1.2	-4.3	-3.9	0.8	2.6	1.2	5.1	0.4	-5.2
St. Vincent	..	..	..	..	..	..	..	..	17.0	-8.0	-4.1
Trinidad and Tobago	-0.2	-6.1	3.5	2.2	-1.7	-5.3	-2.0	-1.1	-1.9	-4.4	-0.3
Uruguay	-3.6	-1.0	1.2	-1.6	3.4	1.1	2.8	-0.1	-0.5	-2.7	-0.9
Venezuela	..	..	..	..	..	-13.2	-7.3	-9.2	-0.2	8.5	-4.1
MIDDLE EAST AND NORTH AFRICA	..	..	..	..	..	..	..	..	..	..	..
Algeria	-0.7	-5.0	5.0	-2.2	-6.8	-3.1	1.6	-4.1	-0.7	3.0	-2.7
Egypt, Arab Rep.	-4.2	0.3	-1.1	-3.6	-16.9	-8.1	10.3	-0.5	-1.7	-9.1	-0.8
Iran, Islamic Rep.	4.6	-1.1	3.2	1.1	-3.4	-8.4	0.7	-3.7	-1.2	1.5	-10.5
Jordan	..	..	..	..	..	..	..	..	..	..	..
Morocco	-2.5	0.6	3.9	-1.0	-2.4	-13.7	-6.2	-2.9	6.7	-1.1	3.5
Oman	..	..	..	..	..	..	..	..	..	..	..
Saudi Arabia	..	..	..	..	..	..	..	..	..	..	..
Syrian Arab Rep.	..	..	..	..	..	..	-1.3	-14.8	5.5	-2.0	-0.5
Tunisia	-3.1	4.7	-0.3	-2.3	-2.2	-3.5	0.7	-3.8	-1.2	0.5	-2.2
EUROPE	..	..	..	..	..	..	..	..	..	..	..
Bulgaria	..	..	..	..	..	..	..	..	..	..	..
Czechoslovakia	..	..	..	..	..	..	..	..	..	..	..
Greece	0.0	-0.3	-0.6	-3.9	4.1	0.1	1.0	-1.5	0.9	-0.5	3.1
Hungary	..	-6.5	7.0	3.1	-6.4	-1.0	0.9	3.1	-5.1	5.6	0.6
Malta	-5.0	9.4	9.2	13.5	-0.9	15.1	-0.3	-1.2	8.3	4.9	-0.4
Poland	..	..	..	..	..	..	..	..	..	..	..
Portugal	-0.8	-2.4	0.5	-3.5	-6.0	6.4	-1.0	-3.2	1.5	1.7	-0.4
Romania	..	..	..	..	..	..	..	..	..	..	..
Turkey	-1.4	-2.4	-1.9	1.3	-4.5	-2.2	-0.2	-2.1	7.5	0.3	-0.1
Yugoslavia	-7.2	-2.6	6.2	-2.2	-6.8	0.9	6.7	-6.4	0.4	-3.6	5.3
Low- and middle-income economies	**-0.7**	**-0.8**	**2.2**	**-0.5**	**-3.3**	**-1.3**	**1.1**	**-1.6**	**-0.6**	**0.1**	**-2.1**
Low-income economies	-1.2	0.2	1.8	-0.1	-2.3	-1.0	0.6	-2.2	-2.1	1.1	-2.0
Low-income Africa	0.0	-2.6	3.6	-0.5	-4.7	-7.1	-0.7	-7.4	-4.6	13.4	-7.0
China and India	-1.2	0.3	0.6	-0.7	-0.3	1.1	0.5	-1.5	-1.2	-0.8	-0.8
Other low-income	-2.1	2.2	3.4	2.1	-5.8	-1.6	1.9	0.4	-2.2	-3.2	-1.1
Middle-income economies	..	..	..	..	..	..	..	..	..	..	..
High-income economies	**-0.2**	**0.0**	**-0.2**	**-0.4**	**0.8**	**0.6**	**-0.4**	**0.2**	**0.1**	**-0.2**	**0.8**
OECD members	-0.2	0.0	-0.2	-0.3	0.8	0.6	-0.4	0.2	0.1	-0.3	0.9
Japan	-0.5	0.5	-0.5	-1.5	1.1	0.9	0.7	0.7	-0.6	-0.7	2.2
United States	0.2	-0.4	-0.2	0.2	0.8	0.7	-1.1	-0.8	0.1	0.4	1.4
WORLD	**-0.2**	**0.0**	**0.1**	**-0.3**	**0.4**	**0.3**	**-0.1**	**-0.1**	**0.1**	**-0.1**	**0.4**

1981	1982	1983	1984	1985	1986	1987	1988	1989	1990	1991	
0.1	*3.7*	*4.5*	*0.3*	*0.4*	*-0.6*	*0.4*	*0.2*	*0.5*	*-0.4*	*-1.8*	*LATIN AMERICA AND CARIBBEAN*
2.1	7.4	1.3	-0.7	2.7	-2.6	-0.6	3.5	2.2	2.3	-5.5	Argentina
-6.7	2.9	1.3	-1.5	-2.9	0.1	-0.4	..	..	..	..	Bahamas
..	..	..	..	..	..	..	..	..	..	..	Barbados
..	..	..	..	..	..	..	..	..	..	..	Belize
-7.2	9.3	-0.7	2.4	-6.7	2.6	-2.1	3.2	2.1	2.0	0.1	Bolivia
2.5	-0.3	2.4	2.1	0.7	-2.6	1.8	1.3	0.0	-1.2	-0.3	Brazil
-8.6	16.6	4.9	-2.4	5.3	0.6	-1.7	-1.5	-2.4	2.3	2.2	Chile
-2.6	-1.5	1.5	1.9	2.9	2.5	0.6	-0.8	2.2	2.4	-2.1	Colombia
12.2	3.3	-4.1	0.4	-2.8	-4.0	0.2	2.4	-0.6	-0.6	3.2	Costa Rica
7.0	2.9	0.3	4.1	-2.8	-2.2	-2.4	3.1	-6.7	8.9	2.6	Dominican Rep.
4.5	-3.3	8.9	3.4	1.0	2.2	-8.1	10.5	-2.0	1.2	2.5	Ecuador
-0.2	1.6	1.6	-1.6	-1.0	-1.8	2.1	-1.6	-3.8	6.2	-1.0	El Salvador
..	..	..	..	-0.4	-17.9	-5.9	4.1	-1.9	6.9	..	Grenada
-2.3	4.3	2.6	-2.0	3.2	0.1	-6.5	0.1	0.8	2.8	-0.6	Guatemala
-4.8	18.7	-1.1	12.6	-4.6	-0.1	9.0	1.1	2.1	-13.8	-13.7	Guyana
-3.7	5.1	-1.7	1.1	-0.1	0.0	-1.4	0.1	-0.5	-2.5	0.8	Haiti
4.8	5.3	-1.8	-4.0	0.5	1.6	-0.7	0.5	1.0	-0.6	0.7	Honduras
-2.1	-3.4	2.3	-2.1	-2.0	8.5	-2.5	-1.6	-9.4	9.8	1.9	Jamaica
-2.8	12.2	7.4	-0.9	-2.2	2.5	1.3	-3.8	-2.6	-3.4	-2.9	Mexico
3.6	3.1	-0.8	-3.7	-1.9	-0.3	-0.6	-0.2	-0.9	-1.0	0.3	Nicaragua
-1.1	2.6	3.2	-4.8	1.8	2.2	0.8	9.6	-4.3	-7.4	0.4	Panama
0.8	3.7	14.0	-6.3	0.4	-2.4	-4.0	3.9	9.6	-1.1	-1.4	Paraguay
-2.9	0.3	4.2	3.8	1.6	-3.4	-2.5	0.4	4.4	-2.0	-0.3	Peru
5.8	-10.2	5.7	6.1	1.4	-11.0	-5.7	..	..	..	..	St. Vincent
1.6	-7.0	1.0	5.9	1.2	-3.7	9.7	6.2	0.3	2.5	-7.5	Trinidad and Tobago
0.9	0.9	6.9	2.2	1.6	-1.5	-5.0	2.0	2.2	2.5	-2.4	Uruguay
-3.9	-6.3	15.6	-5.0	-0.1	2.8	-2.1	-4.1	9.3	4.2	-6.7	Venezuela
..	..	..	..	..	..	..	..	..	..	..	*MIDDLE EAST AND NORTH AFRICA*
-3.1	1.8	-0.4	0.3	0.5	3.1	3.2	1.3	0.2	1.1	0.2	Algeria
-3.2	4.9	1.4	-4.8	-0.6	5.3	6.6	0.5	0.4	0.6	2.4	Egypt, Arab Rep.
-2.3	7.7	-4.7	-0.3	1.8	1.7	0.1	3.4	-0.3	..	..	Iran, Islamic Rep.
..	..	..	4.0	1.3	-5.9	4.7	-0.6	7.9	-10.8	6.5	Jordan
-0.5	0.1	4.9	-0.5	0.9	-1.4	0.1	2.4	-4.5	0.7	-1.5	Morocco
..	..	..	..	..	..	..	..	..	..	..	Oman
..	..	..	..	..	..	..	..	..	..	..	Saudi Arabia
2.8	5.7	0.8	-0.2	-7.7	10.7	-3.1	5.8	-2.7	2.2	..	Syrian Arab Rep.
-4.9	-2.9	1.5	-1.9	7.3	2.4	6.0	2.6	-4.8	-3.2	1.1	Tunisia
2.0	*2.6*	*2.3*	*1.0*	*0.6*	*-1.2*	*-0.1*	*0.2*	*-1.9*	*-3.1*	*..*	*EUROPE*
..	..	..	2.7	-3.3	-3.9	0.1	2.5	-0.8	-1.5	2.8	Bulgaria
2.6	1.4	0.7	1.3	0.9	-1.4	-0.4	0.8	-2.1	-5.8	9.2	Czechoslovakia
-1.8	-2.8	-0.3	2.8	-2.9	1.6	-1.1	-0.3	-2.8	-1.9	..	Greece
1.2	2.6	2.1	2.1	-1.0	-1.9	0.7	2.4	-0.2	0.9	-2.9	Hungary
-3.0	-9.1	4.8	-0.4	-2.3	4.8	-0.9	-4.9	-1.7	..	..	Malta
0.6	3.7	0.8	0.8	-1.2	-0.1	0.2	0.3	-0.4	5.6	-6.6	Poland
-1.8	-0.5	6.5	4.4	2.1	-3.1	-5.4	-4.5	-1.9	..	..	Portugal
8.8	12.0	12.1	-4.8	8.0	1.4	-8.5	-10.5	-13.2	10.4		Romania
3.3	3.2	-0.5	-1.3	0.6	-2.5	0.9	3.8	-0.3	-5.6	3.3	Turkey
3.2	2.5	0.6	1.9	1.4	-2.2	1.6	1.8	-0.6	-3.8		Yugoslavia
-0.8	**3.0**	**2.0**	**0.7**	**0.1**	**0.8**	**1.1**	**0.2**	**-0.6**	**-0.3**	**-0.5**	**Low- and middle-income economies**
-3.0	1.8	1.0	0.4	-2.2	1.6	2.1	-0.3	0.0	1.1	-0.3	Low-income economies
-12.2	6.3	6.4	3.7	1.2	1.5	5.0	0.2	0.7	-0.3	-0.2	Low-income Africa
0.3	1.4	-0.4	-0.2	-3.0	1.2	1.4	-1.1	-0.2	2.1	-0.6	China and India
-4.6	-0.1	0.9	0.1	-1.8	2.4	2.4	1.7	0.5	-1.4	0.8	Other low-income
..	..	..	..	..	..	..	..	..	..	..	Middle-income economies
0.7	**0.0**	**-0.1**	**-0.1**	**0.1**	**-0.6**	**-0.3**	**-0.1**	**0.1**	**0.3**	**..**	**High-income economies**
0.8	0.0	-0.1	-0.2	0.1	-0.6	-0.4	-0.1	0.0	0.3	..	OECD members
1.2	0.3	0.7	0.8	0.7	-0.7	-0.5	-0.6	-0.5	0.1	..	Japan
-0.2	-0.4	-1.1	-1.5	-0.3	-0.3	0.2	0.8	0.4	0.4	..	United States
0.5	**0.4**	**0.3**	**0.1**	**0.2**	**-0.3**	**-0.1**	**0.1**	**0.0**	**0.3**	**..**	**WORLD**

Table 13. Gross domestic investment: percentage of gross domestic product

Percentage points	1970	1971	1972	1973	1974	1975	1976	1977	1978	1979	1980
SUB-SAHARAN AFRICA	*16.7*	*18.8*	*19.5*	*19.8*	*19.6*	*23.3*	*25.9*	*26.0*	*23.5*	*21.0*	*21.9*
Excluding Nigeria	*17.7*	*18.9*	*18.8*	*18.7*	*21.3*	*22.0*	*21.7*	*22.3*	*19.8*	*19.2*	*20.1*
Benin	11.6	10.3	13.4	13.1	18.2	19.3	16.7	17.8	16.1	19.0	15.2
Botswana	42.2	47.7	52.5	49.9	51.7	47.7	42.0	31.3	39.6	38.3	41.0
Burkina Faso	12.3	17.9	20.8	24.8	30.7	27.8	27.5	23.5	22.0	19.7	18.2
Burundi	4.5	7.6	3.2	5.3	4.1	7.6	9.1	11.1	14.0	14.9	13.9
Cameroon	16.0	16.6	18.2	19.9	17.1	20.0	17.6	21.8	22.7	21.7	18.9
Cape Verde	..	..	..	19.7	16.7	16.0	27.2	38.7	34.6	46.6	41.9
Central African Rep.	18.9	19.7	19.2	22.1	14.6	13.9	12.1	11.7	11.0	9.7	7.0
Chad	18.1	17.8	16.5	-3.8	20.7	23.0	19.1	20.8	18.2	..	..
Comoros	..	..	..	..	..	..	..	..	..	..	..
Congo	24.2	26.6	29.1	32.0	35.1	39.1	31.0	26.6	27.3	26.0	35.8
Côte d'Ivoire	22.5	21.8	20.9	23.2	22.0	22.4	23.0	27.3	29.8	28.0	28.2
Equatorial Guinea	19.9	20.4	20.8	18.0	16.6	15.0	13.2	13.5	..	..	..
Ethiopia	11.5	11.8	12.7	11.4	9.9	10.4	9.6	8.8	7.5	8.7	10.0
Gabon	32.0	32.0	48.1	37.6	51.8	62.7	73.5	58.1	35.0	32.9	27.5
Gambia, The	4.8	6.4	8.0	8.2	4.4	12.2	11.4	14.8	31.6	27.1	26.2
Ghana	14.2	14.1	7.1	9.0	13.0	12.7	8.9	11.1	5.4	6.5	5.6
Guinea-Bissau	29.6	28.0	22.8	20.9	16.8	15.4	16.3	19.8	21.7	21.8	29.6
Kenya	24.4	23.9	22.3	25.8	25.8	18.1	20.2	23.7	29.8	22.3	29.2
Lesotho	11.4	15.8	15.2	18.6	17.7	18.7	36.1	25.0	25.9	34.6	42.4
Liberia	22.2	20.1	21.2	14.5	19.7	34.0	31.5	32.8	29.7	30.1	27.3
Madagascar	9.9	11.2	8.8	9.1	8.7	8.1	8.1	8.1	9.6	16.1	15.0
Malawi	25.7	19.2	24.4	22.4	27.3	33.7	26.3	24.7	38.4	30.2	24.7
Mali	16.2	17.0	18.1	17.9	14.3	16.5	14.2	16.5	16.9	16.4	17.0
Mauritania	22.0	22.8	30.4	8.6	16.1	34.5	42.4	39.1	31.0	25.5	36.2
Mauritius	9.9	14.5	15.3	24.9	25.2	26.3	31.8	30.0	30.7	31.2	20.7
Mozambique	..	..	..	..	..	..	..	..	..	..	18.9
Namibia											33.2
Niger	9.8	7.8	11.1	14.9	15.1	14.3	14.2	19.7	23.0	25.8	36.6
Nigeria	14.8	18.7	21.1	22.4	17.0	25.2	31.5	31.0	28.8	23.4	23.9
Rwanda	7.0	9.1	9.6	9.4	10.5	13.7	13.8	15.1	16.6	12.0	16.1
Senegal	15.7	16.2	17.0	18.9	22.2	17.8	16.5	17.5	17.4	14.4	15.3
Seychelles	..	..	..	..	..	..	38.9	40.0	43.3	32.9	38.3
Sierra Leone	16.6	15.3	11.7	11.7	15.8	15.7	11.3	13.1	11.3	13.4	16.2
Somalia	11.7	11.9	13.6	14.3	26.9	22.5	29.9	21.4	28.7	23.0	42.4
Sudan	0.0	11.8	9.2	11.7	18.4	17.5	23.2	17.1	14.4	13.2	15.1
Swaziland	19.2	19.9	22.3	23.4	26.9	17.8	29.6	27.0	43.9	39.7	40.7
Tanzania	22.5	26.4	21.8	21.1	22.0	21.1	22.9	26.1	25.2	26.1	23.0
Togo	15.1	18.9	20.7	21.7	16.4	27.7	24.9	34.3	52.7	48.8	30.1
Uganda	0.0	0.0	0.0	0.0	0.0	0.0	0.0	0.0	0.0	0.0	6.1
Zaire	14.9	18.4	18.6	16.7	17.1	17.8	14.5	21.4	11.9	12.7	10.0
Zambia	28.2	37.1	35.3	29.2	36.7	40.6	23.7	24.7	23.9	14.1	23.3
Zimbabwe	20.4	22.4	26.4	25.4	27.5	26.3	17.9	19.1	11.9	12.7	18.8
SOUTH ASIA	*16.3*	*17.0*	*15.9*	*17.0*	*17.8*	*18.2*	*19.3*	*19.0*	*21.0*	*21.6*	*20.5*
Bangladesh	11.3	8.2	4.7	8.7	7.4	6.1	9.9	11.5	11.5	11.2	14.9
Bhutan	..	..	..	..	..	..	..	..	..	..	31.0
India	17.1	18.5	17.1	18.3	19.8	20.8	20.9	19.8	22.3	22.9	20.9
Nepal	6.0	7.8	7.3	9.2	8.8	14.5	15.1	16.0	18.3	15.8	18.3
Pakistan	15.8	15.6	14.2	12.9	13.4	16.2	17.2	19.3	17.9	17.9	18.5
Sri Lanka	18.9	17.1	17.3	13.7	15.7	15.6	16.2	14.4	20.0	25.8	33.8
EAST ASIA AND PACIFIC	*26.6*	*27.1*	*25.6*	*27.3*	*27.8*	*28.8*	*27.2*	*27.7*	*31.0*	*33.1*	*30.4*
China	28.5	29.0	27.1	29.0	28.9	30.3	28.5	29.0	33.4	34.9	32.2
Fiji	22.2	24.8	24.0	22.2	18.9	20.6	21.5	23.2	22.8	30.1	31.8
Indonesia	15.8	18.4	21.8	20.8	19.5	23.7	24.1	23.4	23.9	26.6	24.3
Korea, Rep.	24.7	25.1	20.8	24.5	31.6	27.1	25.3	27.3	31.4	35.5	31.7
Malaysia	22.4	22.4	23.3	25.5	30.8	25.3	23.6	25.8	26.7	28.9	30.4
Mongolia	..	..	..	..	..	..	..	..	..	..	46.2
Papua New Guinea	41.6	42.8	27.8	15.5	17.4	20.0	18.6	21.6	22.6	23.5	25.2
Philippines	21.3	21.0	20.8	21.8	26.9	30.9	32.9	30.6	30.6	33.2	29.1
Solomon Islands	..	..	..	..	..	..	..	..	..	..	36.4
Thailand	25.6	24.2	21.7	27.0	26.6	26.7	24.0	26.9	28.2	27.2	26.4
Tonga	..	..	..	..	..	27.6	19.7	20.2	29.5	31.2	28.7
Vanuatu	..	..	..	..	..	..	..	..	..	..	..
Western Samoa	..	..	..	..	..	..	..	..	..	46.4	33.1

1981	1982	1983	1984	1985	1986	1987	1988	1989	1990	1991	
22.0	*19.9*	*15.8*	*12.8*	*13.1*	*16.7*	*15.9*	*15.7*	*15.9*	*16.1*	..	*SUB-SAHARAN AFRICA*
20.1	*19.4*	*16.6*	*15.6*	*16.4*	*17.5*	*16.6*	*16.5*	*16.6*	*16.8*	..	*Excluding Nigeria*
15.7	27.6	17.3	12.8	15.8	14.7	14.2	15.5	12.2	..	..	Benin
43.6	44.2	29.4	24.4	30.1	17.9	6.3	10.3	23.9	..	..	Botswana
17.0	21.6	20.6	17.0	25.9	22.9	20.0	22.2	22.8	19.9	..	Burkina Faso
17.0	14.5	22.8	18.4	13.9	11.6	22.7	15.0	16.7	19.3	..	Burundi
24.7	23.4	24.4	20.8	24.9	30.8	24.1	15.7	18.5	16.5	9.0	Cameroon
45.3	52.9	48.8	44.0	45.1	45.8	44.3	41.7	42.3	37.0	..	Cape Verde
8.7	6.7	11.8	12.3	14.5	12.2	13.7	11.5	11.2	11.1	..	Central African Rep.
..	..	3.1	5.4	8.2	9.1	12.3	7.8	9.0	10.3	..	Chad
..	..	29.0	45.8	29.6	23.6	23.3	16.0	13.9	14.7	..	Comoros
48.2	59.7	38.4	30.4	30.3	29.5	19.7	18.6	16.0	15.9	11.8	Congo
25.9	23.2	20.6	10.9	14.6	12.2	11.7	15.1	10.3	9.8	10.2	Côte d'Ivoire
..	..	..	..	9.3	12.7	24.2	21.0	21.3	24.3	..	Equatorial Guinea
10.4	11.8	11.2	12.8	14.0	12.7	14.6	15.3	13.3	..	..	Ethiopia
36.4	35.0	35.2	33.0	38.3	45.5	25.5	33.0	34.6	25.9	..	Gabon
24.5	20.6	17.3	19.2	15.8	20.4	18.5	18.0	22.0	20.7	..	Gambia, The
4.6	3.4	3.7	6.9	9.6	9.4	10.4	10.9	13.5	15.1	..	Ghana
25.7	28.3	22.7	30.0	32.0	24.3	33.3	34.2	35.6	22.4	..	Guinea-Bissau
27.7	21.8	20.8	20.7	26.0	21.8	24.3	25.0	24.6	23.7	..	Kenya
42.9	49.7	33.6	41.6	50.0	45.4	44.9	46.2	60.0	71.1	..	Lesotho
16.3	14.3	11.8	10.2	8.7	9.7	..	..	..	..	..	Liberia
11.5	8.5	8.4	8.6	8.5	9.0	10.1	13.3	13.5	16.9	..	Madagascar
17.6	21.4	22.8	12.9	18.6	12.3	15.4	18.7	20.3	19.1	..	Malawi
17.5	17.6	14.6	15.2	19.5	22.9	23.1	24.7	26.0	26.5	..	Mali
41.9	47.1	17.8	25.1	24.3	23.0	20.5	17.7	14.7	14.5	..	Mauritania
25.3	18.2	17.5	22.0	23.5	21.9	25.3	30.6	30.8	30.3	..	Mauritius
20.3	19.3	10.0	10.6	6.9	9.7	24.0	33.4	35.5	37.1	..	Mozambique
30.8	23.1	17.8	17.2	14.0	12.7	15.9	20.2	16.6	..	..	Namibia
20.3	18.2	12.8	3.2	12.7	10.1	9.2	11.0	9.5	9.2	..	Niger
24.4	20.6	14.8	9.6	9.0	15.1	13.7	13.5	13.9	14.6	16.9	Nigeria
13.3	17.8	13.5	15.8	17.3	15.9	15.6	15.7	15.6	12.5	..	Rwanda
11.9	11.3	11.9	11.7	9.8	11.0	11.7	12.5	10.8	12.7	..	Senegal
32.6	32.3	21.2	21.7	22.7	22.8	18.6	20.0	19.8	21.2	..	Seychelles
19.1	13.4	14.3	12.7	10.0	11.2	10.4	11.6	11.4	11.5	..	Sierra Leone
27.6	29.3	22.4	24.2	29.8	25.2	33.3	23.9	30.3	15.5	..	Somalia
14.3	22.8	16.0	13.8	4.5	12.8	10.3	10.0	9.1	9.3	..	Sudan
31.0	32.2	35.0	31.6	29.6	22.2	15.3	16.6	..	..	..	Swaziland
20.6	21.0	13.6	15.3	15.7	19.5	22.5	19.8	24.7	..	..	Tanzania
30.2	26.3	22.1	21.2	28.8	24.0	20.2	20.2	21.4	22.5	..	Togo
6.0	7.9	9.1	8.8	9.9	12.5	12.9	10.1	9.9	12.3	..	Uganda
10.5	8.3	9.3	10.5	12.5	13.2	14.2	14.4	14.5	11.5	..	Zaire
19.3	16.8	13.8	14.7	14.9	23.8	13.9	11.4	9.9	14.3	..	Zambia
23.1	21.2	15.9	19.0	19.8	18.4	18.5	16.9	18.2	21.0	24.8	Zimbabwe
23.7	*22.1*	*20.3*	*20.2*	*22.5*	*21.7*	*21.4*	*22.2*	*21.7*	*21.4*	*19.2*	*SOUTH ASIA*
15.9	15.3	13.4	12.2	12.8	12.3	12.5	12.0	12.2	11.8	11.7	Bangladesh
38.5	40.4	39.8	36.3	45.4	40.5	30.2	38.5	..	..	..	Bhutan
25.0	22.9	20.7	21.1	24.0	23.0	22.7	23.9	23.6	23.2	21.7	India
17.6	17.1	19.6	18.7	22.9	21.0	21.8	21.4	22.0	18.2	21.2	Nepal
18.8	19.3	18.8	18.3	18.3	18.8	19.1	18.0	18.9	18.6	..	Pakistan
27.8	29.9	28.3	26.0	23.4	23.3	22.9	22.3	21.4	22.3	..	Sri Lanka
29.4	*29.1*	*30.0*	*30.0*	*33.4*	*33.2*	*33.0*	*34.1*	*35.7*	*36.9*	*36.3*	*EAST ASIA AND PACIFIC*
29.2	29.7	30.4	32.3	40.1	40.4	39.1	39.6	39.0	39.1	40.4	China
34.3	25.6	21.1	18.9	19.1	18.2	14.9	13.0	12.8	18.7	..	Fiji
29.6	27.5	28.7	26.2	28.0	28.3	31.4	31.5	35.2	36.5	36.6	Indonesia
29.5	28.6	28.8	29.8	29.3	28.8	29.2	29.8	34.5	37.3	..	Korea, Rep.
35.0	37.3	37.8	33.6	27.6	26.0	23.2	26.0	28.8	32.3	35.7	Malaysia
62.0	63.3	51.3	50.7	58.4	66.4	45.7	42.1	46.0	29.9	..	Mongolia
27.2	32.2	29.4	27.0	19.8	19.9	20.7	27.5	23.5	25.0	..	Papua New Guinea
27.5	27.9	29.6	21.8	15.3	16.0	18.0	18.4	21.9	21.7	16.7	Philippines
33.9	30.0	36.8	23.0	26.3	26.9	27.3	38.6	..	..	..	Solomon Islands
26.3	23.1	25.9	24.9	24.0	21.8	23.9	28.8	31.5	36.8	..	Thailand
25.4	24.9	31.2	33.9	36.1	..	..	..	..	..	..	Tonga
..	..	25.7	23.9	28.3	34.5	35.3	30.7	37.1	..	..	Vanuatu
38.8	25.2	27.4	29.5	30.6	28.4	35.2	29.5	31.3	41.2	..	Western Samoa

Table 13. Gross domestic investment: percentage of gross domestic product (cont'd.)

Percentage points	1970	1971	1972	1973	1974	1975	1976	1977	1978	1979	1980
LATIN AMERICA AND CARIBBEAN	*21.4*	*20.9*	*20.6*	*21.2*	*23.2*	*25.1*	*23.7*	*24.2*	*24.6*	*23.8*	*24.4*
Argentina	21.6	21.1	20.9	18.1	19.4	25.8	26.8	27.2	24.4	22.7	22.2
Bahamas	..	..	..	..	..	..	..	12.5	11.3	12.8	18.3
Barbados	26.1	23.1	22.3	22.2	22.8	19.2	27.0	19.5	22.9	23.5	25.3
Belize	..	..	..	..	..	..	..	..	..	..	..
Bolivia	23.8	24.1	29.6	29.1	21.4	36.9	28.3	27.3	24.0	20.0	14.8
Brazil	20.5	21.1	21.2	23.2	25.4	26.8	23.1	22.1	23.0	22.8	23.3
Chile	16.5	14.5	12.2	7.9	21.2	13.1	12.8	14.4	17.8	17.8	21.0
Colombia	20.2	19.4	18.1	18.3	21.5	17.0	17.6	18.8	18.3	18.2	19.1
Costa Rica	20.5	24.3	22.0	24.0	26.7	21.6	23.7	24.3	23.5	25.3	26.6
Dominican Rep.	19.1	17.9	19.7	22.1	23.3	24.5	22.5	21.8	23.7	25.4	25.1
Ecuador	18.2	23.2	20.0	19.5	22.5	26.7	23.8	26.5	28.4	25.3	26.1
El Salvador	12.9	15.6	14.2	18.3	22.6	22.1	19.6	23.4	23.8	18.1	13.3
Grenada	..	..	..	..	..	..	..	..	..	..	32.9
Guatemala	12.8	14.4	12.1	13.7	18.6	16.1	21.4	20.0	21.6	18.7	15.9
Guyana	22.8	18.6	19.8	27.2	26.4	33.1	37.4	29.1	20.5	31.0	29.8
Haiti	11.4	11.4	13.9	15.9	16.5	14.7	15.8	15.5	16.8	18.7	16.9
Honduras	20.9	17.1	15.9	19.1	26.2	19.0	19.2	23.1	27.2	26.5	24.5
Jamaica	31.5	32.1	27.3	31.5	24.3	25.8	18.2	12.2	15.0	19.2	15.9
Mexico	21.3	18.9	19.0	20.0	21.8	22.3	21.0	21.6	22.3	24.7	27.2
Nicaragua	18.4	17.7	13.1	24.2	31.5	21.3	18.7	26.8	13.3	-5.7	16.8
Panama	27.8	30.4	31.8	33.6	33.6	30.8	31.6	23.7	26.6	28.1	27.7
Paraguay	14.7	14.6	15.1	19.0	21.0	24.1	24.6	24.7	27.2	28.6	31.7
Peru	15.5	17.9	15.2	20.3	25.9	24.7	21.9	19.2	19.4	21.7	27.5
St. Vincent	..	..	..	..	..	..	..	28.1	28.8	35.0	40.3
Trinidad and Tobago	25.9	34.0	31.3	26.0	21.8	27.3	24.6	26.7	30.2	29.1	30.6
Uruguay	16.1	17.7	17.2	17.5	15.9	18.9	21.0	21.5	22.7	24.0	24.2
Venezuela	32.9	32.2	33.2	31.0	26.1	32.8	36.2	43.1	43.9	33.2	26.4
MIDDLE EAST AND NORTH AFRICA	*19.1*	*19.2*	*21.0*	*21.0*	*22.4*	*28.4*	*28.4*	*28.6*	*25.7*	*23.4*	*26.9*
Algeria	36.4	35.5	34.3	40.3	39.7	45.2	43.1	46.8	52.1	42.5	39.1
Egypt, Arab Rep.	13.9	13.2	12.3	13.1	22.5	33.4	28.4	29.2	31.7	32.8	27.5
Iran, Islamic Rep.	18.9	21.4	22.7	19.5	18.3	28.8	28.5	27.3	22.0	20.4	32.5
Jordan	..	..	..	..	..	..	..	..	..	..	..
Morocco	18.5	17.9	15.3	16.9	20.6	25.2	28.1	34.2	25.4	24.5	24.2
Oman	13.8	28.5	29.8	26.2	30.6	35.6	35.9	30.6	28.9	26.0	22.3
Saudi Arabia	16.1	11.9	12.4	13.8	9.3	13.2	20.9	25.4	33.1	27.8	20.7
Syrian Arab Rep.	13.8	14.9	20.2	12.5	25.0	25.0	31.4	35.5	27.4	26.2	27.5
Tunisia	21.1	21.5	22.7	21.3	25.8	28.0	30.7	30.5	30.8	29.4	29.4
EUROPE	..	..	..	..	..	..	..	..	..	..	*30.5*
Bulgaria	..	..	..	..	..	..	..	..	..	..	34.0
Czechoslovakia	..	..	..	..	..	..	..	..	..	..	32.6
Greece	28.1	27.9	29.6	35.8	29.3	27.0	26.3	26.4	27.7	30.1	25.0
Hungary	33.6	37.7	31.7	29.7	35.8	37.8	35.9	37.2	41.3	34.0	30.7
Malta	32.7	29.0	25.0	22.1	27.1	23.5	27.5	26.0	23.4	25.5	24.6
Poland	..	..	..	..	..	..	..	..	..	..	26.3
Portugal	26.2	26.3	28.9	29.7	28.5	24.3	25.9	29.0	30.5	29.5	34.1
Romania	..	..	..	..	..	..	..	..	..	..	..
Turkey	19.8	17.8	20.9	19.0	21.6	23.2	25.1	25.2	18.7	18.6	21.9
Yugoslavia	32.3	32.8	28.1	28.4	30.2	33.5	31.9	35.8	34.3	38.3	39.9
Low- and middle-income economies	**22.4**	**22.8**	**22.2**	**23.2**	**24.1**	**26.2**	**25.7**	**26.1**	**26.6**	**26.6**	**26.7**
Low-income economies	21.1	21.9	21.3	22.6	22.4	24.5	24.5	24.6	26.6	27.3	25.7
Low-income Africa	16.0	18.2	18.6	18.6	17.9	21.9	24.9	25.3	22.9	20.2	21.2
China and India	24.1	25.0	23.4	25.1	25.4	26.9	25.5	25.3	29.2	30.6	28.1
Other low-income	14.3	14.0	14.7	15.2	16.5	19.5	21.2	21.7	22.4	24.1	23.2
Middle-income economies	23.4	23.3	22.7	23.3	24.4	26.5	26.0	26.8	27.0	26.2	26.7
High-income economies	**23.3**	**23.2**	**23.5**	**25.1**	**24.8**	**21.8**	**22.8**	**23.0**	**23.4**	**23.8**	**23.0**
OECD members	23.2	23.2	23.5	25.0	24.8	21.8	22.8	22.9	23.4	23.7	23.0
Japan	39.0	35.8	35.5	38.1	37.3	32.8	31.8	30.8	30.9	32.5	32.2
United States	17.8	19.0	19.6	20.3	19.5	16.9	18.4	20.1	21.4	20.9	18.9
WORLD	**23.2**	**23.2**	**23.3**	**24.7**	**24.6**	**22.7**	**23.4**	**23.7**	**24.2**	**24.4**	**23.8**

1981	1982	1983	1984	1985	1986	1987	1988	1989	1990	1991	
24.3	*21.9*	*17.5*	*16.9*	*18.3*	*17.6*	*20.2*	*20.9*	*21.7*	*18.8*	..	*LATIN AMERICA AND CARIBBEAN*
18.8	15.9	17.3	11.3	8.5	8.8	13.7	12.4	9.0	8.4	..	Argentina
18.8	21.5	20.3	16.3	19.2	18.4	18.8	..	..	..	..	Bahamas
27.6	22.6	19.9	16.2	15.4	16.0	16.0	17.5	18.4	17.0	..	Barbados
27.2	24.6	18.9	23.5	20.7	19.8	24.5	30.4	33.9	26.4	..	Belize
13.9	13.8	8.7	7.3	10.2	7.9	11.1	12.1	11.3	11.4	..	Bolivia
23.1	21.1	16.7	15.7	19.2	19.1	22.3	22.8	24.9	21.7	..	Brazil
22.7	11.3	9.8	13.6	13.7	14.6	16.9	17.0	20.3	20.2	..	Chile
20.6	20.5	19.9	19.0	19.0	18.0	20.0	22.0	20.5	19.1	..	Colombia
29.0	24.7	24.2	22.7	25.9	25.2	27.1	24.7	26.4	29.3	24.7	Costa Rica
23.6	20.0	21.1	21.3	20.0	19.7	25.2	22.8	20.2	13.8	16.0	Dominican Rep.
23.2	25.2	17.6	17.2	18.2	20.9	22.7	21.5	21.6	19.3	22.7	Ecuador
14.2	13.2	12.1	12.0	10.8	13.3	12.4	12.8	15.3	11.8	12.0	El Salvador
47.9	50.9	41.6	32.0	33.4	39.0	34.3	32.9	30.0	29.7	..	Grenada
17.0	14.1	11.1	11.6	11.5	10.3	13.9	13.7	13.5	12.1	12.9	Guatemala
29.5	24.2	21.0	27.4	29.8	33.8	31.9	21.1	32.0	46.8	..	Guyana
19.1	16.6	16.3	15.9	14.2	10.9	12.9	12.5	12.4	10.9	..	Haiti
20.7	13.5	14.9	19.0	18.0	14.2	14.7	13.0	12.3	12.8	12.1	Honduras
20.3	20.9	22.3	23.1	25.3	19.2	23.2	26.7	30.3	29.6	25.9	Jamaica
27.4	22.9	20.8	19.9	21.2	18.2	19.2	21.0	22.8	19.6	25.5	Mexico
23.6	18.8	22.5	22.2	23.1	16.9	15.8	..	..	..	..	Nicaragua
30.1	27.7	21.4	16.7	15.4	16.7	17.5	6.9	2.6	16.3	14.2	Panama
31.6	27.9	21.4	22.9	22.0	25.0	25.1	24.4	23.8	22.0	..	Paraguay
31.4	31.3	23.5	22.2	21.6	22.4	22.8	26.1	20.6	22.9	20.7	Peru
33.2	28.8	25.5	27.9	28.2	28.2	30.7	24.0	..	..	..	St. Vincent
27.6	28.3	26.0	21.6	19.4	22.2	19.9	17.1	19.1	16.6	..	Trinidad and Tobago
21.4	19.8	14.3	12.1	11.4	11.4	14.3	13.0	11.1	11.8	..	Uruguay
24.4	27.7	12.2	17.5	18.5	20.9	24.6	28.0	12.7	9.3	..	Venezuela
29.8	*21.7*	*26.2*	*22.7*	*22.2*	*26.1*	*23.6*	*22.0*	*22.9*	*22.8*	..	*MIDDLE EAST AND NORTH AFRICA*
37.0	37.3	37.6	35.1	33.2	33.5	30.0	30.4	31.1	33.0	32.0	Algeria
29.5	30.1	28.7	27.5	26.7	23.7	18.0	24.2	23.3	21.9	..	Egypt, Arab Rep.
34.4	13.3	25.9	18.6	18.2	24.3	23.6	19.3	22.8	20.8	..	Iran, Islamic Rep.
..	..	33.9	29.7	25.6	21.9	22.3	22.8	19.9	18.9	..	Jordan
26.1	28.2	24.0	25.3	25.0	22.8	21.1	21.1	24.0	25.7	24.5	Morocco
23.0	26.6	26.5	30.0	27.6	32.1	18.0	16.6	..	..	..	Oman
21.7	23.7	26.0	33.0	20.9	19.9	19.0	20.9	21.6	17.2	..	Saudi Arabia
23.2	23.7	23.6	23.7	23.8	22.2	18.0	14.0	17.2	14.2	..	Syrian Arab Rep.
32.3	31.7	29.6	32.0	26.6	23.5	20.6	19.4	22.7	26.6	..	Tunisia
28.9	*28.8*	*27.0*	*27.0*	*27.5*	*28.9*	*25.6*	*28.1*	*30.1*	*25.2*	..	*EUROPE*
35.5	33.5	32.9	33.2	32.2	35.9	32.9	34.4	33.2	29.4	21.4	Bulgaria
28.9	29.2	29.0	29.0	28.8	30.2	29.3	28.1	27.7	30.0	18.6	Czechoslovakia
25.4	21.1	21.9	20.1	21.5	19.3	17.2	18.8	19.5	18.8	..	Greece
29.7	28.5	26.5	25.7	25.0	26.9	26.7	24.7	25.7	23.0	23.4	Hungary
27.1	31.5	30.0	28.9	28.1	25.5	27.5	28.8	29.6	..	..	Malta
18.5	28.0	25.0	26.3	27.7	28.9	28.8	32.6	38.5	30.5	22.4	Poland
36.1	37.0	29.1	23.2	21.7	23.3	27.7	29.8	30.4	31.5	..	Portugal
..	..	..	..	..	..	31.8	28.4	26.7	34.3	13.5	Romania
22.0	20.6	19.6	19.5	21.0	24.4	25.4	24.0	22.7	23.1	22.9	Turkey
38.9	35.6	35.7	37.2	38.8	38.4	21.0	37.7	44.0	21.5	..	Yugoslavia
26.9	**24.4**	**23.5**	**22.5**	**23.8**	**24.5**	**24.4**	**25.5**	**26.8**	**25.1**	..	**Low- and middle-income economies**
26.0	25.0	24.0	24.0	27.4	27.9	27.7	29.2	29.5	28.9	29.5	Low-income economies
20.7	18.4	14.2	11.3	11.1	14.9	15.2	15.2	15.4	16.0	..	Low-income Africa
27.6	27.0	26.4	27.9	33.3	32.6	31.6	33.0	33.1	32.1	33.1	China and India
26.3	25.3	25.3	23.5	24.1	23.2	23.1	24.2	25.5	26.2	..	Other low-income
26.8	24.0	23.3	22.4	21.7	22.6	22.4	23.4	25.2	23.0	..	Middle-income economies
22.3	**20.4**	**20.1**	**21.4**	**20.8**	**20.8**	**21.2**	**22.0**	**22.4**	**22.0**	..	**High-income economies**
22.2	20.3	19.9	21.3	20.7	20.7	21.1	21.9	22.3	21.9	..	OECD members
31.1	29.9	28.1	28.0	28.2	27.8	28.7	30.6	31.7	33.2	..	Japan
19.7	16.8	17.0	19.8	18.7	18.1	17.9	17.3	17.1	16.0	..	United States
23.4	**21.4**	**20.9**	**21.7**	**21.4**	**21.5**	**21.7**	**22.6**	**23.2**	**22.5**	..	**WORLD**

Table 14. Gross domestic savings: percentage of gross domestic product

Percentage points	1970	1971	1972	1973	1974	1975	1976	1977	1978	1979	1980
SUB-SAHARAN AFRICA	*15.5*	*15.1*	*16.8*	*18.4*	*21.9*	*16.6*	*20.5*	*19.5*	*15.1*	*16.7*	*19.7*
Excluding Nigeria	*18.2*	*15.4*	*15.7*	*17.0*	*18.8*	*14.1*	*16.7*	*16.4*	*12.1*	*11.7*	*13.2*
Benin	5.3	3.9	3.2	5.8	4.8	1.7	-0.4	0.9	0.0	1.6	-5.1
Botswana	1.7	14.7	27.5	28.0	27.6	22.5	22.9	14.3	12.3	22.6	28.5
Burkina Faso	2.4	4.1	6.7	8.9	15.5	5.7	9.7	1.9	2.5	-0.4	-3.1
Burundi	3.6	1.9	-0.2	3.0	-1.7	-3.1	6.2	11.4	5.5	4.4	4.9
Cameroon	17.6	12.5	12.6	16.6	19.7	17.1	12.9	19.1	18.2	14.5	15.7
Cape Verde	..	..	..	-23.4	-12.7	-12.5	-22.4	-27.1	-32.4	-23.3	-8.0
Central African Rep.	3.6	6.5	5.6	7.9	5.8	-5.7	4.1	1.5	-0.7	-1.7	-9.6
Chad	9.8	10.5	9.7	-14.8	8.8	6.8	4.5	2.3	1.8	..	..
Comoros	..	..	..	..	..	..	..	..	..	..	..
Congo	1.2	6.5	5.6	20.2	28.8	11.3	4.8	6.9	10.0	24.7	35.7
Côte d'Ivoire	29.2	25.6	25.4	25.7	29.3	22.6	28.5	33.6	28.8	24.9	22.2
Equatorial Guinea	10.5	17.4	11.2	2.8	0.1	7.2	7.7	7.8	..	..	..
Ethiopia	11.2	9.9	10.8	13.4	13.3	7.5	8.7	5.7	1.9	3.4	4.9
Gabon	43.7	46.0	48.9	38.7	66.0	64.3	73.0	58.4	49.9	54.0	60.6
Gambia, The	5.1	-3.6	3.8	-1.9	3.3	15.2	-4.1	4.9	-10.6	10.8	0.7
Ghana	12.8	9.6	12.6	14.1	9.6	13.7	8.5	10.0	4.0	6.6	4.9
Guinea-Bissau	3.4	-2.2	-8.5	-13.8	-17.4	-5.4	-6.4	-3.5	-5.8	-10.7	-6.0
Kenya	23.6	17.4	20.2	24.5	18.5	13.5	20.9	27.0	20.0	16.4	18.1
Lesotho	-32.2	-42.6	-49.9	-45.9	-66.0	-70.4	-83.3	-74.5	-47.4	-66.2	-59.7
Liberia	42.0	38.1	40.6	32.6	31.9	38.4	34.2	25.6	24.6	26.9	27.3
Madagascar	7.5	4.6	4.8	4.5	4.0	3.1	5.8	4.5	2.7	0.3	-1.4
Malawi	10.8	7.1	9.7	12.4	16.4	17.0	17.8	20.1	20.5	12.6	10.8
Mali	10.2	9.7	8.0	4.5	-15.5	-4.4	3.5	9.3	-2.5	-2.0	-1.9
Mauritania	29.7	30.4	27.5	9.8	5.8	13.0	2.9	-1.3	0.0	-0.6	6.9
Mauritius	11.2	10.1	17.5	22.8	31.1	27.3	24.9	19.3	18.4	19.5	10.5
Mozambique	..	..	..	..	..	..	..	..	..	..	0.5
Namibia	..	..	..	..	..	..	..	..	..	..	37.6
Niger	2.5	4.5	4.8	6.7	-1.6	2.6	2.1	10.0	17.7	17.5	22.6
Nigeria	12.0	15.9	20.3	23.0	27.6	20.7	25.8	24.1	19.8	23.4	27.3
Rwanda	3.3	2.5	1.6	7.6	1.3	5.2	9.0	11.7	7.6	10.3	4.2
Senegal	11.1	8.9	13.3	8.8	15.6	12.5	8.4	11.3	4.7	4.2	-0.4
Seychelles	..	..	..	..	..	..	22.9	36.0	42.0	26.9	27.1
Sierra Leone	14.6	14.1	11.8	11.0	8.6	6.4	2.8	6.6	3.9	0.7	-0.8
Somalia	6.5	5.3	8.8	1.4	4.3	8.1	16.1	-17.5	-1.6	-28.2	-12.9
Sudan	0.0	10.2	7.6	11.9	14.5	6.1	13.2	10.7	6.3	6.6	3.4
Swaziland	25.1	31.4	30.2	38.1	49.5	33.9	37.7	23.7	22.1	6.6	7.4
Tanzania	20.5	21.7	18.3	14.9	7.4	8.6	20.7	22.8	10.0	13.3	9.8
Togo	25.9	25.8	21.5	21.9	53.5	17.4	25.6	23.4	39.8	22.6	24.8
Uganda	0.0	0.0	0.0	0.0	0.0	0.0	0.0	0.0	0.0	0.0	-0.4
Zaire	12.2	12.0	11.0	11.5	10.9	7.9	4.4	6.8	2.9	2.9	10.2
Zambia	45.1	35.0	36.9	45.0	46.1	21.0	28.8	22.1	20.5	23.1	19.3
Zimbabwe	..	..	..	..	..	25.1	21.8	21.5	15.4	12.5	15.8
SOUTH ASIA	*14.3*	*15.0*	*14.5*	*15.9*	*15.6*	*16.0*	*18.0*	*18.0*	*18.1*	*17.5*	*15.2*
Bangladesh	7.2	3.8	-3.4	3.4	0.7	0.9	-3.0	6.2	1.6	1.5	2.1
Bhutan	..	..	..	..	..	..	..	..	..	..	7.9
India	16.4	17.5	16.7	17.7	18.7	20.4	21.7	20.3	21.1	20.7	17.4
Nepal	2.6	4.0	5.1	5.4	3.7	10.0	11.7	13.5	13.4	11.6	11.1
Pakistan	9.0	8.7	9.2	10.1	6.4	4.9	7.9	9.5	8.6	5.8	6.9
Sri Lanka	15.8	15.1	15.7	12.5	8.2	8.1	13.9	18.1	15.3	13.8	11.2
EAST ASIA AND PACIFIC	*25.6*	*26.5*	*25.8*	*28.2*	*27.5*	*27.8*	*27.5*	*28.5*	*30.4*	*32.4*	*30.7*
China	28.7	29.9	28.1	29.8	28.8	30.6	29.0	29.5	33.2	34.7	32.2
Fiji	18.9	17.0	14.7	8.7	13.7	20.0	16.8	20.4	18.4	24.7	26.9
Indonesia	13.9	16.8	22.6	22.5	27.9	25.9	26.3	28.2	26.3	33.6	37.1
Korea, Rep.	15.0	14.8	16.1	21.6	20.6	18.5	24.1	27.5	28.5	28.2	24.3
Malaysia	26.6	23.9	22.0	31.0	31.1	25.8	33.7	33.1	32.2	37.8	32.9
Mongolia	..	..	..	..	..	..	..	..	..	..	26.6
Papua New Guinea	6.1	5.9	10.8	25.5	24.5	13.9	19.6	20.3	19.1	23.4	15.1
Philippines	21.9	21.1	21.0	26.7	24.6	24.8	26.9	27.6	26.4	28.1	24.2
Solomon Islands	..	..	..	..	..	..	..	..	..	..	6.7
Thailand	21.2	21.3	20.7	25.6	24.3	22.1	21.5	21.5	23.9	20.5	20.1
Tonga	..	..	..	..	..	-1.9	-10.0	-3.1	-9.6	-12.6	-5.7
Vanuatu	..	..	..	..	..	..	..	..	..	..	..
Western Samoa	..	..	..	..	..	..	..	..	..	-17.3	-4.5

1981	1982	1983	1984	1985	1986	1987	1988	1989	1990	1991	
13.0	*11.5*	*10.8*	*12.3*	*13.1*	*12.5*	*12.6*	*11.5*	*13.4*	*15.5*	*12.7*	*SUB-SAHARAN AFRICA*
11.3	*11.7*	*11.1*	*13.5*	*13.5*	*13.0*	*11.7*	*11.0*	*11.1*	*11.8*	*..*	*Excluding Nigeria*
-12.1	7.0	0.7	5.4	7.8	3.8	3.5	5.0	5.2	..	..	Benin
22.4	7.8	16.8	23.8	28.4	38.6	34.0	35.8	37.1	..	..	Botswana
-4.1	-1.0	-0.2	-0.6	3.2	2.9	4.1	7.3	5.2	4.6	..	Burkina Faso
3.8	-2.7	6.6	5.8	3.8	1.1	6.9	1.6	4.4	1.1	..	Burundi
22.3	23.1	28.8	32.7	35.9	31.5	19.6	12.9	20.3	18.6	9.1	Cameroon
-3.9	-3.4	-4.3	-10.9	-11.4	-12.0	4.5	1.3	4.0	13.2	..	Cape Verde
-1.9	-6.8	-1.2	-0.3	-0.3	-1.7	-1.2	-0.6	0.2	-1.7	..	Central African Rep.
..	..	-8.6	-3.4	-19.3	-22.1	-17.7	-13.4	-13.5	-15.4	..	Chad
..	..	2.8	-10.8	-9.1	-3.5	-9.2	-10.7	-4.9	-6.2	..	Comoros
30.1	46.5	44.6	46.4	31.1	15.6	22.8	18.8	28.6	23.5	5.4	Congo
18.8	20.3	18.9	22.4	27.8	19.7	16.1	18.0	13.4	14.2	16.4	Côte d'Ivoire
..	..	..	..	1.0	2.9	-1.4	-7.2	-3.3	-6.3	..	Equatorial Guinea
3.6	2.0	2.7	2.4	2.8	2.8	3.6	4.5	5.9	..	..	Ethiopia
59.0	56.9	53.0	51.9	51.9	28.2	26.4	27.0	41.4	44.6	..	Gabon
4.2	9.8	4.3	4.9	6.4	5.2	6.9	7.1	8.3	9.0	..	Gambia, The
4.0	3.7	3.3	6.6	7.6	7.7	8.2	10.7	6.0	..	..	Ghana
1.2	-5.2	-3.6	-8.3	-11.0	-1.3	3.6	-5.9	-14.4	-11.2	..	Guinea-Bissau
19.6	18.1	20.4	19.4	24.9	21.9	19.2	19.8	18.8	18.4	..	Kenya
-68.3	-73.5	-99.0	-94.1	-78.4	-75.7	-75.8	-56.9	-50.9	-41.1	..	Lesotho
18.8	12.5	10.0	14.4	14.3	18.4	..	..	..	..	..	Liberia
0.2	-1.0	1.4	3.7	2.6	4.4	4.7	6.6	9.1	8.2	..	Madagascar
11.8	15.1	15.2	14.8	12.9	10.1	13.0	9.2	4.5	9.8	..	Malawi
-0.3	0.5	-4.8	-3.4	-14.2	-1.2	6.2	7.0	10.3	10.3	..	Mali
12.6	3.0	-12.1	-1.9	8.8	15.4	13.7	6.1	7.9	2.8	..	Mauritania
14.8	15.4	17.1	18.7	21.6	28.6	27.4	25.5	23.1	21.4	..	Mauritius
0.0	-3.3	-10.8	-6.2	-3.1	-1.1	-12.1	-16.4	-16.6	-11.8	..	Mozambique
11.6	6.4	3.1	4.1	16.1	16.6	3.8	13.2	15.4	..	..	Namibia
8.7	7.8	7.5	-1.6	2.4	5.6	4.5	6.7	2.4	2.0	..	Niger
15.2	11.4	10.3	10.9	12.6	11.7	17.6	14.5	23.4	29.5	25.7	Nigeria
1.4	5.2	4.4	8.8	8.2	8.3	6.3	6.4	6.3	3.8	..	Rwanda
-7.5	-1.0	-0.4	2.2	-1.4	5.6	6.1	7.5	5.5	8.7	..	Senegal
17.0	8.8	-1.0	8.2	7.2	..	..	..	..	..	..	Seychelles
4.4	1.9	7.5	11.1	8.0	9.6	11.1	9.0	4.9	5.1	..	Sierra Leone
-16.0	-12.8	-26.6	-22.3	16.8	2.8	8.8	6.5	-6.9	21.5	..	Somalia
1.0	8.3	1.5	6.2	-3.8	5.3	6.9	1.4	2.1	1.9	..	Sudan
1.4	2.0	-1.1	-4.6	-3.2	11.4	15.7	14.8	..	..	..	Swaziland
12.1	13.6	8.4	7.2	7.4	5.5	0.1	-5.4	-5.9	..	..	Tanzania
23.5	17.7	20.9	19.1	20.0	12.3	11.6	10.6	13.9	11.1	..	Togo
-0.6	1.2	3.9	6.2	7.8	8.4	6.1	0.8	-0.2	-0.7	..	Uganda
8.0	7.1	8.6	12.6	14.4	13.9	12.2	12.2	11.9	5.4	..	Zaire
6.8	8.0	15.2	16.5	15.4	22.6	18.0	18.7	3.5	17.0	..	Zambia
15.8	15.3	12.8	19.5	21.0	22.7	22.5	22.2	20.5	21.1	19.3	Zimbabwe
18.6	*17.2*	*16.2*	*16.2*	*17.7*	*17.5*	*17.8*	*18.1*	*18.0*	*17.6*	*16.3*	*SOUTH ASIA*
3.4	1.1	1.2	1.6	1.9	2.4	3.6	2.8	2.0	1.9	4.3	Bangladesh
7.0	9.3	8.4	7.4	13.6	13.8	18.1	18.7	..	..	..	Bhutan
21.8	20.2	18.5	18.7	20.9	20.3	20.1	20.8	21.0	20.4	19.8	India
10.9	9.9	8.5	9.9	14.0	11.7	12.4	11.6	9.8	9.3	..	Nepal
8.5	8.1	8.4	7.7	6.7	8.8	12.3	10.6	11.6	11.5	..	Pakistan
11.7	11.5	13.5	20.0	11.7	11.8	12.6	11.8	12.0	14.5	..	Sri Lanka
28.7	*28.7*	*29.2*	*30.4*	*31.9*	*33.2*	*35.5*	*36.0*	*36.0*	*37.5*	*35.6*	*EAST ASIA AND PACIFIC*
30.1	31.8	31.6	32.8	36.1	37.5	39.3	38.7	38.4	42.6	42.6	China
19.9	19.2	15.7	17.9	18.7	20.4	17.6	15.6	15.0	17.4	..	Fiji
33.7	27.9	29.0	29.7	29.8	27.3	32.9	34.0	37.6	37.4	36.5	Indonesia
24.5	26.0	28.3	29.9	30.5	34.8	37.3	38.3	37.3	36.7	..	Korea, Rep.
28.8	28.6	32.1	35.5	32.7	32.1	37.3	36.3	33.9	32.3	30.2	Malaysia
27.8	30.7	21.5	23.1	28.0	30.3	16.6	14.1	12.9	2.9	..	Mongolia
6.7	8.5	12.2	13.3	9.5	12.0	14.1	18.7	11.3	9.9	..	Papua New Guinea
24.1	22.1	23.1	20.9	17.4	19.9	18.4	19.8	19.5	16.0	12.8	Philippines
1.7	15.5	15.2	19.2	7.5	-0.6	-5.0	-3.0	..	..	..	Solomon Islands
20.0	21.4	18.7	20.6	21.2	23.9	24.5	27.3	29.2	33.6	..	Thailand
-12.7	-15.9	-9.7	-2.1	-15.9	..	..	..	..	..	..	Tonga
..	..	12.0	18.5	6.9	3.0	5.9	6.0	9.1	..	..	Vanuatu
-16.2	-9.2	-2.4	-2.2	-5.1	-15.0	-15.3	-19.9	-23.0	-23.5	..	Western Samoa

Table 14. Gross domestic savings: percentage of gross domestic product (cont'd.)

Percentage points	1970	1971	1972	1973	1974	1975	1976	1977	1978	1979	1980
LATIN AMERICA AND CARIBBEAN	*20.7*	*19.6*	*19.5*	*21.2*	*22.2*	*22.6*	*22.4*	*23.0*	*22.7*	*22.6*	*23.1*
Argentina	21.6	20.3	21.4	20.6	20.2	25.6	31.2	30.3	28.3	23.0	20.0
Bahamas	..	..	..	..	..	..	..	29.0	26.5	21.5	25.8
Barbados	7.0	10.4	9.0	10.6	15.8	9.2	8.3	4.8	15.0	13.9	19.3
Belize	..	..	..	..	..	..	..	..	..	..	..
Bolivia	24.2	21.3	26.9	28.7	30.1	30.8	26.3	24.6	16.6	16.8	18.8
Brazil	20.1	19.4	19.6	22.0	19.5	22.9	20.7	21.4	21.8	20.7	21.1
Chile	17.1	13.5	8.7	6.1	21.8	11.1	17.1	12.6	14.5	15.0	16.8
Colombia	18.4	15.4	17.7	19.3	20.4	18.8	20.7	22.4	21.1	19.9	19.7
Costa Rica	13.8	13.9	15.6	17.9	11.9	13.2	17.7	18.8	15.6	15.0	16.2
Dominican Rep.	11.8	9.7	14.9	18.3	12.1	22.2	15.2	17.6	16.8	19.0	15.4
Ecuador	13.6	13.7	16.4	22.7	27.6	20.3	22.4	23.5	22.8	25.9	25.9
El Salvador	13.2	13.7	15.3	15.5	14.2	17.0	20.0	24.3	14.6	17.9	14.2
Grenada	..	..	..	..	..	..	..	..	..	..	0.0
Guatemala	13.6	13.0	12.5	14.4	15.3	14.3	15.4	18.2	15.8	14.2	13.1
Guyana	22.2	22.4	18.5	10.5	28.3	33.0	12.5	13.5	20.5	21.6	19.3
Haiti	7.5	8.0	9.0	11.2	9.3	6.5	6.9	6.6	7.9	8.8	8.1
Honduras	14.7	16.3	17.0	18.2	14.3	10.0	14.8	18.6	22.6	22.4	17.3
Jamaica	27.4	25.0	19.0	21.9	14.1	15.4	9.4	13.6	18.3	18.4	15.7
Mexico	18.7	17.1	17.4	18.1	18.9	19.0	18.8	20.6	20.7	22.3	24.9
Nicaragua	16.0	15.5	18.9	14.5	18.0	12.2	19.9	21.1	16.6	8.2	-2.3
Panama	24.5	26.6	26.9	29.6	24.2	23.5	24.6	20.1	21.9	19.3	24.4
Paraguay	13.5	12.0	15.0	19.7	18.7	18.6	21.2	21.7	23.5	23.1	18.3
Peru	17.4	17.0	14.6	18.3	18.4	13.6	13.7	12.4	20.0	30.3	27.5
St. Vincent	..	..	..	..	..	..	..	-15.5	7.7	-1.8	-2.5
Trinidad and Tobago	27.0	28.8	24.7	31.7	46.3	45.1	40.3	39.3	34.6	34.8	42.1
Uruguay	14.8	16.6	17.7	18.9	13.3	15.4	20.4	18.7	20.4	19.7	18.7
Venezuela	37.0	37.7	36.1	39.3	48.1	39.7	36.9	36.2	32.7	34.5	33.3
MIDDLE EAST AND NORTH AFRICA	*20.9*	*20.2*	*21.8*	*25.3*	*31.7*	*26.7*	*30.1*	*27.1*	*22.3*	*26.5*	*27.1*
Algeria	29.3	26.1	29.1	34.0	43.0	36.0	39.0	35.6	37.5	40.8	43.1
Egypt, Arab Rep.	9.4	8.1	6.6	8.0	5.7	12.3	16.7	18.5	16.4	14.2	15.2
Iran, Islamic Rep.	24.9	25.4	26.5	35.0	44.2	37.7	39.0	31.6	23.6	33.6	29.3
Jordan	..	..	..	..	..	..	..	..	..	..	..
Morocco	14.5	15.2	14.6	15.6	20.0	14.3	8.7	13.8	11.7	11.6	13.7
Oman	67.8	62.1	45.5	38.8	56.6	52.5	52.2	44.9	38.5	46.4	47.3
Saudi Arabia	46.7	55.5	60.4	67.4	80.2	75.7	67.9	63.2	54.9	43.7	53.4
Syrian Arab Rep.	10.2	9.9	14.7	8.8	15.3	12.5	16.6	13.0	11.1	9.3	10.3
Tunisia	16.6	19.5	21.6	18.8	26.2	23.2	22.7	20.3	21.1	24.4	24.0
EUROPE	..	..	..	..	..	..	..	..	..	..	*26.3*
Bulgaria	..	..	..	..	..	..	..	..	..	..	39.0
Czechoslovakia	..	..	..	..	..	..	..	..	..	..	32.7
Greece	19.7	19.8	21.2	24.8	19.8	17.0	18.0	18.0	20.6	22.4	19.7
Hungary	31.3	31.4	33.0	34.2	31.3	30.3	31.8	32.7	32.1	30.7	28.5
Malta	2.7	3.3	2.0	2.5	-1.7	10.0	15.8	11.6	16.3	20.3	19.2
Poland	..	..	..	..	..	..	..	..	..	..	23.4
Portugal	19.6	19.2	24.2	22.7	13.2	11.9	12.5	14.0	18.1	18.7	19.0
Romania	..	..	..	..	..	..	..	..	..	..	..
Turkey	17.5	14.3	18.1	16.8	15.2	15.0	18.3	17.1	15.1	15.4	14.1
Yugoslavia	27.1	26.5	25.6	24.8	20.5	25.7	29.3	29.6	29.5	31.4	35.6
Low- and middle-income economies	**21.2**	**21.1**	**21.4**	**23.4**	**24.2**	**23.4**	**24.5**	**24.6**	**24.1**	**25.5**	**25.5**
Low-income economies	20.0	20.7	20.6	22.3	22.1	22.0	22.7	23.0	23.6	25.1	24.6
Low-income Africa	14.4	14.2	16.0	17.5	19.9	14.4	18.6	17.6	13.4	15.5	18.9
China and India	24.0	25.2	23.9	25.4	24.8	26.9	26.2	25.9	28.7	29.7	26.8
Other low-income	10.1	9.8	11.3	13.4	14.9	14.3	17.3	20.2	18.4	20.7	23.9
Middle-income economies	22.1	21.5	22.1	24.6	27.3	26.6	27.3	27.4	25.8	26.3	27.7
High-income economies	**23.8**	**24.0**	**24.3**	**25.5**	**24.6**	**22.5**	**22.9**	**23.0**	**23.9**	**23.6**	**22.6**
OECD members	23.8	23.9	24.2	25.4	24.3	22.3	22.6	22.8	23.8	23.3	22.3
Japan	40.3	38.5	37.8	38.1	36.6	32.8	32.6	32.5	32.6	31.6	31.3
United States	18.2	19.0	19.3	20.5	19.3	17.8	18.2	18.8	20.2	19.9	18.3
WORLD	**23.4**	**23.5**	**23.8**	**25.2**	**24.9**	**23.1**	**23.6**	**23.7**	**24.2**	**24.2**	**23.6**

1981	1982	1983	1984	1985	1986	1987	1988	1989	1990	1991	
22.7	21.8	21.6	22.2	23.1	19.9	22.8	23.7	24.7	21.5	..	*LATIN AMERICA AND CARIBBEAN*
18.3	19.1	22.1	15.5	15.2	11.1	13.7	16.5	17.0	15.8	..	Argentina
23.9	27.7	28.9	21.6	24.7	24.3	24.3	..	..	..	..	Bahamas
12.6	16.4	14.6	16.9	19.3	18.3	16.5	19.5	16.4	12.0	..	Barbados
14.7	7.9	6.8	16.1	10.1	17.8	21.9	24.4	22.2	20.3	..	Belize
11.8	17.8	11.5	10.4	8.5	5.0	4.8	6.6	7.6	8.4	..	Bolivia
22.7	20.4	19.1	21.4	24.4	21.6	25.6	28.0	28.1	23.4	..	Brazil
12.4	9.4	12.5	12.6	16.5	18.4	21.0	24.2	24.0	23.2	..	Chile
17.1	16.2	17.1	18.4	20.3	24.8	24.0	24.4	24.7	25.5	..	Colombia
24.1	27.6	23.4	23.1	24.1	26.1	23.0	22.7	22.8	21.5	21.2	Costa Rica
19.4	15.1	17.2	24.0	14.5	15.3	15.2	16.8	14.0	9.1	12.9	Dominican Rep.
24.2	22.9	21.6	23.7	24.1	21.0	16.4	19.4	19.7	22.4	20.3	Ecuador
8.1	8.2	6.6	5.2	3.3	10.1	5.3	6.3	4.9	0.6	1.4	El Salvador
6.7	1.7	-1.4	2.8	4.2	4.8	6.4	10.3	2.9	4.1	..	Grenada
10.5	10.2	9.5	9.4	10.5	11.8	7.5	7.9	8.4	8.0	9.1	Guatemala
7.6	9.1	2.5	18.2	12.9	19.7	18.3	16.7	19.4	33.9	..	Guyana
3.8	6.4	5.9	6.8	6.1	5.1	5.0	4.5	4.6	1.1	..	Haiti
14.4	11.6	11.2	12.3	13.5	12.8	11.8	9.6	9.0	5.8	6.5	Honduras
11.6	9.5	13.2	16.2	14.3	24.7	25.4	33.3	25.1	29.6	27.2	Jamaica
24.9	27.9	30.3	27.7	26.3	22.8	26.3	23.3	23.7	19.1	22.2	Mexico
4.2	8.7	11.9	9.2	16.1	8.8	13.8	..	..	..	..	Nicaragua
25.8	23.5	21.8	15.0	15.9	20.3	19.4	20.8	12.2	17.4	16.4	Panama
19.9	18.2	22.7	19.5	16.6	16.1	14.5	20.3	29.7	23.3	..	Paraguay
25.4	25.6	22.4	25.9	26.3	20.2	20.0	25.4	21.7	23.2	19.0	Peru
6.1	-2.1	3.9	14.4	22.1	17.2	10.1	5.5	..	..	..	St. Vincent
37.3	20.9	16.0	19.9	23.6	15.0	21.3	22.0	27.0	32.7	..	Trinidad and Tobago
17.6	16.8	16.4	17.3	17.0	17.3	16.7	17.7	17.5	19.5	..	Uruguay
29.3	25.1	20.5	28.7	27.7	19.9	25.1	21.0	25.7	29.3	..	Venezuela
26.9	23.0	25.4	21.2	21.5	23.7	..	..	..	..	..	*MIDDLE EAST AND NORTH AFRICA*
40.7	39.2	39.7	37.4	36.4	29.4	31.9	30.0	31.0	38.2	38.0	Algeria
14.1	15.2	17.8	14.0	14.5	13.8	6.6	8.2	5.7	4.8	..	Egypt, Arab Rep.
29.3	18.8	26.2	18.3	18.1	22.2	22.5	18.5	19.1	20.0	..	Iran, Islamic Rep.
..	..	-10.2	-9.3	-10.2	-3.9	-1.2	0.1	5.2	-8.6	..	Jordan
11.5	13.8	15.2	14.7	16.1	16.5	16.7	20.6	18.5	19.6	17.3	Morocco
49.6	42.0	42.1	42.7	40.2	18.0	..	..	..	..	..	Oman
62.2	39.1	24.0	20.2	13.0	9.1	11.7	16.9	22.3	29.4	..	Saudi Arabia
5.9	12.6	10.2	12.1	11.2	11.2	4.8	4.7	12.2	13.6	..	Syrian Arab Rep.
23.9	21.2	21.0	20.3	20.4	16.2	19.6	19.8	18.6	19.3	..	Tunisia
25.1	26.4	25.1	26.1	26.5	27.7	24.6	28.5	29.4	21.5	..	*EUROPE*
36.5	34.6	33.1	34.7	31.8	32.3	31.1	34.1	33.2	27.9	22.1	Bulgaria
30.3	31.3	30.5	31.1	31.8	31.4	30.7	31.0	29.1	28.0	18.2	Czechoslovakia
18.9	10.8	11.6	11.8	9.9	10.8	9.9	12.3	10.8	8.2	..	Greece
28.6	29.3	28.4	28.9	27.1	25.5	26.2	27.3	29.0	26.9	24.0	Hungary
18.7	15.3	15.0	13.7	12.3	15.4	18.2	18.7	18.7	..	..	Malta
16.3	30.0	26.8	28.3	29.0	30.3	31.2	35.3	42.7	38.7	23.6	Poland
15.9	16.8	16.8	15.0	18.3	20.8	21.1	20.2	20.7	21.2	..	Portugal
..	..	..	..	..	..	36.0	35.3	31.3	25.2	4.8	Romania
16.6	17.3	15.3	15.3	17.8	21.5	23.4	26.1	21.7	18.3	19.3	Turkey
36.4	35.5	35.9	38.0	40.6	40.1	23.9	43.8	47.1	20.7	..	Yugoslavia
24.2	**23.1**	**23.4**	**23.5**	**24.2**	**24.0**	**25.1**	**26.4**	**27.3**	**25.4**	..	**Low- and middle-income economies**
22.8	21.9	21.7	22.4	23.8	24.0	25.4	26.3	27.1	27.9	28.0	Low-income economies
11.0	9.0	8.1	9.3	9.9	9.1	10.2	9.2	10.8	13.5	12.0	Low-income Africa
26.8	27.1	26.2	27.3	29.7	29.8	30.5	31.2	31.6	32.9	33.6	China and India
22.7	19.4	20.0	19.6	19.0	17.5	18.5	19.5	20.8	21.1	21.2	Other low-income
27.8	24.7	24.2	23.7	23.7	23.2	24.2	25.8	26.9	24.3	..	Middle-income economies
22.4	**20.5**	**20.2**	**21.1**	**20.6**	**21.0**	**21.2**	**22.1**	**22.4**	**22.2**	..	**High-income economies**
22.1	20.3	20.0	20.9	20.4	21.0	21.1	22.0	22.2	22.1	..	OECD members
31.9	30.7	29.8	30.8	31.5	31.8	31.8	32.9	33.1	33.9	..	Japan
19.0	16.0	15.2	16.8	15.6	14.8	14.5	14.9	15.3	14.5	..	United States
23.4	**21.3**	**20.9**	**21.6**	**21.3**	**21.6**	**21.9**	**22.8**	**23.3**	**22.8**	..	**WORLD**

Table 15. Private consumption: percentage of gross domestic product

Percentage points	1970	1971	1972	1973	1974	1975	1976	1977	1978	1979	1980
SUB-SAHARAN AFRICA	*73.3*	*72.9*	*70.6*	*68.9*	*67.0*	*70.3*	*67.2*	*66.8*	*70.0*	*69.4*	*66.6*
Excluding Nigeria	*70.3*	*71.7*	*71.3*	*70.4*	*69.1*	*72.6*	*70.6*	*70.9*	*74.8*	*75.0*	*72.4*
Benin	85.0	86.1	86.7	84.3	86.5	89.1	91.8	90.7	91.7	90.4	96.5
Botswana	78.0	66.9	57.0	59.7	55.5	58.0	57.1	61.6	62.3	57.2	51.6
Burkina Faso	90.4	88.5	85.8	82.7	75.9	80.9	79.8	87.6	87.0	89.1	93.5
Burundi	86.6	87.5	87.2	85.4	89.1	91.6	85.1	77.5	80.7	82.8	87.8
Cameroon	70.5	75.3	75.3	71.8	69.2	72.0	76.4	71.1	72.0	76.3	75.5
Cape Verde	..	..	..	114.7	100.4	96.6	102.7	101.5	110.0	100.3	93.3
Central African Rep.	75.3	73.6	74.6	71.5	75.4	88.5	82.2	86.0	86.4	86.2	94.5
Chad	63.6	62.1	62.6	84.0	63.7	67.9	71.8	73.7	72.8	..	..
Comoros											
Congo	81.8	76.3	77.0	62.3	53.4	70.7	77.5	73.7	67.1	54.9	46.8
Côte d'Ivoire	57.3	58.5	59.0	58.5	54.5	60.4	55.3	52.7	54.9	56.9	60.0
Equatorial Guinea	67.3	59.7	63.7	71.8	75.6	65.6	63.6	63.3	..	..	..
Ethiopia	78.9	80.3	78.5	75.9	76.1	79.4	76.9	80.2	81.1	82.0	79.9
Gabon	36.6	35.3	33.4	45.7	24.7	23.5	16.5	23.5	36.5	33.9	26.1
Gambia, The	84.1	90.7	83.4	88.5	84.2	71.1	90.0	80.5	90.7	74.5	79.2
Ghana	74.4	77.4	74.8	75.0	78.2	73.3	79.2	77.4	84.7	83.1	83.9
Guinea-Bissau	76.7	80.5	85.7	89.3	92.2	82.5	81.5	85.0	84.7	88.5	77.0
Kenya	60.2	64.7	62.2	59.0	64.4	68.2	61.6	55.8	60.5	64.4	62.1
Lesotho	120.4	126.1	133.1	132.1	149.9	151.2	163.9	157.2	129.7	144.8	123.9
Liberia	46.9	49.5	47.5	56.0	57.7	51.5	54.1	60.7	60.7	58.4	56.4
Madagascar	79.4	80.5	81.6	83.3	84.8	86.1	83.0	84.5	85.4	87.4	89.3
Malawi	72.8	78.0	76.4	74.2	69.4	68.9	68.1	66.4	62.7	68.4	69.9
Mali	79.9	80.2	80.4	87.1	103.8	94.1	88.7	81.5	92.2	92.1	91.5
Mauritania	56.2	55.1	53.2	71.5	76.9	67.3	65.2	65.3	65.3	70.9	67.8
Mauritius	75.3	76.6	69.4	66.4	59.4	61.6	62.8	67.2	67.9	67.3	75.5
Mozambique	..	..	..	..	..	..	..	..	..	..	76.2
Namibia	..	..	..	..	..	..	..	..	..	..	45.9
Niger	88.8	87.2	85.9	84.7	93.5	86.6	84.9	75.7	70.7	71.1	67.1
Nigeria	79.8	75.9	69.9	66.7	63.8	66.7	62.6	61.2	63.0	61.9	59.9
Rwanda	88.0	87.6	87.8	81.0	86.7	78.2	74.3	71.0	76.6	76.6	83.3
Senegal	74.0	75.4	71.7	75.5	69.7	72.2	75.9	72.6	76.9	76.7	78.4
Seychelles	..	..	..	..	..	..	54.8	40.3	32.8	46.8	44.2
Sierra Leone	73.6	76.9	79.3	78.4	81.0	82.5	86.8	83.9	87.1	90.0	92.4
Somalia	83.2	85.0	70.8	79.1	71.1	71.6	67.0	103.4	82.8	88.5	97.3
Sudan	0.0	68.8	74.8	69.6	71.0	80.1	74.3	77.4	82.2	80.9	80.6
Swaziland	54.2	52.2	49.7	43.3	30.2	49.4	44.5	55.7	56.1	73.3	67.9
Tanzania	68.8	66.7	69.2	70.5	75.4	74.1	63.0	62.3	72.6	70.3	77.1
Togo	58.3	55.2	58.2	59.8	32.4	60.9	51.9	58.8	41.4	52.0	52.8
Uganda	..	..	..	..	..	..	..	..	..	..	..
Zaire	73.7	74.8	77.7	78.1	77.4	80.5	86.0	83.5	87.9	87.7	81.5
Zambia	39.4	41.4	39.7	33.3	34.9	51.4	44.8	51.5	55.6	53.1	55.2
Zimbabwe	..	..	..	..	..	62.1	63.5	61.1	65.6	68.5	64.5
SOUTH ASIA	*76.6*	*76.5*	*76.9*	*76.5*	*76.0*	*75.2*	*72.5*	*72.8*	*72.6*	*72.8*	*75.3*
Bangladesh	79.5	96.2	103.4	92.7	94.6	95.9	98.9	88.7	93.5	92.2	91.6
Bhutan	..	..	..	..	..	..	..	..	..	..	67.3
India	74.8	72.8	74.0	73.9	72.8	70.2	68.6	70.6	69.6	69.6	73.0
Nepal	..	..	..	..	..	82.4	80.8	79.2	79.2	79.9	82.2
Pakistan	80.9	80.9	78.8	78.3	83.8	84.4	81.3	79.3	80.6	83.8	83.1
Sri Lanka	72.3	72.4	71.8	76.5	80.2	82.6	76.1	73.3	75.2	77.1	80.3
EAST ASIA AND PACIFIC	*65.5*	*64.2*	*65.1*	*63.1*	*63.9*	*63.1*	*63.1*	*62.1*	*60.1*	*58.0*	*59.4*
China	63.7	62.3	64.0	62.7	63.7	61.9	63.3	62.8	59.2	56.9	59.5
Fiji	67.1	68.5	70.8	78.7	74.3	68.0	69.6	64.1	65.3	58.4	57.2
Indonesia	78.1	74.7	69.1	67.8	65.0	65.1	64.3	61.9	63.0	56.8	52.3
Korea, Rep.	75.5	75.5	73.7	70.0	69.7	70.5	65.1	61.9	61.2	62.0	64.2
Malaysia	57.7	59.2	58.5	53.2	53.4	56.5	50.9	50.2	51.7	48.3	50.5
Mongolia	..	..	..	..	..	..	..	..	..	..	..
Papua New Guinea	63.8	63.3	58.9	47.2	46.3	52.6	50.1	53.7	55.3	53.9	60.9
Philippines	68.8	69.6	68.8	63.8	65.4	64.5	62.3	62.2	63.6	62.5	66.7
Solomon Islands	..	..	..	..	..	..	..	..	..	..	70.2
Thailand	67.5	67.1	68.4	64.7	66.4	67.6	67.5	67.9	64.9	67.5	67.5
Tonga	..	..	..	..	..	88.9	90.9	87.8	94.9	97.6	91.0
Vanuatu	..	..	..	..	..	..	..	..	..	..	..
Western Samoa	..	..	..	..	..	..	..	..	..	98.6	86.8

1981	1982	1983	1984	1985	1986	1987	1988	1989	1990	1991	
72.8	*73.0*	*73.4*	*71.3*	*72.4*	*71.6*	*71.3*	*71.8*	*70.5*	*67.8*	..	*SUB-SAHARAN AFRICA*
74.1	*73.7*	*74.5*	*70.9*	*70.9*	*71.9*	*72.6*	*72.5*	*72.2*	..	..	*Excluding Nigeria*
103.0	82.5	84.9	81.0	79.7	82.4	81.9	83.1	81.8	..	..	Benin
51.9	61.6	54.4	48.3	44.9	37.6	42.1	41.6	43.3	..	..	Botswana
94.4	86.6	85.2	87.0	84.8	84.1	82.5	80.0	81.7	82.5	..	Burkina Faso
80.2	87.7	80.2	81.2	83.4	83.4	77.3	82.9	81.5	83.8	..	Burundi
68.9	68.2	62.3	57.9	55.1	59.7	69.5	75.8	67.9	69.7	82.8	Cameroon
88.8	84.3	83.6	88.0	87.7	84.6	72.1	74.5	76.4	..	..	Cape Verde
86.9	90.9	84.3	86.0	86.5	86.7	87.7	87.3	86.5	88.1	..	Central African Rep.
..	..	100.0	89.2	102.7	102.3	95.1	95.5	92.2	92.4	..	Chad
..	..	68.7	82.5	79.5	75.9	82.7	81.4	75.9	76.2	..	Comoros
56.5	40.0	39.8	38.8	52.5	59.4	56.6	60.1	52.8	56.6	65.2	Congo
63.8	62.5	64.2	62.3	56.8	65.7	67.8	61.3	68.1	67.6	66.3	Côte d'Ivoire
				75.5	68.2	73.3	70.6	68.8	72.1	..	Equatorial Guinea
80.7	81.8	80.0	79.2	77.7	78.3	77.1	71.9	68.3	..	..	Ethiopia
26.7	27.3	29.8	29.9	29.5	46.5	49.9	51.7	41.7	38.0	..	Gabon
72.8	70.4	75.1	76.9	77.1	72.1	73.1	76.0	75.0	74.7	..	Gambia, The
87.2	89.8	90.8	86.1	83.0	81.2	81.8	79.4	83.7	..	..	Ghana
70.3	75.7	78.1	83.6	86.8	87.6	84.8	89.1	100.3	98.6	..	Guinea-Bissau
61.9	63.5	61.2	63.3	57.6	59.7	62.3	61.8	62.5	63.2	..	Kenya
134.8	141.6	167.3	164.5	145.3	141.8	144.9	128.0	124.8	117.6	..	Lesotho
61.9	65.9	70.9	68.6	64.7	64.5	..	..	..	..	..	Liberia
88.2	90.3	89.0	86.7	87.7	86.8	86.2	85.3	82.1	83.2	..	Madagascar
70.3	67.4	68.4	69.5	69.4	70.1	67.9	74.5	79.2	74.8	..	Malawi
90.4	89.7	93.9	92.6	102.4	90.3	82.8	82.4	79.2	79.6	..	Mali
65.7	79.1	93.7	84.7	76.4	71.0	73.1	79.9	78.9	87.5	..	Mauritania
71.3	70.8	69.5	68.5	66.9	60.9	61.1	61.9	64.7	66.5	..	Mauritius
74.3	79.7	82.2	80.2	80.6	75.7	96.0	99.0	96.4	91.6	..	Mozambique
63.2	66.3	67.3	65.1	55.6	54.0	62.6	56.4	56.2	..	..	Namibia
80.4	80.5	81.1	91.4	86.8	82.9	83.8	82.9	85.5	..	..	Niger
71.2	72.0	71.8	71.3	73.9	72.5	69.8	73.0	67.6	59.2	62.7	Nigeria
78.6	81.9	83.9	81.0	80.5	79.7	80.7	80.7	79.4	77.8	..	Rwanda
87.0	82.8	82.4	79.3	84.6	79.0	78.3	77.8	79.3	77.0	..	Senegal
51.2	56.2	68.2	61.2	58.2	..	..	..	..	..	..	Seychelles
88.6	89.5	83.6	82.0	84.8	83.8	82.8	80.8	85.4	85.0	..	Sierra Leone
93.9	99.5	106.8	105.3	64.7	73.6	66.7	72.9	81.6	..	..	Somalia
83.0	81.0	89.3	84.1	94.2	81.1	80.2	84.6	83.3	83.9	..	Sudan
71.9	72.3	77.7	77.1	81.1	65.7	63.1	63.5	..	..	..	Swaziland
75.4	72.6	78.2	77.2	77.2	79.7	88.4	95.5	95.4	..	..	Tanzania
57.4	63.1	61.9	64.3	63.4	67.7	67.4	71.4	68.5	70.4	..	Togo
..	..	93.0	84.1	83.2	83.0	86.2	91.7	93.3	93.9	..	Uganda
81.9	83.4	83.8	80.9	77.9	78.1	77.9	75.1	79.3	..	..	Zaire
64.9	64.3	60.7	58.3	60.7	50.5	59.8	66.0	83.9	67.6	..	Zambia
67.0	65.0	68.9	59.2	57.6	55.8	52.4	52.6	56.6	52.9	57.0	Zimbabwe
71.8	*72.7*	*73.6*	*73.3*	*71.2*	*70.7*	*70.1*	*69.7*	*68.2*	*68.2*	*66.3*	*SOUTH ASIA*
89.9	91.8	93.1	91.8	90.8	89.4	89.0	89.1	88.5	89.2	86.7	Bangladesh
70.9	69.3	66.8	68.2	63.0	65.6	64.3	66.9	..	..	..	Bhutan
68.6	69.5	71.4	70.7	67.9	67.9	67.6	67.2	67.0	67.5	68.6	India
82.1	81.6	81.3	80.9	76.1	78.1	76.6	76.0	78.4	79.0	..	Nepal
81.3	81.6	80.2	80.3	81.2	78.5	74.2	73.9	71.6	73.4	..	Pakistan
80.9	80.4	78.5	72.2	78.3	78.0	77.6	78.6	77.6	76.0	..	Sri Lanka
61.2	*60.9*	*60.9*	*59.6*	*58.1*	*56.5*	*54.8*	*54.6*	*54.5*	*50.3*	*49.2*	*EAST ASIA AND PACIFIC*
61.8	60.0	60.3	58.4	55.6	53.7	52.3	53.3	53.5	49.2	49.2	China
63.7	62.5	64.0	62.9	62.2	62.3	64.9	69.8	69.0	66.7	..	Fiji
55.3	60.5	60.6	60.2	59.0	61.7	57.7	57.0	53.0	53.8	54.5	Indonesia
63.9	62.5	61.0	60.1	59.4	55.1	52.8	51.5	52.5	..	..	Korea, Rep.
53.1	53.1	52.1	49.8	52.0	51.0	47.3	49.4	52.2	54.1	55.4	Malaysia
..	..	..	56.1	51.1	45.3	58.9	61.9	63.9	72.7	..	Mongolia
66.2	64.7	64.5	63.5	67.0	64.8	63.3	60.2	64.0	65.8	..	Papua New Guinea
67.1	68.8	68.6	72.1	75.0	72.1	73.2	71.3	71.2	74.5	77.2	Philippines
74.7	61.2	60.8	57.3	64.4	67.3	74.1	69.2	..	..	..	Solomon Islands
67.2	65.2	68.3	66.1	64.7	62.9	63.7	62.3	61.0	56.7	..	Thailand
98.6	98.1	94.3	86.2	98.2	..	..	..	..	..	..	Tonga
..	..	52.0	48.5	57.2	59.2	60.2	60.9	61.0	..	..	Vanuatu
97.2	90.6	88.2	85.6	87.3	95.2	95.5	99.8	102.3	101.1	..	Western Samoa

Table 15. Private consumption: percentage of gross domestic product (cont'd.)

Percentage points	1970	1971	1972	1973	1974	1975	1976	1977	1978	1979	1980
LATIN AMERICA AND CARIBBEAN	*69.2*	*69.9*	*70.0*	*68.3*	*67.4*	*66.5*	*66.9*	*66.7*	*66.8*	*66.9*	*66.3*
Argentina	68.2	69.1	68.9	67.5	66.2	61.3	59.0	60.3	60.1	65.6	66.8
Bahamas	..	..	..	..	..	..	..	55.7	58.1	65.9	61.7
Barbados	79.9	76.1	77.9	74.9	72.3	74.2	74.4	77.9	68.0	70.5	63.3
Belize	..	..	..	..	..	..	..	..	..	..	..
Bolivia	66.2	68.5	63.1	61.5	60.6	58.7	63.0	63.6	70.6	68.0	67.1
Brazil	68.6	69.6	69.7	67.5	70.7	66.5	68.8	69.2	68.6	69.5	69.7
Chile	70.1	71.3	75.2	80.8	62.4	73.2	68.9	72.8	71.1	70.7	70.7
Colombia	72.4	73.7	72.8	71.3	70.9	72.3	71.1	69.9	70.3	70.8	70.2
Costa Rica	73.7	72.2	70.0	68.2	73.8	71.6	66.3	65.2	67.6	66.9	65.5
Dominican Rep.	76.6	80.1	76.2	73.4	78.0	71.6	80.9	78.3	77.5	73.4	77.0
Ecuador	75.3	76.0	73.5	67.0	59.8	65.2	63.6	61.7	63.4	61.2	59.6
El Salvador	76.1	76.1	74.1	74.1	74.9	71.8	68.0	64.5	72.5	68.9	71.8
Grenada	..	..	..	..	..	..	..	..	..	..	72.4
Guatemala	78.4	80.0	80.0	79.2	78.1	78.9	77.8	75.3	77.0	78.7	78.9
Guyana	60.8	59.6	62.0	64.7	54.7	47.4	59.3	60.7	56.2	52.2	51.8
Haiti	83.0	81.8	81.8	80.3	83.3	84.5	84.7	85.1	82.7	81.7	81.9
Honduras	73.8	71.8	71.0	71.6	74.0	77.7	72.3	68.9	65.7	65.9	69.4
Jamaica	60.9	62.6	67.3	61.8	68.0	66.2	69.8	65.7	61.7	62.3	64.0
Mexico	74.8	76.0	74.8	73.6	72.9	71.6	71.3	69.6	69.4	67.7	65.1
Nicaragua	74.5	74.8	71.6	77.3	74.3	78.6	70.5	69.4	71.0	74.0	82.5
Panama	60.6	57.7	55.2	53.1	57.7	57.3	55.7	60.0	58.4	60.5	56.5
Paraguay	77.5	79.5	77.0	73.8	75.8	75.1	72.5	72.1	69.8	71.2	75.7
Peru	70.4	70.6	72.3	68.8	70.1	74.1	74.1	73.5	68.8	61.0	61.3
St. Vincent	..	..	..	..	..	..	..	91.0	67.6	77.7	78.3
Trinidad and Tobago	60.0	55.3	59.3	54.0	42.3	42.6	47.5	47.9	52.0	51.3	45.9
Uruguay	69.4	66.6	69.2	66.6	71.6	70.6	65.2	68.5	66.8	68.3	68.6
Venezuela	51.9	50.6	52.2	49.6	42.0	48.9	50.8	51.5	55.6	54.3	54.9
MIDDLE EAST AND NORTH AFRICA	*60.1*	*59.2*	*58.3*	*56.1*	*48.6*	*51.3*	*49.4*	*53.0*	*55.1*	*51.4*	*49.8*
Algeria	55.8	57.0	55.3	51.4	46.3	51.1	48.5	51.1	48.5	45.6	43.2
Egypt, Arab Rep.	65.9	66.0	66.6	63.8	73.5	62.9	58.5	62.0	63.1	68.7	69.2
Iran, Islamic Rep.	59.1	55.9	53.5	47.5	35.1	39.0	39.7	49.3	53.7	47.1	49.8
Jordan	..	..	..	..	..	..	..	..	..	..	..
Morocco	73.4	72.5	73.0	72.7	68.0	69.4	68.9	65.6	67.5	67.0	67.9
Oman	19.4	17.1	24.9	24.0	8.7	15.9	20.5	26.8	32.8	26.1	27.7
Saudi Arabia	33.7	28.0	24.5	19.5	9.9	12.9	14.5	16.8	24.2	27.5	26.6
Syrian Arab Rep.	72.3	72.3	67.6	69.7	66.9	66.4	63.3	67.4	69.0	69.1	66.5
Tunisia	66.5	64.8	63.9	66.0	60.6	62.2	62.1	63.5	62.5	60.4	61.5
EUROPE	*..*	*..*	*..*	*..*	*..*	*..*	*..*	*..*	*..*	*..*	*59.5*
Bulgaria	..	..	..	..	..	..	..	..	..	..	44.7
Czechoslovakia	..	..	..	..	..	..	..	..	..	..	48.0
Greece	67.6	67.7	66.6	63.8	66.4	67.8	66.9	66.0	63.4	61.3	63.9
Hungary	58.4	58.1	57.2	56.3	58.2	59.2	58.1	57.4	57.4	58.8	61.2
Malta	77.8	76.8	78.7	77.8	81.3	71.6	66.6	71.9	67.1	63.2	64.7
Poland	..	..	..	..	..	..	..	..	..	..	67.4
Portugal	66.5	67.3	62.5	64.5	72.6	73.1	73.7	72.0	68.0	67.5	66.6
Romania	..	..	..	..	..	..	..	..	..	..	..
Turkey	69.7	72.3	69.9	70.7	73.3	72.7	69.0	69.4	71.4	71.0	73.4
Yugoslavia	55.2	56.9	57.5	59.2	62.1	56.1	53.2	52.9	53.0	51.5	48.8
Low- and middle-income economies	**67.9**	**67.6**	**67.3**	**65.7**	**64.3**	**64.0**	**62.9**	**62.7**	**63.0**	**61.5**	**61.5**
Low-income economies	70.4	69.5	69.9	68.7	69.1	68.4	67.3	67.0	66.2	64.6	65.4
Low-income Africa	75.4	74.6	72.5	71.0	69.6	72.9	69.5	69.1	72.1	71.1	68.0
China and India	67.9	66.3	67.7	66.8	67.3	64.9	65.4	65.9	63.1	61.4	64.4
Other low-income	75.0	76.4	74.9	72.5	74.7	74.9	70.8	68.2	69.8	68.2	65.5
Middle-income economies	66.0	66.0	65.2	63.2	59.8	59.2	58.5	58.4	59.4	58.5	57.4
High-income economies	**59.9**	**59.8**	**59.7**	**58.8**	**59.0**	**60.2**	**60.1**	**60.2**	**59.7**	**59.9**	**60.3**
OECD members	59.9	59.8	59.7	58.9	59.2	60.4	60.3	60.4	59.8	60.1	60.6
Japan	52.3	53.6	54.0	53.6	54.3	57.1	57.5	57.7	57.7	58.7	58.8
United States	63.0	62.9	62.7	62.0	62.7	63.6	63.7	63.6	62.8	63.1	64.1
WORLD	**61.4**	**61.3**	**61.1**	**60.1**	**59.9**	**60.7**	**60.4**	**60.4**	**60.1**	**60.0**	**60.2**

1981	1982	1983	1984	1985	1986	1987	1988	1989	1990	1991	
66.3	*67.1*	*67.5*	*67.7*	*66.3*	*69.1*	*66.3*	*65.6*	*63.0*	*66.2*	..	*LATIN AMERICA AND CARIBBEAN*
68.0	69.8	64.8	73.5	73.8	77.1	79.9	77.7	77.3	80.0	..	Argentina
62.3	59.1	57.4	65.4	62.9	63.5	63.7	..	..	..	..	Bahamas
70.6	67.1	69.0	66.2	61.9	64.0	66.4	63.1	67.2	..	..	Barbados
64.6	68.5	69.0	62.1	67.2	60.9	58.8	56.5	59.0	61.9	..	Belize
77.4	65.8	70.4	66.0	78.2	83.5	83.2	79.0	78.1	77.1	..	Bolivia
68.0	69.6	71.2	70.4	65.8	67.8	62.3	59.4	57.6	60.9	..	Brazil
74.5	75.3	73.3	73.0	69.3	68.9	67.6	65.3	66.1	67.1	..	Chile
72.5	72.9	71.9	70.6	69.0	65.3	66.1	65.5	64.9	64.5		Colombia
60.1	57.8	61.5	61.3	60.1	58.6	62.0	61.7	60.2	60.4	60.9	Costa Rica
71.0	75.2	73.7	67.6	77.5	72.5	75.4	73.9	78.2	83.8	80.1	Dominican Rep.
61.6	63.1	65.9	64.1	64.5	66.9	70.7	69.1	71.2	69.5	69.7	Ecuador
76.0	76.1	77.5	78.8	81.2	77.9	81.0	80.9	82.9	88.0	87.6	El Salvador
68.0	74.5	76.6	74.1	72.8	73.9	72.7	71.3	72.2	74.2	..	Grenada
81.6	82.0	82.9	82.9	82.6	81.1	84.6	84.2	83.6	85.0	84.4	Guatemala
63.4	63.8	66.3	63.7	69.0	61.9	65.9	55.1	58.6	49.5	..	Guyana
85.0	82.2	83.4	82.4	82.0	84.5	84.8	85.8	85.3	90.2	..	Haiti
72.0	74.5	74.3	73.0	71.6	70.2	71.3	74.0	74.6	79.6	78.8	Honduras
67.8	68.6	66.7	67.4	70.2	59.4	59.4	50.6	60.7	55.8	58.9	Jamaica
64.4	61.6	60.9	63.1	64.5	68.2	65.1	68.4	65.8	69.5	66.9	Mexico
73.9	67.9	56.7	55.4	48.2	55.8	52.0	..	..	..	..	Nicaragua
53.3	54.0	56.7	63.0	62.8	57.7	57.5	54.6	66.1	61.0	62.2	Panama
73.4	74.9	69.9	75.0	77.8	78.6	80.3	75.0	64.6	70.3	..	Paraguay
63.2	61.8	65.0	62.9	62.4	68.2	67.3	65.0	68.6	70.8	72.5	Peru
70.5	78.6	73.0	63.7	58.0	67.3	..	..	..	..	..	St. Vincent
49.9	62.8	66.7	61.2	53.3	61.5	57.1	58.3	55.5	51.7	..	Trinidad and Tobago
68.0	67.5	69.1	69.1	68.5	68.3	70.1	69.1	68.9	67.3	..	Uruguay
57.9	62.4	67.6	61.0	61.8	68.9	64.7	68.4	64.7	62.1	..	Venezuela
53.5	*57.2*	*56.3*	*60.3*	*60.6*	*62.9*	*60.5*	*61.2*	*60.9*	*60.9*	..	*MIDDLE EAST AND NORTH AFRICA*
45.5	46.0	45.4	47.7	47.9	52.7	49.5	51.3	49.5	43.5	45.9	Algeria
66.9	67.0	65.0	67.9	68.2	69.6	79.4	78.3	81.8	83.5	..	Egypt, Arab Rep.
50.6	64.0	58.5	67.2	67.1	64.7	64.8	68.1	69.7	68.8	..	Iran, Islamic Rep.
..	..	84.3	81.7	83.5	77.5	74.5	73.7	69.6	84.8	..	Jordan
69.4	67.9	68.1	69.8	68.1	68.2	67.6	63.9	65.6	64.6	67.9	Morocco
25.8	31.9	31.4	30.8	33.9	51.5	..	..	..	..	..	Oman
22.1	32.3	42.4	45.3	50.5	51.7	49.2	48.9	46.7	39.3	..	Saudi Arabia
73.4	65.4	67.8	63.4	65.1	67.3	77.3	82.0	71.4	71.9	..	Syrian Arab Rep.
61.3	62.3	62.2	63.2	63.0	66.4	64.1	64.3	64.4	64.4	..	Tunisia
60.6	*59.7*	*61.2*	*60.5*	*60.0*	*58.7*	*58.1*	*58.1*	*57.5*	*64.6*	..	*EUROPE*
46.9	48.2	50.1	49.4	50.7	49.5	51.1	48.7	48.9	54.5	67.1	Bulgaria
49.2	48.6	49.0	48.0	47.9	47.8	48.0	47.9	49.3	51.1	63.5	Czechoslovakia
63.2	70.9	69.6	68.7	69.7	69.8	70.4	67.5	68.5	70.9	..	Greece
61.3	60.8	61.5	61.4	62.8	63.9	63.5	61.1	60.7	62.5	62.9	Hungary
64.0	66.2	67.0	68.9	70.0	67.1	63.9	63.9	63.5	..	..	Malta
74.2	61.8	64.4	62.4	61.8	60.6	59.8	56.5	51.3	53.8	67.1	Poland
69.3	68.8	68.6	70.5	67.5	65.6	65.5	66.5	66.2	65.6	..	Portugal
						60.7	61.1	64.6	70.1	87.1	Romania
72.4	71.8	74.5	75.6	73.6	69.6	67.5	65.2	66.7	67.6	64.7	Turkey
48.6	49.4	49.8	48.3	46.1	46.3	43.0	47.9	46.1	72.4	..	Yugoslavia
63.2	**63.8**	**63.7**	**63.7**	**62.8**	**63.2**	**61.7**	**61.6**	**60.4**	**62.0**	..	**Low- and middle-income economies**
66.9	67.3	67.7	66.6	65.4	64.8	63.8	63.4	62.2	60.9	60.2	Low-income economies
75.3	75.8	76.1	74.8	76.4	75.8	75.9	76.8	76.1	72.2	..	Low-income Africa
64.5	63.9	64.8	63.3	60.8	60.1	59.3	59.2	58.7	57.2	56.8	China and India
66.3	69.4	69.1	69.4	69.4	70.8	70.9	69.6	66.1	66.0	..	Other low-income
58.3	60.0	60.4	61.3	61.0	62.2	60.3	60.4	59.2	61.8	..	Middle-income economies
60.4	**61.8**	**62.2**	**61.6**	**62.1**	**61.9**	**61.9**	**61.5**	**61.4**	**61.4**	..	**High-income economies**
60.7	62.0	62.5	61.9	62.3	62.0	62.0	61.5	61.5	61.4	..	OECD members
58.1	59.4	60.2	59.4	58.9	58.6	58.7	57.9	57.7	57.1	..	Japan
63.5	65.6	66.4	65.2	66.0	66.5	66.9	66.8	66.7	67.4	..	United States
60.5	**61.9**	**62.3**	**62.0**	**62.2**	**62.1**	**61.9**	**61.5**	**61.2**	**61.4**	..	**WORLD**

Table 16. Current account balance before official transfers

Percentage of GDP	1970	1971	1972	1973	1974	1975	1976	1977	1978	1979	1980
SUB-SAHARAN AFRICA	..	..	..	..	..	..	..	..	..	..	..
Excluding Nigeria	..	..	..	..	..	..	..	..	..	..	..
Benin	-7.0	-7.0	-10.8	-7.3	-12.1	-15.6	-18.1	-17.0	-16.3	-11.4	-7.9
Botswana	-41.8	-37.6	-34.7	-24.6	-7.1	-12.2	-8.9	-14.6	-28.9	-14.3	-23.2
Burkina Faso	-5.2	-8.0	-8.8	-10.1	-14.5	-18.4	-13.5	-18.3	-16.4	-15.6	-15.2
Burundi	-1.0	-5.8	-3.6	-2.1	-5.6	-10.6	-2.5	-1.7	-9.9	-9.9	-13.9
Cameroon	-4.1	-5.0	-7.6	-2.0	-1.7	-7.2	-4.8	-3.7	-4.5	-2.7	-6.4
Cape Verde	..	..	..	..	..	..	..	-28.3	-35.2	-37.3	-17.7
Central African Rep.	-13.4	-12.1	-12.2	-11.6	-18.1	-22.7	-9.7	-11.3	-12.6	-14.5	-17.6
Chad	-10.0	-9.6	-9.1	-13.4	-13.7	-22.0	-14.9	-19.9	-20.8	-6.2	-2.2
Comoros	..	..	..	..	..	..	..	..	..	..	..
Congo	-19.4	-24.5	-28.1	-16.6	-19.8	-37.2	-35.6	-28.8	-26.4	-11.9	-13.5
Côte d'Ivoire	-5.1	-9.2	-8.5	-10.9	-3.5	-10.8	-6.0	-3.5	-11.1	-15.2	-17.5
Equatorial Guinea	..	-4.6	..	-1.8	..	..	..	..	..	..	..
Ethiopia	-2.4	-3.0	-0.3	2.6	0.8	-3.0	-0.3	-2.7	-5.1	-4.8	-4.5
Gabon	-4.7	2.4	-7.1	-9.1	12.7	1.4	0.3	2.5	1.6	7.0	8.2
Gambia, The	0.1	-4.8	-2.2	-7.0	-0.9	6.1	-15.1	-7.2	-31.2	-25.2	-47.8
Ghana	-3.4	-6.4	4.3	4.4	-6.9	-0.1	-3.8	-4.5	-3.0	1.0	-1.2
Guinea-Bissau	..	..	..	..	..	..	..	..	..	..	..
Kenya	-5.4	-10.3	-5.1	-6.6	-11.9	-8.6	-4.6	-0.8	-13.9	-9.3	-13.8
Lesotho	-1.4	-7.1	-15.5	-12.6	-22.9	-14.1	-27.4	-20.3	-16.4	-27.1	-31.8
Liberia	-6.6	-4.7	-3.8	-2.2	-8.5	6.3	4.3	-5.4	-3.9	-1.7	0.9
Madagascar	-3.8	-6.6	-3.8	-4.0	-4.8	-6.1	-4.5	-3.7	-5.8	-14.0	-15.4
Malawi	-15.8	-11.2	-14.1	-8.4	-7.7	-14.1	-10.3	-10.9	-22.5	-29.5	-25.0
Mali	-6.4	-7.6	-8.3	-15.6	-28.0	-19.6	-9.5	-5.8	-17.3	-14.6	-14.4
Mauritania	-6.4	-4.8	-8.7	-9.2	-5.3	-30.5	-45.5	-46.3	-43.7	-37.3	-35.4
Mauritius	2.4	-3.3	3.3	-0.5	6.8	1.8	-5.5	-10.5	-12.4	-12.8	-11.5
Mozambique	..	..	..	..	..	..	..	..	..	..	-17.5
Namibia											
Niger	-5.0	-2.0	-4.5	-6.3	-12.0	-6.7	-12.3	-13.2	-18.0	-13.2	-16.9
Nigeria	-3.3	-3.0	-2.2	-0.1	15.8	0.2	-0.8	-1.9	-6.6	2.4	5.7
Rwanda	-5.6	-9.0	-11.4	-2.6	-11.8	-11.7	-5.7	-6.0	-16.0	-7.5	-13.4
Senegal	-7.7	-10.5	-6.9	-14.4	-10.8	-9.4	-9.6	-8.1	-15.9	-14.0	-17.4
Seychelles	1.1	-18.2	-24.1	-23.9	-14.8	-18.6	-19.3	-17.4	-16.1	-16.7	-20.4
Sierra Leone	-4.7	-5.8	-2.8	-7.4	-14.5	-11.1	-10.6	-10.2	-16.1	-20.6	-19.0
Somalia	-5.5	-4.9	-5.4	-12.7	-21.4	-14.1	-13.5	-27.8	-16.4	-44.7	-46.2
Sudan	0.0	-1.9	-2.3	1.2	-8.1	-11.0	-8.1	-4.5	-6.5	-6.0	-9.6
Swaziland	..	..	..	..	10.6	11.7	8.1	-0.4	-26.6	-37.9	-38.9
Tanzania	-2.8	-7.3	-4.8	-6.8	-15.1	-11.8	-2.5	-4.6	-15.3	-10.8	-12.2
Togo	-5.4	-8.6	-13.1	-10.1	16.6	-19.1	-9.8	-16.7	-32.7	-33.4	-15.9
Uganda	0.0	0.0	0.0	0.0	0.0	0.0	0.0	0.0	0.0	0.0	-9.6
Zaire	-2.9	-5.4	-6.6	-4.5	-5.0	-7.0	-9.7	-13.0	2.0	1.1	-3.9
Zambia	6.0	-14.9	-11.2	4.6	0.3	-29.5	-5.0	-9.2	-11.4	0.1	-14.0
Zimbabwe	-1.7	-4.1	-0.7	-1.3	-3.4	-6.7	-0.7	..	..	..	-5.6
SOUTH ASIA	..	..	..	..	..	..	..	..	..	..	..
Bangladesh	-3.5	-4.8	-9.5	-6.2	-5.9	-7.0	-11.9	-6.2	-8.0	-7.3	-11.1
Bhutan											
India	-1.0	-1.2	-0.7	-0.7	-1.0	-0.1	1.3	1.4	-0.3	-0.7	-1.7
Nepal	-2.9	-3.2	-1.2	-2.7	-4.7	-2.8	-1.1	0.0	-3.5	-3.0	-5.1
Pakistan	-7.0	-5.6	-3.1	-2.0	-6.2	-10.4	-7.1	-7.0	-3.4	-5.7	-4.8
Sri Lanka	-3.1	-2.3	-1.9	-1.3	-5.0	-4.9	-1.8	2.0	-4.5	-11.0	-19.7
EAST ASIA AND PACIFIC	..	..	..	..	..	..	..	..	..	..	..
China	-0.1	-0.1	-0.1	0.4	-0.5	-0.2	0.2	0.3	0.1	0.0	0.3
Fiji	-8.2	-12.7	-12.5	-15.2	-5.9	-4.1	-7.5	-4.0	-4.6	-7.8	-5.0
Indonesia	-3.9	-4.2	-3.3	-3.1	2.0	-3.5	-2.3	-0.2	-2.6	1.7	3.6
Korea, Rep.	-7.9	-9.3	-3.9	-2.5	-11.1	-9.3	-1.6	-0.1	-2.2	-6.5	-8.6
Malaysia	0.0	-2.8	-4.8	1.1	-5.6	-5.3	5.0	3.1	0.5	4.2	-1.3
Mongolia	..	..	..	..	..	..	..	..	..	..	-21.1
Papua New Guinea	-37.0	-41.3	-18.0	2.4	-0.1	-10.2	-6.9	-7.9	-15.8	-7.6	-22.7
Philippines	-2.1	-1.4	-1.3	3.3	-2.6	-7.2	-7.2	-4.4	-5.4	-5.9	-6.3
Solomon Islands	..	..	..	..	..	-39.9	-17.0	-8.7	-18.1	-7.0	-27.0
Thailand	-4.2	-2.9	-1.0	-0.7	-0.8	-4.4	-2.7	-5.6	-4.9	-7.8	-6.9
Tonga	..	..	..	..	..	..	..	..	-2.4	-5.0	-5.8
Vanuatu	..	..	..	..	..	..	..	..	..	..	..
Western Samoa	..	..	..	..	..	..	..	..	-31.2	-39.9	-26.7

1981	1982	1983	1984	1985	1986	1987	1988	1989	1990	1991	
..	..	..	..	..	..	..	..	..	..	..	*SUB-SAHARAN AFRICA*
..	..	..	..	..	..	..	..	..	..	..	*Excluding Nigeria*
-21.6	-30.9	-9.4	-11.8	-4.0	-7.0	-6.2	-7.7	-6.2	..	..	Benin
-34.1	-19.5	-13.4	-9.9	3.8	4.9	34.2	0.2	9.9	-6.6	..	Botswana
-14.1	-18.0	-15.9	-12.5	-15.6	-12.7	-11.5	-11.3	-14.4	-12.1	..	Burkina Faso
-13.0	-17.7	-16.9	-16.8	-10.5	-11.7	-17.9	-14.5	-13.1	-18.5	-17.4	Burundi
-6.1	-5.3	-1.7	1.8	4.0	-5.7	-9.8	-7.2	-1.8	-2.5	-4.0	Cameroon
-30.7	-35.8	-37.7	-34.2	-33.6	-20.8	-11.9	-13.1	-9.1	-5.4	..	Cape Verde
-11.2	-15.3	-16.3	-15.4	-16.6	-19.1	-19.1	-16.7	-19.0	-19.9	..	Central African Rep.
-3.3	-7.4	-13.0	-12.1	-30.3	-33.1	-32.5	-23.9	-27.8	-27.0	..	Chad
..	-26.3	-27.9	-59.7	-40.3	-29.1	-30.3	-22.9	-17.9	-19.6	..	Comoros
-25.3	-16.7	-20.9	7.7	-9.3	-35.7	-12.6	-23.0	-5.5	-6.8	-23.9	Congo
-16.9	-13.8	-14.1	-1.5	0.6	-3.9	-10.7	-11.5	-13.2	-12.2	-11.4	Côte d'Ivoire
..	..	..	..	9.9	-13.9	-44.3	-51.3	-46.1	-43.5	..	Equatorial Guinea
-6.4	-9.0	-7.0	-8.6	-8.8	-6.5	-9.1	-9.9	-5.7	-5.1	..	Ethiopia
9.7	7.9	2.0	2.5	-4.8	-31.2	-17.8	-17.6	-5.1	4.7	-1.9	Gabon
-49.2	-26.0	-25.8	-1.2	-0.4	-1.8	-10.1	-3.7	-7.8	-3.5	..	Gambia, The
-12.0	-4.8	-6.1	-4.1	-5.4	-2.9	-4.3	-5.0	-6.1	-7.1	-6.6	Ghana
..	-48.0	-44.0	-47.3	-48.1	-58.7	-39.1	-50.8	-60.6	-44.4	..	Guinea-Bissau
-9.9	-5.5	-2.7	-3.9	-3.6	-2.6	-8.0	-8.4	-10.4	-7.8	-7.1	Kenya
-34.6	-23.7	-25.2	-29.2	-34.3	-30.2	-24.7	-37.1	-44.0	-26.4	..	Lesotho
0.6	-8.0	-20.3	-9.6	-3.1	-7.5	-14.3	..	..	..	..	Liberia
-12.4	-11.0	-9.2	-9.2	-9.0	-8.4	-10.1	-12.6	-11.4	-10.5	0.0	Madagascar
-15.6	-13.1	-13.8	-6.1	-13.2	-10.1	-7.2	-10.0	-12.8	-8.7	-10.1	Malawi
-17.4	-16.6	-18.8	-18.5	-31.1	-22.7	-16.4	-16.9	-14.5	-14.9	..	Mali
-35.3	-49.4	-37.9	-29.9	-35.0	-36.7	-26.3	-20.6	-13.8	-18.9	..	Mauritania
-14.1	-5.8	-2.9	-6.2	-4.0	5.1	2.1	-4.1	-5.3	-5.2	-2.1	Mauritius
-20.3	-23.5	-22.2	-18.8	-13.0	-14.0	-47.6	-52.5	-58.9	-54.4	-65.8	Mozambique
..	..	..	..	..	..	..	..	..	..	..	Namibia
-15.8	-19.5	-11.1	-9.9	-19.2	-6.6	-10.7	-9.7	-11.9	-9.8	..	Niger
-7.4	-9.4	-5.5	0.2	3.2	0.9	-0.2	-0.7	3.0	6.3	-0.9	Nigeria
-13.1	-13.6	-10.7	-8.9	-10.3	-9.6	-11.7	-11.1	-10.6	-10.5	..	Rwanda
-25.8	-17.3	-18.6	-17.6	-16.8	-12.1	-11.6	-9.5	-9.2	-8.2	-8.5	Senegal
-20.5	-34.1	-27.5	-18.7	-19.9	-23.9	-18.0	-20.2	-18.7	-14.0	..	Seychelles
-14.0	-16.1	-3.4	-4.4	-1.0	9.5	-6.7	-1.0	-2.7	-15.1	..	Sierra Leone
-30.1	-44.0	-39.5	-42.3	-35.2	-46.4	-45.2	-30.4	-44.6	-37.1	..	Somalia
-12.2	-16.5	-11.7	-8.8	-6.2	-6.1	-4.4	-10.8	-10.6	-14.3	..	Sudan
-26.8	-34.5	-33.6	-31.5	-25.0	-7.3	6.1	2.0	-18.7	-14.0	..	Swaziland
-8.7	-9.8	-6.2	-7.8	-7.3	-11.2	-21.5	-23.2	-29.4	-39.9	-31.9	Tanzania
-11.8	-18.9	-14.5	-6.8	-12.9	-15.0	-12.7	-9.4	-8.1	-12.8	..	Togo
-9.4	-6.6	-4.7	-3.3	-2.1	-2.1	-6.0	-8.4	-12.9	-14.4	-10.3	Uganda
-6.8	-5.5	-4.7	-6.3	-6.8	-7.4	-11.3	-9.1	-10.1	-11.4	..	Zaire
-19.1	-15.3	-9.3	-6.0	-17.9	-22.4	-12.4	-9.8	-6.7	-15.7	..	Zambia
-11.3	-11.0	-8.1	-3.7	-3.1	-1.0	-0.6	0.8	-1.0	-4.3	-12.0	Zimbabwe
..	..	..	..	..	..	..	..	..	..	..	*SOUTH ASIA*
-10.0	-12.3	-8.9	-6.7	-8.4	-6.9	-5.5	-5.8	-6.7	-6.9	-4.2	Bangladesh
..	..	-54.3	-46.7	-49.7	-44.6	-25.8	-25.6	-19.0	-13.3	..	Bhutan
-1.9	-1.6	-1.5	-1.8	-2.8	-2.6	-2.5	-3.2	-3.0	-3.5	-2.6	India
-4.6	-6.0	-8.8	-6.9	-7.2	-7.6	-7.1	-8.6	-9.7	-10.2	-10.9	Nepal
-3.6	-5.0	-1.8	-3.2	-5.4	-3.9	-2.2	-4.4	-4.8	-4.7	-4.6	Pakistan
-13.7	-14.5	-12.1	-3.4	-9.8	-9.1	-7.4	-8.4	-8.5	-5.8	-5.7	Sri Lanka
..	..	..	..	..	..	..	..	..	..	..	*EAST ASIA AND PACIFIC*
1.1	2.4	1.6	1.0	-3.9	-2.8	0.0	-1.0	-1.1	3.3	2.1	China
-16.3	-9.5	-8.1	-3.9	-4.0	-1.9	-2.4	-0.3	0.1	-1.3	..	Fiji
-0.9	-5.8	-7.5	-2.2	-2.2	-5.1	-3.0	-1.8	-1.4	-2.3	-5.1	Indonesia
-6.8	-3.6	-2.0	-1.5	-1.0	4.3	7.5	8.2	2.4	-0.9	-3.4	Korea, Rep.
-10.0	-13.5	-11.7	-5.0	-2.1	-0.6	8.1	5.0	-0.8	-4.1	-3.7	Malaysia
-34.7	-33.4	-31.1	-29.1	-32.2	-36.2	-29.5	-29.0	-34.5	-28.8	..	Mongolia
-32.1	-31.4	-24.6	-22.8	-15.4	-12.1	-13.4	-15.3	-16.3	-17.2	..	Papua New Guinea
-6.3	-9.1	-9.1	-5.0	-0.8	2.5	-1.9	-1.7	-4.3	-7.0	-3.4	Philippines
-34.1	-18.2	-14.4	-3.4	-20.3	-26.8	-26.9	-36.8	-40.1	-34.8	..	Solomon Islands
-7.7	-3.1	-7.6	-5.4	-4.4	0.2	-1.0	-3.1	-3.9	-9.0	..	Thailand
-10.0	5.7	-24.1	-9.4	-7.3	-3.2	-0.9	-21.1	-12.1	-1.7	..	Tonga
..	-23.3	-17.4	-7.1	-19.1	-21.2	-30.9	-19.6	-17.1	..	..	Vanuatu
-27.4	-18.3	-12.1	-12.9	-10.8	-4.4	-5.5	-7.1	-4.8	-10.3	..	Western Samoa

Table 16. Current account balance before official transfers (cont'd.)

Percentage of GDP	1970	1971	1972	1973	1974	1975	1976	1977	1978	1979	1980
LATIN AMERICA AND CARIBBEAN	..	..	..	..	..	..	..	..	..	..	..
Argentina	-0.7	-1.6	-0.9	1.8	..	-3.3	1.7	2.7	4.3	-1.0	-8.4
Bahamas	..	..	..	-22.1	-19.8	6.4	12.4	8.5	4.1	0.4	-2.6
Barbados	-23.7	-18.0	-19.4	-18.9	-14.2	-10.4	-15.1	-11.0	-6.1	-5.8	-3.1
Belize	..	..	..	..	..	..	..	..	..	..	..
Bolivia	0.2	-0.7	-1.0	0.2	7.7	-8.1	-3.3	-5.9	-15.1	-16.1	-1.7
Brazil	-2.0	-3.4	-2.9	-2.7	-7.2	-5.7	-4.3	-2.9	-3.5	-4.7	-5.5
Chile	-1.2	-2.0	-3.9	-2.8	-2.7	-6.9	1.3	-4.2	-7.2	-5.8	-7.3
Colombia	-4.6	-6.2	-2.5	-0.8	-3.1	-1.4	1.0	1.9	1.0	1.6	-0.6
Costa Rica	-7.8	-11.0	-8.3	-7.3	-16.0	-11.1	-8.4	-7.4	-10.3	-13.7	-13.6
Dominican Rep.	-6.9	-7.8	-2.4	-4.2	-8.3	-2.2	-3.3	-2.9	-6.6	-6.5	-10.2
Ecuador	-7.3	-10.2	-4.5	-0.5	0.6	-5.5	-0.6	-5.7	-9.6	-7.0	-5.7
El Salvador	0.7	-1.4	0.8	-3.4	-8.6	-5.3	0.8	0.8	-9.5	0.4	0.0
Grenada	..	..	..	..	..	..	..	..	..	..	-19.8
Guatemala	-0.4	-2.4	-0.5	0.3	-3.2	-1.8	-1.8	-0.7	-4.5	-3.0	-2.1
Guyana	..	-2.7	-5.3	-21.1	-2.2	-4.6	-31.7	-22.0	-4.6	-16.0	-21.4
Haiti	1.0	-6.2	-6.5	-7.8	-11.0	-17.2	-15.6	-7.1	-8.4	-8.4	-9.4
Honduras	-9.3	-3.6	-2.0	-4.2	-11.9	-11.1	-8.5	-8.3	-9.0	-9.3	-13.0
Jamaica	-10.6	-10.7	-10.6	-12.7	-3.5	-10.1	-10.3	-1.4	-2.3	-6.1	-6.5
Mexico	-2.9	-2.0	-2.0	-2.4	-3.8	-4.4	-3.7	-2.2	-3.0	-3.9	-5.5
Nicaragua	-5.5	-5.7	2.0	-8.9	-17.7	-12.7	-2.7	-9.2	-1.7	5.7	-25.8
Panama	-7.7	-7.8	-9.2	-9.0	-14.9	-10.3	-10.2	-8.8	-9.7	-12.9	-10.6
Paraguay	-3.2	-3.9	-1.2	-2.0	-4.1	-5.6	-4.2	-2.8	-4.6	-6.2	-13.5
Peru	2.0	-0.9	-0.7	-2.8	-5.6	-9.6	-8.0	-6.9	-2.0	3.9	-1.2
St. Vincent	..	..	..	..	..	..	..	..	0.0	-14.9	-23.2
Trinidad and Tobago	-12.7	-18.1	-10.9	-1.8	13.9	14.0	11.0	6.0	1.7	-0.3	5.7
Uruguay	-2.4	-2.7	2.2	0.6	-3.6	-5.6	-2.3	-4.2	-2.7	-5.1	-7.3
Venezuela	-0.7	0.0	-0.6	4.4	19.4	6.8	0.8	-7.1	-11.9	0.6	6.8
MIDDLE EAST AND NORTH AFRICA	..	..	..	..	..	..	..	..	..	..	..
Algeria	-3.3	-3.5	-2.5	-5.1	4.3	-10.8\	-5.1	-11.1	-13.5	-4.9	0.5
Egypt, Arab Rep.	-5.9	-5.7	-5.3	-5.8	-17.7	-21.2	-10.2	-9.9	-9.2	-10.6	-1.9
Iran, Islamic Rep.	-4.4	-0.9	-2.3	0.6	26.9	9.2	11.5	3.5	0.2	13.3	-2.6
Jordan	..	..	..	..	..	..	..	..	..	..	..
Morocco	-4.1	-2.2	0.3	1.0	2.5	-6.3	-15.1	-16.9	-10.5	-9.8	-8.1
Oman	..	..	..	..	9.4	-7.2	-0.6	0.3	-2.5	9.9	14.0
Saudi Arabia	3.9	21.9	32.9	27.6	85.9	44.1	37.9	27.3	2.5	18.5	40.9
Syrian Arab Rep.	-3.4	-3.1	-0.5	-0.8	-4.8	-8.2	-15.4	-17.0	-8.6	-6.9	-9.7
Tunisia	-6.1	-1.2	-1.6	-3.7	0.6	-4.9	-10.3	-12.3	-8.5	-5.1	-5.3
EUROPE	..	..	..	..	..	..	..	..	..	..	..
Bulgaria	..	..	..	..	..	..	..	..	..	..	3.7
Czechoslovakia	..	..	..	..	..	..	..	..	..	..	-0.4
Greece	-4.3	-3.1	-3.2	-7.3	-6.1	-4.2	-4.2	..	-3.0	-4.9	..
Hungary	..	..	..	..	..	..	..	..	..	..	..
Malta	-12.9	-4.9	3.7	7.9	-3.4	11.3	9.9	5.9	7.6	2.7	1.8
Poland	..	..	..	..	..	..	..	..	..	..	-6.2
Portugal	-2.6	2.1	..	..	..	-4.9	..	..	..	-0.3	-4.3
Romania	..	..	..	..	..	..	..	..	..	..	..
Turkey	-0.5	-0.2	1.2	3.1	-2.0	-4.7	-4.9	-6.6	-2.4	-2.1	-6.0
Yugoslavia	-2.8	-2.7	2.7	2.4	-3.6	-2.1	0.5	-2.9	-2.3	-5.3	-3.2
Low- and middle-income economies	..	..	..	..	..	..	..	..	..	..	..
Low-income economies	..	..	..	..	..	..	..	..	..	..	..
Low-income Africa	..	..	..	..	..	..	..	..	..	..	..
China and India	..	..	..	..	..	..	..	..	..	..	..
Other low-income	..	..	..	..	..	..	..	..	..	..	..
Middle-income economies	..	..	..	..	..	..	..	..	..	..	..
High-income economies	..	..	..	..	..	..	..	..	..	..	..
OECD members	..	..	..	..	..	..	..	..	..	..	..
Japan	1.1	2.6	2.3	0.0	-1.0	-0.1	0.7	1.6	1.7	-0.8	-0.9
United States	0.5	0.1	-0.2	0.7	0.6	1.4	0.5	-0.5	-0.5	0.2	0.3
WORLD	..	..	..	..	..	..	..	..	..	..	..

1981	1982	1983	1984	1985	1986	1987	1988	1989	1990	1991	
..	..	..	..	..	..	..	..	..	..	..	*LATIN AMERICA AND CARIBBEAN*
-8.2	-4.1	-3.8	-3.2	-1.4	-3.6	-5.3	-1.7	-2.2	1.7	..	Argentina
-6.5	-5.4	-3.0	-3.0	-7.2	-1.6	-6.6	-5.1	-5.9	-6.6	..	Bahamas
-11.9	-4.2	-4.4	1.8	4.1	-0.7	-2.8	0.9	1.4	-5.1	..	Barbados
..	..	..	-7.5	-2.0	0.0	-2.5	-4.6	-8.9	..	..	Belize
-13.5	-6.4	-7.0	-8.6	-11.5	-12.0	-12.2	-9.7	-8.9	-7.6	-8.3	Bolivia
-4.5	-5.8	-3.4	0.0	-0.1	-2.0	-0.5	1.3	0.2	-0.6	-0.6	Brazil
-14.7	-9.7	-5.9	-11.3	-8.4	-7.0	-4.6	-1.3	-3.6	-3.4	-2.0	Chile
-5.4	-7.8	-7.8	-3.7	-5.2	1.1	0.9	-0.5	-0.5	1.0	3.7	Colombia
-15.6	-10.5	-10.4	-7.1	-7.7	-7.7	-4.4	-9.8	-8.5	-10.8	-11.9	-5.8	Costa Rica
-5.8	-6.3	-6.4	-7.4	-7.0	-4.2	-8.5	-3.7	-5.9	-3.7	-3.6	Dominican Rep.
-7.3	-9.8	-1.5	-2.8	0.3	-5.3	-12.0	-6.0	-5.6	-2.2	-5.7	Ecuador
-7.9	-6.8	-5.4	-5.9	-6.2	-3.0	-4.8	-5.0	-8.1	-6.7	-5.4	El Salvador
-35.5	-42.0	-31.4	-20.1	-21.9	-27.5	-21.7	-15.2	-14.1	..	..	Grenada
-6.7	-4.6	-2.5	-4.0	-2.5	-0.6	-7.5	-6.3	-5.2	-4.4	-3.2	Guatemala
-31.6	-28.9	-32.9	-22.6	-20.4	-28.8	-35.5	-24.3	-17.5	-55.0	..	Guyana
-15.2	-10.8	-10.7	-10.0	-9.5	-6.5	-6.8	-7.7	-7.6	-5.7	..	Haiti
-11.6	-8.7	-8.4	-12.0	-9.6	-7.7	-8.4	-9.0	-10.0	-14.5	-13.8	Honduras
-12.3	-14.2	-11.1	-15.7	-18.3	-3.1	-6.5	-1.1	-11.6	-9.7	-9.4	Jamaica
-6.4	-3.7	3.6	2.3	0.2	-1.4	2.6	-1.5	-2.0	-2.7	-4.5	Mexico
-26.6	-23.0	-23.4	-22.8	-29.1	-29.3	-23.8	..	..	..	..	Nicaragua
-0.6	-3.5	7.1	1.6	3.0	4.5	1.7	14.4	4.1	-0.6	-6.9	Panama
-11.3	-9.1	2.9	-1.9	-5.5	-9.5	-11.5	-5.1	5.3	1.9	-0.9	Paraguay
-7.5	-6.9	-5.5	-1.8	0.0	-5.1	-6.1	-6.4	0.6	-2.5	-5.3	Peru
-8.0	-17.3	-6.1	-3.5	0.3	3.6	-13.4	-3.4	-10.9	..	..	St. Vincent
5.8	-7.3	-12.5	-6.4	-1.2	-8.8	-4.8	-2.5	-1.4	8.5	..	Trinidad and Tobago
-4.2	-2.7	-1.4	-2.9	-2.8	0.3	-2.3	-0.2	1.9	2.6	..	Uruguay
5.2	-5.3	5.5	7.8	5.4	-3.7	-2.9	-9.6	5.0	17.0	3.8	Venezuela
..	..	..	..	..	..	..	..	..	..	..	*MIDDLE EAST AND NORTH AFRICA*
0.2	-0.4	-0.2	0.2	1.7	-3.5	0.2	-3.8	-2.2	2.7	2.9	Algeria
-9.1	-9.1	-5.4	-8.2	-9.3	-9.4	-5.2	-4.0	-8.1	-7.2	-7.2	Egypt, Arab Rep.
						-1.7	-1.3	-2.1	-0.3	-7.8	Iran, Islamic Rep.
..	..	-24.3	-19.3	-20.3	-11.4	-7.8	-14.1	-16.8	-29.3	-23.7	Jordan
-12.7	-13.2	-7.1	-8.5	-7.8	-2.2	-0.1	0.7	-4.7	-2.1	-3.8	Morocco
15.0	5.9	4.3	1.0	0.1	-14.2	9.5	-4.6	..	..	..	Oman
29.5	9.0	-11.8	-14.8	-11.2	-12.0	-8.8	-6.4	-8.5	0.3	..	Saudi Arabia
-13.9	-10.1	-12.2	-11.6	-13.2	-9.5	-9.3	-6.5	8.9	11.9	..	Syrian Arab Rep.
-5.2	-8.7	-7.6	-10.1	-7.7	-7.5	-1.0	0.9	-3.7	-5.7	..	Tunisia
..	..	..	..	..	..	..	..	..	..	..	*EUROPE*
0.4	0.7	0.1	1.6	-0.5	-3.9	-2.6	-1.8	-2.4	-4.4	-7.5	Bulgaria
0.6	1.6	2.0	2.5	2.5	1.0	1.4	3.0	1.9	-2.6	-1.2	Czechoslovakia
-6.9	-6.4	-7.8	-8.4	-12.4	-7.8	-6.3	-5.5	-9.5	-9.6	..	Greece
..	-2.3	-0.9	0.2	-2.2	-5.7	-2.6	-2.0	-1.9	0.7	-1.7	Hungary
3.0	-1.9	-3.3	-2.2	-4.1	-0.9	0.2	0.0	-2.7	..	..	Malta
-8.0	-3.0	-2.1	-1.4	-1.4	-1.5	-0.6	-0.2	-1.8	4.3	-1.8	Poland
..	..	..	-2.9	1.5	3.2	0.2	-4.3	-1.5	-2.0	..	Portugal
..	..	..	..	..	..	..	..	..	..	-8.9	Romania
-3.4	-2.0	-4.2	-3.3	-2.3	-2.9	-1.7	1.8	0.7	-3.5	-2.2	Turkey
..	..	0.6	1.1	1.8	1.7	1.9	4.0	3.1	-2.7	..	Yugoslavia
..	..	..	..	..	..	..	..	..	..	..	**Low- and middle-income economies**
..	..	..	..	..	..	..	..	..	..	..	Low-income economies
..	..	..	..	..	..	..	..	..	..	..	Low-income Africa
..	..	..	..	..	..	..	..	..	..	..	China and India
..	..	..	..	..	..	..	..	..	..	..	Other low-income
..	..	..	..	..	..	..	..	..	..	..	Middle-income economies
..	..	..	..	..	..	..	..	..	..	..	**High-income economies**
..	..	..	..	..	..	..	..	..	..	..	OECD members
0.5	0.7	1.9	2.9	3.8	4.4	3.7	2.9	2.1	1.4	..	Japan
0.5	0.1	-0.9	-2.4	-2.7	-3.1	-3.3	-2.4	-1.8	-1.3	..	United States
..	..	..	..	..	..	..	..	..	..	..	**WORLD**

Table 17. Value of merchandise exports

Millions of US dollars	1970	1971	1972	1973	1974	1975	1976	1977	1978	1979	1980
SUB-SAHARAN AFRICA	..	..	..	..	..	..	..	..	..	..	..
Excluding Nigeria	..	..	..	..	..	..	..	..	..	..	..
Benin	..	..	..	..	..	..	..	..	..	..	..
Botswana	..	..	..	..	..	..	..	..	..	..	..
Burkina Faso	18.2	15.9	20.3	25.4	36.0	43.5	53.3	55.2	42.4	76.8	90.2
Burundi	..	..	..	..	..	..	..	..	..	..	..
Cameroon	225.9	206.0	217.8	352.5	476.6	446.3	510.8	663.0	762.2	1,128.6	1,320.9
Cape Verde	..	..	..	..	..	..	..	..	..	..	..
Central African Rep.	..	..	..	..	..	..	..	..	..	..	..
Chad	..	..	..	..	..	..	..	..	..	..	..
Comoros	..	..	..	..	..	..	..	..	..	..	..
Congo	30.8	39.5	52.4	85.4	228.1	178.7	181.8	181.7	308.3	509.3	955.3
Côte d'Ivoire	468.8	455.6	552.9	860.6	1,214.3	1,181.6	1,630.8	2,154.8	2,322.9	2,506.8	2,978.9
Equatorial Guinea	..	..	..	..	..	..	..	..	..	..	..
Ethiopia	117.8	123.8	165.3	233.9	262.4	215.2	274.6	333.4	309.2	421.8	424.4
Gabon	121.0	177.8	193.1	289.5	944.5	941.9	1,136.3	1,218.2	1,106.2	1,849.6	2,189.3
Gambia, The	..	..	..	..	..	..	..	..	..	..	..
Ghana	..	..	..	..	..	..	..	..	..	..	..
Guinea-Bissau	..	..	..	..	..	..	..	..	..	..	..
Kenya	200.5	204.9	253.6	349.2	456.2	456.0	761.5	1,161.0	955.8	1,030.7	1,313.4
Lesotho	..	..	..	..	..	..	..	..	..	..	..
Liberia	212.6	222.4	244.0	323.8	399.8	393.9	457.1	447.4	487.5	536.6	597.0
Madagascar	144.8	146.8	163.8	202.7	244.2	301.4	282.5	347.3	399.3	407.5	386.5
Malawi	48.4	60.3	68.9	85.5	106.7	121.1	154.0	190.8	177.1	216.2	269.5
Mali	..	..	..	..	..	..	..	..	..	..	..
Mauritania	..	..	..	..	..	..	..	..	..	..	..
Mauritius	67.5	63.9	105.5	135.7	309.9	294.6	260.0	304.9	320.2	393.1	420.3
Mozambique	156.7	160.4	175.0	226.6	296.0	201.7	..	129.0	..	397.8	511.3
Namibia	..	..	..	..	..	..	..	..	..	..	..
Niger	31.6	38.4	54.3	62.8	52.6	91.2	133.9	160.1	282.9	448.0	579.7
Nigeria	1,227.9	1,793.2	2,161.1	3,448.0	9,177.6	7,983.4	10,557.0	11,834.6	9,958.6	16,360.8	25,057.5
Rwanda	..	..	..	..	..	..	..	..	..	..	..
Senegal	160.6	124.9	215.9	194.7	390.7	462.4	485.2	622.8	420.8	533.3	476.7
Seychelles	..	..	..	..	..	..	..	..	..	..	..
Sierra Leone	101.5	98.5	114.8	128.6	141.4	140.1	103.0	122.5	167.4	216.2	228.1
Somalia	31.4	34.5	43.1	54.2	62.0	88.6	94.6	63.0	106.6	111.8	132.6
Sudan	291.8	328.7	357.5	412.3	438.8	424.0	572.9	661.0	481.3	581.2	584.2
Swaziland	..	..	..	..	..	..	..	..	..	..	..
Tanzania	236.1	243.0	283.8	318.2	355.2	343.2	484.0	550.8	472.3	500.3	527.7
Togo	54.6	56.4	49.6	61.4	189.1	124.8	105.2	159.4	240.5	218.4	334.8
Uganda	..	..	..	..	..	..	..	..	..	..	..
Zaire	735.4	688.0	737.7	1,001.3	1,381.5	864.8	809.3	1,110.0	899.4	2,004.1	2,506.9
Zambia	994.5	672.0	750.5	1,136.2	1,399.4	805.1	1,036.2	895.4	867.3	1,372.0	1,329.7
Zimbabwe	..	..	..	..	..	..	..	..	..	14.1	433.3
SOUTH ASIA	..	..	..	..	..	..	..	..	..	..	..
Bangladesh	..	..	..	..	367.6	264.8	361.7	435.0	552.8	661.6	740.4
Bhutan	..	..	..	..	..	..	..	..	..	..	..
India	2,012.6	2,036.7	2,414.9	2,961.1	3,898.7	4,354.8	5,322.7	5,980.1	6,167.4	6,995.7	7,510.6
Nepal	..	..	..	..	..	..	..	..	..	..	..
Pakistan	695.3	660.3	686.8	941.2	1,091.0	1,031.3	1,144.2	1,152.8	1,446.9	2,036.3	2,588.0
Sri Lanka	331.6	323.7	323.4	405.3	519.7	557.7	565.2	760.3	843.9	977.7	1,043.0
EAST ASIA AND PACIFIC	..	..	..	..	..	..	..	..	..	..	..
China	2,307.3	2,782.5	3,692.5	5,876.1	7,107.9	7,689.0	6,943.4	7,519.6	9,954.9	13,614.1	18,099.3
Fiji	..	..	..	..	..	..	..	..	..	..	..
Indonesia	1,055.1	1,199.5	1,777.7	3,210.9	7,426.3	7,130.2	8,556.3	10,852.6	11,643.2	15,590.1	21,908.9
Korea, Rep.	829.6	1,060.0	1,615.8	3,214.9	4,452.6	5,070.6	7,693.0	9,986.0	12,654.1	14,951.7	17,445.8
Malaysia	1,686.6	1,638.8	1,721.6	3,039.7	4,234.2	3,846.6	5,294.8	6,079.3	7,386.7	11,075.1	12,939.2
Mongolia	..	..	..	..	..	..	..	..	..	..	..
Papua New Guinea	..	..	..	..	..	..	..	..	..	..	..
Philippines	1,059.7	1,116.3	1,028.7	1,795.7	2,648.1	2,216.1	2,484.7	3,065.4	3,327.3	4,572.2	5,750.9
Solomon Islands	..	..	..	..	..	..	..	..	..	..	..
Thailand	685.2	801.8	1,039.1	1,526.8	2,402.5	2,162.2	2,950.2	3,450.9	3,996.3	5,207.1	6,369.1
Tonga	3.0	2.5	2.4	4.6	6.6	5.8	3.8	6.9	5.5	6.8	7.9
Vanuatu	..	..	..	..	..	..	..	..	..	..	..
Western Samoa	..	..	..	..	..	..	..	..	..	..	..

1981	1982	1983	1984	1985	1986	1987	1988	1989	1990	1991	
..	..	..	..	..	..	..	..	..	..	..	*SUB-SAHARAN AFRICA*
..	..	..	..	..	..	..	..	..	..	..	*Excluding Nigeria*
..	..	..	..	..	..	..	..	..	..	..	Benin
..	..	..	..	..	..	..	..	..	..	..	Botswana
75.0	56.2	57.0	..	..	83.0	155.0	140.8	130.0	160.0	..	Burkina Faso
..	..	..	..	..	..	..	..	..	..	..	Burundi
..	1,028.9	..	872.7	716.2	780.8	829.4	923.7	1,281.6	1,200.0	..	Cameroon
..	..	..	..	..	..	..	..	..	..	..	Cape Verde
..	..	..	..	..	..	..	..	..	..	..	Central African Rep.
..	..	..	..	..	..	..	..	..	..	..	Chad
..	..	..	..	..	..	..	..	..	..	..	Comoros
1,128.0	1,264.2	1,066.2	1,182.6	1,087.2	776.9	1,010.1	959.9	1,165.0	1,130.0	..	Congo
2,535.2	2,287.9	2,067.7	2,710.4	2,668.9	3,351.0	3,091.6	2,774.8	2,800.0	2,600.0	..	Côte d'Ivoire
..	..	..	..	..	..	..	..	..	..	..	Equatorial Guinea
378.0	404.3	402.3	416.7	337.5	464.4	370.7	421.1	440.3	297.5	..	Ethiopia
2,200.7	2,160.6	2,000.2	2,011.4	1,951.4	1,270.6	1,287.7	1,195.6	1,626.0	2,471.1	..	Gabon
..	..	..	..	..	..	..	..	..	..	..	Gambia, The
..	..	..	..	..	..	..	..	..	..	..	Ghana
..	..	..	..	..	..	..	..	..	..	..	Guinea-Bissau
1,146.9	937.7	947.3	1,075.8	956.8	1,168.0	916.3	1,034.0	967.5	1,033.3	..	Kenya
..	..	..	..	..	..	..	..	..	..	..	Lesotho
523.6	472.6	422.6	449.1	435.6	408.4	382.2	400.0	450.0	500.0	..	Liberia
324.4	329.5	310.3	339.9	286.7	316.6	331.1	273.7	304.7	334.6	..	Madagascar
261.6	238.6	239.2	302.2	242.1	248.3	278.5	293.5	269.3	411.7	..	Malawi
..	..	..	..	..	..	..	..	..	..	..	Mali
..	..	..	..	..	..	..	..	..	..	..	Mauritania
316.1	358.6	360.8	375.4	435.8	673.0	880.3	1,001.3	986.8	1,182.1	..	Mauritius
359.0	305.5	239.8	..	..	..	..	..	..	..	..	Mozambique
..	..	..	..	..	..	..	..	..	..	..	Namibia
454.8	256.2	261.6	203.4	205.4	267.6	427.7	423.3	430.0	435.0	..	Niger
18,048.9	15,974.0	10,659.0	12,005.2	13,112.7	5,899.5	7,365.0	6,875.2	7,871.1	13,670.8	..	Nigeria
..	..	..	..	..	..	..	..	..	..	..	Rwanda
560.8	547.9	618.0	634.0	562.0	624.8	604.6	591.2	750.9	782.6	..	Senegal
..	..	..	..	..	..	..	..	..	..	..	Seychelles
205.2	127.6	90.7	147.1	131.0	121.3	136.8	102.4	138.3	138.1	..	Sierra Leone
152.0	199.3	149.9	122.7	43.1	98.3	104.0	113.9	120.0	130.0	..	Somalia
500.8	561.8	601.1	628.7	369.1	333.3	532.4	509.0	671.7	400.0	..	Sudan
..	..	..	..	..	..	..	..	..	..	..	Swaziland
552.7	401.0	425.0	376.7	283.9	340.0	288.1	274.6	305.7	300.3	..	Tanzania
206.4	251.5	225.6	191.3	190.1	203.7	243.6	242.3	245.1	300.0	..	Togo
..	..	..	..	..	..	..	..	..	..	..	Uganda
2,029.9	1,530.2	1,387.9	1,005.5	949.3	1,100.7	674.4	1,120.2	1,254.3	999.1	..	Zaire
975.7	861.5	825.4	..	..	..	..	..	..	..	..	Zambia
656.3	636.3	672.2	1,004.1	954.5	1,018.8	..	..	..	..	..	Zimbabwe
..	..	..	..	..	..	..	..	..	..	..	*SOUTH ASIA*
659.6	671.1	788.9	934.4	973.7	954.5	1,194.5	1,291.0	1,304.9	1,674.5	..	Bangladesh
..	..	..	..	..	..	..	..	..	..	..	Bhutan
7,866.9	8,468.3	9,424.9	9,827.3	8,949.5	9,751.7	12,039.9	13,815.2	15,847.7	17,967.3	..	India
..	..	..	..	..	..	..	..	..	..	..	Nepal
2,737.7	2,347.8	3,061.9	2,556.2	2,707.6	3,302.9	4,105.1	4,484.7	4,698.2	5,590.1	..	Pakistan
1,007.5	994.8	1,051.8	1,435.5	1,246.2	1,159.2	1,326.0	1,475.4	1,558.4	1,983.9	..	Sri Lanka
..	..	..	..	..	..	..	..	..	..	..	*EAST ASIA AND PACIFIC*
21,566.4	21,891.7	22,184.5	24,871.4	27,554.7	31,446.9	39,437.1	47,515.9	52,538.1	62,063.0	..	China
..	..	..	..	..	..	..	..	..	..	..	Fiji
22,260.4	22,293.3	21,145.2	21,887.8	18,586.7	14,786.7	16,860.9	18,901.0	21,772.9	25,553.2	..	Indonesia
21,199.8	21,850.0	24,436.9	29,247.9	30,282.7	34,701.6	47,171.8	60,697.0	62,283.4	64,837.1	..	Korea, Rep.
11,733.9	12,026.7	14,099.9	16,483.6	15,632.4	13,830.3	17,910.6	21,109.7	25,038.4	29,408.9	..	Malaysia
..	..	..	..	..	..	..	..	..	..	..	Mongolia
..	..	..	..	..	..	..	..	..	..	..	Papua New Guinea
5,712.1	5,012.0	4,966.7	5,265.9	4,588.8	4,730.0	5,651.4	6,994.4	7,771.4	8,681.3	..	Philippines
..	..	..	..	..	..	..	..	..	..	..	Solomon Islands
6,848.8	6,796.6	6,274.7	7,279.1	7,056.1	8,786.5	11,629.5	15,902.5	20,088.5	23,002.4	..	Thailand
7.6	3.7	5.5	8.8	5.0	5.8	6.7	7.5	9.7	11.9	..	Tonga
..	..	..	..	..	..	..	..	..	..	..	Vanuatu
..	..	..	..	..	..	..	..	..	..	..	Western Samoa

Table 17. Value of merchandise exports (cont'd.)

Millions of US dollars	1970	1971	1972	1973	1974	1975	1976	1977	1978	1979	1980
LATIN AMERICA AND CARIBBEAN	..	..	..	..	..	..	..	..	..	..	..
Argentina	1,773.2	1,740.3	1,941.1	3,266.0	3,930.7	2,961.3	3,911.9	5,641.7	6,394.2	7,807.8	8,019.2
Bahamas											
Barbados	30.5	28.3	33.4	43.2	61.8	87.7	68.7	75.3	93.4	119.5	149.5
Belize	..	..	..	..	..	..	..	..	..	..	..
Bolivia	225.4	215.9	240.4	314.5	647.8	530.1	637.1	747.9	720.9	811.3	1,036.2
Brazil	2,738.7	2,903.8	3,991.2	6,199.2	7,950.9	8,669.5	10,128.0	12,120.2	12,658.6	15,244.4	20,132.1
Chile	1,233.6	961.2	855.4	1,249.4	2,480.6	1,648.7	2,208.5	2,138.4	2,462.1	4,229.3	4,583.9
Colombia	727.7	689.1	863.4	1,175.5	1,416.7	1,464.9	1,744.6	2,443.0	3,038.3	3,300.4	3,945.0
Costa Rica	231.2	225.4	280.9	344.5	440.3	494.1	600.4	839.5	919.4	934.3	1,031.5
Dominican Rep.											
Ecuador	189.9	199.1	326.3	531.9	1,123.5	973.9	1,257.5	1,436.3	1,557.5	2,104.2	2,480.2
El Salvador	228.3	228.4	277.3	358.3	462.5	513.4	720.7	972.8	801.0	1,031.7	1,073.6
Grenada											
Guatemala	290.2	283.1	328.1	436.1	572.1	623.4	760.3	1,160.2	1,111.6	1,160.9	1,486.1
Guyana	..	..	..	..	..	..	..	..	..	..	..
Haiti	..	..	..				..		..		
Honduras	169.7	182.8	193.1	246.8	253.3	293.3	391.8	510.7	601.8	720.9	813.4
Jamaica	334.9	330.2	356.4	382.5	718.4	769.4	617.8	762.8	736.6	808.9	942.4
Mexico	1,205.4	1,320.5	1,844.6	2,631.5	2,957.2	2,993.1	3,467.8	4,284.4	6,300.7	8,817.0	15,442.0
Nicaragua	174.8	183.4	246.3	274.7	377.0	371.5	538.5	633.0	646.0	566.6	413.8
Panama	109.5	116.5	122.6	137.8	210.5	286.4	236.7	249.5	244.3	291.6	353.4
Paraguay	64.0	65.2	86.2	126.8	169.7	174.1	181.3	278.9	257.0	305.2	310.2
Peru	1,044.4	892.9	944.4	1,049.5	1,517.4	1,314.6	1,296.1	1,647.4	1,805.3	3,379.6	3,265.5
St. Vincent											
Trinidad and Tobago	481.5	520.4	557.6	695.7	2,037.7	1,772.7	2,219.3	2,179.8	2,042.7	2,610.4	4,077.0
Uruguay	232.5	205.5	214.1	321.5	381.0	381.2	536.0	598.5	681.9	787.2	1,059.0
Venezuela	3,196.7	3,109.8	2,953.1	4,761.7	11,248.3	8,990.6	9,443.4	9,626.6	9,270.3	14,267.1	19,292.8
MIDDLE EAST AND NORTH AFRICA	..	..	..	..	..	..	..	..	..	..	..
Algeria	1,009.0	856.7	1,305.9	1,906.0	4,259.8	4,290.8	4,971.9	5,809.4	6,125.5	9,863.3	15,623.6
Egypt, Arab Rep.	761.7	789.3	825.2	1,116.7	1,515.7	1,401.9	1,521.7	1,708.3	1,737.2	1,839.7	3,046.0
Iran, Islamic Rep.											
Jordan	26.1	24.7	35.3	42.4	122.7	125.6	149.2	183.1	209.3	274.7	401.5
Morocco	487.9	499.1	633.6	876.6	1,706.4	1,543.0	1,262.1	1,299.9	1,511.3	1,958.6	2,403.4
Oman	206.2	221.1	241.5	344.0	1,211.3	1,436.5	1,566.0	1,573.0	1,512.5	2,279.8	3,747.7
Saudi Arabia	2,423.7	3,845.3	5,490.7	9,089.4	35,561.7	29,669.0	38,282.4	43,458.2	40,715.3	63,419.2	109,112.7
Syrian Arab Rep.	203.0	194.6	287.3	351.1	783.7	930.0	1,055.1	1,063.0	1,060.3	1,645.1	2,107.3
Tunisia	182.5	215.8	310.9	385.5	914.2	856.2	788.8	929.1	1,126.1	1,790.7	2,233.7
EUROPE	..	..	..	..	..	..	..	..	..	..	..
Bulgaria										..	10,372.1
Czechoslovakia	4,091.0	4,420.0	4,915.3	6,035.4	7,053.4	8,382.5	9,035.1	10,302.4	11,740.0	13,197.5	14,891.1
Greece	642.5	662.5	870.9	1,454.1	2,029.7	2,278.3	2,558.2	2,757.3	3,375.3	3,877.4	5,141.7
Hungary	2,316.6	2,500.4	3,291.7	4,478.7	5,128.6	6,093.1	4,932.2	5,839.5	6,433.5	7,937.8	8,676.7
Malta	29.3	36.3	56.4	86.9	110.5	131.5	187.9	246.7	304.3	381.6	431.7
Poland	3,827.0	4,064.0	5,053.0	6,586.0	8,568.0	10,468.0	11,161.0	12,586.0	14,245.0	17,297.0	16,997.0
Portugal	949.2	1,052.6	1,293.8	1,861.7	2,302.0	1,939.7	1,820.4	2,013.4	2,410.5	3,353.8	4,629.0
Romania									..	..	
Turkey	588.5	676.6	885.0	1,317.1	1,537.8	1,401.1	1,960.2	1,753.0	2,288.2	2,261.2	2,909.6
Yugoslavia	1,679.1	1,835.7	2,237.3	3,020.0	3,804.6	4,072.2	4,895.9	4,896.4	5,546.0	6,799.5	8,977.5
Low- and middle-income economies	..	..	..	..	..	..	..	..	..	..	..
Low-income economies	..	..	..	..	..	..	..	..	..	..	..
Low-income Africa	..	..	..	..	..	..	..	..	..	..	..
China and India	..	..	..	..	..	..	..	..	..	..	..
Other low-income	..	..	..	..	..	..	..	..	..	..	..
Middle-income economies	..	..	..	..	..	..	..	..	..	..	..
High-income economies	..	..	..	..	..	..	..	..	..	..	..
OECD members	..	..	..	..	..	..	..	..	..	..	..
Japan	..	..	..	..	..	..	..	..	..	..	..
United States	..	..	..	..	..	..	..	..	..	..	..
WORLD	..	..	..	..	..	..	..	..	..	..	..

68

1981	1982	1983	1984	1985	1986	1987	1988	1989	1990	1991	
..	..	..	..	..	..	..	..	..	..	..	*LATIN AMERICA AND CARIBBEAN*
9,141.3	7,623.2	7,836.1	8,107.4	8,396.0	6,852.2	6,360.2	9,134.2	9,565.4	12,352.5	..	Argentina
										..	Bahamas
147.7	190.8	289.2	272.0	214.9	209.1	160.3	173.4	187.6	213.4	..	Barbados
										..	Belize
983.4	895.5	817.6	781.4	672.8	636.3	569.8	597.5	819.2	922.9	..	Bolivia
23,292.4	20,173.0	21,897.8	26,975.9	25,594.2	22,382.5	26,228.6	33,759.3	34,289.8	31,243.1	..	Brazil
3,744.8	3,579.0	3,619.6	3,547.2	3,665.0	4,157.5	4,845.2	6,794.2	8,191.0	8,579.0	..	Chile
2,955.5	3,073.9	3,080.9	3,483.1	3,551.9	5,107.9	5,024.4	5,026.2	5,739.4	6,765.8	..	Colombia
1,010.5	876.8	844.5	951.3	941.0	1,089.8	1,113.8	1,245.7	1,414.6	1,457.4	..	Costa Rica
										..	Dominican Rep.
2,167.9	2,290.8	2,225.6	2,582.5	2,902.8	2,184.2	2,020.7	2,192.5	2,353.8	2,714.3	..	Ecuador
796.7	699.4	844.1	615.0	610.9	706.3	612.7	608.8	497.2	550.0	..	El Salvador
										..	Grenada
1,114.8	1,083.8	1,118.4	1,094.6	974.5	1,072.6	899.2	1,067.9	1,126.2	1,211.4	..	Guatemala
										..	Guyana
										..	Haiti
712.5	655.7	660.1	703.7	699.4	771.1	761.0	868.7	1,196.7	915.8	..	Honduras
975.7	717.0	717.3	732.1	535.1	567.2	692.3	811.6	969.7	1,347.2	..	Jamaica
20,035.6	21,170.4	24,642.3	26,563.3	24,364.5	12,708.2	20,531.6	20,408.7	22,974.8	26,714.3	..	Mexico
475.9	390.7	428.8	386.7	274.6	233.6	299.9	235.7	321.8	378.7	..	Nicaragua
319.4	310.2	302.6	257.6	301.2	325.2	338.2	292.5	297.2	321.4	..	Panama
295.5	329.8	258.2	334.5	303.9	232.5	353.4	509.8	1,009.4	958.7	..	Paraguay
2,335.5	2,755.8	2,009.5	2,460.4	2,852.1	1,798.0	2,152.3	2,506.5	3,488.9	3,276.6	..	Peru
										..	St. Vincent
3,760.8	3,085.5	2,352.7	2,173.4	2,160.9	1,385.7	1,462.4	1,412.0	1,578.1	2,080.4	..	Trinidad and Tobago
1,216.7	1,024.2	1,008.4	924.9	852.7	1,082.1	1,191.1	1,442.6	1,596.4	1,695.7	..	Uruguay
17,518.0	16,307.5	14,476.9	15,742.7	16,022.7	8,612.9	10,506.0	9,552.7	12,667.7	17,219.9	..	Venezuela
..	..	..	..	..	..	..	..	..	..	..	*MIDDLE EAST AND NORTH AFRICA*
13,296.2	11,475.9	11,158.4	11,885.7	10,149.1	7,830.6	8,185.9	8,164.0	10,801.7	12,730.0	..	Algeria
3,232.2	3,120.2	3,214.8	3,139.9	1,838.2	2,214.3	2,037.2	2,120.4	2,647.8	2,985.3	..	Egypt, Arab Rep.
										..	Iran, Islamic Rep.
509.8	528.3	439.9	677.8	649.0	645.1	730.3	884.8	1,117.9	1,146.3	..	Jordan
2,320.3	2,058.6	2,062.1	2,171.9	2,165.1	2,427.6	2,806.9	3,625.4	3,336.5	4,262.9	..	Morocco
4,695.7	4,438.1	4,551.6	4,177.0	4,794.8	2,773.5	3,776.1	3,268.3	3,932.8	458.4	..	Oman
119,913.2	79,124.9	45,860.8	37,544.7	26,907.8	20,184.7	23,198.9	23,727.4	27,735.3	31,065.4	..	Saudi Arabia
2,102.9	2,026.4	1,922.9	1,853.5	1,637.3	1,326.2	3,870.6	1,344.6	3,005.8	4,172.5	..	Syrian Arab Rep.
2,503.7	1,983.5	1,871.5	1,796.3	1,627.3	1,759.6	2,152.4	2,392.9	2,932.4	3,498.3	..	Tunisia
..	..	..	..	..	..	..	..	..	..	..	*EUROPE*
										..	Bulgaria
14,782.4	15,693.5	16,476.6	17,152.9	17,474.0	20,457.0	23,016.4	22,818.5	21,579.3	17,949.6	..	Czechoslovakia
4,249.5	4,296.7	4,412.2	4,864.2	4,536.2	5,660.2	6,489.3	5,155.6	7,353.1	8,053.1	..	Greece
8,712.2	8,798.6	8,721.7	8,560.3	8,554.9	9,156.8	9,570.9	9,930.7	9,604.6	9,587.6	..	Hungary
397.4	364.8	327.7	358.1	362.2	460.4	551.4	656.8	797.5	1,125.7	..	Malta
13,249.0	11,213.5	11,571.8	11,647.0	11,489.4	12,073.7	12,204.8	13,960.4	13,466.1	13,626.8	..	Poland
4,180.0	4,170.9	4,601.5	5,207.7	5,685.4	7,159.9	9,166.7	10,989.6	12,797.7	16,415.7	..	Portugal
										..	Romania
4,701.9	5,747.5	5,670.6	7,133.6	7,958.0	7,456.7	10,189.7	11,662.0	11,626.1	12,959.3	..	Turkey
10,928.9	10,752.3	9,913.5	10,254.5	10,641.5	10,297.5	11,396.7	12,579.3	13,343.5	14,364.6	..	Yugoslavia
..	..	..	..	..	..	..	..	..	..	..	**Low- and middle-income economies**
..	..	..	..	..	..	..	..	..	..	..	Low-income economies
..	..	..	..	..	..	..	..	..	..	..	Low-income Africa
..	..	..	..	..	..	..	..	..	..	..	China and India
..	..	..	..	..	..	..	..	..	..	..	Other low-income
..	..	..	..	..	..	..	..	..	..	..	Middle-income economies
..	..	..	..	..	..	..	..	..	..	..	**High-income economies**
..	..	..	..	..	..	..	..	..	..	..	OECD members
..	..	..	..	..	..	..	..	..	..	..	Japan
..	..	..	..	..	..	..	..	..	..	..	United States
..	..	..	..	..	..	..	..	..	..	..	**WORLD**

Table 18. Value of merchandise imports

Millions of US dollars	1970	1971	1972	1973	1974	1975	1976	1977	1978	1979	1980
SUB-SAHARAN AFRICA	..	..	..	..	..	..	..	..	..	..	..
Excluding Nigeria	..	..	..	..	..	..	..	..	..	..	..
Benin	..	..	..	..	..	..	..	..	..	..	..
Botswana	..	..	..	..	..	..	..	..	..	..	..
Burkina Faso	46.7	49.7	60.7	78.8	144.5	151.2	144.6	209.2	227.9	307.4	358.0
Burundi	..	..	..	..	..	..	..	..	..	..	..
Cameroon	242.1	249.5	298.8	334.7	437.3	598.3	594.7	746.9	1,008.5	1,270.6	1,538.4
Cape Verde	..	..	..	..	..	..	..	..	..	..	..
Central African Rep.	..	..	..	..	..	..	..	..	..	..	..
Chad	..	..	..	..	..	..	..	..	..	..	..
Comoros	..	..	..	..	..	..	..	..	..	..	..
Congo	57.2	78.9	89.7	125.1	123.3	164.8	167.6	183.1	242.0	266.4	418.1
Côte d'Ivoire	387.2	398.1	452.8	713.5	966.7	1,126.5	1,295.4	1,751.5	2,309.6	2,388.9	2,552.1
Equatorial Guinea	..	..	..	..	..	..	..	..	..	..	..
Ethiopia	173.1	187.7	189.4	213.1	272.9	294.0	353.2	391.4	505.3	567.4	721.4
Gabon	79.8	90.9	133.3	158.5	331.9	446.3	497.4	705.8	564.3	532.1	673.6
Gambia, The	..	..	..	..	..	..	..	..	..	..	..
Ghana	..	..	..	..	..	..	..	..	..	..	..
Guinea-Bissau	..	..	..	..	..	..	..	..	..	..	..
Kenya	397.4	514.8	496.1	587.6	986.6	910.8	971.8	1,285.6	1,705.9	1,655.5	2,122.0
Lesotho	..	..	..	..	..	..	..	..	..	..	..
Liberia	149.7	162.2	178.6	193.5	288.4	331.2	399.2	463.5	480.9	506.5	534.1
Madagascar	170.4	213.2	202.2	202.9	281.0	366.9	289.9	353.0	460.1	698.4	676.5
Malawi	85.6	109.0	130.0	142.2	187.6	250.5	205.6	232.4	338.2	397.6	440.2
Mali	..	..	..	..	..	..	..	..	..	..	..
Mauritania	..	..	..	..	..	..	..	..	..	..	..
Mauritius	75.6	83.1	119.9	169.6	308.5	330.7	357.5	444.9	498.4	576.1	619.3
Mozambique	323.2	335.3	327.0	464.7	463.6	417.1	..	277.7	..	270.2	550.1
Namibia	..	..	..	..	..	..	..	..	..	..	..
Niger	58.4	53.0	65.7	86.8	96.4	98.9	127.1	196.3	305.9	461.7	607.7
Nigeria	1,059.0	1,510.5	1,504.9	1,861.7	2,780.6	6,041.2	8,194.6	11,020.2	12,762.8	10,274.3	13,408.0
Rwanda	..	..	..	..	..	..	..	..	..	..	..
Senegal	192.4	217.8	278.5	359.0	497.4	581.4	644.0	762.3	756.1	931.2	1,037.9
Seychelles	..	..	..	..	..	..	..	..	..	..	..
Sierra Leone	116.9	113.1	121.0	157.7	161.1	159.3	166.3	180.0	278.1	193.7	268.3
Somalia	45.1	62.5	75.6	108.1	142.8	154.7	155.7	227.6	241.3	245.7	348.0
Sudan	311.1	355.2	353.5	479.5	655.8	957.0	951.8	982.6	878.0	915.8	1,499.3
Swaziland	..	..	..	..	..	..	..	..	..	..	..
Tanzania	271.5	337.9	363.4	447.4	760.1	718.2	645.3	730.1	1,141.3	1,076.7	1,211.4
Togo	64.5	70.0	84.8	100.5	119.1	173.9	185.6	284.3	450.8	518.5	549.6
Uganda	..	..	..	..	..	..	..	..	..	..	..
Zaire	533.0	620.0	766.4	781.9	940.0	932.8	840.3	852.3	796.7	826.4	1,117.1
Zambia	477.0	558.9	563.4	532.0	787.3	928.7	655.1	671.2	628.3	750.2	1,100.1
Zimbabwe	..	..	..	..	..	..	..	..	..	21.9	192.9
SOUTH ASIA	..	..	..	..	..	..	..	..	..	..	..
Bangladesh	..	..	..	..	905.5	1,039.2	958.0	911.6	1,333.1	1,537.1	1,979.5
Bhutan	..	..	..	..	..	..	..	..	..	..	..
India	2,093.7	2,405.8	2,230.4	3,146.1	5,167.1	6,289.5	5,404.9	6,423.0	7,561.6	9,114.0	13,818.7
Nepal	..	..	..	..	..	..	..	..	..	..	..
Pakistan	1,170.9	925.9	681.8	965.9	1,729.4	2,153.1	2,182.9	2,454.6	3,160.5	4,061.3	5,350.5
Sri Lanka	386.6	328.1	336.4	422.3	688.1	744.6	552.1	701.1	942.1	1,449.2	2,035.4
EAST ASIA AND PACIFIC	..	..	..	..	..	..	..	..	..	..	..
China	2,278.8	2,128.5	2,850.7	5,207.6	7,791.1	7,925.6	6,660.1	7,148.2	11,130.9	15,620.6	19,941.3
Fiji	103.9	128.1	158.2	203.5	273.1	267.3	262.7	306.2	366.3	469.6	561.3
Indonesia	1,002.0	1,104.3	1,561.7	2,295.1	3,858.2	4,769.7	5,673.5	6,182.6	6,654.5	7,183.4	10,834.4
Korea, Rep.	1,983.3	2,394.1	2,522.0	4,240.3	6,844.3	7,271.0	8,764.5	10,803.1	14,966.0	20,296.1	22,228.2
Malaysia	1,400.6	1,442.4	1,611.2	2,440.7	4,110.6	3,524.6	3,814.2	4,537.8	5,888.8	7,835.0	10,734.7
Mongolia	..	..	..	..	..	..	..	..	..	..	..
Papua New Guinea	..	..	..	..	..	..	..	..	..	..	..
Philippines	1,210.4	1,318.7	1,387.8	1,789.5	3,467.6	3,776.2	3,953.3	4,269.8	5,143.3	6,613.0	8,294.6
Solomon Islands	..	..	..	..	..	..	..	..	..	..	..
Thailand	1,293.4	1,287.0	1,484.4	2,073.3	3,155.5	3,279.4	3,571.9	4,613.2	5,314.2	7,131.8	9,450.3
Tonga	6.2	7.1	8.9	11.3	17.1	17.0	14.3	19.6	25.6	29.3	34.3
Vanuatu	..	..	..	..	..	..	..	..	..	..	..
Western Samoa	13.6	13.4	19.5	21.4	26.2	36.8	27.5	45.7	52.5	72.5	62.5

1981	1982	1983	1984	1985	1986	1987	1988	1989	1990	1991	
..	..	..	..	..	..	..	..	..	..	..	*SUB-SAHARAN AFRICA*
..	..	..	..	..	..	..	..	..	..	..	*Excluding Nigeria*
..	..	..	..	..	..	..	..	..	..	..	Benin
										..	Botswana
337.5	346.2	287.5	211.4	0.0	405.0	434.0	453.0	400.0	480.0	..	Burkina Faso
									..		Burundi
1,430.5	1,243.2	1,187.6	1,106.9	1,282.6	1,704.7	1,749.0	1,271.0	1,273.3	1,300.0	..	Cameroon
..	..	..	..	..		..	..	..	..	..	Cape Verde
..	..	..	..	..		..	..	..	..	..	Central African Rep.
..	..	..	..	..		..	..	..	..	..	Chad
..	..	..	..	..		..	..	..	..	..	Comoros
667.5	830.1	629.0	598.6	580.2	578.6	529.3	564.0	524.0	570.0	..	Congo
2,393.1	2,183.7	1,813.5	1,507.2	1,733.8	2,047.5	2,242.3	2,081.3	2,000.0	2,100.0	..	Côte d'Ivoire
										..	Equatorial Guinea
737.3	784.9	876.0	942.6	988.6	1,100.8	1,101.2	1,085.0	950.6	1,081.4	..	Ethiopia
834.4	798.5	685.6	723.6	854.7	866.3	732.0	791.2	751.7	760.3	..	Gabon
..	..	..	..	..		..	..	..	..	..	Gambia, The
..	..	..	..	..		..	..	..	..	..	Ghana
..	..	..	..	..		..	..	..	..	..	Guinea-Bissau
2,081.3	1,603.0	1,379.1	1,469.4	1,457.4	1,649.8	1,737.8	1,986.7	2,150.3	2,123.5	..	Kenya
										..	Lesotho
477.4	428.4	411.6	363.2	284.4	234.8	307.6	350.0	400.0	450.0	..	Liberia
473.0	439.0	411.5	412.2	465.1	373.6	302.1	363.9	450.0	480.0	..	Madagascar
350.1	311.7	310.4	268.8	295.2	256.8	296.1	421.7	506.9	576.2	..	Malawi
..	..	..	..	..		..	..	..	..	..	Mali
..	..	..	..	..		..	..	..	..	..	Mauritania
554.0	464.2	441.7	470.6	525.8	677.2	1,012.3	1,283.1	1,325.7	1,616.0	..	Mauritius
649.3	625.2	500.1	..	..	..	..	..	..	..	..	Mozambique
										..	Namibia
509.7	322.8	209.3	184.9	231.7	219.0	239.2	219.3	225.0	230.0	..	Niger
20,455.2	11,131.2	9,028.9	5,868.0	6,204.6	4,028.2	3,907.9	4,726.9	4,190.1	5,687.7	..	Nigeria
..	..	..	..	..		..	..	..	..	..	Rwanda
1,077.4	991.9	1,025.3	980.9	825.7	960.9	1,023.4	1,079.6	1,534.0	1,620.4	..	Senegal
										..	Seychelles
199.7	161.1	165.7	126.5	153.4	125.7	129.9	160.4	182.3	146.2	..	Sierra Leone
512.9	330.1	352.3	342.6	235.5	303.8	132.0	323.5	350.0	360.0	..	Somalia
1,518.7	1,294.0	1,424.0	1,146.7	760.0	960.9	929.0	1,060.4	1,170.0	600.0	..	Sudan
..	..	..	..	..		..	..	..	..	..	Swaziland
905.8	955.9	654.1	847.2	1,028.0	849.5	923.4	814.1	843.3	934.9	..	Tanzania
435.8	393.4	296.8	271.1	288.0	311.8	423.6	487.4	471.9	700.0	..	Togo
..	..	..	..	..		..	..	..	..	..	Uganda
1,019.1	912.5	841.7	685.5	791.1	875.4	756.2	762.7	849.9	887.7	..	Zaire
1,061.8	839.2	560.8	..	..	..	..	..	..	..	..	Zambia
456.2	489.3	450.7	959.3	896.6	985.3	..	..	..	1,851.4	..	Zimbabwe
..	..	..	..	..	..	..	..	..	..	..	*SOUTH ASIA*
1,802.7	1,742.1	1,502.4	2,041.6	2,420.5	1,983.9	2,572.7	3,042.8	3,650.4	3,646.0	..	Bangladesh
										..	Bhutan
14,456.9	14,774.3	15,284.2	14,411.6	16,223.6	15,721.7	17,153.8	19,350.7	20,570.8	23,692.1	..	India
										..	Nepal
5,412.7	5,232.8	5,341.0	5,873.1	5,890.4	5,376.8	5,829.3	6,617.3	7,119.3	7,377.1	..	Pakistan
1,803.8	1,769.9	1,788.4	1,847.4	1,786.3	1,831.6	2,021.3	2,238.5	2,197.8	2,689.0	..	Sri Lanka
..	..	..	..	..	..	..	..	..	..	..	*EAST ASIA AND PACIFIC*
21,572.3	18,900.9	21,349.4	26,184.7	42,895.1	43,411.1	43,215.6	55,268.3	59,140.1	53,345.2	..	China
631.1	513.7	483.2	448.8	440.6	434.2	377.1	460.6	582.7	740.7	..	Fiji
13,008.3	16,530.4	16,346.3	13,864.6	10,256.1	10,718.4	12,370.3	13,248.5	16,359.5	21,836.9	..	Indonesia
26,028.3	24,236.1	26,173.8	30,608.6	31,118.7	31,518.0	40,925.3	51,810.7	61,347.5	69,584.9	..	Korea, Rep.
11,508.1	12,363.4	13,229.0	13,952.9	12,515.1	10,731.4	12,588.8	16,232.0	22,466.8	29,250.6	..	Malaysia
..	..	..	..	..		..	..	..	..	..	Mongolia
										..	Papua New Guinea
8,477.7	8,262.3	7,977.4	6,424.3	5,444.6	5,392.5	7,189.6	8,729.1	11,179.7	13,079.6	..	Philippines
..	..	..	..	..		..	..	..	..	..	Solomon Islands
10,055.0	8,526.7	10,278.9	10,518.0	9,238.7	9,124.0	12,955.1	20,224.8	25,783.2	33,129.4	..	Thailand
40.2	41.6	31.3	41.1	41.2	39.8	47.9	55.5	54.1	61.7	..	Tonga
..	..	..	..	..		..	..	..	..	..	Vanuatu
68.3	41.9	52.6	50.8	51.3	47.1	61.8	75.7	77.0	85.1	..	Western Samoa

Table 18. Value of merchandise imports (cont'd.)

Millions of US dollars	1970	1971	1972	1973	1974	1975	1976	1977	1978	1979	1980
LATIN AMERICA AND CARIBBEAN	..	..	..	..	..	..	..	..	..	..	..
Argentina	1,688.6	1,845.5	1,904.3	2,235.3	3,634.8	3,945.3	3,028.5	4,158.4	3,832.3	6,692.4	10,539.2
Bahamas	..	..	..	..	..	..	..	..	..	..	..
Barbados	117.3	121.8	141.7	167.6	204.0	216.4	236.6	271.6	312.4	420.8	517.1
Belize	..	..	..	..	..	..	..	..	..	..	..
Bolivia	159.2	169.6	178.6	230.2	366.2	574.0	593.5	586.3	769.5	841.5	654.6
Brazil	2,844.6	3,695.8	4,775.6	6,992.1	14,162.7	13,578.3	13,713.5	13,254.4	15,016.2	19,731.4	24,948.8
Chile	930.1	979.8	945.2	1,102.4	1,910.4	1,533.6	1,643.0	1,906.3	2,553.6	4,229.3	5,123.1
Colombia	843.0	929.4	858.9	1,061.5	1,597.2	1,494.8	1,708.1	2,028.3	2,836.3	3,233.2	4,662.6
Costa Rica	316.7	349.7	372.8	455.3	719.7	694.0	800.3	1,059.3	1,211.7	1,446.1	1,596.4
Dominican Rep.	..	..	..	..	..	..	..	..	..	..	..
Ecuador	272.9	338.5	325.0	396.4	781.3	984.6	951.5	1,165.4	1,498.6	1,599.7	2,215.3
El Salvador	213.6	247.4	278.1	373.8	563.4	598.0	717.9	942.5	1,023.9	1,012.0	975.9
Grenada	..	..	..	..	..	..	..	..	..	..	..
Guatemala	284.3	303.3	327.7	427.4	700.5	732.6	838.4	1,052.5	1,260.7	1,361.8	1,559.1
Guyana	..	..	..	..	..	..	..	..	..	..	..
Haiti	..	..	..	..	..	..	..	..	..	..	..
Honduras	220.7	193.4	192.8	262.2	380.1	404.3	453.1	579.4	699.2	825.8	1,008.7
Jamaica	525.4	550.5	620.2	664.4	935.5	1,122.5	911.2	858.8	879.9	991.5	1,177.7
Mexico	2,460.7	2,407.2	2,935.0	4,145.6	6,057.2	6,571.6	6,032.7	5,588.8	8,053.0	12,586.5	19,591.2
Nicaragua	197.9	209.6	218.0	326.4	559.0	516.9	532.1	761.9	596.0	360.2	881.9
Panama	357.0	395.8	440.4	502.2	822.4	892.1	848.3	858.9	942.4	1,183.8	1,447.5
Paraguay	75.2	83.5	79.8	122.3	194.4	212.0	219.9	308.1	382.4	520.9	614.7
Peru	621.7	749.6	796.3	1,024.2	1,595.3	2,379.6	1,798.0	1,598.3	1,356.3	1,475.5	2,573.3
St. Vincent	..	..	..	..	..	..	..	..	..	..	..
Trinidad and Tobago	543.4	662.8	762.0	792.2	1,846.5	1,488.4	1,976.3	1,808.5	1,979.9	2,104.6	3,177.7
Uruguay	232.9	222.1	186.8	284.8	461.1	516.5	599.0	668.8	715.7	1,173.2	1,651.9
Venezuela	1,640.1	1,833.4	2,139.3	2,473.9	3,739.3	5,807.3	6,019.1	9,749.2	10,582.1	9,598.4	10,669.2
MIDDLE EAST AND NORTH AFRICA	..	..	..	..	..	..	..	..	..	..	..
Algeria	1,257.1	1,227.4	1,492.4	2,258.7	4,035.5	5,974.1	5,306.5	7,101.9	8,666.7	8,406.7	10,524.5
Egypt, Arab Rep.	786.6	919.8	898.3	914.4	2,350.7	3,933.7	3,861.7	4,815.3	6,726.6	3,837.4	4,860.0
Iran, Islamic Rep.	..	..	..	..	..	..	..	..	..	..	..
Jordan	184.5	214.6	267.0	327.9	486.6	730.8	1,022.1	1,381.1	1,498.8	1,948.6	2,394.4
Morocco	684.3	697.0	764.4	1,098.2	1,900.8	2,547.3	2,592.9	3,168.5	2,950.3	3,673.5	4,182.4
Oman	18.2	33.1	48.8	116.8	392.5	670.5	667.3	874.5	947.4	1,246.4	1,732.0
Saudi Arabia	692.1	805.6	1,125.4	1,977.5	2,847.9	4,141.2	8,408.8	14,288.7	20,177.2	24,384.3	29,957.1
Syrian Arab Rep.	350.0	438.3	539.4	613.2	1,229.4	1,669.1	1,959.1	2,656.0	2,443.8	3,324.0	4,095.8
Tunisia	304.6	341.9	458.5	605.6	1,120.1	1,417.8	1,525.7	1,820.9	2,157.7	2,842.2	3,508.7
EUROPE	..	..	..	..	..	..	..	..	..	..	..
Bulgaria	..	..	..	..	..	..	..	..	..	..	9,649.9
Czechoslovakia	4,228.0	4,444.0	4,662.4	6,137.4	7,532.2	9,105.5	9,706.3	11,186.6	12,604.2	14,360.1	15,148.2
Greece	1,958.3	2,098.1	2,345.8	3,473.1	4,385.2	5,321.4	6,050.6	6,852.5	7,654.5	9,593.8	10,531.3
Hungary	2,505.1	2,989.6	3,153.9	3,966.2	5,574.9	7,177.9	5,516.8	6,509.0	7,967.4	8,659.2	9,211.5
Malta	160.5	156.1	174.2	239.5	357.3	374.9	420.9	512.7	569.1	753.3	935.7
Poland	4,154.0	4,456.0	5,965.0	8,597.0	11,669.0	13,666.0	14,992.0	15,463.0	16,714.0	18,852.0	19,089.0
Portugal	1,589.8	1,823.8	2,227.2	3,072.8	4,640.6	3,863.0	4,316.0	4,964.0	5,228.6	6,508.7	9,292.9
Romania	..	..	..	..	..	..	..	..	..	..	..
Turkey	885.8	1,088.2	1,507.9	2,049.4	3,719.7	4,640.4	4,993.1	5,693.9	4,479.3	4,946.1	7,572.5
Yugoslavia	2,874.0	3,297.1	3,232.7	4,782.7	7,519.9	7,698.9	7,366.7	8,972.9	9,769.5	14,037.3	15,064.3
Low- and middle-income economies	..	..	..	..	..	..	..	..	..	..	..
Low-income economies	..	..	..	..	..	..	..	..	..	..	..
Low-income Africa	..	..	..	..	..	..	..	..	..	..	..
China and India	..	..	..	..	..	..	..	..	..	..	..
Other low-income	..	..	..	..	..	..	..	..	..	..	..
Middle-income economies	..	..	..	..	..	..	..	..	..	..	..
High-income economies	..	..	..	..	..	..	..	..	..	..	..
OECD members	..	..	..	..	..	..	..	..	..	..	..
Japan	..	..	..	..	..	..	..	..	..	..	..
United States	..	..	..	..	..	..	..	..	..	..	..
WORLD	..	..	..	..	..	..	..	..	..	..	..

1981	1982	1983	1984	1985	1986	1987	1988	1989	1990	1991	
..	..	..	..	..	..	..	..	..	..	..	*LATIN AMERICA AND CARIBBEAN*
9,430.2	5,336.9	4,504.1	4,584.6	3,814.1	4,723.4	5,817.8	5,321.5	4,200.5	4,076.7	..	Argentina
										..	Bahamas
591.1	549.8	605.2	665.2	601.9	593.2	514.9	578.7	673.5	698.5	..	Barbados
										..	Belize
904.0	485.8	531.2	416.6	690.9	674.0	766.3	590.5	619.9	715.7	..	Bolivia
24,072.5	21,061.3	16,783.9	15,208.3	14,328.8	15,555.0	16,577.8	16,054.4	19,173.2	22,459.0	..	Brazil
6,277.2	3,076.5	2,694.8	3,190.9	2,743.8	2,964.0	3,793.2	4,730.8	6,495.7	7,023.0	..	Chile
5,199.2	5,463.1	4,966.9	4,492.4	4,130.7	3,852.1	4,228.0	5,005.3	5,010.5	5,589.5	..	Colombia
1,274.2	945.2	982.7	1,086.2	1,098.2	1,145.2	1,377.1	1,409.8	1,717.4	2,026.1	..	Costa Rica
										..	Dominican Rep.
1,906.8	1,736.7	1,500.3	1,715.7	1,808.3	1,805.6	1,890.9	1,713.5	1,859.7	1,861.9	..	Ecuador
1,044.5	944.8	818.5	1,314.0	1,104.5	924.2	987.2	1,007.0	1,151.6	1,200.0	..	El Salvador
										..	Grenada
1,688.3	1,420.4	1,154.3	1,472.2	1,296.7	1,035.5	1,448.6	1,557.0	1,664.0	1,625.9	..	Guatemala
										..	Guyana
										..	Haiti
944.9	689.9	823.0	813.4	873.7	755.6	863.0	932.9	875.6	1,028.4	..	Honduras
1,487.0	1,373.3	1,529.9	1,145.7	1,143.4	967.6	1,233.9	1,434.3	1,805.0	1,685.2	..	Jamaica
24,853.0	14,909.5	10,797.4	14,458.0	16,151.8	9,335.1	12,757.7	19,557.1	22,786.9	28,062.9	..	Mexico
994.2	774.9	806.3	825.9	1,066.5	774.5	922.4	718.3	642.4	750.0	..	Nicaragua
1,561.9	1,567.8	1,412.5	1,411.8	1,383.3	1,253.7	1,304.8	794.6	964.1	1,538.6	..	Panama
599.7	672.0	545.9	585.8	501.5	578.1	595.3	573.9	775.8	1,112.9	..	Paraguay
3,159.5	2,940.2	2,234.3	1,881.4	1,767.4	2,365.8	3,002.7	3,109.2	2,565.9	3,229.5	..	Peru
										..	St. Vincent
3,124.6	3,698.0	2,582.0	1,919.1	1,533.0	1,369.8	1,218.7	1,127.0	1,222.4	1,261.6	..	Trinidad and Tobago
1,633.1	1,110.0	787.5	775.7	707.8	870.0	1,141.9	1,176.9	1,239.7	1,414.5	..	Uruguay
11,811.0	13,390.6	6,146.4	6,872.0	7,418.2	7,666.7	8,711.1	11,476.2	7,029.6	6,363.5	..	Venezuela
..	..	..	..	..	..	..	..	..	..	..	*MIDDLE EAST AND NORTH AFRICA*
11,302.3	10,679.4	10,331.9	10,263.2	9,813.5	9,234.4	7,028.7	7,396.7	8,924.2	10,432.9	..	Algeria
8,839.5	9,078.0	10,275.4	10,765.8	5,495.3	8,679.9	7,596.2	8,657.3	7,447.5	10,340.0	..	Egypt, Arab Rep.
										..	Iran, Islamic Rep.
3,146.3	3,217.5	3,016.3	2,688.7	2,593.2	2,412.7	2,690.9	2,746.7	2,156.4	2,662.8	..	Jordan
4,352.6	4,315.3	3,596.6	3,906.7	3,849.6	3,790.2	4,228.7	4,772.4	5,491.9	6,918.4	..	Morocco
2,288.2	2,682.5	2,492.3	2,748.2	3,152.7	2,384.1	1,812.6	2,148.5	2,177.9	2,608.2	..	Oman
35,041.5	40,472.6	38,910.7	33,472.6	23,439.5	19,078.6	19,927.0	21,608.3	20,257.9	24,069.4	..	Saudi Arabia
5,039.8	4,014.1	4,542.3	4,115.6	3,967.0	2,716.3	7,112.1	2,230.7	2,097.5	2,399.7	..	Syrian Arab Rep.
3,770.9	3,395.7	3,099.5	3,114.9	2,586.9	2,897.7	3,021.7	3,680.9	4,366.0	5,471.1	..	Tunisia
..	..	..	..	..	..	..	..	..	..	..	*EUROPE*
										..	Bulgaria
14,633.8	15,492.3	16,324.1	17,078.0	17,547.7	21,088.9	23,283.7	21,840.8	21,351.7	19,861.6	..	Czechoslovakia
8,780.6	10,012.2	9,499.6	9,611.0	10,137.9	11,240.5	12,908.1	11,976.8	16,103.1	19,700.9	..	Greece
9,123.3	8,835.9	8,480.7	8,083.9	8,142.8	9,582.6	9,854.7	9,309.4	8,817.9	8,646.4	..	Hungary
850.8	783.3	727.3	710.8	751.0	879.7	1,116.5	1,331.4	1,494.0	1,960.1	..	Malta
15,475.5	10,243.8	10,589.8	10,547.3	10,836.4	11,208.4	10,843.7	12,243.3	10,277.3	9,780.8	..	Poland
9,946.0	9,605.1	8,256.7	7,975.3	7,649.7	9,393.3	13,437.5	17,884.8	19,043.2	25,332.6	..	Portugal
											Romania
8,864.3	8,793.5	8,548.1	10,662.8	11,340.5	11,104.8	14,162.6	14,335.3	15,788.4	22,300.1	..	Turkey
15,757.0	14,099.9	12,154.5	11,996.0	12,162.9	11,749.1	12,549.0	13,151.8	14,799.0	18,911.0	..	Yugoslavia
..	..	..	..	..	..	..	..	..	..	..	**Low- and middle-income economies**
..	..	..	..	..	..	..	..	..	..	..	Low-income economies
..	..	..	..	..	..	..	..	..	..	..	Low-income Africa
..	..	..	..	..	..	..	..	..	..	..	China and India
..	..	..	..	..	..	..	..	..	..	..	Other low-income
..	..	..	..	..	..	..	..	..	..	..	Middle-income economies
..	..	..	..	..	..	..	..	..	..	..	**High-income economies**
..	..	..	..	..	..	..	..	..	..	..	OECD members
..	..	..	..	..	..	..	..	..	..	..	Japan
..	..	..	..	..	..	..	..	..	..	..	United States
..	..	..	..	..	..	..	..	..	..	..	**WORLD**

Table 19. Growth of merchandise exports

Average annual growth (percent)	1970	1971	1972	1973	1974	1975	1976	1977	1978	1979	1980
SUB-SAHARAN AFRICA	..	..	..	..	..	..	..	..	..	..	..
Excluding Nigeria	..	..	..	..	..	..	..	..	..	..	..
Benin	..	..	..	..	..	..	..	..	..	..	..
Botswana	..	..	..	..	..	..	..	..	..	..	..
Burkina Faso	-15.8	-20.4	16.3	-21.5	39.6	44.0	-2.2	3.6	-29.4	53.9	8.8
Burundi	..	..	..	..	..	..	..	..	..	..	..
Cameroon	-1.1	1.9	-3.7	10.4	10.2	5.7	-24.9	-5.5	24.8	47.4	5.8
Cape Verde	..	..	..	..	..	..	..	..	..	..	..
Central African Rep.	..	..	..	..	..	..	..	..	..	..	..
Chad	..	..	..	..	..	..	..	..	..	..	..
Comoros	..	..	..	..	..	..	..	..	..	..	..
Congo	-33.8	24.7	38.5	123.8	23.2	-19.8	-7.2	-16.4	-17.9	164.1	21.5
Côte d'Ivoire	-2.8	5.4	16.6	5.4	6.5	9.8	-6.1	-5.4	13.9	-5.3	20.5
Equatorial Guinea	..	..	..	..	..	..	..	..	..	..	..
Ethiopia	-16.6	15.5	9.9	4.5	11.4	-14.6	-29.2	-19.5	22.0	17.9	10.6
Gabon	-14.2	31.5	-19.9	28.4	27.8	4.2	9.6	-0.5	-14.8	22.4	-22.0
Gambia, The	..	..	..	..	..	..	..	..	..	..	..
Ghana	..	..	..	..	..	..	..	..	..	..	..
Guinea-Bissau	..	..	..	..	..	..	..	..	..	..	..
Kenya	10.6	-5.3	2.9	-1.7	-20.1	9.3	34.3	14.4	-7.0	-8.6	11.0
Lesotho	..	..	..	..	..	..	..	..	..	..	..
Liberia	-0.8	13.6	9.7	-6.4	11.6	-8.5	10.7	-7.2	14.7	-11.9	-1.6
Madagascar	16.4	-2.6	2.5	-4.5	-8.9	32.6	-33.6	-11.0	30.0	-9.9	-4.4
Malawi	-0.5	15.7	8.3	0.6	-19.3	13.7	39.7	2.2	-4.4	5.4	1.8
Mali	..	..	..	..	..	..	..	..	..	..	..
Mauritania	..	..	..	..	..	..	..	..	..	..	..
Mauritius	-5.0	1.3	18.9	8.2	1.3	-23.0	21.3	7.7	7.5	10.9	-5.0
Mozambique	..	..	..	..	..	..	..	..	..	..	..
Namibia	..	..	..	..	..	..	..	..	..	..	..
Niger	21.9	27.5	26.5	3.1	-39.7	60.1	41.4	14.5	54.8	48.9	31.5
Nigeria	76.3	39.3	16.5	12.3	-28.4	-9.5	22.2	0.6	-17.7	17.4	-3.8
Rwanda	..	..	..	..	..	..	..	..	..	..	..
Senegal	23.2	-20.0	46.4	-27.1	6.6	28.3	10.6	18.8	-30.9	8.6	-25.1
Seychelles	..	..	..	..	..	..	..	..	..	..	..
Sierra Leone	1.6	-0.8	10.9	-20.6	-23.2	11.5	-35.4	-8.5	46.4	8.6	1.7
Somalia	-7.7	7.3	6.9	-3.0	38.3	56.1	-9.5	-31.8	28.4	-21.9	23.5
Sudan	16.6	-1.1	-2.2	-29.5	-2.4	14.1	4.7	17.2	-29.8	9.9	-12.1
Swaziland	..	..	..	..	..	..	..	..	..	..	..
Tanzania	-2.5	-1.7	11.7	-27.0	-29.5	4.7	10.3	-8.4	-8.0	-9.2	2.8
Togo	20.3	9.0	-13.3	-7.3	11.0	-28.8	-1.4	45.7	70.7	-17.6	20.7
Uganda	..	..	..	..	..	..	..	..	..	..	..
Zaire	4.6	22.7	11.4	-27.5	10.7	-7.0	-17.7	26.3	-21.0	71.6	18.9
Zambia	-2.0	-12.2	11.7	-9.5	5.3	-5.8	15.0	-7.7	-6.4	9.4	-11.9
Zimbabwe	..	..	..	..	..	..	..	..	..	..	..
SOUTH ASIA	..	..	..	..	..	..	..	..	..	..	..
Bangladesh	..	..	..	..	..	-24.2	36.9	10.6	20.3	4.1	8.8
Bhutan	..	..	..	..	..	..	..	..	..	..	..
India	-14.8	1.5	12.4	0.8	-1.2	6.1	24.8	2.1	-3.6	0.3	-9.1
Nepal	..	..	..	..	..	..	..	..	..	..	..
Pakistan	4.0	-11.2	-7.2	-20.8	-5.8	17.6	8.9	-13.9	13.3	24.3	12.1
Sri Lanka	17.2	-7.3	-3.5	8.4	-6.0	11.1	-7.7	0.4	20.0	3.9	-21.3
EAST ASIA AND PACIFIC	..	..	..	..	..	..	..	..	..	..	..
China	-4.6	14.3	12.1	14.2	4.4	21.2	-15.2	-0.2	27.6	16.6	11.6
Fiji	..	..	..	..	..	..	..	..	..	..	..
Indonesia	1.6	6.4	58.2	22.6	-16.7	3.9	7.1	12.9	6.3	-6.5	-2.9
Korea, Rep.	23.7	21.1	49.3	60.7	10.4	12.2	34.7	27.9	13.8	-0.8	10.0
Malaysia	5.0	1.0	-9.2	6.1	-5.6	7.3	23.9	-2.0	7.2	15.9	-1.0
Mongolia	..	..	..	..	..	..	..	..	..	..	..
Papua New Guinea	..	..	..	..	..	..	..	..	..	..	..
Philippines	23.1	8.9	-14.5	10.9	-7.8	14.7	10.0	16.2	1.8	7.1	15.4
Solomon Islands	..	..	..	..	..	..	..	..	..	..	..
Thailand	8.3	19.7	21.2	-0.4	2.1	3.4	41.0	7.9	-2.1	11.3	10.0
Tonga	..	..	..	..	..	..	..	..	..	..	..
Vanuatu	..	..	..	..	..	..	..	..	..	..	..
Western Samoa	..	..	..	..	..	..	..	..	..	..	..

1981	1982	1983	1984	1985	1986	1987	1988	1989	1990	1991	
..	..	..	..	..	..	..	..	..	..	..	*SUB-SAHARAN AFRICA*
..	..	..	..	..	..	..	..	..	..	..	*Excluding Nigeria*
..	..	..	..	..	..	..	..	..	..	..	Benin
..	..	..	..	..	..	..	..	..	..	..	Botswana
-8.9	-15.9	-7.6	..		..	55.5	-8.7	-16.8	6.5	..	Burkina Faso
..	..	..	..							..	Burundi
..	..	..	..	-14.5	39.4	4.2	1.0	26.1	-10.9	..	Cameroon
..	..	..	..	..	..	..	..	..	..	..	Cape Verde
..	..	..	..	..	..	..	..	..	..	..	Central African Rep.
..	..	..	..	..	..	..	..	..	..	..	Chad
..	..	..	..	..	..	..	..	..	..	..	Comoros
10.0	22.7	-8.6	12.2	-4.5	12.7	5.5	18.5	-3.5	-21.0	..	Congo
-1.4	-5.9	-11.6	22.0	4.1	20.0	0.8	-16.5	15.5	-6.4	..	Côte d'Ivoire
..	..	..	..	..	..	..	..	..	..	..	Equatorial Guinea
3.3	4.3	1.1	-5.6	-16.7	11.4	8.7	0.5	16.4	-29.3	..	Ethiopia
-5.8	6.2	1.3	2.0	2.2	-7.5	-16.1	4.5	13.3	..	..	Gabon
..	..	..	..	..	..	..	..	..	..	..	Gambia, The
..	..	..	..	..	..	..	..	..	..	..	Ghana
..	..	..	..	..	..	..	..	..	..	..	Guinea-Bissau
-8.4	-11.1	0.8	2.8	2.2	11.2	-5.6	7.9	-0.5	2.6	..	Kenya
..	..	..	..	..	..	..	..	..	..	..	Lesotho
-0.8	-10.6	-6.5	9.4	2.6	-5.2	-12.9	-2.1	2.0	-0.3	..	Liberia
-5.1	0.2	-4.0	4.7	-17.6	-3.4	26.0	-26.0	24.6	4.9	..	Madagascar
8.8	-2.2	3.4	23.3	1.7	-7.9	12.3	-8.2	-4.4	46.2	..	Malawi
..	..	..	..	..	..	..	..	..	..	..	Mali
..	..	..	..	..	..	..	..	..	..	..	Mauritania
-19.9	23.1	2.9	10.4	..	-87.2	13.8	3.7	-6.2	3.0	..	Mauritius
-36.9	7.6	-25.2	..	..	..	..	..	..	..	..	Mozambique
..	..	..	..	..	..	..	..	..	..	..	Namibia
-23.1	-41.9	1.6	-21.4	2.0	40.1	77.8	-5.4	21.6	-9.5	..	Niger
-34.5	-2.2	-27.6	14.4	20.3	-19.9	3.5	9.4	0.0	35.4	..	Nigeria
..	..	..	..	..	..	..	..	..	..	..	Rwanda
10.4	14.3	14.9	0.1	-2.5	17.6	-9.5	-6.2	25.9	-15.1	..	Senegal
..	..	..	..	..	..	..	..	..	..	..	Seychelles
-5.7	-35.6	-28.3	58.0	-6.2	-11.2	11.3	-28.1	124.1	-7.2	..	Sierra Leone
24.1	36.5	-27.8	-12.5	-63.2	131.7	-5.5	0.9	46.0	..	..	Somalia
-11.5	30.3	-3.3	7.1	-27.7	-0.8	37.8	-7.2	14.8	-47.1	..	Sudan
..	..	..	..	..	..	..	..	..	..	..	Swaziland
18.8	-25.4	6.2	-14.6	-18.9	3.5	-8.2	-11.8	14.6	..	..	Tanzania
-38.7	38.4	-2.9	-19.8	13.4	9.9	25.0	-9.6	1.4	5.7	..	Togo
..	..	..	..	..	..	..	..	..	..	..	Uganda
-4.3	-16.9	-12.7	-26.5	-2.1	8.0	-39.2	25.9	-3.0	-27.7	..	Zaire
-9.7	3.7	-10.5	..	..	..	..	..	..	..	..	Zambia
63.4	10.8	-0.7	53.0	4.8	8.3					..	Zimbabwe
..	..	..	..	..	..	..	..	..	..	..	*SOUTH ASIA*
-7.5	2.1	18.9	10.4	-2.7	14.3	16.2	0.5	4.6	13.4	..	Bangladesh
..	..	..	..	..	..	..	..	..	..	..	Bhutan
-4.3	13.9	7.3	1.8	-3.9	6.2	14.6	9.1	14.4	8.6	..	India
..	..	..	..	..	..	..	..	..	..	..	Nepal
6.3	-5.5	29.7	-13.3	14.5	23.9	9.2	4.3	10.6	14.8	..	Pakistan
28.5	4.5	-2.6	20.4	7.9	-2.5	6.7	3.5	8.0	10.9	..	Sri Lanka
..	..	..	..	..	..	..	..	..	..	..	*EAST ASIA AND PACIFIC*
17.8	8.3	6.8	12.1	16.1	13.7	10.7	12.1	5.9	1.9	..	China
..	..	..	..	..	..	..	..	..	..	..	Fiji
-4.5	9.3	4.0	4.9	-10.4	16.7	-5.5	2.4	8.4	10.2	..	Indonesia
19.4	7.3	15.0	18.5	6.5	16.6	25.2	12.9	-4.0	4.4	..	Korea, Rep.
-0.4	13.6	15.6	12.7	4.5	8.7	7.0	9.0	20.1	15.6	..	Malaysia
..	..	..	..	..	..	..	..	..	..	..	Mongolia
..	..	..	..	..	..	..	..	..	..	..	Papua New Guinea
7.6	-2.6	-7.2	0.3	-2.2	6.2	1.1	7.4	13.2	15.0	..	Philippines
..	..	..	..	..	..	..	..	..	..	..	Solomon Islands
18.2	19.5	-9.5	21.9	6.0	11.3	20.5	21.6	21.6	9.7	..	Thailand
..	..	..	..	..	..	..	..	..	..	..	Tonga
..	..	..	..	..	..	..	..	..	..	..	Vanuatu
..	..	..	..	..	..	..	..	..	..	..	Western Samoa

Table 19. Growth of merchandise exports (cont'd.)

Average annual growth (percent)	1970	1971	1972	1973	1974	1975	1976	1977	1978	1979	1980
LATIN AMERICA AND CARIBBEAN	..	..	..	..	..	..	..	..	..	..	..
Argentina	2.6	-4.7	-0.3	16.7	1.3	-21.2	31.4	42.1	5.4	0.5	-6.7
Bahamas	..	..	..	..	..	..	..	..	..	..	..
Barbados	-7.1	-6.4	-10.4	-16.5	-29.4	50.4	-8.7	9.6	19.5	-0.8	-11.3
Belize	..	..	..	..	..	..	..	..	..	..	..
Bolivia	-14.6	15.0	15.3	-8.2	-0.9	-3.4	9.8	-3.6	-11.1	-13.0	8.2
Brazil	8.7	6.3	24.9	6.5	5.1	15.1	1.8	-1.9	11.5	8.3	23.3
Chile	15.2	-2.0	-12.7	-15.0	71.2	0.6	24.1	2.2	9.9	24.6	-2.8
Colombia	-0.7	-4.7	4.2	5.5	-11.4	8.8	-20.8	0.5	45.9	-2.2	18.0
Costa Rica	11.9	7.3	8.4	-1.7	7.2	11.1	-4.3	10.6	20.2	-11.2	4.9
Dominican Rep.	..	..	..	..	..	..	..	..	..	..	..
Ecuador	24.7	16.7	145.4	115.4	-28.3	-11.4	11.0	-9.0	8.2	10.0	-13.0
El Salvador	-10.4	5.1	11.7	-1.1	8.0	17.6	-12.4	0.2	1.9	12.4	4.5
Grenada	..	..	..	..	..	..	..	..	..	..	..
Guatemala	-1.9	1.6	3.8	0.0	5.9	17.6	-10.4	21.8	9.4	-6.3	17.8
Guyana	..	..	..	..	..	..	..	..	..	..	..
Haiti	..	..	..	..	..	..	..	..	..	..	..
Honduras	-0.4	-1.0	-5.6	0.9	-15.4	13.1	6.0	9.2	24.2	0.1	7.1
Jamaica	27.0	-2.6	-1.2	-15.3	13.3	10.0	-20.9	9.4	-5.2	-3.6	1.1
Mexico	-12.8	-1.8	23.9	6.2	-9.2	12.0	3.1	19.9	53.2	16.2	35.7
Nicaragua	1.3	4.7	23.8	-22.4	16.4	13.2	5.1	1.2	10.2	-23.6	-32.1
Panama	-7.7	-4.0	-17.7	-15.2	-17.8	42.5	-29.4	-2.2	-3.5	-7.3	-6.6
Paraguay	9.8	-6.2	21.3	-15.4	31.3	19.7	-5.6	40.8	-8.3	1.6	-4.1
Peru	15.2	-5.3	-7.8	-33.0	20.8	24.9	-20.6	16.9	16.8	50.3	-16.0
St. Vincent	..	..	..	..	..	..	..	..	..	..	..
Trinidad and Tobago	1.3	-16.3	-3.8	-8.1	-21.4	-11.6	19.0	-9.9	-7.9	-9.6	-2.2
Uruguay	13.2	-13.0	-19.5	-1.3	20.3	14.1	28.2	6.8	-0.4	-5.3	24.5
Venezuela	1.4	-24.9	-15.3	15.4	-40.8	-18.1	-2.4	-6.4	-4.5	7.6	-16.3
MIDDLE EAST AND NORTH AFRICA	..	..	..	..	..	..	..	..	..	..	..
Algeria	11.4	-30.5	48.1	3.5	-39.3	3.1	9.1	8.2	4.4	12.8	-2.5
Egypt, Arab Rep.	18.9	-10.5	-3.4	-11.7	-22.5	5.4	6.6	9.2	6.4	-12.7	10.3
Iran, Islamic Rep.	..	..	..	..	..	..	..	..	..	..	..
Jordan	-27.1	-3.8	35.6	1.5	58.0	-7.0	45.9	20.2	8.5	9.3	31.0
Morocco	0.2	-1.1	18.6	12.2	6.0	-18.7	9.1	1.1	8.9	9.6	6.5
Oman	..	..	..	..	..	..	..	..	..	..	..
Saudi Arabia	21.7	20.1	27.2	17.3	-5.0	-14.5	20.5	3.7	-7.3	8.2	5.2
Syrian Arab Rep.	20.2	-4.2	14.6	-7.6	27.4	35.0	0.1	-7.6	-0.8	18.1	-14.6
Tunisia	6.1	4.5	30.2	-0.1	14.8	7.2	-10.2	5.5	21.8	16.5	-9.4
EUROPE	..	..	..	..	..	..	..	..	..	..	..
Bulgaria	..	..	..	..	..	..	..	..	..	..	..
Czechoslovakia	..	..	..	..	..	..	..	..	..	..	..
Greece	13.5	2.7	24.0	48.5	0.8	12.6	3.8	-0.5	18.8	-6.7	14.9
Hungary	..	7.4	19.0	12.8	-0.9	8.6	-19.7	12.6	1.4	12.4	1.1
Malta	-5.3	1.2	30.4	14.8	-10.7	19.7	36.5	21.1	14.7	4.5	0.6
Poland	..	..	..	..	..	..	5.4	9.7	4.1	12.6	10.3
Portugal	12.0	1.3	5.8	7.8	1.6	-22.6	-0.7	8.9	2.9	16.9	14.2
Romania	..	..	..	..	..	..	..	..	..	..	..
Turkey	6.7	11.1	36.9	12.6	-12.3	-7.9	27.6	-13.5	20.0	-18.2	19.1
Yugoslavia	6.9	7.7	13.2	6.5	-1.5	3.1	19.1	-2.5	0.7	1.7	15.3
Low- and middle-income economies	..	..	..	..	..	..	..	..	..	..	..
Low-income economies	..	..	..	..	..	..	..	..	..	..	..
Low-income Africa	..	..	..	..	..	..	..	..	..	..	..
China and India	..	..	..	..	..	..	..	..	..	..	..
Other low-income	..	..	..	..	..	..	..	..	..	..	..
Middle-income economies	..	..	..	..	..	..	..	..	..	..	..
High-income economies	..	..	..	..	..	..	..	..	..	..	..
OECD members	..	..	..	..	..	..	..	..	..	..	..
Japan	..	..	..	..	..	..	..	..	..	..	..
United States	..	..	..	..	..	..	..	..	..	..	..
WORLD	..	..	..	..	..	..	..	..	..	..	..

1981	1982	1983	1984	1985	1986	1987	1988	1989	1990	1991	
..	..	..	..	..	..	..	..	..	..	..	*LATIN AMERICA AND CARIBBEAN*
16.1	-6.3	-1.1	5.0	11.9	-15.0	-12.1	24.5	-0.2	15.9	..	Argentina
											Bahamas
4.9	59.4	56.2	-0.7	-17.0	-5.5	-13.5	-10.1	-3.6	0.9	..	Barbados
											Belize
0.2	-1.1	-6.1	-2.8	-10.0	17.5	3.8	-13.7	26.0	23.2	..	Bolivia
19.6	-5.2	13.2	22.3	2.1	-17.9	14.5	17.8	-5.9	-19.1	..	Brazil
-5.8	9.2	-4.1	6.1	6.6	14.0	-0.6	5.9	10.4	-0.8	..	Chile
-18.0	2.0	4.0	10.0	4.4	31.5	25.4	-5.0	27.5	13.2	..	Colombia
4.5	-9.7	-4.8	16.2	-0.5	0.9	12.6	-1.7	13.7	-3.3	..	Costa Rica
											Dominican Rep.
-15.3	12.9	1.1	19.0	15.5	4.2	-17.3	23.8	-8.9	-1.6	..	Ecuador
-14.5	-14.5	24.5	-30.3	1.6	-8.7	18.0	-14.0	-23.4	..	..	El Salvador
											Grenada
-15.1	1.7	3.2	-2.0	-6.4	-6.7	-5.1	4.1	9.5	2.5	..	Guatemala
											Guyana
										..	Haiti
-5.6	-5.5	-1.9	11.6	1.5	-0.2	9.0	-2.8	34.1	-27.4	..	Honduras
5.9	-20.5	1.6	4.5	-25.6	-3.3	21.4	11.3	5.5	51.6	..	Jamaica
22.2	12.7	25.7	9.1	-5.8	-30.7	30.7	0.9	1.7	-0.3	..	Mexico
31.1	-15.0	7.6	-8.2	-23.0	-24.1	43.2	-27.5	32.0	..	..	Nicaragua
-3.8	0.9	-3.8	-12.9	20.4	17.6	4.0	-27.6	2.4	2.1	..	Panama
2.0	23.9	-28.7	30.6	10.5	-18.2	36.5	21.4	66.5	-5.3	..	Paraguay
-22.4	35.1	-25.8	24.9	21.4	-32.5	5.6	-3.0	24.3	0.5	..	Peru
											St. Vincent
-16.3	-9.1	-16.9	-5.3	1.9	4.9	-13.3	6.7	0.4	16.9	..	Trinidad and Tobago
18.1	-5.8	1.9	-7.5	-2.6	22.9	-5.9	14.9	3.4	3.5	..	Uruguay
-18.0	2.7	-3.0	11.5	6.2	-6.5	0.3	5.4	6.0	10.2	..	Venezuela
..	..	..	..	..	..	..	..	..	..	..	*MIDDLE EAST AND NORTH AFRICA*
-23.9	-4.6	6.8	9.3	-12.2	36.1	-7.6	21.3	10.0	-4.3	..	Algeria
-0.9	6.5	5.5	2.1	-29.6	58.5	-16.6	-7.5	36.9	-3.9	..	Egypt, Arab Rep.
											Iran, Islamic Rep.
30.1	11.1	-12.4	54.3	-0.5	-5.9	9.5	13.8	24.3	4.6	..	Jordan
1.2	-0.8	7.2	4.1	4.2	4.5	6.9	16.2	9.1	6.8	..	Morocco
										..	Oman
-2.3	-27.1	-36.4	-16.3	-26.2	37.3	-8.2	13.3	-1.6	-13.0	..	Saudi Arabia
-7.8	7.2	0.9	-1.1	-7.1	21.9	133.6	-61.1	84.0	23.7	..	Syrian Arab Rep.
9.6	-9.0	2.8	1.4	-5.6	14.7	11.6	4.5	19.2	3.7	..	Tunisia
..	..	..	..	..	..	..	..	..	..	..	*EUROPE*
..	..	..	..	..	..	..	..	..	..	..	Bulgaria
..	..	..	..	..	..	..	..	..	..	..	Czechoslovakia
-12.4	3.5	8.5	16.5	-2.2	20.9	4.8	-27.6	26.3	-1.8	..	Greece
2.6	7.4	9.5	5.9	-0.4	-2.2	3.7	33.6	-1.9	-2.9	..	Hungary
1.7	-16.8	7.9	12.6	2.6	8.4	9.5	9.8	23.2	17.6	..	Malta
-17.8	-13.2	11.0	9.4	1.3	4.8	4.9	9.1	0.1	8.3	..	Poland
0.8	14.8	18.1	12.9	8.0	18.4	4.6	12.1	10.0	..	..	Portugal
											Romania
67.6	34.3	-0.9	30.3	16.4	-13.2	21.9	5.9	-30.4	7.5	..	Turkey
18.1	-4.6	-7.4	6.9	7.2	-5.8	0.9	-0.3	-6.2	1.2	..	Yugoslavia
..	..	..	..	..	..	..	..	..	..	..	**Low- and middle-income economies**
..	..	..	..	..	..	..	..	..	..	..	Low-income economies
..	..	..	..	..	..	..	..	..	..	..	Low-income Africa
..	..	..	..	..	..	..	..	..	..	..	China and India
..	..	..	..	..	..	..	..	..	..	..	Other low-income
..	..	..	..	..	..	..	..	..	..	..	Middle-income economies
..	..	..	..	..	..	..	..	..	..	..	**High-income economies**
..	..	..	..	..	..	..	..	..	..	..	OECD members
..	..	..	..	..	..	..	..	..	..	..	Japan
..	..	..	..	..	..	..	..	..	..	..	United States
..	..	..	..	..	..	..	..	..	..	..	**WORLD**

Table 20. Growth of merchandise imports

Average annual growth (percent)	1970	1971	1972	1973	1974	1975	1976	1977	1978	1979	1980
SUB-SAHARAN AFRICA	..	..	..	..	..	..	..	..	..	..	..
Excluding Nigeria	..	..	..	..	..	..	..	..	..	..	..
Benin	..	..	..	..	..	..	..	..	..	..	..
Botswana	..	..	..	..	..	..	..	..	..	..	..
Burkina Faso	-2.3	-4.5	8.7	-5.9	10.4	6.5	-3.5	34.3	-2.5	16.5	0.0
Burundi	..	..	..	..	..	..	..	..	..	..	..
Cameroon	10.9	-5.0	7.6	-9.9	-13.1	29.7	-2.4	14.8	18.9	9.7	4.9
Cape Verde	..	..	..	..	..	..	..	..	..	..	..
Central African Rep.	..	..	..	..	..	..	..	..	..	..	..
Chad	..	..	..	..	..	..	..	..	..	..	..
Comoros	..	..	..	..	..	..	..	..	..	..	..
Congo	-35.4	30.1	4.3	14.8	-25.2	25.4	1.0	-4.4	23.5	-7.3	37.8
Côte d'Ivoire	9.4	-7.5	10.7	15.5	-0.4	12.3	12.7	22.4	15.9	-11.4	-8.2
Equatorial Guinea	..	..	..	..	..	..	..	..	..	..	..
Ethiopia	10.4	1.1	-12.6	-7.9	-19.7	3.7	15.8	2.4	12.8	-2.6	6.1
Gabon	-4.1	5.7	34.1	-1.1	66.2	24.0	7.9	28.4	-29.2	-18.0	16.2
Gambia, The	..	..	..	..	..	..	..	..	..	..	..
Ghana	..	..	..	..	..	..	..	..	..	..	..
Guinea-Bissau	..	..	..	..	..	..	..	..	..	..	..
Kenya	13.4	6.8	-4.3	-9.5	4.4	-8.2	1.5	18.4	17.5	-17.7	5.0
Lesotho	..	..	..	..	..	..	..	..	..	..	..
Liberia	43.4	0.2	-2.6	-13.4	0.6	7.7	20.4	6.2	-5.0	-11.1	-13.6
Madagascar	-6.2	7.0	-6.5	-21.8	-16.1	33.7	-22.1	8.9	15.7	28.5	-18.0
Malawi	9.2	32.4	6.7	-14.1	-18.1	24.6	-17.5	3.7	30.2	0.1	-5.9
Mali	..	..	..	..	..	..	..	..	..	..	..
Mauritania	..	..	..	..	..	..	..	..	..	..	..
Mauritius	-2.7	-5.2	37.7	3.8	14.2	7.4	9.1	16.0	-1.2	-0.7	-7.4
Mozambique	..	..	..	..	..	..	..	..	..	..	..
Namibia	..	..	..	..	..	..	..	..	..	..	..
Niger	13.6	-0.5	14.6	4.0	-33.7	-1.2	29.1	37.4	47.9	28.0	9.2
Nigeria	24.2	15.5	-8.5	2.8	17.3	101.2	36.7	23.3	1.8	-29.0	14.7
Rwanda	..	..	..	..	..	..	..	..	..	..	..
Senegal	-15.9	8.3	12.5	-3.0	-9.0	18.9	12.8	8.3	-9.7	5.3	-7.6
Seychelles	..	..	..	..	..	..	..	..	..	..	..
Sierra Leone	-5.7	-3.8	-3.9	-4.1	-6.1	-29.7	5.2	0.7	40.4	-42.6	16.3
Somalia	-10.9	13.6	11.7	9.4	-8.2	0.7	3.8	34.4	-3.6	-13.8	25.0
Sudan	9.4	-4.2	-12.2	1.6	-14.8	38.9	1.2	-4.5	-18.2	-9.7	37.9
Swaziland	..	..	..	..	..	..	..	..	..	..	..
Tanzania	24.5	10.3	-0.7	-0.1	-2.5	-12.2	-4.2	1.3	37.3	-19.3	-4.4
Togo	9.5	3.0	12.4	-3.7	-18.9	32.1	6.6	37.5	51.4	-1.5	-11.1
Uganda	..	..	..	..	..	..	..	..	..	..	..
Zaire	-10.6	0.1	10.2	-20.7	-18.3	-4.6	-10.0	-7.3	-17.5	-11.9	18.0
Zambia	1.5	-7.1	-13.4	-17.6	-9.6	13.2	-30.3	-6.2	-13.9	-1.5	23.0
Zimbabwe	..	..	..	..	..	..	..	..	..	..	..
SOUTH ASIA	..	..	..	..	..	..	..	..	..	..	..
Bangladesh	..	..	..	..	..	18.5	-0.6	-6.3	31.5	-4.7	9.4
Bhutan	..	..	..	..	..	..	..	..	..	..	..
India	12.5	12.8	-10.8	10.1	-7.2	16.6	-12.5	9.7	9.2	0.8	18.7
Nepal	..	..	..	..	..	..	..	..	..	..	..
Pakistan	10.3	-23.2	-35.0	8.8	12.4	25.9	2.0	0.6	20.8	4.4	12.7
Sri Lanka	-24.4	-25.5	-11.4	24.0	-9.3	8.6	-15.1	26.8	13.7	25.8	11.4
EAST ASIA AND PACIFIC	..	..	..	..	..	..	..	..	..	..	..
China	16.3	-10.5	23.5	27.2	24.5	5.4	-18.8	4.7	37.9	19.5	14.4
Fiji	14.1	3.9	9.7	-4.1	-14.7	-4.0	-4.7	8.5	7.3	6.2	0.2
Indonesia	18.3	8.2	27.4	14.2	26.4	19.4	21.6	4.7	-6.5	-6.6	25.8
Korea, Rep.	10.2	12.3	-2.5	18.3	9.3	8.4	16.6	15.1	23.6	10.8	-9.5
Malaysia	11.0	-8.7	-15.3	10.2	11.9	-16.4	7.7	9.4	15.7	12.1	16.7
Mongolia	..	..	..	..	..	..	..	..	..	..	..
Papua New Guinea	..	..	..	..	..	..	..	..	..	..	..
Philippines	0.5	-3.1	-6.6	-2.0	13.8	5.2	3.1	0.3	8.5	4.7	3.0
Solomon Islands	..	..	..	..	..	..	..	..	..	..	..
Thailand	5.6	-7.9	3.8	11.7	-6.1	0.3	5.7	18.3	4.8	9.1	8.7
Tonga	..	..	..	..	..	..	..	..	..	..	..
Vanuatu	..	..	..	..	..	..	..	..	..	..	..
Western Samoa	..	..	..	..	..	..	..	..	..	..	..

1981	1982	1983	1984	1985	1986	1987	1988	1989	1990	1991	
..	..	..	..	..	..	..	..	..	..	..	*SUB-SAHARAN AFRICA*
..	..	..	..	..	..	..	..	..	..	..	*Excluding Nigeria*
..	..	..	..	..	..	..	..	..	..	..	Benin
..	..	..	..					..	..	..	Botswana
-8.9	8.2	-14.2	-24.9	..	..	-0.4	-2.7	-15.9	6.2	..	Burkina Faso
											Burundi
-8.0	-10.0	-2.2	-4.9	15.7	19.9	2.3	-36.7	-4.6	-12.2	..	Cameroon
											Cape Verde
..	..	..	..		..	..	..	..	..	..	Central African Rep.
	..	..	..	..	..		..		..	..	Chad
									..	..	Comoros
58.2	30.3	-21.8	-2.7	-2.9	-6.0	-14.6	0.2	-11.5	-3.2	..	Congo
-8.5	-2.5	-13.9	-16.0	17.4	23.1	0.2	-8.8	-5.1	-7.5	..	Côte d'Ivoire
											Equatorial Guinea
-0.9	10.6	15.9	9.1	5.7	1.3	4.0	7.0	-14.9	-6.0	..	Ethiopia
24.4	-1.7	-11.9	7.1	17.9	-10.5	-19.4	1.1	-8.6	..	..	Gabon
											Gambia, The
..	..	..	..		..		..	..	..	..	Ghana
											Guinea-Bissau
-5.9	-18.4	-10.6	6.3	2.5	24.4	-7.8	23.8	8.7	-9.0	..	Kenya
										..	Lesotho
-13.8	-1.9	0.1	-8.9	-19.8	-11.8	19.4	16.4	8.8	-2.2	..	Liberia
-31.3	-1.5	-3.2	0.4	15.0	-5.8	-26.1	29.4	24.7	-3.6	..	Madagascar
-22.7	-7.8	2.8	-11.4	10.0	-18.0	5.2	33.6	17.2	0.7	..	Malawi
..	..	..	..		..		..		..	..	Mali
										..	Mauritania
-12.9	-10.1	-1.6	9.0	13.5	23.2	35.9	24.3	-1.5	11.3	..	Mauritius
18.0	3.3	-18.1						..		..	Mozambique
									..	..	Namibia
-17.0	-32.6	-33.3	-11.4	28.8	-5.7	3.8	-15.9	0.5	-10.3	..	Niger
52.0	-44.4	-14.8	-33.3	5.4	-42.5	-3.1	5.7	-10.8	23.5	..	Nigeria
..	..	..	..					..	..	..	Rwanda
0.4	2.4	7.3	-2.3	-11.4	11.0	4.6	2.9	42.5	-11.5	..	Senegal
										..	Seychelles
-25.7	-15.2	6.3	-21.4	21.7	-22.1	-3.0	19.1	47.0	-23.5	..	Sierra Leone
46.3	-32.3	8.7	-0.5	-30.3	16.4	-59.0	140.1	56.8	..	..	Somalia
3.7	-4.4	10.0	-18.2	-30.1	17.2	-6.9	12.8	0.3	-57.3	..	Sudan
..	..	..	..		..	..	..	..	..	..	Swaziland
-27.9	12.6	-29.3	31.9	22.9	-18.2	1.5	-13.9	9.3	..	..	Tanzania
-18.8	-3.5	-23.0	-7.7	13.1	-1.1	35.6	7.9	0.7	36.6	..	Togo
..	..	..	..		..		..	..	..	..	Uganda
-9.8	-6.7	-6.0	-16.4	16.4	1.4	-21.3	-1.8	6.3	9.5	..	Zaire
-5.3	-17.5	-31.3	..	..	..					..	Zambia
129.3	13.9	-5.2	117.7	-5.0	3.2	..	..	..	..	..	Zimbabwe
..	..	..	..	..	..	..	..	..	..	..	*SOUTH ASIA*
-10.5	3.1	-11.7	36.4	25.4	-12.1	20.2	6.6	19.9	-10.0	..	Bangladesh
								..		..	Bhutan
1.3	10.3	6.2	-5.6	14.9	-1.7	1.1	7.2	6.7	5.6	..	India
..	..	..	..							..	Nepal
-0.4	2.1	4.7	7.7	4.9	0.0	-1.6	16.9	4.5	-4.7	..	Pakistan
-12.6	4.6	6.5	6.9	-3.1	4.9	2.1	9.6	-5.9	-4.0	..	Sri Lanka
..	..	..	..	..	..	..	..	..	..	..	*EAST ASIA AND PACIFIC*
10.8	-5.0	9.5	24.9	64.9	-10.7	-9.2	14.8	10.9	-17.6	..	China
9.6	-14.0	-2.1	-5.4	-1.0	0.1	-19.8	22.3	24.0	5.0	..	Fiji
19.3	33.7	2.6	-13.1	-24.7	13.7	-4.0	-2.3	13.3	42.9	..	Indonesia
16.5	-0.3	10.7	18.3	4.5	8.5	10.7	15.9	14.6	13.4	..	Korea, Rep.
6.1	12.9	9.6	8.2	-9.3	-17.6	5.9	18.5	36.8	24.5	..	Malaysia
..	..	..	..	..	..		..		..	..	Mongolia
									..	..	Papua New Guinea
-1.5	2.4	0.2	-17.3	-13.9	6.1	16.2	17.7	25.6	4.2	..	Philippines
									..	..	Solomon Islands
3.5	-11.2	24.9	4.5	-10.6	1.6	24.0	40.1	20.1	23.1	..	Thailand
..	..	..	..	..	..		..		..	..	Tonga
											Vanuatu
..	..	..	..	..	..	..	..	..	..	..	Western Samoa

Table 20. Growth of merchandise imports (cont'd.)

Average annual growth (percent)	1970	1971	1972	1973	1974	1975	1976	1977	1978	1979	1980
LATIN AMERICA AND CARIBBEAN	..	..	..	..	..	..	..	..	..	..	..
Argentina	-6.0	8.2	-17.1	7.1	10.3	2.6	-24.8	24.4	-18.6	47.4	33.6
Bahamas	..	..	..	..	..	..	..	..	..	..	..
Barbados	5.2	-2.7	2.3	-5.2	-13.9	3.4	3.3	5.2	2.6	13.1	5.8
Belize	..	..	..	..	..	..	..	..	..	..	..
Bolivia	-7.9	0.1	-4.6	2.9	22.8	50.2	4.3	-8.6	15.2	-5.2	-29.1
Brazil	20.9	18.4	14.6	15.2	13.3	-4.8	0.3	-9.3	4.8	4.4	-2.4
Chile	-6.1	5.2	-12.7	-17.7	8.2	-14.2	-0.2	13.4	21.0	38.6	-1.2
Colombia	16.0	4.9	-17.4	-1.4	19.9	-10.1	12.9	11.8	25.6	-1.8	25.7
Costa Rica	21.0	3.5	0.9	2.1	4.5	-7.8	11.7	21.8	2.2	2.3	-5.2
Dominican Rep.	..	..	..	..	..	..	..	..	..	..	..
Ecuador	6.6	20.4	-18.6	-15.4	56.4	7.4	-4.8	12.3	12.6	-6.9	26.0
El Salvador	-11.7	21.5	-1.3	11.9	4.1	-1.4	17.8	23.1	-4.7	-15.9	-15.4
Grenada	..	..	..	..	..	..	..	..	..	..	..
Guatemala	8.4	12.9	9.2	1.7	9.1	-1.3	11.8	16.3	6.7	-10.5	-0.8
Guyana	..	..	..	..	..	..	..	..	..	..	..
Haiti	..	..	..	..	..	..	..	..	..	..	..
Honduras	14.1	-15.2	-6.8	6.2	-9.8	0.3	6.0	18.7	7.2	0.5	4.9
Jamaica	13.2	5.1	0.0	-13.7	-14.3	17.1	-18.8	-9.0	-8.7	-6.4	-6.6
Mexico	10.7	-5.5	12.8	20.5	-7.1	2.7	-8.5	-15.6	27.8	33.2	39.8
Nicaragua	9.6	-0.5	-6.3	17.0	14.0	-11.2	0.1	32.3	-28.9	-48.5	102.7
Panama	7.9	-9.7	-2.8	-4.9	-14.6	8.4	-12.1	-7.6	-4.2	3.0	-1.9
Paraguay	7.8	-9.1	-11.4	6.7	2.4	1.6	2.4	18.7	21.6	11.8	-3.5
Peru	-6.4	22.0	4.8	-0.7	6.6	41.9	-23.0	-15.5	-31.9	-7.7	56.0
St. Vincent	..	..	..	..	..	..	..	..	..	..	..
Trinidad and Tobago	12.7	-8.6	-0.2	-22.0	-16.0	-27.3	31.2	-19.9	-1.2	-22.2	21.0
Uruguay	26.4	-19.4	-18.6	-1.0	4.6	9.8	12.2	-3.0	3.7	23.5	15.7
Venezuela	8.7	1.9	5.9	-6.0	20.3	45.1	2.7	49.9	-4.7	-21.1	0.5
MIDDLE EAST AND NORTH AFRICA	..	..	..	..	..	..	..	..	..	..	..
Algeria	22.3	-2.7	3.4	18.0	34.9	38.0	-10.5	24.2	8.8	-16.0	12.3
Egypt, Arab Rep.	22.5	-4.6	-14.4	-35.4	78.1	75.1	0.1	17.2	21.3	-51.8	14.0
Iran, Islamic Rep.	..	..	..	..	..	..	..	..	..	..	..
Jordan	-6.1	7.5	4.7	-8.3	5.4	52.8	39.5	24.8	-2.3	9.2	4.9
Morocco	15.5	-3.9	1.3	4.5	13.5	29.6	4.8	14.1	-13.3	4.1	-6.4
Oman	..	..	..	..	..	..	..	..	..	..	..
Saudi Arabia	-11.8	10.9	26.7	41.4	16.0	35.6	102.8	56.3	23.1	5.1	11.5
Syrian Arab Rep.	-15.7	2.3	3.1	-10.9	40.6	32.0	18.2	28.9	-18.6	18.2	-0.4
Tunisia	21.8	-0.1	37.3	0.5	20.1	21.7	8.2	10.6	6.3	13.0	2.9
EUROPE	..	..	..	..	..	..	..	..	..	..	..
Bulgaria	..	..	..	..	..	..	..	..	..	..	..
Czechoslovakia	..	..	..	..	..	..	..	..	..	..	..
Greece	15.9	-3.7	10.9	22.5	-22.4	18.6	6.6	0.6	3.7	2.9	-8.6
Hungary	..	16.7	-4.7	2.8	10.0	11.7	-21.8	8.4	12.6	-3.3	-1.2
Malta	4.7	-7.7	7.2	1.4	4.5	0.0	8.7	11.3	-0.9	10.7	10.4
Poland	..	..	..	..	..	..	4.7	-2.0	-0.1	1.7	-5.1
Portugal	22.5	-2.4	3.8	1.5	3.0	-16.4	8.4	6.8	-2.4	3.8	18.1
Romania	..	..	..	..	..	..	..	..	..	..	..
Turkey	11.6	24.1	21.5	7.7	8.2	19.1	9.6	6.3	-24.4	-11.5	18.4
Yugoslavia	29.5	9.2	-13.0	24.3	3.6	-0.5	-7.5	10.6	0.2	19.3	-8.7
Low- and middle-income economies	..	..	..	..	..	..	..	..	..	..	..
Low-income economies	..	..	..	..	..	..	..	..	..	..	..
Low-income Africa	..	..	..	..	..	..	..	..	..	..	..
China and India	..	..	..	..	..	..	..	..	..	..	..
Other low-income	..	..	..	..	..	..	..	..	..	..	..
Middle-income economies	..	..	..	..	..	..	..	..	..	..	..
High-income economies	..	..	..	..	..	..	..	..	..	..	..
OECD members	..	..	..	..	..	..	..	..	..	..	..
Japan	..	..	..	..	..	..	..	..	..	..	..
United States	..	..	..	..	..	..	..	..	..	..	..
WORLD	..	..	..	..	..	..	..	..	..	..	..

1981	1982	1983	1984	1985	1986	1987	1988	1989	1990	1991	
..	..	..	..	..	..	..	..	..	..	..	*LATIN AMERICA AND CARIBBEAN*
-10.7	-41.4	-13.4	4.1	-16.8	22.6	11.8	-16.3	-21.8	-11.4	..	Argentina
									..	..	Bahamas
13.2	-3.0	12.7	11.4	-7.7	-2.1	-18.3	9.1	13.0	-5.3	..	Barbados
								..		..	Belize
37.9	-44.3	10.7	-20.7	65.7	-11.8	8.5	-28.4	0.0	5.1	..	Bolivia
-8.4	-5.8	-16.2	-7.0	-4.0	25.8	-8.0	6.6	13.7	3.1	..	Brazil
22.0	-48.3	-10.6	20.6	-12.9	-0.5	16.8	13.9	30.8	7.1	..	Chile
10.4	9.8	-7.5	-7.7	-6.6	-13.3	-1.5	8.9	-2.6	16.6	..	Colombia
-21.1	-22.7	6.3	12.3	1.9	-0.4	8.8	3.5	15.8	15.3	..	Costa Rica
..	..										Dominican Rep.
-15.4	-4.5	-12.3	15.7	6.0	-11.1	-4.6	-15.5	14.7	-8.6	..	Ecuador
4.7	-5.8	-10.4	64.9	-15.3	-22.5	-1.9	-0.1	8.6	..	..	El Salvador
									..	..	Grenada
3.7	-10.9	-15.5	29.8	-11.2	-19.6	23.2	3.0	8.3	-10.8	..	Guatemala
..	..										Guyana
							..		..	..	Haiti
-8.4	-24.4	23.4	0.9	7.8	-15.4	5.1	11.8	-10.1	-3.1	..	Honduras
21.8	-0.8	14.9	-23.5	2.0	-11.1	16.3	6.6	21.6	-15.0	..	Jamaica
27.6	-37.9	-26.4	36.8	13.8	-48.1	22.7	41.9	13.1	18.9	..	Mexico
10.1	-18.3	7.3	4.6	30.4	-29.7	10.5	-21.2	-13.5	..	..	Nicaragua
4.9	5.1	-6.6	1.7	-1.3	-11.5	-11.1	-26.2	28.7	36.7	..	Panama
-4.0	17.5	-17.9	4.8	-8.1	12.3	-6.3	9.1	1.2	30.9	..	Paraguay
22.7	-2.8	-22.4	-14.0	-5.7	18.9	21.2	-5.2	-41.1	19.2	..	Peru
								..		..	St. Vincent
-5.2	25.7	-28.1	-23.9	-18.3	-19.3	-15.2	-8.0	-0.3	9.5	..	Trinidad and Tobago
-3.6	-28.8	-26.1	0.3	-6.9	33.9	11.6	-0.4	6.0	5.1	..	Uruguay
11.6	17.8	-54.0	13.4	10.1	-7.5	4.1	18.2	-25.6	2.0	..	Venezuela
..	..	..	..	..	..	..	..	..	..	..	*MIDDLE EAST AND NORTH AFRICA*
8.5	-1.8	-1.4	0.7	-2.3	-13.5	-25.7	-5.1	19.5	6.8	..	Algeria
85.4	8.8	13.0	6.0	-48.1	51.7	-17.1	-1.5	-20.7	10.5	..	Egypt, Arab Rep.
								..		..	Iran, Islamic Rep.
30.2	7.8	-3.8	-8.2	-1.9	-1.9	1.9	-0.3	-16.9	26.0	..	Jordan
4.4	6.2	-14.5	9.9	1.7	6.7	0.6	3.6	7.2	12.4	..	Morocco
		..							..	..	Oman
17.5	19.1	-2.6	-11.7	-29.6	-27.1	-3.0	-2.0	-10.7	-4.9	..	Saudi Arabia
20.4	-14.7	18.6	-7.5	-1.4	-26.0	132.7	-74.4	-10.4	5.2	..	Syrian Arab Rep.
7.2	-4.4	-7.0	2.4	-15.3	10.4	-2.9	12.3	16.8	8.4	..	Tunisia
..	..	..	..	..	..	..	..	..	..	..	*EUROPE*
..	..	..	..	..	..	..	..	..	..	..	Bulgaria
..	..	..	..	..	..	..	..	..	..	..	Czechoslovakia
-17.3	19.1	-1.9	3.3	7.8	13.8	4.9	-19.3	21.1	18.7	..	Greece
0.2	-0.1	4.0	0.2	1.0	2.1	3.3	3.0	-1.3	-4.3	..	Hungary
-8.9	-3.8	-5.4	-0.4	6.8	10.9	16.8	13.7	13.9	5.0	..	Malta
-10.9	-28.7	5.2	8.6	8.0	4.9	4.5	10.9	1.6	-12.3	..	Poland
6.1	3.2	-12.8	-1.0	0.3	30.3	21.9	33.0	-0.8	..	..	Portugal
..	..										Romania
12.8	5.8	1.7	27.5	8.8	8.9	15.0	-2.2	-29.6	38.9	..	Turkey
3.6	-5.7	-11.5	0.4	4.0	6.3	-9.5	7.2	6.1	20.1	..	Yugoslavia
..	..	..	..	..	..	..	..	..	..	..	**Low- and middle-income economies**
..	..	..	..	..	..	..	..	..	..	..	Low-income economies
..	..	..	..	..	..	..	..	..	..	..	Low-income Africa
..	..	..	..	..	..	..	..	..	..	..	China and India
..	..	..	..	..	..	..	..	..	..	..	Other low-income
..	..	..	..	..	..	..	..	..	..	..	Middle-income economies
..	..	..	..	..	..	..	..	..	..	..	**High-income economies**
..	..	..	..	..	..	..	..	..	..	..	OECD members
..	..	..	..	..	..	..	..	..	..	..	Japan
..	..	..	..	..	..	..	..	..	..	..	United States
..	..	..	..	..	..	..	..	..	..	..	**WORLD**

Country Pages

ALGERIA	1970	1971	1972	1973	1974	1975	1976	1977	1978	1979	1980
CURRENT GNP PER CAPITA (US $)	360	340	430	500	670	870	1,060	1,180	1,380	1,650	1,940
POPULATION (thousands)	13,746	14,169	14,609	15,064	15,534	16,018	16,516	17,030	17,559	18,105	18,669
USE AND ORIGIN OF RESOURCES					*(Billions of current Algerian Dinars)*						
Gross National Product (GNP)	23.51	24.77	30.27	34.33	55.26	60.93	72.83	85.72	102.48	124.02	157.91
Net Factor Income from Abroad	-0.56	-0.28	-0.15	-0.26	-0.30	-0.64	-1.24	-1.52	-2.35	-4.21	-4.60
GDP at Market Prices	24.07	25.04	30.41	34.59	55.56	61.57	74.07	87.24	104.83	128.22	162.51
Resource Balance	-1.70	-2.34	-1.59	-2.17	1.83	-5.69	-3.03	-9.78	-15.26	-2.17	6.46
Exports of Goods & NF Services	5.31	4.57	6.16	8.75	21.40	20.71	24.36	26.55	26.69	39.91	55.80
Imports of Goods & NF Services	7.01	6.91	7.76	10.92	19.57	26.40	27.39	36.33	41.95	42.08	49.34
Domestic Absorption	25.77	27.39	32.01	36.76	53.73	67.26	77.11	97.02	120.10	130.40	156.04
Private Consumption, etc.	13.44	14.28	16.81	17.79	25.72	31.45	35.93	44.62	50.88	58.48	70.18
General Gov't Consumption	3.58	4.22	4.76	5.03	5.93	7.97	9.25	11.59	14.60	17.48	22.35
Gross Domestic Investment	8.75	8.89	10.44	13.94	22.08	27.84	31.93	40.81	54.62	54.43	63.51
Fixed Investment	8.16	8.34	9.81	12.42	16.96	23.97	31.36	38.43	50.79	50.37	54.88
Indirect Taxes, net	1.65	1.45	1.89	2.05	10.31	11.43	14.04	17.13	20.57	23.59	30.36
GDP at factor cost	22.42	23.60	28.53	32.55	45.25	50.15	60.04	70.11	84.26	104.63	132.15
Agriculture	2.43	2.62	2.83	2.73	4.05	6.08	6.97	6.98	8.72	11.14	13.25
Industry	9.27	8.95	12.61	15.94	24.09	23.07	30.01	35.85	41.97	52.81	70.94
Manufacturing	3.37	3.47	4.09	4.78	3.72	4.32	5.72	6.53	8.84	10.67	12.47
Services, etc.	10.72	12.03	13.09	13.87	17.12	21.00	23.06	27.28	33.57	40.68	47.96
Gross Domestic Saving	7.05	6.54	8.85	11.77	23.91	22.15	28.90	31.03	39.36	52.26	69.98
Gross National Saving	7.46	7.37	9.71	12.85	24.94	22.91	29.26	30.66	38.18	49.26	66.44
					(Billions of 1987 Algerian Dinars)						
Gross National Product	135.14	126.43	152.35	156.55	168.49	176.18	189.75	199.68	216.94	230.52	233.68
GDP at Market Prices	138.42	127.86	153.18	157.84	169.53	178.17	193.14	203.38	222.08	238.52	240.67
Resource Balance	13.98	7.00	13.44	10.13	-0.62	-5.94	-3.04	-10.96	-12.41	-5.83	-12.32
Exports of Goods & NF Services	32.32	23.94	33.19	34.95	32.85	33.05	34.17	34.00	36.09	38.64	33.66
Imports of Goods & NF Services	18.34	16.94	19.75	24.82	33.47	38.99	37.21	44.97	48.51	44.46	45.98
Domestic Absorption	98.30	102.38	119.23	129.09	163.34	183.36	194.62	220.55	240.89	247.22	267.80
Private Consumption, etc.	50.82	53.72	63.11	63.94	80.10	89.04	96.22	106.74	106.61	116.99	129.09
General Gov't Consumption	14.99	16.68	18.73	18.64	19.18	24.73	26.64	29.46	33.01	36.21	42.51
Gross Domestic Investment	32.49	31.98	37.39	46.51	64.06	69.58	71.75	84.34	101.27	94.01	96.20
Fixed Investment	31.28	31.05	36.20	42.78	51.53	62.67	73.76	83.13	99.29	91.41	91.52
GDP at factor cost	127.64	119.28	142.35	147.21	135.95	143.01	154.40	160.99	175.07	190.70	191.29
Agriculture	11.54	12.04	12.08	11.11	14.47	18.64	18.20	16.79	18.75	20.43	22.99
Industry	63.07	50.94	74.84	79.09	63.08	59.57	67.79	73.66	81.79	85.06	86.39
Manufacturing	11.33	11.14	12.83	14.72	10.88	11.61	14.64	15.91	19.40	22.04	23.32
Services, etc.	53.03	56.29	55.43	57.02	58.41	64.81	68.42	70.54	74.53	85.21	81.92
Memo Items:											
Capacity to Import	13.89	11.20	15.69	19.89	36.60	30.59	33.10	32.86	30.86	42.17	52.00
Terms of Trade Adjustment	-18.43	-12.75	-17.50	-15.06	3.75	-2.46	-1.08	-1.14	-5.23	3.53	18.35
Gross Domestic Income	119.98	115.11	135.68	142.78	173.28	175.71	192.06	202.23	216.85	242.05	259.01
Gross National Income	116.70	113.68	134.85	141.49	172.24	173.72	188.67	198.54	211.70	234.05	252.03
DOMESTIC PRICES/DEFLATORS					*(Index 1987 = 100)*						
Overall (GDP)	17.4	19.6	19.9	21.9	32.8	34.6	38.4	42.9	47.2	53.8	67.5
Domestic Absorption	26.2	26.8	26.8	28.5	32.9	36.7	39.6	44.0	49.9	52.7	58.3
Agriculture	21.0	21.7	23.4	24.6	28.0	32.6	38.3	41.6	46.5	54.5	57.7
Industry	14.7	17.6	16.8	20.2	38.2	38.7	44.3	48.7	51.3	62.1	82.1
Manufacturing	29.7	31.1	31.9	32.4	34.2	37.3	39.1	41.0	45.5	48.4	53.5
Consumer Price Index	23.8	24.4	25.3	26.9	28.1	30.7	33.4	37.4	43.8	48.9	53.5
MANUFACTURING ACTIVITY											
Employment (1987=100)	..	..	..	..	..	..	..	..	..	..	..
Real Earnings per Empl. (1987=100)	..	..	..	..	..	..	..	..	..	..	..
Real Output per Empl. (1987=100)											
Earnings as % of Value Added	45.2	46.4	45.1	44.9	53.9	55.6	54.5	54.8	52.7	54.5	55.8
MONETARY HOLDINGS					*(Billions of current Algerian Dinars)*						
Money Supply, Broadly Defined	13.45	14.59	19.00	21.42	27.12	35.44	45.88	55.24	72.07	86.29	103.83
Money	11.63	12.95	16.75	18.92	24.25	31.97	41.07	48.55	62.21	72.21	84.43
Currency Outside Banks	4.74	5.70	7.05	8.82	10.45	12.74	17.24	20.57	27.37	35.40	42.34
Demand Deposits	6.89	7.25	9.70	10.11	13.80	19.23	23.83	27.98	34.84	36.81	42.09
Quasi-Money	1.83	1.64	2.25	2.50	2.87	3.47	4.81	6.69	9.86	14.08	19.40
					(Millions of current Algerian Dinars)						
GOVERNMENT DEFICIT (-) OR SURPLUS	..	..	..	..	1,534	..	..	..	..	..	..
Current Revenue	..	..	..	..		..	..	..	..	..	..
Current Expenditure	..	..	..	..	8,501	..	..	..	..	..	..
Current Budget Balance	..	..	..	..		..	..	..	..	..	..
Capital Receipts	..	..	..	..		..	..	..	..	..	..
Capital Payments	..	..	..	..	13,382	..	..	..	..	..	..

1981	1982	1983	1984	1985	1986	1987	1988	1989	1990 estimate	Notes	ALGERIA
2,240	2,430	2,420	2,470	2,590	2,650	2,690	2,470	2,280	2,060	..	**CURRENT GNP PER CAPITA (US $)**
19,254	19,862	20,495	21,173	21,848	22,497	23,124	23,753	24,396	25,056	..	**POPULATION (thousands)**
											USE AND ORIGIN OF RESOURCES
			(Billions of current Algerian Dinars)								
186.06	201.52	227.89	257.19	284.83	289.83	305.27	304.85	359.94	452.20	..	Gross National Product (GNP)
-5.41	-6.03	-5.87	-6.66	-6.77	-6.72	-7.44	-11.91	-14.40	-18.70	..	Net Factor Income from Abroad
191.47	207.55	233.75	263.86	291.60	296.55	312.71	316.76	374.34	470.90	..	GDP at Market Prices
7.10	3.99	5.06	6.02	9.28	-12.09	5.95	-1.32	-0.60	24.70	..	Resource Balance
66.18	64.22	65.34	67.69	68.63	38.71	45.83	49.81	76.10	120.00	..	Exports of Goods & NF Services
59.08	60.23	60.29	61.67	59.35	50.80	39.89	51.13	76.70	95.30	..	Imports of Goods & NF Services
184.37	203.56	228.69	257.84	282.32	308.64	306.76	318.07	374.94	446.20	..	Domestic Absorption
87.18	95.56	106.18	125.83	139.72	156.41	154.88	162.56	185.30	205.00	..	Private Consumption, etc.
26.35	30.66	34.69	39.48	45.83	52.89	58.00	59.31	73.04	85.80	..	General Gov't Consumption
70.84	77.34	87.82	92.53	96.77	99.33	93.88	96.20	116.60	155.40	..	Gross Domestic Investment
63.04	71.49	80.32	87.48	92.77	101.33	92.88	96.10	111.50	153.40	..	Fixed Investment
37.65	39.35	43.32	51.77	53.19	52.96	59.13	55.80	68.83	93.32	..	Indirect Taxes, net
153.82	168.20	190.43	212.09	238.41	243.59	253.58	260.96	305.51	377.59	..	GDP at factor cost
16.58	16.47	16.97	18.28	23.95	26.07	31.50	38.37	47.07	47.37	..	Agriculture
81.93	88.40	100.80	112.71	120.81	111.63	109.93	108.48	128.74	176.82	..	Industry
14.63	16.58	19.91	26.13	29.08	34.77	34.31	32.77	34.98	44.61	..	Manufacturing
55.31	63.33	72.67	81.09	93.64	105.88	112.14	114.11	129.70	153.39	..	Services, etc.
77.94	81.33	92.88	98.55	106.05	87.25	99.83	94.88	116.00	180.10	..	Gross Domestic Saving
73.84	76.90	88.14	92.82	101.12	84.12	94.92	85.26	105.67	164.37	..	Gross National Saving
			(Billions of 1987 Algerian Dinars)								
240.45	256.13	271.01	286.80	303.62	306.94	305.27	294.43	304.14	298.45	..	Gross National Product
247.90	263.86	278.07	294.31	310.89	314.20	312.71	304.70	316.70	310.23	H	GDP at Market Prices
-19.72	-15.36	-16.32	-15.46	-13.88	-4.11	5.95	10.13	10.77	14.36	..	Resource Balance
33.76	37.20	39.51	41.76	43.06	43.49	45.83	47.35	50.52	53.70	..	Exports of Goods & NF Services
53.47	52.57	55.82	57.22	56.93	47.60	39.89	37.21	39.74	39.35	..	Imports of Goods & NF Services
285.14	291.76	309.42	322.77	328.55	325.01	306.76	302.65	313.04	301.95	..	Domestic Absorption
139.93	143.71	152.62	160.86	164.40	166.54	154.88	154.57	159.21	151.09	..	Private Consumption, etc.
45.44	47.99	50.53	53.51	56.29	57.31	58.00	59.27	62.18	60.31	..	General Gov't Consumption
99.76	100.06	106.27	108.39	107.85	101.16	93.88	88.81	91.65	90.55	..	Gross Domestic Investment
94.41	97.09	102.08	105.75	107.91	103.51	92.88	88.30	88.57	90.25	..	Fixed Investment
195.18	208.60	222.54	233.41	249.72	255.80	253.58	250.74	258.55	247.32	..	GDP at factor cost
23.03	21.19	20.72	22.19	28.03	29.53	31.50	29.90	33.63	27.92	..	Agriculture
85.80	94.75	102.28	106.10	110.33	112.75	109.93	111.75	111.57	113.20	..	Industry
25.95	27.92	30.99	33.40	35.40	35.85	34.31	33.44	32.40	31.70	..	Manufacturing
86.36	92.66	99.53	105.12	111.37	113.52	112.14	109.09	113.35	106.20	..	Services, etc.
											Memo Items:
59.90	56.05	60.51	62.80	65.84	36.27	45.83	36.26	39.43	49.54	..	Capacity to Import
26.14	18.85	21.00	21.04	22.78	-7.21	0.00	-11.09	-11.09	-4.16	..	Terms of Trade Adjustment
274.05	282.71	299.07	315.35	333.67	306.98	312.71	293.61	305.61	306.07	..	Gross Domestic Income
266.60	274.97	292.01	307.84	326.40	299.73	305.27	283.34	293.05	294.29	..	Gross National Income
			(Index 1987 = 100)								**DOMESTIC PRICES/DEFLATORS**
77.2	78.7	84.1	89.7	93.8	94.4	100.0	104.0	118.2	151.8	..	Overall (GDP)
64.7	69.8	73.9	79.9	85.9	95.0	100.0	105.1	119.8	147.8	..	Domestic Absorption
72.0	77.7	81.9	82.4	85.4	88.3	100.0	128.4	140.0	169.7	..	Agriculture
95.5	93.3	98.6	106.2	109.5	99.0	100.0	97.1	115.4	156.2	..	Industry
56.4	59.4	64.3	78.2	82.1	97.0	100.0	98.0	108.0	140.7	..	Manufacturing
61.3	65.4	69.3	75.0	82.8	93.1	100.0	105.9	115.8	135.0	..	Consumer Price Index
											MANUFACTURING ACTIVITY
..	..	..	..	..	..	..	..	..	..	..	Employment (1987=100)
..	..	..	..	..	..	..	..	..	..	..	Real Earnings per Empl. (1987=100)
..	..	..	..	..	..	..	..	..	..	..	Real Output per Empl. (1987=100)
..	..	..	..	..	..	..	..	..	..	..	Earnings as % of Value Added
			(Billions of current Algerian Dinars)								**MONETARY HOLDINGS**
121.23	154.12	185.02	216.63	249.46	257.68	295.89	339.14	366.26	408.07	D	Money Supply, Broadly Defined
97.92	125.30	152.76	180.43	202.23	204.82	223.91	252.21	250.01	270.08	..	Money
48.06	49.16	60.02	67.46	76.64	89.36	96.87	109.75	119.87	134.94	..	Currency Outside Banks
49.87	76.14	92.74	112.97	125.59	115.46	127.04	142.45	130.14	135.14	..	Demand Deposits
23.31	28.82	32.26	36.20	47.23	52.87	71.98	86.94	116.25	137.99	..	Quasi-Money
			(Millions of current Algerian Dinars)								**GOVERNMENT DEFICIT (-) OR SURPLUS**
..	..	..	..	..	..	..	..	..	..	..	Current Revenue
..	..	..	..	..	..	..	..	..	..	..	Current Expenditure
..	..	..	..	..	..	..	..	..	..	..	Current Budget Balance
..	..	..	..	..	..	..	..	..	..	..	Capital Receipts
..	..	..	..	..	..	..	..	..	..	..	Capital Payments

ALGERIA	1970	1971	1972	1973	1974	1975	1976	1977	1978	1979	1980
FOREIGN TRADE (CUSTOMS BASIS)					*(Millions of current US dollars)*						
Value of Exports, fob	1,009	857	1,306	1,906	4,260	4,291	4,972	5,809	6,126	9,863	15,624
Nonfuel Primary Products	232	142	165	262	234	233	274	195	206	184	194
Fuels	709	641	1,074	1,582	3,941	3,964	4,654	5,577	5,885	9,640	15,381
Manufactures	68	73	67	62	86	94	44	38	35	40	49
Value of Imports, cif	1,257	1,227	1,492	2,259	4,036	5,974	5,307	7,102	8,667	8,407	10,525
Nonfuel Primary Products	233	263	353	473	1,040	1,520	1,109	1,520	1,726	1,878	2,718
Fuels	27	43	34	36	60	102	84	97	130	165	259
Manufactures	998	922	1,105	1,749	2,936	4,353	4,113	5,485	6,812	6,364	7,548
					(Index 1987 = 100)						
Terms of Trade	34.7	42.2	37.0	40.7	113.0	103.0	110.2	110.4	99.4	123.0	179.3
Export Prices, fob	10.4	12.7	13.1	18.4	67.9	66.4	70.5	76.1	76.9	109.8	178.4
Import Prices, cif	30.0	30.1	35.4	45.4	60.1	64.4	64.0	69.0	77.4	89.3	99.5
BALANCE OF PAYMENTS					*(Millions of current US dollars)*						
Exports of Goods & Services	1,129	935	1,348	2,133	5,268	4,854	5,536	6,384	6,735	10,109	14,500
Merchandise, fob	1,010	816	1,224	1,950	4,944	4,501	5,221	6,009	6,340	9,484	13,652
Nonfactor Services	98	107	106	160	176	281	235	288	326	468	476
Factor Services	21	11	18	23	148	73	80	87	69	156	372
Imports of Goods & Services	1,487	1,339	1,740	2,914	5,015	6,888	6,822	8,988	10,588	12,061	14,552
Merchandise, fob	1,078	996	1,303	2,141	3,667	5,452	4,693	6,198	7,293	7,805	9,596
Nonfactor Services	245	246	326	513	715	1,009	1,299	1,532	1,959	2,391	2,715
Factor Services	164	97	111	259	633	427	830	1,259	1,336	1,865	2,241
Long-Term Interest	10	17	52	69	220	217	348	417	614	1,253	1,436
Private Current Transfers, net	195	225	224	337	319	355	386	278	295	313	277
Workers' Remittances	211	238	272	332	351	412	433	349	393	417	406
Curr. A/C Bal before Off. Transf.	-163	-180	-167	-444	572	-1,678	-900	-2,327	-3,558	-1,639	225
Net Official Transfers	37	222	41	-2	-396	20	18	4	20	8	24
Curr. A/C Bal after Off. Transf.	-125	42	-126	-445	176	-1,658	-882	-2,323	-3,538	-1,631	249
Long-Term Capital, net	59	4	199	1,015	529	1,373	1,740	1,897	3,647	2,432	897
Direct Investment	45	-151	17	50	358	85	184	173	135	10	315
Long-Term Loans	279	257	281	1,366	350	1,308	1,644	2,496	4,208	2,834	916
Disbursements	313	310	420	1,599	842	1,560	2,084	3,142	5,112	4,397	3,398
Repayments	35	53	138	233	492	252	440	646	904	1,563	2,481
Other Long-Term Capital	-265	-102	-100	-402	-179	-19	-87	-772	-696	-412	-334
Other Capital, net	-16	-46	2	14	-141	-49	-235	79	-16	-317	195
Change in Reserves	83	0	-75	-583	-564	334	-622	347	-93	-484	-1,341
Memo Item:					*(Algerian Dinars per US dollar)*						
Conversion Factor (Annual Avg)	4.940	4.910	4.480	3.960	4.180	3.950	4.160	4.150	3.970	3.850	3.840
EXTERNAL DEBT (Total)				*(Millions of US dollars), outstanding at end of year*							
	945	1,261	1,550	2,991	3,416	4,633	6,149	10,618	15,750	18,519	19,377
Long-Term Debt (by debtor)	945	1,261	1,550	2,991	3,416	4,633	6,149	8,932	13,765	16,586	17,052
Central Bank, incl. IMF credit	20	51	236	948	887	1,222	1,448	1,831	2,844	3,173	3,076
Central Government	438	484	487	623	703	695	687	752	837	1,027	1,017
Rest of General Government	0	0	0	0	0	0	0	0	0	0	1
Non-financial Public Enterprises	487	725	828	1,420	1,826	2,715	4,015	6,349	10,084	12,386	12,958
Priv. Sector, incl non-guaranteed	0	0	0	0	0	0	0	0	0	0	0
Short-Term Debt	0	0	0	0	0	0	0	1,686	1,985	1,933	2,325
Memo Items:					*(Millions of US dollars)*						
Int'l Reserves Excluding Gold	147.9	298.6	285.1	912.2	1,454.3	1,128.3	1,764.9	1,683.6	1,980.5	2,658.8	3,772.6
Gold Holdings (at market price)	204.4	238.7	355.1	614.1	1,020.4	767.4	737.3	907.1	1,249.1	2,858.5	3,291.2
SOCIAL INDICATORS											
Total Fertility Rate	7.4	7.4	7.4	7.3	7.3	7.3	7.2	7.2	7.0	6.9	6.7
Infant Mortality Rate	139.2	135.6	132.0	128.0	124.0	120.0	116.0	112.0	107.2	102.4	97.6
Life Expectancy at Birth	53.3	53.9	54.5	55.1	55.7	56.3	56.9	57.5	58.1	58.7	59.3
Urban Population, % of total	39.5	39.7	39.8	40.0	40.1	40.3	40.9	41.5	42.2	42.8	43.4
Food Prod. per capita (1987=100)	131.4	127.7	115.8	108.3	110.8	123.6	107.3	84.8	85.9	87.7	100.2
Labor Force, Agriculture (%)	47.3	45.5	43.8	42.1	40.6	39.2	37.4	35.7	34.1	32.6	31.1
Labor Force, Female (%)	6.0	6.3	6.5	6.7	6.9	7.1	7.3	7.6	7.8	8.0	8.2
Primary Schl. Enroll. Ratio	76.0	..	..	..	..	93.0	..	95.0	95.0	95.0	94.0
Primary Schl. Enroll. Ratio, Female	58.0	..	..	..	..	75.0	..	79.0	80.0	81.0	81.0
Secondary Schl. Enroll. Ratio	11.0	..	..	..	..	20.0	23.0	27.0	29.0	31.0	33.0

1981	1982	1983	1984	1985	1986	1987	1988	1989	1990 estimate	Notes	ALGERIA
				(Millions of current US dollars)							**FOREIGN TRADE (CUSTOMS BASIS)**
13,296	11,476	11,158	11,886	10,149	7,831	8,186	8,164	10,802	12,730	..	Value of Exports, fob
202	148	105	110	98	88	71	105	138	195	..	Nonfuel Primary Products
13,027	11,239	10,971	11,592	9,898	7,636	7,974	7,741	10,242	11,941	..	Fuels
67	89	82	184	153	107	141	318	421	594	..	Manufactures
11,302	10,679	10,332	10,263	9,814	9,234	7,029	7,397	8,924	10,433	..	Value of Imports, cif
2,865	2,658	2,728	2,537	3,050	2,540	2,384	2,594	3,130	3,659	..	Nonfuel Primary Products
230	165	214	211	184	274	160	171	206	241	..	Fuels
8,207	7,856	7,390	7,515	6,579	6,420	4,484	4,632	5,589	6,534	..	Manufactures
				(Index 1987 = 100)							
202.7	190.7	176.9	174.7	173.6	90.5	100.0	74.1	88.2	99.2	..	Terms of Trade
199.6	180.6	164.4	160.3	155.9	88.4	100.0	82.2	98.8	121.7	..	Export Prices, fob
98.4	94.7	93.0	91.7	89.8	97.6	100.0	110.9	112.0	122.7	..	Import Prices, cif
				(Millions of current US dollars)							**BALANCE OF PAYMENTS**
15,072	14,366	13,608	13,570	13,756	8,785	9,704	8,162	10,141	13,535	f	Exports of Goods & Services
14,117	13,509	12,742	12,792	13,034	8,065	9,029	7,620	9,534	12,964	..	Merchandise, fob
474	528	679	599	531	549	565	470	496	498	..	Nonfactor Services
481	328	186	179	191	172	110	71	111	73	..	Factor Services
15,291	14,878	13,931	13,676	13,120	11,779	10,080	10,592	11,762	12,448	f	Imports of Goods & Services
10,088	9,889	9,516	9,235	8,811	7,879	6,616	6,675	8,372	8,777	..	Merchandise, fob
2,720	2,670	2,436	2,583	2,573	2,035	1,455	1,347	1,231	1,328	..	Nonfactor Services
2,483	2,319	1,979	1,859	1,736	1,865	2,009	2,571	2,159	2,343	..	Factor Services
1,361	1,427	1,274	1,376	1,409	1,564	1,576	1,811	1,887	1,914	..	Long-Term Interest
304	347	237	186	367	765	522	385	535	332	..	Private Current Transfers, net
447	507	392	329	313	358	487	379	345	352	..	Workers' Remittances
85	-165	-86	80	1,004	-2,229	146	-2,045	-1,087	1,419	..	Curr. A/C Bal before Off. Transf.
5	-18	1	-5	11	-1	-5	5	6	1	..	Net Official Transfers
90	-183	-85	74	1,015	-2,230	141	-2,040	-1,081	1,420	..	Curr. A/C Bal after Off. Transf.
6	-956	-852	-404	-36	353	21	764	715	-926	f	Long-Term Capital, net
-1	-65	-14	-14	-2	11	-11	8	4	-4	..	Direct Investment
246	-338	206	567	484	960	735	1,432	-197	-589	..	Long-Term Loans
2,798	2,617	3,523	4,175	3,988	4,545	4,575	5,912	5,024	5,568	..	Disbursements
2,552	2,955	3,317	3,608	3,504	3,585	3,840	4,480	5,221	6,156	..	Repayments
-239	-553	-1,044	-958	-518	-617	-703	-676	907	-333	..	Other Long-Term Capital
24	69	517	-3	42	379	-514	316	-407	-411	f	Other Capital, net
-120	1,070	421	333	-1,020	1,498	352	960	774	-84	..	Change in Reserves
				(Algerian Dinars per US dollar)							**Memo Item:**
4.320	4.590	4.790	4.980	5.030	4.700	4.850	5.910	7.610	8.960	..	Conversion Factor (Annual Avg)
				(Millions of US dollars), outstanding at end of year							
18,397	17,728	16,285	15,944	18,374	22,796	24,748	25,074	26,063	26,806	..	**EXTERNAL DEBT (Total)**
16,090	14,977	14,328	14,185	16,512	19,644	23,432	23,454	24,223	24,986	..	Long-Term Debt (by debtor)
2,981	2,854	2,661	4,119	6,652	9,821	12,255	13,697	14,421	15,358	..	Central Bank, incl. IMF credit
1,062	1,037	1,062	830	1,035	1,231	1,976	2,469	2,595	2,845	..	Central Government
3	42	125	277	324	295	243	20	11	15	..	Rest of General Government
12,044	11,044	10,481	8,958	8,501	8,297	8,958	7,260	7,183	6,736	..	Non-financial Public Enterprises
0	0	0	0	0	0	0	7	14	31	..	Priv. Sector, incl non-guaranteed
2,307	2,751	1,957	1,759	1,862	3,152	1,315	1,620	1,840	1,820	..	Short-Term Debt
				(Millions of US dollars)							**Memo Items:**
3,695.4	2,422.0	1,880.4	1,464.2	2,819.0	1,660.2	1,640.5	900.2	847.0	724.8	..	Int'l Reserves Excluding Gold
2,219.3	2,550.8	2,129.8	1,721.2	1,825.6	2,182.3	2,702.6	2,290.4	2,238.7	1,978.7	..	Gold Holdings (at market price)
											SOCIAL INDICATORS
6.5	6.4	6.2	6.0	5.8	5.7	5.5	5.4	5.2	5.1	..	Total Fertility Rate
92.8	88.0	85.2	82.4	79.6	76.8	74.0	71.5	69.0	66.5	..	Infant Mortality Rate
59.9	60.5	61.2	61.9	62.6	63.3	64.0	64.5	64.9	65.4	..	Life Expectancy at Birth
44.2	45.0	45.9	46.7	47.5	48.3	49.2	50.0	50.9	51.7	..	Urban Population, % of total
88.8	76.5	79.8	83.8	101.2	96.4	100.0	86.4	87.4	91.0	..	Food Prod. per capita (1987=100)
..	..	..	..	..	..	..	..	..	..	..	Labor Force, Agriculture (%)
8.4	8.5	8.7	8.8	8.9	9.1	9.2	9.3	9.5	9.6	..	Labor Force, Female (%)
..	94.0	94.0	94.0	92.0	95.0	96.0	95.0	94.0	95.0	..	Primary Schl. Enroll. Ratio
81.0	81.0	82.0	83.0	82.0	85.0	87.0	86.0	86.0	88.0	..	Primary Schl. Enroll. Ratio, Female
..	..	43.0	47.0	50.0	53.0	55.0	60.0	61.0	..	..	Secondary Schl. Enroll. Ratio

ANTIGUA AND BARBUDA	1970	1971	1972	1973	1974	1975	1976	1977	1978	1979	1980
CURRENT GNP PER CAPITA (US $)	..	..	..	..	..	..	..	..	..	..	..
POPULATION (thousands)	66	67	68	69	70	71	72	73	74	75	75
USE AND ORIGIN OF RESOURCES					*(Millions of current Eastern Caribbean Dollars)*						
Gross National Product (GNP)	91.70	95.90	109.30	118.20	131.50	142.10	135.10	162.20	182.70	229.30	299.80
Net Factor Income from Abroad	0.00	0.00	0.00	0.00	0.00	0.00	0.00	-0.30	-2.20	-4.90	-3.20
GDP at Market Prices	91.70	95.90	109.30	118.20	131.50	142.10	135.10	162.50	184.90	234.20	303.00
Resource Balance	..	..	..	..	..	..	..	..	..	-75.10	-74.80
Exports of Goods & NFServices	..	..	..	..	..	..	..	..	..	135.50	281.10
Imports of Goods & NFServices	..	..	..	..	..	..	..	..	..	210.60	355.90
Domestic Absorption	..	..	..	..	..	..	..	..	..	..	..
Private Consumption, etc.	..	..	..	..	..	..	..	..	..	..	..
General Gov't Consumption	..	..	..	..	..	..	..	..	..	..	..
Gross Domestic Investment	..	..	..	..	..	..	..	..	..	..	..
Fixed Investment	..	..	..	..	..	..	..	..	..	..	..
Indirect Taxes, net	..	..	..	..	..	..	..	20.50	25.60	16.80	45.80
GDP at factor cost	..	..	..	..	..	..	..	142.00	159.30	217.40	257.20
Agriculture	..	..	..	..	..	..	..	..	..	..	18.30
Industry	..	..	..	..	..	..	..	..	..	..	46.60
Manufacturing	..	..	..	..	..	..	..	..	..	..	13.70
Services, etc.	..	..	..	..	..	..	..	..	..	..	192.30
Gross Domestic Saving	..	..	..	..	..	..	..	..	..	..	..
Gross National Saving	..	..	..	..	..	..	..	..	..	..	..
					(Millions of 1987 Eastern Caribbean Dollars)						
Gross National Product	..	..	..	..	..	..	..	..	..	..	480.37
GDP at Market Prices	..	..	..	..	..	..	..	..	..	..	485.33
Resource Balance	..	..	..	..	..	..	..	..	..	..	..
Exports of Goods & NFServices	..	..	..	..	..	..	..	..	..	..	..
Imports of Goods & NFServices	..	..	..	..	..	..	..	..	..	..	..
Domestic Absorption	..	..	..	..	..	..	..	..	..	..	..
Private Consumption, etc.	..	..	..	..	..	..	..	..	..	..	..
General Gov't Consumption	..	..	..	..	..	..	..	..	..	..	..
Gross Domestic Investment	..	..	..	..	..	..	..	..	..	..	..
Fixed Investment	..	..	..	..	..	..	..	..	..	..	..
GDP at factor cost	..	..	..	..	..	..	..	302.07	343.37	366.23	412.60
Agriculture	..	..	..	..	..	..	..	34.32	45.84	36.41	36.41
Industry	..	..	..	..	..	..	..	42.00	51.60	55.60	71.80
Manufacturing	..	..	..	..	..	..	..	10.54	11.82	13.67	16.24
Services, etc.	..	..	..	..	..	..	..	225.75	245.93	274.22	304.39
Memo Items:											
Capacity to Import	..	..	..	..	..	..	..	..	..	..	..
Terms of Trade Adjustment	..	..	..	..	..	..	..	..	..	..	..
Gross Domestic Income	..	..	..	..	..	..	..	..	..	..	..
Gross National Income	..	..	..	..	..	..	..	..	..	..	..
DOMESTIC PRICES/DEFLATORS					*(Index 1987 = 100)*						
Overall (GDP)	..	..	..	..	..	..	..	..	..	..	62.4
Domestic Absorption	..	..	..	..	..	..	..	..	..	..	..
Agriculture	..	..	..	..	..	..	..	..	..	..	50.3
Industry	..	..	..	..	..	..	..	..	..	..	64.9
Manufacturing	..	..	..	..	..	..	..	..	..	..	84.4
Consumer Price Index	..	..	..	..	..	..	..	..	..	..	..
MANUFACTURING ACTIVITY											
Employment (1987=100)	..	..	..	..	..	..	..	..	..	..	..
Real Earnings per Empl. (1987=100)	..	..	..	..	..	..	..	..	..	..	..
Real Output per Empl. (1987=100)	..	..	..	..	..	..	..	..	..	..	..
Earnings as % of Value Added	..	..	..	..	..	..	..	..	..	..	..
MONETARY HOLDINGS					*(Millions of current Eastern Caribbean Dollars)*						
Money Supply, Broadly Defined	..	..	..	..	..	98.02	106.49	102.53	113.21	130.74	145.37
Money	..	..	..	..	..	18.97	24.26	30.91	29.37	34.81	38.57
Currency Outside Banks	..	..	..	..	..	10.77	11.92	13.15	15.13	17.09	15.26
Demand Deposits	..	..	..	..	..	8.20	12.35	17.76	14.24	17.72	23.31
Quasi-Money	..	..	..	..	..	79.05	82.23	71.61	83.84	95.93	106.79
GOVERNMENT DEFICIT (-) OR SURPLUS					*(Millions of current Eastern Caribbean Dollars)*						
Current Revenue	..	..	..	..	..	..	..	..	..	..	..
Current Expenditure	..	..	..	..	..	..	..	..	..	..	..
Current Budget Balance	..	..	..	..	..	..	..	..	..	..	..
Capital Receipts	..	..	..	..	..	..	..	..	..	..	..
Capital Payments	..	..	..	..	..	..	..	..	..	..	..

1981	1982	1983	1984	1985	1986	1987	1988	1989	1990 estimate	Notes	ANTIGUA AND BARBUDA
..	1,780	2,030	2,260	2,540	2,980	3,080	3,640	4,080	4,600	..	**CURRENT GNP PER CAPITA (US $)**
75	75	75	76	76	76	77	77	78	79	..	**POPULATION (thousands)**
											USE AND ORIGIN OF RESOURCES
			(Millions of current Eastern Caribbean Dollars)								
334.90	364.20	419.90	469.20	536.90	628.60	667.10	840.82	904.64	1,007.65	..	Gross National Product (GNP)
-5.40	-10.00	-2.70	-1.10	-7.30	-24.30	-93.20	-95.58	-110.16	-122.85	..	Net Factor Income from Abroad
340.30	374.20	422.60	470.30	544.20	652.90	760.30	936.40	1,014.80	1,130.50	..	GDP at Market Prices
-110.90	-127.70	-50.50	-36.50	-93.40	-374.50	-239.50	..	..	..	..	Resource Balance
280.60	272.70	268.10	451.70	482.30	540.20	594.50					Exports of Goods & NF Services
391.50	400.40	318.60	488.20	575.70	914.70	834.00					Imports of Goods & NF Services
..	..	..	..	..	..	..	..	..	..	..	Domestic Absorption
..	..	..	..	..	..	..	..	..	..	..	Private Consumption, etc.
..	..	..	..	..	..	..	..	..	..	..	General Gov't Consumption
..	..	..	..	..	..	..	..	..	..	..	Gross Domestic Investment
..	..	..	..	..	..	..	..	..	..	..	Fixed Investment
50.90	57.10	66.50	65.90	79.40	115.80	129.50	148.00	153.50	163.80	..	Indirect Taxes, net
289.40	317.10	356.10	404.40	464.80	537.10	630.80	788.40	861.30	966.70	..	GDP at factor cost
18.60	19.70	21.80	19.30	23.20	24.60	29.60	34.30	37.10	40.90	..	Agriculture
53.40	46.30	50.70	63.10	77.80	101.90	131.40	173.20	201.10	228.40	..	Industry
14.60	16.80	17.60	19.30	20.30	21.50	23.50	27.90	30.50	34.70	..	Manufacturing
217.40	251.10	283.60	322.00	363.80	410.60	469.80	580.90	623.10	697.40	..	Services, etc.
..	..	..	..	..	..	..	..	..	..	..	Gross Domestic Saving
..	..	..	..	..	..	..	..	..	..	..	Gross National Saving
			(Millions of 1987 Eastern Caribbean Dollars)								
500.06	499.80	547.80	577.46	616.23	688.46	667.10	723.73	738.22	763.15	..	Gross National Product
508.36	513.23	551.18	579.16	627.43	705.16	760.30	806.15	828.25	856.35	..	GDP at Market Prices
..	..	..	..	..	..	..	..	..	..	..	Resource Balance
..	..	..	..	..	..	..	..	..	..	..	Exports of Goods & NF Services
..	..	..	..	..	..	..	..	..	..	..	Imports of Goods & NF Services
..	..	..	..	..	..	..	..	..	..	..	Domestic Absorption
..	..	..	..	..	..	..	..	..	..	..	Private Consumption, etc.
..	..	..	..	..	..	..	..	..	..	..	General Gov't Consumption
..	..	..	..	..	..	..	..	..	..	..	Gross Domestic Investment
..	..	..	..	..	..	..	..	..	..	..	Fixed Investment
432.89	435.21	465.13	498.38	536.10	580.30	630.80	678.76	702.97	732.34	..	GDP at factor cost
32.48	30.65	30.39	24.36	24.88	26.46	29.60	31.17	31.96	33.27	..	Agriculture
81.60	67.80	68.40	74.60	87.00	108.00	131.40	146.20	162.20	168.00	..	Industry
19.80	19.80	20.22	21.08	21.65	22.50	23.50	23.93	24.64	25.35	..	Manufacturing
318.81	336.76	366.34	399.42	424.22	445.84	469.80	501.39	508.81	531.07	..	Services, etc.
											Memo Items:
..	..	..	..	..	..	..	..	..	..		Capacity to Import
..	..	..	..	..	..	..	..	..	..		Terms of Trade Adjustment
..	..	..	..	..	..	..	..	..	..		Gross Domestic Income
..	..	..	..	..	..	..	..	..	..		Gross National Income
											DOMESTIC PRICES/DEFLATORS
			(Index 1987 = 100)								
66.9	72.9	76.7	81.2	86.7	92.6	100.0	116.2	122.5	132.0	..	Overall (GDP)
..	..	..	..	..	..	..	..	..	..	..	Domestic Absorption
57.3	64.3	71.7	79.2	93.2	93.0	100.0	110.0	116.1	122.9	..	Agriculture
65.4	68.3	74.1	84.6	89.4	94.4	100.0	118.5	124.0	136.0	..	Industry
73.7	84.9	87.0	91.6	93.8	95.5	100.0	116.6	123.8	136.9	..	Manufacturing
..	..	..	..	..	..	..	..	..	..		Consumer Price Index
											MANUFACTURING ACTIVITY
..	..	..	..	..	..	..	..	..	..		Employment (1987=100)
..	..	..	..	..	..	..	..	..	..		Real Earnings per Empl. (1987=100)
..	..	..	..	..	..	..	..	..	..		Real Output per Empl. (1987=100)
..	..	..	..	..	..	..	..	..	..		Earnings as % of Value Added
											MONETARY HOLDINGS
			(Millions of current Eastern Caribbean Dollars)								
168.54	191.25	236.80	286.08	319.92	378.13	449.44	499.84	566.12	593.07	..	Money Supply, Broadly Defined
43.16	41.70	51.10	58.40	68.45	87.37	110.62	128.19	141.09	156.74	..	Money
16.27	16.32	17.47	23.97	26.50	32.46	42.24	51.31	61.47	57.52	..	Currency Outside Banks
26.89	25.38	33.62	34.44	41.95	54.91	68.39	76.88	79.63	99.22	..	Demand Deposits
125.38	149.55	185.71	227.68	251.47	290.76	338.82	371.64	425.03	436.34	..	Quasi-Money
			(Millions of current Eastern Caribbean Dollars)								
											GOVERNMENT DEFICIT (-) OR SURPLUS
..	..	..	..	..	..	..	..	..	..		Current Revenue
..	..	..	..	..	..	..	..	..	..		Current Expenditure
..	..	..	..	..	..	..	..	..	..		Current Budget Balance
..	..	..	..	..	..	..	..	..	..		Capital Receipts
..	..	..	..	..	..	..	..	..	..		Capital Payments

ANTIGUA AND BARBUDA	1970	1971	1972	1973	1974	1975	1976	1977	1978	1979	1980

FOREIGN TRADE (CUSTOMS BASIS)
(Millions of current US dollars)

	1970	1971	1972	1973	1974	1975	1976	1977	1978	1979	1980
Value of Exports, fob	..	..	..	..	..	..	..	..	..	..	..
Nonfuel Primary Products	..	..	..	..	..	..	..	..	..	..	..
Fuels	..	..	..	..	..	..	..	..	..	..	..
Manufactures	..	..	..	..	..	..	..	..	..	..	..
Value of Imports, cif	..	..	..	..	..	..	..	..	..	..	..
Nonfuel Primary Products	..	..	..	..	..	..	..	..	..	..	..
Fuels	..	..	..	..	..	..	..	..	..	..	..
Manufactures	..	..	..	..	..	..	..	..	..	..	..

Terms of Trade *(Index 1987 = 100)*

	1970	1971	1972	1973	1974	1975	1976	1977	1978	1979	1980
Export Prices, fob	..	..	..	..	..	..	..	..	..	..	..
Import Prices, cif	..	..	..	..	..	..	..	..	..	..	..

BALANCE OF PAYMENTS
(Millions of current US dollars)

	1970	1971	1972	1973	1974	1975	1976	1977	1978	1979	1980
Exports of Goods & Services	..	..	..	..	..	..	..	31.60	42.20	51.00	106.90
Merchandise, fob	..	..	..	..	..	..	..	6.60	12.60	12.00	59.50
Nonfactor Services	..	..	..	..	..	..	..	24.70	29.50	38.20	44.60
Factor Services	..	..	..	..	..	..	..	0.30	0.10	0.80	2.80
Imports of Goods & Services	..	..	..	..	..	..	..	44.00	49.60	80.60	135.80
Merchandise, fob	..	..	..	..	..	..	..	37.00	42.09	67.72	114.72
Nonfactor Services	..	..	..	..	..	..	..	6.50	7.01	10.28	17.09
Factor Services	..	..	..	..	..	..	..	0.50	0.50	2.60	4.00
Long-Term Interest	..	..	..	..	..	..	..	..	..	..	..
Private Current Transfers, net	..	..	..	..	..	..	..	1.20	3.70	8.20	7.00
Workers' Remittances	..	..	..	..	..	..	..	..	..	..	..
Curr. A/C Bal before Off. Transf.	..	..	..	..	..	..	..	-11.20	-3.70	-21.40	-21.90
Net Official Transfers	..	..	..	..	..	..	..	1.60	1.50	1.90	3.10
Curr. A/C Bal after Off. Transf.	..	..	..	..	..	..	..	-9.60	-2.20	-19.50	-18.80
Long-Term Capital, net	..	..	..	..	..	..	..	8.84	3.50	17.43	23.57
Direct Investment	..	..	..	..	..	..	..	2.20	-6.90	8.50	19.60
Long-Term Loans	..	..	..	..	..	..	..	..	..	..	..
Disbursements	..	..	..	..	..	..	..	..	..	..	..
Repayments	..	..	..	..	..	..	..	..	..	..	..
Other Long-Term Capital	..	..	..	..	..	..	..	6.64	10.40	8.93	3.97
Other Capital, net	..	..	..	..	..	..	..	-3.71	-0.53	7.43	-7.98
Change in Reserves	..	..	..	..	..	..	-2.35	4.46	-0.77	-5.36	3.21

Memo Item:
(Eastern Caribbean Dollars per US dollar)

	1970	1971	1972	1973	1974	1975	1976	1977	1978	1979	1980
Conversion Factor (Annual Avg)	2.000	1.970	1.920	1.960	2.050	2.170	2.610	2.700	2.700	2.700	2.700

EXTERNAL DEBT (Total)
(Millions of US dollars), outstanding at end of year

	1970	1971	1972	1973	1974	1975	1976	1977	1978	1979	1980
EXTERNAL DEBT (Total)	..	..	..	..	..	..	..	..	..	..	..
Long-Term Debt (by debtor)	..	..	..	..	..	..	..	..	..	..	..
Central Bank, incl. IMF credit	..	..	..	..	..	..	..	..	..	..	..
Central Government	..	..	..	..	..	..	..	..	..	..	..
Rest of General Government	..	..	..	..	..	..	..	..	..	..	..
Non-financial Public Enterprises	..	..	..	..	..	..	..	..	..	..	..
Priv. Sector, incl non-guaranteed	..	..	..	..	..	..	..	..	..	..	..
Short-Term Debt	..	..	..	..	..	..	..	..	..	..	..

Memo Items:
(Thousands of US dollars)

	1970	1971	1972	1973	1974	1975	1976	1977	1978	1979	1980
Int'l Reserves Excluding Gold	..	..	..	..	..	7,316	9,666	5,104	5,973	11,233	7,817
Gold Holdings (at market price)	..	..	..	..	..	..	..	..	..	..	..

SOCIAL INDICATORS

	1970	1971	1972	1973	1974	1975	1976	1977	1978	1979	1980
Total Fertility Rate	..	..	2.6	2.6	2.5	2.4	2.4	2.3	2.2	2.2	2.1
Infant Mortality Rate	..	..	..	..	..	..	..	..	..	..	31.5
Life Expectancy at Birth	66.9	67.3	67.8	68.2	68.7	69.1	69.6	70.0	70.4	70.9	71.3
Urban Population, % of total	33.7	33.1	32.5	32.0	31.4	30.8	30.8	30.8	30.8	30.8	30.8
Food Prod. per capita (1987=100)	79.8	121.9	74.4	74.5	73.5	70.7	72.7	74.6	86.8	75.0	84.5
Labor Force, Agriculture (%)	..	..	..	..	..	..	..	..	..	..	..
Labor Force, Female (%)	..	..	..	..	..	..	..	..	..	..	..
Primary Schl. Enroll. Ratio	..	..	..	..	..	..	..	..	..	..	..
Primary Schl. Enroll. Ratio, Female	..	..	..	..	..	..	..	..	..	..	..
Secondary Schl. Enroll. Ratio	..	..	..	..	..	..	..	..	..	..	..

1981	1982	1983	1984	1985	1986	1987	1988	1989	1990 estimate	Notes	ANTIGUA AND BARBUDA
				(Millions of current US dollars)							**FOREIGN TRADE (CUSTOMS BASIS)**
..	..	..	..	..	..	..	..	..	..	..	Value of Exports, fob
..	..	..	..	..	..	..	..	..	..	..	Nonfuel Primary Products
..	..	..	..	..	..	..	..	..	..	..	Fuels
..	..	..	..	..	..	..	..	..	..	..	Manufactures
..	..	..	..	..	..	..	..	..	..	..	Value of Imports, cif
..	..	..	..	..	..	..	..	..	..	..	Nonfuel Primary Products
..	..	..	..	..	..	..	..	..	..	..	Fuels
..	..	..	..	..	..	..	..	..	..	..	Manufactures
				(Index 1987 = 100)							
..	..	..	..	..	..	..	..	..	..	..	Terms of Trade
..	..	..	..	..	..	..	..	..	..	..	Export Prices, fob
..	..	..	..	..	..	..	..	..	..	..	Import Prices, cif
				(Millions of current US dollars)							**BALANCE OF PAYMENTS**
107.10	107.60	104.30	172.40	181.00	203.10	222.80	296.98	334.62	358.95	..	Exports of Goods & Services
51.40	49.30	36.50	35.20	28.30	30.90	28.50	30.13	31.63	33.23	..	Merchandise, fob
52.50	51.70	62.80	132.10	150.30	169.70	191.70	263.65	299.39	321.11	..	Nonfactor Services
3.20	6.60	5.00	5.10	2.40	2.50	2.60	3.20	3.60	4.60	..	Factor Services
150.20	158.60	124.00	186.30	218.30	346.90	324.80	398.29	453.63	475.05	..	Imports of Goods & Services
125.26	126.72	99.72	150.17	174.80	284.15	258.25	274.79	317.02	325.93	..	Merchandise, fob
19.74	21.59	18.28	30.63	38.40	55.55	50.65	67.34	75.65	81.76	..	Nonfactor Services
5.20	10.30	6.00	5.50	5.10	7.20	15.90	56.16	60.96	67.37	..	Factor Services
..	..	..	..	..	..	..	..	..	..		Long-Term Interest
7.80	8.70	10.60	12.50	13.50	14.50	17.00	18.92	22.82	19.82	..	Private Current Transfers, net
..	..	..	..	..	..	..	..	..	..		Workers' Remittances
-35.30	-42.30	-9.10	-1.40	-23.80	-129.30	-85.00	-82.39	-96.19	-96.28	..	Curr. A/C Bal before Off. Transf.
2.60	0.70	..	2.00	0.70	2.70	1.70	1.80	0.70	0.80	..	Net Official Transfers
-32.70	-41.60	-9.10	0.60	-23.10	-126.60	-83.30	-80.59	-95.49	-95.48	..	Curr. A/C Bal after Off. Transf.
36.71	30.40	-1.10	-0.40	10.80	121.90	76.60	66.17	51.35	71.17	..	Long-Term Capital, net
22.40	23.00	5.00	4.40	15.60	17.70	29.20	59.46	60.76	84.69	..	Direct Investment
..	..	..	..	..	..	..	..	..	..		Long-Term Loans
..	..	..	..	..	..	..	..	..	..		Disbursements
..	..	..	..	..	..	..	..	..	..		Repayments
14.31	7.40	-6.10	-4.80	-4.80	104.20	47.40	6.71	-9.41	-13.51	..	Other Long-Term Capital
-4.39	12.40	11.60	6.90	15.60	13.90	11.19	14.81	47.14	24.11	..	Other Capital, net
0.38	-1.20	-1.40	-7.10	-3.30	-9.20	-4.49	-0.40	-3.00	0.20	..	Change in Reserves
				(Eastern Caribbean Dollars per US dollar)							**Memo Item:**
2.700	2.700	2.700	2.700	2.700	2.700	2.700	2.700	2.700	2.700	..	Conversion Factor (Annual Avg)
				(Millions of US dollars), outstanding at end of year							**EXTERNAL DEBT (Total)**
..	..	..	..	..	..	..	..	..	..	..	Long-Term Debt (by debtor)
..	..	..	..	..	..	..	..	..	..	..	Central Bank, incl. IMF credit
..	..	..	..	..	..	..	..	..	..	..	Central Government
..	..	..	..	..	..	..	..	..	..	..	Rest of General Government
..	..	..	..	..	..	..	..	..	..	..	Non-financial Public Enterprises
..	..	..	..	..	..	..	..	..	..	..	Priv. Sector, incl non-guaranteed
..	..	..	..	..	..	..	..	..	..	..	Short-Term Debt
				(Thousands of US dollars)							**Memo Items:**
7,336	8,520	9,930	15,440	16,580	28,260	25,600	28,030	28,070	27,500	..	Int'l Reserves Excluding Gold
..	..	..	..	..	..	..	..	..	..	..	Gold Holdings (at market price)
											SOCIAL INDICATORS
2.1	2.0	2.0	2.0	1.9	1.9	1.9	1.9	1.9	1.9	..	Total Fertility Rate
30.1	28.7	27.3	25.8	24.4	23.0	21.6	20.8	20.0	19.2	..	Infant Mortality Rate
71.8	72.2	72.4	72.6	72.8	72.9	73.1	73.3	73.5	73.7	..	Life Expectancy at Birth
30.8	30.8	30.8	30.8	30.8	31.0	31.3	31.5	31.8	32.0	..	Urban Population, % of total
82.9	82.2	82.9	79.9	98.7	99.1	100.0	100.1	98.8	99.3	..	Food Prod. per capita (1987=100)
..	..	..	..	..	..	..	..	..	..	..	Labor Force, Agriculture (%)
..	..	..	..	..	..	..	..	..	..	..	Labor Force, Female (%)
..	..	..	..	..	..	..	..	..	..	..	Primary Schl. Enroll. Ratio
..	..	..	..	..	..	..	..	..	..	..	Primary Schl. Enroll. Ratio, Female
..	..	..	..	..	..	..	..	..	..	..	Secondary Schl. Enroll. Ratio

ARGENTINA	1970	1971	1972	1973	1974	1975	1976	1977	1978	1979	1980
CURRENT GNP PER CAPITA (US $)	1,020	1,070	1,050	1,240	1,630	1,810	1,680	1,610	1,570	1,800	1,970
POPULATION (thousands)	23,962	24,348	24,757	25,183	25,617	26,052	26,489	26,928	27,367	27,803	28,237

USE AND ORIGIN OF RESOURCES

(Billions of current Argentine Australes)

	1970	1971	1972	1973	1974	1975	1976	1977	1978	1979	1980
Gross National Product (GNP)	8.70E-6	1.24E-5	2.04E-5	3.51E-5	4.82E-5	1.42E-4	7.49E-4	2.07E-3	5.17E-3	1.41E-2	2.80E-2
Net Factor Income from Abroad	-1.00E-7	1.00E-7	-2.00E-7	-3.00E-7	-3.00E-7	-1.60E-6	-9.80E-6	-2.70E-5	-5.91E-5	-1.43E-4	-3.33E-4
GDP at Market Prices	8.80E-6	1.23E-5	2.06E-5	3.54E-5	4.85E-5	1.43E-4	7.59E-4	2.09E-3	5.23E-3	1.43E-2	2.83E-2
Resource Balance	0.00E+0	-1.00E-7	1.00E-7	9.00E-7	4.00E-7	-3.00E-7	3.33E-5	6.50E-5	2.05E-4	3.50E-5	-6.16E-4
Exports of Goods & NFServices	8.00E-7	1.00E-6	2.00E-6	3.60E-6	4.50E-6	1.13E-5	9.39E-5	2.73E-4	6.10E-4	1.26E-3	1.94E-3
Imports of Goods & NFServices	8.00E-7	1.10E-6	1.90E-6	2.70E-6	4.10E-6	1.16E-5	6.06E-5	2.08E-4	4.05E-4	1.22E-3	2.56E-3
Domestic Absorption	8.80E-6	1.24E-5	2.05E-5	3.45E-5	4.81E-5	1.44E-4	7.26E-4	2.03E-3	5.03E-3	1.42E-2	2.90E-2
Private Consumption, etc.	6.00E-6	8.50E-6	1.42E-5	2.39E-5	3.21E-5	8.78E-5	4.48E-4	1.26E-3	3.14E-3	9.34E-3	1.89E-2
General Gov't Consumption	9.00E-7	1.30E-6	2.00E-6	4.20E-6	6.60E-6	1.88E-5	7.42E-5	1.97E-4	6.09E-4	1.64E-3	3.74E-3
Gross Domestic Investment	1.90E-6	2.60E-6	4.30E-6	6.40E-6	9.40E-6	3.70E-5	2.04E-4	5.69E-4	1.28E-3	3.24E-3	6.28E-3
Fixed Investment	1.90E-6	2.60E-6	4.30E-6	6.40E-6	9.40E-6	3.70E-5	2.04E-4	5.69E-4	1.28E-3	2.99E-3	5.78E-3
Indirect Taxes, net	1.00E-6	1.40E-6	2.40E-6	4.00E-6	5.50E-6	1.63E-5	8.65E-5	2.39E-4	5.97E-4	1.26E-3	3.23E-3
GDP at factor cost	7.80E-6	1.09E-5	1.82E-5	3.14E-5	4.30E-5	1.27E-4	6.73E-4	1.85E-3	4.64E-3	1.30E-2	2.51E-2
Agriculture	1.02E-6	1.60E-6	2.70E-6	5.00E-6	5.90E-6	1.13E-5	7.38E-5	2.03E-4	4.70E-4	1.33E-3	2.16E-3
Industry	2.96E-6	4.40E-6	7.30E-6	1.19E-5	1.65E-5	5.58E-5	3.01E-4	7.79E-4	1.90E-3	4.95E-3	9.28E-3
Manufacturing	2.10E-6	3.30E-6	5.60E-6	9.00E-6	1.23E-5	4.11E-5	2.22E-4	5.76E-4	1.34E-3	3.50E-3	6.27E-3
Services, etc.	3.82E-6	4.90E-6	8.20E-6	1.45E-5	2.06E-5	5.99E-5	2.98E-4	8.72E-4	2.27E-3	6.70E-3	1.37E-2
Gross Domestic Saving	1.90E-6	2.50E-6	4.40E-6	7.30E-6	9.80E-6	3.67E-5	2.37E-4	6.34E-4	1.48E-3	3.27E-3	5.67E-3
Gross National Saving	1.80E-6	2.60E-6	4.20E-6	7.00E-6	..	3.51E-5	2.28E-4	6.08E-4	1.43E-3	3.13E-3	5.34E-3

(Millions of 1987 Argentine Australes)

	1970	1971	1972	1973	1974	1975	1976	1977	1978	1979	1980
Gross National Product	135,000	142,000	142,000	147,000	155,000	154,000	154,000	164,000	158,000	169,000	172,000
GDP at Market Prices	139,000	145,000	148,000	153,000	162,000	161,000	160,000	171,000	165,000	177,000	181,000
Resource Balance	-2,760	-5,070	-4,260	-2,930	-3,580	-4,710	836	28	2,070	-5,940	-16,600
Exports of Goods & NFServices	9,110	8,200	8,370	9,540	9,560	8,670	11,400	14,500	15,800	15,300	14,500
Imports of Goods & NFServices	11,900	13,300	12,600	12,500	13,100	13,400	10,600	14,500	13,700	21,200	31,100
Domestic Absorption	141,000	150,000	152,000	156,000	165,000	166,000	160,000	171,000	163,000	183,000	197,000
Private Consumption, etc.	103,000	108,000	110,000	115,000	124,000	123,000	115,000	118,000	117,000	132,000	143,000
General Gov't Consumption	6,820	7,130	7,000	7,450	8,030	8,040	8,400	8,760	9,040	9,540	9,670
Gross Domestic Investment	31,100	34,500	34,900	33,200	33,600	34,200	36,600	44,200	37,200	41,000	44,800
Fixed Investment	30,800	33,300	33,700	31,300	32,500	32,600	36,000	43,500	37,900	40,500	42,700
GDP at factor cost	122,000	128,000	130,000	135,000	143,000	142,000	142,000	151,000	146,000	156,000	159,000
Agriculture	13,800	14,000	14,300	15,800	16,300	15,800	16,600	17,000	17,500	18,000	17,000
Industry	59,500	63,400	65,600	66,400	70,400	69,800	70,100	76,000	70,100	75,600	74,700
Manufacturing	..	..	..	..	..	..	..	..	..	..	..
Services, etc.	48,800	50,200	50,300	52,800	55,900	56,300	54,800	57,800	58,100	62,600	67,600

Memo Items:

	1970	1971	1972	1973	1974	1975	1976	1977	1978	1979	1980
Capacity to Import	11,900	12,100	13,300	16,600	14,400	13,000	16,400	19,000	20,700	21,900	23,600
Terms of Trade Adjustment	2,760	3,870	4,930	7,080	4,860	4,360	4,970	4,500	4,880	6,540	9,090
Gross Domestic Income	141,000	149,000	153,000	160,000	167,000	165,000	165,000	175,000	170,000	184,000	190,000
Gross National Income	138,000	145,000	147,000	154,000	160,000	159,000	159,000	168,000	163,000	176,000	181,000

DOMESTIC PRICES/DEFLATORS

(Index 1987 = 100)

	1970	1971	1972	1973	1974	1975	1976	1977	1978	1979	1980
Overall (GDP)	6.35E-6	8.50E-6	1.40E-5	2.31E-5	3.00E-5	8.91E-5	4.73E-4	1.22E-3	3.17E-3	8.05E-3	1.57E-2
Domestic Absorption	6.22E-6	8.28E-6	1.35E-5	2.21E-5	2.91E-5	8.67E-5	4.55E-4	1.19E-3	3.08E-3	7.77E-3	1.47E-2
Agriculture	7.40E-6	1.14E-5	1.89E-5	3.15E-5	3.62E-5	7.14E-5	4.45E-4	1.20E-3	2.69E-3	7.42E-3	1.27E-2
Industry	4.97E-6	6.94E-6	1.11E-5	1.79E-5	2.34E-5	8.00E-5	4.29E-4	1.02E-3	2.70E-3	6.55E-3	1.24E-2
Manufacturing	..	..	..	..	..	..	..	..	..	..	..
Consumer Price Index	6.51E-6	8.77E-6	1.39E-5	2.24E-5	2.77E-5	7.83E-5	4.26E-4	1.17E-3	3.24E-3	8.40E-3	1.69E-2

MANUFACTURING ACTIVITY

	1970	1971	1972	1973	1974	1975	1976	1977	1978	1979	1980
Employment (1987=100)	145	149	152	158	167	172	166	155	140	137	126
Real Earnings per Empl. (1987=100)	91	99	94	102	119	123	80	78	77	87	98
Real Output per Empl. (1987=100)	57	55	57	59	57	53	55	63	62	71	74
Earnings as % of Value Added	30	31	28	32	36	32	20	20	21	23	26

MONETARY HOLDINGS

(Billions of current Argentine Australes)

	1970	1971	1972	1973	1974	1975	1976	1977	1978	1979	1980
Money Supply, Broadly Defined	2.55E-10	3.00E-10	5.30E-10	9.70E-10	1.50E-9	3.60E-9	1.59E-8	5.17E-8	1.46E-7	4.35E-7	8.23E-7
Money	1.76E-10	2.00E-10	3.30E-10	5.70E-10	9.00E-10	2.80E-9	1.05E-8	2.26E-8	5.87E-8	1.40E-7	2.75E-7
Currency Outside Banks	7.62E-11	1.00E-10	1.30E-10	2.70E-10	4.00E-10	1.20E-9	4.10E-9	1.07E-8	3.33E-8	7.87E-8	1.64E-7
Demand Deposits	1.00E-10	1.00E-10	2.00E-10	3.00E-10	5.00E-10	1.60E-9	6.40E-9	1.19E-8	2.54E-8	6.09E-8	1.10E-7
Quasi-Money	7.92E-11	1.00E-10	2.00E-10	4.00E-10	6.00E-10	8.00E-10	5.40E-9	2.91E-8	8.78E-8	2.96E-7	5.48E-7

GOVERNMENT DEFICIT (-) OR SURPLUS

(Millions of current Argentine Australes)

	1970	1971	1972	1973	1974	1975	1976	1977	1978	1979	1980
Current Revenue	..	..	..	..	..	..	..	..	..	..	-1
Current Expenditure	..	..	..	..	..	..	..	..	1	3	6
Current Budget Balance	..	..	..	..	..	..	..	..	1	3	7
Capital Receipts	..	..	..	..	..	..	..	..	0	0	-1
Capital Payments	..	..	..	..	..	..	..	..	0	..	..
										0	1

1981	1982	1983	1984	1985	1986	1987	1988	1989	1990 estimate	Notes	ARGENTINA
1,960	1,880	1,970	2,150	2,130	2,380	2,400	2,560	2,160	2,400	A	CURRENT GNP PER CAPITA (US $)
28,666	29,090	29,508	29,922	30,331	30,735	31,133	31,526	31,913	32,293	..	POPULATION (thousands)
											USE AND ORIGIN OF RESOURCES
				(Billions of current Argentine Australes)							
5.31E-2	1.35E-1	6.26E-1	5.0	36.0	70.0	164.0	773.0	23,018.0	485,000.0	..	Gross National Product (GNP)
-1.64E-3	-1.26E-2	-5.71E-2	-0.4	-3.0	-4.0	-9.0	-48.0	-2,562.0	-29,407.0	..	Net Factor Income from Abroad
5.48E-2	1.48E-1	6.83E-1	5.0	40.0	74.0	173.0	821.0	25,580.0	514,000.0	..	GDP at Market Prices
-2.37E-4	4.76E-3	3.33E-2	0.2	3.0	2.0	0.0	34.0	2,038.0	37,898.0	..	Resource Balance
5.17E-3	1.99E-2	1.00E-1	0.7	6.0	8.0	18.0	107.0	4,769.0	72,412.0	..	Exports of Goods & NF Services
5.41E-3	1.51E-2	6.69E-2	0.5	4.0	7.0	18.0	73.0	2,731.0	34,514.0	..	Imports of Goods & NF Services
5.50E-2	1.43E-1	6.49E-1	5.0	37.0	73.0	173.0	787.0	23,542.0	477,000.0	..	Domestic Absorption
3.72E-2	1.03E-1	4.42E-1	4.0	29.0	57.0	138.0	638.0	19,781.0	411,000.0	..	Private Consumption, etc.
7.47E-3	1.65E-2	8.91E-2	0.6	4.0	9.0	11.0	48.0	1,458.0	21,605.0	..	General Gov't Consumption
1.03E-2	2.34E-2	1.18E-1	0.6	3.0	7.0	24.0	101.0	2,303.0	43,408.0	..	Gross Domestic Investment
1.04E-2	2.15E-2	1.17E-1	0.6	4.0	7.0	24.0	98.0	2,312.0	40,171.0	..	Fixed Investment
6.24E-3	1.68E-2	7.78E-2	0.6	5.0	8.0	20.0	94.0	2,915.0	58,621.0	..	Indirect Taxes, net
4.85E-2	1.31E-1	6.05E-1	5.0	35.0	66.0	153.0	728.0	22,665.0	456,000.0	..	GDP at factor cost
4.38E-3	1.54E-2	7.65E-2	0.6	4.0	8.0	19.0	94.0	3,008.0	66,138.0	..	Agriculture
1.74E-2	4.98E-2	2.63E-1	2.0	15.0	29.0	67.0	309.0	9,560.0	181,000.0	..	Industry
1.16E-2	3.71E-2	1.86E-1	1.0	11.0	20.0	..	..	..	..	..	Manufacturing
2.67E-2	6.56E-2	2.65E-1	2.0	15.0	29.0	67.0	325.0	10,097.0	209,000.0	..	Services, etc.
1.00E-2	2.82E-2	1.51E-1	0.8	6.0	8.0	24.0	136.0	4,341.0	81,306.0	..	Gross Domestic Saving
8.38E-3	1.56E-2	9.42E-2	0.4	3.0	4.0	15.0	87.0	1,782.0	52,245.0	..	Gross National Saving
				(Millions of 1987 Argentine Australes)							
158,000	148,000	152,000	155,000	149,000	161,000	164,000	159,000	149,000	150,000	..	Gross National Product
168,000	159,000	163,000	167,000	159,000	169,000	173,000	168,000	161,000	160,000	I f	GDP at Market Prices
-12,800	-333	1,660	589	5,090	994	0	5,980	9,590	13,300	..	Resource Balance
15,300	15,900	17,100	17,000	19,100	17,600	18,000	21,400	22,400	26,100	..	Exports of Goods & NF Services
28,100	16,200	15,400	16,400	14,000	16,600	18,000	15,400	12,800	12,800	..	Imports of Goods & NF Services
181,000	159,000	162,000	167,000	154,000	168,000	173,000	162,000	151,000	147,000	..	Domestic Absorption
137,000	122,000	128,000	135,000	127,000	137,000	138,000	131,000	132,000	130,000	..	Private Consumption, etc.
9,820	9,120	9,370	9,570	9,400	9,900	11,000	8,500	4,230	2,970	..	General Gov't Consumption
34,300	27,500	24,600	21,800	17,500	20,700	23,700	22,000	14,800	13,900	..	Gross Domestic Investment
35,100	25,500	24,100	22,000	19,400	20,900	24,000	20,800	14,700	12,800	..	Fixed Investment
148,000	140,000	144,000	147,000	140,000	149,000	153,000	148,000	141,000	140,000	I f	GDP at factor cost
17,300	18,500	18,800	19,400	19,200	18,700	19,000	19,200	18,600	20,500	..	Agriculture
65,100	60,600	64,100	64,700	59,600	65,900	67,000	63,700	58,900	56,200	..	Industry
..	..	..	..	..	..	..	..	..	..	..	Manufacturing
65,800	60,900	61,100	63,100	61,300	64,100	67,000	64,900	63,500	63,400	..	Services, etc.
											Memo Items:
26,900	21,300	23,100	24,500	24,400	20,700	18,000	22,600	22,300	26,800	..	Capacity to Import
11,600	5,430	6,010	7,510	5,260	3,180	0	1,200	-60	735	..	Terms of Trade Adjustment
180,000	164,000	169,000	175,000	164,000	172,000	173,000	169,000	161,000	161,000	..	Gross Domestic Income
169,000	153,000	158,000	163,000	155,000	164,000	164,000	160,000	149,000	151,000	..	Gross National Income
											DOMESTIC PRICES/DEFLATORS
				(Index 1987 = 100)							
3.26E-2	9.30E-2	4.18E-1	3.0	25.0	44.0	100.0	490.0	15,919.0	322,000.0	..	Overall (GDP)
3.04E-2	8.98E-2	4.01E-1	3.0	24.0	43.0	100.0	487.0	15,580.0	325,000.0	..	Domestic Absorption
2.53E-2	8.32E-2	4.06E-1	3.0	23.0	45.0	100.0	490.0	16,200.0	322,000.0	..	Agriculture
2.68E-2	8.21E-2	4.10E-1	3.0	26.0	43.0	100.0	485.0	16,221.0	321,000.0	..	Industry
..	..	..	..	..	..	..	..	..	..	..	Manufacturing
3.45E-2	9.13E-2	4.05E-1	3.0	23.0	43.0	100.0	443.0	14,085.0	340,000.0	..	Consumer Price Index
											MANUFACTURING ACTIVITY
109	103	107	110	105	101	100	101	..	..	J	Employment (1987=100)
90	80	103	125	103	108	100	95	..	..	J	Real Earnings per Empl. (1987=100)
72	74	77	69	64	76	100	92	..	..	J	Real Output per Empl. (1987=100)
23	16	19	25	21	21	19	18	..	..	J	Earnings as % of Value Added
				(Billions of current Argentine Australes)						*	MONETARY HOLDINGS
1.75E-6	4.59E-6	2.30E-5	1.64E-4	8.43E-4	1.78E-3	4.84E-3	2.60E-2	0.596	7.000	..	Money Supply, Broadly Defined
4.67E-7	1.62E-6	7.50E-6	4.51E-5	3.03E-4	5.60E-4	1.26E-3	5.51E-3	0.231	3.000	..	Money
3.02E-7	8.74E-7	4.63E-6	3.13E-5	2.02E-4	3.99E-4	9.26E-4	4.32E-3	0.182	2.000	..	Currency Outside Banks
1.65E-7	7.50E-7	2.87E-6	1.38E-5	1.01E-4	1.61E-4	3.32E-4	1.19E-3	0.049	0.448	..	Demand Deposits
1.28E-6	2.97E-6	1.55E-5	1.19E-4	5.40E-4	1.22E-3	3.58E-3	2.05E-2	0.365	4.000	..	Quasi-Money
				(Millions of current Argentine Australes)						E	GOVERNMENT DEFICIT (-) OR SURPLUS
-5	-11	-87	-267	-2,924	-1,964	-6,675	-20,871	..	..	..	Current Revenue
9	23	106	783	8,286	15,176	32,431	103,000	..	..	..	Current Expenditure
10	26	134	805	8,583	14,704	32,665	107,000	..	..	..	Current Budget Balance
-1	-3	-28	-22	-297	472	-234	-4,878	..	..	..	Capital Receipts
..	..	..	..	..	3	196	309	..	..	..	Capital Payments
4	8	59	245	2,627	2,439	6,637	16,302	..	..		

	1970	1971	1972	1973	1974	1975	1976	1977	1978	1979	1980
FOREIGN TRADE (CUSTOMS BASIS)					*(Millions of current US dollars)*						
Value of Exports, fob	1,773	1,740	1,941	3,266	3,931	2,961	3,912	5,642	6,394	7,808	8,019
Nonfuel Primary Products	1,519	1,468	1,540	2,527	2,958	2,224	2,919	4,265	4,669	5,871	5,883
Fuels	8	9	6	6	12	15	20	28	52	49	278
Manufactures	247	264	395	733	961	723	973	1,349	1,674	1,888	1,859
Value of Imports, cif	1,689	1,846	1,904	2,235	3,635	3,945	3,029	4,158	3,832	6,692	10,539
Nonfuel Primary Products	374	390	411	552	780	763	511	615	566	1,096	1,299
Fuels	80	123	72	170	528	522	536	682	477	1,109	1,086
Manufactures	1,234	1,332	1,422	1,514	2,327	2,660	1,982	2,861	2,790	4,488	8,155
					(Index 1987 = 100)						
Terms of Trade	169.3	172.6	155.2	204.0	164.4	148.5	146.3	134.4	127.6	130.9	122.2
Export Prices, fob	43.1	44.4	49.7	71.6	85.0	81.3	81.7	82.9	89.1	108.2	119.1
Import Prices, cif	25.5	25.7	32.0	35.1	51.7	54.7	55.8	61.7	69.8	82.7	97.5
BALANCE OF PAYMENTS					*(Millions of current US dollars)*						
Exports of Goods & Services	2,148	2,131	2,318	3,747	4,714	3,587	4,691	6,738	7,836	9,916	11,202
Merchandise, fob	1,773	1,740	1,941	3,266	3,930	2,961	3,918	5,651	6,401	7,810	8,021
Nonfactor Services	331	360	359	433	623	537	691	937	1,083	1,366	1,872
Factor Services	44	31	17	48	161	89	82	150	352	740	1,309
Imports of Goods & Services	2,308	2,518	2,541	3,047	4,596	4,878	4,058	5,643	6,048	10,486	15,999
Merchandise, fob	1,499	1,653	1,685	1,978	3,216	3,510	2,765	3,799	3,488	6,028	9,394
Nonfactor Services	487	512	460	564	808	813	703	913	1,473	2,745	3,687
Factor Services	322	354	395	505	572	555	590	931	1,473	2,745	3,687
Long-Term Interest	338	343	367	461	511	495	470	551	754	957	1,337
Private Current Transfers, net	0	0	0	0	..	6	24	32	48	35	23
Workers' Remittances	..	..	..	..	..	..	..	..	..	..	..
Curr. A/C Bal before Off. Transf.	-160	-387	-223	700	118	-1,286	657	1,127	1,836	-535	-4,774
Net Official Transfers	-3	-3	-4	11	..	-1	-6	-1	20	22	0
Curr. A/C Bal after Off. Transf.	-163	-390	-227	711	118	-1,287	651	1,126	1,856	-513	-4,774
Long-Term Capital, net	120	338	187	42	-2	-285	805	473	1,390	2,994	4,255
Direct Investment	11	11	10	10	10	..	..	143	227	147	568
Long-Term Loans	135	343	265	320	464	-52	1,119	426	1,278	4,566	2,855
Disbursements	907	1,068	1,027	1,234	1,460	920	2,173	1,577	3,316	5,865	4,708
Repayments	772	726	761	915	996	972	1,053	1,151	2,038	1,299	1,853
Other Long-Term Capital	-26	-16	-88	-288	-476	-233	-314	-96	-115	-1,719	832
Other Capital, net	119	-393	-25	90	-41	494	-538	246	-1,111	1,679	-2,186
Change in Reserves	-76	445	65	-842	-75	1,078	-918	-1,845	-2,135	-4,160	2,705
Memo Item:					*(Argentine Australes per US dollar)*						
Conversion Factor (Annual Avg)	3.79E-7	4.52E-7	5.00E-7	5.00E-7	5.00E-7	3.66E-6	1.40E-5	4.08E-5	7.96E-5	1.32E-4	1.84E-4
Additional Conversion Factor	3.80E-7	5.00E-7	8.00E-7	9.00E-7	9.00E-7	3.70E-6	2.00E-5	5.00E-5	1.22E-4	2.79E-4	4.99E-4
EXTERNAL DEBT (Total)					*(Millions of US dollars), outstanding at end of year*						
	5,171	5,564	6,028	6,429	6,789	8,171	9,880	11,445	13,276	20,950	27,157
Long-Term Debt (by debtor)	5,171	5,564	6,028	6,429	6,789	6,873	8,258	8,721	9,848	14,039	16,774
Central Bank, incl. IMF credit	105	86	416	625	411	526	1,227	1,007	118	174	170
Central Government	702	894	943	905	1,117	1,087	1,447	1,391	1,988	2,819	3,480
Rest of General Government	65	47	41	43	36	30	42	42	71	277	475
Non-financial Public Enterprises	875	956	955	1,137	1,391	1,385	1,536	1,876	2,793	2,718	3,399
Priv. Sector, incl non-guaranteed	3,424	3,581	3,673	3,719	3,835	3,846	4,007	4,405	4,878	8,051	9,250
Short-Term Debt	0	0	0	0	0	1,297	1,622	2,724	3,428	6,911	10,383
Memo Items:					*(Millions of US dollars)*						
Int'l Reserves Excluding Gold	532.6	192.4	313.3	1,148.7	1,144.3	287.8	1,444.9	3,153.8	4,966.5	9,388.0	6,719.5
Gold Holdings (at market price)	149.2	111.9	259.1	448.6	745.3	560.4	538.5	690.2	966.8	2,238.5	2,577.3
SOCIAL INDICATORS											
Total Fertility Rate	3.1	3.1	3.1	3.2	3.2	3.3	3.3	3.4	3.3	3.3	3.2
Infant Mortality Rate	51.8	50.4	49.0	47.4	45.8	44.2	42.6	41.0	40.0	39.0	38.0
Life Expectancy at Birth	66.8	67.0	67.3	67.6	67.9	68.1	68.4	68.7	68.9	69.1	69.3
Urban Population, % of total	78.4	78.9	79.3	79.8	80.2	80.7	81.1	81.6	82.0	82.5	82.9
Food Prod. per capita (1987=100)	100.4	91.7	88.2	92.0	94.7	96.3	105.0	103.5	111.2	110.9	100.3
Labor Force, Agriculture (%)	16.0	15.7	15.4	15.1	14.8	14.5	14.2	13.9	13.6	13.3	13.0
Labor Force, Female (%)	24.9	25.1	25.3	25.6	25.8	26.0	26.2	26.3	26.5	26.7	26.9
Primary Schl. Enroll. Ratio	105.0	..	..	..	..	106.0	109.0	111.0	..	112.0	106.0
Primary Schl. Enroll. Ratio, Female	106.0	..	..	..	..	106.0	109.0	111.0	..	..	106.0
Secondary Schl. Enroll. Ratio	44.0	..	..	..	..	54.0	57.0	56.0	56.0	..	56.0

* The data for monetary holdings, such as money supply, money and quasi-money are in billions of new pesos (equivalent to 10,000 australes)

1981	1982	1983	1984	1985	1986	1987	1988	1989	1990 estimate	Notes	ARGENTINA
											FOREIGN TRADE (CUSTOMS BASIS)
				(Millions of current US dollars)							
9,141	7,623	7,836	8,107	8,396	6,852	6,360	9,134	9,565	12,353	..	Value of Exports, fob
6,724	5,228	6,219	6,353	5,988	4,894	4,262	6,102	5,876	7,588	..	Nonfuel Primary Products
620	548	334	332	614	154	85	139	324	418	..	Fuels
1,798	1,847	1,283	1,423	1,795	1,804	2,013	2,893	3,365	4,346	..	Manufactures
9,430	5,337	4,504	4,585	3,814	4,723	5,818	5,322	4,201	4,077	..	Value of Imports, cif
1,039	722	626	694	492	812	813	677	597	580	..	Nonfuel Primary Products
1,022	682	463	478	462	424	664	500	370	359	..	Fuels
7,370	3,933	3,414	3,413	2,860	3,488	4,341	4,145	3,233	3,138	..	Manufactures
				(Index 1987 = 100)							
119.8	110.4	117.7	118.6	109.8	104.3	100.0	105.5	109.6	111.5	..	Terms of Trade
117.0	104.2	108.2	106.7	98.7	94.7	100.0	115.3	121.0	134.8	..	Export Prices, fob
97.7	94.4	92.0	89.9	89.9	90.8	100.0	109.3	110.4	120.9	..	Import Prices, cif
											BALANCE OF PAYMENTS
				(Millions of current US dollars)							
11,805	9,755	9,764	9,909	10,329	8,841	8,406	11,360	12,042	15,075	..	Exports of Goods & Services
9,143	7,623	7,835	8,100	8,396	6,852	6,360	9,134	9,573	12,354	..	Merchandise, fob
1,710	1,562	1,453	1,507	1,643	1,581	1,780	2,009	2,186	2,435	..	Nonfactor Services
952	570	476	302	290	408	266	217	283	286	..	Factor Services
16,495	12,142	12,216	12,406	11,281	11,702	12,633	12,932	13,355	13,357	..	Imports of Goods & Services
8,431	4,859	4,119	4,118	3,518	4,406	5,343	4,892	3,864	3,726	..	Merchandise, fob
3,180	1,655	1,700	1,843	1,767	2,080	2,286	2,414	2,390	2,704	..	Nonfactor Services
4,884	5,628	6,397	6,445	5,996	5,216	5,004	5,626	7,101	6,927	..	Factor Services
2,044	2,435	2,419	3,280	4,396	3,707	3,660	2,781	1,519	2,273	..	Long-Term Interest
-22	34	16	2	0	2	-8	0	8	71	..	Private Current Transfers, net
..	..	..	..	..	..	..	..	..	..	..	Workers' Remittances
-4,712	-2,353	-2,436	-2,495	-952	-2,859	-4,235	-1,572	-1,305	1,789	..	Curr. A/C Bal before Off. Transf.
0	0	0	0	0	0	0	0	0	..	..	Net Official Transfers
-4,712	-2,353	-2,436	-2,495	-952	-2,859	-4,235	-1,572	-1,305	1,789	..	Curr. A/C Bal after Off. Transf.
9,754	3,784	1,717	-322	4,790	2,275	2,459	1,228	4,747	1,218	..	Long-Term Capital, net
730	197	183	268	919	574	-19	1,147	1,028	2,036	..	Direct Investment
6,396	5,759	1,465	-3	2,567	645	1,641	491	-434	-749	..	Long-Term Loans
8,346	7,054	2,832	821	3,584	2,688	3,182	1,889	1,079	914	..	Disbursements
1,950	1,294	1,367	824	1,017	2,043	1,541	1,398	1,512	1,664	..	Repayments
2,628	-2,172	69	-587	1,304	1,056	837	-410	4,153	-69	..	Other Long-Term Capital
-8,313	-2,062	-1,587	2,789	-2,590	-299	-267	2,264	-4,715	404	..	Other Capital, net
3,271	631	2,306	28	-1,248	883	2,043	-1,920	1,273	-3,411	..	Change in Reserves
											Memo Item:
				(Argentine Australes per US dollar)							
4.40E-4	2.59E-3	1.05E-2	0.068	0.602	0.943	2.100	8.800	423.300	4,875.900	..	Conversion Factor (Annual Avg)
9.50E-4	2.59E-3	1.05E-2	0.068	0.602	0.943	2.100	8.800	423.300	4,876.000	..	Additional Conversion Factor
				(Millions of US dollars), outstanding at end of year							
35,657	43,634	45,920	48,857	50,945	52,451	58,458	58,735	64,776	61,144	..	**EXTERNAL DEBT (Total)**
22,736	27,113	37,006	38,138	44,215	48,041	54,927	53,021	56,360	51,029	..	Long-Term Debt (by debtor)
251	5,068	12,995	13,852	26,952	30,504	41,335	39,685	42,200	35,763	..	Central Bank, incl. IMF credit
4,238	4,485	2,625	2,422	4,889	5,313	6,814	6,695	7,998	9,114	..	Central Government
479	433	504	509	379	345	163	144	117	99	..	Rest of General Government
2,978	2,922	3,266	4,672	4,195	4,345	2,872	2,937	2,663	2,690	..	Non-financial Public Enterprises
14,790	14,205	17,616	16,683	7,799	7,533	3,743	3,560	3,382	3,364	..	Priv. Sector, incl non-guaranteed
12,921	16,521	8,913	10,718	6,730	4,410	3,531	5,714	8,416	10,115	..	Short-Term Debt
											Memo Items:
				(Millions of US dollars)							
3,268.4	2,506.4	1,172.4	1,242.6	3,273.0	2,718.0	1,617.0	3,363.5	1,463.3	4,592.3	..	Int'l Reserves Excluding Gold
1,737.9	1,997.6	1,667.9	1,347.9	1,429.6	1,709.4	2,117.0	1,794.0	1,753.6	1,629.7	..	Gold Holdings (at market price)
											SOCIAL INDICATORS
3.2	3.1	3.1	3.1	3.1	3.0	3.0	2.9	2.9	2.8	..	Total Fertility Rate
37.0	36.0	35.2	34.4	33.6	32.8	32.0	31.0	30.1	29.1	..	Infant Mortality Rate
69.5	69.7	69.8	70.0	70.2	70.4	70.6	70.8	71.0	71.2	..	Life Expectancy at Birth
83.3	83.6	84.0	84.3	84.7	85.0	85.3	85.7	86.0	86.3	..	Urban Population, % of total
108.2	108.0	101.7	106.4	106.2	105.3	100.0	103.3	93.9	99.2	..	Food Prod. per capita (1987=100)
..	..	..	..	..	..	..	..			..	Labor Force, Agriculture (%)
27.0	27.1	27.2	27.4	27.5	27.6	27.7	27.8	28.0	28.1	..	Labor Force, Female (%)
..	108.0	107.0	107.0	107.0	109.0	110.0	111.0	..	..	..	Primary Schl. Enroll. Ratio
107.0	107.0	107.0	107.0	108.0	109.0	110.0	114.0			..	Primary Schl. Enroll. Ratio, Female
..	..	60.0	65.0	71.0	71.0	74.0	..	..	..	..	Secondary Schl. Enroll. Ratio

AUSTRALIA	1970	1971	1972	1973	1974	1975	1976	1977	1978	1979	1980
CURRENT GNP PER CAPITA (US $)	3,130	3,370	3,730	4,580	5,740	7,130	7,780	7,850	8,540	9,210	10,470
POPULATION (thousands)	12,507	12,937	13,177	13,380	13,723	13,893	14,033	14,192	14,358	14,514	14,692
USE AND ORIGIN OF RESOURCES	*(Billions of current Australian Dollars)*										
Gross National Product (GNP)	34.63	38.78	44.23	53.18	64.16	75.80	86.58	94.08	106.95	120.99	138.03
Net Factor Income from Abroad	-0.48	-0.51	-0.55	-0.41	-0.51	-0.84	-1.05	-1.21	-1.52	-1.94	-2.13
GDP at Market Prices	35.12	39.29	44.78	53.59	64.67	76.64	87.64	95.29	108.47	122.93	140.17
Resource Balance	-0.02	0.44	1.62	0.00	-0.27	0.30	-0.54	-0.96	-1.10	0.87	-2.57
Exports of Goods & NFServices	5.07	5.67	7.01	7.88	10.09	11.20	13.38	14.21	16.86	21.96	22.51
Imports of Goods & NFServices	5.08	5.23	5.38	7.88	10.36	10.90	13.92	15.18	17.96	21.09	25.07
Domestic Absorption	35.13	38.85	43.16	53.59	64.94	76.35	88.18	96.26	109.57	122.06	142.73
Private Consumption, etc.	20.66	23.13	26.08	31.56	38.12	44.55	50.73	56.87	63.22	71.03	82.00
General Gov't Consumption	4.90	5.60	6.35	7.93	10.66	13.20	15.31	17.17	19.02	21.34	24.99
Gross Domestic Investment	9.57	10.13	10.73	14.10	16.16	18.60	22.14	22.22	27.33	29.69	35.74
Fixed Investment	9.13	10.11	11.00	12.93	15.14	18.44	21.01	22.65	25.98	28.85	35.24
Indirect Taxes, net	3.23	3.67	4.11	5.10	6.21	8.02	9.03	9.56	11.09	13.14	15.01
GDP at factor cost	31.88	35.63	40.68	48.48	58.46	68.62	78.61	85.74	97.38	109.80	125.16
Agriculture	2.03	2.31	3.14	4.28	3.74	3.86	4.31	4.22	6.67	7.67	7.32
Industry	13.70	15.13	16.78	19.60	23.70	27.94	31.61	34.30	38.07	43.77	51.07
Manufacturing	8.53	9.23	10.15	11.81	13.82	15.86	17.83	19.11	20.83	23.56	27.12
Services, etc.	19.38	21.86	24.86	29.70	37.23	44.84	51.71	56.78	63.72	71.50	81.78
Gross Domestic Saving	9.55	10.57	12.35	14.09	15.89	18.89	21.60	21.26	26.22	30.56	33.17
Gross National Saving	9.14	10.11	11.86	13.68	15.36	17.99	20.49	20.03	24.73	28.71	31.28
	(Billions of 1987 Australian Dollars)										
Gross National Product	171.64	180.59	188.42	196.93	200.63	205.72	211.56	213.25	224.17	227.96	235.07
GDP at Market Prices	174.09	183.01	190.85	198.53	202.29	208.08	214.19	216.02	227.38	231.67	238.77
Resource Balance	-2.72	0.26	0.87	-7.85	-6.85	-3.75	-5.33	-3.28	-4.23	-1.70	-6.73
Exports of Goods & NFServices	23.19	25.45	26.15	24.61	26.43	27.50	29.38	30.04	31.90	34.28	32.58
Imports of Goods & NFServices	25.91	25.19	25.28	32.46	33.28	31.25	34.70	33.32	36.13	35.97	39.30
Domestic Absorption	176.81	182.75	189.98	206.37	209.15	211.84	219.52	219.30	231.61	233.37	245.49
Private Consumption, etc.	100.89	106.37	112.93	120.53	123.63	125.11	127.83	131.05	134.40	136.19	142.12
General Gov't Consumption	26.05	27.28	28.17	30.29	32.84	35.23	36.50	37.76	39.23	39.98	41.73
Gross Domestic Investment	49.86	49.10	48.88	55.55	52.67	51.49	55.19	50.49	57.98	57.21	61.64
Fixed Investment	47.86	49.54	50.19	51.86	49.13	51.40	52.33	51.77	55.00	55.50	60.89
GDP at factor cost	157.85	165.82	172.84	178.88	182.30	185.90	191.77	194.28	204.05	206.62	212.90
Agriculture	..	..	..	..	9.68	10.54	10.84	10.47	12.81	11.17	9.74
Industry	..	..	..	..	70.32	70.55	73.48	73.25	75.81	77.90	80.37
Manufacturing	..	..	..	..	40.53	40.10	41.09	40.91	42.59	44.44	45.35
Services, etc.	..	..	..	..	122.29	127.00	129.87	132.30	138.76	142.61	148.66
Memo Items:											
Capacity to Import	25.82	27.31	32.91	32.45	32.41	32.10	33.35	31.20	33.91	37.45	35.28
Terms of Trade Adjustment	2.63	1.87	6.76	7.83	5.98	4.60	3.98	1.17	2.01	3.18	2.70
Gross Domestic Income	176.72	184.88	197.61	206.36	208.27	212.69	218.17	217.19	229.39	234.85	241.47
Gross National Income	174.27	182.45	195.18	204.77	206.61	210.32	215.54	214.41	226.18	231.13	237.77
DOMESTIC PRICES/DEFLATORS	*(Index 1987 = 100)*										
Overall (GDP)	20.2	21.5	23.5	27.0	32.0	36.8	40.9	44.1	47.7	53.1	58.7
Domestic Absorption	19.9	21.3	22.7	26.0	31.1	36.0	40.2	43.9	47.3	52.3	58.1
Agriculture	..	..	..	..	38.7	36.6	39.7	40.3	52.1	68.7	75.1
Industry	..	..	..	..	33.7	39.6	43.0	46.8	50.2	56.2	63.5
Manufacturing	..	..	..	..	34.1	39.6	43.4	46.7	48.9	53.0	59.8
Consumer Price Index	21.1	22.4	23.7	25.9	29.8	34.3	39.0	43.8	47.2	51.5	56.7
MANUFACTURING ACTIVITY											
Employment (1987=100)	125.8	126.2	126.1	125.5	129.4	121.2	116.8	114.3	111.4	111.4	112.2
Real Earnings per Empl. (1987=100)	75.8	77.9	81.7	83.1	86.2	95.2	96.6	97.7	98.4	96.9	97.5
Real Output per Empl. (1987=100)	..	..	..	..	62.9	64.9	66.6	71.4	75.9	80.7	84.0
Earnings as % of Value Added	52.5	53.9	54.1	54.3	54.5	56.0	55.9	54.8	54.9	54.0	52.1
MONETARY HOLDINGS	*(Billions of current Australian Dollars)*										
Money Supply, Broadly Defined	15.70	17.07	20.42	24.71	26.96	32.55	52.67	58.13	65.90	74.83	87.42
Money	5.45	5.75	6.90	8.05	7.99	9.81	10.68	11.39	12.71	14.66	17.22
Currency Outside Banks	1.33	1.48	1.66	1.96	2.36	2.76	3.13	3.55	3.96	4.37	4.98
Demand Deposits	4.12	4.27	5.23	6.09	5.64	7.05	7.55	7.84	8.75	10.29	12.25
Quasi-Money	10.25	11.32	13.53	16.66	18.97	22.75	41.99	46.74	53.19	60.17	70.20
GOVERNMENT DEFICIT (-) OR SURPLUS	*(Millions of current Australian Dollars)*										
	-260	-78	130	-409	-241	-2,482	-3,609	-2,702	-3,290	-3,132	-2,085
Current Revenue	7,308	8,219	9,087	9,691	12,253	15,725	18,818	22,046	24,179	26,310	30,556
Current Expenditure	5,844	6,597	7,374	8,431	9,982	13,623	17,980	21,021	24,069	26,460	29,735
Current Budget Balance	1,464	1,622	1,713	1,260	2,271	2,102	838	1,025	110	-150	821
Capital Receipts	15	22	44	49	43	21	35	32	39	26	28
Capital Payments	1,739	1,722	1,627	1,718	2,555	4,605	4,482	3,758	3,440	3,009	2,934

1981	1982	1983	1984	1985	1986	1987	1988	1989	1990 estimate	Notes	AUSTRALIA
11,710	11,810	12,160	12,260	11,680	11,370	11,690	13,270	15,430	16,680	..	CURRENT GNP PER CAPITA (US $)
14,927	15,178	15,369	15,544	15,758	15,974	16,249	16,532	16,811	17,086	..	POPULATION (thousands)

USE AND ORIGIN OF RESOURCES

(Billions of current Australian Dollars)

1981	1982	1983	1984	1985	1986	1987	1988	1989	1990	Notes	
155.17	168.05	189.98	209.55	232.42	256.00	289.19	326.32	354.84	362.25	C f	Gross National Product (GNP)
-2.96	-3.58	-4.64	-6.51	-7.67	-8.62	-10.24	-13.52	-17.09	-17.33		Net Factor Income from Abroad
158.13	171.63	194.62	216.06	240.09	264.63	299.43	339.83	371.93	379.58	C	GDP at Market Prices
-5.70	-3.81	-2.60	-4.75	-7.39	-4.87	-2.44	-7.12	-7.59	-0.91	..	Resource Balance
23.30	25.16	28.59	34.75	38.69	43.15	50.26	53.98	59.61	65.06	..	Exports of Goods & NFServices
29.00	28.97	31.19	39.50	46.09	48.02	52.70	61.10	67.20	65.97	..	Imports of Goods & NFServices
163.82	175.44	197.21	220.81	247.49	269.50	301.87	346.95	379.52	380.49	..	Domestic Absorption
92.21	104.31	115.50	128.38	141.97	158.17	178.54	202.22	223.85	231.57	..	Private Consumption, etc.
28.53	32.44	35.91	40.21	44.72	48.71	52.63	56.34	61.55	67.44	..	General Gov't Consumption
43.09	38.69	45.80	52.22	60.80	62.62	70.69	88.40	94.12	81.48	..	Gross Domestic Investment
41.53	41.13	44.37	51.12	59.33	64.01	71.08	84.50	89.19	82.74	..	Fixed Investment
17.08	19.42	22.42	25.80	28.48	31.70	37.00	40.91	44.43	45.11	..	Indirect Taxes, net
141.05	152.20	172.20	190.26	211.61	232.93	262.43	298.92	327.50	334.47	B C	GDP at factor cost
7.65	5.91	9.34	9.38	9.30	10.17	12.18	14.30	..	..	..	Agriculture
56.21	60.53	67.86	75.43	83.25	87.39	96.40	106.79	..	..	..	Industry
30.30	31.13	35.03	38.37	41.49	44.23	50.16	57.34			..	Manufacturing
94.27	105.18	117.42	131.25	147.54	167.06	190.85	218.74	..	..	..	Services, etc.
37.39	34.88	43.20	47.47	53.40	57.75	68.25	81.28	86.53	80.57	..	Gross Domestic Saving
34.69	31.60	39.02	41.47	46.71	50.35	59.72	69.95	72.13	65.72	..	Gross National Saving

(Billions of 1987 Australian Dollars)

1981	1982	1983	1984	1985	1986	1987	1988	1989	1990	Notes	
240.26	234.41	248.98	259.84	269.65	276.97	289.19	297.43	306.05	303.70	C f	Gross National Product
244.89	239.46	255.12	267.98	278.48	286.14	299.43	310.13	321.23	318.46	C	GDP at Market Prices
-10.77	-6.94	-6.21	-7.89	-6.20	-1.00	-2.44	-14.58	-14.28	-4.76	..	Resource Balance
32.96	33.06	35.86	40.72	43.13	46.92	50.26	50.68	54.40	61.47	..	Exports of Goods & NFServices
43.73	40.00	42.07	48.61	49.32	47.93	52.70	65.27	68.68	66.23	..	Imports of Goods & NFServices
255.66	246.40	261.33	275.87	284.68	287.14	301.87	324.71	335.50	323.22	..	Domestic Absorption
146.58	148.62	154.54	161.83	165.15	169.82	178.54	188.22	195.89	193.51	..	Private Consumption, etc.
42.08	43.26	45.13	47.72	49.90	51.15	52.63	53.21	55.23	57.42	..	General Gov't Consumption
67.00	54.53	61.66	66.32	69.63	66.18	70.69	83.28	84.39	72.29	..	Gross Domestic Investment
64.89	57.93	59.54	65.08	68.18	67.71	71.08	79.54	80.40	73.54	..	Fixed Investment
218.22	212.08	225.47	235.75	245.71	252.42	262.43	271.71	281.82	280.06	B C	GDP at factor cost
11.41	8.84	12.80	12.87	12.41	12.85	12.18	12.47	..	..	..	Agriculture
82.17	77.50	79.61	85.49	90.45	90.15	96.40	102.30	..	..	..	Industry
46.47	42.65	43.29	45.51	46.63	47.32	50.16	52.95			..	Manufacturing
151.31	153.11	162.70	169.62	175.62	183.14	190.85	195.36	..	..	..	Services, etc.

Memo Items:

1981	1982	1983	1984	1985	1986	1987	1988	1989	1990	Notes	
35.14	34.74	38.57	42.77	41.41	43.07	50.26	57.66	60.92	65.31	..	Capacity to Import
2.18	1.68	2.71	2.05	-1.72	-3.86	0.00	6.98	6.52	3.84	..	Terms of Trade Adjustment
247.07	241.14	257.83	270.03	276.76	282.28	299.43	317.11	327.75	322.31	..	Gross Domestic Income
242.44	236.08	251.69	261.89	267.93	273.11	289.19	304.41	312.57	307.54	..	Gross National Income

DOMESTIC PRICES/DEFLATORS

(Index 1987 = 100)

1981	1982	1983	1984	1985	1986	1987	1988	1989	1990	Notes	
64.6	71.7	76.3	80.6	86.2	92.5	100.0	109.6	115.8	119.2	..	Overall (GDP)
64.1	71.2	75.5	80.0	86.9	93.9	100.0	106.8	113.1	117.7	..	Domestic Absorption
67.1	66.9	72.9	72.9	74.9	79.1	100.0	114.7	..	..	..	Agriculture
68.4	78.1	85.2	88.2	92.0	96.9	100.0	104.4	..	..	..	Industry
65.2	73.0	80.9	84.3	89.0	93.5	100.0	108.3	..	..	..	Manufacturing
62.2	69.2	76.2	79.2	84.5	92.2	100.0	107.2	115.3	123.7	..	Consumer Price Index

MANUFACTURING ACTIVITY

1981	1982	1983	1984	1985	1986	1987	1988	1989	1990	Notes	
112.4	112.2	102.5	98.5	99.7	99.8	100.0	103.6	..	..	..	Employment (1987=100)
99.1	101.8	103.5	104.1	103.6	101.5	100.0	100.2	..	..	..	Real Earnings per Empl. (1987=100)
87.6	86.0	84.4	89.8	94.4	97.9	100.0	101.7	..	..	..	Real Output per Empl. (1987=100)
52.3	54.1	55.9	51.0	48.9	48.0	47.1	46.5	..	..	..	Earnings as % of Value Added

MONETARY HOLDINGS

(Billions of current Australian Dollars)

1981	1982	1983	1984	1985	1986	1987	1988	1989	1990	Notes	
99.14	111.32	124.46	138.24	159.81	175.22	195.49	230.25	270.58	287.51	D	Money Supply, Broadly Defined
18.06	18.03	20.80	22.49	23.30	25.95	31.22	40.47	43.51	46.70		Money
5.53	6.02	6.88	7.86	8.63	9.54	10.84	12.27	13.02	14.34	..	Currency Outside Banks
12.53	12.01	13.91	14.64	14.67	16.41	20.38	28.20	30.50	32.36	..	Demand Deposits
81.08	93.28	103.67	115.75	136.51	149.27	164.27	189.78	227.06	240.81	..	Quasi-Money

GOVERNMENT DEFICIT (-) OR SURPLUS

(Millions of current Australian Dollars)

1981	1982	1983	1984	1985	1986	1987	1988	1989	1990	Notes	
-1,078	-590	-4,601	-8,014	-6,817	-5,827	-3,331	1,441	5,255	6,808	C	GOVERNMENT DEFICIT (-) OR SURPLUS
35,959	41,775	45,764	50,288	59,146	66,425	74,427	82,492	90,060	98,705	..	Current Revenue
34,043	38,894	45,831	53,357	60,629	66,846	72,543	77,386	80,614	88,049	..	Current Expenditure
1,916	2,881	-67	-3,069	-1,483	-421	1,884	5,106	9,446	10,656	..	Current Budget Balance
285	39	64	79	136	233	268	745	318	246	..	Capital Receipts
3,279	3,510	4,598	5,024	5,470	5,639	5,483	4,410	4,509	4,094	..	Capital Payments

AUSTRALIA	1970	1971	1972	1973	1974	1975	1976	1977	1978	1979	1980
FOREIGN TRADE (CUSTOMS BASIS)					*(Millions of current US dollars)*						
Value of Exports, fob	4,482	4,930	6,123	9,311	10,777	11,646	12,911	13,057	14,189	18,379	21,279
Nonfuel Primary Products	3,386	3,644	4,556	6,752	7,500	8,075	8,618	8,555	8,295	11,370	13,321
Fuels	250	317	388	588	952	1,383	1,648	1,777	2,010	2,250	2,370
Manufactures	846	969	1,180	1,971	2,325	2,188	2,645	2,724	3,883	4,759	5,588
Value of Imports, cif	4,482	4,632	4,556	6,812	11,087	9,831	11,088	12,154	14,018	16,342	19,870
Nonfuel Primary Products	544	541	566	900	1,343	978	1,166	1,384	1,467	1,687	2,024
Fuels	245	221	214	279	933	960	1,060	1,225	1,274	1,740	2,749
Manufactures	3,694	3,871	3,776	5,632	8,810	7,892	8,861	9,545	11,276	12,914	15,097
					(Index 1987 = 100)						
Terms of Trade	150.0	131.5	148.8	178.5	163.2	135.4	140.2	127.9	118.5	122.7	124.4
Export Prices, fob	37.2	37.5	46.7	70.6	88.2	78.3	83.5	84.0	87.5	106.5	124.3
Import Prices, cif	24.8	28.5	31.4	39.6	54.0	57.8	59.6	65.7	73.8	86.8	99.9
BALANCE OF PAYMENTS					*(Millions of current US dollars)*						
Exports of Goods & Services	5,705	6,267	7,751	11,329	13,533	14,468	15,574	15,851	17,358	22,480	26,323
Merchandise, fob	4,623	5,064	6,276	9,271	10,765	11,691	12,976	13,197	14,115	18,578	21,560
Nonfactor Services	902	967	1,107	1,399	2,001	2,178	2,087	2,126	2,621	3,142	3,736
Factor Services	180	236	369	658	767	599	511	528	622	760	1,028
Imports of Goods & Services	6,467	7,075	7,205	10,770	16,089	15,120	17,327	18,732	21,648	24,891	30,510
Merchandise, fob	4,108	4,476	4,294	6,464	10,631	9,481	10,943	12,174	14,025	16,060	20,191
Nonfactor Services	1,357	1,517	1,697	2,449	3,492	3,501	3,921	4,109	4,724	5,224	6,201
Factor Services	1,001	1,082	1,214	1,857	1,966	2,138	2,462	2,450	2,899	3,607	4,117
Long-Term Interest	..	..	..	..	..	..	..	..	..	..	..
Private Current Transfers, net	80	56	66	-11	-32	-82	-72	-21	24	104	275
Workers' Remittances	..	..	..	..	..	..	..	..	..	..	..
Curr. A/C Bal before Off. Transf.	-682	-752	612	548	-2,588	-734	-1,825	-2,902	-4,266	-2,306	-3,912
Net Official Transfers	-95	-82	-150	-141	-248	-331	-185	-231	-294	-354	-336
Curr. A/C Bal after Off. Transf.	-777	-833	462	407	-2,836	-1,065	-2,010	-3,133	-4,560	-2,660	-4,248
Long-Term Capital, net	1,045	1,881	1,721	-963	866	812	1,502	2,191	3,300	2,476	4,152
Direct Investment	778	1,045	926	-112	1,088	295	777	873	1,442	1,111	1,365
Long-Term Loans	..	..	..	..	..	..	..	..	..	..	..
Disbursements	..	..	..	..	..	..	..	..	..	..	..
Repayments	..	..	..	..	..	..	..	..	..	..	..
Other Long-Term Capital	267	836	795	-852	-222	517	725	1,318	1,859	1,365	2,787
Other Capital, net	77	322	534	237	337	-621	124	-213	1,173	-517	694
Change in Reserves	-345	-1,369	-2,717	319	1,633	874	384	1,155	87	701	-598
Memo Item:					*(Australian Dollars per US dollar)*						
Conversion Factor (Annual Avg)	0.890	0.880	0.840	0.700	0.700	0.760	0.820	0.900	0.870	0.890	0.880
EXTERNAL DEBT (Total)					*(Millions US dollars), outstanding at end of year*						
Long-Term Debt (by debtor)	..	..	..	..	..	..	..	..	..	..	..
Central Bank, incl. IMF credit	..	..	..	..	..	..	..	..	..	..	..
Central Government	..	..	..	..	..	..	..	..	..	..	..
Rest of General Government	..	..	..	..	..	..	..	..	..	..	..
Non-financial Public Enterprises	..	..	..	..	..	..	..	..	..	..	..
Priv. Sector, incl non-guaranteed	..	..	..	..	..	..	..	..	..	..	..
Short-Term Debt	..	..	..	..	..	..	..	..	..	..	..
Memo Items:					*(Millions of US dollars)*						
Int'l Reserves Excluding Gold	1,454.0	3,034.0	5,860.0	5,386.0	3,953.0	2,954.0	2,870.0	2,058.0	2,062.0	1,424.0	1,690.0
Gold Holdings (at market price)	255.0	324.0	480.0	827.0	1,376.0	1,035.0	992.0	1,262.0	1,761.0	4,062.0	4,677.0
SOCIAL INDICATORS											
Total Fertility Rate	2.9	3.0	2.7	2.5	2.4	2.2	2.1	2.0	2.0	1.9	1.9
Infant Mortality Rate	17.9	17.3	16.7	16.5	16.1	14.2	13.8	12.4	12.1	11.3	10.7
Life Expectancy at Birth	71.4	71.5	71.7	72.1	72.4	72.8	73.1	73.5	73.8	74.2	74.5
Urban Population, % of total	85.2	85.3	85.5	85.6	85.8	85.9	85.9	85.9	85.8	85.8	85.8
Food Prod. per capita (1987=100)	96.3	100.2	99.7	108.6	97.9	105.5	111.7	107.8	124.9	117.1	98.7
Labor Force, Agriculture (%)	8.1	7.9	7.8	7.7	7.6	7.4	7.3	7.2	7.1	7.0	6.9
Labor Force, Female (%)	31.2	31.9	32.6	33.2	33.8	34.4	35.1	35.7	36.4	37.0	37.5
Primary Schl. Enroll. Ratio	115.0	..	..	..	..	107.0	108.0	109.0	111.0	111.0	111.0
Primary Schl. Enroll. Ratio, Female	115.0	..	..	..	..	107.0	108.0	109.0	111.0	111.0	110.0
Secondary Schl. Enroll. Ratio	82.0	..	..	..	..	87.0	88.0	88.0	87.0	86.0	71.0

1981	1982	1983	1984	1985	1986	1987	1988	1989	1990 estimate	Notes	AUSTRALIA
											FOREIGN TRADE (CUSTOMS BASIS)
21,443	21,067	19,190	22,117	21,735	21,048	24,165	29,766	33,205	35,973	..	Value of Exports, fob
12,891	12,816	10,754	12,684	11,853	12,217	13,888	15,798	17,320	16,333	..	Nonfuel Primary Products
3,284	3,838	4,444	5,387	5,849	4,805	5,060	4,964	5,120	6,636	..	Fuels
5,268	4,413	3,992	4,046	4,033	4,026	5,217	9,003	10,764	13,004	..	Manufactures
23,486	23,672	19,116	22,659	23,094	24,340	26,834	33,157	39,869	39,740	..	Value of Imports, cif
2,064	1,903	1,794	2,089	2,007	2,101	2,450	3,082	3,412	3,224	..	Nonfuel Primary Products
3,192	3,417	2,070	2,042	1,560	1,125	1,306	1,326	2,040	2,181	..	Fuels
18,230	18,352	15,252	18,528	19,526	21,114	23,078	28,750	34,416	34,334	..	Manufactures

(Index 1987 = 100)

1981	1982	1983	1984	1985	1986	1987	1988	1989	1990	Notes	
119.1	112.6	113.7	116.2	111.0	99.3	100.0	114.5	122.0	114.7	..	Terms of Trade
116.0	104.7	101.7	101.6	94.9	91.4	100.0	124.8	133.3	141.2	..	Export Prices, fob
97.3	93.0	89.4	87.4	85.5	92.1	100.0	109.0	109.2	123.1	..	Import Prices, cif

(Millions of current US dollars)

1981	1982	1983	1984	1985	1986	1987	1988	1989	1990	Notes	
											BALANCE OF PAYMENTS
26,552	26,411	25,130	29,076	27,960	28,584	34,818	43,884	48,681	53,054	..	Exports of Goods & Services
21,214	20,793	19,501	22,769	22,275	22,187	26,270	32,780	36,339	38,905	..	Merchandise, fob
4,304	4,518	4,249	4,546	4,138	4,704	5,928	8,043	8,476	9,995	..	Nonfactor Services
1,034	1,099	1,381	1,761	1,547	1,692	2,621	3,061	3,866	4,154	..	Factor Services
34,921	34,674	31,053	37,729	37,379	38,542	43,881	55,759	68,571	69,719	..	Imports of Goods & Services
23,538	23,406	19,470	23,653	23,592	24,264	26,749	33,892	40,329	38,965	..	Merchandise, fob
6,985	7,138	6,486	7,385	7,062	7,061	7,992	9,830	12,113	12,840	..	Nonfactor Services
4,397	4,130	5,097	6,691	6,725	7,217	9,139	12,037	16,128	17,914	..	Factor Services
..	..	..	..	..	..	..	..	..	..	..	Long-Term Interest
298	300	412	451	686	817	1,196	1,706	2,124	1,939	..	Private Current Transfers, net
..	..	..	..	..	..	..	..	..	..	..	Workers' Remittances
-8,071	-7,963	-5,510	-8,202	-8,733	-9,141	-7,867	-10,168	-17,766	-14,725	..	Curr. A/C Bal before Off. Transf.
-399	-496	-437	-458	-263	-225	-178	-232	-182	-98	..	Net Official Transfers
-8,470	-8,459	-5,947	-8,660	-8,995	-9,366	-8,044	-10,401	-17,948	-14,823	..	Curr. A/C Bal after Off. Transf.
6,448	11,994	7,496	6,397	7,462	9,621	7,580	12,978	13,865	7,448	..	Long-Term Capital, net
1,551	1,610	2,464	-1,033	396	351	-2,061	2,025	4,253	5,334	..	Direct Investment
..	..	..	..	..	..	..	..	..	..	..	Long-Term Loans
..	..	..	..	..	..	..	..	..	..	..	Disbursements
..	..	..	..	..	..	..	..	..	..	..	Repayments
4,897	10,384	5,032	7,429	7,066	9,270	9,641	10,954	9,611	2,114	..	Other Long-Term Capital
1,879	1,367	1,517	956	-749	450	835	2,673	4,711	9,100	..	Other Capital, net
143	-4,902	-3,065	1,307	2,282	-705	-371	-5,251	-628	-1,725	..	Change in Reserves

(Australian Dollars per US dollar)

1981	1982	1983	1984	1985	1986	1987	1988	1989	1990	Notes	
											Memo Item:
0.870	0.990	1.110	1.140	1.430	1.500	1.430	1.280	1.260	1.280	..	Conversion Factor (Annual Avg)

(Millions US dollars), outstanding at end of year

1981	1982	1983	1984	1985	1986	1987	1988	1989	1990	Notes	
										..	**EXTERNAL DEBT (Total)**
..	..	..	..	..	..	..	..	..	..	..	Long-Term Debt (by debtor)
..	..	..	..	..	..	..	..	..	..	..	Central Bank, incl. IMF credit
..	..	..	..	..	..	..	..	..	..	..	Central Government
..	..	..	..	..	..	..	..	..	..	..	Rest of General Government
..	..	..	..	..	..	..	..	..	..	..	Non-financial Public Enterprises
..	..	..	..	..	..	..	..	..	..	..	Priv. Sector, incl non-guaranteed
..	..	..	..	..	..	..	..	..	..	..	Short-Term Debt

(Millions of US dollars)

1981	1982	1983	1984	1985	1986	1987	1988	1989	1990	Notes	
											Memo Items:
1,671.0	6,371.0	8,962.0	7,441.0	5,768.0	7,246.0	8,744.0	13,598.0	13,780.0	16,264.0	..	Int'l Reserves Excluding Gold
3,153.0	3,624.0	3,026.0	2,445.0	2,593.0	3,100.0	3,840.0	3,255.0	3,181.0	3,054.0	..	Gold Holdings (at market price)
											SOCIAL INDICATORS
2.0	2.0	2.0	2.0	1.9	1.9	1.9	1.9	1.9	1.9	..	Total Fertility Rate
9.9	10.3	9.6	9.2	9.9	9.9	8.0	7.7	7.5	7.2	..	Infant Mortality Rate
74.9	75.2	75.4	75.6	75.8	75.9	76.1	76.3	76.5	76.7	..	Life Expectancy at Birth
85.7	85.7	85.6	85.6	85.5	85.5	85.5	85.5	85.5	85.5	..	Urban Population, % of total
104.6	91.8	113.3	105.9	102.6	103.3	100.0	102.6	99.1	104.1	..	Food Prod. per capita (1987=100)
..	..	..	..	..	..	..	..	..	..	..	Labor Force, Agriculture (%)
37.6	37.6	37.7	37.7	37.8	37.9	37.9	38.0	38.1	38.1	..	Labor Force, Female (%)
..	..	108.0	108.0	106.0	106.0	105.0	106.0	106.0	..	..	Primary Schl. Enroll. Ratio
107.0	106.0	108.0	107.0	105.0	106.0	105.0	105.0	105.0	..	..	Primary Schl. Enroll. Ratio, Female
..	..	90.0	94.0	79.0	97.0	81.0	82.0	82.0	..	..	Secondary Schl. Enroll. Ratio

AUSTRIA	1970	1971	1972	1973	1974	1975	1976	1977	1978	1979	1980
CURRENT GNP PER CAPITA (US $)	1,960	2,180	2,520	3,110	3,950	4,740	5,370	6,110	6,870	8,450	9,990
POPULATION (thousands)	7,426	7,460	7,510	7,553	7,564	7,556	7,552	7,559	7,553	7,550	7,553

USE AND ORIGIN OF RESOURCES *(Billions of current Austrian Schillings)*

	1970	1971	1972	1973	1974	1975	1976	1977	1978	1979	1980
Gross National Product (GNP)	373.9	417.7	476.8	540.1	615.6	652.5	719.7	789.3	833.9	910.7	986.4
Net Factor Income from Abroad	-2.0	-1.9	-2.7	-3.4	-3.0	-3.6	-5.1	-6.9	-8.4	-7.8	-8.4
GDP at Market Prices	375.9	419.6	479.5	543.5	618.6	656.1	724.8	796.2	842.3	918.5	994.7
Resource Balance	3.7	3.0	2.7	2.0	-2.1	4.2	-11.1	-21.5	0.3	-3.9	-19.4
Exports of Goods & NFServices	116.8	128.6	146.4	165.9	204.2	209.0	236.3	256.9	280.8	327.7	366.2
Imports of Goods & NFServices	113.1	125.7	143.7	163.9	206.3	204.8	247.3	278.4	280.4	331.6	385.7
Domestic Absorption	372.2	416.6	476.8	541.5	620.6	651.9	735.8	817.6	842.0	922.4	1,014.1
Private Consumption, etc.	205.3	230.0	259.8	291.8	330.6	368.3	410.2	456.9	468.8	511.7	552.5
General Gov't Consumption	55.2	62.0	70.1	81.9	97.4	113.0	127.8	138.7	154.1	166.0	178.7
Gross Domestic Investment	111.7	124.7	146.9	167.8	192.6	170.6	197.8	222.0	219.0	244.8	282.9
Fixed Investment	97.2	116.9	144.9	155.0	175.7	174.9	188.7	212.9	215.6	231.9	255.5
Indirect Taxes, net	55.2	62.4	74.6	88.0	94.0	92.6	98.7	112.6	112.7	124.3	132.8
GDP at factor cost	320.7	357.2	404.9	455.4	524.6	563.6	626.0	683.6	729.6	794.3	861.9
Agriculture	25.8	25.1	28.2	31.4	33.1	33.1	36.4	36.0	39.3	40.3	44.3
Industry	170.5	190.8	219.2	231.4	265.1	268.4	294.0	318.9	334.8	368.2	393.4
Manufacturing	126.7	140.9	158.2	166.7	190.6	187.7	208.7	223.0	234.7	260.2	276.7
Services, etc.	179.6	203.7	232.1	280.7	320.3	354.7	394.3	441.3	468.2	510.1	557.0
Gross Domestic Saving	115.4	127.6	149.6	169.8	190.5	174.8	186.8	200.6	219.4	240.9	263.5
Gross National Saving	113.7	126.0	146.2	164.8	184.6	168.8	179.9	191.7	211.0	233.7	254.4

(Billions of 1987 Austrian Schillings)

	1970	1971	1972	1973	1974	1975	1976	1977	1978	1979	1980
Gross National Product	942.0	988.5	1,048.3	1,100.2	1,145.3	1,139.6	1,189.9	1,240.8	1,240.7	1,301.4	1,339.5
GDP at Market Prices	946.9	993.0	1,054.3	1,107.2	1,150.8	1,145.9	1,198.2	1,251.5	1,253.2	1,312.5	1,350.6
Resource Balance	-0.5	-0.2	-4.9	-15.7	-6.7	0.3	-18.0	-25.2	-1.2	-1.4	-5.5
Exports of Goods & NFServices	215.4	229.2	252.5	266.2	294.8	287.7	319.5	333.0	357.4	399.1	419.9
Imports of Goods & NFServices	215.9	229.5	257.4	281.9	301.4	287.4	337.5	358.3	358.6	400.5	425.3
Domestic Absorption	947.4	993.2	1,059.1	1,122.9	1,157.4	1,145.6	1,216.2	1,276.8	1,254.4	1,313.9	1,356.1
Private Consumption, etc.	508.6	540.7	572.6	602.9	622.7	643.1	668.7	703.4	695.6	725.1	734.9
General Gov't Consumption	175.8	181.6	189.1	194.7	205.8	214.0	223.1	230.4	238.0	245.1	251.6
Gross Domestic Investment	262.9	270.9	297.5	325.3	328.9	288.6	324.3	343.0	320.8	343.7	369.6
Fixed Investment	234.8	267.1	299.6	300.6	312.5	297.1	308.4	324.1	310.9	321.8	331.4
GDP at factor cost	807.2	844.5	888.8	924.9	976.0	984.1	1,035.5	1,075.8	1,085.9	1,136.0	1,173.5
Agriculture	37.6	34.8	35.0	37.2	38.7	40.6	42.0	40.5	43.1	44.0	45.8
Industry	358.5	382.3	409.8	432.5	448.4	429.2	449.2	471.0	471.5	497.7	507.8
Manufacturing	246.2	260.6	280.4	295.0	305.1	286.9	305.0	320.3	323.4	344.2	352.4
Services, etc.	550.8	576.0	609.5	637.5	663.6	676.1	707.0	740.1	738.5	770.8	797.0

Memo Items:

	1970	1971	1972	1973	1974	1975	1976	1977	1978	1979	1980
Capacity to Import	222.9	234.9	262.2	285.4	298.4	293.3	322.4	330.7	359.0	395.8	403.9
Terms of Trade Adjustment	7.5	5.7	9.8	19.2	3.6	5.6	2.9	-2.4	1.6	-3.3	-15.9
Gross Domestic Income	954.4	998.7	1,064.0	1,126.3	1,154.4	1,151.5	1,201.1	1,249.1	1,254.8	1,309.2	1,334.7
Gross National Income	949.5	994.2	1,058.1	1,119.4	1,148.9	1,145.3	1,192.8	1,238.4	1,242.3	1,298.1	1,323.5

DOMESTIC PRICES/DEFLATORS *(Index 1987 = 100)*

	1970	1971	1972	1973	1974	1975	1976	1977	1978	1979	1980
Overall (GDP)	39.7	42.3	45.5	49.1	53.8	57.3	60.5	63.6	67.2	70.0	73.6
Domestic Absorption	39.3	41.9	45.0	48.2	53.6	56.9	60.5	64.0	67.1	70.2	74.8
Agriculture	68.5	72.3	80.6	84.2	85.4	81.4	86.7	89.0	91.2	91.5	96.8
Industry	47.6	49.9	53.5	53.5	59.1	62.5	65.4	67.7	71.0	74.0	77.5
Manufacturing	51.5	54.1	56.4	56.5	62.5	65.4	68.4	69.6	72.6	75.6	78.5
Consumer Price Index	41.6	43.5	46.3	49.8	54.5	59.1	63.4	66.9	69.3	71.9	76.4

MANUFACTURING ACTIVITY

	1970	1971	1972	1973	1974	1975	1976	1977	1978	1979	1980
Employment (1987=100)	102.3	107.2	109.7	111.9	110.8	105.0	109.4	109.4	108.3	109.0	109.0
Real Earnings per Empl. (1987=100)	63.4	65.9	69.1	72.9	76.8	80.0	79.3	82.2	85.7	86.9	88.2
Real Output per Empl. (1987=100)	56.9	58.0	60.8	64.5	72.1	73.0	74.6	78.1	79.3	82.8	88.2
Earnings as % of Value Added	47.1	47.7	48.5	52.0	51.5	56.2	55.9	58.4	58.4	57.3	58.6

MONETARY HOLDINGS *(Billions of current Austrian Schillings)*

	1970	1971	1972	1973	1974	1975	1976	1977	1978	1979	1980
Money Supply, Broadly Defined	215.1	247.0	285.8	323.2	363.6	430.5	503.2	548.9	627.4	678.3	765.0
Money	64.8	73.7	89.2	95.9	101.4	115.9	125.5	127.3	137.9	125.4	145.1
Currency Outside Banks	34.0	37.3	42.9	46.1	48.7	52.3	55.2	58.7	63.2	67.0	71.6
Demand Deposits	30.8	36.4	46.4	49.8	52.7	63.5	70.4	68.6	74.7	58.4	73.4
Quasi-Money	150.4	173.3	196.6	227.3	262.3	314.6	377.6	421.6	489.5	552.8	620.0

GOVERNMENT DEFICIT (-) OR SURPLUS *(Billions of current Austrian Schillings)*

	1970	1971	1972	1973	1974	1975	1976	1977	1978	1979	1980
GOVERNMENT DEFICIT (-) OR SURPLUS	-1.80	0.24	-0.85	-8.96	-9.76	-26.34	-34.06	-30.21	-34.92	-35.31	-33.57
Current Revenue	110.06	124.63	142.93	163.80	189.51	205.49	226.70	254.14	290.01	317.76	346.98
Current Expenditure	99.94	111.72	126.44	144.72	171.27	203.15	230.63	255.66	291.79	314.92	338.12
Current Budget Balance	10.12	12.91	16.49	19.08	18.24	2.34	-3.93	-1.52	-1.78	2.84	8.86
Capital Receipts	0.27	0.14	0.17	0.17	0.21	0.27	0.37	0.42	0.40	0.40	0.43
Capital Payments	12.19	12.81	17.51	28.21	28.21	28.95	30.50	29.11	33.54	38.55	42.86

1981	1982	1983	1984	1985	1986	1987	1988	1989	1990 estimate	Notes	AUSTRIA
10,120	9,800	9,300	9,090	9,040	9,870	11,950	15,430	17,250	18,980	..	**CURRENT GNP PER CAPITA (US $)**
7,565	7,574	7,552	7,552	7,555	7,565	7,573	7,595	7,618	7,712	..	**POPULATION (thousands)**
											USE AND ORIGIN OF RESOURCES
					(Billions of current Austrian Schillings)						
1,047.2	1,125.1	1,192.4	1,268.2	1,341.4	1,410.5	1,468.5	1,548.0	1,649.5	1,775.3	..	Gross National Product (GNP)
-8.8	-8.4	-8.8	-8.6	-7.1	-12.0	-12.9	-13.7	-14.4	-14.1		Net Factor Income from Abroad
1,056.0	1,133.5	1,201.2	1,276.8	1,348.4	1,422.5	1,481.4	1,561.7	1,663.9	1,789.4		GDP at Market Prices
-14.0	18.8	15.8	1.9	2.3	13.2	7.2	8.9	14.9	20.3	..	Resource Balance
404.5	431.2	449.7	497.6	549.1	523.0	527.1	587.5	664.6	734.8		Exports of Goods & NF Services
418.5	412.4	433.9	495.7	546.8	509.8	519.8	578.6	649.7	714.5		Imports of Goods & NF Services
1,069.9	1,114.7	1,185.5	1,274.8	1,346.1	1,409.3	1,474.2	1,552.8	1,649.0	1,769.1		Domestic Absorption
596.5	640.2	694.8	733.2	775.5	804.4	837.8	880.1	928.3	991.9	..	Private Consumption, etc.
195.2	214.3	226.9	237.8	255.0	270.7	280.4	288.4	302.9	321.2	..	General Gov't Consumption
278.2	260.2	263.7	303.9	315.6	334.3	355.9	384.3	417.9	456.0	..	Gross Domestic Investment
267.9	262.9	269.6	282.9	304.4	324.0	342.1	371.2	402.6	435.1		Fixed Investment
142.3	150.7	161.7	180.2	186.7	188.0	197.8	209.8	226.3	240.8		Indirect Taxes, net
913.7	982.8	1,039.5	1,096.6	1,161.7	1,234.5	1,283.6	1,351.9	1,437.6	1,548.6	B	GDP at factor cost
43.4	43.7	44.1	48.7	45.0	47.3	48.7	49.0	51.5	..	..	Agriculture
410.4	436.6	454.7	471.3	497.6	521.1	536.9	572.3	611.5		..	Industry
288.9	308.1	322.8	340.1	362.8	377.4	383.5	413.7	444.0			Manufacturing
602.1	653.2	702.4	756.8	805.9	854.1	895.7	940.5	1,000.9	..		Services, etc.
264.2	279.0	279.5	305.8	317.9	347.4	363.2	393.2	432.8	476.2		Gross Domestic Saving
254.6	270.0	270.0	296.8	309.7	335.5	350.1	380.0	417.6	463.4	..	Gross National Saving
					(Billions of 1987 Austrian Schillings)						
1,334.7	1,351.3	1,376.8	1,396.3	1,432.7	1,445.0	1,468.5	1,526.9	1,583.9	1,663.3	..	Gross National Product
1,345.6	1,361.1	1,386.8	1,405.6	1,440.1	1,457.2	1,481.4	1,540.5	1,597.7	1,676.5	..	GDP at Market Prices
18.2	44.2	36.0	21.8	26.7	18.2	7.2	5.6	15.5	17.3	..	Resource Balance
440.3	452.2	466.6	495.0	529.2	514.8	527.1	574.1	632.9	694.4	..	Exports of Goods & NF Services
422.1	408.0	430.6	473.3	502.5	496.6	519.8	568.5	617.3	677.1	..	Imports of Goods & NF Services
1,327.4	1,317.0	1,350.8	1,383.8	1,413.5	1,439.0	1,474.2	1,534.9	1,582.2	1,659.2	..	Domestic Absorption
737.9	750.9	785.1	781.6	799.8	813.7	837.8	864.6	888.6	919.5	..	Private Consumption, etc.
257.2	263.1	268.9	269.5	274.8	279.3	280.4	281.4	283.6	287.8	..	General Gov't Consumption
332.3	302.9	296.7	332.7	339.0	346.0	355.9	388.9	410.1	451.9	..	Gross Domestic Investment
326.8	300.2	298.4	304.7	320.0	331.8	342.1	362.8	382.5	400.5	..	Fixed Investment
1,169.6	1,184.3	1,203.3	1,210.4	1,244.3	1,265.5	1,283.6	1,332.8	1,380.3	1,450.2	B	GDP at factor cost
44.2	50.2	48.2	50.6	48.2	48.7	48.7	50.8	50.0	..	..	Agriculture
498.6	493.7	498.8	508.4	524.5	528.7	536.9	562.3	591.3	..	..	Industry
347.8	349.2	354.8	365.0	379.0	381.0	383.5	405.0	429.0	..		Manufacturing
802.8	817.2	839.8	846.6	867.4	879.9	895.7	927.4	956.4	..	..	Services, etc.
											Memo Items:
408.0	426.6	446.3	475.1	504.6	509.5	527.1	577.2	631.5	696.3	..	Capacity to Import
-32.3	-25.6	-20.4	-19.9	-24.5	-5.4	0.0	3.2	-1.4	1.9	..	Terms of Trade Adjustment
1,313.3	1,335.6	1,366.4	1,385.7	1,415.6	1,451.9	1,481.4	1,543.7	1,596.3	1,678.4	..	Gross Domestic Income
1,302.4	1,325.7	1,356.4	1,376.4	1,408.2	1,439.7	1,468.5	1,530.1	1,582.5	1,665.3	..	Gross National Income
					(Index 1987 = 100)						**DOMESTIC PRICES/DEFLATORS**
78.5	83.3	86.6	90.8	93.6	97.6	100.0	101.4	104.1	106.7	..	Overall (GDP)
80.6	84.6	87.8	92.1	95.2	97.9	100.0	101.2	104.2	106.6	..	Domestic Absorption
98.3	87.1	91.7	96.2	93.3	97.2	100.0	96.5	103.0		..	Agriculture
82.3	88.4	91.2	92.7	94.9	98.6	100.0	101.8	103.4	..	..	Industry
83.1	88.2	91.0	93.2	95.7	99.1	100.0	102.2	103.5	..		Manufacturing
81.6	86.0	88.9	94.0	97.0	98.6	100.0	101.9	104.5	107.9	..	Consumer Price Index
											MANUFACTURING ACTIVITY
106.6	103.5	104.2	103.2	103.5	102.1	100.0	100.3	101.4	..	..	Employment (1987=100)
90.0	91.8	91.9	91.2	93.3	96.9	100.0	105.2	..	..	..	Real Earnings per Empl. (1987=100)
91.9	93.6	95.5	100.4	102.4	99.2	100.0	104.4			..	Real Output per Empl. (1987=100)
58.5	58.2	56.7	55.5	55.6	56.0	55.8	56.5			..	Earnings as % of Value Added
					(Billions of current Austrian Schillings)						**MONETARY HOLDINGS**
843.6	936.1	984.7	1,047.3	1,110.2	1,205.9	1,296.5	1,371.9	1,469.3	1,611.2	..	Money Supply, Broadly Defined
141.6	153.3	170.4	176.4	181.9	193.5	213.5	232.2	235.0	247.3	..	Money
73.2	75.7	84.1	83.9	84.5	87.9	93.0	98.7	102.6	106.6	..	Currency Outside Banks
68.5	77.5	86.3	92.5	97.4	105.7	120.5	133.5	132.4	140.6	..	Demand Deposits
702.0	782.8	814.3	870.9	928.3	1,012.4	1,083.0	1,139.7	1,234.3	1,363.9	..	Quasi-Money
					(Billions of current Austrian Schillings)						
-32.52	-54.53	-71.84	-58.22	-63.33	-84.22	-81.55	-78.40	-62.84	-77.72	E	**GOVERNMENT DEFICIT (-) OR SURPLUS**
382.46	397.57	417.64	456.97	476.12	497.45	516.35	557.07	583.53	627.78	..	Current Revenue
370.13	405.34	433.57	461.64	484.60	520.81	550.50	568.13	590.23	631.64	..	Current Expenditure
12.33	-7.77	-15.93	-4.67	-8.48	-23.36	-34.15	-11.06	-6.70	-3.86	..	Current Budget Balance
0.47	0.51	0.53	0.46	0.58	0.84	0.72	0.97	1.19	1.63	..	Capital Receipts
45.32	47.27	56.44	54.01	55.43	61.70	48.12	68.31	57.33	75.49	..	Capital Payments

AUSTRIA	1970	1971	1972	1973	1974	1975	1976	1977	1978	1979	1980
FOREIGN TRADE (CUSTOMS BASIS)					*(Millions of current US dollars)*						
Value of Exports, fob	2,857	3,169	3,883	5,285	7,161	7,518	8,507	9,808	12,174	15,478	17,478
Nonfuel Primary Products	493	519	619	868	1,068	943	1,232	1,378	1,745	2,327	2,723
Fuels	72	64	77	113	144	155	159	189	191	223	274
Manufactures	2,291	2,586	3,187	4,303	5,950	6,420	7,116	8,241	10,238	12,928	14,481
Value of Imports, cif	3,549	4,189	5,216	7,121	9,023	9,392	11,523	14,248	15,975	20,231	24,415
Nonfuel Primary Products	777	819	950	1,392	1,743	1,622	1,898	2,339	2,567	3,266	3,781
Fuels	294	340	370	533	1,096	1,187	1,409	1,465	1,715	2,499	3,781
Manufactures	2,479	3,029	3,896	5,196	6,184	6,584	8,216	10,444	11,694	14,465	16,852
					(Index 1987 = 100)						
Terms of Trade	131.3	122.3	119.0	122.7	100.8	109.0	99.6	97.0	104.6	105.0	96.6
Export Prices, fob	25.3	26.8	30.0	39.0	47.8	54.0	51.7	56.0	66.5	79.7	84.7
Import Prices, cif	19.3	21.9	25.2	31.8	47.4	49.6	51.9	57.7	63.6	75.8	87.7
BALANCE OF PAYMENTS					*(Millions of current US dollars)*						
Exports of Goods & Services	4,331	5,037	6,173	8,543	11,270	12,454	13,748	16,273	20,598	26,005	31,315
Merchandise, fob	2,837	3,143	3,842	5,238	7,504	7,553	8,468	9,728	12,189	15,454	17,027
Nonfactor Services	1,358	1,723	2,155	3,040	3,222	4,289	4,646	5,795	7,406	8,966	11,749
Factor Services	136	170	177	265	544	611	634	750	1,002	1,584	2,538
Imports of Goods & Services	4,415	5,132	6,296	8,710	11,306	12,545	14,753	18,333	21,294	27,175	32,951
Merchandise, fob	3,516	4,076	4,969	6,804	8,812	9,508	11,048	13,553	15,472	19,726	23,644
Nonfactor Services	687	811	1,033	1,465	1,787	2,217	2,789	3,614	4,243	5,277	6,124
Factor Services	212	246	294	440	707	820	916	1,166	1,579	2,172	3,182
Long-Term Interest	..	..	..	..	..	..	..	..	..	..	..
Private Current Transfers, net	11	9	-30	-82	-157	-137	-103	-122	2	53	-58
Workers' Remittances	13	19	27	40	66	73	89	103	136	177	215
Curr. A/C Bal before Off. Transf.	-73	-87	-152	-249	-193	-228	-1,108	-2,183	-695	-1,118	-1,694
Net Official Transfers	-2	-4	-5	-5	-10	-3	-11	-17	-11	-23	-31
Curr. A/C Bal after Off. Transf.	-75	-91	-157	-254	-203	-231	-1,119	-2,200	-706	-1,141	-1,725
Long-Term Capital, net	14	-18	78	-227	403	1,062	-72	604	1,404	-521	550
Direct Investment	104	107	107	122	157	53	35	11	53	103	139
Long-Term Loans	..	..	..	..	..	..	..	..	..	..	..
Disbursements	..	..	..	..	..	..	..	..	..	..	..
Repayments	..	..	..	..	..	..	..	..	..	..	..
Other Long-Term Capital	-90	-125	-29	-349	245	1,009	-107	593	1,351	-624	411
Other Capital, net	242	482	445	310	188	341	1,076	1,251	652	640	2,516
Change in Reserves	-181	-373	-366	171	-388	-1,172	116	344	-1,350	1,022	-1,341
Memo Item:					*(Austrian Schillings per US dollar)*						
Conversion Factor (Annual Avg)	26.000	24.960	23.120	19.580	18.690	17.420	17.940	16.530	14.520	13.370	12.940
EXTERNAL DEBT (Total)					*(Millions US dollars), outstanding at end of year*						
Long-Term Debt (by debtor)	..	..	..	..	..	..	..	..	..	..	..
Central Bank, incl. IMF credit	..	..	..	..	..	..	..	..	..	..	..
Central Government	..	..	..	..	..	..	..	..	..	..	..
Rest of General Government	..	..	..	..	..	..	..	..	..	..	..
Non-financial Public Enterprises	..	..	..	..	..	..	..	..	..	..	..
Priv. Sector, incl non-guaranteed	..	..	..	..	..	..	..	..	..	..	..
Short-Term Debt	..	..	..	..	..	..	..	..	..	..	..
Memo Items:					*(Millions of US dollars)*						
Int'l Reserves Excluding Gold	1,044	1,547	1,927	1,992	2,535	3,583	3,561	3,351	5,047	4,075	5,281
Gold Holdings (at market price)	762	909	1,353	2,344	3,894	2,928	2,814	3,463	4,758	10,808	12,445
SOCIAL INDICATORS											
Total Fertility Rate	2.3	2.2	2.1	2.0	1.9	1.8	1.7	1.6	1.6	1.7	1.7
Infant Mortality Rate	25.9	26.1	25.2	23.8	23.5	20.5	18.2	16.9	14.9	14.8	13.9
Life Expectancy at Birth	70.3	70.4	70.6	70.8	71.1	71.4	71.7	72.0	72.2	72.4	72.7
Urban Population, % of total	51.7	52.0	52.3	52.6	52.9	53.2	53.5	53.8	54.2	54.5	54.8
Food Prod. per capita (1987=100)	82.8	82.0	80.1	83.8	86.6	89.2	89.3	88.2	91.4	93.0	97.7
Labor Force, Agriculture (%)	14.8	14.2	13.6	13.0	12.5	11.9	11.3	10.7	10.1	9.6	9.0
Labor Force, Female (%)	38.7	38.9	39.1	39.3	39.5	39.6	39.8	39.9	40.1	40.2	40.4
Primary Schl. Enroll. Ratio	104.0	..	..	..	..	102.0	102.0	100.0	100.0	99.0	99.0
Primary Schl. Enroll. Ratio, Female	103.0	..	..	..	..	101.0	102.0	100.0	99.0	98.0	98.0
Secondary Schl. Enroll. Ratio	72.0	..	..	..	..	74.0	75.0	72.0	72.0	72.0	73.0

1981	1982	1983	1984	1985	1986	1987	1988	1989	1990 estimate	Notes	AUSTRIA
											FOREIGN TRADE (CUSTOMS BASIS)
				(Millions of current US dollars)							
15,840	15,690	15,423	15,712	17,102	22,517	27,163	31,082	32,444	41,876	..	Value of Exports, fob
2,310	2,116	2,137	2,175	2,128	2,622	3,100	3,663	3,927	4,683	..	Nonfuel Primary Products
276	241	217	234	346	273	479	396	407	416	..	Fuels
13,255	13,333	13,070	13,304	14,628	19,622	23,583	27,023	28,110	36,778	..	Manufactures
21,013	19,514	19,322	19,573	20,803	26,793	32,638	36,609	38,854	49,960	..	Value of Imports, cif
3,229	3,002	2,866	3,072	3,139	3,796	4,340	5,019	5,320	6,073	..	Nonfuel Primary Products
3,920	3,150	2,667	2,955	3,090	2,320	2,358	2,078	2,221	3,163	..	Fuels
13,863	13,363	13,788	13,546	14,574	20,678	25,939	29,512	31,313	40,725	..	Manufactures
				(Index 1987 = 100)							
86.2	89.9	87.8	84.4	87.2	100.0	100.0	94.8	89.6	92.1	..	Terms of Trade
73.8	72.8	69.0	64.9	65.6	80.7	100.0	102.9	93.7	108.6	..	Export Prices, fob
85.6	81.0	78.6	76.9	75.3	80.7	100.0	108.6	104.6	117.9	..	Import Prices, cif
											BALANCE OF PAYMENTS
				(Millions of current US dollars)							
28,720	28,628	27,826	27,919	30,106	38,473	46,617	53,405	57,522	73,280	..	Exports of Goods & Services
15,603	15,363	15,155	15,471	16,683	21,565	26,558	30,056	31,832	40,252	..	Merchandise, fob
9,920	10,078	10,039	9,540	10,194	13,081	15,508	17,943	18,814	23,790	..	Nonfactor Services
3,197	3,187	2,632	2,908	3,229	3,827	4,551	5,406	6,876	9,239	..	Factor Services
30,096	27,913	27,498	28,122	30,286	38,344	46,966	53,827	57,334	72,322	..	Imports of Goods & Services
20,646	18,814	18,794	19,485	21,089	26,176	31,702	36,358	38,437	48,234	..	Merchandise, fob
5,708	5,418	5,586	5,302	5,631	7,538	9,688	10,946	10,931	13,711	..	Nonfactor Services
3,742	3,682	3,118	3,335	3,567	4,630	5,576	6,523	7,965	10,377	..	Factor Services
..	..	..	..	..	..	..	..	..	..	..	Long-Term Interest
-57	-37	-38	-22	-55	2	-10	38	-57	108	..	Private Current Transfers, net
198	201	188	176	184	269	365	410	420	573	..	Workers' Remittances
-1,433	677	290	-226	-235	130	-358	-384	131	1,067	..	Curr. A/C Bal before Off. Transf.
-30	-36	-44	-39	-39	-44	-71	-74	-72	-109	..	Net Official Transfers
-1,464	641	246	-264	-273	86	-429	-458	59	958	..	Curr. A/C Bal after Off. Transf.
814	-557	-1,343	-308	-313	-1,656	893	599	399	-2,313	..	Long-Term Capital, net
117	129	104	92	195	-39	145	190	-66	-746	..	Direct Investment
..	..	..	..	..	..	..	..	..	..	..	Long-Term Loans
..	..	..	..	..	..	..	..	..	..	..	Disbursements
..	..	..	..	..	..	..	..	..	..	..	Repayments
698	-687	-1,447	-400	-508	-1,617	748	408	465	-1,567	..	Other Long-Term Capital
1,028	124	606	642	674	2,299	-60	254	538	1,319	..	Other Capital, net
-379	-208	491	-70	-88	-728	-404	-395	-996	36	..	Change in Reserves
											Memo Item:
				(Austrian Schillings per US dollar)							
15.930	17.060	17.960	20.010	20.690	15.270	12.640	12.350	13.230	11.370	..	Conversion Factor (Annual Avg)
											EXTERNAL DEBT (Total)
				(Millions US dollars), outstanding at end of year							
..	..	..	..	..	..	..	..	..	..	..	Long-Term Debt (by debtor)
..	..	..	..	..	..	..	..	..	..	..	Central Bank, incl. IMF credit
..	..	..	..	..	..	..	..	..	..	..	Central Government
..	..	..	..	..	..	..	..	..	..	..	Rest of General Government
..	..	..	..	..	..	..	..	..	..	..	Non-financial Public Enterprises
..	..	..	..	..	..	..	..	..	..	..	Priv. Sector, incl non-guaranteed
..	..	..	..	..	..	..	..	..	..	..	Short-Term Debt
											Memo Items:
				(Millions of US dollars)							
5,285	5,300	4,515	4,244	4,767	6,162	7,532	7,368	8,598	9,376	..	Int'l Reserves Excluding Gold
8,392	9,649	8,060	6,516	6,912	8,265	10,237	8,675	8,284	7,851	..	Gold Holdings (at market price)
											SOCIAL INDICATORS
1.6	1.6	1.6	1.5	1.5	1.5	1.5	1.5	1.5	1.5	..	Total Fertility Rate
12.6	12.8	12.0	11.5	11.2	10.3	9.9	9.5	9.2	8.8	..	Infant Mortality Rate
72.9	73.1	73.5	73.9	74.3	74.7	75.1	75.4	75.7	76.0	..	Life Expectancy at Birth
55.1	55.4	55.8	56.1	56.4	56.8	57.2	57.6	58.0	58.4	..	Urban Population, % of total
93.2	104.5	99.8	102.4	99.2	101.6	100.0	102.5	98.9	98.6	..	Food Prod. per capita (1987=100)
..	..	..	..	..	..	..	..	..	..	..	Labor Force, Agriculture (%)
40.3	40.3	40.3	40.2	40.2	40.2	40.1	40.1	40.1	40.1	..	Labor Force, Female (%)
..	98.0	98.0	97.0	100.0	100.0	103.0	104.0	104.0		..	Primary Schl. Enroll. Ratio
98.0	98.0	97.0	97.0	99.0	100.0	102.0	103.0	103.0		..	Primary Schl. Enroll. Ratio, Female
..	74.0	74.0	76.0	78.0	79.0	79.0	80.0	82.0		..	Secondary Schl. Enroll. Ratio

BAHAMAS, THE	1970	1971	1972	1973	1974	1975	1976	1977	1978	1979	1980
CURRENT GNP PER CAPITA (US $)	2,700	2,900	2,900	3,260	2,950	2,730	3,000	3,330	3,670	5,100	5,830
POPULATION (thousands)	171	174	178	181	185	189	193	197	201	206	210
USE AND ORIGIN OF RESOURCES				*(Millions of current Bahamian Dollars)*							
Gross National Product (GNP)	475.3	505.2	520.6	591.1	557.2	525.3	565.7	628.2	702.7	1,016.4	1,221.7
Net Factor Income from Abroad	-64.2	-68.2	-70.3	-79.8	-75.2	-70.9	-76.4	-84.8	-129.7	-123.4	-113.6
GDP at Market Prices	539.5	573.4	590.9	670.9	632.4	596.2	642.1	713.0	832.4	1,139.8	1,335.3
Resource Balance	..	..	..	..	..	..	..	117.7	126.1	98.8	100.2
Exports of Goods & NF Services	..	..	..	..	..	..	..	589.3	688.1	785.0	939.8
Imports of Goods & NF Services	..	..	..	..	..	..	..	471.6	562.0	686.2	839.6
Domestic Absorption	..	..	..	..	..	..	..	595.3	706.3	1,041.0	1,235.1
Private Consumption, etc.	..	..	..	..	..	..	..	396.8	483.5	751.0	823.9
General Gov't Consumption	..	..	..	..	..	..	..	109.3	128.4	143.8	167.0
Gross Domestic Investment	..	..	..	..	..	..	..	89.2	94.4	146.2	244.2
Fixed Investment	..	..	..	..	..	..	..	81.3	85.9	135.3	212.9
Indirect Taxes, net	..	..	..	..	..	..	..	..	..	125.9	146.6
GDP at factor cost	..	..	..	..	..	..	..	..	..	1,013.9	1,188.7
Agriculture	..	..	..	..	..	..	..	..	..	..	..
Industry	..	..	..	..	..	..	..	..	..	..	..
Manufacturing	..	..	..	..	..	..	..	..	..	..	..
Services, etc.	..	..	..	..	..	..	..	..	..	..	..
Gross Domestic Saving	..	..	..	..	..	..	..	206.9	220.5	245.0	344.4
Gross National Saving	..	..	..	..	..	..	..	103.5	68.6	105.8	211.1
				(Millions of 1987 Bahamian Dollars)							
Gross National Product	1,446.3	1,469.9	1,418.5	1,525.9	1,270.3	1,082.0	1,138.2	1,242.4	1,359.7	1,854.2	2,025.4
GDP at Market Prices	1,636.0	1,662.6	1,604.5	1,725.9	1,436.7	1,224.1	1,287.5	1,405.4	1,604.7	2,023.9	2,155.6
Resource Balance	..	..	..	..	..	..	..	269.9	331.1	295.4	322.0
Exports of Goods & NF Services	..	..	..	..	..	..	..	1,011.6	1,115.5	1,156.7	1,273.4
Imports of Goods & NF Services	..	..	..	..	..	..	..	741.8	784.4	861.3	951.4
Domestic Absorption	..	..	..	..	..	..	..	1,135.5	1,273.6	1,728.5	1,833.6
Private Consumption, etc.	..	..	..	..	..	..	..	766.7	886.7	1,271.0	1,253.9
General Gov't Consumption	..	..	..	..	..	..	..	209.9	232.1	238.5	247.1
Gross Domestic Investment	..	..	..	..	..	..	..	159.0	154.7	219.0	332.6
Fixed Investment	..	..	..	..	..	..	..	144.9	140.8	202.6	289.8
GDP at factor cost	..	..	..	..	..	..	..	..	..	1,824.2	1,948.6
Agriculture	..	..	..	..	..	..	..	..	..	..	..
Industry	..	..	..	..	..	..	..	..	..	..	..
Manufacturing	..	..	..	..	..	..	..	..	..	..	..
Services, etc.	..	..	..	..	..	..	..	..	..	..	..
Memo Items:											
Capacity to Import	..	..	..	..	..	..	..	926.9	960.4	985.3	1,065.0
Terms of Trade Adjustment	..	..	..	..	..	..	..	-84.7	-155.1	-171.4	-208.5
Gross Domestic Income	..	..	..	..	..	..	..	1,320.6	1,449.6	1,852.5	1,947.1
Gross National Income	..	..	..	..	..	..	..	1,157.7	1,204.6	1,682.8	1,817.0
DOMESTIC PRICES/DEFLATORS				*(Index 1987 = 100)*							
Overall (GDP)	33.0	34.5	36.8	38.9	44.0	48.7	49.9	50.7	51.9	56.3	61.9
Domestic Absorption	..	..	..	..	..	..	..	52.4	55.5	60.2	67.4
Agriculture	..	..	..	..	..	..	..	..	..	..	..
Industry	..	..	..	..	..	..	..	..	..	..	..
Manufacturing	..	..	..	..	..	..	..	..	..	..	..
Consumer Price Index	32.7	34.2	36.5	38.5	43.6	48.1	50.2	51.8	54.9	59.9	67.2
MANUFACTURING ACTIVITY											
Employment (1987=100)	..	..	..	..	..	..	..	..	..	..	..
Real Earnings per Empl. (1987=100)	..	..	..	..	..	..	..	..	..	..	..
Real Output per Empl. (1987=100)	..	..	..	..	..	..	..	..	..	..	..
Earnings as % of Value Added	..	..	..	..	..	..	..	39.8	93.8	45.3	42.6
MONETARY HOLDINGS				*(Millions of current Bahamian Dollars)*							
Money Supply, Broadly Defined	183.6	189.2	204.5	252.9	254.2	276.9	356.8	338.3	388.2	456.9	520.3
Money	80.5	68.8	84.9	80.4	77.8	73.7	77.5	89.5	107.1	138.3	136.3
Currency Outside Banks	17.8	15.3	21.3	20.2	19.3	20.1	20.5	23.3	26.5	29.8	33.4
Demand Deposits	62.7	53.5	63.6	60.2	58.5	53.6	57.0	66.2	80.6	108.5	102.9
Quasi-Money	103.1	120.4	119.6	172.5	176.4	203.2	279.3	248.8	281.1	318.6	384.0
GOVERNMENT DEFICIT (-) OR SURPLUS				*(Millions of current Bahamian Dollars)*							
Current Revenue	..	..	..	1.90	-40.10	-0.40	-6.90	-9.80	-13.60	6.70	18.90
Current Expenditure	..	..	..	107.60	118.00	137.20	152.10	156.00	185.20	226.50	270.40
Current Budget Balance	..	..	..	97.30	103.00	113.40	127.70	140.70	149.80	180.40	228.10
Capital Receipts	..	..	..	10.30	15.00	23.80	24.40	15.30	35.40	46.10	42.30
Capital Payments	..	..	..	..	..	..	..	..	..	..	..
	..	..	..	8.40	55.10	24.20	31.30	25.10	49.00	39.40	23.40

1981	1982	1983	1984	1985	1986	1987	1988	1989	1990 estimate	Notes	BAHAMAS, THE
5,650	6,600	7,110	8,190	8,950	9,530	10,360	10,630	11,070	11,420	..	**CURRENT GNP PER CAPITA (US $)**
214	219	224	229	232	236	240	245	250	255	..	**POPULATION (thousands)**
											USE AND ORIGIN OF RESOURCES
			(Millions of current Bahamian Dollars)								
1,287.7	1,463.4	1,609.5	1,892.6	2,158.1	2,309.2	2,551.9	2,649.6	2,799.7	2,933.4	..	Gross National Product (GNP)
-138.8	-114.9	-123.3	-148.5	-162.6	-163.3	-162.1	-168.3	-177.8	-186.3	..	Net Factor Income from Abroad
1,426.5	1,578.3	1,732.8	2,041.1	2,320.7	2,472.5	2,714.0	2,817.9	2,977.5	3,119.7	..	GDP at Market Prices
71.5	98.4	148.2	107.8	128.1	146.2	149.8	..	..	..	..	Resource Balance
961.2	1,038.3	1,153.5	1,297.9	1,503.6	1,577.9	1,664.3					Exports of Goods & NFServices
889.7	939.9	1,005.3	1,190.1	1,375.5	1,431.7	1,514.5					Imports of Goods & NFServices
1,355.0	1,479.9	1,584.5	1,933.3	2,192.6	2,326.3	2,564.2					Domestic Absorption
888.9	932.2	994.3	1,335.6	1,458.6	1,570.7	1,727.7					Private Consumption, etc.
197.3	208.9	238.0	264.0	289.1	300.1	326.4					General Gov't Consumption
268.8	338.8	352.2	333.7	444.9	455.5	510.1					Gross Domestic Investment
238.9	298.7	310.7	326.5	407.8	425.2	508.1					Fixed Investment
152.6	157.0	179.0	254.0	303.1	322.8	335.4	..	..	..	..	Indirect Taxes, net
1,273.9	1,421.3	1,553.8	1,787.1	2,017.6	2,149.7	2,378.6	..	..	..	..	GDP at factor cost
..	..	..	41.7	44.2	44.8	49.6	..	..	..	..	Agriculture
..	..	..	246.6	279.6	301.0	344.6	..	..	..	..	Industry
											Manufacturing
..	..	..	1,498.8	1,693.8	1,803.9	1,984.4	..	..	..	..	Services, etc.
340.3	437.2	500.5	441.5	573.0	601.7	659.9					Gross Domestic Saving
187.6	304.6	366.9	278.4	395.8	424.4	480.0					Gross National Saving
			(Millions of 1987 Bahamian Dollars)								
1,780.4	1,952.0	2,009.9	2,281.8	2,385.0	2,462.2	2,551.9	2,541.8	2,548.2	2,552.5		Gross National Product
1,956.7	2,088.0	2,163.1	2,469.8	2,588.6	2,635.2	2,714.0	2,681.2	2,687.9	2,692.4		GDP at Market Prices
177.9	234.2	260.9	229.5	158.4	160.5	149.8	..	..	..		Resource Balance
1,166.1	1,265.9	1,376.1	1,551.5	1,643.5	1,686.4	1,664.3	..	..	..		Exports of Goods & NFServices
988.2	1,031.6	1,115.2	1,322.0	1,485.1	1,526.0	1,514.5	..	..	..		Imports of Goods & NFServices
1,778.8	1,853.8	1,902.2	2,240.2	2,430.2	2,474.7	2,564.2	..	..	..		Domestic Absorption
1,180.4	1,184.6	1,205.7	1,559.0	1,628.3	1,680.7	1,727.7					Private Consumption, etc.
262.7	262.3	287.0	306.4	321.4	319.9	326.4					General Gov't Consumption
335.8	406.9	409.4	374.8	480.5	474.1	510.1					Gross Domestic Investment
298.3	358.8	360.9	366.6	440.4	442.5	508.1					Fixed Investment
1,762.0	1,900.7	1,957.0	2,184.5	2,263.8	2,299.3	2,378.6	..	..	..		GDP at factor cost
..	..	..	..	..	..	..	..	..	..		Agriculture
..	..	..	..	..	..	..	..	..	..		Industry
..	..	..	..	..	..	..	..	..	..		Manufacturing
..	..	..	..	..	..	..	..	..	..		Services, etc.
											Memo Items:
1,067.6	1,139.6	1,279.5	1,441.7	1,623.4	1,681.8	1,664.3	..	..	..		Capacity to Import
-98.5	-126.2	-96.5	-109.8	-20.1	-4.6	0.0	..	..	..		Terms of Trade Adjustment
1,858.2	1,961.8	2,066.6	2,360.0	2,568.5	2,630.5	2,714.0	..	..	..		Gross Domestic Income
1,681.9	1,825.7	1,913.4	2,172.0	2,364.9	2,457.6	2,551.9	..	..	..		Gross National Income
			(Index 1987 = 100)								**DOMESTIC PRICES/DEFLATORS**
72.9	75.6	80.1	82.6	89.6	93.8	100.0	105.1	110.8	115.9	..	Overall (GDP)
76.2	79.8	83.3	86.3	90.2	94.0	100.0	..	..	..	..	Domestic Absorption
..	..	..	..	..	..	..	..	..	..	..	Agriculture
..	..	..	..	..	..	..	..	..	..	..	Industry
..	..	..	..	..	..	..	..	..	..		Manufacturing
74.6	79.1	82.3	85.5	89.5	94.3	100.0	104.1	109.8	114.9	..	Consumer Price Index
											MANUFACTURING ACTIVITY
..	..	..	..	..	..	..	..	..	..		Employment (1987=100)
..	..	..	..	..	..	..	..	..	..		Real Earnings per Empl. (1987=100)
..	..	..	..	..	..	..	..	..	..		Real Output per Empl. (1987=100)
100.1	81.0	41.0	..	..	39.1	..	..	..	..		Earnings as % of Value Added
			(Millions of current Bahamian Dollars)								**MONETARY HOLDINGS**
583.4	684.7	792.6	857.9	937.9	1,065.6	1,241.3	1,323.6	1,417.2	1,521.4	D	Money Supply, Broadly Defined
143.5	159.7	176.9	187.7	208.1	249.2	277.7	297.1	298.3	327.5	..	Money
37.4	41.1	45.5	51.0	57.8	65.0	74.8	78.8	79.5	80.2	..	Currency Outside Banks
106.1	118.6	131.4	136.7	150.3	184.2	202.9	218.3	218.8	247.3	..	Demand Deposits
439.9	525.0	615.7	670.2	729.8	816.4	963.6	1,026.5	1,118.9	1,193.9	..	Quasi-Money
			(Millions of current Bahamian Dollars)								**GOVERNMENT DEFICIT (-) OR SURPLUS**
-33.90	-45.10	-52.20	14.40	4.50	-17.40	..	..	..	..		Current Revenue
314.20	311.30	337.90	376.70	430.60	451.20	..	..	..	..		Current Expenditure
261.40	289.00	318.10	343.80	385.00	436.00	..	..	..	..		Current Budget Balance
52.80	22.30	19.80	32.90	45.60	15.20	..	..	..	..		Capital Receipts
..	..	..	..	..	..	..	..	..	..		Capital Payments
86.70	67.40	72.00	18.50	41.10	32.60	..	..	..	..		

BAHAMAS, THE

	1970	1971	1972	1973	1974	1975	1976	1977	1978	1979	1980
FOREIGN TRADE (CUSTOMS BASIS)					*(Millions of current US dollars)*						
Value of Exports, fob	..	..	..	..	..	..	..	..	..	..	..
Nonfuel Primary Products											
Fuels	..	..	..								
Manufactures	..	..	..								
Value of Imports, cif	..	..	..					..	..		
Nonfuel Primary Products	..	..	..								
Fuels	..	..	..								
Manufactures	..	..	..					..	..		
Terms of Trade					*(Index 1987 = 100)*						
Terms of Trade	..	..	..	..	..			..	..		..
Export Prices, fob	..	..	..							..	
Import Prices, cif	..	..	..	..				..			
BALANCE OF PAYMENTS					*(Millions of current US dollars)*						
Exports of Goods & Services	..	..	..	593.7	696.0	712.8	694.0	712.4	836.4	952.7	1,160.1
Merchandise, fob		..	..	95.0	122.8	117.3	149.3	135.9	146.4	170.5	200.5
Nonfactor Services		..	..	374.8	444.0	470.7	540.2	572.5	683.1	771.3	946.6
Factor Services		..	..	123.9	129.2	124.8	4.5	4.0	6.9	10.9	13.0
Imports of Goods & Services	..	..	..	721.5	800.8	659.9	597.6	633.1	780.4	932.9	1,174.5
Merchandise, fob			..	388.8	411.1	340.6	389.5	390.4	467.9	597.5	800.8
Nonfactor Services			..	120.6	140.2	130.4	127.0	152.7	175.3	188.0	223.1
Factor Services			..	212.1	249.5	188.8	81.1	90.0	137.2	147.4	150.6
Long-Term Interest	..	..	..								
Private Current Transfers, net			..	-20.3	-20.1	-14.9	-16.5	-18.6	-22.2	-15.8	-19.7
Workers' Remittances	..										
Curr. A/C Bal before Off. Transf.			..	-148.1	-125.0	38.0	79.9	60.7	33.8	4.0	-34.1
Net Official Transfers				3.0	2.4	4.7	4.9	5.4	7.5	11.8	17.8
Curr. A/C Bal after Off. Transf.			..	-145.1	-122.5	42.7	84.8	66.1	41.3	15.8	-16.3
Long-Term Capital, net		..	..	90.6	113.0	37.7	9.6	40.7	-25.3	8.8	9.5
Direct Investment				79.4	111.1	48.8	14.6	31.4	-1.1	9.6	4.1
Long-Term Loans	..	..	..					..			..
Disbursements	..	..	..								
Repayments	..	..	..	..							
Other Long-Term Capital			..	11.2	1.9	-11.1	-5.0	9.3	-24.2	-0.8	5.4
Other Capital, net	..	..	..	61.6	16.0	-76.7	-100.3	-87.7	-25.0	-9.8	17.5
Change in Reserves	4.4	-7.8	-7.6	-7.2	-6.5	-3.7	5.9	-19.1	9.0	-14.8	-10.7
Memo Item:					*(Bahamian Dollars per US dollar)*						
Conversion Factor (Annual Avg)	1.000	1.000	1.000	1.000	1.000	1.000	1.000	1.000	1.000	1.000	1.000
EXTERNAL DEBT (Total)					*(Millions of US dollars), outstanding at end of year*						
Long-Term Debt (by debtor)	..	..	..	..			..			..	..
Central Bank, incl. IMF credit	..	..	..	..						..	..
Central Government	..	..	..	..						..	..
Rest of General Government	..	..	..	..						..	..
Non-financial Public Enterprises	..	..	..	..						..	..
Priv. Sector, incl non-guaranteed	..	..	..	..						..	..
Short-Term Debt	..	..	..	..						..	..
Memo Items:					*(Millions of US dollars)*						
Int'l Reserves Excluding Gold	21.7	29.5	37.1	43.2	49.8	53.3	47.4	67.1	58.1	77.5	92.3
Gold Holdings (at market price)	..	..	..				..		1.4	2.9	8.8	..
SOCIAL INDICATORS											
Total Fertility Rate	3.4	3.4	3.4	3.4	3.4	3.4	3.4	3.4	3.3	3.3	3.3
Infant Mortality Rate	35.0	32.0	29.0	27.3	25.5	34.2	24.7	27.7	32.5	25.9	30.0
Life Expectancy at Birth	65.2	65.3	65.5	65.6	65.8	65.9	66.0	66.2	66.3	66.4	66.6
Urban Population, % of total	58.0	58.3	58.5	58.8	59.0	59.3	59.6	59.8	60.1	60.3	60.6
Food Prod. per capita (1987=100)	101.2	75.0	85.2	67.2	81.8	84.9	95.0	88.8	90.9	87.9	105.0
Labor Force, Agriculture (%)	..	..	..								..
Labor Force, Female (%)	..	..	..	..							..
Primary Schl. Enroll. Ratio	..	..	..	..							..
Primary Schl. Enroll. Ratio, Female	..	..	..	..							..
Secondary Schl. Enroll. Ratio	..	..	..	..							..

FOREIGN TRADE (CUSTOMS BASIS)

(Millions of current US dollars)

1981	1982	1983	1984	1985	1986	1987	1988	1989	1990 est.	Notes	
..	..	..	..	..	..	..	..	..	..	..	Value of Exports, fob
..	..	..	..	..	..	..	..	..	..	..	Nonfuel Primary Products
..	..	..	..	..	..	..	..	..	..	..	Fuels
..	..	..	..	..	..	..	..	..	..	..	Manufactures
..	..	..	..	..	..	..	..	..	..	..	Value of Imports, cif
..	..	..	..	..	..	..	..	..	..	..	Nonfuel Primary Products
..	..	..	..	..	..	..	..	..	..	..	Fuels
..	..	..	..	..	..	..	..	..	..	..	Manufactures

(Index 1987 = 100)

1981	1982	1983	1984	1985	1986	1987	1988	1989	1990 est.	Notes	
..	..	..	..	..	..	..	..	..	..	..	Terms of Trade
..	..	..	..	..	..	..	..	..	..	..	Export Prices, fob
..	..	..	..	..	..	..	..	..	..	..	Import Prices, cif

BALANCE OF PAYMENTS

(Millions of current US dollars)

1981	1982	1983	1984	1985	1986	1987	1988	1989	1990 est.	Notes	
1,160.6	1,158.8	1,263.3	1,327.8	1,536.3	1,607.2	1,662.5	1,628.4	1,765.9	1,813.3	..	Exports of Goods & Services
176.2	212.7	225.1	261.9	295.8	293.4	273.1	273.6	259.2	300.9	..	Merchandise, fob
967.4	922.3	1,022.9	1,047.1	1,220.1	1,294.3	1,371.3	1,339.5	1,490.6	1,497.4	..	Nonfactor Services
17.0	23.8	15.3	18.8	20.4	19.5	18.1	15.3	16.1	15.0	..	Factor Services
1,239.9	1,225.8	1,304.9	1,374.1	1,688.3	1,633.6	1,824.9	1,742.2	1,924.7	2,009.1	..	Imports of Goods & Services
796.7	754.5	822.1	866.2	1,096.2	1,012.8	1,154.7	1,058.9	1,203.5	1,228.8	..	Merchandise, fob
267.0	312.5	325.5	320.3	385.0	413.8	464.8	497.4	525.7	590.8	..	Nonfactor Services
176.2	158.8	157.3	187.6	207.1	207.0	205.4	185.9	195.5	189.5	..	Factor Services
..	..	..	..	..	..	..	..	..	..	..	Long-Term Interest
-13.9	-17.7	-10.3	-14.6	-14.6	-14.0	-17.8	-28.9	-17.9	-10.7	..	Private Current Transfers, net
..	..	..	..	..	..	..	..	..	..	..	Workers' Remittances
-93.2	-84.7	-51.9	-60.9	-166.6	-40.4	-180.2	-142.7	-176.7	-206.5	..	Curr. A/C Bal before Off. Transf.
11.1	21.5	17.4	15.4	17.9	13.7	14.2	14.4	18.9	21.3	..	Net Official Transfers
-82.1	-63.2	-34.5	-45.5	-148.7	-26.7	-166.0	-128.3	-157.8	-185.2	..	Curr. A/C Bal after Off. Transf.
145.6	74.8	19.3	-6.8	-35.8	-0.8	-27.0	24.0	46.5	28.1	..	Long-Term Capital, net
34.4	2.8	-6.0	-4.9	-30.2	-13.2	10.8	36.7	25.0	-16.3	..	Direct Investment
..	..	..	..	..	..	..	..	..	..	..	Long-Term Loans
..	..	..	..	..	..	..	..	..	..	..	Disbursements
..	..	..	..	..	..	..	..	..	..	..	Repayments
111.2	72.0	25.3	-1.9	-5.6	12.4	-37.8	-12.7	21.5	44.4	..	Other Long-Term Capital
-58.2	2.4	25.8	91.4	203.9	75.1	133.4	105.1	98.1	168.8	..	Other Capital, net
-5.3	-14.0	-10.6	-39.1	-19.4	-47.6	59.6	-0.8	13.2	-11.7	..	Change in Reserves

(Bahamian Dollars per US dollar)

1981	1982	1983	1984	1985	1986	1987	1988	1989	1990 est.	Notes	Memo Item:
1.000	1.000	1.000	1.000	1.000	1.000	1.000	1.000	1.000	1.000	..	Conversion Factor (Annual Avg)

EXTERNAL DEBT (Total)

(Millions of US dollars), outstanding at end of year

1981	1982	1983	1984	1985	1986	1987	1988	1989	1990 est.	Notes	
..	..	..	..	..	..	..	..	..	..	..	Long-Term Debt (by debtor)
..	..	..	..	..	..	..	..	..	..	..	Central Bank, incl. IMF credit
..	..	..	..	..	..	..	..	..	..	..	Central Government
..	..	..	..	..	..	..	..	..	..	..	Rest of General Government
..	..	..	..	..	..	..	..	..	..	..	Non-financial Public Enterprises
..	..	..	..	..	..	..	..	..	..	..	Priv. Sector, incl non-guaranteed
..	..	..	..	..	..	..	..	..	..	..	Short-Term Debt

(Millions of US dollars)

1981	1982	1983	1984	1985	1986	1987	1988	1989	1990 est.	Notes	Memo Items:
100.2	113.5	122.0	161.1	182.5	231.5	170.1	172.0	146.8	158.2	..	Int'l Reserves Excluding Gold
..	..	..	..	..	..	..	..	..	..	..	Gold Holdings (at market price)

SOCIAL INDICATORS

1981	1982	1983	1984	1985	1986	1987	1988	1989	1990 est.	Notes	
3.3	3.2	3.0	2.8	2.7	2.5	2.3	2.3	2.2	2.2	..	Total Fertility Rate
22.3	33.2	21.6	22.9	26.7	27.3	27.9	26.9	25.9	25.0	..	Infant Mortality Rate
66.7	66.8	67.0	67.3	67.5	67.7	68.0	68.3	68.6	69.0	..	Life Expectancy at Birth
60.9	61.3	61.6	62.0	62.3	62.7	63.1	63.5	63.9	64.3	..	Urban Population, % of total
104.4	99.5	99.3	106.9	95.6	99.7	100.0	98.3	92.7	91.2	..	Food Prod. per capita (1987=100)
..	..	..	..	..	..	..	..	..	..	..	Labor Force, Agriculture (%)
..	..	..	..	..	..	..	..	..	..	..	Labor Force, Female (%)
..	..	..	..	..	..	..	..	..	..	..	Primary Schl. Enroll. Ratio
..	..	..	..	..	..	..	..	..	..	..	Primary Schl. Enroll. Ratio, Female
..	..	..	..	..	..	..	..	..	..	..	Secondary Schl. Enroll. Ratio

BAHRAIN	1970	1971	1972	1973	1974	1975	1976	1977	1978	1979	1980
CURRENT GNP PER CAPITA (US $)	..	..	..	..							
POPULATION (thousands)	210	216	227	238	250	262	275	289	303	319	334
USE AND ORIGIN OF RESOURCES					*(Millions of current Bahrain Dinars)*						
Gross National Product (GNP)	..	..	..	..	..	..	..	..	..	..	1,111.5
Net Factor Income from Abroad	..	..	..	..	..	..	..	..	..	..	-46.6
GDP at Market Prices	..	..	..	..	..	..	..	..	..	..	1,158.1
Resource Balance	..	..	..	..	..	..	..	..	..	..	102.7
Exports of Goods & NFServices	..	..	..	..	..	..	..	..	..	..	1,437.3
Imports of Goods & NFServices	..	..	..	..	..	..	..	..	..	..	1,334.6
Domestic Absorption	..	..	..	..	..	..	..	..	..	..	1,055.4
Private Consumption, etc.	..	..	..	..	..	..	..	..	..	..	370.3
General Gov't Consumption	..	..	..	..	..	..	..	..	..	..	150.9
Gross Domestic Investment	..	..	..	..	..	..	..	..	..	..	534.2
Fixed Investment	..	..	..	..	..	..	..	..	..	..	356.9
Indirect Taxes, net	..	..	..	..	..	..	..	..	..	..	40.3
GDP at factor cost	..	..	..	..	..	..	..	..	..	..	1,117.8
Agriculture	..	..	..	..	..	..	..	..	..	..	11.4
Industry	..	..	..	..	..	..	..	..	..	..	684.3
Manufacturing	..	..	..	..	..	..	..	..	..	..	187.9
Services, etc.	..	..	..	..	..	..	..	..	..	..	462.4
Gross Domestic Saving	..	..	..	..	..	..	..	..	..	..	636.9
Gross National Saving	..	..	..	..	..	..	..	..	..	..	555.1
					(Millions of 1987 Bahrain Dinars)						
Gross National Product	..	..	..	..	..	..	..	..	..	..	1,161.8
GDP at Market Prices	..	..	..	..	..	..	..	..	..	..	1,210.7
Resource Balance	..	..	..	..	..	..	..	..	..	..	5.8
Exports of Goods & NFServices	..	..	..	..	..	..	..	..	..	..	1,020.6
Imports of Goods & NFServices	..	..	..	..	..	..	..	..	..	..	1,014.7
Domestic Absorption	..	..	..	..	..	..	..	..	..	..	1,154.7
Private Consumption, etc.	..	..	..	..	..	..	..	..	..	..	437.5
General Gov't Consumption	..	..	..	..	..	..	..	..	..	..	177.4
Gross Domestic Investment	..	..	..	..	..	..	..	..	..	..	539.8
Fixed Investment	..	..	..	..	..	..	..	..	..	..	280.3
GDP at factor cost	..	..	..	..	..	..	..	..	..	..	1,188.1
Agriculture	..	..	..	..	..	..	..	..	..	..	12.4
Industry	..	..	..	..	..	..	..	..	..	..	664.0
Manufacturing	..	..	..	..	..	..	..	..	..	..	136.4
Services, etc.	..	..	..	..	..	..	..	..	..	..	513.5
Memo Items:											
Capacity to Import	..	..	..	..	..	..	..	..	..	..	1,092.8
Terms of Trade Adjustment	..	..	..	..	..	..	..	..	..	..	72.2
Gross Domestic Income	..	..	..	..	..	..	..	..	..	..	1,282.9
Gross National Income	..	..	..	..	..	..	..	..	..	..	1,234.0
DOMESTIC PRICES/DEFLATORS					*(Index 1987 = 100)*						
Overall (GDP)	..	..	..	..	..	..	..	..	..	..	95.7
Domestic Absorption	..	..	..	..	..	..	..	..	..	..	91.4
Agriculture	..	..	..	..	..	..	..	..	..	..	91.8
Industry	..	..	..	..	..	..	..	..	..	..	103.1
Manufacturing	..	..	..	..	..	..	..	..	..	..	137.8
Consumer Price Index	26.2	27.8	29.2	33.3	41.5	48.2	59.0	69.5	80.5	82.2	85.4
MANUFACTURING ACTIVITY											
Employment (1987=100)	..	..	..	..	..	..	..	..	..	..	..
Real Earnings per Empl. (1987=100)	..	..	..	..	..	..	..	..	..	..	..
Real Output per Empl. (1987=100)	..	..	..	..	..	..	..	..	..	..	..
Earnings as % of Value Added	..	..	..	..	..	..	..	..	..	..	..
MONETARY HOLDINGS					*(Millions of current Bahrain Dinars)*						
Money Supply, Broadly Defined	56.4	73.1	87.9	99.6	145.8	184.2	303.8	355.5	402.3	411.9	524.1
Money	37.9	48.6	55.2	59.4	61.3	77.8	127.9	152.5	171.3	186.1	192.2
Currency Outside Banks	18.9	21.2	23.8	14.9	16.9	24.0	34.2	43.8	44.1	49.9	58.3
Demand Deposits	19.1	27.3	31.4	44.5	44.4	53.8	93.7	108.7	127.2	136.2	133.9
Quasi-Money	18.5	24.6	32.7	40.3	84.5	106.5	175.9	203.0	231.0	225.8	331.8
GOVERNMENT DEFICIT (-) OR SURPLUS					*(Millions of current Bahrain Dinars)*						
	..	..	..	..	39.60	5.50	-36.20	-12.90	-30.60	22.10	68.00
Current Revenue	..	..	..	..	117.50	129.00	186.70	255.10	273.90	304.30	445.70
Current Expenditure	..	..	..	..	38.20	61.60	78.40	100.20	137.00	156.80	191.60
Current Budget Balance	..	..	..	..	79.30	67.40	108.30	154.90	136.90	147.50	254.10
Capital Receipts	..	..	..	..						..	..
Capital Payments	..	..	..	..	39.70	61.90	144.50	167.80	167.50	125.40	186.10

1981	1982	1983	1984	1985	1986	1987	1988	1989	1990 estimate	Notes	BAHRAIN
..	8,830	9,440	9,680	8,380	7,710	6,840	6,360	6,380		..	CURRENT GNP PER CAPITA (US $)
353	374	390	407	425	442	458	473	489	503	..	POPULATION (thousands)

(Millions of current Bahrain Dinars) — **USE AND ORIGIN OF RESOURCES**

1981	1982	1983	1984	1985	1986	1987	1988	1989	1990	Notes	
1,288.9	1,332.8	1,343.6	1,411.0	1,283.2	1,085.1	1,084.1	1,094.9	1,135.0	..	..	Gross National Product (GNP)
-15.0	-38.0	-60.8	-57.5	-109.7	-113.1	-107.7	-168.0	-175.0	..	..	Net Factor Income from Abroad
1,303.9	1,370.8	1,404.4	1,468.5	1,392.9	1,198.2	1,191.8	1,262.9	1,310.0	..	..	GDP at Market Prices
145.0	167.3	52.4	38.8	159.3	205.7	138.3	143.5	..	..	..	Resource Balance
1,709.8	1,631.0	1,357.8	1,416.9	1,392.3	1,143.1	1,232.6	1,139.0	..	..	..	Exports of Goods & NF Services
1,564.8	1,463.7	1,305.4	1,378.1	1,233.0	937.4	1,094.3	995.5	..	..	..	Imports of Goods & NF Services
1,158.9	1,203.5	1,352.0	1,429.7	1,233.6	992.5	1,053.5	1,119.4	..	..	..	Domestic Absorption
427.7	472.9	481.6	502.2	450.5	408.3	453.5	514.2	..	..	..	Private Consumption, etc.
188.6	233.3	254.5	302.2	312.8	312.4	310.9	339.9	..	..	..	General Gov't Consumption
542.6	497.3	615.9	625.3	470.3	271.8	289.1	265.3	..	..	..	Gross Domestic Investment
380.5	451.9	576.1	647.0	487.8	390.8	359.2	344.8	..	..	..	Fixed Investment
50.2	60.4	62.7	58.5	44.9	26.6	28.3	33.2	..	..		Indirect Taxes, net
1,253.7	1,310.4	1,341.7	1,410.0	1,348.0	1,171.6	1,163.5	1,229.7	..	..	..	GDP at factor cost
13.2	14.5	16.2	16.4	16.4	16.4	16.0	15.4	..	..	..	Agriculture
753.7	724.9	676.8	719.7	696.6	521.5	524.7	544.6	..	..	..	Industry
202.3	170.1	167.2	182.8	138.8	166.1	191.0	235.3	..	..	..	Manufacturing
537.0	631.4	711.4	732.4	679.9	660.3	651.1	702.9	..	..	..	Services, etc.
687.6	664.6	668.3	664.1	629.6	477.5	427.4	408.8	..	..		Gross Domestic Saving
632.5	582.4	569.1	559.4	431.6	264.9	228.1	168.2	..	..		Gross National Saving

(Millions of 1987 Bahrain Dinars)

1981	1982	1983	1984	1985	1986	1987	1988	1989	1990	Notes	
1,134.4	1,036.1	1,084.9	1,140.4	1,054.5	1,103.3	1,084.1	1,105.2	1,132.8	..	..	Gross National Product
1,147.8	1,065.7	1,133.9	1,186.9	1,144.9	1,219.0	1,191.8	1,274.3	1,306.2	..	H	GDP at Market Prices
-11.8	15.9	-14.2	29.8	111.3	201.4	138.3	133.3	..	..	..	Resource Balance
1,109.3	1,055.9	972.3	1,087.0	1,073.0	1,258.8	1,232.6	1,267.8	..	..	..	Exports of Goods & NF Services
1,121.1	1,040.0	986.4	1,057.3	961.7	1,057.4	1,094.3	1,134.5	..	..	..	Imports of Goods & NF Services
1,119.6	1,039.3	1,123.6	1,139.8	1,029.3	1,009.0	1,053.5	1,146.8	..	..	..	Domestic Absorption
437.6	463.9	462.1	472.0	437.0	402.1	453.5	514.8	..	..	..	Private Consumption, etc.
192.8	221.5	231.6	258.1	274.0	301.4	310.9	335.9	..	..	..	General Gov't Consumption
489.2	353.8	429.9	409.7	318.3	305.6	289.1	296.1	..	..	..	Gross Domestic Investment
282.9	329.8	420.3	488.5	422.9	381.2	359.2	342.5	..	..	..	Fixed Investment
1,107.7	1,006.3	1,071.3	1,130.7	1,099.6	1,192.5	1,163.5	1,232.9	..	..	..	GDP at factor cost
12.7	15.1	15.1	15.4	15.1	15.0	16.0	16.6	..	..	..	Agriculture
599.7	463.6	486.7	529.7	521.1	576.7	524.7	543.2	..	..	..	Industry
144.7	148.2	137.9	149.0	124.9	202.6	191.0	199.6	..	..	..	Manufacturing
520.0	586.1	632.1	641.8	608.8	627.3	651.1	714.5	..	..	..	Services, etc.

Memo Items:

1981	1982	1983	1984	1985	1986	1987	1988	1989	1990	Notes	
1,224.9	1,158.9	1,026.0	1,087.0	1,086.0	1,289.4	1,232.6	1,298.1	..	..	..	Capacity to Import
115.6	103.0	53.8	0.0	13.0	30.6	0.0	30.3	..	..	..	Terms of Trade Adjustment
1,263.4	1,168.7	1,187.7	1,186.9	1,157.9	1,249.6	1,191.8	1,304.6	..	..	..	Gross Domestic Income
1,250.0	1,139.1	1,138.7	1,140.4	1,067.5	1,133.9	1,084.1	1,135.5	..	..	..	Gross National Income

(Index 1987 = 100) — **DOMESTIC PRICES/DEFLATORS**

1981	1982	1983	1984	1985	1986	1987	1988	1989	1990	Notes	
113.6	128.6	123.9	123.7	121.7	98.3	100.0	99.1	100.3	..	..	Overall (GDP)
103.5	115.8	120.3	125.4	119.8	98.4	100.0	97.6	..	..	..	Domestic Absorption
104.0	96.2	107.4	106.2	108.8	109.4	100.0	92.5	..	..	..	Agriculture
125.7	156.4	139.1	135.9	133.7	90.4	100.0	100.3	..	..	..	Industry
139.8	114.8	121.3	122.7	111.1	82.0	100.0	117.9	..	..	..	Manufacturing
95.1	103.6	106.6	107.0	104.2	101.8	100.0	100.3	101.8	102.7	..	Consumer Price Index

MANUFACTURING ACTIVITY

1981	1982	1983	1984	1985	1986	1987	1988	1989	1990	Notes	
..	..	..	..	..	..						Employment (1987=100)
..	..	..	..	..	..						Real Earnings per Empl. (1987=100)
..	..	..	..	..	..						Real Output per Empl. (1987=100)
..	..	..	..	..	..						Earnings as % of Value Added

(Millions of current Bahrain Dinars) — **MONETARY HOLDINGS**

1981	1982	1983	1984	1985	1986	1987	1988	1989	1990	Notes	
730.5	780.2	843.1	827.8	903.3	885.2	968.5	1,007.6	1,052.4	930.7	..	Money Supply, Broadly Defined
248.8	266.9	250.0	239.3	243.1	235.7	246.7	238.9	234.7	258.6	..	Money
63.3	70.5	73.5	78.2	79.0	80.0	84.1	84.4	84.8	105.3	..	Currency Outside Banks
185.4	196.5	176.5	161.1	164.2	155.7	162.6	154.5	149.9	153.3	..	Demand Deposits
481.8	513.3	593.1	588.5	660.2	649.5	721.8	768.7	817.8	672.2	..	Quasi-Money

(Millions of current Bahrain Dinars) — **GOVERNMENT DEFICIT (-) OR SURPLUS**

1981	1982	1983	1984	1985	1986	1987	1988	1989	1990	Notes	
110.80	32.10	-96.20	-23.00	13.70	-51.90	-122.20	49.10	-115.80	105.70		
536.60	554.20	490.50	523.00	541.40	459.80	414.00	395.50	440.80	495.00	..	Current Revenue
230.90	298.70	313.20	328.60	344.20	354.50	300.00	331.90	354.40	374.10	..	Current Expenditure
305.70	255.50	177.30	194.40	197.20	105.30	114.00	63.60	86.40	120.90	..	Current Budget Balance
..	..	..	..	..	..	..	2.70	0.20	0.20	..	Capital Receipts
194.90	223.40	273.50	217.40	183.50	157.20	236.20	17.20	202.40	15.40	..	Capital Payments

FOREIGN TRADE (CUSTOMS BASIS)

(Millions of current US dollars)

	1970	1971	1972	1973	1974	1975	1976	1977	1978	1979	1980
Value of Exports, fob	..	..	..	..	..	..	..	..	..	..	..
Nonfuel Primary Products	..	..	..	..	..	..	..	..	..	..	..
Fuels	..	..	..	..	..	..	..	..	..	..	..
Manufactures	..	..	..	..	..	..	..	..	..	..	..
Value of Imports, cif	..	..	..	..	..	..	..	..	..	..	..
Nonfuel Primary Products	..	..	..	..	..	..	..	..	..	..	..
Fuels	..	..	..	..	..	..	..	..	..	..	..
Manufactures	..	..	..	..	..	..	..	..	..	..	..

(Index 1987 = 100)

	1970	1971	1972	1973	1974	1975	1976	1977	1978	1979	1980
Terms of Trade	..	..	..	..	..	..	..	..	..	..	..
Export Prices, fob	..	..	..	..	..	..	..	..	..	..	..
Import Prices, cif	..	..	..	..	..	..	..	..	..	..	..

BALANCE OF PAYMENTS

(Millions of current US dollars)

	1970	1971	1972	1973	1974	1975	1976	1977	1978	1979	1980
Exports of Goods & Services	246.0	300.0	392.0	541.0	1,436.0	1,404.8	1,786.2	2,181.0	2,362.9	2,924.9	4,080.1
Merchandise, fob	218.0	265.0	348.0	479.0	1,272.0	1,203.0	1,517.9	1,848.9	1,891.8	2,499.1	3,433.1
Nonfactor Services	15.0	19.0	24.0	34.0	89.0	156.3	201.5	255.8	364.2	313.7	332.9
Factor Services	13.0	16.0	20.0	28.0	75.0	45.5	66.7	76.3	106.9	112.2	314.1
Imports of Goods & Services	291.0	356.0	425.0	607.0	1,324.0	1,531.5	2,062.7	2,502.7	2,710.0	3,152.1	3,983.6
Merchandise, fob	247.0	303.0	361.0	516.0	1,126.0	1,090.0	1,510.1	1,837.0	1,873.3	2,094.8	2,987.5
Nonfactor Services	40.0	48.0	58.0	83.0	180.0	179.3	243.2	296.2	342.8	369.7	473.7
Factor Services	4.0	5.0	6.0	8.0	18.0	262.2	309.4	369.5	494.0	687.6	522.3
Long-Term Interest	..	..	..	..	..	..	..	..	..	..	..
Private Current Transfers, net	-44.0	-54.0	-63.0	-92.0	-198.0	-76.4	-84.9	-101.1	-131.1	-93.5	-93.4
Workers' Remittances	..	..	..	..	..	..	..	..	..	..	..
Curr. A/C Bal before Off. Transf.	-89.0	-110.0	-96.0	-158.0	-86.0	-203.0	-361.5	-422.8	-478.3	-320.7	3.2
Net Official Transfers	0.0	0.0	0.0	0.0	0.0	..	1.3	98.8	90.6	98.0	181.2
Curr. A/C Bal after Off. Transf.	-89.0	-110.0	-96.0	-158.0	-86.0	-203.0	-360.2	-324.0	-387.7	-222.7	184.3
Long-Term Capital, net	73.2	57.2	44.5	-13.8	56.2	88.0	279.8	402.1	146.3	170.6	10.3
Direct Investment	..	..	..	..	..	..	..	..	23.0	145.2	-418.0
Long-Term Loans	..	..	..	..	..	..	..	..	..	..	..
Disbursements	..	..	..	..	..	..	..	..	..	..	..
Repayments	..	..	..	..	..	..	..	..	..	..	..
Other Long-Term Capital	73.2	57.2	44.5	-13.8	56.2	88.0	279.8	402.1	123.4	25.4	428.4
Other Capital, net	19.0	76.0	49.0	152.0	97.0	284.0	227.0	-10.8	223.1	173.7	148.3
Change in Reserves	-3.2	-23.2	2.5	19.8	-67.2	-168.9	-146.6	-67.3	18.2	-121.6	-343.0

Memo Item:

(Bahrain Dinars per US dollar)

	1970	1971	1972	1973	1974	1975	1976	1977	1978	1979	1980
Conversion Factor (Annual Avg)	0.480	0.470	0.440	0.400	0.390	0.400	0.400	0.400	0.390	0.380	0.380

EXTERNAL DEBT (Total)

(Millions of US dollars), outstanding at end of year

	1970	1971	1972	1973	1974	1975	1976	1977	1978	1979	1980
Long-Term Debt (by debtor)	..	..	..	..	..	..	..	..	..	..	..
Central Bank, incl. IMF credit	..	..	..	..	..	..	..	..	..	..	..
Central Government	..	..	..	..	..	..	..	..	..	..	..
Rest of General Government	..	..	..	..	..	..	..	..	..	..	..
Non-financial Public Enterprises	..	..	..	..	..	..	..	..	..	..	..
Priv. Sector, incl non-guaranteed	..	..	..	..	..	..	..	..	..	..	..
Short-Term Debt	..	..	..	..	..	..	..	..	..	..	..

Memo Items:

(Millions of US dollars)

	1970	1971	1972	1973	1974	1975	1976	1977	1978	1979	1980
Int'l Reserves Excluding Gold	62.8	86.0	83.5	64.0	131.3	289.5	436.4	503.9	493.4	613.9	953.4
Gold Holdings (at market price)	8.9	10.3	15.4	26.6	44.4	21.0	20.2	24.7	33.9	76.8	88.4

SOCIAL INDICATORS

	1970	1971	1972	1973	1974	1975	1976	1977	1978	1979	1980
Total Fertility Rate	6.4	6.2	5.9	5.9	5.8	5.7	5.6	5.5	5.4	5.4	5.3
Infant Mortality Rate	64.2	59.6	55.0	53.4	51.8	50.2	48.6	47.0	45.4	43.8	42.2
Life Expectancy at Birth	62.1	62.8	63.5	63.9	64.2	64.6	65.0	65.3	65.7	66.1	66.5
Urban Population, % of total	78.7	78.8	78.9	79.0	79.1	79.2	79.5	79.7	80.0	80.2	80.5
Food Prod. per capita (1987=100)	..	..	..	..	..	..	..	..	..	..	..
Labor Force, Agriculture (%)	7.2	6.7	6.2	5.7	5.3	5.0	4.4	3.9	3.6	3.3	3.0
Labor Force, Female (%)	4.9	6.0	6.9	7.8	8.5	9.2	9.8	10.2	10.5	10.8	11.1
Primary Schl. Enroll. Ratio	99.0	..	..	..	..	96.0	..	97.0	99.0	102.0	104.0
Primary Schl. Enroll. Ratio, Female	84.0	..	..	..	..	85.0	..	87.0	90.0	93.0	97.0
Secondary Schl. Enroll. Ratio	51.0	..	..	..	..	52.0	..	50.0	52.0	54.0	65.0

1981	1982	1983	1984	1985	1986	1987	1988	1989	1990 estimate	Notes	BAHRAIN
				(Millions of current US dollars)							**FOREIGN TRADE (CUSTOMS BASIS)**
..	..	..	..	..	..	..	..	..	..	..	Value of Exports, fob
..	..	..	..	..	..	..	..	..	..	..	Nonfuel Primary Products
..	..	..	..	..	..	..	..	..	..	..	Fuels
..	..	..	..	..	..	..	..	..	..	..	Manufactures
									..	..	Value of Imports, cif
..	..	..	..	..	..	..	..	..	..	..	Nonfuel Primary Products
..	..	..	..	..	..	..	..	..	..	..	Fuels
..	..	..	..	..	..	..	..	..	..	..	Manufactures
				(Index 1987 = 100)							
..	..	..	..	..	..	..	..	..	..	..	Terms of Trade
..	..	..	..	..	..	..	..	..	..	..	Export Prices, fob
..	..	..	..	..	..	..	..	..	..	..	Import Prices, cif
				(Millions of current US dollars)							**BALANCE OF PAYMENTS**
5,055.9	4,752.4	3,901.9	4,353.5	4,130.9	3,241.8	3,575.8	3,573.9	4,198.1	..	..	Exports of Goods & Services
4,177.1	3,695.0	3,119.4	3,204.0	2,896.8	2,199.5	2,429.5	2,411.4	2,831.1	..	..	Merchandise, fob
360.9	567.6	366.8	813.8	911.4	764.4	864.1	899.5	872.9	..	..	Nonfactor Services
517.8	489.9	415.7	335.5	322.6	277.9	282.2	263.0	494.1	..	..	Factor Services
4,714.1	4,398.9	3,839.6	4,134.0	3,977.4	3,166.8	3,645.7	3,557.4	4,123.7	..	..	Imports of Goods & Services
3,559.3	3,167.8	2,935.6	3,131.7	2,796.0	2,164.6	2,442.3	2,334.0	2,820.2	..	..	Merchandise, fob
610.1	729.8	499.5	555.1	488.6	327.1	525.0	529.3	559.8	..	..	Nonfactor Services
544.7	501.3	404.5	447.3	692.8	675.0	678.5	694.1	743.6	..	..	Factor Services
..	..	..	..	..	..	..	..	..	..	..	Long-Term Interest
-106.6	-117.6	-102.1	-125.5	-234.8	-264.6	-243.6	-193.1	-195.7	..	..	Private Current Transfers, net
..	..	..	..	..	..	..	..	..	..	..	Workers' Remittances
235.1	235.9	-39.9	93.9	-81.4	-189.6	-313.6	-176.6	-121.3	..	..	Curr. A/C Bal before Off. Transf.
194.4	189.6	142.6	124.5	120.2	120.7	113.3	366.5	102.1	..	..	Net Official Transfers
429.5	425.6	102.7	218.4	38.8	-68.9	-200.3	189.9	-19.1	..	..	Curr. A/C Bal after Off. Transf.
-2.9	-94.9	41.2	151.3	4.5	-86.4	-63.3	205.1	93.6	..	..	Long-Term Capital, net
	28.5	64.1	140.7	101.3	-31.9	-35.9	222.1	180.9	..	..	Direct Investment
..	..	..	..	..	..	..	..	..	..	..	Long-Term Loans
..	..	..	..	..	..	..	..	..	..	..	Disbursements
..	..	..	..	..	..	..	..	..	..	..	Repayments
-2.9	-123.4	-22.9	10.6	-96.8	-54.5	-27.4	-17.0	-87.2	..	..	Other Long-Term Capital
162.7	-335.0	-252.4	-379.8	314.1	-24.1	-86.0	-295.2	-262.9	..	..	Other Capital, net
-589.3	4.4	108.5	10.1	-357.4	179.4	349.6	-99.7	188.5	-180.0	..	Change in Reserves
				(Bahrain Dinars per US dollar)							**Memo Item:**
0.380	0.380	0.380	0.380	0.380	0.380	0.380	0.380	0.380	..	..	Conversion Factor (Annual Avg)
				(Millions of US dollars), outstanding at end of year							
..	..	..	..	..	..	..	..	..	..	..	**EXTERNAL DEBT (Total)**
..	..	..	..	..	..	..	..	..	..	..	Long-Term Debt (by debtor)
..	..	..	..	..	..	..	..	..	..	..	Central Bank, incl. IMF credit
..	..	..	..	..	..	..	..	..	..	..	Central Government
..	..	..	..	..	..	..	..	..	..	..	Rest of General Government
..	..	..	..	..	..	..	..	..	..	..	Non-financial Public Enterprises
..	..	..	..	..	..	..	..	..	..	..	Priv. Sector, incl non-guaranteed
..	..	..	..	..	..	..	..	..	..	..	Short-Term Debt
				(Millions of US dollars)							**Memo Items:**
1,544.1	1,534.8	1,426.4	1,302.4	1,659.7	1,489.4	1,148.5	1,251.7	1,050.0	1,234.9	..	Int'l Reserves Excluding Gold
59.6	68.5	57.2	46.2	49.0	58.6	72.6	61.5	60.1	57.8	..	Gold Holdings (at market price)
											SOCIAL INDICATORS
5.2	5.1	5.1	5.0	5.0	4.9	4.9	4.8	4.8	4.7	..	Total Fertility Rate
40.6	39.0	38.2	37.4	36.6	35.8	35.0	34.0	32.9	31.9	..	Infant Mortality Rate
66.8	67.2	67.4	67.7	67.9	68.1	68.3	68.6	68.8	69.1	..	Life Expectancy at Birth
80.7	81.0	81.2	81.5	81.7	82.0	82.2	82.5	82.7	83.0	..	Urban Population, % of total
..	..	..	..	..	..	..	..	..	..	..	Food Prod. per capita (1987=100)
..	..	..	..	..	..	..	..	..	..	..	Labor Force, Agriculture (%)
11.0	10.9	10.9	10.8	10.8	10.7	10.6	10.6	10.5	10.4	..	Labor Force, Female (%)
..	104.0	108.0	110.0	112.0	111.0	111.0	110.0	..	..	..	Primary Schl. Enroll. Ratio
..	99.0	104.0	108.0	110.0	111.0	109.0	108.0	..	..	..	Primary Schl. Enroll. Ratio, Female
..	78.0	77.0	82.0	84.0	85.0	84.0	84.0	..	..	..	Secondary Schl. Enroll. Ratio

BANGLADESH	1970	1971	1972	1973	1974	1975	1976	1977	1978	1979	1980
CURRENT GNP PER CAPITA (US $)	100	100	80	80	100	130	130	120	110	130	150
POPULATION (thousands)	66,671	68,598	70,629	72,699	74,704	76,582	78,323	79,969	81,582	83,225	84,969

USE AND ORIGIN OF RESOURCES *(Billions of current Bangladesh Taka)*

	1970	1971	1972	1973	1974	1975	1976	1977	1978	1979	1980
Gross National Product (GNP)	32.01	30.99	27.70	46.38	73.34	126.85	110.32	109.28	147.15	173.83	200.66
Net Factor Income from Abroad	0.28	0.11	-0.04	0.12	0.06	-0.06	-0.13	-0.48	-0.48	-0.33	0.22
GDP at Market Prices	31.73	30.88	27.74	46.26	73.28	126.91	110.45	109.76	147.63	174.16	200.43
Resource Balance	-1.33	-1.37	-2.23	-2.46	-4.87	-6.61	-14.24	-5.86	-14.65	-16.87	-25.57
Exports of Goods & NFServices	2.64	1.94	1.57	3.02	2.71	3.67	5.24	7.73	8.21	10.64	11.34
Imports of Goods & NFServices	3.97	3.31	3.81	5.48	7.58	10.28	19.48	13.59	22.86	27.51	36.91
Domestic Absorption	33.06	32.25	29.97	48.72	78.15	133.51	124.69	115.62	162.28	191.04	226.01
Private Consumption, etc.	25.22	29.71	28.67	42.87	69.34	121.69	109.25	97.39	138.04	160.58	183.52
General Gov't Consumption	4.24	0.00	0.00	1.82	3.40	4.02	4.49	5.59	7.20	10.94	12.68
Gross Domestic Investment	3.60	2.54	1.30	4.03	5.40	7.80	10.95	12.65	17.05	19.51	29.80
Fixed Investment	..	..	..	..	..	..	..	..	..	..	29.80
Indirect Taxes, net	1.10	1.07	0.96	1.07	2.11	1.79	6.07	5.49	7.17	8.91	10.35
GDP at factor cost	30.63	29.81	26.78	45.19	71.17	125.11	104.38	104.27	140.47	165.25	190.08
Agriculture	17.38	15.82	16.60	26.20	41.50	78.62	57.34	53.67	80.09	91.35	99.50
Industry	3.44	2.99	2.08	5.60	9.80	14.73	15.96	18.36	21.13	27.32	31.94
Manufacturing	2.51	2.31	1.50	3.94	6.78	8.94	10.25	12.32	14.63	17.17	22.01
Services, etc.	10.92	12.08	9.06	14.46	21.98	33.55	37.15	37.73	46.42	55.49	68.99
Gross Domestic Saving	2.27	1.17	-0.93	1.57	0.53	1.20	-3.29	6.79	2.40	2.64	4.23
Gross National Saving	..	1.35	-0.90	1.96	0.75	1.56	-2.98	7.23	3.61	4.53	7.70

(Billions of 1987 Bangladesh Taka)

	1970	1971	1972	1973	1974	1975	1976	1977	1978	1979	1980
Gross National Product	333.86	318.46	280.06	282.65	320.41	316.57	331.02	334.42	358.94	380.15	385.48
GDP at Market Prices	331.62	317.10	279.45	281.47	319.16	315.16	329.22	332.62	357.03	378.21	383.51
Resource Balance	-31.56	-25.91	-29.10	0.38	-26.89	-21.79	-29.49	-11.01	-32.92	-31.44	-49.90
Exports of Goods & NFServices	19.49	14.11	10.88	20.20	16.81	20.08	18.83	24.72	26.42	26.24	27.06
Imports of Goods & NFServices	51.05	40.02	39.97	19.83	43.69	41.87	48.32	35.73	59.34	57.68	76.97
Domestic Absorption	363.18	343.01	308.55	281.09	346.05	336.95	358.71	343.63	389.96	409.65	433.41
Private Consumption, etc.	309.63	302.36	290.52	245.66	312.43	307.09	327.12	305.92	342.03	359.63	363.40
General Gov't Consumption	0.00	0.00	0.00	0.00	0.00	0.00	0.00	0.00	0.00	0.00	0.00
Gross Domestic Investment	53.55	40.65	18.03	35.43	33.62	29.86	31.60	37.71	47.92	50.02	70.01
Fixed Investment	..	..	..	..	..	..	..	..	..	..	..
GDP at factor cost	..	..	..	..	..	..	..	..	..	..	..
Agriculture	174.17	166.31	148.51	148.91	159.76	151.28	160.36	154.52	170.72	172.55	174.22
Industry	50.64	40.70	21.70	36.82	49.53	46.41	44.45	50.36	51.45	62.32	59.10
Manufacturing	33.68	28.55	15.65	25.93	36.43	32.45	32.23	35.98	36.41	40.48	41.07
Services, etc.	103.00	103.65	98.59	90.35	104.57	114.08	120.99	125.09	131.34	140.23	147.85

Memo Items:

	1970	1971	1972	1973	1974	1975	1976	1977	1978	1979	1980
Capacity to Import	33.93	23.47	16.52	10.94	15.63	14.96	13.00	20.32	21.30	22.30	23.65
Terms of Trade Adjustment	14.44	9.36	5.64	-9.27	-1.18	-5.11	-5.82	-4.41	-5.11	-3.93	-3.42
Gross Domestic Income	346.06	326.47	285.10	272.20	317.98	310.05	323.40	328.22	351.92	374.28	380.09
Gross National Income	348.30	327.82	285.70	273.38	319.24	311.45	325.20	330.02	353.83	376.22	382.06

DOMESTIC PRICES/DEFLATORS *(Index 1987 = 100)*

	1970	1971	1972	1973	1974	1975	1976	1977	1978	1979	1980
Overall (GDP)	9.6	9.7	9.9	16.4	23.0	40.3	33.5	33.0	41.4	46.0	52.3
Domestic Absorption	9.1	9.4	9.7	17.3	22.6	39.6	34.8	33.6	41.6	46.6	52.1
Agriculture	10.0	9.5	11.2	17.6	26.0	52.0	35.8	34.7	46.9	52.9	57.1
Industry	6.8	7.3	9.6	15.2	19.8	31.7	35.9	36.5	41.1	43.8	54.0
Manufacturing	7.4	8.1	9.6	15.2	18.6	27.5	31.8	34.2	40.2	42.4	53.6
Consumer Price Index	8.1	8.1	11.4	17.0	26.3	32.0	32.8	34.3	36.1	41.4	47.0

MANUFACTURING ACTIVITY

	1970	1971	1972	1973	1974	1975	1976	1977	1978	1979	1980
Employment (1987=100)	46.4	52.9	44.4	41.2	75.9	80.2	82.6	81.3	88.5	90.1	92.6
Real Earnings per Empl. (1987=100)	132.9	140.5	106.4	83.0	75.1	68.6	73.4	73.7	85.9	100.5	106.2
Real Output per Empl. (1987=100)	137.0	105.5	77.6	71.3	69.9	69.4	79.8	90.0	82.9	91.9	90.7
Earnings as % of Value Added	26.4	33.8	35.0	30.0	35.6	32.7	32.4	27.0	29.6	34.5	31.3

MONETARY HOLDINGS *(Billions of current Bangladesh Taka)*

	1970	1971	1972	1973	1974	1975	1976	1977	1978	1979	1980
Money Supply, Broadly Defined	..	..	..	..	13.99	14.74	17.47	21.61	27.30	33.40	33.56
Money	..	..	..	..	8.39	8.28	9.22	11.67	14.64	18.36	20.17
Currency Outside Banks	..	..	..	3.21	4.10	3.62	3.82	4.90	6.33	7.11	8.27
Demand Deposits	..	..	..	..	4.29	4.66	5.40	6.76	8.31	11.24	11.90
Quasi-Money	..	..	..	..	5.60	6.46	8.25	9.94	12.67	15.05	13.39

(Millions of current Bangladesh Taka)

	1970	1971	1972	1973	1974	1975	1976	1977	1978	1979	1980
GOVERNMENT DEFICIT (-) OR SURPLUS	..	..	..	-864.00	-330.00	1,444.00	-3,728.00	209.00	4,274.00	874.00	4,976.00
Current Revenue	..	..	..	4,022.00	5,970.00	11,863.00	10,763.00	15,912.00	21,672.00	24,098.00	28,068.00
Current Expenditure	..	..	..	..	..	..	..	..	..	..	..
Current Budget Balance	..	..	..	..	..	..	..	..	..	..	..
Capital Receipts	..	..	..	..	..	..	..	..	..	..	..
Capital Payments	..	..	..	..	..	..	..	..	..	..	..

1981	1982	1983	1984	1985	1986	1987	1988	1989	1990 estimate	Notes	BANGLADESH
170	170	160	150	160	160	170	180	190	210	..	**CURRENT GNP PER CAPITA (US $)**
86,879	88,920	91,064	93,254	95,456	97,676	99,915	102,163	104,412	106,656	..	**POPULATION (thousands)**
											USE AND ORIGIN OF RESOURCES
			(Billions of current Bangladesh Taka)								
233.72	258.38	290.84	350.91	404.55	462.45	535.44	592.92	655.29	746.11	C f	Gross National Product (GNP)
-0.37	-1.95	-2.59	-1.61	-2.38	-3.78	-3.77	-4.22	-4.30	-4.29	f	Net Factor Income from Abroad
234.08	260.33	293.43	352.52	406.93	466.23	539.20	597.14	659.60	750.41	C	GDP at Market Prices
-29.17	-37.08	-35.71	-37.32	-44.34	-46.14	-48.27	-55.16	-67.61	-72.87	..	Resource Balance
15.25	16.85	21.36	26.01	30.28	31.17	39.84	46.44	51.37	62.68	..	Exports of Goods & NFServices
44.42	53.93	57.07	63.32	74.62	77.31	88.11	101.60	118.98	135.55	..	Imports of Goods & NFServices
263.26	297.41	329.14	389.83	451.28	512.37	587.47	652.30	727.21	823.28	..	Domestic Absorption
210.38	239.01	273.20	323.66	368.75	417.02	479.74	531.89	584.07	671.05	..	Private Consumption, etc.
15.64	18.56	16.73	23.10	29.79	38.08	40.15	48.55	62.43	65.17	..	General Gov't Consumption
37.23	39.84	39.21	43.08	52.73	57.27	67.58	71.86	80.71	87.05	..	Gross Domestic Investment
37.23	39.84	39.21	43.08	52.73	57.27	67.58	71.86	80.71	87.05	..	Fixed Investment
13.46	13.82	15.47	18.85	21.79	25.52	30.08	32.70	37.60	46.01	..	Indirect Taxes, net
220.62	246.51	277.96	333.66	385.14	440.71	509.12	564.44	622.00	704.40	B C	GDP at factor cost
93.62	103.59	116.42	148.40	169.97	188.38	219.76	231.62	245.39	285.98	..	Agriculture
39.02	44.74	49.40	57.77	64.98	72.34	80.02	89.64	101.59	116.16	..	Industry
25.19	27.92	32.76	37.73	40.11	43.56	47.63	50.44	55.61	64.51	f	Manufacturing
101.44	112.00	127.60	146.34	171.98	205.51	239.42	275.87	312.61	348.28	..	Services, etc.
8.06	2.76	3.50	5.77	8.39	11.12	19.31	16.69	13.10	14.18		Gross Domestic Saving
14.51	10.19	16.37	20.05	19.36	25.16	38.16	37.48	35.75	37.61		Gross National Saving
			(Billions of 1987 Bangladesh Taka)								
421.82	437.48	457.70	478.55	493.37	513.81	535.44	550.58	564.50	600.10	C f	Gross National Product
419.86	435.64	455.84	477.52	496.30	517.95	539.20	554.49	568.17	603.50	C	GDP at Market Prices
-42.44	-39.96	-36.91	-41.70	-58.62	-42.91	-48.27	-51.98	-52.65	-50.00	..	Resource Balance
31.09	33.05	33.84	34.35	32.49	36.98	39.84	46.06	50.51	54.54	..	Exports of Goods & NFServices
73.53	73.01	70.75	76.05	91.11	79.88	88.11	98.04	103.15	104.54	..	Imports of Goods & NFServices
462.30	475.60	492.75	519.22	554.92	560.86	587.47	606.47	620.81	653.50	..	Domestic Absorption
390.13	404.95	409.81	428.40	451.29	457.52	479.74	492.97	504.72	544.80	..	Private Consumption, etc.
0.00	0.00	26.27	31.50	36.71	41.88	40.15	45.01	53.22	44.66	..	General Gov't Consumption
72.17	70.65	56.66	59.33	66.92	61.46	67.58	68.49	62.87	64.04	..	Gross Domestic Investment
..	..	..	..	..	..	..	..	..	..	..	Fixed Investment
..	..	..	..	469.71	489.28	509.12	524.04	535.63	566.43	B C	GDP at factor cost
179.41	191.39	199.85	209.80	211.93	218.89	219.76	218.08	215.75	232.36	..	Agriculture
61.00	62.02	62.93	69.98	72.13	74.04	80.02	84.25	88.32	94.35	..	Industry
39.82	39.92	40.68	43.73	43.03	44.15	47.63	47.93	49.27	52.84	f	Manufacturing
180.01	181.84	193.07	197.73	212.24	225.02	239.42	252.17	264.10	276.79	..	Services, etc.
											Memo Items:
25.24	22.82	26.48	31.24	36.97	32.20	39.84	44.81	44.54	48.34	..	Capacity to Import
-5.85	-10.23	-7.36	-3.11	4.48	-4.77	0.00	-1.25	-5.97	-6.20	..	Terms of Trade Adjustment
414.01	425.41	448.48	474.40	500.78	513.18	539.20	553.25	562.19	597.30	..	Gross Domestic Income
415.97	427.25	450.34	475.44	497.85	509.04	535.44	549.33	558.52	593.90	..	Gross National Income
			(Index 1987 = 100)								**DOMESTIC PRICES/DEFLATORS**
55.8	59.8	64.4	73.8	82.0	90.0	100.0	107.7	116.1	124.3	..	Overall (GDP)
56.9	62.5	66.8	75.1	81.3	91.4	100.0	107.6	117.1	126.0	..	Domestic Absorption
52.2	54.1	58.3	70.7	80.2	86.1	100.0	106.2	113.7	123.1	..	Agriculture
64.0	72.1	78.5	82.6	90.1	97.7	100.0	106.4	115.0	123.1	..	Industry
63.3	69.9	80.5	86.3	93.2	98.7	100.0	105.2	112.9	122.1	f	Manufacturing
54.6	61.4	67.2	74.3	82.2	91.3	100.0	109.3	120.3	130.0	..	Consumer Price Index
											MANUFACTURING ACTIVITY
98.5	102.1	100.8	101.4	105.2	104.9	100.0	96.8			J	Employment (1987=100)
102.2	93.0	91.4	94.0	95.3	105.2	100.0	100.3			J	Real Earnings per Empl. (1987=100)
84.5	86.2	80.6	91.7	92.1	94.4	100.0	106.8			J	Real Output per Empl. (1987=100)
34.0	32.2	28.7	26.9	29.8	29.7	29.7	27.9			J	Earnings as % of Value Added
			(Billions of current Bangladesh Taka)								**MONETARY HOLDINGS**
43.93	45.97	58.98	83.86	105.34	123.38	138.71	164.08	190.78	234.21	..	Money Supply, Broadly Defined
22.72	23.34	31.64	42.27	45.95	50.00	51.00	53.16	60.00	65.74	..	Money
9.14	9.74	13.44	17.25	17.67	19.03	22.49	25.28	27.29	29.95	..	Currency Outside Banks
13.57	13.59	18.19	25.02	28.28	30.97	28.51	27.88	32.72	35.78	..	Demand Deposits
21.21	22.64	27.35	41.59	59.39	73.39	87.71	110.92	130.78	168.47	..	Quasi-Money
			(Millions of current Bangladesh Taka)								
-7,396.00	3,135.00	9,003.00	2,873.00	-5,924.00	-2,601.00	-6,625.00	-5,881.00	-2,828.00	..	C	**GOVERNMENT DEFICIT (-) OR SURPLUS**
30,078.00	41,232.00	44,257.00	44,355.00	48,124.00	59,562.00	62,381.00	67,868.00	95,664.00	..	..	Current Revenue
..	..	..	..	..	..	..	74,938.00	98,341.00	..	..	Current Expenditure
..	..	..	..	..	..	..	-7,070.00	-2,677.00	..	..	Current Budget Balance
..	..	..	..	..	..	..			..	..	Capital Receipts
..	..	..	..	..	..	..	-1,189.00	151.00	..	..	Capital Payments

BANGLADESH	1970	1971	1972	1973	1974	1975	1976	1977	1978	1979	1980
FOREIGN TRADE (CUSTOMS BASIS)					*(Millions of current US dollars)*						
Value of Exports, fob	..	..	..	..	367.6	264.8	361.7	435.0	552.8	661.6	740.4
Nonfuel Primary Products	..	..	..	..	151.1	84.2	138.0	177.9	199.7	..	230.6
Fuels	..	..	..	..	0.1	0.2	1.4	6.7	6.7	..	0.0
Manufactures	..	..	..	..	216.4	180.3	222.4	250.4	346.4	436.7	509.7
Value of Imports, cif	..	..	..	..	905.5	1,039.2	958.0	911.6	1,333.1	1,537.1	1,979.5
Nonfuel Primary Products	..	..	..	..	544.7	631.1	458.5	213.8	463.6	509.7	642.5
Fuels	..	..	..	..	34.0	78.6	120.0	217.2	193.9	176.3	188.0
Manufactures	..	..	..	..	326.8	329.5	379.5	480.6	675.6	851.0	1,149.0
					(Index 1987 = 100)						
Terms of Trade	..	..	136.7	145.7	98.4	96.5	103.8	111.1	105.5	100.3	87.7
Export Prices, fob	..	..	47.7	57.8	77.0	73.2	73.1	79.4	83.9	96.5	99.3
Import Prices, cif	..	..	34.9	39.6	78.3	75.9	70.4	71.5	79.5	96.2	113.3
BALANCE OF PAYMENTS					*(Millions of current US dollars)*						
Exports of Goods & Services	526.0	344.0	355.0	411.7	417.5	439.5	450.9	488.6	598.6	765.1	976.4
Merchandise, fob	420.0	295.0	260.0	354.2	369.7	344.0	371.9	404.6	489.8	609.7	722.3
Nonfactor Services	61.0	40.0	76.0	43.1	34.4	82.5	62.9	59.4	82.2	113.8	162.6
Factor Services	45.0	9.0	19.0	14.4	13.4	13.0	16.1	24.6	26.6	41.6	91.5
Imports of Goods & Services	769.8	664.9	800.8	816.7	984.1	1,477.8	1,361.4	988.0	1,489.7	1,738.8	2,622.1
Merchandise, fob	660.0	570.0	683.0	780.0	925.0	1,403.0	1,275.0	875.0	1,349.0	1,556.0	2,372.0
Nonfactor Services	105.0	94.0	113.0	35.0	48.7	56.3	51.1	57.5	82.0	118.9	172.8
Factor Services	4.8	0.9	4.8	1.7	10.4	18.5	35.3	55.5	58.7	63.9	77.3
Long-Term Interest	0.0	0.0	0.0	4.1	9.2	16.6	28.2	29.7	37.0	40.4	46.9
Private Current Transfers, net	9.8	9.9	9.8	34.3	19.4	35.0	28.8	60.2	113.1	142.9	210.1
Workers' Remittances	0.0	0.0	0.0	0.0	0.0	8.5	15.5	44.8	102.1	127.0	197.4
Curr. A/C Bal before Off. Transf.	-234.0	-311.0	-436.0	-370.7	-547.2	-1,003.3	-881.7	-439.2	-778.0	-830.8	-1,435.6
Net Official Transfers	120.0	160.0	210.0	431.0	173.8	382.3	244.7	264.8	392.6	553.2	592.1
Curr. A/C Bal after Off. Transf.	-114.0	-151.0	-226.0	60.3	-373.4	-621.0	-637.0	-174.4	-385.4	-277.6	-843.5
Long-Term Capital, net	160.0	140.0	95.0	95.5	190.9	506.0	504.9	256.8	456.4	474.1	682.8
Direct Investment	..	..	..	0.0	0.0	0.0	0.0	0.0	0.0	0.0	0.0
Long-Term Loans	0.0	0.0	59.8	308.9	502.0	550.0	256.9	273.8	432.8	516.9	595.7
Disbursements	0.0	0.0	59.8	315.1	517.9	605.4	297.2	316.1	486.9	592.6	658.3
Repayments	0.0	0.0	0.0	6.2	15.9	55.4	40.3	42.3	54.1	75.7	62.6
Other Long-Term Capital	160.0	140.0	35.2	-213.4	-311.1	-44.0	248.0	-17.0	23.6	-42.8	87.1
Other Capital, net	0.0	0.0	65.3	-252.4	89.9	160.0	-1.6	47.9	-118.9	-49.3	-42.9
Change in Reserves	-46.0	11.0	65.7	96.6	92.6	-45.0	133.7	-130.3	47.9	-147.2	203.6
Memo Item:					*(Bangladesh Taka per US dollar)*						
Conversion Factor (Annual Avg)	4.760	4.760	6.030	7.780	7.970	8.880	14.850	15.470	15.120	15.220	15.480
					(Millions of US dollars), outstanding at end of year						
EXTERNAL DEBT (Total)	15	15	161	496	1,253	1,812	2,117	2,456	3,026	3,196	4,056
Long-Term Debt (by debtor)	15	15	161	495	1,253	1,810	2,111	2,425	2,949	3,080	3,844
Central Bank, incl. IMF credit	0	0	68	75	169	212	298	282	328	373	451
Central Government	15	15	93	401	1,059	1,561	1,798	2,126	2,604	2,688	3,371
Rest of General Government	..	..	..	..	..	..	..	..	..	..	..
Non-financial Public Enterprises	0	0	0	18	25	36	15	17	18	19	22
Priv. Sector, incl non-guaranteed	0	0	0	0	0	0	0	0	0	0	0
Short-Term Debt	0	0	0	1	0	2	6	31	77	116	212
Memo Items:					*(Millions of US dollars)*						
Int'l Reserves Excluding Gold	..	..	270.5	143.2	138.2	148.3	288.9	232.7	315.2	386.3	299.6
Gold Holdings (at market price)	..	..	..	..	..	..	..	8.8	6.0	27.4	31.5
SOCIAL INDICATORS											
Total Fertility Rate	7.0	7.0	7.0	6.9	6.7	6.6	6.4	6.3	6.2	6.2	6.1
Infant Mortality Rate	140.0	140.0	140.0	139.4	138.8	138.2	137.6	137.0	135.2	133.4	131.6
Life Expectancy at Birth	44.9	44.9	44.9	45.2	45.6	46.0	46.4	46.8	47.1	47.5	47.9
Urban Population, % of total	7.6	7.9	8.3	8.6	9.0	9.3	9.7	10.1	10.5	10.9	11.3
Food Prod. per capita (1987=100)	121.7	109.0	104.4	112.8	106.3	114.9	107.0	112.4	113.2	109.0	109.4
Labor Force, Agriculture (%)	81.4	80.7	80.0	79.4	78.7	78.1	77.4	76.7	76.1	75.4	74.8
Labor Force, Female (%)	5.4	5.5	5.6	5.7	5.7	5.8	5.9	6.0	6.1	6.2	6.3
Primary Schl. Enroll. Ratio	54.0	..	..	..	..	73.0	70.0	69.0	65.0	64.0	62.0
Primary Schl. Enroll. Ratio, Female	35.0	..	..	..	..	51.0	54.0	53.0	50.0	48.0	46.0
Secondary Schl. Enroll. Ratio	..	..	..	..	..	26.0	21.0	21.0	18.0	15.0	18.0

1981	1982	1983	1984	1985	1986	1987	1988	1989	1990 estimate	Notes	BANGLADESH
				(Millions of current US dollars)							**FOREIGN TRADE (CUSTOMS BASIS)**
659.6	671.1	788.9	934.4	973.7	954.5	1,194.5	1,291.0	1,304.9	1,674.5	..	Value of Exports, fob
211.9	239.0	274.6	311.0	303.8	310.0	300.5	324.8	328.3	421.3	..	Nonfuel Primary Products
0.0	15.0	29.3	17.5	24.8	8.4	15.2	16.4	16.6	21.3	..	Fuels
447.6	417.0	485.0	605.9	645.0	636.2	878.7	949.7	960.0	1,231.9	..	Manufactures
1,802.7	1,742.1	1,502.4	2,041.6	2,420.5	1,983.9	2,572.7	3,042.8	3,650.4	3,646.0	..	Value of Imports, cif
559.2	584.3	461.6	802.8	789.6	519.8	918.5	1,086.4	1,303.3	1,301.7	..	Nonfuel Primary Products
134.8	212.2	160.2	189.2	400.2	372.6	352.4	416.8	500.0	499.4	..	Fuels
1,108.7	945.6	880.7	1,049.6	1,230.7	1,091.5	1,301.7	1,539.6	1,847.1	1,844.9	..	Manufactures
				(Index 1987 = 100)							
82.9	88.2	89.3	96.1	108.9	100.2	100.0	96.9	93.5	95.4	..	Terms of Trade
95.6	95.3	94.2	101.0	108.2	92.8	100.0	107.5	103.9	117.6	..	Export Prices, fob
115.2	108.0	105.5	105.1	99.4	92.7	100.0	111.0	111.0	123.3	..	Import Prices, cif
				(Millions of current US dollars)							**BALANCE OF PAYMENTS**
984.9	874.0	926.0	1,090.0	1,220.0	1,079.0	1,335.8	1,541.1	1,676.7	1,971.0	C f	Exports of Goods & Services
710.7	626.0	686.0	811.0	934.0	819.0	1,074.0	1,231.0	1,286.0	1,524.0	..	Merchandise, fob
222.3	214.0	213.0	222.4	228.0	223.9	226.6	255.2	311.9	379.4	..	Nonfactor Services
51.9	34.0	27.0	56.6	58.0	36.1	35.2	54.9	78.8	67.6	..	Factor Services
2,792.4	2,890.0	2,652.0	2,664.0	3,011.2	2,749.1	3,033.1	3,440.6	3,888.2	4,314.0	C f	Imports of Goods & Services
2,533.0	2,572.0	2,309.0	2,353.0	2,647.0	2,364.0	2,620.0	2,987.0	3,375.0	3,759.0	..	Merchandise, fob
184.8	187.0	208.0	190.0	216.6	222.9	256.3	265.7	326.1	357.0	..	Nonfactor Services
74.6	131.0	135.0	121.0	147.6	162.2	156.8	187.9	187.1	198.0	..	Factor Services
54.8	59.1	65.4	72.0	90.9	108.4	138.3	140.7	138.7	158.6	..	Long-Term Interest
379.0	424.0	628.0	626.8	476.8	586.0	731.0	788.0	835.4	802.0	f	Private Current Transfers, net
362.3	368.3	575.7	526.6	363.7	497.4	617.4	737.0	771.0	761.0		Workers' Remittances
-1,428.5	-1,592.0	-1,098.0	-947.2	-1,314.4	-1,084.1	-966.3	-1,111.5	-1,376.1	-1,541.0	..	Curr. A/C Bal before Off. Transf.
584.4	697.3	720.0	708.0	700.8	962.6	656.9	823.0	672.9	765.9	f	Net Official Transfers
-844.1	-894.7	-378.0	-239.2	-613.6	-121.5	-309.4	-288.5	-703.2	-775.1	..	Curr. A/C Bal after Off. Transf.
553.0	499.8	551.5	470.2	546.2	152.4	681.1	652.0	839.8	867.7	C f	Long-Term Capital, net
0.0	0.0	0.0	0.2	-0.4	2.1	2.4	0.0	0.0		..	Direct Investment
467.4	578.5	476.0	511.3	558.6	917.0	785.8	710.0	836.6	846.2	..	Long-Term Loans
547.2	671.9	538.5	596.0	668.5	1,067.2	950.4	908.4	1,010.8	1,120.8	..	Disbursements
79.8	93.4	62.5	84.7	109.9	150.2	164.6	198.4	174.2	274.6	..	Repayments
85.6	-78.7	75.5	-41.3	-12.0	-766.7	-107.1	-58.0	3.2	21.5	..	Other Long-Term Capital
-107.8	-112.6	35.8	124.0	-9.6	97.1	-168.7	-219.0	-32.0	-318.8	C f	Other Capital, net
398.9	507.5	-209.3	-355.0	77.0	-128.0	-203.0	-144.5	-104.6	226.2	..	Change in Reserves
				(Bangladesh Taka per US dollar)							**Memo Item:**
16.350	20.040	23.760	24.950	26.000	29.890	30.630	31.250	32.140	32.790	..	Conversion Factor (Annual Avg)
			(Millions of US dollars), outstanding at end of year								
4,455	5,019	5,435	5,632	6,629	8,032	9,891	10,387	10,709	12,245	..	**EXTERNAL DEBT (Total)**
4,227	4,810	5,265	5,499	6,494	7,907	9,817	10,337	10,641	12,089	..	Long-Term Debt (by debtor)
486	571	584	477	540	568	875	868	738	641	..	Central Bank, incl. IMF credit
3,720	4,217	4,661	5,005	5,937	7,295	8,919	9,450	9,888	11,410	..	Central Government
..	..	..	..	..	..	..	..	..	..	..	Rest of General Government
21	23	20	17	17	44	23	19	15	38	..	Non-financial Public Enterprises
0	0	0	0	0	0	0	0	0	..	..	Priv. Sector, incl non-guaranteed
228	209	170	133	135	125	74	50	68	156	..	Short-Term Debt
				(Millions of US dollars)							**Memo Items:**
138.4	182.6	524.1	389.9	336.5	409.1	843.1	1,046.1	501.5	628.6	..	Int'l Reserves Excluding Gold
21.3	24.4	21.4	16.5	17.5	20.9	25.9	30.4	30.6	30.9	..	Gold Holdings (at market price)
											SOCIAL INDICATORS
6.1	6.0	5.8	5.6	5.4	5.2	5.0	4.9	4.7	4.6	..	Total Fertility Rate
129.8	128.0	124.4	120.8	117.2	113.6	110.0	108.2	106.4	104.5	..	Infant Mortality Rate
48.3	48.6	49.1	49.5	49.9	50.3	50.8	51.0	51.3	51.6	..	Life Expectancy at Birth
11.8	12.3	12.7	13.2	13.7	14.2	14.8	15.3	15.9	16.4	..	Urban Population, % of total
105.6	106.6	106.3	103.7	104.5	102.9	100.0	97.9	108.7	105.1	..	Food Prod. per capita (1987=100)
..	..	..	..	..	..	..	..	..	..	..	Labor Force, Agriculture (%)
6.4	6.5	6.6	6.7	6.8	6.9	7.0	7.1	7.2	7.3	..	Labor Force, Female (%)
60.0	61.0	62.0	62.0	60.0	60.0	59.0	70.0	70.0	..	..	Primary Schl. Enroll. Ratio
50.0	51.0	47.0	51.0	50.0	50.0	49.0	64.0	64.0	..	..	Primary Schl. Enroll. Ratio, Female
..	..	18.0	19.0	18.0	18.0	18.0	18.0	17.0	..	..	Secondary Schl. Enroll. Ratio

BARBADOS	1970	1971	1972	1973	1974	1975	1976	1977	1978	1979	1980
CURRENT GNP PER CAPITA (US $)	750	830	910	1,040	1,220	1,520	1,740	1,960	2,250	2,670	3,130
POPULATION (thousands)	239	240	242	243	245	246	246	247	248	247	249
USE AND ORIGIN OF RESOURCES					*(Millions of current Barbados Dollars)*						
Gross National Product (GNP)	361.6	402.1	444.6	554.6	704.2	809.8	877.8	989.9	1,115.4	1,345.3	1,683.2
Net Factor Income from Abroad	-1.4	-0.8	-3.8	-3.3	5.1	-2.6	4.4	-3.7	3.3	-3.1	4.7
GDP at Market Prices	363.0	402.9	448.4	557.9	699.1	812.4	873.4	993.6	1,112.1	1,348.4	1,678.5
Resource Balance	-69.4	-51.0	-59.5	-64.7	-49.0	-81.5	-163.8	-146.4	-87.8	-130.0	-100.2
Exports of Goods & NF Services	216.0	246.7	290.8	336.5	435.6	409.3	395.1	503.0	645.6	867.8	1,129.4
Imports of Goods & NF Services	285.4	297.7	350.3	401.2	484.6	490.8	558.9	649.4	733.4	997.8	1,229.6
Domestic Absorption	432.4	453.9	507.9	622.6	748.1	893.9	1,037.2	1,140.0	1,199.9	1,478.4	1,778.7
Private Consumption, etc.	289.9	306.7	349.3	417.9	505.2	602.9	649.9	773.8	755.7	950.9	1,062.0
General Gov't Consumption	47.7	54.2	58.8	80.8	83.4	134.8	151.4	172.1	189.7	210.3	292.4
Gross Domestic Investment	94.8	93.0	99.8	123.9	159.5	156.2	235.9	194.1	254.5	317.2	424.3
Fixed Investment	94.8	93.0	99.8	123.9	159.5	156.2	235.9	194.1	254.5	317.2	424.3
Indirect Taxes, net	43.1	47.7	53.3	59.0	58.7	111.8	85.4	103.5	127.6	152.2	194.7
GDP at factor cost	319.9	355.2	395.1	498.9	640.4	700.6	788.0	890.1	984.5	1,196.2	1,483.8
Agriculture	35.1	33.4	39.0	51.7	68.5	93.4	76.8	91.8	91.7	109.8	152.2
Industry	62.5	69.7	76.5	92.2	125.8	130.1	153.9	181.2	210.1	252.1	331.8
Manufacturing	25.4	29.6	34.2	43.8	62.6	71.9	84.8	102.6	112.4	136.4	169.0
Services, etc.	222.3	252.1	279.6	355.0	446.1	477.1	557.3	617.1	682.7	834.3	999.8
Gross Domestic Saving	25.4	42.0	40.3	59.2	110.5	74.7	72.1	47.7	166.7	187.2	324.1
Gross National Saving	31.8	48.8	45.1	67.2	128.7	85.8	98.2	69.6	199.1	218.1	372.0
					(Millions of 1987 Barbados Dollars)						
Gross National Product	2,026.1	2,122.1	2,148.5	2,181.1	2,107.0	2,168.5	2,187.0	2,260.7	2,415.9	2,588.4	2,724.9
GDP at Market Prices	2,058.6	2,152.0	2,192.5	2,220.2	2,116.3	2,201.4	2,201.9	2,296.2	2,437.1	2,625.3	2,749.6
Resource Balance	..	..	..	..	..	..	..	..	..	..	..
Exports of Goods & NF Services	..	..	..	..	..	..	..	..	..	..	..
Imports of Goods & NF Services	..	..	..	..	..	..	..	..	..	..	..
Domestic Absorption	..	..	..	..	..	..	..	..	..	..	..
Private Consumption, etc.	..	..	..	..	..	..	..	..	..	..	..
General Gov't Consumption	..	..	..	..	..	..	..	..	..	..	..
Gross Domestic Investment	..	..	..	..	..	..	..	..	..	..	..
Fixed Investment	..	..	..	..	..	..	..	..	..	..	..
GDP at factor cost	1,766.2	1,848.4	1,883.7	1,935.5	1,889.7	1,850.3	1,936.5	2,005.1	2,102.9	2,270.4	2,369.4
Agriculture	269.6	243.0	204.4	214.5	203.0	196.1	210.1	214.5	214.5	232.0	244.7
Industry	374.3	377.2	396.1	423.3	402.5	398.0	462.3	439.3	465.2	527.6	551.3
Manufacturing	175.5	191.3	211.3	226.5	215.8	238.9	279.2	274.0	280.6	319.9	326.8
Services, etc.	1,122.2	1,228.2	1,283.2	1,297.7	1,284.3	1,256.2	1,264.1	1,351.3	1,423.2	1,510.8	1,573.4
Memo Items:											
Capacity to Import	..	..	..	..	..	..	..	..	..	..	..
Terms of Trade Adjustment	..	..	..	..	..	..	..	..	..	..	..
Gross Domestic Income	..	..	..	..	..	..	..	..	..	..	..
Gross National Income	..	..	..	..	..	..	..	..	..	..	..
DOMESTIC PRICES/DEFLATORS					*(Index 1987 = 100)*						
Overall (GDP)	17.6	18.7	20.5	25.1	33.0	36.9	39.7	43.3	45.6	51.4	61.0
Domestic Absorption	..	..	..	..	..	..	..	..	..	..	..
Agriculture	13.0	13.7	19.1	24.1	33.8	47.6	36.6	42.8	42.7	47.3	62.2
Industry	16.7	18.5	19.3	21.8	31.3	32.7	33.3	41.2	45.2	47.8	60.2
Manufacturing	14.5	15.5	16.2	19.3	29.0	30.1	30.4	37.4	40.1	42.6	51.7
Consumer Price Index	17.4	18.7	21.0	24.5	34.0	40.9	43.0	46.6	51.0	57.7	66.0
MANUFACTURING ACTIVITY											
Employment (1987=100)	77.2	87.8	92.0	97.9	86.9	90.3	95.9	108.6	87.0	96.3	83.9
Real Earnings per Empl. (1987=100)	79.4	77.0	79.3	75.9	68.9	60.7	63.4	63.1	70.6	64.0	83.0
Real Output per Empl. (1987=100)	108.6	101.3	108.9	106.9	105.9	107.1	113.0	91.8	112.1	114.1	138.7
Earnings as % of Value Added	56.7	54.9	51.9	51.1	46.9	53.1	56.2	61.7	51.6	53.7	63.0
MONETARY HOLDINGS					*(Millions of current Barbados Dollars)*						
Money Supply, Broadly Defined	193.9	228.5	240.1	203.8	249.3	275.7	309.4	342.1	427.2	546.0	627.2
Money	55.7	62.5	67.8	74.1	88.5	106.5	113.7	135.7	160.7	222.2	244.8
Currency Outside Banks	21.2	21.4	23.7	26.9	34.1	41.8	46.9	55.6	65.8	80.2	101.5
Demand Deposits	34.5	41.1	44.1	47.2	54.4	64.7	66.8	80.0	94.9	142.0	143.3
Quasi-Money	138.2	166.0	172.3	129.7	160.7	169.2	195.7	206.4	266.5	323.8	382.4
GOVERNMENT DEFICIT (-) OR SURPLUS					*(Millions of current Barbados Dollars)*						
GOVERNMENT DEFICIT (-) OR SURPLUS	..	..	-8.00	-33.80	-22.00	-20.00	-58.50	-62.80	-4.30	-20.90	-60.90
Current Revenue	..	..	119.50	138.60	177.50	214.20	230.30	267.00	330.00	377.50	476.00
Current Expenditure	..	..	102.00	139.10	161.00	185.30	227.20	244.60	261.00		393.10
Current Budget Balance	..	..	17.50	-0.50	16.50	28.90	3.10	22.40	69.00	..	82.90
Capital Receipts	..	..	..	..	..	..	..	..	..	..	..
Capital Payments	..	..	25.50	33.30	38.50	48.90	61.60	85.20	73.30	..	143.80

1981	1982	1983	1984	1985	1986	1987	1988	1989	1990 estimate	Notes	BARBADOS
3,510	3,760	4,010	4,420	4,640	5,170	5,330	5,880	6,410	6,540	..	**CURRENT GNP PER CAPITA (US $)**
250	251	252	253	253	254	255	256	257	257	..	POPULATION (thousands)
				(Millions of current Barbados Dollars)							**USE AND ORIGIN OF RESOURCES**
1,904.6	1,984.8	2,082.6	2,280.5	2,392.3	2,568.8	2,824.5	3,077.2	3,503.8	3,385.3	..	Gross National Product (GNP)
0.0	-5.2	-30.1	-22.3	-28.8	-77.2	-89.2	-19.8	54.4	-140.6	..	Net Factor Income from Abroad
1,904.6	1,990.0	2,112.7	2,302.8	2,421.1	2,646.0	2,913.7	3,097.0	3,449.4	3,525.9	..	GDP at Market Prices
-285.5	-124.7	-112.6	15.9	95.2	61.2	15.5	61.3	-68.2	-174.9	..	Resource Balance
1,072.5	1,215.5	1,353.7	1,573.8	1,558.7	1,495.9	1,340.1	1,536.8	1,732.7	1,762.5	..	Exports of Goods & NF Services
1,358.0	1,340.2	1,466.3	1,557.9	1,463.5	1,434.7	1,324.6	1,475.5	1,800.9	1,937.4	..	Imports of Goods & NF Services
2,190.1	2,114.7	2,225.2	2,286.9	2,325.9	2,584.9	2,898.2	3,035.6	3,517.6	3,700.8	..	Domestic Absorption
1,343.9	1,335.2	1,457.9	1,525.4	1,497.8	1,692.3	1,934.0	1,955.0	2,318.0	..	f	Private Consumption, etc.
321.2	329.0	346.1	387.6	456.3	468.8	497.5	537.3	564.2	..	..	General Gov't Consumption
525.0	450.5	421.2	373.9	371.8	423.8	466.7	543.3	635.4	599.4	f	Gross Domestic Investment
525.0	450.5	421.2	373.9	371.8	423.8	466.7	449.6	..	..	..	Fixed Investment
198.4	205.8	213.7	228.2	229.3	348.7	414.8	431.6	522.6	558.2	..	Indirect Taxes, net
1,706.2	1,784.2	1,899.0	2,074.6	2,191.8	2,297.3	2,498.9	2,665.4	2,926.8	2,967.7	B	GDP at factor cost
128.9	122.0	135.6	139.2	150.1	213.2	207.4	199.9	193.0	..	..	Agriculture
379.7	388.4	440.4	493.2	449.2	473.3	537.5	549.0	611.3	..	..	Industry
189.7	205.5	238.7	264.1	231.7	238.9	276.8	261.2	289.6	..	f	Manufacturing
1,197.6	1,273.8	1,323.0	1,442.2	1,592.5	1,610.8	1,754.0	1,916.5	2,122.5	..	..	Services, etc.
239.5	325.8	308.7	389.8	467.0	484.9	482.2	604.7	567.2	424.5		Gross Domestic Saving
287.9	355.0	312.2	400.7	467.7	445.1	431.2	644.6	685.8	..		Gross National Saving
				(Millions of 1987 Barbados Dollars)							
2,630.1	2,491.2	2,467.0	2,569.9	2,593.0	2,850.2	2,824.5	3,012.6	3,006.3	2,917.6		Gross National Product
2,661.3	2,527.6	2,532.9	2,616.4	2,623.5	2,896.7	2,913.7	3,115.1	3,226.8	3,138.7	..	GDP at Market Prices
											Resource Balance
..	..	..	..	..	..		..	..	..		Exports of Goods & NF Services
..	..	..	..	..	..		..	..	..		Imports of Goods & NF Services
											Domestic Absorption
..	..	..	..	..	..		..	..	..		Private Consumption, etc.
..	..	..	..	..	..		..	..	..		General Gov't Consumption
..	..	..	..	..	..		..	..	..		Gross Domestic Investment
..	..	..	..	..	..		..	..	..		Fixed Investment
2,324.1	2,209.4	2,219.3	2,299.1	2,318.8	2,439.7	2,498.9	2,586.8	2,680.1	2,588.6	B	GDP at factor cost
202.7	197.9	205.3	224.9	223.7	233.5	207.4	195.3	177.8	186.1	..	Agriculture
545.5	508.7	525.0	538.5	511.3	543.9	537.5	574.6	606.3	577.8	..	Industry
315.1	298.2	305.1	311.6	282.0	296.4	276.8	295.4	310.9	303.0	f	Manufacturing
1,576.0	1,502.7	1,488.9	1,535.8	1,583.8	1,662.3	1,754.0	1,817.0	1,896.0	1,824.7	..	Services, etc.
											Memo Items:
..	..	..	..	..	..	..	..	..	..		Capacity to Import
..	..	..	..	..	..	..	..	..	..		Terms of Trade Adjustment
..	..	..	..	..	..	..	..	..	..		Gross Domestic Income
..	..	..	..	..	..	..	..	..	..		Gross National Income
				(Index 1987 = 100)							**DOMESTIC PRICES/DEFLATORS**
71.6	78.7	83.4	88.0	92.3	91.3	100.0	99.4	106.9	112.3	..	Overall (GDP)
..	..	..	..	..	..		..	..	..	..	Domestic Absorption
63.6	61.6	66.0	61.9	67.1	91.3	100.0	102.4	108.6	..	..	Agriculture
69.6	76.4	83.9	91.6	87.9	87.0	100.0	95.5	100.8	..	..	Industry
60.2	68.9	78.2	84.8	82.2	80.6	100.0	88.4	93.1		..	Manufacturing
75.6	83.4	87.8	91.9	95.5	96.8	100.0	104.9	111.3	114.8	..	Consumer Price Index
											MANUFACTURING ACTIVITY
89.6	117.6	125.9	122.2	98.7	107.8	100.0	..	..	..	G	Employment (1987=100)
79.6	81.8	86.3	96.0	102.2	100.5	100.0	..	..	..	G	Real Earnings per Empl. (1987=100)
127.7	106.8	99.6	107.3	117.7	118.8	100.0	..	..	..	G	Real Output per Empl. (1987=100)
60.2	69.8	64.0	67.5	77.9	71.8	69.0	..	..	..		Earnings as % of Value Added
				(Millions of current Barbados Dollars)							**MONETARY HOLDINGS**
732.1	790.1	860.1	918.2	1,033.2	1,168.4	1,408.4	1,571.1	1,637.2	1,823.0	D	Money Supply, Broadly Defined
249.6	251.5	312.9	305.7	353.5	395.4	466.9	524.8	459.0	526.2	..	Money
111.2	110.6	114.1	118.1	123.5	137.4	156.6	171.3	182.7	192.8	..	Currency Outside Banks
138.3	140.9	198.7	187.6	230.0	258.0	310.3	353.4	276.3	333.4	..	Demand Deposits
482.5	538.6	547.2	612.4	679.7	773.1	941.4	1,046.4	1,178.1	1,296.8	..	Quasi-Money
				(Millions of current Barbados Dollars)							
-128.80	-76.10	-25.70	-91.00	-71.40	-79.70	-213.80	-88.70	-32.80	..	C F	**GOVERNMENT DEFICIT (-) OR SURPLUS**
512.20	572.50	636.90	666.10	748.50	775.10	844.20	1,036.70	1,121.50	..	..	Current Revenue
484.90	513.90	532.30	613.60	674.90	698.30	860.20	900.40	953.30	..	..	Current Expenditure
27.30	58.60	104.60	52.50	73.60	76.80	-16.00	136.30	168.20	..	..	Current Budget Balance
0.70	..	..	..	..	..	0.20	..	..	..	..	Capital Receipts
156.80	134.70	130.30	143.50	145.00	156.50	198.00	225.00	201.00	..	..	Capital Payments

BARBADOS	1970	1971	1972	1973	1974	1975	1976	1977	1978	1979	1980
FOREIGN TRADE (CUSTOMS BASIS)					*(Millions of current US dollars)*						
Value of Exports, fob	30.52	28.30	33.41	43.17	61.75	87.72	68.69	75.28	93.38	119.53	149.52
Nonfuel Primary Products	22.38	21.08	21.48	25.33	39.10	61.39	35.80	37.51	37.41	43.26	70.69
Fuels	0.39	0.07	0.20	0.34	1.02	1.08	0.66	0.26	0.51	0.24	0.26
Manufactures	7.75	7.15	11.73	17.50	21.63	25.25	32.23	37.50	55.46	76.03	78.56
Value of Imports, cif	117.27	121.84	141.66	167.62	203.96	216.39	236.58	271.61	312.35	420.75	517.09
Nonfuel Primary Products	32.64	35.12	42.39	51.83	60.89	59.73	65.90	71.05	82.89	93.93	111.00
Fuels	6.50	7.97	8.29	11.13	32.35	36.54	30.79	36.01	36.23	59.17	79.42
Manufactures	78.14	78.75	90.98	104.66	110.72	120.13	139.90	164.55	193.23	267.66	326.67
					(Index 1987 = 100)						
Terms of Trade	100.9	93.6	108.5	134.5	192.9	177.5	144.0	131.9	122.2	132.4	160.8
Export Prices, fob	26.2	26.0	34.2	52.9	107.2	101.3	86.9	86.9	90.2	116.5	164.3
Import Prices, cif	26.0	27.7	31.5	39.3	55.6	57.1	60.4	65.9	73.8	87.9	102.1
BALANCE OF PAYMENTS					*(Millions of current US dollars)*						
Exports of Goods & Services	101.65	110.74	125.23	149.35	189.80	220.78	210.21	260.02	329.54	441.55	572.66
Merchandise, fob	35.75	33.27	37.68	47.93	67.31	94.45	76.11	85.36	110.97	131.51	180.78
Nonfactor Services	59.15	71.65	81.04	92.38	112.46	114.05	123.82	166.73	206.78	294.39	371.35
Factor Services	6.75	5.82	6.51	9.03	10.03	12.28	10.28	7.92	11.78	15.66	20.53
Imports of Goods & Services	148.65	151.25	174.99	208.96	244.64	269.39	287.01	327.34	377.47	497.64	619.75
Merchandise, fob	106.90	112.16	128.04	152.56	185.51	197.02	219.09	250.20	288.02	379.11	480.78
Nonfactor Services	34.65	31.04	37.11	44.25	46.80	56.09	59.19	64.88	75.97	95.71	118.33
Factor Services	7.10	8.05	9.84	12.15	12.32	16.29	8.73	12.26	13.47	22.82	20.63
Long-Term Interest	..	..	..	..	..	..	..	..	..	..	..
Private Current Transfers, net	3.90	3.85	4.48	5.77	6.38	6.78	10.83	12.76	14.47	16.90	21.48
Workers' Remittances	..	..	..	..	..	..	..	..	..	..	..
Curr. A/C Bal before Off. Transf.	-43.10	-36.66	-45.28	-53.85	-48.46	-41.83	-65.98	-54.56	-33.46	-39.18	-25.61
Net Official Transfers	1.30	1.52	2.03	1.53	0.63	0.50	1.80	3.19	2.19	4.97	-0.05
Curr. A/C Bal after Off. Transf.	-41.80	-35.14	-43.25	-52.32	-47.83	-41.33	-64.18	-51.38	-31.27	-34.21	-25.66
Long-Term Capital, net	11.10	16.36	19.62	24.81	1.85	20.89	22.96	35.03	11.88	-7.51	22.77
Direct Investment	8.45	14.79	17.23	4.80	2.24	22.13	5.94	4.48	8.90	5.07	2.19
Long-Term Loans											
Disbursements	..	..	..	..	..	..	..	..	..	..	..
Repayments	..	..	..	..	..	..	..	..	..	..	..
Other Long-Term Capital	2.65	1.57	2.39	20.01	-0.39	-1.24	17.02	30.55	2.98	-12.58	20.58
Other Capital, net	24.85	30.48	26.70	27.10	39.32	29.15	29.21	17.99	40.47	46.50	20.52
Change in Reserves	5.85	-11.70	-3.07	0.41	6.66	-8.70	12.02	-1.64	-21.08	-4.79	-17.64
Memo Item:					*(Barbados Dollars per US dollar)*						
Conversion Factor (Annual Avg)	2.000	1.970	1.920	1.960	2.050	2.020	2.000	2.010	2.010	2.010	2.010
EXTERNAL DEBT (Total)	..	..	..	*(Millions of US dollars), outstanding at end of year*					..	..	..
Long-Term Debt (by debtor)	..	..	..						..	..	..
Central Bank, incl. IMF credit	..	..	..						..	..	..
Central Government	..	..	..						..	..	..
Rest of General Government	..	..	..						..	..	..
Non-financial Public Enterprises	..	..	..						..	..	..
Priv. Sector, incl non-guaranteed	..	..	..						..	..	..
Short-Term Debt	..	..	..						..	..	..
Memo Items:					*(Millions of US dollars)*						
Int'l Reserves Excluding Gold	16.58	18.86	27.99	32.37	39.15	39.58	27.98	37.01	59.84	66.12	78.92
Gold Holdings (at market price)	..	..	..	..	..	..	..	..	..	..	1.65
SOCIAL INDICATORS											
Total Fertility Rate	3.0	2.9	2.7	2.6	2.5	2.4	2.3	2.2	2.1	2.1	2.0
Infant Mortality Rate	38.2	35.6	33.0	31.8	30.6	29.4	28.2	27.0	25.0	23.0	21.0
Life Expectancy at Birth	68.7	69.0	69.4	69.8	70.1	70.5	70.9	71.2	71.6	71.9	72.3
Urban Population, % of total	37.4	37.6	37.9	38.1	38.4	38.6	38.9	39.2	39.5	39.8	40.1
Food Prod. per capita (1987=100)	142.7	128.8	113.6	111.8	109.5	102.3	106.8	116.1	114.7	122.4	135.1
Labor Force, Agriculture (%)	18.2	17.2	16.3	15.5	14.7	14.0	13.1	12.2	11.4	10.6	9.9
Labor Force, Female (%)	39.9	40.7	41.4	42.1	42.7	43.3	44.2	45.0	45.8	46.5	47.2
Primary Schl. Enroll. Ratio	102.0	..	..	..	..	103.0	109.0	116.0	122.0	115.0	100.0
Primary Schl. Enroll. Ratio, Female	101.0	..	..	..	..	103.0	111.0	116.0	122.0	114.0	100.0
Secondary Schl. Enroll. Ratio	69.0	..	..	..	..	77.0	77.0	81.0	81.0	85.0	90.0

1981	1982	1983	1984	1985	1986	1987	1988	1989	1990 estimate	Notes	BARBADOS
											FOREIGN TRADE (CUSTOMS BASIS)
				(Millions of current US dollars)							
147.67	190.79	289.16	272.00	214.90	209.13	160.33	173.42	187.57	213.40	..	Value of Exports, fob
44.57	53.40	35.92	42.37	34.31	40.71	47.98	27.02	44.53	58.64	..	Nonfuel Primary Products
0.22	0.46	1.00	0.90	0.00	0.03	28.95	0.57	36.33	58.74	..	Fuels
102.88	136.93	252.23	228.72	180.59	168.38	83.39	145.83	106.71	96.02	..	Manufactures
591.11	549.75	605.22	665.19	601.93	593.22	514.86	578.70	673.45	698.46	..	Value of Imports, cif
119.52	109.04	107.84	113.54	106.78	112.17	120.81	130.94	152.38	150.45	..	Nonfuel Primary Products
94.56	89.03	60.68	90.64	105.62	60.75	55.43	60.99	70.97	99.92	..	Fuels
377.04	351.69	436.69	461.01	389.53	420.30	338.62	386.77	450.10	448.09	..	Manufactures
				(Index 1987 = 100)							
149.9	126.8	125.9	120.8	117.3	119.9	100.0	116.8	127.2	131.0	..	Terms of Trade
154.6	125.4	121.6	115.2	109.6	112.8	100.0	120.3	134.9	152.1	..	Export Prices, fob
103.1	98.8	96.6	95.3	93.5	94.1	100.0	103.0	106.1	116.1	..	Import Prices, cif
											BALANCE OF PAYMENTS
				(Millions of current US dollars)							
555.46	626.31	698.35	827.28	794.71	760.35	688.31	803.26	921.84	916.56	f	Exports of Goods & Services
162.78	208.22	272.16	339.73	300.45	244.27	131.41	144.83	146.92	151.34	..	Merchandise, fob
370.16	396.11	405.01	458.66	464.82	476.91	523.44	627.65	739.82	729.92	..	Nonfactor Services
22.52	21.98	21.18	28.89	29.43	39.18	33.46	30.78	35.10	35.32	..	Factor Services
692.04	685.13	761.00	822.80	759.96	787.80	748.22	818.72	930.29	1,045.98	f	Imports of Goods & Services
527.17	507.03	571.47	606.22	559.19	522.60	458.36	517.87	599.26	705.72	..	Merchandise, fob
133.50	144.68	148.66	165.47	149.06	194.70	208.22	229.95	263.36	262.35	..	Nonfactor Services
31.37	33.41	40.87	51.11	51.71	70.50	81.64	70.90	67.67	77.90	..	Factor Services
..	..	..	..	..	..	..	..	..	..	..	Long-Term Interest
24.06	17.10	16.71	16.51	14.67	18.59	18.99	29.68	31.92	..	..	Private Current Transfers, net
..	..	..	..	..	..	..	..	..	..	..	Workers' Remittances
-112.51	-41.71	-45.94	20.98	49.42	-8.85	-40.92	14.22	23.47	-89.21	..	Curr. A/C Bal before Off. Transf.
-6.12	6.07	3.98	-1.84	-9.15	-6.96	-12.48	-12.03	-26.10	..	..	Net Official Transfers
-118.63	-35.65	-41.96	19.14	40.27	-15.81	-53.40	2.19	-2.64	-89.21	..	Curr. A/C Bal after Off. Transf.
70.60	8.05	21.68	-19.39	11.49	12.33	69.41	26.35	0.94	-66.64	f	Long-Term Capital, net
7.16	4.13	2.24	-1.49	2.59	4.97	4.57	10.54	5.37	5.61	..	Direct Investment
..	..	..	..	..	..	..	..	..	..	..	Long-Term Loans
..	..	..	..	..	..	..	..	..	..	..	Disbursements
..	..	..	..	..	..	..	..	..	..	..	Repayments
63.44	3.93	19.44	-17.90	8.90	7.36	64.83	15.81	-4.42	-72.25	..	Other Long-Term Capital
69.27	29.38	9.56	-13.34	-29.50	23.58	-9.79	9.45	-40.67	167.40	f	Other Capital, net
-21.24	-1.79	10.73	13.59	-22.25	-20.10	-6.22	-37.99	42.36	-11.55		Change in Reserves
											Memo Item:
				(Barbados Dollars per US dollar)							
2.010	2.010	2.010	2.010	2.010	2.010	2.010	2.010	2.010	2.010	..	Conversion Factor (Annual Avg)
			(Millions of US dollars), outstanding at end of year								**EXTERNAL DEBT (Total)**
..	..	..	..	..	..	..	..	..	..		Long-Term Debt (by debtor)
..	..	..	..	..	..	..	..	..	..		Central Bank, incl. IMF credit
..	..	..	..	..	..	..	..	..	..		Central Government
..	..	..	..	..	..	..	..	..	..		Rest of General Government
..	..	..	..	..	..	..	..	..	..		Non-financial Public Enterprises
..	..	..	..	..	..	..	..	..	..		Priv. Sector, incl non-guaranteed
..	..	..	..	..	..	..	..	..	..		Short-Term Debt
				(Millions of US dollars)							**Memo Items:**
100.56	121.60	123.28	132.52	139.77	151.71	145.21	135.46	109.47	117.54	..	Int'l Reserves Excluding Gold
2.41	2.77	2.31	1.87	1.98	2.37	2.93	2.49	2.43	..	..	Gold Holdings (at market price)
											SOCIAL INDICATORS
2.0	1.9	1.9	1.9	1.8	1.8	1.8	1.8	1.8	1.8	..	Total Fertility Rate
19.0	17.0	15.1	13.1	12.9	12.6	12.0	11.5	11.0	10.4	..	Infant Mortality Rate
72.6	72.9	73.2	73.5	73.8	74.1	74.3	74.6	74.9	75.1	..	Life Expectancy at Birth
40.5	40.9	41.4	41.8	42.2	42.7	43.2	43.7	44.2	44.7	..	Urban Population, % of total
116.3	109.5	99.6	102.2	100.1	109.4	100.0	102.5	95.6	97.2	..	Food Prod. per capita (1987=100)
..	..	..	..	..	..	..	..	..	..	..	Labor Force, Agriculture (%)
47.2	47.2	47.2	47.2	47.2	47.2	47.3	47.3	47.3	47.3	..	Labor Force, Female (%)
101.0	103.0	108.0	110.0	..	..	..	..	..	..	..	Primary Schl. Enroll. Ratio
99.0	99.0	107.0	108.0	..	..	..	..	..	..	..	Primary Schl. Enroll. Ratio, Female
89.0	89.0	91.0	93.0	..	..	..	..	..	..	..	Secondary Schl. Enroll. Ratio

BELGIUM	1970	1971	1972	1973	1974	1975	1976	1977	1978	1979	1980
CURRENT GNP PER CAPITA (US $)	2,670	2,910	3,330	4,070	5,080	5,940	6,840	7,610	8,760	10,420	12,140
POPULATION (thousands)	9,638	9,673	9,709	9,738	9,768	9,795	9,811	9,822	9,830	9,837	9,847
USE AND ORIGIN OF RESOURCES	*(Billions of current Belgian Francs)*										
Gross National Product (GNP)	1,271.7	1,390.0	1,555.2	1,762.1	2,065.5	2,280.8	2,592.7	2,793.3	2,993.1	3,180.2	3,425.0
Net Factor Income from Abroad	9.6	8.0	9.8	7.1	8.7	9.7	13.8	8.0	5.6	-8.6	-26.2
GDP at Market Prices	1,262.1	1,382.0	1,545.4	1,755.0	2,056.8	2,271.1	2,578.9	2,785.3	2,987.5	3,188.8	3,451.1
Resource Balance	30.8	30.4	53.8	38.6	12.1	9.1	10.9	-18.1	-23.5	-59.6	-87.6
Exports of Goods & NF Services	654.5	698.7	789.1	975.8	1,260.2	1,220.1	1,456.9	1,543.7	1,597.4	1,863.9	2,170.2
Imports of Goods & NF Services	623.7	668.3	735.3	937.2	1,248.1	1,211.0	1,446.0	1,561.8	1,620.9	1,923.5	2,257.8
Domestic Absorption	1,231.3	1,351.6	1,491.6	1,716.4	2,044.7	2,262.0	2,568.0	2,803.4	3,011.0	3,248.4	3,538.8
Private Consumption, etc.	755.2	833.1	930.2	1,063.4	1,230.3	1,390.4	1,571.6	1,724.5	1,838.9	2,002.4	2,171.9
General Gov't Consumption	169.4	194.7	224.3	255.3	302.3	373.6	423.4	467.3	520.1	561.1	613.9
Gross Domestic Investment	306.7	323.9	337.1	397.8	512.0	498.0	573.0	611.6	651.9	684.9	753.0
Fixed Investment	286.2	304.8	329.7	375.6	467.4	511.1	568.7	603.0	647.5	661.1	728.3
Indirect Taxes, net	130.6	140.9	141.8	151.8	181.5	188.0	217.7	233.5	252.2	262.7	289.5
GDP at factor cost	1,131.5	1,241.1	1,403.6	1,603.2	1,875.3	2,083.2	2,361.2	2,551.7	2,735.3	2,926.1	3,161.6
Agriculture	..	..	..	..	..	63.4	73.2	66.1	73.0	69.6	73.1
Industry	..	..	..	..	..	841.9	947.4	1,006.0	1,046.5	1,111.4	1,175.6
Manufacturing	..	..	..	..	..	605.0	681.4	714.9	740.5	793.3	833.8
Services, etc.	..	..	..	..	..	1,365.9	1,558.3	1,713.1	1,868.0	2,007.8	2,202.4
Gross Domestic Saving	337.5	354.3	390.9	436.4	524.1	507.1	583.9	593.5	628.4	625.3	665.4
Gross National Saving	..	..	..	..	..	..	..	..	..	..	..
	(Billions of 1987 Belgian Francs)										
Gross National Product	3,341.0	3,456.9	3,641.6	3,847.8	4,005.7	3,946.1	4,170.7	4,179.8	4,289.7	4,360.1	4,525.6
GDP at Market Prices	3,314.3	3,436.0	3,617.4	3,831.2	3,987.9	3,928.6	4,147.5	4,167.2	4,281.2	4,372.6	4,561.2
Resource Balance	-98.8	-84.4	-62.7	-173.5	-198.8	-159.2	-163.5	-242.9	-259.8	-339.6	-246.5
Exports of Goods & NF Services	1,962.7	2,051.8	2,278.6	2,601.2	2,698.9	2,477.1	2,795.7	2,857.9	2,922.9	3,128.9	3,207.2
Imports of Goods & NF Services	2,061.4	2,136.2	2,341.3	2,774.7	2,897.7	2,636.3	2,959.2	3,100.8	3,182.7	3,468.5	3,453.7
Domestic Absorption	3,413.1	3,520.5	3,680.1	4,004.7	4,186.7	4,087.7	4,311.0	4,410.1	4,541.1	4,712.2	4,807.7
Private Consumption, etc.	2,093.3	2,187.2	2,314.1	2,516.3	2,588.8	2,586.9	2,717.7	2,794.7	2,861.2	3,010.5	3,054.6
General Gov't Consumption	535.3	565.0	598.2	630.2	651.7	681.0	706.1	722.1	765.8	784.8	796.7
Gross Domestic Investment	784.4	768.3	767.8	858.3	946.2	819.9	887.2	893.3	914.1	917.0	956.4
Fixed Investment	740.5	726.4	751.1	803.8	859.6	843.5	877.2	877.6	901.9	877.3	917.7
GDP at factor cost	2,952.3	3,069.0	3,267.6	3,477.1	3,616.3	3,588.9	3,782.1	3,799.8	3,900.9	3,991.6	4,167.9
Agriculture	..	..	..	..	..	77.6	74.5	77.4	86.7	86.4	89.6
Industry	..	..	..	..	..	1,238.9	1,334.0	1,354.5	1,387.3	1,425.3	1,459.7
Manufacturing	..	..	..	..	..	823.5	896.0	902.1	926.0	964.9	983.2
Services, etc.	..	..	..	..	..	2,612.0	2,739.1	2,735.4	2,807.3	2,860.9	3,011.9
Memo Items:											
Capacity to Import	2,163.2	2,233.4	2,512.6	2,889.0	2,925.8	2,656.1	2,981.5	3,064.9	3,136.6	3,361.0	3,319.7
Terms of Trade Adjustment	200.6	181.6	234.0	287.8	226.9	179.0	185.8	207.0	213.7	232.1	112.5
Gross Domestic Income	3,514.9	3,617.6	3,851.4	4,119.0	4,214.8	4,107.5	4,333.3	4,374.2	4,494.9	4,604.7	4,673.7
Gross National Income	3,541.5	3,638.5	3,875.6	4,135.5	4,232.6	4,125.1	4,356.5	4,386.8	4,503.4	4,592.3	4,638.1
DOMESTIC PRICES/DEFLATORS	*(Index 1987 = 100)*										
Overall (GDP)	38.1	40.2	42.7	45.8	51.6	57.8	62.2	66.8	69.8	72.9	75.7
Domestic Absorption	36.1	38.4	40.5	42.9	48.8	55.3	59.6	63.6	66.3	68.9	73.6
Agriculture	..	..	..	..	..	81.6	98.3	85.5	84.2	80.5	81.6
Industry	..	..	..	..	..	68.0	71.0	74.3	75.4	78.0	80.5
Manufacturing	..	..	..	..	..	73.5	76.0	79.2	80.0	82.2	84.8
Consumer Price Index	34.0	35.5	37.4	40.0	45.1	50.8	55.5	59.4	62.1	64.9	69.2
MANUFACTURING ACTIVITY											
Employment (1987=100)	152.8	153.3	151.5	146.2	147.8	138.7	133.1	128.0	122.5	119.2	116.5
Real Earnings per Empl. (1987=100)	61.6	66.2	70.7	76.1	80.8	83.3	87.6	90.0	92.2	95.7	97.7
Real Output per Empl. (1987=100)	40.3	43.9	46.1	55.0	60.9	57.3	65.6	0.0	0.0	0.0	79.8
Earnings as % of Value Added	46.4	48.4	47.5	46.1	46.9	49.7	49.1	48.8	48.8	49.1	49.9
MONETARY HOLDINGS	*(Millions of current Belgian Francs)*										
Money Supply, Broadly Defined	741.2	838.6	971.0	1,101.0	1,200.2	1,384.4	1,554.1	1,686.8	1,818.7	1,935.6	1,996.6
Money	378.1	420.3	484.2	520.3	552.6	639.4	684.1	741.0	784.4	804.1	806.1
Currency Outside Banks	183.2	196.4	216.8	231.5	248.9	281.2	299.5	327.4	349.7	359.0	364.2
Demand Deposits	194.9	223.9	267.4	288.8	303.7	358.2	384.6	413.6	434.7	445.1	441.9
Quasi-Money	363.1	418.3	486.8	580.7	647.6	745.0	870.0	945.8	1,034.3	1,131.5	1,190.5
	(Billions of current Belgian Francs)										
GOVERNMENT DEFICIT (-) OR SURPLUS	-21	-40	-68	-62	-47	-109	-148	-168	-209	-248	-282
Current Revenue	449	495	556	650	781	927	1,060	1,183	1,300	1,398	1,510
Current Expenditure	417	463	545	635	742	940	1,091	1,226	1,360	1,494	1,610
Current Budget Balance	32	32	10	15	38	-13	-32	-43	-60	-97	-99
Capital Receipts	1	1	0	1	1	1	0	1	1	1	1
Capital Payments	54	72	79	77	86	97	116	126	150	151	183

1981	1982	1983	1984	1985	1986	1987	1988	1989	1990 estimate	Notes	BELGIUM
11,770	10,490	9,120	8,490	8,230	9,080	11,090	14,200	15,890	17,560	..	**CURRENT GNP PER CAPITA (US $)**
9,852	9,856	9,856	9,853	9,858	9,862	9,870	9,902	9,938	9,956	..	**POPULATION (thousands)**
											USE AND ORIGIN OF RESOURCES
			(Billions of current Belgian Francs)								
3,547.5	3,830.6	4,059.5	4,369.3	4,661.6	4,921.4	5,148.7	5,478.8	5,965.1	6,352.1	..	Gross National Product (GNP)
-30.0	-58.4	-62.8	-59.7	-76.4	-64.6	-56.8	-63.9	-50.9	-77.2	..	Net Factor Income from Abroad
3,577.5	3,889.0	4,122.3	4,429.0	4,738.0	4,986.0	5,205.5	5,542.7	6,016.0	6,429.3	..	GDP at Market Prices
-58.0	-39.2	74.6	76.2	119.0	200.6	163.7	213.2	206.5	206.8	..	Resource Balance
2,439.0	2,794.3	3,078.9	3,505.2	3,644.9	3,527.8	3,616.0	4,039.2	4,641.9	4,777.5	..	Exports of Goods & NFServices
2,497.0	2,833.5	3,004.3	3,429.0	3,525.9	3,327.2	3,452.3	3,826.0	4,435.4	4,570.7	..	Imports of Goods & NFServices
3,635.5	3,928.2	4,047.7	4,352.8	4,619.0	4,785.4	5,041.8	5,329.5	5,809.5	6,222.5	..	Domestic Absorption
2,333.9	2,550.0	2,686.9	2,873.4	3,105.1	3,196.5	3,354.9	3,499.5	3,744.0	3,978.8	..	Private Consumption, etc.
663.7	700.6	721.5	755.1	808.9	839.3	844.6	845.1	873.6	920.2	..	General Gov't Consumption
637.9	677.6	639.3	724.4	705.0	749.5	842.3	984.9	1,191.9	1,323.5	..	Gross Domestic Investment
642.9	672.1	669.0	709.0	741.3	782.9	834.1	981.6	1,173.8	1,307.3	..	Fixed Investment
301.8	338.1	351.7	368.6	391.2	403.8	466.1	492.2	554.5	582.9	..	Indirect Taxes, net
3,275.7	3,550.9	3,770.6	4,060.4	4,346.8	4,582.1	4,739.4	5,050.4	5,461.4	5,846.4	B	GDP at factor cost
81.4	91.0	102.4	105.0	105.1	106.5	100.8	105.4	123.3	..	..	Agriculture
1,126.8	1,246.0	1,314.1	1,378.4	1,490.8	1,536.6	1,567.1	1,698.1	1,862.8		..	Industry
808.5	912.1	966.0	1,027.0	1,115.1	1,157.5	1,185.5	1,280.4	1,400.5		..	Manufacturing
2,369.4	2,552.0	2,705.8	2,945.7	3,142.1	3,342.8	3,537.6	3,739.2	4,029.9		..	Services, etc.
579.9	638.4	713.9	800.6	824.0	950.1	1,006.0	1,198.1	1,398.4	1,530.3	..	Gross Domestic Saving
..	..	..	..			..				..	Gross National Saving
			(Billions of 1987 Belgian Francs)								
4,478.5	4,515.6	4,532.1	4,636.4	4,661.6	4,743.5	4,857.0	5,093.0	5,295.2	5,474.1	..	Gross National Product
4,516.3	4,584.1	4,601.8	4,699.5	4,738.0	4,807.6	4,912.6	5,154.8	5,342.6	5,543.5	..	GDP at Market Prices
-63.4	-25.8	108.2	104.4	119.0	57.2	-23.8	-0.2	-64.7	-47.1	..	Resource Balance
3,289.6	3,332.3	3,423.4	3,605.6	3,644.9	3,850.3	4,103.7	4,456.4	4,783.1	5,005.2	..	Exports of Goods & NFServices
3,353.0	3,358.1	3,315.2	3,501.2	3,525.9	3,793.1	4,127.5	4,456.6	4,847.8	5,052.3	..	Imports of Goods & NFServices
4,579.7	4,609.9	4,493.6	4,595.1	4,619.0	4,750.4	4,936.4	5,155.0	5,407.3	5,590.6	..	Domestic Absorption
3,021.2	3,061.4	3,010.2	3,044.9	3,105.1	3,179.6	3,280.5	3,381.8	3,492.8	3,582.4	..	Private Consumption, etc.
798.7	787.7	788.4	790.0	808.9	822.8	825.5	817.7	811.1	818.7	..	General Gov't Consumption
759.8	760.8	694.9	760.1	705.0	748.0	830.3	955.6	1,103.4	1,189.4	..	Gross Domestic Investment
769.9	756.7	723.4	736.0	741.3	774.0	817.5	941.6	1,077.9	1,167.5	..	Fixed Investment
4,136.1	4,187.3	4,211.4	4,310.3	4,346.8	4,406.7	4,456.2	4,678.6	4,826.4	5,019.7	B	GDP at factor cost
93.6	99.4	97.3	106.4	105.1	110.3	102.0	108.4	108.8	..	..	Agriculture
1,396.2	1,415.9	1,460.0	1,477.9	1,490.8	1,496.1	1,536.7	1,637.0	1,717.1	..	..	Industry
979.8	1,017.8	1,077.0	1,105.9	1,115.1	1,116.2	1,143.2	1,216.9	1,273.3	..	..	Manufacturing
3,026.5	3,068.9	3,044.5	3,115.2	3,142.1	3,201.2	3,273.9	3,409.3	3,516.6		..	Services, etc.
											Memo Items:
3,275.1	3,311.6	3,397.5	3,579.0	3,644.9	4,021.8	4,323.2	4,704.9	5,073.5	5,280.9	..	Capacity to Import
-14.5	-20.7	-25.9	-26.6	0.0	171.5	219.5	248.5	290.4	275.7	..	Terms of Trade Adjustment
4,501.8	4,563.5	4,575.9	4,672.9	4,738.0	4,979.1	5,132.1	5,403.3	5,633.0	5,819.2	..	Gross Domestic Income
4,464.0	4,494.9	4,506.2	4,609.8	4,661.6	4,914.9	5,076.5	5,341.5	5,585.6	5,749.8	..	Gross National Income
											DOMESTIC PRICES/DEFLATORS
			(Index 1987 = 100)								
79.2	84.8	89.6	94.2	100.0	103.7	106.0	107.5	112.6	116.0	..	Overall (GDP)
79.4	85.2	90.1	94.7	100.0	100.7	102.1	103.4	107.4	111.3	..	Domestic Absorption
86.9	91.5	105.2	98.7	100.0	96.6	98.8	97.2	113.3		..	Agriculture
80.7	88.0	90.0	93.3	100.0	102.7	102.0	103.7	108.5	..	..	Industry
82.5	89.6	89.7	92.9	100.0	103.7	103.7	105.2	110.0	..	..	Manufacturing
74.5	81.0	87.2	92.7	97.2	98.5	100.0	101.2	104.3	107.9	..	Consumer Price Index
											MANUFACTURING ACTIVITY
110.8	106.7	103.8	103.0	101.1	101.3	100.0	..	..	..	..	Employment (1987=100)
98.3	97.5	95.1	93.8	93.1	97.3	100.0	..	..	..	..	Real Earnings per Empl. (1987=100)
83.0	84.9	90.4	92.2	91.9	94.3	100.0	..	..	..	..	Real Output per Empl. (1987=100)
53.2	49.4	47.7	46.5	46.2	46.3	46.2	..	..		..	Earnings as % of Value Added
											MONETARY HOLDINGS
			(Millions of current Belgian Francs)								
2,110.3	2,237.2	2,411.7	2,527.4	2,657.6	2,931.4	3,174.9	3,381.2	3,721.8	3,839.7	D	Money Supply, Broadly Defined
823.5	855.8	929.8	932.5	962.4	1,037.3	1,086.0	1,145.9	1,207.4	1,217.0	..	Money
370.1	369.5	383.3	381.9	379.9	400.5	410.7	415.0	422.6	408.6	..	Currency Outside Banks
453.4	486.3	546.5	550.6	582.5	636.8	675.3	730.9	784.8	808.4	..	Demand Deposits
1,286.8	1,381.4	1,481.9	1,594.9	1,695.2	1,894.1	2,088.9	2,235.3	2,514.4	2,622.7	..	Quasi-Money
											GOVERNMENT DEFICIT (-) OR SURPLUS
			(Billions of current Belgian Francs)								
-447	-432	-516	-596	-538	-492	-396	-364	-380	..	..	Current Revenue
1,598	1,783	1,858	2,042	2,203	2,279	2,380	2,461	2,584	..	..	Current Expenditure
1,841	2,011	2,167	2,325	2,457	2,563	2,595	2,643	2,790	..	..	Current Budget Balance
-243	-228	-308	-283	-254	-284	-215	-182	-206	..	..	Capital Receipts
1	2	2	1	1	1	1	1	1	..	..	Capital Payments
205	206	209	314	285	209	182	182	174	..		

BELGIUM	1970	1971	1972	1973	1974	1975	1976	1977	1978	1979	1980
FOREIGN TRADE (CUSTOMS BASIS)					*(Millions of current US dollars)*						
Value of Exports, fob	11,609	12,391	16,044	22,393	28,126	28,760	32,783	37,450	44,793	56,083	63,967
Nonfuel Primary Products	2,451	2,330	2,914	4,366	5,286	4,873	5,559	6,447	7,382	9,201	11,217
Fuels	310	332	466	639	938	1,393	1,572	2,012	1,912	3,526	5,310
Manufactures	8,849	9,729	12,663	17,388	21,902	22,495	25,652	28,991	35,498	43,357	47,440
Value of Imports, cif	11,362	12,856	15,589	21,916	29,446	30,191	35,161	40,140	48,268	60,186	71,192
Nonfuel Primary Products	3,577	3,530	4,125	6,086	7,720	7,215	8,514	9,346	10,733	13,536	15,764
Fuels	1,035	1,223	1,567	1,899	4,219	4,323	4,982	5,637	5,986	8,555	12,361
Manufactures	6,751	8,103	9,897	13,931	17,507	18,652	21,666	25,157	31,549	38,095	43,068
					(Index 1987 = 100)						
Terms of Trade	157.5	139.9	150.8	145.7	117.1	115.4	113.1	109.5	113.6	114.6	108.0
Export Prices, fob	32.6	32.4	37.7	50.1	62.4	63.0	63.9	67.1	77.7	94.5	103.9
Import Prices, cif	20.7	23.1	25.0	34.4	53.3	54.6	56.5	61.3	68.4	82.5	96.2
BALANCE OF PAYMENTS					*(Millions of current US dollars)*						
Exports of Goods & Services	12,358	13,600	17,173	24,741	33,732	33,832	37,334	46,240	56,441	73,952	88,925
Merchandise, fob	9,062	9,804	12,789	18,425	24,215	23,077	26,065	31,224	38,204	49,186	55,155
Nonfactor Services	2,176	2,501	2,920	3,940	5,266	6,178	6,734	9,622	10,712	13,063	15,158
Factor Services	1,120	1,295	1,463	2,377	4,251	4,576	4,534	5,393	7,525	11,703	18,612
Imports of Goods & Services	11,487	12,790	15,665	23,038	32,522	33,037	36,379	46,172	56,511	76,136	92,625
Merchandise, fob	8,598	9,589	11,998	17,545	24,193	23,905	27,307	34,203	40,848	53,813	60,310
Nonfactor Services	1,857	2,040	2,431	3,368	4,438	5,064	5,207	7,159	8,795	10,966	13,493
Factor Services	1,032	1,162	1,236	2,125	3,890	4,068	3,865	4,809	6,869	11,357	18,823
Long-Term Interest	..	..	..	..	..	..	..	..	..	..	..
Private Current Transfers, net	33	44	34	62	10	-108	-196	-163	-284	-345	-374
Workers' Remittances	154	186	199	280	294	286	263	322	461	471	534
Curr. A/C Bal before Off. Transf.	9.04E+8	8.53E+8	1.54E+9	1.77E+9	1.22E+9	6.87E+8	7.59E+8	-9.47E+7	-3.55E+8	-2.53E+9	-4.07E+9
Net Official Transfers	-187	-206	-234	-370	-389	-506	-324	-459	-468	-552	-857
Curr. A/C Bal after Off. Transf.	717	647	1,308	1,395	831	181	435	-554	-823	-3,080	-4,931
Long-Term Capital, net	-363	-546	-898	-731	-211	-280	149	-313	-270	511	3,986
Direct Investment	140	221	209	450	658	717	520	810	876	-211	1,349
Long-Term Loans	..	..	..	..	..	..	..	..	..	..	..
Disbursements	..	..	..	..	..	..	..	..	..	..	..
Repayments	..	..	..	..	..	..	..	..	..	..	..
Other Long-Term Capital	-503	-767	-1,107	-1,180	-869	-997	-371	-1,123	-1,146	722	2,637
Other Capital, net	-123	281	178	329	-1,182	78	-1,860	422	1,078	-531	1,368
Change in Reserves	-230	-382	-588	-994	562	21	1,276	445	15	3,100	-423
Memo Item:					*(Belgian Francs per US dollar)*						
Conversion Factor (Annual Avg)	50.00	48.87	44.01	38.98	38.95	36.78	38.61	35.84	31.49	29.32	29.24
EXTERNAL DEBT (Total)					*(Millions of US dollars), outstanding at end of year*						
Long-Term Debt (by debtor)	..	..	..	..	..	..	..	..	..	..	..
Central Bank, incl. IMF credit	..	..	..	..	..	..	..	..	..	..	..
Central Government	..	..	..	..	..	..	..	..	..	..	..
Rest of General Government	..	..	..	..	..	..	..	..	..	..	..
Non-financial Public Enterprises	..	..	..	..	..	..	..	..	..	..	..
Priv. Sector, incl non-guaranteed	..	..	..	..	..	..	..	..	..	..	..
Short-Term Debt	..	..	..	..	..	..	..	..	..	..	..
Memo Items:					*(Millions of US dollars)*						
Int'l Reserves Excluding Gold	1,377	1,797	2,232	3,319	3,538	4,069	3,491	3,956	3,966	5,443	7,823
Gold Holdings (at market price)	1,570	1,925	2,796	4,734	7,865	5,915	5,683	7,002	9,625	17,516	20,151
SOCIAL INDICATORS											
Total Fertility Rate	2.2	2.2	2.1	1.9	1.8	1.7	1.7	1.7	1.7	1.7	1.7
Infant Mortality Rate	21.1	20.4	18.8	17.7	17.4	16.1	15.3	13.6	13.3	12.3	12.1
Life Expectancy at Birth	71.2	71.3	71.4	71.6	71.8	71.9	72.1	72.3	72.6	72.9	73.2
Urban Population, % of total	94.3	94.4	94.4	94.5	94.5	94.6	94.8	94.9	95.1	95.2	95.4
Food Prod. per capita (1987=100)	87.8	91.3	87.9	91.6	97.6	89.8	85.4	87.6	89.8	95.9	93.2
Labor Force, Agriculture (%)	4.8	4.6	4.4	4.2	4.0	3.8	3.6	3.4	3.2	3.0	2.8
Labor Force, Female (%)	30.5	30.8	31.2	31.5	31.9	32.2	32.6	32.9	33.2	33.6	33.9
Primary Schl. Enroll. Ratio	103.0	..	..	..	..	102.0	101.0	102.0	101.0	101.0	104.0
Primary Schl. Enroll. Ratio, Female	104.0	..	..	..	..	102.0	102.0	102.0	101.0	101.0	113.0
Secondary Schl. Enroll. Ratio	81.0	..	..	..	..	84.0	85.0	85.0	87.0	87.0	91.0

FOREIGN TRADE (CUSTOMS BASIS)

(Millions of current US dollars)

1981	1982	1983	1984	1985	1986	1987	1988	1989	1990 est.	Notes	BELGIUM
55,228	51,695	51,676	51,416	53,316	68,649	82,951	88,953	100,737	118,002	f	Value of Exports, fob
9,693	8,994	8,707	9,108	9,017	11,013	13,174	14,862	16,867	18,007	..	Nonfuel Primary Products
4,961	4,440	4,292	4,016	3,439	3,295	3,058	3,135	3,413	4,049	..	Fuels
40,574	38,261	38,676	38,293	40,860	54,342	66,719	70,957	80,457	95,946	..	Manufactures
61,417	57,213	53,654	54,746	55,561	68,025	82,598	91,097	99,336	119,725	f	Value of Imports, cif
13,361	12,253	11,828	12,148	11,933	13,667	15,997	18,526	19,617	21,306	..	Nonfuel Primary Products
12,523	11,886	9,450	10,242	9,257	7,233	7,688	6,646	7,627	9,623	..	Fuels
35,533	33,074	32,376	32,357	34,371	47,126	58,913	65,926	72,091	88,796	..	Manufactures

(Index 1987 = 100)

1981	1982	1983	1984	1985	1986	1987	1988	1989	1990 est.	Notes	BELGIUM
96.4	94.6	94.2	91.0	93.7	103.8	100.0	95.8	96.7	95.7	f	Terms of Trade
90.6	83.6	80.8	76.0	76.6	88.2	100.0	105.3	113.7	130.1	f	Export Prices, fob
94.0	88.4	85.8	83.6	81.8	84.9	100.0	110.0	117.5	135.9	f	Import Prices, cif

BALANCE OF PAYMENTS

(Millions of current US dollars)

1981	1982	1983	1984	1985	1986	1987	1988	1989	1990 est.	Notes	BELGIUM
87,258	82,097	76,701	77,366	80,803	101,196	124,352	141,609	161,837	204,721	f	Exports of Goods & Services
48,597	46,061	45,662	46,213	47,336	59,955	76,088	85,496	89,988	108,762	..	Merchandise, fob
14,276	12,964	12,493	11,995	12,443	17,288	20,409	22,565	24,598	31,610	..	Nonfactor Services
24,384	23,072	18,546	19,159	21,024	23,953	27,856	33,547	47,252	64,349	..	Factor Services
90,186	83,515	76,097	76,590	79,479	97,195	120,132	136,259	156,922	198,158	f	Imports of Goods & Services
53,204	49,508	47,478	47,431	47,808	59,399	76,268	84,273	89,020	108,132	..	Merchandise, fob
12,367	10,525	9,775	9,816	10,400	13,742	16,036	18,407	21,030	25,854	..	Nonfactor Services
24,615	23,482	18,843	19,344	21,270	24,055	27,828	33,579	46,872	64,172	..	Factor Services
..	..	..	..	..	..	..	..	..	..		Long-Term Interest
-409	-250	-181	-176	-129	-212	-114	41	47	-595	f	Private Current Transfers, net
455	388	394	358	385	482	554	628	585	1,005	..	Workers' Remittances
-3.34E+9	-1.67E+9	4.22E+8	6.01E+8	1.20E+9	3.79E+9	4.11E+9	5.39E+9	4.96E+9	5.97E+9	..	Curr. A/C Bal before Off. Transf.
-831	-927	-918	-656	-527	-734	-1,313	-1,796	-1,765	-1,418	..	Net Official Transfers
-4,168	-2,594	-495	-55	669	3,055	2,794	3,594	3,197	4,548	..	Curr. A/C Bal after Off. Transf.
3,747	1,473	-2,339	-2,228	-4,558	-6,777	-1,960	-3,839	-2,437	141	f	Long-Term Capital, net
1,283	1,403	935	96	755	-993	-427	1,428	245	1,831	..	Direct Investment
..	..	..	..	..	..	..	..	..	..	..	Long-Term Loans
..	..	..	..	..	..	..	..	..	..	..	Disbursements
..	..	..	..	..	..	..	..	..	..	..	Repayments
2,464	70	-3,274	-2,324	-5,313	-5,784	-1,532	-5,268	-2,683	-1,691	..	Other Long-Term Capital
-1,888	347	2,468	2,893	4,117	4,113	1,439	141	-3,078	-3,646	..	Other Capital, net
2,309	774	366	-611	-228	-392	-2,273	104	2,319	-1,043	..	Change in Reserves

(Belgian Francs per US dollar)

1981	1982	1983	1984	1985	1986	1987	1988	1989	1990 est.	Notes	BELGIUM
											Memo Item:
37.13	45.69	51.13	57.78	59.38	44.67	37.33	36.77	39.40	33.42	..	Conversion Factor (Annual Avg)

(Millions of US dollars), outstanding at end of year

1981	1982	1983	1984	1985	1986	1987	1988	1989	1990 est.	Notes	BELGIUM
..	..	..	..	..	..	..	..	..	..	..	**EXTERNAL DEBT (Total)**
..	..	..	..	..	..	..	..	..	..	..	Long-Term Debt (by debtor)
..	..	..	..	..	..	..	..	..	..	..	Central Bank, incl. IMF credit
..	..	..	..	..	..	..	..	..	..	..	Central Government
..	..	..	..	..	..	..	..	..	..	..	Rest of General Government
..	..	..	..	..	..	..	..	..	..	..	Non-financial Public Enterprises
..	..	..	..	..	..	..	..	..	..	..	Priv. Sector, incl non-guaranteed
..	..	..	..	..	..	..	..	..	..	..	Short-Term Debt

(Millions of US dollars)

1981	1982	1983	1984	1985	1986	1987	1988	1989	1990 est.	Notes	BELGIUM
											Memo Items:
4,952	3,927	4,714	4,564	4,849	5,538	9,620	9,333	10,766	12,151	..	Int'l Reserves Excluding Gold
13,588	15,618	13,041	10,539	11,178	13,362	16,279	13,813	12,121	11,637	..	Gold Holdings (at market price)

SOCIAL INDICATORS

1981	1982	1983	1984	1985	1986	1987	1988	1989	1990 est.	Notes	BELGIUM
1.7	1.6	1.6	1.6	1.5	1.5	1.6	1.6	1.6	1.6	..	Total Fertility Rate
11.5	11.1	10.5	10.7	9.8	9.6	9.7	9.4	9.1	8.9	..	Infant Mortality Rate
73.6	73.9	74.2	74.5	74.8	75.1	75.4	75.7	76.0	76.2	..	Life Expectancy at Birth
95.6	95.8	95.9	96.1	96.3	96.4	96.5	96.7	96.8	96.9	..	Urban Population, % of total
97.7	94.2	90.6	97.6	97.0	103.9	100.0	103.8	103.3	102.9	f	Food Prod. per capita (1987=100)
..	..	..	..	..	..	..	..	..	..	..	Labor Force, Agriculture (%)
33.9	33.9	33.9	33.8	33.8	33.8	33.8	33.8	33.7	33.7	..	Labor Force, Female (%)
..	98.0	97.0	97.0	99.0	100.0	101.0	..	..	..	..	Primary Schl. Enroll. Ratio
100.0	98.0	97.0	98.0	99.0	100.0	101.0	..	..	..	..	Primary Schl. Enroll. Ratio, Female
..	89.0	92.0	97.0	98.0	98.0	99.0	..	..	..	..	Secondary Schl. Enroll. Ratio

BELIZE	1970	1971	1972	1973	1974	1975	1976	1977	1978	1979	1980
CURRENT GNP PER CAPITA (US $)	430	470	520	570	660	790	840	870	910	1,090	1,170
POPULATION (thousands)	120	122	123	125	127	129	131	134	137	140	144
USE AND ORIGIN OF RESOURCES					*(Millions of current Belize Dollars)*						
Gross National Product (GNP)	86.00	93.40	101.00	121.00	158.00	191.50	197.40	224.10	259.00	293.00	333.80
Net Factor Income from Abroad	-2.90	-3.70	-4.70	-6.70	-18.50	-22.20	-18.70	-11.20	-13.60	-10.60	-14.20
GDP at Market Prices	88.90	97.10	105.70	127.70	176.50	213.70	216.10	235.30	272.60	303.60	348.00
Resource Balance	..	..	..	..	..	..	..	..	..	..	..
Exports of Goods & NFServices	..	..	..	..	..	..	..	..	..	..	..
Imports of Goods & NFServices	..	..	..	..	..	..	..	..	..	..	..
Domestic Absorption	..	..	..	..	..	..	..	..	..	..	..
Private Consumption, etc.	..	..	..	..	..	..	..	..	..	..	..
General Gov't Consumption	..	..	..	..	..	..	..	..	..	..	..
Gross Domestic Investment	..	..	..	..	..	..	..	..	..	..	..
Fixed Investment	..	..	..	..	..	..	..	..	..	..	..
Indirect Taxes, net	..	..	..	..	..	..	..	..	20.70	26.70	39.90
GDP at factor cost	..	..	..	..	..	..	..	..	251.90	276.90	308.10
Agriculture	..	..	..	..	..	..	..	..	79.00	85.20	91.70
Industry	..	..	..	..	..	..	..	..	62.10	60.70	73.60
Manufacturing	..	..	..	..	..	..	..	..	45.10	41.90	50.10
Services, etc.	..	..	..	..	..	..	..	..	110.80	131.00	142.80
Gross Domestic Saving	..	..	..	..	..	..	..	..	..	..	..
Gross National Saving	..	..	..	..	..	..	..	..	..	..	..
					(Millions of 1987 Belize Dollars)						
Gross National Product	228.19	242.05	260.09	268.90	274.77	288.27	318.70	339.39	365.51	403.61	414.50
GDP at Market Prices	222.14	230.94	254.53	268.16	304.52	315.46	315.35	335.84	362.44	385.26	399.23
Resource Balance	..	..	..	..	..	..	..	..	..	..	..
Exports of Goods & NFServices	..	..	..	..	..	..	..	..	..	..	..
Imports of Goods & NFServices	..	..	..	..	..	..	..	..	..	..	..
Domestic Absorption	..	..	..	..	..	..	..	..	..	..	..
Private Consumption, etc.	..	..	..	..	..	..	..	..	..	..	..
General Gov't Consumption	..	..	..	..	..	..	..	..	..	..	..
Gross Domestic Investment	..	..	..	..	..	..	..	..	..	..	..
Fixed Investment	..	..	..	..	..	..	..	..	..	..	..
GDP at factor cost	..	..	..	254.61	273.06	284.10	275.29	316.79	321.93	332.68	345.48
Agriculture	..	..	..	57.59	62.53	64.66	58.38	77.80	82.07	80.72	81.50
Industry	..	..	..	48.97	56.20	59.54	60.99	67.89	74.12	76.90	85.02
Manufacturing	..	..	..	33.49	39.15	39.91	38.71	46.76	48.94	46.44	52.63
Services, etc.	..	..	..	148.05	154.33	159.89	155.93	171.10	165.75	175.07	178.95
Memo Items:											
Capacity to Import	..	..	..	..	..	..	..	..	..	..	..
Terms of Trade Adjustment	..	..	..	..	..	..	..	..	..	..	..
Gross Domestic Income	..	..	..	..	..	..	..	..	..	..	..
Gross National Income	..	..	..	..	..	..	..	..	..	..	..
DOMESTIC PRICES/DEFLATORS					*(Index 1987 = 100)*						
Overall (GDP)	40.0	42.0	41.5	47.6	58.0	67.7	68.5	70.1	75.2	78.8	87.2
Domestic Absorption	..	..	..	..	..	..	..	..	..	..	..
Agriculture	..	..	..	..	..	..	..	..	96.3	105.6	112.5
Industry	..	..	..	..	..	..	..	..	83.8	78.9	86.6
Manufacturing	..	..	..	..	..	..	..	..	92.2	90.2	95.2
Consumer Price Index	..	..	..	..	..	..	..	..	..	..	72.4
MANUFACTURING ACTIVITY											
Employment (1987=100)											
Real Earnings per Empl. (1987=100)	..	..	..	..	..	..	..	..	..	..	..
Real Output per Empl. (1987=100)	..	..	..	..	..	..	..	..	..	..	..
Earnings as % of Value Added	..	..	..	..	..	..	..	..	..	..	..
MONETARY HOLDINGS					*(Millions of current Belize Dollars)*						
Money Supply, Broadly Defined	..	..	..	..	..	..	71.58	73.43	92.93	95.94	108.20
Money	..	..	..	..	..	..	21.30	24.69	36.01	36.89	41.65
Currency Outside Banks	..	..	..	..	..	..	11.27	12.55	16.72	16.67	17.51
Demand Deposits	..	..	..	..	..	..	10.03	12.14	19.29	20.22	24.14
Quasi-Money	..	..	..	..	..	..	50.28	48.74	56.92	59.04	66.55
GOVERNMENT DEFICIT (-) OR SURPLUS					*(Thousands of current Belize Dollars)*						
Current Revenue	..	..	..	..	..	..	..	-12,112	-2,613	-5,018	-5,916
Current Expenditure	..	..	..	..	..	..	..	49,880	62,000	71,001	84,972
Current Budget Balance	..	..	..	..	..	..	..	38,574	43,735	51,599	65,414
Capital Receipts	..	..	..	..	..	..	..	11,306	18,265	19,402	19,558
Capital Payments	..	..	..	..	..	..	..	200	491	684	281
	..	..	..	..	..	..	..	23,618	21,369	25,104	25,755

1981	1982	1983	1984	1985	1986	1987	1988	1989	1990 estimate	Notes	BELIZE
1,220	1,140	1,090	1,120	1,140	1,200	1,370	1,560	1,780	1,990	..	CURRENT GNP PER CAPITA (US $)
148	152	157	162	166	171	175	179	184	188	..	POPULATION (thousands)
											USE AND ORIGIN OF RESOURCES
			(Millions of current Belize Dollars)								
350.60	327.00	336.80	372.50	361.20	404.70	496.20	562.80	636.40	724.30	..	Gross National Product (GNP)
-3.80	-10.40	-11.00	-21.20	-22.80	-19.80	-14.80	-14.40	-22.40	-22.60	..	Net Factor Income from Abroad
354.40	337.40	347.80	393.70	384.00	424.50	511.00	577.20	658.80	746.90	..	GDP at Market Prices
-44.50	-56.20	-42.00	-29.20	-40.70	-8.40	-13.10	-34.40	-76.70	-45.80	..	Resource Balance
206.00	172.00	185.50	224.30	212.00	247.20	289.70	343.30	367.00	415.50	..	Exports of Goods & NFServices
250.50	228.20	227.50	253.50	252.70	255.60	302.80	377.70	443.70	461.30	..	Imports of Goods & NFServices
398.90	393.60	389.80	422.90	424.70	432.90	524.10	611.60	735.50	792.70	..	Domestic Absorption
229.00	231.20	239.90	244.60	258.00	258.70	300.50	326.40	388.90	462.30	..	Private Consumption, etc.
73.40	79.50	84.20	85.60	87.10	90.20	98.40	110.00	123.50	132.90	..	General Gov't Consumption
96.50	82.90	65.70	92.70	79.60	84.00	125.20	175.20	223.10	197.50	..	Gross Domestic Investment
93.50	79.90	68.70	81.70	71.60	80.00	119.20	169.10	223.10	197.50	..	Fixed Investment
45.00	45.80	45.40	54.70	57.10	68.20	84.10	102.00	117.70	130.00	..	Indirect Taxes, net
309.40	291.60	302.40	339.00	326.90	356.30	426.90	475.20	541.10	616.90	B	GDP at factor cost
86.20	67.50	67.90	72.90	69.40	73.40	95.20	104.10	118.80	135.10	..	Agriculture
66.40	56.90	55.50	73.60	68.00	73.30	97.60	112.10	127.60	153.00	..	Industry
42.60	31.90	37.50	45.00	37.70	37.70	54.70	60.60	60.80	64.10	..	Manufacturing
156.80	167.20	179.00	192.50	189.50	209.60	234.10	259.00	294.70	328.80	..	Services, etc.
52.00	26.70	23.70	63.50	38.90	75.60	112.10	140.80	146.40	151.70	..	Gross Domestic Saving
..	..	..	74.10	55.30	86.50	127.70	156.90	165.40	..	..	Gross National Saving
			(Millions of 1987 Belize Dollars)								
420.33	391.86	384.52	393.48	406.86	431.69	496.20	548.87	616.47	693.50	..	Gross National Product
404.94	398.19	395.65	416.80	425.43	440.04	511.00	559.81	634.68	711.98	..	GDP at Market Prices
..	..	..	..	..	..	..	..	..	..	..	Resource Balance
..	..	..	..	..	..	..	..	..	..	..	Exports of Goods & NFServices
..	..	..	..	..	..	..	..	..	..	..	Imports of Goods & NFServices
..	..	..	..	..	..	..	..	..	..	..	Domestic Absorption
..	..	..	..	..	..	..	..	..	..	..	Private Consumption, etc.
..	..	..	..	..	..	..	..	..	..	..	General Gov't Consumption
..	..	..	..	..	..	..	..	..	..	..	Gross Domestic Investment
..	..	..	..	..	..	..	..	..	..	..	Fixed Investment
354.33	355.67	348.96	358.50	366.80	477.24	426.90	461.11	523.08	593.45	B	GDP at factor cost
81.17	84.87	79.93	81.84	80.83	77.35	95.20	94.30	105.42	119.45	..	Agriculture
87.92	85.14	82.58	81.91	82.02	85.36	97.60	107.62	129.54	155.02	..	Industry
54.70	54.05	53.50	48.94	49.37	50.57	54.70	54.48	60.03	62.31	..	Manufacturing
185.25	185.66	186.45	194.75	203.95	314.53	234.10	259.19	288.12	318.98	..	Services, etc.
											Memo Items:
..	..	..	..	..	..	..	..	..	..	..	Capacity to Import
..	..	..	..	..	..	..	..	..	..	..	Terms of Trade Adjustment
..	..	..	..	..	..	..	..	..	..	..	Gross Domestic Income
..	..	..	..	..	..	..	..	..	..	..	Gross National Income
											DOMESTIC PRICES/DEFLATORS
			(Index 1987 = 100)								
87.5	84.7	87.9	94.5	90.3	96.5	100.0	103.1	103.8	104.9	..	Overall (GDP)
..	..	..	..	..	..	..	..	..	..	..	Domestic Absorption
106.2	79.5	84.9	89.1	85.9	94.9	100.0	110.4	112.7	113.1	..	Agriculture
75.5	66.8	67.2	89.9	82.9	85.9	100.0	104.2	98.5	98.7	..	Industry
77.9	59.0	70.1	92.0	76.4	74.6	100.0	111.2	101.3	102.9	..	Manufacturing
80.5	86.0	90.3	93.7	97.1	98.0	100.0	103.2	105.4	108.5	..	Consumer Price Index
											MANUFACTURING ACTIVITY
..	..	..	..	..	..	..	..	..	..	..	Employment (1987=100)
..	..	..	..	..	..	..	..	..	..	..	Real Earnings per Empl. (1987=100)
..	..	..	..	..	..	..	..	..	..	..	Real Output per Empl. (1987=100)
..	..	..	..	..	..	..	..	..	..	..	Earnings as % of Value Added
											MONETARY HOLDINGS
			(Millions of current Belize Dollars)								
117.81	125.07	148.16	154.63	167.73	199.10	241.65	252.11	287.27	330.80	..	Money Supply, Broadly Defined
39.56	39.40	42.41	50.01	58.61	71.03	84.30	81.78	99.87	105.99	..	Money
19.01	20.61	21.53	22.77	22.64	25.90	29.56	34.11	40.44	43.46	..	Currency Outside Banks
20.55	18.79	20.88	27.24	35.97	45.13	54.74	47.67	59.43	62.53	..	Demand Deposits
78.25	85.67	105.75	104.62	109.12	128.06	157.35	170.33	187.40	224.80	..	Quasi-Money
			(Thousands of current Belize Dollars)								
..	..	..	-5,214	-11,044	..	..	..	..	..	C F	GOVERNMENT DEFICIT (-) OR SURPLUS
88,794	97,638	95,521	97,884	103,113	..	..	..	..	..	..	Current Revenue
77,910	83,958	84,038	93,569	99,891	..	..	..	..	..	..	Current Expenditure
10,884	13,680	11,483	4,315	3,222	..	..	..	..	..	..	Current Budget Balance
288	302	341	511	157	..	..	..	..	..	..	Capital Receipts
..	..	..	10,040	14,423	..	..	..	..	..	..	Capital Payments

FOREIGN TRADE (CUSTOMS BASIS)

(Millions of current US dollars)

	1970	1971	1972	1973	1974	1975	1976	1977	1978	1979	1980
Value of Exports, fob	..	..	..	..	..	..	..	..	..	..	..
Nonfuel Primary Products	..	..	..	..	..	..	..	..	..	..	..
Fuels	..	..	..	..	..	..	..	..	..	..	..
Manufactures	..	..	..	..	..	..	..	..	..	..	..
Value of Imports, cif	..	..	..	..	..	..	..	..	..	..	..
Nonfuel Primary Products	..	..	..	..	..	..	..	..	..	..	..
Fuels	..	..	..	..	..	..	..	..	..	..	..
Manufactures	..	..	..	..	..	..	..	..	..	..	..

(Index 1987 = 100)

	1970	1971	1972	1973	1974	1975	1976	1977	1978	1979	1980
Terms of Trade	..	..	..	..	..	..	..	..	..	..	..
Export Prices, fob	..	..	..	..	..	..	..	..	..	..	..
Import Prices, cif	..	..	..	..	..	..	..	..	..	..	..

BALANCE OF PAYMENTS

(Millions of current US dollars)

	1970	1971	1972	1973	1974	1975	1976	1977	1978	1979	1980
Exports of Goods & Services	..	..	..	..	..	..	..	..	..	..	..
Merchandise, fob	..	..	..	..	..	..	..	..	..	..	..
Nonfactor Services	..	..	..	..	..	..	..	..	..	..	..
Factor Services	..	..	..	..	..	..	..	..	..	..	..
Imports of Goods & Services	..	..	..	..	..	..	..	..	..	..	..
Merchandise, fob	..	..	..	..	..	..	..	..	..	..	..
Nonfactor Services	..	..	..	..	..	..	..	..	..	..	..
Factor Services	..	..	..	..	..	..	..	..	..	..	..
Long-Term Interest	0.00	0.00	0.00	0.30	0.20	0.30	0.20	0.30	0.30	0.60	0.90
Private Current Transfers, net	..	..	..	..	..	..	..	..	..	..	..
Workers' Remittances	..	..	..	..	..	..	..	..	..	..	..
Curr. A/C Bal before Off. Transf.	..	..	..	..	..	..	..	..	..	..	..
Net Official Transfers	..	..	..	..	..	..	..	..	..	..	..
Curr. A/C Bal after Off. Transf.	..	..	..	..	..	..	..	..	..	..	..
Long-Term Capital, net	..	..	..	..	..	..	..	..	..	..	..
Direct Investment	..	..	..	..	..	..	..	..	..	..	..
Long-Term Loans	4.30	0.00	0.00	-0.20	0.40	0.20	4.90	4.30	8.70	11.10	13.20
Disbursements	4.30	0.00	0.00	0.00	0.60	0.40	5.10	4.50	8.80	11.30	13.70
Repayments	0.00	0.00	0.00	0.20	0.20	0.20	0.20	0.20	0.10	0.20	0.50
Other Long-Term Capital	..	..	..	..	..	..	..	..	..	..	..
Other Capital, net	..	..	..	..	..	..	..	..	..	..	..
Change in Reserves	..	..	..	..	..	..	..	-2.53	-5.96	3.51	-2.21

Memo Item:

(Belize Dollars per US dollar)

	1970	1971	1972	1973	1974	1975	1976	1977	1978	1979	1980
Conversion Factor (Annual Avg)	1.670	1.640	1.600	1.630	1.710	1.810	2.230	2.000	2.000	2.000	2.000

EXTERNAL DEBT (Total)

(Millions of US dollars), outstanding at end of year

	1970	1971	1972	1973	1974	1975	1976	1977	1978	1979	1980
EXTERNAL DEBT (Total)	4.10	4.30	5.10	4.80	5.30	4.80	9.20	20.70	33.20	71.70	62.90
Long-Term Debt (by debtor)	4.10	4.30	5.10	4.80	5.30	4.80	9.20	13.70	22.20	33.70	46.90
Central Bank, incl. IMF credit	0.00	0.00	0.00	0.00	0.00	0.20	4.10	4.90	6.40	8.20	9.20
Central Government	4.10	4.30	5.10	4.80	4.70	4.00	4.50	8.10	11.30	14.20	18.20
Rest of General Government	..	..	..	..	..	..	..	..	..	..	..
Non-financial Public Enterprises	0.00	0.00	0.00	0.00	0.60	0.60	0.60	0.70	4.50	11.30	19.50
Priv. Sector, incl non-guaranteed	0.00	0.00	0.00	0.00	0.00	0.00	0.00	0.00	0.00	0.00	0.00
Short-Term Debt	0.00	0.00	0.00	0.00	0.00	0.00	0.00	7.00	11.00	38.00	16.00

Memo Items:

(Thousands of US dollars)

	1970	1971	1972	1973	1974	1975	1976	1977	1978	1979	1980
Int'l Reserves Excluding Gold	..	..	..	..	..	..	5,491	8,021	13,978	10,463	12,676
Gold Holdings (at market price)	..	..	..	..	..	..	..	..	..	..	..

SOCIAL INDICATORS

	1970	1971	1972	1973	1974	1975	1976	1977	1978	1979	1980
Total Fertility Rate	6.9	6.4	6.3	6.3	6.2	6.1	6.0	5.9	5.8	5.8	5.7
Infant Mortality Rate	..	..	..	..	..	..	..	..	..	..	..
Life Expectancy at Birth	58.9	59.4	59.9	60.5	61.0	61.5	62.0	62.5	63.1	63.6	64.1
Urban Population, % of total	50.9	50.6	50.3	50.0	49.7	49.4	49.4	49.4	49.4	49.4	49.4
Food Prod. per capita (1987=100)	71.4	77.4	80.5	85.6	91.5	82.8	76.8	90.2	97.7	87.5	99.4
Labor Force, Agriculture (%)	..	..	..	..	..	..	..	..	..	..	..
Labor Force, Female (%)	..	..	..	..	..	..	..	..	..	..	..
Primary Schl. Enroll. Ratio	..	..	..	..	..	..	..	..	..	..	..
Primary Schl. Enroll. Ratio, Female	..	..	..	..	..	..	..	..	..	..	..
Secondary Schl. Enroll. Ratio	..	..	..	..	..	..	..	..	..	..	..

1981	1982	1983	1984	1985	1986	1987	1988	1989	1990 estimate	Notes	BELIZE
				(Millions of current US dollars)							**FOREIGN TRADE (CUSTOMS BASIS)**
..	..	..	..	..	..	..	..	..	..	..	Value of Exports, fob
..	..	..	..	..	..	..	..	..	..	..	Nonfuel Primary Products
..	..	..	..	..	..	..	..	..	..	..	Fuels
..	..	..	..	..	..	..	..	..	..	..	Manufactures
..	..	..	..	..	..	..	..	..	..	..	Value of Imports, cif
..	..	..	..	..	..	..	..	..	..	..	Nonfuel Primary Products
..	..	..	..	..	..	..	..	..	..	..	Fuels
..	..	..	..	..	..	..	..	..	..	..	Manufactures
				(Index 1987 = 100)							
..	..	..	..	..	..	..	..	..	..	..	Terms of Trade
..	..	..	..	..	..	..	..	..	..	..	Export Prices, fob
..	..	..	..	..	..	..	..	..	..	..	Import Prices, cif
				(Millions of current US dollars)							**BALANCE OF PAYMENTS**
..	..	..	129.90	131.15	144.60	164.70	201.85	219.95	..	..	Exports of Goods & Services
..	..	..	93.20	90.15	92.60	102.85	119.40	124.40	..	..	Merchandise, fob
..	..	..	35.40	38.10	42.35	55.40	71.55	82.95	..	..	Nonfactor Services
..	..	..	1.30	2.90	9.65	6.45	10.90	12.60	..	..	Factor Services
..	..	..	160.50	154.50	160.05	186.25	230.35	270.10	..	..	Imports of Goods & Services
..	..	..	116.30	113.80	108.30	126.95	161.30	188.50	..	..	Merchandise, fob
..	..	..	29.30	27.35	38.90	45.70	53.15	62.30	..	..	Nonfactor Services
..	..	..	14.90	13.35	12.85	13.60	15.90	19.30	..	..	Factor Services
1.80	2.50	2.60	3.30	5.90	4.70	4.00	4.00	6.40	6.50	..	Long-Term Interest
..	..	..	15.90	19.60	15.35	15.20	15.25	20.70	..	..	Private Current Transfers, net
..	..	..	17.65	20.65	16.85	15.85	12.90	17.90	..	..	Workers' Remittances
..	..	..	-14.70	-3.75	-0.10	-6.35	-13.25	-29.45	..	..	Curr. A/C Bal before Off. Transf.
..	..	..	9.40	12.80	12.05	15.75	10.60	10.40	..	..	Net Official Transfers
..	..	..	-5.30	9.05	11.95	9.40	-2.65	-19.05	..	..	Curr. A/C Bal after Off. Transf.
..	..	..	-0.10	10.40	8.25	7.40	23.30	29.90	..	..	Long-Term Capital, net
..	..	..	-3.70	3.70	4.60	6.85	14.00	18.65	..	..	Direct Investment
11.10	9.20	15.20	6.00	14.40	-0.10	4.20	8.70	12.60	8.40	..	Long-Term Loans
12.50	11.70	18.60	8.70	24.50	8.70	12.20	17.40	19.50	18.60	..	Disbursements
1.40	2.50	3.40	2.70	10.10	8.80	8.00	8.70	6.90	10.20	..	Repayments
..	..	..	-2.40	-7.70	3.75	-3.65	0.60	-1.35		..	Other Long-Term Capital
..	..	..	1.31	-17.13	-8.40	-4.93	1.12	4.66	..	..	Other Capital, net
2.34	0.53	4.31	4.09	-2.32	-11.80	-11.87	-21.77	-15.51	-12.68	..	Change in Reserves
				(Belize Dollars per US dollar)							**Memo Item:**
2.000	2.000	2.000	2.000	2.000	2.000	2.000	2.000	2.000	2.000	..	Conversion Factor (Annual Avg)
				(Millions of US dollars), outstanding at end of year							**EXTERNAL DEBT (Total)**
60.30	69.60	100.00	97.10	118.20	120.60	136.80	139.30	143.80	158.00	..	Long-Term Debt (by debtor)
56.10	62.20	78.20	79.20	105.10	108.90	122.40	134.20	139.00	152.20	..	Central Bank, incl. IMF credit
10.10	11.20	18.00	21.40	31.10	33.30	35.30	32.30	25.70	24.60	..	Central Government
24.80	28.30	35.70	36.50	57.40	62.00	71.60	71.90	83.50	95.60	..	Rest of General Government
..	..	..	..	..	..	..	..	..	..	..	Non-financial Public Enterprises
21.20	22.70	24.50	21.30	16.60	13.60	15.50	22.20	22.10	20.90	..	Priv. Sector, incl non-guaranteed
0.00	0.00	0.00	0.00	0.00	0.00	0.00	7.80	7.70	11.10	..	Short-Term Debt
4.20	7.40	21.80	17.90	13.10	11.70	14.40	5.10	4.80	5.80	..	
				(Thousands of US dollars)							**Memo Items:**
10,335	9,838	9,306	6,072	14,813	26,897	36,415	51,657	59,880	69,782	..	Int'l Reserves Excluding Gold
..	..	..	..	..	..	..	..	..	..	..	Gold Holdings (at market price)
											SOCIAL INDICATORS
5.6	5.5	5.4	5.3	5.2	5.1	5.0	4.9	4.8	4.7	..	Total Fertility Rate
..	60.0	58.0	56.0	54.0	52.0	50.0	48.2	46.4	44.6	..	Infant Mortality Rate
64.6	65.1	65.5	65.8	66.1	66.4	66.7	67.1	67.5	67.9	..	Life Expectancy at Birth
49.5	49.6	49.8	49.9	50.0	50.3	50.6	51.0	51.3	51.6	..	Urban Population, % of total
97.1	100.4	93.4	93.0	88.7	89.8	100.0	90.9	92.0	96.1	..	Food Prod. per capita (1987=100)
..	..	..	..	..	..	..	..	..	..	..	Labor Force, Agriculture (%)
..	..	..	..	..	..	..	..	..	..	..	Labor Force, Female (%)
..	..	..	..	..	..	..	..	..	..	..	Primary Schl. Enroll. Ratio
..	..	..	..	..	..	..	..	..	..	..	Primary Schl. Enroll. Ratio, Female
..	..	..	..	..	..	..	..	..	..	..	Secondary Schl. Enroll. Ratio

BENIN	1970	1971	1972	1973	1974	1975	1976	1977	1978	1979	1980
CURRENT GNP PER CAPITA (US $)	130	130	140	160	180	200	220	240	260	320	390
POPULATION (thousands)	2,657	2,727	2,800	2,875	2,951	3,029	3,107	3,189	3,275	3,367	3,464

USE AND ORIGIN OF RESOURCES *(Billions of current CFA Francs)*

	1970	1971	1972	1973	1974	1975	1976	1977	1978	1979	1980
Gross National Product (GNP)	91.52	91.41	102.86	111.92	132.95	144.81	166.99	184.17	209.70	252.44	296.29
Net Factor Income from Abroad	-0.69	-0.86	-0.55	-0.50	-0.55	-0.26	0.10	-0.10	0.10	0.10	-0.61
GDP at Market Prices	92.22	92.26	103.41	112.42	133.51	145.06	166.88	184.27	209.60	252.34	296.90
Resource Balance	-5.81	-5.92	-10.51	-8.23	-17.87	-25.56	-28.52	-30.97	-33.60	-44.06	-60.21
Exports of Goods & NFServices	20.34	23.85	21.62	25.59	27.78	30.63	31.51	43.33	50.34	64.24	68.25
Imports of Goods & NFServices	26.15	29.77	32.13	33.82	45.65	56.19	60.03	74.30	83.94	108.30	128.46
Domestic Absorption	98.03	98.18	113.92	120.65	151.38	170.62	195.41	215.24	243.20	296.40	357.11
Private Consumption, etc.	78.36	79.42	89.61	94.75	115.54	129.20	153.28	167.22	192.10	228.15	286.45
General Gov't Consumption	8.98	9.27	10.49	11.20	11.50	13.42	14.34	15.31	17.43	20.25	25.66
Gross Domestic Investment	10.69	9.49	13.82	14.70	24.34	28.00	27.79	32.71	33.67	48.00	45.00
Fixed Investment	..	..	..	..	..	..	..	..	..	..	..
Indirect Taxes, net	7.53	8.33	8.74	9.24	9.07	10.18	13.34	15.89	15.89	18.20	22.26
GDP at factor cost	84.69	83.93	94.67	103.18	124.44	134.88	153.55	168.38	193.71	234.14	274.64
Agriculture	33.50	31.70	35.40	37.80	42.10	44.30	55.40	58.70	72.40	88.30	105.20
Industry	10.79	12.44	14.36	16.07	22.81	23.45	21.54	23.14	29.36	33.67	36.46
Manufacturing	..	10.54	11.46	12.57	17.01	17.75	15.34	16.64	22.56	22.37	23.66
Services, etc.	47.92	48.13	53.65	58.55	68.60	77.31	89.94	102.43	107.84	130.37	155.24
Gross Domestic Saving	4.88	3.57	3.31	6.47	6.47	2.44	-0.73	1.74	0.07	3.94	-15.21
Gross National Saving	4.19	3.21	3.55	6.71	7.01	5.38	5.75	10.97	12.52	19.16	0.00

(Billions of 1987 CFA Francs)

	1970	1971	1972	1973	1974	1975	1976	1977	1978	1979	1980
Gross National Product	277.98	273.43	291.79	303.58	312.02	296.78	300.82	315.07	320.38	341.05	362.13
GDP at Market Prices	287.71	283.53	301.32	313.26	321.80	305.37	308.82	323.80	328.93	350.18	372.74
Resource Balance	-50.96	-56.32	-63.08	-66.55	-68.85	-76.75	-69.63	-77.88	-79.52	-94.83	-119.41
Exports of Goods & NFServices	55.35	70.87	74.18	68.99	68.35	68.80	66.34	71.03	77.90	105.86	117.34
Imports of Goods & NFServices	106.31	127.19	137.26	135.54	137.20	145.55	135.97	148.91	157.42	200.69	236.75
Domestic Absorption	338.66	339.84	364.40	379.81	390.66	382.12	378.44	401.68	408.46	445.01	492.15
Private Consumption, etc.	258.25	259.94	268.55	280.29	278.41	272.14	272.69	307.24	316.81	329.61	343.71
General Gov't Consumption	55.07	55.33	60.24	63.45	59.42	57.10	51.88	44.86	44.83	48.38	56.84
Gross Domestic Investment	25.35	24.58	35.61	36.07	52.83	52.87	53.88	49.58	46.81	67.01	91.60
Fixed Investment	..	..	..	..	..	..	..	..	..	..	..
GDP at factor cost	264.28	258.01	275.91	287.62	299.89	283.85	284.10	295.81	304.01	324.91	344.70
Agriculture	105.52	101.67	105.15	119.74	102.52	96.97	107.87	107.40	118.68	124.32	128.17
Industry	31.72	29.42	33.55	32.60	41.82	36.14	31.67	36.19	33.92	36.57	36.11
Manufacturing	..	..	..	27.06	32.57	28.61	23.78	29.67	27.26	24.36	24.07
Services, etc.	151.28	153.39	163.47	161.94	177.87	174.03	171.72	182.34	178.41	191.57	212.48

Memo Items:

	1970	1971	1972	1973	1974	1975	1976	1977	1978	1979	1980
Capacity to Import	82.69	101.90	92.36	102.55	83.49	79.34	71.37	86.84	94.41	119.04	125.78
Terms of Trade Adjustment	27.34	31.02	18.18	33.57	15.14	10.54	5.03	15.81	16.51	13.18	8.44
Gross Domestic Income	315.04	314.55	319.50	346.82	336.95	315.91	313.85	339.61	345.44	363.36	381.18
Gross National Income	305.32	304.45	309.97	337.15	327.17	307.32	305.85	330.88	336.89	354.23	370.57

DOMESTIC PRICES/DEFLATORS *(Index 1987 = 100)*

	1970	1971	1972	1973	1974	1975	1976	1977	1978	1979	1980
Overall (GDP)	32.1	32.5	34.3	35.9	41.5	47.5	54.0	56.9	63.7	72.1	79.7
Domestic Absorption	28.9	28.9	31.3	31.8	38.7	44.7	51.6	53.6	59.5	66.6	72.6
Agriculture	31.7	31.2	33.7	31.6	41.1	45.7	51.4	54.7	61.0	71.0	82.1
Industry	34.0	42.3	42.8	49.3	54.5	64.9	68.0	63.9	86.5	92.1	101.0
Manufacturing	..	..	..	46.5	52.2	62.0	64.5	56.1	82.7	91.8	98.3
Consumer Price Index	..	..	..	..	..	..	..	..	..	..	..

MANUFACTURING ACTIVITY

	1970	1971	1972	1973	1974	1975	1976	1977	1978	1979	1980
Employment (1987=100)	..	..	..	..	..	..	..	..	..	..	..
Real Earnings per Empl. (1987=100)	..	..	..	..	..	..	..	..	..	..	..
Real Output per Empl. (1987=100)	..	..	..	..	..	..	..	..	..	..	..
Earnings as % of Value Added	..	..	..	..	19.2	20.9	24.3	23.9	25.1	25.4	24.8

MONETARY HOLDINGS *(Millions of current CFA Francs)*

	1970	1971	1972	1973	1974	1975	1976	1977	1978	1979	1980
Money Supply, Broadly Defined	10,028	12,263	13,897	14,786	18,449	31,859	30,631	34,918	39,017	40,741	61,407
Money	9,631	11,521	12,709	12,325	15,730	26,869	25,631	29,318	31,017	33,741	45,407
Currency Outside Banks	4,510	4,966	5,801	6,017	6,067	8,446	9,364	9,924	7,955	13,255	17,047
Demand Deposits	5,121	6,555	6,908	6,308	9,663	18,423	16,267	19,394	23,062	20,486	28,360
Quasi-Money	397	742	1,188	2,461	2,719	4,990	5,000	5,600	8,000	7,000	16,000

GOVERNMENT DEFICIT (-) OR SURPLUS *(Millions of current CFA Francs)*

	1970	1971	1972	1973	1974	1975	1976	1977	1978	1979	1980
Current Revenue	..	..	..	..	..	..	..	1,434	5,052	-1,010	..
Current Expenditure	..	..	..	..	..	..	..	41,982	40,695	45,898	..
Current Budget Balance	..	..	..	..	..	..	..	22,416	18,853	26,315	..
Capital Receipts	..	..	..	..	..	..	15	13	12	7	..
Capital Payments	..	..	..	..	..	..	..	18,145	16,802	20,600	..

1981	1982	1983	1984	1985	1986	1987	1988	1989	1990 estimate	Notes	BENIN
420	400	320	300	280	280	310	340	340	..		**CURRENT GNP PER CAPITA (US $)**
3,568	3,678	3,794	3,916	4,043	4,174	4,310	4,450	4,593	4,740	..	**POPULATION (thousands)**
											USE AND ORIGIN OF RESOURCES
				(Billions of current CFA Francs)							
347.67	414.63	412.33	451.96	456.86	451.28	456.80	472.80	475.63	504.20	f	Gross National Product (GNP)
-3.17	-1.97	-5.07	-7.34	-12.94	-11.32	-12.80	-9.50	-14.07	-14.60	..	Net Factor Income from Abroad
350.84	416.60	417.40	459.30	469.80	462.60	469.60	482.30	489.70	518.80	f	GDP at Market Prices
-97.56	-86.00	-69.30	-34.00	-37.50	-50.40	-50.30	-50.40	-34.10	-49.20	..	Resource Balance
81.23	107.60	83.50	130.70	156.50	129.50	128.70	142.50	107.50	145.40	..	Exports of Goods & NFServices
178.79	193.60	152.80	164.70	194.00	179.90	179.00	192.90	141.60	194.60	..	Imports of Goods & NFServices
448.40	502.60	486.70	493.30	507.30	513.00	519.90	532.70	523.80	568.00	..	Domestic Absorption
361.27	343.90	354.20	372.00	374.30	381.20	384.60	400.80	400.70	425.10	..	Private Consumption, etc.
32.13	43.70	60.20	62.60	58.80	63.80	68.70	57.30	63.60	64.30	..	General Gov't Consumption
55.00	115.00	72.30	58.70	74.20	68.00	66.60	74.60	59.50	78.60	..	Gross Domestic Investment
..	112.70	69.40	57.30	63.00	68.20	66.70	72.70	72.00	78.60	..	Fixed Investment
32.70	41.10	31.60	27.60	38.30	40.00	38.80	31.40	21.80	26.00	..	Indirect Taxes, net
318.14	375.50	385.80	431.70	431.50	422.60	430.80	450.90	467.90	492.80	..	GDP at factor cost
114.60	135.40	138.40	153.00	148.20	154.70	155.70	167.20	182.70	187.40	..	Agriculture
45.29	63.00	64.10	78.40	78.60	59.60	61.30	67.40	68.60	76.00	..	Industry
23.29	37.90	36.20	36.40	37.10	34.80	34.70	41.70	42.90	45.30	..	Manufacturing
190.94	218.20	214.90	227.90	243.00	248.30	252.60	247.70	238.40	255.40	..	Services, etc.
-42.56	29.00	3.00	24.70	36.70	17.60	16.30	24.20	25.40	29.40	..	Gross Domestic Saving
-11.22	59.72	6.93	34.05	51.66	33.88	27.90	39.00	32.32	33.80	..	Gross National Saving
				(Billions of 1987 CFA Francs)							
392.86	405.45	385.94	411.91	426.94	443.11	456.80	456.47	435.99	453.85	..	Gross National Product
407.02	418.34	401.00	433.34	465.79	477.24	469.60	484.92	475.94	494.45	I	GDP at Market Prices
-130.98	-103.81	-78.12	-52.68	-51.84	-50.87	-50.30	-59.42	-31.25	-41.53	..	Resource Balance
128.13	94.94	68.87	94.49	116.90	123.17	128.70	127.06	94.18	95.07	..	Exports of Goods & NFServices
259.11	198.74	146.99	147.17	168.74	174.04	179.00	186.48	125.43	136.60	..	Imports of Goods & NFServices
537.99	522.14	479.12	486.01	517.63	528.11	519.90	544.34	507.19	535.98	..	Domestic Absorption
371.75	325.08	327.89	356.62	374.65	390.10	384.60	403.89	397.87	416.35	..	Private Consumption, etc.
62.01	47.92	63.89	64.91	60.20	64.60	68.70	57.23	52.20	40.51	..	General Gov't Consumption
104.23	149.15	87.35	64.48	82.78	73.41	66.60	83.22	57.12	79.11	..	Gross Domestic Investment
..	..	85.84	67.39	72.20	76.10	66.70	83.32	72.89	81.27	..	Fixed Investment
368.71	376.90	370.56	407.25	427.75	436.02	430.80	453.42	454.84	469.74	I	GDP at factor cost
118.96	121.22	121.22	144.35	155.81	164.53	155.70	174.94	186.19	188.71	..	Agriculture
43.00	57.79	55.53	60.21	65.73	61.22	61.30	60.80	58.46	62.89	..	Industry
22.62	36.83	32.67	30.64	35.86	32.86	34.70	37.21	37.50	38.57	..	Manufacturing
250.66	240.04	224.25	228.78	244.26	251.49	252.60	249.18	231.29	242.85	..	Services, etc.
											Memo Items:
117.72	110.46	80.33	116.79	136.12	125.28	128.70	137.76	95.23	102.06	..	Capacity to Import
-10.41	15.52	11.46	22.30	19.22	2.11	0.00	10.70	1.04	6.99	..	Terms of Trade Adjustment
396.61	433.86	412.46	455.63	485.02	479.35	469.60	495.62	476.98	501.44	..	Gross Domestic Income
382.45	420.97	397.40	434.20	446.16	445.22	456.80	467.17	437.04	460.84	..	Gross National Income
											DOMESTIC PRICES/DEFLATORS
				(Index 1987 = 100)							
86.2	99.6	104.1	106.0	100.9	96.9	100.0	99.5	102.9	104.9	..	Overall (GDP)
83.3	96.3	101.6	101.5	98.0	97.1	100.0	97.9	103.3	106.0	..	Domestic Absorption
96.3	111.7	114.2	106.0	95.1	94.0	100.0	95.6	98.1	99.3	..	Agriculture
105.3	109.0	115.4	130.2	119.6	97.4	100.0	110.9	117.4	120.8	..	Industry
103.0	102.9	110.8	118.8	103.5	105.9	100.0	112.1	114.4	117.5	..	Manufacturing
..	..	..	..	..	..	..	..	..	..	..	Consumer Price Index
											MANUFACTURING ACTIVITY
..	..	..	..	..	..	..	..	..	..	..	Employment (1987=100)
..	..	..	..	..	..	..	..	..	..	..	Real Earnings per Empl. (1987=100)
..	..	..	..	..	..	..	..	..	..	..	Real Output per Empl. (1987=100)
25.0	..	..	..	..	..	..	..	..	..	..	Earnings as % of Value Added
											MONETARY HOLDINGS
				(Millions of current CFA Francs)							
75,436	98,438	97,000	110,610	111,620	109,142	96,814	97,862	104,192	134,024	..	Money Supply, Broadly Defined
60,436	83,438	82,000	89,489	87,090	78,926	61,844	71,954	84,372	104,551	..	Money
28,103	28,844	22,511	26,954	20,262	26,166	19,606	23,685	36,391	41,074	..	Currency Outside Banks
32,333	54,594	59,489	62,535	66,828	52,760	42,238	48,269	47,981	63,477	..	Demand Deposits
15,000	15,000	15,000	21,121	24,530	30,216	34,970	25,908	19,820	29,473	..	Quasi-Money
											GOVERNMENT DEFICIT (-) OR SURPLUS
				(Millions of current CFA Francs)							
..	..	..	..	..	..	..	..	..	..	..	Current Revenue
..	..	..	..	..	..	..	..	..	..	..	Current Expenditure
..	..	..	..	..	..	..	..	..	..	..	Current Budget Balance
..	..	..	..	..	..	..	..	..	..	..	Capital Receipts
..	..	..	..	..	..	..	..	..	..	..	Capital Payments

BENIN	1970	1971	1972	1973	1974	1975	1976	1977	1978	1979	1980

FOREIGN TRADE (CUSTOMS BASIS) *(Millions of current US dollars)*

Value of Exports, fob	..	..	..	..	..	..	..	..	..	..	..
Nonfuel Primary Products	..	..	..	..	..	..	..	..	..	..	..
Fuels	..	..	..	..	..	..	..	..	..	..	..
Manufactures	..	..	..	..	..	..	..	..	..	..	..
Value of Imports, cif	..	..	..	..	..	..	..	..	..	..	..
Nonfuel Primary Products	..	..	..	..	..	..	..	..	..	..	..
Fuels	..	..	..	..	..	..	..	..	..	..	..
Manufactures	..	..	..	..	..	..	..	..	..	..	..

(Index 1987 = 100)

Terms of Trade	..	..	..	..	..	..	..	..	..	..	..
Export Prices, fob	..	..	..	..	..	..	..	..	..	..	..
Import Prices, cif	..	..	..	..	..	..	..	..	..	..	..

BALANCE OF PAYMENTS *(Millions of current US dollars)*

	1970	1971	1972	1973	1974	1975	1976	1977	1978	1979	1980
Exports of Goods & Services	71.50	83.75	84.79	115.40	119.07	147.73	119.88	165.03	168.16	182.31	241.30
Merchandise, fob	58.00	69.71	67.31	92.99	92.99	116.10	85.86	129.06	125.56	132.91	163.95
Nonfactor Services	11.90	12.24	15.31	18.95	22.01	28.13	30.83	32.55	38.67	43.36	62.29
Factor Services	1.60	1.81	2.17	3.46	4.07	3.50	3.19	3.42	3.93	6.05	15.06
Imports of Goods & Services	94.60	108.92	132.13	155.45	190.69	268.28	272.70	330.40	373.93	388.65	427.78
Merchandise, fob	66.00	78.43	94.35	115.52	148.27	205.64	208.57	255.51	284.77	288.96	312.24
Nonfactor Services	24.50	25.58	33.44	36.48	40.64	57.88	60.98	71.27	85.49	94.91	108.59
Factor Services	4.10	4.91	4.34	3.46	1.79	4.76	3.16	3.61	3.67	4.78	6.95
Long-Term Interest	0.40	0.90	0.50	0.40	0.70	0.80	0.90	0.90	2.00	3.10	2.90
Private Current Transfers, net	0.00	1.81	3.15	3.34	4.55	14.93	26.71	37.97	54.73	71.08	74.88
Workers' Remittances	2.20	4.01	5.65	6.56	7.31	17.59	28.04	39.18	56.24	72.92	77.00
Curr. A/C Bal before Off. Transf.	-23.10	-23.37	-44.19	-36.72	-67.07	-105.63	-126.11	-127.39	-151.04	-135.26	-111.59
Net Official Transfers	20.10	21.46	35.61	22.41	37.79	52.25	61.30	70.73	60.71	83.41	75.87
Curr. A/C Bal after Off. Transf.	-3.00	-1.91	-8.58	-14.31	-29.27	-53.38	-64.82	-56.66	-90.33	-51.85	-35.72
Long-Term Capital, net	7.60	8.83	8.69	11.68	19.04	17.71	17.89	17.24	26.57	31.93	24.13
Direct Investment	6.70	2.81	4.78	3.46	-2.34	1.89	2.45	3.13	0.75	3.37	4.32
Long-Term Loans	1.00	5.00	4.30	9.20	11.50	11.40	23.80	30.20	34.20	147.50	56.10
Disbursements	2.40	7.70	6.70	11.10	16.90	16.70	27.20	33.20	37.40	150.90	61.90
Repayments	1.40	2.70	2.40	1.90	5.40	5.30	3.40	3.00	3.20	3.40	5.80
Other Long-Term Capital	-0.10	1.02	-0.39	-0.97	9.89	4.42	-8.36	-16.09	-8.39	-118.94	-36.29
Other Capital, net	1.66	-1.11	2.28	4.17	10.69	15.81	52.09	39.55	57.30	16.29	4.11
Change in Reserves	-6.26	-5.81	-2.39	-1.55	-0.46	19.85	-5.17	-0.12	6.47	3.63	7.49

Memo Item: *(CFA Francs per US dollar)*

	1970	1971	1972	1973	1974	1975	1976	1977	1978	1979	1980
Conversion Factor (Annual Avg)	277.710	277.130	252.210	222.700	240.500	214.320	238.980	245.670	225.640	212.720	211.300

EXTERNAL DEBT (Total) *(Millions of US dollars), outstanding at end of year*

	1970	1971	1972	1973	1974	1975	1976	1977	1978	1979	1980
EXTERNAL DEBT (Total)	40.5	48.0	43.5	56.1	70.3	80.4	101.9	161.8	233.2	396.4	417.3
Long-Term Debt (by debtor)	40.5	48.0	43.5	56.1	70.3	80.4	101.9	134.8	171.8	299.0	343.9
Central Bank, incl. IMF credit	1.5	2.7	2.8	3.1	3.9	4.2	3.8	6.3	15.6	15.9	28.7
Central Government	26.8	33.8	29.5	41.3	49.9	60.8	82.2	109.9	117.4	132.9	176.2
Rest of General Government	0.0	0.0	0.0	0.0	0.0	0.0	0.0	0.0	0.0	0.0	0.0
Non-financial Public Enterprises	12.2	11.5	11.2	11.7	16.5	15.4	15.9	18.6	38.8	150.2	139.0
Priv. Sector, incl non-guaranteed	..	..	..	..	..	..	..	..	..	..	..
Short-Term Debt	0.0	0.0	0.0	0.0	0.0	0.0	0.0	27.0	61.4	97.4	73.4

Memo Items: *(Thousands of US dollars)*

	1970	1971	1972	1973	1974	1975	1976	1977	1978	1979	1980
Int'l Reserves Excluding Gold	15,510.0	24,596.0	28,416.5	33,081.0	34,602.6	15,034.9	19,231.4	20,359.6	15,515.2	14,241.3	8,145.8
Gold Holdings (at market price)	..	..	..	..	..	..	..	923.7	1,898.4	5,683.2	6,543.4

SOCIAL INDICATORS

	1970	1971	1972	1973	1974	1975	1976	1977	1978	1979	1980
Total Fertility Rate	6.9	6.9	6.9	6.8	6.7	6.6	6.6	6.5	6.5	6.5	6.5
Infant Mortality Rate	154.6	152.8	151.0	146.8	142.6	138.4	134.2	130.0	128.0	126.0	124.0
Life Expectancy at Birth	44.0	44.2	44.5	44.8	45.0	45.3	45.6	45.8	46.2	46.7	47.1
Urban Population, % of total	18.2	19.5	20.9	22.2	23.6	24.9	26.2	27.5	28.9	30.2	31.5
Food Prod. per capita (1987=100)	107.3	104.2	103.3	105.0	95.5	91.8	107.2	100.8	109.6	111.3	101.6
Labor Force, Agriculture (%)	80.9	79.8	78.6	77.6	76.5	75.6	74.4	73.3	72.2	71.2	70.2
Labor Force, Female (%)	47.9	48.0	48.1	48.2	48.3	48.4	48.6	48.7	48.8	48.8	48.9
Primary Schl. Enroll. Ratio	36.0	..	..	..	..	50.0	..	52.0	58.0	60.0	64.0
Primary Schl. Enroll. Ratio, Female	22.0	..	..	..	..	31.0	..	33.0	37.0	40.0	41.0
Secondary Schl. Enroll. Ratio	5.0	..	..	..	..	9.0	..	11.0	11.0	12.0	16.0

1981	1982	1983	1984	1985	1986	1987	1988	1989	1990 estimate	Notes	BENIN
											FOREIGN TRADE (CUSTOMS BASIS)
(Millions of current US dollars)											
..	..	..	..	..	..	..	..	..	..	..	Value of Exports, fob
..	..	..	..	..	..	..	..	..	..	..	Nonfuel Primary Products
..	..	..	..	..	..	..	..	..	..	..	Fuels
..	..	..	..	..	..	..	..	..	..	..	Manufactures
..	..	..	..	..	..	..	..	..	..	..	Value of Imports, cif
..	..	..	..	..	..	..	..	..	..	..	Nonfuel Primary Products
..	..	..	..	..	..	..	..	..	..	..	Fuels
..	..	..	..	..	..	..	..	..	..	..	Manufactures
(Index 1987 = 100)											
..	..	..	..	..	..	..	..	..	..	..	Terms of Trade
..	..	..	..	..	..	..	..	..	..	..	Export Prices, fob
..	..	..	..	..	..	..	..	..	..	..	Import Prices, cif
(Millions of current US dollars)											**BALANCE OF PAYMENTS**
256.00	214.50	241.70	234.80	367.50	378.60	458.50	476.80	306.00	380.50	f	Exports of Goods & Services
184.00	143.60	175.80	170.30	301.20	303.90	364.10	376.70	217.90	263.70	..	Merchandise, fob
71.80	70.60	65.60	64.50	61.80	71.80	91.10	100.10	88.10	115.00	..	Nonfactor Services
0.20	0.30	0.30	0.00	4.50	2.90	3.30	0.00	0.00	1.80	..	Factor Services
661.30	706.20	367.90	396.60	471.20	551.60	636.10	683.00	467.20	603.00	f	Imports of Goods & Services
522.40	575.70	250.80	266.20	326.80	402.80	463.90	508.20	316.80	428.20	..	Merchandise, fob
135.50	124.20	103.50	100.80	118.30	119.50	139.80	149.50	111.70	135.20	..	Nonfactor Services
3.40	6.30	13.60	29.60	26.10	29.30	32.40	25.30	38.70	39.60	..	Factor Services
3.10	6.00	13.20	16.80	13.60	21.70	14.90	7.60	12.20	4.70	..	Long-Term Interest
127.00	99.50	23.60	38.20	62.10	79.70	81.20	81.60	65.80	69.80	f	Private Current Transfers, net
127.00	99.50	23.60	38.20	62.10	79.70	81.20	81.60	65.80	69.80	..	Workers' Remittances
-278.30	-392.20	-102.60	-123.60	-41.60	-93.30	-96.40	-124.60	-95.40	-152.70	..	Curr. A/C Bal before Off. Transf.
81.70	64.50	55.10	38.00	29.10	34.60	58.50	72.50	107.50	58.80	..	Net Official Transfers
-196.60	-327.70	-47.50	-85.60	-12.50	-58.70	-37.90	-52.10	12.10	-93.90	..	Curr. A/C Bal after Off. Transf.
100.60	213.00	159.70	71.90	16.90	13.00	13.10	-11.20	91.60	127.90	f	Long-Term Capital, net
2.10	-0.50	-0.50	-0.50	0.70	1.20	1.30	1.30	1.30	1.80	..	Direct Investment
100.30	219.90	91.80	16.80	11.90	42.80	56.30	46.30	144.40	90.00	..	Long-Term Loans
107.20	228.50	102.60	37.80	38.00	71.40	69.50	56.50	151.30	95.10	..	Disbursements
6.90	8.60	10.80	21.00	26.10	28.60	13.20	10.20	6.90	5.10	..	Repayments
-1.80	-6.40	68.40	55.60	4.30	-31.00	-44.50	-58.80	-54.10	36.10	..	Other Long-Term Capital
180.30	-35.30	-113.20	21.90	-18.20	49.70	-51.40	62.30	-7.80	72.90	f	Other Capital, net
-84.30	150.00	1.00	-8.20	13.80	-4.00	76.20	1.00	-95.90	-106.90	..	Change in Reserves
(CFA Francs per US dollar)											**Memo Item:**
271.730	328.620	381.070	436.960	449.260	346.300	300.540	297.850	319.010	..	..	Conversion Factor (Annual Avg)
(Millions of US dollars), outstanding at end of year											
485.8	665.3	706.5	674.3	812.3	941.7	1,140.5	1,059.9	1,177.0	1,427.2	..	**EXTERNAL DEBT (Total)**
401.4	587.1	624.1	587.2	668.8	773.4	934.5	912.9	1,056.5	1,270.7	..	Long-Term Debt (by debtor)
28.1	29.6	28.0	25.8	27.9	26.5	26.5	20.6	18.4	17.3	..	Central Bank, incl. IMF credit
198.4	343.5	381.9	369.4	413.4	480.1	579.4	596.7	731.4	912.4	..	Central Government
0.0	0.0	0.0	0.0	0.0	0.0	0.0	0.0	0.0	0.0	..	Rest of General Government
174.9	214.0	214.2	192.0	227.5	266.8	328.6	295.6	306.7	341.0	..	Non-financial Public Enterprises
..	..	..	..	..	..	..	..	..	..	..	Priv. Sector, incl non-guaranteed
84.4	78.2	82.4	87.1	143.5	168.3	206.0	147.0	120.5	156.5	..	Short-Term Debt
(Thousands of US dollars)											**Memo Items:**
57,641.5	4,943.4	3,674.7	2,452.3	4,102.6	3,899.0	3,595.0	4,225.8	3,399.6	64,911.4	..	Int'l Reserves Excluding Gold
4,412.3	5,071.6	4,234.6	3,422.1	3,629.7	4,339.0	5,373.5	4,553.8	4,451.1	4,273.5	..	Gold Holdings (at market price)
											SOCIAL INDICATORS
6.5	6.5	6.5	6.5	6.5	6.5	6.5	6.4	6.4	6.3	..	Total Fertility Rate
122.0	120.0	119.2	118.4	117.5	116.7	115.9	114.9	113.9	112.9	..	Infant Mortality Rate
47.6	48.0	48.5	48.9	49.4	49.8	50.3	50.3	50.4	50.5	..	Life Expectancy at Birth
32.1	32.7	33.4	34.0	34.6	35.4	36.2	36.7	37.2	37.7	..	Urban Population, % of total
96.3	93.4	90.4	112.8	112.2	114.9	100.0	115.7	117.7	114.3	..	Food Prod. per capita (1987=100)
..	..	..	..	..	..	..	..	..	..	..	Labor Force, Agriculture (%)
48.8	48.7	48.5	48.4	48.3	48.1	47.9	47.7	47.6	47.4	..	Labor Force, Female (%)
..	70.0	67.0	67.0	67.0	..	66.0	65.0	..	..	..	Primary Schl. Enroll. Ratio
..	45.0	44.0	44.0	44.0	..	44.0	44.0	..	..	..	Primary Schl. Enroll. Ratio, Female
..	22.0	21.0	20.0	17.0	16.0	..	..	..	..	..	Secondary Schl. Enroll. Ratio

BHUTAN	1970	1971	1972	1973	1974	1975	1976	1977	1978	1979	1980
CURRENT GNP PER CAPITA (US $)	..	..	..	..	..	..	..	..	..	..	..
POPULATION (thousands)	976	989	1,002	1,016	1,031	1,047	1,067	1,090	1,115	1,140	1,165

USE AND ORIGIN OF RESOURCES *(Millions of current Bhutanese Ngultrum)*

	1970	1971	1972	1973	1974	1975	1976	1977	1978	1979	1980
Gross National Product (GNP)	..	..	..	..	..	..	..	..	..	..	912.9
Net Factor Income from Abroad	..	..	..	..	..	..	..	..	..	..	-200.0
GDP at Market Prices	..	..	..	..	..	..	..	..	..	..	1,112.9
Resource Balance	..	..	..	..	..	..	..	..	..	..	-256.7
Exports of Goods & NFServices	..	..	..	..	..	..	..	..	..	..	145.4
Imports of Goods & NFServices	..	..	..	..	..	..	..	..	..	..	402.1
Domestic Absorption	..	..	..	..	..	..	..	..	..	..	1,369.6
Private Consumption, etc.	..	..	..	..	..	..	..	..	..	..	748.6
General Gov't Consumption	..	..	..	..	..	..	..	..	..	..	275.9
Gross Domestic Investment	..	..	..	..	..	..	..	..	..	..	345.1
Fixed Investment	..	..	..	..	..	..	..	..	..	..	330.4
Indirect Taxes, net	..	..	..	..	..	..	..	..	..	..	17.9
GDP at factor cost	..	..	..	..	..	..	..	..	..	..	1,095.0
Agriculture	..	..	..	..	..	..	..	..	..	..	621.4
Industry	..	..	..	..	..	..	..	..	..	..	133.6
Manufacturing	..	..	..	..	..	..	..	..	..	..	35.8
Services, etc.	..	..	..	..	..	..	..	..	..	..	340.0
Gross Domestic Saving	..	..	..	..	..	..	..	..	..	..	88.4
Gross National Saving	..	..	..	..	..	..	..	..	..	..	..

(Millions of 1987 Bhutanese Ngultrum)

	1970	1971	1972	1973	1974	1975	1976	1977	1978	1979	1980
Gross National Product	..	..	..	..	..	..	..	..	..	..	1,621.6
GDP at Market Prices	..	..	..	..	..	..	..	..	..	..	1,980.6
Resource Balance	..	..	..	..	..	..	..	..	..	..	..
Exports of Goods & NFServices	..	..	..	..	..	..	..	..	..	..	..
Imports of Goods & NFServices	..	..	..	..	..	..	..	..	..	..	..
Domestic Absorption	..	..	..	..	..	..	..	..	..	..	..
Private Consumption, etc.	..	..	..	..	..	..	..	..	..	..	..
General Gov't Consumption	..	..	..	..	..	..	..	..	..	..	..
Gross Domestic Investment	..	..	..	..	..	..	..	..	..	..	667.5
Fixed Investment	..	..	..	..	..	..	..	..	..	..	632.7
GDP at factor cost	..	..	..	..	..	..	..	..	..	..	1,948.6
Agriculture	..	..	..	..	..	..	..	..	..	..	1,089.7
Industry	..	..	..	..	..	..	..	..	..	..	254.8
Manufacturing	..	..	..	..	..	..	..	..	..	..	69.8
Services, etc.	..	..	..	..	..	..	..	..	..	..	604.1

Memo Items:

	1970	1971	1972	1973	1974	1975	1976	1977	1978	1979	1980
Capacity to Import	..	..	..	..	..	..	..	..	..	..	..
Terms of Trade Adjustment	..	..	..	..	..	..	..	..	..	..	..
Gross Domestic Income	..	..	..	..	..	..	..	..	..	..	..
Gross National Income	..	..	..	..	..	..	..	..	..	..	..

DOMESTIC PRICES/DEFLATORS *(Index 1987 = 100)*

	1970	1971	1972	1973	1974	1975	1976	1977	1978	1979	1980
Overall (GDP)	..	..	..	..	..	..	..	..	..	..	56.2
Domestic Absorption	..	..	..	..	..	..	..	..	..	..	..
Agriculture	..	..	..	..	..	..	..	..	..	..	57.0
Industry	..	..	..	..	..	..	..	..	..	..	52.4
Manufacturing	..	..	..	..	..	..	..	..	..	..	51.3
Consumer Price Index	..	..	..	..	..	..	..	..	..	..	55.0

MANUFACTURING ACTIVITY

	1970	1971	1972	1973	1974	1975	1976	1977	1978	1979	1980
Employment (1987=100)	..	..	..	..	..	..	..	..	..	..	..
Real Earnings per Empl. (1987=100)	..	..	..	..	..	..	..	..	..	..	..
Real Output per Empl. (1987=100)	..	..	..	..	..	..	..	..	..	..	..
Earnings as % of Value Added	..	..	..	..	..	..	..	..	..	..	..

MONETARY HOLDINGS *(Millions of current Bhutanese Ngultrum)*

	1970	1971	1972	1973	1974	1975	1976	1977	1978	1979	1980
Money Supply, Broadly Defined	..	..	..	..	..	..	..	..	..	..	65.3
Money	..	..	..	..	..	..	..	..	..	..	..
Currency Outside Banks	..	..	..	..	..	..	..	..	..	..	..
Demand Deposits	..	..	..	..	..	..	..	..	..	..	..
Quasi-Money	..	..	..	..	..	..	..	..	..	..	..

(Millions of current Bhutanese Ngultrum)

GOVERNMENT DEFICIT (-) OR SURPLUS

	1970	1971	1972	1973	1974	1975	1976	1977	1978	1979	1980
	..	..	..	..	..	..	..	..	..	..	..
Current Revenue	..	..	..	..	..	..	..	..	..	..	..
Current Expenditure	..	..	..	..	..	..	..	..	..	..	..
Current Budget Balance	..	..	..	..	..	..	..	..	..	..	..
Capital Receipts	..	..	..	..	..	..	..	..	..	..	..
Capital Payments	..	..	..	..	..	..	..	..	..	..	..

1981	1982	1983	1984	1985	1986	1987	1988	1989	1990 estimate	Notes	BHUTAN
..	110	110	130	130	140	180	190	190	190	..	**CURRENT GNP PER CAPITA (US $)**
1,188	1,212	1,237	1,261	1,286	1,313	1,343	1,373	1,403	1,433		**POPULATION (thousands)**

(Millions of current Bhutanese Ngultrum)

USE AND ORIGIN OF RESOURCES

1981	1982	1983	1984	1985	1986	1987	1988	1989	1990	Notes	
1,031.6	1,200.1	1,332.2	1,717.7	1,941.7	2,334.6	3,258.0	3,596.6	4,019.6	4,517.9	..	Gross National Product (GNP)
-269.7	-321.6	-456.1	-387.8	-449.7	-467.0	-349.5	-344.3	-389.5	-441.6		Net Factor Income from Abroad
1,301.3	1,521.7	1,788.3	2,105.5	2,391.4	2,801.6	3,607.5	3,940.9	4,409.1	4,959.5		GDP at Market Prices
-408.8	-474.4	-561.2	-608.7	-760.3	-747.3	-435.1	-782.9	-805.1	-619.3		Resource Balance
207.4	213.2	227.8	290.2	367.5	550.5	767.5	1,200.8	1,555.0	1,781.8		Exports of Goods & NFServices
616.2	687.6	789.0	898.9	1,127.8	1,297.8	1,202.6	1,983.7	2,360.1	2,401.0		Imports of Goods & NFServices
1,710.0	1,996.0	2,350.0	2,714.3	3,151.7	3,548.9	4,042.6	4,723.8	..	..		Domestic Absorption
922.2	1,053.8	1,195.1	1,435.8	1,506.3	1,837.5	2,320.8	2,636.7				Private Consumption, etc.
287.3	326.7	442.9	513.2	560.9	576.3	633.6	568.7				General Gov't Consumption
500.5	615.5	712.0	765.3	1,084.5	1,135.1	1,088.2	1,518.4				Gross Domestic Investment
425.8	555.7	690.7	754.9	1,002.9	1,103.1	1,249.7	1,508.0				Fixed Investment
21.2	23.6	34.8	45.6	41.8	43.0	76.7	82.8	..	..		Indirect Taxes, net
1,280.1	1,498.1	1,753.5	2,059.9	2,349.6	2,758.6	3,530.8	3,858.1	4,281.1	4,815.7		GDP at factor cost
676.7	804.3	934.2	1,117.6	1,236.2	1,399.2	1,623.5	1,746.3	1,924.3	2,089.4		Agriculture
217.9	274.5	352.0	415.2	445.8	538.6	968.6	963.5	1,087.4	1,322.9		Industry
63.5	70.1	96.5	109.5	128.3	137.1	204.7	226.5	302.5	473.8		Manufacturing
385.5	419.3	467.3	527.1	667.6	820.8	938.7	1,148.3	1,269.4	1,403.4		Services, etc.
91.8	141.2	150.3	156.5	324.2	387.8	653.1	735.5	..	..		Gross Domestic Saving
..	..	-305.8	-231.3	-125.5	-79.2	303.6	391.2	..	..		Gross National Saving

(Millions of 1987 Bhutanese Ngultrum)

1981	1982	1983	1984	1985	1986	1987	1988	1989	1990	Notes	
1,724.6	1,806.0	1,849.1	2,169.3	2,227.7	2,514.4	3,258.0	3,396.8	3,482.9	3,604.6		Gross National Product
2,179.8	2,294.4	2,486.9	2,663.1	2,748.1	3,021.8	3,607.5	3,722.4	3,820.8	3,957.4		GDP at Market Prices
..	..	..	..	..	..	..	..	..	..		Resource Balance
..	..	..	..	..	..	..	..	..	..		Exports of Goods & NFServices
..	..	..	..	..	..	..	..	..	..		Imports of Goods & NFServices
..	..	..	..	..	..	..	..	..	..		Domestic Absorption
..	..	..	..	..	..	..	..	..	..		Private Consumption, etc.
..	..	..	..	..	..	..	..	..	..		General Gov't Consumption
875.6	998.3	1,062.3	974.1	1,311.0	1,109.3	1,088.2	1,525.9	..	..		Gross Domestic Investment
737.6	894.3	1,023.2	947.5	1,195.7	1,055.9	1,249.7	1,501.5				Fixed Investment
2,144.0	2,258.6	2,438.3	2,605.1	2,699.9	2,975.1	3,530.8	3,644.2	3,759.7	3,889.8		GDP at factor cost
1,115.5	1,213.9	1,301.5	1,414.3	1,462.3	1,544.9	1,623.5	1,647.9	1,656.9	1,651.6		Agriculture
384.7	443.4	501.6	499.1	501.6	563.3	968.6	966.1	1,018.2	1,137.2		Industry
115.2	116.2	122.6	131.0	147.0	138.4	204.7	215.0	289.6	416.4		Manufacturing
643.8	601.3	635.2	691.8	736.0	866.8	938.7	1,030.2	1,084.7	1,100.9		Services, etc.

Memo Items:

1981	1982	1983	1984	1985	1986	1987	1988	1989	1990	Notes	
..	..	..	..	..	..	..	..	..	..		Capacity to Import
..	..	..	..	..	..	..	..	..	..		Terms of Trade Adjustment
..	..	..	..	..	..	..	..	..	..		Gross Domestic Income
..	..	..	..	..	..	..	..	..	..		Gross National Income

(Index 1987 = 100)

DOMESTIC PRICES/DEFLATORS

1981	1982	1983	1984	1985	1986	1987	1988	1989	1990	Notes	
59.7	66.3	71.9	79.1	87.0	92.7	100.0	105.9	115.4	125.3		Overall (GDP)
..	..	..	..	..	..	..	..	..	..		Domestic Absorption
60.7	66.3	71.8	79.0	84.5	90.6	100.0	106.0	116.1	126.5		Agriculture
56.6	61.9	70.2	83.2	88.9	95.6	100.0	99.7	106.8	116.3		Industry
55.1	60.3	78.7	83.6	87.3	99.0	100.0	105.3	104.5	113.8		Manufacturing
60.5	66.4	78.4	83.9	85.5	94.0	100.0	110.1	119.7	..		Consumer Price Index

MANUFACTURING ACTIVITY

1981	1982	1983	1984	1985	1986	1987	1988	1989	1990	Notes	
..	..	..	..	..	..	..	..	..	..		Employment (1987=100)
..	..	..	..	..	..	..	..	..	..		Real Earnings per Empl. (1987=100)
..	..	..	..	..	..	..	..	..	..		Real Output per Empl. (1987=100)
..	..	..	..	..	..	..	..	..	..		Earnings as % of Value Added

(Millions of current Bhutanese Ngultrum)

MONETARY HOLDINGS

1981	1982	1983	1984	1985	1986	1987	1988	1989	1990	Notes	
74.3	85.7	324.6	367.0	464.0	498.6	552.5	723.7	976.5	1,078.8		Money Supply, Broadly Defined
..	..	177.2	209.8	261.7	277.0	316.8	412.1	546.3	539.5		Money
..	..	22.1	46.2	70.4	90.7	103.5	149.1	188.1	194.1		Currency Outside Banks
..	..	155.1	163.6	191.3	186.3	213.3	263.0	358.2	345.4		Demand Deposits
..	..	147.4	157.2	202.3	221.6	235.7	311.6	430.2	539.3		Quasi-Money

(Millions of current Bhutanese Ngultrum)

1981	1982	1983	1984	1985	1986	1987	1988	1989	1990	Notes	
..	10.0	-23.0	32.0	-207.0	-98.0	..	32.0	-432.0	-327.0		**GOVERNMENT DEFICIT (-) OR SURPLUS**
..	498.0	673.0	787.0	966.0	1,116.0	..	1,762.0	1,494.0	1,616.0		Current Revenue
..	213.0	223.0	304.0	441.0	423.0	..	775.0	940.0	1,037.0		Current Expenditure
..	285.0	450.0	482.0	525.0	693.0	..	987.0	554.0	580.0		Current Budget Balance
..	1.0	2.0	4.0	4.0	7.0	..	10.0	7.0	7.0		Capital Receipts
..	275.0	476.0	454.0	736.0	798.0	..	965.0	992.0	913.0		Capital Payments

BHUTAN	1970	1971	1972	1973	1974	1975	1976	1977	1978	1979	1980
FOREIGN TRADE (CUSTOMS BASIS)				*(Thousands of current US dollars)*							
Value of Exports, fob	..	..	..	..	..	..	..	..	..	..	..
Nonfuel Primary Products	..	..	..	..	..	..	..	..	..	..	..
Fuels	..	..	..	..	..	..	..	..	..	..	..
Manufactures	..	..	..	..	..	..	..	..	..	..	..
Value of Imports, cif	..	..	..	..	..	..	..	..	..	..	..
Nonfuel Primary Products	..	..	..	..	..	..	..	..	..	..	..
Fuels	..	..	..	..	..	..	..	..	..	..	..
Manufactures	..	..	..	..	..	..	..	..	..	..	..
Terms of Trade					*(Index 1987 = 100)*						
Export Prices, fob	..	..	..	..	..	..	..	..	..	..	..
Import Prices, cif	..	..	..	..	..	..	..	..	..	..	..
BALANCE OF PAYMENTS					*(Millions of current US dollars)*						
Exports of Goods & Services	..	..	..	..	..	..	..	..	..	..	..
Merchandise, fob	..	..	..	..	..	..	..	..	..	..	..
Nonfactor Services	..	..	..	..	..	..	..	..	..	..	..
Factor Services	..	..	..	..	..	..	..	..	..	..	..
Imports of Goods & Services	..	..	..	..	..	..	..	..	..	..	..
Merchandise, fob	..	..	..	..	..	..	..	..	..	..	..
Nonfactor Services	..	..	..	..	..	..	..	..	..	..	..
Factor Services	..	..	..	..	..	..	..	..	..	..	..
Long-Term Interest	0.00	0.00	0.00	0.00	0.00	0.00	0.00	0.00	0.00	0.00	0.00
Private Current Transfers, net	..	..	..	..	..	..	..	..	..	..	..
Workers' Remittances	..	..	..	..	..	..	..	..	..	..	..
Curr. A/C Bal before Off. Transf.	..	..	..	..	..	..	..	..	..	..	..
Net Official Transfers	..	..	..	..	..	..	..	..	..	..	0.00
Curr. A/C Bal after Off. Transf.	..	..	..	..	..	..	..	..	..	..	..
Long-Term Capital, net	..	..	..	..	..	..	..	..	..	..	..
Direct Investment	..	..	..	..	..	..	..	..	..	..	..
Long-Term Loans	0.00	0.00	0.00	0.00	0.00	0.00	0.00	0.00	0.00	0.00	0.00
Disbursements	0.00	0.00	0.00	0.00	0.00	0.00	0.00	0.00	0.00	0.00	0.00
Repayments	0.00	0.00	0.00	0.00	0.00	0.00	0.00	0.00	0.00	0.00	0.00
Other Long-Term Capital	..	..	..	..	..	..	..	..	..	..	..
Other Capital, net	..	..	..	..	..	..	..	..	..	..	..
Change in Reserves	..	..	..	..	..	..	..	..	..	..	..
Memo Item:					*(Bhutanese Ngultrum per US dollar)*						
Conversion Factor (Annual Avg)	7.500	7.500	7.590	7.740	8.100	8.380	8.960	8.740	8.190	8.130	7.860
				(Thousands of US dollars), outstanding at end of year							
EXTERNAL DEBT (Total)	0	0	0	0	0	0	0	0	0	0	0
Long-Term Debt (by debtor)	0	0	0	0	0	0	0	0	0	0	0
Central Bank, incl. IMF credit	..	..	..	..	..	..	..	..	..	..	..
Central Government	0	0	0	0	0	0	0	0	0	0	0
Rest of General Government	..	..	..	..	..	..	..	..	..	..	..
Non-financial Public Enterprises	..	..	..	..	..	..	..	..	..	..	..
Priv. Sector, incl non-guaranteed	..	..	..	..	..	..	..	..	..	..	..
Short-Term Debt	0	0	0	0	0	0	0	0	0	0	0
Memo Items:					*(Thousands of US dollars)*						
Int'l Reserves Excluding Gold	..	..	..	..	..	..	..	..	..	..	..
Gold Holdings (at market price)	..	..	..	..	..	..	..	..	..	..	..
SOCIAL INDICATORS											
Total Fertility Rate	5.8	5.8	5.7	5.7	5.7	5.7	5.7	5.6	5.6	5.6	5.6
Infant Mortality Rate	157.4	155.2	153.0	151.8	150.6	149.4	148.2	147.0	145.4	143.8	142.2
Life Expectancy at Birth	41.6	41.9	42.3	42.8	43.3	43.8	44.3	44.8	45.0	45.3	45.5
Urban Population, % of total	3.1	3.2	3.3	3.3	3.4	3.5	3.6	3.7	3.7	3.8	3.9
Food Prod. per capita (1987=100)	83.9	84.4	85.0	85.2	85.8	86.3	86.8	87.2	88.1	88.6	89.9
Labor Force, Agriculture (%)	94.1	93.9	93.8	93.6	93.4	93.3	93.1	92.9	92.7	92.6	92.4
Labor Force, Female (%)	34.8	34.7	34.6	34.5	34.4	34.3	34.1	34.0	33.9	33.8	33.7
Primary Schl. Enroll. Ratio	6.0	..	..	..	..	..	9.0	10.0	10.0	11.0	16.0
Primary Schl. Enroll. Ratio, Female	1.0	..	..	..	..	..	5.0	6.0	6.0	7.0	..
Secondary Schl. Enroll. Ratio	1.0	..	..	..	..	1.0	1.0	..	1.0	1.0	..

1981	1982	1983	1984	1985	1986	1987	1988	1989	1990 est.	Notes	BHUTAN
			(Thousands of current US dollars)								**FOREIGN TRADE (CUSTOMS BASIS)**
..	..	..	..	..	..	..	..	..	..	..	Value of Exports, fob
..	..	..	..	..	..	..	..	..	..	..	Nonfuel Primary Products
..	..	..	..	..	..	..	..	..	..	..	Fuels
..	..	..	..	..	..	..	..	..	..	..	Manufactures
..	..	..	..	..	..	..	..	..	..	..	Value of Imports, cif
..	..	..	..	..	..	..	..	..	..	..	Nonfuel Primary Products
..	..	..	..	..	..	..	..	..	..	..	Fuels
..	..	..	..	..	..	..	..	..	..	..	Manufactures
			(Index 1987 = 100)								
..	..	..	..	..	..	..	..	..	..	..	Terms of Trade
..	..	..	..	..	..	..	..	..	..	..	Export Prices, fob
..	..	..	..	..	..	..	..	..	..	..	Import Prices, cif
			(Millions of current US dollars)								**BALANCE OF PAYMENTS**
..	..	..	..	..	..	..	..	..	..	..	Exports of Goods & Services
..	17.20	15.80	18.90	21.00	28.30	48.90	62.00	76.20	78.60	..	Merchandise, fob
..	..	9.00	10.60	10.70	12.50	13.70	14.30	19.60	23.20	..	Nonfactor Services
..	..									..	Factor Services
..	..	..	116.10	127.70	139.90	134.30	148.90	147.40	139.40	..	Imports of Goods & Services
..	66.70	69.90	69.80	84.60	93.90	89.00	103.90	107.10	107.30	..	Merchandise, fob
..	..	51.10	46.20	42.80	45.60	44.70	43.50	38.40	29.90	..	Nonfactor Services
			0.10	0.30	0.40	0.60	1.50	1.90	2.20	..	Factor Services
0.00	0.00	0.00	0.00	0.00	0.20	0.50	0.70	1.30	2.30	..	Long-Term Interest
..	..	0.00	0.00	0.00	0.00	0.00	0.00	0.00		..	Private Current Transfers, net
..	..									..	Workers' Remittances
..	..	-96.20	-86.60	-96.00	-99.10	-71.70	-72.60	-51.60	-37.60	..	Curr. A/C Bal before Off. Transf.
..	..	67.50	58.20	69.70	75.80	72.30	69.50	62.80	57.00	..	Net Official Transfers
..	..	-28.70	-28.40	-26.30	-23.30	0.60	-3.10	11.20	19.40	..	Curr. A/C Bal after Off. Transf.
0.30	0.80	0.70	1.10	5.50	11.40	16.30	29.60	9.90	16.50	..	Long-Term Capital, net
..	..	..	..	..	..	..	..	..		..	Direct Investment
0.30	0.80	0.70	1.10	5.50	11.40	15.90	28.00	8.30	3.90	..	Long-Term Loans
0.30	0.80	0.70	1.10	5.50	11.40	15.90	28.60	11.20	8.30	..	Disbursements
0.00	0.00	0.00	0.00	0.00	0.00	0.00	0.60	2.90	4.40	..	Repayments
0.00	0.00	0.00	0.00	0.00	0.00	0.40	1.60	1.60	12.60	..	Other Long-Term Capital
..	..	0.00	0.00	0.00	0.00	0.00	0.00	0.00		..	Other Capital, net
..	..	28.00	27.30	20.80	11.90	-16.90	-26.50	-21.10	-35.90	..	Change in Reserves
			(Bhutanese Ngultrum per US dollar)								**Memo Item:**
8.660	9.460	10.100	11.360	12.370	12.610	12.960	13.920	16.230	17.500	..	Conversion Factor (Annual Avg)
			(Thousands of US dollars), outstanding at end of year								**EXTERNAL DEBT (Total)**
300	1,100	1,800	2,700	8,800	21,000	40,200	66,200	75,500	83,400	..	Long-Term Debt (by debtor)
300	1,100	1,800	2,700	8,800	21,000	40,200	66,200	73,500	80,400	..	Central Bank, incl. IMF credit
..	..	..	..	..	..	..	..	..		..	Central Government
300	1,100	1,800	2,700	8,800	21,000	40,200	66,200	73,500	80,400	..	Rest of General Government
..	..	..	..	..	..	..	..	..		..	Non-financial Public Enterprises
..	..	..	..	..	..	..	..	..		..	Priv. Sector, incl non-guaranteed
..	..	..	0	0	0	0	0	..		..	
0	0	0	0	0	0	0	0	2,000	3,000	..	Short-Term Debt
			(Thousands of US dollars)								**Memo Items:**
31,114.0	35,510.0	40,221.0	44,813.0	50,303.0	61,002.0	74,940.0	94,120.0	98,510.0	86,014.0	..	Int'l Reserves Excluding Gold
..	..	..	..	..	..	..	..	..		..	Gold Holdings (at market price)
											SOCIAL INDICATORS
5.6	5.5	5.5	5.5	5.5	5.5	5.5	5.5	5.5	5.5	..	Total Fertility Rate
140.6	139.0	136.6	134.2	131.9	129.5	127.1	125.6	124.0	122.5	..	Infant Mortality Rate
45.7	45.9	46.3	46.7	47.1	47.6	48.0	48.2	48.4	48.7	..	Life Expectancy at Birth
4.0	4.1	4.3	4.4	4.5	4.7	4.8	5.0	5.1	5.3	..	Urban Population, % of total
93.0	92.6	93.6	99.9	93.2	92.7	100.0	83.4	83.3	85.2	..	Food Prod. per capita (1987=100)
..	..	..	..	..	..	..	..	..		..	Labor Force, Agriculture (%)
33.5	33.3	33.2	33.0	32.9	32.7	32.6	32.4	32.3	32.1	..	Labor Force, Female (%)
..	22.0	24.0	26.0	27.0	24.0	25.0	26.0	..	..	..	Primary Schl. Enroll. Ratio
..	15.0	16.0	18.0	19.0	17.0	..	20.0	..	..	..	Primary Schl. Enroll. Ratio, Female
..	3.0	4.0	4.0	4.0	4.0	4.0	5.0	..	..	..	Secondary Schl. Enroll. Ratio

BOLIVIA	1970	1971	1972	1973	1974	1975	1976	1977	1978	1979	1980
CURRENT GNP PER CAPITA (US $)	230	250	270	290	320	360	400	410	440	460	490
POPULATION (thousands)	4,325	4,431	4,540	4,653	4,771	4,894	5,022	5,156	5,295	5,437	5,581

USE AND ORIGIN OF RESOURCES

(Millions of current Bolivianos)

	1970	1971	1972	1973	1974	1975	1976	1977	1978	1979	1980
Gross National Product (GNP)	1.19E-2	1.31E-2	1.66E-2	2.51E-2	4.17E-2	4.75E-2	5.45E-2	6.23E-2	7.27E-2	8.55E-2	1.16E-1
Net Factor Income from Abroad	-2.84E-4	-1.79E-4	-3.09E-4	-4.88E-4	-8.22E-4	-7.92E-4	-8.96E-4	-1.68E-3	-2.33E-3	-3.93E-3	-7.20E-3
GDP at Market Prices	1.21E-2	1.33E-2	1.69E-2	2.56E-2	4.25E-2	4.83E-2	5.54E-2	6.40E-2	7.50E-2	8.95E-2	1.23E-1
Resource Balance	5.13E-5	-3.71E-4	-4.58E-4	-1.00E-4	3.68E-3	-2.93E-3	-1.09E-3	-1.72E-3	-5.55E-3	-2.84E-3	4.87E-3
Exports of Goods & NFServices	2.99E-3	2.80E-3	3.56E-3	7.06E-3	1.49E-2	1.26E-2	1.52E-2	1.74E-2	1.71E-2	2.20E-2	2.56E-2
Imports of Goods & NFServices	2.94E-3	3.18E-3	4.02E-3	7.16E-3	1.13E-2	1.55E-2	1.63E-2	1.91E-2	2.26E-2	2.48E-2	2.07E-2
Domestic Absorption	1.21E-2	1.37E-2	1.74E-2	2.57E-2	3.88E-2	5.12E-2	5.65E-2	6.57E-2	8.06E-2	9.23E-2	1.18E-1
Private Consumption, etc.	8.03E-3	9.11E-3	1.07E-2	1.57E-2	2.58E-2	2.84E-2	3.49E-2	4.07E-2	5.30E-2	6.08E-2	8.26E-2
General Gov't Consumption	1.17E-3	1.35E-3	1.70E-3	2.49E-3	3.95E-3	5.04E-3	5.93E-3	7.57E-3	9.54E-3	1.36E-2	1.73E-2
Gross Domestic Investment	2.88E-3	3.20E-3	5.00E-3	7.45E-3	9.10E-3	1.78E-2	1.57E-2	1.75E-2	1.80E-2	1.79E-2	1.82E-2
Fixed Investment	2.20E-3	2.43E-3	3.57E-3	5.63E-3	7.41E-3	1.25E-2	1.25E-2	1.41E-2	1.60E-2	1.66E-2	1.76E-2
Indirect Taxes, net	..	..	..	..	..	..	..	..	..	..	..
GDP at factor cost	..	..	..	..	..	..	..	..	..	..	..
Agriculture	2.41E-3	2.70E-3	3.33E-3	5.09E-3	8.88E-3	9.82E-3	1.10E-2	1.24E-2	1.39E-2	1.63E-2	2.26E-2
Industry	3.91E-3	3.98E-3	5.84E-3	9.81E-3	1.69E-2	1.55E-2	1.82E-2	2.11E-2	2.44E-2	2.83E-2	4.27E-2
Manufacturing	1.61E-3	1.77E-3	2.16E-3	3.26E-3	5.18E-3	5.94E-3	7.04E-3	8.16E-3	9.36E-3	1.18E-2	1.80E-2
Services, etc.	5.82E-3	6.61E-3	7.75E-3	1.07E-2	1.67E-2	2.29E-2	2.62E-2	3.04E-2	3.67E-2	4.49E-2	5.76E-2
Gross Domestic Saving	2.93E-3	2.83E-3	4.55E-3	7.35E-3	1.28E-2	1.49E-2	1.46E-2	1.57E-2	1.25E-2	1.50E-2	2.30E-2
Gross National Saving	2.67E-3	2.68E-3	4.30E-3	6.95E-3	1.20E-2	1.41E-2	1.38E-2	1.41E-2	1.03E-2	1.13E-2	1.61E-2

(Millions of 1987 Bolivianos)

	1970	1971	1972	1973	1974	1975	1976	1977	1978	1979	1980
Gross National Product	6,370	6,740	7,080	7,440	7,810	8,370	8,870	9,160	9,420	9,290	9,040
GDP at Market Prices	6,530	6,850	7,220	7,600	7,990	8,520	9,040	9,420	9,730	9,730	9,640
Resource Balance	-566	-675	-755	-629	-412	-896	-710	-725	-876	-834	-356
Exports of Goods & NFServices	1,250	1,390	1,540	1,710	1,690	1,620	1,790	1,760	1,700	1,730	1,330
Imports of Goods & NFServices	1,810	2,070	2,290	2,340	2,100	2,510	2,500	2,480	2,580	2,560	1,690
Domestic Absorption	7,090	7,520	7,970	8,230	8,400	9,410	9,750	10,100	10,600	10,600	9,990
Private Consumption, etc.	3,720	3,790	3,500	4,050	4,160	3,700	4,390	4,620	5,010	5,310	5,660
General Gov't Consumption	745	812	901	1,010	1,100	1,220	1,290	1,330	1,370	1,600	1,560
Gross Domestic Investment	2,630	2,920	3,570	3,170	3,140	4,500	4,070	4,190	4,230	3,650	2,770
Fixed Investment	1,910	2,110	2,350	2,300	2,500	3,010	3,150	3,330	3,640	3,350	2,710
GDP at factor cost	..	..	..	..	..	..	..	..	..	..	..
Agriculture	1,710	1,820	1,920	2,010	2,080	2,250	2,360	2,350	2,390	2,470	2,510
Industry	2,950	3,100	3,360	3,900	3,880	3,910	4,070	4,170	4,070	3,810	3,820
Manufacturing	1,040	1,080	1,160	1,220	1,360	1,440	1,560	1,670	1,750	1,720	1,730
Services, etc.	1,990	2,080	2,140	2,100	2,370	2,660	2,890	3,120	3,400	3,530	3,430

Memo Items:

	1970	1971	1972	1973	1974	1975	1976	1977	1978	1979	1980
Capacity to Import	1,840	1,830	2,030	2,310	2,790	2,040	2,330	2,260	1,950	2,270	2,080
Terms of Trade Adjustment	597	434	494	596	1,100	421	543	501	244	541	752
Gross Domestic Income	7,130	7,280	7,710	8,190	9,090	8,940	9,580	9,920	9,970	10,300	10,400
Gross National Income	6,960	7,180	7,570	8,040	8,910	8,790	9,420	9,660	9,670	9,830	9,800

DOMESTIC PRICES/DEFLATORS

(Index 1987 = 100)

	1970	1971	1972	1973	1974	1975	1976	1977	1978	1979	1980
Overall (GDP)	1.86E-4	1.94E-4	2.34E-4	3.36E-4	5.32E-4	5.67E-4	6.13E-4	6.80E-4	7.71E-4	9.19E-4	1.28E-3
Domestic Absorption	1.70E-4	1.82E-4	2.18E-4	3.12E-4	4.62E-4	5.44E-4	5.79E-4	6.48E-4	7.60E-4	8.74E-4	1.18E-3
Agriculture	1.40E-4	1.49E-4	1.73E-4	2.53E-4	4.26E-4	4.37E-4	4.67E-4	5.31E-4	5.81E-4	6.58E-4	8.99E-4
Industry	1.32E-4	1.28E-4	1.74E-4	2.52E-4	4.35E-4	3.97E-4	4.46E-4	5.06E-4	6.00E-4	7.44E-4	1.12E-3
Manufacturing	1.55E-4	1.64E-4	1.86E-4	2.67E-4	3.81E-4	4.11E-4	4.50E-4	4.88E-4	5.35E-4	6.88E-4	1.04E-3
Consumer Price Index	2.28E-4	2.36E-4	2.51E-4	3.31E-4	5.38E-4	5.81E-4	6.07E-4	6.56E-4	7.24E-4	8.67E-4	1.28E-3

MANUFACTURING ACTIVITY

	1970	1971	1972	1973	1974	1975	1976	1977	1978	1979	1980
Employment (1987=100)	48.5	46.0	48.5	56.7	69.4	72.3	69.3	68.5	61.9	65.3	70.0
Real Earnings per Empl. (1987=100)	209.5	232.3	246.4	231.1	193.3	196.4	216.9	230.9	237.6	240.6	201.7
Real Output per Empl. (1987=100)	185.7	210.4	215.4	201.0	188.6	187.6	212.4	243.5	323.2	281.6	285.4
Earnings as % of Value Added	43.4	43.3	42.1	40.2	42.2	41.8	39.4	38.6	32.6	34.2	29.7

MONETARY HOLDINGS

(Thousands of current Bolivianos)

	1970	1971	1972	1973	1974	1975	1976	1977	1978	1979	1980
Money Supply, Broadly Defined	2.00	2.00	3.00	4.00	5.00	7.00	10.00	13.00	14.00	17.00	23.00
Money	2.00	2.00	2.00	3.00	4.00	5.00	6.00	8.00	9.00	10.00	15.00
Currency Outside Banks	1.00	1.00	2.00	2.00	3.00	3.00	4.00	5.00	6.00	7.00	9.00
Demand Deposits	0.38	0.48	0.61	0.90	2.00	2.00	3.00	3.00	3.00	3.00	5.00
Quasi-Money	0.38	0.49	0.63	0.81	1.00	2.00	3.00	5.00	6.00	6.00	8.00

GOVERNMENT DEFICIT (-) OR SURPLUS

(Thousands of current Bolivianos)

	1970	1971	1972	1973	1974	1975	1976	1977	1978	1979	1980
Current Revenue	..	..	..	..	..	..	..	..	..	..	..
Current Expenditure	..	..	..	..	..	..	..	..	..	..	..
Current Budget Balance	..	..	..	..	..	..	..	..	..	..	..
Capital Receipts	..	..	..	..	..	..	..	..	..	..	..
Capital Payments	..	..	..	..	..	..	..	..	..	..	..

1981	1982	1983	1984	1985	1986	1987	1988	1989	1990 estimate	Notes	BOLIVIA
560	530	490	460	430	450	530	620	640	630	A	**CURRENT GNP PER CAPITA (US $)**
5,728	5,878	6,031	6,185	6,342	6,501	6,663	6,828	6,997	7,171	..	**POPULATION (thousands)**
											USE AND ORIGIN OF RESOURCES
				(Millions of current Bolivianos)							
1.60E-1	3.45E-1	1.30E+0	1.87E+1	2,061.2	6,870.4	8,324.1	9,773.7	11,434.4	13,453.1	..	Gross National Product (GNP)
-9.88E-3	-2.98E-2	-9.85E-2	-1.30E+0	-191.3	-591.9	-531.8	-621.0	-671.0	-771.1	..	Net Factor Income from Abroad
1.70E-1	3.75E-1	1.40E+0	2.00E+1	2,252.4	7,462.2	8,855.9	10,394.7	12,105.4	14,224.2	..	GDP at Market Prices
-3.63E-3	1.50E-2	3.83E-2	6.35E-1	-38.2	-213.6	-550.5	-567.9	-445.8	-434.3	..	Resource Balance
2.50E-2	6.06E-2	1.96E-1	2.40E+0	321.9	1,349.9	1,341.3	1,581.7	2,337.7	3,039.9	..	Exports of Goods & NF Services
2.86E-2	4.56E-2	1.58E-1	1.80E+0	360.1	1,563.5	1,891.8	2,149.6	2,783.5	3,474.2	..	Imports of Goods & NF Services
1.74E-1	3.60E-1	1.30E+0	1.93E+1	2,290.6	7,675.9	9,406.5	10,962.6	12,551.2	14,658.5	..	Domestic Absorption
1.32E-1	2.47E-1	9.56E-1	1.32E+1	1,761.5	6,233.3	7,366.2	8,214.1	9,459.7	10,968.7	..	Private Consumption, etc.
1.85E-2	6.15E-2	2.46E-1	4.70E+0	300.4	855.5	1,060.4	1,493.0	1,725.6	2,066.8	..	General Gov't Consumption
2.36E-2	5.18E-2	1.18E-1	1.40E+0	228.7	587.1	979.9	1,255.5	1,365.9	1,623.0	..	Gross Domestic Investment
1.87E-2	5.18E-2	1.17E-1	1.70E+0	162.8	705.5	911.0	1,271.9	1,463.9	1,693.1		Fixed Investment
..	..	..	..	..	..	..	..	..	..		Indirect Taxes, net
..	..	..	..	..	..	..	..	..	..	B	GDP at factor cost
2.85E-2	7.84E-2	3.70E-1	7.00E+0	832.1	2,453.5	2,817.9	3,390.3	2,663.2	3,393.1	..	Agriculture
5.21E-2	1.44E-1	4.12E-1	6.10E+0	817.0	2,385.5	2,689.5	3,367.6	3,837.4	4,553.9	..	Industry
2.45E-2	3.35E-2	1.41E-1	2.10E+0	343.6	1,188.5	1,352.6	1,666.8	1,575.9	1,805.3	..	Manufacturing
8.97E-2	1.53E-1	5.75E-1	6.80E+0	603.3	2,623.3	3,348.6	3,636.8	5,604.8	6,277.2	..	Services, etc.
2.00E-2	6.68E-2	1.56E-1	2.10E+0	190.5	373.5	429.4	687.6	920.1	1,188.7	..	Gross Domestic Saving
1.05E-2	3.81E-2	6.69E-2	8.64E-1	8.0	-182.8	-65.5	96.4	304.5	486.1	..	Gross National Saving
				(Millions of 1987 Bolivianos)							
9,140	8,520	8,190	8,320	8,090	7,950	8,320	8,660	8,950	9,240	..	Gross National Product
9,730	9,300	8,890	8,980	8,910	8,630	8,860	9,190	9,450	9,740	..	GDP at Market Prices
-1,050	-144	-214	-4	-604	-372	-551	-266	-75	114	..	Resource Balance
1,280	1,300	1,300	1,260	1,180	1,380	1,340	1,420	1,760	1,980	..	Exports of Goods & NF Services
2,320	1,450	1,520	1,260	1,790	1,750	1,890	1,690	1,840	1,860	..	Imports of Goods & NF Services
10,800	9,450	9,100	8,980	9,520	9,000	9,410	9,460	9,530	9,630	..	Domestic Absorption
6,800	5,840	6,470	6,720	7,580	7,320	7,370	7,150	7,310	7,360	..	Private Consumption, etc.
1,230	1,540	1,420	1,320	947	1,020	1,060	1,280	1,260	1,320	..	General Gov't Consumption
2,740	2,060	1,220	939	994	661	980	1,030	948	947	..	Gross Domestic Investment
2,190	2,080	1,220	1,040	772	820	911	1,050	1,090	1,030	..	Fixed Investment
..	..	..	..	..	..	..	..	..	..	B	GDP at factor cost
2,490	2,660	2,200	2,620	2,820	2,720	2,820	2,890	2,840	2,890	..	Agriculture
3,730	3,460	3,340	3,140	2,870	2,650	2,690	3,020	3,290	3,520	..	Industry
1,590	1,400	1,400	1,410	1,290	1,320	1,350	1,430	1,480	1,520	..	Manufacturing
3,570	3,340	3,350	3,210	3,220	3,260	3,350	3,290	3,320	3,330	..	Services, etc.
											Memo Items:
2,030	1,920	1,880	1,720	1,600	1,510	1,340	1,240	1,540	1,630	..	Capacity to Import
751	620	582	456	414	133	0	-180	-219	-347	..	Terms of Trade Adjustment
10,500	9,920	9,470	9,430	9,330	8,760	8,860	9,010	9,230	9,390	..	Gross Domestic Income
9,890	9,140	8,780	8,780	8,500	8,080	8,320	8,480	8,730	8,890	..	Gross National Income
											DOMESTIC PRICES/DEFLATORS
				(Index 1987 = 100)							
1.75E-3	4.03E-3	1.53E-2	0.2	25.3	86.5	100.0	113.1	128.1	146.0	..	Overall (GDP)
1.61E-3	3.81E-3	1.45E-2	0.2	24.1	85.3	100.0	115.9	131.8	152.3	..	Domestic Absorption
1.15E-3	2.95E-3	1.68E-2	0.3	29.5	90.1	100.0	117.5	93.6	117.4	..	Agriculture
1.40E-3	4.16E-3	1.23E-2	0.2	28.5	90.0	100.0	111.6	116.8	129.5	..	Industry
1.54E-3	2.40E-3	1.01E-2	0.1	26.5	90.1	100.0	116.9	106.8	119.1	..	Manufacturing
1.69E-3	3.77E-3	1.42E-2	0.2	23.2	87.3	100.0	116.0	133.6	156.5	..	Consumer Price Index
											MANUFACTURING ACTIVITY
70.2	79.1	82.0	89.2	94.0	99.5	100.0	106.1	..	..	G	Employment (1987=100)
196.7	134.2	184.2	231.8	127.9	82.9	100.0	92.2	..	..	G	Real Earnings per Empl. (1987=100)
224.8	258.0	218.1	226.5	118.6	92.0	100.0	97.5	..	..	G	Real Output per Empl. (1987=100)
27.3	25.9	32.3	37.8	26.1	23.8	27.5	25.8	..	..	..	Earnings as % of Value Added
											MONETARY HOLDINGS
				(Thousands of current Bolivianos)							
29.0	97.0	265.0	4,053.0	287,000	817,000	1,180,000	1,680,000	..	..	..	Money Supply, Broadly Defined
18.0	58.0	178.0	3,370.0	..	..	..	..	..	..	..	Money
11.0	39.0	125.0	2,888.0	..	..	..	..	..	..	..	Currency Outside Banks
7.0	19.0	53.0	482.0	..	..	..	..	..	..	..	Demand Deposits
12.0	39.0	88.0	684.0	..	..	..	..	..	..	..	Quasi-Money
				(Thousands of current Bolivianos)							
..	-100	-200	-6,200	-1,030,000	-5,500	66,700	-79,300	-184,000	-262,000	C F	**GOVERNMENT DEFICIT (-) OR SURPLUS**
..	..	..	700	233,000	1,010,000	1,180,000	1,440,000	1,750,000	2,270,000	..	Current Revenue
..	100	200	6,800	1,240,000	911,000	1,080,000	1,250,000	1,650,000	2,150,000	..	Current Expenditure
..	-100	-200	-6,100	-1,010,000	103,000	92,500	185,000	96,000	124,000	..	Current Budget Balance
..	..	..	..	..	..	..	3,100	..	1,000	..	Capital Receipts
..	0	0	100	19,100	108,000	25,800	268,000	280,000	388,000	..	Capital Payments

BOLIVIA	1970	1971	1972	1973	1974	1975	1976	1977	1978	1979	1980
FOREIGN TRADE (CUSTOMS BASIS)					*(Millions of current US dollars)*						
Value of Exports, fob	225.42	215.89	240.36	314.55	647.83	530.10	637.11	747.94	720.92	811.28	1,036.16
Nonfuel Primary Products	208.25	186.38	195.86	247.12	440.07	356.85	453.38	568.99	586.25	661.25	760.47
Fuels	10.21	23.88	41.58	58.57	193.22	153.98	167.52	138.87	122.18	113.11	245.13
Manufactures	6.95	5.64	2.92	8.86	14.54	19.27	16.21	40.08	12.50	36.91	30.56
Value of Imports, cif	159.15	169.63	178.61	230.20	366.20	573.99	593.45	586.28	769.48	841.54	654.56
Nonfuel Primary Products	35.40	39.92	41.61	55.52	88.32	109.26	98.11	92.72	119.45	131.45	141.56
Fuels	1.97	2.12	1.59	2.40	3.81	12.56	10.70	8.46	10.89	7.08	3.58
Manufactures	121.78	127.58	135.41	172.29	274.07	452.17	484.65	485.10	639.15	703.02	509.43
					(Index 1987 = 100)						
Terms of Trade	136.5	106.8	93.4	106.4	170.7	138.5	152.9	172.2	163.9	183.8	197.7
Export Prices, fob	40.6	33.8	32.6	46.5	96.7	81.9	89.6	109.1	118.3	153.0	180.5
Import Prices, cif	29.7	31.6	34.9	43.7	56.6	59.1	58.6	63.4	72.2	83.2	91.3
BALANCE OF PAYMENTS					*(Millions of current US dollars)*						
Exports of Goods & Services	207.1	202.3	223.0	294.1	597.7	494.6	636.2	700.7	706.0	873.4	1,045.7
Merchandise, fob	190.4	181.6	201.3	260.8	556.5	444.7	563.0	634.3	627.3	759.8	942.2
Nonfactor Services	14.2	16.1	21.2	26.1	36.9	40.9	60.4	60.8	76.2	105.2	87.9
Factor Services	2.5	4.5	0.5	7.2	4.3	9.0	12.8	5.6	2.5	8.4	15.6
Imports of Goods & Services	206.8	211.8	240.1	297.0	474.3	667.5	706.9	833.6	1,064.5	1,321.6	1,111.6
Merchandise, fob	135.2	144.3	153.2	193.2	324.1	469.9	512.3	579.0	723.9	738.4	574.4
Nonfactor Services	43.7	45.5	64.1	71.3	118.2	147.8	145.7	180.0	221.8	390.7	256.5
Factor Services	27.9	22.0	22.8	32.4	32.0	49.9	48.9	74.6	118.8	192.5	280.7
Long-Term Interest	7.2	8.2	12.5	17.0	18.5	25.5	39.4	60.6	89.5	129.2	173.2
Private Current Transfers, net	1.5	2.1	4.9	4.9	3.0	3.4	3.2	2.3	5.5	10.5	12.7
Workers' Remittances	..	..	..	..	..	..	..	..	..	..	0.0
Curr. A/C Bal before Off. Transf.	1.8	-7.4	-12.2	2.0	126.4	-139.9	-64.3	-130.6	-353.0	-437.7	-53.2
Net Official Transfers	2.4	5.0	8.6	10.5	10.6	9.7	10.8	12.7	21.5	40.7	46.8
Curr. A/C Bal after Off. Transf.	4.2	-2.4	-3.6	12.5	137.0	-130.2	-53.5	-117.9	-331.5	-397.0	-6.4
Long-Term Capital, net	33.2	55.9	92.8	37.0	100.1	158.9	215.2	325.1	273.4	249.0	276.8
Direct Investment	-75.9	1.9	-10.5	4.6	25.9	53.4	-8.1	-1.2	11.5	35.0	46.5
Long-Term Loans	38.8	47.6	95.9	7.8	73.4	116.1	247.5	345.3	284.1	222.6	311.5
Disbursements	57.7	66.9	126.9	41.1	127.1	170.3	321.5	451.1	562.8	384.3	456.8
Repayments	18.9	19.3	31.0	33.3	53.7	54.2	74.0	105.8	278.7	161.7	145.3
Other Long-Term Capital	70.3	6.4	7.5	24.5	0.8	-10.6	-24.2	-19.0	-22.2	-8.6	-81.2
Other Capital, net	-38.4	-54.7	-88.0	-52.7	-113.2	-68.8	-105.9	-145.3	-13.2	106.5	-422.6
Change in Reserves	1.0	1.3	-1.3	3.2	-123.8	40.0	-55.8	-61.9	71.3	41.5	152.2
Memo Item:					*(Bolivianos per US dollar)*						
Conversion Factor (Annual Avg)	1.19E-5	1.19E-5	1.33E-5	2.00E-5	2.00E-5	2.00E-5	2.00E-5	2.00E-5	2.00E-5	2.04E-5	2.45E-5
Additional Conversion Factor	1.19E-5	1.19E-5	1.33E-5	2.00E-5	2.60E-5	2.00E-5	2.80E-5	2.90E-5	3.20E-5	3.30E-5	4.00E-5
EXTERNAL DEBT (Total)				*(Millions of US dollars), outstanding at end of year*							
	497.3	547.2	644.9	674.2	747.9	856.5	1,090.3	1,733.3	2,161.9	2,550.6	2,699.9
Long-Term Debt (by debtor)	497.3	547.2	644.9	674.2	747.9	856.5	1,090.3	1,448.3	1,797.9	2,022.6	2,399.9
Central Bank, incl. IMF credit	8.7	12.8	24.2	42.9	46.0	50.4	40.0	52.8	133.9	159.1	266.6
Central Government	302.9	312.0	356.3	371.4	418.4	459.5	587.9	735.0	812.0	907.0	1,178.1
Rest of General Government	0.1	0.7	2.5	4.1	3.3	2.1	2.5	23.2	47.4	53.1	55.6
Non-financial Public Enterprises	133.2	180.6	216.6	212.0	230.8	267.2	360.7	520.5	611.1	680.9	686.3
Priv. Sector, incl non-guaranteed	52.4	41.1	45.3	43.8	49.4	77.3	99.2	116.8	193.5	222.5	213.3
Short-Term Debt	0.0	0.0	0.0	0.0	0.0	0.0	0.0	285.0	364.0	528.0	300.0
Memo Items:					*(Millions of US dollars)*						
Int'l Reserves Excluding Gold	33.00	40.00	44.00	55.00	176.00	140.00	151.00	211.00	170.00	178.00	106.00
Gold Holdings (at market price)	14.00	17.00	26.00	46.00	76.00	57.00	56.00	99.00	146.00	350.00	447.00
SOCIAL INDICATORS											
Total Fertility Rate	6.5	6.5	6.5	6.4	6.4	6.3	6.2	6.1	6.0	5.9	5.8
Infant Mortality Rate	153.4	152.2	151.0	147.0	143.0	139.0	135.0	131.0	126.6	122.2	117.8
Life Expectancy at Birth	46.1	46.4	46.7	47.6	48.4	49.3	50.1	51.0	52.0	53.1	54.1
Urban Population, % of total	40.8	40.9	41.1	41.2	41.4	41.5	42.1	42.6	43.2	43.7	44.3
Food Prod. per capita (1987=100)	88.6	88.1	93.8	96.3	97.5	101.6	102.7	97.5	95.0	93.8	94.4
Labor Force, Agriculture (%)	52.1	51.5	50.9	50.3	49.8	49.2	48.6	48.0	47.5	46.9	46.4
Labor Force, Female (%)	21.5	21.6	21.7	21.8	21.9	22.0	22.1	22.2	22.3	22.4	22.5
Primary Schl. Enroll. Ratio	76.0	..	..	..	..	85.0	89.0	89.0	..	..	84.0
Primary Schl. Enroll. Ratio, Female	62.0	..	..	..	..	76.0	76.0	..	..	..	78.0
Secondary Schl. Enroll. Ratio	24.0	..	..	..	..	31.0	30.0	32.0	..	..	36.0

1981	1982	1983	1984	1985	1986	1987	1988	1989	1990 estimate	Notes	BOLIVIA
											FOREIGN TRADE (CUSTOMS BASIS)
983.43	895.52	817.59	781.36	672.77	636.32	569.79	597.46	819.19	922.92	..	Value of Exports, fob
609.82	473.12	390.48	389.17	295.49	285.56	297.28	359.55	578.59	651.85	..	Nonfuel Primary Products
336.06	398.43	420.07	389.01	374.45	332.59	256.06	218.93	201.24	226.72	..	Fuels
37.54	23.97	7.04	3.19	2.82	18.16	16.45	18.98	39.37	44.35	..	Manufactures
904.03	485.84	531.24	416.56	690.87	674.03	766.29	590.50	619.94	715.70	..	Value of Imports, cif
154.60	104.09	122.55	84.07	143.93	105.38	156.52	79.01	82.95	95.76	..	Nonfuel Primary Products
15.70	9.10	5.01	2.16	3.31	3.22	3.34	5.53	5.80	6.70	..	Fuels
733.73	372.65	403.68	330.32	543.63	565.43	606.43	505.96	531.19	613.24	..	Manufactures

(Millions of current US dollars) — heading above Value of Exports

(Index 1987 = 100)

1981	1982	1983	1984	1985	1986	1987	1988	1989	1990	Notes	BOLIVIA
187.0	178.5	175.7	174.7	167.0	121.5	100.0	112.8	116.8	97.3	..	Terms of Trade
171.0	157.4	153.1	150.6	144.1	116.0	100.0	121.4	132.1	120.8	..	Export Prices, fob
91.4	88.2	87.2	86.2	86.3	95.5	100.0	107.7	113.0	124.1	..	Import Prices, cif

(Millions of current US dollars) — **BALANCE OF PAYMENTS**

1981	1982	1983	1984	1985	1986	1987	1988	1989	1990	Notes	BOLIVIA
1,021.6	918.4	899.0	848.0	737.4	684.2	666.4	689.0	890.7	995.5	f	Exports of Goods & Services
912.4	827.7	755.1	724.5	623.4	545.5	518.7	542.5	723.5	830.8	..	Merchandise, fob
93.0	82.3	103.0	93.5	96.5	121.1	131.5	128.3	143.3	145.9	..	Nonfactor Services
16.2	8.4	40.9	30.0	17.5	17.6	16.2	18.2	23.9	18.8	..	Factor Services
1,525.9	1,136.8	1,143.3	1,110.7	1,099.3	1,168.4	1,210.4	1,128.7	1,310.7	1,356.3	f	Imports of Goods & Services
827.7	496.0	496.0	412.3	462.8	596.5	646.3	590.9	729.5	775.6	..	Merchandise, fob
316.8	218.7	241.6	250.5	243.6	243.7	266.4	251.2	295.0	306.7	..	Nonfactor Services
381.4	422.1	405.7	447.9	392.9	328.2	297.7	286.6	286.2	274.0	..	Factor Services
179.7	190.8	205.3	213.4	157.2	98.5	76.7	96.6	93.3	130.5	..	Long-Term Interest
13.3	16.7	40.2	21.8	19.7	18.5	18.0	12.7	20.6	21.6	..	Private Current Transfers, net
0.5	0.5	0.5	0.5	0.3	0.5	0.6	0.8	0.8	2.0	..	Workers' Remittances
-491.0	-201.7	-204.1	-240.9	-342.2	-465.7	-526.0	-427.0	-399.4	-339.2	..	Curr. A/C Bal before Off. Transf.
26.2	28.8	66.0	66.7	60.3	81.7	103.3	171.6	135.7	145.0	..	Net Official Transfers
-464.8	-172.9	-138.1	-174.2	-281.9	-384.0	-422.7	-255.4	-263.7	-194.2	..	Curr. A/C Bal after Off. Transf.
459.0	25.9	288.2	-144.2	-229.8	-54.0	23.2	266.2	228.0	264.9	f	Long-Term Capital, net
75.6	31.0	6.9	7.0	10.0	10.0	36.4	-12.0	-25.4	43.9	..	Direct Investment
251.4	185.0	45.4	60.3	-37.3	224.9	169.0	172.0	243.1	101.8	..	Long-Term Loans
379.6	309.0	152.2	210.6	137.1	328.5	256.7	330.8	381.6	293.7	..	Disbursements
128.2	124.0	106.8	150.3	174.4	103.6	87.7	158.8	138.5	191.9	..	Repayments
132.0	-190.1	235.9	-211.5	-202.5	-288.9	-182.2	106.2	10.3	119.2	..	Other Long-Term Capital
-191.4	32.6	121.3	471.9	534.9	603.4	385.5	-39.7	-140.6	49.9	f	Other Capital, net
197.2	114.5	-271.4	-153.5	-23.2	-165.5	14.0	28.9	176.3	-120.6	..	Change in Reserves

(Bolivianos per US dollar) — **Memo Item:**

1981	1982	1983	1984	1985	1986	1987	1988	1989	1990	Notes	BOLIVIA
2.45E-5	6.41E-5	2.32E-4	0.003	0.440	1.920	2.050	2.350	2.690	3.170	..	Conversion Factor (Annual Avg)
4.70E-5	1.19E-4	4.68E-4	0.007	0.758	1.920	2.050	2.350	2.690	3.170	..	Additional Conversion Factor

(Millions of US dollars), outstanding at end of year

1981	1982	1983	1984	1985	1986	1987	1988	1989	1990	Notes	BOLIVIA
3,218.6	3,328.5	4,069.3	4,317.0	4,804.6	5,574.9	5,835.7	4,901.5	4,135.5	4,276.1	..	**EXTERNAL DEBT (Total)**
2,915.8	3,092.1	3,758.0	3,808.0	4,148.5	4,817.6	5,006.5	4,548.9	3,880.6	4,116.8	..	Long-Term Debt (by debtor)
269.2	273.4	280.1	281.7	257.0	443.3	378.5	349.2	349.2	330.3	..	Central Bank, incl. IMF credit
1,741.9	1,882.0	2,407.0	2,539.7	2,661.4	3,146.0	3,722.6	3,446.6	2,790.4	3,042.0	..	Central Government
58.9	59.5	61.0	61.3	61.5	48.5	48.3	35.3	34.7	30.9	..	Rest of General Government
660.0	653.3	552.4	508.2	535.3	556.0	591.4	466.8	454.7	486.8	..	Non-financial Public Enterprises
185.8	223.9	457.5	417.1	633.3	623.8	265.7	250.9	251.6	226.8	..	Priv. Sector, incl non-guaranteed
302.8	236.4	311.3	509.0	656.1	757.3	829.2	352.6	254.9	159.3	..	Short-Term Debt

(Millions of US dollars) — **Memo Items:**

1981	1982	1983	1984	1985	1986	1987	1988	1989	1990	Notes	BOLIVIA
100.00	156.00	160.00	252.00	200.00	164.00	97.00	106.00	205.00	167.00	..	Int'l Reserves Excluding Gold
329.00	407.00	349.00	281.00	292.00	350.00	433.00	367.00	358.00	344.00	..	Gold Holdings (at market price)

SOCIAL INDICATORS

1981	1982	1983	1984	1985	1986	1987	1988	1989	1990	Notes	BOLIVIA
5.6	5.5	5.4	5.3	5.2	5.1	5.0	4.9	4.9	4.8	..	Total Fertility Rate
113.4	109.0	106.8	104.6	102.5	100.3	98.1	96.0	94.0	91.9	..	Infant Mortality Rate
55.2	56.2	56.8	57.3	57.8	58.3	58.8	59.2	59.6	60.0	..	Life Expectancy at Birth
45.0	45.7	46.3	47.0	47.7	48.4	49.1	49.8	50.5	51.2	..	Urban Population, % of total
97.4	99.1	81.7	95.7	101.5	96.8	100.0	102.5	99.4	108.7	..	Food Prod. per capita (1987=100)
								..	..	..	Labor Force, Agriculture (%)
22.9	23.2	23.5	23.9	24.2	24.5	24.9	25.2	25.5	25.8	..	Labor Force, Female (%)
86.0	85.0	87.0	91.0	..	87.0	91.0	81.0	81.0	..	..	Primary Schl. Enroll. Ratio
78.0	..	81.0	85.0	..	82.0	85.0	..	77.0	..	..	Primary Schl. Enroll. Ratio, Female
34.0	35.0	35.0	37.0	..	37.0	37.0	34.0	34.0	..	..	Secondary Schl. Enroll. Ratio

BOTSWANA	1970	1971	1972	1973	1974	1975	1976	1977	1978	1979	1980
CURRENT GNP PER CAPITA (US $)	130	150	190	240	340	350	420	430	490	600	780
POPULATION (thousands)	624	647	673	699	727	755	783	811	840	870	902

USE AND ORIGIN OF RESOURCES *(Millions of current Botswana Pula)*

	1970	1971	1972	1973	1974	1975	1976	1977	1978	1979	1980
Gross National Product (GNP)	58.6	71.9	88.3	129.5	180.3	188.1	248.0	290.7	328.4	470.3	655.0
Net Factor Income from Abroad	-1.3	-6.1	-15.3	-21.1	-8.0	-24.9	-25.9	-24.4	-31.9	-45.8	-54.5
GDP at Market Prices	59.9	78.0	103.6	150.6	188.3	213.0	273.9	315.1	360.3	516.1	709.5
Resource Balance	-24.3	-25.7	-25.9	-33.0	-45.4	-53.8	-52.3	-53.5	-98.1	-81.0	-88.4
Exports of Goods & NFServices	13.6	20.4	39.8	55.2	76.4	93.8	135.2	155.5	161.1	275.9	357.8
Imports of Goods & NFServices	37.9	46.1	65.7	88.2	121.8	147.6	187.5	209.0	259.2	356.9	446.2
Domestic Absorption	84.2	103.7	129.5	183.6	233.7	266.8	326.2	368.6	458.4	597.1	797.9
Private Consumption, etc.	46.7	52.2	59.1	89.9	104.6	123.6	156.5	194.2	224.6	295.2	366.3
General Gov't Consumption	12.2	14.3	16.0	18.6	31.7	41.5	54.7	75.7	91.3	104.3	140.7
Gross Domestic Investment	25.3	37.2	54.4	75.1	97.4	101.7	115.0	98.7	142.5	197.6	290.9
Fixed Investment	17.3	30.3	54.5	64.3	79.6	57.3	79.1	77.8	110.1	162.9	248.8
Indirect Taxes, net	4.0	5.6	11.2	12.0	14.2	18.1	22.9	29.2	40.9	61.6	102.0
GDP at factor cost	55.9	72.4	92.4	138.6	174.1	194.9	251.0	285.9	319.4	454.5	607.5
Agriculture	19.8	25.7	34.2	49.7	62.4	61.2	65.7	74.4	71.7	81.7	83.3
Industry	16.5	21.5	28.6	41.6	49.5	60.5	84.4	91.8	107.3	193.1	291.3
Manufacturing	3.5	4.6	6.1	8.9	10.1	15.5	20.9	25.3	24.4	42.8	29.2
Services, etc.	23.6	30.8	40.8	59.3	76.4	91.3	123.8	148.9	181.3	241.3	334.9
Gross Domestic Saving	1.0	11.5	28.5	42.1	52.0	47.9	62.7	45.2	44.4	116.6	202.5
Gross National Saving	0.4	8.3	20.9	34.2	72.5	17.5	41.6	26.0	17.8	72.5	146.9

(Millions of 1987 Botswana Pula)

	1970	1971	1972	1973	1974	1975	1976	1977	1978	1979	1980
Gross National Product	305.6	343.5	427.5	520.9	703.1	640.6	758.9	790.6	935.7	1,035.8	1,204.6
GDP at Market Prices	320.2	380.1	502.7	612.7	734.9	725.3	834.3	852.9	1,011.2	1,132.1	1,305.8
Resource Balance	-247.7	-213.2	-176.7	-239.8	-240.4	-240.6	-169.7	-136.5	-124.4	-195.1	-250.4
Exports of Goods & NFServices	100.7	150.9	275.3	313.3	378.2	388.8	522.5	530.1	633.6	740.1	716.3
Imports of Goods & NFServices	348.4	364.2	451.9	553.1	618.5	629.4	692.2	666.6	758.0	935.3	966.7
Domestic Absorption	567.9	593.3	679.4	852.5	975.3	965.9	1,004.0	989.4	1,135.6	1,327.2	1,556.2
Private Consumption, etc.	385.9	367.0	392.1	518.2	562.7	583.3	606.4	610.3	678.1	832.8	943.7
General Gov't Consumption	74.3	78.8	88.1	85.8	159.2	160.2	183.4	220.5	240.1	228.6	269.6
Gross Domestic Investment	107.6	147.6	199.2	248.5	253.3	222.4	214.2	158.5	217.3	265.8	342.9
Fixed Investment	..	..	..	..	395.0	243.0	277.1	233.5	313.2	404.5	537.3
GDP at factor cost	..	..	..	..			..				
Agriculture	78.3	92.5	122.5	149.2	207.1	184.0	186.5	194.7	182.1	181.7	174.8
Industry	106.9	121.6	160.8	196.2	231.5	236.0	293.0	282.3	422.4	446.8	512.0
Manufacturing	25.7	30.9	40.7	50.2	56.7	79.8	102.3	112.7	105.5	142.0	95.1
Services, etc.	144.7	177.2	234.2	285.6	321.1	327.2	375.9	399.3	422.7	521.5	636.7

Memo Items:

	1970	1971	1972	1973	1974	1975	1976	1977	1978	1979	1980
Capacity to Import	125.0	161.2	273.8	346.2	388.0	400.0	499.1	496.0	471.1	723.0	775.2
Terms of Trade Adjustment	24.3	10.2	-1.5	32.8	9.8	11.2	-23.4	-34.1	-162.5	-17.1	58.9
Gross Domestic Income	344.5	390.3	501.2	645.5	744.7	736.5	810.9	818.7	848.7	1,114.9	1,364.7
Gross National Income	329.9	353.8	426.0	553.8	712.9	651.8	735.5	756.5	773.3	1,018.7	1,263.5

DOMESTIC PRICES/DEFLATORS *(Index 1987 = 100)*

	1970	1971	1972	1973	1974	1975	1976	1977	1978	1979	1980
Overall (GDP)	18.7	20.5	20.6	24.6	25.6	29.4	32.8	36.9	35.6	45.6	54.3
Domestic Absorption	14.8	17.5	19.1	21.5	24.0	27.6	32.5	37.3	40.4	45.0	51.3
Agriculture	25.3	27.8	27.9	33.3	30.1	33.3	35.2	38.2	39.4	45.0	47.7
Industry	15.4	17.7	17.8	21.2	21.4	25.6	28.8	32.5	25.4	43.2	56.9
Manufacturing	13.6	14.9	15.0	17.7	17.8	19.4	20.4	22.4	23.1	30.1	30.7
Consumer Price Index	..	..	..	..	25.2	28.2	31.5	35.6	38.9	43.4	49.3

MANUFACTURING ACTIVITY

	1970	1971	1972	1973	1974	1975	1976	1977	1978	1979	1980
Employment (1987=100)	..	15.7	18.0	19.4	22.4	26.2	29.1	28.2	30.3	37.3	37.3
Real Earnings per Empl. (1987=100)	..	..	..	..	..	..	..	..	..	..	..
Real Output per Empl. (1987=100)	..	..	..	..	..	..	..	..	..	..	..
Earnings as % of Value Added	..	..	27.6	..	39.6	51.6	20.6	37.1	50.4	29.7	49.2

MONETARY HOLDINGS *(Millions of current Botswana Pula)*

	1970	1971	1972	1973	1974	1975	1976	1977	1978	1979	1980
Money Supply, Broadly Defined	..	..	..	..	..	..	86.2	108.6	120.9	199.0	236.9
Money	..	..	..	..	..	..	43.5	58.2	60.9	82.1	90.6
Currency Outside Banks	..	..	..	..	..	..	10.4	12.4	15.8	17.9	24.4
Demand Deposits	..	..	..	..	..	..	33.1	45.8	45.2	64.2	66.2
Quasi-Money	..	..	..	..	..	..	42.7	50.4	60.0	116.9	146.3

(Millions of current Botswana Pula)

	1970	1971	1972	1973	1974	1975	1976	1977	1978	1979	1980
GOVERNMENT DEFICIT (-) OR SURPLUS	..	-11.2	-21.0	-14.1	-5.7	1.2	-20.8	-4.6	-6.9	21.4	-1.3
Current Revenue	..	19.2	28.9	45.6	65.9	89.3	84.0	115.1	160.1	242.3	299.9
Current Expenditure	..	18.1	20.2	26.0	36.0	46.8	63.5	75.8	100.0	137.0	178.6
Current Budget Balance	..	1.1	8.7	19.6	29.9	42.5	20.6	39.4	60.1	105.2	121.3
Capital Receipts	..	0.0					0.8	0.3	0.7	0.9	1.8
Capital Payments	..	12.3	29.7	33.7	35.6	41.2	42.1	44.3	67.7	84.8	124.4

1981	1982	1983	1984	1985	1986	1987	1988	1989	1990 estimate	Notes	BOTSWANA
1,040	1,020	1,070	1,080	960	970	1,030	1,200	1,610	2,040	..	**CURRENT GNP PER CAPITA (US $)**
933	966	1,000	1,035	1,070	1,106	1,142	1,179	1,217	1,254	..	**POPULATION (thousands)**
			(Millions of current Botswana Pula)								**USE AND ORIGIN OF RESOURCES**
771.1	781.8	996.3	1,171.3	1,432.5	1,957.0	2,316.8	2,881.6	4,409.7	4,830.0	C	Gross National Product (GNP)
-19.1	-11.1	-53.4	-130.8	-228.2	-278.1	-330.7	-516.3	-578.2	-396.0	..	Net Factor Income from Abroad
790.2	792.9	1,049.7	1,302.1	1,660.7	2,235.1	2,647.5	3,397.9	4,987.9	5,226.0	C f	GDP at Market Prices
-167.7	-288.5	-131.5	-7.8	-27.9	463.5	733.8	865.1	654.5	..	..	Resource Balance
398.0	349.9	618.3	772.3	970.3	1,591.6	2,132.9	2,674.9	3,173.5	..	..	Exports of Goods & NFServices
565.7	638.4	749.8	780.1	998.2	1,128.1	1,399.1	1,809.8	2,519.0			Imports of Goods & NFServices
957.9	1,081.4	1,181.2	1,309.9	1,688.6	1,771.6	1,913.7	2,532.8	4,333.4			Domestic Absorption
409.8	488.4	571.2	629.3	746.3	840.1	1,115.7	1,412.3	2,159.7	..	..	Private Consumption, etc.
203.2	242.6	301.9	362.8	443.1	531.8	630.4	770.7	979.8	..	..	General Gov't Consumption
344.9	350.4	308.1	317.8	499.2	399.7	167.6	349.8	1,193.9	..	..	Gross Domestic Investment
306.6	304.6	320.3	337.6	484.0	411.9	550.5	743.0	1,114.5	..	..	Fixed Investment
120.6	118.8	131.9	165.4	155.0	..	..	..	..			Indirect Taxes, net
669.6	674.1	917.8	1,136.7	1,505.7	2,037.4	..	..	..	..	B C f	GDP at factor cost
90.5	87.8	77.2	76.1	82.9	94.0	107.0	136.2	149.1	..		Agriculture
310.6	270.7	440.4	590.7	814.2	1,183.3	1,251.6	1,645.3	2,851.5	..		Industry
49.3	71.2	78.7	82.0	88.0	125.9	161.9	166.8	309.4	..		Manufacturing
389.1	434.4	532.1	635.3	763.6	957.8	1,288.9	1,616.4	1,987.3	..		Services, etc.
177.2	61.9	176.6	310.0	471.3	863.2	901.4	1,214.9	1,848.4	..		Gross Domestic Saving
156.7	50.6	122.8	169.7	237.1	580.2	582.1	666.6	1,208.5	..		Gross National Saving
			(Millions of 1987 Botswana Pula)								
1,371.1	1,369.4	1,650.8	1,894.1	1,950.2	2,119.5	2,316.8	2,414.5	2,827.1	3,283.0	C	Gross National Product
1,402.1	1,386.4	1,719.5	2,048.1	2,219.3	2,400.0	2,647.5	2,890.6	3,277.9	3,562.9	C	GDP at Market Prices
-192.5	-313.8	176.2	501.4	202.8	617.7	733.8	525.0	-193.5	..		Resource Balance
871.3	776.8	1,280.3	1,581.6	1,534.3	1,844.6	2,132.9	2,158.7	1,811.6	..		Exports of Goods & NFServices
1,063.7	1,090.6	1,104.0	1,080.2	1,331.5	1,226.9	1,399.1	1,633.7	2,005.1	..		Imports of Goods & NFServices
1,594.5	1,700.3	1,543.3	1,546.7	2,016.5	1,782.3	1,913.7	2,365.6	3,471.4	..		Domestic Absorption
932.0	991.3	895.1	857.6	1,113.7	916.8	1,115.7	1,380.9	2,078.8	..		Private Consumption, etc.
313.5	371.7	414.6	459.9	537.5	583.8	630.4	710.9	809.7	..		General Gov't Consumption
349.1	337.2	233.6	229.2	365.3	281.6	167.6	273.8	582.8	..		Gross Domestic Investment
571.7	534.3	457.2	453.7	647.0	489.4	550.5	650.7	848.1	..		Fixed Investment
..	..	..	..	..	..	..	..			B C	GDP at factor cost
157.4	150.6	126.1	106.8	98.2	111.6	107.0	125.3	125.3	..		Agriculture
606.4	564.7	840.0	1,118.0	1,151.4	1,195.7	1,251.6	1,308.2	1,514.7	..		Industry
120.5	149.2	138.1	143.3	116.6	147.9	161.9	170.0	179.5	..		Manufacturing
649.9	684.9	753.5	823.3	969.7	1,092.7	1,288.9	1,457.2	1,638.0	..		Services, etc.
											Memo Items:
748.4	597.7	910.4	1,069.4	1,294.3	1,730.9	2,132.9	2,414.7	2,526.0	..		Capacity to Import
-122.9	-179.0	-369.9	-512.2	-240.0	-113.7	0.0	255.9	714.4	..		Terms of Trade Adjustment
1,279.2	1,207.4	1,349.7	1,535.9	1,979.3	2,286.3	2,647.5	3,146.6	3,992.4	..		Gross Domestic Income
1,248.2	1,190.3	1,281.0	1,381.9	1,710.2	2,005.9	2,316.8	2,670.5	3,541.6	..		Gross National Income
			(Index 1987 = 100)								**DOMESTIC PRICES/DEFLATORS**
56.4	57.2	61.0	63.6	74.8	93.1	100.0	117.5	152.2	146.7	..	Overall (GDP)
60.1	63.6	76.5	84.7	83.7	99.4	100.0	107.1	124.8	..		Domestic Absorption
57.5	58.3	61.2	71.3	84.4	84.2	100.0	108.7	119.0	..		Agriculture
51.2	47.9	52.4	52.8	70.7	99.0	100.0	125.8	188.3	..		Industry
40.9	47.7	57.0	57.2	75.5	85.1	100.0	98.1	172.4	..		Manufacturing
57.5	63.9	70.5	76.6	82.8	91.1	100.0	108.4	120.9	134.7	..	Consumer Price Index
											MANUFACTURING ACTIVITY
44.9	56.1	66.0	66.0	68.0	83.0	100.0	111.6		..	G	Employment (1987=100)
..	..	..	..	..	..	..	..	..	..	G	Real Earnings per Empl. (1987=100)
..	..	..	..	..	..	..	..	..	..	G	Real Output per Empl. (1987=100)
46.5	35.6	37.2	41.1	39.3	35.9	..	..	..	..		Earnings as % of Value Added
			(Millions of current Botswana Pula)								**MONETARY HOLDINGS**
226.5	245.6	316.3	368.9	557.4	606.2	1,013.3	1,228.3	1,797.3	1,545.9	..	Money Supply, Broadly Defined
114.8	127.4	137.3	150.6	188.2	243.4	312.1	406.5	506.5	586.1	..	Money
29.6	29.0	30.2	35.2	43.4	58.5	68.6	95.8	117.6	143.7	..	Currency Outside Banks
85.1	98.4	107.2	115.4	144.8	184.9	243.6	310.7	388.9	442.4	..	Demand Deposits
111.7	118.2	178.9	218.3	369.2	362.7	701.2	821.9	1,290.8	959.8	..	Quasi-Money
			(Millions of current Botswana Pula)								
-18.3	-20.1	103.2	188.3	413.8	539.8	502.4	789.7	554.3	..	C	**GOVERNMENT DEFICIT (-) OR SURPLUS**
311.4	385.7	554.5	787.9	1,116.3	1,508.4	1,798.5	2,513.8	2,724.8	..	..	Current Revenue
211.9	270.1	316.1	416.3	497.6	727.5	962.5	1,358.7	1,379.6	..	..	Current Expenditure
99.5	115.6	238.4	371.6	618.8	780.9	836.0	1,155.1	1,345.2	..	..	Current Budget Balance
3.7	1.9	1.7	3.2	4.4	3.6	4.4	7.1	11.1	..	..	Capital Receipts
121.5	137.6	136.9	186.5	209.3	244.7	338.0	372.5	802.0	..	..	Capital Payments

	1970	1971	1972	1973	1974	1975	1976	1977	1978	1979	1980
FOREIGN TRADE (CUSTOMS BASIS)					*(Millions of current US dollars)*						
Value of Exports, fob	..	..	..	..	..	..	..	..	..	..	..
Nonfuel Primary Products	..	..	..	..	..	..	..	..	..	..	..
Fuels	..	..	..	..	..	..	..	..	..	..	..
Manufactures	..	..	..	..	..	..	..	..	..	..	..
Value of Imports, cif	..	..	..	..	..	..	..	..	..	..	..
Nonfuel Primary Products	..	..	..	..	..	..	..	..	..	..	..
Fuels	..	..	..	..	..	..	..	..	..	..	..
Manufactures	..	..	..	..	..	..	..	..	..	..	..
					(Index 1987 = 100)						
Terms of Trade	..	..	..	..	..	..	..	..	..	..	..
Export Prices, fob	..	..	..	..	..	..	..	..	..	..	..
Import Prices, cif	..	..	..	..	..	..	..	..	..	..	..
BALANCE OF PAYMENTS					*(Millions of current US dollars)*						
Exports of Goods & Services	58.0	85.0	102.0	157.0	159.0	219.9	275.9	311.3	332.8	575.6	747.5
Merchandise, fob	26.0	38.0	57.0	92.0	120.0	142.0	169.7	191.6	223.4	442.2	544.5
Nonfactor Services	31.0	46.0	43.0	63.0	36.0	30.8	46.8	51.4	50.5	61.1	100.9
Factor Services	1.0	1.0	2.0	2.0	3.0	47.1	59.3	68.3	58.9	72.3	102.2
Imports of Goods & Services	94.0	130.0	161.0	225.0	221.0	273.6	310.5	370.7	465.4	666.6	953.5
Merchandise, fob	57.0	78.0	98.0	137.0	165.0	181.2	180.2	226.4	295.0	442.1	602.5
Nonfactor Services	34.0	46.0	50.0	70.0	41.0	46.7	78.4	89.9	101.8	128.3	177.0
Factor Services	3.0	6.0	13.0	18.0	15.0	45.7	51.9	54.4	68.6	96.2	174.0
Long-Term Interest	0.4	0.6	1.2	2.2	3.0	3.4	3.2	3.5	4.6	5.8	6.7
Private Current Transfers, net	1.0	4.0	10.0	19.0	42.0	-7.4	5.5	6.2	6.4	2.1	-1.4
Workers' Remittances	..	..	..	..	..	..	..	..	..	..	..
Curr. A/C Bal before Off. Transf.	-35.0	-41.0	-49.0	-49.0	-20.0	-37.9	-29.1	-53.2	-126.2	-89.0	-207.4
Net Official Transfers	5.0	4.0	10.0	1.0	2.0	2.3	14.4	32.3	14.7	35.0	64.6
Curr. A/C Bal after Off. Transf.	-30.0	-37.0	-39.0	-48.0	-18.0	-35.6	-14.7	-20.9	-111.5	-54.0	-142.8
Long-Term Capital, net	15.0	92.0	156.0	142.0	124.0	50.2	19.8	-10.5	67.7	99.9	135.6
Direct Investment	6.0	38.0	60.0	53.0	46.0	-38.3	11.2	12.0	40.8	127.9	109.2
Long-Term Loans	5.5	15.4	44.9	41.4	18.2	21.0	24.8	13.4	7.7	12.1	21.2
Disbursements	5.7	15.7	45.3	41.7	18.5	24.7	25.9	15.8	11.3	15.6	27.2
Repayments	0.2	0.3	0.4	0.3	0.3	3.7	1.1	2.4	3.6	3.5	6.0
Other Long-Term Capital	3.5	38.6	51.1	47.6	59.8	67.4	-16.2	-35.8	19.2	-40.1	5.2
Other Capital, net	15.5	-55.0	-64.0	-94.0	-55.0	..	66.8	49.1	83.0	70.1	97.7
Change in Reserves	-0.5	0.0	-53.0	0.0	-51.0	..	-71.9	-17.7	-39.3	-116.0	-90.4
Memo Item:					*(Botswana Pula per US dollar)*						
Conversion Factor (Annual Avg)	0.720	0.710	0.730	0.760	0.670	0.680	0.830	0.860	0.820	0.830	0.790
EXTERNAL DEBT (Total)				*(Millions of US dollars), outstanding at end of year*							
EXTERNAL DEBT (Total)	17.40	33.20	74.80	114.90	134.10	147.30	165.20	183.80	123.50	127.70	133.20
Long-Term Debt (by debtor)	17.40	33.20	74.80	114.90	134.10	147.30	165.20	180.80	120.50	110.70	129.20
Central Bank, incl. IMF credit	0.00	0.00	0.00	0.00	0.00	0.00	0.00	0.00	0.00	0.00	0.00
Central Government	17.40	33.20	74.80	114.90	134.10	147.30	165.20	178.70	117.90	107.80	117.10
Rest of General Government	..	..	..	..	..	..	..	..	..	..	..
Non-financial Public Enterprises	0.00	0.00	0.00	0.00	0.00	0.00	0.00	2.10	2.60	2.90	12.10
Priv. Sector, incl non-guaranteed	0.00	0.00	0.00	0.00	0.00	0.00	0.00	0.00	0.00	0.00	0.00
Short-Term Debt	0.00	0.00	0.00	0.00	0.00	0.00	0.00	3.00	3.00	17.00	4.00
Memo Items:					*(Millions of US dollars)*						
Int'l Reserves Excluding Gold	..	..	..	..	..	..	74.9	100.1	150.6	267.3	343.7
Gold Holdings (at market price)	..	..	..	..	..	..	..	..	..	..	..
SOCIAL INDICATORS											
Total Fertility Rate	6.9	6.9	6.9	6.9	6.8	6.8	6.7	6.7	6.7	6.7	6.7
Infant Mortality Rate	101.0	98.0	95.0	92.4	89.8	87.2	84.6	82.0	75.6	69.2	62.8
Life Expectancy at Birth	49.7	50.1	50.5	50.9	51.3	51.7	52.1	52.5	55.0	57.4	59.8
Urban Population, % of total	8.4	9.1	9.8	10.6	11.3	12.0	12.6	13.2	13.9	14.5	15.1
Food Prod. per capita (1987=100)	239.4	254.1	241.9	219.3	218.6	203.0	220.7	201.3	156.0	194.9	142.7
Labor Force, Agriculture (%)	85.5	83.8	82.3	80.8	79.4	78.1	76.3	74.7	73.2	71.7	70.3
Labor Force, Female (%)	43.8	43.1	42.5	41.8	41.3	40.7	40.1	39.5	38.9	38.4	37.8
Primary Schl. Enroll. Ratio	65.0	..	..	..	..	72.0	82.0	89.0	91.0	95.0	98.0
Primary Schl. Enroll. Ratio, Female	67.0	..	..	..	..	79.0	90.0	98.0	101.0	105.0	106.0
Secondary Schl. Enroll. Ratio	7.0	..	..	..	..	16.0	18.0	20.0	21.0	21.0	21.0

1981	1982	1983	1984	1985	1986	1987	1988	1989	1990 estimate	Notes	BOTSWANA
				(Millions of current US dollars)							**FOREIGN TRADE (CUSTOMS BASIS)**
..	..	..	..	..	..	..	..	..	..	..	Value of Exports, fob
..	..	..	..	..	..	..	..	..	..	..	Nonfuel Primary Products
..	..	..	..	..	..	..	..	..	..	..	Fuels
..	..	..	..	..	..	..	..	..	..	..	Manufactures
..	..	..	..	..	..	..	..	..	..	..	Value of Imports, cif
..	..	..	..	..	..	..	..	..	..	..	Nonfuel Primary Products
..	..	..	..	..	..	..	..	..	..	..	Fuels
..	..	..	..	..	..	..	..	..	..	..	Manufactures
				(Index 1987 = 100)							
..	..	..	..	..	..	..	..	..	..	..	Terms of Trade
..	..	..	..	..	..	..	..	..	..	..	Export Prices, fob
..	..	..	..	..	..	..	..	..	..	..	Import Prices, cif
				(Millions of current US dollars)							**BALANCE OF PAYMENTS**
604.4	645.5	836.0	877.6	888.8	1,069.1	1,883.5	1,799.4	2,174.9	2,250.3	..	Exports of Goods & Services
401.3	460.6	640.3	677.7	727.6	852.5	1,586.6	1,469.0	1,819.7	1,753.0	..	Merchandise, fob
97.0	102.5	113.0	107.2	76.3	100.0	125.1	110.3	110.5	134.1	..	Nonfactor Services
106.0	82.4	82.7	92.7	84.9	116.5	171.8	220.1	244.8	363.2	..	Factor Services
948.6	813.3	965.2	982.8	846.5	1,009.3	1,393.5	1,778.8	1,896.5	2,388.3	..	Imports of Goods & Services
687.1	579.8	615.3	583.4	493.8	608.4	803.9	986.9	1,184.9	1,606.2	..	Merchandise, fob
176.5	155.8	186.9	173.1	119.1	138.7	186.8	219.1	213.0	268.1	..	Nonfactor Services
85.0	77.7	163.1	226.2	233.6	262.2	402.8	572.8	498.6	514.0	..	Factor Services
6.8	9.8	12.9	15.3	20.5	27.8	33.5	34.0	33.0	36.4	..	Long-Term Interest
-1.7	-0.2	-0.4	-7.3	-3.2	-2.6	6.8	-17.5	-30.6	-40.9	..	Private Current Transfers, net
..	..	..	..	..	..	..	..	..	..		Workers' Remittances
-345.9	-168.0	-129.6	-112.5	39.2	57.1	496.8	3.1	247.8	-178.8	..	Curr. A/C Bal before Off. Transf.
50.9	23.3	47.3	42.6	42.1	53.8	166.7	184.6	250.5	316.2	..	Net Official Transfers
-295.0	-144.7	-82.3	-69.9	81.3	110.9	663.5	187.6	498.3	137.3	..	Curr. A/C Bal after Off. Transf.
121.7	105.8	64.0	114.8	105.0	99.6	-84.3	39.9	106.5	160.2	..	Long-Term Capital, net
88.3	21.1	22.5	61.9	52.1	70.4	113.6	39.9	98.2	148.3	..	Direct Investment
25.8	55.1	25.4	59.8	41.4	17.0	63.5	14.3	28.8	-37.1	..	Long-Term Loans
27.8	59.1	37.3	76.6	68.1	34.4	99.4	52.5	64.4	24.7	..	Disbursements
2.0	4.0	11.9	16.8	26.7	17.4	35.9	38.2	35.6	61.8	..	Repayments
7.5	29.6	16.1	-6.9	11.5	12.2	-261.4	-14.3	-20.6	48.9	..	Other Long-Term Capital
99.5	93.8	142.0	79.4	68.0	96.4	-17.7	154.7	-28.3	9.7	..	Other Capital, net
73.8	-54.9	-123.6	-124.3	-254.3	-306.9	-561.5	-382.3	-576.5	-307.2	..	Change in Reserves
											Memo Item:
				(Botswana Pula per US dollar)							
0.780	0.920	1.090	1.140	1.610	1.910	1.820	1.690	1.990	1.930	..	Conversion Factor (Annual Avg)
				(Millions of US dollars), outstanding at end of year							
157.60	203.10	225.60	260.70	333.60	387.00	513.30	501.60	512.90	515.60	..	**EXTERNAL DEBT (Total)**
149.60	200.10	221.60	255.70	331.60	383.90	509.00	497.80	509.30	509.80		Long-Term Debt (by debtor)
0.00	0.00	0.00	0.50	1.10	1.40	1.40	1.20	1.10	1.30		Central Bank, incl. IMF credit
130.00	181.40	198.90	200.10	232.50	264.00	364.70	367.10	393.70	397.90		Central Government
..	..	..	..	..	..	..	..	..	..		Rest of General Government
16.90	16.30	20.90	53.80	96.60	117.10	141.50	128.60	114.00	110.60		Non-financial Public Enterprises
2.70	2.40	1.80	1.30	1.40	1.40	1.40	0.90	0.50	..		Priv. Sector, incl non-guaranteed
8.00	3.00	4.00	5.00	2.00	3.10	4.30	3.80	3.60	5.80		Short-Term Debt
				(Millions of US dollars)							**Memo Items:**
253.4	293.0	395.7	474.3	783.2	1,197.7	2,057.1	2,258.1	2,841.1	3,385.3	..	Int'l Reserves Excluding Gold
..	..	..	..	..	..	..	..	..	..	..	Gold Holdings (at market price)
											SOCIAL INDICATORS
6.7	6.8	6.5	6.2	5.9	5.6	5.3	5.1	4.9	4.7	..	Total Fertility Rate
56.4	50.0	48.3	46.7	45.0	43.4	41.7	40.4	39.1	37.7	..	Infant Mortality Rate
62.3	64.7	65.1	65.5	65.9	66.3	66.7	66.9	67.1	67.4	..	Life Expectancy at Birth
16.2	17.2	18.3	19.3	20.4	22.2	24.0	25.2	26.3	27.5	..	Urban Population, % of total
175.7	176.1	156.5	144.1	131.6	120.4	100.0	132.0	128.1	122.9	..	Food Prod. per capita (1987=100)
..	..	..	..	..	..	..	..	..	..		Labor Force, Agriculture (%)
37.5	37.2	36.9	36.6	36.3	36.0	35.7	35.4	35.2	34.9	..	Labor Force, Female (%)
	96.0	99.0	103.0	110.0	112.0	115.0	111.0	111.0	115.0	..	Primary Schl. Enroll. Ratio
110.0	104.0	106.0	109.0	115.0	115.0	118.0	114.0	114.0	117.0	..	Primary Schl. Enroll. Ratio, Female
	21.0	21.0	27.0	31.0	32.0	33.0	35.0	37.0	..	..	Secondary Schl. Enroll. Ratio

BRAZIL	1970	1971	1972	1973	1974	1975	1976	1977	1978	1979	1980
CURRENT GNP PER CAPITA (US $)	450	500	570	710	880	1,070	1,300	1,470	1,640	1,870	2,060
POPULATION (millions)	96	98	101	103	106	108	111	113	116	119	121
USE AND ORIGIN OF RESOURCES	*(Billions of current Brazilian Cruzados)*										
Gross National Product (GNP)	1.92E-4	2.58E-4	3.44E-4	4.81E-4	7.07E-4	9.91E-4	1.60E-3	2.45E-3	3.54E-3	5.90E-3	1.20E-2
Net Factor Income from Abroad	-1.84E-6	-2.46E-6	-3.31E-6	-4.47E-6	-6.18E-6	-1.43E-5	-2.48E-5	-4.02E-5	-8.38E-5	-1.63E-4	-4.05E-4
GDP at Market Prices	1.94E-4	2.60E-4	3.47E-4	4.85E-4	7.14E-4	1.00E-3	1.63E-3	2.49E-3	3.63E-3	6.06E-3	1.24E-2
Resource Balance	-8.16E-7	-4.48E-6	-5.50E-6	-5.97E-6	-4.19E-5	-3.99E-5	-3.90E-5	-1.66E-5	-4.31E-5	-1.24E-4	-2.79E-4
Exports of Goods & NF Services	1.37E-5	1.67E-5	2.52E-5	4.02E-5	5.72E-5	7.58E-5	1.15E-4	1.81E-4	2.42E-4	4.32E-4	1.12E-3
Imports of Goods & NF Services	1.45E-5	2.12E-5	3.07E-5	4.61E-5	9.91E-5	1.16E-4	1.54E-4	1.97E-4	2.85E-4	5.56E-4	1.40E-3
Domestic Absorption	1.95E-4	2.65E-4	3.53E-4	4.91E-4	7.55E-4	1.04E-3	1.67E-3	2.51E-3	3.67E-3	6.18E-3	1.27E-2
Private Consumption, etc.	1.33E-4	1.81E-4	2.42E-4	3.28E-4	5.05E-4	6.68E-4	1.12E-3	1.72E-3	2.49E-3	4.21E-3	8.63E-3
General Gov't Consumption	2.20E-5	2.87E-5	3.73E-5	5.07E-5	6.95E-5	1.07E-4	1.71E-4	2.35E-4	3.50E-4	5.90E-4	1.14E-3
Gross Domestic Investment	3.99E-5	5.49E-5	7.35E-5	1.13E-4	1.81E-4	2.70E-4	3.77E-4	5.50E-4	8.33E-4	1.38E-3	2.89E-3
Fixed Investment	3.66E-5	5.14E-5	7.05E-5	1.04E-4	1.63E-4	2.45E-4	3.66E-4	5.32E-4	8.05E-4	1.39E-3	2.83E-3
Indirect Taxes, net	3.10E-5	3.73E-5	5.15E-5	6.95E-5	9.34E-5	1.18E-4	1.94E-4	2.96E-4	4.17E-4	6.14E-4	1.20E-3
GDP at factor cost	1.63E-4	2.23E-4	2.96E-4	4.16E-4	6.20E-4	8.87E-4	1.43E-3	2.19E-3	3.21E-3	5.45E-3	1.12E-2
Agriculture	2.02E-5	2.86E-5	3.84E-5	5.56E-5	8.01E-5	1.07E-4	1.87E-4	3.22E-4	3.73E-4	6.00E-4	1.23E-3
Industry	6.25E-5	8.51E-5	1.14E-4	1.62E-4	2.48E-4	3.56E-4	5.70E-4	8.48E-4	1.29E-3	2.21E-3	4.90E-3
Manufacturing	4.79E-5	6.50E-5	8.69E-5	1.24E-4	1.89E-4	2.69E-4	4.36E-4	6.44E-4	9.86E-4	1.69E-3	3.75E-3
Services, etc.	8.06E-5	1.09E-4	1.44E-4	1.98E-4	2.92E-4	4.23E-4	6.78E-4	1.02E-3	1.55E-3	2.63E-3	5.05E-3
Gross Domestic Saving	3.91E-5	5.04E-5	6.80E-5	1.07E-4	1.39E-4	2.30E-4	3.37E-4	5.33E-4	7.90E-4	1.25E-3	2.61E-3
Gross National Saving	3.72E-5	4.79E-5	6.46E-5	1.02E-4	1.33E-4	2.16E-4	3.13E-4	..	7.07E-4	1.09E-3	2.21E-3
	(Millions of 1987 Brazilian Cruzados)										
Gross National Product	4,268	4,751	5,334	6,103	6,659	6,966	7,641	7,985	8,182	8,700	9,441
GDP at Market Prices	4,319	4,807	5,398	6,174	6,732	7,083	7,777	8,135	8,398	8,966	9,783
Resource Balance	-136	-215	-248	-318	-503	-420	-411	-351	-331	-353	-244
Exports of Goods & NF Services	242	255	317	362	370	413	412	410	465	508	623
Imports of Goods & NF Services	378	470	564	679	873	833	823	761	796	861	867
Domestic Absorption	4,455	5,023	5,646	6,492	7,235	7,504	8,188	8,485	8,729	9,319	10,027
Private Consumption, etc.	2,814	3,176	3,537	3,936	4,365	4,309	4,920	5,262	5,386	5,903	6,294
General Gov't Consumption	492	536	581	653	654	753	811	767	809	875	876
Gross Domestic Investment	1,149	1,311	1,527	1,903	2,217	2,441	2,457	2,457	2,534	2,541	2,857
Fixed Investment	1,102	1,271	1,483	1,795	2,033	2,231	2,387	2,359	2,471	2,567	2,803
GDP at factor cost	3,875	4,315	4,846	5,546	6,047	6,358	6,981	7,304	7,525	8,033	8,802
Agriculture	509	561	583	583	589	631	647	725	705	739	809
Industry	1,675	1,873	2,141	2,508	2,718	2,848	3,181	3,280	3,648	3,896	4,257
Manufacturing	1,235	1,382	1,575	1,836	1,979	2,054	2,303	2,356	2,614	2,794	3,048
Services, etc.	1,691	1,881	2,122	2,454	2,740	2,879	3,153	3,299	3,172	3,398	3,735
Memo Items:											
Capacity to Import	356	370	463	591	504	546	614	697	675	668	694
Terms of Trade Adjustment	115	116	147	230	134	133	202	287	211	161	71
Gross Domestic Income	4,433	4,923	5,545	6,404	6,866	7,216	7,979	8,421	8,608	9,127	9,854
Gross National Income	4,382	4,866	5,481	6,333	6,792	7,099	7,843	8,272	8,393	8,861	9,512
DOMESTIC PRICES/DEFLATORS	*(Index 1987 = 100)*										
Overall (GDP)	4.50E-3	5.41E-3	6.43E-3	7.86E-3	1.06E-2	1.42E-2	2.09E-2	3.06E-2	4.32E-2	0.07	0.13
Domestic Absorption	4.38E-3	5.27E-3	6.25E-3	7.57E-3	1.04E-2	1.39E-2	2.04E-2	2.95E-2	4.20E-2	0.07	0.13
Agriculture	3.96E-3	5.11E-3	6.59E-3	9.53E-3	1.36E-2	1.70E-2	2.88E-2	4.44E-2	5.28E-2	0.08	0.15
Industry	3.73E-3	4.54E-3	5.31E-3	6.47E-3	9.14E-3	1.25E-2	1.79E-2	2.59E-2	3.53E-2	0.06	0.12
Manufacturing	3.88E-3	4.71E-3	5.52E-3	6.75E-3	9.58E-3	1.31E-2	1.89E-2	2.73E-2	3.77E-2	0.06	0.12
Consumer Price Index	..	..	..	..	..	..	..	..	..	..	..
MANUFACTURING ACTIVITY											
Employment (1987=100)	49.7	52.8	57.4	74.7	79.1	82.5	87.8	92.7	98.3	102.0	106.9
Real Earnings per Empl. (1987=100)	61.0	68.2	77.4	79.1	84.3	80.8	88.3	89.8	94.0	98.1	90.7
Real Output per Empl. (1987=100)	57.1	58.1	64.4	69.2	75.7	81.7	79.6	77.8	79.4	78.7	80.8
Earnings as % of Value Added	22.3	23.6	25.4	23.3	21.9	18.9	20.1	20.9	21.2	20.7	17.2
MONETARY HOLDINGS	*(Millions of current Brazilian Cruzados)*										
Money Supply, Broadly Defined	..	0.061	0.090	0.127	0.175	0.276	0.416	0.636	0.959	1.700	2.900
Money	0.035	0.046	0.059	0.087	0.117	0.169	0.231	0.319	0.434	0.759	1.300
Currency Outside Banks	0.007	0.009	0.012	0.016	0.022	0.031	0.046	0.065	0.093	0.167	0.290
Demand Deposits	0.028	0.037	0.047	0.071	0.095	0.138	0.185	0.254	0.341	0.592	0.998
Quasi-Money	..	0.015	0.031	0.040	0.058	0.107	0.185	0.317	0.525	0.917	1.600
GOVERNMENT DEFICIT (-) OR SURPLUS	*(Billions of current Brazilian Cruzados)*										
	..	..	..	..	..	..	..	..	-1.00E-4	..	-3.00E-4
Current Revenue	..	..	1.00E-4	1.00E-4	1.00E-4	2.00E-4	3.00E-4	6.00E-4	8.00E-4	1.40E-3	2.80E-3
Current Expenditure	..	..	..	..	1.00E-4	1.00E-4	2.00E-4	4.00E-4	6.00E-4	1.00E-3	2.30E-3
Current Budget Balance	..	..	..	0.00E+0	1.00E-4	1.00E-4	2.00E-4	2.00E-4	4.00E-4	5.00E-4	
Capital Receipts	..	..	..	..	..	..	..	..	..	..	..
Capital Payments	..	..	..	0.00E+0	1.00E-4	1.00E-4	2.00E-4	3.00E-4	4.00E-4	8.00E-4	

1981	1982	1983	1984	1985	1986	1987	1988	1989	1990 estimate	Notes	BRAZIL
2,030	2,050	1,820	1,700	1,630	1,780	1,910	2,040	2,400	2,680	..	**CURRENT GNP PER CAPITA (US $)**
124	127	130	133	136	139	141	144	147	150	..	**POPULATION (millions)**
				(Billions of current Brazilian Cruzados)							**USE AND ORIGIN OF RESOURCES**
0.024	0.048	0.110	0.364	1.000	3.000	11.000	83	1,228	31,557	f	Gross National Product (GNP)
-0.001	-0.003	-0.007	-0.022	-0.074	-0.163	-0.436	-3	-38	-796		Net Factor Income from Abroad
0.025	0.051	0.117	0.386	1.000	4.000	12.000	86	1,266	32,353	f	GDP at Market Prices
0.000	0.000	0.003	0.022	0.071	0.090	0.377	4	41	573	..	Resource Balance
0.002	0.004	0.013	0.052	0.169	0.323	1.000	9	105	2,345	..	Exports of Goods & NF Services
0.002	0.004	0.011	0.031	0.098	0.233	0.714	5	64	1,772	..	Imports of Goods & NF Services
0.025	0.051	0.114	0.364	1.000	4.000	11.000	82	1,226	31,780	..	Domestic Absorption
0.017	0.035	0.084	0.272	0.909	2.000	7.000	51	730	19,710	..	Private Consumption, etc.
0.002	0.005	0.011	0.032	0.136	0.391	1.000	11	181	5,058	..	General Gov't Consumption
0.006	0.011	0.020	0.061	0.265	0.699	3.000	20	315	7,012	..	Gross Domestic Investment
0.006	0.011	0.021	0.065	0.234	0.699	3.000	20	315	7,012	..	Fixed Investment
0.003	0.005	0.012	0.034	0.124	0.403	1.000	8	112	4,073	..	Indirect Taxes, net
0.022	0.045	0.105	0.352	1.000	3.000	10.000	78	1,154	28,281	f	GDP at factor cost
0.002	0.004	0.012	0.040	0.145	0.364	1.000	8	99	2,888	..	Agriculture
0.010	0.021	0.046	0.161	0.570	1.000	5.000	34	495	10,928	..	Industry
0.007	0.016	0.035	0.119	0.425	1.000	3.000	24	342	7,430	..	Manufacturing
0.010	0.021	0.048	0.151	0.543	1.000	5.000	36	561	14,464	..	Services, etc.
0.006	0.010	0.022	0.083	0.337	0.789	3.000	24	355	7,585	..	Gross Domestic Saving
0.005	0.008	0.016	0.061	0.264	0.627	3.000	21	318	6,852	..	Gross National Saving
				(Millions of 1987 Brazilian Cruzados)							
8,933	8,867	8,521	8,991	9,749	10,644	11,100	11,007	11,316	10,838	..	Gross National Product
9,353	9,407	9,086	9,574	10,334	11,163	11,537	11,510	11,887	11,385	f	GDP at Market Prices
-4	-28	195	384	452	179	377	528	527	386	..	Resource Balance
755	686	784	956	1,024	915	1,091	1,234	1,297	1,233	..	Exports of Goods & NF Services
760	714	589	572	572	736	714	706	770	847	..	Imports of Goods & NF Services
9,357	9,434	8,891	9,190	9,883	10,984	11,160	10,982	11,360	10,999	..	Domestic Absorption
6,027	6,262	6,303	6,627	6,813	7,247	7,183	7,051	7,130	6,949	..	Private Consumption, etc.
849	915	840	750	953	1,134	1,403	1,482	1,752	1,771	..	General Gov't Consumption
2,481	2,258	1,748	1,813	2,116	2,603	2,573	2,449	2,478	2,280	..	Gross Domestic Investment
2,456	2,290	1,922	1,945	2,116	2,603	2,573	2,449	2,478	2,280	..	Fixed Investment
8,415	8,464	8,175	8,615	9,299	10,050	10,383	10,356	10,696	10,242	..	GDP at factor cost
874	870	865	894	983	904	1,039	1,048	1,078	1,038	..	Agriculture
3,881	3,881	3,655	3,896	4,218	4,714	4,764	4,641	4,774	4,421	..	Industry
2,732	2,727	2,568	2,726	2,953	3,287	3,318	3,205	3,296	3,010	..	Manufacturing
3,661	3,713	3,656	3,826	4,098	4,432	4,580	4,667	4,844	4,784	..	Services, etc.
											Memo Items:
730	656	747	978	987	1,021	1,091	1,351	1,258	1,121	..	Capacity to Import
-25	-29	-37	22	-36	106	0	117	-39	-112	..	Terms of Trade Adjustment
9,328	9,377	9,049	9,596	10,298	11,269	11,537	11,627	11,849	11,273	..	Gross Domestic Income
8,907	8,838	8,484	9,012	9,713	10,750	11,100	11,124	11,278	10,726	..	Gross National Income
				(Index 1987 = 100)							**DOMESTIC PRICES/DEFLATORS**
0.26	0.54	1.3	4.0	13.4	32.8	100.00	748.90	10,653.0	284,000	..	Overall (GDP)
0.26	0.54	1.3	4.0	13.3	32.5	100.00	743.90	10,790.2	289,000	..	Domestic Absorption
0.27	0.47	1.3	4.5	14.8	40.2	100.00	755.10	9,165.6	278,000	..	Agriculture
0.25	0.53	1.3	4.1	13.5	31.2	100.00	735.80	10,366.1	247,000	..	Industry
0.27	0.58	1.4	4.4	14.4	32.7	100.00	755.60	10,389.0	247,000	..	Manufacturing
..	..	..	..	..	..	..	..	..	..	..	Consumer Price Index
											MANUFACTURING ACTIVITY
92.1	90.9	82.8	87.6	95.5	106.2	100.0	98.1			G	Employment (1987=100)
103.2	111.6	102.8	95.3	98.7	102.5	100.0	98.6			G	Real Earnings per Empl. (1987=100)
83.8	78.7	91.2	93.3	91.8	91.9	100.0	94.0			G	Real Output per Empl. (1987=100)
18.3	19.4	16.1	13.7	14.5	16.5	15.1	15.0			..	Earnings as % of Value Added
				(Millions of current Brazilian Cruzados)							**MONETARY HOLDINGS**
6.300	13.1	36.3	127.0	467.9	..	..	..	..	..	D	Money Supply, Broadly Defined
2.400	4.0	8.0	24.4	106.1	456.5	1,439.9	..	..	..	..	Money
0.523	1.0	1.9	6.2	23.8	85.1	253.3	2,131.3	41,102.0	989,000.0	..	Currency Outside Banks
1.800	3.0	6.2	18.2	82.3	371.4	1,186.6	..	..	..	..	Demand Deposits
3.900	9.2	28.3	102.6	361.7						..	Quasi-Money
				(Billions of current Brazilian Cruzados)							
-0.001	-0.001	-0.005	-0.019	-0.154	-0.488	-1.400	-13.200	-204.400		E	**GOVERNMENT DEFICIT (-) OR SURPLUS**
0.006	0.013	0.030	0.091	0.363	0.829	4.000	37.100	1,139.800	..	..	Current Revenue
0.005	0.010	0.024	0.078	0.349	1.000	3.000	28.000	506.100	..	..	Current Expenditure
0.001	0.003	0.006	0.012	0.014	-0.171	1.000	9.000	633.800	..	..	Current Budget Balance
0.000	0.000	0.001	0.001	0.005	0.000	0.027	0.221	31.000	..	..	Capital Receipts
0.002	0.004	0.012	0.032	0.173	0.317	2.400	22.500	869.100	..	..	Capital Payments

BRAZIL	1970	1971	1972	1973	1974	1975	1976	1977	1978	1979	1980
FOREIGN TRADE (CUSTOMS BASIS)					*(Millions of current US dollars)*						
Value of Exports, fob	2,739	2,904	3,991	6,199	7,951	8,669	10,128	12,120	12,659	15,244	20,132
Nonfuel Primary Products	2,335	2,350	3,167	4,779	5,769	6,098	7,377	8,763	8,128	9,140	12,005
Fuels	16	24	40	84	111	201	251	217	196	228	358
Manufactures	388	530	784	1,337	2,071	2,371	2,500	3,141	4,335	5,876	7,770
Value of Imports, cif	2,845	3,696	4,776	6,992	14,163	13,578	13,714	13,254	15,016	19,731	24,949
Nonfuel Primary Products	531	591	690	1,287	2,199	1,607	1,922	1,832	2,435	3,642	4,010
Fuels	351	523	643	1,054	3,372	3,551	4,332	4,502	4,937	7,314	10,749
Manufactures	1,962	2,581	3,443	4,652	8,591	8,421	7,459	6,920	7,645	8,776	10,190
					(Index 1987 = 100)						
Terms of Trade	190.8	173.4	169.3	194.4	132.6	124.7	142.2	162.7	140.9	124.5	102.9
Export Prices, fob	40.0	39.9	44.0	64.1	78.2	74.1	85.1	103.7	97.2	108.0	115.6
Import Prices, cif	21.0	23.0	26.0	33.0	59.0	59.4	59.8	63.8	69.0	86.8	112.4
BALANCE OF PAYMENTS					*(Millions of current US dollars)*						
Exports of Goods & Services	3,117	3,334	4,508	7,037	9,371	9,939	11,283	13,510	14,489	17,998	23,275
Merchandise, fob	2,739	2,891	3,941	6,093	7,814	8,492	9,961	11,923	12,473	15,244	20,132
Nonfactor Services	320	388	421	603	824	926	887	1,080	1,191	1,464	1,725
Factor Services	58	55	145	341	734	521	435	507	825	1,290	1,418
Imports of Goods & Services	3,975	4,985	6,204	9,222	16,934	16,950	17,841	18,622	21,597	28,493	36,250
Merchandise, fob	2,507	3,256	4,193	6,154	12,562	12,042	12,347	12,023	13,631	17,961	22,955
Nonfactor Services	788	939	1,151	1,626	2,354	2,281	2,340	2,623	2,863	3,763	4,833
Factor Services	680	790	860	1,442	2,019	2,627	3,154	3,976	5,103	6,769	8,462
Long-Term Interest	224	297	425	748	1,472	2,056	1,720	2,027	3,131	4,760	6,333
Private Current Transfers, net	-3	-7	-17	11	4	13	7	..	69	12	127
Workers' Remittances	..	..	..	..	..	..	..	..	..	5	4
Curr. A/C Bal before Off. Transf.	-861	-1,658	-1,713	-2,174	-7,560	-6,998	-6,551	-5,116	-7,039	-10,483	-12,848
Net Official Transfers	24	20	23	17	-2	-10	-3	4	3	5	42
Curr. A/C Bal after Off. Transf.	-837	-1,638	-1,690	-2,158	-7,562	-7,008	-6,554	-5,112	-7,036	-10,478	-12,806
Long-Term Capital, net	1,217	1,668	3,543	4,100	6,231	4,936	6,108	6,040	10,088	6,460	6,207
Direct Investment	407	536	570	1,341	1,268	1,190	1,372	1,687	1,882	2,223	1,544
Long-Term Loans	1,340	1,434	3,555	2,664	6,292	4,827	5,640	5,827	9,528	5,827	4,623
Disbursements	1,796	1,999	4,313	3,814	8,212	7,068	8,164	9,496	14,728	12,341	11,456
Repayments	456	564	758	1,150	1,920	2,242	2,524	3,668	5,200	6,514	6,833
Other Long-Term Capital	-530	-302	-583	95	-1,329	-1,081	-904	-1,474	-1,322	-1,590	40
Other Capital, net	114	453	579	354	347	1,007	3,118	-407	1,576	1,231	2,893
Change in Reserves	-494	-483	-2,431	-2,296	984	1,065	-2,672	-521	-4,628	2,787	3,706
Memo Item:					*(Brazilian Cruzados per US dollar)*						
Conversion Factor (Annual Avg)	4.59E-6	5.29E-6	5.93E-6	6.13E-6	6.79E-6	8.13E-6	1.07E-5	1.41E-5	1.81E-5	2.69E-5	5.27E-5
				(Billions of US dollars), outstanding at end of year							
EXTERNAL DEBT (Total)	5.13	6.64	10.18	12.95	19.43	23.77	29.06	41.43	53.85	60.71	70.98
Long-Term Debt (by debtor)	5.13	6.64	10.18	12.95	19.43	23.77	29.06	35.44	46.78	52.08	57.43
Central Bank, incl. IMF credit	0.39	0.51	0.70	1.15	2.06	2.68	3.06	3.58	5.07	5.33	6.41
Central Government	1.42	1.55	2.08	2.50	3.26	3.52	3.83	4.44	5.65	7.31	7.77
Rest of General Government	0.12	0.17	0.26	0.40	0.59	0.95	1.45	1.42	1.74	2.31	2.61
Non-financial Public Enterprises	1.39	1.82	2.64	3.36	4.81	6.29	8.58	11.78	16.41	19.34	21.98
Priv. Sector, incl non-guaranteed	1.81	2.58	4.51	5.52	8.71	10.34	12.13	14.22	17.90	17.79	18.67
Short-Term Debt	0.00	0.00	0.00	0.00	0.00	0.00	0.00	5.99	7.07	8.63	13.55
Memo Items:					*(Millions of US dollars)*						
Int'l Reserves Excluding Gold	1,141.7	1,696.2	4,132.8	6,359.9	5,215.7	3,980.4	6,488.0	7,192.0	11,826.4	8,966.3	5,769.3
Gold Holdings (at market price)	48.2	57.7	86.1	149.0	247.5	186.1	178.8	249.9	363.6	872.4	1,105.9
SOCIAL INDICATORS											
Total Fertility Rate	4.9	4.8	4.7	4.6	4.5	4.4	4.3	4.2	4.1	4.1	4.0
Infant Mortality Rate	94.6	92.8	91.0	88.6	86.2	83.8	81.4	79.0	77.4	75.8	74.2
Life Expectancy at Birth	59.0	59.4	59.8	60.2	60.6	61.0	61.4	61.8	62.1	62.5	62.8
Urban Population, % of total	55.8	56.9	58.0	59.0	60.1	61.2	62.2	63.2	64.2	65.2	66.2
Food Prod. per capita (1987=100)	78.7	78.2	80.9	79.7	82.9	84.7	88.4	90.9	84.3	85.3	93.3
Labor Force, Agriculture (%)	44.9	43.3	41.8	40.4	39.1	37.9	36.4	34.9	33.6	32.3	31.2
Labor Force, Female (%)	21.7	22.3	22.9	23.4	23.9	24.4	25.0	25.5	26.0	26.5	26.9
Primary Schl. Enroll. Ratio	..	82.0	..	..	..	88.0	..	89.0	92.0	97.0	99.0
Primary Schl. Enroll. Ratio, Female	..	82.0	..	..	..	87.0	..	88.0	91.0	96.0	97.0
Secondary Schl. Enroll. Ratio	26.0	17.0	..	..	..	26.0	30.0	32.0	32.0	32.0	34.0

1981	1982	1983	1984	1985	1986	1987	1988	1989	1990 estimate	Notes	BRAZIL
											FOREIGN TRADE (CUSTOMS BASIS)
				(Millions of current US dollars)							
23,292	20,173	21,898	26,976	25,594	22,382	26,229	33,759	34,290	31,243	..	Value of Exports, fob
12,650	10,758	11,828	13,705	12,506	10,772	12,079	14,863	14,703	14,047	..	Nonfuel Primary Products
1,178	1,444	1,158	1,824	1,624	699	946	894	850	678	..	Fuels
9,465	7,971	8,911	11,447	11,464	10,911	13,203	18,003	18,736	16,518	..	Manufactures
24,073	21,061	16,784	15,208	14,329	15,555	16,578	16,054	19,173	22,459	..	Value of Imports, cif
3,197	2,646	2,043	2,168	2,116	3,502	2,585	2,136	3,850	4,509	..	Nonfuel Primary Products
12,159	11,276	9,381	8,036	6,766	4,165	5,397	4,836	4,317	5,057	..	Fuels
8,716	7,140	5,360	5,005	5,447	7,887	8,595	9,082	11,006	12,892	..	Manufactures
				(Index 1987 = 100)							
94.5	93.0	93.7	96.8	91.7	113.2	100.0	120.3	123.6	122.7	..	Terms of Trade
111.8	102.2	97.9	98.6	91.7	97.7	100.0	109.2	117.9	132.9	..	Export Prices, fob
118.3	109.9	104.5	101.9	100.0	86.3	100.0	90.8	95.4	108.3	..	Import Prices, cif
				(Millions of current US dollars)							**BALANCE OF PAYMENTS**
26,923	23,469	24,341	30,205	29,309	25,131	28,730	36,823	38,817	35,551	f	Exports of Goods & Services
23,276	20,173	21,898	27,002	25,634	22,348	26,210	33,773	34,375	31,414	..	Merchandise, fob
2,246	1,794	1,713	1,936	2,079	1,812	1,947	2,273	3,120	1,825	..	Nonfactor Services
1,401	1,502	730	1,267	1,596	971	573	777	1,322	2,312	..	Factor Services
38,873	39,773	31,286	30,334	29,737	30,522	30,250	32,758	38,036	39,463	f	Imports of Goods & Services
22,091	19,395	15,429	13,916	13,168	14,044	15,052	14,605	18,263	20,424	..	Merchandise, fob
5,109	5,366	4,105	3,679	3,760	4,355	4,275	5,254	5,847	3,434	..	Nonfactor Services
11,673	15,012	11,752	12,739	12,809	12,123	10,923	12,899	13,926	15,605	..	Factor Services
7,993	9,391	8,032	7,636	7,463	6,431	6,427	11,749	4,365	2,683	..	Long-Term Interest
189	-10	106	161	139	89	113	107	226	929	..	Private Current Transfers, net
14	6	2	4	2	0	0	0	..	..	..	Workers' Remittances
-11,761	-16,314	-6,839	32	-289	-5,302	-1,407	4,172	1,007	-2,983	..	Curr. A/C Bal before Off. Transf.
10	2	2	10	16	-2	-43	-13	18	..	..	Net Official Transfers
-11,751	-16,312	-6,837	42	-273	-5,304	-1,450	4,159	1,025	-2,983	..	Curr. A/C Bal after Off. Transf.
11,647	8,011	7,744	8,080	1,105	-265	-995	451	-3,025	-2,777	f	Long-Term Capital, net
2,313	2,534	1,373	1,556	1,267	177	1,087	2,794	744	510	..	Direct Investment
8,721	8,005	4,617	5,392	514	135	-847	2,243	-1,992	-165	..	Long-Term Loans
16,137	15,543	8,336	9,919	2,521	3,444	2,475	5,778	3,026	3,561	..	Disbursements
7,415	7,538	3,719	4,527	2,007	3,308	3,321	3,535	5,018	3,726	..	Repayments
613	-2,528	1,754	1,132	-676	-577	-1,235	-4,586	-1,777	-3,122	..	Other Long-Term Capital
657	1,466	-1,493	-3,244	-958	1,941	4,085	-2,972	2,602	6,436	f	Other Capital, net
-553	6,835	586	-4,878	126	3,628	-1,640	-1,638	-602	-676	..	Change in Reserves
											Memo Item:
				(Brazilian Cruzados per US dollar)							
9.31E-5	1.80E-4	5.77E-4	0.0019	0.0062	0.0137	0.0392	0.2620	2.8300	68.3000	..	Conversion Factor (Annual Avg)
				(Billions of US dollars), outstanding at end of year							**EXTERNAL DEBT (Total)**
80.93	92.90	98.27	105.25	105.97	113.55	123.67	115.67	111.31	116.17	..	Long-Term Debt (by debtor)
65.56	75.37	83.91	94.13	96.35	103.87	110.01	104.75	92.73	91.69	..	Central Bank, incl. IMF credit
7.54	8.48	17.06	24.39	20.27	25.86	31.47	60.59	53.55	48.83	..	Central Government
7.60	8.10	9.48	11.65	14.50	19.83	23.32	18.24	19.43	20.36	..	Rest of General Government
3.12	3.28	3.46	3.96	5.41	5.50	5.27	1.00	0.98	1.13	..	Non-financial Public Enterprises
25.51	30.36	30.53	33.03	37.25	36.44	33.96	12.81	12.16	13.00	..	Priv. Sector, incl non-guaranteed
21.79	25.16	23.39	21.10	18.92	16.23	15.99	12.11	6.61	8.37	..	Short-Term Debt
15.37	17.53	14.36	11.13	9.61	9.68	13.66	10.92	18.58	24.48	..	
				(Millions of US dollars)							**Memo Items:**
6,603.5	3,927.9	4,355.1	11,507.9	10,604.6	5,803.0	6,299.2	6,971.8	7,535.4	7,440.6	..	Int'l Reserves Excluding Gold
876.1	69.4	206.4	452.9	1,013.4	950.7	1,177.8	1,118.3	1,193.4	1,759.1	..	Gold Holdings (at market price)
											SOCIAL INDICATORS
3.9	3.8	3.8	3.7	3.6	3.6	3.5	3.4	3.3	3.2	..	Total Fertility Rate
72.6	71.0	69.4	67.8	66.2	64.6	63.0	61.2	59.3	57.5	..	Infant Mortality Rate
63.1	63.4	63.7	64.0	64.3	64.6	64.9	65.3	65.7	66.2	..	Life Expectancy at Birth
67.2	68.1	69.1	70.0	71.0	71.8	72.6	73.3	74.1	74.9	..	Urban Population, % of total
92.1	95.9	92.7	93.0	99.8	92.5	100.0	103.1	106.3	101.0	..	Food Prod. per capita (1987=100)
..	..	..	..	..	..	..	..	..	..	..	Labor Force, Agriculture (%)
27.0	27.0	27.1	27.1	27.2	27.2	27.3	27.3	27.4	27.4	..	Labor Force, Female (%)
..	..	103.0	103.0	101.0	103.0	101.0	104.0	105.0	..	..	Primary Schl. Enroll. Ratio
..	..	99.0	..	..	..	..	..	..	..	..	Primary Schl. Enroll. Ratio, Female
..	..	35.0	35.0	36.0	37.0	37.0	38.0	39.0	..	..	Secondary Schl. Enroll. Ratio

147

BULGARIA	1970	1971	1972	1973	1974	1975	1976	1977	1978	1979	1980
CURRENT GNP PER CAPITA (US $)	..	..	..	..	..	..	..	..	..	..	..
POPULATION (thousands)	8,490	8,536	8,576	8,621	8,679	8,721	8,759	8,804	8,814	8,826	8,862
USE AND ORIGIN OF RESOURCES					*(Millions of current Bulgarian Leva)*						
Gross National Product (GNP)	..	..	..	..	..	..	..	..	..	..	25,383
Net Factor Income from Abroad											-408
GDP at Market Prices	..	..	..	..	..	..	..	..	..	..	25,791
Resource Balance	..	..	..	..	..	..	..	..	..	..	1,294
Exports of Goods & NFServices	..	..	..	..	..	..	..	..	..	..	9,209
Imports of Goods & NFServices	..	..	..	..	..	..	..	..	..	..	7,915
Domestic Absorption	..	..	..	..	..	..	..	..	..	..	24,497
Private Consumption, etc.	..	..	..	..	..	..	..	..	..	..	11,526
General Gov't Consumption	..	..	..	..	..	..	..	..	..	..	4,202
Gross Domestic Investment	..	..	..	..	..	..	..	..	..	..	8,768
Fixed Investment	..	..	..	..	..	..	..	..	..	..	7,289
Indirect Taxes, net	..	..	..	..	..	..	..	..	..	..	339
GDP at factor cost	..	..	..	..	..	..	..	..	..	..	25,452
Agriculture	..	..	..	..	..	..	..	..	..	..	3,719
Industry	..	..	..	..	..	..	..	..	..	..	13,869
Manufacturing	..	..	..	..	..	..	..	..	..	..	..
Services, etc.	..	..	..	..	..	..	..	..	..	..	8,204
Gross Domestic Saving	..	..	..	..	..	..	..	..	..	..	10,062
Gross National Saving	..	..	..	..	..	..	..	..	..	..	..
					(Millions of 1987 Bulgarian Leva)						
Gross National Product	..	..	..	..	..	..	..	..	..	..	27,627
GDP at Market Prices	..	..	..	..	..	..	..	..	..	..	28,118
Resource Balance	..	..	..	..	..	..	..	..	..	..	
Exports of Goods & NFServices	..	..	..	..	..	..	..	..	..	..	..
Imports of Goods & NFServices	..	..	..	..	..	..	..	..	..	..	..
Domestic Absorption	..	..	..	..	..	..	..	..	..	..	..
Private Consumption, etc.	..	..	..	..	..	..	..	..	..	..	..
General Gov't Consumption	..	..	..	..	..	..	..	..	..	..	4,569
Gross Domestic Investment	..	..	..	..	..	..	..	..	..	..	9,533
Fixed Investment	..	..	..	..	..	..	..	..	..	..	7,925
GDP at factor cost	..	..	..	..	..	..	..	..	..	..	27,748
Agriculture	..	..	..	..	..	..	..	..	..	..	5,046
Industry	..	..	..	..	..	..	..	..	..	..	14,630
Manufacturing	..	..	..	..	..	..	..	..	..	..	..
Services, etc.	..	..	..	..	..	..	..	..	..	..	8,627
Memo Items:											
Capacity to Import	..	..	..	..	..	..	..	..	..	..	..
Terms of Trade Adjustment	..	..	..	..	..	..	..	..	..	..	..
Gross Domestic Income	..	..	..	..	..	..	..	..	..	..	..
Gross National Income	..	..	..	..	..	..	..	..	..	..	..
DOMESTIC PRICES/DEFLATORS					*(Index 1987 = 100)*						
Overall (GDP)	..	..	..	..	..	..	..	..	..	..	91.7
Domestic Absorption	..	..	..	..	..	..	..	..	..	..	..
Agriculture	..	..	..	..	..	..	..	..	..	..	73.7
Industry	..	..	..	..	..	..	..	..	..	..	94.8
Manufacturing	..	..	..	..	..	..	..	..	..	..	..
Consumer Price Index	..	..	..	..	..	..	..	..	..	..	..
MANUFACTURING ACTIVITY											
Employment (1987=100)	80.2	82.3	84.3	86.1	89.5	91.0	91.9	92.7	93.5	94.6	95.8
Real Earnings per Empl. (1987=100)	..	..	..	..	..	..	..	..	..	..	..
Real Output per Empl. (1987=100)	..	..	..	..	..	..	..	..	..	..	..
Earnings as % of Value Added	..	..	..	..	..	..	..	..	..	..	..
MONETARY HOLDINGS					*(Millions of current Bulgarian Leva)*						
Money Supply, Broadly Defined	..	..	..	..	..	..	..	..	..	..	..
Money	..	..	..	..	..	..	..	..	..	..	..
Currency Outside Banks	..	..	..	..	..	..	..	..	..	..	..
Demand Deposits	..	..	..	..	..	..	..	..	..	..	..
Quasi-Money	..	..	..	..	..	..	..	..	..	..	..
					(Millions of current Bulgarian Leva)						
GOVERNMENT DEFICIT (-) OR SURPLUS	..	..	..	..	..	..	..	..	..	..	..
Current Revenue	..	..	..	..	..	..	..	..	..	..	..
Current Expenditure	..	..	..	..	..	..	..	..	..	..	..
Current Budget Balance	..	..	..	..	..	..	..	..	..	..	..
Capital Receipts	..	..	..	..	..	..	..	..	..	..	..
Capital Payments	..	..	..	..	..	..	..	..	..	..	..

1981	1982	1983	1984	1985	1986	1987	1988	1989	1990 estimate	Notes	BULGARIA
..	2,450	2,260	2,150	2,040	2,170	2,560	2,760	2,710	2,250	..	**CURRENT GNP PER CAPITA (US $)**
8,878	8,894	8,909	8,925	8,941	8,957	8,971	8,981	8,989	8,823	..	**POPULATION (thousands)**
				(Millions of current Bulgarian Leva)							**USE AND ORIGIN OF RESOURCES**
27,546	28,781	29,674	31,605	32,480	34,194	36,123	37,629	38,397	40,529	..	Gross National Product (GNP)
-272	-232	-141	-66	-115	-230	-408	-717	-1,078	-1,471	..	Net Factor Income from Abroad
27,818	29,013	29,815	31,671	32,595	34,424	36,531	38,345	39,475	42,000	..	GDP at Market Prices
295	309	57	489	-134	-1,216	-670	-128	-3	-657	..	Resource Balance
9,823	9,947	11,009	12,075	13,519	13,944	14,892	17,481	17,190	16,751	..	Exports of Goods & NFServices
9,529	9,637	10,953	11,586	13,653	15,161	15,561	17,609	17,193	17,409	..	Imports of Goods & NFServices
27,523	28,704	29,758	31,182	32,729	35,640	37,201	38,473	39,478	42,657	..	Domestic Absorption
13,057	13,976	14,945	15,630	16,510	17,048	18,685	18,688	19,305	22,875	..	Private Consumption, etc.
4,595	4,997	5,006	5,036	5,724	6,242	6,497	6,587	7,069	7,426	..	General Gov't Consumption
9,872	9,730	9,807	10,516	10,495	12,350	12,020	13,197	13,104	12,356	..	Gross Domestic Investment
7,690	7,973	7,975	8,112	8,613	9,291	9,817	10,260	10,328	9,145	..	Fixed Investment
677	-22	31	51	151	585	-1,212	-1,881	-1,217	-1,917	..	Indirect Taxes, net
27,141	29,035	29,783	31,620	32,445	33,838	37,743	40,226	40,692	43,917	..	GDP at factor cost
4,625	4,984	4,317	5,008	3,869	4,447	4,309	4,394	4,457	7,356	..	Agriculture
14,448	16,802	17,984	18,988	20,382	22,035	22,454	23,379	23,432	21,688	..	Industry
..	..	..								..	Manufacturing
8,745	7,228	7,513	7,675	8,344	7,942	9,768	10,572	11,586	12,956	..	Services, etc.
10,167	10,040	9,863	11,005	10,361	11,134	11,350	13,070	13,101	11,699	..	Gross Domestic Saving
..	..	..		10,321	10,967	11,036	12,439	12,088	10,501	..	Gross National Saving
				(Millions of 1987 Bulgarian Leva)							
29,156	29,760	31,049	32,174	32,917	34,241	36,123	36,949	36,533	32,117	..	Gross National Product
29,493	30,050	31,242	32,275	33,067	34,464	36,531	37,484	37,274	32,957	..	GDP at Market Prices
..	..	827	1,658	581	-696	-670	240	-54	-619	..	Resource Balance
..	..	13,730	16,598	15,935	13,131	14,892	12,909	11,672	9,874	..	Exports of Goods & NFServices
..	..	12,903	14,940	15,354	13,827	15,561	12,669	11,725	10,493	..	Imports of Goods & NFServices
..	..	30,415	30,617	32,486	35,160	37,201	37,244	37,328	33,576	..	Domestic Absorption
..	..	14,947	14,810	16,038	16,556	18,684	17,903	18,222	18,051	..	Private Consumption, etc.
4,858	5,185	5,228	5,118	5,805	6,246	6,497	6,440	6,695	5,828	..	General Gov't Consumption
10,439	10,095	10,240	10,689	10,643	12,358	12,020	12,902	12,411	9,697	..	Gross Domestic Investment
8,131	8,272	8,327	8,245	8,734	9,297	9,817	10,030	9,781	7,177	..	Fixed Investment
28,776	30,073	31,209	32,223	32,914	33,879	37,743	39,323	38,427	34,462	..	GDP at factor cost
5,271	5,577	4,666	5,211	4,136	5,048	4,309	4,235	4,153	3,877	..	Agriculture
15,430	16,872	18,161	19,275	20,257	21,309	22,454	23,000	24,258	20,308	..	Industry
..	..	..	..		..		..	..	..	..	Manufacturing
8,981	7,845	8,415	7,790	8,674	8,108	9,768	10,249	8,862	8,773	..	Services, etc.
											Memo Items:
..	..	12,969	15,571	15,204	12,718	14,892	12,577	11,723	10,097	..	Capacity to Import
..	..	-761	-1,028	-731	-413	0	-332	52	223	..	Terms of Trade Adjustment
..	..	30,482	31,247	32,335	34,051	36,531	37,152	37,326	33,180	..	Gross Domestic Income
..	..	30,288	31,146	32,185	33,827	36,123	36,617	36,584	32,339	..	Gross National Income
				(Index 1987 = 100)							**DOMESTIC PRICES/DEFLATORS**
94.3	96.5	95.4	98.1	98.6	99.9	100.0	102.3	105.9	127.4	..	Overall (GDP)
..	..	97.8	101.8	100.7	101.4	100.0	103.3	105.8	127.0	..	Domestic Absorption
87.7	89.4	92.5	96.1	93.5	88.1	100.0	103.7	107.3	189.8	..	Agriculture
93.6	99.6	99.0	98.5	100.6	103.4	100.0	101.6	96.6	106.8	..	Industry
..	..	..	..		..	..	..	..		..	Manufacturing
..	..	..	..	..	..	..	..	..		..	Consumer Price Index
											MANUFACTURING ACTIVITY
97.2	98.3	98.1	98.7	100.0	100.9	100.0	101.8			..	Employment (1987=100)
..	..	..	..	..	..	..	..	..	..	..	Real Earnings per Empl. (1987=100)
..	..	..	..	..	..	..	..	..	..	..	Real Output per Empl. (1987=100)
..	..	..	..	..	..	..	..			..	Earnings as % of Value Added
				(Millions of current Bulgarian Leva)							**MONETARY HOLDINGS**
..	..	..	..	..	..	..	..	..	..	..	Money Supply, Broadly Defined
..	..	..	..	..	13,213	15,469	17,260	19,855	21,643	..	Money
..	..	..	..	..	3,378	4,014	4,731	5,969	7,666	..	Currency Outside Banks
..	..	..	..	..	9,835	11,455	12,529	13,886	13,977	..	Demand Deposits
..	..	..	..	..	..	..	..	..	..	..	Quasi-Money
				(Millions of current Bulgarian Leva)							
..	..	..	..	..	..	-1,915	-2,099	-594	..	..	**GOVERNMENT DEFICIT (-) OR SURPLUS**
..	..	..	..	..	..	28,409	28,679	30,123	..	..	Current Revenue
..	..	..	..	..	..	26,043	26,762	27,356	..	..	Current Expenditure
..	..	..	..	..	..	2,366	1,916	2,767	..	..	Current Budget Balance
..	..	..	..	..	..				..	..	Capital Receipts
..	..	..	..	..	..	4,281	4,015	3,361	..	..	Capital Payments

BULGARIA	1970	1971	1972	1973	1974	1975	1976	1977	1978	1979	1980
FOREIGN TRADE (CUSTOMS BASIS)				*(Millions of current US dollars)*							
Value of Exports, fob	..	..	..	..	..	..	..	..	..	..	10,372
Nonfuel Primary Products	..	..	..	..	..	..	..	..	..	..	..
Fuels	..	..	..	..	..	..	..	..	..	..	..
Manufactures	..	..	..	..	..	..	..	..	..	..	..
Value of Imports, cif	..	..	..	..	..	..	..	..	..	..	9,650
Nonfuel Primary Products	..	..	..	..	..	..	..	..	..	..	..
Fuels	..	..	..	..	..	..	..	..	..	..	..
Manufactures	..	..	..	..	..	..	..	..	..	..	..
					(Index 1987 = 100)						
Terms of Trade	..	..	..	..	..	..	..	..	..	..	..
Export Prices, fob	..	..	..	..	..	..	..	..	..	..	..
Import Prices, cif	..	..	..	..	..	..	..	..	..	..	..
BALANCE OF PAYMENTS					*(Millions of current US dollars)*						
Exports of Goods & Services	..	..	..	..	..	..	..	..	..	..	9,443.00
Merchandise, fob	..	..	..	..	..	..	..	..	..	..	8,091.00
Nonfactor Services	..	..	..	..	..	..	..	..	..	..	1,211.00
Factor Services	..	..	..	..	..	..	..	..	..	..	141.00
Imports of Goods & Services	..	..	..	..	..	..	..	..	..	..	8,547.00
Merchandise, fob	..	..	..	..	..	..	..	..	..	..	7,445.00
Nonfactor Services	..	..	..	..	..	..	..	..	..	..	549.00
Factor Services	..	..	..	..	..	..	..	..	..	..	553.00
Long-Term Interest	0.00	0.00	0.00	0.00	1.10	1.80	1.50	1.90	3.60	7.20	23.30
Private Current Transfers, net	..	..	..	..	..	..	..	..	..	..	58.00
Workers' Remittances	..	..	..	..	..	..	..	..	..	..	..
Curr. A/C Bal before Off. Transf.	..	..	..	..	..	..	..	..	..	..	954.00
Net Official Transfers	..	..	..	..	..	..	..	..	..	..	0.00
Curr. A/C Bal after Off. Transf.	..	..	..	..	..	..	..	..	..	..	954.00
Long-Term Capital, net	..	..	..	..	..	..	..	..	..	..	-523.00
Direct Investment	..	..	..	..	..	..	..	..	..	..	..
Long-Term Loans	0.00	0.00	4.60	7.30	2.60	1.30	9.50	1.30	9.60	11.30	216.50
Disbursements	0.00	0.00	4.60	7.30	2.60	1.30	9.50	1.30	9.60	11.30	221.90
Repayments	0.00	0.00	0.00	0.00	0.00	0.00	0.00	0.00	0.00	0.00	5.40
Other Long-Term Capital	..	..	..	..	..	..	..	..	..	..	-739.50
Other Capital, net	..	..	..	..	..	..	..	..	..	..	-196.00
Change in Reserves	..	..	..	..	..	..	..	..	..	..	-235.00
Memo Item:					*(Bulgarian Leva per US dollar)*						
Conversion Factor (Annual Avg)	..	..	..	..	..	..	..	..	1.340	1.300	1.290
				(Millions of US dollars), outstanding at end of year							
EXTERNAL DEBT (Total)	0	0	5	13	19	20	31	38	56	68	272
Long-Term Debt (by debtor)	0	0	5	13	19	20	31	38	56	68	272
Central Bank, incl. IMF credit	0	0	5	13	19	20	31	38	56	68	272
Central Government	..	..	..	..	..	..	..	..	..	..	..
Rest of General Government	..	..	..	..	..	..	..	..	..	..	..
Non-financial Public Enterprises	..	..	..	..	..	..	..	..	..	..	..
Priv. Sector, incl non-guaranteed	..	..	..	..	..	..	..	..	..	..	..
Short-Term Debt	0	0	0	0	0	0	0	0	0	0	0
Memo Items:					*Millions US dollars)*						
Int'l Reserves Excluding Gold	..	..	..	..	..	..	..	..	..	..	..
Gold Holdings (at market price)	..	..	..	..	..	..	..	..	..	..	..
SOCIAL INDICATORS											
Total Fertility Rate	2.2	2.1	2.0	2.1	2.3	2.2	2.2	2.2	2.1	2.1	2.1
Infant Mortality Rate	27.3	24.9	26.2	26.2	25.5	23.1	23.5	23.7	22.2	21.2	20.2
Life Expectancy at Birth	71.1	71.2	71.2	71.2	71.2	71.1	71.1	71.1	71.1	71.2	71.3
Urban Population, % of total	51.8	52.9	54.1	55.2	56.4	57.5	58.2	59.0	59.7	60.5	61.2
Food Prod. per capita (1987=100)	94.0	95.6	100.8	98.5	88.7	94.2	102.4	95.9	100.2	107.6	101.5
Labor Force, Agriculture (%)	34.8	33.1	31.4	29.8	28.1	26.5	24.8	23.2	21.5	19.8	18.1
Labor Force, Female (%)	44.2	44.5	44.8	45.1	45.4	45.6	45.8	45.9	46.0	46.1	46.3
Primary Schl. Enroll. Ratio	101.0	..	..	..	..	99.0	99.0	99.0	97.0	96.0	98.0
Primary Schl. Enroll. Ratio, Female	100.0	..	..	..	..	99.0	99.0	98.0	96.0	95.0	98.0
Secondary Schl. Enroll. Ratio	79.0	..	..	..	..	89.0	90.0	90.0	89.0	87.0	84.0

1981	1982	1983	1984	1985	1986	1987	1988	1989	1990 estimate	Notes	BULGARIA
					(Millions of current US dollars)						**FOREIGN TRADE (CUSTOMS BASIS)**
..	..	..	..	..	..	..	..	..	..	..	Value of Exports, fob
..	..	..	..	..	..	..	..	..	..	..	Nonfuel Primary Products
..	..	..	..	..	..	..	..	..	..	..	Fuels
..	..	..	..	..	..	..	..	..	..	..	Manufactures
..	..	..	..	..	..	..	..	..	..	..	Value of Imports, cif
..	..	..	..	..	..	..	..	..	..	..	Nonfuel Primary Products
..	..	..	..	..	..	..	..	..	..	..	Fuels
..	..	..	..	..	..	..	..	..	..	..	Manufactures
					(Index 1987 = 100)						
..	..	..	..	..	..	..	..	..	..	..	Terms of Trade
..	..	..	..	..	..	..	..	..	..	..	Export Prices, fob
..	..	..	..	..	..	..	..	..	..	..	Import Prices, cif
					(Millions of current US dollars)						**BALANCE OF PAYMENTS**
9,518.00	9,261.00	10,049.00	11,117.00	11,520.00	9,958.00	11,570.00	10,551.00	9,618.00	7,070.00	..	Exports of Goods & Services
8,052.00	7,894.00	8,829.00	9,671.00	10,313.00	8,862.00	10,297.00	9,283.00	8,268.00	6,113.00		Merchandise, fob
1,284.00	1,207.00	1,059.00	1,273.00	1,047.00	958.00	1,158.00	1,186.00	1,223.00	837.00		Nonfactor Services
182.00	160.00	161.00	173.00	160.00	138.00	115.00	82.00	127.00	120.00		Factor Services
9,486.00	9,186.00	10,122.00	10,663.00	11,729.00	10,976.00	12,398.00	11,056.00	10,464.00	8,905.00	..	Imports of Goods & Services
8,360.00	8,184.00	9,235.00	9,849.00	10,818.00	10,045.00	11,308.00	9,889.00	8,960.00	7,427.00		Merchandise, fob
683.00	630.00	598.00	581.00	654.00	631.00	661.00	656.00	785.00	600.00		Nonfactor Services
443.00	372.00	289.00	233.00	257.00	300.00	429.00	511.00	719.00	878.00		Factor Services
54.80	163.80	151.10	236.40	216.70	283.00	384.70	466.20	706.10	455.70		Long-Term Interest
90.00	102.00	109.00	81.00	73.00	67.00	108.00	103.00	77.00	125.00		Private Current Transfers, net
..	..	..	..	..	..	..	..	..	..		Workers' Remittances
122.00	177.00	36.00	535.00	-136.00	-951.00	-720.00	-402.00	-769.00	-1,710.00		Curr. A/C Bal before Off. Transf.
0.00	0.00	0.00	0.00	0.00	0.00	0.00	0.00	0.00	..		Net Official Transfers
122.00	177.00	36.00	535.00	-136.00	-951.00	-720.00	-402.00	-769.00	-1,710.00		Curr. A/C Bal after Off. Transf.
-622.00	-555.00	-351.00	-51.00	185.00	597.00	-69.00	1,554.00	319.00	-4,089.00		Long-Term Capital, net
..	..	..	..	..	0.00	0.00	0.00	0.00	4.00		Direct Investment
591.80	458.10	781.80	1,161.80	571.50	659.60	532.70	2,137.40	707.10	-390.80		Long-Term Loans
603.90	474.60	805.50	1,213.10	2,037.10	3,140.80	2,779.50	4,225.70	3,037.20	436.80		Disbursements
12.10	16.50	23.70	51.30	1,465.60	2,481.20	2,246.80	2,088.30	2,330.10	827.60		Repayments
-1,213.80	-1,013.10	-1,132.80	-1,212.80	-386.50	-62.60	-601.70	-583.40	-388.10	-3,702.20		Other Long-Term Capital
139.00	504.00	527.00	-67.00	249.00	-531.00	292.00	-495.00	16.00	4,921.00		Other Capital, net
361.00	-126.00	-212.00	-417.00	-298.00	885.00	497.00	-657.00	434.00	878.00		Change in Reserves
					(Bulgarian Leva per US dollar)						**Memo Item:**
1.390	1.470	1.760	1.820	1.860	1.700	1.280	1.670	1.820	2.110	..	Conversion Factor (Annual Avg)
				(Millions of US dollars), outstanding at end of year							
852	1,297	2,046	3,139	3,994	5,244	7,072	9,128	10,213	10,927	..	**EXTERNAL DEBT (Total)**
852	1,297	2,046	3,139	3,944	5,184	6,721	8,499	9,359	9,564		Long-Term Debt (by debtor)
852	1,297	2,046	3,139	3,944	5,184	6,721	8,499	9,359	9,564		Central Bank, incl. IMF credit
..	..	..	..	..	..	..	..	..	..		Central Government
..	..	..	..	..	..	..	..	..	..		Rest of General Government
..	..	..	..	..	..	..	..	..	..		Non-financial Public Enterprises
..	..	..	..	..	..	..	..	..	..		Priv. Sector, incl non-guaranteed
0	0	0	0	50	60	351	629	854	1,363		Short-Term Debt
					Millions US dollars)						**Memo Items:**
..	..	..	..	..	..	..	..	..	..		Int'l Reserves Excluding Gold
..	..	..	..	..	..	..	..	..	..		Gold Holdings (at market price)
											SOCIAL INDICATORS
2.0	2.0	2.0	2.0	1.9	2.0	1.9	1.9	1.9	1.9	..	Total Fertility Rate
19.5	18.2	16.8	16.2	15.4	14.5	14.7	14.2	13.7	13.1	..	Infant Mortality Rate
71.3	71.4	71.5	71.6	71.8	71.9	72.0	72.2	72.4	72.7	..	Life Expectancy at Birth
61.9	62.5	63.2	63.8	64.5	65.1	65.8	66.4	67.1	67.7	..	Urban Population, % of total
110.2	118.5	103.9	113.1	92.5	109.5	100.0	101.1	108.8	98.1	..	Food Prod. per capita (1987=100)
										..	Labor Force, Agriculture (%)
46.2	46.2	46.2	46.2	46.2	46.3	46.3	46.3	46.3	46.4	..	Labor Force, Female (%)
..	102.0	102.0	102.0	102.0	104.0	104.0	104.0	97.0	..	..	Primary Schl. Enroll. Ratio
99.0	102.0	101.0	102.0	102.0	103.0	103.0	103.0	96.0	..	..	Primary Schl. Enroll. Ratio, Female
..	82.0	86.0	92.0	102.0	75.0	76.0	75.0	75.0	..	..	Secondary Schl. Enroll. Ratio

BURKINA FASO	1970	1971	1972	1973	1974	1975	1976	1977	1978	1979	1980
CURRENT GNP PER CAPITA (US $)	80	80	90	100	120	130	150	160	170	210	240
POPULATION (thousands)	5,633	5,741	5,848	5,959	6,076	6,202	6,341	6,487	6,639	6,798	6,962

USE AND ORIGIN OF RESOURCES *(Billions of current CFA Francs)*

	1970	1971	1972	1973	1974	1975	1976	1977	1978	1979	1980
Gross National Product (GNP)	116.69	122.64	134.16	140.22	166.69	182.89	213.91	253.45	292.39	327.96	360.50
Net Factor Income from Abroad	4.30	4.80	4.80	6.80	6.30	4.30	6.90	6.90	-3.00	-2.00	-1.00
GDP at Market Prices	112.40	117.84	129.36	133.42	160.39	178.59	207.01	246.55	295.39	329.96	361.50
Resource Balance	-11.20	-16.25	-18.27	-21.20	-24.37	-39.40	-36.87	-53.30	-57.55	-66.28	-76.89
Exports of Goods & NFServices	7.32	7.74	9.87	10.04	15.91	15.66	20.25	23.40	26.30	32.44	38.58
Imports of Goods & NFServices	18.52	24.00	28.14	31.24	40.28	55.05	57.12	76.70	83.85	98.72	115.47
Domestic Absorption	123.60	134.10	147.63	154.63	184.76	217.99	243.88	299.85	352.94	396.24	438.40
Private Consumption, etc.	101.59	104.26	110.96	110.29	121.72	144.43	165.16	216.08	256.95	294.06	337.97
General Gov't Consumption	8.14	8.76	9.79	11.24	13.81	23.91	21.85	25.77	30.92	37.11	34.76
Gross Domestic Investment	13.86	21.08	26.88	33.10	49.23	49.65	56.86	58.00	65.07	65.07	65.67
Fixed Investment	..	..	..	..	..	..	..	..	..	59.57	59.27
Indirect Taxes, net	4.30	6.49	6.48	7.66	9.03	10.47	14.26	18.44	20.01	13.50	16.00
GDP at factor cost	108.09	111.35	122.88	125.76	151.37	168.12	192.75	228.11	275.38	316.46	345.50
Agriculture	33.64	35.34	40.45	38.44	48.46	50.56	58.87	68.68	87.20	95.01	100.79
Industry	29.79	34.09	35.98	41.71	43.97	55.31	65.37	62.66	75.60	81.33	85.44
Manufacturing	18.02	19.71	22.82	24.38	28.53	31.12	35.27	38.90	43.57	50.31	51.17
Services, etc.	44.67	41.93	46.45	45.61	58.94	62.25	68.51	96.76	112.58	140.12	159.27
Gross Domestic Saving	2.66	4.82	8.61	11.90	24.86	10.25	19.99	4.70	7.52	-1.21	-11.22
Gross National Saving	11.40	15.60	19.08	26.67	38.18	21.51	35.62	21.45	16.85	14.46	11.40

(Billions of 1987 CFA Francs)

	1970	1971	1972	1973	1974	1975	1976	1977	1978	1979	1980
Gross National Product	398.15	404.04	417.02	424.25	454.18	459.43	502.87	507.77	512.68	545.03	546.11
GDP at Market Prices	382.46	387.19	401.34	403.07	436.62	448.61	486.53	493.75	517.54	548.30	547.79
Resource Balance	-48.39	-64.16	-58.74	-66.67	-66.39	-88.06	-79.81	-109.69	-89.50	-75.17	-98.94
Exports of Goods & NFServices	35.04	35.44	47.67	44.00	47.26	46.44	42.78	44.81	65.43	81.15	73.13
Imports of Goods & NFServices	83.42	99.60	106.41	110.67	113.64	134.50	122.58	154.51	154.93	156.33	172.07
Domestic Absorption	430.85	451.35	460.08	469.74	503.01	536.67	566.34	603.44	607.04	623.47	646.73
Private Consumption, etc.	360.99	364.18	352.35	347.36	369.29	389.34	418.55	467.64	467.60	494.28	521.90
General Gov't Consumption	29.26	30.00	34.81	37.03	39.26	53.70	53.33	49.63	50.37	55.09	49.22
Gross Domestic Investment	40.60	57.17	72.92	85.35	94.46	93.63	94.46	86.17	89.07	74.10	75.61
Fixed Investment	..	..	..	..	..	..	..	..	..	71.07	72.30
GDP at factor cost	364.22	368.67	384.75	383.26	415.66	425.79	457.01	461.02	486.97	524.39	517.86
Agriculture	172.74	174.82	174.30	164.53	189.21	187.67	194.87	183.56	193.84	181.35	185.84
Industry	102.57	106.63	108.78	123.01	108.64	131.43	145.59	120.96	130.23	126.42	131.67
Manufacturing	58.76	60.45	66.10	69.49	70.62	74.01	76.83	77.96	80.79	83.68	91.41
Services, etc.	88.90	87.22	101.67	95.72	117.81	106.68	116.54	156.50	162.91	216.61	200.35

Memo Items:

	1970	1971	1972	1973	1974	1975	1976	1977	1978	1979	1980
Capacity to Import	32.96	32.14	37.32	35.56	44.89	38.25	43.46	47.14	48.60	51.37	57.49
Terms of Trade Adjustment	-2.08	-3.31	-10.34	-8.44	-2.37	-8.19	0.68	2.32	-16.83	-29.79	-15.64
Gross Domestic Income	380.39	383.89	391.00	394.63	434.26	440.42	487.21	496.07	500.71	518.52	532.14
Gross National Income	396.07	400.73	406.68	415.81	451.82	451.23	503.55	510.09	495.85	515.25	530.47

DOMESTIC PRICES/DEFLATORS *(Index 1987 = 100)*

	1970	1971	1972	1973	1974	1975	1976	1977	1978	1979	1980
Overall (GDP)	29.4	30.4	32.2	33.1	36.7	39.8	42.5	49.9	57.1	60.2	66.0
Domestic Absorption	28.7	29.7	32.1	32.9	36.7	40.6	43.1	49.7	58.1	63.6	67.8
Agriculture	19.5	20.2	23.2	23.4	25.6	26.9	30.2	37.4	45.0	52.4	54.2
Industry	29.0	32.0	33.1	33.9	40.5	42.1	44.9	51.8	58.0	64.3	64.9
Manufacturing	30.7	32.6	34.5	35.1	40.4	42.0	45.9	49.9	53.9	60.1	56.0
Consumer Price Index	31.5	32.2	31.2	33.6	36.6	43.4	39.8	51.7	56.0	64.3	72.2

MANUFACTURING ACTIVITY

	1970	1971	1972	1973	1974	1975	1976	1977	1978	1979	1980
Employment (1987=100)	..	..	..	..	..	..	..	..	..	..	..
Real Earnings per Empl. (1987=100)	..	..	..	..	..	..	..	..	..	..	..
Real Output per Empl. (1987=100)	..	..	..	..	..	..	..	..	..	..	..
Earnings as % of Value Added	..	..	..	..	11.1	13.3	15.4	17.5	20.7	22.8	23.0

MONETARY HOLDINGS *(Billions of current CFA Francs)*

	1970	1971	1972	1973	1974	1975	1976	1977	1978	1979	1980
Money Supply, Broadly Defined	9.36	9.93	10.59	14.49	17.53	24.32	31.55	35.57	42.52	46.24	53.22
Money	9.14	9.47	9.89	13.50	16.38	22.50	27.55	30.78	34.40	34.76	41.67
Currency Outside Banks	5.74	5.65	5.77	7.13	8.51	10.65	12.85	14.75	13.50	17.36	19.90
Demand Deposits	3.40	3.82	4.11	6.36	7.86	11.85	14.71	16.03	20.90	17.41	21.77
Quasi-Money	0.23	0.46	0.71	0.99	1.16	1.82	4.00	4.79	8.12	11.48	11.55

GOVERNMENT DEFICIT (-) OR SURPLUS *(Millions of current CFA Francs)*

	1970	1971	1972	1973	1974	1975	1976	1977	1978	1979	1980
GOVERNMENT DEFICIT (-) OR SURPLUS	..	..	..	354	2,212	-1,664	-1,272	4,313	1,495	-5,622	879
Current Revenue	..	..	..	12,850	15,971	16,644	21,728	31,384	32,542	35,550	43,109
Current Expenditure	..	..	..	10,255	11,457	14,487	17,503	22,343	27,203	34,661	35,305
Current Budget Balance	..	..	..	2,595	4,514	2,157	4,225	9,041	5,339	889	7,804
Capital Receipts	..	..	..	12	2	18	37	30	..	1	30
Capital Payments	..	..	..	2,253	2,304	3,839	5,534	4,758	3,844	6,512	6,955

1981	1982	1983	1984	1985	1986	1987	1988	1989	1990 estimate	Notes	BURKINA FASO
250	250	220	190	190	210	240	300	310	330	..	**CURRENT GNP PER CAPITA (US $)**
7,132	7,308	7,491	7,681	7,881	8,090	8,308	8,535	8,771	9,016	..	**POPULATION (thousands)**
											USE AND ORIGIN OF RESOURCES
				(Billions of current CFA Francs)							
425.08	508.45	536.98	563.40	642.80	699.10	746.60	816.80	822.80	861.40	f	Gross National Product (GNP)
-3.00	-3.00	-4.00	-2.50	-0.40	-4.20	-4.30	-3.90	-4.90	-2.10	..	Net Factor Income from Abroad
428.09	511.45	540.98	565.90	643.20	703.30	750.90	820.70	827.70	863.50	..	GDP at Market Prices
-90.15	-115.28	-112.61	-99.90	-146.20	-140.50	-118.80	-122.40	-145.40	-132.90	..	Resource Balance
47.34	49.97	50.85	73.40	73.10	65.40	79.60	84.60	81.20	96.40	..	Exports of Goods & NFServices
137.49	165.25	163.46	173.30	219.30	205.90	198.40	207.00	226.60	229.30	..	Imports of Goods & NFServices
518.23	626.73	653.59	665.80	789.40	843.80	869.70	943.10	973.10	996.40	..	Domestic Absorption
404.22	443.02	461.12	492.50	545.20	591.80	619.50	656.70	676.10	712.50	..	Private Consumption, etc.
41.27	73.46	81.03	76.90	77.70	90.80	100.30	104.00	108.20	111.70	..	General Gov't Consumption
72.74	110.25	111.45	96.40	166.50	161.20	149.90	182.40	188.80	172.20	..	Gross Domestic Investment
68.64	102.25	108.45	97.60	134.50	162.40	201.70	184.30	156.80	149.30	..	Fixed Investment
17.70	22.00	18.00	18.50	25.20	26.90	26.90	27.90	29.20	31.80	..	Indirect Taxes, net
410.38	489.45	522.98	547.40	618.00	676.40	724.00	792.80	798.50	831.70	..	GDP at factor cost
125.04	137.94	146.41	158.06	206.00	225.00	233.00	275.00	278.00	264.20	..	Agriculture
95.84	114.99	131.39	134.80	140.00	159.00	182.00	203.00	204.00	199.80	..	Industry
59.30	70.71	83.16	82.12	88.00	94.00	107.00	112.00	115.00	118.50	..	Manufacturing
189.50	236.52	245.17	254.53	272.00	292.40	309.00	314.80	316.50	367.70	..	Services, etc.
-17.41	-5.03	-1.17	-3.50	20.30	20.70	31.10	60.00	43.40	39.30	..	Gross Domestic Saving
12.26	21.13	28.76	25.24	65.79	71.79	63.81	89.87	69.60	68.20	..	Gross National Saving
				(Billions of 1987 CFA Francs)							
567.66	625.62	631.61	622.67	677.96	737.56	746.60	793.66	789.15	802.20	I	Gross National Product
570.94	630.49	636.49	625.40	678.35	741.91	750.90	797.37	793.95	804.13	..	GDP at Market Prices
-101.81	-109.20	-101.46	-82.97	-128.17	-145.57	-118.80	-128.16	-132.31	-127.26	..	Resource Balance
82.75	71.20	55.81	63.51	62.34	68.32	79.60	75.14	75.56	91.01	..	Exports of Goods & NFServices
184.56	180.40	157.27	146.48	190.51	213.89	198.40	203.30	207.88	218.27	..	Imports of Goods & NFServices
672.75	739.69	737.96	708.37	806.51	887.48	869.70	925.53	926.27	931.39	..	Domestic Absorption
543.15	558.22	567.44	534.09	559.07	605.11	619.50	651.38	646.14	658.96	..	Private Consumption, etc.
54.14	82.78	79.42	81.66	83.83	92.96	100.30	98.10	103.31	105.52	..	General Gov't Consumption
75.46	98.69	91.10	92.62	163.61	189.42	149.90	176.05	176.82	166.92	..	Gross Domestic Investment
75.01	97.44	93.06	94.65	134.77	175.25	201.70	176.15	151.55	155.06	..	Fixed Investment
541.41	599.00	611.48	604.94	651.75	713.54	724.00	770.26	765.92	774.50	..	GDP at factor cost
200.84	206.44	207.04	204.84	219.59	243.32	233.00	265.15	257.59	248.94	..	Agriculture
129.75	140.17	141.27	143.74	151.70	167.95	182.00	187.72	183.01	190.85	..	Industry
83.89	93.15	93.73	92.86	94.12	101.52	107.00	108.13	106.57	111.98	..	Manufacturing
210.82	252.39	263.17	256.35	280.45	302.27	309.00	317.39	325.32	334.71	..	Services, etc.
											Memo Items:
63.55	54.55	48.92	62.04	63.50	67.94	79.60	83.09	74.49	91.76	..	Capacity to Import
-19.20	-16.65	-6.89	-1.47	1.16	-0.38	0.00	7.95	-1.07	0.75	..	Terms of Trade Adjustment
551.74	613.84	629.61	623.93	679.51	741.53	750.90	805.32	792.88	804.88	..	Gross Domestic Income
548.46	608.97	624.73	621.21	679.12	737.18	746.60	801.61	788.08	802.95	..	Gross National Income
											DOMESTIC PRICES/DEFLATORS
				(Index 1987 = 100)							
75.0	81.1	85.0	90.5	94.8	94.8	100.0	102.9	104.3	107.4	..	Overall (GDP)
77.0	84.7	88.6	94.0	97.9	95.1	100.0	101.9	105.1	107.0	..	Domestic Absorption
62.3	66.8	70.7	77.2	93.8	92.5	100.0	103.7	107.9	106.1	..	Agriculture
73.9	82.0	93.0	93.8	92.3	94.7	100.0	108.1	111.5	104.7	..	Industry
70.7	75.9	88.7	88.4	93.5	92.6	100.0	103.6	107.9	105.8	..	Manufacturing
77.7	87.0	94.3	98.9	105.7	102.9	100.0	104.4	103.9	103.4	..	Consumer Price Index
											MANUFACTURING ACTIVITY
..	..	..	..	..	..	..	..	..	..	..	Employment (1987=100)
..	..	..	..	..	..	..	..	..	..	..	Real Earnings per Empl. (1987=100)
..	..	..	..	..	..	..	..	..	..	..	Real Output per Empl. (1987=100)
21.2	19.8	18.3	..	..	..	..	..	..	..	..	Earnings as % of Value Added
				(Billions of current CFA Francs)							
											MONETARY HOLDINGS
63.72	71.38	80.06	92.77	93.32	114.19	127.51	148.69	154.17	153.49	..	Money Supply, Broadly Defined
48.83	54.36	60.33	66.50	69.54	85.43	91.18	100.87	105.27	103.63	..	Money
24.83	27.03	31.74	31.24	30.97	43.43	43.71	49.31	53.28	58.69	..	Currency Outside Banks
24.00	27.34	28.60	35.26	38.57	42.00	47.47	51.56	52.00	44.94	..	Demand Deposits
14.89	17.01	19.72	26.26	23.78	28.77	36.33	47.83	48.89	49.87	..	Quasi-Money
				(Millions of current CFA Francs)							
-4,674	-6,185	562	-3,350	6,339	-747	1,976	..	..	..	F	**GOVERNMENT DEFICIT (-) OR SURPLUS**
48,674	54,527	54,540	63,071	71,488	79,162	89,924	..	..	..	..	Current Revenue
41,140	55,354	47,987	60,854	56,639	71,690	..	..	..	..	..	Current Expenditure
7,534	-827	6,553	2,217	14,849	7,472	..	..	..	..	..	Current Budget Balance
46	33	..	17	100	78	40	..	..	..	..	Capital Receipts
12,254	5,391	5,991	5,584	8,610	8,297	..	..	..	..	..	Capital Payments

BURKINA FASO	1970	1971	1972	1973	1974	1975	1976	1977	1978	1979	1980
FOREIGN TRADE (CUSTOMS BASIS)					*(Millions of current US dollars)*						
Value of Exports, fob	18.20	15.87	20.35	25.38	36.05	43.53	53.32	55.24	42.42	76.76	90.23
Nonfuel Primary Products	17.40	14.91	18.60	23.91	33.10	40.70	..	52.11	39.18	66.80	80.40
Fuels	0.00	0.00	0.00	0.13	0.01	0.00	..	0.03	0.06	0.44	0.10
Manufactures	0.80	0.95	1.74	1.34	2.94	2.83	3.13	3.09	3.18	9.52	9.72
Value of Imports, cif	46.66	49.66	60.75	78.79	144.49	151.23	144.63	209.21	227.86	307.39	357.96
Nonfuel Primary Products	12.67	14.04	18.07	23.65	53.22	36.74	32.39	48.98	70.95	77.20	83.09
Fuels	3.82	4.39	5.20	5.57	9.37	13.37	11.35	17.75	19.39	34.82	47.30
Manufactures	30.16	31.22	37.48	49.57	81.90	101.12	100.90	142.48	137.52	195.37	227.57
					(Index 1987 = 100)						
Terms of Trade	216.6	212.8	208.5	240.3	147.2	125.6	158.6	147.2	143.4	145.6	135.1
Export Prices, fob	43.6	47.7	52.6	83.5	84.9	71.2	89.2	89.2	97.1	114.1	123.3
Import Prices, cif	20.1	22.4	25.2	34.8	57.7	56.7	56.2	60.6	67.7	78.4	91.3
BALANCE OF PAYMENTS					*(Millions of current US dollars)*						
Exports of Goods & Services	30.80	33.20	45.06	58.41	84.37	95.19	106.49	118.53	136.46	181.37	225.24
Merchandise, fob	24.60	24.57	36.05	44.23	65.98	73.49	83.06	94.83	107.81	132.70	160.59
Nonfactor Services	4.10	6.12	6.30	8.46	9.36	14.31	17.02	17.49	23.72	41.57	49.10
Factor Services	2.10	2.51	2.71	5.72	9.04	7.39	6.41	6.21	4.93	7.10	15.55
Imports of Goods & Services	67.70	88.96	112.48	154.86	210.50	281.31	260.37	341.98	406.14	506.83	596.37
Merchandise, fob	44.90	58.07	74.37	104.31	147.76	187.79	167.45	220.69	255.40	312.13	368.33
Nonfactor Services	20.70	27.88	34.09	44.59	51.44	74.06	77.00	94.88	134.71	178.38	208.40
Factor Services	2.10	3.01	4.02	5.96	11.29	19.46	15.93	26.40	16.03	16.31	19.63
Long-Term Interest	0.40	0.50	0.50	0.80	1.10	1.50	1.60	1.70	2.60	4.50	6.30
Private Current Transfers, net	16.00	21.56	22.47	35.76	29.15	32.47	36.51	40.12	54.64	83.07	111.82
Workers' Remittances	18.00	20.96	26.17	35.53	33.65	46.25	49.93	59.66	77.95	109.53	150.27
Curr. A/C Bal before Off. Transf.	-20.90	-34.20	-44.95	-60.68	-96.97	-153.65	-117.37	-183.32	-215.05	-242.39	-259.31
Net Official Transfers	29.40	35.00	48.42	63.18	91.72	99.35	84.85	100.33	155.51	185.87	210.58
Curr. A/C Bal after Off. Transf.	8.50	0.80	3.47	2.50	-5.26	-54.30	-32.51	-82.99	-59.54	-56.52	-48.73
Long-Term Capital, net	1.34	2.14	-5.48	17.69	13.03	19.04	18.69	40.18	27.76	64.04	53.46
Direct Investment	0.40	0.80	-1.00	4.19	2.41	-0.38	2.05	4.60	0.39	1.13	0.02
Long-Term Loans	-0.10	1.40	4.10	9.20	13.30	17.50	24.20	41.60	34.30	62.40	54.80
Disbursements	1.70	2.90	5.60	11.50	15.80	21.20	27.30	45.40	38.80	67.10	65.40
Repayments	1.80	1.50	1.50	2.30	2.50	3.70	3.10	3.80	4.50	4.70	10.60
Other Long-Term Capital	1.04	-0.06	-8.58	4.31	-2.68	1.92	-7.56	-6.03	-6.93	0.51	-1.36
Other Capital, net	2.26	-1.14	4.31	-8.81	8.54	29.00	15.30	24.37	7.21	13.11	6.19
Change in Reserves	-12.10	-1.80	-2.31	-11.39	-16.31	6.26	-1.47	18.44	24.57	-20.63	-10.92
Memo Item:					*(CFA Francs per US dollar)*						
Conversion Factor (Annual Avg)	277.710	277.130	252.210	222.700	240.500	214.320	238.980	245.670	225.640	212.720	211.300
EXTERNAL DEBT (Total)	20.70	23.60	20.00	31.20	47.20	62.50	85.20	164.40	262.70	295.00	330.40
				(Millions of US dollars), outstanding at end of year							
Long-Term Debt (by debtor)	20.70	23.60	20.00	31.20	47.20	62.50	85.20	134.40	184.70	257.00	295.40
Central Bank, incl. IMF credit	0.00	0.00	0.00	0.00	0.00	0.00	0.00	0.00	6.10	11.40	15.40
Central Government	16.60	16.90	10.30	16.40	24.90	39.60	59.00	99.60	137.40	190.90	229.40
Rest of General Government	0.10	0.10	0.10	0.10	0.00	0.00	0.00	0.00	0.00	0.00	0.00
Non-financial Public Enterprises	1.00	1.10	1.10	2.60	4.20	5.10	5.80	11.80	12.40	25.20	24.80
Priv. Sector, incl non-guaranteed	3.00	5.50	8.50	12.10	18.10	17.80	20.40	23.00	28.80	29.50	25.80
Short-Term Debt	0.00	0.00	0.00	0.00	0.00	0.00	0.00	30.00	78.00	38.00	35.00
Memo Items:					*(Millions of US dollars)*						
Int'l Reserves Excluding Gold	36.4	43.0	47.5	62.6	83.6	76.5	71.4	56.2	36.3	61.6	68.2
Gold Holdings (at market price)	..	..	..	..	..	..	..	0.9	1.9	5.7	6.6
SOCIAL INDICATORS											
Total Fertility Rate	6.4	6.4	6.4	6.4	6.4	6.5	6.5	6.5	6.5	6.5	6.5
Infant Mortality Rate	177.8	175.4	173.0	170.8	168.6	166.4	164.2	162.0	159.4	156.8	154.2
Life Expectancy at Birth	40.4	40.8	41.2	41.6	42.0	42.4	42.8	43.2	43.6	44.0	44.4
Urban Population, % of total	5.7	5.8	5.9	6.1	6.2	6.3	6.4	6.6	6.7	6.9	7.0
Food Prod. per capita (1987=100)	102.6	97.8	90.4	78.9	86.7	94.7	84.5	84.8	89.0	92.2	83.5
Labor Force, Agriculture (%)	88.3	88.1	87.9	87.8	87.6	87.5	87.3	87.1	87.0	86.8	86.7
Labor Force, Female (%)	48.3	48.3	48.2	48.2	48.2	48.1	48.1	48.0	47.9	47.9	47.8
Primary Schl. Enroll. Ratio	13.0	..	..	..	..	16.0	15.0	16.0	17.0	18.0	18.0
Primary Schl. Enroll. Ratio, Female	10.0	..	..	..	..	12.0	11.0	12.0	12.0	13.0	14.0
Secondary Schl. Enroll. Ratio	1.0	..	..	..	..	2.0	2.0	2.0	2.0	3.0	3.0

1981	1982	1983	1984	1985	1986	1987	1988	1989	1990 estimate	Notes	BURKINA FASO
											FOREIGN TRADE (CUSTOMS BASIS)
				(Millions of current US dollars)							
74.98	56.20	56.97	..	..	82.99	155.00	140.84	130.00	160.00	..	Value of Exports, fob
63.95	48.42	50.99	..	..	74.28	138.73	126.06	116.36	143.21	..	Nonfuel Primary Products
0.13	0.00	0.00	..	..	0.00	0.00	0.00	0.00	0.00	..	Fuels
10.90	7.77	5.98	..	..	8.71	16.27	14.78	13.64	16.79	..	Manufactures
337.55	346.18	287.52	211.38	..	405.00	434.00	453.05	400.00	480.00	..	Value of Imports, cif
93.66	97.89	82.82	60.89	..	116.66	125.02	130.50	115.22	138.27	..	Nonfuel Primary Products
52.50	57.01	49.22	36.19	..	69.33	74.30	77.56	68.48	82.17	..	Fuels
191.39	191.28	155.47	114.30	..	219.00	234.68	244.99	216.30	259.56	..	Manufactures
				(Index 1987 = 100)							
119.1	112.0	126.9	..	..	89.6	100.0	92.7	98.0	100.2	..	Terms of Trade
112.5	100.3	110.0	..	..	83.3	100.0	99.5	110.4	127.6	..	Export Prices, fob
94.5	89.6	86.7	..	..	93.0	100.0	107.3	112.7	127.3	..	Import Prices, cif
				(Millions of current US dollars)							**BALANCE OF PAYMENTS**
209.10	183.69	156.54	174.99	172.52	200.80	278.84	298.14	268.33	369.20		Exports of Goods & Services
159.36	126.43	112.93	140.87	135.56	149.00	229.92	249.12	215.67	304.19		Merchandise, fob
40.86	48.25	37.72	27.12	27.13	39.67	34.94	34.92	39.50	49.58		Nonfactor Services
8.88	9.02	5.89	7.01	9.83	12.13	13.98	14.10	13.17	15.43		Factor Services
552.21	553.11	471.78	408.80	498.68	618.92	688.44	722.18	738.85	866.07		Imports of Goods & Services
348.44	359.86	308.90	270.11	352.80	437.48	475.15	486.83	501.56	593.18		Merchandise, fob
185.08	173.97	146.90	124.27	129.35	147.84	185.00	208.16	208.77	249.39		Nonfactor Services
18.69	19.28	15.97	14.43	16.53	33.61	28.28	27.20	28.53	23.51		Factor Services
6.10	7.50	7.60	5.90	9.80	11.90	14.30	13.50	15.70	9.80		Long-Term Interest
120.22	88.73	89.04	71.48	102.14	159.64	123.14	113.37	97.49	113.86		Private Current Transfers, net
153.32	110.27	113.16	90.19	125.88	191.74	173.36	161.83	141.06	165.28		Workers' Remittances
-222.89	-280.68	-226.20	-162.33	-224.03	-258.47	-286.46	-310.67	-373.04	-383.01		Curr. A/C Bal before Off. Transf.
180.80	188.61	166.10	158.87	163.88	237.74	235.55	261.40	460.94	272.45		Net Official Transfers
-42.09	-92.07	-60.10	-3.46	-60.15	-20.74	-50.91	-49.27	87.90	-110.56	..	Curr. A/C Bal after Off. Transf.
37.22	56.23	78.93	45.08	43.18	52.93	85.12	70.55	-206.27	75.83	..	Long-Term Capital, net
2.43	1.95	1.98	1.67	-1.43	3.14	5.99	1.68	1.57	1.60	..	Direct Investment
60.80	65.20	81.80	41.40	40.50	74.40	94.80	72.90	81.80	60.50	..	Long-Term Loans
68.40	72.90	89.30	53.60	55.40	93.10	109.10	94.10	97.60	78.70	..	Disbursements
7.60	7.70	7.50	12.20	14.90	18.70	14.30	21.20	15.80	18.20	..	Repayments
-26.01	-10.92	-4.85	2.01	4.11	-24.61	-15.67	-4.03	-289.64	13.73	..	Other Long-Term Capital
19.15	35.64	17.51	-6.87	22.51	33.87	2.31	14.64	55.64	36.29		Other Capital, net
-14.29	0.20	-36.35	-34.76	-5.54	-66.06	-36.53	-35.92	62.74	-1.57		Change in Reserves
				(CFA Francs per US dollar)							**Memo Item:**
271.730	328.620	381.070	436.960	449.260	346.300	300.540	297.850	319.010	272.260	..	Conversion Factor (Annual Avg)
				(Millions of US dollars), outstanding at end of year							**EXTERNAL DEBT (Total)**
328.10	351.90	397.30	410.00	511.10	639.90	827.80	845.20	717.30	833.80		Long-Term Debt (by debtor)
293.10	319.90	370.20	380.00	466.30	584.90	750.10	769.90	648.80	749.90		Central Bank, incl. IMF credit
14.00	13.70	14.40	12.90	13.20	12.10	10.80	8.00	5.60	5.60		Central Government
232.70	271.20	315.70	327.50	404.20	520.70	681.50	714.50	604.80	709.10		Rest of General Government
0.00	0.00	0.00	0.00	0.00	0.00	0.00	0.00	0.00	..		Non-financial Public Enterprises
26.40	28.30	35.00	35.80	45.20	49.00	54.70	45.10	36.70	33.80		Priv. Sector, incl non-guaranteed
20.00	6.70	5.10	3.80	3.70	3.10	3.10	2.30	1.70	1.40		Short-Term Debt
35.00	32.00	27.10	30.00	44.80	55.00	77.70	75.30	68.50	83.90		
				(Millions of US dollars)							**Memo Items:**
70.8	61.8	85.0	106.3	139.5	233.5	322.6	320.9	265.5	300.5	..	Int'l Reserves Excluding Gold
4.5	5.1	4.2	3.4	3.6	4.3	5.4	4.6	4.5	4.3	..	Gold Holdings (at market price)
											SOCIAL INDICATORS
6.5	6.5	6.5	6.5	6.5	6.5	6.5	6.5	6.5	6.5	..	Total Fertility Rate
151.6	149.0	146.8	144.5	142.3	140.0	137.8	136.6	135.5	134.3	..	Infant Mortality Rate
44.8	45.2	45.6	46.0	46.4	46.8	47.2	47.4	47.5	47.7	..	Life Expectancy at Birth
7.2	7.4	7.5	7.7	7.9	8.2	8.5	8.7	8.8	9.0	..	Urban Population, % of total
89.2	87.4	87.8	86.0	101.3	111.1	100.0	108.9	101.2	91.2	..	Food Prod. per capita (1987=100)
..	..	..	..	..	..	..	..	..	..	..	Labor Force, Agriculture (%)
47.7	47.5	47.3	47.2	47.0	46.9	46.7	46.5	46.4	46.2	..	Labor Force, Female (%)
..	24.0	26.0	26.0	29.0	31.0	32.0	34.0	35.0	..	..	Primary Schl. Enroll. Ratio
17.0	18.0	19.0	19.0	21.0	23.0	24.0	25.0	27.0	..	..	Primary Schl. Enroll. Ratio, Female
..	3.0	4.0	4.0	5.0	5.0	6.0	7.0	7.0	..	..	Secondary Schl. Enroll. Ratio

BURUNDI	1970	1971	1972	1973	1974	1975	1976	1977	1978	1979	1980
CURRENT GNP PER CAPITA (US $)	70	90	80	80	90	100	120	140	150	170	200
POPULATION (thousands)	3,350	3,420	3,494	3,569	3,644	3,720	3,789	3,861	3,938	4,022	4,114
USE AND ORIGIN OF RESOURCES					*(Billions of current Burundi Francs)*						
Gross National Product (GNP)	20.59	21.33	20.60	23.69	26.48	32.47	37.70	48.35	53.62	69.51	82.14
Net Factor Income from Abroad	-0.65	-0.79	-1.00	-0.67	-0.71	-0.68	-0.97	-1.23	-1.30	-0.91	-0.63
GDP at Market Prices	21.24	22.12	21.60	24.36	27.19	33.15	38.68	49.58	54.92	70.42	82.78
Resource Balance	-0.20	-1.27	-0.72	-0.56	-1.57	-3.56	-1.13	0.15	-4.68	-7.44	-12.24
Exports of Goods & NFServices	2.27	1.87	2.53	2.68	2.65	2.74	5.31	8.67	6.43	9.98	7.29
Imports of Goods & NFServices	2.47	3.14	3.26	3.25	4.22	6.30	6.44	8.52	11.11	17.43	19.53
Domestic Absorption	21.44	23.39	22.32	24.92	28.76	36.71	39.81	49.43	59.60	77.87	95.01
Private Consumption, etc.	18.40	19.37	18.84	20.80	24.24	30.37	32.92	38.42	44.31	58.31	72.64
General Gov't Consumption	2.08	2.34	2.79	2.82	3.42	3.83	3.37	5.50	7.58	9.05	10.88
Gross Domestic Investment	0.96	1.68	0.69	1.29	1.10	2.51	3.52	5.52	7.71	10.50	11.49
Fixed Investment	0.85	1.12	1.14	1.39	1.77	3.07	3.52	5.52	7.71	10.50	11.49
Indirect Taxes, net	1.59	1.44	1.50	1.66	2.00	2.20	3.17	6.38	6.11	7.89	6.22
GDP at factor cost	19.65	20.69	20.09	22.69	25.19	30.95	35.50	43.20	48.81	62.54	76.56
Agriculture	13.88	14.33	13.12	15.42	16.59	20.32	23.00	27.39	29.64	37.91	47.66
Industry	2.00	2.16	2.33	2.83	3.30	4.17	4.54	6.00	7.86	10.36	9.66
Manufacturing	1.43	1.62	1.77	2.27	2.58	2.84	3.16	3.88	4.53	6.55	5.70
Services, etc.	3.77	4.20	4.64	4.44	5.30	6.45	7.96	9.81	11.32	14.26	19.24
Gross Domestic Saving	0.76	0.41	-0.03	0.73	-0.47	-1.04	2.38	5.67	3.03	3.06	-0.74
Gross National Saving	0.17	-0.32	-0.98	0.12	-1.09	-1.61	1.61	4.72	2.05	2.35	-1.02
					(Billions of 1987 Burundi Francs)						
Gross National Product	53.98	78.03	71.92	78.90	78.47	79.50	85.26	94.87	94.35	96.99	98.52
GDP at Market Prices	55.95	80.90	75.25	81.19	80.60	81.16	87.60	97.64	96.73	98.34	99.32
Resource Balance	-5.77	-8.63	-6.17	-6.09	-7.63	-10.53	-10.55	-15.83	-14.71	-17.99	-18.50
Exports of Goods & NFServices	7.57	7.38	9.15	8.28	7.69	9.08	7.77	6.64	9.37	10.46	7.38
Imports of Goods & NFServices	13.34	16.01	15.32	14.38	15.31	19.61	18.32	22.47	24.09	28.45	25.88
Domestic Absorption	61.72	89.52	81.41	87.28	88.22	91.68	98.15	113.47	111.44	116.33	117.81
Private Consumption, etc.	46.71	69.98	67.24	70.68	67.69	73.60	79.28	85.17	79.13	84.52	87.01
General Gov't Consumption	10.19	10.86	11.51	11.15	11.34	11.43	8.94	13.71	15.25	14.35	14.12
Gross Domestic Investment	4.82	8.69	2.67	5.45	9.20	6.65	9.93	14.59	17.06	17.45	16.69
Fixed Investment	..	..	..	..	..	..	..	..	..	..	16.69
GDP at factor cost	51.02	76.07	70.49	76.16	75.24	76.26	81.09	86.17	86.92	88.59	91.84
Agriculture	33.15	49.17	44.28	49.60	47.62	49.81	51.63	53.74	52.30	53.08	53.76
Industry	3.00	8.23	8.04	8.19	8.49	8.54	9.43	11.73	13.07	13.18	14.51
Manufacturing	6.18	6.77	6.61	6.82	7.05	7.02	7.47	7.81	8.36	8.69	9.29
Services, etc.	20.59	17.60	17.75	16.95	17.91	16.54	18.74	19.74	20.96	21.72	23.19
Memo Items:											
Capacity to Import	12.27	9.53	11.92	11.88	9.62	8.54	15.10	22.87	13.94	16.30	9.66
Terms of Trade Adjustment	4.70	2.15	2.77	3.60	1.93	-0.54	7.33	16.23	4.57	5.84	2.28
Gross Domestic Income	60.65	83.04	78.02	84.78	82.53	80.62	94.93	113.87	101.30	104.18	101.60
Gross National Income	58.68	80.18	74.69	82.49	80.40	78.96	92.58	111.09	98.92	102.84	100.81
DOMESTIC PRICES/DEFLATORS					*(Index 1987 = 100)*						
Overall (GDP)	38.0	27.3	28.7	30.0	33.7	40.8	44.1	50.8	56.8	71.6	83.3
Domestic Absorption	34.7	26.1	27.4	28.6	32.6	40.0	40.6	43.6	53.5	66.9	80.6
Agriculture	41.9	29.1	29.6	31.1	34.9	40.8	44.6	51.0	56.7	71.4	88.7
Industry	66.6	26.2	29.0	34.6	38.8	48.8	48.2	51.2	60.1	78.6	66.6
Manufacturing	23.1	24.0	26.7	33.3	36.6	40.5	42.4	49.7	54.2	75.4	61.3
Consumer Price Index	19.9	20.7	21.4	22.7	26.3	30.4	32.5	34.7	43.1	58.8	60.3
MANUFACTURING ACTIVITY											
Employment (1987=100)	..	..	..	..	..	..	..	..	..	..	..
Real Earnings per Empl. (1987=100)	..	..	..	..	..	..	..	..	..	..	..
Real Output per Empl. (1987=100)	..	..	..	..	..	..	..	..	..	..	..
Earnings as % of Value Added	..	29.5	28.8	26.7	26.5	28.7	25.6	25.5	19.3	13.2	14.4
MONETARY HOLDINGS					*(Millions of current Burundi Francs)*						
Money Supply, Broadly Defined	2,138	2,444	2,440	2,988	3,451	3,350	4,713	6,550	8,902	9,477	12,859
Money	2,001	2,321	2,310	2,825	3,307	3,208	4,548	6,154	8,406	9,058	10,016
Currency Outside Banks	1,192	1,333	1,370	1,548	1,873	1,709	2,411	3,225	4,542	4,876	4,971
Demand Deposits	809	988	940	1,277	1,434	1,499	2,137	2,930	3,864	4,182	5,044
Quasi-Money	138	124	131	163	144	141	165	396	496	419	2,844
GOVERNMENT DEFICIT (-) OR SURPLUS					*(Millions of current Burundi Francs)*						
	..	..	..	..	-86	-1,081	-237	-791	-1,610	-3,758	-3,234
Current Revenue	..	..	..	4,719	5,658	5,729	8,435	9,821	10,970	12,471	14,708
Current Expenditure	..	..	..	..	..	..	..	..	..	..	..
Current Budget Balance	..	..	..	..	..	..	..	..	..	..	..
Capital Receipts	..	..	..	1	2	17	2	21	5	9	12
Capital Payments	..	..	..	..	..	..	..	..	..	..	..

1981	1982	1983	1984	1985	1986	1987	1988	1989	1990 estimate	Notes	BURUNDI
250	250	240	230	250	250	240	240	220	210	..	CURRENT GNP PER CAPITA (US $)
4,214	4,324	4,443	4,567	4,696	4,830	4,970	5,116	5,268	5,427	..	POPULATION (thousands)
											USE AND ORIGIN OF RESOURCES
					(Billions of current Burundi Francs)						
86.95	90.51	99.79	116.61	136.42	134.80	136.00	149.31	171.06	186.45	..	Gross National Product (GNP)
-0.26	-0.69	-0.87	-1.56	-2.37	-2.40	-3.51	-3.15	-2.80	-2.56	..	Net Factor Income from Abroad
87.21	91.20	100.66	118.17	138.79	137.20	139.51	152.46	173.86	189.01	..	GDP at Market Prices
-11.53	-15.66	-16.37	-14.83	-13.91	-14.40	-22.03	-20.47	-21.49	-34.32	..	Resource Balance
7.89	9.24	8.99	13.44	14.59	17.02	13.64	19.13	16.82	14.69	..	Exports of Goods & NFServices
19.42	24.90	25.36	28.27	28.49	31.42	35.67	39.60	38.31	49.01	..	Imports of Goods & NFServices
98.74	106.86	117.03	133.00	152.70	151.60	161.54	172.92	195.34	223.33	..	Domestic Absorption
69.93	79.99	80.71	95.93	115.82	114.43	107.79	126.45	141.75	158.43	..	Private Consumption, etc.
13.98	13.69	13.34	15.36	17.64	21.20	22.14	23.63	24.50	28.44	..	General Gov't Consumption
14.83	13.18	22.98	21.71	19.24	15.98	31.61	22.85	29.10	36.47	..	Gross Domestic Investment
11.83	13.80	19.44	20.78	19.85	19.18	29.16	16.89	20.49	18.04	..	Fixed Investment
4.52	6.83	6.62	10.75	12.60	14.08	11.55	16.89	20.49	18.04		Indirect Taxes, net
82.70	84.37	94.04	107.42	126.19	123.12	127.95	135.57	153.37	170.97	..	GDP at factor cost
50.71	47.98	53.83	64.59	77.66	72.06	70.68	73.20	86.37	95.33	..	Agriculture
11.09	13.04	14.58	14.87	16.41	16.64	21.67	23.40	24.10	26.45	..	Industry
6.38	7.52	8.41	9.26	10.17	10.79	14.51	16.33	16.25	17.88	..	Manufacturing
20.90	23.36	25.63	27.96	32.13	34.43	35.60	38.97	42.91	49.19	..	Services, etc.
3.30	-2.48	6.61	6.88	5.33	1.57	9.58	2.38	7.61	2.15	..	Gross Domestic Saving
3.46	-3.00	6.05	5.73	4.17	0.05	6.95	0.62	6.18	1.31	..	Gross National Saving
					(Billions of 1987 Burundi Francs)						
111.05	109.40	113.31	113.14	125.84	129.71	136.00	143.23	146.20	151.22	..	Gross National Product
111.40	110.23	114.32	114.70	128.08	132.13	139.51	146.26	148.53	153.60	..	GDP at Market Prices
-13.21	-17.71	-21.71	-19.06	-16.18	-20.59	-22.03	-20.22	-15.33	-16.83	..	Resource Balance
11.73	12.66	11.40	13.04	14.69	12.76	13.64	15.07	14.64	14.65	..	Exports of Goods & NFServices
24.94	30.38	33.11	32.09	30.87	33.36	35.67	35.29	29.96	31.48	..	Imports of Goods & NFServices
124.61	127.94	136.03	133.76	144.26	152.72	161.54	166.48	163.85	170.43	..	Domestic Absorption
87.34	94.63	90.54	92.16	104.52	113.56	107.79	123.09	118.87	122.91	..	Private Consumption, etc.
16.88	16.08	15.67	16.80	18.82	22.10	22.14	21.48	20.33	21.65	..	General Gov't Consumption
20.39	17.23	29.81	24.80	20.92	17.06	31.61	21.91	24.65	25.87	..	Gross Domestic Investment
16.27	18.04	25.23	23.74	21.59	20.45	29.16	22.02	24.80	25.53	..	Fixed Investment
103.74	101.63	105.67	105.53	118.28	122.17	127.95	130.20	130.20	139.03	..	GDP at factor cost
61.34	56.69	59.17	57.04	64.52	67.19	70.68	71.80	70.24	73.87	f	Agriculture
15.90	17.37	17.94	18.21	19.91	20.17	21.67	21.79	21.95	23.20	f	Industry
9.63	10.36	10.46	11.48	12.65	13.20	14.51	14.72	14.41	15.15	..	Manufacturing
25.94	27.61	28.55	30.28	33.85	34.81	35.60	36.61	38.02	41.97	..	Services, etc.
											Memo Items:
10.14	11.27	11.74	15.26	15.80	18.07	13.64	17.05	13.16	9.44	..	Capacity to Import
-1.60	-1.40	0.33	2.22	1.12	5.30	0.00	1.98	-1.48	-5.22	..	Terms of Trade Adjustment
109.80	108.83	114.66	116.92	129.19	137.43	139.51	148.24	147.05	148.38	..	Gross Domestic Income
109.45	108.00	113.65	115.36	126.96	135.01	136.00	145.21	144.72	146.00	..	Gross National Income
											DOMESTIC PRICES/DEFLATORS
					(Index 1987 = 100)						
78.3	82.7	88.0	103.0	108.4	103.8	100.0	104.2	117.1	123.1	..	Overall (GDP)
79.2	83.5	86.0	99.4	105.8	99.3	100.0	103.9	119.2	131.0	..	Domestic Absorption
82.7	84.6	91.0	113.2	120.4	107.2	100.0	101.9	123.0	129.1	..	Agriculture
69.7	75.0	81.3	81.6	82.4	82.5	100.0	107.4	109.8	114.0	..	Industry
66.2	72.6	80.4	80.6	80.4	81.7	100.0	110.9	112.8	118.0	..	Manufacturing
67.5	71.4	77.3	88.5	91.7	93.4	100.0	104.5	116.7	124.9	..	Consumer Price Index
											MANUFACTURING ACTIVITY
..	..	..	..	..	..	..	..	..	..	..	Employment (1987=100)
..	..	..	..	..	..	..	..	..	..	..	Real Earnings per Empl. (1987=100)
..	..	..	..	..	..	..	..	..	..	..	Real Output per Empl. (1987=100)
..	..	18.1	..	..	..	..	..	..	..	..	Earnings as % of Value Added
											MONETARY HOLDINGS
					(Millions of current Burundi Francs)						
15,874	15,305	19,439	20,206	24,183	24,347	24,854	28,241	31,968	35,381	..	Money Supply, Broadly Defined
12,463	10,827	13,845	14,762	18,453	19,909	19,786	20,507	21,112	23,233	..	Money
7,059	6,419	7,262	7,498	7,253	8,008	8,734	9,605	9,868	10,766	..	Currency Outside Banks
5,404	4,408	6,583	7,264	11,200	11,901	11,052	10,902	11,243	12,467	..	Demand Deposits
3,411	4,478	5,593	5,444	5,730	4,438	5,067	7,735	10,856	12,148	..	Quasi-Money
					(Millions of current Burundi Francs)						
											GOVERNMENT DEFICIT (-) OR SURPLUS
-4,933	-6,110	-12,575	-10,906	-8,332	-5,690	..	..	..	..	..	Current Revenue
16,096	18,061	17,075	22,401	25,190	29,120	..	..	..	..	..	Current Expenditure
10,060	..	..	..	..	..	..	..	..	..	..	Current Budget Balance
6,036	..	..	..	..	..	..	..	..	..	..	Capital Receipts
22	..	..	..	..	..	..	..	..	..	..	Capital Payments
10,991	..	..	..	..	..	..	..	..	..	..	

BURUNDI	1970	1971	1972	1973	1974	1975	1976	1977	1978	1979	1980
FOREIGN TRADE (CUSTOMS BASIS)					*(Millions of current US dollars)*						
Value of Exports, fob	..	..	..	..	..	..	..	..	..	..	..
Nonfuel Primary Products	..	..	..	..	..	..	..	..	..	..	..
Fuels	..	..	..	..	..	..	..	..	..	..	..
Manufactures	..	..	..	..	..	..	..	..	..	..	..
Value of Imports, cif	..	..	..	..	..	..	..	..	..	..	..
Nonfuel Primary Products	..	..	..	..	..	..	..	..	..	..	..
Fuels	..	..	..	..	..	..	..	..	..	..	..
Manufactures	..	..	..	..	..	..	..	..	..	..	..
					(Index 1987 = 100)						
Terms of Trade	..	..	..	..	..	..	..	..	..	..	..
Export Prices, fob	..	..	..	..	..	..	..	..	..	..	..
Import Prices, cif	..	..	..	..	..	..	..	..	..	..	..
BALANCE OF PAYMENTS					*(Millions of current US dollars)*						
Exports of Goods & Services	26.50	22.00	29.70	34.80	34.90	35.90	62.80	98.90	78.70	115.50	92.00
Merchandise, fob	24.50	19.60	26.60	31.10	31.30	32.30	56.90	93.20	69.50	102.00	66.30
Nonfactor Services	1.40	1.70	2.40	2.70	2.40	2.50	4.60	3.10	4.40	6.60	14.70
Factor Services	0.60	0.70	0.70	1.00	1.20	1.10	1.30	2.60	4.80	6.90	11.00
Imports of Goods & Services	29.50	37.40	39.20	42.00	55.40	81.90	76.40	111.60	142.60	194.90	223.70
Merchandise, fob	22.40	29.90	31.30	31.40	43.10	61.70	58.20	76.30	96.50	145.00	168.00
Nonfactor Services	5.80	5.90	5.90	9.50	10.50	18.30	16.60	18.40	26.90	32.80	37.70
Factor Services	1.30	1.60	2.00	1.10	1.80	1.90	1.60	16.90	19.20	17.10	18.00
Long-Term Interest	0.20	0.20	0.30	0.20	0.20	0.40	0.50	0.60	0.90	1.30	1.90
Private Current Transfers, net	0.60	0.70	0.60	0.70	1.10	1.50	2.30	3.20	3.60	2.20	4.00
Workers' Remittances	..	..	..	..	..	..	..	..	..	..	..
Curr. A/C Bal before Off. Transf.	-2.40	-14.70	-8.90	-6.50	-19.40	-44.50	-11.30	-9.50	-60.30	-77.20	-127.70
Net Official Transfers	4.70	5.50	4.70	5.90	8.70	11.80	18.20	25.70	29.00	17.80	32.00
Curr. A/C Bal after Off. Transf.	2.30	-9.20	-4.20	-0.60	-10.70	-32.70	6.90	16.20	-31.30	-59.40	-95.70
Long-Term Capital, net	7.60	7.00	6.20	11.50	16.30	31.50	15.30	31.80	45.40	64.00	77.00
Direct Investment	0.20	..	..	..	0.20	..	..	..	..	..	1.10
Long-Term Loans	1.00	0.10	-1.00	0.30	1.50	9.30	2.80	15.50	17.10	31.70	34.70
Disbursements	1.40	0.50	0.60	1.00	2.20	10.90	5.10	17.90	19.00	34.60	39.00
Repayments	0.40	0.40	1.60	0.70	0.70	1.60	2.30	2.40	1.90	2.90	4.30
Other Long-Term Capital	6.40	6.90	7.20	11.20	14.60	22.20	12.50	16.30	28.30	32.30	41.20
Other Capital, net	-6.37	4.67	2.41	-8.38	-12.97	16.39	-3.86	-2.79	-26.35	-11.49	20.57
Change in Reserves	-3.53	-2.47	-4.41	-2.52	7.37	-15.19	-18.34	-45.21	12.25	6.89	-1.87
Memo Item:					*(Burundi Francs per US dollar)*						
Conversion Factor (Annual Avg)	87.500	87.500	87.500	80.030	78.750	78.750	86.250	90.000	90.000	90.000	90.000
EXTERNAL DEBT (Total)	15.10	13.60	6.90	7.70	*(Millions of US dollars), outstanding at end of year* 9.40	19.30	22.40	47.20	74.70	136.20	165.70
Long-Term Debt (by debtor)	15.10	13.60	6.90	7.70	9.40	19.30	22.40	42.20	69.70	123.20	153.70
Central Bank, incl. IMF credit	7.70	5.80	0.00	0.00	0.00	2.40	3.40	8.10	14.90	35.20	40.40
Central Government	5.00	5.30	5.30	5.80	7.10	13.00	15.90	32.10	50.70	82.00	110.40
Rest of General Government	..	..	..	..	..	..	..	..	..	..	..
Non-financial Public Enterprises	0.90	0.90	0.00	0.00	0.00	2.00	1.10	0.00	1.90	2.40	1.70
Priv. Sector, incl non-guaranteed	1.50	1.60	1.60	1.90	2.30	1.90	2.00	2.00	2.20	3.60	1.20
Short-Term Debt	0.00	0.00	0.00	0.00	0.00	0.00	0.00	5.00	5.00	13.00	12.00
Memo Items:					*(Thousands of US dollars)*						
Int'l Reserves Excluding Gold	15,360.0	17,685.0	18,487.0	21,483.0	14,189.0	30,713.0	49,030.0	94,406.0	81,304.0	89,987.0	94,502.0
Gold Holdings (at market price)	36.0	42.0	62.0	108.0	179.0	135.0	129.0	1,500.0	2,055.0	6,738.0	10,152.0
SOCIAL INDICATORS											
Total Fertility Rate	6.4	6.4	6.4	6.4	6.4	6.5	6.5	6.5	6.5	6.5	6.5
Infant Mortality Rate	137.0	136.0	135.0	134.0	133.0	132.0	131.0	130.0	127.4	124.8	122.2
Life Expectancy at Birth	43.0	43.0	43.0	43.2	43.4	43.6	43.8	44.0	44.3	44.6	44.9
Urban Population, % of total	2.4	2.6	2.7	2.9	3.0	3.2	3.4	3.6	3.9	4.1	4.3
Food Prod. per capita (1987=100)	100.6	102.3	93.0	104.1	91.0	105.4	106.4	105.2	101.8	96.1	96.4
Labor Force, Agriculture (%)	93.5	93.4	93.3	93.3	93.2	93.1	93.0	93.0	92.9	92.8	92.7
Labor Force, Female (%)	49.7	49.7	49.6	49.6	49.5	49.5	49.4	49.3	49.3	49.2	49.1
Primary Schl. Enroll. Ratio	30.0	..	..	..	..	22.0	..	23.0	23.0	25.0	27.0
Primary Schl. Enroll. Ratio, Female	20.0	..	..	..	..	17.0	..	18.0	18.0	20.0	21.0
Secondary Schl. Enroll. Ratio	2.0	..	..	..	..	3.0	2.0	2.0	3.0	3.0	3.0

1981	1982	1983	1984	1985	1986	1987	1988	1989	1990 estimate	Notes	BURUNDI
					(Millions of current US dollars)						**FOREIGN TRADE (CUSTOMS BASIS)**
..	..	..	..	..	..	..	..	..	..		Value of Exports, fob
..	..	..	..	..	..	..	..	..	..		Nonfuel Primary Products
..	..	..	..	..	..	..	..	..	..		Fuels
..	..	..	..	..	..	..	..	..	..		Manufactures
..	..	..	..	..	..	..	..	..	..		Value of Imports, cif
..	..	..	..	..	..	..	..	..	..		Nonfuel Primary Products
..	..	..	..	..	..	..	..	..	..		Fuels
..	..	..	..	..	..	..	..	..	..		Manufactures
					(Index 1987 = 100)						
..	..	..	..	..	..	..	..	..	..		Terms of Trade
..	..	..	..	..	..	..	..	..	..		Export Prices, fob
..	..	..	..	..	..	..	..	..	..		Import Prices, cif
					(Millions of current US dollars)						**BALANCE OF PAYMENTS**
97.00	108.20	98.60	102.70	128.36	142.94	113.17	139.16	117.45	97.35	f	Exports of Goods & Services
74.90	87.80	80.60	87.80	113.65	129.14	98.34	124.36	93.25	72.55	..	Merchandise, fob
12.80	14.90	16.10	13.40	13.16	11.74	11.91	11.92	15.32	16.58	..	Nonfactor Services
9.30	5.50	1.90	1.50	1.56	2.07	2.92	2.88	8.89	8.22	..	Factor Services
227.80	289.60	284.40	272.40	258.98	290.88	322.55	306.76	269.98	312.12	f	Imports of Goods & Services
161.00	214.00	184.00	184.00	149.70	165.31	159.17	166.06	151.41	188.63	..	Merchandise, fob
37.40	43.90	72.10	60.00	89.34	102.86	132.04	114.87	92.06	100.35	..	Nonfactor Services
29.40	31.70	28.30	28.40	19.94	22.71	31.34	25.83	26.51	23.15	..	Factor Services
1.60	2.30	3.30	8.10	8.80	12.30	15.40	16.80	15.00	12.20		Long-Term Interest
4.60	1.90	3.30	3.40	9.98	7.67	7.16	9.87	8.60	10.05		Private Current Transfers, net
..	..	..	..	..	..	..	..	..	..		Workers' Remittances
-126.20	-179.50	-182.50	-166.30	-120.63	-140.26	-202.21	-157.73	-143.94	-204.72	..	Curr. A/C Bal before Off. Transf.
37.40	15.10	26.70	40.60	78.47	102.69	105.73	87.16	132.37	148.33	..	Net Official Transfers
-88.80	-164.40	-155.80	-125.70	-42.16	-37.58	-96.48	-70.57	-11.57	-56.40	..	Curr. A/C Bal after Off. Transf.
65.00	93.00	143.00	111.00	55.40	61.65	115.89	79.31	64.01	62.32	f	Long-Term Capital, net
0.60	1.50	0.40	0.90	0.54	1.52	1.37	1.20	0.52	1.25	..	Direct Investment
26.10	51.80	104.70	74.50	59.10	82.40	117.00	80.20	85.10	66.80	..	Long-Term Loans
29.70	55.10	108.30	82.30	71.50	98.80	141.30	103.70	108.70	94.30	..	Disbursements
3.60	3.30	3.60	7.80	12.40	16.40	24.30	23.50	23.60	27.50	..	Repayments
38.30	39.70	37.90	35.60	-4.24	-22.27	-2.48	-2.08	-21.61	-5.73	..	Other Long-Term Capital
-10.88	40.37	15.89	13.01	-0.56	0.13	-26.69	-5.91	-17.17	-9.92	..	Other Capital, net
34.68	31.03	-3.09	1.69	-12.68	-24.21	7.27	-2.83	-35.26	3.99		Change in Reserves
											Memo Item:
					(Burundi Francs per US dollar)						
90.000	90.000	92.950	119.710	120.690	114.170	123.560	140.400	158.670	171.260	..	Conversion Factor (Annual Avg)
					(Millions of US dollars), outstanding at end of year						**EXTERNAL DEBT (Total)**
178.70	227.40	307.80	348.00	455.10	570.50	769.70	800.70	888.90	905.60	..	Long-Term Debt (by debtor)
168.70	211.40	297.80	336.00	423.50	546.40	732.40	788.00	872.40	892.20	..	Central Bank, incl. IMF credit
36.70	35.50	30.40	21.40	21.40	30.40	30.30	42.60	53.00	53.90	..	Central Government
129.70	173.10	257.50	305.70	392.30	505.40	695.30	739.90	814.90	836.60	..	Rest of General Government
..	..	..	..	..	..	..	..	..	..	..	Non-financial Public Enterprises
1.70	1.30	1.40	1.20	1.60	1.90	2.00	2.90	2.90	1.70	..	Priv. Sector, incl non-guaranteed
0.60	1.50	8.50	7.70	8.20	8.70	4.80	2.60	1.60	..	..	Short-Term Debt
10.00	16.00	10.00	12.00	31.60	24.10	37.30	12.70	16.50	13.40	..	
					(Thousands of US dollars)						**Memo Items:**
61,300.0	29,489.0	26,939.0	19,731.0	29,472.0	69,073.0	60,732.0	69,384.0	99,621.0	105,038.0	..	Int'l Reserves Excluding Gold
6,846.0	7,869.0	6,570.0	5,310.0	5,632.0	6,732.0	8,337.0	7,065.0	6,906.0	6,630.0	..	Gold Holdings (at market price)
											SOCIAL INDICATORS
6.5	6.5	6.6	6.6	6.7	6.7	6.8	6.8	6.8	6.8	..	Total Fertility Rate
119.6	117.0	115.6	114.2	112.7	111.3	109.9	108.9	107.9	107.0	..	Infant Mortality Rate
45.2	45.5	45.8	46.2	46.5	46.9	47.2	47.1	47.0	46.8	..	Life Expectancy at Birth
4.4	4.5	4.7	4.8	4.9	5.1	5.2	5.3	5.4	5.5	..	Urban Population, % of total
100.5	97.7	93.3	89.1	97.7	98.7	100.0	96.5	89.1	82.8	..	Food Prod. per capita (1987=100)
..	..	..	..	..	..	..	..	..	..		Labor Force, Agriculture (%)
49.0	48.8	48.6	48.4	48.3	48.1	47.9	47.7	47.5	47.3	..	Labor Force, Female (%)
..	..	44.0	49.0	53.0	60.0	69.0	71.0	..	..	..	Primary Schl. Enroll. Ratio
25.0	..	35.0	40.0	44.0	51.0	60.0	..	..	..	..	Primary Schl. Enroll. Ratio, Female
..	..	3.0	4.0	4.0	4.0	4.0	..	..	..	..	Secondary Schl. Enroll. Ratio

CAMEROON	1970	1971	1972	1973	1974	1975	1976	1977	1978	1979	1980
CURRENT GNP PER CAPITA (US $)	180	180	180	210	270	310	360	410	500	600	760
POPULATION (thousands)	6,506	6,667	6,840	7,026	7,226	7,439	7,670	7,912	8,165	8,429	8,701
USE AND ORIGIN OF RESOURCES					*(Billions of current CFA Francs)*						
Gross National Product (GNP)	304.8	316.5	347.2	390.9	477.2	563.7	639.7	773.9	987.5	1,167.1	1,427.3
Net Factor Income from Abroad	-13.4	-24.1	-30.4	-32.9	-42.1	-48.6	-52.8	-60.1	-64.7	-92.0	-141.6
GDP at Market Prices	318.2	340.6	377.6	423.8	519.3	612.3	692.5	834.0	1,052.2	1,259.1	1,568.9
Resource Balance	4.9	-14.1	-21.5	-14.0	13.7	-17.5	-32.7	-22.9	-47.0	-90.2	-49.1
Exports of Goods & NFServices	83.4	78.4	77.0	87.7	132.1	138.9	156.8	209.0	248.9	265.4	378.0
Imports of Goods & NFServices	78.5	92.5	98.5	101.7	118.4	156.4	189.5	231.9	295.9	355.6	427.1
Domestic Absorption	313.3	354.7	399.1	437.8	505.6	629.8	725.2	856.9	1,099.2	1,349.3	1,618.0
Private Consumption, etc.	224.2	256.5	284.2	304.5	359.6	440.8	528.9	593.2	757.6	960.4	1,185.3
General Gov't Consumption	38.1	41.5	46.0	49.0	57.3	66.7	74.5	81.9	102.8	116.3	136.8
Gross Domestic Investment	51.0	56.7	68.9	84.3	88.7	122.3	121.8	181.8	238.8	272.6	295.9
Fixed Investment	..	..	..	..	..	100.3	118.8	163.5	204.7	251.7	282.4
Indirect Taxes, net	20.4	18.4	29.6	46.9	70.7	96.5	116.0	80.4	108.2	83.5	118.2
GDP at factor cost	297.8	322.2	348.0	376.9	448.6	515.8	576.5	753.6	944.0	1,175.6	1,450.7
Agriculture	99.8	105.6	120.7	130.5	153.4	178.3	191.2	280.6	329.9	388.1	437.0
Industry	59.3	65.5	71.2	78.9	92.8	111.7	131.3	153.4	167.9	259.9	406.0
Manufacturing	32.6	35.2	39.2	43.4	51.0	63.0	73.0	74.7	86.7	101.9	124.1
Services, etc.	159.1	169.5	185.7	214.4	273.1	322.3	370.0	400.0	554.4	611.1	725.9
Gross Domestic Saving	55.9	42.6	47.4	70.3	102.4	104.8	89.1	158.9	191.8	182.4	246.8
Gross National Saving	40.5	16.4	14.4	31.7	55.6	51.5	32.3	98.4	124.3	83.4	88.4
					(Billions of 1987 CFA Francs)						
Gross National Product	1,268.1	1,265.0	1,282.6	1,359.2	1,495.4	1,489.7	1,562.8	1,694.1	1,975.0	2,215.7	2,513.0
GDP at Market Prices	1,320.1	1,369.9	1,401.9	1,478.5	1,637.2	1,624.9	1,695.2	1,838.6	2,108.6	2,388.8	2,762.2
Resource Balance	-89.7	-180.0	-160.7	-108.7	-65.6	-127.1	-123.0	-222.2	-163.2	-149.6	-86.5
Exports of Goods & NFServices	307.2	301.8	316.9	325.2	369.7	331.6	384.9	339.1	446.8	529.7	665.5
Imports of Goods & NFServices	396.9	481.9	477.6	433.9	435.3	458.7	508.0	561.3	610.0	679.4	751.9
Domestic Absorption	1,409.8	1,549.9	1,562.6	1,587.2	1,702.8	1,752.0	1,818.2	2,060.8	2,271.9	2,538.4	2,848.7
Private Consumption, etc.	1,092.7	1,197.5	1,174.4	1,169.2	1,278.4	1,299.9	1,362.0	1,542.6	1,566.6	1,841.2	2,086.9
General Gov't Consumption	143.5	140.2	160.8	175.4	201.8	191.9	214.9	186.9	215.5	228.1	240.9
Gross Domestic Investment	173.6	212.2	227.3	242.7	222.6	260.2	241.3	331.3	489.8	469.1	521.0
Fixed Investment	..	..	..	..	..	..	..	..	..	..	..
GDP at factor cost	..	..	..	..	..	..	..	..	..	..	..
Agriculture	490.6	497.0	525.8	546.4	572.9	579.9	587.6	595.4	617.9	710.2	769.3
Industry	214.9	240.9	232.6	242.3	255.5	264.8	285.1	337.4	372.7	535.3	714.8
Manufacturing	108.8	123.6	125.2	125.4	127.7	138.2	147.1	167.0	192.5	199.5	218.4
Services, etc.	614.6	632.0	643.4	689.7	808.9	780.2	822.4	905.8	1,118.1	1,143.2	1,278.1
Memo Items:											
Capacity to Import	421.7	408.4	373.4	374.2	485.6	407.4	420.3	505.8	513.1	507.1	665.5
Terms of Trade Adjustment	114.5	106.6	56.4	49.0	116.0	75.8	35.4	166.8	66.3	-22.7	0.0
Gross Domestic Income	1,434.6	1,476.5	1,458.3	1,527.5	1,753.2	1,700.7	1,730.6	2,005.4	2,175.0	2,366.1	2,762.3
Gross National Income	1,382.6	1,371.6	1,339.0	1,408.2	1,611.4	1,565.5	1,598.2	1,860.9	2,041.3	2,193.0	2,513.0
DOMESTIC PRICES/DEFLATORS					*(Index 1987 = 100)*						
Overall (GDP)	24.1	24.9	26.9	28.7	31.7	37.7	40.9	45.4	49.9	52.7	56.8
Domestic Absorption	22.2	22.9	25.5	27.6	29.7	35.9	39.9	41.6	48.4	53.2	56.8
Agriculture	20.3	21.2	23.0	23.9	26.8	30.7	32.5	47.1	53.4	54.6	56.8
Industry	27.6	27.2	30.6	32.6	36.3	42.2	46.0	45.5	45.1	48.5	56.8
Manufacturing	30.0	28.5	31.3	34.6	39.9	45.6	49.6	44.7	45.0	51.1	56.8
Consumer Price Index	19.4	20.2	21.8	24.1	28.2	32.1	35.2	40.4	45.5	48.5	53.1
MANUFACTURING ACTIVITY											
Employment (1987=100)	..	..	..	..	..	..	..	..	..	..	..
Real Earnings per Empl. (1987=100)	..	..	..	..	..	..	..	..	..	..	..
Real Output per Empl. (1987=100)	..	..	..	..	..	..	..	..	..	..	..
Earnings as % of Value Added	29.5	31.0	25.3	..	32.6	39.0	39.8	40.6	39.6	37.0	34.6
MONETARY HOLDINGS					*(Billions of current CFA Francs)*						
Money Supply, Broadly Defined	45.47	51.60	57.37	70.33	94.44	105.69	132.48	183.50	212.31	260.09	315.42
Money	38.40	43.60	47.19	55.38	72.89	76.05	94.57	126.62	146.95	184.25	208.23
Currency Outside Banks	19.55	20.90	21.88	25.91	30.99	32.23	36.90	48.92	58.47	68.24	78.08
Demand Deposits	18.85	22.70	25.31	29.48	41.90	43.82	57.67	77.70	88.48	116.01	130.15
Quasi-Money	7.07	8.00	10.18	14.95	21.56	29.64	37.91	56.87	65.37	75.84	107.18
GOVERNMENT DEFICIT (-) OR SURPLUS					*(Billions of current CFA Francs)*						
	..	..	..	..	..	-12.98	-15.85	-3.02	4.07	31.72	7.24
Current Revenue	..	..	..	..	..	90.96	109.61	132.75	178.78	222.43	230.74
Current Expenditure	..	..	..	..	..	73.36	77.73	95.92	124.42	133.90	148.68
Current Budget Balance	..	..	..	..	..	17.60	31.88	36.83	54.36	88.53	82.06
Capital Receipts	..	..	..	..	..						
Capital Payments	..	..	..	..	..	30.58	47.73	39.85	50.29	56.81	74.82

1981	1982	1983	1984	1985	1986	1987	1988	1989	1990 estimate	Notes	CAMEROON
900	900	870	820	810	890	920	990	1,010	960	..	**CURRENT GNP PER CAPITA (US $)**
8,982	9,270	9,565	9,864	10,166	10,471	10,780	11,093	11,413	11,739	..	**POPULATION (thousands)**
			(Billions of current CFA Francs)								**USE AND ORIGIN OF RESOURCES**
1,800.4	2,158.1	2,609.5	3,059.6	3,595.9	3,949.0	3,818.0	3,568.0	3,393.3	3,186.0	C	Gross National Product (GNP)
-179.6	-145.3	-175.0	-213.0	-243.0	-217.0	-151.0	-127.0	-101.7	-160.0	..	Net Factor Income from Abroad
1,980.0	2,303.4	2,784.5	3,272.6	3,838.9	4,166.0	3,969.0	3,695.0	3,495.0	3,346.0	C	GDP at Market Prices
-45.9	-6.0	121.8	390.3	422.1	28.6	-177.3	-102.0	61.7	69.0	..	Resource Balance
516.0	599.0	797.0	1,085.0	1,318.0	985.0	666.0	611.0	686.0	709.4	..	Exports of Goods & NFServices
561.9	605.0	675.2	694.7	895.9	956.4	843.3	713.0	624.3	640.4	..	Imports of Goods & NFServices
2,025.9	2,309.4	2,662.7	2,882.3	3,416.8	4,137.4	4,146.3	3,797.0	3,433.3	3,277.0	..	Domestic Absorption
1,365.2	1,571.4	1,734.3	1,894.7	2,116.2	2,488.8	2,756.6	2,800.0	2,374.6	2,332.7	..	Private Consumption, etc.
172.3	199.3	248.3	306.4	345.3	364.0	433.0	417.0	412.0	391.0	..	General Gov't Consumption
488.4	538.7	680.1	681.2	955.3	1,284.6	956.7	580.0	646.7	553.3	..	Gross Domestic Investment
441.4	507.2	654.5	661.8	939.0	1,255.2	950.3	..	..	..	..	Fixed Investment
..	..	..	..	121.0	144.3	186.6	165.6	154.3	183.0	..	Indirect Taxes, net
..	..	..	..	3,717.9	4,021.7	3,782.4	3,529.4	3,340.7	3,163.0	B C	GDP at factor cost
527.4	633.9	656.0	758.7	790.4	907.9	976.0	954.0	939.0	891.0	..	Agriculture
617.9	810.4	1,085.9	1,333.4	1,317.4	1,373.1	1,137.0	1,055.0	945.0	930.0	..	Industry
173.7	247.0	290.9	358.5	422.5	536.6	522.8	498.2	456.2	..	..	Manufacturing
834.7	859.1	1,042.6	1,180.5	1,731.1	1,885.0	1,856.0	1,686.0	1,611.0	1,525.0	..	Services, etc.
442.5	532.7	801.9	1,071.5	1,377.4	1,313.2	779.4	478.0	708.4	622.3	..	Gross Domestic Saving
248.8	363.5	597.0	830.7	1,119.6	1,073.2	588.4	308.0	580.2	439.4	..	Gross National Saving
			(Billions of 1987 CFA Francs)								
2,838.2	2,999.5	3,235.1	3,416.1	3,678.2	4,025.1	3,818.0	3,536.3	3,415.1	3,309.3	C	Gross National Product
3,118.9	3,201.4	3,449.7	3,651.2	3,930.5	4,246.1	3,969.0	3,662.1	3,538.3	3,451.4	C	GDP at Market Prices
-72.2	-8.3	150.9	435.4	432.0	29.0	-177.3	-101.1	64.4	71.1	..	Resource Balance
812.8	832.5	987.3	1,210.3	1,349.3	1,003.8	666.0	605.6	696.5	731.7	..	Exports of Goods & NFServices
885.0	840.8	836.4	775.0	917.2	974.8	843.3	706.7	632.0	660.6	..	Imports of Goods & NFServices
3,191.1	3,209.7	3,298.8	3,215.8	3,498.4	4,217.1	4,146.3	3,763.2	3,473.9	3,380.3	..	Domestic Absorption
2,177.3	2,171.6	2,183.3	2,122.8	2,328.5	2,536.7	2,756.6	2,775.1	2,576.3	2,540.1	..	Private Consumption, etc.
278.3	288.5	314.5	342.0	352.0	371.0	433.0	413.3	476.7	475.3	..	General Gov't Consumption
735.4	749.7	801.1	751.1	818.0	1,309.3	956.7	574.8	421.0	365.0	..	Gross Domestic Investment
..	..	..	..	..	..	..	..	..	..	..	Fixed Investment
..	..	..	..	..	..	..	..	..	..	B C	GDP at factor cost
870.5	903.8	835.3	909.1	807.5	925.3	976.0	945.4	926.5	945.2	..	Agriculture
934.1	1,086.7	1,312.4	1,368.5	1,270.5	1,399.5	1,137.0	1,045.6	1,251.8	1,183.7	..	Industry
289.6	389.8	415.7	410.0	473.9	547.1	522.8	493.6	..	..	..	Manufacturing
1,314.3	1,210.9	1,301.9	1,373.6	1,852.5	1,921.3	1,856.0	1,671.1	1,360.0	1,322.6	..	Services, etc.
											Memo Items:
812.7	832.5	987.3	1,210.4	1,349.4	1,004.0	666.0	605.6	694.5	731.7	..	Capacity to Import
-0.1	0.0	0.0	0.1	0.1	0.1	0.0	0.0	-2.0	0.1	..	Terms of Trade Adjustment
3,118.8	3,201.4	3,449.7	3,651.2	3,930.6	4,246.2	3,969.0	3,662.1	3,536.4	3,451.5	..	Gross Domestic Income
2,838.1	2,999.5	3,235.2	3,416.1	3,678.4	4,025.2	3,818.0	3,536.3	3,413.2	3,309.4	..	Gross National Income
			(Index 1987 = 100)								**DOMESTIC PRICES/DEFLATORS**
63.5	71.9	80.7	89.6	97.7	98.1	100.0	100.9	98.8	96.9	..	Overall (GDP)
63.5	71.9	80.7	89.6	97.7	98.1	100.0	100.9	98.8	96.9	..	Domestic Absorption
60.6	70.1	78.5	83.5	97.9	98.1	100.0	100.9	101.3	94.3	..	Agriculture
66.1	74.6	82.7	97.4	103.7	98.1	100.0	100.9	75.5	78.6	..	Industry
60.0	63.4	70.0	87.4	89.2	98.1	100.0	100.9	..	..	..	Manufacturing
58.8	66.6	77.7	86.5	87.6	94.4	100.0	108.6	108.6	..	..	Consumer Price Index
											MANUFACTURING ACTIVITY
..	..	..	..	..	..	..	..	..	..		Employment (1987=100)
..	..	..	..	..	..	..	..	..	..		Real Earnings per Empl. (1987=100)
..	..	..	..	..	..	..	..	..	..		Real Output per Empl. (1987=100)
35.5	34.0	32.1	30.2								Earnings as % of Value Added
			(Billions of current CFA Francs)								**MONETARY HOLDINGS**
405.61	483.41	612.42	736.23	864.52	831.04	677.72	715.81	761.03	753.25	..	Money Supply, Broadly Defined
258.92	298.48	377.06	410.76	426.68	447.97	387.01	421.98	452.40	418.63	..	Money
101.81	107.59	127.63	134.41	148.30	167.65	171.11	166.12	162.85	155.98	..	Currency Outside Banks
157.11	190.89	249.43	276.35	278.38	280.31	215.90	255.87	289.55	262.65	..	Demand Deposits
146.69	184.92	235.35	325.47	437.84	383.07	290.71	293.82	308.64	334.62	..	Quasi-Money
			(Billions of current CFA Francs)								
-58.50	-55.22	33.87	52.91	30.51	26.02	-136.71	36.62	-110.24	..	C	**GOVERNMENT DEFICIT (-) OR SURPLUS**
314.54	389.21	668.14	795.32	885.68	912.22	731.18	613.00	601.54	..	..	Current Revenue
248.42	256.44	344.57	428.84	466.19	556.20	493.98	458.78	445.54	..	..	Current Expenditure
66.12	132.77	323.57	366.48	419.49	356.02	237.20	154.22	156.00	..	..	Current Budget Balance
	1.23	3.69	0.09		11.64	11.60	20.20	0.11	..	..	Capital Receipts
124.62	189.22	293.39	313.66	388.98	341.64	385.46	137.80	266.35	..	..	Capital Payments

CAMEROON	1970	1971	1972	1973	1974	1975	1976	1977	1978	1979	1980
FOREIGN TRADE (CUSTOMS BASIS)					*(Millions of current US dollars)*						
Value of Exports, fob	225.9	206.0	217.8	352.5	476.6	446.3	510.8	663.0	762.2	1,128.6	1,320.9
Nonfuel Primary Products	206.6	185.9	195.7	319.1	432.9	397.7	459.3	632.7	706.8	794.9	865.6
Fuels	0.0	0.1	0.4	0.6	1.0	1.4	2.0	0.5	24.9	266.3	405.2
Manufactures	19.3	20.1	21.7	32.8	42.6	47.2	49.6	29.9	30.6	67.4	50.1
Value of Imports, cif	242.1	249.5	298.8	334.7	437.3	598.3	594.7	746.9	1,008.5	1,270.6	1,538.4
Nonfuel Primary Products	32.9	37.2	39.7	47.6	67.3	76.4	67.2	102.3	113.2	152.7	157.0
Fuels	13.1	15.3	17.8	21.4	42.4	60.2	53.2	67.2	72.4	137.1	179.3
Manufactures	196.0	197.0	241.3	265.7	327.6	461.7	474.3	577.4	822.9	980.8	1,202.1
					(Index 1987 = 100)						
Terms of Trade	179.8	148.3	146.3	172.4	140.7	118.2	176.8	222.0	180.1	157.6	151.0
Export Prices, fob	43.2	38.7	42.5	62.2	76.3	67.7	103.1	141.6	130.5	131.1	145.0
Import Prices, cif	24.0	26.1	29.0	36.1	54.2	57.2	58.3	63.8	72.4	83.2	96.0
BALANCE OF PAYMENTS					*(Millions of current US dollars)*						
Exports of Goods & Services	279.3	294.3	320.0	521.2	583.8	672.3	721.2	979.0	1,318.6	1,718.0	1,827.7
Merchandise, fob	218.7	235.7	239.3	409.5	493.2	512.0	584.2	809.1	1,095.8	1,354.1	1,418.1
Nonfactor Services	56.7	51.7	75.0	108.1	86.8	147.9	133.7	161.8	206.5	351.5	388.6
Factor Services	3.9	6.9	5.6	3.6	3.7	12.4	3.3	8.1	16.3	12.4	21.0
Imports of Goods & Services	319.4	347.6	417.8	531.5	601.9	848.4	851.2	1,103.6	1,506.0	1,843.8	2,226.2
Merchandise, fob	190.8	223.1	257.6	310.6	389.9	540.3	554.9	719.2	951.5	1,270.8	1,452.3
Nonfactor Services	122.4	114.2	146.4	194.1	175.7	249.4	251.9	335.1	464.1	464.7	589.4
Factor Services	6.2	10.3	13.8	26.8	36.3	58.8	44.4	49.3	90.4	108.3	184.5
Long-Term Interest	4.9	6.1	7.1	11.1	13.1	17.2	20.9	31.1	48.3	71.3	119.2
Private Current Transfers, net	-7.2	-7.4	-10.2	-25.6	-19.4	-22.1	-16.7	-1.5	-12.2	-32.7	-79.5
Workers' Remittances	..	..	..	..	..	..	..	..	..	3.5	11.0
Curr. A/C Bal before Off. Transf.	-47.3	-60.8	-108.0	-35.9	-37.5	-198.3	-146.7	-126.1	-199.7	-158.4	-478.0
Net Official Transfers	17.5	16.3	16.4	19.2	20.6	45.8	54.7	33.7	13.3	32.7	82.9
Curr. A/C Bal after Off. Transf.	-29.8	-44.4	-91.6	-16.7	-17.0	-152.5	-92.1	-92.4	-186.4	-125.7	-395.1
Long-Term Capital, net	42.4	36.8	17.0	51.5	32.1	59.4	112.9	111.2	121.6	279.7	615.2
Direct Investment	16.0	1.7	3.3	-0.7	13.5	25.3	8.2	4.3	33.7	59.9	105.2
Long-Term Loans	33.1	26.0	69.8	31.1	41.8	104.6	162.6	320.7	281.3	507.5	497.8
Disbursements	39.5	35.3	81.2	50.0	60.3	132.3	189.9	357.4	353.3	599.4	611.8
Repayments	6.4	9.3	11.4	18.9	18.5	27.7	27.3	36.7	72.0	91.9	114.0
Other Long-Term Capital	-6.7	9.1	-56.0	21.1	-23.2	-70.5	-57.9	-213.8	-193.3	-287.7	12.2
Other Capital, net	-8.6	7.7	44.6	-44.1	-34.6	75.2	-72.2	-20.9	70.4	-80.0	-74.9
Change in Reserves	-4.0	-0.1	30.0	9.3	19.4	17.9	51.4	2.1	-5.7	-74.1	-145.2
Memo Item:					*(CFA Francs per US dollar)*						
Conversion Factor (Annual Avg)	274.330	277.710	265.390	240.960	230.050	222.420	225.090	247.780	238.590	216.650	209.210
					(Millions of US dollars), outstanding at end of year						
EXTERNAL DEBT (Total)	140.4	174.1	215.5	259.0	316.3	420.1	590.7	1,056.8	1,478.2	2,116.7	2,512.7
Long-Term Debt (by debtor)	140.4	174.1	215.5	259.0	315.1	419.4	590.7	945.4	1,314.1	1,877.8	2,242.2
Central Bank, incl. IMF credit	0.0	0.0	0.5	1.0	10.1	23.1	65.7	80.2	125.1	130.5	116.0
Central Government	69.8	83.4	66.7	92.1	117.2	183.0	283.7	415.4	559.2	748.7	885.1
Rest of General Government	0.2	0.1	0.1	0.0	0.0	0.0	0.0	0.0	0.0	0.0	0.0
Non-financial Public Enterprises	47.7	65.8	117.2	133.4	144.5	172.7	198.6	403.8	541.1	811.0	995.9
Priv. Sector, incl non-guaranteed	22.7	24.8	31.0	32.5	43.3	40.6	42.7	46.0	88.7	187.6	245.2
Short-Term Debt	0.0	0.0	0.0	0.0	1.2	0.7	0.0	111.4	164.1	238.9	270.5
Memo Items:					*(Millions of US dollars)*						
Int'l Reserves Excluding Gold	80.8	73.6	43.6	51.2	78.5	28.8	43.8	42.4	52.3	125.7	188.9
Gold Holdings (at market price)	..	..	..	..	..	..	..	2.5	3.4	15.2	17.5
SOCIAL INDICATORS											
Total Fertility Rate	5.8	5.9	6.0	6.1	6.2	6.3	6.4	6.5	6.5	6.5	6.5
Infant Mortality Rate	125.8	122.4	119.0	117.4	115.8	114.2	112.6	111.0	109.4	107.8	106.2
Life Expectancy at Birth	48.9	49.8	50.6	50.9	51.2	51.5	51.8	52.1	52.4	52.7	53.0
Urban Population, % of total	20.3	21.6	22.9	24.3	25.6	26.9	27.9	28.8	29.8	30.7	31.7
Food Prod. per capita (1987=100)	129.8	132.5	134.8	134.5	138.8	135.5	126.5	125.3	117.0	116.8	112.3
Labor Force, Agriculture (%)	83.4	82.0	80.6	79.2	77.9	76.7	75.2	73.8	72.5	71.1	69.9
Labor Force, Female (%)	37.5	37.3	37.1	36.9	36.7	36.5	36.3	36.1	35.9	35.7	35.5
Primary Schl. Enroll. Ratio	89.0	..	..	..	..	97.0	99.0	101.0	103.0	104.0	98.0
Primary Schl. Enroll. Ratio, Female	75.0	..	..	..	..	87.0	88.0	91.0	93.0	94.0	89.0
Secondary Schl. Enroll. Ratio	7.0	..	..	..	..	13.0	15.0	16.0	17.0	18.0	18.0

1981	1982	1983	1984	1985	1986	1987	1988	1989	1990 estimate	Notes	CAMEROON
						(Millions of current US dollars)					**FOREIGN TRADE (CUSTOMS BASIS)**
..	1,028.9	..	872.7	716.2	780.8	829.4	923.7	1,281.6	1,200.0	..	Value of Exports, fob
..	468.0	..	575.5	472.3	573.5	532.3	609.1	845.2	791.3	..	Nonfuel Primary Products
..	483.2	..	157.3	129.1	77.3	145.2	166.4	230.9	216.2	..	Fuels
..	77.7	..	139.9	114.8	130.0	151.9	148.1	205.5	192.4	..	Manufactures
1,430.5	1,243.2	1,187.6	1,106.9	1,282.6	1,704.7	1,749.0	1,271.0	1,273.3	1,300.0	..	Value of Imports, cif
237.3	145.8	222.8	188.9	218.9	290.9	287.5	216.9	229.6	221.9	..	Nonfuel Primary Products
104.3	45.3	25.3	18.2	21.1	28.1	24.0	20.9	18.0	21.4	..	Fuels
1,088.9	1,052.1	939.5	899.8	1,042.6	1,385.7	1,437.5	1,033.2	1,025.7	1,056.7	..	Manufactures
						(Index 1987 = 100)					
148.3	144.3	141.7	145.6	139.4	98.4	100.0	96.1	100.6	90.9	..	Terms of Trade
144.0	135.3	129.8	130.7	125.4	98.1	100.0	110.2	121.2	127.4	..	Export Prices, fob
97.1	93.7	91.5	89.8	89.9	99.7	100.0	114.7	120.5	140.1	..	Import Prices, cif
						(Millions of current US dollars)					**BALANCE OF PAYMENTS**
2,218.3	2,032.6	2,259.6	2,588.3	2,819.0	2,897.1	2,255.4	2,097.0	2,166.9	2,335.3	C f	Exports of Goods & Services
1,763.1	1,617.1	1,829.6	2,080.2	2,337.0	2,292.8	1,826.7	1,645.1	1,807.2	1,909.2	..	Merchandise, fob
430.5	402.4	417.3	461.3	461.0	551.5	389.3	406.2	374.1	449.8	..	Nonfactor Services
24.7	13.1	12.7	46.9	21.0	52.8	39.4	45.7	-14.4	-23.7	..	Factor Services
2,676.5	2,368.6	2,311.2	2,380.0	2,458.0	3,441.1	3,347.8	2,865.8	2,287.3	2,528.8	C f	Imports of Goods & Services
1,611.4	1,285.4	1,166.2	1,194.7	1,088.0	1,477.0	1,734.0	1,484.0	1,275.4	1,371.5	..	Merchandise, fob
776.5	753.6	737.5	718.9	810.0	1,284.7	1,072.0	909.8	703.7	758.2	..	Nonfactor Services
288.6	329.6	407.4	466.4	560.0	679.4	541.8	472.0	308.2	399.1	..	Factor Services
137.3	150.6	139.1	166.1	136.2	188.7	178.4	192.3	114.2	189.8	..	Long-Term Interest
-52.0	-72.8	-78.5	-63.7	-33.0	-66.4	-133.1	-144.4	-83.1	-84.1	..	Private Current Transfers, net
21.1	17.3	25.6	14.2	1.0	2.0	3.0	3.4	2.7	3.1	..	Workers' Remittances
-510.2	-408.8	-130.1	144.6	328.0	-610.4	-1,225.5	-913.2	-203.5	-277.6	..	Curr. A/C Bal before Off. Transf.
62.6	57.0	75.1	56.5	0.0	0.0	0.0	0.0	0.0	..	..	Net Official Transfers
-447.6	-351.8	-55.0	201.1	328.0	-610.4	-1,225.5	-913.2	-203.5	-277.6	..	Curr. A/C Bal after Off. Transf.
441.0	262.9	297.7	73.9	-157.8	84.5	91.6	287.0	521.8	597.6	C f	Long-Term Capital, net
30.5	27.6	57.8	92.1	21.0	0.0	31.0	34.0	31.7	33.2	..	Direct Investment
328.0	166.9	341.9	210.0	-157.8	84.5	91.6	288.1	580.6	559.7	..	Long-Term Loans
452.6	362.8	508.9	407.0	306.5	509.2	488.4	662.8	768.2	817.0	..	Disbursements
124.6	195.9	167.0	197.0	464.3	424.7	396.8	374.7	187.6	257.3	..	Repayments
82.5	68.4	-102.0	-228.2	-21.0	0.0	-31.0	-35.1	-90.5	4.7	..	Other Long-Term Capital
-94.7	37.7	-35.4	-491.5	-131.6	324.9	587.1	579.2	-435.6	-243.5	C f	Other Capital, net
101.3	51.2	-207.3	216.5	-38.6	201.0	546.8	47.0	117.3	-76.5	..	Change in Reserves
						(CFA Francs per US dollar)					**Memo Item:**
235.270	296.680	354.660	409.520	471.130	386.600	318.660	291.710	315.360	300.660	..	Conversion Factor (Annual Avg)
				(Millions of US dollars), outstanding at end of year							
2,548.3	2,716.7	2,738.9	2,721.6	2,939.9	3,709.8	4,039.0	4,227.6	4,785.9	6,023.4	..	**EXTERNAL DEBT (Total)**
2,303.0	2,320.3	2,411.0	2,339.5	2,411.2	2,926.2	3,316.7	3,462.0	4,239.4	5,135.5	..	Long-Term Debt (by debtor)
91.9	78.1	64.1	51.3	51.3	44.0	39.8	119.7	123.9	132.5	..	Central Bank, incl. IMF credit
911.9	955.1	991.9	995.8	1,232.7	1,534.9	1,848.9	2,093.7	3,099.7	4,109.6	..	Central Government
0.0	0.0	0.0	0.0	0.0	0.0	0.0	0.0	0.0	..	..	Rest of General Government
981.7	872.5	782.4	650.3	708.0	804.0	869.5	746.7	519.8	532.8	..	Non-financial Public Enterprises
317.5	414.6	572.6	642.1	419.2	543.3	558.5	501.9	496.0	360.6	..	Priv. Sector, incl non-guaranteed
245.3	396.4	327.9	382.1	528.7	783.6	722.3	765.6	546.5	887.9	..	Short-Term Debt
						(Millions of US dollars)					**Memo Items:**
85.2	67.2	159.1	53.9	132.5	59.0	63.8	175.9	79.9	25.5	..	Int'l Reserves Excluding Gold
11.8	13.6	11.3	9.3	9.8	11.7	14.5	12.3	12.0	11.6	..	Gold Holdings (at market price)
											SOCIAL INDICATORS
6.5	6.5	6.4	6.3	6.1	6.0	5.9	5.9	5.9	5.8	..	Total Fertility Rate
104.6	103.0	101.2	99.4	97.5	95.7	93.9	92.0	90.2	88.3	..	Infant Mortality Rate
53.3	53.6	54.1	54.6	55.1	55.7	56.2	56.5	56.7	57.0	..	Life Expectancy at Birth
32.6	33.5	34.5	35.4	36.3	37.6	38.8	39.6	40.4	41.2	..	Urban Population, % of total
112.3	107.9	103.1	102.3	106.1	110.5	100.0	103.0	100.6	98.7	..	Food Prod. per capita (1987=100)
..	..	..	..	..	..	..	..	..	..	..	Labor Force, Agriculture (%)
35.2	35.0	34.8	34.6	34.4	34.2	33.9	33.7	33.5	33.3	..	Labor Force, Female (%)
105.0	107.0	106.0	107.0	102.0	103.0	104.0	..	101.0	..	..	Primary Schl. Enroll. Ratio
96.0	98.0	96.0	97.0	93.0	95.0	96.0	..	93.0	..	..	Primary Schl. Enroll. Ratio, Female
19.0	21.0	22.0	23.0	23.0	25.0	26.0	..	26.0	..	..	Secondary Schl. Enroll. Ratio

CANADA	1970	1971	1972	1973	1974	1975	1976	1977	1978	1979	1980
CURRENT GNP PER CAPITA (US $)	3,870	4,300	4,810	5,530	6,440	7,260	8,310	8,850	9,420	9,940	10,600
POPULATION (thousands)	21,324	21,592	21,822	22,072	22,364	22,697	22,993	23,273	23,517	23,747	24,043

USE AND ORIGIN OF RESOURCES *(Billions of current Canadian Dollars)*

	1970	1971	1972	1973	1974	1975	1976	1977	1978	1979	1980
Gross National Product (GNP)	87.11	95.04	106.32	124.69	148.72	167.57	192.76	211.52	233.63	266.94	299.90
Net Factor Income from Abroad	-1.35	-1.51	-1.46	-1.73	-2.24	-2.54	-3.54	-4.57	-5.95	-7.16	-7.83
GDP at Market Prices	88.46	96.55	107.79	126.42	150.96	170.11	196.29	216.09	239.58	274.09	307.73
Resource Balance	2.25	1.64	0.96	1.74	0.44	-2.41	-1.03	-0.07	1.10	1.79	5.65
Exports of Goods & NFServices	20.08	21.17	23.74	29.77	37.81	38.95	44.25	51.18	61.15	75.07	87.58
Imports of Goods & NFServices	17.83	19.53	22.78	28.02	37.37	41.36	45.28	51.25	60.05	73.28	81.93
Domestic Absorption	86.21	94.91	106.83	124.68	150.52	172.51	197.32	216.16	238.48	272.30	302.08
Private Consumption, etc.	50.57	54.81	62.12	71.19	83.79	96.15	110.13	120.81	135.65	151.72	170.36
General Gov't Consumption	16.39	18.16	20.05	22.77	27.35	33.15	38.15	43.26	47.20	52.15	59.10
Gross Domestic Investment	19.25	21.94	24.66	30.72	39.37	43.21	49.04	52.09	55.63	68.43	72.62
Fixed Investment	19.01	21.57	23.88	28.86	35.78	41.84	46.71	50.23	54.58	63.44	72.29
Indirect Taxes, net	11.09	12.05	13.63	15.31	17.87	17.09	20.99	23.19	24.82	26.64	27.27
GDP at factor cost	77.37	84.50	94.16	111.11	133.09	153.02	175.30	192.90	214.76	247.46	280.46
Agriculture	3.39	3.53	3.73	5.82	6.97	7.58	7.73	7.60	9.19	10.85	11.70
Industry	28.08	30.58	33.96	41.19	49.74	54.61	62.03	69.10	75.69	89.88	101.55
Manufacturing	17.58	19.14	21.40	25.15	29.65	31.43	35.16	38.46	43.59	51.08	55.04
Services, etc.	45.89	50.39	56.47	64.11	76.38	90.83	105.54	116.20	129.88	146.73	167.21
Gross Domestic Saving	21.50	23.58	25.62	32.46	39.81	40.81	48.01	52.02	56.73	70.22	78.27
Gross National Saving	20.23	22.25	24.33	30.97	37.99	38.65	44.90	47.80	51.06	63.50	70.51

(Billions of 1987 Canadian Dollars)

	1970	1971	1972	1973	1974	1975	1976	1977	1978	1979	1980
Gross National Product	280.54	296.88	314.16	337.04	350.48	359.00	380.06	392.34	408.35	422.82	429.46
GDP at Market Prices	284.80	301.46	318.36	341.66	355.79	364.42	387.02	400.72	418.53	434.07	440.80
Resource Balance	12.83	12.61	10.66	9.49	0.92	-1.62	-0.45	4.84	10.25	5.56	3.70
Exports of Goods & NFServices	58.66	61.71	66.55	73.57	72.11	67.23	74.35	80.95	91.99	96.62	99.25
Imports of Goods & NFServices	45.82	49.11	55.89	64.09	71.19	68.85	74.80	76.11	81.74	91.06	95.56
Domestic Absorption	271.97	288.86	307.70	332.18	354.86	366.04	387.47	395.87	408.27	428.51	437.10
Private Consumption, etc.	157.70	167.88	181.54	195.15	206.84	213.83	228.92	232.99	242.92	251.59	255.31
General Gov't Consumption	64.19	66.98	68.76	72.81	76.82	81.87	83.52	87.32	88.74	89.37	91.90
Gross Domestic Investment	50.08	53.99	57.41	64.22	71.21	70.34	75.03	75.56	76.61	87.56	89.89
Fixed Investment	48.91	52.75	55.03	60.49	64.51	68.25	71.41	72.89	75.15	81.57	89.80
GDP at factor cost	250.32	265.36	279.64	301.29	313.91	328.24	345.94	358.42	376.18	392.20	401.31
Agriculture	11.80	13.45	12.02	13.22	11.94	12.81	13.95	14.10	13.99	13.05	13.69
Industry	102.10	106.52	114.73	128.44	128.80	120.60	128.87	132.54	133.59	140.44	137.92
Manufacturing	55.85	59.40	64.19	71.09	73.23	68.34	73.35	76.01	79.47	82.45	78.75
Services, etc.	132.79	141.36	148.78	156.24	170.63	193.48	201.40	210.18	227.70	238.06	249.54

Memo Items:

	1970	1971	1972	1973	1974	1975	1976	1977	1978	1979	1980
Capacity to Import	51.60	53.23	58.24	68.07	72.02	64.85	73.10	76.00	83.24	93.29	102.14
Terms of Trade Adjustment	-7.06	-8.48	-8.31	-5.50	-0.09	-2.39	-1.25	-4.95	-8.75	-3.33	2.89
Gross Domestic Income	277.74	292.98	310.05	336.16	355.70	362.03	385.77	395.77	409.77	430.74	443.68
Gross National Income	273.49	288.40	305.85	331.54	350.40	356.61	378.81	387.40	399.60	419.49	432.35

DOMESTIC PRICES/DEFLATORS *(Index 1987 = 100)*

	1970	1971	1972	1973	1974	1975	1976	1977	1978	1979	1980
Overall (GDP)	31.1	32.0	33.9	37.0	42.4	46.7	50.7	53.9	57.2	63.1	69.8
Domestic Absorption	31.7	32.9	34.7	37.5	42.4	47.1	50.9	54.6	58.4	63.5	69.1
Agriculture	28.7	26.2	31.1	44.0	58.4	59.2	55.4	53.9	65.7	83.1	85.5
Industry	27.5	28.7	29.6	32.1	38.6	45.3	48.1	52.1	56.7	64.0	73.6
Manufacturing	31.5	32.2	33.3	35.4	40.5	46.0	47.9	50.6	54.9	61.9	69.9
Consumer Price Index	29.7	30.5	32.0	34.4	38.2	42.3	45.5	49.1	53.5	58.4	64.3

MANUFACTURING ACTIVITY

	1970	1971	1972	1973	1974	1975	1976	1977	1978	1979	1980
Employment (1987=100)	88.0	87.6	90.1	94.1	96.0	93.7	93.7	91.6	96.2	99.7	99.6
Real Earnings per Empl. (1987=100)	83.9	87.5	89.8	90.6	92.5	93.3	98.7	101.2	99.6	99.8	99.8
Real Output per Empl. (1987=100)	0.0	0.0	0.0	0.0	0.0	0.0	0.0	0.0	0.0	0.0	0.0
Earnings as % of Value Added	53.0	52.3	51.6	49.5	46.6	49.5	51.2	50.4	48.8	46.8	47.4

MONETARY HOLDINGS *(Billions of current Canadian Dollars)*

	1970	1971	1972	1973	1974	1975	1976	1977	1978	1979	1980
Money Supply, Broadly Defined	46.31	49.92	55.83	70.32	83.72	97.62	116.83	135.48	159.57	188.43	211.37
Money	15.57	17.61	19.77	21.50	21.83	25.97	26.36	29.10	31.12	31.56	34.75
Currency Outside Banks	3.56	3.99	4.56	5.20	5.86	6.78	7.32	8.08	8.95	9.45	10.40
Demand Deposits	12.01	13.63	15.21	16.30	15.97	19.19	19.04	21.01	22.17	22.11	24.35
Quasi-Money	30.74	32.30	36.05	48.82	61.90	71.65	90.47	106.38	128.44	156.86	176.62

GOVERNMENT DEFICIT (-) OR SURPLUS *(Billions of current Canadian Dollars)*

	1970	1971	1972	1973	1974	1975	1976	1977	1978	1979	1980
GOVERNMENT DEFICIT (-) OR SURPLUS	..	-1.72	..	..	-1.97	-5.70	-6.30	-9.41	-11.95	-10.56	-10.73
Current Revenue	..	18.14	..	..	31.62	34.89	37.72	38.24	41.64	48.22	57.49
Current Expenditure	..	..	..	..	28.87	34.85	38.41	43.71	49.15	54.62	64.75
Current Budget Balance	..	..	..	..	2.75	0.04	-0.69	-5.47	-7.52	-6.40	-7.25
Capital Receipts	..	..	..	..						..	..
Capital Payments	..	..	..	..	4.72	5.74	5.61	3.94	4.44	4.16	3.48

1981	1982	1983	1984	1985	1986	1987	1988	1989	1990 estimate	Notes	CANADA
11,780	11,960	12,730	13,670	14,140	14,210	15,070	16,760	18,870	20,370	..	**CURRENT GNP PER CAPITA (US $)**
24,342	24,583	24,787	24,978	25,165	25,353	25,625	25,950	26,219	26,522	..	**POPULATION (thousands)**
			(Billions of current Canadian Dollars)								**USE AND ORIGIN OF RESOURCES**
342.12	359.15	390.63	427.82	460.01	485.02	530.33	581.02	622.26	641.28	..	Gross National Product (GNP)
-11.34	-12.67	-11.60	-13.49	-14.33	-16.40	-16.44	-18.95	-21.14	-23.95	..	Net Factor Income from Abroad
353.45	371.82	402.23	441.31	474.34	501.43	546.78	599.97	643.41	665.24	..	GDP at Market Prices
3.88	14.05	13.61	15.40	11.53	4.75	4.91	4.82	0.11	2.05	..	Resource Balance
96.88	96.65	103.44	126.03	134.92	138.12	145.42	159.66	163.28	168.93	..	Exports of Goods & NFServices
93.00	82.60	89.83	110.63	123.39	133.37	140.50	154.84	163.16	166.88	..	Imports of Goods & NFServices
349.57	357.77	388.62	425.91	462.81	496.68	541.86	595.15	643.29	663.19	..	Domestic Absorption
193.67	207.75	225.97	247.57	271.05	292.68	316.51	345.33	372.93	392.53	..	Private Consumption, etc.
68.60	78.44	84.31	88.88	95.27	99.88	105.57	113.73	121.87	131.44	..	General Gov't Consumption
87.30	71.57	78.33	89.46	96.48	104.12	119.79	136.09	148.49	139.21	..	Gross Domestic Investment
86.12	81.33	81.23	84.70	94.20	101.56	116.72	132.96	146.42	142.56	D	Fixed Investment
36.46	38.91	40.13	42.71	47.21	53.83	59.72	67.51	74.49	75.10	..	Indirect Taxes, net
317.00	332.91	362.09	398.60	427.13	447.60	487.06	532.46	568.92	590.13	..	GDP at factor cost
13.22	12.63	12.08	13.60	13.34	14.73	15.70	..	..	..	..	Agriculture
113.45	112.32	123.82	138.92	149.60	147.91	163.87			..	..	Industry
61.65	57.84	65.26	75.50	81.67	86.79	94.61			..	..	Manufacturing
190.33	207.97	226.19	246.07	264.19	284.96	307.49			..	..	Services, etc.
91.18	85.63	91.94	104.86	108.01	108.87	124.70	140.90	148.61	141.26	..	Gross Domestic Saving
80.03	73.27	80.37	91.41	93.69	92.52	108.78	122.77	128.37	118.20	..	Gross National Saving
			(Billions of 1987 Canadian Dollars)								
442.34	427.23	443.21	470.60	493.03	508.06	530.33	554.26	567.00	567.61	..	Gross National Product
457.16	442.36	456.45	485.48	508.37	525.08	546.78	572.49	586.54	588.99	..	GDP at Market Prices
-0.09	13.38	11.94	14.63	12.46	9.17	4.91	0.46	-6.75	-2.00	..	Resource Balance
103.62	101.36	107.85	126.94	134.51	140.51	145.42	158.85	159.83	165.96	..	Exports of Goods & NFServices
103.71	87.98	95.91	112.32	122.04	131.33	140.50	158.39	166.58	167.97	..	Imports of Goods & NFServices
457.25	428.98	444.51	470.85	495.90	515.91	541.86	572.03	593.28	590.99	..	Domestic Absorption
261.82	251.57	260.45	277.88	292.53	304.40	316.51	331.70	341.93	345.61	..	Private Consumption, etc.
94.21	96.45	97.81	99.07	102.17	103.78	105.57	109.80	113.01	116.49	..	General Gov't Consumption
101.22	80.96	86.25	93.90	101.20	107.74	119.79	130.53	138.34	128.89	..	Gross Domestic Investment
100.38	89.35	88.71	90.60	99.17	105.33	116.72	128.85	136.06	131.63	..	Fixed Investment
409.49	395.84	410.64	438.35	457.84	469.22	487.06	507.54	517.72	521.98	..	GDP at factor cost
14.61	15.02	15.23	15.09	14.64	16.69	15.70	13.21	14.70	..	..	Agriculture
140.74	129.80	135.96	147.41	156.17	156.31	163.87	172.68	173.81	..	..	Industry
81.65	71.12	75.72	85.48	90.30	90.97	94.61	99.25	99.70	..	..	Manufacturing
253.79	251.05	259.45	275.85	287.03	296.22	307.49	321.65	329.21		..	Services, etc.
											Memo Items:
108.03	102.95	110.44	127.96	133.45	136.01	145.42	163.32	166.69	170.03	..	Capacity to Import
4.42	1.59	2.59	1.01	-1.06	-4.50	0.00	4.47	6.86	4.07	..	Terms of Trade Adjustment
461.57	443.95	459.04	486.49	507.31	520.59	546.78	576.96	593.40	593.05	..	Gross Domestic Income
446.76	428.82	445.80	471.61	491.97	503.57	530.33	558.73	573.86	571.68	..	Gross National Income
			(Index 1987 = 100)								**DOMESTIC PRICES/DEFLATORS**
77.3	84.1	88.1	90.9	93.3	95.5	100.0	104.8	109.7	112.9	..	Overall (GDP)
76.5	83.4	87.4	90.5	93.3	96.3	100.0	104.0	108.4	112.2	..	Domestic Absorption
90.5	84.1	79.3	90.2	91.1	88.2	100.0	..	..	..	..	Agriculture
80.6	86.5	91.1	94.2	95.8	94.6	100.0	..	..	..	..	Industry
75.5	81.3	86.2	88.3	90.4	95.4	100.0	..	..	..	..	Manufacturing
72.3	80.1	84.8	88.5	92.0	95.8	100.0	104.0	109.2	114.4	..	Consumer Price Index
											MANUFACTURING ACTIVITY
99.3	91.4	89.8	92.3	94.9	97.0	100.0	101.6	102.2	..	..	Employment (1987=100)
99.5	99.1	100.3	101.8	102.2	101.2	100.0	103.3	104.3	..	..	Real Earnings per Empl. (1987=100)
0.0	0.0	0.0	0.0	0.0	0.0	0.0	0.0	..	..	..	Real Output per Empl. (1987=100)
47.3	51.3	48.5	45.8	45.6	45.3	43.7	43.6	43.5	..	..	Earnings as % of Value Added
			(Billions of current Canadian Dollars)								**MONETARY HOLDINGS**
243.41	257.06	264.82	283.64	303.60	332.52	364.44	403.72	457.60	494.76	D	Money Supply, Broadly Defined
36.75	39.82	44.09	52.44	68.91	80.22	85.20	90.12	95.45	96.22	..	Money
10.71	11.62	12.80	13.50	14.61	15.59	16.92	18.24	19.64	20.05	..	Currency Outside Banks
26.04	28.20	31.30	38.94	54.31	64.63	68.27	71.88	75.80	76.17	..	Demand Deposits
206.66	217.24	220.73	231.20	234.69	252.30	279.25	313.60	362.16	398.54	..	Quasi-Money
			(Billions of current Canadian Dollars)								
-8.43	-20.81	-25.16	-28.87	-28.68	-20.11	-14.00	-13.51	-18.17	..	C E	**GOVERNMENT DEFICIT (-) OR SURPLUS**
72.28	73.24	77.33	85.30	91.10	99.23	111.66	119.36	127.41	..	..	Current Revenue
74.84	88.02	97.02	108.78	115.06	117.13	124.94	130.94	143.08	..	..	Current Expenditure
-2.56	-14.78	-19.69	-23.48	-23.96	-17.90	-13.28	-11.58	-15.67	..	..	Current Budget Balance
..	..	..	..	..	..	..	..	..	..	..	Capital Receipts
5.87	6.03	5.47	5.39	4.72	2.21	0.72	1.93	2.50	..	..	Capital Payments

CANADA	1970	1971	1972	1973	1974	1975	1976	1977	1978	1979	1980
FOREIGN TRADE (CUSTOMS BASIS)					*(Millions of current US dollars)*						
Value of Exports, fob	16,185	17,675	20,178	25,207	32,783	32,300	38,370	41,293	44,080	55,117	63,105
Nonfuel Primary Products	6,918	7,214	7,981	10,627	13,045	11,904	14,250	15,076	15,343	19,718	23,500
Fuels	978	1,262	1,734	2,466	5,179	5,334	5,300	5,171	4,815	7,281	9,010
Manufactures	8,288	9,199	10,463	12,115	14,559	15,063	18,821	21,046	23,922	28,119	30,595
Value of Imports, cif	13,348	15,458	18,923	23,316	32,296	33,954	37,934	39,485	41,697	52,622	57,707
Nonfuel Primary Products	1,979	2,143	2,547	3,463	4,646	4,526	5,012	5,188	5,414	6,927	8,323
Fuels	749	907	1,085	1,324	3,391	4,090	4,103	3,920	3,770	4,884	7,143
Manufactures	10,620	12,409	15,291	18,530	24,260	25,338	28,819	30,377	32,513	40,811	42,241
					(Index 1987 = 100)						
Terms of Trade	117.1	106.2	101.4	122.0	92.6	101.4	104.3	93.4	89.8	89.5	90.1
Export Prices, fob	33.0	33.0	34.9	52.6	56.9	65.6	70.2	69.3	74.7	88.4	101.6
Import Prices, cif	28.2	31.1	34.4	43.1	61.5	64.7	67.3	74.2	83.2	98.7	112.8
BALANCE OF PAYMENTS					*(Billions of current US dollars)*						
Exports of Goods & Services	20.19	21.95	25.03	31.00	40.13	39.99	46.46	49.80	55.62	66.37	77.99
Merchandise, fob	16.71	18.30	21.20	26.55	34.48	34.02	40.01	43.19	48.16	57.65	67.48
Nonfactor Services	2.48	2.66	2.80	3.21	4.18	4.27	4.80	4.91	5.40	6.46	7.41
Factor Services	1.00	0.98	1.04	1.23	1.48	1.70	1.64	1.70	2.06	2.26	3.11
Imports of Goods & Services	19.31	21.82	25.53	30.99	41.97	44.87	51.15	54.19	59.85	70.93	79.86
Merchandise, fob	13.66	15.63	19.03	23.37	32.39	34.29	38.13	40.05	43.98	53.47	59.48
Nonfactor Services	3.36	3.71	3.99	4.65	5.82	6.38	7.64	8.16	8.63	9.09	10.58
Factor Services	2.29	2.48	2.51	2.97	3.76	4.20	5.37	5.98	7.24	8.37	9.80
Long-Term Interest	..	..	..	..	..	..	..	..	..	..	..
Private Current Transfers, net	0.08	0.17	0.18	0.24	0.43	0.38	0.43	0.33	0.24	0.37	0.05
Workers' Remittances	..	..	..	..	..	..	..	..	..	..	..
Curr. A/C Bal before Off. Transf.	0.96	0.30	-0.32	0.25	-1.41	-4.51	-4.26	-4.07	-3.99	-4.19	-1.81
Net Official Transfers	0.05	0.06	0.05	0.06	0.08	-0.07	0.11	-0.03	-0.29	0.05	0.28
Curr. A/C Bal after Off. Transf.	1.01	0.36	-0.28	0.31	-1.32	-4.57	-4.15	-4.10	-4.29	-4.14	-1.53
Long-Term Capital, net	0.52	0.27	1.33	0.22	0.89	3.76	7.75	3.36	3.12	2.44	-0.20
Direct Investment	0.51	0.73	0.34	-0.14	0.08	-0.15	-1.06	-0.47	-1.43	-0.73	-3.17
Long-Term Loans	..	..	..	..	..	..	..	..	..	..	..
Disbursements	..	..	..	..	..	..	..	..	..	..	..
Repayments	..	..	..	..	..	..	..	..	..	..	..
Other Long-Term Capital	0.01	-0.45	0.99	0.36	0.82	3.91	8.81	3.83	4.55	3.17	2.97
Other Capital, net	-1.27	-0.90	-1.09	-0.56	0.62	0.97	-3.07	-0.60	0.97	0.76	1.08
Change in Reserves	-0.25	0.26	0.04	0.04	-0.18	-0.16	-0.53	1.35	0.19	0.94	0.66
Memo Item:					*(Canadian Dollars per US dollar)*						
Conversion Factor (Annual Avg)	1.050	1.010	0.990	1.000	0.980	1.020	0.990	1.060	1.140	1.170	1.170
					(Millions US dollars), outstanding at end of year						
EXTERNAL DEBT (Total)	..	..	..	..	..	..	..	..	..	..	..
Long-Term Debt (by debtor)	..	..	..	..	..	..	..	..	..	..	..
Central Bank, incl. IMF credit	..	..	..	..	..	..	..	..	..	..	..
Central Government	..	..	..	..	..	..	..	..	..	..	..
Rest of General Government	..	..	..	..	..	..	..	..	..	..	..
Non-financial Public Enterprises	..	..	..	..	..	..	..	..	..	..	..
Priv. Sector, incl non-guaranteed	..	..	..	..	..	..	..	..	..	..	..
Short-Term Debt	..	..	..	..	..	..	..	..	..	..	..
Memo Items:					*(Millions of US dollars)*						
Int'l Reserves Excluding Gold	3,888	4,839	5,216	4,841	4,885	4,385	4,924	3,653	3,544	2,856	3,041
Gold Holdings (at market price)	844	990	1,424	2,464	4,094	3,079	2,913	3,630	5,001	11,356	12,369
SOCIAL INDICATORS											
Total Fertility Rate	2.3	2.1	2.0	1.9	1.8	1.8	1.8	1.8	1.8	1.8	1.8
Infant Mortality Rate	18.8	17.5	17.1	15.5	15.0	14.2	13.4	12.3	11.9	10.9	10.4
Life Expectancy at Birth	72.5	72.6	72.8	73.0	73.2	73.4	73.6	73.8	74.1	74.4	74.7
Urban Population, % of total	75.7	75.7	75.7	75.6	75.6	75.6	75.6	75.6	75.7	75.7	75.7
Food Prod. per capita (1987=100)	73.7	85.7	81.8	80.7	73.7	81.4	90.4	89.7	93.0	83.5	88.6
Labor Force, Agriculture (%)	7.8	7.5	7.2	7.0	6.7	6.5	6.2	6.0	5.7	5.5	5.3
Labor Force, Female (%)	32.5	33.4	34.2	35.0	35.7	36.4	37.2	37.9	38.6	39.2	39.8
Primary Schl. Enroll. Ratio	101.0	..	..	..	..	99.0	100.0	100.0	101.0	101.0	100.0
Primary Schl. Enroll. Ratio, Female	100.0	..	..	..	..	99.0	100.0	100.0	100.0	100.0	100.0
Secondary Schl. Enroll. Ratio	65.0	..	..	..	..	91.0	91.0	89.0	88.0	88.0	89.0

1981	1982	1983	1984	1985	1986	1987	1988	1989	1990 estimate	Notes	CANADA
				(Millions of current US dollars)							**FOREIGN TRADE (CUSTOMS BASIS)**
68,281	66,977	72,142	84,844	85,737	84,381	92,886	111,364	114,066	125,056	..	Value of Exports, fob
23,258	21,311	22,465	24,280	22,191	22,676	26,851	31,643	31,788	32,900	..	Nonfuel Primary Products
9,451	9,601	9,926	11,117	12,047	8,146	9,382	10,158	10,604	12,558	..	Fuels
35,573	36,065	39,751	49,446	51,499	53,559	56,653	69,563	71,674	79,597	..	Manufactures
65,405	54,470	60,363	72,934	75,404	79,631	86,810	105,922	113,230	115,881	..	Value of Imports, cif
8,405	7,106	7,627	8,512	7,911	8,578	9,142	10,938	11,921	12,191	..	Nonfuel Primary Products
8,090	5,480	4,212	4,703	4,569	3,763	4,248	4,211	5,378	7,286	..	Fuels
48,911	41,884	48,524	59,719	62,925	67,290	73,420	90,773	95,931	96,405	..	Manufactures
				(Index 1987 = 100)							
96.6	100.6	104.9	109.4	109.5	101.2	100.0	107.4	110.4	108.8	..	Terms of Trade
105.3	104.0	105.7	107.2	106.1	99.6	100.0	111.3	116.4	117.3	..	Export Prices, fob
109.0	103.4	100.7	98.0	96.8	98.4	100.0	103.6	105.5	107.9	..	Import Prices, cif
				(Billions of current US dollars)							**BALANCE OF PAYMENTS**
84.14	82.74	88.46	102.16	104.33	104.98	115.76	139.05	146.22	152.74	..	Exports of Goods & Services
72.52	70.49	75.68	88.62	89.65	89.03	98.05	116.06	123.02	129.05	..	Merchandise, fob
8.29	7.81	8.24	8.64	9.14	10.39	11.65	13.76	14.89	15.76	..	Nonfactor Services
3.33	4.44	4.54	4.90	5.54	5.55	6.06	9.24	8.31	7.93	..	Factor Services
90.36	81.67	86.83	100.76	106.39	113.35	124.46	150.50	163.96	171.46	..	Imports of Goods & Services
65.94	55.50	60.71	72.66	77.07	81.35	89.09	106.64	116.28	119.09	..	Merchandise, fob
11.63	11.46	12.17	12.79	13.27	14.64	16.90	19.18	21.51	23.90	..	Nonfactor Services
12.78	14.71	13.95	15.32	16.04	17.35	18.47	24.68	26.17	28.47	..	Factor Services
..	..	..	..	..	..	..	..	..	..		Long-Term Interest
0.15	0.25	0.03	0.02	0.01	0.04	0.39	0.66	0.77	0.76	..	Private Current Transfers, net
..	..	..	..	..	..	..	..	..	..		Workers' Remittances
-6.06	1.32	1.66	1.42	-2.05	-8.33	-8.31	-10.79	-16.98	-17.95	..	Curr. A/C Bal before Off. Transf.
0.32	0.25	0.05	-0.20	-0.22	0.14	-0.45	-0.45	-0.50	-0.86	..	Net Official Transfers
-5.74	1.57	1.71	1.22	-2.28	-8.19	-8.75	-11.24	-17.48	-18.82	..	Curr. A/C Bal after Off. Transf.
2.03	5.77	0.17	2.99	3.31	12.67	8.16	10.01	19.91	16.08	..	Long-Term Capital, net
-8.68	-2.28	-3.77	-0.84	-4.85	-2.65	-3.55	-2.26	-0.74	4.90	..	Direct Investment
..	..	..	..	..	..	..	..	..	..		Long-Term Loans
..	..	..	..	..	..	..	..	..	..	..	Disbursements
..	..	..	..	..	..	..	..	..	..	..	Repayments
10.71	8.04	3.95	3.82	8.16	15.31	11.71	12.27	20.64	11.18	..	Other Long-Term Capital
3.86	-7.92	-1.43	-5.07	-1.11	-4.00	3.93	8.78	-2.14	3.36	..	Other Capital, net
-0.15	0.58	-0.45	0.87	0.07	-0.48	-3.34	-7.56	-0.29	-0.63	..	Change in Reserves
				(Canadian Dollars per US dollar)							**Memo Item:**
1.200	1.230	1.230	1.300	1.370	1.390	1.330	1.230	1.180	1.170	..	Conversion Factor (Annual Avg)
			(Millions US dollars), outstanding at end of year								
..	..	..	..	..	..	..	..	..	..	..	**EXTERNAL DEBT (Total)**
..	..	..	..	..	..	..	..	..	..	..	Long-Term Debt (by debtor)
..	..	..	..	..	..	..	..	..	..	..	Central Bank, incl. IMF credit
..	..	..	..	..	..	..	..	..	..	..	Central Government
..	..	..	..	..	..	..	..	..	..	..	Rest of General Government
..	..	..	..	..	..	..	..	..	..	..	Non-financial Public Enterprises
..	..	..	..	..	..	..	..	..	..	..	Priv. Sector, incl non-guaranteed
..	..	..	..	..	..	..	..	..	..	..	Short-Term Debt
				(Millions of US dollars)							**Memo Items:**
3,492	3,000	3,465	2,491	2,503	3,251	7,277	15,391	16,055	17,845	..	Int'l Reserves Excluding Gold
8,134	9,258	7,695	6,208	6,575	7,710	8,965	7,031	6,457	5,684	..	Gold Holdings (at market price)
											SOCIAL INDICATORS
1.7	1.7	1.7	1.6	1.7	1.7	1.7	1.7	1.7	1.7	..	Total Fertility Rate
9.6	9.1	8.5	8.1	7.9	7.9	7.3	7.1	6.9	6.6	..	Infant Mortality Rate
75.0	75.4	75.6	75.9	76.2	76.4	76.7	76.9	77.2	77.4	..	Life Expectancy at Birth
75.8	76.0	76.1	76.3	76.4	76.5	76.7	76.8	77.0	77.1	..	Urban Population, % of total
95.1	101.6	94.5	94.3	97.6	106.2	100.0	88.4	95.4	104.6	..	Food Prod. per capita (1987=100)
..	..	..	..	..	..	..	..	..	..	..	Labor Force, Agriculture (%)
39.8	39.8	39.8	39.8	39.8	39.8	39.8	39.8	39.8	39.8	..	Labor Force, Female (%)
..	107.0	106.0	106.0	105.0	105.0	105.0	105.0	105.0	..	..	Primary Schl. Enroll. Ratio
106.0	106.0	105.0	105.0	104.0	104.0	104.0	104.0	105.0	..	..	Primary Schl. Enroll. Ratio, Female
..	99.0	102.0	103.0	103.0	103.0	104.0	105.0	105.0	..	..	Secondary Schl. Enroll. Ratio

CAPE VERDE	1970	1971	1972	1973	1974	1975	1976	1977	1978	1979	1980
CURRENT GNP PER CAPITA (US $)	..	..	200	230	290	310	350	320	330	360	530
POPULATION (thousands)	267	270	273	275	277	278	279	280	282	285	289
USE AND ORIGIN OF RESOURCES				*(Millions of current Cape Verde Escudos)*							
Gross National Product (GNP)	1,434	1,497	1,743	1,701	2,133	2,367	2,367	2,567	3,081	3,651	5,748
Net Factor Income from Abroad	-51	-53	-61	-60	-75	-83	-83	-91	-108	-129	33
GDP at Market Prices	1,484	1,549	1,805	1,761	2,209	2,450	2,450	2,658	3,190	3,779	5,715
Resource Balance	..	..	..	-758	-649	-697	-1,216	-1,748	-2,134	-2,642	-2,851
Exports of Goods & NFServices	..	..	..	364	317	266	197	88	316	529	976
Imports of Goods & NFServices	..	..	..	1,121	967	964	1,412	1,836	2,450	3,171	3,827
Domestic Absorption	..	..	..	2,519	2,858	3,148	3,666	4,406	5,324	6,422	8,566
Private Consumption, etc.	..	..	..	2,019	2,218	2,367	2,515	2,698	3,508	3,791	5,332
General Gov't Consumption	..	..	..	154	272	390	484	680	713	868	842
Gross Domestic Investment	..	..	..	346	369	391	667	1,028	1,102	1,763	2,392
Fixed Investment	..	..	..	..	..	..	..	..	..	..	2,214
Indirect Taxes, net	90	100	104	110	117	122	120	137	204	228	468
GDP at factor cost	1,394	1,449	1,701	1,652	2,092	2,328	2,330	2,521	2,986	3,551	5,247
Agriculture	..	..	..	214	223	304	405	429	592	821	1,068
Industry	..	..	..	421	392	433	490	454	650	757	962
Manufacturing	..	..	..	..	..	..	..	..	..	..	291
Services, etc.	..	..	..	1,126	1,593	1,713	1,555	1,775	1,948	2,202	3,685
Gross Domestic Saving	..	..	..	-412	-281	-306	-549	-720	-1,032	-880	-459
Gross National Saving	..	..	..	..	..	..	..	-13	-312	-55	1,170
				(Millions of 1987 Cape Verde Escudos)							
Gross National Product	6,491	6,038	5,760	5,719	5,857	5,395	6,348	6,390	7,070	7,847	11,250
GDP at Market Prices	7,438	6,920	6,601	6,553	6,373	6,573	6,570	6,613	7,317	8,122	11,183
Resource Balance	..	..	..	-1,751	-1,221	-1,320	-2,732	-4,384	-4,355	-4,659	-4,736
Exports of Goods & NFServices	..	..	..	2,807	1,964	1,429	1,500	428	1,344	1,395	1,984
Imports of Goods & NFServices	..	..	..	4,558	3,184	2,749	4,232	4,812	5,699	6,054	6,720
Domestic Absorption	..	..	..	8,304	7,593	7,894	9,302	10,997	11,673	12,781	15,919
Private Consumption, etc.	..	..	..	6,228	5,016	5,353	5,866	6,240	7,546	7,793	9,892
General Gov't Consumption	..	..	..	535	943	1,113	1,245	1,623	1,387	1,388	1,578
Gross Domestic Investment	..	..	..	1,541	1,634	1,427	2,190	3,135	2,740	3,600	4,449
Fixed Investment	..	..	..	..	..	..	..	..	..	..	..
GDP at factor cost	..	..	..	..	..	..	..	..	..	..	10,266
Agriculture	..	..	..	..	..	..	..	..	..	..	2,200
Industry	..	..	..	..	..	..	..	..	..	..	1,821
Manufacturing	..	..	..	..	..	..	..	..	..	..	717
Services, etc.	..	..	..	..	..	..	..	..	..	..	7,162
Memo Items:											
Capacity to Import	..	..	..	1,478	1,045	760	589	229	735	1,009	1,713
Terms of Trade Adjustment	..	..	..	-1,329	-919	-669	-911	-199	-609	-386	-270
Gross Domestic Income	..	..	..	5,224	5,454	5,904	5,660	6,415	6,708	7,736	10,913
Gross National Income	..	..	..	4,390	4,939	4,726	5,437	6,191	6,461	7,461	10,980
DOMESTIC PRICES/DEFLATORS				*(Index 1987 = 100)*							
Overall (GDP)	20.0	22.4	27.3	26.9	34.7	37.3	37.3	40.2	43.6	46.5	51.1
Domestic Absorption	..	..	..	30.3	37.6	39.9	39.4	40.1	45.6	50.2	53.8
Agriculture	..	..	..	..	..	..	..	..	..	..	48.5
Industry	..	..	..	..	..	..	..	..	..	..	52.9
Manufacturing	..	..	..	..	..	..	..	..	..	..	40.5
Consumer Price Index	..	..	..	..	..	..	..	..	..	..	..
MANUFACTURING ACTIVITY											
Employment (1987=100)	..	..	..	..	..	..	..	..	..	..	..
Real Earnings per Empl. (1987=100)	..	..	..	..	..	..	..	..	..	..	..
Real Output per Empl. (1987=100)	..	..	..	..	..	..	..	..	..	..	..
Earnings as % of Value Added	..	..	..	..	..	..	..	..	..	..	..
MONETARY HOLDINGS				*(Millions of current Cape Verde Escudos)*							
Money Supply, Broadly Defined	..	..	..	..	..	..	1,022	1,441	1,674	1,966	2,563
Money	..	..	..	..	..	..	1,000	1,411	1,615	1,823	2,302
Currency Outside Banks	..	..	..	..	..	..	465	537	638	736	872
Demand Deposits	..	..	..	..	..	..	536	874	977	1,086	1,430
Quasi-Money	..	..	..	..	..	..	21	30	59	143	261
GOVERNMENT DEFICIT (-) OR SURPLUS				*(Millions of current Cape Verde Escudos)*							
Current Revenue	..	..	..	..	..	..	..	..	..	..	..
Current Expenditure	..	..	..	..	..	..	..	..	..	..	..
Current Budget Balance	..	..	..	..	..	..	..	..	..	..	..
Capital Receipts	..	..	..	..	..	..	..	..	..	..	..
Capital Payments	..	..	..	..	..	..	..	..	..	..	..

1981	1982	1983	1984	1985	1986	1987	1988	1989	1990 estimate	Notes	CAPE VERDE
530	510	490	460	450	480	570	700	780	890	..	**CURRENT GNP PER CAPITA (US $)**
294	300	308	316	324	333	341	351	361	371	..	**POPULATION (thousands)**
				(Millions of current Cape Verde Escudos)							**USE AND ORIGIN OF RESOURCES**
6,601	8,036	9,620	10,875	12,315	15,082	16,798	18,920	21,993	26,353	..	Gross National Product (GNP)
-191	-163	-309	-334	-310	-204	-180	-34	-70	139	..	Net Factor Income from Abroad
6,792	8,199	9,929	11,209	12,625	15,286	16,978	18,954	22,062	26,214	..	GDP at Market Prices
-3,343	-4,612	-5,279	-6,155	-7,137	-8,837	-6,758	-7,656	-8,447	-6,232	..	Resource Balance
1,458	1,879	2,445	2,552	2,856	2,691	3,745	3,183	3,188	4,493	..	Exports of Goods & NFServices
4,801	6,491	7,724	8,707	9,993	11,527	10,503	10,839	11,636	10,725	..	Imports of Goods & NFServices
10,135	12,811	15,209	17,364	19,761	24,122	23,736	26,610	30,509	32,446	..	Domestic Absorption
6,029	6,910	8,304	9,859	11,066	12,926	12,244	14,130	16,855	..	..	Private Consumption, etc.
1,028	1,566	2,055	2,570	2,999	4,194	3,973	4,585	4,326	..	..	General Gov't Consumption
3,078	4,335	4,850	4,935	5,696	7,002	7,519	7,895	9,328	9,701	..	Gross Domestic Investment
3,271	4,222	4,840	4,966	5,958	6,440				..	..	Fixed Investment
552	616	715	834	876	1,088	1,215	1,305	1,436	..	..	Indirect Taxes, net
6,240	7,583	9,214	10,375	11,749	14,197	15,763	17,649	20,626	..	B	GDP at factor cost
1,093	1,035	1,255	1,376	1,720	2,182	2,548	2,759	3,180	..	..	Agriculture
1,156	1,292	1,656	1,925	2,189	2,624	2,898	3,170	3,773	..	..	Industry
289	389	524	604	807	1,005	1,270	1,520	1,931	..	..	Manufacturing
4,542	5,872	7,017	7,908	8,716	10,480	11,533	13,026	15,109	..	..	Services, etc.
-265	-277	-429	-1,220	-1,441	-1,835	762	239	881	3,469	..	Gross Domestic Saving
1,303	1,426	1,750	279	285	261	3,048	3,059	4,188	6,647	..	Gross National Saving
				(Millions of 1987 Cape Verde Escudos)							
11,834	12,249	13,280	13,800	15,093	15,648	16,799	17,484	18,420	19,350	..	Gross National Product
12,128	12,470	13,658	14,176	15,412	15,861	16,978	17,517	18,483	19,222	..	GDP at Market Prices
-4,231	-5,372	-5,372	-5,879	-5,894	-7,842	-6,758	-7,124	-6,400	-6,956	..	Resource Balance
2,449	2,628	3,184	2,983	3,439	3,060	3,745	3,028	3,143	3,210	..	Exports of Goods & NFServices
6,679	8,000	8,556	8,862	9,332	10,902	10,503	10,152	9,543	10,167	..	Imports of Goods & NFServices
16,358	17,842	19,030	20,055	21,306	23,702	23,736	24,641	24,882	26,178	..	Domestic Absorption
9,772	9,671	10,517	11,336	12,075	12,584	12,244	12,774	13,090	..	..	Private Consumption, etc.
1,741	2,316	2,715	3,030	3,415	4,092	3,973	4,109	3,862	..	..	General Gov't Consumption
4,845	5,855	5,798	5,690	5,816	7,027	7,519	7,758	7,930	8,247	..	Gross Domestic Investment
..	..	..	..	..	..	..	..	..	..	..	Fixed Investment
11,140	11,532	12,672	13,120	14,343	14,731	15,763	16,311	17,279	..	B	GDP at factor cost
2,078	1,647	1,638	1,670	2,129	2,282	2,548	2,650	2,752	..	..	Agriculture
2,017	2,020	2,361	2,348	2,694	2,743	2,898	3,044	3,288	..	..	Industry
607	740	869	835	1,096	1,050	1,270	1,461	1,607	..	..	Manufacturing
8,033	8,804	9,660	10,159	10,589	10,836	11,533	11,823	12,443	..	..	Services, etc.
											Memo Items:
2,028	2,316	2,708	2,597	2,668	2,545	3,745	2,981	2,615	4,259	..	Capacity to Import
-421	-312	-476	-386	-771	-516	0	-47	-528	1,049	..	Terms of Trade Adjustment
11,707	12,158	13,181	13,790	14,642	15,345	16,978	17,470	17,954	20,271	..	Gross Domestic Income
11,413	11,937	12,803	13,415	14,322	15,132	16,799	17,437	17,891	20,398	..	Gross National Income
				(Index 1987 = 100)							**DOMESTIC PRICES/DEFLATORS**
56.0	65.8	72.7	79.1	81.9	96.4	100.0	108.2	119.4	136.4	..	Overall (GDP)
62.0	71.8	79.9	86.6	92.7	101.8	100.0	108.0	122.6	123.9	..	Domestic Absorption
52.6	62.8	76.7	82.4	80.8	95.6	100.0	104.1	115.6	..	..	Agriculture
57.3	64.0	70.2	82.0	81.3	95.7	100.0	104.1	114.7	..	..	Industry
47.6	52.6	60.3	72.4	73.6	95.7	100.0	104.1	120.2	..	..	Manufacturing
..	..	74.1	82.4	86.9	96.3	100.0	..	..	..	..	Consumer Price Index
											MANUFACTURING ACTIVITY
..	..	..	..	..	..	..	..	..	..	..	Employment (1987=100)
..	..	..	..	..	..	..	..	..	..	..	Real Earnings per Empl. (1987=100)
..	..	..	..	..	..	..	..	..	..	..	Real Output per Empl. (1987=100)
..	..	..	..	..	..	..	..	..	..	..	Earnings as % of Value Added
				(Millions of current Cape Verde Escudos)							**MONETARY HOLDINGS**
3,047	3,854	4,598	5,413	6,520	7,859	8,466	9,951	11,255	12,970	..	Money Supply, Broadly Defined
2,553	3,228	3,956	4,202	4,843	5,621	5,710	6,038	6,411	6,926	..	Money
1,041	1,252	1,333	1,434	1,628	1,826	1,956	2,219	2,490	2,842	..	Currency Outside Banks
1,512	1,976	2,623	2,768	3,215	3,794	3,755	3,819	3,920	4,084	..	Demand Deposits
494	626	642	1,211	1,676	2,238	2,755	3,913	4,845	6,044	..	Quasi-Money
				(Millions of current Cape Verde Escudos)							**GOVERNMENT DEFICIT (-) OR SURPLUS**
..	..	..	..	..	..	..	..	..	..	..	Current Revenue
..	..	..	..	..	..	..	..	..	..	..	Current Expenditure
..	..	..	..	..	..	..	..	..	..	..	Current Budget Balance
..	..	..	..	..	..	..	..	..	..	..	Capital Receipts
..	..	..	..	..	..	..	..	..	..	..	Capital Payments

CAPE VERDE	1970	1971	1972	1973	1974	1975	1976	1977	1978	1979	1980
FOREIGN TRADE (CUSTOMS BASIS)					*(Millions of current US dollars)*						
Value of Exports, fob	..	..	..	..	..	..	..	..	..	..	..
Nonfuel Primary Products	..	..	..	..	..	..	..	..	..	..	..
Fuels	..	..	..	..	..	..	..	..	..	..	..
Manufactures	..	..	..	..	..	..	..	..	..	..	..
Value of Imports, cif	..	..	..	..	..	..	..	..	..	..	..
Nonfuel Primary Products	..	..	..	..	..	..	..	..	..	..	..
Fuels	..	..	..	..	..	..	..	..	..	..	..
Manufactures	..	..	..	..	..	..	..	..	..	..	..
					(Index 1987 = 100)						
Terms of Trade	..	..	..	..	..	..	..	..	..	..	..
Export Prices, fob	..	..	..	..	..	..	..	..	..	..	..
Import Prices, cif	..	..	..	..	..	..	..	..	..	..	..
BALANCE OF PAYMENTS					*(Thousands of current US dollars)*						
Exports of Goods & Services	..	..	..	..	..	..	..	3.33	8.65	14.44	22.68
Merchandise, fob	..	..	..	..	..	..	..	1.24	3.07	4.12	9.12
Nonfactor Services	..	..	..	..	..	..	..	0.96	4.68	8.19	10.08
Factor Services	..	..	..	..	..	..	..	1.13	0.90	2.12	3.48
Imports of Goods & Services	..	..	..	..	..	..	..	48.88	63.63	77.55	87.53
Merchandise, fob	..	..	..	..	..	..	..	45.08	58.75	71.25	79.97
Nonfactor Services	..	..	..	..	..	..	..	3.66	4.62	5.48	7.47
Factor Services	..	..	..	..	..	..	..	0.14	0.26	0.83	0.09
Long-Term Interest	0.00	0.00	0.00	0.00	0.00	0.00	0.10	0.10	0.10	0.10	0.10
Private Current Transfers, net	..	..	..	..	..	..	..	23.43	23.35	25.46	39.74
Workers' Remittances	..	..	..	..	..	..	..	24.28	23.60	24.01	40.06
Curr. A/C Bal before Off. Transf.	..	..	..	..	..	..	..	-22.11	-31.62	-37.65	-25.12
Net Official Transfers	..	..	..	..	..	..	..	27.95	23.05	36.64	29.44
Curr. A/C Bal after Off. Transf.	..	..	..	..	..	..	..	5.84	-8.57	-1.02	4.32
Long-Term Capital, net	..	..	..	..	..	..	..	2.35	1.56	0.80	2.36
Direct Investment	..	..	..	..	..	..	..	..	..	..	..
Long-Term Loans	0.00	0.00	0.00	0.00	0.00	0.50	11.30	2.30	1.40	3.10	3.20
Disbursements	0.00	0.00	0.00	0.00	0.00	0.50	11.30	2.30	1.50	3.20	3.30
Repayments	0.00	0.00	0.00	0.00	0.00	0.00	0.00	0.00	0.10	0.10	0.10
Other Long-Term Capital	..	..	..	..	..	..	..	0.05	0.16	-2.30	-0.84
Other Capital, net	..	..	..	..	..	..	..	-20.06	3.76	-10.58	-12.82
Change in Reserves	..	..	..	..	..	..	..	11.87	3.25	10.80	6.14
Memo Item:					*(Cape Verde Escudos per US dollar)*						
Conversion Factor (Annual Avg)	28.750	28.310	27.050	24.520	25.410	25.540	30.230	34.050	35.500	37.430	40.170
				(Millions of US dollars), outstanding at end of year							
EXTERNAL DEBT (Total)	0.0	0.0	0.0	0.0	0.0	0.5	11.7	13.7	19.9	18.8	20.8
Long-Term Debt (by debtor)	0.0	0.0	0.0	0.0	0.0	0.5	11.7	13.7	14.9	17.8	20.8
Central Bank, incl. IMF credit	..	..	..	..	..	..	..	..	..	..	..
Central Government	0.0	0.0	0.0	0.0	0.0	0.5	11.7	13.7	14.9	17.8	20.8
Rest of General Government	..	..	..	..	..	..	..	..	..	..	..
Non-financial Public Enterprises	0.0	0.0	0.0	0.0	0.0	0.0	0.0	0.0	0.0	0.0	0.0
Priv. Sector, incl non-guaranteed	..	..	..	..	..	..	..	..	..	..	..
Short-Term Debt	0.0	0.0	0.0	0.0	0.0	0.0	0.0	0.0	5.0	1.0	0.0
Memo Items:					*(Thousands of US dollars)*						
Int'l Reserves Excluding Gold	..	..	..	..	..	..	32,695	42,024	39,368	42,322	42,401
Gold Holdings (at market price)	..	..	..	..	..	..	..	..	..	..	..
SOCIAL INDICATORS											
Total Fertility Rate	7.0	7.0	7.0	6.9	6.9	6.8	6.8	6.7	6.6	6.5	6.5
Infant Mortality Rate	86.0	84.0	82.0	79.6	77.2	74.8	72.4	70.0	66.4	62.8	59.2
Life Expectancy at Birth	56.7	57.1	57.5	58.0	58.5	59.0	59.5	60.0	60.8	61.6	62.4
Urban Population, % of total	19.6	20.0	20.3	20.7	21.0	21.4	21.8	22.2	22.6	23.0	23.4
Food Prod. per capita (1987=100)	71.5	59.5	57.4	55.0	54.3	56.1	61.9	54.5	64.1	57.9	85.2
Labor Force, Agriculture (%)	64.1	62.8	61.6	60.3	59.1	58.0	56.7	55.4	54.1	52.9	51.7
Labor Force, Female (%)	23.6	24.0	24.4	24.8	25.2	25.6	26.0	26.5	26.9	27.3	27.7
Primary Schl. Enroll. Ratio	66.0	..	..	..	..	145.0	..	..	..	..	116.0
Primary Schl. Enroll. Ratio, Female	..	..	..	..	..	138.0	..	..	..	..	111.0
Secondary Schl. Enroll. Ratio	..	..	..	..	..	8.0	..	..	..	..	8.0

1981	1982	1983	1984	1985	1986	1987	1988	1989	1990 estimate	Notes	CAPE VERDE
				(Millions of current US dollars)							**FOREIGN TRADE (CUSTOMS BASIS)**
..	..	..	..	..	..	..	..	..	..	..	Value of Exports, fob
..	..	..	..	..	..	..	..	..	..	..	Nonfuel Primary Products
..	..	..	..	..	..	..	..	..	..	..	Fuels
..	..	..	..	..	..	..	..	..	..	..	Manufactures
..	..	..	..	..	..	..	..	..	..	..	Value of Imports, cif
..	..	..	..	..	..	..	..	..	..	..	Nonfuel Primary Products
..	..	..	..	..	..	..	..	..	..	..	Fuels
..	..	..	..	..	..	..	..	..	..	..	Manufactures
				(Index 1987 = 100)							
..	..	..	..	..	..	..	..	..	..	..	Terms of Trade
..	..	..	..	..	..	..	..	..	..	..	Export Prices, fob
..	..	..	..	..	..	..	..	..	..	..	Import Prices, cif
				(Thousands of current US dollars)							**BALANCE OF PAYMENTS**
26.53	33.09	38.10	32.28	32.84	40.81	57.08	48.51	67.16	86.50	..	Exports of Goods & Services
6.26	3.97	3.30	6.93	6.12	5.06	12.18	4.95	11.19	13.00	..	Merchandise, fob
17.39	27.45	33.48	23.73	24.81	32.21	39.08	36.36	45.56	48.60	..	Nonfactor Services
2.88	1.66	1.32	1.62	1.90	3.54	5.82	7.19	10.41	24.90	..	Factor Services
105.43	115.46	124.99	99.04	101.31	109.23	118.88	122.58	136.16	150.20	..	Imports of Goods & Services
85.90	96.71	104.59	82.47	86.74	85.93	92.83	101.78	110.21	121.80	f	Merchandise, fob
17.17	12.62	12.20	10.45	8.60	15.50	18.32	13.99	19.99	25.10	..	Nonfactor Services
2.36	6.13	8.19	6.12	5.98	7.79	7.73	6.81	5.95	3.30	..	Factor Services
0.20	0.90	2.00	3.00	2.60	2.00	3.40	3.50	2.10	1.80	f	Long-Term Interest
36.13	32.02	34.71	21.60	22.21	28.68	34.03	39.60	43.31	43.40	..	Private Current Transfers, net
31.60	25.85	20.55	20.62	20.76	26.70	31.64	35.65	40.24	43.40	..	Workers' Remittances
-42.76	-50.35	-52.17	-45.16	-46.26	-39.74	-27.77	-34.48	-25.69	-20.30	f	Curr. A/C Bal before Off. Transf.
21.15	35.52	38.82	38.74	37.32	42.20	46.94	38.71	35.67	12.40	f	Net Official Transfers
-21.61	-14.84	-13.35	-6.42	-8.94	2.46	19.17	4.23	9.99	-7.90	..	Curr. A/C Bal after Off. Transf.
18.69	19.89	15.03	10.16	13.87	7.02	5.42	-1.84	5.44	5.70	f	Long-Term Capital, net
						2.78	0.41	-0.60	2.10	..	Direct Investment
20.70	22.30	16.50	14.60	19.60	9.10	4.60	6.70	6.80	6.00	..	Long-Term Loans
20.80	22.90	17.50	16.90	21.70	11.50	8.20	10.20	9.90	9.10	..	Disbursements
0.10	0.60	1.00	2.30	2.10	2.40	3.60	3.50	3.10	3.10	..	Repayments
-2.01	-2.41	-1.47	-4.44	-5.73	-2.08	-1.97	-8.95	-0.76	-2.40	..	Other Long-Term Capital
10.54	8.03	11.76	-11.82	13.37	-29.84	8.20	0.16	-37.00	4.43	f	Other Capital, net
-7.62	-13.08	-13.44	8.07	-18.30	20.35	-32.78	-2.55	21.57	-2.23	..	Change in Reserves
				(Cape Verde Escudos per US dollar)							**Memo Item:**
48.690	58.290	71.690	84.880	91.630	80.140	72.470	72.070	77.980	70.030	..	Conversion Factor (Annual Avg)
			(Millions of US dollars), outstanding at end of year								
39.4	59.0	71.7	77.0	99.6	119.2	137.8	133.8	135.3	152.0	..	**EXTERNAL DEBT (Total)**
39.4	59.0	71.7	77.0	98.6	112.3	127.2	129.0	132.1	144.3	..	Long-Term Debt (by debtor)
..	..	..	..	..	..	..	..	..	..	..	Central Bank, incl. IMF credit
22.0	29.4	34.2	45.2	64.1	75.1	94.8	100.2	105.4	117.5	..	Central Government
..	..	..	..	..	..	..	..	..	..	..	Rest of General Government
17.4	29.6	37.5	31.8	34.5	37.2	32.4	28.8	26.7	26.8	..	Non-financial Public Enterprises
..	..	..	..	..	..	..	..	..	..	..	Priv. Sector, incl non-guaranteed
0.0	0.0	0.0	0.0	1.0	6.9	10.6	4.8	3.2	7.7	..	Short-Term Debt
				(Thousands of US dollars)							**Memo Items:**
37,829	42,739	45,902	40,990	55,358	56,360	80,730	81,333	74,738	76,969	..	Int'l Reserves Excluding Gold
..	..	..	..	..	..	..	..	..	..	..	Gold Holdings (at market price)
											SOCIAL INDICATORS
6.4	6.3	6.2	6.0	5.9	5.7	5.6	5.5	5.5	5.4	..	Total Fertility Rate
55.6	52.0	50.4	48.8	47.2	45.6	44.0	42.9	41.8	40.8	..	Infant Mortality Rate
63.2	64.0	64.4	64.8	65.1	65.5	65.9	66.1	66.2	66.3	..	Life Expectancy at Birth
23.9	24.4	24.9	25.4	25.9	26.6	27.3	27.8	28.2	28.7	..	Urban Population, % of total
59.1	57.4	49.6	58.3	54.9	71.3	100.0	88.7	79.4	76.7	..	Food Prod. per capita (1987=100)
..	..	..	..	..	..	..	..	..	..	..	Labor Force, Agriculture (%)
28.0	28.2	28.4	28.6	28.8	28.9	29.0	29.0	29.1	29.1	..	Labor Force, Female (%)
..	106.0	110.0	109.0	113.0	..	114.0	115.0	116.0	..	..	Primary Schl. Enroll. Ratio
..	102.0	107.0	107.0	111.0	..	110.0	111.0	..	..	..	Primary Schl. Enroll. Ratio, Female
..	..	10.0	11.0	13.0	..	16.0	18.0	20.0	..	..	Secondary Schl. Enroll. Ratio

CENTRAL AFRICAN REPUBLIC	1970	1971	1972	1973	1974	1975	1976	1977	1978	1979	1980
CURRENT GNP PER CAPITA (US $)	110	100	110	120	150	170	200	230	260	280	320
POPULATION (thousands)	1,879	1,902	1,928	1,958	1,993	2,034	2,085	2,140	2,198	2,258	2,320
USE AND ORIGIN OF RESOURCES					*(Billions of current CFA Francs)*						
Gross National Product (GNP)	49.60	52.60	55.50	57.00	71.90	80.50	107.10	123.60	136.40	151.10	168.90
Net Factor Income from Abroad	-0.10	-0.10	-0.10	-0.10	-0.10	-0.10	0.10	0.10	0.10	0.20	0.50
GDP at Market Prices	49.70	52.70	55.60	57.10	72.00	80.60	107.00	123.50	136.30	150.90	168.40
Resource Balance	-7.60	-7.00	-7.60	-8.10	-6.30	-15.80	-8.50	-12.50	-15.90	-17.10	-28.00
Exports of Goods & NF Services	13.90	13.90	12.10	14.40	19.00	18.40	25.40	32.70	33.70	35.20	44.00
Imports of Goods & NF Services	21.50	20.90	19.70	22.50	25.30	34.20	33.90	45.20	49.60	52.30	72.00
Domestic Absorption	57.30	59.70	63.20	65.20	78.30	96.40	115.50	136.00	152.20	168.00	196.40
Private Consumption, etc.	37.40	38.80	41.50	40.80	54.30	71.30	88.00	106.20	117.80	130.10	159.10
General Gov't Consumption	10.50	10.50	11.00	11.80	13.50	13.90	14.60	15.40	19.40	23.30	25.50
Gross Domestic Investment	9.40	10.40	10.70	12.60	10.50	11.20	12.90	14.40	15.00	14.60	11.80
Fixed Investment	..	..	..	..	..	..	..	14.50	12.50	16.70	11.70
Indirect Taxes, net	2.90	3.30	3.90	4.50	4.90	5.10	5.80	7.20	7.20	8.10	9.90
GDP at factor cost	46.80	49.40	51.70	52.60	67.10	75.50	101.20	116.30	129.10	142.80	158.50
Agriculture	16.60	18.40	19.90	20.60	26.50	28.50	40.60	46.80	51.30	55.80	63.40
Industry	12.20	13.30	14.10	14.10	15.10	17.30	20.50	22.90	28.80	32.20	31.80
Manufacturing	3.20	3.30	3.80	4.10	5.20	5.70	6.20	7.60	10.80	11.80	11.40
Services, etc.	18.00	17.70	17.70	17.90	25.50	29.70	40.10	46.60	49.00	54.80	63.30
Gross Domestic Saving	1.80	3.40	3.10	4.50	4.20	-4.60	4.40	1.90	-0.90	-2.50	-16.20
Gross National Saving	0.62	1.85	1.88	3.23	2.25	-7.33	2.02	-0.48	-3.80	-4.06	-19.22
					(Billions of 1987 CFA Francs)						
Gross National Product	250.78	252.08	258.61	264.42	280.04	280.81	295.03	305.59	312.87	305.12	291.46
GDP at Market Prices	249.02	251.30	257.28	263.04	278.54	279.30	292.56	303.05	310.56	302.30	288.45
Resource Balance	-50.36	-45.82	-44.52	-39.33	-2.78	-3.41	-11.89	-37.45	-42.64	-34.90	-48.50
Exports of Goods & NF Services	47.06	48.31	43.29	50.82	72.16	87.21	71.95	68.39	66.72	68.60	82.40
Imports of Goods & NF Services	97.42	94.14	87.81	90.16	74.94	90.62	83.83	105.85	109.36	103.50	130.90
Domestic Absorption	299.38	297.13	301.80	302.37	281.32	282.71	304.45	340.50	353.20	337.20	336.95
Private Consumption, etc.	171.19	171.06	177.17	172.28	184.56	195.58	217.28	256.00	260.18	244.50	255.50
General Gov't Consumption	79.67	75.72	74.28	77.51	63.88	59.93	58.13	55.26	64.59	68.54	64.59
Gross Domestic Investment	48.52	50.35	50.35	52.58	32.89	27.21	29.03	29.24	28.42	24.16	16.85
Fixed Investment	..	..	..	..	..	..	..	29.29	23.63	27.47	16.56
GDP at factor cost	231.04	232.09	236.07	239.12	257.09	259.48	269.34	283.52	286.91	279.85	274.90
Agriculture	92.95	95.97	96.43	97.13	101.08	103.40	106.89	108.75	112.23	110.61	108.98
Industry	27.37	27.06	30.85	31.96	34.97	34.81	32.91	36.23	41.45	39.08	39.56
Manufacturing	..	..	..	..	..	..	..	..	..	..	..
Services, etc.	119.58	118.35	111.91	111.91	123.26	123.57	133.99	142.88	134.30	131.84	127.24
Memo Items:											
Capacity to Import	62.98	62.61	53.94	57.70	56.28	48.76	62.81	76.57	74.30	69.66	80.00
Terms of Trade Adjustment	15.92	14.29	10.64	6.88	-15.88	-38.46	-9.13	8.18	7.58	1.06	-2.41
Gross Domestic Income	264.94	265.60	267.92	269.92	262.66	240.84	283.43	311.23	318.14	303.36	286.04
Gross National Income	266.70	266.37	269.25	271.30	264.16	242.35	285.89	313.77	320.45	306.18	289.05
DOMESTIC PRICES/DEFLATORS					*(Index 1987 = 100)*						
Overall (GDP)	20.0	21.0	21.6	21.7	25.8	28.9	36.6	40.8	43.9	49.9	58.4
Domestic Absorption	19.1	20.1	20.9	21.6	27.8	34.1	37.9	39.9	43.1	49.8	58.3
Agriculture	17.9	19.2	20.6	21.2	26.2	27.6	38.0	43.0	45.7	50.4	58.2
Industry	44.6	49.2	45.7	44.1	43.2	49.7	62.3	63.2	69.5	82.4	80.4
Manufacturing	..	..	..	..	..	..	..	..	..	..	..
Consumer Price Index	..	..	..	..	..	..	..	..	..	..	..
MANUFACTURING ACTIVITY											
Employment (1987=100)	..	..	..	..	..	..	..	..	..	..	..
Real Earnings per Empl. (1987=100)	..	..	..	..	..	..	..	..	..	..	..
Real Output per Empl. (1987=100)	..	..	..	..	..	..	..	..	..	..	..
Earnings as % of Value Added	..	..	..	30.1	27.3	31.4	31.6	30.8	49.6	..	47.9
MONETARY HOLDINGS					*(Millions of current CFA Francs)*						
Money Supply, Broadly Defined	8,381	8,365	9,768	10,427	13,629	13,682	19,346	20,487	22,508	27,104	36,617
Money	7,547	7,547	8,917	9,213	12,477	12,274	17,075	18,200	20,517	26,131	34,612
Currency Outside Banks	4,958	4,901	5,528	5,752	7,380	7,482	8,957	11,160	13,358	17,938	24,367
Demand Deposits	2,589	2,646	3,389	3,461	5,097	4,792	8,118	7,040	7,159	8,193	10,245
Quasi-Money	834	818	851	1,214	1,152	1,408	2,271	2,287	1,991	973	2,005
					(Millions of current CFA Francs)						
GOVERNMENT DEFICIT (-) OR SURPLUS											
Current Revenue	..	..	..	..	..	..	..	..	..	..	..
Current Expenditure	..	..	..	..	..	..	..	..	..	..	..
Current Budget Balance	..	..	..	..	..	..	..	..	..	..	..
Capital Receipts	..	..	..	..	..	..	..	..	..	..	..
Capital Payments	..	..	..	..	..	..	..	..	..	..	..

1981	1982	1983	1984	1985	1986	1987	1988	1989	1990 estimate	Notes	CENTRAL AFRICAN REPUBLIC
330	340	280	280	270	290	310	370	380	390	..	**CURRENT GNP PER CAPITA (US $)**
2,383	2,445	2,509	2,576	2,646	2,719	2,795	2,873	2,953	3,035	..	**POPULATION (thousands)**
				(Billions of current CFA Francs)							**USE AND ORIGIN OF RESOURCES**
190.10	244.60	247.50	274.50	311.20	338.60	308.50	321.40	336.80	347.30	..	Gross National Product (GNP)
1.30	-1.30	-3.50	-4.20	-5.00	-4.30	-5.80	-6.60	-6.80	-7.00	..	Net Factor Income from Abroad
188.80	245.90	251.00	278.70	316.20	342.90	314.30	328.00	343.60	354.30	..	GDP at Market Prices
-20.00	-33.20	-32.80	-35.00	-46.50	-47.60	-46.70	-39.70	-37.60	-45.60	..	Resource Balance
48.50	54.60	60.50	65.40	79.80	64.30	59.10	58.30	68.10	61.10	..	Exports of Goods & NFServices
68.50	87.80	93.30	100.40	126.30	111.90	105.80	98.00	105.70	106.70	..	Imports of Goods & NFServices
208.80	279.10	283.80	313.70	362.70	390.50	361.00	367.70	381.20	399.90	..	Domestic Absorption
164.00	223.60	211.70	239.70	273.40	297.30	275.70	286.30	297.30	312.20	f	Private Consumption, etc.
28.30	39.10	42.40	39.70	43.60	51.30	42.30	43.60	45.50	48.30	..	General Gov't Consumption
16.50	16.40	29.70	34.30	45.70	41.90	43.00	37.80	38.40	39.40	f	Gross Domestic Investment
15.20	15.70	26.30	33.80	49.10	41.70	42.80	37.50	38.00	39.20	..	Fixed Investment
11.10	14.10	13.70	18.70	22.40	25.80	21.38	21.69	22.04	22.67	..	Indirect Taxes, net
177.70	231.80	237.30	260.00	293.80	317.10	292.92	306.31	321.56	331.63	..	GDP at factor cost
70.50	96.60	95.80	109.27	117.30	132.10	124.68	132.75	137.09	140.31	..	Agriculture
33.60	30.35	34.83	39.00	40.30	38.90	41.96	43.65	51.14	54.76	..	Industry
13.20	17.90	20.60	21.70	21.52	20.51	..	..	..	..	..	Manufacturing
73.60	104.85	106.67	111.73	136.20	146.10	126.28	129.90	133.32	136.56	..	Services, etc.
-3.50	-16.80	-3.10	-0.70	-0.80	-5.70	-3.70	-1.90	0.80	-6.20	..	Gross Domestic Saving
-5.97	-23.68	-12.25	-9.79	-11.11	-16.74	-16.63	-16.72	-13.94	-20.96	..	Gross National Saving
				(Billions of 1987 CFA Francs)							
286.37	303.58	280.67	307.00	318.21	320.44	308.50	318.41	326.79	329.27	..	Gross National Product
281.98	303.05	282.87	309.20	321.14	325.32	314.30	324.95	333.38	335.91	..	GDP at Market Prices
-26.63	-37.45	-32.74	-36.53	-38.03	-51.47	-46.70	-39.33	-36.48	-43.23	..	Resource Balance
85.54	68.39	70.06	70.48	73.20	64.21	59.10	57.76	66.08	57.93	..	Exports of Goods & NFServices
112.17	105.85	102.80	107.02	111.23	115.68	105.80	97.09	102.56	101.16	..	Imports of Goods & NFServices
308.60	340.50	315.61	345.74	359.17	376.79	361.00	364.28	369.87	379.14	..	Domestic Absorption
225.66	256.00	225.35	248.86	258.32	281.77	275.70	283.65	288.43	295.99	f	Private Consumption, etc.
62.44	55.26	47.01	49.16	51.32	50.96	42.30	43.18	44.18	45.80	..	General Gov't Consumption
20.51	29.24	43.25	47.71	49.54	44.06	43.00	37.45	37.26	37.35	f	Gross Domestic Investment
18.38	27.88	38.18	47.01	52.13	43.68	42.80	37.15	36.87	37.16	..	Fixed Investment
271.26	283.52	264.39	289.36	300.49	300.31	292.92	303.46	312.00	314.42	..	GDP at factor cost
107.12	108.75	104.33	114.09	118.28	127.68	124.68	131.52	133.01	133.03	..	Agriculture
36.39	36.23	39.56	40.66	42.09	40.38	41.96	43.25	49.62	51.92	..	Industry
..	..	..	..	..	..	..	..	..	..	..	Manufacturing
130.31	142.88	120.50	134.60	140.12	132.25	126.28	128.69	129.36	129.47	..	Services, etc.
											Memo Items:
79.42	65.82	66.66	69.71	70.28	66.47	59.10	57.76	66.08	57.93	..	Capacity to Import
-6.12	-2.57	-3.40	-0.77	-2.92	2.26	0.00	0.00	0.00	0.00	..	Terms of Trade Adjustment
275.85	300.48	279.47	308.43	318.22	327.58	314.30	324.95	333.38	335.91	..	Gross Domestic Income
280.24	301.01	277.27	306.23	315.29	322.70	308.50	318.41	326.79	329.27	..	Gross National Income
				(Index 1987 = 100)							**DOMESTIC PRICES/DEFLATORS**
67.0	81.1	88.7	90.1	98.5	105.4	100.0	100.9	103.1	105.5	..	Overall (GDP)
67.7	82.0	89.9	90.7	101.0	103.6	100.0	100.9	103.1	105.5	..	Domestic Absorption
65.8	88.8	91.8	95.8	99.2	103.5	100.0	100.9	103.1	105.5	..	Agriculture
92.3	83.8	88.1	95.9	95.8	96.3	100.0	100.9	103.1	105.5	..	Industry
..	..	..	..	..	..	..	..	..	..	..	Manufacturing
71.5	81.0	92.9	95.2	105.2	107.5	100.0	96.0	96.7	96.7	..	Consumer Price Index
											MANUFACTURING ACTIVITY
..	..	..	..	..	..	..	..	..	..	..	Employment (1987=100)
..	..	..	..	..	..	..	..	..	..	..	Real Earnings per Empl. (1987=100)
..	..	..	..	..	..	..	..	..	..	..	Real Output per Empl. (1987=100)
45.4	62.6	56.2	..	48.8	85.3	..	..	..	..	J	Earnings as % of Value Added
				(Millions of current CFA Francs)							**MONETARY HOLDINGS**
45,329	43,286	47,928	52,114	56,545	58,356	60,025	57,057	64,409	62,027	..	Money Supply, Broadly Defined
42,322	40,557	44,779	48,244	51,536	52,186	53,548	49,739	56,657	54,556	..	Money
31,956	31,218	34,313	37,236	37,147	40,606	41,462	38,709	42,236	41,840	..	Currency Outside Banks
10,366	9,339	10,466	11,008	14,389	11,580	12,086	11,030	14,421	12,716	..	Demand Deposits
3,007	2,729	3,149	3,870	5,009	6,170	6,477	7,318	7,752	7,471	..	Quasi-Money
				(Millions of current CFA Francs)							**GOVERNMENT DEFICIT (-) OR SURPLUS**
-6,671	..	..	..	..	..	..	..	..	..	..	
35,036	..	..	42,129	44,944	43,228	73,162	73,534	..	..	..	Current Revenue
34,977	..	..	39,661	43,198	46,130	50,935	49,710	..	..	..	Current Expenditure
59	..	..	2,468	1,746	-2,902	22,227	23,824	..	..	..	Current Budget Balance
15	..	..	..	..	..	..	..	..	..	..	Capital Receipts
7,179	..	..	27,767	44,065	42,367	36,180	34,140	..	..	..	Capital Payments

CENTRAL AFRICAN REPUBLIC	1970	1971	1972	1973	1974	1975	1976	1977	1978	1979	1980
FOREIGN TRADE (CUSTOMS BASIS)					*(Millions of current US dollars)*						
Value of Exports, fob	..	..	..	..	..	..	..	..	..	..	..
Nonfuel Primary Products	..	..	..	..	..	..	..	..	..	..	..
Fuels	..	..	..	..	..	..	..	..	..	..	..
Manufactures	..	..	..	..	..	..	..	..	..	..	..
Value of Imports, cif	..	..	..	..	..	..	..	..	..	..	..
Nonfuel Primary Products	..	..	..	..	..	..	..	..	..	..	..
Fuels	..	..	..	..	..	..	..	..	..	..	..
Manufactures	..	..	..	..	..	..	..	..	..	..	..
					(Index 1987 = 100)						
Terms of Trade	..	..	..	..	..	..	..	..	..	..	..
Export Prices, fob	..	..	..	..	..	..	..	..	..	..	..
Import Prices, cif	..	..	..	..	..	..	..	..	..	..	..
BALANCE OF PAYMENTS					*(Millions of current US dollars)*						
Exports of Goods & Services	60.80	60.38	57.98	78.08	78.89	80.98	101.60	130.62	146.67	159.83	205.38
Merchandise, fob	43.40	43.93	40.50	54.96	57.37	54.03	69.50	104.50	110.29	122.24	147.20
Nonfactor Services	17.00	16.05	16.83	22.65	20.69	25.98	30.59	23.36	32.69	35.00	53.83
Factor Services	0.40	0.40	0.65	0.48	0.84	0.97	1.50	2.76	3.69	2.59	4.35
Imports of Goods & Services	80.80	78.23	80.45	102.52	125.19	154.08	134.50	177.49	209.48	254.24	329.22
Merchandise, fob	39.60	44.83	46.25	50.67	62.90	82.93	75.85	103.89	119.03	132.90	185.11
Nonfactor Services	39.00	30.49	31.49	48.28	59.05	68.24	56.46	70.24	87.92	113.34	142.33
Factor Services	2.20	2.91	2.71	3.58	3.25	2.91	2.19	3.36	2.53	8.01	1.79
Long-Term Interest	0.70	0.60	0.60	1.20	1.20	2.10	0.90	1.20	1.40	0.40	0.40
Private Current Transfers, net	-3.90	-5.22	-4.45	-5.25	-7.70	-12.26	-10.39	-10.11	-13.29	-8.28	-16.67
Workers' Remittances	..	..	..	..	..	..	..	..	..	..	..
Curr. A/C Bal before Off. Transf.	-23.90	-23.07	-26.93	-29.68	-54.00	-85.35	-43.29	-56.98	-76.10	-102.69	-140.51
Net Official Transfers	12.40	14.14	28.01	26.70	39.45	48.08	48.78	38.09	51.78	86.86	97.46
Curr. A/C Bal after Off. Transf.	-11.50	-8.93	1.09	-2.98	-14.55	-37.27	5.48	-18.89	-24.32	-15.82	-43.05
Long-Term Capital, net	-0.10	6.82	-3.04	-0.36	18.04	20.03	16.63	9.79	11.19	37.98	46.57
Direct Investment	0.90	0.30	1.19	-0.48	5.65	4.25	3.46	-2.93	4.75	22.43	5.34
Long-Term Loans	-0.60	2.50	14.90	15.80	6.10	9.80	9.30	21.20	19.10	12.80	24.20
Disbursements	1.80	4.10	16.00	19.30	9.60	13.40	11.20	24.30	21.70	13.10	25.20
Repayments	2.40	1.60	1.10	3.50	3.50	3.60	1.90	3.10	2.60	0.30	1.00
Other Long-Term Capital	-0.40	4.02	-19.13	-15.68	6.29	5.98	3.86	-8.48	-12.66	2.75	17.03
Other Capital, net	10.18	-0.93	2.05	3.29	-5.90	16.79	-10.76	14.10	7.61	-3.81	6.96
Change in Reserves	1.41	3.03	-0.10	0.05	2.41	0.45	-11.35	-4.99	5.52	-18.35	-10.47
Memo Item:					*(CFA Francs per US dollar)*						
Conversion Factor (Annual Avg)	277.710	277.130	252.480	222.890	240.700	214.310	238.950	245.680	225.650	212.720	211.280
				(Millions of US dollars), outstanding at end of year							
EXTERNAL DEBT (Total)	24.10	28.10	36.30	55.20	67.10	77.00	90.30	125.80	135.20	149.80	194.60
Long-Term Debt (by debtor)	24.10	28.10	36.30	55.20	67.10	77.00	90.30	115.80	126.20	133.80	170.00
Central Bank, incl. IMF credit	0.00	0.00	0.00	0.00	3.30	5.70	11.10	11.60	20.40	17.90	23.50
Central Government	12.60	15.10	18.10	26.00	29.30	37.30	35.70	44.00	62.90	72.70	98.10
Rest of General Government	0.10	0.10	0.00	0.00	0.00	0.00	0.00	0.00	0.00	0.00	0.00
Non-financial Public Enterprises	8.90	10.40	15.60	26.70	32.20	32.20	41.70	58.40	41.30	41.60	47.00
Priv. Sector, incl non-guaranteed	2.50	2.50	2.60	2.50	2.30	1.80	1.80	1.80	1.60	1.60	1.40
Short-Term Debt	0.00	0.00	0.00	0.00	0.00	0.00	0.00	10.00	9.00	16.00	24.60
Memo Items:					*(Millions of US dollars)*						
Int'l Reserves Excluding Gold	1.4	0.2	1.7	1.8	1.7	3.8	18.8	25.4	24.1	44.1	55.0
Gold Holdings (at market price)	..	..	..	..	..	..	..	0.9	1.9	5.8	6.7
SOCIAL INDICATORS											
Total Fertility Rate	4.9	4.9	5.0	5.1	5.2	5.3	5.4	5.5	5.5	5.5	5.5
Infant Mortality Rate	139.2	135.6	132.0	130.0	128.0	126.0	124.0	122.0	120.4	118.8	117.2
Life Expectancy at Birth	42.4	42.9	43.4	43.8	44.3	44.7	45.1	45.5	45.9	46.4	46.8
Urban Population, % of total	30.4	31.2	31.9	32.7	33.4	34.2	35.0	35.8	36.7	37.5	38.3
Food Prod. per capita (1987=100)	104.9	107.6	108.9	111.5	118.7	121.1	113.6	114.1	108.5	110.5	112.4
Labor Force, Agriculture (%)	82.9	81.8	80.8	79.7	78.7	77.7	76.6	75.5	74.4	73.4	72.4
Labor Force, Female (%)	49.1	49.0	48.9	48.8	48.7	48.6	48.5	48.4	48.2	48.1	48.0
Primary Schl. Enroll. Ratio	64.0	..	..	..	..	73.0	..	70.0	69.0	70.0	71.0
Primary Schl. Enroll. Ratio, Female	41.0	..	..	..	..	51.0	..	47.0	48.0	49.0	51.0
Secondary Schl. Enroll. Ratio	4.0	..	..	..	..	8.0	9.0	10.0	10.0	11.0	14.0

1981	1982	1983	1984	1985	1986	1987	1988	1989	1990 estimate	Notes	CENTRAL AFRICAN REPUBLIC
				(Millions of current US dollars)							**FOREIGN TRADE (CUSTOMS BASIS)**
..	..	..	..	..	..	..	..	..	..	..	Value of Exports, fob
..	..	..	..	..	..	..	..	..	..	..	Nonfuel Primary Products
..	..	..	..	..	..	..	..	..	..	..	Fuels
..	..	..	..	..	..	..	..	..	..	..	Manufactures
..	..	..	..	..	..	..	..	..	..	..	Value of Imports, cif
..	..	..	..	..	..	..	..	..	..	..	Nonfuel Primary Products
..	..	..	..	..	..	..	..	..	..	..	Fuels
..	..	..	..	..	..	..	..	..	..	..	Manufactures
				(Index 1987 = 100)							
..	..	..	..	..	..	..	..	..	..	..	Terms of Trade
..	..	..	..	..	..	..	..	..	..	..	Export Prices, fob
..	..	..	..	..	..	..	..	..	..	..	Import Prices, cif
				(Millions of current US dollars)							**BALANCE OF PAYMENTS**
177.39	170.93	162.17	151.94	184.49	188.33	197.70	198.60	214.20	224.90	f	Exports of Goods & Services
117.69	124.41	123.40	114.43	131.05	129.49	127.09	133.60	148.00	151.00		Merchandise, fob
51.72	41.55	35.67	34.78	46.79	56.00	67.84	62.00	65.60	73.50	..	Nonfactor Services
7.97	4.97	3.10	2.73	6.66	2.84	2.77	3.00	0.60	0.40	..	Factor Services
241.32	268.34	254.98	238.83	289.82	357.81	374.02	354.50	394.00	456.00	f	Imports of Goods & Services
144.56	149.71	137.52	140.06	167.75	201.00	197.67	178.30	185.90	211.60	f	Merchandise, fob
92.09	106.40	103.67	86.38	108.05	141.65	154.42	150.90	186.20	218.20	..	Nonfactor Services
4.67	12.24	13.79	12.39	14.03	15.16	21.93	25.30	21.90	26.20	..	Factor Services
0.90	2.30	6.60	5.60	6.60	9.20	8.40	7.30	7.10	8.70	..	Long-Term Interest
-13.89	-16.98	-14.83	-11.20	-11.81	-19.46	-23.71	-27.60	-24.90	-28.50	..	Private Current Transfers, net
..	..	..	..	..	..	..	..	..	..	..	Workers' Remittances
-77.82	-114.39	-107.64	-98.09	-117.15	-188.94	-200.03	-183.50	-204.70	-259.60	..	Curr. A/C Bal before Off. Transf.
73.64	71.75	78.33	64.64	68.53	102.42	124.80	168.60	129.70	162.90	..	Net Official Transfers
-4.18	-42.64	-29.31	-33.45	-48.62	-86.52	-75.23	-14.90	-75.00	-96.70	..	Curr. A/C Bal after Off. Transf.
15.00	2.19	35.77	49.79	55.38	94.01	85.08	26.80	32.70	64.40	f	Long-Term Capital, net
5.78	8.81	4.03	4.90	2.39	6.90	9.33	-13.10	-11.90	..	..	Direct Investment
27.80	15.60	18.50	27.60	42.50	71.70	84.40	77.80	60.40	115.50	..	Long-Term Loans
30.50	18.00	29.50	36.10	47.50	78.00	93.70	82.00	66.20	121.00	..	Disbursements
2.70	2.40	11.00	8.50	5.00	6.30	9.30	4.20	5.80	5.50	..	Repayments
-18.58	-22.22	13.24	17.29	10.50	15.41	-8.65	-37.90	-15.80	-51.10	..	Other Long-Term Capital
-6.89	24.88	-8.43	-9.02	-26.92	-3.72	-2.03	-3.83	59.16	37.02	..	Other Capital, net
-3.93	15.57	1.97	-7.32	20.15	-3.76	-7.82	-8.07	-16.86	-4.72	..	Change in Reserves
				(CFA Francs per US dollar)							**Memo Item:**
271.730	328.600	381.060	436.960	449.260	346.300	300.530	297.850	319.010	272.260	..	Conversion Factor (Annual Avg)
			(Millions of US dollars), outstanding at end of year								
233.40	252.20	258.30	264.90	348.00	467.90	626.10	670.90	715.60	901.20	..	**EXTERNAL DEBT (Total)**
213.90	232.80	243.40	251.30	329.80	439.40	596.60	633.40	677.60	852.80	..	Long-Term Debt (by debtor)
37.70	37.70	40.00	35.10	39.00	41.80	51.90	50.30	35.30	37.60	..	Central Bank, incl. IMF credit
146.90	147.80	159.70	184.20	245.70	334.30	458.70	503.70	557.50	708.10	..	Central Government
0.00	0.00	0.00	0.00	0.00	0.00	0.00	0.00	0.00	..	..	Rest of General Government
29.30	47.30	43.70	30.80	43.30	61.40	84.00	77.50	83.00	105.10	..	Non-financial Public Enterprises
0.00	0.00	0.00	1.20	1.80	1.90	2.00	1.90	1.80	2.00	..	Priv. Sector, incl non-guaranteed
19.50	19.40	14.90	13.60	18.20	28.50	29.50	37.50	38.00	48.40	..	Short-Term Debt
				(Millions of US dollars)							**Memo Items:**
69.3	46.4	46.8	52.7	49.6	65.4	96.7	108.5	113.1	118.6	..	Int'l Reserves Excluding Gold
4.5	5.2	4.4	3.4	3.6	4.3	5.4	4.6	4.5	4.3	..	Gold Holdings (at market price)
											SOCIAL INDICATORS
5.5	5.5	5.6	5.6	5.7	5.7	5.8	5.8	5.8	5.8	..	Total Fertility Rate
115.6	114.0	112.0	110.0	107.9	105.9	103.9	103.0	102.1	101.1	..	Infant Mortality Rate
47.3	47.7	48.1	48.6	49.0	49.4	49.9	49.7	49.5	49.3	..	Life Expectancy at Birth
39.1	40.0	40.8	41.7	42.5	43.6	44.6	45.3	46.0	46.7	..	Urban Population, % of total
113.4	113.2	110.5	100.4	95.9	106.4	100.0	102.7	101.9	100.0	..	Food Prod. per capita (1987=100)
..	..	..	..	..	..	..	..	..	..	..	Labor Force, Agriculture (%)
47.8	47.6	47.4	47.1	46.9	46.7	46.4	46.2	46.0	45.7	..	Labor Force, Female (%)
..	74.0	77.0	79.0	74.0	63.0	63.0	64.0	..	..	..	Primary Schl. Enroll. Ratio
52.0	51.0	55.0	57.0	57.0	48.0	48.0	48.0	..	..	..	Primary Schl. Enroll. Ratio, Female
..	..	16.0	16.0	16.0	13.0	12.0	11.0	..	..	..	Secondary Schl. Enroll. Ratio

CHAD	1970	1971	1972	1973	1974	1975	1976	1977	1978	1979	1980
CURRENT GNP PER CAPITA (US $)	100	90	100	100	120	150	150	160	170	150	160
POPULATION (thousands)	3,652	3,723	3,796	3,871	3,949	4,030	4,113	4,199	4,288	4,381	4,477

USE AND ORIGIN OF RESOURCES					*(Billions of current CFA Francs)*						
Gross National Product (GNP)	91.30	97.28	104.86	101.84	110.86	129.73	145.07	160.36	175.04	148.56	152.76
Net Factor Income from Abroad	0.00	0.00	1.00	0.30	0.30	-0.70	-0.60	-1.40	-1.90	-1.82	-0.87
GDP at Market Prices	91.30	97.28	103.86	101.54	110.56	130.43	145.67	161.76	176.94	150.39	153.63
Resource Balance	-7.50	-7.10	-7.10	-11.20	-13.20	-21.20	-21.30	-29.90	-29.00	-36.00	-26.00
Exports of Goods & NFServices	21.10	22.00	21.50	22.70	28.90	26.70	33.30	35.30	41.30	38.00	37.00
Imports of Goods & NFServices	28.60	29.10	28.60	33.90	42.10	47.90	54.60	65.20	70.30	74.00	63.00
Domestic Absorption	98.80	104.38	110.96	112.74	123.76	151.63	166.97	191.66	205.94	186.38	179.63
Private Consumption, etc.	58.05	60.42	64.98	85.32	70.39	88.62	104.62	119.23	128.83	..	..
General Gov't Consumption	24.27	26.61	28.79	31.30	30.46	32.97	34.48	38.83	44.89	..	..
Gross Domestic Investment	16.48	17.34	17.19	-3.87	22.92	30.04	27.87	33.60	32.22	..	..
Fixed Investment	..	..	..	..	..	..	..	..	..	..	..
Indirect Taxes, net	7.40	7.60	6.20	5.80	7.10	6.70	7.30	1.28	1.46	0.95	0.49
GDP at factor cost	83.90	89.68	97.66	95.74	103.46	123.73	138.37	160.48	175.48	149.43	153.14
Agriculture	39.52	42.23	45.82	43.21	47.34	56.24	60.80	66.99	74.50	72.40	81.96
Industry	15.17	16.20	17.73	19.82	21.87	25.77	26.71	29.24	30.81	20.89	18.15
Manufacturing	14.17	15.20	16.49	18.29	20.10	23.70	24.22	26.28	27.41	..	..
Services, etc.	36.61	38.84	40.31	38.51	41.36	48.42	58.16	65.53	71.63	57.10	53.51
Gross Domestic Saving	8.98	10.24	10.09	-15.07	9.72	8.84	6.57	3.70	3.22	-36.00	-26.00
Gross National Saving	7.26	8.32	8.92	-16.82	7.85	6.40	4.98	-1.15	-1.25	-39.80	-27.74

					(Billions of 1987 CFA Francs)						
Gross National Product	214.95	210.20	212.42	195.22	204.84	221.40	228.30	232.36	230.79	181.18	171.33
GDP at Market Prices	214.25	209.51	211.72	194.58	204.23	222.63	229.27	234.39	233.29	183.27	172.30
Resource Balance	-31.83	-30.02	-35.11	-47.66	-50.02	-44.55	-39.26	-43.32	-37.99	-30.58	-29.21
Exports of Goods & NFServices	50.08	53.28	45.82	47.15	34.63	39.43	51.15	51.15	49.17	46.22	41.68
Imports of Goods & NFServices	81.91	83.30	80.93	94.81	84.65	83.98	90.41	94.47	87.17	76.80	70.89
Domestic Absorption	246.08	239.53	246.83	242.23	254.25	267.18	268.53	277.71	271.28	213.85	201.51
Private Consumption, etc.	..	..	..	..	..	..	..	..	..	..	..
General Gov't Consumption	..	..	..	..	..	..	..	..	..	..	..
Gross Domestic Investment	..	..	..	..	..	..	..	..	..	..	..
Fixed Investment	..	..	..	..	..	..	..	..	..	..	..
GDP at factor cost	..	..	..	..	..	..	..	232.54	231.36	182.11	171.75
Agriculture	98.68	96.26	99.49	86.31	89.00	96.80	95.73	96.94	98.23	88.23	91.92
Industry	32.96	33.47	33.95	34.19	35.95	38.72	42.02	42.37	40.62	25.46	20.36
Manufacturing	..	..	..	..	..	..	..	..	..	..	..
Services, etc.	82.60	79.77	78.29	74.07	79.27	87.11	91.52	95.08	94.45	69.58	60.02

Memo Items:											
Capacity to Import	60.43	62.98	60.84	63.49	58.11	46.81	55.14	51.15	51.21	39.44	41.64
Terms of Trade Adjustment	10.35	9.70	15.02	16.33	23.48	7.38	3.99	0.00	2.03	-6.78	-0.05
Gross Domestic Income	224.59	219.20	226.74	210.91	227.71	230.01	233.26	234.39	235.32	176.49	172.25
Gross National Income	225.30	219.90	227.44	211.55	228.32	228.78	232.29	232.36	232.82	174.40	171.28

DOMESTIC PRICES/DEFLATORS					*(Index 1987 = 100)*						
Overall (GDP)	42.6	46.4	49.1	52.2	54.1	58.6	63.5	69.0	75.8	82.1	89.2
Domestic Absorption	40.2	43.6	45.0	46.5	48.7	56.8	62.2	69.0	75.9	87.2	89.1
Agriculture	40.0	43.9	46.1	50.1	53.2	58.1	63.5	69.1	75.8	82.1	89.2
Industry	46.0	48.4	52.2	58.0	60.8	66.6	63.6	69.0	75.8	82.1	89.2
Manufacturing	..	..	..	..	..	..	..	..	..	..	..
Consumer Price Index	..	..	..	..	..	..	..	..	..	..	..

MANUFACTURING ACTIVITY											
Employment (1987=100)	..	..	..	..	..	..	..	..	..	..	..
Real Earnings per Empl. (1987=100)	..	..	..	..	..	..	..	..	..	..	..
Real Output per Empl. (1987=100)	..	..	..	..	..	..	..	..	..	..	..
Earnings as % of Value Added	..	..	..	..	..	13.5	..	..	..	..	..

MONETARY HOLDINGS					*(Millions of current CFA Francs)*						
Money Supply, Broadly Defined	9,195	9,782	10,125	10,660	15,122	16,687	20,830	23,709	29,419	33,236	28,142
Money	8,603	9,269	9,635	9,796	14,133	15,513	19,494	22,508	27,565	31,572	26,478
Currency Outside Banks	5,311	6,196	6,903	6,487	8,527	10,883	12,999	14,365	16,492	22,539	17,445
Demand Deposits	3,292	3,073	2,732	3,309	5,606	4,630	6,495	8,143	11,073	9,033	9,033
Quasi-Money	592	513	490	864	989	1,174	1,336	1,201	1,854	1,664	1,664

GOVERNMENT DEFICIT (-) OR SURPLUS					*(Millions of current CFA Francs)*						
	..	..	-2,783	-3,910	-2,543	-2,130	-2,848	..	..	..	..
Current Revenue	..	..	12,852	13,450	16,707	18,191	20,292	..	..	..	..
Current Expenditure	..	..	12,554	14,164	15,571	15,371	19,085	..	..	..	..
Current Budget Balance	..	..	298	-714	1,136	2,820	1,207	..	..	..	..
Capital Receipts	..	..						..	..	..	..
Capital Payments	..	..	3,081	3,196	3,679	4,950	4,055	..	..	..	..

1981	1982	1983	1984	1985	1986	1987	1988	1989	1990 estimate	Notes	CHAD
160	150	140	130	150	150	140	180	190	190	..	**CURRENT GNP PER CAPITA (US $)**
4,577	4,680	4,788	4,901	5,018	5,140	5,268	5,400	5,538	5,680	..	**POPULATION (thousands)**
				(Billions of current CFA Francs)							**USE AND ORIGIN OF RESOURCES**
167.58	192.78	222.18	278.66	325.45	257.21	241.15	309.61	319.72	298.76	..	Gross National Product (GNP)
-0.16	-0.22	-1.10	-4.00	-2.45	-3.06	-3.06	-3.97	-4.02	-1.47	..	Net Factor Income from Abroad
167.74	193.00	223.29	282.66	327.90	260.26	244.21	313.58	323.74	300.23	..	GDP at Market Prices
-18.00	-19.00	-26.00	-25.00	-90.11	-81.26	-73.34	-66.58	-72.58	-77.11	..	Resource Balance
36.00	18.00	52.00	72.00	55.29	49.55	54.04	66.35	71.48	76.45	..	Exports of Goods & NFServices
54.00	37.00	78.00	97.00	145.40	130.82	127.39	132.94	144.06	153.56	..	Imports of Goods & NFServices
185.74	212.00	249.29	307.66	418.00	341.53	317.56	380.16	396.32	377.34	..	Domestic Absorption
..	197.00	223.25	252.12	336.72	266.35	232.22	299.51	298.51	277.56	..	Private Consumption, etc.
..	15.00	19.19	40.23	54.51	51.43	55.33	56.11	68.80	68.89	..	General Gov't Consumption
..	..	6.85	15.32	26.77	23.75	30.00	24.53	29.01	30.89	..	Gross Domestic Investment
..	..	6.85	15.32	26.77	23.75	30.00	24.53	29.01	30.89	..	Fixed Investment
0.73	0.85	5.37	12.81	13.23	10.68	12.37	17.02	17.65	19.10	..	Indirect Taxes, net
167.01	192.15	217.92	269.85	314.67	249.58	231.84	296.56	306.09	281.13	B	GDP at factor cost
78.80	90.00	101.29	107.42	141.30	96.17	90.02	128.76	116.01	113.32	f	Agriculture
26.35	32.00	38.90	58.03	54.88	49.77	45.33	54.19	64.61	50.74	..	Industry
..	..	36.77	54.34	49.52	44.77	40.19	48.47	56.76	42.00	..	Manufacturing
62.59	71.00	83.10	117.21	131.72	114.32	108.87	130.62	143.12	136.17	..	Services, etc.
-18.00	-19.00	-19.15	-9.68	-63.34	-57.51	-43.34	-42.05	-43.57	-46.22	..	Gross Domestic Saving
-18.32	-19.43	-21.34	-14.42	-62.72	-62.44	-49.36	-51.12	-54.02	-51.19	..	Gross National Saving
				(Billions of 1987 CFA Francs)							
173.82	183.07	210.97	213.30	261.55	249.79	241.15	283.58	286.15	279.30	..	Gross National Product
173.98	183.28	212.02	216.37	263.52	252.76	244.21	287.21	289.83	280.67	..	GDP at Market Prices
-17.87	-28.98	-24.69	-19.13	-72.42	-78.92	-73.34	-60.98	-64.94	-72.09	..	Resource Balance
37.58	20.29	49.38	55.11	44.43	48.13	54.04	60.78	63.99	71.47	..	Exports of Goods & NFServices
55.45	49.27	74.06	74.25	116.85	127.05	127.39	121.76	128.93	143.55	..	Imports of Goods & NFServices
191.85	212.26	236.71	235.50	335.93	331.68	317.55	348.20	354.77	352.76	..	Domestic Absorption
..	..	211.98	192.98	270.61	258.67	232.22	274.33	267.21	259.49	..	Private Consumption, etc.
..	..	18.22	30.79	43.81	49.94	55.33	51.40	61.59	64.39	..	General Gov't Consumption
..	..	6.50	11.73	21.51	23.07	30.00	22.47	25.97	28.88	..	Gross Domestic Investment
..	..	..	..	..	..	..	..	..	..	..	Fixed Investment
173.23	182.46	206.92	206.56	252.89	242.38	231.84	271.63	274.03	263.11	B	GDP at factor cost
81.74	85.91	96.18	82.23	113.56	93.40	90.02	117.94	103.83	113.09	f	Agriculture
27.33	30.26	36.93	43.31	44.10	48.34	45.33	49.64	57.82	39.50	..	Industry
..	..	34.91	41.60	39.80	43.48	40.19	44.39	50.80	31.20	..	Manufacturing
64.91	67.12	78.91	90.83	105.86	111.02	108.87	119.64	128.18	128.08	..	Services, etc.
											Memo Items:
36.97	23.97	49.38	55.11	44.43	48.13	54.04	60.78	63.97	71.47	..	Capacity to Import
-0.62	3.68	0.00	0.00	0.00	0.00	0.00	0.00	-0.02	0.00	..	Terms of Trade Adjustment
173.37	186.97	212.02	216.36	263.52	252.76	244.21	287.21	289.81	280.67	..	Gross Domestic Income
173.20	186.75	210.97	213.30	261.55	249.79	241.15	283.58	286.14	279.30	..	Gross National Income
				(Index 1987 = 100)							**DOMESTIC PRICES/DEFLATORS**
96.4	105.3	105.3	130.6	124.4	103.0	100.0	109.2	111.7	107.0	..	Overall (GDP)
96.8	99.9	105.3	130.6	124.4	103.0	100.0	109.2	111.7	107.0	..	Domestic Absorption
96.4	104.8	105.3	130.6	124.4	103.0	100.0	109.2	111.7	100.2	..	Agriculture
96.4	105.8	105.3	134.0	124.4	103.0	100.0	109.2	111.7	128.5	..	Industry
..	..	105.3	130.6	124.4	103.0	100.0	109.2	111.7	134.6	..	Manufacturing
..	..	96.7	116.3	122.3	106.4	100.0	115.5	109.8	110.5	..	Consumer Price Index
											MANUFACTURING ACTIVITY
..	..	..	..	..	..	..	..	..	..	..	Employment (1987=100)
..	..	..	..	..	..	..	..	..	..	..	Real Earnings per Empl. (1987=100)
..	..	..	..	..	..	..	..	..	..	..	Real Output per Empl. (1987=100)
..	..	..	..	..	..	..	..	..	..	..	Earnings as % of Value Added
				(Millions of current CFA Francs)							**MONETARY HOLDINGS**
33,162	34,649	42,389	67,759	71,898	72,714	75,381	65,481	70,770	69,086	..	Money Supply, Broadly Defined
31,680	33,163	40,753	65,125	68,344	69,138	70,596	61,573	66,459	66,340	..	Money
22,143	23,609	29,196	44,925	47,354	46,665	46,702	40,272	43,055	46,810	..	Currency Outside Banks
9,537	9,554	11,557	20,200	20,990	22,473	23,894	21,301	23,404	19,530	..	Demand Deposits
1,482	1,486	1,636	2,634	3,554	3,576	4,785	3,908	4,311	2,746	..	Quasi-Money
				(Millions of current CFA Francs)							
..	..	2,019	..	..	-3,757	..	..	..	..	..	**GOVERNMENT DEFICIT (-) OR SURPLUS**
..	..	14,120	18,072	..	21,535	..	..	..	..	..	Current Revenue
..	..	..	..	..	..	..	..	..	..	..	Current Expenditure
..	..	..	..	..	..	..	..	..	..	..	Current Budget Balance
..	..	..	..	..	..	..	..	..	..	..	Capital Receipts
..	..	..	..	..	..	..	..	..	..	..	Capital Payments

CHAD	1970	1971	1972	1973	1974	1975	1976	1977	1978	1979	1980

FOREIGN TRADE (CUSTOMS BASIS)

(Millions of current US dollars)

Value of Exports, fob	..	..	..	..	..	..	..	..	..	..	..
Nonfuel Primary Products	..	..	..	..	..	..	..	..	..	..	..
Fuels	..	..	..	..	..	..	..	..	..	..	..
Manufactures	..	..	..	..	..	..	..	..	..	..	..
Value of Imports, cif	..	..	..	..	..	..	..	..	..	..	..
Nonfuel Primary Products	..	..	..	..	..	..	..	..	..	..	..
Fuels	..	..	..	..	..	..	..	..	..	..	..
Manufactures	..	..	..	..	..	..	..	..	..	..	..

(Index 1987 = 100)

Terms of Trade	..	..	..	..	..	..	..	..	..	..	..
Export Prices, fob	..	..	..	..	..	..	..	..	..	..	..
Import Prices, cif	..	..	..	..	..	..	..	..	..	..	..

BALANCE OF PAYMENTS

(Millions of current US dollars)

Exports of Goods & Services	69.80	73.22	78.39	93.82	109.44	104.42	128.61	132.38	..	..	..
Merchandise, fob	39.80	42.33	39.85	48.76	70.47	57.92	100.79	106.55	98.95	88.27	70.99
Nonfactor Services	28.80	29.99	37.24	43.27	37.16	44.32	25.86	24.19	20.59	4.60	0.38
Factor Services	1.20	0.90	1.30	1.79	1.80	2.19	1.96	1.64	..	..	..
Imports of Goods & Services	96.50	100.10	107.05	145.80	163.32	229.96	215.20	249.56	271.17	127.06	83.17
Merchandise, fob	52.50	53.06	58.52	73.55	82.74	126.15	115.34	142.20	163.38	64.09	55.28
Nonfactor Services	41.70	44.53	45.82	68.55	76.97	100.90	97.56	103.42	104.13	54.41	24.21
Factor Services	2.30	2.51	2.71	3.70	3.61	2.91	2.31	3.94	3.66	8.56	3.68
Long-Term Interest	0.40	0.90	0.70	0.50	0.70	1.40	0.80	0.60	0.70	0.20	0.00
Private Current Transfers, net	-6.20	-6.92	-8.58	-9.18	-9.02	-8.13	-4.16	-14.03	-11.37	-9.29	-4.11
Workers' Remittances	..	..	..	..	..	..	..	..	..	..	..
Curr. A/C Bal before Off. Transf.	-32.90	-33.80	-37.24	-61.16	-62.90	-133.68	-90.75	-131.21	-163.00	-43.49	-15.91
Net Official Transfers	34.50	37.11	37.35	54.36	58.69	73.33	85.55	102.69	116.56	41.94	28.21
Curr. A/C Bal after Off. Transf.	1.60	3.31	0.11	-6.80	-4.21	-60.34	-5.20	-28.52	-46.44	-1.55	12.31
Long-Term Capital, net	3.60	7.32	-13.14	4.65	14.67	37.76	58.65	33.05	34.57	-3.97	-4.17
Direct Investment	0.60	0.30	-0.11	6.08	13.83	20.28	26.78	21.15	33.09	-1.29	-0.43
Long-Term Loans	3.30	9.00	-1.20	10.60	23.50	18.00	6.50	37.00	38.50	22.60	2.60
Disbursements	5.80	14.80	2.40	13.40	26.10	23.10	10.20	39.80	41.00	24.40	5.20
Repayments	2.50	5.80	3.60	2.80	2.60	5.10	3.70	2.80	2.50	1.80	2.60
Other Long-Term Capital	-0.30	-1.98	-11.83	-12.03	-22.66	-0.52	25.36	-25.10	-37.02	-25.28	-6.34
Other Capital, net	-8.48	-3.89	10.51	-6.53	-0.07	10.21	-39.74	-8.55	5.76	3.16	-13.17
Change in Reserves	3.28	-6.75	2.52	8.67	-10.39	12.38	-13.71	4.02	6.10	2.36	5.03

Memo Item:

(CFA Francs per US dollar)

Conversion Factor (Annual Avg)	277.710	277.130	252.480	222.890	240.700	214.310	238.950	245.680	225.650	212.720	211.280

(Millions of US dollars), outstanding at end of year

EXTERNAL DEBT (Total)	34.90	46.60	35.80	46.90	74.80	90.70	100.20	145.60	210.80	236.70	218.30
Long-Term Debt (by debtor)	34.90	46.60	35.80	46.90	74.80	90.70	100.20	141.60	196.80	223.70	207.70
Central Bank, incl. IMF credit	6.00	6.90	6.50	5.40	8.40	8.00	13.50	14.10	20.40	20.00	16.40
Central Government	23.10	35.00	24.80	29.90	51.50	69.50	73.20	87.00	104.90	120.70	117.20
Rest of General Government	0.30	0.20	0.20	0.10	0.10	0.10	0.00	0.00	0.00	0.00	0.00
Non-financial Public Enterprises	5.50	4.50	4.30	11.50	14.80	13.10	13.50	40.50	71.50	83.00	74.10
Priv. Sector, incl non-guaranteed	0.00	0.00	0.00	0.00	0.00	0.00	0.00	0.00	0.00	0.00	0.00
Short-Term Debt	0.00	0.00	0.00	0.00	0.00	0.00	0.00	4.00	14.00	13.00	10.60

Memo Items:

(Thousands of US dollars)

Int'l Reserves Excluding Gold	2,309.0	11,224.0	10,075.0	1,471.0	15,267.0	3,059.0	23,274.0	18,783.0	11,790.0	11,267.0	5,053.0
Gold Holdings (at market price)	..	..	..	..	..	..	..	924.0	1,921.0	5,837.0	6,720.0

SOCIAL INDICATORS

Total Fertility Rate	6.0	6.0	6.0	6.0	5.9	5.9	5.9	5.9	5.9	5.9	5.9
Infant Mortality Rate	171.2	168.6	166.0	163.6	161.2	158.8	156.4	154.0	151.8	149.6	147.4
Life Expectancy at Birth	38.2	38.6	39.0	39.4	39.8	40.2	40.6	41.0	41.4	41.8	42.2
Urban Population, % of total	11.3	12.2	13.2	14.1	15.1	16.0	16.8	17.7	18.5	19.4	20.2
Food Prod. per capita (1987=100)	132.1	127.3	118.7	107.9	107.7	112.1	113.1	112.8	117.8	117.3	119.5
Labor Force, Agriculture (%)	90.2	89.4	88.7	88.0	87.4	86.7	86.0	85.3	84.6	83.9	83.3
Labor Force, Female (%)	23.0	22.9	22.9	22.8	22.7	22.7	22.6	22.6	22.5	22.4	22.4
Primary Schl. Enroll. Ratio	35.0	..	..	..	..	35.0	35.0	..	..	..	..
Primary Schl. Enroll. Ratio, Female	17.0	..	..	..	..	18.0	19.0	..	..	..	..
Secondary Schl. Enroll. Ratio	2.0	..	..	..	..	3.0	3.0	..	..	..	..

(Millions of current US dollars)

											FOREIGN TRADE (CUSTOMS BASIS)
..	..	..	..	..	..	..	..	..	..	..	Value of Exports, fob
..	..	..	..	..	..	..	..	..	..	..	Nonfuel Primary Products
..	..	..	..	..	..	..	..	..	..	..	Fuels
..	..	..	..	..	..	..	..	..	..	..	Manufactures
..	..	..	..	..	..	..	..	..	..	..	Value of Imports, cif
..	..	..	..	..	..	..	..	..	..	..	Nonfuel Primary Products
..	..	..	..	..	..	..	..	..	..	..	Fuels
..	..	..	..	..	..	..	..	..	..	..	Manufactures

(Index 1987 = 100)

..	..	..	..	..	..	..	..	..	..	..	Terms of Trade
..	..	..	..	..	..	..	..	..	..	..	Export Prices, fob
..	..	..	..	..	..	..	..	..	..	..	Import Prices, cif

(Millions of current US dollars)

											BALANCE OF PAYMENTS
..	61.99	106.84	147.85	99.49	146.64	182.71	226.77	198.98	237.33	f	Exports of Goods & Services
83.41	57.72	78.22	109.68	61.84	98.60	109.45	145.89	155.36	193.30	..	Merchandise, fob
4.11	2.36	24.24	36.84	32.60	44.50	70.38	78.74	42.30	34.09	..	Nonfactor Services
..	1.91	4.38	1.33	5.04	3.54	2.88	2.14	1.32	9.94	..	Factor Services
107.60	104.73	180.09	224.69	327.44	390.12	436.92	461.79	461.02	522.27	f	Imports of Goods & Services
81.21	81.69	99.15	128.33	166.29	212.06	225.91	228.40	240.30	262.65	..	Merchandise, fob
25.32	22.09	77.61	90.07	153.86	165.70	197.96	217.92	209.96	244.25	..	Nonfactor Services
1.07	0.95	3.34	6.29	7.29	12.37	13.06	15.46	10.76	15.37	..	Factor Services
0.10	0.20	0.20	0.30	2.10	1.70	3.10	3.50	1.70	3.30	..	Long-Term Interest
-0.59	-0.66	-2.83	-1.68	6.85	-5.39	-9.84	-17.13	-20.18	-12.84	..	Private Current Transfers, net
..	..	..	..	0.03	1.23	1.35	0.35	0.79	0.04	..	Workers' Remittances
-20.67	-43.40	-76.08	-78.52	-221.11	-248.88	-264.05	-252.15	-282.22	-297.78	..	Curr. A/C Bal before Off. Transf.
44.11	61.92	114.06	87.57	133.87	189.51	238.52	277.65	230.95	218.75	..	Net Official Transfers
23.44	18.53	37.98	9.05	-87.24	-59.37	-25.53	25.51	-51.28	-79.03	f	Curr. A/C Bal after Off. Transf.
-1.93	-1.11	-18.13	4.36	67.51	49.28	55.76	68.87	80.99	132.26	f	Long-Term Capital, net
-0.11	-0.12	-0.09	9.19	53.39	27.77	0.17	-12.55	6.19	19.19	..	Direct Investment
9.10	3.60	13.70	7.50	-0.30	28.50	40.50	58.10	76.60	92.60	..	Long-Term Loans
9.70	4.60	13.90	10.50	9.80	31.50	42.80	60.50	80.00	95.80	..	Disbursements
0.60	1.00	0.20	3.00	10.10	3.00	2.30	2.40	3.40	3.20	..	Repayments
-10.92	-4.58	-31.74	-12.33	14.42	-6.99	15.10	23.32	-1.81	20.47	..	Other Long-Term Capital
-22.97	-14.84	-2.48	10.54	-2.09	-4.99	-13.68	-108.03	4.68	-59.50	f	Other Capital, net
1.46	-2.58	-17.37	-23.95	21.82	15.08	-16.56	13.64	-34.39	6.27	..	Change in Reserves

(CFA Francs per US dollar)

											Memo Item:
271.730	328.600	381.060	436.960	449.260	346.300	300.530	297.850	319.010	272.260	..	Conversion Factor (Annual Avg)

(Millions of US dollars), outstanding at end of year

											EXTERNAL DEBT (Total)
201.40	168.00	168.60	157.80	186.00	237.30	320.00	357.40	368.50	491.60	..	Long-Term Debt (by debtor)
190.60	160.50	163.20	155.00	165.80	206.40	282.00	320.00	340.80	461.00	..	Central Bank, incl. IMF credit
16.90	14.70	13.80	9.30	13.00	11.90	21.10	18.00	24.80	31.60	..	Central Government
118.00	118.00	125.60	122.50	124.10	145.10	180.80	221.70	288.30	388.40	..	Rest of General Government
0.00	0.00	0.00	0.00	0.00	0.00	0.00	0.30	0.40	0.60	..	Non-financial Public Enterprises
55.70	27.80	23.80	23.20	28.70	49.40	76.30	74.50	27.10	40.20	..	Priv. Sector, incl non-guaranteed
0.00	0.00	0.00	0.00	0.00	0.00	3.80	5.50	0.20	0.20	..	Short-Term Debt
10.80	7.50	5.40	2.80	20.20	30.90	38.00	37.40	27.70	30.60	..	

(Thousands of US dollars)

											Memo Items:
7,315.0	12,405.0	27,999.0	44,162.0	33,460.0	15,910.0	52,108.0	63,083.0	111,733.0	127,781.0	..	Int'l Reserves Excluding Gold
4,532.0	5,209.0	4,349.0	3,422.0	3,630.0	4,339.0	5,374.0	4,554.0	4,451.0	4,274.0	..	Gold Holdings (at market price)

											SOCIAL INDICATORS
5.9	5.9	5.9	5.9	5.9	5.9	5.9	5.9	5.9	6.0	..	Total Fertility Rate
145.2	143.0	140.8	138.6	136.3	134.1	131.9	129.5	127.1	124.6	..	Infant Mortality Rate
42.6	43.0	43.5	44.0	44.5	45.0	45.5	46.0	46.5	47.0	..	Life Expectancy at Birth
21.1	22.0	22.9	23.8	24.7	25.9	27.1	27.9	28.7	29.5	..	Urban Population, % of total
112.8	111.1	112.8	92.2	105.0	102.0	100.0	102.9	95.8	99.1	..	Food Prod. per capita (1987=100)
..	..	..	..	..	..	..	..	..	..	..	Labor Force, Agriculture (%)
22.2	22.1	22.0	21.8	21.7	21.6	21.5	21.3	21.2	21.1	..	Labor Force, Female (%)
..	..	..	38.0	43.0	43.0	51.0	50.0	57.0	..	..	Primary Schl. Enroll. Ratio
..	..	..	21.0	24.0	24.0	29.0	30.0	35.0	..	..	Primary Schl. Enroll. Ratio, Female
..	..	..	6.0	..	6.0	6.0	6.0	7.0	..	..	Secondary Schl. Enroll. Ratio

CHILE	1970	1971	1972	1973	1974	1975	1976	1977	1978	1979	1980
CURRENT GNP PER CAPITA (US $)	840	990	1,080	1,090	1,140	860	880	1,030	1,330	1,690	2,100
POPULATION (thousands)	9,504	9,680	9,853	10,023	10,189	10,350	10,508	10,661	10,815	10,975	11,145

USE AND ORIGIN OF RESOURCES *(Billions of current Chilean Pesos)*

	1970	1971	1972	1973	1974	1975	1976	1977	1978	1979	1980
Gross National Product (GNP)	9.60E-2	1.26E-1	2.32E-1	1.10E+0	9.10E+0	34.1	124.5	281.9	476.5	752.7	1,043.4
Net Factor Income from Abroad	-2.40E-3	-1.50E-3	-2.90E-3	-1.22E-2	-1.44E-1	-1.4	-4.2	-5.9	-11.0	-19.5	-31.9
GDP at Market Prices	9.84E-2	1.27E-1	2.34E-1	1.10E+0	9.20E+0	35.4	128.7	287.8	487.5	772.2	1,075.3
Resource Balance	6.00E-4	-1.30E-3	-8.20E-3	-2.13E-2	6.23E-2	-0.7	5.6	-5.2	-16.3	-21.9	-44.7
Exports of Goods & NF Services	1.48E-2	1.44E-2	2.36E-2	1.60E-1	1.90E+0	9.0	32.3	59.3	100.4	179.7	245.4
Imports of Goods & NF Services	1.42E-2	1.57E-2	3.18E-2	1.82E-1	1.80E+0	9.7	26.8	64.5	116.7	201.6	290.1
Domestic Absorption	9.78E-2	1.28E-1	2.43E-1	1.20E+0	9.10E+0	36.1	123.1	293.0	503.8	794.1	1,120.0
Private Consumption, etc.	6.90E-2	9.05E-2	1.76E-1	9.27E-1	5.70E+0	25.9	88.7	209.5	346.6	546.3	760.5
General Gov't Consumption	1.26E-2	1.94E-2	3.77E-2	1.51E-1	1.40E+0	5.6	18.0	41.9	70.3	110.4	133.9
Gross Domestic Investment	1.62E-2	1.84E-2	2.86E-2	9.07E-2	1.90E+0	4.6	16.4	41.5	86.8	137.4	225.6
Fixed Investment	1.48E-2	1.85E-2	3.07E-2	1.47E-1	1.60E+0	6.3	17.1	38.3	71.6	115.0	178.9
Indirect Taxes, net	1.04E-2	1.24E-2	2.00E-2	1.20E-1	1.40E+0	5.0	17.7	41.3	67.4	95.8	129.8
GDP at factor cost	8.80E-2	1.15E-1	2.15E-1	1.00E+0	7.80E+0	30.5	111.0	246.5	420.1	676.4	945.5
Agriculture	6.70E-3	1.03E-2	1.95E-2	7.64E-2	5.23E-1	2.3	10.9	28.3	37.1	56.1	77.7
Industry	4.07E-2	4.90E-2	8.86E-2	4.70E-1	4.50E+0	13.5	51.4	103.9	175.5	288.0	401.1
Manufacturing	2.51E-2	3.10E-2	5.48E-2	3.11E-1	2.70E+0	7.2	29.9	62.6	109.2	164.0	230.5
Services, etc.	5.10E-2	6.77E-2	1.26E-1	6.00E-1	4.20E+0	19.6	66.4	155.6	274.9	428.1	596.4
Gross Domestic Saving	1.68E-2	1.71E-2	2.04E-2	6.94E-2	2.00E+0	3.9	22.0	36.3	70.5	115.5	180.9
Gross National Saving	1.44E-2	1.56E-2	1.76E-2	5.77E-2	1.90E+0	2.6	18.2	32.2	61.9	99.3	151.5

(Billions of 1987 Chilean Pesos)

	1970	1971	1972	1973	1974	1975	1976	1977	1978	1979	1980
Gross National Product	2,877.2	3,181.1	3,144.5	2,976.4	2,984.3	2,534.9	2,640.3	2,937.4	3,176.0	3,428.8	3,680.4
GDP at Market Prices	2,958.5	3,228.9	3,193.4	3,017.7	3,042.3	2,640.4	2,735.2	3,003.3	3,254.1	3,524.6	3,800.5
Resource Balance	-503.6	-577.5	-669.8	-605.3	-475.1	-79.8	22.8	-124.4	-193.0	-306.3	-405.0
Exports of Goods & NF Services	401.8	405.1	343.9	353.5	515.9	528.1	656.7	734.8	817.0	932.5	1,065.9
Imports of Goods & NF Services	905.4	982.7	1,013.7	958.8	991.1	607.8	633.9	859.2	1,010.0	1,238.9	1,470.8
Domestic Absorption	3,462.1	3,806.5	3,863.2	3,623.0	3,517.5	2,720.2	2,712.4	3,127.7	3,447.1	3,831.0	4,205.5
Private Consumption, etc.	2,418.8	2,735.3	2,942.1	2,743.8	2,260.8	1,905.9	1,898.0	2,236.5	2,427.3	2,616.7	2,832.8
General Gov't Consumption	390.3	438.8	463.8	471.9	517.2	463.9	463.5	481.3	513.8	560.9	515.4
Gross Domestic Investment	653.0	632.3	457.3	407.4	739.5	350.4	350.9	409.9	505.9	653.4	857.3
Fixed Investment	588.3	574.6	459.2	431.5	514.0	396.9	338.1	390.4	458.2	535.4	652.6
GDP at factor cost	..	..	..	..	..	..	..	..	..	..	..
Agriculture	..	..	..	..	..	..	..	..	..	..	..
Industry	..	..	..	..	..	..	..	..	..	..	..
Manufacturing	..	..	..	..	..	..	..	..	..	..	..
Services, etc.	..	..	..	..	..	..	..	..	..	..	..

Memo Items:

	1970	1971	1972	1973	1974	1975	1976	1977	1978	1979	1980
Capacity to Import	943.7	901.3	752.3	846.3	1,025.1	564.1	765.9	790.1	868.9	1,104.5	1,244.2
Terms of Trade Adjustment	541.9	496.2	408.4	492.8	509.1	36.0	109.1	55.3	51.9	172.0	178.3
Gross Domestic Income	3,500.4	3,725.1	3,601.8	3,510.6	3,551.5	2,676.4	2,844.3	3,058.6	3,306.0	3,696.6	3,978.8
Gross National Income	3,419.1	3,677.3	3,552.9	3,469.2	3,493.4	2,570.9	2,749.5	2,992.8	3,227.9	3,600.7	3,858.6

DOMESTIC PRICES/DEFLATORS *(Index 1987 = 100)*

	1970	1971	1972	1973	1974	1975	1976	1977	1978	1979	1980
Overall (GDP)	3.33E-3	3.93E-3	7.34E-3	3.80E-2	3.02E-1	1.30E+0	4.7	9.6	15.0	21.9	28.3
Domestic Absorption	2.82E-3	3.37E-3	6.28E-3	3.22E-2	2.60E-1	1.30E+0	4.5	9.4	14.6	20.7	26.6
Agriculture	..	..	..	..	..	..	..	..	..	..	..
Industry	..	..	..	..	..	..	..	..	..	..	..
Manufacturing	..	..	..	..	..	..	..	..	..	..	..
Consumer Price Index	..	..	..	..	..	..	..	..	..	..	..

MANUFACTURING ACTIVITY

	1970	1971	1972	1973	1974	1975	1976	1977	1978	1979	1980
Employment (1987=100)	111.9	113.5	119.1	121.5	116.5	108.4	100.8	103.9	101.9	100.4	94.9
Real Earnings per Empl. (1987=100)	40.9	53.3	59.3	42.1	52.8	51.9	61.4	66.1	78.3	91.1	101.4
Real Output per Empl. (1987=100)	..	..	..	..	..	..	..	..	..	..	..
Earnings as % of Value Added	18.6	22.8	29.6	16.3	12.1	12.3	14.6	17.5	17.9	18.2	18.4

MONETARY HOLDINGS *(Billions of current Chilean Pesos)*

	1970	1971	1972	1973	1974	1975	1976	1977	1978	1979	1980
Money Supply, Broadly Defined	1.50E-2	3.03E-2	7.41E-2	3.22E-1	1.28E+0	5.20E+0	26.770	53.400	103.410	172.160	278.660
Money	1.00E-2	2.13E-2	5.41E-2	2.29E-1	8.37E-1	2.98E+0	10.600	19.800	34.990	56.570	87.000
Currency Outside Banks	4.38E-3	8.97E-3	2.82E-2	9.57E-2	3.49E-1	1.36E+0	4.480	9.300	16.390	24.870	35.560
Demand Deposits	5.65E-3	1.23E-2	2.59E-2	1.33E-1	4.87E-1	1.62E+0	6.120	10.500	18.610	31.690	51.440
Quasi-Money	4.98E-3	9.03E-3	2.00E-2	9.30E-2	4.41E-1	2.22E+0	16.170	33.600	68.420	115.600	191.650

GOVERNMENT DEFICIT (-) OR SURPLUS *(Billions of current Chilean Pesos)*

	1970	1971	1972	1973	1974	1975	1976	1977	1978	1979	1980
	..	..	-0.03	-0.08	-0.49	0.05	1.80	-3.20	-0.52	37.20	58.20
Current Revenue	..	..	0.07	0.32	2.60	12.30	39.70	89.10	154.20	252.40	358.70
Current Expenditure	..	..	0.08	0.31	2.10	9.70	33.10	81.40	135.60	195.10	272.30
Current Budget Balance	..	..	-0.01	0.01	0.47	2.60	6.50	7.70	18.60	57.30	86.50
Capital Receipts	..	..	..	0.01	0.04	0.12	1.40	2.40	3.20	11.10	8.40
Capital Payments	..	..	0.02	0.10	1.00	2.70	6.20	13.30	22.30	31.20	36.60

1981	1982	1983	1984	1985	1986	1987	1988	1989	1990 estimate	Notes	CHILE
2,610	2,220	1,910	1,700	1,420	1,330	1,360	1,510	1,780	1,940	..	**CURRENT GNP PER CAPITA (US $)**
11,325	11,515	11,713	11,916	12,121	12,329	12,538	12,748	12,961	13,173	..	**POPULATION (thousands)**
											USE AND ORIGIN OF RESOURCES
			(Billions of current Chilean Pesos)								
1,220.3	1,149.0	1,430.7	1,710.6	2,291.2	2,882.1	3,787.0	4,940.8	6,265.2	7,937.5	..	Gross National Product (GNP)
-52.8	-90.1	-127.0	-182.8	-285.4	-364.0	-372.8	-470.2	-514.2	-540.4	..	Net Factor Income from Abroad
1,273.1	1,239.1	1,557.7	1,893.4	2,576.6	3,246.1	4,159.8	5,411.0	6,779.4	8,477.9	f	GDP at Market Prices
-131.6	-23.5	42.4	-20.1	71.1	124.0	170.6	389.0	252.0	250.7	..	Resource Balance
209.0	239.9	374.5	459.5	749.2	994.2	1,394.3	2,022.0	2,567.3	3,105.9	..	Exports of Goods & NF Services
340.6	263.4	332.1	479.6	678.1	870.2	1,223.7	1,633.0	2,315.3	2,855.2	..	Imports of Goods & NF Services
1,404.7	1,262.6	1,515.4	1,913.5	2,505.5	3,122.1	3,989.2	5,022.0	6,527.6	8,227.1	..	Domestic Absorption
948.3	932.7	1,141.9	1,381.7	1,785.2	2,237.3	2,811.0	3,534.8	4,482.2	5,686.1	..	Private Consumption, etc.
167.4	190.1	220.7	273.8	367.1	410.7	475.1	568.5	667.0	825.0	..	General Gov't Consumption
289.0	139.9	152.8	258.0	353.2	474.1	703.1	918.7	1,378.4	1,716.0	..	Gross Domestic Investment
236.8	181.4	186.5	233.8	366.4	472.7	666.8	882.7	1,249.9	1,650.6	..	Fixed Investment
181.5	168.2	..	..	..	..	..	..	..	..	..	Indirect Taxes, net
1,091.7	1,070.9	..	..	..	..	..	..	..	..	B f	GDP at factor cost
80.7	69.4	88.8	..	..	..	..	..	..	..	..	Agriculture
466.4	438.5	604.2	..	..	..	..	..	..	..	..	Industry
284.2	233.5	320.8	..	..	..	..	..	..	..	..	Manufacturing
726.0	731.3	864.7	..	..	..	..	..	..	..	..	Services, etc.
157.4	116.4	195.2	237.9	424.3	598.1	873.7	1,307.7	1,630.2	1,966.8	..	Gross Domestic Saving
106.0	28.3	72.4	59.7	146.5	241.9	515.2	852.9	1,131.5	1,442.9	..	Gross National Saving
			(Billions of 1987 Chilean Pesos)								
3,838.0	3,195.2	3,143.4	3,295.3	3,326.6	3,506.3	3,787.0	4,078.9	4,540.0	4,704.2	..	Gross National Product
4,011.8	3,441.0	3,417.9	3,634.6	3,723.6	3,934.4	4,159.8	4,466.9	4,911.9	5,017.6	f	GDP at Market Prices
-731.4	-67.4	102.9	20.5	213.5	235.8	170.6	106.5	0.0	113.3	..	Resource Balance
970.5	1,016.2	1,022.6	1,092.0	1,167.2	1,281.6	1,394.3	1,479.7	1,718.7	1,842.2	..	Exports of Goods & NF Services
1,701.9	1,083.6	919.7	1,071.5	953.7	1,045.8	1,223.7	1,373.2	1,718.8	1,728.9	..	Imports of Goods & NF Services
4,743.1	3,508.4	3,315.0	3,614.1	3,510.2	3,698.6	3,989.2	4,360.4	4,912.0	4,904.3	..	Domestic Absorption
3,197.9	2,653.0	2,526.5	2,592.3	2,524.3	2,653.9	2,811.0	3,099.0	3,397.3	3,408.2	..	Private Consumption, etc.
499.2	492.6	489.5	497.1	495.8	485.4	475.1	498.1	501.5	509.5	..	General Gov't Consumption
1,046.0	362.7	299.0	524.7	490.1	559.3	703.1	763.3	1,013.2	986.5	..	Gross Domestic Investment
762.0	503.4	428.5	467.0	536.0	573.9	666.8	738.1	891.8	953.9	..	Fixed Investment
..	..	..	..	..	..	..	..	..	..	B f	GDP at factor cost
..	..	..	..	..	..	..	..	..	..	..	Agriculture
..	..	..	..	..	..	..	..	..	..	..	Industry
..	..	..	..	..	..	..	..	..	..	..	Manufacturing
..	..	..	..	..	..	..	..	..	..	..	Services, etc.
											Memo Items:
1,044.3	986.9	1,037.1	1,026.7	1,053.7	1,194.9	1,394.3	1,700.4	1,905.8	1,880.7	..	Capacity to Import
73.9	-29.3	14.5	-65.4	-113.5	-86.8	0.0	220.6	187.1	38.5	..	Terms of Trade Adjustment
4,085.6	3,411.7	3,432.3	3,569.2	3,610.1	3,847.6	4,159.8	4,687.5	5,099.1	5,056.1	..	Gross Domestic Income
3,911.8	3,165.9	3,157.9	3,229.9	3,213.1	3,419.5	3,787.0	4,299.5	4,727.1	4,742.7	..	Gross National Income
			(Index 1987 = 100)								
											DOMESTIC PRICES/DEFLATORS
31.7	36.0	45.6	52.1	69.2	82.5	100.0	121.1	138.0	169.0	..	Overall (GDP)
29.6	36.0	45.7	52.9	71.4	84.4	100.0	115.2	132.9	167.8	..	Domestic Absorption
..	..	..	..	..	..	..	..	..	..	..	Agriculture
..	..	..	..	..	..	..	..	..	..	..	Industry
..	..	..	..	..	..	..	..	..	..	..	Manufacturing
..	..	..	..	..	..	..	..	..	..	..	Consumer Price Index
											MANUFACTURING ACTIVITY
88.3	69.8	69.5	77.4	85.1	97.3	100.0	101.2	..	..	..	Employment (1987=100)
122.3	126.2	114.1	106.8	98.0	99.6	100.0	106.0	..	..	..	Real Earnings per Empl. (1987=100)
..	..	..	..	..	..	..	..	..	..	..	Real Output per Empl. (1987=100)
23.0	20.3	17.1	15.4	13.7	16.6	16.8	16.6	..	..	..	Earnings as % of Value Added
			(Billions of current Chilean Pesos)								
											MONETARY HOLDINGS
359.030	484.410	588.470	720.280	1,060.950	1,329.090	1,793.670	2,280.170	2,990.480	3,695.710	..	Money Supply, Broadly Defined
82.460	92.410	113.000	130.400	148.410	214.910	229.160	385.540	441.580	517.570	..	Money
44.490	42.960	51.880	64.180	79.460	108.480	135.690	181.560	221.800	285.480	..	Currency Outside Banks
37.980	49.450	61.120	66.220	68.950	106.430	93.470	203.980	219.780	232.090	..	Demand Deposits
276.560	392.000	475.480	589.880	912.540	1,114.180	1,564.510	1,894.630	2,548.900	3,178.140	..	Quasi-Money
			(Billions of current Chilean Pesos)								
33.00	-12.20	-40.90	-56.20	-60.70	-31.40	20.00	-12.20	..	..	..	**GOVERNMENT DEFICIT (-) OR SURPLUS**
406.40	368.30	429.00	544.10	745.90	914.30	1,194.00	1,534.30	..	..	..	Current Revenue
341.40	395.00	463.00	563.00	725.80	861.50	1,064.40	1,413.80	..	..	..	Current Expenditure
64.90	-26.70	-34.00	-18.90	20.10	52.80	129.60	120.50	..	..	..	Current Budget Balance
13.00	6.10	3.10	3.30	6.20	6.60	11.60	16.00	..	..	..	Capital Receipts
44.90	-8.40	10.10	40.50	87.00	90.90	121.20	148.70	..	..	..	Capital Payments

CHILE	1970	1971	1972	1973	1974	1975	1976	1977	1978	1979	1980
FOREIGN TRADE (CUSTOMS BASIS)					*(Millions of current US dollars)*						
Value of Exports, fob	1,233.6	961.2	855.4	1,249.4	2,480.6	1,648.7	2,208.5	2,138.4	2,462.1	4,229.3	4,583.9
Nonfuel Primary Products	1,178.4	909.8	806.9	1,200.9	2,351.3	1,469.0	1,943.3	1,842.8	2,154.3	3,845.6	4,079.7
Fuels	0.4	0.9	2.8	2.6	20.0	14.3	34.6	58.6	41.8	54.9	59.4
Manufactures	54.8	50.5	45.7	45.9	109.3	165.4	230.5	237.0	266.0	328.8	444.8
Value of Imports, cif	930.1	979.8	945.2	1,102.4	1,910.4	1,533.6	1,643.0	1,906.3	2,553.6	4,229.3	5,123.1
Nonfuel Primary Products	199.3	253.2	311.0	365.9	757.9	359.1	535.2	340.0	557.2	711.0	947.9
Fuels	57.7	89.2	86.0	80.6	272.9	303.4	193.3	382.2	428.7	897.6	944.6
Manufactures	673.1	637.4	548.2	655.9	879.6	871.1	914.5	1,184.1	1,567.7	2,620.8	3,230.6
					(Index 1987 = 100)						
Terms of Trade	305.9	242.7	223.8	271.4	196.5	138.8	139.5	129.2	122.3	141.1	128.4
Export Prices, fob	68.0	54.0	55.1	94.7	109.8	72.5	78.3	74.2	77.7	107.1	119.4
Import Prices, cif	22.2	22.3	24.6	34.9	55.9	52.3	56.1	57.4	63.5	75.9	93.0
BALANCE OF PAYMENTS					*(Millions of current US dollars)*						
Exports of Goods & Services	1,274.0	1,142.4	984.7	1,467.5	2,351.2	1,842.0	2,425.0	2,621.0	2,984.0	4,746.0	6,276.0
Merchandise, fob	1,113.0	1,000.0	851.2	1,316.1	2,151.5	1,590.0	2,116.0	2,186.0	2,460.0	3,835.0	4,705.0
Nonfactor Services	134.0	130.4	132.5	146.6	175.6	248.0	297.0	417.0	481.0	785.0	1,263.0
Factor Services	27.0	12.0	1.1	4.8	24.1	4.0	12.0	18.0	43.0	126.0	308.0
Imports of Goods & Services	1,371.0	1,347.0	1,463.5	1,760.8	2,657.8	2,344.0	2,325.0	3,268.0	4,169.0	6,040.0	8,360.0
Merchandise, fob	867.0	926.8	1,011.9	1,329.2	1,901.4	1,520.0	1,473.0	2,151.0	2,886.0	4,190.0	5,469.0
Nonfactor Services	281.0	289.9	302.9	317.1	461.8	529.0	507.0	720.0	735.0	1,027.0	1,554.0
Factor Services	223.0	130.4	148.7	114.4	294.6	295.0	345.0	397.0	548.0	823.0	1,337.0
Long-Term Interest	104.4	108.5	50.0	64.9	114.2	195.4	253.6	264.8	384.3	582.6	918.3
Private Current Transfers, net	2.0	3.0	5.4	4.8	6.0	4.0	32.0	80.0	75.0	88.0	64.0
Workers' Remittances	..	..	..	..	..	..	..	..	..	..	..
Curr. A/C Bal before Off. Transf.	-95.0	-201.6	-473.4	-288.5	-300.7	-498.0	132.0	-567.0	-1,110.0	-1,206.0	-2,020.0
Net Official Transfers	4.0	4.0	2.2	9.5	8.4	8.0	16.0	16.0	22.0	17.0	49.0
Curr. A/C Bal after Off. Transf.	-91.0	-197.6	-471.2	-279.0	-292.2	-490.0	148.0	-551.0	-1,088.0	-1,189.0	-1,971.0
Long-Term Capital, net	140.0	-114.3	107.5	-63.2	16.8	172.0	46.0	49.0	1,510.0	1,685.1	2,242.0
Direct Investment	-79.0	-66.2	-1.1	-4.8	-556.8	50.0	-1.0	16.0	177.0	233.0	170.0
Long-Term Loans	448.2	-57.0	165.1	186.4	509.7	44.7	13.6	195.9	1,136.6	1,466.4	2,089.4
Disbursements	655.3	222.7	291.6	358.1	760.6	464.6	653.9	995.4	2,232.6	2,784.5	3,551.2
Repayments	207.1	279.7	126.5	171.7	250.9	419.9	640.3	799.5	1,096.0	1,318.1	1,461.8
Other Long-Term Capital	-229.2	8.9	-56.5	-244.8	64.0	77.3	33.4	-162.9	196.4	-14.3	-17.4
Other Capital, net	37.3	53.0	226.7	388.5	154.6	92.6	84.4	633.3	307.6	551.3	974.2
Change in Reserves	-86.3	258.9	137.0	-46.3	120.8	225.4	-278.4	-131.3	-729.6	-1,047.4	-1,245.2
Memo Item:					*(Chilean Pesos per US dollar)*						
Conversion Factor (Annual Avg)	0.0120	0.0124	0.0195	0.1110	0.8320	4.9100	13.0500	21.5300	31.6600	37.2500	39.0000
				(Millions of US dollars), outstanding at end of year							
EXTERNAL DEBT (Total)	2,570	2,618	3,050	3,275	4,522	4,762	4,849	5,884	7,374	9,361	12,081
Long-Term Debt (by debtor)	2,570	2,618	3,050	3,275	4,522	4,762	4,849	5,020	6,273	7,726	9,521
Central Bank, incl. IMF credit	75	122	366	443	774	950	1,123	1,093	1,337	1,577	1,404
Central Government	719	715	945	939	1,573	1,681	1,541	1,440	1,293	1,193	1,105
Rest of General Government	1	1	1	1	0	0	0	0	0	0	0
Non-financial Public Enterprises	1,171	1,255	1,244	1,384	1,528	1,384	1,301	1,392	1,945	2,068	2,191
Priv. Sector, incl non-guaranteed	604	525	495	508	647	745	882	1,095	1,697	2,888	4,821
Short-Term Debt	0	0	0	0	0	0	0	864	1,101	1,635	2,560
Memo Items:					*(Millions of US dollars)*						
Int'l Reserves Excluding Gold	341.8	170.1	96.8	121.6	41.1	55.9	405.1	426.5	1,040.2	1,938.3	3,123.2
Gold Holdings (at market price)	49.9	58.7	87.9	154.5	268.2	181.9	180.0	225.0	314.1	780.3	1,004.5
SOCIAL INDICATORS											
Total Fertility Rate	4.0	3.8	3.6	3.5	3.3	3.2	3.0	2.9	2.9	2.9	2.8
Infant Mortality Rate	78.0	74.0	70.0	65.4	60.8	56.2	51.6	47.0	42.4	37.8	33.2
Life Expectancy at Birth	62.4	63.0	63.6	64.3	65.0	65.7	66.4	67.2	67.9	68.7	69.5
Urban Population, % of total	75.2	75.8	76.5	77.1	77.8	78.4	79.0	79.5	80.1	80.6	81.2
Food Prod. per capita (1987=100)	94.8	92.1	83.7	75.0	87.9	92.2	88.5	93.8	89.6	96.7	95.6
Labor Force, Agriculture (%)	23.2	22.5	21.7	21.0	20.4	19.7	19.0	18.3	17.7	17.0	16.5
Labor Force, Female (%)	22.4	22.9	23.4	23.9	24.4	24.8	25.3	25.9	26.3	26.8	27.2
Primary Schl. Enroll. Ratio	107.0	..	..	..	..	118.0	116.0	117.0	118.0	119.0	109.0
Primary Schl. Enroll. Ratio, Female	107.0	..	..	..	..	118.0	116.0	117.0	117.0	118.0	108.0
Secondary Schl. Enroll. Ratio	39.0	..	..	..	..	48.0	49.0	50.0	52.0	55.0	53.0

1981	1982	1983	1984	1985	1986	1987	1988	1989	1990 estimate	Notes	CHILE
											FOREIGN TRADE (CUSTOMS BASIS)
(Millions of current US dollars)											
3,744.8	3,579.0	3,619.6	3,547.2	3,665.0	4,157.5	4,845.2	6,794.2	8,191.0	8,579.0	..	Value of Exports, fob
3,376.9	3,242.1	3,305.2	3,219.1	3,365.8	3,769.9	4,353.4	6,112.8	7,369.5	7,718.6	..	Nonfuel Primary Products
67.4	71.4	59.7	45.4	17.4	2.5	6.8	12.0	14.5	15.2	..	Fuels
300.5	265.5	254.8	282.6	281.8	385.2	485.0	669.4	807.0	845.2	..	Manufactures
6,277.2	3,076.5	2,694.8	3,190.9	2,743.8	2,964.0	3,793.2	4,730.7	6,495.7	7,023.0	..	Value of Imports, cif
954.2	588.5	629.5	597.4	366.2	303.0	372.9	481.1	504.2	545.2	..	Nonfuel Primary Products
917.1	570.5	578.8	591.8	529.0	440.5	467.3	579.9	806.1	871.5	..	Fuels
4,405.9	1,917.5	1,486.5	2,001.6	1,848.6	2,220.5	2,953.1	3,669.7	5,185.4	5,606.3	..	Manufactures
(Index 1987 = 100)											
110.9	102.4	110.2	103.7	101.9	93.4	100.0	120.9	125.7	131.5		Terms of Trade
103.6	90.7	95.7	88.4	85.7	85.3	100.0	132.4	144.5	152.6	..	Export Prices, fob
93.4	88.6	86.8	85.2	84.1	91.3	100.0	109.5	115.0	116.1	..	Import Prices, cif
(Millions of current US dollars)											**BALANCE OF PAYMENTS**
5,614.0	5,154.0	4,831.0	4,636.0	4,669.0	5,349.0	6,492.0	8,451.0	9,857.0	10,542.0		Exports of Goods & Services
3,836.0	3,706.0	3,831.0	3,650.0	3,804.0	4,199.0	5,224.0	7,052.0	8,080.0	8,310.0		Merchandise, fob
1,172.0	936.0	797.0	664.0	664.0	922.0	1,085.0	1,214.0	1,536.0	1,876.0		Nonfactor Services
606.0	512.0	203.0	322.0	201.0	228.0	183.0	185.0	241.0	356.0		Factor Services
10,455.0	7,567.0	6,045.0	6,854.0	6,058.0	6,570.0	7,426.0	8,795.0	10,839.0	11,531.0		Imports of Goods & Services
6,513.0	3,643.0	2,845.0	3,288.0	2,954.0	3,099.0	3,994.0	4,833.0	6,502.0	7,037.0		Merchandise, fob
1,741.0	1,377.0	1,204.0	1,181.0	967.0	1,318.0	1,506.0	1,808.0	2,114.0	2,283.0		Nonfactor Services
2,201.0	2,547.0	1,996.0	2,385.0	2,137.0	2,153.0	1,926.0	2,154.0	2,223.0	2,211.0		Factor Services
1,419.8	1,942.8	1,361.1	1,983.0	1,637.4	1,404.8	1,389.4	1,007.4	1,286.3	1,348.1		Long-Term Interest
36.0	41.0	54.0	47.0	47.0	40.0	65.0	63.0	58.0	54.0	..	Private Current Transfers, net
..	..	..	..	..	..	..	..	..	..		Workers' Remittances
-4,805.0	-2,372.0	-1,160.0	-2,171.0	-1,342.0	-1,181.0	-869.0	-281.0	-924.0	-935.0	..	Curr. A/C Bal before Off. Transf.
72.0	68.0	43.0	60.0	14.0	44.0	61.0	114.0	157.0	145.0	..	Net Official Transfers
-4,733.0	-2,304.0	-1,117.0	-2,111.0	-1,328.0	-1,137.0	-808.0	-167.0	-767.0	-790.0	..	Curr. A/C Bal after Off. Transf.
3,579.0	1,659.0	-3.0	3,516.0	900.0	804.0	833.0	1,310.0	645.0	2,027.0	..	Long-Term Capital, net
362.0	384.0	132.0	67.0	62.0	57.0	97.0	109.0	259.0	587.0	..	Direct Investment
3,400.0	1,428.1	1,048.8	1,207.2	1,120.6	811.0	597.5	1,232.1	671.2	1,506.3	..	Long-Term Loans
5,198.6	2,678.3	1,961.7	1,651.3	1,450.0	1,171.2	937.7	1,686.5	1,503.8	2,251.8	..	Disbursements
1,798.6	1,250.2	912.9	444.1	329.4	360.2	340.2	454.4	832.6	745.5	..	Repayments
-183.0	-153.1	-1,183.8	2,241.8	-282.6	-64.0	138.5	-31.1	-285.2	-66.3	..	Other Long-Term Capital
1,221.0	-513.2	579.0	-1,386.3	329.7	106.1	33.3	-409.5	561.7	1,131.2	..	Other Capital, net
-67.0	1,158.2	541.0	-18.7	98.3	226.9	-58.3	-733.5	-439.7	-2,368.2	..	Change in Reserves
(Chilean Pesos per US dollar)											**Memo Item:**
39.0000	50.9100	78.8400	98.6600	161.0800	193.0200	219.5400	245.0500	267.1600	305.0600	..	Conversion Factor (Annual Avg)
(Millions of US dollars), outstanding at end of year											
15,664	17,315	17,928	19,737	20,384	21,144	21,471	19,580	18,018	19,114	..	**EXTERNAL DEBT (Total)**
12,675	13,977	15,329	17,823	18,716	19,455	19,455	17,378	15,045	15,758	..	Long-Term Debt (by debtor)
1,000	1,177	3,139	4,572	5,314	5,479	4,924	4,076	3,162	2,774	..	Central Bank, incl. IMF credit
982	965	998	3,905	5,887	7,995	9,769	9,219	7,389	7,155	..	Central Government
0	0	0	0	0	0	0	0	0	..	..	Rest of General Government
2,429	3,001	2,964	2,808	2,721	2,495	2,271	1,709	1,559	1,558	..	Non-financial Public Enterprises
8,263	8,834	8,228	6,537	4,793	3,486	2,491	2,374	2,934	4,271	..	Priv. Sector, incl non-guaranteed
2,989	3,338	2,599	1,914	1,668	1,689	2,017	2,202	2,973	3,356	..	Short-Term Debt
(Millions of US dollars)											**Memo Items:**
3,213.3	1,815.0	2,036.3	2,303.2	2,449.9	2,351.3	2,504.2	3,160.5	3,628.6	6,068.5	..	Int'l Reserves Excluding Gold
676.5	782.2	583.3	471.4	500.0	701.7	876.7	748.3	702.6	715.3	..	Gold Holdings (at market price)
											SOCIAL INDICATORS
2.8	2.8	2.8	2.8	2.7	2.7	2.7	2.6	2.6	2.5	..	Total Fertility Rate
28.6	24.0	22.8	21.6	20.5	19.3	18.1	17.6	17.1	16.5	..	Infant Mortality Rate
70.2	71.0	71.1	71.2	71.3	71.4	71.5	71.7	71.8	72.0	..	Life Expectancy at Birth
81.7	82.2	82.8	83.3	83.8	84.2	84.6	85.1	85.5	85.9	..	Urban Population, % of total
101.5	98.8	93.3	96.9	94.9	98.6	100.0	104.6	112.5	114.7	..	Food Prod. per capita (1987=100)
											Labor Force, Agriculture (%)
27.4	27.6	27.7	27.8	28.0	28.1	28.2	28.3	28.4	28.5	..	Labor Force, Female (%)
..	108.0	108.0	107.0	106.0	105.0	103.0	102.0	100.0	98.0	..	Primary Schl. Enroll. Ratio
..	106.0	107.0	106.0	104.0	104.0	..	101.0	99.0	97.0	..	Primary Schl. Enroll. Ratio, Female
..	58.0	63.0	66.0	67.0	68.0	70.0	74.0	75.0	..	..	Secondary Schl. Enroll. Ratio

CHINA	1970	1971	1972	1973	1974	1975	1976	1977	1978	1979	1980
CURRENT GNP PER CAPITA (US $)	130	130	130	150	160	180	170	190	220	260	300
POPULATION (millions)	818	841	862	882	900	916	931	944	956	969	981

USE AND ORIGIN OF RESOURCES *(Billions of current Chinese Yuan)*

	1970	1971	1972	1973	1974	1975	1976	1977	1978	1979	1980
Gross National Product (GNP)	229.5	247.5	254.5	267.1	279.6	298.1	289.0	314.8	358.8	399.8	447.0
Net Factor Income from Abroad	0.0	0.0	0.0	-9.0	0.0	0.0	0.0	0.0	0.0	1.4	0.3
GDP at Market Prices	229.5	247.5	254.5	276.1	279.6	298.1	289.0	314.8	358.8	398.4	446.7
Resource Balance	0.5	2.2	2.6	2.2	-0.4	0.7	1.6	1.8	-0.6	-1.0	0.2
Exports of Goods & NFServices	6.2	7.5	9.1	12.8	15.2	15.6	14.7	15.3	17.7	23.4	30.1
Imports of Goods & NFServices	5.7	5.3	6.5	10.6	15.6	14.9	13.1	13.5	18.3	24.4	29.9
Domestic Absorption	229.0	245.3	251.9	273.9	280.0	297.4	287.4	313.0	359.5	399.3	446.5
Private Consumption, etc.	146.2	154.1	162.9	173.1	178.2	184.4	183.0	197.7	212.3	226.5	265.7
General Gov't Consumption	17.5	19.5	20.0	20.7	20.9	22.5	22.1	24.0	27.3	33.8	36.9
Gross Domestic Investment	65.4	71.7	69.0	80.1	80.9	90.4	82.2	91.2	119.8	139.0	143.8
Fixed Investment	..	..	..	..	..	..	..	..	96.3	100.7	107.4
Indirect Taxes, net	..								..	..	..
GDP at factor cost	..	..	..					..	..		..
Agriculture	78.3	81.2	81.4	89.2	92.7	95.3	95.9	94.1	101.9	125.5	135.8
Industry	88.0	99.3	104.0	112.4	112.8	127.5	122.2	137.7	160.4	176.5	199.2
Manufacturing	67.8	76.7	79.9	85.8	83.3	94.1	86.9	99.5	118.8	131.8	146.4
Services, etc.	63.2	66.9	69.1	74.5	74.1	75.2	70.9	82.9	96.5	96.4	111.7
Gross Domestic Saving	65.9	73.9	71.6	82.3	80.6	91.1	83.8	93.0	119.1	138.0	144.0
Gross National Saving	65.9	73.9	71.6	73.3	80.6	91.1	83.8	93.0	120.2	140.5	145.3

(Billions of 1987 Chinese Yuan)

	1970	1971	1972	1973	1974	1975	1976	1977	1978	1979	1980
Gross National Product	335.04	360.44	372.96	404.04	408.30	442.07	418.20	451.06	507.60	546.16	587.66
GDP at Market Prices	335.05	360.44	372.96	404.04	408.31	442.07	418.17	451.07	507.59	544.18	587.27
Resource Balance	1.01	9.66	9.91	7.05	-1.80	4.67	3.69	0.27	-15.25	-19.90	-20.48
Exports of Goods & NFServices	28.12	33.56	39.53	44.38	42.21	49.38	41.19	40.37	41.70	53.21	65.69
Imports of Goods & NFServices	27.11	23.90	29.62	37.33	44.01	44.71	37.50	40.10	56.95	73.11	86.17
Domestic Absorption	334.04	350.78	363.05	396.99	410.11	437.40	414.47	450.80	522.84	564.07	607.75
Private Consumption, etc.	218.33	222.83	237.43	254.48	265.62	276.56	265.60	286.10	313.28	329.11	371.21
General Gov't Consumption	26.26	29.30	30.12	31.09	31.09	33.46	32.77	34.66	39.14	47.22	49.60
Gross Domestic Investment	89.44	98.65	95.50	111.43	113.39	127.39	116.11	130.03	170.42	187.75	186.94
Fixed Investment	..	..	..	..	..	..	..	..	134.63	135.97	139.57
GDP at factor cost	..	..						..	..		..
Agriculture	156.71	160.20	158.01	171.79	178.67	182.39	184.15	180.20	189.97	202.13	198.49
Industry	99.35	112.82	118.83	129.09	130.39	148.37	142.42	161.99	188.31	203.56	225.75
Manufacturing	69.81	79.38	83.17	89.76	87.81	99.79	92.28	106.73	127.17	152.15	165.96
Services, etc.	78.99	87.41	96.12	103.16	99.25	111.31	91.60	108.88	129.31	138.48	163.03

Memo Items:

	1970	1971	1972	1973	1974	1975	1976	1977	1978	1979	1980
Capacity to Import	29.64	34.06	41.28	45.10	42.93	46.73	42.15	45.35	54.96	70.17	86.75
Terms of Trade Adjustment	1.52	0.50	1.75	0.73	0.72	-2.66	0.96	4.98	13.26	16.96	21.06
Gross Domestic Income	336.57	360.94	374.71	404.77	409.03	439.42	419.13	456.05	520.85	561.14	608.33
Gross National Income	336.56	360.94	374.70	404.76	409.03	439.41	419.16	456.05	520.86	563.12	608.72

DOMESTIC PRICES/DEFLATORS *(Index 1987 = 100)*

	1970	1971	1972	1973	1974	1975	1976	1977	1978	1979	1980
Overall (GDP)	68.5	68.7	68.2	68.3	68.5	67.4	69.1	69.8	70.7	73.2	76.1
Domestic Absorption	68.6	69.9	69.4	69.0	68.3	68.0	69.3	69.4	68.8	70.8	73.5
Agriculture	50.0	50.7	51.5	51.9	51.9	52.2	52.1	52.2	53.6	62.1	68.4
Industry	88.6	88.0	87.5	87.1	86.5	86.0	85.8	85.0	85.2	86.7	88.3
Manufacturing	97.2	96.6	96.0	95.6	94.9	94.3	94.1	93.3	93.5	86.6	88.2
Consumer Price Index	..	..	..	..	..	61.7	61.9	63.5	64.0	65.3	70.1

MANUFACTURING ACTIVITY

	1970	1971	1972	1973	1974	1975	1976	1977	1978	1979	1980
Employment (1987=100)	..	..	..	..	..	..	..	..	..	..	..
Real Earnings per Empl. (1987=100)	..	..	..	..	..	..	..	..	..	..	..
Real Output per Empl. (1987=100)	..	..	..	..	..	..	..	..	..	..	..
Earnings as % of Value Added	..	..	..	..	..	..	..	..	..	..	..

MONETARY HOLDINGS *(Billions of current Chinese Yuan)*

	1970	1971	1972	1973	1974	1975	1976	1977	1978	1979	1980
Money Supply, Broadly Defined	..	..	..	..	..	..	..	85.84	88.97	132.78	167.11
Money	..	..	..	..	..	..	..	58.01	58.04	92.15	114.88
Currency Outside Banks	..	..	..	..	..	..	..	19.54	21.20	26.77	34.62
Demand Deposits	..	..	..	..	..	..	..	38.47	36.84	65.38	80.26
Quasi-Money	..	..	..	..	..	..	..	27.83	30.93	40.63	52.23

GOVERNMENT DEFICIT (-) OR SURPLUS *(Millions of current Chinese Yuan)*

	1970	1971	1972	1973	1974	1975	1976	1977	1978	1979	1980
Current Revenue	..	..	..	..	..	..	..	..	..	..	..
Current Expenditure	..	..	..	..	..	..	..	..	..	..	..
Current Budget Balance	..	..	..	..	..	..	..	..	..	..	..
Capital Receipts	..	..	..	..	..	..	..	..	..	..	..
Capital Payments	..	..	..	..	..	..	..	..	..	..	..

1981	1982	1983	1984	1985	1986	1987	1988	1989	1990 estimate	Notes	CHINA
320	320	320	330	320	300	300	330	350	370	..	**CURRENT GNP PER CAPITA (US $)**
994	1,009	1,023	1,037	1,051	1,067	1,084	1,102	1,119	1,134	..	**POPULATION (millions)**
											USE AND ORIGIN OF RESOURCES
				(Billions of current Chinese Yuan)							
477.3	519.3	580.9	696.2	856.8	969.6	1,130.1	1,398.4	1,578.9	1,740.0	..	Gross National Product (GNP)
0.3	0.4	1.1	2.4	0.8	-0.3	-2.9	-2.6	-6.9	-5.4	..	Net Factor Income from Abroad
477.0	518.9	579.8	693.8	855.9	969.9	1,133.0	1,401.0	1,585.8	1,745.4	f	GDP at Market Prices
4.1	10.9	7.1	3.5	-34.8	-27.7	2.3	-13.1	-10.7	61.6	..	Resource Balance
41.6	47.4	49.3	67.1	89.3	120.4	163.1	192.6	211.8	316.8	..	Exports of Goods & NF Services
37.5	36.5	42.3	63.6	124.1	148.2	160.8	205.7	222.6	255.2	..	Imports of Goods & NF Services
472.9	508.0	572.5	690.3	890.7	997.7	1,130.7	1,414.1	1,596.6	1,683.8	..	Domestic Absorption
294.9	311.4	349.3	405.1	475.5	521.1	592.9	747.3	848.6	858.5	..	Private Consumption, etc.
38.7	42.5	47.2	61.1	71.7	84.8	94.9	111.7	129.1	143.3	..	General Gov't Consumption
139.3	154.1	176.0	224.2	343.6	391.7	443.0	555.2	618.9	682.1	..	Gross Domestic Investment
96.1	123.0	143.0	183.3	254.3	302.0	364.1	449.7	413.8	445.1	..	Fixed Investment
..	..	..	..	..	..	..	..	..	..		Indirect Taxes, net
										B f	GDP at factor cost
154.6	175.9	195.9	229.0	254.2	276.4	321.8	383.9	425.0	480.0	..	Agriculture
205.1	216.4	236.4	278.2	344.9	396.7	460.0	578.6	659.7	726.1	..	Industry
148.7	157.3	170.5	204.2	255.3	316.6	368.0	476.8	548.2	662.2	..	Manufacturing
117.3	126.6	147.5	186.6	256.8	296.8	351.2	438.5	501.1	539.3	..	Services, etc.
143.4	165.1	183.3	227.7	308.8	364.0	445.3	542.1	608.2	743.7	..	Gross Domestic Saving
144.5	166.5	185.3	230.8	310.1	364.6	443.2	541.0	602.1	739.2	..	Gross National Saving
				(Billions of 1987 Chinese Yuan)							
614.09	667.53	736.29	843.42	944.48	1,021.43	1,130.10	1,240.86	1,279.95	1,338.79	..	Gross National Product
613.75	667.04	734.51	840.56	943.60	1,021.75	1,133.04	1,243.17	1,285.65	1,343.13	f	GDP at Market Prices
-12.87	2.51	0.15	-3.20	-43.84	-18.84	2.26	-12.93	-27.45	21.26	..	Resource Balance
80.50	86.68	86.94	101.43	111.32	138.29	163.11	188.15	198.11	216.84	..	Exports of Goods & NF Services
93.37	84.16	86.79	104.63	155.16	157.13	160.85	201.08	225.56	195.57	..	Imports of Goods & NF Services
626.61	664.53	734.36	843.76	987.44	1,040.58	1,130.78	1,256.11	1,313.10	1,321.87	..	Domestic Absorption
398.56	412.87	453.19	500.76	533.85	543.08	592.92	659.58	697.88	670.34	..	Private Consumption, etc.
50.89	55.80	60.62	74.40	76.62	86.19	94.91	98.98	106.26	117.10	..	General Gov't Consumption
177.17	195.86	220.55	268.60	376.98	411.31	443.00	497.55	508.97	534.42	..	Gross Domestic Investment
122.23	156.35	179.19	219.61	279.05	317.07	364.09	402.99	340.28	348.75	..	Fixed Investment
										B f	GDP at factor cost
212.58	237.46	257.64	291.13	296.08	307.03	321.78	332.07	343.03	366.70	..	Agriculture
229.59	243.37	267.21	307.03	367.21	402.46	460.01	555.24	597.43	647.02	..	Industry
166.50	176.95	192.71	225.45	271.78	321.22	368.01	457.64	499.78	537.12	..	Manufacturing
171.57	186.22	209.66	242.40	280.31	312.26	351.25	355.87	345.19	329.42	..	Services, etc.
											Memo Items:
103.55	109.41	101.33	110.43	111.67	127.75	163.11	188.27	214.69	242.75	..	Capacity to Import
23.04	22.73	14.39	9.00	0.35	-10.54	0.00	0.12	16.58	25.92	..	Terms of Trade Adjustment
636.79	689.78	748.90	849.57	943.95	1,011.21	1,133.04	1,243.30	1,302.23	1,369.05	..	Gross Domestic Income
637.13	690.26	750.67	852.43	944.83	1,010.89	1,130.10	1,240.98	1,296.52	1,364.71	..	Gross National Income
											DOMESTIC PRICES/DEFLATORS
				(Index 1987 = 100)							
77.7	77.8	78.9	82.5	90.7	94.9	100.0	112.7	123.3	130.0	..	Overall (GDP)
75.5	76.4	78.0	81.8	90.2	95.9	100.0	112.6	121.6	127.4	..	Domestic Absorption
72.7	74.1	76.0	78.6	85.9	90.0	100.0	115.6	123.9	130.9	..	Agriculture
89.3	88.9	88.5	90.6	93.9	98.6	100.0	104.2	110.4	112.2	..	Industry
89.3	88.9	88.5	90.6	93.9	98.6	100.0	104.2	109.7	123.3	..	Manufacturing
71.9	73.4	74.8	76.8	85.9	91.9	100.0	120.7	140.4	..	..	Consumer Price Index
											MANUFACTURING ACTIVITY
..	..	..	..	..	..	..	..	..	..		Employment (1987=100)
..	..	..	..	..	..	..	..	..	..		Real Earnings per Empl. (1987=100)
..	..	..	..	..	..	..	..	..	..		Real Output per Empl. (1987=100)
..	..	..		13.3	14.5	..	..	..	..		Earnings as % of Value Added
				(Billions of current Chinese Yuan)							**MONETARY HOLDINGS**
197.77	226.57	271.28	359.85	487.49	634.86	795.74	960.21	1,139.31	1,468.19	..	Money Supply, Broadly Defined
134.52	148.84	174.89	244.94	301.73	385.90	457.40	548.74	583.42	700.95	..	Money
39.63	43.91	52.98	79.21	98.78	121.84	145.45	213.26	234.21	264.12	..	Currency Outside Banks
94.89	104.93	121.91	165.73	202.95	264.06	311.95	335.48	349.21	436.83	..	Demand Deposits
63.25	77.73	96.39	114.91	185.76	248.96	338.34	411.47	555.89	767.24	..	Quasi-Money
				(Millions of current Chinese Yuan)							
											GOVERNMENT DEFICIT (-) OR SURPLUS
..	..	..	..	..	..	..	..	..	..	..	Current Revenue
..	..	..	..	..	..	..	..	..	..	..	Current Expenditure
..	..	..	..	..	..	..	..	..	..	..	Current Budget Balance
..	..	..	..	..	..	..	..	..	..	..	Capital Receipts
..	..	..	..	..	..	..	..	..	..	..	Capital Payments

CHINA	1970	1971	1972	1973	1974	1975	1976	1977	1978	1979	1980
FOREIGN TRADE (CUSTOMS BASIS)					*(Millions of current US dollars)*						
Value of Exports, fob	2,307	2,783	3,692	5,876	7,108	7,689	6,943	7,520	9,955	13,614	18,099
Nonfuel Primary Products	495	597	792	1,260	1,525	1,649	1,489	1,613	2,135	2,920	3,882
Fuels	188	227	301	479	579	627	566	613	811	1,110	1,475
Manufactures	1,624	1,959	2,600	4,137	5,004	5,413	4,888	5,294	7,008	9,584	12,742
Value of Imports, cif	2,279	2,128	2,851	5,208	7,791	7,926	6,660	7,148	11,131	15,621	19,941
Nonfuel Primary Products	382	357	477	872	1,305	1,327	1,116	1,197	1,864	2,616	3,340
Fuels	28	26	35	64	95	97	82	88	136	191	244
Manufactures	1,869	1,746	2,338	4,272	6,391	6,501	5,463	5,863	9,130	12,813	16,357
					(Index 1987 = 100)						
Terms of Trade	113.0	114.4	124.8	121.2	116.8	108.1	111.2	117.7	108.2	108.0	115.4
Export Prices, fob	34.0	35.9	42.5	59.2	68.6	61.2	65.1	70.7	73.3	86.0	102.5
Import Prices, cif	30.1	31.4	34.0	48.8	58.7	56.6	58.5	60.0	67.8	79.6	88.8
BALANCE OF PAYMENTS					*(Millions of current US dollars)*						
Exports of Goods & Services	..	..	..	..	..	..	..	8,770	10,749	15,353	20,597
Merchandise, fob	2,309	2,803	3,652	5,677	7,108	7,689	6,943	8,050	9,750	13,660	18,188
Nonfactor Services	128	81	132	103	128	139	440	500	763	1,388	1,897
Factor Services	..	..	..	..	..	..	..	220	236	305	512
Imports of Goods & Services	..	..	..	..	..	..	..	8,286	11,134	16,030	20,267
Merchandise, fob	2,280	2,144	2,819	5,031	7,791	7,926	6,660	7,627	9,986	14,379	18,294
Nonfactor Services	238	862	1,099	220	168	171	465	521	904	1,301	1,656
Factor Services	..	..	..	..	..	..	..	138	244	350	317
Long-Term Interest	0	0	0	0	0	0	0	0	0	61	317
Private Current Transfers, net	0	0	0	0	0	0	0	0	597	656	640
Workers' Remittances	..	..	..	..	..	..	..	..	597	656	640
Curr. A/C Bal before Off. Transf.	-81	-122	-134	529	-723	-269	258	484	212	-21	970
Net Official Transfers	0	0	0	0	0	0	0	-70	0	-30	-70
Curr. A/C Bal after Off. Transf.	-81	-122	-134	529	-723	-269	258	414	212	-51	900
Long-Term Capital, net	..	..	..	..	..	..	..	-990	-830	822	1,830
Direct Investment									..	..	57
Long-Term Loans	0	0	0	0	0	0	0	0	583	1,779	1,927
Disbursements	0	0	0	0	0	0	0	0	583	1,779	2,539
Repayments	0	0	0	0	0	0	0	0	0	0	613
Other Long-Term Capital	..	..	..	..	..	..	..	-990	-1,413	-957	-154
Other Capital, net	..	..	..	..	..	..	..	670	-130	-168	-2,063
Change in Reserves	..	..	..	..	..	..	..	-94	748	-603	-667
Memo Item:					*(Chinese Yuan per US dollar)*						
Conversion Factor (Annual Avg)	2.460	2.460	2.250	1.990	1.960	1.860	1.940	1.860	1.680	1.550	1.500
EXTERNAL DEBT (Total)	0	0	0	0	*(Millions of US dollars), outstanding at end of year*						
EXTERNAL DEBT (Total)	0	0	0	0	0	0	0	0	623	2,183	4,504
Long-Term Debt (by debtor)	0	0	0	0	0	0	0	0	623	2,183	4,504
Central Bank, incl. IMF credit	0	0	0	0	0	0	0	0	0	76	363
Central Government	0	0	0	0	0	0	0	0	27	226	576
Rest of General Government	0	0	0	0	0	0	0	0	0	0	0
Non-financial Public Enterprises	0	0	0	0	0	0	0	0	596	1,861	3,406
Priv. Sector, incl non-guaranteed	0	0	0	0	0	0	0	0	0	19	160
Short-Term Debt	0	0	0	0	0	0	0	0	0	0	0
Memo Items:					*(Millions of US dollars)*						
Int'l Reserves Excluding Gold	..	..	..	..	..	..	..	2,345.0	1,557.0	2,154.0	2,545.0
Gold Holdings (at market price)	..	..	..	..	..	..	..	2,111.0	2,893.0	6,554.0	7,546.0
SOCIAL INDICATORS											
Total Fertility Rate	5.8	5.1	4.9	4.4	3.8	3.4	2.9	2.7	2.6	2.3	2.5
Infant Mortality Rate	69.0	66.0	61.0	56.0	51.0	46.0	41.0	39.0	38.0	43.0	41.0
Life Expectancy at Birth	61.7	62.5	63.2	63.8	64.3	64.8	65.2	65.6	66.1	66.5	66.9
Urban Population, % of total	17.5	17.4	17.3	17.2	17.2	17.3	17.4	17.5	17.8	18.5	19.2
Food Prod. per capita (1987=100)	68.1	69.6	67.7	71.4	70.1	70.7	69.3	68.4	73.7	77.8	77.7
Labor Force, Agriculture (%)	78.3	77.9	77.5	77.0	76.7	76.3	75.8	75.4	75.0	74.6	74.2
Labor Force, Female (%)	41.7	41.8	42.0	42.1	42.3	42.4	42.6	42.7	42.9	43.0	43.2
Primary Schl. Enroll. Ratio	89.0	..	..	..	..	126.0	..	106.0	124.0	122.0	112.0
Primary Schl. Enroll. Ratio, Female	..	..	..	..	..	115.0	..	..	114.0	112.0	103.0
Secondary Schl. Enroll. Ratio	24.0	..	..	..	..	47.0	..	83.0	63.0	56.0	46.0

1981	1982	1983	1984	1985	1986	1987	1988	1989	1990 estimate	Notes	CHINA
											FOREIGN TRADE (CUSTOMS BASIS)
				(Millions of current US dollars)							
21,566	21,892	22,185	24,871	27,555	31,447	39,437	47,516	52,538	62,063	..	Value of Exports, fob
4,626	4,695	4,758	5,766	5,910	6,745	9,301	11,268	11,268	11,318	..	Nonfuel Primary Products
1,758	1,784	1,808	5,726	2,246	2,563	4,518	3,918	4,282	5,159	..	Fuels
15,183	15,412	15,618	13,380	19,399	22,139	25,619	32,329	36,987	45,586	..	Manufactures
21,572	18,901	21,349	26,185	42,895	43,411	43,216	55,268	59,140	53,345	..	Value of Imports, cif
3,613	3,166	4,757	5,834	7,185	7,271	7,238	10,430	11,478	9,228	..	Nonfuel Primary Products
264	231	108	132	525	531	529	775	1,647	1,269	..	Fuels
17,695	15,504	16,485	20,219	35,185	35,609	35,448	44,063	46,015	42,848	..	Manufactures
				(Index 1987 = 100)							
119.5	121.4	111.7	113.8	109.3	96.8	100.0	96.5	104.4	110.6	..	Terms of Trade
103.6	97.1	92.1	92.2	87.9	88.3	100.0	107.5	112.2	130.1	..	Export Prices, fob
86.7	80.0	82.5	81.0	80.4	91.2	100.0	111.4	107.4	117.6	..	Import Prices, cif
				(Millions of current US dollars)							**BALANCE OF PAYMENTS**
25,110	26,083	26,505	30,948	31,883	35,869	44,850	53,257	57,649	67,771	f	Exports of Goods & Services
22,010	22,330	22,230	26,129	27,350	30,942	39,437	47,518	52,537	62,063	..	Merchandise, fob
2,403	2,736	2,747	2,801	3,060	3,941	4,386	4,235	3,750	4,157	..	Nonfactor Services
697	1,017	1,528	2,018	1,473	986	1,027	1,504	1,362	1,551	..	Factor Services
22,551	20,103	22,212	28,407	43,448	43,982	45,033	57,478	62,347	56,501	f	Imports of Goods & Services
20,185	17,680	19,616	25,135	38,745	39,343	39,629	50,687	54,231	48,922	..	Merchandise, fob
1,827	1,600	1,775	2,275	3,507	3,561	3,587	4,588	4,909	4,428	..	Nonfactor Services
539	823	821	997	1,196	1,078	1,817	2,203	3,207	3,151	..	Factor Services
518	541	523	610	586	644	1,125	1,610	2,508	2,534	..	Long-Term Interest
464	530	436	305	171	255	249	416	238	195	..	Private Current Transfers, net
464	541	446	317	180	208	166	129	76	108	..	Workers' Remittances
3,023	6,510	4,729	2,846	-11,394	-7,858	66	-3,805	-4,460	11,935	..	Curr. A/C Bal before Off. Transf.
108	-44	75	137	72	124	-25	3	143	65	..	Net Official Transfers
3,131	6,466	4,804	2,983	-11,322	-7,734	41	-3,802	-4,317	12,000	..	Curr. A/C Bal after Off. Transf.
523	453	1,097	1,471	4,264	6,934	5,815	7,053	3,212	3,900	f	Long-Term Capital, net
265	386	543	1,124	1,031	1,425	1,669	2,344	2,613	2,613	..	Direct Investment
596	535	986	1,071	4,006	4,851	6,131	6,781	6,023	6,249	..	Long-Term Loans
1,800	1,838	2,375	2,357	5,302	6,725	8,047	9,130	8,424	9,620	..	Disbursements
1,204	1,302	1,389	1,287	1,297	1,874	1,916	2,349	2,401	3,371	..	Repayments
-338	-468	-432	-724	-773	658	-1,985	-2,072	-5,424	-4,962	..	Other Long-Term Capital
-1,447	-828	-2,334	-3,247	1,770	-1,345	-1,630	-1,588	-625	-4,330	f	Other Capital, net
-2,207	-6,091	-3,567	-1,207	5,288	2,145	-4,226	-1,663	1,730	-11,570	..	Change in Reserves
				(Chinese Yuan per US dollar)							**Memo Item:**
1.700	1.890	1.980	2.320	2.940	3.450	3.720	3.720	3.760	4.780	..	Conversion Factor (Annual Avg)
				(Millions of US dollars), outstanding at end of year							
5,797	8,358	9,609	12,082	16,722	23,746	35,303	42,406	44,847	52,555	..	**EXTERNAL DEBT (Total)**
5,797	6,058	5,625	6,482	10,303	17,670	27,082	33,600	37,940	45,788	..	Long-Term Debt (by debtor)
1,461	1,533	1,149	1,287	3,178	5,727	10,141	13,820	15,772	18,914	..	Central Bank, incl. IMF credit
989	1,575	2,105	2,583	4,344	6,195	8,258	8,797	9,007	10,714	..	Central Government
0	0	0	1	12	35	43	37	35	37	..	Rest of General Government
3,163	2,781	2,065	2,382	1,961	3,401	5,969	8,448	10,882	14,013	..	Non-financial Public Enterprises
185	169	307	229	808	2,312	2,671	2,498	2,244	2,111	..	Priv. Sector, incl non-guaranteed
0	2,300	3,984	5,600	6,419	6,076	8,221	8,806	6,907	6,766	..	Short-Term Debt
				(Millions of US dollars)							**Memo Items:**
5,058.0	11,349.0	14,987.0	17,366.0	12,728.0	11,453.0	16,305.0	18,541.0	17,960.0	29,586.0	..	Int'l Reserves Excluding Gold
5,048.0	5,803.0	4,845.0	3,915.0	4,153.0	4,964.0	6,148.0	5,210.0	5,093.0	4,890.0	..	Gold Holdings (at market price)
											SOCIAL INDICATORS
3.0	2.3	2.3	2.2	2.4	2.5	2.6	2.6	2.5	2.5	..	Total Fertility Rate
41.0	39.0	37.6	36.2	34.8	33.4	32.0	31.0	29.9	28.9	..	Infant Mortality Rate
67.4	67.8	68.1	68.5	68.8	69.1	69.5	69.7	69.9	70.2	..	Life Expectancy at Birth
19.4	20.2	23.5	31.9	36.6	41.4	46.6	49.6	52.8	56.2	..	Urban Population, % of total
78.9	84.1	88.7	94.1	94.5	97.4	100.0	100.8	102.7	108.2	..	Food Prod. per capita (1987=100)
..	..	..	..	..	..	..	..	..	..	..	Labor Force, Agriculture (%)
43.2	43.2	43.2	43.2	43.2	43.2	43.2	43.2	43.2	43.2	..	Labor Force, Female (%)
..	112.0	113.0	118.0	124.0	129.0	132.0	134.0	135.0	..	..	Primary Schl. Enroll. Ratio
106.0	101.0	102.0	107.0	114.0	120.0	124.0	126.0	128.0	..	..	Primary Schl. Enroll. Ratio, Female
..	36.0	35.0	37.0	39.0	42.0	43.0	44.0	44.0	..	..	Secondary Schl. Enroll. Ratio

COLOMBIA	1970	1971	1972	1973	1974	1975	1976	1977	1978	1979	1980
CURRENT GNP PER CAPITA (US $)	340	360	390	430	500	550	610	690	850	1,030	1,190
POPULATION (thousands)	21,360	21,871	22,350	22,812	23,282	23,776	24,291	24,828	25,384	25,951	26,525

USE AND ORIGIN OF RESOURCES
(Billions of current Colombian Pesos)

	1970	1971	1972	1973	1974	1975	1976	1977	1978	1979	1980
Gross National Product (GNP)	129	152	185	238	317	397	521	708	902	1,182	1,568
Net Factor Income from Abroad	-3	-4	-4	-5	-5	-8	-11	-8	-8	-7	-11
GDP at Market Prices	133	156	190	243	322	405	532	716	909	1,189	1,579
Resource Balance	-2	-6	-1	2	-4	7	17	26	26	21	10
Exports of Goods & NFServices	19	20	27	37	47	64	91	121	151	181	256
Imports of Goods & NFServices	21	26	28	35	50	57	74	95	125	160	246
Domestic Absorption	135	162	190	241	326	398	515	690	884	1,168	1,569
Private Consumption, etc.	96	115	138	173	229	293	378	500	640	841	1,109
General Gov't Consumption	12	17	18	23	28	36	44	55	78	111	159
Gross Domestic Investment	27	30	34	44	69	69	93	134	166	216	301
Fixed Investment	24	27	30	38	53	62	85	104	140	183	265
Indirect Taxes, net	10	11	13	17	22	32	50	75	99	123	158
GDP at factor cost	123	145	177	227	300	373	483	641	810	1,066	1,421
Agriculture	33	37	46	59	79	97	126	179	210	255	306
Industry	37	43	55	74	98	118	164	217	273	351	499
Manufacturing	27	32	41	55	75	94	129	171	211	267	367
Services, etc.	63	76	89	110	146	190	242	320	427	583	775
Gross Domestic Saving	24	24	33	47	66	76	110	161	192	237	311
Gross National Saving	21	20	29	42	61	69	101	154	186	234	307

(Billions of 1987 Colombian Pesos)

	1970	1971	1972	1973	1974	1975	1976	1977	1978	1979	1980
Gross National Product	4,036.8	4,289.1	4,615.9	4,933.3	5,246.4	5,335.1	5,582.3	5,852.1	6,355.3	6,728.0	7,029.2
GDP at Market Prices	4,126.6	4,373.6	4,707.8	5,024.0	5,312.1	5,425.5	5,683.9	5,916.1	6,415.8	6,761.9	7,041.1
Resource Balance	-41.5	-109.2	9.9	17.0	-7.6	171.9	68.3	-36.0	-10.3	60.0	-66.3
Exports of Goods & NFServices	607.8	638.3	721.7	742.6	702.5	803.9	778.3	743.3	930.3	1,008.1	1,059.5
Imports of Goods & NFServices	649.3	747.4	711.8	725.6	710.1	632.1	710.0	779.2	940.7	948.0	1,125.8
Domestic Absorption	4,168.1	4,482.8	4,697.9	5,007.0	5,319.8	5,253.7	5,615.6	5,952.0	6,426.2	6,701.9	7,107.3
Private Consumption, etc.	2,867.8	3,050.7	3,310.8	3,489.3	3,602.9	3,754.8	4,002.6	4,131.9	4,468.9	4,681.5	4,856.2
General Gov't Consumption	347.1	438.1	417.4	459.9	449.4	459.8	477.2	499.8	545.6	613.2	690.9
Gross Domestic Investment	953.2	993.9	969.7	1,057.8	1,267.5	1,039.1	1,135.8	1,320.3	1,411.6	1,407.2	1,560.2
Fixed Investment	806.0	845.1	828.5	900.5	978.7	941.2	1,030.8	1,038.0	1,135.0	1,178.3	1,333.5
GDP at factor cost	3,772.6	4,004.9	4,340.4	4,671.8	4,896.2	4,994.8	5,208.9	5,404.5	5,740.5	5,987.0	6,317.5
Agriculture	878.9	886.1	955.3	977.9	1,032.2	1,088.6	1,125.2	1,162.0	1,256.3	1,317.1	1,346.3
Industry	1,338.0	1,432.8	1,576.7	1,728.7	1,820.4	1,822.9	1,903.7	1,931.7	2,078.8	2,188.7	2,266.6
Manufacturing	841.1	912.8	1,010.6	1,096.9	1,188.2	1,202.9	1,255.7	1,273.8	1,400.8	1,486.4	1,504.5
Services, etc.	1,909.7	2,054.7	2,175.8	2,317.4	2,459.6	2,514.0	2,655.1	2,822.4	3,080.8	3,256.1	3,428.2

Memo Items:

	1970	1971	1972	1973	1974	1975	1976	1977	1978	1979	1980
Capacity to Import	572.3	566.5	689.2	777.0	660.6	713.5	871.0	995.7	1,133.4	1,072.9	1,170.6
Terms of Trade Adjustment	-35.5	-71.8	-32.5	34.4	-41.9	-90.4	92.7	252.4	203.0	64.9	111.1
Gross Domestic Income	4,091.1	4,301.9	4,675.3	5,058.4	5,270.2	5,335.1	5,776.7	6,168.5	6,618.9	6,826.8	7,152.1
Gross National Income	4,001.3	4,217.3	4,583.4	4,967.7	5,204.5	5,244.7	5,675.0	6,104.5	6,558.3	6,792.9	7,140.3

DOMESTIC PRICES/DEFLATORS
(Index 1987 = 100)

	1970	1971	1972	1973	1974	1975	1976	1977	1978	1979	1980
Overall (GDP)	3.2	3.6	4.0	4.8	6.1	7.5	9.4	12.1	14.2	17.6	22.4
Domestic Absorption	3.2	3.6	4.1	4.8	6.1	7.6	9.2	11.6	13.8	17.4	22.1
Agriculture	3.8	4.1	4.8	6.0	7.6	8.9	11.2	15.4	16.7	19.4	22.7
Industry	2.7	3.0	3.5	4.3	5.4	6.5	8.6	11.2	13.1	16.0	22.0
Manufacturing	3.3	3.5	4.0	5.0	6.3	7.8	10.2	13.4	15.1	18.0	24.4
Consumer Price Index	3.7	4.0	4.5	5.5	6.8	8.4	10.1	13.4	15.8	19.7	24.9

MANUFACTURING ACTIVITY

	1970	1971	1972	1973	1974	1975	1976	1977	1978	1979	1980
Employment (1987=100)	71.2	73.3	79.5	87.7	92.8	94.7	97.4	100.9	103.6	107.0	106.9
Real Earnings per Empl. (1987=100)	89.9	94.3	92.0	84.1	81.6	80.0	82.3	80.5	95.8	92.2	87.6
Real Output per Empl. (1987=100)	59.7	65.2	64.2	61.6	67.7	63.9	63.5	60.3	66.1	73.0	69.6
Earnings as % of Value Added	24.9	24.0	23.3	23.0	19.9	20.6	19.8	19.6	22.4	19.7	18.4

MONETARY HOLDINGS
(Billions of current Colombian Pesos)

	1970	1971	1972	1973	1974	1975	1976	1977	1978	1979	1980
Money Supply, Broadly Defined	28.9	32.0	40.2	53.1	65.6	97.4	135.1	181.8	240.0	301.5	447.2
Money	22.4	25.1	31.9	41.6	49.1	58.9	79.4	103.5	132.9	165.9	212.4
Currency Outside Banks	..	..	..	..	..	..	..	..	53.7	67.3	84.1
Demand Deposits	..	..	..	..	..	..	..	..	79.2	98.6	128.3
Quasi-Money	6.5	7.0	8.4	11.4	16.5	38.5	55.8	78.3	107.1	135.6	234.8

GOVERNMENT DEFICIT (-) OR SURPLUS
(Billions of current Colombian Pesos)

	1970	1971	1972	1973	1974	1975	1976	1977	1978	1979	1980
	..	-2.5	-4.7	-5.6	-4.1	-0.9	5.3	4.5	6.2	-9.2	-27.8
Current Revenue	..	17.3	20.1	25.2	34.2	51.3	63.6	84.0	110.8	139.0	189.4
Current Expenditure	..	11.5	13.3	14.7	22.3	34.5	38.3	51.7	74.2	124.3	164.9
Current Budget Balance	..	5.8	6.8	10.5	11.9	16.8	25.3	32.3	36.6	14.7	24.5
Capital Receipts	..	..	..	..	..	..	..	0.1	0.1	..	0.1
Capital Payments	..	8.3	11.5	16.1	16.0	17.7	20.0	27.9	30.5	23.9	52.4

1981	1982	1983	1984	1985	1986	1987	1988	1989	1990 estimate	Notes	COLOMBIA
1,330	1,390	1,390	1,380	1,270	1,230	1,200	1,220	1,230	1,260	..	**CURRENT GNP PER CAPITA (US $)**
27,107	27,699	28,295	28,891	29,481	30,066	30,646	31,219	31,785	32,345	..	**POPULATION (thousands)**

USE AND ORIGIN OF RESOURCES

(Billions of current Colombian Pesos)

1981	1982	1983	1984	1985	1986	1987	1988	1989	1990 est.	Notes	
1,960	2,446	2,978	3,728	4,760	6,486	8,395	11,246	14,329	19,459	..	Gross National Product (GNP)
-22	-51	-76	-128	-206	-302	-429	-486	-860	-1,196	..	Net Factor Income from Abroad
1,983	2,497	3,054	3,857	4,966	6,788	8,824	11,731	15,189	20,654	..	GDP at Market Prices
-71	-107	-85	-22	64	465	356	285	648	1,311	..	Resource Balance
235	273	319	458	686	1,279	1,496	1,911	2,711	4,131	..	Exports of Goods & NF Services
306	379	404	481	622	814	1,140	1,626	2,063	2,820	..	Imports of Goods & NF Services
2,053	2,604	3,139	3,879	4,902	6,323	8,468	11,446	14,541	19,344	..	Domestic Absorption
1,438	1,820	2,197	2,722	3,425	4,436	5,835	7,684	9,862	13,322	..	Private Consumption, etc.
207	273	335	426	531	666	868	1,182	1,573	2,071	..	General Gov't Consumption
409	512	608	731	946	1,222	1,765	2,580	3,107	3,951	..	Gross Domestic Investment
350	436	525	654	870	1,204	1,537	2,288	2,894	3,674	..	Fixed Investment
167	215	254	361	517	799	1,033	1,278	..	..	..	Indirect Taxes, net
1,815	2,283	2,800	3,496	4,449	5,989	7,791	10,453	..	..	B	GDP at factor cost
382	469	572	671	844	1,186	1,594	1,965	2,454	3,454	..	Agriculture
607	771	962	1,283	1,718	2,455	3,066	4,254	5,639	6,576	..	Industry
423	530	641	853	1,080	1,526	1,793	2,482	3,128	4,332	..	Manufacturing
994	1,257	1,520	1,902	2,404	3,146	4,164	5,513	7,096	10,625	..	Services, etc.
338	405	523	709	1,009	1,687	2,121	2,865	3,755	5,262	..	Gross Domestic Saving
329	365	458	610	868	1,540	1,936	2,671	3,244	4,575	..	Gross National Saving

(Billions of 1987 Colombian Pesos)

1981	1982	1983	1984	1985	1986	1987	1988	1989	1990 est.	Notes	
7,135.7	7,135.2	7,220.1	7,416.0	7,480.4	7,958.5	8,394.9	8,816.6	9,015.6	9,380.7	..	Gross National Product
7,190.9	7,262.2	7,378.4	7,641.0	7,892.0	8,374.3	8,824.3	9,185.2	9,482.3	9,877.1	..	GDP at Market Prices
-246.8	-355.4	-247.9	-108.1	109.8	305.6	355.9	285.0	483.0	707.6	..	Resource Balance
934.2	919.6	911.4	1,005.3	1,149.6	1,387.6	1,495.7	1,499.5	1,636.2	1,932.3	..	Exports of Goods & NF Services
1,180.9	1,275.0	1,159.3	1,113.4	1,039.8	1,082.0	1,139.8	1,214.5	1,153.2	1,224.7	..	Imports of Goods & NF Services
7,437.7	7,617.6	7,626.4	7,749.1	7,782.1	8,068.7	8,468.4	8,900.2	8,999.3	9,169.4	..	Domestic Absorption
4,954.4	5,006.8	5,060.0	5,259.4	5,422.7	5,630.6	5,835.4	6,040.3	6,215.6	6,359.5	..	Private Consumption, etc.
716.6	749.9	745.4	776.1	811.1	822.4	868.4	953.9	992.3	1,037.0	..	General Gov't Consumption
1,766.7	1,860.9	1,820.9	1,713.6	1,548.4	1,615.7	1,764.6	1,906.0	1,791.3	1,772.9	..	Gross Domestic Investment
1,417.1	1,459.0	1,476.2	1,494.6	1,416.5	1,524.8	1,537.2	1,704.4	1,688.9	1,670.3	..	Fixed Investment
6,486.8	6,525.6	6,647.7	6,852.9	7,065.2	7,386.9	7,791.3	8,177.1	..	..	B	GDP at factor cost
1,389.4	1,363.1	1,401.3	1,425.9	1,449.4	1,498.3	1,594.0	1,638.1	1,712.2	1,826.9	..	Agriculture
2,246.1	2,237.0	2,313.0	2,472.1	2,619.6	2,890.0	3,066.3	3,181.4	3,311.8	3,478.8	..	Industry
1,464.7	1,443.6	1,460.1	1,547.5	1,593.2	1,688.0	1,792.9	1,826.9	1,880.2	2,004.3	..	Manufacturing
3,555.4	3,662.1	3,664.1	3,742.9	3,823.0	3,986.0	4,164.0	4,365.6	4,458.3	4,571.3	..	Services, etc.

Memo Items:

1981	1982	1983	1984	1985	1986	1987	1988	1989	1990 est.	Notes	
907.7	916.0	915.8	1,061.7	1,146.2	1,699.5	1,495.7	1,427.4	1,515.4	1,793.8	..	Capacity to Import
-26.4	-3.6	4.4	56.4	-3.4	311.8	0.0	-72.1	-120.8	-138.5	..	Terms of Trade Adjustment
7,164.4	7,258.6	7,382.9	7,697.4	7,888.6	8,686.2	8,824.3	9,113.1	9,361.5	9,738.6	..	Gross Domestic Income
7,109.3	7,131.6	7,224.6	7,472.4	7,477.0	8,270.3	8,394.9	8,744.5	8,894.8	9,242.2	..	Gross National Income

DOMESTIC PRICES/DEFLATORS

(Index 1987 = 100)

1981	1982	1983	1984	1985	1986	1987	1988	1989	1990 est.	Notes	
27.6	34.4	41.4	50.5	62.9	81.1	100.0	127.7	160.2	209.1	..	Overall (GDP)
27.6	34.2	41.2	50.1	63.0	78.4	100.0	128.6	161.6	211.0	..	Domestic Absorption
27.5	34.4	40.8	47.1	58.2	79.2	100.0	119.9	143.3	189.0	..	Agriculture
27.0	34.5	41.6	51.9	65.6	85.0	100.0	133.7	170.3	189.0	..	Industry
28.9	36.7	43.9	55.1	67.8	90.4	100.0	135.9	166.4	216.1	..	Manufacturing
31.7	39.5	47.4	55.0	68.2	81.1	100.0	128.1	161.2	208.2	..	Consumer Price Index

MANUFACTURING ACTIVITY

1981	1982	1983	1984	1985	1986	1987	1988	1989	1990 est.	Notes	
103.8	101.2	97.8	95.7	92.6	94.6	100.0	99.5	..	..	..	Employment (1987=100)
88.7	90.7	95.0	102.7	101.5	101.5	100.0	100.6	..	..	..	Real Earnings per Empl. (1987=100)
73.7	70.8	74.8	79.8	89.1	88.1	100.0	105.3	..	..	..	Real Output per Empl. (1987=100)
19.0	20.5	21.0	19.9	17.9	15.9	16.6	14.7	..	..	..	Earnings as % of Value Added

MONETARY HOLDINGS

(Billions of current Colombian Pesos)

1981	1982	1983	1984	1985	1986	1987	1988	1989	1990 est.	Notes	
615.3	773.9	1,010.3	1,243.7	1,495.3	..	1,815.3	2,198.4	..	..	D	Money Supply, Broadly Defined
256.4	321.4	396.7	492.4	545.3	..	1,019.6	1,282.0	..	..	..	Money
101.6	130.3	167.7	211.7	186.7	..	418.8	530.7	..	..	..	Currency Outside Banks
154.7	191.1	229.1	280.7	358.5	..	600.7	751.4	..	..	..	Demand Deposits
359.0	452.5	613.6	751.3	950.1	..	795.7	916.4	..	..	..	Quasi-Money

(Billions of current Colombian Pesos)

1981	1982	1983	1984	1985	1986	1987	1988	1989	1990 est.	Notes	
-60.4	-118.1	-127.9	-166.5	-158.2	-107.4	-61.0	-156.3	-286.7	..	F	**GOVERNMENT DEFICIT (-) OR SURPLUS**
229.2	283.4	347.9	428.6	587.1	828.7	1,138.7	1,505.1	1,944.4	..	..	Current Revenue
218.0	302.7	381.0	506.5	567.9	730.9	975.0	1,315.8	1,800.4	..	..	Current Expenditure
11.2	-19.3	-33.1	-77.9	19.2	97.8	163.7	189.3	144.0	..	..	Current Budget Balance
0.2	..	0.1	0.1	0.8	0.9	12.2	2.6	1.4	..	..	Capital Receipts
71.8	98.8	94.9	88.7	178.2	206.1	236.9	348.2	432.1	..	..	Capital Payments

COLOMBIA	1970	1971	1972	1973	1974	1975	1976	1977	1978	1979	1980
FOREIGN TRADE (CUSTOMS BASIS)					*(Millions of current US dollars)*						
Value of Exports, fob	727.7	689.1	863.4	1,175.5	1,416.7	1,464.9	1,744.6	2,443.0	3,038.3	3,300.4	3,945.0
Nonfuel Primary Products	595.8	527.4	625.5	804.6	901.3	1,053.8	1,289.8	1,881.6	2,377.5	2,453.7	3,028.9
Fuels	73.2	70.2	65.3	61.9	117.2	105.6	71.0	95.8	130.9	131.8	112.4
Manufactures	58.7	91.5	172.6	309.0	398.2	305.5	383.8	465.6	529.8	714.9	803.8
Value of Imports, cif	843.0	929.4	858.9	1,061.5	1,597.2	1,494.8	1,708.1	2,028.3	2,836.3	3,233.2	4,662.6
Nonfuel Primary Products	131.8	166.7	147.0	224.4	367.4	257.7	342.0	398.0	488.5	561.1	825.4
Fuels	8.8	11.0	5.5	4.5	4.4	15.3	42.7	137.7	206.3	325.8	567.7
Manufactures	702.4	751.7	706.5	832.7	1,225.4	1,221.8	1,323.4	1,492.6	2,141.6	2,346.4	3,269.5
					(Index 1987 = 100)						
Terms of Trade	108.8	102.8	110.6	113.8	123.4	112.6	167.3	219.5	168.0	160.9	142.2
Export Prices, fob	32.3	32.1	38.6	49.8	67.7	64.3	96.7	134.7	114.8	127.6	129.3
Import Prices, cif	29.7	31.2	34.9	43.7	54.9	57.1	57.8	61.4	68.3	79.3	91.0
BALANCE OF PAYMENTS					*(Millions of current US dollars)*						
Exports of Goods & Services	1,019.0	996.9	1,228.3	1,588.0	1,947.9	2,180.4	2,849.8	3,502.0	4,099.5	4,851.0	5,860.4
Merchandise, fob	788.0	754.2	978.6	1,262.6	1,494.5	1,683.2	2,201.9	2,660.0	3,155.4	3,441.0	3,986.3
Nonfactor Services	189.0	214.6	223.7	279.0	363.2	422.2	558.8	717.9	770.6	1,091.0	1,331.0
Factor Services	42.0	28.1	26.1	46.5	90.2	75.0	89.2	124.1	173.4	319.0	543.2
Imports of Goods & Services	1,348.0	1,485.0	1,454.3	1,677.3	2,350.7	2,400.3	2,738.0	3,172.6	3,914.1	4,514.9	6,231.3
Merchandise, fob	802.0	902.5	849.6	982.7	1,511.4	1,414.9	1,654.0	1,969.7	2,552.2	2,977.8	4,283.4
Nonfactor Services	324.0	381.0	376.7	431.4	557.6	592.4	639.2	766.2	851.9	940.9	1,159.5
Factor Services	222.0	201.4	228.0	263.2	281.8	392.9	444.7	436.7	510.1	596.2	788.4
Long-Term Interest	59.2	67.1	81.1	103.4	133.0	135.6	156.9	153.8	195.3	251.7	309.9
Private Current Transfers, net	-4.0	0.0	8.7	11.9	18.4	30.0	39.0	39.5	44.1	99.0	164.0
Workers' Remittances	6.0	8.0	8.7	11.9	15.6	18.0	42.0	42.0	43.8	63.0	68.0
Curr. A/C Bal before Off. Transf.	-333.0	-488.1	-217.3	-77.4	-384.4	-189.9	150.9	368.9	229.4	435.0	-206.8
Net Official Transfers	40.0	34.1	26.1	22.7	32.5	18.2	12.0	6.5	28.8	3.0	1.0
Curr. A/C Bal after Off. Transf.	-293.0	-454.0	-191.2	-54.7	-351.9	-171.7	162.9	375.4	258.1	438.0	-205.8
Long-Term Capital, net	227.0	194.3	263.6	285.4	228.4	302.1	79.1	225.0	108.0	755.4	815.4
Direct Investment	39.0	40.1	17.4	22.7	34.9	33.1	14.0	43.0	66.0	103.0	51.1
Long-Term Loans	115.2	185.2	282.6	243.4	117.6	326.8	149.4	186.3	50.7	679.2	808.3
Disbursements	252.6	356.7	469.8	449.7	400.8	505.3	366.0	411.5	335.2	1,130.2	1,071.2
Repayments	137.4	171.5	187.2	206.3	283.2	178.5	216.6	225.2	284.5	451.0	262.9
Other Long-Term Capital	72.8	-31.1	-36.4	19.4	75.9	-57.7	-84.3	-4.3	-8.7	-26.8	-44.0
Other Capital, net	82.5	241.8	88.1	-69.5	29.1	-68.2	372.2	47.7	202.9	302.8	309.0
Change in Reserves	-16.5	18.0	-160.5	-161.3	94.4	-62.3	-614.2	-648.1	-569.0	-1,496.2	-918.6
Memo Item:					*(Colombian Pesos per US dollar)*						
Conversion Factor (Annual Avg)	18.440	19.930	21.870	23.640	26.060	30.930	34.690	36.770	39.100	42.550	47.280
EXTERNAL DEBT (Total)				*(Millions of US dollars), outstanding at end of year*							
	1,635	1,837	2,067	2,320	2,446	2,746	2,882	5,053	5,102	5,869	6,940
Long-Term Debt (by debtor)	1,635	1,837	2,067	2,320	2,446	2,746	2,882	3,089	3,175	3,857	4,603
Central Bank, incl. IMF credit	202	219	190	200	214	209	212	224	258	309	375
Central Government	638	710	860	1,036	1,108	1,258	1,250	1,245	1,272	1,638	2,033
Rest of General Government	172	182	209	258	294	313	344	369	369	358	399
Non-financial Public Enterprises	259	297	337	390	464	544	628	809	868	1,039	1,229
Priv. Sector, incl non-guaranteed	363	428	470	436	366	421	448	441	409	513	568
Short-Term Debt	0	0	0	0	0	0	0	1,964	1,927	2,012	2,337
Memo Items:					*(Millions of US dollars)*						
Int'l Reserves Excluding Gold	189.1	188.0	309.0	516.2	431.1	474.7	1,100.8	1,747.2	2,366.4	3,843.8	4,830.8
Gold Holdings (at market price)	18.2	17.5	27.8	48.2	80.0	157.9	190.4	285.5	443.2	1,186.3	1,642.9
SOCIAL INDICATORS											
Total Fertility Rate	5.3	5.0	4.7	4.6	4.5	4.4	4.2	4.1	4.0	3.9	3.8
Infant Mortality Rate	76.6	74.8	73.0	70.2	67.4	64.6	61.8	59.0	55.4	51.8	48.2
Life Expectancy at Birth	61.0	61.3	61.6	62.1	62.6	63.0	63.5	64.0	64.6	65.3	65.9
Urban Population, % of total	57.2	57.9	58.6	59.3	60.0	60.7	61.3	62.0	62.6	63.3	63.9
Food Prod. per capita (1987=100)	88.9	92.4	90.9	88.2	92.5	98.8	103.1	100.2	103.7	105.6	103.2
Labor Force, Agriculture (%)	39.3	38.7	38.2	37.7	37.2	36.7	36.2	35.7	35.2	34.7	34.2
Labor Force, Female (%)	21.3	21.4	21.5	21.6	21.8	21.9	22.0	22.1	22.2	22.3	22.5
Primary Schl. Enroll. Ratio	108.0	..	..	..	..	118.0	..	125.0	129.0	133.0	118.0
Primary Schl. Enroll. Ratio, Female	110.0	..	..	..	..	120.0	..	127.0	131.0	135.0	120.0
Secondary Schl. Enroll. Ratio	25.0	..	..	..	..	39.0	..	43.0	45.0	48.0	41.0

1981	1982	1983	1984	1985	1986	1987	1988	1989	1990 estimate	Notes	COLOMBIA
											FOREIGN TRADE (CUSTOMS BASIS)
			(Millions of current US dollars)								
2,955.5	3,073.9	3,080.9	3,483.1	3,551.9	5,107.9	5,024.4	5,026.2	5,739.4	6,765.8	..	Value of Exports, fob
2,072.1	2,093.7	2,034.3	2,354.2	2,316.8	3,650.3	2,307.2	2,463.3	2,431.8	2,866.6	..	Nonfuel Primary Products
45.7	228.9	451.5	517.8	578.3	665.0	1,634.2	1,294.2	1,858.1	2,190.4	..	Fuels
837.6	751.2	595.1	611.1	656.8	792.7	1,083.0	1,268.7	1,449.5	1,708.7	..	Manufactures
5,199.2	5,463.1	4,966.9	4,492.4	4,130.7	3,852.1	4,228.0	5,005.3	5,010.5	5,589.5	..	Value of Imports, cif
819.3	875.8	799.1	765.7	683.4	627.9	663.2	806.1	769.2	858.1	..	Nonfuel Primary Products
730.7	663.1	648.4	474.1	484.4	153.2	121.3	180.9	243.2	271.4	..	Fuels
3,649.1	3,924.2	3,519.5	3,252.6	2,962.9	3,070.9	3,443.4	4,018.3	3,998.0	4,460.0	..	Manufactures
			(Index 1987 = 100)								
128.6	137.0	134.3	140.8	139.7	142.0	100.0	96.8	84.3	91.8	..	Terms of Trade
118.2	120.5	116.1	119.4	116.6	127.5	100.0	105.3	94.3	98.2	..	Export Prices, fob
91.9	87.9	86.5	84.8	83.4	89.8	100.0	108.7	111.8	106.9	..	Import Prices, cif
											BALANCE OF PAYMENTS
			(Millions of current US dollars)								
5,014.1	4,974.2	4,103.0	5,328.0	4,616.0	6,614.0	7,029.0	7,008.0	7,620.0	8,911.0	f	Exports of Goods & Services
3,157.7	3,113.8	2,970.0	4,273.0	3,650.0	5,331.0	5,661.0	5,343.0	6,031.0	7,105.0	..	Merchandise, fob
1,131.4	1,309.1	814.0	894.0	826.0	1,097.0	1,155.0	1,395.0	1,285.0	1,446.0	..	Nonfactor Services
725.0	551.3	319.0	161.0	140.0	186.0	213.0	270.0	304.0	360.0	..	Factor Services
7,217.4	8,197.3	7,270.0	7,028.0	6,886.0	7,016.0	7,694.0	8,188.0	8,713.0	9,519.0	f	Imports of Goods & Services
4,730.1	5,357.6	4,464.0	4,027.0	3,673.0	3,409.0	3,793.0	4,516.0	4,557.0	5,088.0	..	Merchandise, fob
1,284.1	1,335.1	1,290.0	1,288.0	1,420.0	1,677.0	1,699.0	1,660.0	1,604.0	1,691.0	..	Nonfactor Services
1,203.2	1,504.7	1,516.0	1,713.0	1,793.0	1,930.0	2,202.0	2,012.0	2,552.0	2,740.0	..	Factor Services
460.8	704.5	625.0	620.3	867.4	978.1	1,184.0	1,213.4	1,383.7	1,341.1	..	Long-Term Interest
241.3	167.2	145.0	289.0	455.0	801.0	1,009.0	975.0	912.0	1,014.0	..	Private Current Transfers, net
99.0	71.0	63.0	71.0	105.0	393.0	616.0	448.0	459.0	488.0	..	Workers' Remittances
-1,962.0	-3,056.0	-3,022.0	-1,411.0	-1,815.0	399.0	344.0	-205.0	-181.0	406.0	..	Curr. A/C Bal before Off. Transf.
0.7	2.2	19.0	10.0	6.0	-16.0	-8.0	-11.0	-14.0	-15.0	..	Net Official Transfers
-1,961.3	-3,053.8	-3,003.0	-1,401.0	-1,809.0	383.0	336.0	-216.0	-195.0	391.0	..	Curr. A/C Bal after Off. Transf.
1,579.8	1,615.1	1,527.7	1,822.0	2,350.0	2,469.0	191.0	834.0	653.0	194.0	f	Long-Term Capital, net
228.0	337.0	513.7	561.0	1,016.0	642.0	293.0	159.0	547.0	471.0	..	Direct Investment
1,401.1	1,255.1	1,048.6	1,357.6	1,329.5	1,632.5	-105.0	618.9	105.8	-167.6	..	Long-Term Loans
1,774.6	1,653.0	1,662.2	2,039.6	2,083.3	2,753.4	1,307.3	2,343.7	2,257.1	2,003.4	..	Disbursements
373.5	397.9	613.6	682.0	753.8	1,120.9	1,412.3	1,724.8	2,151.3	2,171.0	..	Repayments
-49.3	23.0	-34.6	-96.6	4.5	194.5	3.0	56.1	0.2	-109.4	..	Other Long-Term Capital
321.3	588.9	-369.3	-805.7	-386.1	-1,556.0	-136.0	-424.0	-95.0	55.0	f	Other Capital, net
60.1	849.8	1,844.6	384.7	-154.9	-1,296.0	-391.0	-194.0	-363.0	-640.0	..	Change in Reserves
											Memo Item:
			(Colombian Pesos per US dollar)								
54.490	64.090	78.850	100.820	142.310	194.260	242.610	299.170	382.570	502.260	..	Conversion Factor (Annual Avg)
			(Millions of US dollars), outstanding at end of year								
8,716	10,306	11,412	12,039	14,245	15,362	17,008	16,995	16,878	17,241	..	**EXTERNAL DEBT (Total)**
5,942	7,182	8,152	9,171	11,141	13,766	15,352	15,384	15,261	15,803	..	Long-Term Debt (by debtor)
397	414	458	391	468	639	993	879	809	788	..	Central Bank, incl. IMF credit
2,516	2,792	2,894	3,238	3,821	4,544	4,765	4,996	5,330	5,812	..	Central Government
551	655	790	839	1,166	1,379	1,689	1,706	1,720	1,772	..	Rest of General Government
1,513	2,029	2,591	2,899	3,636	5,082	5,754	5,721	5,656	5,892	..	Non-financial Public Enterprises
965	1,292	1,419	1,804	2,051	2,123	2,150	2,082	1,746	1,539	..	Priv. Sector, incl non-guaranteed
2,774	3,124	3,260	2,868	3,104	1,597	1,656	1,610	1,617	1,438	..	Short-Term Debt
			(Millions of US dollars)								**Memo Items:**
4,740.5	3,861.4	1,900.9	1,364.1	1,595.0	2,695.8	3,086.1	3,247.8	3,616.1	4,211.5	..	Int'l Reserves Excluding Gold
1,338.0	1,744.0	1,611.1	421.4	602.3	785.3	330.2	452.1	246.2	241.0	..	Gold Holdings (at market price)
											SOCIAL INDICATORS
3.6	3.5	3.4	3.3	3.1	3.0	2.9	2.8	2.7	2.7	..	Total Fertility Rate
44.6	41.0	40.8	40.6	40.4	40.2	40.0	39.1	38.2	37.4	..	Infant Mortality Rate
66.5	67.2	67.4	67.6	67.8	68.0	68.2	68.4	68.6	68.8	..	Life Expectancy at Birth
64.5	65.1	65.8	66.4	67.0	67.6	68.2	68.8	69.4	70.0	..	Urban Population, % of total
104.6	101.1	96.4	98.1	97.4	101.4	100.0	104.7	112.5	110.2	..	Food Prod. per capita (1987=100)
..	..	..	..	..	..	..	..	..	..	..	Labor Force, Agriculture (%)
22.4	22.4	22.3	22.3	22.2	22.2	22.1	22.0	22.0	21.9	..	Labor Force, Female (%)
..	..	..	..	107.0	..	106.0	106.0	107.0	..	..	Primary Schl. Enroll. Ratio
..	..	..	..	109.0	..	107.0	107.0	108.0	..	..	Primary Schl. Enroll. Ratio, Female
..	..	..	..	46.0	..	52.0	52.0	52.0	..	..	Secondary Schl. Enroll. Ratio

COMOROS	1970	1971	1972	1973	1974	1975	1976	1977	1978	1979	1980
CURRENT GNP PER CAPITA (US $)	100	110	110	140	150	170	190	200	220	260	340
POPULATION (thousands)	266	272	279	285	292	298	304	310	316	324	333

USE AND ORIGIN OF RESOURCES *(Millions of current Comorian Francs)*

	1970	1971	1972	1973	1974	1975	1976	1977	1978	1979	1980
Gross National Product (GNP)	6,856	8,041	8,539	9,447	14,305	12,797	12,361	13,771	16,494	19,656	25,551
Net Factor Income from Abroad	..	..	..	..	..	..	..	..	..	..	..
GDP at Market Prices	..	..	..	..	..	..	..	..	..	..	..
Resource Balance	..	..	..	..	..	..	..	..	..	..	..
Exports of Goods & NFServices	..	..	..	..	..	..	..	..	..	..	..
Imports of Goods & NFServices	..	..	..	..	..	..	..	..	..	..	..
Domestic Absorption	..	..	..	..	..	..	..	..	..	..	..
Private Consumption, etc.	..	..	..	..	..	..	..	..	..	..	..
General Gov't Consumption	..	..	..	..	..	..	..	..	..	..	..
Gross Domestic Investment	..	..	..	..	..	..	..	..	..	..	..
Fixed Investment	..	..	..	..	..	..	..	..	..	..	..
Indirect Taxes, net	..	..	..	..	..	..	..	..	..	..	..
GDP at factor cost	..	..	..	..	..	..	..	..	..	..	..
Agriculture	..	..	..	..	..	..	..	..	..	..	..
Industry	..	..	..	..	..	..	..	..	..	..	..
Manufacturing	..	..	..	..	..	..	..	..	..	..	..
Services, etc.	..	..	..	..	..	..	..	..	..	..	..
Gross Domestic Saving	..	..	..	..	..	..	..	..	..	..	..
Gross National Saving	..	..	..	..	..	..	..	..	..	..	..
Gross National Product	34,968	38,477	39,721	43,699	38,129	34,291	34,291	35,814	37,121	38,442	45,141
GDP at Market Prices	..	..	..	..	..	..	..	..	..	..	..
Resource Balance	..	..	..	..	..	..	..	..	..	..	..
Exports of Goods & NFServices	..	..	..	..	..	..	..	..	..	..	..
Imports of Goods & NFServices	..	..	..	..	..	..	..	..	..	..	..
Domestic Absorption	..	..	..	..	..	..	..	..	..	..	..
Private Consumption, etc.	..	..	..	..	..	..	..	..	..	..	..
General Gov't Consumption	..	..	..	..	..	..	..	..	..	..	..
Gross Domestic Investment	..	..	..	..	..	..	..	..	..	..	..
Fixed Investment	..	..	..	..	..	..	..	..	..	..	..
GDP at factor cost	..	..	..	..	..	..	..	..	..	..	..
Agriculture	..	..	..	..	..	..	..	..	..	..	..
Industry	..	..	..	..	..	..	..	..	..	..	..
Manufacturing	..	..	..	..	..	..	..	..	..	..	..
Services, etc.	..	..	..	..	..	..	..	..	..	..	..

Memo Items:

	1970	1971	1972	1973	1974	1975	1976	1977	1978	1979	1980
Capacity to Import	..	..	..	..	..	..	..	..	..	..	..
Terms of Trade Adjustment	..	..	..	..	..	..	..	..	..	..	..
Gross Domestic Income	..	..	..	..	..	..	..	..	..	..	..
Gross National Income	..	..	..	..	..	..	..	..	..	..	..

DOMESTIC PRICES/DEFLATORS *(Index 1987 = 100)*

	1970	1971	1972	1973	1974	1975	1976	1977	1978	1979	1980
Overall (GDP)	..	..	..	..	..	..	..	..	..	..	..
Domestic Absorption	..	..	..	..	..	..	..	..	..	..	..
Agriculture	..	..	..	..	..	..	..	..	..	..	..
Industry	..	..	..	..	..	..	..	..	..	..	..
Manufacturing	..	..	..	..	..	..	..	..	..	..	..
Consumer Price Index	..	..	..	..	..	..	..	..	..	..	..

MANUFACTURING ACTIVITY

	1970	1971	1972	1973	1974	1975	1976	1977	1978	1979	1980
Employment (1987=100)	..	..	..	..	..	..	..	..	..	..	..
Real Earnings per Empl. (1987=100)	..	..	..	..	..	..	..	..	..	..	..
Real Output per Empl. (1987=100)	..	..	..	..	..	..	..	..	..	..	..
Earnings as % of Value Added	..	..	..	..	..	..	..	..	..	..	..

MONETARY HOLDINGS *(Millions of current Comorian Francs)*

	1970	1971	1972	1973	1974	1975	1976	1977	1978	1979	1980
Money Supply, Broadly Defined	..	..	..	..	..	..	..	..	..	..	..
Money	..	..	..	..	..	..	..	..	..	..	..
Currency Outside Banks	..	..	..	..	..	..	..	..	..	..	..
Demand Deposits	..	..	..	..	..	..	..	..	..	..	..
Quasi-Money	..	..	..	..	..	..	..	..	..	..	..

(Millions of current Comorian Francs)

GOVERNMENT DEFICIT (-) OR SURPLUS

	1970	1971	1972	1973	1974	1975	1976	1977	1978	1979	1980
GOVERNMENT DEFICIT (-) OR SURPLUS	..	..	..	..	..	..	..	..	..	..	..
Current Revenue	..	..	..	..	..	..	..	..	..	..	..
Current Expenditure	..	..	..	..	..	..	..	..	..	..	..
Current Budget Balance	..	..	..	..	..	..	..	..	..	..	1,071
Capital Receipts	..	..	..	..	..	..	..	..	..	..	..
Capital Payments	..	..	..	..	..	..	..	..	..	..	..

1981	1982	1983	1984	1985	1986	1987	1988	1989	1990 estimate	Notes	COMOROS
380	350	330	310	300	320	370	440	460	480	..	**CURRENT GNP PER CAPITA (US $)**
343	355	367	381	395	410	425	441	458	475	..	**POPULATION (thousands)**
				(Millions of current Comorian Francs)							**USE AND ORIGIN OF RESOURCES**
30,115	36,150	42,321	46,832	51,262	56,117	59,335	61,251	63,252	67,143	..	Gross National Product (GNP)
..	-1,609	-175	-136	-350	-153	-337	-417	-432	-109	..	Net Factor Income from Abroad
..	37,759	42,496	46,968	51,612	56,270	59,672	61,668	63,684	67,252	..	GDP at Market Prices
..	..	-11,135	-26,587	-19,966	-15,255	-19,382	-16,424	-11,936	-14,058	..	Resource Balance
..	..	8,426	4,236	8,943	9,251	6,431	7,700	11,355	9,633	..	Exports of Goods & NFServices
..	..	19,561	30,823	28,909	24,506	25,813	24,124	23,291	23,691	..	Imports of Goods & NFServices
..	..	53,631	73,555	71,578	71,525	79,054	78,092	75,620	81,310	..	Domestic Absorption
..	..	29,207	38,727	41,016	42,700	49,335	50,170	48,327	51,227	..	Private Consumption, etc.
..	..	12,084	13,305	15,310	15,552	15,819	18,085	18,447	20,189	..	General Gov't Consumption
..	..	12,340	21,523	15,252	13,273	13,900	9,837	8,846	9,894	..	Gross Domestic Investment
..	..	11,366	15,740	13,410	11,773	9,838	7,704	7,246	7,394	..	Fixed Investment
..	..	..	..	..	..	..	..	..	..	..	Indirect Taxes, net
..	..	..	..	..	..	..	..	..	..	B	GDP at factor cost
..	13,724	14,861	16,266	18,640	21,049	21,363	24,606	26,174	..	..	Agriculture
..	5,236	6,038	7,195	7,261	7,286	8,413	6,351	6,495	..	..	Industry
..	1,431	1,516	1,716	1,893	2,062	2,148	2,424	2,420	..	..	Manufacturing
..	18,799	21,597	23,507	25,711	27,935	29,896	30,711	31,015	..	..	Services, etc.
..	..	1,205	-5,064	-4,714	-1,982	-5,482	-6,587	-3,090	-4,164	..	Gross Domestic Saving
..	..	208	-6,502	-5,369	-2,835	-5,540	-6,075	-2,675	-2,775	..	Gross National Saving
49,969	49,640	53,284	55,637	56,965	58,380	59,335	59,680	59,775	60,672		Gross National Product
..	..	53,505	55,792	57,346	58,541	59,672	60,084	60,190	61,092		GDP at Market Prices
..	..	-14,883	-26,727	-20,755	-17,435	-19,382	..	..	..	..	Resource Balance
..	..	5,789	4,051	6,765	7,112	6,431	..	..	..	..	Exports of Goods & NFServices
..	..	20,672	30,779	27,521	24,547	25,813	..	..	..	..	Imports of Goods & NFServices
..	..	68,387	82,519	78,102	75,976	79,054	..	..	..	..	Domestic Absorption
..	..	36,552	43,595	45,054	44,463	49,335	..	..	..	..	Private Consumption, etc.
..	..	14,185	14,875	16,193	15,358	15,819	16,882	18,035	..	..	General Gov't Consumption
..	..	17,650	24,049	16,855	16,154	13,900	9,620	8,405	9,397	..	Gross Domestic Investment
..	..	16,439	17,533	14,818	14,203	9,838	7,534	6,884	6,635	..	Fixed Investment
..	..	..	..	..	..	..	..	..	..	B	GDP at factor cost
..	..	17,331	17,992	18,922	19,547	21,363	22,030	22,581	..	..	Agriculture
..	..	9,132	9,770	9,420	9,461	8,413	7,463	6,977	..	..	Industry
..	..	1,721	1,846	1,935	2,072	2,148	2,222	2,110	..	..	Manufacturing
..	..	27,042	28,030	29,005	29,533	29,896	30,591	30,632	..	..	Services, etc.
											Memo Items:
..	..	8,905	4,230	8,514	9,266	6,431	..	..	..	..	Capacity to Import
..	..	3,115	179	1,748	2,155	0	..	..	..	..	Terms of Trade Adjustment
..	..	56,620	55,971	59,094	60,696	59,672	..	..	..	..	Gross Domestic Income
..	..	56,399	55,816	58,714	60,535	59,335	..	..	..	..	Gross National Income
				(Index 1987 = 100)							**DOMESTIC PRICES/DEFLATORS**
..	..	79.4	84.2	90.0	96.1	100.0	102.6	105.8	110.1	..	Overall (GDP)
..	..	78.4	89.1	91.6	94.1	100.0	..	..	..	..	Domestic Absorption
..	..	85.7	90.4	98.5	107.7	100.0	111.7	115.9	..	..	Agriculture
..	..	66.1	73.6	77.1	77.0	100.0	85.1	93.1	..	..	Industry
..	..	88.1	92.9	97.8	99.5	100.0	109.1	114.7	..	..	Manufacturing
..	..	..	..	..	..	..	..	..	..	..	Consumer Price Index
											MANUFACTURING ACTIVITY
..	..	..	..	..	..	..	..	..	..		Employment (1987=100)
..	..	..	..	..	..	..	..	..	..		Real Earnings per Empl. (1987=100)
..	..	..	..	..	..	..	..	..	..		Real Output per Empl. (1987=100)
..	..	..	..	..	..	..	..	..	..		Earnings as % of Value Added
				(Millions of current Comorian Francs)							**MONETARY HOLDINGS**
..	6,370	8,521	7,213	8,192	8,664	10,847	12,438	14,864	15,462	..	Money Supply, Broadly Defined
..	5,202	7,292	6,254	7,177	7,232	7,812	8,879	10,256	10,888	..	Money
..	2,434	3,427	3,142	3,448	3,118	3,151	3,688	3,618	4,274	..	Currency Outside Banks
..	2,768	3,865	3,112	3,729	4,114	4,661	5,191	6,638	6,614	..	Demand Deposits
..	1,168	1,229	959	1,015	1,432	3,035	3,559	4,608	4,574	..	Quasi-Money
				(Millions of current Comorian Francs)							**GOVERNMENT DEFICIT (-) OR SURPLUS**
..	-4,084	-6,353	-8,586	-8,126	-4,816	-7,395	..	..	..	..	Current Revenue
..	9,551	13,501	16,111	16,017	18,509	13,709	..	..	..	..	Current Expenditure
1,228	9,362	12,208	14,585	15,324	17,921	14,986	..	..	..	..	Current Budget Balance
..	189	1,293	1,526	693	588	-1,277	..	..	..	..	Capital Receipts
..	..	..	..	..	..	..	..	..	..	..	Capital Payments
..	4,273	7,645	10,113	8,819	5,404	6,118	..	..	..	..	

COMOROS	1970	1971	1972	1973	1974	1975	1976	1977	1978	1979	1980

FOREIGN TRADE (CUSTOMS BASIS) *(Thousands of current US dollars)*

Value of Exports, fob	..	..	..	..	..	..	..	..	..	..	..
Nonfuel Primary Products	..	..	..	..	..	..	..	..	..	..	..
Fuels					..			..			
Manufactures	..				..			..			..
Value of Imports, cif				..		..			..		
Nonfuel Primary Products					..			..	..		
Fuels	..							..			..
Manufactures	..			..					..		..

(Index 1987 = 100)

Terms of Trade				..		..			..		
Export Prices, fob	..				..				..		..
Import Prices, cif	..								..		..

BALANCE OF PAYMENTS *(Thousands of current US dollars)*

Exports of Goods & Services	..	..	..	..	..	..	..	..	..	..	14.06
Merchandise, fob	..	..	..	..	..	..	..	..	..	..	11.19
Nonfactor Services	..	..	..	..	..	..	..	..	..	..	2.24
Factor Services	..	..	..	..	..	..	..	..	..	..	0.63
Imports of Goods & Services	..	..	..	..	..	..	..	..	..	..	34.33
Merchandise, fob	..	..	..	..	..	..	..	..	..	..	22.37
Nonfactor Services	..	..	..	..	..	..	..	..	..	..	11.92
Factor Services	..	..	..	..	..	..	..	..	..	..	0.04
Long-Term Interest	0.00	0.00	0.00	0.00	0.00	0.10	0.10	0.10	0.10	0.20	0.30
Private Current Transfers, net	..	..	..	..	..	..	..	..	..	..	0.10
Workers' Remittances	..	..	..	..	..	..	..	..	..	..	1.62
Curr. A/C Bal before Off. Transf.	..	..	..	..	..	..	..	..	..	..	-20.17
Net Official Transfers	..	..	..	..	..	..	..	..	..	..	11.26
Curr. A/C Bal after Off. Transf.	..	..	..	..	..	..	..	..	..	..	-8.91
Long-Term Capital, net	..	..	..	..	..	..	..	..	..	..	16.23
Direct Investment	..	..	..	..	..	..	..	..	..	..	..
Long-Term Loans	0.00	0.00	0.20	0.00	2.30	0.50	14.20	4.30	3.50	10.10	13.00
Disbursements	0.00	0.00	0.30	0.10	2.40	0.90	14.60	4.60	3.60	10.10	13.00
Repayments	0.00	0.00	0.10	0.10	0.10	0.40	0.40	0.30	0.10	0.00	0.00
Other Long-Term Capital	..	..	..	..	..	..	..	..	..	..	3.23
Other Capital, net	..	..	..	..	..	..	..	..	..	..	-10.82
Change in Reserves	..	..	..	..	..	..	..	0.00	..	0.00	3.51

Memo Item: *(Comorian Francs per US dollar)*

Conversion Factor (Annual Avg)	277.710	277.130	252.210	222.700	240.500	214.320	238.980	225.670	225.640	212.720	211.280

EXTERNAL DEBT (Total) *(Millions of US dollars), outstanding at end of year*

EXTERNAL DEBT (Total)	1.20	1.20	1.50	1.70	4.30	4.70	18.50	24.40	28.90	39.50	44.00
Long-Term Debt (by debtor)	1.20	1.20	1.50	1.70	4.30	4.70	18.50	23.40	27.90	38.50	43.00
Central Bank, incl. IMF credit	0.00	0.00	0.00	0.00	0.00	0.00	0.00	0.00	0.00	0.00	0.00
Central Government	1.20	1.20	1.40	1.50	4.10	4.60	18.40	23.30	27.80	38.30	43.00
Rest of General Government	0.00	0.00	0.00	0.00	0.00	0.00	0.00	0.00	0.00	0.00	0.00
Non-financial Public Enterprises	0.00	0.00	0.10	0.20	0.20	0.10	0.10	0.10	0.10	0.20	0.00
Priv. Sector, incl non-guaranteed	..	..	..	..	..	..	..	..	..	..	..
Short-Term Debt	0.00	0.00	0.00	0.00	0.00	0.00	0.00	1.00	1.00	1.00	1.00

Memo Items: *(Thousands of US dollars)*

Int'l Reserves Excluding Gold	..	..	..	..	..	..	..	..	..	..	6,373
Gold Holdings (at market price)	..	..	..	..	..	..	..	..	..	..	

SOCIAL INDICATORS

Total Fertility Rate	7.0	7.0	7.0	7.0	7.0	7.0	7.0	7.0	7.0	7.0	7.0
Infant Mortality Rate	141.0	138.0	135.0	132.0	129.0	126.0	123.0	120.0	117.8	115.6	113.4
Life Expectancy at Birth	46.5	47.0	47.5	48.0	48.5	49.0	49.5	50.0	50.4	50.8	51.2
Urban Population, % of total	19.4	19.8	20.1	20.5	20.8	21.2	21.6	22.0	22.4	22.8	23.2
Food Prod. per capita (1987=100)	147.0	146.3	140.9	146.8	141.5	132.4	127.4	120.1	117.5	114.0	117.3
Labor Force, Agriculture (%)	86.7	86.2	85.8	85.5	85.1	84.8	84.4	84.0	83.6	83.3	83.0
Labor Force, Female (%)	42.8	42.8	42.7	42.7	42.6	42.6	42.5	42.5	42.5	42.4	42.4
Primary Schl. Enroll. Ratio	34.0	..	..	46.0	..	..	..	..	..	..	87.0
Primary Schl. Enroll. Ratio, Female	21.0	..	..	29.0	..	..	..	..	..	..	74.0
Secondary Schl. Enroll. Ratio	3.0	..	..	7.0	..	..	..	..	..	..	22.0

1981	1982	1983	1984	1985	1986	1987	1988	1989	1990 estimate	Notes	COMOROS

(Thousands of current US dollars)

FOREIGN TRADE (CUSTOMS BASIS)

1981	1982	1983	1984	1985	1986	1987	1988	1989	1990 est.	Notes	COMOROS
..	..	..	..	..	..	..	..	..	..	..	Value of Exports, fob
..	..	..	..	..	..	..	..	..	..	..	Nonfuel Primary Products
..	..	..	..	..	..	..	..	..	..	..	Fuels
..	..	..	..	..	..	..	..	..	..	..	Manufactures
..	..	..	..	..	..	..	..	..	..	..	Value of Imports, cif
..	..	..	..	..	..	..	..	..	..	..	Nonfuel Primary Products
..	..	..	..	..	..	..	..	..	..	..	Fuels
..	..	..	..	..	..	..	..	..	..	..	Manufactures

(Index 1987 = 100)

1981	1982	1983	1984	1985	1986	1987	1988	1989	1990 est.	Notes	COMOROS
..	..	..	..	..	..	..	..	..	..	..	Terms of Trade
..	..	..	..	..	..	..	..	..	..	..	Export Prices, fob
..	..	..	..	..	..	..	..	..	..	..	Import Prices, cif

(Thousands of current US dollars)

BALANCE OF PAYMENTS

1981	1982	1983	1984	1985	1986	1987	1988	1989	1990 est.	Notes	COMOROS
18.33	23.41	23.38	10.73	20.48	28.63	27.84	40.09	39.89	38.15	..	Exports of Goods & Services
16.42	19.58	19.47	7.05	15.69	20.37	11.60	21.48	18.05	17.93	..	Merchandise, fob
1.10	2.56	2.64	2.65	4.22	6.76	14.44	16.85	17.55	16.86	..	Nonfactor Services
0.81	1.27	1.27	1.04	0.57	1.50	1.80	1.76	4.30	3.35	..	Factor Services
50.76	51.23	52.38	71.91	66.08	73.94	88.87	90.56	78.20	92.17	..	Imports of Goods & Services
24.89	25.10	28.80	32.65	28.22	28.54	44.15	44.29	35.65	45.23	..	Merchandise, fob
25.31	25.41	21.85	37.66	35.89	42.27	41.80	42.29	39.61	42.73	..	Nonfactor Services
0.56	0.71	1.73	1.61	1.97	3.13	2.92	3.97	2.94	4.21	..	Factor Services
0.40	0.80	1.20	1.60	1.50	0.80	0.90	0.30	0.70	0.50	..	Long-Term Interest
0.48	-2.40	-2.16	-2.98	-0.68	-2.02	0.93	3.12	2.66	5.50	..	Private Current Transfers, net
1.22	2.37	1.84	2.14	4.23	4.76	6.80	7.38	7.89	9.94	..	Workers' Remittances
-31.95	-30.23	-31.16	-64.16	-46.28	-47.34	-60.11	-47.32	-35.65	-48.52	..	Curr. A/C Bal before Off. Transf.
23.79	19.27	20.11	31.44	32.02	31.65	38.74	40.80	41.06	39.23	..	Net Official Transfers
-8.16	-10.96	-11.05	-32.72	-14.26	-15.69	-21.37	-6.52	5.41	-9.29	..	Curr. A/C Bal after Off. Transf.
10.60	19.15	16.01	25.89	20.01	20.51	18.12	5.84	6.89	0.19	..	Long-Term Capital, net
..	..	..	..	..	..	7.55	3.77	3.27	-0.71	..	Direct Investment
11.00	16.20	17.80	23.10	21.80	23.10	12.70	8.30	5.20	8.10	..	Long-Term Loans
11.10	16.30	18.10	24.10	22.20	24.20	13.10	8.30	5.20	8.20	..	Disbursements
0.10	0.10	0.30	1.00	0.40	1.10	0.40	0.00	0.00	0.10	..	Repayments
-0.40	2.95	-1.79	2.79	-1.79	-2.59	-2.13	-6.23	-1.57	-7.20	..	Other Long-Term Capital
1.06	-4.48	-2.88	0.97	0.37	-1.34	12.04	4.24	-6.95	4.24	..	Other Capital, net
-3.51	-3.71	-2.08	5.85	-6.12	-3.48	-8.79	-3.56	-5.35	4.85	..	Change in Reserves

(Comorian Francs per US dollar)

Memo Item:

1981	1982	1983	1984	1985	1986	1987	1988	1989	1990 est.	Notes	COMOROS
271.730	328.600	381.060	436.960	449.260	346.300	300.530	297.850	319.010	272.260	..	Conversion Factor (Annual Avg)

(Millions of US dollars), outstanding at end of year

1981	1982	1983	1984	1985	1986	1987	1988	1989	1990 est.	Notes	COMOROS
54.50	68.70	85.60	104.30	133.30	166.10	202.90	198.70	175.50	189.90	..	**EXTERNAL DEBT (Total)**
52.50	67.70	83.60	101.30	129.30	158.50	187.70	187.40	162.30	177.20	..	Long-Term Debt (by debtor)
0.00	0.00	0.00	0.00	0.00	0.00	0.20	0.40	0.20	0.50	..	Central Bank, incl. IMF credit
52.50	66.50	81.40	96.40	119.60	144.30	164.40	161.90	158.10	171.50	..	Central Government
0.00	0.00	0.00	0.00	0.00	0.00	0.00	0.00	0.00	..	..	Rest of General Government
0.00	1.20	2.20	4.90	9.70	14.20	23.10	25.10	4.00	5.20	..	Non-financial Public Enterprises
..	..	..	..	..	..	..	..	..	..	..	Priv. Sector, incl non-guaranteed
2.00	1.00	2.00	3.00	4.00	7.60	15.20	11.30	13.20	12.70	..	Short-Term Debt

(Thousands of US dollars)

Memo Items:

1981	1982	1983	1984	1985	1986	1987	1988	1989	1990 est.	Notes	COMOROS
8,392	10,831	10,794	3,509	11,748	17,546	30,674	23,541	30,773	29,695	..	Int'l Reserves Excluding Gold
..		221	176	186	223	276	234	229	219	..	Gold Holdings (at market price)

SOCIAL INDICATORS

1981	1982	1983	1984	1985	1986	1987	1988	1989	1990 est.	Notes	COMOROS
7.0	7.0	7.0	7.0	7.0	7.0	7.0	6.9	6.9	6.8	..	Total Fertility Rate
111.2	109.0	107.0	105.0	102.9	100.9	98.9	96.6	94.2	91.9	..	Infant Mortality Rate
51.6	52.0	52.4	52.8	53.2	53.6	54.0	54.4	54.8	55.2	..	Life Expectancy at Birth
23.6	24.0	24.5	24.9	25.3	26.0	26.6	27.0	27.4	27.8	..	Urban Population, % of total
98.6	101.2	105.9	96.4	98.6	101.5	100.0	99.0	97.1	95.6	..	Food Prod. per capita (1987=100)
..	..	..	..	..	..	..	..	..	..	..	Labor Force, Agriculture (%)
42.2	42.0	41.8	41.6	41.4	41.2	41.0	40.8	40.6	40.4	..	Labor Force, Female (%)
..	90.0	..	..	82.0	75.0	75.0	..	75.0	..	..	Primary Schl. Enroll. Ratio
..	..	..	..	72.0	67.0	67.0	..	67.0	..	..	Primary Schl. Enroll. Ratio, Female
..	..	..	..	28.0	27.0	17.0	..	17.0	..	..	Secondary Schl. Enroll. Ratio

CONGO	1970	1971	1972	1973	1974	1975	1976	1977	1978	1979	1980
CURRENT GNP PER CAPITA (US $)	240	260	290	340	430	530	520	490	530	650	850
POPULATION (thousands)	1,208	1,239	1,271	1,304	1,340	1,380	1,424	1,472	1,522	1,575	1,630

USE AND ORIGIN OF RESOURCES *(Billions of current CFA Francs)*

	1970	1971	1972	1973	1974	1975	1976	1977	1978	1979	1980
Gross National Product (GNP)	74.20	86.70	101.90	114.00	135.70	157.90	170.60	178.70	185.60	234.60	325.70
Net Factor Income from Abroad	-1.80	-2.00	-1.60	-6.80	-5.20	-6.50	-9.70	-9.30	-12.70	-20.40	-34.70
GDP at Market Prices	76.00	88.70	103.50	120.80	140.90	164.40	180.30	188.00	198.30	255.00	360.40
Resource Balance	-17.50	-17.80	-24.30	-14.20	-8.80	-45.80	-47.20	-37.00	-34.40	-3.10	-0.40
Exports of Goods & NFServices	26.40	28.90	29.30	38.20	75.00	59.00	72.80	85.70	86.70	120.90	216.30
Imports of Goods & NFServices	43.90	46.70	53.60	52.40	83.80	104.80	120.00	122.70	121.10	124.00	216.70
Domestic Absorption	93.50	106.50	127.80	135.00	149.70	210.20	227.50	225.00	232.70	258.10	360.80
Private Consumption, etc.	62.20	67.70	79.70	75.20	75.20	116.30	139.70	138.60	133.00	139.90	168.50
General Gov't Consumption	12.90	15.20	18.00	21.20	25.10	29.60	31.90	36.40	45.50	52.00	63.40
Gross Domestic Investment	18.40	23.60	30.10	38.60	49.40	64.30	55.90	50.00	54.20	66.20	128.90
Fixed Investment	..	..	..	..	47.30	61.50	53.60	48.90	46.40	56.40	118.70
Indirect Taxes, net	9.70	11.80	11.90	12.90	14.50	21.60	21.00	26.70	21.80	35.40	17.50
GDP at factor cost	66.30	76.90	91.60	107.90	126.40	142.80	159.30	161.30	176.50	219.60	342.90
Agriculture	13.60	15.20	17.00	19.00	21.30	23.80	24.30	29.00	31.80	36.50	42.10
Industry	18.20	19.40	22.00	26.70	35.80	53.30	67.80	59.50	58.50	92.80	168.00
Manufacturing	..	..	..	..	..	..	..	..	18.60	21.50	27.00
Services, etc.	44.20	54.10	64.50	75.10	83.80	87.30	88.20	99.50	108.00	125.70	150.30
Gross Domestic Saving	0.90	5.80	5.80	24.40	40.60	18.50	8.70	13.00	19.80	63.10	128.50
Gross National Saving	-2.07	1.55	0.99	15.90	21.62	4.95	-8.72	-4.53	4.10	35.97	80.20

(Billions of 1987 CFA Francs)

	1970	1971	1972	1973	1974	1975	1976	1977	1978	1979	1980
Gross National Product	217.82	235.27	257.87	267.39	301.00	333.78	337.21	301.62	315.80	348.12	403.88
GDP at Market Prices	228.02	245.96	267.41	289.60	318.34	351.02	359.13	320.32	339.81	380.52	452.11
Resource Balance	-140.80	-137.87	-134.71	-131.56	-128.19	-140.89	-125.29	-94.71	-78.32	-22.70	-65.30
Exports of Goods & NFServices	113.07	117.04	121.23	125.42	129.82	130.05	134.01	148.56	162.89	170.16	207.19
Imports of Goods & NFServices	253.87	254.91	255.94	256.98	258.01	270.94	259.30	243.27	241.21	192.86	272.49
Domestic Absorption	375.66	393.50	415.18	438.07	461.95	502.73	486.86	422.04	424.76	409.47	520.12
Private Consumption, etc.	219.75	217.12	215.34	211.32	204.01	207.31	244.81	213.28	240.20	212.24	254.99
General Gov't Consumption	56.11	59.37	62.88	66.38	70.39	74.15	72.40	72.15	76.15	80.91	91.69
Gross Domestic Investment	99.80	117.00	136.96	160.36	187.55	221.27	169.65	136.62	108.40	116.31	173.44
Fixed Investment	..	..	..	..	..	..	..	..	..	..	..
GDP at factor cost	..	..	..	..	..	..	..	..	..	361.79	425.25
Agriculture	48.55	50.26	52.21	54.16	56.11	58.07	55.38	57.58	57.33	60.99	65.63
Industry	58.29	58.86	62.85	71.98	89.90	113.60	124.78	99.85	104.32	129.86	162.01
Manufacturing	..	..	..	..	..	..	..	..	27.87	27.87	32.39
Services, etc.	121.18	136.84	152.35	163.46	172.33	179.35	178.96	162.88	178.15	189.67	224.48

Memo Items:

	1970	1971	1972	1973	1974	1975	1976	1977	1978	1979	1980
Capacity to Import	152.67	157.75	139.91	187.34	230.92	152.53	157.31	169.91	172.69	188.04	271.99
Terms of Trade Adjustment	39.60	40.71	18.68	61.92	101.09	22.49	23.30	21.35	9.80	17.88	64.79
Gross Domestic Income	267.62	286.67	286.09	351.52	419.43	373.51	382.43	341.67	349.61	398.40	516.91
Gross National Income	257.42	275.98	276.55	329.31	402.09	356.27	360.51	322.97	325.60	366.00	468.68

DOMESTIC PRICES/DEFLATORS *(Index 1987 = 100)*

	1970	1971	1972	1973	1974	1975	1976	1977	1978	1979	1980
Overall (GDP)	33.3	36.1	38.7	41.7	44.3	46.8	50.2	58.7	58.4	67.0	79.7
Domestic Absorption	24.9	27.1	30.8	30.8	32.4	41.8	46.7	53.3	54.8	63.0	69.4
Agriculture	28.0	30.2	32.6	35.1	38.0	41.0	43.9	50.4	55.5	59.8	64.2
Industry	31.2	33.0	35.0	37.1	39.8	46.9	54.3	59.6	56.1	71.5	103.7
Manufacturing	..	..	..	..	..	..	..	..	66.7	77.1	83.4
Consumer Price Index	24.5	25.5	28.0	28.9	30.5	35.8	38.4	43.8	48.4	52.3	56.1

MANUFACTURING ACTIVITY

	1970	1971	1972	1973	1974	1975	1976	1977	1978	1979	1980
Employment (1987=100)	..	..	..	..	..	..	..	..	..	..	..
Real Earnings per Empl. (1987=100)	..	..	..	..	..	..	..	..	..	..	..
Real Output per Empl. (1987=100)	..	..	..	..	..	..	..	..	..	..	..
Earnings as % of Value Added	33.8	35.1	40.6	44.3	49.8	46.7	43.8	..	..	..	..

MONETARY HOLDINGS *(Billions of current CFA Francs)*

	1970	1971	1972	1973	1974	1975	1976	1977	1978	1979	1980
Money Supply, Broadly Defined	13.40	14.90	15.90	18.48	25.60	29.07	33.89	34.50	36.89	44.91	61.41
Money	12.47	13.74	14.65	17.07	23.73	26.91	31.27	30.63	32.96	39.61	54.34
Currency Outside Banks	5.42	6.38	7.77	8.88	11.61	14.03	15.05	15.86	16.31	18.96	22.85
Demand Deposits	7.05	7.36	6.88	8.18	12.12	12.88	16.21	14.76	16.65	20.65	31.50
Quasi-Money	0.92	1.16	1.26	1.42	1.87	2.16	2.62	3.87	3.92	5.30	7.06

(Billions of current CFA Francs)

	1970	1971	1972	1973	1974	1975	1976	1977	1978	1979	1980
GOVERNMENT DEFICIT (-) OR SURPLUS	-1.09	-2.40	..	..	..	..	..	..	..	..	-18.76
Current Revenue	16.70	17.61	18.80	19.60	43.77	47.83	46.92	..	..	..	159.93
Current Expenditure	16.11	17.66	..	..	..	..	..	..	..	..	..
Current Budget Balance	0.59	-0.05	..	..	..	..	..	..	..	..	..
Capital Receipts	0.01	..	..	0.50	0.35	..	1.38	..	..	..	0.07
Capital Payments	1.69	2.35	..	..	..	..	..	..	..	..	..

1981	1982	1983	1984	1985	1986	1987	1988	1989	1990 estimate	Notes	CONGO
1,100	1,320	1,240	1,150	1,040	940	960	930	970	1,010	..	**CURRENT GNP PER CAPITA (US $)**
1,688	1,748	1,810	1,874	1,938	2,003	2,069	2,137	2,205	2,276	..	**POPULATION (thousands)**
											USE AND ORIGIN OF RESOURCES
				(Billions of current CFA Francs)							
501.20	654.10	732.90	871.00	867.60	652.10	613.85	567.86	676.25	684.40	..	Gross National Product (GNP)
-40.50	-55.90	-66.30	-87.50	-103.20	11.70	-76.67	-91.10	-98.66	-97.22	..	Net Factor Income from Abroad
541.70	710.00	799.20	958.50	970.80	640.41	690.52	658.96	774.91	781.62	..	GDP at Market Prices
-97.90	-94.00	49.40	153.40	7.60	-88.60	21.50	1.30	97.50	59.40	..	Resource Balance
314.30	392.40	463.10	590.70	551.30	255.10	288.20	267.70	368.10	380.50	..	Exports of Goods & NFServices
412.20	486.40	413.70	437.30	543.70	343.70	266.70	266.40	270.60	321.10	..	Imports of Goods & NFServices
639.60	804.00	749.80	805.10	963.20	729.01	669.02	657.66	677.41	722.22	..	Domestic Absorption
305.90	284.10	318.40	372.10	509.50	380.61	390.72	396.26	408.91	442.62	..	Private Consumption, etc.
72.80	95.80	124.20	141.70	159.70	159.80	142.10	138.70	144.60	155.40	..	General Gov't Consumption
260.90	424.10	307.20	291.30	294.00	188.60	136.20	122.70	123.90	124.20	..	Gross Domestic Investment
239.70	404.70	302.90	277.30	276.90	182.90	144.00	129.20	126.70	129.20	..	Fixed Investment
21.80	30.30	29.00	37.10	34.20	28.00	25.50	29.20	29.40	26.62	..	Indirect Taxes, net
519.90	679.70	770.20	921.40	936.60	612.41	665.02	629.76	745.51	755.00	B	GDP at factor cost
42.70	55.80	60.60	66.30	72.30	77.42	82.43	91.38	101.38	103.46	..	Agriculture
275.70	373.20	434.20	542.40	523.40	209.07	247.14	197.15	299.49	303.76	..	Industry
34.30	33.90	44.10	46.50	54.60	61.77	59.76	56.92	55.33	56.49	f	Manufacturing
223.30	281.00	304.40	349.80	375.10	353.91	360.95	370.43	374.04	374.40	..	Services, etc.
163.00	330.10	356.60	444.70	301.60	100.00	157.70	124.00	221.40	183.60	..	Gross Domestic Saving
113.73	258.67	274.64	337.55	181.57	97.50	63.95	16.03	113.24	74.91	..	Gross National Saving
				(Billions of 1987 CFA Francs)							
470.85	583.30	625.95	656.75	647.54	604.75	613.85	605.66	632.48	637.76	..	Gross National Product
515.16	649.64	699.93	748.67	739.71	689.03	690.52	702.84	724.72	728.31	H	GDP at Market Prices
-176.16	-338.53	-170.60	-127.69	-149.75	-62.49	21.50	56.88	85.28	34.90	..	Resource Balance
226.37	247.06	289.70	318.07	297.41	287.07	288.20	325.77	350.39	330.28	..	Exports of Goods & NFServices
402.53	585.58	460.30	445.76	447.16	349.56	266.70	268.89	265.11	295.38	..	Imports of Goods & NFServices
714.39	998.19	874.95	878.89	888.57	748.10	669.02	645.72	638.82	678.97	..	Domestic Absorption
304.60	448.38	371.86	398.59	413.76	385.60	390.72	392.11	398.80	308.83	..	Private Consumption, etc.
95.95	120.34	140.09	157.50	168.21	164.70	142.10	137.41	140.43	270.14	..	General Gov't Consumption
313.84	429.47	363.00	322.80	306.60	197.80	136.20	116.20	99.60	100.00	..	Gross Domestic Investment
..	..	..	..	293.06	193.96	144.00	122.76	112.45	109.21	..	Fixed Investment
487.84	613.47	665.07	705.26	700.65	660.13	665.02	674.08	697.59	703.90	B H	GDP at factor cost
68.51	71.94	75.18	73.92	74.46	75.07	82.43	87.91	92.76	96.02	..	Agriculture
155.85	219.34	257.68	279.79	266.24	243.27	247.14	254.50	278.11	280.30	..	Industry
38.81	41.35	54.39	57.68	63.23	59.33	59.76	63.63	66.42	66.75	f	Manufacturing
290.79	358.36	367.07	394.96	399.01	370.69	360.95	360.43	353.85	351.99	..	Services, etc.
											Memo Items:
306.92	472.42	515.27	602.13	453.41	259.45	288.20	270.20	360.63	350.02	..	Capacity to Import
80.56	225.36	225.56	284.06	156.00	-27.62	0.00	-55.57	10.24	19.74	..	Terms of Trade Adjustment
595.71	875.00	925.50	1,032.72	895.71	661.40	690.52	647.26	734.96	748.05	..	Gross Domestic Income
551.41	808.67	851.51	940.81	803.54	577.12	613.85	550.09	642.72	657.50	..	Gross National Income
				(Index 1987 = 100)							**DOMESTIC PRICES/DEFLATORS**
105.2	109.3	114.2	128.0	131.2	92.9	100.0	93.8	106.9	107.3	..	Overall (GDP)
89.5	80.5	85.7	91.6	108.4	97.4	100.0	101.8	106.0	106.4	..	Domestic Absorption
62.3	77.6	80.6	89.7	97.1	103.1	100.0	104.0	109.3	107.7	..	Agriculture
176.9	170.1	168.5	193.9	196.6	85.9	100.0	77.5	107.7	108.4	..	Industry
88.4	82.0	81.1	80.6	86.4	104.1	100.0	89.4	83.3	84.6	..	Manufacturing
65.6	74.1	79.8	90.0	95.5	97.8	100.0	103.7	108.0	..	..	Consumer Price Index
											MANUFACTURING ACTIVITY
..	..	..	..	..	..	..	..	..	..	..	Employment (1987=100)
..	..	..	..	..	..	..	..	..	..	..	Real Earnings per Empl. (1987=100)
..	..	..	..	..	..	..	..	..	..	..	Real Output per Empl. (1987=100)
34.3	45.1	42.0	53.7	48.5						..	Earnings as % of Value Added
				(Billions of current CFA Francs)							**MONETARY HOLDINGS**
92.12	115.95	113.83	122.26	147.49	130.49	138.46	136.44	141.40	167.94	..	Money Supply, Broadly Defined
75.11	97.60	90.49	101.34	111.86	97.51	102.33	97.54	96.59	121.04	..	Money
30.64	43.19	42.92	43.68	48.14	49.39	55.26	51.20	49.91	66.20	..	Currency Outside Banks
44.47	54.41	47.58	57.66	63.73	48.11	47.08	46.34	46.67	54.84	..	Demand Deposits
17.01	18.35	23.33	20.92	35.62	32.99	36.13	38.91	44.81	46.90	..	Quasi-Money
				(Billions of current CFA Francs)							
13.62	-93.38	-26.65	..	..	..	..	..	..	..	E F	**GOVERNMENT DEFICIT (-) OR SURPLUS**
215.00	262.85	284.00									Current Revenue
118.35	176.36	181.34									Current Expenditure
96.65	86.49	102.66									Current Budget Balance
0.05	0.04	0.01									Capital Receipts
96.30	179.91	129.32									Capital Payments

CONGO	1970	1971	1972	1973	1974	1975	1976	1977	1978	1979	1980
FOREIGN TRADE (CUSTOMS BASIS)					*(Millions of current US dollars)*						
Value of Exports, fob	30.8	39.5	52.4	85.4	228.1	178.7	181.8	181.7	308.3	509.3	955.3
Nonfuel Primary Products	21.6	25.5	29.5	29.9	51.9	26.8	21.3	53.8	23.2	36.7	35.8
Fuels	0.3	0.5	2.6	28.2	158.0	131.2	136.8	99.1	253.1	433.7	855.7
Manufactures	9.0	13.5	20.3	27.3	18.2	20.8	23.6	28.9	31.9	38.8	63.7
Value of Imports, cif	57.2	78.9	89.7	125.1	123.3	164.8	167.6	183.1	242.0	266.4	418.2
Nonfuel Primary Products	12.1	13.6	17.4	19.2	22.0	28.7	29.2	40.7	58.1	75.5	89.9
Fuels	1.2	2.0	2.4	3.5	10.6	13.0	15.1	2.7	19.4	17.2	57.9
Manufactures	44.0	63.4	70.0	102.4	90.7	123.1	123.3	139.7	164.6	173.7	270.3
					(Index 1987 = 100)						
Terms of Trade	127.4	123.4	108.4	65.0	106.9	98.1	106.8	111.7	103.9	113.5	153.8
Export Prices, fob	37.5	38.4	36.9	26.9	58.2	56.9	62.3	74.5	74.2	96.3	148.6
Import Prices, cif	29.4	31.2	34.0	41.3	54.4	58.0	58.4	66.7	71.4	84.9	96.6
BALANCE OF PAYMENTS					*(Millions of current US dollars)*						
Exports of Goods & Services	80.2	105.1	115.2	173.0	304.9	276.9	293.1	348.6	380.4	568.7	1,029.3
Merchandise, fob	58.0	75.3	78.1	122.2	261.2	230.8	221.6	266.7	308.2	495.7	910.6
Nonfactor Services	22.0	28.2	34.7	47.7	41.3	43.0	68.5	77.2	68.8	69.7	110.6
Factor Services	0.2	1.6	2.4	3.1	2.4	3.2	3.1	4.8	3.4	3.3	8.0
Imports of Goods & Services	129.0	175.5	217.8	255.5	363.8	529.2	529.5	535.2	599.3	679.1	1,194.9
Merchandise, fob	72.0	98.6	119.2	126.8	193.4	272.0	235.1	234.1	282.1	363.0	545.2
Nonfactor Services	50.0	68.3	89.9	105.3	152.1	224.9	254.1	258.6	259.2	219.8	480.1
Factor Services	7.0	8.6	8.7	23.4	18.3	32.4	40.3	42.5	58.0	96.3	169.6
Long-Term Interest	3.0	3.0	2.9	4.6	5.6	9.2	11.8	11.9	8.2	33.0	37.4
Private Current Transfers, net	-4.2	-8.1	-12.7	-7.6	-57.2	-32.9	-32.3	-33.5	-13.3	-31.7	-64.4
Workers' Remittances	0.8	..	..	..	..	..	..	..	..	..	0.8
Curr. A/C Bal before Off. Transf.	-53.0	-78.5	-115.3	-90.1	-116.2	-285.2	-268.7	-220.1	-232.2	-142.1	-230.0
Net Official Transfers	8.0	11.8	17.5	11.8	23.1	36.3	41.3	26.7	51.6	42.7	63.3
Curr. A/C Bal after Off. Transf.	-45.0	-66.7	-97.8	-78.3	-93.1	-248.9	-227.3	-193.3	-180.6	-99.4	-166.7
Long-Term Capital, net	59.0	58.1	85.7	74.4	72.6	159.3	138.5	135.7	172.5	72.6	242.4
Direct Investment	30.0	48.7	66.3	68.3	46.1	15.4	1.4	2.0	4.1	16.5	40.0
Long-Term Loans	12.6	16.8	22.4	29.1	57.9	112.7	34.4	47.6	144.6	151.7	455.9
Disbursements	18.4	22.3	27.1	36.5	70.6	132.6	45.9	69.5	156.9	195.1	491.1
Repayments	5.8	5.5	4.7	7.4	12.7	19.9	11.5	21.9	12.3	43.4	35.2
Other Long-Term Capital	16.4	-7.5	-3.1	-23.0	-31.3	31.2	102.8	86.1	23.8	-95.5	-253.5
Other Capital, net	-12.2	8.3	10.2	0.2	39.2	79.2	84.3	49.3	-2.0	54.8	-16.6
Change in Reserves	-1.8	0.3	2.0	3.7	-18.7	10.4	4.5	8.4	10.1	-28.1	-59.1
Memo Item:					*(CFA Francs per US dollar)*						
Conversion Factor (Annual Avg)	277.710	277.130	252.480	222.890	240.700	214.310	238.950	245.680	225.650	212.720	211.280
					(Millions of US dollars), outstanding at end of year						
EXTERNAL DEBT (Total)	118.8	141.5	164.0	196.0	268.1	364.6	388.9	594.8	798.7	1,062.3	1,510.7
Long-Term Debt (by debtor)	118.5	140.8	162.5	192.6	263.5	359.3	381.1	465.2	674.1	869.7	1,264.6
Central Bank, incl. IMF credit	0.6	0.5	0.3	2.3	3.8	10.3	14.5	31.9	46.6	53.8	47.3
Central Government	73.8	93.2	111.5	138.5	202.7	290.0	302.4	365.0	545.4	706.4	844.6
Rest of General Government	0.3	0.3	0.2	0.5	0.5	0.3	0.3	0.2	0.3	0.2	0.2
Non-financial Public Enterprises	14.5	19.0	24.2	26.7	33.6	30.4	39.1	43.3	58.8	74.4	88.4
Priv. Sector, incl non-guaranteed	29.3	27.8	26.3	24.6	22.9	28.3	24.8	24.8	23.0	34.9	284.1
Short-Term Debt	0.3	0.7	1.5	3.4	4.6	5.3	7.8	129.6	124.6	192.6	246.1
Memo Items:					*(Thousands of US dollars)*						
Int'l Reserves Excluding Gold	8,884.8	10,820.1	10,338.0	7,858.0	24,101.2	13,814.5	12,168.2	13,530.0	9,429.1	42,232.5	85,899.0
Gold Holdings (at market price)	..	..	..	..	..	..	..	923.7	1,921.0	5,836.8	6,720.3
SOCIAL INDICATORS											
Total Fertility Rate	5.9	6.0	6.0	6.0	6.0	6.0	6.0	6.0	6.0	6.0	6.0
Infant Mortality Rate	126.1	125.5	125.0	125.0	125.0	124.9	124.9	124.9	124.7	124.5	124.4
Life Expectancy at Birth	45.8	46.2	46.6	47.0	47.4	47.8	48.2	48.6	49.0	49.4	49.8
Urban Population, % of total	32.8	33.0	33.2	33.4	33.6	33.8	34.2	34.6	35.0	35.4	35.8
Food Prod. per capita (1987=100)	117.2	119.7	113.8	114.3	108.6	108.9	106.6	104.8	100.8	102.4	101.7
Labor Force, Agriculture (%)	65.0	64.7	64.5	64.2	64.0	63.7	63.4	63.2	62.9	62.7	62.4
Labor Force, Female (%)	40.2	40.2	40.1	40.1	40.0	40.0	40.0	39.9	39.9	39.8	39.8
Primary Schl. Enroll. Ratio	..	..	..	..	133.0	..	..	..	..	..	..
Primary Schl. Enroll. Ratio, Female	..	..	..	..	..	..	..	..	..	..	..
Secondary Schl. Enroll. Ratio	..	..	..	..	33.0	..	..	..	..	..	..

1981	1982	1983	1984	1985	1986	1987	1988	1989	1990 estimate	Notes	CONGO
											FOREIGN TRADE (CUSTOMS BASIS)
											(Millions of current US dollars)
1,128.0	1,264.2	1,066.2	1,182.6	1,087.2	776.9	1,010.1	959.9	1,165.0	1,130.0	..	Value of Exports, fob
145.9	121.4	50.9	55.1	35.3	65.7	85.4	81.1	98.4	95.5	..	Nonfuel Primary Products
899.6	1,066.3	957.9	1,085.1	1,013.9	692.1	900.0	855.2	1,037.9	1,006.8	..	Fuels
82.5	76.5	57.5	42.5	38.1	19.1	24.8	23.6	28.6	27.7	..	Manufactures
667.5	830.2	629.0	598.6	580.2	578.6	529.3	564.0	524.0	570.0	..	Value of Imports, cif
85.4	89.9	100.8	122.6	120.0	117.5	107.5	114.6	106.5	115.8	..	Nonfuel Primary Products
80.4	60.9	14.5	22.5	18.0	9.9	9.1	9.7	9.0	9.8	..	Fuels
501.7	679.4	513.7	453.5	442.3	451.2	412.7	439.7	408.6	444.4	..	Manufactures
											(Index 1987 = 100)
163.6	156.5	149.1	150.7	145.4	86.9	100.0	75.4	90.3	98.7	..	Terms of Trade
159.5	145.7	134.4	132.9	127.9	81.1	100.0	80.2	100.8	123.8	..	Export Prices, fob
97.5	93.1	90.1	88.2	88.0	93.3	100.0	106.3	111.6	125.4	..	Import Prices, cif
											BALANCE OF PAYMENTS
											(Millions of current US dollars)
1,173.3	1,205.7	1,159.4	1,355.2	1,228.6	783.8	1,004.4	942.9	1,228.0	1,451.9	f	Exports of Goods & Services
1,072.7	1,108.5	1,066.2	1,268.4	1,144.8	672.6	876.7	843.2	1,138.0	1,349.6	..	Merchandise, fob
84.0	77.6	87.8	80.3	74.7	103.1	97.2	92.3	83.1	95.3	..	Nonfactor Services
16.6	19.6	5.4	6.5	9.1	8.1	30.5	7.5	7.0	7.0	..	Factor Services
1,645.7	1,519.2	1,556.2	1,142.4	1,392.8	1,403.4	1,238.2	1,396.2	1,330.8	1,606.3	f	Imports of Goods & Services
803.6	663.8	649.5	617.6	630.1	512.4	419.9	522.7	534.0	424.6	..	Merchandise, fob
713.3	697.3	727.4	391.3	525.6	656.8	532.1	560.1	480.6	678.6	..	Nonfactor Services
128.8	158.0	179.3	133.5	237.2	234.2	286.2	313.3	316.2	503.1	..	Factor Services
94.3	94.2	97.3	98.8	132.5	92.2	83.3	83.9	94.2	104.1	..	Long-Term Interest
-32.3	-47.2	-41.1	-45.0	-37.5	-41.0	-56.8	-56.6	-29.8	-42.1	..	Private Current Transfers, net
..	..	..	..	..	..	..	..	..	..		Workers' Remittances
-504.6	-360.7	-437.9	167.9	-201.7	-660.6	-290.6	-509.9	-132.6	-196.5	..	Curr. A/C Bal before Off. Transf.
43.9	29.2	37.0	42.3	40.4	59.9	67.9	64.4	51.7	73.5	..	Net Official Transfers
-460.7	-331.5	-400.9	210.2	-161.3	-600.7	-222.7	-445.5	-80.9	-123.0	f	Curr. A/C Bal after Off. Transf.
135.5	451.2	175.0	-55.4	27.8	-56.3	173.2	8.8	-234.4	110.5	f	Long-Term Capital, net
30.8	35.3	56.1	34.9	12.7	22.4	43.4	9.1	-1.1	-1.1	..	Direct Investment
237.3	502.9	278.6	210.2	205.4	123.4	154.3	333.2	-37.5	-5.6	..	Long-Term Loans
342.8	627.1	494.8	454.1	456.3	366.1	460.6	614.2	141.7	134.2	..	Disbursements
105.5	124.2	216.2	243.9	250.9	242.7	306.3	281.0	179.2	139.8	..	Repayments
-132.7	-87.0	-159.7	-300.6	-190.2	-202.2	-24.6	-333.5	-195.8	117.2	..	Other Long-Term Capital
387.8	-201.3	193.6	-163.2	132.0	647.6	44.5	438.7	318.2	13.2	f	Other Capital, net
-62.6	81.6	32.3	8.4	1.5	9.5	5.0	-2.1	-2.9	-0.7	..	Change in Reserves
											Memo Item:
											(CFA Francs per US dollar)
271.730	328.600	381.060	436.960	449.260	346.300	300.530	297.850	319.010	272.260	..	Conversion Factor (Annual Avg)
											(Millions of US dollars), outstanding at end of year
1,487.4	1,952.7	2,014.3	2,054.6	3,030.9	3,481.8	4,350.8	4,161.0	4,325.7	5,118.3	..	**EXTERNAL DEBT (Total)**
1,371.6	1,767.0	1,842.7	1,861.2	2,351.8	2,781.1	3,450.7	3,565.3	3,556.0	4,391.1	..	Long-Term Debt (by debtor)
34.6	31.3	115.2	93.0	110.9	121.7	146.4	131.5	110.3	105.5	..	Central Bank, incl. IMF credit
889.1	1,140.9	1,140.5	1,206.2	1,515.2	1,927.3	2,617.4	2,736.8	2,792.5	3,688.6	..	Central Government
0.1	0.1	0.1	6.1	7.6	2.8	2.4	1.7	1.7	1.6	..	Rest of General Government
99.4	122.1	163.0	171.9	225.8	238.6	252.2	211.6	190.7	143.6	..	Non-financial Public Enterprises
348.4	472.6	423.9	384.0	492.3	490.7	432.3	483.7	460.8	451.8	..	Priv. Sector, incl non-guaranteed
115.8	185.7	171.6	193.4	679.1	700.7	900.1	595.7	769.7	727.2	..	Short-Term Debt
											Memo Items:
											(Thousands of US dollars)
123,369.0	37,014.5	7,360.1	4,113.8	3,963.4	6,818.5	3,398.1	14,606.8	15,821.5	21,993.9	..	Int'l Reserves Excluding Gold
4,531.5	5,208.7	4,349.1	3,422.1	3,629.7	4,339.0	5,373.5	4,553.8	4,451.1	4,273.5	..	Gold Holdings (at market price)
											SOCIAL INDICATORS
6.0	6.0	6.1	6.2	6.3	6.4	6.5	6.5	6.5	6.6	..	Total Fertility Rate
124.2	124.0	123.0	122.0	121.0	120.0	119.0	118.0	117.0	116.0	..	Infant Mortality Rate
50.2	50.6	51.0	51.4	51.8	52.2	52.5	52.7	52.8	53.0	..	Life Expectancy at Birth
36.2	36.7	37.1	37.6	38.0	38.7	39.3	39.7	40.1	40.5	..	Urban Population, % of total
103.1	103.4	101.7	102.2	100.9	99.4	100.0	99.3	94.1	95.2	..	Food Prod. per capita (1987=100)
..	..	..	..	..	..	..	..	..	..	..	Labor Force, Agriculture (%)
39.7	39.6	39.5	39.4	39.3	39.2	39.1	39.0	38.9	38.8	..	Labor Force, Female (%)
..	..	..	..	..	..	..	..	..	..	..	Primary Schl. Enroll. Ratio
..	..	..	..	..	..	..	..	..	..	..	Primary Schl. Enroll. Ratio, Female
..	..	..	..	..	..	..	..	..	..	..	Secondary Schl. Enroll. Ratio

COSTA RICA	1970	1971	1972	1973	1974	1975	1976	1977	1978	1979	1980
CURRENT GNP PER CAPITA (US $)	560	610	660	750	860	950	1,070	1,320	1,560	1,790	1,960
POPULATION (thousands)	1,727	1,775	1,823	1,871	1,919	1,968	2,017	2,066	2,116	2,167	2,218

USE AND ORIGIN OF RESOURCES *(Billions of current Costa Rican Colones)*

	1970	1971	1972	1973	1974	1975	1976	1977	1978	1979	1980
Gross National Product (GNP)	6.43	7.04	7.96	9.88	12.89	16.28	20.08	25.70	29.31	33.31	39.42
Net Factor Income from Abroad	-0.09	-0.10	-0.25	-0.28	-0.33	-0.52	-0.60	-0.63	-0.88	-1.28	-1.99
GDP at Market Prices	6.52	7.14	8.22	10.16	13.22	16.80	20.68	26.33	30.19	34.58	41.41
Resource Balance	-0.44	-0.74	-0.53	-0.62	-1.96	-1.43	-1.24	-1.44	-2.37	-3.55	-4.28
Exports of Goods & NFServices	1.84	1.94	2.52	3.16	4.43	5.05	5.98	8.13	8.51	9.31	10.96
Imports of Goods & NFServices	2.28	2.69	3.05	3.78	6.39	6.48	7.22	9.57	10.88	12.86	15.25
Domestic Absorption	6.97	7.88	8.74	10.78	15.17	18.23	21.92	27.77	32.56	38.14	45.69
Private Consumption, etc.	4.81	5.15	5.75	6.93	9.75	12.04	13.72	17.17	20.41	23.14	27.14
General Gov't Consumption	0.82	0.99	1.18	1.42	1.89	2.56	3.31	4.21	5.07	6.24	7.54
Gross Domestic Investment	1.34	1.74	1.81	2.44	3.53	3.64	4.89	6.39	7.08	8.75	11.00
Fixed Investment	1.27	1.58	1.80	2.25	3.17	3.69	4.85	5.89	6.95	9.05	9.89
Indirect Taxes, net	0.73	0.77	0.74	1.00	1.45	2.12	2.57	3.41	4.00	4.22	4.86
GDP at factor cost	5.80	6.37	7.47	9.17	11.77	14.69	18.11	22.92	26.19	30.37	36.54
Agriculture	1.47	1.44	1.60	1.96	2.52	3.42	4.21	5.76	6.16	6.40	7.37
Industry	1.58	1.82	2.14	2.71	3.64	4.60	5.68	6.89	7.87	9.15	11.17
Manufacturing	..	1.35	1.57	2.05	2.75	3.43	4.07	5.00	5.66	6.33	7.70
Services, etc.	3.48	3.88	4.47	5.49	7.05	8.79	10.79	13.68	16.16	19.04	22.87
Gross Domestic Saving	0.90	1.00	1.28	1.82	1.58	2.21	3.65	4.95	4.71	5.20	6.72
Gross National Saving	0.83	0.92	1.05	1.58	1.32	1.77	3.15	4.46	3.97	4.07	4.90

(Millions of 1987 Costa Rican Colones)

	1970	1971	1972	1973	1974	1975	1976	1977	1978	1979	1980
Gross National Product	146,030	156,086	166,423	179,847	190,792	192,978	202,734	221,389	233,578	243,498	242,774
GDP at Market Prices	146,793	156,758	169,590	182,728	192,556	196,419	207,090	225,577	239,540	251,405	253,284
Resource Balance	-13,471	-13,893	-7,318	-7,268	-9,018	-5,498	-12,021	-24,375	-24,749	-25,246	-24,997
Exports of Goods & NFServices	36,534	39,652	46,418	49,801	53,417	52,364	55,202	59,704	65,638	67,777	64,833
Imports of Goods & NFServices	50,005	53,545	53,736	57,069	62,435	57,862	67,223	84,079	90,387	93,023	89,831
Domestic Absorption	160,263	170,651	176,909	189,996	201,574	201,917	219,111	249,952	264,289	276,651	278,281
Private Consumption, etc.	104,894	106,155	113,520	118,174	123,629	126,401	129,696	145,127	158,332	161,503	157,448
General Gov't Consumption	23,661	25,167	26,938	28,570	30,981	32,736	35,291	38,380	39,787	42,856	43,480
Gross Domestic Investment	31,708	39,330	36,451	43,252	46,964	42,780	54,125	66,445	66,169	72,291	77,354
Fixed Investment	26,002	30,260	31,679	34,361	37,709	37,244	46,068	51,795	56,007	64,568	58,487
GDP at factor cost	..	..	..	..	..	..	..	..	..	236,169	239,288
Agriculture	33,644	35,196	37,104	39,200	38,536	39,706	39,903	40,782	43,474	43,689	43,472
Industry	33,482	36,836	41,432	44,961	50,158	51,937	56,472	62,420	67,131	71,109	71,934
Manufacturing	..	..	..	34,161	38,506	39,725	42,031	47,382	51,267	525,705	53,054
Services, etc.	79,667	84,726	91,054	98,567	103,862	104,777	110,715	122,375	128,935	136,606	137,878

Memo Items:

	1970	1971	1972	1973	1974	1975	1976	1977	1978	1979	1980
Capacity to Import	40,330	38,767	44,415	47,715	43,307	45,124	55,666	71,431	70,694	67,336	64,601
Terms of Trade Adjustment	3,796	-884	-2,003	-2,086	-10,110	-7,240	464	11,727	5,056	-441	-233
Gross Domestic Income	150,588	155,874	167,587	180,642	182,446	189,180	207,554	237,304	244,596	250,964	253,051
Gross National Income	149,826	155,201	164,420	177,761	180,682	185,738	203,199	233,115	238,634	243,056	242,541

DOMESTIC PRICES/DEFLATORS *(Index 1987 = 100)*

	1970	1971	1972	1973	1974	1975	1976	1977	1978	1979	1980
Overall (GDP)	4.4	4.6	4.8	5.6	6.9	8.6	10.0	11.7	12.6	13.8	16.3
Domestic Absorption	4.3	4.6	4.9	5.7	7.5	9.0	10.0	11.1	12.3	13.8	16.4
Agriculture	4.4	4.1	4.3	5.0	6.5	8.6	10.6	14.1	14.2	14.6	17.0
Industry	4.7	4.9	5.2	6.0	7.3	8.9	10.0	11.0	11.7	12.9	15.5
Manufacturing	..	..	..	6.0	7.1	8.6	9.7	10.6	11.0	1.2	14.5
Consumer Price Index	6.1	6.3	6.6	7.6	9.9	11.7	12.1	12.6	13.3	14.6	17.2

MANUFACTURING ACTIVITY

	1970	1971	1972	1973	1974	1975	1976	1977	1978	1979	1980
Employment (1987=100)	..	..	..	..	..	..	..	..	..	..	..
Real Earnings per Empl. (1987=100)	..	..	..	..	..	..	..	..	..	..	..
Real Output per Empl. (1987=100)	..	..	..	..	..	..	..	..	..	..	..
Earnings as % of Value Added	41.4	41.9	41.8	40.0	38.4	39.5	40.1	38.6	40.0	40.5	42.9

MONETARY HOLDINGS *(Billions of current Costa Rican Colones)*

	1970	1971	1972	1973	1974	1975	1976	1977	1978	1979	1980
Money Supply, Broadly Defined	1.28	1.81	2.17	2.64	3.45	4.90	6.59	8.66	11.07	14.87	17.24
Money	1.01	1.32	1.50	1.87	2.15	2.77	3.41	4.50	5.62	6.23	7.27
Currency Outside Banks	0.38	0.43	0.52	0.64	0.73	0.85	1.12	1.41	1.70	1.95	2.26
Demand Deposits	0.63	0.88	0.98	1.23	1.41	1.92	2.29	3.09	3.92	4.27	5.02
Quasi-Money	0.27	0.49	0.66	0.77	1.30	2.13	3.18	4.16	5.44	8.64	9.96

(Millions of current Costa Rican Colones)

	1970	1971	1972	1973	1974	1975	1976	1977	1978	1979	1980
GOVERNMENT DEFICIT (-) OR SURPLUS	..	..	-360	-380	-90	-370	-700	-820	-1,510	-2,340	-3,060
Current Revenue	..	..	1,260	1,620	2,450	3,030	3,650	4,390	5,750	6,320	7,380
Current Expenditure	..	..	1,260	1,570	2,000	2,750	3,500	4,170	5,870	7,040	8,810
Current Budget Balance	..	..	0	50	450	280	150	220	-120	-720	-1,430
Capital Receipts	..	..	..	..	..	..	..	..	..	..	..
Capital Payments	..	..	360	430	540	650	850	1,040	1,390	1,620	1,630

1981	1982	1983	1984	1985	1986	1987	1988	1989	1990 estimate	Notes	COSTA RICA
1,530	1,150	1,060	1,250	1,400	1,550	1,650	1,680	1,760	1,900	..	**CURRENT GNP PER CAPITA (US $)**
2,270	2,322	2,375	2,431	2,489	2,546	2,606	2,672	2,736	2,807	..	**POPULATION (thousands)**
				(Billions of current Costa Rican Colones)							**USE AND ORIGIN OF RESOURCES**
50.67	81.42	115.64	149.21	183.79	231.48	265.97	323.57	395.03	494.27	..	Gross National Product (GNP)
-6.43	-16.09	-13.67	-13.80	-14.13	-15.10	-18.57	-26.09	-31.61	-27.95	..	Net Factor Income from Abroad
57.10	97.51	129.31	163.01	197.92	246.58	284.53	349.66	426.63	522.22	..	GDP at Market Prices
-2.80	2.85	-0.96	0.60	-3.47	2.09	-11.70	-7.05	-15.09	-40.37	..	Resource Balance
24.71	43.96	46.60	56.00	60.81	77.28	90.07	120.65	149.14	176.39	..	Exports of Goods & NFServices
27.51	41.11	47.57	55.40	64.28	75.19	101.77	127.70	164.23	216.76	..	Imports of Goods & NFServices
59.91	94.66	130.28	162.41	201.39	244.49	296.23	356.71	441.72	562.59	..	Domestic Absorption
34.34	56.40	79.48	99.91	118.97	144.38	176.48	215.79	256.92	315.43	..	Private Consumption, etc.
8.99	14.19	19.53	25.50	31.18	37.95	42.65	54.63	72.28	94.33	..	General Gov't Consumption
16.58	24.07	31.27	37.00	51.24	62.16	77.11	86.29	112.52	152.84	..	Gross Domestic Investment
13.74	19.81	23.27	32.68	38.24	46.02	56.31	66.21	87.22	115.47	..	Fixed Investment
6.78	11.31	18.62	23.91	26.69	32.10	22.60	0.00	..	25.00	..	Indirect Taxes, net
50.32	86.19	110.69	139.10	171.23	214.48	261.93	349.66	426.63	497.22	B	GDP at factor cost
13.14	23.88	28.45	34.57	37.34	51.53	51.42	62.77	73.19	83.81	..	Agriculture
15.20	25.10	37.00	48.01	57.13	68.11	78.46	95.15	114.55	133.78	..	Industry
10.82	19.83	28.26	36.67	43.71	52.57	60.70	74.31	86.80	100.00	f	Manufacturing
28.76	48.52	63.87	80.43	103.44	126.94	154.66	191.74	238.89	304.63	..	Services, etc.
13.77	26.92	30.31	37.60	47.77	64.25	65.41	79.24	97.43	112.46	..	Gross Domestic Saving
7.93	11.94	17.57	25.22	35.78	51.24	49.27	56.18	69.02	88.89	..	Gross National Saving
				(Millions of 1987 Costa Rican Colones)							
233,070	209,800	219,530	238,818	242,051	255,063	265,967	273,868	286,981	308,387	..	Gross National Product
247,561	230,296	236,697	255,287	257,427	271,607	284,533	294,413	311,158	323,092	..	GDP at Market Prices
5,871	13,926	4,466	5,356	-1,799	-12,136	-11,701	-4,842	-6,477	-8,265	..	Resource Balance
72,042	68,111	67,217	74,796	71,809	74,415	90,067	97,971	112,667	121,191	..	Exports of Goods & NFServices
66,171	54,185	62,751	69,440	73,608	86,550	101,768	102,813	119,143	129,456	..	Imports of Goods & NFServices
241,689	216,370	232,231	249,931	259,226	283,743	296,234	299,255	317,635	331,357	..	Domestic Absorption
152,480	140,467	145,630	156,584	161,368	167,280	176,475	183,132	194,854	202,952	..	Private Consumption, etc.
41,041	39,995	38,820	40,332	40,741	41,732	42,652	43,933	45,469	46,607	..	General Gov't Consumption
48,169	35,908	47,781	53,015	57,117	74,730	77,107	72,190	77,312	81,799	..	Gross Domestic Investment
43,919	31,705	34,327	43,303	45,631	51,037	56,313	54,255	62,614	71,192	..	Fixed Investment
234,944	220,867	222,242	241,522	241,269	248,806	261,933	..	..		B	GDP at factor cost
45,688	43,539	45,280	49,829	47,075	49,344	51,417	53,781	57,717	59,968	..	Agriculture
68,910	59,618	62,052	69,047	70,099	74,673	78,456	79,967	84,067	86,039	..	Industry
52,789	46,771	47,613	52,563	53,620	57,534	60,698	62,035	64,393	66,260	f	Manufacturing
132,963	127,139	129,366	136,410	140,253	147,591	154,660	160,666	169,374	177,085	..	Services, etc.
											Memo Items:
59,430	57,936	61,479	70,192	69,635	88,951	90,067	97,137	108,197	105,344	..	Capacity to Import
-12,612	-10,175	-5,738	-4,604	-2,174	14,536	0	-835	-4,469	-15,847	..	Terms of Trade Adjustment
234,948	220,121	230,959	250,683	255,253	286,143	284,533	293,579	306,689	307,246	..	Gross Domestic Income
220,458	199,625	213,791	234,214	239,877	269,599	265,967	273,033	282,512	292,540	..	Gross National Income
				(Index 1987 = 100)							**DOMESTIC PRICES/DEFLATORS**
23.1	42.3	54.6	63.9	76.9	90.8	100.0	118.8	137.1	161.6	..	Overall (GDP)
24.8	43.7	56.1	65.0	77.7	86.2	100.0	119.2	139.1	169.8	..	Domestic Absorption
28.8	54.9	62.8	69.4	79.3	104.4	100.0	116.7	126.8	139.8	..	Agriculture
22.1	42.1	59.6	69.5	81.5	91.2	100.0	119.0	136.3	155.5	..	Industry
20.5	42.4	59.4	69.8	81.5	91.4	100.0	119.8	134.8	150.9	..	Manufacturing
23.6	44.8	59.4	66.5	76.5	85.6	100.0	120.8	140.8	167.6	..	Consumer Price Index
											MANUFACTURING ACTIVITY
..	..	..	..	..	92.3	100.0	102.5		..	..	Employment (1987=100)
..	..	..	..	..	100.2	100.0	92.8		..	..	Real Earnings per Empl. (1987=100)
..	..	..	..	..	105.8	100.0	100.8		..	G	Real Output per Empl. (1987=100)
..	..	..	..	..	29.6	32.8	30.6		..	..	Earnings as % of Value Added
				(Billions of current Costa Rican Colones)							**MONETARY HOLDINGS**
32.27	40.99	56.14	65.76	76.00	92.16	107.15	150.23	174.83	222.95	..	Money Supply, Broadly Defined
10.83	18.45	25.62	30.13	32.44	42.49	42.61	65.27	63.97	66.48	..	Money
3.50	5.44	6.94	8.59	9.94	13.24	14.78	24.73	21.92	27.51	..	Currency Outside Banks
7.33	13.01	18.68	21.54	22.50	29.25	27.83	40.53	42.05	38.98	..	Demand Deposits
21.44	22.55	30.52	35.63	43.56	49.67	64.53	84.96	110.86	156.46	..	Quasi-Money
				(Millions of current Costa Rican Colones)							
-1,640	-860	-2,600	-1,200	-2,470	-11,040	-8,290	10	-9,060	-16,410	F	**GOVERNMENT DEFICIT (-) OR SURPLUS**
10,190	17,030	28,110	36,380	41,010	54,560	70,080	87,720	104,060	120,250	..	Current Revenue
10,620	17,490	27,000	33,080	36,970	53,700	67,330	74,230	93,200	118,580	..	Current Expenditure
-430	-460	1,110	3,300	4,040	860	2,750	13,490	10,860	1,670	..	Current Budget Balance
							10	30	480	470	..	Capital Receipts
1,210	400	3,710	4,500	6,510	11,900	11,050	13,510	20,400	18,550	..	Capital Payments

COSTA RICA	1970	1971	1972	1973	1974	1975	1976	1977	1978	1979	1980
FOREIGN TRADE (CUSTOMS BASIS)					*(Millions of current US dollars)*						
Value of Exports, fob	231.2	225.4	280.9	344.5	440.3	494.1	600.4	839.5	919.4	934.3	1,031.5
Nonfuel Primary Products	184.7	172.4	221.1	264.1	321.5	364.2	428.5	635.5	655.3	705.2	671.4
Fuels	1.0	1.8	0.6	0.4	0.6	0.3	0.8	0.8	0.9	0.8	6.2
Manufactures	45.5	51.2	59.2	79.9	118.2	129.6	171.2	203.3	263.1	228.3	353.9
Value of Imports, cif	316.7	349.7	372.8	455.3	719.7	694.0	800.3	1,059.3	1,211.7	1,446.1	1,596.4
Nonfuel Primary Products	44.6	51.6	48.8	61.0	108.7	89.2	95.0	115.1	122.8	152.5	198.0
Fuels	12.3	15.8	20.1	31.5	65.1	73.8	73.9	102.2	117.7	189.5	245.7
Manufactures	259.8	282.4	303.8	362.8	545.9	531.0	631.4	842.0	971.3	1,104.1	1,152.7
					(Index 1987 = 100)						
Terms of Trade	153.8	131.0	142.6	148.8	117.4	113.3	139.4	162.1	132.0	129.5	117.1
Export Prices, fob	39.5	35.9	41.3	51.5	61.4	62.0	78.8	99.6	90.7	103.8	109.3
Import Prices, cif	25.7	27.4	28.9	34.6	52.3	54.7	56.5	61.4	68.7	80.2	93.3
BALANCE OF PAYMENTS					*(Millions of current US dollars)*						
Exports of Goods & Services	277.9	281.4	344.2	418.8	539.6	600.5	710.6	969.1	1,025.0	1,111.3	1,218.6
Merchandise, fob	231.0	225.3	278.8	344.8	440.2	493.1	592.4	827.8	863.9	942.1	1,000.9
Nonfactor Services	45.9	55.5	64.1	71.4	95.2	103.2	112.6	130.9	143.8	156.1	196.9
Factor Services	1.0	0.7	1.3	2.6	4.2	4.2	5.7	10.4	17.3	13.1	20.8
Imports of Goods & Services	357.9	403.3	450.8	537.9	815.4	827.8	925.2	1,210.5	1,404.8	1,681.7	1,897.0
Merchandise, fob	286.8	317.2	337.1	412.1	648.9	627.2	695.4	925.1	1,049.4	1,257.2	1,375.2
Nonfactor Services	54.3	68.3	74.8	82.4	120.5	130.4	148.6	195.3	224.8	261.7	282.5
Factor Services	16.8	17.8	38.9	43.4	45.9	70.2	81.3	90.1	130.6	162.8	239.3
Long-Term Interest	14.2	15.3	17.7	23.6	31.2	36.9	41.0	51.5	84.6	116.2	170.6
Private Current Transfers, net	3.4	3.5	4.0	7.0	8.7	9.5	11.2	15.4	15.9	16.5	19.8
Workers' Remittances	..	..	..	..	..	..	..	..	..	..	..
Curr. A/C Bal before Off. Transf.	-76.6	-118.4	-102.6	-112.1	-267.1	-217.8	-203.4	-226.0	-363.9	-553.9	-658.6
Net Official Transfers	2.5	3.9	2.6	-0.1	1.0	0.1	2.0	0.4	0.7	-4.3	-5.3
Curr. A/C Bal after Off. Transf.	-74.1	-114.4	-100.0	-112.2	-266.1	-217.7	-201.5	-225.6	-363.2	-558.2	-663.9
Long-Term Capital, net	43.8	57.1	80.1	92.4	135.9	238.0	217.4	298.8	352.7	354.7	402.2
Direct Investment	26.4	22.1	25.8	37.7	46.3	69.0	60.7	62.5	47.0	42.4	48.1
Long-Term Loans	18.9	35.1	53.1	61.4	83.6	157.8	156.3	247.6	211.6	198.8	372.6
Disbursements	59.9	78.1	103.3	118.2	157.8	260.1	275.9	399.0	515.3	464.9	535.7
Repayments	41.0	43.0	50.2	56.8	74.2	102.3	119.6	151.4	303.7	266.1	163.1
Other Long-Term Capital	-1.5	-0.1	1.2	-6.7	6.0	11.2	0.4	-11.3	94.1	113.5	-18.5
Other Capital, net	15.0	63.5	23.6	46.2	79.4	-18.3	35.8	33.3	-16.6	120.5	223.7
Change in Reserves	15.3	-6.1	-3.7	-26.4	50.8	-2.0	-51.8	-106.4	27.1	83.0	38.0
Memo Item:					*(Costa Rican Colones per US dollar)*						
Conversion Factor (Annual Avg)	6.630	6.630	6.630	6.650	7.930	8.570	8.570	8.570	8.570	8.570	8.570
				(Millions of US dollars), outstanding at end of year							
EXTERNAL DEBT (Total)	246.0	282.6	339.2	401.6	508.5	684.4	842.8	1,317.2	1,679.0	2,109.8	2,738.5
Long-Term Debt (by debtor)	246.0	282.6	339.2	401.6	508.5	684.4	842.8	1,094.2	1,395.0	1,756.8	2,163.5
Central Bank, incl. IMF credit	27.0	28.6	33.3	39.8	79.5	131.6	176.3	262.2	281.3	478.4	666.6
Central Government	50.0	65.3	87.9	110.2	120.6	147.3	174.1	213.1	317.7	410.6	505.2
Rest of General Government	0.9	4.4	5.1	5.4	4.5	7.3	6.5	5.8	5.2	4.3	3.2
Non-financial Public Enterprises	54.4	62.8	72.6	85.3	110.6	153.6	194.9	247.7	334.6	418.9	535.8
Priv. Sector, incl non-guaranteed	113.7	121.5	140.3	160.9	193.3	244.6	291.0	365.4	456.2	444.6	452.7
Short-Term Debt	0.0	0.0	0.0	0.0	0.0	0.0	0.0	223.0	284.0	353.0	575.0
Memo Items:					*(Millions of US dollars)*						
Int'l Reserves Excluding Gold	14.2	27.2	40.6	48.5	42.1	48.8	95.4	190.5	193.9	118.6	145.6
Gold Holdings (at market price)	2.2	2.6	3.9	6.7	11.1	8.4	8.0	12.1	18.1	44.5	51.3
SOCIAL INDICATORS											
Total Fertility Rate	4.9	4.6	4.3	4.3	4.2	4.1	4.0	3.9	3.8	3.7	3.7
Infant Mortality Rate	61.5	56.5	54.4	44.8	37.5	37.8	33.1	27.9	23.8	23.3	20.1
Life Expectancy at Birth	67.1	67.6	68.1	68.6	69.2	69.7	70.3	70.8	71.3	71.9	72.4
Urban Population, % of total	39.7	40.0	40.3	40.7	41.0	41.3	41.7	42.0	42.4	42.7	43.1
Food Prod. per capita (1987=100)	100.9	104.9	106.6	108.1	104.0	116.8	118.9	118.3	113.7	113.5	107.4
Labor Force, Agriculture (%)	42.6	41.2	39.9	38.7	37.6	36.6	35.2	34.0	32.8	31.8	30.8
Labor Force, Female (%)	18.0	18.4	18.8	19.1	19.4	19.7	20.0	20.4	20.7	21.0	21.3
Primary Schl. Enroll. Ratio	110.0	..	..	..	..	107.0	108.0	109.0	107.0	107.0	105.0
Primary Schl. Enroll. Ratio, Female	109.0	..	..	..	..	106.0	108.0	108.0	107.0	106.0	104.0
Secondary Schl. Enroll. Ratio	28.0	..	..	..	..	42.0	43.0	44.0	..	48.0	48.0

1981	1982	1983	1984	1985	1986	1987	1988	1989	1990 estimate	Notes	COSTA RICA
				(Millions of current US dollars)							**FOREIGN TRADE (CUSTOMS BASIS)**
1,010.5	876.8	844.5	951.3	941.0	1,089.8	1,113.8	1,245.7	1,414.6	1,457.4	..	Value of Exports, fob
676.4	620.9	602.4	709.4	701.7	837.0	816.2	912.9	1,036.6	1,068.0	..	Nonfuel Primary Products
12.5	8.0	14.7	18.1	17.0	14.8	11.8	13.2	15.0	15.4	..	Fuels
321.6	247.9	227.4	223.7	222.2	238.0	285.8	319.6	363.0	374.0	..	Manufactures
1,274.2	945.2	982.7	1,086.2	1,098.2	1,145.2	1,377.1	1,409.8	1,717.4	2,026.1	..	Value of Imports, cif
157.9	114.0	143.1	153.3	130.1	142.7	169.7	173.7	211.7	249.7	..	Nonfuel Primary Products
205.3	188.9	189.2	166.7	182.2	120.4	141.2	144.5	176.1	207.7	..	Fuels
911.0	642.3	650.4	766.3	785.9	882.1	1,066.2	1,091.5	1,329.7	1,568.7	..	Manufactures
				(Index 1987 = 100)							
108.5	108.7	112.4	110.8	111.1	121.8	100.0	115.0	109.2	113.8	..	Terms of Trade
102.4	98.4	99.6	96.5	96.0	110.2	100.0	113.8	113.6	121.1	..	Export Prices, fob
94.4	90.5	88.6	87.1	86.4	90.4	100.0	98.9	104.1	106.4	..	Import Prices, cif
				(Millions of current US dollars)							**BALANCE OF PAYMENTS**
1,199.3	1,143.4	1,172.6	1,313.7	1,270.2	1,440.2	1,492.3	1,658.8	1,951.2	2,047.3	f	Exports of Goods & Services
1,002.6	869.0	852.5	997.5	939.1	1,084.8	1,106.7	1,180.7	1,333.4	1,365.6	..	Merchandise, fob
172.9	247.7	280.2	278.5	281.3	310.0	344.5	439.4	507.9	584.5	..	Nonfactor Services
23.8	26.7	39.9	37.7	49.8	45.4	41.1	38.7	109.9	97.2	..	Factor Services
1,639.1	1,451.0	1,524.1	1,605.7	1,614.9	1,672.1	1,974.7	2,092.7	2,557.5	2,773.8	f	Imports of Goods & Services
1,090.6	804.9	894.3	992.9	1,001.0	1,045.2	1,245.2	1,278.6	1,572.0	1,833.3	..	Merchandise, fob
213.4	237.5	249.9	255.0	274.0	296.0	382.9	416.6	486.5	550.4	..	Nonfactor Services
335.1	408.6	379.9	357.8	339.9	330.9	346.6	397.5	499.0	390.1	..	Factor Services
135.4	109.4	529.5	244.5	343.0	217.0	144.9	188.9	132.6	171.2	..	Long-Term Interest
27.2	29.6	22.9	31.9	42.6	37.4	38.7	40.0	39.2	47.8	..	Private Current Transfers, net
..	..	..	..	..	0.0	0.0	0.0	..	..	..	Workers' Remittances
-409.0	-273.0	-326.0	-260.1	-302.1	-194.5	-443.7	-393.9	-567.1	-678.7	..	Curr. A/C Bal before Off. Transf.
-0.1	6.3	46.1	109.0	176.1	114.5	187.3	215.4	152.2	164.9	..	Net Official Transfers
-409.1	-266.7	-279.9	-151.1	-126.0	-80.0	-256.4	-178.5	-414.9	-513.8	..	Curr. A/C Bal after Off. Transf.
217.6	22.1	1,175.3	67.4	343.4	-55.9	-363.1	-98.0	59.7	529.5	f	Long-Term Capital, net
66.2	26.5	55.3	52.0	65.2	57.4	75.8	121.4	95.2	108.7	..	Direct Investment
198.8	122.2	292.2	103.3	176.7	2.0	41.7	48.0	-16.0	-62.5	..	Long-Term Loans
376.9	243.2	429.8	240.3	320.7	203.1	124.1	167.1	125.6	206.6	..	Disbursements
178.1	121.0	137.6	137.0	144.0	201.1	82.4	119.1	141.6	269.1	..	Repayments
-47.4	-126.6	827.8	-87.9	101.5	-115.3	-480.6	-267.4	-19.5	483.4	..	Other Long-Term Capital
146.8	358.0	-823.0	79.8	-103.1	228.8	662.3	510.7	505.0	-212.5	f	Other Capital, net
44.8	-113.4	-72.4	3.9	-114.3	-92.9	-42.8	-234.2	-149.8	196.8	..	Change in Reserves
				(Costa Rican Colones per US dollar)							**Memo Item:**
21.760	37.410	41.090	44.530	50.450	55.990	62.780	75.800	81.500	91.580	..	Conversion Factor (Annual Avg)
				(Millions of US dollars), outstanding at end of year							
3,300.2	3,640.9	4,177.3	3,988.0	4,398.9	4,574.8	4,720.1	4,543.7	4,603.2	3,772.0	..	**EXTERNAL DEBT (Total)**
2,680.4	2,865.4	3,682.1	3,652.8	4,022.2	4,102.6	4,141.2	3,948.0	3,898.4	3,391.7	..	Long-Term Debt (by debtor)
1,086.4	1,148.7	1,254.0	1,243.6	1,250.1	1,127.1	1,091.6	992.5	1,002.8	1,348.3	..	Central Bank, incl. IMF credit
547.8	658.9	1,523.2	1,563.4	1,944.2	2,112.0	2,118.4	2,041.4	2,090.7	1,309.9	..	Central Government
2.2	2.2	1.5	1.1	18.0	13.6	13.5	24.2	19.5	19.1	..	Rest of General Government
640.1	632.6	533.7	510.4	498.9	538.4	613.4	571.7	481.1	410.3	..	Non-financial Public Enterprises
403.9	423.0	369.7	334.3	311.0	311.5	304.3	318.2	304.3	304.1	..	Priv. Sector, incl non-guaranteed
619.8	775.5	495.2	335.2	376.7	472.2	578.9	595.7	704.8	380.3	..	Short-Term Debt
				(Millions of US dollars)							**Memo Items:**
131.4	226.1	311.3	405.0	506.4	523.4	488.9	668.0	742.6	520.6	..	Int'l Reserves Excluding Gold
11.5	23.7	33.4	7.1	19.0	27.1	30.3	8.7	3.3	4.3	..	Gold Holdings (at market price)
											SOCIAL INDICATORS
3.6	3.5	3.5	3.4	3.4	3.3	3.3	3.2	3.1	3.1	..	Total Fertility Rate
17.9	19.3	18.6	18.9	18.6	18.2	17.9	17.4	16.9	16.5	..	Infant Mortality Rate
73.0	73.5	73.8	74.0	74.2	74.4	74.6	74.8	75.0	75.2	..	Life Expectancy at Birth
43.5	43.8	44.2	44.5	44.9	45.3	45.8	46.2	46.7	47.1	..	Urban Population, % of total
103.7	95.7	95.6	99.5	101.9	101.6	100.0	97.3	98.2	98.7	..	Food Prod. per capita (1987=100)
..	..	..	..	..	..	..	..	..	..	..	Labor Force, Agriculture (%)
21.4	21.4	21.5	21.6	21.6	21.7	21.7	21.7	21.7	21.8	..	Labor Force, Female (%)
..	103.0	102.0	98.0	97.0	98.0	98.0	100.0	100.0	..	..	Primary Schl. Enroll. Ratio
105.0	102.0	100.0	97.0	96.0	97.0	97.0	99.0	99.0	..	..	Primary Schl. Enroll. Ratio, Female
..	46.0	44.0	41.0	40.0	41.0	41.0	41.0	41.0	..	..	Secondary Schl. Enroll. Ratio

COTE D'IVOIRE	1970	1971	1972	1973	1974	1975	1976	1977	1978	1979	1980
CURRENT GNP PER CAPITA (US $)	270	280	290	310	390	510	560	630	830	1,010	1,180
POPULATION (thousands)	5,510	5,742	5,982	6,231	6,489	6,755	7,037	7,323	7,612	7,902	8,194
USE AND ORIGIN OF RESOURCES					*(Billions of current CFA Francs)*						
Gross National Product (GNP)	380.3	407.2	433.8	509.5	679.6	767.2	1,006.9	1,406.9	1,610.5	1,742.4	2,102.7
Net Factor Income from Abroad	-22.0	-29.0	-32.3	-49.6	-59.4	-67.3	-107.1	-132.3	-172.3	-202.5	-118.9
GDP at Market Prices	402.3	436.2	466.1	559.1	739.0	834.5	1,114.0	1,539.2	1,782.8	1,944.9	2,221.6
Resource Balance	26.8	16.5	21.0	14.1	54.1	1.2	61.2	96.9	-16.3	-59.5	-134.6
Exports of Goods & NF Services	143.9	140.5	156.2	199.9	337.7	306.5	465.0	656.1	651.1	673.0	756.0
Imports of Goods & NF Services	117.1	124.0	135.2	185.8	283.6	305.3	403.8	559.2	667.4	732.5	890.6
Domestic Absorption	375.5	419.7	445.1	545.0	684.9	833.3	1,052.8	1,442.3	1,799.1	2,004.4	2,356.2
Private Consumption, etc.	230.4	255.1	275.1	327.3	402.5	504.2	616.4	811.9	978.1	1,106.7	1,333.6
General Gov't Consumption	54.6	69.5	72.7	88.1	119.7	141.8	180.3	209.7	290.4	353.8	395.9
Gross Domestic Investment	90.5	95.1	97.3	129.6	162.7	187.3	256.1	420.7	530.6	543.9	626.7
Fixed Investment	83.1	91.5	94.2	121.9	143.6	183.9	247.2	397.6	528.8	527.1	581.8
Indirect Taxes, net	83.9	79.1	83.8	110.2	164.5	149.8	299.8	501.5	448.6	448.4	429.4
GDP at factor cost	318.4	357.1	382.3	448.9	574.5	684.7	814.2	1,037.7	1,334.2	1,496.5	1,792.2
Agriculture	128.2	134.7	138.9	173.6	188.2	235.7	272.7	373.5	461.4	513.5	597.9
Industry	74.4	85.9	92.0	99.2	118.9	142.2	182.3	233.3	293.8	331.8	357.4
Manufacturing	41.4	45.1	51.7	56.8	75.6	78.4	104.8	117.6	137.0	158.1	195.6
Services, etc.	115.8	136.5	151.4	176.1	267.4	306.8	359.2	430.9	579.0	651.2	836.9
Gross Domestic Saving	117.3	111.6	118.3	143.7	216.8	188.5	317.3	517.6	514.3	484.4	492.1
Gross National Saving	79.9	64.3	63.4	66.7	123.9	81.8	141.0	300.6	238.6	159.3	222.0
					(Billions of 1987 CFA Francs)						
Gross National Product	1,451.4	1,606.6	1,711.6	1,749.9	1,900.1	2,106.0	2,154.0	2,119.8	2,383.3	2,450.4	2,635.0
GDP at Market Prices	1,582.2	1,765.5	1,879.0	1,959.0	2,080.0	2,291.9	2,423.9	2,419.9	2,755.9	2,836.5	2,814.3
Resource Balance	55.1	76.8	133.4	11.5	62.8	52.0	-32.3	-306.0	-415.0	-360.4	-332.3
Exports of Goods & NF Services	547.5	579.4	648.7	635.2	729.0	699.9	782.1	720.1	761.5	778.8	878.1
Imports of Goods & NF Services	492.4	502.6	515.3	623.7	666.2	648.0	814.4	1,026.1	1,176.5	1,139.3	1,210.4
Domestic Absorption	1,527.1	1,688.7	1,745.6	1,947.4	2,017.1	2,239.9	2,456.2	2,726.0	3,170.9	3,197.0	3,146.6
Private Consumption, etc.	935.5	1,046.6	1,119.8	1,195.2	1,245.6	1,418.2	1,455.4	1,446.6	1,667.6	1,712.8	1,344.3
General Gov't Consumption	225.7	278.0	276.3	313.2	341.4	379.4	442.3	476.6	568.9	615.2	772.6
Gross Domestic Investment	365.9	364.1	349.4	439.0	430.1	442.3	558.5	802.9	934.4	868.9	1,029.7
Fixed Investment	330.9	346.7	334.7	407.6	372.8	432.4	534.3	764.2	931.3	841.0	955.9
GDP at factor cost	1,185.5	1,376.6	1,462.2	1,506.6	1,621.8	1,848.5	1,774.9	1,625.6	2,013.5	2,114.9	2,112.0
Agriculture	693.2	746.5	750.6	796.9	712.5	779.4	826.4	790.4	865.6	869.0	981.3
Industry	224.5	272.2	291.2	280.6	275.2	315.0	364.0	400.3	476.8	515.0	560.4
Manufacturing	..	..	..	..	..	..	..	..	..	..	..
Services, etc.	267.8	357.9	420.4	429.1	634.1	754.1	584.5	434.8	671.1	730.9	570.3
Memo Items:											
Capacity to Import	605.1	569.5	595.4	671.0	793.2	650.5	937.8	1,203.9	1,147.7	1,046.7	1,027.5
Terms of Trade Adjustment	57.6	-9.9	-53.3	35.8	64.3	-49.4	155.7	483.8	386.2	267.9	149.4
Gross Domestic Income	1,639.8	1,755.6	1,825.6	1,994.8	2,144.2	2,242.4	2,579.7	2,903.8	3,142.1	3,104.4	2,963.7
Gross National Income	1,509.0	1,596.6	1,658.3	1,785.7	1,964.3	2,056.5	2,309.7	2,603.7	2,769.6	2,718.3	2,784.4
DOMESTIC PRICES/DEFLATORS					*(Index 1987 = 100)*						
Overall (GDP)	25.4	24.7	24.8	28.5	35.5	36.4	46.0	63.6	64.7	68.6	78.9
Domestic Absorption	24.6	24.9	25.5	28.0	34.0	37.2	42.9	52.9	56.7	62.7	74.9
Agriculture	18.5	18.0	18.5	21.8	26.4	30.2	33.0	47.3	53.3	59.1	60.9
Industry	33.1	31.6	31.6	35.4	43.2	45.1	50.1	58.3	61.6	64.4	63.8
Manufacturing	..	..	..	..	..	..	..	..	..	..	..
Consumer Price Index	22.8	22.5	22.5	25.0	29.4	32.7	36.7	46.8	52.8	61.6	70.6
MANUFACTURING ACTIVITY											
Employment (1987=100)	..	..	..	..	..	..	..	..	..	..	..
Real Earnings per Empl. (1987=100)	..	..	..	..	..	..	..	..	..	..	..
Real Output per Empl. (1987=100)	..	..	..	..	..	..	..	..	..	..	..
Earnings as % of Value Added	27.1	26.2	25.6	27.6	25.0	29.8	29.7	26.1	29.3	30.5	30.3
MONETARY HOLDINGS					*(Billions of current CFA Francs)*						
Money Supply, Broadly Defined	106.78	117.60	122.83	147.91	223.21	244.56	349.75	524.49	581.61	566.16	581.82
Money	83.54	92.08	103.16	117.94	162.81	179.84	260.10	383.08	415.55	433.78	438.73
Currency Outside Banks	39.83	46.95	51.48	57.02	77.47	89.63	106.74	137.27	164.47	193.71	210.94
Demand Deposits	43.71	45.13	51.68	60.92	85.34	90.21	153.36	245.81	251.08	240.07	227.79
Quasi-Money	23.24	25.52	19.67	29.97	60.40	64.72	89.65	141.41	166.06	132.38	143.09
					(Billions of current CFA Francs)						
GOVERNMENT DEFICIT (-) OR SURPLUS	..	..	..	..	..	..	..	..	..	-168.30	-233.19
Current Revenue	..	..	..	..	..	..	..	..	..	467.11	517.40
Current Expenditure	..	..	..	..	..	..	..	..	..	..	409.57
Current Budget Balance	..	..	..	..	..	..	..	..	..	..	107.83
Capital Receipts	..	..	..	..	..	..	..	..	..	..	0.16
Capital Payments	..	..	..	..	..	..	..	..	..	..	341.18

1981	1982	1983	1984	1985	1986	1987	1988	1989	1990 estimate	Notes	COTE D'IVOIRE
1,150	1,000	800	700	670	730	780	850	810	750	..	**CURRENT GNP PER CAPITA (US $)**
8,487	8,778	9,078	9,400	9,755	10,138	10,548	10,980	11,433	11,902	..	**POPULATION (thousands)**
				(Billions of current CFA Francs)							**USE AND ORIGIN OF RESOURCES**
2,150.8	2,319.8	2,388.1	2,661.9	2,838.7	3,005.3	2,846.8	2,809.5	2,655.6	2,386.9	..	Gross National Product (GNP)
-140.7	-166.7	-193.8	-207.4	-299.1	-239.0	-271.0	-257.7	-291.9	-318.5	f	Net Factor Income from Abroad
2,291.5	2,486.5	2,581.9	2,869.3	3,137.8	3,244.3	3,117.8	3,067.2	2,947.5	2,705.4	..	GDP at Market Prices
-162.8	-72.2	-43.2	330.2	414.3	242.3	137.7	86.6	88.9	119.6	f	Resource Balance
806.0	905.7	942.8	1,314.1	1,437.9	1,273.6	1,103.5	982.2	1,027.5	991.6	..	Exports of Goods & NFServices
968.8	977.9	986.0	983.9	1,023.6	1,031.3	965.8	895.6	938.6	872.0	..	Imports of Goods & NFServices
2,454.3	2,558.7	2,625.1	2,539.1	2,723.5	3,002.0	2,980.1	2,980.6	2,858.6	2,585.8	..	Domestic Absorption
1,462.0	1,553.9	1,658.5	1,787.8	1,783.0	2,129.9	2,114.0	1,880.6	2,007.7	1,829.0	..	Private Consumption, etc.
398.0	427.8	435.0	438.0	483.0	476.4	501.3	635.7	546.2	491.5	..	General Gov't Consumption
594.3	577.0	531.6	313.3	457.5	395.7	364.8	464.3	304.7	265.3	..	Gross Domestic Investment
558.4	538.7	469.5	352.6	420.7	421.0	333.4	365.2	294.5	263.6	..	Fixed Investment
373.5	450.1	502.8	728.4	792.9	696.3	772.4	733.1	686.8	633.3	..	Indirect Taxes, net
1,918.0	2,036.4	2,079.1	2,140.9	2,344.9	2,548.0	2,345.4	2,334.1	2,260.7	2,072.1	..	GDP at factor cost
655.8	650.2	633.8	788.4	833.5	881.3	945.8	995.7	1,002.8	967.7	..	Agriculture
375.8	462.9	487.8	506.8	618.0	647.6	651.8	612.3	571.6	556.1	..	Industry
201.0	263.5	301.6	334.2	399.2	412.3	..	..	..	..	..	Manufacturing
886.4	923.3	957.5	845.7	893.4	1,019.1	747.8	726.1	686.3	548.3	..	Services, etc.
431.5	504.8	488.4	643.5	871.8	638.0	502.5	550.9	393.6	384.9	..	Gross Domestic Saving
156.4	209.5	172.8	308.9	447.4	251.0	80.9	140.0	-48.1	-80.6	..	Gross National Saving
				(Billions of 1987 CFA Francs)							
2,726.9	2,756.1	2,703.1	2,683.5	2,737.0	2,902.2	2,846.8	2,819.0	2,768.6	2,677.7	..	Gross National Product
2,935.2	2,981.6	2,945.8	2,912.7	3,063.5	3,156.8	3,117.8	3,067.1	3,036.8	2,958.9	I	GDP at Market Prices
-210.5	-70.7	-51.6	129.1	145.3	15.0	137.7	174.9	301.7	471.5	f	Resource Balance
939.1	952.6	876.3	966.2	962.3	1,089.3	1,103.5	1,084.8	1,216.0	1,363.0	..	Exports of Goods & NFServices
1,149.6	1,023.3	927.9	837.1	817.0	1,074.4	965.8	909.8	914.3	891.5	..	Imports of Goods & NFServices
3,145.6	3,052.3	2,997.4	2,783.6	2,918.2	3,141.8	2,980.1	2,892.1	2,735.2	2,487.4	..	Domestic Absorption
1,676.5	1,724.2	1,752.8	1,964.6	1,940.1	2,219.0	2,114.0	1,845.7	1,950.6	1,782.1	..	Private Consumption, etc.
659.3	628.8	607.4	513.7	550.7	509.4	501.3	595.5	506.8	459.7	..	General Gov't Consumption
809.9	699.3	637.1	305.3	427.5	413.4	364.8	450.9	277.8	245.6	..	Gross Domestic Investment
760.9	652.9	562.6	343.5	393.0	439.8	333.4	354.6	268.5	244.1	..	Fixed Investment
2,244.5	2,282.1	2,281.8	2,189.3	2,304.7	2,372.2	2,345.4	2,310.2	2,291.3	2,234.9	..	GDP at factor cost
1,001.8	988.1	879.0	903.5	988.8	966.1	945.8	1,000.6	1,065.7	1,110.4	..	Agriculture
616.2	524.0	540.2	555.3	573.0	606.9	651.8	608.1	580.1	523.3	..	Industry
..	..	..	..	..	..	..	..	..	..	..	Manufacturing
626.4	770.0	862.7	730.5	742.9	799.3	747.8	701.5	645.4	601.3	..	Services, etc.
											Memo Items:
956.4	947.8	887.3	1,118.0	1,147.7	1,326.8	1,103.5	997.8	1,000.9	1,013.8	..	Capacity to Import
17.3	-4.9	11.0	151.8	185.4	237.5	0.0	-87.0	-215.1	-349.2	..	Terms of Trade Adjustment
2,952.5	2,976.7	2,956.8	3,064.5	3,248.9	3,394.2	3,117.8	2,980.1	2,821.8	2,609.7	..	Gross Domestic Income
2,744.2	2,751.3	2,714.0	2,835.4	2,922.4	3,139.7	2,846.8	2,732.1	2,553.5	2,328.5	..	Gross National Income
				(Index 1987 = 100)							**DOMESTIC PRICES/DEFLATORS**
78.1	83.4	87.6	98.5	102.4	102.8	100.0	100.0	97.1	91.4	..	Overall (GDP)
78.0	83.8	87.6	91.2	93.3	95.6	100.0	103.1	104.5	104.0	..	Domestic Absorption
65.5	65.8	72.1	87.3	84.3	91.2	100.0	99.5	94.1	87.2	..	Agriculture
61.0	88.3	90.3	91.3	107.8	106.7	100.0	100.7	98.5	106.3	..	Industry
..	..	..	..	..	..	..	..	..	..	..	Manufacturing
76.9	82.5	87.4	91.1	92.8	99.6	100.0	107.0	..	..	..	Consumer Price Index
											MANUFACTURING ACTIVITY
..	..	..	..	..	..	..	..	..	..	..	Employment (1987=100)
..	..	..	..	..	..	..	..	..	..	..	Real Earnings per Empl. (1987=100)
..	..	..	..	..	..	..	..	..	..	..	Real Output per Empl. (1987=100)
33.0	31.0	..	..	..	..	..	..	..	..	..	Earnings as % of Value Added
				(Billions of current CFA Francs)							**MONETARY HOLDINGS**
639.65	660.34	691.95	826.05	939.44	963.90	929.95	944.00	867.72	845.41	..	Money Supply, Broadly Defined
464.39	460.31	488.01	574.57	620.18	636.43	598.58	577.96	511.21	526.40	..	Money
229.83	219.13	231.99	278.71	307.07	317.66	304.71	298.45	254.14	270.74	..	Currency Outside Banks
234.56	241.18	256.02	295.86	313.11	318.77	293.87	279.51	257.07	255.66	..	Demand Deposits
175.26	200.03	203.94	251.48	319.26	327.47	331.37	366.04	356.51	319.01	..	Quasi-Money
				(Billions of current CFA Francs)							**GOVERNMENT DEFICIT (-) OR SURPLUS**
..	..	..	-90.03	..	..	..	..	..	..	..	Current Revenue
..	..	..	816.10	559.17	..	..	..	..	..	..	Current Revenue
..	..	..	748.50	540.01	..	..	..	..	..	..	Current Expenditure
..	..	..	67.60	19.16	..	..	..	..	..	..	Current Budget Balance
..	..	..			..	..	..	..	..	..	Capital Receipts
..	..	..	157.63	92.45	..	..	..	..	..	..	Capital Payments

205

COTE D'IVOIRE	1970	1971	1972	1973	1974	1975	1976	1977	1978	1979	1980
FOREIGN TRADE (CUSTOMS BASIS)					*(Millions of current US dollars)*						
Value of Exports, fob	468.8	455.6	552.9	860.6	1,214.3	1,181.6	1,630.8	2,154.8	2,322.9	2,506.8	2,978.9
Nonfuel Primary Products	437.9	424.8	488.7	769.4	1,069.7	974.3	1,446.1	1,912.3	2,081.6	2,182.4	2,754.0
Fuels	2.9	2.5	11.4	19.6	45.3	66.9	63.0	81.9	86.0	112.4	70.0
Manufactures	28.0	28.4	52.8	71.6	99.3	140.4	121.7	160.5	155.3	212.0	154.9
Value of Imports, cif	387.2	398.1	452.8	713.5	966.7	1,126.5	1,295.4	1,751.5	2,309.6	2,388.9	2,552.1
Nonfuel Primary Products	70.8	74.0	90.5	160.6	189.7	191.2	206.8	286.8	358.1	417.4	401.2
Fuels	18.4	19.1	29.0	33.1	137.6	156.6	166.4	199.9	221.3	272.7	413.7
Manufactures	298.0	305.0	333.3	519.8	639.3	778.7	922.2	1,264.7	1,730.2	1,698.8	1,737.1
					(Index 1987 = 100)						
Terms of Trade	120.6	100.0	101.3	109.7	106.8	91.2	131.3	166.1	138.1	134.9	114.3
Export Prices, fob	33.5	30.8	32.1	47.4	62.8	55.7	81.8	114.3	108.1	123.2	121.5
Import Prices, cif	27.8	30.8	31.7	43.2	58.8	61.0	62.3	68.8	78.3	91.4	106.3
BALANCE OF PAYMENTS					*(Millions of current US dollars)*						
Exports of Goods & Services	565.7	576.3	696.9	995.3	1,445.7	1,503.4	1,998.3	2,779.2	3,086.6	3,292.6	3,639.7
Merchandise, fob	497.1	496.0	595.7	861.8	1,253.0	1,238.9	1,735.1	2,412.1	2,615.9	2,722.8	3,012.6
Nonfactor Services	53.5	65.4	84.4	116.9	167.3	225.8	235.2	324.8	410.4	510.5	564.2
Factor Services	15.1	14.9	16.8	16.6	25.4	38.7	28.0	42.3	60.3	59.2	63.0
Imports of Goods & Services	583.6	654.8	765.2	1,145.5	1,414.1	1,740.6	1,988.4	2,656.4	3,507.3	4,104.0	4,760.5
Merchandise, fob	375.1	400.4	460.2	701.1	894.4	1,012.1	1,161.3	1,597.2	2,042.9	2,233.4	2,613.6
Nonfactor Services	145.6	173.0	228.3	324.5	397.6	548.8	640.9	822.7	1,095.2	1,351.1	1,521.2
Factor Services	62.9	81.4	76.7	119.9	122.1	179.6	186.2	236.5	369.1	519.5	625.7
Long-Term Interest	12.1	16.0	19.0	28.9	42.5	59.1	71.0	110.9	189.5	257.3	383.1
Private Current Transfers, net	-55.5	-66.0	-89.4	-123.1	-139.3	-183.8	-289.6	-344.8	-458.2	-576.3	-715.6
Workers' Remittances	..	..	..	..	..	..	..	..	..	..	..
Curr. A/C Bal before Off. Transf.	-73.4	-144.5	-157.6	-273.4	-107.7	-421.0	-279.7	-221.9	-879.0	-1,387.7	-1,836.4
Net Official Transfers	35.5	39.0	61.0	54.0	46.7	42.0	30.5	45.2	40.3	4.7	9.9
Curr. A/C Bal after Off. Transf.	-37.9	-105.5	-96.6	-219.3	-61.0	-379.0	-249.2	-176.7	-838.6	-1,383.0	-1,826.5
Long-Term Capital, net	69.4	96.8	25.2	219.9	173.7	270.2	276.2	570.7	839.3	715.0	1,032.8
Direct Investment	30.7	15.7	18.7	51.0	32.6	69.1	44.8	14.7	83.3	74.7	94.7
Long-Term Loans	51.2	82.5	42.5	205.9	109.5	308.5	270.3	724.6	832.6	706.4	1,119.9
Disbursements	81.7	114.2	84.5	252.6	190.9	391.7	396.5	905.8	1,085.6	1,108.2	1,675.3
Repayments	30.5	31.7	42.0	46.7	81.4	83.2	126.2	181.2	253.0	401.8	555.4
Other Long-Term Capital	-12.5	-1.5	-36.0	-37.0	31.6	-107.4	-38.9	-168.6	-76.6	-66.1	-181.8
Other Capital, net	3.6	-11.7	-0.3	-6.9	-51.1	16.4	3.0	-275.3	165.4	339.1	681.9
Change in Reserves	-35.1	20.5	71.8	6.3	-61.6	92.4	-30.0	-118.7	-166.1	328.9	111.8
Memo Item:					*(CFA Francs per US dollar)*						
Conversion Factor (Annual Avg)	277.710	277.130	252.210	222.700	240.500	214.320	238.980	245.670	225.640	212.720	211.300
					(Millions of US dollars), outstanding at end of year						
EXTERNAL DEBT (Total)	267	366	413	615	756	1,040	1,298	2,559	3,819	4,755	5,847
Long-Term Debt (by debtor)	267	366	413	615	756	1,040	1,298	2,081	3,090	3,898	4,788
Central Bank, incl. IMF credit	17	17	20	28	52	64	102	101	154	157	195
Central Government	177	265	281	342	362	539	626	1,136	1,679	2,237	2,721
Rest of General Government	1	1	1	0	0	0	0	0	0	0	0
Non-financial Public Enterprises	61	70	100	213	293	356	480	670	939	1,237	1,409
Priv. Sector, incl non-guaranteed	11	14	13	32	49	81	90	174	318	267	464
Short-Term Debt	0	0	0	0	0	0	0	478	729	857	1,059
Memo Items:					*(Thousands of US dollars)*						
Int'l Reserves Excluding Gold	118,840	89,433	87,178	88,373	65,667	102,760	76,403	184,808	447,966	147,031	19,704
Gold Holdings (at market price)	..	..	..	..	..	..	..	3,695	7,571	22,784	26,233
SOCIAL INDICATORS											
Total Fertility Rate	7.4	7.4	7.4	7.4	7.4	7.4	7.4	7.4	7.4	7.4	7.4
Infant M. ality Rate	134.6	131.8	129.0	126.4	123.8	121.2	118.6	116.0	113.8	111.6	109.4
Life Expectancy at Birth	44.5	45.0	45.5	46.0	46.5	47.0	47.5	48.0	49.1	50.2	51.3
Urban Population, % of total	27.4	28.3	29.3	30.2	31.2	32.1	33.2	34.4	35.5	36.7	37.8
Food Prod. per capita (1987=100)	83.8	89.2	82.0	83.4	88.8	99.1	93.3	94.0	96.4	100.5	99.4
Labor Force, Agriculture (%)	76.5	75.2	74.0	72.9	71.9	70.9	69.6	68.4	67.3	66.3	65.2
Labor Force, Female (%)	38.1	37.8	37.4	37.1	36.9	36.6	36.2	35.9	35.5	35.2	34.9
Primary Schl. Enroll. Ratio	58.0	..	..	..	..	62.0	64.0	66.0	70.0	72.0	79.0
Primary Schl. Enroll. Ratio, Female	45.0	..	..	..	..	47.0	64.0	..	..	..	63.0
Secondary Schl. Enroll. Ratio	9.0	..	..	..	..	13.0	13.0	14.0	17.0	20.0	19.0

1981	1982	1983	1984	1985	1986	1987	1988	1989	1990 estimate	Notes	COTE D'IVOIRE
				(Millions of current US dollars)							**FOREIGN TRADE (CUSTOMS BASIS)**
2,535.2	2,287.9	2,067.7	2,710.4	2,668.9	3,351.0	3,091.6	2,774.8	2,800.0	2,600.0	..	Value of Exports, fob
2,081.8	1,743.3	1,595.9	2,065.2	2,136.3	2,553.2	2,355.6	2,114.2	2,133.4	1,981.0	..	Nonfuel Primary Products
191.2	298.0	236.8	353.1	259.1	436.5	402.7	361.4	364.7	338.7	..	Fuels
262.2	246.7	235.0	292.2	273.5	361.3	333.3	299.1	301.9	280.3	..	Manufactures
2,393.1	2,183.7	1,813.5	1,507.2	1,733.8	2,047.5	2,242.3	2,081.3	2,000.0	2,100.0	..	Value of Imports, cif
545.1	469.1	413.5	298.3	343.2	405.2	443.8	411.9	395.8	415.6	..	Nonfuel Primary Products
527.5	469.0	336.4	331.5	381.3	450.3	493.2	457.7	439.9	461.9	..	Fuels
1,320.5	1,245.6	1,063.6	877.4	1,009.3	1,191.9	1,305.3	1,211.6	1,164.3	1,222.5	..	Manufactures
				(Index 1987 = 100)							
96.3	98.6	104.5	113.5	109.6	119.5	100.0	105.7	91.2	79.7	..	Terms of Trade
104.8	100.5	102.8	110.4	104.4	109.3	100.0	107.5	93.9	93.2	..	Export Prices, fob
108.9	101.9	98.3	97.3	95.3	91.5	100.0	101.7	103.1	117.0	..	Import Prices, cif
				(Millions of current US dollars)							**BALANCE OF PAYMENTS**
2,915.4	2,843.8	2,538.2	3,032.8	3,199.5	3,726.2	3,563.6	3,402.4	3,337.2	3,683.9	f	Exports of Goods & Services
2,435.1	2,347.2	2,066.3	2,624.8	2,761.0	3,187.4	2,949.7	2,774.2	2,807.8	3,120.1	..	Merchandise, fob
434.3	450.7	425.1	370.3	398.9	471.3	535.7	556.7	494.3	519.7	..	Nonfactor Services
46.0	46.0	46.7	37.3	39.6	67.6	78.2	71.5	35.1	44.1	..	Factor Services
3,847.6	3,498.4	3,173.7	2,842.6	2,878.7	3,667.6	4,172.9	4,069.5	4,089.6	4,354.2	f	Imports of Goods & Services
2,067.9	1,789.7	1,635.2	1,487.3	1,409.9	1,639.9	1,863.7	1,696.2	1,720.3	1,701.3	..	Merchandise, fob
1,215.9	1,155.5	983.3	823.9	763.0	1,311.9	1,349.9	1,338.3	1,426.0	1,563.2	..	Nonfactor Services
563.8	553.2	555.3	531.4	705.8	715.8	959.3	1,035.1	943.2	1,089.8	..	Factor Services
444.0	551.1	519.0	573.7	634.1	771.8	518.0	444.4	429.1	399.2	..	Long-Term Interest
-494.6	-391.4	-319.6	-291.1	-278.9	-427.4	-501.1	-514.4	-469.6	-539.9	..	Private Current Transfers, net
..	..	..	..	..	..	..	..	..	..	..	Workers' Remittances
-1,426.8	-1,045.9	-955.2	-100.9	41.8	-368.8	-1,110.4	-1,181.5	-1,221.9	-1,210.2	..	Curr. A/C Bal before Off. Transf.
15.5	29.8	26.5	28.1	26.0	71.0	143.1	61.1	73.7	106.5	..	Net Official Transfers
-1,411.3	-1,016.1	-928.7	-72.8	67.9	-297.7	-967.3	-1,120.4	-1,148.3	-1,103.7	..	Curr. A/C Bal after Off. Transf.
921.1	898.6	533.5	346.0	241.5	153.6	344.7	587.6	263.6	236.2	f	Long-Term Capital, net
32.8	47.5	37.5	21.7	29.2	70.7	87.5	56.1	78.4	-47.7	..	Direct Investment
809.9	1,504.5	506.3	941.6	728.5	458.6	691.3	583.5	564.9	917.2	..	Long-Term Loans
1,421.0	2,105.9	1,116.1	1,430.4	1,286.1	1,223.5	1,491.0	1,202.2	1,245.2	1,726.1	..	Disbursements
611.1	601.4	609.8	488.8	557.6	764.9	799.7	618.7	680.3	808.9	..	Repayments
78.5	-653.3	-10.3	-617.3	-516.2	-375.7	-434.1	-52.0	-379.6	-633.3	..	Other Long-Term Capital
113.1	-32.4	250.5	-299.5	-282.8	234.1	763.6	603.9	990.6	758.6	f	Other Capital, net
377.1	149.9	144.7	26.2	-26.6	-90.0	-141.1	-71.1	-106.0	108.9	..	Change in Reserves
				(CFA Francs per US dollar)							**Memo Item:**
271.730	328.620	381.070	436.960	449.260	346.300	300.540	297.850	319.010	272.260	..	Conversion Factor (Annual Avg)
			(Millions of US dollars), outstanding at end of year								
6,651	7,862	7,819	8,106	9,745	11,087	13,554	13,993	15,613	17,956	..	**EXTERNAL DEBT (Total)**
5,486	6,756	6,933	7,467	9,012	10,283	12,177	12,155	12,790	14,853	..	Long-Term Debt (by debtor)
560	677	802	759	796	800	736	615	465	519	..	Central Bank, incl. IMF credit
2,971	3,619	3,507	3,633	4,534	5,433	7,100	7,036	7,491	9,305	..	Central Government
0	0	0	0	0	0	0	0	0	..	..	Rest of General Government
1,319	1,263	1,228	1,068	1,103	1,087	1,072	800	759	655	..	Non-financial Public Enterprises
636	1,196	1,395	2,008	2,580	2,963	3,269	3,704	4,074	4,375	..	Priv. Sector, incl non-guaranteed
1,165	1,106	886	639	732	804	1,377	1,839	2,823	3,103	..	Short-Term Debt
				(Thousands of US dollars)							**Memo Items:**
17,847	2,195	19,721	5,367	4,732	19,556	8,902	10,418	14,986	3,988	..	Int'l Reserves Excluding Gold
17,689	20,332	16,977	13,719	14,552	17,395	21,542	18,256	17,844	17,132	..	Gold Holdings (at market price)
											SOCIAL INDICATORS
7.4	7.4	7.3	7.2	7.0	6.9	6.8	6.8	6.7	6.7	..	Total Fertility Rate
107.2	105.0	103.2	101.4	99.5	97.7	95.9	95.5	95.0	94.6	..	Infant Mortality Rate
52.4	53.5	53.9	54.4	54.9	55.4	55.9	55.7	55.5	55.3	..	Life Expectancy at Birth
37.8	37.7	37.7	37.6	37.6	38.3	39.0	39.5	39.9	40.4	..	Urban Population, % of total
100.0	92.0	88.9	102.9	100.1	98.9	100.0	107.9	99.4	95.4	..	Food Prod. per capita (1987=100)
..	..	..	..	..	..	..	..	..	..	..	Labor Force, Agriculture (%)
34.9	34.8	34.8	34.7	34.7	34.6	34.5	34.4	34.3	34.2	..	Labor Force, Female (%)
..	..	..	76.0	75.0	..	..	..	..	..	..	Primary Schl. Enroll. Ratio
..	..	..	63.0	62.0	..	..	..	..	..	..	Primary Schl. Enroll. Ratio, Female
..	19.0	19.0	20.0	20.0	19.0	20.0	..	..	..	..	Secondary Schl. Enroll. Ratio

CYPRUS	1970	1971	1972	1973	1974	1975	1976	1977	1978	1979	1980
CURRENT GNP PER CAPITA (US $)	..	..	..	..	..	..	..	..	..	..	..
POPULATION (thousands)	615	614	613	611	610	609	611	614	618	623	629

USE AND ORIGIN OF RESOURCES *(Millions of current Cyprus Pounds)*

	1970	1971	1972	1973	1974	1975	1976	1977	1978	1979	1980
Gross National Product (GNP)	..	..	..	..	..	259.0	336.2	431.6	516.0	638.2	772.3
Net Factor Income from Abroad	..	..	..	..	..	2.0	2.3	8.5	9.5	8.4	12.0
GDP at Market Prices	..	..	..	..	..	257.0	333.9	423.1	506.5	629.8	760.3
Resource Balance	..	..	..	..	..	-54.5	-43.0	-84.4	-104.3	-120.2	-135.4
Exports of Goods & NFServices	..	..	..	..	..	91.2	166.1	202.3	214.4	281.4	344.1
Imports of Goods & NFServices	..	..	..	..	..	145.7	209.1	286.7	318.7	401.6	479.5
Domestic Absorption	..	..	..	..	..	311.5	376.9	507.5	610.8	750.0	895.7
Private Consumption, etc.	..	..	..	..	..	208.7	233.7	300.7	356.0	425.6	504.3
General Gov't Consumption	..	..	..	..	..	44.9	54.5	59.2	66.3	80.5	103.9
Gross Domestic Investment	..	..	..	..	..	57.9	88.7	147.6	188.5	243.9	287.5
Fixed Investment	..	..	..	..	..	50.5	70.3	124.6	170.4	219.5	260.0
Indirect Taxes, net	..	..	..	..	..	..	..	..	..	..	..
GDP at factor cost	..	..	..	..	..	..	..	..	..	..	..
Agriculture	..	..	..	..	..	40.4	53.1	55.9	55.3	64.5	72.9
Industry	..	..	..	..	..	64.7	96.3	131.1	167.8	209.2	255.8
Manufacturing	..	..	..	..	..	36.8	57.6	75.2	92.6	110.8	133.4
Services, etc.	..	..	..	..	..	151.9	184.5	236.1	283.4	356.1	431.6
Gross Domestic Saving	..	..	..	..	..	3.4	45.7	63.2	84.2	123.7	152.1
Gross National Saving	..	..	..	..	..	10.5	53.4	77.6	102.1	141.1	175.6

(Millions of 1987 Cyprus Pounds)

	1970	1971	1972	1973	1974	1975	1976	1977	1978	1979	1980
Gross National Product	..	..	..	..	..	706.5	848.0	997.9	1,072.9	1,172.7	1,243.2
GDP at Market Prices	..	..	..	..	..	701.1	841.9	978.2	1,053.2	1,157.2	1,223.9
Resource Balance	..	..	..	..	..	-113.3	-113.4	-159.7	-166.8	-180.1	-168.0
Exports of Goods & NFServices	..	..	..	..	..	172.9	285.7	349.4	370.9	447.8	496.2
Imports of Goods & NFServices	..	..	..	..	..	286.1	399.1	509.1	537.7	627.9	664.2
Domestic Absorption	..	..	..	..	..	814.4	955.3	1,137.9	1,220.0	1,337.3	1,391.9
Private Consumption, etc.	..	..	..	..	..	533.4	597.1	666.9	705.2	755.6	777.7
General Gov't Consumption	..	..	..	..	..	134.2	155.7	157.4	155.9	162.7	176.6
Gross Domestic Investment	..	..	..	..	..	146.8	202.6	313.5	358.9	418.9	437.7
Fixed Investment	..	..	..	..	..	125.2	164.0	269.5	327.1	380.5	400.4
GDP at factor cost	..	..	..	..	..	..	..	..	..	..	..
Agriculture	..	..	..	..	..	104.0	112.8	113.0	109.2	113.2	119.6
Industry	..	..	..	..	..	198.4	261.8	327.2	363.0	400.8	420.1
Manufacturing	..	..	..	..	..	105.0	136.8	158.0	171.7	187.3	202.2
Services, etc.	..	..	..	..	..	399.7	468.8	540.0	583.1	645.4	686.4

Memo Items:

	1970	1971	1972	1973	1974	1975	1976	1977	1978	1979	1980
Capacity to Import	..	..	..	..	..	179.1	317.0	359.2	361.7	440.0	476.7
Terms of Trade Adjustment	..	..	..	..	..	6.2	31.3	9.8	-9.1	-7.9	-19.6
Gross Domestic Income	..	..	..	..	..	707.4	873.3	988.0	1,044.1	1,149.3	1,204.3
Gross National Income	..	..	..	..	..	712.8	879.3	1,007.7	1,063.7	1,164.9	1,223.7

DOMESTIC PRICES/DEFLATORS *(Index 1987 = 100)*

	1970	1971	1972	1973	1974	1975	1976	1977	1978	1979	1980
Overall (GDP)	..	..	..	..	..	36.7	39.7	43.3	48.1	54.4	62.1
Domestic Absorption	..	..	..	..	..	38.2	39.5	44.6	50.1	56.1	64.4
Agriculture	..	..	..	..	..	38.8	47.1	49.5	50.6	57.0	61.0
Industry	..	..	..	..	..	32.6	36.8	40.1	46.2	52.2	60.9
Manufacturing	..	..	..	..	..	35.1	42.1	47.6	53.9	59.2	66.0
Consumer Price Index	32.7	34.1	35.8	38.5	41.0	46.9	48.7	52.2	56.1	61.4	69.7

MANUFACTURING ACTIVITY

	1970	1971	1972	1973	1974	1975	1976	1977	1978	1979	1980
Employment (1987=100)	57.6	60.1	66.2	67.6	54.7	46.5	54.4	67.5	76.5	82.1	86.6
Real Earnings per Empl. (1987=100)	41.6	42.2	45.9	50.2	56.3	49.4	50.3	54.8	59.6	67.3	73.0
Real Output per Empl. (1987=100)	..	..	..	..	..	85.5	92.6	85.9	78.9	84.4	93.4
Earnings as % of Value Added	37.8	35.7	35.1	37.0	40.6	36.2	30.0	32.6	34.8	38.3	37.6

MONETARY HOLDINGS *(Millions of current Cyprus Pounds)*

	1970	1971	1972	1973	1974	1975	1976	1977	1978	1979	1980
Money Supply, Broadly Defined	120.4	145.0	175.2	197.0	228.5	229.7	275.1	316.0	363.3	433.5	501.2
Money	42.6	46.7	57.4	60.8	67.0	62.1	80.0	85.9	100.8	129.5	153.3
Currency Outside Banks	18.4	21.8	26.3	29.7	35.8	33.7	39.3	43.2	51.2	64.0	75.9
Demand Deposits	24.2	25.0	31.2	31.1	31.3	28.3	40.7	42.8	49.6	65.5	77.4
Quasi-Money	77.8	98.3	117.7	136.1	161.4	167.6	195.1	230.1	262.5	304.0	347.9

GOVERNMENT DEFICIT (-) OR SURPLUS *(Millions of current Cyprus Pounds)*

	1970	1971	1972	1973	1974	1975	1976	1977	1978	1979	1980
GOVERNMENT DEFICIT (-) OR SURPLUS	1.42	0.45	-4.39	-12.15	-20.90	-20.38	-24.90	-12.71	-28.84	-41.64	-70.01
Current Revenue	41.25	46.97	52.35	60.31	61.12	66.82	78.70	106.72	113.31	136.58	173.63
Current Expenditure	31.94	37.29	45.34	60.95	72.23	76.18	83.93	91.84	100.95	129.25	165.09
Current Budget Balance	9.31	9.68	7.01	-0.64	-11.11	-9.36	-5.23	14.88	12.36	7.33	8.54
Capital Receipts	0.12	0.06	0.03	0.11	0.03	0.07	0.07	0.09	0.19	0.19	0.14
Capital Payments	8.01	9.29	11.53	11.62	9.82	11.09	19.74	27.68	41.39	49.16	78.69

1981	1982	1983	1984	1985	1986	1987	1988	1989	1990 estimate	Notes	CYPRUS
..	..	..	..	..	4,480	5,300	6,450	7,230	8,020	..	**CURRENT GNP PER CAPITA (US $)**
637	645	653	660	666	673	680	687	695	702	..	**POPULATION (thousands)**
			(Millions of current Cyprus Pounds)								**USE AND ORIGIN OF RESOURCES**
887.6	1,037.1	1,136.4	1,339.5	1,485.2	1,600.8	1,780.1	1,994.5	2,245.3	2,480.6	..	Gross National Product (GNP)
11.6	12.2	-0.3	2.5	5.0	2.8	1.0	1.8	13.0	14.8	..	Net Factor Income from Abroad
876.0	1,024.9	1,136.7	1,337.0	1,480.2	1,598.0	1,779.1	1,992.7	2,232.3	2,465.8	..	GDP at Market Prices
-114.5	-136.5	-154.2	-166.4	-149.6	-54.2	-3.9	-50.4	-127.6	-59.9	..	Resource Balance
440.2	521.9	573.0	731.0	722.4	721.0	841.8	959.3	1,156.3	1,284.4	..	Exports of Goods & NFServices
554.7	658.4	727.2	897.4	872.0	775.2	845.7	1,009.7	1,283.9	1,344.3	..	Imports of Goods & NFServices
990.5	1,161.4	1,290.9	1,503.4	1,629.8	1,652.2	1,783.0	2,043.1	2,359.9	2,525.6	..	Domestic Absorption
566.3	684.2	776.0	864.6	971.6	1,011.3	1,085.8	1,235.7	1,383.7	1,549.7	..	Private Consumption, etc.
128.0	152.1	172.6	189.5	208.5	225.9	246.3	275.0	299.3	340.9	..	General Gov't Consumption
296.2	325.1	342.3	449.3	449.7	415.0	450.9	532.4	676.9	635.0	..	Gross Domestic Investment
275.9	304.7	316.0	412.5	403.0	384.0	414.3	475.2	609.9	590.0	..	Fixed Investment
..	..	..	..	..	..	..	..	..	..	..	Indirect Taxes, net
..	..	..	..	..	..	..	..	..	..	B	GDP at factor cost
81.1	95.0	89.8	119.6	111.0	117.3	132.3	143.2	156.3	166.9	..	Agriculture
283.9	316.3	342.0	388.2	420.9	439.7	487.6	547.0	597.8	656.3	..	Industry
154.2	174.5	187.9	215.2	231.9	240.5	273.9	309.1	334.0	359.1	..	Manufacturing
511.0	613.6	704.9	829.2	948.3	1,041.0	1,159.2	1,302.5	1,478.2	1,642.6	..	Services, etc.
181.7	188.6	188.1	282.9	300.1	360.8	447.0	482.0	549.3	575.2	..	Gross Domestic Saving
204.8	212.6	200.1	298.1	318.7	375.9	460.7	495.3	573.6	600.0	..	Gross National Saving
			(Millions of 1987 Cyprus Pounds)								
1,272.2	1,347.7	1,405.8	1,532.5	1,607.1	1,665.4	1,780.1	1,931.8	2,080.7	2,195.0	..	Gross National Product
1,255.6	1,331.5	1,406.2	1,529.6	1,601.7	1,662.5	1,779.1	1,930.1	2,068.9	2,182.0	I	GDP at Market Prices
-114.7	-157.1	-149.5	-182.4	-147.8	-61.8	-3.9	-26.9	-87.0	-37.6	..	Resource Balance
566.1	610.9	660.8	760.6	752.3	739.7	841.8	954.1	1,107.8	1,186.9	..	Exports of Goods & NFServices
680.9	768.0	810.3	942.9	900.1	801.5	845.7	980.9	1,194.8	1,224.5	..	Imports of Goods & NFServices
1,370.3	1,488.6	1,555.7	1,712.0	1,749.5	1,724.2	1,783.0	1,956.9	2,155.9	2,219.6	..	Domestic Absorption
782.6	880.6	937.6	994.6	1,051.0	1,065.1	1,085.8	1,191.3	1,286.5	1,381.8	..	Private Consumption, etc.
189.7	197.1	209.4	217.4	225.7	233.8	246.3	263.7	273.4	298.0	..	General Gov't Consumption
398.0	410.8	408.7	500.0	472.8	425.2	450.9	501.9	596.0	539.7	..	Gross Domestic Investment
374.6	388.7	380.2	462.2	426.5	396.3	414.3	447.2	534.3	501.0	..	Fixed Investment
..	..	..	..	..	..	..	..	..	..	B	GDP at factor cost
118.7	119.2	117.9	128.9	128.6	127.9	132.3	146.8	151.6	150.3	..	Agriculture
406.3	415.2	423.4	444.1	450.2	456.6	487.6	518.8	541.0	566.6	..	Industry
215.0	227.9	232.3	247.2	252.8	253.5	273.9	292.6	301.3	311.4	..	Manufacturing
731.8	797.8	864.8	956.6	1,023.0	1,078.0	1,159.2	1,264.5	1,376.2	1,465.1	..	Services, etc.
											Memo Items:
540.3	608.8	638.5	768.1	745.7	745.5	841.8	932.0	1,076.1	1,170.0	..	Capacity to Import
-25.8	-2.2	-22.3	7.5	-6.7	5.7	0.0	-22.1	-31.7	-17.0	..	Terms of Trade Adjustment
1,229.8	1,329.4	1,383.9	1,537.1	1,595.1	1,668.2	1,779.1	1,908.0	2,037.1	2,165.1	..	Gross Domestic Income
1,246.4	1,345.6	1,383.5	1,540.0	1,600.4	1,671.1	1,780.1	1,909.7	2,049.0	2,178.1	..	Gross National Income
			(Index 1987 = 100)								**DOMESTIC PRICES/DEFLATORS**
69.8	77.0	80.8	87.4	92.4	96.1	100.0	103.2	107.9	113.0	..	Overall (GDP)
72.3	78.0	83.0	87.8	93.2	95.8	100.0	104.4	109.5	113.8	..	Domestic Absorption
68.3	79.7	76.1	92.8	86.3	91.7	100.0	97.6	103.1	111.1	..	Agriculture
69.9	76.2	80.8	87.4	93.5	96.3	100.0	105.4	110.5	115.8	..	Industry
71.7	76.6	80.9	87.1	91.7	94.9	100.0	105.6	110.9	115.3	..	Manufacturing
77.2	82.2	86.3	91.5	96.1	97.3	100.0	103.4	107.3	112.2	..	Consumer Price Index
											MANUFACTURING ACTIVITY
90.6	92.0	92.6	95.9	98.5	95.9	100.0	105.5	..	..	J	Employment (1987=100)
78.6	85.3	89.2	91.2	93.5	97.3	100.0	103.7	..	..	J	Real Earnings per Empl. (1987=100)
99.4	99.8	101.7	103.8	100.8	97.9	100.0	100.1	..	..	J	Real Output per Empl. (1987=100)
44.0	46.1	47.6	46.7	46.9	46.4	44.8	45.0	..	..	J	Earnings as % of Value Added
			(Millions of current Cyprus Pounds)								**MONETARY HOLDINGS**
601.4	709.5	791.1	899.4	992.3	1,095.5	1,238.4	1,456.1	1,686.2	1,969.6	..	Money Supply, Broadly Defined
188.3	218.5	248.4	259.4	285.3	282.5	314.0	358.9	385.0	429.1	..	Money
89.5	101.6	115.9	122.2	127.9	130.7	142.6	157.6	169.1	183.5	..	Currency Outside Banks
98.8	116.8	132.6	137.1	157.4	151.9	171.5	201.3	215.9	245.6	..	Demand Deposits
413.1	491.0	542.7	640.1	707.0	813.0	924.4	1,097.1	1,301.1	1,540.5	..	Quasi-Money
			(Millions of current Cyprus Pounds)								**GOVERNMENT DEFICIT (-) OR SURPLUS**
-46.75	-48.48	-81.34	-73.11	-65.40	-58.07	-75.06	-63.78	-31.16	-59.01	..	
203.22	252.19	288.66	344.07	389.86	426.40	460.59	535.76	632.29	710.12	..	Current Revenue
212.44	249.35	301.24	337.18	362.92	381.09	425.54	481.26	529.58	606.83	..	Current Expenditure
-9.22	2.84	-12.58	6.89	26.94	45.31	35.05	54.50	102.71	103.29	..	Current Budget Balance
0.12	0.16	0.75	0.28	0.24	0.69	1.12	0.30	0.32	0.34	..	Capital Receipts
37.65	51.48	69.51	80.28	92.58	104.07	111.23	118.58	134.19	162.64	..	Capital Payments

CYPRUS	1970	1971	1972	1973	1974	1975	1976	1977	1978	1979	1980
FOREIGN TRADE (CUSTOMS BASIS)					*(Millions of current US dollars)*						
Value of Exports, fob	108.5	114.8	133.8	173.1	152.2	151.2	256.8	317.5	343.7	456.3	532.8
Nonfuel Primary Products	91.4	95.6	110.4	138.5	114.8	91.5	151.4	175.2	172.9	205.6	209.6
Fuels	0.0	0.0	0.5	0.1	0.6	0.6	9.9	5.9	8.3	23.1	27.9
Manufactures	17.0	19.2	22.9	34.5	36.8	59.1	95.5	136.5	162.5	227.6	295.3
Value of Imports, cif	235.1	259.0	315.4	449.0	406.1	305.5	429.8	619.1	748.2	999.8	1,195.1
Nonfuel Primary Products	46.8	50.1	63.7	119.6	93.0	85.6	114.1	129.9	153.4	190.6	214.4
Fuels	16.8	20.8	22.0	25.1	52.3	48.8	65.2	86.3	83.1	125.5	222.5
Manufactures	171.5	188.2	229.7	304.3	260.8	171.1	250.5	402.8	511.8	683.7	758.2
					(Index 1987 = 100)						
Terms of Trade	178.9	153.2	138.8	122.7	102.1	108.2	104.2	105.7	101.9	101.7	95.2
Export Prices, fob	42.5	40.0	41.4	50.0	58.1	63.4	62.7	69.3	75.1	89.7	97.4
Import Prices, cif	23.8	26.1	29.8	40.8	57.0	58.6	60.2	65.5	73.7	88.2	102.3
BALANCE OF PAYMENTS					*(Millions of current US dollars)*						
Exports of Goods & Services	229.2	264.6	329.9	423.2	365.5	301.0	459.4	565.4	658.6	896.6	1,107.2
Merchandise, fob	102.4	109.0	121.9	163.6	142.4	142.3	250.2	304.3	326.6	421.5	489.2
Nonfactor Services	111.3	140.9	191.2	236.4	192.5	133.3	179.8	214.6	271.2	400.9	520.3
Factor Services	15.5	14.6	16.8	23.2	30.5	25.4	29.5	46.5	60.8	74.2	97.7
Imports of Goods & Services	268.0	298.7	373.8	516.3	498.9	410.5	533.5	728.1	888.3	1,183.3	1,421.9
Merchandise, fob	206.3	227.4	281.4	402.1	379.1	301.2	397.8	558.8	683.8	906.2	1,079.2
Nonfactor Services	47.9	58.0	78.4	92.7	99.7	89.2	111.6	143.6	169.5	226.6	279.0
Factor Services	13.8	13.3	14.0	21.5	20.1	20.0	24.1	25.7	35.1	50.5	63.7
Long-Term Interest	2.4	2.8	2.4	3.0	3.8	4.9	5.3	8.6	13.4	24.8	29.3
Private Current Transfers, net	13.7	16.3	16.1	12.0	17.3	13.8	13.2	14.5	22.5	25.4	32.6
Workers' Remittances	..	..	..	..	..	10.9	16.3	17.3	25.7	29.3	..
Curr. A/C Bal before Off. Transf.	-25.1	-17.8	-27.8	-81.1	-116.1	-95.7	-60.9	-148.2	-207.2	-261.3	-282.1
Net Official Transfers	3.4	2.7	2.6	2.9	43.7	58.4	47.5	58.3	45.0	46.3	40.8
Curr. A/C Bal after Off. Transf.	-21.7	-15.0	-25.2	-78.2	-72.4	-37.3	-13.4	-89.9	-162.2	-215.0	-241.3
Long-Term Capital, net	24.8	27.2	34.9	47.6	45.7	13.5	62.6	77.7	143.5	127.5	217.2
Direct Investment	20.2	29.6	36.4	37.2	32.4	18.1	32.4	41.4	57.0	70.5	85.0
Long-Term Loans	4.3	-17.3	-0.8	16.7	17.1	4.7	18.0	58.4	65.7	52.2	108.3
Disbursements	7.4	6.8	4.3	22.0	21.9	9.8	27.3	67.7	78.1	67.7	138.5
Repayments	3.1	24.1	5.1	5.3	4.8	5.1	9.3	9.3	12.4	15.5	30.2
Other Long-Term Capital	0.3	14.9	-0.7	-6.3	-3.8	-9.3	12.2	-22.1	20.8	4.8	24.0
Other Capital, net	25.3	38.8	19.0	15.5	-14.5	-8.7	-4.4	35.4	37.5	75.4	61.1
Change in Reserves	-28.4	-51.0	-28.7	15.1	41.2	32.5	-44.8	-23.2	-18.7	12.0	-37.1
Memo Item:					*(Cyprus Pounds per US dollar)*						
Conversion Factor (Annual Avg)	0.420	0.410	0.380	0.350	0.360	0.370	0.410	0.410	0.370	0.350	0.350
				(Millions of US dollars), outstanding at end of year							
EXTERNAL DEBT (Total)	56.0	41.2	39.9	57.2	84.0	85.8	144.4	275.3	370.2	462.5	545.4
Long-Term Debt (by debtor)	56.0	41.2	39.9	57.2	84.0	85.8	144.4	214.3	284.2	349.5	437.4
Central Bank, incl. IMF credit	0.0	0.0	0.0	0.0	7.8	9.5	50.0	52.3	42.9	50.0	39.0
Central Government	26.0	10.1	10.5	17.6	21.3	26.1	52.1	96.9	144.2	179.2	256.2
Rest of General Government	0.0	0.0	0.6	2.0	3.0	3.1	3.3	3.3	3.3	3.2	3.4
Non-financial Public Enterprises	29.3	30.3	27.5	36.2	48.4	43.4	35.3	55.8	81.9	96.8	110.1
Priv. Sector, incl non-guaranteed	0.7	0.8	1.3	1.4	3.5	3.7	3.7	6.0	11.9	20.3	28.7
Short-Term Debt	0.0	0.0	0.0	0.0	0.0	0.0	0.0	61.0	86.0	113.0	108.0
Memo Items:					*(Millions of US dollars)*						
Int'l Reserves Excluding Gold	194.0	268.7	303.3	288.7	250.1	197.7	274.5	313.5	345.7	353.1	368.3
Gold Holdings (at market price)	16.0	18.7	27.8	48.0	79.8	60.0	57.7	72.6	100.1	235.0	270.6
SOCIAL INDICATORS											
Total Fertility Rate	2.4	2.3	2.2	2.2	2.2	2.2	2.2	2.2	2.2	2.2	2.3
Infant Mortality Rate	29.0	29.0	29.0	27.2	25.4	23.6	21.8	20.0	19.2	18.4	17.6
Life Expectancy at Birth	71.0	71.2	71.4	71.9	72.3	72.8	73.2	73.7	74.0	74.2	74.4
Urban Population, % of total	40.8	41.3	41.8	42.4	42.9	43.4	44.0	44.6	45.1	45.7	46.3
Food Prod. per capita (1987=100)	120.7	141.9	137.5	104.5	115.2	85.9	90.7	92.5	95.9	99.5	100.0
Labor Force, Agriculture (%)	38.5	37.2	35.9	34.7	33.4	32.3	31.0	29.7	28.4	27.2	26.0
Labor Force, Female (%)	33.6	33.7	33.8	33.9	34.0	34.1	34.2	34.4	34.5	34.6	34.8
Primary Schl. Enroll. Ratio	..	..	..	..	..	..	..	..	..	..	104.0
Primary Schl. Enroll. Ratio, Female	..	..	..	..	..	..	..	..	..	..	104.0
Secondary Schl. Enroll. Ratio	..	..	..	..	..	..	..	..	..	..	95.0

1981	1982	1983	1984	1985	1986	1987	1988	1989	1990 est.	Notes	CYPRUS
											FOREIGN TRADE (CUSTOMS BASIS)
			(Millions of current US dollars)								
559.0	554.0	494.2	575.0	476.3	506.4	621.2	505.5	497.9	572.4	..	Value of Exports, fob
215.6	228.5	178.8	217.8	169.1	201.4	219.4	175.7	195.0	247.7	..	Nonfuel Primary Products
31.7	38.5	41.4	36.2	38.6	29.8	32.3	6.2	8.9	10.9	..	Fuels
311.7	286.9	274.0	320.9	268.6	275.2	369.5	323.6	293.9	313.8	..	Manufactures
1,101.4	1,206.8	1,207.8	1,350.8	1,233.5	1,263.4	1,463.3	1,825.7	2,255.7	2,532.6	..	Value of Imports, cif
212.5	217.2	242.8	242.2	221.0	238.8	250.8	306.4	357.7	446.1	..	Nonfuel Primary Products
238.7	246.7	227.7	247.9	224.0	161.1	182.5	167.6	219.5	270.8	..	Fuels
650.1	742.8	737.3	860.6	788.6	863.6	1,030.1	1,351.7	1,678.5	1,815.8	..	Manufactures
				(Index 1987 = 100)							
92.5	92.4	92.1	90.6	92.7	100.7	100.0	104.1	103.8	103.0	..	Terms of Trade
95.7	91.0	88.8	85.7	86.2	90.4	100.0	107.5	106.4	116.5	..	Export Prices, fob
103.5	98.5	96.4	94.6	93.0	89.8	100.0	103.3	102.5	113.2	..	Import Prices, cif
											BALANCE OF PAYMENTS
			(Millions of current US dollars)								
1,180.3	1,246.6	1,225.7	1,384.6	1,328.9	1,564.2	1,942.2	2,273.7	2,595.9	3,167.6	..	Exports of Goods & Services
507.6	499.2	438.1	522.6	416.9	451.6	566.4	645.5	717.3	846.5	..	Merchandise, fob
570.4	632.1	684.7	752.1	796.3	983.1	1,234.5	1,468.4	1,692.4	2,082.6	..	Nonfactor Services
102.3	115.3	102.9	110.0	115.6	129.5	141.3	159.9	186.2	238.5	..	Factor Services
1,390.7	1,474.2	1,484.5	1,630.9	1,530.8	1,620.2	1,894.2	2,317.5	2,768.7	3,162.5	..	Imports of Goods & Services
1,042.6	1,090.3	1,093.5	1,224.9	1,121.9	1,141.6	1,326.8	1,666.9	2,072.1	2,304.7	..	Merchandise, fob
273.4	294.3	287.5	300.3	301.5	354.5	428.2	494.6	534.9	653.5	..	Nonfactor Services
74.7	89.6	103.5	105.7	107.4	124.1	139.3	156.0	161.7	204.3	..	Factor Services
41.5	49.5	62.6	66.1	67.5	78.6	95.1	93.7	100.7	105.6	..	Long-Term Interest
27.3	24.8	23.4	21.6	22.2	23.7	26.4	24.6	22.9	21.9	..	Private Current Transfers, net
..	..	..	..	..	..	..	0.0	..	..	..	Workers' Remittances
-183.2	-202.8	-235.5	-224.7	-179.7	-32.2	74.4	-19.1	-149.9	26.9	..	Curr. A/C Bal before Off. Transf.
35.4	46.7	50.9	21.9	18.6	21.6	17.5	27.4	17.0	18.7	..	Net Official Transfers
-147.8	-156.1	-184.6	-202.8	-161.1	-10.6	91.9	8.4	-132.9	45.7	..	Curr. A/C Bal after Off. Transf.
188.6	220.0	136.3	204.5	113.6	171.2	45.9	51.2	333.3	111.3	..	Long-Term Capital, net
78.3	71.5	68.4	52.7	58.0	46.3	52.0	62.1	69.9	129.9	..	Direct Investment
104.7	134.4	66.8	151.1	73.3	131.8	22.3	-31.6	104.0	-20.9	..	Long-Term Loans
139.4	184.1	134.3	212.0	166.8	245.8	199.3	150.8	316.8	91.5	..	Disbursements
34.7	49.7	67.5	60.9	93.5	114.0	177.0	182.4	212.8	112.4	..	Repayments
5.6	14.1	1.2	0.7	-17.6	-6.9	-28.3	20.7	159.4	2.3	..	Other Long-Term Capital
47.1	76.3	89.9	94.2	17.9	-1.1	-74.1	11.1	28.1	-157.0	..	Other Capital, net
-88.0	-140.2	-41.7	-95.9	29.6	-159.5	-63.7	-70.7	-228.5	0.0	..	Change in Reserves
											Memo Item:
			(Cyprus Pounds per US dollar)								
0.420	0.480	0.530	0.590	0.610	0.520	0.480	0.470	0.490	0.460	..	Conversion Factor (Annual Avg)
											EXTERNAL DEBT (Total)
		(Millions of US dollars), outstanding at end of year									
622.5	729.7	860.1	1,022.6	1,349.3	1,618.5	2,015.8	2,042.3	2,105.2	..	..	
511.5	622.7	660.1	764.6	940.3	1,197.5	1,418.6	1,323.8	1,433.2	..	..	Long-Term Debt (by debtor)
25.2	13.6	5.7	3.1	0.0	0.0	0.0	0.0	0.0	..	..	Central Bank, incl. IMF credit
304.0	405.7	446.2	503.8	605.4	876.0	1,072.2	1,023.3	1,013.2	..	..	Central Government
3.2	3.1	2.9	2.5	2.8	3.0	3.4	3.0	2.5	..	..	Rest of General Government
135.3	154.4	159.0	215.6	278.1	269.8	300.3	264.8	379.3	..	..	Non-financial Public Enterprises
43.8	45.9	46.3	39.6	54.0	48.7	42.7	33.7	38.2	..	..	Priv. Sector, incl non-guaranteed
111.0	107.0	200.0	258.0	409.0	421.0	597.2	718.5	672.0	..	..	Short-Term Debt
											Memo Items:
			(Millions of US dollars)								
426.4	523.2	519.1	540.6	595.3	752.8	873.5	927.9	1,124.0	1,506.9	..	Int'l Reserves Excluding Gold
182.5	209.7	175.1	141.5	150.1	179.4	222.2	188.3	184.1	176.7	..	Gold Holdings (at market price)
											SOCIAL INDICATORS
2.3	2.4	2.4	2.4	2.4	2.4	2.4	2.4	2.3	2.3	..	Total Fertility Rate
16.8	16.0	15.1	14.2	13.3	12.4	11.5	11.0	10.5	10.0	..	Infant Mortality Rate
74.7	74.9	75.1	75.2	75.4	75.5	75.7	75.9	76.2	76.5	..	Life Expectancy at Birth
46.9	47.6	48.2	48.9	49.5	50.2	50.8	51.5	52.1	52.8	..	Urban Population, % of total
96.8	100.7	95.4	104.4	101.4	95.6	100.0	108.8	116.2	111.8	..	Food Prod. per capita (1987=100)
..	..	..	..	..	..	..	..	..	..	..	Labor Force, Agriculture (%)
34.9	34.9	35.0	35.1	35.2	35.3	35.3	35.4	35.5	35.6	..	Labor Force, Female (%)
..	..	96.0	98.0	103.0	106.0	106.0	104.0	103.0	..	..	Primary Schl. Enroll. Ratio
..	..	95.0	97.0	102.0	106.0	105.0	103.0	103.0	..	..	Primary Schl. Enroll. Ratio, Female
..	..	98.0	97.0	94.0	91.0	87.0	87.0	88.0	..	..	Secondary Schl. Enroll. Ratio

CZECHOSLOVAKIA	1970	1971	1972	1973	1974	1975	1976	1977	1978	1979	1980
CURRENT GNP PER CAPITA (US $)	..	..	..	..	..	..	..	..	..	..	..
POPULATION (thousands)	14,334	14,390	14,465	14,560	14,686	14,802	14,918	15,031	15,138	15,211	15,262
USE AND ORIGIN OF RESOURCES					*(Billions of current Czechoslovakian Koruny)*						
Gross National Product (GNP)	..	..	..	..	..	..	..	..	..	..	580.2
Net Factor Income from Abroad	..	..	..	..	..	..	..	..	..	..	-6.6
GDP at Market Prices	..	..	..	..	..	..	..	..	..	..	586.8
Resource Balance	..	..	..	..	..	..	..	..	..	..	0.3
Exports of Goods & NF Services	..	..	..	..	..	..	..	..	..	..	198.7
Imports of Goods & NF Services	..	..	..	..	..	..	..	..	..	..	198.4
Domestic Absorption	..	..	..	..	..	..	..	..	..	..	586.5
Private Consumption, etc.	..	..	..	..	..	..	..	..	..	..	281.6
General Gov't Consumption	..	..	..	..	..	..	..	..	..	..	113.6
Gross Domestic Investment	..	..	..	..	..	..	..	..	..	..	191.3
Fixed Investment	..	..	..	..	..	..	..	..	..	..	155.4
Indirect Taxes, net	..										..
GDP at factor cost											..
Agriculture	..									..	39.6
Industry											350.2
Manufacturing											..
Services, etc.	..										197.0
Gross Domestic Saving	..									..	191.6
Gross National Saving	..	..	..							..	185.4
Gross National Product					*(Billions of 1987 Czechoslovakian Koruny)*						
Gross National Product	..	..	..	..	..	..	..	..	..	..	637.24
GDP at Market Prices										..	644.61
Resource Balance										..	-22.65
Exports of Goods & NF Services	..									..	183.33
Imports of Goods & NF Services										..	205.98
Domestic Absorption	..	..	..	..	..	..	..	..	..	..	667.27
Private Consumption, etc.										..	313.26
General Gov't Consumption										..	125.95
Gross Domestic Investment										..	228.06
Fixed Investment	..									..	191.71
GDP at factor cost										..	..
Agriculture	..	..								..	47.75
Industry	..									..	362.92
Manufacturing											..
Services, etc.	..									..	232.92
Memo Items:											
Capacity to Import	..	..	..	..	..	..	..	..	..	..	206.29
Terms of Trade Adjustment	..									..	22.96
Gross Domestic Income	..	..								..	667.58
Gross National Income	..	..								..	660.20
DOMESTIC PRICES/DEFLATORS					*(Index 1987 = 100)*						
Overall (GDP)	..	..	..	..	..	..	..	..	..	..	91.0
Domestic Absorption	..	..	..							..	87.9
Agriculture										..	82.9
Industry	..									..	96.5
Manufacturing										..	..
Consumer Price Index	80.5	80.2	79.9	80.2	80.6	81.2	81.8	82.9	84.2	87.5	90.0
MANUFACTURING ACTIVITY											
Employment (1987=100)	92.0	92.2	92.7	93.4	93.9	94.6	95.1	95.8	96.3	97.0	97.0
Real Earnings per Empl. (1987=100)	78.3	81.2	84.4	86.9	89.6	92.3	94.4	96.6	98.2	97.1	96.6
Real Output per Empl. (1987=100)	..		..	..	..		..		..	..	77.5
Earnings as % of Value Added	49.1	47.7	47.3	45.2	42.8	42.5	42.4	33.9	33.3	33.1	32.5
MONETARY HOLDINGS					*(Millions of current Czechoslovakian Koruny)*						
Money Supply, Broadly Defined	133.95	..	..	..	..	225.43	..	..	..	..	311.98
Money	107.95	..	..	..	..	164.83	..	..	..	..	207.08
Currency Outside Banks	17.85	..	..	..	..	27.73	..	..	..	..	41.58
Demand Deposits	90.10	..	..	..	..	137.10	..	..	..	..	165.50
Quasi-Money	26.00	..	..	..	..	60.60	..	..	..	..	104.90
GOVERNMENT DEFICIT (-) OR SURPLUS					*(Millions of current Czechoslovakian Koruny)*						
Current Revenue	..	..	..	..	..	..	..	..	..	..	..
Current Expenditure	..	..	..	..	..	..	..	..	..	..	..
Current Budget Balance	..	..	..	..	..	..	..	..	..	..	..
Capital Receipts	..	..	..	..	..	..	..	..	..	..	..
Capital Payments	..	..	..	..	..	..	..	..	..	..	..

1981	1982	1983	1984	1985	1986	1987	1988	1989	1990 estimate	Notes	CZECHOSLOVAKIA
..	2,980	3,000	2,860	2,740	2,790	3,030	3,360	3,460	3,140	..	**CURRENT GNP PER CAPITA (US $)**
15,314	15,366	15,415	15,459	15,500	15,532	15,565	15,597	15,629	15,662	..	**POPULATION (thousands)**
				(Billions of current Czechoslovakian Koruny)							**USE AND ORIGIN OF RESOURCES**
570.2	596.0	611.1	648.7	674.1	692.8	709.3	737.8	758.2	792.9	..	Gross National Product (GNP)
-8.1	-5.4	-3.4	-3.8	-2.9	-1.9	-1.8	-2.2	-1.3	-5.2	..	Net Factor Income from Abroad
578.3	601.4	614.5	652.5	677.0	694.7	711.1	740.0	759.5	798.1	..	GDP at Market Prices
7.6	12.4	9.6	14.0	20.4	8.2	10.2	21.8	10.8	-16.0	..	Resource Balance
179.8	193.2	198.3	227.7	245.3	246.1	250.8	261.9	260.0	265.0	..	Exports of Goods & NF Services
172.2	180.8	188.7	213.7	224.9	237.9	240.6	240.1	249.2	281.0	..	Imports of Goods & NF Services
570.7	589.0	604.9	638.5	656.6	686.5	700.9	718.2	748.7	814.1	..	Domestic Absorption
284.5	292.3	301.2	313.3	324.3	332.2	341.3	354.2	374.3	408.2	..	Private Consumption, etc.
118.8	120.8	125.6	136.0	137.2	144.6	151.4	156.1	164.2	166.1	..	General Gov't Consumption
167.4	175.9	178.1	189.2	195.1	209.7	208.2	207.9	210.2	239.8	..	Gross Domestic Investment
154.8	161.7	162.7	176.5	180.9	191.5	184.5	197.3	201.0	208.5	..	Fixed Investment
..	..	..	..	..	..	..	..	..	..	..	Indirect Taxes, net
										..	GDP at factor cost
34.5	43.2	45.8	47.3	44.0	46.8	46.3	46.9	59.9	..	..	Agriculture
332.2	348.0	360.7	374.6	389.8	399.6	409.6	425.2	427.6	..	..	Industry
..	..	..	..	..	..	..	..	..	..	..	Manufacturing
211.6	210.2	208.0	230.6	243.2	248.3	255.2	267.9	272.0	..	..	Services, etc.
175.0	188.3	187.7	203.2	215.5	217.9	218.4	229.7	221.0	223.8	..	Gross Domestic Saving
167.3	183.4	184.6	199.9	213.2	216.8	217.9	228.9	221.7	223.3	..	Gross National Saving
				(Billions of 1987 Czechoslovakian Koruny)							Gross National Product
636.28	643.99	661.51	674.98	690.43	703.97	709.30	727.26	737.64	708.23	..	GDP at Market Prices
645.31	649.82	665.19	678.91	693.38	705.88	711.10	729.45	738.93	713.10	..	
-5.94	2.90	7.73	16.66	23.02	13.02	10.20	15.62	-0.04	-42.85	..	Resource Balance
187.08	197.51	207.23	230.43	244.96	245.41	250.80	260.37	251.97	245.92	..	Exports of Goods & NF Services
193.01	194.61	199.50	213.76	221.94	232.39	240.60	244.75	252.01	288.77	..	Imports of Goods & NF Services
651.24	646.93	657.46	662.24	670.36	692.87	700.90	713.83	738.97	755.95	..	Domestic Absorption
316.43	309.79	320.27	324.76	328.37	333.18	341.30	354.86	362.27	374.90	..	Private Consumption, etc.
126.27	133.83	143.81	148.33	148.52	152.75	151.40	157.91	164.38	159.04	..	General Gov't Consumption
208.55	203.30	193.37	189.15	193.48	206.93	208.20	201.06	212.31	222.01	..	Gross Domestic Investment
194.39	186.02	176.95	178.81	180.42	189.72	184.50	192.92	205.90	206.71	..	Fixed Investment
										..	GDP at factor cost
42.50	46.30	46.41	50.10	46.97	47.87	46.30	46.64	47.08	..	..	Agriculture
368.19	361.23	366.61	378.20	390.32	398.11	409.60	424.14	428.36	..	..	Industry
..	..	..	..	..	..	..	..	..	..	..	Manufacturing
232.80	241.87	252.18	250.61	256.10	259.90	255.20	258.67	263.49	..	..	Services, etc.
											Memo Items:
201.53	207.96	209.65	227.77	242.07	240.40	250.80	266.98	262.94	272.33	..	Capacity to Import
14.46	10.45	2.42	-2.66	-2.89	-5.01	0.00	6.61	10.96	26.41	..	Terms of Trade Adjustment
659.76	660.27	667.61	676.25	690.49	700.88	711.10	736.06	749.89	739.51	..	Gross Domestic Income
650.74	654.43	663.92	672.32	687.54	698.96	709.30	733.87	748.60	734.64	..	Gross National Income
				(Index 1987 = 100)							**DOMESTIC PRICES/DEFLATORS**
89.6	92.5	92.4	96.1	97.6	98.4	100.0	101.4	102.8	111.9	..	Overall (GDP)
87.6	91.0	92.0	96.4	97.9	99.1	100.0	100.6	101.3	107.7	..	Domestic Absorption
81.2	93.3	98.7	94.4	93.7	97.8	100.0	100.6	127.2	..	..	Agriculture
90.2	96.3	98.4	99.0	99.9	100.4	100.0	100.2	99.8	..	..	Industry
..	..	..	..	..	..	..	..	..	..	..	Manufacturing
90.8	95.4	96.3	97.2	99.4	99.9	100.0	100.1	101.5	111.7	..	Consumer Price Index
											MANUFACTURING ACTIVITY
98.1	98.6	98.8	99.3	99.7	100.2	100.0	99.7	98.9	..	..	Employment (1987=100)
97.8	95.3	96.6	97.9	97.7	98.4	100.0	101.9	..	..	..	Real Earnings per Empl. (1987=100)
85.6	85.9	86.2	93.1	95.4	97.2	100.0	101.7			..	Real Output per Empl. (1987=100)
42.7	42.8	41.4	41.8	40.7	41.4	39.9	38.9	..	..	..	Earnings as % of Value Added
				(Millions of current Czechoslovakian Koruny)							**MONETARY HOLDINGS**
335.47	363.40	386.73	413.15	431.09	447.60	474.62	529.35	554.42	550.65	..	Money Supply, Broadly Defined
220.87	236.61	245.73	257.55	260.39	261.30	270.72	309.46	317.72	291.15	..	Money
43.27	46.11	49.33	52.05	53.99	56.20	58.62	62.46	68.02	73.65	..	Currency Outside Banks
177.60	190.50	196.40	205.50	206.40	205.10	212.10	247.00	249.70	217.50	..	Demand Deposits
114.60	126.80	141.00	155.60	170.70	186.30	203.90	219.90	236.70	259.50	..	Quasi-Money
				(Millions of current Czechoslovakian Koruny)							
..	..	..	..	..	..	..	..	-28,800	-56,400	..	**GOVERNMENT DEFICIT (-) OR SURPLUS**
..	..	..	..	..	..	..	..	431,200	432,000	..	Current Revenue
..	..	..	..	..	..	..	..	387,400	429,100	..	Current Expenditure
..	..	..	..	..	..	..	..	43,800	2,900	..	Current Budget Balance
..	..	..	..	..	..	..	..			..	Capital Receipts
..	..	..	..	..	..	..	..	72,600	59,300	..	Capital Payments

CZECHOSLOVAKIA	1970	1971	1972	1973	1974	1975	1976	1977	1978	1979	1980
FOREIGN TRADE (CUSTOMS BASIS)				*(Millions of current US dollars)*							
Value of Exports, fob	4,091	4,420	4,915	6,035	7,053	8,383	9,035	10,302	11,740	13,198	14,891
Nonfuel Primary Products	384	415	462	565	761	707	694	763	963	1,153	1,438
Fuels	150	162	180	228	283	448	439	495	481	667	899
Manufactures	3,557	3,843	4,274	5,243	6,010	7,227	7,902	9,044	10,296	11,378	12,554
Value of Imports, cif	4,228	4,444	4,662	6,137	7,532	9,106	9,706	11,187	12,604	14,360	15,148
Nonfuel Primary Products	1,387	1,458	1,530	1,939	2,385	2,526	2,663	2,983	2,985	3,564	3,871
Fuels	423	445	467	596	649	1,215	1,363	1,694	2,119	2,592	2,847
Manufactures	2,417	2,541	2,666	3,603	4,498	5,365	5,681	6,510	7,500	8,205	8,429
					(Index 1987 = 100)						
Terms of Trade	..	..	..	..	..	..	..	..	..	..	..
Export Prices, fob											
Import Prices, cif	..	..	..	..	..	..	..	..	..	..	..
BALANCE OF PAYMENTS					*(Millions of current US dollars)*						
Exports of Goods & Services	3,234	3,518	4,164	5,146	6,201	7,221	7,634	9,457	11,017	12,819	6,173
Merchandise, fob	2,775	3,046	3,587	4,403	5,272	6,071	6,401	8,011	9,159	10,810	5,237
Nonfactor Services	400	421	510	660	817	957	1,122	1,329	1,666	1,761	574
Factor Services	58	51	68	83	111	194	112	117	191	247	363
Imports of Goods & Services	3,078	3,318	3,801	5,057	6,383	7,669	7,990	10,150	11,522	13,113	6,684
Merchandise, fob	2,704	2,935	3,403	4,499	5,667	6,666	7,989	8,874	9,924	11,273	5,226
Nonfactor Services	312	360	378	534	684	774	-145	1,081	1,254	1,320	633
Factor Services	62	23	20	24	32	229	146	195	345	520	825
Long-Term Interest	0	0	0	0	0	0	0	0	0	0	0
Private Current Transfers, net	0	-2	-1	-2	-3	-5	19	21	22	35	28
Workers' Remittances	..	..	..	..	..	..	..	..	..	..	..
Curr. A/C Bal before Off. Transf.	156	199	362	87	-184	-453	-336	-672	-483	-259	-177
Net Official Transfers	-10	-1	-3	-11	-20	-30	-24	-18	-16	-21	-30
Curr. A/C Bal after Off. Transf.	146	197	360	76	-205	-484	-360	-689	-499	-280	-207
Long-Term Capital, net	-50	-34	-14	110	21	180	328	304	-94	148	362
Direct Investment	..	..	..	..	..	..	..	..	..	..	..
Long-Term Loans	0	0	0	0	0	0	0	0	0	0	0
Disbursements	0	0	0	0	0	0	0	0	0	0	0
Repayments	0	0	0	0	0	0	0	0	0	0	0
Other Long-Term Capital	-50	-34	-14	110	21	180	328	304	-94	148	362
Other Capital, net	-59	-71	-271	-102	345	181	207	499	974	578	202
Change in Reserves	-38	-92	-74	-84	-161	123	-175	-113	-382	-447	-357
Memo Item:					*(Czechoslovakian Koruny per US dollar)*						
Conversion Factor (Annual Avg)	27.000	..	..	..	..	..	..	..	..	..	14.260
EXTERNAL DEBT (Total)				*Millions US dollars), outstanding at end of year*							
Long-Term Debt (by debtor)	..	..	..	..	..	..	..	..	..	..	..
Central Bank, incl. IMF credit	..	..	..	..	..	..	..	..	..	..	..
Central Government	..	..	..	..	..	..	..	..	..	..	..
Rest of General Government	..	..	..	..	..	..	..	..	..	..	..
Non-financial Public Enterprises	..	..	..	..	..	..	..	..	..	..	..
Priv. Sector, incl non-guaranteed	..	..	..	..	..	..	..	..	..	..	..
Short-Term Debt	..	..	..	..	..	..	..	..	..	..	..
Memo Items:					*(Millions of US dollars)*						
Int'l Reserves Excluding Gold	..	..	..	..	..	..	..	..	..	..	1,839.3
Gold Holdings (at market price)	69.0	80.5	119.8	207.2	344.3	259.1	248.9	304.7	417.4	945.7	1,799.3
SOCIAL INDICATORS											
Total Fertility Rate	2.1	2.1	2.2	2.4	2.5	2.5	2.4	2.4	2.4	2.3	2.2
Infant Mortality Rate	22.1	21.7	21.6	21.3	20.5	20.8	21.0	19.6	18.7	17.7	18.4
Life Expectancy at Birth	70.0	70.0	70.0	70.1	70.2	70.3	70.4	70.5	70.5	70.5	70.6
Urban Population, % of total	55.2	56.4	57.7	58.9	60.2	61.4	62.6	63.8	65.1	66.3	67.5
Food Prod. per capita (1987=100)	74.0	76.8	78.4	84.9	85.8	82.7	81.5	88.6	90.8	81.2	88.6
Labor Force, Agriculture (%)	16.9	16.5	16.2	15.8	15.5	15.1	14.7	14.4	14.0	13.6	13.3
Labor Force, Female (%)	43.8	44.1	44.4	44.7	45.0	45.3	45.5	45.7	45.9	46.1	46.3
Primary Schl. Enroll. Ratio	98.0	..	..	..	..	96.0	97.0	96.0	94.0	92.0	92.0
Primary Schl. Enroll. Ratio, Female	98.0	..	..	..	..	97.0	97.0	96.0	95.0	93.0	92.0
Secondary Schl. Enroll. Ratio	31.0	..	..	..	..	35.0	36.0	38.0	40.0	43.0	89.0

	1981	1982	1983	1984	1985	1986	1987	1988	1989	1990 estimate	Notes
FOREIGN TRADE (CUSTOMS BASIS)											
(Millions of current US dollars)											
Value of Exports, fob	14,782	15,694	16,477	17,153	17,474	20,457	23,016	22,818	21,579	17,950	..
Nonfuel Primary Products	1,102	1,134	1,044	1,108	1,636	1,254	2,155	2,136	2,020	1,680	..
Fuels	709	799	791	795	659	724	868	861	814	677	..
Manufactures	12,971	13,760	14,641	15,250	15,179	18,479	19,994	19,822	18,745	15,592	..
Value of Imports, cif	14,634	15,492	16,324	17,078	17,548	21,089	23,284	21,841	21,352	19,862	..
Nonfuel Primary Products	3,373	3,369	3,190	3,187	2,965	3,564	3,935	3,691	3,608	3,356	..
Fuels	3,431	4,376	4,931	5,293	5,337	6,414	7,081	6,643	6,494	6,041	..
Manufactures	7,829	7,747	8,203	8,598	9,245	11,111	12,268	11,507	11,250	10,465	..
(Index 1987 = 100)											
Terms of Trade	..	..	..	..	..	..	..	..	..	..	..
Export Prices, fob	..	..	..	..	..	..	..	..	..	..	..
Import Prices, cif	..	..	..	..	..	..	..	..	..	..	..
BALANCE OF PAYMENTS											
(Millions of current US dollars)											
Exports of Goods & Services	13,886	14,198	14,538	14,246	14,367	16,323	18,234	18,273	17,581	14,802	..
Merchandise, fob	11,479	11,868	11,948	11,595	11,667	13,532	15,228	15,070	14,216	11,634	..
Nonfactor Services	2,033	2,020	2,321	2,394	2,437	2,510	2,685	2,846	2,864	2,662	..
Factor Services	374	310	269	257	263	281	321	357	501	506	..
Imports of Goods & Services	13,672	13,525	13,678	13,300	13,435	15,921	17,620	16,826	16,756	16,238	..
Merchandise, fob	11,229	11,566	11,552	11,174	11,406	13,852	15,391	14,784	14,073	13,056	..
Nonfactor Services	1,459	1,256	1,618	1,643	1,597	1,659	1,780	1,528	2,093	2,423	..
Factor Services	984	703	508	483	432	410	449	514	590	759	..
Long-Term Interest	0	2	6	3	300	240	224	273	297	365	..
Private Current Transfers, net	30	36	19	29	34	53	95	94	130	261	..
Workers' Remittances	..	..	..	..	..	..	..	..	..	..	..
Curr. A/C Bal before Off. Transf.	244	709	879	975	966	455	709	1,541	955	-1,175	..
Net Official Transfers	-19	-152	-31	-20	-29	-41	-27	-29	-23	-52	..
Curr. A/C Bal after Off. Transf.	225	557	848	955	937	414	682	1,512	932	-1,227	..
Long-Term Capital, net	276	-74	-409	-618	-799	-389	213	-279	-551	681	..
Direct Investment									255	188	..
Long-Term Loans	22	52	21	69	-338	-111	549	615	458	882	..
Disbursements	22	52	21	71	469	787	1,547	1,716	1,617	1,866	..
Repayments	0	0	0	2	807	898	997	1,101	1,159	984	..
Other Long-Term Capital	254	-126	-430	-687	-461	-278	-336	-894	-1,264	-389	..
Other Capital, net	-1,388	-647	-326	-179	-237	231	-640	-1,024	187	-586	..
Change in Reserves	887	164	-113	-158	99	-256	-255	-209	-568	1,132	..
Memo Item:											
(Czechoslovakian Koruny per US dollar)											
Conversion Factor (Annual Avg)	13.250	13.730	14.150	16.600	17.180	15.000	13.680	14.360	15.050	17.950	..
EXTERNAL DEBT (Total)											
Millions US dollars), outstanding at end of year											
Long-Term Debt (by debtor)	..	..	..	..	..	..	..	..	..	..	..
Central Bank, incl. IMF credit	..	..	..	..	..	..	..	..	..	..	..
Central Government	..	..	..	..	..	..	..	..	..	..	..
Rest of General Government	..	..	..	..	..	..	..	..	..	..	..
Non-financial Public Enterprises	..	..	..	..	..	..	..	..	..	..	..
Priv. Sector, incl non-guaranteed	..	..	..	..	..	..	..	..	..	..	..
Short-Term Debt	..	..	..	..	..	..	..	..	..	..	..
Memo Items:											
(Millions of US dollars)											
Int'l Reserves Excluding Gold	955.9	776.0	803.0	966.3	854.3	1,115.2	1,382.0	1,583.0	2,156.5	1,102.0	..
Gold Holdings (at market price)	1,248.2	1,668.1	1,470.2	1,205.1	1,244.8	1,475.2	1,771.9	1,530.2	1,452.8	957.5	..
SOCIAL INDICATORS											
Total Fertility Rate	2.1	2.1	2.1	2.1	2.1	2.0	2.0	2.0	2.0	2.0	..
Infant Mortality Rate	16.8	16.2	15.7	15.3	14.0	13.6	13.1	12.8	12.4	12.1	..
Life Expectancy at Birth	70.6	70.6	70.7	70.8	70.9	71.0	71.2	71.3	71.4	71.5	..
Urban Population, % of total	68.6	69.7	70.9	72.0	73.1	74.0	74.9	75.7	76.6	77.5	..
Food Prod. per capita (1987=100)	88.1	93.1	96.6	102.0	98.9	98.3	100.0	102.5	103.2	102.1	..
Labor Force, Agriculture (%)	..	..	..	..	..	..	..	..	..		..
Labor Force, Female (%)	46.3	46.4	46.4	46.4	46.4	46.5	46.5	46.5	46.6	46.6	..
Primary Schl. Enroll. Ratio	91.0	89.0	88.0	99.0	99.0	98.0	96.0	94.0	92.0	..	..
Primary Schl. Enroll. Ratio, Female	91.0	89.0	88.0	100.0	99.0	98.0	96.0	94.0	93.0	..	..
Secondary Schl. Enroll. Ratio						84.0	81.0	82.0	85.0	87.0	..

DENMARK	1970	1971	1972	1973	1974	1975	1976	1977	1978	1979	1980
CURRENT GNP PER CAPITA (US $)	3,120	3,450	3,990	4,810	5,760	6,910	8,030	8,930	10,010	11,880	13,130
POPULATION (thousands)	4,929	4,963	4,992	5,022	5,045	5,060	5,073	5,088	5,104	5,117	5,123

USE AND ORIGIN OF RESOURCES

(Billions of current Danish Kroner)

	1970	1971	1972	1973	1974	1975	1976	1977	1978	1979	1980
Gross National Product (GNP)	118.41	130.71	149.98	172.03	192.35	214.59	249.26	276.24	306.78	340.31	364.50
Net Factor Income from Abroad	-0.21	-0.41	-0.75	-0.83	-1.28	-1.66	-1.96	-3.07	-4.60	-6.59	-9.28
GDP at Market Prices	118.63	131.12	150.73	172.86	193.63	216.26	251.22	279.31	311.38	346.89	373.79
Resource Balance	-3.56	-2.42	0.89	-3.29	-5.67	-2.03	-11.69	-10.19	-6.73	-9.80	-3.95
Exports of Goods & NFServices	33.10	36.18	40.83	49.31	61.48	65.05	72.45	80.46	86.52	101.44	122.26
Imports of Goods & NFServices	36.66	38.60	39.94	52.61	67.16	67.08	84.14	90.66	93.25	111.25	126.21
Domestic Absorption	122.18	133.54	149.84	176.15	199.30	218.29	262.90	289.50	318.11	356.70	377.74
Private Consumption, etc.	68.08	73.16	80.44	94.20	105.22	119.94	142.13	158.90	174.89	195.81	208.81
General Gov't Consumption	23.67	27.87	32.08	36.81	45.25	53.18	60.52	66.77	76.25	86.83	99.73
Gross Domestic Investment	30.43	32.51	37.32	45.14	48.83	45.16	60.25	63.84	66.97	74.05	69.19
Fixed Investment	29.28	31.75	37.01	42.81	46.46	45.59	57.68	61.66	67.49	72.47	70.31
Indirect Taxes, net	17.30	19.25	21.89	23.76	23.98	27.54	33.09	39.11	46.32	54.58	57.80
GDP at factor cost	101.33	111.87	128.84	149.10	169.65	188.71	218.12	240.20	265.06	292.32	315.99
Agriculture	6.61	7.16	8.56	10.52	11.44	10.93	12.30	14.56	16.78	16.07	17.82
Industry	35.06	37.92	43.34	48.52	53.83	58.99	66.29	71.11	77.26	83.48	93.59
Manufacturing	21.97	23.55	26.65	30.91	34.96	39.05	43.97	47.64	51.41	56.98	64.31
Services, etc.	59.66	66.79	76.94	90.06	104.38	118.80	139.53	154.53	171.02	192.76	204.58
Gross Domestic Saving	26.87	30.09	38.22	41.85	43.15	43.13	48.56	53.64	60.24	64.25	65.24
Gross National Saving	26.59	29.64	37.35	40.95	41.70	41.27	46.32	50.51	55.46	57.31	55.45

(Billions of 1987 Danish Kroner)

	1970	1971	1972	1973	1974	1975	1976	1977	1978	1979	1980
Gross National Product	473.81	486.71	511.91	528.48	523.18	518.73	551.71	559.13	565.07	582.55	577.08
GDP at Market Prices	474.69	488.23	514.48	531.06	526.60	522.75	556.04	565.37	573.74	593.94	591.63
Resource Balance	-33.38	-26.32	-22.01	-30.82	-20.11	-15.05	-32.66	-27.02	-25.52	-21.85	-1.57
Exports of Goods & NFServices	108.63	114.67	121.07	130.53	135.10	132.69	138.12	143.80	145.50	157.66	165.79
Imports of Goods & NFServices	142.01	140.99	143.08	161.35	155.21	147.74	170.77	170.81	171.02	179.51	167.36
Domestic Absorption	508.08	514.56	536.49	561.88	546.71	537.80	588.70	592.38	599.25	615.79	593.21
Private Consumption, etc.	282.82	282.75	288.91	299.28	292.66	303.73	324.42	329.16	331.80	336.75	327.65
General Gov't Consumption	103.22	108.85	115.11	119.70	123.91	126.40	132.04	135.22	143.59	152.01	158.51
Gross Domestic Investment	122.04	122.96	132.47	142.89	130.14	107.67	132.23	128.01	123.86	127.03	107.05
Fixed Investment	118.28	120.57	131.73	136.30	124.23	108.85	127.49	124.37	125.75	125.19	109.41
GDP at factor cost	402.18	413.80	436.05	454.43	460.45	454.57	481.07	484.57	485.65	498.87	500.69
Agriculture	16.93	19.20	19.78	18.32	22.31	20.86	18.77	21.34	21.84	21.95	22.86
Industry	121.50	124.34	134.28	134.98	133.19	127.16	133.38	134.21	134.75	137.85	142.38
Manufacturing	77.96	79.55	86.37	91.15	92.56	90.32	94.65	95.07	94.80	100.19	104.71
Services, etc.	262.55	267.93	278.99	300.97	304.04	306.31	329.67	329.11	329.00	339.19	335.03

Memo Items:

	1970	1971	1972	1973	1974	1975	1976	1977	1978	1979	1980
Capacity to Import	128.23	132.15	146.27	151.25	142.09	143.27	147.05	151.61	158.67	163.69	162.13
Terms of Trade Adjustment	19.60	17.48	25.20	20.72	6.99	10.57	8.93	7.81	13.17	6.03	-3.66
Gross Domestic Income	494.30	505.72	539.69	551.78	533.59	533.33	564.97	573.18	586.91	599.97	587.97
Gross National Income	493.42	504.19	537.12	549.20	530.17	529.30	560.65	566.94	578.24	588.58	573.42

DOMESTIC PRICES/DEFLATORS

(Index 1987 = 100)

	1970	1971	1972	1973	1974	1975	1976	1977	1978	1979	1980
Overall (GDP)	25.0	26.9	29.3	32.6	36.8	41.4	45.2	49.4	54.3	58.4	63.2
Domestic Absorption	24.0	26.0	27.9	31.4	36.5	40.6	44.7	48.9	53.1	57.9	63.7
Agriculture	39.1	37.3	43.3	57.4	51.3	52.4	65.5	68.3	76.8	73.2	78.0
Industry	28.9	30.5	32.3	35.9	40.4	46.4	49.7	53.0	57.3	60.6	65.7
Manufacturing	28.2	29.6	30.9	33.9	37.8	43.2	46.5	50.1	54.2	56.9	61.4
Consumer Price Index	24.8	26.2	28.0	30.6	35.2	38.6	42.1	46.8	51.5	56.4	63.4

MANUFACTURING ACTIVITY

	1970	1971	1972	1973	1974	1975	1976	1977	1978	1979	1980
Employment (1987=100)	103.9	100.6	102.0	105.8	102.3	92.9	93.5	95.6	95.2	96.4	94.5
Real Earnings per Empl. (1987=100)	76.3	81.8	84.0	85.9	91.3	96.6	99.2	97.5	96.6	97.7	97.1
Real Output per Empl. (1987=100)	68.1	70.5	74.4	77.8	86.3	81.5	87.9	92.7	92.7	97.7	104.3
Earnings as % of Value Added	56.4	58.1	56.6	57.0	59.1	59.1	57.4	57.5	57.6	57.7	56.8

MONETARY HOLDINGS

(Billions of current Danish Kroner)

	1970	1971	1972	1973	1974	1975	1976	1977	1978	1979	1980
Money Supply, Broadly Defined	54.39	59.21	67.12	76.27	82.70	104.99	117.30	128.19	136.44	150.38	167.99
Money	27.47	29.61	33.64	37.59	39.36	49.86	52.34	56.08	65.06	71.88	77.51
Currency Outside Banks	4.87	4.92	5.56	5.99	6.04	7.63	8.44	9.91	10.75	11.57	12.36
Demand Deposits	22.60	24.69	28.08	31.60	33.32	42.23	43.90	46.17	54.31	60.31	65.15
Quasi-Money	26.92	29.60	33.48	38.68	43.34	55.12	64.96	72.11	71.38	78.50	90.48

GOVERNMENT DEFICIT (-) OR SURPLUS

(Billions of current Danish Kroner)

	1970	1971	1972	1973	1974	1975	1976	1977	1978	1979	1980
	2.95	3.57	4.09	6.14	1.34	-4.35	-0.52	-2.73	-1.07	-2.58	-10.00
Current Revenue	41.83	47.63	53.57	58.64	67.27	71.24	83.17	91.70	106.80	122.09	135.23
Current Expenditure	35.39	40.34	45.67	48.38	61.01	69.79	77.44	88.35	101.61	118.61	137.09
Current Budget Balance	6.44	7.29	7.90	10.26	6.25	1.45	5.73	3.35	5.19	3.48	-1.86
Capital Receipts	0.11	0.09	0.19	0.15	0.21	0.16	1.00	0.21	0.62	0.61	3.67
Capital Payments	3.60	3.81	4.00	4.28	5.13	5.96	7.25	6.29	6.87	6.67	11.81

1981	1982	1983	1984	1985	1986	1987	1988	1989	1990 estimate	Notes	DENMARK
12,840	12,120	11,390	11,150	11,310	12,640	15,120	18,860	20,740	22,680	..	CURRENT GNP PER CAPITA (US $)
5,122	5,118	5,114	5,112	5,114	5,121	5,127	5,130	5,132	5,140		POPULATION (thousands)
											USE AND ORIGIN OF RESOURCES
				(Billions of current Danish Kroner)							
395.11	446.65	494.11	541.42	588.90	639.00	672.34	707.79	744.42	777.08		Gross National Product (GNP)
-12.69	-17.82	-18.43	-23.86	-26.17	-27.49	-27.57	-27.73	-31.59	-33.37	..	Net Factor Income from Abroad
407.79	464.47	512.54	565.28	615.07	666.50	699.91	735.52	776.02	810.45		GDP at Market Prices
2.99	2.00	10.17	7.11	2.09	-3.00	12.86	22.61	27.34	43.85		Resource Balance
149.04	168.92	186.31	207.52	225.57	213.56	220.08	237.71	266.41	283.03		Exports of Goods & NF Services
146.05	166.93	176.14	200.41	223.48	216.55	207.23	215.10	239.07	239.17		Imports of Goods & NF Services
404.80	462.47	502.37	558.17	612.99	669.49	687.05	712.91	748.67	766.59		Domestic Absorption
228.57	255.64	279.96	307.89	337.21	366.75	377.88	393.08	409.71	424.08		Private Consumption, etc.
113.22	131.10	140.54	146.18	155.48	159.36	176.21	188.55	194.64	200.81		General Gov't Consumption
63.02	75.73	81.86	104.10	120.29	143.39	132.96	131.27	144.32	141.70		Gross Domestic Investment
63.82	74.61	82.05	97.25	115.19	138.37	138.03	134.77	141.32	143.62		Fixed Investment
62.67	67.05	74.67	83.61	94.56	110.82	113.96	115.26	115.12	116.01	..	Indirect Taxes, net
345.12	397.41	437.87	481.68	520.52	555.68	585.95	620.26	660.89	694.44		GDP at factor cost
20.96	26.27	24.94	31.00	30.10	30.00	27.34	28.13	31.93	..	..	Agriculture
95.58	110.50	121.59	136.17	148.87	163.22	171.82	177.65	185.77		..	Industry
67.15	76.26	86.04	97.50	105.07	111.70	113.87	118.76	122.38		..	Manufacturing
228.57	260.64	291.34	314.50	341.55	362.45	386.79	414.49	443.20	..	..	Services, etc.
66.01	77.73	92.03	111.22	122.38	140.39	145.82	153.89	171.67	185.56	..	Gross Domestic Saving
52.44	59.58	72.75	87.29	95.63	111.99	117.87	125.56	140.66	151.90		Gross National Saving
				(Billions of 1987 Danish Kroner)							
568.51	581.50	597.19	618.82	645.04	668.73	672.34	677.34	683.11	697.12	..	Gross National Product
586.34	604.21	619.12	645.67	673.31	697.58	699.91	703.62	711.72	726.42	..	GDP at Market Prices
14.83	13.10	19.03	16.24	11.30	-2.01	12.86	25.96	31.20	48.18	..	Resource Balance
179.38	183.87	192.80	199.49	209.39	209.45	220.08	236.11	250.20	271.85	..	Exports of Goods & NF Services
164.55	170.77	173.77	183.25	198.09	211.46	207.23	210.15	219.00	223.66	..	Imports of Goods & NF Services
571.51	591.11	600.09	629.43	662.01	699.58	687.05	677.66	680.52	678.23	..	Domestic Absorption
322.32	326.92	335.98	346.45	362.65	381.11	377.88	376.81	374.63	380.72		Private Consumption, etc.
162.68	167.69	167.62	166.93	171.14	171.97	176.21	176.53	174.28	173.64		General Gov't Consumption
86.51	96.51	96.49	116.06	128.22	146.50	132.96	124.33	131.61	123.88		Gross Domestic Investment
88.39	94.65	96.40	108.82	122.49	143.44	138.03	128.94	129.25	126.75		Fixed Investment
498.12	518.76	530.28	551.57	571.17	581.28	585.95	594.40	607.46	624.65	..	GDP at factor cost
24.75	27.23	24.89	29.88	29.75	28.69	27.34	29.00	30.70	..	..	Agriculture
133.22	136.27	142.51	150.87	160.36	171.57	171.82	170.73	173.76		..	Industry
101.39	103.00	109.92	115.07	118.73	118.73	113.87	114.32	115.73		..	Manufacturing
339.82	354.70	362.88	370.83	381.06	381.02	386.79	394.67	403.00	..	..	Services, etc.
											Memo Items:
167.92	172.81	183.81	189.75	199.94	208.53	220.08	232.24	244.05	264.67		Capacity to Import
-11.46	-11.06	-8.99	-9.73	-9.45	-0.92	0.00	-3.87	-6.15	-7.17		Terms of Trade Adjustment
574.88	593.15	610.12	635.94	663.86	696.66	699.91	699.76	705.57	719.24		Gross Domestic Income
557.05	570.43	588.20	609.08	635.59	667.81	672.34	673.48	676.96	689.95		Gross National Income
				(Index 1987 = 100)							DOMESTIC PRICES/DEFLATORS
69.5	76.9	82.8	87.5	91.4	95.5	100.0	104.5	109.0	111.6	..	Overall (GDP)
70.8	78.2	83.7	88.7	92.6	95.7	100.0	105.2	110.0	113.0	..	Domestic Absorption
84.7	96.5	100.2	103.8	101.2	104.6	100.0	97.0	104.0	..	..	Agriculture
71.7	81.1	85.3	90.3	92.8	95.1	100.0	104.1	106.9		..	Industry
66.2	74.0	78.3	84.7	88.5	94.1	100.0	103.9	105.7		..	Manufacturing
70.8	78.0	83.4	88.6	92.7	96.2	100.0	104.6	109.6	112.4	..	Consumer Price Index
											MANUFACTURING ACTIVITY
89.9	89.5	89.3	93.7	100.4	102.4	100.0	97.0	96.7		..	Employment (1987=100)
94.9	96.1	96.9	95.4	93.7	96.9	100.0	102.0	104.2	..	..	Real Earnings per Empl. (1987=100)
111.4	110.8	115.8	116.0	113.0	109.0	100.0	105.8	..	..	..	Real Output per Empl. (1987=100)
55.1	54.4	52.5	51.7	51.8	52.7	53.3	52.2	52.7	..	..	Earnings as % of Value Added
				(Billions of current Danish Kroner)							MONETARY HOLDINGS
186.21	206.82	264.31	309.79	366.67	401.19	427.31	450.95	456.90	486.72	..	Money Supply, Broadly Defined
88.03	91.67	113.30	128.08	156.49	167.97	188.45	225.11	226.11	244.48		Money
13.57	14.18	15.42	16.37	17.57	18.82	19.82	21.39	22.38	22.58		Currency Outside Banks
74.46	77.48	97.89	111.71	138.92	149.15	168.63	203.72	203.74	221.90		Demand Deposits
98.18	115.16	151.00	181.71	210.18	233.23	238.86	225.83	230.79	242.24		Quasi-Money
				(Billions of current Danish Kroner)						E	GOVERNMENT DEFICIT (-) OR SURPLUS
-24.69	-37.52	-35.15	-22.24	-3.73	30.08	27.41	15.62	4.90	-2.75		Current Revenue
148.10	166.21	192.19	223.32	251.18	283.31	294.34	304.86	312.95	316.37	..	Current Expenditure
162.04	191.50	213.75	233.94	242.58	243.69	257.56	278.30	296.40	308.95		Current Budget Balance
-13.94	-25.30	-21.56	-10.62	8.60	39.62	36.77	26.56	16.55	7.42		Capital Receipts
0.23	0.27	0.39	0.38	0.33	2.34	1.31	1.15	0.92	3.02		Capital Payments
10.99	12.50	13.99	11.99	12.66	11.88	10.68	12.09	12.56	13.19	..	

DENMARK	1970	1971	1972	1973	1974	1975	1976	1977	1978	1979	1980
FOREIGN TRADE (CUSTOMS BASIS)					*(Millions of current US dollars)*						
Value of Exports, fob	3,285	3,601	4,312	6,116	7,683	8,663	8,980	9,911	11,676	14,342	16,407
Nonfuel Primary Products	1,429	1,556	1,831	2,654	3,085	3,479	3,577	4,014	4,961	5,906	6,589
Fuels	82	81	89	132	288	292	335	317	298	562	566
Manufactures	1,774	1,963	2,392	3,330	4,310	4,892	5,068	5,580	6,417	7,874	9,252
Value of Imports, cif	4,385	4,582	5,027	7,714	9,857	10,326	12,404	13,227	14,777	18,412	19,315
Nonfuel Primary Products	869	849	967	1,486	1,761	1,640	2,133	2,539	2,847	3,464	3,664
Fuels	459	557	549	821	1,889	1,920	2,038	2,227	2,303	3,603	4,328
Manufactures	3,057	3,177	3,511	5,407	6,206	6,766	8,232	8,461	9,627	11,345	11,323
					(Index 1987 = 100)						
Terms of Trade	146.7	146.7	144.9	147.8	104.5	104.2	103.8	100.3	106.5	108.5	97.1
Export Prices, fob	29.4	32.1	36.9	49.4	54.7	57.1	60.4	64.2	75.4	92.0	97.9
Import Prices, cif	20.0	21.9	25.5	33.4	52.3	54.8	58.3	64.1	70.7	84.8	100.8
BALANCE OF PAYMENTS					*(Millions of current US dollars)*						
Exports of Goods & Services	4,549	5,152	6,230	8,711	10,895	12,124	12,894	14,487	17,134	16,486	19,245
Merchandise, fob	3,317	3,610	4,363	6,191	7,703	8,652	9,053	10,011	11,807	14,574	16,786
Nonfactor Services	1,148	1,462	1,769	2,353	2,968	3,223	3,586	4,113	4,785	4,710	4,904
Factor Services	84	80	98	167	224	249	255	363	543	1,912	2,459
Imports of Goods & Services	5,050	5,525	6,203	9,409	12,033	12,690	15,026	16,594	19,187	21,295	23,057
Merchandise, fob	4,077	4,322	4,793	7,380	9,490	9,956	11,931	12,726	14,163	17,966	18,809
Nonfactor Services	844	1,052	1,191	1,703	2,061	2,159	2,480	2,958	3,596	3,180	3,583
Factor Services	129	151	218	326	482	574	616	911	1,429	3,329	4,248
Long-Term Interest	..	..	..	..	..	..	..	..	..	..	..
Private Current Transfers, net	-9	-6	-17	-11	-29	-34	-47	-11	-32	-67	-89
Workers' Remittances	..	..	..	..	..	..	..	..	..	..	..
Curr. A/C Bal before Off. Transf.	-510	-379	10	-709	-1,167	-600	-2,179	-2,118	-2,085	-3,338	-2,578
Net Official Transfers	-34	-45	-73	241	186	110	265	396	583	366	112
Curr. A/C Bal after Off. Transf.	-544	-424	-63	-468	-981	-490	-1,914	-1,722	-1,502	-2,972	-2,466
Long-Term Capital, net	111	376	266	511	344	134	1,863	2,478	2,435	933	2,546
Direct Investment	75	73	16	114	..	188	-254	-85	56	103	-92
Long-Term Loans	..	..	..	..	..	..	..	..	..	..	..
Disbursements	..	..	..	..	..	..	..	..	..	..	..
Repayments	..	..	..	..	..	..	..	..	..	..	..
Other Long-Term Capital	36	303	250	397	344	-54	2,117	2,564	2,379	829	2,638
Other Capital, net	444	226	-112	399	199	313	70	-39	564	1,967	-4
Change in Reserves	-11	-178	-91	-443	438	42	-19	-717	-1,496	72	-77
Memo Item:					*(Danish Kroner per US dollar)*						
Conversion Factor (Annual Avg)	7.500	7.420	6.950	6.050	6.090	5.750	6.050	6.000	5.510	5.260	5.640
EXTERNAL DEBT (Total)					*(Millions US dollars), outstanding at end of year*						
Long-Term Debt (by debtor)	..	..	..	..	..	..	..	..	..	..	..
Central Bank, incl. IMF credit	..	..	..	..	..	..	..	..	..	..	..
Central Government	..	..	..	..	..	..	..	..	..	..	..
Rest of General Government	..	..	..	..	..	..	..	..	..	..	..
Non-financial Public Enterprises	..	..	..	..	..	..	..	..	..	..	..
Priv. Sector, incl non-guaranteed	..	..	..	..	..	..	..	..	..	..	..
Short-Term Debt	..	..	..	..	..	..	..	..	..	..	..
Memo Items:					*(Millions of US dollars)*						
Int'l Reserves Excluding Gold	419	653	786	1,247	858	803	841	1,589	3,129	3,236	3,387
Gold Holdings (at market price)	69	79	118	204	338	254	244	318	447	840	960
SOCIAL INDICATORS											
Total Fertility Rate	1.9	2.0	2.0	1.9	1.9	1.9	1.7	1.7	1.7	1.6	1.5
Infant Mortality Rate	14.2	13.5	12.2	11.5	10.7	10.4	10.2	8.7	8.8	8.8	8.4
Life Expectancy at Birth	73.3	73.4	73.6	73.7	73.8	74.0	74.1	74.2	74.2	74.3	74.3
Urban Population, % of total	79.7	80.1	80.5	81.0	81.4	81.8	82.2	82.6	82.9	83.3	83.7
Food Prod. per capita (1987=100)	75.2	78.8	76.1	76.2	85.6	80.3	76.0	84.1	83.5	86.1	86.8
Labor Force, Agriculture (%)	11.2	10.8	10.4	10.0	9.6	9.2	8.8	8.4	8.0	7.7	7.3
Labor Force, Female (%)	36.0	36.9	37.7	38.5	39.3	40.0	40.8	41.6	42.4	43.2	43.9
Primary Schl. Enroll. Ratio	96.0	..	..	..	..	104.0	101.0	99.0	98.0	98.0	96.0
Primary Schl. Enroll. Ratio, Female	97.0	..	..	..	..	..	102.0	100.0	99.0	98.0	95.0
Secondary Schl. Enroll. Ratio	78.0	..	..	..	..	80.0	80.0	83.0	99.0	102.0	105.0

1981	1982	1983	1984	1985	1986	1987	1988	1989	1990 estimate	Notes	DENMARK
											FOREIGN TRADE (CUSTOMS BASIS)
				(Millions of current US dollars)							
15,697	14,953	15,601	15,486	16,469	20,558	24,697	27,815	27,997	34,801	..	Value of Exports, fob
6,304	6,110	5,899	5,748	5,967	7,581	8,924	9,369	9,284	11,051	..	Nonfuel Primary Products
505	385	779	801	903	643	734	613	840	1,158	..	Fuels
8,888	8,458	8,922	8,936	9,599	12,334	15,039	17,834	17,873	22,592	..	Manufactures
17,521	16,834	16,179	16,536	17,985	22,726	25,334	26,458	26,592	31,562	..	Value of Imports, cif
3,323	3,017	3,066	3,052	3,036	3,997	4,642	4,978	4,933	5,538	..	Nonfuel Primary Products
4,216	3,790	3,163	2,999	3,097	2,009	1,996	1,672	1,915	2,195	..	Fuels
9,982	10,027	9,950	10,485	11,852	16,719	18,696	19,807	19,743	23,829	..	Manufactures
				(Index 1987 = 100)							
90.9	90.8	91.8	89.6	92.7	98.0	100.0	103.6	102.3	104.1	..	Terms of Trade
90.3	84.7	83.2	79.0	79.6	89.0	100.0	108.0	114.1	132.6	..	Export Prices, fob
99.3	93.3	90.6	88.1	85.8	90.9	100.0	104.3	111.6	127.4	..	Import Prices, cif
											BALANCE OF PAYMENTS
				(Millions of current US dollars)							
23,176	22,241	22,511	22,444	24,019	29,674	36,170	40,840	43,275	55,481	..	Exports of Goods & Services
16,136	15,685	16,210	16,079	17,123	21,307	25,695	27,537	28,728	35,740	..	Merchandise, fob
5,853	5,410	5,310	5,208	5,487	6,372	7,848	9,710	9,894	12,997	..	Nonfactor Services
1,187	1,146	991	1,157	1,409	1,995	2,627	3,592	4,652	6,743	..	Factor Services
24,891	24,315	23,499	24,149	26,651	33,886	38,951	41,873	44,024	53,884	..	Imports of Goods & Services
17,064	16,479	15,974	16,285	17,887	22,357	24,900	25,654	26,304	31,174	..	Merchandise, fob
4,663	4,538	4,511	4,465	4,794	6,066	7,302	8,427	8,638	10,413	..	Nonfactor Services
3,164	3,298	3,013	3,399	3,970	5,464	6,750	7,791	9,082	12,297	..	Factor Services
..	..	..	..	..	..	..	..	..	..	..	Long-Term Interest
-124	-39	-94	-7	-55	-112	-56	-88	80	-46	..	Private Current Transfers, net
..	..	..	..	..	..	..	..	..	..	..	Workers' Remittances
-1,839	-2,113	-1,082	-1,712	-2,687	-4,324	-2,838	-1,121	-669	1,551	..	Curr. A/C Bal before Off. Transf.
-37	-146	-94	76	-80	-166	-164	-131	-223	-10	..	Net Official Transfers
-1,875	-2,259	-1,176	-1,637	-2,767	-4,490	-3,001	-1,252	-892	1,541	..	Curr. A/C Bal after Off. Transf.
1,349	2,398	2,466	1,900	4,337	3,144	6,559	2,382	-3,790	6,066	..	Long-Term Capital, net
-39	52	-97	-88	-195	-491	-534	-217	-976	-271	..	Direct Investment
..	..	..	..	..	..	..	..	..	..	..	Long-Term Loans
..	..	..	..	..	..	..	..	..	..	..	Disbursements
..	..	..	..	..	..	..	..	..	..	..	Repayments
1,388	2,346	2,562	1,988	4,533	3,636	7,093	2,599	-2,814	6,336	..	Other Long-Term Capital
-187	-436	85	-631	-48	-633	886	186	860	-4,233	..	Other Capital, net
713	297	-1,375	367	-1,522	1,979	-4,443	-1,316	3,821	-3,374	..	Change in Reserves
											Memo Item:
				(Danish Kroner per US dollar)							
7.120	8.330	9.140	10.360	10.600	8.090	6.840	6.730	7.310	6.190		Conversion Factor (Annual Avg)
											EXTERNAL DEBT (Total)
				(Millions US dollars), outstanding at end of year							
..	..	..	..	..	..	..	..	..	..	..	Long-Term Debt (by debtor)
..	..	..	..	..	..	..	..	..	..	..	Central Bank, incl. IMF credit
..	..	..	..	..	..	..	..	..	..	..	Central Government
..	..	..	..	..	..	..	..	..	..	..	Rest of General Government
..	..	..	..	..	..	..	..	..	..	..	Non-financial Public Enterprises
..	..	..	..	..	..	..	..	..	..	..	Priv. Sector, incl non-guaranteed
..	..	..	..	..	..	..	..	..	..	..	Short-Term Debt
											Memo Items:
				(Millions of US dollars)							
2,548	2,266	3,621	3,009	5,429	4,964	10,066	10,765	6,397	10,591	..	Int'l Reserves Excluding Gold
648	744	621	502	533	637	788	668	657	634	..	Gold Holdings (at market price)
											SOCIAL INDICATORS
1.4	1.4	1.4	1.4	1.4	1.5	1.5	1.5	1.5	1.5	..	Total Fertility Rate
7.9	8.2	7.7	7.7	7.9	8.2	8.3	8.2	8.1	7.9	..	Infant Mortality Rate
74.3	74.3	74.4	74.5	74.6	74.7	74.8	75.0	75.1	75.3	..	Life Expectancy at Birth
84.1	84.4	84.8	85.1	85.5	85.8	86.1	86.4	86.7	87.0	..	Urban Population, % of total
88.0	95.4	91.1	107.6	105.7	104.2	100.0	104.9	109.3	115.2	..	Food Prod. per capita (1987=100)
..	..	..	..	..	..	..	..	..	..	..	Labor Force, Agriculture (%)
44.0	44.0	44.1	44.2	44.2	44.3	44.4	44.5	44.5	44.6	..	Labor Force, Female (%)
..	98.0	99.0	98.0	98.0	99.0	99.0	97.0	98.0	..	..	Primary Schl. Enroll. Ratio
98.0	98.0	99.0	99.0	98.0	99.0	99.0	97.0	98.0	..	..	Primary Schl. Enroll. Ratio, Female
..	105.0	103.0	103.0	105.0	107.0	107.0	109.0	..	..	..	Secondary Schl. Enroll. Ratio

DJIBOUTI	1970	1971	1972	1973	1974	1975	1976	1977	1978	1979	1980
CURRENT GNP PER CAPITA (US $)	..		..		..			..		..	..
POPULATION (thousands)	168	183	199	214	229	243	257	270	282	293	304
USE AND ORIGIN OF RESOURCES				*(Millions of current Djibouti Francs)*							
Gross National Product (GNP)	..	..	..	..	..	..	..	..	..	..	..
Net Factor Income from Abroad	..	..	..	..	..	..	..	..	..	..	..
GDP at Market Prices	..	..	..	..	..	..	..	..	..	..	..
Resource Balance	..	..	..	..	..	..	..	..	..	..	..
Exports of Goods & NFServices	..	..	..	..	..	..	..	..	..	..	..
Imports of Goods & NFServices	..	..	..	..	..	..	..	..	..	..	..
Domestic Absorption	..	..	..	..	..	..	..	..	..	..	..
Private Consumption, etc.	..	..	..	..	..	..	..	..	..	..	..
General Gov't Consumption	..	..	..	..	..	..	..	..	..	..	..
Gross Domestic Investment	..	..	..	..	..	..	..	..	..	..	..
Fixed Investment	..	..	..	..	..	..	..	..	..	..	..
Indirect Taxes, net	..	..	..	..	..	..	..	..	..	..	..
GDP at factor cost	..	..	..	..	..	..	..	..	..	..	..
Agriculture	..	..	..	..	..	..	..	..	..	..	..
Industry	..	..	..	..	..	..	..	..	..	..	..
Manufacturing	..	..	..	..	..	..	..	..	..	..	..
Services, etc.	..	..	..	..	..	..	..	..	..	..	..
Gross Domestic Saving	..	..	..	..	..	..	..	..	..	..	..
Gross National Saving	..	..	..	..	..	..	..	..	..	..	..
				(Millions of 1987 Djibouti Francs)							
Gross National Product	..	..	..	..	..	..	..	..	..	..	..
GDP at Market Prices	..	..	..	..	..	..	..	..	..	..	..
Resource Balance											
Exports of Goods & NFServices	..	..	..	..	..	..	..	..	..	..	..
Imports of Goods & NFServices	..	..	..	..	..	..	..	..	..	..	..
Domestic Absorption	..	..	..	..	..	..	..	..	..	..	..
Private Consumption, etc.	..	..	..	..	..	..	..	..	..	..	..
General Gov't Consumption	..	..	..	..	..	..	..	..	..	..	..
Gross Domestic Investment	..	..	..	..	..	..	..	..	..	..	..
Fixed Investment	..	..	..	..	..	..	..	..	..	..	..
GDP at factor cost	..	..	..	..	..	..	..	..	..	..	..
Agriculture	..	..	..	..	..	..	..	..	..	..	..
Industry	..	..	..	..	..	..	..	..	..	..	..
Manufacturing	..	..	..	..	..	..	..	..	..	..	..
Services, etc.	..	..	..	..	..	..	..	..	..	..	..
Memo Items:											
Capacity to Import	..	..	..	..	..	..	..	..	..	..	..
Terms of Trade Adjustment	..	..	..	..	..	..	..	..	..	..	..
Gross Domestic Income	..	..	..	..	..	..	..	..	..	..	..
Gross National Income	..	..	..	..	..	..	..	..	..	..	..
DOMESTIC PRICES/DEFLATORS				*(Index 1987 = 100)*							
Overall (GDP)	..	..	..	..	..	..	..	..	..	..	..
Domestic Absorption	..	..	..	..	..	..	..	..	..	..	..
Agriculture	..	..	..	..	..	..	..	..	..	..	..
Industry	..	..	..	..	..	..	..	..	..	..	..
Manufacturing	..	..	..	..	..	..	..	..	..	..	..
Consumer Price Index	..	..	..	..	..	..	..	..	..	67.0	75.1
MANUFACTURING ACTIVITY											
Employment (1987=100)											
Real Earnings per Empl. (1987=100)	..	..							..		..
Real Output per Empl. (1987=100)	..	..							..		
Earnings as % of Value Added	..	..							..		
MONETARY HOLDINGS				*(Millions of current Djibouti Francs)*							
Money Supply, Broadly Defined	..	..		..	..	..	..	..	..	..	..
Money	..	..		..	..	..	..	..	..	..	..
Currency Outside Banks									..		..
Demand Deposits	..	..		..					..		..
Quasi-Money	..								..		
GOVERNMENT DEFICIT (-) OR SURPLUS				*(Millions of current Djibouti Francs)*							
Current Revenue	..	..	..	..	..	..	..	..	..	1,872	4,062
Current Expenditure	..	..	..	..	..	..	..	..	..	22,351	31,382
Current Budget Balance	..	..	..	..	..	..	..	..	..	14,540	..
Capital Receipts	..	..	..	..	..	..	..	..	..	7,811	..
Capital Payments	..	..	..	..	..	..	..	..	..	5,939	..

1981	1982	1983	1984	1985	1986	1987	1988	1989	1990 estimate	Notes	DJIBOUTI
..	..	..	..	..	..	..	..	..	..		**CURRENT GNP PER CAPITA (US $)**
314	323	333	343	..	..	..	..	..	..		**POPULATION (thousands)**
											USE AND ORIGIN OF RESOURCES
			(Millions of current Djibouti Francs)								
..	..	..	60,363	62,138	66,797	69,107	..	..	..	..	Gross National Product (GNP)
..	..	..	2,185	2,064	2,340	2,751	..	..	..	..	Net Factor Income from Abroad
..	..	..	58,178	60,074	64,457	66,356	70,267	71,716	..	..	GDP at Market Prices
..	..	..	-18,509	-16,682	-12,562	-12,888	-14,109	-16,527	..	..	Resource Balance
..	..	..	28,585	26,825	29,184	31,703	33,730	33,475	..	..	Exports of Goods & NFServices
..	..	..	47,094	43,507	41,746	44,591	47,839	50,002	..	..	Imports of Goods & NFServices
..	..	..	76,687	76,756	77,019	79,244	84,376	88,243	..	..	Domestic Absorption
..	..	..	38,671	38,958	41,192	43,275	49,474	50,929	..	..	Private Consumption, etc.
..	..	..	21,442	23,508	25,419	23,609	23,989	24,065	..	..	General Gov't Consumption
..	..	..	16,574	14,290	10,408	12,360	10,913	13,249	..	..	Gross Domestic Investment
..	..	..	15,194	12,780	11,788	11,530	10,103	12,466	..	..	Fixed Investment
..	..	..	10,670	10,619	10,056	10,629	10,937	10,917	..	..	Indirect Taxes, net
..	..	..	47,508	49,455	54,401	55,727	59,330	60,799	..	..	GDP at factor cost
..	..	..	1,331	1,345	1,497	1,596	1,684	1,698	..	..	Agriculture
..	..	..	8,524	9,128	10,100	10,019	10,631	11,031	..	..	Industry
..	..	..	2,001	2,014	2,433	2,740	2,906	2,990	..	..	Manufacturing
..	..	..	37,653	38,982	42,804	44,112	47,015	48,070	..	..	Services, etc.
..	..	..	-1,935	-2,392	-2,154	-528	-3,196	-3,278	..	..	Gross Domestic Saving
..	..	..	-1,687	-2,496	-1,947	179	..	..	..	..	Gross National Saving
			(Millions of 1987 Djibouti Francs)								
..	..	..	74,706.00	74,196.00	69,176.00	69,107.00	..	..	..	..	Gross National Product
..	..	..	72,000.00	71,726.00	66,751.00	66,356.00	66,940.00	66,409.00	..	..	GDP at Market Prices
..	..	..	-23,049.00	-20,216.00	-13,076.00	-12,888.00	-11,456.00	-13,696.00	..	..	Resource Balance
..	..	..	35,595.00	32,509.00	30,381.00	31,703.00	32,131.00	30,987.00	..	..	Exports of Goods & NFServices
..	..	..	58,644.00	52,724.00	43,457.00	44,591.00	43,586.00	44,683.00	..	..	Imports of Goods & NFServices
..	..	..	95,049.00	91,941.00	79,827.00	79,244.00	78,396.00	80,105.00	..	..	Domestic Absorption
..	..	..	48,371.00	47,330.00	42,827.00	43,275.00	..	..	..	..	Private Consumption, etc.
..	..	..	26,700.00	28,489.00	26,461.00	23,609.00	..	..	..	..	General Gov't Consumption
..	..	..	19,978.00	16,122.00	10,538.00	12,360.00	10,393.00	12,262.00	..	..	Gross Domestic Investment
..	..	..	18,315.00	14,419.00	11,936.00	11,530.00	..	..	..	..	Fixed Investment
..	..	..	58,713.00	58,856.00	56,282.00	55,727.00	56,524.00	56,305.00	..	..	GDP at factor cost
..	..	..	1,745.00	1,747.00	1,629.00	1,596.00	1,604.00	1,572.00	..	..	Agriculture
..	..	..	10,079.00	9,868.00	10,094.00	10,019.00	10,145.00	10,243.00	..	..	Industry
..	..	..	2,549.00	2,525.00	2,679.00	2,740.00	2,768.00	2,768.00	..	..	Manufacturing
..	..	..	46,889.00	47,241.00	44,560.00	44,112.00	44,775.00	44,490.00	..	..	Services, etc.
											Memo Items:
..	..	..	35,596.00	32,508.00	30,380.00	31,703.00	30,732.00	29,914.00	..	..	Capacity to Import
..	..	..	1.00	-1.00	-1.00	0.00	-1,399.00	-1,073.00	..	..	Terms of Trade Adjustment
..	..	..	72,001.00	71,725.00	66,750.00	66,356.00	65,541.00	65,336.00	..	..	Gross Domestic Income
..	..	..	74,707.00	74,196.00	69,175.00	69,107.00	..	..	..	..	Gross National Income
											DOMESTIC PRICES/DEFLATORS
			(Index 1987 = 100)								
..	..	..	80.8	83.8	96.6	100.0	105.0	108.0	..	..	Overall (GDP)
..	..	..	80.7	83.5	96.5	100.0	107.6	110.2	..	..	Domestic Absorption
..	..	..	76.3	77.0	91.9	100.0	105.0	108.0	..	..	Agriculture
..	..	..	84.6	92.5	100.1	100.0	104.8	107.7	..	..	Industry
..	..	..	78.5	79.8	90.8	100.0	105.0	108.0	..	..	Manufacturing
79.4	77.4	78.1	79.6	81.3	96.1	100.0	..	..	..	..	Consumer Price Index
											MANUFACTURING ACTIVITY
..	..	..	..	..	..	..	..	..	..	..	Employment (1987=100)
..	..	..	..	..	..	..	..	..	..	..	Real Earnings per Empl. (1987=100)
..	..	..	..	..	..	..	..	..	..	..	Real Output per Empl. (1987=100)
..	..	..	..	..	..	..	..	..	..	..	Earnings as % of Value Added
											MONETARY HOLDINGS
			(Millions of current Djibouti Francs)								
..	..	..	38,198	45,227	50,340	51,677	55,457	56,803	58,824	..	Money Supply, Broadly Defined
..	..	..	19,934	20,533	23,290	25,331	27,066	25,184	27,362	..	Money
..	..	..	6,671	6,686	7,180	8,013	8,439	8,197	9,035	..	Currency Outside Banks
..	..	..	13,263	13,847	16,110	17,318	18,627	16,987	18,327	..	Demand Deposits
..	..	..	18,264	24,694	27,050	26,346	28,391	31,619	31,462	..	Quasi-Money
			(Millions of current Djibouti Francs)							F	**GOVERNMENT DEFICIT (-) OR SURPLUS**
5,268	2,798	4,587	2,729	922	-1,470	..	-733	..	..		Current Revenue
23,154	27,801	28,622	25,117	23,930	23,428	..	21,501	..	..		Current Expenditure
12,285	18,764	18,784	19,645	20,497	21,559	19,824	21,326	..	..		Current Budget Balance
10,869	9,037	9,838	5,472	3,433	1,869	..	175	..	..		Capital Receipts
5,601	6,238	5,251	2,743	2,511	3,339	1,603	908	..	..		Capital Payments

DJIBOUTI	1970	1971	1972	1973	1974	1975	1976	1977	1978	1979	1980
FOREIGN TRADE (CUSTOMS BASIS)					*(Millions of current US dollars)*						
Value of Exports, fob	..	..	..	..	..	..	..	..	..	..	..
Nonfuel Primary Products	..	..	..	..	..	..	..	..	..	..	..
Fuels	..	..	..	..	..	..	..	..	..	..	..
Manufactures	..	..	..	..	..	..	..	..	..	..	..
Value of Imports, cif	..	..	..	..	..	..	..	..	..	..	..
Nonfuel Primary Products	..	..	..	..	..	..	..	..	..	..	..
Fuels	..	..	..	..	..	..	..	..	..	..	..
Manufactures	..	..	..	..	..	..	..	..	..	..	..
Terms of Trade					*(Index 1987 = 100)*						
Export Prices, fob	..	..	..	..	..	..	..	..	..	..	..
Import Prices, cif	..	..	..	..	..	..	..	..	..	..	..
BALANCE OF PAYMENTS					*(Millions of current US dollars)*						
Exports of Goods & Services	..	..	..	..	..	..	..	..	..	..	..
Merchandise, fob	..	..	..	..	..	..	..	..	..	..	..
Nonfactor Services	..	..	..	..	..	..	..	..	..	..	..
Factor Services	..	..	..	..	..	..	..	..	..	..	..
Imports of Goods & Services	..	..	..	..	..	..	..	..	..	..	..
Merchandise, fob	..	..	..	..	..	..	..	..	..	..	..
Nonfactor Services	..	..	..	..	..	..	..	..	..	..	..
Factor Services	..	..	..	..	..	..	..	..	..	..	..
Long-Term Interest	0.0	0.1	0.1	0.2	0.2	0.4	0.7	0.8	0.8	0.9	0.9
Private Current Transfers, net	..	..	..	..	..	..	..	..	..	..	..
Workers' Remittances	..	..	..	..	..	..	..	..	..	..	..
Curr. A/C Bal before Off. Transf.	..	..	..	..	..	..	..	..	..	..	..
Net Official Transfers	..	..	..	..	..	..	..	..	..	..	..
Curr. A/C Bal after Off. Transf.	..	..	..	..	..	..	..	..	..	..	..
Long-Term Capital, net	..	..	..	..	..	..	..	..	..	..	..
Direct Investment	..	..	..	..	..	..	..	..	..	..	..
Long-Term Loans	1.3	-0.1	2.7	0.5	1.5	4.3	6.5	1.0	-0.6	-1.3	8.0
Disbursements	1.4	0.0	2.9	0.7	1.7	4.7	7.2	1.7	0.4	0.0	10.2
Repayments	0.1	0.1	0.2	0.2	0.2	0.4	0.7	0.7	1.0	1.3	2.2
Other Long-Term Capital	..	..	..	..	..	..	..	..	..	..	..
Other Capital, net	..	..	..	..	..	..	..	..	..	..	..
Change in Reserves	..	..	..	..	..	..	..	..	..	..	..
Memo Item:					*(Djibouti Francs per US dollar)*						
Conversion Factor (Annual Avg)	214.390	213.780	197.470	179.940	177.720	177.720	177.720	177.720	177.720	177.720	177.720
EXTERNAL DEBT (Total)				*(Millions of US dollars), outstanding at end of year*							
	2.6	2.6	5.4	6.2	8.2	12.3	17.2	27.2	25.1	25.5	31.9
Long-Term Debt (by debtor)	2.6	2.6	5.4	6.2	8.2	12.3	17.2	19.2	21.1	20.5	25.9
Central Bank, incl. IMF credit	..	..	..	..	..	..	..	..	..	..	..
Central Government	2.1	2.2	2.1	2.1	2.1	2.0	1.9	3.2	3.4	3.2	3.6
Rest of General Government	0.0	0.0	0.0	0.0	0.0	0.6	1.0	1.1	1.2	1.1	0.9
Non-financial Public Enterprises	0.5	0.4	3.3	4.1	6.1	9.7	14.3	14.9	16.5	16.2	21.4
Priv. Sector, incl non-guaranteed	..	..	..	..	..	..	..	..	..	..	..
Short-Term Debt	0.0	0.0	0.0	0.0	0.0	0.0	0.0	8.0	4.0	5.0	6.0
Memo Items:					*(Thousands of US dollars)*						
Int'l Reserves Excluding Gold	..	..	..	..	..	..	..	..	..	..	..
Gold Holdings (at market price)	..	..	..	..	..	..	..	..	..	..	..
SOCIAL INDICATORS											
Total Fertility Rate	6.6	6.6	6.6	6.6	6.6	6.6	6.6	6.6	6.6	6.6	6.6
Infant Mortality Rate	158.8	156.4	154.0	151.8	149.6	147.4	145.2	143.0	140.8	138.6	136.4
Life Expectancy at Birth	40.2	40.6	41.0	41.4	41.8	42.2	42.6	43.0	43.4	43.8	44.2
Urban Population, % of total	62.0	63.3	64.6	65.9	67.2	68.5	69.5	70.6	71.6	72.7	73.7
Food Prod. per capita (1987=100)	..	..	..	..	..	..	..	..	..	..	..
Labor Force, Agriculture (%)	..	..	..	..	..	..	..	..	..	..	..
Labor Force, Female (%)	..	..	..	..	..	..	..	..	..	..	..
Primary Schl. Enroll. Ratio	..	..	..	..	..	..	..	..	..	..	..
Primary Schl. Enroll. Ratio, Female	..	..	..	..	..	..	..	..	..	..	..
Secondary Schl. Enroll. Ratio	..	..	..	..	..	..	..	..	..	..	..

1981	1982	1983	1984	1985	1986	1987	1988	1989	1990 estimate	Notes	DJIBOUTI
			(Millions of current US dollars)								**FOREIGN TRADE (CUSTOMS BASIS)**
..	..	..	..	..	..	..	..	..	..		Value of Exports, fob
..	..	..	..	..	..	..	..	..	..		Nonfuel Primary Products
..	..	..	..	..	..	..	..	..	..		Fuels
..	..	..	..	..	..	..	..	..	..		Manufactures
											Value of Imports, cif
..	..	..	..	..	..	..	..	..	..		Nonfuel Primary Products
..	..	..	..	..	..	..	..	..	..		Fuels
..	..	..	..	..	..	..	..	..	..		Manufactures
			(Index 1987 = 100)								
..	..	..	..	..	..	..	..	..	..		Terms of Trade
..	..	..	..	..	..	..	..	..	..		Export Prices, fob
..	..	..	..	..	..	..	..	..	..		Import Prices, cif
			(Millions of current US dollars)								**BALANCE OF PAYMENTS**
..	..	..	174.2	164.9	180.5	197.3	203.0	201.9	..	..	Exports of Goods & Services
..	..	..	27.0	29.9	32.3	39.9	41.9	41.1	..	..	Merchandise, fob
..	..	..	133.9	121.1	131.9	138.5	147.8	147.2	..	..	Nonfactor Services
..	..	..	13.4	14.0	16.3	18.9	13.3	13.6	..	..	Factor Services
..	..	..	266.1	247.2	238.0	254.3	273.1	285.1	..	..	Imports of Goods & Services
..	..	..	238.5	219.3	207.4	222.3	239.2	249.3	..	..	Merchandise, fob
..	..	..	26.4	25.5	27.5	28.6	30.0	32.1	..	..	Nonfactor Services
..	..	..	1.1	2.4	3.1	3.4	3.9	3.7	..	..	Factor Services
1.0	0.8	1.2	1.3	2.2	3.0	3.4	3.9	2.4	2.0	..	Long-Term Interest
..	..	..	-10.9	-12.2	-12.0	-11.5	-1.1	-1.0	..	..	Private Current Transfers, net
..	..	..	..	..	..	..	..	14.3	14.6	..	Workers' Remittances
..	..	..	-102.8	-94.5	-69.5	-68.5	-71.2	-71.4	-88.2	..	Curr. A/C Bal before Off. Transf.
..	..	..	45.7	52.4	48.3	53.8	46.9	48.8	63.5	..	Net Official Transfers
..	..	..	-57.1	-42.1	-21.2	-14.7	-24.3	-22.6	-24.7	..	Curr. A/C Bal after Off. Transf.
..	..	..	52.2	31.8	38.5	33.1	12.2	4.1	28.7	..	Long-Term Capital, net
..	..	..	..	..	..	..	..	0.0	..	..	Direct Investment
-0.8	7.3	12.5	38.7	29.7	19.2	20.9	12.2	4.1	6.6	..	Long-Term Loans
1.4	9.7	15.6	41.7	31.6	23.4	30.2	21.7	13.2	14.4	..	Disbursements
2.2	2.4	3.1	3.0	1.9	4.2	9.3	9.5	9.1	7.8	..	Repayments
..	..	..	13.5	2.1	19.3	12.2	0.0	0.0	22.1	..	Other Long-Term Capital
..	..	..	-5.5	16.1	-14.8	-8.7	20.2	20.6	..	..	Other Capital, net
..	..	..	10.4	-5.8	-2.5	-9.7	-8.1	-2.1	..	..	Change in Reserves
			(Djibouti Francs per US dollar)								**Memo Item:**
177.720	177.720	177.720	177.720	177.720	177.720	177.720	177.720	177.720	177.720	..	Conversion Factor (Annual Avg)
			(Millions of US dollars), outstanding at end of year								
29.8	32.5	45.6	85.7	144.0	125.2	183.4	184.6	180.0	194.7	..	**EXTERNAL DEBT (Total)**
19.8	24.5	33.6	61.7	96.0	119.2	154.4	158.3	132.8	144.7	..	Long-Term Debt (by debtor)
..	..	..	..	..	..	..	..	..	..		Central Bank, incl. IMF credit
3.3	4.1	6.3	15.0	28.5	39.9	63.6	75.4	74.3	79.7	..	Central Government
0.6	0.5	0.3	0.0	0.0	0.0	0.0	0.0	0.0	..	..	Rest of General Government
15.9	19.9	27.0	46.7	67.5	79.3	90.8	82.9	58.5	65.0	..	Non-financial Public Enterprises
..	..	..	..	..	..	..	..	..	..		Priv. Sector, incl non-guaranteed
10.0	8.0	12.0	24.0	48.0	6.0	29.0	26.3	47.2	50.0	..	Short-Term Debt
			(Thousands of US dollars)								**Memo Items:**
..	..	..	44,934	50,941	53,616	63,526	64,361	59,153	93,639	..	Int'l Reserves Excluding Gold
..	..	..	..	..	..	..	..	..	..		Gold Holdings (at market price)
											SOCIAL INDICATORS
6.6	6.6	6.6	6.6	6.6	6.6	6.6	6.6	6.6	6.6	..	Total Fertility Rate
134.2	132.0	130.0	128.0	126.0	124.0	122.0	119.8	117.6	115.3	..	Infant Mortality Rate
44.6	45.0	45.4	45.8	46.2	46.6	47.0	47.5	48.0	48.5	..	Life Expectancy at Birth
74.5	75.3	76.1	76.9	77.7	78.4	79.2	79.7	80.2	80.7	..	Urban Population, % of total
..	..	..	..	..	..	..	..	..	..		Food Prod. per capita (1987=100)
..	..	..	..	..	..	..	..	..	..		Labor Force, Agriculture (%)
..	..	..	..	..	..	..	..	..	..		Labor Force, Female (%)
..	..	..	..	43.0	45.0	46.0	46.0	47.0	..	..	Primary Schl. Enroll. Ratio
..	..	..	..	36.0	37.0	38.0	39.0	39.0	..	..	Primary Schl. Enroll. Ratio, Female
..	..	..	..	14.0	14.0	15.0	15.0	16.0	..	..	Secondary Schl. Enroll. Ratio

DOMINICA	1970	1971	1972	1973	1974	1975	1976	1977	1978	1979	1980
CURRENT GNP PER CAPITA (US $)	290	320	340	350	350	380	420	470	560	500	700
POPULATION (thousands)	68	69	70	70	71	71	71	72	72	73	73

USE AND ORIGIN OF RESOURCES *(Millions of current East Caribbean Dollars)*

	1970	1971	1972	1973	1974	1975	1976	1977	1978	1979	1980
Gross National Product (GNP)	40.30	43.00	45.60	49.60	56.90	60.20	74.30	98.24	109.80	112.50	158.50
Net Factor Income from Abroad	0.00	0.00	0.00	0.00	0.00	0.00	0.00	0.00	0.00	-0.30	0.80
GDP at Market Prices	40.30	43.00	45.60	49.60	56.90	60.20	74.30	98.24	109.80	112.80	157.70
Resource Balance	..	..	..	..	..	..	..	..	..	-62.40	-109.40
Exports of Goods & NF Services	..	..	..	..	..	..	..	..	..	51.00	41.30
Imports of Goods & NF Services	..	..	..	..	..	..	..	..	..	113.40	150.70
Domestic Absorption	..	..	..	..	..	..	..	..	..	175.20	267.10
Private Consumption, etc.	..	..	..	..	..	..	..	..	..	..	..
General Gov't Consumption	..	..	..	..	..	..	..	..	..	..	..
Gross Domestic Investment	..	..	..	..	..	..	..	..	..	..	..
Fixed Investment	..	..	..	..	..	..	..	..	..	..	..
Indirect Taxes, net	..	..	..	..	..	..	..	13.40	14.40	7.00	14.00
GDP at factor cost	..	..	..	..	..	..	..	84.84	95.40	105.80	143.70
Agriculture	..	..	..	..	..	..	..	31.93	35.50	34.78	44.05
Industry	..	..	..	..	..	..	..	12.51	14.23	15.57	30.05
Manufacturing	..	..	..	..	..	..	..	4.24	5.85	5.02	6.93
Services, etc.	..	..	..	..	..	..	..	40.40	45.67	55.45	69.60
Gross Domestic Saving	..	..	..	..	..	..	..	..	..	..	..
Gross National Saving	..	..	..	..	..	..	..	..	..	..	..

(Millions of 1987 East Caribbean Dollars)

	1970	1971	1972	1973	1974	1975	1976	1977	1978	1979	1980
Gross National Product	245.67	260.47	264.80	252.96	220.63	206.97	214.25	223.68	249.83	188.96	225.57
GDP at Market Prices	246.96	261.84	266.19	254.29	221.79	208.05	215.38	224.85	251.15	190.34	225.61
Resource Balance	..	..	..	..	..	..	..	..	..	..	..
Exports of Goods & NF Services	..	..	..	..	..	..	..	..	..	..	..
Imports of Goods & NF Services	..	..	..	..	..	..	..	..	..	..	..
Domestic Absorption	..	..	..	..	..	..	..	..	..	..	..
Private Consumption, etc.	..	..	..	..	..	..	..	..	..	..	..
General Gov't Consumption	..	..	..	..	..	..	..	..	..	..	..
Gross Domestic Investment	..	..	..	..	..	..	..	..	..	..	..
Fixed Investment	..	..	..	..	..	..	..	..	..	..	..
GDP at factor cost	..	..	..	..	..	..	..	194.72	218.72	178.47	205.29
Agriculture	..	..	..	..	..	..	..	68.78	76.49	52.04	50.97
Industry	..	..	..	..	..	..	..	22.40	25.50	24.82	36.69
Manufacturing	..	..	..	..	..	..	..	7.89	10.89	9.03	11.54
Services, etc.	..	..	..	..	..	..	..	99.68	112.63	101.58	118.58

Memo Items:

	1970	1971	1972	1973	1974	1975	1976	1977	1978	1979	1980
Capacity to Import	..	..	..	..	..	..	..	..	..	..	..
Terms of Trade Adjustment	..	..	..	..	..	..	..	..	..	..	..
Gross Domestic Income	..	..	..	..	..	..	..	..	..	..	..
Gross National Income	..	..	..	..	..	..	..	..	..	..	..

DOMESTIC PRICES/DEFLATORS *(Index 1987 = 100)*

	1970	1971	1972	1973	1974	1975	1976	1977	1978	1979	1980
Overall (GDP)	16.3	16.4	17.1	19.5	25.7	28.9	34.5	43.7	43.7	59.3	69.9
Domestic Absorption	..	..	..	..	..	..	..	..	..	..	..
Agriculture	..	..	..	..	..	..	..	46.4	46.4	66.8	86.4
Industry	..	..	..	..	..	..	..	55.8	55.8	62.7	81.9
Manufacturing	..	..	..	..	..	..	..	53.7	53.7	55.6	60.0
Consumer Price Index	18.0	18.7	19.4	21.7	29.2	35.0	38.8	72.3	45.7	..	71.6

MANUFACTURING ACTIVITY

	1970	1971	1972	1973	1974	1975	1976	1977	1978	1979	1980
Employment (1987=100)	..	..	..	..	..	..	..	..	..	..	..
Real Earnings per Empl. (1987=100)	..	..	..	..	..	..	..	..	..	..	..
Real Output per Empl. (1987=100)	..	..	..	..	..	..	..	..	..	..	..
Earnings as % of Value Added	..	..	..	..	..	..	..	..	..	..	..

MONETARY HOLDINGS *(Millions of current East Caribbean Dollars)*

	1970	1971	1972	1973	1974	1975	1976	1977	1978	1979	1980
Money Supply, Broadly Defined	..	..	..	..	..	36.65	41.25	45.15	53.94	77.60	79.47
Money	..	..	..	..	..	8.54	9.36	11.53	17.49	30.09	27.11
Currency Outside Banks	..	..	..	..	..	2.77	3.65	4.81	5.15	7.33	7.48
Demand Deposits	..	..	..	..	..	5.77	5.70	6.72	12.34	22.75	19.63
Quasi-Money	..	..	..	..	..	28.11	31.89	33.63	36.45	47.52	52.36

GOVERNMENT DEFICIT (-) OR SURPLUS *(Thousands of current East Caribbean Dollars)*

	1970	1971	1972	1973	1974	1975	1976	1977	1978	1979	1980
Current Revenue	..	..	..	..	..	..	-4,490	200	-2,720	-8,110	..
Current Expenditure	..	..	..	..	..	..	21,660	30,970	43,280	52,080	..
Current Budget Balance	..	..	..	..	..	..	19,460	23,740	35,190	37,810	..
Capital Receipts	..	..	..	..	..	..	2,200	7,230	8,090	14,270	..
Capital Payments	..	..	..	..	..	..	20	30	20	50	..
	..	..	..	..	..	..	6,710	7,060	10,830	22,430	..

1981	1982	1983	1984	1985	1986	1987	1988	1989	1990 estimate	Notes	DOMINICA
940	1,020	1,020	1,140	1,220	1,410	1,610	1,840	1,890	2,200	..	CURRENT GNP PER CAPITA (US $)
75	74	74	74	74	73	73	73	73	72	..	POPULATION (thousands)
											USE AND ORIGIN OF RESOURCES
			(Millions of current East Caribbean Dollars)								
182.50	196.90	208.00	233.80	252.30	289.90	323.60	372.90	384.30	431.20	..	Gross National Product (GNP)
1.30	0.50	-5.70	-8.70	-15.90	-16.50	-18.60	-21.60	-28.40	-28.10	..	Net Factor Income from Abroad
181.20	196.40	213.70	242.50	268.20	306.40	342.20	394.50	412.70	459.30	..	GDP at Market Prices
-79.60	-51.30	-37.00	-54.50	-58.30	-16.50	-35.10	-58.50	-144.70	-124.47	..	Resource Balance
61.60	84.00	97.20	108.00	114.00	157.10	177.60	208.30	179.00	222.21	..	Exports of Goods & NFServices
141.20	135.30	134.20	162.50	172.30	173.60	212.70	266.80	323.70	346.68	..	Imports of Goods & NFServices
260.80	247.70	250.70	297.00	326.50	322.90	377.30	453.00	557.40	583.80	..	Domestic Absorption
..	..	..	152.80	182.80	191.40	229.90	275.90	332.30	369.30	..	Private Consumption, etc.
..	..	..	57.20	61.40	66.80	72.60	79.30	86.10	91.40	..	General Gov't Consumption
..	..	..	87.00	82.30	64.70	74.80	97.80	139.00	123.10	..	Gross Domestic Investment
..	..	..	87.00	82.30	64.70	74.80	97.80	139.00	..	..	Fixed Investment
28.30	32.80	33.30	39.80	44.90	53.10	60.40	70.20	66.50	78.00	..	Indirect Taxes, net
152.90	163.60	180.40	202.70	223.30	253.30	281.80	324.30	346.20	381.30	..	GDP at factor cost
48.48	49.78	52.50	56.80	62.39	76.64	82.59	95.90	89.55	97.43	..	Agriculture
30.97	33.48	33.26	36.95	37.07	36.76	41.87	53.69	62.45	69.62	..	Industry
10.23	13.39	14.12	12.36	14.37	16.88	18.30	20.99	24.53	27.04	..	Manufacturing
73.45	80.34	94.64	108.95	123.84	139.90	157.34	174.71	194.20	214.25	..	Services, etc.
..	..	..	32.50	24.00	48.20	39.70	39.30	-5.70	-1.40		Gross Domestic Saving
..	..	..	40.81	25.65	49.80	41.60	40.40	-4.15	5.50		Gross National Saving
			(Millions of 1987 East Caribbean Dollars)								
261.77	270.17	263.66	278.99	278.65	302.27	323.60	347.96	332.65	363.37	..	Gross National Product
261.43	270.82	272.86	289.41	296.23	319.46	342.20	368.21	357.32	386.92	..	GDP at Market Prices
										..	Resource Balance
..	..	..	..	..	..	..	..	..	..	..	Exports of Goods & NFServices
..	..	..	..	..	..	..	..	..	..	..	Imports of Goods & NFServices
										..	Domestic Absorption
..	..	..	..	..	..	..	..	..	..	..	Private Consumption, etc.
..	..	..	..	..	..	..	..	..	..	..	General Gov't Consumption
..	..	..	..	..	..	..	..	..	..	..	Gross Domestic Investment
..	..	..	..	..	..	..	..	..	..	..	Fixed Investment
220.61	225.82	230.35	241.80	246.52	264.04	281.80	302.39	299.56	318.29	..	GDP at factor cost
62.30	63.74	64.28	67.79	66.09	78.63	82.59	88.10	74.99	81.08	..	Agriculture
35.69	35.73	35.41	40.53	40.31	38.23	41.87	49.96	52.70	55.66	..	Industry
13.59	15.95	16.27	14.65	16.57	17.28	18.30	20.16	21.37	22.43	..	Manufacturing
121.56	125.61	130.67	133.48	140.12	147.17	157.34	164.32	171.87	181.54	..	Services, etc.
											Memo Items:
..	..	..	..	..	..	..	..	..	..	..	Capacity to Import
..	..	..	..	..	..	..	..	..	..	..	Terms of Trade Adjustment
..	..	..	..	..	..	..	..	..	..	..	Gross Domestic Income
..	..	..	..	..	..	..	..	..	..	..	Gross National Income
			(Index 1987 = 100)								**DOMESTIC PRICES/DEFLATORS**
69.3	72.5	78.3	83.8	90.5	95.9	100.0	107.1	115.5	118.7	..	Overall (GDP)
..	..	..	..	..	..	..	..	..	..	..	Domestic Absorption
77.8	78.1	81.7	83.8	94.4	97.5	100.0	108.8	119.4	120.2	..	Agriculture
86.8	93.7	93.9	91.2	92.0	96.1	100.0	107.5	118.5	125.1	..	Industry
75.3	83.9	86.8	84.4	86.7	97.7	100.0	104.1	114.8	120.5	..	Manufacturing
81.1	84.7	88.2	90.2	93.5	96.1	100.0	102.9	109.9	111.5	..	Consumer Price Index
											MANUFACTURING ACTIVITY
..	..	..	..	..	..	..	..	..	..	..	Employment (1987=100)
..	..	..	..	..	..	..	..	..	..	..	Real Earnings per Empl. (1987=100)
..	..	..	..	..	..	..	..	..	..	..	Real Output per Empl. (1987=100)
..	..	..	..	..	..	..	..	..	..	..	Earnings as % of Value Added
			(Millions of current East Caribbean Dollars)								**MONETARY HOLDINGS**
81.29	96.26	105.71	122.59	128.20	147.27	190.85	184.26	206.13	253.57	..	Money Supply, Broadly Defined
26.44	25.41	25.40	32.40	31.22	37.03	58.67	57.19	56.08	69.92	..	Money
7.73	6.58	6.39	12.22	9.64	6.64	20.77	22.83	20.69	24.96	..	Currency Outside Banks
18.71	18.83	19.01	20.18	21.58	30.39	37.89	34.37	35.39	44.96	..	Demand Deposits
54.84	70.85	80.31	90.19	96.98	110.24	132.18	127.06	150.05	183.65	..	Quasi-Money
			(Thousands of current East Caribbean Dollars)							C	**GOVERNMENT DEFICIT (-) OR SURPLUS**
..	..	..	..	..	..	..	..	..	..		Current Revenue
..	..	..	..	..	..	..	..	..	..		Current Expenditure
..	..	..	..	..	..	..	..	..	..		Current Budget Balance
..	..	..	..	..	..	..	..	..	..		Capital Receipts
..	..	..	..	..	..	..	..	..	..		Capital Payments

DOMINICA	1970	1971	1972	1973	1974	1975	1976	1977	1978	1979	1980
FOREIGN TRADE (CUSTOMS BASIS)					*(Thousands of current US dollars)*						
Value of Exports, fob	5,905	6,139	7,026	8,544	10,475	12,458	11,142	11,704	15,704	9,149	9,338
Nonfuel Primary Products	..	..	..	..	9,515	10,492	..	..	..	..	..
Fuels	..	..	..	..	1	1					
Manufactures	700	781	1,055	1,283	958	1,966	1,350	1,757	2,792	2,503	5,069
Value of Imports, cif	15,757	16,510	16,440	16,147	19,459	20,847	19,110	21,356	28,433	22,210	47,678
Nonfuel Primary Products	4,858	5,142	6,108	5,910	7,588	7,972	7,700	8,347	10,393	7,843	15,451
Fuels	428	412	549	692	1,166	1,272	1,397	1,420	1,656	1,385	4,202
Manufactures	10,472	10,956	9,783	9,545	10,705	11,603	10,013	11,589	16,384	12,983	28,024
					(Index 1987 = 100)						
Terms of Trade	..	..	..	..	..	..	..	..	..	..	..
Export Prices, fob	..	..	..	..	..	..	..	..	..	..	..
Import Prices, cif	..	..	..	..	..	..	..	..	..	..	..
BALANCE OF PAYMENTS					*(Thousands of current US dollars)*						
Exports of Goods & Services	..	..	..	..	..	..	14,002	15,300	19,200	19,600	16,300
Merchandise, fob	..	..	..	..	..	..	11,099	12,000	15,900	9,800	10,100
Nonfactor Services	..	..	..	..	..	..	2,501	3,000	3,100	9,500	5,600
Factor Services	..	..	..	..	..	..	402	300	200	300	600
Imports of Goods & Services	..	..	..	..	..	..	19,299	22,500	29,700	40,700	55,000
Merchandise, fob	..	..	..	..	..	..	17,272	19,907	25,907	35,818	48,359
Nonfactor Services	..	..	..	..	..	..	1,828	2,293	3,393	4,481	6,341
Factor Services	..	..	..	..	..	..	199	300	400	400	300
Long-Term Interest	0	0	100	100	100	200	200	200	200	200	300
Private Current Transfers, net	..	..	..	..	..	..	1,300	1,700	3,600	6,800	6,300
Workers' Remittances	..	..	..	..	..	..	1,300	3,200	5,800	8,700	8,600
Curr. A/C Bal before Off. Transf.	..	..	..	..	..	..	-3,997	-5,500	-6,900	-14,300	-32,400
Net Official Transfers	..	..	..	..	..	..	2,899	4,000	5,600	20,600	18,100
Curr. A/C Bal after Off. Transf.	..	..	..	..	..	..	-1,098	-1,500	-1,300	6,300	-14,300
Long-Term Capital, net	..	..	..	..	..	..	1,499	2,000	1,100	600	1,467
Direct Investment	..	..	..	..	..	..	..	..	..	..	..
Long-Term Loans	600	500	500	1,100	1,800	700	900	2,500	1,600	2,700	1,000
Disbursements	600	500	500	1,100	1,800	700	900	2,500	1,600	2,800	1,700
Repayments	0	0	0	0	0	0	0	0	0	100	700
Other Long-Term Capital	..	..	..	..	..	..	599	-500	-500	-2,100	467
Other Capital, net	..	..	..	..	..	..	-4	459	296	-1,341	8,889
Change in Reserves	..	..	..	..	..	..	-398	-959	-96	-5,559	3,944
Memo Item:					*(East Caribbean Dollars per US dollar)*						
Conversion Factor (Annual Avg)	2.000	1.970	1.920	1.960	2.050	2.170	2.610	2.700	2.700	2.700	2.700
EXTERNAL DEBT (Total)				*(Millions of US dollars), outstanding at end of year*							
	1	1	1	3	4	5	5	8	9	13	14
Long-Term Debt (by debtor)	1	1	1	3	4	5	5	8	9	13	14
Central Bank, incl. IMF credit	0	0	0	0	0	0	1	1	1	1	1
Central Government	1	1	1	3	4	4	4	7	8	11	12
Rest of General Government	..	..	..	..	..	..	..	..	..	..	..
Non-financial Public Enterprises	0	0	0	0	0	0	0	0	0	0	1
Priv. Sector, incl non-guaranteed	..	..	..	..	..	..	..	..	..	..	..
Short-Term Debt	0	0	0	0	0	0	0	0	0	0	0
Memo Items:					*(Thousands of US dollars)*						
Int'l Reserves Excluding Gold	..	..	..	..	..	345	1,173	2,230	1,925	9,836	5,078
Gold Holdings (at market price)	..	..	..	..	..	..	..	..	..	..	..
SOCIAL INDICATORS											
Total Fertility Rate	..	..	5.5	5.3	5.1	4.9	4.7	4.5	4.3	4.1	3.9
Infant Mortality Rate	..	..	..	38.7	28.1	26.9	24.0	27.0	21.9	12.3	12.6
Life Expectancy at Birth	..	..	..	..	..	..	..	..	..	..	..
Urban Population, % of total	..	..	..	..	..	..	..	..	..	..	..
Food Prod. per capita (1987=100)	78.2	75.4	75.8	72.1	77.5	81.4	90.9	92.6	100.5	76.8	68.3
Labor Force, Agriculture (%)	..	..	..	..	..	..	..	..	..	..	..
Labor Force, Female (%)	..	..	..	..	..	..	..	..	..	..	..
Primary Schl. Enroll. Ratio	..	..	..	..	..	..	..	..	..	..	..
Primary Schl. Enroll. Ratio, Female	..	..	..	..	..	..	..	..	..	..	..
Secondary Schl. Enroll. Ratio	..	..	..	..	..	..	..	..	..	..	..

1981	1982	1983	1984	1985	1986	1987	1988	1989	1990 est.	Notes	DOMINICA
				(Thousands of current US dollars)							**FOREIGN TRADE (CUSTOMS BASIS)**
18,727	24,450	26,770	25,641	26,257	38,901	45,027	54,508	43,583	55,033	..	Value of Exports, fob
..	11,318	..	..	..	..	..	41,860	28,965	36,575	..	Nonfuel Primary Products
..	0	..	..	..	..	..	0	0	..	..	Fuels
8,113	13,132	10,942	9,055	9,273	9,485	10,083	12,648	14,618	18,458	..	Manufactures
49,668	47,478	45,078	57,815	55,324	55,810	66,376	87,531	107,074	117,922	..	Value of Imports, cif
16,556	15,826	14,003	16,376	15,671	16,563	19,045	24,165	26,507	29,192	..	Nonfuel Primary Products
4,265	4,077	3,743	6,327	6,055	4,192	4,356	4,886	5,683	6,259	..	Fuels
28,847	27,575	27,332	35,111	33,599	35,055	42,975	58,480	74,884	82,471	..	Manufactures
				(Index 1987 = 100)							Terms of Trade
..	..	..	..	..	..	..	..	..	..	..	Export Prices, fob
..	..	..	..	..	..	..	..	..	..	..	Import Prices, cif
				(Thousands of current US dollars)							**BALANCE OF PAYMENTS**
24,400	32,700	37,259	..	..	59,848	67,389	80,778	72,419	97,233	..	Exports of Goods & Services
19,700	25,100	27,800	25,600	28,400	44,574	49,267	57,030	46,296	59,852	..	Merchandise, fob
3,700	6,600	8,200	11,800	10,200	13,296	15,444	19,418	22,522	33,382	..	Nonfactor Services
1,000	1,000	1,259	..	..	1,978	2,678	4,330	3,600	4,000	..	Factor Services
52,600	50,900	51,404	62,100	65,700	68,693	80,711	101,259	128,067	144,778	..	Imports of Goods & Services
45,178	43,178	42,815	50,722	52,000	49,000	58,704	77,000	94,218	103,926	..	Merchandise, fob
6,922	6,922	6,885	9,478	11,800	15,185	17,444	18,481	25,830	31,593	..	Nonfactor Services
500	800	1,704	1,900	1,900	4,507	4,563	5,778	8,019	9,259	..	Factor Services
200	400	200	300	600	900	1,100	1,300	1,200	1,400	..	Long-Term Interest
5,800	4,600	5,000	6,300	6,500	6,704	7,593	8,407	11,093	12,963	..	Private Current Transfers, net
8,500	7,500	9,400	10,800	11,100	9,259	10,741	11,741	12,330	9,370	..	Workers' Remittances
-22,400	-13,600	-9,144	-18,400	-20,600	-2,141	-5,730	-12,074	-44,556	-34,581	..	Curr. A/C Bal before Off. Transf.
9,598	5,795	7,394	11,298	14,299	9,526	10,636	9,472	7,737	8,780	..	Net Official Transfers
-12,802	-7,805	-1,750	-7,102	-6,301	7,385	4,907	-2,602	-36,818	-25,802	..	Curr. A/C Bal after Off. Transf.
2,678	8,356	6,000	7,100	7,500	8,852	17,411	15,296	26,522	22,111	..	Long-Term Capital, net
..	200	200	2,300	3,000	2,667	8,630	6,889	8,907	8,370	..	Direct Investment
1,700	7,800	3,100	15,900	3,400	800	6,000	2,900	7,900	8,700	..	Long-Term Loans
2,100	8,300	3,400	16,500	4,200	2,100	7,500	4,700	10,400	11,300	..	Disbursements
400	500	300	600	800	1,300	1,500	1,800	2,500	2,600	..	Repayments
978	356	2,700	-11,100	1,100	5,385	2,781	5,507	9,715	5,041	..	Other Long-Term Capital
1,611	-2,086	-8,626	5,765	-1,675	-10,159	-13,647	-13,732	10,502	8,370	..	Other Capital, net
8,514	1,536	4,376	-5,763	476	-6,078	-8,671	1,038	-206	-4,680	..	Change in Reserves
				(East Caribbean Dollars per US dollar)							**Memo Item:**
2.700	2.700	2.700	2.700	2.700	2.700	2.700	2.700	2.700	2.700	..	Conversion Factor (Annual Avg)
				(Millions of US dollars), outstanding at end of year							**EXTERNAL DEBT (Total)**
14	20	34	47	52	54	67	69	73	84	..	Long-Term Debt (by debtor)
14	20	34	47	52	54	67	66	71	82	..	Long-Term Debt (by debtor)
2	2	13	13	13	13	16	13	10	9	..	Central Bank, incl. IMF credit
11	17	19	32	36	39	49	51	58	71	..	Central Government
..	..	..	..	..	..	..	..	..	..	..	Rest of General Government
2	2	2	3	3	2	2	2	2	2	..	Non-financial Public Enterprises
..	..	..	..	..	..	..	..	..	..	..	Priv. Sector, incl non-guaranteed
0	0	0	0	0	0	0	3	2	2	..	Short-Term Debt
				(Thousands of US dollars)							**Memo Items:**
3,057	4,329	1,479	5,250	3,271	9,593	18,427	14,064	11,684	14,463	..	Int'l Reserves Excluding Gold
..	..	..	..	..	..	..	..	..	..	..	Gold Holdings (at market price)
											SOCIAL INDICATORS
3.7	3.5	3.4	3.4	3.3	3.2	3.1	3.0	2.9	2.8	..	Total Fertility Rate
10.2	20.0	13.9	14.9	15.9	17.0	17.9	17.4	16.9	16.4	..	Infant Mortality Rate
..	73.5	73.6	73.7	73.8	74.0	74.1	74.4	74.6	74.9	..	Life Expectancy at Birth
..	..	..	..	..	..	..	..	..	..	..	Urban Population, % of total
79.8	83.4	83.4	84.6	86.5	100.8	100.0	108.2	93.9	99.7	..	Food Prod. per capita (1987=100)
..	..	..	..	..	..	..	..	..	..	..	Labor Force, Agriculture (%)
..	..	..	..	..	..	..	..	..	..	..	Labor Force, Female (%)
..	..	..	..	..	..	..	..	..	..	..	Primary Schl. Enroll. Ratio
..	..	..	..	..	..	..	..	..	..	..	Primary Schl. Enroll. Ratio, Female
..	..	..	..	..	..	..	..	..	..	..	Secondary Schl. Enroll. Ratio

DOMINICAN REPUBLIC	1970	1971	1972	1973	1974	1975	1976	1977	1978	1979	1980
CURRENT GNP PER CAPITA (US $)	330	370	430	490	570	660	760	840	900	1,000	1,090
POPULATION (thousands)	4,423	4,548	4,672	4,797	4,922	5,048	5,175	5,301	5,429	5,561	5,697
USE AND ORIGIN OF RESOURCES					*(Millions of current Dominican Pesos)*						
Gross National Product (GNP)	1,476	1,664	2,027	2,351	2,920	3,598	3,945	4,508	4,771	5,551	6,419
Net Factor Income from Abroad	-9	-2	40	6	-5	-2	-6	-80	-3	52	-212
GDP at Market Prices	1,485	1,666	1,987	2,345	2,926	3,599	3,951	4,587	4,774	5,499	6,631
Resource Balance	-109	-135	-96	-89	-331	-83	-289	-191	-326	-349	-648
Exports of Goods & NFServices	256	275	411	513	730	998	825	918	828	1,135	1,271
Imports of Goods & NFServices	365	410	506	602	1,060	1,080	1,114	1,109	1,154	1,484	1,919
Domestic Absorption	1,595	1,802	2,083	2,434	3,256	3,682	4,240	4,778	5,100	5,848	7,279
Private Consumption, etc.	1,139	1,335	1,514	1,722	2,282	2,578	3,197	3,590	3,699	4,034	5,109
General Gov't Consumption	172	169	178	194	292	222	152	189	271	420	504
Gross Domestic Investment	284	298	392	518	683	882	891	1,000	1,130	1,394	1,666
Fixed Investment	246	294	427	498	644	803	789	939	1,032	1,335	1,584
Indirect Taxes, net	160	181	205	229	398	432	386	450	403	456	507
GDP at factor cost	1,325	1,486	1,782	2,116	2,528	3,167	3,565	4,138	4,371	5,043	6,124
Agriculture	345	371	409	521	648	773	753	921	886	1,027	1,336
Industry	388	450	549	658	833	1,139	1,238	1,353	1,383	1,651	1,876
Manufacturing	275	306	347	399	545	752	815	871	874	929	1,015
Services, etc.	752	846	1,029	1,166	1,445	1,688	1,960	2,313	2,505	2,821	3,419
Gross Domestic Saving	175	162	296	429	353	799	602	808	804	1,045	1,018
Gross National Saving	196	176	365	464	381	832	719	865	947	1,274	989
					(Millions of 1987 Dominican Pesos)						
Gross National Product	8,183.5	9,129.1	10,302.0	11,420.9	12,058.9	12,645.5	13,489.4	14,057.9	14,480.1	15,179.1	15,513.9
GDP at Market Prices	8,397.5	9,315.4	10,283.7	11,609.9	12,279.4	12,869.4	13,735.7	14,402.8	14,737.4	15,373.0	16,312.1
Resource Balance	-1,105.0	-1,240.4	-1,528.8	-1,429.2	-2,434.3	-1,339.5	-1,366.5	-1,386.9	-1,355.2	-1,089.7	-3,020.9
Exports of Goods & NFServices	2,151.8	2,223.3	2,555.4	2,515.9	2,032.4	3,098.6	2,718.5	2,656.3	2,485.6	3,036.4	4,708.9
Imports of Goods & NFServices	3,256.8	3,463.7	4,084.2	3,945.1	4,466.6	4,438.1	4,085.1	4,043.2	3,840.8	4,126.1	7,729.7
Domestic Absorption	9,502.5	10,555.8	11,812.5	13,039.1	14,713.6	14,208.9	15,102.2	15,789.7	16,092.6	16,462.7	19,332.9
Private Consumption, etc.	6,911.5	7,760.5	8,788.2	9,426.2	10,241.1	9,730.9	11,103.0	11,433.7	11,506.0	11,366.9	13,619.4
General Gov't Consumption	990.9	920.0	915.4	937.3	1,285.9	1,033.0	776.0	872.8	1,009.3	1,226.5	1,503.6
Gross Domestic Investment	1,600.1	1,875.3	2,108.9	2,675.6	3,186.7	3,445.0	3,223.2	3,483.3	3,577.3	3,869.4	4,209.9
Fixed Investment	1,415.6	1,896.2	2,252.6	2,671.6	2,932.4	3,291.0	3,029.7	3,326.7	3,308.9	3,761.9	4,006.6
GDP at factor cost	7,499.1	8,314.4	9,231.3	10,488.1	10,620.6	11,328.4	12,397.7	12,994.2	13,498.5	14,101.9	15,068.3
Agriculture	2,319.3	2,443.6	2,536.3	2,755.4	2,756.0	2,686.8	2,884.4	2,934.8	3,068.5	3,102.0	3,258.6
Industry	1,992.8	2,348.5	2,745.7	3,311.3	3,481.7	3,760.9	4,045.2	4,240.2	4,179.2	4,509.2	4,629.3
Manufacturing	1,293.9	1,461.2	1,581.0	1,791.5	1,876.5	2,013.3	2,149.0	2,270.3	2,267.4	2,371.7	2,490.1
Services, etc.	4,085.3	4,523.3	5,001.6	5,543.2	6,041.7	6,421.6	6,806.1	7,227.9	7,489.8	7,761.8	8,424.2
Memo Items:											
Capacity to Import	2,281.5	2,319.5	3,313.2	3,361.3	3,074.0	4,098.0	3,027.0	3,346.2	2,755.8	3,154.8	5,119.6
Terms of Trade Adjustment	129.7	96.3	757.8	845.4	1,041.6	999.4	308.5	689.9	270.2	118.4	410.7
Gross Domestic Income	8,527.2	9,411.7	11,041.4	12,455.3	13,321.0	13,868.7	14,044.2	15,092.7	15,007.6	15,491.5	16,722.8
Gross National Income	8,313.1	9,225.4	11,059.8	12,266.3	13,100.5	13,644.9	13,798.0	14,747.8	14,750.3	15,297.5	15,924.6
DOMESTIC PRICES/DEFLATORS					*(Index 1987 = 100)*						
Overall (GDP)	17.7	17.9	19.3	20.2	23.8	28.0	28.8	31.8	32.4	35.8	40.7
Domestic Absorption	16.8	17.1	17.6	18.7	22.1	25.9	28.1	30.3	31.7	35.5	37.7
Agriculture	14.9	15.2	16.1	18.9	23.5	28.8	26.1	31.4	28.9	33.1	41.0
Industry	19.5	19.1	20.0	19.9	23.9	30.3	30.6	31.9	33.1	36.6	40.5
Manufacturing	21.3	21.0	22.0	22.3	29.0	37.4	37.9	38.3	38.5	39.2	40.8
Consumer Price Index	13.8	14.3	15.5	17.9	20.2	23.1	24.9	28.1	29.1	31.8	37.1
MANUFACTURING ACTIVITY											
Employment (1987=100)	..	..	..	..	..	..	..	..	..	..	..
Real Earnings per Empl. (1987=100)	..	..	..	..	..	..	..	..	..	..	..
Real Output per Empl. (1987=100)	..	..	..	..	..	..	..	..	..	..	..
Earnings as % of Value Added	35.3	33.2	34.4	30.5	26.5	24.2	22.7	22.1	23.4	25.8	26.9
MONETARY HOLDINGS					*(Millions of current Dominican Pesos)*						
Money Supply, Broadly Defined	289.8	356.1	442.4	559.8	798.8	947.0	997.5	1,158.3	1,183.7	1,392.1	1,494.1
Money	171.7	188.1	222.5	260.1	364.2	379.7	390.4	460.0	458.0	598.4	579.6
Currency Outside Banks	81.2	83.5	98.9	116.2	140.6	157.7	172.3	203.2	223.9	273.5	274.9
Demand Deposits	90.5	104.6	123.6	143.9	223.6	222.1	218.2	256.8	234.0	324.9	304.7
Quasi-Money	118.1	168.0	220.0	299.7	434.6	567.3	607.2	698.4	725.7	793.7	914.5
					(Millions of current Dominican Pesos)						
GOVERNMENT DEFICIT (-) OR SURPLUS	..	..	-3.2	-20.6	-41.8	56.3	-10.6	-0.1	-70.4	-315.0	-172.9
Current Revenue	..	..	348.2	386.0	499.1	684.2	616.8	671.3	679.2	731.9	945.9
Current Expenditure	..	..	215.4	234.1	275.8	302.2	344.3	390.1	460.0	630.9	752.8
Current Budget Balance	..	..	132.8	151.9	223.3	382.0	272.5	281.2	219.2	101.0	193.1
Capital Receipts	..	..	13.3	11.5	14.2	10.4	5.4	6.6	15.5	7.8	9.6
Capital Payments	..	..	149.3	184.0	279.3	336.1	288.5	287.9	305.1	423.8	375.6

1981	1982	1983	1984	1985	1986	1987	1988	1989	1990 estimate	Notes	DOMINICAN REPUBLIC
1,210	1,260	1,210	990	790	740	770	740	790	830	A	CURRENT GNP PER CAPITA (US $)
5,837	5,982	6,129	6,275	6,416	6,554	6,688	6,819	6,948	7,074	..	POPULATION (thousands)
											USE AND ORIGIN OF RESOURCES
				(Millions of current Dominican Pesos)							
6,990	7,709	8,325	9,690	13,274	15,064	18,468	26,789	40,593	58,001	..	Gross National Product (GNP)
-277	-255	-297	-665	-699	-717	-1,068	-1,564	-1,800	-2,554	..	Net Factor Income from Abroad
7,267	7,964	8,622	10,355	13,973	15,781	19,536	28,353	42,393	60,555	..	GDP at Market Prices
-305	-391	-336	280	-771	-700	-1,950	-1,694	-2,650	-2,861	..	Resource Balance
1,513	1,142	1,242	3,780	4,088	4,041	5,432	10,067	13,089	16,844	..	Exports of Goods & NFServices
1,818	1,533	1,578	3,500	4,859	4,741	7,382	11,761	15,739	19,705	..	Imports of Goods & NFServices
7,572	8,355	8,958	10,075	14,744	16,481	21,486	30,047	45,043	63,416	..	Domestic Absorption
5,163	5,986	6,356	7,002	10,833	11,447	14,735	20,964	33,135	50,769	..	Private Consumption, etc.
693	779	786	871	1,112	1,925	1,832	2,627	3,339	4,268	..	General Gov't Consumption
1,716	1,590	1,816	2,202	2,799	3,109	4,919	6,456	8,569	8,379	..	Gross Domestic Investment
1,655	1,491	1,754	2,169	2,747	3,024	4,801	6,368	8,469	8,291	..	Fixed Investment
541	473	574	789	1,170	1,569	1,986	2,948	3,857	4,288	..	Indirect Taxes, net
6,726	7,491	8,048	9,566	12,803	14,212	17,550	25,405	38,536	56,267	B	GDP at factor cost
1,350	1,411	1,485	1,915	2,754	3,088	3,655	5,173	7,558	10,551	..	Agriculture
2,008	2,278	2,503	2,928	3,604	4,208	5,784	8,307	12,096	16,125	..	Industry
1,133	1,455	1,527	1,708	1,902	2,254	2,866	3,979	5,866	8,050	..	Manufacturing
3,909	4,275	4,634	5,512	7,615	8,485	10,097	14,873	22,739	33,879	..	Services, etc.
1,411	1,199	1,480	2,482	2,028	2,409	2,969	4,762	5,919	5,518	..	Gross Domestic Saving
1,311	1,134	1,378	2,022	2,082	2,395	2,901	4,963	6,024	5,648	..	Gross National Saving
				(Millions of 1987 Dominican Pesos)							
16,018.8	16,374.3	17,024.1	17,267.2	16,865.0	17,309.1	18,468.0	18,727.7	19,651.7	18,881.9	..	Gross National Product
16,985.9	17,293.7	18,060.8	18,109.1	17,651.2	18,178.8	19,536.0	19,670.4	20,458.8	19,407.2	..	GDP at Market Prices
-1,872.2	-1,385.9	-1,336.6	-601.9	-1,115.0	-1,511.3	-1,950.0	-1,337.7	-2,665.3	-849.2	..	Resource Balance
5,028.4	4,355.7	4,574.3	4,809.8	4,742.5	4,809.8	5,432.0	6,071.1	6,205.6	6,693.3	..	Exports of Goods & NFServices
6,900.6	5,741.6	5,911.0	5,411.7	5,857.5	6,321.1	7,382.0	7,408.8	8,870.9	7,542.5	..	Imports of Goods & NFServices
18,858.1	18,679.5	19,397.5	18,711.0	18,766.2	19,690.1	21,486.0	21,008.1	23,124.1	20,256.4	..	Domestic Absorption
13,185.8	13,653.8	14,049.6	13,211.4	13,349.0	13,988.0	14,735.0	13,678.9	15,361.9	13,162.1	..	Private Consumption, etc.
1,912.7	1,941.4	1,999.1	1,993.3	2,079.7	2,229.5	1,832.0	2,010.6	1,993.3	2,074.0	..	General Gov't Consumption
3,759.6	3,084.2	3,348.8	3,506.3	3,337.5	3,472.6	4,919.0	5,318.6	5,768.9	5,020.3	..	Gross Domestic Investment
3,667.0	2,861.0	3,223.7	3,500.0	3,287.0	3,402.2	4,801.0	5,296.1	5,785.4	5,037.0	..	Fixed Investment
15,725.7	16,273.5	16,864.2	16,735.8	16,181.4	16,377.8	17,550.0	17,625.2	18,596.3	18,033.8	B	GDP at factor cost
3,433.3	3,587.8	3,702.0	3,702.0	3,574.4	3,547.5	3,655.0	3,608.0	3,688.6	3,460.2	..	Agriculture
4,778.1	4,552.3	4,978.2	4,998.8	4,624.1	4,906.4	5,784.0	5,671.1	5,912.3	5,250.3	..	Industry
2,560.6	2,640.5	2,668.7	2,602.9	2,419.7	2,588.8	2,866.0	2,776.7	2,837.8	2,584.1	..	Manufacturing
8,774.5	9,153.6	9,380.6	9,408.3	9,452.8	9,724.9	10,097.0	10,391.4	10,857.9	10,696.8	..	Services, etc.
											Memo Items:
5,742.9	4,277.1	4,652.3	5,844.6	4,928.0	5,387.8	5,432.0	6,341.6	7,377.3	6,447.4	..	Capacity to Import
714.5	-78.6	78.0	1,034.9	185.5	578.0	0.0	270.6	1,171.7	-245.9	..	Terms of Trade Adjustment
17,700.4	17,215.1	18,138.8	19,144.0	17,836.8	18,756.8	19,536.0	19,941.0	21,630.5	19,161.3	..	Gross Domestic Income
16,733.3	16,295.8	17,102.2	18,302.1	17,050.6	17,887.1	18,468.0	18,998.2	20,823.4	18,636.0	..	Gross National Income
				(Index 1987 = 100)							DOMESTIC PRICES/DEFLATORS
42.8	46.1	47.7	57.2	79.2	86.8	100.0	144.1	207.2	312.0	..	Overall (GDP)
40.2	44.7	46.2	53.8	78.6	83.7	100.0	143.0	194.8	313.1	..	Domestic Absorption
39.3	39.3	40.1	51.7	77.0	87.0	100.0	143.4	204.9	304.9	..	Agriculture
42.0	50.0	50.3	58.6	77.9	85.8	100.0	146.5	204.6	307.1	..	Industry
44.2	55.1	57.2	65.6	78.6	87.1	100.0	143.3	206.7	311.5	..	Manufacturing
39.9	43.0	45.0	57.2	78.6	86.3	100.0	144.4	210.0	334.9	..	Consumer Price Index
											MANUFACTURING ACTIVITY
..	..	..	..	..	..	..	..	..	..	..	Employment (1987=100)
..	..	..	..	..	..	..	..	..	..	..	Real Earnings per Empl. (1987=100)
..	..	..	..	..	..	..	..	..	..	..	Real Output per Empl. (1987=100)
25.9	23.0	22.8	..	..	..	..	..	..	..	..	Earnings as % of Value Added
				(Millions of current Dominican Pesos)							MONETARY HOLDINGS
1,723.6	1,994.2	2,211.8	2,768.5	3,394.7	5,107.2	6,020.5	8,761.9	11,370.5	15,277.5	D	Money Supply, Broadly Defined
660.5	731.5	781.4	1,159.5	1,355.2	1,988.6	2,609.4	4,168.3	5,284.5	7,340.7	..	Money
323.8	357.8	414.7	592.8	677.2	937.4	1,312.8	1,876.3	2,682.9	3,733.3	..	Currency Outside Banks
336.7	373.6	366.7	566.7	678.0	1,051.2	1,296.6	2,292.1	2,601.7	3,607.3	..	Demand Deposits
1,063.1	1,262.7	1,430.4	1,609.0	2,039.5	3,118.5	3,411.1	4,593.5	6,086.0	7,936.8	..	Quasi-Money
				(Millions of current Dominican Pesos)							GOVERNMENT DEFICIT (-) OR SURPLUS
-181.4	-246.6	-216.4	-114.4	-262.0	76.9	-147.4	-563.3	18.7	..	..	
984.1	818.6	986.3	1,262.5	1,717.9	2,447.9	3,067.6	4,795.1	6,138.6	..	..	Current Revenue
809.1	824.4	908.0	1,061.2	1,468.1	1,699.4	1,580.2	2,317.0	3,128.7	..	..	Current Expenditure
175.0	-5.8	78.3	201.3	249.8	748.5	1,487.4	2,478.1	3,009.9	..	..	Current Budget Balance
10.2	7.7	14.0	19.3	11.4	9.4	17.5	19.7	41.4	..	..	Capital Receipts
366.6	248.5	308.7	335.0	523.2	681.0	1,652.3	3,061.1	3,032.6	..	..	Capital Payments

DOMINICAN REPUBLIC	1970	1971	1972	1973	1974	1975	1976	1977	1978	1979	1980
FOREIGN TRADE (CUSTOMS BASIS)					*(Millions of current US dollars)*						
Value of Exports, fob	..	..	..	..	..	..	..	..	..	..	..
Nonfuel Primary Products	..	..	..	..	..	..	..	..	..	..	..
Fuels	..	..	..	..	..	..	..	..	..	..	..
Manufactures	..	..	..	..	..	..	..	..	..	..	..
Value of Imports, cif	..	..	..	..	..	..	..	..	..	..	..
Nonfuel Primary Products	..	..	..	..	..	..	..	..	..	..	..
Fuels	..	..	..	..	..	..	..	..	..	..	..
Manufactures	..	..	..	..	..	..	..	..	..	..	..
					(Index 1987 = 100)						
Terms of Trade	..	..	..	..	..	..	..	..	..	..	..
Export Prices, fob	..	..	..	..	..	..	..	..	..	..	..
Import Prices, cif	..	..	..	..	..	..	..	..	..	..	..
BALANCE OF PAYMENTS					*(Millions of current US dollars)*						
Exports of Goods & Services	258.5	291.7	412.6	516.4	735.2	1,015.2	853.1	939.5	848.8	1,166.8	1,313.2
Merchandise, fob	214.0	240.7	347.6	442.1	636.8	893.8	716.4	780.5	675.5	868.6	962.0
Nonfactor Services	43.0	49.5	63.5	71.5	93.4	116.2	127.8	146.7	152.5	266.3	309.4
Factor Services	1.5	1.5	1.5	2.8	5.0	5.2	8.9	12.3	20.8	31.9	41.8
Imports of Goods & Services	391.6	438.5	490.2	643.6	1,011.2	1,127.0	1,108.1	1,207.7	1,310.5	1,703.9	2,170.7
Merchandise, fob	278.0	309.7	337.7	421.9	673.0	772.7	763.6	849.3	862.4	1,137.5	1,519.7
Nonfactor Services	86.2	98.5	104.1	142.0	243.4	236.3	226.4	247.7	291.6	346.8	399.0
Factor Services	27.4	30.3	48.4	79.7	94.8	118.0	118.1	110.7	156.5	219.6	252.0
Long-Term Interest	12.6	13.5	16.3	20.0	23.5	32.8	34.3	48.4	61.1	77.9	120.7
Private Current Transfers, net	30.4	16.3	29.0	28.8	33.2	34.2	122.9	136.1	146.3	177.0	183.1
Workers' Remittances	25.1	14.5	24.0	24.0	26.8	28.0	112.0	123.6	131.6	161.3	183.1
Curr. A/C Bal before Off. Transf.	-102.7	-130.5	-48.6	-98.4	-242.8	-77.6	-132.1	-132.1	-315.4	-360.1	-674.4
Net Official Transfers	0.8	1.1	1.6	1.8	1.8	4.8	2.9	3.5	3.5	28.8	4.7
Curr. A/C Bal after Off. Transf.	-101.9	-129.4	-47.0	-96.6	-241.0	-72.8	-129.2	-128.6	-311.9	-331.3	-669.7
Long-Term Capital, net	109.5	81.5	82.2	69.6	161.3	159.2	167.5	218.9	160.4	160.3	346.3
Direct Investment	71.6	65.0	43.5	34.5	53.6	63.9	60.0	71.5	63.6	17.1	62.7
Long-Term Loans	33.0	37.9	44.1	35.1	107.8	95.3	115.3	137.0	119.7	124.0	346.5
Disbursements	59.9	70.6	75.6	76.8	151.6	157.7	188.7	226.9	223.0	351.4	481.5
Repayments	26.9	32.7	31.5	41.7	43.8	62.4	73.4	89.9	103.3	227.4	135.0
Other Long-Term Capital	4.9	-21.4	-5.4	0.0	-0.1	0.0	-7.8	10.4	-22.9	19.2	-62.9
Other Capital, net	-12.6	63.2	-30.0	59.9	79.6	-93.1	-60.9	-47.7	115.1	126.5	138.4
Change in Reserves	5.0	-15.3	-5.2	-32.9	0.1	6.7	22.6	-42.6	36.4	44.5	185.0
Memo Item:					*(Dominican Pesos per US dollar)*						
Conversion Factor (Annual Avg)	1.000	1.000	1.000	1.000	1.000	1.000	1.000	1.000	1.000	1.000	1.000
				(Millions of US dollars), outstanding at end of year							
EXTERNAL DEBT (Total)	359.7	402.8	439.4	470.3	577.5	672.7	811.5	1,121.1	1,334.3	1,603.8	2,002.2
Long-Term Debt (by debtor)	359.7	402.8	439.4	470.3	577.5	672.7	811.5	957.1	1,079.3	1,286.8	1,521.8
Central Bank, incl. IMF credit	32.9	40.8	38.1	49.6	52.5	61.3	109.3	178.8	226.7	307.1	317.0
Central Government	146.4	152.4	172.6	179.1	182.6	186.7	186.6	205.6	293.4	445.1	589.8
Rest of General Government	0.0	0.0	0.0	1.3	2.9	2.3	2.7	2.0	1.3	0.6	0.1
Non-financial Public Enterprises	24.2	19.1	33.5	44.6	77.8	109.6	173.4	212.0	208.2	195.7	326.0
Priv. Sector, incl non-guaranteed	156.2	190.5	195.2	195.7	261.7	312.8	339.5	358.7	349.7	338.3	288.9
Short-Term Debt	0.0	0.0	0.0	0.0	0.0	0.0	0.0	164.0	255.0	317.0	480.4
Memo Items:					*(Millions of US dollars)*						
Int'l Reserves Excluding Gold	29.1	52.8	55.3	84.3	87.1	112.6	123.5	180.1	154.1	238.6	201.8
Gold Holdings (at market price)	3.2	3.8	5.6	9.7	16.0	12.1	11.6	17.2	23.5	57.9	77.2
SOCIAL INDICATORS											
Total Fertility Rate	6.3	6.1	5.8	5.6	5.4	5.1	4.9	4.7	4.6	4.4	4.3
Infant Mortality Rate	90.0	85.0	80.0	79.0	78.0	77.0	76.0	75.0	73.6	72.2	70.8
Life Expectancy at Birth	58.7	59.3	59.9	60.3	60.8	61.2	61.6	62.1	62.5	62.9	63.3
Urban Population, % of total	40.3	41.3	42.3	43.3	44.3	45.3	46.3	47.4	48.4	49.5	50.5
Food Prod. per capita (1987=100)	118.5	122.5	122.0	120.9	120.0	112.4	118.6	116.9	118.9	114.9	108.4
Labor Force, Agriculture (%)	54.8	53.7	52.8	51.9	51.0	50.2	49.2	48.2	47.3	46.5	45.7
Labor Force, Female (%)	10.9	11.1	11.2	11.4	11.5	11.7	11.8	12.0	12.1	12.2	12.4
Primary Schl. Enroll. Ratio	100.0	..	..	..	..	104.0	..	95.0	102.0	104.0	118.0
Primary Schl. Enroll. Ratio, Female	100.0	..	..	..	..	..	..	96.0	..	..	..
Secondary Schl. Enroll. Ratio	21.0	..	..	..	..	36.0	..	..	38.0	39.0	42.0

(Millions of current US dollars)

FOREIGN TRADE (CUSTOMS BASIS)

1981	1982	1983	1984	1985	1986	1987	1988	1989	1990 estimate	Notes	DOMINICAN REPUBLIC
..	..	..	..	..	..	..	..	..	..	..	Value of Exports, fob
..	..	..	..	..	..	..	..	..	..		Nonfuel Primary Products
..	..	..	..	..	..	..	..	..	..		Fuels
..	..	..	..	..	..	..	..	..	..		Manufactures
..	..	..	..	..	..	..	..	..	..		Value of Imports, cif
..	..	..	..	..	..	..	..	..	..		Nonfuel Primary Products
..	..	..	..	..	..	..	..	..	..		Fuels
..	..	..	..	..	..	..	..	..	..		Manufactures

(Index 1987 = 100)

1981	1982	1983	1984	1985	1986	1987	1988	1989	1990	Notes	
..	..	..	..	..	..	..	..	..	..		Terms of Trade
..	..	..	..	..	..	..	..	..	..		Export Prices, fob
..	..	..	..	..	..	..	..	..	..		Import Prices, cif

(Millions of current US dollars)

BALANCE OF PAYMENTS

1981	1982	1983	1984	1985	1986	1987	1988	1989	1990	Notes	
1,524.3	1,146.1	1,236.8	1,342.7	1,344.4	1,424.9	1,571.1	1,844.3	2,077.9	2,016.9	..	Exports of Goods & Services
1,187.9	767.6	785.3	835.4	738.5	721.9	711.2	889.5	924.5	734.5	..	Merchandise, fob
324.6	374.1	444.6	501.5	584.3	686.0	848.3	946.3	1,143.4	1,270.6	..	Nonfactor Services
11.8	4.4	6.9	5.8	21.6	17.0	11.6	8.5	10.0	11.8	..	Factor Services
2,123.3	1,793.1	1,872.8	1,920.1	1,901.1	1,897.8	2,262.6	2,304.6	2,774.5	2,593.9	..	Imports of Goods & Services
1,451.7	1,257.3	1,282.2	1,257.1	1,285.9	1,351.7	1,591.5	1,607.9	1,964.0	1,792.8	..	Merchandise, fob
366.7	277.3	286.6	299.5	274.5	284.3	360.5	366.8	464.8	440.2	..	Nonfactor Services
304.9	258.5	304.0	363.5	340.7	261.8	310.6	329.9	345.7	360.9	..	Factor Services
143.7	126.0	130.5	111.8	139.0	184.8	108.2	154.6	94.0	59.5	..	Long-Term Interest
176.3	190.0	195.0	205.0	242.0	242.0	260.0	288.8	300.5	314.8	..	Private Current Transfers, net
182.9	190.0	195.0	205.0	242.0	230.3	277.4	292.9	305.8	314.9	..	Workers' Remittances
-422.7	-457.0	-441.0	-372.4	-314.7	-230.9	-431.5	-171.5	-396.1	-262.2	..	Curr. A/C Bal before Off. Transf.
16.7	15.0	20.0	60.0	114.3	29.0	95.4	64.8	83.8	55.8	..	Net Official Transfers
-406.0	-442.0	-421.0	-312.4	-200.4	-201.9	-336.1	-106.7	-312.3	-206.4	..	Curr. A/C Bal after Off. Transf.
240.9	176.5	8.0	68.7	-174.2	-194.4	-259.3	-165.3	86.8	-155.1	..	Long-Term Capital, net
79.7	-1.4	22.0	68.5	37.0	50.0	89.0	106.1	110.0	132.8	..	Direct Investment
162.4	275.0	70.5	217.9	166.6	93.4	61.4	56.9	99.1	46.5	..	Long-Term Loans
298.8	455.1	257.6	309.6	251.0	195.3	159.4	163.5	212.7	141.1	..	Disbursements
136.4	180.1	187.1	91.7	84.4	101.9	98.0	106.6	113.6	94.6	..	Repayments
-1.2	-97.1	-84.5	-217.7	-377.8	-337.8	-409.7	-328.3	-122.3	-334.4	..	Other Long-Term Capital
47.8	-193.3	375.7	328.1	496.7	487.4	480.7	401.6	113.1	511.8	..	Other Capital, net
117.3	458.8	37.3	-84.4	-122.1	-91.1	114.7	-129.6	112.4	-150.3	..	Change in Reserves

Memo Item:

(Dominican Pesos per US dollar)

1981	1982	1983	1984	1985	1986	1987	1988	1989	1990	Notes	
1.000	1.090	1.260	2.060	3.110	2.900	3.840	6.110	6.340	8.520	..	Conversion Factor (Annual Avg)

(Millions of US dollars), outstanding at end of year

1981	1982	1983	1984	1985	1986	1987	1988	1989	1990	Notes	
2,293.8	2,519.0	2,928.1	3,111.8	3,502.4	3,687.4	3,923.6	3,991.7	4,104.0	4,399.6	..	**EXTERNAL DEBT (Total)**
1,655.9	1,989.8	2,630.1	2,740.7	3,138.6	3,380.3	3,636.7	3,617.5	3,562.0	3,611.0		Long-Term Debt (by debtor)
348.6	371.9	1,050.4	1,008.1	1,099.0	1,369.3	1,485.9	1,465.9	1,370.1	1,332.7		Central Bank, incl. IMF credit
693.5	917.5	966.7	1,091.0	1,495.9	1,552.7	1,700.2	1,723.9	1,755.1	1,814.6		Central Government
0.0	0.0	0.0	0.0	0.0	0.0	0.0	0.0	0.0	..	Rest of General Government
349.6	418.0	399.6	449.0	360.3	283.8	289.6	281.3	303.2	335.7		Non-financial Public Enterprises
264.2	282.4	213.4	192.6	183.4	174.5	161.0	146.4	133.6	128.0		Priv. Sector, incl non-guaranteed
637.9	529.2	298.0	371.1	363.8	307.1	286.9	374.2	542.0	788.6		Short-Term Debt

Memo Items:

(Millions of US dollars)

1981	1982	1983	1984	1985	1986	1987	1988	1989	1990	Notes	
225.2	129.0	171.3	253.5	340.1	376.3	182.2	254.0	164.0	61.6	..	Int'l Reserves Excluding Gold
56.5	41.6	29.4	5.6	5.9	7.0	8.7	7.4	7.2	6.9	..	Gold Holdings (at market price)

SOCIAL INDICATORS

1981	1982	1983	1984	1985	1986	1987	1988	1989	1990	Notes	
4.1	4.0	3.9	3.8	3.7	3.6	3.5	3.4	3.3	3.2	..	Total Fertility Rate
69.4	68.0	66.6	65.2	63.8	62.4	61.0	59.3	57.6	55.9	..	Infant Mortality Rate
63.7	64.1	64.5	64.8	65.2	65.6	65.9	66.3	66.6	67.0	..	Life Expectancy at Birth
51.5	52.6	53.6	54.7	55.7	56.6	57.6	58.5	59.5	60.4	..	Urban Population, % of total
107.3	112.0	112.6	110.0	102.8	100.3	100.0	99.0	103.2	96.1	..	Food Prod. per capita (1987=100)
..	..	..	..	..	..	..	..	..	..		Labor Force, Agriculture (%)
12.7	13.0	13.2	13.5	13.7	14.0	14.3	14.5	14.7	15.0	..	Labor Force, Female (%)
..	109.0	112.0	126.0	126.0	101.0	98.0	95.0		..	..	Primary Schl. Enroll. Ratio
..	115.0	117.0	124.0	129.0	103.0	98.0	96.0	..	..	..	Primary Schl. Enroll. Ratio, Female
..	50.0	50.0	50.0	51.0	74.0	..	..	..	..	..	Secondary Schl. Enroll. Ratio

ECUADOR	1970	1971	1972	1973	1974	1975	1976	1977	1978	1979	1980
CURRENT GNP PER CAPITA (US $)	290	290	300	370	430	540	680	790	930	1,080	1,260
POPULATION (thousands)	6,051	6,240	6,433	6,628	6,829	7,035	7,246	7,463	7,683	7,904	8,123

USE AND ORIGIN OF RESOURCES	*(Billions of current Ecuadoran Sucres)*										
Gross National Product (GNP)	34.3	39.1	45.2	58.7	87.1	105.3	128.9	158.9	185.8	224.0	278.8
Net Factor Income from Abroad	-0.7	-0.9	-1.7	-3.5	-5.7	-2.5	-4.1	-7.5	-5.5	-9.9	-14.5
GDP at Market Prices	35.0	40.0	46.9	62.2	92.8	107.7	132.9	166.4	191.3	234.0	293.3
Resource Balance	-1.6	-3.8	-1.7	2.0	4.8	-7.0	-1.8	-5.0	-10.8	1.3	-0.7
Exports of Goods & NFServices	4.9	6.0	8.8	15.5	33.6	28.2	34.2	41.3	40.8	60.6	73.8
Imports of Goods & NFServices	6.5	9.8	10.5	13.5	28.8	35.2	36.0	46.3	51.6	59.3	74.5
Domestic Absorption	36.6	43.8	48.5	60.2	88.0	114.7	134.7	171.4	202.1	232.7	294.1
Private Consumption, etc.	26.4	30.4	34.4	41.7	55.5	70.3	84.5	102.6	121.2	143.3	174.9
General Gov't Consumption	3.9	4.1	4.7	6.4	11.6	15.6	18.6	24.7	26.5	30.1	42.6
Gross Domestic Investment	6.4	9.3	9.4	12.1	20.8	28.8	31.6	44.1	54.4	59.3	76.6
Fixed Investment	5.8	8.7	8.4	10.9	16.9	24.9	29.5	39.3	50.1	55.4	69.3
Indirect Taxes, net	3.8	4.6	5.5	7.7	10.4	10.7	10.6	13.4	16.5	19.1	24.4
GDP at factor cost	31.3	35.4	41.4	54.5	82.4	97.0	122.4	152.9	174.9	214.9	268.9
Agriculture	8.4	9.2	10.5	12.2	17.4	19.3	22.6	27.7	28.5	31.7	35.6
Industry	8.6	10.7	13.1	20.1	35.4	36.5	47.0	57.3	66.1	90.3	111.7
Manufacturing	6.4	7.5	8.8	10.8	14.3	17.2	22.9	29.9	36.3	44.9	51.8
Services, etc.	18.0	20.1	23.2	29.9	40.0	51.9	63.3	81.4	96.8	112.0	146.1
Gross Domestic Saving	4.8	5.5	7.7	14.1	25.6	21.8	29.8	39.1	43.7	60.6	75.9
Gross National Saving	4.3	4.8	6.2	10.8	20.3	19.7	25.9	31.7	38.4	50.7	61.4

	(Billions of 1987 Ecuadoran Sucres)										
Gross National Product	663.53	704.89	811.47	1,020.65	1,075.14	1,177.71	1,281.70	1,368.20	1,460.80	1,518.58	1,576.20
GDP at Market Prices	680.11	725.29	845.41	1,085.14	1,148.52	1,208.98	1,325.99	1,410.25	1,508.54	1,590.44	1,663.26
Resource Balance	-130.12	-166.08	-49.58	104.73	-38.05	-137.03	-94.06	-193.67	-200.57	-182.14	-247.67
Exports of Goods & NFServices	99.81	111.30	219.11	387.70	369.34	338.26	366.85	348.48	359.70	377.69	368.80
Imports of Goods & NFServices	229.92	277.38	268.69	282.97	407.39	475.30	460.91	542.15	560.27	559.83	616.48
Domestic Absorption	810.23	891.37	894.99	980.41	1,186.57	1,346.01	1,420.05	1,603.92	1,709.11	1,772.58	1,910.93
Private Consumption, etc.	515.82	542.72	576.20	628.64	685.82	756.99	836.90	897.77	945.05	1,012.44	1,083.49
General Gov't Consumption	82.41	80.55	85.15	93.14	142.68	169.42	185.40	223.07	223.51	234.84	256.02
Gross Domestic Investment	212.00	268.10	233.64	258.63	358.07	419.61	397.75	483.08	540.55	525.29	571.43
Fixed Investment	205.97	260.80	213.95	242.02	306.38	377.88	383.36	442.72	501.54	499.98	530.63
GDP at factor cost	603.44	638.42	744.01	950.88	1,019.54	1,087.81	1,220.56	1,296.07	1,378.66	1,460.96	1,524.76
Agriculture	157.88	165.79	172.45	174.26	189.88	194.29	199.90	204.61	196.72	202.33	213.03
Industry	151.18	171.69	263.02	440.46	431.19	427.41	491.19	501.42	550.54	587.78	584.49
Manufacturing	131.71	138.25	151.01	164.92	182.10	209.81	237.45	265.74	287.45	315.33	326.82
Services, etc.	371.06	387.82	409.94	470.42	527.45	587.28	634.89	704.22	761.28	800.34	865.74

Memo Items:											
Capacity to Import	173.64	169.97	225.42	325.09	474.67	381.12	437.70	483.67	443.24	572.04	610.44
Terms of Trade Adjustment	73.84	58.66	6.30	-62.61	105.33	42.85	70.85	135.19	83.54	194.35	241.64
Gross Domestic Income	753.95	783.96	851.71	1,022.53	1,253.85	1,251.83	1,396.84	1,545.44	1,592.08	1,784.79	1,904.90
Gross National Income	737.37	763.56	817.78	958.03	1,180.47	1,220.57	1,352.55	1,503.40	1,544.34	1,712.92	1,817.84

DOMESTIC PRICES/DEFLATORS	*(Index 1987 = 100)*										
Overall (GDP)	5.1	5.5	5.5	5.7	8.1	8.9	10.0	11.8	12.7	14.7	17.6
Domestic Absorption	4.5	4.9	5.4	6.1	7.4	8.5	9.5	10.7	11.8	13.1	15.4
Agriculture	5.3	5.5	6.1	7.0	9.2	10.0	11.3	13.5	14.5	15.6	16.7
Industry	5.7	6.2	5.0	4.6	8.2	8.5	9.6	11.4	12.0	15.4	19.1
Manufacturing	4.8	5.5	5.8	6.6	7.8	8.2	9.7	11.3	12.6	14.2	15.8
Consumer Price Index	5.7	6.2	6.6	7.5	9.3	10.7	11.8	13.4	14.9	16.5	18.6

MANUFACTURING ACTIVITY											
Employment (1987=100)	43.7	45.9	48.9	53.8	60.8	68.4	74.1	80.0	90.7	97.8	103.4
Real Earnings per Empl. (1987=100)	60.2	63.1	65.8	64.5	61.7	63.7	68.1	68.1	68.4	73.5	101.8
Real Output per Empl. (1987=100)	73.2	72.4	73.4	75.7	81.1	80.0	83.3	88.7	89.4	87.1	88.0
Earnings as % of Value Added	26.7	25.7	28.0	27.4	24.8	29.1	26.3	25.4	21.4	24.8	39.4

MONETARY HOLDINGS	*(Billions of current Ecuadoran Sucres)*										
Money Supply, Broadly Defined	7.73	8.89	10.97	14.43	21.03	23.08	28.81	35.96	39.74	52.18	66.17
Money	5.99	6.72	8.38	11.30	16.87	18.34	22.81	29.88	32.92	41.95	53.58
Currency Outside Banks	2.33	2.41	2.89	3.62	4.78	5.39	7.57	9.13	10.27	12.34	15.29
Demand Deposits	3.66	4.30	5.49	7.68	12.09	12.96	15.24	20.75	22.65	29.61	38.30
Quasi-Money	1.75	2.18	2.59	3.13	4.17	4.74	6.01	6.09	6.82	10.23	12.59

GOVERNMENT DEFICIT (-) OR SURPLUS	*(Millions of current Ecuadoran Sucres)*										
	..	..	..	124	-3	-666	-2,160	-5,388	-2,296	-1,520	-4,119
Current Revenue	..	..	..	7,973	11,390	12,391	14,653	16,452	19,057	23,078	37,549
Current Expenditure	..	..	..	..	..	..	..	..	..	..	34,872
Current Budget Balance	..	..	..	..	..	..	..	..	..	..	2,677
Capital Receipts	..	..	..	..	..	..	..	..	..	..	..
Capital Payments	..	..	..	..	..	..	..	..	..	..	6,796

1981	1982	1983	1984	1985	1986	1987	1988	1989	1990 estimate	Notes	ECUADOR
1,490	1,500	1,320	1,170	1,180	1,160	1,090	1,080	1,010	980	A	**CURRENT GNP PER CAPITA (US $)**
8,341	8,558	8,775	8,990	9,205	9,420	9,635	9,850	10,066	10,284	..	**POPULATION (thousands)**
				(Billions of current Ecuadoran Sucres)							**USE AND ORIGIN OF RESOURCES**
330.4	384.8	518.5	740.1	1,028.2	1,271.6	1,672.2	2,812.9	4,942.0	7,703.1	..	Gross National Product (GNP)
-18.3	-30.9	-41.8	-72.6	-81.8	-111.6	-122.3	-206.8	-383.2	-646.6	..	Net Factor Income from Abroad
348.7	415.7	560.3	812.6	1,109.9	1,383.2	1,794.5	3,019.7	5,325.2	8,349.7	..	GDP at Market Prices
3.5	-9.5	22.4	52.4	65.3	2.2	-112.2	-63.3	-104.8	255.8	..	Resource Balance
75.9	87.6	133.1	209.9	296.9	314.7	431.5	859.1	1,500.7	2,585.5	..	Exports of Goods & NFServices
72.4	97.0	110.6	157.4	231.7	312.5	543.7	922.4	1,605.5	2,329.7	..	Imports of Goods & NFServices
345.2	425.2	537.8	760.2	1,044.7	1,381.0	1,906.7	3,083.0	5,429.9	8,094.3	..	Domestic Absorption
214.7	262.2	369.3	520.6	715.7	925.8	1,269.4	2,086.9	3,791.1	5,807.0	..	Private Consumption, etc.
49.7	58.1	70.1	99.6	127.3	166.7	230.4	346.9	487.1	676.5	..	General Gov't Consumption
80.8	104.8	98.4	140.0	201.7	288.5	406.8	649.2	1,151.8	1,610.8	..	Gross Domestic Investment
77.6	94.2	93.0	125.2	178.3	260.0	406.6	642.9	1,110.1	1,527.4	..	Fixed Investment
32.6	35.7	46.7	67.7	128.4	156.5	204.5	350.6	652.5	957.8	..	Indirect Taxes, net
316.0	380.0	513.6	744.9	981.6	1,226.8	1,590.0	2,669.1	4,672.6	7,391.9	B	GDP at factor cost
41.6	50.4	73.0	110.0	148.0	208.7	274.6	432.8	728.2	1,101.4	..	Agriculture
137.0	167.6	227.5	335.6	451.8	485.9	579.2	1,083.7	2,085.7	3,466.2	..	Industry
60.0	73.9	103.6	168.0	210.3	274.2	350.3	644.8	1,209.7	1,903.5	..	Manufacturing
170.0	197.8	259.8	367.0	510.2	688.6	940.7	1,503.2	2,511.2	3,782.1	..	Services, etc.
84.3	95.4	120.9	192.4	267.0	290.7	294.7	585.9	1,047.0	1,866.2	..	Gross Domestic Saving
65.9	64.5	79.1	119.8	185.2	179.1	172.4	379.1	663.8	1,219.6	..	Gross National Saving
				(Billions of 1987 Ecuadoran Sucres)							
1,635.51	1,615.74	1,581.78	1,611.01	1,713.97	1,762.70	1,672.21	1,857.31	1,857.55	1,896.93	..	Gross National Product
1,731.10	1,750.47	1,713.96	1,784.03	1,859.72	1,914.81	1,794.50	1,985.90	1,996.57	2,042.71	f	GDP at Market Prices
-173.16	-230.75	-74.93	-16.93	1.53	43.34	-112.16	76.82	37.26	61.66	..	Resource Balance
386.23	367.07	376.04	423.17	473.84	514.58	431.54	565.33	547.36	578.50	..	Exports of Goods & NFServices
559.39	597.81	450.96	440.10	472.31	471.23	543.70	488.51	510.10	516.85	..	Imports of Goods & NFServices
1,904.27	1,981.22	1,788.89	1,800.96	1,858.19	1,871.46	1,906.66	1,909.08	1,959.31	1,981.05	..	Domestic Absorption
1,147.28	1,160.59	1,158.22	1,184.84	1,222.03	1,224.81	1,269.41	1,283.25	1,317.40	1,347.18	..	Private Consumption, etc.
262.25	263.48	247.53	238.52	228.53	226.64	230.42	234.22	226.62	228.79	..	General Gov't Consumption
494.74	557.15	383.14	377.60	407.63	420.02	406.83	391.62	415.28	405.08	..	Gross Domestic Investment
492.20	495.61	366.05	349.48	373.50	389.61	406.60	386.35	394.92	386.59	..	Fixed Investment
1,569.07	1,599.88	1,572.15	1,636.23	1,645.59	1,698.90	1,589.97	1,755.67	1,752.08	1,808.47	B	GDP at factor cost
227.59	232.15	199.89	221.16	242.98	267.88	274.58	295.46	305.10	316.81	..	Agriculture
626.76	628.29	670.37	690.41	716.41	724.22	579.20	725.92	701.41	712.68	..	Industry
355.50	360.68	355.79	349.21	350.03	344.31	350.26	357.36	350.23	359.34	..	Manufacturing
876.75	890.03	843.70	872.45	900.34	922.71	940.71	964.53	990.05	1,013.22	..	Services, etc.
											Memo Items:
586.15	539.51	542.46	586.73	605.35	474.60	431.54	454.97	476.80	573.60	..	Capacity to Import
199.92	172.45	166.43	163.56	131.51	-39.98	0.00	-110.35	-70.56	-4.91	..	Terms of Trade Adjustment
1,931.02	1,922.92	1,880.39	1,947.59	1,991.23	1,874.83	1,794.50	1,875.55	1,926.01	2,037.80	..	Gross Domestic Income
1,835.43	1,788.19	1,748.21	1,774.57	1,845.47	1,722.73	1,672.21	1,746.96	1,786.99	1,892.03	..	Gross National Income
				(Index 1987 = 100)							**DOMESTIC PRICES/DEFLATORS**
20.1	23.7	32.7	45.6	59.7	72.2	100.0	152.1	266.7	408.8	..	Overall (GDP)
18.1	21.5	30.1	42.2	56.2	73.8	100.0	161.5	277.1	408.6	..	Domestic Absorption
18.3	21.7	36.5	49.7	60.9	77.9	100.0	146.5	238.7	347.6	..	Agriculture
21.9	26.7	33.9	48.6	63.1	67.1	100.0	149.3	297.4	486.4	..	Industry
16.9	20.5	29.1	48.1	60.1	79.6	100.0	180.4	345.4	529.7	..	Manufacturing
21.7	25.2	37.4	49.0	62.8	77.2	100.0	158.2	277.9	412.7	..	Consumer Price Index
											MANUFACTURING ACTIVITY
95.3	92.8	87.2	87.7	89.6	94.1	100.0	101.6	..	..	J	Employment (1987=100)
109.2	110.7	95.0	95.9	99.5	104.7	100.0	96.5	..	..	J	Real Earnings per Empl. (1987=100)
96.5	99.5	100.7	93.5	91.4	96.2	100.0	88.4	..	..	J	Real Output per Empl. (1987=100)
43.3	52.8	34.8	36.8	39.7	37.5	36.1	34.6	..	..	J	Earnings as % of Value Added
				(Billions of current Ecuadoran Sucres)							**MONETARY HOLDINGS**
75.70	93.63	118.01	169.28	216.96	268.20	383.90	621.58	882.37	1,357.18	..	Money Supply, Broadly Defined
61.81	73.13	95.15	129.06	153.18	183.40	246.19	372.61	539.81	852.90	..	Money
17.41	20.52	25.42	35.31	42.70	54.60	74.78	123.96	176.29	272.75	..	Currency Outside Banks
44.39	52.61	69.72	93.74	110.47	128.80	171.41	248.65	363.53	580.15	..	Demand Deposits
13.90	20.50	22.87	40.22	63.79	84.80	137.71	248.97	342.55	504.28	..	Quasi-Money
				(Millions of current Ecuadoran Sucres)							**GOVERNMENT DEFICIT (-) OR SURPLUS**
-16,837	-18,480	-14,047	-6,785	21,971	-31,031	-40,997	-1,372	97,000	155,000		Current Revenue
39,297	45,996	60,187	99,872	189,472	186,907	236,762	411,242	832,000	1.36M		Current Revenue
43,135	49,336	..	..	..	..	..	..	646,000	988,000		Current Expenditure
-3,838	-3,340	..	..	..	..	..	..	186,000	372,000		Current Budget Balance
..	..	..	..	..	17	..	..	..	..		Capital Receipts
12,999	15,140	..	..	..	..	..	..	89,000	217,000		Capital Payments

ECUADOR	1970	1971	1972	1973	1974	1975	1976	1977	1978	1979	1980
FOREIGN TRADE (CUSTOMS BASIS)					*(Millions of current US dollars)*						
Value of Exports, fob	189.9	199.1	326.3	531.9	1,123.5	973.9	1,257.5	1,436.3	1,557.5	2,104.2	2,480.2
Nonfuel Primary Products	185.7	193.0	259.0	236.1	405.3	364.3	492.0	692.9	800.2	868.6	841.4
Fuels	0.9	2.0	59.9	282.7	696.7	588.0	740.4	713.3	718.4	1,178.2	1,564.5
Manufactures	3.3	4.0	7.4	13.0	21.5	21.6	25.1	30.1	38.9	57.4	74.3
Value of Imports, cif	272.9	338.5	325.0	396.4	781.3	984.6	951.5	1,165.4	1,498.6	1,599.7	2,215.3
Nonfuel Primary Products	27.2	39.1	44.3	57.0	99.1	115.2	112.0	125.5	164.2	193.5	268.0
Fuels	17.1	28.4	21.4	12.1	137.6	20.5	11.3	10.4	13.6	20.4	28.3
Manufactures	228.7	271.0	259.2	327.3	544.6	848.9	828.2	1,029.5	1,320.8	1,385.8	1,919.1
					(Index 1987 = 100)						
Terms of Trade	211.6	184.5	104.4	54.8	128.1	106.8	122.4	140.7	123.4	132.3	163.0
Export Prices, fob	44.2	39.7	26.5	20.1	59.1	57.8	67.3	84.4	84.5	103.9	140.6
Import Prices, cif	20.9	21.5	25.4	36.6	46.1	54.1	55.0	60.0	68.5	78.5	86.3
BALANCE OF PAYMENTS					*(Millions of current US dollars)*						
Exports of Goods & Services	258.9	265.7	367.0	633.0	1,333.2	1,126.7	1,431.8	1,626.2	1,738.4	2,472.9	2,975.0
Merchandise, fob	234.9	238.0	323.2	584.7	1,225.4	1,012.8	1,307.2	1,400.8	1,529.2	2,150.5	2,520.0
Nonfactor Services	23.7	27.0	41.7	42.3	82.5	96.9	111.4	201.9	174.3	260.2	367.0
Factor Services	0.3	0.7	2.1	6.0	25.4	17.0	13.2	23.5	34.9	62.2	88.0
Imports of Goods & Services	388.8	437.7	459.7	653.3	1,326.6	1,379.0	1,469.1	2,005.8	2,482.6	3,133.0	3,646.8
Merchandise, fob	249.6	306.8	284.1	397.5	875.2	1,006.3	1,047.9	1,360.5	1,704.0	2,096.8	2,241.8
Nonfactor Services	109.7	94.4	107.8	111.6	225.1	288.6	263.9	413.7	462.7	556.4	681.9
Factor Services	29.5	36.5	67.7	144.2	226.3	84.1	157.3	231.6	315.9	479.8	723.1
Long-Term Interest	10.1	10.8	13.8	20.1	25.2	31.5	41.8	68.9	135.7	268.7	365.3
Private Current Transfers, net	7.7	7.9	7.8	8.3	15.8	13.5	7.9	0.4	12.0	0.4	0.0
Workers' Remittances	..	..	..	..	..	..	..	..	..	..	..
Curr. A/C Bal before Off. Transf.	-122.2	-164.1	-84.9	-11.9	22.4	-238.8	-29.4	-379.2	-732.2	-659.7	-671.8
Net Official Transfers	9.2	7.8	7.5	18.5	15.3	18.8	22.8	35.8	28.9	29.4	30.2
Curr. A/C Bal after Off. Transf.	-113.0	-156.3	-77.4	6.6	37.6	-220.0	-6.6	-343.4	-703.3	-630.3	-641.6
Long-Term Capital, net	110.4	180.6	159.4	77.1	105.2	199.7	157.0	591.0	782.0	566.7	763.0
Direct Investment	88.6	162.1	80.8	52.3	76.8	95.3	-19.9	34.5	48.6	63.4	70.0
Long-Term Loans	21.4	19.9	84.1	29.0	86.1	241.1	159.8	633.2	577.3	572.9	747.8
Disbursements	47.6	53.9	121.3	71.5	176.3	305.2	270.1	760.8	768.1	1,424.8	1,282.7
Repayments	26.2	34.0	37.2	42.5	90.2	64.1	110.3	127.6	190.8	851.9	534.9
Other Long-Term Capital	0.4	-1.3	-5.5	-4.2	-57.7	-136.7	17.1	-76.7	156.1	-69.6	-54.8
Other Capital, net	8.6	-35.7	-13.0	8.5	-33.2	-43.7	23.0	-126.3	-88.4	89.0	124.9
Change in Reserves	-6.0	11.3	-68.9	-92.2	-109.7	64.0	-173.4	-121.3	9.7	-25.4	-246.3
Memo Item:					*(Ecuadoran Sucres per US dollar)*						
Conversion Factor (Annual Avg)	20.920	25.000	25.000	25.000	25.000	25.000	25.000	25.000	25.000	25.000	25.000
				(Millions of US dollars), outstanding at end of year							
EXTERNAL DEBT (Total)	256	270	358	382	471	709	870	2,374	3,976	4,525	5,997
Long-Term Debt (by debtor)	256	270	358	382	471	709	870	1,518	2,778	3,376	4,422
Central Bank, incl. IMF credit	27	19	23	15	17	27	44	69	126	100	101
Central Government	89	99	161	173	136	213	256	608	1,330	1,673	2,125
Rest of General Government	35	38	41	47	58	60	65	97	100	115	135
Non-financial Public Enterprises	47	48	53	60	74	107	175	260	566	600	832
Priv. Sector, incl non-guaranteed	58	65	80	87	185	301	331	485	657	888	1,228
Short-Term Debt	0	0	0	0	0	0	0	856	1,198	1,149	1,575
Memo Items:					*(Millions of US dollars)*						
Int'l Reserves Excluding Gold	55.2	37.1	121.1	210.4	318.6	253.4	477.4	623.1	635.8	722.0	1,013.0
Gold Holdings (at market price)	20.4	23.3	23.1	43.3	72.0	54.1	52.0	66.0	92.0	212.1	244.2
SOCIAL INDICATORS											
Total Fertility Rate	6.3	6.2	6.1	5.9	5.8	5.7	5.5	5.4	5.3	5.2	5.0
Infant Mortality Rate	99.8	97.4	95.0	91.0	87.0	83.0	79.0	75.0	73.0	71.0	69.0
Life Expectancy at Birth	58.1	58.5	58.9	59.4	59.9	60.4	60.9	61.4	62.0	62.6	63.1
Urban Population, % of total	39.5	40.1	40.7	41.2	41.8	42.4	43.3	44.2	45.2	46.1	47.0
Food Prod. per capita (1987=100)	124.3	121.0	113.6	111.4	119.2	116.7	114.7	116.5	109.7	106.7	109.4
Labor Force, Agriculture (%)	50.6	49.3	48.0	46.8	45.6	44.5	43.2	41.9	40.8	39.6	38.6
Labor Force, Female (%)	16.3	16.6	16.9	17.2	17.4	17.7	18.1	18.4	18.7	19.0	19.3
Primary Schl. Enroll. Ratio	97.0	..	..	..	..	104.0	104.0	106.0	108.0	112.0	113.0
Primary Schl. Enroll. Ratio, Female	95.0	..	..	..	..	102.0	102.0	104.0	106.0	109.0	111.0
Secondary Schl. Enroll. Ratio	22.0	..	..	..	..	40.0	..	..	..	49.0	51.0

1981	1982	1983	1984	1985	1986	1987	1988	1989	1990 estimate	Notes	ECUADOR
											FOREIGN TRADE (CUSTOMS BASIS)
				(Millions of current US dollars)							
2,167.9	2,290.8	2,225.6	2,582.5	2,902.8	2,184.2	2,020.7	2,192.5	2,353.8	2,714.3	..	Value of Exports, fob
753.4	749.6	559.7	764.3	1,055.5	1,241.0	1,149.7	1,166.8	1,145.3	1,320.7	..	Nonfuel Primary Products
1,341.7	1,471.9	1,644.5	1,797.4	1,824.7	912.4	817.0	975.7	1,147.5	1,323.2	..	Fuels
72.8	69.3	21.4	20.8	22.7	30.7	54.0	50.0	61.0	70.4	..	Manufactures
1,906.8	1,736.7	1,500.3	1,715.7	1,808.3	1,805.6	1,890.9	1,713.5	1,859.7	1,861.9	..	Value of Imports, cif
178.1	182.0	230.6	309.2	378.8	216.6	210.7	225.3	291.5	291.9	..	Nonfuel Primary Products
250.7	28.1	24.5	26.9	103.1	75.4	31.6	61.7	80.3	80.4	..	Fuels
1,478.1	1,526.6	1,245.1	1,379.6	1,326.4	1,513.6	1,648.5	1,426.5	1,487.8	1,489.6	..	Manufactures
				(Index 1987 = 100)							
165.3	162.2	158.3	156.1	152.7	98.2	100.0	81.7	101.7	108.9		Terms of Trade
145.1	135.8	130.5	127.3	123.8	89.4	100.0	87.6	103.3	121.1		Export Prices, fob
87.8	83.7	82.4	81.5	81.1	91.1	100.0	107.3	101.5	111.2		Import Prices, cif
											BALANCE OF PAYMENTS
				(Millions of current US dollars)							
2,995.0	2,739.0	2,688.0	2,971.0	3,327.0	2,654.0	2,465.0	2,657.0	2,895.0	3,256.0	..	Exports of Goods & Services
2,527.0	2,327.0	2,348.0	2,621.0	2,905.0	2,186.0	2,021.0	2,202.0	2,354.0	2,714.0	..	Merchandise, fob
398.6	386.0	315.0	291.0	393.0	444.0	434.0	446.0	519.0	520.0	..	Nonfactor Services
69.4	26.0	25.0	59.0	29.0	24.0	10.0	9.0	22.0	22.0	..	Factor Services
4,018.0	3,955.0	2,846.0	3,255.0	3,293.0	3,252.0	3,728.0	3,259.0	3,464.0	3,492.0	..	Imports of Goods & Services
2,353.0	2,187.0	1,421.0	1,567.0	1,611.0	1,643.0	2,054.0	1,583.0	1,693.0	1,711.0	..	Merchandise, fob
806.3	722.0	457.0	507.0	594.0	579.0	620.0	586.0	603.0	626.0	..	Nonfactor Services
858.7	1,046.0	968.0	1,181.0	1,088.0	1,030.0	1,054.0	1,090.0	1,168.0	1,155.0	..	Factor Services
539.4	764.7	540.7	842.2	745.1	680.5	259.4	288.0	417.7	413.2	..	Long-Term Interest
0.0	0.0	0.0	0.0	0.0	0.0	0.0	0.0	0.0	..		Private Current Transfers, net
..	..	..	..	..	..	..	..	..	..		Workers' Remittances
-1,023.0	-1,216.0	-158.0	-284.0	34.0	-598.0	-1,263.0	-602.0	-569.0	-236.0	..	Curr. A/C Bal before Off. Transf.
25.0	20.0	24.0	20.0	80.0	45.0	132.0	97.0	97.0	100.0	..	Net Official Transfers
-998.0	-1,196.0	-134.0	-264.0	114.0	-553.0	-1,131.0	-505.0	-472.0	-136.0	..	Curr. A/C Bal after Off. Transf.
1,076.8	164.0	904.0	552.0	518.0	1,576.0	365.0	180.0	466.0	-383.0	..	Long-Term Capital, net
60.0	40.0	50.0	50.0	62.0	70.0	75.0	80.0	80.0	82.0		Direct Investment
1,275.0	-114.1	97.6	630.0	384.8	808.3	368.6	356.1	462.9	164.5		Long-Term Loans
2,080.4	1,060.5	293.9	852.7	656.1	1,183.6	715.8	908.7	927.3	659.7		Disbursements
805.4	1,174.6	196.3	222.7	271.3	375.3	347.2	552.6	464.4	495.2		Repayments
-258.2	238.1	756.4	-128.0	71.2	697.7	-78.6	-256.1	-76.9	-629.5		Other Long-Term Capital
-446.4	586.2	-730.9	-296.1	-502.1	-1,278.5	703.4	388.8	212.6	877.1	..	Other Capital, net
367.6	445.8	-39.1	8.1	-129.9	255.5	62.6	-63.8	-206.6	-358.1	..	Change in Reserves
											Memo Item:
				(Ecuadoran Sucres per US dollar)							Conversion Factor (Annual Avg)
25.000	33.400	52.900	79.500	91.500	122.790	170.460	301.610	526.350	767.750		
				(Millions of US dollars), outstanding at end of year							
7,665	7,705	7,595	8,304	8,703	9,334	10,474	10,745	11,315	12,105	..	**EXTERNAL DEBT (Total)**
5,644	5,514	6,429	7,021	7,713	8,831	9,579	9,552	9,908	10,282	..	Long-Term Debt (by debtor)
119	151	422	500	834	1,135	1,202	1,064	1,051	922	..	Central Bank, incl. IMF credit
2,759	2,487	4,213	5,316	5,752	6,379	7,018	7,420	7,743	8,218	..	Central Government
211	196	185	158	149	147	152	140	185	183	..	Rest of General Government
1,026	992	894	787	804	1,069	1,097	799	763	788	..	Non-financial Public Enterprises
1,530	1,689	715	260	174	101	111	128	166	171	..	Priv. Sector, incl non-guaranteed
2,021	2,191	1,166	1,283	989	503	895	1,194	1,407	1,823	..	Short-Term Debt
				(Millions of US dollars)							**Memo Items:**
632.4	304.2	644.5	611.2	718.2	644.2	491.1	397.6	540.4	838.5	..	Int'l Reserves Excluding Gold
164.7	189.3	158.0	127.7	135.5	161.9	200.5	170.0	166.1	170.6	..	Gold Holdings (at market price)
											SOCIAL INDICATORS
4.9	4.8	4.7	4.5	4.4	4.2	4.1	4.0	3.9	3.7	..	Total Fertility Rate
67.0	65.0	63.6	62.2	60.8	59.4	58.0	56.9	55.8	54.8	..	Infant Mortality Rate
63.7	64.3	64.5	64.8	65.0	65.2	65.4	65.7	65.9	66.1	..	Life Expectancy at Birth
47.9	48.8	49.8	50.7	51.6	52.5	53.4	54.2	55.1	56.0	..	Urban Population, % of total
105.7	104.1	88.1	92.3	100.2	101.8	100.0	106.7	106.0	107.4	..	Food Prod. per capita (1987=100)
..	..	..	..	..	..	..	..	..	..	..	Labor Force, Agriculture (%)
19.3	19.3	19.3	19.3	19.3	19.3	19.3	19.3	19.3	19.3	..	Labor Force, Female (%)
115.0	116.0	117.0	114.0	116.0	118.0	117.0	..	..	..	..	Primary Schl. Enroll. Ratio
113.0	112.0	117.0	..	116.0	117.0	116.0	..	..	..	..	Primary Schl. Enroll. Ratio, Female
53.0	55.0	52.0	55.0	55.0	56.0	56.0	..	..	..	..	Secondary Schl. Enroll. Ratio

EGYPT, ARAB REPUBLIC OF	1970	1971	1972	1973	1974	1975	1976	1977	1978	1979	1980
CURRENT GNP PER CAPITA (US $)	230	250	260	280	280	320	360	410	410	440	500
POPULATION (thousands)	33,053	33,648	34,253	34,886	35,561	36,289	37,080	37,942	38,869	39,850	40,875

USE AND ORIGIN OF RESOURCES *(Millions of current Egyptian Pounds)*

	1970	1971	1972	1973	1974	1975	1976	1977	1978	1979	1980
Gross National Product (GNP)	3,033	3,212	3,363	3,757	4,282	5,107	6,555	8,102	9,358	11,957	15,446
Net Factor Income from Abroad	-26	-29	-26	-49	-57	-111	-172	-242	-437	-748	-1,051
GDP at Market Prices	3,058	3,241	3,390	3,806	4,339	5,218	6,727	8,344	9,795	12,705	16,497
Resource Balance	-140	-165	-196	-197	-726	-1,101	-789	-894	-1,496	-2,364	-2,038
Exports of Goods & NFServices	434	447	452	532	890	1,053	1,498	1,876	2,130	3,777	5,034
Imports of Goods & NFServices	573	612	649	729	1,616	2,154	2,287	2,770	3,626	6,141	7,072
Domestic Absorption	3,198	3,406	3,586	4,003	5,065	6,319	7,516	9,238	11,291	15,069	18,535
Private Consumption, etc.	2,016	2,139	2,259	2,429	3,191	3,280	3,936	5,176	6,178	8,724	11,411
General Gov't Consumption	756	839	909	1,074	899	1,298	1,670	1,628	2,012	2,172	2,585
Gross Domestic Investment	427	429	418	500	975	1,741	1,910	2,434	3,101	4,173	4,539
Fixed Investment	353	363	378	462	685	1,282	1,471	1,873	2,685	3,763	4,062
Indirect Taxes, net	432	449	388	342	142	162	562	810	774	604	757
GDP at factor cost	2,627	2,792	3,002	3,464	4,197	5,056	6,165	7,534	9,021	12,101	15,740
Agriculture	773	814	933	1,062	1,280	1,468	1,744	2,038	2,286	2,530	2,875
Industry	740	787	804	852	1,052	1,360	1,615	2,051	2,583	4,337	5,789
Manufacturing	..	..	..	..	746	880	993	1,120	1,319	1,650	1,928
Services, etc.	1,114	1,191	1,265	1,550	1,865	2,228	2,806	3,445	4,152	5,234	7,076
Gross Domestic Saving	287	263	222	303	249	640	1,121	1,540	1,605	1,809	2,501
Gross National Saving	276	251	243	308	282	707	1,278	1,673	1,878	2,835	3,404

(Millions of 1987 Egyptian Pounds)

	1970	1971	1972	1973	1974	1975	1976	1977	1978	1979	1980
Gross National Product	13,737	14,430	14,804	15,556	16,153	17,635	20,280	22,855	24,269	25,799	28,390
GDP at Market Prices	14,212	14,807	15,191	15,965	16,582	18,258	21,077	23,829	25,659	27,685	30,678
Resource Balance	-3,525	-3,489	-3,655	-4,200	-6,896	-8,234	-6,347	-6,457	-6,872	-9,203	-9,424
Exports of Goods & NFServices	3,477	3,429	3,603	3,422	3,558	4,387	5,595	6,134	6,149	5,931	6,940
Imports of Goods & NFServices	7,002	6,918	7,258	7,622	10,454	12,621	11,942	12,591	13,021	15,134	16,364
Domestic Absorption	17,737	18,296	18,846	20,165	23,478	26,492	27,424	30,286	32,531	36,888	40,102
Private Consumption, etc.	..	..	..	..	16,605	16,627	17,288	20,004	21,222	25,107	28,157
General Gov't Consumption	..	..	..	..	3,367	4,381	4,668	4,116	4,445	4,110	4,383
Gross Domestic Investment	2,004	1,757	1,812	2,381	3,506	5,484	5,468	6,166	6,864	7,671	7,562
Fixed Investment	..	..	..	..	2,306	3,780	3,942	4,441	5,564	6,475	6,335
GDP at factor cost	11,871	12,407	12,956	14,214	14,994	16,617	19,061	21,202	23,220	25,487	28,279
Agriculture	5,368	5,438	5,877	6,052	6,070	6,443	6,532	6,350	6,704	6,978	7,222
Industry	3,806	3,952	3,999	3,930	3,780	4,408	5,064	6,157	7,135	7,772	8,871
Manufacturing	..	..	..	..	..	..	..	..	..	..	..
Services, etc.	3,784	4,056	4,223	5,129	6,045	6,648	8,213	9,175	9,776	11,062	12,354

Memo Items:

	1970	1971	1972	1973	1974	1975	1976	1977	1978	1979	1980
Capacity to Import	5,296	5,050	5,064	5,562	5,757	6,170	7,822	8,527	7,649	9,308	11,649
Terms of Trade Adjustment	1,819	1,621	1,461	2,140	2,199	1,783	2,227	2,393	1,500	3,377	4,709
Gross Domestic Income	16,031	16,429	16,652	18,105	18,781	20,041	23,304	26,223	27,159	31,062	35,387
Gross National Income	15,556	16,051	16,265	17,697	18,353	19,418	22,507	25,248	25,769	29,176	33,099

DOMESTIC PRICES/DEFLATORS *(Index 1987 = 100)*

	1970	1971	1972	1973	1974	1975	1976	1977	1978	1979	1980
Overall (GDP)	21.5	21.9	22.3	23.8	26.2	28.6	31.9	35.0	38.2	45.9	53.8
Domestic Absorption	18.0	18.6	19.0	19.9	21.6	23.9	27.4	30.5	34.7	40.9	46.2
Agriculture	14.4	15.0	15.9	17.6	21.1	22.8	26.7	32.1	34.1	36.3	39.8
Industry	19.4	19.9	20.1	21.7	27.8	30.9	31.9	33.3	36.2	55.8	65.3
Manufacturing	..	..	..	..	..	..	..	..	..	..	..
Consumer Price Index	14.3	14.7	15.0	15.8	17.4	19.1	21.1	23.7	26.4	29.0	35.0

MANUFACTURING ACTIVITY

	1970	1971	1972	1973	1974	1975	1976	1977	1978	1979	1980
Employment (1987=100)	..	..	..	..	..	..	..	..	..	..	..
Real Earnings per Empl. (1987=100)	..	..	..	..	..	..	..	..	..	..	..
Real Output per Empl. (1987=100)	..	..	..	..	..	..	..	..	..	..	..
Earnings as % of Value Added	53.7	50.3	50.5	49.5	42.9	52.8	53.4	48.6	54.8	54.1	57.0

MONETARY HOLDINGS *(Millions of current Egyptian Pounds)*

	1970	1971	1972	1973	1974	1975	1976	1977	1978	1979	1980
Money Supply, Broadly Defined	1,053	1,084	1,255	1,536	2,000	2,430	3,061	4,103	5,212	6,844	10,364
Money	783	846	989	1,205	1,503	1,863	2,239	2,943	3,553	4,354	6,775
Currency Outside Banks	525	559	631	777	948	1,156	1,388	1,749	2,184	2,657	3,398
Demand Deposits	258	288	358	428	555	707	851	1,194	1,369	1,697	3,377
Quasi-Money	270	238	266	331	498	567	822	1,160	1,659	2,490	3,589

GOVERNMENT DEFICIT (-) OR SURPLUS *(Millions of current Egyptian Pounds)*

	1970	1971	1972	1973	1974	1975	1976	1977	1978	1979	1980
	..	..	..	..	..	-938	-1,557	-1,114	-1,246	-1,964	-1,928
Current Revenue	..	..	..	..	..	2,235	2,424	3,301	3,778	4,363	7,271
Current Expenditure	..	..	..	..	..	2,418	2,662	3,209	3,488	4,516	6,519
Current Budget Balance	..	..	..	..	..	-183	-238	92	290	-153	752
Capital Receipts	..	..	..	..	..	54	105	147	42	323	170
Capital Payments	..	..	..	..	..	809	1,424	1,353	1,578	2,134	2,850

1981	1982	1983	1984	1985	1986	1987	1988	1989	1990 estimate	Notes	EGYPT, ARAB REPUBLIC OF
550	600	620	640	660	670	690	660	640	610	A	CURRENT GNP PER CAPITA (US $)
41,943	43,048	44,185	45,342	46,511	47,664	48,798	49,910	50,999	52,061	..	POPULATION (thousands)
				(Millions of current Egyptian Pounds)							USE AND ORIGIN OF RESOURCES
16,088	19,332	22,557	26,585	29,995	34,280	40,782	49,753	60,317	70,530	C	Gross National Product (GNP)
-1,232	-1,449	-1,613	-1,919	-3,136	-4,076	-4,466	-4,800	-5,260	-8,377	..	Net Factor Income from Abroad
17,320	20,781	24,170	28,504	33,132	38,356	45,249	54,553	65,577	78,907	C	GDP at Market Prices
-2,673	-3,096	-2,646	-3,837	-4,018	-3,783	-5,178	-8,736	-11,504	-13,489	..	Resource Balance
5,780	5,618	6,159	6,371	6,598	6,034	8,006	12,944	14,010	18,922	..	Exports of Goods & NFServices
8,453	8,714	8,805	10,208	10,616	9,817	13,184	21,680	25,514	32,411	..	Imports of Goods & NFServices
19,993	23,877	26,816	32,341	37,150	42,139	50,427	63,289	77,081	92,396	..	Domestic Absorption
11,588	13,923	15,712	19,367	22,600	26,706	35,947	42,729	53,623	65,888	..	Private Consumption, etc.
3,294	3,704	4,160	5,140	5,712	6,340	6,330	7,373	8,189	9,232	..	General Gov't Consumption
5,111	6,250	6,944	7,834	8,838	9,093	8,150	13,187	15,269	17,276	..	Gross Domestic Investment
4,702	6,150	7,144	7,634	8,338	8,593	8,050	13,037	15,029	16,916	..	Fixed Investment
768	684	929	1,103	1,180	2,125	3,218	2,499	4,532	6,254	..	Indirect Taxes, net
16,552	20,097	23,241	27,401	31,952	36,231	42,031	52,054	61,045	72,653	C	GDP at factor cost
3,326	3,932	4,564	5,494	6,386	7,531	8,640	10,052	11,345	13,324	..	Agriculture
6,245	6,521	6,970	8,024	9,125	9,715	12,329	15,614	18,053	21,450	..	Industry
2,144	2,670	3,068	3,624	4,316	4,805	..	..	..	..	..	Manufacturing
6,981	9,644	11,707	13,883	16,441	18,985	21,062	26,388	31,647	37,879	..	Services, etc.
2,438	3,154	4,298	3,997	4,820	5,310	2,972	4,451	3,765	3,787	..	Gross Domestic Saving
2,767	3,198	4,919	4,848	4,149	3,331	629	2,036	1,533	1,251	..	Gross National Saving
				(Millions of 1987 Egyptian Pounds)							
29,313	32,633	35,231	37,340	38,492	39,086	40,783	43,082	44,764	44,710	C	Gross National Product
31,894	35,302	38,020	40,336	42,999	44,137	45,249	47,023	48,421	49,652	C	GDP at Market Prices
-10,402	-8,843	-8,341	-10,163	-10,385	-8,085	-5,178	-4,939	-4,755	-4,449	..	Resource Balance
6,838	6,126	6,784	7,199	7,494	7,528	8,006	8,870	9,157	9,644	..	Exports of Goods & NFServices
17,240	14,969	15,125	17,362	17,879	15,613	13,184	13,809	13,912	14,093	..	Imports of Goods & NFServices
42,296	44,145	46,361	50,499	53,384	52,222	50,427	51,962	53,176	54,101	..	Domestic Absorption
28,806	29,744	31,086	33,604	35,609	35,823	35,947	36,976	38,020	38,890	..	Private Consumption, etc.
5,309	5,187	5,711	6,354	6,435	6,481	6,330	6,356	6,528	6,711	..	General Gov't Consumption
8,181	9,214	9,564	10,541	11,340	9,918	8,150	8,630	8,628	8,500	..	Gross Domestic Investment
7,046	8,487	9,223	9,612	10,006	8,721	8,050	8,530	8,490	8,321	..	Fixed Investment
29,421	32,787	35,316	37,468	39,940	40,997	42,031	43,723	45,015	46,102	C	GDP at factor cost
7,349	7,645	7,866	8,031	8,288	8,463	8,640	8,856	9,033	9,187	..	Agriculture
9,196	9,408	10,057	10,990	11,857	12,057	12,329	12,876	12,726	13,291	..	Industry
..	..	..	..	..	..	..	..	..	..	..	Manufacturing
13,005	15,829	17,393	18,447	19,795	20,477	21,062	21,991	23,256	23,624	..	Services, etc.
											Memo Items:
11,788	9,651	10,580	10,836	11,112	9,597	8,006	8,245	7,639	8,228	..	Capacity to Import
4,950	3,525	3,796	3,637	3,618	2,069	0	-625	-1,518	-1,416	..	Terms of Trade Adjustment
36,844	38,827	41,816	43,973	46,617	46,206	45,249	46,398	46,903	48,236	..	Gross Domestic Income
34,264	36,157	39,026	40,977	42,110	41,154	40,783	42,457	43,246	43,294	..	Gross National Income
				(Index 1987 = 100)							DOMESTIC PRICES/DEFLATORS
54.3	58.9	63.6	70.7	77.1	86.9	100.0	116.0	135.4	158.9	..	Overall (GDP)
47.3	54.1	57.8	64.0	69.6	80.7	100.0	121.8	145.0	170.8	..	Domestic Absorption
45.3	51.4	58.0	68.4	77.1	89.0	100.0	113.5	125.6	145.0	..	Agriculture
67.9	69.3	69.3	73.0	77.0	80.6	100.0	121.3	141.9	161.4	..	Industry
..	..	..	..	..	..	..	..	..	..	..	Manufacturing
38.6	44.3	51.4	60.2	67.4	83.5	100.0	117.7	142.7	166.6	..	Consumer Price Index
											MANUFACTURING ACTIVITY
..	..	..	..	..	..	..	..	..	..	..	Employment (1987=100)
..	..	..	..	..	..	..	..	..	..	..	Real Earnings per Empl. (1987=100)
..	..	..	..	..	..	..	..	..	..	..	Real Output per Empl. (1987=100)
63.8	59.4	61.6	59.5	56.0	56.4	..	..	..	..	..	Earnings as % of Value Added
				(Millions of current Egyptian Pounds)							MONETARY HOLDINGS
13,566	17,792	21,817	25,929	30,676	37,102	44,878	54,549	64,093	82,508	..	Money Supply, Broadly Defined
7,646	9,552	10,933	12,443	14,696	15,973	18,241	20,579	22,471	26,205	..	Money
4,291	5,503	6,475	7,097	8,284	8,803	9,537	10,406	10,934	12,410	..	Currency Outside Banks
3,355	4,049	4,457	5,346	6,411	7,170	8,704	10,173	11,537	13,795	..	Demand Deposits
5,920	8,240	10,885	13,486	15,980	21,129	26,637	33,970	41,622	56,303	..	Quasi-Money
				(Millions of current Egyptian Pounds)							
-1,096	-3,554	-2,364	-3,258	-3,439	-4,655	-2,613	-4,716	-4,126	..	C F	GOVERNMENT DEFICIT (-) OR SURPLUS
7,893	9,116	10,714	11,951	13,245	15,214	16,590	19,459	22,348	..	..	Current Revenue
6,333	9,347	9,637	12,519	12,891	15,054	15,008	18,957	20,116	..	..	Current Expenditure
1,560	-231	1,077	-568	354	160	1,582	502	2,232	..	..	Current Budget Balance
188	601	363	395	655	668	1,261	1,005	1,276	..	..	Capital Receipts
2,844	3,924	3,804	3,085	4,448	5,483	5,456	6,223	7,634	..	..	Capital Payments

EGYPT, ARAB REPUBLIC OF	1970	1971	1972	1973	1974	1975	1976	1977	1978	1979	1980
FOREIGN TRADE (CUSTOMS BASIS)					*(Millions of current US dollars)*						
Value of Exports, fob	762	789	825	1,117	1,516	1,402	1,522	1,708	1,737	1,840	3,046
Nonfuel Primary Products	519	562	516	721	988	792	761	866	752	702	756
Fuels	36	7	54	113	129	132	381	413	482	765	1,957
Manufactures	207	220	256	283	399	478	380	429	504	373	334
Value of Imports, cif	787	920	898	914	2,351	3,934	3,862	4,815	6,727	3,837	4,860
Nonfuel Primary Products	274	370	361	372	1,225	1,703	1,344	1,586	2,224	1,256	1,940
Fuels	74	71	60	24	66	272	221	109	101	31	53
Manufactures	439	479	478	518	1,060	1,958	2,296	3,120	4,401	2,550	2,868
					(Index 1987 = 100)						
Terms of Trade	139.5	131.7	125.0	121.6	147.5	135.5	140.6	135.9	112.9	115.9	156.6
Export Prices, fob	29.4	34.0	36.8	56.5	98.9	86.8	88.3	90.8	86.9	105.4	158.2
Import Prices, cif	21.1	25.8	29.5	46.4	67.0	64.1	62.8	66.8	76.9	91.0	101.0
BALANCE OF PAYMENTS					*(Millions of current US dollars)*						
Exports of Goods & Services	962	1,005	1,017	1,304	2,338	2,589	3,391	4,001	4,243	5,707	6,516
Merchandise, fob	817	851	813	1,000	1,818	1,875	2,169	2,346	2,558	3,987	3,854
Nonfactor Services	143	153	203	300	433	628	1,150	1,542	1,541	1,414	2,393
Factor Services	2	1	1	4	87	86	72	113	144	306	270
Imports of Goods & Services	1,447	1,518	1,592	1,986	4,165	5,471	5,596	6,417	7,419	10,156	9,745
Merchandise, fob	1,084	1,131	1,170	1,429	3,618	4,608	4,659	5,110	5,998	7,817	6,814
Nonfactor Services	297	312	352	429	341	533	523	769	614	964	2,343
Factor Services	66	74	69	128	206	330	414	538	807	1,375	588
Long-Term Interest	40	28	46	58	64	105	98	296	369	263	405
Private Current Transfers, net	33	38	110	123	231	456	842	960	1,815	2,534	2,791
Workers' Remittances	29	27	104	117	189	366	755	897	1,761	2,445	2,696
Curr. A/C Bal before Off. Transf.	-452	-474	-465	-559	-1,596	-2,426	-1,363	-1,456	-1,361	-1,915	-438
Net Official Transfers	304	268	290	579	1,261	986	705	382	291	72	2
Curr. A/C Bal after Off. Transf.	-148	-207	-174	20	-335	-1,440	-658	-1,074	-1,070	-1,843	-436
Long-Term Capital, net	2	20	304	204	66	955	1,009	2,499	1,933	2,195	966
Direct Investment	..	..	..	..	87	225	444	477	387	1,375	541
Long-Term Loans	-29	221	42	79	92	2,285	1,055	2,494	1,859	1,946	2,475
Disbursements	199	408	328	487	360	2,513	1,265	2,728	2,107	2,221	2,888
Repayments	227	188	287	408	268	229	211	234	248	274	413
Other Long-Term Capital	31	-201	262	126	-113	-1,555	-490	-472	-313	-1,126	-2,051
Other Capital, net	134	128	-115	-54	90	59	157	-73	113	262	168
Change in Reserves	12	58	-14	-171	179	426	-508	-1,352	-976	-614	-698
Memo Item:					*(Egyptian Pounds per US dollar)*						
Conversion Factor (Annual Avg)	0.400	0.390	0.390	0.400	0.480	0.460	0.500	0.570	0.660	0.700	0.720
					(Millions of US dollars), outstanding at end of year						
EXTERNAL DEBT (Total)	1,567	1,841	1,830	2,069	2,261	4,393	5,616	12,750	14,061	16,402	20,976
Long-Term Debt (by debtor)	1,567	1,841	1,830	2,069	2,261	4,393	5,616	8,463	10,753	12,926	16,948
Central Bank, incl. IMF credit	302	261	246	420	526	1,947	2,430	2,838	3,028	3,062	2,900
Central Government	948	1,230	1,197	1,289	1,271	1,925	2,399	4,390	5,871	7,252	10,744
Rest of General Government	5	13	10	7	5	2	1	14	21	30	67
Non-financial Public Enterprises	312	337	377	351	454	513	761	1,162	1,756	2,396	2,971
Priv. Sector, incl non-guaranteed	0	0	0	1	5	5	26	60	77	187	267
Short-Term Debt	0	0	0	0	0	0	0	4,287	3,308	3,476	4,027
Memo Items:					*(Millions of US dollars)*						
Int'l Reserves Excluding Gold	74.1	57.1	51.5	259.6	251.8	193.9	239.6	430.7	491.7	529.5	1,046.0
Gold Holdings (at market price)	91.0	106.1	157.8	273.0	453.6	341.1	327.7	401.2	558.9	1,265.7	1,433.7
SOCIAL INDICATORS											
Total Fertility Rate	5.9	5.7	5.5	5.5	5.4	5.4	5.3	5.3	5.2	5.1	5.1
Infant Mortality Rate	144.0	145.0	146.0	143.2	140.4	137.6	134.8	132.0	129.4	126.8	124.2
Life Expectancy at Birth	51.1	51.6	52.1	52.5	52.9	53.3	53.7	54.1	54.6	55.1	55.5
Urban Population, % of total	42.2	42.5	42.7	43.0	43.2	43.5	43.6	43.6	43.7	43.7	43.8
Food Prod. per capita (1987=100)	88.9	90.6	89.6	89.7	89.6	90.1	90.4	86.0	85.2	86.2	84.0
Labor Force, Agriculture (%)	52.0	51.3	50.6	50.0	49.4	48.8	48.1	47.5	46.8	46.2	45.7
Labor Force, Female (%)	7.1	7.3	7.4	7.5	7.7	7.8	8.0	8.1	8.3	8.5	8.6
Primary Schl. Enroll. Ratio	72.0	..	..	..	..	71.0	73.0	73.0	74.0	75.0	78.0
Primary Schl. Enroll. Ratio, Female	57.0	..	..	..	..	57.0	57.0	57.0	58.0	61.0	65.0
Secondary Schl. Enroll. Ratio	35.0	..	..	..	..	43.0	45.0	47.0	49.0	50.0	54.0

1981	1982	1983	1984	1985	1986	1987	1988	1989	1990 estimate	Notes	EGYPT, ARAB REPUBLIC OF
											FOREIGN TRADE (CUSTOMS BASIS)
				(Millions of current US dollars)							
3,232	3,120	3,215	3,140	1,838	2,214	2,037	2,120	2,648	2,985	..	Value of Exports, fob
870	795	830	895	400	636	609	668	809	912	..	Nonfuel Primary Products
2,087	2,068	2,005	1,808	1,253	1,134	728	703	807	910	..	Fuels
276	256	380	437	186	444	700	749	1,032	1,164	..	Manufactures
8,839	9,078	10,275	10,766	5,495	8,680	7,596	8,657	7,448	10,340	..	Value of Imports, cif
3,566	3,292	3,220	3,610	1,935	3,116	2,600	3,016	3,056	4,242	..	Nonfuel Primary Products
265	371	584	484	208	296	211	220	171	238	..	Fuels
5,008	5,415	6,471	6,672	3,353	5,268	4,786	5,421	4,220	5,860	..	Manufactures
				(Index 1987 = 100)							
170.8	164.0	160.0	155.0	131.2	95.7	100.0	97.2	81.8	75.4	..	Terms of Trade
169.3	153.4	149.9	143.5	119.3	90.7	100.0	112.5	102.6	120.5	..	Export Prices, fob
99.1	93.5	93.7	92.6	91.0	94.7	100.0	115.7	125.5	157.6	..	Import Prices, cif
				(Millions of current US dollars)							**BALANCE OF PAYMENTS**
6,936	6,806	7,156	7,393	7,433	7,028	6,492	8,189	8,613	9,071	..	Exports of Goods & Services
3,999	3,847	3,740	3,958	3,928	3,576	2,264	3,274	2,914	3,145	..	Merchandise, fob
2,537	2,491	2,943	2,889	2,938	2,917	3,403	3,951	4,324	4,767	..	Nonfactor Services
401	468	474	546	568	534	825	964	1,375	1,159	..	Factor Services
11,303	11,271	11,870	13,854	14,164	13,380	11,379	12,832	14,919	16,549	..	Imports of Goods & Services
7,918	8,418	8,869	10,201	10,516	9,525	7,952	9,841	10,201	11,416	..	Merchandise, fob
2,487	1,714	1,896	2,086	2,091	2,300	2,145	1,848	2,175	2,268	..	Nonfactor Services
898	1,139	1,104	1,567	1,558	1,555	1,282	1,142	2,543	2,865	..	Factor Services
648	654	889	911	998	1,116	574	1,093	1,295	1,143	..	Long-Term Interest
2,230	2,133	3,191	3,956	3,522	2,995	3,033	3,406	3,556	3,768	..	Private Current Transfers, net
2,181	2,082	3,165	3,931	3,496	2,973	3,012	3,384	3,532	3,743	..	Workers' Remittances
-2,136	-2,332	-1,522	-2,504	-3,209	-3,357	-1,854	-1,237	-2,750	-3,710	..	Curr. A/C Bal before Off. Transf.
1	527	601	686	1,097	1,209	974	698	756	1,110	..	Net Official Transfers
-2,135	-1,806	-921	-1,819	-2,112	-2,148	-880	-539	-1,994	-2,600	..	Curr. A/C Bal after Off. Transf.
2,129	2,847	3,064	2,329	2,395	1,840	1,276	1,438	-143	519	..	Long-Term Capital, net
747	885	966	1,275	1,289	1,275	869	973	124	136	..	Direct Investment
2,256	3,715	2,837	2,533	2,491	1,821	1,748	1,722	700	396	..	Long-Term Loans
2,810	4,413	3,667	3,573	3,993	3,125	2,619	3,147	2,444	2,294	..	Disbursements
555	698	830	1,039	1,502	1,305	871	1,425	1,744	1,898	..	Repayments
-874	-1,753	-739	-1,479	-1,386	-1,255	-1,341	-1,257	-967	-13	..	Other Long-Term Capital
175	-980	-1,254	-385	107	721	350	-564	1,993	2,337	..	Other Capital, net
-169	-61	-889	-125	-390	-413	-746	-336	144	-256	..	Change in Reserves
											Memo Item:
				(Egyptian Pounds per US dollar)							
0.740	0.810	0.860	0.930	0.960	1.070	1.270	1.760	1.940	2.230	..	Conversion Factor (Annual Avg)
				(Millions of US dollars), outstanding at end of year							**EXTERNAL DEBT (Total)**
23,897	29,389	32,459	35,501	41,836	46,041	50,783	52,027	51,159	39,885	..	
20,257	24,321	27,252	29,713	35,610	38,834	44,460	45,326	43,513	35,367	..	Long-Term Debt (by debtor)
2,613	2,836	2,880	2,705	2,639	2,728	3,225	3,121	3,706	1,112	..	Central Bank, incl. IMF credit
13,834	16,922	19,178	21,610	26,076	27,887	32,801	33,582	31,139	24,353	..	Central Government
81	89	105	98	112	126	136	122	113	114	..	Rest of General Government
3,405	4,006	4,462	4,720	5,995	7,103	7,139	7,244	7,329	8,600	..	Non-financial Public Enterprises
325	469	627	579	789	990	1,159	1,257	1,227	1,187	..	Priv. Sector, incl non-guaranteed
3,640	5,068	5,207	5,788	6,226	7,207	6,323	6,700	7,646	4,518	..	Short-Term Debt
				(Millions of US dollars)							**Memo Items:**
716.2	698.1	771.1	736.2	792.1	829.0	1,378.3	1,263.4	1,520.1	2,683.6	..	Int'l Reserves Excluding Gold
966.7	1,111.2	927.8	749.8	795.3	950.7	1,177.3	997.7	975.2	936.3	..	Gold Holdings (at market price)
											SOCIAL INDICATORS
5.0	5.0	4.8	4.7	4.6	4.5	4.4	4.3	4.2	4.0	..	Total Fertility Rate
121.6	119.0	109.8	100.6	91.5	82.3	73.1	70.7	68.3	65.9	..	Infant Mortality Rate
56.0	56.5	57.0	57.5	58.0	58.5	59.0	59.4	59.8	60.2	..	Life Expectancy at Birth
43.8	43.8	43.9	43.9	43.9	44.5	45.0	45.6	46.1	46.7	..	Urban Population, % of total
83.6	87.2	89.8	88.7	93.1	96.7	100.0	100.1	97.6	100.5	..	Food Prod. per capita (1987=100)
..	..	..	..	..	..	..	..	..	..	..	Labor Force, Agriculture (%)
8.8	8.9	9.1	9.2	9.3	9.5	9.7	9.8	9.9	10.1	..	Labor Force, Female (%)
..	82.0	84.0	86.0	91.0	88.0	96.0	96.0	97.0	..	..	Primary Schl. Enroll. Ratio
..	70.0	73.0	76.0	82.0	79.0	85.0	88.0	89.0	..	..	Primary Schl. Enroll. Ratio, Female
..	57.0	59.0	60.0	66.0	68.0	69.0	68.0	81.0	..	..	Secondary Schl. Enroll. Ratio

EL SALVADOR	1970	1971	1972	1973	1974	1975	1976	1977	1978	1979	1980
CURRENT GNP PER CAPITA (US $)	290	300	310	330	380	430	500	580	700	760	750
POPULATION (thousands)	3,588	3,696	3,798	3,894	3,989	4,085	4,181	4,278	4,371	4,455	4,525
USE AND ORIGIN OF RESOURCES					*(Millions of current Salvadoran Colones)*						
Gross National Product (GNP)	2,549	2,679	2,855	3,294	3,891	4,412	5,689	7,095	7,562	8,547	8,789
Net Factor Income from Abroad	-22	-25	-27	-37	-53	-66	-17	-72	-130	-60	-128
GDP at Market Prices	2,571	2,704	2,882	3,332	3,944	4,478	5,706	7,167	7,692	8,607	8,917
Resource Balance	8	-50	32	-94	-332	-228	21	62	-713	-15	82
Exports of Goods & NFServices	643	669	842	1,003	1,284	1,485	2,178	2,767	2,328	3,182	3,046
Imports of Goods & NFServices	635	719	810	1,096	1,615	1,713	2,157	2,705	3,041	3,197	2,964
Domestic Absorption	2,563	2,754	2,850	3,425	4,275	4,706	5,685	7,105	8,405	8,622	8,835
Private Consumption, etc.	1,957	2,057	2,135	2,467	2,954	3,214	3,880	4,622	5,575	5,933	6,405
General Gov't Consumption	276	275	308	349	429	501	686	805	996	1,133	1,247
Gross Domestic Investment	331	422	408	609	892	991	1,120	1,679	1,834	1,556	1,183
Fixed Investment	298	359	474	521	719	1,031	1,145	1,520	1,652	1,512	1,210
Indirect Taxes, net	196	199	223	268	329	353	562	848	645	855	642
GDP at factor cost	2,375	2,505	2,659	3,064	3,615	4,125	5,144	6,319	7,047	7,752	8,275
Agriculture	731	729	728	922	999	1,028	1,614	2,374	2,049	2,508	2,480
Industry	600	644	712	769	915	1,115	1,246	1,488	1,664	1,851	1,846
Manufacturing	485	519	563	611	707	831	933	1,047	1,205	1,338	1,339
Services, etc.	1,240	1,331	1,442	1,640	2,030	2,335	2,845	3,305	3,979	4,248	4,591
Gross Domestic Saving	339	372	440	515	561	762	1,140	1,741	1,122	1,541	1,265
Gross National Saving	348	387	435	507	551	760	1,184	1,744	1,104	1,593	1,181
					(Millions of 1987 Salvadoran Colones)						
Gross National Product	17,939.2	18,794.9	19,797.1	20,731.0	22,049.6	23,204.5	24,324.0	25,523.1	27,072.3	26,913.1	24,452.6
GDP at Market Prices	17,787.6	18,644.1	19,643.9	20,613.7	21,954.9	23,128.6	23,989.8	25,388.7	27,083.1	26,650.2	24,389.0
Resource Balance	-1,330.7	-1,487.2	-1,263.0	-2,476.5	-2,421.7	-1,513.9	-3,218.7	-6,181.8	-5,616.2	-3,170.5	-1,835.2
Exports of Goods & NFServices	3,520.7	3,827.2	4,485.7	4,314.5	4,601.7	5,157.4	4,670.0	4,122.6	4,968.3	6,764.5	5,782.2
Imports of Goods & NFServices	4,851.3	5,314.3	5,748.8	6,791.0	7,023.4	6,671.3	7,888.7	10,304.4	10,584.5	9,935.0	7,617.3
Domestic Absorption	19,118.3	20,131.3	20,906.9	23,090.2	24,376.5	24,642.6	27,208.5	31,570.5	32,699.4	29,820.8	26,224.2
Private Consumption, etc.	15,361.1	15,981.7	16,683.9	17,918.9	18,419.9	18,951.9	20,811.6	23,261.4	23,956.6	22,408.8	20,469.2
General Gov't Consumption	1,520.2	1,431.3	1,679.3	1,872.8	1,800.3	1,958.1	2,266.1	2,379.2	2,640.5	2,705.8	2,555.2
Gross Domestic Investment	2,237.0	2,718.4	2,543.7	3,298.4	4,156.4	3,732.5	4,130.8	5,929.9	6,102.2	4,706.2	3,199.8
Fixed Investment	1,968.6	2,231.6	2,932.3	2,667.8	3,051.7	3,945.5	4,066.4	5,148.7	5,285.5	4,459.3	3,209.8
GDP at factor cost	..	..	..	..	..	..	..	..	..	..	..
Agriculture	2,730.4	2,832.7	2,874.5	2,925.4	3,225.0	3,427.4	3,157.0	3,270.7	3,729.1	3,862.7	3,661.6
Industry	3,775.8	4,069.3	4,381.2	4,579.4	4,847.5	5,354.8	5,666.1	6,240.0	6,436.8	6,254.4	5,534.5
Manufacturing	3,258.9	3,486.4	3,620.2	3,879.7	4,105.8	4,297.6	4,673.8	4,918.4	5,141.5	4,883.5	4,358.6
Services, etc.	11,281.4	11,742.1	12,388.1	13,108.9	13,882.4	14,346.4	15,166.6	15,878.0	16,917.3	16,533.1	15,193.0
Memo Items:											
Capacity to Import	4,912.5	4,943.3	5,974.4	6,210.7	5,581.7	5,783.1	7,964.8	10,539.8	8,104.0	9,889.3	7,827.3
Terms of Trade Adjustment	1,391.8	1,116.2	1,488.7	1,896.2	980.0	625.7	3,294.8	6,417.2	3,135.8	3,124.9	2,045.1
Gross Domestic Income	19,179.5	19,760.3	21,132.6	22,509.9	22,934.9	23,754.4	27,284.5	31,805.9	30,218.9	29,775.1	26,434.1
Gross National Income	19,331.1	19,911.1	21,285.8	22,627.2	23,029.6	23,830.2	27,618.7	31,940.3	30,208.0	30,037.9	26,497.7
DOMESTIC PRICES/DEFLATORS					*(Index 1987 = 100)*						
Overall (GDP)	14.5	14.5	14.7	16.2	18.0	19.4	23.8	28.2	28.4	32.3	36.6
Domestic Absorption	13.4	13.7	13.6	14.8	17.5	19.1	20.9	22.5	25.7	28.9	33.7
Agriculture	26.8	25.7	25.3	31.5	31.0	30.0	51.1	72.6	54.9	64.9	67.7
Industry	15.9	15.8	16.3	16.8	18.9	20.8	22.0	23.9	25.9	29.6	33.3
Manufacturing	14.9	14.9	15.5	15.7	17.2	19.3	20.0	21.3	23.4	27.4	30.7
Consumer Price Index	11.1	11.2	11.3	12.1	14.1	16.8	18.0	20.1	22.8	26.1	30.6
MANUFACTURING ACTIVITY											
Employment (1987=100)	..	..	..	..	..	..	..	..	..	..	..
Real Earnings per Empl. (1987=100)	..	..	..	..	..	..	..	..	..	..	..
Real Output per Empl. (1987=100)	..	..	..	..	..	..	..	..	..	..	..
Earnings as % of Value Added	28.0	25.3	23.3	24.6	23.3	22.6	22.5	19.2	25.2	29.0	31.4
MONETARY HOLDINGS					*(Millions of current Salvadoran Colones)*						
Money Supply, Broadly Defined	595.5	658.2	807.1	957.6	1,116.3	1,352.7	1,770.4	2,003.6	2,241.4	2,445.7	2,563.2
Money	295.3	315.4	389.6	466.0	556.6	648.1	916.7	988.3	1,086.9	1,320.9	1,428.5
Currency Outside Banks	136.1	145.2	174.9	201.1	240.6	252.9	379.6	432.0	500.5	743.0	718.7
Demand Deposits	159.2	170.2	214.7	264.9	316.0	395.3	537.1	556.3	586.4	578.0	709.9
Quasi-Money	300.2	342.8	417.5	491.5	559.7	704.6	853.7	1,015.3	1,154.4	1,124.8	1,134.7
					(Millions of current Salvadoran Colones)						
GOVERNMENT DEFICIT (-) OR SURPLUS	..	-18.9	..	..	..	..	..	..	..	..	..
Current Revenue	..	336.4	..	..	..	..	..	..	..	..	..
Current Expenditure	..	278.1	..	..	..	..	..	..	..	..	..
Current Budget Balance	..	58.3	..	..	..	..	..	..	..	..	..
Capital Receipts	..	..	..	..	..	..	..	..	..	..	..
Capital Payments	..	77.2	..	..	..	..	..	..	..	..	..

1981	1982	1983	1984	1985	1986	1987	1988	1989	1990 estimate	Notes	EL SALVADOR
750	740	760	820	840	830	860	970	1,070	1,110	A	**CURRENT GNP PER CAPITA (US $)**
4,582	4,626	4,664	4,709	4,767	4,846	4,934	5,008	5,107	5,213	..	POPULATION (thousands)
			(Millions of current Salvadoran Colones)								**USE AND ORIGIN OF RESOURCES**
8,427	8,660	9,795	11,251	13,834	19,128	22,778	26,856	31,551	40,114	..	Gross National Product (GNP)
-219	-306	-357	-406	-497	-635	-363	-510	-679	-943	..	Net Factor Income from Abroad
8,647	8,966	10,152	11,657	14,331	19,763	23,141	27,366	32,230	41,057	..	GDP at Market Prices
-527	-454	-550	-791	-1,084	-630	-1,645	-1,772	-3,369	-4,584	..	Resource Balance
2,383	2,188	2,486	2,536	3,199	5,130	4,395	4,327	4,267	6,528	..	Exports of Goods & NFServices
2,909	2,642	3,036	3,327	4,283	5,760	6,040	6,099	7,636	11,113	..	Imports of Goods & NFServices
9,173	9,420	10,702	12,448	15,415	20,393	24,786	29,138	35,599	45,641	..	Domestic Absorption
6,574	6,821	7,871	9,184	11,640	15,392	18,744	22,151	26,729	36,141	..	Private Consumption, etc.
1,369	1,414	1,607	1,869	2,220	2,382	3,181	3,484	3,930	4,649	..	General Gov't Consumption
1,231	1,185	1,224	1,394	1,554	2,619	2,860	3,503	4,940	4,851	..	Gross Domestic Investment
1,173	1,131	1,180	1,336	1,723	2,619	3,152	3,417	4,293	4,834	..	Fixed Investment
661	..	..	..	..	..	..	..	..	..	..	Indirect Taxes, net
7,986	..	..	..	..	..	..	..	..	..	B	GDP at factor cost
2,106	2,075	2,160	2,320	2,611	3,996	3,198	3,801	3,767	4,599	..	Agriculture
1,847	1,896	2,175	2,492	3,139	4,051	5,252	5,670	6,879	8,784	..	Industry
1,359	1,382	1,572	1,837	2,346	3,059	4,045	4,808	5,836	7,647	..	Manufacturing
4,693	4,995	5,817	6,846	8,582	11,716	14,690	17,895	21,584	27,674	..	Services, etc.
704	731	673	604	471	1,989	1,215	1,731	1,571	266	..	Gross Domestic Saving
583	646	560	493	297	2,080	1,754	2,231	2,075	1,689	..	Gross National Saving
			(Millions of 1987 Salvadoran Colones)								
22,236.2	20,829.6	20,952.8	21,423.7	21,931.0	22,156.8	22,777.6	23,645.4	23,863.4	24,578.7	..	Gross National Product
22,395.2	21,159.2	21,294.8	21,772.5	22,284.7	22,518.7	23,140.6	23,854.0	24,095.1	24,821.8	..	GDP at Market Prices
-1,876.1	-1,512.4	-1,166.4	-1,503.5	-1,716.8	-2,107.6	-1,645.5	-2,026.2	-2,930.1	-1,435.5	..	Resource Balance
4,922.7	4,349.0	4,866.8	4,652.8	4,473.3	3,910.0	4,394.6	3,981.8	3,444.7	4,962.7	..	Exports of Goods & NFServices
6,798.8	5,861.5	6,033.2	6,156.3	6,190.1	6,017.6	6,040.1	6,008.0	6,374.8	6,398.2	..	Imports of Goods & NFServices
24,271.3	22,671.7	22,461.2	23,276.0	24,001.5	24,626.3	24,786.1	25,880.2	27,025.2	26,257.2	..	Domestic Absorption
18,549.6	17,254.4	17,272.5	17,883.8	18,566.6	18,551.3	18,744.3	19,229.6	19,528.3	19,978.5	..	Private Consumption, etc.
2,645.3	2,637.5	2,660.5	2,788.7	2,977.4	3,088.7	3,181.3	3,260.5	3,222.4	3,252.1	..	General Gov't Consumption
3,076.4	2,779.7	2,528.2	2,603.5	2,457.5	2,986.3	2,860.5	3,390.1	4,274.4	3,026.7	..	Gross Domestic Investment
2,863.2	2,591.8	2,382.8	2,438.3	2,686.8	2,889.0	3,152.0	3,226.5	3,564.7	2,949.1	..	Fixed Investment
..	..	..	..	..	..	..	..	..	..	B	GDP at factor cost
3,428.3	3,267.6	3,164.0	3,269.4	3,230.2	3,133.5	3,198.4	3,167.9	3,182.7	3,419.5	..	Agriculture
4,974.3	4,626.7	4,739.1	4,766.6	4,959.2	5,088.8	5,252.0	4,628.1	4,768.6	4,781.6	..	Industry
3,903.5	3,575.6	3,647.0	3,694.6	3,832.9	3,928.1	4,044.8	..	..	..	..	Manufacturing
13,992.6	13,264.9	13,391.6	13,736.6	14,095.3	14,296.4	14,690.2	16,058.0	16,143.7	16,620.6	..	Services, etc.
											Memo Items:
5,567.7	4,854.2	4,939.7	4,693.0	4,623.7	5,359.4	4,394.6	4,262.5	3,562.1	3,758.8	..	Capacity to Import
645.0	505.2	72.9	40.2	150.4	1,449.4	0.0	280.7	117.4	-1,204.0	..	Terms of Trade Adjustment
23,040.2	21,664.4	21,367.7	21,812.7	22,435.2	23,968.1	23,140.6	24,134.7	24,212.5	23,617.8	..	Gross Domestic Income
22,881.2	21,334.8	21,025.7	21,463.9	22,081.4	23,606.2	22,777.6	23,926.1	23,980.8	23,374.7	..	Gross National Income
			(Index 1987 = 100)								**DOMESTIC PRICES/DEFLATORS**
38.6	42.4	47.7	53.5	64.3	87.8	100.0	114.7	133.8	165.4	..	Overall (GDP)
37.8	41.5	47.6	53.5	64.2	82.8	100.0	112.6	131.7	173.8	..	Domestic Absorption
61.4	63.5	68.3	71.0	80.8	127.5	100.0	120.0	118.4	134.5	..	Agriculture
37.1	41.0	45.9	52.3	63.3	79.6	100.0	122.5	144.3	183.7	..	Industry
34.8	38.6	43.1	49.7	61.2	77.9	100.0	..	..	..	..	Manufacturing
35.1	39.3	44.5	49.6	60.7	80.1	100.0	119.8	140.9	174.7	..	Consumer Price Index
											MANUFACTURING ACTIVITY
..	..	..	..	..	..	..	..	..	..	G J	Employment (1987=100)
..	..	..	..	..	..	..	..	..	..	G J	Real Earnings per Empl. (1987=100)
..	..	..	..	..	..	..	..	..	..	G J	Real Output per Empl. (1987=100)
30.1	25.3	21.9	21.3	19.5						J	Earnings as % of Value Added
			(Millions of current Salvadoran Colones)								**MONETARY HOLDINGS**
2,834.1	3,232.5	3,575.3	4,235.5	5,374.4	6,904.5	7,371.0	8,218.7	9,130.2	12,019.8	..	Money Supply, Broadly Defined
1,437.2	1,633.0	1,595.9	1,830.4	2,306.3	2,757.7	2,762.4	2,996.2	3,370.3	4,153.0	..	Money
703.0	731.9	724.4	836.3	1,079.8	1,156.5	1,298.0	1,326.2	1,727.1	1,856.2	..	Currency Outside Banks
734.1	901.1	871.5	994.1	1,226.5	1,601.2	1,464.4	1,670.0	1,643.2	2,296.8	..	Demand Deposits
1,397.0	1,599.5	1,979.4	2,405.1	3,068.1	4,146.8	4,608.6	5,222.5	5,759.9	7,866.8	..	Quasi-Money
			(Millions of current Salvadoran Colones)								
..	..	..	..	..	..	..	..	..	..		**GOVERNMENT DEFICIT (-) OR SURPLUS**
..	..	..	..	..	..	..	..	..	..	..	Current Revenue
..	..	..	..	..	..	..	..	..	..	..	Current Expenditure
..	..	..	..	..	..	..	..	..	..	..	Current Budget Balance
..	..	..	..	..	..	..	..	..	..	..	Capital Receipts
..	..	..	..	..	..	..	..	..	..	..	Capital Payments

EL SALVADOR	1970	1971	1972	1973	1974	1975	1976	1977	1978	1979	1980
FOREIGN TRADE (CUSTOMS BASIS)	*(Millions of current US dollars)*										
Value of Exports, fob	228.3	228.4	277.3	358.3	462.5	513.4	720.7	972.8	801.0	1,031.7	1,073.6
Nonfuel Primary Products	161.8	153.9	192.7	247.0	318.1	368.5	540.8	770.5	634.4	771.7	850.3
Fuels	1.1	1.1	1.6	1.9	3.9	6.3	6.0	6.6	5.6	8.7	7.4
Manufactures	65.5	73.4	83.0	109.3	140.5	138.5	173.9	195.6	161.0	251.3	215.9
Value of Imports, cif	213.6	247.4	278.1	373.8	563.4	598.0	717.9	942.5	1,023.9	1,012.0	975.9
Nonfuel Primary Products	38.9	41.0	42.2	63.1	88.6	94.5	110.1	135.5	158.9	173.6	210.2
Fuels	5.2	13.1	12.8	21.5	52.4	50.3	52.6	92.3	80.1	95.4	173.2
Manufactures	169.4	193.4	223.1	289.2	422.4	453.2	555.2	714.7	785.0	743.0	592.5
	(Index 1987 = 100)										
Terms of Trade	145.9	145.7	138.9	151.2	124.9	109.4	172.0	217.1	153.9	150.0	131.1
Export Prices, fob	40.2	38.2	41.5	54.3	64.9	61.2	98.1	132.1	106.7	122.3	121.8
Import Prices, cif	27.5	26.2	29.9	35.9	52.0	56.0	57.0	60.8	69.4	81.5	92.9
BALANCE OF PAYMENTS	*(Millions of current US dollars)*										
Exports of Goods & Services	260.5	271.4	339.3	402.3	518.7	600.0	899.6	1,126.4	959.6	1,355.7	1,270.8
Merchandise, fob	236.1	243.9	301.7	358.4	464.5	533.0	744.6	973.5	801.6	1,132.3	1,075.3
Nonfactor Services	19.8	23.7	34.1	39.6	49.2	60.3	117.4	115.1	121.4	133.5	140.1
Factor Services	4.6	3.8	3.5	4.4	5.1	6.7	37.6	37.8	36.6	89.9	55.4
Imports of Goods & Services	266.1	302.9	339.0	459.8	671.2	720.4	905.2	1,135.1	1,296.8	1,385.7	1,289.1
Merchandise, fob	194.7	226.0	249.7	339.8	522.2	550.7	681.0	861.0	951.1	954.7	897.0
Nonfactor Services	57.2	62.5	73.1	99.5	109.2	122.6	171.4	208.6	256.8	300.6	273.5
Factor Services	14.2	14.4	16.2	20.5	39.8	47.0	52.8	65.5	88.8	130.3	118.6
Long-Term Interest	9.1	9.6	10.9	14.6	16.9	18.8	26.3	31.3	37.0	41.2	35.5
Private Current Transfers, net	12.4	16.1	8.9	11.8	17.2	25.1	24.4	30.4	44.9	44.9	17.4
Workers' Remittances	..	..	..	..	..	..	..	33.6	45.3	49.2	10.9
Curr. A/C Bal before Off. Transf.	6.8	-15.3	9.2	-45.7	-135.3	-95.2	18.8	21.6	-292.3	14.9	-1.0
Net Official Transfers	1.9	1.1	3.1	1.8	1.1	2.3	4.8	9.2	6.5	6.5	31.6
Curr. A/C Bal after Off. Transf.	8.7	-14.2	12.4	-43.9	-134.2	-92.9	23.6	30.8	-285.8	21.4	30.6
Long-Term Capital, net	6.0	21.1	62.2	37.0	193.1	138.7	72.7	38.3	175.7	78.4	148.4
Direct Investment	3.7	7.0	6.6	6.0	20.1	13.1	12.9	18.6	23.4	-10.0	5.9
Long-Term Loans	9.2	18.9	46.7	3.3	94.1	52.3	73.5	41.9	74.0	27.1	74.4
Disbursements	31.3	48.5	73.9	46.5	140.5	132.1	134.7	136.5	134.6	90.0	109.5
Repayments	22.1	29.6	27.2	43.2	46.4	79.8	61.2	94.6	60.6	62.9	35.1
Other Long-Term Capital	-6.9	-4.9	8.9	27.7	79.0	73.2	-13.7	-22.3	78.3	61.2	68.2
Other Capital, net	-12.5	-13.9	-59.6	-3.5	-44.2	-16.1	-12.0	-28.2	165.6	-233.6	-259.9
Change in Reserves	-2.2	7.1	-15.0	10.4	-14.7	-29.7	-84.3	-40.9	-55.4	133.8	80.9
Memo Item:	*(Salvadoran Colones per US dollar)*										
Conversion Factor (Annual Avg)	2.500	2.500	2.500	2.500	2.500	2.500	2.500	2.500	2.500	2.500	2.500
	(Millions of US dollars), outstanding at end of year										
EXTERNAL DEBT (Total)	182.6	206.1	252.0	244.3	360.3	412.2	480.4	723.4	910.1	886.4	911.2
Long-Term Debt (by debtor)	182.6	206.1	252.0	244.3	360.3	412.2	480.4	507.4	581.1	608.4	691.2
Central Bank, incl. IMF credit	31.0	36.0	37.6	18.3	100.3	79.4	59.0	58.3	71.6	88.4	138.3
Central Government	34.4	38.9	53.6	60.7	62.4	68.8	83.8	104.2	147.9	200.1	254.7
Rest of General Government	..	..	..	..	..	..	..	..	..	..	..
Non-financial Public Enterprises	28.9	28.8	27.4	27.7	34.9	68.5	133.2	97.0	100.5	105.3	122.5
Priv. Sector, incl non-guaranteed	88.3	102.4	133.4	137.6	162.7	195.5	204.4	247.9	261.1	214.6	175.7
Short-Term Debt	0.0	0.0	0.0	0.0	0.0	0.0	0.0	216.0	329.0	278.0	220.0
Memo Items:	*(Millions of US dollars)*										
Int'l Reserves Excluding Gold	45.4	46.2	63.9	41.3	77.6	107.0	185.4	211.3	268.1	142.6	77.7
Gold Holdings (at market price)	18.5	21.5	31.5	54.5	90.6	68.1	65.5	82.6	113.2	260.2	304.0
SOCIAL INDICATORS											
Total Fertility Rate	6.3	6.2	6.1	6.0	5.9	5.9	5.8	5.7	5.6	5.5	5.4
Infant Mortality Rate	103.0	100.0	97.0	94.0	91.0	88.0	85.0	82.0	79.6	77.2	74.8
Life Expectancy at Birth	57.6	58.2	58.7	58.5	58.2	57.9	57.7	57.4	57.4	57.3	57.3
Urban Population, % of total	39.4	39.6	39.8	40.0	40.2	40.4	40.6	40.8	41.1	41.3	41.5
Food Prod. per capita (1987=100)	100.7	103.1	96.3	106.4	107.0	113.3	113.3	109.5	121.2	119.3	111.0
Labor Force, Agriculture (%)	56.0	54.5	53.1	51.8	50.6	49.4	48.0	46.7	45.5	44.3	43.2
Labor Force, Female (%)	20.4	20.9	21.4	21.8	22.2	22.6	23.1	23.6	24.1	24.5	24.9
Primary Schl. Enroll. Ratio	85.0	..	..	..	..	75.0	..	76.0	78.0	79.0	75.0
Primary Schl. Enroll. Ratio, Female	83.0	..	..	..	..	74.0	..	76.0	77.0	79.0	75.0
Secondary Schl. Enroll. Ratio	22.0	..	..	..	..	19.0	21.0	23.0	25.0	26.0	24.0

1981	1982	1983	1984	1985	1986	1987	1988	1989	1990 estimate	Notes	EL SALVADOR
				(Millions of current US dollars)							**FOREIGN TRADE (CUSTOMS BASIS)**
796.7	699.4	844.1	615.0	610.9	706.3	612.7	608.8	497.2	550.0	..	Value of Exports, fob
468.2	399.5	605.9	445.5	438.3	594.9	466.2	463.2	378.3	418.5	..	Nonfuel Primary Products
21.3	12.4	7.2	16.6	15.4	7.7	7.9	7.8	6.4	7.1	..	Fuels
307.2	287.5	231.0	153.0	157.3	103.6	138.6	137.8	112.5	124.5	..	Manufactures
1,044.5	944.8	818.5	1,314.0	1,104.5	924.2	987.2	1,007.0	1,151.6	1,200.0	..	Value of Imports, cif
214.2	200.0	198.9	208.5	209.6	154.6	190.6	194.5	222.4	231.7	..	Nonfuel Primary Products
218.0	232.5	76.4	497.1	268.5	204.5	113.0	115.2	131.8	137.3	..	Fuels
612.4	512.4	543.1	608.4	626.5	565.0	683.6	697.3	797.4	830.9	..	Manufactures
				(Index 1987 = 100)							
111.3	119.0	119.3	128.1	126.2	148.1	100.0	113.2	114.5	..	..	Terms of Trade
105.6	108.4	105.0	109.8	107.4	136.0	100.0	115.5	123.1	..	..	Export Prices, fob
94.9	91.1	88.0	85.7	85.1	91.8	100.0	102.1	107.5	..	..	Import Prices, cif
				(Millions of current US dollars)							**BALANCE OF PAYMENTS**
970.2	867.8	930.8	954.2	951.4	1,055.9	950.7	962.8	803.0	903.4	f	Exports of Goods & Services
798.0	699.6	758.0	725.9	679.0	777.9	589.6	610.6	497.5	580.2	..	Merchandise, fob
126.4	118.5	137.8	167.7	226.7	245.2	320.2	331.5	288.0	304.6	..	Nonfactor Services
45.8	49.8	35.0	60.6	45.7	32.7	40.9	20.6	17.5	18.6	..	Factor Services
1,281.0	1,195.0	1,230.3	1,315.3	1,323.6	1,322.3	1,353.7	1,437.6	1,506.0	1,609.2	f	Imports of Goods & Services
898.4	799.8	832.2	914.5	895.0	902.3	938.7	966.5	1,079.8	1,180.0	..	Merchandise, fob
262.6	250.3	242.0	238.9	289.4	278.7	278.5	338.0	287.4	286.5	..	Nonfactor Services
120.0	144.9	156.0	161.9	139.3	141.3	136.5	133.0	138.8	142.7	..	Factor Services
39.0	44.0	69.4	78.4	81.2	80.7	82.9	72.7	60.6	74.9	..	Long-Term Interest
39.2	88.4	97.4	118.0	129.4	149.6	180.5	202.1	236.8	345.4	..	Private Current Transfers, net
42.2	77.7	92.5	114.2	126.2	138.6	167.4	194.4	225.0	346.0	..	Workers' Remittances
-271.6	-238.8	-202.1	-243.1	-242.9	-116.9	-222.6	-272.7	-466.2	-360.4	..	Curr. A/C Bal before Off. Transf.
21.2	119.0	174.1	189.6	214.2	233.7	358.4	298.5	282.4	223.2	..	Net Official Transfers
-250.4	-119.8	-28.0	-53.5	-28.7	116.9	135.8	25.8	-183.8	-137.2	..	Curr. A/C Bal after Off. Transf.
185.5	189.3	316.7	83.8	99.4	66.1	-36.7	29.2	217.1	-15.8	f	Long-Term Capital, net
-5.7	-1.0	28.1	12.4	12.4	24.1	18.3	17.0	14.4	..	..	Direct Investment
201.4	249.3	270.9	147.4	68.9	3.8	6.6	29.4	139.9	-15.7	..	Long-Term Loans
239.0	303.9	378.9	278.3	206.3	139.4	131.2	143.0	236.3	109.0	..	Disbursements
37.6	54.6	108.0	130.9	137.4	135.6	124.6	113.6	96.4	124.7	..	Repayments
-10.2	-59.0	17.7	-75.9	18.1	38.2	-61.6	-17.2	62.8	-0.1	..	Other Long-Term Capital
-19.2	-62.1	-259.5	-37.2	-49.7	-124.5	-20.9	-79.8	3.0	275.4	f	Other Capital, net
84.2	-7.4	-29.3	6.9	-21.0	-58.4	-78.2	24.8	-36.3	-122.4	..	Change in Reserves
				(Salvadoran Colones per US dollar)							**Memo Item:**
2.500	2.570	2.730	2.820	3.670	5.000	5.000	5.000	5.600	7.600	..	Conversion Factor (Annual Avg)
				(Millions of US dollars), outstanding at end of year							
1,130.1	1,442.4	1,739.9	1,826.0	1,854.4	1,850.3	1,975.5	1,986.8	2,070.5	2,132.5	..	**EXTERNAL DEBT (Total)**
918.1	1,236.4	1,645.9	1,715.0	1,770.8	1,723.4	1,761.2	1,743.5	1,862.8	1,923.8	..	Long-Term Debt (by debtor)
242.4	383.4	594.2	583.3	511.5	405.8	352.4	294.8	303.3	273.3	..	Central Bank, incl. IMF credit
386.2	564.9	771.3	889.2	1,008.6	1,076.5	1,160.3	1,225.6	1,363.7	1,445.5	..	Central Government
..	..	..	..	..	..	..	..	..	..	..	Rest of General Government
125.2	136.4	138.8	107.4	116.6	115.1	125.3	116.1	106.2	127.0	..	Non-financial Public Enterprises
164.3	151.7	141.6	135.1	134.1	126.0	123.2	107.0	89.6	78.0	..	Priv. Sector, incl non-guaranteed
212.0	206.0	94.0	111.0	83.6	126.9	214.3	243.3	207.7	208.7	..	Short-Term Debt
				(Millions of US dollars)							**Memo Items:**
71.9	108.5	160.2	165.8	179.6	169.7	186.1	161.6	265.9	414.8	..	Int'l Reserves Excluding Gold
205.0	235.6	178.8	144.7	153.4	183.4	227.1	192.5	188.2	180.6	..	Gold Holdings (at market price)
											SOCIAL INDICATORS
5.3	5.2	5.1	5.0	4.8	4.7	4.6	4.5	4.4	4.2	..	Total Fertility Rate
72.4	70.0	67.8	65.6	63.4	61.2	59.0	57.0	55.0	52.9	..	Infant Mortality Rate
57.2	57.2	58.2	59.2	60.1	61.1	62.1	62.6	63.1	63.6	..	Life Expectancy at Birth
41.7	42.0	42.2	42.5	42.7	43.0	43.4	43.7	44.1	44.4	..	Urban Population, % of total
101.7	94.6	97.1	108.1	106.1	108.1	100.0	106.4	108.6	106.7	..	Food Prod. per capita (1987=100)
..	..	..	..	..	..	..	..	..	..	..	Labor Force, Agriculture (%)
24.9	25.0	25.0	25.0	25.1	25.1	25.1	25.1	25.1	25.1	..	Labor Force, Female (%)
..	..	73.0	74.0	..	..	79.0	80.0	78.0	..	..	Primary Schl. Enroll. Ratio
..	..	73.0	75.0	..	..	81.0	81.0	78.0	..	..	Primary Schl. Enroll. Ratio, Female
..	23.0	26.0	27.0	..	..	29.0	29.0	26.0	..	..	Secondary Schl. Enroll. Ratio

EQUATORIAL GUINEA	1970	1971	1972	1973	1974	1975	1976	1977	1978	1979	1980
CURRENT GNP PER CAPITA (US $)	..							..	..	..	..
POPULATION (thousands)	288	293	297	302	308	313	318	324	330	335	341
USE AND ORIGIN OF RESOURCES					*(Millions of current CFA Francs)*						
Gross National Product (GNP)	4,680	4,541	4,194	4,743	5,453	6,010	6,961	7,929	..	..	..
Net Factor Income from Abroad	37	29	-11	12	21	23	27	30	..	..	..
GDP at Market Prices	4,643	4,512	4,205	4,731	5,432	5,987	6,935	7,899	..	..	..
Resource Balance	-436	-136	-403	-720	-896	-469	-380	-447	..	..	..
Exports of Goods & NFServices	1,658	2,096	1,463	1,814	2,300	2,573	3,259	3,713	..	..	..
Imports of Goods & NFServices	2,094	2,233	1,866	2,533	3,196	3,042	3,640	4,161	..	..	..
Domestic Absorption	5,079	4,648	4,608	5,450	6,328	6,456	7,315	8,346	..	..	..
Private Consumption, etc.	3,125	2,693	2,679	3,397	4,108	3,927	4,414	5,000	..	..	..
General Gov't Consumption	1,031	1,035	1,053	1,201	1,316	1,632	1,988	2,281	..	..	..
Gross Domestic Investment	923	920	876	853	904	897	913	1,065	..	..	..
Fixed Investment	..	..	..	..	..	..	..	..	..	..	..
Indirect Taxes, net	..	..	..	..	..	..	..	..	..	..	..
GDP at factor cost	4,293	4,174	3,890	4,376	4,942	..	..	..	..	..	..
Agriculture	..	..	..	..	..	..	..	..	..	..	..
Industry	..	..	..	..	..	..	..	..	..	..	..
Manufacturing	..	..	..	..	..	..	.	..	..	..	..
Services, etc.	..	..	..	..	..	..	..	..	..	..	..
Gross Domestic Saving	487	784	473	134	7	428	533	618	..	..	..
Gross National Saving	386	712	373	137	..	..	..	..	..	..	..
Gross National Product	..	..	..	..	..	..	..	..	..	..	..
GDP at Market Prices	..	..	..	..	..	..	..	..	..	..	..
Resource Balance	..	..	..	..	..	..	..	..	..	..	..
Exports of Goods & NFServices	..	..	..	..	..	..	..	..	..	..	..
Imports of Goods & NFServices	..	..	..	..	..	..	..	..	..	..	..
Domestic Absorption	..	..	..	..	..	..	..	..	..	..	..
Private Consumption, etc.	..	..	..	..	..	..	..	..	..	..	..
General Gov't Consumption	..	..	..	..	..	..	..	..	..	..	..
Gross Domestic Investment	..	..	..	..	..	..	..	..	..	..	..
Fixed Investment	..	..	..	..	..	..	..	..	..	..	..
GDP at factor cost	..	..	..	..	..	..	..	..	..	..	..
Agriculture	..	..	..	..	..	..	..	..	..	..	..
Industry	..	..	..	..	..	..	..	..	..	..	..
Manufacturing	..	..	..	..	..	..	..	..	..	..	..
Services, etc.	..	..	..	..	..	..	..	..	..	..	..
Memo Items:											
Capacity to Import	..	..	..	..	..	..	..	..	..	..	..
Terms of Trade Adjustment	..	..	..	..	..	..	..	..	..	..	..
Gross Domestic Income	..	..	..	..	..	..	..	..	..	..	..
Gross National Income	..	..	..	..	..	..	..	..	..	..	..
DOMESTIC PRICES/DEFLATORS					*(Index 1987 = 100)*						
Overall (GDP)	..	..	..	..	..	..	..	..	..	..	..
Domestic Absorption	..	..	..	..	..	..	..	..	..	..	..
Agriculture	..	..	..	..	..	..	..	..	..	..	..
Industry	..	..	..	..	..	..	..	..	..	..	..
Manufacturing	..	..	..	..	..	..	..	..	..	..	..
Consumer Price Index	..	..	..	..	..	..	..	..	..	..	..
MANUFACTURING ACTIVITY											
Employment (1987=100)	..	..	..	..	..	..	..	..	..	..	..
Real Earnings per Empl. (1987=100)	..	..	..	..	..	..	..	..	..	..	..
Real Output per Empl. (1987=100)	..	..	..	..	..	..	..	..	..	..	..
Earnings as % of Value Added	..	..	..	..	..	..	..	..	..	..	..
MONETARY HOLDINGS					*(Millions of current CFA Francs)*						
Money Supply, Broadly Defined	..	..	..	..	..	..	..	..	..	..	..
Money	..	..	..	..	..	..	..	..	..	..	..
Currency Outside Banks	..	..	..	..	..	..	..	..	..	..	..
Demand Deposits	..	..	..	..	..	..	..	..	..	..	..
Quasi-Money	..	..	..	..	..	..	..	..	..	..	..
					(Millions of current CFA Francs)						
GOVERNMENT DEFICIT (-) OR SURPLUS	..	..	..	..	..	..	..	..	..	..	..
Current Revenue	..	..	..	..	..	..	..	..	..	..	..
Current Expenditure	..	..	..	..	..	..	..	..	..	..	..
Current Budget Balance	..	..	..	..	..	..	..	..	..	..	..
Capital Receipts	..	..	..	..	..	..	..	..	..	..	..
Capital Payments	..	..	..	..	..	..	..	..	..	..	..

1981	1982	1983	1984	1985	1986	1987	1988	1989	1990 estimate	Notes	EQUATORIAL GUINEA
..	..	..	..	..	..	270	310	310	330	..	**CURRENT GNP PER CAPITA (US $)**
347	353	359	366	373	381	389	398	407	417	..	**POPULATION (thousands)**
				(Millions of current CFA Francs)							**USE AND ORIGIN OF RESOURCES**
..	..	..	..	38,575	34,806	34,614	36,944	37,772	39,550	..	Gross National Product (GNP)
..	..	..	..	-1,871	-1,315	-1,326	-1,563	-1,754	-1,551	..	Net Factor Income from Abroad
..	..	..	..	40,446	36,121	35,940	38,507	39,526	41,101	..	GDP at Market Prices
..	-7,910	-2,869	-7,166	-3,368	-3,529	-9,180	-10,847	-9,761	-12,566	..	Resource Balance
..	3,296	5,163	9,438	10,776	12,145	13,425	15,228	13,111	11,560	..	Exports of Goods & NFServices
..	11,206	8,032	16,604	14,144	15,674	22,605	26,075	22,872	24,126	..	Imports of Goods & NFServices
..	..	..	..	43,814	39,650	45,120	49,354	49,287	53,667	..	Domestic Absorption
..	..	..	..	30,554	24,625	26,351	27,184	27,188	29,627	..	Private Consumption, etc.
..	..	..	..	9,498	10,455	10,080	14,100	13,662	14,051	..	General Gov't Consumption
..	..	..	..	3,762	4,570	8,689	8,070	8,437	9,989	..	Gross Domestic Investment
..	..	..	..	3,762	4,570	8,689	8,070	8,437	9,989	..	Fixed Investment
..	..	..	..	2,328	2,064	1,880	1,529	1,414	1,562	..	Indirect Taxes, net
..	..	..	..	38,118	34,057	34,062	36,978	38,217	39,851	..	GDP at factor cost
..	..	..	..	24,887	21,643	20,932	21,044	21,642	22,257	..	Agriculture
..	..	..	..	2,789	2,302	2,645	3,306	3,516	3,849	..	Industry
..	..	..	..	..	..	..	..	..	..	..	Manufacturing
..	..	..	..	10,442	10,112	10,485	12,628	13,059	13,745	..	Services, etc.
..	..	..	..	394	1,041	-491	-2,777	-1,324	-2,577	..	Gross Domestic Saving
..	..	..	..	-623	973	-2,578	-5,466	-3,700	-1,923	,.	Gross National Saving
..	..	..	..	33,667.7	33,427.8	34,616.0	36,316.6	36,129.2	37,260.6	..	Gross National Product
..	..	..	..	34,566.9	34,425.5	35,942.0	37,857.4	37,662.3	38,827.4	..	GDP at Market Prices
..	..	..	..	-3,627.6	-3,819.6	-9,180.0	-10,407.0	-7,534.4	-10,282.0	..	Resource Balance
..	..	..	..	9,228.1	12,281.6	13,425.0	14,713.8	13,104.9	12,227.7	..	Exports of Goods & NFServices
..	..	..	..	12,855.8	16,101.3	22,605.0	25,121.1	20,639.3	22,509.6	..	Imports of Goods & NFServices
..	..	..	..	38,194.5	38,245.2	45,122.0	48,264.7	45,196.7	49,109.3	..	Domestic Absorption
..	..	..	..	24,654.0	23,048.3	26,353.0	26,889.3	24,776.0	26,929.1	..	Private Consumption, etc.
..	..	..	..	10,261.5	10,736.9	10,080.0	13,689.6	12,840.4	12,820.9	..	General Gov't Consumption
..	..	..	..	3,279.0	4,460.0	8,689.0	7,685.8	7,580.3	9,359.3	..	Gross Domestic Investment
..	..	..	..	3,279.0	4,460.0	8,689.0	7,685.8	7,580.3	9,359.3	..	Fixed Investment
..	..	..	..	32,458.7	32,365.3	34,062.0	36,407.6	36,418.0	37,416.5	..	GDP at factor cost
..	..	..	..	18,994.2	19,766.6	20,932.0	20,963.3	21,072.4	21,718.9	..	Agriculture
..	..	..	..	2,806.0	2,328.1	2,645.0	3,175.2	3,293.9	3,444.8	..	Industry
..	..	..	..	..	..	..	..	..	..	..	Manufacturing
..	..	..	..	10,658.5	10,270.7	10,485.0	12,269.1	12,051.7	12,252.7	..	Services, etc.
											Memo Items:
..	..	..	..	9,794.5	12,476.1	13,425.0	14,670.9	11,831.2	10,785.5	..	Capacity to Import
..	..	..	..	566.4	194.4	0.0	-42.9	-1,273.8	-1,442.2	..	Terms of Trade Adjustment
..	..	..	..	35,133.3	34,620.0	35,942.0	37,814.5	36,388.6	37,385.1	..	Gross Domestic Income
..	..	..	..	34,234.0	33,622.2	34,616.0	36,273.7	34,855.4	35,818.4	..	Gross National Income
				(Index 1987 = 100)							**DOMESTIC PRICES/DEFLATORS**
..	..	..	..	117.0	104.9	100.0	101.7	104.9	105.9	..	Overall (GDP)
..	..	..	..	114.7	103.7	100.0	102.3	109.0	109.3	..	Domestic Absorption
..	..	..	..	131.0	109.5	100.0	100.4	102.7	102.5	..	Agriculture
..	..	..	..	99.4	98.9	100.0	104.1	106.7	111.7	..	Industry
..	..	..	..	..	..	..	..	..	..	..	Manufacturing
..	..	..	..	139.6	114.8	100.0	102.3	108.4	109.6	..	Consumer Price Index
											MANUFACTURING ACTIVITY
..	..	..	..	..	..	..	..	..	..	..	Employment (1987=100)
..	..	..	..	..	..	..	..	..	..	..	Real Earnings per Empl. (1987=100)
..	..	..	..	..	..	..	..	..	..	..	Real Output per Empl. (1987=100)
..	..	..	..	..	..	..	..	..	..	..	Earnings as % of Value Added
				(Millions of current CFA Francs)							**MONETARY HOLDINGS**
..	..	..	..	8,972.0	10,539.0	9,434.0	5,602.0	7,883.0	3,791.0	..	Money Supply, Broadly Defined
..	..	..	..	8,047.0	9,919.0	9,004.0	5,224.0	7,250.0	3,126.0	..	Money
..	..	..	..	5,239.0	7,475.0	6,687.0	1,964.0	4,790.0	900.0	..	Currency Outside Banks
..	..	..	..	2,808.0	2,444.0	2,317.0	3,260.0	2,460.0	2,226.0	..	Demand Deposits
..	..	..	..	925.0	620.0	430.0	378.0	633.0	665.0	..	Quasi-Money
				(Millions of current CFA Francs)							**GOVERNMENT DEFICIT (-) OR SURPLUS**
..	..	..	..	..	..	..	..	..	..	..	Current Revenue
..	..	..	..	..	..	..	..	..	..	..	Current Expenditure
..	..	..	..	..	..	..	..	..	..	..	Current Budget Balance
..	..	..	..	..	..	..	..	..	..	..	Capital Receipts
..	..	..	..	..	..	..	..	..	..	..	Capital Payments

EQUATORIAL GUINEA	1970	1971	1972	1973	1974	1975	1976	1977	1978	1979	1980
FOREIGN TRADE (CUSTOMS BASIS)					*(Thousands of current US dollars)*						
Value of Exports, fob	..	..	..	..	..	..	..	..	..	..	..
Nonfuel Primary Products	..	..	..	..	..	..	..	..	..	..	..
Fuels	..	..	..	..	..	..	..	..	..	..	..
Manufactures	..	..	..	..	..	..	..	..	..	..	..
Value of Imports, cif	..	..	..	..	..	..	..	..	..	..	..
Nonfuel Primary Products	..	..	..	..	..	..	..	..	..	..	..
Fuels	..	..	..	..	..	..	..	..	..	..	..
Manufactures	..	..	..	..	..	..	..	..	..	..	..
					(Index 1987 = 100)						
Terms of Trade	..	..	..	..	..	..	..	..	..	..	..
Export Prices, fob	..	..	..	..	..	..	..	..	..	..	..
Import Prices, cif	..	..	..	..	..	..	..	..	..	..	..
BALANCE OF PAYMENTS					*(Thousands of current US dollars)*						
Exports of Goods & Services	27.0	31.0	23.0	22.0	37.0	..	..	..	..	..	..
Merchandise, fob	25.0	28.0	19.0	19.0	34.0	..	..	..	..	..	15.0
Nonfactor Services	1.0	2.0	3.0	3.0	2.0	..	..	..	..	..	0.0
Factor Services	1.0	1.0	0.0	0.0	1.0	..	..	..	..	..	..
Imports of Goods & Services	31.0	32.0	29.0	..	21.0	..	..	..	..	..	..
Merchandise, fob	21.0	25.0	24.0	18.0	14.0	..	..	..	..	..	58.0
Nonfactor Services	9.0	7.0	5.0	5.0	6.0	..	..	..	..	..	0.0
Factor Services	1.0	0.0	1.0	..	1.0	..	..	..	..	..	..
Long-Term Interest	0.0	0.0	0.0	0.0	0.0	0.0	0.0	0.0	0.0	0.0	0.0
Private Current Transfers, net	-2.0	-1.0	-1.0	0.0	..	..	..	..	..	..	..
Workers' Remittances	..	..	..	..	..	..	..	..	..	..	..
Curr. A/C Bal before Off. Transf.	-6.0	-3.0	-8.0	-1.0	16.0	..	..	..	..	..	-43.0
Net Official Transfers	..	1.0	..	0.0	..	..	..	..	..	..	..
Curr. A/C Bal after Off. Transf.	-6.0	-2.0	-8.0	-1.0	16.0	..	..	..	..	..	-43.0
Long-Term Capital, net	2.0	2.0	4.0	1.0	1.0	..	..	..	..	..	24.0
Direct Investment	..	..	..	..	..	..	..	..	..	..	..
Long-Term Loans	0.0	4.0	5.0	5.0	4.0	1.0	2.0	2.0	-1.0	1.0	18.0
Disbursements	0.0	4.0	5.0	5.0	4.0	1.0	2.0	3.0	0.0	2.0	20.0
Repayments	0.0	0.0	0.0	0.0	0.0	0.0	0.0	1.0	1.0	1.0	2.0
Other Long-Term Capital	2.0	-2.0	0.0	-4.0	-3.0	..	..	..	..	..	6.0
Other Capital, net	6.0	-3.0	-3.0	7.0	-6.0	..	..	..	..	..	6.0
Change in Reserves	-2.0	3.0	7.0	-6.0	-11.0	0.0	-2.0	2.0	0.0	2.0	13.0
Memo Item:					*(CFA Francs per US dollar)*						
Conversion Factor (Annual Avg)	70.000	69.470	64.270	58.260	57.690	57.410	66.900	75.960	76.670	68.340	110.630
					(Millions of US dollars), outstanding at end of year						
EXTERNAL DEBT (Total)	5.0	9.1	13.9	19.8	25.8	25.2	28.4	49.4	39.2	40.6	75.6
Long-Term Debt (by debtor)	5.0	9.1	13.9	19.8	25.8	25.2	28.4	34.4	37.2	38.6	68.6
Central Bank, incl. IMF credit	5.0	5.0	5.0	5.0	5.0	5.0	5.0	7.1	7.2	7.0	21.1
Central Government	0.0	4.1	8.9	14.8	20.8	20.2	23.4	27.3	30.0	31.6	35.6
Rest of General Government	..	..	..	..	..	..	..	..	..	..	..
Non-financial Public Enterprises	..	..	..	..	..	..	..	..	..	..	..
Priv. Sector, incl non-guaranteed	0.0	0.0	0.0	0.0	0.0	0.0	0.0	0.0	0.0	0.0	11.9
Short-Term Debt	0.0	0.0	0.0	0.0	0.0	0.0	0.0	15.0	2.0	2.0	7.0
Memo Items:					*(Thousands of US dollars)*						
Int'l Reserves Excluding Gold	..	..	..	..	..	..	..	..	..	..	..
Gold Holdings (at market price)	..	..	..	..	..	..	..	..	..	..	..
SOCIAL INDICATORS											
Total Fertility Rate	5.0	5.0	5.0	5.0	5.0	5.0	5.0	5.0	5.0	5.0	5.0
Infant Mortality Rate	165.2	162.6	160.0	157.8	155.6	153.4	151.2	149.0	146.6	144.2	141.8
Life Expectancy at Birth	39.5	39.8	40.2	40.5	40.9	41.2	41.5	41.9	42.2	42.5	42.9
Urban Population, % of total	26.7	26.8	26.9	26.9	27.0	27.1	27.2	27.2	27.3	27.3	27.4
Food Prod. per capita (1987=100)											
Labor Force, Agriculture (%)	75.0	74.1	73.1	72.2	71.3	70.5	69.5	68.5	67.6	66.7	65.8
Labor Force, Female (%)	41.8	41.8	41.7	41.7	41.6	41.6	41.5	41.5	41.4	41.3	41.3
Primary Schl. Enroll. Ratio	76.0	..	..	78.0	..	..	..	..	..	..	135.0
Primary Schl. Enroll. Ratio, Female	67.0	..	..	69.0	..	..	..	..	..	..	..
Secondary Schl. Enroll. Ratio	16.0	..	..	..	..	11.0	..	..	..	..	..

				(Thousands of current US dollars)							**FOREIGN TRADE (CUSTOMS BASIS)**
..	..	..	..	..	..	..	..	..	..	..	Value of Exports, fob
..	..	..	..	..	..	..	..	..	..	..	Nonfuel Primary Products
..	..	..	..	..	..	..	..	..	..	..	Fuels
..	..	..	..	..	..	..	..	..	..	..	Manufactures
..	..	..	..	..	..	..	..	..	..	..	Value of Imports, cif
..	..	..	..	..	..	..	..	..	..	..	Nonfuel Primary Products
..	..	..	..	..	..	..	..	..	..	..	Fuels
..	..	..	..	..	..	..	..	..	..	..	Manufactures
				(Index 1987 = 100)							
..	..	..	..	..	..	..	..	..	..	..	Terms of Trade
..	..	..	..	..	..	..	..	..	..	..	Export Prices, fob
..	..	..	..	..	..	..	..	..	..	..	Import Prices, cif
				(Thousands of current US dollars)							**BALANCE OF PAYMENTS**
..	..	18.0	22.0	25.0	37.0	47.0	53.0	41.0	45.0	..	Exports of Goods & Services
16.0	15.0	18.0	21.0	24.0	35.0	38.0	45.0	33.0	37.0	..	Merchandise, fob
0.0	0.0	0.0	0.0	0.0	1.0	6.0	6.0	6.0	5.0	..	Nonfactor Services
..	..	0.0	0.0	0.0	2.0	2.0	2.0	2.0	3.0	..	Factor Services
..	..	33.0	37.0	35.0	55.0	95.0	113.0	94.0	119.0	..	Imports of Goods & Services
49.0	50.0	27.0	36.0	25.0	27.0	48.0	57.0	44.0	63.0	..	Merchandise, fob
0.0	0.0	0.0	0.0	6.0	22.0	41.0	49.0	43.0	47.0	..	Nonfactor Services
..	..	6.0	1.0	4.0	6.0	7.0	8.0	8.0	9.0	..	Factor Services
0.0	0.0	0.0	0.0	1.0	1.0	3.0	2.0	0.0	1.0	..	Long-Term Interest
..	0.0	0.0	0.0	2.0	4.0	-3.0	-4.0	-2.0	8.0	..	Private Current Transfers, net
..	..	..	..	..	..	..	..	..	..	..	Workers' Remittances
-33.0	-35.0	-15.0	-16.0	-9.0	-15.0	-53.0	-66.0	-57.0	-66.0	..	Curr. A/C Bal before Off. Transf.
..	5.0	6.0	7.0	8.0	20.0	29.0	50.0	40.0	47.0	..	Net Official Transfers
-33.0	-30.0	-9.0	-8.0	-1.0	5.0	-24.0	-17.0	-17.0	-19.0	..	Curr. A/C Bal after Off. Transf.
16.0	30.0	8.0	0.0	3.0	1.0	13.0	14.0	15.0	6.0	..	Long-Term Capital, net
..	..	..	..	0.0	0.0	0.0	0.0	0.0	10.0	..	Direct Investment
16.0	30.0	11.0	0.0	8.0	18.0	18.0	20.0	19.0	9.0	..	Long-Term Loans
20.0	33.0	12.0	1.0	9.0	20.0	24.0	22.0	19.0	10.0	..	Disbursements
4.0	3.0	2.0	1.0	1.0	1.0	7.0	1.0	0.0	1.0	..	Repayments
0.0	0.0	-3.0	0.0	-5.0	-18.0	-4.0	-7.0	-4.0	-14.0	..	Other Long-Term Capital
9.0	1.0	0.0	15.0	1.0	-5.0	7.0	5.0	1.0	15.0	..	Other Capital, net
9.0	0.0	1.0	-6.0	1.0	-1.0	4.0	-3.0	1.0	-2.0	..	Change in Reserves
				(CFA Francs per US dollar)							**Memo Item:**
184.630	219.720	286.860	321.520	449.260	346.300	300.530	297.850	319.010	272.260	..	Conversion Factor (Annual Avg)
				(Millions of US dollars), outstanding at end of year							
92.4	116.9	122.4	116.4	132.2	158.5	195.7	210.6	226.8	237.5	..	**EXTERNAL DEBT (Total)**
85.0	106.3	110.1	93.2	125.7	150.4	184.7	198.7	211.9	211.9	..	Long-Term Debt (by debtor)
27.4	32.5	36.4	28.1	21.7	19.9	21.6	24.1	18.8	16.7	..	Central Bank, incl. IMF credit
37.7	54.1	56.7	49.3	98.9	124.6	156.0	167.8	190.9	192.7	..	Central Government
..	..	..	..	..	..	..	..	..	..	..	Rest of General Government
..	..	..	..	..	..	..	..	..	..	..	Non-financial Public Enterprises
19.9	19.7	17.0	15.8	5.1	5.9	7.1	6.8	2.2	2.5	..	Priv. Sector, incl non-guaranteed
7.4	10.6	12.3	23.2	6.5	8.1	11.0	11.9	14.9	25.6	..	Short-Term Debt
				(Thousands of US dollars)							**Memo Items:**
..	2,773.6	1,300.0	1,381.0	3,465.5	2,676.4	568.6	5,503.3	816.3	706.7	..	Int'l Reserves Excluding Gold
..	..	..	..	..	..	..	..	..	..	..	Gold Holdings (at market price)
											SOCIAL INDICATORS
5.0	5.0	5.1	5.2	5.3	5.4	5.5	5.5	5.5	5.5	..	Total Fertility Rate
139.4	137.0	135.0	133.0	130.9	128.9	126.9	124.7	122.5	120.4	..	Infant Mortality Rate
43.2	43.5	43.9	44.3	44.7	45.0	45.4	45.9	46.3	46.8	..	Life Expectancy at Birth
27.5	27.5	27.6	27.6	27.7	27.9	28.2	28.4	28.5	28.7	..	Urban Population, % of total
..	..	..	..	..	..	..	..	..	..	..	Food Prod. per capita (1987=100)
..	..	..	..	..	..	..	..	..	..	..	Labor Force, Agriculture (%)
41.2	41.0	40.9	40.8	40.6	40.5	40.4	40.2	40.1	39.9	..	Labor Force, Female (%)
128.0	134.0	147.0	..	..	..	..	..	..	..	..	Primary Schl. Enroll. Ratio
..	..	..	..	..	..	..	..	..	..	..	Primary Schl. Enroll. Ratio, Female
..	14.0	..	..	..	..	..	..	..	..	..	Secondary Schl. Enroll. Ratio

ETHIOPIA	1970	1971	1972	1973	1974	1975	1976	1977	1978	1979	1980
CURRENT GNP PER CAPITA (US $)	60	70	70	70	80	90	90	90	100	110	120
POPULATION (thousands)	28,937	29,646	30,412	31,224	32,074	32,954	33,860	34,790	35,741	36,716	37,717

USE AND ORIGIN OF RESOURCES *(Millions of current Ethiopian Birr)*

	1970	1971	1972	1973	1974	1975	1976	1977	1978	1979	1980
Gross National Product (GNP)	4,441	4,691	4,712	4,955	5,513	5,516	5,993	6,851	7,295	7,982	8,518
Net Factor Income from Abroad	-20	-19	-32	-50	-38	-35	-3	-4	0	-5	14
GDP at Market Prices	4,461	4,710	4,744	5,005	5,551	5,551	5,996	6,855	7,295	7,987	8,505
Resource Balance	-14	-88	-93	101	189	-164	-58	-216	-405	-425	-440
Exports of Goods & NF Services	489	468	487	653	827	683	760	840	866	943	1,178
Imports of Goods & NF Services	504	556	580	552	638	847	818	1,056	1,271	1,368	1,619
Domestic Absorption	4,475	4,798	4,837	4,905	5,362	5,715	6,054	7,071	7,700	8,413	8,945
Private Consumption, etc.	3,519	3,783	3,726	3,798	4,227	4,405	4,610	5,497	5,915	6,546	6,798
General Gov't Consumption	443	461	508	538	586	730	866	968	1,240	1,168	1,293
Gross Domestic Investment	512	554	603	569	549	580	578	606	545	699	854
Fixed Investment	512	554	603	569	549	580	578	606	545	699	854
Indirect Taxes, net	288	301	327	376	410	421	474	690	749	901	880
GDP at factor cost	4,173	4,409	4,417	4,629	5,141	5,130	5,522	6,164	6,546	7,086	7,625
Agriculture	2,327	2,405	2,286	2,331	2,605	2,450	2,768	3,227	3,497	3,656	3,907
Industry	602	672	707	748	796	855	824	892	894	1,046	1,189
Manufacturing	372	420	440	464	508	569	586	636	636	758	830
Services, etc.	1,244	1,333	1,424	1,550	1,739	1,825	1,930	2,046	2,154	2,383	2,528
Gross Domestic Saving	498	467	510	670	739	416	520	390	140	274	413
Gross National Saving	472	443	485	644	738	411	561	420	171	317	468

(Millions of 1980 Ethiopian Birr)

	1970	1971	1972	1973	1974	1975	1976	1977	1978	1979	1980
Gross National Product	6,377.2	6,644.5	6,963.2	7,160.6	7,272.4	7,288.6	7,531.4	7,736.9	7,655.8	8,142.5	8,518.3
GDP at Market Prices	6,406.5	6,672.2	7,010.3	7,233.8	7,323.9	7,334.8	7,534.7	7,741.2	7,656.0	8,147.8	8,504.8
Resource Balance	-190.7	-182.5	-203.0	25.0	158.4	-184.9	-25.3	-225.3	-400.7	-376.6	-440.5
Exports of Goods & NF Services	766.2	823.3	815.6	945.2	1,126.5	1,038.5	1,133.5	1,158.9	1,016.5	995.4	1,178.0
Imports of Goods & NF Services	956.9	1,005.7	1,018.7	920.2	968.1	1,223.3	1,158.7	1,384.2	1,417.2	1,372.1	1,618.5
Domestic Absorption	6,597.2	6,854.7	7,213.3	7,208.8	7,165.5	7,519.7	7,560.0	7,966.5	8,056.7	8,524.5	8,945.3
Private Consumption, etc.	5,174.9	5,361.1	5,504.5	5,544.2	5,610.0	5,716.3	5,453.9	5,835.5	6,123.9	6,588.8	6,798.1
General Gov't Consumption	630.3	648.1	746.5	774.4	770.8	968.6	1,092.7	1,096.4	1,304.8	1,190.4	1,293.2
Gross Domestic Investment	792.0	845.5	962.3	890.1	784.7	834.7	1,013.3	1,034.6	627.9	745.2	854.0
Fixed Investment	..	..	..	..	..	834.7	1,013.3	1,034.6	627.9	745.2	854.0
GDP at factor cost	5,980.2	6,230.8	6,509.4	6,669.6	6,761.3	6,752.5	6,911.8	6,926.8	6,834.4	7,219.3	7,624.7
Agriculture	3,470.7	3,540.7	3,666.6	3,693.1	3,672.8	3,601.8	3,700.8	3,688.0	3,640.5	3,728.3	3,906.9
Industry	871.7	955.0	997.7	1,027.0	1,019.7	1,005.0	966.5	978.7	947.2	1,085.9	1,189.4
Manufacturing	567.5	619.7	645.1	677.2	670.4	662.7	652.3	657.4	657.8	772.2	830.0
Services, etc.	1,637.8	1,735.2	1,845.0	1,949.5	2,068.8	2,145.6	2,244.5	2,260.2	2,246.7	2,405.1	2,528.4
Memo Items:											
Capacity to Import	929.6	847.1	855.3	1,088.1	1,255.6	986.3	1,076.6	1,100.7	965.5	945.5	1,178.0
Terms of Trade Adjustment	163.4	23.8	39.7	142.9	129.1	-52.2	-56.9	-58.2	-51.0	-50.0	0.0
Gross Domestic Income	6,569.9	6,696.0	7,050.0	7,376.7	7,453.0	7,282.6	7,477.9	7,683.0	7,604.9	8,097.8	8,504.8
Gross National Income	6,540.5	6,668.3	7,002.9	7,303.5	7,401.5	7,236.4	7,474.5	7,678.7	7,604.7	8,092.6	8,518.3

DOMESTIC PRICES/DEFLATORS *(Index 1980 = 100)*

	1970	1971	1972	1973	1974	1975	1976	1977	1978	1979	1980
Overall (GDP)	69.6	70.6	67.7	69.2	75.8	75.7	79.6	88.5	95.3	98.0	100.0
Domestic Absorption	67.8	70.0	67.1	68.0	74.8	76.0	80.1	88.8	95.6	98.7	100.0
Agriculture	67.1	67.9	62.3	63.1	70.9	68.0	74.8	87.5	96.1	98.1	100.0
Industry	69.0	70.3	70.8	72.9	78.1	85.1	85.3	91.1	94.4	96.4	100.0
Manufacturing	65.6	67.7	68.2	68.5	75.7	85.9	89.8	96.7	96.7	98.2	100.0
Consumer Price Index	31.9	32.1	30.1	32.8	35.6	38.0	48.8	56.9	65.0	75.5	78.9

MANUFACTURING ACTIVITY

	1970	1971	1972	1973	1974	1975	1976	1977	1978	1979	1980
Employment (1987=100)	52.4	54.2	56.3	57.8	60.5	63.3	62.3	65.7	69.3	78.6	80.6
Real Earnings per Empl. (1987=100)	132.3	139.5	152.4	148.2	143.8	139.1	122.0	114.0	102.4	92.3	94.5
Real Output per Empl. (1987=100)	53.4	56.9	60.7	65.0	65.1	55.7	60.4	57.8	55.4	70.6	87.0
Earnings as % of Value Added	23.8	24.0	23.5	23.6	23.3	21.7	23.0	25.3	25.3	20.6	18.0

MONETARY HOLDINGS *(Millions of current Ethiopian Birr)*

	1970	1971	1972	1973	1974	1975	1976	1977	1978	1979	1980
Money Supply, Broadly Defined	639.7	651.3	755.9	981.8	1,134.6	1,243.9	1,402.9	1,651.9	1,861.4	2,107.9	2,196.5
Money	453.2	436.7	490.7	618.5	753.9	942.1	953.0	1,178.7	1,378.2	1,571.9	1,568.3
Currency Outside Banks	323.2	303.8	339.5	403.8	532.9	689.0	574.6	769.4	894.7	1,012.4	1,029.2
Demand Deposits	130.0	132.9	151.2	214.7	221.0	253.1	378.4	409.3	483.5	559.5	539.1
Quasi-Money	186.5	214.6	265.2	363.3	380.7	301.8	449.9	473.2	483.2	536.0	628.2

(Millions of current Ethiopian Birr)

	1970	1971	1972	1973	1974	1975	1976	1977	1978	1979	1980
GOVERNMENT DEFICIT (-) OR SURPLUS	..	..	-64.2	-49.2	-43.8	-226.2	-325.1	-232.5	-421.9	-254.5	-380.5
Current Revenue	..	..	586.2	651.1	716.2	804.8	853.2	1,093.6	1,252.8	1,601.3	1,764.4
Current Expenditure	..	..	545.2	581.2	646.9	848.1	966.7	1,090.9	1,405.6	1,595.7	1,858.8
Current Budget Balance	..	..	41.0	69.9	69.3	-43.3	-113.5	2.7	-152.8	5.6	-94.4
Capital Receipts	..	..	0.8	1.6	1.4	1.7	1.9	2.7	3.3	3.3	6.8
Capital Payments	..	..	106.0	120.7	114.5	184.6	213.5	237.9	272.4	263.4	292.9

1981	1982	1983	1984	1985	1986	1987	1988	1989	1990 estimate	Notes	ETHIOPIA
120	120	120	120	110	120	120	120	120	120	..	**CURRENT GNP PER CAPITA (US $)**
38,744	39,793	40,889	42,067	43,350	44,732	46,210	47,781	49,441	51,180	..	**POPULATION (thousands)**
			(Millions of current Ethiopian Birr)								**USE AND ORIGIN OF RESOURCES**
8,888	9,149	10,003	9,961	9,821	10,768	11,101	11,633	12,323	12,415	C	Gross National Product (GNP)
-15	-18	-28	-40	-68	-64	-95	-134	-169	-170	..	Net Factor Income from Abroad
8,903	9,167	10,031	10,001	9,890	10,832	11,196	11,767	12,491	12,585	C	GDP at Market Prices
-603	-900	-848	-1,044	-1,104	-1,078	-1,229	-1,274	-929	-822	..	Resource Balance
1,147	1,059	1,142	1,266	1,136	1,390	1,290	1,317	1,556	1,390	..	Exports of Goods & NFServices
1,750	1,959	1,990	2,310	2,240	2,467	2,519	2,591	2,485	2,212	..	Imports of Goods & NFServices
9,506	10,067	10,879	11,045	10,993	11,910	12,425	13,041	13,420	13,407	..	Domestic Absorption
7,185	7,499	8,027	7,920	7,687	8,487	8,628	8,459	8,536	..	f	Private Consumption, etc.
1,400	1,487	1,733	1,841	1,924	2,045	2,164	2,777	3,223	..	..	General Gov't Consumption
922	1,082	1,119	1,284	1,382	1,378	1,633	1,805	1,661	..	f	Gross Domestic Investment
922	1,082	1,119	1,234	1,382	1,378	1,633	1,805	1,661	..	..	Fixed Investment
806	871	948	1,057	979	1,115	1,196	1,279	1,282	1,221	..	Indirect Taxes, net
8,097	8,297	9,083	8,944	8,910	9,718	9,999	10,488	11,209	11,364	C	GDP at factor cost
4,072	4,062	4,389	4,070	3,916	4,354	4,318	4,327	4,666	4,700	..	Agriculture
1,258	1,297	1,402	1,476	1,495	1,596	1,737	1,775	1,843	1,877	..	Industry
871	902	984	1,009	1,023	1,073	1,167	1,200	1,230	1,271	..	Manufacturing
2,767	2,938	3,292	3,397	3,500	3,767	3,944	4,386	4,701	4,787	..	Services, etc.
318	182	271	240	279	301	404	531	732	..	..	Gross Domestic Saving
355	257	419	422	510	670	615	641	953	..	..	Gross National Saving
			(Millions of 1980 Ethiopian Birr)								
8,665.9	8,800.3	9,240.2	9,023.5	8,361.1	8,928.5	9,723.6	10,048.8	10,266.9	9,851.7	C	Gross National Product
8,680.1	8,817.7	9,266.2	9,059.0	8,420.3	8,985.0	9,811.6	10,171.3	10,415.1	9,984.7	C	GDP at Market Prices
-524.0	-812.4	-798.8	-805.3	-1,074.4	-1,426.9	..	..	..	-510.2	..	Resource Balance
1,166.7	1,114.7	1,218.9	1,415.6	1,128.9	1,054.7	..	..	..	1,152.5	..	Exports of Goods & NFServices
1,690.8	1,927.1	2,017.7	2,220.8	2,203.3	2,481.6	..	..	..	1,662.6	..	Imports of Goods & NFServices
9,204.1	9,630.1	10,065.0	9,864.3	9,494.6	10,411.9	..	..	..	10,494.9	..	Domestic Absorption
6,888.6	7,072.2	7,275.5	6,952.7	6,857.6	7,641.4	..	..	..	..	f	Private Consumption, etc.
1,369.8	1,435.5	1,609.6	1,687.7	1,706.3	1,764.3	..	..	..	..	..	General Gov't Consumption
945.7	1,122.4	1,179.8	1,224.0	930.7	1,006.1	..	..	..	1,399.6	f	Gross Domestic Investment
945.7	1,122.4	1,179.8	1,224.0	930.7	1,006.1	..	..	..	1,399.6	..	Fixed Investment
7,858.2	7,948.8	8,371.9	8,061.1	7,491.7	7,994.3	8,714.5	9,022.3	9,289.7	8,969.3	C	GDP at factor cost
4,002.8	3,951.4	4,137.8	3,728.5	3,122.4	3,410.5	3,901.9	3,871.8	4,094.9	3,952.6	..	Agriculture
1,230.2	1,268.2	1,334.3	1,404.6	1,414.3	1,467.1	1,532.7	1,552.3	1,578.8	1,502.4	..	Industry
866.9	900.6	951.3	983.0	993.2	1,036.8	1,087.4	1,112.1	1,133.7	1,087.9	..	Manufacturing
2,625.3	2,729.2	2,899.8	2,928.1	2,955.1	3,116.6	3,279.9	3,598.2	3,616.1	3,514.3	..	Services, etc.
											Memo Items:
1,107.9	1,041.7	1,157.9	1,217.4	1,117.7	1,397.6	..	..	..	1,045.1	..	Capacity to Import
-58.8	-73.1	-61.0	-198.1	-11.2	342.9	..	..	..	-107.4	..	Terms of Trade Adjustment
8,621.3	8,744.6	9,205.2	8,860.9	8,409.1	9,327.9	..	..	..	9,877.3	..	Gross Domestic Income
8,607.1	8,727.2	9,179.3	8,825.4	8,349.9	9,271.4	..	..	..	9,744.3	..	Gross National Income
			(Index 1980 = 100)								**DOMESTIC PRICES/DEFLATORS**
102.6	104.0	108.3	110.4	117.5	120.6	114.1	115.7	119.9	126.0	..	Overall (GDP)
103.3	104.5	108.1	112.0	115.8	114.4	..	..	..	127.7	..	Domestic Absorption
101.7	102.8	106.1	109.2	125.4	127.7	110.7	111.7	113.9	118.9	..	Agriculture
102.3	102.2	105.1	105.1	105.7	108.8	113.3	114.4	116.7	124.9	..	Industry
100.5	100.1	103.5	102.7	103.0	103.5	107.4	107.9	108.5	116.8	..	Manufacturing
83.7	88.6	88.0	95.4	113.6	102.5	100.0	107.1	115.5	121.4	f	Consumer Price Index
											MANUFACTURING ACTIVITY
83.2	86.1	87.6	94.4	92.6	95.6	100.0	103.8	..	..	G J	Employment (1987=100)
91.6	89.1	96.1	89.2	80.9	91.6	100.0	96.8	..	..	G J	Real Earnings per Empl. (1987=100)
91.4	97.6	96.8	95.3	99.5	99.4	100.0	100.2	..	..	G J	Real Output per Empl. (1987=100)
18.7	19.0	19.7	19.7	20.3	19.2	19.5	19.5	..	..	J	Earnings as % of Value Added
			(Millions of current Ethiopian Birr)								**MONETARY HOLDINGS**
2,438.3	2,689.4	3,198.4	3,449.0	3,994.0	4,467.8	4,754.4	5,291.4	6,048.3	7,167.0	..	Money Supply, Broadly Defined
1,719.9	1,892.3	2,142.2	2,309.3	2,702.2	3,272.8	3,341.4	3,721.6	4,321.9	5,272.7	..	Money
1,039.2	1,149.9	1,250.5	1,272.1	1,417.6	1,640.2	1,744.1	1,962.4	2,340.5	3,081.0	..	Currency Outside Banks
680.7	742.4	891.7	1,037.1	1,284.6	1,632.6	1,597.3	1,759.2	1,981.3	2,191.7	..	Demand Deposits
718.4	797.1	1,056.1	1,139.7	1,291.8	1,195.0	1,413.0	1,569.8	1,726.5	1,894.4	..	Quasi-Money
			(Millions of current Ethiopian Birr)								
-334.2	-491.5	-1,352.3	-621.5	-868.8	-813.1	-754.9	..	..	..	C F	**GOVERNMENT DEFICIT (-) OR SURPLUS**
1,974.5	2,117.8	2,402.7	2,522.4	2,885.8	3,160.9	3,154.6	..	..	..	..	Current Revenue
1,969.9	2,180.7	2,766.8	2,492.0	3,078.6	3,109.0	3,063.3	..	..	..	..	Current Expenditure
4.6	-62.9	-364.1	30.4	-192.8	51.9	91.3	..	..	..	..	Current Budget Balance
7.6	9.1	15.0	14.5	11.5	12.6	15.2	..	..	..	..	Capital Receipts
346.4	437.7	1,003.2	666.4	687.5	877.6	861.4	..	..	..	..	Capital Payments

ETHIOPIA	1970	1971	1972	1973	1974	1975	1976	1977	1978	1979	1980
FOREIGN TRADE (CUSTOMS BASIS)					*(Millions of current US dollars)*						
Value of Exports, fob	117.8	123.8	165.3	233.9	262.4	215.2	274.6	333.4	309.2	421.8	424.4
Nonfuel Primary Products	114.4	119.7	161.0	225.8	251.5	202.3	265.6	324.8	294.6	399.4	392.0
Fuels	1.4	2.0	1.1	1.6	4.7	7.2	7.0	6.2	12.1	20.3	31.5
Manufactures	2.0	2.1	3.2	6.5	6.2	5.6	2.1	2.4	2.5	2.1	1.0
Value of Imports, cif	173.1	187.7	189.4	213.1	272.9	294.0	353.2	391.4	505.3	567.4	721.4
Nonfuel Primary Products	21.4	22.1	20.4	24.8	28.7	28.3	32.1	33.2	46.9	60.0	80.3
Fuels	13.4	17.7	15.7	20.0	38.7	51.3	53.3	62.0	60.3	110.2	178.5
Manufactures	138.2	147.9	153.3	168.3	205.5	214.4	267.9	296.2	398.1	397.2	462.6
					(Index 1987 = 100)						
Terms of Trade	166.2	140.8	148.3	164.4	103.7	95.9	166.6	232.2	154.2	154.9	117.6
Export Prices, fob	37.7	34.3	41.7	56.5	56.9	54.6	98.5	148.5	112.9	130.7	118.9
Import Prices, cif	22.7	24.4	28.1	34.4	54.8	57.0	59.1	64.0	73.2	84.4	101.1
BALANCE OF PAYMENTS					*(Millions of current US dollars)*						
Exports of Goods & Services	185.3	194.4	247.2	347.7	390.4	346.4	384.6	422.3	430.8	465.4	590.5
Merchandise, fob	122.3	126.4	165.6	239.0	266.7	230.0	260.4	312.2	324.0	359.9	459.2
Nonfactor Services	56.5	63.3	78.1	100.0	103.2	100.0	106.8	93.4	94.2	95.5	109.9
Factor Services	6.5	4.7	3.6	8.7	20.4	16.4	17.4	16.7	12.6	10.0	21.4
Imports of Goods & Services	225.5	248.7	256.7	297.9	386.8	442.7	413.9	528.7	626.5	672.5	796.6
Merchandise, fob	144.3	158.9	157.8	178.8	249.7	275.9	278.2	368.0	470.9	589.0	691.9
Nonfactor Services	67.0	73.4	76.3	90.6	105.6	133.4	117.0	142.3	142.9	71.0	89.8
Factor Services	14.2	16.4	22.6	28.5	31.5	33.4	18.7	18.5	12.7	12.5	14.9
Long-Term Interest	6.3	7.0	8.1	8.9	9.7	11.0	10.4	11.3	12.4	13.0	16.9
Private Current Transfers, net	-2.6	-1.8	2.8	11.3	18.2	15.0	21.2	16.6	14.8	23.3	20.0
Workers' Remittances	..	..	..	..	..	..	..	..	..	..	..
Curr. A/C Bal before Off. Transf.	-42.8	-56.2	-6.6	61.2	21.8	-81.3	-8.1	-89.9	-180.9	-183.8	-186.1
Net Official Transfers	10.6	10.9	14.8	14.2	33.7	29.7	29.4	42.6	53.2	59.7	59.9
Curr. A/C Bal after Off. Transf.	-32.2	-45.2	8.1	75.3	55.4	-51.6	21.3	-47.3	-127.7	-124.1	-126.2
Long-Term Capital, net	16.5	36.3	32.1	53.4	50.9	68.6	59.9	50.6	36.7	70.6	150.0
Direct Investment	3.9	5.7	9.7	30.9	28.9	19.3	4.3	5.8	..	..	..
Long-Term Loans	12.7	31.2	19.6	24.2	24.8	62.1	60.2	38.3	48.3	94.6	84.4
Disbursements	27.6	44.4	32.9	37.3	36.2	76.5	73.9	52.1	63.0	110.2	101.7
Repayments	14.9	13.2	13.3	13.1	11.4	14.4	13.7	13.8	14.7	15.6	17.3
Other Long-Term Capital	-0.1	-0.6	2.9	-1.7	-2.8	-12.8	-4.6	6.5	-11.6	-24.0	65.6
Other Capital, net	12.6	3.0	-9.1	-23.1	-16.6	-23.6	-37.4	-76.8	58.8	8.1	-64.1
Change in Reserves	3.1	5.9	-31.2	-105.6	-89.7	6.6	-43.7	73.5	32.2	45.4	40.3
Memo Item:					*(Ethiopian Birr per US dollar)*						
Conversion Factor (Annual Avg)	2.500	2.490	2.300	2.100	2.070	2.070	2.070	2.070	2.070	2.070	2.070
					(Millions of US dollars), outstanding at end of year						
EXTERNAL DEBT (Total)	169.0	204.0	226.1	256.2	283.2	343.6	402.1	500.2	563.0	728.7	804.4
Long-Term Debt (by debtor)	169.0	204.0	226.1	256.2	283.2	343.6	402.1	447.2	511.0	664.7	747.9
Central Bank, incl. IMF credit	2.4	2.5	2.3	2.1	1.7	4.5	5.1	6.3	22.3	79.8	86.8
Central Government	96.0	135.2	162.0	193.2	217.2	273.1	336.9	383.0	422.9	503.7	550.6
Rest of General Government	10.9	11.6	11.6	10.8	9.8	9.0	6.9	6.2	5.1	4.8	3.9
Non-financial Public Enterprises	52.1	48.2	44.1	43.9	48.4	51.6	48.4	47.4	56.7	72.8	103.3
Priv. Sector, incl non-guaranteed	7.6	6.5	6.1	6.2	6.1	5.4	4.8	4.3	4.0	3.6	3.3
Short-Term Debt	0.0	0.0	0.0	0.0	0.0	0.0	0.0	53.0	52.0	64.0	56.5
Memo Items:					*(Thousands of US dollars)*						
Int'l Reserves Excluding Gold	63,300	59,294	83,204	166,027	263,550	276,684	294,735	213,316	152,926	172,727	80,129
Gold Holdings (at market price)	8,446	10,340	16,160	28,848	51,288	38,569	37,056	47,176	64,636	146,432	182,156
SOCIAL INDICATORS											
Total Fertility Rate	5.8	5.8	5.8	5.8	5.9	5.9	6.0	6.0	6.3	6.6	6.9
Infant Mortality Rate	157.8	156.4	155.0	153.8	152.6	151.4	150.2	149.0	151.0	153.0	155.0
Life Expectancy at Birth	43.3	43.4	43.5	43.7	43.9	44.1	44.3	44.5	44.1	43.8	43.5
Urban Population, % of total	8.6	8.8	9.0	9.1	9.3	9.5	9.7	9.9	10.1	10.3	10.5
Food Prod. per capita (1987=100)	134.0	125.6	123.9	122.8	114.3	116.7	113.4	108.3	115.7	124.1	117.0
Labor Force, Agriculture (%)	85.0	84.4	83.9	83.4	82.9	82.4	81.8	81.3	80.8	80.3	79.8
Labor Force, Female (%)	40.0	39.9	39.8	39.8	39.7	39.7	39.6	39.5	39.5	39.4	39.3
Primary Schl. Enroll. Ratio	16.0	..	..	..	..	24.0	25.0	24.0	29.0	37.0	35.0
Primary Schl. Enroll. Ratio, Female	10.0	..	..	..	..	15.0	..	..	18.0	25.0	25.0
Secondary Schl. Enroll. Ratio	4.0	..	..	..	..	6.0	8.0	7.0	9.0	10.0	9.0

1981	1982	1983	1984	1985	1986	1987	1988	1989	1990 estimate	Notes	ETHIOPIA
											FOREIGN TRADE (CUSTOMS BASIS)
378.0	404.3	402.3	416.7	337.5	464.4	370.7	421.1	440.3	297.5	..	Value of Exports, fob
343.0	370.0	366.5	382.0	300.7	449.7	340.2	396.7	414.8	280.2	..	Nonfuel Primary Products
29.9	30.9	33.2	30.8	33.1	10.7	21.3	12.7	13.3	9.0	..	Fuels
5.2	3.3	2.6	3.8	3.7	4.0	9.2	11.7	12.3	8.3	..	Manufactures
737.3	784.9	876.0	942.6	988.6	1,100.8	1,101.2	1,085.0	950.6	1,081.4	..	Value of Imports, cif
95.3	103.9	151.4	129.2	328.6	304.4	164.6	215.9	142.1	161.6	..	Nonfuel Primary Products
171.0	193.3	169.1	174.0	146.2	102.3	109.2	107.2	94.3	107.3	..	Fuels
470.9	487.8	555.5	639.3	513.8	694.2	827.4	761.9	714.2	812.5	..	Manufactures
				(Index 1987 = 100)							
98.3	104.7	107.0	119.1	116.6	131.0	100.0	122.7	107.0	84.5	..	Terms of Trade
102.5	105.1	103.4	113.5	110.3	136.2	100.0	113.0	101.5	96.9	..	Export Prices, fob
104.3	100.4	96.6	95.3	94.6	104.0	100.0	92.1	94.8	114.7	..	Import Prices, cif
			(Millions of current US dollars)								**BALANCE OF PAYMENTS**
564.6	537.6	577.5	626.5	558.5	688.4	640.0	648.0	758.3	676.7	C f	Exports of Goods & Services
411.3	375.8	391.5	449.2	359.0	455.3	391.1	380.6	443.5	365.6	..	Merchandise, fob
142.8	135.7	160.2	162.5	189.9	216.0	232.2	255.5	308.3	306.1	..	Nonfactor Services
10.5	26.1	25.8	14.8	9.6	17.1	16.7	11.9	6.5	5.0	..	Factor Services
863.0	981.2	1,000.9	1,149.7	1,124.4	1,240.3	1,279.7	1,328.5	1,288.6	1,155.6	C f	Imports of Goods & Services
743.6	848.4	856.3	1,026.4	974.7	1,067.9	1,080.3	1,098.6	1,019.3	881.0	..	Merchandise, fob
101.8	97.9	105.2	89.3	107.1	124.1	136.6	153.1	181.4	187.6	..	Nonfactor Services
17.6	34.9	39.4	34.0	42.6	48.3	62.8	76.8	87.9	87.0	..	Factor Services
16.8	21.4	23.7	30.9	34.9	45.7	52.3	77.7	71.8	44.4	..	Long-Term Interest
24.7	45.2	84.9	107.2	145.0	209.5	148.1	118.5	187.9	171.3	..	Private Current Transfers, net
..	..	..	..	..	..	..	..	..	..	..	Workers' Remittances
-273.7	-398.4	-338.5	-416.0	-420.9	-342.4	-491.6	-562.0	-342.4	-307.6	..	Curr. A/C Bal before Off. Transf.
59.9	67.5	92.5	161.9	298.3	293.2	211.8	187.8	209.2	162.0	..	Net Official Transfers
-213.8	-330.9	-246.0	-254.1	-122.6	-49.2	-279.8	-374.2	-133.2	-145.6	..	Curr. A/C Bal after Off. Transf.
161.6	309.2	203.6	180.3	162.3	268.1	187.8	312.5	245.0	188.0	C f	Long-Term Capital, net
..	..	..	..	..	..	..	..	..	..	..	Direct Investment
287.9	80.3	201.5	201.0	282.4	235.8	308.0	305.3	131.8	133.1	..	Long-Term Loans
313.3	113.1	245.1	251.7	348.5	343.7	436.1	465.4	306.0	276.7	..	Disbursements
25.4	32.8	43.6	50.7	66.1	107.9	128.1	160.1	174.2	143.6	..	Repayments
-126.3	228.9	2.1	-20.7	-120.1	32.3	-120.2	7.2	113.2	54.9	C	Other Long-Term Capital
-7.0	81.7	-29.1	31.5	7.9	-53.7	70.9	-123.5	-122.8	-301.1	C f	Other Capital, net
59.2	-60.0	71.5	42.3	-47.6	-165.2	21.1	185.2	11.0	258.7	..	Change in Reserves
											Memo Item:
2.070	2.070	2.070	2.070	2.070	2.070	2.070	2.070	2.070	2.070		Conversion Factor (Annual Avg)
			(Millions of US dollars), outstanding at end of year								**EXTERNAL DEBT (Total)**
1,138.6	1,239.1	1,386.6	1,524.1	1,869.3	2,214.9	2,708.4	2,978.5	3,023.7	3,250.3	..	Long-Term Debt (by debtor)
1,079.7	1,170.7	1,324.0	1,456.8	1,792.0	2,131.6	2,610.8	2,845.7	2,916.4	3,122.6	..	Central Bank, incl. IMF credit
151.2	166.1	138.7	102.6	76.1	90.4	85.4	63.2	36.8	19.5	..	Central Bank, incl. IMF credit
764.2	843.8	1,020.2	1,095.0	1,373.6	1,678.4	2,079.0	2,300.8	2,467.4	2,743.0	..	Central Government
2.0	0.0	0.0	0.0	0.0	0.0	0.0	0.0	0.0	..	..	Rest of General Government
159.4	158.2	162.8	254.0	337.4	358.7	443.1	479.3	410.5	359.2	..	Non-financial Public Enterprises
2.9	2.6	2.3	5.2	4.9	4.1	3.3	2.4	1.7	0.9	..	Priv. Sector, incl non-guaranteed
58.9	68.4	62.6	67.3	77.3	83.3	97.6	132.8	107.3	127.7	..	Short-Term Debt
			(Thousands of US dollars)								**Memo Items:**
266,705	181,841	125,874	44,341	147,998	250,500	122,688	64,227	46,053	20,156	..	Int'l Reserves Excluding Gold
103,350	95,492	79,734	64,435	68,343	81,698	101,177	85,742	76,992	35,035	..	Gold Holdings (at market price)
											SOCIAL INDICATORS
7.2	7.5	7.5	7.5	7.5	7.5	7.5	7.5	7.5	7.5	..	Total Fertility Rate
157.0	159.0	154.6	150.1	145.7	141.2	136.8	135.1	133.3	131.6	..	Infant Mortality Rate
43.1	42.8	43.6	44.5	45.3	46.2	47.1	47.4	47.7	48.0	..	Life Expectancy at Birth
10.7	10.9	11.2	11.4	11.6	12.0	12.3	12.5	12.7	12.9	..	Urban Population, % of total
113.2	121.4	110.6	99.0	102.7	109.2	100.0	99.4	99.8	99.7	..	Food Prod. per capita (1987=100)
..	..	..	..	..	..	..	..	..	..	..	Labor Force, Agriculture (%)
39.1	39.0	38.8	38.6	38.4	38.2	38.0	37.8	37.6	37.4	..	Labor Force, Female (%)
..	40.0	39.0	34.0	36.0	36.0	40.0	38.0	..	..	..	Primary Schl. Enroll. Ratio
32.0	29.0	29.0	28.0	28.0	28.0	31.0	30.0			..	Primary Schl. Enroll. Ratio, Female
..	10.0	11.0	12.0	12.0	14.0	14.0	15.0	..	..	..	Secondary Schl. Enroll. Ratio

FIJI	1970	1971	1972	1973	1974	1975	1976	1977	1978	1979	1980
CURRENT GNP PER CAPITA (US $)	400	450	520	660	840	1,030	1,190	1,290	1,350	1,580	1,750
POPULATION (thousands)	520	531	543	554	565	576	587	599	610	622	634

USE AND ORIGIN OF RESOURCES

(Millions of current Fiji Dollars)

	1970	1971	1972	1973	1974	1975	1976	1977	1978	1979	1980
Gross National Product (GNP)	183.6	201.8	252.1	333.7	448.2	556.4	622.5	651.5	697.7	839.7	969.1
Net Factor Income from Abroad	-8.2	-10.1	-9.2	-4.6	-1.8	-6.0	-1.0	-8.6	-4.5	-12.5	-14.6
GDP at Market Prices	191.8	211.9	261.3	338.3	450.0	562.4	623.5	660.1	702.2	852.2	983.7
Resource Balance	-6.2	-16.5	-24.3	-45.6	-23.5	-3.6	-29.5	-18.2	-31.0	-46.3	-48.6
Exports of Goods & NFServices	92.8	105.5	119.9	153.2	221.1	241.8	235.1	289.9	299.5	385.8	470.0
Imports of Goods & NFServices	99.0	122.0	144.2	198.8	244.6	245.4	264.6	308.1	330.5	432.1	518.6
Domestic Absorption	198.0	228.4	285.6	383.9	473.5	566.0	653.0	678.3	733.2	898.5	1,032.3
Private Consumption, etc.	128.7	145.1	185.1	266.3	334.4	382.5	433.7	423.0	458.2	497.7	562.4
General Gov't Consumption	26.8	30.7	37.9	42.4	54.0	67.5	85.3	102.3	115.1	143.9	156.7
Gross Domestic Investment	42.5	52.6	62.6	75.2	85.1	116.0	134.0	153.0	159.9	256.9	313.2
Fixed Investment	34.8	45.9	53.1	65.7	74.2	103.4	119.5	128.9	149.8	197.3	249.8
Indirect Taxes, net	22.9	27.3	30.8	37.7	39.5	47.0	52.9	54.4	59.2	72.8	82.7
GDP at factor cost	168.9	184.6	230.5	300.6	410.5	515.4	570.6	605.7	643.0	779.4	901.0
Agriculture	48.2	45.7	57.6	75.7	105.0	132.0	147.0	141.3	141.1	168.0	199.5
Industry	39.8	39.8	52.4	66.6	91.0	115.0	128.0	125.4	126.1	167.9	198.3
Manufacturing	23.7	21.1	27.0	31.6	48.0	60.0	67.0	69.4	70.8	98.5	107.6
Services, etc.	80.9	99.1	120.5	158.3	214.5	268.4	295.6	339.0	375.8	443.5	503.2
Gross Domestic Saving	36.3	36.1	38.3	29.6	61.6	112.4	104.5	134.8	128.9	210.6	264.6
Gross National Saving	27.1	25.7	29.8	24.3	58.0	104.4	99.1	122.6	121.0	191.0	248.1

(Millions of 1987 Fiji Dollars)

	1970	1971	1972	1973	1974	1975	1976	1977	1978	1979	1980
Gross National Product	841.49	902.40	977.77	1,110.15	1,150.60	1,149.19	1,182.01	1,249.88	1,282.24	1,427.05	1,404.18
GDP at Market Prices	880.31	943.95	1,014.13	1,128.85	1,158.21	1,164.12	1,195.94	1,266.34	1,290.00	1,447.59	1,424.73
Resource Balance	5.00	-17.26	-35.08	-64.97	-97.25	-130.04	-168.32	-151.07	-155.22	-162.05	-165.71
Exports of Goods & NFServices	426.36	474.13	512.20	569.68	540.37	495.26	472.04	551.79	548.56	656.48	642.77
Imports of Goods & NFServices	421.35	491.39	547.28	634.65	637.62	625.30	640.36	702.86	703.78	818.53	808.49
Domestic Absorption	875.30	961.21	1,049.21	1,193.82	1,255.46	1,294.16	1,364.25	1,417.42	1,445.22	1,609.64	1,590.44
Private Consumption, etc.	574.28	626.51	672.79	797.31	880.92	885.01	922.44	961.81	965.24	994.93	944.32
General Gov't Consumption	101.66	109.57	123.40	124.29	130.40	143.51	173.51	183.75	186.44	223.26	220.21
Gross Domestic Investment	199.36	225.13	253.02	272.21	244.14	265.64	268.31	271.86	293.54	391.44	425.91
Fixed Investment	176.24	215.02	236.33	259.44	228.49	252.20	255.22	259.03	279.33	337.81	384.23
GDP at factor cost	753.34	804.04	867.93	979.16	1,004.65	1,005.57	1,032.65	1,094.43	1,114.19	1,248.38	1,227.76
Agriculture	213.31	201.68	200.10	212.78	205.38	206.44	214.36	248.89	245.72	287.81	269.14
Industry	215.60	215.60	231.90	253.90	243.11	231.47	238.67	265.33	265.11	307.43	311.66
Manufacturing	88.66	81.04	84.61	87.41	90.53	90.99	98.77	107.95	115.57	136.41	125.68
Services, etc.	324.43	386.75	435.94	512.48	556.16	567.66	579.62	580.22	603.36	653.13	646.95

Memo Items:

	1970	1971	1972	1973	1974	1975	1976	1977	1978	1979	1980
Capacity to Import	394.97	424.93	455.05	489.08	576.36	616.13	568.96	661.34	637.76	730.82	732.72
Terms of Trade Adjustment	-31.39	-49.20	-57.15	-80.60	35.99	120.87	96.92	109.55	89.21	74.34	89.95
Gross Domestic Income	848.91	894.75	956.99	1,048.25	1,194.20	1,284.99	1,292.86	1,375.90	1,379.21	1,521.93	1,514.68
Gross National Income	810.09	853.20	920.63	1,029.55	1,186.59	1,270.06	1,278.94	1,359.43	1,371.45	1,501.39	1,494.13

DOMESTIC PRICES/DEFLATORS

(Index 1987 = 100)

	1970	1971	1972	1973	1974	1975	1976	1977	1978	1979	1980
Overall (GDP)	21.8	22.4	25.8	30.0	38.9	48.3	52.1	52.1	54.4	58.9	69.0
Domestic Absorption	22.6	23.8	27.2	32.2	37.7	43.7	47.9	47.9	50.7	55.8	64.9
Agriculture	22.6	22.7	28.8	35.6	51.1	63.9	68.6	56.8	57.4	58.4	74.1
Industry	18.5	18.5	22.6	26.2	37.4	49.7	53.6	47.3	47.6	54.6	63.6
Manufacturing	26.7	26.0	31.9	36.1	53.0	65.9	67.8	64.3	61.3	72.2	85.6
Consumer Price Index	22.3	24.3	29.7	32.9	37.7	42.6	47.5	50.8	54.0	58.2	66.6

MANUFACTURING ACTIVITY

	1970	1971	1972	1973	1974	1975	1976	1977	1978	1979	1980
Employment (1987=100)	63.4	64.0	63.9	69.6	75.9	71.2	86.0	85.5	85.6	90.2	96.2
Real Earnings per Empl. (1987=100)	..	..	..	..	..	..	..	..	..	..	..
Real Output per Empl. (1987=100)	..	..	..	..	..	..	..	..	..	..	..
Earnings as % of Value Added	43.6	59.4	50.1	42.6	37.1	37.5	48.4	46.0	54.6	41.4	43.0

MONETARY HOLDINGS

(Millions of current Fiji Dollars)

	1970	1971	1972	1973	1974	1975	1976	1977	1978	1979	1980
Money Supply, Broadly Defined	65.47	77.96	95.44	108.11	150.46	191.27	193.88	230.05	247.45	298.30	335.13
Money	37.34	42.74	52.32	56.55	69.06	84.02	85.38	84.05	98.45	112.32	100.68
Currency Outside Banks	11.16	13.07	14.95	17.19	21.52	27.34	30.70	34.02	38.79	45.24	44.06
Demand Deposits	26.18	29.67	37.37	39.36	47.54	56.68	54.68	50.03	59.66	67.08	56.63
Quasi-Money	28.14	35.22	43.12	51.57	81.39	107.25	108.49	146.00	149.00	185.98	234.45

GOVERNMENT DEFICIT (-) OR SURPLUS

(Millions of current Fiji Dollars)

	1970	1971	1972	1973	1974	1975	1976	1977	1978	1979	1980
	-5.25	-3.23	-4.02	-11.16	-16.04	-7.65	-23.62	-35.18	-30.57	-24.78	-29.54
Current Revenue	43.36	50.17	55.08	68.20	80.02	109.32	124.07	134.11	157.04	194.00	224.35
Current Expenditure	39.12	46.08	44.17	55.60	70.03	87.17	108.47	119.38	140.00	165.32	193.63
Current Budget Balance	4.24	4.09	10.91	12.60	9.99	22.15	15.60	14.73	17.04	28.68	30.72
Capital Receipts	..	..	..	..	..	..	..	..	..	..	..
Capital Payments	9.49	7.32	14.93	23.76	26.03	29.80	39.22	49.91	47.61	53.46	60.26

1981	1982	1983	1984	1985	1986	1987	1988	1989	1990 estimate	Notes	FIJI
2,000	1,870	1,700	1,770	1,640	1,760	1,620	1,580	1,700	1,780	..	**CURRENT GNP PER CAPITA (US $)**
646	659	672	686	700	711	719	728	736	744	..	**POPULATION (thousands)**
											USE AND ORIGIN OF RESOURCES
				(Millions of current Fiji Dollars)							
1,046.9	1,079.5	1,106.3	1,234.2	1,265.2	1,419.0	1,399.0	1,492.0	1,737.0	1,994.0	..	Gross National Product (GNP)
-9.3	-33.8	-35.9	-41.3	-50.9	-42.0	-46.0	-46.0	-54.0	-46.0	..	Net Factor Income from Abroad
1,056.2	1,113.3	1,142.2	1,275.5	1,316.1	1,461.0	1,445.0	1,538.0	1,791.0	2,040.0	f	GDP at Market Prices
-152.2	-71.3	-62.0	-13.6	-5.0	32.0	40.0	40.0	39.0	-27.0	..	Resource Balance
454.4	481.3	498.1	546.2	584.0	609.0	658.0	852.0	1,115.0	1,277.0	..	Exports of Goods & NFServices
606.6	552.6	560.1	559.8	589.0	577.0	618.0	812.0	1,076.0	1,304.0	..	Imports of Goods & NFServices
1,208.4	1,184.6	1,204.2	1,289.1	1,321.1	1,429.0	1,405.0	1,498.0	1,752.0	2,067.0	..	Domestic Absorption
673.1	696.3	731.1	802.8	818.0	910.0	938.0	1,073.0	1,236.0	1,360.0	..	Private Consumption, etc.
173.1	203.8	231.6	245.0	252.0	253.0	252.0	225.0	286.0	325.0	..	General Gov't Consumption
362.2	284.5	241.5	241.3	251.1	266.0	215.0	200.0	230.0	382.0	..	Gross Domestic Investment
280.5	262.6	239.2	218.0	239.1	215.0	210.0	188.0	223.0	357.0	..	Fixed Investment
102.5	92.8	110.4	123.6	139.0	124.9	159.8	152.9	193.0	222.0	..	Indirect Taxes, net
953.7	1,020.5	1,031.8	1,151.9	1,177.1	1,336.1	1,285.2	1,385.1	1,598.0	1,818.0	f	GDP at factor cost
189.7	206.8	189.9	220.2	215.7	277.1	304.9	279.6	389.8	367.0	..	Agriculture
202.6	217.6	203.4	216.4	229.5	267.1	268.5	283.6	344.6	372.2	..	Industry
100.1	108.9	94.4	112.5	111.3	136.6	130.5	137.2	165.0	180.1	..	Manufacturing
561.4	596.1	638.5	715.3	731.9	791.9	711.8	821.9	863.7	1,078.8	..	Services, etc.
210.0	213.2	179.5	227.7	246.1	298.0	255.0	240.0	269.0	355.0	..	Gross Domestic Saving
193.2	176.6	141.6	182.3	184.5	250.0	183.2	188.8	195.6	276.1	..	Gross National Saving
				(Millions of 1987 Fiji Dollars)							
1,503.31	1,383.81	1,323.65	1,435.25	1,385.38	1,516.07	1,399.00	1,416.36	1,596.02	1,686.01	..	Gross National Product
1,514.73	1,424.52	1,364.00	1,479.88	1,432.16	1,545.66	1,445.00	1,458.66	1,644.55	1,725.19	f	GDP at Market Prices
-208.58	-105.26	-89.27	-27.39	-16.18	25.93	40.00	-115.00	-159.22	-238.62	..	Resource Balance
631.16	642.77	631.16	673.42	672.09	686.36	658.00	797.52	1,008.79	1,063.99	..	Exports of Goods & NFServices
839.74	748.03	720.43	700.81	688.26	660.43	618.00	912.51	1,168.02	1,302.61	..	Imports of Goods & NFServices
1,723.31	1,529.79	1,453.26	1,507.27	1,448.34	1,519.73	1,405.00	1,573.65	1,803.77	1,963.81	..	Domestic Absorption
1,058.42	968.24	915.15	991.30	957.94	986.07	938.00	1,200.33	1,365.29	1,412.20	..	Private Consumption, etc.
213.20	236.91	255.59	262.24	246.79	254.51	252.00	199.37	244.28	255.05	..	General Gov't Consumption
451.68	324.63	282.52	253.74	243.61	279.14	215.00	173.95	194.21	296.56	..	Gross Domestic Investment
383.43	331.78	287.37	254.01	243.16	281.94	210.00	184.88	213.01	313.49	..	Fixed Investment
1,300.84	1,286.41	1,236.06	1,337.46	1,273.81	1,375.24	1,285.20	1,296.93	1,462.06	1,534.00	f	GDP at factor cost
304.02	309.30	253.29	318.64	274.96	327.62	304.90	298.03	331.32	342.42	..	Agriculture
331.34	311.87	289.02	295.16	274.85	306.59	268.50	255.80	296.01	310.61	..	Industry
138.28	134.39	120.86	141.54	123.35	147.14	130.50	129.41	144.50	151.96	..	Manufacturing
665.48	665.23	693.75	723.66	724.01	741.03	711.80	743.09	834.73	880.98	..	Services, etc.
											Memo Items:
629.04	651.52	640.68	683.78	682.42	697.06	658.00	957.47	1,210.35	1,275.64	..	Capacity to Import
-2.12	8.74	9.52	10.37	10.34	10.70	0.00	159.95	201.56	211.65	..	Terms of Trade Adjustment
1,512.61	1,433.27	1,373.52	1,490.25	1,442.50	1,556.35	1,445.00	1,618.61	1,846.11	1,936.84	..	Gross Domestic Income
1,501.19	1,392.55	1,333.17	1,445.61	1,395.72	1,526.77	1,399.00	1,576.31	1,797.57	1,897.66	..	Gross National Income
				(Index 1987 = 100)							**DOMESTIC PRICES/DEFLATORS**
69.7	78.2	83.7	86.2	91.9	94.5	100.0	105.4	108.9	118.2	..	Overall (GDP)
70.1	77.4	82.9	85.5	91.2	94.0	100.0	95.2	97.1	105.3	..	Domestic Absorption
62.4	66.9	75.0	69.1	78.4	84.6	100.0	93.8	117.6	107.2	..	Agriculture
61.1	69.8	70.4	73.3	83.5	87.1	100.0	110.9	116.4	119.8	..	Industry
72.4	81.0	78.1	79.5	90.2	92.8	100.0	106.0	114.2	118.5	..	Manufacturing
74.0	79.2	84.6	89.0	93.0	94.6	100.0	111.8	118.7	128.4	f	Consumer Price Index
											MANUFACTURING ACTIVITY
88.9	92.3	96.4	105.1	100.6	103.4	100.0	..	..	..	..	Employment (1987=100)
..	..	..	..	..	..	..	..	..	..	..	Real Earnings per Empl. (1987=100)
..	..	..	..	..	..	..	..	..	..	..	Real Output per Empl. (1987=100)
48.4	47.0	55.1	55.9	58.6						..	Earnings as % of Value Added
				(Millions of current Fiji Dollars)							**MONETARY HOLDINGS**
352.58	381.20	432.22	480.07	489.37	574.98	598.18	721.32	789.20	988.24	..	Money Supply, Broadly Defined
118.43	123.55	134.76	135.97	137.79	172.10	168.31	272.92	263.58	265.35	..	Money
48.73	52.77	58.73	61.03	61.76	63.13	64.91	67.73	77.98	86.02	..	Currency Outside Banks
69.71	70.79	76.04	74.93	76.03	108.97	103.40	205.19	185.59	179.33	..	Demand Deposits
234.15	257.64	297.46	344.11	351.59	402.88	429.87	448.40	525.62	722.89	..	Quasi-Money
				(Millions of current Fiji Dollars)							**GOVERNMENT DEFICIT (-) OR SURPLUS**
-45.26	-70.33	-43.29	-38.73	-35.44	-70.57	-73.92	-11.89	-54.66	-46.49	..	Current Revenue
262.85	264.80	293.65	329.16	339.69	340.06	336.18	389.84	459.99	539.06	..	Current Revenue
213.38	244.57	281.47	316.74	318.49	327.30	349.41	333.66	386.02	431.86	..	Current Expenditure
49.47	20.23	12.18	12.42	21.20	12.76	-13.23	56.18	73.97	107.20	..	Current Budget Balance
..	..	..	..	..	..	..	..	..	..	..	Capital Receipts
94.73	90.56	55.47	51.15	56.64	83.33	60.69	68.07	128.63	153.69	..	Capital Payments

FIJI	1970	1971	1972	1973	1974	1975	1976	1977	1978	1979	1980
FOREIGN TRADE (CUSTOMS BASIS)					*(Millions of current US dollars)*						
Value of Exports, fob	..	..	..	..	..	..	..	..	..	..	..
Nonfuel Primary Products	..	..	..	..	..	..	..	..	..	..	..
Fuels	..	..	..	..	..	..	..	..	..	..	..
Manufactures	..	..	..	..	..	..	..	..	..	..	..
Value of Imports, cif	103.91	128.09	158.15	203.45	273.06	267.34	262.68	306.22	366.26	469.64	561.26
Nonfuel Primary Products	24.93	30.28	37.54	49.68	64.87	57.86	58.25	72.18	89.57	94.79	98.35
Fuels	11.45	13.42	15.71	18.20	42.90	46.58	42.17	59.03	63.90	86.58	129.46
Manufactures	67.52	84.39	104.90	135.58	165.30	162.90	162.26	175.01	212.80	288.26	333.45
Terms of Trade					*(Index 1987 = 100)*						
Export Prices, fob	..	..	..	..	..	..	..	..	..	..	..
Import Prices, cif	..	..	..	..	..	..	..	..	..	..	..
BALANCE OF PAYMENTS					*(Millions of current US dollars)*						
Exports of Goods & Services	109.00	126.58	151.13	198.37	286.23	295.16	264.89	325.51	369.52	475.46	600.11
Merchandise, fob	62.10	63.39	71.01	82.73	142.75	157.60	120.86	164.47	184.47	242.40	343.31
Nonfactor Services	44.40	59.38	74.37	108.60	130.13	126.03	137.73	153.09	176.20	219.00	233.74
Factor Services	2.50	3.81	5.75	7.03	13.35	11.53	6.30	7.96	8.86	14.05	23.06
Imports of Goods & Services	125.90	157.57	191.63	262.39	316.78	320.78	311.96	350.55	403.27	546.39	657.83
Merchandise, fob	92.50	113.34	139.19	194.68	234.52	230.93	226.80	258.50	298.17	412.38	492.96
Nonfactor Services	21.20	28.69	35.61	54.96	66.63	62.41	67.45	75.30	90.93	106.62	124.64
Factor Services	12.20	15.55	16.83	12.76	15.63	27.44	17.71	16.75	14.17	27.39	40.23
Long-Term Interest	1.10	0.80	1.20	1.80	3.80	4.00	4.20	4.80	6.40	6.30	9.50
Private Current Transfers, net	-1.20	-0.40	0.87	-0.83	-2.29	-2.43	-4.89	-3.97	-4.02	-8.51	-2.33
Workers' Remittances	..	..	..	..	..	..	..	..	..	..	..
Curr. A/C Bal before Off. Transf.	-18.10	-31.39	-39.63	-64.85	-32.83	-28.05	-51.95	-29.00	-37.77	-79.45	-60.04
Net Official Transfers	3.80	3.81	7.71	6.68	3.97	1.70	1.34	2.92	2.01	13.19	35.19
Curr. A/C Bal after Off. Transf.	-14.30	-27.58	-31.92	-58.18	-28.86	-26.35	-50.62	-26.08	-35.76	-66.26	-24.86
Long-Term Capital, net	15.50	14.14	27.90	43.16	49.07	45.41	15.33	36.26	1.18	55.52	74.10
Direct Investment	6.40	6.52	8.47	13.23	12.03	10.93	..	..	..	10.17	34.22
Long-Term Loans	0.70	3.40	6.10	24.80	9.30	9.00	10.30	19.10	-3.90	23.00	67.00
Disbursements	2.30	4.10	7.30	26.50	12.40	12.40	14.60	24.00	8.00	30.50	78.20
Repayments	1.60	0.70	1.20	1.70	3.10	3.40	4.30	4.90	11.90	7.50	11.20
Other Long-Term Capital	8.40	4.22	13.33	5.12	27.74	25.48	5.03	17.16	5.08	22.35	-27.12
Other Capital, net	-0.70	22.66	28.23	23.25	13.68	30.75	12.90	6.32	13.03	16.20	-9.00
Change in Reserves	-0.50	-9.22	-24.21	-8.23	-33.88	-49.81	22.39	-16.50	21.54	-5.46	-40.24
Memo Item:					*(Fiji Dollars per US dollar)*						
Conversion Factor (Annual Avg)	0.870	0.860	0.830	0.790	0.810	0.820	0.900	0.920	0.850	0.840	0.820
EXTERNAL DEBT (Total)	11.70	14.80	20.80	47.20	*(Millions of US dollars), outstanding at end of year*						
					54.50	59.30	63.90	120.40	103.20	141.40	280.90
Long-Term Debt (by debtor)	11.70	14.80	20.80	47.20	54.50	59.30	63.90	94.40	93.20	118.40	244.90
Central Bank, incl. IMF credit	0.00	0.00	0.00	0.00	1.20	1.40	1.90	9.70	10.20	10.20	1.80
Central Government	11.70	13.70	14.60	37.00	41.40	46.20	51.30	73.10	72.00	81.20	112.80
Rest of General Government	..	..	..	..	..	..	..	..	..	..	..
Non-financial Public Enterprises	0.00	1.10	6.20	10.20	11.90	11.70	10.70	11.60	11.00	27.00	65.40
Priv. Sector, incl non-guaranteed	0.00	0.00	0.00	0.00	0.00	0.00	0.00	0.00	0.00	0.00	64.90
Short-Term Debt	0.00	0.00	0.00	0.00	0.00	0.00	0.00	26.00	10.00	23.00	36.00
Memo Items:					*(Millions of US dollars)*						
Int'l Reserves Excluding Gold	27.4	39.6	69.4	74.0	109.2	148.6	116.3	147.1	134.7	136.5	167.5
Gold Holdings (at market price)	..	..	..	..	..	..	..	0.9	1.9	5.7	6.5
SOCIAL INDICATORS											
Total Fertility Rate	4.1	3.9	3.7	3.7	3.7	3.6	3.6	3.6	3.6	3.6	3.5
Infant Mortality Rate	49.0	47.0	45.0	43.4	41.8	40.2	38.6	37.0	36.0	35.0	34.0
Life Expectancy at Birth	57.3	57.7	58.1	58.5	58.9	59.2	59.6	60.0	60.4	60.8	61.1
Urban Population, % of total	34.8	35.2	35.6	35.9	36.3	36.7	37.5	37.5	37.9	38.3	38.7
Food Prod. per capita (1987=100)	151.5	136.9	122.4	123.1	112.7	108.8	105.9	116.7	115.5	136.2	122.1
Labor Force, Agriculture (%)	51.5	50.9	50.3	49.7	49.1	48.6	48.1	47.6	47.1	46.6	46.2
Labor Force, Female (%)	11.9	12.5	13.1	13.7	14.2	14.7	15.3	15.9	16.4	16.9	17.4
Primary Schl. Enroll. Ratio	105.0	..	..	..	..	115.0	112.0	110.0	110.0	109.0	120.0
Primary Schl. Enroll. Ratio, Female	103.0	..	..	..	..	115.0	111.0	110.0	110.0	108.0	120.0
Secondary Schl. Enroll. Ratio	52.0	..	..	..	..	66.0	55.0	58.0	60.0	62.0	55.0

1981	1982	1983	1984	1985	1986	1987	1988	1989	1990 estimate	Notes	FIJI
											FOREIGN TRADE (CUSTOMS BASIS)
..	..	..	..	..	..	..	..	..	..	..	Value of Exports, fob
..	..	..	..	..	..	..	..	..	..	..	Nonfuel Primary Products
..	..	..	..	..	..	..	..	..	..	..	Fuels
..	..	..	..	..	..	..	..	..	..	..	Manufactures
631.08	513.70	483.16	448.77	440.62	434.20	377.13	460.62	582.66	740.74	..	Value of Imports, cif
112.05	94.35	96.38	88.83	89.11	84.68	84.15	102.78	130.01	165.28	..	Nonfuel Primary Products
162.02	146.70	112.21	98.78	100.19	72.33	61.65	75.30	95.25	121.09	..	Fuels
357.01	272.65	274.57	261.16	251.32	277.18	231.33	282.54	357.40	454.36	..	Manufactures

(Index 1987 = 100)

1981	1982	1983	1984	1985	1986	1987	1988	1989	1990 estimate	Notes	FIJI
..	..	..	..	..	..	..	..	..	..	..	Terms of Trade
..	..	..	..	..	..	..	..	..	..	..	Export Prices, fob
..	..	..	..	..	..	..	..	..	..	..	Import Prices, cif

(Millions of current US dollars)

1981	1982	1983	1984	1985	1986	1987	1988	1989	1990 estimate	Notes	FIJI
											BALANCE OF PAYMENTS
561.42	543.50	511.28	526.26	523.34	554.91	546.96	618.52	783.50	932.17	..	Exports of Goods & Services
278.39	251.39	217.05	227.87	207.68	245.70	303.56	345.62	399.36	494.26	..	Merchandise, fob
252.24	269.58	273.56	277.47	301.29	290.09	222.36	244.49	346.97	398.24	..	Nonfactor Services
30.78	22.53	20.67	20.92	14.37	19.12	21.04	28.42	37.17	39.67	..	Factor Services
753.97	653.74	600.60	568.15	559.34	573.71	554.52	617.88	769.70	927.98	..	Imports of Goods & Services
544.86	440.23	421.19	390.70	382.57	368.32	329.05	395.26	495.21	591.12	..	Merchandise, fob
167.51	154.76	130.39	128.33	131.13	155.81	173.94	175.37	222.27	253.91	..	Nonfactor Services
41.60	58.76	49.01	49.12	45.64	49.58	51.53	47.25	52.22	82.94	..	Factor Services
16.50	22.30	23.00	24.30	24.60	25.20	26.00	24.80	31.70	31.10	..	Long-Term Interest
-8.80	-2.99	-1.99	-3.78	-9.29	-5.27	-20.78	-3.62	-13.05	-22.21	..	Private Current Transfers, net
..	..	..	0.00	..	..	0.00	19.10	..	..	..	Workers' Remittances
-201.35	-113.23	-91.31	-45.66	-45.28	-24.06	-28.34	-2.98	0.74	-18.02	..	Curr. A/C Bal before Off. Transf.
25.86	20.47	26.68	18.77	32.96	14.75	10.32	33.69	28.36	24.95	..	Net Official Transfers
-175.49	-92.76	-64.63	-26.89	-12.32	-9.31	-18.02	30.71	29.11	6.93	..	Curr. A/C Bal after Off. Transf.
104.01	75.96	58.73	28.52	1.71	-23.59	-51.90	5.02	-50.24	-11.61	..	Long-Term Capital, net
34.62	35.91	32.02	23.04	0.86	-13.98	-27.79	-1.58	-15.00	30.46	..	Direct Investment
70.60	44.90	41.00	17.00	2.70	-12.90	-18.60	6.80	-30.60	-42.10	..	Long-Term Loans
80.10	56.80	55.50	43.70	33.90	18.40	18.10	43.50	26.60	30.00	..	Disbursements
9.50	11.90	14.50	26.70	31.20	31.30	36.70	36.70	57.20	72.10	..	Repayments
-1.21	-4.86	-14.29	-11.52	-1.85	3.29	-5.51	-0.20	-4.64	0.03	..	Other Long-Term Capital
47.89	-5.35	-0.35	5.86	5.77	60.76	7.00	76.37	7.47	40.55	..	Other Capital, net
23.59	22.16	6.26	-7.49	4.84	-27.87	62.92	-112.09	13.66	-35.87	..	Change in Reserves

(Fiji Dollars per US dollar)

1981	1982	1983	1984	1985	1986	1987	1988	1989	1990 estimate	Notes	FIJI
											Memo Item:
0.850	0.930	1.020	1.080	1.150	1.130	1.240	1.430	1.480	1.480	..	Conversion Factor (Annual Avg)

(Millions of US dollars), outstanding at end of year

1981	1982	1983	1984	1985	1986	1987	1988	1989	1990 estimate	Notes	FIJI
372.20	401.90	437.40	413.30	443.70	440.80	466.20	466.60	405.20	399.00	..	**EXTERNAL DEBT (Total)**
333.20	379.90	411.40	391.30	424.70	420.80	444.70	435.20	391.20	387.00	..	Long-Term Debt (by debtor)
1.80	16.70	15.70	14.50	15.80	9.90	12.80	10.60	7.20	5.50	..	Central Bank, incl. IMF credit
140.90	149.40	148.40	142.00	145.30	155.90	171.70	177.40	163.20	177.80	..	Central Government
..	..	..	..	..	..	..	..	..	..	..	Rest of General Government
94.80	114.20	142.30	136.00	155.60	153.50	156.50	146.20	123.00	109.00	..	Non-financial Public Enterprises
95.70	99.60	105.00	98.80	108.00	101.50	103.70	101.00	97.80	94.70	..	Priv. Sector, incl non-guaranteed
39.00	22.00	26.00	22.00	19.00	20.00	21.50	31.40	14.00	12.00	..	Short-Term Debt

(Millions of US dollars)

1981	1982	1983	1984	1985	1986	1987	1988	1989	1990 estimate	Notes	FIJI
											Memo Items:
135.1	126.9	115.8	117.4	130.8	171.1	132.2	233.4	211.6	260.8	..	Int'l Reserves Excluding Gold
4.4	5.1	4.2	3.4	3.6	4.3	0.4	0.3	0.3	0.3	..	Gold Holdings (at market price)
											SOCIAL INDICATORS
3.5	3.5	3.5	3.4	3.4	3.3	3.3	3.2	3.1	3.1	..	Total Fertility Rate
33.0	32.0	31.0	30.0	29.0	28.0	27.0	26.1	25.1	24.2	..	Infant Mortality Rate
61.5	61.9	62.3	62.7	63.0	63.4	63.8	64.1	64.4	64.7	..	Life Expectancy at Birth
39.2	39.7	40.2	40.7	41.2	41.8	42.3	42.9	43.4	44.0	..	Urban Population, % of total
129.9	131.7	97.6	135.7	111.8	128.5	100.0	103.8	114.5	114.1	..	Food Prod. per capita (1987=100)
..	..	..	..	..	..	..	..	..	..	..	Labor Force, Agriculture (%)
17.7	18.0	18.3	18.6	18.9	19.2	19.4	19.7	19.9	20.2	..	Labor Force, Female (%)
..	..	..	122.0	122.0	122.0	..	..	..	125.0	..	Primary Schl. Enroll. Ratio
..	..	..	121.0	122.0	122.0	..	..	..	..	..	Primary Schl. Enroll. Ratio, Female
..	..	..	53.0	51.0	52.0	..	..	..	..	..	Secondary Schl. Enroll. Ratio

FINLAND	1970	1971	1972	1973	1974	1975	1976	1977	1978	1979	1980
CURRENT GNP PER CAPITA (US $)	2,380	2,550	2,910	3,520	4,360	5,400	6,160	6,700	7,280	8,580	10,110
POPULATION (thousands)	4,606	4,616	4,640	4,666	4,691	4,711	4,726	4,739	4,753	4,765	4,780
USE AND ORIGIN OF RESOURCES					*(Billions of current Finnish Markkaa)*						
Gross National Product (GNP)	45.32	49.76	57.98	70.55	89.01	102.77	115.79	127.31	140.68	164.12	189.36
Net Factor Income from Abroad	-0.43	-0.50	-0.65	-0.82	-1.04	-1.52	-1.86	-2.48	-2.69	-2.77	-3.24
GDP at Market Prices	45.74	50.26	58.63	71.36	90.05	104.29	117.64	129.79	143.38	166.89	192.60
Resource Balance	-0.56	-0.91	0.15	-0.45	-3.30	-6.17	-2.29	2.25	5.65	2.60	-1.53
Exports of Goods & NFServices	11.75	12.23	14.95	18.15	24.80	24.76	29.54	36.97	43.04	52.55	63.49
Imports of Goods & NFServices	12.31	13.14	14.80	18.60	28.09	30.92	31.82	34.73	37.39	49.95	65.02
Domestic Absorption	46.31	51.17	58.48	71.81	93.35	110.46	119.93	127.54	137.73	164.29	194.13
Private Consumption, etc.	26.09	28.57	33.50	40.63	48.55	57.66	66.91	69.84	79.33	91.44	103.42
General Gov't Consumption	6.61	7.62	8.96	10.69	13.69	17.80	21.31	24.00	26.34	29.87	34.89
Gross Domestic Investment	13.60	14.98	16.01	20.49	31.12	34.99	31.71	33.71	32.06	42.98	55.82
Fixed Investment	12.01	13.82	16.36	20.57	26.86	32.67	33.18	35.49	34.84	39.26	49.13
Indirect Taxes, net	4.74	5.43	6.37	7.72	8.37	8.87	10.22	12.57	14.88	16.59	19.49
GDP at factor cost	41.00	44.83	52.26	63.64	81.69	95.42	107.42	117.22	128.50	150.30	173.12
Agriculture	5.06	5.55	5.78	6.80	8.34	10.15	10.69	11.48	11.88	13.91	16.74
Industry	16.34	17.37	20.92	26.05	34.99	38.74	42.04	45.26	50.10	59.42	67.97
Manufacturing	10.87	11.58	13.83	17.18	23.66	25.20	28.45	30.27	34.55	41.76	48.48
Services, etc.	19.60	21.91	25.56	30.79	38.36	46.52	54.69	60.49	66.51	76.97	88.41
Gross Domestic Saving	13.04	14.07	16.16	20.04	27.82	28.83	29.42	35.95	37.70	45.58	54.29
Gross National Saving	12.62	13.60	15.52	19.23	26.80	27.29	27.53	33.43	34.95	42.74	50.97
					(Billions of 1987 Finnish Markkaa)						
Gross National Product	224.36	228.69	246.11	262.45	269.98	271.48	271.76	271.33	277.54	298.49	314.80
GDP at Market Prices	226.41	230.90	248.78	265.41	273.04	275.48	276.14	276.64	282.82	303.47	319.99
Resource Balance	-4.83	-5.12	-0.39	-3.61	-8.18	-16.77	-8.99	0.96	9.27	4.07	4.50
Exports of Goods & NFServices	48.78	48.17	55.13	59.15	58.77	50.56	57.01	65.97	71.87	78.16	84.73
Imports of Goods & NFServices	53.61	53.29	55.53	62.75	66.95	67.33	66.01	65.01	62.60	74.09	80.24
Domestic Absorption	231.24	236.02	249.17	269.02	281.22	292.24	285.13	275.68	273.55	299.40	315.50
Private Consumption, etc.	119.93	123.07	136.53	146.55	140.21	150.32	158.15	149.48	151.98	160.64	163.24
General Gov't Consumption	37.40	39.56	42.62	45.01	47.03	50.28	53.14	55.38	57.67	59.85	62.39
Gross Domestic Investment	73.91	73.40	70.02	77.46	93.97	91.64	73.84	70.82	63.90	78.91	89.87
Fixed Investment	64.54	66.97	71.34	77.41	80.12	84.88	77.39	74.69	69.51	71.61	79.08
GDP at factor cost	202.70	205.83	221.69	236.47	247.83	251.92	251.81	249.49	253.38	273.28	288.39
Agriculture	24.74	24.50	23.85	23.58	22.59	21.85	22.22	22.55	22.40	25.19	26.93
Industry	71.91	72.31	80.14	86.00	89.12	87.25	86.52	86.35	88.80	95.79	102.93
Manufacturing	45.95	46.71	51.99	55.35	57.81	54.85	56.05	55.17	57.50	63.70	68.98
Services, etc.	105.40	108.57	116.97	126.18	135.80	143.24	143.56	140.90	142.35	152.38	158.23
Memo Items:											
Capacity to Import	51.15	49.58	56.09	61.24	59.10	53.90	61.26	69.22	72.05	77.94	78.35
Terms of Trade Adjustment	2.37	1.42	0.95	2.09	0.33	3.34	4.25	3.24	0.18	-0.22	-6.38
Gross Domestic Income	228.78	232.32	249.73	267.50	273.37	278.82	280.39	279.89	283.01	303.26	313.61
Gross National Income	226.72	230.11	247.06	264.53	270.31	274.82	276.01	274.57	277.72	298.27	308.41
DOMESTIC PRICES/DEFLATORS					*(Index 1987 = 100)*						
Overall (GDP)	20.2	21.8	23.6	26.9	33.0	37.9	42.6	46.9	50.7	55.0	60.2
Domestic Absorption	20.0	21.7	23.5	26.7	33.2	37.8	42.1	46.3	50.3	54.9	61.5
Agriculture	20.5	22.7	24.2	28.8	36.9	46.5	48.1	50.9	53.1	55.2	62.2
Industry	22.7	24.0	26.1	30.3	39.3	44.4	48.6	52.4	56.4	62.0	66.0
Manufacturing	23.7	24.8	26.6	31.0	40.9	45.9	50.8	54.9	60.1	65.6	70.3
Consumer Price Index	21.4	22.8	24.4	27.1	31.6	37.2	42.5	47.9	51.6	55.5	61.9
MANUFACTURING ACTIVITY											
Employment (1987=100)	99.1	101.9	104.8	109.1	112.4	111.4	110.9	107.8	104.7	108.4	113.9
Real Earnings per Empl. (1987=100)	63.6	66.6	71.8	74.9	78.5	81.7	82.7	78.9	80.3	83.6	84.4
Real Output per Empl. (1987=100)	57.3	57.4	61.2	61.1	63.8	61.3	62.9	64.2	67.0	72.6	78.7
Earnings as % of Value Added	47.1	50.3	50.2	48.9	44.1	49.5	50.1	49.2	45.3	43.4	44.1
MONETARY HOLDINGS					*(Billions of current Finnish Markkaa)*						
Money Supply, Broadly Defined	19.48	21.98	25.71	29.67	34.90	42.70	46.67	51.99	59.92	70.75	81.41
Money	3.45	4.03	4.96	6.11	7.27	9.77	9.60	9.87	11.50	14.09	14.98
Currency Outside Banks	1.29	1.48	1.55	1.78	2.15	2.51	2.54	2.84	3.48	3.91	4.30
Demand Deposits	2.16	2.55	3.41	4.33	5.12	7.26	7.06	7.03	8.01	10.18	10.67
Quasi-Money	16.04	17.96	20.75	23.56	27.63	32.93	37.07	42.12	48.43	56.66	66.43
					(Billions of current Finnish Markkaa)						
GOVERNMENT DEFICIT (-) OR SURPLUS	..	..	0.72	2.04	0.76	-2.32	-0.03	-1.94	-2.64	-4.10	-4.15
Current Revenue	..	..	15.64	19.51	23.69	29.08	36.53	39.60	40.95	45.79	52.89
Current Expenditure	..	..	11.82	13.84	18.38	24.73	29.18	33.02	36.61	42.61	48.19
Current Budget Balance	..	..	3.82	5.67	5.30	4.35	7.35	6.58	4.34	3.18	4.71
Capital Receipts	..	..	0.00	0.01	0.01	0.02	0.03	0.03	0.11	0.03	0.07
Capital Payments	..	..	3.11	3.64	4.56	6.69	7.41	8.55	7.10	7.32	8.93

1981	1982	1983	1984	1985	1986	1987	1988	1989	1990 estimate	Notes	FINLAND
11,040	11,360	10,880	10,790	10,960	12,110	14,570	18,630	22,110	24,520	..	**CURRENT GNP PER CAPITA (US $)**
4,800	4,827	4,856	4,882	4,902	4,918	4,933	4,951	4,962	4,986	..	**POPULATION (thousands)**
			(Billions of current Finnish Markkaa)								**USE AND ORIGIN OF RESOURCES**
213.65	239.58	267.77	301.17	327.99	350.18	383.93	433.45	484.62	509.14	..	Gross National Product (GNP)
-4.83	-6.14	-6.88	-7.19	-6.99	-7.38	-7.67	-8.09	-12.31	-15.64	..	Net Factor Income from Abroad
218.48	245.72	274.65	308.36	334.99	357.57	391.60	441.54	496.93	524.78	..	GDP at Market Prices
3.11	2.04	1.37	8.05	3.28	5.74	2.26	-1.12	-9.29	-7.20	..	Resource Balance
72.36	75.80	82.74	94.19	98.17	95.63	100.03	108.75	116.70	119.14	..	Exports of Goods & NFServices
69.25	73.76	81.36	86.14	94.89	89.90	97.77	109.87	126.00	126.35	..	Imports of Goods & NFServices
215.37	243.68	273.27	300.30	331.71	351.83	389.34	442.65	506.23	531.98	..	Domestic Absorption
117.21	132.68	150.07	165.63	183.88	196.53	215.62	239.87	264.59	278.32	..	Private Consumption, etc.
40.83	46.66	53.33	59.74	68.22	74.00	81.34	88.73	97.81	110.64	..	General Gov't Consumption
57.33	64.34	69.87	74.94	79.61	81.30	92.38	114.05	143.83	143.02	..	Gross Domestic Investment
55.33	62.25	70.05	73.43	80.05	83.51	93.27	111.05	137.40	138.07	..	Fixed Investment
22.46	25.45	28.10	33.74	37.46	41.19	45.91	55.65	62.46	63.95	..	Indirect Taxes, net
196.01	220.27	246.55	274.62	297.53	316.37	345.69	385.89	434.48	460.83	..	GDP at factor cost
17.41	19.41	21.06	23.30	24.13	23.74	22.43	24.46	27.71	..	..	Agriculture
76.08	83.43	92.81	102.31	107.43	111.83	124.43	138.49	155.25	..	..	Industry
53.09	57.23	63.28	70.65	74.59	76.64	85.71	93.80	101.08	..	..	Manufacturing
102.52	117.43	132.68	149.01	165.97	180.80	198.83	222.93	251.52	..	..	Services, etc.
60.44	66.38	71.25	82.99	82.89	87.04	94.64	112.94	134.53	135.82	..	Gross Domestic Saving
55.57	60.11	64.24	75.67	75.86	78.86	86.26	104.48	121.14	118.86	..	Gross National Saving
			(Billions of 1987 Finnish Markkaa)								
318.00	328.11	337.95	348.78	361.28	368.85	383.93	405.12	423.94	423.48	..	Gross National Product
324.95	336.31	346.40	356.96	368.84	376.57	391.60	412.78	434.89	436.71	..	GDP at Market Prices
12.42	9.58	9.41	13.48	9.09	7.73	2.26	-4.91	-12.86	-9.80	..	Resource Balance
88.92	87.95	90.11	95.00	96.16	97.46	100.03	103.72	105.34	107.19	..	Exports of Goods & NFServices
76.49	78.37	80.70	81.53	87.06	89.73	97.77	108.64	118.20	116.99	..	Imports of Goods & NFServices
312.52	326.73	336.99	343.49	359.75	368.84	389.34	417.69	447.75	446.52	..	Domestic Absorption
163.78	172.07	179.22	183.82	196.04	204.50	215.62	228.61	237.77	240.83	..	Private Consumption, etc.
65.07	67.38	69.88	71.83	75.54	77.87	81.34	83.26	85.39	89.17	..	General Gov't Consumption
83.67	87.28	87.88	87.84	88.18	86.47	92.38	105.83	124.60	116.52	..	Gross Domestic Investment
80.79	84.37	87.80	85.95	88.45	88.46	93.27	103.07	117.57	111.69	..	Fixed Investment
292.53	302.31	311.88	318.57	328.34	333.49	345.69	360.10	379.35	382.84	..	GDP at factor cost
24.82	25.06	26.33	26.67	26.45	24.92	22.43	24.33	26.14	..	..	Agriculture
105.27	107.57	111.24	114.11	118.19	119.41	124.43	129.84	135.90	..	..	Industry
71.25	72.24	74.54	77.54	80.59	81.66	85.71	89.04	91.82	..	..	Manufacturing
162.25	169.77	174.30	177.79	183.70	189.16	198.83	205.92	217.32	..	..	Services, etc.
											Memo Items:
79.92	80.53	82.06	89.15	90.07	95.45	100.03	107.53	109.48	110.32	..	Capacity to Import
-8.99	-7.41	-8.05	-5.85	-6.08	-2.00	0.00	3.81	4.14	3.13	..	Terms of Trade Adjustment
315.96	328.90	338.35	351.11	362.76	374.57	391.60	416.59	439.04	439.85	..	Gross Domestic Income
309.01	320.69	329.90	342.93	355.20	366.85	383.93	408.93	428.09	426.62	..	Gross National Income
			(Index 1987 = 100)								**DOMESTIC PRICES/DEFLATORS**
67.2	73.1	79.3	86.4	90.8	95.0	100.0	107.0	114.3	120.2	..	Overall (GDP)
68.9	74.6	81.1	87.4	92.2	95.4	100.0	106.0	113.1	119.1	..	Domestic Absorption
70.1	77.5	80.0	87.4	91.2	95.3	100.0	100.5	106.0	..	..	Agriculture
72.3	77.6	83.4	89.7	90.9	93.7	100.0	106.7	114.2	..	..	Industry
74.5	79.2	84.9	91.1	92.6	93.9	100.0	105.3	110.1	..	..	Manufacturing
69.4	76.0	82.4	88.2	93.4	96.1	100.0	105.1	112.1	118.9	..	Consumer Price Index
											MANUFACTURING ACTIVITY
113.7	111.5	109.2	107.8	106.3	101.9	100.0	97.4	99.5	..	..	Employment (1987=100)
86.1	87.0	88.1	90.3	93.0	96.7	100.0	103.3		..	..	Real Earnings per Empl. (1987=100)
83.1	84.4	87.6	91.3	96.3	97.6	100.0	104.8		..	..	Real Output per Empl. (1987=100)
45.4	45.6	44.4	42.6	43.3	49.1	45.7	44.0		..	..	Earnings as % of Value Added
			(Billions of current Finnish Markkaa)								**MONETARY HOLDINGS**
94.38	107.06	121.34	140.25	165.59	178.73	200.25	246.38	269.76	283.33	..	Money Supply, Broadly Defined
17.19	19.92	21.43	24.95	27.69	27.84	30.34	35.92	41.44	44.43	..	Money
4.82	5.17	5.63	5.88	6.14	6.36	7.26	8.42	8.77	9.56	..	Currency Outside Banks
12.36	14.75	15.80	19.07	21.55	21.48	23.08	27.50	32.67	34.87	..	Demand Deposits
77.19	87.14	99.91	115.30	137.90	150.90	169.91	210.46	228.31	238.90	..	Quasi-Money
			(Billions of current Finnish Markkaa)								
-1.97	-5.07	-7.96	-3.11	-2.70	0.39	-6.69	1.75	8.55	0.73	E	**GOVERNMENT DEFICIT (-) OR SURPLUS**
62.50	70.01	78.34	88.88	100.40	113.27	116.53	137.17	155.43	164.07	..	Current Revenue
55.47	65.39	76.53	82.35	92.59	101.09	110.74	119.08	130.57		..	Current Expenditure
7.02	4.62	1.81	6.53	7.82	12.18	5.79	18.09	24.87		..	Current Budget Balance
0.04	0.07	0.21	0.15	0.08	0.13	0.56	0.11	0.08		..	Capital Receipts
9.04	9.75	9.98	9.79	10.60	11.91	13.04	16.44	16.40		..	Capital Payments

FINLAND	1970	1971	1972	1973	1974	1975	1976	1977	1978	1979	1980
FOREIGN TRADE (CUSTOMS BASIS)					*(Millions of current US dollars)*						
Value of Exports, fob	2,306	2,356	2,947	3,719	5,522	5,489	6,339	7,668	8,572	11,175	14,140
Nonfuel Primary Products	750	727	814	1,057	1,435	1,230	1,497	1,818	1,936	2,838	3,658
Fuels	19	5	6	10	47	23	100	165	223	303	618
Manufactures	1,538	1,624	2,127	2,652	4,040	4,236	4,741	5,686	6,413	8,034	9,864
Value of Imports, cif	2,637	2,796	3,198	4,210	6,850	7,600	7,391	7,608	7,865	11,390	15,632
Nonfuel Primary Products	488	443	524	720	1,113	1,196	1,098	1,218	1,276	1,735	2,272
Fuels	302	383	420	527	1,504	1,447	1,586	1,794	1,746	3,018	4,546
Manufactures	1,847	1,970	2,254	2,963	4,233	4,957	4,708	4,596	4,842	6,637	8,814
					(Index 1987 = 100)						
Terms of Trade	121.4	127.1	127.9	114.2	88.9	98.9	94.8	91.5	92.2	97.2	89.1
Export Prices, fob	24.1	27.1	30.8	36.5	47.6	55.7	55.3	58.2	63.5	81.6	92.5
Import Prices, cif	19.8	21.3	24.1	31.9	53.5	56.3	58.3	63.6	68.9	83.9	103.9
BALANCE OF PAYMENTS					*(Millions of current US dollars)*						
Exports of Goods & Services	2,773	2,908	3,613	4,725	6,576	6,742	7,680	9,211	10,590	13,717	17,332
Merchandise, fob	2,294	2,352	2,929	3,820	5,487	5,508	6,295	7,609	8,504	11,100	14,070
Nonfactor Services	411	464	571	768	845	1,095	1,246	1,452	1,859	2,246	2,729
Factor Services	68	91	113	137	244	139	139	150	227	372	533
Imports of Goods & Services	3,008	3,247	3,740	5,096	7,768	8,849	8,752	9,267	9,864	13,776	18,621
Merchandise, fob	2,471	2,628	2,985	4,070	6,367	7,224	6,960	7,167	7,408	10,734	14,727
Nonfactor Services	371	421	506	685	920	1,072	1,172	1,337	1,575	1,961	2,492
Factor Services	166	198	250	341	481	553	620	762	881	1,080	1,401
Long-Term Interest	..	..	..	..	..	..	..	..	..	..	..
Private Current Transfers, net	2	6	1	1	5	-2	-8	-12	-15	-16	-20
Workers' Remittances	..	..	..	..	..	..	..	..	..	..	..
Curr. A/C Bal before Off. Transf.	-233	-333	-126	-370	-1,187	-2,109	-1,081	-67	711	-75	-1,308
Net Official Transfers	-7	-8	9	-15	-23	-34	-37	-38	-36	-94	-102
Curr. A/C Bal after Off. Transf.	-240	-341	-117	-386	-1,210	-2,143	-1,117	-105	674	-169	-1,410
Long-Term Capital, net	79	378	333	69	236	1,313	947	439	851	126	-150
Direct Investment	-34	-21	-24	-2	6	42	27	-24	-29	-97	-109
Long-Term Loans	..	..	..	..	..	..	..	..	..	..	..
Disbursements	..	..	..	..	..	..	..	..	..	..	..
Repayments	..	..	..	..	..	..	..	..	..	..	..
Other Long-Term Capital	113	399	357	71	230	1,270	920	463	880	223	-41
Other Capital, net	255	155	-195	131	948	605	62	-291	-814	434	1,839
Change in Reserves	-94	-193	-21	186	27	225	108	-43	-710	-391	-280
Memo Item:					*(Finnish Markkaa per US dollar)*						
Conversion Factor (Annual Avg)	4.200	4.180	4.150	3.820	3.770	3.680	3.860	4.030	4.120	3.900	3.730
EXTERNAL DEBT (Total)					*(Millions US dollars), outstanding at end of year*						
Long-Term Debt (by debtor)	..	..	..	..	..	..	..	..	..	..	..
Central Bank, incl. IMF credit	..	..	..	..	..	..	..	..	..	..	..
Central Government	..	..	..	..	..	..	..	..	..	..	..
Rest of General Government	..	..	..	..	..	..	..	..	..	..	..
Non-financial Public Enterprises	..	..	..	..	..	..	..	..	..	..	..
Priv. Sector, incl non-guaranteed	..	..	..	..	..	..	..	..	..	..	..
Short-Term Debt	..	..	..	..	..	..	..	..	..	..	..
Memo Items:					*(Millions of US dollars)*						
Int'l Reserves Excluding Gold	424.6	623.1	667.6	574.3	595.9	433.2	462.1	531.1	1,222.9	1,540.0	1,870.2
Gold Holdings (at market price)	30.8	60.9	90.6	92.4	153.6	115.5	111.0	149.2	213.6	504.9	581.3
SOCIAL INDICATORS											
Total Fertility Rate	1.8	1.7	1.6	1.5	1.6	1.7	1.7	1.7	1.7	1.6	1.7
Infant Mortality Rate	13.2	12.6	12.0	11.5	11.0	9.5	9.8	9.0	7.5	7.6	7.6
Life Expectancy at Birth	70.3	70.5	70.7	71.0	71.3	71.6	71.9	72.2	72.5	72.9	73.2
Urban Population, % of total	50.3	51.9	53.5	55.1	56.7	58.3	58.6	58.9	59.2	59.5	59.8
Food Prod. per capita (1987=100)	99.9	106.0	104.3	98.1	100.9	105.0	113.5	103.2	104.6	109.0	109.0
Labor Force, Agriculture (%)	19.6	18.8	18.1	17.3	16.5	15.8	15.0	14.3	13.5	12.8	12.0
Labor Force, Female (%)	43.7	43.9	44.2	44.5	44.7	45.0	45.3	45.6	45.9	46.1	46.4
Primary Schl. Enroll. Ratio	82.0	..	..	..	..	102.0	101.0	100.0	98.0	97.0	96.0
Primary Schl. Enroll. Ratio, Female	79.0	..	..	..	..	101.0	100.0	100.0	98.0	96.0	96.0
Secondary Schl. Enroll. Ratio	102.0	..	..	..	..	89.0	91.0	93.0	96.0	97.0	98.0

1981	1982	1983	1984	1985	1986	1987	1988	1989	1990 estimate	Notes	FINLAND
				(Millions of current US dollars)							**FOREIGN TRADE (CUSTOMS BASIS)**
14,007	13,127	12,510	13,498	13,609	16,325	20,039	21,639	23,265	26,718	..	Value of Exports, fob
3,363	2,529	2,530	2,804	2,530	2,742	3,500	3,788	4,138	4,157	..	Nonfuel Primary Products
591	532	646	743	580	395	444	369	218	392	..	Fuels
10,052	10,066	9,334	9,950	10,499	13,188	16,095	17,482	18,908	22,169	..	Manufactures
14,190	13,380	12,846	12,435	13,226	15,325	19,860	20,911	24,611	27,098	..	Value of Imports, cif
1,925	1,945	1,725	1,762	1,761	2,044	2,539	2,873	3,157	3,156	..	Nonfuel Primary Products
4,357	3,654	3,454	3,101	3,218	2,345	2,672	2,013	2,433	3,183	..	Fuels
7,909	7,781	7,667	7,572	8,247	10,936	14,650	16,025	19,021	20,759	..	Manufactures
				(Index 1987 = 100)							
84.6	87.3	84.4	85.1	85.3	96.6	100.0	101.9	104.1	98.2	..	Terms of Trade
87.4	84.3	78.6	77.4	76.1	87.5	100.0	112.6	118.8	135.7	..	Export Prices, fob
103.2	96.5	93.2	91.0	89.2	90.6	100.0	110.5	114.2	138.2	..	Import Prices, cif
				(Millions of current US dollars)							**BALANCE OF PAYMENTS**
17,259	16,136	15,225	16,397	16,780	19,789	24,136	28,188	29,493	34,873	..	Exports of Goods & Services
13,662	12,842	12,172	13,087	13,351	16,005	19,079	21,826	22,882	26,089	..	Merchandise, fob
2,908	2,719	2,525	2,433	2,423	2,752	3,543	3,975	4,111	4,883	..	Nonfactor Services
689	576	528	877	1,006	1,032	1,515	2,388	2,500	3,901	..	Factor Services
17,626	16,930	16,211	16,246	17,415	20,087	25,375	30,372	34,525	40,478	..	Imports of Goods & Services
13,285	12,627	12,010	11,596	12,473	14,363	17,700	20,686	23,101	25,322	..	Merchandise, fob
2,533	2,447	2,438	2,582	2,812	3,235	4,411	5,350	6,046	7,538	..	Nonfactor Services
1,809	1,855	1,763	2,069	2,130	2,489	3,264	4,335	5,378	7,619	..	Factor Services
..	..	..	..	..	..	..	..	..	..		Long-Term Interest
-10	-27	-23	-22	-7	-157	-162	-87	-252	-342	..	Private Current Transfers, net
..	..	..	..	..	..	..	..	..	..		Workers' Remittances
-377	-820	-1,009	129	-642	-455	-1,400	-2,270	-5,285	-5,947	..	Curr. A/C Bal before Off. Transf.
-106	-108	-121	-153	-169	-236	-328	-425	-510	-735	..	Net Official Transfers
-483	-929	-1,129	-24	-811	-691	-1,729	-2,695	-5,796	-6,682	..	Curr. A/C Bal after Off. Transf.
589	401	547	371	669	-415	-418	725	1,523	7,434	..	Long-Term Capital, net
-29	-77	-54	-356	-235	-470	-885	-2,092	-2,620	-2,606	..	Direct Investment
..	..	..	..	..	..	..	..	..	..	..	Long-Term Loans
..	..	..	..	..	..	..	..	..	..	..	Disbursements
..	..	..	..	..	..	..	..	..	..	..	Repayments
618	478	601	727	904	56	467	2,817	4,144	10,040	..	Other Long-Term Capital
-330	727	355	1,471	729	-1,174	6,169	2,225	3,215	3,183	..	Other Capital, net
224	-200	228	-1,817	-586	2,280	-4,022	-255	1,058	-3,935	..	Change in Reserves
				(Finnish Markkaa per US dollar)							**Memo Item:**
4.320	4.820	5.570	6.010	6.200	5.070	4.400	4.180	4.290	3.820	..	Conversion Factor (Annual Avg)
			(Millions US dollars), outstanding at end of year								
											EXTERNAL DEBT (Total)
..	..	..	..	..	..	..	..	..	..	..	Long-Term Debt (by debtor)
..	..	..	..	..	..	..	..	..	..	..	Central Bank, incl. IMF credit
..	..	..	..	..	..	..	..	..	..	..	Central Government
..	..	..	..	..	..	..	..	..	..	..	Rest of General Government
..	..	..	..	..	..	..	..	..	..	..	Non-financial Public Enterprises
..	..	..	..	..	..	..	..	..	..	..	Priv. Sector, incl non-guaranteed
..	..	..	..	..	..	..	..	..	..	..	Short-Term Debt
				(Millions of US dollars)							**Memo Items:**
1,483.7	1,517.5	1,237.7	2,754.3	3,749.9	1,787.1	6,417.5	6,369.2	5,111.1	9,644.1	..	Int'l Reserves Excluding Gold
504.5	580.2	484.5	391.6	625.2	747.4	946.4	802.1	802.8	770.9	..	Gold Holdings (at market price)
											SOCIAL INDICATORS
1.7	1.8	1.8	1.8	1.8	1.8	1.8	1.8	1.8	1.8	..	Total Fertility Rate
6.5	6.0	6.2	6.3	6.3	6.5	6.5	6.4	6.3	6.3	..	Infant Mortality Rate
73.5	73.9	74.1	74.3	74.5	74.7	74.9	75.1	75.4	75.6	..	Life Expectancy at Birth
59.8	59.8	59.8	59.8	59.8	59.8	59.8	59.7	59.7	59.7	..	Urban Population, % of total
98.5	110.1	119.2	117.4	113.6	113.0	100.0	102.3	112.2	117.0	..	Food Prod. per capita (1987=100)
..	..	..	..	..	..	..	..	..	..	..	Labor Force, Agriculture (%)
46.5	46.5	46.6	46.6	46.6	46.7	46.8	46.9	46.9	47.0	..	Labor Force, Female (%)
..	100.0	102.0	103.0	102.0	102.0	101.0	100.0	99.0	..	..	Primary Schl. Enroll. Ratio
98.0	99.0	102.0	102.0	102.0	103.0	101.0	100.0	99.0	..	..	Primary Schl. Enroll. Ratio, Female
..	98.0	101.0	103.0	104.0	104.0	106.0	109.0	112.0	..	..	Secondary Schl. Enroll. Ratio

FRANCE	1970	1971	1972	1973	1974	1975	1976	1977	1978	1979	1980
CURRENT GNP PER CAPITA (US $)	2,990	3,160	3,470	4,210	5,060	5,970	6,690	7,490	8,400	10,010	11,850
POPULATION (thousands)	50,772	51,251	51,701	52,118	52,460	52,699	52,909	53,145	53,376	53,606	53,880
USE AND ORIGIN OF RESOURCES					*(Billions of current French Francs)*						
Gross National Product (GNP)	796.8	887.1	990.1	1,132.2	1,307.1	1,470.3	1,703.5	1,921.7	2,187.3	2,489.7	2,820.9
Net Factor Income from Abroad	3.3	2.9	2.1	2.3	4.1	2.4	2.9	3.9	4.8	8.6	12.6
GDP at Market Prices	793.5	884.2	987.9	1,129.8	1,303.0	1,467.9	1,700.6	1,917.8	2,182.6	2,481.1	2,808.3
Resource Balance	4.2	9.6	10.3	9.8	-13.1	17.5	-12.5	2.4	29.1	14.8	-34.4
Exports of Goods & NFServices	125.4	145.2	165.1	198.6	269.6	279.8	333.0	392.9	445.5	526.9	604.4
Imports of Goods & NFServices	121.2	135.6	154.9	188.7	282.7	262.3	345.4	390.5	416.4	512.1	638.8
Domestic Absorption	789.3	874.6	977.7	1,120.0	1,316.0	1,450.3	1,713.0	1,915.4	2,153.5	2,466.3	2,842.7
Private Consumption, etc.	459.6	511.1	570.3	645.0	749.6	862.3	993.5	1,117.1	1,264.0	1,442.0	1,653.3
General Gov't Consumption	116.6	131.9	146.8	167.7	200.2	243.4	287.8	329.5	383.7	436.7	509.3
Gross Domestic Investment	213.1	231.5	260.6	307.3	366.2	344.6	431.7	468.8	505.9	587.6	680.1
Fixed Investment	192.9	218.3	244.5	285.2	336.1	354.3	407.2	439.3	488.4	555.1	645.8
Indirect Taxes, net	103.0	113.6	127.9	142.6	159.8	177.6	212.8	224.3	263.6	311.7	357.0
GDP at factor cost	690.5	770.6	860.1	987.2	1,143.2	1,290.3	1,487.7	1,693.5	1,919.0	2,169.4	2,451.3
Agriculture	..	..	..	..	..	..	..	91.2	104.5	118.5	119.0
Industry	..	..	..	..	..	..	..	679.8	766.5	859.8	947.3
Manufacturing	..	..	..	..	..	..	..	496.4	564.3	635.6	679.5
Services, etc.	..	..	..	..	..	..	..	1,146.8	1,311.6	1,502.9	1,742.0
Gross Domestic Saving	217.3	241.1	270.8	317.1	353.2	362.2	419.3	471.2	534.9	602.4	645.7
Gross National Saving	216.9	239.3	268.4	314.5	351.7	358.0	415.4	468.2	531.5	601.2	647.9
					(Billions of 1987 French Francs)						
Gross National Product	3,594.9	3,733.3	3,868.0	4,047.8	4,151.4	4,111.3	4,292.0	4,384.7	4,534.8	4,685.7	4,753.4
GDP at Market Prices	3,579.8	3,720.8	3,859.4	4,039.0	4,138.0	4,104.3	4,284.3	4,375.4	4,524.5	4,668.9	4,731.9
Resource Balance	-60.9	-50.3	-65.3	-89.7	-37.7	24.5	-33.5	20.1	46.0	27.0	29.4
Exports of Goods & NFServices	464.7	510.4	572.4	635.5	693.2	685.7	744.1	803.8	857.1	922.9	945.4
Imports of Goods & NFServices	525.6	560.8	637.7	725.2	731.0	661.2	777.5	783.7	811.1	895.8	916.0
Domestic Absorption	3,640.7	3,771.1	3,924.7	4,128.6	4,175.7	4,079.8	4,317.8	4,355.4	4,478.5	4,641.9	4,702.5
Private Consumption, etc.	2,169.2	2,242.9	2,330.5	2,413.2	2,433.6	2,487.5	2,588.6	2,604.5	2,707.7	2,776.8	2,803.0
General Gov't Consumption	612.5	636.6	659.0	681.3	689.6	719.8	749.7	767.6	806.8	831.2	851.7
Gross Domestic Investment	859.0	891.7	935.2	1,034.1	1,052.5	872.5	979.4	983.3	964.0	1,033.8	1,047.8
Fixed Investment	813.0	872.3	920.9	987.3	995.6	928.1	953.6	938.7	960.0	990.8	1,018.0
GDP at factor cost	3,124.5	3,248.0	3,360.9	3,523.8	3,641.6	3,614.7	3,756.0	3,867.8	3,978.9	4,083.5	4,142.4
Agriculture	..	..	..	..	..	..	..	136.0	150.3	162.8	159.6
Industry	..	..	..	..	..	..	..	1,503.4	1,533.4	1,563.5	1,570.1
Manufacturing	..	..	..	..	..	..	..	1,126.6	1,150.9	1,178.7	1,171.0
Services, etc.	..	..	..	..	..	..	..	2,736.0	2,840.8	2,942.6	3,002.2
Memo Items:											
Capacity to Import	543.7	600.5	680.0	763.0	697.2	705.4	749.4	788.5	867.7	921.8	866.7
Terms of Trade Adjustment	79.0	90.0	107.6	127.5	3.9	19.7	5.4	-15.3	10.6	-1.1	-78.7
Gross Domestic Income	3,658.9	3,810.8	3,967.0	4,166.5	4,141.9	4,124.1	4,289.7	4,360.1	4,535.1	4,667.8	4,653.2
Gross National Income	3,674.0	3,823.3	3,975.6	4,175.3	4,155.3	4,131.0	4,297.3	4,369.4	4,545.4	4,684.6	4,674.7
DOMESTIC PRICES/DEFLATORS					*(Index 1987 = 100)*						
Overall (GDP)	22.2	23.8	25.6	28.0	31.5	35.8	39.7	43.8	48.2	53.1	59.3
Domestic Absorption	21.7	23.2	24.9	27.1	31.5	35.5	39.7	44.0	48.1	53.1	60.5
Agriculture	..	..	..	..	..	..	..	67.1	69.5	72.8	74.6
Industry	..	..	..	..	..	..	..	45.2	50.0	55.0	60.3
Manufacturing	..	..	..	..	..	..	..	44.1	49.0	53.9	58.0
Consumer Price Index	23.8	25.2	26.7	28.7	32.6	36.4	39.9	43.7	47.6	52.8	59.8
MANUFACTURING ACTIVITY											
Employment (1987=100)	121.8	123.6	125.5	128.7	130.4	126.7	125.5	125.1	123.4	121.3	119.6
Real Earnings per Empl. (1987=100)	..	..	..	..	..	..	..	..	..	..	..
Real Output per Empl. (1987=100)	66.4	69.5	72.4	76.3	79.4	75.7	81.1	80.5	79.9	85.4	92.2
Earnings as % of Value Added	..	..	..	..	..	..	..	66.7	64.8	64.1	68.4
MONETARY HOLDINGS					*(Billions of current French Francs)*						
Money Supply, Broadly Defined	489.7	577.6	681.4	783.9	916.3	1,075.2	1,228.5	1,443.5	1,634.4	1,868.3	2,044.9
Money	232.5	259.9	299.0	327.9	377.7	425.2	457.0	507.8	665.9	751.4	801.2
Currency Outside Banks	75.9	78.0	84.0	89.5	97.8	106.6	116.1	121.5	131.9	139.2	143.8
Demand Deposits	156.6	181.9	215.0	238.4	279.9	318.6	340.9	386.3	534.0	612.2	657.4
Quasi-Money	257.2	317.7	382.4	456.0	538.6	650.0	771.5	935.7	968.5	1,116.9	1,243.7
GOVERNMENT DEFICIT (-) OR SURPLUS					*(Billions of current French Francs)*						
	..	..	6.8	4.7	5.8	-37.8	-17.1	-22.3	-29.6	-37.0	-2.0
Current Revenue	..	..	333.8	372.9	457.5	516.4	627.8	699.0	793.2	942.1	1,124.3
Current Expenditure	..	..	299.0	335.3	414.0	502.7	578.0	669.2	784.2	905.1	1,050.9
Current Budget Balance	..	..	34.8	37.6	43.5	13.7	49.8	29.8	9.0	37.0	73.4
Capital Receipts	..	..	0.8	2.6	2.2	1.6	3.8	2.9	0.9	1.0	0.8
Capital Payments	..	..	30.1	30.7	39.3	52.8	64.4	50.6	51.2	64.9	71.0

1981	1982	1983	1984	1985	1986	1987	1988	1989	1990 estimate	Notes	FRANCE
12,420	11,890	10,630	9,950	9,750	10,780	12,970	16,240	17,910	19,520	..	**CURRENT GNP PER CAPITA (US $)**
54,182	54,480	54,728	54,947	55,170	55,394	55,630	55,884	56,160	56,440	..	**POPULATION (thousands)**
				(Billions of current French Francs)							**USE AND ORIGIN OF RESOURCES**
3,175.1	3,628.0	3,994.8	4,338.4	4,674.5	5,052.7	5,324.2	5,711.6	6,126.1	6,467.3	..	Gross National Product (GNP)
10.3	2.0	-11.7	-23.5	-25.7	-16.6	-12.5	-11.6	-9.9	-16.8	..	Net Factor Income from Abroad
3,164.8	3,626.0	4,006.5	4,361.9	4,700.1	5,069.3	5,336.7	5,723.2	6,136.1	6,484.1	..	GDP at Market Prices
-30.5	-69.2	-6.7	28.4	31.3	52.3	7.0	3.5	9.6	-2.4	..	Resource Balance
714.3	790.4	900.7	1,053.3	1,123.9	1,074.1	1,101.4	1,220.5	1,412.1	1,467.0	..	Exports of Goods & NF Services
744.8	859.5	907.4	1,025.0	1,092.6	1,021.8	1,094.3	1,217.0	1,402.5	1,469.4	..	Imports of Goods & NF Services
3,195.3	3,695.2	4,013.2	4,333.6	4,668.8	5,017.0	5,329.6	5,719.7	6,126.5	6,486.5	..	Domestic Absorption
1,907.2	2,200.8	2,435.5	2,651.3	2,871.1	3,062.8	3,249.5	3,448.1	3,679.0	3,911.6	..	Private Consumption, etc.
595.0	701.3	782.1	854.3	910.3	959.5	1,004.7	1,059.2	1,106.4	1,170.0	..	General Gov't Consumption
693.0	793.1	795.5	827.9	887.4	994.7	1,075.4	1,212.4	1,341.1	1,404.9	..	Gross Domestic Investment
700.5	774.3	809.6	840.4	905.3	977.5	1,054.8	1,177.2	1,295.9	1,373.1	..	Fixed Investment
390.2	460.8	506.0	554.9	599.9	627.6	667.4	738.9	788.6	825.3	..	Indirect Taxes, net
2,774.7	3,165.2	3,500.5	3,807.0	4,100.2	4,441.7	4,669.2	4,984.3	5,347.4	5,658.8	B	GDP at factor cost
130.9	166.2	169.6	175.2	182.3	189.5	189.3	189.1	215.2	..	..	Agriculture
1,029.8	1,148.4	1,256.6	1,338.7	1,434.0	1,536.8	1,585.2	1,694.7	1,787.1	..	..	Industry
733.5	821.5	901.0	956.3	1,033.1	1,120.1	1,146.8	1,230.6	1,309.3	..	..	Manufacturing
2,004.0	2,311.4	2,580.3	2,848.0	3,083.8	3,343.0	3,562.2	3,839.5	4,133.8	..	..	Services, etc.
662.6	723.9	788.8	856.3	918.7	1,047.0	1,082.5	1,215.9	1,350.7	1,402.5	..	Gross Domestic Saving
660.5	713.0	763.8	824.0	881.3	1,018.3	1,056.2	1,189.8	1,323.7	1,364.1	..	Gross National Saving
				(Billions of 1987 French Francs)							
4,802.6	4,903.5	4,922.8	4,983.3	5,073.2	5,206.2	5,324.2	5,530.6	5,732.4	5,874.7	..	Gross National Product
4,786.9	4,900.6	4,936.9	5,009.5	5,100.4	5,223.3	5,336.7	5,541.8	5,741.7	5,890.1	..	GDP at Market Prices
84.1	46.0	105.8	149.4	132.3	54.2	7.0	1.9	30.1	17.9	..	Resource Balance
979.2	961.8	997.0	1,064.1	1,085.4	1,071.0	1,101.4	1,188.8	1,312.7	1,380.2	..	Exports of Goods & NF Services
895.1	915.8	891.3	914.7	953.1	1,016.8	1,094.3	1,186.9	1,282.6	1,362.3	..	Imports of Goods & NF Services
4,702.8	4,854.6	4,831.1	4,860.1	4,968.1	5,169.1	5,329.6	5,539.9	5,711.6	5,872.2	..	Domestic Absorption
2,859.2	2,950.2	2,981.9	3,011.9	3,073.5	3,175.1	3,249.5	3,344.9	3,441.4	3,536.9	..	Private Consumption, etc.
878.1	910.8	929.2	940.3	961.4	977.5	1,004.7	1,033.2	1,035.1	1,070.4	..	General Gov't Consumption
965.5	993.6	920.0	907.9	933.3	1,016.4	1,075.4	1,161.8	1,235.1	1,264.9	..	Gross Domestic Investment
998.9	986.5	953.9	929.3	960.8	1,004.9	1,054.8	1,146.4	1,231.5	1,275.2	..	Fixed Investment
4,215.2	4,297.2	4,330.8	4,390.6	4,465.0	4,578.1	4,669.2	4,825.4	5,005.2	5,141.0	B	GDP at factor cost
158.6	185.1	176.0	184.2	185.7	187.0	189.3	188.8	194.8	..	..	Agriculture
1,570.1	1,575.7	1,584.7	1,565.7	1,565.7	1,576.5	1,585.2	1,640.7	1,688.2	..	..	Industry
1,163.0	1,173.1	1,177.9	1,156.3	1,151.8	1,149.8	1,146.8	1,184.2	1,228.3	..	..	Manufacturing
3,058.3	3,139.8	3,176.2	3,259.6	3,349.0	3,459.8	3,562.2	3,712.4	3,858.6	..	..	Services, etc.
											Memo Items:
858.5	842.1	884.7	940.1	980.4	1,068.9	1,101.4	1,190.3	1,291.4	1,360.1	..	Capacity to Import
-120.8	-119.7	-112.4	-124.1	-105.0	-2.2	0.0	1.5	-21.3	-20.1	..	Terms of Trade Adjustment
4,666.2	4,780.9	4,824.5	4,885.4	4,995.4	5,221.1	5,336.7	5,543.3	5,720.3	5,870.0	..	Gross Domestic Income
4,681.9	4,783.8	4,810.5	4,859.2	4,968.2	5,204.1	5,324.2	5,532.1	5,711.1	5,854.6	..	Gross National Income
				(Index 1987 = 100)							**DOMESTIC PRICES/DEFLATORS**
66.1	74.0	81.2	87.1	92.2	97.1	100.0	103.3	106.9	110.1	..	Overall (GDP)
67.9	76.1	83.1	89.2	94.0	97.1	100.0	103.2	107.3	110.5	..	Domestic Absorption
82.6	89.8	96.4	95.1	98.2	101.3	100.0	100.2	110.5	..	..	Agriculture
65.6	72.9	79.3	85.5	91.6	97.5	100.0	103.3	105.9	..	..	Industry
63.1	70.0	76.5	82.7	89.7	97.4	100.0	103.9	106.6	..	..	Manufacturing
67.8	75.8	83.1	89.3	94.4	96.8	100.0	102.7	106.3	109.9	..	Consumer Price Index
											MANUFACTURING ACTIVITY
115.5	113.9	111.5	108.0	104.8	102.8	100.0	98.1	98.3	..	..	Employment (1987=100)
..	..	..	..	..	..	..	..	..	..	..	Real Earnings per Empl. (1987=100)
96.9	98.6	99.3	103.6	104.2	97.6	100.0	107.0	..	..	..	Real Output per Empl. (1987=100)
70.2	70.1	68.7	68.2	66.3	..	..	..	..	..	..	Earnings as % of Value Added
				(Billions of current French Francs)							**MONETARY HOLDINGS**
2,271.0	2,536.7	2,817.8	3,443.4	3,338.3	3,573.7	4,095.4	4,452.0	4,836.8	..	D	Money Supply, Broadly Defined
899.8	985.0	1,108.4	1,219.2	1,312.4	1,406.8	1,471.1	1,531.6	1,633.3	1,702.5	..	Money
160.9	177.1	191.7	198.8	207.3	214.1	221.8	235.7	246.4	259.0	..	Currency Outside Banks
738.9	807.9	916.7	1,020.4	1,105.1	1,192.7	1,249.3	1,295.9	1,386.9	1,443.5	..	Demand Deposits
1,371.2	1,551.7	1,709.4	2,224.2	2,025.9	2,166.9	2,624.3	2,920.4	3,203.5	..	..	Quasi-Money
				(Billions of current French Francs)							
-73.2	-121.9	-140.7	-116.3	-127.7	-170.2	-64.5	-134.2	-113.9	-140.9	..	**GOVERNMENT DEFICIT (-) OR SURPLUS**
1,287.7	1,496.0	1,672.6	1,835.2	1,979.4	2,100.8	2,228.0	2,365.8	2,522.3	2,666.9	..	Current Revenue
1,264.7	1,499.1	1,698.9	1,862.7	2,013.7	2,131.1	2,219.3	2,337.7	2,465.0	2,626.5	..	Current Expenditure
23.0	-3.1	-26.3	-27.5	-34.3	-30.3	8.8	28.1	57.3	40.4	..	Current Budget Balance
1.3	3.0	1.2	2.3	1.9	2.1	5.2	7.9	3.2	12.1	..	Capital Receipts
88.4	139.7	106.4	108.9	109.1	137.6	94.6	138.3	139.6	167.1	..	Capital Payments

FRANCE	1970	1971	1972	1973	1974	1975	1976	1977	1978	1979	1980
FOREIGN TRADE (CUSTOMS BASIS)					*(Billions of current US dollars)*						
Value of Exports, fob	17.74	20.42	25.84	35.66	45.14	51.60	55.46	63.36	76.49	97.96	110.87
Nonfuel Primary Products	4.11	4.83	6.38	9.20	11.09	10.82	11.65	12.89	16.21	20.25	24.73
Fuels	0.38	0.45	0.58	0.76	1.21	1.41	1.61	1.89	2.05	3.49	4.49
Manufactures	13.25	15.13	18.88	25.70	32.84	39.38	42.20	48.58	58.24	74.22	81.65
Value of Imports, cif	18.92	21.14	26.72	37.05	52.17	53.61	64.02	70.28	81.86	106.71	134.33
Nonfuel Primary Products	5.60	5.60	6.88	9.97	12.16	12.17	13.95	16.47	18.69	22.52	25.61
Fuels	2.29	2.93	3.53	4.58	11.94	12.26	14.37	15.09	15.94	22.95	35.73
Manufactures	11.04	12.60	16.30	22.50	28.07	29.17	35.70	38.71	47.24	61.24	73.00
					(Index 1987 = 100)						
Terms of Trade	164.7	157.9	156.6	157.3	111.5	122.4	114.4	107.3	112.5	111.2	102.3
Export Prices, fob	29.4	30.9	34.7	47.3	54.6	61.3	60.4	62.6	72.4	87.8	97.1
Import Prices, cif	17.9	19.6	22.1	30.0	49.0	50.1	52.8	58.3	64.3	79.0	94.9
BALANCE OF PAYMENTS					*(Billions of current US dollars)*						
Exports of Goods & Services	25.29	28.92	35.78	49.97	63.51	73.31	78.68	90.51	114.20	144.87	171.82
Merchandise, fob	17.95	20.43	25.89	34.87	44.00	49.91	53.92	61.18	74.56	94.28	107.52
Nonfactor Services	5.61	6.72	7.81	11.34	14.17	18.07	19.21	22.70	30.01	35.81	42.89
Factor Services	1.73	1.78	2.08	3.76	5.34	5.34	5.56	6.63	9.63	14.78	21.42
Imports of Goods & Services	24.61	27.49	34.24	46.79	65.09	67.94	79.60	88.10	103.86	135.71	171.86
Merchandise, fob	17.69	19.57	24.83	34.44	48.80	48.78	58.91	64.47	74.45	97.50	120.93
Nonfactor Services	5.38	6.24	7.23	9.01	11.47	13.65	14.98	17.37	20.70	25.27	31.65
Factor Services	1.54	1.69	2.18	3.35	4.82	5.52	5.71	6.26	8.71	12.93	19.27
Long-Term Interest	..	..	..	..	..	..	..	..	..	..	..
Private Current Transfers, net	-0.66	-0.85	-0.90	-1.11	-1.15	-1.53	-1.41	-1.41	-1.82	-2.30	-2.45
Workers' Remittances	0.13	0.15	0.18	0.20	0.21	0.24	0.24	0.27	0.34	0.40	0.45
Curr. A/C Bal before Off. Transf.	0.02	0.58	0.64	2.07	-2.73	3.85	-2.33	1.01	8.52	6.86	-2.49
Net Official Transfers	-0.22	-0.42	-0.74	-0.64	-1.12	-1.10	-1.04	-1.42	-1.45	-1.72	-1.71
Curr. A/C Bal after Off. Transf.	-0.20	0.16	-0.10	1.44	-3.86	2.74	-3.37	-0.41	7.06	5.14	-4.21
Long-Term Capital, net	0.10	0.01	-0.65	-2.48	-0.26	-1.50	-2.19	0.89	-3.43	-5.20	-8.48
Direct Investment	0.25	0.13	0.09	0.19	1.34	0.23	-0.66	0.89	0.57	0.60	0.19
Long-Term Loans	..	..	..	..	..	..	..	..	..	..	..
Disbursements	..	..	..	..	..	..	..	..	..	..	..
Repayments	..	..	..	..	..	..	..	..	..	..	..
Other Long-Term Capital	-0.15	-0.12	-0.74	-2.67	-1.60	-1.73	-1.53	0.00	-4.00	-5.80	-8.67
Other Capital, net	1.91	3.11	2.36	-0.85	3.77	2.27	2.52	0.20	-0.63	1.81	18.75
Change in Reserves	-1.81	-3.28	-1.61	1.89	0.35	-3.51	3.04	-0.68	-3.00	-1.75	-6.06
Memo Item:					*(French Francs per US dollar)*						
Conversion Factor (Annual Avg)	5.550	5.540	5.050	4.460	4.810	4.290	4.780	4.910	4.510	4.250	4.230
					(Millions US dollars), outstanding at end of year						
EXTERNAL DEBT (Total)	..	..	..	..	..	..	..	..	..	..	..
Long-Term Debt (by debtor)	..	..	..	..	..	..	..	..	..	..	..
Central Bank, incl. IMF credit	..	..	..	..	..	..	..	..	..	..	..
Central Government	..	..	..	..	..	..	..	..	..	..	..
Rest of General Government	..	..	..	..	..	..	..	..	..	..	..
Non-financial Public Enterprises	..	..	..	..	..	..	..	..	..	..	..
Priv. Sector, incl non-guaranteed	..	..	..	..	..	..	..	..	..	..	..
Short-Term Debt	..	..	..	..	..	..	..	..	..	..	..
Memo Items:					*(Millions of US dollars)*						
Int'l Reserves Excluding Gold	1,428	4,428	6,189	4,268	4,526	8,457	5,620	5,872	9,278	17,579	27,340
Gold Holdings (at market price)	3,771	4,392	6,535	11,327	18,824	14,156	13,613	16,770	23,050	41,941	48,252
SOCIAL INDICATORS											
Total Fertility Rate	2.5	2.5	2.4	2.3	2.1	1.9	1.8	1.9	1.8	1.9	1.9
Infant Mortality Rate	18.2	17.2	16.0	15.4	14.6	13.8	12.5	11.4	10.7	10.0	10.0
Life Expectancy at Birth	72.0	72.2	72.3	72.6	72.9	73.2	73.5	73.8	74.0	74.1	74.3
Urban Population, % of total	71.0	71.4	71.8	72.2	72.6	73.0	73.1	73.1	73.2	73.2	73.3
Food Prod. per capita (1987=100)	83.9	85.2	83.5	90.0	90.4	84.7	83.7	82.5	87.7	93.4	95.2
Labor Force, Agriculture (%)	13.6	13.1	12.6	12.1	11.6	11.1	10.6	10.1	9.6	9.1	8.6
Labor Force, Female (%)	36.2	36.5	36.8	37.1	37.4	37.7	38.0	38.4	38.7	39.0	39.3
Primary Schl. Enroll. Ratio	117.0	..	..	..	..	109.0	109.0	111.0	112.0	112.0	111.0
Primary Schl. Enroll. Ratio, Female	117.0	..	..	..	..	109.0	110.0	111.0	111.0	111.0	110.0
Secondary Schl. Enroll. Ratio	74.0	..	..	..	..	82.0	83.0	83.0	83.0	84.0	85.0

1981	1982	1983	1984	1985	1986	1987	1988	1989	1990 estimate	Notes	FRANCE
											FOREIGN TRADE (CUSTOMS BASIS)
				(Billions of current US dollars)							
101.25	92.36	91.14	93.16	97.46	119.07	143.08	161.70	172.56	209.49	..	Value of Exports, fob
22.85	20.08	20.49	20.89	21.46	25.39	30.21	35.25	37.43	42.95	..	Nonfuel Primary Products
4.72	3.66	3.46	3.40	3.75	3.19	3.17	3.34	3.78	4.94	..	Fuels
73.68	68.62	67.19	68.87	72.24	90.49	109.70	123.11	131.35	161.60	..	Manufactures
120.28	115.45	105.27	103.61	107.59	127.85	157.52	176.75	190.19	232.52	..	Value of Imports, cif
21.68	20.28	19.53	19.56	19.57	23.65	27.72	31.90	33.76	37.80	..	Nonfuel Primary Products
34.67	30.83	25.75	24.91	23.95	16.14	16.93	14.60	16.83	22.28	..	Fuels
63.93	64.35	59.99	59.15	64.08	88.06	112.87	130.24	139.59	172.45	..	Manufactures
				(Index 1987 = 100)							
91.6	91.5	91.9	92.2	95.9	100.1	100.0	103.6	102.3	102.4	..	Terms of Trade
86.1	80.6	78.1	76.4	77.7	87.1	100.0	111.3	117.7	135.7	..	Export Prices, fob
94.0	88.2	85.0	82.8	81.0	86.9	100.0	107.5	115.1	132.6	..	Import Prices, cif
				(Billions of current US dollars)							**BALANCE OF PAYMENTS**
168.78	153.77	145.28	147.70	154.28	187.80	221.00	247.97	271.22	339.50	..	Exports of Goods & Services
100.87	91.50	89.71	92.21	95.93	119.36	141.66	160.18	170.75	206.55	..	Merchandise, fob
41.25	36.45	34.77	34.65	36.04	43.51	50.89	55.81	63.07	78.96	..	Nonfactor Services
26.66	25.81	20.80	20.85	22.31	24.93	28.46	31.98	37.39	53.99	..	Factor Services
169.36	161.23	146.63	145.68	151.69	180.78	220.04	244.74	266.68	339.17	..	Imports of Goods & Services
110.84	107.29	98.46	96.87	101.20	121.44	150.32	168.73	181.45	220.51	..	Merchandise, fob
33.01	27.78	25.52	25.13	25.45	32.18	38.92	42.03	45.91	61.05	..	Nonfactor Services
25.50	26.16	22.65	23.69	25.03	27.16	30.80	33.99	39.33	57.61	..	Factor Services
..	..	..	..	..	..	..	..	..	..	..	Long-Term Interest
-2.27	-1.96	-1.74	-1.01	-1.31	-1.74	-2.30	-2.44	-2.67	-3.98	..	Private Current Transfers, net
0.35	0.32	0.34	0.34	0.23	0.32	0.40	0.44	0.54	0.81	..	Workers' Remittances
-2.84	-9.42	-3.09	1.01	1.28	5.28	-1.33	0.79	1.86	-3.65	..	Curr. A/C Bal before Off. Transf.
-1.97	-2.66	-2.08	-1.88	-1.32	-2.85	-3.11	-4.29	-5.70	-6.23	..	Net Official Transfers
-4.81	-12.08	-5.17	-0.88	-0.03	2.43	-4.45	-3.50	-3.84	-9.88	..	Curr. A/C Bal after Off. Transf.
-8.89	0.85	9.31	4.37	3.23	-7.47	2.21	-1.07	7.74	2.99	..	Long-Term Capital, net
-2.08	-1.26	0.01	0.28	0.35	-2.15	-4.07	-6.01	-9.12	-22.05	..	Direct Investment
..	..	..	..	..	..	..	..	..	..	..	Long-Term Loans
..	..	..	..	..	..	..	..	..	..	..	Disbursements
..	..	..	..	..	..	..	..	..	..	..	Repayments
-6.81	2.11	9.30	4.10	2.87	-5.32	6.28	4.94	16.85	25.03	..	Other Long-Term Capital
8.93	7.63	0.02	-0.71	-0.81	6.46	-6.09	4.48	-6.37	18.71	..	Other Capital, net
4.77	3.61	-4.17	-2.79	-2.38	-1.42	8.33	0.10	2.47	-11.82	..	Change in Reserves
											Memo Item:
				(French Francs per US dollar)							
5.430	6.570	7.620	8.740	8.990	6.930	6.010	5.960	6.380	5.450	..	Conversion Factor (Annual Avg)
			(Millions US dollars), outstanding at end of year								
..	..	..	..	..	..	..	..	..	..	..	**EXTERNAL DEBT (Total)**
..	..	..	..	..	..	..	..	..	..	..	Long-Term Debt (by debtor)
..	..	..	..	..	..	..	..	..	..	..	Central Bank, incl. IMF credit
..	..	..	..	..	..	..	..	..	..	..	Central Government
..	..	..	..	..	..	..	..	..	..	..	Rest of General Government
..	..	..	..	..	..	..	..	..	..	..	Non-financial Public Enterprises
..	..	..	..	..	..	..	..	..	..	..	Priv. Sector, incl non-guaranteed
..	..	..	..	..	..	..	..	..	..	..	Short-Term Debt
				(Millions of US dollars)							**Memo Items:**
22,262	16,531	19,851	20,940	26,589	31,454	33,050	25,365	24,611	36,778	..	Int'l Reserves Excluding Gold
32,536	37,398	31,227	25,235	26,766	31,996	39,625	33,580	32,823	31,513	..	Gold Holdings (at market price)
											SOCIAL INDICATORS
1.9	1.9	1.8	1.8	1.8	1.8	1.8	1.8	1.8	1.8	..	Total Fertility Rate
9.7	9.5	9.1	8.3	8.3	8.0	7.8	7.6	7.3	7.1	..	Infant Mortality Rate
74.4	74.6	74.9	75.2	75.4	75.7	76.0	76.3	76.6	76.8	..	Life Expectancy at Birth
73.4	73.4	73.5	73.5	73.6	73.7	73.9	74.0	74.2	74.3	..	Urban Population, % of total
92.8	97.9	92.5	101.4	99.0	96.9	100.0	98.5	95.4	96.6	..	Food Prod. per capita (1987=100)
..	..	..	..	..	..	..	..	..	..	..	Labor Force, Agriculture (%)
39.4	39.4	39.5	39.6	39.6	39.7	39.7	39.8	39.8	39.9	..	Labor Force, Female (%)
..	109.0	108.0	106.0	109.0	111.0	113.0	114.0	113.0	..	..	Primary Schl. Enroll. Ratio
109.0	108.0	107.0	105.0	107.0	110.0	113.0	113.0	111.0	..	..	Primary Schl. Enroll. Ratio, Female
..	88.0	90.0	89.0	90.0	91.0	92.0	94.0	97.0	..	..	Secondary Schl. Enroll. Ratio

GABON	1970	1971	1972	1973	1974	1975	1976	1977	1978	1979	1980
CURRENT GNP PER CAPITA (US $)	670	700	740	850	1,530	2,620	4,180	3,810	2,950	3,200	3,830
POPULATION (thousands)	504	525	550	578	607	637	668	698	728	761	797

USE AND ORIGIN OF RESOURCES

(Billions of current CFA Francs)

	1970	1971	1972	1973	1974	1975	1976	1977	1978	1979	1980
Gross National Product (GNP)	84.9	98.5	101.3	148.3	341.3	429.6	676.4	653.0	488.0	567.7	814.7
Net Factor Income from Abroad	-4.6	-6.6	-7.2	-12.8	-30.4	-32.8	-42.7	-37.2	-51.2	-76.9	-89.5
GDP at Market Prices	89.5	105.1	108.5	161.1	371.7	462.4	719.1	690.2	539.2	644.6	904.2
Resource Balance	10.5	14.7	0.9	1.9	53.1	7.5	-3.7	2.3	80.0	135.9	299.2
Exports of Goods & NFServices	44.5	69.7	79.3	94.8	213.9	229.0	327.8	356.1	333.0	377.0	585.2
Imports of Goods & NFServices	34.0	55.0	78.4	92.9	160.8	221.5	331.5	353.8	253.0	241.1	286.0
Domestic Absorption	79.0	90.4	107.6	159.2	318.6	454.9	722.8	687.9	459.2	508.7	605.0
Private Consumption, etc.	32.8	37.1	36.2	73.6	91.8	108.6	118.3	162.2	196.6	218.6	236.4
General Gov't Consumption	17.6	19.7	19.2	25.1	34.4	56.5	76.0	124.9	73.8	77.9	119.6
Gross Domestic Investment	28.6	33.6	52.2	60.5	192.4	289.8	528.5	400.8	188.8	212.2	249.0
Fixed Investment	27.2	32.2	51.5	52.3	156.3	258.2	435.5	338.0	224.0	203.1	241.2
Indirect Taxes, net	13.5	9.7	5.3	13.5	20.3	31.9	38.5	50.8	38.7	37.8	55.7
GDP at factor cost	76.0	95.4	103.2	147.6	351.4	430.5	680.6	639.4	500.5	606.8	848.5
Agriculture	16.6	14.5	14.2	18.7	30.5	29.6	36.0	37.7	35.1	48.0	61.1
Industry	42.6	47.9	55.6	77.1	235.5	288.0	448.4	402.1	311.8	398.1	546.4
Manufacturing	6.1	7.5	8.4	10.7	13.6	19.7	27.8	32.6	32.2	32.3	41.2
Services, etc.	30.3	42.7	38.7	65.3	105.7	144.8	234.7	250.4	192.3	198.5	296.7
Gross Domestic Saving	39.1	48.3	53.1	62.4	245.5	297.3	524.8	403.1	268.8	348.1	548.2
Gross National Saving	32.5	39.2	42.8	45.3	209.1	255.7	470.0	349.7	199.8	238.5	425.4

(Billions of 1987 CFA Francs)

	1970	1971	1972	1973	1974	1975	1976	1977	1978	1979	1980
Gross National Product	630.22	681.66	758.17	762.23	1,058.73	1,261.24	1,708.44	1,492.47	1,124.74	1,117.42	1,136.54
GDP at Market Prices	545.26	601.20	669.36	737.52	1,028.74	1,226.16	1,662.99	1,453.75	1,104.13	1,109.37	1,137.69
Resource Balance	59.86	65.73	53.10	54.67	-41.65	-70.02	-61.04	-71.75	53.83	29.64	-3.57
Exports of Goods & NFServices	209.48	221.72	235.87	237.44	356.73	440.74	513.75	496.34	515.10	423.44	453.77
Imports of Goods & NFServices	149.62	155.99	182.77	182.77	398.38	510.76	574.78	568.09	461.26	393.81	457.34
Domestic Absorption	485.41	535.47	616.27	682.85	1,070.39	1,296.17	1,724.02	1,525.49	1,050.29	1,079.73	1,141.26
Private Consumption, etc.	262.05	283.32	304.00	355.93	297.94	307.77	361.68	397.55	549.58	499.69	501.86
General Gov't Consumption	73.54	80.81	107.43	90.82	109.02	167.84	188.35	210.96	151.94	149.26	197.35
Gross Domestic Investment	149.82	171.34	204.84	236.10	663.43	820.56	1,174.00	916.99	348.77	430.78	442.06
Fixed Investment	..	..	..	..	..	..	..	..	..	..	426.59
GDP at factor cost	..	..	..	..	..	..	..	..	..	..	1,069.97
Agriculture	..	..	..	..	..	..	..	..	..	..	101.13
Industry	..	..	..	..	..	..	..	..	..	..	496.34
Manufacturing	..	..	..	..	..	..	..	..	..	..	64.33
Services, etc.	..	..	..	..	..	..	..	..	..	..	501.29

Memo Items:

	1970	1971	1972	1973	1974	1975	1976	1977	1978	1979	1980
Capacity to Import	195.82	197.68	184.87	186.51	529.93	528.05	568.37	571.78	607.12	615.78	935.80
Terms of Trade Adjustment	-13.65	-24.04	-51.00	-50.93	173.21	87.31	54.62	75.44	92.02	192.34	482.03
Gross Domestic Income	531.61	577.16	618.36	686.59	1,201.95	1,313.47	1,717.61	1,529.19	1,196.15	1,301.71	1,619.72
Gross National Income	616.56	657.62	707.17	711.30	1,231.94	1,348.55	1,763.06	1,567.91	1,216.77	1,309.75	1,618.57

DOMESTIC PRICES/DEFLATORS

(Index 1987 = 100)

	1970	1971	1972	1973	1974	1975	1976	1977	1978	1979	1980
Overall (GDP)	16.4	17.5	16.2	21.8	36.1	37.7	43.2	47.5	48.8	58.1	79.5
Domestic Absorption	16.3	16.9	17.5	23.3	29.8	35.1	41.9	45.1	43.7	47.1	53.0
Agriculture	..	..	..	..	..	..	..	..	..	..	60.4
Industry	..	..	..	..	..	..	..	..	..	..	110.1
Manufacturing	..	..	..	..	..	..	..	..	..	..	64.0
Consumer Price Index	19.8	20.5	21.3	22.6	25.3	32.5	39.0	44.4	49.2	53.1	59.7

MANUFACTURING ACTIVITY

	1970	1971	1972	1973	1974	1975	1976	1977	1978	1979	1980
Employment (1987=100)	..	..	..	..	..	..	..	..	..	..	..
Real Earnings per Empl. (1987=100)	..	..	..	..	..	..	..	..	..	..	..
Real Output per Empl. (1987=100)	..	..	..	..	..	..	..	..	..	..	..
Earnings as % of Value Added	..	..	40.1	39.8	45.1	48.6	44.5	42.3	44.5	..	50.4

MONETARY HOLDINGS

(Billions of current CFA Francs)

	1970	1971	1972	1973	1974	1975	1976	1977	1978	1979	1980
Money Supply, Broadly Defined	13.49	15.33	19.71	26.11	44.00	70.95	132.49	129.58	112.78	122.35	152.07
Money	12.53	14.50	18.41	22.84	38.11	58.97	104.06	95.76	89.84	85.42	93.96
Currency Outside Banks	4.98	5.81	7.00	9.14	15.29	21.71	32.73	30.51	30.48	29.86	34.93
Demand Deposits	7.55	8.69	11.41	13.70	22.82	37.26	71.33	65.26	59.37	55.56	59.03
Quasi-Money	0.95	0.83	1.30	3.27	5.89	11.98	28.43	33.82	22.94	36.93	58.11

GOVERNMENT DEFICIT (-) OR SURPLUS

(Billions of current CFA Francs)

	1970	1971	1972	1973	1974	1975	1976	1977	1978	1979	1980
GOVERNMENT DEFICIT (-) OR SURPLUS	..	..	..	-17.63	-15.46	-36.97	-158.13	..	..	-3.50	55.10
Current Revenue	..	..	..	38.82	89.16	167.31	188.43	..	..	275.00	353.50
Current Expenditure	..	..	..	..	..	..	..	..	..	..	330.30
Current Budget Balance	..	..	..	..	..	..	..	..	..	..	23.20
Capital Receipts	..	..	..	0.05	0.03	0.08	0.63	..	..	..	0.30
Capital Payments	..	..	..	..	..	..	..	..	..	..	-31.60

1981	1982	1983	1984	1985	1986	1987	1988	1989	1990 estimate	Notes	GABON
4,390	4,190	3,730	3,710	3,380	3,310	2,790	3,010	3,160	3,470	..	**CURRENT GNP PER CAPITA (US $)**
835	875	916	957	997	1,023	1,050	1,077	1,105	1,136	..	**POPULATION (thousands)**
				(Billions of current CFA Francs)							**USE AND ORIGIN OF RESOURCES**
960.4	1,086.0	1,179.9	1,458.3	1,536.2	1,116.1	937.2	956.0	1,131.6	1,234.7	..	Gross National Product (GNP)
-89.1	-102.9	-112.4	-97.9	-109.6	-84.2	-83.6	-82.8	-137.8	-138.3	..	Net Factor Income from Abroad
1,049.5	1,188.9	1,292.3	1,556.2	1,645.8	1,200.3	1,020.8	1,038.8	1,269.4	1,373.0	..	GDP at Market Prices
237.9	260.7	229.8	294.0	224.7	-208.4	9.6	-62.2	85.7	257.5	..	Resource Balance
665.0	732.3	792.5	919.6	935.7	475.8	421.2	377.7	560.2	711.8	..	Exports of Goods & NFServices
427.1	471.6	562.7	625.6	711.0	684.2	411.6	439.9	474.5	454.3	..	Imports of Goods & NFServices
811.6	928.2	1,062.5	1,262.2	1,421.1	1,408.7	1,011.2	1,101.0	1,183.7	1,115.5	..	Domestic Absorption
280.6	325.1	385.5	464.8	484.7	558.3	509.0	537.5	528.9	521.9	..	Private Consumption, etc.
149.5	186.8	222.3	284.4	306.3	303.9	242.2	220.6	215.4	238.5	..	General Gov't Consumption
381.5	416.3	454.7	513.0	630.1	546.5	260.0	342.9	439.4	355.1	..	Gross Domestic Investment
347.1	384.5	469.4	487.1	613.3	543.4	272.5	367.3	439.4	340.4	..	Fixed Investment
64.0	74.3	78.2	86.7	104.9	91.5	63.2	66.0	62.0	58.2	..	Indirect Taxes, net
985.5	1,114.6	1,214.1	1,469.5	1,540.9	1,108.8	957.6	972.8	1,207.4	1,314.8	B	GDP at factor cost
64.2	72.8	84.0	95.0	102.2	108.6	107.4	108.0	114.6	123.1	..	Agriculture
613.0	720.9	734.5	929.0	979.2	510.1	447.8	387.8	566.0	656.6	..	Industry
42.3	51.0	57.9	83.6	85.4	83.6	70.4	71.4	67.9	72.0	..	Manufacturing
372.3	395.2	473.8	532.2	564.4	581.6	465.6	543.0	588.8	593.3	..	Services, etc.
619.4	677.0	684.5	807.0	854.8	338.1	269.6	280.7	525.1	612.6	..	Gross Domestic Saving
505.0	546.6	535.9	668.7	696.1	195.3	141.6	151.6	344.2	434.3	..	Gross National Saving
				(Billions of 1987 CFA Francs)							
1,156.70	1,085.13	1,104.61	1,188.33	1,135.92	1,150.44	937.20	1,020.93	1,011.78	1,050.92	..	Gross National Product
1,163.03	1,147.85	1,188.32	1,274.75	1,243.47	1,232.09	1,020.80	1,105.45	1,164.54	1,219.75	..	GDP at Market Prices
-236.24	-181.02	-251.07	-161.42	-211.17	-227.46	9.60	21.58	98.32	323.83	..	Resource Balance
421.01	413.46	431.04	532.28	495.51	449.85	421.20	451.95	535.05	725.30	..	Exports of Goods & NFServices
657.25	594.48	682.10	693.70	706.68	677.32	411.60	430.38	436.73	401.48	..	Imports of Goods & NFServices
1,399.27	1,328.87	1,439.38	1,436.17	1,454.65	1,459.55	1,011.20	1,083.87	1,066.22	895.92	..	Domestic Absorption
518.73	480.77	566.96	506.28	473.79	604.25	509.00	588.65	443.31	377.19	..	Private Consumption, etc.
234.36	245.77	297.66	325.15	318.01	300.94	242.20	234.66	213.72	218.78	..	General Gov't Consumption
646.18	602.32	574.76	604.74	662.85	554.36	260.00	260.56	409.18	299.95	..	Gross Domestic Investment
588.50	554.67	591.93	571.95	642.87	549.93	272.50	284.21	408.38	286.81	..	Fixed Investment
1,092.52	1,077.82	1,116.74	1,203.90	1,164.31	1,138.17	957.60	1,035.56	1,107.77	1,167.88	B	GDP at factor cost
101.31	98.50	103.00	106.37	111.15	109.55	107.40	115.27	107.31	110.86	..	Agriculture
463.72	486.33	471.20	534.79	535.48	544.88	447.80	429.79	492.34	577.76	..	Industry
63.20	70.40	69.62	79.59	87.74	83.75	70.40	61.12	58.87	56.87	..	Manufacturing
595.79	536.21	614.12	633.59	596.85	577.66	465.60	560.39	564.90	531.13	..	Services, etc.
											Memo Items:
1,023.35	923.11	960.67	1,019.70	930.01	471.01	421.20	369.52	515.60	629.03	..	Capacity to Import
602.34	509.65	529.63	487.43	434.51	21.16	0.00	-82.43	-19.44	-96.27	..	Terms of Trade Adjustment
1,765.37	1,657.49	1,717.94	1,762.17	1,677.98	1,253.25	1,020.80	1,023.02	1,145.10	1,123.48	..	Gross Domestic Income
1,759.04	1,594.78	1,634.24	1,675.76	1,570.43	1,171.60	937.20	938.50	992.33	954.65	..	Gross National Income
				(Index 1987 = 100)							**DOMESTIC PRICES/DEFLATORS**
90.2	103.6	108.8	122.1	132.4	97.4	100.0	94.0	109.0	112.6	..	Overall (GDP)
58.0	69.8	73.8	87.9	97.7	96.5	100.0	101.6	111.0	124.5	..	Domestic Absorption
63.4	73.9	81.6	89.3	92.0	99.1	100.0	93.7	106.8	111.0	..	Agriculture
132.2	148.2	155.9	173.7	182.9	93.6	100.0	90.2	115.0	113.6	..	Industry
66.9	72.4	83.2	105.0	97.3	99.8	100.0	116.8	115.3	126.6	..	Manufacturing
64.9	75.7	83.6	88.5	95.0	101.0	100.0	90.2	96.5	104.8	..	Consumer Price Index
											MANUFACTURING ACTIVITY
..	..	..	..	..	..	..	..	..	..	..	Employment (1987=100)
..	..	..	..	..	..	..	..	..	..	..	Real Earnings per Empl. (1987=100)
..	..	..	..	..	..	..	..	..	..	..	Real Output per Empl. (1987=100)
56.4	57.7									..	Earnings as % of Value Added
				(Billions of current CFA Francs)							**MONETARY HOLDINGS**
176.16	199.64	235.32	272.80	305.97	274.90	238.73	263.04	278.89	287.94	..	Money Supply, Broadly Defined
114.50	125.56	142.59	167.75	176.55	152.39	133.26	163.06	171.17	180.93	..	Money
36.74	43.98	48.39	52.64	55.78	47.39	49.46	48.13	57.50	61.88	..	Currency Outside Banks
77.76	81.58	94.20	115.11	120.77	105.00	83.80	114.93	113.67	119.05	..	Demand Deposits
61.67	74.08	92.73	105.05	129.41	122.51	105.46	99.98	107.72	107.01	..	Quasi-Money
				(Billions of current CFA Francs)							
8.20	35.10	-16.30	3.10	1.10	..	..	..	..	..	F	**GOVERNMENT DEFICIT (-) OR SURPLUS**
422.80	488.10	509.29	606.70	648.40	..	..	..	..	..		Current Revenue
..	..	253.10	290.20	298.50	..	..	..	..	..		Current Expenditure
..	..	256.19	316.50	349.90	..	..	..	..	..		Current Budget Balance
0.40	0.30	0.11	0.10	..	..	..	..	..	..		Capital Receipts
..	..	272.60	313.50	348.80	..	..	..	..	..		Capital Payments

GABON	1970	1971	1972	1973	1974	1975	1976	1977	1978	1979	1980
FOREIGN TRADE (CUSTOMS BASIS)					*(Millions of current US dollars)*						
Value of Exports, fob	121.0	177.9	193.1	289.5	944.5	941.9	1,136.3	1,218.2	1,106.2	1,849.6	2,189.3
Nonfuel Primary Products	58.6	84.2	114.0	147.4	261.5	151.7	229.9	205.1	289.2	360.8	..
Fuels	51.6	80.3	61.5	124.5	654.1	780.7	895.1	987.6	802.0	1,444.5	1,925.4
Manufactures	10.9	13.4	17.6	17.6	28.9	9.5	11.4	25.5	14.9	44.3	..
Value of Imports, cif	79.8	90.9	133.3	158.5	331.9	446.3	497.4	705.9	564.3	532.1	673.6
Nonfuel Primary Products	12.3	13.9	21.0	23.3	47.1	63.4	65.8	99.7	120.6	111.1	138.8
Fuels	1.1	1.1	1.6	1.8	4.2	5.7	3.8	7.7	6.9	8.1	9.2
Manufactures	66.5	75.9	110.8	133.4	280.6	377.2	427.8	598.5	436.8	412.9	525.5
					(Index 1987 = 100)						
Terms of Trade	42.6	44.2	54.8	53.2	107.7	95.0	101.3	98.7	93.3	110.8	154.3
Export Prices, fob	12.3	13.8	18.7	21.8	55.6	53.2	58.5	63.1	67.3	91.9	139.3
Import Prices, cif	28.9	31.2	34.1	41.0	51.6	56.0	57.8	63.9	72.1	82.9	90.3
BALANCE OF PAYMENTS					*(Millions of current US dollars)*						
Exports of Goods & Services	207.9	251.6	310.9	442.6	1,005.4	1,247.3	1,357.7	1,487.0	1,482.9	2,031.2	2,433.9
Merchandise, fob	173.7	225.1	268.0	396.5	956.9	1,149.2	1,217.3	1,300.4	1,308.6	1,815.0	2,084.4
Nonfactor Services	31.4	24.9	40.0	42.3	39.3	85.8	127.0	172.7	169.9	208.8	324.6
Factor Services	2.8	1.7	3.0	3.8	9.1	12.3	13.4	13.9	4.4	7.3	24.9
Imports of Goods & Services	215.8	233.5	329.3	488.9	784.7	1,175.1	1,299.4	1,349.8	1,366.7	1,665.6	1,926.0
Merchandise, fob	99.3	106.9	155.6	231.0	349.7	516.9	527.3	589.2	557.9	554.8	686.1
Nonfactor Services	97.2	101.1	142.0	196.7	299.7	492.7	580.1	595.3	577.7	741.9	789.4
Factor Services	19.3	25.5	31.7	61.2	135.3	165.5	192.0	165.2	231.1	368.8	450.5
Long-Term Interest	2.6	3.4	4.2	10.9	10.7	15.0	25.3	31.0	71.5	101.3	118.7
Private Current Transfers, net	-7.2	-9.0	-12.2	-19.4	-25.0	-41.2	-50.6	-65.8	-79.1	-153.7	-157.5
Workers' Remittances	..	..	..	..	..	..	..	..	..	0.1	0.0
Curr. A/C Bal before Off. Transf.	-15.1	9.1	-30.5	-65.7	195.7	31.1	7.7	71.3	37.1	211.9	350.4
Net Official Transfers	12.5	8.8	26.8	22.7	23.5	42.4	44.6	27.6	36.7	35.8	33.4
Curr. A/C Bal after Off. Transf.	-2.6	18.0	-3.7	-43.0	219.1	73.5	52.3	98.9	73.9	247.6	383.9
Long-Term Capital, net	6.3	18.1	0.9	41.4	116.5	276.5	197.7	-17.5	100.0	31.5	-35.8
Direct Investment	-0.7	15.7	17.4	15.9	76.4	159.9	1.0	14.6	56.5	48.3	23.5
Long-Term Loans	16.6	32.0	79.8	138.2	105.8	328.0	333.4	132.0	-55.7	149.4	-108.5
Disbursements	25.9	47.0	98.0	189.9	135.8	377.4	396.1	228.5	146.3	374.5	170.5
Repayments	9.3	15.0	18.2	51.7	30.0	49.4	62.7	96.5	202.0	225.1	279.0
Other Long-Term Capital	-9.6	-29.7	-96.3	-112.7	-65.6	-211.4	-136.8	-164.1	99.1	-166.2	49.1
Other Capital, net	1.1	-29.0	-1.1	24.4	-284.9	-303.9	-267.1	-192.5	-165.6	-295.5	-252.1
Change in Reserves	-4.8	-7.0	3.9	-22.8	-50.7	-46.0	17.1	111.2	-8.2	16.3	-95.9
Memo Item:					*(CFA Francs per US dollar)*						
Conversion Factor (Annual Avg)	277.710	277.130	252.210	222.700	240.500	214.320	238.980	245.670	225.640	212.720	211.300
EXTERNAL DEBT (Total)					*(Millions of US dollars), outstanding at end of year*						
	90.9	127.5	200.7	346.2	462.0	771.7	1,079.2	1,476.3	1,511.8	1,721.6	1,513.1
Long-Term Debt (by debtor)	90.9	127.5	200.7	346.2	462.0	771.7	1,079.2	1,255.3	1,297.8	1,480.6	1,285.1
Central Bank, incl. IMF credit	16.1	18.9	22.6	21.6	25.7	25.3	20.1	18.5	27.7	36.2	32.4
Central Government	35.7	71.1	134.5	265.7	341.0	567.8	850.6	1,010.5	1,021.4	1,139.4	997.3
Rest of General Government	0.1	1.3	4.2	3.2	2.3	1.1	0.1	0.0	10.6	8.8	6.9
Non-financial Public Enterprises	13.3	16.3	24.9	29.9	52.2	104.6	136.2	156.9	174.0	247.3	215.2
Priv. Sector, incl non-guaranteed	25.7	19.9	14.5	25.8	40.8	72.9	72.2	69.4	64.1	48.9	33.3
Short-Term Debt	0.0	0.0	0.0	0.0	0.0	0.0	0.0	221.0	214.0	241.0	228.0
Memo Items:					*(Thousands of US dollars)*						
Int'l Reserves Excluding Gold	14,740	25,387	23,227	47,858	103,293	146,069	116,155	9,905	22,574	20,135	107,503
Gold Holdings (at market price)	..	..	..	..	..	..	..	1,056	2,147	6,451	7,428
SOCIAL INDICATORS											
Total Fertility Rate	4.2	4.2	4.3	4.3	4.3	4.3	4.4	4.4	4.4	4.4	4.5
Infant Mortality Rate	138.0	135.0	132.0	130.0	128.0	126.0	124.0	122.0	120.0	118.0	116.0
Life Expectancy at Birth	44.2	44.6	45.0	45.4	45.8	46.3	46.7	47.1	47.6	48.0	48.4
Urban Population, % of total	25.6	26.6	27.6	28.6	29.6	30.6	31.6	32.7	33.7	34.8	35.8
Food Prod. per capita (1987=100)	137.1	134.5	129.6	124.9	122.8	120.8	119.0	118.6	120.9	121.0	119.6
Labor Force, Agriculture (%)	79.6	79.2	78.8	78.4	78.0	77.5	77.1	76.7	76.3	75.9	75.4
Labor Force, Female (%)	40.0	40.0	39.9	39.8	39.8	39.7	39.6	39.6	39.5	39.4	39.4
Primary Schl. Enroll. Ratio	85.0	..	..	..	..	102.0	..	..	..	..	..
Primary Schl. Enroll. Ratio, Female	81.0	..	..	..	..	100.0	..	..	..	..	..
Secondary Schl. Enroll. Ratio	8.0	..	..	..	..	17.0	..	..	..	..	..

1981	1982	1983	1984	1985	1986	1987	1988	1989	1990 estimate	Notes	GABON
											FOREIGN TRADE (CUSTOMS BASIS)
			(Millions of current US dollars)								
2,200.7	2,160.6	2,000.2	2,011.4	1,951.4	1,270.6	1,287.7	1,195.6	1,626.0	2,471.1	..	Value of Exports, fob
279.5	254.0	291.4	293.1	284.3	185.1	187.6	174.2	236.9	360.0	..	Nonfuel Primary Products
1,816.3	1,828.3	1,589.4	1,598.3	1,550.7	1,009.6	1,023.2	950.1	1,292.1	1,963.6	..	Fuels
104.9	78.3	119.4	120.0	116.4	75.8	76.8	71.3	97.0	147.4	..	Manufactures
834.5	798.5	685.6	723.6	854.7	866.3	732.0	791.2	751.7	760.3	..	Value of Imports, cif
146.9	146.5	134.7	142.2	167.9	170.2	143.8	155.5	147.7	149.4	..	Nonfuel Primary Products
22.3	8.2	12.1	12.8	15.1	15.3	12.9	14.0	13.3	13.4	..	Fuels
665.3	643.8	538.8	568.7	671.7	680.8	575.3	621.8	590.7	597.5	..	Manufactures
			(Index 1987 = 100)								
165.4	156.9	147.2	147.3	139.6	86.8	100.0	83.1	95.9	..	..	Terms of Trade
148.7	137.4	125.6	123.8	117.6	82.8	100.0	88.8	106.6	..	..	Export Prices, fob
89.9	87.6	85.3	84.1	84.2	95.4	100.0	106.9	111.2	..	..	Import Prices, cif
			(Millions of current US dollars)								**BALANCE OF PAYMENTS**
2,533.0	2,350.7	2,218.3	2,203.4	2,119.1	1,215.9	1,417.2	1,424.0	1,934.0	2,634.9	..	Exports of Goods & Services
2,200.2	2,160.4	2,000.1	2,017.8	1,951.4	1,074.2	1,286.4	1,195.6	1,626.0	2,471.1	..	Merchandise, fob
307.6	170.3	200.8	137.8	138.5	123.6	114.8	213.3	289.0	141.8	..	Nonfactor Services
25.2	20.0	17.3	47.7	29.2	18.1	16.0	15.1	19.0	22.0	..	Factor Services
2,064.6	1,982.1	2,056.8	2,023.6	2,185.9	2,126.5	1,874.4	1,881.5	2,103.6	2,251.5	..	Imports of Goods & Services
841.2	722.6	725.5	733.2	854.7	979.1	731.8	791.2	751.7	760.3	..	Merchandise, fob
868.2	926.1	1,031.5	1,018.5	1,058.3	882.7	883.9	797.6	900.8	960.8	..	Nonfactor Services
355.2	333.3	299.8	271.8	272.8	264.7	258.7	292.7	451.1	530.4	..	Factor Services
87.5	94.9	52.6	60.8	56.8	51.2	42.8	74.7	102.0	74.8	..	Long-Term Interest
-93.1	-83.6	-95.1	-92.5	-109.2	-169.1	-147.8	-155.5	-135.2	-146.9	..	Private Current Transfers, net
0.2	0.1	0.3	0.1	0.1	0.2	0.3	0.1	0.2	..	..	Workers' Remittances
375.3	285.0	66.4	87.4	-176.0	-1,079.7	-605.1	-613.0	-201.5	236.5	..	Curr. A/C Bal before Off. Transf.
28.0	24.3	5.6	25.3	13.5	22.3	24.4	11.2	9.3	-12.1	..	Net Official Transfers
403.3	309.4	72.0	112.7	-162.5	-1,057.4	-580.6	-601.8	-192.2	224.4	..	Curr. A/C Bal after Off. Transf.
-95.9	92.9	71.8	172.6	212.6	570.1	533.5	639.0	258.4	7.3	..	Long-Term Capital, net
47.5	127.0	106.1	4.8	11.1	103.7	82.2	121.4	-38.6	-77.1	..	Direct Investment
-161.1	-91.5	-58.9	56.4	133.1	328.5	187.6	223.5	72.3	108.1	..	Long-Term Loans
60.8	95.5	103.1	249.9	301.0	451.7	210.7	251.4	128.6	160.9	..	Disbursements
221.9	187.0	162.0	193.5	167.9	123.2	23.1	27.9	56.3	52.8	..	Repayments
17.8	57.5	24.6	111.4	68.4	137.9	263.8	294.1	224.7	-23.6	..	Other Long-Term Capital
-189.6	-255.8	-233.3	-246.0	-99.0	355.7	-89.5	-56.7	-101.7	-2.6	..	Other Capital, net
-117.8	-146.5	89.5	-39.2	48.9	131.7	136.6	19.5	35.5	-229.2	..	Change in Reserves
			(CFA Francs per US dollar)								**Memo Item:**
271.730	328.620	381.070	436.960	449.260	346.300	300.540	297.850	319.010	272.260	..	Conversion Factor (Annual Avg)
			(Millions of US dollars), outstanding at end of year								
1,134.9	1,000.0	913.7	920.1	1,206.6	1,940.1	2,542.8	2,799.3	3,180.5	3,647.2	..	**EXTERNAL DEBT (Total)**
987.8	827.0	680.6	669.1	944.6	1,461.0	2,137.3	2,397.1	2,618.2	3,084.9	..	Long-Term Debt (by debtor)
26.7	23.6	16.5	9.0	10.1	44.1	67.9	137.1	138.3	143.4	..	Central Bank, incl. IMF credit
775.1	671.7	569.8	591.5	845.1	1,278.1	1,894.7	2,105.5	2,326.7	2,761.6	..	Central Government
3.3	0.7	0.5	0.3	0.0	0.0	0.0	0.0	0.0	..	..	Rest of General Government
164.4	122.6	88.1	65.4	86.6	136.1	172.3	152.8	151.4	177.9	..	Non-financial Public Enterprises
18.3	8.4	5.7	2.9	2.8	2.7	2.4	1.7	1.8	2.0	..	Priv. Sector, incl non-guaranteed
147.1	173.0	233.1	251.0	262.0	479.1	405.5	402.2	562.3	562.3	..	Short-Term Debt
			(Thousands of US dollars)								**Memo Items:**
198,854	311,885	186,898	199,450	192,546	126,350	11,999	67,435	34,426	273,765	..	Int'l Reserves Excluding Gold
5,009	5,757	4,807	3,885	4,120	4,925	6,100	5,169	5,053	4,851	..	Gold Holdings (at market price)
											SOCIAL INDICATORS
4.5	4.5	4.7	4.9	5.1	5.3	5.5	5.6	5.7	5.7	..	Total Fertility Rate
114.0	112.0	110.2	108.4	106.5	104.7	102.9	100.8	98.7	96.7	..	Infant Mortality Rate
48.9	49.3	49.9	50.6	51.2	51.8	52.4	52.7	53.0	53.4	..	Life Expectancy at Birth
36.8	37.8	38.9	39.9	40.9	42.1	43.3	44.1	44.9	45.7	..	Urban Population, % of total
112.3	109.0	105.8	103.9	100.1	101.2	100.0	100.9	98.2	96.8	..	Food Prod. per capita (1987=100)
..	..	..	..	..	..	..	..	..	..	..	Labor Force, Agriculture (%)
39.2	39.0	38.7	38.5	38.3	38.1	37.9	37.7	37.5	37.3	..	Labor Force, Female (%)
..	..	..	..	..	..	..	..	..	..	..	Primary Schl. Enroll. Ratio
..	..	..	..	..	..	..	..	..	..	..	Primary Schl. Enroll. Ratio, Female
..	..	..	..	..	..	..	..	..	..	..	Secondary Schl. Enroll. Ratio

GAMBIA, THE	1970	1971	1972	1973	1974	1975	1976	1977	1978	1979	1980
CURRENT GNP PER CAPITA (US $)	100	120	130	140	200	210	230	250	260	350	350
POPULATION (thousands)	463	476	489	502	517	533	552	571	591	612	634
USE AND ORIGIN OF RESOURCES					*(Millions of current Gambian Dalasis)*						
Gross National Product (GNP)	111.8	108.5	117.7	128.8	196.0	220.5	274.0	347.3	355.3	401.5	390.2
Net Factor Income from Abroad	-4.0	-4.7	-5.9	-3.6	0.6	-0.6	-4.3	-7.7	-6.5	-18.9	-19.2
GDP at Market Prices	115.8	113.2	123.6	132.4	195.4	221.1	278.3	355.0	361.8	420.4	409.4
Resource Balance	0.3	-11.3	-5.2	-13.4	-2.1	6.7	-43.2	-35.1	-152.7	-68.6	-104.5
Exports of Goods & NFServices	38.3	35.8	44.1	45.7	82.0	104.2	100.9	131.8	109.6	163.8	190.8
Imports of Goods & NFServices	38.0	47.1	49.4	59.1	84.2	97.5	144.0	166.9	262.4	232.4	295.3
Domestic Absorption	115.5	124.5	128.8	145.8	197.5	214.4	321.5	390.1	514.5	489.0	513.9
Private Consumption, etc.	97.4	102.7	103.1	117.2	164.6	157.1	250.4	285.7	328.2	313.0	324.1
General Gov't Consumption	12.6	14.6	15.8	17.7	24.3	30.3	39.3	52.0	72.0	61.9	82.4
Gross Domestic Investment	5.6	7.2	9.9	10.9	8.6	27.0	31.7	52.4	114.3	114.1	107.4
Fixed Investment	..	..	..	..	..	..	..	..	..	..	107.4
Indirect Taxes, net	14.4	10.6	11.7	12.7	14.7	17.6	33.1	46.5	46.9	60.9	42.1
GDP at factor cost	101.4	102.6	111.9	119.7	180.7	203.5	245.2	308.5	314.9	359.5	367.3
Agriculture	33.0	36.5	39.9	42.6	63.0	70.5	92.5	103.8	96.5	112.3	111.9
Industry	9.4	9.4	10.2	10.9	16.3	20.8	27.2	33.3	43.0	48.1	59.9
Manufacturing	3.4	3.4	3.6	3.9	5.8	6.6	11.8	14.3	13.6	13.8	26.7
Services, etc.	59.0	56.7	61.8	66.2	101.4	112.2	125.5	171.4	175.4	199.1	195.5
Gross Domestic Saving	5.9	-4.1	4.6	-2.5	6.5	33.7	-11.4	17.3	-38.4	45.5	2.9
Gross National Saving	2.4	-8.2	-0.2	-5.4	7.4	32.7	-12.9	11.8	-44.7	24.9	-10.1
					(Millions of 1987 Gambian Dalasis)						
Gross National Product	548.18	606.32	645.99	691.91	854.12	831.17	903.28	923.42	875.63	1,000.38	898.69
GDP at Market Prices	567.29	632.69	678.33	709.84	850.60	832.40	915.21	942.69	889.95	1,043.68	941.86
Resource Balance	-404.73	-579.09	-552.75	-556.61	-403.50	-402.27	-763.16	-856.74	-1,560.90	-899.95	-1,154.00
Exports of Goods & NFServices	353.16	299.20	380.94	386.69	434.90	528.46	554.65	531.97	410.64	539.00	630.64
Imports of Goods & NFServices	757.89	878.29	933.69	943.29	838.40	930.74	1,317.80	1,388.71	1,971.53	1,438.95	1,784.65
Domestic Absorption	972.01	1,211.78	1,231.08	1,266.45	1,254.10	1,234.68	1,678.37	1,799.43	2,450.85	1,943.63	2,095.87
Private Consumption, etc.	883.96	1,108.96	1,111.94	1,143.68	1,141.82	1,053.92	1,493.66	1,570.74	2,050.20	1,579.37	1,663.23
General Gov't Consumption	65.76	74.33	81.06	87.79	74.48	80.91	80.91	87.94	113.79	144.53	187.81
Gross Domestic Investment	22.28	28.49	38.08	34.98	37.80	99.85	103.80	140.75	286.86	219.73	244.83
Fixed Investment	..	..	..	..	..	..	..	..	..	..	244.83
GDP at factor cost	488.14	544.05	583.52	610.30	731.31	685.57	724.33	733.34	705.97	819.14	776.04
Agriculture	172.59	192.42	206.11	215.79	258.53	242.47	246.01	245.07	211.31	222.83	207.81
Industry	53.28	59.59	64.03	66.83	80.15	74.78	75.71	77.82	100.95	94.46	110.11
Manufacturing	21.98	24.32	26.19	27.36	32.73	30.16	34.37	33.44	34.37	4.44	-4.44
Services, etc.	262.28	292.04	313.38	327.68	392.63	368.32	402.60	410.45	393.71	501.85	458.12
Memo Items:											
Capacity to Import	763.60	667.58	834.88	729.39	817.11	994.65	922.93	1,096.45	823.89	1,014.18	1,153.10
Terms of Trade Adjustment	410.44	368.38	453.94	342.70	382.21	466.18	368.28	564.48	413.25	475.18	522.46
Gross Domestic Income	977.73	1,001.07	1,132.27	1,052.54	1,232.81	1,298.59	1,283.49	1,507.17	1,303.20	1,518.86	1,464.32
Gross National Income	958.62	974.70	1,099.92	1,034.61	1,236.33	1,297.35	1,271.56	1,487.90	1,288.88	1,475.56	1,421.15
DOMESTIC PRICES/DEFLATORS					*(Index 1987 = 100)*						
Overall (GDP)	20.4	17.9	18.2	18.7	23.0	26.6	30.4	37.7	40.7	40.3	43.5
Domestic Absorption	11.9	10.3	10.5	11.5	15.8	17.4	19.2	21.7	21.0	25.2	24.5
Agriculture	19.1	19.0	19.4	19.7	24.4	29.1	37.6	42.4	45.7	50.4	53.8
Industry	17.6	15.8	15.9	16.3	20.3	27.8	35.9	42.8	42.6	50.9	54.4
Manufacturing	15.5	14.0	13.7	14.3	17.7	21.9	34.3	42.8	39.6	310.6	-601.0
Consumer Price Index	10.3	10.6	11.5	12.3	13.5	17.0	19.9	22.3	24.3	25.8	27.5
MANUFACTURING ACTIVITY											
Employment (1987=100)	..	..	..	..	..	..	..	..	..	..	..
Real Earnings per Empl. (1987=100)	..	..	..	..	..	..	..	..	..	..	..
Real Output per Empl. (1987=100)	..	..	..	..	..	..	..	..	..	..	..
Earnings as % of Value Added	..	..	..	..	..	43.2	43.7	40.8	60.8	40.5	25.3
MONETARY HOLDINGS					*(Millions of current Gambian Dalasis)*						
Money Supply, Broadly Defined	19.36	19.44	27.07	38.42	42.24	47.90	69.91	61.45	89.68	82.19	90.70
Money	16.45	16.36	22.78	31.80	33.03	37.34	49.42	39.80	57.78	57.78	61.28
Currency Outside Banks	12.12	12.73	14.94	25.21	24.06	27.15	32.08	19.79	34.53	36.53	36.76
Demand Deposits	4.33	3.63	7.84	6.59	8.97	10.19	17.34	20.01	23.25	21.25	24.52
Quasi-Money	2.91	3.08	4.29	6.62	9.21	10.56	20.49	21.65	31.90	24.41	29.42
					(Millions of current Gambian Dalasis)						
GOVERNMENT DEFICIT (-) OR SURPLUS	..	..	..	0.30	-2.79	-6.61	-6.65	-26.49	-35.85	-38.42	-18.32
Current Revenue	..	..	19.37	22.87	26.94	35.02	47.46	64.56	102.57	88.71	109.00
Current Expenditure	..	..	..	18.04	20.70	30.93	39.91	54.45	61.61	62.66	68.17
Current Budget Balance	..	..	..	4.83	6.24	4.09	7.55	10.11	40.96	26.05	40.83
Capital Receipts	..	..	0.01	0.02	0.01	0.02	0.04	0.03	0.20	0.15	0.05
Capital Payments	..	..	..	4.55	9.04	10.72	14.24	36.63	77.01	64.62	59.20

1981	1982	1983	1984	1985	1986	1987	1988	1989	1990 estimate	Notes	GAMBIA, THE
360	360	290	250	210	170	190	210	240	260	..	**CURRENT GNP PER CAPITA (US $)**
656	678	701	724	748	772	797	823	849	875	..	**POPULATION (thousands)**
				(Millions of current Gambian Dalasis)							**USE AND ORIGIN OF RESOURCES**
436.9	495.6	550.3	607.6	734.5	861.6	1,073.1	1,322.4	1,591.1	1,829.5	C	Gross National Product (GNP)
-24.5	-32.3	-48.2	-65.1	-124.9	-216.6	-177.8	-167.1	-201.9	-179.8	..	Net Factor Income from Abroad
461.4	527.9	598.5	672.7	859.4	1,078.2	1,250.9	1,489.5	1,793.0	2,009.3	C	GDP at Market Prices
-94.0	-57.4	-77.7	-96.0	-80.7	-163.6	-144.7	-162.6	-245.8	-236.6	..	Resource Balance
192.0	246.6	322.1	327.8	443.3	755.0	787.5	996.2	1,218.9	1,362.7	..	Exports of Goods & NFServices
286.0	304.0	399.8	423.8	524.0	918.6	932.2	1,158.8	1,464.7	1,599.3	..	Imports of Goods & NFServices
555.4	585.3	676.2	768.7	940.1	1,241.8	1,395.6	1,652.1	2,038.8	2,245.9	..	Domestic Absorption
335.7	371.4	449.2	517.3	662.9	776.9	914.0	1,132.4	1,345.6	1,500.4	..	Private Consumption, etc.
106.5	104.9	123.3	122.3	141.1	245.4	250.5	251.0	298.7	329.0	..	General Gov't Consumption
113.2	109.0	103.7	129.1	136.1	219.5	231.1	268.7	394.5	416.5	..	Gross Domestic Investment
113.2	109.0	103.7	129.1	136.1	219.5	231.1	268.7	394.5	416.5	..	Fixed Investment
53.6	66.3	77.6	96.4	141.8	166.5	210.4	328.0	354.0	244.9	..	Indirect Taxes, net
407.8	461.6	520.9	576.3	717.6	911.6	1,040.5	1,161.5	1,439.0	1,764.4	C	GDP at factor cost
154.8	195.9	167.8	188.2	246.9	322.0	361.7	396.2	493.6	544.9	..	Agriculture
48.8	45.7	77.3	89.3	71.1	95.5	110.3	119.4	167.3	200.5	..	Industry
22.7	23.3	51.6	58.7	44.1	57.0	65.0	66.4	99.9	113.3	..	Manufacturing
204.2	220.0	275.8	298.8	399.6	494.1	568.5	645.9	778.1	1,019.0	..	Services, etc.
19.2	51.6	26.0	33.1	55.4	55.9	86.4	106.1	148.7	179.9	..	Gross Domestic Saving
1.8	25.9	-15.1	-14.4	-45.0	-86.4	4.0	24.7	-2.5	111.5	..	Gross National Saving
				(Millions of 1987 Gambian Dalasis)							
984.02	1,112.29	1,019.91	1,031.70	985.04	941.54	1,073.10	1,201.89	1,260.61	1,350.60	C	Gross National Product
1,037.69	1,169.76	1,107.98	1,141.24	1,148.30	1,180.08	1,250.90	1,348.80	1,416.87	1,478.56	C I	GDP at Market Prices
-685.23	-483.69	-169.15	-358.33	-274.75	-386.48	-144.70	-286.25	-233.43	-211.86	..	Resource Balance
787.50	854.36	802.93	524.25	571.50	541.29	787.50	728.36	837.00	877.18	..	Exports of Goods & NFServices
1,472.73	1,338.04	972.08	882.58	846.25	927.77	932.20	1,014.61	1,070.43	1,089.04	..	Imports of Goods & NFServices
1,722.93	1,653.45	1,277.13	1,499.57	1,423.05	1,566.57	1,395.60	1,635.06	1,650.30	1,690.43	..	Domestic Absorption
1,238.73	1,189.20	862.63	1,078.33	1,060.36	1,055.17	914.00	1,178.58	1,114.55	1,160.38	..	Private Consumption, etc.
234.70	227.70	225.11	204.91	184.70	269.93	250.50	220.45	230.81	233.92	..	General Gov't Consumption
249.49	236.54	189.39	216.33	177.99	241.46	231.10	236.02	304.94	296.13	..	Gross Domestic Investment
249.49	236.54	189.39	216.33	177.99	241.46	231.10	236.02	304.94	296.13	..	Fixed Investment
848.07	955.50	897.08	926.35	914.47	991.62	1,040.50	1,052.15	1,125.70	1,143.52	C I	GDP at factor cost
295.76	357.14	281.71	301.35	314.46	350.13	361.70	362.69	386.02	352.96	..	Agriculture
87.49	76.88	92.07	89.27	89.67	102.82	110.30	106.42	126.19	128.53	..	Industry
41.85	45.13	59.62	55.65	55.65	61.49	65.00	59.90	72.01	72.72	..	Manufacturing
464.82	521.47	523.30	535.73	510.35	538.67	568.50	583.04	613.49	662.03	..	Services, etc.
											Memo Items:
988.69	1,085.40	783.16	682.65	715.92	762.54	787.50	872.24	890.80	927.93	..	Capacity to Import
201.19	231.04	-19.77	158.40	144.42	221.25	0.00	143.88	53.80	50.75	..	Terms of Trade Adjustment
1,238.88	1,400.81	1,088.21	1,299.64	1,292.72	1,401.33	1,250.90	1,492.69	1,470.66	1,529.31	..	Gross Domestic Income
1,185.21	1,343.33	1,000.14	1,190.11	1,129.46	1,162.79	1,073.10	1,345.78	1,314.41	1,401.35	..	Gross National Income
				(Index 1987 = 100)							**DOMESTIC PRICES/DEFLATORS**
44.5	45.1	54.0	58.9	74.8	91.4	100.0	110.4	126.5	135.9	..	Overall (GDP)
32.2	35.4	52.9	51.3	66.1	79.3	100.0	101.0	123.5	132.9	..	Domestic Absorption
52.3	54.9	59.6	62.5	78.5	92.0	100.0	109.2	127.9	154.4	..	Agriculture
55.8	59.4	84.0	100.0	79.3	92.9	100.0	112.2	132.6	156.0	..	Industry
54.2	51.6	86.5	105.5	79.3	92.7	100.0	110.8	138.7	155.8	..	Manufacturing
29.2	32.4	35.8	43.7	51.7	81.0	100.0	111.7	120.9	135.7	..	Consumer Price Index
											MANUFACTURING ACTIVITY
..	..	..	..	..	..	..	..	..	..	J	Employment (1987=100)
..	..	..	..	..	..	..	..	..	..	J	Real Earnings per Empl. (1987=100)
..	..	..	..	..	..	..	..	..	..	J	Real Output per Empl. (1987=100)
25.8	31.7	..	..	..	..	..	..	..	..	J	Earnings as % of Value Added
				(Millions of current Gambian Dalasis)							**MONETARY HOLDINGS**
109.66	127.02	160.96	169.78	256.95	275.64	343.53	394.19	476.18	516.09	..	Money Supply, Broadly Defined
76.97	87.22	100.32	99.58	162.10	166.49	197.83	213.52	260.25	296.19	..	Money
42.62	55.92	57.18	58.38	85.67	91.18	95.02	111.99	134.78	152.17	..	Currency Outside Banks
34.35	31.30	43.14	41.20	76.43	75.31	102.81	101.53	125.47	144.02	..	Demand Deposits
32.69	39.80	60.64	70.20	94.85	109.15	145.70	180.67	215.93	219.90	..	Quasi-Money
				(Millions of current Gambian Dalasis)							
-50.10	-33.86	-35.74	-41.82	-3.78	-80.19	-30.14	-97.11	-55.08	-11.11	C	**GOVERNMENT DEFICIT (-) OR SURPLUS**
97.39	135.03	108.28	141.19	154.75	214.98	330.69	326.76	397.50	475.93	..	Current Revenue
84.86	119.74	114.63	133.46	134.40	173.93	195.26	231.69	280.74	372.91	..	Current Expenditure
12.53	15.29	-6.35	7.73	20.35	41.05	135.43	95.07	116.76	103.02	..	Current Budget Balance
0.03	0.04	1.24	0.11	0.65	3.15	0.68	0.07	0.22	0.75	..	Capital Receipts
62.66	49.19	30.63	49.66	24.78	124.39	166.25	192.25	172.06	114.88	..	Capital Payments

	1970	1971	1972	1973	1974	1975	1976	1977	1978	1979	1980
FOREIGN TRADE (CUSTOMS BASIS)					*(Millions of current US dollars)*						
Value of Exports, fob	..	..	..	..	..	..	..	..	..	..	..
Nonfuel Primary Products	..	..	..	..	..	..	..	..	..	..	..
Fuels	..	..	..	..	..	..	..	..	..	..	..
Manufactures	..	..	..	..	..	..	..	..	..	..	..
Value of Imports, cif	..	..	..	..	..	..	..	..	..	..	..
Nonfuel Primary Products	..	..	..	..	..	..	..	..	..	..	..
Fuels	..	..	..	..	..	..	..	..	..	..	..
Manufactures	..	..	..	..	..	..	..	..	..	..	..
					(Index 1987 = 100)						
Terms of Trade	..	..	..	..	..	..	..	..	..	..	..
Export Prices, fob	..	..	..	..	..	..	..	..	..	..	..
Import Prices, cif	..	..	..	..	..	..	..	..	..	..	..
BALANCE OF PAYMENTS					*(Millions of current US dollars)*						
Exports of Goods & Services	20.00	21.26	26.82	29.14	54.23	68.88	56.42	67.83	55.28	78.18	..
Merchandise, fob	17.76	18.31	21.57	20.64	43.73	56.69	43.72	53.47	40.08	53.75	48.29
Nonfactor Services	1.50	2.06	4.17	6.66	9.20	9.42	10.09	12.29	13.27	22.51	17.96
Factor Services	0.74	0.89	1.07	1.84	1.30	2.77	2.61	2.07	1.93	1.92	..
Imports of Goods & Services	20.22	24.29	28.79	35.06	55.43	61.95	75.73	80.47	111.83	136.43	181.45
Merchandise, fob	15.92	19.13	21.80	26.57	41.37	47.35	59.54	62.64	81.00	94.74	137.69
Nonfactor Services	2.43	2.86	4.09	5.88	11.44	12.24	15.31	17.40	26.15	37.27	41.56
Factor Services	1.87	2.31	2.90	2.61	2.62	2.36	0.88	0.43	4.68	4.42	2.20
Long-Term Interest	0.00	0.00	0.00	0.00	0.10	0.00	0.00	0.10	0.20	0.30	0.40
Private Current Transfers, net	0.26	0.29	0.53	0.38	0.20	-0.23	1.27	0.98	0.09	-0.88	3.62
Workers' Remittances	..	..	..	..	..	..	..	..	..	..	..
Curr. A/C Bal before Off. Transf.	0.04	-2.74	-1.44	-5.54	-1.00	6.70	-18.03	-11.65	-56.46	-59.13	-111.58
Net Official Transfers	0.41	1.77	1.24	1.44	6.69	4.59	1.37	3.88	12.88	25.99	37.66
Curr. A/C Bal after Off. Transf.	0.45	-0.97	-0.21	-4.10	5.69	11.29	-16.66	-7.78	-43.59	-33.14	-73.92
Long-Term Capital, net	1.28	1.69	3.76	4.64	4.32	1.87	2.47	4.34	10.14	16.56	3.73
Direct Investment	0.11	1.71	1.66	1.41	1.21	0.11	0.94	..	2.00	11.68	..
Long-Term Loans	0.70	0.10	2.30	1.50	3.30	2.40	3.40	9.00	14.80	22.70	50.80
Disbursements	0.80	0.30	2.60	1.80	3.70	2.80	3.70	9.50	15.00	22.90	51.20
Repayments	0.10	0.20	0.30	0.30	0.40	0.40	0.30	0.50	0.20	0.20	0.40
Other Long-Term Capital	0.47	-0.12	-0.20	1.73	-0.20	-0.64	-1.86	-4.66	-6.66	-17.83	-47.07
Other Capital, net	-0.12	0.95	-1.84	10.14	-5.48	0.85	7.09	4.69	20.24	0.75	63.89
Change in Reserves	-1.61	-1.66	-1.72	-10.68	-4.52	-14.01	7.10	-1.26	13.21	15.83	6.30
Memo Item:					*(Gambian Dalasis per US dollar)*						
Conversion Factor (Annual Avg)	2.080	1.970	1.920	1.680	1.700	2.010	2.340	2.190	2.000	1.790	1.750
EXTERNAL DEBT (Total)				*(Millions of US dollars), outstanding at end of year*							
	5.10	5.50	7.40	8.90	12.20	13.40	15.50	38.00	49.70	81.20	136.80
Long-Term Debt (by debtor)	5.10	5.50	7.40	8.90	12.20	13.40	15.50	31.00	39.70	61.20	113.50
Central Bank, incl. IMF credit	0.00	0.00	0.00	0.00	0.00	0.00	0.00	5.20	15.20	13.70	16.20
Central Government	5.10	5.50	7.40	8.90	12.20	13.40	14.30	22.90	23.90	42.50	82.70
Rest of General Government	..	..	..	..	..	..	..	..	..	..	..
Non-financial Public Enterprises	0.00	0.00	0.00	0.00	0.00	0.00	1.20	2.90	0.60	3.40	11.20
Priv. Sector, incl non-guaranteed	0.00	0.00	0.00	0.00	0.00	0.00	0.00	0.00	0.00	1.60	3.40
Short-Term Debt	0.00	0.00	0.00	0.00	0.00	0.00	0.00	7.00	10.00	20.00	23.30
Memo Items:					*(Thousands of US dollars)*						
Int'l Reserves Excluding Gold	8,110	10,939	11,385	16,241	28,046	28,552	20,635	24,395	26,072	1,929	5,670
Gold Holdings (at market price)	..	..	..	..	..	..	..	..	..	..	..
SOCIAL INDICATORS											
Total Fertility Rate	6.5	6.5	6.5	6.5	6.5	6.5	6.5	6.5	6.5	6.5	6.5
Infant Mortality Rate	184.6	181.8	179.0	176.4	173.8	171.2	168.6	166.0	163.6	161.2	158.8
Life Expectancy at Birth	36.1	36.5	36.9	37.3	37.7	38.1	38.5	38.9	39.3	39.8	40.2
Urban Population, % of total	15.0	15.3	15.6	16.0	16.3	16.6	16.9	17.2	17.6	17.9	18.2
Food Prod. per capita (1987=100)	192.2	199.8	167.6	196.8	191.7	194.3	176.1	127.6	157.4	94.9	91.5
Labor Force, Agriculture (%)	86.6	86.3	86.1	85.8	85.6	85.3	85.1	84.8	84.5	84.3	84.0
Labor Force, Female (%)	42.7	42.7	42.6	42.6	42.6	42.6	42.5	42.5	42.4	42.3	42.3
Primary Schl. Enroll. Ratio	24.0	..	..	..	..	33.0	31.0	33.0	37.0	42.0	51.0
Primary Schl. Enroll. Ratio, Female	15.0	..	..	..	..	21.0	20.0	21.0	24.0	28.0	35.0
Secondary Schl. Enroll. Ratio	7.0	..	..	..	..	10.0	11.0	11.0	11.0	12.0	11.0

1981	1982	1983	1984	1985	1986	1987	1988	1989	1990 estimate	Notes	GAMBIA, THE
					(Millions of current US dollars)						**FOREIGN TRADE (CUSTOMS BASIS)**
..	..	..	..	..	..	..	..	..	..	..	Value of Exports, fob
..	..	..	..	..	..	..	..	..	..	..	Nonfuel Primary Products
..	..	..	..	..	..	..	..	..	..	..	Fuels
..	..	..	..	..	..	..	..	..	..	..	Manufactures
..	..		..		..	..	..	..	..	..	Value of Imports, cif
..	..		..		..	..	..	..	..	..	Nonfuel Primary Products
..	..		..		..	..	..	..	..	..	Fuels
..	..		..		..	..	..	..	..	..	Manufactures
					(Index 1987 = 100)						
..	..	..		..		..	..	..	..	..	Terms of Trade
..	..	..		..		..	..	..	..	..	Export Prices, fob
..	..	..		..		..	..	..	..	..	Import Prices, cif
					(Millions of current US dollars)						**BALANCE OF PAYMENTS**
..	83.84	81.96	118.45	87.22	93.56	124.70	146.71	167.93	181.99	..	Exports of Goods & Services
45.13	58.56	54.55	90.73	62.80	64.87	74.51	83.06	100.20	110.62	..	Merchandise, fob
20.16	24.32	27.19	27.73	24.42	28.69	49.37	62.21	65.73	69.78	..	Nonfactor Services
..	0.96	0.22	0.00	0.00	0.00	0.81	1.44	2.01	1.59	..	Factor Services
173.00	141.99	137.29	125.32	94.18	106.99	158.48	168.46	191.76	205.37	..	Imports of Goods & Services
128.69	94.41	89.70	99.43	74.84	84.57	94.95	105.92	125.35	140.51	..	Merchandise, fob
41.59	36.17	29.92	25.88	19.30	21.48	44.32	48.17	50.60	51.83	..	Nonfactor Services
2.72	11.41	17.66	0.01	0.05	0.94	19.21	14.37	15.81	13.04	..	Factor Services
2.10	2.10	1.70	1.40	0.50	4.70	5.00	4.80	4.10	12.10	..	Long-Term Interest
3.55	2.89	2.69	4.91	6.29	10.71	13.49	12.78	6.68	14.13	..	Private Current Transfers, net
..	..	0.00	0.00	0.00	0.00	0.00	..	..	..	..	Workers' Remittances
-104.17	-55.27	-52.63	-1.95	-0.68	-2.73	-18.68	-7.85	-17.15	-9.24	..	Curr. A/C Bal before Off. Transf.
54.66	32.80	19.65	10.02	7.97	6.94	36.18	41.91	33.87	44.97	..	Net Official Transfers
-49.51	-22.46	-32.98	8.07	7.29	4.21	17.50	34.07	16.72	35.72	..	Curr. A/C Bal after Off. Transf.
14.18	17.76	-5.43	-10.13	1.98	-9.78	33.83	11.49	12.88	6.65	..	Long-Term Capital, net
2.28	..	..	0.50	2.20	6.10	1.48	1.17	14.79	9.30	..	Direct Investment
39.30	21.00	8.80	10.40	13.30	31.80	28.60	8.80	20.70	-3.70	..	Long-Term Loans
39.90	29.40	13.70	13.80	13.80	35.30	37.10	15.00	27.80	24.40	..	Disbursements
0.60	8.40	4.90	3.40	0.50	3.50	8.50	6.20	7.10	28.10	..	Repayments
-27.41	-3.24	-14.23	-21.03	-13.52	-47.68	3.76	1.52	-22.60	1.05	..	Other Long-Term Capital
45.47	-19.76	29.59	3.97	-8.67	8.49	-36.75	-27.30	-36.27	-31.42	..	Other Capital, net
-10.14	24.46	8.82	-1.91	-0.60	-2.92	-14.58	-18.25	6.67	-10.95	..	Change in Reserves
					(Gambian Dalasis per US dollar)						**Memo Item:**
2.180	2.480	2.940	4.110	4.990	7.310	6.750	7.030	8.130	7.650	..	Conversion Factor (Annual Avg)
				(Millions of US dollars), outstanding at end of year							
176.00	207.00	211.80	230.00	245.30	270.20	326.80	321.50	340.60	352.10	..	**EXTERNAL DEBT (Total)**
157.50	187.40	186.90	184.60	209.60	241.70	303.40	307.50	328.30	349.00	..	Long-Term Debt (by debtor)
25.30	40.00	35.10	32.90	33.00	29.50	37.80	34.60	37.70	44.90	..	Central Bank, incl. IMF credit
117.40	122.00	125.60	126.70	150.20	192.80	248.80	265.80	284.00	301.50	..	Central Government
..	..	..	..	..	..	..	..	..	..	..	Rest of General Government
11.30	20.20	21.60	21.00	21.80	16.40	13.80	4.90	4.80	0.80	..	Non-financial Public Enterprises
3.50	5.20	4.60	4.00	4.60	3.00	3.00	2.20	1.80	1.80	..	Priv. Sector, incl non-guaranteed
18.50	19.60	24.90	45.40	35.70	28.50	23.40	14.00	12.30	3.10	..	Short-Term Debt
					(Thousands of US dollars)						**Memo Items:**
3,948	8,387	2,918	2,259	1,734	13,563	25,757	19,049	20,589	55,387	..	Int'l Reserves Excluding Gold
..	..	..	..	..	..	..	..	..	..	..	Gold Holdings (at market price)
											SOCIAL INDICATORS
6.5	6.5	6.5	6.5	6.5	6.5	6.5	6.5	6.5	6.5	..	Total Fertility Rate
156.4	154.0	151.8	149.6	147.3	145.1	142.9	140.7	138.5	136.2	..	Infant Mortality Rate
40.6	41.0	41.5	42.0	42.5	42.9	43.4	43.7	44.0	44.2	..	Life Expectancy at Birth
18.7	19.1	19.6	20.0	20.5	21.2	21.9	22.3	22.8	23.2	..	Urban Population, % of total
126.9	153.4	114.3	110.1	84.8	106.1	100.0	89.1	104.4	75.4	..	Food Prod. per capita (1987=100)
..	..	..	..	..	..	..	..	..	..	..	Labor Force, Agriculture (%)
42.1	41.9	41.7	41.5	41.3	41.1	40.9	40.7	40.5	40.3	..	Labor Force, Female (%)
..	62.0	68.0	..	68.0	67.0	65.0	61.0	64.0	..	..	Primary Schl. Enroll. Ratio
41.0	45.0	51.0	..	52.0	52.0	51.0	47.0	53.0	..	..	Primary Schl. Enroll. Ratio, Female
..	17.0	..	..	17.0	17.0	16.0	..	..	..	..	Secondary Schl. Enroll. Ratio

GERMANY	1970	1971	1972	1973	1974	1975	1976	1977	1978	1979	1980
CURRENT GNP PER CAPITA (US $)	2,850	3,240	3,830	4,750	5,710	6,670	7,460	8,230	9,490	11,540	13,270
POPULATION (thousands) *	77,719	78,363	78,715	78,956	78,979	78,679	78,317	78,166	78,083	78,104	78,303

USE AND ORIGIN OF RESOURCES
(Billions of current Deutsche Mark)

	1970	1971	1972	1973	1974	1975	1976	1977	1978	1979	1980
Gross National Product (GNP)	675.7	750.4	824.6	918.8	983.7	1,027.7	1,123.8	1,195.6	1,289.4	1,393.8	1,477.4
Net Factor Income from Abroad	0.4	0.6	1.5	1.6	-0.2	1.1	3.3	0.3	5.9	5.4	5.4
GDP at Market Prices	675.3	749.7	823.1	917.3	983.9	1,026.6	1,120.5	1,195.3	1,283.6	1,388.4	1,472.0
Resource Balance	13.7	13.4	16.7	26.9	43.8	30.1	25.4	28.6	32.4	9.3	-6.9
Exports of Goods & NF Services	143.0	155.7	169.8	200.4	260.0	253.5	287.8	304.5	318.3	348.2	389.1
Imports of Goods & NF Services	129.3	142.3	153.1	173.5	216.2	223.4	262.4	275.9	285.9	338.9	396.0
Domestic Absorption	661.6	736.3	806.5	890.3	940.2	996.6	1,095.1	1,166.7	1,251.2	1,379.1	1,478.9
Private Consumption, etc.	368.8	409.0	452.0	495.6	533.6	583.5	631.9	682.1	725.9	781.3	837.0
General Gov't Consumption	106.5	126.8	141.0	163.1	190.1	210.1	221.9	235.1	253.1	273.5	298.0
Gross Domestic Investment	186.3	200.6	213.5	231.6	216.4	203.0	241.3	249.4	272.1	324.3	343.9
Fixed Investment	172.1	196.1	209.2	219.3	212.7	209.4	225.7	242.4	264.9	301.3	332.1
Indirect Taxes, net	77.3	86.1	94.4	102.4	106.2	109.9	119.8	127.9	137.9	152.0	162.8
GDP at factor cost	598.0	663.7	728.7	814.8	877.8	916.7	1,000.7	1,067.4	1,145.7	1,236.4	1,309.2
Agriculture	21.8	22.7	24.7	26.6	25.9	28.5	31.1	31.8	32.2	30.9	30.2
Industry	333.7	360.9	387.5	430.9	455.6	454.8	500.1	528.7	560.9	606.1	629.3
Manufacturing	259.5	277.7	296.3	333.2	355.4	354.0	389.3	413.5	437.3	469.1	480.6
Services, etc.	319.8	366.1	410.9	459.7	502.4	543.4	589.4	634.8	690.5	751.5	812.5
Gross Domestic Saving	200.0	214.0	230.1	258.6	260.2	233.1	266.8	278.0	304.5	333.6	337.0
Gross National Saving	194.6	207.3	223.8	251.4	250.5	224.9	260.4	269.2	300.8	329.2	331.7

(Billions of 1987 Deutsche Mark)

	1970	1971	1972	1973	1974	1975	1976	1977	1978	1979	1980
Gross National Product	1,396.7	1,437.0	1,497.8	1,571.5	1,572.8	1,552.5	1,638.1	1,680.3	1,738.2	1,807.8	1,826.7
GDP at Market Prices	1,396.0	1,435.9	1,495.2	1,569.0	1,573.3	1,551.0	1,633.4	1,680.1	1,730.4	1,800.9	1,820.3
Resource Balance	22.0	12.7	16.2	35.5	75.2	47.7	48.5	52.2	44.6	28.1	35.5
Exports of Goods & NF Services	269.0	281.3	300.5	332.8	373.7	349.7	383.2	398.2	409.9	427.4	449.7
Imports of Goods & NF Services	247.0	268.6	284.3	297.2	298.5	302.0	334.7	346.0	365.3	399.3	414.2
Domestic Absorption	1,374.0	1,423.2	1,479.0	1,533.4	1,498.1	1,503.3	1,584.9	1,627.8	1,685.8	1,772.8	1,784.7
Private Consumption, etc.	748.8	785.4	819.6	846.2	852.7	876.3	907.2	948.4	980.5	1,007.7	1,018.8
General Gov't Consumption	256.1	269.2	280.4	294.4	306.1	317.9	322.8	327.2	339.9	351.5	360.6
Gross Domestic Investment	369.1	368.6	379.1	392.8	339.2	309.1	354.8	352.2	365.3	413.7	405.4
Fixed Investment	342.5	363.1	372.7	371.7	335.6	318.2	329.9	342.4	357.1	381.6	390.5
GDP at factor cost	1,237.2	1,270.6	1,323.0	1,393.8	1,405.8	1,386.5	1,461.0	1,502.7	1,545.4	1,605.8	1,623.9
Agriculture	25.6	25.1	24.4	26.3	27.5	26.0	25.7	27.2	28.0	26.7	27.1
Industry	661.8	673.0	698.1	735.7	724.4	687.9	737.4	752.1	765.2	801.3	800.9
Manufacturing	504.8	509.9	526.6	560.1	556.2	530.3	570.9	582.7	593.4	620.9	620.9
Services, etc.	708.7	737.7	772.6	807.0	821.4	837.0	870.4	900.8	937.2	972.9	992.2

Memo Items:

	1970	1971	1972	1973	1974	1975	1976	1977	1978	1979	1980
Capacity to Import	273.3	294.0	315.3	343.4	358.9	342.6	367.2	381.9	406.7	410.2	407.0
Terms of Trade Adjustment	4.2	12.7	14.8	10.6	-14.8	-7.0	-16.1	-16.4	-3.2	-17.1	-42.7
Gross Domestic Income	1,400.2	1,448.5	1,509.9	1,579.6	1,558.5	1,544.0	1,617.3	1,663.7	1,727.2	1,783.8	1,777.6
Gross National Income	1,401.0	1,449.7	1,512.5	1,582.1	1,558.0	1,545.4	1,622.0	1,664.0	1,735.0	1,790.7	1,784.0

DOMESTIC PRICES/DEFLATORS
(Index 1987 = 100)

	1970	1971	1972	1973	1974	1975	1976	1977	1978	1979	1980
Overall (GDP)	48.4	52.2	55.1	58.5	62.5	66.2	68.6	71.1	74.2	77.1	80.9
Domestic Absorption	48.1	51.7	54.5	58.1	62.8	66.3	69.1	71.7	74.2	77.8	82.9
Agriculture	85.2	90.5	101.3	101.3	94.3	109.3	121.1	116.9	115.0	115.6	111.5
Industry	50.4	53.6	55.5	58.6	62.9	66.1	67.8	70.3	73.3	75.6	78.6
Manufacturing	51.4	54.5	56.3	59.5	63.9	66.8	68.2	71.0	73.7	75.6	77.4
Consumer Price Index	50.3	53.0	55.9	59.8	63.9	67.7	70.7	73.3	75.2	78.3	82.6

MANUFACTURING ACTIVITY

	1970	1971	1972	1973	1974	1975	1976	1977	1978	1979	1980
Employment (1987=100)	121.7	120.7	118.2	119.0	115.9	108.1	105.5	106.2	105.5	105.9	107.3
Real Earnings per Empl. (1987=100)	64.9	68.3	70.8	74.3	77.9	79.0	82.5	85.3	87.9	89.8	90.7
Real Output per Empl. (1987=100)	58.2	58.9	61.7	65.0	69.6	70.1	78.5	86.5	87.3	93.5	97.5
Earnings as % of Value Added	46.3	47.4	47.7	47.9	49.1	49.4	47.7	48.5	48.2	47.9	50.3

MONETARY HOLDINGS
(Billions of current Deutsche Mark)

	1970	1971	1972	1973	1974	1975	1976	1977	1978	1979	1980
Money Supply, Broadly Defined	373.0	423.4	483.4	529.5	569.1	634.0	683.5	752.2	827.4	873.0	914.4
Money	103.7	116.9	133.4	135.7	150.2	171.7	177.3	198.6	227.5	234.1	243.4
Currency Outside Banks	36.9	40.3	45.7	47.4	51.5	56.5	60.6	67.5	76.2	79.9	84.0
Demand Deposits	66.8	76.6	87.7	88.2	98.7	115.2	116.7	131.1	151.3	154.3	159.4
Quasi-Money	269.4	306.6	350.0	393.8	418.8	462.3	506.2	553.6	599.9	638.9	671.1

GOVERNMENT DEFICIT (-) OR SURPLUS
(Billions of current Deutsche Mark)

	1970	1971	1972	1973	1974	1975	1976	1977	1978	1979	1980
	6.94	6.37	5.83	12.43	-6.43	-37.16	-31.21	-25.57	-26.49	-27.63	-26.91
Current Revenue	166.10	186.69	208.22	242.26	260.36	272.99	302.23	329.27	352.40	377.62	425.69
Current Expenditure	143.54	161.62	184.78	208.38	241.54	283.61	303.65	325.23	348.84	371.51	415.25
Current Budget Balance	22.56	25.07	23.44	33.88	18.82	-10.62	-1.42	4.04	3.56	6.11	10.44
Capital Receipts	0.12	0.10	0.12	0.13	0.12	0.10	0.32	0.10	0.12	0.12	0.14
Capital Payments	15.74	18.80	17.73	21.58	25.37	26.64	30.11	29.71	30.17	33.86	37.49

1981	1982	1983	1984	1985	1986	1987	1988	1989	1990 estimate	Notes	GERMANY
13,230	12,220	11,400	11,170	10,920	11,920	14,280	18,320	20,520	22,360	..	**CURRENT GNP PER CAPITA (US $)**
78,418	78,335	78,122	77,846	77,698	77,728	77,840	78,144	78,752	79,479	..	**POPULATION (thousands) ***

(Billions of current Deutsche Mark) — **USE AND ORIGIN OF RESOURCES**

1981	1982	1983	1984	1985	1986	1987	1988	1989	1990 estimate	Notes	GERMANY
1,539.6	1,590.3	1,675.7	1,763.3	1,834.5	1,936.1	2,003.0	2,108.0	2,245.2	2,425.5	..	Gross National Product (GNP)
4.6	2.2	7.2	12.4	11.3	10.8	12.5	12.0	24.3	21.0	..	Net Factor Income from Abroad
1,535.0	1,588.1	1,668.5	1,750.9	1,823.2	1,925.3	1,990.5	2,096.0	2,220.9	2,404.5	..	GDP at Market Prices
12.3	38.1	33.5	43.3	63.9	99.9	100.0	109.7	120.4	133.3	..	Resource Balance
441.1	474.4	479.6	536.3	592.7	580.5	576.6	619.8	701.4	769.1	..	Exports of Goods & NF Services
428.8	436.3	446.1	493.1	528.9	480.6	476.7	510.1	581.0	635.9	..	Imports of Goods & NF Services
1,522.7	1,550.0	1,635.0	1,707.6	1,759.3	1,825.4	1,890.5	1,986.3	2,100.5	2,271.3	..	Domestic Absorption
883.5	916.1	959.3	1,001.2	1,036.5	1,066.4	1,108.0	1,153.7	1,209.6	1,299.2	..	Private Consumption, etc.
318.4	326.4	336.4	350.4	365.7	382.6	397.3	412.4	418.8	443.1	..	General Gov't Consumption
320.7	307.4	339.3	356.0	357.1	376.4	385.2	420.2	472.1	529.0	..	Gross Domestic Investment
331.3	323.5	340.8	350.7	355.8	373.5	385.8	409.9	451.4	509.5	..	Fixed Investment
169.2	172.4	182.7	189.8	192.4	194.9	200.7	209.4	231.5	254.4	..	Indirect Taxes, net
1,365.8	1,415.7	1,485.9	1,561.1	1,630.8	1,730.4	1,789.8	1,886.6	1,989.4	2,150.2	B	GDP at factor cost
31.6	36.1	32.1	34.6	32.1	33.6	30.3	32.9	35.9	..	..	Agriculture
639.1	652.9	682.5	708.5	742.5	785.5	791.6	825.8	..	..	..	Industry
487.8	499.8	523.0	545.7	581.2	619.0	622.6	651.0	690.5	..	..	Manufacturing
864.3	899.0	954.0	1,007.8	1,048.5	1,106.3	1,168.6	1,237.3	..	..	..	Services, etc.
333.1	345.5	372.8	399.3	420.9	476.3	485.2	529.9	592.5	662.2	..	Gross Domestic Saving
326.7	336.9	369.0	400.3	421.7	476.8	487.8	530.9	606.3	672.2	..	Gross National Saving

(Billions of 1987 Deutsche Mark)

1981	1982	1983	1984	1985	1986	1987	1988	1989	1990 estimate	Notes	GERMANY
1,828.6	1,809.7	1,842.4	1,898.3	1,932.8	1,974.3	2,003.0	2,075.2	2,154.8	2,251.4	..	Gross National Product
1,823.4	1,807.5	1,834.8	1,885.4	1,921.4	1,963.3	1,990.5	2,063.3	2,131.1	2,231.7	..	GDP at Market Prices
81.6	103.1	93.3	112.1	132.5	116.6	100.0	106.4	126.3	130.8	..	Resource Balance
482.1	499.9	496.6	537.1	577.7	574.1	576.6	607.4	669.6	730.4	..	Exports of Goods & NF Services
400.4	396.8	403.3	425.0	445.1	457.5	476.7	501.0	543.3	599.7	..	Imports of Goods & NF Services
1,741.8	1,704.3	1,741.5	1,773.3	1,788.8	1,846.7	1,890.5	1,956.9	2,004.8	2,101.0	..	Domestic Absorption
1,015.4	1,002.2	1,014.3	1,028.7	1,042.7	1,076.4	1,108.0	1,136.7	1,153.0	1,202.3	..	Private Consumption, etc.
367.1	363.8	364.6	373.8	381.5	391.2	397.3	405.9	399.1	407.4	..	General Gov't Consumption
359.2	338.3	362.6	370.9	364.6	379.1	385.2	414.3	452.7	491.3	..	Gross Domestic Investment
371.4	351.8	363.6	364.7	364.9	377.9	385.8	403.7	432.1	470.3	..	Fixed Investment
1,630.6	1,618.9	1,641.1	1,689.0	1,726.3	1,766.6	1,789.8	1,856.9	1,909.2	1,994.7	B	GDP at factor cost
27.3	32.2	29.3	31.9	30.2	32.7	30.3	32.4	32.1	..	..	Agriculture
784.3	762.5	772.0	787.4	803.3	806.7	791.6	814.5	..	..	..	Industry
611.5	596.9	603.6	620.1	641.0	641.1	622.6	640.9	670.7	..	..	Manufacturing
1,011.8	1,012.8	1,033.5	1,066.2	1,087.8	1,123.9	1,168.6	1,216.5	..	..	..	Services, etc.

Memo Items:

1981	1982	1983	1984	1985	1986	1987	1988	1989	1990 estimate	Notes	GERMANY
411.9	431.5	433.6	462.3	498.9	552.6	576.6	608.8	655.9	725.3	..	Capacity to Import
-70.1	-68.4	-63.0	-74.8	-78.8	-21.5	0.0	1.3	-13.7	-5.1	..	Terms of Trade Adjustment
1,753.3	1,739.0	1,771.8	1,810.6	1,842.6	1,941.8	1,990.5	2,064.7	2,117.4	2,226.6	..	Gross Domestic Income
1,758.5	1,741.3	1,779.4	1,823.4	1,854.0	1,952.7	2,003.0	2,076.5	2,141.1	2,246.4	..	Gross National Income

(Index 1987 = 100) — **DOMESTIC PRICES/DEFLATORS**

1981	1982	1983	1984	1985	1986	1987	1988	1989	1990 estimate	Notes	GERMANY
84.2	87.9	90.9	92.9	94.9	98.1	100.0	101.6	104.2	107.7	..	Overall (GDP)
87.4	90.9	93.9	96.3	98.4	98.8	100.0	101.5	104.8	108.1	..	Domestic Absorption
115.7	112.3	109.5	108.4	106.4	102.5	100.0	101.6	111.8	..	..	Agriculture
81.5	85.6	88.4	90.0	92.4	97.4	100.0	101.4	..	..	..	Industry
79.8	83.7	86.6	88.0	90.7	96.6	100.0	101.6	102.9	..	..	Manufacturing
87.8	92.4	95.5	97.7	99.9	99.8	100.0	101.3	104.1	106.9	..	Consumer Price Index

MANUFACTURING ACTIVITY

1981	1982	1983	1984	1985	1986	1987	1988	1989	1990 estimate	Notes	GERMANY
104.7	100.9	97.6	96.7	98.1	100.0	100.0	99.9	100.5	..	G	Employment (1987=100)
90.0	89.3	90.1	91.1	92.9	96.8	100.0	102.6	..	..	G	Real Earnings per Empl. (1987=100)
101.2	102.1	105.2	111.5	114.2	103.4	100.0	105.3	..	..	G	Real Output per Empl. (1987=100)
44.5	43.9	43.0	41.9	41.7	42.6	42.7	41.8	..	..	..	Earnings as % of Value Added

(Billions of current Deutsche Mark) — **MONETARY HOLDINGS**

1981	1982	1983	1984	1985	1986	1987	1988	1989	1990 estimate	Notes	GERMANY
950.0	1,012.4	1,067.7	1,120.8	1,199.7	1,268.0	1,333.1	1,404.5	1,472.5	1,728.0	D	Money Supply, Broadly Defined
239.6	256.7	278.2	294.7	314.5	340.2	365.7	408.3	431.6	551.4	..	Money
84.2	88.6	96.4	99.8	103.9	112.1	124.1	142.6	147.9	158.6	..	Currency Outside Banks
155.4	168.1	181.8	195.0	210.6	228.1	241.6	265.7	283.7	392.8	..	Demand Deposits
710.4	755.6	789.6	826.1	885.3	927.7	967.4	996.2	1,040.9	1,176.7	..	Quasi-Money

(Billions of current Deutsche Mark)

1981	1982	1983	1984	1985	1986	1987	1988	1989	1990 estimate	Notes	GERMANY
-36.31	-32.02	-32.95	-32.31	-20.00	-17.56	-21.57	-37.28	-1.66	-31.12	E	**GOVERNMENT DEFICIT (-) OR SURPLUS**
451.53	480.43	493.75	527.00	554.19	575.41	591.35	607.51	657.83	699.20	..	Current Revenue
450.59	475.39	489.50	518.86	533.64	553.70	578.35	610.15	624.33	682.75	..	Current Expenditure
0.94	5.04	4.25	8.14	20.55	21.71	13.00	-2.64	33.50	16.45	..	Current Budget Balance
0.17	0.30	0.24	0.21	0.24	0.25	0.19	0.36	0.27	0.27	..	Capital Receipts
36.97	36.20	37.59	38.27	38.35	35.54	34.74	31.18	37.06	47.84	..	Capital Payments

GERMANY	1970	1971	1972	1973	1974	1975	1976	1977	1978	1979	1980
FOREIGN TRADE (CUSTOMS BASIS)					*(Billions of current US dollars)*						
Value of Exports, fob	34.19	39.04	46.21	67.44	89.17	90.02	102.03	117.93	142.09	171.44	191.64
Nonfuel Primary Products	2.73	3.00	3.62	5.96	8.20	7.57	8.70	10.45	12.33	15.91	19.05
Fuels	1.01	1.16	1.21	1.72	3.08	2.81	2.93	3.12	4.51	5.69	7.14
Manufactures	30.45	34.88	41.38	59.76	77.88	79.64	90.40	104.36	125.25	149.84	165.45
Value of Imports, cif	29.81	34.34	39.76	54.50	68.98	74.21	87.78	100.70	120.67	157.68	185.92
Nonfuel Primary Products	10.84	11.10	12.71	17.72	20.52	20.38	23.64	26.89	29.86	36.19	41.79
Fuels	2.63	3.50	3.67	6.21	13.31	13.10	15.83	17.23	19.54	30.96	41.90
Manufactures	16.34	19.74	23.38	30.57	35.15	40.73	48.31	56.58	71.27	90.53	102.22
					(Index 1987 = 100)						
Terms of Trade	124.8	125.4	122.8	135.4	99.0	105.3	103.6	100.8	107.9	104.0	93.2
Export Prices, fob	25.5	27.4	30.8	41.7	49.1	54.0	55.6	59.5	70.1	81.9	87.2
Import Prices, cif	20.4	21.9	25.1	30.8	49.6	51.3	53.7	59.1	65.0	78.8	93.5
BALANCE OF PAYMENTS					*(Billions of current US dollars)*						
Exports of Goods & Services	42.97	48.01	56.95	81.05	106.74	110.36	123.40	141.14	172.67	206.98	233.94
Merchandise, fob	34.32	37.31	44.79	65.09	86.99	87.65	98.46	113.29	136.04	163.91	183.22
Nonfactor Services	6.21	7.67	8.63	11.14	13.84	16.48	17.99	20.36	25.95	29.44	34.93
Factor Services	2.45	3.03	3.53	4.82	5.91	6.24	6.95	7.49	10.69	13.63	15.79
Imports of Goods & Services	39.48	44.06	51.98	70.77	90.27	98.98	112.48	129.52	154.53	201.29	235.04
Merchandise, fob	28.62	30.64	36.39	49.39	65.14	70.77	82.45	93.84	111.93	147.43	174.53
Nonfactor Services	7.90	9.62	11.25	15.66	18.04	21.42	22.86	26.37	32.51	39.58	44.35
Factor Services	2.96	3.80	4.34	5.72	7.10	6.79	7.18	9.31	10.08	14.28	16.16
Long-Term Interest	..	..	..	..	..	..	..	..	..	..	..
Private Current Transfers, net	-1.59	-2.10	-2.43	-3.27	-3.65	-3.75	-3.84	-3.94	-4.79	-5.30	-5.85
Workers' Remittances	..	..	..	..	..	..	..	..	..	..	..
Curr. A/C Bal before Off. Transf.	1.90	1.85	2.54	7.02	12.81	7.63	7.08	7.67	13.36	0.39	-6.96
Net Official Transfers	-1.05	-0.92	-1.41	-1.97	-2.36	-3.39	-3.59	-3.91	-4.50	-6.31	-7.44
Curr. A/C Bal after Off. Transf.	0.85	0.93	1.13	5.05	10.46	4.24	3.50	3.76	8.86	-5.93	-14.39
Long-Term Capital, net	0.25	0.93	0.71	2.19	-2.27	-7.17	-0.74	-5.35	-1.38	6.64	3.03
Direct Investment	-0.30	0.11	0.04	0.39	0.21	-1.31	-1.23	-1.25	-2.01	-2.81	-3.60
Long-Term Loans	..	..	..	..	..	..	..	..	..	..	..
Disbursements	..	..	..	..	..	..	..	..	..	..	..
Repayments	..	..	..	..	..	..	..	..	..	..	..
Other Long-Term Capital	0.55	0.82	0.67	1.80	-2.49	-5.86	0.49	-4.10	0.63	9.45	6.63
Other Capital, net	4.95	2.95	2.78	2.25	-8.88	1.84	0.81	4.45	2.21	-3.80	-4.28
Change in Reserves	-6.05	-4.81	-4.62	-9.48	0.69	1.09	-3.56	-2.86	-9.69	3.09	15.65
Memo Item:					*(Deutsche Mark per US dollar)*						
Conversion Factor (Annual Avg)	3.660	3.490	3.190	2.670	2.590	2.460	2.520	2.320	2.010	1.830	1.820
					(Millions US dollars), outstanding at end of year						
EXTERNAL DEBT (Total)	..	..	..	..	..	..	..	..	..	..	..
Long-Term Debt (by debtor)	..	..	..	..	..	..	..	..	..	..	..
Central Bank, incl. IMF credit	..	..	..	..	..	..	..	..	..	..	..
Central Government	..	..	..	..	..	..	..	..	..	..	..
Rest of General Government	..	..	..	..	..	..	..	..	..	..	..
Non-financial Public Enterprises	..	..	..	..	..	..	..	..	..	..	..
Priv. Sector, incl non-guaranteed	..	..	..	..	..	..	..	..	..	..	..
Short-Term Debt	..	..	..	..	..	..	..	..	..	..	..
Memo Items:					*(Millions of US dollars)*						
Int'l Reserves Excluding Gold	9,630	14,231	19,326	28,206	27,359	26,216	30,019	34,708	48,474	52,549	48,592
Gold Holdings (at market price)	4,249	5,081	7,616	13,202	21,935	16,495	15,848	19,513	26,812	48,769	56,110
SOCIAL INDICATORS											
Total Fertility Rate *	2.1	1.9	1.8	1.7	1.6	1.5	1.5	1.5	1.5	1.6	1.6
Infant Mortality Rate *	22.5	21.9	21.4	20.6	19.7	18.9	17.3	15.6	14.5	13.5	12.4
Life Expectancy at Birth *	70.5	70.5	70.5	70.8	71.1	71.4	71.7	72.0	72.2	72.4	72.6
Urban Population, % of total *	79.7	80.0	80.4	80.7	81.1	81.4	81.6	81.9	82.1	82.4	82.6
Food Prod. per capita (1987=100)	67.9	64.0	72.5	72.7	82.6	74.5	70.1	76.1	81.0	84.7	81.6
Labor Force, Agriculture (%)	9.5	9.3	9.1	8.9	8.7	8.6	8.4	8.2	8.0	7.8	7.7
Labor Force, Female (%)	40.1	40.2	40.3	40.4	40.5	40.6	40.8	40.9	41.0	41.1	41.3
Primary Schl. Enroll. Ratio *	..	..	..	..	..	101.0	..	..	..	..	101.0
Primary Schl. Enroll. Ratio, Female *	..	..	..	..	..	101.0	..	..	..	..	101.0
Secondary Schl. Enroll. Ratio *	..	..	..	..	..	87.0	..	..	..	..	90.0

Note: Data refer to the Federal Republic of Germany before unification for all indicators except those marked with an asteriks.

1981	1982	1983	1984	1985	1986	1987	1988	1989	1990 estimate	Notes	GERMANY
											FOREIGN TRADE (CUSTOMS BASIS)
											(Billions of current US dollars)
175.28	175.46	168.75	171.01	183.33	242.40	293.79	322.56	340.63	397.91	..	Value of Exports, fob
17.27	16.21	16.12	16.71	16.97	21.05	24.68	28.63	30.44	33.45	..	Nonfuel Primary Products
6.97	6.47	5.63	5.55	5.06	3.88	3.89	4.15	4.46	5.32	..	Fuels
151.04	152.77	147.00	148.75	161.30	217.47	265.22	289.78	305.72	359.14	..	Manufactures
162.69	154.05	152.01	152.87	157.60	189.65	227.33	249.00	268.60	341.25	..	Value of Imports, cif
34.59	32.73	32.23	32.82	32.97	39.73	45.15	50.66	53.53	60.61	..	Nonfuel Primary Products
39.80	36.43	32.40	31.17	31.35	21.88	21.96	19.13	20.43	28.14	..	Fuels
88.30	84.90	87.37	88.88	93.28	128.04	160.21	179.20	194.63	252.49	..	Manufactures
											(Index 1987=100)
82.6	86.0	85.7	78.8	82.2	96.4	100.0	98.6	95.9	97.3	..	Terms of Trade
75.8	74.1	71.7	64.4	65.5	84.3	100.0	103.1	107.6	123.8	..	Export Prices, fob
91.7	86.2	83.7	81.7	79.7	87.4	100.0	104.5	112.2	127.3	..	Import Prices, cif
											BALANCE OF PAYMENTS
											(Billions of current US dollars)
215.45	215.61	207.85	209.50	223.79	298.50	360.92	395.84	425.22	524.18	..	Exports of Goods & Services
166.82	165.81	159.90	161.38	173.66	231.02	278.49	308.63	324.94	391.58	..	Merchandise, fob
33.15	33.76	31.71	30.99	32.43	41.74	48.53	48.60	51.95	64.29	..	Nonfactor Services
15.49	16.04	16.24	17.12	17.70	25.73	33.90	38.62	48.33	68.31	..	Factor Services
207.91	199.92	192.60	189.52	196.76	245.90	298.35	327.02	349.77	454.63	..	Imports of Goods & Services
150.74	141.08	138.47	139.24	145.08	175.27	208.28	228.81	247.15	320.00	..	Merchandise, fob
40.41	40.11	37.94	35.11	35.79	47.16	57.70	61.84	62.56	79.53	..	Nonfactor Services
16.76	18.73	16.19	15.17	15.89	23.47	32.37	36.38	40.06	55.11	..	Factor Services
..	..	..	..	..	..	..	..	..	..	..	Long-Term Interest
-4.85	-4.47	-4.32	-4.00	-3.58	-4.73	-5.53	-6.27	-5.59	-6.77	..	Private Current Transfers, net
..	..	..	..	..	..	..	..	..	..	..	Workers' Remittances
2.69	11.22	10.94	15.98	23.45	47.86	57.03	62.55	69.87	62.77	..	Curr. A/C Bal before Off. Transf.
-6.26	-6.33	-5.67	-6.51	-6.58	-8.08	-11.11	-12.32	-12.97	-15.97	..	Net Official Transfers
-3.57	4.89	5.27	9.47	16.87	39.78	45.93	50.23	56.90	46.80	..	Curr. A/C Bal after Off. Transf.
3.55	-5.95	-3.22	-6.81	-4.59	14.67	-12.73	-51.81	-12.65	-40.80	..	Long-Term Capital, net
-3.54	-1.65	-1.59	-3.76	-4.45	-9.01	-7.26	-10.19	-7.54	-21.09	..	Direct Investment
..	..	..	..	..	..	..	..	..	..	..	Long-Term Loans
..	..	..	..	..	..	..	..	..	..	..	Disbursements
..	..	..	..	..	..	..	..	..	..	..	Repayments
7.09	-4.30	-1.64	-3.05	-0.14	23.67	-5.46	-41.62	-5.12	-19.70	..	Other Long-Term Capital
1.58	3.99	-3.28	-3.80	-11.38	-52.90	-12.85	-16.85	-54.86	-0.54	..	Other Capital, net
-1.56	-2.92	1.23	1.13	-0.89	-1.54	-20.35	18.43	10.62	-5.47	..	Change in Reserves
											Memo Item:
											(Deutsche Mark per US dollar)
2.260	2.430	2.550	2.850	2.940	2.170	1.800	1.760	1.880	1.620	..	Conversion Factor (Annual Avg)
											EXTERNAL DEBT (Total)
											(Millions US dollars), outstanding at end of year
..	..	..	..	..	..	..	..	..	..	..	Long-Term Debt (by debtor)
..	..	..	..	..	..	..	..	..	..	..	Central Bank, incl. IMF credit
..	..	..	..	..	..	..	..	..	..	..	Central Government
..	..	..	..	..	..	..	..	..	..	..	Rest of General Government
..	..	..	..	..	..	..	..	..	..	..	Non-financial Public Enterprises
..	..	..	..	..	..	..	..	..	..	..	Priv. Sector, incl non-guaranteed
..	..	..	..	..	..	..	..	..	..	..	Short-Term Debt
											Memo Items:
											(Millions of US dollars)
43,719	44,762	42,674	40,141	44,380	51,734	78,756	58,528	60,709	67,902	..	Int'l Reserves Excluding Gold
37,835	43,489	36,312	29,345	31,125	37,207	46,078	39,048	38,168	36,645	..	Gold Holdings (at market price)
											SOCIAL INDICATORS
1.5	1.5	1.5	1.4	1.4	1.5	1.5	1.5	1.5	1.5	..	Total Fertility Rate *
11.8	11.1	10.4	9.8	9.1	8.7	8.4	8.1	7.8	7.5	..	Infant Mortality Rate *
72.9	73.1	73.5	74.0	74.4	74.8	75.3	75.6	75.9	76.2	..	Life Expectancy at Birth *
82.8	83.0	83.2	83.4	83.6	83.7	83.8	83.8	83.9	84.0	..	Urban Population, % of total *
85.3	80.1	78.8	90.4	99.9	97.3	100.0	95.1	96.0	93.8	..	Food Prod. per capita (1987=100)
..	..	..	..	..	..	..	..	..	..	..	Labor Force, Agriculture (%)
41.2	41.1	41.0	40.9	40.8	40.8	40.7	40.6	40.6	40.5	..	Labor Force, Female (%)
..	..	..	..	99.0	..	103.0	103.0	..	..	..	Primary Schl. Enroll. Ratio *
..	..	..	..	99.0	..	103.0	104.0	..	..	..	Primary Schl. Enroll. Ratio, Female *
..	..	..	..	94.0	..	96.0	97.0	..	..	..	Secondary Schl. Enroll. Ratio *

GHANA	1970	1971	1972	1973	1974	1975	1976	1977	1978	1979	1980
CURRENT GNP PER CAPITA (US $)	250	270	250	260	290	280	280	300	350	380	410
POPULATION (thousands)	8,614	8,877	9,138	9,388	9,621	9,835	10,023	10,177	10,322	10,501	10,740

USE AND ORIGIN OF RESOURCES

(Millions of current Ghanaian Cedis)

	1970	1971	1972	1973	1974	1975	1976	1977	1978	1979	1980
Gross National Product (GNP)	2,214	2,454	2,779	3,475	4,629	5,241	6,478	11,123	20,938	28,123	42,670
Net Factor Income from Abroad	-45	-47	-37	-26	-31	-42	-48	-40	-48	-99	-182
GDP at Market Prices	2,259	2,500	2,815	3,501	4,660	5,283	6,526	11,163	20,986	28,222	42,852
Resource Balance	-31	-112	154	177	-162	49	-22	-118	-279	20	-295
Exports of Goods & NF Services	482	394	583	751	854	1,023	1,025	1,172	1,754	3,170	3,628
Imports of Goods & NF Services	513	506	428	574	1,016	973	1,047	1,289	2,033	3,150	3,923
Domestic Absorption	2,290	2,612	2,661	3,324	4,822	5,234	6,548	11,281	21,265	28,202	43,147
Private Consumption, etc.	1,680	1,935	2,106	2,626	3,645	3,873	5,170	8,637	17,766	23,454	35,953
General Gov't Consumption	290	324	355	382	569	688	799	1,409	2,371	2,903	4,784
Gross Domestic Investment	320	353	200	316	608	672	580	1,235	1,128	1,845	2,410
Fixed Investment	271	311	244	268	555	614	642	1,049	1,062	1,899	2,613
Indirect Taxes, net	309	301	303	281	418	541	672	867	1,398	1,524	1,524
GDP at factor cost	1,950	2,199	2,512	3,220	4,242	4,742	5,854	10,296	19,588	26,698	41,328
Agriculture	1,051	1,104	1,313	1,715	2,383	2,518	3,300	6,274	12,742	16,924	24,820
Industry	412	457	499	651	845	1,110	1,254	1,768	2,524	3,466	5,086
Manufacturing	258	275	306	409	502	737	857	1,204	1,813	2,447	3,346
Services, etc.	797	940	1,003	1,135	1,432	1,655	1,972	3,121	5,721	7,832	12,946
Gross Domestic Saving	289	241	354	493	446	721	558	1,117	849	1,865	2,115
Gross National Saving	233	185	314	459	410	708	505	1,070	792	1,759	1,924

(Millions of 1987 Ghanaian Cedis)

	1970	1971	1972	1973	1974	1975	1976	1977	1978	1979	1980
Gross National Product	640,148	676,745	659,976	682,479	732,782	634,551	612,597	624,723	686,095	674,592	676,721
GDP at Market Prices	654,846	690,530	669,939	689,354	739,901	641,100	618,708	629,989	691,929	680,402	684,213
Resource Balance	8,967	35,169	128,095	69,232	-19,886	9,430	28,345	-34,110	-26,958	-2,313	-35,954
Exports of Goods & NF Services	236,075	220,927	256,432	255,221	200,340	196,572	206,356	154,955	148,227	145,709	125,909
Imports of Goods & NF Services	227,108	185,758	128,337	185,989	220,226	187,142	178,011	189,065	175,185	148,022	161,863
Domestic Absorption	645,879	655,361	541,845	620,122	759,787	631,671	590,363	664,099	718,887	682,715	720,167
Private Consumption, etc.	483,897	493,519	425,898	498,626	593,703	481,167	457,976	481,379	557,594	534,857	569,764
General Gov't Consumption	58,268	53,182	58,718	46,959	57,972	58,370	59,727	76,869	90,374	74,266	83,253
Gross Domestic Investment	103,714	108,661	57,229	74,537	108,113	92,133	72,660	105,851	70,919	73,592	67,151
Fixed Investment	87,773	96,662	63,713	63,754	98,710	83,745	78,679	94,273	79,949	74,692	70,459
GDP at factor cost	..	..	..	..	..	..	..	..	..	..	..
Agriculture	354,043	370,848	385,080	377,403	410,659	328,804	323,385	305,876	364,150	377,873	386,099
Industry	148,830	150,876	135,662	162,186	161,264	159,866	155,587	161,898	149,796	128,516	128,948
Manufacturing	89,028	83,545	75,911	93,816	88,477	96,662	92,294	95,311	91,966	76,475	75,425
Services, etc.	176,820	191,821	176,016	179,653	194,929	182,431	169,723	192,448	201,212	190,234	185,825

Memo Items:

	1970	1971	1972	1973	1974	1975	1976	1977	1978	1979	1980
Capacity to Import	213,421	144,678	174,591	243,341	185,111	196,581	174,255	171,777	151,161	148,962	149,691
Terms of Trade Adjustment	-22,654	-76,249	-81,841	-11,880	-15,228	9	-32,102	16,822	2,934	3,253	23,782
Gross Domestic Income	632,192	614,281	588,099	677,474	724,672	641,109	586,606	646,811	694,863	683,655	707,995
Gross National Income	617,493	600,497	578,135	670,599	717,554	634,560	580,496	641,545	689,029	677,845	700,503

DOMESTIC PRICES/DEFLATORS

(Index 1987 = 100)

	1970	1971	1972	1973	1974	1975	1976	1977	1978	1979	1980
Overall (GDP)	0.3	0.4	0.4	0.5	0.6	0.8	1.1	1.8	3.0	4.1	6.3
Domestic Absorption	0.4	0.4	0.5	0.5	0.6	0.8	1.1	1.7	3.0	4.1	6.0
Agriculture	0.3	0.3	0.3	0.5	0.6	0.8	1.0	2.1	3.5	4.5	6.4
Industry	0.3	0.3	0.4	0.4	0.5	0.7	0.8	1.1	1.7	2.7	3.9
Manufacturing	0.3	0.3	0.4	0.4	0.6	0.8	0.9	1.3	2.0	3.2	4.4
Consumer Price Index	0.2	0.2	0.3	0.3	0.4	0.5	0.7	1.6	2.7	4.2	6.3

MANUFACTURING ACTIVITY

	1970	1971	1972	1973	1974	1975	1976	1977	1978	1979	1980
Employment (1987=100)	..	..	..	..	..	..	..	..	..	..	..
Real Earnings per Empl. (1987=100)	..	..	..	..	..	..	..	..	..	..	..
Real Output per Empl. (1987=100)	..	..	..	..	..	..	..	..	..	..	..
Earnings as % of Value Added	23.0	22.0	22.1	19.5	21.2	20.5	17.1	17.1	21.8	18.3	20.0

MONETARY HOLDINGS

(Millions of current Ghanaian Cedis)

	1970	1971	1972	1973	1974	1975	1976	1977	1978	1979	1980
Money Supply, Broadly Defined	427	475	668	794	1,005	1,386	1,903	3,044	5,131	5,942	7,949
Money	306	321	463	564	697	1,009	1,429	2,393	4,126	4,680	6,085
Currency Outside Banks	151	159	239	245	336	486	707	1,157	2,122	2,459	3,521
Demand Deposits	155	162	223	319	361	523	722	1,236	2,004	2,221	2,564
Quasi-Money	121	154	205	230	308	377	474	651	1,005	1,262	1,864

GOVERNMENT DEFICIT (-) OR SURPLUS

(Millions of current Ghanaian Cedis)

	1970	1971	1972	1973	1974	1975	1976	1977	1978	1979	1980
GOVERNMENT DEFICIT (-) OR SURPLUS	..	..	-161	-187	-196	-401	-736	-1,057	-1,897	-1,800	-1,808
Current Revenue	..	..	422	392	584	810	870	1,171	1,393	2,600	2,951
Current Expenditure	..	..	440	453	624	910	1,102	1,361	2,541	3,500	4,179
Current Budget Balance	..	..	-18	-61	-40	-100	-232	-190	-1,148	-900	-1,228
Capital Receipts	..	..	..	..	..	..	..	..	..	..	..
Capital Payments	..	..	143	126	156	301	504	867	749	900	580

1981	1982	1983	1984	1985	1986	1987	1988	1989	1990 estimate	Notes	GHANA
410	380	350	370	370	390	390	400	380	390	A	**CURRENT GNP PER CAPITA (US $)**
11,030	11,366	11,747	12,168	12,620	13,073	13,526	13,977	14,425	14,870	..	**POPULATION (thousands)**
				(Millions of current Ghanaian Cedis)							**USE AND ORIGIN OF RESOURCES**
72,404	86,226	182,398	266,919	337,279	498,797	725,476	1,024,670	1,389,030	2,009,070	..	Gross National Product (GNP)
-222	-225	-1,640	-3,642	-5,769	-12,576	-20,524	-26,527	-28,189	-36,550	..	Net Factor Income from Abroad
72,626	86,451	184,038	270,561	343,048	511,373	746,000	1,051,200	1,417,210	2,045,620	..	GDP at Market Prices
-412	308	-797	-710	-6,641	-8,518	-16,924	-2,845	-106,928	-88,578	..	Resource Balance
3,454	2,886	10,225	20,161	33,185	81,847	157,819	217,724	292,003	..	..	Exports of Goods & NFServices
3,866	2,578	11,022	20,871	39,826	90,365	174,743	220,569	398,931	..	..	Imports of Goods & NFServices
73,038	86,143	184,835	271,271	349,689	519,891	762,924	1,054,040	1,524,140	2,134,200	..	Domestic Absorption
63,333	77,620	167,147	233,023	284,620	415,420	610,394	834,306	1,186,740	1,670,270	..	Private Consumption, etc.
6,384	5,603	10,787	19,641	32,241	56,596	74,690	104,818	145,454	154,167	..	General Gov't Consumption
3,321	2,920	6,901	18,607	32,828	47,875	77,840	114,917	191,946	309,766	..	Gross Domestic Investment
3,430	3,053	6,922	18,542	32,689	47,535	77,286	114,130	190,950	..	..	Fixed Investment
2,867	2,937	..	..	..	..	..	..	..	..	..	Indirect Taxes, net
69,759	83,514	..	..	..	..	..	..	..	..	B	GDP at factor cost
38,553	49,572	109,927	133,232	154,003	244,317	377,481	521,529	693,974	972,323	..	Agriculture
6,654	5,401	12,199	28,631	57,209	87,723	121,744	174,140	237,013	322,171	..	Industry
4,338	3,117	7,101	17,306	39,562	57,021	73,720	100,535	141,815	187,524	..	Manufacturing
27,419	31,478	61,912	108,698	131,836	179,333	246,775	355,527	486,227	751,131	..	Services, etc.
2,909	3,228	6,104	17,897	26,187	39,357	60,916	112,072	85,019	221,188		Gross Domestic Saving
2,675	3,000	4,448	15,014	22,190	33,213	71,384	120,429	111,397	250,524		Gross National Saving
				(Millions of 1987 Ghanaian Cedis)							Gross National Product
657,402	614,691	587,801	635,323	664,017	694,134	725,476	767,768	810,344	825,423		GDP at Market Prices
664,118	621,009	593,399	645,398	678,197	712,979	746,000	787,359	826,577	848,338	I	Resource Balance
-24,996	45,939	-5,578	-2,695	-16,728	-13,270	-16,924	-2,314	-63,638	-65,561	..	Resource Balance
114,760	132,253	71,701	78,621	83,619	125,909	157,819	166,085	173,582	184,539	..	Exports of Goods & NFServices
139,756	86,314	77,279	81,316	100,348	139,179	174,743	168,399	237,220	250,100	..	Imports of Goods & NFServices
689,114	575,070	598,977	648,093	694,925	726,249	762,924	789,674	890,215	913,899	..	Domestic Absorption
531,547	442,301	468,041	521,156	556,984	591,559	610,394	627,802	691,992	712,182	..	Private Consumption, etc.
96,309	85,627	83,931	73,079	70,790	72,062	74,690	79,098	85,711	82,490	..	General Gov't Consumption
61,258	47,143	47,005	53,858	67,151	62,628	77,840	82,774	112,512	119,227	..	Gross Domestic Investment
62,266	48,065	46,972	53,527	66,772	62,129	77,286	82,202	111,833	..	..	Fixed Investment
..	..	..	..	..	..	..	..	..	..	B I	GDP at factor cost
376,175	355,676	330,867	362,988	365,338	377,350	377,481	391,060	407,643	397,850	..	Agriculture
108,345	90,047	79,242	86,445	101,573	109,354	121,744	130,677	136,008	141,771	..	Industry
60,865	48,403	43,025	48,535	60,340	67,030	73,720	77,393	79,754	81,722	..	Manufacturing
188,581	179,102	183,290	195,965	211,285	226,275	246,775	265,622	282,926	308,717	..	Services, etc.
											Memo Items:
124,862	96,626	71,691	78,550	83,615	126,060	157,819	166,227	173,636	..	..	Capacity to Import
10,102	-35,626	-10	-71	-5	151	0	142	55	..	..	Terms of Trade Adjustment
674,220	585,382	593,389	645,327	678,192	713,130	746,000	787,502	826,631	..	..	Gross Domestic Income
667,504	579,064	587,791	635,252	664,012	694,285	725,476	767,910	810,399	..	..	Gross National Income
				(Index 1987 = 100)							**DOMESTIC PRICES/DEFLATORS**
10.9	13.9	31.0	41.9	50.6	71.7	100.0	133.5	171.5	241.1	..	Overall (GDP)
10.6	15.0	30.9	41.9	50.3	71.6	100.0	133.5	171.2	233.5	..	Domestic Absorption
10.2	13.9	33.2	36.7	42.2	64.7	100.0	133.4	170.2	244.4	..	Agriculture
6.1	6.0	15.4	33.1	56.3	80.2	100.0	133.3	174.3	227.2	..	Industry
7.1	6.4	16.5	35.7	65.6	85.1	100.0	129.9	177.8	229.5	..	Manufacturing
13.7	16.7	37.3	52.1	57.4	71.5	100.0	131.4	164.5	225.8	..	Consumer Price Index
											MANUFACTURING ACTIVITY
..	..	..	..	..	..	..	..	..	..	..	Employment (1987=100)
..	..	..	..	..	..	..	..	..	..	..	Real Earnings per Empl. (1987=100)
..	..	..	..	..	..	..	..	..	..	..	Real Output per Empl. (1987=100)
20.6	20.5	17.6	11.0	12.9	14.3	..	..	..	..	..	Earnings as % of Value Added
				(Millions of current Ghanaian Cedis)							**MONETARY HOLDINGS**
12,029	14,837	20,804	31,962	46,718	69,112	105,970	155,010	239,750	271,640	..	Money Supply, Broadly Defined
9,413	11,203	16,717	26,849	38,308	55,156	84,170	122,030	186,390	206,440	..	Money
6,049	6,957	10,389	17,631	22,557	32,348	48,980	67,880	82,920	80,050	..	Currency Outside Banks
3,364	4,246	6,328	9,218	15,750	22,808	35,190	54,150	103,470	126,390	..	Demand Deposits
2,616	3,634	4,086	5,113	8,410	13,957	21,800	32,980	53,360	65,200	..	Quasi-Money
				(Millions of current Ghanaian Cedis)						C F	**GOVERNMENT DEFICIT (-) OR SURPLUS**
-4,707	-4,848	-4,933	-4,843	-7,579	299	4,059	3,911	..	..		Current Revenue
3,279	4,856	10,242	22,642	40,311	73,626	111,046	153,791	..	..		Current Expenditure
6,330	8,603	13,401	23,326	38,461	60,834	80,703	111,002	..	..		Current Budget Balance
-3,051	-3,747	-3,159	-684	1,850	12,792	30,343	42,789	..	..		Capital Receipts
1,656	1,101	1,774	4,159	9,429	12,493	26,284	38,878	..	..		Capital Payments

GHANA	1970	1971	1972	1973	1974	1975	1976	1977	1978	1979	1980
FOREIGN TRADE (CUSTOMS BASIS)					*(Millions of current US dollars)*						
Value of Exports, fob	..	..	..	..	..	..	..	..	..	..	..
Nonfuel Primary Products	..	..	..	..	..	..	..	..	..	..	..
Fuels	..	..	..	..	..	..	..	..	..	..	..
Manufactures	..	..	..	..	..	..	..	..	..	..	..
Value of Imports, cif	..	..	..	..	..	..	..	..	..	..	..
Nonfuel Primary Products	..	..	..	..	..	..	..	..	..	..	..
Fuels	..	..	..	..	..	..	..	..	..	..	..
Manufactures	..	..	..	..	..	..	..	..	..	..	..
					(Index 1987 = 100)						
Terms of Trade											
Export Prices, fob	..	..	..	..	..	..	..	..	..	..	..
Import Prices, cif	..	..	..	..	..	..	..	..	..	..	..
BALANCE OF PAYMENTS					*(Millions of current US dollars)*						
Exports of Goods & Services	476.5	389.3	442.9	653.8	746.5	895.4	894.0	1,020.4	997.4	1,164.6	1,213.1
Merchandise, fob	427.0	334.6	384.3	585.0	679.0	801.0	779.0	889.6	892.8	1,065.7	1,103.6
Nonfactor Services	45.4	51.9	54.9	62.0	63.3	90.0	112.4	128.3	103.3	97.0	106.7
Factor Services	4.1	2.8	3.6	6.8	4.2	4.4	2.5	2.5	1.3	1.9	2.8
Imports of Goods & Services	542.5	535.4	347.9	539.6	942.1	922.3	994.8	1,158.6	1,101.6	1,121.4	1,263.5
Merchandise, fob	375.1	368.2	222.9	372.1	708.2	650.5	690.3	860.2	780.3	803.1	908.3
Nonfactor Services	127.5	127.9	100.0	144.8	207.1	231.0	260.3	261.0	292.6	258.1	266.4
Factor Services	39.9	39.3	25.0	22.7	26.8	40.8	44.3	37.4	28.7	60.2	88.8
Long-Term Interest	12.2	15.3	7.0	12.1	13.0	19.4	18.7	15.6	23.9	29.9	30.9
Private Current Transfers, net	-10.0	-8.7	-2.9	-6.3	-3.6	24.3	-4.3	-6.1	-5.1	-2.6	-3.3
Workers' Remittances	..	..	..	..	..	..	..	..	..	1.3	0.5
Curr. A/C Bal before Off. Transf.	-76.0	-154.9	92.1	107.9	-199.3	-2.7	-105.1	-144.4	-109.3	40.6	-53.7
Net Official Transfers	8.3	9.0	16.2	18.8	27.8	20.3	31.0	64.6	63.4	81.4	82.9
Curr. A/C Bal after Off. Transf.	-67.7	-145.8	108.2	126.7	-171.5	17.6	-74.0	-79.7	-45.9	122.0	29.2
Long-Term Capital, net	102.1	65.0	41.3	31.5	8.4	92.4	-13.4	89.0	93.6	85.6	64.1
Direct Investment	67.8	30.6	11.5	14.4	10.5	70.9	-18.3	19.2	9.7	-2.8	15.6
Long-Term Loans	27.7	24.7	34.1	21.0	17.0	-3.9	11.3	92.5	68.8	95.0	143.0
Disbursements	41.8	37.9	41.5	32.1	31.1	31.1	44.8	115.0	113.0	139.1	220.0
Repayments	14.1	13.2	7.4	11.1	14.1	35.0	33.5	22.5	44.2	44.1	77.0
Other Long-Term Capital	6.6	9.7	-4.4	-4.0	-19.0	25.5	-6.4	-22.8	15.1	-6.6	-94.5
Other Capital, net	-41.0	87.6	-84.3	-82.9	103.1	-112.6	28.1	100.2	37.9	-238.6	-189.0
Change in Reserves	6.6	-6.7	-65.2	-75.3	59.9	2.5	59.3	-109.4	-85.5	31.0	95.7
Memo Item:					*(Ghanaian Cedis per US dollar)*						
Conversion Factor (Annual Avg)	1.020	1.030	1.330	1.160	1.150	1.150	1.150	1.150	1.760	2.750	2.750
Additional Conversion Factor	1.020	1.030	1.320	1.420	1.610	1.880	2.360	3.500	5.730	7.020	9.640
					(Millions of US dollars), outstanding at end of year						
EXTERNAL DEBT (Total)	572	544	602	756	738	728	717	1,074	1,286	1,290	1,407
Long-Term Debt (by debtor)	567	537	585	731	729	722	714	849	919	1,087	1,276
Central Bank, incl. IMF credit	46	20	2	0	0	45	45	47	66	130	105
Central Government	340	342	405	481	555	520	510	624	666	762	929
Rest of General Government	..	..	..	..	..	..	..	..	..	..	..
Non-financial Public Enterprises	170	164	168	166	99	82	74	82	106	133	190
Priv. Sector, incl non-guaranteed	11	11	10	83	75	76	85	97	81	61	53
Short-Term Debt	5	7	16	26	9	6	3	224	367	204	131
Memo Items:					*(Millions of US dollars)*						
Int'l Reserves Excluding Gold	36.60	36.11	93.66	176.08	71.49	124.72	91.74	148.59	277.16	289.11	180.44
Gold Holdings (at market price)	5.98	6.98	10.38	17.96	29.84	22.44	21.56	32.99	49.49	112.13	149.14
SOCIAL INDICATORS											
Total Fertility Rate	6.7	6.7	6.6	6.6	6.6	6.6	6.5	6.5	6.5	6.5	6.5
Infant Mortality Rate	110.6	108.8	107.0	106.0	105.0	104.0	103.0	102.0	101.2	100.4	99.6
Life Expectancy at Birth	49.2	49.6	50.0	50.2	50.4	50.6	50.8	51.0	51.2	51.4	51.6
Urban Population, % of total	29.0	29.2	29.3	29.5	29.6	29.8	30.0	30.2	30.3	30.5	30.7
Food Prod. per capita (1987=100)	149.6	153.4	136.4	134.3	146.0	135.0	115.4	102.1	100.0	102.8	101.8
Labor Force, Agriculture (%)	58.4	58.1	57.8	57.6	57.3	57.1	56.8	56.6	56.3	56.1	55.8
Labor Force, Female (%)	42.2	42.2	42.1	42.0	41.9	41.9	41.8	41.7	41.6	41.5	41.4
Primary Schl. Enroll. Ratio	64.0	..	..	..	..	71.0	71.0	71.0	71.0	69.0	80.0
Primary Schl. Enroll. Ratio, Female	54.0	..	..	..	..	62.0	62.0	61.0	62.0	60.0	71.0
Secondary Schl. Enroll. Ratio	14.0	..	..	..	..	37.0	36.0	36.0	36.0	36.0	41.0

1981	1982	1983	1984	1985	1986	1987	1988	1989	1990 estimate	Notes	GHANA
											FOREIGN TRADE (CUSTOMS BASIS)
			(Millions of current US dollars)								
..	..	..	..	..	..	..	..	..	..	..	Value of Exports, fob
..	..	..	..	..	..	..	..	..	..	..	Nonfuel Primary Products
..	..	..	..	..	..	..	..	..	..	..	Fuels
..	..	..	..	..	..	..	..	..	..	..	Manufactures
..	..	..	..	..	..	..	..	..	..	..	Value of Imports, cif
..	..	..	..	..	..	..	..	..	..	..	Nonfuel Primary Products
..	..	..	..	..	..	..	..	..	..	..	Fuels
..	..	..	..	..	..	..	..	..	..	..	Manufactures
			(Index 1987 = 100)								
..	..	..	..	..	..	..	..	..	..	..	Terms of Trade
..	..	..	..	..	..	..	..	..	..	..	Export Prices, fob
..	..	..	..	..	..	..	..	..	..	..	Import Prices, cif
			(Millions of current US dollars)								**BALANCE OF PAYMENTS**
831.8	713.9	477.6	611.7	676.0	818.5	906.1	958.7	889.1	983.7	..	Exports of Goods & Services
710.7	607.0	439.1	565.9	632.4	773.4	826.8	881.0	807.2	890.6	..	Merchandise, fob
119.1	103.9	38.2	43.8	38.0	39.7	72.4	71.4	75.5	79.3	..	Nonfactor Services
2.0	3.0	0.3	2.0	5.6	5.4	6.9	6.3	6.4	13.8	..	Factor Services
1,335.6	905.0	724.1	812.8	952.3	1,056.1	1,327.8	1,393.0	1,410.0	1,627.9	..	Imports of Goods & Services
954.3	588.7	499.7	533.0	668.7	712.5	951.5	993.4	1,002.2	1,198.9	..	Merchandise, fob
291.6	224.7	134.4	162.9	167.5	227.6	237.5	255.0	270.7	295.4	..	Nonfactor Services
89.7	91.6	90.0	116.9	116.1	116.0	138.8	144.6	137.1	133.6	..	Factor Services
30.5	29.7	43.8	29.2	30.5	45.5	56.2	71.5	61.8	59.4	..	Long-Term Interest
-4.2	-1.2	-1.8	21.1	32.6	72.1	201.6	172.4	202.1	201.9	..	Private Current Transfers, net
0.8	0.9	0.4	4.5	0.4	0.6	0.7	6.0	6.0	6.0	..	Workers' Remittances
-508.0	-192.3	-248.3	-180.0	-243.7	-165.5	-220.1	-261.9	-318.8	-442.3	..	Curr. A/C Bal before Off. Transf.
87.2	83.7	74.2	141.2	109.5	122.5	123.2	196.1	220.2	213.8	..	Net Official Transfers
-420.8	-108.6	-174.1	-38.8	-134.2	-43.0	-96.9	-65.8	-98.6	-228.5	..	Curr. A/C Bal after Off. Transf.
93.7	128.1	33.8	204.2	45.1	146.3	232.4	183.9	180.2	334.2	..	Long-Term Capital, net
16.3	16.3	2.4	2.0	5.6	4.3	4.7	5.0	15.0	14.8	..	Direct Investment
75.9	56.6	80.0	41.5	124.4	292.3	257.2	255.3	224.9	257.1	..	Long-Term Loans
114.8	98.3	151.9	106.1	191.6	377.7	367.3	400.4	380.3	387.9	..	Disbursements
38.9	41.7	71.9	64.6	67.2	85.4	110.1	145.1	155.4	130.8	..	Repayments
1.6	55.2	-48.6	160.7	-84.9	-150.3	-29.5	-76.4	-59.7	62.3	..	Other Long-Term Capital
291.1	-20.7	-115.4	-232.7	149.5	-133.5	-69.7	52.2	78.4	-1.7	..	Other Capital, net
35.9	1.3	255.7	67.3	-60.4	30.2	-65.8	-170.3	-160.0	-104.0	..	Change in Reserves
			(Ghanaian Cedis per US dollar)								**Memo Item:**
2.750	2.750	8.830	35.990	54.370	89.200	153.730	202.350	270.000	326.330	..	Conversion Factor (Annual Avg)
17.200	21.420	45.360	61.320	76.160	89.290	147.000	202.350	270.000	326.330	..	Additional Conversion Factor
			(Millions of US dollars), outstanding at end of year								**EXTERNAL DEBT (Total)**
1,546	1,475	1,650	1,941	2,229	2,732	3,271	3,058	3,151	3,498	..	Long-Term Debt (by debtor)
1,260	1,267	1,558	1,699	2,040	2,545	3,152	2,987	3,105	3,448	..	Central Bank, incl. IMF credit
85	75	331	516	706	882	1,005	867	799	793	..	Central Government
908	905	942	926	1,051	1,350	1,797	1,798	2,024	2,385	..	Rest of General Government
..	..	..	..	..	..	..	..	..	..	..	Non-financial Public Enterprises
217	231	237	204	223	245	276	256	220	208	..	Priv. Sector, incl non-guaranteed
50	56	47	53	60	67	74	65	62	62	..	Short-Term Debt
286	208	93	242	189	187	119	72	47	50	..	
			(Millions of US dollars)								**Memo Items:**
145.60	138.89	144.81	301.56	478.50	512.96	195.13	221.32	347.31	218.84	..	Int'l Reserves Excluding Gold
122.83	175.45	146.50	135.65	73.58	111.02	136.52	89.02	88.62	90.48	..	Gold Holdings (at market price)
											SOCIAL INDICATORS
6.5	6.5	6.5	6.5	6.4	6.4	6.4	6.3	6.3	6.2	..	Total Fertility Rate
98.8	98.0	96.4	94.8	93.1	91.5	89.9	88.2	86.4	84.7	..	Infant Mortality Rate
51.8	52.0	52.4	52.8	53.2	53.6	54.0	54.2	54.4	54.6	..	Life Expectancy at Birth
30.9	31.0	31.2	31.3	31.5	31.9	32.3	32.5	32.8	33.0	..	Urban Population, % of total
99.1	90.0	82.7	116.5	102.3	101.1	100.0	105.2	101.8	87.4	..	Food Prod. per capita (1987=100)
..	..	..	..	..	..	..	..	..	..	..	Labor Force, Agriculture (%)
41.2	41.0	40.9	40.7	40.6	40.4	40.2	40.0	39.9	39.7	..	Labor Force, Female (%)
..	77.0	78.0	76.0	76.0	72.0	71.0	73.0	75.0	..	..	Primary Schl. Enroll. Ratio
68.0	67.0	68.0	66.0	..	63.0	63.0	66.0	67.0	..	..	Primary Schl. Enroll. Ratio, Female
..	38.0	38.0	41.0	40.0	39.0	40.0	39.0	..	..	..	Secondary Schl. Enroll. Ratio

GREECE	1970	1971	1972	1973	1974	1975	1976	1977	1978	1979	1980
CURRENT GNP PER CAPITA (US $)	1,170	1,300	1,460	1,720	1,940	2,370	2,650	2,850	3,270	3,860	4,370
POPULATION (thousands)	8,793	8,831	8,889	8,929	8,962	9,047	9,167	9,309	9,430	9,548	9,643

USE AND ORIGIN OF RESOURCES *(Billions of current Greek Drachmas)*

	1970	1971	1972	1973	1974	1975	1976	1977	1978	1979	1980
Gross National Product (GNP)	304.4	338.2	387.3	497.2	582.1	691.4	849.9	994.0	1,193.8	1,472.2	1,767.5
Net Factor Income from Abroad	5.5	7.9	9.6	13.1	17.9	19.2	24.9	30.3	32.4	43.5	56.6
GDP at Market Prices	298.9	330.3	377.7	484.2	564.2	672.2	824.9	963.7	1,161.4	1,428.8	1,710.9
Resource Balance	-25.0	-26.8	-31.4	-53.2	-53.9	-67.2	-67.9	-81.0	-81.7	-111.3	-91.2
Exports of Goods & NF Services	30.0	34.1	44.3	68.9	90.8	113.3	145.1	162.3	204.4	249.6	357.7
Imports of Goods & NF Services	55.0	60.9	75.7	122.1	144.7	180.6	213.1	243.3	286.1	360.8	448.9
Domestic Absorption	323.9	357.1	409.1	537.3	618.1	739.4	892.9	1,044.7	1,243.1	1,540.0	1,802.2
Private Consumption, etc.	202.2	223.5	251.5	308.7	374.7	456.0	551.8	636.1	736.6	875.8	1,093.9
General Gov't Consumption	37.7	41.4	45.9	55.4	78.1	102.0	124.3	153.8	185.2	233.5	280.0
Gross Domestic Investment	84.0	92.2	111.7	173.2	165.4	181.3	216.7	254.7	321.4	430.7	428.2
Fixed Investment	70.7	83.3	104.8	135.7	125.5	140.0	175.0	221.4	278.0	369.2	413.7
Indirect Taxes, net	40.9	42.9	47.7	55.9	56.9	79.0	96.2	119.1	144.7	183.6	187.2
GDP at factor cost	258.0	287.4	330.0	428.2	507.3	593.2	728.7	844.6	1,016.7	1,245.2	1,523.7
Agriculture	47.1	52.3	61.5	87.3	100.4	111.0	136.2	141.5	177.1	198.2	270.1
Industry	81.0	91.7	106.7	142.0	155.2	178.9	222.8	263.8	312.9	401.3	474.3
Manufacturing	49.3	55.6	61.9	86.2	102.6	118.1	146.5	165.3	191.3	238.5	297.0
Services, etc.	130.0	143.4	161.8	198.9	251.8	303.3	369.8	439.3	526.7	645.8	779.4
Gross Domestic Saving	59.0	65.4	80.3	120.0	111.4	114.1	148.8	173.8	239.7	319.4	337.0
Gross National Saving	74.8	87.4	107.0	154.8	148.6	156.8	202.9	238.0	308.1	406.0	439.9

(Billions of 1987 Greek Drachmas)

	1970	1971	1972	1973	1974	1975	1976	1977	1978	1979	1980
Gross National Product	3,751.9	4,039.2	4,398.6	4,731.7	4,567.2	4,813.6	5,116.3	5,294.8	5,632.4	5,829.1	5,963.1
GDP at Market Prices	3,666.2	3,927.2	4,275.9	4,589.0	4,440.0	4,706.3	4,990.8	5,141.3	5,491.2	5,675.2	5,794.8
Resource Balance	-343.9	-355.3	-380.6	-546.4	-359.2	-355.9	-310.0	-382.5	-337.4	-366.3	-191.8
Exports of Goods & NF Services	352.6	394.4	484.7	597.9	598.6	662.3	770.8	784.4	913.0	973.8	1,041.3
Imports of Goods & NF Services	696.5	749.7	865.3	1,144.3	957.9	1,018.2	1,080.8	1,167.0	1,250.4	1,340.0	1,233.1
Domestic Absorption	4,010.1	4,282.5	4,656.5	5,135.4	4,799.3	5,062.2	5,300.8	5,523.9	5,828.6	6,041.5	5,986.6
Private Consumption, etc.	2,209.5	2,376.5	2,566.8	2,602.9	2,622.6	2,815.7	2,981.7	3,131.4	3,285.9	3,287.7	3,309.5
General Gov't Consumption	561.1	588.8	622.1	664.5	744.7	833.6	876.4	933.6	966.3	1,022.8	1,024.8
Gross Domestic Investment	1,239.5	1,317.2	1,467.6	1,868.0	1,432.0	1,412.9	1,442.7	1,459.0	1,576.4	1,731.0	1,652.3
Fixed Investment	1,048.2	1,195.0	1,379.2	1,484.8	1,105.1	1,107.5	1,183.0	1,275.0	1,351.4	1,470.4	1,375.2
GDP at factor cost	3,108.5	3,356.1	3,662.4	3,967.2	3,906.6	4,107.2	4,342.5	4,452.3	4,744.1	4,897.8	5,017.2
Agriculture	673.8	696.7	738.0	733.1	768.5	812.3	801.4	742.1	819.2	767.7	866.2
Industry	934.1	1,047.5	1,176.2	1,319.3	1,173.3	1,241.0	1,356.6	1,421.5	1,510.9	1,601.7	1,563.0
Manufacturing	548.0	607.2	655.1	770.1	748.2	789.2	868.0	880.4	938.2	990.0	991.4
Services, etc.	1,500.6	1,611.9	1,748.3	1,914.8	1,964.8	2,054.0	2,184.5	2,288.7	2,414.1	2,528.5	2,588.0

Memo Items:

	1970	1971	1972	1973	1974	1975	1976	1977	1978	1979	1980
Capacity to Import	379.8	419.9	506.2	645.8	600.8	639.2	736.2	778.6	893.3	926.7	982.5
Terms of Trade Adjustment	27.2	25.4	21.5	47.9	2.2	-23.1	-34.6	-5.8	-19.8	-47.0	-58.8
Gross Domestic Income	3,693.4	3,952.6	4,297.4	4,636.9	4,442.2	4,683.2	4,956.2	5,135.5	5,471.4	5,628.2	5,736.0
Gross National Income	3,779.1	4,064.6	4,420.1	4,779.6	4,569.4	4,790.5	5,081.8	5,289.0	5,612.7	5,782.1	5,904.3

DOMESTIC PRICES/DEFLATORS *(Index 1987 = 100)*

	1970	1971	1972	1973	1974	1975	1976	1977	1978	1979	1980
Overall (GDP)	8.2	8.4	8.8	10.6	12.7	14.3	16.5	18.7	21.2	25.2	29.5
Domestic Absorption	8.1	8.3	8.8	10.5	12.9	14.6	16.8	18.9	21.3	25.5	30.1
Agriculture	7.0	7.5	8.3	11.9	13.1	13.7	17.0	19.1	21.6	25.8	31.2
Industry	8.7	8.8	9.1	10.8	13.2	14.4	16.4	18.6	20.7	25.1	30.3
Manufacturing	9.0	9.2	9.5	11.2	13.7	15.0	16.9	18.8	20.4	24.1	30.0
Consumer Price Index	7.2	7.4	7.7	8.9	11.3	12.8	14.6	16.3	18.4	21.9	27.3

MANUFACTURING ACTIVITY

	1970	1971	1972	1973	1974	1975	1976	1977	1978	1979	1980
Employment (1987=100)	78.4	81.9	84.6	89.6	94.8	97.7	104.2	106.0	106.9	107.8	108.8
Real Earnings per Empl. (1987=100)	63.3	66.2	70.3	72.5	70.9	77.2	84.6	90.6	94.0	99.1	97.6
Real Output per Empl. (1987=100)	50.4	52.1	55.9	60.9	64.6	68.5	69.2	71.6	79.1	86.7	89.4
Earnings as % of Value Added	31.5	31.7	32.9	29.8	31.6	35.9	37.6	38.9	39.0	39.0	39.0

MONETARY HOLDINGS *(Billions of current Greek Drachmas)*

	1970	1971	1972	1973	1974	1975	1976	1977	1978	1979	1980
Money Supply, Broadly Defined	139.0	170.5	212.1	250.0	301.4	375.4	472.2	586.2	797.3	947.4	1,159.8
Money	54.6	63.6	75.9	93.7	112.2	130.6	159.6	186.6	228.2	265.4	308.8
Currency Outside Banks	39.1	43.3	50.8	65.3	80.6	92.2	112.3	133.4	161.8	184.7	211.8
Demand Deposits	15.5	20.4	25.1	28.4	31.6	38.5	47.3	53.2	66.4	80.8	97.0
Quasi-Money	84.4	106.8	136.2	156.3	189.2	244.8	312.6	399.6	569.1	682.0	851.0

(Billions of current Greek Drachmas)

	1970	1971	1972	1973	1974	1975	1976	1977	1978	1979	1980
GOVERNMENT DEFICIT (-) OR SURPLUS	..	..	-6.5	-13.0	-23.4	-26.1	-32.4	-47.4	-49.8	-55.3	-85.5
Current Revenue	..	..	98.5	123.0	143.7	179.5	239.5	283.9	348.9	427.3	524.7
Current Expenditure	..	..	77.7	100.4	132.4	163.0	215.9	256.5	321.7	407.1	532.2
Current Budget Balance	..	..	20.8	22.6	11.3	16.6	23.7	27.4	27.2	20.2	-7.5
Capital Receipts	..	..	1.6	0.5	1.2	0.5	0.6	0.5	0.9	1.4	1.6
Capital Payments	..	..	28.9	36.1	36.0	43.2	56.7	75.4	77.9	76.9	79.6

1981	1982	1983	1984	1985	1986	1987	1988	1989	1990 estimate	Notes	GREECE
4,470	4,320	3,950	3,810	3,610	3,670	3,980	4,780	5,380	5,990	..	**CURRENT GNP PER CAPITA (US $)**
9,729	9,790	9,847	9,896	9,934	9,964	9,984	10,004	10,033	10,062	..	**POPULATION (thousands)**
											USE AND ORIGIN OF RESOURCES
			(Billions of current Greek Drachmas)								
2,109.1	2,632.4	3,109.6	3,807.6	4,584.0	5,429.8	6,164.7	7,445.3	8,713.2	10,542.2	..	Gross National Product (GNP)
59.0	57.8	30.4	1.9	-33.8	-67.8	-63.3	-56.7	-85.2	-73.6	..	Net Factor Income from Abroad
2,050.1	2,574.7	3,079.2	3,805.7	4,617.8	5,497.6	6,228.0	7,502.0	8,798.4	10,615.8	..	GDP at Market Prices
-133.7	-265.3	-315.9	-314.5	-535.9	-470.2	-456.6	-489.8	-770.0	-1,132.2	..	Resource Balance
422.4	473.0	609.5	824.6	977.6	1,233.1	1,536.8	1,800.9	2,069.5	2,300.6	..	Exports of Goods & NFServices
556.1	738.3	925.4	1,139.1	1,513.5	1,703.3	1,993.4	2,290.7	2,839.5	3,432.8	f	Imports of Goods & NFServices
2,183.8	2,839.9	3,395.1	4,120.2	5,153.7	5,967.8	6,684.7	7,991.8	9,568.3	11,748.0	f	Domestic Absorption
1,294.6	1,825.4	2,142.5	2,614.1	3,220.7	3,839.1	4,384.1	5,062.8	6,023.4	7,528.0	..	Private Consumption, etc.
368.5	471.2	579.4	742.8	942.1	1,067.2	1,229.4	1,517.5	1,828.6	2,220.0	..	General Gov't Consumption
520.6	543.3	673.2	763.3	990.9	1,061.5	1,071.2	1,411.5	1,716.3	2,000.0	f	Gross Domestic Investment
456.3	513.5	624.0	702.9	880.4	1,018.1	1,045.8	1,282.3	1,630.5	2,000.0	f	Fixed Investment
190.1	264.0	346.0	443.1	481.0	642.0	794.2	955.3	943.3	1,438.0	..	Indirect Taxes, net
1,860.0	2,310.7	2,733.2	3,362.6	4,136.8	4,855.6	5,433.8	6,546.7	7,855.1	9,177.8	..	GDP at factor cost
329.3	424.4	462.8	591.4	713.8	788.1	851.9	1,079.4	1,337.3	..	..	Agriculture
570.4	672.7	812.3	982.9	1,210.7	1,443.9	1,553.9	1,824.8	2,130.2	..	..	Industry
361.3	422.6	503.1	614.8	752.5	907.4	971.1	1,148.7	1,346.7	..	..	Manufacturing
960.2	1,213.5	1,458.2	1,788.3	2,212.2	2,623.6	3,028.0	3,642.5	4,387.6	..	..	Services, etc.
386.9	278.0	357.3	448.8	455.0	591.3	614.5	921.7	946.4	867.8	..	Gross Domestic Saving
505.5	405.2	469.7	554.1	531.3	660.0	736.7	1,108.0	1,085.5	1,082.2	..	Gross National Saving
			(Billions of 1987 Greek Drachmas)								
5,945.2	5,935.3	5,866.8	5,996.0	6,137.9	6,189.9	6,164.7	6,426.7	6,592.3	6,644.9	..	Gross National Product
5,795.2	5,822.4	5,827.9	5,993.9	6,177.3	6,262.5	6,228.0	6,480.6	6,662.9	6,683.9	I	GDP at Market Prices
-298.5	-458.9	-476.1	-312.9	-485.8	-384.7	-456.6	-475.8	-656.2	-783.6	..	Resource Balance
979.6	908.9	981.7	1,148.0	1,163.1	1,326.3	1,536.8	1,654.4	1,710.8	1,704.9	..	Exports of Goods & NFServices
1,278.1	1,367.8	1,457.8	1,460.9	1,648.9	1,711.0	1,993.4	2,130.2	2,367.0	2,488.6	f	Imports of Goods & NFServices
6,093.7	6,281.3	6,304.0	6,306.8	6,663.1	6,647.2	6,684.6	6,956.4	7,319.1	7,467.6	f	Domestic Absorption
3,581.7	3,835.2	3,838.1	3,871.3	4,074.8	4,200.6	4,384.0	4,342.4	4,644.1	4,808.8	..	Private Consumption, etc.
1,094.7	1,119.8	1,150.6	1,185.7	1,223.5	1,213.0	1,229.4	1,309.7	1,379.5	1,379.5	..	General Gov't Consumption
1,417.3	1,326.3	1,315.4	1,249.7	1,364.8	1,233.5	1,071.2	1,304.3	1,295.5	1,279.2	f	Gross Domestic Investment
1,272.0	1,247.5	1,231.2	1,161.5	1,220.8	1,145.2	1,045.8	1,139.3	1,237.2	1,286.1	f	Fixed Investment
5,023.0	5,055.1	5,060.9	5,212.4	5,386.3	5,466.9	5,433.8	5,678.1	5,856.1	5,886.9	I	GDP at factor cost
852.1	872.5	794.9	850.4	866.2	887.7	851.9	903.4	934.9	887.7	..	Agriculture
1,539.4	1,504.2	1,506.8	1,525.6	1,581.6	1,583.5	1,553.9	1,638.1	1,678.5	1,691.2	..	Industry
988.5	967.2	950.4	961.9	995.9	995.0	971.1	1,014.5	1,036.7	1,039.0	..	Manufacturing
2,631.5	2,678.4	2,759.2	2,836.5	2,938.5	2,995.7	3,028.0	3,136.5	3,242.7	3,308.0	..	Services, etc.
											Memo Items:
970.7	876.3	960.2	1,057.6	1,065.1	1,238.7	1,536.8	1,674.7	1,725.1	1,667.8	..	Capacity to Import
-8.9	-32.6	-21.5	-90.4	-98.0	-87.6	0.0	20.3	14.3	-37.1	..	Terms of Trade Adjustment
5,786.3	5,789.9	5,806.4	5,903.5	6,079.2	6,174.9	6,228.0	6,501.0	6,677.2	6,646.8	..	Gross Domestic Income
5,936.4	5,902.7	5,845.3	5,905.6	6,039.8	6,102.2	6,164.7	6,447.0	6,606.6	6,607.7	..	Gross National Income
			(Index 1987 = 100)								**DOMESTIC PRICES/DEFLATORS**
35.4	44.2	52.8	63.5	74.8	87.8	100.0	115.8	132.1	158.8	..	Overall (GDP)
35.8	45.2	53.9	65.3	77.3	89.8	100.0	114.9	130.7	157.3	..	Domestic Absorption
38.6	48.6	58.2	69.5	82.4	88.8	100.0	119.5	143.0	..	..	Agriculture
37.1	44.7	53.9	64.4	76.5	91.2	100.0	111.4	126.9	..	..	Industry
36.5	43.7	52.9	63.9	75.6	91.2	100.0	113.2	129.9	..	..	Manufacturing
34.0	41.1	49.4	58.5	69.8	85.9	100.0	113.5	129.1	155.4	..	Consumer Price Index
											MANUFACTURING ACTIVITY
109.3	105.3	102.2	102.2	101.3	101.3	100.0	..	..	..	..	Employment (1987=100)
96.4	105.6	104.0	109.4	109.6	108.3	100.0	..	..	..	..	Real Earnings per Empl. (1987=100)
92.3	89.9	92.7	95.0	99.7	101.5	100.0	..	..	..	..	Real Output per Empl. (1987=100)
39.8	44.9	42.8	43.2	42.4	42.8	43.0	..	..	..	..	Earnings as % of Value Added
			(Billions of current Greek Drachmas)								**MONETARY HOLDINGS**
1,536.7	1,973.3	2,374.3	3,070.3	3,851.6	4,579.7	6,960.1	8,508.1	10,212.9	..	D	Money Supply, Broadly Defined
377.4	459.1	525.6	630.9	743.3	896.0	1,057.7	1,205.7	1,486.4	1,848.1	..	Money
263.7	305.2	348.2	408.2	513.5	550.1	641.4	754.9	988.7	1,190.1	..	Currency Outside Banks
113.7	153.9	177.4	222.7	229.8	345.9	416.2	450.8	497.8	658.0	..	Demand Deposits
1,159.3	1,514.2	1,848.7	2,439.4	3,108.3	3,683.7	5,902.4	7,302.3	8,726.5	..	..	Quasi-Money
			(Billions of current Greek Drachmas)								**GOVERNMENT DEFICIT (-) OR SURPLUS**
-223.7	-477.5	-160.9	-534.0	-661.3	..	..	..	..	..	..	Current Revenue
600.8	871.6	1,192.7	1,368.0	1,671.3	..	..	..	..	..	..	Current Expenditure
728.4	1,206.4	1,162.2	1,661.0	2,033.7	..	..	..	..	..	..	Current Budget Balance
-127.6	-334.8	30.6	-293.0	-362.4	..	..	..	..	..	..	Capital Receipts
2.3	3.6	0.2	4.2	3.6	..	..	..	..	..	..	Capital Payments
98.4	146.3	191.7	245.2	302.5	..	..	..	..	..	..	

GREECE	1970	1971	1972	1973	1974	1975	1976	1977	1978	1979	1980
FOREIGN TRADE (CUSTOMS BASIS)					*(Millions of current US dollars)*						
Value of Exports, fob	643	662	871	1,454	2,030	2,278	2,558	2,757	3,375	3,877	5,142
Nonfuel Primary Products	414	454	549	713	942	1,024	1,156	1,251	1,512	1,646	1,901
Fuels	6	6	11	203	183	252	150	133	321	459	800
Manufactures	222	202	311	537	905	1,003	1,253	1,373	1,543	1,773	2,441
Value of Imports, cif	1,958	2,098	2,346	3,473	4,385	5,321	6,051	6,852	7,655	9,594	10,531
Nonfuel Primary Products	399	448	486	813	981	991	982	1,134	1,231	1,620	1,725
Fuels	135	153	231	427	974	1,178	1,234	1,041	1,429	2,036	2,464
Manufactures	1,425	1,496	1,629	2,233	2,429	3,152	3,835	4,678	4,995	5,938	6,343
					(Index 1987 = 100)						
Terms of Trade	162.3	146.4	153.9	143.1	121.7	118.6	120.2	115.7	110.7	111.9	107.6
Export Prices, fob	39.8	39.9	42.3	47.6	65.9	65.7	71.0	76.9	79.2	97.6	112.6
Import Prices, cif	24.5	27.3	27.5	33.2	54.1	55.4	59.0	66.5	71.6	87.2	104.7
BALANCE OF PAYMENTS					*(Millions of current US dollars)*						
Exports of Goods & Services	1,100	1,314	1,692	2,401	3,254	3,647	4,202	4,833	5,905	7,680	8,374
Merchandise, fob	612	627	835	1,230	1,774	1,960	2,228	2,522	2,999	3,932	4,093
Nonfactor Services	471	668	818	1,105	1,370	1,559	1,838	2,193	2,742	3,495	4,029
Factor Services	17	19	39	66	111	129	136	118	164	253	252
Imports of Goods & Services	1,868	2,129	2,664	4,323	5,041	5,272	5,940	6,833	7,842	10,732	11,670
Merchandise, fob	1,509	1,727	2,161	3,582	4,125	4,320	4,922	5,686	6,498	8,948	9,650
Nonfactor Services	267	307	392	591	690	720	738	859	1,001	1,340	1,475
Factor Services	92	95	112	149	226	232	280	288	343	444	545
Long-Term Interest	..	..	..	..	..	..	..	..	..	..	..
Private Current Transfers, net	344	469	572	732	642	733	800	922	981	1,164	1,087
Workers' Remittances	333	457	560	715	625	716	777	899	951	1,137	1,066
Curr. A/C Bal before Off. Transf.	-424	-346	-401	-1,190	-1,145	-891	-938	-1,078	-956	-1,888	-2,209
Net Official Transfers	2	2	1	1	2	15	10	..	1	1	
Curr. A/C Bal after Off. Transf.	-422	-344	-400	-1,189	-1,143	-877	-928	-1,078	-955	-1,887	-2,209
Long-Term Capital, net	280	236	496	795	759	789	544	862	1,040	1,331	1,994
Direct Investment	50	42	55	62	67	24	305	387	428	613	672
Long-Term Loans											
Disbursements	..	..	..	..	..	..	..	..	..	..	..
Repayments	..	..	..	..	..	..	..	..	..	..	..
Other Long-Term Capital	230	193	441	733	692	765	239	475	612	718	1,322
Other Capital, net	119	292	375	382	227	-96	312	387	49	513	78
Change in Reserves	23	-184	-472	11	156	183	72	-171	-134	43	137
Memo Item:					*(Greek Drachmas per US dollar)*						
Conversion Factor (Annual Avg)	30.000	30.000	30.000	29.630	30.000	32.050	36.520	36.840	36.740	37.040	42.620
EXTERNAL DEBT (Total)					*(Millions of US dollars), outstanding at end of year*						
Long-Term Debt (by debtor)	..	..	..	..	..	..	..	..	..	..	..
Central Bank, incl. IMF credit	..	..	..	..	..	..	..	..	..	..	..
Central Government	..	..	..	..	..	..	..	..	..	..	..
Rest of General Government	..	..	..	..	..	..	..	..	..	..	..
Non-financial Public Enterprises	..	..	..	..	..	..	..	..	..	..	..
Priv. Sector, incl non-guaranteed	..	..	..	..	..	..	..	..	..	..	..
Short-Term Debt	..	..	..	..	..	..	..	..	..	..	..
Memo Items:					*(Millions of US dollars)*						
Int'l Reserves Excluding Gold	193.6	412.4	898.8	898.9	781.7	963.6	880.6	1,048.3	1,305.0	1,342.8	1,345.9
Gold Holdings (at market price)	124.4	122.4	226.8	393.1	673.3	509.0	492.0	615.3	852.0	1,949.7	2,260.7
SOCIAL INDICATORS											
Total Fertility Rate	2.3	2.3	2.3	2.3	2.4	2.4	2.4	2.3	2.3	2.3	2.2
Infant Mortality Rate	29.6	26.9	27.3	24.1	23.9	24.0	22.5	20.4	19.3	18.7	17.9
Life Expectancy at Birth	71.8	72.1	72.4	72.6	72.9	73.2	73.4	73.7	73.9	74.1	74.4
Urban Population, % of total	52.5	53.1	53.6	54.2	54.7	55.3	55.8	56.2	56.7	57.1	57.6
Food Prod. per capita (1987=100)	83.5	81.6	85.5	87.4	95.9	100.6	95.8	92.1	97.9	93.9	104.7
Labor Force, Agriculture (%)	42.2	41.1	40.0	38.8	37.7	36.6	35.4	34.2	33.1	32.0	30.9
Labor Force, Female (%)	25.7	25.7	25.8	25.8	25.9	25.9	25.9	26.0	26.0	26.0	26.1
Primary Schl. Enroll. Ratio	107.0	..	..	..	..	104.0	104.0	103.0	103.0	100.0	103.0
Primary Schl. Enroll. Ratio, Female	106.0	..	..	..	..	104.0	103.0	103.0	103.0	99.0	103.0
Secondary Schl. Enroll. Ratio	63.0	..	..	..	..	78.0	80.0	81.0	81.0	81.0	81.0

1981	1982	1983	1984	1985	1986	1987	1988	1989	1990 estimate	Notes	GREECE
											FOREIGN TRADE (CUSTOMS BASIS)
											(Millions of current US dollars)
4,249	4,297	4,412	4,864	4,536	5,660	6,489	5,156	7,353	8,053	..	Value of Exports, fob
1,580	1,680	1,913	1,998	1,749	2,241	2,579	1,885	3,126	3,112	..	Nonfuel Primary Products
404	462	306	492	546	371	436	275	411	588	..	Fuels
2,266	2,154	2,194	2,374	2,241	3,048	3,474	2,995	3,816	4,353	..	Manufactures
8,781	10,012	9,500	9,611	10,138	11,240	12,908	11,977	16,103	19,701	..	Value of Imports, cif
1,613	1,916	1,880	1,845	1,948	2,633	3,307	3,023	3,732	4,267	..	Nonfuel Primary Products
1,933	2,871	2,606	2,626	2,993	1,959	1,786	609	1,038	1,527	..	Fuels
5,234	5,225	5,013	5,140	5,197	6,648	7,815	8,345	11,333	13,906	..	Manufactures
											(Index 1987 = 100)
100.6	102.6	100.4	97.0	94.4	100.0	100.0	95.5	97.1	105.1	..	Terms of Trade
106.2	103.7	98.2	92.9	88.5	91.4	100.0	109.7	124.0	138.2	..	Export Prices, fob
105.6	101.1	97.8	95.8	93.7	91.3	100.0	115.0	127.6	131.5	..	Import Prices, cif
											BALANCE OF PAYMENTS
											(Millions of current US dollars)
9,183	7,891	7,166	7,333	7,111	7,905	10,216	11,378	11,185	13,333	..	Exports of Goods & Services
4,772	4,141	4,106	4,394	4,293	4,513	5,612	5,933	5,994	6,365	..	Merchandise, fob
4,065	3,492	2,930	2,756	2,664	3,286	4,419	5,176	4,908	6,653	..	Nonfactor Services
346	258	130	183	154	106	185	269	283	315	..	Factor Services
12,828	11,382	10,811	11,097	12,053	11,948	14,474	15,985	17,729	21,588	..	Imports of Goods & Services
10,149	8,910	8,400	8,624	9,346	8,936	11,112	12,005	13,377	16,543	..	Merchandise, fob
1,773	1,612	1,446	1,320	1,417	1,589	1,736	2,188	2,424	3,006	..	Nonfactor Services
906	860	965	1,153	1,290	1,423	1,626	1,792	1,928	2,039	..	Factor Services
..	..	..	..	..	..	..	..	..	..		Long-Term Interest
1,076	1,039	931	917	797	975	1,370	1,713	1,381	1,817	..	Private Current Transfers, net
1,057	1,016	912	898	775	942	1,334	1,675	1,350	1,775	..	Workers' Remittances
-2,569	-2,452	-2,714	-2,847	-4,145	-3,068	-2,888	-2,894	-5,163	-6,438	..	Curr. A/C Bal before Off. Transf.
161	560	836	715	869	1,392	1,665	1,936	2,602	2,901	..	Net Official Transfers
-2,408	-1,892	-1,878	-2,132	-3,276	-1,676	-1,223	-958	-2,561	-3,537	..	Curr. A/C Bal after Off. Transf.
1,589	1,239	2,110	1,773	2,766	2,151	1,387	1,438	1,941	2,975	..	Long-Term Capital, net
520	436	439	485	447	471	683	907	752	1,005	..	Direct Investment
..	..	..	..	..	..	..	..	..	..		Long-Term Loans
..	..	..	..	..	..	..	..	..	..		Disbursements
..	..	..	..	..	..	..	..	..	..		Repayments
1,069	803	1,671	1,288	2,319	1,680	704	531	1,189	1,970		Other Long-Term Capital
661	541	-132	490	369	-205	642	668	279	602	..	Other Capital, net
158	112	-100	-131	141	-270	-806	-1,148	341	-40	..	Change in Reserves
											Memo Item:
											(Greek Drachmas per US dollar)
55.410	66.800	88.060	112.720	138.120	139.980	135.430	141.860	162.420	158.510	..	Conversion Factor (Annual Avg)
											EXTERNAL DEBT (Total)
											(Millions of US dollars), outstanding at end of year
..	..	..	..	..	..	..	..	..	..	..	Long-Term Debt (by debtor)
..	..	..	..	..	..	..	..	..	..		Central Bank, incl. IMF credit
..	..	..	..	..	..	..	..	..	..		Central Government
..	..	..	..	..	..	..	..	..	..		Rest of General Government
..	..	..	..	..	..	..	..	..	..		Non-financial Public Enterprises
..	..	..	..	..	..	..	..	..	..		Priv. Sector, incl non-guaranteed
..	..	..	..	..	..	..	..	..	..		Short-Term Debt
											Memo Items:
											(Millions of US dollars)
1,022.0	861.1	900.5	954.2	868.0	1,518.7	2,681.4	3,619.4	3,223.5	3,412.1	..	Int'l Reserves Excluding Gold
1,531.6	1,769.1	1,480.2	1,265.9	1,348.2	1,293.1	1,617.9	1,392.8	1,361.4	1,309.0	..	Gold Holdings (at market price)
											SOCIAL INDICATORS
2.1	2.0	1.9	1.8	1.7	1.6	1.5	1.5	1.5	1.5	..	Total Fertility Rate
16.3	15.1	14.6	14.3	14.1	12.2	12.6	12.2	11.8	11.3	..	Infant Mortality Rate
74.6	74.8	74.9	75.0	75.0	75.7	76.4	76.6	76.9	77.1	..	Life Expectancy at Birth
58.1	58.6	59.0	59.5	60.0	60.5	61.0	61.5	62.0	62.5	..	Urban Population, % of total
106.3	107.3	102.7	105.9	108.5	102.0	100.0	105.9	110.4	96.5	..	Food Prod. per capita (1987=100)
..	..	..	..	..	..	..	..	..	..	..	Labor Force, Agriculture (%)
26.1	26.2	26.3	26.3	26.4	26.4	26.5	26.5	26.6	26.7	..	Labor Force, Female (%)
104.0	105.0	105.0	105.0	104.0	102.0	102.0	..	..	..		Primary Schl. Enroll. Ratio
104.0	105.0	105.0	105.0	104.0	102.0	102.0	..	..	..	..	Primary Schl. Enroll. Ratio, Female
84.0	84.0	85.0	88.0	90.0	95.0	97.0	..	..		..	Secondary Schl. Enroll. Ratio

GRENADA	1970	1971	1972	1973	1974	1975	1976	1977	1978	1979	1980
CURRENT GNP PER CAPITA (US $)	..	..		..	..	..	..	..		..	
POPULATION (thousands)	..	..		..	..	..	..	..		..	87
USE AND ORIGIN OF RESOURCES				*(Millions of current Eastern Caribbean Dollars)*							
Gross National Product (GNP)	..	..	..	..	..	..	..	..	..	..	163.80
Net Factor Income from Abroad	..	..		..	..	..	..	..		..	-5.90
GDP at Market Prices	..	..		..	..	..	..	..		..	169.70
Resource Balance	..	..		..	..	..	..	..		..	-55.90
Exports of Goods & NF Services	..	..		..	..	..	..	..		..	106.90
Imports of Goods & NF Services	..	..		..	..	..	..	..		..	162.80
Domestic Absorption	..	..		..	..	..	..	..		..	225.60
Private Consumption, etc.	..	..		..	..	..	..	..		..	122.90
General Gov't Consumption	..	..		..	..	..	..	..		..	46.80
Gross Domestic Investment	..	..		..	..	..	..	..		..	55.90
Fixed Investment	..	..		..	..	..	..	..		..	55.90
Indirect Taxes, net	..	..		..	..	..	..	..		..	..
GDP at factor cost	..	..		..	..	..	..	..		..	167.60
Agriculture	..	..		..	..	..	..	..		..	41.40
Industry	..	..		..	..	..	..	..		..	21.80
Manufacturing	..	..		..	..	..	..	..		..	6.60
Services, etc.	..	..		..	..	..	..	..		..	104.40
Gross Domestic Saving	..	..		..	..	..	..	..		..	0.00
Gross National Saving	..	..		..	..	..	..	..		..	25.15
				(Millions of 1987 Eastern Caribbean Dollars)							
Gross National Product	..	..		..	..	..	..	..		..	..
GDP at Market Prices	..	..		..	..	..	..	..		..	..
Resource Balance	..	..		..	..	..	..	..		..	
Exports of Goods & NF Services	..	..		..	..	..	..	..		..	
Imports of Goods & NF Services	..	..		..	..	..	..	..		..	
Domestic Absorption	..	..		..	..	..	..	..		..	
Private Consumption, etc.	..	..		..	..	..	..	..		..	
General Gov't Consumption	..	..		..	..	..	..	..		..	
Gross Domestic Investment	..	..		..	..	..	..	..		..	
Fixed Investment	..	..		..	..	..	..	..		..	..
GDP at factor cost	..	..	..	..	..	..	..	..		..	240.18
Agriculture	..	..		..	..	..	..	..		..	62.15
Industry	..	..		..	..	..	..	..		..	34.61
Manufacturing	..	..		..	..	..	..	..		..	10.32
Services, etc.	..	..		..	..	..	..	..		..	143.42
Memo Items:											
Capacity to Import	..	..		..	..	..	..	..	..	..	..
Terms of Trade Adjustment	..	..		..	..	..	..	..	..	..	..
Gross Domestic Income	..	..		..	..	..	..	..	..	..	..
Gross National Income	..	..	..	..	..	..	..	..	..	..	..
DOMESTIC PRICES/DEFLATORS				*(Index 1987 = 100)*							
Overall (GDP)	..	..		..	..	..	..	..		..	
Domestic Absorption	..	..		..	..	..	..	..		..	
Agriculture	..	..		..	..	..	..	..		..	66.6
Industry	..	..		..	..	..	..	..		..	63.0
Manufacturing	..	..		..	..	..	..	..		..	64.0
Consumer Price Index	..	..		..	..	..	33.1	39.2	46.3	56.3	68.2
MANUFACTURING ACTIVITY											
Employment (1987=100)	..	..		..	..	..	..	..	..	..	..
Real Earnings per Empl. (1987=100)	..	..		..	..	..	..	..	..	..	..
Real Output per Empl. (1987=100)	..	..		..	..	..	..	..	..	..	..
Earnings as % of Value Added	..	..		..	..	..	..	..	..	..	..
MONETARY HOLDINGS				*(Millions of current Eastern Caribbean Dollars)*							
Money Supply, Broadly Defined	42.68	45.41	53.91	55.48	54.48	66.67	79.28	88.07	104.13	123.40	130.95
Money	10.81	11.87	14.31	15.62	15.78	19.38	26.70	29.51	38.04	45.65	48.45
Currency Outside Banks	6.09	6.90	8.28	8.39	9.71	12.65	15.32	18.33	23.67	28.50	32.58
Demand Deposits	4.72	4.97	6.03	7.23	6.07	6.73	11.38	11.18	14.37	17.15	15.86
Quasi-Money	31.87	33.54	39.60	39.86	38.69	47.29	52.58	58.55	66.09	77.75	82.51
GOVERNMENT DEFICIT (-) OR SURPLUS				*(Thousands of current Eastern Caribbean Dollars)*							
					-5,250	-5,080	-6,370	-1,660			
Current Revenue	..	..	..	..	18,620	21,120	29,750	35,110	..	..	..
Current Expenditure	..	..		..	19,380	22,760	33,250	31,120	..	..	..
Current Budget Balance	..	..		..	-760	-1,640	-3,500	3,990			
Capital Receipts	..	..		..	80	130	60	130	..	..	..
Capital Payments	..	..		..	4,570	3,570	2,930	5,780	..	..	..

1981	1982	1983	1984	1985	1986	1987	1988	1989	1990 est.	Notes	GRENADA
..	..	..	..	..	1,350	1,560	1,770	1,970	2,190	..	**CURRENT GNP PER CAPITA (US $)**
88	91	92	93	94	90	90	91	91	91	..	**POPULATION (thousands)**
			(Millions of current Eastern Caribbean Dollars)								**USE AND ORIGIN OF RESOURCES**
187.10	202.60	210.30	273.20	307.10	345.90	399.20	441.40	491.20	538.70	..	Gross National Product (GNP)
-13.50	-13.50	-11.90	-4.10	-5.10	-4.90	-6.20	-8.10	-13.20	-11.30	..	Net Factor Income from Abroad
200.60	216.10	222.20	277.30	312.20	350.80	405.40	449.50	504.40	550.00	..	GDP at Market Prices
-82.60	-106.40	-95.50	-80.70	-91.00	-119.90	-113.10	-101.80	-136.90	-141.00	..	Resource Balance
106.90	103.10	104.80	107.50	142.80	182.80	212.00	226.80	227.10	243.90	..	Exports of Goods & NFServices
189.50	209.50	200.30	188.20	233.80	302.70	325.10	328.60	364.00	384.90	..	Imports of Goods & NFServices
283.20	322.50	317.70	358.00	403.20	470.50	518.50	551.30	641.30	691.00	..	Domestic Absorption
136.40	161.10	170.20	205.40	227.40	259.20	294.70	320.30	364.10	408.30	..	Private Consumption, etc.
50.80	51.40	55.00	64.00	71.60	74.70	84.90	83.00	125.70	119.30	..	General Gov't Consumption
96.00	110.00	92.50	88.60	104.20	136.80	138.90	148.00	151.50	163.40	..	Gross Domestic Investment
96.00	110.00	92.50	88.60	104.20	136.80	138.90	148.00	151.50	163.40	..	Fixed Investment
..	..	..	..	66.00	68.80	84.90	99.30	109.10	128.00	..	Indirect Taxes, net
180.90	196.60	204.50	223.40	246.20	282.00	320.50	350.20	395.30	422.00	..	GDP at factor cost
44.80	40.70	41.30	44.90	44.20	52.90	69.50	72.00	73.70	71.30	..	Agriculture
29.70	35.50	32.80	32.70	39.10	45.20	54.20	63.40	74.20	81.80	..	Industry
8.70	10.20	10.50	9.80	12.50	13.20	16.00	18.40	20.80	22.60	..	Manufacturing
106.40	120.40	130.40	145.80	162.90	183.90	196.80	214.80	247.40	268.90	..	Services, etc.
13.40	3.60	-3.00	7.90	13.20	16.90	25.80	46.20	14.60	22.40	..	Gross Domestic Saving
27.98	19.80	23.98	32.42	35.96	40.08	51.46	79.41	47.30	..	..	Gross National Saving
			(Millions of 1987 Eastern Caribbean Dollars)								
..	..	..	335.47	358.84	370.82	399.20	424.86	442.69	470.60	..	Gross National Product
..	..	..	339.52	363.89	375.72	405.40	432.58	454.08	479.65	..	GDP at Market Prices
..	..	..	-24.44	-25.96	-90.92	-113.10	-96.30	-104.43	-72.88	..	Resource Balance
..	..	..	177.22	217.28	216.29	212.00	219.58	228.81	256.51	..	Exports of Goods & NFServices
..	..	..	201.66	243.24	307.21	325.10	315.89	333.24	329.39	..	Imports of Goods & NFServices
..	..	..	363.97	389.85	466.64	518.50	528.89	558.50	552.52	..	Domestic Absorption
..	..	..	206.50	213.95	249.30	294.70	308.79	332.29	341.23	..	Private Consumption, etc.
..	..	..	68.87	76.40	79.73	84.90	81.99	90.71	83.39	..	General Gov't Consumption
..	..	..	88.60	99.50	137.60	138.90	138.10	135.50	127.90	..	Gross Domestic Investment
..	..	..		99.50	137.60	138.90	138.10	135.50	127.90	..	Fixed Investment
244.67	255.88	260.30	275.39	287.06	301.95	320.50	336.92	355.47	372.97	..	GDP at factor cost
65.98	59.40	60.77	68.73	64.30	63.99	69.50	71.03	72.71	72.10	..	Agriculture
42.47	45.99	40.24	38.36	42.70	47.16	54.20	61.24	69.57	75.90	..	Industry
12.41	13.80	13.45	11.36	13.57	13.68	16.00	17.62	19.71	21.33	..	Manufacturing
136.22	150.49	159.29	168.29	180.06	190.80	196.80	204.65	213.19	224.96	..	Services, etc.
											Memo Items:
..	..	..	115.19	148.56	185.52	212.00	218.02	207.91	208.72	..	Capacity to Import
..	..	..	-62.03	-68.71	-30.77	0.00	-1.56	-20.90	-47.79	..	Terms of Trade Adjustment
..	..	..	277.49	295.18	344.95	405.40	431.02	433.17	431.86	..	Gross Domestic Income
..	..	..	273.44	290.13	340.05	399.20	423.30	421.79	422.81	..	Gross National Income
			(Index 1987 = 100)								**DOMESTIC PRICES/DEFLATORS**
..	..	..	81.7	85.8	93.4	100.0	103.9	111.1	114.7	..	Overall (GDP)
..	..	..	98.4	103.4	100.9	100.0	104.2	114.8	125.1	..	Domestic Absorption
67.9	68.5	68.0	65.3	68.7	82.7	100.0	101.4	101.4	98.9	..	Agriculture
69.9	77.2	81.5	85.2	91.6	95.8	100.0	103.5	106.7	107.8	..	Industry
70.1	73.9	78.1	86.3	92.1	96.5	100.0	104.4	105.5	105.9	..	Manufacturing
81.0	87.3	92.6	97.8	100.4	100.9	100.0	104.0	109.8	..	..	Consumer Price Index
											MANUFACTURING ACTIVITY
..	..	..	..	..	..	..	..	..	..	..	Employment (1987=100)
..	..	..	..	..	..	..	..	..	..	..	Real Earnings per Empl. (1987=100)
..	..	..	..	..	..	..	..	..	..	..	Real Output per Empl. (1987=100)
..	..	..	..	..	..	..	..	..	..	..	Earnings as % of Value Added
			(Millions of current Eastern Caribbean Dollars)								**MONETARY HOLDINGS**
141.16	146.61	146.96	148.42	177.21	226.95	253.55	299.63	322.25	354.42	..	Money Supply, Broadly Defined
53.32	59.57	58.10	50.71	54.12	69.34	74.31	83.00	87.99	91.09	..	Money
37.41	39.95	41.36	20.58	25.07	30.69	33.07	35.13	31.40	38.05	..	Currency Outside Banks
15.91	19.62	16.74	30.13	29.05	38.65	41.24	47.87	56.59	53.04	..	Demand Deposits
87.83	87.03	88.86	97.71	123.09	157.61	179.24	216.63	234.26	263.32	..	Quasi-Money
			(Thousands of current Eastern CaribbeanDollars)								
..	..	..	..	..	..	..	..	..	..	..	**GOVERNMENT DEFICIT (-) OR SURPLUS**
..	..	..	..	..	..	..	..	..	..	..	Current Revenue
..	..	..	..	..	..	..	..	..	..	..	Current Expenditure
..	..	..	..	..	..	..	..	..	..	..	Current Budget Balance
..	..	..	..	..	..	..	..	..	..	..	Capital Receipts
..	..	..	..	..	..	..	..	..	..	..	Capital Payments

GRENADA	1970	1971	1972	1973	1974	1975	1976	1977	1978	1979	1980
FOREIGN TRADE (CUSTOMS BASIS)				*(Thousands of current US dollars)*							
Value of Exports, fob	..	..	..	..	..	..	..	..	..	..	..
Nonfuel Primary Products	..	..	..	..	..	..	..	..	..	..	..
Fuels	..	..	..	..	..	..	..	..	..	..	..
Manufactures	..	..	..	..	..	..	..	..	..	..	..
Value of Imports, cif	..	..	..	..	..	..	..	..	..	..	..
Nonfuel Primary Products	..	..	..	..	..	..	..	..	..	..	..
Fuels	..	..	..	..	..	..	..	..	..	..	..
Manufactures	..	..	..	..	..	..	..	..	..	..	..
Terms of Trade					*(Index 1987 = 100)*						
Export Prices, fob	..	..	..	..	..	..	..	..	..	..	..
Import Prices, cif	..	..	..	..	..	..	..	..	..	..	..
BALANCE OF PAYMENTS					*(Millions of current US dollars)*						
Exports of Goods & Services	..	..	..	..	..	..	..	29.16	33.60	41.35	39.10
Merchandise, fob	..	..	..	..	..	..	..	14.26	16.90	21.40	17.40
Nonfactor Services	..	..	..	..	..	..	..	14.60	16.40	19.15	20.60
Factor Services	..	..	..	..	..	..	..	0.30	0.30	0.80	1.10
Imports of Goods & Services	..	..	..	..	..	..	..	33.09	40.35	55.66	63.06
Merchandise, fob	..	..	..	..	..	..	..	28.54	33.35	42.64	48.79
Nonfactor Services	..	..	..	..	..	..	..	4.35	6.60	12.42	11.07
Factor Services	..	..	..	..	..	..	..	0.20	0.40	0.60	3.20
Long-Term Interest	0.10	0.20	0.50	0.50	0.40	0.40	0.40	0.40	0.30	0.40	0.50
Private Current Transfers, net	..	..	..	..	..	..	..	4.50	7.00	6.30	11.50
Workers' Remittances	..	..	..	..	..	..	..	..	..	..	..
Curr. A/C Bal before Off. Transf.	..	..	..	..	..	..	..	0.57	0.25	-8.01	-12.46
Net Official Transfers	..	..	..	..	..	..	..	0.74	0.80	6.90	12.73
Curr. A/C Bal after Off. Transf.	..	..	..	..	..	..	..	1.31	1.05	-1.11	0.27
Long-Term Capital, net	..	..	..	..	..	..	..	1.49	2.29	2.21	1.21
Direct Investment	..	..	..	..	..	..	..	-0.10	1.40		
Long-Term Loans	3.00	0.20	-0.20	0.20	0.60	0.80	-0.20	1.60	2.40	1.10	0.10
Disbursements	3.00	0.40	0.00	0.40	0.90	1.20	0.90	1.80	3.20	1.40	1.00
Repayments	0.00	0.20	0.20	0.20	0.30	0.40	1.10	0.20	0.80	0.30	0.90
Other Long-Term Capital	..	..	..	..	..	..	..	-0.01	-1.51	1.11	1.11
Other Capital, net	..	..	..	..	..	..	..	-2.93	-1.54	1.43	0.11
Change in Reserves	-5.32	-0.51	0.22	0.60	-0.36	0.51	-3.34	0.13	-1.79	-2.53	-1.60
Memo Item:					*(Eastern Caribbean Dollars per US dollar)*						
Conversion Factor (Annual Avg)	2.000	1.970	1.920	1.960	2.050	2.170	2.610	2.700	2.700	2.700	2.700
EXTERNAL DEBT (Total)				*(Thousands of US dollars), outstanding at end of year*							
	7,600	8,000	7,800	7,800	8,200	8,900	8,800	11,700	14,600	17,700	16,600
Long-Term Debt (by debtor)	7,600	8,000	7,800	7,800	8,200	8,900	8,800	10,700	13,600	15,700	15,600
Central Bank, incl. IMF credit	0	0	0	0	0	900	1,400	1,700	2,700	3,200	2,800
Central Government	7,600	8,000	7,800	7,800	8,200	7,500	6,600	8,100	9,900	10,800	11,100
Rest of General Government	..	..	..	..	..	..	..	..	..	..	..
Non-financial Public Enterprises	0	0	0	0	0	500	800	900	1,000	1,700	1,700
Priv. Sector, incl non-guaranteed	..	..	..	..	..	..	..	..	..	..	..
Short-Term Debt	0	0	0	0	0	0	0	1,000	1,000	2,000	1,000
Memo Items:					*(Thousands of US dollars)*						
Int'l Reserves Excluding Gold	5,316	5,821	5,604	5,004	5,363	5,036	8,113	7,650	9,703	12,220	12,909
Gold Holdings (at market price)	..	..	..	..	..	..	..	..	..	..	..
SOCIAL INDICATORS											
Total Fertility Rate	4.6	4.5	4.5	4.4	4.3	4.3	4.2	4.1	4.0	3.9	3.8
Infant Mortality Rate	32.8	36.9	41.0	40.8	40.6	40.4	40.2	40.0	39.8	39.6	39.4
Life Expectancy at Birth	64.9	65.1	65.3	65.5	65.7	65.9	66.1	66.3	66.5	66.7	66.9
Urban Population, % of total	..	..	..	..	..	..	..	..	..	..	..
Food Prod. per capita (1987=100)	103.8	95.6	89.2	88.7	86.6	87.3	99.1	96.6	100.1	105.8	96.3
Labor Force, Agriculture (%)	..	..	..	..	..	..	..	..	..	..	..
Labor Force, Female (%)	..	..	..	..	..	..	..	..	..	..	..
Primary Schl. Enroll. Ratio	..	..	..	..	..	..	..	..	..	..	..
Primary Schl. Enroll. Ratio, Female	..	..	..	..	..	..	..	..	..	..	..
Secondary Schl. Enroll. Ratio	..	..	..	..	..	..	..	..	..	..	..

	1981	1982	1983	1984	1985	1986	1987	1988	1989	1990 estimate	Notes
(Thousands of current US dollars)											
FOREIGN TRADE (CUSTOMS BASIS)											
Value of Exports, fob	..	..	..	..	..	..	..	..	..	..	..
Nonfuel Primary Products	..	..	..	..	..	..	..	..	..	..	..
Fuels	..	..	..	..	..	..	..	..	..	..	..
Manufactures	..	..	..	..	..	..	..	..	..	..	..
Value of Imports, cif										..	..
Nonfuel Primary Products	..	..	..	..	..	..	..	..	..	..	..
Fuels	..	..	..	..	..	..	..	..	..	..	..
Manufactures	..	..	..	..	..	..	..	..	..	..	..
(Index 1987 = 100)											
Terms of Trade	..	..	..	..	..	..	..	..	..	..	..
Export Prices, fob	..	..	..	..	..	..	..	..	..	..	..
Import Prices, cif	..	..	..	..	..	..	..	..	..	..	..
(Millions of current US dollars)											
BALANCE OF PAYMENTS											
Exports of Goods & Services	39.00	38.30	39.60	41.20	54.09	69.29	80.04	85.51	85.99	..	..
Merchandise, fob	19.00	18.50	19.30	18.20	22.30	28.80	31.60	32.81	27.90	..	..
Nonfactor Services	18.70	18.30	18.60	21.60	30.59	38.89	46.94	51.20	56.99	..	..
Factor Services	1.30	1.50	1.70	1.40	1.20	1.60	1.50	1.50	1.10		..
Imports of Goods & Services	75.76	82.90	79.80	72.40	89.73	115.43	124.43	126.10	129.35	..	..
Merchandise, fob	56.07	59.03	57.88	51.12	65.56	85.97	92.80	94.50	92.48	..	..
Nonfactor Services	13.39	17.37	15.82	18.38	21.07	26.07	27.73	27.20	30.87	..	..
Factor Services	6.30	6.50	6.10	2.90	3.10	3.40	3.90	4.40	6.00	..	..
Long-Term Interest	0.40	0.60	0.80	1.10	1.10	1.00	1.90	2.40	1.10	1.10	..
Private Current Transfers, net	10.40	11.00	14.40	10.60	10.32	10.40	11.80	15.30	17.00	..	..
Workers' Remittances	..	..		..	..	..		..	..	..	..
Curr. A/C Bal before Off. Transf.	-26.36	-33.60	-25.80	-20.60	-25.32	-35.74	-32.59	-25.29	-26.36	..	..
Net Official Transfers	12.49	15.90	10.90	24.40	27.90	25.50	8.19	5.20	12.20	..	..
Curr. A/C Bal after Off. Transf.	-13.87	-17.70	-14.90	3.80	2.58	-10.24	-24.40	-20.09	-14.16	..	..
Long-Term Capital, net	7.61	10.74	15.91	8.04	4.91	10.95	23.90	23.81	11.50	..	..
Direct Investment		1.90	2.50	2.80	4.11	5.00	12.70	13.00	10.00	..	..
Long-Term Loans	7.00	12.40	13.20	2.80	1.10	3.90	8.20	5.20	5.70	13.50	..
Disbursements	7.50	13.00	16.20	4.70	2.90	6.50	10.70	8.20	6.40	14.60	..
Repayments	0.50	0.60	3.00	1.90	1.80	2.60	2.50	3.00	0.70	1.10	..
Other Long-Term Capital	0.61	-3.56	0.21	2.44	-0.30	2.05	3.00	5.61	-4.20		..
Other Capital, net	2.50	4.97	-0.92	-11.30	1.46	1.23	3.82	-9.23	1.46	..	..
Change in Reserves	3.76	1.99	-0.09	-0.54	-8.95	-1.94	-3.32	5.51	1.20	-2.51	..
(Eastern Caribbean Dollars per US dollar)											
Memo Item:											
Conversion Factor (Annual Avg)	2.700	2.700	2.700	2.700	2.700	2.700	2.700	2.700	2.700	2.700	..
(Thousands of US dollars), outstanding at end of year											
EXTERNAL DEBT (Total)	29,900	40,000	53,200	50,100	52,500	56,600	70,900	80,200	83,100	103,800	..
Long-Term Debt (by debtor)	27,900	38,000	50,700	48,300	50,900	54,400	67,700	70,900	72,600	91,100	..
Central Bank, incl. IMF credit	8,300	7,000	7,700	6,200	4,200	2,600	2,100	1,100	500	..	..
Central Government	17,600	28,600	39,100	37,700	41,900	46,300	59,400	64,000	66,600	86,000	..
Rest of General Government	..	..	..	..	..	..	..	..	..	..	..
Non-financial Public Enterprises	2,000	2,400	3,900	4,400	4,800	5,500	6,200	5,800	5,500	5,100	..
Priv. Sector, incl non-guaranteed	..	..	..	..	..	..	..	..	..	..	..
Short-Term Debt	2,000	2,000	2,500	1,800	1,600	2,200	3,200	9,300	10,500	12,700	..
(Thousands of US dollars)											
Memo Items:											
Int'l Reserves Excluding Gold	16,097	9,233	14,142	14,234	20,812	20,565	22,740	16,923	15,442	17,579	..
Gold Holdings (at market price)	..	..	..	..	..	..	..	..	..	..	..
SOCIAL INDICATORS											
Total Fertility Rate	3.7	3.6	3.6	3.5	3.4	3.4	3.3	3.2	3.1	3.1	..
Infant Mortality Rate	39.2	39.0	38.0	37.0	36.0	35.0	34.0	32.9	31.8	30.8	..
Life Expectancy at Birth	67.2	67.4	67.6	67.8	68.1	68.3	68.6	69.0	69.3	69.7	..
Urban Population, % of total	..	..	..	..	..	..	..	..	..	..	..
Food Prod. per capita (1987=100)	108.0	96.0	91.2	99.4	89.9	92.9	100.0	95.9	95.0	93.9	..
Labor Force, Agriculture (%)	..	..	..	..	..	..	..	..	..	..	..
Labor Force, Female (%)	..	..	..	..	..	..	..	..	..	..	..
Primary Schl. Enroll. Ratio	..	..	..	..	..	..	..	..	..	..	..
Primary Schl. Enroll. Ratio, Female	..	..	..	..	..	..	..	..	..	..	..
Secondary Schl. Enroll. Ratio	..	..	..	..	..	..	..	..	..	..	..

GUATEMALA	1970	1971	1972	1973	1974	1975	1976	1977	1978	1979	1980
CURRENT GNP PER CAPITA (US $)	360	380	390	430	500	570	660	790	900	1,030	1,120
POPULATION (thousands)	5,246	5,393	5,544	5,699	5,859	6,023	6,192	6,365	6,543	6,727	6,917

USE AND ORIGIN OF RESOURCES *(Millions of current Guatemalan Quetzales)*

	1970	1971	1972	1973	1974	1975	1976	1977	1978	1979	1980
Gross National Product (GNP)	1,862	1,941	2,054	2,521	3,112	3,577	4,292	5,448	6,044	6,890	7,808
Net Factor Income from Abroad	-42	-44	-47	-48	-50	-69	-74	-33	-26	-12	-71
GDP at Market Prices	1,904	1,985	2,101	2,569	3,161	3,646	4,365	5,481	6,071	6,903	7,879
Resource Balance	15	-28	8	17	-103	-66	-262	-99	-351	-311	-215
Exports of Goods & NFServices	354	343	397	536	708	792	942	1,340	1,304	1,474	1,748
Imports of Goods & NFServices	339	371	389	519	811	858	1,204	1,439	1,655	1,784	1,963
Domestic Absorption	1,889	2,013	2,093	2,552	3,264	3,712	4,628	5,579	6,422	7,213	8,094
Private Consumption, etc.	1,493	1,588	1,682	2,034	2,470	2,875	3,396	4,127	4,675	5,432	6,217
General Gov't Consumption	151	139	157	167	207	250	297	355	435	488	627
Gross Domestic Investment	244	285	255	352	588	587	934	1,098	1,312	1,294	1,250
Fixed Investment	239	264	272	357	468	571	900	1,039	1,218	1,286	1,294
Indirect Taxes, net	132	138	144	170	227	252	316	492	536	543	597
GDP at factor cost	1,772	1,847	1,958	2,399	2,935	3,394	4,049	4,988	5,535	6,360	7,282
Agriculture	..	..	..	..	..	..	..	..	..	..	..
Industry	..	..	..	..	..	..	..	..	..	..	..
Manufacturing	..	..	..	..	..	..	..	..	..	..	..
Services, etc.	..	..	..	..	..	..	..	..	..	..	..
Gross Domestic Saving	259	257	263	369	485	521	672	1,000	961	983	1,035
Gross National Saving	234	240	246	364	492	530	796	1,061	1,050	1,094	1,073

(Millions of 1987 Guatemalan Quetzales)

	1970	1971	1972	1973	1974	1975	1976	1977	1978	1979	1980
Gross National Product	10,181.3	10,734.5	11,521.3	12,365.4	13,183.0	13,408.5	14,417.8	15,683.1	16,464.7	17,245.7	17,808.2
GDP at Market Prices	10,429.2	11,011.5	11,819.0	12,620.6	13,425.2	13,687.0	14,698.1	15,845.9	16,637.6	17,419.5	18,076.9
Resource Balance	-1,321.2	-1,458.7	-890.6	-991.6	-1,369.6	-1,029.2	-2,119.7	-2,429.8	-2,706.4	-1,838.2	-1,101.8
Exports of Goods & NFServices	2,345.9	2,443.6	2,794.1	3,061.9	3,265.3	3,373.1	3,595.5	3,819.3	3,815.2	4,198.3	4,414.6
Imports of Goods & NFServices	3,667.2	3,902.2	3,684.7	4,053.5	4,634.9	4,402.4	5,715.2	6,249.1	6,521.7	6,036.5	5,516.4
Domestic Absorption	11,750.4	12,470.2	12,709.5	13,612.2	14,794.8	14,716.2	16,817.7	18,275.7	19,344.1	19,257.8	19,178.7
Private Consumption, etc.	9,385.2	9,892.5	10,374.5	10,971.8	11,437.8	11,709.0	12,854.9	13,905.7	14,561.5	14,914.3	15,183.3
General Gov't Consumption	676.4	626.3	692.5	693.1	725.9	799.7	888.6	948.3	1,008.1	1,071.1	1,199.3
Gross Domestic Investment	1,688.8	1,951.3	1,642.5	1,947.4	2,631.1	2,207.5	3,074.3	3,421.7	3,774.5	3,272.4	2,796.1
Fixed Investment	1,723.0	1,869.3	1,858.7	2,070.7	2,032.1	2,224.5	3,053.1	3,335.9	3,581.7	3,395.1	3,066.3
GDP at factor cost	..	..	..	..	..	..	..	..	..	..	..
Agriculture	..	..	..	..	..	..	..	..	..	..	..
Industry	..	..	..	..	..	..	..	..	..	..	..
Manufacturing	..	..	..	..	..	..	..	..	..	..	..
Services, etc.	..	..	..	..	..	..	..	..	..	..	..

Memo Items:

	1970	1971	1972	1973	1974	1975	1976	1977	1978	1979	1980
Capacity to Import	3,830.8	3,607.8	3,758.5	4,189.4	4,046.6	4,063.7	4,469.7	5,820.5	5,137.3	4,985.1	4,911.5
Terms of Trade Adjustment	1,484.8	1,164.2	964.4	1,127.5	781.2	690.6	874.2	2,001.2	1,322.1	786.8	496.9
Gross Domestic Income	11,914.0	12,175.7	12,783.3	13,748.1	14,206.4	14,377.6	15,572.3	17,847.1	17,959.8	18,206.4	18,573.8
Gross National Income	11,666.1	11,898.7	12,485.7	13,492.9	13,964.2	14,099.1	15,292.0	17,684.3	17,786.8	18,032.5	18,305.0

DOMESTIC PRICES/DEFLATORS *(Index 1987 = 100)*

	1970	1971	1972	1973	1974	1975	1976	1977	1978	1979	1980
Overall (GDP)	18.3	18.0	17.8	20.4	23.5	26.6	29.7	34.6	36.5	39.6	43.6
Domestic Absorption	16.1	16.1	16.5	18.7	22.1	25.2	27.5	30.5	33.2	37.5	42.2
Agriculture	..	..	..	..	..	..	..	..	..	..	..
Industry	..	..	..	..	..	..	..	..	..	..	..
Manufacturing	..	..	..	..	..	..	..	..	..	..	..
Consumer Price Index	18.2	18.1	18.2	20.7	24.1	27.3	30.2	33.9	36.7	40.9	45.3

MANUFACTURING ACTIVITY

	1970	1971	1972	1973	1974	1975	1976	1977	1978	1979	1980
Employment (1987=100)	..	90.1	96.5	91.8	99.5	102.0	108.2	114.9	122.6	124.4	128.7
Real Earnings per Empl. (1987=100)	..	134.3	138.0	141.4	127.9	127.7	114.5	101.2	102.3	113.9	112.8
Real Output per Empl. (1987=100)	..	..	..	..	..	..	..	..	..	..	..
Earnings as % of Value Added	..	26.7	29.9	27.0	24.4	24.0	21.0	18.3	18.3	21.5	22.5

MONETARY HOLDINGS *(Millions of current Guatemalan Quetzales)*

	1970	1971	1972	1973	1974	1975	1976	1977	1978	1979	1980
Money Supply, Broadly Defined	343.7	383.3	476.9	579.8	668.3	808.5	1,051.8	1,249.1	1,423.6	1,537.2	1,692.4
Money	172.8	178.9	214.4	264.3	305.4	353.6	493.8	594.1	664.0	734.9	752.8
Currency Outside Banks	96.5	99.0	114.1	137.3	158.3	175.4	236.6	284.4	324.6	365.4	381.0
Demand Deposits	76.3	79.9	100.3	127.0	147.1	178.2	257.2	309.7	339.4	369.5	371.8
Quasi-Money	170.9	204.4	262.5	315.5	362.9	454.9	558.0	655.0	759.6	802.3	939.6

(Millions of current Guatemalan Quetzales)

GOVERNMENT DEFICIT (-) OR SURPLUS	1970	1971	1972	1973	1974	1975	1976	1977	1978	1979	1980
	..	..	-45.15	-37.94	-45.57	-30.59	-111.25	-51.19	-71.15	-149.12	-307.28
Current Revenue	..	..	183.17	212.22	279.64	327.38	409.08	589.26	661.24	666.14	883.29
Current Expenditure	..	..	153.74	170.80	213.04	262.49	310.86	392.54	465.50	525.37	728.98
Current Budget Balance	..	..	29.43	41.42	66.60	64.89	98.22	196.72	195.74	140.77	154.31
Capital Receipts	..	..					0.56	0.23	0.25	0.29	1.35
Capital Payments	..	..	74.58	79.36	112.17	95.48	210.03	248.14	267.14	290.18	462.94

1981	1982	1983	1984	1985	1986	1987	1988	1989	1990 estimate	Notes	GUATEMALA
1,200	1,190	1,170	1,180	1,200	1,050	950	890	920	900	A	**CURRENT GNP PER CAPITA (US $)**
7,113	7,315	7,524	7,739	7,963	8,194	8,434	8,681	8,935	9,197	..	**POPULATION (thousands)**
				(Millions of current Guatemalan Quetzales)							**USE AND ORIGIN OF RESOURCES**
8,505	8,596	8,937	9,267	10,966	15,402	17,239	20,074	23,082	33,189	..	Gross National Product (GNP)
-103	-121	-113	-203	-214	-436	-472	-471	-563	-1,052	..	Net Factor Income from Abroad
8,607	8,717	9,050	9,470	11,180	15,838	17,711	20,545	23,645	34,241	..	GDP at Market Prices
-560	-340	-141	-204	-116	231	-1,141	-1,198	-1,215	-1,431	..	Resource Balance
1,471	1,289	1,176	1,231	1,336	2,542	2,807	3,308	4,070	7,091	..	Exports of Goods & NFServices
2,032	1,629	1,317	1,435	1,452	2,311	3,948	4,507	5,285	8,522	..	Imports of Goods & NFServices
9,168	9,057	9,191	9,673	11,296	15,607	18,852	21,743	24,860	35,672	..	Domestic Absorption
7,022	7,149	7,501	7,852	9,233	12,846	14,989	17,289	19,762	29,119	..	Private Consumption, etc.
680	675	688	726	777	1,124	1,400	1,640	1,906	2,394	..	General Gov't Consumption
1,466	1,233	1,002	1,096	1,285	1,637	2,464	2,815	3,192	4,158	..	Gross Domestic Investment
1,443	1,309	950	912	1,225	1,593	2,188	2,747	3,224	4,109	..	Fixed Investment
561	539	461	437	586	..	..	..	..	..	..	Indirect Taxes, net
8,047	8,178	8,589	9,033	10,594		..	..	..	..	B	GDP at factor cost
..	..	..			..	4,601	5,367	6,154	8,872	..	Agriculture
..	..	..	..	..		3,515	4,092	4,700	6,669	..	Industry
..	..	..	..	..	..	..	..	..	..	..	Manufacturing
..	..	..	..	..	..	9,595	11,086	12,791	18,701	..	Services, etc.
905	893	861	892	1,170	1,868	1,322	1,616	1,977	2,728	..	Gross Domestic Saving
892	834	778	718	975	1,527	1,102	1,516	1,918	2,464	..	Gross National Saving
				(Millions of 1987 Guatemalan Quetzales)							
17,880.4	17,222.9	16,790.7	16,698.8	16,752.0	16,617.4	17,238.6	17,979.1	18,704.5	19,297.0	..	Gross National Product
18,193.9	17,551.6	17,100.2	17,185.1	17,080.4	17,103.7	17,711.0	18,401.0	19,126.4	19,701.2	..	GDP at Market Prices
-1,511.5	-720.6	-266.6	-605.1	-47.6	-31.4	-1,141.5	-1,132.3	-976.3	-440.8	..	Resource Balance
3,778.6	3,459.3	3,083.0	2,983.3	3,078.2	2,644.3	2,807.0	2,965.0	3,378.6	3,720.3	..	Exports of Goods & NFServices
5,290.1	4,179.8	3,349.6	3,588.4	3,125.8	2,675.7	3,948.5	4,097.3	4,354.9	4,161.1	..	Imports of Goods & NFServices
19,705.3	18,272.2	17,366.8	17,790.2	17,128.0	17,135.1	18,852.5	19,533.3	20,102.7	20,142.0	..	Domestic Absorption
15,228.3	14,428.5	13,967.6	14,224.6	14,029.3	13,964.0	14,989.2	15,624.6	16,111.1	16,347.0	..	Private Consumption, etc.
1,252.6	1,237.0	1,238.0	1,270.9	1,244.0	1,308.6	1,399.6	1,470.1	1,505.1	1,563.8	..	General Gov't Consumption
3,224.4	2,606.7	2,161.1	2,294.7	1,854.7	1,862.5	2,463.7	2,438.6	2,486.5	2,231.1	..	Gross Domestic Investment
3,304.6	2,942.9	2,120.9	1,931.8	1,808.5	1,882.5	2,188.3	2,465.3	2,602.6	2,333.8	..	Fixed Investment
..	..	16,229.1	16,392.1	16,185.1	..	..	..	..	..	B	GDP at factor cost
..	..	4,333.5	4,403.9	4,415.5	4,380.6	4,601.1	4,806.5	4,980.4	5,149.7	..	Agriculture
..	..	3,506.3	3,395.2	3,356.8	3,438.2	3,515.0	3,664.5	3,803.6	3,842.5	..	Industry
..	..	..	..	..	..	..	..	..	..	..	Manufacturing
..	..	9,260.4	9,386.1	9,308.1	9,284.8	9,594.9	9,930.0	10,342.5	10,709.0	..	Services, etc.
											Memo Items:
3,830.5	3,307.4	2,991.0	3,079.5	2,876.4	2,943.4	2,807.0	3,007.9	3,353.5	3,462.4	..	Capacity to Import
51.9	-151.8	-92.0	96.2	-201.8	299.1	0.0	42.9	-25.0	-257.9	..	Terms of Trade Adjustment
18,245.8	17,399.8	17,008.2	17,281.3	16,878.6	17,402.7	17,711.0	18,443.9	19,101.4	19,443.3	..	Gross Domestic Income
17,932.3	17,071.1	16,698.7	16,795.0	16,550.2	16,916.4	17,238.6	18,022.0	18,679.5	19,039.1	..	Gross National Income
				(Index 1987 = 100)							**DOMESTIC PRICES/DEFLATORS**
47.3	49.7	52.9	55.1	65.5	92.6	100.0	111.7	123.6	173.8	..	Overall (GDP)
46.5	49.6	52.9	54.4	65.9	91.1	100.0	111.3	123.7	177.1	..	Domestic Absorption
..	..	..	..	..	..	100.0	111.7	123.6	172.3	..	Agriculture
..	..	..	..	..	..	100.0	111.7	123.6	173.6	..	Industry
..	..	..	..	..	..	..	..	..	..	..	Manufacturing
50.5	50.7	53.0	54.8	65.0	89.0	100.0	110.8	123.5	174.3	..	Consumer Price Index
											MANUFACTURING ACTIVITY
119.6	118.7	114.4	114.7	114.0	106.9	100.0	144.9	..	..	G	Employment (1987=100)
121.0	123.8	121.9	124.3	115.9	95.6	100.0	99.8	..	..	G	Real Earnings per Empl. (1987=100)
..	..	..	..	..	..	100.0	109.9	..	..	..	Real Output per Empl. (1987=100)
21.9	25.9	23.0	23.7	22.3	22.0	19.4	18.9	..	..	..	Earnings as % of Value Added
				(Millions of current Guatemalan Quetzales)							**MONETARY HOLDINGS**
1,906.7	2,190.7	2,155.1	2,399.1	3,192.9	3,875.1	4,167.8	4,995.0	5,800.6	7,296.3	..	Money Supply, Broadly Defined
775.9	786.6	833.8	869.4	1,346.5	1,608.4	1,765.6	2,019.0	2,437.8	3,241.5	..	Money
405.2	404.6	437.9	460.9	697.8	804.6	931.2	1,069.0	1,329.2	1,897.1	..	Currency Outside Banks
370.7	382.0	395.9	408.5	648.7	803.8	834.4	950.0	1,108.6	1,344.4	..	Demand Deposits
1,130.8	1,404.1	1,321.3	1,529.7	1,846.4	2,266.7	2,402.2	2,976.0	3,362.8	4,054.8	..	Quasi-Money
				(Millions of current Guatemalan Quetzales)							**GOVERNMENT DEFICIT (-) OR SURPLUS**
-535.40	-416.91	-317.99	-360.72	-201.61	-91.55	-133.72	-218.13	-408.25	..	F	
895.89	880.88	874.00	664.38	862.25	1,461.88	1,851.91	2,291.24	2,427.14	..	..	Current Revenue
818.27	804.67	888.20	761.03	819.93	1,230.61	1,723.94	2,088.86	2,436.89	..	..	Current Expenditure
77.62	76.21	-14.20	-96.65	42.32	231.27	127.97	202.38	-9.75	..	..	Current Budget Balance
2.65	0.59	..	0.16	0.24	..	0.02	0.09	0.07	..	..	Capital Receipts
615.67	493.71	303.79	264.23	244.17	322.82	261.71	420.60	398.57	..	..	Capital Payments

GUATEMALA	1970	1971	1972	1973	1974	1975	1976	1977	1978	1979	1980
FOREIGN TRADE (CUSTOMS BASIS)				*(Millions of current US dollars)*							
Value of Exports, fob	290.2	283.1	328.1	436.1	572.1	623.4	760.3	1,160.2	1,111.6	1,160.9	1,486.1
Nonfuel Primary Products	208.9	204.9	241.7	318.8	418.7	468.1	580.8	957.2	881.8	892.6	1,111.4
Fuels	0.1	0.2	0.1	0.1	0.4	0.4	0.3	0.2	0.3	0.4	15.6
Manufactures	81.2	78.1	86.3	117.2	153.0	154.9	179.2	202.8	229.5	268.0	359.1
Value of Imports, cif	284.3	303.3	327.7	427.4	700.5	732.6	838.4	1,052.5	1,260.7	1,361.8	1,559.1
Nonfuel Primary Products	40.7	41.1	40.0	52.3	86.1	86.8	77.3	90.0	119.8	134.9	174.4
Fuels	6.2	15.3	25.0	31.5	94.0	103.3	106.0	148.4	160.7	145.9	377.4
Manufactures	237.4	246.9	262.7	343.7	520.4	542.5	655.1	814.1	980.2	1,080.9	1,007.3
				(Index 1987 = 100)							
Terms of Trade	139.2	141.5	159.7	165.6	136.5	119.4	158.7	184.1	143.7	132.7	125.0
Export Prices, fob	40.4	38.8	43.4	57.7	71.4	66.2	90.1	112.9	98.8	110.1	119.6
Import Prices, cif	29.1	27.5	27.2	34.8	52.3	55.4	56.8	61.3	68.8	83.0	95.7
BALANCE OF PAYMENTS				*(Millions of current US dollars)*							
Exports of Goods & Services	353.7	342.2	397.7	541.7	720.1	797.5	1,007.7	1,369.6	1,349.1	1,552.0	1,834.0
Merchandise, fob	297.1	286.9	335.9	442.0	582.3	641.0	760.4	1,160.2	1,092.4	1,221.4	1,519.8
Nonfactor Services	52.4	51.8	58.1	89.9	119.7	141.9	208.3	161.0	183.6	228.0	210.8
Factor Services	4.2	3.6	3.7	9.8	18.2	14.6	39.0	48.4	73.1	102.6	103.4
Imports of Goods & Services	379.1	416.7	439.2	576.4	878.6	941.0	1,284.1	1,500.7	1,735.2	1,884.2	2,107.1
Merchandise, fob	266.6	290.0	294.8	391.4	631.5	672.4	950.7	1,087.0	1,283.8	1,401.7	1,472.6
Nonfactor Services	70.1	81.2	95.1	129.3	181.0	188.0	250.4	338.3	360.7	382.5	486.1
Factor Services	42.4	45.5	49.3	55.7	66.1	80.6	83.0	75.4	90.7	100.0	148.4
Long-Term Interest	7.0	8.6	8.6	10.2	11.1	12.5	14.6	20.0	32.7	48.2	59.5
Private Current Transfers, net	17.4	26.3	31.2	43.2	56.6	78.3	197.7	93.9	115.0	123.2	108.6
Workers' Remittances	..	..	..	..	..	..	..	..	..	..	36.6
Curr. A/C Bal before Off. Transf.	-8.0	-48.2	-10.3	8.5	-101.9	-65.2	-78.7	-37.2	-271.1	-209.0	-164.5
Net Official Transfers	0.1	-1.0	-1.2	-0.7	-1.2	-0.5	1.2	1.9	0.6	3.4	1.2
Curr. A/C Bal after Off. Transf.	-7.9	-49.2	-11.5	7.7	-103.1	-65.7	-77.5	-35.3	-270.5	-205.6	-163.3
Long-Term Capital, net	53.6	39.2	25.5	49.4	58.1	146.3	83.2	198.2	263.2	241.5	238.1
Direct Investment	29.4	28.6	15.9	34.8	47.4	80.0	12.5	97.5	127.2	117.0	110.7
Long-Term Loans	21.2	13.9	5.6	28.4	29.2	49.8	45.2	108.9	156.3	184.1	92.5
Disbursements	43.2	36.4	44.4	47.2	60.7	72.3	74.4	141.8	202.7	248.9	170.1
Repayments	22.0	22.5	38.8	18.8	31.5	22.5	29.2	32.9	46.4	64.8	77.6
Other Long-Term Capital	3.0	-3.3	4.1	-13.9	-18.5	16.5	25.5	-8.2	-20.3	-59.6	34.9
Other Capital, net	-30.3	20.1	25.0	23.8	33.8	23.6	213.8	18.8	75.6	-61.6	-332.7
Change in Reserves	-15.4	-10.1	-39.0	-81.0	11.2	-104.2	-219.5	-181.7	-68.3	25.7	257.9
Memo Item:				*(Guatemalan Quetzales per US dollar)*							
Conversion Factor (Annual Avg)	1.000	1.000	1.000	1.000	1.000	1.000	1.000	1.000	1.000	1.000	1.000
EXTERNAL DEBT (Total)	120.4	134.2	139.8	165.9	195.1	243.3	288.5	652.2	813.0	1,039.7	1,165.9
Long-Term Debt (by debtor)	120.4	134.2	139.8	165.9	195.1	243.3	288.5	397.2	554.0	738.7	830.9
Central Bank, incl. IMF credit	16.4	14.9	12.0	6.3	7.0	9.7	7.1	6.1	8.3	16.4	44.9
Central Government	66.9	64.4	63.8	71.9	66.6	80.1	92.8	139.3	207.4	271.1	336.8
Rest of General Government	4.4	3.2	0.3	1.5	5.4	6.1	7.1	8.7	8.2	8.5	7.3
Non-financial Public Enterprises	17.6	30.4	33.0	36.1	41.1	47.4	56.5	63.1	80.1	130.7	159.8
Priv. Sector, incl non-guaranteed	15.1	21.3	30.7	50.1	75.0	100.0	125.0	180.0	250.0	312.0	282.1
Short-Term Debt	0.0	0.0	0.0	0.0	0.0	0.0	0.0	255.0	259.0	301.0	335.0
Memo Items:				*(Millions of US dollars)*							
Int'l Reserves Excluding Gold	60.8	74.7	116.3	191.3	181.3	283.8	491.0	668.9	741.5	696.3	444.7
Gold Holdings (at market price)	18.7	21.6	31.9	55.2	91.7	68.9	66.2	83.6	116.3	267.4	307.9
SOCIAL INDICATORS											
Total Fertility Rate	6.5	6.5	6.5	6.4	6.4	6.4	6.4	6.4	6.3	6.3	6.2
Infant Mortality Rate	100.2	97.6	95.0	93.2	91.4	89.6	87.8	86.0	84.2	82.4	80.6
Life Expectancy at Birth	52.5	53.2	54.0	54.5	55.0	55.4	55.9	56.4	56.9	57.4	58.0
Urban Population, % of total	35.5	35.7	36.0	36.2	36.5	36.8	37.0	37.1	37.3	37.4	
Food Prod. per capita (1987=100)	112.3	112.4	115.6	116.7	113.4	116.6	119.8	118.6	115.8	108.6	107.7
Labor Force, Agriculture (%)	61.3	60.8	60.4	59.9	59.5	59.1	58.6	58.1	57.7	57.3	56.8
Labor Force, Female (%)	13.1	13.2	13.3	13.3	13.4	13.5	13.5	13.6	13.7	13.7	13.8
Primary Schl. Enroll. Ratio	57.0	..	..	..	..	61.0	61.0	63.0	65.0	67.0	71.0
Primary Schl. Enroll. Ratio, Female	51.0	..	..	..	..	56.0	56.0	58.0	60.0	61.0	65.0
Secondary Schl. Enroll. Ratio	8.0	..	..	..	..	12.0	13.0	13.0	14.0	16.0	18.0

1981	1982	1983	1984	1985	1986	1987	1988	1989	1990 estimate	Notes	GUATEMALA
				(Millions of current US dollars)							**FOREIGN TRADE (CUSTOMS BASIS)**
1,114.8	1,083.8	1,118.4	1,094.6	974.5	1,072.6	899.2	1,067.9	1,126.2	1,211.4	..	Value of Exports, fob
768.4	763.7	773.4	812.5	758.0	859.1	669.5	795.1	838.6	902.0	..	Nonfuel Primary Products
21.8	33.3	67.2	26.2	16.4	29.5	16.3	19.4	20.5	22.0	..	Fuels
324.6	286.8	277.7	255.9	200.1	184.0	213.3	253.3	267.2	287.4	..	Manufactures
1,688.3	1,420.4	1,154.3	1,472.2	1,296.7	1,035.5	1,448.6	1,557.0	1,664.0	1,625.9	..	Value of Imports, cif
150.0	159.6	143.5	148.5	158.1	197.9	271.2	291.5	311.5	304.4	..	Nonfuel Primary Products
638.7	273.5	195.2	485.7	463.6	173.9	185.2	199.1	212.7	207.9	..	Fuels
899.6	987.3	815.6	838.0	675.1	663.6	992.2	1,066.5	1,139.7	1,113.6	..	Manufactures
				(Index 1987 = 100)							
105.7	107.0	111.2	113.0	108.3	128.6	100.0	109.3	106.7	102.3	..	Terms of Trade
105.7	101.1	101.1	100.9	96.0	113.2	100.0	114.1	109.9	115.3	..	Export Prices, fob
100.0	94.5	90.9	89.3	88.6	88.1	100.0	104.4	103.0	112.7	..	Import Prices, cif
				(Millions of current US dollars)							**BALANCE OF PAYMENTS**
1,525.9	1,312.2	1,205.0	1,261.2	1,191.3	1,203.2	1,167.3	1,300.7	1,454.8	1,585.0	f	Exports of Goods & Services
1,291.3	1,170.4	1,091.7	1,132.2	1,059.7	1,043.8	977.9	1,073.3	1,126.1	1,211.5	..	Merchandise, fob
154.8	107.5	80.2	96.0	101.1	123.3	158.3	195.8	297.7	364.3	..	Nonfactor Services
79.8	34.3	33.1	33.0	30.5	36.1	31.1	31.6	31.0	9.2	..	Factor Services
2,189.5	1,774.0	1,459.5	1,667.3	1,457.3	1,295.9	1,803.1	1,939.0	2,071.7	2,095.4	f	Imports of Goods & Services
1,540.0	1,284.3	1,056.0	1,182.2	1,076.7	875.7	1,333.2	1,413.2	1,484.4	1,428.0	..	Merchandise, fob
483.7	341.5	257.5	245.3	180.0	170.0	259.5	317.9	376.9	465.7	..	Nonfactor Services
165.8	148.2	146.0	239.8	200.6	250.2	210.4	207.9	210.4	201.7	..	Factor Services
63.5	76.8	88.9	94.9	116.0	156.6	154.1	117.2	108.8	85.4	..	Long-Term Interest
89.5	61.9	29.8	28.0	18.9	50.6	101.0	141.7	178.8	175.7	..	Private Current Transfers, net
28.1	19.2	9.8	9.1	5.9	15.2	30.5	42.7	68.6	..	..	Workers' Remittances
-574.1	-399.9	-224.7	-378.1	-247.1	-42.1	-534.8	-496.6	-438.1	-334.7	..	Curr. A/C Bal before Off. Transf.
1.4	0.8	0.8	0.7	0.8	24.5	92.3	82.6	71.0	55.5	..	Net Official Transfers
-572.7	-399.1	-223.9	-377.4	-246.3	-17.6	-442.5	-414.0	-367.1	-279.2	..	Curr. A/C Bal after Off. Transf.
397.7	339.4	283.5	194.0	241.7	44.6	136.8	108.0	125.7	214.7	f	Long-Term Capital, net
127.1	77.1	45.0	38.0	61.8	68.8	150.2	329.7	76.2	84.6	..	Direct Investment
279.7	278.7	225.0	92.6	142.0	20.9	-68.5	-7.9	5.9	56.9	..	Long-Term Loans
344.3	337.3	313.5	254.3	294.4	175.4	85.0	207.8	162.4	147.2	..	Disbursements
64.6	58.6	88.5	161.7	152.4	154.5	153.5	215.7	156.5	90.3	..	Repayments
-9.1	-16.4	13.5	63.4	37.9	-45.1	55.1	-213.8	43.6	73.2	..	Other Long-Term Capital
-126.3	21.3	-50.0	200.0	111.8	81.9	251.7	167.1	310.1	52.4	f	Other Capital, net
301.3	38.4	-9.6	-16.6	-107.2	-108.9	54.0	138.9	-68.7	12.1	..	Change in Reserves
				(Guatemalan Quetzales per US dollar)							**Memo Item:**
1.000	1.000	1.000	1.000	1.150	2.190	2.500	2.620	2.820	4.490		Conversion Factor (Annual Avg)
				(Millions of US dollars), outstanding at end of year							
1,264.3	1,537.2	1,799.5	2,353.3	2,653.4	2,768.2	2,768.8	2,604.9	2,593.9	2,776.8	..	**EXTERNAL DEBT (Total)**
1,127.9	1,417.5	1,680.3	2,202.3	2,387.8	2,457.3	2,486.7	2,309.4	2,274.0	2,372.2	..	Long-Term Debt (by debtor)
272.2	385.6	563.0	1,141.8	1,183.4	1,114.1	1,048.3	840.2	776.4	752.5	..	Central Bank, incl. IMF credit
424.8	517.4	603.0	624.2	696.4	782.7	845.6	909.9	910.5	992.4	..	Central Government
6.7	6.6	5.8	4.8	3.8	3.3	2.2	1.6	1.3	1.5	..	Rest of General Government
213.8	339.3	353.6	325.5	397.2	435.7	471.8	441.9	460.2	496.1	..	Non-financial Public Enterprises
210.4	168.6	154.9	106.0	107.0	121.5	118.8	115.8	125.6	129.7	..	Priv. Sector, incl non-guaranteed
136.4	119.7	119.2	151.0	265.6	310.9	282.1	295.5	319.9	404.6	..	Short-Term Debt
				(Millions of US dollars)							**Memo Items:**
149.7	112.2	210.0	274.4	300.9	362.1	287.8	201.2	306.0	282.0	..	Int'l Reserves Excluding Gold
207.6	238.6	199.3	161.0	170.8	204.2	253.1	214.6	217.5	79.8	..	Gold Holdings (at market price)
											SOCIAL INDICATORS
6.2	6.1	6.0	5.9	5.8	5.7	5.6	5.5	5.5	5.4	..	Total Fertility Rate
78.8	77.0	75.2	73.4	71.6	69.8	68.0	66.0	64.0	62.1	..	Infant Mortality Rate
58.5	59.0	59.6	60.2	60.8	61.4	62.0	62.4	62.8	63.2	..	Life Expectancy at Birth
37.5	37.7	37.8	38.0	38.1	38.4	38.6	38.9	39.1	39.4	..	Urban Population, % of total
110.7	113.3	109.6	106.1	106.8	102.2	100.0	99.7	98.1	100.5	..	Food Prod. per capita (1987=100)
..	..	..	..	..	..	..	..	..	..	..	Labor Force, Agriculture (%)
14.1	14.4	14.6	14.9	15.1	15.4	15.6	15.9	16.1	16.4	..	Labor Force, Female (%)
..	70.0	75.0	76.0	76.0	76.0	77.0	79.0		..	..	Primary Schl. Enroll. Ratio
..	65.0	69.0	..	70.0	70.0			..	..	..	Primary Schl. Enroll. Ratio, Female
..	17.0	17.0	19.0	19.0	20.0	21.0	..	..	..	..	Secondary Schl. Enroll. Ratio

GUINEA-BISSAU	1970	1971	1972	1973	1974	1975	1976	1977	1978	1979	1980
CURRENT GNP PER CAPITA (US $)	..	..	160	160	170	190	170	160	170	170	130
POPULATION (thousands)	526	537	552	573	598	628	662	701	742	779	809

USE AND ORIGIN OF RESOURCES *(Millions of current Guinea-Bissau Pesos)*

	1970	1971	1972	1973	1974	1975	1976	1977	1978	1979	1980
Gross National Product (GNP)	2,810	2,749	3,070	3,428	3,904	4,615	4,492	4,368	5,234	5,801	5,223
Net Factor Income from Abroad	0	0	0	0	0	101	-316	-232	-299	-84	-33
GDP at Market Prices	2,810	2,749	3,070	3,428	3,904	4,513	4,808	4,600	5,533	5,885	5,257
Resource Balance	-736	-829	-960	-1,188	-1,336	-937	-1,090	-1,072	-1,523	-1,917	-1,869
Exports of Goods & NFServices	112	114	134	208	196	234	254	428	472	527	439
Imports of Goods & NFServices	848	943	1,094	1,396	1,532	1,171	1,343	1,500	1,995	2,444	2,308
Domestic Absorption	3,546	3,578	4,030	4,616	5,240	5,450	5,897	5,672	7,056	7,802	7,126
Private Consumption, etc.	2,155	2,213	2,632	3,061	3,598	3,722	3,918	3,909	4,686	5,208	4,046
General Gov't Consumption	560	595	699	839	985	1,033	1,197	853	1,169	1,309	1,525
Gross Domestic Investment	831	770	698	716	656	695	782	910	1,200	1,285	1,555
Fixed Investment	..	..	..	..	..	..	..	..	..	..	..
Indirect Taxes, net	125	128	134	168	178	107	169	159	202	336	321
GDP at factor cost	2,685	2,621	2,936	3,259	3,726	4,406	4,639	4,441	5,332	5,549	4,935
Agriculture	1,333	1,233	1,405	1,470	1,615	2,156	2,312	2,123	2,856	3,036	2,328
Industry	597	607	689	836	995	1,145	747	1,041	1,106	1,169	1,033
Manufacturing	597	..	..	..	..	..	..	..	..	..	..
Services, etc.	880	909	975	1,122	1,293	1,212	1,749	1,436	1,571	1,680	1,895
Gross Domestic Saving	95	-59	-262	-472	-680	-242	-308	-162	-322	-632	-314
Gross National Saving	..	..	..	..	..	..	..	..	..	..	..

(Millions of 1987 Guinea-Bissau Pesos)

	1970	1971	1972	1973	1974	1975	1976	1977	1978	1979	1980
Gross National Product	60,745.8	61,409.0	64,054.8	66,632.2	69,523.1	76,234.0	72,465.6	68,003.4	77,250.2	80,881.4	66,126.3
GDP at Market Prices	60,738.6	61,401.8	64,047.3	66,624.3	69,514.9	74,342.7	77,879.3	71,846.6	81,641.3	82,018.8	66,539.9
Resource Balance	-41,194.0	-42,003.0	-46,245.0	-44,106.0	-41,906.0	-24,091.0	-21,814.0	-18,855.0	-19,849.0	-20,581.0	-15,859.0
Exports of Goods & NFServices	7,393.1	7,115.4	7,756.6	10,664.0	9,415.4	14,765.5	12,320.2	15,038.1	13,680.4	13,680.4	16,943.5
Imports of Goods & NFServices	48,587.3	49,118.6	54,001.3	54,769.5	51,321.0	38,856.9	34,134.1	33,892.9	33,529.9	34,261.6	32,802.3
Domestic Absorption	101,933.0	103,405.0	110,292.0	110,730.0	111,421.0	98,434.2	99,693.2	90,701.4	101,491.0	102,600.0	82,398.7
Private Consumption, etc.	39,662.0	49,618.8	62,051.8	69,421.6	76,728.0	65,351.4	63,084.8	53,015.9	51,727.6	43,683.8	38,130.7
General Gov't Consumption	7,468.7	7,643.2	8,536.0	8,884.3	9,377.4	8,994.6	10,171.5	7,150.8	9,326.7	8,854.6	9,012.2
Gross Domestic Investment	54,802.1	46,143.0	39,704.2	32,424.0	25,315.1	24,088.1	26,437.0	30,534.8	40,436.5	50,061.6	35,255.8
Fixed Investment	..	..	..	..	..	..	..	..	..	..	..
GDP at factor cost	..	..	..	..	..	..	..	..	..	..	..
Agriculture	40,210.2	37,030.6	40,089.1	39,750.5	41,139.0	41,725.2	44,994.5	39,172.5	44,883.0	41,291.3	25,808.1
Industry	12,435.7	11,472.8	12,369.1	11,957.0	12,095.7	14,298.9	8,876.6	11,651.0	15,911.8	15,906.4	13,839.2
Manufacturing	..	..	..	..	..	..	..	..	..	..	..
Services, etc.	8,440.6	10,190.6	9,978.9	11,420.7	12,770.2	15,157.0	20,821.2	18,514.5	17,649.7	22,803.4	27,578.3

Memo Items:

	1970	1971	1972	1973	1974	1975	1976	1977	1978	1979	1980
Capacity to Import	6,437.8	5,952.4	6,601.4	8,149.3	6,562.1	7,764.8	6,442.5	9,672.7	7,941.3	7,387.8	6,243.6
Terms of Trade Adjustment	-955.3	-1,163.0	-1,155.1	-2,514.7	-2,853.3	-7,000.8	-5,877.7	-5,365.4	-5,739.2	-6,292.6	-10,700.0
Gross Domestic Income	59,783.3	60,238.7	62,892.1	64,109.6	66,661.6	67,342.0	72,001.7	66,481.2	75,902.2	75,726.2	55,840.0
Gross National Income	59,790.5	60,246.0	62,899.7	64,117.5	66,669.9	69,233.2	66,587.9	62,638.0	71,511.0	74,588.8	55,426.4

DOMESTIC PRICES/DEFLATORS *(Index 1987 = 100)*

	1970	1971	1972	1973	1974	1975	1976	1977	1978	1979	1980
Overall (GDP)	4.6	4.5	4.8	5.1	5.6	6.1	6.2	6.4	6.8	7.2	7.9
Domestic Absorption	3.5	3.5	3.7	4.2	4.7	5.5	5.9	6.3	7.0	7.6	8.6
Agriculture	3.3	3.3	3.5	3.7	3.9	5.2	5.1	5.4	6.4	7.4	9.0
Industry	4.8	5.3	5.6	7.0	8.2	8.0	8.4	8.9	7.0	7.3	7.5
Manufacturing	..	..	..	..	..	..	..	..	..	..	..
Consumer Price Index	..	..	..	..	..	..	..	..	..	..	..

MANUFACTURING ACTIVITY

	1970	1971	1972	1973	1974	1975	1976	1977	1978	1979	1980
Employment (1987=100)	..	..	..	..	..	..	..	..	..	..	..
Real Earnings per Empl. (1987=100)	..	..	..	..	..	..	..	..	..	..	..
Real Output per Empl. (1987=100)	..	..	..	..	..	..	..	..	..	..	..
Earnings as % of Value Added	..	..	..	..	..	..	..	..	..	..	..

MONETARY HOLDINGS *(Millions of current Guinea-Bissau Pesos)*

	1970	1971	1972	1973	1974	1975	1976	1977	1978	1979	1980
Money Supply, Broadly Defined	..	..	..	..	..	..	..	..	..	..	..
Money	..	..	..	..	..	..	..	..	..	..	..
Currency Outside Banks	..	..	..	..	..	..	..	..	..	..	..
Demand Deposits	..	..	..	..	..	..	..	..	..	..	..
Quasi-Money	..	..	..	..	..	..	..	..	..	..	..

GOVERNMENT DEFICIT (-) OR SURPLUS *(Millions of current Guinea-Bissau Pesos)*

	1970	1971	1972	1973	1974	1975	1976	1977	1978	1979	1980
Current Revenue	..	..	..	..	..	..	..	..	..	..	..
Current Expenditure	..	..	..	..	..	..	..	..	..	..	..
Current Budget Balance	..	..	..	..	..	..	..	..	..	..	..
Capital Receipts	..	..	..	..	..	..	..	..	..	..	..
Capital Payments	..	..	..	..	..	..	..	..	..	..	..

1981	1982	1983	1984	1985	1986	1987	1988	1989	1990 estimate	Notes	GUINEA-BISSAU
170	190	200	190	180	160	170	170	180	180	A	**CURRENT GNP PER CAPITA (US $)**
824	839	854	870	886	903	921	939	959	980	..	**POPULATION (thousands)**

(Millions of current Guinea-Bissau Pesos)

1981	1982	1983	1984	1985	1986	1987	1988	1989	1990	Notes	
											USE AND ORIGIN OF RESOURCES
6,567	7,944	9,578	16,644	24,942	46,544	89,563	167,800	302,500	404,060	..	Gross National Product (GNP)
-71	-117	-24	-56	-296	-423	-2,777	-3,900	-4,000	-22,281	..	Net Factor Income from Abroad
6,638	8,061	9,602	16,700	25,238	46,967	92,340	171,700	306,500	426,341	f	GDP at Market Prices
-1,628	-2,696	-2,520	-6,398	-10,866	-11,993	-27,461	-69,000	-153,200	-143,186	..	Resource Balance
743	632	577	2,270	2,488	3,588	13,387	28,800	46,900	96,791	..	Exports of Goods & NF Services
2,371	3,328	3,097	8,668	13,354	15,580	40,848	97,800	200,100	239,977	..	Imports of Goods & NF Services
8,266	10,757	12,122	23,098	36,104	58,960	119,800	240,700	459,700	569,528	..	Domestic Absorption
4,666	6,106	7,502	13,965	21,909	41,135	78,275	152,904	307,500	420,242	f	Private Consumption, etc.
1,891	2,373	2,444	4,124	6,116	6,423	10,776	29,000	43,200	53,719	..	General Gov't Consumption
1,709	2,278	2,176	5,009	8,079	11,402	30,749	58,796	109,000	95,566	f	Gross Domestic Investment
..	..	..	..	..	..	..	..	..	..	..	Fixed Investment
499	506	..			1,544	3,037	5,359	9,500	14,069	..	Indirect Taxes, net
6,139	7,555	..	..		45,423	89,303	166,341	297,000	412,272	B f	GDP at factor cost
3,271	3,769	4,075	6,933	10,719	21,271	43,756	78,400	144,000	197,396	..	Agriculture
1,057	1,161	1,100	2,359	3,592	9,309	14,417	27,400	48,500	67,362	..	Industry
					5,400	10,530	18,540	31,900		..	Manufacturing
2,311	3,130	4,427	7,408	10,927	16,387	34,167	65,900	114,000	161,583	..	Services, etc.
81	-418	-344	-1,389	-2,787	-591	3,289	-10,204	-44,200	-47,620	..	Gross Domestic Saving
..	-1,093	-827	-1,961	-3,626	-1,320	-607	-12,437	-46,026	-67,279	..	Gross National Saving

(Millions of 1987 Guinea-Bissau Pesos)

1981	1982	1983	1984	1985	1986	1987	1988	1989	1990	Notes	
78,241.1	81,346.3	79,744.5	84,079.1	86,976.0	86,238.3	89,563.2	96,510.9	102,285.0	101,197.0	..	Gross National Product
79,112.6	82,620.9	79,964.7	84,367.2	87,996.5	87,115.9	92,339.9	98,617.1	103,550.0	106,697.0	f	GDP at Market Prices
-18,360.0	-31,469.0	-30,538.0	-33,462.0	-38,630.0	-36,698.0	-27,461.0	-31,418.0	-42,553.0	-28,829.0	..	Resource Balance
12,143.7	10,869.1	10,064.3	13,758.3	9,960.5	11,017.0	13,387.1	14,529.3	15,144.5	26,502.9	..	Exports of Goods & NF Services
30,503.2	42,337.8	40,602.3	47,220.5	48,590.1	47,715.3	40,847.6	45,947.6	57,698.0	55,332.4	..	Imports of Goods & NF Services
97,472.2	114,090.0	110,503.0	117,829.0	126,626.0	123,814.0	119,800.0	130,035.0	146,103.0	135,527.0	..	Domestic Absorption
58,612.6	65,044.5	62,386.7	68,091.8	72,309.7	69,387.4	78,275.2	81,448.1	80,370.5	86,095.4	f	Private Consumption, etc.
9,419.4	11,331.5	11,535.8	11,143.5	11,823.2	11,953.1	10,776.2	11,566.9	14,635.0	14,122.8	..	General Gov't Consumption
29,440.2	37,713.7	36,580.2	38,594.0	42,493.1	42,473.7	30,749.0	37,020.3	51,097.7	35,308.4	f	Gross Domestic Investment
..	..	..	..	..	..	..	..	..	..	..	Fixed Investment
..	..	..	..		84,242.5	89,302.9	95,537.8	100,339.0	103,037.0	B f	GDP at factor cost
33,127.5	35,015.1	34,316.1	35,413.6	37,786.7	39,475.8	43,755.6	45,178.1	48,715.4	49,933.3	..	Agriculture
13,278.9	14,474.3	14,226.8	18,506.7	19,447.8	17,275.9	14,417.2	15,789.4	16,408.2	16,900.5	..	Industry
..	..	..	..		10,048.6	10,530.0	10,651.4	10,779.5		..	Manufacturing
33,032.1	33,288.7	31,421.8	30,446.9	30,762.0	30,364.2	34,167.1	37,649.5	38,426.1	39,863.3	..	Services, etc.
											Memo Items:
9,558.8	8,040.1	7,564.6	12,366.2	9,052.9	10,987.1	13,387.1	13,530.6	13,523.4	22,317.4	..	Capacity to Import
-2,584.9	-2,829.0	-2,499.7	-1,392.1	-907.6	-29.9	0.0	-998.7	-1,621.1	-4,185.5	..	Terms of Trade Adjustment
76,527.7	79,791.9	77,465.0	82,975.1	87,088.9	87,085.9	92,339.9	97,618.4	101,929.0	102,512.0	..	Gross Domestic Income
75,656.3	78,517.3	77,244.7	82,687.0	86,068.4	86,208.3	89,563.2	95,512.2	100,664.0	97,011.8	..	Gross National Income

(Index 1987 = 100)

1981	1982	1983	1984	1985	1986	1987	1988	1989	1990	Notes	
											DOMESTIC PRICES/DEFLATORS
8.4	9.8	12.0	19.8	28.7	53.9	100.0	174.1	296.0	399.6	..	Overall (GDP)
8.5	9.4	11.0	19.6	28.5	47.6	100.0	185.1	314.6	420.2	..	Domestic Absorption
9.9	10.8	11.9	19.6	28.4	53.9	100.0	173.5	295.6	395.3	..	Agriculture
8.0	8.0	7.7	12.7	18.5	53.9	100.0	173.5	295.6	398.6	..	Industry
..	..	..	..		53.7	100.0	174.1	295.9		..	Manufacturing
..	..	..	..	..	..			..	..	..	Consumer Price Index
											MANUFACTURING ACTIVITY
	..	..	..	..	..		..	..			Employment (1987=100)
..	..	..	..	..	..		..	..			Real Earnings per Empl. (1987=100)
..	..	..	..	..			..	..			Real Output per Empl. (1987=100)
..	..	..	..	..	..		..	..			Earnings as % of Value Added

(Millions of current Guinea-Bissau Pesos)

1981	1982	1983	1984	1985	1986	1987	1988	1989	1990	Notes	
											MONETARY HOLDINGS
..	2,779	3,402	4,541	6,433	8,753	22,395	38,650	..	..	..	Money Supply, Broadly Defined
..	..	..	..	..	8,650	16,724	30,859	..	..	..	Money
..	..	..	..	..	5,468	9,309	15,976	..	..	..	Currency Outside Banks
..	..	..	..	..	3,183	7,416	14,883	..	..	..	Demand Deposits
..	..	..	..	..	102	5,671	7,792	..	..	..	Quasi-Money

(Millions of current Guinea-Bissau Pesos)

1981	1982	1983	1984	1985	1986	1987	1988	1989	1990	Notes	
											GOVERNMENT DEFICIT (-) OR SURPLUS
..	..	-2,215	-4,615	-7,163	-7,530	-17,893	-31,557	-53,558	..	..	Current Revenue
..	..	2,510	5,141	8,406	11,494	34,583	59,035	148,109	..	..	Current Expenditure
..	..	2,311	3,602	5,581	8,363	15,694	29,180	73,428	..	..	Current Budget Balance
..	..	199	1,539	2,825	3,131	18,889	29,855	74,681	..	..	Capital Receipts
..	..	5	7	7	9	13	14	58	..	..	Capital Payments
..	..	2,398	6,031	9,531	10,670	36,795	61,426	..	..	..	Capital Payments

GUINEA-BISSAU	1970	1971	1972	1973	1974	1975	1976	1977	1978	1979	1980
FOREIGN TRADE (CUSTOMS BASIS)					*(Thousands of current US dollars)*						
Value of Exports, fob	..	..	..	..	..	..	..	..	..	..	..
Nonfuel Primary Products	..	..	..	..	..	..	..	..	..	..	..
Fuels	..	..	..	..	..	..	..	..	..	..	..
Manufactures	..	..	..	..	..	..	..	..	..	..	..
Value of Imports, cif	..	..	..	..	..	..	..	..	..	..	..
Nonfuel Primary Products	..	..	..	..	..	..	..	..	..	..	..
Fuels	..	..	..	..	..	..	..	..	..	..	..
Manufactures	..	..	..	..	..	..	..	..	..	..	..
					(Index 1987 = 100)						
Terms of Trade	..	..	..	..	..	..	..	..	..	..	..
Export Prices, fob	..	..	..	..	..	..	..	..	..	..	..
Import Prices, cif	..	..	..	..	..	..	..	..	..	..	..
BALANCE OF PAYMENTS					*(Millions of current US dollars)*						
Exports of Goods & Services	..	..	..	..	..	..	..	..	..	..	..
Merchandise, fob	..	..	..	..	..	..	..	..	..	..	..
Nonfactor Services	..	..	..	..	..	..	..	..	..	..	..
Factor Services	..	..	..	..	..	..	..	..	..	..	..
Imports of Goods & Services	..	..	..	..	..	..	..	..	..	..	..
Merchandise, fob	..	..	..	..	..	..	..	..	..	..	..
Nonfactor Services	..	..	..	..	..	..	..	..	..	..	..
Factor Services	..	..	..	..	..	..	..	..	..	..	..
Long-Term Interest	0.00	0.00	0.00	0.00	0.00	0.00	0.00	0.00	0.20	1.00	1.10
Private Current Transfers, net	..	..	..	..	..	..	..	..	..	..	..
Workers' Remittances	..	..	..	..	..	..	..	..	..	..	..
Curr. A/C Bal before Off. Transf.	..	..	..	..	..	..	..	..	..	..	..
Net Official Transfers	..	..	..	..	..	..	..	..	..	..	..
Curr. A/C Bal after Off. Transf.	..	..	..	..	..	..	..	..	..	..	..
Long-Term Capital, net	..	..	..	..	..	..	..	..	..	..	..
Direct Investment	..	..	..	..	..	..	..	..	..	..	..
Long-Term Loans	0.00	0.00	0.00	0.00	0.00	8.40	12.70	9.30	20.60	17.80	66.20
Disbursements	0.00	0.00	0.00	0.00	0.00	8.40	12.70	9.60	21.40	19.20	69.20
Repayments	0.00	0.00	0.00	0.00	0.00	0.00	0.00	0.30	0.80	1.40	3.00
Other Long-Term Capital	..	..	..	..	..	..	..	..	..	..	..
Other Capital, net	..	..	..	..	..	..	..	..	..	..	..
Change in Reserves	..	..	..	..	..	..	..	-0.93	0.98	1.82	-0.01
Memo Item:					*(Guinea-Bissau Pesos per US dollar)*						
Conversion Factor (Annual Avg)	28.80	28.30	27.10	24.50	25.40	25.50	30.20	33.60	35.00	34.10	33.80
Additional Conversion Factor	35.69	35.00	35.00	38.35	39.52	41.41	42.78	40.01	45.11	49.65	49.86
EXTERNAL DEBT (Total)				*(Millions of US dollars), outstanding at end of year*							
EXTERNAL DEBT (Total)	0.0	0.0	0.0	0.0	0.0	7.9	19.7	28.8	53.9	71.7	134.1
Long-Term Debt (by debtor)	0.0	0.0	0.0	0.0	0.0	7.9	19.6	27.5	48.4	67.9	129.0
Central Bank, incl. IMF credit	0.0	0.0	0.0	0.0	0.0	0.0	0.0	0.0	0.0	6.4	17.4
Central Government	0.0	0.0	0.0	0.0	0.0	7.9	19.6	27.2	48.0	58.5	108.6
Rest of General Government	..	..	..	..	..	..	..	..	..	..	..
Non-financial Public Enterprises	0.0	0.0	0.0	0.0	0.0	0.0	0.0	0.3	0.4	3.0	3.0
Priv. Sector, incl non-guaranteed	..	..	..	..	..	..	..	..	..	..	..
Short-Term Debt	0.0	0.0	0.0	0.0	0.0	0.1	1.3	5.5	3.8	5.1	
Memo Items:					*(Thousands of US dollars)*						
Int'l Reserves Excluding Gold	..	..	..	..	..	..	..	..	..	..	..
Gold Holdings (at market price)	..	..	..	..	..	..	..	..	..	..	..
SOCIAL INDICATORS											
Total Fertility Rate	5.9	5.9	5.9	5.9	5.9	6.0	6.0	6.0	6.0	6.0	6.0
Infant Mortality Rate	186.6	184.8	183.0	181.6	180.2	178.8	177.4	176.0	173.4	170.8	168.2
Life Expectancy at Birth	35.5	35.5	35.6	35.7	35.8	35.8	35.9	36.0	36.3	36.7	37.0
Urban Population, % of total	15.1	15.3	15.4	15.6	15.7	15.9	16.1	16.3	16.4	16.6	16.8
Food Prod. per capita (1987=100)	109.1	97.5	99.5	96.5	94.0	101.9	110.0	81.4	86.8	83.5	79.7
Labor Force, Agriculture (%)	84.1	83.9	83.7	83.6	83.4	83.2	83.0	82.8	82.6	82.5	82.3
Labor Force, Female (%)	42.6	42.6	42.6	42.6	42.6	42.6	42.6	42.6	42.6	42.6	42.6
Primary Schl. Enroll. Ratio	39.0	..	..	..	..	64.0	..	..	106.0	98.0	68.0
Primary Schl. Enroll. Ratio, Female	23.0	..	..	..	..	39.0	41.0	..	..	..	42.0
Secondary Schl. Enroll. Ratio	8.0	..	..	..	..	3.0	..	..	..	..	6.0

1981	1982	1983	1984	1985	1986	1987	1988	1989	1990 est.	Notes	
											FOREIGN TRADE (CUSTOMS BASIS)
				(Thousands of current US dollars)							
..	..	..	..	..	..	..	..	..	..	..	Value of Exports, fob
..	..	..	..	..	..	..	..	..	..	..	Nonfuel Primary Products
..	..	..	..	..	..	..	..	..	..	..	Fuels
..	..	..	..	..	..	..	..	..	..	..	Manufactures
..	..	..	..	..	..	..	..	..	..	..	Value of Imports, cif
..	..	..	..	..	..	..	..	..	..	..	Nonfuel Primary Products
..	..	..	..	..	..	..	..	..	..	..	Fuels
..	..	..	..	..	..	..	..	..	..	..	Manufactures
				(Index 1987 = 100)							
..	..	..	..	..	..	..	..	..	..	..	Terms of Trade
..	..	..	..	..	..	..	..	..	..	..	Export Prices, fob
..	..	..	..	..	..	..	..	..	..	..	Import Prices, cif
				(Millions of current US dollars)							**BALANCE OF PAYMENTS**
..	17.40	15.30	25.40	18.10	17.70	23.90	25.80	25.80	44.20	f	Exports of Goods & Services
..	11.80	8.60	17.40	11.60	9.70	15.40	15.90	14.20	17.70	..	Merchandise, fob
..	5.60	6.70	8.00	6.50	8.00	8.50	9.90	11.60	26.50	..	Nonfactor Services
..	0.00	0.00	0.00	0.00	0.00	0.00	0.00	0.00		..	Factor Services
..	82.90	76.40	86.00	90.50	80.10	80.40	100.30	122.90	122.00	f	Imports of Goods & Services
..	61.50	58.40	60.10	59.50	51.20	44.70	58.90	69.00	68.20	..	Merchandise, fob
..	18.20	14.90	21.80	25.70	22.40	28.10	30.80	41.60	41.30	..	Nonfactor Services
..	3.20	3.10	4.10	5.30	6.50	7.60	10.60	12.30	12.50	..	Factor Services
1.30	1.00	0.70	0.70	1.80	0.70	4.50	3.10	3.40	3.40	..	Long-Term Interest
..	-14.00	-10.90	-4.90	-3.40	-1.50	-2.00	1.50	1.20	1.20	..	Private Current Transfers, net
..	..	..	..	..	..	..	1.50	0.00		..	Workers' Remittances
..	-79.50	-72.00	-65.50	-75.80	-63.90	-58.50	-73.00	-95.90	-76.60	..	Curr. A/C Bal before Off. Transf.
..	44.50	43.00	29.30	30.50	43.50	45.60	44.00	58.30	61.20	..	Net Official Transfers
..	-35.00	-29.00	-36.20	-45.30	-20.40	-12.90	-29.00	-37.60	-15.40	..	Curr. A/C Bal after Off. Transf.
..	18.90	16.70	36.50	63.00	17.90	64.20	29.20	33.70	25.30	f	Long-Term Capital, net
..	..	..	..	..	..	..	..	0.00	0.60	..	Direct Investment
16.50	16.60	15.80	29.30	57.70	20.80	39.10	33.40	35.60	33.10	..	Long-Term Loans
19.10	18.20	17.40	30.90	60.30	23.20	43.00	36.10	40.00	34.90	..	Disbursements
2.60	1.60	1.60	1.60	2.60	2.40	3.90	2.70	4.40	1.80	..	Repayments
..	2.30	0.90	7.20	5.30	-2.90	25.10	-4.20	-1.90	-8.40	..	Other Long-Term Capital
..	0.20	-0.70	0.00	-1.10	-1.70	-40.20	12.20	1.93	-9.90	f	Other Capital, net
3.12	15.90	13.00	-0.30	-16.60	4.20	-11.10	-12.40	1.97	0.00	..	Change in Reserves
				(Guinea-Bissau Pesos per US dollar)							**Memo Item:**
37.30	39.90	42.10	105.30	159.60	204.00	559.30	1,111.10	1,811.40	2,185.40	..	Conversion Factor (Annual Avg)
42.90	48.70	58.70	120.60	160.00	373.30	559.33	1,111.06	1,811.42	2,190.00	..	Additional Conversion Factor
				(Millions of US dollars), outstanding at end of year							**EXTERNAL DEBT (Total)**
140.6	158.2	186.2	242.6	307.7	336.0	437.4	455.1	498.3	592.6	..	Long-Term Debt (by debtor)
136.0	143.1	148.7	192.8	266.9	312.9	406.8	419.7	465.4	549.5	..	Central Bank, incl. IMF credit
17.0	18.5	16.5	43.5	42.9	42.1	43.1	45.0	46.9	47.3	..	Central Government
114.6	119.2	127.2	145.1	219.2	265.7	360.4	374.2	418.1	501.9	..	Rest of General Government
..	..	..	..	..	..	..	..	..	..	..	Non-financial Public Enterprises
4.4	5.4	5.0	4.2	4.8	5.1	3.3	0.5	0.4	0.3	..	Priv. Sector, incl non-guaranteed
..	..	..	..	..	..	..	..	..	..	..	
4.6	15.1	37.5	49.8	40.8	23.1	30.6	35.4	32.9	43.1	..	Short-Term Debt
				(Thousands of US dollars)							**Memo Items:**
..	..	..	..	..	30,015.00	9,822.00	14,711.00	..	..	..	Int'l Reserves Excluding Gold
..	..	..	..	..	..	..	..	..	..	..	Gold Holdings (at market price)
											SOCIAL INDICATORS
6.0	6.0	6.0	6.0	6.0	6.0	6.0	6.0	6.0	6.0	..	Total Fertility Rate
165.6	163.0	160.6	158.2	155.7	153.3	150.9	150.1	149.2	148.4	..	Infant Mortality Rate
37.3	37.7	38.0	38.2	38.5	38.8	39.0	39.0	38.9	38.8	..	Life Expectancy at Birth
17.1	17.3	17.6	17.8	18.1	18.6	19.0	19.3	19.6	19.9	..	Urban Population, % of total
87.4	95.0	82.5	95.6	93.2	97.6	100.0	98.6	99.2	97.9	..	Food Prod. per capita (1987=100)
..	..	..	..	..	..	..	..	..	..	..	Labor Force, Agriculture (%)
42.4	42.3	42.1	42.0	41.8	41.6	41.4	41.2	41.0	40.8	..	Labor Force, Female (%)
66.0	63.0	62.0	64.0	..	61.0	59.0	59.0	..	..	..	Primary Schl. Enroll. Ratio
40.0	40.0	40.0	43.0	..	43.0	41.0	42.0	..	..	..	Primary Schl. Enroll. Ratio, Female
8.0	10.0	11.0	11.0	..	7.0	6.0	7.0	..	..	..	Secondary Schl. Enroll. Ratio

GUYANA	1970	1971	1972	1973	1974	1975	1976	1977	1978	1979	1980
CURRENT GNP PER CAPITA (US $)	380	410	400	410	510	640	650	610	610	640	720
POPULATION (thousands)	670	680	692	706	719	730	739	745	750	754	760
USE AND ORIGIN OF RESOURCES				*(Millions of current Guyana Dollars)*							
Gross National Product (GNP)	493.1	528.1	577.1	613.1	905.4	1,154.5	1,075.3	1,057.5	1,203.1	1,249.0	1,399.4
Net Factor Income from Abroad	-42.5	-36.0	-22.2	-31.7	-49.3	-33.0	-60.9	-67.1	-64.5	-77.0	-108.6
GDP at Market Prices	535.6	564.1	599.3	644.8	954.7	1,187.5	1,136.2	1,124.6	1,267.6	1,326.0	1,508.0
Resource Balance	-2.9	21.0	-7.8	-107.7	18.4	-0.3	-283.2	-175.0	-0.2	-124.9	-158.4
Exports of Goods & NFServices	302.4	329.5	344.4	336.5	652.5	889.2	750.7	710.9	799.7	793.1	1,041.9
Imports of Goods & NFServices	305.3	308.5	352.2	444.2	634.1	889.5	1,033.9	885.9	799.9	918.0	1,200.3
Domestic Absorption	538.5	543.1	607.1	752.5	936.3	1,187.8	1,419.0	1,299.7	1,267.9	1,451.0	1,666.4
Private Consumption, etc.	325.7	336.3	371.3	417.3	522.0	562.3	673.7	682.7	711.9	692.0	781.4
General Gov't Consumption	90.9	101.7	116.9	159.7	162.2	232.9	320.1	290.0	296.0	348.0	436.0
Gross Domestic Investment	121.9	105.1	118.9	175.5	252.1	392.6	425.2	327.0	260.0	411.0	449.0
Fixed Investment	112.6	102.8	108.3	154.8	198.1	350.3	381.0	290.0	242.0	325.0	404.0
Indirect Taxes, net	65.6	65.7	68.6	68.4	84.9	90.0	97.8	105.3	132.0	147.0	172.0
GDP at factor cost	470.0	498.4	530.7	576.4	869.8	1,097.5	1,038.4	1,019.3	1,135.6	1,179.0	1,336.0
Agriculture	90.1	101.7	104.2	106.3	264.1	341.4	236.0	210.8	256.6	263.5	312.0
Industry	189.3	190.6	196.3	191.8	287.8	376.9	364.9	364.0	391.0	400.5	478.0
Manufacturing	57.0	61.3	63.9	64.3	120.3	161.6	134.9	122.9	137.5	146.0	162.0
Services, etc.	190.6	206.1	230.2	278.3	317.9	379.2	437.5	444.5	488.0	515.0	546.0
Gross Domestic Saving	119.0	126.1	111.1	67.8	270.5	392.3	142.4	151.9	259.7	286.0	290.6
Gross National Saving	75.5	89.7	89.4	34.3	216.1	349.0	70.3	75.8	195.8	209.5	184.5
Gross National Product	3,292.1	3,560.1	3,457.0	3,478.2	3,786.1	4,221.7	4,176.8	4,057.7	4,037.3	3,936.4	3,944.4
GDP at Market Prices	3,781.2	3,892.8	3,782.2	3,840.7	4,145.0	4,472.6	4,535.4	4,414.4	4,348.0	4,257.7	4,332.9
Resource Balance	-1,642.2	-1,143.8	-1,383.2	-2,527.2	-1,974.1	-3,303.3	-3,783.8	-2,518.2	-1,044.0	-1,234.8	-1,654.4
Exports of Goods & NFServices	5,074.2	5,246.0	4,854.3	4,560.4	4,396.6	4,516.0	4,343.7	3,757.5	4,088.4	3,673.0	3,777.6
Imports of Goods & NFServices	6,716.4	6,389.8	6,237.5	7,087.6	6,370.7	7,819.4	8,127.5	6,275.7	5,132.4	4,907.8	5,432.0
Domestic Absorption	5,423.4	5,036.6	5,165.4	6,367.8	6,119.1	7,776.0	8,319.2	6,932.6	5,392.0	5,492.5	5,987.3
Private Consumption, etc.	2,671.1	2,604.4	3,028.9	3,351.8	3,357.7	3,206.7	4,035.9	3,782.1	3,040.9	2,558.1	3,004.7
General Gov't Consumption	472.6	487.8	512.2	585.8	574.8	806.9	1,054.7	882.0	782.2	780.4	857.0
Gross Domestic Investment	2,279.7	1,944.4	1,624.4	2,430.3	2,186.6	3,762.4	3,228.6	2,268.5	1,568.8	2,154.0	2,125.6
Fixed Investment	..	..	..	..	..	..	2,448.3	1,701.9	1,234.7	1,449.5	1,626.2
GDP at factor cost	3,234.7	3,343.5	3,239.7	3,329.3	3,602.2	3,932.9	3,994.7	3,876.6	3,772.5	3,711.2	3,772.9
Agriculture	803.4	852.8	774.5	774.5	898.1	865.2	898.1	868.5	943.4	877.5	881.6
Industry	1,503.2	1,550.3	1,456.1	1,421.8	1,541.7	1,683.0	1,614.5	1,558.8	1,443.2	1,417.5	1,464.6
Manufacturing	391.1	459.6	444.9	420.4	528.0	581.8	596.4	600.8	616.0	640.4	645.3
Services, etc.	928.1	940.4	1,009.1	1,133.0	1,162.4	1,384.8	1,482.0	1,449.3	1,385.8	1,416.2	1,426.6
Memo Items:											
Capacity to Import	6,652.6	6,824.8	6,099.4	5,369.1	6,555.5	7,816.7	5,901.3	5,036.0	5,131.1	4,240.1	4,715.2
Terms of Trade Adjustment	1,578.4	1,578.8	1,245.1	808.7	2,159.0	3,300.7	1,557.6	1,278.5	1,042.7	567.1	937.6
Gross Domestic Income	5,359.6	5,471.6	5,027.2	4,649.4	6,304.0	7,773.3	6,093.0	5,692.9	5,390.7	4,824.8	5,270.4
Gross National Income	4,870.5	5,138.9	4,702.1	4,286.9	5,945.1	7,522.4	5,734.4	5,336.2	5,079.9	4,503.5	4,882.0
DOMESTIC PRICES/DEFLATORS					*(Index 1987 = 100)*						
Overall (GDP)	14.2	14.5	15.8	16.8	23.0	26.6	25.1	25.5	29.2	31.1	34.8
Domestic Absorption	9.9	10.8	11.8	11.8	15.3	15.3	17.1	18.7	23.5	26.4	27.8
Agriculture	11.2	11.9	13.5	13.7	29.4	39.5	26.3	24.3	27.2	30.0	35.4
Industry	12.6	12.3	13.5	13.5	18.7	22.4	22.6	23.4	27.1	28.3	32.6
Manufacturing	14.6	13.3	14.4	15.3	22.8	27.8	22.6	20.5	22.3	22.8	25.1
Consumer Price Index	11.2	11.3	11.8	12.7	14.9	16.1	17.6	19.0	21.9	25.8	29.4
MANUFACTURING ACTIVITY											
Employment (1987=100)	..	..	..	..	..	..	..	..	..	..	..
Real Earnings per Empl. (1987=100)	..	..	..	..	..	..	..	..	..	..	..
Real Output per Empl. (1987=100)	..	..	..	..	..	..	..	..	..	..	..
Earnings as % of Value Added	..	..	..	..	..	..	..	..	..	..	..
MONETARY HOLDINGS					*(Millions of current Guyana Dollars)*						
Money Supply, Broadly Defined	173.9	202.0	246.3	291.8	339.1	475.8	523.8	646.1	716.3	770.8	929.4
Money	61.4	69.4	87.5	100.6	133.1	207.4	221.5	284.9	300.4	288.2	328.1
Currency Outside Banks	37.3	40.7	48.1	55.6	63.6	91.6	105.2	142.8	156.4	148.3	167.0
Demand Deposits	24.1	28.7	39.4	44.9	69.5	115.8	116.3	142.1	143.9	139.9	161.1
Quasi-Money	112.5	132.5	158.8	191.2	205.9	268.4	302.3	361.2	415.9	482.6	601.4
					(Millions of current Guyana Dollars)						
GOVERNMENT DEFICIT (-) OR SURPLUS	-24.30	-33.00	-39.20	-104.70	-22.20	-77.50	-313.10	-133.40	-128.70	-232.40	-440.20
Current Revenue	143.30	140.10	162.50	177.40	322.80	503.10	399.10	380.50	404.20	480.50	539.70
Current Expenditure	..	..	..	199.50	258.80	302.80	388.60	391.20	402.50	450.20	605.40
Current Budget Balance	..	..	..	-22.10	64.00	200.30	10.50	-10.70	1.70	30.30	-65.70
Capital Receipts	0.80	0.60	0.90	2.40	..	..	..	..	0.20	0.30	..
Capital Payments	..	..	..	85.00	86.20	277.80	323.60	122.70	130.60	263.00	374.50

1981	1982	1983	1984	1985	1986	1987	1988	1989	1990 estimate	Notes	GUYANA
740	620	550	500	540	550	430	400	420	330	..	**CURRENT GNP PER CAPITA (US $)**
766	773	780	786	790	792	793	795	796	798	..	**POPULATION (thousands)**
			(Millions of current Guyana Dollars)								**USE AND ORIGIN OF RESOURCES**
1,443.6	1,299.2	1,295.5	1,491.8	1,778.6	1,806.9	2,633.8	3,192.0	7,466.5	9,761.7	..	Gross National Product (GNP)
-153.4	-146.8	-172.5	-171.2	-171.4	-363.1	-871.2	-946.0	-434.5	-2,886.0	..	Net Factor Income from Abroad
1,597.0	1,446.0	1,468.0	1,663.0	1,950.0	2,170.0	3,505.0	4,138.0	7,901.0	12,647.7	..	GDP at Market Prices
-350.2	-219.0	-272.7	-152.9	-330.3	-306.3	-477.0	-184.0	-997.0	-1,635.7	..	Resource Balance
1,031.9	794.4	675.3	938.0	1,047.7	1,056.0	2,676.1	2,602.0	6,662.0	3,326.6	..	Exports of Goods & NF Services
1,382.1	1,013.4	948.0	1,090.9	1,378.0	1,362.3	3,153.1	2,786.0	7,659.0	4,962.3	..	Imports of Goods & NF Services
1,947.2	1,665.0	1,740.7	1,815.9	2,280.4	2,476.6	3,982.0	4,322.0	8,898.0	14,283.0	..	Domestic Absorption
1,012.2	923.0	973.7	1,058.9	1,346.4	1,342.6	2,311.0	2,282.0	4,629.0	6,263.0	..	Private Consumption, etc.
464.0	392.0	458.0	301.0	352.0	401.0	552.0	1,165.0	1,737.0	2,100.0	..	General Gov't Consumption
471.0	350.0	309.0	456.0	582.0	733.0	1,119.0	875.0	2,532.0	5,920.0	..	Gross Domestic Investment
441.0	350.0	309.0	456.0	466.0	595.0	946.0	746.0	1,949.0	4,341.0	..	Fixed Investment
247.0	196.0	268.0	259.0	314.0	333.0	441.0	560.0	1,024.0	1,060.0	..	Indirect Taxes, net
1,350.0	1,250.0	1,200.0	1,404.0	1,636.0	1,837.0	3,064.0	3,578.0	6,877.0	11,587.7		GDP at factor cost
300.0	292.0	291.0	347.0	439.0	490.0	894.0	878.0	2,008.0	3,188.0	..	Agriculture
412.0	362.0	273.0	348.0	397.0	501.0	955.0	1,115.0	2,568.0	4,041.0	f	Industry
201.0	179.0	158.0	183.0	227.0	271.0	440.0	543.0	1,136.0	1,386.0	..	Manufacturing
638.0	596.0	636.0	709.0	800.0	846.0	1,215.0	1,585.0	2,301.0	4,358.7	f	Services, etc.
120.8	131.0	36.3	303.1	251.6	426.4	642.0	691.0	1,535.0	4,284.7		Gross Domestic Saving
-20.6	-33.4	-149.0	135.9	71.6	81.7	-183.3	-231.0	1,293.3	..		Gross National Saving
			(Millions of 1987 Guyana Dollars)								
3,936.6	3,384.3	3,113.6	2,816.2	2,955.0	2,999.4	2,633.8	2,516.2	3,172.4	2,487.0	..	Gross National Product
4,408.8	3,811.0	3,558.5	3,557.0	3,592.7	3,645.7	3,505.0	3,367.3	3,360.4	3,321.3	I	GDP at Market Prices
-1,864.5	-1,041.0	-1,084.3	-636.9	-801.6	-806.9	-477.0	-439.8	-369.0	-833.3		Resource Balance
3,554.0	2,726.3	2,545.6	2,731.6	2,774.4	2,565.1	2,676.1	2,358.4	2,208.9	2,161.8		Exports of Goods & NF Services
5,418.6	3,767.3	3,629.9	3,368.5	3,576.0	3,372.0	3,153.1	2,798.2	2,577.9	2,995.1		Imports of Goods & NF Services
6,273.3	4,852.0	4,642.8	4,193.8	4,394.3	4,452.6	3,982.0	3,807.0	3,729.4	4,154.6		Domestic Absorption
3,571.9	2,993.6	2,967.4	2,346.7	2,659.9	2,077.8	2,311.0	2,465.4	2,278.7	2,574.2		Private Consumption, etc.
746.6	522.8	530.1	278.3	282.8	508.8	552.0	480.8	386.6	314.2		General Gov't Consumption
1,954.8	1,335.6	1,145.4	1,568.8	1,451.5	1,865.9	1,119.0	860.8	1,064.2	1,266.2		Gross Domestic Investment
1,559.3	1,129.1	968.3	1,326.3	1,047.5	1,577.5	946.0	727.7	899.6	1,070.4		Fixed Investment
3,762.3	3,370.0	3,052.0	3,119.0	3,154.2	3,160.5	3,064.0	3,002.7	2,916.4	2,857.9	I	GDP at factor cost
902.2	889.9	856.9	885.8	885.8	918.7	894.0	832.2	836.3	704.5	..	Agriculture
1,434.6	1,160.6	916.5	937.9	976.4	946.4	955.0	942.2	865.1	925.0	f	Industry
684.4	596.4	498.7	469.3	454.7	454.7	440.0	425.3	391.4	342.2	..	Manufacturing
1,425.4	1,319.6	1,278.6	1,295.3	1,292.0	1,295.3	1,215.0	1,228.4	1,215.0	1,228.4	f	Services, etc.
											Memo Items:
4,045.6	2,953.2	2,585.7	2,896.3	2,718.9	2,613.8	2,676.1	2,613.4	2,242.3	2,007.9	..	Capacity to Import
491.6	226.8	40.2	164.7	-55.6	48.7	0.0	255.0	33.5	-154.0	..	Terms of Trade Adjustment
4,900.3	4,037.9	3,598.7	3,721.7	3,537.1	3,694.4	3,505.0	3,622.2	3,393.8	3,167.3	..	Gross Domestic Income
4,428.2	3,611.2	3,153.7	2,980.9	2,899.4	3,048.1	2,633.8	2,771.2	3,205.9	2,333.0	..	Gross National Income
			(Index 1987 = 100)								**DOMESTIC PRICES/DEFLATORS**
36.2	37.9	41.3	46.8	54.3	59.5	100.0	122.9	235.1	380.8	..	Overall (GDP)
31.0	34.3	37.5	43.3	51.9	55.6	100.0	113.5	238.6	343.8	..	Domestic Absorption
33.3	32.8	34.0	39.2	49.6	53.3	100.0	105.5	240.1	452.5	..	Agriculture
28.7	31.2	29.8	37.1	40.7	52.9	100.0	118.3	296.9	436.9	..	Industry
29.4	30.0	31.7	39.0	49.9	59.6	100.0	127.7	290.5	405.0	..	Manufacturing
35.9	43.5	50.0	62.6	72.0	77.7	100.0	139.9				Consumer Price Index
											MANUFACTURING ACTIVITY
..	..	..	..	..	..	..	..	..	..		Employment (1987=100)
..	..	..	..	..	..	..	..	..	..		Real Earnings per Empl. (1987=100)
..	..	..	..	..	..	..	..	..	..		Real Output per Empl. (1987=100)
..	..	..	..	..	..	..	..	..	..		Earnings as % of Value Added
			(Millions of current Guyana Dollars)								**MONETARY HOLDINGS**
1,085.5	1,384.2	1,671.7	1,991.0	2,431.0	2,906.5	4,331.8	5,407.0	8,867.7	13,177.5	D	Money Supply, Broadly Defined
350.8	436.0	508.9	618.6	739.6	880.8	1,332.5	2,095.2	2,922.6	4,261.9	..	Money
186.0	231.0	268.9	335.8	421.6	508.8	726.2	1,057.8	1,506.0	2,211.4	..	Currency Outside Banks
164.7	205.0	240.0	282.8	318.0	372.0	606.4	1,037.4	1,416.7	2,050.4	..	Demand Deposits
734.7	948.2	1,162.8	1,372.4	1,691.4	2,025.7	2,999.3	3,312.0	5,945.0	8,915.6	..	Quasi-Money
			(Millions of current Guyana Dollars)								**GOVERNMENT DEFICIT (-) OR SURPLUS**
-453.00	-884.10	-465.60	-748.80	-823.80	..	..	..	..	..	..	Current Revenue
666.40	651.00	673.00	1,019.20	959.40	..	..	..	..	..	..	Current Revenue
794.70	759.60	887.10	1,260.40	1,096.90	..	..	..	..	..	..	Current Expenditure
-128.30	-108.60	-214.10	-241.20	-137.50	..	..	..	..	..	..	Current Budget Balance
..	..	..	..	3.20	..	..	..	..	..	..	Capital Receipts
324.70	775.50	251.50	507.60	689.50	..	..	..	..	..	..	Capital Payments

GUYANA	1970	1971	1972	1973	1974	1975	1976	1977	1978	1979	1980
FOREIGN TRADE (CUSTOMS BASIS)					*(Millions of current US dollars)*						
Value of Exports, fob	..	..	..	..	..	..	..	..	..	..	..
Nonfuel Primary Products	..	..	..	..	..	..	..	..	..	..	..
Fuels	..	..	..	..	..	..	..	..	..	..	..
Manufactures	..	..	..	..	..	..	..	..	..	..	..
Value of Imports, cif	..	..	..	..	..	..	..	..	..	..	..
Nonfuel Primary Products	..	..	..	..	..	..	..	..	..	..	..
Fuels	..	..	..	..	..	..	..	..	..	..	..
Manufactures	..	..	..	..	..	..	..	..	..	..	..
					(Index 1987 = 100)						
Terms of Trade	..	..	..	..	..	..	..	..	..	..	..
Export Prices, fob	..	..	..	..	..	..	..	..	..	..	..
Import Prices, cif	..	..	..	..	..	..	..	..	..	..	..
BALANCE OF PAYMENTS					*(Millions of current US dollars)*						
Exports of Goods & Services	146.60	163.19	163.83	157.60	293.08	371.77	294.75	..	..	314.94	410.51
Merchandise, fob	129.00	145.93	143.64	135.66	270.11	351.38	279.51	259.33	295.61	292.71	388.86
Nonfactor Services	16.60	16.45	18.78	20.50	21.65	18.94	13.62	16.16	18.16	18.55	19.76
Factor Services	1.00	0.80	1.41	1.43	1.32	1.46	1.62	..	..	3.69	1.88
Imports of Goods & Services	167.90	170.61	179.14	221.38	300.30	390.35	431.44	369.10	336.86	398.24	538.23
Merchandise, fob	119.90	120.36	128.87	159.39	230.31	305.84	330.89	286.71	253.49	288.78	386.43
Nonfactor Services	31.10	31.29	38.22	48.52	49.79	64.11	75.04	60.75	60.08	71.37	107.33
Factor Services	16.90	18.96	12.05	13.47	20.20	20.40	25.51	21.65	23.29	38.08	44.47
Long-Term Interest	3.40	3.60	6.40	8.10	8.70	10.30	19.80	15.20	17.30	25.20	26.60
Private Current Transfers, net	-0.50	-0.20	0.22	-0.83	-2.29	-4.37	-4.39	-3.53	0.24	0.20	0.98
Workers' Remittances	..	..	..	..	..	..	..	..	..	..	..
Curr. A/C Bal before Off. Transf.	-21.80	-7.62	-15.09	-64.61	-9.50	-22.95	-141.08	-97.14	-22.86	-83.10	-126.75
Net Official Transfers	..	1.00	-1.19	0.12	-1.20	-1.70	-1.73	-0.39	-6.71	0.20	-1.76
Curr. A/C Bal after Off. Transf.	-21.80	-6.62	-16.29	-64.49	-10.70	-24.65	-142.81	-97.53	-29.57	-82.90	-128.51
Long-Term Capital, net	17.10	6.94	8.82	18.22	43.10	89.85	44.79	41.33	32.82	14.31	74.47
Direct Investment	9.00	-55.77	2.50	8.23	1.32	0.85	-26.09	-1.76	..	0.59	0.59
Long-Term Loans	11.60	14.10	8.80	16.10	29.70	98.50	56.90	42.50	27.40	32.80	70.70
Disbursements	13.80	15.50	11.20	21.10	35.00	105.00	70.00	59.20	59.70	98.90	113.30
Repayments	2.20	1.40	2.40	5.00	5.30	6.50	13.10	16.70	32.30	66.10	42.60
Other Long-Term Capital	-3.50	48.61	-2.47	-6.11	12.08	-9.50	13.98	0.60	5.42	-19.07	3.18
Other Capital, net	2.45	1.39	15.65	20.22	13.64	-15.45	10.07	44.78	13.27	11.62	10.75
Change in Reserves	2.25	-1.71	-8.19	26.05	-46.03	-49.75	87.95	11.42	-16.52	56.97	43.29
Memo Item:					*(Guyana Dollars per US dollar)*						
Conversion Factor (Annual Avg)	2.000	1.980	2.090	2.110	2.230	2.360	2.550	2.550	2.550	2.550	2.550
				(Millions of US dollars), outstanding at end of year							
EXTERNAL DEBT (Total)	82.7	156.4	157.7	178.1	219.8	305.8	394.3	492.2	574.2	640.2	794.3
Long-Term Debt (by debtor)	82.7	156.4	157.7	178.1	219.8	305.8	394.3	448.2	501.2	574.2	684.3
Central Bank, incl. IMF credit	0.0	2.2	0.0	4.7	6.1	0.0	22.5	26.8	48.4	63.0	98.0
Central Government	62.3	130.0	133.8	149.4	184.4	246.3	290.1	311.5	328.4	376.6	442.3
Rest of General Government	..	..	..	..	..	..	..	..	..	..	..
Non-financial Public Enterprises	11.9	15.2	15.6	15.8	21.0	52.3	72.3	94.9	106.7	116.2	119.5
Priv. Sector, incl non-guaranteed	8.5	9.0	8.3	8.2	8.3	7.2	9.4	15.0	17.7	18.4	24.5
Short-Term Debt	0.0	0.0	0.0	0.0	0.0	0.0	0.0	44.0	73.0	66.0	110.0
Memo Items:					*(Thousands of US dollars)*						
Int'l Reserves Excluding Gold	20,400.0	26,156.0	36,750.3	13,973.7	62,572.1	100,497.0	27,282.9	22,976.2	58,265.7	17,528.0	12,700.0
Gold Holdings (at market price)	..	..	..	..	..	..	..	..	..	..	..
SOCIAL INDICATORS											
Total Fertility Rate	5.4	5.1	4.9	4.7	4.5	4.3	4.1	3.9	3.8	3.7	3.5
Infant Mortality Rate	80.2	79.6	79.0	76.6	74.2	71.8	69.4	67.0	66.2	65.4	64.6
Life Expectancy at Birth	59.7	59.8	60.0	60.1	60.3	60.4	60.6	60.7	60.8	60.9	61.0
Urban Population, % of total	29.4	29.4	29.5	29.5	29.6	29.6	29.8	30.0	30.1	30.3	30.5
Food Prod. per capita (1987=100)	113.8	118.8	107.8	104.0	123.5	118.8	106.2	121.3	127.5	109.6	108.5
Labor Force, Agriculture (%)	31.9	31.3	30.8	30.2	29.8	29.3	28.7	28.2	27.7	27.2	26.8
Labor Force, Female (%)	20.7	21.2	21.6	22.0	22.4	22.8	23.1	23.5	23.8	24.1	24.4
Primary Schl. Enroll. Ratio	98.0	..	..	..	..	95.0	99.0	98.0	98.0	102.0	102.0
Primary Schl. Enroll. Ratio, Female	96.0	..	..	..	..	95.0	98.0	98.0	97.0	101.0	101.0
Secondary Schl. Enroll. Ratio	55.0	..	..	..	..	54.0	61.0	61.0	60.0	59.0	66.0

FOREIGN TRADE (CUSTOMS BASIS)

(Millions of current US dollars)

Item	1981	1982	1983	1984	1985	1986	1987	1988	1989	1990 est.	Notes
Value of Exports, fob	..	..	..	..	..	..	..	..	..	..	..
Nonfuel Primary Products	..	..	..	..	..	..	..	..	..	..	..
Fuels	..	..	..	..	..	..	..	..	..	..	..
Manufactures	..	..	..	..	..	..	..	..	..	..	..
Value of Imports, cif	..	..	..	..	..	..	..	..	..	..	..
Nonfuel Primary Products	..	..	..	..	..	..	..	..	..	..	..
Fuels	..	..	..	..	..	..	..	..	..	..	..
Manufactures	..	..	..	..	..	..	..	..	..	..	..

(Index 1987 = 100)

Item	1981	1982	1983	1984	1985	1986	1987	1988	1989	1990 est.	Notes
Terms of Trade	..	..	..	..	..	..	..	..	..	..	..
Export Prices, fob	..	..	..	..	..	..	..	..	..	..	..
Import Prices, cif	..	..	..	..	..	..	..	..	..	..	..

BALANCE OF PAYMENTS

(Millions of current US dollars)

Item	1981	1982	1983	1984	1985	1986	1987	1988	1989	1990 est.	Notes
Exports of Goods & Services	372.44	264.37	225.20	246.37	..	247.40	274.60	260.50	257.00	247.65	..
Merchandise, fob	346.42	241.43	193.33	216.88	214.02	217.40	232.20	208.90	208.70	194.32	..
Nonfactor Services	22.97	22.60	31.53	29.23	48.00	29.80	42.10	51.30	47.80	50.81	..
Factor Services	3.06	0.33	0.33	0.26	..	0.20	0.30	0.30	0.50	2.52	..
Imports of Goods & Services	556.12	397.91	381.69	345.63	353.43	404.10	412.80	373.50	321.90	438.07	..
Merchandise, fob	399.64	254.17	225.73	201.64	209.09	259.50	261.90	215.60	221.70	280.77	..
Nonfactor Services	98.88	94.47	98.13	99.05	104.03	59.40	61.30	63.00	84.20	82.04	..
Factor Services	57.60	49.28	57.82	44.95	40.32	85.20	89.60	94.90	16.00	75.26	..
Long-Term Interest	35.90	21.60	24.40	19.40	11.50	16.30	14.40	12.10	11.30	72.80	..
Private Current Transfers, net	4.27	-5.87	-4.27	1.04	-2.02	4.30	4.70	2.40	7.10	..	..
Workers' Remittances	..	2.30	1.17	..	..	..	..	..	..	..	..
Curr. A/C Bal before Off. Transf.	-179.41	-139.41	-160.75	-98.22	-93.42	-146.40	-127.60	-100.50	-50.90	-176.07	..
Net Official Transfers	-4.08	-1.90	3.27	3.60	-3.20	6.00	5.90	10.10	6.90	10.00	..
Curr. A/C Bal after Off. Transf.	-183.50	-141.31	-157.49	-94.62	-96.62	-140.40	-121.70	-90.40	-44.00	-166.07	..
Long-Term Capital, net	114.88	10.17	-32.93	-27.73	-36.02	-2.80	-11.40	-18.00	39.90	159.32	..
Direct Investment	-1.78	4.43	4.73	4.49	1.81	-12.00	5.40	4.70	9.20	5.00	..
Long-Term Loans	96.50	52.70	32.60	12.70	48.70	52.30	34.50	23.80	29.30	87.70	..
Disbursements	139.80	75.70	54.60	27.00	60.40	65.40	46.00	32.70	44.80	151.80	..
Repayments	43.30	23.00	22.00	14.30	11.70	13.10	11.50	8.90	15.50	64.10	..
Other Long-Term Capital	20.16	-46.97	-70.27	-44.92	-86.53	-43.10	-51.30	-46.50	1.40	66.62	..
Other Capital, net	50.83	130.75	190.74	146.25	137.15	145.73	132.52	104.01	14.47	53.69	..
Change in Reserves	17.79	0.40	-0.32	-23.90	-4.50	-2.53	0.58	4.39	-10.37	-46.93	..

(Guyana Dollars per US dollar)

Memo Item:

Item	1981	1982	1983	1984	1985	1986	1987	1988	1989	1990 est.	Notes
Conversion Factor (Annual Avg)	2.810	3.000	3.000	3.830	4.250	4.270	9.760	10.000	27.160	39.530	..

(Millions of US dollars), outstanding at end of year

Item	1981	1982	1983	1984	1985	1986	1987	1988	1989	1990 est.	Notes
EXTERNAL DEBT (Total)	873.3	956.0	1,205.5	1,268.0	1,485.0	1,618.3	1,719.2	1,722.4	1,861.9	1,960.1	..
Long-Term Debt (by debtor)	764.2	797.9	806.8	779.7	870.8	959.0	1,071.3	1,088.8	1,590.3	1,776.1	..
Central Bank, incl. IMF credit	112.7	114.7	109.5	104.5	115.4	127.3	154.1	173.6	172.5	162.2	..
Central Government	529.9	568.0	590.0	582.0	654.8	699.9	765.7	775.8	1,325.1	1,544.2	..
Rest of General Government	..	..	..	..	..	..	..	..	..	..	..
Non-financial Public Enterprises	100.8	87.2	75.0	61.5	58.7	87.6	104.0	92.4	61.9	37.9	..
Priv. Sector, incl non-guaranteed	20.8	28.0	32.3	31.7	41.9	44.2	47.5	47.0	30.8	31.8	..
Short-Term Debt	109.1	158.1	398.7	488.3	614.2	659.3	647.9	633.6	271.6	184.0	..

(Thousands of US dollars)

Memo Items:

Item	1981	1982	1983	1984	1985	1986	1987	1988	1989	1990 est.	Notes
Int'l Reserves Excluding Gold	6,910.5	10,557.1	6,490.0	5,850.0	6,470.0	9,000.0	8,430.0	4,040.0	13,350.0	28,679.8	..
Gold Holdings (at market price)	..	..	..	..	..	..	..	..	..	..	..

SOCIAL INDICATORS

Item	1981	1982	1983	1984	1985	1986	1987	1988	1989	1990 est.	Notes
Total Fertility Rate	3.4	3.3	3.2	3.2	3.2	3.1	3.1	3.0	2.9	2.8	..
Infant Mortality Rate	63.8	63.0	61.6	60.2	58.7	57.3	55.9	54.3	52.7	51.0	..
Life Expectancy at Birth	61.1	61.2	61.6	62.0	62.4	62.8	63.2	63.5	63.8	64.2	..
Urban Population, % of total	30.8	31.2	31.5	31.9	32.2	32.7	33.2	33.6	34.1	34.6	..
Food Prod. per capita (1987=100)	114.7	116.5	103.3	107.3	102.8	109.9	100.0	98.3	98.3	94.5	..
Labor Force, Agriculture (%)	..	..	..	..	..	..	..	..	..	..	..
Labor Force, Female (%)	24.5	24.6	24.7	24.7	24.8	24.9	24.9	24.9	25.0	25.0	..
Primary Schl. Enroll. Ratio	99.0	95.0	102.0	101.0	103.0	106.0	..	..	..	..	..
Primary Schl. Enroll. Ratio, Female	99.0	..	101.0	101.0	101.0	104.0	..	..	..	..	..
Secondary Schl. Enroll. Ratio	60.0	57.0	55.0	58.0	63.0	64.0	..	..	..	..	..

HAITI	1970	1971	1972	1973	1974	1975	1976	1977	1978	1979	1980
CURRENT GNP PER CAPITA (US $)	90	100	100	110	130	150	170	180	200	220	250
POPULATION (thousands)	4,535	4,614	4,694	4,774	4,855	4,937	5,020	5,103	5,189	5,277	5,370

USE AND ORIGIN OF RESOURCES *(Millions of current Haitian Gourdes)*

	1970	1971	1972	1973	1974	1975	1976	1977	1978	1979	1980
Gross National Product (GNP)	1,954	2,207	2,354	2,821	3,460	3,573	4,359	4,878	4,928	5,531	7,230
Net Factor Income from Abroad	-18	-20	-22	-22	-30	-35	-36	-61	-73	-66	-79
GDP at Market Prices	1,972	2,227	2,377	2,843	3,489	3,608	4,395	4,939	5,001	5,597	7,309
Resource Balance	-77	-76	-117	-132	-249	-297	-391	-440	-443	-557	-649
Exports of Goods & NF Services	272	304	296	350	422	528	736	905	1,018	1,094	1,580
Imports of Goods & NF Services	349	380	413	483	672	825	1,128	1,345	1,461	1,651	2,229
Domestic Absorption	2,049	2,303	2,494	2,976	3,739	3,905	4,786	5,379	5,444	6,154	7,958
Private Consumption, etc.	1,636	1,821	1,944	2,283	2,908	3,048	3,721	4,201	4,135	4,573	5,984
General Gov't Consumption	188	227	219	241	257	326	372	411	469	532	736
Gross Domestic Investment	225	254	331	451	574	532	694	767	840	1,049	1,238
Fixed Investment	..	..	..	..	..	..	..	..	..	..	..
Indirect Taxes, net	..	..	..	..	..	..	..	..	..	..	320
GDP at factor cost	..	..	..	..	..	..	..	..	..	..	6,989
Agriculture	..	..	..	..	..	..	..	..	..	..	..
Industry	..	..	..	..	..	..	..	..	..	..	..
Manufacturing	..	..	..	..	..	..	..	..	..	..	..
Services, etc.	..	..	..	..	..	..	..	..	..	..	..
Gross Domestic Saving	148	178	213	319	325	234	303	327	397	492	589
Gross National Saving	204	145	198	273	266	27	77	421	467	596	770

(Millions of 1976 Haitian Gourdes)

	1970	1971	1972	1973	1974	1975	1976	1977	1978	1979	1980
Gross National Product	3,453.0	3,748.0	3,794.5	3,849.4	4,094.8	4,010.5	4,359.0	4,360.1	4,558.5	4,908.0	5,284.6
GDP at Market Prices	3,504.0	3,800.0	3,852.5	3,898.4	4,144.8	4,048.7	4,395.0	4,416.0	4,628.0	4,966.0	5,342.0
Resource Balance	-177.0	-165.0	-203.0	-142.0	-164.0	-209.4	-391.0	-551.6	-517.2	-397.1	-410.3
Exports of Goods & NF Services	412.0	491.0	520.0	610.0	649.0	654.1	736.5	726.9	797.8	893.8	1,133.0
Imports of Goods & NF Services	589.0	656.0	723.0	752.0	813.0	863.5	1,127.5	1,278.5	1,315.0	1,290.9	1,543.3
Domestic Absorption	3,681.0	3,965.0	4,055.5	4,040.4	4,308.8	4,258.1	4,786.0	4,967.6	5,145.2	5,363.0	5,752.3
Private Consumption, etc.	2,981.0	3,202.0	3,274.5	3,232.4	3,486.8	3,321.3	3,720.8	3,865.9	3,898.8	3,969.3	4,265.9
General Gov't Consumption	403.0	460.0	423.0	391.0	359.0	356.2	371.5	382.9	448.8	464.6	552.4
Gross Domestic Investment	297.0	303.0	358.0	417.0	463.0	580.6	693.7	718.8	797.6	929.1	934.0
Fixed Investment	282.0	286.0	341.0	400.0	446.0	580.6	693.7	718.8	797.6	929.1	934.0
GDP at factor cost	..	..	..	..	..	..	..	..	..	..	5,108.0
Agriculture	1,409.0	1,499.1	1,491.4	1,476.9	1,614.2	1,596.2	1,675.0	1,575.0	1,604.0	1,708.0	1,723.0
Industry	592.7	646.6	690.8	761.7	856.7	823.9	996.0	1,061.0	1,128.0	1,234.0	1,361.0
Manufacturing	422.0	447.0	486.0	507.0	556.0	546.0	664.0	721.0	772.0	851.0	970.0
Services, etc.	1,502.3	1,654.3	1,670.3	1,659.8	1,673.9	1,628.6	1,724.0	1,780.0	1,896.0	2,024.0	2,258.0

Memo Items:

	1970	1971	1972	1973	1974	1975	1976	1977	1978	1979	1980
Capacity to Import	459.0	524.6	517.6	545.5	510.9	552.8	736.5	860.3	916.3	855.4	1,094.1
Terms of Trade Adjustment	47.0	33.6	-2.4	-64.5	-138.1	-101.3	0.0	133.4	118.5	-38.4	-38.9
Gross Domestic Income	3,551.0	3,833.6	3,850.1	3,833.9	4,006.7	3,947.4	4,395.0	4,549.4	4,746.5	4,927.6	5,303.1
Gross National Income	3,500.0	3,781.6	3,792.1	3,784.9	3,956.7	3,909.2	4,359.0	4,493.5	4,677.0	4,869.6	5,245.6

DOMESTIC PRICES/DEFLATORS *(Index 1976 = 100)*

	1970	1971	1972	1973	1974	1975	1976	1977	1978	1979	1980
Overall (GDP)	56.3	58.6	61.7	72.9	84.2	89.1	100.0	111.8	108.1	112.7	136.8
Domestic Absorption	55.7	58.1	61.5	73.6	86.8	91.7	100.0	108.3	105.8	114.7	138.3
Agriculture	..	..	..	..	..	..	..	..	..	..	..
Industry	..	..	..	..	..	..	..	..	..	..	..
Manufacturing	..	..	..	..	..	..	..	..	..	..	..
Consumer Price Index	25.7	28.2	29.1	35.7	41.0	47.9	51.3	54.6	53.1	60.1	70.8

MANUFACTURING ACTIVITY

	1970	1971	1972	1973	1974	1975	1976	1977	1978	1979	1980
Employment (1987=100)	32.0	34.0	40.7	46.1	51.6	60.0	63.8	73.2	72.5	80.9	86.2
Real Earnings per Empl. (1987=100)	92.0	96.1	84.5	69.7	62.2	52.9	60.9	59.4	71.7	72.9	65.2
Real Output per Empl. (1987=100)	..	..	..	..	..	..	..	..	..	..	..
Earnings as % of Value Added	..	..	..	..	..	..	..	..	..	..	..

MONETARY HOLDINGS *(Millions of current Haitian Gourdes)*

	1970	1971	1972	1973	1974	1975	1976	1977	1978	1979	1980
Money Supply, Broadly Defined	248.6	290.0	381.6	487.3	583.7	734.8	1,015.2	1,216.8	1,431.5	1,872.7	1,938.2
Money	190.6	214.6	271.2	332.8	342.4	402.6	549.6	629.1	717.8	1,107.8	945.4
Currency Outside Banks	114.6	126.1	147.7	172.9	182.7	189.5	243.2	265.5	311.4	418.5	418.1
Demand Deposits	76.0	88.5	123.5	159.9	159.7	213.0	306.4	363.6	406.4	689.3	527.3
Quasi-Money	58.0	75.4	110.3	154.5	241.3	332.2	465.6	587.8	713.7	764.9	992.8

(Millions of current Haitian Gourdes)

GOVERNMENT DEFICIT (-) OR SURPLUS	1970	1971	1972	1973	1974	1975	1976	1977	1978	1979	1980
	..	..	..	..	..	..	..	..	..	-225.7	-341.7
Current Revenue	..	..	..	..	..	..	..	..	..	823.8	926.5
Current Expenditure	..	..	309.9	313.8	422.1	527.5	641.8	757.7	666.5	878.2	1,012.5
Current Budget Balance	..	..	..	..	..	..	..	..	..	-54.4	-86.0
Capital Receipts	..	..	..	..	..	..	..	..	..	..	..
Capital Payments	..	..	31.6	29.4	27.9	107.8	174.3	229.4	255.0	171.3	255.7

1981	1982	1983	1984	1985	1986	1987	1988	1989	1990 estimate	Notes	HAITI
270	270	280	290	320	340	360	360	360	370	..	**CURRENT GNP PER CAPITA (US $)**
5,467	5,568	5,673	5,780	5,889	6,000	6,114	6,230	6,349	6,472	..	**POPULATION (thousands)**
				(Millions of current Haitian Gourdes)							**USE AND ORIGIN OF RESOURCES**
7,270	7,341	8,026	8,983	9,974	11,134	10,739	10,957	11,623	12,089	C	Gross National Product (GNP)
-74	-84	-122	-99	-73	-84	-73	-97	-124	-1,721	..	Net Factor Income from Abroad
7,344	7,425	8,148	9,082	10,047	11,218	10,812	11,054	11,747	13,811	C	GDP at Market Prices
-1,124	-755	-848	-821	-821	-658	-856	-882	-913	-1,358	..	Resource Balance
1,243	1,465	1,427	1,587	1,520	1,458	1,412	1,382	1,442	1,700	..	Exports of Goods & NF Services
2,367	2,220	2,276	2,408	2,341	2,116	2,268	2,264	2,355	3,058	f	Imports of Goods & NF Services
8,468	8,180	8,996	9,903	10,868	11,876	11,668	11,936	12,660	15,169	..	Domestic Absorption
6,240	6,102	6,794	7,488	8,241	9,484	9,172	9,486	10,026	12,455	..	Private Consumption, etc.
826	848	871	974	1,197	1,168	1,096	1,067	1,176	1,205	..	General Gov't Consumption
1,402	1,230	1,331	1,441	1,431	1,225	1,400	1,384	1,458	1,509	f	Gross Domestic Investment
..	..	1,331	1,441	1,431	1,225	1,400	1,209	..	..	f	Fixed Investment
332	542	645	713	912	1,027	920	876	930	684	..	Indirect Taxes, net
7,012	6,883	7,503	8,369	9,135	10,191	9,892	10,178	10,818	13,127	B C	GDP at factor cost
..	..	..	..	..	..	..	..	..	..	..	Agriculture
..	..	..	..	..	..	..	..	..	..	..	Industry
..	..	..	..	..	..	..	..	..	..	..	Manufacturing
..	..	..	..	..	..	..	..	..	..	..	Services, etc.
278	475	483	620	609	567	544	501	545	151	..	Gross Domestic Saving
528	639	592	746	779	743	752	722	718	-1,337	..	Gross National Saving
				(Millions of 1976 Haitian Gourdes)							
5,145.0	4,963.1	4,981.2	5,016.6	5,044.4	5,074.4	5,056.0	4,968.3	4,930.6	4,937.2	C	Gross National Product
5,196.0	5,018.0	5,056.0	5,071.0	5,081.0	5,113.0	5,090.8	5,012.6	4,983.9	4,839.0	C	GDP at Market Prices
-659.6	-330.8	-437.9	-366.8	-372.1	-375.1	-465.0	-457.5	-490.9	-636.0	..	Resource Balance
862.6	1,058.4	958.1	1,017.1	956.0	868.4	836.0	829.0	824.5	1,007.0	..	Exports of Goods & NF Services
1,522.2	1,389.2	1,396.0	1,383.9	1,328.1	1,243.5	1,301.0	1,286.5	1,315.4	1,643.0	f	Imports of Goods & NF Services
5,855.5	5,348.7	5,493.9	5,437.9	5,453.1	5,488.1	5,556.0	5,470.0	5,474.8	5,475.0	..	Domestic Absorption
4,249.5	3,938.4	4,061.4	3,944.7	4,021.3	4,236.3	4,309.5	4,258.1	4,249.9	..	..	Private Consumption, etc.
562.0	533.6	508.2	526.1	596.5	537.8	500.0	473.0	493.3	..	..	General Gov't Consumption
1,044.0	876.7	924.3	967.1	835.3	714.0	746.5	738.9	731.6	745.0	f	Gross Domestic Investment
1,044.0	876.7	924.3	967.1	835.3	714.0	746.5	738.9	731.6	745.0	f	Fixed Investment
4,961.0	4,652.0	4,656.0	4,673.0	4,620.0	4,645.0	4,657.8	4,615.3	4,589.4	..	BC	GDP at factor cost
1,699.0	1,627.0	1,566.0	1,621.0	1,629.0	1,671.0	1,666.0	1,635.2	1,602.4	..	..	Agriculture
1,249.0	1,223.0	1,221.0	1,177.0	1,190.0	1,149.0	1,141.0	1,141.4	1,159.0	..	..	Industry
856.0	843.0	888.0	836.0	812.0	789.0	773.0	766.8	778.8	..	..	Manufacturing
2,248.0	2,168.0	2,269.0	2,273.0	2,262.0	2,293.0	2,283.8	2,236.0	2,222.5	..	..	Services, etc.
											Memo Items:
799.4	916.5	875.6	912.1	862.1	856.7	809.9	785.2	805.4	913.4	..	Capacity to Import
-63.2	-141.9	-82.5	-105.0	-93.9	-11.7	-26.1	-43.8	-19.1	-93.6	..	Terms of Trade Adjustment
5,132.8	4,876.1	4,973.5	4,966.0	4,987.1	5,101.3	5,064.7	4,968.8	4,964.8	4,745.4	..	Gross Domestic Income
5,081.8	4,821.2	4,898.7	4,911.6	4,950.5	5,062.7	5,029.9	4,924.5	4,911.5	4,843.6	..	Gross National Income
				(Index 1976 = 100)							**DOMESTIC PRICES/DEFLATORS**
141.3	148.0	161.2	179.1	197.7	219.4	212.4	220.5	235.7	285.4	..	Overall (GDP)
144.6	152.9	163.8	182.1	199.3	216.4	210.0	218.2	231.2	277.1	..	Domestic Absorption
..	..	..	..	..	..	..	..	..	..	..	Agriculture
..	..	..	..	..	..	..	..	..	..	..	Industry
..	..	..	..	..	..	..	..	..	..	..	Manufacturing
78.5	84.2	92.9	98.8	109.3	112.9	100.0	104.1	111.3	135.2	f	Consumer Price Index
											MANUFACTURING ACTIVITY
88.3	95.7	105.4	97.1	99.5	109.3	100.0	94.7	..	..	..	Employment (1987=100)
73.5	75.5	70.2	70.0	67.7	75.7	100.0	102.6	..	..	..	Real Earnings per Empl. (1987=100)
..	..	..	..	..	..	..	..	..	..	..	Real Output per Empl. (1987=100)
..	..	..	..	..	..	..	..	..	..	..	Earnings as % of Value Added
				(Millions of current Haitian Gourdes)							**MONETARY HOLDINGS**
2,175.0	2,247.0	2,347.7	2,606.1	1,442.4	3,276.5	3,693.6	3,312.9	4,558.8	..	..	Money Supply, Broadly Defined
1,166.5	1,164.3	1,174.7	1,388.0	1,076.1	1,789.9	2,097.9	1,635.2	2,633.6	..	..	Money
487.4	565.6	599.5	691.0	763.2	829.1	979.5	205.0	1,458.8	..	..	Currency Outside Banks
679.1	598.7	575.2	697.0	312.9	960.8	1,118.3	1,430.2	1,174.8	..	..	Demand Deposits
1,008.5	1,082.7	1,173.0	1,218.1	366.4	1,486.7	1,595.7	1,677.7	1,925.3	..	..	Quasi-Money
				(Millions of current Haitian Gourdes)							
..	-236.3	-72.5	-91.7	120.9	-191.1	-795.5	..	..	..	C	**GOVERNMENT DEFICIT (-) OR SURPLUS**
..	1,113.3	1,345.9	1,590.8	1,929.7	1,596.8	1,262.3	..	..	..	..	Current Revenue
1,299.7	1,205.4	1,406.8	..	1,798.5	1,709.8	1,959.3	..	..	..	..	Current Expenditure
..	-92.1	-60.9	..	131.2	-113.0	-697.0	..	..	..	..	Current Budget Balance
..	..	..	..	..	..	..	..	..	..	..	Capital Receipts
160.4	144.2	11.6	..	10.3	82.1	98.5	..	..	..	..	Capital Payments

HAITI	1970	1971	1972	1973	1974	1975	1976	1977	1978	1979	1980

FOREIGN TRADE (CUSTOMS BASIS) *(Millions of current US dollars)*

Value of Exports, fob	..	..	..	..	..	..	..	..	..	..	..
Nonfuel Primary Products	..	..	..	..	..	..	..	..	..	..	..
Fuels	..	..	..	..	..	..	..	..	..	..	..
Manufactures	..	..	..	..	..	..	..	..	..	..	..
Value of Imports, cif	..	..	..	..	..	..	..	..	..	..	..
Nonfuel Primary Products	..	..	..	..	..	..	..	..	..	..	..
Fuels	..	..	..	..	..	..	..	..	..	..	..
Manufactures	..	..	..	..	..	..	..	..	..	..	..

(Index 1987 = 100)

Terms of Trade	..	..	..	..	..	..	..	..	..	..	..
Export Prices, fob	..	..	..	..	..	..	..	..	..	..	..
Import Prices, cif	..	..	..	..	..	..	..	..	..	..	..

BALANCE OF PAYMENTS *(Millions of current US dollars)*

	1970	1971	1972	1973	1974	1975	1976	1977	1978	1979	1980
Exports of Goods & Services	53.00	..	..	52.92	59.24	67.70	129.44	175.40	213.26	215.54	308.78
Merchandise, fob	39.10	29.72	26.42	31.06	37.22	41.82	99.68	137.64	149.92	137.98	215.80
Nonfactor Services	13.80	18.80	21.02	21.62	21.78	25.58	28.76	36.44	61.30	74.94	89.88
Factor Services	0.10	..	..	0.24	0.24	0.30	1.00	1.32	2.04	2.62	3.10
Imports of Goods & Services	63.80	73.34	79.82	92.76	130.14	157.02	229.08	276.40	325.80	343.96	498.36
Merchandise, fob	41.90	47.22	51.76	58.52	87.32	111.70	164.20	199.92	207.46	220.06	319.00
Nonfactor Services	18.30	20.96	22.66	27.68	34.76	37.88	56.70	63.12	101.62	107.88	161.96
Factor Services	3.60	5.16	5.40	6.56	8.06	7.44	8.18	13.36	16.72	16.02	17.40
Long-Term Interest	0.40	0.30	0.30	0.50	0.50	1.20	1.50	3.80	4.50	3.50	5.10
Private Current Transfers, net	14.80	-2.80	1.40	-4.72	-5.72	-34.48	-37.88	30.92	28.72	34.10	52.10
Workers' Remittances	16.50	1.32	2.44	1.70	2.44	2.60	3.66	75.02	76.00	84.78	106.44
Curr. A/C Bal before Off. Transf.	4.00	-27.62	-30.98	-44.56	-76.62	-123.80	-137.52	-70.08	-83.82	-94.32	-137.48
Net Official Transfers	7.10	5.74	7.48	8.76	11.20	13.44	31.92	32.58	39.18	41.76	36.64
Curr. A/C Bal after Off. Transf.	11.10	-21.88	-23.50	-35.80	-65.42	-110.36	-105.60	-37.50	-44.64	-52.56	-100.84
Long-Term Capital, net	2.60	2.70	15.26	1.30	10.34	36.12	33.92	67.98	40.08	61.18	80.34
Direct Investment	2.80	3.40	4.06	6.98	7.94	2.64	7.78	8.00	10.00	12.00	13.00
Long-Term Loans	0.90	-1.20	1.10	-2.20	4.80	10.80	35.40	48.10	38.50	35.90	31.80
Disbursements	4.30	3.00	4.60	3.00	10.40	17.10	44.10	63.10	52.60	44.40	47.10
Repayments	3.40	4.20	3.50	5.20	5.60	6.30	8.70	15.00	14.10	8.50	15.30
Other Long-Term Capital	-1.10	0.50	10.10	-3.48	-2.40	22.68	-9.26	11.88	-8.42	13.28	35.54
Other Capital, net	-12.47	27.24	16.41	34.61	44.20	61.29	82.79	-18.18	18.66	-0.47	-8.69
Change in Reserves	-1.23	-8.06	-8.17	-0.11	10.88	12.95	-11.11	-12.30	-14.10	-8.15	29.19

Memo Item: *(Haitian Gourdes per US dollar)*

	1970	1971	1972	1973	1974	1975	1976	1977	1978	1979	1980
Conversion Factor (Annual Avg)	5.000	5.000	5.000	5.000	5.000	5.000	5.000	5.000	5.000	5.000	5.000

(Millions of US dollars), outstanding at end of year

	1970	1971	1972	1973	1974	1975	1976	1977	1978	1979	1980
EXTERNAL DEBT (Total)	42.90	39.90	43.40	41.00	49.50	69.60	102.60	156.40	201.00	254.10	302.40
Long-Term Debt (by debtor)	42.90	39.90	43.40	41.00	49.50	69.60	102.60	148.40	195.00	235.10	288.40
Central Bank, incl. IMF credit	2.90	1.20	0.00	0.00	4.00	17.50	25.40	33.70	56.60	70.20	99.70
Central Government	35.90	35.10	36.80	34.00	32.10	38.70	53.30	88.50	111.00	132.00	152.90
Rest of General Government	..	..	..	..	..	..	..	..	..	..	..
Non-financial Public Enterprises	4.10	3.60	6.60	7.00	13.40	13.40	23.90	26.20	27.40	32.90	28.40
Priv. Sector, incl non-guaranteed	0.00	0.00	0.00	0.00	0.00	0.00	0.00	0.00	0.00	0.00	7.40
Short-Term Debt	0.00	0.00	0.00	0.00	0.00	0.00	0.00	8.00	6.00	19.00	14.00

Memo Items: *(Thousands of US dollars)*

	1970	1971	1972	1973	1974	1975	1976	1977	1978	1979	1980
Int'l Reserves Excluding Gold	4,300	10,387	17,882	17,032	19,700	12,430	27,941	33,844	38,638	55,015	16,226
Gold Holdings (at market price)	..	..	..	..	289	217	208	926	2,195	9,118	10,498

SOCIAL INDICATORS

	1970	1971	1972	1973	1974	1975	1976	1977	1978	1979	1980
Total Fertility Rate	5.9	5.8	5.8	5.7	5.6	5.5	5.4	5.4	5.3	5.3	5.2
Infant Mortality Rate	141.0	138.0	135.0	132.2	129.4	126.6	123.8	121.0	118.4	115.8	113.2
Life Expectancy at Birth	47.6	48.0	48.5	48.9	49.4	49.8	50.2	50.7	51.1	51.5	51.9
Urban Population, % of total	19.8	20.2	20.6	20.9	21.3	21.7	22.1	22.5	22.9	23.3	23.7
Food Prod. per capita (1987=100)	97.9	99.2	100.5	100.6	101.5	100.9	101.9	98.2	101.7	102.5	99.4
Labor Force, Agriculture (%)	74.4	73.9	73.5	73.0	72.6	72.2	71.7	71.3	70.8	70.4	70.0
Labor Force, Female (%)	46.6	46.3	46.1	45.8	45.6	45.4	45.1	44.8	44.5	44.2	44.0
Primary Schl. Enroll. Ratio	..	53.0	..	..	..	60.0	61.0	60.0	60.0	64.0	76.0
Primary Schl. Enroll. Ratio, Female	..	..	..	..	..	..	..	..	55.0	59.0	70.0
Secondary Schl. Enroll. Ratio	..	6.0	..	..	..	8.0	10.0	11.0	12.0	12.0	14.0

1981	1982	1983	1984	1985	1986	1987	1988	1989	1990 estimate	Notes	HAITI
				(Millions of current US dollars)							**FOREIGN TRADE (CUSTOMS BASIS)**
..	..	..	..	..	..	..	..	..	..		Value of Exports, fob
..	..	..	..	..	..	..	..	..	..		Nonfuel Primary Products
..	..	..	..	..	..	..	..	..	..		Fuels
..	..	..	..	..	..	..	..	..	..		Manufactures
..	..	..	..	..	..	..	..	..	..		Value of Imports, cif
..	..	..	..	..	..	..	..	..	..		Nonfuel Primary Products
..	..	..	..	..	..	..	..	..	..		Fuels
..	..	..	..	..	..	..	..	..	..		Manufactures
				(Index 1987 = 100)							
..	..	..	..	..	..	..	..	..	..		Terms of Trade
..	..	..	..	..	..	..	..	..	..		Export Prices, fob
..	..	..	..	..	..	..	..	..	..		Import Prices, cif
				(Millions of current US dollars)							**BALANCE OF PAYMENTS**
245.66	278.48	294.54	323.54	342.28	296.62	325.60	281.10	241.38	227.06	C	Exports of Goods & Services
151.12	177.14	186.56	214.58	223.00	190.78	210.12	180.38	148.26	139.00		Merchandise, fob
90.40	97.72	103.28	104.46	114.18	101.28	110.28	94.48	88.48	83.54		Nonfactor Services
4.14	3.62	4.70	4.50	5.10	4.56	5.20	6.24	4.64	4.52		Factor Services
533.80	488.75	516.07	549.56	581.97	493.42	527.82	514.30	478.24	432.06	C	Imports of Goods & Services
360.14	301.92	325.90	337.86	344.70	303.24	311.18	283.86	259.26	224.82		Merchandise, fob
156.46	169.14	171.32	189.10	212.38	170.24	190.52	197.12	188.84	177.68		Nonfactor Services
17.20	17.69	18.85	22.60	24.89	19.94	26.12	33.32	30.14	29.56		Factor Services
5.60	6.30	6.10	6.20	7.00	7.40	8.60	8.10	9.20	5.60		Long-Term Interest
64.78	49.70	46.40	45.00	48.54	52.02	56.24	63.42	59.34	46.80		Private Current Transfers, net
126.62	97.04	89.88	90.00	95.78	105.42	113.16	124.10	122.80	111.00		Workers' Remittances
-223.36	-160.57	-175.13	-181.02	-191.15	-144.78	-145.98	-169.78	-177.52	-158.20		Curr. A/C Bal before Off. Transf.
74.56	62.00	64.00	78.00	96.50	99.84	114.82	129.46	114.94	103.00		Net Official Transfers
-148.80	-98.57	-111.13	-103.02	-94.65	-44.94	-31.16	-40.32	-62.58	-55.20		Curr. A/C Bal after Off. Transf.
111.10	84.56	85.29	90.39	53.79	39.19	57.66	23.41	32.89	36.74	C	Long-Term Capital, net
8.34	7.08	8.42	4.46	4.92	4.82	4.68	10.10	9.36	8.20		Direct Investment
101.60	57.50	34.50	48.90	55.50	32.40	75.80	35.10	14.20	31.00		Long-Term Loans
116.70	65.90	41.80	58.60	66.10	39.30	90.00	50.20	28.90	36.80		Disbursements
15.10	8.40	7.30	9.70	10.60	6.90	14.20	15.10	14.70	5.80		Repayments
1.16	19.98	42.37	37.03	-6.63	1.97	-22.82	-21.79	9.33	-2.46		Other Long-Term Capital
-0.47	-5.71	-3.10	-8.53	43.44	26.06	-25.17	38.05	28.99	43.60	C	Other Capital, net
38.17	19.73	28.94	21.17	-2.58	-20.31	-1.33	-21.13	0.69	-25.14		Change in Reserves
				(Haitian Gourdes per US dollar)							**Memo Item:**
5.000	5.000	5.000	5.000	5.000	5.000	5.000	5.000	5.000	5.000		Conversion Factor (Annual Avg)
			(Millions of US dollars), outstanding at end of year								
423.00	536.10	569.40	664.40	717.30	710.30	844.20	818.10	802.50	873.60		**EXTERNAL DEBT (Total)**
399.00	463.10	523.40	575.70	617.90	654.30	753.80	730.60	725.70	782.90		Long-Term Debt (by debtor)
122.90	148.00	186.10	204.80	211.80	196.50	201.30	172.60	170.80	170.10		Central Bank, incl. IMF credit
228.00	261.10	286.60	324.30	360.20	411.90	510.30	518.70	528.30	583.00		Central Government
..	..	..	..	..	..	..	..	..	..		Rest of General Government
41.10	48.50	45.80	42.40	41.10	40.00	38.60	36.30	26.60	29.80		Non-financial Public Enterprises
7.00	5.50	4.90	4.20	4.80	5.90	3.60	3.00	0.00			Priv. Sector, incl non-guaranteed
24.00	73.00	46.00	88.70	99.40	56.00	90.40	87.50	76.80	90.70		Short-Term Debt
				(Thousands of US dollars)							**Memo Items:**
24,047	4,225	8,968	12,978	6,388	15,879	16,999	12,994	12,597	3,171		Int'l Reserves Excluding Gold
7,079	8,136	6,794	5,490	5,823	6,961	8,621	7,364	7,232	6,997		Gold Holdings (at market price)
											SOCIAL INDICATORS
5.2	5.2	5.1	5.1	5.1	5.0	5.0	4.9	4.9	4.8		Total Fertility Rate
110.6	108.0	105.9	103.7	101.6	99.4	97.3	96.4	95.6	94.7		Infant Mortality Rate
52.3	52.7	53.0	53.2	53.5	53.7	54.0	54.1	54.2	54.4		Life Expectancy at Birth
24.1	24.5	25.0	25.4	25.8	26.3	26.8	27.2	27.7	28.2		Urban Population, % of total
98.3	97.7	99.5	100.1	100.7	100.2	100.0	96.0	94.3	90.9		Food Prod. per capita (1987=100)
..	..	..	..	..	..	..	..	..	..		Labor Force, Agriculture (%)
43.7	43.5	43.3	43.1	42.8	42.6	42.3	42.1	41.9	41.6		Labor Force, Female (%)
67.0	81.0	87.0	92.0	96.0	83.0	84.0	..	..	..		Primary Schl. Enroll. Ratio
63.0	76.0	82.0	85.0	90.0	80.0	81.0	..	..	..		Primary Schl. Enroll. Ratio, Female
12.0	15.0	17.0	20.0	18.0	19.0	19.0	..	..	..		Secondary Schl. Enroll. Ratio

HONDURAS	1970	1971	1972	1973	1974	1975	1976	1977	1978	1979	1980
CURRENT GNP PER CAPITA (US $)	270	280	290	310	340	360	400	460	530	600	640
POPULATION (thousands)	2,627	2,706	2,792	2,884	2,980	3,081	3,186	3,296	3,411	3,533	3,662

USE AND ORIGIN OF RESOURCES

(Millions of current Honduran Lempiras)

	1970	1971	1972	1973	1974	1975	1976	1977	1978	1979	1980
Gross National Product (GNP)	1,400.8	1,413.0	1,551.0	1,759.0	2,042.0	2,190.0	2,580.0	3,201.0	3,627.0	4,184.0	4,781.0
Net Factor Income from Abroad	-45.2	-49.0	-55.0	-66.0	-27.0	-58.0	-116.0	-138.0	-171.0	-241.0	-307.0
GDP at Market Prices	1,446.0	1,462.0	1,606.0	1,825.0	2,069.0	2,248.0	2,696.0	3,339.0	3,798.0	4,425.0	5,088.0
Resource Balance	-89.6	-12.0	17.0	-16.0	-247.0	-202.0	-120.0	-148.0	-175.0	-184.0	-370.0
Exports of Goods & NFServices	403.6	434.0	470.0	588.0	665.0	690.0	909.0	1,163.0	1,380.0	1,679.0	1,886.0
Imports of Goods & NFServices	493.2	446.0	453.0	604.0	912.0	892.0	1,029.0	1,311.0	1,555.0	1,863.0	2,256.0
Domestic Absorption	1,535.6	1,474.0	1,589.0	1,841.0	2,316.0	2,450.0	2,816.0	3,487.0	3,973.0	4,609.0	5,458.0
Private Consumption, etc.	1,067.6	1,049.0	1,140.0	1,307.0	1,532.0	1,746.0	1,950.0	2,300.0	2,497.0	2,915.0	3,532.0
General Gov't Consumption	166.0	175.0	193.0	186.0	242.0	278.0	348.0	417.0	442.0	520.0	678.0
Gross Domestic Investment	302.0	250.0	256.0	348.0	542.0	426.0	518.0	770.0	1,034.0	1,174.0	1,248.0
Fixed Investment	268.0	253.0	245.0	325.0	433.0	476.0	550.0	711.0	941.0	1,004.0	1,235.0
Indirect Taxes, net	139.0	143.0	151.0	170.0	199.0	221.0	286.0	407.0	426.0	496.0	539.0
GDP at factor cost	1,307.0	1,319.0	1,455.0	1,655.0	1,870.0	2,027.0	2,410.0	2,932.0	3,372.0	3,929.0	4,549.0
Agriculture	424.0	413.0	450.0	511.0	550.0	554.0	688.0	898.0	945.0	1,038.0	1,132.0
Industry	290.0	299.0	329.0	397.0	474.0	505.0	560.0	679.0	836.0	978.0	1,143.0
Manufacturing	181.0	196.0	221.0	261.0	294.0	319.0	363.0	443.0	520.0	606.0	687.0
Services, etc.	593.0	607.0	676.0	747.0	846.0	968.0	1,162.0	1,355.0	1,591.0	1,913.0	2,274.0
Gross Domestic Saving	212.4	238.0	273.0	332.0	295.0	224.0	398.0	622.0	859.0	990.0	878.0
Gross National Saving	173.0	195.2	224.5	272.9	295.1	175.8	288.6	491.7	696.9	762.8	586.0

(Millions of 1987 Honduran Lempiras)

	1970	1971	1972	1973	1974	1975	1976	1977	1978	1979	1980
Gross National Product	3,994.7	4,140.4	4,387.9	4,726.0	4,855.9	4,915.7	5,311.9	5,842.9	6,305.3	6,677.3	6,720.9
GDP at Market Prices	4,134.7	4,294.0	4,548.7	4,907.7	4,863.5	4,986.3	5,508.4	6,084.2	6,591.8	7,007.6	7,101.6
Resource Balance	-326.2	-21.3	35.8	-93.2	-378.6	-211.1	-351.2	-658.8	-619.3	-475.3	-660.2
Exports of Goods & NFServices	1,129.4	1,278.6	1,281.0	1,411.4	1,271.6	1,321.0	1,335.1	1,331.5	1,621.8	1,902.7	1,802.8
Imports of Goods & NFServices	1,455.6	1,300.0	1,245.2	1,504.6	1,650.2	1,532.0	1,686.2	1,990.3	2,241.1	2,378.0	2,463.0
Domestic Absorption	4,460.9	4,315.3	4,512.9	5,000.8	5,242.1	5,197.3	5,859.6	6,743.0	7,211.1	7,482.9	7,761.8
Private Consumption, etc.	3,100.6	3,091.3	3,268.8	3,627.0	3,508.5	3,660.4	4,137.2	4,650.8	4,768.1	4,935.7	5,199.3
General Gov't Consumption	539.2	557.2	591.0	545.2	626.8	670.6	793.9	841.7	879.5	923.3	1,018.8
Gross Domestic Investment	821.0	666.8	653.2	828.6	1,106.8	866.4	928.4	1,250.4	1,563.4	1,623.9	1,543.8
Fixed Investment	722.3	662.7	621.0	768.4	871.2	948.6	971.0	1,139.2	1,401.3	1,370.1	1,505.6
GDP at factor cost	3,712.1	3,867.1	4,113.6	4,424.5	4,389.0	4,492.6	4,918.8	5,336.2	5,846.8	6,389.0	6,344.0
Agriculture	987.5	1,076.8	1,097.8	1,160.8	1,057.1	986.2	1,096.5	1,162.1	1,240.9	1,342.0	1,331.5
Industry	807.9	832.0	894.0	1,016.3	1,068.0	1,073.1	1,124.8	1,272.9	1,440.0	1,669.1	1,557.1
Manufacturing	470.2	501.3	553.7	624.2	627.4	652.0	697.9	792.9	851.9	907.6	881.4
Services, etc.	1,916.8	1,958.4	2,121.9	2,247.4	2,264.0	2,433.3	2,697.6	2,901.1	3,165.9	3,377.9	3,455.4

Memo Items:

	1970	1971	1972	1973	1974	1975	1976	1977	1978	1979	1980
Capacity to Import	1,191.2	1,265.0	1,291.9	1,464.8	1,203.3	1,185.1	1,489.6	1,765.6	1,988.9	2,143.1	2,059.1
Terms of Trade Adjustment	61.8	-13.6	10.9	53.3	-68.3	-135.9	154.5	434.1	367.1	240.4	256.3
Gross Domestic Income	4,196.4	4,280.3	4,559.7	4,961.0	4,795.2	4,850.4	5,662.9	6,518.3	6,958.8	7,248.1	7,357.9
Gross National Income	4,056.5	4,126.7	4,398.8	4,779.3	4,787.5	4,779.9	5,466.5	6,277.0	6,672.3	6,917.8	6,977.2

DOMESTIC PRICES/DEFLATORS

(Index 1987 = 100)

	1970	1971	1972	1973	1974	1975	1976	1977	1978	1979	1980
Overall (GDP)	35.0	34.0	35.3	37.2	42.5	45.1	48.9	54.9	57.6	63.1	71.6
Domestic Absorption	34.4	34.2	35.2	36.8	44.2	47.1	48.1	51.7	55.1	61.6	70.3
Agriculture	42.9	38.4	41.0	44.0	52.0	56.2	62.7	77.3	76.2	77.3	85.0
Industry	35.9	35.9	36.8	39.1	44.4	47.1	49.8	53.3	58.1	58.6	73.4
Manufacturing	38.5	39.1	39.9	41.8	46.9	48.9	52.0	55.9	61.0	66.8	77.9
Consumer Price Index	30.8	31.5	32.7	34.4	38.8	42.0	44.1	47.8	50.5	56.7	66.9

MANUFACTURING ACTIVITY

	1970	1971	1972	1973	1974	1975	1976	1977	1978	1979	1980
Employment (1987=100)	..	44.8	42.8	49.3	53.4	57.6	61.3	66.9	73.1	80.3	86.2
Real Earnings per Empl. (1987=100)	..	98.8	105.3	104.1	99.8	95.0	..	..	..	..	..
Real Output per Empl. (1987=100)	..	78.7	89.2	95.3	98.2	95.3	..	..	..	..	..
Earnings as % of Value Added	..	37.5	36.9	37.3	38.0	37.5	..	..	..	..	..

MONETARY HOLDINGS

(Millions of current Honduran Lempiras)

	1970	1971	1972	1973	1974	1975	1976	1977	1978	1979	1980
Money Supply, Broadly Defined	300.3	333.1	378.5	460.6	474.4	532.0	692.6	839.4	1,008.6	1,107.2	1,212.3
Money	158.9	169.4	192.9	238.4	242.4	262.7	361.0	411.3	480.4	545.6	610.3
Currency Outside Banks	76.8	80.2	90.1	112.2	108.8	114.8	173.3	193.2	215.4	270.1	274.6
Demand Deposits	82.1	89.2	102.8	126.2	133.6	147.9	187.7	218.1	265.0	275.5	335.7
Quasi-Money	141.4	163.7	185.6	222.2	232.0	269.3	331.6	428.1	528.2	561.6	602.0

GOVERNMENT DEFICIT (-) OR SURPLUS

(Millions of current Honduran Lempiras)

	1970	1971	1972	1973	1974	1975	1976	1977	1978	1979	1980
GOVERNMENT DEFICIT (-) OR SURPLUS	..	..	..	-44.70	-8.20	-18.40	-63.40	-64.00			
Current Revenue	172.80	179.40	205.60	241.80	278.00	308.30	390.40	476.90	519.10	631.60	748.20
Current Expenditure	..	..	186.20	198.10	201.60	235.50	288.40	..	..	..	..
Current Budget Balance	..	..	19.40	43.70	76.40	72.80	102.00	..	..	..	..
Capital Receipts	..	..	1.00	0.10	0.10	1.30	..	..	..	..	..
Capital Payments	..	..	65.10	52.00	94.90	137.50	166.00	..	..	..	..

1981	1982	1983	1984	1985	1986	1987	1988	1989	1990 estimate	Notes	HONDURAS
690	680	690	720	740	760	820	830	740	590	A	**CURRENT GNP PER CAPITA (US $)**
3,798	3,941	4,089	4,237	4,383	4,528	4,672	4,815	4,959	5,105	..	POPULATION (thousands)

(Millions of current Honduran Lempiras)

USE AND ORIGIN OF RESOURCES

1981	1982	1983	1984	1985	1986	1987	1988	1989	1990	Notes	
5,247.0	5,359.0	5,731.0	6,106.0	6,628.0	7,090.0	7,653.0	8,413.0	9,060.3	10,518.3	..	Gross National Product (GNP)
-306.0	-403.0	-304.0	-356.0	-380.0	-506.0	-475.0	-524.0	-721.7	-1,141.7	..	Net Factor Income from Abroad
5,553.0	5,762.0	6,035.0	6,462.0	7,008.0	7,596.0	8,128.0	8,937.0	9,782.0	11,660.0	..	GDP at Market Prices
-354.0	-105.0	-223.0	-437.0	-319.0	-105.0	-237.0	-305.0	-323.0	-819.0	..	Resource Balance
1,771.0	1,537.0	1,606.0	1,699.0	1,811.0	2,022.0	1,945.0	2,333.0	3,199.0	4,669.0	..	Exports of Goods & NFServices
2,125.0	1,642.0	1,829.0	2,136.0	2,130.0	2,127.0	2,182.0	2,638.0	3,522.0	5,488.0	..	Imports of Goods & NFServices
5,907.0	5,867.0	6,258.0	6,899.0	7,327.0	7,701.0	8,365.0	9,242.0	10,105.0	12,479.0	..	Domestic Absorption
3,998.0	4,291.0	4,484.0	4,716.0	5,017.0	5,329.0	5,798.0	6,611.0	7,297.0	9,282.0	..	Private Consumption, etc.
758.0	800.0	877.0	952.0	1,046.0	1,297.0	1,371.0	1,465.0	1,607.0	1,703.0	..	General Gov't Consumption
1,151.0	776.0	897.0	1,231.0	1,264.0	1,075.0	1,196.0	1,166.0	1,201.0	1,494.0	..	Gross Domestic Investment
1,051.0	966.0	1,073.0	1,246.0	1,252.0	1,088.0	1,035.0	1,141.0	1,306.0	1,344.0	..	Fixed Investment
597.0	577.0	616.0	705.0	842.0	829.0	945.0	1,036.0	1,095.0	1,625.0	..	Indirect Taxes, net
4,956.0	5,185.0	5,419.0	5,757.0	6,166.0	6,767.0	7,183.0	7,901.0	8,687.0	10,035.0	..	GDP at factor cost
1,166.0	1,186.0	1,226.0	1,253.0	1,328.0	1,495.0	1,518.0	1,630.0	1,779.0	2,327.0	..	Agriculture
1,180.0	1,335.0	1,392.0	1,502.0	1,540.0	1,658.0	1,707.0	1,935.0	2,153.0	2,377.0	..	Industry
726.0	766.0	832.0	913.0	926.0	962.0	1,055.0	1,232.0	1,369.0	1,559.0	..	Manufacturing
2,610.0	2,664.0	2,801.0	3,002.0	3,298.0	3,614.0	3,958.0	4,336.0	4,755.0	5,331.0	..	Services, etc.
797.0	671.0	674.0	794.0	945.0	970.0	959.0	861.0	878.0	675.0	..	Gross Domestic Saving
508.8	286.0	389.4	458.6	589.8	490.0	516.0	372.0	188.3	-361.8	..	Gross National Saving

(Millions of 1987 Honduran Lempiras)

1981	1982	1983	1984	1985	1986	1987	1988	1989	1990	Notes	
6,889.2	6,604.7	6,709.8	6,874.4	7,088.9	7,165.9	7,653.0	8,049.3	8,137.7	7,862.1	..	Gross National Product
7,209.6	7,064.2	7,046.2	7,238.5	7,499.2	7,716.7	8,128.0	8,566.8	8,768.0	8,669.8	..	GDP at Market Prices
-319.3	62.8	-61.7	-342.2	-302.6	-185.5	-237.0	-199.6	-116.9	-172.1	..	Resource Balance
1,843.9	1,626.5	1,781.6	1,811.0	1,859.2	1,940.3	1,945.0	2,015.5	2,108.4	2,053.1	..	Exports of Goods & NFServices
2,163.3	1,563.7	1,843.3	2,153.2	2,161.8	2,125.8	2,182.0	2,215.1	2,225.2	2,225.2	..	Imports of Goods & NFServices
7,528.9	7,001.4	7,107.9	7,580.7	7,801.8	7,902.2	8,365.0	8,766.4	8,884.8	8,841.9	..	Domestic Absorption
5,191.9	5,219.9	5,149.6	5,199.1	5,373.6	5,460.1	5,798.0	6,206.7	6,352.7	6,336.8	..	Private Consumption, etc.
1,042.7	1,008.8	1,020.8	1,058.6	1,114.3	1,329.2	1,371.0	1,422.7	1,452.6	1,365.0	..	General Gov't Consumption
1,294.3	772.6	937.4	1,323.0	1,313.9	1,112.8	1,196.0	1,137.0	1,079.6	1,140.1	..	Gross Domestic Investment
1,163.1	960.5	1,100.5	1,317.9	1,282.2	1,108.0	1,035.0	1,099.0	1,146.7	1,018.6	..	Fixed Investment
6,427.6	6,350.1	6,320.0	6,442.3	6,591.0	6,859.2	7,183.0	7,557.1	7,742.5	7,570.8	..	GDP at factor cost
1,382.7	1,374.9	1,365.7	1,382.7	1,423.5	1,457.6	1,518.0	1,545.6	1,579.7	1,583.7	..	Agriculture
1,424.5	1,496.9	1,526.1	1,617.4	1,601.9	1,684.6	1,707.0	1,822.4	1,874.1	1,774.2	..	Industry
860.1	828.9	873.2	946.9	930.5	958.3	1,055.0	1,143.5	1,163.1	1,163.1	..	Manufacturing
3,620.4	3,478.4	3,428.1	3,442.1	3,565.6	3,717.0	3,958.0	4,189.1	4,288.7	4,213.0	..	Services, etc.

Memo Items:

1981	1982	1983	1984	1985	1986	1987	1988	1989	1990	Notes	
1,802.9	1,463.7	1,618.6	1,712.7	1,838.1	2,020.9	1,945.0	1,959.0	2,021.2	1,893.2	..	Capacity to Import
-41.0	-162.8	-163.1	-98.4	-21.2	80.6	0.0	-56.5	-87.2	-160.0	..	Terms of Trade Adjustment
7,168.5	6,901.4	6,883.1	7,140.2	7,478.1	7,797.2	8,128.0	8,510.3	8,680.8	8,509.8	..	Gross Domestic Income
6,848.2	6,441.9	6,546.7	6,776.0	7,067.8	7,246.5	7,653.0	7,992.8	8,050.5	7,702.2	..	Gross National Income

(Index 1987 = 100)

DOMESTIC PRICES/DEFLATORS

1981	1982	1983	1984	1985	1986	1987	1988	1989	1990	Notes	
77.0	81.6	85.6	89.3	93.4	98.4	100.0	104.3	111.6	134.5	..	Overall (GDP)
78.5	83.8	88.0	91.0	93.9	97.5	100.0	105.4	113.7	141.1	..	Domestic Absorption
84.3	86.3	89.8	90.6	93.3	102.6	100.0	105.5	112.6	146.9	..	Agriculture
82.8	89.2	91.2	92.9	96.1	98.4	100.0	106.2	114.9	134.0	..	Industry
84.4	92.4	95.3	96.4	99.5	100.4	100.0	107.7	117.7	134.0	..	Manufacturing
73.2	79.8	86.4	90.5	93.5	97.6	100.0	104.5	114.8	141.6	..	Consumer Price Index

MANUFACTURING ACTIVITY

1981	1982	1983	1984	1985	1986	1987	1988	1989	1990	Notes	
92.5	99.5	95.3	96.4	100.3	97.9	100.0	104.8	..	..	G	Employment (1987=100)
..	..	92.9	98.4	97.4	98.4	100.0	102.7	..	..	G	Real Earnings per Empl. (1987=100)
..	..	84.6	93.0	88.0	91.5	100.0	102.8	..	..	G	Real Output per Empl. (1987=100)
..	..	39.3	39.8	41.2	41.2	40.6	39.5	..	..	..	Earnings as % of Value Added

(Millions of current Honduran Lempiras)

MONETARY HOLDINGS

1981	1982	1983	1984	1985	1986	1987	1988	1989	1990	Notes	
1,320.9	1,579.2	1,851.7	2,056.4	2,009.5	2,203.0	2,707.7	3,085.3	3,513.8	4,256.0	D	Money Supply, Broadly Defined
637.4	716.9	814.9	846.0	855.6	955.3	1,119.1	1,252.6	1,523.7	1,969.8	..	Money
302.2	313.6	361.9	383.5	410.2	425.8	491.5	570.3	676.0	882.4	..	Currency Outside Banks
335.2	403.3	453.0	462.5	445.4	529.5	627.6	682.3	847.7	1,087.4	..	Demand Deposits
683.5	862.3	1,036.8	1,210.4	1,153.9	1,247.7	1,588.6	1,832.7	1,990.1	2,286.2	..	Quasi-Money

(Millions of current Honduran Lempiras)

GOVERNMENT DEFICIT (-) OR SURPLUS

1981	1982	1983	1984	1985	1986	1987	1988	1989	1990	Notes	
..	..	..	..	..	..	..	..	..	..	F	
741.20	..	..	..	..	..	..	..	..	..	..	Current Revenue
..	..	..	..	..	..	..	..	..	..	..	Current Expenditure
..	..	..	..	..	..	..	..	..	..	..	Current Budget Balance
..	..	..	..	..	..	..	..	..	..	..	Capital Receipts
..	..	..	..	..	..	..	..	..	..	..	Capital Payments

HONDURAS	1970	1971	1972	1973	1974	1975	1976	1977	1978	1979	1980
FOREIGN TRADE (CUSTOMS BASIS)					*(Millions of current US dollars)*						
Value of Exports, fob	169.7	182.8	193.1	246.8	253.3	293.3	391.8	510.7	601.8	720.9	813.4
Nonfuel Primary Products	149.8	174.8	183.5	228.6	211.0	249.5	351.9	461.0	541.6	640.0	707.9
Fuels	6.3	3.0	3.4	4.1	14.5	12.3	1.1	0.6	0.0	0.3	3.8
Manufactures	13.7	5.1	6.2	14.0	27.8	31.5	38.8	49.1	60.2	80.6	101.7
Value of Imports, cif	220.7	193.4	192.8	262.2	380.1	404.3	453.1	579.4	699.2	825.8	1,008.7
Nonfuel Primary Products	28.4	21.3	24.2	30.1	46.2	60.4	56.6	64.9	79.2	84.7	119.6
Fuels	14.7	17.4	19.2	26.1	63.4	68.5	48.2	69.3	76.0	106.8	160.7
Manufactures	177.6	154.6	149.4	206.1	270.5	275.3	348.3	445.2	544.0	634.3	728.4
					(Index 1987 = 100)						
Terms of Trade	146.6	154.4	161.5	159.6	120.5	116.3	138.6	153.6	129.5	131.9	119.3
Export Prices, fob	33.4	36.4	40.7	51.6	62.6	64.0	80.7	96.4	91.5	109.4	115.2
Import Prices, cif	22.8	23.6	25.2	32.3	51.9	55.1	58.2	62.7	70.6	83.0	96.6
BALANCE OF PAYMENTS					*(Millions of current US dollars)*						
Exports of Goods & Services	198.8	217.7	237.4	297.6	336.8	350.9	463.4	593.9	706.5	859.2	967.5
Merchandise, fob	178.2	194.6	212.1	266.6	300.3	309.6	411.7	529.9	626.1	756.5	850.2
Nonfactor Services	18.3	20.9	22.8	27.1	31.5	34.7	42.0	50.8	61.3	81.5	91.3
Factor Services	2.3	2.3	2.5	3.9	4.9	6.5	9.6	13.2	19.1	21.2	25.8
Imports of Goods & Services	269.2	247.2	256.7	339.0	474.6	480.6	581.3	736.6	881.0	1,071.8	1,305.8
Merchandise, fob	203.4	178.0	176.5	243.4	387.5	372.3	432.5	550.1	654.5	783.5	954.1
Nonfactor Services	40.9	42.1	50.3	58.5	67.8	73.2	81.5	104.6	122.1	147.0	172.5
Factor Services	24.9	27.1	29.9	37.1	19.3	35.1	67.4	81.9	104.3	141.3	179.1
Long-Term Interest	3.5	5.0	6.4	9.7	12.1	16.2	21.8	30.6	43.3	60.0	83.0
Private Current Transfers, net	2.9	3.1	3.3	3.5	13.5	4.9	3.3	3.8	4.4	6.9	7.5
Workers' Remittances	..	..	..	..	..	..	..	..	..	..	..
Curr. A/C Bal before Off. Transf.	-67.5	-26.4	-16.0	-38.0	-122.9	-124.9	-114.7	-138.9	-170.0	-205.6	-330.8
Net Official Transfers	3.7	3.7	3.3	3.5	19.0	12.8	9.9	10.3	12.8	13.5	14.0
Curr. A/C Bal after Off. Transf.	-63.8	-22.7	-12.7	-34.6	-103.9	-112.1	-104.8	-128.7	-157.2	-192.1	-316.8
Long-Term Capital, net	40.1	35.3	23.5	32.3	63.3	131.5	103.7	148.8	175.5	170.1	257.7
Direct Investment	8.4	7.3	3.0	6.6	-1.1	7.0	5.3	8.9	13.1	28.2	5.8
Long-Term Loans	32.2	29.2	24.5	4.2	67.7	98.7	98.4	139.7	161.7	149.7	258.0
Disbursements	38.5	37.7	37.6	21.0	89.2	127.5	135.8	199.7	236.2	268.8	345.2
Repayments	6.3	8.5	13.1	16.8	21.5	28.8	37.4	60.0	74.5	119.1	87.2
Other Long-Term Capital	-0.5	-1.2	-4.1	21.5	-3.3	25.8	0.0	0.1	0.7	-7.8	-6.1
Other Capital, net	11.3	-13.6	1.0	10.8	23.7	34.5	38.9	46.4	-8.7	42.1	-18.7
Change in Reserves	12.3	0.9	-11.8	-8.6	17.0	-53.9	-37.9	-66.5	-9.6	-20.1	77.8
Memo Item:					*(Honduran Lempiras per US dollar)*						
Conversion Factor (Annual Avg)	2.000	2.000	2.000	2.000	2.000	2.000	2.000	2.000	2.000	2.000	2.000
				(Millions of US dollars), outstanding at end of year							
EXTERNAL DEBT (Total)	109.4	138.5	163.9	196.0	281.0	379.5	478.1	752.4	932.6	1,182.1	1,470.2
Long-Term Debt (by debtor)	109.4	138.5	163.9	196.0	281.0	379.5	478.1	603.4	759.6	918.1	1,198.0
Central Bank, incl. IMF credit	7.2	6.5	5.9	6.7	27.1	52.9	68.6	55.1	55.8	75.7	83.2
Central Government	67.0	79.0	94.7	105.0	126.6	177.7	209.0	262.4	346.7	422.9	564.9
Rest of General Government	0.0	0.0	0.0	0.0	0.0	0.3	3.7	4.6	6.8	6.8	6.8
Non-financial Public Enterprises	16.0	16.7	18.7	21.9	38.1	51.2	70.7	114.1	141.8	161.9	176.2
Priv. Sector, incl non-guaranteed	19.2	36.3	44.6	62.4	89.2	97.4	126.1	167.2	208.5	250.8	366.9
Short-Term Debt	0.0	0.0	0.0	0.0	0.0	0.0	0.0	149.0	173.0	264.0	272.2
Memo Items:					*(Thousands of US dollars)*						
Int'l Reserves Excluding Gold	20,130	21,774	35,087	41,656	44,302	96,969	130,830	179,772	184,436	209,170	149,826
Gold Holdings (at market price)	116	135	201	348	578	435	418	2,276	3,119	7,066	9,432
SOCIAL INDICATORS											
Total Fertility Rate	7.4	7.4	7.4	7.2	7.1	6.9	6.7	6.6	6.5	6.4	6.3
Infant Mortality Rate	115.2	112.6	110.0	107.0	104.0	101.0	98.0	95.0	92.4	89.8	87.2
Life Expectancy at Birth	52.7	53.3	54.0	54.7	55.4	56.2	56.9	57.7	58.5	59.4	60.2
Urban Population, % of total	28.9	29.6	30.3	30.9	31.6	32.3	33.0	33.7	34.5	35.2	35.9
Food Prod. per capita (1987=100)	129.9	137.8	140.5	132.0	117.5	102.0	111.1	115.9	123.8	111.0	123.4
Labor Force, Agriculture (%)	64.9	64.4	64.0	63.5	63.1	62.7	62.2	61.7	61.3	60.9	60.5
Labor Force, Female (%)	14.2	14.4	14.5	14.7	14.8	14.9	15.1	15.3	15.4	15.6	15.7
Primary Schl. Enroll. Ratio	87.0	..	..	..	..	88.0	88.0	..	89.0	89.0	93.0
Primary Schl. Enroll. Ratio, Female	87.0	..	..	..	..	86.0	88.0	..	89.0	85.0	94.0
Secondary Schl. Enroll. Ratio	14.0	..	..	..	..	16.0	17.0	19.0	23.0	..	30.0

1981	1982	1983	1984	1985	1986	1987	1988	1989	1990 estimate	Notes	HONDURAS
											FOREIGN TRADE (CUSTOMS BASIS)
				(Millions of current US dollars)							
712.5	655.7	660.1	703.7	699.4	771.1	761.0	868.7	1,196.7	915.8	..	Value of Exports, fob
626.9	597.5	598.3	652.1	666.3	741.6	724.9	805.4	1,109.6	849.1	..	Nonfuel Primary Products
2.4	0.6	4.0	4.7	5.9	0.4	1.6	3.0	4.1	3.1	..	Fuels
83.2	57.6	57.8	46.9	27.1	29.1	34.5	60.3	83.1	63.6	..	Manufactures
944.9	689.9	823.0	813.4	873.7	755.6	863.0	932.9	875.6	1,028.4	..	Value of Imports, cif
114.5	79.6	96.4	105.0	94.4	96.5	100.0	146.9	137.8	161.9	..	Nonfuel Primary Products
149.4	150.3	184.1	100.6	226.3	127.4	155.9	147.0	138.0	162.1	..	Fuels
681.0	460.0	542.4	607.8	552.9	531.7	607.1	639.0	599.8	704.4	..	Manufactures
				(Index 1987 = 100)							
108.2	109.2	115.8	113.0	111.1	120.0	100.0	121.5	119.5	103.9	..	Terms of Trade
107.0	104.2	106.9	102.1	100.0	110.4	100.0	117.5	120.7	127.1	..	Export Prices, fob
98.8	95.4	92.3	90.3	90.0	92.0	100.0	96.7	100.9	122.4	..	Import Prices, cif
				(Millions of current US dollars)							**BALANCE OF PAYMENTS**
903.2	783.5	815.0	863.2	918.2	1,022.1	981.9	1,028.8	1,105.4	1,080.0	f	Exports of Goods & Services
783.8	676.5	698.7	737.0	789.6	891.2	844.3	893.0	966.7	943.3	..	Merchandise, fob
99.8	90.4	102.3	110.3	113.8	117.8	125.5	123.6	125.8	128.9	..	Nonfactor Services
19.6	16.5	13.9	15.8	14.8	13.1	12.0	12.1	12.9	7.8	..	Factor Services
1,233.4	1,041.8	1,078.7	1,259.6	1,267.9	1,327.7	1,338.0	1,392.7	1,452.0	1,502.6	f	Imports of Goods & Services
898.6	680.7	756.3	884.8	879.2	874.1	893.9	916.6	964.0	1,014.0	..	Merchandise, fob
162.0	142.3	156.1	181.2	183.5	187.4	193.8	201.8	208.7	214.0	..	Nonfactor Services
172.8	218.8	166.3	193.6	205.2	266.2	250.3	274.2	279.3	277.0	..	Factor Services
95.9	111.6	96.7	88.1	100.5	114.0	93.6	128.7	46.1	181.8	..	Long-Term Interest
8.9	9.0	9.7	10.3	12.4	13.0	16.0	17.5	16.0	25.5	..	Private Current Transfers, net
..	..	..	..	..	..	..	..	..	..	..	Workers' Remittances
-321.3	-249.3	-254.0	-386.2	-337.3	-292.5	-340.1	-346.5	-330.7	-397.1	..	Curr. A/C Bal before Off. Transf.
18.6	21.0	34.8	69.7	133.2	145.3	115.3	117.5	56.0	207.6	..	Net Official Transfers
-302.7	-228.3	-219.2	-316.5	-204.1	-147.2	-224.8	-229.0	-274.6	-189.5	..	Curr. A/C Bal after Off. Transf.
222.0	134.0	147.7	261.5	219.8	31.0	78.6	66.8	7.2	263.5	f	Long-Term Capital, net
-3.6	13.8	21.0	20.4	27.5	30.0	38.8	46.8	37.3	43.5	..	Direct Investment
233.0	163.8	169.9	186.0	265.6	113.8	86.2	132.9	106.5	149.6	..	Long-Term Loans
330.3	256.2	253.7	269.6	347.5	219.0	255.5	308.3	176.9	337.3	..	Disbursements
97.3	92.4	83.8	83.6	81.9	105.2	169.3	175.4	70.4	187.7	..	Repayments
-7.4	-43.5	-43.2	55.0	-73.3	-112.8	-46.4	-112.9	-136.7	70.4	..	Other Long-Term Capital
6.9	10.0	28.1	39.9	-33.0	146.0	223.7	183.2	222.3	-55.2	f	Other Capital, net
73.8	84.2	43.4	15.0	17.4	-29.8	-77.4	-21.1	45.1	-18.8	..	Change in Reserves
											Memo Item:
				(Honduran Lempiras per US dollar)							
2.000	2.000	2.000	2.000	2.000	2.000	2.000	2.330	2.970	4.260	..	Conversion Factor (Annual Avg)
				(Millions of US dollars), outstanding at end of year							
1,702.7	1,841.9	2,124.9	2,283.5	2,728.1	2,973.2	3,302.3	3,304.6	3,332.9	3,480.1	..	**EXTERNAL DEBT (Total)**
1,461.2	1,690.2	1,983.1	2,084.8	2,425.3	2,612.3	2,894.9	2,894.2	2,941.5	3,257.9	..	Long-Term Debt (by debtor)
130.6	203.8	250.0	223.7	267.6	237.3	201.1	189.1	263.0	259.4	..	Central Bank, incl. IMF credit
670.0	821.5	986.3	1,141.0	1,368.4	1,556.4	1,836.6	1,949.3	2,009.8	2,445.8	..	Central Government
6.8	6.1	5.3	5.0	4.2	3.8	3.2	3.1	1.9	1.9	..	Rest of General Government
238.2	261.3	319.1	329.4	415.3	468.4	526.4	453.7	398.2	338.7	..	Non-financial Public Enterprises
415.6	397.5	422.4	385.7	369.8	346.4	327.6	299.0	268.6	212.1	..	Priv. Sector, incl non-guaranteed
241.5	151.7	141.8	198.7	302.8	360.9	407.4	410.4	391.4	222.2	..	Short-Term Debt
											Memo Items:
				(Thousands of US dollars)							
101,018	112,228	113,617	128,157	105,800	111,300	106,000	50,000	21,100	40,414	..	Int'l Reserves Excluding Gold
6,360	7,310	6,104	4,933	5,232	6,254	7,746	6,564	6,416	6,160	..	Gold Holdings (at market price)
											SOCIAL INDICATORS
6.2	6.2	6.0	5.9	5.8	5.7	5.6	5.5	5.4	5.2	..	Total Fertility Rate
84.6	82.0	79.4	76.8	74.2	71.6	69.0	67.4	65.8	64.3	..	Infant Mortality Rate
61.1	61.9	62.3	62.7	63.1	63.5	63.9	64.3	64.6	64.9	..	Life Expectancy at Birth
36.7	37.4	38.2	38.9	39.7	40.5	41.3	42.1	42.9	43.7	..	Urban Population, % of total
126.2	115.6	101.6	99.1	97.1	93.1	100.0	100.7	100.4	97.6	..	Food Prod. per capita (1987=100)
..	..	..	..	..	..	..	..	..	..	..	Labor Force, Agriculture (%)
16.1	16.4	16.7	17.0	17.3	17.6	18.0	18.3	18.6	18.8	..	Labor Force, Female (%)
..	99.0	101.0	100.0	102.0	106.0	..	108.0	..	..	..	Primary Schl. Enroll. Ratio
..	98.0	100.0	101.0	103.0	108.0	..	109.0	..	..	..	Primary Schl. Enroll. Ratio, Female
..	32.0	33.0	32.0	35.0	32.0					..	Secondary Schl. Enroll. Ratio

HONG KONG	1970	1971	1972	1973	1974	1975	1976	1977	1978	1979	1980
CURRENT GNP PER CAPITA (US $)	900	1,020	1,220	1,570	1,900	2,180	2,700	3,200	3,750	4,260	5,210
POPULATION (thousands)	3,942	4,012	4,089	4,173	4,263	4,360	4,443	4,510	4,597	4,979	5,039

USE AND ORIGIN OF RESOURCES

(Billions of current Hong Kong Dollars)

	1970	1971	1972	1973	1974	1975	1976	1977	1978	1979	1980
Gross National Product (GNP)	..	..	..	..	..	..	..	..	..	..	..
Net Factor Income from Abroad	..	..	..	..	..	..	..	..	..	..	..
GDP at Market Prices	21.88	25.18	30.38	39.10	44.58	46.46	59.34	68.90	81.16	107.05	137.08
Resource Balance	0.78	-0.06	1.17	0.96	0.32	0.48	4.05	1.60	-2.90	-3.11	-6.30
Exports of Goods & NF Services	20.33	22.42	25.48	33.29	38.52	38.51	53.16	57.11	68.64	95.19	120.40
Imports of Goods & NF Services	19.55	22.48	24.31	32.33	38.21	38.02	49.11	55.51	71.54	98.31	126.71
Domestic Absorption	21.10	25.24	29.21	38.14	44.26	45.98	55.29	67.31	84.06	110.16	143.38
Private Consumption, etc.	14.78	17.04	19.62	26.18	29.74	31.20	35.36	43.33	54.16	66.89	85.26
General Gov't Consumption	1.64	1.74	2.11	2.59	3.20	3.53	4.03	4.72	5.55	6.83	8.83
Gross Domestic Investment	4.68	6.45	7.48	9.38	11.33	11.26	15.91	19.26	24.35	36.44	49.29
Fixed Investment	4.51	6.26	7.25	9.08	10.65	10.53	12.93	17.56	22.29	33.19	45.55
Indirect Taxes, net	1.06	1.18	1.50	1.69	1.59	1.92	2.42	2.86	3.52	4.06	5.20
GDP at factor cost	20.82	23.99	28.88	37.41	42.99	44.54	56.91	66.04	77.64	102.99	131.88
Agriculture	0.38	0.41	0.44	0.53	0.54	0.53	0.64	0.72	0.86	0.99	1.11
Industry	7.56	8.55	9.98	12.07	12.51	13.39	17.36	20.11	24.31	32.33	41.04
Manufacturing	6.14	6.70	7.73	9.37	9.44	10.34	13.70	15.65	18.33	24.72	30.55
Services, etc.	12.89	15.04	18.46	24.81	29.94	30.62	38.91	45.21	52.47	69.67	89.74
Gross Domestic Saving	5.46	6.39	8.65	10.34	11.64	11.74	19.95	20.86	21.46	33.33	42.99
Gross National Saving	5.46	6.39	8.65	10.34	11.64	11.74	19.95	20.86	21.46	33.33	42.99

(Billions of 1987 Hong Kong Dollars)

	1970	1971	1972	1973	1974	1975	1976	1977	1978	1979	1980
Gross National Product	..	..	..	..	..	..	..	..	..	..	..
GDP at Market Prices	89.89	96.45	107.06	120.65	123.31	123.55	144.68	162.77	178.22	199.01	220.64
Resource Balance	6.70	1.07	4.31	4.94	7.88	5.19	10.09	6.41	-2.11	-2.31	-8.85
Exports of Goods & NF Services	75.52	78.72	85.59	94.71	90.78	91.22	116.87	121.35	136.99	161.63	185.39
Imports of Goods & NF Services	68.82	77.65	81.29	89.77	82.90	86.03	106.79	114.93	139.10	163.94	194.24
Domestic Absorption	83.18	95.38	102.75	115.71	115.43	118.36	134.60	156.36	180.33	201.33	229.50
Private Consumption, etc.	53.08	59.91	64.23	72.91	71.55	73.56	79.22	93.23	110.62	120.99	136.24
General Gov't Consumption	7.66	7.79	8.42	9.23	10.06	10.69	11.39	12.54	13.91	15.22	16.39
Gross Domestic Investment	22.45	27.68	30.10	33.57	33.82	34.10	43.99	50.59	55.80	65.12	76.87
Fixed Investment	21.71	26.89	29.22	32.58	32.11	32.74	37.31	46.95	51.62	59.39	71.12
GDP at factor cost	85.53	91.98	101.73	115.38	118.92	118.53	138.84	156.14	170.53	191.46	212.33
Agriculture	..	..	..	..	..	..	..	..	..	..	..
Industry	..	..	..	..	..	..	..	..	..	..	..
Manufacturing	..	..	..	..	..	..	..	..	..	..	..
Services, etc.	..	..	..	..	..	..	..	..	..	..	..

Memo Items:

	1970	1971	1972	1973	1974	1975	1976	1977	1978	1979	1980
Capacity to Import	71.56	77.45	85.19	92.44	83.59	87.12	115.59	118.25	133.47	158.75	184.58
Terms of Trade Adjustment	-3.96	-1.27	-0.40	-2.28	-7.20	-4.10	-1.29	-3.10	-3.52	-2.88	-0.81
Gross Domestic Income	85.92	95.17	106.66	118.38	116.11	119.46	143.39	159.67	174.70	196.13	219.84
Gross National Income	85.92	95.17	106.66	118.38	116.11	119.46	143.39	159.67	174.70	196.13	219.84

DOMESTIC PRICES/DEFLATORS

(Index 1987 = 100)

	1970	1971	1972	1973	1974	1975	1976	1977	1978	1979	1980
Overall (GDP)	24.3	26.1	28.4	32.4	36.2	37.6	41.0	42.3	45.5	53.8	62.1
Domestic Absorption	25.4	26.5	28.4	33.0	38.3	38.8	41.1	43.0	46.6	54.7	62.5
Agriculture	..	..	..	..	..	..	..	..	..	..	..
Industry	..	..	..	..	..	..	..	..	..	..	..
Manufacturing	..	..	..	..	..	..	..	..	..	..	..
Consumer Price Index	26.1	27.0	28.7	33.9	38.8	39.9	41.4	43.7	46.2	51.6	59.3

MANUFACTURING ACTIVITY

	1970	1971	1972	1973	1974	1975	1976	1977	1978	1979	1980
Employment (1987=100)	58.2	59.8	61.3	69.1	64.3	73.3	85.6	83.9	84.2	94.3	99.2
Real Earnings per Empl. (1987=100)	..	..	..	56.6	51.4	53.0	57.8	62.0	77.4	77.8	74.3
Real Output per Empl. (1987=100)	..	..	..	..	..	..	..	..	..	..	..
Earnings as % of Value Added	..	..	..	53.2	53.5	52.5	51.3	53.2	55.6	51.3	52.0

MONETARY HOLDINGS

(Billions of current Hong Kong Dollars)

	1970	1971	1972	1973	1974	1975	1976	1977	1978	1979	1980
Money Supply, Broadly Defined	..	..	..	..	..	..	..	..	70.15	79.73	110.36
Money	..	..	..	..	..	..	..	..	20.11	20.85	24.12
Currency Outside Banks	..	..	..	..	..	..	..	..	..	..	..
Demand Deposits	..	..	..	..	..	..	..	..	..	..	..
Quasi-Money	..	..	..	..	..	..	..	..	50.04	58.88	86.23

GOVERNMENT DEFICIT (-) OR SURPLUS

(Millions of current Hong Kong Dollars)

	1970	1971	1972	1973	1974	1975	1976	1977	1978	1979	1980
Current Revenue	..	..	..	..	..	..	..	..	..	..	..
Current Expenditure	..	..	..	..	..	..	..	..	..	..	..
Current Budget Balance	..	..	..	..	..	..	..	..	..	..	..
Capital Receipts	..	..	..	..	..	..	..	..	..	..	..
Capital Payments	..	..	..	..	..	..	..	..	..	..	..

1981	1982	1983	1984	1985	1986	1987	1988	1989	1990 estimate	Notes	HONG KONG
6,080	6,330	6,140	6,330	6,090	6,900	8,190	9,310	10,300	11,490	f	**CURRENT GNP PER CAPITA (US $)**
5,120	5,202	5,285	5,370	5,456	5,533	5,613	5,681	5,761	5,801	..	**POPULATION (thousands)**
					(Billions of current Hong Kong Dollars)						**USE AND ORIGIN OF RESOURCES**
..	..	..	..	..	..	..	..	..	..		Gross National Product (GNP)
..	..	..	..	..	..	..	..	..	..		Net Factor Income from Abroad
164.97	186.33	207.56	248.73	261.19	300.82	369.27	434.02	490.81	546.06	f	GDP at Market Prices
-9.24	-6.77	-4.18	10.45	14.84	14.05	22.72	21.97	40.05	29.36	..	Resource Balance
149.32	157.99	197.62	265.29	281.00	330.82	448.87	578.56	667.96	747.00	..	Exports of Goods & NF Services
158.56	164.76	201.81	254.84	266.16	316.77	426.14	556.59	627.92	717.64	..	Imports of Goods & NF Services
174.22	193.10	211.75	238.28	246.36	286.77	346.55	412.05	450.76	516.69	..	Domestic Absorption
102.45	118.93	138.83	158.60	169.86	191.68	221.76	255.86	284.58	321.27	..	Private Consumption, etc.
12.40	14.91	16.72	18.29	19.92	22.97	25.78	30.01	36.30	44.20	..	General Gov't Consumption
59.36	59.26	56.20	61.38	56.58	72.12	99.02	126.18	129.88	151.23	..	Gross Domestic Investment
55.41	57.86	51.87	55.58	55.12	65.94	89.27	112.05	127.37	144.93	..	Fixed Investment
6.12	6.23	8.10	9.89	12.33	14.75	18.65	21.45	25.40	..	..	Indirect Taxes, net
158.86	180.10	199.46	238.83	248.86	286.07	350.63	412.57	465.41	..	f	GDP at factor cost
1.12	1.23	1.24	1.27	1.24	1.33	1.36	1.44	1.42	..	..	Agriculture
50.45	52.84	61.47	73.74	72.16	85.07	102.11	113.51	122.04	..	..	Industry
36.05	36.39	44.14	55.54	53.07	62.78	75.76	83.18	86.06	..	..	Manufacturing
107.28	126.02	136.75	163.82	175.47	199.67	247.16	297.62	341.96	..	..	Services, etc.
50.12	52.49	52.01	71.83	71.42	86.17	121.74	148.15	169.93	180.59	..	Gross Domestic Saving
50.12	52.49	52.01	71.83	71.42	86.17	121.74	..	..	..	..	Gross National Saving
					(Billions of 1987 Hong Kong Dollars)						
..	..	..	..	..	..	..	..	..	..		Gross National Product
241.42	248.70	264.86	289.97	289.64	324.09	369.27	398.38	407.59	417.45	f	GDP at Market Prices
-8.15	-7.48	-1.29	10.86	8.60	14.45	22.72	23.46	32.02	20.72	..	Resource Balance
211.05	207.85	236.59	283.26	298.43	344.03	448.87	557.77	612.61	666.52	..	Exports of Goods & NF Services
219.20	215.33	237.89	272.40	289.83	329.57	426.14	534.31	580.59	645.80	..	Imports of Goods & NF Services
249.56	256.18	266.15	279.11	281.04	309.64	346.55	374.92	375.57	396.74	..	Domestic Absorption
146.28	154.58	166.83	176.82	183.58	200.22	221.76	240.13	247.07	256.69	..	Private Consumption, etc.
20.03	21.14	22.26	22.87	23.29	24.74	25.78	27.10	28.70	30.89	..	General Gov't Consumption
83.25	80.47	77.06	79.42	74.17	84.68	99.02	107.69	99.79	109.17	..	Gross Domestic Investment
77.43	78.72	72.13	73.28	72.66	77.93	89.27	95.05	96.37	102.58	..	Fixed Investment
232.51	240.43	254.66	278.44	275.94	308.28	350.63	378.70	386.64	..	f	GDP at factor cost
..	..	..	..	..	..	..	..	..	..	..	Agriculture
..	..	..	..	..	..	..	..	..	..	..	Industry
..	..	..	..	..	..	..	..	..	..	..	Manufacturing
..	..	..	..	..	..	..	..	..	..	..	Services, etc.
											Memo Items:
206.42	206.48	232.95	283.57	305.99	344.19	448.87	555.40	617.62	672.23	..	Capacity to Import
-4.63	-1.37	-3.64	0.31	7.56	0.16	0.00	-2.36	5.01	5.71	..	Terms of Trade Adjustment
236.79	247.33	261.22	290.28	297.20	324.26	369.27	396.01	412.59	423.16	..	Gross Domestic Income
236.79	247.33	261.22	290.28	297.20	324.26	369.27	396.01	412.59	423.16	..	Gross National Income
					(Index 1987 = 100)						**DOMESTIC PRICES/DEFLATORS**
68.3	74.9	78.4	85.8	90.2	92.8	100.0	108.9	120.4	130.8	..	Overall (GDP)
69.8	75.4	79.6	85.4	87.7	92.6	100.0	109.9	120.0	130.2	..	Domestic Absorption
..	..	..	..	..	..	..	..	..	..	..	Agriculture
..	..	..	..	..	..	..	..	..	..	..	Industry
..	..	..	..	..	..	..	..	..	..	..	Manufacturing
67.5	74.6	82.0	88.9	92.0	95.0	100.0	107.4	117.8	129.3	..	Consumer Price Index
											MANUFACTURING ACTIVITY
105.5	94.8	99.2	101.2	96.2	99.8	100.0	102.9	..	..	G	Employment (1987=100)
74.0	75.7	75.9	80.5	84.3	91.8	100.0	102.0	..	..	G	Real Earnings per Empl. (1987=100)
..	..	..	..	..	..	..	..	..	..	G	Real Output per Empl. (1987=100)
51.5	51.6	48.4	59.0	63.2	59.5	56.8	56.3	..	..	..	Earnings as % of Value Added
					(Billions of current Hong Kong Dollars)						**MONETARY HOLDINGS**
135.74	..	..	..	..	..	..	..	..	..	D	Money Supply, Broadly Defined
25.06	..	..	..	..	..	..	..	..	..	..	Money
..	..	..	..	..	..	..	..	..	..	..	Currency Outside Banks
..	..	..	..	..	..	..	..	..	..	..	Demand Deposits
110.68	..	..	..	..	..	..	..	..	..	..	Quasi-Money
					(Millions of current Hong Kong Dollars)						**GOVERNMENT DEFICIT (-) OR SURPLUS**
..	..	..	..	..	..	..	..	..	..	..	Current Revenue
..	..	..	..	..	..	..	..	..	..	..	Current Expenditure
..	..	..	..	..	..	..	..	..	..	..	Current Budget Balance
..	..	..	..	..	..	..	..	..	..	..	Capital Receipts
..	..	..	..	..	..	..	..	..	..	..	Capital Payments

HONG KONG	1970	1971	1972	1973	1974	1975	1976	1977	1978	1979	1980
FOREIGN TRADE (CUSTOMS BASIS)				*(Millions of current US dollars)*							
Value of Exports, fob	2,037	2,300	2,733	3,784	4,506	4,612	6,691	7,514	8,684	11,160	13,672
Nonfuel Primary Products	..	..	..	..		134	..	247	270	346	459
Fuels	..	..	..	..		0	..	0	0	10	18
Manufactures	1,954	2,221	2,642	3,659	4,348	4,477	6,497	7,267	8,414	10,804	13,194
Value of Imports, cif	2,905	3,387	3,895	5,631	6,710	6,757	8,909	10,457	13,451	17,137	22,027
Nonfuel Primary Products	835	964	1,076	1,581	1,926	2,005	2,398	2,629	3,015	3,398	4,145
Fuels	85	109	120	153	419	429	552	643	666	979	1,217
Manufactures	1,985	2,314	2,700	3,897	4,364	4,323	5,960	7,186	9,770	12,760	16,665
					(Index 1987 = 100)						
Terms of Trade	107.5	115.7	126.3	141.1	137.2	119.7	123.0	113.7	95.6	97.1	94.6
Export Prices, fob	27.6	31.8	38.6	54.6	68.6	62.4	66.9	67.3	64.1	75.9	82.7
Import Prices, cif	25.7	27.5	30.5	38.7	50.0	52.1	54.4	59.1	67.0	78.2	87.5
BALANCE OF PAYMENTS				*(Millions of current US dollars)*							
Exports of Goods & Services	3,474	3,888	4,708	6,783	8,201	8,509	11,651	13,241	15,986	20,935	24,190
Merchandise, fob	2,514	2,872	3,442	5,041	5,969	6,027	8,512	9,624	11,517	15,181	19,731
Nonfactor Services	840	879	1,078	1,413	1,687	1,753	2,377	2,637	3,149	3,850	3,686
Factor Services	120	137	188	329	545	729	762	980	1,320	1,904	773
Imports of Goods & Services	3,249	3,785	4,354	6,394	7,870	7,940	10,412	12,396	16,049	20,736	25,448
Merchandise, fob	2,910	3,394	3,866	5,633	6,785	6,774	8,915	10,476	13,516	17,262	22,453
Nonfactor Services	316	366	447	635	807	907	1,145	1,443	1,769	2,393	2,643
Factor Services	23	25	41	126	278	259	352	477	764	1,081	352
Long-Term Interest	..	..	..	..	..	..	..	..	..	..	..
Private Current Transfers, net	0	0	0	0	0	0	0	0	0	0	0
Workers' Remittances	..	..	..	..	..	..	..	..	..	..	..
Curr. A/C Bal before Off. Transf.	225	103	354	389	331	569	1,239	845	-63	199	-1,258
Net Official Transfers	0	0	0	0	0	0	0	0	0	0	0
Curr. A/C Bal after Off. Transf.	225	103	354	389	331	569	1,239	845	-63	199	-1,258
Long-Term Capital, net	-1	-1	-1	0	16	4	41	88	29	103	329
Direct Investment	..	..	..	..	..	..	..	..	..	..	250
Long-Term Loans	..	..	..	..	..	..	..	..	..	..	
Disbursements	..	..	..	..	..	..	..	..	..	..	
Repayments	..	..	..	..	..	..	..	..	..	..	
Other Long-Term Capital	-1	-1	-1	0	16	4	41	88	29	103	79
Other Capital, net	..	..	..	..	..	..	..	..	..	..	250
Change in Reserves	..	..	..	..	..	..	..	..	..	..	679
Memo Item:				*(Hong Kong Dollars per US dollar)*							
Conversion Factor (Annual Avg)	6.060	5.980	5.640	5.150	5.030	4.940	4.900	4.660	4.680	5.000	4.980
EXTERNAL DEBT (Total)				*(Millions of US dollars), outstanding at end of year*							
Long-Term Debt (by debtor)	..	..	..	..	..	..	..	..	..	..	..
Central Bank, incl. IMF credit	..	..	..	..	..	..	..	..	..	..	..
Central Government	..	..	..	..	..	..	..	..	..	..	..
Rest of General Government	..	..	..	..	..	..	..	..	..	..	..
Non-financial Public Enterprises	..	..	..	..	..	..	..	..	..	..	..
Priv. Sector, incl non-guaranteed	..	..	..	..	..	..	..	..	..	..	..
Short-Term Debt	..	..	..	..	..	..	..	..	..	..	..
Memo Items:				*Millions US dollars)*							
Int'l Reserves Excluding Gold	..	..	..	..	..	..	..	..	..	..	..
Gold Holdings (at market price)	..	..	..	..	..	..	..	..	..	..	..
SOCIAL INDICATORS											
Total Fertility Rate	3.3	3.1	2.9	2.8	2.7	2.5	2.4	2.3	2.2	2.1	2.0
Infant Mortality Rate	19.4	18.2	17.0	16.9	16.8	14.9	13.7	13.5	11.8	12.3	11.2
Life Expectancy at Birth	70.0	70.0	70.0	71.0	71.3	71.5	71.8	72.1	72.7	73.4	74.1
Urban Population, % of total	89.7	89.9	90.1	90.2	90.4	90.6	90.8	91.0	91.2	91.4	91.6
Food Prod. per capita (1987=100)	238.7	226.2	244.5	191.0	189.7	151.3	131.5	152.9	144.5	167.4	132.6
Labor Force, Agriculture (%)	0.0	0.0	0.0	0.0	0.0	0.0	0.0	0.0	0.0	0.0	0.0
Labor Force, Female (%)	..	..									..
Primary Schl. Enroll. Ratio	117.0	..	..	..	..	119.0	114.0	115.0	113.0	111.0	106.0
Primary Schl. Enroll. Ratio, Female	115.0	..	..	..	..	117.0	112.0	113.0	111.0	109.0	105.0
Secondary Schl. Enroll. Ratio	36.0	..	..	..	..	49.0	52.0	54.0	57.0	60.0	64.0

|---|---|---|---|---|---|---|---|---|---|---|---|
				(Millions of current US dollars)							**FOREIGN TRADE (CUSTOMS BASIS)**
14,310	13,665	14,261	17,639	16,599	19,734	25,036	27,882	28,731	29,002	..	Value of Exports, fob
429	392	529	542	543	552	718	896	980	1,118	..	Nonfuel Primary Products
18	18	22	40	57	59	64	67	86	100	..	Fuels
13,863	13,255	13,710	17,057	16,000	19,123	24,254	26,919	27,665	27,784	..	Manufactures
24,671	23,461	24,009	28,567	29,580	35,366	48,462	63,894	72,154	82,494	..	Value of Imports, cif
4,303	4,383	4,415	4,731	4,840	5,306	6,757	8,532	9,109	9,603	..	Nonfuel Primary Products
1,955	1,884	1,595	1,568	1,384	1,135	1,215	1,219	1,728	2,010	..	Fuels
18,414	17,194	17,999	22,268	23,355	28,925	40,491	54,143	61,316	70,882	..	Manufactures
				(Index 1987 = 100)							
103.7	102.5	94.5	94.3	97.4	102.3	100.0	99.2	100.5	..	..	Terms of Trade
90.7	86.4	78.4	77.0	78.2	90.9	100.0	108.3	113.9	..	..	Export Prices, fob
87.4	84.3	82.9	81.6	80.3	88.9	100.0	109.3	113.3	..	..	Import Prices, cif
				(Millions of current US dollars)							**BALANCE OF PAYMENTS**
26,646	26,039	27,199	33,968	36,187	42,116	53,168	..	..	..	..	Exports of Goods & Services
21,791	20,986	22,119	28,325	30,186	35,449	45,835	..	..	..	..	Merchandise, fob
4,001	4,184	4,265	4,594	4,800	5,372	5,923	..	..	..	..	Nonfactor Services
854	869	815	1,049	1,201	1,295	1,410	..	..	..	..	Factor Services
28,269	27,126	27,756	32,555	34,318	40,564	51,969	..	..	..	..	Imports of Goods & Services
24,838	23,685	24,304	28,754	29,861	35,564	46,559	..	..	..	..	Merchandise, fob
3,027	3,036	3,046	3,354	3,928	4,423	4,769	..	..	..	..	Nonfactor Services
404	405	406	447	529	577	641	..	..	..	..	Factor Services
..	..	..	..	..	..	..	..	..	..	..	Long-Term Interest
0	0	0	0	0	0	0	..	..	..	..	Private Current Transfers, net
..	..	..	..	..	..	..	..	..	..	..	Workers' Remittances
-1,623	-1,087	-557	1,413	1,869	1,552	1,199	..	..	..	..	Curr. A/C Bal before Off. Transf.
0	0	0	0	0	0	0	..	..	..	..	Net Official Transfers
-1,623	-1,087	-557	1,413	1,869	1,552	1,199	..	..	..	..	Curr. A/C Bal after Off. Transf.
125	208	206	224	270	295	321	..	..	..	..	Long-Term Capital, net
300	200	200	243	257	282	282	..	..	..	..	Direct Investment
..	..	..	..	..	..	..	..	..	..	..	Long-Term Loans
..	..	..	..	..	..	..	..	..	..	..	Disbursements
..	..	..	..	..	..	..	..	..	..	..	Repayments
-175	8	6	-19	13	13	39	..	..	..	..	Other Long-Term Capital
300	200	200	243	257	282	0	..	..	..	..	Other Capital, net
1,198	679	151	-1,880	-2,396	-2,129	-1,520	..	..	..	..	Change in Reserves
				(Hong Kong Dollars per US dollar)							**Memo Item:**
5.590	6.070	7.270	7.820	7.790	7.800	7.800	7.810	7.800	7.790	..	Conversion Factor (Annual Avg)
			(Millions of US dollars), outstanding at end of year								**EXTERNAL DEBT (Total)**
..	..	..	..	..	..	..	..	..	..	..	Long-Term Debt (by debtor)
..	..	..	..	..	..	..	..	..	..	..	Central Bank, incl. IMF credit
..	..	..	..	..	..	..	..	..	..	..	Central Government
..	..	..	..	..	..	..	..	..	..	..	Rest of General Government
..	..	..	..	..	..	..	..	..	..	..	Non-financial Public Enterprises
..	..	..	..	..	..	..	..	..	..	..	Priv. Sector, incl non-guaranteed
..	..	..	..	..	..	..	..	..	..	..	Short-Term Debt
				Millions US dollars)							**Memo Items:**
..	..	..	..	..	..	..	..	..	..	..	Int'l Reserves Excluding Gold
..	..	..	..	..	..	..	..	..	..	..	Gold Holdings (at market price)
											SOCIAL INDICATORS
1.9	1.8	1.7	1.7	1.6	1.6	1.5	1.5	1.5	1.5	..	Total Fertility Rate
9.7	9.9	9.4	8.8	8.3	7.9	7.4	7.1	6.9	6.6	..	Infant Mortality Rate
74.7	75.4	75.5	75.5	76.0	76.5	77.0	77.2	77.5	77.7	..	Life Expectancy at Birth
91.9	92.1	92.4	92.6	92.9	93.1	93.4	93.6	93.9	94.1	..	Urban Population, % of total
170.2	124.8	115.8	126.4	169.9	84.8	100.0	111.7	129.4	133.2	..	Food Prod. per capita (1987=100)
..	..	..	..	..	..	..	..	..	..	..	Labor Force, Agriculture (%)
..											Labor Force, Female (%)
106.0	106.0	106.0	104.0	104.0	104.0	105.0	..	..	..	..	Primary Schl. Enroll. Ratio
105.0	105.0	105.0	104.0	103.0	103.0	104.0	..	..	..	..	Primary Schl. Enroll. Ratio, Female
66.0	67.0	68.0	72.0	72.0	73.0	73.0	..	..	..	..	Secondary Schl. Enroll. Ratio

HUNGARY	1970	1971	1972	1973	1974	1975	1976	1977	1978	1979	1980
CURRENT GNP PER CAPITA (US $)	..	..	..	..	..	..	..	1,320	1,500	1,680	1,930
POPULATION (thousands)	10,337	10,365	10,394	10,436	10,471	10,532	10,589	10,637	10,673	10,698	10,710

USE AND ORIGIN OF RESOURCES *(Billions of current Hungarian Forint)*

	1970	1971	1972	1973	1974	1975	1976	1977	1978	1979	1980
Gross National Product (GNP)	..	..	..	..	..	475.2	524.4	574.9	619.7	668.7	708.4
Net Factor Income from Abroad						-7.5	-4.5	-7.1	-10.0	-13.6	-12.6
GDP at Market Prices	332.6	360.8	391.0	429.0	449.0	482.7	528.9	582.0	629.7	682.3	721.0
Resource Balance	-7.7	-22.5	4.7	19.6	-19.9	-36.0	-21.3	-26.3	-57.7	-22.3	-15.6
Exports of Goods & NFServices	100.2	108.4	133.4	163.9	186.8	200.2	205.2	240.6	243.9	283.3	281.8
Imports of Goods & NFServices	107.9	130.9	128.6	144.2	206.7	236.2	226.5	266.9	301.6	305.6	297.4
Domestic Absorption	340.2	383.3	386.2	409.4	468.8	518.7	550.2	608.3	687.4	704.6	736.6
Private Consumption, etc.	194.1	209.6	223.5	241.7	261.4	286.0	307.3	334.0	361.7	401.2	441.2
General Gov't Consumption	34.4	37.8	38.6	40.5	46.9	50.3	53.2	57.8	65.8	71.3	74.1
Gross Domestic Investment	111.7	135.9	124.1	127.2	160.5	182.4	189.7	216.5	259.9	232.1	221.3
Fixed Investment	100.3	113.1	116.8	123.1	139.2	161.0	168.2	197.7	214.4	220.8	207.7
Indirect Taxes, net	..	..	..	..	..	..	..	..	..	..	..
GDP at factor cost	..	..	..	..	..	..	..	..	..	..	..
Agriculture	60.6	69.1	70.7	82.3	84.7	86.4	94.7	105.4	107.8	108.8	123.5
Industry	150.5	163.8	178.6	200.5	224.9	247.8	259.1	285.6	308.5	332.4	296.8
Manufacturing											243.4
Services, etc.	121.5	128.0	141.7	146.2	139.4	148.5	175.1	191.0	213.4	241.1	300.7
Gross Domestic Saving	104.0	113.4	128.9	146.8	140.7	146.4	168.4	190.2	202.2	209.8	205.7
Gross National Saving	..	..	..	..	..	142.2	166.8	184.9	195.9	197.8	194.6

Gross National Product *(Billions of 1987 Hungarian Forint)*

	1970	1971	1972	1973	1974	1975	1976	1977	1978	1979	1980
Gross National Product	..	..	..	786.14	830.91	882.26	920.39	980.06	1,022.74	1,034.52	1,037.26
GDP at Market Prices	655.40	697.41	741.94	797.74	844.02	897.60	929.89	993.46	1,040.63	1,056.93	1,057.32
Resource Balance	-90.22	-132.75	-83.68	-60.86	-111.92	-120.05	-111.80	-83.26	-134.15	-75.64	-69.25
Exports of Goods & NFServices	138.81	149.66	185.07	216.81	224.65	234.87	253.91	293.58	299.45	338.86	340.83
Imports of Goods & NFServices	229.04	282.42	268.75	277.67	336.57	354.92	365.71	376.83	433.60	414.50	410.09
Domestic Absorption	745.63	830.16	825.62	858.60	955.94	1,017.65	1,041.69	1,076.72	1,174.78	1,132.58	1,126.57
Private Consumption, etc.	481.44	509.40	529.99	560.81	632.74	622.49	636.89	643.38	666.57	677.47	682.78
General Gov't Consumption	83.10	88.56	89.03	90.73	92.14	95.48	98.96	99.81	101.97	106.98	107.12
Gross Domestic Investment	181.08	232.19	206.61	207.06	231.06	299.68	305.84	333.52	406.24	348.13	336.68
Fixed Investment	168.71	202.98	201.09	207.81	233.49	263.71	263.71	300.16	315.43	317.81	300.52
GDP at factor cost	..	..	..	..	..	..	..	..	..	..	..
Agriculture	120.56	128.31	131.61	138.77	142.63	145.83	140.15	157.32	158.80	156.70	162.51
Industry	250.63	267.87	285.43	307.88	333.55	357.09	377.79	401.82	423.67	445.53	438.15
Manufacturing											
Services, etc.	284.21	300.74	325.06	351.34	368.51	396.25	415.07	436.49	461.29	458.09	459.40

Memo Items:

	1970	1971	1972	1973	1974	1975	1976	1977	1978	1979	1980
Capacity to Import	212.71	233.90	278.67	315.40	304.24	300.83	331.32	339.70	350.64	384.25	388.57
Terms of Trade Adjustment	73.90	84.23	93.60	98.59	79.59	65.96	77.40	46.12	51.20	45.40	47.74
Gross Domestic Income	729.30	781.64	835.55	896.33	923.62	963.56	1,007.30	1,039.59	1,091.83	1,102.33	1,105.06
Gross National Income	..	..	..	884.73	910.50	948.21	997.79	1,026.19	1,073.94	1,079.92	1,085.00

DOMESTIC PRICES/DEFLATORS *(Index 1987 = 100)*

	1970	1971	1972	1973	1974	1975	1976	1977	1978	1979	1980
Overall (GDP)	50.7	51.7	52.7	53.8	53.2	53.8	56.9	58.6	60.5	64.6	68.2
Domestic Absorption	45.6	46.2	46.8	47.7	49.0	51.0	52.8	56.5	58.5	62.2	65.4
Agriculture	50.2	53.9	53.7	59.3	59.4	59.2	67.6	67.0	67.9	69.4	76.0
Industry	60.0	61.1	62.6	65.1	67.4	69.4	68.6	71.1	72.8	74.6	67.7
Manufacturing	..	..	..	..	..	..	..	..	..	..	..
Consumer Price Index	..	..	42.6	44.0	44.8	46.5	49.0	50.9	53.3	58.0	63.4

MANUFACTURING ACTIVITY

	1970	1971	1972	1973	1974	1975	1976	1977	1978	1979	1980
Employment (1987=100)	124.7	122.6	122.0	123.9	125.4	124.9	116.3	116.2	116.3	114.4	111.3
Real Earnings per Empl. (1987=100)	..	..	70.9	74.9	78.9	80.9	91.5	93.8	96.5	93.2	89.1
Real Output per Empl. (1987=100)	36.7	39.8	42.5	44.3	47.2	52.7	61.9	65.0	68.5	71.9	89.1
Earnings as % of Value Added	27.9	26.0	25.0	24.9	24.0	23.2	24.6	28.5	28.9	27.2	33.7

MONETARY HOLDINGS *(Billions of current Hungarian Forint)*

	1970	1971	1972	1973	1974	1975	1976	1977	1978	1979	1980
Money Supply, Broadly Defined	..	..	..	..	..	..	..	..	..	..	..
Money	..	..	..	..	..	..	..	..	..	..	..
Currency Outside Banks	..	..	..	..	..	..	..	..	..	..	..
Demand Deposits	..	..	..	..	..	..	..	..	..	..	..
Quasi-Money	..	..	..	..	..	..	..	..	..	..	..

GOVERNMENT DEFICIT (-) OR SURPLUS *(Billions of current Hungarian Forint)*

	1970	1971	1972	1973	1974	1975	1976	1977	1978	1979	1980
Current Revenue	..	..	..	..	..	..	..	..	..	..	..
Current Expenditure	..	..	..	..	..	..	..	..	..	..	..
Current Budget Balance	..	..	..	..	..	..	..	..	..	..	..
Capital Receipts	..	..	..	..	..	..	..	..	..	..	..
Capital Payments	..	..	..	..	..	..	..	..	..	..	..

1981	1982	1983	1984	1985	1986	1987	1988	1989	1990 estimate	Notes	HUNGARY
2,150	2,220	2,120	2,030	1,930	2,010	2,250	2,480	2,620	2,780	..	CURRENT GNP PER CAPITA (US $)
10,713	10,711	10,700	10,679	10,657	10,640	10,621	10,596	10,576	10,553	..	POPULATION (thousands)
											USE AND ORIGIN OF RESOURCES
				(Billions of current Hungarian Forint)							
751.5	807.1	863.3	937.7	990.2	1,043.4	1,178.2	1,397.0	1,648.1	1,987.9	..	Gross National Product (GNP)
-28.4	-40.8	-33.1	-40.7	-43.5	-45.4	-48.2	-55.2	-82.3	-93.0	..	Net Factor Income from Abroad
779.9	847.9	896.4	978.4	1,033.7	1,088.8	1,226.4	1,452.2	1,730.4	2,080.9	..	GDP at Market Prices
-8.2	6.8	17.1	30.9	21.4	-15.4	-5.9	38.7	57.4	80.1	..	Resource Balance
308.2	321.8	360.7	402.0	436.2	431.6	464.4	530.4	620.9	685.1	..	Exports of Goods & NFServices
316.4	315.0	343.6	371.1	414.8	447.0	470.3	491.7	563.5	605.0	..	Imports of Goods & NFServices
788.1	841.1	879.3	947.5	1,012.3	1,104.2	1,232.3	1,413.5	1,673.0	2,000.8		Domestic Absorption
477.7	515.1	551.2	600.5	649.3	695.5	778.5	886.8	1,050.4	1,300.0	..	Private Consumption, etc.
79.1	84.2	90.9	95.2	104.6	116.0	126.3	168.5	177.7	222.0	..	General Gov't Consumption
231.3	241.8	237.2	251.8	258.4	292.7	327.5	358.2	444.9	478.8	..	Gross Domestic Investment
206.7	213.9	220.1	225.4	232.1	261.2	303.5	295.6	348.4	369.6	..	Fixed Investment
..	..	..	..	..	..	..	..	..	..	..	Indirect Taxes, net
..	..	..	..	..	..	..	..	..	..	B	GDP at factor cost
136.8	148.5	152.9	166.1	166.6	182.6	189.2	209.8	235.5	258.6	..	Agriculture
323.8	350.1	369.3	400.8	425.9	440.0	494.6	527.4	629.9	657.7	..	Industry
268.3	290.0	303.8	329.7	351.9	361.0	402.3	430.3	515.3	552.3	..	Manufacturing
319.3	349.3	374.2	411.5	441.2	466.2	542.6	715.0	865.0	1,164.6	..	Services, etc.
223.1	248.6	254.3	282.7	279.8	277.3	321.6	396.9	502.3	558.9		Gross Domestic Saving
196.4	210.1	223.6	245.2	239.6	235.5	278.3	347.6	427.7	512.4		Gross National Saving
				(Billions of 1987 Hungarian Forint)							
1,057.00	1,064.03	1,084.78	1,108.13	1,106.77	1,124.81	1,178.20	1,174.01	1,163.10	1,121.77	..	Gross National Product
1,098.44	1,118.82	1,127.20	1,156.87	1,156.02	1,173.48	1,226.40	1,220.87	1,222.37	1,175.28	..	GDP at Market Prices
-56.64	-28.34	-5.09	19.01	7.82	-14.36	-5.90	23.94	21.38	32.68	..	Resource Balance
360.18	373.39	400.12	428.58	452.14	442.25	464.40	496.37	502.36	500.20	..	Exports of Goods & NFServices
416.82	401.73	405.21	409.58	444.32	456.61	470.30	472.43	480.98	467.53	..	Imports of Goods & NFServices
1,155.08	1,147.16	1,132.29	1,137.87	1,148.20	1,187.84	1,232.30	1,196.93	1,200.99	1,142.60		Domestic Absorption
714.15	715.54	711.18	722.86	738.35	744.95	778.50	746.26	759.68	726.07	..	Private Consumption, etc.
111.51	113.37	113.66	115.08	120.09	125.87	126.30	133.64	125.86	131.89	..	General Gov't Consumption
329.42	318.24	307.45	299.92	289.76	317.02	327.50	317.04	315.44	284.64	..	Gross Domestic Investment
288.10	283.57	274.28	264.44	256.58	274.52	303.50	278.11	290.62	266.82	..	Fixed Investment
..	..	..	..	..	..	..	..	..	..	B	GDP at factor cost
169.06	187.59	187.72	196.50	188.46	195.14	189.20	204.16	204.06	187.13	..	Agriculture
468.69	474.48	483.74	489.97	477.81	475.93	494.60	457.35	451.28	411.74	..	Industry
..	..	..	..	..	..	..	..	..	..		Manufacturing
463.02	456.74	455.73	470.40	489.75	502.41	542.60	559.36	567.03	576.41	..	Services, etc.
											Memo Items:
406.01	410.40	425.37	443.68	467.24	440.88	464.40	509.61	529.97	529.42	..	Capacity to Import
45.84	37.01	25.26	15.10	15.10	-1.37	0.00	13.24	27.62	29.22	..	Terms of Trade Adjustment
1,144.27	1,155.83	1,152.45	1,171.97	1,171.12	1,172.11	1,226.40	1,234.11	1,249.99	1,204.50	..	Gross Domestic Income
1,102.84	1,101.04	1,110.03	1,123.23	1,121.88	1,123.44	1,178.20	1,187.25	1,190.72	1,151.00	..	Gross National Income
											DOMESTIC PRICES/DEFLATORS
				(Index 1987 = 100)							
71.0	75.8	79.5	84.6	89.4	92.8	100.0	118.9	141.6	177.1	..	Overall (GDP)
68.2	73.3	77.7	83.3	88.2	93.0	100.0	118.1	139.3	175.1	..	Domestic Absorption
80.9	79.2	81.5	84.5	88.4	93.6	100.0	102.8	115.4	138.2	..	Agriculture
69.1	73.8	76.3	81.8	89.1	92.5	100.0	115.3	139.6	159.7	..	Industry
..	..	..	..	..	..	..	..	..	..		Manufacturing
66.3	70.9	75.5	82.0	87.8	92.4	100.0	116.3	136.0	174.4	..	Consumer Price Index
											MANUFACTURING ACTIVITY
108.8	106.1	102.1	101.4	102.8	102.1	100.0	97.2	92.6	..	..	Employment (1987=100)
92.5	91.7	90.6	94.9	96.9	98.9	100.0	111.0	..	..	..	Real Earnings per Empl. (1987=100)
96.0	96.5	101.8	103.0	98.5	98.9	100.0	98.8		..	..	Real Output per Empl. (1987=100)
32.9	32.5	32.1	32.6	33.5	34.2	32.8	39.3		..	..	Earnings as % of Value Added
											MONETARY HOLDINGS
				(Billions of current Hungarian Forint)							
..	..	..	..	..	554.37	595.10	..	..	..	..	Money Supply, Broadly Defined
..	187.61	192.22	200.86	239.70	266.45	306.62	301.99	354.98	449.13	..	Money
..	84.87	94.79	105.42	116.75	130.88	153.77	164.45	180.62	209.79	..	Currency Outside Banks
..	102.74	97.43	95.44	122.95	135.57	152.85	137.54	174.36	239.34	..	Demand Deposits
..	..	..	..	..	287.92	288.48	..	..	..	..	Quasi-Money
				(Billions of current Hungarian Forint)							
-22.10	-16.10	-6.40	15.70	-10.10	-30.90	-40.30	-3.20	-32.60	16.70	..	**GOVERNMENT DEFICIT (-) OR SURPLUS**
416.80	438.70	484.50	535.20	538.70	606.80	660.40	789.90	923.40	1,105.90		Current Revenue
380.00	399.00	438.60	463.40	491.70	592.20	651.50	738.70	893.40	1,048.20		Current Expenditure
36.80	39.70	45.90	71.80	47.00	14.60	8.90	51.20	30.00	57.70		Current Budget Balance
1.30	..	1.00	..	0.30	..	..	..	3.20	..		Capital Receipts
60.20	55.80	53.30	56.10	57.40	45.50	49.20	54.40	65.80	41.00		Capital Payments

HUNGARY	1970	1971	1972	1973	1974	1975	1976	1977	1978	1979	1980
FOREIGN TRADE (CUSTOMS BASIS)					*(Millions of current US dollars)*						
Value of Exports, fob	2,317	2,500	3,292	4,479	5,129	6,093	4,932	5,840	6,434	7,938	8,677
Nonfuel Primary Products	720	758	967	1,395	1,586	1,712	1,457	1,722	1,822	2,163	2,548
Fuels	30	29	46	50	58	123	146	179	222	333	420
Manufactures	1,567	1,713	2,279	3,033	3,485	4,258	3,328	3,939	4,390	5,441	5,709
Value of Imports, cif	2,505	2,990	3,154	3,966	5,575	7,178	5,517	6,509	7,967	8,659	9,212
Nonfuel Primary Products	733	788	825	1,083	1,498	1,651	1,275	1,514	1,640	1,732	1,958
Fuels	222	257	299	375	473	970	683	803	1,083	1,384	1,512
Manufactures	1,551	1,945	2,030	2,508	3,604	4,557	3,558	4,192	5,244	5,543	5,741
Terms of Trade	139.3	136.8	136.7	134.9	*(Index 1987 = 100)* 122.0	115.8	118.8	114.7	114.7	112.0	112.5
Export Prices, fob	50.5	50.7	56.1	67.6	78.2	85.5	86.2	90.7	98.5	108.1	116.8
Import Prices, cif	36.2	37.1	41.0	50.2	64.1	73.8	72.6	79.0	85.9	96.5	103.8
BALANCE OF PAYMENTS					*(Millions of current US dollars)*						
Exports of Goods & Services	2,144	2,108	2,707	3,683	4,628	5,333	5,518	6,473	7,275	8,678	10,176
Merchandise, fob	1,819	1,864	2,421	3,327	4,021	4,765	5,042	5,877	6,565	7,949	8,877
Nonfactor Services	307	229	262	313	538	492	386	504	603	625	806
Factor Services	18	15	24	43	69	77	90	92	107	103	493
Imports of Goods & Services	2,204	2,498	2,672	3,501	5,046	6,059	6,208	7,330	8,812	9,662	10,801
Merchandise, fob	1,921	2,206	2,325	2,957	4,421	5,277	5,528	6,496	7,752	8,509	9,020
Nonfactor Services	204	212	253	415	444	534	482	569	688	669	900
Factor Services	79	80	93	129	181	248	198	264	372	484	881
Long-Term Interest	0	0	0	0	0	0	0	0	8	25	635
Private Current Transfers, net	36	42	60	73	80	75	69	44	99	42	48
Workers' Remittances	..	..	..	..	..	..	..	..	..	..	..
Curr. A/C Bal before Off. Transf.	-25	-347	95	256	-339	-651	-620	-813	-1,437	-942	-577
Net Official Transfers	..	..	..	..	..	..	..	..	..	..	..
Curr. A/C Bal after Off. Transf.	-25	-347	95	256	-339	-651	-620	-813	-1,437	-942	-577
Long-Term Capital, net	..	217	137	5	143	413	419	637	1,143	943	778
Direct Investment	..	..	..	..	..	..	..	-6	-4	6	0
Long-Term Loans	0	0	0	0	0	0	2	43	272	275	728
Disbursements	0	0	0	0	0	0	2	43	272	377	1,552
Repayments	0	0	0	0	0	0	0	0	0	103	824
Other Long-Term Capital	..	217	137	5	143	413	417	600	875	662	51
Other Capital, net	..	..	-59	30	416	124	136	242	426	-167	283
Change in Reserves	..	..	-172	-290	-220	114	66	-67	-132	166	-484
Memo Item:					*(Hungarian Forint per US dollar)*						
Conversion Factor (Annual Avg)	60.000	59.820	55.260	48.970	46.750	43.970	41.570	40.960	37.910	35.580	32.530
EXTERNAL DEBT (Total)					*(Millions of US dollars), outstanding at end of year*						
	0	0	0	0	0	0	2	45	8,248	8,861	9,756
Long-Term Debt (by debtor)	0	0	0	0	0	0	2	45	4,825	5,689	6,409
Central Bank, incl. IMF credit	0	0	0	0	0	0	2	45	4,825	5,689	6,409
Central Government	0	0	0	0	0	0	0	0	0	0	0
Rest of General Government	..	..	..	..	..	..	..	..	..	..	..
Non-financial Public Enterprises	0	0	0	0	0	0	0	0	0	0	0
Priv. Sector, incl non-guaranteed	..	..	..	..	..	..	..	..	..	..	..
Short-Term Debt	0	0	0	0	0	0	0	0	3,423	3,172	3,347
Memo Items:					*(Millions of US dollars)*						
Int'l Reserves Excluding Gold	..	..	..	..	..	..	..	..	..	..	..
Gold Holdings (at market price)	..	63.1	108.4	204.3	248.0	133.4	178.1	211.5	447.0	909.8	1,219.7
SOCIAL INDICATORS											
Total Fertility Rate	2.0	1.9	1.9	2.0	2.3	2.4	2.3	2.2	2.1	2.0	1.9
Infant Mortality Rate	35.9	35.1	33.2	33.8	34.3	32.8	29.8	26.2	24.4	23.7	23.1
Life Expectancy at Birth	69.8	69.8	69.9	69.9	69.9	69.9	70.0	70.0	69.9	69.8	69.7
Urban Population, % of total	45.6	46.4	47.2	48.0	48.8	49.6	50.4	51.2	52.0	52.8	53.6
Food Prod. per capita (1987=100)	64.5	72.5	76.9	81.5	82.6	84.8	80.6	86.9	88.9	86.3	94.6
Labor Force, Agriculture (%)	25.1	24.4	23.7	23.0	22.3	21.7	21.0	20.3	19.6	18.9	18.2
Labor Force, Female (%)	39.8	40.3	40.7	41.1	41.6	42.0	42.4	42.7	43.1	43.5	43.9
Primary Schl. Enroll. Ratio	97.0	..	..	..	..	99.0	99.0	98.0	97.0	96.0	96.0
Primary Schl. Enroll. Ratio, Female	97.0	..	..	..	..	99.0	99.0	98.0	97.0	96.0	97.0
Secondary Schl. Enroll. Ratio	63.0	..	..	..	..	63.0	..	..	..	70.0	69.0

	1981	1982	1983	1984	1985	1986	1987	1988	1989	1990 estimate	Notes	HUNGARY
FOREIGN TRADE (CUSTOMS BASIS)												
(Millions of current US dollars)												
Value of Exports, fob	8,712	8,799	8,722	8,560	8,555	9,157	9,571	9,931	9,605	9,588	..	
Nonfuel Primary Products	2,708	2,615	2,476	2,404	2,252	2,340	2,386	2,686	2,759	3,022	..	
Fuels	413	581	806	739	437	368	402	298	275	296	..	
Manufactures	5,591	5,603	5,440	5,418	5,866	6,450	6,783	6,947	6,570	6,269	..	
Value of Imports, cif	9,123	8,836	8,481	8,084	8,143	9,583	9,855	9,309	8,818	8,646	..	
Nonfuel Primary Products	1,850	1,461	1,472	1,430	1,343	1,630	1,635	1,646	1,439	1,296	..	
Fuels	1,518	1,843	1,939	1,821	1,796	1,952	1,675	1,286	1,036	1,229	..	
Manufactures	5,755	5,531	5,069	4,833	5,004	6,000	6,545	6,377	6,343	6,121	..	
(Index 1987 = 100)												
Terms of Trade	111.5	108.2	106.1	103.4	104.1	98.8	100.0	84.7	87.0	87.4	..	
Export Prices, fob	114.4	107.6	97.4	90.3	90.7	99.2	100.0	77.7	76.6	78.7	..	
Import Prices, cif	102.6	99.5	91.8	87.3	87.1	100.4	100.0	91.7	88.0	90.1	..	
BALANCE OF PAYMENTS												
(Millions of current US dollars)												
Exports of Goods & Services	10,335	10,421	10,378	10,688	10,012	11,024	12,030	12,159	12,799	11,302	f	
Merchandise, fob	8,901	9,038	8,978	9,090	8,578	9,198	9,965	9,989	10,494	8,989	..	
Nonfactor Services	1,191	1,264	1,268	1,439	1,229	1,565	1,822	1,932	2,075	2,060	..	
Factor Services	244	119	132	159	205	261	243	238	231	252	..	
Imports of Goods & Services	11,276	11,018	10,614	10,715	10,532	12,465	12,812	12,849	13,501	11,807	f	
Merchandise, fob	8,855	8,628	8,544	8,310	8,130	9,663	9,887	9,406	9,450	8,555	..	
Nonfactor Services	1,057	1,158	1,163	1,396	1,330	1,550	1,655	2,112	2,425	1,560	..	
Factor Services	1,365	1,232	907	1,009	1,072	1,252	1,270	1,331	1,625	1,693	..	
Long-Term Interest	704	890	777	840	825	938	1,068	1,123	1,479	1,571	..	
Private Current Transfers, net	48	63	56	66	65	78	105	118	130	736	..	
Workers' Remittances	..	0	0	0	0	0	0	0	..	..	..	
Curr. A/C Bal before Off. Transf.	-893	-534	-180	39	-455	-1,363	-677	-572	-571	230	..	
Net Official Transfers	..	0	0	0	0	0	0	0	0	..	..	
Curr. A/C Bal after Off. Transf.	-893	-534	-180	39	-455	-1,363	-677	-572	-571	230	..	
Long-Term Capital, net	990	290	297	1,749	1,600	844	226	289	1,292	225	f	
Direct Investment	2	..	..	..	..	..	..	..	180	337	..	
Long-Term Loans	772	467	26	1,341	1,933	1,186	1,198	715	1,631	340	..	
Disbursements	1,916	1,702	1,523	3,102	4,513	4,105	3,364	2,565	3,372	2,573	..	
Repayments	1,143	1,235	1,496	1,761	2,580	2,919	2,167	1,850	1,741	2,233	..	
Other Long-Term Capital	216	-177	271	408	-333	-342	-972	-426	-519	-452	..	
Other Capital, net	-540	-529	702	-1,046	-629	495	-698	246	-153	-893	f	
Change in Reserves	443	773	-819	-742	-516	24	1,149	37	-568	438	..	
Memo Item:												
(Hungarian Forint per US dollar)												
Conversion Factor (Annual Avg)	34.310	36.630	42.670	48.040	50.120	45.830	46.970	50.410	59.070	63.210	..	
EXTERNAL DEBT (Total)												
(Millions of US dollars), outstanding at end of year												
Long-Term Debt (by debtor)	9,781	10,216	10,745	10,983	13,954	16,907	19,584	19,602	20,390	21,316	..	
Central Bank, incl. IMF credit	6,933	6,955	6,842	8,006	10,936	13,413	16,482	16,239	17,084	18,375	..	
Central Government	6,927	6,949	6,832	7,888	10,768	13,152	16,149	15,820	16,565	17,702	..	
Rest of General Government	0	0	0	12	42	108	168	298	421	584	..	
Non-financial Public Enterprises	..	..	..	..	..	..	..	..	..	..	..	
Priv. Sector, incl non-guaranteed	5	6	9	106	126	153	164	122	98	90	..	
Short-Term Debt	2,848	3,261	3,904	2,977	3,019	3,494	3,103	3,363	3,307	2,940	..	
Memo Items:												
(Millions of US dollars)												
Int'l Reserves Excluding Gold	..	..	1,231.2	1,560.0	2,153.1	2,302.0	1,634.3	1,467.2	1,246.0	1,070.3	..	
Gold Holdings (at market price)	669.8	295.2	584.5	636.0	760.9	917.1	794.4	653.5	600.3	115.5	..	
SOCIAL INDICATORS												
Total Fertility Rate	1.9	1.8	1.8	1.7	1.8	1.8	1.8	1.8	1.8	1.8	..	
Infant Mortality Rate	20.6	19.7	19.0	20.2	20.4	19.0	17.0	16.5	16.0	15.4	..	
Life Expectancy at Birth	69.6	69.6	69.7	69.8	69.9	70.0	70.2	70.3	70.5	70.7	..	
Urban Population, % of total	54.4	55.2	55.9	56.7	57.5	58.3	59.0	59.8	60.5	61.3	..	
Food Prod. per capita (1987=100)	91.4	102.3	96.3	102.6	98.7	99.5	100.0	106.3	105.5	95.8	..	
Labor Force, Agriculture (%)	..	..	..	..	..	..	..	..	..	..	..	
Labor Force, Female (%)	44.0	44.1	44.2	44.3	44.4	44.5	44.6	44.7	44.8	44.9	..	
Primary Schl. Enroll. Ratio	..	99.0	99.0	99.0	98.0	98.0	97.0	96.0	94.0	..	..	
Primary Schl. Enroll. Ratio, Female	..	99.0	99.0	99.0	99.0	98.0	97.0	97.0	94.0	..	..	
Secondary Schl. Enroll. Ratio	..	73.0	73.0	73.0	72.0	70.0	70.0	71.0	76.0	..	..	

ICELAND	1970	1971	1972	1973	1974	1975	1976	1977	1978	1979	1980
CURRENT GNP PER CAPITA (US $)	2,420	2,820	3,370	4,220	5,570	6,360	7,100	8,230	9,930	11,800	13,580
POPULATION (thousands)	204	206	209	212	215	218	220	222	224	226	228

USE AND ORIGIN OF RESOURCES

(Billions of current Icelandic Kronur)

	1970	1971	1972	1973	1974	1975	1976	1977	1978	1979	1980
Gross National Product (GNP)	0.43	0.55	0.69	0.96	1.40	1.98	2.79	4.05	6.32	9.37	15.09
Net Factor Income from Abroad	0.00	-0.01	-0.01	-0.01	-0.02	-0.05	-0.07	-0.09	-0.16	-0.24	-0.41
GDP at Market Prices	0.44	0.56	0.70	0.97	1.42	2.03	2.87	4.14	6.48	9.62	15.50
Resource Balance	0.01	-0.03	-0.01	-0.01	-0.14	-0.17	0.03	-0.01	0.24	0.18	0.10
Exports of Goods & NFServices	0.21	0.22	0.26	0.37	0.47	0.72	1.05	1.44	2.48	3.81	5.75
Imports of Goods & NFServices	0.20	0.25	0.27	0.38	0.61	0.88	1.02	1.45	2.24	3.63	5.65
Domestic Absorption	0.43	0.59	0.71	0.99	1.55	2.20	2.84	4.15	6.24	9.44	15.40
Private Consumption, etc.	0.27	0.34	0.42	0.56	0.85	1.19	1.63	2.34	3.66	5.50	8.85
General Gov't Consumption	0.06	0.07	0.10	0.14	0.23	0.33	0.45	0.65	1.07	1.64	2.55
Gross Domestic Investment	0.10	0.18	0.18	0.29	0.48	0.67	0.76	1.16	1.51	2.30	4.01
Fixed Investment	0.10	0.16	0.19	0.29	0.45	0.64	0.78	1.09	1.55	2.25	3.93
Indirect Taxes, net	0.08	0.10	0.13	0.19	0.30	0.42	0.60	0.84	1.24	1.80	3.03
GDP at factor cost	0.36	0.46	0.57	0.78	1.12	1.61	2.27	3.30	5.24	7.82	12.47
Agriculture	..	..	..	0.10	0.15	0.19	0.26	0.43	0.70	1.02	1.57
Industry	..	..	..	0.29	0.36	0.52	0.77	1.07	1.56	2.42	3.98
Manufacturing	..	..	..	0.17	0.19	0.28	0.44	0.63	0.92	1.51	2.41
Services, etc.	..	..	..	0.39	0.61	0.90	1.24	1.80	2.97	4.38	6.92
Gross Domestic Saving	0.11	0.14	0.17	0.27	0.34	0.51	0.79	1.15	1.75	2.48	4.10
Gross National Saving	0.11	0.14	0.17	0.26	0.33	0.46	0.72	..	1.59	2.23	3.68

(Millions of 1987 Icelandic Kronur)

	1970	1971	1972	1973	1974	1975	1976	1977	1978	1979	1980
Gross National Product	86,694	98,182	103,468	109,461	116,196	116,091	122,750	134,149	142,905	150,517	159,166
GDP at Market Prices	87,436	98,868	104,585	110,627	117,569	118,621	125,710	136,871	146,367	154,116	163,114
Resource Balance	5,808	-3,472	700	-3,158	-9,210	-2,458	3,853	-263	5,006	7,136	7,186
Exports of Goods & NFServices	32,633	29,947	34,291	37,262	36,270	37,221	42,085	45,836	52,784	56,092	57,606
Imports of Goods & NFServices	26,826	33,419	33,591	40,420	45,479	39,679	38,231	46,099	47,777	48,956	50,420
Domestic Absorption	81,629	102,340	103,885	113,785	126,779	121,079	121,857	137,134	141,361	146,980	155,928
Private Consumption, etc.	52,050	59,124	66,371	68,143	71,927	66,246	74,081	80,844	87,516	90,044	93,838
General Gov't Consumption	13,023	14,014	16,047	17,410	18,886	20,649	21,685	22,155	23,731	25,026	25,558
Gross Domestic Investment	16,556	29,203	21,467	28,231	35,966	34,184	26,091	34,135	30,114	31,910	36,532
Fixed Investment	17,045	24,714	24,528	29,501	32,451	29,575	28,666	32,120	31,096	31,160	35,571
GDP at factor cost	73,131	82,182	85,363	88,600	93,194	95,236	100,115	109,060	118,495	126,342	132,695
Agriculture	..	..	..	12,705	13,453	13,962	13,034	14,121	16,170	15,819	17,778
Industry	..	..	..	33,570	33,085	33,096	36,695	39,002	39,046	40,393	43,892
Manufacturing	..	..	..	19,306	19,413	19,342	21,459	24,374	24,766	26,503	28,668
Services, etc.	..	..	..	42,852	47,071	48,573	50,780	56,294	63,520	70,175	71,275

Memo Items:

	1970	1971	1972	1973	1974	1975	1976	1977	1978	1979	1980
Capacity to Import	28,369	29,008	32,505	38,886	35,343	32,261	39,316	45,813	52,892	51,369	51,295
Terms of Trade Adjustment	-4,264	-939	-1,786	1,624	-927	-4,960	-2,768	-23	108	-4,723	-6,311
Gross Domestic Income	83,172	97,928	102,799	112,250	116,642	113,661	122,942	136,848	146,475	149,394	156,803
Gross National Income	82,430	97,243	101,682	111,085	115,269	111,131	119,982	134,127	143,013	145,794	152,855

DOMESTIC PRICES/DEFLATORS

(Index 1987 = 100)

	1970	1971	1972	1973	1974	1975	1976	1977	1978	1979	1980
Overall (GDP)	0.5	0.6	0.7	0.9	1.2	1.7	2.3	3.0	4.4	6.2	9.5
Domestic Absorption	0.5	0.6	0.7	0.9	1.2	1.8	2.3	3.0	4.4	6.4	9.9
Agriculture	..	..	..	0.8	1.1	1.4	2.0	3.1	4.3	6.5	8.8
Industry	..	..	..	0.9	1.1	1.6	2.1	2.8	4.0	6.0	9.1
Manufacturing	..	..	..	0.9	1.0	1.5	2.0	2.6	3.7	5.7	8.4
Consumer Price Index	0.6	0.6	0.7	0.8	1.1	1.7	2.2	2.9	4.2	6.2	9.8

MANUFACTURING ACTIVITY

	1970	1971	1972	1973	1974	1975	1976	1977	1978	1979	1980
Employment (1987=100)	67.6	71.0	73.0	72.3	73.4	75.8	78.4	82.1	83.8	87.4	90.8
Real Earnings per Empl. (1987=100)	60.2	63.4	78.1	88.0	92.2	78.6	76.8	84.5	91.2	97.4	88.1
Real Output per Empl. (1987=100)	0.0	0.0	0.0	87.0	110.8	100.2	98.1	107.0	114.3	114.1	118.7
Earnings as % of Value Added	58.0	59.8	61.6	59.4	61.3	60.0	56.6	58.7	58.9	54.6	50.5

MONETARY HOLDINGS

(Millions of current Icelandic Kronur)

	1970	1971	1972	1973	1974	1975	1976	1977	1978	1979	1980
Money Supply, Broadly Defined	173	209	247	327	420	542	720	1,038	1,540	2,421	4,003
Money	46	57	69	96	125	167	208	305	430	629	1,010
Currency Outside Banks	14	17	21	27	35	44	57	88	124	160	224
Demand Deposits	32	39	48	69	90	123	151	217	306	469	786
Quasi-Money	126	152	178	231	296	375	513	732	1,110	1,792	2,993

GOVERNMENT DEFICIT (-) OR SURPLUS

(Millions of current Icelandic Kronur)

	1970	1971	1972	1973	1974	1975	1976	1977	1978	1979	1980
	..	..	-18	-30	-66	-122	-69	-173	-156	-193	-193
Current Revenue	..	..	194	285	415	579	763	1,068	1,717	2,626	4,089
Current Expenditure	..	..	154	212	344	496	595	862	1,435	2,243	3,388
Current Budget Balance	..	..	39	74	71	83	168	205	282	383	700
Capital Receipts	..	..	..	0	2	9	10	4	3	4	2
Capital Payments	..	..	57	104	140	213	247	382	441	580	895

	1981	1982	1983	1984	1985	1986	1987	1988	1989	1990 estimate	Notes
CURRENT GNP PER CAPITA (US $)	14,830	14,530	12,350	11,750	11,680	13,390	16,880	20,150	21,450	22,050	..
POPULATION (thousands)	231	234	237	239	241	243	246	250	252	255	..

USE AND ORIGIN OF RESOURCES

(Billions of current Icelandic Kronur)

	1981	1982	1983	1984	1985	1986	1987	1988	1989	1990	Notes
Gross National Product (GNP)	23.53	36.64	62.77	82.95	113.51	152.37	201.90	246.31	287.38	326.70	..
Net Factor Income from Abroad	-0.81	-1.49	-3.07	-4.55	-5.58	-6.23	-6.20	-8.33	-13.22	-14.61	..
GDP at Market Prices	24.34	38.13	65.84	87.51	119.09	158.60	208.10	254.64	300.59	341.31	..
Resource Balance	-0.21	-1.61	1.80	0.42	0.77	6.78	-1.03	-0.91	8.60	5.39	..
Exports of Goods & NF Services	8.72	12.71	27.08	34.29	49.82	63.12	73.47	84.13	108.97	125.60	..
Imports of Goods & NF Services	8.94	14.33	25.27	33.87	49.05	56.34	74.50	85.04	100.37	120.21	..
Domestic Absorption	24.55	39.75	64.03	87.08	118.32	151.81	209.13	255.55	291.99	335.92	..
Private Consumption, etc.	14.33	22.94	39.42	53.89	74.71	96.93	131.71	158.20	181.00	207.80	..
General Gov't Consumption	4.04	6.64	11.56	14.06	20.14	27.29	36.79	47.47	56.37	63.75	..
Gross Domestic Investment	6.18	10.16	13.06	19.14	23.48	27.59	40.63	49.88	54.62	64.37	..
Fixed Investment	5.93	9.25	14.13	18.36	24.46	29.68	41.04	48.03	55.51	66.20	..
Indirect Taxes, net	5.02	7.81	12.28	17.67	22.85	29.74	41.53	51.07	59.33	67.74	..
GDP at factor cost	19.32	30.32	53.56	69.83	96.24	128.86	166.57	203.57	241.27	273.58	..
Agriculture	2.30	2.93	5.13	7.21	11.43	15.84	21.13	25.20	..	..	..
Industry	6.09	9.80	16.66	23.45	30.14	40.41	53.67	63.50	..	..	..
Manufacturing	3.70	5.52	9.06	13.10	17.22	24.08	32.74	37.54	..	..	..
Services, etc.	10.93	17.59	31.77	39.17	54.67	72.62	91.77	114.87			..
Gross Domestic Saving	5.97	8.55	14.86	19.57	24.25	34.37	39.60	48.97	63.23	69.76	..
Gross National Saving	5.15	7.01	11.78	15.08	18.72	28.38	33.43	40.67	50.06	55.51	..

(Millions of 1987 Icelandic Kronur)

	1981	1982	1983	1984	1985	1986	1987	1988	1989	1990	Notes
Gross National Product	164,525	166,582	158,552	164,027	170,759	184,347	201,896	199,752	194,878	195,215	..
GDP at Market Prices	169,823	173,014	166,065	172,738	178,847	191,728	208,099	206,504	203,781	203,866	..
Resource Balance	4,561	-712	7,738	4,796	5,998	9,976	-1,030	-735	7,327	5,326	..
Exports of Goods & NF Services	58,338	52,744	58,167	59,912	66,478	70,609	73,466	71,431	72,333	71,180	..
Imports of Goods & NF Services	53,776	53,455	50,429	55,115	60,481	60,632	74,496	72,166	65,007	65,855	..
Domestic Absorption	165,262	173,726	158,326	167,942	172,849	181,752	209,129	207,240	196,455	198,540	..
Private Consumption, etc.	100,127	105,372	98,162	101,838	106,042	114,184	131,712	126,965	120,481	120,517	..
General Gov't Consumption	27,435	29,132	30,497	30,547	32,444	34,683	36,791	38,327	39,250	39,913	..
Gross Domestic Investment	37,699	39,222	29,667	35,557	34,363	32,886	40,626	41,948	36,724	38,110	..
Fixed Investment	35,915	35,734	31,350	34,221	34,910	34,493	41,042	40,499	37,075	38,750	..
GDP at factor cost	136,151	138,885	135,968	138,930	145,752	156,492	166,568	165,128	164,207	164,115	..
Agriculture	18,050	17,484	15,717	17,472	20,451	20,666	21,130	21,787	..	..	..
Industry	45,073	45,394	44,510	47,480	47,557	49,622	53,673	51,564	..	..	..
Manufacturing	29,631	28,525	26,741	28,632	28,894	30,333	32,736	30,274	..	..	..
Services, etc.	73,271	76,132	75,740	73,978	77,745	86,205	91,765	91,777	..	..	..

Memo Items:

	1981	1982	1983	1984	1985	1986	1987	1988	1989	1990	Notes
Capacity to Import	52,501	47,430	54,026	55,805	61,428	67,932	73,466	71,393	70,578	68,808	..
Terms of Trade Adjustment	-5,837	-5,313	-4,141	-4,106	-5,051	-2,677	0	-38	-1,755	-2,372	..
Gross Domestic Income	163,986	167,701	161,924	168,632	173,796	189,052	208,099	206,466	202,026	201,493	..
Gross National Income	158,688	161,268	154,410	159,920	165,708	181,670	201,896	199,715	193,123	192,843	..

DOMESTIC PRICES/DEFLATORS

(Index 1987 = 100)

	1981	1982	1983	1984	1985	1986	1987	1988	1989	1990	Notes
Overall (GDP)	14.3	22.0	39.6	50.7	66.6	82.7	100.0	123.3	147.5	167.4	..
Domestic Absorption	14.9	22.9	40.4	51.9	68.5	83.5	100.0	123.3	148.6	169.2	..
Agriculture	12.8	16.8	32.7	41.3	55.9	76.6	100.0	115.7	..	..	..
Industry	13.5	21.6	37.4	49.4	63.4	81.4	100.0	123.2	..	..	..
Manufacturing	12.5	19.3	33.9	45.7	59.6	79.4	100.0	124.0	..	..	..
Consumer Price Index	14.7	22.2	41.0	52.9	69.7	84.9	100.0	125.8	151.9	175.4	..

MANUFACTURING ACTIVITY

	1981	1982	1983	1984	1985	1986	1987	1988	1989	1990	Notes
Employment (1987=100)	92.3	92.7	93.6	95.7	95.9	97.0	100.0	101.3	..	..	G
Real Earnings per Empl. (1987=100)	90.7	93.5	78.2	75.0	81.2	85.3	100.0	..	..	..	G
Real Output per Empl. (1987=100)	118.6	120.3	108.3	108.6	110.9	102.7	100.0	..	..	..	G
Earnings as % of Value Added	54.3	51.9	57.4	52.7	56.1	58.0	65.1	..	..	..	..

MONETARY HOLDINGS

(Millions of current Icelandic Kronur)

	1981	1982	1983	1984	1985	1986	1987	1988	1989	1990	Notes
Money Supply, Broadly Defined	6,868	10,856	19,448	26,031	38,453	52,003	70,423	116,358	111,201	127,856	..
Money	1,628	2,076	3,698	5,282	6,722	9,674	12,883	15,177	19,673	24,816	..
Currency Outside Banks	406	527	770	966	1,251	1,734	2,244	2,639	3,045	3,174	..
Demand Deposits	1,222	1,549	2,928	4,316	5,471	7,940	10,639	12,538	16,628	21,642	..
Quasi-Money	5,240	8,780	15,750	20,749	31,731	42,328	57,540	101,181	91,528	103,040	..

(Millions of current Icelandic Kronur)

	1981	1982	1983	1984	1985	1986	1987	1988	1989	1990	Notes
GOVERNMENT DEFICIT (-) OR SURPLUS	-172	-958	-1,998	-1,610	-4,719	-7,639	-2,677	..	..	..	E
Current Revenue	6,623	10,762	17,492	23,630	31,231	41,671	55,012	..	..	..	
Current Expenditure	5,342	9,017	16,505	19,665	28,644	42,939	49,882	..	..	..	
Current Budget Balance	1,281	1,745	987	3,964	2,587	-1,268	5,129	..	..	..	
Capital Receipts	1	10	21	4	25	267	242	..	..	..	
Capital Payments	1,454	2,713	3,006	5,578	7,331	6,639	8,048	..	..	..	

ICELAND

ICELAND	1970	1971	1972	1973	1974	1975	1976	1977	1978	1979	1980
FOREIGN TRADE (CUSTOMS BASIS)					*(Millions of current US dollars)*						
Value of Exports, fob	146.9	150.1	191.4	290.7	329.3	307.5	404.0	512.6	640.9	790.8	931.2
Nonfuel Primary Products	..	..	..	..	..	..	..	..	..	..	..
Fuels	..	..	..	..	..	..	..	..	..	..	..
Manufactures	5.2	6.9	9.8	13.5	19.0	16.7	24.3	32.9	32.4	51.9	78.1
Value of Imports, cif	157.1	220.7	233.4	327.2	524.5	488.3	470.0	606.9	673.5	825.0	1,000.1
Nonfuel Primary Products	34.0	39.5	42.6	48.4	76.4	73.6	77.5	88.0	97.5	114.4	148.3
Fuels	14.5	17.9	17.9	26.0	63.6	62.0	57.7	77.9	79.2	161.8	167.3
Manufactures	108.6	163.3	172.9	252.9	384.6	352.7	334.8	441.1	496.8	548.8	684.5
Terms of Trade	198.3	176.4	165.5	178.9	*(Index 1987 = 100)* 136.2	104.8	122.1	136.3	132.6	124.9	131.4
Export Prices, fob	36.6	39.0	40.8	55.0	64.3	52.8	63.6	77.7	83.7	91.3	115.7
Import Prices, cif	18.5	22.1	24.6	30.8	47.2	50.4	52.1	57.0	63.1	73.2	88.1
BALANCE OF PAYMENTS					*(Millions of current US dollars)*						
Exports of Goods & Services	234.8	251.7	294.9	414.9	476.0	491.1	577.7	729.5	908.2	1,084.3	1,213.5
Merchandise, fob	146.2	150.8	191.7	291.0	329.4	306.5	402.0	512.6	640.3	779.6	919.8
Nonfactor Services	85.1	97.2	99.8	118.9	140.7	182.5	172.5	212.1	262.0	292.8	279.8
Factor Services	3.5	3.7	3.4	5.0	5.9	2.1	3.2	4.8	5.9	11.9	13.9
Imports of Goods & Services	232.3	300.7	320.9	447.3	637.0	593.1	600.8	777.8	888.2	1,102.6	1,288.4
Merchandise, fob	143.5	200.6	215.5	326.0	476.7	441.9	427.9	564.7	618.4	754.1	899.9
Nonfactor Services	71.3	85.0	84.0	93.2	125.3	118.3	117.2	149.8	192.1	253.5	262.8
Factor Services	17.5	15.1	21.4	28.0	35.0	32.9	55.7	63.3	77.7	95.0	125.7
Long-Term Interest	..	..	..	..	..	..	..	..	..	..	..
Private Current Transfers, net	0.0	-0.1	0.8	1.7	1.4	0.5	1.1	..	-0.3	-1.4	-3.0
Workers' Remittances	..	..	..	..	..	..	..	..	..	..	..
Curr. A/C Bal before Off. Transf.	2.5	-49.0	-25.3	-30.8	-159.6	-101.5	-22.0	-47.6	19.7	-19.7	-77.9
Net Official Transfers	-0.4	..	-0.5	14.5	-0.8	-1.2	-0.8	-0.7	-0.8	-1.5	-1.2
Curr. A/C Bal after Off. Transf.	2.1	-49.0	-25.8	-16.2	-160.4	-102.7	-22.8	-48.3	18.9	-21.2	-79.1
Long-Term Capital, net	-2.9	53.2	24.1	22.9	109.0	134.3	64.7	111.7	78.1	94.9	153.0
Direct Investment	4.5	19.8	2.8	-1.5	13.2	42.4	4.5	4.2	8.1	3.1	22.3
Long-Term Loans	..	..	..	..	..	..	..	..	..	..	..
Disbursements	..	..	..	..	..	..	..	..	..	..	..
Repayments	..	..	..	..	..	..	..	..	..	..	..
Other Long-Term Capital	-7.4	33.4	21.3	24.4	95.7	92.0	60.2	107.5	70.0	91.8	130.7
Other Capital, net	21.6	10.1	13.2	9.3	-16.8	-50.2	-38.4	-47.2	-45.7	-37.0	-39.7
Change in Reserves	-20.8	-14.2	-11.5	-16.0	68.3	18.6	-3.5	-16.2	-51.3	-36.7	-34.2
Memo Item:					*(Icelandic Kronur per US dollar)*						
Conversion Factor (Annual Avg)	0.880	0.880	0.880	0.900	1.000	1.540	1.820	1.990	2.710	3.530	4.800
EXTERNAL DEBT (Total)					*(Millions US dollars), outstanding at end of year*						
Long-Term Debt (by debtor)	..	..	..	..	..	..	..	..	..	..	..
Central Bank, incl. IMF credit	..	..	..	..	..	..	..	..	..	..	..
Central Government	..	..	..	..	..	..	..	..	..	..	..
Rest of General Government	..	..	..	..	..	..	..	..	..	..	..
Non-financial Public Enterprises	..	..	..	..	..	..	..	..	..	..	..
Priv. Sector, incl non-guaranteed	..	..	..	..	..	..	..	..	..	..	..
Short-Term Debt	..	..	..	..	..	..	..	..	..	..	..
Memo Items:					*(Millions of US dollars)*						
Int'l Reserves Excluding Gold	52.72	68.85	83.05	98.40	47.25	45.60	79.38	98.34	135.83	161.94	173.81
Gold Holdings (at market price)	1.08	1.27	1.88	3.26	5.59	4.21	4.04	6.43	9.94	25.09	28.89
SOCIAL INDICATORS											
Total Fertility Rate	2.8	2.9	3.1	2.9	2.7	2.6	2.5	2.3	2.4	2.4	2.5
Infant Mortality Rate	13.2	12.9	11.3	9.6	11.7	12.5	7.7	9.5	11.3	9.5	7.7
Life Expectancy at Birth	74.0	74.1	74.3	74.7	75.1	75.5	75.9	76.3	76.4	76.5	76.6
Urban Population, % of total	84.9	85.3	85.7	86.0	86.4	86.8	87.1	87.4	87.6	87.9	88.2
Food Prod. per capita (1987=100)	105.1	104.7	112.0	111.8	117.8	118.5	110.8	107.9	115.1	114.1	108.5
Labor Force, Agriculture (%)	17.2	16.4	15.7	15.0	14.3	13.6	12.9	12.2	11.5	10.8	10.2
Labor Force, Female (%)	34.0	34.9	35.8	36.6	37.4	38.1	38.9	39.7	40.4	41.1	41.8
Primary Schl. Enroll. Ratio	97.0	..	..	..	..	100.0	99.0	..	96.0	96.0	99.0
Primary Schl. Enroll. Ratio, Female	100.0	..	..	..	..	102.0	100.0	..	..	..	..
Secondary Schl. Enroll. Ratio	80.0	..	..	..	..	80.0	83.0	..	83.0	80.0	85.0

FOREIGN TRADE (CUSTOMS BASIS)

(Millions of current US dollars)

1981	1982	1983	1984	1985	1986	1987	1988	1989	1990 est.	Notes	ICELAND
894.6	684.9	748.4	744.2	813.8	1,095.8	1,375.1	1,431.1	1,401.2	1,586.4	..	Value of Exports, fob
							1,248.5	1,251.6	1,449.1	..	Nonfuel Primary Products
..	..	..	..	..	..		0.0	0.0	0.0	..	Fuels
69.6	65.8	71.3	93.0	80.7	100.6	127.8	182.6	149.6	137.3	..	Manufactures
1,021.0	941.6	815.3	843.6	904.0	1,115.3	1,581.4	1,587.7	1,400.5	1,659.2	..	Value of Imports, cif
144.2	134.1	130.5	128.5	128.0	147.9	179.7	188.3	185.3	206.4	..	Nonfuel Primary Products
168.1	146.3	132.5	132.9	142.1	107.1	117.3	101.2	122.6	163.9	..	Fuels
708.7	661.1	552.3	582.2	633.9	860.4	1,284.3	1,298.2	1,092.5	1,288.9	..	Manufactures

(Index 1987 = 100)

1981	1982	1983	1984	1985	1986	1987	1988	1989	1990 est.	Notes	
129.6	118.2	119.5	111.7	104.1	97.1	100.0	100.9	100.8	107.2	..	Terms of Trade
110.9	95.9	94.0	85.6	78.7	82.6	100.0	104.9	136.8	161.5	..	Export Prices, fob
85.5	81.1	78.7	76.7	75.6	85.1	100.0	103.9	135.7	150.6	..	Import Prices, cif

BALANCE OF PAYMENTS

(Millions of current US dollars)

1981	1982	1983	1984	1985	1986	1987	1988	1989	1990 est.	Notes	
1,221.6	1,054.3	1,100.0	1,106.0	1,224.4	1,569.7	1,945.8	1,983.2	1,950.9	2,212.7	..	Exports of Goods & Services
896.4	685.5	742.0	743.2	814.0	1,096.8	1,376.1	1,425.4	1,401.5	1,588.6	..	Merchandise, fob
302.8	340.6	342.5	347.1	394.3	453.2	541.9	531.6	516.9	585.0	..	Nonfactor Services
22.4	28.2	15.5	15.7	16.1	19.7	27.8	26.2	32.5	39.1	..	Factor Services
1,366.2	1,312.4	1,154.9	1,238.1	1,339.7	1,556.5	2,136.0	2,203.5	2,031.8	2,372.8	..	Imports of Goods & Services
925.5	837.6	721.6	756.6	814.3	1,000.0	1,428.2	1,439.4	1,267.3	1,509.1	..	Merchandise, fob
282.0	308.5	280.7	310.9	362.9	373.6	509.9	535.6	494.8	568.6	..	Nonfactor Services
158.7	166.3	152.6	170.6	162.5	182.9	197.9	228.5	269.7	295.1	..	Factor Services
..	..	..	..	..	..	..	..	..	..	..	Long-Term Interest
-1.6	-3.4	-0.6	2.1	1.3	5.7	0.9	0.7	0.9	6.1	..	Private Current Transfers, net
..	..	..	..	..	..	..	..	..	..	..	Workers' Remittances
-146.2	-261.5	-55.5	-130.0	-114.0	18.9	-189.3	-219.6	-80.0	-154.0	..	Curr. A/C Bal before Off. Transf.
-1.7	-1.7	-1.4	-1.3	-1.1	-1.7	-1.7	-1.9	-3.9	-6.3	..	Net Official Transfers
-147.9	-263.2	-56.9	-131.3	-115.1	17.2	-191.0	-221.5	-83.9	-160.3	..	Curr. A/C Bal after Off. Transf.
191.3	214.1	93.5	113.0	155.3	156.7	178.1	207.8	259.7	254.9	..	Long-Term Capital, net
53.0	35.8	-23.4	13.7	23.6	6.4	1.7	-15.9	-35.6	-0.6	..	Direct Investment
..	..	..	..	..	..	..	..	..	..	..	Long-Term Loans
										..	Disbursements
										..	Repayments
138.3	178.3	116.9	99.3	131.7	150.3	176.4	223.7	295.3	255.5	..	Other Long-Term Capital
28.5	-46.5	-25.7	3.1	23.9	-75.0	-5.2	14.9	-121.2	-20.2	..	Other Capital, net
-71.9	95.6	-10.9	15.2	-64.1	-98.9	18.1	-1.2	-54.6	-74.4	..	Change in Reserves

(Icelandic Kronur per US dollar)

Memo Item:

1981	1982	1983	1984	1985	1986	1987	1988	1989	1990 est.	Notes	
7.220	12.350	24.840	31.690	41.510	41.100	38.680	43.010	57.040	58.280	..	Conversion Factor (Annual Avg)

(Millions US dollars), outstanding at end of year

EXTERNAL DEBT (Total)

1981	1982	1983	1984	1985	1986	1987	1988	1989	1990 est.	Notes	
..	..	..	..	..	..	..	..	..	..	..	Long-Term Debt (by debtor)
..	..	..	..	..	..	..	..	..	..	..	Central Bank, incl. IMF credit
..	..	..	..	..	..	..	..	..	..	..	Central Government
..	..	..	..	..	..	..	..	..	..	..	Rest of General Government
..	..	..	..	..	..	..	..	..	..	..	Non-financial Public Enterprises
..	..	..	..	..	..	..	..	..	..	..	Priv. Sector, incl non-guaranteed
..	..	..	..	..	..	..	..	..	..	..	Short-Term Debt

(Millions of US dollars)

Memo Items:

1981	1982	1983	1984	1985	1986	1987	1988	1989	1990 est.	Notes	
229.53	145.17	149.29	127.60	205.54	309.84	311.31	290.74	337.32	436.12	..	Int'l Reserves Excluding Gold
19.48	22.39	18.69	15.11	16.02	19.15	23.72	20.10	19.65	18.87	..	Gold Holdings (at market price)

SOCIAL INDICATORS

1981	1982	1983	1984	1985	1986	1987	1988	1989	1990 est.	Notes	
2.4	2.3	2.2	2.1	1.9	1.9	2.1	2.1	2.1	2.1	..	Total Fertility Rate
7.2	6.7	6.2	6.1	5.7	5.4	7.2	7.1	7.0	7.0	..	Infant Mortality Rate
76.7	76.8	76.9	77.1	77.2	77.4	77.5	77.7	77.9	78.0	..	Life Expectancy at Birth
88.4	88.7	88.9	89.2	89.4	89.6	89.8	90.1	90.3	90.5	..	Urban Population, % of total
108.3	106.3	106.3	102.3	106.3	104.1	100.0	87.9	84.9	84.8	..	Food Prod. per capita (1987=100)
..	..	..	..	..	..	..	..	..	..	..	Labor Force, Agriculture (%)
41.9	42.0	42.1	42.2	42.3	42.3	42.4	42.5	42.6	42.7	..	Labor Force, Female (%)
..	99.0	101.0	100.0	99.0	99.0	101.0	102.0	101.0	..	..	Primary Schl. Enroll. Ratio
..	101.0	102.0	..	99.0	100.0	102.0	..	..	..	..	Primary Schl. Enroll. Ratio, Female
..	88.0	88.0	89.0	91.0	94.0	94.0	96.0	99.0	..	..	Secondary Schl. Enroll. Ratio

INDIA	1970	1971	1972	1973	1974	1975	1976	1977	1978	1979	1980
CURRENT GNP PER CAPITA (US $)	110	110	110	130	140	170	160	170	190	200	240
POPULATION (millions)	548	560	573	586	600	613	628	642	657	672	687

USE AND ORIGIN OF RESOURCES *(Billions of current Indian Rupees)*

	1970	1971	1972	1973	1974	1975	1976	1977	1978	1979	1980
Gross National Product (GNP)	429.8	460.5	507.8	618.1	730.7	785.9	847.7	959.8	1,042.0	1,146.2	1,362.9
Net Factor Income from Abroad	-1.8	-2.1	-2.2	-2.0	-1.6	-1.7	-1.2	-0.9	0.1	2.6	2.8
GDP at Market Prices	431.6	462.6	510.0	620.1	732.3	787.6	848.9	960.7	1,041.9	1,143.6	1,360.1
Resource Balance	-3.2	-4.3	-2.1	-3.3	-8.0	-3.0	6.5	4.8	-12.5	-25.3	-48.4
Exports of Goods & NF Services	16.1	17.7	21.5	26.5	36.5	48.9	60.8	66.1	68.8	80.6	89.0
Imports of Goods & NF Services	19.3	22.0	23.6	29.8	44.5	51.9	54.3	61.3	81.3	105.9	137.4
Domestic Absorption	434.8	466.7	512.1	623.3	740.4	790.6	842.5	955.9	1,054.4	1,168.8	1,408.3
Private Consumption, etc.	322.6	336.7	377.6	458.5	533.2	552.7	582.5	678.1	725.0	795.7	993.0
General Gov't Consumption	38.4	44.6	47.3	51.6	62.4	73.8	82.3	87.6	97.2	111.7	130.8
Gross Domestic Investment	73.8	85.5	87.2	113.3	144.8	164.1	177.8	190.2	232.2	261.4	284.5
Fixed Investment	63.0	70.8	81.3	90.7	110.0	133.3	153.0	172.2	188.8	213.1	262.8
Indirect Taxes, net	34.6	40.1	45.3	50.5	62.0	75.6	83.6	87.2	103.1	119.1	135.8
GDP at factor cost	397.1	422.5	464.7	569.5	670.4	712.0	765.4	873.5	938.8	1,024.4	1,224.3
Agriculture	179.4	183.2	201.5	265.6	291.0	288.4	294.6	348.8	358.5	370.9	466.5
Industry	87.0	96.1	106.0	123.1	154.4	169.0	191.7	216.5	243.4	273.8	317.1
Manufacturing	59.5	66.0	73.3	88.7	114.0	118.6	131.2	147.0	169.2	193.8	216.4
Services, etc.	130.7	143.2	157.2	180.8	225.1	254.6	279.0	308.2	336.9	379.7	440.7
Gross Domestic Saving	70.6	81.3	85.2	110.0	136.7	161.1	184.2	194.9	219.7	236.2	236.3
Gross National Saving	69.4	80.1	83.7	109.3	137.1	163.3	189.1	203.5	229.2	253.9	261.6

(Billions of 1987 Indian Rupees)

	1970	1971	1972	1973	1974	1975	1976	1977	1978	1979	1980
Gross National Product	1,728.0	1,754.1	1,744.0	1,805.2	1,832.4	2,001.7	2,038.5	2,185.7	2,314.9	2,198.1	2,343.0
GDP at Market Prices	1,737.5	1,765.0	1,754.3	1,814.2	1,835.9	2,004.5	2,040.1	2,186.9	2,313.1	2,191.7	2,336.7
Resource Balance	-18.0	-38.1	-21.6	-33.3	-12.0	1.4	22.9	-18.7	-8.9	-25.2	-55.5
Exports of Goods & NF Services	85.1	85.4	95.9	100.3	106.2	117.8	139.5	134.4	144.2	153.2	155.8
Imports of Goods & NF Services	103.0	123.5	117.5	133.6	118.3	116.4	116.6	153.2	153.2	178.4	211.3
Domestic Absorption	1,755.4	1,803.1	1,775.9	1,847.5	1,847.9	2,003.1	2,017.2	2,205.7	2,322.1	2,217.0	2,392.2
Private Consumption, etc.	1,239.7	1,237.4	1,234.1	1,257.2	1,257.9	1,372.2	1,347.7	1,512.4	1,544.8	1,445.7	1,626.2
General Gov't Consumption	153.7	169.6	170.2	168.5	160.6	177.4	191.4	197.3	211.9	224.9	236.8
Gross Domestic Investment	362.0	396.1	371.6	421.8	429.3	453.6	478.0	496.0	565.4	546.4	529.2
Fixed Investment	315.0	334.6	351.9	348.3	337.6	370.2	416.9	456.8	461.1	447.7	496.5
GDP at factor cost	1,565.1	1,580.5	1,574.4	1,646.8	1,665.9	1,816.0	1,838.6	1,976.0	2,084.7	1,976.3	2,118.0
Agriculture	694.4	681.3	647.1	693.7	683.2	771.2	726.7	799.6	818.0	713.5	805.5
Industry	362.9	373.3	387.3	394.7	402.5	424.7	462.2	493.2	536.7	520.1	538.2
Manufacturing	221.7	228.9	237.9	248.5	255.7	261.1	284.0	301.7	339.0	328.1	328.7
Services, etc.	507.9	525.9	539.9	558.4	580.3	620.0	649.8	683.2	730.0	742.6	774.4

Memo Items:

	1970	1971	1972	1973	1974	1975	1976	1977	1978	1979	1980
Capacity to Import	85.9	99.3	107.0	118.8	97.0	109.7	130.5	165.2	129.6	135.8	136.9
Terms of Trade Adjustment	0.9	13.9	11.1	18.5	-9.2	-8.1	-9.0	30.7	-14.6	-17.4	-18.9
Gross Domestic Income	1,738.3	1,778.9	1,765.4	1,832.7	1,826.6	1,996.4	2,031.1	2,217.7	2,298.5	2,174.3	2,317.8
Gross National Income	1,728.9	1,768.0	1,755.1	1,823.7	1,823.2	1,993.5	2,029.5	2,216.5	2,300.3	2,180.7	2,324.1

DOMESTIC PRICES/DEFLATORS *(Index 1987 = 100)*

	1970	1971	1972	1973	1974	1975	1976	1977	1978	1979	1980
Overall (GDP)	24.8	26.2	29.1	34.2	39.9	39.3	41.6	43.9	45.0	52.2	58.2
Domestic Absorption	24.8	25.9	28.8	33.7	40.1	39.5	41.8	43.3	45.4	52.7	58.9
Agriculture	25.8	26.9	31.1	38.3	42.6	37.4	40.5	43.6	43.8	52.0	57.9
Industry	24.0	25.7	27.4	31.2	38.4	39.8	41.5	43.9	45.4	52.6	58.9
Manufacturing	26.8	28.8	30.8	35.7	44.6	45.4	46.2	48.7	49.9	59.1	65.8
Consumer Price Index	25.6	26.4	28.1	32.8	42.2	44.6	41.2	44.6	45.8	48.6	54.2

MANUFACTURING ACTIVITY

	1970	1971	1972	1973	1974	1975	1976	1977	1978	1979	1980
Employment (1987=100)	71.0	75.2	75.9	78.5	80.9	85.0	87.4	93.1	95.3	101.5	104.6
Real Earnings per Empl. (1987=100)	70.7	78.3	79.6	72.1	66.4	67.0	73.1	72.2	75.7	79.0	77.1
Real Output per Empl. (1987=100)	48.0	47.9	49.9	47.0	48.0	50.8	55.1	55.9	60.5	57.0	57.7
Earnings as % of Value Added	46.5	60.8	54.2	47.8	43.6	47.2	43.3	49.9	48.6	49.5	50.7

MONETARY HOLDINGS *(Billions of current Indian Rupees)*

	1970	1971	1972	1973	1974	1975	1976	1977	1978	1979	1980
Money Supply, Broadly Defined	109.0	126.9	145.3	172.6	192.8	218.2	271.5	322.1	388.3	455.9	527.7
Money	67.6	76.5	86.2	101.0	111.3	122.3	152.8	178.5	157.6	176.9	204.6
Currency Outside Banks	41.6	45.6	49.1	57.8	61.4	64.4	73.2	84.2	94.6	108.0	126.3
Demand Deposits	26.1	30.8	37.1	43.3	49.9	57.9	79.6	94.3	63.1	68.9	78.3
Quasi-Money	41.4	50.4	59.2	71.5	81.5	95.8	118.8	143.6	230.7	279.0	323.1

GOVERNMENT DEFICIT (-) OR SURPLUS *(Billions of current Indian Rupees)*

	1970	1971	1972	1973	1974	1975	1976	1977	1978	1979	1980
GOVERNMENT DEFICIT (-) OR SURPLUS	..	..	..	..	-23.6	-32.0	-36.9	-37.9	-50.8	-63.0	-88.6
Current Revenue	..	..	..	..	75.8	93.6	104.2	115.6	130.9	146.2	163.6
Current Expenditure	..	..	..	..	65.6	80.8	92.6	101.7	116.4	140.0	159.1
Current Budget Balance	..	..	..	..	10.3	12.8	11.6	13.8	14.5	6.3	4.5
Capital Receipts	..	..	..	..	0.5	0.9	1.1	1.2	1.4	1.6	1.9
Capital Payments	..	..	..	..	34.3	45.7	49.6	52.9	66.7	70.8	95.0

1981	1982	1983	1984	1985	1986	1987	1988	1989	1990 estimate	Notes	INDIA
270	280	280	280	280	290	310	340	350	350	..	**CURRENT GNP PER CAPITA (US $)**
703	718	734	750	765	782	799	816	833	850	..	**POPULATION (millions)**
											USE AND ORIGIN OF RESOURCES
				(Billions of current Indian Rupees)							
1,598.1	1,774.8	2,064.6	2,296.7	2,600.2	2,893.6	3,294.2	3,906.7	4,372.6	5,032.3	C f	Gross National Product (GNP)
0.5	-6.5	-11.3	-17.2	-19.0	-26.1	-32.0	-43.2	-55.1	-70.4	..	Net Factor Income from Abroad
1,597.6	1,781.3	2,075.9	2,313.9	2,619.2	2,919.7	3,326.2	3,949.9	4,427.7	5,102.7	C f	GDP at Market Prices
-52.3	-48.1	-47.5	-54.2	-81.3	-80.2	-85.9	-120.9	-113.9	-141.9	..	Resource Balance
101.7	108.6	127.6	157.1	156.3	174.9	210.3	263.7	348.5	407.2	..	Exports of Goods & NFServices
154.0	156.7	175.0	211.3	237.6	255.1	296.2	384.6	462.4	549.1	..	Imports of Goods & NFServices
1,650.3	1,829.3	2,123.5	2,368.3	2,700.1	2,999.9	3,412.5	4,070.7	4,542.0	5,244.6	..	Domestic Absorption
1,096.7	1,238.8	1,481.5	1,636.9	1,778.9	1,981.4	2,248.3	2,655.0	2,967.4	3,444.7	..	Private Consumption, etc.
153.5	182.7	211.4	243.5	291.7	346.3	410.3	472.0	530.7	617.4	..	General Gov't Consumption
400.1	407.8	430.6	487.9	629.5	672.3	753.9	943.7	1,044.0	1,182.5	..	Gross Domestic Investment
314.6	357.7	399.9	455.7	542.6	612.6	708.4	832.1	948.4	1,038.2	..	Fixed Investment
165.4	187.4	208.7	228.1	284.4	329.2	383.5	432.6	476.3	533.9	..	Indirect Taxes, net
1,432.2	1,593.9	1,867.2	2,085.8	2,334.8	2,590.5	2,942.7	3,517.3	3,951.4	4,568.8	C f	GDP at factor cost
526.9	561.5	675.0	719.9	772.8	825.2	924.6	1,147.6	1,232.6	1,401.8	..	Agriculture
382.0	433.9	507.4	578.5	654.4	734.8	835.9	979.3	1,134.0	1,325.2	..	Industry
252.6	280.7	330.5	372.4	417.8	461.7	528.5	624.6	740.6	878.2	..	Manufacturing
523.3	598.5	684.8	787.4	907.6	1,030.5	1,182.2	1,390.4	1,584.8	1,841.8	..	Services, etc.
347.4	359.8	383.0	433.5	548.6	592.1	667.6	822.9	929.6	1,040.6	..	Gross Domestic Saving
367.9	378.1	398.9	444.6	556.9	595.3	670.5	816.6	911.2	1,005.2	..	Gross National Saving
				(Billions of 1987 Indian Rupees)							
2,491.7	2,575.2	2,760.4	2,858.4	3,011.8	3,139.6	3,294.2	3,612.1	3,793.7	3,969.1	C	Gross National Product
2,489.4	2,583.6	2,775.5	2,878.6	3,034.0	3,170.5	3,326.2	3,650.7	3,834.3	4,013.2	C I	GDP at Market Prices
-67.3	-55.1	-64.7	-62.4	-96.2	-107.0	-85.9	-110.2	-77.7	-71.2	..	Resource Balance
157.4	159.0	169.0	185.4	180.6	194.6	210.3	233.5	261.8	272.0	..	Exports of Goods & NFServices
224.7	214.1	233.7	247.7	276.8	301.6	296.2	343.7	339.5	343.2	..	Imports of Goods & NFServices
2,556.7	2,638.7	2,840.2	2,941.0	3,130.2	3,277.5	3,412.1	3,761.0	3,912.0	4,084.4	..	Domestic Absorption
1,641.8	1,733.7	1,955.4	2,015.1	2,053.8	2,184.7	2,247.9	2,451.9	2,572.0	2,698.3	..	Private Consumption, etc.
247.3	272.9	285.1	307.4	342.5	377.4	410.3	433.1	453.3	479.1	..	General Gov't Consumption
667.6	632.1	599.7	618.5	733.8	715.4	753.9	875.9	886.6	907.0	..	Gross Domestic Investment
530.6	553.6	559.9	581.6	623.0	647.2	708.4	763.8	799.0	808.9	..	Fixed Investment
2,247.1	2,316.8	2,506.3	2,603.3	2,709.9	2,815.7	2,942.7	3,248.7	3,416.4	3,587.6	C I	GDP at factor cost
853.1	842.7	933.8	934.1	936.7	920.9	924.6	1,066.9	1,093.0	1,129.1	..	Agriculture
581.1	608.6	661.8	701.4	733.7	785.1	835.9	903.8	965.1	1,027.0	..	Industry
355.1	378.3	415.8	442.7	460.5	492.8	528.5	572.7	614.9	662.3	..	Manufacturing
812.9	865.5	910.7	967.8	1,039.5	1,109.8	1,182.2	1,278.0	1,358.3	1,431.5	..	Services, etc.
											Memo Items:
148.4	148.4	170.3	184.2	182.0	206.7	210.3	235.7	255.9	254.5	..	Capacity to Import
-9.0	-10.6	1.3	-1.1	1.5	12.2	0.0	2.2	-5.9	-17.5	..	Terms of Trade Adjustment
2,480.4	2,573.0	2,776.8	2,877.5	3,035.4	3,182.7	3,326.2	3,652.9	3,828.3	3,995.7	..	Gross Domestic Income
2,482.7	2,564.6	2,761.7	2,857.3	3,013.2	3,151.7	3,294.2	3,614.3	3,787.8	3,951.7	..	Gross National Income
											DOMESTIC PRICES/DEFLATORS
				(Index 1987 = 100)							
64.2	68.9	74.8	80.4	86.3	92.1	100.0	108.2	115.5	127.1	..	Overall (GDP)
64.6	69.3	74.8	80.5	86.3	91.5	100.0	108.2	116.1	128.4	..	Domestic Absorption
61.8	66.6	72.3	77.1	82.5	89.6	100.0	107.6	112.8	124.2	..	Agriculture
65.7	71.3	76.7	82.5	89.2	93.6	100.0	108.4	117.5	129.0	..	Industry
71.1	74.2	79.5	84.1	90.7	93.7	100.0	109.1	120.4	132.6	..	Manufacturing
61.3	66.1	73.9	80.1	84.5	91.9	100.0	109.4	116.1	126.5	..	Consumer Price Index
											MANUFACTURING ACTIVITY
104.2	107.0	103.9	102.7	98.4	97.6	100.0	..	..	..	G	Employment (1987=100)
75.7	80.5	85.3	91.4	93.0	94.8	100.0	..	..	..	G	Real Earnings per Empl. (1987=100)
64.1	69.9	71.9	78.6	87.2	92.9	100.0	..	..	..	G	Real Output per Empl. (1987=100)
47.9	48.6	48.1	50.3	48.1	49.4	49.4	..	..	..	..	Earnings as % of Value Added
											MONETARY HOLDINGS
				(Billions of current Indian Rupees)							
618.0	720.9	840.4	988.4	1,152.5	1,356.0	1,575.4	1,859.0	2,149.4	2,413.4	D	Money Supply, Broadly Defined
232.5	273.7	308.6	365.6	412.4	478.7	543.2	632.8	746.9	836.4	..	Money
137.4	157.4	181.3	218.1	239.4	268.0	315.6	356.4	434.5	501.9	..	Currency Outside Banks
95.0	116.3	127.2	147.5	173.0	210.7	227.6	276.3	312.4	334.5	..	Demand Deposits
385.5	447.2	531.9	622.8	740.1	877.3	1,032.2	1,226.2	1,402.5	1,577.1	..	Quasi-Money
				(Billions of current Indian Rupees)							
-87.3	-107.3	-133.3	-175.8	-222.5	-272.0	-278.8	-320.6	-371.5	-368.6	C E	**GOVERNMENT DEFICIT (-) OR SURPLUS**
196.3	225.9	254.9	297.0	361.3	420.1	477.8	557.6	675.4	754.3	..	Current Revenue
181.3	213.3	248.5	301.9	370.9	444.3	515.8	608.9	725.7	808.4	..	Current Expenditure
15.0	12.7	6.4	-4.9	-9.6	-24.2	-38.0	-51.2	-50.3	-54.1	..	Current Budget Balance
3.4	3.1	3.6	3.9	4.8	5.0	7.9	5.7	8.9	9.0	..	Capital Receipts
105.7	123.1	143.3	174.8	217.7	252.8	248.7	275.1	330.2	323.4	..	Capital Payments

INDIA	1970	1971	1972	1973	1974	1975	1976	1977	1978	1979	1980
FOREIGN TRADE (CUSTOMS BASIS)					*(Millions of current US dollars)*						
Value of Exports, fob	2,013	2,037	2,415	2,961	3,899	4,355	5,323	5,980	6,167	6,996	7,511
Nonfuel Primary Products	949	932	1,072	1,353	1,839	2,354	2,486	2,590	2,415	2,874	3,054
Fuels	17	11	16	40	26	39	35	34	24	20	32
Manufactures	1,047	1,094	1,327	1,569	2,034	1,962	2,801	3,356	3,729	4,102	4,424
Value of Imports, cif	2,094	2,406	2,230	3,146	5,167	6,290	5,405	6,423	7,562	9,114	13,819
Nonfuel Primary Products	838	773	594	1,009	1,475	2,025	1,933	1,998	1,910	1,745	2,302
Fuels	162	245	266	436	1,446	1,419	1,390	1,640	1,973	3,023	6,168
Manufactures	1,095	1,387	1,371	1,701	2,247	2,846	2,082	2,784	3,678	4,345	5,349
					(Index 1987 = 100)						
Terms of Trade	133.6	130.9	132.9	126.2	95.0	95.8	95.6	97.0	96.4	91.1	84.2
Export Prices, fob	31.4	31.3	33.0	40.2	53.6	56.4	55.2	60.8	65.0	73.5	86.8
Import Prices, cif	23.5	23.9	24.9	31.9	56.4	58.9	57.8	62.6	67.5	80.7	103.1
BALANCE OF PAYMENTS					*(Millions of current US dollars)*						
Exports of Goods & Services	2,140	2,380	2,828	3,454	4,688	5,784	7,009	8,031	8,858	10,776	12,364
Merchandise, fob	1,870	2,090	2,460	3,020	3,990	4,830	5,740	6,340	6,770	7,680	8,332
Nonfactor Services	270	290	330	380	580	820	1,060	1,380	1,610	2,300	2,949
Factor Services	0	0	38	54	118	134	209	311	478	796	1,083
Imports of Goods & Services	2,814	3,240	3,372	4,133	5,886	6,315	6,425	7,578	10,360	13,590	18,135
Merchandise, fob	2,290	2,680	2,780	3,500	5,210	5,480	5,390	6,470	9,010	11,860	15,892
Nonfactor Services	280	280	270	320	360	510	690	690	890	1,260	1,516
Factor Services	244	280	322	313	316	325	345	418	460	470	727
Long-Term Interest	193	219	241	255	268	263	279	303	379	395	532
Private Current Transfers, net	83	112	97	159	258	470	692	1,077	1,150	1,852	2,860
Workers' Remittances	80	110	138	185	277	490	707	1,088	1,173	1,872	2,786
Curr. A/C Bal before Off. Transf.	-591	-748	-447	-520	-940	-61	1,276	1,530	-352	-962	-2,911
Net Official Transfers	206	400	109	91	118	342	377	432	449	577	643
Curr. A/C Bal after Off. Transf.	-385	-348	-338	-429	-822	281	1,653	1,962	97	-385	-2,268
Long-Term Capital, net	582	604	462	487	796	1,255	948	994	736	840	1,771
Direct Investment	0	0	0	0	0	0	0	0	0	0	8
Long-Term Loans	594	622	494	542	868	1,342	1,043	820	592	658	1,424
Disbursements	908	959	865	953	1,395	1,881	1,577	1,387	1,259	1,369	2,180
Repayments	314	336	371	412	526	539	534	567	667	712	756
Other Long-Term Capital	-12	-18	-32	-55	-72	-87	-95	174	144	182	339
Other Capital, net	-35	-52	-118	-28	-642	-961	-699	-575	898	-129	-863
Change in Reserves	-162	-204	-6	-30	668	-575	-1,902	-2,381	-1,731	-326	1,360
Memo Item:					*(Indian Rupees per US dollar)*						
Conversion Factor (Annual Avg)	7.500	7.440	7.710	7.790	7.980	8.650	8.940	8.560	8.210	8.080	7.890
					(Millions of US dollars), outstanding at end of year						
EXTERNAL DEBT (Total)	7,937	8,892	9,805	10,575	12,235	13,234	13,971	15,504	16,461	17,892	20,610
Long-Term Debt (by debtor)	7,937	8,892	9,805	10,575	12,235	13,234	13,971	15,072	15,810	17,194	19,684
Central Bank, incl. IMF credit	0	0	0	75	620	813	481	172	26	1,076	2,402
Central Government	5,927	6,702	7,530	8,100	9,049	9,823	10,896	12,089	12,788	13,167	14,063
Rest of General Government	70	71	68	62	58	46	42	41	36	32	27
Non-financial Public Enterprises	1,395	1,552	1,609	1,685	1,712	1,727	1,680	1,856	1,917	1,892	2,135
Priv. Sector, incl non-guaranteed	545	568	598	653	796	824	872	915	1,043	1,026	1,058
Short-Term Debt	0	0	0	0	0	0	0	432	651	698	926
Memo Items:					*(Millions of US dollars)*						
Int'l Reserves Excluding Gold	763.3	942.4	916.3	848.8	1,027.7	1,089.1	2,791.7	4,872.0	6,426.3	7,204.0	6,858.0
Gold Holdings (at market price)	259.9	303.4	451.3	780.5	1,296.9	975.3	937.0	1,213.4	1,889.8	4,382.9	5,065.9
SOCIAL INDICATORS											
Total Fertility Rate	5.8	5.7	5.6	5.5	5.4	5.3	5.3	5.2	5.1	5.0	5.0
Infant Mortality Rate	139.0	137.0	135.0	133.2	131.4	129.6	127.8	126.0	122.8	119.6	116.4
Life Expectancy at Birth	47.5	48.0	48.4	49.1	49.7	50.4	51.1	51.7	52.4	53.0	53.7
Urban Population, % of total	19.8	20.1	20.4	20.7	21.0	21.3	21.7	22.0	22.4	22.7	23.1
Food Prod. per capita (1987=100)	94.0	92.8	86.1	91.7	85.3	94.8	92.4	98.1	98.5	91.1	93.0
Labor Force, Agriculture (%)	71.7	71.5	71.3	71.1	70.9	70.7	70.5	70.3	70.1	69.9	69.7
Labor Force, Female (%)	29.7	29.4	29.2	28.9	28.7	28.5	28.2	27.9	27.7	27.4	27.2
Primary Schl. Enroll. Ratio	73.0	..	..	..	..	79.0	79.0	78.0	76.0	81.0	83.0
Primary Schl. Enroll. Ratio, Female	56.0	..	..	..	..	62.0	63.0	64.0	61.0	65.0	67.0
Secondary Schl. Enroll. Ratio	26.0	..	..	..	..	26.0	26.0	27.0	28.0	30.0	32.0

1981	1982	1983	1984	1985	1986	1987	1988	1989	1990 estimate	Notes	INDIA
											FOREIGN TRADE (CUSTOMS BASIS)
				(Millions of current US dollars)							
7,867	8,468	9,425	9,827	8,950	9,752	12,040	13,815	15,848	17,967	f	Value of Exports, fob
3,136	3,033	3,093	3,094	3,200	3,300	3,326	3,334	3,825	4,337	..	Nonfuel Primary Products
34	1,254	1,539	1,531	540	328	507	356	408	462	..	Fuels
4,698	4,181	4,793	5,203	5,210	6,124	8,207	10,125	11,615	13,168	..	Manufactures
14,457	14,774	15,284	14,412	16,224	15,722	17,154	19,351	20,571	23,692	f	Value of Imports, cif
2,460	2,618	3,089	2,767	3,059	2,786	3,349	3,922	3,645	4,199	..	Nonfuel Primary Products
6,308	2,225	4,689	4,586	4,298	2,367	3,281	3,263	3,097	3,567	..	Fuels
5,689	9,931	7,507	7,058	8,867	10,568	10,524	12,166	13,828	15,926	..	Manufactures
				(Index 1987 = 100)							
89.3	91.0	97.0	99.5	96.2	100.1	100.0	100.0	100.6	96.4	f	Terms of Trade
95.0	89.8	93.1	95.4	90.4	92.8	100.0	105.2	105.5	110.2	..	Export Prices, fob
106.4	98.6	96.0	96.0	94.0	92.7	100.0	105.2	104.8	114.3	..	Import Prices, cif
											BALANCE OF PAYMENTS
				(Millions of current US dollars)							
12,306	11,801	12,819	13,709	13,318	14,178	16,661	18,615	21,308	22,884	C f	Exports of Goods & Services
8,697	8,389	9,090	9,769	9,461	10,460	12,644	14,262	16,850	18,485	..	Merchandise, fob
2,697	2,887	3,280	3,447	3,310	3,217	3,571	3,956	4,063	4,200	..	Nonfactor Services
912	525	449	493	547	501	446	397	395	199	..	Factor Services
18,107	17,473	18,517	19,716	21,518	22,496	25,756	29,946	31,452	34,712	C f	Imports of Goods & Services
15,552	14,387	14,782	15,424	17,295	17,728	19,812	23,339	24,414	27,214	..	Merchandise, fob
1,696	1,884	2,192	2,350	2,124	2,222	3,027	3,225	3,338	3,377	..	Nonfactor Services
859	1,202	1,543	1,942	2,099	2,546	2,917	3,382	3,700	4,121	..	Factor Services
599	787	975	1,043	1,372	1,793	2,181	2,627	3,024	3,409	..	Long-Term Interest
2,314	2,625	2,691	2,496	2,207	2,327	2,698	2,654	2,256	2,000	..	Private Current Transfers, net
2,333	2,525	2,568	2,509	2,219	2,339	2,724	2,225	2,186	1,947	..	Workers' Remittances
-3,487	-3,047	-3,007	-3,511	-5,993	-5,991	-6,397	-8,677	-7,888	-9,828	..	Curr. A/C Bal before Off. Transf.
497	399	367	453	359	403	410	406	500	524	..	Net Official Transfers
-2,990	-2,648	-2,640	-3,058	-5,634	-5,588	-5,987	-8,271	-7,388	-9,304	..	Curr. A/C Bal after Off. Transf.
2,004	2,702	2,907	3,573	4,282	4,936	5,950	7,300	6,923	4,799	C f	Long-Term Capital, net
10	65	63	62	160	208	181	287	350	253	..	Direct Investment
1,629	1,966	1,907	2,697	2,544	2,903	3,777	4,364	4,230	2,925	..	Long-Term Loans
2,376	2,898	2,991	3,788	3,853	5,192	5,669	6,314	6,165	5,406	..	Disbursements
747	932	1,083	1,091	1,309	2,289	1,893	1,949	1,935	2,480	..	Repayments
365	671	937	814	1,578	1,825	1,992	2,649	2,343	1,621	..	Other Long-Term Capital
-2,063	-1,517	-691	-319	2,164	1,372	780	749	622	1,707	C f	Other Capital, net
3,049	1,463	424	-196	-812	-720	-743	222	-157	2,798	..	Change in Reserves
				(Indian Rupees per US dollar)							**Memo Item:**
8.930	9.630	10.310	11.890	12.240	12.790	12.970	14.480	16.660	17.950	..	Conversion Factor (Annual Avg)
			(Millions of US dollars), outstanding at end of year								
22,633	27,462	32,025	34,048	41,210	48,538	55,856	58,524	64,374	70,115	..	**EXTERNAL DEBT (Total)**
21,429	25,571	29,389	31,192	38,081	45,241	52,337	54,752	59,685	65,208	..	Long-Term Debt (by debtor)
3,182	5,537	7,597	7,838	10,016	11,907	13,435	13,919	15,008	17,226	..	Central Bank, incl. IMF credit
14,440	15,617	16,725	17,075	20,456	24,066	27,967	28,757	30,829	33,479	..	Central Government
22	18	15	18	21	19	74	63	125	215	..	Rest of General Government
2,143	2,564	2,993	4,063	5,080	6,514	7,537	8,520	10,028	10,494	..	Non-financial Public Enterprises
1,643	1,835	2,059	2,198	2,508	2,735	3,323	3,493	3,694	3,793	..	Priv. Sector, incl non-guaranteed
1,204	1,891	2,636	2,856	3,129	3,297	3,519	3,772	4,689	4,908	..	Short-Term Debt
				(Millions of US dollars)							**Memo Items:**
4,461.0	4,965.0	5,847.0	6,110.0	6,657.0	6,730.0	6,391.0	4,959.0	4,108.0	1,521.0	..	Int'l Reserves Excluding Gold
3,416.0	3,926.4	3,278.5	2,693.6	3,072.8	4,084.4	5,058.2	4,286.5	4,189.9	4,116.5	..	Gold Holdings (at market price)
											SOCIAL INDICATORS
4.9	4.8	4.7	4.6	4.5	4.4	4.3	4.2	4.1	3.9	..	Total Fertility Rate
113.2	110.0	107.6	105.3	102.9	100.6	98.2	96.1	94.0	91.9	..	Infant Mortality Rate
54.3	55.0	55.6	56.1	56.7	57.3	57.9	58.3	58.7	59.0	..	Life Expectancy at Birth
23.5	23.9	24.2	24.6	25.0	25.4	25.8	26.2	26.6	27.0	..	Urban Population, % of total
98.1	93.9	104.6	104.0	104.0	102.4	100.0	110.6	114.1	112.2	..	Food Prod. per capita (1987=100)
..	..	..	..	..	..	..	..	..	..	..	Labor Force, Agriculture (%)
27.0	26.8	26.6	26.4	26.2	26.0	25.8	25.6	25.4	25.2	..	Labor Force, Female (%)
82.0	85.0	92.0	93.0	96.0	98.0	99.0	99.0	98.0	..	..	Primary Schl. Enroll. Ratio
66.0	69.0	75.0	76.0	80.0	81.0	83.0	83.0	82.0	..	..	Primary Schl. Enroll. Ratio, Female
34.0	35.0	35.0	37.0	38.0	39.0	40.0	41.0	43.0	..	..	Secondary Schl. Enroll. Ratio

INDONESIA	1970	1971	1972	1973	1974	1975	1976	1977	1978	1979	1980
CURRENT GNP PER CAPITA (US $)	80	90	90	110	150	210	270	320	370	400	470
POPULATION (millions)	118	120	123	126	130	133	136	139	142	145	148

USE AND ORIGIN OF RESOURCES	(Billions of current Indonesian Rupiahs)										
Gross National Product (GNP)	3,540	3,878	4,756	7,002	10,984	13,004	16,122	19,749	23,540	32,860	46,903
Net Factor Income from Abroad	15	3	-60	-124	-315	-338	-200	-336	-462	-1,484	-2,011
GDP at Market Prices	3,525	3,875	4,816	7,126	11,300	13,341	16,321	20,084	24,002	34,345	48,914
Resource Balance	-69	-59	38	122	943	292	357	969	587	2,402	6,277
Exports of Goods & NFServices	458	563	815	1,449	3,255	3,097	3,870	4,824	5,317	10,147	16,162
Imports of Goods & NFServices	528	622	776	1,328	2,312	2,805	3,513	3,855	4,730	7,746	9,886
Domestic Absorption	3,594	3,934	4,778	7,004	10,357	13,050	15,964	19,116	23,416	31,943	42,637
Private Consumption, etc.	2,754	2,894	3,328	4,833	7,342	8,687	10,500	12,422	15,126	19,516	25,595
General Gov't Consumption	282	328	398	688	809	1,206	1,530	1,997	2,556	3,277	5,148
Gross Domestic Investment	558	712	1,052	1,483	2,206	3,157	3,934	4,696	5,734	9,150	11,894
Fixed Investment	..	..	..	..	..	..	..	..	..	7,668	10,550
Indirect Taxes, net	188	229	236	328	447	520	635	846	1,029	1,305	1,635
GDP at factor cost	3,337	3,646	4,580	6,798	10,853	12,821	15,686	19,238	22,973	33,040	47,278
Agriculture	1,584	1,656	1,848	2,726	3,517	4,026	4,840	5,940	6,745	9,374	11,725
Industry	659	806	1,215	1,891	3,862	4,466	5,560	6,880	8,578	12,944	20,405
Manufacturing	363	357	521	756	1,036	1,308	1,691	2,115	2,816	4,003	6,353
Services, etc.	1,282	1,414	1,753	2,509	3,920	4,850	5,921	7,265	8,680	12,027	16,783
Gross Domestic Saving	489	653	1,090	1,605	3,149	3,449	4,292	5,665	6,320	11,551	18,171
Gross National Saving	504	656	1,030	1,481	2,833	3,111	4,092	5,330	5,858	10,067	16,160

	(Billions of 1987 Indonesian Rupiahs)										
Gross National Product	39,658	42,428	45,151	49,093	52,463	55,126	59,290	64,339	69,165	73,016	79,303
GDP at Market Prices	43,842	46,901	49,853	54,171	58,331	61,259	65,491	71,368	76,882	81,616	88,093
Resource Balance	8,443	9,130	11,457	12,640	11,349	9,533	11,189	12,961	11,353	10,134	9,909
Exports of Goods & NFServices	12,576	14,551	17,637	20,924	22,298	21,757	25,461	27,868	28,146	28,790	30,382
Imports of Goods & NFServices	4,133	5,421	6,181	8,285	10,949	12,225	14,272	14,907	16,793	18,657	20,473
Domestic Absorption	32,786	34,575	36,057	39,975	45,413	50,321	52,365	56,215	63,493	69,517	76,088
Private Consumption, etc.	25,411	25,943	26,084	27,986	32,252	34,701	35,750	36,929	41,163	44,808	49,698
General Gov't Consumption	2,556	2,763	2,987	3,812	3,413	4,451	4,776	5,559	6,539	7,323	8,765
Gross Domestic Investment	4,819	5,869	6,985	8,177	9,747	11,169	11,839	13,727	15,792	17,386	17,625
Fixed Investment	..	..	..	..	..	..	..	..	..	16,975	21,450
GDP at factor cost	..	..	..	..	..	..	..	..	..	..	..
Agriculture	15,197	16,121	16,372	17,898	18,565	18,565	19,443	19,688	20,705	22,082	23,610
Industry	13,367	13,929	16,925	20,556	22,011	22,208	25,079	28,442	29,396	30,538	32,888
Manufacturing	2,557	2,638	3,036	3,499	4,064	4,565	5,006	5,696	6,654	7,754	9,516
Services, etc.	13,752	15,058	15,740	15,839	17,857	20,681	20,929	22,911	26,599	28,919	31,509

Memo Items:											
Capacity to Import	3,590	4,907	6,487	9,045	15,413	13,496	15,725	18,653	18,877	24,441	33,472
Terms of Trade Adjustment	-8,986	-9,645	-11,150	-11,879	-6,885	-8,261	-9,736	-9,215	-9,269	-4,350	3,090
Gross Domestic Income	34,856	37,256	38,702	42,292	51,446	52,998	55,754	62,153	67,612	77,266	91,182
Gross National Income	30,672	32,783	34,001	37,214	45,578	46,864	49,554	55,124	59,895	68,666	82,393

DOMESTIC PRICES/DEFLATORS	(Index 1987 = 100)										
Overall (GDP)	8.0	8.3	9.7	13.2	19.4	21.8	24.9	28.1	31.2	42.1	55.5
Domestic Absorption	11.0	11.4	13.3	17.5	22.8	25.9	30.5	34.0	36.9	45.9	56.0
Agriculture	10.4	10.3	11.3	15.2	18.9	21.7	24.9	30.2	32.6	42.5	49.7
Industry	4.9	5.8	7.2	9.2	17.5	20.1	22.2	24.2	29.2	42.4	62.0
Manufacturing	14.2	13.5	17.2	21.6	25.5	28.7	33.8	37.1	42.3	51.6	66.8
Consumer Price Index	11.3	11.8	12.6	16.5	23.2	27.6	33.0	36.7	39.7	46.1	54.4

MANUFACTURING ACTIVITY											
Employment (1987=100)	..	..	..	..	..	..	..	..	..	..	..
Real Earnings per Empl. (1987=100)	..	..	..	..	..	..	..	..	..	..	..
Real Output per Empl. (1987=100)	..	..	..	..	..	..	..	..	..	..	..
Earnings as % of Value Added	26.4	23.0	23.5	20.9	23.9	20.5	21.6	20.6	20.3	19.6	16.4

MONETARY HOLDINGS	(Billions of current Indonesian Rupiahs)										
Money Supply, Broadly Defined	330	468	696	994	1,454	2,022	2,651	3,133	3,822	5,159	7,707
Money	250	319	474	671	942	1,274	1,601	2,006	2,488	3,316	5,011
Currency Outside Banks	155	198	269	375	497	650	779	979	1,240	1,545	2,169
Demand Deposits	96	121	205	296	445	625	822	1,027	1,248	1,771	2,842
Quasi-Money	80	148	222	323	512	747	1,050	1,127	1,334	1,842	2,696

GOVERNMENT DEFICIT (-) OR SURPLUS	(Billions of current Indonesian Rupiahs)										
	..	..	-117	-163	-167	-468	-693	-393	-754	-764	-1,102
Current Revenue	..	..	644	1,020	1,832	2,300	2,968	3,634	4,378	7,050	10,406
Current Expenditure	..	..	413	695	1,282	1,519	1,809	2,113	2,570	3,959	5,731
Current Budget Balance	..	..	231	325	550	781	1,159	1,521	1,808	3,091	4,675
Capital Receipts	..	..	..	..	..	..	..	..	..	..	..
Capital Payments	..	..	348	488	718	1,249	1,852	1,914	2,562	3,855	5,777

1981	1982	1983	1984	1985	1986	1987	1988	1989	1990 estimate	Notes	INDONESIA
550	610	610	590	550	530	500	490	510	570	..	**CURRENT GNP PER CAPITA (US $)**
151	154	157	160	163	166	169	172	175	178	..	**POPULATION (millions)**
											USE AND ORIGIN OF RESOURCES
			(Billions of current Indonesian Rupiahs)								
56,496	59,611	74,304	85,719	93,063	98,558	118,810	135,208	159,362	188,443	..	Gross National Product (GNP)
-1,925	-3,036	-3,319	-4,166	-3,934	-4,125	-6,007	-6,897	-8,133	-9,278	..	Net Factor Income from Abroad
58,421	62,646	77,623	89,885	96,997	102,683	124,817	142,105	167,495	197,721	..	GDP at Market Prices
2,367	253	221	3,154	1,699	-1,026	1,919	3,495	4,108	1,712	..	Resource Balance
16,401	15,324	19,847	22,999	21,534	20,010	29,875	34,666	42,503	51,197	..	Exports of Goods & NFServices
14,034	15,071	19,626	19,845	19,835	21,036	27,956	31,171	38,395	49,485	..	Imports of Goods & NFServices
56,054	62,393	77,402	86,731	95,298	103,709	122,898	138,610	163,387	196,009	..	Domestic Absorption
32,293	37,924	47,064	54,066	57,201	63,355	71,988	81,044	88,751	106,312	..	Private Consumption, etc.
6,452	7,229	8,077	9,122	10,893	11,329	11,764	12,756	15,698	17,543	..	General Gov't Consumption
17,309	17,241	22,261	23,543	27,204	29,025	39,146	44,810	58,938	72,154	..	Gross Domestic Investment
14,135	15,822	19,468	20,136	22,367	24,782	30,980	36,803	45,650	55,538	..	Fixed Investment
1,752	2,133	2,547	..	..	..	..	..	..	..	..	Indirect Taxes, net
56,669	60,514	75,076	..	..	..	..	..	..	..	B	GDP at factor cost
13,649	15,001	17,765	20,420	22,513	24,871	29,116	34,278	39,547	43,062	..	Agriculture
24,076	23,745	30,915	35,162	34,772	34,648	45,252	51,452	62,606	79,435	..	Industry
7,067	7,482	9,896	13,113	15,503	17,185	21,150	26,252	30,573	38,602	..	Manufacturing
20,696	23,901	28,943	34,304	39,712	43,164	50,450	56,375	65,342	75,224	..	Services, etc.
19,676	17,494	22,482	26,697	28,903	27,999	41,065	48,305	63,046	73,866		Gross Domestic Saving
17,751	14,458	19,172	22,585	25,037	23,965	35,199	41,575	55,209	64,870		Gross National Saving
			(Billions of 1987 Indonesian Rupiahs)								
85,887	86,740	94,346	101,169	104,754	112,113	118,810	127,157	137,118	147,143	..	Gross National Product
94,632	94,301	102,608	109,576	112,479	119,004	124,817	132,061	141,930	152,157	H	GDP at Market Prices
-2,494	-5,123	-3,998	-461	-3,695	-1,351	1,919	7,459	7,849	2,706		Resource Balance
24,899	22,656	23,030	24,537	22,622	26,064	29,875	30,188	32,319	35,135	..	Exports of Goods & NFServices
27,393	27,779	27,028	24,998	26,317	27,415	27,956	22,729	24,470	32,429	..	Imports of Goods & NFServices
96,656	99,268	106,725	110,358	116,836	120,768	122,898	124,706	134,344	150,054	..	Domestic Absorption
54,748	58,158	64,905	67,496	68,193	69,685	71,988	74,782	77,885	85,576	..	Private Consumption, etc.
9,628	10,494	10,299	10,651	11,464	11,783	11,764	12,654	13,981	14,457	..	General Gov't Consumption
32,280	30,616	31,521	32,211	37,179	39,300	39,146	37,270	42,478	50,021	..	Gross Domestic Investment
24,210	25,693	26,690	25,085	26,893	29,369	30,980	34,550	39,166	45,493	..	Fixed Investment
..	..	..	..	..	..	..	..	..	..	B H	GDP at factor cost
24,744	25,009	25,576	26,653	27,786	28,505	29,116	30,542	31,668	32,545	..	Agriculture
34,564	31,856	36,913	40,497	40,334	43,017	45,252	47,622	51,519	56,425	..	Industry
10,264	10,387	12,892	15,736	17,496	19,122	21,150	23,687	25,841	29,021	..	Manufacturing
35,317	37,878	40,120	42,426	44,359	47,482	50,450	53,898	58,743	63,188	..	Services, etc.
											Memo Items:
32,013	28,246	27,332	28,971	28,571	26,078	29,875	25,278	27,088	33,551	..	Capacity to Import
7,114	5,589	4,302	4,434	5,949	13	0	-4,910	-5,230	-1,584	..	Terms of Trade Adjustment
101,747	99,890	106,911	114,010	118,428	119,017	124,817	127,151	136,700	150,573	..	Gross Domestic Income
93,002	92,329	98,648	105,603	110,703	112,126	118,810	122,247	131,888	145,559	..	Gross National Income
			(Index 1987 = 100)								
61.7	66.4	75.6	82.0	86.2	86.3	100.0	107.6	118.0	129.9	..	Overall (GDP)
58.0	62.9	72.5	78.6	81.6	85.9	100.0	111.1	121.6	130.6	..	Domestic Absorption
55.2	60.0	69.5	76.6	81.0	87.3	100.0	112.2	124.9	132.3	..	Agriculture
69.7	74.5	83.8	86.8	86.2	80.5	100.0	108.0	121.5	140.8	..	Industry
68.9	72.0	76.8	83.3	88.6	89.9	100.0	110.8	118.3	133.0	..	Manufacturing
61.1	66.9	74.8	82.6	86.5	91.6	100.0	108.0	115.0	123.5	..	Consumer Price Index
											MANUFACTURING ACTIVITY
..	..	..	..	..	..	..	..	..	..	J	Employment (1987=100)
..	..	..	..	..	..	..	..	..	..	J	Real Earnings per Empl. (1987=100)
..	..	..	..	..	..	..	..	..	..	J	Real Output per Empl. (1987=100)
17.7	19.8	20.0	17.5	19.0	19.0	..	..	..	..	J	Earnings as % of Value Added
			(Billions of current Indonesian Rupiahs)								
											MONETARY HOLDINGS
9,705	11,074	14,670	17,937	23,177	27,615	33,904	42,072	58,526	84,629	..	Money Supply, Broadly Defined
6,474	7,120	7,576	8,581	10,124	11,631	12,705	14,392	20,558	23,819	..	Money
2,546	2,934	3,340	3,712	4,460	5,338	5,802	6,245	7,908	9,094	..	Currency Outside Banks
3,929	4,185	4,236	4,869	5,663	6,293	6,903	8,146	12,651	14,725	..	Demand Deposits
3,231	3,954	7,093	9,356	13,054	15,984	21,200	27,681	37,967	60,810	..	Quasi-Money
			(Billions of current Indonesian Rupiahs)								
-1,172	-1,191	-1,862	1,219	-948	-3,621	-1,037	-4,388	-3,362	..	C	**GOVERNMENT DEFICIT (-) OR SURPLUS**
13,763	12,815	15,511	18,724	20,347	21,324	24,781	24,088	29,093	..	..	Current Revenue
6,882	6,996	8,412	9,429	11,426	13,560	13,507	14,480	17,638	..	..	Current Expenditure
6,881	5,819	7,099	9,295	8,921	7,764	11,274	9,608	11,455	..	..	Current Budget Balance
..	..	..	..	..	..	..	..	..	..	..	Capital Receipts
8,053	7,010	8,961	8,076	9,869	11,385	12,311	13,996	14,817	..	..	Capital Payments

INDONESIA	1970	1971	1972	1973	1974	1975	1976	1977	1978	1979	1980
FOREIGN TRADE (CUSTOMS BASIS)					*(Millions of current US dollars)*						
Value of Exports, fob	1,055	1,199	1,778	3,211	7,426	7,130	8,556	10,853	11,643	15,590	21,909
Nonfuel Primary Products	694	700	827	1,533	2,145	1,704	2,419	3,283	3,431	4,936	5,633
Fuels	346	478	913	1,609	5,211	5,339	6,014	7,379	7,986	10,165	15,743
Manufactures	15	22	37	69	70	88	124	191	225	488	533
Value of Imports, cif	1,002	1,104	1,562	2,295	3,858	4,770	5,673	6,183	6,655	7,183	10,834
Nonfuel Primary Products	131	144	217	341	765	823	1,098	1,313	1,550	1,602	2,021
Fuels	26	29	40	42	185	257	440	735	583	797	1,754
Manufactures	845	931	1,305	1,912	2,908	3,690	4,135	4,135	4,522	4,784	7,060
					(Index 1987 = 100)						
Terms of Trade	46.6	48.9	41.3	47.2	98.7	88.1	100.9	108.9	95.6	118.4	142.9
Export Prices, fob	14.7	15.7	14.7	21.6	60.1	55.5	62.2	69.9	70.6	101.0	146.2
Import Prices, cif	31.4	32.0	35.6	45.8	60.9	63.0	61.7	64.2	73.8	85.3	102.3
BALANCE OF PAYMENTS					*(Millions of current US dollars)*						
Exports of Goods & Services	..	..	..	3,306	7,464	7,025	8,774	10,929	11,327	15,552	22,241
Merchandise, fob	1,173	1,311	1,793	3,215	7,265	6,888	8,613	10,763	11,035	15,154	21,795
Nonfactor Services	16	28	45	52	71	93	111	114	234	315	327
Factor Services	..	..	..	38	127	44	50	51	58	83	119
Imports of Goods & Services	1,565	1,757	2,222	3,836	6,915	8,160	9,696	11,004	12,754	14,602	19,432
Merchandise, fob	1,116	1,230	1,445	2,663	4,634	5,469	6,815	7,478	8,386	9,245	12,624
Nonfactor Services	316	355	430	544	952	1,306	1,669	1,840	2,349	2,889	3,477
Factor Services	133	173	347	629	1,329	1,385	1,212	1,686	2,018	2,468	3,330
Long-Term Interest	46	57	86	118	186	322	489	610	720	1,049	1,182
Private Current Transfers, net	0	0	0	0	0	0	0	0	0	0	0
Workers' Remittances	..	..	..	..	..	..	..	..	..	..	..
Curr. A/C Bal before Off. Transf.	-376	-418	-385	-530	548	-1,135	-922	-75	-1,427	950	2,810
Net Official Transfers	66	46	51	55	49	27	15	24	14	30	201
Curr. A/C Bal after Off. Transf.	-310	-372	-334	-476	598	-1,109	-907	-51	-1,413	980	3,011
Long-Term Capital, net	290	377	501	521	492	2,244	2,262	1,491	1,596	1,320	2,153
Direct Investment	83	139	207	15	-49	476	344	235	279	226	180
Long-Term Loans	516	529	976	1,288	1,507	2,264	2,153	1,356	862	655	1,613
Disbursements	636	691	1,190	1,615	2,017	2,945	3,004	2,727	2,975	2,670	3,245
Repayments	120	162	215	327	510	682	851	1,372	2,113	2,016	1,632
Other Long-Term Capital	-309	-291	-683	-783	-966	-496	-235	-100	455	440	360
Other Capital, net	-3	-35	211	295	-401	-1,986	-453	-444	-11	-856	-2,558
Change in Reserves	23	30	-377	-341	-688	851	-902	-996	-171	-1,444	-2,606
Memo Item:					*(Indonesian Rupiahs per US dollar)*						
Conversion Factor (Annual Avg)	365.000	393.400	415.000	415.000	415.000	415.000	415.000	415.000	442.000	623.100	627.000
EXTERNAL DEBT (Total)				*(Millions of US dollars), outstanding at end of year*							
	3,096	4,248	5,243	6,563	8,211	10,372	12,634	16,477	18,053	18,631	20,944
Long-Term Debt (by debtor)	3,096	4,248	5,243	6,563	8,211	10,372	12,634	14,552	16,267	16,523	18,169
Central Bank, incl. IMF credit	139	136	116	23	0	575	626	486	108	92	89
Central Government	2,408	3,272	3,658	4,237	4,845	5,763	7,524	9,345	11,359	11,704	13,135
Rest of General Government	1	1	1	1	2	0	0	0	0	0	0
Non-financial Public Enterprises	86	188	554	1,017	1,521	1,664	1,860	1,879	1,760	1,588	1,804
Priv. Sector, incl non-guaranteed	463	651	914	1,286	1,844	2,369	2,624	2,842	3,040	3,140	3,142
Short-Term Debt	0	0	0	0	0	0	0	1,925	1,786	2,108	2,775
Memo Items:					*(Millions of US dollars)*						
Int'l Reserves Excluding Gold	156.0	185.3	572.2	804.7	1,489.5	584.3	1,496.5	2,508.7	2,626.1	4,061.8	5,391.7
Gold Holdings (at market price)	4.3	2.5	7.9	6.4	10.6	8.0	7.7	27.9	50.6	143.4	1,411.3
SOCIAL INDICATORS											
Total Fertility Rate	5.5	5.4	5.4	5.3	5.1	5.0	4.9	4.8	4.6	4.5	4.3
Infant Mortality Rate	118.0	116.0	114.0	112.2	110.4	108.6	106.8	105.0	103.0	101.0	99.0
Life Expectancy at Birth	47.4	48.2	49.0	49.7	50.5	51.2	51.9	52.7	53.3	54.0	54.7
Urban Population, % of total	17.1	17.6	18.0	18.5	18.9	19.4	20.0	20.5	21.1	21.6	22.2
Food Prod. per capita (1987=100)	73.3	72.4	71.5	76.5	77.8	75.8	75.0	75.4	78.7	80.8	87.0
Labor Force, Agriculture (%)	66.3	65.3	64.4	63.5	62.6	61.8	60.8	59.8	58.9	58.0	57.2
Labor Force, Female (%)	30.2	30.4	30.5	30.6	30.7	30.8	31.0	31.1	31.2	31.2	31.3
Primary Schl. Enroll. Ratio	80.0	..	..	..	..	86.0	84.0	90.0	99.0	107.0	107.0
Primary Schl. Enroll. Ratio, Female	73.0	..	..	..	..	78.0	79.0	83.0	92.0	99.0	100.0
Secondary Schl. Enroll. Ratio	16.0	..	..	..	..	20.0	20.0	21.0	22.0	24.0	29.0

1981	1982	1983	1984	1985	1986	1987	1988	1989	1990 estimate	Notes	INDONESIA
											FOREIGN TRADE (CUSTOMS BASIS)
				(Millions of current US dollars)							
22,260	22,293	21,145	21,888	18,587	14,787	16,861	18,901	21,773	25,553	..	Value of Exports, fob
3,763	3,053	3,382	3,839	3,753	3,825	4,383	5,811	6,057	5,252	..	Nonfuel Primary Products
17,764	18,373	16,146	15,683	12,378	8,097	8,259	7,467	8,759	11,239	..	Fuels
733	868	1,618	2,365	2,455	2,864	4,219	5,623	6,957	9,061	..	Manufactures
13,008	16,530	16,346	13,865	10,256	10,718	12,370	13,248	16,360	21,837	..	Value of Imports, cif
2,243	1,971	2,025	1,796	1,531	1,634	1,933	2,251	2,852	3,070	..	Nonfuel Primary Products
1,726	3,549	4,140	2,704	1,286	1,105	1,125	956	1,262	1,947	..	Fuels
9,039	11,010	10,181	9,365	7,439	7,979	9,313	10,041	12,245	16,821	..	Manufactures
				(Index 1987 = 100)							
151.1	145.6	137.8	139.2	134.3	99.6	100.0	99.9	97.5	111.1		Terms of Trade
155.5	142.4	129.9	128.2	121.5	82.9	100.0	109.5	116.4	123.9		Export Prices, fob
102.9	97.8	94.3	92.1	90.5	83.2	100.0	109.6	119.4	111.5		Import Prices, cif
				(Millions of current US dollars)							**BALANCE OF PAYMENTS**
24,878	21,274	19,866	22,152	20,139	15,972	18,832	21,370	25,411	29,455		Exports of Goods & Services
23,348	19,747	18,689	20,754	18,527	14,396	17,206	19,509	22,974	26,832		Merchandise, fob
449	504	546	570	844	844	1,065	1,369	1,875	2,061		Nonfactor Services
1,081	1,023	631	828	768	732	561	492	562	562		Factor Services
25,694	26,732	26,318	24,175	22,150	20,142	21,187	23,021	26,858	32,038		Imports of Goods & Services
16,542	17,854	17,726	15,047	12,705	11,938	12,532	13,831	16,310	20,734		Merchandise, fob
4,998	4,862	4,311	4,239	5,135	4,256	4,440	4,606	5,439	5,988		Nonfactor Services
4,154	4,016	4,281	4,889	4,310	3,948	4,215	4,584	5,109	5,316		Factor Services
1,428	1,554	1,613	2,044	2,028	2,388	2,617	2,920	2,952	3,021		Long-Term Interest
0	0	10	53	61	71	86	99	167	153	..	Private Current Transfers, net
..	..	10	53	61	71	86	99	167	153		Workers' Remittances
-816	-5,458	-6,442	-1,970	-1,950	-4,099	-2,269	-1,552	-1,280	-2,430		Curr. A/C Bal before Off. Transf.
250	134	104	114	27	188	171	155	172	61		Net Official Transfers
-566	-5,324	-6,338	-1,856	-1,923	-3,911	-2,098	-1,397	-1,108	-2,369		Curr. A/C Bal after Off. Transf.
2,151	5,096	5,323	2,981	1,880	2,882	2,511	1,809	3,016	3,882		Long-Term Capital, net
133	225	292	222	310	258	385	576	682	964		Direct Investment
2,055	2,468	3,889	2,664	1,249	1,640	2,331	2,072	2,815	5,031		Long-Term Loans
3,845	4,410	5,915	4,920	4,285	4,958	6,435	7,298	8,028	10,148		Disbursements
1,790	1,942	2,026	2,256	3,036	3,317	4,104	5,226	5,213	5,117		Repayments
-37	2,403	1,142	95	321	984	-205	-839	-481	-2,113		Other Long-Term Capital
-1,959	-1,625	1,198	-144	553	26	217	-525	-1,459	760		Other Capital, net
374	1,853	-183	-981	-510	1,003	-630	113	-449	-2,273		Change in Reserves
				(Indonesian Rupiahs per US dollar)							**Memo Item:**
631.800	661.400	909.300	1,025.900	1,110.600	1,282.600	1,643.800	1,685.700	1,770.100	1,842.800	..	Conversion Factor (Annual Avg)
			(Millions of US dollars), outstanding at end of year								
22,762	26,304	29,978	31,861	36,673	42,974	52,080	52,775	54,637	67,908	..	**EXTERNAL DEBT (Total)**
19,487	21,518	25,339	26,453	30,624	36,508	45,720	46,048	46,662	54,873	..	Long-Term Debt (by debtor)
73	57	486	441	69	68	727	623	608	494	..	Central Bank, incl. IMF credit
14,037	16,565	19,914	20,986	25,824	32,005	40,502	41,015	41,124	44,970	..	Central Government
0	0	0	0	0	0	0	0	0	..	..	Rest of General Government
1,799	1,696	1,539	1,226	921	607	386	234	81	4	..	Non-financial Public Enterprises
3,579	3,200	3,400	3,800	3,810	3,828	4,105	4,176	4,849	9,405	..	Priv. Sector, incl non-guaranteed
3,274	4,787	4,639	5,408	6,049	6,466	6,360	6,727	7,975	13,035	..	Short-Term Debt
				(Millions of US dollars)							**Memo Items:**
5,014.2	3,144.5	3,718.4	4,773.0	4,974.2	4,051.3	5,592.3	5,048.3	5,453.5	7,459.1	..	Int'l Reserves Excluding Gold
1,233.8	1,418.2	1,184.2	957.0	1,015.0	1,213.4	1,502.6	1,273.4	1,245.9	1,197.7	..	Gold Holdings (at market price)
											SOCIAL INDICATORS
4.2	4.1	3.9	3.8	3.6	3.5	3.3	3.2	3.1	3.1	..	Total Fertility Rate
97.0	95.0	90.2	85.4	80.6	75.8	71.0	67.7	64.5	61.2	..	Infant Mortality Rate
55.3	56.0	56.8	57.7	58.5	59.3	60.2	60.7	61.3	61.8	..	Life Expectancy at Birth
23.0	23.8	24.6	25.4	26.2	..	..	28.8	29.6	30.5	..	Urban Population, % of total
89.8	87.4	92.9	97.6	97.6	101.4	100.0	103.0	106.2	107.9	..	Food Prod. per capita (1987=100)
..	..				..	..					Labor Force, Agriculture (%)
31.3	31.3	31.3	31.3	31.3			31.2	31.2	31.2	..	Labor Force, Female (%)
111.0	113.0	115.0	118.0	117.0	117.0	117.0	118.0			..	Primary Schl. Enroll. Ratio
105.0	109.0	112.0	115.0	114.0	114.0	114.0	115.0			..	Primary Schl. Enroll. Ratio, Female
31.0	35.0	37.0	39.0	41.0	46.0	48.0	47.0	..	..	..	Secondary Schl. Enroll. Ratio

IRAN, ISLAMIC REPUBLIC OF	1970	1971	1972	1973	1974	1975	1976	1977	1978	1979	1980
CURRENT GNP PER CAPITA (US $)	380	430	510	690	950	1,320	1,890	2,170	1,970	2,080	1,990
POPULATION (thousands)	28,429	29,300	30,213	31,167	32,164	33,206	34,294	35,431	36,617	37,848	39,124
USE AND ORIGIN OF RESOURCES				*(Billions of current Iranian Rials)*							
Gross National Product (GNP)	798	968	1,235	1,836	3,079	3,497	4,692	5,850	5,344	6,391	6,628
Net Factor Income from Abroad	-86	-46	-29	-24	-11	-15	-5	-98	-186	55	6
GDP at Market Prices	884	1,014	1,264	1,861	3,090	3,512	4,697	5,948	5,530	6,335	6,622
Resource Balance	53	41	48	289	802	313	492	259	86	840	-209
Exports of Goods & NFServices	211	255	328	643	1,478	1,440	1,787	1,751	1,189	1,762	880
Imports of Goods & NFServices	158	214	280	355	676	1,127	1,295	1,491	1,103	923	1,089
Domestic Absorption	832	973	1,217	1,572	2,288	3,199	4,205	5,688	5,444	5,496	6,830
Private Consumption, etc.	523	567	677	883	1,084	1,369	1,863	2,933	2,972	2,982	3,301
General Gov't Consumption	142	189	253	325	639	817	1,004	1,134	1,255	1,223	1,380
Gross Domestic Investment	167	217	287	363	564	1,013	1,338	1,622	1,217	1,290	2,150
Fixed Investment	167	217	287	363	530	999	1,589	1,790	1,696	1,191	1,407
Indirect Taxes, net	57	65	74	77	19	80	126	185	175	-3	161
GDP at factor cost	827	949	1,190	1,784	3,071	3,432	4,571	5,762	5,354	6,338	6,460
Agriculture	161	173	202	234	303	334	426	459	543	768	1,080
Industry	351	412	511	920	1,878	1,997	2,538	2,761	2,166	2,634	2,137
Manufacturing	114	138	171	232	313	383	490	493	437	454	662
Services, etc.	315	364	477	629	889	1,102	1,606	2,542	2,645	2,937	3,243
Gross Domestic Saving	220	258	335	652	1,367	1,326	1,830	1,881	1,303	2,130	1,941
Gross National Saving	134	212	306	627	1,356	1,311	1,824	1,783	1,117	2,185	1,948
				(Billions of 1987 Iranian Rials)							
Gross National Product	13,191	14,323	16,343	19,157	19,918	20,380	24,004	25,557	21,174	19,282	15,549
GDP at Market Prices	14,428	14,740	16,644	19,136	19,870	20,348	23,909	25,506	21,150	19,205	15,493
Resource Balance	3,565	3,405	3,877	4,055	3,400	1,737	1,876	1,002	690	1,007	-1,000
Exports of Goods & NFServices	4,483	4,600	5,301	5,716	5,624	5,051	5,627	5,122	3,485	3,015	956
Imports of Goods & NFServices	918	1,195	1,424	1,662	2,225	3,314	3,751	4,120	2,795	2,008	1,956
Domestic Absorption	10,863	11,335	12,767	15,081	16,471	18,611	22,033	24,505	20,460	18,197	16,493
Private Consumption, etc.	7,387	7,616	8,033	9,682	9,137	8,741	10,882	13,806	11,831	10,475	7,625
General Gov't Consumption	1,542	1,668	2,193	2,576	3,847	4,385	5,143	4,811	4,800	3,833	3,501
Gross Domestic Investment	1,934	2,050	2,541	2,823	3,487	5,485	6,008	5,887	3,829	3,890	5,368
Fixed Investment	1,870	1,982	2,456	2,729	3,163	5,224	7,055	6,419	5,545	3,439	3,357
GDP at factor cost	14,077	14,308	16,372	18,547	19,733	19,880	23,259	24,701	20,470	19,194	15,101
Agriculture	2,115	2,197	2,317	2,450	2,593	2,770	2,922	2,799	2,842	3,047	3,081
Industry	5,907	5,410	6,181	6,818	6,966	6,677	7,417	7,248	5,532	4,486	2,785
Manufacturing	703	794	937	1,102	1,304	1,518	1,743	1,498	1,302	1,156	1,396
Services, etc.	6,056	6,702	7,874	9,280	10,174	10,433	12,920	14,655	12,096	11,661	9,236
Memo Items:											
Capacity to Import	1,223	1,426	1,665	3,014	4,867	4,234	5,176	4,837	3,012	3,835	1,581
Terms of Trade Adjustment	-3,260	-3,174	-3,636	-2,703	-758	-817	-451	-285	-473	820	625
Gross Domestic Income	11,168	11,565	13,008	16,434	19,113	19,531	23,458	25,221	20,678	20,025	16,118
Gross National Income	9,931	11,148	12,708	16,455	19,161	19,563	23,553	25,272	20,701	20,102	16,174
DOMESTIC PRICES/DEFLATORS				*(Index 1987 = 100)*							
Overall (GDP)	6.1	6.9	7.6	9.7	15.6	17.3	19.6	23.3	26.1	33.0	42.7
Domestic Absorption	7.7	8.6	9.5	10.4	13.9	17.2	19.1	23.2	26.6	30.2	41.4
Agriculture	7.6	7.9	8.7	9.6	11.7	12.1	14.6	16.4	19.1	25.2	35.1
Industry	5.9	7.6	8.3	13.5	27.0	29.9	34.2	38.1	39.2	58.7	76.7
Manufacturing	16.2	17.4	18.3	21.0	24.0	25.2	28.1	32.9	33.6	39.3	47.4
Consumer Price Index	9.6	10.0	10.6	11.6	13.3	15.0	16.7	21.3	23.8	26.3	31.7
MANUFACTURING ACTIVITY											
Employment (1987=100)	..	..	..	..	..	..	..	..	..	..	..
Real Earnings per Empl. (1987=100)	..	..	..	..	..	..	..	..	..	..	..
Real Output per Empl. (1987=100)	..	..	..	..	..	..	..	..	..	..	..
Earnings as % of Value Added	24.7	24.7	25.0	25.8	23.1	27.4	29.8	30.9	..	70.4	55.5
MONETARY HOLDINGS				*(Billions of current Iranian Rials)*							
Money Supply, Broadly Defined	250	310	419	546	779	1,050	1,511	1,905	2,351	3,186	4,025
Money	128	155	214	278	381	458	668	822	1,078	1,689	2,258
Currency Outside Banks	37	42	56	70	102	148	206	252	511	769	1,108
Demand Deposits	92	113	158	208	280	310	462	570	567	920	1,150
Quasi-Money	121	155	204	268	398	592	843	1,083	1,273	1,497	1,767
GOVERNMENT DEFICIT (-) OR SURPLUS	-54	-31	-57	-13	*(Billions of current Iranian Rials)* 140	12	-38	-262	-450	-231	-915
Current Revenue	189	275	323	491	1,427	1,627	1,896	2,193	1,736	1,781	1,430
Current Expenditure	152	203	253	338	982	1,152	1,284	1,472	1,563	1,602	1,838
Current Budget Balance	37	72	70	154	445	475	611	721	173	178	-408
Capital Receipts	..	..	..	..	..	..	..	..	..	..	..
Capital Payments	91	103	127	167	305	463	649	983	623	410	507

1981	1982	1983	1984	1985	1986	1987	1988	1989	1990 estimate	Notes	IRAN, ISLAMIC REPUBLIC OF
2,540	3,140	3,530	3,750	3,990	3,960	3,650	3,070	2,580	2,490	A	CURRENT GNP PER CAPITA (US $)
40,450	41,832	43,276	44,787	46,374	48,051	49,824	51,698	53,681	55,779	..	POPULATION (thousands)
											USE AND ORIGIN OF RESOURCES
			(Billions of current Iranian Rials)								
8,380	11,152	14,021	15,151	16,522	18,107	21,280	23,598	28,139	36,463	C	Gross National Product (GNP)
31	0	-7	-11	-34	-18	10	10	15	21	..	Net Factor Income from Abroad
8,349	11,152	14,028	15,162	16,556	18,125	21,270	23,588	28,124	36,442	C	GDP at Market Prices
-424	613	35	-35	-15	-382	-229	-176	-1,033	-263	..	Resource Balance
876	1,864	1,885	1,570	1,251	553	1,697	1,928	2,831	5,551	..	Exports of Goods & NF Services
1,300	1,251	1,851	1,605	1,266	935	1,926	2,104	3,864	5,814	..	Imports of Goods & NF Services
8,773	10,539	13,993	15,197	16,571	18,507	21,499	23,764	29,157	36,705		Domestic Absorption
4,224	7,143	8,207	10,195	11,111	11,736	13,776	16,075	19,593	25,088		Private Consumption, etc.
1,676	1,910	2,151	2,190	2,443	2,371	2,707	3,140	3,163	4,048		General Gov't Consumption
2,873	1,486	3,634	2,813	3,018	4,400	5,016	4,549	6,401	7,569		Gross Domestic Investment
1,575	1,821	2,879	3,098	2,841	2,606	2,658	2,933	3,382	4,086		Fixed Investment
125	204	447	561	608	613	665	540	721	..	Indirect Taxes, net
8,224	10,948	13,581	14,601	15,948	17,512	20,605	23,048	27,402	35,624	C	GDP at factor cost
1,502	2,000	2,223	2,606	2,848	3,734	4,813	4,776	5,774	7,517	..	Agriculture
2,612	3,900	4,588	4,522	4,274	3,456	3,917	4,165	5,170	7,339	..	Industry
928	1,065	1,212	1,375	1,365	1,393	1,542	1,787	2,202	2,707	..	Manufacturing
4,110	5,047	6,770	7,473	8,826	10,323	11,875	14,107	16,458	20,768	..	Services, etc.
2,449	2,100	3,669	2,778	3,003	4,018	4,787	4,373	5,368	7,306	..	Gross Domestic Saving
						4,797	4,383	5,383	7,327	..	Gross National Saving
			(Billions of 1987 Iranian Rials)								
16,825	19,338	21,301	22,354	23,483	21,640	21,280	19,905	20,496	22,485	C	Gross National Product
16,757	19,273	21,222	22,292	23,453	21,608	21,270	19,894	20,475	22,538	C	GDP at Market Prices
-1,357	-59	-974	-1,041	-645	-240	-229	494	437	..	..	Resource Balance
859	2,023	2,079	1,687	1,529	1,335	1,697	1,617	1,610	..	..	Exports of Goods & NF Services
2,216	2,082	3,053	2,727	2,174	1,576	1,926	1,123	1,172	..	..	Imports of Goods & NF Services
18,113	19,332	22,196	23,333	24,098	21,849	21,499	19,400	20,038			Domestic Absorption
8,214	12,730	12,297	15,362	15,879	13,427	13,776	12,967	13,248			Private Consumption, etc.
3,653	3,624	3,596	3,392	3,575	2,856	2,707	2,793	2,420			General Gov't Consumption
6,247	2,977	6,303	4,579	4,644	5,566	5,016	3,640	4,369			Gross Domestic Investment
3,423	3,506	4,832	4,868	4,229	3,243	2,658	2,288	2,282			Fixed Investment
16,492	18,904	20,532	21,463	22,596	20,885	20,605	19,434	19,963	21,940	C	GDP at factor cost
3,420	3,751	3,881	4,163	4,497	4,690	4,813	4,292	4,549	4,754	..	Agriculture
3,152	4,113	4,466	4,265	4,243	3,834	3,918	3,979	4,428	4,851	..	Industry
1,759	1,484	1,667	1,892	1,838	1,709	1,542	1,480	1,584	1,696	..	Manufacturing
9,920	11,041	12,186	13,035	13,856	12,361	11,875	11,162	10,987	12,335	..	Services, etc.
											Memo Items:
1,494	3,103	3,110	2,668	2,148	932	1,697	1,029	859	..	..	Capacity to Import
634	1,080	1,031	981	619	-403	0	-589	-751	..	..	Terms of Trade Adjustment
17,391	20,352	22,253	23,274	24,072	21,205	21,270	19,305	19,724	..	..	Gross Domestic Income
17,459	20,418	22,331	23,335	24,102	21,236	21,280	19,317	19,745	..	..	Gross National Income
			(Index 1987 = 100)								DOMESTIC PRICES/DEFLATORS
49.8	57.9	66.1	68.0	70.6	83.9	100.0	118.6	137.4	161.7	..	Overall (GDP)
48.4	54.5	63.0	65.1	68.8	84.7	100.0	122.5	145.5		..	Domestic Absorption
43.9	53.3	57.3	62.6	63.3	79.6	100.0	111.3	126.9	158.1	..	Agriculture
82.9	94.8	102.7	106.0	100.7	90.1	100.0	104.7	116.8	151.3	..	Industry
52.8	71.8	72.7	72.7	74.3	81.5	100.0	120.8	139.0	159.6	..	Manufacturing
39.3	46.7	55.9	62.9	65.7	77.8	100.0	128.7	157.4	169.4	..	Consumer Price Index
											MANUFACTURING ACTIVITY
..	..	..	..	..	..	..	..	..	..	..	Employment (1987=100)
..	..	..	..	..	..	..	..	..	..	..	Real Earnings per Empl. (1987=100)
..	..	..	..	..	..	..	..	..	..	..	Real Output per Empl. (1987=100)
45.2	54.0	54.3	55.0	..	..	..	..	..	..	..	Earnings as % of Value Added
			(Billions of current Iranian Rials)								MONETARY HOLDINGS
4,683	5,884	6,983	8,045	10,965	9,848	11,745	14,106	..	20,392	..	Money Supply, Broadly Defined
2,637	3,293	3,922	..		5,509	6,462	7,118	..	9,729	..	Money
1,248	1,465	1,757	..		2,354	2,712	3,068	..	3,518	..	Currency Outside Banks
1,389	1,828	2,165	..	..	3,155	3,750	4,050	..	6,211	..	Demand Deposits
2,046	2,591	3,061	..		4,339	5,283	6,988	..	10,663	..	Quasi-Money
			(Billions of current Iranian Rials)								GOVERNMENT DEFICIT (-) OR SURPLUS
-841	-603	-842	-597	-594	-1,353	-1,419	-2,104	-1,131	..	C	
1,923	2,698	2,994	2,989	2,964	2,017	2,511	2,501	3,625	..	..	Current Revenue
2,169	2,422	2,739	2,754	2,846	2,755	3,255	3,919	3,893	..	..	Current Expenditure
-246	276	255	235	117	-738	-744	-1,418	-269	..	..	Current Budget Balance
..	..	..	..	..	..	..	..	..	..	..	Capital Receipts
594	879	1,097	832	712	615	675	687	863	..	..	Capital Payments

	1970	1971	1972	1973	1974	1975	1976	1977	1978	1979	1980
FOREIGN TRADE (CUSTOMS BASIS)					*(Millions of current US dollars)*						
Value of Exports, fob	..	..	..	..	..	..	..	..	..	..	..
Nonfuel Primary Products	..	..	..	..	..	..	..	..	..	..	..
Fuels	..	..	..	..	..	..	..	..	..	..	..
Manufactures	..	..	..	..	..	..	..	..	..	..	..
Value of Imports, cif	..	..	..	..	..	..	..	..	..	..	..
Nonfuel Primary Products	..	..	..	..	..	..	..	..	..	..	..
Fuels	..	..	..	..	..	..	..	..	..	..	..
Manufactures	..	..	..	..	..	..	..	..	..	..	..
Terms of Trade					*(Index 1987 = 100)*						
Export Prices, fob	..	..	..	..	..	..	..	..	..	..	..
Import Prices, cif	..	..	..	..	..	..	..	..	..	..	..
BALANCE OF PAYMENTS					*(Millions of current US dollars)*						
Exports of Goods & Services	2,613	3,957	4,284	6,770	22,711	22,904	27,980	28,544	21,879	26,991	14,073
Merchandise, fob	2,417	3,724	3,966	6,122	21,356	20,432	24,719	24,076	17,675	24,171	12,338
Nonfactor Services	186	223	303	598	959	1,770	2,651	3,699	3,104	1,580	731
Factor Services	10	10	15	50	396	702	610	769	1,100	1,240	1,004
Imports of Goods & Services	3,124	4,079	4,676	6,614	10,410	18,178	20,303	25,603	21,760	15,008	16,509
Merchandise, fob	1,658	2,069	2,591	3,985	7,257	12,898	13,860	16,718	11,803	8,521	10,888
Nonfactor Services	561	686	815	1,317	2,409	4,572	5,773	8,201	9,177	5,690	5,223
Factor Services	905	1,324	1,270	1,311	744	708	670	684	780	797	398
Long-Term Interest	0	0	0	0	0	0	0	0	0	0	432
Private Current Transfers, net	0	0	0	-1	-1	-1	0	0	0	0	0
Workers' Remittances	..	..	..	..	..	..	..	..	..	..	..
Curr. A/C Bal before Off. Transf.	-511	-122	-392	155	12,299	4,724	7,677	2,941	119	11,983	-2,436
Net Official Transfers	4	4	4	-1	-32	-17	-17	-125	-15	-15	-2
Curr. A/C Bal after Off. Transf.	-507	-118	-388	154	12,267	4,707	7,660	2,816	104	11,968	-2,438
Long-Term Capital, net	462	740	622	1,189	-1,939	-2,869	-925	1,706	-73	-2,000	-6,533
Direct Investment	25	65	91	561	324	141	..	..	..	..	..
Long-Term Loans	0	0	0	0	0	0	0	0	0	0	-267
Disbursements	0	0	0	0	0	0	0	0	0	0	264
Repayments	0	0	0	0	0	0	0	0	0	0	531
Other Long-Term Capital	437	675	531	627	-2,262	-3,010	-925	1,706	-73	-2,000	-6,266
Other Capital, net	-192	-235	250	-1,312	-3,172	-1,771	-4,322	-2,432	-746	-6,899	-876
Change in Reserves	237	-387	-485	-30	-7,156	-67	-2,413	-2,090	715	-3,069	9,847
Memo Item:					*(Iranian Rials per US dollar)*						
Conversion Factor (Annual Avg)	75.750	75.750	75.750	68.880	67.630	68.170	70.540	70.580	70.480	70.480	71.570
EXTERNAL DEBT (Total)					*(Millions of US dollars), outstanding at end of year*						
EXTERNAL DEBT (Total)	0	0	0	0	0	0	0	0	0	0	4,508
Long-Term Debt (by debtor)	0	0	0	0	0	0	0	0	0	0	4,508
Central Bank, incl. IMF credit	0	0	0	0	0	0	0	0	0	0	172
Central Government	0	0	0	0	0	0	0	0	0	0	1,198
Rest of General Government	..	..	..	..	..	..	..	..	..	..	..
Non-financial Public Enterprises	0	0	0	0	0	0	0	0	0	0	..
Priv. Sector, incl non-guaranteed	..	..	..	..	..	..	..	..	..	..	3,138
Short-Term Debt	0	0	0	0	0	0	0	0	0	0	0
Memo Items:					*(Millions of US dollars)*						
Int'l Reserves Excluding Gold	77.0	479.3	818.3	1,078.5	8,223.2	8,743.6	8,681.3	12,105.8	11,977.2	15,209.6	10,222.9
Gold Holdings (at market price)	139.9	163.3	242.9	420.2	697.2	524.3	503.7	623.4	863.4	1,998.1	2,907.4
SOCIAL INDICATORS											
Total Fertility Rate	6.7	6.6	6.5	6.4	6.3	6.2	6.1	6.1	6.1	6.1	6.1
Infant Mortality Rate	131.2	126.6	122.0	120.0	118.0	116.0	114.0	112.0	110.2	108.4	106.6
Life Expectancy at Birth	54.8	55.3	55.9	56.4	57.0	57.5	58.0	58.6	58.9	59.1	59.4
Urban Population, % of total	41.0	41.9	42.9	43.8	44.8	45.7	46.5	47.3	48.0	48.8	49.6
Food Prod. per capita (1987=100)	72.4	70.1	75.0	75.1	77.4	80.2	84.4	80.1	83.7	77.3	78.2
Labor Force, Agriculture (%)	43.8	42.9	42.1	41.3	40.6	39.9	39.1	38.4	37.6	37.0	36.4
Labor Force, Female (%)	13.3	13.5	13.7	13.9	14.1	14.3	14.5	14.8	15.0	15.2	15.3
Primary Schl. Enroll. Ratio	72.0	..	..	..	..	93.0	98.0	101.0	..	..	87.0
Primary Schl. Enroll. Ratio, Female	52.0	..	..	..	..	71.0	77.0	80.0	..	..	..
Secondary Schl. Enroll. Ratio	27.0	..	..	..	..	45.0	48.0	42.0	..	..	..

	1981	1982	1983	1984	1985	1986	1987	1988	1989	1990 estimate	Notes
FOREIGN TRADE (CUSTOMS BASIS)											
(Millions of current US dollars)											
Value of Exports, fob	..	..	..	..	..	..	..	..	..	..	..
Nonfuel Primary Products	..	..	..	..	..	..	..	..	..	..	..
Fuels	..	..	..	..	..	..	..	..	..	..	..
Manufactures	..	..	..	..	..	..	..	..	..	..	..
Value of Imports, cif	..	..	..	..	..	..	..	..	..	..	..
Nonfuel Primary Products	..	..	..	..	..	..	..	..	..	..	..
Fuels	..	..	..	..	..	..	..	..	..	..	..
Manufactures	..	..	..	..	..	..	..	..	..	..	..
(Index 1987=100)											
Terms of Trade	..	..	..	..	..	..	..	..	..	..	..
Export Prices, fob	..	..	..	..	..	..	..	..	..	..	..
Import Prices, cif	..	..	..	..	..	..	..	..	..	..	..
BALANCE OF PAYMENTS											
(Millions of current US dollars)											
Exports of Goods & Services	13,282	21,573	22,842	18,156	14,938	7,778	11,076	11,176	13,879	18,704	..
Merchandise, fob	11,831	20,452	21,507	17,087	14,175	7,171	10,639	10,709	13,081	17,812	..
Nonfactor Services	556	509	540	475	370	242	231	244	446	522	..
Factor Services	895	612	795	594	393	365	206	223	352	370	..
Imports of Goods & Services	16,728	15,840	22,484	18,570	15,414	12,933	13,552	12,868	16,442	19,089	..
Merchandise, fob	13,138	12,552	18,027	14,729	12,006	10,585	11,197	10,448	13,331	15,900	..
Nonfactor Services	3,315	3,061	4,273	3,698	3,308	2,282	2,289	2,338	3,007	3,121	..
Factor Services	275	227	184	143	100	66	66	82	104	68	..
Long-Term Interest	221	182	115	79	58	61	38	62	44	28	..
Private Current Transfers, net	..	..		..		..	0	0	0	..	..
Workers' Remittances	..	..		..		..	..	..	..	..	..
Curr. A/C Bal before Off. Transf.	-3,446	5,733	358	-414	-476	-5,155	-2,476	-1,692	-2,563	-385	..
Net Official Transfers							0	0	0	..	..
Curr. A/C Bal after Off. Transf.	-3,446	5,733	358	-414	-476	-5,155	-2,476	-1,692	-2,563	-385	..
Long-Term Capital, net	-947	-2,186	-835	-663	-570	-1,258	-1,079	-37	831	8	..
Direct Investment	..	..		..		..	..	..	..	..	..
Long-Term Loans	-428	-272	-451	-365	-267	-279	-203	-178	-124	-86	..
Disbursements	95	209	94	5	87	42	11	157	0	139	..
Repayments	522	481	544	370	354	321	214	335	124	225	..
Other Long-Term Capital	-520	-1,914	-384	-298	-303	-979	-876	141	955	94	..
Other Capital, net	4,023	1,340	-772	-3,059	1,601	5,199	3,331	1,458	1,843	385	..
Change in Reserves	370	-4,887	1,249	4,136	-555	1,214	224	271	-111	-8	..
Memo Item:											
(Iranian Rials per US dollar)											
Conversion Factor (Annual Avg)	80.030	84.450	87.230	91.900	87.730	76.550	144.910	177.970	226.000	307.000	..
EXTERNAL DEBT (Total)											
(Millions of US dollars), outstanding at end of year											
Long-Term Debt (by debtor)	3,793	8,237	7,107	5,160	6,057	5,825	6,144	5,831	6,519	9,021	..
Central Bank, incl. IMF credit	3,793	3,468	2,968	2,457	2,390	2,413	2,280	2,055	1,862	1,797	..
Central Government	141	117	100	73	74	70	46	16	8	2	..
Rest of General Government	1,005	884	779	667	653	672	638	572	526	504	..
Non-financial Public Enterprises	..	..		..		..	..	..	..	..	..
Priv. Sector, incl non-guaranteed	2,647	2,467	2,089	1,717	1,664	1,671	1,596	1,467	1,327	1,290	..
Short-Term Debt	0	4,769	4,139	2,703	3,667	3,413	3,864	3,776	4,657	7,224	..
Memo Items:											
(Millions of US dollars)											
Int'l Reserves Excluding Gold	1,605.4	5,701.2	..	..	..	..	..	..	..	..	..
Gold Holdings (at market price)	2,407.7	2,706.2	..	..	..	..	..	..	..	..	..
SOCIAL INDICATORS											
Total Fertility Rate	6.2	6.2	6.2	6.3	6.3	6.4	6.4	6.3	6.3	6.2	..
Infant Mortality Rate	104.8	103.0	101.0	99.0	97.0	95.0	93.0	91.4	89.8	88.3	..
Life Expectancy at Birth	59.7	59.9	60.3	60.8	61.2	61.6	62.0	62.3	62.6	62.9	..
Urban Population, % of total	50.3	51.0	51.8	52.5	53.2	53.9	54.6	55.3	56.0	56.7	..
Food Prod. per capita (1987=100)	87.3	86.5	84.9	89.8	95.4	100.1	100.0	89.8	80.3	83.4	..
Labor Force, Agriculture (%)	..	..		..		..	..	..	..	..	..
Labor Force, Female (%)	15.7	15.9	16.2	16.5	16.7	17.0	17.3	17.5	17.8	18.0	..
Primary Schl. Enroll. Ratio	..	97.0	102.0	103.0	98.0	..	103.0	105.0	109.0	..	..
Primary Schl. Enroll. Ratio, Female	..	82.0	89.0	92.0	88.0	..	94.0	97.0	101.0	..	..
Secondary Schl. Enroll. Ratio	..	39.0	40.0	42.0	45.0	46.0	48.0	51.0	53.0	..	..

IRELAND	1970	1971	1972	1973	1974	1975	1976	1977	1978	1979	1980
CURRENT GNP PER CAPITA (US $)	1,290	1,420	1,680	2,090	2,370	2,650	2,680	3,000	3,430	4,120	5,050
POPULATION (thousands)	2,950	2,978	3,024	3,073	3,124	3,177	3,228	3,272	3,314	3,368	3,401

USE AND ORIGIN OF RESOURCES	*(Millions of current Irish Pounds)*										
Gross National Product (GNP)	1,648	1,880	2,267	2,714	3,007	3,796	4,617	5,595	6,529	7,634	9,003
Net Factor Income from Abroad	28	27	30	13	19	4	-36	-108	-228	-283	-358
GDP at Market Prices	1,620	1,853	2,237	2,701	2,987	3,792	4,653	5,703	6,757	7,917	9,361
Resource Balance	-130	-135	-120	-185	-437	-230	-370	-520	-670	-1,299	-1,261
Exports of Goods & NFServices	599	669	773	1,026	1,272	1,619	2,152	2,817	3,374	3,936	4,639
Imports of Goods & NFServices	728	804	893	1,211	1,708	1,849	2,522	3,337	4,043	5,235	5,900
Domestic Absorption	1,750	1,988	2,357	2,886	3,424	4,022	5,023	6,223	7,426	9,216	10,622
Private Consumption, etc.	1,116	1,261	1,454	1,738	2,044	2,432	3,002	3,658	4,309	5,170	6,158
General Gov't Consumption	237	283	343	423	513	705	839	973	1,156	1,431	1,860
Gross Domestic Investment	396	444	561	725	867	885	1,182	1,592	1,962	2,614	2,604
Fixed Investment	368	438	530	682	736	862	1,164	1,412	1,869	2,414	2,677
Indirect Taxes, net	236	272	320	375	376	389	593	532	482	525	830
GDP at factor cost	1,385	1,581	1,918	2,326	2,611	3,403	4,060	5,171	6,275	7,392	8,530
Agriculture	233	258	349	436	419	589	705	958	1,084	1,055	991
Industry	509	581	706	872	1,033	1,214	1,414	1,812	2,246	2,706	..
Manufacturing	327	370	451	566	680	773	911	1,198	1,488	1,767	..
Services, etc.	643	742	863	1,017	1,160	1,599	1,941	2,401	2,944	3,631	..
Gross Domestic Saving	267	310	441	540	430	655	812	1,072	1,292	1,315	1,343
Gross National Saving	326	370	506	592	492	705	825	1,016	1,121	1,078	1,045

	(Millions of 1987 Irish Pounds)										
Gross National Product	10,776	10,750	11,322	12,573	13,127	13,796	13,863	14,831	15,650	16,109	16,579
GDP at Market Prices	10,575	10,575	11,146	12,495	13,027	13,764	13,956	15,102	16,187	16,685	17,199
Resource Balance	-932	-995	-1,096	-1,600	-1,442	-575	-945	-1,034	-1,379	-2,017	-1,228
Exports of Goods & NFServices	3,367	3,505	3,632	4,028	4,056	4,363	4,717	5,379	6,041	6,432	6,841
Imports of Goods & NFServices	4,299	4,500	4,728	5,628	5,499	4,937	5,662	6,413	7,420	8,449	8,069
Domestic Absorption	11,507	11,570	12,242	14,094	14,470	14,339	14,901	16,136	17,566	18,701	18,427
Private Consumption, etc.	7,107	6,943	7,074	8,313	8,528	8,918	8,953	9,606	10,433	10,771	10,972
General Gov't Consumption	1,904	2,068	2,224	2,374	2,554	2,776	2,848	2,907	3,137	3,281	3,514
Gross Domestic Investment	2,496	2,559	2,944	3,407	3,388	2,645	3,100	3,623	3,995	4,650	3,941
Fixed Investment	2,312	2,518	2,715	3,154	2,787	2,687	3,051	3,175	3,774	4,288	4,085
GDP at factor cost	..	..	..	..	..	..	..	..	..	..	..
Agriculture	2,377	2,454	3,018	3,005	1,762	1,577	2,856	3,214	3,366	3,743	2,762
Industry	..	..	..	..	..	..	..	..	..	..	..
Manufacturing	..	..	..	..	..	..	..	..	..	..	..
Services, etc.	..	..	..	..	..	..	..	..	..	..	..

Memo Items:											
Capacity to Import	3,535	3,745	4,093	4,770	4,093	4,323	4,832	5,414	6,191	6,353	6,344
Terms of Trade Adjustment	167	240	461	742	37	-40	115	35	150	-80	-497
Gross Domestic Income	10,742	10,815	11,608	13,237	13,064	13,725	14,071	15,137	16,337	16,605	16,702
Gross National Income	10,943	10,989	11,783	13,315	13,163	13,757	13,978	14,866	15,800	16,029	16,082

DOMESTIC PRICES/DEFLATORS	*(Index 1987 = 100)*										
Overall (GDP)	15.3	17.5	20.1	21.6	22.9	27.6	33.3	37.8	41.7	47.4	54.4
Domestic Absorption	15.2	17.2	19.3	20.5	23.7	28.1	33.7	38.6	42.3	49.3	57.6
Agriculture	9.8	10.5	11.6	14.5	23.8	37.4	24.7	29.8	32.2	28.2	35.9
Industry	..	..	..	..	..	..	..	..	..	..	..
Manufacturing	..	..	..	..	..	..	..	..	..	..	..
Consumer Price Index	14.5	15.8	17.2	19.2	22.4	27.1	32.0	36.3	39.1	44.3	52.4

MANUFACTURING ACTIVITY											
Employment (1987=100)	105.6	104.8	105.5	111.4	112.2	103.9	105.3	109.1	110.5	121.4	120.5
Real Earnings per Empl. (1987=100)	60.3	63.8	67.7	71.7	74.6	79.3	78.8	80.3	87.3	88.8	90.0
Real Output per Empl. (1987=100)	13.1	11.5	11.4	16.1	16.6	20.2	27.0	24.4	30.2	30.0	110.6
Earnings as % of Value Added	48.7	48.5	48.5	46.4	45.3	46.0	42.0	42.4	41.1	42.3	43.6

MONETARY HOLDINGS	*(Millions of current Irish Pounds)*										
Money Supply, Broadly Defined	1,084	1,177	1,352	1,682	2,033	2,456	2,770	3,261	4,142	4,914	5,954
Money	415	440	518	572	624	748	875	1,072	1,367	1,479	1,686
Currency Outside Banks	155	173	191	219	245	292	342	390	476	582	663
Demand Deposits	260	267	327	354	380	456	533	682	892	896	1,023
Quasi-Money	669	738	834	1,109	1,409	1,708	1,895	2,189	2,775	3,435	4,268

GOVERNMENT DEFICIT (-) OR SURPLUS	*(Millions of current Irish Pounds)*										
	-89	-98	-125	-183	-357	-472	-470	-534	-768	-944	-1,224
Current Revenue	506	598	695	842	956	1,209	1,629	1,933	2,256	2,728	3,550
Current Expenditure	481	560	663	810	987	1,406	1,750	2,065	2,531	3,081	3,950
Current Budget Balance	25	38	32	32	-31	-197	-121	-132	-275	-353	-400
Capital Receipts	..	..	..	..	..	..	..	..	..	..	..
Capital Payments	114	136	157	215	326	275	349	402	493	591	824

1981	1982	1983	1984	1985	1986	1987	1988	1989	1990 estimate	Notes	IRELAND
5,590	5,530	5,120	4,980	4,910	5,280	6,480	7,920	8,890	10,360	..	**CURRENT GNP PER CAPITA (US $)**
3,443	3,480	3,504	3,529	3,540	3,541	3,543	3,538	3,515	3,503	..	**POPULATION (thousands)**
			(Millions of current Irish Pounds)								**USE AND ORIGIN OF RESOURCES**
10,854	12,455	13,595	14,768	15,824	16,920	18,306	19,273	21,268	22,911	..	Gross National Product (GNP)
-505	-928	-1,184	-1,639	-1,966	-1,957	-1,957	-2,542	-3,040	-2,782	..	Net Factor Income from Abroad
11,359	13,382	14,779	16,407	17,790	18,877	20,263	21,815	24,308	25,693	..	GDP at Market Prices
-1,614	-981	-413	-45	342	491	1,318	1,968	2,303	2,079	..	Resource Balance
5,504	6,433	7,752	9,770	10,738	10,352	11,785	13,533	15,991	15,940	..	Exports of Goods & NF Services
7,117	7,415	8,164	9,815	10,397	9,860	10,468	11,565	13,688	13,861	..	Imports of Goods & NF Services
12,973	14,364	15,192	16,452	17,448	18,386	18,945	19,847	22,005	23,614	..	Domestic Absorption
7,490	8,001	8,814	9,652	10,598	11,311	11,999	12,762	13,728	14,231	..	Private Consumption, etc.
2,260	2,646	2,857	3,067	3,301	3,542	3,594	3,577	3,713	4,021	..	General Gov't Consumption
3,222	3,716	3,521	3,733	3,550	3,533	3,352	3,508	4,564	5,362	..	Gross Domestic Investment
3,368	3,547	3,419	3,516	3,387	3,394	3,339	3,637	4,422	4,895	..	Fixed Investment
1,225	1,568	1,773	1,874	1,817	1,988	2,108	2,145	3,021	2,641	..	Indirect Taxes, net
10,134	11,815	13,006	14,533	15,973	16,889	18,155	19,670	21,287	23,052	..	GDP at factor cost
1,143	1,386	1,570	1,814	1,719	1,659	1,948	2,246	..	..	..	Agriculture
..	1,773	1,663	1,753	1,756	1,712	1,769	..	..	..	..	Industry
..	679	569	676	692	685	709	..	..	..	..	Manufacturing
..	8,655	9,773	10,966	12,498	13,518	14,438	..	..	..	..	Services, etc.
1,609	2,735	3,108	3,688	3,891	4,024	4,669	5,476	6,867	7,441	..	Gross Domestic Saving
1,164	1,871	1,970	2,019	1,906	2,022	2,603	2,854	3,760	4,619	..	Gross National Saving
			(Millions of 1987 Irish Pounds)								
17,030	16,956	16,694	17,050	17,360	17,315	18,306	18,708	19,692	21,593	..	Gross National Product
17,770	18,176	18,132	18,908	19,486	19,346	20,263	21,166	22,519	24,121	..	GDP at Market Prices
-1,232	-590	-192	337	664	424	1,318	1,933	2,043	2,553	..	Resource Balance
6,975	7,361	8,130	9,479	10,102	10,394	11,785	12,809	14,102	15,339	..	Exports of Goods & NF Services
8,207	7,951	8,322	9,142	9,439	9,970	10,468	10,876	12,060	12,786	..	Imports of Goods & NF Services
19,003	18,767	18,324	18,571	18,822	18,921	18,945	19,233	20,476	21,567	..	Domestic Absorption
11,174	10,605	10,661	10,920	11,448	11,575	11,999	12,525	13,003	13,237	..	Private Consumption, etc.
3,525	3,640	3,626	3,601	3,667	3,759	3,594	3,403	3,335	3,452	..	General Gov't Consumption
4,304	4,522	4,037	4,050	3,708	3,588	3,352	3,306	4,138	4,878	..	Gross Domestic Investment
4,475	4,322	3,921	3,822	3,527	3,417	3,339	3,450	3,996	4,377	..	Fixed Investment
..	..	15,978	16,783	17,521	17,283	18,155	19,099	19,711	21,725	..	GDP at factor cost
3,415	2,895	2,295	2,221	2,093	1,686	1,948	..	..	..	..	Agriculture
..	..	1,899	1,925	1,795	1,900	1,769	..	..	..	..	Industry
..	..	654	726	707	690	709	..	..	..	..	Manufacturing
..	..	11,785	12,637	13,633	13,697	14,438	..	..	..	..	Services, etc.
											Memo Items:
6,346	6,899	7,901	9,100	9,749	10,466	11,785	12,726	14,089	14,704	..	Capacity to Import
-628	-462	-229	-379	-354	72	0	-83	-13	-636	..	Terms of Trade Adjustment
17,142	17,714	17,903	18,529	19,132	19,418	20,263	21,083	22,505	23,485	..	Gross Domestic Income
16,402	16,494	16,465	16,671	17,006	17,387	18,306	18,625	19,678	20,957	..	Gross National Income
			(Index 1987 = 100)								**DOMESTIC PRICES/DEFLATORS**
63.9	73.6	81.5	86.8	91.3	97.6	100.0	103.1	107.9	106.5	..	Overall (GDP)
68.3	76.5	82.9	88.6	92.7	97.2	100.0	103.2	107.5	109.5	..	Domestic Absorption
33.5	47.9	68.4	81.7	82.1	98.4	100.0	..	..	..	..	Agriculture
..	..	87.6	91.0	97.8	90.1	100.0	..	..	..	..	Industry
..	..	87.0	93.1	97.8	99.4	100.0	..	..	..	..	Manufacturing
63.1	73.9	81.6	88.6	93.4	97.0	100.0	102.2	106.3	109.9	..	Consumer Price Index
											MANUFACTURING ACTIVITY
118.8	114.2	107.8	104.6	100.0	98.8	100.0	102.6	..	..	G	Employment (1987=100)
86.6	84.4	86.6	88.7	92.0	94.2	100.0	106.8	..	..	G	Real Earnings per Empl. (1987=100)
108.8	64.4	77.2	88.6	91.8	98.8	100.0	..	..	..	G	Real Output per Empl. (1987=100)
41.2	39.6	35.8	33.2	32.5	33.1	32.1	31.3	..	..	..	Earnings as % of Value Added
			(Millions of current Irish Pounds)								**MONETARY HOLDINGS**
6,832	7,043	7,486	8,257	8,750	8,620	9,559	9,654	10,749	12,259	D	Money Supply, Broadly Defined
1,743	1,838	2,048	2,245	2,289	2,382	2,640	2,826	3,112	3,346	..	Money
739	811	907	923	970	1,025	1,107	1,212	1,310	1,317	..	Currency Outside Banks
1,004	1,027	1,142	1,322	1,318	1,357	1,532	1,614	1,802	2,029	..	Demand Deposits
5,088	5,205	5,438	6,012	6,461	6,238	6,919	6,828	7,637	8,913	..	Quasi-Money
			(Millions of current Irish Pounds)								**GOVERNMENT DEFICIT (-) OR SURPLUS**
-1,662	-1,984	-1,849	-1,756	-2,078	-2,119	-1,947	-1,017	..	..	F	
4,427	5,607	6,516	7,188	7,674	8,119	8,770	9,380	..	..	..	Current Revenue
5,046	6,484	7,357	7,960	8,781	9,280	9,841	9,834	..	..	..	Current Expenditure
-619	-877	-841	-772	-1,107	-1,161	-1,071	-454	..	..	..	Current Budget Balance
..	..	..	..	..	..	..	..	..	..	..	Capital Receipts
1,043	1,107	1,008	984	971	958	876	563	..	..	..	Capital Payments

IRELAND	1970	1971	1972	1973	1974	1975	1976	1977	1978	1979	1980
FOREIGN TRADE (CUSTOMS BASIS)					*(Millions of current US dollars)*						
Value of Exports, fob	998	1,282	1,581	2,131	2,629	3,179	3,313	4,400	5,681	7,173	8,473
Nonfuel Primary Products	577	684	814	1,079	1,243	1,661	1,546	1,951	2,565	3,059	3,509
Fuels	15	15	14	16	35	42	22	29	23	34	55
Manufactures	406	583	753	1,036	1,352	1,475	1,745	2,420	3,093	4,080	4,909
Value of Imports, cif	1,568	1,835	2,102	2,793	3,813	3,769	4,192	5,381	7,102	9,850	11,133
Nonfuel Primary Products	344	355	426	599	802	726	793	1,023	1,218	1,662	1,862
Fuels	127	166	158	190	531	531	562	678	718	1,187	1,647
Manufactures	1,097	1,314	1,517	2,004	2,481	2,512	2,837	3,680	5,166	7,001	7,624
					(Index 1987 = 100)						
Terms of Trade	140.1	148.0	144.4	131.2	99.7	97.6	97.8	92.7	97.8	100.1	90.5
Export Prices, fob	30.2	34.9	39.9	47.8	52.4	53.6	55.7	57.8	69.1	83.9	87.9
Import Prices, cif	21.5	23.6	27.6	36.4	52.6	54.9	56.9	62.3	70.6	83.8	97.2
BALANCE OF PAYMENTS					*(Millions of current US dollars)*						
Exports of Goods & Services	1,539	1,754	2,101	2,730	3,319	3,947	4,248	5,286	6,942	8,683	10,418
Merchandise, fob	1,092	1,271	1,580	2,090	2,479	3,032	3,326	4,229	5,604	6,949	8,229
Nonfactor Services	306	331	331	397	508	568	561	715	896	1,169	1,381
Factor Services	141	152	190	243	331	347	360	343	442	565	808
Imports of Goods & Services	1,842	2,065	2,376	3,196	4,311	4,462	4,992	6,396	8,677	11,929	13,754
Merchandise, fob	1,524	1,711	1,958	2,617	3,561	3,518	3,935	5,049	6,669	9,269	10,452
Nonfactor Services	220	239	269	350	407	550	572	739	1,024	1,372	1,593
Factor Services	98	115	149	229	342	395	485	608	984	1,288	1,710
Long-Term Interest	..	..	..	..	..	..	..	..	..	..	..
Private Current Transfers, net	75	82	89	97	101	102	88	92	109	93	123
Workers' Remittances	..	..	..	..	..	..	..	..	..	..	..
Curr. A/C Bal before Off. Transf.	-228	-229	-186	-370	-892	-413	-656	-1,018	-1,626	-3,153	-3,213
Net Official Transfers	30	29	36	116	203	290	228	495	777	1,053	1,081
Curr. A/C Bal after Off. Transf.	-198	-200	-150	-254	-688	-124	-428	-522	-849	-2,100	-2,132
Long-Term Capital, net	102	-15	33	277	218	388	655	195	965	854	1,326
Direct Investment	32	25	31	52	51	158	173	136	375	337	286
Long-Term Loans	..	..	..	..	..	..	..	..	..	..	..
Disbursements	..	..	..	..	..	..	..	..	..	..	..
Repayments	..	..	..	..	..	..	..	..	..	..	..
Other Long-Term Capital	70	-40	1	224	167	230	483	59	590	518	1,039
Other Capital, net	88	423	204	-21	603	86	102	735	27	659	1,519
Change in Reserves	8	-209	-87	-1	-132	-350	-329	-408	-142	586	-712
Memo Item:					*(Irish Pounds per US dollar)*						
Conversion Factor (Annual Avg)	0.420	0.410	0.400	0.410	0.430	0.450	0.560	0.570	0.520	0.490	0.490
EXTERNAL DEBT (Total)	..	..	..	..	*(Millions US dollars), outstanding at end of year*						
Long-Term Debt (by debtor)	..	..	..	..	..	..	..	..	..	..	..
Central Bank, incl. IMF credit	..	..	..	..	..	..	..	..	..	..	..
Central Government	..	..	..	..	..	..	..	..	..	..	..
Rest of General Government	..	..	..	..	..	..	..	..	..	..	..
Non-financial Public Enterprises	..	..	..	..	..	..	..	..	..	..	..
Priv. Sector, incl non-guaranteed	..	..	..	..	..	..	..	..	..	..	..
Short-Term Debt	..	..	..	..	..	..	..	..	..	..	..
Memo Items:					*(Millions of US dollars)*						
Int'l Reserves Excluding Gold	680.7	978.0	1,109.4	1,007.2	1,247.2	1,512.6	1,818.5	2,351.1	2,668.4	2,212.0	2,860.3
Gold Holdings (at market price)	17.1	19.9	29.7	48.1	83.4	62.7	60.2	78.0	101.0	196.2	210.7
SOCIAL INDICATORS											
Total Fertility Rate	3.9	4.0	3.9	3.7	3.6	3.4	3.3	3.3	3.2	3.2	3.2
Infant Mortality Rate	19.5	18.0	18.0	18.0	17.8	17.5	15.5	15.5	14.9	12.8	11.1
Life Expectancy at Birth	71.1	71.1	71.3	71.4	71.6	71.7	71.9	72.0	72.2	72.5	72.7
Urban Population, % of total	51.7	52.1	52.5	52.8	53.2	53.6	53.9	54.3	54.6	55.0	55.3
Food Prod. per capita (1987=100)	72.8	81.6	77.8	73.9	84.5	96.1	84.0	93.8	99.4	89.7	97.9
Labor Force, Agriculture (%)	26.3	25.5	24.7	23.9	23.1	22.4	21.6	20.8	20.0	19.3	18.6
Labor Force, Female (%)	26.3	26.5	26.8	27.0	27.2	27.5	27.6	27.7	27.8	28.0	28.1
Primary Schl. Enroll. Ratio	106.0	..	..	..	..	103.0	106.0	105.0	104.0	100.0	100.0
Primary Schl. Enroll. Ratio, Female	106.0	..	..	..	..	103.0	105.0	105.0	104.0	100.0	100.0
Secondary Schl. Enroll. Ratio	74.0	..	..	..	..	86.0	91.0	92.0	92.0	90.0	90.0

1981	1982	1983	1984	1985	1986	1987	1988	1989	1990 estimate	Notes	IRELAND
											FOREIGN TRADE (CUSTOMS BASIS)
7,784	8,060	8,609	9,627	10,399	12,604	15,970	18,736	20,693	23,796	..	Value of Exports, fob
2,913	2,782	2,772	2,907	3,016	3,732	4,900	5,461	5,645	5,984	..	Nonfuel Primary Products
51	51	99	116	132	98	115	103	103	156	..	Fuels
4,820	5,227	5,737	6,604	7,251	8,773	10,955	13,173	14,945	17,656	..	Manufactures
10,595	9,696	9,169	9,658	10,049	11,564	13,614	15,558	17,419	20,716	..	Value of Imports, cif
1,846	1,610	1,591	1,634	1,700	2,020	2,272	2,582	2,657	3,065	..	Nonfuel Primary Products
1,556	1,435	1,237	1,198	1,195	981	1,005	868	962	1,339	..	Fuels
7,193	6,651	6,342	6,825	7,154	8,563	10,336	12,108	13,800	16,312	..	Manufactures
				(Index 1987 = 100)							
96.3	78.3	80.7	82.7	97.1	100.5	100.0	101.4	100.1	95.4	..	Terms of Trade
90.8	69.6	70.1	69.8	80.0	91.6	100.0	111.4	120.7	127.6	..	Export Prices, fob
94.3	88.9	86.8	84.5	82.4	91.2	100.0	109.9	120.5	133.7	..	Import Prices, cif
				(Millions of current US dollars)							**BALANCE OF PAYMENTS**
9,681	9,864	10,197	11,249	12,189	14,864	18,617	21,926	24,376	28,929	..	Exports of Goods & Services
7,696	7,933	8,438	9,421	10,131	12,365	15,569	18,392	20,355	23,359	..	Merchandise, fob
1,209	1,219	1,174	1,166	1,302	1,621	2,029	2,260	2,354	3,110	..	Nonfactor Services
776	712	584	663	756	878	1,020	1,274	1,667	2,460	..	Factor Services
13,120	12,633	12,242	13,086	13,925	16,837	19,552	22,821	25,429	30,112	..	Imports of Goods & Services
9,950	9,096	8,690	9,183	9,500	11,224	12,948	14,563	16,348	19,382	..	Merchandise, fob
1,435	1,375	1,372	1,372	1,471	1,966	2,522	2,955	2,962	3,489	..	Nonfactor Services
1,734	2,162	2,179	2,531	2,954	3,647	4,083	5,302	6,120	7,242	..	Factor Services
..	..	..	..	..	..	..	..	..	..		Long-Term Interest
97	91	57	-33	-21	-61	-162	-121	-94	-66	..	Private Current Transfers, net
..	..	..	..	..	..	..	..	..	..		Workers' Remittances
-3,342	-2,677	-1,988	-1,870	-1,757	-2,034	-1,098	-1,016	-1,147	-1,249	..	Curr. A/C Bal before Off. Transf.
741	743	769	833	1,068	1,352	1,471	1,659	1,671	2,683	..	Net Official Transfers
-2,601	-1,935	-1,219	-1,038	-690	-682	373	644	524	1,433	..	Curr. A/C Bal after Off. Transf.
1,690	1,661	995	800	835	1,050	827	-261	-1,215	-3,001	..	Long-Term Capital, net
203	242	170	121	164	-43	89	92	85	99	..	Direct Investment
..	..	..	..	..	..	..	..	..	..		Long-Term Loans
..	..	..	..	..	..	..	..	..	..		Disbursements
..	..	..	..	..	..	..	..	..	..		Repayments
1,486	1,419	825	679	672	1,093	738	-352	-1,300	-3,100	..	Other Long-Term Capital
904	395	412	195	-97	-464	-315	211	-247	2,317	..	Other Capital, net
8	-121	-188	43	-48	96	-885	-593	937	-750	..	Change in Reserves
				(Irish Pounds per US dollar)							**Memo Item:**
0.620	0.700	0.800	0.920	0.950	0.740	0.670	0.660	0.710	0.600	..	Conversion Factor (Annual Avg)
				(Millions US dollars), outstanding at end of year							
..	..	..	..	..	..	..	..	..	..	..	**EXTERNAL DEBT (Total)**
..	..	..	..	..	..	..	..	..	..	..	Long-Term Debt (by debtor)
..	..	..	..	..	..	..	..	..	..	..	Central Bank, incl. IMF credit
..	..	..	..	..	..	..	..	..	..	..	Central Government
..	..	..	..	..	..	..	..	..	..	..	Rest of General Government
..	..	..	..	..	..	..	..	..	..	..	Non-financial Public Enterprises
..	..	..	..	..	..	..	..	..	..	..	Priv. Sector, incl non-guaranteed
..	..	..	..	..	..	..	..	..	..	..	Short-Term Debt
				(Millions of US dollars)							**Memo Items:**
2,651.3	2,622.1	2,639.6	2,352.4	2,939.6	3,236.3	4,796.2	5,086.8	4,057.4	5,223.4	..	Int'l Reserves Excluding Gold
142.6	164.3	137.1	110.8	117.5	140.5	173.9	147.4	144.0	138.3	..	Gold Holdings (at market price)
											SOCIAL INDICATORS
3.1	3.0	2.8	2.6	2.5	2.4	2.3	2.3	2.2	2.2	..	Total Fertility Rate
10.3	10.5	10.1	9.6	8.8	8.9	7.9	7.7	7.4	7.2	..	Infant Mortality Rate
72.9	73.1	73.2	73.4	73.5	73.6	73.8	74.0	74.2	74.4	..	Life Expectancy at Birth
55.5	55.7	55.9	56.1	56.3	56.5	56.6	56.8	56.9	57.1	..	Urban Population, % of total
81.8	87.6	91.1	98.2	98.7	99.9	100.0	95.9	94.5	102.5	..	Food Prod. per capita (1987=100)
..	..	..	..	..	..	..	..	..	..	..	Labor Force, Agriculture (%)
28.3	28.4	28.6	28.8	28.9	29.0	29.1	29.2	29.3	29.4	..	Labor Force, Female (%)
99.0	100.0	99.0	100.0	100.0	101.0	101.0	101.0	..	..	..	Primary Schl. Enroll. Ratio
100.0	100.0	99.0	100.0	100.0	101.0	101.0	101.0	..	..	..	Primary Schl. Enroll. Ratio, Female
92.0	94.0	96.0	97.0	98.0	98.0	98.0	97.0	..	..	..	Secondary Schl. Enroll. Ratio

ISRAEL	1970	1971	1972	1973	1974	1975	1976	1977	1978	1979	1980
CURRENT GNP PER CAPITA (US $)	1,830	2,090	2,440	2,670	3,320	3,890	4,080	4,090	4,260	4,740	5,400
POPULATION (thousands)	2,974	3,069	3,148	3,278	3,377	3,455	3,533	3,613	3,690	3,786	3,878

USE AND ORIGIN OF RESOURCES *(Millions of current Israel New Sheqalims)*

	1970	1971	1972	1973	1974	1975	1976	1977	1978	1979	1980
Gross National Product (GNP)	2.00E+0	2.00E+0	3.00E+0	4.00E+0	6.00E+0	8.00E+0	1.10E+1	1.50E+1	25	47	112
Net Factor Income from Abroad	-3.52E-2	-4.28E-2	-5.70E-2	-1.11E-1	-1.57E-1	-2.80E-1	-3.52E-1	-3.60E-1	-1	-2	-4
GDP at Market Prices	2.00E+0	2.00E+0	3.00E+0	4.00E+0	6.00E+0	8.00E+0	1.10E+1	1.60E+1	26	49	116
Resource Balance	-3.83E-1	-3.95E-1	-3.64E-1	-9.63E-1	-1.00E+0	-2.00E+0	-2.00E+0	-2.00E+0	-4	-7	-13
Exports of Goods & NF Services	4.88E-1	6.80E-1	8.68E-1	1.00E+0	2.00E+0	2.00E+0	3.00E+0	6.00E+0	11	19	46
Imports of Goods & NF Services	8.71E-1	1.00E+0	1.00E+0	2.00E+0	3.00E+0	4.00E+0	5.00E+0	7.00E+0	15	26	59
Domestic Absorption	2.00E+0	3.00E+0	4.00E+0	5.00E+0	7.00E+0	1.10E+1	1.30E+1	1.80E+1	30	56	129
Private Consumption, etc.	1.00E+0	1.00E+0	2.00E+0	2.00E+0	3.00E+0	5.00E+0	6.00E+0	9.00E+0	15	28	59
General Gov't Consumption	6.73E-1	7.94E-1	9.29E-1	2.00E+0	2.00E+0	3.00E+0	4.00E+0	5.00E+0	9	15	45
Gross Domestic Investment	5.37E-1	7.43E-1	9.73E-1	1.00E+0	2.00E+0	2.00E+0	3.00E+0	4.00E+0	6	12	25
Fixed Investment	5.02E-1	6.94E-1	9.19E-1	1.00E+0	2.00E+0	2.00E+0	3.00E+0	3.00E+0	6	12	24
Indirect Taxes, net	..			..							..
GDP at factor cost	..		..		..				..		
Agriculture	1.03E-1	1.26E-1	1.51E-1	1.86E-1	2.85E-1	3.98E-1	5.68E-1	7.76E-1	1	2	5
Industry	5.89E-1	7.45E-1	9.71E-1	1.00E+0	2.00E+0	2.00E+0	3.00E+0	4.00E+0	8	14	24
Manufacturing	..	..	..								
Services, etc.	..										
Gross Domestic Saving	1.54E-1	3.47E-1	6.09E-1	3.27E-1	5.02E-1	4.15E-1	7.80E-1	2.00E+0	2	5	12
Gross National Saving	2.75E-1	5.13E-1	8.48E-1	6.94E-1	6.74E-1	6.16E-1	1.00E+0	2.00E+0	3	6	14

(Millions of 1987 Israel New Sheqalims)

	1970	1971	1972	1973	1974	1975	1976	1977	1978	1979	1980
Gross National Product	26,561.2	29,544.7	33,666.9	34,496.7	36,884.1	37,928.9	38,409.1	38,764.4	40,524.0	42,792.1	46,040.1
GDP at Market Prices	27,339.7	30,408.4	34,562.5	35,717.7	38,160.7	39,427.2	39,946.0	39,942.8	41,868.4	44,500.0	47,557.7
Resource Balance	-5,174.7	-4,985.2	-4,016.3	-8,290.5	-7,479.2	-8,256.0	-6,343.1	-4,705.7	-5,657.9	-5,110.3	-3,167.4
Exports of Goods & NF Services	6,071.9	7,535.3	8,514.4	8,980.9	9,499.1	9,667.7	11,168.8	12,394.2	13,056.6	13,512.6	14,286.1
Imports of Goods & NF Services	11,246.5	12,520.5	12,530.7	17,271.4	16,978.3	17,923.7	17,511.9	17,099.9	18,714.6	18,622.9	17,453.4
Domestic Absorption	32,514.4	35,393.6	38,578.7	44,008.3	45,639.9	47,683.1	46,289.1	44,648.5	47,526.4	49,610.3	50,725.0
Private Consumption, etc.	13,880.0	14,872.8	16,843.5	16,870.6	18,609.9	18,456.6	19,959.2	21,423.3	22,911.8	25,078.6	23,382.0
General Gov't Consumption	10,614.1	10,752.1	10,547.4	15,326.5	15,751.0	17,354.6	15,664.1	13,565.1	14,700.5	13,427.4	17,649.1
Gross Domestic Investment	8,020.2	9,768.8	11,187.8	11,811.2	11,279.0	11,872.0	10,665.7	9,660.1	9,914.1	11,104.3	9,693.9
Fixed Investment	7,540.8	9,164.9	10,426.7	11,541.4	11,179.9	11,225.2	10,020.4	8,879.1	9,388.9	10,525.8	9,647.8
GDP at factor cost	..	..	..	..	..		..		..	..	
Agriculture	..			..						..	
Industry	..	..	..		..		..		..	..	
Manufacturing	..										
Services, etc.	..	..	..							..	

Memo Items:

	1970	1971	1972	1973	1974	1975	1976	1977	1978	1979	1980
Capacity to Import	6,302.9	7,918.3	8,828.4	9,150.1	9,306.7	9,355.1	11,111.1	12,817.5	13,532.2	13,550.9	13,687.3
Terms of Trade Adjustment	231.0	383.0	314.0	169.3	-192.4	-312.6	-57.7	423.3	475.5	38.2	-598.8
Gross Domestic Income	27,570.7	30,791.4	34,876.5	35,887.0	37,968.3	39,114.6	39,888.3	40,366.1	42,344.0	44,538.2	46,958.9
Gross National Income	26,792.2	29,927.7	33,980.9	34,666.0	36,691.7	37,616.3	38,351.4	39,187.7	40,999.5	42,830.3	45,441.3

DOMESTIC PRICES/DEFLATORS *(Index 1987 = 100)*

	1970	1971	1972	1973	1974	1975	1976	1977	1978	1979	1980
Overall (GDP)	0.01	0.01	0.01	0.01	0.02	0.02	0.03	0.04	0.06	0.11	0.24
Domestic Absorption	0.01	0.01	0.01	0.01	0.02	0.02	0.03	0.04	0.06	0.11	0.25
Agriculture	..	..	..		..				..	..	..
Industry	..								..		..
Manufacturing	..		..								..
Consumer Price Index	..								..	..	..

MANUFACTURING ACTIVITY

	1970	1971	1972	1973	1974	1975	1976	1977	1978	1979	1980
Employment (1987=100)	67.5	71.8	75.8	80.3	82.2	80.9	81.5	82.9	85.6	89.5	85.5
Real Earnings per Empl. (1987=100)	41.8	42.4	45.0	42.3	41.7	47.9	53.0	55.7	53.6	95.6	108.1
Real Output per Empl. (1987=100)	..	..	..						..	..	..
Earnings as % of Value Added	36.2	36.7	36.9	36.5	33.4	35.4	37.5	36.4	24.0	51.1	53.5

MONETARY HOLDINGS *(Millions of current Israel New Sheqalims)*

	1970	1971	1972	1973	1974	1975	1976	1977	1978	1979	1980
Money Supply, Broadly Defined	0.27	0.16	2.00	3.00	3.00	4.00	7.00	11.00	19	38	93
Money	0.13	0.16	0.20	1.00	1.00	1.00	2.00	2.00	3	3	8
Currency Outside Banks	0.13	0.16	0.20	0.28	0.33	0.42	0.51	0.69	1	1	3
Demand Deposits	0.00	0.00	0.00	1.00	1.00	1.00	1.00	1.00	2	2	5
Quasi-Money	0.14	0.00	2.00	2.00	2.00	3.00	5.00	9.00	16	35	85

GOVERNMENT DEFICIT (-) OR SURPLUS *(Millions of current Israel New Sheqalims)*

	1970	1971	1972	1973	1974	1975	1976	1977	1978	1979	1980
GOVERNMENT DEFICIT (-) OR SURPLUS	..	..	-0.5	-0.8	-1.0	-2.0	-2.0	-3.0	-3.0	-7.0	-18.0
Current Revenue	..	..	1.0	2.0	3.0	4.0	6.0	9.0	14.0	31.0	70.0
Current Expenditure	..	..	1.0	2.0	3.0	5.0	7.0	10.0	15.0	32.0	78.0
Current Budget Balance	..	..	-0.3	-0.5	-0.7	-0.7	-0.8	-1.0	-0.7	-2.0	-8.0
Capital Receipts	..	..									
Capital Payments	..	..	0.2	0.3	0.6	0.9	1.0	1.0	2.0	5.0	10.0

1981	1982	1983	1984	1985	1986	1987	1988	1989	1990 estimate	Notes	ISRAEL
6,250	6,510	6,780	6,680	6,570	6,780	7,590	8,970	9,790	10,920	..	**CURRENT GNP PER CAPITA (US $)**
3,956	4,031	4,105	4,170	4,233	4,305	4,375	4,431	4,509	4,659	..	**POPULATION (thousands)**
											USE AND ORIGIN OF RESOURCES
				(Millions of current Israel New Sheqalims)							
270	621	1,604	7,710	29,133	46,244	59,295	71,748	86,022	105,000	f	Gross National Product (GNP)
-6	-14	-35	-333	-1,129	-1,522	-1,817	-1,801	-2,191	-2,634		Net Factor Income from Abroad
276	635	1,639	8,043	30,262	47,766	61,112	73,549	88,213	107,000	f	GDP at Market Prices
-35	-76	-177	-696	-2,022	-2,541	-5,609	-4,696	-3,293	-6,795	..	Resource Balance
106	213	508	2,886	12,123	16,759	21,383	23,488	30,238	34,063	..	Exports of Goods & NF Services
141	289	686	3,582	14,145	19,300	26,992	28,184	33,531	40,858	f	Imports of Goods & NF Services
311	712	1,816	8,739	32,284	50,307	66,721	78,245	91,506	114,000	..	Domestic Absorption
145	343	909	4,158	16,544	27,732	36,071	43,284	51,679	63,172	..	Private Consumption, etc.
110	229	547	2,925	10,475	13,946	19,755	22,820	25,953	31,464	..	General Gov't Consumption
56	140	360	1,656	5,265	8,629	10,895	12,141	13,874	19,425	..	Gross Domestic Investment
58	135	355	1,556	5,275	7,871	10,967	12,467	13,856	18,396	..	Fixed Investment
..	..	..	..	..	..	..	..	..	..	..	Indirect Taxes, net
										..	GDP at factor cost
12	20	45	250	1,062	1,509	1,753	1,757	..	..	..	Agriculture
64	146	371	1,853	6,385	9,135	12,028	14,314			..	Industry
..	..	..	..	..	..	..	..	..	..	..	Manufacturing
..	..	..	..	..	..	..	..	..	..	..	Services, etc.
21	64	183	960	3,243	6,088	5,286	7,445	10,581	12,630	..	Gross Domestic Saving
29	71	193	852	3,088	6,326	5,652	7,475	11,412	13,992	..	Gross National Saving
				(Millions of 1987 Israel New Sheqalims)							
48,916.5	49,820.2	51,581.3	50,959.3	52,994.7	55,556.5	59,295.0	60,545.2	60,792.3	64,099.9	f	Gross National Product
50,006.1	50,910.5	52,697.8	53,174.0	55,007.6	57,393.2	61,112.0	62,099.7	62,352.0	65,721.1	f	GDP at Market Prices
-4,109.0	-5,230.8	-6,064.4	-4,112.5	-2,516.8	-3,353.1	-5,609.0	-5,421.5	-2,871.5	-4,511.8	..	Resource Balance
14,984.0	14,533.3	14,860.6	16,896.0	18,335.2	19,297.7	21,383.0	20,908.6	21,836.7	22,062.4	..	Exports of Goods & NF Services
19,093.0	19,764.1	20,925.0	21,008.6	20,852.0	22,650.8	26,992.0	26,330.1	24,708.1	26,574.2	..	Imports of Goods & NF Services
54,115.1	56,141.3	58,762.2	57,286.5	57,524.5	60,746.3	66,721.0	67,521.2	65,223.5	70,233.0	..	Domestic Absorption
26,132.9	27,961.6	30,233.8	28,586.8	29,249.5	33,281.6	36,071.0	37,439.1	37,154.0	39,007.8	..	Private Consumption, etc.
18,795.0	17,636.7	16,927.8	17,924.6	18,643.3	16,874.1	19,755.0	19,392.0	17,666.6	18,330.9	..	General Gov't Consumption
9,187.2	10,542.9	11,600.6	10,775.1	9,630.7	10,590.6	10,895.0	10,690.0	10,402.8	12,894.3	..	Gross Domestic Investment
10,034.6	10,544.5	11,874.1	10,533.8	9,715.2	9,658.9	10,967.0	10,916.7	10,319.1	11,969.6	..	Fixed Investment
										..	GDP at factor cost
..	..	..	..	..	..	..	..	..	..	..	Agriculture
..	..	..	..	..	..	..	..	..	..	..	Industry
..	..	..	..	..	..	..	..	..	..	..	Manufacturing
..	..	..	..	..	..	..	..	..	..	..	Services, etc.
											Memo Items:
14,356.7	14,540.0	15,510.9	16,926.5	17,871.2	19,668.6	21,383.0	21,943.0	22,281.6	22,154.7	..	Capacity to Import
-627.3	6.7	650.3	30.5	-463.9	371.0	0.0	1,034.4	444.9	92.3	..	Terms of Trade Adjustment
49,378.8	50,917.2	53,348.1	53,204.4	54,543.7	57,764.2	61,112.0	63,134.1	62,796.9	65,813.5	..	Gross Domestic Income
48,289.2	49,826.9	52,231.6	50,989.8	52,530.8	55,927.5	59,295.0	61,579.6	61,237.2	64,192.2	..	Gross National Income
											DOMESTIC PRICES/DEFLATORS
				(Index 1987 = 100)							
0.55	1.20	3.10	15.10	55.00	83.20	100.00	118.40	141.50	163.20	..	Overall (GDP)
0.57	1.30	3.10	15.30	56.10	82.80	100.00	115.90	140.30	162.40	..	Domestic Absorption
..	..	..	..	..	..	..	..	..	..	..	Agriculture
..	..	..	..	..	..	..	..	..	..	..	Industry
..	..	..	..	..	..	..	..	..	..	..	Manufacturing
..	..	..	..	..	..	..	..	..	..	..	Consumer Price Index
											MANUFACTURING ACTIVITY
87.8	91.2	93.4	93.4	96.7	96.9	100.0	95.0	89.2	..	J	Employment (1987=100)
111.0	113.1	136.6	70.6	110.0	69.8	100.0	78.3	..	..	J	Real Earnings per Empl. (1987=100)
..	..	..	..	..	..	..	..	..	..	..	Real Output per Empl. (1987=100)
52.0	64.3	65.6	51.3	58.7	39.8	63.3	42.7	..	..	J	Earnings as % of Value Added
											MONETARY HOLDINGS
				(Millions of current Israel New Sheqalims)							
224	543	1,671	10,190	27,361	33,039	42,037	51,390	62,216	74,303	..	Money Supply, Broadly Defined
13	28	68	305	1,051	2,238	3,346	3,723	5,374	7,023	..	Money
4	9	25	123	481	974	1,365	1,643	2,224	2,817	..	Currency Outside Banks
9	20	43	182	570	1,264	1,981	2,080	3,150	4,206	..	Demand Deposits
211	515	1,603	9,885	26,310	30,801	38,691	47,667	56,842	67,280	..	Quasi-Money
				(Millions of current Israel New Sheqalims)							
-58.0	-101.0	-412.0	-1,440.0	-951.0	333.0	-2,000.0	-5,897.0	-3,512.0	-4,540.0	C	**GOVERNMENT DEFICIT (-) OR SURPLUS**
158.0	381.0	1,108.0	5,791.0	20,949.0	29,104.0	33,055.0	34,355.0	40,336.0	49,293.0	..	Current Revenue
190.0	424.0	1,319.0	6,587.0	19,267.0	25,792.0	31,548.0	33,868.0	40,705.0	50,001.0	..	Current Expenditure
-32.0	-42.0	-211.0	-796.0	1,682.0	3,312.0	1,507.0	488.0	-369.0	-709.0	..	Current Budget Balance
..	..	..	..	..	..	..	247.0	..	500.0	..	Capital Receipts
26.0	58.0	202.0	644.0	2,634.0	2,979.0	3,507.0	6,631.0	3,143.0	4,332.0	..	Capital Payments

ISRAEL	1970	1971	1972	1973	1974	1975	1976	1977	1978	1979	1980
FOREIGN TRADE (CUSTOMS BASIS)					*(Millions of current US dollars)*						
Value of Exports, fob	776	960	1,149	1,509	1,825	1,941	2,416	3,083	3,924	4,553	5,540
Nonfuel Primary Products	229	263	286	320	394	455	535	630	730	898	988
Fuels	0	0	0	0	0	0	0	0	0	1	1
Manufactures	547	697	863	1,189	1,431	1,486	1,880	2,453	3,195	3,654	4,551
Value of Imports, cif	1,451	1,808	1,973	2,988	4,237	4,173	4,132	4,845	5,871	7,448	8,023
Nonfuel Primary Products	326	372	390	593	862	926	848	948	1,030	1,345	1,348
Fuels	71	90	98	209	630	639	682	739	776	1,339	2,124
Manufactures	1,054	1,345	1,485	2,186	2,745	2,608	2,603	3,158	4,064	4,764	4,551
					(Index 1987 = 100)						
Terms of Trade	159.7	154.7	135.9	134.2	128.8	131.3	126.8	120.6	116.2	116.2	111.1
Export Prices, fob	39.6	42.3	40.9	48.0	67.9	71.4	70.4	73.0	78.5	93.0	106.3
Import Prices, cif	24.8	27.3	30.1	35.8	52.7	54.4	55.5	60.6	67.6	80.0	95.7
BALANCE OF PAYMENTS					*(Millions of current US dollars)*						
Exports of Goods & Services	1,402	1,874	2,120	2,697	3,563	3,688	4,397	5,459	6,619	8,075	9,858
Merchandise, fob	808	1,002	1,219	1,563	2,004	2,178	2,669	3,403	4,074	4,802	5,870
Nonfactor Services	498	703	709	821	1,109	1,083	1,299	1,557	1,921	2,278	2,709
Factor Services	96	169	192	313	450	427	429	499	624	995	1,279
Imports of Goods & Services	2,614	3,096	3,219	5,263	6,756	7,537	7,466	7,818	9,712	11,590	13,458
Merchandise, fob	1,931	2,205	2,287	3,965	4,995	5,520	5,248	5,364	6,693	7,884	8,976
Nonfactor Services	438	593	549	759	967	1,079	1,269	1,462	1,780	2,068	2,241
Factor Services	245	298	383	539	794	938	949	992	1,239	1,638	2,241
Long-Term Interest	..	..	..	..	..	..	..	..	..	..	..
Private Current Transfers, net	446	550	708	1,139	740	759	776	803	825	1,001	1,060
Workers' Remittances	..	..	..	..	..	..	..	..	..	..	..
Curr. A/C Bal before Off. Transf.	-766	-672	-391	-1,427	-2,453	-3,090	-2,293	-1,556	-2,268	-2,514	-2,540
Net Official Transfers	204	240	341	1,050	990	1,332	1,657	1,269	1,400	1,836	1,965
Curr. A/C Bal after Off. Transf.	-562	-432	-50	-377	-1,463	-1,758	-636	-287	-868	-678	-575
Long-Term Capital, net	677	626	731	999	601	1,027	1,234	1,005	1,016	1,254	1,237
Direct Investment	40	53	114	149	84	43	41	75	32	10	48
Long-Term Loans	..	..	..	..	..	..	..	..	..	..	..
Disbursements	..	..	..	..	..	..	..	..	..	..	..
Repayments	..	..	..	..	..	..	..	..	..	..	..
Other Long-Term Capital	637	573	617	850	517	984	1,193	930	984	1,244	1,189
Other Capital, net	-108	17	-133	-74	20	575	-414	-504	797	-365	-121
Change in Reserves	-7	-211	-548	-548	842	156	-184	-214	-945	-211	-541
Memo Item:					*(Israel New Sheqalims per US dollar)*						
Conversion Factor (Annual Avg)	0.00035	0.00038	0.00042	0.00042	0.00045	0.00063	0.00079	0.00104	0.00174	0.00254	0.00512
				(Millions of US dollars), outstanding at end of year							
EXTERNAL DEBT (Total)	..	..	..	..	..	..	..	..	..	..	..
Long-Term Debt (by debtor)	..	..	..	..	..	..	..	..	..	..	..
Central Bank, incl. IMF credit	..	..	..	..	..	..	..	..	..	..	..
Central Government	..	..	..	..	..	..	..	..	..	..	..
Rest of General Government	..	..	..	..	..	..	..	..	..	..	..
Non-financial Public Enterprises	..	..	..	..	..	..	..	..	..	..	..
Priv. Sector, incl non-guaranteed	..	..	..	..	..	..	..	..	..	..	..
Short-Term Debt	..	..	..	..	..	..	..	..	..	..	..
Memo Items:					*(Millions of US dollars)*						
Int'l Reserves Excluding Gold	405.20	689.80	1,178.90	1,768.30	1,153.40	1,137.10	1,328.30	1,521.60	2,625.10	3,063.50	3,351.40
Gold Holdings (at market price)	46.30	54.10	74.20	123.10	205.00	154.40	148.60	192.00	264.60	630.30	703.90
SOCIAL INDICATORS											
Total Fertility Rate	3.8	3.8	3.8	3.7	3.6	3.6	3.5	3.4	3.4	3.3	3.2
Infant Mortality Rate	25.3	23.0	24.2	22.8	23.4	22.9	20.1	18.1	16.3	15.9	15.1
Life Expectancy at Birth	71.2	71.7	71.1	71.7	71.7	72.0	73.0	73.2	73.1	73.0	72.9
Urban Population, % of total	84.2	84.7	85.2	85.6	86.1	86.6	87.0	87.4	87.8	88.2	88.6
Food Prod. per capita (1987=100)	91.4	98.9	106.6	100.5	105.8	106.6	106.7	107.0	106.0	99.5	95.8
Labor Force, Agriculture (%)	9.7	9.3	8.9	8.6	8.2	7.9	7.6	7.2	6.9	6.5	6.2
Labor Force, Female (%)	30.0	30.4	30.8	31.1	31.5	31.8	32.2	32.5	32.8	33.2	33.5
Primary Schl. Enroll. Ratio	96.0	..	..	..	..	97.0	96.0	97.0	96.0	96.0	95.0
Primary Schl. Enroll. Ratio, Female	95.0	..	..	..	..	97.0	97.0	97.0	97.0	97.0	..
Secondary Schl. Enroll. Ratio	57.0	..	..	..	..	66.0	66.0	67.0	68.0	71.0	73.0

1981	1982	1983	1984	1985	1986	1987	1988	1989	1990 estimate	Notes	ISRAEL
											FOREIGN TRADE (CUSTOMS BASIS)
					(Millions of current US dollars)						
5,664	5,280	5,112	5,803	6,256	7,135	8,475	9,734	10,735	12,047	..	Value of Exports, fob
1,074	1,034	989	1,065	1,044	1,083	1,237	1,295	1,318	1,518	..	Nonfuel Primary Products
0	0	0	1	1	1	1	55	61	80	..	Fuels
4,590	4,246	4,122	4,738	5,212	6,052	7,236	8,384	9,357	10,449	..	Manufactures
7,894	8,013	8,500	8,289	8,184	9,481	11,752	12,874	13,101	15,197	..	Value of Imports, cif
1,492	1,305	1,249	1,321	1,222	1,333	1,486	1,751	1,860	1,969	..	Nonfuel Primary Products
2,049	1,858	1,495	1,450	1,343	764	997	925	1,087	1,344	..	Fuels
4,354	4,850	5,755	5,518	5,619	7,384	9,269	10,198	10,154	11,884	..	Manufactures
					(Index 1987 = 100)						
105.4	106.7	105.9	105.0	104.6	103.1	100.0	102.7	102.0	103.0	..	Terms of Trade
102.2	97.7	95.4	92.5	90.7	92.7	100.0	107.4	113.9	123.8	..	Export Prices, fob
97.0	91.5	90.1	88.1	86.7	89.9	100.0	104.6	111.6	120.2	..	Import Prices, cif
											BALANCE OF PAYMENTS
					(Millions of current US dollars)						
10,556	10,370	10,276	10,644	10,960	11,920	14,093	15,567	16,880	18,495	..	Exports of Goods & Services
6,027	5,667	5,655	6,319	6,751	7,839	9,310	10,355	11,169	12,260	..	Merchandise, fob
2,700	2,565	2,732	2,846	3,064	2,966	3,596	3,839	4,103	4,379	..	Nonfactor Services
1,829	2,138	1,889	1,479	1,145	1,115	1,187	1,373	1,608	1,856	..	Factor Services
14,613	14,728	14,925	15,206	14,838	15,655	19,725	20,739	20,639	23,582	..	Imports of Goods & Services
9,468	8,844	8,804	8,820	9,115	9,711	13,030	13,424	12,933	15,150	..	Merchandise, fob
2,539	2,823	3,032	3,040	2,650	2,921	3,514	3,937	4,350	4,902	..	Nonfactor Services
2,606	3,061	3,089	3,346	3,073	3,023	3,181	3,378	3,356	3,530	..	Factor Services
..	..	..	..	..	..	..	..	..	..		Long-Term Interest
1,313	880	809	767	826	1,183	1,369	1,145	1,577	1,982	..	Private Current Transfers, net
..	..	..	..	..	..	..	..	..	..		Workers' Remittances
-2,744	-3,478	-3,840	-3,795	-3,052	-2,552	-4,263	-4,027	-2,182	-3,105	..	Curr. A/C Bal before Off. Transf.
1,787	1,583	1,899	2,514	4,172	4,197	3,400	3,370	3,286	3,807	..	Net Official Transfers
-957	-1,895	-1,941	-1,281	1,120	1,645	-863	-657	1,104	702	..	Curr. A/C Bal after Off. Transf.
1,144	1,119	2,342	1,066	-69	347	430	-628	-15	-568	..	Long-Term Capital, net
4	-122	-31	19	48	46	173	133	105	-137	..	Direct Investment
..	..	..	..	..	..	..	..	..	..		Long-Term Loans
..	..	..	..	..	..	..	..	..	..		Disbursements
..	..	..	..	..	..	..	..	..	..		Repayments
1,140	1,241	2,373	1,047	-117	301	257	-761	-120	-431	..	Other Long-Term Capital
363	1,690	-900	-293	-660	-1,000	1,094	123	307	425	..	Other Capital, net
-550	-914	499	508	-391	-992	-661	1,162	-1,396	-559	..	Change in Reserves
											Memo Item:
				(Israel New Sheqalims per US dollar)							
0.01140	0.02430	0.05620	0.29300	1.18000	1.49000	1.59000	1.60000	1.92000	2.02000	..	Conversion Factor (Annual Avg)
			(Millions of US dollars), outstanding at end of year								
..	..	..	..	..	..	..	..	..	..		**EXTERNAL DEBT (Total)**
..	..	..	..	..	..	..	..	..	..		Long-Term Debt (by debtor)
..	..	..	..	..	..	..	..	..	..	..	Central Bank, incl. IMF credit
..	..	..	..	..	..	..	..	..	..		Central Government
..	..	..	..	..	..	..	..	..	..		Rest of General Government
..	..	..	..	..	..	..	..	..	..		Non-financial Public Enterprises
..	..	..	..	..	..	..	..	..	..		Priv. Sector, incl non-guaranteed
..	..	..	..	..	..	..	..	..	..	..	Short-Term Debt
											Memo Items:
					(Millions of US dollars)						
3,496.70	3,839.30	3,651.20	3,060.30	3,680.20	4,659.60	5,876.10	4,015.60	5,276.20	6,275.10		Int'l Reserves Excluding Gold
474.20	495.30	387.20	313.50	332.60	397.50	492.30	417.60	407.80	323.00		Gold Holdings (at market price)
											SOCIAL INDICATORS
3.2	3.1	3.1	3.1	3.1	3.0	3.0	2.9	2.9	2.8	..	Total Fertility Rate
15.5	13.9	14.4	12.8	12.3	11.4	11.4	11.0	10.6	10.2	..	Infant Mortality Rate
73.7	74.5	74.7	74.9	75.1	75.3	75.6	75.8	76.0	76.2	..	Life Expectancy at Birth
88.9	89.3	89.6	90.0	90.3	90.6	90.8	91.1	91.3	91.6	..	Urban Population, % of total
93.0	99.0	103.7	100.5	101.1	92.7	100.0	91.6	90.8	90.6	..	Food Prod. per capita (1987=100)
..	..	..	..	..	..	..	..	..	..		Labor Force, Agriculture (%)
33.5	33.5	33.5	33.5	33.5	33.5	33.6	33.6	33.6	33.7	..	Labor Force, Female (%)
..	97.0	98.0	97.0	97.0	95.0	96.0	97.0	93.0	..	..	Primary Schl. Enroll. Ratio
..	97.0	99.0	99.0	98.0	97.0	97.0	97.0	95.0	..	..	Primary Schl. Enroll. Ratio, Female
..	73.0	74.0	81.0	80.0	83.0	83.0	82.0	83.0	..	..	Secondary Schl. Enroll. Ratio

ITALY	1970	1971	1972	1973	1974	1975	1976	1977	1978	1979	1980
CURRENT GNP PER CAPITA (US $)	2,000	2,150	2,380	2,840	3,370	3,690	4,030	4,390	4,890	6,080	7,480
POPULATION (thousands)	53,822	54,074	54,381	54,751	55,111	55,441	55,718	55,955	56,155	56,318	56,434

USE AND ORIGIN OF RESOURCES					*(Billions of current Italian Lire)*						
Gross National Product (GNP)	67,489	73,332	80,146	97,009	122,094	138,213	174,355	214,175	253,515	310,679	388,459
Net Factor Income from Abroad	311	338	336	271	-96	-419	-514	-223	-21	845	790
GDP at Market Prices	67,178	72,994	79,810	96,738	122,190	138,632	174,869	214,398	253,536	309,834	387,669
Resource Balance	62	502	590	-1,958	-5,074	-88	-2,028	2,299	5,673	3,423	-10,469
Exports of Goods & NFServices	11,041	12,355	14,110	16,833	24,637	28,467	38,563	49,838	59,392	75,153	84,953
Imports of Goods & NFServices	10,979	11,853	13,520	18,791	29,711	28,555	40,591	47,539	53,719	71,730	95,422
Domestic Absorption	67,116	72,492	79,220	98,696	127,264	138,720	176,897	212,099	247,863	306,411	398,138
Private Consumption, etc.	39,992	43,660	47,951	58,484	73,637	85,972	106,383	129,209	150,848	185,051	236,603
General Gov't Consumption	8,709	10,634	12,082	13,936	16,805	19,563	23,438	29,529	35,850	44,962	57,013
Gross Domestic Investment	18,415	18,198	19,187	26,276	36,822	33,185	47,076	53,361	61,165	76,398	104,522
Fixed Investment	16,532	17,475	18,465	24,063	31,664	34,568	41,776	50,323	57,657	70,767	94,062
Indirect Taxes, net	5,830	6,076	6,110	7,181	9,011	6,894	10,240	13,543	15,356	16,618	22,496
GDP at factor cost	61,348	66,918	73,700	89,557	113,179	131,738	164,629	200,855	238,180	293,216	365,173
Agriculture	5,242	5,415	5,507	7,216	8,395	10,007	11,642	13,919	16,326	19,265	22,305
Industry	27,719	29,795	31,788	38,736	50,160	57,455	72,449	87,125	101,087	122,314	151,321
Manufacturing	18,183	19,536	21,054	26,056	34,919	38,425	51,467	61,816	71,317	87,803	107,810
Services, etc.	34,217	37,784	42,515	50,786	63,635	71,170	90,778	113,354	136,123	168,255	214,043
Gross Domestic Saving	18,477	18,700	19,777	24,318	31,748	33,097	45,048	55,660	66,838	79,821	94,053
Gross National Saving	19,104	19,384	20,478	24,955	32,024	33,064	44,968	56,165	67,757	81,844	96,016

					(Billions of 1987 Italian Lire)						
Gross National Product	603,132	611,684	626,929	671,607	705,475	684,508	728,995	754,702	782,886	832,515	867,530
GDP at Market Prices	600,110	608,613	624,035	669,486	705,845	686,434	730,976	755,300	782,744	830,003	865,535
Resource Balance	-8,465	-5,152	-5,315	-11,289	-6,725	10,145	7,824	20,172	27,373	26,276	7,656
Exports of Goods & NFServices	86,663	92,734	101,520	105,522	111,720	113,768	125,338	139,913	153,032	166,412	152,186
Imports of Goods & NFServices	95,128	97,886	106,835	116,810	118,445	103,622	117,515	119,741	125,659	140,136	144,530
Domestic Absorption	608,575	613,765	629,350	680,775	712,570	676,289	723,153	735,128	755,371	803,727	857,878
Private Consumption, etc.	344,594	354,212	362,977	389,411	406,507	408,479	428,202	443,596	457,706	489,088	517,454
General Gov't Consumption	98,675	103,790	109,044	112,000	114,656	117,407	119,884	123,524	127,898	131,715	134,504
Gross Domestic Investment	165,307	155,764	157,330	179,364	191,407	150,403	175,067	168,008	169,767	182,924	205,921
Fixed Investment	153,696	153,953	155,975	169,629	173,090	160,397	160,473	163,433	164,463	173,854	188,985
GDP at factor cost	547,302	557,123	575,237	619,647	655,245	653,465	689,463	708,686	736,371	787,017	817,455
Agriculture	33,979	33,964	31,084	33,025	33,413	34,877	33,549	33,273	33,940	35,975	37,316
Industry	210,235	210,298	218,052	237,984	254,363	236,710	256,149	265,475	273,776	293,187	308,861
Manufacturing	115,623	117,161	123,575	138,983	148,510	140,075	160,737	166,481	174,332	191,752	201,989
Services, etc.	355,897	364,351	374,898	398,477	418,068	414,847	441,278	456,552	475,028	500,842	519,358
Memo Items:											
Capacity to Import	95,665	102,032	111,497	104,639	98,217	103,303	111,643	125,532	138,929	146,823	128,673
Terms of Trade Adjustment	9,002	9,298	9,977	-883	-13,503	-10,464	-13,695	-14,381	-14,103	-19,589	-23,513
Gross Domestic Income	609,113	617,911	634,012	668,603	692,342	675,969	717,282	740,919	768,642	810,414	842,022
Gross National Income	612,134	620,981	636,907	670,724	691,972	674,043	715,300	740,321	768,784	812,926	844,017

DOMESTIC PRICES/DEFLATORS					*(Index 1987 = 100)*						
Overall (GDP)	11.2	12.0	12.8	14.4	17.3	20.2	23.9	28.4	32.4	37.3	44.8
Domestic Absorption	11.0	11.8	12.6	14.5	17.9	20.5	24.5	28.9	32.8	38.1	46.4
Agriculture	15.4	15.9	17.7	21.9	25.1	28.7	34.7	41.8	48.1	53.6	59.8
Industry	13.2	14.2	14.6	16.3	19.7	24.3	28.3	32.8	36.9	41.7	49.0
Manufacturing	15.7	16.7	17.0	18.7	23.5	27.4	32.0	37.1	40.9	45.8	53.4
Consumer Price Index	12.7	13.3	14.0	15.6	18.5	21.7	25.3	29.9	33.6	38.5	46.7

MANUFACTURING ACTIVITY											
Employment (1987=100)	114.5	121.3	121.0	124.5	125.0	124.7	122.6	120.8	117.8	117.8	116.0
Real Earnings per Empl. (1987=100)	65.6	70.3	71.8	77.0	80.2	82.5	86.5	90.9	93.8	96.4	96.9
Real Output per Empl. (1987=100)	39.1	38.6	41.7	50.3	57.9	52.3	60.8	62.3	64.8	73.1	77.4
Earnings as % of Value Added	41.4	43.6	42.7	39.1	36.9	39.7	36.9	39.4	39.7	37.9	37.5

MONETARY HOLDINGS					*(Billions of current Italian Lire)*						
Money Supply, Broadly Defined	56,679	66,630	79,313	95,562	110,273	135,769	163,683	199,846	246,066	298,115	336,601
Money	29,885	35,567	42,229	52,460	57,194	64,011	76,311	92,702	116,763	145,069	164,616
Currency Outside Banks	8,502	9,567	11,789	13,557	14,981	13,215	14,255	16,105	19,044	21,665	25,357
Demand Deposits	21,383	26,000	30,440	38,903	42,213	50,796	62,056	76,597	97,719	123,404	139,259
Quasi-Money	26,794	31,063	37,084	43,102	53,079	71,758	87,372	107,144	129,303	153,046	171,985

GOVERNMENT DEFICIT (-) OR SURPLUS					*(Billions of current Italian Lire)*						
	..	..	..	-8,421	-12,086	-21,492	-19,805	-24,349	-21,151	-27,452	-41,480
Current Revenue	..	..	..	24,431	31,594	36,722	48,554	61,380	76,365	94,591	123,676
Current Expenditure	..	..	..	26,129	32,728	41,838	52,372	63,195	80,829	103,944	145,723
Current Budget Balance	..	..	..	-1,698	-1,134	-5,116	-3,818	-1,815	-4,464	-9,353	-22,047
Capital Receipts	..	..	..	8	2	1	12	16	7	8	8
Capital Payments	..	..	..	6,731	10,954	16,377	15,999	22,550	16,694	18,107	19,441

1981	1982	1983	1984	1985	1986	1987	1988	1989	1990 estimate	Notes	ITALY
8,010	7,900	7,540	7,590	7,700	8,580	10,450	13,420	15,180	16,860	..	**CURRENT GNP PER CAPITA (US $)**
56,508	56,640	56,836	57,005	57,141	57,246	57,345	57,452	57,541	57,663	..	**POPULATION (thousands)**

(Billions of current Italian Lire)

USE AND ORIGIN OF RESOURCES

1981	1982	1983	1984	1985	1986	1987	1988	1989	1990 estimate	Notes	ITALY
461,844	541,472	629,240	721,024	805,202	892,996	977,081	1.08433M	1.18223M	1.29098M	..	Gross National Product (GNP)
-2,186	-3,652	-4,196	-4,736	-5,378	-6,907	-6,722	-7,504	-10,494	-15,858	..	Net Factor Income from Abroad
464,030	545,124	633,436	725,760	810,580	899,903	983,803	1.09184M	1.19273M	1.30683M	..	GDP at Market Prices
-8,989	-5,897	4,508	-2,040	-3,291	13,699	6,439	2,002	-651	307	..	Resource Balance
108,344	125,125	140,016	165,197	185,022	181,961	191,841	210,046	243,046	274,472	..	Exports of Goods & NFServices
117,333	131,022	135,508	167,237	188,313	168,262	185,402	208,044	243,697	274,165	..	Imports of Goods & NFServices
473,019	551,021	628,928	727,800	813,871	886,204	977,364	1.08983M	1.19338M	1.30653M	..	Domestic Absorption
284,030	335,448	387,170	443,268	498,048	551,868	606,889	670,883	739,970	808,153	..	Private Consumption, etc.
74,156	87,386	103,568	118,034	133,265	145,960	163,880	184,291	199,486	226,539	..	General Gov't Consumption
114,833	128,187	138,190	166,498	182,558	188,376	206,595	234,661	253,920	271,834	..	Gross Domestic Investment
110,683	121,734	134,842	152,603	167,593	177,654	194,102	219,252	241,005	264,341	..	Fixed Investment
25,604	30,150	39,303	44,520	49,811	56,778	69,155	84,485	95,910	112,878	..	Indirect Taxes, net
438,426	514,974	594,133	681,240	760,769	843,125	914,648	1.00735M	1.09681M	1.19396M	B	GDP at factor cost
24,812	27,944	33,304	33,847	36,485	38,804	40,363	39,756	42,074	..	..	Agriculture
174,658	200,927	226,273	255,420	280,746	307,715	331,341	368,493	399,156	..	..	Industry
123,878	141,022	155,950	176,217	195,238	211,465	227,005	255,834	276,802	..	..	Manufacturing
264,560	316,253	373,859	436,493	493,349	553,385	612,099	683,588	751,495		..	Services, etc.
105,844	122,290	142,698	164,458	179,267	202,075	213,034	236,663	253,269	272,141		Gross Domestic Saving
105,296	120,623	140,637	162,276	176,419	197,353	207,969	231,045	244,559	257,321		Gross National Saving

(Billions of 1987 Italian Lire)

1981	1982	1983	1984	1985	1986	1987	1988	1989	1990 estimate	Notes	ITALY
865,679	864,787	873,506	897,343	920,735	946,628	977,081	1.01679M	1.04568M	1.06242M		Gross National Product
869,515	870,413	879,178	903,076	926,721	953,929	983,803	1.02384M	1.05495M	1.07555M	..	GDP at Market Prices
19,285	17,591	23,543	18,694	17,731	14,457	6,439	2,154	3,524	6,365		Resource Balance
161,765	159,785	163,898	176,445	181,852	183,900	191,841	201,544	219,688	239,810		Exports of Goods & NFServices
142,481	142,194	140,355	157,752	164,121	169,443	185,402	199,390	216,164	233,444	..	Imports of Goods & NFServices
850,230	852,822	855,635	884,383	908,990	939,472	977,364	1.02169M	1.05143M	1.06919M		Domestic Absorption
526,575	529,803	533,951	543,667	559,836	583,616	606,889	633,468	654,994	670,130		Private Consumption, etc.
137,590	141,193	146,067	149,336	154,424	158,375	163,880	168,543	170,068	171,699		General Gov't Consumption
186,066	181,826	175,617	191,380	194,729	197,481	206,595	219,675	226,365	227,358		Gross Domestic Investment
183,080	174,497	173,458	179,687	180,850	184,854	194,102	207,581	217,040	223,537		Fixed Investment
824,060	824,232	826,052	849,177	871,271	893,906	914,648	944,522	970,219	982,606	B	GDP at factor cost
37,530	36,542	39,588	38,149	38,318	39,086	40,363	38,993	40,023	..		Agriculture
304,466	300,296	299,378	307,197	313,543	320,532	331,341	351,361	361,154	..		Industry
198,487	197,026	198,600	207,492	213,673	218,563	227,005	243,963	251,232	..		Manufacturing
527,518	533,575	540,212	557,730	574,860	594,311	612,099	633,486	653,774	..		Services, etc.

Memo Items:

1981	1982	1983	1984	1985	1986	1987	1988	1989	1990 estimate	Notes	ITALY
131,565	135,794	145,024	155,827	161,253	183,239	191,841	201,309	215,586	233,706	..	Capacity to Import
-30,200	-23,991	-18,874	-20,618	-20,599	-662	0	-235	-4,101	-6,104	..	Terms of Trade Adjustment
839,314	846,422	860,304	882,458	906,122	953,267	983,803	1.0236M	1.05085M	1.06945M	..	Gross Domestic Income
835,479	840,796	854,633	876,725	900,135	945,966	977,081	1.01656M	1.04158M	1.05632M	..	Gross National Income

(Index 1987 = 100)

DOMESTIC PRICES/DEFLATORS

1981	1982	1983	1984	1985	1986	1987	1988	1989	1990 estimate	Notes	ITALY
53.4	62.6	72.0	80.4	87.5	94.3	100.0	106.6	113.1	121.5	..	Overall (GDP)
55.6	64.6	73.5	82.3	89.5	94.3	100.0	106.7	113.5	122.2	..	Domestic Absorption
66.1	76.5	84.1	88.7	95.2	99.3	100.0	102.0	105.1	..	..	Agriculture
57.4	66.9	75.6	83.1	89.5	96.0	100.0	104.9	110.5	..	..	Industry
62.4	71.6	78.5	84.9	91.4	96.8	100.0	104.9	110.2	..	..	Manufacturing
55.8	65.0	74.6	82.6	90.2	95.5	100.0	105.1	111.7	118.8	..	Consumer Price Index

MANUFACTURING ACTIVITY

1981	1982	1983	1984	1985	1986	1987	1988	1989	1990 estimate	Notes	ITALY
111.0	104.5	107.7	107.9	100.1	98.9	100.0	99.8	..	..		Employment (1987=100)
97.8	96.8	94.3	100.4	97.9	97.1	100.0	105.6	..	..		Real Earnings per Empl. (1987=100)
80.0	81.5	85.4	93.6	99.0	97.5	100.0	107.2	..	..		Real Output per Empl. (1987=100)
37.7	38.4	45.2	45.7	42.4	41.6	40.7	40.9	..	..		Earnings as % of Value Added

(Billions of current Italian Lire)

MONETARY HOLDINGS

1981	1982	1983	1984	1985	1986	1987	1988	1989	1990 estimate	Notes	ITALY
372,080	444,509	498,237	563,250	629,382	695,766	762,305	846,730	953,817	1.05863M	D	Money Supply, Broadly Defined
181,044	212,029	239,210	269,575	297,951	331,039	357,151	386,037	433,334	467,463	..	Money
29,712	33,263	37,338	41,202	45,009	48,203	52,646	56,980	67,473	69,337	..	Currency Outside Banks
151,332	178,766	201,872	228,373	252,942	282,836	304,505	329,057	365,861	398,126	..	Demand Deposits
191,036	232,480	259,027	293,675	331,431	364,727	405,154	460,693	520,483	591,167	..	Quasi-Money

(Billions of current Italian Lire)

1981	1982	1983	1984	1985	1986	1987	1988	1989	1990 estimate	Notes	ITALY
-52,017	-54,081	-71,513	-95,325	-108,216	-128,056	-146,631	-115,338	-125,287	-134,434	F	**GOVERNMENT DEFICIT (-) OR SURPLUS**
145,292	186,105	230,751	253,130	278,495	334,360	361,513	400,103	452,624	508,080	..	Current Revenue
..	..	..	..	..	392,322	437,537	456,089	507,600	573,532	..	Current Expenditure
..	..	..	..	..	-57,962	-76,024	-55,986	-54,976	-65,452	..	Current Budget Balance
..	..	..	..	..	41	147	1,416	1,791	1,233	..	Capital Receipts
..	..	..	..	..	70,135	70,754	60,768	72,102	70,215	..	Capital Payments

ITALY	1970	1971	1972	1973	1974	1975	1976	1977	1978	1979	1980
FOREIGN TRADE (CUSTOMS BASIS)					*(Billions of current US dollars)*						
Value of Exports, fob	13.21	15.11	18.55	22.22	30.25	34.83	36.97	45.06	56.05	72.24	77.64
Nonfuel Primary Products	1.56	1.77	2.18	2.52	3.32	3.79	3.78	4.90	5.26	7.36	7.45
Fuels	0.67	0.82	0.82	1.26	2.36	2.03	2.10	2.53	3.29	4.75	4.40
Manufactures	10.98	12.52	15.55	18.44	24.57	29.01	31.08	37.63	47.49	60.13	65.80
Value of Imports, cif	14.94	15.97	19.28	27.79	40.68	37.93	42.79	46.68	55.11	76.16	98.12
Nonfuel Primary Products	5.93	6.13	7.56	11.16	13.82	12.52	13.81	14.86	17.32	23.48	26.00
Fuels	2.09	2.69	2.90	3.92	10.83	10.26	11.05	12.00	13.35	18.35	27.34
Manufactures	6.91	7.15	8.82	12.71	16.03	15.15	17.93	19.82	24.45	34.33	44.78
					(Index 1987 = 100)						
Terms of Trade	142.2	140.2	136.0	123.1	91.3	104.1	93.0	95.5	97.2	93.4	88.3
Export Prices, fob	25.2	26.8	30.7	38.6	47.4	53.8	51.4	57.1	63.7	78.3	89.2
Import Prices, cif	17.7	19.1	22.6	31.3	51.9	51.6	55.2	59.8	65.5	83.8	101.0
BALANCE OF PAYMENTS					*(Billions of current US dollars)*						
Exports of Goods & Services	18.88	21.38	25.99	31.23	40.87	45.52	47.64	58.43	73.02	95.13	105.26
Merchandise, fob	13.12	14.97	18.44	22.07	30.02	34.51	36.84	44.80	55.50	71.39	77.02
Nonfactor Services	4.13	4.58	5.37	6.34	7.16	8.26	8.43	10.75	13.43	17.51	19.92
Factor Services	1.63	1.83	2.18	2.82	3.69	2.75	2.37	2.88	4.09	6.24	8.32
Imports of Goods & Services	18.28	20.05	24.42	33.98	48.87	46.34	50.79	56.17	66.39	90.11	116.69
Merchandise, fob	13.50	14.85	18.39	26.03	38.53	35.66	41.08	44.93	52.59	72.38	93.96
Nonfactor Services	3.44	3.66	4.14	5.30	6.25	6.99	6.57	7.85	9.54	12.30	15.17
Factor Services	1.35	1.53	1.89	2.65	4.10	3.69	3.14	3.40	4.27	5.44	7.56
Long-Term Interest	..	..	..	..	..	..	..	..	..	..	..
Private Current Transfers, net	0.51	0.56	0.63	0.63	0.57	0.59	0.52	0.83	1.11	1.42	1.37
Workers' Remittances	0.45	0.52	0.58	0.62	0.54	0.52	0.46	0.71	0.93	1.15	1.24
Curr. A/C Bal before Off. Transf.	1.10	1.90	2.20	-2.12	-7.43	-0.23	-2.62	3.09	7.73	6.44	-10.05
Net Official Transfers	-0.30	-0.29	-0.15	-0.34	-0.57	-0.29	-0.22	-0.60	-1.48	-0.93	0.23
Curr. A/C Bal after Off. Transf.	0.80	1.60	2.06	-2.46	-8.00	-0.52	-2.84	2.49	6.25	5.50	-9.82
Long-Term Capital, net	0.38	-0.08	-1.10	3.11	1.70	-0.36	-0.39	0.29	1.04	-0.40	3.41
Direct Investment	0.50	0.12	0.41	0.37	0.40	0.29	-0.06	0.58	0.35	-0.18	-0.16
Long-Term Loans	..	..	..	..	..	..	..	..	..	..	..
Disbursements	..	..	..	..	..	..	..	..	..	..	..
Repayments	..	..	..	..	..	..	..	..	..	..	..
Other Long-Term Capital	-0.12	-0.20	-1.51	2.74	1.31	-0.66	-0.32	-0.29	0.69	-0.22	3.57
Other Capital, net	-0.79	-0.04	-1.81	-0.80	5.14	-2.43	5.11	3.07	-3.53	-2.23	7.33
Change in Reserves	-0.39	-1.48	0.85	0.15	1.16	3.32	-1.88	-5.85	-3.76	-2.87	-0.92
Memo Item:					*(Italian Lire per US dollar)*						
Conversion Factor (Annual Avg)	625.000	619.900	583.200	583.000	650.300	652.800	832.300	882.400	848.700	830.900	856.400
EXTERNAL DEBT (Total)	..	..	..	*(Millions US dollars), outstanding at end of year*		..	..	..	..	..	..
Long-Term Debt (by debtor)	..	..	..	..	..	..	..	..	..	..	..
Central Bank, incl. IMF credit	..	..	..	..	..	..	..	..	..	..	..
Central Government	..	..	..	..	..	..	..	..	..	..	..
Rest of General Government	..	..	..	..	..	..	..	..	..	..	..
Non-financial Public Enterprises	..	..	..	..	..	..	..	..	..	..	..
Priv. Sector, incl non-guaranteed	..	..	..	..	..	..	..	..	..	..	..
Short-Term Debt	..	..	..	..	..	..	..	..	..	..	..
Memo Items:					*(Millions of US dollars)*						
Int'l Reserves Excluding Gold	2,465	3,689	2,954	2,953	3,406	1,306	3,223	8,104	11,109	18,197	23,126
Gold Holdings (at market price)	3,082	3,595	5,346	9,259	15,383	11,568	11,114	13,676	18,786	34,157	39,302
SOCIAL INDICATORS											
Total Fertility Rate	2.4	2.4	2.4	2.3	2.3	2.2	2.1	2.0	1.9	1.8	1.7
Infant Mortality Rate	29.6	28.5	27.0	26.2	22.9	21.1	19.5	18.1	17.1	15.7	14.6
Life Expectancy at Birth	71.7	71.9	72.1	72.3	72.4	72.6	72.7	73.6	74.0	74.3	74.7
Urban Population, % of total	64.3	64.6	64.8	65.1	65.3	65.6	65.8	66.0	66.2	66.4	66.6
Food Prod. per capita (1987=100)	89.3	88.7	82.3	89.6	91.7	92.3	88.5	90.3	91.4	96.8	101.9
Labor Force, Agriculture (%)	18.8	18.1	17.4	16.7	16.1	15.4	14.7	14.0	13.4	12.7	12.0
Labor Force, Female (%)	28.7	29.0	29.2	29.5	29.8	30.1	30.4	30.7	30.9	31.2	31.5
Primary Schl. Enroll. Ratio	110.0	..	..	..	..	106.0	105.0	103.0	102.0	102.0	100.0
Primary Schl. Enroll. Ratio, Female	109.0	..	..	..	..	106.0	104.0	103.0	102.0	102.0	100.0
Secondary Schl. Enroll. Ratio	61.0	..	..	..	..	70.0	72.0	73.0	73.0	73.0	72.0

1981	1982	1983	1984	1985	1986	1987	1988	1989	1990 estimate	Notes	ITALY
											FOREIGN TRADE (CUSTOMS BASIS)
				(Billions of current US dollars)							
75.25	73.44	72.67	73.36	78.94	97.82	116.58	127.90	140.47	168.52	..	Value of Exports, fob
7.75	7.13	6.78	7.07	7.96	9.36	10.45	11.90	12.39	14.15	..	Nonfuel Primary Products
4.72	4.99	3.89	3.32	3.69	2.73	2.84	2.10	2.35	3.36	..	Fuels
62.77	61.31	62.00	62.96	67.29	85.72	103.29	113.90	125.73	151.02	..	Manufactures
89.00	83.83	78.32	81.97	88.59	99.77	122.21	135.50	149.43	176.15	..	Value of Imports, cif
20.66	20.54	19.64	20.72	22.69	25.73	30.70	34.49	37.32	39.79	..	Nonfuel Primary Products
30.74	27.15	24.54	23.18	23.72	17.34	16.66	11.68	14.57	18.76	..	Fuels
37.59	36.14	34.14	38.08	42.18	56.71	74.85	89.32	97.54	117.61	..	Manufactures
				(Index 1987 = 100)							
73.7	82.5	82.1	81.7	83.7	99.7	100.0	95.0	94.5	97.3		Terms of Trade
74.2	77.7	74.5	72.3	72.0	86.6	100.0	106.1	114.6	134.0		Export Prices, fob
100.8	94.1	90.8	88.5	86.0	86.9	100.0	111.7	121.2	137.8		Import Prices, cif
											BALANCE OF PAYMENTS
				(Billions of current US dollars)							
101.53	98.91	97.08	99.55	103.36	128.91	156.14	169.85	188.85	227.27	..	Exports of Goods & Services
76.18	72.87	72.09	73.84	76.07	96.72	116.18	127.42	140.12	169.94	..	Merchandise, fob
16.74	17.41	17.97	18.13	19.30	23.14	29.33	30.49	33.86	35.65	..	Nonfactor Services
8.61	8.62	7.01	7.58	7.98	9.05	10.64	11.94	14.87	21.68	..	Factor Services
112.14	106.41	97.18	103.67	107.92	124.36	156.68	174.83	197.50	237.63	..	Imports of Goods & Services
88.32	81.78	74.60	79.65	82.16	92.19	116.52	128.78	142.29	169.22	..	Merchandise, fob
13.16	13.05	12.51	13.28	14.53	17.70	23.55	27.13	31.89	32.82	..	Nonfactor Services
10.67	11.58	10.07	10.73	11.24	14.47	16.62	18.92	23.33	35.59	..	Factor Services
..	..	..	..	..	..	..	..	..	..	..	Long-Term Interest
1.44	1.47	1.41	1.45	1.33	1.47	1.28	1.45	1.30	0.87	..	Private Current Transfers, net
1.16	1.19	1.14	1.11	1.08	1.21	1.21	1.23	1.38	1.18	..	Workers' Remittances
-9.17	-6.04	1.30	-2.67	-3.24	6.01	0.74	-3.53	-7.36	-9.49	..	Curr. A/C Bal before Off. Transf.
-0.44	-0.24	0.21	0.27	-0.17	-2.88	-2.01	-2.66	-3.53	-3.25	..	Net Official Transfers
-9.61	-6.28	1.52	-2.39	-3.41	3.13	-1.27	-6.19	-10.89	-12.73	..	Curr. A/C Bal after Off. Transf.
8.41	5.02	0.82	0.68	2.24	-2.90	3.08	7.44	15.22	21.73	..	Long-Term Capital, net
-0.25	-0.38	-0.95	-0.69	-0.87	-2.85	1.75	1.27	0.53	-0.67	..	Direct Investment
..	..	..	..	..	..	..	..	..	..	..	Long-Term Loans
..	..	..	..	..	..	..	..	..	..	..	Disbursements
..	..	..	..	..	..	..	..	..	..	..	Repayments
8.67	5.41	1.77	1.37	3.11	-0.05	1.32	6.17	14.69	22.39	..	Other Long-Term Capital
0.45	-3.30	3.47	4.35	-6.27	2.21	3.63	6.21	6.80	1.41	..	Other Capital, net
0.74	4.56	-5.81	-2.64	7.44	-2.44	-5.43	-7.47	-11.13	-10.40	..	Change in Reserves
											Memo Item:
				(Italian Lire per US dollar)							
1,136.800	1,352.500	1,518.900	1,757.000	1,909.400	1,490.800	1,296.100	1,301.600	1,372.100	1,198.100	..	Conversion Factor (Annual Avg)
				(Millions US dollars), outstanding at end of year							
											EXTERNAL DEBT (Total)
..	..	..	..	..	..	..	..	..	..	..	Long-Term Debt (by debtor)
..	..	..	..	..	..	..	..	..	..	..	Central Bank, incl. IMF credit
..	..	..	..	..	..	..	..	..	..	..	Central Government
..	..	..	..	..	..	..	..	..	..	..	Rest of General Government
..	..	..	..	..	..	..	..	..	..	..	Non-financial Public Enterprises
..	..	..	..	..	..	..	..	..	..	..	Priv. Sector, incl non-guaranteed
..	..	..	..	..	..	..	..	..	..	..	Short-Term Debt
											Memo Items:
				(Millions of US dollars)							
20,134	14,091	20,105	20,795	15,595	19,987	30,214	34,715	46,720	62,927	..	Int'l Reserves Excluding Gold
26,501	30,462	25,435	20,555	21,801	26,062	32,275	27,352	26,735	25,668	..	Gold Holdings (at market price)
											SOCIAL INDICATORS
1.6	1.6	1.5	1.5	1.4	1.3	1.3	1.3	1.3	1.3	..	Total Fertility Rate
14.1	13.0	12.3	11.4	10.5	10.2	9.8	9.4	9.0	8.7	..	Infant Mortality Rate
75.1	75.5	75.7	76.0	76.3	76.6	76.8	77.1	77.3	77.5	..	Life Expectancy at Birth
66.8	67.0	67.2	67.4	67.6	67.9	68.1	68.4	68.6	68.9	..	Urban Population, % of total
99.3	97.2	105.8	97.1	96.5	97.5	100.0	94.7	96.8	89.5	..	Food Prod. per capita (1987=100)
..	..	..	..	..	..	..	..	..	..	..	Labor Force, Agriculture (%)
31.5	31.6	31.6	31.7	31.7	31.8	31.8	31.9	31.9	31.9	..	Labor Force, Female (%)
..	100.0	99.0	97.0	96.0	95.0	95.0	95.0	96.0		..	Primary Schl. Enroll. Ratio
..	100.0	99.0	97.0	96.0	95.0	95.0	95.0	96.0		..	Primary Schl. Enroll. Ratio, Female
..	73.0	73.0	72.0	73.0	74.0	75.0	76.0	78.0		..	Secondary Schl. Enroll. Ratio

JAMAICA	1970	1971	1972	1973	1974	1975	1976	1977	1978	1979	1980
CURRENT GNP PER CAPITA (US $)	720	770	910	960	1,090	1,260	1,330	1,440	1,420	1,250	1,130
POPULATION (thousands)	1,869	1,896	1,925	1,956	1,986	2,013	2,038	2,060	2,081	2,105	2,133

USE AND ORIGIN OF RESOURCES *(Millions of current Jamaica Dollars)*

	1970	1971	1972	1973	1974	1975	1976	1977	1978	1979	1980
Gross National Product (GNP)	1,120	1,208	1,414	1,692	2,211	2,620	2,627	2,856	3,586	3,922	4,331
Net Factor Income from Abroad	-51	-74	-25	-27	52	20	-69	-98	-152	-358	-442
GDP at Market Prices	1,171	1,282	1,439	1,720	2,159	2,600	2,696	2,954	3,737	4,280	4,773
Resource Balance	-49	-91	-119	-165	-221	-269	-239	41	120	-35	-8
Exports of Goods & NF Services	389	434	472	543	770	917	783	879	1,516	2,132	2,510
Imports of Goods & NF Services	438	525	591	707	991	1,186	1,022	839	1,395	2,167	2,517
Domestic Absorption	1,220	1,374	1,558	1,885	2,380	2,869	2,935	2,913	3,617	4,315	4,781
Private Consumption, etc.	713	803	968	1,063	1,469	1,722	1,882	1,940	2,305	2,668	3,055
General Gov't Consumption	137	159	197	280	386	477	562	612	750	825	966
Gross Domestic Investment	369	412	393	542	525	670	491	361	562	823	759
Fixed Investment	367	356	367	448	478	610	451	349	499	748	690
Indirect Taxes, net	98	114	125	146	180	239	237	216	272	358	387
GDP at factor cost	1,073	1,169	1,314	1,574	1,980	2,362	2,460	2,739	3,465	3,922	4,386
Agriculture	78	102	107	120	154	191	214	249	297	308	392
Industry	499	511	533	633	820	956	992	1,092	1,485	1,725	1,826
Manufacturing	184	207	242	287	387	444	491	545	638	702	794
Services, etc.	593	670	799	968	1,185	1,453	1,490	1,613	1,956	2,246	2,554
Gross Domestic Saving	320	320	274	377	304	401	253	402	683	787	752
Gross National Saving	292	268	276	381	387	441	185	318	553	553	455

(Millions of 1987 Jamaica Dollars)

	1970	1971	1972	1973	1974	1975	1976	1977	1978	1979	1980
Gross National Product	15,764.4	16,009.3	18,218.2	18,353.7	18,426.9	18,012.0	16,184.6	15,590.6	15,531.1	14,564.6	13,526.4
GDP at Market Prices	16,434.6	16,939.4	18,475.6	18,547.2	17,943.5	17,803.9	16,547.8	16,088.6	16,156.3	15,824.2	14,848.8
Resource Balance	-162.3	-345.8	-368.0	-576.6	-800.0	-1,924.0	-1,372.6	-332.9	51.8	127.6	593.2
Exports of Goods & NF Services	6,015.6	6,575.1	6,817.5	6,736.7	6,692.4	5,953.9	5,159.8	5,244.1	5,674.1	6,286.6	5,832.2
Imports of Goods & NF Services	6,177.9	6,920.9	7,185.5	7,313.2	7,492.4	7,877.9	6,532.4	5,577.0	5,622.3	6,159.0	5,239.1
Domestic Absorption	16,596.9	17,285.2	18,843.6	19,123.7	18,743.5	19,727.9	17,920.4	16,421.4	16,104.5	15,696.6	14,255.7
Private Consumption, etc.	7,910.9	8,552.0	10,801.8	8,431.8	10,147.4	10,403.2	10,426.4	10,603.4	9,658.1	9,445.4	8,961.5
General Gov't Consumption	1,408.5	1,429.9	1,607.0	2,034.1	2,116.9	2,150.9	2,445.9	2,471.1	2,566.5	2,534.1	2,438.2
Gross Domestic Investment	7,277.4	7,303.3	6,434.8	8,657.9	6,479.2	7,173.8	5,048.2	3,346.9	3,879.9	3,717.0	2,855.9
Fixed Investment	7,420.5	6,570.0	6,141.6	7,232.2	6,043.0	6,702.7	4,786.9	3,329.9	3,551.0	3,381.7	2,603.2
GDP at factor cost	15,100.2	15,476.2	16,905.4	17,009.7	16,494.7	16,208.8	15,121.3	14,931.8	14,997.4	14,514.2	13,652.4
Agriculture	845.6	958.2	975.3	839.3	879.9	894.7	901.0	927.3	1,016.4	911.3	872.5
Industry	8,592.3	8,830.1	9,348.2	9,310.0	9,194.5	8,825.6	7,804.0	7,335.2	7,250.0	7,016.7	6,350.6
Manufacturing	3,669.3	3,754.6	4,193.8	4,220.1	4,077.9	4,170.6	3,987.3	3,691.4	3,518.7	3,338.6	2,963.7
Services, etc.	7,345.0	7,491.0	8,453.0	8,698.2	8,162.4	8,325.6	7,988.2	7,914.5	7,933.1	7,955.8	7,643.2

Memo Items:

	1970	1971	1972	1973	1974	1975	1976	1977	1978	1979	1980
Capacity to Import	5,486.8	5,717.3	5,735.0	5,609.5	5,822.6	6,090.6	5,007.5	5,849.0	6,107.5	6,058.7	5,223.3
Terms of Trade Adjustment	-528.8	-857.7	-1,082.4	-1,127.2	-869.7	136.7	-152.3	604.9	433.4	-228.0	-609.0
Gross Domestic Income	15,905.7	16,081.6	17,393.2	17,420.0	17,073.8	17,940.6	16,395.5	16,693.5	16,589.6	15,596.2	14,239.8
Gross National Income	15,235.6	15,151.6	17,135.8	17,226.5	17,557.2	18,148.7	16,032.4	16,195.5	15,964.5	14,336.6	12,917.4

DOMESTIC PRICES/DEFLATORS *(Index 1987 = 100)*

	1970	1971	1972	1973	1974	1975	1976	1977	1978	1979	1980
Overall (GDP)	7.1	7.6	7.8	9.3	12.0	14.6	16.3	18.4	23.1	27.0	32.1
Domestic Absorption	7.3	7.9	8.3	9.9	12.7	14.5	16.4	17.7	22.5	27.5	33.5
Agriculture	9.2	10.6	10.9	14.2	17.5	21.4	23.8	26.8	29.2	33.8	45.0
Industry	5.8	5.8	5.7	6.8	8.9	10.8	12.7	14.9	20.5	24.6	28.8
Manufacturing	5.0	5.5	5.8	6.8	9.5	10.6	12.3	14.8	18.1	21.0	26.8
Consumer Price Index	7.2	7.5	8.0	9.4	11.9	14.0	15.4	17.1	23.0	29.7	37.8

MANUFACTURING ACTIVITY

	1970	1971	1972	1973	1974	1975	1976	1977	1978	1979	1980
Employment (1987=100)	..	..	..	..	..	..	..	..	..	..	..
Real Earnings per Empl. (1987=100)	..	..	..	..	..	..	..	..	..	..	..
Real Output per Empl. (1987=100)	..	..	..	..	..	..	..	..	..	..	..
Earnings as % of Value Added	42.6	41.5	44.2	46.5	42.5	46.3	47.7	45.9	46.3	45.9	46.6

MONETARY HOLDINGS *(Millions of current Jamaica Dollars)*

	1970	1971	1972	1973	1974	1975	1976	1977	1978	1979	1980
Money Supply, Broadly Defined	393	492	581	667	868	962	1,030	1,145	1,353	1,538	1,842
Money	127	160	173	218	258	322	339	474	570	629	717
Currency Outside Banks	46	58	72	82	102	127	138	182	173	220	260
Demand Deposits	80	102	101	136	156	195	200	292	397	410	457
Quasi-Money	266	332	408	448	609	640	691	671	783	909	1,126

(Millions of current Jamaica Dollars)

	1970	1971	1972	1973	1974	1975	1976	1977	1978	1979	1980
GOVERNMENT DEFICIT (-) OR SURPLUS	..	..	..	..	..	-253.0	-394.9	-496.5	-514.1	-542.6	-739.3
Current Revenue	..	..	..	..	..	681.9	709.9	734.1	1,129.7	1,148.5	1,381.9
Current Expenditure	..	..	..	..	..	585.1	740.2	814.2	..	..	..
Current Budget Balance	..	..	..	..	..	96.8	-30.3	-80.1	..	..	..
Capital Receipts	..	..	..	..	..	0.1			..	1.4	..
Capital Payments	..	..	..	..	..	349.9	364.6	416.4	..	..	..

1981	1982	1983	1984	1985	1986	1987	1988	1989	1990 estimate	Notes	JAMAICA
1,250	1,320	1,340	1,140	910	850	950	1,140	1,390	1,500	A	CURRENT GNP PER CAPITA (US $)
2,166	2,203	2,242	2,279	2,311	2,339	2,364	2,385	2,404	2,420	..	POPULATION (thousands)
											USE AND ORIGIN OF RESOURCES
						(Millions of current Jamaica Dollars)					
5,040	5,628	6,595	8,338	9,626	11,547	13,818	16,655	20,145	25,034	..	Gross National Product (GNP)
-267	-239	-398	-1,021	-1,577	-1,841	-2,184	-2,093	-2,080	-3,472	..	Net Factor Income from Abroad
5,307	5,867	6,993	9,358	11,202	13,388	16,002	18,748	22,225	28,506	..	GDP at Market Prices
-463	-667	-636	-651	-1,239	737	362	1,235	-1,142	-5	..	Resource Balance
2,580	2,310	2,451	5,185	6,845	7,680	8,936	11,335	12,327	16,678	..	Exports of Goods & NF Services
3,043	2,977	3,087	5,836	8,084	6,944	8,573	10,100	13,469	16,683	..	Imports of Goods & NF Services
5,770	6,534	7,629	10,009	12,441	12,652	15,640	17,513	23,366	28,511	..	Domestic Absorption
3,598	4,022	4,666	6,304	7,862	7,957	9,499	9,491	13,493	15,900	..	Private Consumption, etc.
1,095	1,288	1,406	1,541	1,741	2,121	2,436	3,016	3,150	4,178	..	General Gov't Consumption
1,077	1,224	1,557	2,164	2,837	2,574	3,705	5,007	6,723	8,433	..	Gross Domestic Investment
954	1,168	1,436	1,981	2,581	2,432	3,545	4,865	6,538	8,362	..	Fixed Investment
517	643	592	934	1,470	1,940	2,467	..	..	..	..	Indirect Taxes, net
4,790	5,225	6,401	8,424	9,733	11,448	13,536	..	..	..	B	GDP at factor cost
398	396	451	544	672	820	963	1,066	1,204	1,502	..	Agriculture
1,887	1,977	2,449	3,525	4,182	5,464	6,591	8,108	9,949	13,084	..	Industry
886	1,054	1,399	1,732	2,241	2,907	3,426	3,759	4,497	5,698	..	Manufacturing
3,023	3,494	4,093	5,289	6,349	7,104	8,448	9,574	11,072	13,920	..	Services, etc.
614	557	921	1,513	1,599	3,311	4,067	6,242	5,582	8,428	..	Gross Domestic Saving
567	557	705	810	873	2,081	2,526	6,545	5,223	5,876	..	Gross National Saving
						(Millions of 1987 Jamaica Dollars)					
14,539.4	14,800.5	14,902.2	13,918.4	12,844.2	12,925.9	13,817.7	14,214.6	15,706.7	15,959.3	..	Gross National Product
15,199.4	15,329.4	15,694.1	15,471.1	14,733.4	15,033.6	16,002.1	16,300.1	17,331.7	18,053.7	I	GDP at Market Prices
284.0	-233.0	123.7	-203.6	-505.6	744.5	362.3	105.4	-1,434.1	271.0	..	Resource Balance
5,820.1	5,198.0	5,157.2	6,791.4	7,573.3	8,107.6	8,935.6	9,966.0	10,002.5	10,588.9	..	Exports of Goods & NF Services
5,536.1	5,431.1	5,033.5	6,995.0	8,079.0	7,363.1	8,573.3	9,860.6	11,436.6	10,317.9	..	Imports of Goods & NF Services
14,915.4	15,562.5	15,570.3	15,674.7	15,239.1	14,289.1	15,639.8	16,194.7	18,765.8	17,782.6	..	Domestic Absorption
8,906.9	9,274.4	9,172.3	9,805.1	9,464.6	9,019.1	9,499.1	9,211.7	11,130.8	..	..	Private Consumption, etc.
2,491.4	2,584.6	2,558.8	2,379.5	2,301.7	2,349.9	2,436.0	2,655.3	2,506.7	..	..	General Gov't Consumption
3,517.2	3,703.5	3,839.2	3,490.0	3,472.8	2,920.1	3,704.7	4,327.7	5,128.4	4,874.2	..	Gross Domestic Investment
3,051.9	3,562.4	3,510.6	3,098.6	3,026.6	2,741.0	3,544.7	4,241.0	5,032.1	4,923.4	..	Fixed Investment
13,722.6	13,648.4	14,367.8	13,920.2	12,788.9	12,850.7	13,535.6	..	..	..	B	GDP at factor cost
891.9	821.6	881.0	969.6	935.3	915.9	963.3	911.3	872.5	975.3	..	Agriculture
6,405.6	6,293.4	6,478.5	6,244.1	5,904.3	6,127.5	6,590.6	6,807.0	7,832.0	8,321.0	..	Industry
2,986.8	3,211.2	3,273.3	3,136.4	3,152.2	3,223.8	3,426.0	3,494.5	3,740.9	3,894.7	..	Manufacturing
7,906.9	8,223.0	8,334.6	8,257.4	7,893.8	7,990.3	8,448.2	8,581.8	8,627.2	8,757.4	..	Services, etc.
											Memo Items:
4,694.1	4,213.6	3,996.1	6,215.2	6,840.9	8,144.2	8,935.6	11,066.3	10,467.2	10,314.8	..	Capacity to Import
-1,126.0	-984.4	-1,161.0	-576.2	-732.4	36.6	0.0	1,100.3	464.8	-274.1	..	Terms of Trade Adjustment
14,073.4	14,345.0	14,533.0	14,894.9	14,001.1	15,070.2	16,002.1	17,400.4	17,796.5	17,779.5	..	Gross Domestic Income
13,413.4	13,816.1	13,741.2	13,342.2	12,111.9	12,962.5	13,817.7	15,314.9	16,171.5	15,685.2	..	Gross National Income
											DOMESTIC PRICES/DEFLATORS
						(Index 1987 = 100)					
34.9	38.3	44.6	60.5	76.0	89.1	100.0	115.0	128.2	157.9	..	Overall (GDP)
38.7	42.0	49.0	63.9	81.6	88.5	100.0	108.1	124.5	160.3	..	Domestic Absorption
44.6	48.2	51.1	56.1	71.8	89.5	100.0	116.9	138.0	154.0	..	Agriculture
29.5	31.4	37.8	56.5	70.8	89.2	100.0	119.1	127.0	157.2	..	Industry
29.7	32.8	42.7	55.2	71.1	90.2	100.0	107.6	120.2	146.3	..	Manufacturing
42.7	45.4	50.7	64.8	81.5	93.8	100.0	108.3	123.8	151.0	..	Consumer Price Index
											MANUFACTURING ACTIVITY
..	..	..	..	..	..	..	..	..	..	..	Employment (1987=100)
..	..	..	..	..	..	..	..	..	..	..	Real Earnings per Empl. (1987=100)
..	..	..	..	..	..	..	..	..	..	..	Real Output per Empl. (1987=100)
..	..	..	..	..	..	..	..	..	..	..	Earnings as % of Value Added
											MONETARY HOLDINGS
						(Millions of current Jamaica Dollars)					
2,358	3,015	3,897	4,692	5,997	7,579	8,859	11,910	13,051	15,563	D	Money Supply, Broadly Defined
775	876	1,066	1,319	1,520	2,140	2,252	3,445	3,153	4,016	..	Money
282	316	375	436	540	729	844	1,288	1,378	1,640	..	Currency Outside Banks
492	560	691	882	980	1,410	1,407	2,157	1,775	2,376	..	Demand Deposits
1,584	2,139	2,831	3,373	4,477	5,439	6,607	8,466	9,898	11,547	..	Quasi-Money
						(Millions of current Jamaica Dollars)					
-720.6	-893.3	-1,389.9	-547.0	-963.4	..	..	..	..	..	C	GOVERNMENT DEFICIT (-) OR SURPLUS
1,671.7	1,719.4	1,840.8	2,872.2	3,740.8	..	..	..	..	..		Current Revenue
..	..	2,476.9	2,648.0	3,830.5	..	..	..	..	..		Current Expenditure
..	..	-636.1	224.2	-89.7	..	..	..	..	..		Current Budget Balance
..	..	..	10.0	..	..	..	..	..	..		Capital Receipts
..	..	753.8	781.2	873.7	..	..	..	..	..		Capital Payments

JAMAICA	1970	1971	1972	1973	1974	1975	1976	1977	1978	1979	1980
FOREIGN TRADE (CUSTOMS BASIS)					*(Millions of current US dollars)*						
Value of Exports, fob	334.9	330.2	356.4	382.5	718.4	769.4	617.8	762.8	736.6	808.9	942.4
Nonfuel Primary Products	171.3	170.2	180.6	184.3	292.1	339.4	256.6	322.1	286.4	354.6	333.8
Fuels	8.7	9.2	9.9	9.1	10.5	11.6	16.4	17.4	18.8	31.9	18.0
Manufactures	154.9	150.8	165.8	189.2	415.8	418.4	344.7	423.2	431.4	422.4	590.7
Value of Imports, cif	525.4	550.5	620.2	664.4	935.5	1,122.5	911.2	858.8	879.9	991.5	1,177.7
Nonfuel Primary Products	112.0	119.0	155.6	180.9	262.8	271.4	250.5	219.3	240.6	208.7	270.1
Fuels	33.7	52.8	56.0	72.5	195.5	215.3	207.3	249.6	212.5	317.4	445.5
Manufactures	379.8	378.7	408.6	410.9	477.3	635.8	453.4	389.9	426.8	465.4	462.1
					(Index 1987 = 100)						
Terms of Trade	120.1	122.0	118.2	120.6	121.7	115.6	117.4	127.9	116.2	109.9	99.6
Export Prices, fob	30.7	31.1	34.0	43.0	71.4	69.5	70.5	79.6	81.1	92.4	106.4
Import Prices, cif	25.6	25.5	28.7	35.7	58.7	60.1	60.1	62.2	69.8	84.1	106.9
BALANCE OF PAYMENTS					*(Millions of current US dollars)*						
Exports of Goods & Services	537.2	558.6	630.0	649.1	1,056.2	1,122.1	942.9	1,007.0	1,169.8	1,220.9	1,421.6
Merchandise, fob	341.4	343.6	376.7	392.1	752.3	808.6	656.4	737.8	831.1	818.2	962.7
Nonfactor Services	157.9	174.9	206.3	199.3	238.0	242.1	222.2	211.8	281.9	346.9	396.1
Factor Services	37.9	40.0	47.0	57.7	65.9	71.4	64.3	57.4	56.8	55.8	62.8
Imports of Goods & Services	712.6	752.3	855.5	924.1	1,172.9	1,432.6	1,251.4	1,069.2	1,245.6	1,439.9	1,678.3
Merchandise, fob	449.0	475.5	528.6	570.4	811.4	969.6	791.6	666.7	750.1	882.5	1,038.2
Nonfactor Services	141.0	147.7	171.8	184.2	246.5	315.3	311.9	224.3	282.2	315.0	347.7
Factor Services	122.6	129.1	155.1	169.5	115.0	147.6	147.9	178.2	213.3	242.4	292.4
Long-Term Interest	63.5	61.4	63.1	80.9	101.7	109.9	96.1	98.8	98.4	104.5	121.1
Private Current Transfers, net	26.9	27.0	35.5	34.7	33.9	22.7	2.0	15.1	15.2	70.0	81.7
Workers' Remittances	28.8	35.9	52.1	50.8	48.8	47.4	47.5	41.0	26.5	48.7	50.6
Curr. A/C Bal before Off. Transf.	-148.5	-166.8	-190.0	-240.3	-82.9	-287.8	-306.5	-47.1	-60.6	-149.0	-175.0
Net Official Transfers	-4.4	-5.4	-6.7	-7.3	-9.0	5.0	3.9	5.0	10.6	10.1	9.0
Curr. A/C Bal after Off. Transf.	-152.9	-172.2	-196.7	-247.6	-91.9	-282.8	-302.6	-42.1	-50.0	-138.9	-166.0
Long-Term Capital, net	160.7	186.8	124.8	202.0	225.6	227.8	94.2	51.5	-95.5	-25.3	231.0
Direct Investment	161.4	174.4	97.2	71.5	23.3	-1.8	-0.6	-9.7	-26.6	-26.4	27.7
Long-Term Loans	9.7	26.2	34.6	149.5	229.2	193.2	-218.0	79.6	-313.0	72.0	251.4
Disbursements	179.9	200.3	216.2	334.5	426.8	401.7	345.6	260.7	263.4	234.6	352.8
Repayments	170.2	174.1	181.6	185.0	197.6	208.5	563.6	181.1	576.4	162.6	101.4
Other Long-Term Capital	-10.4	-13.8	-7.0	-19.1	-26.9	36.5	312.8	-18.4	244.1	-70.9	-48.1
Other Capital, net	7.0	17.4	46.5	-3.4	-71.0	-19.6	2.1	-43.5	89.0	5.0	-2.4
Change in Reserves	-14.9	-31.9	25.4	49.1	-62.8	74.5	206.3	34.1	56.5	159.2	-62.6
Memo Item:					*(Jamaica Dollars per US dollar)*						
Conversion Factor (Annual Avg)	0.830	0.820	0.800	0.910	0.910	0.910	0.910	0.910	1.450	1.760	1.780
					(Millions of US dollars), outstanding at end of year						
EXTERNAL DEBT (Total)	982.0	1,013.1	1,041.1	1,205.6	1,434.7	1,614.1	1,449.5	1,678.6	1,423.4	1,705.8	1,903.5
Long-Term Debt (by debtor)	982.0	1,013.1	1,041.1	1,205.6	1,434.7	1,614.1	1,449.5	1,575.6	1,343.4	1,599.8	1,805.5
Central Bank, incl. IMF credit	3.2	3.8	4.3	23.9	63.6	74.1	187.9	212.5	286.3	453.1	505.6
Central Government	124.4	136.9	150.1	195.8	283.7	373.0	505.4	557.7	697.8	827.6	972.8
Rest of General Government	..	..	..	..	..	..	..	..	..	..	..
Non-financial Public Enterprises	30.5	42.0	55.5	105.5	137.0	196.2	242.7	239.8	212.7	198.9	191.8
Priv. Sector, incl non-guaranteed	823.9	830.4	831.2	880.4	950.4	970.8	513.5	565.6	146.6	120.2	135.3
Short-Term Debt	0.0	0.0	0.0	0.0	0.0	0.0	0.0	103.0	80.0	106.0	98.0
Memo Items:					*(Millions of US dollars)*						
Int'l Reserves Excluding Gold	139.19	179.05	159.69	127.45	190.39	125.58	32.39	47.78	58.82	63.81	105.00
Gold Holdings (at market price)	..	..	..	..	..	..	..	1.86	..	5.79	..
SOCIAL INDICATORS											
Total Fertility Rate	5.3	5.2	5.0	4.8	4.6	4.4	4.2	4.0	3.9	3.8	3.7
Infant Mortality Rate	43.2	42.6	42.0	38.8	35.6	32.4	29.2	26.0	24.4	22.8	21.2
Life Expectancy at Birth	67.7	68.2	68.6	68.9	69.2	69.5	69.8	70.1	70.3	70.6	70.8
Urban Population, % of total	41.5	42.0	42.5	43.1	43.6	44.1	44.6	45.2	45.7	46.3	46.8
Food Prod. per capita (1987=100)	120.8	126.4	122.4	112.5	114.5	108.0	109.4	107.7	116.1	106.8	103.0
Labor Force, Agriculture (%)	33.2	33.0	32.7	32.5	32.3	32.1	31.9	31.8	31.6	31.4	31.3
Labor Force, Female (%)	42.5	43.0	43.4	43.8	44.2	44.6	44.9	45.2	45.5	45.8	46.0
Primary Schl. Enroll. Ratio	119.0	..	..	..	..	97.0	97.0	98.0	99.0	99.0	103.0
Primary Schl. Enroll. Ratio, Female	119.0	..	..	..	..	98.0	97.0	98.0	100.0	100.0	104.0
Secondary Schl. Enroll. Ratio	46.0	..	..	..	..	58.0	58.0	58.0	60.0	60.0	67.0

1981	1982	1983	1984	1985	1986	1987	1988	1989	1990 estimate	Notes	JAMAICA
											FOREIGN TRADE (CUSTOMS BASIS)
				(Millions of current US dollars)							
975.7	717.0	717.3	732.1	535.1	567.2	692.3	811.6	969.7	1,347.2	..	Value of Exports, fob
303.4	267.8	283.8	325.6	222.3	254.8	304.3	319.1	381.2	529.6	..	Nonfuel Primary Products
26.4	26.2	28.8	18.3	27.9	17.7	13.6	18.8	22.5	31.2	..	Fuels
645.9	423.0	404.7	388.1	284.9	294.6	374.4	473.8	566.0	786.4	..	Manufactures
1,487.0	1,373.3	1,529.9	1,145.7	1,143.4	967.6	1,233.9	1,434.3	1,805.0	1,685.2	..	Value of Imports, cif
328.1	313.9	315.6	271.2	237.9	228.1	260.8	328.1	412.9	385.5	..	Nonfuel Primary Products
494.4	398.8	457.5	345.9	366.8	198.6	237.0	195.0	245.5	229.2	..	Fuels
664.5	660.6	756.9	528.6	538.6	541.0	736.1	911.1	1,146.6	1,070.5	..	Manufactures
				(Index 1987 = 100)							
93.8	93.2	94.6	94.4	94.7	109.0	100.0	96.6	105.8	88.3	..	Terms of Trade
104.0	96.1	94.6	92.4	90.8	99.4	100.0	105.4	119.3	109.4	..	Export Prices, fob
110.9	103.2	100.0	97.9	95.8	91.2	100.0	109.1	112.8	123.9	..	Import Prices, cif
											BALANCE OF PAYMENTS
				(Millions of current US dollars)							
1,499.8	1,371.1	1,332.2	1,335.2	1,266.2	1,411.0	1,633.4	1,773.8	1,989.2	2,270.0		Exports of Goods & Services
974.0	767.4	685.7	702.3	568.6	589.5	708.4	883.0	996.5	1,125.0	..	Merchandise, fob
426.3	477.3	534.0	561.7	603.4	734.6	812.3	768.4	881.8	1,133.0	..	Nonfactor Services
99.5	126.4	112.5	71.2	94.2	86.9	112.7	122.4	110.9	12.0	..	Factor Services
1,960.9	1,924.8	1,788.8	1,787.9	1,789.0	1,597.5	1,941.1	2,249.2	2,738.5	2,784.0		Imports of Goods & Services
1,296.7	1,208.9	1,124.2	1,037.0	1,004.2	837.4	1,065.1	1,240.3	1,568.9	1,842.0	..	Merchandise, fob
385.1	394.4	369.4	379.7	372.6	366.1	406.9	522.0	655.9	442.0	..	Nonfactor Services
279.1	321.5	295.2	371.2	412.2	394.0	469.1	486.9	513.7	500.0	..	Factor Services
109.7	140.3	157.0	194.4	211.6	224.7	204.6	190.6	172.4	226.9	..	Long-Term Interest
123.3	134.5	94.7	80.4	153.2	111.6	117.2	436.5	299.5	128.0		Private Current Transfers, net
62.7	74.5	41.6	26.1	92.3	54.0	58.8	67.7	117.2	..	..	Workers' Remittances
-337.8	-419.2	-361.9	-372.3	-369.6	-74.9	-190.5	-38.9	-449.8	-386.0		Curr. A/C Bal before Off. Transf.
1.0	15.8	6.8	40.2	68.0	36.5	54.4	70.0	154.5	115.0	..	Net Official Transfers
-336.8	-403.4	-355.1	-332.1	-301.6	-38.4	-136.1	31.1	-295.3	-271.0		Curr. A/C Bal after Off. Transf.
116.8	349.1	137.5	390.0	131.8	-182.9	255.6	12.4	246.7	46.0		Long-Term Capital, net
-11.5	-15.8	-18.7	12.2	-9.0	-4.6	53.4	-12.0	57.1	90.0	..	Direct Investment
292.6	445.4	381.8	297.2	289.5	-31.1	115.8	62.5	59.1	-45.0		Long-Term Loans
464.7	560.2	506.7	396.4	450.2	231.4	356.7	319.8	291.2	263.5	..	Disbursements
172.1	114.8	124.9	99.2	160.7	262.5	240.9	257.3	232.1	308.5	..	Repayments
-164.3	-80.5	-225.6	80.6	-148.7	-147.2	86.4	-38.1	130.5	1.0	..	Other Long-Term Capital
-46.2	4.1	109.1	-37.7	209.8	336.4	45.4	87.7	71.3	338.7		Other Capital, net
266.2	50.3	108.4	-20.1	-40.1	-115.1	-164.9	-131.1	-22.7	-113.7		Change in Reserves
				(Jamaica Dollars per US dollar)							**Memo Item:**
1.930	1.990	2.150	3.940	5.560	5.480	5.490	5.490	5.740	7.180	..	Conversion Factor (Annual Avg)
			(Millions of US dollars), outstanding at end of year								
2,299.7	2,846.2	3,411.7	3,566.0	4,068.1	4,187.0	4,696.4	4,532.4	4,536.5	4,598.2		**EXTERNAL DEBT (Total)**
2,207.7	2,748.2	3,161.7	3,315.6	3,881.5	4,003.4	4,465.2	4,244.3	4,152.0	4,263.8		Long-Term Debt (by debtor)
846.0	1,051.7	1,191.1	1,193.7	1,311.5	1,288.2	1,179.4	962.1	852.1	837.6	..	Central Bank, incl. IMF credit
1,119.2	1,434.3	1,590.7	1,766.2	2,183.8	2,332.5	2,851.1	2,833.5	2,867.2	3,034.7	..	Central Government
..	..	..	..	..	..	..	..	..	..	..	Rest of General Government
165.3	150.4	248.3	247.9	292.6	292.7	350.6	376.7	371.9	342.3	..	Non-financial Public Enterprises
77.2	111.8	131.6	107.8	93.6	90.0	84.1	72.0	60.8	49.2	..	Priv. Sector, incl non-guaranteed
92.0	98.0	250.0	250.4	186.6	183.6	231.2	288.1	384.5	334.4	..	Short-Term Debt
				(Millions of US dollars)							**Memo Items:**
85.17	108.97	63.20	96.93	161.30	98.42	174.30	147.20	107.50	168.16	..	Int'l Reserves Excluding Gold
..	..	..	..	..	..	..	..	..	..	..	Gold Holdings (at market price)
											SOCIAL INDICATORS
3.6	3.6	3.4	3.3	3.2	3.1	3.0	2.9	2.8	2.8	..	Total Fertility Rate
19.6	18.0	17.8	17.6	17.4	17.2	17.0	16.6	16.2	15.7	..	Infant Mortality Rate
71.1	71.3	71.6	71.8	72.1	72.3	72.5	72.8	73.0	73.2	..	Life Expectancy at Birth
47.3	47.8	48.4	48.9	49.4	50.0	50.6	51.1	51.7	52.3	..	Urban Population, % of total
96.8	92.5	94.5	104.6	97.2	99.0	100.0	100.2	93.7	95.9	..	Food Prod. per capita (1987=100)
..	..	..	..	..	..	..	..	..	..	..	Labor Force, Agriculture (%)
46.0	45.9	45.9	45.8	45.8	45.8	45.8	45.8	45.8	45.7	..	Labor Force, Female (%)
104.0	106.0	106.0	..	100.0	..	101.0	104.0	105.0		..	Primary Schl. Enroll. Ratio
..	108.0	107.0	..	101.0	..	102.0	105.0	105.0	..	..	Primary Schl. Enroll. Ratio, Female
60.0	60.0	59.0	..	59.0	..	62.0	61.0	..	..	..	Secondary Schl. Enroll. Ratio

JAPAN	1970	1971	1972	1973	1974	1975	1976	1977	1978	1979	1980
CURRENT GNP PER CAPITA (US $)	1,950	2,140	2,540	3,230	3,860	4,530	4,990	5,650	7,000	8,630	9,830
POPULATION (millions)	104	106	107	108	110	112	113	114	115	116	117

USE AND ORIGIN OF RESOURCES *(Billions of current Japanese Yen)*

	1970	1971	1972	1973	1974	1975	1976	1977	1978	1979	1980
Gross National Product (GNP)	73,188	80,592	92,401	112,520	133,997	148,170	166,417	185,530	204,474	221,825	240,098
Net Factor Income from Abroad	-157	-109	6	23	-247	-158	-156	-92	70	279	-79
GDP at Market Prices	73,345	80,701	92,395	112,497	134,244	148,328	166,573	185,622	204,404	221,546	240,177
Resource Balance	941	2,198	2,134	30	-999	63	1,335	3,041	3,555	-2,002	-2,149
Exports of Goods & NF Services	7,926	9,452	9,779	11,291	18,258	18,982	22,582	24,308	22,729	25,627	32,887
Imports of Goods & NF Services	6,985	7,254	7,645	11,261	19,257	18,919	21,247	21,267	19,174	27,629	35,036
Domestic Absorption	72,404	78,503	90,261	112,467	135,243	148,265	165,238	182,581	200,849	223,548	242,326
Private Consumption, etc.	38,333	43,230	49,901	60,308	72,912	84,763	95,784	107,076	117,923	130,078	141,324
General Gov't Consumption	5,455	6,421	7,537	9,336	12,240	14,890	16,417	18,243	19,752	21,486	23,568
Gross Domestic Investment	28,616	28,852	32,823	42,823	50,091	48,612	53,037	57,262	63,174	71,984	77,434
Fixed Investment	26,043	27,637	31,524	40,938	46,695	48,136	51,945	55,982	62,147	70,171	75,821
Indirect Taxes, net	4,397	4,808	5,425	6,709	7,131	7,529	8,689	10,421	11,199	13,258	14,095
GDP at factor cost	68,948	75,893	86,970	105,788	127,113	140,799	157,884	175,201	193,205	208,288	226,082
Agriculture	4,488	4,274	5,050	6,675	7,506	8,141	8,870	9,402	9,441	9,623	8,847
Industry	34,230	37,282	42,135	52,185	59,956	62,901	70,747	76,862	85,200	92,071	100,681
Manufacturing	26,402	28,430	31,918	39,568	45,137	44,801	51,101	55,412	60,545	64,815	70,232
Services, etc.	34,627	39,145	45,210	53,637	66,782	77,286	86,956	99,358	109,763	119,852	130,649
Gross Domestic Saving	29,557	31,050	34,957	42,853	49,092	48,675	54,372	60,303	66,729	69,982	75,285
Gross National Saving	29,389	30,927	34,924	42,850	48,817	48,488	54,175	60,195	66,744	70,211	75,152

(Billions of 1987 Japanese Yen)

	1970	1971	1972	1973	1974	1975	1976	1977	1978	1979	1980
Gross National Product	174,355	182,074	197,529	212,962	210,958	217,001	226,172	236,672	248,401	262,482	271,406
GDP at Market Prices	174,733	182,326	197,518	212,927	211,376	217,249	226,401	236,803	248,320	262,149	271,504
Resource Balance	-2,235	-1,429	-2,379	-5,433	-3,065	-1,184	390	1,890	458	-1,335	4,357
Exports of Goods & NF Services	10,746	12,465	12,980	13,659	16,821	16,658	19,425	21,701	21,644	22,580	26,413
Imports of Goods & NF Services	12,981	13,894	15,359	19,092	19,886	17,843	19,035	19,810	21,187	23,916	22,057
Domestic Absorption	176,967	183,755	199,896	218,360	214,440	218,433	226,012	234,913	247,862	263,484	267,148
Private Consumption, etc.	100,283	106,075	115,641	125,067	124,843	131,519	135,785	141,447	148,668	157,575	161,141
General Gov't Consumption	17,066	17,965	18,936	19,944	20,582	22,190	23,182	24,128	25,357	26,460	27,333
Gross Domestic Investment	59,618	59,715	65,320	73,350	69,015	64,725	67,045	69,338	73,836	79,449	78,674
Fixed Investment	55,171	57,598	63,189	70,540	64,667	64,051	65,787	67,603	72,876	77,403	77,413
GDP at factor cost	163,863	170,957	185,369	199,694	199,916	206,076	214,433	223,284	234,362	246,296	255,868
Agriculture	9,079	8,642	9,819	10,311	10,219	10,186	9,659	9,410	9,427	9,566	8,642
Industry	70,466	74,678	81,134	88,774	85,273	86,037	91,141	93,103	98,114	105,202	108,808
Manufacturing	43,247	45,384	50,039	56,328	54,670	52,651	57,794	59,988	62,653	67,875	71,798
Services, etc.	95,187	99,006	106,565	113,842	115,883	121,026	125,602	134,290	140,778	147,381	154,054

Memo Items:

	1970	1971	1972	1973	1974	1975	1976	1977	1978	1979	1980
Capacity to Import	14,730	18,104	19,646	19,143	18,855	17,902	20,231	22,643	25,115	22,183	20,704
Terms of Trade Adjustment	3,984	5,639	6,666	5,484	2,033	1,244	806	942	3,471	-398	-5,710
Gross Domestic Income	178,716	187,965	204,184	218,411	213,409	218,493	227,208	237,746	251,790	261,751	265,795
Gross National Income	178,338	187,713	204,194	218,446	212,991	218,244	226,978	237,614	251,872	262,085	265,696

DOMESTIC PRICES/DEFLATORS *(Index 1987 = 100)*

	1970	1971	1972	1973	1974	1975	1976	1977	1978	1979	1980
Overall (GDP)	42.0	44.3	46.8	52.8	63.5	68.3	73.6	78.4	82.3	84.5	88.5
Domestic Absorption	40.9	42.7	45.2	51.5	63.1	67.9	73.1	77.7	81.0	84.8	90.7
Agriculture	49.4	49.5	51.4	64.7	73.4	79.9	91.8	99.9	100.1	100.6	102.4
Industry	48.6	49.9	51.9	58.8	70.3	73.1	77.6	82.6	86.8	87.5	92.5
Manufacturing	61.0	62.6	63.8	70.2	82.6	85.1	88.4	92.4	96.6	95.5	97.8
Consumer Price Index	36.7	39.0	40.9	45.7	56.2	62.8	68.7	74.4	77.5	80.4	86.6

MANUFACTURING ACTIVITY

	1970	1971	1972	1973	1974	1975	1976	1977	1978	1979	1980
Employment (1987=100)	103.3	102.0	104.0	105.8	101.5	99.9	99.0	96.3	96.2	96.1	97.0
Real Earnings per Empl. (1987=100)	63.0	68.3	73.2	79.8	83.7	83.0	83.8	85.3	87.0	89.4	88.3
Real Output per Empl. (1987=100)	36.7	38.1	40.3	47.0	54.3	50.9	56.6	60.9	62.2	70.1	82.0
Earnings as % of Value Added	31.8	34.2	34.8	33.4	35.2	40.4	38.6	38.7	37.8	35.6	34.8

MONETARY HOLDINGS *(Billions of current Japanese Yen)*

	1970	1971	1972	1973	1974	1975	1976	1977	1978	1979	1980
Money Supply, Broadly Defined	74,890	92,738	115,669	138,980	158,623	185,068	213,447	241,885	275,360	306,284	337,202
Money	21,360	27,693	34,526	40,311	44,951	49,949	56,179	60,786	68,929	71,020	69,572
Currency Outside Banks	5,098	5,958	7,706	9,113	10,731	11,579	12,858	14,122	16,259	17,052	17,475
Demand Deposits	16,262	21,735	26,820	31,198	34,220	38,370	43,321	46,664	52,670	53,968	52,097
Quasi-Money	53,530	65,045	81,143	98,669	113,672	135,119	157,268	181,099	206,431	235,264	267,630

GOVERNMENT DEFICIT (-) OR SURPLUS *(Billions of current Japanese Yen)*

	1970	1971	1972	1973	1974	1975	1976	1977	1978	1979	1980
	-79	-393	-1,740	-382	-3,357	-7,666	-9,417	-11,916	-15,236	-16,318	-16,872
Current Revenue	7,963	8,741	10,409	14,204	15,993	14,690	16,635	18,560	20,719	24,219	28,043
Current Expenditure	6,343	6,861	8,696	11,075	14,958	17,375	20,539	23,630	27,768	31,657	35,591
Current Budget Balance	1,620	1,880	1,713	3,129	1,035	-2,685	-3,904	-5,070	-7,049	-7,438	-7,548
Capital Receipts	227	276	100	102	24	11	20	33	21	51	62
Capital Payments	1,926	2,549	3,553	3,613	4,416	4,992	5,533	6,879	8,208	8,931	9,386

|---|---|---|---|---|---|---|---|---|---|---|---|
10,350	10,310	10,340	10,570	11,350	13,010	16,020	21,400	24,240	25,890	..	**CURRENT GNP PER CAPITA (US $)**
118	118	119	120	121	121	122	123	123	124	..	**POPULATION (millions)**
											USE AND ORIGIN OF RESOURCES
			(Billions of current Japanese Yen)								
257,416	270,671	282,078	301,048	321,556	335,838	350,479	373,730	398,695	429,173	..	Gross National Product (GNP)
-547	69	311	505	1,137	1,229	2,054	2,302	2,850	3,066	..	Net Factor Income from Abroad
257,963	270,602	281,767	300,543	320,419	334,609	348,425	371,428	395,845	426,107	..	GDP at Market Prices
2,050	2,050	5,017	8,201	10,775	13,299	11,015	8,418	5,584	2,914	..	Resource Balance
37,977	39,391	39,275	45,066	46,307	38,090	36,210	37,483	42,352	47,440	..	Exports of Goods & NFServices
35,927	37,341	34,258	36,865	35,532	24,791	25,195	29,065	36,768	44,526	..	Imports of Goods & NFServices
255,913	268,552	276,750	292,342	309,644	321,310	337,410	363,010	390,261	423,193	..	Domestic Absorption
149,997	160,834	169,687	178,631	188,760	195,969	204,585	215,122	228,445	243,401	..	Private Consumption, etc.
25,585	26,796	27,996	29,449	30,685	32,388	32,975	34,184	36,240	38,275	..	General Gov't Consumption
80,331	80,922	79,067	84,262	90,199	92,953	99,850	113,704	125,576	141,517	..	Gross Domestic Investment
78,908	79,735	78,881	83,251	88,040	91,310	99,160	111,074	122,518	138,786	..	Fixed Investment
15,710	16,505	16,663	19,136	21,250	21,535	24,960	27,469	29,001	31,556	..	Indirect Taxes, net
242,253	254,097	265,104	281,407	299,169	313,074	323,465	343,959	366,844	394,551	B	GDP at factor cost
9,075	9,238	9,516	9,957	10,214	9,975	9,768	9,754	10,221	..	..	Agriculture
108,147	112,143	114,884	123,788	131,318	135,472	141,739	153,104	164,451		..	Industry
74,939	78,468	81,748	89,245	94,673	96,262	99,297	106,650	114,405		..	Manufacturing
140,741	149,221	157,367	166,798	178,887	189,162	196,918	208,570	221,173		..	Services, etc.
82,381	82,972	84,084	92,463	100,974	106,252	110,865	122,122	131,160	144,431	..	Gross Domestic Saving
81,788	83,019	84,352	92,937	102,044	107,382	112,776	124,281	133,873	147,351	..	Gross National Saving
			(Billions of 1987 Japanese Yen)								
280,630	290,199	298,188	311,073	327,204	335,940	350,479	372,398	389,974	411,905	..	Gross National Product
281,244	290,134	297,865	310,559	326,067	334,712	348,425	370,096	387,173	408,965	..	GDP at Market Prices
7,574	8,397	10,478	12,943	15,225	12,812	11,015	8,849	7,110	7,546	..	Resource Balance
29,724	30,001	31,430	36,082	38,041	36,179	36,210	38,753	42,276	46,880	..	Exports of Goods & NFServices
22,151	21,603	20,953	23,139	22,816	23,367	25,195	29,905	35,166	39,334	..	Imports of Goods & NFServices
273,671	281,737	287,388	297,617	310,842	321,900	337,410	361,247	380,063	401,419	..	Domestic Absorption
164,568	172,332	178,906	183,857	191,045	196,971	204,585	213,851	221,488	229,746	..	Private Consumption, etc.
28,643	29,222	30,097	30,905	31,434	32,833	32,975	33,684	34,398	34,883	..	General Gov't Consumption
80,460	80,183	78,385	82,855	88,363	92,096	99,850	113,712	124,177	136,791	..	Gross Domestic Investment
79,265	79,151	78,390	82,041	86,394	90,506	99,160	110,982	120,860	134,013	..	Fixed Investment
264,381	272,789	280,584	291,103	304,822	313,191	323,465	342,636	358,668	378,697	B	GDP at factor cost
8,741	9,170	9,331	9,689	9,663	9,466	9,768	9,456	9,876	..	..	Agriculture
113,324	116,657	118,592	125,609	133,324	131,826	141,739	154,790	163,686	..	..	Industry
75,124	78,475	81,881	88,817	95,091	92,519	99,297	108,476	115,473	..	..	Manufacturing
159,179	164,308	169,943	175,261	183,080	193,420	196,918	205,850	213,611	..	..	Services, etc.
											Memo Items:
23,415	22,789	24,021	28,287	29,735	35,902	36,210	38,566	40,507	41,909	..	Capacity to Import
-6,310	-7,211	-7,409	-7,795	-8,306	-277	0	-188	-1,769	-4,971	..	Terms of Trade Adjustment
274,935	282,923	290,456	302,764	317,761	334,435	348,425	369,909	385,404	403,994	..	Gross Domestic Income
274,321	282,988	290,779	303,278	318,898	335,663	350,479	372,210	388,205	406,933	..	Gross National Income
											DOMESTIC PRICES/DEFLATORS
			(Index 1987 = 100)								
91.7	93.3	94.6	96.8	98.3	100.0	100.0	100.4	102.2	104.2	..	Overall (GDP)
93.5	95.3	96.3	98.2	99.6	99.8	100.0	100.5	102.7	105.4	..	Domestic Absorption
103.8	100.7	102.0	102.8	105.7	105.4	100.0	103.2	103.5	..	..	Agriculture
95.4	96.1	96.9	98.6	98.5	102.8	100.0	98.9	100.5		..	Industry
99.8	100.0	99.8	100.5	99.6	104.0	100.0	98.3	99.1		..	Manufacturing
90.9	93.4	95.1	97.3	99.3	99.9	100.0	100.7	103.0	106.1	..	Consumer Price Index
											MANUFACTURING ACTIVITY
97.9	97.2	98.6	99.7	100.6	101.3	100.0	101.5	101.7		..	Employment (1987=100)
89.6	91.6	92.6	94.0	96.7	98.5	100.0	102.9			..	Real Earnings per Empl. (1987=100)
83.0	86.0	89.8	98.1	102.7	95.5	100.0	108.3			..	Real Output per Empl. (1987=100)
36.2	36.2	36.4	35.1	35.2	36.7	35.4	33.9			..	Earnings as % of Value Added
											MONETARY HOLDINGS
			(Billions of current Japanese Yen)								
376,528	410,689	442,707	476,216	517,999	566,186	618,383	674,813	754,662	805,561	D	Money Supply, Broadly Defined
76,510	80,900	80,802	86,375	88,980	98,214	102,973	111,844	114,474	119,628	..	Money
18,584	19,776	20,575	22,114	23,407	26,198	28,583	31,521	36,681	37,254	..	Currency Outside Banks
57,926	61,124	60,227	64,261	65,573	72,016	74,390	80,323	77,793	82,374	..	Demand Deposits
300,018	329,789	361,905	389,841	429,019	467,972	515,410	562,969	640,188	685,933	..	Quasi-Money
			(Billions of current Japanese Yen)								
-16,826	-17,583	-18,843	-17,290	-15,603	-15,967	-12,195	-9,657	-11,424	..	C E	**GOVERNMENT DEFICIT (-) OR SURPLUS**
31,607	32,973	33,829	36,751	40,203	41,655	47,132	52,076	55,639	..	..	Current Revenue
38,938	41,253	43,550	45,095	47,375	48,820	49,746	52,656	58,219	..	..	Current Expenditure
-7,331	-8,280	-9,721	-8,344	-7,172	-7,165	-2,614	-580	-2,580	..	..	Current Budget Balance
34	65	86	84	158	136	178	154	276	..	..	Capital Receipts
9,529	9,368	9,208	9,030	8,589	8,938	9,759	9,231	9,120	..	..	Capital Payments

JAPAN	1970	1971	1972	1973	1974	1975	1976	1977	1978	1979	1980
FOREIGN TRADE (CUSTOMS BASIS)					*(Billions of current US dollars)*						
Value of Exports, fob	19.32	24.02	28.59	36.93	55.54	55.75	67.20	80.47	97.50	102.96	129.54
Nonfuel Primary Products	1.25	1.34	1.43	1.87	3.18	2.17	2.49	2.80	3.29	3.64	5.01
Fuels	0.05	0.06	0.07	0.09	0.25	0.22	0.12	0.16	0.26	0.36	0.50
Manufactures	18.02	22.61	27.08	34.97	52.11	53.36	64.60	77.51	93.95	98.96	124.03
Value of Imports, cif	18.88	19.71	23.47	38.31	62.09	57.86	64.50	70.56	78.73	110.11	139.89
Nonfuel Primary Products	10.20	10.03	11.72	19.92	24.51	21.75	24.04	26.17	29.14	40.03	42.90
Fuels	3.91	4.75	5.72	8.34	24.92	25.65	28.29	31.15	31.34	45.29	69.99
Manufactures	4.78	4.93	6.04	10.05	12.67	10.46	12.18	13.24	18.26	24.80	27.00
					(Index 1987 = 100)						
Terms of Trade	167.8	158.2	160.4	133.1	88.5	90.7	84.4	85.7	97.3	79.1	64.0
Export Prices, fob	29.8	30.8	34.4	42.8	54.7	53.2	53.2	57.9	70.0	76.0	81.0
Import Prices, cif	17.7	19.5	21.5	32.1	61.8	58.6	62.9	67.5	71.9	96.0	126.7
BALANCE OF PAYMENTS					*(Billions of current US dollars)*						
Exports of Goods & Services	22.95	28.40	34.28	44.72	66.47	68.23	80.49	94.76	114.30	126.26	158.23
Merchandise, fob	18.96	23.55	28.00	36.21	54.40	54.65	65.93	79.16	95.32	101.12	126.74
Nonfactor Services	3.23	3.81	4.60	5.80	8.41	9.83	10.93	11.58	13.29	15.69	19.89
Factor Services	0.76	1.03	1.67	2.72	3.67	3.76	3.62	4.02	5.69	9.45	11.60
Imports of Goods & Services	20.75	22.33	27.18	44.55	70.89	68.55	76.43	83.46	97.08	133.88	167.45
Merchandise, fob	15.00	15.79	19.07	32.56	53.05	49.71	56.13	62.00	71.02	99.38	124.61
Nonfactor Services	4.44	5.05	6.32	9.15	13.11	14.26	15.85	16.71	20.35	26.08	31.03
Factor Services	1.31	1.49	1.79	2.83	4.74	4.57	4.45	4.75	5.71	8.42	11.81
Long-Term Interest	..	..	..	..	..	..	..	..	..	..	..
Private Current Transfers, net	-0.03	-0.04	-0.13	-0.10	-0.10	-0.10	-0.14	-0.06	-0.26	-0.23	-0.24
Workers' Remittances	..	..	..	..	..	..	..	..	..	..	..
Curr. A/C Bal before Off. Transf.	2.17	6.03	6.97	0.08	-4.52	-0.41	3.92	11.24	16.96	-7.85	-9.46
Net Official Transfers	-0.18	-0.22	-0.33	-0.20	-0.20	-0.27	-0.22	-0.33	-0.42	-0.89	-1.29
Curr. A/C Bal after Off. Transf.	1.99	5.80	6.64	-0.13	-4.72	-0.68	3.71	10.91	16.54	-8.74	-10.75
Long-Term Capital, net	-1.46	-0.96	-3.06	-8.36	-3.59	-0.44	-1.44	-6.30	-12.39	-12.62	2.39
Direct Investment	-0.26	-0.15	-0.56	-1.93	-1.67	-1.53	-1.87	-1.63	-2.36	-2.66	-2.11
Long-Term Loans	..	..	..	..	..	..	..	..	..	..	..
Disbursements	..	..	..	..	..	..	..	..	..	..	..
Repayments	..	..	..	..	..	..	..	..	..	..	..
Other Long-Term Capital	-1.20	-0.81	-2.50	-6.43	-1.92	1.09	0.43	-4.67	-10.03	-9.96	4.50
Other Capital, net	0.53	5.42	-0.73	2.14	9.55	0.53	1.53	1.87	5.81	8.22	13.39
Change in Reserves	-1.06	-10.26	-2.85	6.35	-1.25	0.59	-3.80	-6.48	-9.96	13.14	-5.03
Memo Item:					*(Japanese Yen per US dollar)*						
Conversion Factor (Annual Avg)	360.000	349.330	303.170	271.700	292.080	296.790	296.550	268.510	210.440	219.140	226.740
EXTERNAL DEBT (Total)	..	..	..	..	*(Millions US dollars), outstanding at end of year*						
Long-Term Debt (by debtor)	..	..	..	..	..	..	..	..	..	..	..
Central Bank, incl. IMF credit	..	..	..	..	..	..	..	..	..	..	..
Central Government	..	..	..	..	..	..	..	..	..	..	..
Rest of General Government	..	..	..	..	..	..	..	..	..	..	..
Non-financial Public Enterprises	..	..	..	..	..	..	..	..	..	..	..
Priv. Sector, incl non-guaranteed	..	..	..	..	..	..	..	..	..	..	..
Short-Term Debt	..	..	..	..	..	..	..	..	..	..	..
Memo Items:					*(Millions of US dollars)*						
Int'l Reserves Excluding Gold	4,308	14,622	17,564	11,355	12,614	11,950	15,746	22,341	32,407	19,521	24,637
Gold Holdings (at market price)	569	847	1,369	2,369	3,937	2,961	2,845	3,567	5,418	12,405	14,282
SOCIAL INDICATORS											
Total Fertility Rate	2.1	2.2	2.1	2.1	2.1	1.9	1.9	1.8	1.8	1.8	1.8
Infant Mortality Rate	13.1	12.4	11.7	11.3	10.7	10.0	9.3	8.9	8.3	7.8	7.5
Life Expectancy at Birth	71.9	72.8	73.1	73.4	73.7	74.3	74.7	75.1	75.6	75.8	76.0
Urban Population, % of total	71.2	72.1	73.0	73.9	74.8	75.7	75.8	75.9	76.0	76.1	76.2
Food Prod. per capita (1987=100)	98.1	92.5	96.5	94.4	97.2	100.3	93.4	99.5	98.6	99.3	94.5
Labor Force, Agriculture (%)	19.6	18.8	17.9	17.0	16.2	15.4	14.5	13.7	12.8	12.0	11.2
Labor Force, Female (%)	39.0	38.9	38.7	38.6	38.4	38.3	38.2	38.1	37.9	37.8	37.7
Primary Schl. Enroll. Ratio	99.0	..	..	..	..	99.0	99.0	99.0	99.0	101.0	101.0
Primary Schl. Enroll. Ratio, Female	99.0	..	..	..	..	99.0	99.0	99.0	100.0	101.0	101.0
Secondary Schl. Enroll. Ratio	86.0	..	..	..	..	91.0	92.0	93.0	93.0	92.0	93.0

1981	1982	1983	1984	1985	1986	1987	1988	1989	1990 estimate	Notes	JAPAN
											FOREIGN TRADE (CUSTOMS BASIS)
				(Billions of current US dollars)							
151.91	138.58	146.80	170.04	175.86	209.08	229.05	264.77	275.04	286.77	..	Value of Exports, fob
4.72	3.96	4.32	4.38	4.17	4.60	4.94	5.78	5.87	5.99	..	Nonfuel Primary Products
0.55	0.41	0.43	0.50	0.54	0.59	0.78	0.64	1.02	1.34	..	Fuels
146.64	134.21	142.05	165.15	171.14	203.90	223.34	258.35	268.14	279.44	..	Manufactures
140.83	130.32	125.02	134.26	127.51	119.42	146.05	183.25	207.36	231.22	..	Value of Imports, cif
40.13	37.36	37.23	40.25	37.63	40.38	50.07	66.41	71.51	69.80	..	Nonfuel Primary Products
72.56	65.62	58.92	60.34	55.79	36.90	39.14	38.37	43.07	56.75	..	Fuels
28.14	27.34	28.86	33.67	34.09	42.14	56.84	78.47	92.77	104.66	..	Manufactures
				(Index 1987 = 100)							
66.2	66.5	68.2	69.7	71.4	97.6	100.0	100.5	96.0	91.1	..	Terms of Trade
85.3	79.4	78.0	77.9	76.2	91.3	100.0	110.9	118.6	118.4	..	Export Prices, fob
128.9	119.4	114.3	111.8	106.7	93.6	100.0	110.4	123.5	129.9	..	Import Prices, cif
											BALANCE OF PAYMENTS
				(Billions of current US dollars)							
189.30	178.75	183.06	210.44	219.53	259.29	304.28	371.55	413.46	446.31	..	Exports of Goods & Services
149.52	137.66	145.47	168.29	174.02	205.59	224.62	259.77	269.55	280.35	..	Merchandise, fob
23.35	22.00	21.24	22.48	22.47	23.54	28.85	35.03	39.70	40.83	..	Nonfactor Services
16.43	19.09	16.35	19.67	23.04	30.16	50.81	76.75	104.21	125.13	..	Factor Services
182.91	170.52	160.71	173.93	168.71	171.40	213.58	287.82	352.19	404.92	..	Imports of Goods & Services
129.56	119.58	114.01	124.03	118.03	112.77	128.20	164.77	192.66	216.77	..	Merchandise, fob
34.88	32.26	31.88	32.80	32.74	35.45	48.42	63.53	75.01	81.97	..	Nonfactor Services
18.47	18.68	14.82	17.10	17.94	23.18	36.96	59.52	84.52	106.18	..	Factor Services
..	..	..	..	..	..	..	..	..	..	..	Long-Term Interest
-0.21	-0.09	-0.18	-0.13	-0.28	-0.59	-0.99	-1.12	-0.99	-1.01	..	Private Current Transfers, net
..	..	..	..	..	..	..	..	..	..	..	Workers' Remittances
6.18	8.14	22.17	36.38	50.54	87.30	89.71	82.61	60.28	40.38	..	Curr. A/C Bal before Off. Transf.
-1.41	-1.29	-1.37	-1.38	-1.37	-1.47	-2.69	-3.00	-3.29	-4.51	..	Net Official Transfers
4.77	6.85	20.80	35.00	49.17	85.83	87.02	79.61	56.99	35.87	..	Curr. A/C Bal after Off. Transf.
-6.45	-16.25	-18.73	-50.01	-63.26	-132.08	-133.98	-117.09	-93.76	-53.08	..	Long-Term Capital, net
-4.71	-4.10	-3.20	-5.97	-5.81	-14.25	-18.35	-34.73	-45.22	-46.29	..	Direct Investment
..	..	..	..	..	..	..	..	..	..	..	Long-Term Loans
..	..	..	..	..	..	..	..	..	..	..	Disbursements
..	..	..	..	..	..	..	..	..	..	..	Repayments
-1.74	-12.15	-15.53	-44.04	-57.45	-117.83	-115.63	-82.36	-48.54	-6.79	..	Other Long-Term Capital
5.32	4.70	-0.52	17.13	13.51	61.09	84.90	54.00	24.01	10.62	..	Other Capital, net
-3.64	4.70	-1.55	-2.12	0.58	-14.84	-37.94	-16.52	12.76	6.59	..	Change in Reserves
				(Japanese Yen per US dollar)							**Memo Item:**
220.540	249.080	237.510	237.520	238.540	168.520	144.640	128.150	137.960	144.790	..	Conversion Factor (Annual Avg)
				(Millions US dollars), outstanding at end of year							
..	..	..	..	..	..	..	..	..	..	..	**EXTERNAL DEBT (Total)**
..	..	..	..	..	..	..	..	..	..	..	Long-Term Debt (by debtor)
..	..	..	..	..	..	..	..	..	..	..	Central Bank, incl. IMF credit
..	..	..	..	..	..	..	..	..	..	..	Central Government
..	..	..	..	..	..	..	..	..	..	..	Rest of General Government
..	..	..	..	..	..	..	..	..	..	..	Non-financial Public Enterprises
..	..	..	..	..	..	..	..	..	..	..	Priv. Sector, incl non-guaranteed
..	..	..	..	..	..	..	..	..	..	..	Short-Term Debt
				(Millions of US dollars)							**Memo Items:**
28,208	23,334	24,602	26,429	26,719	42,257	80,973	96,728	83,957	78,501	..	Int'l Reserves Excluding Gold
9,631	11,070	9,243	7,469	7,923	9,471	11,729	9,940	9,715	9,328	..	Gold Holdings (at market price)
											SOCIAL INDICATORS
1.7	1.8	1.8	1.8	1.8	1.7	1.7	1.7	1.7	1.6	..	Total Fertility Rate
7.1	6.6	6.2	6.0	5.5	5.5	5.0	4.9	4.7	4.6	..	Infant Mortality Rate
76.4	76.9	76.9	76.9	77.3	77.7	78.2	78.4	78.6	78.8	..	Life Expectancy at Birth
76.3	76.4	76.5	76.6	76.7	76.8	76.8	76.9	76.9	77.0	..	Urban Population, % of total
94.6	98.2	96.1	98.9	100.2	100.2	100.0	96.3	97.7	98.1	..	Food Prod. per capita (1987=100)
											Labor Force, Agriculture (%)
37.8	37.8	37.8	37.8	37.8	37.8	37.8	37.9	37.9	37.9	..	Labor Force, Female (%)
	101.0	101.0	101.0	102.0	102.0	102.0	101.0	102.0		..	Primary Schl. Enroll. Ratio
100.0	101.0	101.0	101.0	102.0	102.0	102.0	101.0	102.0		..	Primary Schl. Enroll. Ratio, Female
	95.0	94.0	94.0	95.0	95.0	95.0	95.0	96.0		..	Secondary Schl. Enroll. Ratio

JORDAN	1970	1971	1972	1973	1974	1975	1976	1977	1978	1979	1980
CURRENT GNP PER CAPITA (US $)	..	..	..	..	..	..	..	..	..	..	..
POPULATION (thousands)	1,508	1,574	1,634	1,690	1,748	1,810	1,876	1,947	2,021	2,099	2,181
USE AND ORIGIN OF RESOURCES					*(Millions of current Jordan Dinars)*						
Gross National Product (GNP)	..	..	..	..	..	..	..	..	..	..	..
Net Factor Income from Abroad	..	..	..	..	..	..	..	..	..	..	..
GDP at Market Prices	..	..	..	..	..	..	..	..	..	..	..
Resource Balance	..	..	..	..	..	..	..	..	..	..	..
Exports of Goods & NFServices	..	..	..	..	..	..	..	..	..	..	..
Imports of Goods & NFServices	..	..	..	..	..	..	..	..	..	..	..
Domestic Absorption	..	..	..	..	..	..	..	..	..	..	..
Private Consumption, etc.	..	..	..	..	..	..	..	..	..	..	..
General Gov't Consumption	..	..	..	..	..	..	..	..	..	..	..
Gross Domestic Investment	..	..	..	..	..	..	..	..	..	..	..
Fixed Investment	..	..	..	..	..	..	..	..	..	..	..
Indirect Taxes, net	..	..	..	..	..	..	..	..	..	..	..
GDP at factor cost	..	..	..	..	..	..	..	..	..	..	..
Agriculture	..	..	..	..	..	..	..	..	..	..	..
Industry	..	..	..	..	..	..	..	..	..	..	..
Manufacturing	..	..	..	..	..	..	..	..	..	..	..
Services, etc.	..	..	..	..	..	..	..	..	..	..	..
Gross Domestic Saving	..	..	..	..	..	..	..	..	..	..	..
Gross National Saving	..	..	..	..	..	..	..	..	..	..	..
					(Millions of 1987 Jordan Dinars)						
Gross National Product	..	..	..	..	..	..	..	..	..	..	..
GDP at Market Prices	..	..	..	..	..	..	..	..	..	..	..
Resource Balance	..	..	..	..	..	..	..	..	..	..	..
Exports of Goods & NFServices	..	..	..	..	..	..	..	..	..	..	..
Imports of Goods & NFServices	..	..	..	..	..	..	..	..	..	..	..
Domestic Absorption	..	..	..	..	..	..	..	..	..	..	..
Private Consumption, etc.	..	..	..	..	..	..	..	..	..	..	..
General Gov't Consumption	..	..	..	..	..	..	..	..	..	..	..
Gross Domestic Investment	..	..	..	..	..	..	..	..	..	..	..
Fixed Investment	..	..	..	..	..	..	..	..	..	..	..
GDP at factor cost	..	..	..	..	..	..	..	..	..	..	..
Agriculture	..	..	..	..	..	..	..	..	..	..	..
Industry	..	..	..	..	..	..	..	..	..	..	..
Manufacturing	..	..	..	..	..	..	..	..	..	..	..
Services, etc.	..	..	..	..	..	..	..	..	..	..	..
Memo Items:											
Capacity to Import	..	..	..	..	..	..	..	..	..	..	..
Terms of Trade Adjustment	..	..	..	..	..	..	..	..	..	..	..
Gross Domestic Income	..	..	..	..	..	..	..	..	..	..	..
Gross National Income	..	..	..	..	..	..	..	..	..	..	..
DOMESTIC PRICES/DEFLATORS					*(Index 1987 = 100)*						
Overall (GDP)	..	..	..	..	..	..	..	..	..	..	..
Domestic Absorption	..	..	..	..	..	..	..	..	..	..	..
Agriculture	..	..	..	..	..	..	..	..	..	..	..
Industry	..	..	..	..	..	..	..	..	..	..	..
Manufacturing	..	..	..	..	..	..	..	..	..	..	..
Consumer Price Index	26.5	27.8	29.9	33.3	39.7	44.5	49.6	56.8	60.7	69.4	77.1
MANUFACTURING ACTIVITY											
Employment (1987=100)	..	25.7	..	..	35.0	43.0	43.7	47.7	55.0	48.7	55.8
Real Earnings per Empl. (1987=100)	..	72.8	..	..	68.1	61.6	63.0	62.7	77.1	97.7	100.8
Real Output per Empl. (1987=100)	..	..	..	..	..	..	..	..	..	..	..
Earnings as % of Value Added	37.2	36.9	..	..	23.5	25.7	25.6	27.1	32.8	29.5	26.9
MONETARY HOLDINGS					*(Millions of current Jordan Dinars)*						
Money Supply, Broadly Defined	129.3	135.1	146.6	176.4	219.8	288.4	387.5	473.9	607.6	767.2	980.3
Money	105.5	108.0	115.0	139.2	172.0	224.7	276.7	329.0	370.5	465.6	580.7
Currency Outside Banks	82.4	83.0	81.5	97.5	115.5	139.0	161.5	188.2	219.5	275.4	351.6
Demand Deposits	23.0	25.0	33.6	41.8	56.5	85.7	115.2	140.8	151.1	190.2	229.1
Quasi-Money	23.8	27.1	31.6	37.2	47.8	63.8	110.8	144.9	237.1	301.6	399.5
GOVERNMENT DEFICIT (-) OR SURPLUS					*(Millions of current Jordan Dinars)*						
Current Revenue	..	..	..	..	-19.37	-21.76	-40.64	-92.59	-160.35	-74.85	-109.90
Current Expenditure	..	..	..	..	125.59	179.35	169.57	259.41	230.82	386.40	414.56
Current Budget Balance	..	..	..	..	101.58	121.89	182.96	190.90	203.58	309.75	305.40
Capital Receipts	..	..	..	..	24.01	57.46	-13.39	68.51	27.24	76.65	109.16
Capital Payments	..	..	..	..	0.05	0.04	0.02	0.02	0.06	0.13	2.79
					43.43	79.26	27.27	161.12	187.65	151.63	221.85

1981	1982	1983	1984	1985	1986	1987	1988	1989	1990 estimate	Notes	JORDAN
..	..	..	..	1,880	2,010	2,080	2,050	1,630	1,240	..	**CURRENT GNP PER CAPITA (US $)**
2,267	2,357	2,451	2,546	2,642	2,739	2,838	2,940	3,045	3,154	..	**POPULATION (thousands)**

(Millions of current Jordan Dinars)

1981	1982	1983	1984	1985	1986	1987	1988	1989	1990 estimate	Notes	JORDAN
											USE AND ORIGIN OF RESOURCES
..	..	1,826.5	1,904.3	1,925.1	2,053.0	2,071.6	2,122.7	2,304.8	2,304.6		Gross National Product (GNP)
..	..	49.2	13.6	-4.8	-17.4	-50.2	-88.6	-78.6	-292.4		Net Factor Income from Abroad
..	..	1,777.3	1,890.7	1,929.9	2,070.4	2,121.8	2,211.3	2,383.4	2,597.0		GDP at Market Prices
..	..	-783.8	-738.0	-690.8	-533.5	-498.3	-501.1	-350.2	-712.3		Resource Balance
..	..	637.2	743.2	778.1	630.3	753.5	912.5	1,350.5	1,696.2		Exports of Goods & NF Services
..	..	1,421.0	1,481.2	1,468.9	1,163.8	1,251.8	1,413.6	1,700.7	2,408.5		Imports of Goods & NF Services
..	..	2,561.1	2,628.7	2,620.7	2,604.3	2,620.1	2,712.4	2,733.6	3,309.3		Domestic Absorption
..	..	1,497.9	1,544.5	1,610.8	1,604.2	1,580.3	1,630.4	1,658.1	2,203.1		Private Consumption, etc.
..	..	461.3	522.8	515.2	546.5	566.3	578.8	601.3	616.5		General Gov't Consumption
..	..	601.9	561.4	494.7	453.6	473.5	503.2	474.2	489.7		Gross Domestic Investment
..	..	548.5	530.4	455.6	423.4	411.8	415.0	437.5	448.0		Fixed Investment
..	..	222.6	213.9	233.7	338.3	327.2	323.2	312.5	390.2		Indirect Taxes, net
..	..	1,554.7	1,676.8	1,696.2	1,732.1	1,794.6	1,888.1	2,070.9	2,206.8		GDP at factor cost
..	..	97.2	79.6	87.4	100.1	125.0	124.0	143.5	167.5		Agriculture
..	..	448.3	504.1	440.1	418.7	435.0	451.5	588.2	581.2		Industry
..	..	197.6	233.7	192.9	180.0	199.6	192.0	252.7	258.5		Manufacturing
..	..	1,009.2	1,093.1	1,168.7	1,213.3	1,234.6	1,312.6	1,339.2	1,458.1		Services, etc.
..	..	-181.9	-176.6	-196.1	-80.3	-24.8	2.1	124.0	-222.6		Gross Domestic Saving
..	..	202.9	232.3	132.6	247.0	176.8	214.1	368.3	-211.0		Gross National Saving

(Millions of 1987 Jordan Dinars)

1981	1982	1983	1984	1985	1986	1987	1988	1989	1990 estimate	Notes	JORDAN
..	..	1,786.2	1,776.5	1,817.6	2,014.9	2,071.6	2,044.9	1,906.3	1,820.4	..	Gross National Product
..	..	1,752.0	1,767.4	1,820.5	2,043.7	2,121.8	2,121.2	1,957.2	1,979.7	H	GDP at Market Prices
..	..	-580.1	-509.3	-486.8	-593.7	-498.3	-512.0	-344.8	-556.9	..	Resource Balance
..	..	605.3	667.7	695.6	605.9	753.5	817.4	911.2	1,002.9	..	Exports of Goods & NF Services
..	..	1,185.4	1,177.1	1,182.5	1,199.6	1,251.8	1,329.3	1,256.0	1,559.8	..	Imports of Goods & NF Services
..	..	2,364.3	2,344.8	2,393.4	2,665.4	2,620.1	2,620.3	2,240.2	2,456.4	..	Domestic Absorption
..	..	1,332.6	1,304.8	1,452.0	1,668.3	1,580.3	1,595.4	1,335.5	1,595.6	..	Private Consumption, etc.
..	..	502.0	569.0	527.0	532.5	566.3	578.8	583.1	574.4	..	General Gov't Consumption
..	..	529.7	470.9	414.4	464.7	473.5	446.2	321.6	286.4	..	Gross Domestic Investment
..	..	474.2	439.2	375.0	434.5	411.8	365.7	296.6	261.9	..	Fixed Investment
..	..	1,560.3	1,622.6	1,698.9	1,737.7	1,794.6	1,772.8	1,549.2	1,507.4	H	GDP at factor cost
..	..	103.4	82.1	93.9	96.9	125.0	152.9	130.0	148.1	..	Agriculture
..	..	408.1	459.4	407.7	429.0	435.0	404.1	455.7	449.0	..	Industry
..	..	200.8	223.8	200.1	192.0	199.6	172.2	217.1	215.3	..	Manufacturing
..	..	1,048.8	1,081.1	1,197.3	1,211.9	1,234.6	1,215.8	963.6	910.3	..	Services, etc.
											Memo Items:
..	..	531.6	590.6	626.4	649.7	753.5	858.1	997.4	1,098.5	..	Capacity to Import
..	..	-73.8	-77.1	-69.2	43.8	0.0	40.7	86.2	95.6	..	Terms of Trade Adjustment
..	..	1,678.2	1,690.2	1,751.2	2,087.5	2,121.8	2,161.9	2,043.5	2,075.3	..	Gross Domestic Income
..	..	1,712.4	1,699.4	1,748.4	2,058.7	2,071.6	2,085.6	1,992.5	1,916.0	..	Gross National Income

(Index 1987 = 100)

1981	1982	1983	1984	1985	1986	1987	1988	1989	1990 estimate	Notes	JORDAN
											DOMESTIC PRICES/DEFLATORS
..	..	101.4	107.0	106.0	101.3	100.0	104.2	121.8	131.2	..	Overall (GDP)
..	..	108.3	112.1	109.5	97.7	100.0	103.5	122.0	134.7	..	Domestic Absorption
..	..	94.0	97.0	93.0	103.3	100.0	81.1	110.4	113.1	..	Agriculture
..	..	109.8	109.7	108.0	97.6	100.0	111.7	129.1	129.4	..	Industry
..	..	98.4	104.4	96.4	93.8	100.0	111.5	116.4	120.1	..	Manufacturing
83.0	89.2	93.7	97.3	100.2	100.2	100.0	106.6	134.0	155.7	..	Consumer Price Index
											MANUFACTURING ACTIVITY
63.8	65.9	71.6	86.6	94.7	96.5	100.0	..	..	..	..	Employment (1987=100)
108.7	113.2	111.8	103.2	100.4	99.5	100.0	..	..	..	..	Real Earnings per Empl. (1987=100)
..	..	112.6	114.6	106.6	99.6	100.0	..	..	..	..	Real Output per Empl. (1987=100)
27.4	28.6	29.5	29.5	31.2	28.4	25.3	..	..	..	..	Earnings as % of Value Added

(Millions of current Jordan Dinars)

1981	1982	1983	1984	1985	1986	1987	1988	1989	1990 estimate	Notes	JORDAN
											MONETARY HOLDINGS
1,183.6	1,406.9	1,617.9	1,762.2	1,879.1	2,078.7	2,404.2	2,778.0	3,237.6	3,505.4	..	Money Supply, Broadly Defined
701.7	787.5	869.4	878.4	848.2	897.1	979.8	1,166.8	1,302.3	1,425.3	..	Money
412.3	470.0	516.0	530.5	531.8	583.9	655.8	811.2	871.1	1,006.2	..	Currency Outside Banks
289.3	317.5	353.4	347.9	316.4	313.2	324.0	355.6	431.2	419.1	..	Demand Deposits
482.0	619.4	748.5	883.8	1,030.9	1,181.7	1,424.4	1,611.2	1,935.4	2,080.1	..	Quasi-Money

(Millions of current Jordan Dinars)

1981	1982	1983	1984	1985	1986	1987	1988	1989	1990 estimate	Notes	JORDAN
											GOVERNMENT DEFICIT (-) OR SURPLUS
-115.91	-128.22	-108.48	-139.70	-153.08	-130.00	-247.84	-208.32	-137.50	..	..	Current Revenue
498.60	542.92	573.82	498.36	599.18	612.90	589.48	629.85	776.63	..	..	Current Expenditure
356.14	451.13	458.34	474.30	523.43	556.10	561.23	644.92	724.22	..	..	Current Budget Balance
142.46	91.79	115.48	24.06	75.75	56.80	28.25	-15.07	52.41	..	..	Capital Receipts
0.37	0.64	..	0.34	0.74	1.40	0.51	0.28	0.36	..	..	Capital Payments
258.74	220.65	223.96	164.10	229.57	188.20	276.60	193.53	190.27	..	..	

JORDAN	1970	1971	1972	1973	1974	1975	1976	1977	1978	1979	1980
FOREIGN TRADE (CUSTOMS BASIS)					*(Millions of current US dollars)*						
Value of Exports, fob	26.1	24.7	35.3	42.4	122.7	125.6	149.2	183.1	209.3	274.7	401.5
Nonfuel Primary Products	21.9	19.0	26.0	30.9	96.3	99.7	115.9	126.0	129.6	177.2	264.8
Fuels	0.0	0.1	0.0	0.5	0.4	0.9	1.9	0.0	0.1	0.0	1.0
Manufactures	4.2	5.6	9.3	11.0	26.0	25.1	31.4	57.0	79.7	97.5	135.7
Value of Imports, cif	184.5	214.6	267.0	327.9	486.6	730.8	1,022.1	1,381.1	1,498.8	1,948.6	2,394.4
Nonfuel Primary Products	64.7	70.4	92.6	112.6	156.2	183.2	297.2	292.8	369.9	459.6	503.1
Fuels	10.5	13.7	12.8	12.6	16.2	77.8	111.9	130.9	153.0	246.7	408.5
Manufactures	109.3	130.5	161.6	202.6	314.2	469.9	613.0	957.4	975.9	1,242.3	1,482.8
					(Index 1987 = 100)						
Terms of Trade	140.7	127.8	113.4	100.3	130.3	146.0	118.5	111.7	106.0	106.9	101.8
Export Prices, fob	37.9	37.3	39.3	46.6	85.2	93.8	76.4	78.0	82.1	98.6	110.0
Import Prices, cif	27.0	29.2	34.7	46.4	65.4	64.3	64.5	69.8	77.5	92.2	108.0
BALANCE OF PAYMENTS					*(Millions of current US dollars)*						
Exports of Goods & Services	123.5	113.1	124.9	189.0	279.7	414.6	590.4	815.3	973.0	1,279.5	1,781.5
Merchandise, fob	34.1	32.0	47.6	73.7	154.3	152.9	206.9	261.5	297.6	402.7	575.1
Nonfactor Services	55.0	51.2	65.0	96.2	98.1	226.4	344.3	462.1	568.6	728.0	997.4
Factor Services	34.4	30.0	12.3	19.2	27.3	35.3	39.2	91.7	106.8	148.8	209.0
Imports of Goods & Services	253.9	275.2	330.1	417.9	609.1	951.2	1,309.4	1,797.3	2,071.8	2,874.2	3,318.2
Merchandise, fob	163.8	190.4	236.6	291.9	430.3	648.2	907.9	1,443.0	1,502.2	1,959.0	2,397.6
Nonfactor Services	88.3	82.1	90.7	122.0	172.3	293.3	387.4	287.5	480.6	786.4	828.4
Factor Services	1.8	2.7	2.8	4.0	6.5	9.7	14.2	66.8	89.0	128.8	92.2
Long-Term Interest	1.8	2.8	2.9	3.1	3.9	7.0	9.4	17.8	31.5	53.1	79.0
Private Current Transfers, net	0.0	0.0	27.2	55.4	82.0	172.0	401.8	971.8	818.2	528.6	594.4
Workers' Remittances	..	..	20.7	44.7	74.8	166.7	410.9	443.7	469.6	540.6	714.6
Curr. A/C Bal before Off. Transf.	-130.4	-162.1	-178.1	-173.5	-247.4	-364.6	-317.2	-10.2	-280.6	-1,066.1	-942.3
Net Official Transfers	110.8	100.3	184.5	186.0	250.9	409.3	353.3	0.0	350.8	1,067.9	1,311.0
Curr. A/C Bal after Off. Transf.	-19.6	-61.8	6.4	12.5	3.4	44.7	36.1	-10.2	70.2	1.8	368.7
Long-Term Capital, net	3.2	21.5	17.1	19.2	32.9	137.6	-44.9	162.9	-59.6	183.7	103.7
Direct Investment	..	..	-1.1	-3.3	3.4	19.4	-10.2	15.0	50.0	15.7	27.4
Long-Term Loans	11.7	23.2	28.0	30.1	51.8	90.1	91.6	227.4	246.6	262.6	266.0
Disbursements	14.5	28.1	35.0	38.6	62.4	104.4	111.1	264.8	294.0	336.6	369.3
Repayments	2.8	4.9	7.0	8.5	10.6	14.3	19.5	37.4	47.4	74.0	103.3
Other Long-Term Capital	-8.5	-1.7	-9.8	-7.6	-22.3	28.1	-126.2	-79.5	-356.2	-94.6	-189.7
Other Capital, net	10.7	1.2	-4.8	7.8	-10.4	-9.4	36.1	53.5	110.4	26.7	-165.6
Change in Reserves	5.7	39.2	-18.7	-39.4	-26.0	-172.9	-27.4	-206.2	-121.0	-212.2	-306.8
Memo Item:					*(Jordan Dinars per US dollar)*						
Conversion Factor (Annual Avg)	0.360	0.360	0.360	0.330	0.320	0.320	0.330	0.330	0.310	0.300	0.300
EXTERNAL DEBT (Total)	119.5	153.8	178.7	214.1	*(Millions of US dollars), outstanding at end of year* 272.4	346.1	436.5	798.3	1,167.5	1,522.6	1,976.8
Long-Term Debt (by debtor)	119.5	153.8	178.7	214.1	272.4	346.1	436.5	686.3	962.5	1,238.6	1,491.1
Central Bank, incl. IMF credit	0.0	4.9	4.9	1.9	0.0	0.0	0.0	0.0	0.0	0.0	0.0
Central Government	110.2	123.5	148.4	186.0	223.3	277.1	357.7	495.9	704.3	903.6	1,021.0
Rest of General Government	3.0	3.0	3.1	3.3	3.3	3.0	7.3	8.8	13.0	15.3	14.5
Non-financial Public Enterprises	5.0	21.2	21.2	21.4	43.8	61.1	61.8	167.9	227.0	299.2	430.0
Priv. Sector, incl non-guaranteed	1.3	1.2	1.1	1.5	2.0	4.9	9.7	13.7	18.2	20.5	25.6
Short-Term Debt	0.0	0.0	0.0	0.0	0.0	0.0	0.0	112.0	205.0	284.0	485.7
Memo Items:					*(Millions of US dollars)*						
Int'l Reserves Excluding Gold	227.8	222.9	241.0	270.7	312.8	458.9	471.5	643.2	885.6	1,166.1	1,142.8
Gold Holdings (at market price)	29.8	34.8	51.7	89.5	148.6	111.8	107.4	133.0	183.3	417.8	601.9
SOCIAL INDICATORS											
Total Fertility Rate	..	..	..	..	..	..	..	7.7	7.5	7.3	7.0
Infant Mortality Rate	..	..	..	..	..	..	..	80.0	77.6	75.2	72.8
Life Expectancy at Birth	54.6	55.6	56.6	57.5	58.4	59.3	60.2	61.2	61.7	62.2	62.7
Urban Population, % of total	..	..	..	..	..	..	..	..	..	..	59.0
Food Prod. per capita (1987=100)	83.8	106.4	115.6	75.4	110.5	74.8	78.5	77.3	94.1	64.6	95.4
Labor Force, Agriculture (%)	27.8	25.9	24.1	22.4	20.7	19.0	17.2	15.5	13.7	12.0	10.2
Labor Force, Female (%)	6.4	6.6	6.7	6.9	7.0	7.1	7.3	7.5	7.6	7.8	7.9
Primary Schl. Enroll. Ratio	..	..	..	..	..	..	..	..	98.0	102.0	104.0
Primary Schl. Enroll. Ratio, Female	..	..	..	..	..	..	..	..	97.0	99.0	102.0
Secondary Schl. Enroll. Ratio	..	..	..	..	..	..	..	..	67.0	74.0	76.0

1981	1982	1983	1984	1985	1986	1987	1988	1989	1990 estimate	Notes	JORDAN
											FOREIGN TRADE (CUSTOMS BASIS)
				(Millions of current US dollars)							
509.8	528.3	439.9	677.8	649.0	645.1	730.3	884.8	1,117.9	1,146.3	..	Value of Exports, fob
292.3	299.1	258.8	350.0	368.0	409.8	380.0	487.7	616.2	631.8	..	Nonfuel Primary Products
0.2	0.1	0.1	0.0	0.0	0.2	0.0	0.9	1.1	1.2	..	Fuels
217.3	229.1	180.9	327.7	280.9	235.1	350.2	396.2	500.6	513.3	..	Manufactures
3,146.3	3,217.5	3,016.3	2,688.7	2,593.2	2,412.7	2,690.9	2,746.7	2,156.4	2,662.8	..	Value of Imports, cif
612.6	666.3	641.9	626.2	591.9	620.5	623.6	648.4	509.0	628.6	..	Nonfuel Primary Products
546.8	682.0	584.2	556.3	567.7	346.0	464.5	430.6	338.0	417.4	..	Fuels
1,986.8	1,869.1	1,790.2	1,506.1	1,433.5	1,446.2	1,602.8	1,667.8	1,309.4	1,616.8	..	Manufactures
				(Index 1987 = 100)							
98.5	96.9	94.4	97.1	95.0	105.9	100.0	104.0	111.9	112.0	..	Terms of Trade
107.4	100.2	95.2	95.1	91.5	96.7	100.0	106.5	108.2	106.1	..	Export Prices, fob
109.0	103.5	100.8	98.0	96.3	91.3	100.0	102.3	96.7	94.8	..	Import Prices, cif
											BALANCE OF PAYMENTS
				(Millions of current US dollars)							
2,214.6	2,208.9	1,930.2	2,038.4	2,075.7	1,903.8	2,283.0	2,471.0	2,391.0	2,580.4	f	Exports of Goods & Services
735.0	750.8	580.2	756.8	789.7	731.8	932.0	1,016.0	1,110.0	1,064.0	..	Merchandise, fob
1,172.8	1,142.5	1,177.0	1,180.6	1,186.0	1,072.0	1,293.0	1,415.0	1,241.0	1,448.9	..	Nonfactor Services
306.8	315.6	173.0	101.0	100.0	100.0	58.0	40.0	40.0	67.5	..	Factor Services
4,865.2	4,941.9	4,042.9	4,018.4	3,912.0	3,566.0	3,517.0	4,112.0	3,656.0	4,185.0	f	Imports of Goods & Services
3,169.7	3,239.0	3,035.9	2,783.7	2,718.0	2,422.0	2,236.0	2,716.0	2,398.4	2,732.0	..	Merchandise, fob
1,049.3	1,051.7	879.0	1,072.7	1,005.0	903.0	1,002.0	1,048.0	833.0	983.0	..	Nonfactor Services
646.2	651.2	128.0	162.0	189.0	241.0	279.0	348.0	425.0	470.0	..	Factor Services
94.3	101.0	139.1	143.4	205.9	238.6	281.5	303.1	253.7	271.5	..	Long-Term Interest
823.8	831.4	924.4	1,028.1	845.0	985.0	744.0	803.0	562.0	458.0	..	Private Current Transfers, net
929.4	975.5	1,110.0	1,237.0	1,021.0	1,184.0	939.0	894.0	623.0	500.0	..	Workers' Remittances
-1,826.8	-1,901.6	-1,188.3	-951.9	-991.3	-677.2	-490.0	-838.0	-703.0	-1,146.6	..	Curr. A/C Bal before Off. Transf.
1,258.2	1,032.4	797.7	681.4	739.0	633.0	599.0	550.0	599.0	393.0	..	Net Official Transfers
-568.6	-869.2	-390.6	-270.5	-252.3	-44.2	109.0	-288.0	-104.0	-753.6	..	Curr. A/C Bal after Off. Transf.
135.0	352.8	426.2	167.6	338.9	147.9	223.0	88.0	-399.0	-363.0	f	Long-Term Capital, net
67.7	90.6	24.3	75.2	14.1	22.6	0.0	0.0	0.0	..	..	Direct Investment
329.6	413.4	568.0	291.2	396.8	620.9	450.2	292.3	828.4	32.2	..	Long-Term Loans
513.3	545.0	744.9	525.7	688.4	977.5	910.3	859.8	1,028.5	381.0	..	Disbursements
183.7	131.6	176.9	234.5	291.6	356.6	460.1	567.5	200.1	348.8	..	Repayments
-262.3	-151.2	-166.1	-198.8	-72.0	-495.6	-227.2	-204.3	-1,227.4	-395.2	..	Other Long-Term Capital
480.1	339.2	103.0	-77.4	67.4	31.3	73.0	-287.0	765.5	1,469.6	f	Other Capital, net
-46.5	177.2	-138.6	180.3	-154.0	-135.0	-405.0	487.0	-262.5	-353.0	..	Change in Reserves
				(Jordan Dinars per US dollar)							Memo Item:
0.330	0.350	0.360	0.380	0.390	0.350	0.340	0.370	0.570	0.660	..	Conversion Factor (Annual Avg)
				(Millions of US dollars), outstanding at end of year							
2,291.2	2,746.6	3,207.1	3,508.3	4,153.4	5,025.8	6,373.3	6,564.1	7,418.2	7,677.6	..	**EXTERNAL DEBT (Total)**
1,762.5	2,137.9	2,634.8	2,831.6	3,460.6	4,260.8	5,050.6	5,389.9	6,499.9	6,580.2	..	Long-Term Debt (by debtor)
0.0	0.0	0.0	0.0	63.0	71.5	181.7	166.5	271.4	252.0	..	Central Bank, incl. IMF credit
1,015.0	1,172.8	1,686.4	1,804.5	2,284.2	2,914.8	3,387.2	3,735.9	4,641.9	4,932.9	..	Central Government
15.1	28.8	28.3	25.7	24.1	21.9	21.0	19.1	16.8	15.1	..	Rest of General Government
705.8	906.3	891.7	976.4	1,060.1	1,220.5	1,423.1	1,435.2	1,517.2	1,322.7	..	Non-financial Public Enterprises
26.6	30.0	28.4	25.0	29.2	32.1	37.6	33.2	52.6	57.5	..	Priv. Sector, incl non-guaranteed
528.7	608.7	572.3	676.7	692.8	765.0	1,322.7	1,174.2	918.3	1,097.4	..	Short-Term Debt
				(Millions of US dollars)							Memo Items:
1,086.7	884.1	824.2	515.0	422.8	437.1	424.7	109.6	470.7	848.8	..	Int'l Reserves Excluding Gold
424.1	493.5	415.8	326.8	347.0	415.9	485.1	304.8	300.0	289.9	..	Gold Holdings (at market price)
											SOCIAL INDICATORS
6.8	6.6	6.6	6.6	6.5	6.5	6.5	6.4	6.3	6.3	..	Total Fertility Rate
70.4	68.0	65.8	63.6	61.3	59.1	56.9	54.9	52.9	51.0	..	Infant Mortality Rate
63.2	63.5	64.0	64.5	65.0	65.5	66.0	66.4	66.8	67.3	..	Life Expectancy at Birth
59.2	59.4	59.6	59.8	60.0	60.2	60.4	60.6	60.8	61.0	..	Urban Population, % of total
88.2	82.8	99.5	88.8	102.7	87.8	100.0	99.9	76.7	72.9	..	Food Prod. per capita (1987=100)
..	..	..	..	..	..	..	..	..	..	..	Labor Force, Agriculture (%)
..	..	..	..	..	..	..	..	..	..	..	Labor Force, Female (%)
8.2	8.5	8.7	8.9	9.1	9.4	9.6	9.9	10.1	10.3	..	Primary Schl. Enroll. Ratio
..	100.0	99.0	..	..	..	..	..	..	..	..	Primary Schl. Enroll. Ratio, Female
100.0	98.0	99.0	..	..	..	..	..	..	..	..	Secondary Schl. Enroll. Ratio
..	78.0	79.0									

KENYA	1970	1971	1972	1973	1974	1975	1976	1977	1978	1979	1980
CURRENT GNP PER CAPITA (US $)	130	160	180	180	210	230	240	270	310	370	420
POPULATION (thousands)	11,498	11,902	12,327	12,773	13,244	13,741	14,258	14,805	15,383	15,992	16,632
USE AND ORIGIN OF RESOURCES					*(Billions of current Kenya Shillings)*						
Gross National Product (GNP)	11.03	12.32	14.62	16.69	20.37	23.01	27.71	35.62	39.17	44.93	52.23
Net Factor Income from Abroad	-0.42	-0.38	-0.43	-0.88	-0.85	-0.93	-1.36	-1.57	-1.82	-1.68	-1.68
GDP at Market Prices	11.45	12.70	15.05	17.57	21.21	23.93	29.07	37.20	40.99	46.60	53.91
Resource Balance	-0.10	-0.83	-0.32	-0.22	-1.53	-1.12	0.20	1.25	-4.00	-2.73	-5.99
Exports of Goods & NFServices	3.42	3.64	4.00	4.81	7.14	7.14	9.43	13.00	11.86	12.00	15.07
Imports of Goods & NFServices	3.51	4.47	4.32	5.04	8.68	8.26	9.23	11.75	15.86	14.73	21.05
Domestic Absorption	11.55	13.53	15.37	17.79	22.75	25.06	28.87	35.95	44.99	49.33	59.90
Private Consumption, etc.	6.89	8.21	9.36	10.37	13.67	16.33	17.91	20.75	24.79	30.00	33.47
General Gov't Consumption	1.86	2.28	2.65	2.89	3.61	4.39	5.08	6.40	8.00	8.95	10.68
Gross Domestic Investment	2.79	3.04	3.36	4.53	5.46	4.34	5.88	8.80	12.20	10.39	15.75
Fixed Investment	2.25	2.88	3.28	3.59	4.06	4.84	5.81	7.80	10.28	10.87	12.42
Indirect Taxes, net	1.07	1.30	1.28	1.78	2.44	2.79	3.51	4.38	5.39	5.94	7.94
GDP at factor cost	10.38	11.40	13.78	15.79	18.78	21.14	25.56	32.81	35.60	40.66	45.97
Agriculture	3.46	3.58	4.85	5.60	6.64	7.22	9.69	13.77	13.14	14.07	14.98
Industry	2.06	2.32	2.81	3.28	3.89	4.28	4.76	5.90	7.15	8.07	9.58
Manufacturing	1.24	1.43	1.56	1.89	2.39	2.54	2.88	3.60	4.39	5.00	5.90
Services, etc.	4.86	5.50	6.12	6.92	8.25	9.64	11.12	13.15	15.31	18.52	21.40
Gross Domestic Saving	2.70	2.21	3.04	4.31	3.93	3.22	6.09	10.05	8.20	7.66	9.77
Gross National Saving	2.20	1.73	2.59	3.37	2.99	2.20	4.56	8.51	6.51	6.06	8.29
					(Millions of 1987 Kenya Shillings)						
Gross National Product	44,499	54,705	64,924	67,278	70,600	71,842	72,657	79,564	84,932	92,372	97,927
GDP at Market Prices	46,575	57,033	67,458	71,389	73,983	74,963	76,598	83,778	89,480	96,193	101,352
Resource Balance	-16,636	-21,882	-17,162	-14,806	-18,802	-11,195	-9,866	-15,258	-25,569	-17,211	-19,980
Exports of Goods & NFServices	21,968	22,973	20,513	22,287	25,665	22,683	23,114	23,759	24,158	23,053	24,305
Imports of Goods & NFServices	38,604	44,855	37,675	37,094	44,467	33,878	32,980	39,017	49,727	40,264	44,285
Domestic Absorption	63,212	78,915	84,620	86,196	92,786	86,158	86,464	99,036	115,049	113,404	121,332
Private Consumption, etc.	27,036	40,981	48,031	43,928	51,145	52,047	48,935	51,711	58,000	64,307	62,070
General Gov't Consumption	9,170	10,547	11,439	11,851	12,862	14,398	15,464	17,352	19,924	21,064	21,542
Gross Domestic Investment	27,006	27,386	25,150	30,417	28,779	19,713	22,066	29,974	37,126	28,033	37,720
Fixed Investment	..	..	..	..	..	..	..	..	..	28,624	29,343
GDP at factor cost	41,217	50,123	58,892	61,591	62,263	64,802	66,356	72,191	76,642	81,988	85,265
Agriculture	16,673	19,362	21,573	22,161	21,620	23,211	23,654	26,018	27,001	27,732	28,030
Industry	6,061	7,654	11,217	12,101	12,198	12,254	12,207	13,776	15,233	15,771	16,612
Manufacturing	3,199	4,142	5,503	6,263	6,591	6,631	6,559	7,601	8,552	9,190	9,671
Services, etc.	18,483	23,107	26,103	27,329	28,445	29,337	30,495	32,397	34,408	38,485	40,623
Memo Items:											
Capacity to Import	37,549	36,506	34,870	35,444	36,615	29,276	33,702	43,174	37,192	32,802	31,690
Terms of Trade Adjustment	15,581	13,533	14,356	13,157	10,950	6,593	10,587	19,415	13,034	9,750	7,385
Gross Domestic Income	62,156	70,566	81,814	84,546	84,934	81,556	87,186	103,193	102,514	105,943	108,737
Gross National Income	60,080	68,238	79,281	80,434	81,550	78,435	83,244	98,979	97,966	102,121	105,312
DOMESTIC PRICES/DEFLATORS					*(Index 1987 = 100)*						
Overall (GDP)	24.6	22.3	22.3	24.6	28.7	31.9	38.0	44.4	45.8	48.4	53.2
Domestic Absorption	18.3	17.2	18.2	20.6	24.5	29.1	33.4	36.3	39.1	43.5	49.4
Agriculture	20.7	18.5	22.5	25.3	30.7	31.1	41.0	52.9	48.7	50.7	53.5
Industry	34.0	30.4	25.1	27.1	31.9	34.9	39.0	42.8	46.9	51.2	57.7
Manufacturing	38.9	34.6	28.3	30.2	36.2	38.3	44.0	47.3	51.3	54.4	61.0
Consumer Price Index	15.8	16.4	17.3	19.0	22.3	26.6	29.6	34.0	39.8	43.0	48.9
MANUFACTURING ACTIVITY											
Employment (1987=100)	37.0	40.8	50.5	56.0	61.7	59.7	64.4	71.7	77.1	82.0	82.4
Real Earnings per Empl. (1987=100)	131.1	123.7	145.8	137.0	137.2	125.2	125.3	112.0	102.6	102.1	97.7
Real Output per Empl. (1987=100)	22.7	27.0	40.1	41.8	46.2	53.1	58.6	68.5	60.0	56.5	53.7
Earnings as % of Value Added	50.2	47.5	48.0	44.4	43.6	44.0	39.4	36.2	38.9	41.6	43.0
MONETARY HOLDINGS					*(Millions of current Kenya Shillings)*						
Money Supply, Broadly Defined	4,005	4,307	4,908	6,120	6,731	8,051	9,820	14,355	16,571	19,253	20,430
Money	2,226	2,371	2,804	3,449	3,755	4,143	5,120	7,333	7,879	9,178	8,434
Currency Outside Banks	697	740	894	982	1,086	1,235	1,625	2,182	2,305	2,673	3,032
Demand Deposits	1,529	1,631	1,909	2,467	2,670	2,908	3,495	5,151	5,573	6,504	5,402
Quasi-Money	1,779	1,936	2,104	2,671	2,975	3,909	4,700	7,022	8,693	10,075	11,997
GOVERNMENT DEFICIT (-) OR SURPLUS					*(Millions of current Kenya Shillings)*						
	..	..	-566	-902	-587	-1,151	-1,709	-1,327	-1,627	-3,015	-2,409
Current Revenue	..	..	2,712	2,827	3,696	4,522	5,325	6,381	9,364	10,100	12,206
Current Expenditure	..	..	2,352	2,618	3,080	4,006	4,848	5,531	7,643	9,400	10,455
Current Budget Balance	..	..	360	209	616	516	477	850	1,721	700	1,751
Capital Receipts	..	..	..	1	..	..	..	2	1	2	2
Capital Payments	..	..	926	1,112	1,203	1,667	2,186	2,179	3,349	3,717	4,162

1981	1982	1983	1984	1985	1986	1987	1988	1989	1990 estimate	Notes	KENYA
430	400	350	320	310	330	340	370	370	370	..	**CURRENT GNP PER CAPITA (US $)**
17,305	18,012	18,745	19,490	20,241	20,999	21,768	22,549	23,345	24,160	..	**POPULATION (thousands)**
											USE AND ORIGIN OF RESOURCES
			(Billions of current Kenya Shillings)								
60.07	67.52	77.11	86.25	97.08	113.29	126.21	144.61	165.07	192.94	..	Gross National Product (GNP)
-1.94	-2.79	-2.54	-3.00	-4.19	-4.97	-4.97	-6.41	-7.26	-7.71	..	Net Factor Income from Abroad
62.02	70.31	79.66	89.25	100.75	117.48	131.18	151.02	172.33	200.65	f	GDP at Market Prices
-5.04	-2.64	-0.36	-1.23	-1.07	0.21	-6.69	-7.79	-9.89	-10.54	..	Resource Balance
15.94	17.55	19.93	23.41	25.50	30.33	27.99	33.30	39.95	50.84	..	Exports of Goods & NF Services
20.97	20.19	20.28	24.64	26.57	30.13	34.68	41.09	49.85	61.39	..	Imports of Goods & NF Services
67.05	72.94	80.02	90.48	101.82	117.28	137.87	158.81	182.23	211.19	..	Domestic Absorption
38.36	44.64	48.77	56.45	58.07	70.19	81.67	93.35	107.71	126.85	..	Private Consumption, etc.
11.53	12.95	14.66	15.51	17.60	21.52	24.35	27.71	32.15	36.83	..	General Gov't Consumption
17.16	15.35	16.59	18.51	26.15	25.57	31.85	37.74	42.36	47.51	..	Gross Domestic Investment
14.49	13.36	14.35	16.14	18.03	23.06	25.73	30.32	33.16	40.61	..	Fixed Investment
8.83	9.32	10.19	11.79	12.37	15.18	18.22	21.58	23.81	27.98	..	Indirect Taxes, net
53.19	60.99	69.47	77.46	88.37	102.30	112.96	129.44	148.52	172.67	f	GDP at factor cost
17.29	20.35	23.77	26.27	28.73	33.80	35.64	40.78	45.43	48.83	..	Agriculture
10.78	12.16	13.46	14.66	16.88	19.01	20.89	24.67	29.20	36.49	..	Industry
6.56	7.45	8.16	9.22	10.37	12.16	13.05	15.06	17.11	19.75	..	Manufacturing
25.12	28.48	32.24	36.53	42.76	49.49	56.43	63.99	73.90	87.36	..	Services, etc.
12.13	12.72	16.23	17.28	25.08	25.77	25.16	29.95	32.47	36.97	..	Gross Domestic Saving
11.08	10.84	14.53	15.15	22.75	22.53	21.38	25.12	27.30	33.10	..	Gross National Saving
			(Millions of 1987 Kenya Shillings)								
102,065	103,204	105,541	107,028	111,473	119,373	126,210	133,066	139,214	146,792	..	Gross National Product
105,475	107,431	109,006	110,854	115,651	123,890	131,182	139,032	145,377	152,709	f	GDP at Market Prices
-11,682	-5,302	-455	-4,525	-925	-2,868	-6,690	-8,544	-8,954	-8,969	..	Resource Balance
23,287	24,028	23,479	23,685	25,276	27,746	27,992	29,271	27,622	29,246	..	Exports of Goods & NF Services
34,969	29,329	23,934	28,210	26,201	30,614	34,682	37,814	36,576	38,215	..	Imports of Goods & NF Services
117,157	112,733	109,461	115,379	116,577	126,759	137,872	147,575	154,331	161,678	..	Domestic Absorption
60,229	64,571	63,324	68,112	61,977	75,875	81,666	88,045	92,852	101,329	..	Private Consumption, etc.
20,382	20,075	21,793	21,796	22,016	23,591	24,354	24,807	25,160	26,317	..	General Gov't Consumption
36,546	28,087	24,344	25,471	32,584	27,293	31,852	34,724	36,319	34,033	..	Gross Domestic Investment
30,815	24,287	20,936	21,576	22,212	24,284	25,734	27,868	27,624	27,653	..	Fixed Investment
90,352	93,927	96,248	97,050	102,014	107,730	112,964	118,817	124,695	130,329	f	GDP at factor cost
29,691	31,878	32,470	31,342	32,598	34,203	35,638	37,311	38,793	40,144	..	Agriculture
17,276	17,568	17,652	18,028	19,085	19,845	20,894	22,015	23,284	24,486	..	Industry
10,018	10,244	10,706	11,165	11,669	12,346	13,050	13,834	14,651	15,416	..	Manufacturing
43,385	44,481	46,126	47,680	50,330	53,682	56,432	59,491	62,618	65,699	..	Services, etc.
											Memo Items:
26,573	25,500	23,512	26,802	25,144	30,823	27,992	30,646	29,317	31,651	..	Capacity to Import
3,286	1,472	33	3,117	-132	3,078	0	1,376	1,694	2,405	..	Terms of Trade Adjustment
108,760	108,903	109,039	113,971	115,519	126,968	131,182	140,407	147,072	155,114	..	Gross Domestic Income
105,351	104,676	105,574	110,145	111,341	122,451	126,210	134,442	140,908	149,198	..	Gross National Income
											DOMESTIC PRICES/DEFLATORS
			(Index 1987 = 100)								
58.8	65.4	73.1	80.5	87.1	94.8	100.0	108.6	118.5	131.4	..	Overall (GDP)
57.2	64.7	73.1	78.4	87.3	92.5	100.0	107.6	118.1	130.6	..	Domestic Absorption
58.2	63.8	73.2	83.8	88.1	98.8	100.0	109.3	117.1	121.6	..	Agriculture
62.4	69.2	76.2	81.3	88.4	95.8	100.0	112.0	125.4	149.0	..	Industry
65.5	72.7	76.3	82.6	88.9	98.5	100.0	108.9	116.8	128.1	..	Manufacturing
54.7	65.9	73.4	80.9	91.5	95.1	100.0	108.3	118.9	132.9	..	Consumer Price Index
											MANUFACTURING ACTIVITY
88.2	86.8	87.9	90.1	93.7	97.1	100.0	102.4	..	..	G	Employment (1987=100)
103.2	99.8	97.2	97.7	91.3	94.8	100.0	103.3	..	..	G	Real Earnings per Empl. (1987=100)
58.5	69.4	71.2	78.2	83.6	88.4	100.0	97.5	..	..	G	Real Output per Empl. (1987=100)
44.5	43.4	44.4	44.7	43.5	43.8	44.1	43.8	..	..		Earnings as % of Value Added
											MONETARY HOLDINGS
			(Millions of current Kenya Shillings)								
23,708	27,585	30,256	35,862	39,488	49,979	55,653	60,064	68,794	84,755	D	Money Supply, Broadly Defined
9,409	10,635	11,473	13,095	12,923	17,522	18,916	19,160	21,647	27,529	..	Money
3,569	3,724	4,083	4,370	5,038	6,371	7,688	8,536	9,655	10,829	..	Currency Outside Banks
5,840	6,911	7,390	8,725	7,885	11,151	11,229	10,624	11,992	16,699	..	Demand Deposits
14,299	16,950	18,783	22,767	26,565	32,457	36,736	40,904	47,147	57,226	..	Quasi-Money
			(Millions of current Kenya Shillings)								
-4,002	-5,463	-3,838	-4,281	-6,245	-5,144	-8,329	-6,242	-11,193	..	..	C	**GOVERNMENT DEFICIT (-) OR SURPLUS**
13,959	15,270	16,620	18,230	20,347	24,129	29,121	34,159	41,490	..	..	Current Revenue
12,851	16,400	17,002	19,339	21,782	25,093	30,004	34,187	43,088	..	..	Current Expenditure
1,108	-1,130	-382	-1,109	-1,435	-964	-883	-28	-1,598	..	..	Current Budget Balance
15	11	2	1	1	2	6	11	18	..	..	Capital Receipts
5,125	4,344	3,458	3,173	4,811	4,182	7,452	6,225	9,613	..	..	Capital Payments

KENYA	1970	1971	1972	1973	1974	1975	1976	1977	1978	1979	1980
FOREIGN TRADE (CUSTOMS BASIS)					*(Millions of current US dollars)*						
Value of Exports, fob	200.5	204.9	253.6	349.2	456.2	456.0	761.5	1,161.0	955.8	1,030.7	1,313.4
Nonfuel Primary Products	151.7	145.1	190.1	267.7	309.5	294.0	476.3	841.5	650.4	681.5	714.4
Fuels	23.4	29.7	31.7	37.1	86.7	101.3	167.2	203.0	180.0	206.9	438.7
Manufactures	25.3	30.1	31.8	44.4	60.0	60.8	117.9	116.5	125.3	142.2	160.3
Value of Imports, cif	397.4	514.8	496.1	587.6	986.6	910.8	971.8	1,285.6	1,705.9	1,655.5	2,122.0
Nonfuel Primary Products	38.8	62.5	64.6	80.1	105.2	80.4	112.0	130.3	172.1	154.2	217.4
Fuels	40.8	46.9	57.1	65.2	227.6	256.9	250.1	286.1	307.5	395.8	718.6
Manufactures	317.9	405.4	374.3	442.3	653.9	573.5	609.8	869.1	1,226.3	1,105.5	1,186.0
Terms of Trade	113.3	100.8	120.4	128.8	131.0	119.1	140.8	167.9	131.6	131.6	123.8
					(Index 1987 = 100)						
Export Prices, fob	24.0	25.9	31.2	43.7	71.4	65.3	81.2	108.2	95.8	113.0	129.7
Import Prices, cif	21.2	25.7	25.9	33.9	54.5	54.9	57.7	64.5	72.8	85.8	104.8
BALANCE OF PAYMENTS					*(Millions of current US dollars)*						
Exports of Goods & Services	505.5	529.0	580.7	706.0	971.4	1,011.1	1,142.9	1,593.9	1,543.6	1,629.4	2,061.3
Merchandise, fob	285.5	293.7	337.4	469.9	581.0	633.2	745.9	1,130.9	956.0	1,031.4	1,261.4
Nonfactor Services	172.8	200.8	207.2	209.2	352.0	321.5	361.7	422.2	540.3	537.5	745.9
Factor Services	47.2	34.5	36.2	26.8	38.4	56.4	35.4	40.8	47.4	60.5	53.9
Imports of Goods & Services	580.1	699.0	686.9	861.9	1,310.6	1,280.0	1,281.7	1,632.8	2,295.1	2,219.0	3,094.7
Merchandise, fob	371.8	478.6	454.3	544.8	897.9	846.9	809.7	1,112.8	1,631.8	1,594.2	2,344.8
Nonfactor Services	138.2	161.3	162.4	188.2	273.4	283.8	294.6	320.9	428.4	376.6	501.6
Factor Services	70.1	59.1	70.2	128.9	139.4	149.3	177.4	199.1	234.9	248.3	248.2
Long-Term Interest	17.4	17.7	19.7	29.1	40.0	45.6	49.6	61.6	86.9	115.3	166.4
Private Current Transfers, net	-11.2	-12.9	-1.4	-8.7	-13.7	-12.5	-19.6	3.4	16.3	10.7	27.2
Workers' Remittances	..	..	..	..	..	..	..	..	..	..	0.0
Curr. A/C Bal before Off. Transf.	-85.8	-182.9	-107.6	-164.6	-353.0	-281.3	-158.4	-35.5	-735.2	-579.0	-1,006.2
Net Official Transfers	36.8	71.2	39.5	38.6	45.1	62.9	34.1	63.1	74.7	80.6	120.2
Curr. A/C Bal after Off. Transf.	-49.0	-111.7	-68.1	-126.0	-307.9	-218.4	-124.2	27.5	-660.5	-498.4	-886.0
Long-Term Capital, net	50.1	36.8	71.9	129.7	184.6	156.3	222.1	189.5	416.5	488.3	532.2
Direct Investment	13.8	12.4	..			15.8	42.1	53.9	32.1	78.1	77.9
Long-Term Loans	47.0	28.8	86.1	184.9	214.6	115.3	203.1	152.6	443.5	370.2	402.4
Disbursements	75.8	63.5	113.7	220.5	271.6	205.1	309.5	376.1	578.2	527.9	603.0
Repayments	28.8	34.7	27.6	35.6	57.0	89.8	106.4	223.5	134.7	157.7	200.6
Other Long-Term Capital	-10.7	-4.4	-14.2	-55.2	-30.0	25.2	-23.1	-17.0	-59.1	40.0	51.9
Other Capital, net	44.3	4.4	20.0	18.0	35.2	24.4	-12.2	59.7	44.0	200.7	152.3
Change in Reserves	-45.4	70.5	-23.8	-21.7	88.1	37.7	-85.7	-276.7	200.1	-190.6	201.5
Memo Item:					*(Kenya Shillings per US dollar)*						
Conversion Factor (Annual Avg)	7.140	7.140	7.140	7.000	7.140	7.340	8.370	8.280	7.730	7.480	7.420
EXTERNAL DEBT (Total)					*(Millions of US dollars), outstanding at end of year*						
	406.1	420.9	491.6	716.4	980.1	1,093.4	1,283.4	1,717.7	2,250.8	2,771.4	3,403.0
Long-Term Debt (by debtor)	406.1	420.9	491.6	716.4	980.1	1,093.4	1,283.4	1,414.7	1,847.8	2,342.4	2,764.9
Central Bank, incl. IMF credit	0.0	0.0	0.0	0.0	40.6	84.2	109.9	79.0	113.1	218.3	287.8
Central Government	284.4	293.9	330.0	384.1	446.3	481.8	533.3	710.9	789.9	1,141.1	1,462.0
Rest of General Government	4.5	5.5	7.1	9.7	10.2	10.6	12.2	11.8	11.3	10.8	10.2
Non-financial Public Enterprises	29.7	40.2	47.8	116.4	131.4	124.5	213.1	341.5	498.7	533.3	567.0
Priv. Sector, incl non-guaranteed	87.5	81.3	106.7	206.2	351.6	392.3	414.9	271.5	434.8	438.9	437.9
Short-Term Debt	0.0	0.0	0.0	0.0	0.0	0.0	0.0	303.0	403.0	429.0	638.1
Memo Items:					*(Millions of US dollars)*						
Int'l Reserves Excluding Gold	219.83	170.95	201.99	233.04	193.28	173.40	275.52	522.39	352.58	627.71	491.70
Gold Holdings (at market price)	..	..	..	0.00	0.01	0.00	0.00	3.39	16.25	40.83	47.01
SOCIAL INDICATORS											
Total Fertility Rate	8.0	8.0	8.0	8.0	8.0	8.1	8.1	8.1	8.1	8.0	8.0
Infant Mortality Rate	102.0	100.0	98.0	96.0	94.0	92.0	90.0	88.0	86.4	84.8	83.2
Life Expectancy at Birth	50.0	50.5	51.0	51.5	52.0	52.5	53.0	53.5	53.9	54.4	54.9
Urban Population, % of total	10.3	10.8	11.3	11.9	12.4	12.9	13.5	14.2	14.8	15.5	16.1
Food Prod. per capita (1987=100)	118.9	116.2	117.1	116.6	112.0	112.9	113.0	118.3	113.5	108.3	100.0
Labor Force, Agriculture (%)	84.8	84.4	84.0	83.6	83.2	82.9	82.5	82.1	81.7	81.3	81.0
Labor Force, Female (%)	42.4	42.3	42.3	42.2	42.2	42.1	42.1	42.0	42.0	41.9	41.9
Primary Schl. Enroll. Ratio	58.0	..	..	..	..	95.0	97.0	95.0	91.0	108.0	115.0
Primary Schl. Enroll. Ratio, Female	48.0	..	..	..	..	87.0	90.0	88.0	85.0	101.0	110.0
Secondary Schl. Enroll. Ratio	9.0	..	..	..	..	13.0	15.0	17.0	18.0	18.0	20.0

1981	1982	1983	1984	1985	1986	1987	1988	1989	1990 estimate	Notes	KENYA
											FOREIGN TRADE (CUSTOMS BASIS)
				(Millions of current US dollars)							
1,146.9	937.7	947.3	1,075.8	956.8	1,168.0	916.3	1,034.0	967.5	1,033.3	..	Value of Exports, fob
649.8	567.6	643.1	839.6	691.9	911.6	676.7	768.0	755.1	806.5		Nonfuel Primary Products
366.7	256.9	194.2	122.9	155.6	133.4	124.3	135.4	110.5	118.0	..	Fuels
130.4	113.2	110.0	113.3	109.2	123.0	115.3	130.5	101.9	108.8		Manufactures
2,081.3	1,603.0	1,379.1	1,469.4	1,457.4	1,649.8	1,737.8	1,986.7	2,150.3	2,123.5		Value of Imports, cif
184.2	167.2	181.0	195.6	194.0	210.4	196.8	207.5	286.3	282.7		Nonfuel Primary Products
776.8	595.3	500.9	465.5	461.7	300.0	348.5	290.3	681.2	672.8	..	Fuels
1,120.4	840.6	697.2	808.2	801.7	1,139.5	1,192.5	1,489.0	1,182.8	1,168.0		Manufactures
				(Index 1987 = 100)							
113.3	110.4	114.9	126.7	113.9	137.4	100.0	113.3	106.9	102.6	..	Terms of Trade
123.7	113.7	114.0	125.9	109.6	120.3	100.0	104.6	98.3	102.4		Export Prices, fob
109.2	103.0	99.2	99.4	96.2	87.6	100.0	92.3	91.9	99.7	..	Import Prices, cif
				(Millions of current US dollars)							**BALANCE OF PAYMENTS**
1,798.6	1,630.0	1,524.8	1,663.1	1,606.6	1,902.3	1,738.6	1,891.8	1,934.6	2,233.3	f	Exports of Goods & Services
1,081.3	935.5	926.6	1,034.5	943.2	1,170.2	908.7	1,017.5	926.1	1,010.5		Merchandise, fob
680.3	672.6	569.6	589.6	625.2	695.1	784.3	854.2	984.6	1,208.6		Nonfactor Services
37.0	21.9	28.7	39.0	38.2	36.9	45.6	20.1	23.9	14.3		Factor Services
2,575.1	2,067.5	1,752.6	1,966.0	1,911.1	2,147.6	2,447.2	2,697.7	2,904.6	3,085.3	f	Imports of Goods & Services
1,834.0	1,467.7	1,197.9	1,348.2	1,269.8	1,454.6	1,622.6	1,802.2	1,963.4	2,008.7		Merchandise, fob
503.0	398.4	341.5	377.0	359.5	415.2	502.9	530.0	598.9	692.5		Nonfactor Services
238.1	201.4	213.2	240.8	281.8	277.8	321.7	365.5	342.3	384.1		Factor Services
162.8	178.5	160.1	164.6	169.4	190.4	209.6	224.6	197.2	226.4	..	Long-Term Interest
98.6	83.3	63.4	60.1	81.5	58.2	72.0	89.0	101.5	167.8		Private Current Transfers, net
0.0	0.0	0.0	0.0	0.0	0.0	0.0	0.0	..	..		Workers' Remittances
-677.9	-354.2	-164.4	-242.8	-223.0	-187.1	-636.6	-716.8	-868.4	-684.2		Curr. A/C Bal before Off. Transf.
119.5	52.1	119.4	119.5	112.7	150.5	142.6	257.1	281.1	206.9		Net Official Transfers
-558.4	-302.1	-44.9	-123.4	-110.3	-36.6	-494.0	-459.8	-587.4	-477.4		Curr. A/C Bal after Off. Transf.
302.4	51.8	109.5	126.6	-45.0	109.0	259.0	331.6	609.8	178.1	f	Long-Term Capital, net
8.3	3.4	9.2	3.9	12.7	27.8	40.7	-1.8	68.8	23.0	..	Direct Investment
221.2	259.4	276.2	111.4	93.6	348.3	345.0	287.8	273.9	356.3		Long-Term Loans
461.9	510.4	537.6	405.6	410.9	666.0	630.9	597.6	624.5	675.6		Disbursements
240.7	251.0	261.4	294.2	317.3	317.7	285.9	309.8	350.6	319.3		Repayments
72.9	-211.0	-175.9	11.3	-151.3	-267.1	-126.7	45.6	267.1	-201.1	..	Other Long-Term Capital
66.9	92.7	34.7	56.4	99.4	56.3	199.1	74.6	141.6	304.8	f	Other Capital, net
189.1	157.6	-99.4	-59.7	56.0	-128.8	35.9	53.6	-164.1	-5.5		Change in Reserves
											Memo Item:
				(Kenya Shillings per US dollar)							
9.050	10.920	13.310	14.410	16.430	16.230	16.450	17.750	20.570	22.910	..	Conversion Factor (Annual Avg)
				(Millions of US dollars), outstanding at end of year							
3,300.0	3,464.7	3,752.8	3,554.9	4,185.9	4,758.4	5,817.4	5,791.3	5,796.0	6,840.5		**EXTERNAL DEBT (Total)**
2,833.7	3,130.4	3,350.5	3,185.6	3,715.6	4,385.0	5,220.3	5,248.9	5,164.9	5,869.9		Long-Term Debt (by debtor)
302.5	449.7	530.5	484.1	598.3	544.5	496.5	535.5	482.7	539.8	..	Central Bank, incl. IMF credit
1,603.0	1,759.7	1,821.3	1,856.4	2,137.4	2,730.7	3,473.0	3,387.9	3,242.4	3,852.1		Central Government
9.5	8.7	8.0	7.1	6.6	5.9	5.4	4.1	2.7	0.2		Rest of General Government
552.9	527.4	493.4	409.7	462.0	644.9	749.0	694.0	805.1	899.9		Non-financial Public Enterprises
365.8	384.9	497.3	428.3	511.3	459.0	496.4	627.4	632.0	577.9		Priv. Sector, incl non-guaranteed
466.3	334.3	402.3	369.3	470.3	373.4	597.1	542.4	631.1	970.6		Short-Term Debt
				(Millions of US dollars)							**Memo Items:**
231.13	211.67	376.00	389.80	390.65	413.32	255.80	263.74	284.65	205.41	..	Int'l Reserves Excluding Gold
31.70	36.44	30.42	24.59	26.08	31.17	38.61	32.72	31.98	30.70	..	Gold Holdings (at market price)
											SOCIAL INDICATORS
8.0	7.9	7.7	7.4	7.2	6.9	6.7	6.6	6.6	6.5	..	Total Fertility Rate
81.6	80.0	78.4	76.8	75.1	73.5	71.9	70.3	68.8	67.2	..	Infant Mortality Rate
55.4	55.9	56.4	56.9	57.4	57.9	58.5	58.6	58.7	58.9	..	Life Expectancy at Birth
16.8	17.5	18.3	19.0	19.7	20.7	21.7	22.3	23.0	23.6	..	Urban Population, % of total
92.9	103.7	98.8	83.5	97.4	105.6	100.0	105.0	103.5	109.9	..	Food Prod. per capita (1987=100)
..	..	..	..	..	..	..	..	..	..	..	Labor Force, Agriculture (%)
41.6	41.4	41.3	41.1	40.9	40.7	40.5	40.3	40.1	39.9	..	Labor Force, Female (%)
..	107.0	105.0	107.0	98.0	97.0	96.0	94.0	..	..	..	Primary Schl. Enroll. Ratio
..	102.0	101.0	104.0	95.0	94.0	94.0	92.0	..	..	..	Primary Schl. Enroll. Ratio, Female
..	18.0	20.0	21.0	21.0	21.0	23.0	23.0	..	..	..	Secondary Schl. Enroll. Ratio

KOREA, REPUBLIC OF	1970	1971	1972	1973	1974	1975	1976	1977	1978	1979	1980
CURRENT GNP PER CAPITA (US $)	270	310	330	390	480	580	740	910	1,190	1,520	1,620
POPULATION (thousands)	31,923	32,596	33,266	33,935	34,606	35,281	35,849	36,412	36,969	37,534	38,124

USE AND ORIGIN OF RESOURCES   *(Billions of current Korean Won)*

	1970	1971	1972	1973	1974	1975	1976	1977	1978	1979	1980
Gross National Product (GNP)	2,777	3,407	4,177	5,356	7,564	10,065	13,818	17,729	23,937	30,741	36,750
Net Factor Income from Abroad	17	-3	-16	-41	-67	-159	-178	-257	-306	-483	-1,291
GDP at Market Prices	2,760	3,410	4,194	5,397	7,631	10,224	13,996	17,985	24,243	31,224	38,041
Resource Balance	-269	-354	-194	-155	-833	-873	-176	37	-726	-2,265	-2,831
Exports of Goods & NFServices	389	524	836	1,602	2,140	2,855	4,446	5,848	7,336	8,563	12,944
Imports of Goods & NFServices	658	878	1,031	1,757	2,973	3,728	4,621	5,811	8,062	10,829	15,774
Domestic Absorption	3,028	3,763	4,388	5,552	8,464	11,097	14,171	17,948	24,969	33,489	40,872
Private Consumption, etc.	2,082	2,573	3,092	3,779	5,321	7,208	9,105	11,125	14,844	19,356	24,414
General Gov't Consumption	263	334	425	452	734	1,121	1,521	1,919	2,501	3,059	4,387
Gross Domestic Investment	683	857	871	1,321	2,408	2,767	3,545	4,904	7,624	11,074	12,071
Fixed Investment	687	765	853	1,243	1,940	2,550	3,365	4,840	7,488	10,191	12,226
Indirect Taxes, net	255	302	332	409	605	986	1,433	1,867	2,620	3,469	4,539
GDP at factor cost	2,505	3,108	3,862	4,988	7,026	9,238	12,563	16,118	21,622	27,755	33,503
Agriculture	718	906	1,096	1,322	1,857	2,504	3,244	3,958	4,890	5,878	5,677
Industry	805	974	1,228	1,728	2,485	3,431	4,856	6,470	9,297	12,502	15,728
Manufacturing	584	725	939	1,356	1,984	2,676	3,869	4,943	6,788	8,949	11,298
Services, etc.	1,237	1,530	1,870	2,346	3,289	4,289	5,896	7,557	10,056	12,845	16,636
Gross Domestic Saving	414	503	677	1,166	1,575	1,894	3,370	4,941	6,898	8,809	9,241
Gross National Saving	461	537	708	1,186	1,571	1,811	3,286	4,767	6,802	8,519	8,192

(Billions of 1987 Korean Won)

	1970	1971	1972	1973	1974	1975	1976	1977	1978	1979	1980
Gross National Product	25,280	27,678	29,238	33,612	36,552	39,057	44,421	49,194	54,641	58,493	55,499
GDP at Market Prices	25,131	27,645	29,258	33,714	36,707	39,519	44,851	49,788	55,232	59,344	57,393
Resource Balance	-2,192	-2,594	-1,419	-1,058	-2,545	-1,384	-236	54	-2,107	-4,467	-1,669
Exports of Goods & NFServices	2,855	3,458	4,703	7,196	7,140	8,499	12,023	14,818	16,677	16,488	18,165
Imports of Goods & NFServices	5,048	6,052	6,122	8,254	9,686	9,883	12,259	14,764	18,784	20,955	19,835
Domestic Absorption	27,323	30,239	30,677	34,772	39,253	40,903	45,088	49,733	57,338	63,812	59,062
Private Consumption, etc.	17,626	19,727	20,319	22,866	24,311	25,666	28,225	29,581	32,292	35,884	34,964
General Gov't Consumption	3,852	4,205	4,448	4,420	5,130	5,718	5,928	6,362	7,148	7,177	7,640
Gross Domestic Investment	5,845	6,307	5,910	7,486	9,811	9,518	10,935	13,790	17,898	20,751	16,458
Fixed Investment	5,194	5,345	5,388	6,684	7,663	8,243	9,832	12,597	16,765	18,203	16,299
GDP at factor cost	22,778	25,167	26,919	31,147	33,788	35,704	40,264	44,629	49,275	52,769	50,546
Agriculture	7,775	8,037	8,200	8,783	9,407	9,800	10,795	11,114	10,014	10,751	8,609
Industry	5,823	6,499	7,079	8,893	10,165	11,387	13,674	15,994	19,460	21,079	20,913
Manufacturing	3,404	4,035	4,582	5,906	6,857	7,680	9,554	11,015	13,364	14,772	14,608
Services, etc.	12,442	14,036	14,860	16,718	17,762	18,921	20,885	23,116	26,042	27,776	28,188

Memo Items:

	1970	1971	1972	1973	1974	1975	1976	1977	1978	1979	1980
Capacity to Import	2,986	3,614	4,967	7,525	6,973	7,569	11,793	14,859	17,091	16,572	16,276
Terms of Trade Adjustment	131	156	265	329	-167	-930	-230	40	414	84	-1,890
Gross Domestic Income	25,261	27,801	29,523	34,043	36,540	38,589	44,622	49,828	55,646	59,428	55,503
Gross National Income	25,410	27,834	29,503	33,941	36,385	38,127	44,192	49,234	55,055	58,577	53,609

DOMESTIC PRICES/DEFLATORS   *(Index 1987 = 100)*

	1970	1971	1972	1973	1974	1975	1976	1977	1978	1979	1980
Overall (GDP)	11.0	12.3	14.3	16.0	20.8	25.9	31.2	36.1	43.9	52.6	66.3
Domestic Absorption	11.1	12.4	14.3	16.0	21.6	27.1	31.4	36.1	43.5	52.5	69.2
Agriculture	9.2	11.3	13.4	15.1	19.7	25.5	30.0	35.6	48.8	54.7	65.9
Industry	13.8	15.0	17.3	19.4	24.5	30.1	35.5	40.5	47.8	59.3	75.2
Manufacturing	17.2	18.0	20.5	23.0	28.9	34.8	40.5	44.9	50.8	60.6	77.3
Consumer Price Index	14.9	16.9	18.8	19.4	24.2	30.3	34.9	38.4	44.0	52.0	67.0

MANUFACTURING ACTIVITY

	1970	1971	1972	1973	1974	1975	1976	1977	1978	1979	1980
Employment (1987=100)	28.0	27.6	32.1	38.2	43.2	47.3	57.3	64.1	70.5	70.7	68.3
Real Earnings per Empl. (1987=100)	30.1	31.5	31.9	38.2	39.7	41.6	46.1	54.1	65.4	72.5	69.3
Real Output per Empl. (1987=100)	24.3	29.6	29.9	37.0	40.7	43.3	44.2	47.1	51.9	54.7	60.3
Earnings as % of Value Added	25.0	23.3	23.5	22.5	23.2	23.6	24.8	26.1	27.1	31.2	29.3

MONETARY HOLDINGS   *(Billions of current Korean Won)*

	1970	1971	1972	1973	1974	1975	1976	1977	1978	1979	1980
Money Supply, Broadly Defined	990	1,224	1,632	2,191	2,682	3,379	4,511	6,256	8,374	10,484	13,622
Money	308	358	519	730	946	1,182	1,544	2,173	2,714	3,275	3,807
Currency Outside Banks	134	162	218	311	411	507	677	953	1,364	1,604	1,856
Demand Deposits	174	196	302	419	535	675	867	1,219	1,349	1,671	1,951
Quasi-Money	683	866	1,112	1,461	1,737	2,197	2,967	4,083	5,660	7,209	9,816

(Billions of current Korean Won)

	1970	1971	1972	1973	1974	1975	1976	1977	1978	1979	1980
GOVERNMENT DEFICIT (-) OR SURPLUS	-21	-10	-161	-27	-165	-201	-192	-316	-300	-545	-849
Current Revenue	440	530	577	675	1,026	1,552	2,314	2,938	4,084	5,376	6,738
Current Expenditure	330	413	537	574	895	1,258	1,790	2,362	3,196	4,205	5,641
Current Budget Balance	110	117	40	101	131	294	524	576	888	1,171	1,097
Capital Receipts	9	8	8	20	13	13	14	20	24	70	96
Capital Payments	140	135	209	148	309	508	730	912	1,212	1,786	2,042

1981	1982	1983	1984	1985	1986	1987	1988	1989	1990 estimate	Notes	KOREA, REPUBLIC OF
1,830	1,930	2,110	2,240	2,320	2,570	2,950	3,600	4,400	5,400	..	**CURRENT GNP PER CAPITA (US $)**
38,723	39,326	39,910	40,406	40,806	41,184	41,575	41,975	42,380	42,793	..	**POPULATION (thousands)**
				(Billions of current Korean Won)							**USE AND ORIGIN OF RESOURCES**
45,528	52,182	61,722	70,084	78,088	90,544	105,630	123,579	141,066	167,668	..	Gross National Product (GNP)
-1,954	-2,261	-2,110	-2,560	-2,758	-2,827	-2,404	-1,730	-1,201	355	..	Net Factor Income from Abroad
47,482	54,443	63,833	72,644	80,847	93,371	108,034	125,309	142,267	167,313	f	GDP at Market Prices
-2,378	-1,404	-300	87	1,018	5,669	8,695	10,681	3,924	-1,082	..	Resource Balance
17,341	18,769	22,748	26,126	27,937	36,034	45,051	51,095	48,714	52,800	..	Exports of Goods & NFServices
19,719	20,174	23,049	26,039	26,919	30,365	36,356	40,414	44,791	53,883	..	Imports of Goods & NFServices
49,860	55,847	64,133	72,557	79,829	87,702	99,339	114,628	138,343	168,395	..	Domestic Absorption
30,352	34,029	38,920	43,629	48,020	51,443	57,044	64,499	74,630	..	..	Private Consumption, etc.
5,515	6,255	6,852	7,263	8,136	9,401	10,708	12,763	14,593	..	..	General Gov't Consumption
13,994	15,563	18,361	21,666	23,673	26,858	31,586	37,366	49,121	62,453	..	Gross Domestic Investment
13,275	15,446	18,669	20,998	22,837	25,764	30,738	36,087	44,778	62,453	..	Fixed Investment
5,658	6,619	8,179	8,752	9,407	10,872	12,548	14,582	16,353	19,232	..	Indirect Taxes, net
41,824	47,824	55,653	63,892	71,439	82,499	95,486	110,727	125,914	148,081	B f	GDP at factor cost
7,431	7,989	8,678	9,392	10,352	10,729	11,353	13,577	14,546	15,120	..	Agriculture
19,305	21,964	26,542	30,847	33,839	40,019	46,963	54,209	62,611	74,550	..	Industry
14,199	15,908	19,106	22,375	24,530	29,566	34,783	39,655	44,460	51,181	..	Manufacturing
20,746	24,490	28,612	32,405	36,656	42,623	49,717	57,523	65,110	77,643	..	Services, etc.
11,615	14,159	18,061	21,753	24,691	32,527	40,281	48,047	53,044	61,370	..	Gross Domestic Saving
9,949	12,225	16,389	19,609	22,415	30,606	38,864	47,344	51,978	61,914	..	Gross National Saving
				(Billions of 1987 Korean Won)							
58,845	63,098	71,269	77,748	83,152	93,822	105,630	118,522	126,966	140,159	..	Gross National Product
61,337	65,853	73,790	80,603	86,177	96,777	108,034	120,197	127,946	139,850	f	GDP at Market Prices
-84	221	1,826	2,112	3,531	6,605	8,695	10,153	952	-2,905	..	Resource Balance
20,912	21,848	26,049	28,119	29,373	37,049	45,051	50,952	48,661	51,484	..	Exports of Goods & NFServices
20,996	21,627	24,223	26,006	25,842	30,445	36,356	40,800	47,709	54,389	..	Imports of Goods & NFServices
61,420	65,632	71,964	78,490	82,647	90,173	99,339	110,045	126,994	142,756	..	Domestic Absorption
36,574	39,404	43,011	46,345	49,112	52,708	57,044	62,387	68,840	75,136	..	Private Consumption, etc.
8,076	8,155	8,434	8,559	9,041	10,016	10,708	11,977	12,629	13,526	..	General Gov't Consumption
16,770	18,073	20,518	23,586	24,494	27,448	31,586	35,681	45,524	54,094	..	Gross Domestic Investment
15,633	17,252	20,320	22,542	23,602	26,175	30,738	34,353	40,597	49,934	..	Fixed Investment
54,040	57,864	64,378	70,920	76,178	85,528	95,486	106,207	113,601	124,158	B f	GDP at factor cost
9,838	10,570	11,388	11,218	11,639	12,176	11,353	12,371	12,172	12,050	..	Agriculture
22,324	24,149	28,242	32,468	34,716	40,316	46,963	52,465	55,919	62,517	..	Industry
16,052	17,127	19,764	23,191	24,840	29,401	34,783	39,322	41,034	44,563	..	Manufacturing
29,446	31,375	34,160	36,916	39,822	44,285	49,717	55,362	59,855	65,283	..	Services, etc.
											Memo Items:
18,463	20,121	23,908	26,093	26,819	36,128	45,051	51,582	51,889	53,296	..	Capacity to Import
-2,449	-1,727	-2,141	-2,026	-2,554	-921	0	630	3,227	1,813	..	Terms of Trade Adjustment
58,888	64,127	71,649	78,577	83,624	95,856	108,034	120,828	131,173	141,663	..	Gross Domestic Income
56,397	61,371	69,128	75,722	80,598	92,901	105,630	119,153	130,194	141,971	..	Gross National Income
				(Index 1987 = 100)							**DOMESTIC PRICES/DEFLATORS**
77.4	82.7	86.5	90.1	93.8	96.5	100.0	104.3	111.2	119.6	..	Overall (GDP)
81.2	85.1	89.1	92.4	96.6	97.3	100.0	104.2	108.9	118.0	..	Domestic Absorption
75.5	75.6	76.2	83.7	88.9	88.1	100.0	109.7	119.5	125.5	..	Agriculture
86.5	91.0	94.0	95.0	97.5	99.3	100.0	103.3	112.0	119.2	..	Industry
88.5	92.9	96.7	96.5	98.8	100.6	100.0	100.8	108.4	114.9	..	Manufacturing
81.3	87.1	90.1	92.2	94.4	97.0	100.0	107.1	113.3	123.0	..	Consumer Price Index
											MANUFACTURING ACTIVITY
68.1	69.9	73.8	78.0	81.2	91.2	100.0	104.7	104.6	..	G	Employment (1987=100)
68.1	71.3	75.5	82.4	86.3	88.8	100.0	106.1	107.2	..	G	Real Earnings per Empl. (1987=100)
68.0	69.9	74.5	83.1	84.4	88.0	100.0	115.0	116.7	..	G	Real Output per Empl. (1987=100)
26.8	27.5	26.3	26.3	27.1	26.2	27.0	26.5	26.0	..	..	Earnings as % of Value Added
				(Billions of current Korean Won)							**MONETARY HOLDINGS**
17,153	21,680	24,972	27,320	32,640	38,892	49,202	62,634	80,616	97,551	D	Money Supply, Broadly Defined
3,982	5,799	6,783	6,821	7,558	8,809	10,107	12,152	14,328	15,905	..	Money
2,025	2,574	2,874	3,109	3,286	3,679	4,443	5,133	6,140	7,011	..	Currency Outside Banks
1,957	3,226	3,909	3,711	4,272	5,130	5,665	7,018	8,188	8,894	..	Demand Deposits
13,170	15,881	18,189	20,499	25,083	30,083	39,095	50,482	66,288	81,646	..	Quasi-Money
				(Billions of current Korean Won)							**GOVERNMENT DEFICIT (-) OR SURPLUS**
-1,585	-1,656	-663	-841	-943	-86	478	2,009	285	-1,090	..	Current Revenue
8,534	9,875	11,418	12,511	13,738	15,721	18,510	22,558	25,502	26,251	..	Current Expenditure
6,931	8,297	9,145	10,213	11,523	12,829	14,325	16,746	20,025	22,268	..	Current Budget Balance
1,603	1,578	2,273	2,298	2,215	2,892	4,185	5,812	5,477	3,983	..	Capital Receipts
71	108	120	93	185	119	148	332	460	567	..	Capital Payments
3,259	3,342	3,056	3,232	3,343	3,097	3,855	4,135	5,652	5,640	..	Capital Payments

KOREA, REPUBLIC OF	1970	1971	1972	1973	1974	1975	1976	1977	1978	1979	1980
FOREIGN TRADE (CUSTOMS BASIS)					*(Millions of current US dollars)*						
Value of Exports, fob	830	1,060	1,616	3,215	4,453	5,071	7,693	9,986	12,654	14,952	17,446
Nonfuel Primary Products	186	183	246	473	558	829	801	1,390	1,434	1,635	1,727
Fuels	9	11	18	35	108	104	145	117	41	18	33
Manufactures	635	866	1,351	2,707	3,787	4,137	6,747	8,480	11,179	13,299	15,686
Value of Imports, cif	1,983	2,394	2,522	4,240	6,844	7,271	8,764	10,803	14,966	20,296	22,228
Nonfuel Primary Products	761	907	860	1,569	2,243	2,199	2,394	2,960	3,748	5,294	5,982
Fuels	136	189	219	312	1,054	1,387	1,747	2,179	2,453	3,779	6,638
Manufactures	1,086	1,298	1,443	2,358	3,547	3,685	4,623	5,664	8,765	11,223	9,608
					(Index 1987 = 100)						
Terms of Trade	155.7	152.8	144.4	125.7	106.8	110.6	120.5	114.2	113.5	110.5	96.7
Export Prices, fob	36.8	38.8	39.6	49.0	61.5	62.4	70.3	71.3	79.4	94.6	100.3
Import Prices, cif	23.6	25.4	27.4	39.0	57.6	56.4	58.3	62.4	70.0	85.6	103.7
BALANCE OF PAYMENTS					*(Millions of current US dollars)*						
Exports of Goods & Services	1,379	1,617	2,226	4,135	5,353	5,882	9,457	13,073	17,161	19,530	22,577
Merchandise, fob	882	1,133	1,676	3,284	4,516	5,003	7,814	10,046	12,711	14,705	17,214
Nonfactor Services	426	429	507	782	723	796	1,525	2,784	4,056	4,390	4,707
Factor Services	71	54	43	70	115	84	118	243	394	435	656
Imports of Goods & Services	2,180	2,633	2,764	4,631	7,600	7,996	10,113	13,284	18,717	24,120	28,347
Merchandise, fob	1,804	2,177	2,251	3,849	6,454	6,674	8,404	10,523	14,491	19,100	21,598
Nonfactor Services	300	336	354	568	818	869	1,190	2,022	3,193	3,502	4,057
Factor Services	76	119	159	214	329	452	519	739	1,033	1,518	2,692
Long-Term Interest	76	101	160	254	240	331	424	517	793	1,123	1,636
Private Current Transfers, net	95	105	119	155	154	158	193	170	434	399	399
Workers' Remittances	..	..	..	..	..	..	..	..	..	..	..
Curr. A/C Bal before Off. Transf.	-706	-911	-418	-342	-2,094	-1,956	-463	-41	-1,122	-4,191	-5,371
Net Official Transfers	83	63	50	36	67	67	153	53	37	40	50
Curr. A/C Bal after Off. Transf.	-623	-848	-368	-306	-2,026	-1,889	-310	12	-1,085	-4,151	-5,321
Long-Term Capital, net	558	641	501	524	891	1,350	1,332	1,400	2,111	3,071	1,987
Direct Investment	66	39	63	93	105	53	75	73	61	16	-7
Long-Term Loans	271	536	622	662	1,019	1,351	1,361	1,604	2,425	3,404	2,426
Disbursements	476	774	906	1,090	1,398	1,769	1,935	2,416	3,687	5,128	3,980
Repayments	205	239	284	428	379	418	575	812	1,262	1,724	1,554
Other Long-Term Capital	221	67	-184	-230	-233	-54	-104	-277	-375	-349	-432
Other Capital, net	113	167	9	132	964	904	291	-42	-295	1,954	3,645
Change in Reserves	-48	40	-141	-350	171	-365	-1,313	-1,370	-731	-874	-311
Memo Item:					*(Korean Won per US dollar)*						
Conversion Factor (Annual Avg)	310.560	347.150	392.890	398.320	404.470	484.000	484.000	484.000	484.000	484.000	607.430
EXTERNAL DEBT (Total)				*(Millions of US dollars), outstanding at end of year*							
	1,991	2,570	3,203	3,924	5,091	6,489	7,983	14,343	17,301	22,886	29,480
Long-Term Debt (by debtor)	1,991	2,570	3,203	3,924	5,091	6,489	7,983	9,886	12,776	15,721	18,919
Central Bank, incl. IMF credit	117	222	230	218	484	817	936	999	949	1,287	1,974
Central Government	183	393	635	846	944	1,040	1,428	1,792	2,158	2,327	2,800
Rest of General Government	21	21	25	25	26	32	46	53	60	63	73
Non-financial Public Enterprises	443	516	664	837	987	1,081	1,270	1,587	2,140	2,691	3,575
Priv. Sector, incl non-guaranteed	1,227	1,419	1,650	1,998	2,650	3,519	4,303	5,455	7,468	9,353	10,497
Short-Term Debt	0	0	0	0	0	0	0	4,457	4,525	7,165	10,561
Memo Items:					*(Millions of US dollars)*						
Int'l Reserves Excluding Gold	606	434	523	885	277	781	1,970	2,967	2,764	2,959	2,925
Gold Holdings (at market price)	4	4	7	12	21	16	15	24	62	151	176
SOCIAL INDICATORS											
Total Fertility Rate	4.3	4.2	4.1	3.8	3.6	3.3	3.1	2.8	2.7	2.6	2.6
Infant Mortality Rate	51.0	49.0	47.0	44.6	42.2	39.8	37.4	35.0	34.0	33.0	32.0
Life Expectancy at Birth	59.9	60.7	61.4	62.3	63.1	63.9	64.7	65.5	66.0	66.4	66.8
Urban Population, % of total	40.7	42.2	43.6	45.1	46.5	48.0	49.8	51.6	53.3	55.1	56.9
Food Prod. per capita (1987=100)	76.8	76.7	76.1	76.6	81.1	89.3	96.7	102.3	107.9	111.2	92.9
Labor Force, Agriculture (%)	49.1	47.7	46.4	45.1	43.9	42.8	41.4	40.1	38.8	37.6	36.4
Labor Force, Female (%)	32.1	32.4	32.6	32.9	33.1	33.3	33.5	33.6	33.8	34.0	34.1
Primary Schl. Enroll. Ratio	103.0	..	..	..	..	107.0	108.0	107.0	109.0	109.0	110.0
Primary Schl. Enroll. Ratio, Female	103.0	..	..	..	..	107.0	109.0	107.0	109.0	109.0	111.0
Secondary Schl. Enroll. Ratio	42.0	..	..	..	..	56.0	61.0	64.0	68.0	75.0	76.0

1981	1982	1983	1984	1985	1986	1987	1988	1989	1990 estimate	Notes	KOREA, REPUBLIC OF
				(Millions of current US dollars)							**FOREIGN TRADE (CUSTOMS BASIS)**
21,200	21,850	24,437	29,248	30,283	34,702	47,172	60,697	62,283	64,837	..	Value of Exports, fob
1,853	1,610	1,661	1,737	1,685	2,153	2,872	3,696	3,722	3,507	..	Nonfuel Primary Products
159	285	536	805	929	618	720	926	652	656	..	Fuels
19,188	19,955	22,240	26,707	27,669	31,931	43,580	56,075	57,910	60,675	..	Manufactures
26,028	24,236	26,174	30,609	31,119	31,518	40,925	51,811	61,347	69,585	..	Value of Imports, cif
6,969	5,440	5,820	6,319	5,910	6,586	8,744	11,848	14,029	14,175	..	Nonfuel Primary Products
7,764	7,592	6,958	7,274	7,333	5,024	5,993	6,429	7,612	11,001	..	Fuels
11,295	11,204	13,396	17,015	17,876	19,908	26,189	33,534	39,706	44,410	..	Manufactures
				(Index 1987 = 100)							
98.0	100.8	100.5	102.7	102.6	108.1	100.0	104.4	108.0	107.7	..	Terms of Trade
102.1	98.1	95.4	96.4	93.7	92.1	100.0	114.0	121.9	121.5	..	Export Prices, fob
104.3	97.3	94.9	93.8	91.3	85.2	100.0	109.2	112.8	112.8	..	Import Prices, cif
				(Millions of current US dollars)							**BALANCE OF PAYMENTS**
27,269	28,356	30,383	33,652	33,106	41,965	56,255	70,900	74,051	77,392	..	Exports of Goods & Services
20,671	20,879	23,204	26,335	26,442	33,913	46,244	59,648	61,408	63,123	..	Merchandise, fob
5,756	6,673	6,470	6,452	5,593	6,866	8,797	9,664	10,326	11,171	..	Nonfactor Services
842	804	709	865	1,071	1,186	1,214	1,588	2,317	3,098	..	Factor Services
32,416	31,505	32,581	35,565	34,571	38,387	47,619	58,187	69,243	79,839	..	Imports of Goods & Services
24,299	23,473	24,967	27,371	26,461	29,707	38,585	48,203	56,811	65,127	..	Merchandise, fob
4,419	4,152	4,151	4,192	4,094	4,598	5,397	6,829	9,354	11,151	..	Nonfactor Services
3,698	3,880	3,463	4,002	4,016	4,082	3,637	3,155	3,078	3,561	..	Factor Services
2,031	2,439	2,280	2,510	2,778	2,863	2,407	2,052	1,938	1,773	..	Long-Term Interest
422	447	566	516	555	1,028	1,199	1,404	200	266	..	Private Current Transfers, net
..	..	..	..	..	..	..	..	..	..		Workers' Remittances
-4,725	-2,702	-1,632	-1,397	-910	4,606	9,835	14,117	5,008	-2,181	..	Curr. A/C Bal before Off. Transf.
79	52	26	25	23	11	19	44	48	9	..	Net Official Transfers
-4,646	-2,650	-1,606	-1,372	-887	4,617	9,854	14,161	5,056	-2,172	..	Curr. A/C Bal after Off. Transf.
3,533	1,797	1,783	2,652	2,229	-2,571	-8,562	-3,407	-3,904	-1,123	..	Long-Term Capital, net
60	-76	-57	73	200	325	418	720	453	-105	..	Direct Investment
3,821	2,423	3,397	3,476	2,649	-1,500	-9,365	-3,072	-2,049	-902	..	Long-Term Loans
5,837	4,564	6,061	6,326	7,101	5,596	4,461	3,928	3,906	4,727	..	Disbursements
2,015	2,141	2,665	2,850	4,452	7,096	13,826	7,000	5,955	5,628	..	Repayments
-348	-550	-1,557	-897	-620	-1,396	385	-1,055	-2,308	-116	..	Other Long-Term Capital
784	858	-413	-720	-1,150	-1,969	812	-1,438	1,968	2,087	..	Other Capital, net
329	-5	236	-560	-192	-77	-2,104	-9,316	-3,120	1,208	..	Change in Reserves
				(Korean Won per US dollar)							**Memo Item:**
681.030	731.080	775.750	805.980	870.020	881.450	822.570	731.470	671.460	707.760	..	Conversion Factor (Annual Avg)
				(Millions of US dollars), outstanding at end of year							
32,989	37,329	40,419	42,099	47,133	46,725	39,808	35,716	32,796	34,014	..	**EXTERNAL DEBT (Total)**
22,763	24,902	28,304	30,674	36,401	37,468	30,517	25,936	22,996	23,214	..	Long-Term Debt (by debtor)
3,260	3,883	4,299	5,354	6,834	6,638	3,878	2,573	1,481	859	..	Central Bank, incl. IMF credit
3,479	4,117	4,756	4,861	5,665	6,512	7,494	6,668	5,965	7,065	..	Central Government
119	133	367	601	840	907	915	854	757	648	..	Rest of General Government
4,110	4,688	5,191	5,658	6,380	6,689	5,594	4,905	4,150	4,606	..	Non-financial Public Enterprises
11,795	12,081	13,692	14,200	16,683	16,724	12,637	10,937	10,643	10,038	..	Priv. Sector, incl non-guaranteed
10,226	12,427	12,115	11,425	10,732	9,256	9,291	9,780	9,800	10,800	..	Short-Term Debt
				(Millions of US dollars)							**Memo Items:**
2,682	2,807	2,347	2,754	2,869	3,320	3,584	12,347	15,214	14,793	..	Int'l Reserves Excluding Gold
120	139	116	95	102	124	155	131	128	123	..	Gold Holdings (at market price)
											SOCIAL INDICATORS
2.5	2.4	2.4	2.4	2.5	2.5	1.8	1.8	1.8	1.8	..	Total Fertility Rate
31.0	30.0	29.6	29.2	28.8	28.4	20.0	19.0	18.1	17.1	..	Infant Mortality Rate
67.3	67.7	68.1	68.4	68.7	69.0	69.3	69.6	69.9	70.2	..	Life Expectancy at Birth
58.5	60.1	61.6	63.2	64.8	66.2	67.7	69.1	70.6	72.0	..	Urban Population, % of total
97.0	100.5	98.9	103.1	109.1	107.7	100.0	105.1	106.8	107.9	..	Food Prod. per capita (1987=100)
..	..	..	..	..	..	..	..	..	..	..	Labor Force, Agriculture (%)
34.1	34.1	34.0	34.0	34.0	34.0	33.9	33.9	33.9	33.8	..	Labor Force, Female (%)
	..	103.0	99.0	97.0	98.0	101.0	104.0	108.0	108.0	..	Primary Schl. Enroll. Ratio
105.0	109.0	104.0	99.0	98.0	99.0	101.0	105.0	109.0	110.0	..	Primary Schl. Enroll. Ratio, Female
..	..	87.0	91.0	90.0	89.0	88.0	87.0	86.0	87.0	..	Secondary Schl. Enroll. Ratio

KUWAIT	1970	1971	1972	1973	1974	1975	1976	1977	1978	1979	1980
CURRENT GNP PER CAPITA (US $)	3,350	3,570	3,670	4,250	6,030	9,070	14,530	14,020	15,290	18,440	17,800
POPULATION (thousands)	744	796	845	894	947	1,007	1,073	1,144	1,218	1,296	1,375

USE AND ORIGIN OF RESOURCES

(Millions of current Kuwaiti Dinars)

	1970	1971	1972	1973	1974	1975	1976	1977	1978	1979	1980
Gross National Product (GNP)	851.3	1,115.8	1,102.4	1,262.1	3,532.0	3,711.0	4,280.7	4,557.6	4,981.3	7,712.9	9,051.2
Net Factor Income from Abroad	-175.0	-266.0	-361.6	-342.0	-281.0	224.0	441.0	506.0	717.0	873.0	1,310.1
GDP at Market Prices	1,026.3	1,381.8	1,464.0	1,604.1	3,813.0	3,487.0	3,839.7	4,051.6	4,264.3	6,839.9	7,741.1
Resource Balance	366.4	658.9	701.8	798.3	2,711.7	1,899.0	1,742.4	1,158.0	1,308.0	3,362.0	3,410.0
Exports of Goods & NF Services	613.9	916.8	1,004.3	1,153.9	3,239.5	2,806.0	2,992.4	2,918.0	3,008.0	5,333.0	6,065.0
Imports of Goods & NF Services	247.5	257.9	302.5	355.6	527.8	907.0	1,250.0	1,760.0	1,700.0	1,971.0	2,655.0
Domestic Absorption	659.9	722.9	762.2	805.8	1,101.3	1,588.0	2,097.3	2,893.6	2,956.3	3,477.8	4,331.0
Private Consumption, etc.	396.2	420.0	427.4	438.6	563.8	758.8	1,029.8	1,362.7	1,477.5	1,780.3	2,388.5
General Gov't Consumption	139.3	173.3	198.6	214.6	279.1	385.5	432.3	586.3	615.9	763.8	864.9
Gross Domestic Investment	124.4	129.6	136.2	152.6	258.4	443.7	635.2	944.6	862.9	933.7	1,077.6
Fixed Investment	126.5	126.6	127.3	145.8	221.7	417.6	563.1	815.2	793.9	789.6	972.6
Indirect Taxes, net	..	..	..	..	..	..	..	..	..	..	..
GDP at factor cost	..	..	..	..	..	..	..	..	..	..	..
Agriculture	2.9	3.2	3.8	4.7	5.9	8.8	10.3	7.7	10.0	11.8	14.0
Industry	689.7	995.3	1,018.3	1,118.7	3,254.1	2,727.8	2,876.5	2,882.3	2,984.3	5,201.1	5,794.6
Manufacturing	42.8	54.2	66.4	80.2	171.2	197.5	234.2	241.3	282.6	566.7	427.3
Services, etc.	333.7	383.3	441.9	480.7	553.0	750.4	952.9	1,161.6	1,270.0	1,627.0	1,932.5
Gross Domestic Saving	490.8	788.5	838.0	950.9	2,970.1	2,342.7	2,377.6	2,102.6	2,170.9	4,295.8	4,487.7
Gross National Saving	253.3	429.9	384.3	388.5	2,327.1	2,486.7	2,726.6	2,502.6	2,768.9	5,021.8	5,610.8

(Millions of 1987 Kuwaiti Dinars)

	1970	1971	1972	1973	1974	1975	1976	1977	1978	1979	1980
Gross National Product	6,093.3	6,409.8	6,364.6	6,527.5	6,879.4	7,189.9	8,188.0	8,209.5	9,159.4	10,107.0	8,174.8
GDP at Market Prices	8,075.7	8,720.6	9,239.1	9,018.4	8,127.7	7,422.1	8,074.4	8,019.9	8,622.0	9,854.6	7,670.1
Resource Balance	5,683.2	6,051.3	6,407.0	5,904.2	5,051.3	4,363.6	4,587.5	3,163.0	3,575.8	4,546.3	1,825.8
Exports of Goods & NF Services	5,999.2	6,362.8	6,762.8	6,311.6	5,558.7	5,137.9	5,592.4	5,233.5	5,613.7	6,770.0	4,678.9
Imports of Goods & NF Services	316.0	311.5	355.7	407.4	507.4	774.3	1,004.9	2,070.5	2,037.9	2,223.8	2,853.0
Domestic Absorption	1,894.5	1,964.3	2,025.1	2,004.9	2,352.3	3,099.3	3,797.0	4,879.5	4,718.3	5,010.7	5,779.9
Private Consumption, etc.	1,053.0	1,049.0	1,031.1	968.6	1,099.9	1,462.9	1,775.2	2,170.6	2,198.2	2,471.6	3,100.6
General Gov't Consumption	478.0	553.1	622.4	666.0	744.9	844.8	930.7	1,123.6	1,164.1	1,201.4	1,279.1
Gross Domestic Investment	363.5	362.1	371.6	370.3	507.6	791.6	1,091.1	1,585.3	1,356.0	1,337.7	1,400.2
Fixed Investment	..	..	..	..	..	..	..	..	..	..	..
GDP at factor cost	..	..	..	..	..	..	..	..	..	..	..
Agriculture	7.1	7.2	6.3	6.8	7.0	8.4	9.2	10.4	12.4	11.4	12.8
Industry	5,646.7	6,071.9	6,295.8	5,921.4	5,246.0	4,614.7	4,947.5	4,765.8	5,161.5	6,005.3	4,188.6
Manufacturing	..	..	..	..	..	..	..	532.6	610.8	607.0	598.2
Services, etc.	1,089.5	1,187.2	1,314.4	1,371.4	1,425.0	1,667.5	1,966.9	2,263.4	2,351.5	2,469.8	2,936.2

Memo Items:

	1970	1971	1972	1973	1974	1975	1976	1977	1978	1979	1980
Capacity to Import	783.7	1,107.4	1,181.1	1,322.0	3,114.0	2,395.6	2,405.7	3,432.7	3,605.9	6,016.9	6,517.3
Terms of Trade Adjustment	-5,215.4	-5,255.4	-5,581.7	-4,989.6	-2,444.7	-2,742.3	-3,186.7	-1,800.8	-2,007.8	-753.1	1,838.5
Gross Domestic Income	2,860.3	3,465.2	3,657.4	4,028.9	5,683.0	4,679.7	4,887.6	6,219.1	6,614.2	9,101.5	9,508.6
Gross National Income	877.9	1,154.5	782.9	1,538.0	4,434.7	4,447.6	5,001.2	6,408.8	7,151.6	9,353.9	10,013.2

DOMESTIC PRICES/DEFLATORS

(Index 1987 = 100)

	1970	1971	1972	1973	1974	1975	1976	1977	1978	1979	1980
Overall (GDP)	12.7	15.8	15.8	17.8	46.9	47.0	47.6	50.5	49.5	69.4	100.9
Domestic Absorption	34.8	36.8	37.6	40.2	46.8	51.2	55.2	59.3	62.7	69.4	74.9
Agriculture	41.1	44.2	60.6	69.6	84.9	104.5	111.9	74.2	80.4	103.9	109.1
Industry	12.2	16.4	16.2	18.9	62.0	59.1	58.1	60.5	57.8	86.6	138.3
Manufacturing	..	..	..	..	..	..	..	45.3	46.3	93.4	71.4
Consumer Price Index	..	..	41.5	44.9	50.7	55.0	57.8	63.6	69.1	74.0	79.1

MANUFACTURING ACTIVITY

	1970	1971	1972	1973	1974	1975	1976	1977	1978	1979	1980
Employment (1987=100)	..	..	..	..	..	..	..	..	..	..	..
Real Earnings per Empl. (1987=100)	..	..	..	..	..	..	..	..	..	..	..
Real Output per Empl. (1987=100)	..	..	..	..	..	..	..	..	..	..	..
Earnings as % of Value Added	12.2	14.5	26.3	27.5	18.1	24.8	19.6	24.6	24.7	19.5	22.2

MONETARY HOLDINGS

(Millions of current Kuwaiti Dinars)

	1970	1971	1972	1973	1974	1975	1976	1977	1978	1979	1980
Money Supply, Broadly Defined	362.1	418.8	493.6	536.3	684.6	891.1	1,220.1	1,568.7	1,950.4	2,262.7	2,857.6
Money	95.2	107.7	142.0	172.4	195.6	290.3	393.7	490.7	636.4	669.4	720.8
Currency Outside Banks	44.8	50.4	57.1	71.1	81.7	101.7	129.1	150.9	177.0	215.9	251.3
Demand Deposits	50.4	57.3	84.9	101.3	113.9	188.6	264.6	339.8	459.4	453.5	469.5
Quasi-Money	266.9	311.1	351.6	363.9	489.0	600.8	826.4	1,078.0	1,314.0	1,593.3	2,136.8

GOVERNMENT DEFICIT (-) OR SURPLUS

(Millions of current Kuwaiti Dinars)

	1970	1971	1972	1973	1974	1975	1976	1977	1978	1979	1980
	..	..	192.0	162.0	1,588.0	..	..	1,514.0	1,134.0	1,753.0	4,545.0
Current Revenue	..	..	608.0	694.0	2,724.0	..	..	2,989.0	3,045.0	3,643.0	6,916.0
Current Expenditure	..	..	303.0	368.0	737.0	..	..	989.0	1,045.0	1,117.0	1,460.0
Current Budget Balance	..	..	305.0	326.0	1,987.0	..	..	2,000.0	2,000.0	2,526.0	5,456.0
Capital Receipts	..	..	1.0	2.0	5.0	..	..	7.0	5.0	4.0	7.0
Capital Payments	..	..	114.0	166.0	404.0	..	..	493.0	871.0	777.0	918.0

1981	1982	1983	1984	1985	1986	1987	1988	1989	1990 estimate	Notes	KUWAIT
20,140	18,980	18,540	17,500	15,010	15,730	14,710	14,660	16,160	..	..	**CURRENT GNP PER CAPITA (US $)**
1,451	1,524	1,593	1,655	1,712	1,791	1,873	1,958	2,048	2,143	..	**POPULATION (thousands)**
				(Millions of current Kuwaiti Dinars)							**USE AND ORIGIN OF RESOURCES**
9,122.8	7,921.3	7,585.2	7,850.8	7,305.3	7,178.0	7,658.5	7,564.0	9,365.5	..	..	Gross National Product (GNP)
2,137.0	1,709.0	1,451.0	1,470.0	1,387.0	2,180.0	1,504.0	1,978.0	2,449.1	..	..	Net Factor Income from Abroad
6,985.8	6,212.3	6,134.2	6,380.8	5,918.3	4,998.0	6,154.5	5,586.0	6,916.4	..	..	GDP at Market Prices
2,167.0	133.0	533.0	825.0	534.0	-249.0	961.5	267.0	840.4	..	..	Resource Balance
4,855.0	3,386.0	3,596.0	3,862.0	3,463.0	2,403.0	3,275.5	2,746.9	3,887.4	..	..	Exports of Goods & NF Services
2,688.0	3,253.0	3,063.0	3,037.0	2,929.0	2,652.0	2,314.0	2,479.9	3,047.0	..	..	Imports of Goods & NF Services
4,818.9	6,079.3	5,601.2	5,555.8	5,384.2	5,247.0	5,193.0	5,319.0	6,076.0	..	..	Domestic Absorption
2,663.9	3,317.0	2,795.7	2,878.7	2,668.4	2,677.0	2,813.0	3,008.0	3,206.0	..	..	Private Consumption, etc.
993.2	1,197.2	1,298.7	1,356.6	1,457.2	1,451.0	1,369.0	1,351.0	1,578.0	..	..	General Gov't Consumption
1,161.8	1,565.1	1,506.8	1,320.5	1,258.6	1,119.0	1,011.0	960.0	1,292.0	..	..	Gross Domestic Investment
1,072.8	1,436.0	1,525.1	1,306.3	1,295.5	1,096.0	..	..	..	..	..	Fixed Investment
..	..										Indirect Taxes, net
..	..	..	..	..	..	..	..	..	..	B	GDP at factor cost
24.0	28.5	28.4	34.9	39.3	51.5	56.7	63.8	70.0	..	..	Agriculture
4,798.7	3,335.6	3,688.4	3,975.5	3,559.4	2,554.4	2,841.3	2,646.0	3,842.6	..	..	Industry
415.1	307.9	374.9	300.3	377.2	555.5	586.6	583.0	597.0	..	..	Manufacturing
2,163.1	2,848.2	2,417.4	2,370.4	2,319.6	2,392.1	3,256.5	2,876.2	3,003.8	..	..	Services, etc.
3,328.7	1,698.1	2,039.8	2,145.5	1,792.7	870.0	1,972.5	1,227.0	2,132.4	..	..	Gross Domestic Saving
5,273.7	3,155.1	3,238.8	3,330.5	2,865.7	2,735.0	3,169.5	2,876.0	4,203.5	..	..	Gross National Saving
			(Millions of 1987 Kuwaiti Dinars)								
7,290.4	6,213.5	6,636.3	6,914.5	6,509.6	7,700.3	7,658.5	8,309.8	9,333.1	..	..	Gross National Product
6,098.1	5,327.8	5,858.2	6,122.3	5,758.1	6,148.0	6,154.5	6,698.6	7,400.4	..	H	GDP at Market Prices
784.1	-429.3	-37.5	183.2	-5.2	1,042.5	961.5	1,275.8	1,837.4	..	..	Resource Balance
3,444.0	2,450.5	2,902.1	3,188.5	2,906.3	3,263.9	3,275.5	3,588.2	4,505.7	..	..	Exports of Goods & NF Services
2,660.0	2,879.7	2,939.6	3,005.3	2,911.5	2,221.4	2,314.0	2,312.4	2,668.4	..	..	Imports of Goods & NF Services
5,906.4	6,996.2	6,294.9	6,223.1	5,937.4	4,851.0	5,193.0	4,473.7	3,551.8	..	..	Domestic Absorption
3,224.9	3,722.0	2,997.5	3,049.4	2,787.6	2,213.6	2,813.0	2,252.5	934.8	..	..	Private Consumption, etc.
1,269.3	1,447.7	1,518.3	1,565.3	1,616.6	1,520.6	1,369.0	1,281.8	1,416.3	..	..	General Gov't Consumption
1,412.2	1,826.5	1,779.1	1,608.5	1,533.2	1,116.7	1,011.0	939.4	1,200.7	..	..	Gross Domestic Investment
..	..	..	..	..	..	..	..	..	..	..	Fixed Investment
..	..	..	..	..	..	..	..	..	..	B H	GDP at factor cost
20.9	23.5	27.1	34.2	39.7	53.3	56.7	60.6	63.8	..	..	Agriculture
2,957.9	2,280.0	2,819.7	3,027.5	2,751.1	3,227.5	2,841.3	2,888.9	4,390.8	..	..	Industry
581.5	631.6	627.1	611.7	640.6	647.5	586.6	589.0	590.7	..	..	Manufacturing
3,099.1	3,338.4	3,011.4	3,060.6	2,967.4	2,867.2	3,256.5	3,749.1	2,945.8	..	..	Services, etc.
											Memo Items:
4,804.3	2,997.5	3,451.1	3,821.7	3,442.3	2,012.8	3,275.5	2,561.4	3,404.3	..	..	Capacity to Import
1,360.3	547.0	549.1	633.2	536.0	-1,251.0	0.0	-1,026.9	-1,101.4	..	..	Terms of Trade Adjustment
7,458.4	5,874.8	6,407.3	6,755.5	6,294.1	4,896.9	6,154.5	5,671.7	6,299.0	..	..	Gross Domestic Income
8,650.7	6,760.5	7,185.4	7,547.7	7,045.6	6,449.2	7,658.5	7,283.0	8,231.7	..	..	Gross National Income
				(Index 1987 = 100)							**DOMESTIC PRICES/DEFLATORS**
114.6	116.6	104.7	104.2	102.8	81.3	100.0	83.4	93.5	..	..	Overall (GDP)
81.6	86.9	89.0	89.3	90.7	108.2	100.0	118.9	171.1	..	..	Domestic Absorption
115.1	121.3	104.7	102.1	99.1	96.7	100.0	105.3	109.8	..	..	Agriculture
162.2	146.3	130.8	131.3	129.4	79.1	100.0	91.6	87.5	..	..	Industry
71.4	48.7	59.8	49.1	58.9	85.8	100.0	99.0	101.1	..	..	Manufacturing
84.9	91.5	95.8	97.0	98.4	99.3	100.0	101.5	104.9	..	..	Consumer Price Index
											MANUFACTURING ACTIVITY
..	..	..	..	..	..	..	..	..	..	G J	Employment (1987=100)
..	..	..	..	..	..	..	..	..	..	G J	Real Earnings per Empl. (1987=100)
..	..	..	..	..	..	..	..	..	..	G J	Real Output per Empl. (1987=100)
27.5	41.7	37.6	51.1	43.0	28.4	..	..	..	..	J	Earnings as % of Value Added
			(Millions of current Kuwaiti Dinars)								**MONETARY HOLDINGS**
3,866.0	4,182.7	4,367.8	4,475.8	4,435.3	4,546.9	4,762.1	5,067.5	5,276.8	..	..	Money Supply, Broadly Defined
1,290.2	1,247.6	1,179.6	968.1	943.9	979.3	1,035.7	958.0	938.8	..	..	Money
284.7	342.7	340.6	325.1	327.9	337.1	338.3	342.5	334.1	..	..	Currency Outside Banks
1,005.5	904.9	839.0	643.0	616.0	642.2	697.4	615.5	604.7	..	..	Demand Deposits
2,575.8	2,935.1	3,188.2	3,507.7	3,491.4	3,567.6	3,726.4	4,109.5	4,338.0	..	..	Quasi-Money
			(Millions of current Kuwaiti Dinars)								
3,025.0	566.0	492.0	780.0	501.0	1,690.0	-997.0	-545.0	-673.0	..	C	**GOVERNMENT DEFICIT (-) OR SURPLUS**
6,338.0	4,272.0	4,145.0	4,358.0	3,794.0	4,744.0	1,649.0	2,134.0	2,210.0	..	..	Current Revenue
1,696.0	1,915.0	2,161.0	2,042.0	2,158.0	2,009.0	1,906.0	2,018.0	2,258.0	..	..	Current Expenditure
4,642.0	2,357.0	1,984.0	2,316.0	1,636.0	2,735.0	-257.0	116.0	-48.0	..	..	Current Budget Balance
13.0	8.0	10.0	9.0	12.0	7.0	..	19.0	18.0	..	..	Capital Receipts
1,630.0	1,799.0	1,502.0	1,545.0	1,147.0	1,052.0	740.0	680.0	643.0	..	..	Capital Payments

KUWAIT	1970	1971	1972	1973	1974	1975	1976	1977	1978	1979	1980
FOREIGN TRADE (CUSTOMS BASIS)					*(Millions of current US dollars)*						
Value of Exports, fob	1,901.4	2,572.7	3,056.4	3,784.7	10,954.1	9,186.0	9,838.2	9,753.9	10,427.5	18,415.9	20,434.6
Nonfuel Primary Products	22.6	23.2	28.4	45.5	48.1	46.4	71.2	76.4	84.1	134.3	154.6
Fuels	1,787.4	2,433.4	2,859.7	3,495.1	10,361.5	8,407.5	8,831.4	8,618.4	9,233.7	16,528.7	18,156.5
Manufactures	91.5	116.1	168.3	244.1	544.5	732.1	935.6	1,059.1	1,109.7	1,752.9	2,123.5
Value of Imports, cif	625.1	650.5	797.0	1,042.2	1,553.5	2,388.2	3,329.5	4,845.0	4,598.0	5,203.8	6,554.2
Nonfuel Primary Products	135.8	148.8	178.5	229.3	314.1	443.2	539.7	680.4	778.8	947.9	1,129.0
Fuels	4.4	6.0	7.9	9.7	18.7	14.1	24.9	34.6	27.2	36.1	49.9
Manufactures	484.9	495.7	610.6	803.2	1,220.7	1,930.9	2,764.9	4,130.0	3,792.0	4,219.8	5,375.3
					(Index 1987 = 100)						
Terms of Trade	24.5	30.5	31.4	37.1	119.6	109.8	118.9	120.0	104.9	128.0	183.9
Export Prices, fob	7.2	9.4	10.6	15.1	60.5	60.5	65.7	72.3	72.6	102.3	161.2
Import Prices, cif	29.5	30.8	33.7	40.7	50.6	55.1	55.3	60.2	69.2	79.9	87.6
BALANCE OF PAYMENTS					*(Millions of current US dollars)*						
Exports of Goods & Services	1,809	2,668	3,153	4,660	12,212	10,289	11,864	12,151	13,837	22,872	27,344
Merchandise, fob	1,693	2,272	2,558	3,826	10,959	8,485	9,621	9,562	10,234	18,114	20,633
Nonfactor Services	26	275	185	275	486	521	612	625	702	1,183	1,225
Factor Services	90	121	410	559	767	1,283	1,631	1,965	2,901	3,575	5,487
Imports of Goods & Services	781	841	1,509	2,038	2,514	3,289	4,398	6,341	6,475	7,552	10,463
Merchandise, fob	625	652	797	1,052	1,552	2,400	3,300	4,735	4,326	4,870	6,756
Nonfactor Services	69	73	317	477	621	759	975	1,406	1,854	2,265	3,067
Factor Services	87	116	395	509	341	131	123	199	295	416	640
Long-Term Interest	..	..	..	..	..	..	..	..	..	..	..
Private Current Transfers, net	-175	-260	-280	-743	-1,235	-276	-315	-370	-433	-532	-692
Workers' Remittances	..	..	..	..	..	..	..	..	..	..	..
Curr. A/C Bal before Off. Transf.	853	1,567	1,364	1,879	8,463	6,723	7,152	5,440	6,930	14,788	16,190
Net Official Transfers	0	0	0	0	0	-793	-222	-879	-800	-756	-888
Curr. A/C Bal after Off. Transf.	853	1,567	1,364	1,879	8,463	5,930	6,929	4,561	6,130	14,032	15,302
Long-Term Capital, net	-40	-90	27	24	126	-1,083	-913	-614	-505	-868	-37
Direct Investment	..	-8	-40	-54	-484	-93	-109	-52	-95	-188	-407
Long-Term Loans	..	..	..	..	..	..	..	..	..	..	..
Disbursements	..	..	..	..	..	..	..	..	..	..	..
Repayments	..	..	..	..	..	..	..	..	..	..	..
Other Long-Term Capital	-40	-82	67	78	610	-990	-804	-562	-411	-680	370
Other Capital, net	-792	-1,402	-1,316	-1,794	-7,728	-4,533	-5,769	-3,004	-6,067	-12,798	-14,219
Change in Reserves	-21	-75	-75	-109	-861	-315	-247	-943	443	-366	-1,045
Memo Item:					*(Kuwaiti Dinars per US dollar)*						
Conversion Factor (Annual Avg)	0.360	0.360	0.330	0.300	0.290	0.290	0.290	0.290	0.280	0.280	0.270
EXTERNAL DEBT (Total)	..	..	..	..	*(Millions of US dollars), outstanding at end of year*						
Long-Term Debt (by debtor)	..	..	..	..	..	..	..	..	..	..	..
Central Bank, incl. IMF credit	..	..	..	..	..	..	..	..	..	..	..
Central Government	..	..	..	..	..	..	..	..	..	..	..
Rest of General Government	..	..	..	..	..	..	..	..	..	..	..
Non-financial Public Enterprises	..	..	..	..	..	..	..	..	..	..	..
Priv. Sector, incl non-guaranteed	..	..	..	..	..	..	..	..	..	..	..
Short-Term Debt	..	..	..	..	..	..	..	..	..	..	..
Memo Items:					*(Millions of US dollars)*						
Int'l Reserves Excluding Gold	117.1	193.7	269.0	380.8	1,249.2	1,491.5	1,701.8	2,883.1	2,500.4	2,870.1	3,928.5
Gold Holdings (at market price)	92.0	108.2	161.0	319.5	653.5	559.3	751.6	414.2	570.7	1,300.0	1,496.7
SOCIAL INDICATORS											
Total Fertility Rate	7.1	7.0	6.9	6.7	6.5	6.3	6.1	5.9	5.7	5.5	5.3
Infant Mortality Rate	47.8	45.4	43.0	41.2	39.4	37.6	35.8	34.0	31.5	29.1	26.6
Life Expectancy at Birth	66.1	66.7	67.3	67.7	68.2	68.6	69.1	69.5	70.0	70.4	70.8
Urban Population, % of total	77.8	79.0	80.2	81.4	82.6	83.8	85.1	86.4	87.6	88.9	90.2
Food Prod. per capita (1987=100)	..	..	..	..	..	..	..	..	..	..	..
Labor Force, Agriculture (%)	1.8	1.8	1.8	1.8	1.8	1.8	1.8	1.8	1.9	1.9	1.9
Labor Force, Female (%)	8.1	9.1	10.0	10.8	11.5	12.2	12.4	12.6	12.8	12.9	13.0
Primary Schl. Enroll. Ratio	89.0	..	..	..	..	92.0	97.0	100.0	98.0	98.0	102.0
Primary Schl. Enroll. Ratio, Female	76.0	..	..	..	..	85.0	92.0	94.0	93.0	95.0	100.0
Secondary Schl. Enroll. Ratio	63.0	..	..	..	..	66.0	74.0	74.0	73.0	74.0	80.0

1981	1982	1983	1984	1985	1986	1987	1988	1989	1990 est.	Notes	KUWAIT
			(Millions of current US dollars)								**FOREIGN TRADE (CUSTOMS BASIS)**
16,299.9	10,861.3	11,540.4	12,274.6	10,593.6	7,243.7	8,271.9	7,765.4	11,501.8	8,300.0	..	Value of Exports, fob
220.5	196.9	156.4	168.2	80.2	54.8	62.6	58.8	130.4	62.8	..	Nonfuel Primary Products
13,626.7	8,216.2	9,127.2	10,160.7	9,412.6	6,436.1	7,349.7	6,899.7	10,469.5	7,374.7	..	Fuels
2,452.7	2,448.2	2,256.7	1,945.8	1,100.9	752.8	859.6	807.0	901.9	862.5	..	Manufactures
6,969.1	8,283.4	7,374.9	6,896.4	6,006.9	5,716.5	5,494.6	6,145.1	6,302.2	4,800.0	..	Value of Imports, cif
1,162.1	1,302.8	1,167.5	1,336.7	1,164.3	1,108.0	1,065.0	1,191.1	1,533.5	930.4	..	Nonfuel Primary Products
39.7	49.5	40.2	39.1	34.1	32.4	31.1	34.8	60.5	27.2	..	Fuels
5,767.3	6,931.2	6,167.2	5,520.6	4,808.5	4,576.1	4,398.4	4,919.2	4,708.3	3,842.4	..	Manufactures
			(Index 1987 = 100)								
205.6	195.5	178.0	179.3	174.6	85.5	100.0	73.0	77.2	..	..	Terms of Trade
178.8	164.7	147.8	145.8	142.3	78.9	100.0	81.8	89.0	..	..	Export Prices, fob
87.0	84.3	83.0	81.3	81.5	92.3	100.0	112.1	115.3	..	..	Import Prices, cif
			(Millions of current US dollars)								**BALANCE OF PAYMENTS**
25,819	18,450	18,029	18,847	16,791	16,380	15,119	16,493	21,550	..	..	Exports of Goods & Services
16,023	10,819	11,473	12,156	10,374	7,216	8,221	7,709	11,383	..	..	Merchandise, fob
1,392	941	868	888	1,137	1,053	1,030	1,158	1,328	..	..	Nonfactor Services
8,404	6,690	5,688	5,803	5,280	8,111	5,867	7,626	8,840	..	..	Factor Services
10,381	12,056	11,191	11,096	10,404	9,728	9,488	10,691	11,607	..	..	Imports of Goods & Services
6,736	7,811	6,889	6,553	5,662	5,265	4,945	5,999	6,624	..	..	Merchandise, fob
2,906	3,491	3,620	3,705	4,076	3,861	4,073	4,204	4,228	..	..	Nonfactor Services
739	754	683	838	665	602	470	487	756	..	..	Factor Services
..	..	..	..	..	..	..	..	..	..	..	Long-Term Interest
-689	-875	-865	-963	-1,044	-1,084	-1,102	-1,179	-1,287	..	..	Private Current Transfers, net
..	..	..	..	..	..	..	..	..	..	..	Workers' Remittances
14,750	5,519	5,973	6,789	5,343	5,568	4,529	4,623	8,656	..	..	Curr. A/C Bal before Off. Transf.
-972	-646	-686	-416	-529	-182	-158	-140	-211	..	..	Net Official Transfers
13,778	4,873	5,287	6,374	4,815	5,386	4,371	4,483	8,445	..	..	Curr. A/C Bal after Off. Transf.
83	-243	-902	-1,074	-712	-1,975	-240	-620	-943	..	..	Long-Term Capital, net
-151	-108	-240	-95	-70	-248	-115	-255	-507	..	..	Direct Investment
..	..	..	..	..	..	..	..	..	..	..	Long-Term Loans
..	..	..	..	..	..	..	..	..	..	..	Disbursements
..	..	..	..	..	..	..	..	..	..	..	Repayments
233	-136	-662	-980	-642	-1,728	-126	-366	-436	..	..	Other Long-Term Capital
-13,574	-2,652	-5,372	-5,331	-3,558	-3,494	-5,977	-5,860	-6,247	..	..	Other Capital, net
-286	-1,978	988	32	-545	83	1,847	1,996	-1,255	..	..	Change in Reserves
			(Kuwaiti Dinars per US dollar)								**Memo Item:**
0.280	0.290	0.290	0.300	0.300	0.290	0.280	0.280	0.290	..	..	Conversion Factor (Annual Avg)
		(Millions of US dollars), outstanding at end of year									
..	..	..	..	..	..	..	..	..	..	..	**EXTERNAL DEBT (Total)**
..	..	..	..	..	..	..	..	..	..	..	Long-Term Debt (by debtor)
..	..	..	..	..	..	..	..	..	..	..	Central Bank, incl. IMF credit
..	..	..	..	..	..	..	..	..	..	..	Central Government
..	..	..	..	..	..	..	..	..	..	..	Rest of General Government
..	..	..	..	..	..	..	..	..	..	..	Non-financial Public Enterprises
..	..	..	..	..	..	..	..	..	..	..	Priv. Sector, incl non-guaranteed
..	..	..	..	..	..	..	..	..	..	..	Short-Term Debt
			(Millions of US dollars)								**Memo Items:**
4,067.5	5,913.2	5,192.1	4,590.2	5,470.7	5,501.1	4,141.6	1,923.5	3,101.9	..	..	Int'l Reserves Excluding Gold
1,009.3	1,160.1	968.6	782.8	830.3	992.5	1,229.1	1,041.6	1,018.1	977.5	..	Gold Holdings (at market price)
											SOCIAL INDICATORS
5.1	4.9	4.7	4.5	4.3	4.1	3.9	3.7	3.6	3.4	..	Total Fertility Rate
24.1	22.8	20.9	19.0	18.4	17.2	16.0	15.3	14.5	13.8	..	Infant Mortality Rate
71.2	71.6	71.9	72.3	72.6	72.9	73.2	73.5	73.8	74.1	..	Life Expectancy at Birth
90.9	91.6	92.3	93.0	93.7	94.1	94.5	94.8	95.2	95.6	..	Urban Population, % of total
..	..	..	..	..	..	..	..	..	..	..	Food Prod. per capita (1987=100)
..	..	..	..	..	..	..	..	..	..	..	Labor Force, Agriculture (%)
13.1	13.2	13.3	13.4	13.4	13.7	14.0	14.2	14.4	14.6	..	Labor Force, Female (%)
..	103.0	104.0	99.0	103.0	101.0	101.0	100.0	..	..	..	Primary Schl. Enroll. Ratio
100.0	101.0	102.0	97.0	102.0	100.0	100.0	99.0	91.0	..	..	Primary Schl. Enroll. Ratio, Female
..	82.0	82.0	86.0	91.0	90.0	90.0	90.0	..	..	..	Secondary Schl. Enroll. Ratio

LAO PDR	1970	1971	1972	1973	1974	1975	1976	1977	1978	1979	1980
CURRENT GNP PER CAPITA (US $)	..	..	..	..	..	..	..	..	..	..	..
POPULATION (thousands)	2,713	2,777	2,844	2,912	2,973	3,024	3,066	3,097	3,125	3,159	3,205
USE AND ORIGIN OF RESOURCES					*(Billions of current Lao Kip)*						
Gross National Product (GNP)	..	..	..	..	..	..	..	..	..	..	..
Net Factor Income from Abroad	..	..	..	..	..	..	..	..	..	..	..
GDP at Market Prices	..	..	..	..	..	..	..	..	..	..	..
Resource Balance	..	..	..	..	..	..	..	..	..	..	..
Exports of Goods & NFServices	..	..	..	..	..	..	..	..	..	..	..
Imports of Goods & NFServices	..	..	..	..	..	..	..	..	..	..	..
Domestic Absorption	..	..	..	..	..	..	..	..	..	..	..
Private Consumption, etc.	..	..	..	..	..	..	..	..	..	..	..
General Gov't Consumption	..	..	..	..	..	..	..	..	..	..	..
Gross Domestic Investment	..	..	..	..	..	..	..	..	..	..	..
Fixed Investment	..	..	..	..	..	..	..	..	..	..	..
Indirect Taxes, net	..	..	..	..	..	..	..	..	..	..	..
GDP at factor cost	..	..	..	..	..	..	..	..	..	..	..
Agriculture	..	..	..	..	..	..	..	..	..	..	..
Industry	..	..	..	..	..	..	..	..	..	..	..
Manufacturing	..	..	..	..	..	..	..	..	..	..	..
Services, etc.	..	..	..	..	..	..	..	..	..	..	..
Gross Domestic Saving	..	..	..	..	..	..	..	..	..	..	..
Gross National Saving	..	..	..	..	..	..	..	..	..	..	..
					..						
Gross National Product	..	..	..	..	..	..	..	..	..	..	..
GDP at Market Prices	..	..	..	..	..	..	..	..	..	..	..
Resource Balance	..	..	..	..	..	..	..	..	..	..	..
Exports of Goods & NFServices	..	..	..	..	..	..	..	..	..	..	..
Imports of Goods & NFServices	..	..	..	..	..	..	..	..	..	..	..
Domestic Absorption	..	..	..	..	..	..	..	..	..	..	..
Private Consumption, etc.	..	..	..	..	..	..	..	..	..	..	..
General Gov't Consumption	..	..	..	..	..	..	..	..	..	..	..
Gross Domestic Investment	..	..	..	..	..	..	..	..	..	..	..
Fixed Investment	..	..	..	..	..	..	..	..	..	..	..
GDP at factor cost	..	..	..	..	..	..	..	..	..	..	..
Agriculture	..	..	..	..	..	..	..	..	..	..	..
Industry	..	..	..	..	..	..	..	..	..	..	..
Manufacturing	..	..	..	..	..	..	..	..	..	..	..
Services, etc.	..	..	..	..	..	..	..	..	..	..	..
Memo Items:											
Capacity to Import	..	..	..	..	..	..	..	..	..	..	..
Terms of Trade Adjustment	..	..	..	..	..	..	..	..	..	..	..
Gross Domestic Income	..	..	..	..	..	..	..	..	..	..	..
Gross National Income	..	..	..	..	..	..	..	..	..	..	..
DOMESTIC PRICES/DEFLATORS					*(Index 1987 = 100)*						
Overall (GDP)	..	..	..	..	..	..	..	..	..	..	..
Domestic Absorption	..	..	..	..	..	..	..	..	..	..	..
Agriculture	..	..	..	..	..	..	..	..	..	..	..
Industry	..	..	..	..	..	..	..	..	..	..	..
Manufacturing	..	..	..	..	..	..	..	..	..	..	..
Consumer Price Index	..	..	..	..	..	..	..	..	..	..	..
MANUFACTURING ACTIVITY											
Employment (1987=100)	..	..	..	..	..	..	..	..	..	..	..
Real Earnings per Empl. (1987=100)	..	..	..	..	..	..	..	..	..	..	..
Real Output per Empl. (1987=100)	..	..	..	..	..	..	..	..	..	..	..
Earnings as % of Value Added	..	..	..	..	..	..	..	..	..	..	..
MONETARY HOLDINGS					*(Millions of current Lao Kip)*						
Money Supply, Broadly Defined	..	..	..	..	..	..	..	..	..	..	..
Money	..	..	..	..	..	..	..	..	..	..	..
Currency Outside Banks	..	..	..	..	..	..	..	..	..	..	..
Demand Deposits	..	..	..	..	..	..	..	..	..	..	..
Quasi-Money	..	..	..	..	..	..	..	..	..	..	..
					(Millions of current Lao Kip)						
GOVERNMENT DEFICIT (-) OR SURPLUS	..	..	..	..	..	..	..	..	..	..	..
Current Revenue	..	..	..	..	..	..	..	..	..	..	..
Current Expenditure	..	..	..	..	..	..	..	..	..	..	..
Current Budget Balance	..	..	..	..	..	..	..	..	..	..	..
Capital Receipts	..	..	..	..	..	..	..	..	..	..	..
Capital Payments	..	..	..	..	..	..	..	..	..	..	..

| --- | --- | --- | --- | --- | --- | --- | --- | --- | --- | --- | --- |
..	..	..	..	..	590	450	260	220	200	..	**CURRENT GNP PER CAPITA (US $)**
3,262	3,330	3,408	3,496	3,594	3,695	3,800	3,909	4,023	4,140	..	**POPULATION (thousands)**
			(Billions of current Lao Kip)								**USE AND ORIGIN OF RESOURCES**
..	..	..	64.67	112.22	177.10	199.16	246.29	449.60	611.22	..	Gross National Product (GNP)
..	..	..	-0.11	-0.10	-0.28	-0.09	-0.86	-1.20	-1.63	..	Net Factor Income from Abroad
..	..	..	64.78	112.33	177.39	199.26	247.14	450.80	612.85	..	GDP at Market Prices
..	..	..	-2.19	-6.06	-6.89	-15.05	-33.13	-59.49	-85.13	..	Resource Balance
..	..	..	1.74	4.32	6.10	11.61	25.68	44.35	61.54	..	Exports of Goods & NFServices
..	..	..	3.94	10.38	12.99	26.65	58.80	103.85	146.67	..	Imports of Goods & NFServices
..	..	..	66.97	118.39	184.28	214.30	280.27	510.30	697.98	..	Domestic Absorption
..	..	..	58.60	100.04	156.91	176.92	214.09	402.96	545.85	..	Private Consumption, etc.
..	..	..	4.51	10.83	15.66	17.88	34.34	52.86	76.55	..	General Gov't Consumption
..	..	..	3.86	7.52	11.71	19.51	31.84	54.47	75.57	..	Gross Domestic Investment
..	..	..	3.86	7.51	11.71	19.51	31.84	54.47	75.57	..	Fixed Investment
..	..	..	..	..	..	..	..	..	..	..	Indirect Taxes, net
..	..	..	..	..	..	..	..	..	..	..	GDP at factor cost
..	..	..	..	..	..	..	..	..	..	..	Agriculture
..	..	..	..	..	..	..	..	..	..	..	Industry
..	..	..	..	..	..	..	..	..	..	..	Manufacturing
..	..	..	..	..	..	..	..	..	..	..	Services, etc.
..	..	..	1.67	1.46	4.82	4.46	-1.29	-5.02	-9.56	..	Gross Domestic Saving
..	..	..	1.65	1.51	4.89	4.98	0.50	-1.38	-4.81	..	Gross National Saving
					..						
..	..	..	182,536	191,917	201,084	199,161	194,950	221,467	236,178	..	Gross National Product
..	..	..	182,859	192,103	201,417	199,256	195,597	222,031	236,769	..	GDP at Market Prices
..	..	..	-12,403	-16,600	-14,454	-15,046	-15,804	-17,342	-16,683	..	Resource Balance
..	..	..	8,824	11,492	11,648	11,606	11,689	13,772	16,071	..	Exports of Goods & NFServices
..	..	..	21,227	28,092	26,102	26,652	27,493	31,113	32,753	..	Imports of Goods & NFServices
..	..	..	195,262	208,703	215,871	214,302	211,400	239,373	253,452	..	Domestic Absorption
..	..	..	155,337	167,097	176,003	176,916	176,772	204,949	219,253	..	Private Consumption, etc.
..	..	..	18,412	21,309	19,584	17,881	17,874	16,302	15,116	..	General Gov't Consumption
..	..	..	21,513	20,297	20,283	19,505	16,754	18,122	19,083	..	Gross Domestic Investment
..	..	..	21,513	20,297	20,283	19,505	16,754	18,122	19,083	..	Fixed Investment
..	..	..	..	..	..	..	..	..	..	..	GDP at factor cost
..	..	..	..	..	..	..	..	..	..	..	Agriculture
..	..	..	..	..	..	..	..	..	..	..	Industry
..	..	..	..	..	..	..	..	..	..	..	Manufacturing
..	..	..	..	..	..	..	..	..	..	..	Services, etc.
											Memo Items:
..	..	..	9,406	11,686	12,252	11,606	12,004	13,288	13,743	..	Capacity to Import
..	..	..	582	193	604	0	315	-483	-2,328	..	Terms of Trade Adjustment
..	..	..	183,441	192,297	202,021	199,256	195,912	221,548	234,441	..	Gross Domestic Income
..	..	..	183,118	192,110	201,688	199,161	195,265	220,984	233,850	..	Gross National Income
			(Index 1987 = 100)								**DOMESTIC PRICES/DEFLATORS**
..	..	..	35.4	58.5	88.1	100.0	126.4	203.0	258.8	..	Overall (GDP)
..	..	..	34.3	56.7	85.4	100.0	132.6	213.2	275.4	..	Domestic Absorption
..	..	..	..	..	..	..	..	..	..	..	Agriculture
..	..	..	..	..	..	..	..	..	..	..	Industry
..	..	..	..	..	..	..	..	..	..	..	Manufacturing
..	..	..	..	..	..	..	..	..	..	..	Consumer Price Index
											MANUFACTURING ACTIVITY
..	..	..	..	..	..	..	..	..	..	..	Employment (1987=100)
..	..	..	..	..	..	..	..	..	..	..	Real Earnings per Empl. (1987=100)
..	..	..	..	..	..	..	..	..	..	..	Real Output per Empl. (1987=100)
..	..	..	..	..	..	..	..	..	..	..	Earnings as % of Value Added
			(Millions of current Lao Kip)								**MONETARY HOLDINGS**
..	..	..	..	2,280	3,876	15,842	21,715	41,114	..	..	Money Supply, Broadly Defined
785	1,205	1,668	1,655	2,226	3,881	6,904	12,102	25,127	..	..	Money
169	236	320	450	635	1,047	2,107	3,486	16,842	..	..	Currency Outside Banks
616	969	1,348	1,205	1,591	2,834	4,797	8,616	8,285	..	..	Demand Deposits
..	..	..	..	54	-5	8,938	9,613	15,987	..	..	Quasi-Money
			(Millions of current Lao Kip)								**GOVERNMENT DEFICIT (-) OR SURPLUS**
..	..	..	..	..	..	..	..	..	..	..	Current Revenue
..	..	..	..	..	..	..	..	..	..	..	Current Expenditure
..	..	..	..	..	..	..	..	..	..	..	Current Budget Balance
..	..	..	..	..	..	..	..	..	..	..	Capital Receipts
..	..	..	..	..	..	..	..	..	..	..	Capital Payments

LAO PDR	1970	1971	1972	1973	1974	1975	1976	1977	1978	1979	1980
FOREIGN TRADE (CUSTOMS BASIS)					*(Thousands of current US dollars)*						
Value of Exports, fob	..	..	..	..	..	..	..	..	..	..	..
Nonfuel Primary Products	..	..	..	..					..	..	..
Fuels	..	..	..	..					..	..	..
Manufactures	..	..	..	..					..	..	..
Value of Imports, cif	..	..	..	..					..	..	..
Nonfuel Primary Products	..	..	..	..					..	..	..
Fuels	..	..	..	..					..	..	..
Manufactures	..	..	..	..					..	..	..
					(Index 1987 = 100)						
Terms of Trade	..	..	..	..	..	..	..	..	..	..	..
Export Prices, fob	..	..	..	..					..	..	..
Import Prices, cif	..	..	..	..					..	..	..
BALANCE OF PAYMENTS					*(Thousands of current US dollars)*						
Exports of Goods & Services	..	..	..	..	..	..	..	..	..	..	..
Merchandise, fob	..	..	..	..					..	..	..
Nonfactor Services	..	..	..	..					..	..	..
Factor Services	..	..	..	..					..	..	..
Imports of Goods & Services	..	..	..	..	..	..	..	..	..	..	..
Merchandise, fob	..	..	..	..					..	..	..
Nonfactor Services	..	..	..	..					..	..	..
Factor Services	..	..	..	..					..	..	..
Long-Term Interest	0.20	0.30	0.40	0.70	0.90	1.00	1.20	1.20	1.80	1.90	1.30
Private Current Transfers, net	..	..	..	..	..	..	..	..	..	..	..
Workers' Remittances	..	..	..	..					..	..	..
Curr. A/C Bal before Off. Transf.	..	..	..	..	..	..	..	..	..	..	..
Net Official Transfers	..	..	..	..					..	..	..
Curr. A/C Bal after Off. Transf.	..	..	..	..					..	..	..
Long-Term Capital, net	..	..	..	..	..	..	..	..	..	..	..
Direct Investment	..	..	..	..					..	..	..
Long-Term Loans	4.40	6.10	2.90	10.90	5.20	25.90	49.80	41.80	43.90	26.80	37.00
Disbursements	5.80	7.70	5.90	15.40	10.00	31.00	54.90	47.80	52.50	38.20	38.10
Repayments	1.40	1.60	3.00	4.50	4.80	5.10	5.10	6.00	8.60	11.40	1.10
Other Long-Term Capital	..	..	..	..					..	..	..
Other Capital, net	..	..	..	..	..	..	..	..	..	..	..
Change in Reserves	0.78	-0.41	2.52	-2.74	-4.20	7.20	3.91	-0.09	5.65	0.47	2.54
Memo Item:					*(Lao Kip per US dollar)*						
Conversion Factor (Annual Avg)	0.120	0.120	0.250	0.300	0.300	0.360	1.630	2.520	4.200	5.710	10.220
					(Millions of US dollars), outstanding at end of year						
EXTERNAL DEBT (Total)	8.3	15.6	18.8	32.6	41.0	64.2	114.5	162.7	225.0	254.7	293.2
Long-Term Debt (by debtor)	8.3	15.6	18.8	32.6	41.0	64.2	114.5	162.7	225.0	254.7	293.2
Central Bank, incl. IMF credit	0.0	0.4	0.4	0.4	0.4	0.4	1.4	1.4	12.9	18.9	22.1
Central Government	8.3	15.2	18.4	32.2	40.6	63.8	113.1	161.3	212.1	235.8	271.1
Rest of General Government	..	..	..	..					..	..	..
Non-financial Public Enterprises	..	..	..	..					..	..	..
Priv. Sector, incl non-guaranteed	..	..	..	..					..	..	..
Short-Term Debt	0.0	0.0	0.0	0.0	0.0	0.0	0.0	0.0	0.0	0.0	0.0
Memo Items:					*(Thousands of US dollars)*						
Int'l Reserves Excluding Gold	6,200	8,317	7,295	10,534	14,810	..	..	..	..	..	13,223
Gold Holdings (at market price)											
SOCIAL INDICATORS											
Total Fertility Rate	6.1	6.1	6.1	6.3	6.4	6.5	6.6	6.7	6.7	6.7	6.7
Infant Mortality Rate	145.8	145.4	145.0	143.0	141.0	139.0	137.0	135.0	132.4	129.8	127.2
Life Expectancy at Birth	40.4	40.4	40.4	41.0	41.7	42.3	42.9	43.5	44.0	44.5	45.0
Urban Population, % of total	9.6	10.0	10.3	10.7	11.0	11.4	11.8	12.2	12.6	13.0	13.4
Food Prod. per capita (1987=100)	79.8	74.2	72.8	73.1	72.8	69.7	59.3	63.1	67.9	79.7	91.4
Labor Force, Agriculture (%)	78.9	78.6	78.2	77.9	77.6	77.3	77.0	76.7	76.4	76.0	75.7
Labor Force, Female (%)	46.4	46.4	46.3	46.3	46.3	46.3	46.3	46.2	46.2	46.2	46.2
Primary Schl. Enroll. Ratio	53.0	..	..	..	..	58.0	92.0	92.0	96.0	96.0	113.0
Primary Schl. Enroll. Ratio, Female	40.0	..	..	..	..		77.0	85.0	85.0	88.0	104.0
Secondary Schl. Enroll. Ratio	3.0	..	..	..	..	7.0	11.0	14.0	16.0	17.0	21.0

1981	1982	1983	1984	1985	1986	1987	1988	1989	1990 estimate	Notes	LAO PDR
				(Thousands of current US dollars)							**FOREIGN TRADE (CUSTOMS BASIS)**
..	..	..	..	..	..	..	..	..	..	..	Value of Exports, fob
..	..	..	..	..	..	..	..	..	..	..	Nonfuel Primary Products
..	..	..	..	..	..	..	..	..	..	..	Fuels
..	..	..	..	..	..	..	..	..	..	..	Manufactures
..	..	..	..	..	..	..	..	..	..	..	Value of Imports, cif
..	..	..	..	..	..	..	..	..	..	..	Nonfuel Primary Products
..	..	..	..	..	..	..	..	..	..	..	Fuels
..	..	..	..	..	..	..	..	..	..	..	Manufactures
				(Index 1987 = 100)							
..	..	..	..	..	..	..	..	..	..	..	Terms of Trade
..	..	..	..	..	..	..	..	..	..	..	Export Prices, fob
..	..	..	..	..	..	..	..	..	..	..	Import Prices, cif
				(Thousands of current US dollars)							**BALANCE OF PAYMENTS**
..	..	..	..	..	..	..	81.04	85.00	..	..	Exports of Goods & Services
..	40.00	40.80	43.80	53.60	55.00	64.30	57.82	54.40	..	..	Merchandise, fob
..	..	..	15.00	21.25	24.35	26.20	22.82	30.60	..	..	Nonfactor Services
..	..	..	..	..	..	..	0.40	0.00	..	..	Factor Services
..	..	..	186.70	221.70	203.50	235.20	205.60	200.60	..	..	Imports of Goods & Services
..	132.20	149.40	161.90	193.20	185.70	216.20	187.99	161.60	..	..	Merchandise, fob
..	..	..	21.70	26.10	16.30	17.60	15.11	3.40	..	..	Nonfactor Services
..	..	..	3.10	2.40	1.50	1.40	2.50	35.60	32.70	..	Factor Services
1.30	1.10	1.20	1.20	0.80	1.60	1.90	2.00	2.50	3.00	..	Long-Term Interest
..	0.20	0.30	2.80	3.50	3.70	3.50	6.74	8.30	9.00	..	Private Current Transfers, net
..	..	..	..	..	..	..	..	..	..	..	Workers' Remittances
..	-99.00	-121.00	-125.00	-143.00	-120.00	-141.00	-118.00	-107.00	-148.00	..	Curr. A/C Bal before Off. Transf.
..	30.80	25.10	42.10	49.60	30.50	27.00	25.50	40.30	42.00	..	Net Official Transfers
..	-68.30	-95.70	-83.00	-93.75	-89.95	-114.20	-92.32	-67.00	-106.30	..	Curr. A/C Bal after Off. Transf.
..	60.20	76.50	30.30	47.70	45.40	56.40	58.70	100.30	73.00	..	Long-Term Capital, net
..	..	..	..	..	..	..	..	..	..	..	Direct Investment
39.10	38.80	41.80	51.20	30.30	100.90	109.10	111.40	124.80	99.40	..	Long-Term Loans
40.00	41.30	44.00	54.50	35.90	106.70	116.70	118.80	133.50	107.40	..	Disbursements
0.90	2.50	2.20	3.30	5.60	5.80	7.60	7.40	8.70	8.00	..	Repayments
..	21.40	34.70	-20.90	17.40	-55.50	-52.70	-52.70	-24.50	-26.40	..	Other Long-Term Capital
..	3.06	30.39	49.08	67.28	53.24	46.43	29.14	-40.59	78.15	..	Other Capital, net
7.56	5.04	-11.19	3.62	-21.23	-8.69	11.37	4.48	7.29	-44.85	..	Change in Reserves
				(Lao Kip per US dollar)							**Memo Item:**
20.000	35.000	35.000	35.000	45.000	95.000	175.120	392.010	583.010	708.570	..	Conversion Factor (Annual Avg)
				(Millions of US dollars), outstanding at end of year							
321.3	354.5	390.6	433.6	476.4	597.3	725.6	823.9	946.8	1,063.3	..	**EXTERNAL DEBT (Total)**
321.3	354.5	390.6	433.6	476.4	597.3	725.6	818.4	945.2	1,061.3	..	Long-Term Debt (by debtor)
20.1	19.1	17.9	15.5	15.4	14.6	13.5	8.5	14.3	14.9	..	Central Bank, incl. IMF credit
301.2	335.4	372.7	418.1	461.0	582.7	712.1	809.9	930.9	1,046.4	..	Central Government
..	..	..	..	..	..	..	..	..	..	..	Rest of General Government
..	..	..	..	..	..	..	..	..	..	..	Non-financial Public Enterprises
..	..	..	..	..	..	..	..	..	..	..	Priv. Sector, incl non-guaranteed
0.0	0.0	0.0	0.0	0.0	0.0	0.0	5.5	1.6	2.0	..	Short-Term Debt
				(Thousands of US dollars)							**Memo Items:**
12,742	7,664	18,847	10,620	25,341	31,998	20,600	16,130	16,143	61,024	..	Int'l Reserves Excluding Gold
..	..	..	..	..	..	..	..	..	..	..	Gold Holdings (at market price)
											SOCIAL INDICATORS
6.7	6.7	6.7	6.7	6.7	6.7	6.7	6.7	6.7	6.7	..	Total Fertility Rate
124.6	122.0	119.6	117.2	114.8	112.4	110.0	107.5	105.0	102.6	..	Infant Mortality Rate
45.5	46.0	46.5	47.0	47.5	48.0	48.5	48.8	49.1	49.5	..	Life Expectancy at Birth
13.9	14.4	14.9	15.4	15.9	16.4	17.0	17.5	18.1	18.6	..	Urban Population, % of total
97.8	95.1	96.2	105.4	109.7	110.2	100.0	91.3	105.7	110.4	..	Food Prod. per capita (1987=100)
..	..	..	..	..	..	..	..	..	..	..	Labor Force, Agriculture (%)
46.0	45.8	45.6	45.5	45.3	45.1	44.9	44.7	44.5	44.3	..	Labor Force, Female (%)
..	109.0	107.0	107.0	111.0	..	111.0	..	..	..	..	Primary Schl. Enroll. Ratio
..	..	92.0	94.0	100.0	..	98.0	..	..	..	..	Primary Schl. Enroll. Ratio, Female
..	22.0	23.0	23.0	23.0	..	27.0	..	..	..	..	Secondary Schl. Enroll. Ratio

LESOTHO	1970	1971	1972	1973	1974	1975	1976	1977	1978	1979	1980
CURRENT GNP PER CAPITA (US $)	100	110	110	150	200	230	250	290	330	360	410
POPULATION (thousands)	1,064	1,087	1,112	1,137	1,165	1,193	1,223	1,254	1,287	1,320	1,355
USE AND ORIGIN OF RESOURCES					*(Millions of current Lesotho Maloti)*						
Gross National Product (GNP)	74.8	76.3	95.8	132.4	158.1	199.7	247.7	308.0	385.1	422.5	491.3
Net Factor Income from Abroad	22.3	25.8	31.5	44.6	60.1	89.1	119.3	139.9	153.3	178.2	205.0
GDP at Market Prices	52.5	50.5	64.3	87.8	98.0	110.6	128.4	168.1	231.8	244.3	286.3
Resource Balance	-22.9	-29.5	-41.9	-56.6	-82.0	-98.6	-153.4	-167.3	-169.9	-246.4	-292.2
Exports of Goods & NFServices	5.7	6.8	10.1	12.8	14.1	14.6	21.3	18.0	36.4	50.0	58.0
Imports of Goods & NFServices	28.6	36.3	52.0	69.4	96.1	113.2	174.7	185.3	206.3	296.4	350.2
Domestic Absorption	75.4	80.0	106.2	144.4	180.0	209.2	281.8	335.4	401.7	490.7	578.5
Private Consumption, etc.	63.2	63.7	85.6	116.0	146.9	167.2	210.5	264.2	300.7	353.7	354.6
General Gov't Consumption	6.2	8.3	10.8	12.1	15.8	21.3	24.9	29.2	40.9	52.4	102.5
Gross Domestic Investment	6.0	8.0	9.8	16.3	17.3	20.7	46.4	42.0	60.1	84.6	121.4
Fixed Investment	5.1	7.1	8.6	10.7	14.5	20.7	45.5	40.3	51.0	73.7	115.6
Indirect Taxes, net	4.7	4.4	5.2	10.9	14.0	13.2	14.3	23.6	46.3	28.8	39.1
GDP at factor cost	47.8	46.1	59.1	76.9	84.0	97.4	114.1	144.5	185.5	215.5	247.2
Agriculture	16.7	12.0	21.0	32.7	31.7	31.7	31.0	49.6	55.2	65.7	58.3
Industry	4.4	4.9	6.0	8.3	11.3	12.9	21.7	22.4	43.5	54.0	71.5
Manufacturing	2.1	2.4	2.8	3.9	4.8	5.6	6.2	7.2	10.1	11.9	16.1
Services, etc.	26.7	29.2	32.1	35.9	41.0	52.8	61.4	72.5	86.8	95.8	117.4
Gross Domestic Saving	-16.9	-21.5	-32.1	-40.3	-64.7	-77.9	-107.0	-125.3	-109.8	-161.8	-170.8
Gross National Saving	26.8	26.5	27.8	50.8	52.5	12.2	13.5	15.9	44.9	18.0	35.8
					(Millions of 1987 Lesotho Maloti)						
Gross National Product	426.33	471.12	506.39	655.20	754.61	808.49	914.17	1,060.49	1,152.23	1,168.19	1,141.08
GDP at Market Prices	268.51	285.01	312.27	405.68	450.23	389.39	432.41	526.72	623.19	641.23	622.11
Resource Balance	-173.75	-214.97	-291.09	-342.27	-403.88	-593.49	-713.71	-737.70	-723.83	-774.19	-812.04
Exports of Goods & NFServices	44.28	53.49	62.92	65.11	63.57	48.01	65.11	46.47	98.43	136.57	127.15
Imports of Goods & NFServices	218.04	268.45	354.01	407.38	467.45	641.50	778.81	784.18	822.26	910.76	939.19
Domestic Absorption	442.26	499.98	603.36	747.95	854.11	982.88	1,146.12	1,264.42	1,347.03	1,415.42	1,434.15
Private Consumption, etc.	371.35	409.11	494.92	604.08	708.09	790.00	892.63	918.57	1,011.97	1,027.92	896.48
General Gov't Consumption	24.56	32.27	40.52	44.47	51.28	67.24	66.34	69.21	90.19	96.28	183.78
Gross Domestic Investment	46.35	58.59	67.92	99.40	94.74	125.64	187.15	276.64	244.87	291.22	353.89
Fixed Investment	..	..	..	..	..	..	..	..	..	..	338.11
GDP at factor cost	229.82	247.81	271.51	338.93	372.96	326.47	364.46	433.11	499.40	518.39	489.11
Agriculture	170.56	175.66	139.95	163.46	200.28	152.15	143.94	180.76	201.16	208.26	129.30
Industry	18.06	12.57	26.06	38.87	46.87	43.90	60.81	97.40	113.40	134.43	163.47
Manufacturing	6.29	3.82	12.36	18.65	19.10	17.75	20.67	19.55	20.00	27.19	36.18
Services, etc.	41.20	59.58	105.50	136.61	125.82	130.42	159.70	154.96	184.83	175.70	196.34
Memo Items:											
Capacity to Import	43.45	50.29	68.76	75.14	68.59	82.74	94.96	76.17	145.08	153.64	155.55
Terms of Trade Adjustment	-0.83	-3.20	5.84	10.03	5.01	34.73	29.85	29.70	46.65	17.06	28.40
Gross Domestic Income	267.68	281.81	318.12	415.71	455.24	424.12	462.26	556.42	669.85	658.29	650.51
Gross National Income	425.50	467.92	512.24	665.23	759.62	843.22	944.02	1,090.19	1,198.89	1,185.25	1,169.49
DOMESTIC PRICES/DEFLATORS					*(Index 1987 = 100)*						
Overall (GDP)	19.6	17.7	20.6	21.6	21.8	28.4	29.7	31.9	37.2	38.1	46.0
Domestic Absorption	17.0	16.0	17.6	19.3	21.1	21.3	24.6	26.5	29.8	34.7	40.3
Agriculture	9.8	6.8	15.0	20.0	15.8	20.8	21.5	27.4	27.4	31.5	45.1
Industry	24.4	39.0	23.0	21.4	24.1	29.4	35.7	23.0	38.4	40.2	43.7
Manufacturing	33.4	62.8	22.7	20.9	25.1	31.5	30.0	36.8	50.5	43.8	44.5
Consumer Price Index	..	..	..	16.0	18.2	20.7	23.1	27.0	30.3	35.2	40.7
MANUFACTURING ACTIVITY											
Employment (1987=100)	..	..	..	..	..	..	..	..	..	..	..
Real Earnings per Empl. (1987=100)	..	..	..	..	..	..	..	..	..	..	..
Real Output per Empl. (1987=100)	..	..	..	..	..	..	..	..	..	..	..
Earnings as % of Value Added	..	..	..	..	..	..	..	..	..	..	26.2
MONETARY HOLDINGS					*(Millions of current Lesotho Maloti)*						
Money Supply, Broadly Defined	..	..	..	..	..	..	..	..	..	..	116.64
Money	..	..	..	..	..	..	..	..	..	..	48.47
Currency Outside Banks	..	..	..	..	..	..	..	..	..	..	6.92
Demand Deposits	..	..	..	..	..	..	..	..	..	..	41.55
Quasi-Money	..	..	..	..	..	..	..	..	..	..	68.17
					(Millions of current Lesotho Maloti)						
GOVERNMENT DEFICIT (-) OR SURPLUS	..	-0.54	-0.85	4.70	8.72	-8.70	-12.85	-2.99	..	..	..
Current Revenue	..	14.88	14.94	23.91	32.04	32.40	40.28	70.08	..	..	..
Current Expenditure	..	11.80	13.08	15.67	16.87	26.76	31.87	43.09	..	..	..
Current Budget Balance	..	3.08	1.86	8.24	15.18	5.64	8.41	26.99	..	..	..
Capital Receipts	..	0.01	0.02	0.00	0.00	0.02	0.10	0.06	..	..	..
Capital Payments	..	3.64	2.73	3.55	6.46	14.35	21.36	30.04	..	..	..

1981	1982	1983	1984	1985	1986	1987	1988	1989	1990 estimate	Notes	LESOTHO
480	550	510	480	390	340	340	410	490	530	..	**CURRENT GNP PER CAPITA (US $)**
1,391	1,427	1,465	1,504	1,545	1,587	1,630	1,675	1,721	1,768	..	**POPULATION (thousands)**
				(Millions of current Lesotho Maloti)							**USE AND ORIGIN OF RESOURCES**
583.2	744.6	814.6	941.6	1,059.0	1,202.8	1,341.2	1,672.5	2,132.5	2,544.7	C	Gross National Product (GNP)
254.8	372.9	423.1	487.2	514.3	583.3	615.4	702.5	939.8	1,088.9	..	Net Factor Income from Abroad
328.4	371.7	391.5	454.4	544.7	619.5	725.8	970.0	1,192.7	1,455.8	C f	GDP at Market Prices
-365.1	-458.0	-518.8	-616.3	-699.5	-750.1	-876.6	-1,000.0	-1,322.2	-1,634.6	..	Resource Balance
58.2	55.4	50.8	60.5	70.2	80.2	123.2	185.9	195.9	209.6	..	Exports of Goods & NF Services
423.3	513.4	569.6	676.8	769.7	830.3	999.8	1,185.9	1,518.1	1,844.2	..	Imports of Goods & NF Services
693.5	829.7	910.3	1,070.7	1,244.2	1,369.6	1,602.4	1,970.0	2,514.9	3,090.3	..	Domestic Absorption
442.8	526.4	655.0	747.3	791.2	878.2	1,051.9	1,241.9	1,488.8	1,712.0	..	Private Consumption, etc.
109.8	118.6	123.9	134.5	180.6	210.2	224.3	279.7	310.7	342.6	..	General Gov't Consumption
140.9	184.7	131.4	188.9	272.4	281.2	326.2	448.4	715.4	1,035.7	..	Gross Domestic Investment
133.2	186.8	130.8	184.5	273.3	276.2	327.0	446.4	712.3	1,031.9	..	Fixed Investment
45.8	64.3	82.6	89.1	93.9	127.0	148.2	187.0	..	..		Indirect Taxes, net
282.6	307.4	308.9	365.3	450.8	492.5	577.6	783.0	..	..	C f	GDP at factor cost
76.6	66.9	73.6	87.6	95.3	93.1	114.0	187.7	..	..	..	Agriculture
73.6	98.4	75.3	96.4	133.2	139.8	174.9	233.3	..	..	..	Industry
20.0	26.9	32.7	42.7	49.6	63.7	82.7	111.8	..	..	..	Manufacturing
132.4	142.1	160.0	181.3	222.3	259.6	288.7	362.0				Services, etc.
-224.2	-273.3	-387.4	-427.4	-427.1	-468.9	-550.4	-551.6	-606.8	-598.8	..	Gross Domestic Saving
32.4	102.5	38.6	64.7	91.3	119.1	65.6	160.9	344.0	502.4	..	Gross National Saving
				(Millions of 1987 Lesotho Maloti)							
1,197.39	1,371.84	1,343.21	1,400.75	1,353.19	1,330.27	1,341.20	1,431.49	1,612.18	1,700.52	C	Gross National Product
628.84	651.88	614.94	661.62	682.57	676.39	725.80	815.05	891.59	962.88	C f	GDP at Market Prices
-898.70	-954.24	-962.42	-983.35	-955.44	-856.04	-876.60	-914.83	-1,044.70	-1,127.20	..	Resource Balance
108.07	109.39	77.60	84.84	85.93	91.19	123.20	153.89	139.86	129.78	..	Exports of Goods & NF Services
1,006.77	1,063.63	1,040.03	1,068.19	1,041.37	947.24	999.80	1,068.72	1,184.58	1,256.99	..	Imports of Goods & NF Services
1,527.54	1,606.12	1,577.36	1,644.97	1,638.01	1,532.44	1,602.40	1,729.88	1,936.31	2,090.10	..	Domestic Absorption
985.23	1,002.90	1,138.25	1,144.30	1,046.78	991.91	1,051.90	1,099.47	1,151.25	1,142.73	..	Private Consumption, etc.
185.21	193.64	192.21	198.66	206.73	221.61	224.30	228.42	222.15	214.80	..	General Gov't Consumption
357.10	409.57	246.91	302.00	384.50	318.91	326.20	401.99	562.91	732.57	..	Gross Domestic Investment
340.75	414.16	246.57	296.00	387.25	312.67	327.00	401.00	562.45	732.39	..	Fixed Investment
489.11	504.54	490.49	506.33	529.41	537.06	577.60	653.73	..	..	C f	GDP at factor cost
137.51	110.01	147.49	118.44	113.33	108.23	114.00	144.16	..	..	..	Agriculture
140.61	183.36	99.68	137.86	163.93	154.78	174.90	204.62	..	..	..	Industry
37.53	46.74	44.50	61.13	63.60	72.81	82.70	98.21	..	..	..	Manufacturing
210.99	211.17	243.32	250.03	252.15	274.04	288.70	304.94	..	..	..	Services, etc.
											Memo Items:
138.42	114.77	92.76	95.49	94.98	91.49	123.20	167.53	152.86	142.86	..	Capacity to Import
30.35	5.38	15.15	10.65	9.04	0.30	0.00	13.64	13.00	13.08	..	Terms of Trade Adjustment
659.19	657.26	630.09	672.27	691.62	676.70	725.80	828.69	904.59	975.97	..	Gross Domestic Income
1,227.74	1,377.22	1,358.37	1,411.40	1,362.24	1,330.58	1,341.20	1,445.13	1,625.18	1,713.60	..	Gross National Income
				(Index 1987 = 100)							**DOMESTIC PRICES/DEFLATORS**
52.2	57.0	63.7	68.7	79.8	91.6	100.0	119.0	133.8	151.2	..	Overall (GDP)
45.4	51.7	57.7	65.1	76.0	89.4	100.0	113.9	129.9	147.9	..	Domestic Absorption
55.7	60.8	49.9	74.0	84.1	86.0	100.0	130.2	..	..	..	Agriculture
52.3	53.7	75.5	69.9	81.3	90.3	100.0	114.0	..	..	..	Industry
53.3	57.5	73.5	69.9	78.0	87.5	100.0	113.8	..	..	..	Manufacturing
45.8	51.3	60.3	66.9	75.8	89.5	100.0	111.5	127.9	142.7	..	Consumer Price Index
											MANUFACTURING ACTIVITY
..	..	..	..	..	..	..	..	..	..		Employment (1987=100)
..	..	..	..	..	..	..	..	..	..		Real Earnings per Empl. (1987=100)
..	..	..	..	..	..	..	..	..	..		Real Output per Empl. (1987=100)
29.7	33.9	26.7	24.0	27.7	..	..	..	..	..		Earnings as % of Value Added
				(Millions of current Lesotho Maloti)							**MONETARY HOLDINGS**
144.20	185.41	217.03	250.32	310.72	352.11	387.08	490.00	555.82	602.63	..	Money Supply, Broadly Defined
58.62	77.17	84.67	103.28	133.14	154.64	156.81	219.88	245.18	264.22	..	Money
10.62	17.77	23.14	23.67	25.23	32.55	33.19	41.87	53.36	59.79	..	Currency Outside Banks
48.00	59.40	61.52	79.60	107.91	122.09	123.62	178.01	191.82	204.43	..	Demand Deposits
85.58	108.24	132.36	147.04	177.58	197.47	230.26	270.12	310.63	338.41	..	Quasi-Money
				(Millions of current Lesotho Maloti)							
..	-27.69	-19.69	-12.65	-27.90	-37.28	-65.06	-47.31	..	..	C	**GOVERNMENT DEFICIT (-) OR SURPLUS**
..	133.07	174.29	239.45	242.45	287.20	320.80	367.28	..	..	..	Current Revenue
..	122.69	142.28	167.52	211.62	257.21	305.36	346.02	..	..	..	Current Expenditure
..	10.38	32.01	71.92	30.84	29.99	15.44	21.26	..	..	..	Current Budget Balance
..	8.29	1.13	0.03	0.04	0.14	0.26	4.91	..	..	..	Capital Receipts
..	46.35	52.82	84.60	58.77	67.40	80.76	73.48	..	..	..	Capital Payments

LESOTHO	1970	1971	1972	1973	1974	1975	1976	1977	1978	1979	1980
FOREIGN TRADE (CUSTOMS BASIS)					*(Millions of current US dollars)*						
Value of Exports, fob	..	..	..	..	..	..	..	..	..	..	..
Nonfuel Primary Products	..	..	..	..	..	..	..	..	..	..	..
Fuels	..	..	..	..	..	..	..	..	..	..	..
Manufactures	..	..	..	..	..	..	..	..	..	..	..
Value of Imports, cif	..	..	..	..	..	..	..	..	..	..	..
Nonfuel Primary Products	..	..	..	..	..	..	..	..	..	..	..
Fuels	..	..	..	..	..	..	..	..	..	..	..
Manufactures	..	..	..	..	..	..	..	..	..	..	..
					(Index 1987 = 100)						
Terms of Trade	117.2	99.8	102.9	118.0	90.8	85.6	86.0	80.7	86.1	88.1	84.9
Export Prices, fob	30.0	29.1	34.2	50.8	57.8	56.4	59.6	60.8	71.3	86.3	92.6
Import Prices, cif	25.6	29.2	33.2	43.1	63.6	65.9	69.3	75.4	82.8	97.9	109.1
BALANCE OF PAYMENTS					*(Millions of current US dollars)*						
Exports of Goods & Services	11.00	16.00	18.00	19.00	26.00	152.53	172.62	199.99	233.34	277.43	363.49
Merchandise, fob	6.00	4.00	8.00	12.00	14.00	13.52	17.94	15.18	33.01	39.07	58.16
Nonfactor Services	2.00	5.00	5.00	6.00	6.00	12.03	11.96	14.14	16.79	18.65	32.23
Factor Services	3.00	7.00	5.00	1.00	6.00	126.98	142.72	170.66	183.54	219.71	273.10
Imports of Goods & Services	42.00	52.00	68.00	102.00	143.00	174.98	214.48	240.70	278.76	358.07	482.39
Merchandise, fob	31.00	37.00	53.00	83.00	113.00	151.45	189.41	210.80	243.11	316.74	424.48
Nonfactor Services	10.00	14.00	14.00	17.00	27.00	19.07	20.93	24.84	29.90	35.27	50.33
Factor Services	1.00	1.00	1.00	2.00	3.00	4.46	4.14	5.06	5.75	6.06	7.58
Long-Term Interest	0.20	0.10	0.20	0.20	0.20	0.20	0.20	0.20	0.40	0.60	1.40
Private Current Transfers, net	30.00	31.00	37.00	67.00	84.00	1.35	1.38	1.50	1.61	1.90	2.05
Workers' Remittances	29.00	30.00	36.00	66.00	85.00	..	..	..	..	..	..
Curr. A/C Bal before Off. Transf.	-1.00	-5.00	-13.00	-16.00	-33.00	-21.10	-40.48	-39.22	-43.82	-78.74	-116.84
Net Official Transfers	19.00	21.00	20.00	30.00	32.00	20.01	6.32	30.02	52.33	78.74	173.17
Curr. A/C Bal after Off. Transf.	18.00	16.00	7.00	14.00	-1.00	-1.08	-34.16	-9.20	8.51	0.00	56.33
Long-Term Capital, net	0.00	0.00	0.00	0.00	2.00	3.92	2.07	9.43	8.63	22.39	33.86
Direct Investment	..	..	..	..	..	..	..	..	..	..	4.49
Long-Term Loans	0.10	0.40	0.40	-0.20	1.90	4.40	2.20	7.20	6.20	17.10	9.80
Disbursements	0.40	0.50	0.50	0.00	2.00	4.50	2.50	7.40	6.90	18.90	13.20
Repayments	0.30	0.10	0.10	0.20	0.10	0.10	0.30	0.20	0.70	1.80	3.40
Other Long-Term Capital	-0.10	-0.40	-0.40	0.20	0.10	-0.48	-0.13	2.23	2.42	5.29	19.56
Other Capital, net	-18.58	-16.00	-7.01	-14.00	-0.86	-2.14	32.04	-0.29	-17.32	-23.28	-47.08
Change in Reserves	0.58	0.00	0.01	0.00	-0.14	-0.70	0.05	0.06	0.19	0.90	-43.10
Memo Item:					*(Lesotho Maloti per US dollar)*						
Conversion Factor (Annual Avg)	0.710	0.720	0.770	0.690	0.680	0.740	0.870	0.870	0.870	0.840	0.780
				(Millions of US dollars), outstanding at end of year							
EXTERNAL DEBT (Total)	8.10	8.60	9.50	8.20	10.20	14.10	16.10	24.00	33.20	52.00	70.70
Long-Term Debt (by debtor)	8.10	8.60	9.50	8.20	10.20	14.10	16.10	24.00	30.20	52.00	62.70
Central Bank, incl. IMF credit	0.00	0.00	0.00	0.00	0.00	0.00	0.00	0.60	0.40	4.70	6.20
Central Government	7.90	8.40	8.90	7.60	9.60	13.60	15.70	23.00	28.30	44.50	54.10
Rest of General Government	..	..	..	..	..	..	..	..	..	..	..
Non-financial Public Enterprises	0.20	0.20	0.60	0.60	0.60	0.50	0.40	0.40	0.30	0.30	0.40
Priv. Sector, incl non-guaranteed	0.00	0.00	0.00	0.00	0.00	0.00	0.00	0.00	1.20	2.50	2.00
Short-Term Debt	0.00	0.00	0.00	0.00	0.00	0.00	0.00	0.00	3.00	0.00	8.00
Memo Items:					*(Thousands of US dollars)*						
Int'l Reserves Excluding Gold	..	..	..	..	..	..	..	..	..	..	50,268
Gold Holdings (at market price)	..	..	..	..	..	..	..	..	..	..	..
SOCIAL INDICATORS											
Total Fertility Rate	5.8	5.8	5.8	5.8	5.8	5.8	5.8	5.8	5.8	5.8	5.8
Infant Mortality Rate	134.0	132.0	130.0	128.6	127.2	125.8	124.4	123.0	120.6	118.2	115.8
Life Expectancy at Birth	49.0	49.1	49.2	49.6	50.0	50.4	50.8	51.2	51.4	51.7	51.9
Urban Population, % of total	8.6	9.0	9.5	9.9	10.4	10.8	11.4	11.9	12.5	13.0	13.6
Food Prod. per capita (1987=100)	136.0	143.2	124.2	133.8	159.7	123.5	107.6	124.3	125.4	114.9	114.6
Labor Force, Agriculture (%)	89.9	89.5	89.1	88.7	88.4	88.0	87.6	87.2	86.9	86.5	86.2
Labor Force, Female (%)	47.9	47.7	47.5	47.3	47.1	46.9	46.6	46.4	46.2	46.0	45.7
Primary Schl. Enroll. Ratio	87.0	..	..	..	..	105.0	105.0	105.0	103.0	104.0	103.0
Primary Schl. Enroll. Ratio, Female	101.0	..	..	..	..	123.0	125.0	125.0	124.0	123.0	120.0
Secondary Schl. Enroll. Ratio	7.0	..	..	..	..	13.0	14.0	14.0	14.0	17.0	18.0

1981	1982	1983	1984	1985	1986	1987	1988	1989	1990 estimate	Notes	LESOTHO
				(Millions of current US dollars)							**FOREIGN TRADE (CUSTOMS BASIS)**
..	..	..	..	..	..	..	..	..	..	..	Value of Exports, fob
..	..	..	..	..	..	..	..	..	..	..	Nonfuel Primary Products
..	..	..	..	..	..	..	..	..	..	..	Fuels
..	..	..	..	..	..	..	..	..	..	..	Manufactures
..	..	..	..	..	..	..	..	..	..	..	Value of Imports, cif
..	..	..	..	..	..	..	..	..	..	..	Nonfuel Primary Products
..	..	..	..	..	..	..	..	..	..	..	Fuels
..	..	..	..	..	..	..	..	..	..	..	Manufactures
				(Index 1987 = 100)							
83.3	83.0	83.4	78.9	85.0	98.2	100.0	97.0	72.1	72.7	..	Terms of Trade
89.1	84.1	83.5	80.1	81.5	95.3	100.0	107.8	92.8	108.5	..	Export Prices, fob
106.9	101.4	100.2	101.5	95.9	97.1	100.0	111.2	128.6	149.3	..	Import Prices, cif
				(Millions of current US dollars)							**BALANCE OF PAYMENTS**
381.41	424.97	454.04	396.18	282.77	314.24	438.81	480.65	479.27	555.04	..	Exports of Goods & Services
45.24	37.35	31.09	28.33	22.43	25.39	46.53	63.69	66.38	59.46	..	Merchandise, fob
34.30	26.22	27.93	24.35	18.34	20.22	27.50	32.07	32.88	40.61	..	Nonfactor Services
301.87	361.40	395.02	343.49	242.01	268.64	364.78	384.89	380.02	454.97	..	Factor Services
512.92	508.73	545.21	489.39	368.53	398.06	527.23	643.41	683.78	708.16	..	Imports of Goods & Services
448.65	446.94	482.54	433.23	324.01	341.55	451.54	559.37	592.57	604.23	..	Merchandise, fob
55.15	46.68	50.22	45.10	35.53	46.20	60.69	68.45	69.48	81.11	..	Nonfactor Services
9.12	15.11	12.45	11.07	9.00	10.30	15.01	15.59	21.73	22.82	..	Factor Services
1.50	4.80	6.10	3.60	4.20	4.40	5.70	7.10	7.30	7.60	..	Long-Term Interest
2.05	2.66	2.60	3.31	1.82	2.05	0.31	4.42	4.20	4.75	..	Private Current Transfers, net
..	..	..	..	..	0.00	..	..	400.10	391.40	..	Workers' Remittances
-129.45	-81.10	-88.57	-89.90	-83.94	-81.76	-88.11	-158.34	-200.31	-148.37	..	Curr. A/C Bal before Off. Transf.
133.73	103.19	129.28	96.35	71.86	78.96	111.76	133.73	210.67	245.79	..	Net Official Transfers
4.27	22.08	40.71	6.45	-12.08	-2.80	23.65	-24.61	10.36	97.42	..	Curr. A/C Bal after Off. Transf.
47.27	49.82	33.56	-0.04	29.38	17.45	40.35	59.07	45.85	34.89	..	Long-Term Capital, net
4.79	3.04	4.80	2.31	4.78	2.06	5.67	20.97	13.37	17.08	..	Direct Investment
17.90	42.40	19.20	11.10	29.30	14.80	40.10	37.40	39.20	37.80	..	Long-Term Loans
20.80	46.90	34.00	28.10	42.90	23.60	48.20	53.00	53.00	52.20	..	Disbursements
2.90	4.50	14.80	17.00	13.60	8.80	8.10	15.60	13.80	14.40	..	Repayments
24.58	4.38	9.56	-13.45	-4.71	0.58	-5.42	0.70	-6.72	-19.99	..	Other Long-Term Capital
-50.95	-63.85	-48.30	1.73	-12.52	-3.13	-64.29	-41.70	-64.81	-115.30	..	Other Capital, net
-0.59	-8.05	-25.98	-8.14	-4.77	-11.51	0.30	7.24	8.61	-17.01	..	Change in Reserves
				(Lesotho Maloti per US dollar)							**Memo Item:**
0.880	1.090	1.110	1.480	2.230	2.290	2.040	2.270	2.620	2.590	..	Conversion Factor (Annual Avg)
				(Millions of US dollars), outstanding at end of year							
83.10	120.50	135.20	136.10	173.00	194.20	255.90	285.10	324.70	389.70	..	**EXTERNAL DEBT (Total)**
77.10	117.50	131.20	132.10	169.00	190.20	251.90	279.10	322.70	386.80	..	Long-Term Debt (by debtor)
5.70	5.40	5.00	4.20	3.90	3.10	2.20	7.20	12.10	17.00	..	Central Bank, incl. IMF credit
69.50	110.50	124.70	125.70	156.80	178.50	239.10	262.80	301.40	360.60	..	Central Government
..	..	..	..	..	..	..	..	..	..	..	Rest of General Government
0.30	0.20	0.30	1.30	7.20	7.50	9.20	7.80	8.10	8.00	..	Non-financial Public Enterprises
1.60	1.40	1.20	0.90	1.10	1.10	1.40	1.30	1.10	1.20	..	Priv. Sector, incl non-guaranteed
6.00	3.00	4.00	4.00	4.00	4.00	4.00	6.00	2.00	2.90	..	Short-Term Debt
				(Thousands of US dollars)							**Memo Items:**
43,396	47,535	66,677	48,576	43,520	60,260	67,531	56,281	48,998	72,374	..	Int'l Reserves Excluding Gold
..	..	..	..	..	..	..	..	..	..	..	Gold Holdings (at market price)
											SOCIAL INDICATORS
5.8	5.8	5.8	5.8	5.8	5.8	5.8	5.7	5.7	5.6	..	Total Fertility Rate
113.4	111.0	108.8	106.6	104.3	102.1	99.9	97.8	95.6	93.5	..	Infant Mortality Rate
52.2	52.5	53.0	53.5	54.1	54.6	55.1	55.5	55.8	56.1	..	Life Expectancy at Birth
14.2	14.8	15.5	16.1	16.7	17.6	18.5	19.1	19.7	20.3	..	Urban Population, % of total
121.6	112.4	109.7	110.5	111.2	102.6	100.0	109.9	96.3	97.2	..	Food Prod. per capita (1987=100)
..	..	..	..	..	..	..	..	..	..	..	Labor Force, Agriculture (%)
45.5	45.3	45.0	44.8	44.6	44.3	44.1	43.8	43.6	43.4	..	Labor Force, Female (%)
..	110.0	111.0	111.0	113.0	112.0	112.0	113.0	110.0	107.0	..	Primary Schl. Enroll. Ratio
..	125.0	125.0	123.0	125.0	123.0	123.0	123.0	119.0	115.0	..	Primary Schl. Enroll. Ratio, Female
..	19.0	21.0	22.0	23.0	24.0	25.0	26.0	26.0	26.0	..	Secondary Schl. Enroll. Ratio

LIBERIA	1970	1971	1972	1973	1974	1975	1976	1977	1978	1979	1980
CURRENT GNP PER CAPITA (US $)	300	310	320	320	370	410	460	500	540	580	580
POPULATION (thousands)	1,394	1,435	1,478	1,521	1,567	1,614	1,663	1,714	1,766	1,822	1,879
USE AND ORIGIN OF RESOURCES					*(Millions of current Liberian Dollars)*						
Gross National Product (GNP)	402.3	424.4	461.9	487.9	613.5	721.0	757.2	866.2	932.9	1,053.9	1,092.9
Net Factor Income from Abroad	-6.1	-5.5	-4.6	-4.7	-4.3	-4.9	-4.6	-6.7	-10.8	-13.7	-23.9
GDP at Market Prices	408.4	429.9	466.5	492.6	617.8	725.9	761.8	872.9	943.7	1,067.6	1,116.8
Resource Balance	81.1	77.5	90.6	89.0	75.1	31.8	20.9	-62.9	-48.6	-33.8	-0.5
Exports of Goods & NFServices	240.1	251.8	274.8	329.9	407.2	403.7	467.1	459.0	500.0	553.6	613.5
Imports of Goods & NFServices	159.0	174.3	184.2	240.9	332.1	371.9	446.2	521.9	548.6	587.4	614.0
Domestic Absorption	327.3	352.4	375.9	403.6	542.7	694.1	740.9	935.8	992.3	1,101.4	1,117.3
Private Consumption, etc.	191.6	212.9	221.8	276.0	356.4	373.9	411.8	529.8	572.8	623.3	630.2
General Gov't Consumption	45.1	53.1	55.4	56.0	64.5	73.2	89.3	120.0	139.0	156.6	182.0
Gross Domestic Investment	90.6	86.4	98.7	71.6	121.8	247.0	239.8	286.0	280.5	321.5	305.1
Fixed Investment	..	..	..	..	..	..	..	..	..	..	..
Indirect Taxes, net	30.0	29.9	35.4	39.4	47.5	49.5	63.0	84.7	103.7	114.2	115.8
GDP at factor cost	378.4	400.0	431.1	453.2	570.3	676.4	698.8	788.2	840.0	953.4	1,001.0
Agriculture	91.2	97.7	97.1	135.6	184.1	179.9	208.4	251.2	288.3	326.8	359.2
Industry	157.2	162.1	184.8	173.5	222.2	305.4	276.1	257.4	247.2	286.0	281.6
Manufacturing	15.2	17.1	18.0	22.6	34.6	36.3	45.2	50.2	53.7	82.0	77.0
Services, etc.	130.0	140.2	149.2	144.1	164.0	191.1	214.3	279.6	304.5	340.6	360.2
Gross Domestic Saving	171.7	163.9	189.3	160.6	196.9	278.8	260.7	223.1	231.9	287.7	304.6
Gross National Saving	152.3	145.3	171.9	138.6	173.2	252.2	233.7	190.9	191.2	242.0	251.7
					(Millions of 1980 Liberian Dollars)						
Gross National Product	898.7	946.2	987.9	963.0	1,008.9	985.8	1,044.5	1,070.1	1,120.9	1,154.5	1,092.9
GDP at Market Prices	913.4	960.2	998.8	972.9	1,016.3	993.4	1,051.7	1,079.0	1,134.1	1,169.8	1,116.8
Resource Balance	135.8	79.5	130.8	141.2	117.2	-67.6	-133.4	-191.4	-115.2	-68.8	-0.5
Exports of Goods & NFServices	675.6	651.8	711.4	746.3	720.7	548.0	592.3	528.3	618.9	610.9	613.5
Imports of Goods & NFServices	539.8	572.3	580.5	605.1	603.5	615.6	725.6	719.7	734.2	679.7	614.0
Domestic Absorption	777.6	880.7	868.0	831.7	899.1	1,061.0	1,185.0	1,270.4	1,249.3	1,238.6	1,117.3
Private Consumption, etc.	409.1	518.5	379.0	561.2	579.6	585.3	695.4	779.7	772.0	718.9	630.2
General Gov't Consumption	150.4	158.4	159.3	133.1	144.1	145.6	154.6	171.0	179.0	191.0	182.0
Gross Domestic Investment	218.1	203.7	329.6	137.5	175.4	330.1	335.0	319.7	298.3	328.7	305.1
Fixed Investment	..	..	..	..	..	..	..	..	..	..	..
GDP at factor cost	842.2	883.6	912.8	887.3	931.8	914.0	961.2	971.4	1,003.9	1,041.7	1,001.0
Agriculture	234.6	245.4	251.4	276.3	292.4	296.7	323.5	331.8	344.4	353.7	359.2
Industry	275.6	284.8	299.3	300.2	320.8	281.1	283.5	264.2	270.4	282.0	281.6
Manufacturing	46.5	50.6	53.9	61.9	77.0	68.4	82.9	86.5	90.9	97.7	77.0
Services, etc.	332.0	353.4	362.0	310.8	318.6	336.3	354.2	375.3	389.2	406.1	360.2
Memo Items:											
Capacity to Import	815.1	826.8	866.0	828.7	740.0	668.3	759.6	633.0	669.1	640.6	613.5
Terms of Trade Adjustment	139.5	175.0	154.7	82.4	19.3	120.3	167.4	104.7	50.2	29.7	0.0
Gross Domestic Income	1,052.9	1,135.1	1,153.5	1,055.3	1,035.6	1,113.7	1,219.0	1,183.6	1,184.3	1,199.5	1,116.8
Gross National Income	1,038.2	1,121.1	1,142.6	1,045.4	1,028.2	1,106.1	1,211.9	1,174.7	1,171.1	1,184.2	1,092.9
DOMESTIC PRICES/DEFLATORS					*(Index 1980 = 100)*						
Overall (GDP)	44.7	44.8	46.7	50.6	60.8	73.1	72.4	80.9	83.2	91.3	100.0
Domestic Absorption	42.1	40.0	43.3	48.5	60.4	65.4	62.5	73.7	79.4	88.9	100.0
Agriculture	38.9	39.8	38.6	49.1	63.0	60.6	64.4	75.7	83.7	92.4	100.0
Industry	57.0	56.9	61.7	57.8	69.3	108.7	97.4	97.4	91.4	101.4	100.0
Manufacturing	32.7	33.8	33.4	36.5	44.9	53.1	54.5	58.1	59.1	83.9	100.0
Consumer Price Index	30.3	30.0	31.2	37.3	44.4	50.6	53.5	56.8	60.9	68.0	78.0
MANUFACTURING ACTIVITY											
Employment (1987=100)	..	..	..	..	..	..	..	..	..	..	..
Real Earnings per Empl. (1987=100)	..	..	..	..	..	..	..	..	..	..	..
Real Output per Empl. (1987=100)	..	..	..	..	..	..	..	..	..	..	..
Earnings as % of Value Added	..	..	..	..	..	..	..	..	..	..	..
MONETARY HOLDINGS					*(Millions of current Liberian Dollars)*						
Money Supply, Broadly Defined	..	..	..	..	75.03	73.92	108.88	122.27	150.97	154.73	114.54
Money	..	..	..	..							
Currency Outside Banks	..	..	..	..	8.48	7.97	8.36	9.24	10.19	11.00	11.35
Demand Deposits	..	..	..	..							
Quasi-Money	..	..	..	..	..	..	..	..	..	..	..
					(Millions of current Liberian Dollars)						
GOVERNMENT DEFICIT (-) OR SURPLUS	..	..	..	..	6.80	3.40	-16.00	-24.20	-56.20	-141.20	-88.30
Current Revenue	..	..	..	..	116.70	129.20	163.70	181.10	197.50	224.10	225.10
Current Expenditure	..	..	..	..	84.60	88.90	111.60	119.30	126.50	152.90	179.70
Current Budget Balance	..	..	..	..	32.10	40.30	52.10	61.80	71.00	71.20	45.40
Capital Receipts	..	..	..	..	0.20	3.10	0.20	0.30	0.20	0.20	0.20
Capital Payments	..	..	..	..	25.50	40.00	68.30	86.30	127.40	212.60	133.90

1981	1982	1983	1984	1985	1986	1987	1988	1989	1990 estimate	Notes	LIBERIA
590	550	500	460	470	450	450	..	..	..	..	**CURRENT GNP PER CAPITA (US $)**
1,939	2,001	2,065	2,132	2,199	2,268	2,339	2,411	2,485	2,561	..	**POPULATION (thousands)**
			(Millions of current Liberian Dollars)								**USE AND ORIGIN OF RESOURCES**
1,073.9	1,049.7	969.5	977.4	1,031.0	1,012.0	1,062.6	..		..	..	Gross National Product (GNP)
-21.1	-72.3	-97.5	-116.6	-64.0	-73.0	-76.7	..		..	..	Net Factor Income from Abroad
1,095.0	1,122.0	1,067.0	1,094.0	1,095.0	1,085.0	1,139.3	..		..	..	GDP at Market Prices
27.1	-20.0	-19.0	45.0	62.0	95.0	..	..		..	..	Resource Balance
588.0	539.0	487.0	471.0	467.0	464.0	..	..		..	..	Exports of Goods & NF Services
560.9	559.0	506.0	426.0	405.0	369.0	..	..		..	..	Imports of Goods & NF Services
1,067.9	1,142.0	1,086.0	1,049.0	1,033.0	990.0	..	..		..	..	Domestic Absorption
677.9	739.0	756.0	750.0	708.0	700.0	..	..		..	..	Private Consumption, etc.
211.0	243.0	204.0	187.0	230.0	185.0	..	..		..	..	General Gov't Consumption
179.0	160.0	126.0	112.0	95.0	105.0	..	..		..	..	Gross Domestic Investment
169.0	130.0	126.0	117.0	97.0	95.0	..	..		..	..	Fixed Investment
103.6	110.2	102.7	100.3	98.0	100.0	..	..		..	..	Indirect Taxes, net
991.4	1,011.8	964.3	993.7	997.0	985.0	..	..		..	..	GDP at factor cost
312.9	326.2	326.4	352.3	364.2	368.0	..	..		..	f	Agriculture
327.2	319.5	293.0	282.8	276.4	273.7	..	..		..	f	Industry
56.5	53.6	49.6	51.2	49.0	46.9	..	..		..	f	Manufacturing
351.3	366.1	344.9	358.6	356.4	343.3	..	..		..	f	Services, etc.
206.1	140.0	107.0	157.0	157.0	200.0	..	..		..	..	Gross Domestic Saving
155.0	22.7	-29.5	-3.2	65.0	101.6	..	..		..	..	Gross National Saving
			(Millions of 1980 Liberian Dollars)								
1,082.5	1,016.8	969.5	935.1	979.4	953.6	944.1	..		..	..	Gross National Product
1,103.1	1,081.3	1,064.3	1,047.2	1,040.4	1,023.0	1,012.8	..		..	..	GDP at Market Prices
69.7	68.4	12.6	38.3	57.3	93.5	..	..		..	..	Resource Balance
612.5	579.6	507.4	511.8	504.5	501.7	..	..		..	..	Exports of Goods & NF Services
542.8	511.2	494.8	473.5	447.2	408.1	..	..		..	..	Imports of Goods & NF Services
1,033.4	1,013.0	1,051.7	1,008.9	983.1	929.5	..	..		..	..	Domestic Absorption
571.5	552.1	660.9	670.5	611.7	605.8	..	..		..	..	Private Consumption, etc.
276.6	303.1	262.6	229.7	279.9	223.5	..	..		..	..	General Gov't Consumption
185.3	157.7	128.3	108.7	91.5	100.2	..	..		..	..	Gross Domestic Investment
..	..	..	..	..	..	..	..		..	..	Fixed Investment
986.5	963.2	950.8	941.4	937.9	919.3	..	..		..	..	GDP at factor cost
345.1	342.6	353.7	364.5	373.3	374.3	..	..		..	f	Agriculture
252.4	234.7	222.1	204.7	198.2	194.6	..	..		..	f	Industry
73.5	66.3	63.4	62.5	59.2	56.3	..	..		..	f	Manufacturing
388.9	385.9	375.1	372.3	366.5	350.4	..	..		..	f	Services, etc.
											Memo Items:
569.0	492.9	476.2	523.5	515.7	513.2	..	..		..	..	Capacity to Import
-43.5	-86.7	-31.1	11.7	11.1	11.5	..	..		..	..	Terms of Trade Adjustment
1,059.6	994.7	1,033.2	1,059.0	1,051.6	1,034.6	..	..		..	..	Gross Domestic Income
1,039.0	930.1	938.3	946.8	990.5	965.2	..	..		..	..	Gross National Income
			(Index 1980 = 100)								**DOMESTIC PRICES/DEFLATORS**
99.3	103.8	100.3	104.5	105.2	106.1	112.5	..		..	..	Overall (GDP)
103.3	112.7	103.3	104.0	105.1	106.5	..	..		..	..	Domestic Absorption
90.7	95.2	92.3	96.7	97.6	98.3	..	..		..	..	Agriculture
129.6	136.1	132.0	138.2	139.5	140.6	..	..		..	..	Industry
76.9	80.8	78.3	81.9	82.7	83.3	..	..		..	..	Manufacturing
83.9	88.9	91.4	92.5	91.6	95.2	100.0	109.6	116.1	..	f	Consumer Price Index
											MANUFACTURING ACTIVITY
..	..	..	..	..	..	..	..		..	G	Employment (1987=100)
..	..	..	..	..	..	..	..		..	G	Real Earnings per Empl. (1987=100)
..	..	..	..	..	..	..	..		..	..	Real Output per Empl. (1987=100)
..	..	..	..	..	..	..	..		..	..	Earnings as % of Value Added
			(Millions of current Liberian Dollars)								**MONETARY HOLDINGS**
100.94	126.69	142.12	144.39	170.75	202.15	233.54	256.54	302.14	..	..	Money Supply, Broadly Defined
..	..	..	..	..	..	..	..		..	..	Money
11.59	15.74	19.83	28.60	46.17	66.06	..	..		..	..	Currency Outside Banks
..	..	..	..	..	..	..	..		..	..	Demand Deposits
..	..	..	..	..	..	..	..		..	..	Quasi-Money
			(Millions of current Liberian Dollars)								
-110.30	-116.60	-102.90	-61.00	-87.10	-90.90	-83.90	-72.20		..	C F	**GOVERNMENT DEFICIT (-) OR SURPLUS**
242.40	278.20	257.20	259.50	228.80	205.40	198.40	212.70		..	..	Current Revenue
211.80	295.40	268.70	244.70	244.10	205.30	226.10	231.60		..	..	Current Expenditure
30.60	-17.20	-11.50	14.80	-15.30	0.10	-27.70	-18.90		..	..	Current Budget Balance
0.10	0.10	5.50	0.20	0.50	0.30	0.20	0.10		..	..	Capital Receipts
141.00	99.50	96.90	76.00	72.30	91.30	56.40	53.40		..	..	Capital Payments

LIBERIA	1970	1971	1972	1973	1974	1975	1976	1977	1978	1979	1980
FOREIGN TRADE (CUSTOMS BASIS)					*(Millions of current US dollars)*						
Value of Exports, fob	212.58	222.37	244.01	323.79	399.76	393.94	457.05	447.43	487.46	536.57	596.98
Nonfuel Primary Products	206.91	216.01	236.85	317.25	393.37	386.30	450.10	439.40	476.54	522.24	569.74
Fuels	0.00	0.00	0.11	0.03	0.22	0.17	0.26	0.01	0.03	0.01	6.95
Manufactures	5.67	6.36	7.05	6.50	6.17	7.46	6.69	8.02	10.89	14.33	20.28
Value of Imports, cif	149.67	162.24	178.56	193.46	288.42	331.21	399.22	463.47	480.95	506.45	534.09
Nonfuel Primary Products	27.38	31.64	32.55	37.54	48.47	50.48	57.24	77.17	87.47	100.48	109.25
Fuels	9.53	11.84	12.03	14.72	56.41	48.34	59.51	68.85	84.54	103.17	152.10
Manufactures	112.76	118.76	133.98	141.20	183.54	232.38	282.47	317.44	308.94	302.80	272.74
					(Index 1987 = 100)						
Terms of Trade	192.3	163.6	144.8	164.2	122.7	123.9	129.7	125.2	108.8	114.8	106.3
Export Prices, fob	52.1	47.9	48.0	68.0	75.2	81.0	84.9	89.6	85.1	106.3	120.2
Import Prices, cif	27.1	29.3	33.1	41.4	61.3	65.4	65.5	71.6	78.2	92.6	113.0
BALANCE OF PAYMENTS					*(Millions of current US dollars)*						
Exports of Goods & Services	..	..	..	..	..	..	..	..	..	..	..
Merchandise, fob	213.70	223.90	243.60	324.00	400.30	394.40	457.00	447.40	486.40	536.60	600.40
Nonfactor Services	3.20	4.10	3.70	5.90	6.90	9.30	10.00	11.60	13.60	17.00	13.10
Factor Services	..										
Imports of Goods & Services	230.70	235.20	252.40	323.40	440.40	336.10	412.10	480.90	506.90	540.10	574.69
Merchandise, fob	149.70	162.40	174.70	193.50	289.40	290.40	358.60	417.30	430.60	457.50	478.00
Nonfactor Services	74.90	67.30	73.10	125.20	146.70	40.80	48.90	56.90	65.50	68.90	72.70
Factor Services	6.10	5.50	4.60	4.70	4.30	4.90	4.60	6.70	10.80	13.70	23.99
Long-Term Interest	6.00	5.90	4.90	5.30	5.00	5.10	5.90	7.20	12.90	22.80	22.70
Private Current Transfers, net	-13.30	-13.10	-12.80	-17.30	-19.40	-21.70	-22.40	-25.50	-29.90	-32.00	-29.00
Workers' Remittances	..										
Curr. A/C Bal before Off. Transf.	-27.10	-20.30	-17.90	-10.80	-52.60	45.90	32.50	-47.40	-36.80	-18.50	9.81
Net Official Transfers	10.80	13.30	9.30	19.60	22.20	27.80	32.30	28.80	29.60	34.70	36.20
Curr. A/C Bal after Off. Transf.	-16.30	-7.00	-8.60	8.80	-30.40	73.70	64.80	-18.60	-7.20	16.20	46.01
Long-Term Capital, net	35.50	30.00	29.20	57.20	50.10	88.40	69.60	83.80	53.50	102.90	70.50
Direct Investment	28.10	20.70	18.70	49.00	45.00	80.80	39.10	44.70	..		
Long-Term Loans	-4.00	1.50	-1.40	-3.80	0.40	8.10	27.80	50.70	68.10	118.80	60.30
Disbursements	7.40	12.30	10.50	8.10	14.90	35.40	43.30	69.70	81.40	170.70	75.50
Repayments	11.40	10.80	11.90	11.90	14.50	27.30	15.50	19.00	13.30	51.90	15.20
Other Long-Term Capital	11.40	7.80	11.90	12.00	4.70	-0.50	2.70	-11.60	-14.60	-15.90	10.20
Other Capital, net	-18.27	-24.21	-20.29	-64.46	-18.10	-161.56	-131.10	-59.22	-58.19	-157.84	-157.16
Change in Reserves	-0.93	1.21	-0.31	-1.54	-1.60	-0.54	-3.30	-5.98	11.89	38.74	40.65
Memo Item:					*(Liberian Dollars per US dollar)*						
Conversion Factor (Annual Avg)	1.000	1.000	1.000	1.000	1.000	1.000	1.000	1.000	1.000	1.000	1.000
				(Millions of US dollars), outstanding at end of year							
EXTERNAL DEBT (Total)	162.3	162.1	159.4	159.1	162.1	178.6	208.5	292.0	443.0	596.5	685.7
Long-Term Debt (by debtor)	162.3	162.0	159.3	159.0	161.9	178.6	208.4	266.9	353.7	521.2	604.6
Central Bank, incl. IMF credit	6.4	2.7	1.0	1.2	2.3	4.9	6.2	11.2	30.1	84.6	106.6
Central Government	142.3	142.1	137.1	129.6	129.3	142.2	168.3	206.5	264.7	360.3	422.5
Rest of General Government	..	..	..	..	..	..	..	..	..	..	..
Non-financial Public Enterprises	13.6	17.2	21.2	28.2	30.3	31.5	33.9	43.7	53.4	72.2	74.1
Priv. Sector, incl non-guaranteed	0.0	0.0	0.0	0.0	0.0	0.0	0.0	5.5	5.5	4.1	1.4
Short-Term Debt	0.0	0.1	0.1	0.1	0.2	0.0	0.1	25.1	89.3	75.3	81.1
Memo Items:					*(Thousands of US dollars)*						
Int'l Reserves Excluding Gold	..	..	..	..	18,719	19,189	17,170	27,345	18,021	54,979	5,450
Gold Holdings (at market price)	..	..	..	..	..	..	..	..	..	..	..
SOCIAL INDICATORS											
Total Fertility Rate	6.5	6.5	6.5	6.5	6.5	6.5	6.5	6.5	6.5	6.5	6.5
Infant Mortality Rate	177.8	179.4	181.0	178.2	175.4	172.6	169.8	167.0	164.2	161.4	158.6
Life Expectancy at Birth	46.5	47.0	47.5	47.9	48.3	48.7	49.1	49.5	49.9	50.3	50.7
Urban Population, % of total	26.0	26.9	27.7	28.6	29.4	30.3	31.2	32.2	33.1	34.1	35.0
Food Prod. per capita (1987=100)	106.5	108.5	107.3	105.7	111.5	107.2	109.3	110.0	107.8	105.9	102.8
Labor Force, Agriculture (%)	77.5	77.2	76.8	76.5	76.2	75.9	75.5	75.2	74.8	74.5	74.2
Labor Force, Female (%)	32.0	32.0	32.0	32.0	32.0	32.0	32.0	31.9	31.9	31.9	31.9
Primary Schl. Enroll. Ratio	56.0	..	..	..	..	62.0	..	..	60.0	71.0	48.0
Primary Schl. Enroll. Ratio, Female	36.0	..	..	..	..	45.0	..	..	46.0	54.0	34.0
Secondary Schl. Enroll. Ratio	10.0	..	..	..	..	17.0	..	..	19.0	23.0	22.0

1981	1982	1983	1984	1985	1986	1987	1988	1989	1990 estimate	Notes	LIBERIA
				(Millions of current US dollars)							**FOREIGN TRADE (CUSTOMS BASIS)**
523.63	472.57	422.58	449.07	435.60	408.44	382.20	400.00	450.00	500.00	..	Value of Exports, fob
510.32	459.10	416.19	444.04	430.73	403.87	377.92	395.52	444.97	494.41	..	Nonfuel Primary Products
0.35	7.41	0.51	0.02	0.02	0.02	0.02	0.02	0.02	0.02	..	Fuels
12.96	6.06	5.87	5.01	4.86	4.55	4.26	4.46	5.02	5.57	..	Manufactures
477.43	428.38	411.62	363.21	284.40	234.82	307.60	350.00	400.00	450.00	..	Value of Imports, cif
114.23	99.51	115.85	97.23	76.13	62.86	82.35	93.70	107.08	120.47	..	Nonfuel Primary Products
129.26	115.10	71.52	71.73	56.16	46.37	60.74	69.12	78.99	88.86	..	Fuels
233.94	213.77	224.25	194.25	152.10	125.59	164.51	187.19	213.93	240.67	..	Manufactures
				(Index 1987 = 100)							
90.7	100.1	99.7	99.9	96.7	102.2	100.0	109.3	114.9	111.4	..	Terms of Trade
106.3	107.3	102.6	99.6	94.1	93.1	100.0	106.9	118.0	131.5	..	Export Prices, fob
117.2	107.2	102.9	99.7	97.4	91.2	100.0	97.8	102.7	118.0	..	Import Prices, cif
				(Millions of current US dollars)							**BALANCE OF PAYMENTS**
..	511.90	461.10	486.20	468.70	466.90	432.60	..	..	..	..	Exports of Goods & Services
529.20	477.40	420.80	446.70	430.40	407.90	374.90	..	..	..	..	Merchandise, fob
11.50	32.70	38.50	36.90	34.60	56.90	52.50	..	..	..	..	Nonfactor Services
..	1.80	1.80	2.60	3.70	2.10	5.20	..	..	..	..	Factor Services
503.71	556.30	638.86	547.33	475.01	522.60	574.20	..	..	..	..	Imports of Goods & Services
423.90	390.20	374.80	325.40	263.80	258.80	311.70	..	..	..	..	Merchandise, fob
58.70	92.00	108.70	92.50	80.20	80.50	74.20	..	..	..	..	Nonfactor Services
21.11	74.10	155.36	129.43	131.01	183.30	188.30	..	..	..	..	Factor Services
17.50	13.50	10.20	10.60	10.10	14.30	6.00	7.30	0.00	..	..	Long-Term Interest
-30.00	-45.00	-39.00	-43.60	-28.00	-25.40	-21.40	..	..	..	..	Private Current Transfers, net
..	..	..	..	..	..	0.00	..	..	..	..	Workers' Remittances
6.99	-89.40	-216.76	-104.73	-34.31	-81.10	-163.00	..	..	..	..	Curr. A/C Bal before Off. Transf.
68.45	92.85	114.15	103.87	91.64	96.40	45.40	..	..	..	..	Net Official Transfers
75.44	3.45	-102.60	-0.86	57.33	15.30	-117.60	..	..	..	..	Curr. A/C Bal after Off. Transf.
43.90	177.90	73.13	71.84	-115.31	-218.66	-188.91	..	..	..	..	Long-Term Capital, net
..	34.80	49.10	36.20	-16.20	-16.50	38.50	..	..	..	..	Direct Investment
73.60	45.70	68.10	91.20	55.20	29.70	27.10	8.00	0.40	..	..	Long-Term Loans
81.60	65.20	77.50	100.10	63.40	43.50	31.90	15.10	0.40	..	..	Disbursements
8.00	19.50	9.40	8.90	8.20	13.80	4.80	7.10	0.00	..	..	Repayments
-29.70	97.40	-44.07	-55.56	-154.31	-231.86	-254.51	..	..	..	..	Other Long-Term Capital
-173.61	-249.74	-7.34	-104.44	62.98	200.76	306.02	..	..	..	..	Other Capital, net
54.28	68.38	36.81	33.47	-5.00	2.60	0.49	-1.30	-10.21	-0.89	..	Change in Reserves
				(Liberian Dollars per US dollar)							**Memo Item:**
1.000	1.000	1.000	1.000	1.000	1.000	1.000	1.000	1.000	1.000	..	Conversion Factor (Annual Avg)
				(Millions of US dollars), outstanding at end of year							
813.4	902.2	1,005.2	1,075.5	1,244.5	1,439.1	1,685.2	1,687.5	1,742.6	1,870.3	..	**EXTERNAL DEBT (Total)**
732.7	823.3	948.3	1,006.3	1,139.8	1,272.0	1,444.5	1,392.3	1,371.5	1,448.7	..	Long-Term Debt (by debtor)
152.1	211.9	249.6	247.7	271.9	301.2	348.8	329.4	319.2	344.3	..	Central Bank, incl. IMF credit
510.6	535.6	609.8	669.7	764.1	850.4	954.4	919.5	908.6	949.1	..	Central Government
..	..	..	..	..	..	..	..	..	..	..	Rest of General Government
70.0	75.8	88.9	88.9	103.8	120.4	141.3	143.4	143.7	155.3	..	Non-financial Public Enterprises
0.0	0.0	0.0	0.0	0.0	0.0	0.0	0.0	0.0	..	..	Priv. Sector, incl non-guaranteed
80.7	78.9	56.9	69.2	104.7	167.1	240.7	295.2	371.1	421.6	..	Short-Term Debt
				(Thousands of US dollars)							**Memo Items:**
8,339	6,471	20,400	3,479	1,522	2,664	513	420	7,869	..	..	Int'l Reserves Excluding Gold
..	..	..	..	..	..	..	..	..	..	..	Gold Holdings (at market price)
											SOCIAL INDICATORS
6.5	6.5	6.5	6.5	6.5	6.5	6.5	6.4	6.4	6.3	..	Total Fertility Rate
155.8	153.0	150.8	148.6	146.3	144.1	141.9	139.8	137.7	135.7	..	Infant Mortality Rate
51.1	51.5	51.8	52.1	52.5	52.8	53.1	53.5	53.9	54.3	..	Life Expectancy at Birth
36.0	37.0	38.1	39.1	40.1	41.6	43.0	44.0	44.9	45.9	..	Urban Population, % of total
105.8	105.5	103.2	100.6	100.4	98.6	100.0	101.2	91.8	71.3	..	Food Prod. per capita (1987=100)
..	..	..	..	..	..	..	..	..	..	..	Labor Force, Agriculture (%)
31.7	31.6	31.4	31.3	31.1	30.9	30.7	30.6	30.4	30.2	..	Labor Force, Female (%)
..	46.0	..	40.0	..	35.0	..	..	..	..	..	Primary Schl. Enroll. Ratio
..	..	..	28.0	..	..	..	..	..	..	..	Primary Schl. Enroll. Ratio, Female
..	..	..	17.0	..	..	..	..	..	..	..	Secondary Schl. Enroll. Ratio

LIBYA	1970	1971	1972	1973	1974	1975	1976	1977	1978	1979	1980
CURRENT GNP PER CAPITA (US $)	1,870	1,840	1,980	2,450	3,210	4,650	6,920	6,790	7,000	8,490	9,740
POPULATION (thousands)	1,986	2,069	2,155	2,247	2,344	2,446	2,554	2,666	2,785	2,910	3,043
USE AND ORIGIN OF RESOURCES					*(Millions of current Libyan Dinars)*						
Gross National Product (GNP)	1,259.6	1,469.2	1,762.4	2,152.5	3,910.3	3,781.5	4,899.8	5,403.1	5,375.9	7,594.7	10,503.9
Net Factor Income from Abroad	-166.8	-157.6	-36.1	-93.7	27.1	1.5	-7.2	-359.9	-312.1	-251.7	-19.3
GDP at Market Prices	1,426.4	1,626.8	1,798.5	2,246.2	3,883.2	3,780.0	4,907.0	5,763.0	5,688.0	7,846.4	10,523.2
Resource Balance	467.0	539.1	445.4	413.8	1,062.0	387.5	1,210.0	1,482.0	779.0	1,979.0	3,658.0
Exports of Goods & NFServices	870.0	975.1	997.8	1,240.3	2,489.9	2,053.2	2,881.4	3,431.0	2,978.0	4,801.0	6,964.0
Imports of Goods & NFServices	403.0	436.0	552.4	826.5	1,427.9	1,665.7	1,671.4	1,949.0	2,199.0	2,822.0	3,306.0
Domestic Absorption	959.4	1,087.7	1,353.1	1,832.4	2,821.2	3,392.5	3,697.0	4,281.0	4,909.0	5,867.4	6,865.2
Private Consumption, etc.	463.9	468.6	543.4	702.8	927.0	1,193.5	1,336.6	1,483.0	1,665.0	1,973.4	2,242.2
General Gov't Consumption	259.9	318.4	359.1	465.4	864.8	1,044.3	1,184.6	1,400.0	1,692.0	1,929.0	2,298.0
Gross Domestic Investment	235.6	300.7	450.6	664.2	1,029.4	1,154.7	1,175.8	1,398.0	1,552.0	1,965.0	2,325.0
Fixed Investment	232.0	288.0	437.0	636.0	971.0	1,055.0	1,226.0	1,368.0	1,532.0	1,855.0	2,230.0
Indirect Taxes, net	42.0	40.3	45.5	63.9	91.2	105.7	138.9	150.0	192.0	243.4	297.9
GDP at factor cost	1,384.4	1,586.5	1,753.0	2,182.3	3,792.0	3,674.3	4,768.1	5,613.0	5,496.0	7,603.0	10,225.3
Agriculture	33.1	33.0	43.6	60.0	64.7	82.9	99.7	90.0	122.0	140.4	164.9
Industry	950.3	1,078.9	1,154.2	1,459.6	2,850.8	2,499.6	3,402.3	4,058.0	3,705.0	5,539.3	7,808.1
Manufacturing	29.1	32.7	46.0	62.8	71.5	86.2	114.8	125.0	149.0	185.8	202.0
Services, etc.	401.0	474.6	555.2	662.7	876.5	1,091.8	1,266.1	1,465.0	1,669.0	1,923.3	2,252.3
Gross Domestic Saving	702.6	839.8	896.0	1,078.0	2,091.4	1,542.2	2,385.8	2,880.0	2,331.0	3,944.0	5,983.0
Gross National Saving	485.8	620.4	759.2	902.4	2,014.9	1,466.8	2,302.4	2,266.0	1,731.2	3,438.0	5,641.4
					(Millions of 1980 Libyan Dinars)						
Gross National Product	7,598.3	7,310.8	7,051.8	6,972.1	6,270.7	6,694.8	8,222.0	8,369.5	8,726.0	10,124.9	10,503.9
GDP at Market Prices	8,604.2	8,094.9	7,196.1	7,275.7	6,227.3	6,692.2	8,234.0	8,927.0	9,232.7	10,460.4	10,523.2
Resource Balance	11,061.3	8,761.8	6,955.4	6,696.6	2,770.8	2,918.1	4,612.9	4,821.9	4,264.4	4,621.8	3,658.0
Exports of Goods & NFServices	11,873.9	9,602.9	7,946.1	8,041.2	5,108.4	5,293.8	6,909.9	7,392.0	7,028.5	7,624.0	6,964.0
Imports of Goods & NFServices	812.5	841.0	990.7	1,344.6	2,337.6	2,375.7	2,296.9	2,570.1	2,764.0	3,002.2	3,306.0
Domestic Absorption	1,647.5	2,007.1	2,312.2	2,621.7	4,246.3	4,504.6	4,747.5	5,300.8	5,848.9	6,433.1	6,865.2
Private Consumption, etc.	303.2	555.0	613.2	775.3	1,164.1	1,330.1	1,456.8	1,529.5	1,872.3	2,076.1	2,242.2
General Gov't Consumption	508.3	604.7	642.7	804.6	1,620.7	1,554.3	1,741.1	2,031.3	2,135.8	2,211.7	2,298.0
Gross Domestic Investment	836.0	847.4	1,056.4	1,041.8	1,461.5	1,620.2	1,549.6	1,740.0	1,840.9	2,145.4	2,325.0
Fixed Investment	..	..	..	..	..	..	..	..	..	..	..
GDP at factor cost	8,787.6	8,281.7	7,351.1	7,411.7	6,282.3	6,744.1	8,270.7	9,014.1	9,249.0	10,194.3	10,225.3
Agriculture	49.9	58.7	78.4	90.2	92.6	110.5	126.2	106.6	136.0	150.6	164.9
Industry	11,137.0	10,124.1	8,534.7	8,307.7	6,350.0	6,463.3	8,198.3	8,835.4	8,765.6	9,453.4	7,808.1
Manufacturing	58.2	64.1	70.4	93.3	85.4	110.2	141.4	154.7	182.8	226.3	202.0
Services, etc.	411.1	512.7	598.9	702.7	832.6	1,013.0	1,151.2	1,311.9	1,435.4	1,656.2	2,252.3
Memo Items:											
Capacity to Import	1,754.1	1,881.0	1,789.4	2,017.9	4,076.2	2,928.3	3,959.8	4,524.3	3,743.2	5,107.6	6,964.0
Terms of Trade Adjustment	-10,120.0	-7,721.9	-6,156.6	-6,023.3	-1,032.2	-2,365.4	-2,950.1	-2,867.7	-3,285.3	-2,516.5	0.0
Gross Domestic Income	-1,515.5	373.0	1,039.4	1,252.4	5,195.1	4,326.8	5,284.0	6,059.3	5,947.5	7,943.9	10,523.2
Gross National Income	-2,521.5	-411.1	895.1	948.7	5,238.4	4,329.4	5,272.0	5,501.8	5,440.8	7,608.4	10,503.9
DOMESTIC PRICES/DEFLATORS					*(Index 1980 = 100)*						
Overall (GDP)	16.6	20.1	25.0	30.9	62.4	56.5	59.6	64.6	61.6	75.0	100.0
Domestic Absorption	58.2	54.2	58.5	69.9	66.4	75.3	77.9	80.8	83.9	91.2	100.0
Agriculture	66.4	56.3	55.6	66.5	69.8	75.0	79.0	84.4	89.7	93.2	100.0
Industry	8.5	10.7	13.5	17.6	44.9	38.7	41.5	45.9	42.3	58.6	100.0
Manufacturing	50.0	51.1	65.3	67.3	83.7	78.2	81.2	80.8	81.5	82.1	100.0
Consumer Price Index	..	..	..	..	..	..	..	..	..	..	..
MANUFACTURING ACTIVITY											
Employment (1987=100)	..	..	..	..	..	..	..	..	..	..	..
Real Earnings per Empl. (1987=100)	..	..	..	..	..	..	..	..	..	..	..
Real Output per Empl. (1987=100)	..	..	..	..	..	..	..	..	..	..	..
Earnings as % of Value Added	37.1	33.9	37.3	36.9	31.1	32.6	30.6	35.3	35.7	47.4	40.9
MONETARY HOLDINGS					*(Millions of current Libyan Dinars)*						
Money Supply, Broadly Defined	320.8	462.9	588.6	810.9	1,334.3	1,360.5	1,694.9	2,128.1	2,373.7	3,199.8	4,104.5
Money	241.1	364.5	413.0	514.0	753.8	867.6	1,139.4	1,443.8	1,687.8	2,247.3	2,898.9
Currency Outside Banks	112.3	120.7	147.4	202.6	262.2	346.0	436.0	585.0	868.5	1,053.7	685.7
Demand Deposits	128.8	243.8	265.6	311.4	491.6	521.6	703.4	858.8	819.3	1,193.6	2,213.2
Quasi-Money	79.7	98.4	175.7	296.8	580.5	492.9	555.6	684.3	685.9	952.5	1,205.7
GOVERNMENT DEFICIT (-) OR SURPLUS					*(Millions of current Libyan Dinars)*						
Current Revenue	..	..	..	..	..	..	..	..	..	..	..
Current Expenditure	..	..	..	..	..	..	..	..	..	..	..
Current Budget Balance	..	..	..	..	..	..	..	..	..	..	..
Capital Receipts	..	..	..	..	..	..	..	..	..	..	..
Capital Payments	..	..	..	..	..	..	..	..	..	..	..

1981	1982	1983	1984	1985	1986	1987	1988	1989	1990 estimate	Notes	LIBYA
9,280	9,270	8,590	7,300	6,760	5,790	5,730	5,330	5,310	..	..	**CURRENT GNP PER CAPITA (US $)**
3,182	3,327	3,476	3,630	3,786	3,942	4,095	4,245	4,395	4,546	..	**POPULATION (thousands)**
											USE AND ORIGIN OF RESOURCES
						(Millions of current Libyan Dinars)					
9,379.0	8,524.1	8,307.2	7,376.5	8,079.2	6,605.3	6,934.9	6,131.1	6,642.0	..	..	Gross National Product (GNP)
32.5	-150.7	-223.8	-197.5	-22.7	-13.9	108.5	92.7	100.4	..	..	Net Factor Income from Abroad
9,346.5	8,674.8	8,531.0	7,574.0	8,101.9	6,619.2	6,826.4	6,038.4	6,541.6	..	..	GDP at Market Prices
1,468.0	1,596.0	1,092.0	..	..	..	..	..	..	..	..	Resource Balance
4,995.0	4,573.0	3,979.0	..	..	..	..	..	..	..	..	Exports of Goods & NFServices
3,527.0	2,977.0	2,887.0	..	..	..	..	..	..	..	..	Imports of Goods & NFServices
7,878.5	7,078.8	7,439.0	..	..	..	..	..	..	..	..	Domestic Absorption
2,478.5	1,655.8	2,172.0	..	..	..	..	..	..	..	..	Private Consumption, etc.
2,539.0	3,005.0	3,113.0	..	..	..	..	..	..	..	..	General Gov't Consumption
2,861.0	2,418.0	2,154.0	..	..	..	..	..	..	..	..	Gross Domestic Investment
2,811.0	2,362.0	2,093.0	..	..	..	..	..	..	..	..	Fixed Investment
385.9	315.6	390.5									Indirect Taxes, net
8,960.6	8,359.2	8,140.5	7,521.7	8,050.2	6,577.0	6,782.9					GDP at factor cost
202.3	220.3	273.8	266.4	283.2	320.0	342.5					Agriculture
6,156.8	5,490.0	5,092.1	4,310.5	4,733.0	3,241.8	3,409.0					Industry
229.1	273.5	294.2	359.9	365.1	401.8	442.5					Manufacturing
2,601.5	2,648.9	2,774.6	2,944.8	3,034.0	3,015.2	3,031.4					Services, etc.
4,329.0	4,014.0	3,246.0	..	..	..	..	..	..	..	..	Gross Domestic Saving
3,896.6	3,390.6	2,416.9	..	..	..	..	..	..	..	..	Gross National Saving
					(Millions of 1980 Libyan Dinars)						
8,574.5	8,119.1	7,957.5	7,330.6	6,840.4	6,249.6	6,158.6	6,198.2	6,238.1	..	..	Gross National Product
8,544.8	8,262.7	8,171.9	7,525.0	6,859.5	6,262.7	6,062.3	6,104.6	6,143.9	..	H	GDP at Market Prices
1,099.8	1,183.7	1,567.4	..	..	..	..	..	..	..	..	Resource Balance
4,491.4	4,426.9	4,426.9	..	..	..	..	..	..	..	..	Exports of Goods & NFServices
3,391.6	3,243.2	2,859.6	..	..	..	..	..	..	..	..	Imports of Goods & NFServices
6,619.4	6,242.6	5,681.8	..	..	..	..	..	..	..	..	Domestic Absorption
2,182.9	2,308.8	2,201.1	..	..	..	..	..	..	..	..	Private Consumption, etc.
2,128.3	2,269.7	2,100.1	..	..	..	..	..	..	..	..	General Gov't Consumption
2,308.2	1,664.1	1,380.7	..	..	..	..	..	..	..	..	Gross Domestic Investment
..	..	..	..	..	..	..	..	..	..	..	Fixed Investment
8,307.2	8,036.7	7,944.3	7,651.0	..	..	..	..	..	..	H	GDP at factor cost
186.0	190.1	222.4	214.1	..	..	..	..	..	..	..	Agriculture
6,051.6	5,764.1	5,496.5	5,160.6	..	..	..	..	..	..	..	Industry
216.1	248.5	262.7	315.7	..	..	..	..	..	..	..	Manufacturing
1,898.3	1,861.9	1,888.8	1,866.8	..	..	..	..	..	..	..	Services, etc.
											Memo Items:
4,803.2	4,982.0	3,941.2	..	..	..	..	..	..	..	..	Capacity to Import
311.8	555.0	-485.7	..	..	..	..	..	..	..	..	Terms of Trade Adjustment
8,856.6	8,817.8	7,686.2	..	..	..	..	..	..	..	..	Gross Domestic Income
8,886.3	8,674.2	7,471.8	..	..	..	..	..	..	..	..	Gross National Income
											DOMESTIC PRICES/DEFLATORS
					(Index 1980 = 100)						
109.4	105.0	104.4	100.7	118.1	105.7	112.6	98.9	106.5	..	..	Overall (GDP)
119.0	113.4	130.9	..	..	..	..	..	..	..	..	Domestic Absorption
108.8	115.9	123.1	124.4	..	..	..	..	..	..	..	Agriculture
101.7	95.2	92.6	83.5	..	..	..	..	..	..	..	Industry
106.0	110.0	112.0	114.0	..	..	..	..	..	..	..	Manufacturing
..	..	..	..	..	..	..	..	..	..	..	Consumer Price Index
											MANUFACTURING ACTIVITY
..	..	..	..	..	..	..	..	..	..	..	Employment (1987=100)
..	..	..	..	..	..	..	..	..	..	..	Real Earnings per Empl. (1987=100)
..	..	..	..	..	..	..	..	..	..	..	Real Output per Empl. (1987=100)
..	..	..	..	..	..	..	..	..	..	J	Earnings as % of Value Added
											MONETARY HOLDINGS
					(Millions of current Libyan Dinars)						
4,646.8	4,305.4	4,126.8	4,175.3	5,053.6	4,811.4	5,073.1	4,754.5	5,156.5	6,201.1	..	Money Supply, Broadly Defined
3,512.2	3,232.3	2,884.5	2,711.3	3,492.2	3,041.4	3,438.6	3,011.6	3,521.4	4,452.2	..	Money
791.1	889.9	838.2	767.5	985.0	1,023.7	1,068.2	899.6	1,131.6	1,461.0	..	Currency Outside Banks
2,721.0	2,342.4	2,046.2	1,943.8	2,507.2	2,017.7	2,370.4	2,112.0	2,389.8	2,991.2	..	Demand Deposits
1,134.7	1,073.1	1,242.3	1,464.0	1,561.4	1,770.0	1,634.5	1,742.9	1,635.0	1,748.9	..	Quasi-Money
					(Millions of current Libyan Dinars)						
											GOVERNMENT DEFICIT (-) OR SURPLUS
..	..	..	..	..	..	..	..	..	..	..	Current Revenue
..	..	..	..	..	..	..	..	..	..	..	Current Expenditure
..	..	..	..	..	..	..	..	..	..	..	Current Budget Balance
..	..	..	..	..	..	..	..	..	..	..	Capital Receipts
..	..	..	..	..	..	..	..	..	..	..	Capital Payments

LIBYA	1970	1971	1972	1973	1974	1975	1976	1977	1978	1979	1980
FOREIGN TRADE (CUSTOMS BASIS)					*(Millions of current US dollars)*						
Value of Exports, fob	2,357	2,688	2,938	3,993	8,265	6,834	9,554	11,411	9,895	16,076	21,910
Nonfuel Primary Products	2	2	7	9	3	0	..	..	0	0	..
Fuels	2,355	2,686	2,931	3,984	8,262	6,834	9,554	11,411	9,867	16,007	21,910
Manufactures	0	0	0	0	0	0	..	..	28	69	..
Value of Imports, cif	554	701	1,043	1,803	2,764	3,542	3,212	3,774	4,603	5,311	6,776
Nonfuel Primary Products	139	178	209	414	610	723	556	824	881	1,013	1,468
Fuels	18	23	23	36	45	69	86	21	36	35	44
Manufactures	397	500	812	1,354	2,110	2,751	2,569	2,928	3,686	4,264	5,265
					(Index 1987 = 100)						
Terms of Trade	52.2	58.4	54.9	64.1	144.2	112.1	117.7	122.3	104.3	138.4	214.6
Export Prices, fob	13.8	16.8	18.0	25.6	73.6	61.6	65.4	73.8	73.0	112.1	190.6
Import Prices, cif	26.4	28.8	32.7	39.9	51.0	54.9	55.6	60.3	70.0	81.0	88.8
BALANCE OF PAYMENTS					*(Millions of current US dollars)*						
Exports of Goods & Services	2,536	2,886	2,695	3,743	8,237	6,793	9,096	10,786	10,370	16,547	23,366
Merchandise, fob	2,397	2,714	2,470	3,528	7,803	6,418	8,748	10,406	9,900	15,981	21,919
Nonfactor Services	42	42	97	101	143	160	167	136	153	143	164
Factor Services	97	129	128	114	291	215	181	244	317	424	1,282
Imports of Goods & Services	1,638	1,838	2,049	3,249	5,118	5,977	5,851	7,690	8,582	11,874	14,018
Merchandise, fob	674	930	1,291	2,011	3,746	4,424	4,277	4,929	5,764	8,647	10,368
Nonfactor Services	400	337	520	811	1,173	1,343	1,368	1,301	1,448	1,953	2,303
Factor Services	564	572	238	427	200	210	206	1,459	1,370	1,273	1,347
Long-Term Interest	..	..	..	..	..	..	..	..	..	..	..
Private Current Transfers, net	-140	-174	-306	-273	-350	-260	-257	-858	-972	-859	-1,089
Workers' Remittances	..	..	..	..	..	..	..	..	..	..	..
Curr. A/C Bal before Off. Transf.	758	874	340	222	2,768	556	2,988	2,238	816	3,814	8,259
Net Official Transfers	-113	-90	-102	-156	-69	-164	-144	-79	-78	-43	-46
Curr. A/C Bal after Off. Transf.	645	783	238	66	2,700	392	2,844	2,159	738	3,771	8,214
Long-Term Capital, net	139	130	-43	-510	-422	-1,524	-1,508	-1,066	-1,068	-930	-1,372
Direct Investment	139	140	-4	-148	-241	-616	-521	-512	-720	-609	-1,136
Long-Term Loans	..	..	..	..	..	..	..	..	..	..	..
Disbursements	..	..	..	..	..	..	..	..	..	..	..
Repayments	..	..	..	..	..	..	..	..	..	..	..
Other Long-Term Capital	0	-10	-39	-362	-182	-908	-987	-554	-348	-321	-236
Other Capital, net	-87	-40	239	-537	48	-765	-178	581	-189	-621	-435
Change in Reserves	-697	-874	-434	982	-2,325	1,897	-1,157	-1,674	519	-2,220	-6,407
Memo Item:					*(Libyan Dinars per US dollar)*						
Conversion Factor (Annual Avg)	0.360	0.360	0.330	0.300	0.300	0.300	0.300	0.300	0.300	0.300	0.300
EXTERNAL DEBT (Total)					*(Millions of US dollars), outstanding at end of year*						
Long-Term Debt (by debtor)	..	..	..	..	..	..	..	..	..	..	..
Central Bank, incl. IMF credit	..	..	..	..	..	..	..	..	..	..	..
Central Government	..	..	..	..	..	..	..	..	..	..	..
Rest of General Government	..	..	..	..	..	..	..	..	..	..	..
Non-financial Public Enterprises	..	..	..	..	..	..	..	..	..	..	..
Priv. Sector, incl non-guaranteed	..	..	..	..	..	..	..	..	..	..	..
Short-Term Debt	..	..	..	..	..	..	..	..	..	..	..
Memo Items:					*(Millions of US dollars)*						
Int'l Reserves Excluding Gold	1,504.8	2,572.8	2,832.2	2,023.8	3,511.1	2,095.0	3,106.4	4,786.4	4,104.8	6,344.4	13,090.5
Gold Holdings (at market price)	91.1	106.3	158.2	273.6	454.6	341.9	328.5	403.8	553.3	1,261.6	1,814.3
SOCIAL INDICATORS											
Total Fertility Rate	7.5	7.6	7.6	7.5	7.5	7.5	7.4	7.4	7.3	7.3	7.3
Infant Mortality Rate	122.2	119.6	117.0	115.0	113.0	111.0	109.0	107.0	105.0	103.0	101.0
Life Expectancy at Birth	51.9	52.4	52.9	53.5	54.1	54.6	55.2	55.8	56.3	56.8	57.3
Urban Population, % of total	35.8	38.0	40.2	42.4	44.6	46.8	48.8	50.7	52.7	54.6	56.6
Food Prod. per capita (1987=100)	86.9	63.8	109.3	124.8	120.5	138.8	142.6	94.0	106.5	115.7	133.6
Labor Force, Agriculture (%)	28.9	27.6	26.5	25.4	24.4	23.5	22.2	21.1	20.0	19.1	18.2
Labor Force, Female (%)	6.4	6.4	6.5	6.6	6.6	6.7	6.8	6.9	7.1	7.2	7.3
Primary Schl. Enroll. Ratio	..	..	..	..	..	..	..	..	..	..	..
Primary Schl. Enroll. Ratio, Female	..	..	..	..	..	..	..	..	..	..	..
Secondary Schl. Enroll. Ratio	..	..	..	..	..	..	..	..	..	..	..

1981	1982	1983	1984	1985	1986	1987	1988	1989	1990 estimate	Notes	LIBYA
											FOREIGN TRADE (CUSTOMS BASIS)
			(Millions of current US dollars)								
15,571	13,951	11,541	11,136	10,841	6,729	8,049	6,908	9,045	14,285	..	Value of Exports, fob
0	0	3	0	0	0	0	0	0	0	..	Nonfuel Primary Products
15,513	13,899	11,333	11,095	10,801	6,704	8,019	6,882	9,012	14,232	..	Fuels
58	52	205	41	40	25	30	26	34	53	..	Manufactures
8,382	7,176	6,586	5,648	4,660	3,789	4,340	4,275	3,794	3,976	..	Value of Imports, cif
1,688	1,311	908	1,082	892	726	831	819	727	761	..	Nonfuel Primary Products
84	104	681	44	36	29	34	33	29	31	..	Fuels
6,611	5,760	4,998	4,523	3,731	3,034	3,475	3,424	3,038	3,184	..	Manufactures
			(Index 1987 = 100)								
239.0	220.0	197.3	196.3	196.1	85.1	100.0	78.8	91.1	97.4	..	Terms of Trade
211.2	187.9	165.4	160.2	160.0	78.5	100.0	79.5	96.6	123.9	..	Export Prices, fob
88.4	85.4	83.8	81.7	81.6	92.3	100.0	101.0	106.0	127.3	..	Import Prices, cif
											BALANCE OF PAYMENTS
			(Millions of current US dollars)								
16,521	14,732	13,185	11,748	10,879	6,443	6,673	6,533	7,849	12,146	..	Exports of Goods & Services
14,731	13,701	12,348	11,028	10,353	5,814	5,828	5,644	7,283	11,362	..	Merchandise, fob
163	163	161	170	63	82	114	128	118	117	..	Nonfactor Services
1,627	868	676	550	463	547	731	761	448	667	..	Factor Services
18,838	14,617	12,726	11,884	8,068	6,072	7,191	7,824	8,388	9,462	..	Imports of Goods & Services
14,563	10,976	8,978	8,464	5,754	4,434	5,391	5,753	6,517	7,582	..	Merchandise, fob
2,757	2,265	2,315	2,202	1,775	1,047	1,437	1,634	1,483	1,387	..	Nonfactor Services
1,517	1,376	1,433	1,218	540	591	364	437	388	493	..	Factor Services
..	..	..	..	..	..	..	..	..	..	..	Long-Term Interest
-1,570	-1,597	-2,045	-1,240	-859	-490	-470	-496	-472	-446	..	Private Current Transfers, net
..	..	..	..	..	..	..	..	..	..	..	Workers' Remittances
-3,888	-1,482	-1,586	-1,376	1,952	-119	-989	-1,786	-1,012	2,239	..	Curr. A/C Bal before Off. Transf.
-76	-78	-58	-81	-45	-36	-56	-37	-16	-35	..	Net Official Transfers
-3,964	-1,560	-1,643	-1,456	1,906	-156	-1,045	-1,823	-1,028	2,203	..	Curr. A/C Bal after Off. Transf.
-1,705	-1,026	-557	-214	-19	-251	-2,953	-430	-391	-937	..	Long-Term Capital, net
-769	-411	-327	-17	119	-177	-213	42	90	54	..	Direct Investment
..	..	..	..	..	..	..	..	..	..	..	Long-Term Loans
..	..	..	..	..	..	..	..	..	..	..	Disbursements
..	..	..	..	..	..	..	..	..	..	..	Repayments
-935	-615	-231	-197	-138	-74	-2,740	-472	-481	-991	..	Other Long-Term Capital
1,532	585	423	-51	475	618	2,998	863	1,711	-107	..	Other Capital, net
4,136	2,001	1,778	1,721	-2,362	-212	1,000	1,390	-292	-1,159	..	Change in Reserves
			(Libyan Dinars per US dollar)								**Memo Item:**
0.300	0.300	0.300	0.300	0.300	0.320	0.290	0.290	0.300	0.280	..	Conversion Factor (Annual Avg)
			(Millions of US dollars), outstanding at end of year								
..	..	..	..	..	..	..	..	..	..	..	**EXTERNAL DEBT (Total)**
..	..	..	..	..	..	..	..	..	..	..	Long-Term Debt (by debtor)
..	..	..	..	..	..	..	..	..	..	..	Central Bank, incl. IMF credit
..	..	..	..	..	..	..	..	..	..	..	Central Government
..	..	..	..	..	..	..	..	..	..	..	Rest of General Government
..	..	..	..	..	..	..	..	..	..	..	Non-financial Public Enterprises
..	..	..	..	..	..	..	..	..	..	..	Priv. Sector, incl non-guaranteed
..	..	..	..	..	..	..	..	..	..	..	Short-Term Debt
			(Millions of US dollars)								**Memo Items:**
9,002.9	7,059.5	5,218.7	3,634.2	5,903.9	5,953.2	5,838.0	4,321.6	4,332.7	5,839.2	..	Int'l Reserves Excluding Gold
1,422.4	1,635.0	1,365.2	1,124.7	1,177.2	1,407.2	1,742.8	1,476.9	1,443.6	1,386.0	..	Gold Holdings (at market price)
											SOCIAL INDICATORS
7.2	7.2	7.1	7.1	7.0	7.0	6.9	6.8	6.7	6.7	..	Total Fertility Rate
99.0	97.0	94.0	91.0	88.0	85.0	82.0	79.3	76.6	74.0	..	Infant Mortality Rate
57.8	58.3	58.8	59.3	59.8	60.3	60.8	61.3	61.9	62.4	..	Life Expectancy at Birth
58.2	59.8	61.3	62.9	64.5	65.6	66.8	67.9	69.1	70.2	..	Urban Population, % of total
130.0	129.3	132.6	119.2	109.0	92.1	100.0	98.4	105.9	93.4	..	Food Prod. per capita (1987=100)
..	..	..	..	..	..	..	..	..	..	..	Labor Force, Agriculture (%)
7.5	7.6	7.8	8.0	8.1	8.3	8.5	8.7	8.9	9.1	..	Labor Force, Female (%)
..	..	..	..	..	..	..	..	..	..	..	Primary Schl. Enroll. Ratio
..	..	..	..	..	..	..	..	..	..	..	Primary Schl. Enroll. Ratio, Female
..	..	..	..	..	..	..	..	..	..	..	Secondary Schl. Enroll. Ratio

LUXEMBOURG	1970	1971	1972	1973	1974	1975	1976	1977	1978	1979	1980
CURRENT GNP PER CAPITA (US $)	3,170	3,440	4,070	4,980	6,420	7,470	8,440	9,240	10,750	12,710	14,920
POPULATION (thousands)	340	345	348	353	357	361	362	362	362	364	365

USE AND ORIGIN OF RESOURCES					*(Billions of current Luxembourg Francs)*						
Gross National Product (GNP)	56.96	58.26	66.62	80.30	99.33	98.61	116.47	122.01	133.51	145.33	160.93
Net Factor Income from Abroad	1.92	2.21	3.42	3.49	5.68	11.87	16.67	19.45	21.30	23.19	28.00
GDP at Market Prices	55.04	56.05	63.21	76.82	93.64	86.74	99.81	102.56	112.21	122.15	132.93
Resource Balance	7.01	1.88	3.61	9.50	19.56	3.40	5.40	3.78	1.09	4.51	-0.86
Exports of Goods & NFServices	48.92	49.40	52.38	68.61	96.10	80.21	87.94	89.08	94.00	111.05	117.66
Imports of Goods & NFServices	41.91	47.52	48.77	59.12	76.54	76.81	82.54	85.30	92.91	106.54	118.51
Domestic Absorption	48.03	54.17	59.59	67.32	74.08	83.35	94.40	98.78	111.12	117.64	133.78
Private Consumption, etc.	27.80	30.74	33.87	37.56	43.19	50.12	56.50	61.09	65.02	70.65	78.08
General Gov't Consumption	5.78	6.56	7.43	8.66	10.73	12.95	14.70	16.29	17.55	19.52	22.18
Gross Domestic Investment	14.45	16.87	18.30	21.10	20.17	20.28	23.20	21.40	28.55	27.47	33.52
Fixed Investment	12.70	15.90	17.56	20.96	23.00	24.06	24.85	25.70	26.99	29.78	36.03
Indirect Taxes, net	4.72	5.36	6.45	7.68	8.27	8.90	9.44	9.59	11.26	11.57	14.03
GDP at factor cost	50.33	50.69	56.76	69.14	85.38	77.85	90.37	92.97	100.96	110.57	118.90
Agriculture	2.12	2.12	2.53	2.95	2.80	2.95	2.81	3.06	3.48	3.62	3.45
Industry	29.44	27.16	30.12	37.92	48.89	36.01	42.55	40.62	44.82	48.79	51.44
Manufacturing	23.79	20.68	22.36	29.40	39.12	25.37	31.76	29.53	33.54	36.87	37.82
Services, etc.	23.49	26.77	30.56	35.94	41.95	47.79	54.44	58.88	63.92	69.74	78.03
Gross Domestic Saving	21.46	18.75	21.91	30.60	39.73	23.67	28.60	25.18	29.64	31.98	32.66
Gross National Saving	..	..	..	..	..	..	..	..	..	..	..

					(Billions of 1987 Luxembourg Francs)						
Gross National Product	152.14	156.10	168.99	182.06	193.53	192.91	203.70	209.65	217.94	223.20	229.04
GDP at Market Prices	144.47	147.94	158.06	171.29	178.52	166.97	171.25	173.96	181.05	185.30	186.89
Resource Balance	-2.20	-6.57	-4.03	-0.17	6.28	-4.49	-4.42	-0.78	-4.03	-0.27	-7.66
Exports of Goods & NFServices	116.33	120.96	127.08	144.89	159.87	134.64	135.95	141.70	146.56	160.41	158.16
Imports of Goods & NFServices	118.53	127.53	131.11	145.06	153.59	139.13	140.37	142.48	150.60	160.68	165.82
Domestic Absorption	146.67	154.51	162.08	171.46	172.24	171.46	175.67	174.74	185.08	185.57	194.55
Private Consumption, etc.	77.20	80.72	85.29	90.99	96.09	99.68	102.85	105.75	108.47	113.04	115.26
General Gov't Consumption	24.63	25.36	26.42	27.33	28.35	29.29	30.11	30.99	31.55	32.25	33.24
Gross Domestic Investment	44.84	48.43	50.37	53.15	47.80	42.49	42.71	38.00	45.06	40.28	46.05
Fixed Investment	40.62	44.95	48.11	53.80	50.05	46.33	44.37	44.34	44.81	46.49	52.40
GDP at factor cost	129.58	132.16	140.25	151.60	159.21	148.44	153.42	156.75	162.04	166.80	166.24
Agriculture	5.21	4.75	5.09	5.22	4.79	5.15	4.48	4.98	5.47	5.41	5.04
Industry	61.96	63.00	68.06	74.16	78.01	65.31	66.48	65.95	68.21	70.06	70.10
Manufacturing	45.29	45.00	47.83	52.88	56.46	45.36	47.40	47.35	49.37	51.14	50.50
Services, etc.	77.30	80.19	84.91	91.91	95.72	96.51	100.29	103.04	107.37	109.83	111.75
Memo Items:											
Capacity to Import	138.36	132.58	140.83	168.37	192.84	145.29	149.56	148.79	152.37	167.48	164.62
Terms of Trade Adjustment	22.03	11.62	13.74	23.48	32.97	10.65	13.60	7.09	5.81	7.07	6.46
Gross Domestic Income	166.50	159.56	171.80	194.77	211.48	177.61	184.85	181.05	186.86	192.37	193.35
Gross National Income	174.17	167.72	182.73	205.54	226.49	203.56	217.30	216.74	223.75	230.27	235.50

DOMESTIC PRICES/DEFLATORS					*(Index 1987 = 100)*						
Overall (GDP)	38.1	37.9	40.0	44.8	52.5	52.0	58.3	59.0	62.0	65.9	71.1
Domestic Absorption	32.7	35.1	36.8	39.3	43.0	48.6	53.7	56.5	60.0	63.4	68.8
Agriculture	40.7	44.6	49.7	56.4	58.5	57.2	62.8	61.4	63.6	66.9	68.4
Industry	47.5	43.1	44.2	51.1	62.7	55.1	64.0	61.6	65.7	69.6	73.4
Manufacturing	52.5	45.9	46.7	55.6	69.3	55.9	67.0	62.4	67.9	72.1	74.9
Consumer Price Index	37.2	38.9	40.9	43.5	47.6	52.7	57.8	61.7	63.6	66.5	70.7

MANUFACTURING ACTIVITY											
Employment (1987=100)	117.2	120.6	123.1	127.7	132.5	129.9	126.7	123.5	116.3	113.4	110.2
Real Earnings per Empl. (1987=100)	73.3	75.1	76.9	79.4	89.4	90.1	87.9	89.5	93.3	94.8	96.5
Real Output per Empl. (1987=100)	34.1	38.9	38.9	40.1	43.0	47.3	42.2	59.9	63.4	72.2	74.3
Earnings as % of Value Added	42.9	55.2	56.8	48.5	46.2	63.6	66.3	76.9	67.4	62.7	65.0

MONETARY HOLDINGS					*(Millions of current Luxembourg Francs)*						
Money Supply, Broadly Defined	..	..	..	..	64	69	80	89	102	117	140
Money	..	..	..	..	24	26	28	32	34	36	38
Currency Outside Banks	..	..	..	..	..	..	..	..	..	..	..
Demand Deposits	..	..	..	..	..	..	..	..	..	..	..
Quasi-Money	..	..	..	..	40	42	52	57	68	81	102

					(Millions of current Luxembourg Francs)						
GOVERNMENT DEFICIT (-) OR SURPLUS	1,024	1,129	969	2,125	4,067	1,008	314	706	3,801	-294	1,673
Current Revenue	17,557	19,841	22,617	27,509	34,341	38,557	44,757	50,523	56,137	58,143	66,339
Current Expenditure	14,296	16,083	18,313	21,187	25,321	32,323	38,013	42,887	45,439	50,397	56,580
Current Budget Balance	3,261	3,758	4,304	6,322	9,020	6,234	6,744	7,636	10,698	7,746	9,759
Capital Receipts	12	3	5	5	16	6	29	9	12	107	13
Capital Payments	2,249	2,632	3,340	4,202	4,969	5,232	6,459	6,939	6,909	8,147	8,571

1981	1982	1983	1984	1985	1986	1987	1988	1989	1990 estimate	Notes	LUXEMBOURG
15,540	15,770	14,660	14,070	14,000	15,290	17,740	22,840	26,210	28,980	..	**CURRENT GNP PER CAPITA (US $)**
366	366	366	366	367	369	371	374	376	378	..	**POPULATION (thousands)**
				(Billions of current Luxembourg Francs)							**USE AND ORIGIN OF RESOURCES**
178.28	218.94	246.88	270.39	288.79	305.58	305.03	334.14	374.99	397.14	..	Gross National Product (GNP)
36.59	60.15	72.19	76.72	83.54	82.27	77.18	85.75	95.95	105.63	..	Net Factor Income from Abroad
141.69	158.79	174.68	193.67	205.26	223.30	227.85	248.39	279.03	291.50	..	GDP at Market Prices
-3.99	-2.50	0.43	3.43	10.81	9.79	-1.84	-0.84	5.93	-1.51	..	Resource Balance
122.76	141.31	157.62	195.76	222.89	224.81	223.84	249.38	285.09	286.84	..	Exports of Goods & NF Services
126.75	143.82	157.18	192.33	212.08	215.02	225.68	250.22	279.16	288.35	..	Imports of Goods & NF Services
145.68	161.29	174.25	190.24	194.44	213.52	229.68	249.23	273.11	293.01	..	Domestic Absorption
86.25	95.76	104.18	112.60	120.52	126.18	134.72	144.74	154.60	166.55	..	Private Consumption, etc.
24.67	26.10	27.56	29.76	32.31	34.96	38.45	40.55	44.26	47.56	..	General Gov't Consumption
34.76	39.44	42.51	47.88	41.61	52.38	56.51	63.93	74.25	78.91	..	Gross Domestic Investment
36.02	39.67	37.09	38.82	36.26	49.43	58.29	66.71	65.39	73.62	..	Fixed Investment
13.86	16.53	20.46	23.62	25.89	28.00	28.77	32.87	38.94	41.95	..	Indirect Taxes, net
127.83	142.26	154.22	170.04	179.37	195.31	199.07	215.52	240.09	249.55	B	GDP at factor cost
3.89	5.41	4.95	5.17	5.24	5.24	5.09	5.28	5.94		..	Agriculture
53.64	61.19	65.08	73.01	77.72	83.55	79.83	89.78	102.82		..	Industry
39.35	46.78	49.83	57.41	61.64	66.02	60.87	68.11	79.11		..	Manufacturing
84.17	92.19	104.66	115.48	122.29	134.51	142.92	153.33	170.27		..	Services, etc.
30.77	36.93	42.95	51.31	52.43	62.17	54.67	63.10	80.17	77.40	..	Gross Domestic Saving
..	..	..	..	..	..	..	..	..	..	..	Gross National Saving
				(Billions of 1987 Luxembourg Francs)							
236.61	262.98	276.34	288.03	299.47	306.81	305.03	324.25	346.11	357.57	..	Gross National Product
185.93	188.03	193.71	205.58	211.54	221.84	227.85	240.31	255.40	261.39	..	GDP at Market Prices
-10.54	-10.54	-4.61	1.26	6.16	1.13	-1.84	-3.28	-2.48	-4.96	..	Resource Balance
150.53	150.06	158.00	186.48	204.26	211.15	223.84	240.80	257.19	262.82	..	Exports of Goods & NF Services
161.07	160.60	162.61	185.22	198.10	210.02	225.68	244.08	259.67	267.78	..	Imports of Goods & NF Services
196.47	198.57	198.31	204.32	205.38	220.72	229.68	243.59	257.89	266.35	..	Domestic Absorption
116.85	117.25	118.66	121.39	125.45	128.66	134.72	140.54	145.45	150.09	..	Private Consumption, etc.
33.71	34.21	34.86	35.61	36.32	37.43	38.45	39.92	40.67	41.96	..	General Gov't Consumption
45.90	47.11	44.80	47.32	43.61	54.62	56.51	63.12	71.76	74.31	..	Gross Domestic Investment
48.52	48.29	42.61	42.66	38.60	50.75	58.29	65.47	61.25	67.01	..	Fixed Investment
166.89	167.38	170.28	180.20	184.29	192.93	199.07	208.14	218.59	223.18	B	GDP at factor cost
5.23	5.96	5.26	5.72	5.40	5.25	5.09	5.03	5.07		..	Agriculture
66.87	66.57	68.06	73.62	76.49	77.86	79.83	88.39	94.36		..	Industry
47.50	48.35	50.03	55.77	58.85	59.88	60.87	67.75	72.75		..	Manufacturing
113.83	115.51	120.38	126.25	129.65	138.73	142.92	146.89	155.97		..	Services, etc.
											Memo Items:
156.00	157.80	163.05	188.52	208.20	219.58	223.84	243.26	265.19	266.38	..	Capacity to Import
5.47	7.74	5.06	2.04	3.94	8.43	0.00	2.46	8.00	3.56	..	Terms of Trade Adjustment
191.40	195.77	198.76	207.63	215.48	230.28	227.85	242.77	263.40	264.95	..	Gross Domestic Income
242.07	270.72	281.39	290.07	303.41	315.25	305.03	326.71	354.10	361.13	..	Gross National Income
				(Index 1987 = 100)							**DOMESTIC PRICES/DEFLATORS**
76.2	84.4	90.2	94.2	97.0	100.7	100.0	103.4	109.3	111.5	..	Overall (GDP)
74.2	81.2	87.9	93.1	94.7	96.7	100.0	102.3	105.9	110.0	..	Domestic Absorption
74.3	90.8	93.9	90.5	97.0	99.9	100.0	105.2	117.1		..	Agriculture
80.2	91.9	95.6	99.2	101.6	107.3	100.0	101.6	109.0		..	Industry
82.8	96.7	99.6	102.9	104.7	110.3	100.0	100.5	108.7		..	Manufacturing
76.4	83.6	90.8	95.9	99.8	100.1	100.0	101.5	104.9	108.8	..	Consumer Price Index
											MANUFACTURING ACTIVITY
109.0	107.4	103.1	101.8	101.4	103.1	100.0	96.8	96.6		..	Employment (1987=100)
93.9	92.7	88.7	91.2	93.8	98.5	100.0	103.4	..	..	..	Real Earnings per Empl. (1987=100)
69.9	72.0	78.8	93.6	100.6	99.2	100.0	113.7	..	..	..	Real Output per Empl. (1987=100)
65.6	57.0	52.1	49.4	50.6	49.9	58.1	53.3	..	..	..	Earnings as % of Value Added
				(Millions of current Luxembourg Francs)							**MONETARY HOLDINGS**
155	155	169	170	198	220	254	295	353	411	..	Money Supply, Broadly Defined
40	41	46	48	45	49	54	59	67	73	..	Money
..	..	..	..	..	..	..	..	..	..	..	Currency Outside Banks
..	..	..	..	..	..	..	..	..	..	..	Demand Deposits
115	114	123	123	153	171	200	236	286	339	..	Quasi-Money
				(Millions of current Luxembourg Francs)							
-3,016	1,152	-3,560	10,253	21,431	16,336	8,081	7,610	9,209	..	..	**GOVERNMENT DEFICIT (-) OR SURPLUS**
72,133	79,548	90,293	96,889	105,115	109,808	113,965	120,912	136,896		..	Current Revenue
62,783	71,537	76,746	80,805	84,645	91,748	96,587	103,432	109,650		..	Current Expenditure
9,350	8,011	13,547	16,084	20,470	18,060	17,378	17,480	27,246		..	Current Budget Balance
98	51	96	171	65	225	210	204	245	..	..	Capital Receipts
10,005	10,491	16,423	11,413	11,657	9,733	10,976	12,722	13,084	..	..	Capital Payments

LUXEMBOURG	1970	1971	1972	1973	1974	1975	1976	1977	1978	1979	1980
FOREIGN TRADE (CUSTOMS BASIS)					*(Millions of current US dollars)*						
Value of Exports, fob	..	..	..	..	..	..	..	..	..	..	..
Nonfuel Primary Products	..	..	..	..	..	..	..	..	..	..	..
Fuels	..	..	..	..	..	..	..	..	..	..	..
Manufactures	..	..	..	..	..	..	..	..	..	..	..
Value of Imports, cif	..	..	..	..	..	..	..	..	..	..	..
Nonfuel Primary Products	..	..	..	..	..	..	..	..	..	..	..
Fuels	..	..	..	..	..	..	..	..	..	..	..
Manufactures	..	..	..	..	..	..	..	..	..	..	..
					(Index 1987 = 100)						
Terms of Trade	..	..	..	..	..	..	..	..	..	..	..
Export Prices, fob	..	..	..	..	..	..	..	..	..	..	..
Import Prices, cif	..	..	..	..	..	..	..	..	..	..	..
BALANCE OF PAYMENTS					*(Millions of current US dollars)*						
Exports of Goods & Services	..	..	..	..	..	..	..	..	..	..	..
Merchandise, fob	..	..	..	..	..	..	..	..	..	..	..
Nonfactor Services	..	..	..	..	..	..	..	..	..	..	..
Factor Services	..	..	..	..	..	..	..	..	..	..	..
Imports of Goods & Services	..	..	..	..	..	..	..	..	..	..	..
Merchandise, fob	..	..	..	..	..	..	..	..	..	..	..
Nonfactor Services	..	..	..	..	..	..	..	..	..	..	..
Factor Services	..	..	..	..	..	..	..	..	..	..	..
Long-Term Interest	..	..	..	..	..	..	..	..	..	..	..
Private Current Transfers, net	..	..	..	..	..	..	..	..	..	..	..
Workers' Remittances	..	..	..	..	..	..	..	..	..	..	..
Curr. A/C Bal before Off. Transf.	..	..	..	..	..	..	..	..	..	..	..
Net Official Transfers	..	..	..	..	..	..	..	..	..	..	..
Curr. A/C Bal after Off. Transf.	..	..	..	..	..	..	..	..	..	..	..
Long-Term Capital, net	..	..	..	..	..	..	..	..	..	..	..
Direct Investment	..	..	..	..	..	..	..	..	..	..	..
Long-Term Loans	..	..	..	..	..	..	..	..	..	..	..
Disbursements	..	..	..	..	..	..	..	..	..	..	..
Repayments	..	..	..	..	..	..	..	..	..	..	..
Other Long-Term Capital	..	..	..	..	..	..	..	..	..	..	..
Other Capital, net	..	..	..	..	..	..	..	..	..	..	..
Change in Reserves	..	..	..	..	..	..	..	..	..	..	..
Memo Item:					*(Luxembourg Francs per US dollar)*						
Conversion Factor (Annual Avg)	50.000	48.870	44.010	38.980	38.950	36.780	38.610	35.840	31.490	29.320	29.240
					(Millions of US dollars), outstanding at end of year						
EXTERNAL DEBT (Total)	..	..	..	..	..	..	..	..	..	..	..
Long-Term Debt (by debtor)	..	..	..	..	..	..	..	..	..	..	..
Central Bank, incl. IMF credit	..	..	..	..	..	..	..	..	..	..	..
Central Government	..	..	..	..	..	..	..	..	..	..	..
Rest of General Government	..	..	..	..	..	..	..	..	..	..	..
Non-financial Public Enterprises	..	..	..	..	..	..	..	..	..	..	..
Priv. Sector, incl non-guaranteed	..	..	..	..	..	..	..	..	..	..	..
Short-Term Debt	..	..	..	..	..	..	..	..	..	..	..
Memo Items:					*(Millions of US dollars)*						
Int'l Reserves Excluding Gold	..	..	..	..	..	..	..	..	..	..	..
Gold Holdings (at market price)	16.43	19.30	28.70	49.65	82.49	62.03	59.60	74.37	102.86	233.03	268.30
SOCIAL INDICATORS											
Total Fertility Rate	2.0	1.9	1.7	1.5	1.6	1.5	1.5	1.4	1.5	1.5	1.5
Infant Mortality Rate	24.9	22.5	14.0	15.3	13.5	14.8	17.9	10.6	10.6	13.0	11.5
Life Expectancy at Birth	70.3	70.5	70.6	70.9	71.1	71.4	71.6	71.9	72.1	72.4	72.7
Urban Population, % of total	67.8	69.0	70.2	71.3	72.5	73.7	74.6	75.6	76.5	77.5	78.4
Food Prod. per capita (1987=100)	..	..	..	..	..	..	..	..	..	..	..
Labor Force, Agriculture (%)	7.9	7.6	7.4	7.1	6.9	6.6	6.4	6.1	5.9	5.6	5.4
Labor Force, Female (%)	26.9	27.3	27.8	28.3	28.7	29.1	29.8	30.5	31.1	31.8	32.4
Primary Schl. Enroll. Ratio	112.0	..	..	..	..	..	98.0	98.0	98.0	94.0	..
Primary Schl. Enroll. Ratio, Female	112.0										
Secondary Schl. Enroll. Ratio	48.0	..	..	..	..	59.0	62.0	64.0	65.0	66.0	71.0

1981	1982	1983	1984	1985	1986	1987	1988	1989	1990 estimate	Notes	LUXEMBOURG
				(Millions of current US dollars)							**FOREIGN TRADE (CUSTOMS BASIS)**
..	..	..	..	..	..	..	..	..	..	f	Value of Exports, fob
..	..	..	..	..	..	..	..	..	..		Nonfuel Primary Products
..	..	..	..	..	..	..	..	..	..		Fuels
..	..	..	..	..	..	..	..	..	..		Manufactures
..	..	..	..	..	..	..	..	..	..	f	Value of Imports, cif
..	..	..	..	..	..	..	..	..	..		Nonfuel Primary Products
..	..	..	..	..	..	..	..	..	..		Fuels
..	..	..	..	..	..	..	..	..	..		Manufactures
				(Index 1987 = 100)							
..	..	..	..	..	..	..	..	..	..	f	Terms of Trade
..	..	..	..	..	..	..	..	..	..	f	Export Prices, fob
..	..	..	..	..	..	..	..	..	..	f	Import Prices, cif
				(Millions of current US dollars)							**BALANCE OF PAYMENTS**
..	..	..	..	..	..	..	..	..	..	f	Exports of Goods & Services
..	..	..	..	..	..	..	..	..	..		Merchandise, fob
..	..	..	..	..	..	..	..	..	..		Nonfactor Services
..	..	..	..	..	..	..	..	..	..		Factor Services
..	..	..	..	..	..	..	..	..	..	f	Imports of Goods & Services
..	..	..	..	..	..	..	..	..	..		Merchandise, fob
..	..	..	..	..	..	..	..	..	..		Nonfactor Services
..	..	..	..	..	..	..	..	..	..		Factor Services
..	..	..	..	..	..	..	..	..	..		Long-Term Interest
..	..	..	..	..	..	..	..	..	..	f	Private Current Transfers, net
..	..	..	..	..	..	..	..	..	..		Workers' Remittances
..	..	..	..	..	..	..	..	..	..		Curr. A/C Bal before Off. Transf.
..	..	..	..	..	..	..	..	..	..		Net Official Transfers
..	..	..	..	..	..	..	..	..	..		Curr. A/C Bal after Off. Transf.
..	..	..	..	..	..	..	..	..	..	f	Long-Term Capital, net
..	..	..	..	..	..	..	..	..	..		Direct Investment
..	..	..	..	..	..	..	..	..	..		Long-Term Loans
..	..	..	..	..	..	..	..	..	..		Disbursements
..	..	..	..	..	..	..	..	..	..		Repayments
..	..	..	..	..	..	..	..	..	..		Other Long-Term Capital
..	..	..	..	..	..	..	..	..	..		Other Capital, net
..	..	..	..	..	..	..	..	..	..		Change in Reserves
				(Luxembourg Francs per US dollar)							**Memo Item:**
37.130	45.690	51.130	57.780	59.380	44.670	37.330	36.770	39.400	33.420	..	Conversion Factor (Annual Avg)
				(Millions of US dollars), outstanding at end of year							**EXTERNAL DEBT (Total)**
..	..	..	..	..	..	..	..	..	..		Long-Term Debt (by debtor)
..	..	..	..	..	..	..	..	..	..		Central Bank, incl. IMF credit
..	..	..	..	..	..	..	..	..	..		Central Government
..	..	..	..	..	..	..	..	..	..		Rest of General Government
..	..	..	..	..	..	..	..	..	..		Non-financial Public Enterprises
..	..	..	..	..	..	..	..	..	..		Priv. Sector, incl non-guaranteed
..	..	..	..	..	..	..	..	..	..		Short-Term Debt
				(Millions of US dollars)							**Memo Items:**
..	..	..	..	..	..	..	..	..	..		Int'l Reserves Excluding Gold
180.91	207.95	173.63	132.29	140.31	167.68	207.65	175.98	172.01	165.15	..	Gold Holdings (at market price)
											SOCIAL INDICATORS
1.6	1.5	1.4	1.4	1.4	1.4	1.5	1.5	1.5	1.5		Total Fertility Rate
13.8	12.1	11.2	11.7	9.0	7.9	9.4	9.1	8.8	8.4	..	Infant Mortality Rate
73.0	73.3	73.5	73.7	73.9	74.1	74.4	74.6	74.8	75.0	..	Life Expectancy at Birth
79.1	79.8	80.4	81.1	81.8	82.3	82.8	83.3	83.8	84.3	..	Urban Population, % of total
..	..	..	..	..	..	..	..	..	..	f	Food Prod. per capita (1987=100)
..	..	..	..	..	..	..	..	..	..		Labor Force, Agriculture (%)
32.4	32.3	32.3	32.3	32.2	32.2	32.1	32.0	31.9	31.9	..	Labor Force, Female (%)
..	..	..	..	..	..	..	..	..	..		Primary Schl. Enroll. Ratio
..	..	..	..	..	..	..	..	..	..		Primary Schl. Enroll. Ratio, Female
..	..	74.0	74.0	75.0	75.0	70.0	..	..	..	..	Secondary Schl. Enroll. Ratio

MADAGASCAR	1970	1971	1972	1973	1974	1975	1976	1977	1978	1979	1980
CURRENT GNP PER CAPITA (US $)	170	170	180	190	230	280	280	300	310	370	430
POPULATION (thousands)	6,752	6,908	7,069	7,237	7,414	7,604	7,814	8,030	8,253	8,481	8,714
USE AND ORIGIN OF RESOURCES					*(Billions of current Malagasy Francs)*						
Gross National Product (GNP)	298.5	321.6	330.0	361.9	456.4	483.4	515.8	572.1	600.4	734.2	844.3
Net Factor Income from Abroad	-10.3	-10.8	-8.1	-6.5	-5.1	-5.9	-5.5	-7.4	-2.0	-2.6	-9.7
GDP at Market Prices	308.8	332.4	338.1	368.4	461.5	489.3	521.3	579.5	602.4	736.8	854.0
Resource Balance	-7.5	-21.9	-13.7	-17.1	-21.6	-24.6	-12.3	-20.9	-41.6	-116.5	-140.0
Exports of Goods & NFServices	59.2	48.0	48.2	52.5	71.7	77.6	79.1	95.3	103.3	107.4	113.9
Imports of Goods & NFServices	66.6	69.9	62.0	69.6	93.3	102.2	91.4	116.2	144.9	223.9	254.0
Domestic Absorption	316.3	354.3	351.8	385.5	483.1	513.9	533.6	600.4	644.0	853.3	994.0
Private Consumption, etc.	245.2	267.8	275.8	306.9	391.5	421.1	432.8	489.7	514.7	644.3	762.8
General Gov't Consumption	40.5	49.2	46.2	45.1	51.7	53.0	58.5	63.9	71.6	90.4	103.4
Gross Domestic Investment	30.6	37.3	29.8	33.5	40.0	39.8	42.4	46.8	57.8	118.6	127.8
Fixed Investment	28.1	32.6	27.9	31.0	33.2	37.6	40.6	46.8	55.6	112.6	123.0
Indirect Taxes, net	32.5	38.2	36.6	39.9	50.0	53.0	56.9	61.7	70.1	83.9	95.9
GDP at factor cost	276.3	294.2	301.5	328.5	411.5	436.3	464.4	517.8	532.3	652.9	758.1
Agriculture	67.5	71.5	75.4	88.0	140.8	148.5	154.7	169.8	171.6	194.3	227.8
Industry	45.0	48.5	51.2	58.9	65.3	69.1	74.6	88.0	91.7	112.1	121.7
Manufacturing	..	..	..	..	..	..	..	..	..	..	..
Services, etc.	163.7	174.2	174.9	181.6	205.4	218.6	235.1	260.0	269.1	346.4	408.6
Gross Domestic Saving	23.1	15.4	16.1	16.5	18.4	15.2	30.1	25.9	16.1	2.1	-12.2
Gross National Saving	5.9	-2.1	0.3	4.9	11.1	4.0	20.4	14.0	10.7	-4.1	-26.3
					(Billions of 1987 Malagasy Francs)						
Gross National Product	2,528.10	2,649.40	2,631.70	2,569.00	2,641.50	2,672.40	2,594.10	2,649.40	2,606.20	2,863.40	2,863.00
GDP at Market Prices	2,620.00	2,741.90	2,699.60	2,618.70	2,671.30	2,704.90	2,621.50	2,683.40	2,613.60	2,871.90	2,894.20
Resource Balance	-539.10	-659.90	-519.00	-517.50	-379.60	-351.90	-229.70	-268.90	-317.30	-593.20	-591.10
Exports of Goods & NFServices	569.90	456.50	450.50	470.50	498.60	585.90	449.50	473.50	523.70	567.80	558.80
Imports of Goods & NFServices	1,109.00	1,116.40	969.40	988.00	878.30	937.80	679.20	742.40	841.00	1,161.10	1,149.90
Domestic Absorption	3,159.10	3,401.80	3,218.50	3,136.20	3,050.90	3,056.80	2,851.20	2,952.30	2,930.90	3,465.10	3,485.30
Private Consumption, etc.	2,675.60	2,832.10	2,748.40	2,670.00	2,574.90	2,589.30	2,421.30	2,535.80	2,501.90	2,840.20	2,868.50
General Gov't Consumption	186.70	219.50	200.00	184.60	176.90	180.60	189.50	190.70	201.60	230.40	241.30
Gross Domestic Investment	296.80	350.20	270.10	281.60	299.10	286.90	240.40	225.90	227.40	394.50	375.40
Fixed Investment	..	..	..	..	..	..	..	..	..	..	..
GDP at factor cost	2,304.70	2,388.10	2,368.00	2,295.90	2,341.90	2,371.40	2,296.10	2,357.40	2,270.80	2,502.30	2,526.00
Agriculture	725.90	711.50	726.30	734.20	801.20	797.20	728.30	751.90	702.60	752.90	771.60
Industry	377.00	343.80	347.40	340.30	362.90	362.90	329.70	339.60	353.70	398.90	388.30
Manufacturing											
Services, etc.	1,201.70	1,332.70	1,294.30	1,221.40	1,177.80	1,211.20	1,238.10	1,265.90	1,214.40	1,350.50	1,366.10
Memo Items:											
Capacity to Import	984.40	767.00	754.60	745.70	674.80	712.00	587.70	609.00	599.60	556.90	515.90
Terms of Trade Adjustment	414.50	310.50	304.20	275.20	176.20	126.10	138.20	135.40	75.90	-10.90	-42.90
Gross Domestic Income	3,034.50	3,052.40	3,003.70	2,893.90	2,847.50	2,831.00	2,759.70	2,818.90	2,689.50	2,860.90	2,851.30
Gross National Income	2,942.60	2,959.90	2,935.80	2,844.20	2,817.70	2,798.50	2,732.30	2,784.80	2,682.10	2,852.40	2,820.10
DOMESTIC PRICES/DEFLATORS					*(Index 1987 = 100)*						
Overall (GDP)	11.8	12.1	12.5	14.1	17.3	18.1	19.9	21.6	23.1	25.7	29.5
Domestic Absorption	10.0	10.4	10.9	12.3	15.8	16.8	18.7	20.3	22.0	24.6	28.5
Agriculture	9.3	10.1	10.4	12.0	17.6	18.6	21.2	22.6	24.4	25.8	29.5
Industry	11.9	14.1	14.7	17.3	18.0	19.0	22.6	25.9	25.9	28.1	31.3
Manufacturing											
Consumer Price Index	12.6	13.2	14.0	14.8	18.1	19.6	20.6	21.2	22.6	25.8	30.5
MANUFACTURING ACTIVITY											
Employment (1987=100)	..	..	..	..	..	..	..	..	..	..	..
Real Earnings per Empl. (1987=100)	..	..	..	..	..	..	..	..	..	..	..
Real Output per Empl. (1987=100)	..	..	..	..	..	..	..	..	..	..	..
Earnings as % of Value Added	35.6	38.5	42.1	41.9	42.5	40.7	40.3	37.5	38.5	36.7	38.2
MONETARY HOLDINGS					*(Billions of current Malagasy Francs)*						
Money Supply, Broadly Defined	57.1	60.6	67.5	70.2	85.1	86.7	100.2	122.4	144.8	169.0	212.2
Money	46.2	47.0	53.3	57.3	67.9	69.4	79.7	100.0	112.8	124.3	151.3
Currency Outside Banks	22.5	22.3	25.4	27.0	31.9	34.0	35.5	42.1	48.2	53.6	70.2
Demand Deposits	23.7	24.7	28.0	30.3	36.1	35.4	44.2	57.9	64.7	70.7	81.1
Quasi-Money	10.9	13.7	14.2	12.9	17.1	17.3	20.5	22.4	32.0	44.8	60.9
					(Millions of current Malagasy Francs)						
GOVERNMENT DEFICIT (-) OR SURPLUS	..	..	-6,729	-7,309	-9,035	..	..	..	..	..	..
Current Revenue	..	..	49,837	54,234	58,246	..	..	..	129,940	168,361	133,025
Current Expenditure	..	..	41,432	46,951	..	..	..	..	..	..	..
Current Budget Balance	..	..	8,405	7,283	..	..	..	..	..	..	..
Capital Receipts	..	..	..	..	..	..	..	..	..	..	..
Capital Payments	..	..	15,134	14,592	..	..	..	..	..	..	..

1981	1982	1983	1984	1985	1986	1987	1988	1989	1990 estimate	Notes	MADAGASCAR
410	400	380	340	310	290	260	240	220	230	..	**CURRENT GNP PER CAPITA (US $)**
8,951	9,189	9,436	9,699	9,985	10,291	10,614	10,954	11,308	11,673	..	**POPULATION (thousands)**
			(Billions of current Malagasy Francs)								**USE AND ORIGIN OF RESOURCES**
951.9	1,198.6	1,463.1	1,611.0	1,808.0	2,099.0	2,557.0	3,197.0	3,661.0	4,388.0	..	Gross National Product (GNP)
-24.9	-34.6	-48.4	-84.0	-85.0	-105.0	-186.0	-240.0	-303.0	-239.0		Net Factor Income from Abroad
976.8	1,233.2	1,511.5	1,695.0	1,893.0	2,204.0	2,743.0	3,437.0	3,964.0	4,627.0	..	GDP at Market Prices
-110.5	-116.4	-105.3	-83.2	-113.0	-102.6	-148.4	-229.7	-177.0	-402.0	..	Resource Balance
112.4	138.4	159.8	223.1	220.0	263.4	433.0	559.8	721.0	708.0	..	Exports of Goods & NF Services
222.9	254.9	265.0	306.3	333.0	366.0	581.4	789.5	898.0	1,110.0	..	Imports of Goods & NF Services
1,087.3	1,349.6	1,616.8	1,778.2	2,005.7	2,306.1	2,891.8	3,666.5	4,141.3	5,029.0	..	Domestic Absorption
861.9	1,113.8	1,345.2	1,469.7	1,659.0	1,912.0	2,364.0	2,930.0	3,254.0	3,850.0	..	Private Consumption, etc.
113.3	131.2	145.1	162.4	184.8	195.0	250.5	279.6	351.0	398.0	..	General Gov't Consumption
112.1	104.6	126.4	146.1	161.8	199.2	277.2	457.0	536.3	781.0	..	Gross Domestic Investment
117.9	97.6	..	..	..	..	..	..	..	..	..	Fixed Investment
109.7	138.5	169.8	190.4	206.7	220.7	349.5	389.0	409.9	520.0	..	Indirect Taxes, net
867.1	1,094.7	1,341.7	1,504.6	1,686.3	1,983.3	2,393.5	3,048.0	3,554.1	4,107.0	B	GDP at factor cost
286.8	374.7	480.1	531.0	593.0	730.0	866.0	1,021.0	1,200.0	1,353.0	..	Agriculture
122.7	146.8	181.1	195.0	225.0	255.0	328.0	401.0	456.0	537.0	..	Industry
..	..	..	175.1	..	..	..	..	..	..	..	Manufacturing
457.6	573.2	680.5	778.6	868.3	998.3	1,199.5	1,626.0	1,898.1	2,217.0	..	Services, etc.
1.6	-11.8	21.2	62.9	49.2	97.0	128.5	227.4	359.0	379.0	..	Gross Domestic Saving
-27.5	-52.3	-31.0	-21.5	-19.8	5.9	-20.9	40.6	131.4	241.8	..	Gross National Saving
			(Billions of 1987 Malagasy Francs)								
2,546.00	2,489.50	2,500.90	2,497.30	2,535.00	2,576.70	2,557.00	2,645.80	2,726.20	2,897.60	..	Gross National Product
2,610.60	2,561.00	2,583.90	2,628.10	2,657.60	2,710.40	2,743.00	2,835.90	2,952.30	3,056.00	..	GDP at Market Prices
-335.70	-336.00	-277.10	-218.10	-239.50	-224.00	-148.40	-160.50	-50.30	-162.20	..	Resource Balance
412.30	382.20	335.10	353.10	341.50	335.10	433.00	411.70	527.10	530.60	..	Exports of Goods & NF Services
748.00	718.20	612.20	571.20	580.90	559.10	581.40	572.20	577.40	692.80	..	Imports of Goods & NF Services
2,946.20	2,897.00	2,861.00	2,846.20	2,897.10	2,934.40	2,891.40	2,996.40	3,002.60	3,218.20	..	Domestic Absorption
2,443.60	2,448.90	2,414.50	2,399.90	2,436.80	2,462.80	2,363.60	2,385.20	2,352.20	2,466.60	..	Private Consumption, etc.
240.90	233.60	234.40	223.50	235.30	233.80	250.50	240.00	261.50	262.60	..	General Gov't Consumption
261.70	214.40	212.10	222.80	225.00	237.70	277.20	371.20	388.90	489.10	..	Gross Domestic Investment
..	..	..	..	..	..	..	..	..	..	..	Fixed Investment
2,278.20	2,234.70	2,254.70	2,293.20	2,318.70	2,365.10	2,393.50	2,475.30	2,575.90	2,667.30	B	GDP at factor cost
737.10	766.70	786.40	811.00	820.90	846.60	866.00	886.90	933.30	947.00	..	Agriculture
300.80	257.70	261.20	293.30	301.30	312.70	328.00	334.10	337.20	358.50	..	Industry
..	..	..	..	..	..	..	..	..	..	..	Manufacturing
1,240.30	1,210.30	1,207.10	1,188.90	1,196.50	1,205.80	1,199.50	1,254.30	1,305.50	1,361.80	..	Services, etc.
											Memo Items:
377.20	390.10	369.10	416.10	383.80	402.30	433.00	405.70	463.60	441.90	..	Capacity to Import
-35.20	7.90	34.00	62.90	42.30	67.20	0.00	-6.00	-63.50	-88.70	..	Terms of Trade Adjustment
2,575.40	2,568.80	2,617.90	2,691.10	2,700.00	2,777.60	2,743.00	2,829.90	2,888.80	2,967.30	..	Gross Domestic Income
2,510.80	2,497.40	2,534.80	2,560.30	2,577.30	2,643.90	2,557.00	2,639.80	2,662.70	2,808.90	..	Gross National Income
			(Index 1987 = 100)								**DOMESTIC PRICES/DEFLATORS**
37.4	48.2	58.5	64.5	71.2	81.3	100.0	121.2	134.3	151.4	..	Overall (GDP)
36.9	46.6	56.5	62.5	69.2	78.6	100.0	122.4	137.9	156.3	..	Domestic Absorption
38.9	48.9	61.1	65.5	72.2	86.2	100.0	115.1	128.6	142.9	..	Agriculture
40.8	57.0	69.3	66.5	74.7	81.5	100.0	120.0	135.3	149.8	..	Industry
..	..	..	..	..	..	..	..	..	..	..	Manufacturing
39.8	52.4	62.5	68.7	76.0	87.0	100.0	126.9	138.3	154.6	..	Consumer Price Index
											MANUFACTURING ACTIVITY
..	..	..	..	..	..	..	..	..	..	J	Employment (1987=100)
..	..	..	..	..	..	..	..	..	..	J	Real Earnings per Empl. (1987=100)
..	..	..	..	..	..	..	..	..	..	J	Real Output per Empl. (1987=100)
49.1	48.2	40.2	35.5	40.0	..	..	..	..	..	J	Earnings as % of Value Added
			(Billions of current Malagasy Francs)								**MONETARY HOLDINGS**
267.0	299.8	293.2	363.3	419.3	511.0	625.4	760.2	984.8	819.6	D	Money Supply, Broadly Defined
193.8	208.0	192.7	239.9	238.6	289.6	371.8	455.0	598.4	574.5	..	Money
83.1	90.4	75.8	89.9	96.2	113.2	140.3	171.2	216.6	214.9	..	Currency Outside Banks
110.7	117.6	116.8	150.0	142.4	176.3	231.5	283.8	381.7	359.5	..	Demand Deposits
73.1	91.8	100.6	123.4	180.7	221.4	253.6	305.2	386.4	245.2	..	Quasi-Money
			(Millions of current Malagasy Francs)								
..	..	..	..	..	..	..	..	..	..		**GOVERNMENT DEFICIT (-) OR SURPLUS**
142,722	145,898	..	..	..	..	..	..	..	..		Current Revenue
..	..	..	..	..	..	..	..	..	..		Current Expenditure
..	..	..	..	..	..	..	..	..	..		Current Budget Balance
..	..	..	..	..	..	..	..	..	..		Capital Receipts
..	..	..	..	..	..	..	..	..	..		Capital Payments

MADAGASCAR	1970	1971	1972	1973	1974	1975	1976	1977	1978	1979	1980
FOREIGN TRADE (CUSTOMS BASIS)					*(Millions of current US dollars)*						
Value of Exports, fob	144.84	146.82	163.81	202.70	244.18	301.42	282.55	347.28	399.32	407.48	386.52
Nonfuel Primary Products	128.70	128.72	148.35	174.95	198.06	263.21	236.98	310.35	362.69	358.34	339.10
Fuels	5.60	5.29	6.54	10.33	23.55	25.89	23.46	13.22	9.62	19.13	23.05
Manufactures	10.54	12.80	8.92	17.43	22.57	12.32	22.11	23.71	27.01	30.01	24.36
Value of Imports, cif	170.40	213.21	202.24	202.93	281.03	366.93	289.93	352.96	460.09	698.44	676.47
Nonfuel Primary Products	25.67	37.28	34.11	43.84	69.90	63.53	48.62	61.26	90.30	130.71	83.80
Fuels	12.56	13.99	17.41	19.40	50.73	73.82	57.67	53.50	63.91	112.09	98.98
Manufactures	132.17	161.94	150.72	139.69	160.40	229.58	183.65	238.19	305.87	455.63	493.69
					(Index 1987 = 100)						
Terms of Trade	118.5	105.5	113.2	114.3	91.5	87.2	121.4	150.0	117.7	112.8	94.9
Export Prices, fob	32.0	33.3	36.2	46.9	62.0	57.7	81.5	112.5	99.5	112.7	111.9
Import Prices, cif	27.0	31.5	32.0	41.1	67.8	66.2	67.1	75.0	84.6	99.9	117.9
BALANCE OF PAYMENTS					*(Millions of current US dollars)*						
Exports of Goods & Services	196.00	205.61	228.00	243.19	287.66	386.96	333.59	387.54	444.40	490.08	518.37
Merchandise, fob	145.00	147.44	166.11	200.28	240.17	319.53	289.02	350.66	405.00	413.78	436.44
Nonfactor Services	49.00	55.16	57.54	36.96	40.17	62.01	40.93	34.76	34.88	73.90	79.47
Factor Services	2.00	3.01	4.34	5.96	7.31	5.41	3.64	2.12	4.52	2.40	2.46
Imports of Goods & Services	213.00	260.77	248.63	287.30	370.87	502.16	413.94	455.92	584.87	958.58	1,121.41
Merchandise, fob	142.00	177.53	168.29	177.63	238.34	331.81	261.77	311.75	404.24	662.42	764.44
Nonfactor Services	64.00	71.21	71.66	95.37	107.39	148.06	131.66	135.38	167.65	265.09	310.63
Factor Services	7.00	12.04	8.69	14.31	25.13	22.30	20.51	8.79	12.98	31.07	46.34
Long-Term Interest	2.00	2.40	2.20	3.40	3.50	4.10	4.60	5.40	7.60	16.30	26.70
Private Current Transfers, net	-25.00	-24.07	-30.40	-22.65	-8.85	-24.50	-17.79	-18.60	-15.11	-16.97	-20.45
Workers' Remittances	..	..	..	..	..	..	..	0.33	0.35	..	0.38
Curr. A/C Bal before Off. Transf.	-42.00	-79.24	-51.03	-66.76	-92.06	-139.70	-98.14	-86.98	-155.59	-485.47	-623.49
Net Official Transfers	52.00	52.15	85.77	56.03	52.43	84.08	70.01	70.99	75.69	58.81	66.78
Curr. A/C Bal after Off. Transf.	10.00	-27.08	34.74	-10.73	-39.63	-55.62	-28.12	-16.00	-79.90	-426.66	-556.71
Long-Term Capital, net	15.00	7.02	-8.69	27.42	24.30	30.66	17.07	22.67	16.71	225.51	374.86
Direct Investment	10.00	-2.01	11.94	10.73	13.71	4.57	1.38	-2.77	-3.68	-6.58	..
Long-Term Loans	5.20	8.50	10.70	20.80	15.40	31.70	17.80	36.60	43.00	314.00	344.80
Disbursements	10.50	14.30	16.20	30.00	22.20	39.40	25.90	45.00	54.00	330.90	375.60
Repayments	5.30	5.80	5.50	9.20	6.80	7.70	8.10	8.40	11.00	16.90	30.80
Other Long-Term Capital	-0.20	0.53	-31.33	-4.11	-4.81	-5.62	-2.11	-11.16	-22.61	-81.91	30.06
Other Capital, net	-10.25	20.06	-23.89	-5.96	-21.54	1.86	21.29	-14.56	65.73	70.40	325.15
Change in Reserves	-14.75	0.00	-2.17	-10.73	36.87	23.11	-10.25	7.88	-2.53	130.75	-143.30
Memo Item:					*(Malagasy Francs per US dollar)*						
Conversion Factor (Annual Avg)	277.700	277.100	252.500	222.900	240.700	214.300	238.900	245.700	225.700	212.700	211.300
					(Millions of US dollars), outstanding at end of year						
EXTERNAL DEBT (Total)	89	103	90	118	143	184	200	291	361	788	1,257
Long-Term Debt (by debtor)	89	103	90	118	143	184	200	245	316	625	1,013
Central Bank, incl. IMF credit	0	1	1	1	5	18	18	20	33	28	91
Central Government	59	70	51	73	91	122	141	166	196	396	594
Rest of General Government	3	2	2	1	1	1	0	0	0	0	0
Non-financial Public Enterprises	17	19	25	31	35	35	33	50	78	185	309
Priv. Sector, incl non-guaranteed	10	11	12	13	11	10	8	9	9	16	18
Short-Term Debt	0	0	0	0	0	0	0	46	45	163	244
Memo Items:					*(Millions of US dollars)*						
Int'l Reserves Excluding Gold	37.1	46.4	52.2	67.9	49.4	35.6	42.2	68.9	59.2	5.0	9.1
Gold Holdings (at market price)	..	..	..	..	..	..	..	..	..	..	..
SOCIAL INDICATORS											
Total Fertility Rate	6.6	6.6	6.6	6.6	6.6	6.6	6.6	6.6	6.6	6.5	6.5
Infant Mortality Rate	181.2	176.6	172.0	167.6	163.2	158.8	154.4	150.0	146.0	142.0	138.0
Life Expectancy at Birth	45.4	45.9	46.5	47.1	47.7	48.3	48.9	49.5	49.6	49.7	49.7
Urban Population, % of total	14.1	14.5	14.9	15.3	15.7	16.1	16.5	17.0	17.4	17.9	18.3
Food Prod. per capita (1987=100)	125.9	119.3	117.0	113.8	126.6	117.7	120.1	113.7	108.9	105.9	112.4
Labor Force, Agriculture (%)	83.7	83.4	83.1	82.8	82.6	82.3	82.0	81.7	81.4	81.1	80.9
Labor Force, Female (%)	41.6	41.6	41.5	41.5	41.5	41.5	41.4	41.4	41.4	41.3	41.3
Primary Schl. Enroll. Ratio	90.0	..	..	..	..	95.0	..	..	100.0	..	142.0
Primary Schl. Enroll. Ratio, Female	82.0	..	..	..	..	88.0	..	..	..	..	139.0
Secondary Schl. Enroll. Ratio	12.0	..	..	..	..	12.0	..	..	..	..	..

1981	1982	1983	1984	1985	1986	1987	1988	1989	1990 estimate	Notes	MADAGASCAR
				(Millions of current US dollars)							**FOREIGN TRADE (CUSTOMS BASIS)**
324.35	329.46	310.30	339.90	286.74	316.64	331.10	273.70	304.70	334.60	..	Value of Exports, fob
274.23	280.14	266.14	299.81	245.88	284.55	297.54	245.96	273.82	300.69	..	Nonfuel Primary Products
25.50	25.37	20.69	7.98	11.32	7.00	7.32	6.05	6.73	7.39	..	Fuels
24.62	23.96	23.48	32.11	29.54	25.09	26.24	21.69	24.15	26.52	..	Manufactures
473.03	438.96	411.46	412.15	465.12	373.64	302.10	363.90	450.00	480.00	..	Value of Imports, cif
82.77	83.97	95.99	63.82	71.23	66.10	70.48	84.90	104.99	111.99	..	Nonfuel Primary Products
50.56	106.35	78.76	113.90	91.54	83.21	57.82	69.65	86.13	91.87	..	Fuels
339.70	248.64	236.71	234.44	302.35	224.34	173.80	209.35	258.88	276.14	..	Manufactures
				(Index 1987 = 100)							
82.4	88.6	89.8	94.2	98.3	131.8	100.0	120.0	108.1	102.4	..	Terms of Trade
98.9	100.3	98.4	103.0	105.4	120.5	100.0	111.7	99.8	104.5	..	Export Prices, fob
120.0	113.2	109.5	109.3	107.2	91.4	100.0	93.1	92.3	102.1	..	Import Prices, cif
				(Millions of current US dollars)							**BALANCE OF PAYMENTS**
397.45	382.06	358.02	395.48	354.26	403.36	431.76	416.20	459.24	488.90	..	Exports of Goods & Services
331.91	327.22	309.93	337.14	291.28	322.99	326.50	284.50	313.37	304.10	..	Merchandise, fob
61.53	49.32	45.21	53.31	58.60	75.08	95.95	118.40	127.54	170.00	..	Nonfactor Services
4.01	5.52	2.88	5.03	4.38	5.29	9.31	13.30	18.33	14.80	..	Factor Services
827.18	752.39	671.51	666.47	636.17	696.67	725.67	761.34	789.24	880.80	..	Imports of Goods & Services
510.80	451.54	378.26	360.12	335.76	331.08	315.25	318.64	314.13	461.30	..	Merchandise, fob
224.05	200.07	172.24	155.30	167.21	205.21	226.29	249.97	257.48	285.10	..	Nonfactor Services
92.34	100.79	121.01	151.06	133.21	160.38	184.14	192.72	217.63	134.40	..	Factor Services
32.20	44.60	29.30	33.10	53.60	59.40	100.90	75.70	112.70	93.30	..	Long-Term Interest
-15.57	-17.01	-8.87	-0.71	24.15	20.54	34.25	37.76	47.04	68.10	..	Private Current Transfers, net
0.22	0.11	0.12	5.64	4.57	4.23	3.36	3.23	3.33	..	..	Workers' Remittances
-445.30	-387.34	-322.36	-271.70	-257.76	-272.77	-259.67	-307.38	-282.97	-323.80	..	Curr. A/C Bal before Off. Transf.
82.25	87.89	75.27	78.30	74.10	131.63	119.87	158.05	155.20	170.80	..	Net Official Transfers
-363.05	-299.45	-247.09	-193.40	-183.66	-141.13	-139.79	-149.33	-127.76	-153.00	..	Curr. A/C Bal after Off. Transf.
280.28	121.32	179.36	188.47	150.37	223.50	240.25	208.84	218.91	90.50	..	Long-Term Capital, net
..	..	..	..	..	..	..	..	6.41	22.40	..	Direct Investment
251.60	222.00	192.50	121.40	123.70	146.20	242.00	178.20	185.30	115.80	..	Long-Term Loans
285.20	254.40	212.60	133.50	169.80	191.20	286.80	249.50	250.40	185.40	..	Disbursements
33.60	32.40	20.10	12.10	46.10	45.00	44.80	71.30	65.10	69.60	..	Repayments
28.68	-100.68	-13.14	67.07	26.67	77.30	-1.75	30.64	27.20	-47.70	..	Other Long-Term Capital
51.66	132.71	47.09	27.76	9.40	-26.98	-58.42	11.30	-54.31	101.08	..	Other Capital, net
31.11	45.42	20.64	-22.82	23.89	-55.38	-42.03	-70.81	-36.84	-38.58	..	Change in Reserves
				(Malagasy Francs per US dollar)							**Memo Item:**
271.700	349.700	430.400	576.600	662.500	676.300	1,069.200	1,407.100	1,603.400	1,494.100	..	Conversion Factor (Annual Avg)
				(Millions of US dollars), outstanding at end of year							
1,613	1,924	2,100	2,190	2,490	3,032	3,695	3,671	3,638	3,938	..	**EXTERNAL DEBT (Total)**
1,523	1,822	1,919	2,040	2,371	2,870	3,504	3,500	3,527	3,821	..	Long-Term Debt (by debtor)
259	351	300	631	820	1,038	1,329	1,249	1,155	1,135	..	Central Bank, incl. IMF credit
774	899	1,023	993	1,083	1,282	1,558	1,648	1,809	2,122	..	Central Government
1	0	0	0	0	0	0	0	0	0	..	Rest of General Government
366	469	503	384	426	493	550	542	486	444	..	Non-financial Public Enterprises
124	103	93	31	42	56	67	62	77	119	..	Priv. Sector, incl non-guaranteed
90	101	181	150	119	162	191	170	111	118	..	Short-Term Debt
				(Millions of US dollars)							**Memo Items:**
26.5	20.0	29.2	58.9	48.4	114.5	185.2	223.7	245.3	92.1	..	Int'l Reserves Excluding Gold
..	..	..	..	..	..	..	..	..	..	..	Gold Holdings (at market price)
											SOCIAL INDICATORS
6.5	6.5	6.5	6.5	6.5	6.5	6.5	6.4	6.4	6.3	..	Total Fertility Rate
134.0	130.0	128.0	126.0	124.0	122.0	120.0	118.6	117.2	115.7	..	Infant Mortality Rate
49.8	49.9	50.0	50.1	50.1	50.2	50.3	50.5	50.7	51.0	..	Life Expectancy at Birth
18.8	19.3	19.9	20.4	20.9	21.9	23.0	23.7	24.3	25.0	..	Urban Population, % of total
108.5	106.1	106.5	107.0	104.5	103.1	100.0	97.2	96.3	94.6	..	Food Prod. per capita (1987=100)
..	..	..	..	..	..	..	..	..	..	..	Labor Force, Agriculture (%)
41.1	40.9	40.7	40.5	40.4	40.1	39.9	39.7	39.5	39.3	..	Labor Force, Female (%)
..	136.0	128.0	118.0	..	..	97.0	97.0	92.0	..	..	Primary Schl. Enroll. Ratio
..	127.0	122.0	114.0	..	..	94.0	94.0	90.0	..	..	Primary Schl. Enroll. Ratio, Female
..	..	37.0	34.0	..	..	21.0	19.0	19.0	..	..	Secondary Schl. Enroll. Ratio

MALAWI	1970	1971	1972	1973	1974	1975	1976	1977	1978	1979	1980
CURRENT GNP PER CAPITA (US $)	60	80	80	90	110	120	120	130	160	170	180
POPULATION (thousands)	4,518	4,652	4,792	4,938	5,089	5,244	5,402	5,563	5,729	5,904	6,091

USE AND ORIGIN OF RESOURCES					(Millions of current Malawi Kwacha)						
Gross National Product (GNP)	236.1	300.3	321.8	364.8	473.9	537.7	594.0	705.0	796.7	829.7	924.0
Net Factor Income from Abroad	-6.0	-3.3	-3.7	0.8	12.4	8.0	-18.0	-23.0	-4.0	-34.8	-81.1
GDP at Market Prices	242.1	303.6	325.5	364.0	461.5	529.7	612.0	728.0	800.7	864.5	1,005.1
Resource Balance	-36.1	-36.5	-47.7	-36.2	-50.5	-88.8	-51.6	-33.7	-143.5	-152.5	-140.3
Exports of Goods & NF Services	58.7	71.2	75.8	100.6	129.3	154.3	186.3	218.4	185.7	200.5	249.7
Imports of Goods & NF Services	94.8	107.7	123.5	136.8	179.8	243.1	237.9	252.1	329.2	353.0	390.0
Domestic Absorption	278.2	340.1	373.2	400.2	512.0	618.5	663.6	761.7	944.2	1,017.0	1,145.4
Private Consumption, etc.	176.3	236.9	248.6	270.0	320.2	365.2	416.6	483.4	502.2	591.6	702.8
General Gov't Consumption	39.6	45.0	45.2	48.7	65.7	74.7	86.3	98.6	134.2	164.0	193.9
Gross Domestic Investment	62.3	58.2	79.4	81.5	126.1	178.6	160.7	179.7	307.8	261.4	248.7
Fixed Investment	..	..	..	74.3	87.3	131.8	135.3	161.6	247.1	231.9	223.1
Indirect Taxes, net	16.5	21.4	22.2	23.2	28.2	35.0	33.7	44.1	58.2	77.7	103.5
GDP at factor cost	225.6	282.2	303.3	340.8	433.3	494.7	578.3	683.9	742.5	786.8	901.6
Agriculture	99.2	125.1	138.4	141.7	178.4	184.2	226.7	285.8	294.9	311.9	335.3
Industry	39.4	44.6	52.9	57.3	73.9	100.6	107.1	127.6	143.5	148.1	172.8
Manufacturing	..	..	..	..	..	64.9	68.8	80.3	84.8	90.8	104.8
Services, etc.	87.0	112.5	112.0	141.8	181.0	209.9	244.5	270.5	304.1	326.8	393.5
Gross Domestic Saving	26.2	21.7	31.7	45.3	75.6	89.8	109.1	146.0	164.3	108.9	108.4
Gross National Saving	18.4	18.7	28.4	47.8	89.3	100.0	91.6	122.5	166.7	79.9	38.1

					(Millions of 1987 Malawi Kwacha)						
Gross National Product	1,236.8	1,460.4	1,548.4	1,606.4	1,767.2	1,852.8	1,847.9	1,936.5	2,193.8	2,212.8	2,130.9
GDP at Market Prices	1,270.4	1,478.8	1,568.3	1,606.0	1,720.2	1,826.5	1,913.8	2,010.5	2,210.7	2,311.0	2,322.9
Resource Balance	-654.0	-669.5	-714.5	-461.0	-521.0	-713.2	-538.6	-454.4	-824.7	-555.5	-541.2
Exports of Goods & NF Services	345.1	378.5	421.1	376.6	409.2	449.2	495.3	512.1	434.4	481.0	640.3
Imports of Goods & NF Services	999.0	1,048.0	1,135.6	837.6	930.2	1,162.3	1,033.8	966.5	1,259.1	1,036.5	1,181.5
Domestic Absorption	1,924.4	2,148.2	2,282.7	2,067.0	2,241.2	2,539.7	2,452.4	2,464.9	3,035.3	2,866.5	2,864.1
Private Consumption, etc.	1,119.3	1,423.7	1,397.6	1,411.3	1,411.1	1,500.9	1,557.7	1,578.1	1,592.2	1,694.6	1,796.6
General Gov't Consumption	157.3	165.6	164.8	162.5	185.5	194.8	204.6	206.1	280.0	314.8	327.9
Gross Domestic Investment	647.7	558.9	720.3	493.2	644.7	843.9	690.1	680.6	1,163.2	857.1	739.6
Fixed Investment	..	..	..	475.7	472.5	659.4	616.2	648.2	988.3	792.2	696.2
GDP at factor cost	1,158.6	1,345.7	1,429.8	1,471.3	1,580.8	1,668.2	1,772.0	1,848.9	2,002.6	2,069.3	2,061.4
Agriculture	502.5	587.2	643.6	603.1	615.5	621.2	694.8	772.8	795.4	820.2	766.6
Industry	219.0	230.3	270.8	267.6	288.3	339.0	328.3	345.0	387.1	389.5	395.1
Manufacturing	..	..	..	..	..	218.5	210.4	218.5	229.3	240.1	239.5
Services, etc.	437.0	528.1	515.4	600.6	676.9	708.0	749.0	731.2	820.2	859.5	899.7

Memo Items:											
Capacity to Import	618.6	692.8	697.0	616.0	668.9	737.8	809.6	837.3	710.3	588.7	756.4
Terms of Trade Adjustment	273.5	314.3	275.9	239.3	259.8	288.6	314.3	325.2	275.8	107.7	116.1
Gross Domestic Income	1,543.9	1,793.1	1,844.1	1,845.3	1,980.0	2,115.1	2,228.2	2,335.7	2,486.5	2,418.7	2,439.1
Gross National Income	1,510.3	1,774.6	1,824.3	1,845.7	2,027.0	2,141.4	2,162.3	2,261.7	2,469.6	2,320.6	2,247.0

DOMESTIC PRICES/DEFLATORS					(Index 1987 = 100)						
Overall (GDP)	19.1	20.5	20.8	22.7	26.8	29.0	32.0	36.2	36.2	37.4	43.3
Domestic Absorption	14.5	15.8	16.3	19.4	22.8	24.4	27.1	30.9	31.1	35.5	40.0
Agriculture	19.7	21.3	21.5	23.5	29.0	29.7	32.6	37.0	37.1	38.0	43.7
Industry	18.0	19.4	19.5	21.4	25.6	29.7	32.6	37.0	37.1	38.0	43.7
Manufacturing	..	..	..	..	..	29.7	32.7	36.8	37.0	37.8	43.8
Consumer Price Index	..	..	..	..	..	..	..	..	..	..	37.9

MANUFACTURING ACTIVITY											
Employment (1987=100)	..	..	..	..	..	..	..	..	..	..	..
Real Earnings per Empl. (1987=100)	..	..	..	..	..	..	..	..	..	..	..
Real Output per Empl. (1987=100)	..	..	..	..	..	..	..	..	..	..	..
Earnings as % of Value Added	36.5	35.0	37.1	41.0	40.4	40.0	..	..	..	43.3	33.1

MONETARY HOLDINGS					(Millions of current Malawi Kwacha)						
Money Supply, Broadly Defined	56.0	66.9	74.3	98.8	133.4	139.1	137.4	178.2	190.2	192.9	219.0
Money	32.7	38.8	40.6	55.1	73.4	73.6	72.8	100.1	93.8	90.6	97.2
Currency Outside Banks	13.3	14.8	17.3	21.3	28.3	27.8	23.1	24.6	29.8	32.3	35.3
Demand Deposits	19.4	24.0	23.3	33.8	45.1	45.8	49.7	75.5	64.0	58.3	61.9
Quasi-Money	23.3	28.1	33.7	43.7	60.0	65.5	64.6	78.2	96.4	102.4	121.8

GOVERNMENT DEFICIT (-) OR SURPLUS					(Millions of current Malawi Kwacha)						
	..	-24.9	-20.0	-20.6	-29.5	-48.6	-37.6	-45.2	-74.3	-75.5	-160.3
Current Revenue	..	51.0	55.0	62.2	72.7	93.4	97.4	125.3	169.0	211.2	235.5
Current Expenditure	..	52.0	56.8	57.9	67.4	79.0	84.5	97.7	139.1	148.9	180.9
Current Budget Balance	..	-1.1	-1.8	4.3	5.2	14.4	12.9	27.6	29.9	62.3	54.6
Capital Receipts	..	0.2	0.3	0.3	0.3	0.3	0.3	0.3	0.3	0.4	0.6
Capital Payments	..	24.1	18.5	25.2	35.0	63.2	50.8	73.1	104.6	138.2	215.5

1981	1982	1983	1984	1985	1986	1987	1988	1989	1990 estimate	Notes	MALAWI
180	190	180	180	170	160	150	160	170	200	..	**CURRENT GNP PER CAPITA (US $)**
6,292	6,502	6,722	6,950	7,188	7,434	7,688	7,952	8,225	8,507	..	**POPULATION (thousands)**
				(Millions of current Malawi Kwacha)							**USE AND ORIGIN OF RESOURCES**
1,033.8	1,171.6	1,361.6	1,628.6	1,854.0	2,084.7	2,488.3	3,280.9	4,250.4	4,920.3	..	Gross National Product (GNP)
-74.3	-74.0	-75.4	-78.8	-90.9	-112.9	-125.7	-137.0	-137.6	-155.7	..	Net Factor Income from Abroad
1,108.1	1,245.6	1,437.0	1,707.4	1,944.9	2,197.6	2,614.0	3,417.9	4,388.0	5,076.0	..	GDP at Market Prices
-64.6	-78.8	-108.8	33.4	-111.0	-47.1	-61.6	-325.9	-690.6	-474.2	..	Resource Balance
284.4	280.2	298.2	484.4	470.5	504.7	665.1	824.3	824.1	1,235.5	..	Exports of Goods & NF Services
349.0	359.0	407.0	451.0	581.5	551.8	726.7	1,150.2	1,514.7	1,709.7	..	Imports of Goods & NF Services
1,172.7	1,324.4	1,545.8	1,674.0	2,055.9	2,244.7	2,675.6	3,743.8	5,078.6	5,550.2	..	Domestic Absorption
779.4	839.8	982.3	1,186.1	1,350.3	1,541.5	1,774.3	2,548.0	3,473.7	3,795.8	..	Private Consumption, etc.
198.0	218.0	235.9	268.0	344.0	433.8	499.2	555.3	716.3	784.4	..	General Gov't Consumption
195.3	266.6	327.6	219.9	361.6	269.4	402.1	640.5	888.6	970.0	..	Gross Domestic Investment
167.8	181.7	197.3	222.7	259.5	264.1	352.9	524.0	699.6	820.0	..	Fixed Investment
107.8	116.1	139.6	178.1	216.0	216.4	268.3	350.3	468.5	542.9	..	Indirect Taxes, net
1,000.3	1,129.5	1,297.4	1,529.3	1,728.9	1,981.2	2,345.7	3,067.6	3,919.5	4,533.1	..	GDP at factor cost
360.3	420.8	487.7	581.8	632.9	721.8	842.9	1,088.6	1,369.4	1,511.2	..	Agriculture
196.4	215.9	247.3	277.9	323.4	360.1	423.2	575.2	763.9	927.5	..	Industry
127.1	139.0	165.2	191.2	213.3	247.1	288.9	377.8	503.1	617.9	..	Manufacturing
443.6	492.8	562.4	669.6	772.6	899.3	1,079.6	1,403.8	1,786.2	2,094.4	..	Services, etc.
130.7	187.8	218.8	253.3	250.6	222.3	340.5	314.6	198.0	495.8	..	Gross Domestic Saving
67.1	126.3	153.1	190.8	178.8	133.8	245.3	216.2	326.1	536.6	..	Gross National Saving
				(Millions of 1987 Malawi Kwacha)							
2,040.6	2,107.7	2,206.0	2,347.8	2,458.4	2,436.2	2,488.3	2,584.1	2,739.9	2,869.9	..	Gross National Product
2,200.4	2,254.6	2,339.1	2,470.6	2,584.0	2,569.5	2,614.0	2,689.0	2,829.6	2,961.8	I	GDP at Market Prices
-391.5	-401.5	-401.5	-183.1	-331.6	-90.5	-61.6	-197.4	-485.4	-358.0	..	Resource Balance
525.7	473.3	488.9	649.2	681.9	657.6	665.1	678.4	577.1	732.0	..	Exports of Goods & NF Services
917.2	874.7	890.4	832.3	1,013.6	748.1	726.7	875.9	1,062.5	1,090.0	..	Imports of Goods & NF Services
2,591.9	2,656.0	2,740.6	2,653.7	2,915.6	2,660.0	2,675.6	2,886.5	3,314.9	3,319.8	..	Domestic Absorption
1,757.0	1,689.3	1,704.4	1,903.2	1,932.9	1,921.5	1,774.3	1,882.9	2,197.8	2,214.4	..	Private Consumption, etc.
314.2	321.3	320.0	346.1	386.8	424.1	499.2	491.9	509.4	517.3	..	General Gov't Consumption
520.8	645.5	716.1	404.4	596.0	314.4	402.1	511.7	607.7	588.0	..	Gross Domestic Investment
472.1	460.1	448.1	434.1	432.1	323.7	352.9	405.3	462.9	492.9	..	Fixed Investment
1,953.5	2,009.6	2,080.3	2,172.8	2,269.4	2,294.2	2,345.7	2,422.8	2,521.3	2,641.6	..	GDP at factor cost
703.7	748.8	781.9	827.3	830.8	835.9	842.9	859.6	880.9	880.7	..	Agriculture
383.6	384.1	396.5	395.1	424.5	417.0	423.2	454.2	491.4	540.5	..	Industry
248.2	247.4	264.9	271.6	280.0	286.2	288.9	298.3	323.7	360.1	..	Manufacturing
866.3	876.8	901.9	950.4	1,014.1	1,041.3	1,079.6	1,109.0	1,148.9	1,220.4	..	Services, etc.
											Memo Items:
747.4	682.7	652.4	893.9	820.1	684.3	665.1	627.7	578.1	787.7	..	Capacity to Import
221.7	209.5	163.4	244.7	138.1	26.6	0.0	-50.7	0.9	55.7	..	Terms of Trade Adjustment
2,422.2	2,464.0	2,502.6	2,715.3	2,722.1	2,596.1	2,614.0	2,638.3	2,830.5	3,017.5	..	Gross Domestic Income
2,262.4	2,317.1	2,369.5	2,592.5	2,596.5	2,462.9	2,488.3	2,533.3	2,740.8	2,925.6	..	Gross National Income
				(Index 1987 = 100)							**DOMESTIC PRICES/DEFLATORS**
50.4	55.2	61.4	69.1	75.3	85.5	100.0	127.1	155.1	171.4	..	Overall (GDP)
45.2	49.9	56.4	63.1	70.5	84.4	100.0	129.7	153.2	167.2	..	Domestic Absorption
51.2	56.2	62.4	70.3	76.2	86.4	100.0	126.6	155.4	171.6	..	Agriculture
51.2	56.2	62.4	70.3	76.2	86.4	100.0	126.6	155.4	171.6	..	Industry
51.2	56.2	62.4	70.4	76.2	86.3	100.0	126.6	155.4	171.6	..	Manufacturing
42.4	46.5	52.8	63.4	70.0	79.9	100.0	133.9	150.6	168.3	..	Consumer Price Index
											MANUFACTURING ACTIVITY
..	..	..	..	..	..	..	..	..	..	G	Employment (1987=100)
..	..	..	..	..	..	..	..	..	..	G	Real Earnings per Empl. (1987=100)
..	..	..	..	..	..	..	..	..	..	G	Real Output per Empl. (1987=100)
34.0	41.7	35.8	25.9	35.4							Earnings as % of Value Added
				(Millions of current Malawi Kwacha)							**MONETARY HOLDINGS**
273.2	317.5	348.0	453.6	407.7	580.7	781.6	862.3	862.0	1,033.6	D	Money Supply, Broadly Defined
114.8	130.8	127.8	154.3	166.9	220.8	298.0	435.9	452.7	482.1	..	Money
39.4	49.5	50.0	56.9	66.0	79.3	107.6	134.6	156.6	159.4	..	Currency Outside Banks
75.4	81.3	77.7	97.4	100.9	141.5	190.4	301.3	296.1	322.7	..	Demand Deposits
158.5	186.6	220.3	299.4	240.8	359.9	483.6	426.3	409.0	551.5	..	Quasi-Money
				(Millions of current Malawi Kwacha)							**GOVERNMENT DEFICIT (-) OR SURPLUS**
-137.7	-95.0	-101.8	-88.3	-162.6	-217.7	-226.1	-204.7	-80.5	..	C	
257.2	271.6	310.7	380.4	460.9	530.9	626.5	804.7	1,099.5	..	..	Current Revenue
263.9	256.2	293.4	320.2	422.5	534.9	667.0	745.2	990.4	..	..	Current Expenditure
-6.7	15.4	17.3	60.1	38.4	-4.1	-40.6	59.5	109.2	..	..	Current Budget Balance
0.4	0.1	0.2	0.4	0.4	0.5	..	0.5	15.7	..	..	Capital Receipts
131.4	110.6	119.3	148.9	201.4	214.2	185.5	264.7	205.3	..	..	Capital Payments

MALAWI	1970	1971	1972	1973	1974	1975	1976	1977	1978	1979	1980
FOREIGN TRADE (CUSTOMS BASIS)					*(Millions of current US dollars)*						
Value of Exports, fob	48.41	60.26	68.88	85.48	106.67	121.09	153.98	190.76	177.09	216.17	269.47
Nonfuel Primary Products	46.60	58.58	67.03	82.62	101.43	114.67	148.05	183.30	169.66	207.68	251.37
Fuels	0.03	0.03	0.04	0.05	0.04	0.04	0.05	0.05	0.07	0.06	0.06
Manufactures	1.78	1.65	1.80	2.81	5.20	6.38	5.88	7.41	7.36	8.43	18.05
Value of Imports, cif	85.62	109.03	129.96	142.16	187.64	250.49	205.60	232.38	338.23	397.59	440.23
Nonfuel Primary Products	17.38	15.92	18.59	24.40	28.41	29.58	26.08	24.43	23.48	33.57	43.69
Fuels	4.71	10.15	11.58	12.71	19.54	24.91	27.78	30.21	40.28	57.96	67.47
Manufactures	63.53	82.95	99.79	105.05	139.69	195.99	151.73	177.74	274.48	306.06	329.08
					(Index 1987 = 100)						
Terms of Trade	181.9	203.4	192.2	186.1	178.4	166.1	152.0	168.9	146.8	144.8	150.6
Export Prices, fob	42.0	45.2	47.8	58.9	91.0	90.8	82.7	100.2	97.3	112.7	138.0
Import Prices, cif	23.1	22.2	24.9	31.7	51.0	54.7	54.4	59.3	66.3	77.9	91.6
BALANCE OF PAYMENTS					*(Millions of current US dollars)*						
Exports of Goods & Services	82.30	100.80	111.83	145.68	185.09	212.60	196.15	..	211.20	258.55	314.74
Merchandise, fob	58.90	71.71	78.61	97.87	119.30	138.66	165.33	199.79	184.53	222.43	280.75
Nonfactor Services	11.50	13.94	15.96	22.29	28.26	35.33	23.44	13.40	25.60	34.77	31.77
Factor Services	11.90	15.14	17.26	25.51	37.52	38.61	7.39	..	1.07	1.35	2.22
Imports of Goods & Services	126.20	142.02	169.59	184.90	228.86	301.59	266.00	..	432.71	577.93	637.86
Merchandise, fob	82.80	93.08	111.50	123.39	166.09	224.98	182.65	182.96	263.94	317.55	307.97
Nonfactor Services	31.00	36.51	42.56	45.42	46.30	59.25	66.15	117.51	119.35	133.19	178.55
Factor Services	12.40	12.44	15.53	16.09	16.48	17.36	17.20	..	49.42	127.19	151.34
Long-Term Interest	3.50	3.80	4.10	6.00	7.70	8.50	8.80	7.20	16.60	24.20	34.50
Private Current Transfers, net	-2.10	0.40	0.54	2.03	1.56	2.55	0.58	-0.55	7.59	7.10	13.30
Workers' Remittances	..	..	..	..	..	..	..	..	..	..	..
Curr. A/C Bal before Off. Transf.	-46.00	-40.82	-57.22	-37.19	-42.21	-86.45	-69.27	-87.83	-213.93	-312.29	-309.82
Net Official Transfers	11.20	7.72	8.14	9.42	6.49	6.80	26.55	26.03	38.87	46.64	50.19
Curr. A/C Bal after Off. Transf.	-34.80	-33.10	-49.07	-27.78	-35.72	-79.65	-42.72	-61.80	-175.05	-265.65	-259.63
Long-Term Capital, net	35.50	32.10	38.11	48.52	69.51	57.19	46.76	57.70	96.12	98.79	180.89
Direct Investment	8.60	9.63	10.10	7.75	22.73	8.62	9.70	5.54	9.13	-1.22	9.48
Long-Term Loans	36.70	24.80	30.30	27.80	25.40	52.00	48.80	83.40	109.90	97.30	120.20
Disbursements	39.60	28.40	34.70	32.70	32.10	60.60	57.80	97.90	129.80	117.00	153.40
Repayments	2.90	3.60	4.40	4.90	6.70	8.60	9.00	14.50	19.90	19.70	33.20
Other Long-Term Capital	-9.80	-2.33	-2.29	12.97	21.38	-3.43	-11.74	-31.24	-22.91	2.71	51.21
Other Capital, net	5.60	-0.40	13.48	13.20	-19.25	4.06	-40.07	55.53	71.97	89.62	62.01
Change in Reserves	-6.30	1.40	-2.52	-33.94	-14.54	18.40	36.03	-51.43	6.96	77.23	16.72
Memo Item:					*(Malawi Kwacha per US dollar)*						
Conversion Factor (Annual Avg)	0.830	0.830	0.800	0.820	0.840	0.860	0.910	0.900	0.840	0.820	0.810
					(Millions of US dollars), outstanding at end of year						
EXTERNAL DEBT (Total)	122.5	140.7	164.5	201.8	229.7	259.9	299.0	448.9	586.1	660.6	820.8
Long-Term Debt (by debtor)	122.5	140.7	164.5	201.8	229.7	259.9	299.0	379.9	511.1	545.6	704.7
Central Bank, incl. IMF credit	0.0	0.0	0.0	0.0	0.0	14.2	37.0	47.7	55.7	83.9	105.7
Central Government	107.4	124.9	144.7	176.0	197.4	216.1	233.8	266.2	347.2	325.1	414.1
Rest of General Government	..	..	..	..	..	..	..	..	..	..	..
Non-financial Public Enterprises	15.1	15.8	19.8	25.8	31.8	29.2	27.1	46.2	68.6	92.3	131.8
Priv. Sector, incl non-guaranteed	0.0	0.0	0.0	0.0	0.5	0.4	1.1	19.8	39.6	44.3	53.1
Short-Term Debt	0.0	0.0	0.0	0.0	0.0	0.0	0.0	69.0	75.0	115.0	116.1
Memo Items:					*(Millions of US dollars)*						
Int'l Reserves Excluding Gold	29.2	31.9	36.2	66.6	81.8	61.5	26.2	87.5	74.8	69.5	68.4
Gold Holdings (at market price)	..	..	..	..	..	..	..	1.1	2.2	6.6	7.6
SOCIAL INDICATORS											
Total Fertility Rate	7.8	7.8	7.8	7.7	7.7	7.7	7.6	7.6	7.6	7.6	7.6
Infant Mortality Rate	193.4	192.2	191.0	188.2	185.4	182.6	179.8	177.0	174.2	171.4	168.6
Life Expectancy at Birth	40.4	40.7	41.0	41.4	41.8	42.2	42.6	43.0	43.4	43.8	44.2
Urban Population, % of total	6.0	6.3	6.7	7.0	7.4	7.7	8.0	8.3	8.5	8.8	9.1
Food Prod. per capita (1987=100)	112.8	136.1	136.6	138.2	132.2	121.5	128.0	133.7	131.4	124.8	119.4
Labor Force, Agriculture (%)	90.5	89.8	89.0	88.3	87.6	87.0	86.2	85.4	84.7	84.0	83.3
Labor Force, Female (%)	45.3	45.2	45.0	44.9	44.8	44.7	44.5	44.3	44.2	44.0	43.9
Primary Schl. Enroll. Ratio	..	..	..	..	..	..	56.0	55.0	55.0	59.0	60.0
Primary Schl. Enroll. Ratio, Female	..	..	..	..	..	..	44.0	44.0	45.0	48.0	48.0
Secondary Schl. Enroll. Ratio	..	..	..	..	..	..	4.0	4.0	4.0	4.0	3.0

1981	1982	1983	1984	1985	1986	1987	1988	1989	1990 estimate	Notes	MALAWI
				(Millions of current US dollars)							**FOREIGN TRADE (CUSTOMS BASIS)**
261.59	238.65	239.20	302.18	242.10	248.30	278.50	293.50	269.30	411.70	..	Value of Exports, fob
240.84	225.22	229.62	293.68	230.00	235.90	264.59	278.84	255.85	391.13	..	Nonfuel Primary Products
0.09	0.06	0.10	0.09	0.05	0.05	0.06	0.06	0.05	0.08	..	Fuels
20.66	13.36	9.49	8.41	12.05	12.35	13.86	14.60	13.40	20.49	..	Manufactures
350.12	311.75	310.45	268.82	295.18	256.80	296.10	421.70	506.90	576.20	..	Value of Imports, cif
46.06	32.08	33.83	30.36	31.53	27.43	31.63	45.05	54.15	61.55	..	Nonfuel Primary Products
59.29	53.33	55.87	44.43	39.09	34.01	39.22	55.85	67.13	76.31	..	Fuels
244.78	226.34	220.75	194.03	224.55	195.36	225.25	320.80	385.62	438.33	..	Manufactures
				(Index 1987 = 100)							
130.7	126.2	126.3	132.3	104.5	109.8	100.0	107.7	100.8	93.4	..	Terms of Trade
123.1	114.8	111.3	114.0	89.9	100.1	100.0	114.8	110.2	115.2	..	Export Prices, fob
94.2	91.0	88.1	86.2	86.0	91.2	100.0	106.6	109.3	123.4	..	Import Prices, cif
				(Millions of current US dollars)							**BALANCE OF PAYMENTS**
317.55	274.28	283.29	349.80	283.17	276.18	322.22	334.75	307.80	469.90	..	Exports of Goods & Services
272.54	239.70	246.18	311.81	245.48	248.41	278.48	296.96	267.60	427.60	..	Merchandise, fob
43.67	33.06	36.01	35.38	32.98	24.45	40.48	28.19	29.70	32.80	..	Nonfactor Services
1.34	1.52	1.11	2.62	4.71	3.33	3.26	9.60	10.50	9.50	..	Factor Services
522.51	440.17	459.75	434.63	443.49	408.42	421.37	483.35	608.00	704.10	..	Imports of Goods & Services
244.28	214.02	216.21	162.02	176.66	154.11	177.61	253.04	245.50	303.40	..	Merchandise, fob
146.77	133.21	141.90	156.29	147.93	139.44	150.95	184.87	302.40	333.20	..	Nonfactor Services
131.46	92.94	101.64	116.32	118.90	114.88	92.81	45.45	60.10	67.50	..	Factor Services
49.30	33.00	30.30	30.10	30.00	36.10	28.50	28.60	28.80	32.60	..	Long-Term Interest
11.95	11.84	8.26	11.53	11.11	13.11	13.81	15.07	96.30	72.00	..	Private Current Transfers, net
..	..	..	..	..	..	..	..	..	..	..	Workers' Remittances
-193.01	-154.05	-168.20	-73.30	-149.21	-119.12	-85.34	-133.53	-203.90	-162.20	..	Curr. A/C Bal before Off. Transf.
47.44	37.33	30.48	25.26	25.20	29.70	30.26	80.52	74.20	82.50	..	Net Official Transfers
-145.57	-116.72	-137.73	-48.04	-124.01	-89.42	-55.08	-53.01	-129.70	-79.70	..	Curr. A/C Bal after Off. Transf.
51.27	9.38	96.19	73.23	5.76	37.61	92.54	171.94	57.00	108.40	..	Long-Term Capital, net
1.12		2.55		0.52		0.09				..	Direct Investment
83.70	42.80	41.00	73.20	22.20	80.20	73.00	78.00	86.40	83.00	..	Long-Term Loans
122.90	73.30	64.60	111.40	68.90	146.00	110.10	112.20	114.60	126.60	..	Disbursements
39.20	30.50	23.60	38.20	46.70	65.80	37.10	34.20	28.20	43.60	..	Repayments
-33.55	-33.42	52.64	0.03	-16.96	-42.59	19.45	93.94	-29.40	25.40	..	Other Long-Term Capital
69.03	89.13	3.17	1.46	97.62	51.10	27.02	-7.44	40.00	13.99	..	Other Capital, net
25.27	18.21	38.37	-26.64	20.63	0.70	-64.48	-111.49	32.70	-42.69	..	Change in Reserves
				(Malawi Kwacha per US dollar)							**Memo Item:**
0.900	1.060	1.170	1.410	1.720	1.860	2.210	2.560	2.760	2.730	..	Conversion Factor (Annual Avg)
				(Millions of US dollars), outstanding at end of year							
812.4	856.9	885.3	875.9	1,017.9	1,161.1	1,372.9	1,344.6	1,394.2	1,543.5	..	**EXTERNAL DEBT (Total)**
762.4	771.1	812.3	833.9	937.3	1,081.0	1,277.8	1,294.4	1,346.2	1,483.9	..	Long-Term Debt (by debtor)
135.1	124.6	128.4	129.0	145.5	133.3	116.9	105.7	100.5	115.0	..	Central Bank, incl. IMF credit
456.8	496.5	567.9	627.3	723.5	884.8	1,089.9	1,125.4	1,176.0	1,303.1	..	Central Government
..	..	..	..	..	..	..	..	..	..	..	Rest of General Government
125.6	113.2	88.7	59.1	53.8	49.2	58.5	52.4	59.6	58.7	..	Non-financial Public Enterprises
44.9	36.8	27.3	18.5	14.5	13.7	12.5	10.9	10.1	7.1	..	Priv. Sector, incl non-guaranteed
50.0	85.8	73.0	42.0	80.6	80.1	95.1	50.2	48.0	59.6	..	Short-Term Debt
				(Millions of US dollars)							**Memo Items:**
49.1	22.7	15.4	56.6	45.0	24.6	51.8	145.6	100.3	137.2	..	Int'l Reserves Excluding Gold
5.1	5.9	4.9	4.0	4.2	5.0	6.2	5.3	5.2	4.9	..	Gold Holdings (at market price)
											SOCIAL INDICATORS
7.6	7.6	7.6	7.6	7.6	7.6	7.6	7.6	7.6	7.6	..	Total Fertility Rate
165.8	163.0	160.4	157.8	155.1	152.5	149.9	149.7	149.5	149.4	..	Infant Mortality Rate
44.6	45.0	45.5	45.9	46.3	46.7	47.1	46.9	46.7	46.4	..	Life Expectancy at Birth
9.4	9.6	9.9	10.1	10.4	10.8	11.1	11.3	11.6	11.8	..	Urban Population, % of total
121.1	122.8	112.8	112.3	106.5	105.1	100.0	102.9	102.1	96.7	..	Food Prod. per capita (1987=100)
..	..	..	..	..	..	..	..	..	..	..	Labor Force, Agriculture (%)
43.6	43.3	43.1	42.9	42.6	42.3	42.0	41.7	41.5	41.2	..	Labor Force, Female (%)
65.0	62.0	60.0	60.0	59.0	61.0	62.0	67.0	..	..	..	Primary Schl. Enroll. Ratio
..	52.0	50.0	51.0	51.0	54.0	55.0	60.0	..	..	..	Primary Schl. Enroll. Ratio, Female
4.0	4.0	4.0	4.0	4.0	4.0	4.0	4.0	..	..	..	Secondary Schl. Enroll. Ratio

MALAYSIA	1970	1971	1972	1973	1974	1975	1976	1977	1978	1979	1980
CURRENT GNP PER CAPITA (US $)	390	410	450	550	700	820	920	1,010	1,150	1,400	1,690
POPULATION (thousands)	10,853	11,128	11,408	11,690	11,974	12,258	12,545	12,837	13,135	13,444	13,764

USE AND ORIGIN OF RESOURCES

(Millions of current Malaysian Ringgit)

	1970	1971	1972	1973	1974	1975	1976	1977	1978	1979	1980
Gross National Product (GNP)	12,517	13,186	14,495	18,916	22,892	22,625	28,261	32,529	36,186	44,354	51,390
Net Factor Income from Abroad	-339	-345	-358	-640	-984	-700	-1,074	-1,249	-1,700	-2,070	-1,918
GDP at Market Prices	12,856	13,531	14,853	19,556	23,876	23,325	29,335	33,778	37,886	46,424	53,308
Resource Balance	539	197	-180	1,071	78	123	2,964	2,461	2,108	4,120	1,334
Exports of Goods & NF Services	5,404	5,250	5,129	7,779	11,060	10,187	14,576	16,240	18,585	26,004	30,676
Imports of Goods & NF Services	4,865	5,053	5,309	6,708	10,982	10,064	11,612	13,779	16,477	21,884	29,342
Domestic Absorption	12,317	13,334	15,033	18,485	23,798	23,202	26,371	31,317	35,778	42,304	51,974
Private Consumption, etc.	7,417	8,016	8,696	10,401	12,746	13,172	14,919	16,941	19,584	22,406	26,946
General Gov't Consumption	2,018	2,284	2,882	3,088	3,701	4,130	4,527	5,671	6,090	6,475	8,811
Gross Domestic Investment	2,882	3,034	3,455	4,996	7,351	5,900	6,925	8,705	10,104	13,423	16,217
Fixed Investment	2,430	2,989	3,553	4,669	6,416	6,199	6,868	8,261	9,381	12,250	16,597
Indirect Taxes, net	1,257	1,867	2,115	2,851	3,730	3,343	4,390	5,447	6,099	7,670	9,139
GDP at factor cost	11,599	11,664	12,738	16,705	20,146	19,982	24,945	28,331	31,787	38,754	44,169
Agriculture	3,667	3,504	3,824	5,155	7,061	6,527	7,857	8,682	9,513	10,988	11,680
Industry	3,246	3,571	4,077	5,296	7,418	7,303	9,477	11,236	13,203	16,736	20,164
Manufacturing	1,531	1,720	1,962	2,941	4,024	3,931	5,203	6,212	7,189	8,992	11,002
Services, etc.	5,943	6,456	6,952	9,105	9,397	9,495	12,001	13,860	15,170	18,700	21,464
Gross Domestic Saving	3,421	3,231	3,275	6,067	7,429	6,023	9,889	11,166	12,212	17,543	17,551
Gross National Saving	2,883	2,696	2,743	5,241	6,320	5,208	8,694	9,804	10,355	15,394	15,539

(Millions of 1980 Malaysian Ringgit)

	1970	1971	1972	1973	1974	1975	1976	1977	1978	1979	1980
Gross National Product	24,152	25,631	28,130	31,067	33,417	34,183	37,897	40,770	43,232	47,231	51,390
GDP at Market Prices	24,985	26,458	28,935	32,313	34,967	35,250	39,382	42,447	45,320	49,613	53,308
Resource Balance	3,387	3,639	4,270	4,611	2,734	5,062	7,022	5,516	4,988	5,385	1,334
Exports of Goods & NF Services	14,453	14,678	14,975	17,100	19,824	19,230	22,491	23,427	25,205	29,733	30,676
Imports of Goods & NF Services	11,066	11,039	10,705	12,489	17,089	14,168	15,470	17,911	20,217	24,348	29,342
Domestic Absorption	21,598	22,819	24,665	27,702	32,233	30,188	32,360	36,931	40,332	44,227	51,974
Private Consumption, etc.	12,549	13,420	14,177	15,327	16,645	16,545	17,306	19,256	21,370	23,537	26,946
General Gov't Consumption	3,377	3,660	4,278	4,474	5,141	5,490	5,956	6,542	6,924	7,043	8,811
Gross Domestic Investment	5,672	5,739	6,209	7,901	10,447	8,154	9,099	11,133	12,038	13,647	16,217
Fixed Investment	4,794	5,696	6,539	7,618	9,283	8,593	9,023	10,340	11,176	13,308	16,597
GDP at factor cost	23,623	23,971	26,074	29,017	31,030	31,737	35,209	37,473	38,414	41,633	44,169
Agriculture	7,381	7,488	8,059	9,008	9,630	9,338	10,481	10,729	10,905	11,532	11,680
Industry	8,669	9,549	10,345	11,410	11,939	11,979	14,095	15,191	16,707	18,899	20,164
Manufacturing	3,659	4,119	4,538	5,560	6,137	6,318	7,487	8,280	9,048	10,073	11,002
Services, etc.	8,934	9,421	10,531	11,895	13,398	13,933	14,806	16,528	17,708	19,182	21,464

Memo Items:

	1970	1971	1972	1973	1974	1975	1976	1977	1978	1979	1980
Capacity to Import	12,292	11,470	10,342	14,483	17,211	14,341	19,418	21,111	22,803	28,932	30,676
Terms of Trade Adjustment	-2,161	-3,209	-4,633	-2,617	-2,613	-4,889	-3,073	-2,317	-2,402	-801	0
Gross Domestic Income	22,824	23,249	24,302	29,696	32,354	30,362	36,309	40,131	42,918	48,811	53,308
Gross National Income	21,991	22,423	23,497	28,451	30,804	29,295	34,825	38,453	40,831	46,429	51,390

DOMESTIC PRICES/DEFLATORS

(Index 1980 = 100)

	1970	1971	1972	1973	1974	1975	1976	1977	1978	1979	1980
Overall (GDP)	51.5	51.1	51.3	60.5	68.3	66.2	74.5	79.6	83.6	93.6	100.0
Domestic Absorption	57.0	58.4	60.9	66.7	73.8	76.9	81.5	84.8	88.7	95.7	100.0
Agriculture	49.7	46.8	47.5	57.2	73.3	69.9	75.0	80.9	87.2	95.3	100.0
Industry	37.4	37.4	39.4	46.4	62.1	61.0	67.2	74.0	79.0	88.6	100.0
Manufacturing	41.8	41.8	43.2	52.9	65.6	62.2	69.5	75.0	79.5	89.3	100.0
Consumer Price Index	44.2	44.9	46.4	51.3	60.2	62.9	64.5	67.6	70.9	73.5	78.4

MANUFACTURING ACTIVITY

	1970	1971	1972	1973	1974	1975	1976	1977	1978	1979	1980
Employment (1987=100)	33.2	36.6	42.8	56.2	57.1	59.6	67.3	70.8	78.2	86.7	96.9
Real Earnings per Empl. (1987=100)	64.2	64.1	61.5	56.3	58.7	60.1	64.2	67.9	67.8	73.1	76.7
Real Output per Empl. (1987=100)	..	..	..	..	..	..	..	..	..	..	..
Earnings as % of Value Added	28.5	30.3	29.3	25.9	26.9	27.4	27.9	27.1	26.2	25.6	28.0

MONETARY HOLDINGS

(Billions of current Malaysian Ringgit)

	1970	1971	1972	1973	1974	1975	1976	1977	1978	1979	1980
Money Supply, Broadly Defined	4.65	5.26	6.56	8.61	13.03	15.20	19.22	22.20	26.56	33.07	41.31
Money	2.07	2.17	2.72	3.74	4.06	4.35	5.26	6.13	7.24	8.49	9.76
Currency Outside Banks	1.00	1.06	1.27	1.72	2.03	2.24	2.63	3.11	3.58	4.09	4.76
Demand Deposits	1.07	1.11	1.45	2.02	2.03	2.11	2.63	3.02	3.66	4.39	5.00
Quasi-Money	2.58	3.09	3.85	4.87	8.97	10.85	13.97	16.08	19.31	24.59	31.55

(Millions of current Malaysian Ringgit)

	1970	1971	1972	1973	1974	1975	1976	1977	1978	1979	1980
GOVERNMENT DEFICIT (-) OR SURPLUS	..	..	-1,359	-1,094	-1,257	-1,827	-1,976	-2,407	-2,356	-1,401	-3,185
Current Revenue	..	..	2,950	3,378	4,748	5,076	6,125	7,766	8,797	10,436	14,016
Current Expenditure	..	..	3,234	3,399	4,446	4,944	5,984	7,252	7,610	8,332	10,217
Current Budget Balance	..	..	-284	-21	302	132	141	514	1,187	2,104	3,799
Capital Receipts	..	..	..	..	11	13	13	28	11	30	37
Capital Payments	..	..	1,075	1,073	1,570	2,037	2,218	3,094	3,384	3,288	7,021

1981	1982	1983	1984	1985	1986	1987	1988	1989	1990 estimate	Notes	MALAYSIA
1,880	1,900	1,900	2,040	1,970	1,840	1,830	1,930	2,120	2,320	..	**CURRENT GNP PER CAPITA (US $)**
14,130	14,510	14,887	15,272	15,682	16,109	16,528	16,942	17,353	17,861	..	**POPULATION (thousands)**
				(Millions of current Malaysian Ringgit)							**USE AND ORIGIN OF RESOURCES**
55,602	59,690	65,530	74,182	71,962	66,814	74,679	85,777	95,600	109,663	..	Gross National Product (GNP)
-2,011	-2,889	-4,411	-5,368	-5,508	-4,780	-4,946	-5,084	-5,863	-4,953	..	Net Factor Income from Abroad
57,613	62,579	69,941	79,550	77,470	71,594	79,625	90,861	101,463	114,616	..	GDP at Market Prices
-3,563	-5,454	-3,998	1,518	3,976	4,364	11,246	9,424	5,097	-80	..	Resource Balance
30,154	31,846	35,795	43,171	42,537	40,305	50,838	61,259	75,030	89,393	..	Exports of Goods & NF Services
33,717	37,300	39,793	41,653	38,561	35,941	39,592	51,835	69,933	89,473	..	Imports of Goods & NF Services
61,176	68,033	73,939	78,032	73,494	67,230	68,379	81,437	96,366	114,696	..	Domestic Absorption
30,594	33,226	36,458	39,594	40,283	36,499	37,685	44,856	52,930	62,030	..	Private Consumption, etc.
10,425	11,469	11,015	11,741	11,844	12,127	12,239	12,997	14,180	15,593	..	General Gov't Consumption
20,157	23,338	26,466	26,697	21,367	18,604	18,455	23,584	29,256	37,073	..	Gross Domestic Investment
20,759	22,745	25,213	25,391	23,124	18,865	18,280	21,922	30,063	37,490	..	Fixed Investment
8,834	8,759	10,310	..	..	..	..	..	..	..		Indirect Taxes, net
48,779	53,820	59,631	..	..	..	..	..	..	..	B	GDP at factor cost
11,962	12,807	13,555	..	..	..	..	..	..	..	..	Agriculture
21,409	21,851	24,835	..	..	..	..	..	..	..	..	Industry
11,542	11,419	12,935	..	..	..	..	..	..	..	..	Manufacturing
24,242	27,921	31,551	..	..	..	..	..	..	..	..	Services, etc.
16,594	17,884	22,468	28,215	25,343	22,968	29,701	33,008	34,353	36,993	..	Gross Domestic Saving
14,457	14,871	17,976	22,700	19,722	18,139	24,930	28,107	28,445	32,084	..	Gross National Saving
				(Millions of 1980 Malaysian Ringgit)							
55,208	57,732	60,011	64,090	63,224	64,882	68,514	75,138	81,675	91,256	..	Gross National Product
56,960	60,355	64,215	69,282	68,449	69,298	73,056	79,683	86,699	95,365	..	GDP at Market Prices
-561	-1,575	-594	2,120	6,337	13,819	17,930	15,288	12,934	10,105	..	Resource Balance
30,421	33,669	37,823	43,036	43,229	48,324	55,359	61,893	73,112	86,516	..	Exports of Goods & NF Services
30,982	35,244	38,417	40,916	36,892	34,505	37,429	46,606	60,177	76,411	..	Imports of Goods & NF Services
57,521	61,929	64,809	67,161	62,112	55,479	55,126	64,395	73,764	85,261	..	Domestic Absorption
28,530	29,333	30,056	31,684	31,598	27,493	27,427	32,231	36,738	41,618	..	Private Consumption, etc.
9,987	10,860	11,357	10,801	10,706	10,842	11,001	11,538	12,415	13,221	..	General Gov't Consumption
19,005	21,737	23,396	24,677	19,808	17,144	16,698	20,625	24,611	30,422	..	Gross Domestic Investment
19,598	21,167	22,866	23,543	21,311	17,395	16,624	19,162	25,271	30,823	..	Fixed Investment
48,190	51,583	53,780	57,612	57,193	60,122	63,783	69,160	75,583	..	B	GDP at factor cost
12,247	13,040	12,956	13,324	13,589	14,155	15,150	15,972	16,928	16,990	..	Agriculture
20,879	22,276	24,594	27,411	26,490	27,661	29,520	33,277	36,947	42,301	..	Industry
11,522	12,167	13,125	14,739	14,175	15,242	17,285	20,326	22,765	26,835	..	Manufacturing
23,834	25,039	26,665	28,547	28,371	27,481	28,386	30,433	32,824	36,075	..	Services, etc.
											Memo Items:
27,708	30,090	34,557	42,407	40,695	38,695	48,061	55,079	64,563	76,343	..	Capacity to Import
-2,713	-3,579	-3,266	-629	-2,534	-9,630	-7,298	-6,814	-8,548	-10,173	..	Terms of Trade Adjustment
54,247	56,776	60,949	68,653	65,916	59,668	65,758	72,868	78,150	85,192	..	Gross Domestic Income
52,495	54,153	56,745	63,461	60,691	55,253	61,216	68,324	73,127	81,082	..	Gross National Income
				(Index 1980 = 100)							**DOMESTIC PRICES/DEFLATORS**
101.1	103.7	108.9	114.8	113.2	103.3	109.0	114.0	117.0	120.2	..	Overall (GDP)
106.4	109.9	114.1	116.2	118.3	121.2	124.0	126.5	130.6	134.5	..	Domestic Absorption
97.7	98.2	104.6	..	..	..	..	..	..	..	..	Agriculture
102.5	98.1	101.0	..	..	..	..	..	..	..	..	Industry
100.2	93.8	98.6	..	..	..	..	..	..	..	..	Manufacturing
86.0	91.0	94.4	98.1	98.4	99.1	100.0	102.0	104.8	107.6	f	Consumer Price Index
											MANUFACTURING ACTIVITY
108.4	100.1	95.1	96.3	91.9	92.4	100.0	111.4	..	..	..	Employment (1987=100)
78.3	85.3	91.4	96.0	103.5	102.4	100.0	107.2	..	..	..	Real Earnings per Empl. (1987=100)
..	..	..	..	..	..	..	..	..	..	..	Real Output per Empl. (1987=100)
30.7	32.1	30.0	28.5	29.9	29.9	29.1	29.6	..	..	..	Earnings as % of Value Added
				(Billions of current Malaysian Ringgit)							**MONETARY HOLDINGS**
49.37	60.90	66.74	77.17	85.12	96.44	99.36	109.02	..	..	D	Money Supply, Broadly Defined
11.01	12.48	13.43	13.36	14.13	14.52	16.37	18.73	21.98	25.41	..	Money
5.10	5.73	6.03	5.97	6.77	7.15	7.97	9.03	9.90	11.22	..	Currency Outside Banks
5.91	6.75	7.41	7.38	7.36	7.38	8.41	9.70	12.07	14.18	..	Demand Deposits
38.36	48.43	53.30	63.81	70.98	81.92	82.99	90.29	..	..	..	Quasi-Money
				(Millions of current Malaysian Ringgit)							
-8,572	-10,100	-6,786	-5,158	-1,951	-6,523	-5,518	-1,140	-2,805	-3,094	F	**GOVERNMENT DEFICIT (-) OR SURPLUS**
15,781	16,595	18,542	20,532	23,352	21,535	19,943	23,302	25,606	31,731	..	Current Revenue
13,686	15,932	16,140	17,525	20,336	21,412	20,722	21,787	24,010	25,949	..	Current Expenditure
2,095	663	2,402	3,007	3,016	123	-779	1,515	1,596	5,782	..	Current Budget Balance
61	33	39	38	105	77	68	53	74	30	..	Capital Receipts
10,728	10,796	9,227	8,203	5,072	6,723	4,807	2,708	4,475	8,906	..	Capital Payments

MALAYSIA	1970	1971	1972	1973	1974	1975	1976	1977	1978	1979	1980
FOREIGN TRADE (CUSTOMS BASIS)	*(Millions of current US dollars)*										
Value of Exports, fob	1,687	1,639	1,722	3,040	4,234	3,847	5,295	6,079	7,387	11,075	12,939
Nonfuel Primary Products	1,438	1,326	1,412	2,511	3,301	2,739	3,706	4,275	4,939	7,088	7,277
Fuels	124	169	118	164	359	419	765	868	1,037	2,020	3,199
Manufactures	125	143	191	364	574	689	824	937	1,410	1,966	2,464
Value of Imports, cif	1,401	1,442	1,611	2,441	4,111	3,525	3,814	4,538	5,889	7,835	10,735
Nonfuel Primary Products	413	384	451	679	1,005	899	885	1,069	1,361	1,595	1,902
Fuels	169	188	131	162	417	424	515	578	632	945	1,627
Manufactures	818	870	1,029	1,600	2,688	2,202	2,414	2,891	3,896	5,295	7,206
	(Index 1987 = 100)										
Terms of Trade	139.3	118.8	104.1	126.1	123.6	102.0	112.8	121.5	122.9	134.0	134.7
Export Prices, fob	24.8	23.9	27.6	45.9	67.7	57.4	63.7	74.7	84.7	109.6	129.4
Import Prices, cif	17.8	20.1	26.5	36.4	54.8	56.2	56.5	61.4	68.9	81.8	96.0
BALANCE OF PAYMENTS	*(Millions of current US dollars)*										
Exports of Goods & Services	1,830	1,793	1,876	3,270	4,733	4,392	5,866	6,841	8,386	12,418	14,836
Merchandise, fob	1,640	1,600	1,680	2,972	4,164	3,784	5,245	6,035	7,311	10,994	12,868
Nonfactor Services	113	106	123	193	408	452	446	549	697	870	1,229
Factor Services	77	87	74	105	162	156	175	257	378	555	739
Imports of Goods & Services	1,763	1,857	2,068	3,103	5,233	4,855	5,246	6,373	8,233	11,482	15,100
Merchandise, fob	1,291	1,375	1,550	2,320	3,939	3,527	3,780	4,516	5,718	7,838	10,462
Nonfactor Services	279	276	309	409	718	872	864	1,086	1,402	2,162	3,026
Factor Services	193	206	208	374	576	456	602	771	1,114	1,482	1,612
Long-Term Interest	25	27	37	54	71	85	156	179	190	344	338
Private Current Transfers, net	-65	-62	-62	-76	-52	-48	-48	-46	-68	-36	-43
Workers' Remittances	..	..	..	..	..	..	..	..	..	..	..
Curr. A/C Bal before Off. Transf.	2	-125	-254	91	-552	-511	572	422	85	901	-307
Net Official Transfers	6	17	7	14	9	15	8	14	23	28	23
Curr. A/C Bal after Off. Transf.	8	-108	-248	105	-543	-496	580	436	108	929	-285
Long-Term Capital, net	96	219	296	218	668	724	568	652	690	925	1,021
Direct Investment	94	100	114	172	571	350	381	406	500	573	934
Long-Term Loans	1	159	221	58	221	756	428	476	402	781	1,111
Disbursements	58	194	269	146	334	893	676	927	1,266	1,256	1,456
Repayments	57	35	48	89	113	137	248	451	864	475	345
Other Long-Term Capital	1	-41	-39	-11	-123	-383	-241	-230	-212	-429	-1,025
Other Capital, net	-90	-47	-22	-99	73	-162	-350	-780	-518	-1,053	-268
Change in Reserves	-14	-64	-27	-224	-198	-65	-798	-308	-279	-802	-468
Memo Item:	*(Malaysian Ringgit per US dollar)*										
Conversion Factor (Annual Avg)	3.060	3.050	2.820	2.440	2.410	2.400	2.540	2.460	2.320	2.190	2.180
	(Millions of US dollars), outstanding at end of year										
EXTERNAL DEBT (Total)	440	614	823	893	1,119	1,843	2,376	3,425	4,167	4,956	6,611
Long-Term Debt (by debtor)	440	614	823	893	1,119	1,843	2,376	2,830	3,356	4,081	5,256
Central Bank, incl. IMF credit	0	0	0	2	10	10	120	13	9	7	4
Central Government	376	490	593	629	696	1,094	1,261	1,647	2,069	2,177	2,840
Rest of General Government	11	12	9	7	16	18	18	15	20	28	41
Non-financial Public Enterprises	4	33	91	91	151	220	316	332	445	872	1,122
Priv. Sector, incl non-guaranteed	50	80	130	164	247	502	661	823	813	998	1,248
Short-Term Debt	0	0	0	0	0	0	0	595	811	874	1,355
Memo Items:	*(Millions of US dollars)*										
Int'l Reserves Excluding Gold	616.3	754.7	907.1	1,275.2	1,547.1	1,456.1	2,404.1	2,783.8	3,243.3	3,914.9	4,387.4
Gold Holdings (at market price)	51.2	72.4	107.7	186.3	309.6	232.8	223.7	287.0	427.1	1,090.6	1,367.6
SOCIAL INDICATORS											
Total Fertility Rate	5.5	5.3	5.1	5.0	4.8	4.6	4.4	4.2	4.2	4.2	4.2
Infant Mortality Rate	45.2	43.6	42.0	40.4	38.8	37.2	35.6	34.0	32.8	31.6	30.4
Life Expectancy at Birth	61.6	62.3	63.0	63.5	63.9	64.4	64.8	65.3	65.8	66.3	66.9
Urban Population, % of total	27.0	27.7	28.5	29.2	30.0	30.7	31.5	32.3	33.0	33.8	34.6
Food Prod. per capita (1987=100)	46.3	50.5	52.6	54.4	59.4	63.3	65.6	66.2	63.9	72.6	77.7
Labor Force, Agriculture (%)	53.8	52.4	51.1	49.9	48.8	47.7	46.3	45.0	43.8	42.6	41.6
Labor Force, Female (%)	31.2	31.7	32.0	32.4	32.7	33.0	33.4	33.7	34.0	34.3	34.6
Primary Schl. Enroll. Ratio	87.0	..	..	..	..	91.0	..	91.0	92.0	92.0	93.0
Primary Schl. Enroll. Ratio, Female	84.0	..	..	..	..	89.0	..	89.0	91.0	90.0	92.0
Secondary Schl. Enroll. Ratio	34.0	..	..	..	..	42.0	47.0	48.0	49.0	51.0	48.0

1981	1982	1983	1984	1985	1986	1987	1988	1989	1990 estimate	Notes	MALAYSIA
											FOREIGN TRADE (CUSTOMS BASIS)
11,734	12,027	14,100	16,484	15,632	13,830	17,911	21,110	25,038	29,409	..	Value of Exports, fob
6,251	5,798	6,534	7,146	6,432	5,518	7,272	8,512	10,096	11,858	..	Nonfuel Primary Products
3,124	3,448	4,048	4,933	4,930	3,160	3,572	3,334	3,955	4,645	..	Fuels
2,359	2,781	3,518	4,404	4,270	5,152	7,066	9,264	10,988	12,905	..	Manufactures
11,508	12,363	13,229	13,953	12,515	10,731	12,589	16,232	22,467	29,251	..	Value of Imports, cif
2,087	2,049	2,149	2,222	1,997	1,774	2,054	2,701	3,738	4,867	..	Nonfuel Primary Products
1,978	1,869	1,824	1,420	1,515	886	900	875	1,211	1,577	..	Fuels
7,443	8,445	9,256	10,312	9,002	8,071	9,635	12,656	17,518	22,807	..	Manufactures

(Index 1987 = 100)

1981	1982	1983	1984	1985	1986	1987	1988	1989	1990 estimate	Notes	MALAYSIA
121.5	115.2	119.7	127.4	117.0	91.5	100.0	99.4	97.0	94.2	..	Terms of Trade
117.8	106.3	107.8	111.8	101.5	82.6	100.0	108.1	106.8	108.5	..	Export Prices, fob
97.0	92.3	90.0	87.8	86.8	90.2	100.0	108.8	110.1	115.2	..	Import Prices, cif

(Millions of current US dollars) — **BALANCE OF PAYMENTS**

1981	1982	1983	1984	1985	1986	1987	1988	1989	1990 estimate	Notes	MALAYSIA
13,879	14,299	16,218	19,067	17,776	16,185	20,983	24,449	28,851	34,863	..	Exports of Goods & Services
11,675	11,966	13,683	16,407	15,133	13,547	17,754	20,852	24,667	28,956	..	Merchandise, fob
1,412	1,683	1,972	2,046	2,052	2,090	2,396	2,507	3,013	4,055	..	Nonfactor Services
792	650	562	614	591	548	834	1,090	1,172	1,852	..	Factor Services
16,331	17,867	19,705	20,700	18,383	16,345	18,485	22,790	29,144	36,612	..	Imports of Goods & Services
11,780	12,719	13,251	13,426	11,556	10,302	11,918	15,306	20,754	27,032	..	Merchandise, fob
2,920	3,351	4,079	4,418	4,048	3,714	3,770	4,453	5,039	5,897	..	Nonfactor Services
1,630	1,797	2,375	2,856	2,779	2,329	2,797	3,032	3,351	3,683	..	Factor Services
515	724	938	1,293	1,475	1,380	1,530	1,544	1,241	1,229	..	Long-Term Interest
-55	-53	-35	-63	-46	-19	69	70	-17	16	..	Private Current Transfers, net
..	..	..	..	..	..	..	..	..	..	..	Workers' Remittances
-2,507	-3,622	-3,523	-1,696	-653	-179	2,567	1,729	-309	-1,733	..	Curr. A/C Bal before Off. Transf.
21	21	26	24	40	56	69	81	97	61	..	Net Official Transfers
-2,486	-3,601	-3,497	-1,671	-613	-123	2,636	1,810	-212	-1,672	..	Curr. A/C Bal after Off. Transf.
2,574	3,605	3,966	3,143	1,582	1,120	-548	-1,224	848	2,588	..	Long-Term Capital, net
1,265	1,397	1,261	797	695	489	423	719	1,668	2,902	..	Direct Investment
2,332	3,915	3,368	2,549	245	429	-624	-1,802	-730	-226	..	Long-Term Loans
2,766	4,510	4,059	3,682	3,893	2,355	2,104	2,169	2,449	2,464	..	Disbursements
434	594	691	1,133	3,647	1,925	2,728	3,971	3,179	2,690	..	Repayments
-1,023	-1,707	-663	-203	642	202	-347	-142	-90	-88	..	Other Long-Term Capital
-540	-267	-485	-986	182	458	-969	-1,016	594	1,037	..	Other Capital, net
452	262	15	-486	-1,151	-1,455	-1,119	430	-1,230	-1,953	..	Change in Reserves

(Malaysian Ringgit per US dollar) — **Memo Item:**

1981	1982	1983	1984	1985	1986	1987	1988	1989	1990 estimate	Notes	MALAYSIA
2.300	2.340	2.320	2.340	2.480	2.580	2.520	2.620	2.710	2.700	..	Conversion Factor (Annual Avg)

(Millions of US dollars), outstanding at end of year

1981	1982	1983	1984	1985	1986	1987	1988	1989	1990 estimate	Notes	MALAYSIA
9,225	13,396	17,753	19,138	20,835	22,709	24,202	21,036	19,166	19,502	..	**EXTERNAL DEBT (Total)**
7,601	11,673	14,726	16,607	18,150	19,997	21,857	19,441	16,893	17,596	..	Long-Term Debt (by debtor)
223	275	391	385	261	153	169	164	151	195	..	Central Bank, incl. IMF credit
4,243	6,396	8,581	9,656	10,703	12,406	13,873	12,551	11,752	12,595	..	Central Government
52	60	127	221	252	263	273	244	194	157	..	Rest of General Government
1,446	1,743	2,895	3,570	3,959	4,262	4,632	3,865	3,088	2,816	..	Non-financial Public Enterprises
1,637	3,198	2,732	2,775	2,976	2,913	2,909	2,617	1,709	1,833	..	Priv. Sector, incl non-guaranteed
1,624	1,723	3,027	2,531	2,685	2,712	2,345	1,595	2,273	1,906	..	Short-Term Debt

(Millions of US dollars) — **Memo Items:**

1981	1982	1983	1984	1985	1986	1987	1988	1989	1990 estimate	Notes	MALAYSIA
4,098.0	3,767.8	3,783.7	3,723.3	4,911.8	6,027.4	7,435.3	6,526.5	7,783.0	9,754.1	..	Int'l Reserves Excluding Gold
926.2	1,064.6	888.9	718.3	765.2	914.7	1,137.6	964.1	950.4	904.8	..	Gold Holdings (at market price)
											SOCIAL INDICATORS
4.2	4.2	4.2	4.1	4.1	4.0	4.0	3.9	3.8	3.8	..	Total Fertility Rate
29.2	28.0	26.0	24.0	22.1	20.1	18.1	17.4	16.7	15.9	..	Infant Mortality Rate
67.4	68.0	68.2	68.5	68.7	69.0	69.2	69.5	69.7	70.0	..	Life Expectancy at Birth
35.4	36.3	37.1	38.0	38.8	39.6	40.5	41.3	42.2	43.0	..	Urban Population, % of total
80.3	88.0	78.4	86.9	94.4	99.7	100.0	106.6	116.7	115.8	..	Food Prod. per capita (1987=100)
..	..	..	..	..	..	..	..	..	..	..	Labor Force, Agriculture (%)
34.7	34.8	34.8	34.9	34.9	34.9	35.0	35.0	35.0	35.1	..	Labor Force, Female (%)
..	94.0	96.0	98.0	101.0	101.0	101.0	99.0	96.0	..	..	Primary Schl. Enroll. Ratio
..	93.0	95.0	97.0	100.0	..	100.0	99.0	96.0	..	..	Primary Schl. Enroll. Ratio, Female
..	49.0	51.0	53.0	53.0	54.0	59.0	57.0	59.0	..	..	Secondary Schl. Enroll. Ratio

MALI	1970	1971	1972	1973	1974	1975	1976	1977	1978	1979	1980
CURRENT GNP PER CAPITA (US $)	70	70	80	80	90	120	140	170	170	210	240
POPULATION (thousands)	5,335	5,450	5,564	5,678	5,791	5,905	6,032	6,165	6,304	6,446	6,590

USE AND ORIGIN OF RESOURCES *(Billions of current CFA Francs)*

	1970	1971	1972	1973	1974	1975	1976	1977	1978	1979	1980
Gross National Product (GNP)	92.39	102.34	115.57	118.10	121.31	165.81	210.07	243.47	262.73	317.59	340.59
Net Factor Income from Abroad	-1.40	-0.30	-0.10	-0.40	-1.00	-2.10	-1.60	0.20	2.50	-2.50	-3.60
GDP at Market Prices	93.79	102.64	115.67	118.50	122.31	167.91	211.68	243.27	260.23	320.09	344.19
Resource Balance	-5.62	-7.43	-11.72	-15.86	-36.53	-34.98	-22.49	-17.59	-50.39	-59.04	-64.82
Exports of Goods & NF Services	12.45	14.61	12.25	12.84	16.47	17.15	24.70	32.94	31.96	40.29	55.58
Imports of Goods & NF Services	18.07	22.04	23.97	28.70	53.00	52.14	47.19	50.52	82.35	99.33	120.40
Domestic Absorption	99.41	110.07	127.39	134.36	158.84	202.90	234.17	260.86	310.62	379.14	409.01
Private Consumption, etc.	74.96	82.31	92.97	103.19	126.97	158.07	187.68	198.24	240.06	294.82	314.80
General Gov't Consumption	9.27	10.36	13.47	9.97	14.33	17.21	16.51	22.43	26.71	31.82	35.82
Gross Domestic Investment	15.19	17.41	20.95	21.21	17.54	27.62	29.98	40.19	43.85	52.49	58.39
Fixed Investment	13.09	15.31	19.05	19.81	15.64	24.02	27.58	37.19	39.85	48.49	58.39
Indirect Taxes, net	6.90	7.90	5.20	5.90	6.00	6.50	10.10	11.50	13.60	16.90	14.50
GDP at factor cost	86.89	94.74	110.47	112.60	116.31	161.41	201.58	231.77	246.63	303.19	329.69
Agriculture	57.51	62.11	68.43	64.84	59.72	102.38	123.71	142.32	143.85	186.68	200.84
Industry	10.17	11.83	13.87	14.71	16.07	18.04	22.06	25.44	27.07	29.97	32.14
Manufacturing	6.85	7.22	9.47	9.57	10.03	11.44	12.10	13.41	13.32	13.79	14.82
Services, etc.	26.11	28.70	33.37	38.94	46.51	47.49	65.90	75.51	89.31	103.44	111.20
Gross Domestic Saving	9.56	9.98	9.23	5.35	-18.99	-7.36	7.49	22.60	-6.54	-6.55	-6.44
Gross National Saving	8.25	11.12	10.66	6.35	-19.00	-6.90	8.31	27.79	3.26	-1.70	-1.49

(Billions of 1987 CFA Francs)

	1970	1971	1972	1973	1974	1975	1976	1977	1978	1979	1980
Gross National Product	286.54	300.04	316.24	307.70	298.94	338.87	386.83	416.63	409.00	445.76	438.94
GDP at Market Prices	291.02	301.03	316.66	308.81	301.35	343.20	389.92	416.36	405.16	449.39	443.67
Resource Balance	-29.46	-23.70	-37.03	-37.84	-62.91	-57.01	-40.32	-26.40	-70.29	-72.45	-69.69
Exports of Goods & NF Services	33.48	45.53	40.95	37.34	40.95	41.60	48.16	59.62	57.00	63.22	79.28
Imports of Goods & NF Services	62.94	69.24	77.98	75.18	103.86	98.61	88.47	86.02	127.29	135.68	148.97
Domestic Absorption	320.49	324.73	353.69	346.65	364.25	400.20	430.23	442.77	475.44	521.84	513.36
Private Consumption, etc.	221.26	218.65	249.77	246.54	278.59	299.32	336.29	324.36	355.26	392.34	385.20
General Gov't Consumption	40.99	45.14	42.21	41.48	39.77	39.95	34.55	43.57	47.29	50.82	52.56
Gross Domestic Investment	58.24	60.94	61.71	58.63	45.90	60.94	59.40	74.83	72.90	78.68	75.60
Fixed Investment	..	..	..	..	..	..	..	..	..	..	..
GDP at factor cost	..	..	..	..	..	..	..	..	..	..	..
Agriculture	192.59	197.08	200.08	178.12	166.65	207.56	237.50	256.46	237.00	274.92	265.94
Industry	36.84	28.95	32.88	33.58	33.58	36.59	38.67	43.30	42.61	35.89	35.66
Manufacturing	..	..	..	..	..	..	..	..	..	..	..
Services, etc.	61.59	75.00	83.70	97.11	101.12	99.05	113.75	116.60	125.55	138.58	142.07

Memo Items:

	1970	1971	1972	1973	1974	1975	1976	1977	1978	1979	1980
Capacity to Import	43.36	45.89	39.86	33.63	32.27	32.44	46.31	56.08	49.40	55.03	68.76
Terms of Trade Adjustment	9.88	0.35	-1.09	-3.71	-8.68	-9.16	-1.85	-3.55	-7.61	-8.20	-10.51
Gross Domestic Income	300.91	301.38	315.57	305.10	292.67	334.04	388.07	412.82	397.55	441.19	433.16
Gross National Income	296.42	300.39	315.15	303.99	290.26	329.71	384.98	413.08	401.40	437.57	428.43

DOMESTIC PRICES/DEFLATORS *(Index 1987 = 100)*

	1970	1971	1972	1973	1974	1975	1976	1977	1978	1979	1980
Overall (GDP)	32.2	34.1	36.5	38.4	40.6	48.9	54.3	58.4	64.2	71.2	77.6
Domestic Absorption	31.0	33.9	36.0	38.8	43.6	50.7	54.4	58.9	65.3	72.7	79.7
Agriculture	29.9	31.5	34.2	36.4	35.8	49.3	52.1	55.5	60.7	67.9	75.5
Industry	27.6	40.9	42.2	43.8	47.9	49.3	57.0	58.8	63.5	83.5	90.1
Manufacturing	..	..	..	..	..	..	..	..	..	..	..
Consumer Price Index	..	..	..	..	..	..	..	..	..	..	..

MANUFACTURING ACTIVITY

	1970	1971	1972	1973	1974	1975	1976	1977	1978	1979	1980
Employment (1987=100)	..	..	..	..	..	..	..	..	..	..	..
Real Earnings per Empl. (1987=100)	..	..	..	..	..	..	..	..	..	..	..
Real Output per Empl. (1987=100)	..	..	..	..	..	..	..	..	..	..	..
Earnings as % of Value Added	45.6	47.8	46.1	49.0	44.2	31.9	30.8	26.1	29.5	29.8	27.6

MONETARY HOLDINGS *(Billions of current CFA Francs)*

	1970	1971	1972	1973	1974	1975	1976	1977	1978	1979	1980
Money Supply, Broadly Defined	13.64	14.68	16.41	17.85	27.13	32.53	36.25	41.82	51.49	60.11	62.80
Money	12.95	13.97	15.62	17.54	27.00	31.95	35.62	40.66	48.48	56.77	59.52
Currency Outside Banks	8.89	9.69	10.52	11.13	15.07	18.70	22.49	27.40	30.70	38.16	40.60
Demand Deposits	4.06	4.29	5.10	6.41	11.93	13.26	13.13	13.26	17.79	18.61	18.92
Quasi-Money	0.70	0.71	0.79	0.31	0.14	0.57	0.63	1.17	3.00	3.34	3.28

(Millions of current CFA Francs)

	1970	1971	1972	1973	1974	1975	1976	1977	1978	1979	1980
GOVERNMENT DEFICIT (-) OR SURPLUS	..	..	..	..	..	..	..	200	-4,000	-9,100	-16,000
Current Revenue	..	..	..	..	..	24,200	27,100	34,700	35,200	36,000	61,400
Current Expenditure	..	..	..	..	..	..	25,200	29,200	33,100	39,600	42,300
Current Budget Balance	..	..	..	..	..	..	1,900	5,500	2,100	-3,600	19,100
Capital Receipts	..	..	..	..	..	..	..	..	..	..	..
Capital Payments	..	..	..	..	..	..	1,900	5,300	6,100	5,500	35,100

1981	1982	1983	1984	1985	1986	1987	1988	1989	1990 estimate	Notes	MALI
240	220	170	160	150	180	200	230	270	270	..	**CURRENT GNP PER CAPITA (US $)**
6,733	6,883	7,041	7,210	7,389	7,579	7,781	7,994	8,220	8,460	..	**POPULATION (thousands)**
				(Billions of current CFA Francs)							**USE AND ORIGIN OF RESOURCES**
361.95	395.65	401.20	454.98	467.00	520.00	562.30	604.10	634.90	657.40	..	Gross National Product (GNP)
-8.85	-7.95	-10.10	-8.52	-8.40	-8.60	-8.40	-8.20	-9.10	-8.70	..	Net Factor Income from Abroad
370.80	403.60	411.30	463.50	475.40	528.60	570.70	612.30	644.00	666.10	..	GDP at Market Prices
-65.90	-69.10	-79.80	-86.40	-160.60	-127.60	-96.00	-108.60	-101.00	-107.50	..	Resource Balance
54.50	61.80	78.60	101.70	98.90	89.00	96.20	93.50	107.30	117.20	..	Exports of Goods & NF Services
120.40	130.90	158.40	188.10	259.50	216.60	192.20	202.10	208.30	224.70	..	Imports of Goods & NF Services
436.70	472.70	491.10	549.90	636.00	656.20	666.70	720.90	745.00	773.60	..	Domestic Absorption
335.30	362.10	386.30	429.30	486.90	477.10	472.30	504.30	510.00	530.50	..	Private Consumption, etc.
36.60	39.60	44.90	50.10	56.20	58.10	62.80	65.10	67.70	66.80	..	General Gov't Consumption
64.80	71.00	59.90	70.50	92.90	121.00	131.60	151.50	167.30	176.30	..	Gross Domestic Investment
64.80	71.40	75.00	84.60	104.40	121.50	120.60	123.80	134.20	144.60	..	Fixed Investment
18.40	16.30	17.50	20.00	20.80	23.30	29.40	26.90	34.80	38.20	..	Indirect Taxes, net
352.40	387.30	393.80	443.50	454.60	505.30	541.30	585.40	609.20	627.90	B	GDP at factor cost
207.00	232.03	219.90	233.42	225.10	273.50	277.00	296.30	301.90	306.30	..	Agriculture
38.27	39.00	45.50	59.90	70.50	67.70	67.60	73.70	78.20	87.90	..	Industry
17.91	19.12	21.96	33.94	40.30	34.70	36.00	40.20	48.70	53.20	..	Manufacturing
125.53	132.57	145.90	170.18	179.80	187.40	226.10	242.30	263.90	271.90	..	Services, etc.
-1.10	1.90	-19.90	-15.90	-67.70	-6.60	35.60	42.90	66.30	68.80		Gross Domestic Saving
-1.15	2.15	-21.10	-15.32	-55.10	0.90	38.20	48.20	73.60	77.30		Gross National Saving
				(Billions of 1987 CFA Francs)							
452.99	485.48	461.22	470.41	468.95	553.52	562.30	576.76	638.37	643.82	..	Gross National Product
464.17	495.15	472.94	479.24	477.39	562.72	570.70	584.60	647.57	652.39	..	GDP at Market Prices
-68.79	-65.89	-75.36	-86.17	-142.79	-103.46	-96.00	-102.26	-88.01	-82.90	..	Resource Balance
75.11	75.48	83.53	88.43	91.48	97.50	96.20	98.61	109.52	118.96	..	Exports of Goods & NF Services
143.90	141.37	158.89	174.60	234.27	200.96	192.20	200.87	197.53	201.86	..	Imports of Goods & NF Services
532.96	561.04	548.30	565.41	620.17	666.18	666.70	686.86	735.57	735.30	..	Domestic Absorption
401.84	424.70	425.17	429.95	463.21	481.52	472.30	476.00	509.23	499.04	..	Private Consumption, etc.
48.31	49.99	56.17	61.23	63.14	63.36	62.80	62.80	66.06	62.24	..	General Gov't Consumption
82.82	86.35	66.96	74.23	93.83	121.30	131.60	148.06	160.28	174.02	..	Gross Domestic Investment
..	..	..	..	..	..	..	..	..	..	..	Fixed Investment
..	..	453.54	458.74	456.59	539.52	541.30	557.70	617.67	621.29	B	GDP at factor cost
261.45	281.74	246.75	226.93	213.46	281.84	277.00	279.66	336.74	331.81	..	Agriculture
45.89	48.19	51.14	60.98	64.84	71.28	67.60	71.09	68.34	75.33	..	Industry
..	..	26.74	34.71	34.54	38.14	36.00	38.23	37.11	35.49	..	Manufacturing
156.83	165.21	175.06	191.33	199.08	209.60	226.10	233.85	242.49	245.26	..	Services, etc.
											Memo Items:
65.14	66.74	78.84	94.40	89.28	82.57	96.20	92.93	101.75	105.29	..	Capacity to Import
-9.97	-8.73	-4.69	5.97	-2.20	-14.92	0.00	-5.68	-7.77	-13.67	..	Terms of Trade Adjustment
454.20	486.41	468.26	485.21	475.19	547.79	570.70	578.93	639.80	638.72	..	Gross Domestic Income
443.02	476.75	456.54	476.38	466.75	538.59	562.30	571.08	630.60	630.15	..	Gross National Income
				(Index 1987 = 100)							**DOMESTIC PRICES/DEFLATORS**
79.9	81.5	87.0	96.7	99.6	93.9	100.0	104.7	99.4	102.1	..	Overall (GDP)
81.9	84.3	89.6	97.3	102.6	98.5	100.0	105.0	101.3	105.2	..	Domestic Absorption
79.2	82.4	89.1	102.9	105.5	97.0	100.0	106.0	89.7	92.3	..	Agriculture
83.4	80.9	89.0	98.2	108.7	95.0	100.0	103.7	114.4	116.7	..	Industry
..	..	82.1	97.8	116.7	91.0	100.0	105.2	131.2	149.9	..	Manufacturing
..	..	..	..	..	..	..	..	..	..	..	Consumer Price Index
											MANUFACTURING ACTIVITY
..	..	..	..	..	..	..	..	..	..	..	Employment (1987=100)
..	..	..	..	..	..	..	..	..	..	..	Real Earnings per Empl. (1987=100)
..	..	..	..	..	..	..	..	..	..	..	Real Output per Empl. (1987=100)
29.5	..	..	..	..	..	..	..	..	..	..	Earnings as % of Value Added
				(Billions of current CFA Francs)							**MONETARY HOLDINGS**
64.69	72.29	87.27	117.39	127.58	135.31	129.92	140.47	141.99	135.04	..	Money Supply, Broadly Defined
60.24	68.32	81.24	107.09	113.77	117.51	109.30	114.44	110.43	98.47	..	Money
40.90	45.00	50.15	50.48	59.76	66.92	60.77	62.19	54.77	46.88	..	Currency Outside Banks
19.34	23.32	31.09	56.61	54.01	50.58	48.53	52.24	55.66	51.60	..	Demand Deposits
4.45	3.98	6.02	10.30	13.81	17.80	20.62	26.03	31.56	36.57	..	Quasi-Money
				(Millions of current CFA Francs)							
-14,700	-31,600	-34,500	-35,000	-46,500	-43,200	-30,900	-27,600	..	..	F	**GOVERNMENT DEFICIT (-) OR SURPLUS**
72,000	83,200	95,100	107,900	119,300	116,700	127,200	149,800	..	..	..	Current Revenue
46,000	49,700	52,800	59,300	75,900	79,400	78,900	76,200	..	..	..	Current Expenditure
26,000	33,500	42,300	48,600	43,400	37,300	48,300	73,600	..	..	..	Current Budget Balance
..	..	..	..	..	..	..	..	..	..	..	Capital Receipts
40,700	65,100	76,800	83,600	83,900	89,900	80,500	79,200	101,200	..	..	Capital Payments

MALI	1970	1971	1972	1973	1974	1975	1976	1977	1978	1979	1980
FOREIGN TRADE (CUSTOMS BASIS)					*(Millions of current US dollars)*						
Value of Exports, fob	..	..	..	..	..	..	..	..	..	..	..
Nonfuel Primary Products	..	..	..	..	..	..	..	..	..	..	..
Fuels	..	..	..	..	..	..	..	..	..	..	..
Manufactures	..	..	..	..	..	..	..	..	..	..	..
Value of Imports, cif	..	..	..	..	..	..	..	..	..	..	..
Nonfuel Primary Products	..	..	..	..	..	..	..	..	..	..	..
Fuels	..	..	..	..	..	..	..	..	..	..	..
Manufactures	..	..	..	..	..	..	..	..	..	..	..
					(Index 1987 = 100)						
Terms of Trade	..	..	..	..	..	..	..	..	..	..	..
Export Prices, fob	..	..	..	..	..	..	..	..	..	..	..
Import Prices, cif	..	..	..	..	..	..	..	..	..	..	..
BALANCE OF PAYMENTS					*(Millions of current US dollars)*						
Exports of Goods & Services	..	..	..	..	..	..	..	..	..	..	262.69
Merchandise, fob	32.80	39.52	45.06	58.53	64.10	71.86	94.37	124.59	94.17	145.73	204.94
Nonfactor Services	17.20	16.05	22.80	18.84	17.56	22.89	17.85	23.89	37.23	45.60	57.74
Factor Services	..	..	..	..	..	..	..	..	..	..	0.00
Imports of Goods & Services	72.00	88.76	112.15	166.42	227.78	260.34	206.57	226.35	363.39	445.89	537.04
Merchandise, fob	37.50	49.15	63.41	106.34	129.16	136.20	111.28	111.12	199.42	270.31	308.36
Nonfactor Services	29.20	33.90	43.43	51.62	90.20	102.47	78.74	95.45	150.67	163.83	211.81
Factor Services	5.30	5.72	5.32	8.46	8.42	21.67	16.55	19.78	13.29	11.75	16.88
Long-Term Interest	0.40	0.50	0.50	0.60	0.80	0.80	0.80	2.30	2.90	3.00	3.30
Private Current Transfers, net	0.30	5.22	6.08	6.32	4.09	11.95	10.15	20.31	32.35	34.55	40.47
Workers' Remittances	5.70	6.72	8.14	9.89	14.19	23.31	17.74	26.50	44.32	54.06	59.40
Curr. A/C Bal before Off. Transf.	-21.70	-27.98	-38.22	-82.73	-142.03	-153.65	-84.20	-57.55	-199.64	-220.01	-233.89
Net Official Transfers	19.80	18.96	26.93	54.36	105.95	97.08	41.98	62.95	100.82	106.71	109.57
Curr. A/C Bal after Off. Transf.	-1.90	-9.03	-11.29	-28.37	-36.08	-56.58	-42.23	5.39	-98.82	-113.29	-124.32
Long-Term Capital, net	3.40	3.11	19.76	9.66	12.51	17.45	25.54	36.67	41.83	81.84	110.61
Direct Investment	..	-0.60	3.37	0.60	..	2.01	-5.04	-4.97	-9.75	-3.06	2.37
Long-Term Loans	22.60	5.70	17.50	14.00	28.50	28.40	29.80	54.10	48.60	64.80	89.00
Disbursements	22.90	6.10	17.90	18.40	30.30	30.80	33.00	58.80	52.70	69.80	95.10
Repayments	0.30	0.40	0.40	4.40	1.80	2.40	3.20	4.70	4.10	5.00	6.10
Other Long-Term Capital	-19.20	-1.99	-1.11	-4.94	-15.99	-12.96	0.79	-12.46	2.98	20.10	19.25
Other Capital, net	-2.96	5.48	-7.37	20.25	27.34	31.13	18.88	-40.71	52.82	37.54	5.75
Change in Reserves	1.46	0.44	-1.10	-1.53	-3.77	7.99	-2.20	-1.36	4.17	-6.09	7.95
Memo Item:					*(CFA Francs per US dollar)*						
Conversion Factor (Annual Avg)	277.710	277.130	252.480	222.890	240.700	214.310	238.950	245.680	225.650	212.720	211.280
				(Millions of US dollars), outstanding at end of year							
EXTERNAL DEBT (Total)	247.3	270.9	268.4	301.1	348.9	356.1	373.8	472.0	567.6	571.1	731.9
Long-Term Debt (by debtor)	246.1	268.9	265.9	299.1	348.3	355.4	372.3	451.6	548.8	546.3	707.8
Central Bank, incl. IMF credit	8.6	8.3	9.0	8.9	16.9	17.0	19.9	19.7	31.5	31.5	40.8
Central Government	232.6	255.5	248.6	276.6	316.1	321.9	331.4	401.7	480.2	494.0	635.1
Rest of General Government	1.2	1.3	0.7	0.6	0.4	0.2	0.0	1.0	1.0	1.2	4.9
Non-financial Public Enterprises	3.7	3.8	7.6	13.0	14.9	16.3	21.0	29.2	36.1	19.6	27.0
Priv. Sector, incl non-guaranteed	0.0	0.0	0.0	0.0	0.0	0.0	0.0	0.0	0.0	0.0	0.0
Short-Term Debt	1.2	2.0	2.5	2.0	0.6	0.7	1.5	20.4	18.8	24.8	24.1
Memo Items:					*(Thousands of US dollars)*						
Int'l Reserves Excluding Gold	900.0	2,068.0	3,749.0	4,226.0	6,110.0	4,196.0	6,895.0	5,380.0	8,161.0	5,986.0	14,536.0
Gold Holdings (at market price)	..	..	..	..	..	..	..	1,569.0	3,214.0	9,639.0	11,098.0
SOCIAL INDICATORS											
Total Fertility Rate	6.5	6.5	6.5	6.5	6.5	6.5	6.5	6.5	6.5	6.6	6.6
Infant Mortality Rate	204.2	203.6	203.0	200.6	198.2	195.8	193.4	191.0	188.8	186.6	184.4
Life Expectancy at Birth	40.4	40.8	41.3	41.7	42.2	42.6	43.1	43.5	43.8	44.1	44.4
Urban Population, % of total	14.3	14.7	15.1	15.4	15.8	16.2	16.4	16.6	16.9	17.1	17.3
Food Prod. per capita (1987=100)	121.3	116.2	98.7	87.5	99.5	111.2	112.5	111.3	113.0	111.6	109.9
Labor Force, Agriculture (%)	89.2	88.8	88.4	88.0	87.7	87.3	86.9	86.6	86.2	85.8	85.5
Labor Force, Female (%)	17.3	17.3	17.4	17.4	17.4	17.5	17.5	17.4	17.4	17.4	17.4
Primary Schl. Enroll. Ratio	22.0	..	..	..	..	24.0	26.0	27.0	27.0	27.0	27.0
Primary Schl. Enroll. Ratio, Female	15.0	..	..	..	..	17.0	19.0	19.0	20.0	..	19.0
Secondary Schl. Enroll. Ratio	5.0	..	..	..	..	7.0	8.0	9.0	9.0	..	9.0

1981	1982	1983	1984	1985	1986	1987	1988	1989	1990 est.	Notes	MALI
											FOREIGN TRADE (CUSTOMS BASIS)
(Millions of current US dollars)											
..	..	..	..	..	..	..	..	..	..	..	Value of Exports, fob
..	..	..	..	..	..	..	..	..	..	..	Nonfuel Primary Products
..	..	..	..	..	..	..	..	..	..	..	Fuels
..	..	..	..	..	..	..	..	..	..	..	Manufactures
..	..	..	..	..	..	..	..	..	..	..	Value of Imports, cif
..	..	..	..	..	..	..	..	..	..	..	Nonfuel Primary Products
..	..	..	..	..	..	..	..	..	..	..	Fuels
..	..	..	..	..	..	..	..	..	..	..	Manufactures
(Index 1987 = 100)											
..	..	..	..	..	..	..	..	..	..	..	Terms of Trade
..	..	..	..	..	..	..	..	..	..	..	Export Prices, fob
..	..	..	..	..	..	..	..	..	..	..	Import Prices, cif
(Millions of current US dollars)											**BALANCE OF PAYMENTS**
200.38	190.20	208.76	232.75	234.70	276.92	342.72	339.44	347.01	440.01	..	Exports of Goods & Services
154.20	145.77	166.77	192.01	176.07	205.60	255.88	251.47	269.27	344.52	..	Merchandise, fob
46.19	44.43	41.99	40.74	57.29	68.15	82.52	83.60	68.96	85.21	..	Nonfactor Services
0.00	0.00	0.00	0.00	1.34	3.18	4.33	4.36	8.78	10.28	..	Factor Services
470.51	419.50	435.31	449.93	610.87	670.51	690.46	731.26	691.83	866.81	..	Imports of Goods & Services
269.02	232.65	240.90	257.76	328.45	338.98	335.40	359.11	338.80	432.45	..	Merchandise, fob
168.92	162.66	166.90	172.95	263.72	306.70	327.08	344.61	321.06	398.36	..	Nonfactor Services
32.58	24.20	27.50	19.22	18.70	24.83	27.97	27.54	31.97	35.99	..	Factor Services
3.40	5.60	6.60	8.30	12.50	12.60	13.50	15.40	13.70	17.10	..	Long-Term Interest
32.38	24.95	23.36	20.83	46.74	46.49	36.60	45.33	51.41	63.17	..	Private Current Transfers, net
47.66	39.41	36.48	32.50	67.00	68.44	88.18	94.34	99.31	121.32	..	Workers' Remittances
-237.74	-204.35	-203.19	-196.36	-329.43	-347.09	-311.14	-346.50	-293.41	-363.62	..	Curr. A/C Bal before Off. Transf.
97.71	89.16	100.51	130.42	196.99	185.67	215.62	256.51	218.49	269.96	..	Net Official Transfers
-140.04	-115.19	-102.69	-65.93	-132.44	-161.42	-95.52	-89.99	-74.92	-93.66	..	Curr. A/C Bal after Off. Transf.
95.61	75.32	86.13	78.10	109.51	140.05	104.15	211.82	251.09	156.83	..	Long-Term Capital, net
3.68	1.52	3.15	10.07	2.89	-8.37	-5.99	0.67	15.05	-6.24	..	Direct Investment
106.30	114.30	147.20	105.10	84.70	161.10	118.40	108.20	146.90	86.90	..	Long-Term Loans
112.40	120.20	154.50	114.90	106.40	178.70	136.60	138.50	168.70	109.60	..	Disbursements
6.10	5.90	7.30	9.80	21.70	17.60	18.20	30.30	21.80	22.70	..	Repayments
-14.37	-40.50	-64.22	-37.07	21.92	-12.68	-8.26	102.95	89.15	76.18	..	Other Long-Term Capital
37.64	13.94	4.07	0.31	10.68	-20.98	5.27	-57.55	-90.88	-17.60	..	Other Capital, net
6.79	25.93	12.49	-12.48	12.25	42.35	-13.90	-64.29	-85.29	-45.57	..	Change in Reserves
(CFA Francs per US dollar)											**Memo Item:**
271.730	328.600	381.060	436.960	449.260	346.300	300.530	297.850	319.010	272.260	..	Conversion Factor (Annual Avg)
(Millions of US dollars), outstanding at end of year											
834.5	879.0	991.8	1,243.9	1,468.2	1,756.1	2,067.2	2,038.7	2,144.9	2,432.6	..	**EXTERNAL DEBT (Total)**
761.9	860.3	970.4	1,174.5	1,399.2	1,677.2	1,991.1	1,984.4	2,098.5	2,375.5	..	Long-Term Debt (by debtor)
36.0	62.3	71.9	86.8	103.7	106.4	97.1	88.4	73.8	90.1	..	Central Bank, incl. IMF credit
698.5	772.6	872.8	1,063.3	1,267.9	1,537.5	1,862.3	1,877.2	2,006.8	2,266.9	..	Central Government
6.4	5.9	4.9	4.7	5.3	5.3	5.0	1.0	1.0	1.2	..	Rest of General Government
21.0	19.5	20.4	17.0	18.8	20.3	17.9	10.1	11.1	11.0	..	Non-financial Public Enterprises
0.0	0.0	0.4	2.7	3.5	7.7	8.8	7.7	5.8	6.3	..	Priv. Sector, incl non-guaranteed
72.6	18.7	21.4	69.4	69.0	78.9	76.1	54.3	46.4	57.1	..	Short-Term Debt
(Thousands of US dollars)											**Memo Items:**
17,386.0	16,727.0	16,234.0	26,641.0	22,517.0	23,311.0	15,849.0	35,973.0	115,820.0	190,518.0	..	Int'l Reserves Excluding Gold
7,483.0	8,602.0	7,182.0	5,804.0	6,156.0	7,359.0	9,114.0	7,723.0	7,549.0	7,248.0	..	Gold Holdings (at market price)
											SOCIAL INDICATORS
6.7	6.7	6.8	6.8	6.9	6.9	7.0	7.0	7.0	7.1	..	Total Fertility Rate
182.2	180.0	177.8	175.5	173.3	171.0	168.8	167.9	166.9	166.0	..	Infant Mortality Rate
44.7	45.0	45.4	45.9	46.3	46.8	47.2	47.4	47.7	47.9	..	Life Expectancy at Birth
17.4	17.6	17.7	17.9	18.0	18.3	18.6	18.8	19.0	19.2	..	Urban Population, % of total
121.3	123.1	117.7	103.0	103.8	109.8	100.0	115.1	113.0	105.7	..	Food Prod. per capita (1987=100)
..	..	..	..	..	..	..	..	..	..	..	Labor Force, Agriculture (%)
17.3	17.2	17.0	16.9	16.8	16.7	16.5	16.4	16.3	16.2	..	Labor Force, Female (%)
24.0	24.0	23.0	24.0	23.0	23.0	23.0	..	23.0	..	..	Primary Schl. Enroll. Ratio
18.0	17.0	17.0	18.0	17.0	17.0	17.0	..	17.0	..	..	Primary Schl. Enroll. Ratio, Female
8.0	7.0	7.0	7.0	7.0	6.0	6.0	..	6.0	..	..	Secondary Schl. Enroll. Ratio

MALTA	1970	1971	1972	1973	1974	1975	1976	1977	1978	1979	1980
CURRENT GNP PER CAPITA (US $)	760	830	900	1,030	1,220	1,540	1,700	1,860	2,090	2,500	3,150
POPULATION (thousands)	326	324	322	322	324	328	334	343	353	360	364
USE AND ORIGIN OF RESOURCES					*(Millions of current Maltese Liri)*						
Gross National Product (GNP)	102.10	105.30	110.50	123.30	144.10	184.10	221.80	258.90	294.60	338.70	422.50
Net Factor Income from Abroad	7.30	7.50	8.30	7.50	12.50	18.30	18.10	19.10	16.90	12.90	30.50
GDP at Market Prices	94.80	97.80	102.20	115.80	131.60	165.80	203.70	239.80	277.70	325.80	392.00
Resource Balance	-28.40	-25.20	-23.50	-22.70	-38.00	-22.40	-23.90	-34.60	-19.90	-16.90	-21.40
Exports of Goods & NFServices	47.10	50.00	53.50	75.30	110.40	137.30	172.70	207.40	229.60	290.80	356.60
Imports of Goods & NFServices	75.50	75.20	77.00	98.00	148.40	159.70	196.60	242.00	249.50	307.70	378.00
Domestic Absorption	123.20	123.00	125.70	138.50	169.60	188.20	227.60	274.40	297.60	342.70	413.40
Private Consumption, etc.	73.80	75.10	80.40	90.10	107.00	118.70	135.70	172.40	186.40	206.00	253.50
General Gov't Consumption	18.40	19.50	19.80	22.80	26.90	30.50	35.90	39.70	46.10	53.70	63.40
Gross Domestic Investment	31.00	28.40	25.50	25.60	35.70	39.00	56.00	62.30	65.10	83.00	96.50
Fixed Investment	27.80	25.50	22.50	22.30	31.20	37.50	54.10	60.00	60.30	78.20	87.10
Indirect Taxes, net	12.60	12.60	12.60	14.90	13.00	12.90	14.30	19.90	26.40	32.10	43.40
GDP at factor cost	82.20	85.20	89.60	100.90	118.60	152.90	189.40	219.90	251.30	293.70	348.60
Agriculture	5.80	6.10	6.70	7.30	8.30	9.20	11.40	12.90	11.40	11.50	13.30
Industry	28.40	26.60	30.30	34.80	44.40	61.80	78.50	91.40	106.40	125.20	146.70
Manufacturing	17.90	17.20	22.00	26.70	33.70	46.70	61.50	72.60	84.40	100.00	115.40
Services, etc.	48.00	52.50	52.60	58.80	65.90	81.90	99.50	115.60	133.50	157.00	188.60
Gross Domestic Saving	2.60	3.20	2.00	2.90	-2.30	16.60	32.10	27.70	45.20	66.10	75.10
Gross National Saving	18.90	19.00	16.80	17.80	18.00	44.10	63.20	63.20	73.20	91.50	117.10
					(Millions of 1987 Maltese Liri)						
Gross National Product	188.28	194.05	204.65	221.70	248.00	300.60	344.68	383.44	420.49	458.53	505.70
GDP at Market Prices	172.94	177.20	187.51	205.82	226.26	270.51	316.55	355.11	394.75	436.16	466.91
Resource Balance	-155.51	-139.31	-123.04	-97.76	-99.63	-65.41	-66.34	-70.26	-40.77	-21.38	-23.19
Exports of Goods & NFServices	127.08	133.29	129.30	167.00	195.39	234.21	271.91	310.94	325.58	380.36	425.83
Imports of Goods & NFServices	282.60	272.60	252.34	264.77	295.02	299.62	338.25	381.21	366.35	401.74	449.02
Domestic Absorption	328.45	316.51	310.55	303.58	325.89	335.92	382.89	425.38	435.51	457.54	490.10
Private Consumption, etc.	198.87	197.23	198.31	198.72	212.26	215.71	237.45	272.72	273.63	279.19	298.68
General Gov't Consumption	42.41	42.41	42.80	43.56	44.90	51.01	59.23	59.99	66.10	72.98	74.32
Gross Domestic Investment	87.16	76.87	69.44	61.30	68.73	69.20	86.21	92.67	95.78	105.36	117.10
Fixed Investment	81.32	71.24	62.81	52.26	56.71	64.21	79.91	85.30	82.49	91.87	92.57
GDP at factor cost	..	..	..	..	..	..	..	..	..	..	..
Agriculture	..	..	..	..	..	..	..	..	..	..	..
Industry	..	..	..	..	..	..	..	..	..	..	..
Manufacturing	..	..	..	..	..	..	..	..	..	..	..
Services, etc.	..	..	..	..	..	..	..	..	..	..	..
Memo Items:											
Capacity to Import	176.30	181.25	175.33	203.44	219.48	257.59	297.13	326.70	337.13	379.68	423.60
Terms of Trade Adjustment	49.21	47.96	46.02	36.43	24.09	23.39	25.22	15.76	11.55	-0.69	-2.23
Gross Domestic Income	222.15	225.16	233.53	242.25	250.34	293.90	341.77	370.87	406.30	435.47	464.68
Gross National Income	237.49	242.01	250.68	258.14	272.08	323.99	369.90	399.20	432.04	457.84	503.47
DOMESTIC PRICES/DEFLATORS					*(Index 1987 = 100)*						
Overall (GDP)	54.8	55.2	54.5	56.3	58.2	61.3	64.4	67.5	70.3	74.7	84.0
Domestic Absorption	37.5	38.9	40.5	45.6	52.0	56.0	59.4	64.5	68.3	74.9	84.4
Agriculture	..	..	..	..	..	..	..	..	..	..	..
Industry	..	..	..	..	..	..	..	..	..	..	..
Manufacturing	..	..	..	..	..	..	..	..	..	..	..
Consumer Price Index	44.0	45.0	46.5	50.1	53.7	58.5	58.8	64.7	67.7	72.6	84.0
MANUFACTURING ACTIVITY											
Employment (1987=100)	65.0	69.5	74.9	81.8	82.2	81.6	88.8	96.9	102.7	107.6	104.5
Real Earnings per Empl. (1987=100)	38.5	42.0	43.7	44.3	49.2	61.9	69.6	70.1	80.8	84.4	89.6
Real Output per Empl. (1987=100)	..	..	..	..	..	..	..	..	..	..	..
Earnings as % of Value Added	47.3	50.7	50.6	48.0	49.6	49.8	44.7	44.4	50.3	49.0	50.4
MONETARY HOLDINGS					*(Millions of current Maltese Liri)*						
Money Supply, Broadly Defined	136.3	157.9	174.8	186.6	205.2	246.8	305.4	336.0	381.9	429.7	463.9
Money	57.7	67.9	80.1	87.2	99.0	123.8	148.3	165.6	194.6	231.6	258.8
Currency Outside Banks	45.9	55.7	62.3	72.7	79.6	98.9	119.6	137.8	155.0	176.3	206.1
Demand Deposits	11.8	12.2	17.8	14.5	19.5	24.9	28.7	27.8	39.6	55.4	52.7
Quasi-Money	78.6	90.0	94.7	99.5	106.2	123.1	157.1	170.3	187.3	198.1	205.1
GOVERNMENT DEFICIT (-) OR SURPLUS					*(Millions of current Maltese Liri)*						
	..	..	-4.8	3.1	4.8	-6.2	4.5	3.5	11.8	..	4.3
Current Revenue	..	..	40.8	57.6	69.4	91.3	102.5	104.9	125.5	..	142.2
Current Expenditure	..	..	37.9	40.9	56.4	63.9	70.6	81.5	87.6	..	106.6
Current Budget Balance	..	..	2.9	16.7	13.1	27.4	32.0	23.4	37.9	..	35.7
Capital Receipts	..	..	0.1	0.0	4.8	0.9	2.6	0.7	0.1	..	1.1
Capital Payments	..	..	7.7	13.6	13.1	34.5	30.0	20.6	26.2	..	32.5

1981	1982	1983	1984	1985	1986	1987	1988	1989	1990 estimate	Notes	MALTA
3,590	3,790	3,510	3,440	3,390	3,580	4,160	5,170	6,010	6,610	..	CURRENT GNP PER CAPITA (US $)
364	362	357	351	344	345	346	348	350	354	..	POPULATION (thousands)
				(Millions of current Maltese Liri)							USE AND ORIGIN OF RESOURCES
477.70	513.80	495.70	506.50	514.80	539.90	579.80	634.80	705.90	767.00	..	Gross National Product (GNP)
41.20	52.00	38.10	45.40	38.80	28.00	30.60	28.30	35.80	38.90	..	Net Factor Income from Abroad
436.50	461.80	457.60	461.10	476.00	511.90	549.20	606.50	670.10	728.10	..	GDP at Market Prices
-36.50	-74.80	-68.50	-70.00	-75.30	-51.50	-51.30	-60.90	-73.30	..	..	Resource Balance
355.90	319.80	307.60	323.50	345.20	370.20	429.60	480.00	543.50	..	..	Exports of Goods & NFServices
392.40	394.60	376.10	393.50	420.50	421.70	480.90	540.90	616.80	..	..	Imports of Goods & NFServices
473.00	536.60	526.10	531.10	551.30	563.40	600.50	667.40	743.40	..	..	Domestic Absorption
279.40	305.80	306.70	317.50	333.20	343.40	351.20	387.60	425.50	..	..	Private Consumption, etc.
75.40	85.20	82.30	80.30	84.30	89.50	98.20	105.20	119.60	..	..	General Gov't Consumption
118.20	145.60	137.10	133.30	133.80	130.50	151.10	174.60	198.30	..	..	Gross Domestic Investment
105.60	120.10	131.60	126.50	125.90	122.30	153.50	166.40	188.40	..	..	Fixed Investment
46.00	44.10	40.50	39.70	45.40	50.10	53.70	63.80	73.29	..	..	Indirect Taxes, net
390.50	417.70	417.10	421.40	430.60	461.80	495.50	542.63	596.85	..	..	GDP at factor cost
15.00	16.80	18.70	19.30	19.40	20.40	21.40	21.10	22.36	..	..	Agriculture
162.10	170.40	164.60	169.40	170.00	188.30	200.00	219.90	..	..	..	Industry
121.40	125.00	120.00	124.70	126.90	134.70	136.40	146.60	163.66	..	..	Manufacturing
213.40	230.50	233.80	232.70	241.20	253.10	274.10	301.63	..	..	..	Services, etc.
81.70	70.80	68.60	63.30	58.50	79.00	99.80	113.70	125.00	..	..	Gross Domestic Saving
135.50	138.10	120.90	123.10	114.20	125.90	152.20	174.30	179.90	..	..	Gross National Saving
				(Millions of 1987 Maltese Liri)							
527.39	545.01	530.47	541.21	547.88	558.33	579.80	623.27	678.72	716.05	..	Gross National Product
482.37	493.39	490.37	494.99	507.79	527.52	549.20	595.41	644.11	679.54	I	GDP at Market Prices
-37.18	-81.19	-57.73	-59.73	-71.31	-46.74	-51.30	-78.13	-88.50	..	..	Resource Balance
377.26	325.14	319.15	332.01	356.63	381.47	429.60	455.99	504.79	..	..	Exports of Goods & NFServices
414.44	406.33	376.88	391.74	427.95	428.22	480.90	534.12	593.29	..	..	Imports of Goods & NFServices
519.55	574.59	548.10	554.72	579.10	574.26	600.50	673.54	732.61	..	..	Domestic Absorption
298.65	301.73	303.98	319.89	342.56	344.67	351.20	383.36	423.50	..	..	Private Consumption, etc.
79.86	84.64	83.68	81.58	86.16	89.98	98.20	104.12	117.31	..	..	General Gov't Consumption
141.04	188.22	160.44	153.26	150.38	139.61	151.10	186.06	191.81	..	..	Gross Domestic Investment
108.50	124.44	144.13	134.05	128.66	117.41	153.50	162.87	164.51	..	..	Fixed Investment
..	..	..	..	..	..	..	..	..	..	..	GDP at factor cost
..	..	..	..	..	..	..	..	..	..	..	Agriculture
..	..	..	..	..	..	..	..	..	..	..	Industry
..	..	..	..	..	..	..	..	..	..	..	Manufacturing
..	..	..	..	..	..	..	..	..	..	..	Services, etc.
											Memo Items:
375.89	329.31	308.24	322.06	351.31	375.92	429.60	473.99	522.78	..	..	Capacity to Import
-1.37	4.17	-10.91	-9.96	-5.32	-5.55	0.00	17.99	18.00	..	..	Terms of Trade Adjustment
481.00	497.56	479.46	485.03	502.47	521.97	549.20	613.40	662.11	..	..	Gross Domestic Income
526.02	549.18	519.56	531.25	542.56	552.78	579.80	641.26	696.72	..	..	Gross National Income
				(Index 1987 = 100)							DOMESTIC PRICES/DEFLATORS
90.5	93.6	93.3	93.2	93.7	97.0	100.0	101.9	104.0	107.1	..	Overall (GDP)
91.0	93.4	96.0	95.7	95.2	98.1	100.0	99.1	101.5	..	..	Domestic Absorption
..	..	..	..	..	..	..	..	..	..	..	Agriculture
..	..	..	..	..	..	..	..	..	..	..	Industry
..	..	..	..	..	..	..	..	..	..	..	Manufacturing
93.7	99.1	98.3	97.8	97.6	99.6	100.0	100.9	101.8	104.8	..	Consumer Price Index
											MANUFACTURING ACTIVITY
101.1	90.9	86.6	90.1	92.6	95.7	100.0	..	..	..	..	Employment (1987=100)
91.4	101.2	102.5	102.3	103.0	101.3	100.0	..	..	..	..	Real Earnings per Empl. (1987=100)
..	..	..	..	..	..	..	..	..	..	..	Real Output per Empl. (1987=100)
53.7	54.0	52.7	51.0	50.0	49.4	49.0	..	..	..	..	Earnings as % of Value Added
				(Millions of current Maltese Liri)							MONETARY HOLDINGS
513.8	544.9	587.5	629.5	662.5	700.9	770.6	837.8	924.1	1,027.5	..	Money Supply, Broadly Defined
293.7	306.3	324.6	325.9	321.2	323.3	354.6	364.0	368.6	384.6	..	Money
239.2	259.7	279.6	283.7	273.3	273.8	300.2	314.3	319.4	330.3	..	Currency Outside Banks
54.6	46.5	45.0	42.2	47.9	49.5	54.4	49.6	49.2	54.3	..	Demand Deposits
220.0	238.7	262.9	303.6	341.3	377.6	416.0	473.8	555.5	642.8	..	Quasi-Money
				(Millions of current Maltese Liri)							
5.6	-7.6	7.3	2.1	-19.2	-19.5	-36.7	-0.2	-31.1	..	F	GOVERNMENT DEFICIT (-) OR SURPLUS
179.1	192.5	197.5	193.7	197.0	189.8	188.7	234.0	238.9	..	..	Current Revenue
134.7	153.0	149.3	151.0	152.4	158.6	170.5	184.8	202.8	..	..	Current Expenditure
44.4	39.5	48.1	42.7	44.5	31.2	18.3	49.3	36.1	..	..	Current Budget Balance
4.0	0.9	2.2	0.1	0.1	0.1	0.1	0.1	0.1	..	..	Capital Receipts
42.9	48.0	43.0	40.7	63.9	50.8	55.1	49.5	67.3	..	..	Capital Payments

MALTA	1970	1971	1972	1973	1974	1975	1976	1977	1978	1979	1980
FOREIGN TRADE (CUSTOMS BASIS)					*(Millions of current US dollars)*						
Value of Exports, fob	29.3	36.3	56.4	86.9	110.5	131.5	187.9	246.7	304.3	381.6	431.7
Nonfuel Primary Products	..	..	..	..	..	..	..	..	..	..	..
Fuels	..	..	..	..	..	..	..	..	..	..	..
Manufactures	23.0	31.0	50.5	74.6	96.5	117.2	167.3	220.5	280.2	349.9	404.0
Value of Imports, cif	160.5	156.1	174.2	239.5	357.3	374.9	420.9	512.7	569.1	753.3	935.7
Nonfuel Primary Products	48.7	52.3	55.6	81.0	109.9	111.5	114.1	132.9	146.1	181.4	223.8
Fuels	7.8	9.6	13.0	14.4	40.4	35.6	37.0	41.4	41.8	49.9	96.2
Manufactures	104.1	94.3	105.6	144.1	207.0	227.7	269.7	338.3	381.2	522.0	615.6
					(Index 1987 = 100)						
Terms of Trade	85.1	98.8	113.0	112.0	111.9	106.1	107.5	106.6	102.3	102.7	102.6
Export Prices, fob	21.4	26.2	31.2	42.0	59.8	59.5	62.3	67.5	72.6	87.2	98.1
Import Prices, cif	25.2	26.6	27.7	37.5	53.5	56.1	57.9	63.4	71.0	84.9	95.6
BALANCE OF PAYMENTS					*(Millions of current US dollars)*						
Exports of Goods & Services	138.9	162.1	204.2	282.5	369.9	451.9	495.1	586.1	705.3	909.1	1,171.9
Merchandise, fob	34.0	47.0	74.4	109.3	154.9	179.8	237.6	300.7	346.4	442.4	509.8
Nonfactor Services	79.0	86.5	97.5	138.3	167.1	208.4	195.9	215.2	280.0	364.6	508.9
Factor Services	25.9	28.6	32.2	35.0	48.0	63.7	61.6	70.1	78.9	102.1	153.1
Imports of Goods & Services	189.8	194.3	211.2	277.9	401.8	427.0	478.4	591.3	679.1	919.7	1,185.2
Merchandise, fob	143.9	142.4	155.9	212.9	313.6	332.4	376.6	456.8	507.3	674.3	884.7
Nonfactor Services	37.5	41.9	44.6	51.5	72.9	79.5	85.4	113.4	138.0	181.9	240.3
Factor Services	8.4	10.1	10.7	13.6	15.3	15.1	16.5	21.1	33.7	63.6	60.2
Long-Term Interest	1.7	2.3	0.4	0.5	1.3	1.3	1.0	1.0	0.9	1.8	1.3
Private Current Transfers, net	21.6	20.4	17.0	20.1	20.2	23.9	30.6	38.8	28.8	34.9	33.3
Workers' Remittances	16.8	13.5	15.2	11.9	10.6	13.5	21.6	24.6	16.3	18.1	22.3
Curr. A/C Bal before Off. Transf.	-29.3	-11.8	10.0	24.7	-11.7	48.9	47.3	33.6	55.0	24.3	20.0
Net Official Transfers	23.7	17.7	15.2	11.9	24.4	17.2	15.3	12.8	24.7	28.5	24.6
Curr. A/C Bal after Off. Transf.	-5.6	5.9	25.2	36.6	12.7	66.0	62.6	46.4	79.7	52.7	44.6
Long-Term Capital, net	2.1	-49.8	-11.5	-40.9	21.0	28.6	41.2	1.9	-8.3	-1.4	23.7
Direct Investment	11.6	11.6	4.5	5.2	10.6	15.9	14.1	18.5	21.5	16.2	26.6
Long-Term Loans	-0.7	-8.0	3.9	1.8	3.7	6.9	17.1	1.5	15.7	7.3	4.9
Disbursements	0.0	7.1	4.7	2.6	5.0	8.3	18.1	2.6	17.1	9.1	6.7
Repayments	0.7	15.1	0.8	0.8	1.3	1.4	1.0	1.1	1.4	1.8	1.8
Other Long-Term Capital	-8.8	-53.3	-19.9	-47.9	6.7	5.8	10.0	-18.1	-45.5	-24.9	-7.8
Other Capital, net	20.0	61.1	58.5	43.7	8.3	18.2	-9.5	11.8	53.8	4.0	-16.9
Change in Reserves	-16.5	-17.2	-72.1	-39.3	-42.0	-112.8	-94.2	-60.1	-125.2	-55.4	-51.4
Memo Item:					*(Maltese Liri per US dollar)*						
Conversion Factor (Annual Avg)	0.420	0.410	0.380	0.370	0.390	0.380	0.430	0.420	0.390	0.360	0.350
EXTERNAL DEBT (Total)	24.90	18.10	21.00	22.40	*(Millions of US dollars), outstanding at end of year* 25.80	30.40	44.90	70.90	89.30	115.40	108.20
Long-Term Debt (by debtor)	24.90	18.10	21.00	22.40	25.80	30.40	44.90	49.90	70.30	82.40	86.20
Central Bank, incl. IMF credit	..	..	..	..	..	..	..	..	..	..	..
Central Government	24.90	18.10	21.00	22.40	25.80	30.40	44.90	49.90	70.30	82.40	86.20
Rest of General Government	..	..	..	..	..	..	..	..	..	..	..
Non-financial Public Enterprises	..	..	..	..	..	..	..	..	..	..	..
Priv. Sector, incl non-guaranteed	..	..	..	..	..	..	..	..	..	..	..
Short-Term Debt	0.00	0.00	0.00	0.00	0.00	0.00	0.00	21.00	19.00	33.00	22.00
Memo Items:					*(Millions of US dollars)*						
Int'l Reserves Excluding Gold	148.2	184.7	261.7	310.4	386.7	485.8	607.8	719.6	925.1	1,012.7	990.1
Gold Holdings (at market price)	10.4	15.4	22.9	39.6	65.8	49.5	47.6	59.4	81.4	187.4	255.8
SOCIAL INDICATORS											
Total Fertility Rate	2.0	2.1	2.0	1.6	1.6	2.3	2.2	2.2	2.1	2.1	2.0
Infant Mortality Rate	27.9	23.9	16.7	23.1	19.9	17.5	15.0	13.5	14.4	15.7	15.2
Life Expectancy at Birth	70.1	70.4	70.6	70.7	70.8	70.8	70.9	71.0	71.1	71.3	71.4
Urban Population, % of total	77.6	78.3	78.9	79.6	80.2	80.9	81.4	81.9	82.5	83.0	83.5
Food Prod. per capita (1987=100)	79.9	79.7	86.5	86.2	82.5	79.5	86.1	94.0	98.6	80.0	83.0
Labor Force, Agriculture (%)	6.9	6.7	6.5	6.4	6.2	6.0	5.9	5.7	5.5	5.4	5.2
Labor Force, Female (%)	21.3	21.3	21.4	21.4	21.5	21.5	21.6	21.6	21.6	21.7	21.7
Primary Schl. Enroll. Ratio	106.0	..	..	..	..	94.0	108.0	110.0	111.0	110.0	103.0
Primary Schl. Enroll. Ratio, Female	106.0	..	..	..	..	92.0	110.0	109.0	111.0	109.0	104.0
Secondary Schl. Enroll. Ratio	50.0	..	..	..	..	75.0	72.0	71.0	70.0	74.0	67.0

1981	1982	1983	1984	1985	1986	1987	1988	1989	1990 estimate	Notes	MALTA
				(Millions of current US dollars)							**FOREIGN TRADE (CUSTOMS BASIS)**
397.4	364.8	327.7	358.1	362.2	460.4	551.4	656.8	797.5	1,125.7	..	Value of Exports, fob
..	..	..	27.6	28.4	28.9	35.6	36.4	40.3	62.4	..	Nonfuel Primary Products
..	..	..	0.0	1.3	0.0	0.1	0.0	0.0	0.0	..	Fuels
369.8	341.1	303.6	330.5	332.4	431.4	515.8	620.4	757.2	1,063.3	..	Manufactures
850.8	783.3	727.3	710.8	751.0	879.7	1,116.5	1,331.4	1,494.0	1,960.1	..	Value of Imports, cif
188.6	172.2	152.7	144.1	144.3	156.9	188.2	221.0	235.5	309.0	..	Nonfuel Primary Products
114.5	114.5	88.5	91.8	90.9	53.4	72.6	61.5	95.1	124.8	..	Fuels
547.7	496.7	486.1	474.9	515.7	669.5	855.7	1,048.8	1,163.4	1,526.3	..	Manufactures
				(Index 1987 = 100)							
93.1	107.3	91.0	89.9	89.5	99.4	100.0	103.4	103.4	99.3	..	Terms of Trade
88.8	98.0	81.6	79.1	78.0	91.5	100.0	108.4	106.9	128.2	..	Export Prices, fob
95.4	91.3	89.7	88.0	87.1	92.0	100.0	104.9	103.3	129.2	..	Import Prices, cif
				(Millions of current US dollars)							**BALANCE OF PAYMENTS**
1,073.4	925.4	821.6	815.6	835.8	1,050.9	1,349.7	1,589.8	1,726.3	..	..	Exports of Goods & Services
470.1	421.0	388.5	410.8	421.6	521.6	631.3	758.3	866.3	..	..	Merchandise, fob
441.7	330.5	300.2	266.1	287.5	382.7	578.9	674.6	669.2	..	..	Nonfactor Services
161.6	174.0	133.0	138.6	126.6	146.6	139.5	156.9	190.8	..	..	Factor Services
1,072.7	983.9	889.6	868.9	913.3	1,111.0	1,409.3	1,688.0	1,833.9	..	..	Imports of Goods & Services
778.1	709.2	659.5	639.2	672.1	786.5	1,024.6	1,222.3	1,327.7	..	..	Merchandise, fob
240.8	243.6	204.9	208.4	217.0	278.6	357.2	410.1	431.0	..	..	Nonfactor Services
53.8	31.1	25.2	21.3	24.3	45.8	27.5	55.6	75.2	..	..	Factor Services
1.1	0.9	1.1	1.3	1.5	2.1	2.2	2.0	2.0	1.8	..	Long-Term Interest
32.6	37.1	32.8	31.2	36.0	48.1	63.1	97.6	54.8	..	..	Private Current Transfers, net
19.4	16.3	17.6	13.9	10.7	10.4	16.5	26.9	40.5	..	..	Workers' Remittances
33.4	-21.4	-35.1	-22.1	-41.6	-12.0	3.5	-0.6	-52.8	..	..	Curr. A/C Bal before Off. Transf.
57.7	37.6	33.5	33.4	18.8	23.2	23.4	68.6	49.6	..	..	Net Official Transfers
91.0	16.3	-1.6	11.3	-22.8	11.2	26.9	68.0	-3.2	..	..	Curr. A/C Bal after Off. Transf.
18.4	7.8	3.2	31.0	-14.9	-46.8	-18.5	-75.9	-20.1	..	..	Long-Term Capital, net
39.0	20.9	24.5	26.2	19.0	21.9	19.4	40.8	51.7	..	..	Direct Investment
8.8	2.5	23.5	5.0	0.6	-8.8	-8.1	-7.3	-4.3	34.1	..	Long-Term Loans
11.4	4.8	32.1	12.2	7.7	3.0	0.3	0.0	3.0	40.7	..	Disbursements
2.6	2.3	8.6	7.2	7.1	11.8	8.4	7.3	7.3	6.6	..	Repayments
-29.5	-15.6	-44.8	-0.2	-34.5	-59.9	-29.8	-109.4	-67.4	..	..	Other Long-Term Capital
38.5	28.1	102.6	-10.4	-29.4	31.1	-12.9	42.7	37.5	..	..	Other Capital, net
-147.8	-52.1	-104.2	-31.9	67.1	4.6	4.5	-34.8	-14.2	-68.2	..	Change in Reserves
				(Maltese Liri per US dollar)							**Memo Item:**
0.390	0.410	0.430	0.460	0.470	0.390	0.350	0.330	0.350	0.320	..	Conversion Factor (Annual Avg)
			(Millions of US dollars), outstanding at end of year								
110.00	122.60	135.80	175.80	185.40	222.20	277.80	369.90	411.10	597.80	..	**EXTERNAL DEBT (Total)**
82.00	76.60	93.80	90.80	99.40	95.20	95.50	84.90	80.10	121.80	..	Long-Term Debt (by debtor)
..	..	..	..	..	..	..	..	..	..	..	Central Bank, incl. IMF credit
82.00	76.60	93.80	90.80	99.40	95.20	95.50	84.90	80.10	121.80	..	Central Government
..	..	..	..	..	..	..	..	..	..	..	Rest of General Government
..	..	..	..	..	..	..	..	..	..	..	Non-financial Public Enterprises
..	..	..	..	..	..	..	..	..	..	..	Priv. Sector, incl non-guaranteed
28.00	46.00	42.00	85.00	86.00	127.00	182.30	285.00	331.00	476.00	..	Short-Term Debt
				(Millions of US dollars)							**Memo Items:**
1,073.8	1,083.6	1,112.3	990.2	986.9	1,145.4	1,414.6	1,364.7	1,355.2	1,431.8	..	Int'l Reserves Excluding Gold
181.3	211.1	180.1	143.7	152.4	182.2	225.6	191.2	90.6	60.4	..	Gold Holdings (at market price)
											SOCIAL INDICATORS
2.0	2.0	2.0	2.0	2.0	2.1	2.1	2.1	2.1	2.1	..	Total Fertility Rate
13.1	13.9	14.1	11.6	13.6	11.8	10.0	9.6	9.3	8.9	..	Infant Mortality Rate
71.5	71.7	71.9	72.1	72.3	72.5	72.8	73.0	73.2	73.4	..	Life Expectancy at Birth
83.9	84.3	84.8	85.2	85.6	85.9	86.3	86.6	87.0	87.3	..	Urban Population, % of total
77.2	89.0	92.4	90.0	98.6	104.0	100.0	94.8	101.7	101.3	..	Food Prod. per capita (1987=100)
..	..	..	..	..	..	..	..	..	..	..	Labor Force, Agriculture (%)
21.8	22.0	22.1	22.2	22.3	22.5	22.7	22.8	23.0	23.2	..	Labor Force, Female (%)
..	..	..	105.0	107.0	107.0	107.0	108.0	..	..	..	Primary Schl. Enroll. Ratio
..	..	..	102.0	104.0	104.0	105.0	107.0	..	..	..	Primary Schl. Enroll. Ratio, Female
..	74.0	76.0	80.0	78.0	77.0	77.0	80.0	..	..	..	Secondary Schl. Enroll. Ratio

MAURITANIA	1970	1971	1972	1973	1974	1975	1976	1977	1978	1979	1980
CURRENT GNP PER CAPITA (US $)	180	170	180	200	260	300	340	360	360	390	440
POPULATION (thousands)	1,221	1,249	1,277	1,307	1,338	1,371	1,407	1,443	1,480	1,516	1,551
USE AND ORIGIN OF RESOURCES	*(Millions of current Mauritanian Ouguiyas)*										
Gross National Product (GNP)	10,878	11,513	12,646	13,913	17,903	19,419	22,089	22,890	23,332	27,464	30,841
Net Factor Income from Abroad	-750	-1,071	-736	-964	-900	-1,095	-1,521	-1,756	-1,800	-2,094	-1,714
GDP at Market Prices	11,628	12,585	13,382	14,877	18,803	20,514	23,610	24,646	25,132	29,558	32,555
Resource Balance	892	950	-379	170	-1,941	-4,395	-9,308	-9,942	-7,795	-7,727	-9,546
Exports of Goods & NFServices	4,746	5,062	8,365	7,064	9,207	7,995	9,083	8,191	8,502	9,945	12,154
Imports of Goods & NFServices	3,854	4,112	8,744	6,894	11,148	12,390	18,391	18,133	16,297	17,672	21,700
Domestic Absorption	10,736	11,635	13,761	14,707	20,744	24,909	32,918	34,588	32,927	37,285	42,101
Private Consumption, etc.	6,537	6,929	7,114	10,638	14,457	13,807	15,403	16,088	16,413	20,954	22,073
General Gov't Consumption	1,640	1,832	2,581	2,785	3,264	4,033	7,512	8,870	8,731	8,793	8,242
Gross Domestic Investment	2,559	2,873	4,065	1,284	3,023	7,069	10,003	9,630	7,783	7,538	11,786
Fixed Investment	..	..	..	2,415	2,050	4,141	9,319	8,499	6,673	7,375	10,187
Indirect Taxes, net	700	752	953	1,400	2,317	2,041	2,461	2,217	1,915	2,100	1,996
GDP at factor cost	10,928	11,833	12,429	13,477	16,486	18,473	21,149	22,429	23,217	27,458	30,559
Agriculture	3,199	3,317	3,463	5,201	5,872	5,467	6,023	6,556	7,158	7,811	9,285
Industry	4,204	4,674	4,420	4,068	5,488	6,296	7,163	6,687	6,082	7,916	7,941
Manufacturing	539	579	630	..	..	..	..	..	..	..	..
Services, etc.	3,524	3,842	4,546	4,208	5,126	6,710	7,963	9,186	9,977	11,731	13,333
Gross Domestic Saving	3,451	3,823	3,686	1,454	1,082	2,674	695	-312	-12	-189	2,240
Gross National Saving	2,373	2,480	2,753	-142	-396	599	-2,105	-3,114	-2,769	-3,756	-762
	(Millions of 1987 Mauritanian Ouguiyas)										
Gross National Product	52,408	51,793	54,317	50,340	56,326	52,162	55,324	54,433	54,493	57,250	60,888
GDP at Market Prices	54,646	55,175	55,893	52,415	57,800	54,093	58,416	57,649	57,397	60,044	62,441
Resource Balance	5,063	5,126	4,935	4,037	-4,653	-13,414	-27,528	-22,708	-13,288	-8,778	-8,055
Exports of Goods & NFServices	16,591	16,852	27,870	20,134	22,046	16,094	17,529	16,620	17,960	20,447	21,542
Imports of Goods & NFServices	11,527	11,726	22,935	16,097	26,699	29,508	45,057	39,327	31,248	29,225	29,597
Domestic Absorption	49,583	50,049	50,957	48,378	62,453	67,507	85,943	80,357	70,685	68,822	70,496
Private Consumption, etc.	38,587	38,655	37,467	35,102	39,459	36,799	41,667	38,356	36,311	38,025	39,434
General Gov't Consumption	7,392	7,556	8,058	9,268	10,255	11,593	19,889	20,311	19,337	17,999	13,256
Gross Domestic Investment	3,604	3,839	5,432	4,008	12,739	19,115	24,377	21,689	15,037	12,798	17,805
Fixed Investment	..	..	..	8,136	9,511	10,429	22,605	19,032	12,598	12,465	14,849
GDP at factor cost	49,478	50,012	50,108	46,490	49,820	48,004	51,758	51,749	52,369	54,380	57,356
Agriculture	18,966	16,486	23,355	19,071	19,007	15,998	16,417	17,368	16,883	17,191	19,171
Industry	10,006	10,592	9,551	9,251	10,673	9,642	10,776	9,600	10,011	11,076	10,355
Manufacturing	..	..	..	..	..	..	..	..	..	..	..
Services, etc.	19,041	20,608	16,826	17,094	18,543	21,136	23,014	23,899	24,404	24,619	27,008
Memo Items:											
Capacity to Import	14,195	14,434	21,941	16,494	22,051	19,041	22,253	17,765	16,302	16,447	16,577
Terms of Trade Adjustment	-2,396	-2,417	-5,929	-3,640	5	2,947	4,724	1,145	-1,658	-4,000	-4,965
Gross Domestic Income	52,250	52,758	49,964	48,775	57,804	57,040	63,139	58,794	55,739	56,044	57,476
Gross National Income	50,012	49,375	48,388	46,700	56,331	55,109	60,047	55,578	52,835	53,250	55,923
DOMESTIC PRICES/DEFLATORS	*(Index 1987 = 100)*										
Overall (GDP)	21.3	22.8	23.9	28.4	32.5	37.9	40.4	42.8	43.8	49.2	52.1
Domestic Absorption	21.7	23.2	27.0	30.4	33.2	36.9	38.3	43.0	46.6	54.2	59.7
Agriculture	16.9	20.1	14.8	27.3	30.9	34.2	36.7	37.7	42.4	45.4	48.4
Industry	42.0	44.1	46.3	44.0	51.4	65.3	66.5	69.7	60.8	71.5	76.7
Manufacturing	..	..	..	..	..	..	..	..	..	..	..
Consumer Price Index	..	..	..	..	..	..	..	..	..	..	..
MANUFACTURING ACTIVITY											
Employment (1987=100)	..	..	..	..	..	..	..	..	..	..	..
Real Earnings per Empl. (1987=100)	..	..	..	..	..	..	..	..	..	..	..
Real Output per Empl. (1987=100)	..	..	..	..	..	..	..	..	..	..	..
Earnings as % of Value Added	..	..	..	..	..	..	..	..	..	..	..
MONETARY HOLDINGS	*(Millions of current Mauritanian Ouguiyas)*										
Money Supply, Broadly Defined	1,252	1,257	1,588	2,024	3,145	3,979	4,813	5,058	5,160	6,293	7,080
Money	1,110	1,132	1,428	1,493	2,451	2,926	3,683	4,095	4,134	5,081	5,677
Currency Outside Banks	445	461	618	629	954	1,214	1,464	1,529	1,728	2,311	2,376
Demand Deposits	665	671	810	864	1,497	1,712	2,219	2,566	2,406	2,770	3,301
Quasi-Money	143	125	160	531	694	1,052	1,131	964	1,025	1,212	1,403
GOVERNMENT DEFICIT (-) OR SURPLUS	*(Millions of current Mauritanian Ouguiyas)*										
	..	..	..	..	..	-532	-2,321	-1,685	-871	-1,464	..
Current Revenue	..	..	..	..	..	7,639	12,059	9,078	8,908	8,984	..
Current Expenditure	..	..	..	..	..	..	..	..	8,648	8,479	..
Current Budget Balance	..	..	..	..	..	..	..	..	260	505	..
Capital Receipts	..	..	..	..	..	3	1	327	862	679	..
Capital Payments	..	..	..	..	..	..	..	..	1,993	2,648	..

1981	1982	1983	1984	1985	1986	1987	1988	1989	1990 estimate	Notes	MAURITANIA
480	450	470	420	410	430	420	470	500	500	..	**CURRENT GNP PER CAPITA (US $)**
1,586	1,620	1,654	1,690	1,729	1,771	1,817	1,865	1,916	1,969	..	**POPULATION (thousands)**
											USE AND ORIGIN OF RESOURCES
			(Millions of current Mauritanian Ouguiyas)								
34,897	36,333	40,904	43,611	51,293	57,976	61,169	68,065	78,316	79,208	..	Gross National Product (GNP)
-1,228	-2,505	-2,308	-2,770	-3,805	-4,723	-8,002	-5,411	-5,184	-5,569	..	Net Factor Income from Abroad
36,125	38,838	43,212	46,381	55,098	62,699	69,171	73,476	83,500	84,777	..	GDP at Market Prices
-10,568	-17,121	-12,934	-12,485	-8,553	-4,727	-4,671	-8,509	-5,621	-9,952	..	Resource Balance
16,506	15,776	20,038	21,437	31,527	34,782	34,689	36,906	41,466	39,867	..	Exports of Goods & NFServices
27,074	32,897	32,972	33,922	40,080	39,509	39,360	45,415	47,087	49,819	..	Imports of Goods & NFServices
46,693	55,959	56,146	58,866	63,651	67,426	73,842	81,985	89,121	94,729	..	Domestic Absorption
23,742	30,705	40,481	39,279	42,102	44,492	50,558	58,717	65,880	74,209	..	Private Consumption, etc.
7,828	6,960	7,970	7,965	8,172	8,537	9,137	10,297	10,990	8,220	..	General Gov't Consumption
15,123	18,294	7,695	11,622	13,377	14,397	14,147	12,971	12,251	12,300	..	Gross Domestic Investment
13,507	15,774	13,540	11,022	13,540	13,576	13,975	11,977	11,270	10,670	..	Fixed Investment
2,875	3,637	4,643	4,897	6,522	6,814	7,250	7,565	8,014	8,188	..	Indirect Taxes, net
33,250	35,201	38,569	41,484	48,576	55,885	61,921	65,911	75,486	76,589	..	GDP at factor cost
10,601	11,657	13,035	11,854	13,994	18,865	22,924	24,970	28,134	19,971	f	Agriculture
8,712	8,228	8,188	10,553	13,126	13,539	13,347	14,273	18,300	22,568	f	Industry
..	..	..	..	..	..	..	..	..	..	f	Manufacturing
13,937	15,316	17,346	19,077	21,456	23,481	25,650	26,668	29,052	34,049	..	Services, etc.
4,555	1,173	-5,239	-863	4,824	9,670	9,476	4,462	6,630	2,348	..	Gross Domestic Saving
2,458	-2,777	-9,026	-4,936	-588	3,237	-48	-2,610	-628	-4,632	..	Gross National Saving
			(Millions of 1987 Mauritanian Ouguiyas)								
64,370	60,887	64,665	59,715	61,081	64,295	61,169	63,850	66,856	65,852	..	Gross National Product
64,817	63,487	66,590	61,763	63,523	67,100	69,171	71,738	74,161	73,063	I	GDP at Market Prices
-10,037	-19,196	-10,790	-10,500	-7,851	-5,304	-4,671	-5,717	-5,831	-6,954	..	Resource Balance
26,513	24,327	31,562	29,488	32,535	34,205	34,689	34,549	35,896	35,107	..	Exports of Goods & NFServices
36,550	43,523	42,352	39,988	40,386	39,509	39,360	40,265	41,727	42,061	..	Imports of Goods & NFServices
74,854	82,683	77,380	72,263	71,374	72,404	73,842	77,455	79,992	80,017	..	Domestic Absorption
41,971	45,546	57,692	50,038	48,357	49,262	50,558	54,959	59,574	62,651	..	Private Consumption, etc.
10,903	9,403	8,788	6,998	7,191	7,695	9,137	9,157	8,309	5,630	..	General Gov't Consumption
21,980	27,734	10,900	15,227	15,826	15,447	14,147	13,340	12,110	11,736	..	Gross Domestic Investment
19,317	23,913	19,179	14,440	16,014	14,566	13,975	12,339	11,189	10,479	..	Fixed Investment
58,588	56,487	59,495	55,136	56,685	60,137	61,921	63,248	65,892	64,425	..	GDP at factor cost
20,881	21,229	24,428	19,923	20,413	22,285	22,924	22,727	23,122	19,766	f	Agriculture
10,350	9,930	9,356	12,501	13,016	13,479	13,347	13,940	15,582	14,803	f	Industry
..	..	..	..	..	..	..	..	..	..	f	Manufacturing
26,668	24,711	25,711	22,712	23,256	24,374	25,650	26,581	27,188	29,856	..	Services, etc.
											Memo Items:
22,283	20,872	25,738	25,270	31,768	34,782	34,689	32,721	36,746	33,659	..	Capacity to Import
-4,230	-3,455	-5,823	-4,217	-767	577	0	-1,827	850	-1,448	..	Terms of Trade Adjustment
60,587	60,032	60,767	57,545	62,756	67,677	69,171	69,911	75,011	71,615	..	Gross Domestic Income
60,140	57,432	58,842	55,497	60,314	64,872	61,169	62,023	67,706	64,404	..	Gross National Income
			(Index 1987 = 100)								**DOMESTIC PRICES/DEFLATORS**
55.7	61.2	64.9	75.1	86.7	93.4	100.0	102.4	112.6	116.0	..	Overall (GDP)
62.4	67.7	72.6	81.5	89.2	93.1	100.0	105.8	111.4	118.4	..	Domestic Absorption
50.8	54.9	53.4	59.5	68.6	84.7	100.0	109.9	121.7	101.0	..	Agriculture
84.2	82.9	87.5	84.4	100.8	100.4	100.0	102.4	117.4	152.5	..	Industry
..	..	..	..	..	..	..	..	..	..	..	Manufacturing
..	..	..	..	..	92.5	100.0	101.3	114.4	122.0	..	Consumer Price Index
											MANUFACTURING ACTIVITY
..	..	..	..	..	..	..	..	..	..	..	Employment (1987=100)
..	..	..	..	..	..	..	..	..	..	..	Real Earnings per Empl. (1987=100)
..	..	..	..	..	..	..	..	..	..	..	Real Output per Empl. (1987=100)
..	..	..	..	..	..	..	..	..	..	..	Earnings as % of Value Added
			(Millions of current Mauritanian Ouguiyas)								**MONETARY HOLDINGS**
9,429	9,572	10,085	11,322	13,848	14,864	17,642	18,003	18,624	22,803	..	Money Supply, Broadly Defined
7,653	7,135	8,090	9,641	12,173	11,392	13,397	14,032	15,062	17,034	..	Money
2,678	2,950	3,024	3,658	4,700	4,418	5,648	5,845	6,040	6,365	..	Currency Outside Banks
4,975	4,185	5,065	5,983	7,473	6,975	7,749	8,187	9,022	10,669	..	Demand Deposits
1,777	2,437	1,995	1,682	1,674	3,471	4,244	3,971	3,562	5,769	..	Quasi-Money
			(Millions of current Mauritanian Ouguiyas)								
..	..	-5,290	-4,378	-9,341	431	-1,266	-2,863	..	..	F	**GOVERNMENT DEFICIT (-) OR SURPLUS**
..	..	8,738	16,566	18,781	19,679	21,864	22,555	..	..		Current Revenue
..	..	9,422	10,463	11,641	12,770	13,454	14,223	..	..		Current Expenditure
..	..	-684	6,103	7,140	6,909	8,410	8,332	..	..		Current Budget Balance
..	..	386	..	..	..	..	..	..	..		Capital Receipts
..	..	4,988	10,481	16,481	6,478	9,676	11,195	..	..		Capital Payments

MAURITANIA	1970	1971	1972	1973	1974	1975	1976	1977	1978	1979	1980
FOREIGN TRADE (CUSTOMS BASIS)					*(Millions of current US dollars)*						
Value of Exports, fob	..	..	..	..	..	..	..	..	..	..	..
Nonfuel Primary Products	..	..	..	..	..	..	..	..	..	..	..
Fuels	..	..	..	..	..	..	..	..	..	..	..
Manufactures	..	..	..	..	..	..	..	..	..	..	..
Value of Imports, cif	..	..	..	..	..	..	..	..	..	..	..
Nonfuel Primary Products	..	..	..	..	..	..	..	..	..	..	..
Fuels	..	..	..	..	..	..	..	..	..	..	..
Manufactures	..	..	..	..	..	..	..	..	..	..	..
					(Index 1987 = 100)						
Terms of Trade	..	..	..	..	..	..	..	..	..	..	..
Export Prices, fob	..	..	..	..	..	..	..	..	..	..	..
Import Prices, cif	..	..	..	..	..	..	..	..	..	..	..
BALANCE OF PAYMENTS					*(Millions of current US dollars)*						
Exports of Goods & Services	104.80	113.60	129.30	141.98	210.22	190.33	205.68	183.03	155.60	203.98	269.76
Merchandise, fob	97.20	102.80	117.30	131.37	187.01	167.32	181.87	157.22	118.58	147.17	196.30
Nonfactor Services	5.70	9.20	10.50	9.66	16.60	18.05	19.46	21.54	33.88	45.45	56.48
Factor Services	1.90	1.60	1.50	0.95	6.61	4.96	4.35	4.28	3.14	11.35	16.99
Imports of Goods & Services	112.30	119.70	148.40	158.55	219.60	312.73	415.84	410.40	372.58	411.94	492.88
Merchandise, fob	72.00	91.60	115.60	119.69	166.57	208.50	272.02	295.52	267.10	286.02	321.27
Nonfactor Services	27.10	12.70	14.80	27.90	41.01	69.18	80.89	67.19	75.26	83.17	127.76
Factor Services	13.20	15.40	18.00	10.97	12.03	35.05	62.92	47.69	30.22	42.75	43.84
Long-Term Interest	0.40	0.80	1.80	2.00	4.30	5.40	7.80	8.90	9.60	15.40	12.80
Private Current Transfers, net	-5.90	-4.90	-3.90	-14.19	-12.75	-22.74	-28.41	-22.95	-20.73	-32.10	-28.05
Workers' Remittances	0.70	0.80	0.60	0.60	4.33	0.44	0.42	0.31	0.56	2.35	5.58
Curr. A/C Bal before Off. Transf.	-13.40	-11.00	-23.00	-30.76	-22.13	-145.14	-238.57	-250.31	-237.70	-240.06	-251.16
Net Official Transfers	8.50	9.80	13.10	45.06	69.39	81.94	152.63	128.08	159.49	143.12	117.91
Curr. A/C Bal after Off. Transf.	-4.90	-1.20	-9.90	14.31	47.26	-63.20	-85.94	-122.23	-78.21	-96.94	-133.25
Long-Term Capital, net	14.70	14.80	9.00	-0.24	26.70	10.07	90.00	55.26	89.12	111.78	128.17
Direct Investment	0.80	7.50	9.80	9.78	1.92	-122.70	1.55	4.12	2.86	63.23	27.09
Long-Term Loans	1.30	10.70	-3.50	44.20	48.10	21.70	114.90	53.80	107.20	36.20	112.50
Disbursements	4.50	13.60	5.60	54.90	57.90	55.90	184.50	85.80	123.80	86.70	129.50
Repayments	3.20	2.90	9.10	10.70	9.80	34.20	69.60	32.00	16.60	50.50	17.00
Other Long-Term Capital	12.60	-3.40	2.70	-54.21	-23.33	111.07	-26.45	-2.67	-20.94	12.35	-11.42
Other Capital, net	-11.57	-10.98	5.31	-7.45	-30.99	-2.06	8.57	16.51	4.86	13.74	-32.89
Change in Reserves	1.77	-2.62	-4.41	-6.62	-42.97	55.19	-12.62	50.46	-15.76	-28.59	37.96
Memo Item:					*(Mauritanian Ouguiyas per US dollar)*						
Conversion Factor (Annual Avg)	55.540	55.430	50.500	44.580	45.330	43.100	45.020	45.590	46.160	45.890	45.910
					(Millions of US dollars), outstanding at end of year						
EXTERNAL DEBT (Total)	26.3	38.9	55.8	104.9	167.6	188.1	406.9	522.4	682.5	717.3	844.1
Long-Term Debt (by debtor)	26.3	38.9	55.8	104.9	167.6	187.9	406.7	480.9	629.0	666.0	779.1
Central Bank, incl. IMF credit	0.3	0.3	0.4	24.5	36.9	35.6	49.2	67.7	121.2	119.3	131.6
Central Government	18.8	26.8	29.4	37.7	74.2	99.7	307.4	350.7	437.9	477.3	581.9
Rest of General Government	0.0	0.0	0.0	0.0	0.0	0.0	0.0	0.0	0.0	0.0	0.0
Non-financial Public Enterprises	7.2	11.8	26.0	42.7	56.5	52.6	50.1	62.5	69.9	69.4	65.6
Priv. Sector, incl non-guaranteed	0.0	0.0	0.0	0.0	0.0	0.0	0.0	0.0	0.0	0.0	0.0
Short-Term Debt	0.0	0.0	0.0	0.0	0.0	0.2	0.2	41.5	53.5	51.3	65.0
Memo Items:					*(Thousands of US dollars)*						
Int'l Reserves Excluding Gold	3,200.0	7,505.0	13,459.0	42,243.0	103,812.0	47,725.0	81,983.0	50,017.0	79,499.0	113,673.0	139,900.0
Gold Holdings (at market price)	..	..	..	..	..	..	..	924.0	1,898.0	4,301.0	6,543.0
SOCIAL INDICATORS											
Total Fertility Rate	6.5	6.5	6.5	6.5	6.5	6.5	6.5	6.5	6.5	6.5	6.5
Infant Mortality Rate	165.8	163.4	161.0	158.6	156.2	153.8	151.4	149.0	146.6	144.2	141.8
Life Expectancy at Birth	39.2	39.6	40.0	40.4	40.8	41.2	41.6	42.0	42.4	42.8	43.2
Urban Population, % of total	13.7	15.0	16.3	17.7	19.0	20.3	22.0	23.8	25.5	27.3	29.0
Food Prod. per capita (1987=100)	143.6	137.3	127.2	107.0	100.8	101.7	109.0	113.9	117.5	116.7	115.4
Labor Force, Agriculture (%)	84.8	83.1	81.6	80.0	78.5	77.1	75.5	73.8	72.3	70.8	69.3
Labor Force, Female (%)	21.5	21.4	21.2	21.1	20.9	20.8	20.6	20.5	20.3	20.2	20.0
Primary Schl. Enroll. Ratio	14.0	..	..	..	..	19.0	23.0	26.0	32.0	32.0	37.0
Primary Schl. Enroll. Ratio, Female	8.0	..	..	..	..	13.0	15.0	17.0	..	24.0	26.0
Secondary Schl. Enroll. Ratio	2.0	..	..	..	..	4.0	4.0	6.0	9.0	9.0	11.0

MAURITANIA

1981	1982	1983	1984	1985	1986	1987	1988	1989	1990 estimate	Notes	
				(Millions of current US dollars)							**FOREIGN TRADE (CUSTOMS BASIS)**
..	..	..	..	..	..	..	..	..	..	..	Value of Exports, fob
..	..	..	..	..	..	..	..	..	..	..	Nonfuel Primary Products
..	..	..	..	..	..	..	..	..	..	..	Fuels
..	..	..	..	..	..	..	..	..	..	..	Manufactures
..	..	..	..	..	..	..	..	..	..	..	Value of Imports, cif
..	..	..	..	..	..	..	..	..	..	..	Nonfuel Primary Products
..	..	..	..	..	..	..	..	..	..	..	Fuels
..	..	..	..	..	..	..	..	..	..	..	Manufactures
				(Index 1987 = 100)							
								..	..	..	Terms of Trade
..	..	..	..	..	..	..	..	..	..	..	Export Prices, fob
..	..	..	..	..	..	..	..	..	..	..	Import Prices, cif
				(Millions of current US dollars)							**BALANCE OF PAYMENTS**
338.95	305.78	354.74	330.28	402.57	444.80	439.44	476.99	487.09	495.10	f	Exports of Goods & Services
269.92	240.03	315.37	293.79	371.53	418.76	402.41	437.61	447.89	432.00	..	Merchandise, fob
48.91	47.25	30.25	28.02	27.09	23.73	34.54	35.25	33.61	58.40	..	Nonfactor Services
20.13	18.51	9.12	8.46	3.96	2.31	2.49	4.13	5.59	4.70	..	Factor Services
585.02	648.22	626.82	527.46	631.77	730.93	665.45	655.57	600.99	676.60	f	Imports of Goods & Services
386.22	426.57	378.24	302.12	333.90	401.20	359.18	348.85	349.33	402.30	..	Merchandise, fob
128.13	157.55	177.17	177.78	201.78	211.15	214.53	217.05	196.04	212.00	..	Nonfactor Services
70.67	64.11	71.41	47.57	96.09	118.59	91.73	89.67	55.63	62.30	..	Factor Services
18.20	22.50	22.70	23.40	27.20	31.60	29.80	32.60	24.50	12.50	..	Long-Term Interest
-17.99	-27.91	-26.98	-20.42	-20.85	-22.99	-20.60	-22.07	-24.97	-17.50	..	Private Current Transfers, net
3.71	2.32	1.22	0.96	0.79	1.86	6.70	9.30	4.78	..	..	Workers' Remittances
-264.06	-370.36	-299.06	-217.61	-250.05	-309.12	-246.61	-200.65	-138.88	-199.00	..	Curr. A/C Bal before Off. Transf.
116.93	93.79	86.04	106.91	134.01	114.86	99.39	104.77	120.29	..	..	Net Official Transfers
-147.13	-276.57	-213.02	-110.69	-116.03	-194.27	-147.22	-95.88	-18.59	-199.00	..	Curr. A/C Bal after Off. Transf.
128.87	166.66	166.53	82.68	98.03	171.79	98.74	76.87	42.85	-12.60	f	Long-Term Capital, net
12.44	14.97	1.37	8.53	6.98	3.13	1.43	0.98	3.47	6.50	..	Direct Investment
124.30	195.40	164.30	96.60	56.20	158.70	98.60	50.80	41.20	51.40	..	Long-Term Loans
160.00	211.20	178.50	115.00	104.60	202.00	162.20	128.80	95.80	79.80	..	Disbursements
35.70	15.80	14.20	18.40	48.40	43.30	63.60	78.00	54.60	28.40	..	Repayments
-7.87	-43.71	0.87	-22.45	34.86	9.96	-1.29	25.08	-1.81	-70.50	..	Other Long-Term Capital
13.30	61.53	14.79	-1.02	-10.85	4.07	-92.52	4.09	-1.36	198.44	f	Other Capital, net
4.96	48.37	31.69	29.04	28.84	18.40	140.99	14.93	-22.91	13.16	..	Change in Reserves
											Memo Item:
				(Mauritanian Ouguiyas per US dollar)							
48.300	51.770	54.810	63.800	77.090	74.380	73.880	75.260	83.050	80.610	..	Conversion Factor (Annual Avg)
				(Millions of US dollars), outstanding at end of year							**EXTERNAL DEBT (Total)**
972.9	1,151.1	1,296.3	1,338.2	1,502.3	1,772.7	2,044.0	2,072.2	2,010.0	2,227.0	..	
874.6	1,058.1	1,188.9	1,211.1	1,394.6	1,655.9	1,924.4	1,890.3	1,845.5	1,967.6	..	Long-Term Debt (by debtor)
143.1	166.8	173.7	165.0	178.8	194.3	244.0	203.8	189.6	196.6	..	Central Bank, incl. IMF credit
634.2	710.9	762.4	787.5	902.6	1,093.7	1,264.9	1,290.4	1,312.0	1,424.2	..	Central Government
0.0	1.9	1.2	0.7	0.6	0.4	0.1	0.0	0.0	..	..	Rest of General Government
97.3	178.5	251.2	255.4	309.4	364.5	413.1	394.1	343.5	346.6	..	Non-financial Public Enterprises
0.0	0.0	0.4	2.5	3.2	3.0	2.3	2.0	0.4	0.2	..	Priv. Sector, incl non-guaranteed
98.3	93.0	107.4	127.1	107.7	116.8	119.6	181.9	164.5	259.4	..	Short-Term Debt
				(Thousands of US dollars)							**Memo Items:**
161,804.0	139,111.0	105,933.0	77,529.0	59,217.0	48,219.0	71,808.0	55,567.0	82,418.0	54,111.0	..	Int'l Reserves Excluding Gold
4,412.0	5,072.0	4,235.0	3,515.0	3,630.0	4,495.0	5,567.0	4,718.0	4,612.0	4,428.0	..	Gold Holdings (at market price)
											SOCIAL INDICATORS
6.5	6.5	6.6	6.6	6.7	6.7	6.8	..	..	..	..	Total Fertility Rate
139.4	137.0	135.0	133.0	130.9	128.9	126.9	125.0	123.0	121.1	..	Infant Mortality Rate
43.6	44.0	44.4	44.8	45.1	45.5	45.9	46.2	46.4	46.6	..	Life Expectancy at Birth
30.8	32.7	34.5	36.4	38.2	40.4	42.5	43.9	45.4	46.8	..	Urban Population, % of total
114.2	108.1	100.4	98.6	100.7	99.5	100.0	100.1	99.3	93.7	..	Food Prod. per capita (1987=100)
..	..	..	..	..	..	..	..	..	..	..	Labor Force, Agriculture (%)
20.3	20.5	20.7	20.9	21.1	21.3	21.6	21.8	22.0	22.2	..	Labor Force, Female (%)
..	37.0	40.0	46.0	49.0	51.0	52.0	51.0	..	..	..	Primary Schl. Enroll. Ratio
..	29.0	32.0	37.0	39.0	41.0	43.0	42.0	..	..	..	Primary Schl. Enroll. Ratio, Female
..	12.0	13.0	15.0	15.0	16.0	16.0	16.0	..	..	..	Secondary Schl. Enroll. Ratio

MAURITIUS	1970	1971	1972	1973	1974	1975	1976	1977	1978	1979	1980
CURRENT GNP PER CAPITA (US $)	280	300	340	430	590	710	860	930	1,020	1,200	1,180
POPULATION (thousands)	829	840	850	860	870	883	898	914	931	948	966

USE AND ORIGIN OF RESOURCES

(Millions of current Mauritian Rupees)

	1970	1971	1972	1973	1974	1975	1976	1977	1978	1979	1980
Gross National Product (GNP)	1,236	1,368	1,681	2,187	3,780	4,021	4,657	5,440	6,258	7,596	8,634
Net Factor Income from Abroad	7	7	2	16	10	17	-47	-2	0	-44	-63
GDP at Market Prices	1,229	1,361	1,679	2,171	3,770	4,004	4,704	5,442	6,258	7,640	8,697
Resource Balance	16	-60	37	-46	222	42	-324	-579	-772	-898	-892
Exports of Goods & NFServices	531	523	759	991	2,124	2,269	2,388	2,656	2,705	3,260	4,450
Imports of Goods & NFServices	515	583	722	1,037	1,902	2,227	2,712	3,235	3,477	4,158	5,342
Domestic Absorption	1,213	1,421	1,642	2,217	3,548	3,962	5,028	6,021	7,030	8,538	9,589
Private Consumption, etc.	925	1,042	1,166	1,441	2,238	2,466	2,956	3,658	4,249	5,144	6,562
General Gov't Consumption	166	182	219	235	360	443	575	733	858	1,009	1,224
Gross Domestic Investment	122	197	257	541	950	1,053	1,497	1,630	1,923	2,385	1,803
Fixed Investment	145	184	229	480	750	1,138	1,287	1,510	1,770	1,965	2,028
Indirect Taxes, net	208	224	247	325	479	546	539	666	764	1,100	1,308
GDP at factor cost	1,020	1,137	1,431	1,846	3,291	3,458	4,165	4,776	5,494	6,540	7,389
Agriculture	165	195	263	368	985	770	938	939	977	1,224	914
Industry	223	262	346	436	712	855	1,041	1,213	1,436	1,697	1,912
Manufacturing	146	168	233	277	505	564	631	699	801	972	1,127
Services, etc.	632	680	823	1,043	1,594	1,833	2,186	2,624	3,081	3,619	4,563
Gross Domestic Saving	138	137	294	495	1,172	1,095	1,173	1,051	1,151	1,487	911
Gross National Saving	153	153	316	537	1,212	1,149	1,153	1,076	1,183	1,475	923

(Millions of 1987 Mauritian Rupees)

	1970	1971	1972	1973	1974	1975	1976	1977	1978	1979	1980
Gross National Product	9,316	9,664	10,392	11,843	12,838	12,921	14,272	15,550	16,438	17,255	15,448
GDP at Market Prices	9,240	9,589	10,353	11,726	12,759	12,814	14,390	15,510	16,389	17,306	15,514
Resource Balance	1,429	714	1,105	1,321	-985	-2,545	-1,833	-1,717	-1,885	-1,616	-550
Exports of Goods & NFServices	6,467	5,872	7,186	8,024	6,905	5,617	7,212	8,182	8,155	8,424	8,565
Imports of Goods & NFServices	5,037	5,158	6,081	6,703	7,890	8,163	9,045	9,899	10,039	10,039	9,116
Domestic Absorption	7,811	8,875	9,247	10,405	13,744	15,359	16,223	17,228	18,274	18,922	16,065
Private Consumption, etc.	5,439	5,717	5,638	5,342	7,697	9,027	9,488	10,439	10,973	11,413	10,727
General Gov't Consumption	1,029	1,123	1,284	1,215	1,439	1,544	2,112	2,218	2,332	2,302	2,317
Gross Domestic Investment	1,342	2,035	2,326	3,847	4,609	4,788	4,623	4,570	4,969	5,206	3,020
Fixed Investment	..	..	..	..	..	..	4,066	4,328	4,647	4,353	3,538
GDP at factor cost	7,662	7,993	8,793	9,958	11,084	11,020	12,669	13,543	14,081	14,592	13,087
Agriculture	2,832	3,049	3,432	3,585	3,534	2,488	2,753	2,753	2,756	2,868	1,887
Industry	1,615	1,707	1,911	2,233	2,796	2,790	3,397	3,717	3,970	4,007	3,622
Manufacturing	1,269	1,312	1,477	1,625	2,060	1,895	2,076	2,191	2,359	2,480	2,306
Services, etc.	3,503	3,606	3,917	4,481	5,082	5,865	6,663	7,201	7,480	7,837	7,551

Memo Items:

	1970	1971	1972	1973	1974	1975	1976	1977	1978	1979	1980
Capacity to Import	5,194	4,627	6,393	6,406	8,811	8,317	7,965	8,128	7,810	7,871	7,593
Terms of Trade Adjustment	-1,273	-1,245	-794	-1,619	1,906	2,699	752	-54	-345	-552	-972
Gross Domestic Income	7,967	8,344	9,559	10,108	14,665	15,513	15,142	15,456	16,045	16,754	14,542
Gross National Income	8,043	8,419	9,598	10,224	14,744	15,620	15,025	15,496	16,094	16,703	14,476

DOMESTIC PRICES/DEFLATORS

(Index 1987 = 100)

	1970	1971	1972	1973	1974	1975	1976	1977	1978	1979	1980
Overall (GDP)	13.3	14.2	16.2	18.5	29.5	31.2	32.7	35.1	38.2	44.1	56.1
Domestic Absorption	15.5	16.0	17.8	21.3	25.8	25.8	31.0	34.9	38.5	45.1	59.7
Agriculture	5.8	6.4	7.7	10.3	27.9	31.0	34.1	34.1	35.4	42.7	48.4
Industry	13.8	15.3	18.1	19.5	25.5	30.6	30.6	32.6	36.2	42.4	52.8
Manufacturing	11.5	12.8	15.8	17.0	24.5	29.8	30.4	31.9	34.0	39.2	48.9
Consumer Price Index	16.4	16.5	17.3	19.7	25.4	29.2	32.9	36.0	39.0	44.7	63.4

MANUFACTURING ACTIVITY

	1970	1971	1972	1973	1974	1975	1976	1977	1978	1979	1980
Employment (1987=100)	12.8	14.5	16.4	20.6	25.7	28.1	35.4	39.0	37.8	39.2	40.1
Real Earnings per Empl. (1987=100)	108.3	109.2	115.4	103.8	97.4	113.3	124.9	128.1	137.4	131.8	108.0
Real Output per Empl. (1987=100)	200.8	190.4	175.0	259.4	225.8	166.7	144.7	143.9	157.3	167.1	144.8
Earnings as % of Value Added	34.3	33.9	32.6	26.3	26.2	34.3	44.7	54.7	53.9	50.5	52.3

MONETARY HOLDINGS

(Millions of current Mauritian Rupees)

	1970	1971	1972	1973	1974	1975	1976	1977	1978	1979	1980
Money Supply, Broadly Defined	489	566	713	921	1,634	2,009	2,163	2,445	2,968	3,218	3,939
Money	230	262	376	467	784	993	1,099	1,219	1,449	1,426	1,720
Currency Outside Banks	105	126	156	201	314	438	588	694	824	725	735
Demand Deposits	125	135	220	266	469	555	511	526	625	701	985
Quasi-Money	259	304	336	455	851	1,015	1,064	1,226	1,519	1,792	2,218

GOVERNMENT DEFICIT (-) OR SURPLUS

(Millions of current Mauritian Rupees)

	1970	1971	1972	1973	1974	1975	1976	1977	1978	1979	1980
Current Revenue	..	..	..	-27	-202	-186	-209	-457	-727	-882	-897
Current Expenditure	..	..	..	355	460	722	1,058	1,173	1,234	1,418	1,813
Current Budget Balance	..	..	..	286	496	669	912	1,176	1,404	1,758	1,972
Capital Receipts	..	..	..	69	-36	53	147	-3	-170	-340	-159
Capital Payments	..	..	..	1	0	1	7	..	..	..	..
				97	166	240	363	454	558	542	737

1981	1982	1983	1984	1985	1986	1987	1988	1989	1990 estimate	Notes	MAURITIUS
1,260	1,210	1,120	1,080	1,100	1,230	1,500	1,830	2,030	2,250	..	**CURRENT GNP PER CAPITA (US $)**
982	995	1,006	1,014	1,020	1,030	1,040	1,051	1,062	1,074	..	**POPULATION (thousands)**
											USE AND ORIGIN OF RESOURCES
				(Millions of current Mauritian Rupees)							
9,949	11,227	12,278	13,734	15,918	18,971	23,043	27,210	31,712	36,775	..	Gross National Product (GNP)
-260	-498	-485	-626	-700	-729	-533	-593	-303	-170	..	Net Factor Income from Abroad
10,209	11,725	12,763	14,360	16,618	19,700	23,576	27,803	32,015	36,945	..	GDP at Market Prices
-1,068	-330	-46	-481	-315	1,312	498	-1,423	-2,474	-3,276	..	Resource Balance
4,566	5,529	5,953	6,989	8,895	11,919	15,639	18,565	21,347	24,864	..	Exports of Goods & NFServices
5,634	5,859	5,999	7,470	9,210	10,607	15,141	19,988	23,821	28,140	..	Imports of Goods & NFServices
11,277	12,055	12,809	14,841	16,933	18,388	23,078	29,226	34,489	40,221	..	Domestic Absorption
7,277	8,301	8,874	9,841	11,118	12,000	14,395	17,215	20,705	24,565	..	Private Consumption, etc.
1,422	1,624	1,706	1,835	1,915	2,068	2,722	3,509	3,930	4,460	..	General Gov't Consumption
2,578	2,130	2,229	3,165	3,900	4,320	5,961	8,502	9,854	11,196	..	Gross Domestic Investment
2,240	2,100	2,300	2,595	3,100	3,890	5,090	7,990	8,565	11,600	..	Fixed Investment
1,444	1,705	2,150	2,310	2,738	3,250	3,881	4,622	5,176	5,875	..	Indirect Taxes, net
8,765	10,020	10,613	12,050	13,880	16,450	19,695	23,181	26,839	31,070	..	GDP at factor cost
1,257	1,530	1,465	1,736	2,123	2,510	2,884	3,067	3,385	3,820	..	Agriculture
2,169	2,462	2,596	3,188	4,056	5,194	6,401	7,541	8,692	10,210	..	Industry
1,377	1,560	1,678	2,183	2,864	3,830	4,841	5,627	6,365	7,450	..	Manufacturing
5,339	6,028	6,552	7,126	7,701	8,746	10,410	12,573	14,762	17,040	..	Services, etc.
1,510	1,800	2,183	2,684	3,585	5,632	6,459	7,079	7,380	7,920	..	Gross Domestic Saving
1,354	1,459	1,888	2,324	3,222	5,306	6,448	7,447	8,118	8,974	..	Gross National Saving
				(Millions of 1987 Mauritian Rupees)							
15,993	16,659	16,754	17,472	18,773	20,693	23,043	24,598	25,889	27,755		Gross National Product
16,345	17,288	17,336	18,166	19,485	21,450	23,576	25,126	26,119	27,872		GDP at Market Prices
-205	1,584	1,447	1,142	1,691	2,057	498	-623	445	686		Resource Balance
7,943	8,859	8,940	9,309	10,421	13,231	15,639	17,531	19,162	20,657		Exports of Goods & NFServices
8,148	7,274	7,493	8,167	8,730	11,174	15,141	18,154	18,717	19,971		Imports of Goods & NFServices
											Domestic Absorption
16,550	15,704	15,889	17,024	17,794	19,393	23,078	25,749	25,673	27,186		Private Consumption, etc.
10,529	10,272	10,444	10,879	11,402	12,127	14,395	16,519	15,843	16,998		General Gov't Consumption
2,324	2,354	2,413	2,503	2,503	2,544	2,722	2,864	3,003	3,137		Gross Domestic Investment
3,696	3,079	3,031	3,643	3,888	4,722	5,961	6,366	6,827	7,051		Fixed Investment
3,285	2,824	2,914	3,093	3,402	4,081	5,090	5,857	6,183	6,385		
13,936	14,782	14,826	15,533	16,668	18,216	19,695	20,844	21,700	23,203		GDP at factor cost
2,301	2,756	2,398	2,416	2,688	2,976	2,884	2,731	2,518	2,738		Agriculture
3,754	3,917	3,928	4,293	4,881	5,695	6,401	6,983	7,430	8,048		Industry
2,507	2,688	2,715	3,046	3,511	4,221	4,841	5,223	5,475	5,928		Manufacturing
7,898	8,181	8,500	8,825	9,099	9,545	10,410	11,129	11,751	12,417		Services, etc.
											Memo Items:
6,604	6,865	7,435	7,641	8,431	12,556	15,639	16,861	16,773	17,646	..	Capacity to Import
-1,340	-1,994	-1,505	-1,668	-1,990	-675	0	-670	-2,389	-3,011	..	Terms of Trade Adjustment
15,005	15,295	15,831	16,499	17,495	20,775	23,576	24,456	23,729	24,861	..	Gross Domestic Income
14,653	14,665	15,249	15,804	16,783	20,018	23,043	23,929	23,499	24,744	..	Gross National Income
											DOMESTIC PRICES/DEFLATORS
				(Index 1987 = 100)							
62.5	67.8	73.6	79.0	85.3	91.8	100.0	110.7	122.6	132.6	..	Overall (GDP)
68.1	76.8	80.6	87.2	95.2	94.8	100.0	113.5	134.3	147.9	..	Domestic Absorption
54.6	55.5	61.1	71.9	79.0	84.3	100.0	112.3	134.4	139.5	..	Agriculture
57.8	62.8	66.1	74.3	83.1	91.2	100.0	108.0	117.0	126.9	..	Industry
54.9	58.0	61.8	71.7	81.6	90.7	100.0	107.7	116.3	125.7	..	Manufacturing
72.6	80.9	85.4	91.7	97.9	99.5	100.0	109.2	123.0	139.6	..	Consumer Price Index
											MANUFACTURING ACTIVITY
40.6	41.8	43.6	51.6	69.7	86.5	100.0	105.5	..	..	G J	Employment (1987=100)
106.9	102.1	103.1	101.3	90.7	92.6	100.0	105.5		..	G J	Real Earnings per Empl. (1987=100)
157.4	163.9	156.6	139.5	115.5	104.3	100.0	98.4	..	..	G J	Real Output per Empl. (1987=100)
48.9	47.8	49.9	47.6	46.2	43.8	43.2	44.7	..	..	J	Earnings as % of Value Added
											MONETARY HOLDINGS
				(Millions of current Mauritian Rupees)							
4,093	5,048	5,556	6,342	8,315	10,706	13,851	17,797	20,542	24,863	D	Money Supply, Broadly Defined
1,533	1,741	1,804	2,050	2,039	2,432	3,304	3,820	4,511	5,578	..	Money
791	875	922	958	1,096	1,305	1,663	2,009	2,404	2,849	..	Currency Outside Banks
742	866	881	1,092	943	1,127	1,640	1,812	2,107	2,729	..	Demand Deposits
2,560	3,307	3,752	4,292	6,277	8,273	10,547	13,977	16,031	19,285	..	Quasi-Money
				(Millions of current Mauritian Rupees)							
-1,293	-1,388	-978	-649	-580	-347	54	87	-468	-196	C F	**GOVERNMENT DEFICIT (-) OR SURPLUS**
2,073	2,289	2,985	3,295	3,758	4,361	5,390	6,681	7,698	8,999	..	Current Revenue
2,471	2,892	3,208	3,360	3,626	3,843	4,147	5,257	6,298	7,373	..	Current Expenditure
-398	-604	-223	-65	132	518	1,244	1,424	1,401	1,626	..	Current Budget Balance
..	..	..	..	..	..	..	..	..	..	..	Capital Receipts
895	785	755	583	712	864	1,190	1,337	1,869	1,822	..	Capital Payments

MAURITIUS	1970	1971	1972	1973	1974	1975	1976	1977	1978	1979	1980
FOREIGN TRADE (CUSTOMS BASIS)					*(Millions of current US dollars)*						
Value of Exports, fob	67.5	63.9	105.5	135.7	309.9	294.6	260.0	304.9	320.2	393.1	420.3
Nonfuel Primary Products	..	..	101.7	125.3	..	..	..	..	..	281.7	305.3
Fuels	..	..	0.0	0.0	..	..	..	..	..	0.1	0.0
Manufactures	1.2	2.3	3.8	10.4	25.5	33.7	47.9	67.8	82.1	111.4	115.0
Value of Imports, cif	75.6	83.1	119.9	169.6	308.5	330.7	357.5	444.9	498.4	576.1	619.3
Nonfuel Primary Products	29.3	30.8	39.0	49.7	111.0	97.4	97.3	121.9	150.9	204.5	194.2
Fuels	5.4	5.3	9.6	11.8	28.4	32.4	31.3	41.7	45.7	9.7	87.5
Manufactures	40.9	46.9	71.3	108.1	169.1	200.9	229.0	281.3	301.8	361.9	337.7
					(Index 1987 = 100)						
Terms of Trade	95.5	76.9	102.0	88.8	125.7	155.5	114.1	115.8	99.8	94.9	91.9
Export Prices, fob	21.7	20.3	28.1	33.4	75.4	93.1	67.7	73.7	72.0	79.7	89.6
Import Prices, cif	22.7	26.3	27.6	37.6	60.0	59.8	59.3	63.6	72.1	84.0	97.5
BALANCE OF PAYMENTS					*(Millions of current US dollars)*						
Exports of Goods & Services	98.2	96.9	144.7	186.2	376.4	379.3	340.1	405.7	445.4	515.4	578.6
Merchandise, fob	69.8	65.5	108.0	138.8	315.2	303.4	264.3	308.0	321.6	381.9	433.7
Nonfactor Services	25.3	28.0	33.7	42.4	56.6	65.8	61.0	92.7	118.2	129.7	139.9
Factor Services	3.1	3.4	3.0	5.0	4.6	10.1	14.8	5.0	5.6	3.8	5.1
Imports of Goods & Services	94.3	106.8	138.0	193.0	336.6	373.2	405.9	496.4	576.3	675.9	718.1
Merchandise, fob	64.8	74.2	98.5	143.4	267.6	278.8	307.6	368.0	418.9	482.8	515.9
Nonfactor Services	27.3	30.0	36.4	46.4	65.5	86.9	89.7	120.7	143.8	172.6	174.0
Factor Services	2.2	2.6	3.1	3.2	3.5	7.5	8.7	7.7	13.6	20.4	28.2
Long-Term Interest	1.7	1.5	1.4	1.2	1.6	1.6	2.5	3.4	9.0	14.9	22.6
Private Current Transfers, net	1.4	1.7	3.8	4.8	5.3	6.1	4.0	4.1	5.2	5.0	9.8
Workers' Remittances	..	..	..	..	..	..	..	..	..	..	..
Curr. A/C Bal before Off. Transf.	5.3	-8.2	10.5	-2.0	45.1	12.1	-38.6	-86.7	-125.6	-155.5	-129.7
Net Official Transfers	2.5	2.8	5.0	2.4	9.3	5.6	2.2	8.4	8.6	7.2	11.1
Curr. A/C Bal after Off. Transf.	7.8	-5.4	15.5	0.4	54.4	17.7	-36.4	-78.3	-117.0	-148.3	-118.7
Long-Term Capital, net	1.8	0.3	1.6	0.6	5.7	6.6	8.5	13.6	65.5	77.3	67.6
Direct Investment	1.6	1.2	-1.2	-3.2	0.6	2.2	2.7	1.5	4.3	-0.7	1.2
Long-Term Loans	0.8	0.1	1.1	7.3	5.8	8.5	7.2	19.5	67.2	74.6	78.5
Disbursements	2.2	2.8	3.1	8.8	7.8	17.1	12.9	27.7	75.1	86.1	97.0
Repayments	1.4	2.7	2.0	1.5	2.0	8.6	5.7	8.2	7.9	11.5	18.5
Other Long-Term Capital	-0.6	-1.0	1.7	-3.5	-0.7	-4.1	-1.4	-7.4	-6.0	3.4	-12.1
Other Capital, net	3.9	3.0	4.2	-4.2	3.5	27.7	-47.9	27.0	30.4	23.9	69.3
Change in Reserves	-13.5	2.1	-21.4	3.2	-63.5	-52.0	75.8	37.7	21.0	47.1	-18.3
Memo Item:					*(Mauritian Rupees per US dollar)*						
Conversion Factor (Annual Avg)	5.560	5.480	5.340	5.440	5.700	6.030	6.680	6.610	6.160	6.310	7.680
EXTERNAL DEBT (Total)	31.7	33.3	35.9	42.3	*(Millions of US dollars), outstanding at end of year*						
	31.7	33.3	35.9	42.3	47.9	52.2	64.9	142.4	251.1	373.2	467.3
Long-Term Debt (by debtor)	31.7	33.3	35.9	42.3	47.9	52.2	64.9	101.4	190.1	306.2	420.1
Central Bank, incl. IMF credit	0.0	0.0	0.0	0.0	0.0	4.1	6.8	28.1	44.9	84.0	123.1
Central Government	30.6	32.1	31.5	33.0	38.8	39.8	40.4	55.4	120.0	188.8	255.3
Rest of General Government	..	..	..	..	..	..	..	..	..		
Non-financial Public Enterprises	1.1	1.2	1.3	1.7	2.2	1.8	3.4	5.5	10.1	10.3	17.7
Priv. Sector, incl non-guaranteed	0.0	0.0	3.1	7.6	6.9	6.5	14.3	12.4	15.1	23.1	24.0
Short-Term Debt	0.0	0.0	0.0	0.0	0.0	0.0	0.0	41.0	61.0	67.0	47.2
Memo Items:					*(Millions of US dollars)*						
Int'l Reserves Excluding Gold	46.2	51.7	70.1	66.8	131.1	166.0	89.5	66.3	45.8	29.2	90.7
Gold Holdings (at market price)	..	..	..	..	..	..	..	1.6	7.4	19.3	22.2
SOCIAL INDICATORS											
Total Fertility Rate	3.6	3.4	3.3	3.2	3.2	3.1	3.1	3.1	2.9	2.8	2.7
Infant Mortality Rate	59.8	57.4	55.0	51.6	48.2	44.8	41.4	38.0	36.0	34.0	32.0
Life Expectancy at Birth	62.4	62.7	62.9	63.3	63.7	64.1	64.5	64.9	65.3	65.6	66.0
Urban Population, % of total	42.0	42.3	42.6	42.8	43.1	43.4	43.3	43.2	43.1	43.0	42.9
Food Prod. per capita (1987=100)	97.4	99.4	113.6	111.8	108.0	81.2	112.1	104.0	104.9	105.2	78.1
Labor Force, Agriculture (%)	34.0	33.4	32.8	32.2	31.6	31.0	30.3	29.6	29.0	28.5	27.9
Labor Force, Female (%)	20.0	20.4	20.7	21.1	21.4	21.8	22.0	22.3	22.5	22.7	22.9
Primary Schl. Enroll. Ratio	94.0	..	..	..	..	107.0	..	109.0	109.0	103.0	98.0
Primary Schl. Enroll. Ratio, Female	93.0	..	..	..	..	106.0	..	107.0	107.0	102.0	98.0
Secondary Schl. Enroll. Ratio	30.0	..	..	..	..	39.0	43.0	46.0	48.0	50.0	43.0

1981	1982	1983	1984	1985	1986	1987	1988	1989	1990 estimate	Notes	MAURITIUS
											FOREIGN TRADE (CUSTOMS BASIS)
				(Millions of current US dollars)							
316.1	358.6	360.8	375.4	435.8	673.0	880.3	1,001.3	986.8	1,182.1	..	Value of Exports, fob
..	246.9	251.4	261.6	303.7	469.0	613.4	697.8	687.6	823.7	..	Nonfuel Primary Products
..	0.0	0.0	0.0	0.0	0.0	0.0	0.0	0.0	0.0	..	Fuels
114.8	111.7	109.4	113.8	132.1	204.0	266.9	303.5	299.1	358.3	..	Manufactures
554.0	464.2	441.7	470.6	525.8	677.2	1,012.3	1,283.1	1,325.7	1,616.0	..	Value of Imports, cif
181.0	156.5	133.0	141.7	158.4	204.0	304.9	386.5	399.3	486.7	..	Nonfuel Primary Products
100.0	86.1	83.0	88.4	98.8	127.2	190.1	241.0	249.0	303.5	..	Fuels
273.0	221.6	225.7	240.5	268.2	346.0	517.3	655.6	677.4	825.7	..	Manufactures
				(Index 1987 = 100)							
84.0	83.0	83.9	80.9	83.2	95.7	100.0	107.6	107.8	114.5	..	Terms of Trade
84.2	77.5	75.8	71.4	72.3	87.0	100.0	109.7	115.3	134.0	..	Export Prices, fob
100.2	93.4	90.4	88.3	86.9	90.9	100.0	101.9	106.9	117.1	..	Import Prices, cif
											BALANCE OF PAYMENTS
				(Millions of current US dollars)							
508.6	510.7	508.5	506.7	580.8	892.7	1,223.8	1,402.2	1,447.5	1,753.0	..	Exports of Goods & Services
327.1	366.1	368.5	374.1	433.0	675.2	891.4	997.9	993.1	1,186.2	..	Merchandise, fob
174.2	140.7	137.5	129.7	145.9	211.8	318.4	377.7	403.4	510.7	..	Nonfactor Services
7.3	4.0	2.5	2.9	1.9	5.7	14.0	26.6	51.0	56.1	..	Factor Services
681.3	587.4	556.7	590.2	645.4	847.7	1,226.6	1,558.6	1,627.5	1,963.5	..	Imports of Goods & Services
478.2	396.7	385.9	415.5	458.8	617.1	907.6	1,165.7	1,204.2	1,466.5	..	Merchandise, fob
150.3	141.0	126.9	126.6	139.4	170.9	263.6	322.3	352.4	420.4	..	Nonfactor Services
52.8	49.7	43.9	48.0	47.3	59.7	55.4	70.6	70.9	76.6	..	Factor Services
35.4	34.8	28.5	27.1	28.1	29.9	33.6	42.3	42.2	41.0	..	Long-Term Interest
11.6	14.4	16.2	19.3	21.8	29.9	40.6	71.5	68.2	82.4	..	Private Current Transfers, net
..	..	..	..	..	0.0	..	..	..	..	..	Workers' Remittances
-161.1	-62.2	-32.1	-64.1	-42.8	74.9	37.8	-84.9	-111.7	-128.2	..	Curr. A/C Bal before Off. Transf.
5.1	19.6	8.9	8.9	14.2	19.7	25.4	21.5	7.3	9.0	..	Net Official Transfers
-156.0	-42.6	-23.1	-55.2	-28.6	94.6	63.2	-63.4	-104.4	-119.1	..	Curr. A/C Bal after Off. Transf.
55.9	49.3	-17.4	45.8	25.5	27.8	81.3	148.6	107.5	144.4	..	Long-Term Capital, net
0.7	1.8	1.6	4.9	8.0	7.4	17.1	23.6	35.1	40.5	..	Direct Investment
51.3	46.0	-22.3	43.6	18.4	10.7	74.3	122.2	47.2	91.3	..	Long-Term Loans
73.1	79.1	38.4	95.3	61.0	49.3	123.1	226.2	99.6	150.1	..	Disbursements
21.8	33.1	60.7	51.7	42.6	38.6	48.8	104.0	52.4	58.8	..	Repayments
3.9	1.6	3.3	-2.7	-0.9	9.7	-10.1	2.8	25.2	12.6	..	Other Long-Term Capital
-16.4	-26.7	10.1	28.2	19.7	-1.4	72.2	98.4	142.0	207.0	..	Other Capital, net
116.5	19.9	30.5	-18.8	-16.6	-121.0	-216.7	-183.6	-145.1	-232.2	..	Change in Reserves
											Memo Item:
				(Mauritian Rupees per US dollar)							
8.940	10.870	11.710	13.800	15.440	13.470	12.880	13.440	15.250	14.860	..	Conversion Factor (Annual Avg)
				(Millions of US dollars), outstanding at end of year							
545.1	584.1	561.0	549.1	628.8	670.7	813.5	859.6	834.6	938.5	..	**EXTERNAL DEBT (Total)**
506.1	552.1	512.0	510.1	577.8	632.7	780.5	811.5	802.5	908.2	..	Long-Term Debt (by debtor)
181.0	198.9	202.6	180.3	188.0	194.1	192.7	140.8	100.8	68.5	..	Central Bank, incl. IMF credit
284.8	318.2	282.3	299.2	346.9	385.0	485.3	453.4	440.7	493.4	..	Central Government
..	..	..	..	..	..	..	..	..	..	..	Rest of General Government
16.7	16.6	12.7	17.9	23.1	25.9	49.1	145.6	154.8	198.8	..	Non-financial Public Enterprises
23.6	18.4	14.4	12.7	19.8	27.7	53.4	71.7	106.2	147.5	..	Priv. Sector, incl non-guaranteed
39.0	32.0	49.0	39.0	51.0	38.0	33.0	48.1	32.1	30.3	..	Short-Term Debt
				(Millions of US dollars)							**Memo Items:**
35.1	38.0	17.9	23.6	29.9	136.0	343.5	442.0	517.8	737.6	..	Int'l Reserves Excluding Gold
15.0	17.2	14.3	11.6	12.3	14.7	18.2	21.2	24.6	23.6	..	Gold Holdings (at market price)
											SOCIAL INDICATORS
2.5	2.4	2.3	2.2	2.2	2.1	2.0	2.0	1.9	1.9	..	Total Fertility Rate
30.0	28.0	27.0	26.0	25.0	24.0	23.0	22.2	21.3	20.5	..	Infant Mortality Rate
66.3	66.7	67.1	67.5	68.0	68.4	68.8	69.2	69.5	69.8	..	Life Expectancy at Birth
42.6	42.3	42.0	41.7	41.4	41.2	41.0	40.8	40.7	40.5	..	Urban Population, % of total
89.3	106.8	88.0	84.9	92.4	99.0	100.0	90.8	89.5	92.1	..	Food Prod. per capita (1987=100)
..	..	..	..	..	..	..	..	..	..	..	Labor Force, Agriculture (%)
23.3	23.7	24.1	24.4	24.8	25.1	25.5	25.9	26.2	26.5	..	Labor Force, Female (%)
..	..	..	105.0	103.0	107.0	104.0	102.0	103.0	..	..	Primary Schl. Enroll. Ratio
..	..	..	106.0	104.0	107.0	105.0	104.0	104.0	..	..	Primary Schl. Enroll. Ratio, Female
..	49.0	51.0	51.0	51.0	50.0	51.0	52.0	53.0	..	..	Secondary Schl. Enroll. Ratio

MEXICO	1970	1971	1972	1973	1974	1975	1976	1977	1978	1979	1980
CURRENT GNP PER CAPITA (US $)	820	800	820	940	1,120	1,360	1,500	1,490	1,580	1,810	2,320
POPULATION (thousands)	52,770	54,549	56,386	58,253	60,107	61,918	63,687	65,407	67,089	68,755	70,416

USE AND ORIGIN OF RESOURCES
(Billions of current Mexican Pesos)

	1970	1971	1972	1973	1974	1975	1976	1977	1978	1979	1980
Gross National Product (GNP)	461	508	586	715	930	1,137	1,410	1,899	2,402	3,142	4,317
Net Factor Income from Abroad	-18	-21	-24	-31	-37	-42	-60	-73	-90	-113	-153
GDP at Market Prices	479	529	610	746	966	1,179	1,471	1,972	2,491	3,255	4,470
Resource Balance	-12	-10	-10	-14	-28	-39	-32	-20	-41	-78	-101
Exports of Goods & NFServices	31	33	41	52	67	68	104	170	218	306	479
Imports of Goods & NFServices	43	43	50	66	96	106	136	190	259	383	580
Domestic Absorption	491	538	620	760	994	1,218	1,503	1,991	2,532	3,333	4,572
Private Consumption, etc.	358	402	456	549	704	845	1,048	1,372	1,728	2,205	2,909
General Gov't Consumption	31	36	47	61	80	110	146	193	247	324	449
Gross Domestic Investment	102	100	116	149	210	263	308	426	557	804	1,214
Fixed Investment	95	94	115	143	192	252	309	389	528	770	1,107
Indirect Taxes, net	23	26	30	38	45	67	78	114	147	220	343
GDP at factor cost	456	503	580	708	922	1,112	1,393	1,857	2,344	3,036	4,127
Agriculture	56	61	64	83	107	127	151	201	247	290	368
Industry	141	153	178	216	289	352	438	605	763	1,017	1,464
Manufacturing	106	119	135	165	217	258	317	443	553	717	989
Services, etc.	282	314	368	447	570	700	882	1,166	1,481	1,948	2,638
Gross Domestic Saving	90	91	106	135	182	224	276	407	516	726	1,113
Gross National Saving	72	70	82	105	147	183	217	336	428	616	965

(Billions of 1987 Mexican Pesos)

	1970	1971	1972	1973	1974	1975	1976	1977	1978	1979	1980
Gross National Product	94,361.0	98,194.6	106,256.0	114,857.0	121,598.0	128,369.0	133,270.0	138,109.0	149,470.0	160,541.0	172,997.0
GDP at Market Prices	94,784.5	98,718.4	107,091.0	115,906.0	122,922.0	129,934.0	135,430.0	139,819.0	151,319.0	165,333.0	179,169.0
Resource Balance	-5,482.8	-4,426.1	-4,268.9	-5,325.3	-9,013.3	-10,267.0	-8,516.3	-4,213.7	-6,761.7	-11,935.0	-20,832.0
Exports of Goods & NFServices	9,438.9	9,810.7	11,422.6	12,985.0	13,010.3	11,851.7	13,820.7	15,846.5	17,682.1	19,830.4	21,039.6
Imports of Goods & NFServices	14,921.7	14,236.8	15,691.5	18,310.3	22,023.6	22,118.2	22,337.0	20,060.2	24,443.8	31,764.9	41,872.0
Domestic Absorption	100,267.0	103,144.0	111,360.0	121,232.0	131,936.0	140,200.0	143,946.0	144,032.0	158,081.0	177,267.0	200,001.0
Private Consumption, etc.	68,660.7	72,193.5	76,969.9	81,972.0	86,714.4	91,941.4	95,966.6	96,285.5	104,836.0	115,526.0	126,186.0
General Gov't Consumption	5,696.8	6,302.4	7,147.5	7,865.2	8,362.3	9,543.9	10,151.1	10,036.2	11,033.4	12,101.3	13,243.5
Gross Domestic Investment	25,909.8	24,648.5	27,242.2	31,394.5	36,858.9	38,715.0	37,828.6	37,710.7	42,210.9	49,639.8	60,571.5
Fixed Investment	22,852.6	22,461.3	25,209.8	28,927.1	31,212.9	34,104.9	34,257.9	31,958.0	36,807.0	44,260.0	50,880.6
GDP at factor cost	..	..	..	..	..	..	..	..	..	154,127.0	165,399.0
Agriculture	10,645.2	11,255.1	11,333.5	11,793.9	12,093.4	12,337.2	12,461.9	13,398.6	14,200.6	13,904.1	14,889.8
Industry	32,998.4	33,610.2	36,981.4	41,064.0	44,001.7	46,321.1	48,749.5	49,831.7	55,111.4	61,407.8	67,227.2
Manufacturing	24,236.3	25,172.0	27,637.6	30,536.8	32,474.6	34,109.1	35,827.6	37,099.3	40,734.4	45,064.9	48,305.9
Services, etc.	51,140.9	53,853.0	58,775.8	63,048.4	66,827.3	71,275.6	74,218.7	76,588.5	82,006.9	90,021.0	97,052.0

Memo Items:

	1970	1971	1972	1973	1974	1975	1976	1977	1978	1979	1980
Capacity to Import	10,631.6	11,069.8	12,710.0	14,440.3	15,542.8	14,065.7	17,053.7	17,969.0	20,572.6	25,329.9	34,544.4
Terms of Trade Adjustment	1,192.6	1,259.1	1,287.4	1,455.2	2,532.6	2,214.0	3,233.0	2,122.5	2,890.4	5,499.5	13,504.8
Gross Domestic Income	95,977.1	99,977.4	108,378.0	117,362.0	125,455.0	132,148.0	138,663.0	141,941.0	154,209.0	170,832.0	192,674.0
Gross National Income	95,553.6	99,453.7	107,543.0	116,312.0	124,131.0	130,583.0	136,503.0	140,232.0	152,360.0	166,041.0	186,502.0

DOMESTIC PRICES/DEFLATORS
(Index 1987 = 100)

	1970	1971	1972	1973	1974	1975	1976	1977	1978	1979	1980
Overall (GDP)	0.5	0.5	0.6	0.6	0.8	0.9	1.1	1.4	1.6	2.0	2.5
Domestic Absorption	0.5	0.5	0.6	0.6	0.8	0.9	1.0	1.4	1.6	1.9	2.3
Agriculture	0.5	0.5	0.6	0.7	0.9	1.0	1.2	1.5	1.7	2.1	2.5
Industry	0.4	0.5	0.5	0.5	0.7	0.8	0.9	1.2	1.4	1.7	2.2
Manufacturing	0.4	0.5	0.5	0.5	0.7	0.8	0.9	1.2	1.4	1.6	2.0
Consumer Price Index	0.5	0.5	0.5	0.6	0.7	0.8	1.0	1.2	1.4	1.7	2.2

MANUFACTURING ACTIVITY

	1970	1971	1972	1973	1974	1975	1976	1977	1978	1979	1980
Employment (1987=100)	77.5	79.6	82.2	86.5	89.7	89.9	91.9	92.1	95.8	102.9	108.6
Real Earnings per Empl. (1987=100)	130.9	132.4	134.5	136.6	135.5	139.0	148.5	150.4	146.5	145.0	141.6
Real Output per Empl. (1987=100)	71.9	71.1	74.9	79.4	84.1	87.0	88.5	88.6	93.1	95.2	93.2
Earnings as % of Value Added	44.0	42.7	41.4	40.6	39.2	39.1	40.1	37.6	35.8	34.7	32.9

MONETARY HOLDINGS
(Billions of current Mexican Pesos)

	1970	1971	1972	1973	1974	1975	1976	1977	1978	1979	1980
Money Supply, Broadly Defined	135	150	168	209	245	296	530	566	759	1,029	1,426
Money	54	58	68	84	101	122	158	208	270	361	477
Currency Outside Banks	20	22	27	34	43	53	80	89	115	150	195
Demand Deposits	34	36	41	49	58	70	78	119	155	211	282
Quasi-Money	81	92	100	126	144	173	372	358	489	668	949

GOVERNMENT DEFICIT (-) OR SURPLUS
(Billions of current Mexican Pesos)

	1970	1971	1972	1973	1974	1975	1976	1977	1978	1979	1980
GOVERNMENT DEFICIT (-) OR SURPLUS	..	..	-17	-28	-34	-54	-64	-61	-63	-102	-134
Current Revenue	..	..	58	70	96	134	169	241	323	439	675
Current Expenditure	..	..	48	64	93	124	158	222	276	350	507
Current Budget Balance	..	..	10	6	3	10	11	19	47	89	168
Capital Receipts	..	..	..	..	..	..	..	..	..	..	..
Capital Payments	..	..	27	33	37	64	75	81	110	191	302

1981	1982	1983	1984	1985	1986	1987	1988	1989	1990 estimate	Notes	MEXICO
3,000	2,770	2,290	2,120	2,180	1,890	1,780	1,770	2,080	2,490	..	**CURRENT GNP PER CAPITA (US $)**
72,070	73,719	75,354	76,958	78,524	80,063	81,584	83,098	84,617	86,154	..	**POPULATION (thousands)**
											USE AND ORIGIN OF RESOURCES
				(Billions of current Mexican Pesos)							
5,875	9,082	16,765	27,783	45,105	74,824	183,818	379,313	497,507	647,323	..	Gross National Product (GNP)
-253	-716	-1,114	-1,689	-2,287	-4,712	-9,734	-16,760	-19,203	-21,368	..	Net Factor Income from Abroad
6,128	9,798	17,879	29,472	47,392	79,536	193,552	396,073	516,710	668,691	..	GDP at Market Prices
-155	491	1,713	2,307	2,408	3,630	13,829	9,150	4,410	-3,253	..	Resource Balance
638	1,502	3,397	5,122	7,305	13,655	38,223	65,611	81,058	108,295	..	Exports of Goods & NFServices
793	1,011	1,684	2,815	4,897	10,025	24,394	56,461	76,648	111,548	..	Imports of Goods & NFServices
6,283	9,307	16,166	27,165	44,984	75,906	179,723	386,923	512,300	671,944	..	Domestic Absorption
3,945	6,036	10,881	18,590	30,575	54,209	126,053	270,752	340,022	464,964	..	Private Consumption, etc.
660	1,026	1,574	2,722	4,374	7,208	16,505	32,961	54,460	75,692	..	General Gov't Consumption
1,678	2,245	3,710	5,853	10,035	14,489	37,165	83,210	117,818	131,288	..	Gross Domestic Investment
1,617	2,249	3,137	5,287	9,048	15,415	35,667	75,197	92,620	131,289	..	Fixed Investment
458	858	1,326	2,376	4,428	6,319	18,710	35,567	47,789	62,857	..	Indirect Taxes, net
5,670	8,940	16,553	27,096	42,964	73,217	174,842	360,506	468,921	605,834	B	GDP at factor cost
503	720	1,392	2,533	4,307	7,466	16,676	33,966	44,021	59,272	..	Agriculture
1,956	3,057	6,016	9,860	15,805	26,921	69,909	140,203	164,617	199,744	..	Industry
1,326	2,033	3,772	6,618	11,069	19,646	50,123	106,741	125,875	152,794	f	Manufacturing
3,668	6,021	10,471	17,078	27,280	45,149	106,967	221,904	308,072	409,675	..	Services, etc.
1,523	2,736	5,423	8,159	12,443	18,119	50,994	92,360	122,228	128,035	..	Gross Domestic Saving
1,276	2,033	4,340	6,525	10,240	13,618	41,789	76,502	107,756	112,874	..	Gross National Saving
				(Billions of 1987 Mexican Pesos)							
186,828.0	179,498.0	173,957.0	181,316.0	188,122.0	178,722.0	183,818.0	188,098.0	195,209.0	204,064.0	..	Gross National Product
194,862.0	193,654.0	185,536.0	192,353.0	197,640.0	189,990.0	193,552.0	196,406.0	202,714.0	210,783.0	..	GDP at Market Prices
-25,811.0	-2,042.3	12,192.7	10,434.2	6,280.7	11,309.4	13,829.0	6,552.7	1,403.3	-5,587.5	..	Resource Balance
23,475.5	28,589.2	32,471.7	34,322.9	32,797.1	34,533.9	38,223.0	40,122.5	41,340.5	43,503.8	..	Exports of Goods & NFServices
49,286.2	30,631.5	20,279.0	23,888.7	26,516.5	23,224.5	24,394.0	33,569.7	39,937.2	49,091.2	..	Imports of Goods & NFServices
220,673.0	195,696.0	173,343.0	181,919.0	191,359.0	178,681.0	179,723.0	189,853.0	201,311.0	216,370.0	..	Domestic Absorption
136,597.0	128,189.0	119,609.0	124,851.0	129,938.0	126,503.0	126,053.0	131,626.0	141,051.0	150,991.0	..	Private Consumption, etc.
14,604.2	14,902.3	15,306.7	16,316.1	16,463.7	16,708.7	16,505.0	16,422.4	16,310.2	16,590.6	..	General Gov't Consumption
69,471.1	52,604.7	38,427.1	40,751.8	44,957.2	35,468.9	37,165.0	41,804.4	43,949.5	48,788.4	..	Gross Domestic Investment
59,107.9	49,180.0	35,299.3	37,551.5	40,493.1	35,713.0	35,667.0	37,735.3	40,171.3	45,549.0	..	Fixed Investment
180,280.0	176,668.0	171,753.0	176,828.0	179,179.0	174,883.0	174,842.0	178,776.0	183,992.0	191,017.0	B	GDP at factor cost
15,800.5	15,489.5	15,802.4	16,227.7	16,829.7	16,384.7	16,676.0	16,146.0	15,409.7	15,935.7	..	Agriculture
73,259.0	71,746.9	65,328.9	68,411.3	71,719.3	67,673.3	69,909.0	71,616.8	75,431.8	79,480.9	..	Industry
51,420.4	50,011.2	46,090.6	48,401.4	51,344.2	48,647.8	50,123.0	51,730.1	55,374.2	58,270.9	f	Manufacturing
105,802.0	106,418.0	104,404.0	107,714.0	109,091.0	105,932.0	106,967.0	108,643.0	111,873.0	115,366.0	..	Services, etc.
											Memo Items:
39,654.0	45,524.4	40,902.3	43,465.1	39,555.4	31,633.9	38,223.0	39,010.0	42,235.0	47,659.6	..	Capacity to Import
16,178.5	16,935.2	8,430.6	9,142.2	6,758.3	-2,900.0	0.0	-1,112.5	894.5	4,155.9	..	Terms of Trade Adjustment
211,040.0	210,589.0	193,966.0	201,496.0	204,398.0	187,090.0	193,552.0	195,293.0	203,609.0	214,939.0	..	Gross Domestic Income
203,006.0	196,434.0	182,388.0	190,459.0	194,881.0	175,822.0	183,818.0	186,985.0	196,104.0	208,220.0	..	Gross National Income
				(Index 1987 = 100)							**DOMESTIC PRICES/DEFLATORS**
3.1	5.1	9.6	15.3	24.0	41.9	100.0	201.7	254.9	317.2	..	Overall (GDP)
2.8	4.8	9.3	14.9	23.5	42.5	100.0	203.8	254.5	310.6	..	Domestic Absorption
3.2	4.6	8.8	15.6	25.6	45.6	100.0	210.4	285.7	371.9	..	Agriculture
2.7	4.3	9.2	14.4	22.0	39.8	100.0	195.8	218.2	251.3	..	Industry
2.6	4.1	8.2	13.7	21.6	40.4	100.0	206.3	227.3	262.2	..	Manufacturing
2.8	4.4	8.9	14.7	23.2	43.1	100.0	214.2	257.0	325.5	..	Consumer Price Index
											MANUFACTURING ACTIVITY
114.2	111.6	101.1	99.2	104.1	98.4	100.0	101.6	..	..	J	Employment (1987=100)
145.9	142.4	105.5	102.8	104.7	98.5	100.0	101.5	..	..	J	Real Earnings per Empl. (1987=100)
92.7	90.6	96.0	103.7	107.1	104.5	100.0	105.1	..	..	J	Real Output per Empl. (1987=100)
34.2	34.0	23.8	21.1	20.9	20.0	19.8	19.8	..	..	J	Earnings as % of Value Added
				(Billions of current Mexican Pesos)							**MONETARY HOLDINGS**
2,141	3,330	5,443	9,186	13,255	23,612	58,555	52,717	98,621	173,663	D	Money Supply, Broadly Defined
635	1,031	1,447	2,315	3,462	5,790	12,627	21,191	29,087	47,439	..	Money
283	505	681	1,122	1,738	3,067	7,339	13,201	18,030	24,689	..	Currency Outside Banks
352	526	766	1,193	1,724	2,723	5,288	7,990	11,057	22,750	..	Demand Deposits
1,506	2,299	3,996	6,871	9,793	17,822	45,928	31,526	69,534	126,224	..	Quasi-Money
				(Billions of current Mexican Pesos)							**GOVERNMENT DEFICIT (-) OR SURPLUS**
-392	-1,454	-1,362	-2,095	-3,979	-10,407	-26,224	-40,343	-26,494	5,104	..	Current Revenue
895	1,520	3,222	4,772	7,820	12,642	33,682	67,465	92,837	96,357	..	Current Expenditure
843	2,191	3,660	5,451	9,669	19,670	52,636	97,031	103,795	102,384	..	Current Budget Balance
52	-671	-438	-679	-1,849	-7,028	-18,954	-29,566	-10,958	-6,027	..	Capital Receipts
..	..	..	1	..	1	1	11	4	50	..	Capital Payments
444	783	924	1,417	2,130	3,380	7,271	10,788	15,540	-11,081	..	Capital Payments

MEXICO	1970	1971	1972	1973	1974	1975	1976	1977	1978	1979	1980
FOREIGN TRADE (CUSTOMS BASIS)					*(Millions of current US dollars)*						
Value of Exports, fob	1,205	1,320	1,845	2,631	2,957	2,993	3,468	4,284	6,301	8,817	15,442
Nonfuel Primary Products	775	785	1,174	1,503	1,713	1,599	1,902	2,089	2,793	3,063	3,280
Fuels	38	31	22	25	124	463	554	1,014	1,804	3,859	10,320
Manufactures	392	504	649	1,103	1,120	931	1,012	1,182	1,704	1,894	1,842
Value of Imports, cif	2,461	2,407	2,935	4,146	6,057	6,572	6,033	5,589	8,053	12,586	19,591
Nonfuel Primary Products	397	339	421	793	1,529	1,347	887	1,143	1,548	2,204	4,528
Fuels	78	104	143	293	426	361	343	166	263	313	388
Manufactures	1,986	1,964	2,371	3,060	4,102	4,864	4,802	4,280	6,242	10,069	14,676
					(Index 1987 = 100)						
Terms of Trade	147.8	159.4	166.2	190.6	149.9	128.2	143.7	134.8	114.8	117.8	136.6
Export Prices, fob	37.1	41.4	46.7	62.7	77.6	70.1	78.8	81.2	77.9	93.9	121.2
Import Prices, cif	25.1	26.0	28.1	32.9	51.8	54.7	54.9	60.2	67.9	79.7	88.7
BALANCE OF PAYMENTS					*(Millions of current US dollars)*						
Exports of Goods & Services	2,935	3,171	3,816	4,840	6,368	6,358	7,203	8,211	11,425	16,003	21,994
Merchandise, fob	1,348	1,409	1,717	2,141	2,999	3,007	3,475	4,604	6,246	9,301	15,511
Nonfactor Services	1,397	1,586	1,892	2,463	3,057	3,059	3,364	3,189	4,497	5,830	5,241
Factor Services	190	177	207	236	311	292	363	419	682	872	1,242
Imports of Goods & Services	4,058	4,064	4,797	6,329	9,365	10,541	10,767	10,235	14,788	21,687	33,028
Merchandise, fob	2,236	2,158	2,610	3,656	5,791	6,278	5,771	5,625	7,992	12,131	18,896
Nonfactor Services	1,181	1,238	1,406	1,580	1,817	2,188	2,518	2,040	3,344	4,573	6,221
Factor Services	641	668	781	1,093	1,757	2,075	2,479	2,570	3,452	4,983	7,911
Long-Term Interest	283	312	353	516	813	1,104	1,360	1,588	2,258	3,357	4,580
Private Current Transfers, net	25	26	25	41	57	59	73	88	104	131	245
Workers' Remittances	..	..	..	..	..	..	..	..	..	..	139
Curr. A/C Bal before Off. Transf.	-1,098	-867	-955	-1,448	-2,940	-4,124	-3,492	-1,936	-3,259	-5,553	-10,789
Net Official Transfers	30	31	39	33	65	81	83	82	88	94	39
Curr. A/C Bal after Off. Transf.	-1,068	-835	-916	-1,415	-2,876	-4,042	-3,409	-1,854	-3,171	-5,459	-10,750
Long-Term Capital, net	626	746	827	1,819	3,046	4,656	4,994	4,611	5,118	5,144	10,530
Direct Investment	323	307	301	457	678	609	628	556	824	1,332	2,156
Long-Term Loans	358	453	602	1,819	2,669	3,746	4,504	4,709	4,537	4,081	6,821
Disbursements	1,375	1,502	1,780	3,173	3,979	5,255	6,489	7,819	9,442	12,140	11,581
Repayments	1,017	1,049	1,178	1,354	1,310	1,509	1,985	3,110	4,905	8,059	4,760
Other Long-Term Capital	-55	-14	-76	-456	-301	302	-138	-654	-243	-269	1,553
Other Capital, net	471	219	267	-247	-97	-410	-2,445	-2,135	-1,561	630	1,038
Change in Reserves	-29	-130	-178	-157	-74	-204	860	-622	-386	-315	-818
Memo Item:					*(Mexican Pesos per US dollar)*						
Conversion Factor (Annual Avg)	12.500	12.500	12.500	12.500	12.500	12.500	15.400	22.600	22.800	22.800	23.000
EXTERNAL DEBT (Total)	5.97	6.42	7.03	9.00	11.95	15.61	20.52	31.19	35.71	42.77	57.38
				(Billions of US dollars), outstanding at end of year							
Long-Term Debt (by debtor)	5.97	6.42	7.03	9.00	11.95	15.61	20.52	25.74	30.77	34.75	41.21
Central Bank, incl. IMF credit	1.15	1.42	1.74	2.48	3.17	4.91	7.05	8.86	9.83	10.73	11.58
Central Government	0.35	0.32	0.36	0.45	0.93	1.37	2.58	3.96	4.69	4.31	4.92
Rest of General Government	0.00	0.00	0.00	0.00	0.00	0.00	0.00	0.00	0.00	0.00	0.00
Non-financial Public Enterprises	1.65	1.71	1.76	2.36	3.68	4.53	5.76	7.34	9.77	11.98	15.15
Priv. Sector, incl non-guaranteed	2.81	2.97	3.17	3.71	4.17	4.79	5.13	5.57	6.47	7.73	9.57
Short-Term Debt	0.00	0.00	0.00	0.00	0.00	0.00	0.00	5.45	4.95	8.02	16.16
Memo Items:					*(Millions of US dollars)*						
Int'l Reserves Excluding Gold	568	752	976	1,160	1,238	1,384	1,188	1,649	1,842	2,072	2,960
Gold Holdings (at market price)	188	229	321	520	683	513	216	289	428	1,016	1,215
SOCIAL INDICATORS											
Total Fertility Rate	6.5	6.4	6.4	6.1	5.8	5.5	5.2	4.9	4.8	4.6	4.5
Infant Mortality Rate	74.2	72.6	71.0	68.6	66.2	63.8	61.4	59.0	57.2	55.4	53.6
Life Expectancy at Birth	61.7	62.2	62.6	63.2	63.7	64.3	64.8	65.4	65.8	66.2	66.6
Urban Population, % of total	59.0	59.8	60.5	61.3	62.0	62.8	63.5	64.2	65.0	65.7	66.4
Food Prod. per capita (1987=100)	92.4	92.7	94.5	93.7	91.7	94.6	94.0	99.3	105.5	98.1	102.0
Labor Force, Agriculture (%)	44.1	43.2	42.4	41.6	40.9	40.3	39.4	38.6	37.9	37.2	36.5
Labor Force, Female (%)	17.8	18.9	20.0	20.9	21.8	22.6	23.6	24.6	25.4	26.2	27.0
Primary Schl. Enroll. Ratio	104.0	..	..	..	..	109.0	..	113.0	118.0	120.0	115.0
Primary Schl. Enroll. Ratio, Female	101.0	..	..	..	..	106.0	..	110.0	117.0	119.0	115.0
Secondary Schl. Enroll. Ratio	22.0	..	..	..	..	34.0	37.0	39.0	42.0	44.0	46.0

1981	1982	1983	1984	1985	1986	1987	1988	1989	1990 estimate	Notes	MEXICO
											FOREIGN TRADE (CUSTOMS BASIS)
				(Millions of current US dollars)							
20,036	21,170	24,642	26,563	24,365	12,708	20,532	20,409	22,975	26,714	..	Value of Exports, fob
3,559	2,831	3,147	3,549	3,118	3,846	4,156	4,658	4,858	5,053	..	Nonfuel Primary Products
14,446	16,352	15,862	16,404	14,640	5,567	8,555	6,548	7,784	9,876	..	Fuels
2,030	1,988	5,633	6,609	6,607	3,296	7,821	9,202	10,332	11,786	..	Manufactures
24,853	14,910	10,797	14,458	16,152	9,335	12,758	19,557	22,787	28,063	..	Value of Imports, cif
5,066	2,689	2,938	3,438	3,350	1,963	2,773	4,638	5,500	6,442	..	Nonfuel Primary Products
429	470	246	488	705	458	515	568	908	1,163	..	Fuels
19,358	11,750	7,613	10,531	12,096	6,914	9,469	14,351	16,379	20,458	..	Manufactures
				(Index 1987 = 100)							
146.0	141.7	133.2	134.5	133.4	90.1	100.0	91.2	97.9	110.3	..	Terms of Trade
128.7	120.7	111.7	110.4	107.5	80.9	100.0	98.5	109.0	127.1	..	Export Prices, fob
88.2	85.2	83.9	82.1	80.6	89.8	100.0	108.0	111.3	115.2	..	Import Prices, cif
				(Millions of current US dollars)							**BALANCE OF PAYMENTS**
27,637	27,520	28,578	32,378	29,544	23,684	29,899	32,007	35,969	41,590	..	Exports of Goods & Services
20,102	21,230	22,312	24,196	21,663	16,031	20,565	20,566	22,765	26,773	..	Merchandise, fob
5,893	4,760	4,817	5,847	5,748	5,842	6,955	8,489	10,098	11,616	..	Nonfactor Services
1,642	1,530	1,449	2,335	2,133	1,811	2,289	2,952	3,106	3,201	..	Factor Services
44,001	34,130	23,477	28,594	29,414	25,821	26,579	35,017	42,002	50,318	..	Imports of Goods & Services
23,948	14,435	8,550	11,255	13,212	11,432	12,222	18,898	23,410	29,799	..	Merchandise, fob
8,129	5,711	4,213	4,940	5,170	4,875	5,009	6,049	7,689	9,743	..	Nonfactor Services
11,924	13,984	10,714	12,399	11,032	9,514	9,348	10,070	10,903	10,776	..	Factor Services
6,117	7,769	8,140	10,250	9,382	7,675	7,692	7,542	7,880	5,765	..	Long-Term Interest
246	232	255	325	327	345	384	397	1,922	2,207	..	Private Current Transfers, net
128	98	111	177	173	180	207	209	1,744	2,020	..	Workers' Remittances
-16,118	-6,378	5,356	4,109	457	-1,792	3,704	-2,613	-4,111	-6,521	..	Curr. A/C Bal before Off. Transf.
57	71	47	85	673	119	264	170	153	1,266	..	Net Official Transfers
-16,061	-6,307	5,403	4,194	1,130	-1,673	3,968	-2,443	-3,958	-5,255	..	Curr. A/C Bal after Off. Transf.
18,610	14,645	7,299	2,453	-410	433	4,044	-677	2,298	5,105	..	Long-Term Capital, net
2,835	1,655	461	390	491	1,523	3,246	2,594	3,037	2,632	..	Direct Investment
12,499	7,969	2,356	1,623	-23	545	3,779	-1,483	-241	5,724	..	Long-Term Loans
17,003	12,500	7,188	7,281	5,049	4,968	7,174	4,715	3,960	9,385	..	Disbursements
4,504	4,531	4,831	5,658	5,072	4,423	3,395	6,198	4,201	3,661	..	Repayments
3,276	5,021	4,482	440	-878	-1,635	-2,981	-1,788	-498	-3,251	..	Other Long-Term Capital
-1,274	-13,127	-9,452	-4,497	-3,451	1,152	-2,442	-3,518	1,839	2,453	..	Other Capital, net
-1,275	4,789	-3,250	-2,150	2,731	88	-5,570	6,638	-179	-2,303	..	Change in Reserves
											Memo Item:
				(Mexican Pesos per US dollar)							Conversion Factor (Annual Avg)
24.500	56.400	120.100	167.800	256.900	611.800	1,378.200	2,273.100	2,461.500	2,812.600		
				(Billions of US dollars), outstanding at end of year							
78.22	86.02	92.97	94.82	96.87	100.88	109.46	100.78	95.42	96.81	..	**EXTERNAL DEBT (Total)**
53.23	59.87	82.83	88.38	91.42	94.98	103.66	91.33	85.12	87.16	..	Long-Term Debt (by debtor)
15.31	18.55	15.06	16.32	11.85	15.61	18.92	18.64	19.03	25.60	..	Central Bank, incl. IMF credit
5.57	8.88	32.39	37.38	53.31	53.54	59.66	57.41	53.51	48.14	..	Central Government
0.00	0.00	0.05	0.09	0.01	0.01	0.01	0.00	0.00	0.00	..	Rest of General Government
19.87	22.09	18.84	16.71	9.45	9.70	9.91	9.02	8.40	8.79	..	Non-financial Public Enterprises
12.49	10.35	16.49	17.88	16.79	16.13	15.16	6.25	4.19	4.63	..	Priv. Sector, incl non-guaranteed
24.98	26.15	10.14	6.44	5.45	5.90	5.80	9.46	10.30	9.64	..	Short-Term Debt
				(Millions of US dollars)							**Memo Items:**
4,074	834	3,913	7,272	4,906	5,670	12,464	5,279	6,329	9,863	..	Int'l Reserves Excluding Gold
897	944	881	747	773	1,004	1,228	1,048	411	354	..	Gold Holdings (at market price)
											SOCIAL INDICATORS
4.3	4.2	4.1	4.0	3.8	3.7	3.6	3.5	3.4	3.3	..	Total Fertility Rate
51.8	50.0	48.6	47.2	45.8	44.4	43.0	41.7	40.4	39.2	..	Infant Mortality Rate
67.0	67.4	67.7	68.0	68.3	68.6	68.9	69.2	69.4	69.7	..	Life Expectancy at Birth
67.0	67.7	68.3	69.0	69.6	70.2	70.8	71.4	72.0	72.6	..	Urban Population, % of total
105.7	102.2	103.9	101.6	102.6	102.0	100.0	104.5	104.9	103.9	..	Food Prod. per capita (1987=100)
..	..	..	..	..	..	..	..	..	..	..	Labor Force, Agriculture (%)
27.0	27.0	27.0	27.0	27.0	27.1	27.1	27.1	27.1	27.1	..	Labor Force, Female (%)
..	119.0	119.0	118.0	119.0	119.0	118.0	117.0	114.0	112.0	..	Primary Schl. Enroll. Ratio
118.0	117.0	117.0	116.0	117.0	118.0	116.0	115.0	112.0	..	..	Primary Schl. Enroll. Ratio, Female
..	53.0	55.0	53.0	53.0	53.0	53.0	53.0	53.0	53.0	..	Secondary Schl. Enroll. Ratio

MONGOLIA	1970	1971	1972	1973	1974	1975	1976	1977	1978	1979	1980
CURRENT GNP PER CAPITA (US $)	..	..	..	..	..	..	..	..	..	..	..
POPULATION (thousands)	1,256	1,287	1,317	1,346	1,378	1,412	1,449	1,488	1,530	1,573	1,619

USE AND ORIGIN OF RESOURCES *(Millions of current Mongolian Tughriks)*

	1970	1971	1972	1973	1974	1975	1976	1977	1978	1979	1980
Gross National Product (GNP)	..	..	..	..	..	..	..	..	..	..	5,718
Net Factor Income from Abroad	..	..	..	..	..	..	..	..	..	..	-1,037
GDP at Market Prices	..	..	..	..	..	..	..	..	..	..	6,755
Resource Balance	..	..	..	..	..	..	..	..	..	..	-1,324
Exports of Goods & NFServices	..	..	..	..	..	..	..	..	..	..	1,285
Imports of Goods & NFServices	..	..	..	..	..	..	..	..	..	..	2,609
Domestic Absorption	..	..	..	..	..	..	..	..	..	..	8,079
Private Consumption, etc.	..	..	..	..	..	..	..	..	..	..	..
General Gov't Consumption	..	..	..	..	..	..	..	..	..	..	..
Gross Domestic Investment	..	..	..	..	..	..	..	..	..	..	3,123
Fixed Investment	..	..	..	..	..	..	..	..	..	..	3,104
Indirect Taxes, net	..	..	..	..	..	..	..	..	..	..	..
GDP at factor cost	..	..	..	..	..	..	..	..	..	..	..
Agriculture	..	..	..	..	..	..	..	..	..	..	..
Industry	..	..	..	..	..	..	..	..	..	..	..
Manufacturing	..	..	..	..	..	..	..	..	..	..	..
Services, etc.	..	..	..	..	..	..	..	..	..	..	..
Gross Domestic Saving	..	..	..	..	..	..	..	..	..	..	1,799
Gross National Saving	..	..	..	..	..	..	..	..	..	..	..

(Millions of 1987 Mongolian Tughriks)

	1970	1971	1972	1973	1974	1975	1976	1977	1978	1979	1980
Gross National Product	..	..	..	..	..	..	..	..	..	..	..
GDP at Market Prices	..	..	..	..	..	..	..	..	..	..	6,125
Resource Balance	..	..	..	..	..	..	..	..	..	..	-2,504
Exports of Goods & NFServices	..	..	..	..	..	..	..	..	..	..	1,786
Imports of Goods & NFServices	..	..	..	..	..	..	..	..	..	..	4,290
Domestic Absorption	..	..	..	..	..	..	..	..	..	..	8,629
Private Consumption, etc.	..	..	..	..	..	..	..	..	..	..	..
General Gov't Consumption	..	..	..	..	..	..	..	..	..	..	..
Gross Domestic Investment	..	..	..	..	..	..	..	..	..	..	..
Fixed Investment	..	..	..	..	..	..	..	..	..	..	..
GDP at factor cost	..	..	..	..	..	..	..	..	..	..	..
Agriculture	..	..	..	..	..	..	..	..	..	..	..
Industry	..	..	..	..	..	..	..	..	..	..	..
Manufacturing	..	..	..	..	..	..	..	..	..	..	..
Services, etc.	..	..	..	..	..	..	..	..	..	..	..
Memo Items:											
Capacity to Import	..	..	..	..	..	..	..	..	..	..	2,113
Terms of Trade Adjustment	..	..	..	..	..	..	..	..	..	..	328
Gross Domestic Income	..	..	..	..	..	..	..	..	..	..	6,453
Gross National Income	..	..	..	..	..	..	..	..	..	..	..

DOMESTIC PRICES/DEFLATORS *(Index 1987 = 100)*

	1970	1971	1972	1973	1974	1975	1976	1977	1978	1979	1980
Overall (GDP)	..	..	..	..	..	..	..	..	..	..	110.3
Domestic Absorption	..	..	..	..	..	..	..	..	..	..	93.6
Agriculture	..	..	..	..	..	..	..	..	..	..	..
Industry	..	..	..	..	..	..	..	..	..	..	..
Manufacturing	..	..	..	..	..	..	..	..	..	..	..
Consumer Price Index	..	..	..	..	..	..	..	..	..	..	..

MANUFACTURING ACTIVITY

	1970	1971	1972	1973	1974	1975	1976	1977	1978	1979	1980
Employment (1987=100)	..	..	..	..	..	..	..	..	..	..	..
Real Earnings per Empl. (1987=100)	..	..	..	..	..	..	..	..	..	..	..
Real Output per Empl. (1987=100)	..	..	..	..	..	..	..	..	..	..	..
Earnings as % of Value Added	..	..	..	..	..	..	..	..	..	..	..

MONETARY HOLDINGS *(Millions of current Mongolian Tughriks)*

	1970	1971	1972	1973	1974	1975	1976	1977	1978	1979	1980
Money Supply, Broadly Defined	..	..	..	..	..	..	..	..	..	..	..
Money	..	..	..	..	..	..	..	..	..	..	..
Currency Outside Banks	..	..	..	..	..	..	..	..	..	..	..
Demand Deposits	..	..	..	..	..	..	..	..	..	..	..
Quasi-Money	..	..	..	..	..	..	..	..	..	..	..

GOVERNMENT DEFICIT (-) OR SURPLUS *(Millions of current Mongolian Tughriks)*

	1970	1971	1972	1973	1974	1975	1976	1977	1978	1979	1980
Current Revenue	..	..	..	..	..	..	..	..	..	..	..
Current Expenditure	..	..	..	..	..	..	..	..	..	..	..
Current Budget Balance	..	..	..	..	..	..	..	..	..	..	..
Capital Receipts	..	..	..	..	..	..	..	..	..	..	..
Capital Payments	..	..	..	..	..	..	..	..	..	..	..

1981	1982	1983	1984	1985	1986	1987	1988	1989	1990 estimate	Notes	MONGOLIA
..	..	..	..	..	..	..	..	..	..	..	**CURRENT GNP PER CAPITA (US $)**
1,666	1,714	1,762	1,810	1,856	1,907	1,960	2,014	2,070	2,128	..	**POPULATION (thousands)**
											USE AND ORIGIN OF RESOURCES
*(Millions of current Mongolian Tughriks)*											
6,352	7,106	7,631	7,827	8,155	8,052	8,351	9,013	9,545	9,295	..	Gross National Product (GNP)
-1,074	-1,099	-1,131	-1,168	-1,217	-1,258	-1,359	-1,288	-1,186	-1,219	..	Net Factor Income from Abroad
7,426	8,205	8,762	8,996	9,372	9,310	9,710	10,301	10,731	10,514	..	GDP at Market Prices
-2,540	-2,676	-2,619	-2,481	-2,850	-3,367	-2,829	-2,886	-3,557	-2,836	..	Resource Balance
1,520	1,840	2,023	2,300	2,369	2,624	2,618	2,669	2,496	2,410	..	Exports of Goods & NF Services
4,059	4,516	4,642	4,781	5,219	5,990	5,447	5,555	6,053	5,247	..	Imports of Goods & NF Services
9,965	10,881	11,381	11,477	12,222	12,677	12,539	13,187	14,288	13,351	..	Domestic Absorption
..	..	..	5,046	4,788	4,220	5,718	6,378	6,855	7,646	..	Private Consumption, etc.
			1,869	1,961	2,272	2,384	2,475	2,492	2,562	..	General Gov't Consumption
4,606	5,193	4,499	4,562	5,474	6,184	4,437	4,335	4,941	3,142	..	Gross Domestic Investment
4,289	4,646	3,924	4,282	4,634	4,763	4,552	4,538	4,807	3,380	..	Fixed Investment
..	..	..	2,142	2,172	1,679	1,664	1,630	1,763	1,517	..	Indirect Taxes, net
..	..	..	6,854	7,200	7,631	8,045	8,671	8,968	8,997	..	GDP at factor cost
..	..	..	1,361	1,354	1,664	1,569	1,683	1,832	1,820	..	Agriculture
..	..	..	2,578	2,767	2,975	3,246	3,483	3,681	3,550	..	Industry
..	..	..	..	..	..	..	..	..	..	..	Manufacturing
..	..	..	2,915	3,079	2,993	3,231	3,505	3,456	3,627	..	Services, etc.
2,066	2,517	1,880	2,081	2,623	2,817	1,608	1,449	1,385	306	..	Gross Domestic Saving
..	..	..	..	1,406	1,559	248	160	199	-913	..	Gross National Saving
*(Millions of 1987 Mongolian Tughriks)*											
..	..	..	..	..	..	..	..	..	..	..	Gross National Product
6,638	7,195	7,605	8,199	8,581	9,290	9,710	10,206	10,632	10,413	..	GDP at Market Prices
-3,185	-2,858	-3,260	-2,832	-3,474	-3,113	-2,829	-2,819	-2,198	-2,160	..	Resource Balance
1,956	2,146	2,443	2,535	2,439	2,710	2,618	2,572	2,423	2,186	..	Exports of Goods & NF Services
5,141	5,004	5,703	5,368	5,913	5,824	5,447	5,391	4,621	4,346	..	Imports of Goods & NF Services
9,823	10,054	10,865	11,032	12,055	12,404	12,539	13,024	12,830	12,573	..	Domestic Absorption
..	..	..	4,628	4,518	3,939	5,718	6,305	6,022	7,034	..	Private Consumption, etc.
..	..	..	1,788	1,989	2,315	2,384	2,413	2,144	2,240	..	General Gov't Consumption
..	..	..	4,615	5,548	6,149	4,437	4,306	4,663	3,300	..	Gross Domestic Investment
..	..	..	..	..	..	..	..	..	..	..	Fixed Investment
..	..	..	..	..	7,617	8,045	8,588	8,884	8,878	..	GDP at factor cost
..	..	..	..	..	..	..	..	..	..	..	Agriculture
..	..	..	..	..	..	..	..	..	..	..	Industry
..	..	..	..	..	..	..	..	..	..	..	Manufacturing
..	..	..	..	..	..	..	..	..	..	..	Services, etc.
											Memo Items:
1,925	2,039	2,485	2,582	2,684	2,551	2,618	2,590	1,906	1,997	..	Capacity to Import
-31	-107	42	47	244	-160	0	18	-517	-189	..	Terms of Trade Adjustment
6,607	7,089	7,647	8,246	8,825	9,131	9,710	10,223	10,115	10,224	..	Gross Domestic Income
..	..	..	..	..	..	..	..	..	..	..	Gross National Income
											DOMESTIC PRICES/DEFLATORS
*(Index 1987 = 100)*											
111.9	114.0	115.2	109.7	109.2	100.2	100.0	100.9	100.9	101.0	..	Overall (GDP)
101.5	108.2	104.8	104.0	101.4	102.2	100.0	101.2	111.4	106.2	..	Domestic Absorption
..	..	..	..	..	..	..	..	..	..	..	Agriculture
..	..	..	..	..	..	..	..	..	..	..	Industry
..	..	..	..	..	..	..	..	..	..	..	Manufacturing
..	..	..	..	..	..	..	..	..	..	..	Consumer Price Index
											MANUFACTURING ACTIVITY
..	..	..	..	..	..	..	..	..	..	..	Employment (1987=100)
..	..	..	..	..	..	..	..	..	..	..	Real Earnings per Empl. (1987=100)
..	..	..	..	..	..	..	..	..	..	..	Real Output per Empl. (1987=100)
..	..	..	..	..	..	..	..	..	..	..	Earnings as % of Value Added
											MONETARY HOLDINGS
*(Millions of current Mongolian Tughriks)*											
..	..	..	..	..	..	..	..	..	..	..	Money Supply, Broadly Defined
..	..	..	..	..	..	..	..	..	..	..	Money
..	..	..	..	..	..	..	..	..	..	..	Currency Outside Banks
..	..	..	..	..	..	..	..	..	..	..	Demand Deposits
..	..	..	..	..	..	..	..	..	..	..	Quasi-Money
											GOVERNMENT DEFICIT (-) OR SURPLUS
*(Millions of current Mongolian Tughriks)*											
..	..	..	..	..	..	..	..	..	..	..	Current Revenue
..	..	..	..	..	..	..	..	..	..	..	Current Expenditure
..	..	..	..	..	..	..	..	..	..	..	Current Budget Balance
..	..	..	..	..	..	..	..	..	..	..	Capital Receipts
..	..	..	..	..	..	..	..	..	..	..	Capital Payments

MONGOLIA	1970	1971	1972	1973	1974	1975	1976	1977	1978	1979	1980
FOREIGN TRADE (CUSTOMS BASIS)				*(Millions of current US dollars)*							
Value of Exports, fob	..	..	..	..	..	..	..	..	..	..	..
Nonfuel Primary Products	..	..	..	..	..	..	..	..	..	..	..
Fuels	..	..	..	..	..	..	..	..	..	..	..
Manufactures	..	..	..	..	..	..	..	..	..	..	..
Value of Imports, cif	..	..	..	..	..	..	..	..	..	..	..
Nonfuel Primary Products	..	..	..	..	..	..	..	..	..	..	..
Fuels	..	..	..	..	..	..	..	..	..	..	..
Manufactures	..	..	..	..	..	..	..	..	..	..	..
					(Index 1987 = 100)						
Terms of Trade	..	..	..	..	..	..	..	..	..	..	..
Export Prices, fob	..	..	..	..	..	..	..	..	..	..	..
Import Prices, cif	..	..	..	..	..	..	..	..	..	..	..
BALANCE OF PAYMENTS				*(Millions of current US dollars)*							
Exports of Goods & Services	..	..	..	..	..	..	..	..	..	..	443
Merchandise, fob	..	..	..	..	..	..	..	..	..	..	403
Nonfactor Services	..	..	..	..	..	..	..	..	..	..	41
Factor Services	..	..	..	..	..	..	..	..	..	..	0
Imports of Goods & Services	..	..	..	..	..	..	..	..	..	..	934
Merchandise, fob	..	..	..	..	..	..	..	..	..	..	862
Nonfactor Services	..	..	..	..	..	..	..	..	..	..	38
Factor Services	..	..	..	..	..	..	..	..	..	..	35
Long-Term Interest	..	..	..	..	..	..	..	..	..	..	..
Private Current Transfers, net	..	..	..	..	..	..	..	..	..	..	0
Workers' Remittances	..	..	..	..	..	..	..	..	..	..	0
Curr. A/C Bal before Off. Transf.	..	..	..	..	..	..	..	..	..	..	-491
Net Official Transfers	..	..	..	..	..	..	..	..	..	..	147
Curr. A/C Bal after Off. Transf.	..	..	..	..	..	..	..	..	..	..	-344
Long-Term Capital, net	..	..	..	..	..	..	..	..	..	..	418
Direct Investment	..	..	..	..	..	..	..	..	..	..	..
Long-Term Loans	..	..	..	..	..	..	..	..	..	..	..
Disbursements	..	..	..	..	..	..	..	..	..	..	..
Repayments	..	..	..	..	..	..	..	..	..	..	..
Other Long-Term Capital	..	..	..	..	..	..	..	..	..	..	418
Other Capital, net	..	..	..	..	..	..	..	..	..	..	-74
Change in Reserves	..	..	..	..	..	..	..	..	..	..	0
Memo Item:				*(Mongolian Tughriks per US dollar)*							
Conversion Factor (Annual Avg)	..	..	..	..	..	..	..	..	..	..	..
EXTERNAL DEBT (Total)				*Millions US dollars), outstanding at end of year*							
Long-Term Debt (by debtor)	..	..	..	..	..	..	..	..	..	..	..
Central Bank, incl. IMF credit	..	..	..	..	..	..	..	..	..	..	..
Central Government	..	..	..	..	..	..	..	..	..	..	..
Rest of General Government	..	..	..	..	..	..	..	..	..	..	..
Non-financial Public Enterprises	..	..	..	..	..	..	..	..	..	..	..
Priv. Sector, incl non-guaranteed	..	..	..	..	..	..	..	..	..	..	..
Short-Term Debt	..	..	..	..	..	..	..	..	..	..	..
Memo Items:				*Millions US dollars)*							
Int'l Reserves Excluding Gold	..	..	..	..	..	..	..	..	..	..	..
Gold Holdings (at market price)	..	..	..	..	..	..	..	..	..	..	..
SOCIAL INDICATORS											
Total Fertility Rate	5.8	5.8	5.8	5.7	5.7	5.6	5.6	5.5	5.4	5.4	5.4
Infant Mortality Rate	102.0	100.0	98.0	96.0	94.0	92.0	90.0	88.0	86.0	84.0	82.0
Life Expectancy at Birth	52.7	53.2	53.7	54.2	54.7	55.2	55.7	56.2	56.7	57.2	57.7
Urban Population, % of total	45.1	45.8	46.5	47.3	48.0	48.7	49.2	49.7	50.3	50.8	51.3
Food Prod. per capita (1987=100)	123.8	119.3	122.1	123.2	125.5	137.7	125.5	114.8	124.2	119.0	109.5
Labor Force, Agriculture (%)	47.9	47.0	46.1	45.3	44.6	43.8	42.9	42.1	41.3	40.5	39.8
Labor Force, Female (%)	44.9	45.0	45.0	45.1	45.1	45.2	45.2	45.3	45.3	45.4	45.4
Primary Schl. Enroll. Ratio	113.0	..	..	..	..	108.0	..	106.0	104.0	104.0	108.0
Primary Schl. Enroll. Ratio, Female	..	..	..	..	..	104.0	..	104.0	103.0	102.0	108.0
Secondary Schl. Enroll. Ratio	87.0	..	..	..	..	81.0	..	86.0	87.0	88.0	91.0

1981	1982	1983	1984	1985	1986	1987	1988	1989	1990 estimate	Notes	MONGOLIA
											FOREIGN TRADE (CUSTOMS BASIS)
											(Millions of current US dollars)
..	..	..	..	..	..	..	..	..	..	..	Value of Exports, fob
..	..	..	..	..	..	..	..	..	..	..	Nonfuel Primary Products
..	..	..	..	..	..	..	..	..	..	..	Fuels
..	..	..	..	..	..	..	..	..	..		Manufactures
..	..	..	..	..	..	..	..	..	..	..	Value of Imports, cif
..	..	..	..	..	..	..	..	..	..	..	Nonfuel Primary Products
..	..	..	..	..	..	..	..	..	..	..	Fuels
..	..	..	..	..	..	..	..	..	..	..	Manufactures
											(Index 1987=100)
..	..	..	..	..	..	..	..	..	..	..	Terms of Trade
..	..	..	..	..	..	..	..	..	..	..	Export Prices, fob
..	..	..	..	..	..	..	..	..	..	..	Import Prices, cif
											BALANCE OF PAYMENTS *(Millions of current US dollars)*
477	568	613	650	639	825	906	924	840	521	..	Exports of Goods & Services
438	519	557	596	567	741	817	829	796	468	..	Merchandise, fob
38	49	56	54	72	84	89	94	36	48	..	Nonfactor Services
0	0	0	0	0	0	0	0	8	5	..	Factor Services
1,284	1,414	1,438	1,390	1,452	1,886	1,896	1,956	2,072	1,168	..	Imports of Goods & Services
1,240	1,352	1,362	1,309	1,366	1,839	1,827	1,850	1,912	1,047	..	Merchandise, fob
33	41	44	42	41	45	57	72	104	73	..	Nonfactor Services
11	21	31	39	45	2	12	34	56	49	..	Factor Services
..	..	..	..	..	..	..	..	..	..		Long-Term Interest
0	0	0	0	0	0	0	0	0	..	..	Private Current Transfers, net
0	0	0	0	0	0	0	0	0	..	..	Workers' Remittances
-807	-846	-825	-740	-813	-1,061	-991	-1,033	-1,233	-647	..	Curr. A/C Bal before Off. Transf.
0	0	0	0	0	0	0	0	4	7	..	Net Official Transfers
-807	-846	-825	-740	-813	-1,061	-991	-1,033	-1,229	-640	..	Curr. A/C Bal after Off. Transf.
807	867	741	746	757	1,082	1,093	1,026	1,195	584	..	Long-Term Capital, net
..	..	..	..	..	..	..	..	..	..	..	Direct Investment
..	..	..	..	..	..	..	..	..	..	..	Long-Term Loans
..	..	..	..	..	..	..	..	..	..	..	Disbursements
..	..	..	..	..	..	..	..	..	..	..	Repayments
807	867	741	746	757	1,082	1,093	1,026	1,195	584	..	Other Long-Term Capital
0	-17	80	10	87	-21	-68	12	42	7	..	Other Capital, net
0	-4	3	-16	-31	0	-34	-5	-8	49	..	Change in Reserves
											Memo Item: *(Mongolian Tughriks per US dollar)*
..	..	..	..	..	..	..	..	..	..	..	Conversion Factor (Annual Avg)
											EXTERNAL DEBT (Total) *Millions US dollars), outstanding at end of year*
..	..	..	..	..	..	..	..	..	..	..	Long-Term Debt (by debtor)
..	..	..	..	..	..	..	..	..	..	..	Central Bank, incl. IMF credit
..	..	..	..	..	..	..	..	..	..	..	Central Government
..	..	..	..	..	..	..	..	..	..	..	Rest of General Government
..	..	..	..	..	..	..	..	..	..	..	Non-financial Public Enterprises
..	..	..	..	..	..	..	..	..	..	..	Priv. Sector, incl non-guaranteed
..	..	..	..	..	..	..	..	..	..	..	Short-Term Debt
											Memo Items: *Millions US dollars)*
..	..	..	..	..	..	..	..	..	..	..	Int'l Reserves Excluding Gold
..	..	..	..	..	..	..	..	..	..	..	Gold Holdings (at market price)
											SOCIAL INDICATORS
5.3	5.3	5.2	5.1	5.1	5.1	5.0	4.9	4.8	4.7	..	Total Fertility Rate
80.0	78.0	76.0	74.0	72.0	70.0	68.0	65.9	63.9	61.8	..	Infant Mortality Rate
58.2	58.7	59.2	59.7	60.2	60.7	61.2	61.7	62.1	62.6	..	Life Expectancy at Birth
51.4	51.5	51.6	51.7	51.8	51.9	52.0	52.1	52.2	52.3	..	Urban Population, % of total
108.1	109.1	110.9	103.8	103.7	108.7	100.0	93.7	98.7	96.1	..	Food Prod. per capita (1987=100)
..	..	..	..	..	..	..	..	..	..	..	Labor Force, Agriculture (%)
45.5	45.5	45.5	45.5	45.5	45.5	45.5	45.5	45.5	45.5	..	Labor Force, Female (%)
106.0	107.0	104.0	103.0	..	100.0	..	..	98.0	..	..	Primary Schl. Enroll. Ratio
	108.0	105.0	104.0	..	102.0	..	..	100.0	..	..	Primary Schl. Enroll. Ratio, Female
88.0	87.0	90.0	90.0	..	92.0	..	..	..	..	..	Secondary Schl. Enroll. Ratio

MOROCCO	1970	1971	1972	1973	1974	1975	1976	1977	1978	1979	1980
CURRENT GNP PER CAPITA (US $)	260	280	300	340	410	500	560	600	650	770	930
POPULATION (thousands)	15,310	15,712	16,113	16,511	16,908	17,305	17,702	18,097	18,501	18,926	19,382

USE AND ORIGIN OF RESOURCES *(Billions of current Moroccan Dirhams)*

	1970	1971	1972	1973	1974	1975	1976	1977	1978	1979	1980
Gross National Product (GNP)	19.79	21.74	23.05	25.31	33.33	36.04	40.45	48.90	53.85	60.34	71.74
Net Factor Income from Abroad	-0.23	-0.26	-0.30	-0.32	-0.27	-0.36	-0.56	-0.87	-1.30	-1.71	-2.35
GDP at Market Prices	20.02	22.00	23.35	25.64	33.60	36.39	41.01	49.76	55.15	62.04	74.09
Resource Balance	-0.79	-0.61	-0.15	-0.33	-0.21	-3.96	-7.97	-10.16	-7.55	-7.97	-7.77
Exports of Goods & NFServices	3.53	3.73	4.34	5.34	9.24	8.18	7.59	8.41	9.03	10.55	12.88
Imports of Goods & NFServices	4.32	4.34	4.49	5.67	9.45	12.14	15.56	18.57	16.58	18.53	20.66
Domestic Absorption	20.81	22.61	23.50	25.96	33.81	40.35	48.98	59.93	62.71	70.02	81.86
Private Consumption, etc.	14.70	15.95	17.04	18.65	22.85	25.27	28.24	32.65	37.21	41.59	50.34
General Gov't Consumption	2.41	2.71	2.89	2.99	4.04	5.92	9.21	10.25	11.47	13.23	13.59
Gross Domestic Investment	3.70	3.95	3.57	4.32	6.92	9.17	11.53	17.03	14.03	15.20	17.93
Fixed Investment	2.99	3.27	3.18	3.47	4.93	9.04	12.18	15.90	13.73	14.88	16.48
Indirect Taxes, net	..	..	..	..	..	..	..	..	..	..	..
GDP at factor cost	..	..	..	..	..	..	..	..	..	..	..
Agriculture	3.99	4.81	4.96	5.34	6.87	6.30	7.86	8.15	10.43	11.12	13.65
Industry	5.40	6.00	6.43	7.17	11.74	12.64	13.34	16.20	17.29	20.27	22.92
Manufacturing	3.24	3.58	3.92	4.45	5.25	6.03	6.76	8.24	9.37	10.44	12.47
Services, etc.	10.63	11.19	11.95	13.13	14.99	17.45	19.82	25.41	27.43	30.66	37.51
Gross Domestic Saving	2.91	3.34	3.42	4.00	6.71	5.21	3.56	6.87	6.47	7.22	10.16
Gross National Saving	2.87	3.45	3.61	4.54	7.75	6.80	5.21	8.46	8.09	8.99	11.76

(Millions of 1987 Moroccan Dirhams)

	1970	1971	1972	1973	1974	1975	1976	1977	1978	1979	1980
Gross National Product	71,614	75,612	77,365	80,035	84,755	90,242	99,796	104,257	106,557	110,927	120,769
GDP at Market Prices	73,641	77,791	79,652	82,401	86,841	92,659	102,853	107,896	111,034	116,116	126,683
Resource Balance	-1,786	-1,313	1,699	874	-1,105	-13,033	-18,790	-21,810	-14,560	-15,748	-11,654
Exports of Goods & NFServices	18,503	18,433	21,833	25,054	24,226	20,022	21,421	23,401	24,802	24,924	25,820
Imports of Goods & NFServices	20,289	19,746	20,134	24,180	25,332	33,054	40,211	45,210	39,362	40,672	37,473
Domestic Absorption	75,426	79,103	77,953	81,527	87,946	105,692	121,644	129,705	125,594	131,863	138,336
Private Consumption, etc.	53,710	55,331	57,489	60,406	63,113	66,442	72,914	75,182	80,429	85,034	90,727
General Gov't Consumption	5,726	6,065	6,100	6,220	6,993	9,707	14,041	14,449	15,461	16,726	16,109
Gross Domestic Investment	15,990	17,707	14,363	14,901	17,841	29,542	34,689	40,074	29,704	30,103	31,501
Fixed Investment	14,403	15,812	14,018	13,557	16,566	29,128	34,521	39,344	28,975	29,374	28,985
GDP at factor cost	..	..	..	..	..	..	..	..	..	..	..
Agriculture	17,430	19,173	18,745	16,999	17,355	16,254	18,742	16,432	19,383	19,051	21,720
Industry	24,636	26,544	28,203	29,909	31,886	35,233	38,512	41,578	41,184	44,360	43,794
Manufacturing	..	..	..	..	..	..	..	..	..	..	22,033
Services, etc.	31,575	32,073	32,704	35,494	37,600	41,172	45,600	49,885	50,466	52,705	61,168

Memo Items:

	1970	1971	1972	1973	1974	1975	1976	1977	1978	1979	1980
Capacity to Import	16,579	16,971	19,452	22,793	24,766	22,279	19,613	20,466	21,430	23,167	23,371
Terms of Trade Adjustment	-1,923	-1,463	-2,381	-2,261	540	2,258	-1,808	-2,934	-3,371	-1,756	-2,449
Gross Domestic Income	71,717	76,328	77,271	80,140	87,381	94,917	101,046	104,961	107,663	114,359	124,234
Gross National Income	69,691	74,149	74,984	77,774	85,294	92,500	97,988	101,323	103,186	109,170	118,320

DOMESTIC PRICES/DEFLATORS *(Index 1987 = 100)*

	1970	1971	1972	1973	1974	1975	1976	1977	1978	1979	1980
Overall (GDP)	27.2	28.3	29.3	31.1	38.7	39.3	39.9	46.1	49.7	53.4	58.5
Domestic Absorption	27.6	28.6	30.1	31.8	38.4	38.2	40.3	46.2	49.9	53.1	59.2
Agriculture	22.9	25.1	26.5	31.4	39.6	38.7	41.9	49.6	53.8	58.3	62.9
Industry	21.9	22.6	22.8	24.0	36.8	35.9	34.6	39.0	42.0	45.7	52.3
Manufacturing	..	..	..	..	..	..	..	..	..	..	56.6
Consumer Price Index	24.7	25.7	26.7	27.8	32.7	35.2	38.2	43.0	47.2	51.2	56.0

MANUFACTURING ACTIVITY

	1970	1971	1972	1973	1974	1975	1976	1977	1978	1979	1980
Employment (1987=100)	..	..	..	..	..	..	53.5	57.5	54.1	59.3	65.0
Real Earnings per Empl. (1987=100)	..	..	..	..	..	..	119.5	123.1	129.0	128.0	125.9
Real Output per Empl. (1987=100)	..	..	..	..	..	..	111.6	108.3	116.1	118.0	105.4
Earnings as % of Value Added	..	..	..	..	..	..	44.0	55.1	54.1	54.5	55.0

MONETARY HOLDINGS *(Millions of current Moroccan Dirhams)*

	1970	1971	1972	1973	1974	1975	1976	1977	1978	1979	1980
Money Supply, Broadly Defined	6,510	7,347	8,677	9,998	12,875	15,421	18,153	21,732	25,670	29,677	33,208
Money	5,514	6,193	7,336	8,572	10,869	12,837	15,102	18,002	20,785	23,352	25,312
Currency Outside Banks	2,261	2,461	2,944	3,411	4,063	4,650	5,732	6,650	7,676	9,020	9,807
Demand Deposits	3,254	3,732	4,392	5,161	6,806	8,187	9,370	11,352	13,109	14,332	15,505
Quasi-Money	995	1,154	1,341	1,426	2,006	2,584	3,051	3,730	4,885	6,325	7,896

GOVERNMENT DEFICIT (-) OR SURPLUS *(Millions of current Moroccan Dirhams)*

	1970	1971	1972	1973	1974	1975	1976	1977	1978	1979	1980
	-619	-658	-897	-526	-1,348	-3,341	-7,217	-7,647	-5,773	-6,039	-7,184
Current Revenue	3,857	3,884	4,330	5,151	8,449	9,441	9,424	12,219	13,183	15,562	17,235
Current Expenditure	3,326	3,472	4,035	4,373	7,582	8,025	8,782	10,080	11,403	13,383	16,877
Current Budget Balance	531	412	295	778	867	1,416	642	2,139	1,780	2,179	358
Capital Receipts	5	6	5	13	19	88	177	114	163	241	267
Capital Payments	1,155	1,076	1,197	1,317	2,234	4,845	8,036	9,900	7,716	8,459	7,809

1981	1982	1983	1984	1985	1986	1987	1988	1989	1990 estimate	Notes	MOROCCO
880	860	730	660	610	650	680	830	880	950	..	**CURRENT GNP PER CAPITA (US $)**
19,867	20,378	20,916	21,478	22,061	22,706	23,376	23,960	24,520	25,091	..	**POPULATION (thousands)**
											USE AND ORIGIN OF RESOURCES
				(Billions of current Moroccan Dirhams)							
75.28	88.90	94.66	107.17	121.80	148.46	150.28	173.07	181.73	199.75	..	Gross National Product (GNP)
-3.75	-3.99	-4.48	-5.18	-7.71	-6.27	-6.41	-8.51	-9.84	-8.13	..	Net Factor Income from Abroad
79.03	92.90	99.14	112.35	129.51	154.73	156.69	181.58	191.58	207.88	..	GDP at Market Prices
-11.52	-13.43	-8.74	-11.91	-11.64	-9.80	-6.92	-0.83	-10.60	-12.72	..	Resource Balance
15.94	17.88	21.29	26.77	32.05	32.92	35.40	44.94	42.77	51.98	..	Exports of Goods & NFServices
27.47	31.31	30.03	38.68	43.68	42.72	42.32	45.77	53.37	64.70	..	Imports of Goods & NFServices
90.56	106.33	107.88	124.26	141.14	164.52	163.61	182.41	202.18	220.60	..	Domestic Absorption
54.84	63.11	67.47	78.37	88.19	105.50	105.94	116.12	125.72	134.20	..	Private Consumption, etc.
15.08	17.00	16.63	17.48	20.52	23.75	24.63	28.03	30.41	32.98	..	General Gov't Consumption
20.64	26.22	23.79	28.41	32.43	35.27	33.04	38.26	46.04	53.42	..	Gross Domestic Investment
20.51	25.38	24.23	25.95	29.93	32.99	31.63	37.23	44.17	51.18	..	Fixed Investment
..	..	..	..	..	..	..	..	..	..	..	Indirect Taxes, net
..	..	..	..	..	..	..	..	..	..	B	GDP at factor cost
10.21	14.22	15.03	16.85	21.50	29.53	24.08	31.35	32.65	32.66	..	Agriculture
26.92	29.63	32.95	37.38	43.24	49.94	51.51	60.49	62.55	68.50	..	Industry
14.30	16.09	18.22	20.74	24.03	26.59	28.59	31.89	33.38	37.88	..	Manufacturing
41.90	49.04	51.15	58.11	64.77	75.26	81.10	89.74	96.37	106.72	..	Services, etc.
9.12	12.79	15.04	16.50	20.80	25.48	26.12	37.43	35.44	40.70	..	Gross Domestic Saving
10.47	13.85	16.87	18.78	22.80	31.90	32.91	39.62	37.11	49.15	..	Gross National Saving
				(Millions of 1987 Moroccan Dirhams)							
116,353	128,315	127,682	133,642	140,397	153,981	150,280	164,614	165,684	172,575	..	Gross National Product
123,187	135,049	134,276	139,909	148,664	160,332	156,689	172,682	175,110	180,116	I	GDP at Market Prices
-12,317	-12,227	-5,556	-6,247	-4,949	-7,065	-6,923	-3,095	-10,926	-9,734	..	Resource Balance
25,878	27,136	29,345	30,171	31,451	32,143	35,395	41,964	36,261	44,096	..	Exports of Goods & NFServices
38,195	39,364	34,901	36,418	36,400	39,208	42,318	45,059	47,187	53,830	..	Imports of Goods & NFServices
135,504	147,276	139,832	146,155	153,613	167,397	163,612	175,777	186,036	189,851	..	Domestic Absorption
87,001	92,125	91,345	94,510	97,218	106,663	105,940	114,002	119,827	120,541	..	Private Consumption, etc.
16,908	18,384	17,981	18,904	21,797	24,692	24,629	25,912	25,767	25,563	..	General Gov't Consumption
31,596	36,767	30,505	32,741	34,599	36,042	33,043	35,863	40,442	43,746	..	Gross Domestic Investment
31,464	35,784	31,059	30,519	32,591	33,941	31,632	34,871	38,774	41,899	..	Fixed Investment
..	..	..	..	..	..	..	..	..	..	B	GDP at factor cost
15,505	20,927	18,758	19,450	23,039	31,501	24,075	31,635	32,471	30,273	..	Agriculture
44,925	46,194	46,815	47,464	50,205	50,677	51,511	55,713	54,226	58,240	..	Industry
22,364	23,544	24,534	25,591	27,403	27,732	28,587	30,289	29,416	31,884	..	Manufacturing
62,756	67,929	68,702	72,995	75,421	78,154	81,103	85,335	88,412	91,603	..	Services, etc.
											Memo Items:
22,168	22,481	24,742	25,202	26,704	30,216	35,395	44,240	37,812	43,243	..	Capacity to Import
-3,710	-4,656	-4,603	-4,969	-4,747	-1,927	0	2,276	1,551	-852	..	Terms of Trade Adjustment
119,477	130,394	129,672	134,940	143,917	158,405	156,689	174,958	176,660	179,264	..	Gross Domestic Income
112,644	123,659	123,078	128,673	135,649	152,054	150,280	166,890	167,235	171,723	..	Gross National Income
				(Index 1987 = 100)							**DOMESTIC PRICES/DEFLATORS**
64.2	68.8	73.8	80.3	87.1	96.5	100.0	105.2	109.4	115.4	..	Overall (GDP)
66.8	72.2	77.2	85.0	91.9	98.3	100.0	103.8	108.7	116.2	..	Domestic Absorption
65.8	68.0	80.1	86.6	93.3	93.7	100.0	99.1	100.5	107.9	..	Agriculture
59.9	64.1	70.4	78.8	86.1	98.5	100.0	108.6	115.4	117.6	..	Industry
63.9	68.3	74.3	81.0	87.7	95.9	100.0	105.3	113.5	118.8	..	Manufacturing
63.0	69.6	73.9	83.1	89.6	97.4	100.0	102.4	105.6	112.9	..	Consumer Price Index
											MANUFACTURING ACTIVITY
66.5	68.0	69.6	81.9	86.1	97.3	100.0	114.0		..	..	Employment (1987=100)
120.6	117.5	119.3	103.3	109.3	96.1	100.0	..	..	..	..	Real Earnings per Empl. (1987=100)
107.6	116.2	113.2	96.6	111.0	100.3	100.0	..	..	..	..	Real Output per Empl. (1987=100)
54.3	..	..	..	..	..	..	..	..	..	..	Earnings as % of Value Added
				(Millions of current Moroccan Dirhams)							**MONETARY HOLDINGS**
38,486	43,364	51,267	56,778	66,754	77,445	84,839	97,549	96,853	114,511	D	Money Supply, Broadly Defined
29,016	30,064	34,197	36,779	42,820	50,029	54,489	62,032	68,395	80,914		Money
11,133	12,022	13,636	14,770	16,192	18,694	20,003	21,914	24,814	29,252	..	Currency Outside Banks
17,883	18,042	20,561	22,009	26,628	31,335	34,486	40,118	43,581	51,662	..	Demand Deposits
9,470	13,300	17,071	19,999	23,934	27,416	30,350	35,517	28,458	33,597	..	Quasi-Money
				(Millions of current Moroccan Dirhams)							**GOVERNMENT DEFICIT (-) OR SURPLUS**
-10,557	-10,630	-7,680	-6,762	-9,424	-11,872	-7,025	..	..	..	..	Current Revenue
20,066	24,080	24,220	26,383	29,896	32,757	36,870	..	..	..	..	Current Expenditure
20,755	22,902	24,171	26,156	31,748	34,162	34,573	..	..	..	..	Current Budget Balance
-689	1,178	49	227	-1,852	-1,405	2,297	..	..	..	..	Capital Receipts
352	308	296	301	317	127	219	..	..	..	..	Capital Payments
10,220	12,116	8,025	7,290	7,889	10,594	9,541	..	..	..	..	

MOROCCO	1970	1971	1972	1973	1974	1975	1976	1977	1978	1979	1980
FOREIGN TRADE (CUSTOMS BASIS)					*(Millions of current US dollars)*						
Value of Exports, fob	487.9	499.1	633.6	876.6	1,706.4	1,543.0	1,262.1	1,299.9	1,511.3	1,958.6	2,403.4
Nonfuel Primary Products	438.7	423.6	541.7	741.7	1,501.5	1,336.1	1,041.8	1,007.1	1,145.1	1,427.3	1,721.5
Fuels	1.9	1.8	1.3	4.7	11.9	14.2	17.7	20.3	21.2	70.9	116.5
Manufactures	47.3	73.7	90.6	130.2	193.0	192.8	202.6	272.4	345.0	460.5	565.5
Value of Imports, cif	684.3	697.0	764.4	1,098.2	1,900.8	2,547.3	2,592.9	3,168.5	2,950.3	3,673.5	4,182.4
Nonfuel Primary Products	211.1	241.3	248.3	416.0	711.1	914.9	710.5	778.8	811.6	1,027.1	1,248.7
Fuels	37.4	46.6	54.7	71.2	258.7	276.4	295.2	370.2	428.2	704.1	986.9
Manufactures	435.8	409.2	461.3	611.0	931.0	1,356.0	1,587.2	2,019.5	1,710.5	1,942.3	1,946.8
					(Index 1987 = 100)						
Terms of Trade	129.6	126.5	125.0	112.2	135.1	145.4	112.3	106.7	106.1	105.0	99.5
Export Prices, fob	36.1	37.3	39.9	49.2	90.4	100.6	75.5	76.9	82.1	97.1	111.9
Import Prices, cif	27.8	29.5	31.9	43.9	66.9	69.2	67.2	72.0	77.3	92.4	112.4
BALANCE OF PAYMENTS					*(Millions of current US dollars)*						
Exports of Goods & Services	705.0	745.2	945.7	1,301.8	2,131.1	2,026.1	1,720.2	1,870.9	2,164.4	2,711.3	3,270.4
Merchandise, fob	487.0	499.5	641.7	913.2	1,704.1	1,529.4	1,247.0	1,283.5	1,488.2	1,936.6	2,414.5
Nonfactor Services	203.0	231.7	291.0	374.3	399.3	467.8	448.9	555.4	649.5	734.9	817.0
Factor Services	15.0	14.0	13.0	14.3	27.7	28.9	24.2	32.0	26.6	39.8	38.9
Imports of Goods & Services	902.0	913.7	1,035.8	1,449.6	2,234.5	3,070.1	3,622.5	4,286.4	4,261.5	5,166.4	5,807.1
Merchandise, fob	624.0	636.9	709.0	1,037.1	1,692.1	2,265.5	2,307.6	2,821.0	2,628.7	3,245.3	3,770.0
Nonfactor Services	218.0	211.6	249.7	319.5	453.4	687.6	1,163.5	1,241.4	1,293.0	1,443.6	1,400.5
Factor Services	60.0	65.2	77.1	93.0	89.0	117.0	151.4	224.1	339.8	477.5	636.6
Long-Term Interest	25.0	29.5	35.5	43.7	46.0	56.8	77.2	170.8	293.3	448.6	618.7
Private Current Transfers, net	36.0	74.2	107.5	211.0	299.5	481.9	499.2	545.6	702.0	891.2	1,004.2
Workers' Remittances	63.0	95.3	140.1	250.3	359.6	533.0	547.1	588.9	762.2	947.9	1,053.7
Curr. A/C Bal before Off. Transf.	-161.0	-94.3	17.4	63.2	196.0	-562.1	-1,403.2	-1,869.9	-1,395.1	-1,563.9	-1,532.5
Net Official Transfers	37.0	35.1	30.4	33.4	30.1	33.8	6.1	14.9	57.6	43.3	113.7
Curr. A/C Bal after Off. Transf.	-124.0	-59.2	47.8	96.6	226.1	-528.3	-1,397.1	-1,855.1	-1,337.5	-1,520.6	-1,418.9
Long-Term Capital, net	114.0	109.3	44.5	1.2	40.9	708.9	2,347.9	2,997.7	2,288.8	1,378.8	1,359.5
Direct Investment	20.0	23.1	13.0	-1.2	-20.4	-0.2	38.0	57.1	47.5	38.5	89.4
Long-Term Loans	135.6	124.0	58.0	29.0	161.9	514.6	661.0	1,824.6	994.6	991.5	1,187.7
Disbursements	175.3	185.6	131.6	122.2	265.0	620.3	775.6	1,969.6	1,325.9	1,435.9	1,777.7
Repayments	39.7	61.6	73.6	93.2	103.1	105.7	114.6	145.0	331.3	444.4	590.0
Other Long-Term Capital	-41.6	-37.7	-26.5	-26.6	-100.6	194.5	1,648.9	1,116.1	1,246.7	348.8	82.4
Other Capital, net	26.1	-10.5	-36.5	-95.8	-144.8	-209.0	-968.5	-1,144.4	-979.9	67.8	-189.2
Change in Reserves	-16.1	-39.7	-55.8	-1.9	-122.2	28.4	17.6	1.7	28.6	74.0	248.5
Memo Item:					*(Moroccan Dirhams per US dollar)*						
Conversion Factor (Annual Avg)	5.060	5.050	4.600	4.110	4.370	4.050	4.420	4.500	4.170	3.900	3.940
				(Millions of US dollars), outstanding at end of year							
EXTERNAL DEBT (Total)	754	888	944	1,040	1,246	1,727	2,470	4,958	6,255	8,502	9,707
Long-Term Debt (by debtor)	754	888	944	1,040	1,246	1,727	2,470	4,393	5,706	7,767	8,932
Central Bank, incl. IMF credit	59	41	54	59	65	105	293	524	691	684	835
Central Government	506	626	689	742	807	1,094	1,495	2,438	3,092	4,632	5,411
Rest of General Government	4	4	4	4	3	3	2	1	1	0	0
Non-financial Public Enterprises	153	185	156	180	296	422	537	1,139	1,599	2,047	2,199
Priv. Sector, incl non-guaranteed	32	33	42	55	75	103	143	291	324	404	487
Short-Term Debt	0	0	0	0	0	0	0	565	549	735	775
Memo Items:					*(Millions of US dollars)*						
Int'l Reserves Excluding Gold	119.3	150.7	213.7	240.6	391.0	352.4	467.1	505.3	618.4	557.0	398.6
Gold Holdings (at market price)	22.4	26.2	38.9	67.4	113.4	85.3	81.9	104.3	153.7	360.5	415.0
SOCIAL INDICATORS											
Total Fertility Rate	7.0	6.9	6.9	6.7	6.5	6.3	6.1	5.9	5.8	5.7	5.6
Infant Mortality Rate	128.4	125.2	122.0	119.6	117.2	114.8	112.4	110.0	106.4	102.8	99.2
Life Expectancy at Birth	51.9	52.4	52.9	53.5	54.1	54.6	55.2	55.8	56.3	56.8	57.3
Urban Population, % of total	34.6	35.2	35.8	36.5	37.1	37.7	38.4	39.1	39.7	40.4	41.1
Food Prod. per capita (1987=100)	96.8	107.3	99.3	88.5	99.4	85.8	95.1	78.1	94.0	94.7	93.0
Labor Force, Agriculture (%)	57.6	56.3	55.0	53.8	52.6	51.5	50.1	48.9	47.7	46.6	45.6
Labor Force, Female (%)	13.9	14.5	15.0	15.6	16.0	16.5	16.9	17.3	17.7	18.0	18.4
Primary Schl. Enroll. Ratio	52.0	..	..	..	..	62.0	66.0	69.0	72.0	75.0	83.0
Primary Schl. Enroll. Ratio, Female	36.0	..	..	..	..	45.0	48.0	51.0	54.0	56.0	63.0
Secondary Schl. Enroll. Ratio	13.0	..	..	..	..	16.0	17.0	19.0	20.0	22.0	26.0

FOREIGN TRADE (CUSTOMS BASIS)

(Millions of current US dollars)

Indicator	1981	1982	1983	1984	1985	1986	1987	1988	1989	1990 est.	Notes
Value of Exports, fob	2,320.3	2,058.6	2,062.1	2,171.9	2,165.1	2,427.6	2,806.9	3,625.4	3,336.5	4,262.9	..
Nonfuel Primary Products	1,560.7	1,264.3	1,181.9	1,200.6	1,204.8	1,308.7	1,361.8	1,742.9	1,698.0	2,169.5	..
Fuels	105.0	87.6	81.8	85.9	84.2	61.9	77.0	74.7	86.5	110.5	..
Manufactures	654.6	706.7	798.4	885.3	876.1	1,056.9	1,368.1	1,807.8	1,552.0	1,982.9	..
Value of Imports, cif	4,352.6	4,315.3	3,596.6	3,906.7	3,849.6	3,790.2	4,228.7	4,772.4	5,491.9	6,918.4	..
Nonfuel Primary Products	1,411.0	1,127.1	1,023.4	1,219.3	1,153.4	1,131.2	1,185.1	1,356.6	1,310.0	1,650.3	..
Fuels	1,187.8	1,173.2	988.3	1,021.2	1,075.9	595.2	739.6	628.6	843.5	1,062.6	..
Manufactures	1,753.8	2,015.0	1,584.8	1,666.2	1,620.3	2,063.8	2,304.0	2,787.2	3,338.3	4,205.5	..

(Index 1987 = 100)

Indicator	1981	1982	1983	1984	1985	1986	1987	1988	1989	1990 est.	Notes
Terms of Trade	95.2	91.1	87.3	89.4	88.2	102.6	100.0	102.1	80.2	85.6	..
Export Prices, fob	106.7	95.4	89.1	90.1	86.2	92.5	100.0	111.2	93.8	112.2	..
Import Prices, cif	112.1	104.6	102.0	100.9	97.7	90.1	100.0	108.9	117.0	131.1	..

BALANCE OF PAYMENTS

(Millions of current US dollars)

Indicator	1981	1982	1983	1984	1985	1986	1987	1988	1989	1990 est.	Notes
Exports of Goods & Services	3,083.7	2,944.4	2,931.0	3,016.0	3,160.2	3,575.9	4,192.7	5,405.8	5,012.5	6,321.3	..
Merchandise, fob	2,282.9	2,042.8	2,058.0	2,161.2	2,145.0	2,410.5	2,781.4	3,607.8	3,312.5	4,210.3	..
Nonfactor Services	762.3	875.6	860.6	837.2	993.0	1,148.2	1,392.7	1,778.5	1,659.1	2,024.0	..
Factor Services	38.5	25.9	12.4	17.6	22.3	17.2	18.7	19.5	40.9	87.0	..
Imports of Goods & Services	6,014.0	5,824.3	4,808.7	4,943.1	5,125.1	5,340.6	5,787.6	6,545.0	7,422.5	8,853.1	..
Merchandise, fob	3,839.7	3,815.2	3,300.6	3,568.9	3,513.1	3,477.0	3,850.1	4,359.8	4,991.4	6,281.6	..
Nonfactor Services	1,410.6	1,320.1	865.0	769.2	819.3	1,143.9	1,135.3	1,086.3	1,190.3	1,441.4	..
Factor Services	763.7	689.0	643.1	605.0	792.7	719.8	802.2	1,098.9	1,240.8	1,130.1	..
Long-Term Interest	697.3	614.1	561.4	534.1	493.1	616.0	619.1	821.1	1,104.1	878.4	..
Private Current Transfers, net	987.6	839.8	887.9	847.2	965.4	1,393.8	1,579.3	1,303.2	1,355.5	2,011.9	..
Workers' Remittances	1,013.5	849.2	916.1	871.8	967.2	1,398.3	1,587.2	1,303.4	1,336.5	2,006.4	..
Curr. A/C Bal before Off. Transf.	-1,942.7	-2,040.2	-989.8	-1,080.0	-999.6	-370.9	-15.6	164.0	-1,054.5	-519.9	..
Net Official Transfers	103.6	164.8	100.7	93.5	110.8	160.3	191.2	303.2	264.8	319.7	..
Curr. A/C Bal after Off. Transf.	-1,839.1	-1,875.4	-889.1	-986.5	-888.8	-210.6	175.6	467.2	-789.7	-200.2	..
Long-Term Capital, net	1,291.5	1,298.7	765.5	831.1	621.3	416.7	427.6	493.8	599.9	1,750.1	..
Direct Investment	58.6	79.5	46.1	47.0	20.0	0.5	59.6	84.5	167.1	165.1	..
Long-Term Loans	1,253.8	1,480.6	471.3	970.8	581.8	756.8	819.8	739.6	545.9	602.6	..
Disbursements	1,900.1	2,304.5	1,190.3	1,218.3	1,103.4	1,414.9	1,457.7	1,280.0	1,211.5	1,352.7	..
Repayments	646.3	823.9	719.0	247.5	521.6	658.1	637.9	540.4	665.6	750.1	..
Other Long-Term Capital	-20.9	-261.4	248.1	-186.7	19.5	-340.6	-451.8	-330.3	-113.1	982.4	..
Other Capital, net	131.7	159.2	-105.1	53.5	180.0	112.1	-258.7	-726.5	185.4	-1,356.2	..
Change in Reserves	415.9	417.5	228.7	101.9	87.5	-318.2	-344.5	-234.5	4.4	-193.8	..

Memo Item:

(Moroccan Dirhams per US dollar)

Indicator	1981	1982	1983	1984	1985	1986	1987	1988	1989	1990 est.	Notes
Conversion Factor (Annual Avg)	5.170	6.020	7.110	8.810	10.060	9.100	8.360	8.210	8.490	8.240	..

EXTERNAL DEBT (Total)

(Millions of US dollars), outstanding at end of year

Indicator	1981	1982	1983	1984	1985	1986	1987	1988	1989	1990 est.	Notes
EXTERNAL DEBT (Total)	10,693	12,517	13,363	14,219	16,527	18,152	20,973	20,969	21,660	23,524	..
Long-Term Debt (by debtor)	9,906	11,486	12,232	13,066	15,298	17,130	19,935	20,603	21,360	23,047	..
Central Bank, incl. IMF credit	923	1,278	1,284	1,285	1,514	1,387	1,437	1,235	1,092	1,081	..
Central Government	6,360	7,218	8,029	9,142	10,716	12,519	15,069	16,493	17,515	19,149	..
Rest of General Government	0	0	0	0	0	0	0	0	0	..	..
Non-financial Public Enterprises	2,002	2,206	2,151	1,981	2,235	2,226	2,212	1,741	1,624	1,577	..
Priv. Sector, incl non-guaranteed	622	784	767	657	832	998	1,217	1,134	1,129	1,239	..
Short-Term Debt	786	1,031	1,131	1,153	1,229	1,022	1,038	366	300	477	..

Memo Items:

(Millions of US dollars)

Indicator	1981	1982	1983	1984	1985	1986	1987	1988	1989	1990 est.	Notes
Int'l Reserves Excluding Gold	229.7	217.6	106.7	48.7	115.1	211.4	411.1	547.5	488.5	2,066.5	..
Gold Holdings (at market price)	279.8	321.7	268.6	217.0	230.2	275.2	340.8	288.8	282.3	271.0	..

SOCIAL INDICATORS

Indicator	1981	1982	1983	1984	1985	1986	1987	1988	1989	1990 est.	Notes
Total Fertility Rate	5.5	5.4	5.3	5.2	5.1	4.9	4.8	4.7	4.6	4.5	..
Infant Mortality Rate	95.6	92.0	88.2	84.4	80.6	76.8	73.0	71.1	69.1	67.2	..
Life Expectancy at Birth	57.8	58.3	58.8	59.3	59.8	60.3	60.8	61.1	61.4	61.8	..
Urban Population, % of total	41.8	42.5	43.1	43.8	44.5	45.2	45.9	46.6	47.3	48.0	..
Food Prod. per capita (1987=100)	77.0	97.8	87.5	88.7	98.7	115.9	100.0	117.3	116.0	105.2	..
Labor Force, Agriculture (%)	..	..	..	..	..	..	..	..	..		..
Labor Force, Female (%)	18.7	18.9	19.2	19.5	19.7	19.9	20.1	20.3	20.5	20.7	..
Primary Schl. Enroll. Ratio	83.0	85.0	86.0	79.0	77.0	74.0	71.0	68.0	68.0	..	..
Primary Schl. Enroll. Ratio, Female	63.0	66.0	66.0	61.0	60.0	58.0	56.0	54.0	55.0	..	..
Secondary Schl. Enroll. Ratio	26.0	28.0	29.0	33.0	34.0	36.0	37.0	36.0	36.0	..	..

MOZAMBIQUE	1970	1971	1972	1973	1974	1975	1976	1977	1978	1979	1980
CURRENT GNP PER CAPITA (US $)	..	..	..	..					..	..	..
POPULATION (thousands)	9,390	9,613	9,845	10,087	10,340	10,606	10,888	11,179	11,479	11,787	12,103

USE AND ORIGIN OF RESOURCES — *(Billions of current Mozambique Meticais)*

	1970	1971	1972	1973	1974	1975	1976	1977	1978	1979	1980
Gross National Product (GNP)	..	..	..	..					..	..	77.18
Net Factor Income from Abroad										..	-1.02
GDP at Market Prices	..	..	..	..					..	..	78.20
Resource Balance	..	..	..	..					..	..	-14.41
Exports of Goods & NF Services										..	12.92
Imports of Goods & NF Services										..	27.33
Domestic Absorption	..	..	..	..					..	..	92.61
Private Consumption, etc.										..	59.60
General Gov't Consumption										..	18.24
Gross Domestic Investment										..	14.77
Fixed Investment										..	14.77
Indirect Taxes, net	..	..	..	..					..	..	9.81
GDP at factor cost	..	..	..	..					..	..	68.39
Agriculture										..	36.80
Industry										..	18.67
Manufacturing	..	..	..	..					..	..	..
Services, etc.										..	12.92
Gross Domestic Saving	..	..	..	..					..	..	0.36
Gross National Saving	..	..	..	..					..	..	-1.48

(Millions of 1987 Mozambique Meticais)

	1970	1971	1972	1973	1974	1975	1976	1977	1978	1979	1980
Gross National Product	..	..	..	..					..	..	491,727
GDP at Market Prices	..	..	..	..					..	..	499,177
Resource Balance	..	..	..	..					..	..	-94,708
Exports of Goods & NF Services										..	129,200
Imports of Goods & NF Services										..	223,908
Domestic Absorption	..	..	..	..					..	..	593,885
Private Consumption, etc.										..	383,353
General Gov't Consumption										..	91,200
Gross Domestic Investment										..	119,332
Fixed Investment										..	118,393
GDP at factor cost	..	..	..	..					..	..	453,853
Agriculture										..	252,401
Industry										..	92,882
Manufacturing										..	..
Services, etc.										..	105,801

Memo Items:

	1970	1971	1972	1973	1974	1975	1976	1977	1978	1979	1980
Capacity to Import	..	..	..	..					..	..	105,851
Terms of Trade Adjustment										..	-23,349
Gross Domestic Income										..	475,828
Gross National Income										..	468,378

DOMESTIC PRICES/DEFLATORS — *(Index 1987 = 100)*

	1970	1971	1972	1973	1974	1975	1976	1977	1978	1979	1980
Overall (GDP)	..	..	..	..					..	..	15.7
Domestic Absorption	..	..	..	..					..	..	15.6
Agriculture	..	..	..	..					..	..	14.6
Industry	..	..	..	..					..	..	20.1
Manufacturing	..	..	..	..					..	..	..
Consumer Price Index	..	..	..	..					..	..	..

MANUFACTURING ACTIVITY

	1970	1971	1972	1973	1974	1975	1976	1977	1978	1979	1980
Employment (1987=100)	76.6	78.7	85.0	89.1					..	..	..
Real Earnings per Empl. (1987=100)	..	..	..	..					..	..	..
Real Output per Empl. (1987=100)	..	..	..	..					..	..	..
Earnings as % of Value Added	28.8	40.9	41.2	41.4					..	..	..

MONETARY HOLDINGS — *(Millions of current Mozambique Meticais)*

	1970	1971	1972	1973	1974	1975	1976	1977	1978	1979	1980
Money Supply, Broadly Defined	..	..	..	..					..	..	..
Money	..	..	..	..					..	..	..
Currency Outside Banks	..	..	..	..					..	..	..
Demand Deposits	..	..	..	..					..	..	..
Quasi-Money	..	..	..	..					..	..	..

(Millions of current Mozambique Meticais)

GOVERNMENT DEFICIT (-) OR SURPLUS

	1970	1971	1972	1973	1974	1975	1976	1977	1978	1979	1980
	..	..	..	..					..	..	..
Current Revenue	..	..	..	..					..	..	..
Current Expenditure	..	..	..	..					..	..	..
Current Budget Balance	..	..	..	..					..	..	..
Capital Receipts	..	..	..	..					..	..	..
Capital Payments	..	..	..	..					..	..	..

1981	1982	1983	1984	1985	1986	1987	1988	1989	1990 estimate	Notes	MOZAMBIQUE
..	190	160	180	180	220	150	110	80	80	..	CURRENT GNP PER CAPITA (US $)
12,426	12,757	13,095	13,440	13,791	14,150	14,520	14,900	15,295	15,707	..	POPULATION (thousands)

(Billions of current Mozambique Meticais) — **USE AND ORIGIN OF RESOURCES**

1981	1982	1983	1984	1985	1986	1987	1988	1989	1990	Notes	
79.19	89.24	87.06	104.58	141.45	160.09	364.10	571.90	805.00	1,140.10	..	Gross National Product (GNP)
-1.51	-3.46	-4.34	-3.12	-5.15	-6.81	-59.20	-85.50	-161.20	-197.90	..	Net Factor Income from Abroad
80.70	92.70	91.40	107.70	146.60	166.90	423.30	657.40	966.20	1,338.00	..	GDP at Market Prices
-16.39	-20.95	-18.97	-18.11	-14.62	-18.08	-153.00	-327.70	-503.00	-655.00	..	Resource Balance
13.96	12.70	8.93	6.65	6.17	5.92	51.00	99.40	149.00	213.00	..	Exports of Goods & NF Services
30.35	33.65	27.90	24.76	20.79	24.00	204.00	427.10	652.00	868.00	..	Imports of Goods & NF Services
97.09	113.65	110.37	125.81	161.22	184.98	576.30	985.10	1,469.20	1,993.00	..	Domestic Absorption
59.99	73.85	75.17	86.38	118.22	126.38	406.50	650.50	931.30	1,225.10	..	Private Consumption, etc.
20.70	21.90	26.10	28.00	32.90	42.40	68.00	115.00	195.00	271.00	..	General Gov't Consumption
16.40	17.90	9.10	11.43	10.10	16.20	101.80	219.60	342.90	496.90	..	Gross Domestic Investment
16.40	17.90	9.10	114.30	10.10	16.20	101.80	219.60	342.90	496.90	..	Fixed Investment
9.93	11.00	11.70	11.80	9.00	11.20	38.20	54.70	79.80	109.80	..	Indirect Taxes, net
70.77	81.70	79.70	95.90	137.60	155.70	385.10	602.70	886.40	1,228.20	..	GDP at factor cost
37.50	45.40	42.90	55.10	87.60	98.90	247.60	390.50	574.40	793.40	..	Agriculture
19.20	20.70	21.10	21.50	28.50	34.80	60.10	92.20	135.60	179.30	..	Industry
..	..	..	..	..	..	..	..	..	..	..	Manufacturing
14.07	15.60	15.70	19.30	21.50	22.00	77.40	120.00	176.40	255.50	..	Services, etc.
0.01	-3.05	-9.87	-6.68	-4.52	-1.88	-51.20	-108.10	-160.10	-158.10	..	Gross Domestic Saving
-2.54	-7.40	-15.01	-10.89	-10.75	-9.62	-100.81	-128.39	-225.35	-231.13	..	Gross National Saving

(Millions of 1987 Mozambique Meticais)

1981	1982	1983	1984	1985	1986	1987	1988	1989	1990	Notes	
491,370	465,250	400,976	419,756	379,638	380,575	364,100	423,040	428,530	442,999	..	Gross National Product
501,736	484,514	422,634	433,519	395,566	400,566	423,300	446,156	470,670	479,463	..	GDP at Market Prices
-112,759	-129,976	-124,361	-126,325	-104,370	-150,988	-153,000	-163,312	-176,738	-171,488	..	Resource Balance
115,000	124,000	78,000	49,000	48,016	44,000	51,000	53,282	57,747	64,196	..	Exports of Goods & NF Services
227,759	253,976	202,361	175,325	152,386	194,988	204,000	216,594	234,485	235,684	..	Imports of Goods & NF Services
614,495	614,490	546,995	559,845	499,935	551,554	576,300	609,467	647,408	650,951	..	Domestic Absorption
389,073	407,223	394,016	402,862	373,264	384,989	406,500	412,088	424,505	420,035	..	Private Consumption, etc.
101,000	88,500	94,000	87,500	68,500	78,500	68,000	78,779	95,603	97,316	..	General Gov't Consumption
124,422	118,767	58,979	69,483	58,171	88,065	101,800	118,600	127,300	133,600	..	Gross Domestic Investment
123,443	117,831	58,515	68,935	57,713	87,372	101,800	118,600	127,300	133,600	..	Fixed Investment
455,854	439,924	384,141	394,568	359,918	364,281	385,100	405,871	429,097	436,647	..	GDP at factor cost
252,401	252,401	211,935	231,139	233,197	234,568	247,600	265,433	279,800	283,100	..	Agriculture
93,379	83,445	75,498	65,067	54,636	59,603	60,100	62,800	66,200	64,000	..	Industry
..	..	..	..	..	..	..	..	..	..	..	Manufacturing
107,453	104,147	96,709	98,362	72,085	70,110	77,400	77,638	83,097	89,547	..	Services, etc.

Memo Items:

1981	1982	1983	1984	1985	1986	1987	1988	1989	1990	Notes	
104,762	95,854	64,770	47,089	45,225	48,097	51,000	50,408	53,586	57,835	..	Capacity to Import
-10,238	-28,146	-13,230	-1,911	-2,791	4,097	0	-2,874	-4,161	-6,362	..	Terms of Trade Adjustment
491,498	456,368	409,404	431,608	392,774	404,663	423,300	443,282	466,509	473,102	..	Gross Domestic Income
481,131	437,104	387,746	417,845	376,847	384,673	364,100	420,167	424,369	436,638	..	Gross National Income

(Index 1987 = 100) — **DOMESTIC PRICES/DEFLATORS**

1981	1982	1983	1984	1985	1986	1987	1988	1989	1990	Notes	
16.1	19.1	21.6	24.8	37.1	41.7	100.0	147.3	205.3	279.1	..	Overall (GDP)
15.8	18.5	20.2	22.5	32.2	33.5	100.0	161.6	226.9	306.2	..	Domestic Absorption
14.9	18.0	20.2	23.8	37.6	42.2	100.0	147.1	205.3	280.3	..	Agriculture
20.6	24.8	27.9	33.0	52.2	58.4	100.0	146.8	204.8	280.2	..	Industry
..	..	..	..	..	..	..	..	..	..	..	Manufacturing
..	..	..	..	..	..	..	..	..	..	..	Consumer Price Index

MANUFACTURING ACTIVITY

1981	1982	1983	1984	1985	1986	1987	1988	1989	1990	Notes	
..	..	..	..	..	56.0	100.0	104.2	..	..	..	Employment (1987=100)
..	..	..	..	..	..	..	..	..	..	..	Real Earnings per Empl. (1987=100)
..	..	..	..	..	97.7	100.0	..	..	..	..	Real Output per Empl. (1987=100)
..	..	..	..	..	..	..	..	..	..	..	Earnings as % of Value Added

(Millions of current Mozambique Meticais) — **MONETARY HOLDINGS**

1981	1982	1983	1984	1985	1986	1987	1988	1989	1990	Notes	
..	..	..	..	..	..	..	..	..	..	..	Money Supply, Broadly Defined
..	..	..	..	..	..	..	..	..	..	..	Money
..	..	..	..	..	..	..	..	..	..	..	Currency Outside Banks
..	..	..	..	..	..	..	..	..	..	..	Demand Deposits
..	..	..	..	..	..	..	..	..	..	..	Quasi-Money

(Millions of current Mozambique Meticais) — **GOVERNMENT DEFICIT (-) OR SURPLUS**

1981	1982	1983	1984	1985	1986	1987	1988	1989	1990	Notes	
..	..	..	..	..	..	..	..	..	..	..	Current Revenue
..	..	..	..	..	..	..	..	..	..	..	Current Expenditure
..	..	..	..	..	..	..	..	..	..	..	Current Budget Balance
..	..	..	..	..	..	..	..	..	..	..	Capital Receipts
..	..	..	..	..	..	..	..	..	..	..	Capital Payments

MOZAMBIQUE	1970	1971	1972	1973	1974	1975	1976	1977	1978	1979	1980
FOREIGN TRADE (CUSTOMS BASIS)					*(Millions of current US dollars)*						
Value of Exports, fob	157	160	175	227	296	202	..	129	..	398	511
Nonfuel Primary Products	129	137	157	202	265	173	..	115	..	274	405
Fuels	13	12	10	12	17	22	..	6	..	8	12
Manufactures	15	11	8	12	14	7	..	8	..	116	95
Value of Imports, cif	323	335	327	465	464	417	..	278	..	270	550
Nonfuel Primary Products	51	64	80	84	118	149	..	77	..	77	110
Fuels	27	31	27	31	44	54	..	10	..	17	51
Manufactures	245	241	220	350	302	214	..	191	..	175	389
					(Index 1987 = 100)						
Terms of Trade	..	..	..	..	..	..	..	..	..	..	81.4
Export Prices, fob	..	..	..	..	..	..	..	..	..	..	90.7
Import Prices, cif	..	..	..	..	..	..	..	..	..	..	111.5
BALANCE OF PAYMENTS					*(Millions of current US dollars)*						
Exports of Goods & Services	..	..	..	..	..	..	..	..	..	..	452
Merchandise, fob	..	..	..	..	..	..	..	..	..	..	281
Nonfactor Services	..	..	..	..	..	..	..	..	..	..	118
Factor Services	..	..	..	..	..	..	..	..	..	..	53
Imports of Goods & Services	..	..	..	..	..	..	..	..	..	..	850
Merchandise, fob	..	..	..	..	..	..	..	..	..	..	720
Nonfactor Services	..	..	..	..	..	..	..	..	..	..	124
Factor Services	..	..	..	..	..	..	..	..	..	..	6
Long-Term Interest	..	..	..	..	..	..	..	..	..	..	0
Private Current Transfers, net	..	..	..	..	..	..	..	..	..	..	-25
Workers' Remittances	..	..	..	..	..	..	..	..	..	..	53
Curr. A/C Bal before Off. Transf.	..	..	..	..	..	..	..	..	..	..	-423
Net Official Transfers	..	..	..	..	..	..	..	..	..	..	56
Curr. A/C Bal after Off. Transf.	..	..	..	..	..	..	..	..	..	..	-367
Long-Term Capital, net	..	..	..	..	..	..	..	..	..	..	364
Direct Investment	..	..	..	..	..	..	..	..	..	..	0
Long-Term Loans	..	..	..	..	..	..	..	..	..	..	0
Disbursements	..	..	..	..	..	..	..	..	..	..	0
Repayments	..	..	..	..	..	..	..	..	..	..	0
Other Long-Term Capital	..	..	..	..	..	..	..	..	..	..	364
Other Capital, net	..	..	..	..	..	..	..	..	..	..	-30
Change in Reserves	..	..	..	..	..	..	..	..	..	..	32
Memo Item:					*(Mozambique Meticais per US dollar)*						
Conversion Factor (Annual Avg)	28.750	28.310	27.050	24.520	25.410	25.550	30.230	33.020	33.000	32.560	32.400
EXTERNAL DEBT (Total)					*(Millions of US dollars), outstanding at end of year*						
Long-Term Debt (by debtor)	..	..	..	..	..	..	..	..	..	..	..
Central Bank, incl. IMF credit	..	..	..	..	..	..	..	..	..	..	..
Central Government	..	..	..	..	..	..	..	..	..	..	..
Rest of General Government	..	..	..	..	..	..	..	..	..	..	..
Non-financial Public Enterprises	..	..	..	..	..	..	..	..	..	..	..
Priv. Sector, incl non-guaranteed	..	..	..	..	..	..	..	..	..	..	..
Short-Term Debt	..	..	..	..	..	..	..	..	..	..	..
Memo Items:					*(Millions of US dollars)*						
Int'l Reserves Excluding Gold	..	..	..	..	..	..	..	..	..	..	..
Gold Holdings (at market price)	..	..	..	..	..	..	..	..	..	..	..
SOCIAL INDICATORS											
Total Fertility Rate	6.7	6.6	6.6	6.6	6.6	6.5	6.5	6.5	6.5	6.4	6.4
Infant Mortality Rate	170.8	169.4	168.0	166.4	164.8	163.2	161.6	160.0	158.6	157.2	155.8
Life Expectancy at Birth	40.1	40.6	41.1	41.6	42.0	42.5	43.0	43.5	43.6	43.7	43.8
Urban Population, % of total	5.7	6.3	6.9	7.4	8.0	8.6	9.5	10.4	11.3	12.2	13.1
Food Prod. per capita (1987=100)	162.6	163.2	164.7	168.6	162.2	138.9	138.5	133.0	125.9	124.2	123.7
Labor Force, Agriculture (%)	86.4	86.2	86.0	85.8	85.6	85.5	85.2	85.0	84.8	84.6	84.5
Labor Force, Female (%)	50.2	50.1	50.1	50.1	50.1	50.0	50.0	49.9	49.9	49.9	49.8
Primary Schl. Enroll. Ratio	47.0	..	..	..	..	..	87.0	100.0	102.0	104.0	99.0
Primary Schl. Enroll. Ratio, Female	..	..	..	..	..	..	70.0	82.0	84.0	87.0	84.0
Secondary Schl. Enroll. Ratio	5.0	..	..	..	..	..	3.0	4.0	5.0	6.0	5.0

1981	1982	1983	1984	1985	1986	1987	1988	1989	1990 estimate	Notes	MOZAMBIQUE
											FOREIGN TRADE (CUSTOMS BASIS)
			(Millions of current US dollars)								
359	306	240	..	..	..	..	..	..	..	..	Value of Exports, fob
303	222	161	..	..	..	..	..	..	..	..	Nonfuel Primary Products
5	19	20	..	..	..	..	..	..	..	..	Fuels
51	64	59	..	..	..	..	..	..	..	..	Manufactures
649	625	500	..	..	..	..	..	..	..	..	Value of Imports, cif
113	110	117	..	..	..	..	..	..	..	..	Nonfuel Primary Products
151	167	89	..	..	..	..	..	..	..	..	Fuels
385	348	293	..	..	..	..	..	..	..	..	Manufactures
			(Index 1987 = 100)								
90.5	76.8	82.5	95.4	93.5	108.6	100.0	94.0	91.4	88.7	..	Terms of Trade
100.9	79.8	83.7	94.0	87.5	97.8	100.0	104.6	101.3	104.4	..	Export Prices, fob
111.6	104.0	101.5	98.5	93.5	90.1	100.0	111.3	110.8	117.7	..	Import Prices, cif
											BALANCE OF PAYMENTS
			(Millions of current US dollars)								
459	401	297	214	184	192	176	188	199	230	f	Exports of Goods & Services
281	229	132	96	77	79	97	103	104	127	..	Merchandise, fob
114	108	91	61	66	63	79	85	95	103	..	Nonfactor Services
65	64	75	57	41	50	0	0	0	..	..	Factor Services
894	953	782	664	599	747	902	970	1,092	1,148	f	Imports of Goods & Services
721	752	573	486	381	488	592	694	761	796	..	Merchandise, fob
138	140	121	98	100	104	107	114	115	138	..	Nonfactor Services
36	60	88	81	117	155	203	162	216	213	..	Factor Services
0	0	0	0	17	30	13	22	31	8	..	Long-Term Interest
-29	-24	-20	-26	-25	-23	33	124	129	134	..	Private Current Transfers, net
65	64	75	57	41	50	58	72	71	70	..	Workers' Remittances
-465	-576	-505	-476	-440	-578	-693	-658	-764	-784	..	Curr. A/C Bal before Off. Transf.
57	79	90	168	139	219	304	377	388	448	..	Net Official Transfers
-407	-497	-415	-308	-301	-359	-389	-281	-376	-335	..	Curr. A/C Bal after Off. Transf.
409	395	43	140	143	-52	-92	-126	-55	-84	f	Long-Term Capital, net
0	0	0	0	0	0	6	5	3	9	..	Direct Investment
0	0	82	1,145	348	366	322	134	158	153	..	Long-Term Loans
0	0	82	1,145	379	435	342	154	181	173	..	Disbursements
0	0	0	0	31	69	20	20	23	20	..	Repayments
409	395	-39	-1,005	-204	-418	-420	-265	-216	-246	..	Other Long-Term Capital
-69	-39	357	191	137	434	465	382	415	419	f	Other Capital, net
67	141	15	-23	21	-24	15	25	16	0	..	Change in Reserves
											Memo Item:
			(Mozambique Meticais per US dollar)								
35.350	37.770	40.180	42.440	43.180	40.430	290.730	524.650	744.920	929.090	..	Conversion Factor (Annual Avg)
			(Millions of US dollars), outstanding at end of year								
..	..	82	1,365	2,714	3,329	4,050	4,198	4,503	4,718	..	**EXTERNAL DEBT (Total)**
..	..	82	1,285	2,557	3,036	3,717	3,798	3,952	4,146	..	Long-Term Debt (by debtor)
..	..	0	0	19	18	59	71	83	95	..	Central Bank, incl. IMF credit
..	..	82	1,271	2,177	2,526	3,193	3,323	3,409	3,682	..	Central Government
..	..	..	..	..	..	..	..	..	..	..	Rest of General Government
..	..	0	14	349	481	449	386	449	349	..	Non-financial Public Enterprises
..	..	0	0	13	12	17	18	11	20	..	Priv. Sector, incl non-guaranteed
..	..	0	80	157	293	332	400	552	572	..	Short-Term Debt
			(Millions of US dollars)								
											Memo Items:
..	..	..	..	..	..	..	..	..	..	..	Int'l Reserves Excluding Gold
..	..	..	..	..	..	..	..	..	..	..	Gold Holdings (at market price)
											SOCIAL INDICATORS
6.3	6.3	6.3	6.3	6.3	6.3	6.3	6.3	6.4	6.4	..	Total Fertility Rate
154.4	153.0	150.6	148.2	145.7	143.3	140.9	139.7	138.6	137.4	..	Infant Mortality Rate
43.9	44.0	44.5	45.0	45.5	46.0	46.5	46.6	46.6	46.7	..	Life Expectancy at Birth
14.4	15.6	16.9	18.1	19.4	21.3	23.1	24.3	25.6	26.8	..	Urban Population, % of total
122.0	117.0	107.7	103.4	102.3	103.1	100.0	99.5	100.7	99.1	..	Food Prod. per capita (1987=100)
..	..	..	..	..	..	..	..	..	..	..	Labor Force, Agriculture (%)
49.6	49.3	49.1	48.9	48.7	48.4	48.1	47.9	47.7	47.4	..	Labor Force, Female (%)
94.0	..	84.0	..	86.0	84.0	68.0	..	..	..	..	Primary Schl. Enroll. Ratio
		72.0	..	75.0	74.0	59.0	..	..	..	..	Primary Schl. Enroll. Ratio, Female
5.0	..	6.0	..	7.0	7.0	5.0	..	..	..	..	Secondary Schl. Enroll. Ratio

NAMIBIA	1970	1971	1972	1973	1974	1975	1976	1977	1978	1979	1980
CURRENT GNP PER CAPITA (US $)	..	..	..	..	..		..	..	..	..	..
POPULATION (thousands)	1,016	1,039	1,063	1,087	1,113	1,141	1,171	1,202	1,235	1,269	1,306
USE AND ORIGIN OF RESOURCES					*(Millions of current South African Rand)*						
Gross National Product (GNP)	308.9	364.9	426.2	497.4	585.3	..	..	..	..	..	1,408.7
Net Factor Income from Abroad	..	..	..	..	..	..	..	..	..	..	-152.8
GDP at Market Prices	..	..	..	..	..	..	..	..	..	..	1,561.5
Resource Balance	..	..	..	..	..	..	..	..	..	..	68.7
Exports of Goods & NFServices	..	..	..	..	..	..	..	..	..	..	1,148.9
Imports of Goods & NFServices	..	..	..	..	..	..	..	..	..	..	1,080.2
Domestic Absorption	..	..	..	..	..	..	..	..	..	..	1,492.8
Private Consumption, etc.	..	..	..	..	..	..	..	..	..	..	717.1
General Gov't Consumption	..	..	..	..	..	..	..	..	..	..	257.7
Gross Domestic Investment	..	..	..	..	..	..	..	..	..	..	518.0
Fixed Investment	..	..	..	..	..	..	..	..	..	..	437.1
Indirect Taxes, net	..	..	..	..	..	..	..	..	..	..	117.4
GDP at factor cost	..	..	..	..	..	..	..	..	..	..	1,444.1
Agriculture	..	..	..	..	..	..	..	..	..	..	166.3
Industry	..	..	..	..	..	..	..	..	..	..	763.4
Manufacturing	..	..	..	..	..	..	..	..	..	..	56.5
Services, etc.	..	..	..	..	..	..	..	..	..	..	514.4
Gross Domestic Saving	..	..	..	..	..	..	..	..	..	..	586.7
Gross National Saving	..	..	..	..	..	..	..	..	..	..	..
					(Millions of 1987 South African Rand)						
Gross National Product	..	..	..	..	..	..	..	..	..	..	3,471.6
GDP at Market Prices	..	..	..	..	..	..	..	..	..	..	3,289.1
Resource Balance	..	..	..	..	..	..	..	..	..	..	-481.2
Exports of Goods & NFServices	..	..	..	..	..	..	..	..	..	..	2,225.3
Imports of Goods & NFServices	..	..	..	..	..	..	..	..	..	..	2,706.5
Domestic Absorption	..	..	..	..	..	..	..	..	..	..	3,770.3
Private Consumption, etc.	..	..	..	..	..	..	..	..	..	..	1,732.3
General Gov't Consumption	..	..	..	..	..	..	..	..	..	..	730.6
Gross Domestic Investment	..	..	..	..	..	..	..	..	..	..	1,307.4
Fixed Investment	..	..	..	..	..	..	..	..	..	..	1,124.0
GDP at factor cost	..	..	..	..	..	..	..	..	..	..	3,095.1
Agriculture	..	..	..	..	..	..	..	..	..	..	426.6
Industry	..	..	..	..	..	..	..	..	..	..	1,301.9
Manufacturing	..	..	..	..	..	..	..	..	..	..	144.1
Services, etc.	..	..	..	..	..	..	..	..	..	..	1,294.7
Memo Items:											
Capacity to Import	..	..	..	..	..	..	..	..	..	..	2,878.7
Terms of Trade Adjustment	..	..	..	..	..	..	..	..	..	..	653.3
Gross Domestic Income	..	..	..	..	..	..	..	..	..	..	3,942.5
Gross National Income	..	..	..	..	..	..	..	..	..	..	4,124.9
DOMESTIC PRICES/DEFLATORS					*(Index 1987 = 100)*						
Overall (GDP)	..	..	..	..	..	..	..	..	..	..	47.0
Domestic Absorption	..	..	..	..	..	..	..	..	..	..	40.0
Agriculture	..	..	..	..	..	..	..	..	..	..	39.0
Industry	..	..	..	..	..	..	..	..	..	..	59.0
Manufacturing	..	..	..	..	..	..	..	..	..	..	39.0
Consumer Price Index	..	..	..	..	..	..	..	..	..	..	..
MANUFACTURING ACTIVITY											
Employment (1987=100)											..
Real Earnings per Empl. (1987=100)	..	..	..	..	..	..	..	..	..	..	..
Real Output per Empl. (1987=100)	..	..	..	..	..	..	..	..	..	..	..
Earnings as % of Value Added	..	..	..	..	..	..	..	..	..	..	..
MONETARY HOLDINGS					*(Millions of current South African Rand)*						
Money Supply, Broadly Defined	..	..	..	..	..	..	..	..	..	..	..
Money	..	..	..	..	..	..	..	..	..	..	..
Currency Outside Banks	..	..	..	..	..	..	..	..	..	..	..
Demand Deposits	..	..	..	..	..	..	..	..	..	..	..
Quasi-Money	..	..	..	..	..	..	..	..	..	..	..
					(Millions of current South African Rand)						
GOVERNMENT DEFICIT (-) OR SURPLUS	..	..	..	..	..	..	..	..	..	..	..
Current Revenue	..	..	..	..	..	..	..	..	..	..	..
Current Expenditure	..	..	..	..	..	..	..	..	..	..	..
Current Budget Balance	..	..	..	..	..	..	..	..	..	..	..
Capital Receipts	..	..	..	..	..	..	..	..	..	..	..
Capital Payments	..	..	..	..	..	..	..	..	..	..	..

1981	1982	1983	1984	1985	1986	1987	1988	1989	1990 estimate	Notes	NAMIBIA
..	1,210	1,130	1,030	930	840	830	960	1,030	..	..	**CURRENT GNP PER CAPITA (US $)**
1,344	1,385	1,427	1,471	1,518	1,567	1,618	1,670	1,724	1,780	..	**POPULATION (thousands)**
				(Millions of current South African Rand)							**USE AND ORIGIN OF RESOURCES**
1,507.0	1,661.5	1,802.6	2,000.0	2,444.0	2,866.4	3,205.0	3,908.0	4,608.2	..	..	Gross National Product (GNP)
-102.7	-132.7	-76.4	-112.6	-297.7	-319.7	-196.7	-399.8	-372.2	..	..	Net Factor Income from Abroad
1,609.7	1,794.2	1,879.0	2,112.6	2,741.7	3,186.1	3,401.7	4,307.8	4,980.4	..	..	GDP at Market Prices
-308.9	-300.6	-275.9	-276.1	59.5	121.9	-410.7	-300.4	-60.5	..	..	Resource Balance
983.8	1,061.9	979.5	1,144.7	1,621.8	2,028.3	1,827.3	2,177.7	2,731.4	..	..	Exports of Goods & NF Services
1,292.7	1,362.5	1,255.4	1,420.8	1,562.3	1,906.4	2,238.0	2,478.1	2,791.9	..	..	Imports of Goods & NF Services
1,918.6	2,094.8	2,154.9	2,388.7	2,682.2	3,064.2	3,812.4	4,608.2	5,040.9	..	..	Domestic Absorption
1,017.6	1,189.3	1,264.3	1,375.0	1,523.1	1,719.2	2,130.2	2,431.4	2,798.7	..	..	Private Consumption, etc.
404.7	490.4	557.0	650.0	776.1	938.9	1,142.6	1,307.2	1,414.9	..	..	General Gov't Consumption
496.3	415.1	333.6	363.7	383.0	406.1	539.6	869.6	827.3	..	..	Gross Domestic Investment
437.2	420.8	360.9	326.2	377.6	422.8	501.2	655.2	805.2	..	..	Fixed Investment
103.6	114.6	100.0	142.9	201.1	258.5	289.1	540.6	654.2	..	..	Indirect Taxes, net
1,506.1	1,679.6	1,779.0	1,969.7	2,540.6	2,927.6	3,112.6	3,767.2	4,326.2	..	..	GDP at factor cost
217.3	204.6	166.4	167.4	198.7	228.7	382.5	469.6	489.5	..	..	Agriculture
625.3	656.4	683.4	723.5	1,142.1	1,316.2	1,050.5	1,406.2	1,657.5	..	..	Industry
67.2	82.7	93.5	102.6	113.2	132.0	156.6	179.3	210.3	..	..	Manufacturing
663.5	818.6	929.2	1,078.8	1,199.8	1,382.7	1,679.6	1,891.4	2,179.2	..	..	Services, etc.
187.4	114.5	57.7	87.6	442.5	528.0	128.9	569.2	766.8			Gross Domestic Saving
..	..	..	..	..	..	..	..	..			Gross National Saving
				(Millions of 1987 South African Rand)							
3,216.0	2,988.1	2,890.5	2,867.3	3,051.1	3,193.5	3,205.0	3,385.5	3,362.4	..	..	Gross National Product
3,353.8	3,195.2	3,095.3	3,033.2	3,207.5	3,395.3	3,401.7	3,572.0	3,482.2	..	..	GDP at Market Prices
-803.3	-661.0	-401.5	-546.4	-303.7	-99.6	-410.7	-463.3	-408.4	..	..	Resource Balance
2,071.2	1,984.2	1,796.9	1,761.3	1,849.4	2,067.5	1,827.3	1,723.1	1,738.4	..	..	Exports of Goods & NF Services
2,874.4	2,645.2	2,198.4	2,307.7	2,153.1	2,167.1	2,238.0	2,186.4	2,146.8	..	..	Imports of Goods & NF Services
4,157.1	3,856.1	3,496.9	3,579.6	3,511.2	3,494.9	3,812.4	4,035.3	3,890.6	..	..	Domestic Absorption
2,075.1	2,104.9	1,954.6	1,966.2	1,900.7	1,908.7	2,130.2	2,034.8	2,141.4	..	..	Private Consumption, etc.
947.3	978.4	991.8	1,040.0	1,108.3	1,136.9	1,142.6	1,195.6	1,148.6	..	..	General Gov't Consumption
1,134.7	772.8	550.5	573.4	502.2	449.2	539.6	804.9	600.7	..	..	Gross Domestic Investment
982.1	812.4	611.8	506.9	506.9	477.0	501.2	571.9	596.6	..	..	Fixed Investment
3,078.4	3,021.2	2,924.1	2,895.9	2,908.3	2,998.1	3,112.6	3,168.1	3,197.4	..	..	GDP at factor cost
440.7	399.2	310.7	275.3	299.4	299.6	382.5	387.4	402.5	..	..	Agriculture
1,197.8	1,112.2	1,083.6	1,048.8	1,020.0	1,066.2	1,050.5	1,064.1	1,018.6	..	..	Industry
141.3	156.1	159.4	158.4	152.8	154.3	156.6	158.6	173.2	..	..	Manufacturing
1,414.8	1,514.7	1,529.8	1,571.9	1,589.0	1,632.3	1,679.6	1,716.6	1,776.3	..	..	Services, etc.
											Memo Items:
2,187.6	2,061.6	1,715.3	1,859.2	2,235.1	2,305.7	1,827.3	1,921.3	2,100.3	..	..	Capacity to Import
116.4	77.4	-81.6	98.0	385.7	238.2	0.0	198.3	361.9	..	..	Terms of Trade Adjustment
3,470.2	3,272.6	3,013.7	3,131.1	3,593.2	3,633.5	3,401.7	3,770.2	3,844.1	..	..	Gross Domestic Income
3,332.4	3,065.5	2,808.9	2,965.2	3,436.8	3,431.7	3,205.0	3,583.8	3,724.3	..	..	Gross National Income
				(Index 1987 = 100)							**DOMESTIC PRICES/DEFLATORS**
48.0	56.0	61.0	70.0	85.0	94.0	100.0	121.0	143.0	..	..	Overall (GDP)
46.0	54.0	62.0	67.0	76.0	88.0	100.0	114.0	130.0	..	..	Domestic Absorption
49.0	51.0	54.0	61.0	66.0	76.0	100.0	121.0	122.0	..	..	Agriculture
52.0	59.0	63.0	69.0	112.0	123.0	100.0	132.0	163.0	..	..	Industry
48.0	53.0	59.0	65.0	74.0	86.0	100.0	113.0	121.0	..	..	Manufacturing
..	..	..	..	..	..	..	..	..	..	..	Consumer Price Index
											MANUFACTURING ACTIVITY
..	..	..	..	..	..	..	..	..	..	..	Employment (1987=100)
..	..	..	..	..	..	..	..	..	..	..	Real Earnings per Empl. (1987=100)
..	..	..	..	..	..	..	..	..	..	..	Real Output per Empl. (1987=100)
..	..	..	..	..	..	..	..	..	..	..	Earnings as % of Value Added
				(Millions of current South African Rand)							**MONETARY HOLDINGS**
..	..	..	..	..	..	..	..	..	..	..	Money Supply, Broadly Defined
..	..	..	..	..	..	..	..	..	..	..	Money
..	..	..	..	..	..	..	..	..	..	..	Currency Outside Banks
..	..	..	..	..	..	..	..	..	..	..	Demand Deposits
..	..	..	..	..	..	..	..	..	..	..	Quasi-Money
				(Millions of current South African Rand)							
..	..	..	..	..	201	-142	2	325	-209	C	**GOVERNMENT DEFICIT (-) OR SURPLUS**
..	..	..	..	..	1,604	1,525	1,792	2,289	1,835	..	Current Revenue
..	..	..	..	..	1,160	1,301	1,473	1,739	1,784	..	Current Expenditure
..	..	..	..	..	444	224	319	551	50	..	Current Budget Balance
..	..	..	..	..	3	3	3	3	0	..	Capital Receipts
..	..	..	..	..	247	369	320	229	260	..	Capital Payments

NAMIBIA	1970	1971	1972	1973	1974	1975	1976	1977	1978	1979	1980
FOREIGN TRADE (CUSTOMS BASIS)					*(Millions of current US dollars)*						
Value of Exports, fob	..	..	..	..	..	..	..	..	..	..	..
Nonfuel Primary Products	..	..	..	..	..	..	..	..	..	..	..
Fuels	..	..	..	..	..	..	..	..	..	..	..
Manufactures	..	..	..	..	..	..	..	..	..	..	..
Value of Imports, cif	..	..	..	..	..	..	..	..	..	..	..
Nonfuel Primary Products	..	..	..	..	..	..	..	..	..	..	..
Fuels	..	..	..	..	..	..	..	..	..	..	..
Manufactures	..	..	..	..	..	..	..	..	..	..	..
					(Index 1987 = 100)						
Terms of Trade	..	..	..	..	..	..	..	..	..	..	..
Export Prices, fob	..	..	..	..	..	..	..	..	..	..	..
Import Prices, cif	..	..	..	..	..	..	..	..	..	..	..
BALANCE OF PAYMENTS					*(Millions of current US dollars)*						
Exports of Goods & Services	..	..	..	..	..	..	..	..	..	..	..
Merchandise, fob	..	..	..	..	..	..	..	..	..	..	..
Nonfactor Services	..	..	..	..	..	..	..	..	..	..	..
Factor Services	..	..	..	..	..	..	..	..	..	..	..
Imports of Goods & Services	..	..	..	..	..	..	..	..	..	..	..
Merchandise, fob	..	..	..	..	..	..	..	..	..	..	..
Nonfactor Services	..	..	..	..	..	..	..	..	..	..	..
Factor Services	..	..	..	..	..	..	..	..	..	..	..
Long-Term Interest	..	..	..	..	..	..	..	..	..	..	..
Private Current Transfers, net	..	..	..	..	..	..	..	..	..	..	..
Workers' Remittances	..	..	..	..	..	..	..	..	..	..	..
Curr. A/C Bal before Off. Transf.	..	..	..	..	..	..	..	..	..	..	..
Net Official Transfers	..	..	..	..	..	..	..	..	..	..	..
Curr. A/C Bal after Off. Transf.	..	..	..	..	..	..	..	..	..	..	..
Long-Term Capital, net	..	..	..	..	..	..	..	..	..	..	..
Direct Investment	..	..	..	..	..	..	..	..	..	..	..
Long-Term Loans	..	..	..	..	..	..	..	..	..	..	..
Disbursements	..	..	..	..	..	..	..	..	..	..	..
Repayments	..	..	..	..	..	..	..	..	..	..	..
Other Long-Term Capital	..	..	..	..	..	..	..	..	..	..	..
Other Capital, net	..	..	..	..	..	..	..	..	..	..	..
Change in Reserves	..	..	..	..	..	..	..	..	..	..	..
Memo Item:					*(South African Rand per US dollar)*						
Conversion Factor (Annual Avg)	0.710	0.720	0.770	0.690	0.680	0.740	0.870	0.870	0.870	0.840	0.780
				(Millions of US dollars), outstanding at end of year							
EXTERNAL DEBT (Total)	..	..	..	..	..	..	..	..	..	..	..
Long-Term Debt (by debtor)	..	..	..	..	..	..	..	..	..	..	..
Central Bank, incl. IMF credit	..	..	..	..	..	..	..	..	..	..	..
Central Government	..	..	..	..	..	..	..	..	..	..	..
Rest of General Government	..	..	..	..	..	..	..	..	..	..	..
Non-financial Public Enterprises	..	..	..	..	..	..	..	..	..	..	..
Priv. Sector, incl non-guaranteed	..	..	..	..	..	..	..	..	..	..	..
Short-Term Debt	..	..	..	..	..	..	..	..	..	..	..
Memo Items:					*(Millions of US dollars)*						
Int'l Reserves Excluding Gold	..	..	..	..	..	..	..	..	..	..	..
Gold Holdings (at market price)	..	..	..	..	..	..	..	..	..	..	..
SOCIAL INDICATORS											
Total Fertility Rate	6.0	6.0	6.0	6.0	6.0	6.0	6.0	6.0	6.0	6.0	6.0
Infant Mortality Rate	137.0	136.0	134.0	132.0	131.0	129.0	128.0	126.0	124.0	122.0	120.0
Life Expectancy at Birth	48.0	48.0	49.0	49.0	50.0	50.0	51.0	51.0	52.0	52.0	53.0
Urban Population, % of total	19.0	19.0	19.0	20.0	20.0	21.0	21.0	21.0	22.0	22.0	23.0
Food Prod. per capita (1987=100)	129.0	136.0	149.0	151.0	151.0	118.0	119.0	105.0	107.0	104.0	102.0
Labor Force, Agriculture (%)	51.0	50.0	49.0	49.0	48.0	47.0	46.0	46.0	45.0	44.0	43.0
Labor Force, Female (%)	24.0	24.0	24.0	24.0	24.0	24.0	24.0	24.0	24.0	24.0	24.0
Primary Schl. Enroll. Ratio	..	..	..	..	..	..	..	..	..	..	..
Primary Schl. Enroll. Ratio, Female	..	..	..	..	..	..	..	..	..	..	..
Secondary Schl. Enroll. Ratio	..	..	..	..	..	..	..	..	..	..	..

1981	1982	1983	1984	1985	1986	1987	1988	1989	1990 estimate	Notes	NAMIBIA
											FOREIGN TRADE (CUSTOMS BASIS)
											(Millions of current US dollars)
..	..	..	..	..	..	..	..	..	..	..	Value of Exports, fob
..	..	..	..	..	..	..	..	..	..	..	Nonfuel Primary Products
..	..	..	..	..	..	..	..	..	..	..	Fuels
..	..	..	..	..	..	..	..	..	..	..	Manufactures
..	..	..	..	..	..	..	..	..	..	..	Value of Imports, cif
..	..	..	..	..	..	..	..	..	..	..	Nonfuel Primary Products
..	..	..	..	..	..	..	..	..	..	..	Fuels
..	..	..	..	..	..	..	..	..	..	..	Manufactures
											(Index 1987 = 100)
..	..	..	..	..	..	..	..	..	..	..	Terms of Trade
..	..	..	..	..	..	..	..	..	..	..	Export Prices, fob
..	..	..	..	..	..	..	..	..	..	..	Import Prices, cif
											BALANCE OF PAYMENTS
											(Millions of current US dollars)
..	..	..	..	..	..	..	..	..	..	..	Exports of Goods & Services
..	..	..	..	..	..	..	..	..	..	..	Merchandise, fob
..	..	..	..	..	..	..	..	..	..	..	Nonfactor Services
..	..	..	..	..	..	..	..	..	..	..	Factor Services
..	..	..	..	..	..	..	..	..	..	..	Imports of Goods & Services
..	..	..	..	..	..	..	..	..	..	..	Merchandise, fob
..	..	..	..	..	..	..	..	..	..	..	Nonfactor Services
..	..	..	..	..	..	..	..	..	..	..	Factor Services
..	..	..	..	..	..	..	..	..	..	..	Long-Term Interest
..	..	..	..	..	..	..	..	..	..	..	Private Current Transfers, net
..	..	..	..	..	..	..	..	..	..	..	Workers' Remittances
..	..	..	..	..	..	..	..	..	..	..	Curr. A/C Bal before Off. Transf.
..	..	..	..	..	..	..	..	..	..	..	Net Official Transfers
..	..	..	..	..	..	..	..	..	..	..	Curr. A/C Bal after Off. Transf.
..	..	..	..	..	..	..	..	..	..	..	Long-Term Capital, net
..	..	..	..	..	..	..	..	..	..	..	Direct Investment
..	..	..	..	..	..	..	..	..	..	..	Long-Term Loans
..	..	..	..	..	..	..	..	..	..	..	Disbursements
..	..	..	..	..	..	..	..	..	..	..	Repayments
..	..	..	..	..	..	..	..	..	..	..	Other Long-Term Capital
..	..	..	..	..	..	..	..	..	..	..	Other Capital, net
..	..	..	..	..	..	..	..	..	..	..	Change in Reserves
											Memo Item:
											(South African Rand per US dollar)
0.880	1.090	1.110	1.480	2.230	2.290	2.040	2.270	2.620	2.590	..	Conversion Factor (Annual Avg)
											EXTERNAL DEBT (Total)
											(Millions of US dollars), outstanding at end of year
..	..	..	..	..	..	..	..	..	..	..	Long-Term Debt (by debtor)
..	..	..	..	..	..	..	..	..	..	..	Central Bank, incl. IMF credit
..	..	..	..	..	..	..	..	..	..	..	Central Government
..	..	..	..	..	..	..	..	..	..	..	Rest of General Government
..	..	..	..	..	..	..	..	..	..	..	Non-financial Public Enterprises
..	..	..	..	..	..	..	..	..	..	..	Priv. Sector, incl non-guaranteed
..	..	..	..	..	..	..	..	..	..	..	Short-Term Debt
											Memo Items:
											(Millions of US dollars)
..	..	..	..	..	..	..	..	..	..	..	Int'l Reserves Excluding Gold
..	..	..	..	..	..	..	..	..	..	..	Gold Holdings (at market price)
											SOCIAL INDICATORS
6.0	6.0	6.0	6.0	6.0	6.0	6.0	6.0	6.0	6.0	..	Total Fertility Rate
118.0	116.0	114.0	112.0	110.0	108.0	106.0	104.0	102.0	100.0	..	Infant Mortality Rate
53.0	54.0	54.0	55.0	55.0	56.0	56.0	57.0	57.0	57.0	..	Life Expectancy at Birth
23.0	24.0	24.0	25.0	25.0	26.0	27.0	27.0	27.0	28.0	..	Urban Population, % of total
103.0	97.0	86.0	85.0	87.0	88.0	100.0	96.0	96.0	96.0	..	Food Prod. per capita (1987=100)
..	..	..	..	..	..	..	..	..	..	..	Labor Force, Agriculture (%)
24.0	24.0	24.0	24.0	24.0	24.0	24.0	24.0	24.0	24.0	..	Labor Force, Female (%)
..	..	..	..	..	..	..	..	..	..	..	Primary Schl. Enroll. Ratio
..	..	..	..	..	..	..	..	..	..	..	Primary Schl. Enroll. Ratio, Female
..	..	..	..	..	..	..	..	..	..	..	Secondary Schl. Enroll. Ratio

NEPAL	1970	1971	1972	1973	1974	1975	1976	1977	1978	1979	1980
CURRENT GNP PER CAPITA (US $)	80	80	80	80	100	110	120	120	120	130	130
POPULATION (thousands)	11,350	11,608	11,890	12,195	12,513	12,841	13,178	13,528	13,889	14,260	14,640

USE AND ORIGIN OF RESOURCES					*(Millions of current Nepalese Rupees)*						
Gross National Product (GNP)	8,768	8,938	10,369	9,969	12,808	16,571	17,458	17,354	19,819	22,315	23,501
Net Factor Income from Abroad	0	0	0	0	0	0	64	74	87	100	150
GDP at Market Prices	8,768	8,938	10,369	9,969	12,808	16,571	17,394	17,280	19,732	22,215	23,351
Resource Balance	-298	-333	-234	-375	-653	-740	-592	-437	-967	-929	-1,679
Exports of Goods & NF Services	430	483	587	659	698	1,475	1,874	2,037	2,086	2,618	2,695
Imports of Goods & NF Services	728	816	821	1,034	1,351	2,215	2,466	2,474	3,053	3,547	4,374
Domestic Absorption	9,066	9,271	10,603	10,344	13,461	17,311	17,986	17,717	20,699	23,144	25,030
Private Consumption, etc.	8,543	8,578	9,843	9,429	12,339	13,652	14,060	13,688	15,621	17,741	19,195
General Gov't Consumption	..	..	..	..	..	1,257	1,294	1,260	1,471	1,889	1,565
Gross Domestic Investment	523	693	760	915	1,122	2,402	2,632	2,769	3,607	3,514	4,270
Fixed Investment	..	..	..	..	..	2,223	2,443	2,581	3,294	3,263	3,681
Indirect Taxes, net	55	163	239	204	383	635	805	1,025	1,306	1,436	1,465
GDP at factor cost	8,713	8,775	10,130	9,765	12,425	15,936	16,589	16,255	18,426	20,779	21,886
Agriculture	5,863	5,974	7,035	6,513	8,763	11,435	11,495	10,389	11,616	13,365	13,520
Industry	1,005	817	943	956	1,115	1,303	1,469	1,821	2,199	2,489	2,608
Manufacturing	323	336	409	399	526	664	690	736	794	848	936
Services, etc.	1,845	1,984	2,152	2,296	2,547	3,198	3,625	4,045	4,611	4,925	5,758
Gross Domestic Saving	225	360	526	540	469	1,662	2,040	2,332	2,640	2,585	2,591
Gross National Saving	225	360	526	540	469	1,842	2,446	2,773	2,927	2,975	3,086
						..					
Gross National Product	15,148	14,967	15,434	15,360	16,333	16,571	17,371	17,891	18,698	19,138	18,726
GDP at Market Prices	15,148	14,967	15,434	15,360	16,333	16,571	17,300	17,822	18,607	19,048	18,606
Resource Balance	..	..	..	..	..	..	..	..	..	..	..
Exports of Goods & NF Services	..	..	..	..	..	..	..	..	..	..	..
Imports of Goods & NF Services	..	..	..	..	..	..	..	..	..	..	..
Domestic Absorption	..	..	..	..	..	..	..	..	..	..	..
Private Consumption, etc.	..	..	..	..	..	..	..	..	..	..	..
General Gov't Consumption	..	..	..	..	..	..	..	..	..	..	..
Gross Domestic Investment	..	..	..	..	..	..	..	..	..	..	..
Fixed Investment	..	..	..	..	..	..	..	..	..	..	..
GDP at factor cost	15,053	14,694	15,078	15,046	15,845	15,936	16,500	16,765	17,375	17,816	17,439
Agriculture	10,585	10,660	10,738	10,647	11,246	11,435	11,498	11,017	11,013	11,346	10,803
Industry	..	..	..	..	..	..	..	..	..	..	..
Manufacturing	..	..	..	..	..	..	..	..	..	..	..
Services, etc.	..	..	..	..	..	..	..	..	..	..	..
Memo Items:											
Capacity to Import	..	..	..	..	..	..	..	..	..	..	..
Terms of Trade Adjustment	..	..	..	..	..	..	..	..	..	..	..
Gross Domestic Income	..	..	..	..	..	..	..	..	..	..	..
Gross National Income	..	..	..	..	..	..	..	..	..	..	..

DOMESTIC PRICES/DEFLATORS					*(Index 1975 = 100)*						
Overall (GDP)	57.9	59.7	67.2	64.9	78.4	100.0	100.5	97.0	106.0	116.6	125.5
Domestic Absorption	..	..	..	..	..	..	..	..	..	..	..
Agriculture	55.4	56.0	65.5	61.2	77.9	100.0	100.0	94.3	105.5	117.8	125.2
Industry	..	..	..	..	..	..	..	..	..	..	..
Manufacturing	..	..	..	..	..	..	..	..	..	..	..
Consumer Price Index	23.6	23.2	25.1	28.0	33.5	36.1	34.9	38.4	41.2	42.7	48.9

MANUFACTURING ACTIVITY											
Employment (1987=100)	..	..	..	..	..	..	..	31.3	..	..	..
Real Earnings per Empl. (1987=100)	..	..	..	..	..	..	..	93.9	..	..	..
Real Output per Empl. (1987=100)	..	..	..	..	..	..	..	..	..	..	..
Earnings as % of Value Added	..	..	..	..	..	..	..	24.8	..	..	..

MONETARY HOLDINGS					*(Millions of current Nepalese Rupees)*						
Money Supply, Broadly Defined	931	1,108	1,293	1,663	1,948	2,180	2,811	3,401	4,070	4,712	5,526
Money	699	784	842	1,090	1,290	1,333	1,636	1,932	2,200	2,534	2,864
Currency Outside Banks	525	549	596	747	882	882	996	1,212	1,379	1,627	1,814
Demand Deposits	174	235	245	343	408	451	640	720	821	907	1,050
Quasi-Money	232	324	451	573	658	847	1,175	1,468	1,870	2,178	2,661

GOVERNMENT DEFICIT (-) OR SURPLUS					*(Millions of current Nepalese Rupees)*						
	..	..	-126	-223	-248	-236	-422	-576	-582	-588	-705
Current Revenue	..	..	783	783	975	1,277	1,447	1,683	1,989	2,323	2,620
Current Expenditure	..	..	..	..	..	..	..	..	..	..	..
Current Budget Balance	..	..	..	..	..	..	..	..	..	..	..
Capital Receipts	..	..	..	..	..	..	..	..	..	..	..
Capital Payments	..	..	..	..	..	..	..	..	..	..	..

1981	1982	1983	1984	1985	1986	1987	1988	1989	1990 estimate	Notes	NEPAL
150	160	160	170	170	160	160	170	180	180	..	**CURRENT GNP PER CAPITA (US $)**
15,023	15,423	15,833	16,255	16,682	17,098	17,529	17,976	18,438	18,916	..	**POPULATION (thousands)**
											USE AND ORIGIN OF RESOURCES
			(Millions of current Nepalese Rupees)								
27,428	31,148	33,943	39,438	44,418	50,426	59,225	68,937	78,610	89,030	C	Gross National Product (GNP)
121	160	183	48	2	-2	-21	79	351	319	..	Net Factor Income from Abroad
27,307	30,988	33,760	39,390	44,416	50,428	59,246	68,858	78,259	88,711	C f	GDP at Market Prices
-1,834	-2,236	-3,742	-3,465	-3,946	-4,712	-5,577	-6,715	-9,478	-7,874	..	Resource Balance
3,523	3,592	3,454	4,196	5,371	6,506	7,555	8,749	9,878	7,744	..	Exports of Goods & NF Services
5,357	5,828	7,196	7,661	9,317	11,218	13,132	15,464	19,356	15,618	..	Imports of Goods & NF Services
29,141	33,224	37,502	42,855	48,362	55,140	64,823	75,573	87,737	96,585	..	Domestic Absorption
22,411	25,272	27,458	31,860	33,807	39,408	45,355	52,345	61,372	70,067	..	Private Consumption, etc.
1,922	2,638	3,416	3,644	4,371	5,133	6,570	8,511	9,186	10,394	..	General Gov't Consumption
4,808	5,314	6,628	7,351	10,184	10,599	12,898	14,717	17,179	16,124	..	Gross Domestic Investment
4,299	5,465	6,576	6,907	9,386	9,431	11,825	12,894	14,156	14,050	..	Fixed Investment
1,841	1,951	2,117	2,386	2,861	3,364	3,888	5,258	5,437	6,245	..	Indirect Taxes, net
25,466	29,037	31,643	37,004	41,555	47,064	55,358	63,600	72,822	82,466	C f	GDP at factor cost
15,510	17,715	19,082	22,570	23,927	26,555	30,448	35,477	41,833	49,704	..	Agriculture
3,148	3,733	4,049	4,661	5,917	7,073	8,620	9,602	10,453	11,464	..	Industry
1,049	1,243	1,460	1,816	1,998	2,622	3,065	3,646	3,834	4,320	..	Manufacturing
6,808	7,589	8,512	9,773	11,711	13,436	16,290	18,521	20,536	21,298	..	Services, etc.
2,974	3,078	2,886	3,886	6,238	5,887	7,321	8,002	7,701	8,250	..	Gross Domestic Saving
3,575	3,700	3,673	4,676	7,017	6,836	8,703	9,825	9,632	10,366	..	Gross National Saving
20,242	21,032	20,411	22,294	23,627	24,646	25,605	27,553	28,700	29,667	C	Gross National Product
20,158	20,920	20,297	22,262	23,630	24,645	25,617	27,475	28,536	29,560	C f	GDP at Market Prices
..	..	..	..	..	..	..	..	..	..	..	Resource Balance
..	..	..	..	..	..	..	..	..	..	..	Exports of Goods & NF Services
..	..	..	..	..	..	..	..	..	..	..	Imports of Goods & NF Services
..	..	..	..	..	..	..	..	..	..	..	Domestic Absorption
..	..	..	..	..	..	..	..	..	..	..	Private Consumption, etc.
..	..	..	..	..	..	..	..	..	..	..	General Gov't Consumption
..	..	..	..	..	..	..	..	..	..	..	Gross Domestic Investment
..	..	..	..	..	..	..	..	..	..	..	Fixed Investment
18,799	19,603	19,024	20,914	22,104	23,001	23,935	25,377	26,553	27,480	C f	GDP at factor cost
11,936	12,483	12,348	13,547	13,849	14,559	14,638	15,838	17,068	18,321	..	Agriculture
..	..	..	..	..	..	..	..	..	..	..	Industry
..	..	..	..	..	..	..	..	..	..	..	Manufacturing
..	..	..	..	..	..	..	..	..	..	..	Services, etc.
											Memo Items:
..	..	..	..	..	..	..	..	..	..	..	Capacity to Import
..	..	..	..	..	..	..	..	..	..	..	Terms of Trade Adjustment
..	..	..	..	..	..	..	..	..	..	..	Gross Domestic Income
..	..	..	..	..	..	..	..	..	..	..	Gross National Income
			(Index 1975 = 100)								**DOMESTIC PRICES/DEFLATORS**
135.5	148.1	166.3	176.9	188.0	204.6	231.3	250.6	274.2	300.1	..	Overall (GDP)
..	..	..	..	..	..	..	..	..	..	..	Domestic Absorption
129.9	141.9	154.5	166.6	172.8	182.4	208.0	224.0	245.1	271.3	..	Agriculture
..	..	..	..	..	..	..	..	..	..	..	Industry
..	..	..	..	..	..	..	..	..	..	..	Manufacturing
54.4	60.8	68.3	70.2	75.9	90.3	100.0	109.0	118.6	128.4	f	Consumer Price Index
											MANUFACTURING ACTIVITY
..	52.4	..	..	..	97.7	100.0	..	..	..	..	Employment (1987=100)
..	..	..	..	..	95.3	100.0	..	..	..	..	Real Earnings per Empl. (1987=100)
..	..	..	..	..	..	..	..	..	..	..	Real Output per Empl. (1987=100)
..	..	..	..	..	22.1	25.0	..	..	..	..	Earnings as % of Value Added
			(Millions of current Nepalese Rupees)								**MONETARY HOLDINGS**
6,580	7,987	9,594	10,841	13,014	15,543	19,024	23,219	28,540	33,303	D	Money Supply, Broadly Defined
3,205	3,705	4,366	4,942	5,616	6,951	8,682	9,826	11,720	14,205	..	Money
2,147	2,408	2,783	3,302	3,797	4,787	5,826	6,671	7,905	9,818	..	Currency Outside Banks
1,058	1,297	1,583	1,641	1,819	2,164	2,855	3,155	3,815	4,387	..	Demand Deposits
3,375	4,283	5,228	5,899	7,398	8,592	10,343	13,393	16,820	19,098	..	Quasi-Money
			(Millions of current Nepalese Rupees)								**GOVERNMENT DEFICIT (-) OR SURPLUS**
-728	-1,591	-2,954	-2,985	-3,380	-3,637	-3,902	-4,280	-8,014	-7,013	C F	Current Revenue
3,233	3,626	3,867	4,186	4,759	5,656	7,055	9,202	9,196	10,562	..	Current Expenditure
..	..	..	..	..	3,232	3,732	4,216	5,076	5,914	..	Current Budget Balance
..	..	..	..	14	25	10	14	25	34	..	Capital Receipts
..	..	..	..	..	6,085	7,236	9,280	12,159	11,695	..	Capital Payments

437

NEPAL	1970	1971	1972	1973	1974	1975	1976	1977	1978	1979	1980

FOREIGN TRADE (CUSTOMS BASIS)

(Millions of current US dollars)

	1970	1971	1972	1973	1974	1975	1976	1977	1978	1979	1980
Value of Exports, fob	..	..	..	..	..	..	..	..	..	..	..
Nonfuel Primary Products	..	..	..	..	..	..	..	..	..	..	..
Fuels	..	..	..	..	..	..	..	..	..	..	..
Manufactures	..	..	..	..	..	..	..	..	..	..	..
Value of Imports, cif	..	..	..	..	..	..	..	..	..	..	..
Nonfuel Primary Products	..	..	..	..	..	..	..	..	..	..	..
Fuels	..	..	..	..	..	..	..	..	..	..	..
Manufactures	..	..	..	..	..	..	..	..	..	..	..

(Index 1987 = 100)

	1970	1971	1972	1973	1974	1975	1976	1977	1978	1979	1980
Terms of Trade	..	..	..	..	..	..	..	..	..	..	..
Export Prices, fob	..	..	..	..	..	..	..	..	..	..	..
Import Prices, cif	..	..	..	..	..	..	..	..	..	..	..

BALANCE OF PAYMENTS

(Millions of current US dollars)

	1970	1971	1972	1973	1974	1975	1976	1977	1978	1979	1980
Exports of Goods & Services	71.00	81.00	97.00	106.00	114.00	149.10	162.80	169.70	177.20	223.50	239.40
Merchandise, fob	42.00	48.00	58.00	63.00	66.00	83.80	100.60	95.10	86.40	101.30	96.10
Nonfactor Services	25.00	29.00	35.00	38.00	40.00	55.10	55.30	67.90	82.70	111.80	127.40
Factor Services	4.00	4.00	4.00	5.00	8.00	10.20	6.90	6.70	8.10	10.40	15.90
Imports of Goods & Services	96.10	109.10	109.10	132.20	171.30	209.90	206.90	198.70	248.80	302.70	367.90
Merchandise, fob	75.00	85.00	85.00	103.00	134.00	171.00	168.30	163.60	194.50	236.30	283.30
Nonfactor Services	21.00	24.00	24.00	29.00	37.00	38.40	37.00	34.30	53.20	64.30	81.30
Factor Services	0.10	0.10	0.10	0.20	0.30	0.50	1.60	0.80	1.10	2.10	3.30
Long-Term Interest	0.10	0.10	0.10	0.20	0.30	0.40	0.60	0.80	1.10	1.50	1.90
Private Current Transfers, net	0.00	0.00	0.00	0.00	0.00	16.40	27.40	29.40	16.50	24.20	28.70
Workers' Remittances	..	..	..	..	..	..	0.00	0.00	0.00	0.00	0.00
Curr. A/C Bal before Off. Transf.	-25.10	-28.10	-12.10	-26.20	-57.30	-44.40	-16.70	0.40	-55.10	-55.00	-99.80
Net Official Transfers	24.00	27.00	24.00	17.00	32.00	33.00	21.60	20.10	31.10	48.20	70.30
Curr. A/C Bal after Off. Transf.	-1.10	-1.10	11.90	-9.20	-25.30	-11.40	4.90	20.50	-24.00	-6.80	-29.50
Long-Term Capital, net	-2.00	5.00	4.00	8.00	8.00	8.40	12.10	17.20	20.40	26.80	34.30
Direct Investment	..	..	..	..	..	..	0.00	0.00	0.00	0.00	0.00
Long-Term Loans	-1.60	5.20	3.70	7.80	7.10	8.00	10.80	26.80	31.50	31.10	48.10
Disbursements	0.60	5.30	3.90	8.10	7.60	9.20	11.90	28.80	33.10	32.90	50.20
Repayments	2.20	0.10	0.20	0.30	0.50	1.20	1.10	2.00	1.60	1.80	2.10
Other Long-Term Capital	-0.40	-0.20	0.30	0.20	0.90	0.40	1.30	-9.60	-11.10	-4.30	-13.80
Other Capital, net	16.26	2.10	-14.91	9.31	19.34	-18.00	12.80	-15.30	-2.50	-42.30	-0.20
Change in Reserves	-13.16	-6.00	-0.99	-8.11	-2.04	21.00	-29.80	-22.40	6.10	22.30	-4.60

Memo Item:

(Nepalese Rupees per US dollar)

	1970	1971	1972	1973	1974	1975	1976	1977	1978	1979	1980
Conversion Factor (Annual Avg)	10.130	10.130	10.130	10.280	10.560	10.560	11.970	12.500	12.360	12.000	12.000

EXTERNAL DEBT (Total)

(Millions of US dollars), outstanding at end of year

	1970	1971	1972	1973	1974	1975	1976	1977	1978	1979	1980
EXTERNAL DEBT (Total)	2.8	8.3	11.6	19.5	27.1	33.7	49.5	100.5	112.6	146.3	204.5
Long-Term Debt (by debtor)	2.8	8.3	11.6	19.5	27.1	33.7	49.5	77.5	96.6	134.3	197.5
Central Bank, incl. IMF credit	0.0	0.0	0.0	0.0	0.0	0.0	5.2	7.3	17.2	24.4	41.6
Central Government	1.1	6.3	9.6	15.7	22.3	27.6	37.4	63.5	74.3	105.1	151.2
Rest of General Government	..	..	..	..	..	..	..	..	..	..	..
Non-financial Public Enterprises	0.9	0.9	0.8	0.8	0.8	0.7	0.6	0.0	0.0	0.0	0.0
Priv. Sector, incl non-guaranteed	0.8	1.1	1.2	3.0	4.0	5.4	6.3	6.7	5.1	4.8	4.7
Short-Term Debt	0.0	0.0	0.0	0.0	0.0	0.0	0.0	23.0	16.0	12.0	7.0

Memo Items:

(Millions of US dollars)

	1970	1971	1972	1973	1974	1975	1976	1977	1978	1979	1980
Int'l Reserves Excluding Gold	88.7	96.1	98.4	117.5	121.3	95.7	127.5	139.5	127.4	165.7	177.8
Gold Holdings (at market price)	5.5	6.2	8.8	14.6	24.3	18.3	17.5	21.9	24.7873M	41.2504M	98.8771M

SOCIAL INDICATORS

	1970	1971	1972	1973	1974	1975	1976	1977	1978	1979	1980
Total Fertility Rate	6.4	6.5	6.5	6.5	6.5	6.5	6.5	6.5	6.5	6.4	6.4
Infant Mortality Rate	157.4	155.2	153.0	151.8	150.6	149.4	148.2	147.0	145.4	143.8	142.2
Life Expectancy at Birth	42.4	42.8	43.3	43.8	44.3	44.8	45.3	45.8	46.3	46.8	47.3
Urban Population, % of total	3.9	4.1	4.3	4.4	4.6	4.8	5.1	5.3	5.6	5.8	6.1
Food Prod. per capita (1987=100)	106.6	104.1	97.5	105.5	104.9	106.2	101.6	96.2	96.7	88.8	95.5
Labor Force, Agriculture (%)	93.6	93.6	93.5	93.4	93.4	93.3	93.2	93.2	93.1	93.0	93.0
Labor Force, Female (%)	35.1	35.0	35.0	35.0	34.9	34.9	34.9	34.9	34.9	34.9	34.9
Primary Schl. Enroll. Ratio	26.0	..	..	..	..	51.0	59.0	69.0	77.0	88.0	88.0
Primary Schl. Enroll. Ratio, Female	8.0	..	..	..	..	16.0	24.0	32.0	38.0	49.0	52.0
Secondary Schl. Enroll. Ratio	10.0	..	..	..	..	13.0	12.0	14.0	16.0	19.0	22.0

1981	1982	1983	1984	1985	1986	1987	1988	1989	1990 estimate	Notes	NEPAL
				(Millions of current US dollars)							**FOREIGN TRADE (CUSTOMS BASIS)**
..	..	..	..	..	..	..	..	..	..	..	Value of Exports, fob
..	..	..	..	..	..	..	..	..	..	..	Nonfuel Primary Products
..	..	..	..	..	..	..	..	..	..	..	Fuels
..	..	..	..	..	..	..	..	..	..	..	Manufactures
											Value of Imports, cif
..	..	..	..	..	..	..	..	..	..	..	Nonfuel Primary Products
..	..	..	..	..	..	..	..	..	..	..	Fuels
..	..	..	..	..	..	..	..	..	..	..	Manufactures
				(Index 1987 = 100)							
..	..	..	..	..	..	..	..	..	..	..	Terms of Trade
..	..	..	..	..	..	..	..	..	..	..	Export Prices, fob
..	..	..	..	..	..	..	..	..	..	..	Import Prices, cif
				(Millions of current US dollars)							**BALANCE OF PAYMENTS**
306.90	292.60	264.10	279.70	306.60	332.50	354.60	404.10	407.10	402.50	C f	Exports of Goods & Services
134.40	116.00	82.00	111.50	154.10	156.20	139.10	187.10	166.30	179.20		Merchandise, fob
159.20	161.50	167.40	162.00	147.30	173.10	210.80	208.10	220.90	200.50	..	Nonfactor Services
13.30	15.10	14.70	6.20	5.20	3.20	4.70	8.90	19.90	22.80	..	Factor Services
449.70	471.20	521.20	502.40	527.90	570.90	613.70	746.60	763.90	780.00	C f	Imports of Goods & Services
352.60	381.40	457.20	425.90	435.90	474.30	506.00	629.90	643.60	648.30		Merchandise, fob
93.80	87.10	25.60	30.60	36.70	38.60	43.10	46.70	48.10	52.70	..	Nonfactor Services
3.30	2.70	38.40	45.90	55.30	58.00	64.60	70.00	72.20	79.00	..	Factor Services
2.40	3.10	4.20	5.30	7.60	11.40	15.60	20.70	26.10	26.00	..	Long-Term Interest
38.90	34.90	41.50	45.10	42.60	44.80	64.30	74.90	58.10	61.20	..	Private Current Transfers, net
0.00	0.00	0.00	0.00	0.00	0.00	0.00	0.00	0.00	..	..	Workers' Remittances
-103.90	-143.70	-215.60	-177.60	-178.70	-193.60	-194.80	-267.60	-298.70	-316.30	..	Curr. A/C Bal before Off. Transf.
79.30	94.70	99.90	98.10	79.90	77.50	68.40	65.00	53.70	52.60	..	Net Official Transfers
-24.60	-49.00	-115.70	-79.50	-98.80	-116.10	-126.40	-202.60	-245.00	-263.70	..	Curr. A/C Bal after Off. Transf.
50.90	59.90	59.10	79.30	73.00	96.30	108.60	157.90	237.10	293.80	C f	Long-Term Capital, net
0.00	0.00	0.00	0.00	0.00	0.00	0.00	0.00	0.00	..	..	Direct Investment
64.30	66.40	68.10	88.00	96.20	138.30	170.70	180.20	207.80	135.00	..	Long-Term Loans
66.50	69.00	71.90	92.10	102.10	152.50	186.80	203.00	234.00	166.10	..	Disbursements
2.20	2.60	3.80	4.10	5.90	14.20	16.10	22.80	26.20	31.10	..	Repayments
-13.40	-6.50	-9.00	-8.70	-23.20	-42.00	-62.10	-22.30	29.30	158.80	..	Other Long-Term Capital
-39.30	42.10	12.40	-38.20	-22.00	43.60	32.70	153.90	-9.20	64.50	C f	Other Capital, net
13.00	-53.00	44.20	38.40	47.80	-23.80	-14.90	-109.20	17.10	-94.60	..	Change in Reserves
				(Nepalese Rupees per US dollar)							**Memo Item:**
12.000	12.940	13.800	15.260	17.780	19.800	21.600	22.050	25.320	28.510	..	Conversion Factor (Annual Avg)
				(Millions of US dollars), outstanding at end of year							
278.5	352.9	452.2	470.1	589.6	751.4	995.0	1,171.7	1,359.4	1,620.5	..	**EXTERNAL DEBT (Total)**
256.5	313.9	372.2	446.1	566.6	730.9	976.3	1,148.7	1,341.9	1,600.6	..	Long-Term Debt (by debtor)
37.8	30.5	23.4	15.5	21.8	23.5	43.0	52.7	52.4	43.9	..	Central Bank, incl. IMF credit
214.2	278.6	341.9	412.8	521.4	659.6	840.7	961.7	1,164.7	1,444.2	..	Central Government
..	..	..	..	..	..	..	..	..	..	..	Rest of General Government
0.0	0.5	2.8	13.9	19.6	37.2	82.3	124.8	116.1	105.0	..	Non-financial Public Enterprises
4.5	4.3	4.1	3.9	3.8	10.6	10.3	9.5	8.7	7.5	..	Priv. Sector, incl non-guaranteed
22.0	39.0	80.0	24.0	23.0	20.5	18.7	23.0	17.5	19.9	..	Short-Term Debt
				(Millions of US dollars)							**Memo Items:**
174.0	221.7	170.9	124.6	68.6	101.3	125.1	241.1	229.4	295.3	..	Int'l Reserves Excluding Gold
64.4555M	48.039M	62.9387M	56.4406M	48.074M	52.4615M	67.6743M	66.2976M	56.9936M	58.8	..	Gold Holdings (at market price)
											SOCIAL INDICATORS
6.3	6.3	6.2	6.1	6.0	6.0	5.9	5.8	5.8	5.7	..	Total Fertility Rate
140.6	139.0	136.6	134.2	131.9	129.5	127.1	125.1	123.2	121.2	..	Infant Mortality Rate
47.8	48.3	48.8	49.4	49.9	50.4	51.0	51.3	51.6	52.0	..	Life Expectancy at Birth
6.4	6.7	7.1	7.4	7.7	8.1	8.5	8.8	9.2	9.6	..	Urban Population, % of total
97.3	87.1	102.5	100.4	98.9	91.6	100.0	110.5	108.6	104.4	..	Food Prod. per capita (1987=100)
..	..	..	..	..	..	..	..	..	..	..	Labor Force, Agriculture (%)
34.8	34.7	34.6	34.4	34.3	34.2	34.0	33.8	33.7	33.6	..	Labor Force, Female (%)
..	71.0	77.0	81.0	82.0	82.0	83.0	86.0	..	..	..	Primary Schl. Enroll. Ratio
..	41.0	45.0	49.0	51.0	51.0	53.0	57.0	..	..	..	Primary Schl. Enroll. Ratio, Female
..	21.0	23.0	25.0	26.0	27.0	29.0	30.0	..	..	..	Secondary Schl. Enroll. Ratio

NETHERLANDS	1970	1971	1972	1973	1974	1975	1976	1977	1978	1979	1980
CURRENT GNP PER CAPITA (US $)	2,560	2,850	3,250	4,030	5,080	6,010	6,870	7,760	8,890	10,570	12,010
POPULATION (thousands)	13,039	13,195	13,329	13,439	13,545	13,666	13,774	13,856	13,942	14,038	14,150

USE AND ORIGIN OF RESOURCES *(Billions of current Netherlands Guilders)*

	1970	1971	1972	1973	1974	1975	1976	1977	1978	1979	1980
Gross National Product (GNP)	121.74	136.92	154.96	177.34	201.45	219.94	252.05	275.42	296.33	315.23	336.12
Net Factor Income from Abroad	0.56	0.39	0.70	1.30	1.67	-0.02	0.12	0.49	-0.68	-0.73	-0.62
GDP at Market Prices	121.18	136.53	154.26	176.04	199.78	219.96	251.93	274.93	297.01	315.96	336.74
Resource Balance	-2.11	-0.41	4.25	5.65	5.47	7.38	8.54	3.34	0.11	-1.63	-1.81
Exports of Goods & NFServices	54.30	62.02	69.40	83.41	107.78	109.72	128.47	130.74	133.34	155.06	176.81
Imports of Goods & NFServices	56.41	62.43	65.15	77.76	102.31	102.34	119.93	127.40	133.23	156.69	178.62
Domestic Absorption	123.29	136.94	150.01	170.39	194.31	212.58	243.39	271.59	296.90	317.59	338.55
Private Consumption, etc.	70.82	78.94	88.45	99.83	113.39	128.95	147.99	164.31	179.17	192.43	205.78
General Gov't Consumption	18.66	21.85	24.43	27.42	32.45	38.25	43.47	47.85	52.61	57.17	60.26
Gross Domestic Investment	33.81	36.15	37.13	43.14	48.47	45.38	51.93	59.43	65.12	67.99	72.51
Fixed Investment	31.36	34.64	36.40	40.66	43.85	46.32	48.97	57.89	63.30	66.49	70.79
Indirect Taxes, net	11.55	13.79	15.77	17.02	17.96	20.21	22.77	26.73	29.30	29.80	32.02
GDP at factor cost	109.63	122.74	138.49	159.02	181.82	199.75	229.16	248.20	267.71	286.16	304.72
Agriculture	6.70	6.99	8.01	9.10	8.29	9.75	11.29	11.42	11.77	11.33	11.68
Industry	45.21	50.55	56.93	64.36	73.09	76.96	87.97	92.62	97.71	102.78	110.45
Manufacturing	31.32	34.33	38.46	43.63	50.00	48.23	54.37	55.06	57.95	60.08	60.37
Services, etc.	69.28	78.99	89.32	102.58	118.40	133.25	152.67	170.90	187.53	201.85	214.62
Gross Domestic Saving	31.70	35.74	41.38	48.79	53.94	52.76	60.47	62.77	65.23	66.36	70.70
Gross National Saving	32.02	35.90	41.75	49.60	54.93	52.06	59.74	62.25	63.40	64.44	68.46

(Billions of 1987 Netherlands Guilders)

	1970	1971	1972	1973	1974	1975	1976	1977	1978	1979	1980
Gross National Product	300.40	312.52	323.43	339.58	353.33	350.03	368.16	377.19	384.87	393.99	397.58
GDP at Market Prices	298.99	311.62	321.93	337.02	350.39	350.07	367.99	376.52	385.77	394.91	398.32
Resource Balance	-11.16	-6.95	-1.12	0.19	5.24	6.43	6.73	-0.56	-5.31	-3.38	0.04
Exports of Goods & NFServices	107.79	119.27	131.14	147.01	150.82	146.09	160.52	157.68	162.88	174.95	177.59
Imports of Goods & NFServices	118.95	126.22	132.27	146.82	145.58	139.66	153.80	158.24	168.19	178.33	177.54
Domestic Absorption	310.15	318.57	323.05	336.83	345.15	343.64	361.26	377.08	391.08	398.29	398.27
Private Consumption, etc.	166.25	172.88	180.44	187.35	195.59	203.74	214.36	222.69	231.54	239.19	239.98
General Gov't Consumption	49.13	51.28	51.68	52.10	53.24	55.43	57.70	59.66	61.98	63.74	64.11
Gross Domestic Investment	94.78	94.41	90.93	97.39	96.31	84.48	89.20	94.72	97.56	95.36	94.19
Fixed Investment	79.36	80.57	78.73	82.02	78.74	75.31	73.66	80.85	82.89	81.46	80.70
GDP at factor cost											
Agriculture	9.05	9.38	9.60	10.49	11.15	11.04	11.15	11.60	12.45	12.98	13.33
Industry	..	..	..	..	..	..	..	..	..	..	..
Manufacturing	..	..	..	..	..	..	..	..	..	..	..
Services, etc.	..	..	..	..	..	..	..	..	..	..	..

Memo Items:

	1970	1971	1972	1973	1974	1975	1976	1977	1978	1979	1980
Capacity to Import	114.50	125.40	140.90	157.49	153.36	149.73	164.75	162.39	168.33	176.47	175.74
Terms of Trade Adjustment	6.71	6.12	9.75	10.47	2.54	3.64	4.23	4.71	5.45	1.53	-1.84
Gross Domestic Income	305.70	317.74	331.68	347.50	352.93	353.71	372.22	381.23	391.21	396.44	396.48
Gross National Income	307.11	318.64	333.18	350.05	355.87	353.68	372.38	381.90	390.31	395.52	395.74

DOMESTIC PRICES/DEFLATORS *(Index 1987 = 100)*

	1970	1971	1972	1973	1974	1975	1976	1977	1978	1979	1980
Overall (GDP)	40.5	43.8	47.9	52.2	57.0	62.8	68.5	73.0	77.0	80.0	84.5
Domestic Absorption	39.8	43.0	46.4	50.6	56.3	61.9	67.4	72.0	75.9	79.7	85.0
Agriculture	74.0	74.5	83.5	86.7	74.3	88.3	101.2	98.4	94.5	87.3	87.6
Industry	..	..	..	..	..	..	..	..	..	..	..
Manufacturing	..	..	..	..	..	..	..	..	..	..	..
Consumer Price Index	40.4	43.5	46.8	50.6	55.5	61.1	66.7	71.0	73.9	77.0	82.0

MANUFACTURING ACTIVITY

	1970	1971	1972	1973	1974	1975	1976	1977	1978	1979	1980
Employment (1987=100)	132.0	129.9	125.9	123.8	122.9	118.6	113.6	114.2	111.3	110.3	109.0
Real Earnings per Empl. (1987=100)	75.4	78.8	82.0	87.1	91.1	92.7	95.0	92.6	95.8	97.5	96.5
Real Output per Empl. (1987=100)	62.0	64.9	65.6	73.3	86.0	80.7	87.8	83.8	83.0	89.9	91.4
Earnings as % of Value Added	52.2	52.8	51.6	51.2	50.7	57.1	53.5	55.7	56.8	57.7	57.9

MONETARY HOLDINGS *(Billions of current Netherlands Guilders)*

	1970	1971	1972	1973	1974	1975	1976	1977	1978	1979	1980
Money Supply, Broadly Defined	70.57	80.12	109.68	124.88	141.20	159.51	183.33	207.80	233.78	258.59	273.69
Money	25.95	29.85	35.12	35.14	39.43	47.20	51.05	57.77	60.19	61.87	65.58
Currency Outside Banks	9.95	10.49	11.41	11.92	12.85	14.49	15.89	17.41	18.71	19.98	22.00
Demand Deposits	16.00	19.36	23.71	23.22	26.58	32.70	35.16	40.35	41.47	41.90	43.59
Quasi-Money	44.61	50.27	74.56	89.74	101.77	112.31	132.29	150.03	173.59	196.72	208.11

GOVERNMENT DEFICIT (-) OR SURPLUS *(Billions of current Netherlands Guilders)*

	1970	1971	1972	1973	1974	1975	1976	1977	1978	1979	1980
GOVERNMENT DEFICIT (-) OR SURPLUS	..	..	..	-0.04	-0.04	-6.35	-6.12	-8.37	-9.20	-14.53	-15.56
Current Revenue	..	..	..	77.22	89.71	103.72	119.49	133.01	143.71	154.63	169.42
Current Expenditure	..	..	..	66.75	80.26	97.30	112.61	125.91	139.89	152.45	164.76
Current Budget Balance	..	..	..	10.47	9.45	6.42	6.88	7.10	3.82	2.18	4.66
Capital Receipts	..	..	..	0.05	0.21	0.21	0.23	0.22	0.15	0.13	0.17
Capital Payments	..	..	..	10.56	9.74	12.39	12.40	12.43	12.58	15.16	19.93

1981	1982	1983	1984	1985	1986	1987	1988	1989	1990 estimate	Notes	NETHERLANDS
11,800	10,930	10,070	9,690	9,360	9,990	11,660	14,420	16,030	17,550	..	CURRENT GNP PER CAPITA (US $)
14,247	14,313	14,367	14,424	14,492	14,572	14,665	14,760	14,849	14,943	..	POPULATION (thousands)
											USE AND ORIGIN OF RESOURCES
				(Billions of current Netherlands Guilders)							
351.89	368.48	381.58	399.75	418.86	427.63	429.44	447.40	476.02	509.00	..	Gross National Product (GNP)
-0.96	-0.38	0.56	-0.50	0.68	-0.98	-0.73	-2.42	0.72	0.69	..	Net Factor Income from Abroad
352.85	368.86	381.02	400.25	418.18	428.61	430.17	449.82	475.30	508.31	..	GDP at Market Prices
12.38	15.77	14.56	20.81	20.04	19.51	13.34	19.48	20.31	25.78	..	Resource Balance
204.62	212.60	219.77	248.56	265.54	232.52	226.65	246.23	276.25	287.91	..	Exports of Goods & NFServices
192.24	196.83	205.21	227.75	245.50	213.01	213.31	226.75	255.94	262.13	..	Imports of Goods & NFServices
340.47	353.09	366.46	379.44	398.14	409.10	416.83	430.34	454.99	482.53	..	Domestic Absorption
213.23	221.83	229.86	236.75	247.72	256.15	263.93	268.96	281.18	299.05	..	Private Consumption, etc.
62.75	65.12	66.58	66.39	67.67	68.55	70.59	71.16	72.67	75.40	..	General Gov't Consumption
64.49	66.14	70.02	76.30	82.75	84.40	82.31	90.22	101.14	108.08	..	Gross Domestic Investment
67.58	67.16	69.46	74.31	80.25	86.18	87.10	95.78	103.23	109.14	..	Fixed Investment
32.90	32.70	33.92	35.38	37.19	39.80	40.59	42.06	45.28	50.68	..	Indirect Taxes, net
319.95	336.16	347.10	364.87	380.99	388.81	389.58	407.76	430.02	457.63	B	GDP at factor cost
14.56	15.93	16.12	17.26	17.14	18.45	17.69	18.20	21.12	..	..	Agriculture
116.01	121.25	124.62	133.38	140.42	137.85	128.68	137.19	146.44	..	..	Industry
59.78	64.67	67.46	72.57	75.23	83.21	81.41	89.37	95.91	..	..	Manufacturing
222.29	231.68	240.28	249.61	260.62	272.30	283.80	294.43	307.74	..	..	Services, etc.
76.87	81.91	84.58	97.11	102.79	103.91	95.65	109.70	121.45	133.86	..	Gross Domestic Saving
74.11	79.65	83.52	95.11	101.96	101.08	92.79	105.48	120.17	132.50	..	Gross National Saving
				(Billions of 1987 Netherlands Guilders)							
394.69	389.67	396.03	407.35	419.12	425.87	429.44	439.13	459.91	477.89	..	Gross National Product
395.76	390.08	395.46	407.87	418.45	426.86	430.17	441.49	459.23	477.25	..	GDP at Market Prices
13.99	11.77	11.24	15.96	14.59	14.68	13.34	16.97	15.93	17.15	..	Resource Balance
181.23	180.77	186.76	200.20	210.81	217.96	226.65	244.35	257.81	269.85	..	Exports of Goods & NFServices
167.24	169.00	175.52	184.23	196.22	203.29	213.31	227.38	241.88	252.70	..	Imports of Goods & NFServices
381.77	378.31	384.21	391.90	403.86	412.18	416.83	424.52	443.29	460.10	..	Domestic Absorption
240.34	236.36	237.50	240.18	245.07	253.19	263.93	266.90	269.75	279.15	..	Private Consumption, etc.
65.70	65.99	66.67	66.16	66.99	68.63	70.59	70.72	70.40	70.41	..	General Gov't Consumption
75.73	75.96	80.05	85.56	91.81	90.36	82.31	86.90	103.15	110.55	..	Gross Domestic Investment
72.64	69.53	70.85	74.52	79.53	85.77	87.10	94.19	97.85	101.76	..	Fixed Investment
..	..	..	..	..	..	..	..	..	..	..	GDP at factor cost
15.17	16.29	16.83	17.87	17.37	18.97	17.69	18.64	19.89	..	..	Agriculture
..	..	..	..	..	..	..	..	..	..	..	Industry
..	..	..	..	..	..	..	..	..	..	..	Manufacturing
..	..	..	..	..	..	..	..	..	..	..	Services, etc.
											Memo Items:
178.01	182.54	187.97	201.07	212.24	221.91	226.65	246.91	261.07	277.55	..	Capacity to Import
-3.22	1.77	1.21	0.87	1.43	3.94	0.00	2.56	3.26	7.70	..	Terms of Trade Adjustment
392.54	391.85	396.67	408.73	419.88	430.80	430.17	444.05	462.49	484.96	..	Gross Domestic Income
391.47	391.44	397.24	408.22	420.55	429.82	429.44	441.69	463.17	485.59	..	Gross National Income
											DOMESTIC PRICES/DEFLATORS
				(Index 1987 = 100)							
89.2	94.6	96.3	98.1	99.9	100.4	100.0	101.9	103.5	106.5	..	Overall (GDP)
89.2	93.3	95.4	96.8	98.6	99.3	100.0	101.4	102.6	104.9	..	Domestic Absorption
96.0	97.8	95.8	96.6	98.7	97.3	100.0	97.6	106.2	..	..	Agriculture
..	..	..	..	..	..	..	..	..	..	..	Industry
..	..	..	..	..	..	..	..	..	..	..	Manufacturing
87.6	92.7	95.3	98.4	100.6	100.7	100.0	100.7	101.8	104.3	..	Consumer Price Index
											MANUFACTURING ACTIVITY
105.4	100.9	96.4	95.3	97.2	99.2	100.0	100.5	..	..	..	Employment (1987=100)
95.2	96.5	97.2	95.4	96.1	98.3	100.0	..	..	..	..	Real Earnings per Empl. (1987=100)
92.9	90.8	98.1	106.6	104.9	97.7	100.0	..	..	..	..	Real Output per Empl. (1987=100)
58.8	56.8	54.0	50.1	50.3	47.2	47.0	..	..	..	..	Earnings as % of Value Added
											MONETARY HOLDINGS
				(Billions of current Netherlands Guilders)							
293.69	312.03	327.30	346.85	366.59	386.50	33.48	368.77	409.29	435.55	D	Money Supply, Broadly Defined
64.03	72.30	79.66	85.00	90.77	97.21	103.71	111.31	119.02	124.29	..	Money
22.34	23.39	26.35	27.80	28.60	29.77	32.85	34.61	36.00	36.47	..	Currency Outside Banks
41.70	48.91	53.31	57.20	62.17	67.44	70.86	76.70	83.02	87.82	..	Demand Deposits
229.66	239.73	247.64	261.85	275.82	289.29	239.77	257.46	290.27	311.26	..	Quasi-Money
				(Billions of current Netherlands Guilders)							
-22.97	-28.05	-29.55	-29.92	-23.37	-8.21	-13.77	-19.25	-20.99	-24.70		**GOVERNMENT DEFICIT (-) OR SURPLUS**
179.55	189.95	201.07	206.97	217.79	223.94	225.65	230.73	230.54	242.08	..	Current Revenue
178.65	195.95	206.46	212.41	216.60	222.39	230.46	232.78	238.93	253.15	..	Current Expenditure
0.90	-6.00	-5.39	-5.44	1.19	1.55	-4.81	-2.05	-8.39	-11.07	..	Current Budget Balance
0.19	0.19	0.09	0.18	0.26	0.36	0.29	0.24	0.42	0.23	..	Capital Receipts
23.23	22.58	22.17	24.13	21.18	9.48	10.84	16.37	15.72	15.18	..	Capital Payments

NETHERLANDS	1970	1971	1972	1973	1974	1975	1976	1977	1978	1979	1980
FOREIGN TRADE (CUSTOMS BASIS)				*(Millions of current US dollars)*							
Value of Exports, fob	11,766	13,934	17,351	24,012	32,734	34,957	40,147	43,605	50,149	63,667	73,871
Nonfuel Primary Products	3,842	4,221	5,234	7,385	9,084	10,145	11,298	12,550	14,693	17,852	19,930
Fuels	1,256	1,738	2,077	3,127	5,234	5,960	7,112	7,932	8,023	11,966	16,114
Manufactures	6,668	7,975	10,040	13,501	18,416	18,852	21,737	23,123	27,434	33,849	37,827
Value of Imports, cif	13,393	14,901	17,226	23,753	32,508	34,394	39,452	45,500	53,041	67,282	76,889
Nonfuel Primary Products	3,354	3,484	4,114	6,036	7,825	8,031	9,141	10,679	11,942	14,649	16,602
Fuels	1,458	1,937	2,267	3,151	5,890	6,145	7,682	8,380	8,253	13,358	18,252
Manufactures	8,581	9,481	10,845	14,566	18,792	20,219	22,630	26,440	32,846	39,274	42,036
					(Index 1987 = 100)						
Terms of Trade	128.8	123.7	132.9	159.0	114.1	110.2	110.4	105.0	112.2	123.4	110.6
Export Prices, fob	24.3	25.2	29.8	47.2	58.8	59.0	60.5	63.5	75.6	99.5	106.3
Import Prices, cif	18.9	20.4	22.4	29.7	51.5	53.6	54.8	60.4	67.4	80.6	96.0
BALANCE OF PAYMENTS				*(Billions of current US dollars)*							
Exports of Goods & Services	14.85	17.83	21.75	30.64	43.10	45.31	50.64	55.76	64.13	83.68	97.87
Merchandise, fob	10.88	12.55	15.58	21.95	30.51	32.02	36.36	39.91	45.47	58.61	67.48
Nonfactor Services	2.66	3.74	4.49	6.09	7.97	9.22	9.70	10.75	12.80	14.45	17.21
Factor Services	1.31	1.54	1.69	2.61	4.61	4.07	4.58	5.10	5.86	10.61	13.18
Imports of Goods & Services	15.30	17.87	20.25	28.10	39.70	42.22	46.70	53.73	64.19	82.56	97.63
Merchandise, fob	11.80	13.17	15.14	20.95	29.92	31.12	35.01	40.15	46.96	60.04	68.89
Nonfactor Services	2.35	3.28	3.64	5.01	6.54	7.27	7.95	9.26	11.46	14.01	16.87
Factor Services	1.16	1.42	1.47	2.14	3.24	3.83	3.74	4.32	5.77	8.52	11.87
Long-Term Interest	..	..	..	..	..	..	..	..	..	..	..
Private Current Transfers, net	-0.07	-0.07	-0.10	-0.18	-0.25	-0.27	-0.32	-0.41	-0.53	-0.59	-0.81
Workers' Remittances	..	..	..	..	..	..	..	..	..	..	..
Curr. A/C Bal before Off. Transf.	-0.51	-0.10	1.40	2.36	3.14	2.83	3.61	1.62	-0.59	0.53	-0.58
Net Official Transfers	0.02	0.01	-0.03	0.09	-0.10	-0.44	-0.15	-0.42	-0.63	-0.38	-0.58
Curr. A/C Bal after Off. Transf.	-0.49	-0.10	1.37	2.45	3.04	2.39	3.46	1.20	-1.22	0.15	-1.16
Long-Term Capital, net	0.56	0.46	-0.94	-1.82	-2.16	-1.43	-3.79	-1.90	-2.62	-5.03	-2.09
Direct Investment	-0.02	0.09	-0.12	-0.12	-1.69	-1.21	-1.79	-2.39	-2.33	-4.45	-3.62
Long-Term Loans	..	..	..	..	..	..	..	..	..	..	..
Disbursements	..	..	..	..	..	..	..	..	..	..	..
Repayments	..	..	..	..	..	..	..	..	..	..	..
Other Long-Term Capital	0.57	0.37	-0.82	-1.70	-0.47	-0.22	-2.01	0.48	-0.30	-0.58	1.54
Other Capital, net	0.55	-0.21	0.44	0.09	0.10	-0.65	0.66	1.01	2.92	4.29	4.43
Change in Reserves	-0.62	-0.16	-0.86	-0.72	-0.98	-0.32	-0.33	-0.30	0.92	0.59	-1.18
Memo Item:				*(Netherlands Guilders per US dollar)*							
Conversion Factor (Annual Avg)	3.620	3.500	3.210	2.800	2.690	2.530	2.640	2.450	2.160	2.010	1.990
EXTERNAL DEBT (Total)				*(Millions US dollars), outstanding at end of year*							
Long-Term Debt (by debtor)	..	..	..	..	..	..	..	..	..	..	..
Central Bank, incl. IMF credit	..	..	..	..	..	..	..	..	..	..	..
Central Government	..	..	..	..	..	..	..	..	..	..	..
Rest of General Government	..	..	..	..	..	..	..	..	..	..	..
Non-financial Public Enterprises	..	..	..	..	..	..	..	..	..	..	..
Priv. Sector, incl non-guaranteed	..	..	..	..	..	..	..	..	..	..	..
Short-Term Debt	..	..	..	..	..	..	..	..	..	..	..
Memo Items:				*(Millions of US dollars)*							
Int'l Reserves Excluding Gold	1,454	1,724	2,726	4,253	4,630	4,884	5,178	5,742	5,088	7,591	11,645
Gold Holdings (at market price)	1,908	2,379	3,516	6,098	10,132	7,620	7,321	9,011	12,380	22,514	25,904
SOCIAL INDICATORS											
Total Fertility Rate	..	..	..	..	..	1.7	1.6	1.6	1.6	1.6	1.6
Infant Mortality Rate	12.7	12.1	11.7	11.5	11.3	10.6	10.7	9.5	9.6	8.7	8.6
Life Expectancy at Birth	73.5	73.8	74.0	74.1	74.3	74.4	74.8	75.3	75.4	75.6	75.7
Urban Population, % of total	86.1	86.6	87.0	87.5	87.9	88.4	88.4	88.4	88.4	88.4	88.4
Food Prod. per capita (1987=100)	72.2	73.7	70.5	74.1	79.2	80.4	77.6	79.5	84.1	86.0	87.2
Labor Force, Agriculture (%)	6.8	6.7	6.5	6.4	6.3	6.2	6.0	5.9	5.8	5.6	5.5
Labor Force, Female (%)	26.4	26.9	27.3	27.7	28.2	28.6	29.1	29.6	30.1	30.6	31.0
Primary Schl. Enroll. Ratio	102.0	..	..	..	..	98.0	100.0	100.0	101.0	101.0	100.0
Primary Schl. Enroll. Ratio, Female	102.0	..	..	..	..	99.0	100.0	101.0	102.0	102.0	101.0
Secondary Schl. Enroll. Ratio	75.0	..	..	..	..	88.0	91.0	92.0	92.0	93.0	92.0

1981	1982	1983	1984	1985	1986	1987	1988	1989	1990 estimate	Notes	NETHERLANDS
											FOREIGN TRADE (CUSTOMS BASIS)
				(Millions of current US dollars)							
68,758	66,404	65,676	65,874	68,282	80,555	92,882	103,206	107,799	131,479	..	Value of Exports, fob
18,789	18,001	17,819	17,720	17,638	22,145	26,560	29,332	30,285	35,409	..	Nonfuel Primary Products
16,231	15,669	15,212	14,878	15,495	12,213	10,089	8,690	9,632	12,621	..	Fuels
33,738	32,734	32,645	33,276	35,149	46,197	56,232	65,183	67,883	83,449	..	Manufactures
66,109	62,583	61,585	62,136	65,212	75,580	91,316	99,743	104,220	125,909	..	Value of Imports, cif
14,092	13,381	13,163	13,271	13,341	15,440	18,459	21,354	20,158	22,745	..	Nonfuel Primary Products
17,258	15,986	15,129	14,470	14,181	8,738	9,936	9,055	10,478	12,794	..	Fuels
34,759	33,216	33,294	34,395	37,690	51,402	62,921	69,333	73,584	90,370	..	Manufactures
				(Index 1987 = 100)							
102.5	106.8	101.8	100.4	101.0	101.4	100.0	100.7	99.6	101.9	..	Terms of Trade
97.7	95.3	88.3	84.9	83.0	90.1	100.0	105.9	112.2	129.5	..	Export Prices, fob
95.3	89.2	86.7	84.6	82.2	88.8	100.0	105.2	112.6	127.1	..	Import Prices, cif
											BALANCE OF PAYMENTS
				(Billions of current US dollars)							
92.17	89.23	84.77	86.46	86.96	103.49	123.40	139.11	150.76	177.74	..	Exports of Goods & Services
63.10	60.53	59.04	59.89	62.29	73.10	86.16	97.44	101.57	122.33	..	Merchandise, fob
16.01	15.99	14.19	14.46	14.89	17.21	20.80	22.43	24.70	29.75	..	Nonfactor Services
13.06	12.71	11.53	12.11	9.78	13.19	16.45	19.24	24.49	25.66	..	Factor Services
86.95	82.91	78.73	79.00	81.65	97.57	117.29	130.17	138.90	164.24	..	Imports of Goods & Services
59.22	55.65	54.64	54.34	56.89	66.05	80.99	88.97	93.45	111.86	..	Merchandise, fob
14.84	14.70	13.49	13.64	14.32	17.82	20.64	22.43	22.89	27.07	..	Nonfactor Services
12.90	12.56	10.59	11.02	10.43	13.70	15.66	18.78	22.55	25.30	..	Factor Services
..	..	..	..	..	..	..	..	..	..	..	Long-Term Interest
-0.72	-0.71	-0.57	-0.47	-0.45	-0.75	-1.05	-0.91	-0.94	-1.13	..	Private Current Transfers, net
										..	Workers' Remittances
4.50	5.62	5.47	6.99	4.85	5.17	5.06	8.03	10.92	12.37	..	Curr. A/C Bal before Off. Transf.
-0.95	-0.91	-0.56	-0.66	-0.66	-1.13	-1.23	-1.16	-1.31	-1.98	..	Net Official Transfers
3.55	4.71	4.91	6.33	4.19	4.04	3.83	6.87	9.61	10.39	..	Curr. A/C Bal after Off. Transf.
-2.87	-3.82	-2.88	-5.80	-2.13	-7.49	-2.69	1.35	4.78	-7.16	..	Long-Term Capital, net
-2.83	-2.07	-2.26	-3.28	-1.32	-0.72	-5.80	-1.78	-6.25	-4.07	..	Direct Investment
..	..	..	..	..	..	..	..	..	..	..	Long-Term Loans
										..	Disbursements
										..	Repayments
-0.04	-1.75	-0.62	-2.51	-0.80	-6.77	3.10	3.12	11.03	-3.09	..	Other Long-Term Capital
-1.50	0.89	-2.26	-0.50	-1.31	3.06	1.73	-6.59	-13.93	-2.96	..	Other Capital, net
0.83	-1.78	0.23	-0.04	-0.75	0.39	-2.86	-1.63	-0.45	-0.28	..	Change in Reserves
											Memo Item:
				(Netherlands Guilders per US dollar)							
2.500	2.670	2.850	3.210	3.320	2.450	2.030	1.980	2.120	1.820	..	Conversion Factor (Annual Avg)
										..	**EXTERNAL DEBT (Total)**
				(Millions US dollars), outstanding at end of year							
..	..	..	..	..	..	..	..	..	..	..	Long-Term Debt (by debtor)
..	..	..	..	..	..	..	..	..	..	..	Central Bank, incl. IMF credit
..	..	..	..	..	..	..	..	..	..	..	Central Government
..	..	..	..	..	..	..	..	..	..	..	Rest of General Government
..	..	..	..	..	..	..	..	..	..	..	Non-financial Public Enterprises
..	..	..	..	..	..	..	..	..	..	..	Priv. Sector, incl non-guaranteed
..	..	..	..	..	..	..	..	..	..	..	Short-Term Debt
											Memo Items:
				(Millions of US dollars)							
9,339	10,133	10,171	9,237	10,782	11,191	16,003	16,075	16,509	17,484	..	Int'l Reserves Excluding Gold
17,467	20,077	16,764	13,547	14,369	17,177	21,272	18,027	17,621	16,918	..	Gold Holdings (at market price)
											SOCIAL INDICATORS
1.6	1.5	1.5	1.5	1.5	1.6	1.6	1.6	1.6	1.6	..	Total Fertility Rate
8.3	8.3	8.4	8.3	8.0	7.7	7.6	7.4	7.2	7.1	..	Infant Mortality Rate
75.9	76.1	76.2	76.3	76.4	76.5	76.6	76.7	76.9	77.1	..	Life Expectancy at Birth
88.4	88.4	88.5	88.5	88.5	88.5	88.5	88.5	88.5	88.5	..	Urban Population, % of total
96.2	96.7	94.6	96.9	94.6	102.6	100.0	97.2	104.1	97.8	..	Food Prod. per capita (1987=100)
..	..	..	..	..	..	..	..	..	..	..	Labor Force, Agriculture (%)
31.0	31.0	31.0	31.0	31.0	31.0	31.0	30.9	30.9	30.9	..	Labor Force, Female (%)
99.0	97.0	95.0	95.0	114.0	115.0	115.0	116.0	..	..	..	Primary Schl. Enroll. Ratio
100.0	98.0	96.0	96.0	115.0	116.0	117.0	117.0	..	..	..	Primary Schl. Enroll. Ratio, Female
94.0	97.0	101.0	102.0	104.0	104.0	103.0	103.0	..	..	..	Secondary Schl. Enroll. Ratio

NEW ZEALAND	1970	1971	1972	1973	1974	1975	1976	1977	1978	1979	1980
CURRENT GNP PER CAPITA (US $)	2,190	2,480	2,880	3,580	4,350	4,610	4,590	4,450	4,930	5,930	6,900
POPULATION (thousands)	2,820	2,854	2,902	2,956	3,024	3,087	3,111	3,120	3,121	3,109	3,113

USE AND ORIGIN OF RESOURCES

(Millions of current New Zealand Dollars)

	1970	1971	1972	1973	1974	1975	1976	1977	1978	1979	1980
Gross National Product (GNP)	5,687	6,684	7,641	8,964	9,730	10,866	13,147	14,543	16,447	19,228	22,436
Net Factor Income from Abroad	-41	-46	-54	-37	-82	-165	-265	-337	-410	-459	-511
GDP at Market Prices	5,728	6,730	7,695	9,001	9,812	11,031	13,412	14,880	16,857	19,687	22,947
Resource Balance	-176	55	236	8	-1,227	-764	-292	-253	40	-260	-269
Exports of Goods & NFServices	1,296	1,560	1,946	2,241	2,117	2,666	3,765	4,125	4,687	5,996	7,003
Imports of Goods & NFServices	1,472	1,505	1,710	2,233	3,344	3,430	4,057	4,378	4,647	6,256	7,272
Domestic Absorption	5,904	6,675	7,459	8,993	11,039	11,795	13,704	15,133	16,817	19,947	23,216
Private Consumption, etc.	3,723	4,112	4,595	5,355	6,149	6,996	8,108	9,092	10,301	12,096	14,285
General Gov't Consumption	770	886	1,023	1,176	1,443	1,732	1,937	2,363	2,882	3,314	4,134
Gross Domestic Investment	1,411	1,677	1,841	2,462	3,447	3,067	3,659	3,678	3,634	4,537	4,797
Fixed Investment	1,302	1,514	1,880	2,188	2,695	3,246	3,538	3,545	3,880	4,067	4,754
Indirect Taxes, net	518	554	625	687	679	712	1,057	1,192	1,297	1,646	1,996
GDP at factor cost	5,210	6,176	7,070	8,314	9,133	10,319	12,355	13,688	15,560	18,041	20,951
Agriculture	..	804	1,068	1,128	860	1,163	1,537	1,496	1,607	2,395	2,517
Industry	..	2,216	2,472	2,807	3,347	3,711	4,534	4,750	5,308	6,218	7,100
Manufacturing	..	1,593	1,754	1,970	2,370	2,597	3,228	3,281	3,771	4,442	5,082
Services, etc.	..	3,710	4,155	5,066	5,605	6,157	7,341	8,634	9,942	11,074	13,330
Gross Domestic Saving	1,235	1,732	2,077	2,470	2,220	2,303	3,367	3,425	3,674	4,277	4,528
Gross National Saving	1,190	1,700	2,068	2,489	2,173	2,188	3,136	3,136	3,290	3,888	4,128

(Millions of 1987 New Zealand Dollars)

	1970	1971	1972	1973	1974	1975	1976	1977	1978	1979	1980
Gross National Product	40,389	42,492	44,291	47,578	50,208	49,327	50,276	47,680	47,678	48,807	49,359
GDP at Market Prices	40,586	42,690	44,520	47,682	50,521	49,940	51,158	48,665	48,772	49,887	50,354
Resource Balance	-117	702	77	-2,161	-3,967	65	1,376	1,247	1,357	564	1,770
Exports of Goods & NFServices	8,848	9,493	9,689	9,500	9,243	10,422	11,577	11,571	11,850	12,371	12,763
Imports of Goods & NFServices	8,965	8,791	9,612	11,661	13,210	10,357	10,201	10,324	10,493	11,808	10,993
Domestic Absorption	40,703	41,987	44,443	49,843	54,488	49,875	49,782	47,418	47,414	49,323	48,584
Private Consumption, etc.	25,083	25,555	27,114	29,056	30,011	30,346	29,770	28,393	29,511	30,410	30,339
General Gov't Consumption	6,580	6,739	7,149	7,438	8,052	8,445	8,380	8,721	9,127	9,007	9,089
Gross Domestic Investment	9,040	9,694	10,180	13,348	16,425	11,084	11,633	10,305	8,776	9,907	9,157
Fixed Investment	8,156	8,640	10,139	11,352	12,126	11,471	10,540	9,392	8,932	8,610	8,485
GDP at factor cost	37,061	39,292	40,864	43,906	47,224	47,076	47,452	45,041	45,223	45,886	46,287
Agriculture	..	..	..	..	..	..	..	2,884	2,744	3,108	3,493
Industry	..	..	..	..	..	..	..	13,975	13,749	13,968	13,792
Manufacturing	..	..	..	..	..	..	..	9,567	9,553	9,999	9,849
Services, etc.	..	..	..	..	..	..	..	31,806	32,279	32,811	33,069

Memo Items:

	1970	1971	1972	1973	1974	1975	1976	1977	1978	1979	1980
Capacity to Import	7,893	9,112	10,939	11,703	8,363	8,050	9,467	9,727	10,583	11,317	10,586
Terms of Trade Adjustment	-955	-381	1,250	2,203	-880	-2,372	-2,110	-1,844	-1,267	-1,054	-2,177
Gross Domestic Income	39,631	42,309	45,769	49,884	49,641	47,568	49,048	46,821	47,505	48,833	48,177
Gross National Income	39,434	42,111	45,541	49,780	49,328	46,955	48,166	45,836	46,411	47,752	47,182

DOMESTIC PRICES/DEFLATORS

(Index 1987 = 100)

	1970	1971	1972	1973	1974	1975	1976	1977	1978	1979	1980
Overall (GDP)	14.1	15.8	17.3	18.9	19.4	22.1	26.2	30.6	34.6	39.5	45.6
Domestic Absorption	14.5	15.9	16.8	18.0	20.3	23.6	27.5	31.9	35.5	40.4	47.8
Agriculture	..	..	..	..	..	..	..	51.9	58.6	77.1	72.1
Industry	..	..	..	..	..	..	..	34.0	38.6	44.5	51.5
Manufacturing	..	..	..	..	..	..	..	34.3	39.5	44.4	51.6
Consumer Price Index	13.3	14.7	15.8	17.0	18.9	21.7	25.4	29.0	32.5	37.0	43.3

MANUFACTURING ACTIVITY

	1970	1971	1972	1973	1974	1975	1976	1977	1978	1979	1980
Employment (1987=100)	90.2	91.4	92.8	96.6	102.1	104.7	107.5	110.5	113.4	112.2	111.0
Real Earnings per Empl. (1987=100)	..	..	..	..	..	..	..	..	..	..	..
Real Output per Empl. (1987=100)	..	..	..	..	..	..	..	..	..	..	..
Earnings as % of Value Added	61.8	63.2	61.6	63.4	65.1	66.5	62.7	66.6	65.8	65.4	66.1

MONETARY HOLDINGS

(Millions of current New Zealand Dollars)

	1970	1971	1972	1973	1974	1975	1976	1977	1978	1979	1980
Money Supply, Broadly Defined	3,066	3,351	4,060	5,011	5,236	5,833	6,793	7,807	9,506	11,108	12,400
Money	861	949	1,219	1,545	1,601	1,749	1,910	1,946	2,378	2,458	2,535
Currency Outside Banks	195	212	242	290	336	352	418	460	536	590	577
Demand Deposits	665	737	978	1,255	1,265	1,397	1,491	1,486	1,842	1,868	1,958
Quasi-Money	2,205	2,402	2,841	3,466	3,635	4,083	4,883	5,862	7,127	8,649	9,865

GOVERNMENT DEFICIT (-) OR SURPLUS

(Millions of current New Zealand Dollars)

	1970	1971	1972	1973	1974	1975	1976	1977	1978	1979	1980
	-108	-93	-298	-225	-416	-1,194	-614	-789	-1,502	-1,127	-1,541
Current Revenue	1,614	1,901	2,141	2,626	3,121	3,496	4,277	5,150	5,648	6,823	7,871
Current Expenditure	1,380	1,610	1,978	2,326	2,712	3,474	3,870	4,777	5,914	6,858	8,246
Current Budget Balance	234	291	163	300	409	22	407	373	-266	-35	-375
Capital Receipts	6	7	5	6	3	7	6	3	3	4	6
Capital Payments	348	391	466	531	828	1,223	1,027	1,165	1,239	1,096	1,172

1981	1982	1983	1984	1985	1986	1987	1988	1989	1990 estimate	Notes	NEW ZEALAND
7,790	7,760	7,450	7,150	6,760	7,110	8,160	10,190	11,780	12,310	..	CURRENT GNP PER CAPITA (US $)
3,145	3,183	3,227	3,260	3,290	3,305	3,336	3,292	3,312	3,405	..	POPULATION (thousands)

USE AND ORIGIN OF RESOURCES

(Millions of current New Zealand Dollars)

1981	1982	1983	1984	1985	1986	1987	1988	1989	1990 estimate	Notes	NEW ZEALAND
27,131	30,237	33,108	36,762	42,099	51,111	56,497	61,275	65,853	67,470	C f	Gross National Product (GNP)
-615	-859	-1,276	-2,002	-2,518	-2,768	-3,281	-3,484	-3,932	-4,210	..	Net Factor Income from Abroad
27,746	31,096	34,384	38,764	44,617	53,879	59,778	64,759	69,785	71,680	..	GDP at Market Prices
-919	-1,085	-634	-1,633	-1,642	-318	399	1,558	-1,173	-1,160	..	Resource Balance
8,249	9,265	10,506	13,364	14,028	15,271	16,669	18,176	19,192	20,380	..	Exports of Goods & NFServices
9,168	10,350	11,140	14,997	15,670	15,589	16,270	16,618	20,365	21,540	..	Imports of Goods & NFServices
28,665	32,181	35,018	40,397	46,259	54,197	59,379	63,201	70,958	72,840	..	Domestic Absorption
16,790	18,565	20,162	22,994	26,901	32,247	35,983	39,248	42,948	45,030	..	Private Consumption, etc.
4,988	5,555	5,858	6,334	7,338	8,923	10,122	11,026	11,421	11,860	..	General Gov't Consumption
6,887	8,061	8,998	11,069	12,020	13,027	13,274	12,927	16,589	15,950	..	Gross Domestic Investment
6,597	7,744	8,447	9,721	11,527	12,033	13,303	12,748	14,684	15,230	..	Fixed Investment
2,336	2,685	3,192	3,913	4,490	6,373	8,541	8,921	10,665	11,250	..	Indirect Taxes, net
25,410	28,411	31,192	34,851	40,127	47,506	51,237	55,838	59,120	60,430	B	GDP at factor cost
2,661	2,561	2,969	3,669	3,936	4,360	4,990	5,572	..	..	..	Agriculture
9,033	10,185	10,962	12,645	14,187	16,177	16,562	17,382	..	..	..	Industry
6,517	7,236	7,841	9,126	9,914	11,377	11,480	11,974	..	..	..	Manufacturing
16,052	18,350	20,453	22,450	26,494	33,342	38,226	41,805	..	..	..	Services, etc.
5,968	6,976	8,364	9,436	10,378	12,709	13,673	14,485	15,416	14,790	..	Gross Domestic Saving
5,429	6,330	7,337	7,781	8,151	10,304	10,764	11,473	12,321	11,693	..	Gross National Saving

(Millions of 1987 New Zealand Dollars)

1981	1982	1983	1984	1985	1986	1987	1988	1989	1990 estimate	Notes	NEW ZEALAND
51,719	51,701	52,596	54,642	54,928	56,072	56,497	55,938	56,557	57,008	C f	Gross National Product
52,762	53,038	54,491	57,408	58,012	58,996	59,778	59,153	60,048	60,648	I	GDP at Market Prices
858	844	1,544	972	936	1,263	399	748	-2,218	-1,465	..	Resource Balance
13,058	13,260	13,905	14,982	15,156	15,842	16,669	17,048	16,530	17,921	..	Exports of Goods & NFServices
12,200	12,416	12,362	14,010	14,220	14,579	16,270	16,300	18,748	19,387	..	Imports of Goods & NFServices
51,904	52,194	52,947	56,436	57,075	57,733	59,379	58,404	62,266	62,113	..	Domestic Absorption
31,602	31,204	31,062	32,856	33,924	34,520	35,983	35,285	35,913	35,794	..	Private Consumption, etc.
9,256	9,291	9,500	9,714	9,843	10,040	10,122	10,217	10,247	10,256	..	General Gov't Consumption
11,046	11,699	12,386	13,866	13,309	13,172	13,274	12,902	16,106	16,063	..	Gross Domestic Investment
10,237	10,906	11,483	12,119	12,864	12,302	13,303	12,976	14,524	14,672	..	Fixed Investment
48,627	48,775	49,747	52,002	52,518	52,265	51,237	50,920	50,578	50,929	B	GDP at factor cost
3,479	3,626	3,483	3,464	4,156	4,282	4,990	4,851	4,779	..	..	Agriculture
14,874	15,158	15,691	17,113	16,955	17,214	16,562	16,026	16,248	..	..	Industry
10,699	10,777	11,075	12,249	11,714	11,982	11,480	11,148	11,346	..	..	Manufacturing
34,409	34,253	35,316	36,832	36,901	37,500	38,226	38,275	39,021	..	..	Services, etc.

Memo Items:

1981	1982	1983	1984	1985	1986	1987	1988	1989	1990 estimate	Notes	NEW ZEALAND
10,977	11,114	11,658	12,484	12,730	14,281	16,669	17,828	17,668	18,342	..	Capacity to Import
-2,081	-2,146	-2,247	-2,497	-2,426	-1,561	0	780	1,138	421	..	Terms of Trade Adjustment
50,681	50,892	52,244	54,911	55,585	57,435	59,778	59,933	61,187	61,069	..	Gross Domestic Income
49,638	49,555	50,349	52,145	52,502	54,512	56,497	56,718	57,695	57,429	..	Gross National Income

DOMESTIC PRICES/DEFLATORS

(Index 1987 = 100)

1981	1982	1983	1984	1985	1986	1987	1988	1989	1990 estimate	Notes	NEW ZEALAND
52.6	58.6	63.1	67.5	76.9	91.3	100.0	109.5	116.2	118.2	..	Overall (GDP)
55.2	61.7	66.1	71.6	81.0	93.9	100.0	108.2	114.0	117.3	..	Domestic Absorption
76.5	70.6	85.2	105.9	94.7	101.8	100.0	114.9	..	..	..	Agriculture
60.7	67.2	69.9	73.9	83.7	94.0	100.0	108.5	..	..	..	Industry
60.9	67.1	70.8	74.5	84.6	95.0	100.0	107.4	..	..	..	Manufacturing
49.9	58.0	62.3	66.1	76.3	86.4	100.0	106.4	112.5	119.3	..	Consumer Price Index

MANUFACTURING ACTIVITY

1981	1982	1983	1984	1985	1986	1987	1988	1989	1990 estimate	Notes	NEW ZEALAND
109.9	111.3	112.7	112.8	109.2	108.0	100.0	91.0	82.0	..	G	Employment (1987=100)
..	..	..	..	..	..	..	..	..	..	G	Real Earnings per Empl. (1987=100)
..	..	..	..	..	..	..	..	..	..	G	Real Output per Empl. (1987=100)
64.5	65.5	62.1	56.4	59.1	57.5	..	..	..	..	..	Earnings as % of Value Added

MONETARY HOLDINGS

(Millions of current New Zealand Dollars)

1981	1982	1983	1984	1985	1986	1987	1988	1989	1990 estimate	Notes	NEW ZEALAND
14,456	16,254	18,147	21,478	26,601	31,019					..	Money Supply, Broadly Defined
2,926	3,030	3,426	3,761	4,104	4,668	6,667	14,668	21,407	23,694	..	Money
683	714	739	867	940	1,006	1,059	1,124	1,177	1,032	..	Currency Outside Banks
2,243	2,316	2,687	2,894	3,164	3,661	5,608	13,545	20,231	22,662	..	Demand Deposits
11,530	13,224	14,721	17,717	22,497	26,351					..	Quasi-Money

(Millions of current New Zealand Dollars)

1981	1982	1983	1984	1985	1986	1987	1988	1989	1990 estimate	Notes	NEW ZEALAND
-2,111	-2,389	-3,209	-3,234	-2,082	-1,990	642	1,354	..	2,894	C F	GOVERNMENT DEFICIT (-) OR SURPLUS
9,747	11,204	11,711	13,687	16,891	20,682	26,582	26,983	..	30,750	..	Current Revenue
10,432	12,171	13,313	15,239	17,195	21,443	26,505	27,170	..	31,132	..	Current Expenditure
-685	-967	-1,602	-1,552	-304	-761	77	-187	..	-382	..	Current Budget Balance
6	3	13	18	42	161	86	177	..	116	..	Capital Receipts
1,432	1,425	1,620	1,700	1,820	1,390	-479	-1,364	..	-3,160	..	Capital Payments

NEW ZEALAND	1970	1971	1972	1973	1974	1975	1976	1977	1978	1979	1980
FOREIGN TRADE (CUSTOMS BASIS)					*(Millions of current US dollars)*						
Value of Exports, fob	1,202.6	1,330.7	1,796.0	2,559.4	2,366.6	2,080.8	2,665.3	3,083.2	3,786.5	4,548.0	5,262.4
Nonfuel Primary Products	1,064.5	1,182.1	1,583.0	2,300.9	2,069.7	1,767.6	2,224.4	2,524.6	3,068.3	3,618.1	4,141.1
Fuels	5.8	10.0	15.8	10.5	13.0	26.9	33.6	38.6	40.7	58.6	59.5
Manufactures	132.3	138.5	197.2	248.0	283.8	286.3	407.4	519.9	677.5	871.3	1,061.8
Value of Imports, cif	1,237.6	1,370.8	1,524.3	2,186.4	3,665.7	3,182.7	3,295.1	3,280.2	3,660.0	4,561.7	5,514.7
Nonfuel Primary Products	210.3	206.1	219.4	331.6	505.3	427.9	414.2	426.0	497.6	561.3	644.4
Fuels	83.2	102.0	112.7	157.4	429.6	455.2	481.7	503.0	513.7	727.0	1,238.6
Manufactures	944.1	1,062.7	1,192.2	1,697.4	2,730.8	2,299.6	2,399.2	2,351.2	2,648.8	3,273.3	3,631.7
					(Index 1987 = 100)						
Terms of Trade	128.9	125.1	145.5	158.7	97.5	88.2	96.8	91.8	99.4	105.5	91.6
Export Prices, fob	31.9	33.7	43.3	60.2	56.5	53.3	59.4	61.5	73.7	93.5	96.7
Import Prices, cif	24.7	27.0	29.7	37.9	58.0	60.5	61.4	67.0	74.2	88.6	105.5
BALANCE OF PAYMENTS					*(Millions of current US dollars)*						
Exports of Goods & Services	1,471	1,782	2,358	3,124	3,051	3,282	3,810	4,132	4,988	6,156	6,503
Merchandise, fob	1,235	1,479	1,955	2,511	2,277	2,449	3,009	3,225	4,020	4,988	5,394
Nonfactor Services	188	251	327	491	653	729	698	787	852	1,036	950
Factor Services	48	52	75	122	122	105	103	119	116	132	159
Imports of Goods & Services	1,688	1,810	2,230	3,293	4,894	4,504	4,614	4,814	5,457	7,024	7,487
Merchandise, fob	1,167	1,213	1,457	2,148	3,595	3,095	3,129	3,116	3,418	4,698	5,091
Nonfactor Services	389	460	549	837	1,060	1,008	962	1,144	1,339	1,677	1,700
Factor Services	132	137	225	307	239	401	523	554	701	649	697
Long-Term Interest	..	..	..	..	..	..	..	..	..	..	..
Private Current Transfers, net	-5	16	54	76	49	60	34	47	27	72	108
Workers' Remittances	40	56	66	79	85	95	91	112	122	159	201
Curr. A/C Bal before Off. Transf.	-222	-12	182	-92	-1,793	-1,162	-770	-636	-442	-796	-876
Net Official Transfers	-10	-8	-18	-29	-49	-58	-48	-53	-47	-47	-50
Curr. A/C Bal after Off. Transf.	-232	-20	164	-121	-1,842	-1,220	-818	-689	-488	-843	-926
Long-Term Capital, net	220	202	158	204	1,135	1,054	627	701	577	757	685
Direct Investment	137	98	123	189	231	117	242	122	218	276	71
Long-Term Loans	..	..	..	..	..	..	..	..	..	..	..
Disbursements	..	..	..	..	..	..	..	..	..	..	..
Repayments	..	..	..	..	..	..	..	..	..	..	..
Other Long-Term Capital	83	103	35	15	904	937	385	578	359	481	614
Other Capital, net	30	7	167	-53	214	12	5	192	-289	-41	105
Change in Reserves	-18	-189	-488	-30	493	154	186	-203	201	127	135
Memo Item:					*(New Zealand Dollars per US dollar)*						
Conversion Factor (Annual Avg)	0.890	0.880	0.840	0.740	0.720	0.830	1.000	1.030	0.960	0.980	1.030
EXTERNAL DEBT (Total)				*(Millions US dollars), outstanding at end of year*							
Long-Term Debt (by debtor)	..	..	..	..	..	..	..	..	..	..	..
Central Bank, incl. IMF credit	..	..	..	..	..	..	..	..	..	..	..
Central Government	..	..	..	..	..	..	..	..	..	..	..
Rest of General Government	..	..	..	..	..	..	..	..	..	..	..
Non-financial Public Enterprises	..	..	..	..	..	..	..	..	..	..	..
Priv. Sector, incl non-guaranteed	..	..	..	..	..	..	..	..	..	..	..
Short-Term Debt	..	..	..	..	..	..	..	..	..	..	..
Memo Items:					*(Millions of US dollars)*						
Int'l Reserves Excluding Gold	256.9	492.0	832.2	1,045.1	638.6	426.9	490.8	442.5	451.0	450.7	352.1
Gold Holdings (at market price)	0.8	1.0	1.5	2.5	4.2	3.2	3.0	7.3	14.8	23.2	13.2
SOCIAL INDICATORS											
Total Fertility Rate	3.2	3.2	2.9	2.7	2.6	2.3	2.3	2.2	2.1	2.2	2.1
Infant Mortality Rate	16.7	16.5	15.6	16.2	15.5	15.9	14.0	14.2	13.7	12.4	12.8
Life Expectancy at Birth	71.5	71.6	71.7	71.8	72.0	72.1	72.3	72.4	72.7	72.9	73.2
Urban Population, % of total	81.1	81.4	81.8	82.1	82.5	82.8	82.9	83.0	83.1	83.2	83.3
Food Prod. per capita (1987=100)	88.8	88.0	91.7	90.8	81.5	87.0	96.5	92.4	90.8	90.5	93.2
Labor Force, Agriculture (%)	0.0	0.0	0.0	0.0	0.0	0.0	0.0	0.0	0.0	0.0	0.0
Labor Force, Female (%)	..	..	..	..	..	..	..	..	..	..	..
Primary Schl. Enroll. Ratio	110.0	..	..	..	..	106.0	108.0	108.0	108.0	107.0	111.0
Primary Schl. Enroll. Ratio, Female	109.0	..	..	..	..	106.0	107.0	108.0	108.0	106.0	111.0
Secondary Schl. Enroll. Ratio	77.0	..	..	..	..	81.0	82.0	81.0	80.0	81.0	83.0

1981	1982	1983	1984	1985	1986	1987	1988	1989	1990 estimate	Notes	NEW ZEALAND
											FOREIGN TRADE (CUSTOMS BASIS)
				(Millions of current US dollars)							Value of Exports, fob
5,330.4	5,222.9	5,192.3	5,346.5	5,569.7	5,700.3	6,954.8	8,525.3	8,586.1	9,045.4	..	Value of Exports, fob
4,169.1	4,137.9	4,098.8	4,002.7	4,144.6	4,288.5	5,328.3	6,470.6	6,333.9	6,433.8	..	Nonfuel Primary Products
65.2	14.1	14.0	22.2	92.0	47.8	64.0	118.4	178.8	356.5	..	Fuels
1,096.0	1,070.9	1,079.6	1,321.6	1,333.1	1,364.1	1,562.5	1,936.3	2,073.5	2,255.1	..	Manufactures
5,731.5	5,900.5	5,326.9	6,180.5	5,981.7	6,131.4	7,254.5	7,304.2	8,756.6	9,466.0	..	Value of Imports, cif
620.2	697.8	604.8	699.8	654.1	612.3	762.1	888.8	1,018.2	1,011.7	..	Nonfuel Primary Products
1,112.9	978.6	964.4	829.7	759.8	530.0	484.0	398.4	530.8	730.5	..	Fuels
3,998.5	4,224.0	3,757.7	4,651.0	4,567.9	4,989.1	6,008.4	6,017.1	7,207.6	7,723.8	..	Manufactures
				(Index 1987=100)							
89.2	90.7	92.0	90.6	88.5	89.0	100.0	100.9	99.7	98.6	..	Terms of Trade
92.1	87.8	86.3	82.9	79.5	83.4	100.0	111.0	119.5	118.7	..	Export Prices, fob
103.3	96.8	93.7	91.5	89.9	93.7	100.0	110.0	119.9	120.4	..	Import Prices, cif
											BALANCE OF PAYMENTS
				(Millions of current US dollars)							
7,068	6,874	6,932	7,122	7,365	7,989	10,265	11,961	12,085	12,335	..	Exports of Goods & Services
5,603	5,304	5,282	5,434	5,595	5,836	7,245	8,817	8,853	9,283	..	Merchandise, fob
1,249	1,262	1,395	1,469	1,493	1,775	2,236	2,550	2,412	2,496	..	Nonfactor Services
216	308	255	219	277	378	783	595	819	557	..	Factor Services
8,207	8,648	8,028	9,079	9,192	9,907	12,077	12,736	13,808	14,555	..	Imports of Goods & Services
5,346	5,524	4,937	5,846	5,654	5,741	6,719	6,675	7,873	8,452	..	Merchandise, fob
2,001	2,014	1,907	1,951	1,969	2,335	2,856	3,430	3,421	3,626	..	Nonfactor Services
860	1,110	1,184	1,283	1,570	1,831	2,501	2,632	2,515	2,477	..	Factor Services
..	..	..	..	..	..	..	..	..	..	..	Long-Term Interest
66	160	166	197	144	190	220	309	501	664	..	Private Current Transfers, net
197	215	230	291	322	353	430	501	514	576	..	Workers' Remittances
-1,073	-1,615	-930	-1,761	-1,683	-1,728	-1,592	-466	-1,223	-1,555	..	Curr. A/C Bal before Off. Transf.
-43	-61	-86	-73	-60	-39	-40	-43	-29	-39	..	Net Official Transfers
-1,116	-1,676	-1,016	-1,834	-1,743	-1,767	-1,632	-509	-1,252	-1,594	..	Curr. A/C Bal after Off. Transf.
1,863	2,563	1,297	2,131	1,336	2,536	-1,316	457	350	209	..	Long-Term Capital, net
171	258	108	110	319	-100	-298	178	-147	69	..	Direct Investment
..	..	..	..	..	..	..	..	..	..	..	Long-Term Loans
..	..	..	..	..	..	..	..	..	..	..	Disbursements
..	..	..	..	..	..	..	..	..	..	..	Repayments
1,692	2,305	1,189	2,021	1,017	2,636	-1,017	280	496	140	..	Other Long-Term Capital
-288	-874	-82	1,181	833	1,197	645	120	1,293	2,737	..	Other Capital, net
-460	-13	-199	-1,477	-426	-1,966	2,303	-69	-391	-1,352	..	Change in Reserves
											Memo Item:
				(New Zealand Dollars per US dollar)							
1.150	1.330	1.500	1.760	2.020	1.910	1.690	1.530	1.670	1.680	..	Conversion Factor (Annual Avg)
				(Millions US dollars), outstanding at end of year							
..	..	..	..	..	..	..	..	..	..		**EXTERNAL DEBT (Total)**
..	..	..	..	..	..	..	..	..	..		Long-Term Debt (by debtor)
..	..	..	..	..	..	..	..	..	..		Central Bank, incl. IMF credit
..	..	..	..	..	..	..	..	..	..		Central Government
..	..	..	..	..	..	..	..	..	..		Rest of General Government
..	..	..	..	..	..	..	..	..	..		Non-financial Public Enterprises
..	..	..	..	..	..	..	..	..	..		Priv. Sector, incl non-guaranteed
..	..	..	..	..	..	..	..	..	..		Short-Term Debt
											Memo Items:
				(Millions of US dollars)							
673.9	635.9	777.6	1,786.7	1,595.7	3,771.2	3,259.6	2,836.0	3,026.8	4,128.8	..	Int'l Reserves Excluding Gold
8.9	10.2	8.5	6.9	7.3	8.7	10.8	9.2	0.6	0.6		Gold Holdings (at market price)
											SOCIAL INDICATORS
2.0	1.9	1.9	1.9	..	..	2.0	2.0	2.0	2.0	..	Total Fertility Rate
11.6	11.8	12.5	11.7	10.8	11.2	11.0	10.6	10.2	10.0	..	Infant Mortality Rate
73.5	73.7	73.9	74.1	74.4	74.6	74.8	75.0	75.2	75.4	..	Life Expectancy at Birth
83.4	83.5	83.5	83.6	83.7	83.8	83.9	84.0	84.1	84.2	..	Urban Population, % of total
96.2	96.4	98.2	97.3	104.6	100.7	100.0	100.0	96.4	90.4	..	Food Prod. per capita (1987=100)
..	..	..	..	..	..	..	..	..	..	..	Labor Force, Agriculture (%)
..	..	..	..	..	..	..	..	..	..	..	Labor Force, Female (%)
..	107.0	106.0	107.0	107.0	106.0	107.0	106.0	106.0	..	..	Primary Schl. Enroll. Ratio
..	106.0	105.0	106.0	106.0	106.0	106.0	106.0	105.0	..	..	Primary Schl. Enroll. Ratio, Female
..	82.0	85.0	86.0	85.0	85.0	85.0	87.0	88.0	..	..	Secondary Schl. Enroll. Ratio

NICARAGUA	1970	1971	1972	1973	1974	1975	1976	1977	1978	1979	1980
CURRENT GNP PER CAPITA (US $)	380	390	390	430	560	630	700	780	740	560	650
POPULATION (thousands)	2,053	2,121	2,192	2,265	2,337	2,408	2,478	2,546	2,615	2,689	2,771

USE AND ORIGIN OF RESOURCES *(Millions of current Nicaraguan New Cordobas)*

	1970	1971	1972	1973	1974	1975	1976	1977	1978	1979	1980
Gross National Product (GNP)	5.3	5.6	5.8	7.2	10.2	10.5	12.1	14.2	13.6	13.8	19.4
Net Factor Income from Abroad	-0.2	-0.2	-0.2	-0.3	-0.5	-0.4	-0.5	-0.5	-0.7	-0.7	-1.3
GDP at Market Prices	5.5	5.8	6.1	7.6	10.6	11.0	12.6	14.7	14.3	14.5	20.8
Resource Balance	-0.1	-0.1	0.3	-0.7	-1.4	-1.0	0.1	-0.8	0.5	2.0	-4.0
Exports of Goods & NFServices	1.5	1.5	2.2	2.2	3.1	3.1	4.3	5.0	5.2	6.1	5.0
Imports of Goods & NFServices	1.6	1.7	1.8	2.9	4.5	4.1	4.1	5.9	4.7	4.1	9.0
Domestic Absorption	5.6	5.9	5.7	8.3	12.1	11.9	12.4	15.6	13.8	12.5	24.8
Private Consumption, etc.	4.1	4.3	4.3	5.9	7.9	8.6	8.9	10.2	10.1	10.7	17.2
General Gov't Consumption	0.5	0.6	0.6	0.6	0.8	1.0	1.2	1.4	1.8	2.6	4.1
Gross Domestic Investment	1.0	1.0	0.8	1.8	3.4	2.3	2.4	3.9	1.9	-0.8	3.5
Fixed Investment	0.9	0.9	0.9	1.5	2.5	2.5	2.6	3.6	2.1	1.0	3.0
Indirect Taxes, net	0.4	0.5	0.5	0.8	1.1	1.0	1.2	1.5	1.3	1.3	1.4
GDP at factor cost	5.1	5.3	5.5	6.8	9.6	9.9	11.4	13.3	12.9	13.2	19.4
Agriculture	1.4	1.4	1.5	1.9	2.9	2.5	2.9	3.6	3.7	4.1	4.8
Industry	1.4	1.5	1.7	2.0	2.9	3.3	3.7	4.2	4.2	4.2	6.5
Manufacturing	1.1	1.2	1.3	1.6	2.2	2.5	2.7	3.1	3.3	3.6	5.3
Services, etc.	2.7	2.8	2.9	3.7	4.8	5.2	6.0	7.0	6.4	6.3	9.4
Gross Domestic Saving	0.9	0.9	1.1	1.1	1.9	1.3	2.5	3.1	2.4	1.2	-0.5
Gross National Saving	..	..	..	..	..	..	..	..	..	..	..

(Millions of 1987 Nicaraguan New Cordobas)

	1970	1971	1972	1973	1974	1975	1976	1977	1978	1979	1980
Gross National Product	2,532	2,608	2,648	2,770	3,221	3,273	3,412	3,702	3,360	2,425	2,548
GDP at Market Prices	2,615	2,701	2,756	2,936	3,352	3,347	3,509	3,818	3,517	2,586	2,705
Resource Balance	189	208	338	220	158	320	340	198	372	542	-27
Exports of Goods & NFServices	448	464	609	602	612	657	683	664	724	828	492
Imports of Goods & NFServices	259	257	270	382	454	337	343	466	352	286	519
Domestic Absorption	2,426	2,493	2,417	2,715	3,195	3,027	3,169	3,620	3,145	2,043	2,732
Private Consumption, etc.	1,986	2,040	2,057	2,140	2,425	2,482	2,596	2,784	2,624	1,884	2,043
General Gov't Consumption	128	131	144	134	149	177	196	212	257	275	370
Gross Domestic Investment	312	323	216	442	621	368	376	624	264	-115	319
Fixed Investment	263	272	250	333	417	393	412	546	303	106	268
GDP at factor cost	2,416	2,479	2,526	2,654	3,031	3,044	3,198	3,447	3,202	2,355	2,538
Agriculture	823	854	854	931	1,026	1,044	1,062	1,121	1,199	1,015	822
Industry	538	557	588	614	725	719	757	862	765	506	592
Manufacturing	380	398	416	437	493	505	526	579	580	421	483
Services, etc.	1,254	1,290	1,314	1,391	1,601	1,584	1,690	1,835	1,553	1,065	1,292
Memo Items:											
Capacity to Import	237	237	322	285	310	256	356	400	388	427	291
Terms of Trade Adjustment	-211	-228	-287	-317	-302	-401	-327	-264	-336	-401	-201
Gross Domestic Income	2,404	2,473	2,469	2,618	3,051	2,946	3,181	3,554	3,181	2,184	2,504
Gross National Income	2,321	2,380	2,361	2,452	2,920	2,871	3,084	3,438	3,024	2,024	2,347

DOMESTIC PRICES/DEFLATORS *(Index 1987 = 100)*

	1970	1971	1972	1973	1974	1975	1976	1977	1978	1979	1980
Overall (GDP)	0.2	0.2	0.2	0.3	0.3	0.3	0.4	0.4	0.4	0.6	0.8
Domestic Absorption	0.2	0.2	0.2	0.3	0.4	0.4	0.4	0.4	0.4	0.6	0.9
Agriculture	0.2	0.2	0.2	0.2	0.3	0.2	0.3	0.3	0.3	0.4	0.6
Industry	0.3	0.3	0.3	0.3	0.4	0.5	0.5	0.5	0.5	0.8	1.1
Manufacturing	0.3	0.3	0.3	0.4	0.4	0.5	0.5	0.5	0.6	0.8	1.1
Consumer Price Index	..	..	0.0	0.0	0.1	0.1	0.1	0.1	0.1	0.1	0.1

MANUFACTURING ACTIVITY

	1970	1971	1972	1973	1974	1975	1976	1977	1978	1979	1980
Employment (1987=100)	..	..	..	..	..	..	..	..	..	..	..
Real Earnings per Empl. (1987=100)	..	..	..	..	..	..	..	..	..	..	..
Real Output per Empl. (1987=100)	..	..	..	..	..	..	..	..	..	..	..
Earnings as % of Value Added	15.7	15.3	18.4	15.8	15.7	15.5	16.2	16.7	15.9	21.8	29.1

MONETARY HOLDINGS *(Thousands of current Nicaraguan New Cordobas)*

	1970	1971	1972	1973	1974	1975	1976	1977	1978	1979	1980
Money Supply, Broadly Defined	829	949	1,226	1,734	2,016	2,030	2,699	2,855	2,652	3,427	5,747
Money	578	619	749	1,146	1,313	1,256	1,616	1,699	1,579	2,654	4,102
Currency Outside Banks	251	252	329	411	452	445	636	692	883	1,572	1,964
Demand Deposits	327	367	420	735	862	811	980	1,007	697	1,083	2,139
Quasi-Money	251	330	477	588	703	774	1,084	1,156	1,073	773	1,644

GOVERNMENT DEFICIT (-) OR SURPLUS *(Millions of current Nicaraguan New Cordobas)*

	1970	1971	1972	1973	1974	1975	1976	1977	1978	1979	1980
GOVERNMENT DEFICIT (-) OR SURPLUS	-0.05	-0.14	-0.23	-0.13	-0.62	-0.62	-0.49	-0.99	-0.84	-0.94	-1.42
Current Revenue	0.65	0.72	0.74	1.04	1.46	1.48	1.72	2.05	1.88	2.14	4.97
Current Expenditure	0.54	0.57	0.62	0.67	1.09	1.24	1.36	1.77	2.22	2.80	5.15
Current Budget Balance	0.11	0.15	0.13	0.37	0.37	0.24	0.37	0.28	-0.35	-0.66	-0.18
Capital Receipts	0.02	0.02	0.01	0.02	0.02	0.05	0.04	0.01	0.02	..	0.00
Capital Payments	0.18	0.30	0.38	0.52	1.01	0.91	0.90	1.29	0.51	0.28	1.24

1981	1982	1983	1984	1985	1986	1987	1988	1989	1990 estimate	Notes	NICARAGUA
760	800	810	790	760	760	810	..	..	..	A	**CURRENT GNP PER CAPITA (US $)**
2,860	2,956	3,058	3,164	3,272	3,383	3,497	3,614	3,732	3,853	..	**POPULATION (thousands)**
			(Millions of current Nicaraguan New Cordobas)								**USE AND ORIGIN OF RESOURCES**
23.1	26.6	31.1	41.0	104.5	393.2	2,503.7	..	..	..	..	Gross National Product (GNP)
-1.4	-1.8	-1.8	-4.0	-11.0	-42.6	-192.1					Net Factor Income from Abroad
24.5	28.3	32.9	45.0	115.4	435.7	2,695.9	312,000.0	1.52E+7	1.15E+9	..	GDP at Market Prices
-4.8	-2.9	-3.5	-5.9	-8.1	-35.1	-53.6	-134,000.0	-5.02E+6	-2.61E+8	..	Resource Balance
5.5	4.5	6.4	7.4	17.0	55.7	317.3	59,000.0	5.04E+6	2.67E+8	..	Exports of Goods & NF Services
10.2	7.4	9.9	13.3	25.2	90.8	371.0	193,000.0	1.01E+7	5.29E+8	..	Imports of Goods & NF Services
29.2	31.2	36.4	50.9	123.6	470.8	2,749.5	446,000.0	2.02E+7	1.41E+9	..	Domestic Absorption
18.1	19.2	18.7	25.0	55.6	243.2	1,400.7	262,000.0	1.21E+7	8.41E+8	..	Private Consumption, etc.
5.4	6.6	10.4	15.9	41.2	154.0	922.9	103,000.0	4.09E+6	3.38E+8	..	General Gov't Consumption
5.8	5.3	7.4	10.0	26.7	73.6	425.9	81,000.0	4.01E+6	2.34E+8	..	Gross Domestic Investment
5.2	4.7	6.4	8.7	23.9	60.3	355.4	85,000.0	4.20E+6	2.35E+8	..	Fixed Investment
3.4	4.5	6.6	10.6	24.5	89.3	504.4	..	..	..	..	Indirect Taxes, net
21.1	23.9	26.3	34.4	90.9	346.4	2,191.5	..	..	..	B	GDP at factor cost
5.0	6.1	7.6	11.2	27.3	90.6	778.4	88,852.9	4.48E+6	3.48E+8	..	Agriculture
8.1	9.1	10.1	14.3	40.4	146.2	623.2	66,843.0	3.03E+6	2.30E+8	..	Industry
6.5	7.4	8.0	11.4	31.9	120.7	505.0	54,000.0	2.41E+6	1.83E+8	..	Manufacturing
11.5	13.2	15.2	19.5	47.7	199.0	1,294.3	156,304.0	7.66E+6	5.73E+8	..	Services, etc.
1.0	2.5	3.9	4.2	18.6	38.5	372.3	-53,000.0	-1.01E+6	-2.73E+7	..	Gross Domestic Saving
..	..	..	..	..	..	..	..	..		..	Gross National Saving
			(Millions of 1987 Nicaraguan New Cordobas)								Gross National Product
2,714	2,679	2,819	2,673	2,524	2,469	2,504	1,888	1,916	..	..	
2,850	2,827	2,957	2,896	2,773	2,717	2,696	2,393	2,288	2,302	I	GDP at Market Prices
69	158	134	25	-29	-38	-54	-58	-80	-102	..	Resource Balance
565	520	557	441	389	321	317	306	352	399	..	Exports of Goods & NF Services
496	362	422	416	418	358	371	364	432	501	..	Imports of Goods & NF Services
2,781	2,669	2,823	2,871	2,802	2,755	2,749	2,451	2,368	2,404	..	Domestic Absorption
1,874	1,776	1,713	1,640	1,519	1,443	1,401	1,586	1,685	1,732	..	Private Consumption, etc.
420	491	673	790	845	879	923	564	424	439	..	General Gov't Consumption
487	402	437	441	438	433	426	301	259	233	..	Gross Domestic Investment
429	346	363	371	375	352	355	313	270	227	..	Fixed Investment
2,467	2,391	2,375	2,220	2,180	2,160	2,191	..	..	..	B	GDP at factor cost
900	925	979	926	882	804	778	699	716	730	..	Agriculture
609	591	625	631	612	634	623	431	393	377	..	Industry
497	498	526	528	503	513	505	360	330	319	..	Manufacturing
1,342	1,311	1,354	1,339	1,278	1,279	1,294	1,262	1,179	1,195	..	Services, etc.
											Memo Items:
265	222	273	232	283	220	317	111	217	254	..	Capacity to Import
-300	-298	-283	-208	-106	-101	0	-195	-136	-146	..	Terms of Trade Adjustment
2,551	2,529	2,674	2,687	2,667	2,616	2,696	2,198	2,152	2,157	..	Gross Domestic Income
2,414	2,381	2,536	2,465	2,418	2,369	2,504	1,694	1,780	..	..	Gross National Income
			(Index 1987 = 100)								**DOMESTIC PRICES/DEFLATORS**
0.9	1.0	1.1	1.6	4.2	16.0	100.0	13040.0	662,880	5.00E+7	..	Overall (GDP)
1.1	1.2	1.3	1.8	4.4	17.1	100.0	18198.3	852,373	5.88E+7	..	Domestic Absorption
0.6	0.7	0.8	1.2	3.1	11.3	100.0	12707.6	625,382	4.77E+7	..	Agriculture
1.3	1.5	1.6	2.3	6.6	23.1	100.0	15493.1	770,752	6.10E+7	..	Industry
1.3	1.5	1.5	2.2	6.3	23.5	100.0	15015.9	731,682	5.73E+7	..	Manufacturing
0.2	0.2	0.3	0.4	1.3	9.9	100.0	10305.0			..	Consumer Price Index
											MANUFACTURING ACTIVITY
..	..	..	..	..	..	..	..	..	..	..	Employment (1987=100)
..	..	..	..	..	..	..	..	..	..	..	Real Earnings per Empl. (1987=100)
..	..	..	..	..	..	..	..	..	..	..	Real Output per Empl. (1987=100)
30.6	22.9	18.8	19.7	16.5	..	..	..	..	..	J	Earnings as % of Value Added
			(Thousands of current Nicaraguan New Cordobas)								**MONETARY HOLDINGS**
7,927	9,895	17,240	30,660	74,410	..	..	..	..	..	..	Money Supply, Broadly Defined
5,206	6,546	10,943	20,841	54,771	192,931	1,421,850	..	..	..	..	Money
2,376	3,086	5,426	11,338	28,560	99,100	730,275	..	..	..	..	Currency Outside Banks
2,831	3,460	5,517	9,504	26,211	93,831	691,575	..	..	..	..	Demand Deposits
2,720	3,349	6,297	9,819	19,639	..	..	..	..	..	..	Quasi-Money
			(Millions of current Nicaraguan New Cordobas)								**GOVERNMENT DEFICIT (-) OR SURPLUS**
-2.63	-5.74	-10.30	-10.61	-25.32	-64.18	..	-78,453	-304,000	-1.81E+8	..	Current Revenue
6.93	8.16	11.89	18.08	43.22	163.09	..	76,673	4,563,000	2.21E+8	..	Current Expenditure
7.55	10.83	13.93	21.56	60.79	209.45	..	133,232	4,388,000	3.84E+8	..	Current Budget Balance
-0.62	-2.67	-2.04	-3.48	-17.57	-46.36	..	-56,559	175,000	-1.63E+8	..	Capital Receipts
0.09	0.09	0.08	0.08	0.21	0.77	..		8,000	4.00E+3	..	Capital Payments
2.09	3.16	8.34	7.21	7.96	18.59	..	21,894	487,000	1.80E+7	..	

NICARAGUA	1970	1971	1972	1973	1974	1975	1976	1977	1978	1979	1980
FOREIGN TRADE (CUSTOMS BASIS)					*(Millions of current US dollars)*						
Value of Exports, fob	175	183	246	275	377	371	539	633	646	567	414
Nonfuel Primary Products	146	155	210	230	305	307	449	527	535	497	347
Fuels	0	0	2	1	2	1	2	1	1	5	10
Manufactures	28	28	34	44	71	63	87	105	110	64	57
Value of Imports, cif	198	210	218	326	559	517	532	762	596	360	882
Nonfuel Primary Products	25	26	30	47	58	52	58	73	72	56	149
Fuels	12	16	16	24	61	74	69	105	91	77	176
Manufactures	161	168	172	255	440	391	405	584	434	228	557
					(Index 1987 = 100)						
Terms of Trade	181.7	171.1	167.3	187.8	147.3	123.2	165.3	177.4	149.3	146.0	129.9
Export Prices, fob	43.3	43.4	47.1	67.6	79.7	69.4	95.8	111.2	103.0	118.3	127.1
Import Prices, cif	23.8	25.4	28.1	36.0	54.1	56.3	57.9	62.7	69.0	81.0	97.8
BALANCE OF PAYMENTS					*(Millions of current US dollars)*						
Exports of Goods & Services	218	224	291	323	448	458	630	733	732	683	514
Merchandise, fob	179	187	249	278	381	375	542	636	646	616	450
Nonfactor Services	35	33	37	37	56	72	74	83	74	56	44
Factor Services	5	4	5	7	11	11	14	14	12	11	19
Imports of Goods & Services	263	274	297	446	720	660	678	926	774	595	1,049
Merchandise, fob	179	190	206	328	542	482	485	704	553	389	803
Nonfactor Services	50	48	50	63	105	106	107	137	112	122	103
Factor Services	35	36	42	56	74	71	86	85	109	84	144
Long-Term Interest	7	8	11	18	29	36	41	52	51	37	42
Private Current Transfers, net	3	3	3	28	3	4	1	1	0	1	2
Workers' Remittances	..	..	..	..	..	..	..	..	..	..	..
Curr. A/C Bal before Off. Transf.	-43	-47	17	-96	-269	-198	-48	-192	-34	90	-534
Net Official Transfers	4	2	5	30	12	13	8	11	9	90	122
Curr. A/C Bal after Off. Transf.	-40	-45	22	-66	-257	-185	-39	-182	-25	180	-411
Long-Term Capital, net	46	51	51	112	174	178	37	211	135	123	558
Direct Investment	15	13	10	13	14	11	13	10	7	3	..
Long-Term Loans	28	33	46	98	128	141	53	184	85	96	221
Disbursements	44	55	66	148	147	160	87	230	133	112	266
Repayments	16	23	20	50	20	19	34	46	47	16	45
Other Long-Term Capital	3	6	-6	1	32	26	-29	17	43	23	337
Other Capital, net	2	-1	-49	19	50	49	-1	-26	-184	-305	-348
Change in Reserves	-9	-5	-23	-65	34	-42	4	-3	74	3	202
Memo Item:					*(Nicaraguan New Cordobas per US dollar)*						
Conversion Factor (Annual Avg)	0.010	0.010	0.010	0.010	0.010	0.010	0.010	0.010	0.010	0.010	0.010
					(Millions of US dollars), outstanding at end of year						
EXTERNAL DEBT (Total)	155	191	234	339	465	611	673	1,276	1,429	1,487	2,170
Long-Term Debt (by debtor)	155	191	234	339	465	611	673	849	944	1,142	1,710
Central Bank, incl. IMF credit	59	70	70	104	110	162	172	206	229	332	304
Central Government	37	45	76	134	194	270	279	381	419	503	1,187
Rest of General Government	2	2	1	1	1	1	0	0	0	0	0
Non-financial Public Enterprises	41	51	59	70	94	107	147	172	193	203	176
Priv. Sector, incl non-guaranteed	16	23	29	31	66	71	74	90	103	103	43
Short-Term Debt	0	0	0	0	0	0	0	427	485	345	460
Memo Items:					*(Millions of US dollars)*						
Int'l Reserves Excluding Gold	48.59	58.11	80.11	116.26	104.49	121.59	146.05	148.33	50.77	146.62	64.52
Gold Holdings (at market price)	0.64	0.79	0.58	1.68	3.54	2.52	2.29	4.29	6.10	9.22	10.61
SOCIAL INDICATORS											
Total Fertility Rate	6.9	6.8	6.7	6.6	6.6	6.5	6.4	6.3	6.2	6.2	6.1
Infant Mortality Rate	106.0	103.0	100.0	98.6	97.2	95.8	94.4	93.0	89.6	86.2	82.8
Life Expectancy at Birth	53.5	54.1	54.7	55.0	55.3	55.7	56.0	56.3	57.0	57.7	58.4
Urban Population, % of total	47.0	47.7	48.3	49.0	49.6	50.3	50.9	51.5	52.2	52.8	53.4
Food Prod. per capita (1987=100)	195.0	193.2	191.1	183.6	181.7	199.0	206.1	207.4	219.1	231.2	151.3
Labor Force, Agriculture (%)	51.5	51.0	50.5	50.0	49.5	49.1	48.5	48.0	47.5	47.0	46.6
Labor Force, Female (%)	19.8	20.0	20.1	20.3	20.4	20.6	20.8	21.0	21.2	21.4	21.6
Primary Schl. Enroll. Ratio	80.0	..	..	..	..	82.0	88.0	87.0	84.0	90.0	99.0
Primary Schl. Enroll. Ratio, Female	81.0	..	..	..	..	85.0	90.0	89.0	88.0	93.0	102.0
Secondary Schl. Enroll. Ratio	18.0	..	..	..	..	24.0	28.0	30.0	28.0	30.0	43.0

1981	1982	1983	1984	1985	1986	1987	1988	1989	1990 estimate	Notes	NICARAGUA
											FOREIGN TRADE (CUSTOMS BASIS)
					(Millions of current US dollars)						
476	391	429	387	275	234	300	236	322	379	..	Value of Exports, fob
419	355	394	355	250	220	283	222	303	357	..	Nonfuel Primary Products
9	5	0	0	0	0	0	0	0	0	..	Fuels
47	30	35	32	24	14	17	14	19	22	..	Manufactures
994	775	806	826	1,067	775	922	718	642	750	..	Value of Imports, cif
185	103	115	124	114	112	134	104	93	109	..	Nonfuel Primary Products
199	180	149	146	339	138	165	128	115	134	..	Fuels
610	492	543	556	613	524	624	486	435	507	..	Manufactures
					(Index 1987 = 100)						
111.3	112.7	118.5	118.9	110.7	120.2	100.0	109.7	109.7	..	..	Terms of Trade
111.5	107.7	109.9	107.9	99.5	111.5	100.0	108.4	112.1	..	..	Export Prices, fob
100.2	95.6	92.7	90.7	89.8	92.8	100.0	98.8	102.2	..	..	Import Prices, cif
					(Millions of current US dollars)						**BALANCE OF PAYMENTS**
582	456	505	465	346	288	326	275	347	385	f	Exports of Goods & Services
508	406	452	412	305	258	295	236	290	321	..	Merchandise, fob
45	41	46	48	39	30	30	38	51	53	..	Nonfactor Services
28	9	7	5	2	1	1	2	7	10	..	Factor Services
1,244	1,021	1,091	1,152	1,199	1,091	1,140	1,121	878	956	f	Imports of Goods & Services
922	724	742	735	794	677	734	718	547	592	..	Merchandise, fob
109	103	128	149	130	159	161	138	119	128	..	Nonfactor Services
212	195	221	268	275	254	245	264	212	236	..	Factor Services
91	109	39	35	26	20	14	9	3	5	..	Long-Term Interest
13	8	4	2	14	0	0	0	0	..	..	Private Current Transfers, net
..	..	..	..	..	..	..	..	..	..	..	Workers' Remittances
-649	-557	-583	-685	-839	-803	-814	-845	-531	-571	..	Curr. A/C Bal before Off. Transf.
57	44	76	88	113	115	135	130	169	202	..	Net Official Transfers
-592	-514	-507	-597	-726	-688	-679	-715	-362	-369	..	Curr. A/C Bal after Off. Transf.
676	473	873	618	783	387	80	203	483	440	f	Long-Term Capital, net
..	..	8	..	..	..	..	..	0	..	..	Direct Investment
295	226	270	339	673	770	478	381	567	441	..	Long-Term Loans
365	282	317	369	697	786	502	395	576	445	..	Disbursements
70	55	47	30	24	16	24	14	9	4	..	Repayments
381	247	596	279	110	-383	-398	-177	-84	-1	..	Other Long-Term Capital
-117	0	-223	285	-49	156	618	616	-121	-71	f	Other Capital, net
33	41	-143	-306	-9	145	-20	-104	0	0	..	Change in Reserves
											Memo Item:
				(Nicaraguan New Cordobas per US dollar)							Conversion Factor (Annual Avg)
0.010	0.010	0.010	0.020	0.040	0.160	0.790	..				
				(Millions of US dollars), outstanding at end of year							**EXTERNAL DEBT (Total)**
2,439	2,913	4,058	4,751	5,736	6,730	7,864	8,587	9,568	10,497	..	**EXTERNAL DEBT (Total)**
2,101	2,492	3,380	4,068	4,893	5,726	6,350	6,885	7,508	8,067	..	Long-Term Debt (by debtor)
448	547	1,257	1,558	1,674	1,814	1,869	2,051	2,218	2,269	..	Central Bank, incl. IMF credit
1,421	1,712	1,865	2,269	2,958	3,743	4,274	4,641	5,095	5,575	..	Central Government
0	0	0	0	0	0	0	0	0	..	..	Rest of General Government
189	191	216	195	214	152	190	176	179	207	..	Non-financial Public Enterprises
42	42	42	47	47	17	17	17	16	16	..	Priv. Sector, incl non-guaranteed
338	421	678	683	844	1,004	1,514	1,703	2,060	2,430	..	Short-Term Debt
					(Millions of US dollars)						**Memo Items:**
111.43	171.17	174.70	..	..	..	..	..	..	..	..	Int'l Reserves Excluding Gold
7.15	8.22	45.78	..	..	..	..	..	..	..	..	Gold Holdings (at market price)
											SOCIAL INDICATORS
6.0	5.9	5.9	5.8	5.7	5.6	5.5	5.4	5.4	5.3	..	Total Fertility Rate
79.4	76.0	73.2	70.4	67.6	64.8	62.0	59.7	57.4	55.1	..	Infant Mortality Rate
59.1	59.8	60.5	61.2	61.9	62.6	63.3	63.8	64.2	64.7	..	Life Expectancy at Birth
54.0	54.7	55.3	56.0	56.6	57.2	57.9	58.5	59.2	59.8	..	Urban Population, % of total
137.9	141.1	137.1	132.4	118.6	105.8	100.0	93.9	103.8	103.6	..	Food Prod. per capita (1987=100)
..	..	..	..	..	..	..	..	..	..	..	Labor Force, Agriculture (%)
22.0	22.4	22.8	23.1	23.4	23.8	24.2	24.6	24.9	25.2	..	Labor Force, Female (%)
..	100.0	103.0	99.0	101.0	98.0	99.0	..	95.0	98.0	..	Primary Schl. Enroll. Ratio
..	103.0	106.0	102.0	107.0	103.0	104.0	..	..	..	..	Primary Schl. Enroll. Ratio, Female
..	39.0	44.0	43.0	39.0	42.0	43.0	..	..	..	..	Secondary Schl. Enroll. Ratio

NIGER	1970	1971	1972	1973	1974	1975	1976	1977	1978	1979	1980
CURRENT GNP PER CAPITA (US $)	160	170	160	160	200	230	230	250	300	360	440
POPULATION (thousands)	4,146	4,240	4,343	4,453	4,574	4,704	4,844	4,995	5,158	5,331	5,515

USE AND ORIGIN OF RESOURCES *(Billions of current CFA Francs)*

	1970	1971	1972	1973	1974	1975	1976	1977	1978	1979	1980
Gross National Product (GNP)	177.14	188.28	184.20	206.74	240.60	214.55	247.87	310.08	389.29	431.99	528.00
Net Factor Income from Abroad	-2.50	-2.70	-3.00	-4.20	-6.40	-10.20	-6.50	-7.20	-11.10	-16.70	-8.20
GDP at Market Prices	179.64	190.98	187.20	210.94	247.00	224.75	254.37	317.28	400.40	448.69	536.20
Resource Balance	-13.16	-6.17	-11.76	-17.34	-41.25	-26.40	-30.71	-30.74	-21.21	-37.38	-75.50
Exports of Goods & NF Services	19.35	23.62	26.61	32.73	30.31	43.26	56.63	62.32	90.21	128.06	130.80
Imports of Goods & NF Services	32.52	29.79	38.37	50.07	71.56	69.66	87.34	93.06	111.43	165.44	206.30
Domestic Absorption	192.80	197.16	198.96	228.28	288.25	251.15	285.08	348.02	421.61	486.06	611.70
Private Consumption, etc.	159.52	166.56	160.81	178.58	230.89	194.68	215.92	240.18	283.08	318.95	360.00
General Gov't Consumption	15.59	15.74	17.42	18.19	20.17	24.30	33.01	45.39	46.46	51.20	55.20
Gross Domestic Investment	17.69	14.86	20.72	31.51	37.19	32.17	36.14	62.45	92.07	115.91	196.50
Fixed Investment	..	..	..	..	..	..	..	..	..	..	152.00
Indirect Taxes, net	5.50	6.00	6.50	6.90	9.10	9.60	11.90	19.00	23.90	26.00	27.00
GDP at factor cost	174.14	184.98	180.70	204.04	237.90	215.15	242.47	298.28	376.50	422.69	509.20
Agriculture	116.54	125.02	116.93	127.14	157.57	113.07	119.62	164.31	210.93	218.44	228.20
Industry	12.47	14.13	15.17	19.78	19.11	24.75	32.76	44.38	59.89	84.09	121.60
Manufacturing	8.34	9.17	9.85	13.34	12.12	12.50	14.85	16.29	18.49	19.00	19.80
Services, etc.	50.63	51.84	55.11	64.02	70.32	86.92	101.98	108.59	129.58	146.16	186.40
Gross Domestic Saving	4.53	8.68	8.96	14.17	-4.07	5.77	5.43	31.71	70.85	78.53	121.00
Gross National Saving	0.97	4.37	3.74	6.41	-14.47	-8.50	-5.81	19.06	51.72	51.24	100.83

(Billions of 1987 CFA Francs)

	1970	1971	1972	1973	1974	1975	1976	1977	1978	1979	1980
Gross National Product	600.98	634.96	600.93	496.53	536.32	512.08	525.82	568.16	641.17	679.22	729.73
GDP at Market Prices	612.75	647.58	614.09	509.48	554.15	538.65	542.30	584.38	663.15	710.50	744.89
Resource Balance	20.90	44.93	29.25	31.72	-65.59	47.95	47.00	39.61	75.91	0.81	0.95
Exports of Goods & NF Services	126.36	136.44	144.96	165.89	89.92	175.97	192.25	178.30	237.99	182.17	193.80
Imports of Goods & NF Services	105.45	91.50	115.71	134.18	155.51	128.02	145.26	138.69	162.08	181.36	192.85
Domestic Absorption	599.28	608.26	600.00	516.98	616.06	535.45	549.49	585.57	647.80	738.63	770.98
Private Consumption, etc.	470.08	498.10	470.29	356.95	456.41	388.25	394.35	410.80	452.90	522.13	576.64
General Gov't Consumption	57.95	55.96	56.46	52.99	56.95	62.90	68.84	77.76	72.80	71.32	64.88
Gross Domestic Investment	71.25	54.19	73.26	107.04	102.69	84.30	86.30	97.01	122.10	145.18	129.46
Fixed Investment	..	..	..	..	..	..	..	..	..	..	..
GDP at factor cost	594.04	627.29	592.85	492.95	533.95	515.44	516.59	549.24	623.58	669.61	707.64
Agriculture	286.16	300.96	272.26	183.00	222.02	178.07	162.37	187.48	213.05	200.49	210.81
Industry	59.90	70.70	71.19	82.98	72.18	84.94	97.22	107.53	128.64	174.79	181.67
Manufacturing	..	..	..	..	..	..	..	..	..	..	..
Services, etc.	266.69	275.91	270.65	243.50	259.95	275.65	282.72	289.37	321.46	335.22	352.41

Memo Items:

	1970	1971	1972	1973	1974	1975	1976	1977	1978	1979	1980
Capacity to Import	62.76	72.54	80.25	87.71	65.86	79.50	94.18	92.88	131.22	140.39	122.27
Terms of Trade Adjustment	-63.60	-63.90	-64.71	-78.19	-24.06	-96.47	-98.07	-85.41	-106.77	-41.78	-71.53
Gross Domestic Income	549.15	583.68	549.38	431.29	530.09	442.18	444.23	498.97	556.38	668.72	673.36
Gross National Income	537.38	571.06	536.21	418.34	512.26	415.61	427.74	482.75	534.40	637.43	658.21

DOMESTIC PRICES/DEFLATORS *(Index 1987 = 100)*

	1970	1971	1972	1973	1974	1975	1976	1977	1978	1979	1980
Overall (GDP)	29.3	29.5	30.5	41.4	44.6	41.7	46.9	54.3	60.4	63.2	72.0
Domestic Absorption	32.2	32.4	33.2	44.2	46.8	46.9	51.9	59.4	65.1	65.8	79.3
Agriculture	40.7	41.5	42.9	69.5	71.0	63.5	73.7	87.6	99.0	109.0	108.2
Industry	20.8	20.0	21.3	23.8	26.5	29.1	33.7	41.3	46.6	48.1	66.9
Manufacturing	..	..	..	..	..	..	..	..	..	..	..
Consumer Price Index	27.0	28.1	30.8	34.5	35.6	38.9	48.0	59.2	65.2	69.9	77.1

MANUFACTURING ACTIVITY

	1970	1971	1972	1973	1974	1975	1976	1977	1978	1979	1980
Employment (1987=100)	..	..	..	..	..	..	..	..	50.0	58.0	63.4	65.2
Real Earnings per Empl. (1987=100)	..	..	..	..	..	..	..	116.9	130.4	142.5	148.1
Real Output per Empl. (1987=100)	..	..	..	..	..	..	..	29.7	33.5	38.0	28.4
Earnings as % of Value Added	..	..	..	..	..	..	..	..	43.1	41.2	43.8

MONETARY HOLDINGS *(Billions of current CFA Francs)*

	1970	1971	1972	1973	1974	1975	1976	1977	1978	1979	1980
Money Supply, Broadly Defined	9.60	12.13	12.90	15.50	20.32	22.31	29.24	37.64	54.20	64.51	77.93
Money	8.83	10.57	11.38	13.62	17.64	20.13	24.78	32.33	46.39	57.27	64.59
Currency Outside Banks	4.87	5.96	6.18	6.66	9.39	9.43	13.41	14.85	19.74	27.28	31.05
Demand Deposits	3.96	4.61	5.20	6.96	8.25	10.70	11.36	17.49	26.66	29.99	33.54
Quasi-Money	0.77	1.56	1.52	1.88	2.68	2.17	4.46	5.30	7.81	7.24	13.34

GOVERNMENT DEFICIT (-) OR SURPLUS *(Millions of current CFA Francs)*

	1970	1971	1972	1973	1974	1975	1976	1977	1978	1979	1980
	..	..	..	..	..	..	-5,468	-5,261	-12,622	-12,105	-25,241
Current Revenue	..	..	..	..	..	..	30,485	37,644	50,382	62,553	77,430
Current Expenditure	..	..	..	..	..	..	24,820	27,113	34,937	39,163	50,581
Current Budget Balance	..	..	..	..	..	..	5,665	10,531	15,445	23,390	26,849
Capital Receipts	..	..	..	..	..	..	4	11	7	6	6
Capital Payments	..	..	..	..	..	..	11,137	15,803	28,074	35,501	52,096

1981	1982	1983	1984	1985	1986	1987	1988	1989	1990 estimate	Notes	NIGER
440	380	310	240	230	240	260	300	290	310	..	**CURRENT GNP PER CAPITA (US $)**
5,710	5,916	6,130	6,347	6,563	6,779	6,997	7,216	7,439	7,666	..	**POPULATION (thousands)**
											USE AND ORIGIN OF RESOURCES
			(Billions of current CFA Francs)								
582.10	618.50	649.20	621.10	629.40	622.60	626.50	672.90	633.80	676.45	..	Gross National Product (GNP)
-7.80	-26.90	-28.10	-17.20	-17.70	-20.80	-23.40	-21.30	-18.00	-10.35	..	Net Factor Income from Abroad
589.90	645.40	677.30	638.30	647.10	643.40	649.90	694.20	651.80	686.80	..	GDP at Market Prices
-68.40	-67.20	-36.00	-30.30	-67.10	-28.90	-30.60	-29.50	-46.60	-49.10	..	Resource Balance
146.70	136.60	152.50	132.10	112.60	126.60	120.80	127.20	115.40	110.00	..	Exports of Goods & NF Services
215.10	203.80	188.50	162.40	179.70	155.50	151.40	156.70	162.00	159.10	..	Imports of Goods & NF Services
658.30	712.60	713.30	668.60	714.20	672.30	680.50	723.70	698.40	735.90	..	Domestic Absorption
474.10	519.80	549.50	583.10	561.70	533.20	544.30	575.30	557.50	..	..	Private Consumption, etc.
64.50	75.20	77.20	65.20	70.10	74.00	76.10	72.20	78.90	..	..	General Gov't Consumption
119.70	117.60	86.60	20.30	82.40	65.10	60.10	76.20	62.00	63.00	..	Gross Domestic Investment
137.60	87.10	99.00	62.90	64.10	63.10	63.10	67.00	66.00	..	..	Fixed Investment
27.80	31.30	25.80	26.20	25.60	24.70	21.00	19.10	19.90	..	..	Indirect Taxes, net
562.10	614.10	651.50	612.10	621.50	618.70	628.90	675.10	631.90		B	GDP at factor cost
269.30	293.70	311.10	228.30	237.80	237.90	219.10	270.70	237.20			Agriculture
113.00	114.40	114.50	137.90	135.50	141.80	157.20	102.30	82.40			Industry
23.20	25.60	20.50	44.80	46.20	49.30	56.70	49.60	39.50			Manufacturing
207.60	237.30	251.70	272.10	273.80	263.70	273.60	321.20	332.20			Services, etc.
51.30	50.40	50.60	-10.00	15.30	36.20	29.50	46.70	15.40	13.90	..	Gross Domestic Saving
29.39	6.05	3.73	-46.13	-28.78	0.40	-8.90	15.00	-15.50	-7.80	..	Gross National Saving
			(Billions of 1987 CFA Francs)								
739.67	709.09	695.71	585.37	602.90	641.55	626.50	657.09	636.72	665.19	..	Gross National Product
753.74	744.53	731.04	607.18	625.92	666.15	649.90	682.36	658.14	678.43	H	GDP at Market Prices
-7.85	-55.37	-38.53	-23.24	-61.55	-29.66	-30.60	-13.37	-0.42	-1.63	..	Resource Balance
189.93	146.81	155.91	141.26	127.13	121.28	120.80	124.76	123.83	123.83	..	Exports of Goods & NF Services
197.78	202.18	194.45	164.50	188.68	150.95	151.40	138.13	124.26	125.47	..	Imports of Goods & NF Services
786.23	804.93	776.01	633.38	706.87	707.72	680.50	697.43	661.01	..	..	Domestic Absorption
583.75	621.17	594.08	554.64	555.21	586.86	544.30	543.96	516.37	..	..	Private Consumption, etc.
68.35	70.30	74.98	71.34	70.27	67.53	76.10	77.10	81.01	..	..	General Gov't Consumption
134.14	113.46	106.94	7.39	81.39	53.33	60.10	76.36	63.64	64.70	..	Gross Domestic Investment
..	..	..	..	..	..	..	..	..	..	..	Fixed Investment
718.52	708.57	703.53	582.31	600.63	639.92	628.90	..	..	..	B H	GDP at factor cost
209.01	203.70	226.88	204.18	234.40	252.69	219.10	..	..	..		Agriculture
189.52	182.65	163.15	153.10	149.12	150.61	157.20	..	..	..		Industry
..	..	..	..	..	..	..	..	..	..		Manufacturing
355.20	358.18	341.01	249.90	242.40	262.85	273.60	..	..	..		Services, etc.
											Memo Items:
134.89	135.52	157.31	133.81	118.23	122.89	120.80	112.13	88.52	86.75	..	Capacity to Import
-55.04	-11.30	1.40	-7.45	-8.90	1.61	0.00	-12.63	-35.32	-37.09	..	Terms of Trade Adjustment
698.70	733.23	732.44	599.73	617.02	667.76	649.90	669.73	622.82	641.35	..	Gross Domestic Income
684.63	697.79	697.11	577.92	594.00	643.16	626.50	644.46	601.40	628.11	..	Gross National Income
											DOMESTIC PRICES/DEFLATORS
			(Index 1987 = 100)								
78.3	86.7	92.6	105.1	103.4	96.6	100.0	101.7	99.0	101.2	..	Overall (GDP)
83.7	88.5	91.9	105.6	101.0	95.0	100.0	103.8	105.7	..	..	Domestic Absorption
128.8	144.2	137.1	111.8	101.4	94.1	100.0	..	..	..	..	Agriculture
59.6	62.6	70.2	90.1	90.9	94.1	100.0	..	..	..	..	Industry
							..	..	..	..	Manufacturing
94.8	105.8	103.2	111.8	110.7	107.2	100.0	98.6	95.8	95.1	..	Consumer Price Index
											MANUFACTURING ACTIVITY
..	81.7	118.0	100.6	94.8	94.8	100.0	..	..	..	G	Employment (1987=100)
..	98.6	89.4	85.3	91.2	90.0	100.0	..	..	..	G	Real Earnings per Empl. (1987=100)
..	29.5	91.3	89.9	93.2	94.0	100.0	..	..	..	G	Real Output per Empl. (1987=100)
..	40.5	9.5	8.1	7.8	7.0	6.7	6.3	..	..		Earnings as % of Value Added
											MONETARY HOLDINGS
			(Billions of current CFA Francs)								
94.07	82.98	82.69	101.02	108.13	121.05	114.44	131.79	139.46	133.83	..	Money Supply, Broadly Defined
74.75	70.93	66.55	78.41	80.62	82.99	73.15	82.12	88.20	77.90	..	Money
34.84	35.27	31.53	30.71	33.37	40.46	35.59	42.17	41.81	37.67	..	Currency Outside Banks
39.91	35.66	35.01	47.69	47.25	42.54	37.55	39.95	46.39	40.23	..	Demand Deposits
19.32	12.05	16.14	22.62	27.51	38.06	41.30	49.68	51.26	55.94	..	Quasi-Money
			(Millions of current CFA Francs)								
..	..	..	..	..	..	..	..	..	..	C	**GOVERNMENT DEFICIT (-) OR SURPLUS**
..	..	..	..	..	..	..	..	..	..		Current Revenue
..	..	..	..	..	..	..	..	..	..		Current Expenditure
..	..	..	..	..	..	..	..	..	..		Current Budget Balance
..	..	..	..	..	..	..	..	..	..		Capital Receipts
..	..	..	..	..	..	..	..	..	..		Capital Payments

NIGER	1970	1971	1972	1973	1974	1975	1976	1977	1978	1979	1980
FOREIGN TRADE (CUSTOMS BASIS)				*(Millions of current US dollars)*							
Value of Exports, fob	31.62	38.37	54.31	62.77	52.57	91.23	133.87	160.11	282.87	448.03	579.69
Nonfuel Primary Products	30.44	36.75	50.37	57.77	46.23	83.24	130.49	155.57	277.27	442.62	560.81
Fuels	0.00	0.01	0.01	0.01	0.00	0.02	0.07	0.08	0.00	0.09	6.47
Manufactures	1.18	1.61	3.93	4.99	6.33	7.98	3.31	4.46	5.60	5.32	12.41
Value of Imports, cif	58.37	52.99	65.70	86.77	96.36	98.94	127.09	196.28	305.92	461.71	607.69
Nonfuel Primary Products	10.71	8.31	13.00	19.94	26.03	28.03	15.69	32.35	61.80	83.89	108.45
Fuels	2.32	4.48	5.82	8.25	13.08	12.43	14.70	14.39	43.40	79.18	158.27
Manufactures	45.34	40.20	46.89	58.57	57.26	58.48	96.71	149.55	200.71	298.63	340.97
					(Index 1987 = 100)						
Terms of Trade	182.3	190.0	196.5	173.3	143.7	149.9	156.4	145.3	157.4	142.0	115.9
Export Prices, fob	52.7	50.2	56.1	62.9	87.4	94.8	98.4	102.8	117.3	124.8	122.7
Import Prices, cif	28.9	26.4	28.6	36.3	60.8	63.2	62.9	70.7	74.5	87.9	105.9
BALANCE OF PAYMENTS				*(Millions of current US dollars)*							
Exports of Goods & Services	60.20	73.52	91.31	126.84	107.57	172.13	203.07	231.65	328.45	533.06	643.66
Merchandise, fob	46.70	58.37	71.01	99.54	81.52	138.52	171.64	196.64	287.65	484.95	576.09
Nonfactor Services	12.30	13.44	18.46	23.25	17.86	23.90	23.37	26.03	31.52	35.69	40.56
Factor Services	1.20	1.71	1.85	4.05	8.20	9.71	8.06	8.98	9.28	12.43	27.01
Imports of Goods & Services	88.80	85.96	115.52	170.59	236.24	254.11	313.89	380.13	613.07	839.16	1,016.28
Merchandise, fob	55.10	53.06	67.86	112.06	144.90	147.96	198.39	241.35	410.62	527.04	677.38
Nonfactor Services	31.00	29.89	44.73	54.84	77.06	87.01	103.66	129.29	163.35	242.35	278.96
Factor Services	2.70	3.01	2.93	3.70	14.29	19.14	11.85	9.49	39.10	69.77	59.94
Long-Term Interest	0.80	0.60	0.70	0.70	0.60	2.30	2.40	3.10	24.70	42.00	64.90
Private Current Transfers, net	-3.80	-5.82	-8.79	-15.97	-16.64	-18.99	-19.83	-22.18	-35.59	-49.82	-56.68
Workers' Remittances	..	0.60	1.85	1.79	2.07	3.00	3.36	3.26	4.66	4.59	5.88
Curr. A/C Bal before Off. Transf.	-32.40	-13.64	-33.01	-59.73	-122.84	-70.69	-130.65	-170.31	-320.21	-278.77	-429.30
Net Official Transfers	32.30	30.09	45.06	84.28	95.04	82.74	110.68	74.68	119.25	141.20	153.61
Curr. A/C Bal after Off. Transf.	-0.10	16.45	12.05	24.56	-27.80	12.05	-19.97	-95.63	-200.96	-137.57	-275.69
Long-Term Capital, net	20.80	7.12	6.90	10.13	16.47	36.29	52.22	90.35	156.61	189.33	223.85
Direct Investment	0.40	-5.72	0.76	0.83	6.60	16.38	8.35	9.19	35.90	36.08	43.94
Long-Term Loans	10.80	8.00	11.20	10.50	24.70	23.20	20.30	22.90	126.70	191.50	223.10
Disbursements	12.40	9.60	12.90	12.40	27.20	29.00	27.00	29.00	146.00	224.20	280.60
Repayments	1.60	1.60	1.70	1.90	2.50	5.80	6.70	6.10	19.30	32.70	57.50
Other Long-Term Capital	9.60	4.84	-5.06	-1.20	-14.82	-3.29	23.57	58.26	-5.99	-38.25	-43.19
Other Capital, net	-10.41	-12.73	-12.66	-29.70	4.94	-42.63	5.52	18.67	58.16	-55.29	57.69
Change in Reserves	-10.29	-10.84	-6.30	-4.99	6.39	-5.72	-37.77	-13.39	-13.81	3.52	-5.85
Memo Item:				*(CFA Francs per US dollar)*							
Conversion Factor (Annual Avg)	277.710	277.130	252.480	222.890	240.700	214.310	238.950	245.680	225.650	212.720	211.280
			(Millions of US dollars), outstanding at end of year								
EXTERNAL DEBT (Total)	31.7	41.5	53.9	64.1	91.8	111.2	129.9	170.3	606.2	628.5	862.9
Long-Term Debt (by debtor)	31.7	41.5	53.9	64.1	91.8	111.2	129.9	118.3	356.2	522.5	703.6
Central Bank, incl. IMF credit	3.0	3.4	3.5	3.7	4.0	4.1	3.1	2.6	10.3	16.2	44.1
Central Government	17.5	25.9	37.8	45.7	61.0	79.7	103.0	90.6	144.9	173.7	236.0
Rest of General Government	0.1	0.1	0.1	0.1	0.0	0.0	0.0	0.0	0.0	0.0	0.0
Non-financial Public Enterprises	1.7	1.7	2.4	3.2	2.8	2.9	3.5	6.4	23.4	56.1	106.2
Priv. Sector, incl non-guaranteed	9.4	10.4	10.1	11.4	24.0	24.5	20.3	18.7	177.6	276.5	317.3
Short-Term Debt	0.0	0.0	0.0	0.0	0.0	0.0	0.0	52.0	250.0	106.0	159.3
Memo Items:				*(Millions of US dollars)*							
Int'l Reserves Excluding Gold	18.7	33.6	41.4	50.8	45.5	50.3	82.5	101.1	128.4	131.7	125.9
Gold Holdings (at market price)	..	..	..	..	..	..	..	0.9	1.9	5.7	6.5
SOCIAL INDICATORS											
Total Fertility Rate	7.1	7.1	7.1	7.1	7.1	7.1	7.1	7.1	7.1	7.1	7.1
Infant Mortality Rate	170.0	168.0	166.0	164.2	162.4	160.6	158.8	157.0	154.8	152.6	150.4
Life Expectancy at Birth	38.4	38.7	39.0	39.3	39.6	39.9	40.2	40.5	40.9	41.3	41.7
Urban Population, % of total	8.5	8.9	9.3	9.8	10.2	10.6	11.1	11.6	12.2	12.7	13.2
Food Prod. per capita (1987=100)	195.6	197.2	191.9	121.4	140.5	129.3	150.0	171.2	177.5	174.4	175.7
Labor Force, Agriculture (%)	94.3	93.9	93.6	93.3	93.0	92.7	92.3	92.0	91.7	91.4	91.1
Labor Force, Female (%)	49.0	48.9	48.8	48.7	48.6	48.6	48.4	48.3	48.2	48.1	48.0
Primary Schl. Enroll. Ratio	14.0	..	..	..	..	20.0	21.0	22.0	23.0	..	25.0
Primary Schl. Enroll. Ratio, Female	10.0	..	..	..	..	14.0	15.0	16.0	17.0	..	18.0
Secondary Schl. Enroll. Ratio	1.0	..	..	..	..	2.0	3.0	3.0	4.0	..	5.0

1981	1982	1983	1984	1985	1986	1987	1988	1989	1990 estimate	Notes	NIGER
											FOREIGN TRADE (CUSTOMS BASIS)
			(Millions of current US dollars)								
454.81	256.18	261.59	203.38	205.38	267.59	427.75	423.30	430.00	435.00	..	Value of Exports, fob
440.84	7.25	17.09	197.13	199.07	259.37	414.61	410.29	416.79	421.64	..	Nonfuel Primary Products
3.91	0.05	8.03	1.75	1.77	2.30	3.68	3.64	3.70	3.74	..	Fuels
10.06	248.88	236.47	4.50	4.54	5.92	9.46	9.36	9.51	9.62	..	Manufactures
509.72	322.83	209.27	184.87	231.70	218.99	239.25	219.34	225.00	230.00	..	Value of Imports, cif
138.42	62.81	45.49	30.47	38.18	36.09	39.43	36.15	37.08	37.90	..	Nonfuel Primary Products
75.66	13.53	8.70	13.55	16.99	16.05	17.54	16.08	16.49	16.86	..	Fuels
295.64	246.49	155.07	140.85	176.53	166.85	182.28	167.11	171.42	175.23	..	Manufactures
			(Index 1987 = 100)								
117.0	120.8	124.9	124.0	126.1	117.0	100.0	96.0	78.6	77.0	..	Terms of Trade
125.3	121.5	122.1	120.8	119.6	111.2	100.0	104.6	87.4	97.6	..	Export Prices, fob
107.1	100.6	97.7	97.5	94.8	95.1	100.0	109.0	111.2	126.8	..	Import Prices, cif
			(Millions of current US dollars)								**BALANCE OF PAYMENTS**
542.67	440.73	387.50	348.09	316.39	..	472.49	419.01	368.64	382.00		Exports of Goods & Services
484.63	381.33	335.23	303.27	259.43	331.50	411.93	368.98	310.96	312.00		Merchandise, fob
39.84	41.80	40.33	31.36	38.56	..	52.57	48.35	50.78	62.00		Nonfactor Services
18.20	17.60	11.94	13.46	18.40	..	7.99	1.68	6.90	8.00		Factor Services
873.50	817.59	537.98	461.99	533.76	411.49	654.83	611.05	571.15	587.00		Imports of Goods & Services
591.79	515.33	331.58	269.92	345.64	309.76	409.60	392.48	368.64	433.00		Merchandise, fob
194.12	212.95	153.74	124.20	127.46	84.20	152.73	145.38	139.18	108.00		Nonfactor Services
87.59	89.31	52.67	67.87	60.66	17.53	92.50	73.19	63.32	46.00		Factor Services
66.30	71.60	51.70	37.60	41.40	48.00	71.00	74.00	35.30	22.50		Long-Term Interest
-51.92	-53.11	-49.25	-43.32	-58.72	-43.31	-49.91	-34.92	-40.44	-41.70		Private Current Transfers, net
4.58	3.35	2.98	4.48	2.10	..		10.07	9.72	12.00		Workers' Remittances
-342.08	-382.79	-197.66	-144.57	-276.09	-123.30	-232.25	-226.96	-242.94	-246.70		Curr. A/C Bal before Off. Transf.
160.58	149.98	135.83	145.77	212.11	148.42	142.08	143.70	131.97	182.00		Net Official Transfers
-181.50	-232.81	-61.83	1.20	-63.98	25.12	-90.17	-83.26	-110.97	-64.70		Curr. A/C Bal after Off. Transf.
224.35	37.38	45.55	32.04	49.02	78.83	102.48	95.69	95.92	44.00		Long-Term Capital, net
-6.71	24.93	0.21	-1.05	-9.57	..	..	..	..	..		Direct Investment
323.00	21.20	77.50	42.60	53.10	112.80	144.50	121.00	111.50	110.70		Long-Term Loans
406.70	178.90	160.10	90.30	106.90	176.90	201.50	177.30	167.10	155.00		Disbursements
83.70	157.70	82.60	47.70	53.80	64.10	57.00	56.30	55.60	44.30		Repayments
-91.94	-8.76	-32.16	-9.50	5.49	-33.97	-42.02	-25.31	-15.58	-66.70		Other Long-Term Capital
-40.08	132.13	13.34	-1.98	17.98	-97.46	1.83	26.49	-0.97	43.14		Other Capital, net
-2.77	63.31	2.94	-31.26	-3.02	-6.49	-14.14	-38.91	16.02	-22.44		Change in Reserves
											Memo Item:
			(CFA Francs per US dollar)								
271.730	328.600	381.060	436.960	449.260	346.300	300.530	297.850	319.010	272.260	..	Conversion Factor (Annual Avg)
			(Millions of US dollars), outstanding at end of year								
1,021.8	957.5	949.7	955.8	1,208.2	1,448.3	1,697.3	1,741.7	1,576.3	1,828.7	..	**EXTERNAL DEBT (Total)**
908.0	833.9	883.5	893.0	1,109.3	1,325.5	1,620.8	1,636.6	1,469.8	1,672.1	..	Long-Term Debt (by debtor)
61.6	64.1	112.5	110.5	140.5	165.0	178.8	130.4	119.0	123.2	..	Central Bank, incl. IMF credit
361.6	405.2	472.3	519.5	667.2	837.4	1,085.4	1,175.3	1,041.7	1,232.4	..	Central Government
0.0	0.0	0.0	0.0	0.0	0.0	0.0	0.0	0.0	..	..	Rest of General Government
171.8	124.8	111.6	95.7	97.4	94.4	97.3	71.2	46.8	52.7	..	Non-financial Public Enterprises
313.0	239.8	187.1	167.3	204.2	228.7	259.3	259.7	262.3	263.8	..	Priv. Sector, incl non-guaranteed
113.8	123.6	66.2	62.8	98.9	122.8	76.5	105.1	106.5	156.6	..	Short-Term Debt
			(Millions of US dollars)								**Memo Items:**
105.3	29.6	53.2	88.7	136.4	189.2	248.5	232.1	212.3	222.2	..	Int'l Reserves Excluding Gold
4.4	5.1	4.2	3.4	3.6	4.3	5.4	4.6	4.5	4.3	..	Gold Holdings (at market price)
											SOCIAL INDICATORS
7.1	7.1	7.1	7.1	7.1	7.1	7.1	7.1	7.1	7.2	..	Total Fertility Rate
148.2	146.0	143.8	141.6	139.3	137.1	134.9	132.6	130.2	127.9	..	Infant Mortality Rate
42.1	42.5	42.9	43.3	43.7	44.1	44.5	44.8	45.1	45.5	..	Life Expectancy at Birth
13.8	14.4	15.0	15.6	16.2	17.1	17.9	18.4	19.0	19.5	..	Urban Population, % of total
164.8	157.6	150.2	103.7	108.5	117.3	100.0	131.1	118.7	118.3	..	Food Prod. per capita (1987=100)
..	..	..	..	..	..	..	..	..	..	..	Labor Force, Agriculture (%)
47.9	47.8	47.6	47.5	47.4	47.2	47.1	47.0	46.8	46.7	..	Labor Force, Female (%)
..	..	27.0	26.0	26.0	29.0	26.0	27.0	28.0	..	..	Primary Schl. Enroll. Ratio
..	..	19.0	19.0	18.0	20.0	18.0	19.0	20.0	..	..	Primary Schl. Enroll. Ratio, Female
..	..	6.0	..	5.0	..	6.0	6.0	..	..	..	Secondary Schl. Enroll. Ratio

NIGERIA	1970	1971	1972	1973	1974	1975	1976	1977	1978	1979	1980
CURRENT GNP PER CAPITA (US $)	140	170	210	240	330	400	540	630	660	780	930
POPULATION (thousands)	66,182	67,842	69,563	71,328	73,105	74,884	76,518	78,282	80,220	82,364	84,732

USE AND ORIGIN OF RESOURCES *(Billions of current Nigerian Naira)*

	1970	1971	1972	1973	1974	1975	1976	1977	1978	1979	1980
Gross National Product (GNP)	8.63	9.62	10.18	11.39	18.92	22.42	27.95	32.72	35.22	41.89	48.83
Net Factor Income from Abroad	-0.33	-0.75	-0.85	-0.87	-0.68	-0.53	-0.66	-0.87	-0.84	-1.03	-2.06
GDP at Market Prices	8.96	10.38	11.03	12.25	19.60	22.95	28.61	33.58	36.05	42.91	50.90
Resource Balance	-0.25	-0.29	-0.09	0.07	2.08	-1.03	-1.63	-2.33	-3.24	-0.02	1.75
Exports of Goods & NF Services	0.75	1.12	1.21	1.95	4.94	4.21	5.21	6.74	5.68	8.48	11.79
Imports of Goods & NF Services	1.00	1.41	1.30	1.88	2.86	5.24	6.84	9.06	8.92	8.50	10.04
Domestic Absorption	9.21	10.67	11.13	12.18	17.52	23.98	30.24	35.91	39.29	42.93	49.15
Private Consumption, etc.	7.15	7.87	7.72	8.18	12.50	15.30	17.90	20.55	22.72	26.56	30.48
General Gov't Consumption	0.74	0.85	1.08	1.26	1.70	2.89	3.34	4.94	6.19	6.31	6.53
Gross Domestic Investment	1.33	1.94	2.33	2.75	3.33	5.79	9.01	10.42	10.38	10.06	12.14
Fixed Investment	..	..	..	2.79	3.30	5.60	9.04	10.50	10.46	10.12	12.24
Indirect Taxes, net	0.68	0.32	0.31	0.30	0.31	0.36	0.48	0.52	0.69	0.76	1.73
GDP at factor cost	8.28	10.05	10.73	11.96	19.29	22.59	28.13	33.06	35.36	42.16	49.17
Agriculture	3.42	4.03	4.10	4.20	6.14	7.17	8.19	9.78	10.78	12.08	13.49
Industry	1.14	1.74	2.14	3.00	6.80	6.44	9.08	10.39	11.79	15.94	19.80
Manufacturing	0.30	0.34	0.42	0.48	0.64	1.14	1.42	1.51	2.31	3.71	3.95
Services, etc.	3.72	4.28	4.48	4.76	6.35	8.98	10.86	12.90	12.80	14.13	15.88
Gross Domestic Saving	1.08	1.65	2.24	2.82	5.41	4.76	7.37	8.09	7.14	10.04	13.89
Gross National Saving	0.76	0.88	1.35	1.91	4.67	4.16	6.61	7.11	6.15	8.80	11.60

(Millions of 1987 Nigerian Naira)

	1970	1971	1972	1973	1974	1975	1976	1977	1978	1979	1980
Gross National Product	73,646	78,935	79,303	85,991	98,592	96,863	105,794	111,985	106,034	113,431	115,337
GDP at Market Prices	78,643	87,665	88,527	95,290	105,926	102,518	111,932	118,752	112,228	119,899	124,348
Resource Balance	7,365	2,949	8,902	7,909	1,479	-24,200	-31,213	-48,441	-61,966	-15,552	-38,233
Exports of Goods & NF Services	28,892	31,421	34,371	39,086	40,290	34,624	34,546	51,304	41,218	61,462	55,648
Imports of Goods & NF Services	21,526	28,472	25,469	31,177	38,811	58,825	65,759	99,745	103,183	77,015	93,881
Domestic Absorption	71,278	84,716	79,625	87,381	104,446	126,718	143,145	167,193	174,194	135,452	162,581
Private Consumption, etc.	45,867	52,840	46,230	47,287	63,310	67,139	68,276	79,196	100,917	74,542	99,061
General Gov't Consumption	7,627	8,619	9,093	11,119	11,413	14,896	15,066	21,108	24,099	19,962	16,431
Gross Domestic Investment	17,784	23,258	24,303	28,975	29,723	44,682	59,803	66,889	49,179	40,947	47,090
Fixed Investment	..	..	..	30,638	31,323	46,955	63,122	70,643	51,866	43,153	49,698
GDP at factor cost	74,161	81,950	83,402	90,911	101,990	98,685	107,634	114,309	107,623	115,196	117,490
Agriculture	38,023	40,004	37,092	40,401	44,589	39,958	39,332	42,017	38,385	37,223	39,061
Industry	21,949	29,162	34,793	34,371	40,287	34,784	42,970	45,111	43,441	51,653	50,524
Manufacturing	1,982	1,920	2,379	2,648	2,561	3,165	3,904	4,148	4,718	6,933	7,328
Services, etc.	15,807	17,153	17,712	20,102	21,751	26,242	27,667	29,611	27,928	28,596	30,048

Memo Items:

	1970	1971	1972	1973	1974	1975	1976	1977	1978	1979	1980
Capacity to Import	16,139	22,634	23,681	32,332	67,070	47,249	50,073	74,138	65,748	76,832	110,212
Terms of Trade Adjustment	-12,752	-8,787	-10,690	-6,754	26,779	12,625	15,527	22,834	24,530	15,370	54,564
Gross Domestic Income	65,891	78,878	77,837	88,536	132,705	115,142	127,459	141,586	136,758	135,269	178,912
Gross National Income	60,894	70,148	68,613	79,236	125,371	109,488	121,321	134,819	130,564	128,800	169,901

DOMESTIC PRICES/DEFLATORS *(Index 1987 = 100)*

	1970	1971	1972	1973	1974	1975	1976	1977	1978	1979	1980
Overall (GDP)	11.4	11.8	12.5	12.9	18.5	22.4	25.6	28.3	32.1	35.8	40.9
Domestic Absorption	12.9	12.6	14.0	13.9	16.8	18.9	21.1	21.5	22.6	31.7	30.2
Agriculture	9.0	10.1	11.1	10.4	13.8	17.9	20.8	23.3	28.1	32.5	34.5
Industry	5.2	6.0	6.1	8.7	16.9	18.5	21.1	23.0	27.1	30.9	39.2
Manufacturing	15.3	17.7	17.6	18.2	25.1	35.9	36.4	36.4	49.0	53.5	53.9
Consumer Price Index	8.8	10.2	10.5	11.1	12.5	16.7	20.8	23.6	28.8	32.1	35.4

MANUFACTURING ACTIVITY

	1970	1971	1972	1973	1974	1975	1976	1977	1978	1979	1980
Employment (1987=100)	..	..	..	..	..	..	..	..	..	..	..
Real Earnings per Empl. (1987=100)	..	..	..	..	..	..	..	..	..	..	..
Real Output per Empl. (1987=100)	..	..	..	..	..	..	..	..	..	..	..
Earnings as % of Value Added	17.6	20.1	21.6	21.8	20.7	21.8	24.5	23.6	22.3	..	21.9

MONETARY HOLDINGS *(Millions of current Nigerian Naira)*

	1970	1971	1972	1973	1974	1975	1976	1977	1978	1979	1980
Money Supply, Broadly Defined	979	1,042	1,204	1,508	2,730	4,178	5,843	7,813	7,521	9,849	14,390
Money	643	670	747	926	1,757	2,605	3,864	5,558	5,101	6,147	9,227
Currency Outside Banks	342	355	385	436	570	1,031	1,351	1,941	2,157	2,351	3,186
Demand Deposits	300	316	362	490	1,187	1,575	2,513	3,617	2,943	3,796	6,041
Quasi-Money	337	372	457	582	973	1,572	1,979	2,255	2,420	3,702	5,163

GOVERNMENT DEFICIT (-) OR SURPLUS *(Millions of current Nigerian Naira)*

	1970	1971	1972	1973	1974	1975	1976	1977	1978	1979	1980
GOVERNMENT DEFICIT (-) OR SURPLUS	..	..	-83	189	1,248	-1,436	-1,870	-2,134	-639	..	..
Current Revenue	..	..	1,054	1,830	4,308	4,740	5,449	6,659	5,933	..	..
Current Expenditure	..	..	716	885	..	2,660	2,646	4,063	2,452	..	..
Current Budget Balance	..	..	338	945	..	2,081	2,803	2,596	3,481	..	..
Capital Receipts	..	..	..	..	..	..	..	..	..	..	..
Capital Payments	..	..	420	756	..	3,517	4,673	4,731	4,120	..	..

1981	1982	1983	1984	1985	1986	1987	1988	1989	1990 estimate	Notes	NIGERIA
970	960	850	790	850	580	360	300	270	290	..	**CURRENT GNP PER CAPITA (US $)**
87,352	90,259	93,367	96,534	99,669	102,799	105,938	109,087	112,253	115,456	..	**POPULATION (thousands)**

USE AND ORIGIN OF RESOURCES

(Billions of current Nigerian Naira)

1981	1982	1983	1984	1985	1986	1987	1988	1989	1990	Notes	
52.07	52.18	56.36	62.19	69.77	67.92	97.76	132.07	210.03	261.34	C	Gross National Product (GNP)
1.31	0.22	-0.79	-1.42	-2.59	-5.15	-11.12	-13.18	-20.12	-23.70	..	Net Factor Income from Abroad
50.75	51.95	57.14	63.61	72.36	73.06	108.88	145.24	230.15	285.04	C	GDP at Market Prices
-4.66	-4.79	-2.56	0.85	2.63	-2.49	4.29	1.53	21.79	42.30	..	Resource Balance
9.75	7.57	7.45	9.10	11.49	12.49	31.15	33.51	73.49	112.52	..	Exports of Goods & NF Services
14.41	12.36	10.01	8.24	8.86	14.98	26.86	31.99	51.71	70.23	..	Imports of Goods & NF Services
55.41	56.75	59.70	62.76	69.73	75.55	104.59	143.71	208.37	242.74	..	Domestic Absorption
36.16	37.43	41.04	45.38	53.44	52.96	76.05	105.98	155.49	168.63	f	Private Consumption, etc.
6.86	8.61	10.19	11.28	9.80	11.58	13.63	18.18	20.81	32.37	..	General Gov't Consumption
12.40	10.71	8.47	6.09	6.49	11.01	14.91	19.56	32.07	41.75	f	Gross Domestic Investment
13.02	11.83	9.13	7.25	6.94	10.59	15.97	19.22	31.10	42.16	..	Fixed Investment
0.29	0.38	0.43	0.60	0.99	0.93	2.00	2.56	4.10	5.66	..	Indirect Taxes, net
50.46	51.57	56.71	63.01	71.37	72.13	106.88	142.68	226.05	279.38	C	GDP at factor cost
13.58	15.91	18.84	23.80	26.62	27.89	39.20	57.92	89.26	101.14	..	Agriculture
18.96	17.19	16.86	17.50	20.83	18.76	35.60	43.98	77.47	107.18	..	Industry
4.63	4.93	5.61	4.93	6.24	6.30	7.22	10.73	..	..	..	Manufacturing
17.92	18.47	21.01	21.70	23.91	25.49	32.07	40.77	59.32	71.06	..	Services, etc.
7.74	5.92	5.91	6.95	9.12	8.52	19.21	21.09	53.85	84.04		Gross Domestic Saving
8.78	5.88	4.86	5.30	6.31	3.18	8.00	7.77	33.59	60.34		Gross National Saving

(Millions of 1987 Nigerian Naira)

1981	1982	1983	1984	1985	1986	1987	1988	1989	1990	Notes	
108,191	106,864	100,175	93,022	101,910	96,387	97,756	109,564	115,546	124,700	C	Gross National Product
112,844	111,915	104,638	101,224	111,588	110,881	108,880	119,618	126,828	134,031	C	GDP at Market Prices
-87,235	-66,432	-44,594	-30,231	-24,262	-16,253	4,292	5,127	8,356	8,093	..	Resource Balance
24,799	23,320	24,811	26,063	28,699	34,087	31,155	31,805	35,144	38,425	..	Exports of Goods & NF Services
112,034	89,753	69,404	56,293	52,961	50,339	26,863	26,679	26,788	30,332	..	Imports of Goods & NF Services
200,079	178,347	149,232	131,455	135,850	127,133	104,588	114,491	118,472	125,938	..	Domestic Absorption
128,234	116,471	97,587	92,978	102,289	89,163	76,047	83,714	85,520	88,255	f	Private Consumption, etc.
20,799	22,980	22,081	17,517	14,417	16,176	13,627	14,281	13,799	16,524	..	General Gov't Consumption
51,045	38,896	29,563	20,959	19,144	21,795	14,914	16,496	19,154	21,159	f	Gross Domestic Investment
53,306	43,649	32,380	24,949	20,396	20,984	15,970	16,207	18,580	21,372	..	Fixed Investment
109,843	108,816	101,650	97,117	105,700	107,749	106,881	117,482	125,123	131,588	C	GDP at factor cost
32,630	33,459	33,361	31,747	37,076	40,495	39,204	43,051	45,088	46,922	..	Agriculture
45,403	43,515	37,117	36,931	38,896	36,676	35,604	39,147	42,156	44,855	..	Industry
8,437	9,523	6,722	5,968	7,153	6,874	7,224	8,152			..	Manufacturing
31,993	32,039	31,172	28,438	29,728	30,578	32,073	35,284	37,879	39,811	..	Services, etc.

Memo Items:

1981	1982	1983	1984	1985	1986	1987	1988	1989	1990	Notes	
75,806	54,951	51,677	62,104	68,674	41,983	31,155	27,954	38,074	48,600	..	Capacity to Import
51,007	31,631	26,866	36,042	39,975	7,896	0	-3,852	2,930	10,175	..	Terms of Trade Adjustment
163,851	143,546	131,504	137,266	151,562	118,777	108,880	115,766	129,758	144,206	..	Gross Domestic Income
159,198	138,495	127,042	129,064	141,885	104,283	97,756	105,713	118,476	134,876	..	Gross National Income

DOMESTIC PRICES/DEFLATORS

(Index 1987 = 100)

1981	1982	1983	1984	1985	1986	1987	1988	1989	1990	Notes	
45.0	46.4	54.6	62.8	64.8	65.9	100.0	121.4	181.5	212.7	..	Overall (GDP)
27.7	31.8	40.0	47.7	51.3	59.4	100.0	125.5	175.9	192.7	..	Domestic Absorption
41.6	47.5	56.5	75.0	71.8	68.9	100.0	134.5	198.0	215.5	..	Agriculture
41.8	39.5	45.4	47.4	53.5	51.1	100.0	112.4	183.8	238.9	..	Industry
54.9	51.7	83.5	82.5	87.2	91.6	100.0	131.6			..	Manufacturing
42.7	46.0	56.7	79.1	85.0	89.9	100.0	154.5	232.5	249.6	..	Consumer Price Index

MANUFACTURING ACTIVITY

1981	1982	1983	1984	1985	1986	1987	1988	1989	1990	Notes	
..	..	..	..	..	..	..	..	..	..	..	Employment (1987=100)
..	..	..	..	..	..	..	..	..	..	..	Real Earnings per Empl. (1987=100)
..	..	..	..	..	..	..	..	..	..	..	Real Output per Empl. (1987=100)
30.1	27.7	20.5	25.2	..	..	..	..	..	..	..	Earnings as % of Value Added

MONETARY HOLDINGS

(Millions of current Nigerian Naira)

1981	1982	1983	1984	1985	1986	1987	1988	1989	1990	Notes	
15,239	16,694	19,034	21,243	23,153	23,605	28,895	38,406	42,519	57,554	..	Money Supply, Broadly Defined
9,745	10,049	11,283	12,204	13,227	12,663	14,906	21,446	25,813	34,540	..	Money
3,862	4,223	4,843	4,884	4,910	5,178	6,299	9,414	11,669	14,951	..	Currency Outside Banks
5,883	5,826	6,440	7,321	8,318	7,485	8,608	12,033	14,144	19,589	..	Demand Deposits
5,494	6,645	7,752	9,039	9,926	10,942	13,989	16,960	16,707	23,013	..	Quasi-Money

(Millions of current Nigerian Naira)

1981	1982	1983	1984	1985	1986	1987	1988	1989	1990	Notes	
..	..	..	-2,900	-1,999	-2,773	-9,702	..	..	..	C	**GOVERNMENT DEFICIT (-) OR SURPLUS**
..	..	..	7,344	9,000	12,549	17,375	..	..	..		Current Revenue
..	..	..	6,418	5,797	8,720	17,172	..	..	..		Current Expenditure
..	..	..	926	3,203	3,829	203	..	..	..		Current Budget Balance
..	..	..	..	..	..	..	..	..	..		Capital Receipts
..	..	..	3,826	5,203	6,602	9,905	..	..	..		Capital Payments

NIGERIA	1970	1971	1972	1973	1974	1975	1976	1977	1978	1979	1980
FOREIGN TRADE (CUSTOMS BASIS)					*(Millions of current US dollars)*						
Value of Exports, fob	1,227.9	1,793.2	2,161.1	3,448.0	9,177.6	7,983.4	10,557.0	11,834.6	9,958.6	16,360.8	25,057.5
Nonfuel Primary Products	499.2	436.9	342.1	509.3	606.0	496.0	541.1	749.1	820.8	691.6	684.1
Fuels	714.0	1,335.4	1,793.6	2,889.9	8,537.6	7,448.9	9,956.5	11,013.6	8,990.0	15,559.3	24,274.0
Manufactures	14.7	20.9	25.3	48.8	34.0	38.5	59.5	71.8	147.8	109.9	99.3
Value of Imports, cif	1,059.0	1,510.5	1,504.9	1,861.7	2,780.6	6,041.2	8,194.6	11,020.2	12,762.8	10,274.3	13,408.0
Nonfuel Primary Products	119.5	174.3	197.3	257.9	392.4	750.3	1,024.9	1,633.1	2,099.0	2,053.7	2,282.0
Fuels	33.6	12.6	14.9	20.6	88.7	162.7	279.1	199.2	245.8	235.0	916.9
Manufactures	905.9	1,323.6	1,292.7	1,583.2	2,299.6	5,128.3	6,890.6	9,187.9	10,417.9	7,985.7	10,209.1
					(Index 1987 = 100)						
Terms of Trade	43.6	37.0	35.1	41.5	121.1	107.8	117.5	120.0	107.8	132.9	186.0
Export Prices, fob	11.9	12.5	12.9	18.4	68.2	65.6	71.0	79.1	80.8	113.0	180.0
Import Prices, cif	27.3	33.8	36.8	44.2	56.4	60.9	60.4	65.9	75.0	85.0	96.8
BALANCE OF PAYMENTS					*(Millions of current US dollars)*						
Exports of Goods & Services	1,341.0	2,010.0	2,315.8	3,763.6	10,048.1	9,130.4	10,924.1	13,278.9	11,581.1	18,108.5	27,748.9
Merchandise, fob	1,248.0	1,888.6	2,184.5	3,607.4	9,698.1	8,329.1	10,121.7	12,365.9	10,414.5	16,811.5	25,928.8
Nonfactor Services	83.0	108.3	117.3	131.1	194.8	299.9	359.1	562.7	876.3	1,027.5	1,128.1
Factor Services	10.0	13.0	14.1	25.0	155.1	501.4	443.3	350.3	290.3	269.5	692.0
Imports of Goods & Services	1,772.0	2,418.2	2,636.1	3,718.3	5,052.3	8,961.6	11,125.0	14,107.6	15,067.9	16,050.8	22,043.9
Merchandise, fob	939.0	1,393.1	1,365.8	1,714.3	2,479.8	5,484.3	7,477.8	9,670.1	11,583.1	11,887.3	14,752.8
Nonfactor Services	369.0	454.4	575.4	1,020.5	1,852.1	2,695.4	2,915.2	3,552.0	2,964.9	3,441.4	5,238.0
Factor Services	464.0	570.7	694.9	983.5	720.4	781.9	732.0	885.5	519.9	722.1	2,053.1
Long-Term Interest	27.8	30.1	31.5	38.2	41.7	45.4	44.3	52.1	66.2	257.6	531.2
Private Current Transfers, net	19.0	-25.1	-46.7	-54.8	-91.4	-111.7	-161.6	-178.5	-251.0	-350.2	-410.0
Workers' Remittances	..	..	..	..	..	..	..	20.2	3.1	8.1	12.9
Curr. A/C Bal before Off. Transf.	-412.0	-433.3	-367.0	-9.5	4,904.4	57.1	-362.5	-1,007.1	-3,737.8	1,707.5	5,295.0
Net Official Transfers	44.0	27.1	25.0	1.2	-7.2	-14.6	5.8	-4.7	-18.9	-39.0	-168.2
Curr. A/C Bal after Off. Transf.	-368.0	-406.2	-342.0	-8.3	4,897.1	42.5	-356.7	-1,011.8	-3,756.7	1,668.5	5,126.8
Long-Term Capital, net	205.0	309.9	367.0	306.4	169.6	208.8	-27.7	419.9	1,605.4	1,234.8	-81.8
Direct Investment	205.0	285.8	305.1	373.1	257.4	417.9	339.4	439.2	211.7	304.7	-739.7
Long-Term Loans	13.3	63.2	86.9	-99.0	-41.1	-91.3	-229.8	55.2	1,626.6	1,306.9	1,509.9
Disbursements	81.1	127.6	150.7	91.5	109.2	133.1	126.2	141.3	1,709.3	1,442.0	1,752.5
Repayments	67.8	64.4	63.8	190.5	150.3	224.4	356.0	86.1	82.7	135.1	242.6
Other Long-Term Capital	-13.3	-39.1	-25.0	32.2	-46.7	-117.5	-137.3	-74.5	-232.9	-376.9	-852.0
Other Capital, net	236.0	256.8	-87.4	-96.2	-168.8	-42.1	4.6	-231.2	43.0	301.0	-672.3
Change in Reserves	-73.0	-160.5	62.4	-201.9	-4,898.0	-209.2	379.8	823.0	2,108.4	-3,204.3	-4,372.7
Memo Item:					*(Nigerian Naira per US dollar)*						
Conversion Factor (Annual Avg)	0.710	0.710	0.660	0.660	0.630	0.620	0.630	0.640	0.640	0.600	0.550
					(Millions of US dollars), outstanding at end of year						
EXTERNAL DEBT (Total)	567	651	732	1,205	1,274	1,143	906	3,146	5,091	6,259	8,934
Long-Term Debt (by debtor)	567	651	732	1,205	1,274	1,143	906	985	2,645	3,976	5,381
Central Bank, incl. IMF credit	3	6	8	8	8	7	5	3	2	3	20
Central Government	189	278	372	841	897	772	510	548	2,009	2,927	3,621
Rest of General Government	12	9	6	4	4	2	2	2	2	2	188
Non-financial Public Enterprises	246	247	253	252	257	262	280	299	294	334	455
Priv. Sector, incl non-guaranteed	117	111	94	99	108	101	110	133	338	710	1,097
Short-Term Debt	0	0	0	0	0	0	0	2,161	2,446	2,283	3,553
Memo Items:					*(Millions of US dollars)*						
Int'l Reserves Excluding Gold	202.2	408.3	355.5	558.8	5,602.5	5,585.6	5,179.8	4,232.2	1,886.7	5,547.9	10,234.8
Gold Holdings (at market price)	21.3	23.7	35.2	64.1	106.5	80.1	76.9	103.8	142.2	351.7	405.0
SOCIAL INDICATORS											
Total Fertility Rate	6.9	6.9	6.9	6.9	6.9	6.9	6.9	6.9	6.9	6.9	6.9
Infant Mortality Rate	139.4	137.2	135.0	132.8	130.6	128.4	126.2	124.0	122.0	120.0	118.0
Life Expectancy at Birth	43.7	44.1	44.5	44.9	45.3	45.7	46.1	46.5	46.9	47.3	47.7
Urban Population, % of total	20.0	20.7	21.4	22.0	22.7	23.4	24.1	24.9	25.6	26.4	27.1
Food Prod. per capita (1987=100)	127.8	121.9	110.6	111.7	121.9	106.4	102.6	100.6	96.7	97.1	98.8
Labor Force, Agriculture (%)	71.0	70.6	70.3	70.1	69.8	69.6	69.2	68.9	68.7	68.4	68.1
Labor Force, Female (%)	37.1	37.1	37.1	37.0	37.0	36.9	36.9	36.8	36.8	36.7	36.7
Primary Schl. Enroll. Ratio	37.0	..	..	..	..	51.0	71.0	82.0	92.0	98.0	104.0
Primary Schl. Enroll. Ratio, Female	27.0	..	..	..	..	..	..	70.0	..	..	90.0
Secondary Schl. Enroll. Ratio	4.0	..	..	..	..	8.0	9.0	11.0	12.0	16.0	19.0

1981	1982	1983	1984	1985	1986	1987	1988	1989	1990 estimate	Notes	NIGERIA
											FOREIGN TRADE (CUSTOMS BASIS)
				(Millions of current US dollars)							
18,048.9	15,974.0	10,659.0	12,005.2	13,112.7	5,899.5	7,365.0	6,875.2	7,871.1	13,670.8	..	Value of Exports, fob
441.8	374.1	422.7	350.0	298.0	327.7	167.4	156.3	178.9	310.7	..	Nonfuel Primary Products
17,518.8	15,512.3	10,062.9	11,423.2	12,682.0	5,493.2	7,123.1	6,649.4	7,612.6	13,221.8	..	Fuels
88.2	87.6	173.5	232.0	132.7	78.7	74.5	69.6	79.6	138.3	..	Manufactures
20,455.2	11,131.2	9,028.9	5,868.0	6,204.6	4,028.2	3,907.9	4,726.9	4,190.1	5,687.7	..	Value of Imports, cif
3,704.4	2,301.8	2,322.1	1,548.4	1,502.2	795.4	771.7	933.4	827.4	1,123.1	..	Nonfuel Primary Products
245.2	355.4	73.2	68.1	53.7	21.6	20.9	25.3	22.4	30.5	..	Fuels
16,505.6	8,474.0	6,633.6	4,251.5	4,648.7	3,211.2	3,115.3	3,768.2	3,340.3	4,534.1	..	Manufactures
				(Index 1987 = 100)							
203.8	188.5	182.6	184.5	167.0	83.0	100.0	74.5	85.8	100.2	..	Terms of Trade
197.9	179.0	165.1	162.6	147.6	82.9	100.0	85.3	97.7	125.3	..	Export Prices, fob
97.1	95.0	90.4	88.1	88.4	99.9	100.0	114.5	113.8	125.1	..	Import Prices, cif
				(Millions of current US dollars)							
											BALANCE OF PAYMENTS
19,736.2	12,896.7	10,854.6	12,350.0	13,510.3	6,313.1	7,815.0	7,301.4	8,573.7	14,371.0	..	Exports of Goods & Services
18,115.0	12,162.8	10,343.8	11,859.4	13,114.7	6,014.9	7,544.6	6,897.2	7,870.0	13,827.0	..	Merchandise, fob
901.2	498.9	397.2	425.5	315.6	229.9	224.9	363.7	551.9	174.0	..	Nonfactor Services
719.9	234.9	113.7	65.2	80.0	68.3	45.5	40.6	151.8	370.0	..	Factor Services
25,341.6	19,752.8	14,814.1	11,908.8	10,689.1	5,833.9	7,859.4	7,483.4	7,610.0	12,148.0	..	Imports of Goods & Services
18,946.2	14,893.9	11,432.8	8,867.1	7,498.9	3,701.5	4,096.9	4,271.1	3,692.4	6,918.0	..	Merchandise, fob
4,935.1	3,418.0	2,378.4	1,790.6	1,641.5	1,194.8	870.5	839.6	1,374.2	1,822.0	..	Nonfactor Services
1,460.3	1,441.0	1,002.9	1,251.1	1,548.7	937.6	2,891.9	2,372.7	2,543.5	3,408.0	..	Factor Services
669.3	873.0	997.7	1,248.8	1,298.5	515.2	556.7	1,460.4	1,439.7	1,761.3	..	Long-Term Interest
-441.6	-388.3	-374.4	-300.3	-253.7	-107.8	-19.4	-32.9	-18.6	..	..	Private Current Transfers, net
13.6	12.0	8.4	6.6	9.9	4.5	2.7	2.5	10.2	10.0	..	Workers' Remittances
-6,047.1	-7,244.5	-4,333.8	140.9	2,567.5	371.4	-63.7	-214.9	945.1	2,223.0	..	Curr. A/C Bal before Off. Transf.
-116.7	-40.9	-20.1	-26.4	-1.5	-5.3	-5.1	21.0	145.1	73.0	..	Net Official Transfers
-6,163.8	-7,285.4	-4,353.8	114.5	2,566.0	366.1	-68.8	-193.9	1,090.1	2,296.0	..	Curr. A/C Bal after Off. Transf.
1,335.2	1,522.5	1,828.3	-46.5	-508.0	-961.6	-1,788.3	-2,425.8	-1,170.2	-1,421.9	..	Long-Term Capital, net
546.5	432.5	344.5	199.8	478.3	166.8	602.7	376.9	1,882.2	495.0	..	Direct Investment
2,506.0	2,882.7	1,818.5	-201.5	-1,109.6	98.3	909.4	404.7	1,020.0	-494.1	..	Long-Term Loans
3,140.5	3,723.7	2,980.8	2,023.4	1,659.0	1,346.7	1,358.4	1,051.1	1,543.6	726.6	..	Disbursements
634.5	841.0	1,162.3	2,224.9	2,768.6	1,248.4	449.0	646.4	523.6	1,220.7	..	Repayments
-1,717.2	-1,792.8	-334.7	-44.8	123.3	-1,226.7	-3,300.4	-3,207.4	-4,072.5	-1,422.8	..	Other Long-Term Capital
162.3	3,652.7	2,084.4	414.7	-1,569.4	117.5	1,904.1	2,182.9	1,264.8	945.9	..	Other Capital, net
4,666.3	2,110.2	441.1	-482.8	-488.6	477.9	-46.9	436.8	-1,184.7	-1,820.0	..	Change in Reserves
				(Nigerian Naira per US dollar)							**Memo Item:**
0.620	0.670	0.720	0.770	0.890	1.750	4.020	4.540	7.360	8.040	..	Conversion Factor (Annual Avg)
				(Millions of US dollars), outstanding at end of year							
12,136	12,954	18,539	18,537	19,550	23,580	30,893	31,540	32,768	36,068	..	**EXTERNAL DEBT (Total)**
7,709	10,419	13,481	12,793	14,555	19,861	29,249	29,858	32,067	34,100	..	Long-Term Debt (by debtor)
36	87	2,434	2,012	986	393	439	159	160	181	..	Central Bank, incl. IMF credit
4,268	5,609	5,503	4,830	6,938	13,311	22,794	23,806	27,849	30,381	..	Central Government
581	1,492	2,187	2,639	2,912	3,033	2,769	2,862	1,452	1,524	..	Rest of General Government
1,476	1,917	2,057	1,911	2,303	2,524	2,695	2,494	2,201	1,623	..	Non-financial Public Enterprises
1,347	1,313	1,300	1,400	1,416	600	552	537	406	391	..	Priv. Sector, incl non-guaranteed
4,427	2,535	5,059	5,744	4,995	3,719	1,644	1,682	701	1,968	..	Short-Term Debt
				(Millions of US dollars)							**Memo Items:**
3,895.4	1,612.5	989.9	1,462.3	1,667.2	1,081.4	1,165.3	651.2	1,765.6	3,864.3	..	Int'l Reserves Excluding Gold
273.1	313.9	262.1	211.8	224.7	268.6	332.6	281.8	275.5	264.5	..	Gold Holdings (at market price)
											SOCIAL INDICATORS
6.9	6.9	6.7	6.6	6.4	6.3	6.1	6.1	6.0	6.0	..	Total Fertility Rate
116.0	114.0	112.2	110.4	108.5	106.7	104.9	102.8	100.6	98.5	..	Infant Mortality Rate
48.1	48.5	48.9	49.3	49.7	50.1	50.5	50.8	51.2	51.5	..	Life Expectancy at Birth
27.9	28.7	29.4	30.2	31.0	32.1	33.1	33.8	34.5	35.2	..	Urban Population, % of total
97.5	98.9	92.6	92.2	98.1	101.8	100.0	103.0	105.7	103.4	..	Food Prod. per capita (1987=100)
..	..	..	..	..	..	..	..	..	..	..	Labor Force, Agriculture (%)
36.5	36.3	36.1	35.9	35.7	35.5	35.3	35.1	34.9	34.8	..	Labor Force, Female (%)
91.0	92.1	92.0	81.0	82.0	..	68.0	72.0	70.0	..	..	Primary Schl. Enroll. Ratio
84.0	84.0	81.0	..	73.0	..	59.0	62.0	63.0	..	..	Primary Schl. Enroll. Ratio, Female
22.0	28.0	29.0	..	29.0	..	26.0	21.0	19.0	..	..	Secondary Schl. Enroll. Ratio

NORWAY	1970	1971	1972	1973	1974	1975	1976	1977	1978	1979	1980
CURRENT GNP PER CAPITA (US $)	2,740	3,090	3,560	4,240	5,290	6,610	7,640	8,550	9,500	10,980	12,880
POPULATION (thousands)	3,877	3,903	3,933	3,961	3,985	4,007	4,026	4,043	4,059	4,073	4,091

USE AND ORIGIN OF RESOURCES

(Billions of current Norwegian Kroner)

	1970	1971	1972	1973	1974	1975	1976	1977	1978	1979	1980
Gross National Product (GNP)	79.25	88.36	97.38	110.67	127.88	146.79	167.66	186.80	205.90	229.34	275.53
Net Factor Income from Abroad	-0.62	-0.75	-1.03	-1.19	-1.85	-1.92	-3.05	-4.73	-7.18	-9.33	-9.52
GDP at Market Prices	79.88	89.11	98.40	111.85	129.73	148.70	170.71	191.53	213.08	238.67	285.05
Resource Balance	-1.03	-2.93	0.76	-0.54	-3.76	-9.95	-16.24	-20.50	-1.90	6.25	17.42
Exports of Goods & NFServices	33.40	35.81	40.05	48.73	60.02	62.19	70.17	76.26	87.22	105.41	134.80
Imports of Goods & NFServices	34.43	38.74	39.29	49.27	63.78	72.14	86.41	96.77	89.12	99.15	117.37
Domestic Absorption	80.91	92.04	97.64	112.40	133.49	158.65	186.95	212.04	214.98	232.42	267.62
Private Consumption, etc.	43.05	47.90	52.56	58.29	66.11	77.62	89.49	103.91	110.67	120.10	135.24
General Gov't Consumption	13.53	15.98	17.86	20.39	23.76	28.70	34.09	38.62	43.54	46.59	53.48
Gross Domestic Investment	24.33	28.16	27.22	33.72	43.62	52.33	63.38	69.50	60.77	65.73	78.90
Fixed Investment	21.20	26.45	27.30	32.75	39.60	50.79	62.00	71.07	67.71	66.19	70.80
Indirect Taxes, net	10.45	11.88	12.96	14.36	15.23	17.20	19.39	22.22	21.50	24.36	29.06
GDP at factor cost	69.43	77.22	85.44	97.50	114.50	131.50	151.32	169.32	191.58	214.31	255.98
Agriculture	4.46	5.02	4.93	5.52	6.46	7.12	8.32	9.47	9.81	10.14	10.97
Industry	25.61	28.13	31.50	35.44	42.72	51.39	57.77	62.74	73.06	88.35	112.90
Manufacturing	17.26	18.81	21.12	24.05	28.38	32.27	34.41	35.96	37.53	43.82	45.63
Services, etc.	49.81	55.96	61.98	70.90	80.55	90.20	104.62	119.33	130.20	140.18	161.17
Gross Domestic Saving	23.30	25.23	27.98	33.18	39.86	42.38	47.14	48.99	58.87	71.98	96.33
Gross National Saving	22.90	24.77	27.21	32.17	38.13	40.53	44.10	44.16	51.52	62.38	86.54

(Billions of 1987 Norwegian Kroner)

	1970	1971	1972	1973	1974	1975	1976	1977	1978	1979	1980
Gross National Product	281.87	294.62	309.08	321.49	337.08	351.32	373.39	384.32	397.79	415.20	434.28
GDP at Market Prices	285.05	298.13	313.35	326.02	343.05	356.97	381.14	394.81	412.12	432.80	450.80
Resource Balance	-31.10	-37.91	-23.60	-33.48	-39.65	-46.85	-53.87	-55.46	-18.06	-13.09	-15.28
Exports of Goods & NFServices	91.18	92.22	105.21	113.93	114.70	118.24	131.56	136.34	147.77	151.58	154.76
Imports of Goods & NFServices	122.28	130.13	128.81	147.40	154.35	165.09	185.42	191.80	165.83	164.67	170.03
Domestic Absorption	316.15	336.04	336.95	359.50	382.71	403.82	435.01	450.27	430.17	445.89	466.08
Private Consumption, etc.	166.33	172.30	181.75	187.21	192.25	200.71	213.54	228.40	230.26	237.40	242.07
General Gov't Consumption	53.33	56.55	59.11	62.34	64.84	69.00	74.09	77.75	81.90	84.81	89.41
Gross Domestic Investment	96.48	107.19	96.10	109.95	125.62	134.11	147.38	144.12	118.01	123.68	134.60
Fixed Investment	84.71	100.59	96.47	109.63	115.22	128.95	142.01	147.18	130.68	124.18	122.33
GDP at factor cost	244.46	254.91	269.17	280.64	299.28	312.79	335.55	347.18	368.46	385.49	399.66
Agriculture	13.86	14.61	14.70	14.50	15.91	15.36	15.86	15.98	15.44	15.90	16.22
Industry	74.86	78.22	83.92	87.84	92.76	101.57	110.02	111.23	127.68	138.11	148.00
Manufacturing	67.41	69.80	73.15	77.30	81.17	79.39	79.57	77.92	76.00	78.44	77.58
Services, etc.	196.33	205.30	214.74	223.68	234.38	240.05	255.26	267.60	269.00	278.79	286.59

Memo Items:

	1970	1971	1972	1973	1974	1975	1976	1977	1978	1979	1980
Capacity to Import	118.63	120.27	131.32	145.78	145.26	142.32	150.58	151.16	162.29	175.05	195.28
Terms of Trade Adjustment	27.45	28.05	26.11	31.86	30.55	24.08	19.02	14.82	14.52	23.47	40.52
Gross Domestic Income	312.49	326.18	339.46	357.88	373.61	381.05	400.16	409.63	426.64	456.27	491.32
Gross National Income	309.32	322.68	335.19	353.34	367.63	375.40	392.41	399.14	412.31	438.67	474.80

DOMESTIC PRICES/DEFLATORS

(Index 1987 = 100)

	1970	1971	1972	1973	1974	1975	1976	1977	1978	1979	1980
Overall (GDP)	28.0	29.9	31.4	34.3	37.8	41.7	44.8	48.5	51.7	55.1	63.2
Domestic Absorption	25.6	27.4	29.0	31.3	34.9	39.3	43.0	47.1	50.0	52.1	57.4
Agriculture	32.2	34.4	33.5	38.1	40.6	46.3	52.5	59.3	63.6	63.7	67.6
Industry	34.2	36.0	37.5	40.3	46.1	50.6	52.5	56.4	57.2	64.0	76.3
Manufacturing	25.6	26.9	28.9	31.1	35.0	40.6	43.2	46.2	49.4	55.9	58.8
Consumer Price Index	24.9	26.4	28.4	30.5	33.3	37.2	40.6	44.3	47.9	50.2	55.7

MANUFACTURING ACTIVITY

	1970	1971	1972	1973	1974	1975	1976	1977	1978	1979	1980
Employment (1987=100)	112.1	113.3	113.6	113.6	116.5	115.9	115.8	116.4	114.7	113.3	112.7
Real Earnings per Empl. (1987=100)	73.5	76.9	77.9	80.1	84.0	89.9	93.1	93.8	93.6	92.6	91.7
Real Output per Empl. (1987=100)	64.4	66.0	65.5	70.1	77.4	76.1	78.5	80.6	77.3	79.7	86.6
Earnings as % of Value Added	50.4	52.2	57.2	55.6	54.0	57.7	60.7	63.0	63.8	59.8	60.3

MONETARY HOLDINGS

(Billions of current Norwegian Kroner)

	1970	1971	1972	1973	1974	1975	1976	1977	1978	1979	1980
Money Supply, Broadly Defined	46.70	52.93	59.57	67.61	75.09	86.59	95.66	112.16	126.01	142.83	158.52
Money	17.20	19.21	22.39	25.81	28.87	33.65	32.42	37.00	40.19	43.25	45.56
Currency Outside Banks	7.28	7.99	8.75	9.44	10.77	12.39	14.26	16.08	17.06	17.73	18.82
Demand Deposits	9.92	11.22	13.64	16.37	18.10	21.26	18.16	20.92	23.13	25.52	26.74
Quasi-Money	29.50	33.72	37.18	41.80	46.22	52.94	63.24	75.16	85.83	99.58	112.96

GOVERNMENT DEFICIT (-) OR SURPLUS

(Billions of current Norwegian Kroner)

	1970	1971	1972	1973	1974	1975	1976	1977	1978	1979	1980
GOVERNMENT DEFICIT (-) OR SURPLUS	..	..	-1.44	-1.03	-1.76	-4.72	-10.01	-13.13	-14.47	-14.99	-5.40
Current Revenue	..	..	37.32	42.91	49.02	55.73	66.12	73.86	82.69	92.88	117.80
Current Expenditure	..	..	32.40	36.66	42.51	49.84	61.28	70.19	81.36	90.22	104.40
Current Budget Balance	..	..	4.93	6.24	6.51	5.90	4.84	3.66	1.33	2.67	13.40
Capital Receipts	..	..	0.00	0.00	0.00	0.00	..	..	..	..	0.05
Capital Payments	..	..	6.37	7.27	8.27	10.61	14.85	16.80	15.80	17.66	18.85

1981	1982	1983	1984	1985	1986	1987	1988	1989	1990 estimate	Notes	NORWAY
14,130	14,390	14,150	14,170	14,460	15,410	17,140	19,130	20,640	22,830	..	**CURRENT GNP PER CAPITA (US $)**
4,100	4,115	4,133	4,140	4,153	4,169	4,187	4,209	4,227	4,242	..	**POPULATION (thousands)**
				(Billions of current Norwegian Kroner)							**USE AND ORIGIN OF RESOURCES**
317.09	349.57	389.20	439.37	490.69	504.63	551.93	569.74	605.34	645.59	..	Gross National Product (GNP)
-10.58	-12.70	-13.00	-13.14	-9.51	-9.09	-9.55	-13.54	-17.65	-16.86	..	Net Factor Income from Abroad
327.67	362.27	402.20	452.51	500.20	513.72	561.48	583.28	622.99	662.44	..	GDP at Market Prices
25.82	20.48	31.89	41.23	40.96	-18.38	-11.20	-4.29	26.83	48.04	..	Resource Balance
156.29	165.02	183.92	214.08	235.56	194.66	200.22	213.67	261.53	291.40		Exports of Goods & NF Services
130.47	144.54	152.03	172.85	194.60	213.04	211.43	217.96	234.71	243.36		Imports of Goods & NF Services
301.85	341.79	370.31	411.29	459.24	532.10	572.68	587.56	596.16	614.40		Domestic Absorption
155.20	175.31	192.98	210.92	245.44	278.91	298.05	307.50	311.99	334.05		Private Consumption, etc.
62.62	70.41	78.21	84.10	92.65	101.58	116.04	122.24	131.08	139.29		General Gov't Consumption
84.03	96.07	99.12	116.27	121.14	151.61	158.58	157.83	153.08	141.06		Gross Domestic Investment
91.79	92.26	103.45	117.57	110.04	145.54	157.36	170.35	171.07	125.06		Fixed Investment
33.90	38.08	45.29	52.49	64.10	70.35	75.98	73.21	70.43	72.03		Indirect Taxes, net
293.77	324.18	356.91	400.02	436.10	443.36	485.50	510.06	552.57	590.41	B	GDP at factor cost
12.96	13.44	13.13	15.04	15.15	16.02	17.69	17.69	17.62	..		Agriculture
129.59	142.59	163.11	190.23	206.48	178.31	196.06	197.35	220.35	..		Industry
48.58	51.38	56.72	64.52	70.13	75.65	84.59	89.51	90.20	..		Manufacturing
185.13	206.24	225.95	247.24	278.56	319.39	347.73	368.24	385.02			Services, etc.
109.85	116.55	131.01	157.49	162.11	133.23	147.38	153.54	179.91	189.10		Gross Domestic Saving
99.11	103.48	117.61	144.06	152.03	123.10	136.53	138.91	160.73	171.06		Gross National Saving
				(Billions of 1987 Norwegian Kroner)							
438.65	439.06	460.49	486.59	519.98	544.32	551.93	542.28	531.84	542.61	..	Gross National Product
455.09	456.72	477.53	503.04	531.14	554.27	561.48	554.95	547.30	556.90	..	GDP at Market Prices
-15.67	-22.21	-10.31	-13.46	-12.51	-30.09	-11.20	3.52	23.95	36.75	..	Resource Balance
156.89	156.66	168.52	182.36	194.87	197.90	200.22	211.32	233.75	251.90	..	Exports of Goods & NF Services
172.56	178.86	178.84	195.83	207.38	227.98	211.43	207.80	209.80	215.16	..	Imports of Goods & NF Services
470.76	478.93	487.85	516.50	543.65	584.35	572.68	551.43	523.35	520.16	..	Domestic Absorption
245.42	248.38	255.83	262.07	291.21	304.37	298.05	285.97	267.62	274.68	..	Private Consumption, etc.
94.90	98.62	103.20	105.73	109.18	111.61	116.04	116.61	119.34	122.14	..	General Gov't Consumption
130.43	131.93	128.81	148.71	143.26	168.37	158.58	148.85	136.39	123.34	..	Gross Domestic Investment
144.25	128.37	135.84	150.71	129.69	160.73	157.36	159.87	152.15	108.74	..	Fixed Investment
401.93	403.01	418.17	437.35	455.89	477.31	485.50	486.44	485.59	496.35	B	GDP at factor cost
17.68	18.40	18.22	19.75	17.96	16.91	17.69	17.89	19.18	..	..	Agriculture
146.10	146.62	158.50	172.39	177.67	182.87	196.06	204.29	229.20	..	..	Industry
76.83	76.31	75.75	80.10	83.04	83.00	84.59	80.55	78.39	..	..	Manufacturing
291.31	291.70	300.82	310.90	335.51	354.49	347.73	332.77	298.92			Services, etc.
											Memo Items:
206.71	204.21	216.35	242.53	251.03	208.31	200.22	203.71	233.78	257.63	..	Capacity to Import
49.82	47.55	47.83	60.17	56.16	10.42	0.00	-7.61	0.03	5.73	..	Terms of Trade Adjustment
504.91	504.27	525.36	563.21	587.30	564.68	561.48	547.34	547.33	562.63	..	Gross Domestic Income
488.47	486.61	508.32	546.76	576.14	554.74	551.93	534.67	531.86	548.34	..	Gross National Income
				(Index 1987 = 100)							**DOMESTIC PRICES/DEFLATORS**
72.0	79.3	84.2	90.0	94.2	92.7	100.0	105.1	113.8	119.0	..	Overall (GDP)
64.1	71.4	75.9	79.6	84.5	91.1	100.0	106.6	113.9	118.1	..	Domestic Absorption
73.3	73.0	72.1	76.2	84.3	94.8	100.0	98.9	91.9	..	..	Agriculture
88.7	97.3	102.9	110.3	116.2	97.5	100.0	96.6	96.1	..	..	Industry
63.2	67.3	74.9	80.6	84.5	91.1	100.0	111.1	115.1	..	..	Manufacturing
63.3	70.5	76.4	81.2	85.8	92.0	100.0	106.7	111.6	116.1	..	Consumer Price Index
											MANUFACTURING ACTIVITY
110.8	107.6	100.0	98.8	99.4	100.3	100.0	93.5	92.4	..	..	Employment (1987=100)
89.8	87.8	89.9	92.7	96.2	98.3	100.0	100.8	..	..	..	Real Earnings per Empl. (1987=100)
91.0	91.5	92.2	97.7	105.0	101.0	100.0	104.5	..	..	..	Real Output per Empl. (1987=100)
62.1	62.3	58.9	56.4	58.1	59.9	59.1	56.1	..	..	..	Earnings as % of Value Added
				(Billions of current Norwegian Kroner)							**MONETARY HOLDINGS**
179.99	200.29	222.58	268.10	305.65	312.94	359.74	377.40	409.79	432.70	..	Money Supply, Broadly Defined
52.38	58.81	65.92	82.00	98.65	101.76	152.63	187.11	218.30	237.63	..	Money
20.16	20.93	21.75	22.78	25.05	26.58	28.16	28.52	29.20	29.88	..	Currency Outside Banks
32.22	37.88	44.17	59.22	73.60	75.18	124.48	158.58	189.10	207.75	..	Demand Deposits
127.61	141.48	156.67	186.10	207.00	211.18	207.11	190.30	191.50	195.07	..	Quasi-Money
				(Billions of current Norwegian Kroner)							
6.82	3.89	9.44	8.96	18.28	17.32	0.32	-0.83	-7.80	4.44	E	**GOVERNMENT DEFICIT (-) OR SURPLUS**
141.24	154.68	177.41	194.94	224.09	245.53	256.42	270.98	282.82	310.69	..	Current Revenue
119.72	135.15	150.00	163.32	178.85	199.38	223.22	244.04	264.15	289.18	..	Current Expenditure
21.52	19.53	27.40	31.61	45.24	46.15	33.19	26.94	18.67	21.52	..	Current Budget Balance
0.04	0.10	0.15	0.25	0.39	0.38	0.81	1.51	1.53	1.46	..	Capital Receipts
14.74	15.74	18.11	22.90	27.36	29.21	33.69	29.27	28.00	18.54	..	Capital Payments

NORWAY	1970	1971	1972	1973	1974	1975	1976	1977	1978	1979	1980
FOREIGN TRADE (CUSTOMS BASIS)					*(Millions of current US dollars)*						
Value of Exports, fob	2,457	2,563	3,279	4,680	6,274	7,207	7,917	8,716	10,027	13,466	18,481
Nonfuel Primary Products	1,041	1,061	1,230	1,709	2,061	1,827	2,231	2,424	2,623	3,175	3,615
Fuels	54	58	105	139	401	936	1,501	1,638	2,058	4,863	8,935
Manufactures	1,361	1,444	1,944	2,831	3,812	4,444	4,185	4,654	5,346	5,428	5,931
Value of Imports, cif	3,702	4,083	4,369	6,219	8,414	9,705	11,105	12,870	11,435	13,732	16,952
Nonfuel Primary Products	791	780	827	1,109	1,550	1,528	1,583	1,647	1,667	2,094	2,610
Fuels	285	308	326	479	1,034	955	1,241	1,424	1,353	2,071	2,957
Manufactures	2,627	2,996	3,216	4,631	5,830	7,222	8,281	9,800	8,416	9,568	11,384
					(Index 1987 = 100)						
Terms of Trade	169.0	152.9	144.2	150.6	134.7	130.7	126.6	126.1	120.1	118.7	134.2
Export Prices, fob	36.3	37.4	38.9	51.2	69.6	72.6	71.9	78.6	82.1	96.1	127.9
Import Prices, cif	21.5	24.5	27.0	34.0	51.7	55.5	56.8	62.3	68.3	81.0	95.4
BALANCE OF PAYMENTS					*(Millions of current US dollars)*						
Exports of Goods & Services	4,790	5,204	6,177	8,563	11,157	12,125	13,113	14,564	17,022	21,397	28,252
Merchandise, fob	2,480	2,587	3,307	4,729	6,329	7,270	8,047	9,152	11,033	13,747	18,649
Nonfactor Services	2,166	2,481	2,742	3,631	4,505	4,511	4,744	5,061	5,521	6,992	8,525
Factor Services	144	136	127	203	322	343	323	351	468	659	1,078
Imports of Goods & Services	5,021	5,729	6,216	8,879	12,174	14,444	16,661	19,305	18,757	22,005	26,658
Merchandise, fob	3,633	4,046	4,322	6,262	8,666	10,141	11,608	13,205	11,545	13,601	16,753
Nonfactor Services	1,138	1,364	1,508	2,032	2,540	3,592	4,172	4,860	5,372	5,900	6,901
Factor Services	250	319	385	586	968	710	882	1,240	1,840	2,504	3,004
Long-Term Interest	..	..	..	..	..	..	..	..	..	..	..
Private Current Transfers, net	31	41	39	31	20	12	1	-18	-31	-53	-55
Workers' Remittances	..	..	..	..	..	..	..	4	6	6	13
Curr. A/C Bal before Off. Transf.	-200	-484	0	-285	-997	-2,307	-3,547	-4,759	-1,766	-660	1,539
Net Official Transfers	-42	-41	-59	-79	-121	-171	-199	-275	-337	-384	-441
Curr. A/C Bal after Off. Transf.	-242	-525	-59	-364	-1,118	-2,478	-3,746	-5,034	-2,103	-1,044	1,098
Long-Term Capital, net	138	354	286	850	990	2,577	2,495	4,185	3,187	2,269	-927
Direct Investment	32	62	121	159	198	48	179	643	424	358	-193
Long-Term Loans	..	..	..	..	..	..	..	..	..	..	..
Disbursements	..	..	..	..	..	..	..	..	..	..	..
Repayments	..	..	..	..	..	..	..	..	..	..	..
Other Long-Term Capital	106	292	165	691	792	2,529	2,316	3,542	2,763	1,912	-734
Other Capital, net	175	475	-88	-242	448	242	1,223	727	-447	60	1,711
Change in Reserves	-71	-304	-139	-244	-321	-340	28	121	-637	-1,285	-1,882
Memo Item:					*(Norwegian Kroner per US dollar)*						
Conversion Factor (Annual Avg)	7.140	7.040	6.590	5.770	5.540	5.230	5.460	5.320	5.240	5.060	4.940
				(Millions US dollars), outstanding at end of year							
EXTERNAL DEBT (Total)	..	..	..	..	..	..	..	..	..	..	..
Long-Term Debt (by debtor)	..	..	..	..	..	..	..	..	..	..	..
Central Bank, incl. IMF credit	..	..	..	..	..	..	..	..	..	..	..
Central Government	..	..	..	..	..	..	..	..	..	..	..
Rest of General Government	..	..	..	..	..	..	..	..	..	..	..
Non-financial Public Enterprises	..	..	..	..	..	..	..	..	..	..	..
Priv. Sector, incl non-guaranteed	..	..	..	..	..	..	..	..	..	..	..
Short-Term Debt	..	..	..	..	..	..	..	..	..	..	..
Memo Items:					*(Millions of US dollars)*						
Int'l Reserves Excluding Gold	788	1,118	1,288	1,533	1,887	2,196	2,189	2,196	2,861	4,215	6,048
Gold Holdings (at market price)	25	41	63	110	183	137	132	178	256	606	698
SOCIAL INDICATORS											
Total Fertility Rate	2.5	2.5	2.4	2.2	2.1	2.0	1.9	1.8	1.8	1.8	1.7
Infant Mortality Rate	12.7	12.8	11.8	11.9	10.4	11.0	10.4	9.1	8.6	8.7	8.0
Life Expectancy at Birth	74.2	74.3	74.4	74.6	74.8	75.0	75.1	75.3	75.5	75.6	75.7
Urban Population, % of total	65.4	66.0	66.5	67.1	67.6	68.2	68.7	69.1	69.6	70.0	70.5
Food Prod. per capita (1987=100)	83.2	85.6	84.8	84.9	94.5	87.8	86.3	92.0	96.7	94.7	96.9
Labor Force, Agriculture (%)	11.8	11.4	11.0	10.7	10.3	10.0	9.6	9.3	9.0	8.6	8.3
Labor Force, Female (%)	29.3	30.5	31.7	32.9	33.9	35.0	36.1	37.1	38.2	39.1	40.1
Primary Schl. Enroll. Ratio	89.0	..	..	..	..	101.0	101.0	100.0	100.0	100.0	100.0
Primary Schl. Enroll. Ratio, Female	94.0	..	..	..	..	101.0	101.0	100.0	100.0	100.0	100.0
Secondary Schl. Enroll. Ratio	83.0	..	..	..	..	88.0	89.0	90.0	92.0	94.0	94.0

1981	1982	1983	1984	1985	1986	1987	1988	1989	1990 estimate	Notes	NORWAY
											FOREIGN TRADE (CUSTOMS BASIS)
17,968	17,583	17,972	18,914	19,941	18,230	21,449	22,503	27,030	34,072	..	Value of Exports, fob
3,401	2,877	3,180	3,358	3,227	3,576	4,556	5,735	6,290	7,017	..	Nonfuel Primary Products
9,034	9,135	9,481	10,322	10,698	7,813	8,690	8,218	11,498	16,274	..	Fuels
5,533	5,571	5,311	5,234	6,016	6,841	8,203	8,550	9,242	10,781	..	Manufactures
15,638	15,471	13,494	13,885	15,871	20,298	22,578	23,220	23,632	26,889	..	Value of Imports, cif
2,255	1,930	1,769	1,918	2,124	2,442	2,691	3,240	3,363	5,544	..	Nonfuel Primary Products
2,253	2,030	1,402	1,421	1,452	1,192	1,193	849	895	1,183	..	Fuels
11,130	11,511	10,323	10,546	12,295	16,664	18,694	19,131	19,374	20,161	..	Manufactures

(Index 1987 = 100)

139.0	137.7	131.4	132.9	130.1	105.8	100.0	90.1	88.7	91.4		Terms of Trade
128.6	120.6	111.6	110.0	106.2	97.8	100.0	99.9	106.3	121.7		Export Prices, fob
92.5	87.6	84.9	82.8	81.6	92.4	100.0	110.9	119.8	133.1		Import Prices, cif

(Millions of current US dollars)

											BALANCE OF PAYMENTS
28,690	27,220	26,542	27,828	29,615	29,008	32,776	36,069	41,318	50,759		Exports of Goods & Services
18,494	17,664	18,055	19,115	20,059	18,143	21,191	23,075	27,171	34,138		Merchandise, fob
8,676	7,898	7,061	7,068	7,428	8,100	8,478	9,648	10,616	12,587		Nonfactor Services
1,520	1,658	1,425	1,645	2,128	2,766	3,107	3,346	3,531	4,035		Factor Services
26,028	25,997	23,977	24,403	25,998	32,749	35,899	38,828	40,007	45,578		Imports of Goods & Services
15,459	15,278	13,704	13,957	15,331	20,258	21,951	23,284	23,400	26,513		Merchandise, fob
7,190	7,056	7,060	7,174	7,438	8,497	9,428	10,109	10,509	12,367		Nonfactor Services
3,379	3,663	3,213	3,272	3,229	3,994	4,520	5,435	6,097	6,698		Factor Services
..	..	..	..	..	..	..	..	..	..		Long-Term Interest
-29	-57	-54	-36	-66	-140	-194	-168	-222	-190		Private Current Transfers, net
9	11	9	10	11	11	12	9	17	22		Workers' Remittances
2,633	1,166	2,510	3,389	3,551	-3,880	-3,316	-2,927	1,089	4,991		Curr. A/C Bal before Off. Transf.
-456	-504	-524	-469	-499	-665	-788	-962	-910	-1,208		Net Official Transfers
2,177	662	1,986	2,919	3,052	-4,545	-4,105	-3,889	179	3,783		Curr. A/C Bal after Off. Transf.
-900	292	-1,582	-600	-1,367	2,809	-13	4,567	3,102	-1,977		Long-Term Capital, net
499	136	-27	-781	-1,731	-582	-687	-699	222	-505		Direct Investment
..	..	..	..	..	..	..	..	..	..		Long-Term Loans
..	..	..	..	..	..	..	..	..	..		Disbursements
..	..	..	..	..	..	..	..	..	..		Repayments
-1,399	155	-1,555	181	363	3,391	674	5,266	2,880	-1,472		Other Long-Term Capital
-846	-246	-502	748	1,768	-1,474	3,898	-816	-2,316	-1,389		Other Capital, net
-431	-708	98	-3,068	-3,452	3,211	220	138	-965	-418		Change in Reserves

(Norwegian Kroner per US dollar)

											Memo Item:
5.740	6.450	7.300	8.160	8.600	7.390	6.740	6.520	6.900	6.260	..	Conversion Factor (Annual Avg)

(Millions US dollars), outstanding at end of year

..	..	..	..	..	..	..	..	..	..	..	**EXTERNAL DEBT (Total)**
..	..	..	..	..	..	..	..	..	..	..	Long-Term Debt (by debtor)
..	..	..	..	..	..	..	..	..	..	..	Central Bank, incl. IMF credit
..	..	..	..	..	..	..	..	..	..	..	Central Government
..	..	..	..	..	..	..	..	..	..	..	Rest of General Government
..	..	..	..	..	..	..	..	..	..	..	Non-financial Public Enterprises
..	..	..	..	..	..	..	..	..	..	..	Priv. Sector, incl non-guaranteed
..	..	..	..	..	..	..	..	..	..	..	Short-Term Debt

(Millions of US dollars)

											Memo Items:
6,253	6,874	6,629	9,365	13,917	12,525	14,277	13,268	13,785	15,332	..	Int'l Reserves Excluding Gold
471	541	452	365	387	463	573	486	475	456	..	Gold Holdings (at market price)
											SOCIAL INDICATORS
1.7	1.7	1.7	1.7	1.7	1.7	1.8	1.8	1.8	1.8		Total Fertility Rate
7.5	8.1	7.9	8.2	8.5	7.8	8.4	8.3	8.2	8.1		Infant Mortality Rate
75.9	76.0	76.2	76.3	76.5	76.6	76.8	76.9	77.1	77.3		Life Expectancy at Birth
71.0	71.4	71.9	72.3	72.8	73.2	73.7	74.1	74.6	75.0		Urban Population, % of total
99.6	103.9	99.0	103.9	101.1	97.3	100.0	96.3	97.5	96.7		Food Prod. per capita (1987=100)
..	..	..	..	..	..	..	..	..			Labor Force, Agriculture (%)
40.2	40.3	40.3	40.4	40.5	40.6	40.8	40.9	41.0	41.1		Labor Force, Female (%)
..	98.0	98.0	95.0	94.0	95.0	96.0	97.0	98.0	..	..	Primary Schl. Enroll. Ratio
100.0	99.0	98.0	94.0	94.0	95.0	95.0	96.0	98.0		..	Primary Schl. Enroll. Ratio, Female
..	97.0	96.0	97.0	97.0	95.0	93.0	94.0	98.0		..	Secondary Schl. Enroll. Ratio

OMAN	1970	1971	1972	1973	1974	1975	1976	1977	1978	1979	1980
CURRENT GNP PER CAPITA (US $)	360	370	390	390	550	1,280	2,840	2,860	2,790	3,080	3,660
POPULATION (thousands)	654	670	688	710	736	766	802	843	888	936	984

USE AND ORIGIN OF RESOURCES *(Millions of current Rials Omani)*

	1970	1971	1972	1973	1974	1975	1976	1977	1978	1979	1980
Gross National Product (GNP)	88.6	105.1	111.8	106.7	416.5	589.3	736.4	816.6	835.9	1,152.2	1,843.6
Net Factor Income from Abroad	-18.2	-20.0	-29.0	-62.7	-152.0	-134.9	-147.9	-130.2	-111.0	-137.3	-222.6
GDP at Market Prices	106.8	125.1	140.8	169.4	568.5	724.2	884.3	946.8	946.9	1,289.5	2,066.2
Resource Balance	57.7	42.1	22.0	21.4	147.6	122.1	144.7	135.0	90.8	262.4	516.6
Exports of Goods & NFServices	78.7	82.3	83.6	114.9	419.1	489.2	551.2	552.0	552.0	787.4	1,294.6
Imports of Goods & NFServices	21.0	40.2	61.6	93.5	271.5	367.1	406.5	417.0	461.2	525.0	778.0
Domestic Absorption	49.1	83.0	118.8	148.0	420.9	602.1	739.6	811.8	855.7	1,027.1	1,549.6
Private Consumption, etc.	20.7	21.4	35.1	40.6	49.6	115.1	181.6	253.4	309.9	337.0	572.3
General Gov't Consumption	13.7	26.0	41.7	63.0	197.2	229.0	240.9	268.5	272.3	354.7	516.7
Gross Domestic Investment	14.7	35.6	42.0	44.4	174.1	258.0	317.1	289.9	273.5	335.4	460.6
Fixed Investment	14.7	35.6	42.0	44.4	174.1	258.0	321.2	310.8	281.0	318.0	464.3
Indirect Taxes, net	1.1	1.1	1.6	1.7	2.3	0.5	4.5	4.6	4.6	8.1	12.0
GDP at factor cost	105.7	124.0	139.2	167.7	566.2	723.7	879.8	942.2	942.3	1,281.4	2,054.2
Agriculture	16.6	16.8	17.0	16.7	18.4	20.2	18.3	24.1	30.7	40.3	52.6
Industry	82.5	94.8	100.0	120.0	469.1	561.5	616.7	626.7	584.8	828.1	1,433.1
Manufacturing	0.2	0.2	0.3	0.6	2.0	2.1	4.3	6.7	8.5	9.6	13.4
Services, etc.	7.7	13.5	23.8	32.7	81.0	142.5	249.3	296.0	331.4	421.1	580.5
Gross Domestic Saving	72.4	77.7	64.0	65.8	321.7	380.1	461.8	424.9	364.7	597.8	977.2
Gross National Saving	..	..	..	..	131.4	173.3	238.0	218.1	180.4	374.6	629.6

(Millions of 1987 Rials Omani)

	1970	1971	1972	1973	1974	1975	1976	1977	1978	1979	1980
Gross National Product	710.6	725.7	748.2	649.9	638.4	918.1	1,133.4	1,184.7	1,167.8	1,177.2	1,131.3
GDP at Market Prices	879.1	887.0	974.1	835.3	931.3	1,158.9	1,396.9	1,411.0	1,359.4	1,374.1	1,426.0
Resource Balance	..	..	..	..	..	..	..	..	..	..	..
Exports of Goods & NFServices	..	..	..	..	..	..	..	..	..	..	..
Imports of Goods & NFServices	..	..	..	..	..	..	..	..	..	..	..
Domestic Absorption	..	..	..	..	..	..	..	..	..	..	..
Private Consumption, etc.	..	..	..	..	..	..	..	..	..	..	..
General Gov't Consumption	..	..	..	..	..	..	..	..	..	..	..
Gross Domestic Investment	..	..	..	..	..	..	..	..	386.0	461.0	479.9
Fixed Investment	..	..	..	..	..	..	..	..	..	..	..
GDP at factor cost	..	..	..	..	..	..	..	..	..	..	..
Agriculture	..	..	..	..	..	..	..	..	34.8	46.0	55.5
Industry	..	..	..	..	..	..	..	..	1,123.7	1,077.3	1,075.0
Manufacturing	..	..	..	..	..	..	..	..	11.2	13.9	16.5
Services, etc.	..	..	..	..	..	..	..	..	201.0	250.8	295.5

Memo Items:

	1970	1971	1972	1973	1974	1975	1976	1977	1978	1979	1980
Capacity to Import	..	..	..	..	..	..	..	..	..	..	..
Terms of Trade Adjustment	..	..	..	..	..	..	..	..	..	..	..
Gross Domestic Income	..	..	..	..	..	..	..	..	..	..	..
Gross National Income	..	..	..	..	..	..	..	..	..	..	..

DOMESTIC PRICES/DEFLATORS *(Index 1987 = 100)*

	1970	1971	1972	1973	1974	1975	1976	1977	1978	1979	1980
Overall (GDP)	12.1	14.1	14.5	20.3	61.0	62.5	63.3	67.1	69.7	93.8	144.9
Domestic Absorption	..	..	..	..	..	..	..	..	..	..	..
Agriculture	..	..	..	..	..	..	..	..	88.2	87.6	94.7
Industry	..	..	..	..	..	..	..	..	52.0	76.9	133.3
Manufacturing	..	..	..	..	..	..	..	..	75.6	69.1	81.0
Consumer Price Index	..	..	..	..	..	..	..	..	..	..	..

MANUFACTURING ACTIVITY

	1970	1971	1972	1973	1974	1975	1976	1977	1978	1979	1980
Employment (1987=100)	..	..	..	..	..	..	..	..	..	..	..
Real Earnings per Empl. (1987=100)	..	..	..	..	..	..	..	..	..	..	..
Real Output per Empl. (1987=100)	..	..	..	..	..	..	..	..	..	..	..
Earnings as % of Value Added	..	..	..	..	..	..	..	..	61.4	..	..

MONETARY HOLDINGS *(Millions of current Rials Omani)*

	1970	1971	1972	1973	1974	1975	1976	1977	1978	1979	1980
Money Supply, Broadly Defined	..	..	44.76	46.61	85.24	117.98	164.59	206.56	230.61	246.22	325.01
Money	..	..	18.96	24.95	48.41	71.64	102.12	111.22	114.32	123.14	154.73
Currency Outside Banks	..	..	12.29	15.17	28.88	38.53	47.76	55.07	64.38	74.28	94.80
Demand Deposits	..	..	6.66	9.78	19.52	33.11	54.36	56.16	49.94	48.86	59.93
Quasi-Money	..	..	25.80	21.66	36.83	46.34	62.48	95.33	116.30	123.08	170.28

GOVERNMENT DEFICIT (-) OR SURPLUS *(Millions of current Rials Omani)*

	1970	1971	1972	1973	1974	1975	1976	1977	1978	1979	1980
GOVERNMENT DEFICIT (-) OR SURPLUS	..	..	-17.1	-23.5	-56.4	-37.7	-84.7	58.1	-75.3	85.0	9.1
Current Revenue	..	..	53.0	68.5	311.5	429.5	473.5	575.0	446.3	650.7	825.2
Current Expenditure	..	..	..	62.2	186.5	309.9	369.9	367.7	410.8	420.5	626.3
Current Budget Balance	..	..	..	6.3	125.0	119.6	103.6	207.3	35.5	230.2	198.9
Capital Receipts	..	..	..	..	..	0.8	1.8	1.1	1.3	1.8	3.9
Capital Payments	..	..	..	29.8	181.4	158.1	190.1	150.3	112.1	147.0	193.7

1981	1982	1983	1984	1985	1986	1987	1988	1989	1990 estimate	Notes	OMAN
5,830	7,110	7,220	7,280	7,550	6,680	5,820	4,990	5,220	..	..	**CURRENT GNP PER CAPITA (US $)**
1,033	1,083	1,135	1,188	1,242	1,299	1,358	1,421	1,486	1,554	..	**POPULATION (thousands)**
			(Millions of current Rials Omani)								**USE AND ORIGIN OF RESOURCES**
2,269.4	2,382.7	2,429.9	2,696.7	3,056.9	2,459.7	2,804.5	2,760.0	2,935.6	..	..	Gross National Product (GNP)
-237.5	-226.7	-310.0	-350.2	-399.0	-338.0	-328.1	-201.3	..	..	..	Net Factor Income from Abroad
2,506.9	2,609.4	2,739.9	3,046.9	3,455.9	2,797.7	3,132.6	2,961.3		..	..	GDP at Market Prices
666.9	401.7	427.0	387.0	437.0	-396.0	..	..	..	..	..	Resource Balance
1,621.9	1,527.7	1,470.0	1,532.0	1,722.0	1,060.2			..	..	..	Exports of Goods & NFServices
955.0	1,126.0	1,043.0	1,145.0	1,285.0	1,456.2			..	..	..	Imports of Goods & NFServices
1,840.0	2,207.7	2,312.9	2,659.7	3,018.9	3,193.7	2,407.6	2,626.4	..	..	..	Domestic Absorption
647.7	832.5	859.5	938.5	1,171.7	1,441.9	929.6	1,179.7	..	..	..	Private Consumption, etc.
616.7	681.2	727.8	808.0	894.1	853.4	913.7	956.0	..	..	..	General Gov't Consumption
575.6	694.0	725.6	913.2	953.1	898.4	564.3	490.6	..	..	..	Gross Domestic Investment
569.9	709.2	..	..	..	..	..	..	..	..	..	Fixed Investment
..	..	..	..	..	..	..	..	..	..	..	Indirect Taxes, net
										B	GDP at factor cost
62.1	66.1	80.5	89.0	95.8	89.3	70.6	77.8	..	..		Agriculture
1,683.1	1,651.7	1,663.1	1,800.5	2,049.0	1,206.5	2,465.8	2,361.1		..	..	Industry
24.0	35.9	67.1	92.3	115.9	178.3	111.5	122.7	..	..	..	Manufacturing
761.7	891.6	996.3	1,157.4	1,311.1	1,501.9	596.2	522.4	..	..	..	Services, etc.
1,242.5	1,095.7	1,152.6	1,300.4	1,390.1	502.4	1,289.3	825.5	..	..	..	Gross Domestic Saving
846.0	677.0	602.6	667.2	678.1	-158.6	691.2	331.2	..	..	..	Gross National Saving
			(Millions of 1987 Rials Omani)								
1,410.8	1,566.0	1,842.6	2,116.8	2,457.4	2,768.8	2,804.5	2,732.0	2,825.8	..	..	Gross National Product
1,664.8	1,841.5	2,175.0	2,515.5	2,907.7	3,089.6	3,132.6	..	..	..	..	GDP at Market Prices
..	..	..	..	..	..	..	..	..	..	..	Resource Balance
..	..	..	..	..	..	..	..	..	..	..	Exports of Goods & NFServices
..	..	..	..	..	..	..	..	..	..	..	Imports of Goods & NFServices
..	..	..	..	..	..	..	..	..	..	..	Domestic Absorption
..	..	..	..	..	..	..	..	..	..	..	Private Consumption, etc.
						913.7			..	..	General Gov't Consumption
601.4	814.1	888.1	1,337.1	1,435.9	1,101.2	564.3	..	..	..	..	Gross Domestic Investment
..	..	..	..	..	..	..	..	..	..	..	Fixed Investment
										B	GDP at factor cost
56.3	61.3	72.8	79.8	94.2	83.5	70.6	79.8	..	..	..	Agriculture
1,245.6	1,354.1	1,639.1	1,880.3	2,203.8	2,443.9	2,465.8	..	..	..	..	Industry
27.2	41.3	63.2	89.3	110.3	100.9	111.5	115.4	..	..	..	Manufacturing
362.9	426.1	463.1	555.4	609.7	562.2	596.2	..	..	..	..	Services, etc.
											Memo Items:
..	..	..	..	..	..	..	..	..	..	..	Capacity to Import
..	..	..	..	..	..	..	..	..	..	..	Terms of Trade Adjustment
..	..	..	..	..	..	..	..	..	..	..	Gross Domestic Income
..	..	..	..	..	..	..	..	..	..	..	Gross National Income
			(Index 1987 = 100)								**DOMESTIC PRICES/DEFLATORS**
150.6	141.7	126.0	121.1	118.9	90.6	100.0	..	..	..	..	Overall (GDP)
..	..	..	..	..	..	..	..	..	..	..	Domestic Absorption
110.3	107.8	110.6	111.6	101.7	106.9	100.0	97.5	..	..	..	Agriculture
135.1	122.0	101.5	95.8	93.0	49.4	100.0	..	..	..	..	Industry
88.1	87.0	106.1	103.4	105.1	176.7	100.0	106.4	..	..	..	Manufacturing
..	..	..	..	..	..	..	..	..	..	..	Consumer Price Index
											MANUFACTURING ACTIVITY
..	..	..	..	..	..	..	..	..	..	..	Employment (1987=100)
..	..	..	..	..	..	..	..	..	..	..	Real Earnings per Empl. (1987=100)
..	..	..	..	..	..	..	..	..	..	..	Real Output per Empl. (1987=100)
..	..	..	..	..	..	..	..	..	..	..	Earnings as % of Value Added
			(Millions of current Rials Omani)								**MONETARY HOLDINGS**
450.69	570.87	704.55	774.00	936.96	873.44	919.49	974.10	1,065.78	1,172.03	..	Money Supply, Broadly Defined
212.65	248.79	299.07	283.92	328.60	312.82	335.19	315.29	345.44	390.76	..	Money
116.17	129.81	140.40	149.96	178.52	168.83	180.36	176.27	183.57	214.12	..	Currency Outside Banks
96.48	118.98	158.68	133.96	150.08	143.99	154.83	139.02	161.86	176.64	..	Demand Deposits
238.04	322.08	405.48	490.08	608.36	560.62	584.30	658.81	720.34	781.27	..	Quasi-Money
			(Millions of current Rials Omani)								**GOVERNMENT DEFICIT (-) OR SURPLUS**
48.5	-222.8	-242.3	-346.8	-364.2	-700.2	-146.2	-346.7	-289.5	-32.8	..	
1,123.4	999.0	1,122.2	1,212.1	1,393.2	888.2	1,197.8	1,025.7	1,148.5	1,580.4	..	Current Revenue
787.0	891.2	1,017.4	1,127.1	1,293.4	1,218.1	1,091.8	1,152.8	1,240.5	1,430.9	..	Current Expenditure
336.4	107.8	104.8	85.0	99.8	-329.9	106.0	-127.1	-92.0	149.5	..	Current Budget Balance
2.5	2.2	2.2	2.3	4.4	6.8	1.6	3.5	4.7	6.3	..	Capital Receipts
290.4	332.8	349.3	434.1	468.4	377.1	253.8	223.1	202.2	188.6	..	Capital Payments

OMAN	1970	1971	1972	1973	1974	1975	1976	1977	1978	1979	1980
FOREIGN TRADE (CUSTOMS BASIS)					*(Millions of current US dollars)*						
Value of Exports, fob	206.2	221.1	241.5	344.0	1,211.3	1,436.5	1,566.0	1,573.0	1,512.5	2,279.8	3,747.7
Nonfuel Primary Products	0.9	1.0	1.0	1.7	1.2	3.1	15.7	15.8	15.2	44.3	32.0
Fuels	205.3	220.1	240.5	342.2	1,210.0	1,433.3	1,474.0	1,480.6	1,423.6	2,159.3	3,603.9
Manufactures	0.1	0.0	0.0	0.0	0.0	0.0	76.2	76.6	73.6	76.2	111.8
Value of Imports, cif	18.2	33.1	48.8	116.8	392.5	670.5	667.3	874.5	947.4	1,246.4	1,732.0
Nonfuel Primary Products	0.6	13.6	17.2	33.1	59.8	106.1	111.3	153.5	181.2	234.1	295.1
Fuels	0.8	2.3	2.4	5.1	14.7	31.3	48.1	62.1	79.7	83.8	187.0
Manufactures	16.8	17.2	29.2	78.6	318.1	533.1	508.0	658.9	686.4	928.5	1,249.9
Terms of Trade					*(Index 1987 = 100)*						
Export Prices, fob	..	..	..	..	..	..	..	..	..	..	..
Import Prices, cif	..	..	..	..	..	..	..	..	..	..	..
BALANCE OF PAYMENTS					*(Millions of current US dollars)*						
Exports of Goods & Services	..	..	..	..	1,231.3	1,432.8	1,601.3	1,619.6	1,610.6	2,287.2	3,852.3
Merchandise, fob	..	..	..	..	1,212.2	1,416.3	1,595.8	1,619.6	1,598.1	2,279.7	3,748.1
Nonfactor Services	..	..	..	..	0.0	0.0	0.0	0.0	7.8	7.5	8.7
Factor Services	..	..	..	..	19.1	16.5	5.5	0.0	4.6	0.0	95.5
Imports of Goods & Services	..	..	..	..	965.3	1,374.6	1,397.2	1,389.4	1,468.2	1,669.1	2,650.0
Merchandise, fob	..	..	..	..	551.5	907.9	1,000.0	1,044.0	1,157.2	1,285.2	1,780.0
Nonfactor Services	..	..	..	..	103.6	154.9	176.9	185.9	193.1	234.8	517.7
Factor Services	..	..	..	..	310.1	311.8	220.3	159.5	117.8	149.1	352.3
Long-Term Interest	0.0	0.0	0.0	0.0	3.6	6.5	10.1	25.1	20.2	23.3	43.9
Private Current Transfers, net	..	..	..	..	-110.9	-208.2	-219.7	-221.8	-212.2	-248.7	-361.9
Workers' Remittances	..	..	..	..	0.0	0.0	0.0	0.0	29.0	32.7	34.7
Curr. A/C Bal before Off. Transf.	..	..	..	..	155.2	-150.0	-15.6	8.4	-69.8	369.4	840.5
Net Official Transfers	..	..	..	..	24.0	207.3	52.1	268.4	20.3	179.2	101.9
Curr. A/C Bal after Off. Transf.	..	..	..	..	179.2	57.3	36.5	276.8	-49.5	548.6	942.4
Long-Term Capital, net	..	..	..	..	16.5	245.2	246.4	132.6	136.4	-25.2	39.4
Direct Investment	..	..	..	..	-61.1	106.3	81.4	48.1	86.3	117.5	98.4
Long-Term Loans	0.0	0.0	0.0	43.5	124.1	121.1	76.0	99.3	-55.0	47.7	-81.4
Disbursements	0.0	0.0	0.0	43.5	130.0	142.2	105.9	161.2	65.5	216.2	97.7
Repayments	0.0	0.0	0.0	0.0	5.9	21.1	29.9	61.9	120.5	168.5	179.1
Other Long-Term Capital	..	..	..	..	-46.5	17.9	89.0	-14.8	105.1	-190.4	22.3
Other Capital, net	..	..	..	..	-145.2	-237.0	-226.3	-337.2	-135.4	-368.0	-185.7
Change in Reserves	..	-14.1	-14.1	-5.1	-50.5	-65.5	-56.6	-72.2	48.5	-155.4	-796.1
Memo Item:					*(Rials Omani per US dollar)*						
Conversion Factor (Annual Avg)	0.420	0.420	0.380	0.350	0.350	0.350	0.350	0.350	0.350	0.350	0.350
EXTERNAL DEBT (Total)					*(Millions of US dollars), outstanding at end of year*						
	0.0	0.0	0.0	41.7	175.7	287.4	349.2	654.3	631.4	660.1	598.6
Long-Term Debt (by debtor)	0.0	0.0	0.0	41.7	175.7	287.4	349.2	473.3	449.4	514.1	435.6
Central Bank, incl. IMF credit	..	..	..	..	..	..	..	..	..	..	..
Central Government	0.0	0.0	0.0	41.7	175.7	287.4	349.2	473.3	449.4	514.1	435.6
Rest of General Government	..	..	..	..	..	..	..	..	..	..	..
Non-financial Public Enterprises	0.0	0.0	0.0	0.0	0.0	0.0	0.0	0.0	0.0	0.0	0.0
Priv. Sector, incl non-guaranteed	..	..	..	..	..	..	..	..	..	..	..
Short-Term Debt	0.0	0.0	0.0	0.0	0.0	0.0	0.0	181.0	182.0	146.0	163.0
Memo Items:					*(Millions of US dollars)*						
Int'l Reserves Excluding Gold	10.3	24.4	36.4	47.1	92.9	161.3	219.6	289.6	254.1	415.6	581.4
Gold Holdings (at market price)	2.4	0.6	0.9	1.6	5.6	4.2	6.2	16.7	41.9	95.8	123.1
SOCIAL INDICATORS											
Total Fertility Rate	7.2	7.2	7.2	7.2	7.2	7.2	7.2	7.2	7.2	7.2	7.2
Infant Mortality Rate	159.0	152.0	145.0	137.0	129.0	121.0	113.0	105.0	96.0	87.0	78.0
Life Expectancy at Birth	47.4	48.2	49.0	49.8	50.6	51.4	52.2	53.0	54.2	55.4	56.6
Urban Population, % of total	5.1	5.3	5.5	5.7	5.9	6.1	6.3	6.6	6.8	7.1	7.3
Food Prod. per capita (1987=100)	..	..	..	..	..	..	..	..	..	..	..
Labor Force, Agriculture (%)	56.7	55.9	55.2	54.5	53.8	53.1	52.3	51.5	50.9	50.3	49.8
Labor Force, Female (%)	6.2	6.4	6.6	6.8	6.9	7.1	7.1	7.2	7.2	7.2	7.2
Primary Schl. Enroll. Ratio	3.0	..	..	..	..	44.0	49.0	53.0	57.0	..	60.0
Primary Schl. Enroll. Ratio, Female	1.0	..	..	..	..	24.0	28.0	33.0	37.0	..	42.0
Secondary Schl. Enroll. Ratio	..	..	..	..	..	1.0	2.0	5.0	8.0	..	14.0

1981	1982	1983	1984	1985	1986	1987	1988	1989	1990 estimate	Notes	OMAN
(Millions of current US dollars)											**FOREIGN TRADE (CUSTOMS BASIS)**
4,695.7	4,438.1	4,551.6	4,177.0	4,794.8	2,773.5	3,776.1	3,268.3	3,932.8	458.4	..	Value of Exports, fob
47.1	36.3	47.6	70.5	86.3	85.6	102.5	147.9	154.1	134.8	..	Nonfuel Primary Products
4,420.0	4,099.0	4,202.7	3,810.9	4,447.0	2,486.5	3,460.9	2,875.0	3,506.3	11.5	..	Fuels
228.6	302.8	301.3	295.6	261.5	201.4	212.7	245.3	272.4	312.0	..	Manufactures
2,288.2	2,682.5	2,492.3	2,748.2	3,152.7	2,384.1	1,812.6	2,148.5	2,177.9	2,608.2	..	Value of Imports, cif
347.7	383.5	409.3	456.5	472.6	424.9	413.9	473.4	473.5	521.5	..	Nonfuel Primary Products
299.2	279.3	40.7	43.0	55.2	66.9	55.3	33.7	47.8	109.9	..	Fuels
1,641.3	2,019.8	2,042.4	2,248.7	2,624.8	1,892.3	1,343.4	1,641.4	1,656.6	1,976.8	..	Manufactures
(Index 1987 = 100)											
..	..	..	..	..	..	..	..	..	..	..	Terms of Trade
..	..	..	..	..	..	..	..	..	..	..	Export Prices, fob
..	..	..	..	..	..	..	..	..	..	..	Import Prices, cif
(Millions of current US dollars)											**BALANCE OF PAYMENTS**
4,881.0	4,753.0	4,577.3	4,780.0	5,347.5	3,471.4	4,338.1	3,612.5	4,379.7	5,854.4	..	Exports of Goods & Services
4,695.7	4,423.0	4,255.9	4,421.0	4,971.1	2,861.4	3,804.9	3,342.0	4,046.8	5,487.6	..	Merchandise, fob
8.7	11.6	14.5	14.5	14.5	13.1	13.0	13.0	10.4	10.4	..	Nonfactor Services
176.6	318.5	306.9	344.5	361.9	596.9	520.2	257.5	322.5	356.3	..	Factor Services
3,331.8	3,754.8	3,538.5	3,872.1	4,428.3	3,665.6	2,859.3	3,201.6	3,281.4	3,856.4	..	Imports of Goods & Services
2,296.2	2,582.5	2,360.5	2,639.6	3,027.8	2,309.0	1,768.5	2,106.6	2,130.0	2,518.6	..	Merchandise, fob
620.4	700.9	687.9	672.6	712.8	688.5	481.1	522.8	559.2	706.4	..	Nonfactor Services
415.2	471.3	490.2	559.9	687.6	668.1	609.6	572.2	592.2	631.5	..	Factor Services
34.8	33.5	52.5	85.4	113.6	168.3	185.8	187.1	225.3	176.7	..	Long-Term Interest
-460.3	-555.9	-694.8	-819.3	-906.2	-845.6	-702.2	-762.0	-790.6	-845.3	..	Private Current Transfers, net
40.5	43.4	43.4	43.4	43.4	39.3	39.0	39.0	39.0	39.0	..	Workers' Remittances
1,088.9	442.4	343.9	88.6	13.0	-1,039.8	776.6	-351.1	307.7	1,152.7	..	Curr. A/C Bal before Off. Transf.
144.8	43.4	147.7	211.4	-26.1	0.0	7.8	41.6	15.6	-57.2	..	Net Official Transfers
1,233.6	485.8	491.6	299.9	-13.0	-1,039.8	784.4	-309.5	323.3	1,095.5	..	Curr. A/C Bal after Off. Transf.
192.5	251.6	523.7	575.3	309.2	687.2	-100.1	273.1	161.5	-249.2	..	Long-Term Capital, net
62.5	182.1	154.6	158.1	161.3	140.3	34.9	91.8	112.4	143.6	..	Direct Investment
118.6	203.0	427.9	254.2	520.7	539.6	-102.8	66.3	183.9	-463.1	..	Long-Term Loans
199.0	287.0	510.9	383.0	667.7	764.8	334.2	414.3	558.5	103.7	..	Disbursements
80.4	84.0	83.0	128.8	147.0	225.2	437.0	348.0	374.6	566.8	..	Repayments
11.4	-133.5	-58.8	163.0	-372.8	7.3	-32.2	115.0	-134.7	70.4	..	Other Long-Term Capital
-178.8	7.1	-663.9	-556.6	-174.5	-260.3	-576.2	-430.7	-203.3	-542.4	..	Other Capital, net
-1,247.4	-744.5	-351.4	-318.6	-121.7	612.9	-108.0	467.1	-281.5	-303.9	..	Change in Reserves
(Rials Omani per US dollar)											**Memo Item:**
0.350	0.350	0.350	0.350	0.350	0.380	0.380	0.380	0.380	0.380	..	Conversion Factor (Annual Avg)
(Millions of US dollars), outstanding at end of year											**EXTERNAL DEBT (Total)**
754.2	957.9	1,488.8	1,632.8	2,330.0	2,959.0	2,847.7	2,938.1	2,974.7	2,483.9	..	Long-Term Debt (by debtor)
537.2	723.9	1,131.8	1,339.8	1,908.0	2,463.0	2,442.7	2,486.3	2,626.6	2,205.3	..	Central Bank, incl. IMF credit
..	..	..	..	..	..	..	..	..	..	..	Central Government
537.2	723.8	1,128.3	1,320.4	1,887.2	2,438.2	2,405.2	2,456.3	2,602.2	2,185.1	..	Rest of General Government
..	..	..	..	..	..	..	..	..	..	..	Non-financial Public Enterprises
0.0	0.1	3.5	19.4	20.8	24.8	37.5	30.0	24.4	20.2	..	Priv. Sector, incl non-guaranteed
..	..	..	..	..	..	..	..	..	..	..	Short-Term Debt
217.0	234.0	357.0	293.0	422.0	496.0	405.0	451.8	348.1	278.6	..	
(Millions of US dollars)											**Memo Items:**
744.3	872.4	762.6	900.2	1,090.2	967.9	1,402.2	1,054.2	1,354.3	1,672.4	..	Int'l Reserves Excluding Gold
108.8	127.3	109.9	89.0	94.4	112.9	139.8	118.5	115.8	111.2	..	Gold Holdings (at market price)
											SOCIAL INDICATORS
7.2	7.2	7.2	7.2	7.2	7.2	7.2	7.1	7.1	7.0	..	Total Fertility Rate
69.0	60.0	56.0	52.0	48.0	44.0	40.0	37.8	35.6	33.3	..	Infant Mortality Rate
57.8	59.0	60.0	61.0	62.0	63.0	64.0	64.5	65.1	65.6	..	Life Expectancy at Birth
7.6	7.9	8.2	8.5	8.8	9.2	9.5	9.9	10.2	10.6	..	Urban Population, % of total
..	..	..	..	..	..	..	..	..	..	..	Food Prod. per capita (1987=100)
..	..	..	..	..	..	..	..	..	..	..	Labor Force, Agriculture (%)
7.3	7.4	7.4	7.5	7.5	7.8	7.9	8.1	8.3	8.5	..	Labor Force, Female (%)
..	69.0	75.0	83.0	89.0	94.0	97.0	100.0	102.0	..	..	Primary Schl. Enroll. Ratio
..	53.0	62.0	72.0	80.0	86.0	91.0	95.0	97.0	..	..	Primary Schl. Enroll. Ratio, Female
..	22.0	25.0	29.0	33.0	35.0	38.0	42.0	48.0	..	..	Secondary Schl. Enroll. Ratio

PAKISTAN	1970	1971	1972	1973	1974	1975	1976	1977	1978	1979	1980
CURRENT GNP PER CAPITA (US $)	170	170	160	130	130	130	170	190	220	250	290
POPULATION (thousands)	60,607	62,573	64,610	66,706	68,849	71,033	73,251	75,494	77,779	80,135	82,581

USE AND ORIGIN OF RESOURCES
(Billions of current Pakistan Rupees)

	1970	1971	1972	1973	1974	1975	1976	1977	1978	1979	1980
Gross National Product (GNP)	47.75	50.40	54.16	65.99	86.12	111.32	130.63	148.08	174.62	192.81	231.75
Net Factor Income from Abroad	0.00	-0.08	0.10	-0.88	-0.73	-0.94	-1.42	-1.67	-1.80	-2.30	-2.78
GDP at Market Prices	47.75	50.49	54.06	66.87	86.85	112.27	132.05	149.75	176.42	195.11	234.53
Resource Balance	-3.26	-3.51	-2.66	-1.89	-6.05	-12.71	-12.38	-14.58	-16.32	-23.54	-27.26
Exports of Goods & NFServices	3.71	4.00	4.00	8.93	11.91	12.21	14.17	13.90	16.31	20.86	29.26
Imports of Goods & NFServices	6.97	7.51	6.67	10.83	17.96	24.91	26.54	28.48	32.64	44.40	56.52
Domestic Absorption	51.01	53.99	56.72	68.76	92.90	124.97	144.43	164.33	192.74	218.65	261.79
Private Consumption, etc.	38.62	40.83	42.58	52.39	72.75	94.80	107.32	118.76	142.12	163.54	194.91
General Gov't Consumption	4.85	5.27	6.48	7.72	8.54	11.95	14.34	16.71	19.12	20.24	23.54
Gross Domestic Investment	7.54	7.89	7.66	8.65	11.61	18.22	22.77	28.86	31.50	34.88	43.34
Fixed Investment	6.83	7.04	6.81	7.65	10.61	16.22	22.77	27.86	30.51	33.13	41.34
Indirect Taxes, net	4.40	4.79	4.89	6.08	6.41	7.63	10.63	13.77	16.49	17.07	23.93
GDP at factor cost	43.34	45.70	49.17	60.79	80.44	104.64	121.42	135.98	159.93	178.04	210.60
Agriculture	15.96	16.24	17.93	21.91	28.08	33.53	38.34	43.97	50.57	54.15	62.16
Industry	9.67	10.57	10.63	13.33	17.64	24.53	29.47	31.10	36.46	42.01	52.49
Manufacturing	6.96	7.57	7.77	9.69	12.75	17.48	20.05	20.39	24.02	27.48	33.55
Services, etc.	17.71	18.89	20.61	25.55	34.71	46.58	53.61	60.92	72.90	81.88	95.95
Gross Domestic Saving	4.28	4.39	5.00	6.76	5.57	5.51	10.39	14.27	15.18	11.33	16.08
Gross National Saving	4.67	4.61	6.22	7.32	6.32	6.83	12.46	18.45	25.52	23.85	32.06

(Billions of 1987 Pakistan Rupees)

	1970	1971	1972	1973	1974	1975	1976	1977	1978	1979	1980
Gross National Product	232.32	233.07	235.69	248.64	258.43	269.24	282.75	293.84	317.86	329.03	363.17
GDP at Market Prices	232.20	233.34	235.15	251.90	260.51	271.28	285.58	296.91	320.88	332.67	367.31
Resource Balance	-72.38	-61.42	-36.85	-27.89	-42.14	-35.01	-35.45	-48.18	-49.92	-70.00	-67.63
Exports of Goods & NFServices	34.05	34.35	28.45	30.08	24.88	27.76	31.69	26.12	29.45	33.37	39.88
Imports of Goods & NFServices	106.43	95.77	65.30	57.97	67.03	62.76	67.13	74.29	79.37	103.37	107.51
Domestic Absorption	304.58	294.76	272.00	279.79	302.65	306.28	321.03	345.09	370.80	402.67	434.94
Private Consumption, etc.	231.23	220.68	196.10	200.34	230.30	225.69	236.97	253.93	274.85	303.88	328.96
General Gov't Consumption	24.87	25.53	29.98	31.87	27.08	30.15	32.67	33.61	36.15	36.04	38.14
Gross Domestic Investment	48.48	48.55	45.92	47.58	45.27	50.45	51.38	57.55	59.79	62.75	67.83
Fixed Investment	45.18	44.66	42.16	43.79	42.69	45.62	52.84	56.60	59.05	60.54	65.58
GDP at factor cost	208.38	209.02	211.33	226.34	240.50	252.15	260.70	271.36	292.36	308.75	331.50
Agriculture	77.08	74.71	77.30	78.59	81.88	80.14	83.73	85.84	88.27	91.00	97.01
Industry	43.81	45.26	43.08	47.98	52.40	53.58	56.20	60.14	65.84	70.89	78.68
Manufacturing	30.16	30.93	29.83	33.02	35.48	35.68	36.24	39.00	43.10	46.67	51.58
Services, etc.	87.19	88.68	90.78	99.52	105.90	118.42	120.66	125.18	138.12	146.69	155.45

Memo Items:

	1970	1971	1972	1973	1974	1975	1976	1977	1978	1979	1980
Capacity to Import	56.64	51.03	39.19	47.84	44.45	30.75	35.83	36.26	39.67	48.56	55.65
Terms of Trade Adjustment	22.59	16.69	10.75	17.76	19.57	2.99	4.14	10.14	10.22	15.19	15.77
Gross Domestic Income	254.79	250.03	245.90	269.66	280.08	274.27	289.72	307.05	331.10	347.86	383.08
Gross National Income	254.91	249.75	246.43	266.39	278.00	272.23	286.89	303.99	328.08	344.22	378.94

DOMESTIC PRICES/DEFLATORS
(Index 1987 = 100)

	1970	1971	1972	1973	1974	1975	1976	1977	1978	1979	1980
Overall (GDP)	20.6	21.6	23.0	26.5	33.3	41.4	46.2	50.4	55.0	58.6	63.9
Domestic Absorption	16.7	18.3	20.9	24.6	30.7	40.8	45.0	47.6	52.0	54.3	60.2
Agriculture	20.7	21.7	23.2	27.9	34.3	41.8	45.8	51.2	57.3	59.5	64.1
Industry	22.1	23.4	24.7	27.8	33.7	45.8	52.4	51.7	55.4	59.3	66.7
Manufacturing	23.1	24.5	26.1	29.4	35.9	49.0	55.3	52.3	55.7	58.9	65.0
Consumer Price Index	20.7	21.7	22.8	28.1	35.6	43.1	46.1	50.8	53.9	58.4	65.4

MANUFACTURING ACTIVITY

	1970	1971	1972	1973	1974	1975	1976	1977	1978	1979	1980
Employment (1987=100)	..	..	..	..	..	..	..	..	..	..	..
Real Earnings per Empl. (1987=100)	..	..	..	..	..	..	..	..	..	..	..
Real Output per Empl. (1987=100)	..	..	..	..	..	..	..	..	..	..	..
Earnings as % of Value Added	20.8	21.6	22.0	23.0	24.2	25.5	26.9	23.4	22.7	23.4	20.9

MONETARY HOLDINGS
(Billions of current Pakistan Rupees)

	1970	1971	1972	1973	1974	1975	1976	1977	1978	1979	1980
Money Supply, Broadly Defined	20.75	23.61	27.73	31.56	31.18	37.80	49.97	58.94	70.63	84.12	97.32
Money	14.02	16.49	19.94	22.19	22.52	25.62	34.04	39.97	47.19	56.83	66.67
Currency Outside Banks	8.06	8.16	9.35	10.99	11.43	11.88	13.85	17.35	21.04	26.45	32.48
Demand Deposits	5.95	8.33	10.59	11.20	11.09	13.74	20.19	22.62	26.15	30.38	34.19
Quasi-Money	6.74	7.12	7.80	9.37	8.67	12.18	15.92	18.97	23.44	27.29	30.65

GOVERNMENT DEFICIT (-) OR SURPLUS
(Billions of current Pakistan Rupees)

	1970	1971	1972	1973	1974	1975	1976	1977	1978	1979	1980
GOVERNMENT DEFICIT (-) OR SURPLUS	..	..	..	-4.55	-5.15	-11.47	-12.24	-12.58	-13.25	-18.00	-13.34
Current Revenue	..	..	..	8.74	12.36	14.64	18.79	21.53	26.25	30.35	39.93
Current Expenditure	..	..	..	8.71	12.33	15.89	17.63	19.31	23.89	29.86	33.93
Current Budget Balance	..	..	..	0.04	0.03	-1.25	1.15	2.22	2.37	0.49	6.00
Capital Receipts	..	..	..	..	..	..	..	..	..	..	..
Capital Payments	..	..	..	4.59	5.18	10.21	13.39	14.80	15.61	18.48	19.35

1981	1982	1983	1984	1985	1986	1987	1988	1989	1990 estimate	Notes	PAKISTAN
330	350	350	350	340	340	340	350	370	380	..	CURRENT GNP PER CAPITA (US $)
85,114	87,736	90,452	93,265	96,180	99,199	102,324	105,558	108,900	112,351	..	POPULATION (thousands)

(Billions of current Pakistan Rupees)

USE AND ORIGIN OF RESOURCES

1981	1982	1983	1984	1985	1986	1987	1988	1989	1990	Notes	
275.61	320.77	359.04	413.84	464.48	504.20	560.55	660.82	758.53	848.52	C	Gross National Product (GNP)
-2.58	-3.38	-5.34	-5.97	-7.67	-10.33	-11.93	-14.57	-11.21	-13.93	..	Net Factor Income from Abroad
278.20	324.16	364.39	419.80	472.16	514.53	572.48	675.39	769.74	862.45	C	GDP at Market Prices
-28.49	-36.27	-37.96	-44.58	-54.86	-51.37	-39.27	-50.34	-56.50	-61.28	..	Resource Balance
35.53	34.19	46.04	50.56	52.83	64.94	80.92	96.61	111.66	139.66	..	Exports of Goods & NF Services
64.02	70.46	84.00	95.14	107.70	116.31	120.19	146.94	168.16	200.94	..	Imports of Goods & NF Services
306.69	360.43	402.34	464.38	527.02	565.91	611.75	725.72	826.23	923.73	..	Domestic Absorption
226.20	264.46	292.28	336.94	383.37	403.70	424.72	499.30	551.46	633.40	..	Private Consumption, etc.
28.28	33.52	41.61	50.74	57.13	65.66	77.48	104.75	129.20	129.56	..	General Gov't Consumption
52.21	62.45	68.46	76.70	86.53	96.55	109.54	121.67	145.57	160.77	..	Gross Domestic Investment
47.71	54.59	61.76	69.21	77.92	87.55	100.04	111.27	133.17	146.77	..	Fixed Investment
30.40	32.00	36.00	45.50	47.10	48.20	57.00	74.36	86.61	103.10	..	Indirect Taxes, net
247.80	292.16	328.39	374.30	425.06	466.33	515.48	601.02	683.14	759.35	C	GDP at factor cost
76.40	92.22	99.38	104.55	121.29	128.80	135.31	156.37	184.07	196.07	..	Agriculture
56.01	65.02	72.49	84.98	95.52	108.85	123.83	146.53	163.23	191.69	..	Industry
37.45	44.20	50.20	60.40	67.60	75.88	85.85	100.92	113.49	132.30	..	Manufacturing
115.38	134.92	156.51	184.77	208.25	228.68	256.34	298.12	335.84	371.58	..	Services, etc.
23.71	26.18	30.51	32.12	31.66	45.17	70.27	71.33	89.08	99.49	..	Gross Domestic Saving
43.33	51.41	65.60	68.95	66.80	81.86	102.87	97.48	121.12	133.66	..	Gross National Saving

(Billions of 1987 Pakistan Rupees)

1981	1982	1983	1984	1985	1986	1987	1988	1989	1990	Notes	
393.24	418.42	444.94	467.87	501.44	527.48	560.55	604.37	638.25	671.30	C	Gross National Product
396.46	422.27	450.79	473.89	509.78	537.75	572.48	616.22	646.71	681.19	C	GDP at Market Prices
-40.72	-41.18	-39.05	-47.83	-54.72	-48.20	-39.27	-40.35	-34.96	-32.19	..	Resource Balance
46.92	45.89	57.27	56.22	56.12	72.24	80.92	77.83	87.78	95.75	..	Exports of Goods & NF Services
87.64	87.07	96.32	104.04	110.84	120.43	120.19	118.19	122.74	127.94	..	Imports of Goods & NF Services
437.19	463.45	489.84	521.72	564.50	585.94	611.75	656.57	681.67	713.38	..	Domestic Absorption
324.87	337.33	350.61	371.98	401.52	412.38	424.72	467.58	468.06	501.34	..	Private Consumption, etc.
40.45	43.98	51.92	58.25	62.19	68.42	77.48	80.86	97.36	94.27	..	General Gov't Consumption
71.87	82.13	87.31	91.48	100.79	105.14	109.54	108.13	116.25	117.76	..	Gross Domestic Investment
65.41	71.77	78.83	82.86	91.14	95.70	100.04	98.68	105.98	106.98	..	Fixed Investment
352.66	379.43	405.09	421.41	458.06	487.17	515.48	548.68	574.98	601.62	C	GDP at factor cost
107.15	112.22	117.16	111.51	123.70	131.04	135.31	139.00	148.55	152.63	..	Agriculture
78.59	87.03	91.33	97.77	105.43	113.97	123.83	135.99	142.31	151.30	..	Industry
52.29	59.48	63.66	68.68	74.24	79.84	85.85	94.42	98.16	103.76	..	Manufacturing
166.80	179.97	196.61	212.13	228.92	242.15	256.34	273.69	284.12	297.69	..	Services, etc.

Memo Items:

1981	1982	1983	1984	1985	1986	1987	1988	1989	1990	Notes	
48.64	42.25	52.79	55.29	54.37	67.24	80.92	77.70	81.50	88.92	..	Capacity to Import
1.72	-3.63	-4.48	-0.92	-1.74	-5.00	0.00	-0.13	-6.27	-6.83	..	Terms of Trade Adjustment
398.18	418.63	446.31	472.97	508.03	532.75	572.48	616.08	640.43	674.36	..	Gross Domestic Income
394.96	414.79	440.47	466.95	499.70	522.48	560.55	604.24	631.98	664.47	..	Gross National Income

(Index 1987 = 100)

DOMESTIC PRICES/DEFLATORS

1981	1982	1983	1984	1985	1986	1987	1988	1989	1990	Notes	
70.2	76.8	80.8	88.6	92.6	95.7	100.0	109.6	119.0	126.6	..	Overall (GDP)
70.2	77.8	82.1	89.0	93.4	96.6	100.0	110.5	121.2	129.5	..	Domestic Absorption
71.3	82.2	84.8	93.8	98.1	98.3	100.0	112.5	123.9	128.5	..	Agriculture
71.3	74.7	79.4	86.9	90.6	95.5	100.0	107.7	114.7	126.7	..	Industry
71.6	74.3	78.9	87.9	91.1	95.0	100.0	106.9	115.6	127.5	..	Manufacturing
73.1	77.4	79.4	87.4	92.3	95.5	100.0	108.8	117.4	128.0	..	Consumer Price Index

MANUFACTURING ACTIVITY

1981	1982	1983	1984	1985	1986	1987	1988	1989	1990	Notes	
..	..	..	..	..	..	..	..	..	..	..	Employment (1987=100)
..	..	..	..	..	..	..	..	..	..	..	Real Earnings per Empl. (1987=100)
..	..	..	..	..	..	..	..	..	..	..	Real Output per Empl. (1987=100)
19.6	19.5	21.2	20.3	19.2	19.0	..	..	..	..	..	Earnings as % of Value Added

(Billions of current Pakistan Rupees)

MONETARY HOLDINGS

1981	1982	1983	1984	1985	1986	1987	1988	1989	1990	Notes	
108.54	132.23	159.88	167.31	191.99	222.84	259.40	279.38	300.05	334.99	..	Money Supply, Broadly Defined
72.29	87.34	100.57	105.78	123.06	145.25	173.02	189.83	217.03	254.62	..	Money
34.49	41.15	46.42	52.00	58.68	71.58	81.77	92.17	105.22	125.81	..	Currency Outside Banks
37.80	46.19	54.14	53.78	64.38	73.67	91.25	97.67	111.80	128.81	..	Demand Deposits
36.25	44.89	59.32	61.53	68.92	77.59	86.38	89.54	83.03	80.37	..	Quasi-Money

(Billions of current Pakistan Rupees)

1981	1982	1983	1984	1985	1986	1987	1988	1989	1990	Notes	
-16.14	-15.35	-24.78	-25.93	-33.78	-46.92	-48.78	-42.43	-56.98	-61.03	C E	GOVERNMENT DEFICIT (-) OR SURPLUS
47.96	52.93	59.94	73.00	79.07	94.23	102.33	125.22	151.20	166.29	..	Current Revenue
45.44	45.97	59.25	72.47	82.51	105.72	..	134.78	157.66	174.09	..	Current Expenditure
2.52	6.96	0.68	0.53	-3.44	-11.49	..	-9.56	-6.46	-7.80	..	Current Budget Balance
..	..	..	..	..	..	..	..	..	..	..	Capital Receipts
18.66	22.31	25.47	26.46	30.34	35.43	..	32.87	50.52	53.23	..	Capital Payments

PAKISTAN	1970	1971	1972	1973	1974	1975	1976	1977	1978	1979	1980
FOREIGN TRADE (CUSTOMS BASIS)					*(Millions of current US dollars)*						
Value of Exports, fob	695.3	660.3	686.8	941.2	1,091.0	1,031.3	1,144.2	1,152.8	1,446.9	2,036.3	2,588.0
Nonfuel Primary Products	288.8	287.8	294.7	341.4	485.8	453.0	460.6	422.4	566.8	758.1	1,148.6
Fuels	8.4	7.7	11.0	7.2	24.9	11.1	24.2	49.4	45.4	138.0	184.5
Manufactures	398.1	364.8	381.2	592.6	580.2	567.2	659.5	681.0	834.7	1,140.2	1,254.9
Value of Imports, cif	1,170.9	925.9	681.8	965.9	1,729.4	2,153.1	2,182.9	2,454.6	3,160.5	4,061.3	5,350.5
Nonfuel Primary Products	321.1	232.2	253.7	332.4	535.7	647.4	588.9	602.5	840.3	1,056.3	1,019.8
Fuels	76.0	80.5	53.2	78.2	238.8	385.6	397.0	387.7	597.4	681.9	1,442.2
Manufactures	773.8	613.2	375.0	555.3	955.0	1,120.1	1,196.9	1,464.5	1,722.8	2,323.1	2,888.5
					(Index 1987 = 100)						
Terms of Trade	119.1	123.7	122.2	162.5	125.6	102.1	104.7	109.7	113.9	104.8	101.6
Export Prices, fob	31.8	33.9	38.0	65.8	81.0	65.1	66.3	77.6	86.0	97.3	110.3
Import Prices, cif	26.7	27.4	31.1	40.5	64.5	63.8	63.4	70.8	75.5	92.9	108.6
BALANCE OF PAYMENTS					*(Millions of current US dollars)*						
Exports of Goods & Services	805.0	770.3	742.9	922.5	1,236.3	1,267.6	1,460.2	1,437.2	1,681.0	2,153.7	3,010.5
Merchandise, fob	672.0	661.0	626.8	768.5	1,018.0	978.8	1,161.2	1,131.7	1,282.4	1,644.2	2,340.8
Nonfactor Services	107.0	96.3	106.4	136.6	182.2	252.0	268.9	272.7	364.3	463.1	617.4
Factor Services	26.0	13.0	9.8	17.4	36.2	36.8	30.0	32.8	34.2	46.3	52.3
Imports of Goods & Services	1,591.0	1,432.3	1,157.4	1,191.5	1,932.6	2,671.3	2,758.4	3,089.9	3,507.6	4,763.8	6,042.3
Merchandise, fob	1,210.0	1,081.2	859.9	890.5	1,488.6	2,110.5	2,138.6	2,417.7	2,751.3	3,815.9	4,856.6
Nonfactor Services	261.0	274.8	197.6	200.3	334.2	428.8	445.6	459.4	541.7	669.1	852.6
Factor Services	120.0	76.2	99.9	100.6	109.8	132.1	174.2	212.8	214.6	278.8	333.1
Long-Term Interest	77.5	59.3	75.6	86.4	84.4	102.3	130.5	143.5	183.0	214.0	248.1
Private Current Transfers, net	81.0	65.2	129.2	144.7	149.6	228.9	352.1	590.3	1,225.8	1,496.2	1,894.9
Workers' Remittances	86.0	70.2	130.3	145.8	150.8	220.1	327.7	576.9	1,155.6	1,397.6	1,747.6
Curr. A/C Bal before Off. Transf.	-705.0	-596.8	-285.2	-124.3	-546.7	-1,174.8	-946.1	-1,062.4	-600.8	-1,113.9	-1,136.9
Net Official Transfers	38.0	114.3	44.5	41.9	54.3	105.8	120.4	148.9	111.8	293.5	268.4
Curr. A/C Bal after Off. Transf.	-667.0	-482.4	-240.7	-82.4	-492.4	-1,069.0	-825.7	-913.5	-489.0	-820.4	-868.5
Long-Term Capital, net	429.0	398.2	200.9	240.5	331.7	790.3	808.8	619.4	648.7	367.8	823.3
Direct Investment	23.0	1.0	17.4	6.3	1.2	11.2	21.7	3.5	33.7	33.5	68.1
Long-Term Loans	376.9	546.8	188.5	241.2	710.3	711.4	747.2	573.9	470.5	584.5	708.3
Disbursements	491.9	639.4	294.9	350.5	829.6	866.7	906.8	770.0	686.7	891.5	1,060.9
Repayments	115.0	92.6	106.4	109.3	119.3	155.3	159.6	196.1	216.2	307.0	352.6
Other Long-Term Capital	29.1	-149.6	-5.0	-7.0	-379.8	67.7	39.9	42.0	144.5	-250.2	46.9
Other Capital, net	120.7	32.9	28.8	-11.5	66.6	154.7	26.7	63.4	125.5	122.5	54.6
Change in Reserves	117.3	51.4	11.1	-146.6	94.1	124.0	-9.8	230.7	-285.2	330.1	-9.4
Memo Item:					*(Pakistan Rupees per US dollar)*						
Conversion Factor (Annual Avg)	4.760	4.760	5.810	10.570	9.900	9.900	9.900	9.900	9.900	9.900	9.900
				(Millions of US dollars), outstanding at end of year							
EXTERNAL DEBT (Total)	3,114	3,660	3,927	4,407	4,946	5,553	6,571	7,581	8,338	8,927	9,936
Long-Term Debt (by debtor)	3,114	3,660	3,927	4,407	4,946	5,553	6,571	7,401	8,128	8,486	9,199
Central Bank, incl. IMF credit	46	51	125	163	296	440	553	606	642	573	677
Central Government	2,676	3,117	3,352	3,859	4,271	4,750	5,696	6,396	7,077	7,404	7,741
Rest of General Government	0	0	0	0	1	8	12	23	23	19	18
Non-financial Public Enterprises	244	314	277	235	235	223	206	276	268	341	588
Priv. Sector, incl non-guaranteed	148	178	174	151	144	132	106	100	117	149	175
Short-Term Debt	0	0	0	0	0	0	0	180	210	441	737
Memo Items:					*(Millions of US dollars)*						
Int'l Reserves Excluding Gold	136.2	129.4	220.7	412.0	392.3	340.3	466.2	448.9	407.7	213.0	495.8
Gold Holdings (at market price)	58.3	69.1	103.1	178.3	296.2	222.7	218.0	266.8	388.3	931.0	1,072.0
SOCIAL INDICATORS											
Total Fertility Rate	7.0	7.0	7.0	7.0	7.0	7.0	7.0	7.0	7.0	7.0	7.0
Infant Mortality Rate	142.0	141.0	140.0	138.0	136.0	134.0	132.0	130.0	128.0	126.0	124.0
Life Expectancy at Birth	48.1	48.6	49.0	49.4	49.8	50.2	50.6	51.0	51.6	52.2	52.8
Urban Population, % of total	24.9	25.2	25.5	25.8	26.1	26.4	26.7	27.1	27.4	27.8	28.1
Food Prod. per capita (1987=100)	96.2	93.8	93.8	95.2	95.6	95.0	97.5	100.0	98.8	100.8	100.1
Labor Force, Agriculture (%)	58.9	58.4	58.0	57.6	57.2	56.8	56.3	55.8	55.4	55.0	54.6
Labor Force, Female (%)	9.1	9.3	9.4	9.5	9.7	9.8	9.9	10.1	10.2	10.3	10.4
Primary Schl. Enroll. Ratio	40.0	..	..	..	..	46.0	51.0	50.0	54.0	42.0	39.0
Primary Schl. Enroll. Ratio, Female	22.0	..	..	..	..	28.0	30.0	29.0	30.0	..	27.0
Secondary Schl. Enroll. Ratio	13.0	..	..	..	..	15.0	16.0	..	15.0	14.0	14.0

1981	1982	1983	1984	1985	1986	1987	1988	1989	1990 estimate	Notes	PAKISTAN
											FOREIGN TRADE (CUSTOMS BASIS)
				(Millions of current US dollars)							
2,737.7	2,347.8	3,061.9	2,556.2	2,707.6	3,302.9	4,105.1	4,484.7	4,698.2	5,590.1	..	Value of Exports, fob
1,119.0	815.2	1,051.7	770.0	968.5	1,074.8	1,115.2	1,490.3	1,363.7	1,857.6	..	Nonfuel Primary Products
179.4	139.7	57.0	25.3	38.6	23.8	27.8	21.6	43.0	27.0	..	Fuels
1,439.3	1,392.9	1,953.3	1,761.0	1,700.5	2,204.3	2,962.0	2,972.8	3,291.6	3,705.6	..	Manufactures
5,412.7	5,232.8	5,341.0	5,873.1	5,890.4	5,376.8	5,829.3	6,617.3	7,119.3	7,377.1	..	Value of Imports, cif
1,205.3	1,051.5	1,094.0	1,471.8	1,463.4	1,324.2	1,296.3	1,592.1	1,902.8	1,971.7	..	Nonfuel Primary Products
1,506.2	1,616.8	1,514.1	1,454.6	1,433.2	764.9	1,026.6	940.4	1,215.1	1,259.1	..	Fuels
2,701.2	2,564.5	2,733.0	2,946.7	2,993.8	3,287.7	3,506.3	4,084.8	4,001.4	4,146.3	..	Manufactures
				(Index 1987 = 100)							
99.6	95.4	98.4	92.7	89.7	96.8	100.0	107.9	99.2	94.6	..	Terms of Trade
109.8	99.6	100.2	96.4	89.2	87.9	100.0	104.7	99.2	102.8	..	Export Prices, fob
110.3	104.4	101.8	104.0	99.5	90.8	100.0	97.1	100.0	108.7	..	Import Prices, cif
											BALANCE OF PAYMENTS
				(Millions of current US dollars)							
3,556.7	3,185.4	3,540.4	3,644.7	3,401.8	3,907.3	4,505.7	5,347.2	5,733.3	6,337.8	C f	Exports of Goods & Services
2,811.5	2,319.7	2,635.6	2,668.8	2,460.5	2,944.6	3,491.8	4,373.6	4,645.1	4,936.6		Merchandise, fob
649.7	735.7	784.1	779.8	786.0	850.9	921.8	868.0	949.3	1,292.8	..	Nonfactor Services
95.5	130.0	120.7	196.1	155.3	111.8	92.1	105.6	138.9	108.4	..	Factor Services
6,823.0	7,137.1	7,134.4	7,687.2	7,774.6	7,982.7	7,792.7	9,294.5	9,781.8	10,455.8	C f	Imports of Goods & Services
5,563.5	5,775.0	5,619.8	5,993.8	6,016.4	6,002.2	5,797.6	6,936.3	7,225.5	7,432.0		Merchandise, fob
903.1	911.3	973.0	1,054.6	1,096.8	1,228.1	1,207.9	1,422.6	1,532.5	1,947.6	..	Nonfactor Services
356.4	450.8	541.6	638.8	661.4	752.4	787.2	935.6	1,023.8	1,076.2	..	Factor Services
199.6	252.8	315.4	315.2	310.2	353.5	394.8	436.8	444.5	508.1	..	Long-Term Interest
2,241.9	2,415.7	3,082.8	3,046.6	2,687.8	2,824.4	2,559.5	2,261.9	2,105.6	2,216.0	..	Private Current Transfers, net
2,097.4	2,226.6	2,888.1	2,738.4	2,456.3	2,597.0	2,280.3	2,017.7	1,901.7	1,947.2	..	Workers' Remittances
-1,024.4	-1,536.0	-511.2	-995.9	-1,685.0	-1,251.0	-727.5	-1,685.4	-1,942.9	-1,902.0	..	Curr. A/C Bal before Off. Transf.
275.0	419.3	333.3	307.0	402.6	477.5	393.9	521.3	592.0	539.8	..	Net Official Transfers
-749.4	-1,116.7	-177.9	-688.9	-1,282.4	-773.5	-333.6	-1,164.1	-1,350.9	-1,362.2	..	Curr. A/C Bal after Off. Transf.
504.0	520.3	639.6	434.6	459.6	768.7	439.0	788.7	1,528.4	1,382.2	C f	Long-Term Capital, net
71.5	122.1	26.1	43.3	77.6	150.1	108.1	144.5	170.4	205.0	..	Direct Investment
410.5	1,068.8	235.8	590.0	276.5	509.1	536.9	737.0	1,019.8	909.6	..	Long-Term Loans
768.4	1,401.9	1,023.9	1,196.7	1,010.1	1,202.8	1,295.5	1,582.8	1,826.7	1,811.1	..	Disbursements
357.9	333.1	788.1	606.7	733.6	693.7	758.6	845.8	806.9	901.5	..	Repayments
22.0	-670.6	377.7	-198.7	105.5	109.5	-206.0	-92.8	338.2	267.6	..	Other Long-Term Capital
262.9	64.5	241.8	192.5	-224.8	432.9	187.5	285.2	-257.5	212.8	C f	Other Capital, net
-17.5	531.9	-703.5	61.8	1,047.6	-428.1	-292.9	90.2	80.0	-232.8	..	Change in Reserves
											Memo Item:
				(Pakistan Rupees per US dollar)							
9.900	10.550	12.700	13.480	15.160	16.130	17.160	17.550	19.160	21.390	..	Conversion Factor (Annual Avg)
				(Millions of US dollars), outstanding at end of year							
10,530	11,633	11,927	12,123	13,355	14,896	16,699	16,967	18,309	20,683	..	**EXTERNAL DEBT (Total)**
9,627	10,913	11,130	11,191	12,045	13,033	14,418	14,537	15,538	17,492	..	Long-Term Debt (by debtor)
1,034	1,445	1,643	1,470	1,485	1,284	1,026	664	1,042	949	..	Central Bank, incl. IMF credit
7,835	8,709	8,655	8,839	9,504	10,703	12,358	12,850	13,415	15,468	..	Central Government
14	10	7	4	2	1	1	1	0	0	..	Rest of General Government
543	525	545	599	681	623	580	554	625	617	..	Non-financial Public Enterprises
202	225	280	279	372	422	454	469	455	458	..	Priv. Sector, incl non-guaranteed
903	720	797	932	1,310	1,863	2,280	2,429	2,772	3,191	..	Short-Term Debt
				(Millions of US dollars)							**Memo Items:**
721.5	968.5	1,972.5	1,035.5	807.5	709.1	501.9	394.6	520.5	295.9	..	Int'l Reserves Excluding Gold
733.8	844.3	710.3	575.0	622.0	755.8	939.0	798.1	781.7	750.5	..	Gold Holdings (at market price)
											SOCIAL INDICATORS
7.0	7.0	6.8	6.7	6.5	6.4	6.2	6.1	6.0	5.8	..	Total Fertility Rate
122.0	120.0	117.4	114.8	112.2	109.6	107.0	105.6	104.3	102.9	..	Infant Mortality Rate
53.4	54.0	54.2	54.4	54.6	54.8	55.0	55.3	55.5	55.8	..	Life Expectancy at Birth
28.4	28.8	29.1	29.5	29.8	30.2	30.7	31.1	31.6	32.0	..	Urban Population, % of total
102.7	102.2	101.3	98.9	98.7	103.1	100.0	99.8	104.0	103.1	..	Food Prod. per capita (1987=100)
..	..	..	..	..	..	..	..	..	..	..	Labor Force, Agriculture (%)
10.7	10.9	11.1	11.3	11.4	11.7	11.9	12.1	12.3	12.5	..	Labor Force, Female (%)
	42.0	45.0	49.0	48.0	44.0	40.0	39.0	38.0	..	..	Primary Schl. Enroll. Ratio
	28.0	30.0	34.0	34.0	32.0	28.0	28.0	27.0	..	..	Primary Schl. Enroll. Ratio, Female
	15.0	16.0	17.0	18.0	18.0	19.0	19.0	20.0	..	..	Secondary Schl. Enroll. Ratio

PANAMA	1970	1971	1972	1973	1974	1975	1976	1977	1978	1979	1980
CURRENT GNP PER CAPITA (US $)	680	740	770	840	920	1,030	1,080	1,120	1,290	1,420	1,630
POPULATION (thousands)	1,531	1,574	1,618	1,662	1,705	1,748	1,790	1,831	1,872	1,914	1,956
USE AND ORIGIN OF RESOURCES					*(Millions of current Panamanian Balboas)*						
Gross National Product (GNP)	994.8	1,120.6	1,231.2	1,404.3	1,599.1	1,820.0	1,902.7	2,008.8	2,403.7	2,721.6	3,223.6
Net Factor Income from Abroad	-26.4	-31.3	-33.7	-42.3	-55.0	-20.8	-53.6	-61.0	-48.8	-78.6	-335.2
GDP at Market Prices	1,021.2	1,151.9	1,264.9	1,446.6	1,654.1	1,840.8	1,956.3	2,069.8	2,452.5	2,800.2	3,558.8
Resource Balance	-34.2	-43.4	-62.4	-56.8	-155.3	-134.0	-137.4	-75.8	-113.8	-246.5	-118.1
Exports of Goods & NF Services	388.2	426.4	460.7	528.1	761.8	865.4	837.8	921.1	986.4	1,124.8	1,567.1
Imports of Goods & NF Services	422.4	469.8	523.1	584.9	917.1	999.4	975.2	996.9	1,100.2	1,371.3	1,685.2
Domestic Absorption	1,055.4	1,195.3	1,327.3	1,503.4	1,809.4	1,974.8	2,093.7	2,145.6	2,566.3	3,046.7	3,676.9
Private Consumption, etc.	618.8	665.2	698.3	767.6	954.0	1,054.1	1,088.8	1,242.6	1,431.7	1,693.8	2,009.5
General Gov't Consumption	152.3	180.2	226.5	250.1	299.3	353.3	386.1	412.1	482.9	567.2	680.5
Gross Domestic Investment	284.3	349.9	402.5	485.7	556.1	567.4	618.8	490.9	651.7	785.7	986.9
Fixed Investment	261.9	306.3	372.2	434.8	465.0	535.5	608.6	445.9	606.3	661.2	866.4
Indirect Taxes, net	78.8	90.6	103.1	115.4	136.9	139.6	146.0	181.9	216.0	251.7	268.2
GDP at factor cost	942.4	1,061.3	1,161.8	1,331.2	1,517.2	1,701.2	1,810.3	1,887.9	2,236.5	2,548.5	3,290.6
Agriculture	149.1	164.2	170.9	184.9	184.5	205.6	231.1	263.5	288.5	304.2	320.4
Industry	219.2	247.5	259.8	318.3	364.0	432.1	431.3	424.1	511.9	587.1	735.0
Manufacturing	127.3	135.9	141.0	161.0	202.0	236.0	217.3	234.0	252.6	293.3	356.0
Services, etc.	652.9	740.2	834.2	943.4	1,105.6	1,203.1	1,293.9	1,382.2	1,652.1	1,908.9	2,503.4
Gross Domestic Saving	250.1	306.5	340.1	428.9	400.8	433.4	481.4	415.1	537.9	539.2	868.8
Gross National Saving	212.8	263.0	292.6	363.9	320.2	387.0	400.1	324.2	455.6	421.3	481.4
					(Millions of 1987 Panamanian Balboas)						
Gross National Product	2,477.5	2,715.8	2,845.1	2,997.8	3,074.5	3,178.6	3,190.8	3,222.8	3,567.6	3,714.4	3,952.9
GDP at Market Prices	2,543.5	2,788.1	2,915.9	3,072.3	3,152.0	3,204.4	3,255.8	3,291.1	3,613.9	3,781.2	4,364.0
Resource Balance	-286.2	-369.1	-446.7	-389.6	-482.2	-397.2	-349.2	-196.0	-310.1	-364.7	-132.0
Exports of Goods & NF Services	822.9	857.9	868.7	909.8	973.4	989.9	965.1	1,067.7	1,142.1	1,126.9	1,620.6
Imports of Goods & NF Services	1,109.1	1,226.9	1,315.4	1,299.4	1,455.6	1,387.1	1,314.4	1,263.7	1,452.2	1,491.6	1,752.6
Domestic Absorption	2,829.7	3,157.2	3,362.6	3,461.9	3,634.2	3,601.6	3,605.1	3,487.0	3,924.0	4,145.9	4,496.0
Private Consumption, etc.	1,633.8	1,731.6	1,719.3	1,767.5	1,974.5	1,910.5	1,902.8	2,051.6	2,287.0	2,420.1	2,569.1
General Gov't Consumption	463.2	526.5	614.1	625.9	645.4	712.6	733.0	761.6	795.3	818.4	866.2
Gross Domestic Investment	732.7	899.1	1,029.3	1,068.5	1,014.3	978.5	969.2	673.9	841.7	907.4	1,060.7
Fixed Investment	673.6	774.2	959.6	961.4	860.4	928.5	947.0	629.1	779.8	771.4	939.6
GDP at factor cost	..	..	..	..	..	..	..	..	..	..	4,364.0
Agriculture	352.0	379.4	366.9	370.9	349.2	374.5	394.5	414.4	446.5	427.3	410.1
Industry	565.4	635.6	660.1	734.4	712.4	734.4	761.2	702.6	790.1	849.2	936.3
Manufacturing	294.9	313.7	328.0	348.7	353.3	340.6	349.1	353.3	358.9	398.5	421.9
Services, etc.	1,626.1	1,773.1	1,888.9	1,967.0	2,090.4	2,095.6	2,100.1	2,174.1	2,377.4	2,504.7	3,017.5
Memo Items:											
Capacity to Import	1,019.3	1,113.6	1,158.5	1,173.2	1,209.1	1,201.1	1,129.2	1,167.6	1,302.0	1,223.5	1,629.8
Terms of Trade Adjustment	196.4	255.7	289.8	263.4	235.7	211.2	164.1	99.9	159.9	96.6	9.2
Gross Domestic Income	2,739.9	3,043.8	3,205.7	3,335.7	3,387.7	3,415.6	3,419.9	3,390.9	3,773.8	3,877.8	4,373.2
Gross National Income	2,673.9	2,971.6	3,134.9	3,261.2	3,310.2	3,389.8	3,354.8	3,322.7	3,727.5	3,811.0	3,962.1
DOMESTIC PRICES/DEFLATORS					*(Index 1987 = 100)*						
Overall (GDP)	40.1	41.3	43.4	47.1	52.5	57.4	60.1	62.9	67.9	74.1	81.5
Domestic Absorption	37.3	37.9	39.5	43.4	49.8	54.8	58.1	61.5	65.4	73.5	81.8
Agriculture	42.4	43.3	46.6	49.8	52.8	54.9	58.6	63.6	64.6	71.2	78.1
Industry	38.8	38.9	39.4	43.3	51.1	58.8	56.7	60.4	64.8	69.1	78.5
Manufacturing	43.2	43.3	43.0	46.2	57.2	69.3	62.2	66.2	70.4	73.6	84.4
Consumer Price Index	43.0	43.8	46.2	49.3	57.3	60.7	63.1	66.0	68.8	74.3	84.5
MANUFACTURING ACTIVITY											
Employment (1987=100)	60.2	69.6	71.4	75.5	74.0	73.5	72.6	74.2	77.6	81.7	86.1
Real Earnings per Empl. (1987=100)	88.5	86.7	87.9	87.8	85.6	87.5	89.2	96.5	93.8	92.5	80.8
Real Output per Empl. (1987=100)	76.8	82.0	88.8	93.3	114.2	107.1	117.6	113.6	103.1	119.6	114.2
Earnings as % of Value Added	32.0	32.8	32.8	31.3	29.1	28.1	29.5	32.9	32.8	30.6	25.1
MONETARY HOLDINGS					*(Millions of current Panamanian Balboas)*						
Money Supply, Broadly Defined	256.0	302.0	393.0	445.0	530.0	634.6	682.4	793.7	946.8	1,166.3	1,458.3
Money	100.5	105.4	153.6	161.1	196.3	173.1	190.0	213.2	246.0	301.3	335.3
Currency Outside Banks	..	..	..	..	..	..	..	..	..	..	..
Demand Deposits	..	..	..	..	..	..	..	..	..	..	..
Quasi-Money	155.8	196.8	239.3	283.4	333.9	462.5	492.4	580.5	700.8	865.0	1,123.0
GOVERNMENT DEFICIT (-) OR SURPLUS					*(Millions of current Panamanian Balboas)*						
	..	..	..	-91.0	-119.4	-149.5	-202.7	-119.0	-159.6	-371.8	-197.6
Current Revenue	..	..	..	306.1	391.5	451.7	440.2	546.4	597.6	696.6	966.1
Current Expenditure	..	..	..	304.1	382.3	431.2	479.4	532.8	614.8	795.9	952.3
Current Budget Balance	..	..	..	2.0	9.2	20.5	-39.2	13.6	-17.2	-99.3	13.8
Capital Receipts	..	..	..	..	..	..	..	..	..	..	..
Capital Payments	..	..	..	93.0	128.6	170.0	163.5	132.6	142.4	272.5	211.4

1981	1982	1983	1984	1985	1986	1987	1988	1989	1990 estimate	Notes	PANAMA
1,820	1,950	1,950	1,990	2,060	2,170	2,210	1,800	1,750	1,850	..	CURRENT GNP PER CAPITA (US $)
1,999	2,043	2,088	2,134	2,180	2,227	2,274	2,322	2,370	2,418	..	POPULATION (thousands)

(Millions of current Panamanian Balboas)

1981	1982	1983	1984	1985	1986	1987	1988	1989	1990 estimate	Notes	USE AND ORIGIN OF RESOURCES
3,559.2	3,874.1	3,989.4	4,239.7	4,498.5	4,787.5	4,940.4	4,168.8	4,102.8	4,316.6	..	Gross National Product (GNP)
-318.8	-404.8	-384.3	-325.8	-402.6	-357.6	-369.3	-382.6	-446.0	-434.0	..	Net Factor Income from Abroad
3,878.0	4,278.9	4,373.7	4,565.5	4,901.1	5,145.1	5,309.7	4,551.4	4,548.8	4,750.6	..	GDP at Market Prices
-167.7	-179.8	18.1	-74.8	24.3	187.2	99.5	633.5	434.0	55.2	..	Resource Balance
1,690.5	1,689.6	1,709.5	1,622.1	1,735.2	1,786.5	1,736.3	1,729.0	1,705.1	1,828.7	..	Exports of Goods & NF Services
1,858.2	1,869.4	1,691.4	1,696.9	1,710.9	1,599.3	1,636.8	1,095.5	1,271.1	1,773.5	..	Imports of Goods & NF Services
4,045.4	4,458.7	4,355.6	4,640.3	4,876.6	4,957.9	5,210.2	3,917.9	4,114.7	4,695.3	..	Domestic Absorption
2,065.4	2,311.5	2,480.0	2,878.0	3,080.0	2,970.9	3,055.3	2,484.7	3,008.9	2,896.0	..	Private Consumption, etc.
812.8	962.6	941.5	1,001.3	1,043.6	1,127.8	1,226.9	1,119.5	987.1	1,025.8	..	General Gov't Consumption
1,167.2	1,184.6	934.1	761.0	753.0	859.2	928.0	313.7	118.7	773.5	..	Gross Domestic Investment
1,079.6	1,185.4	917.8	779.9	773.1	896.7	937.0	407.7	329.7	548.5	..	Fixed Investment
281.6	307.9	331.4	353.7	384.7	427.6	444.6	318.8	340.6	355.7	..	Indirect Taxes, net
3,596.4	3,971.0	4,042.3	4,211.8	4,516.4	4,717.5	4,865.1	4,232.6	4,208.2	4,394.9	B	GDP at factor cost
359.3	371.2	408.4	415.9	450.6	478.6	505.5	444.4	462.1	482.1	..	Agriculture
821.9	934.3	833.9	836.9	867.6	915.4	936.6	406.3	404.0	448.1	f	Industry
375.6	394.0	401.0	411.0	420.0	421.8	440.4				..	Manufacturing
2,696.8	2,973.4	3,131.4	3,312.7	3,582.9	3,751.1	3,867.6	3,700.7	3,682.7	3,820.4	..	Services, etc.
999.8	1,004.8	952.2	686.2	777.5	1,046.4	1,027.5	947.2	552.8	828.8	..	Gross Domestic Saving
633.4	545.0	507.8	328.8	344.1	661.7	607.4	524.7	71.0	359.8	..	Gross National Saving

(Millions of 1987 Panamanian Balboas)

1981	1982	1983	1984	1985	1986	1987	1988	1989	1990 estimate	Notes	
4,171.5	4,344.8	4,393.6	4,452.2	4,608.2	4,830.7	4,940.4	4,015.5	3,873.3	4,078.9		Gross National Product
4,545.3	4,798.6	4,816.6	4,794.3	5,020.6	5,191.5	5,309.7	4,476.0	4,415.3	4,577.9		GDP at Market Prices
-178.3	-60.5	90.7	-139.9	-52.0	57.6	99.5	609.2	415.9	90.6	..	Resource Balance
1,570.1	1,687.1	1,682.9	1,575.6	1,689.0	1,769.8	1,736.3	1,687.8	1,676.7	1,708.7	..	Exports of Goods & NF Services
1,748.4	1,747.6	1,592.2	1,715.6	1,741.0	1,712.2	1,636.8	1,078.6	1,260.8	1,618.2	..	Imports of Goods & NF Services
4,723.6	4,859.1	4,725.9	4,934.2	5,072.6	5,133.8	5,210.2	3,866.8	3,999.4	4,487.3	..	Domestic Absorption
2,510.8	2,610.8	2,801.7	3,093.0	3,161.3	3,059.0	3,055.3	2,532.5	2,986.0	3,249.2	..	Private Consumption, etc.
1,018.6	1,099.2	1,045.6	1,059.6	1,076.7	1,168.2	1,226.9	996.7	869.5	888.4	..	General Gov't Consumption
1,194.2	1,149.1	878.5	781.6	834.7	906.6	928.0	337.6	143.8	349.7	..	Gross Domestic Investment
1,096.0	1,145.3	856.5	797.9	852.4	934.9	937.0	426.2	342.6	548.1	..	Fixed Investment
4,545.3	4,798.6	4,816.6	4,794.3	5,020.6	5,170.0	4,865.1	4,161.9	4,082.5	4,233.6	B	GDP at factor cost
444.1	437.3	451.0	458.5	481.4	470.8	505.5	480.0	495.1	511.4	f	Agriculture
940.0	1,026.4	906.4	852.5	873.9	912.1	936.6	608.8	600.2	659.1	f	Industry
408.0	416.8	409.4	407.3	415.4	424.6	440.4	..	..	..	..	Manufacturing
3,161.2	3,335.0	3,459.2	3,483.2	3,665.3	3,808.6	3,867.6	3,387.2	3,319.9	3,407.5	f	Services, etc.

1981	1982	1983	1984	1985	1986	1987	1988	1989	1990 estimate	Notes	Memo Items:
1,590.6	1,579.5	1,609.2	1,639.9	1,765.8	1,912.6	1,736.3	1,702.3	1,691.3	1,668.5	..	Capacity to Import
20.5	-107.6	-73.7	64.3	76.7	142.8	0.0	14.6	14.6	-40.2	..	Terms of Trade Adjustment
4,565.8	4,691.0	4,742.9	4,858.6	5,097.4	5,334.2	5,309.7	4,490.5	4,429.9	4,537.7	..	Gross Domestic Income
4,192.0	4,237.2	4,319.9	4,516.5	4,684.9	4,973.5	4,940.4	4,030.0	3,887.9	4,038.7	..	Gross National Income

(Index 1987 = 100)

1981	1982	1983	1984	1985	1986	1987	1988	1989	1990 estimate	Notes	DOMESTIC PRICES/DEFLATORS
85.3	89.2	90.8	95.2	97.6	99.1	100.0	101.7	103.0	103.8	..	Overall (GDP)
85.6	91.8	92.2	94.0	96.1	96.6	100.0	101.3	102.9	104.6	..	Domestic Absorption
80.9	84.9	90.6	90.7	93.6	101.7	100.0	92.6	93.3	94.3	..	Agriculture
87.4	91.0	92.0	98.2	99.3	100.4	100.0	66.7	67.3	68.0	..	Industry
92.1	94.5	98.0	100.9	101.1	99.3	100.0				..	Manufacturing
90.7	94.6	96.5	98.1	99.1	99.0	100.0	100.4	100.2	100.8	..	Consumer Price Index

1981	1982	1983	1984	1985	1986	1987	1988	1989	1990 estimate	Notes	MANUFACTURING ACTIVITY
93.5	98.3	97.8	99.7	98.8	99.4	100.0	87.9	..	..	..	Employment (1987=100)
87.8	91.6	97.4	101.4	100.7	100.9	100.0	99.2	..	..	..	Real Earnings per Empl. (1987=100)
111.3	107.3	106.9	103.4	99.7	101.1	100.0	92.6	..	..	..	Real Output per Empl. (1987=100)
28.8	34.8	33.2	33.7	34.3	32.8	31.5	36.8	..	..	..	Earnings as % of Value Added

(Millions of current Panamanian Balboas)

1981	1982	1983	1984	1985	1986	1987	1988	1989	1990 estimate	Notes	MONETARY HOLDINGS
1,723.8	1,949.1	1,970.8	2,108.6	2,194.7	2,360.0	2,278.0	1,649.0	1,600.0	2,184.0	D	Money Supply, Broadly Defined
359.7	379.3	372.6	380.7	409.3	449.5	442.1	303.8	306.9	432.8	..	Money
..	..	..	..	..	..	..	..	..	..		Currency Outside Banks
..	..	..	..	..	..	..	..	..	..		Demand Deposits
1,364.1	1,569.8	1,598.2	1,727.9	1,785.4	1,910.4	1,835.6	1,344.7	1,293.3	1,751.6	..	Quasi-Money

(Millions of current Panamanian Balboas)

1981	1982	1983	1984	1985	1986	1987	1988	1989	1990 estimate	Notes	GOVERNMENT DEFICIT (-) OR SURPLUS
-334.6	-482.6	-272.5	-340.0	-155.0	-220.7	-227.9	-283.7	-334.9		..	
1,029.8	1,203.8	1,324.3	1,369.0	1,397.9	1,536.9	1,593.1	1,097.1	996.3			Current Revenue
1,069.9	1,401.1	1,341.7	1,457.5	1,391.8	1,561.4	1,692.9	1,276.3	1,266.2			Current Expenditure
-40.1	-197.3	-17.4	-88.5	6.1	-24.5	-99.8	-179.2	-269.9			Current Budget Balance
			5.1	5.0	2.1		..	..		..	Capital Receipts
294.5	285.3	255.1	256.6	166.1	198.3	128.1	104.4	64.9		..	Capital Payments

PANAMA	1970	1971	1972	1973	1974	1975	1976	1977	1978	1979	1980
FOREIGN TRADE (CUSTOMS BASIS)					*(Millions of current US dollars)*						
Value of Exports, fob	109.5	116.5	122.6	137.8	210.5	286.4	236.7	249.5	244.3	291.6	353.4
Nonfuel Primary Products	84.1	88.5	97.7	107.1	110.8	144.6	148.5	158.3	163.0	188.8	240.0
Fuels	21.5	25.2	21.6	24.4	86.3	128.3	66.3	68.3	60.1	72.4	81.8
Manufactures	3.9	2.9	3.3	6.3	13.4	13.5	21.8	22.9	21.1	30.4	31.5
Value of Imports, cif	357.0	395.8	440.4	502.2	822.4	892.1	848.3	858.9	942.4	1,183.8	1,447.5
Nonfuel Primary Products	41.7	54.9	53.0	64.8	95.9	86.5	87.9	95.0	100.7	134.5	166.1
Fuels	66.4	70.9	73.3	102.0	293.4	360.5	282.1	283.4	230.1	337.6	441.7
Manufactures	249.0	270.0	314.1	335.4	433.2	445.0	478.4	480.5	611.5	711.7	839.6
Terms of Trade	130.1	117.5	131.2	144.9	*(Index 1987 = 100)* 140.3	133.9	144.8	142.4	126.2	133.3	138.9
Export Prices, fob	17.6	19.5	24.9	33.0	61.3	58.6	68.6	73.9	75.0	96.5	125.3
Import Prices, cif	13.5	16.6	19.0	22.8	43.7	43.7	47.3	51.9	59.4	72.4	90.2
BALANCE OF PAYMENTS					*(Millions of current US dollars)*						
Exports of Goods & Services	394.5	446.4	495.5	603.9	1,059.8	1,222.6	1,230.7	1,388.1	1,743.6	2,583.4	7,736.4
Merchandise, fob	130.3	137.8	146.1	161.9	250.9	330.9	269.0	288.5	304.4	355.6	2,267.1
Nonfactor Services	250.3	278.9	303.8	351.6	493.9	512.4	544.9	608.3	633.6	782.4	1,106.2
Factor Services	13.9	29.7	45.6	90.5	315.0	379.4	416.8	491.3	805.6	1,445.4	4,363.1
Imports of Goods & Services	462.7	524.2	598.7	710.9	1,301.0	1,391.8	1,403.0	1,541.1	1,949.2	2,906.7	8,061.7
Merchandise, fob	331.0	363.9	408.7	458.1	760.7	823.1	783.3	790.4	862.1	1,085.7	2,994.5
Nonfactor Services	88.9	100.8	109.9	121.4	150.2	164.4	165.6	200.9	233.1	280.3	639.8
Factor Services	42.8	59.5	80.1	131.4	390.1	404.3	454.1	549.8	854.0	1,540.7	4,427.4
Long-Term Interest	6.9	12.3	17.3	23.6	44.1	41.2	55.9	73.2	122.0	197.8	251.8
Private Current Transfers, net	-10.9	-12.2	-13.8	-22.7	-25.6	-25.6	-27.7	-29.9	-33.5	-39.3	-52.2
Workers' Remittances	..	..	..	..	..	..	..	..	..	..	..
Curr. A/C Bal before Off. Transf.	-79.1	-90.0	-116.9	-129.6	-246.4	-189.4	-200.0	-182.9	-239.1	-362.6	-377.5
Net Official Transfers	14.9	16.5	18.5	18.5	22.0	20.8	23.8	27.5	31.4	51.6	66.7
Curr. A/C Bal after Off. Transf.	-64.2	-73.4	-98.5	-111.1	-224.4	-168.6	-176.2	-155.4	-207.7	-311.0	-310.8
Long-Term Capital, net	119.8	86.2	128.1	147.7	113.4	184.4	722.0	-113.0	451.4	314.0	-720.5
Direct Investment	33.4	21.8	13.4	35.6	34.5	7.6	-10.6	10.9	-2.5	49.8	-46.6
Long-Term Loans	43.8	50.8	100.8	99.9	103.5	213.7	322.0	239.4	549.5	219.3	189.3
Disbursements	67.4	78.9	135.5	163.3	194.9	244.9	366.7	327.6	992.4	409.4	403.9
Repayments	23.6	28.1	34.7	63.4	91.4	31.2	44.7	88.2	442.9	190.1	214.6
Other Long-Term Capital	42.6	13.6	14.0	12.2	-24.6	-36.9	410.7	-363.3	-95.6	44.9	-863.2
Other Capital, net	-56.3	-14.0	-11.3	-39.5	99.1	-38.2	-528.8	261.1	-157.5	-30.1	1,042.6
Change in Reserves	0.6	1.3	-18.3	2.9	11.9	22.4	-17.0	7.3	-86.2	27.1	-11.3
Memo Item:					*(Panamanian Balboas per US dollar)*						
Conversion Factor (Annual Avg)	1.000	1.000	1.000	1.000	1.000	1.000	1.000	1.000	1.000	1.000	1.000
EXTERNAL DEBT (Total)	193.9	244.7	345.4	457.4	*(Millions of US dollars), outstanding at end of year* 573.9	791.2	1,142.5	1,684.3	2,312.7	2,604.3	2,974.0
Long-Term Debt (by debtor)	193.9	244.7	345.4	457.4	573.9	791.2	1,142.5	1,384.3	1,927.7	2,113.3	2,294.0
Central Bank, incl. IMF credit	6.3	12.4	18.3	17.1	26.6	63.9	134.2	170.8	173.9	160.0	157.9
Central Government	145.4	178.6	220.8	305.3	369.4	452.6	573.4	678.6	1,155.9	1,466.0	1,679.2
Rest of General Government	0.0	0.5	11.7	12.5	11.3	9.4	7.6	5.7	2.6	3.1	12.0
Non-financial Public Enterprises	42.2	53.2	94.6	122.5	166.6	265.3	427.3	523.6	589.8	469.7	424.4
Priv. Sector, incl non-guaranteed	0.0	0.0	0.0	0.0	0.0	0.0	0.0	5.6	5.5	14.5	20.5
Short-Term Debt	0.0	0.0	0.0	0.0	0.0	0.0	0.0	300.0	385.0	491.0	680.0
Memo Items:					*(Thousands of US dollars)*						
Int'l Reserves Excluding Gold	15,750	21,022	43,128	41,715	39,316	34,445	78,942	70,866	150,418	118,718	117,383
Gold Holdings (at market price)	..	..	..	..	..	..	..	..	..	..	..
SOCIAL INDICATORS											
Total Fertility Rate	5.2	5.1	4.9	4.8	4.6	4.4	4.2	4.1	3.9	3.8	3.7
Infant Mortality Rate	46.6	44.8	43.0	40.8	38.6	36.4	34.2	32.0	30.8	29.6	28.4
Life Expectancy at Birth	65.5	65.9	66.4	66.9	67.5	68.1	68.6	69.2	69.6	69.9	70.3
Urban Population, % of total	47.6	47.8	48.0	48.3	48.5	48.7	48.9	49.1	49.3	49.5	49.7
Food Prod. per capita (1987=100)	102.9	106.5	103.2	102.0	101.9	105.6	104.9	108.7	106.8	102.8	100.9
Labor Force, Agriculture (%)	41.6	40.5	39.5	38.5	37.5	36.6	35.5	34.5	33.5	32.6	31.7
Labor Force, Female (%)	25.3	25.4	25.5	25.6	25.7	25.8	25.9	25.9	26.0	26.1	26.1
Primary Schl. Enroll. Ratio	99.0	..	..	..	..	114.0	121.0	120.0	118.0	116.0	106.0
Primary Schl. Enroll. Ratio, Female	97.0	..	..	..	..	111.0	120.0	118.0	116.0	113.0	104.0
Secondary Schl. Enroll. Ratio	38.0	..	..	..	..	55.0	60.0	63.0	66.0	66.0	61.0

1981	1982	1983	1984	1985	1986	1987	1988	1989	1990 estimate	Notes	PANAMA
											FOREIGN TRADE (CUSTOMS BASIS)
											(Millions of current US dollars)
319.4	310.2	302.6	257.6	301.2	325.2	338.2	292.5	297.2	321.4	..	Value of Exports, fob
229.6	201.2	236.7	217.5	240.5	275.7	283.2	236.1	238.8	259.4	..	Nonfuel Primary Products
58.4	70.3	36.5	5.6	21.8	0.3	0.2	0.1	0.4	0.1	..	Fuels
31.4	38.7	29.4	34.5	38.8	49.2	54.7	56.3	58.0	61.8	..	Manufactures
1,561.9	1,567.8	1,412.5	1,411.8	1,383.3	1,253.7	1,304.8	794.6	964.1	1,538.6	..	Value of Imports, cif
162.9	164.2	168.1	165.7	185.7	182.7	170.7	129.1	167.5	267.3	..	Nonfuel Primary Products
439.0	417.5	392.3	367.2	293.0	174.1	212.3	145.9	160.4	256.0	..	Fuels
960.0	986.1	852.1	879.0	904.7	896.9	921.8	519.6	636.2	1,015.3	..	Manufactures
											(Index 1987 = 100)
126.7	127.7	134.2	133.3	130.5	117.1	100.0	144.7	152.3	138.1	..	Terms of Trade
117.7	113.2	114.8	112.1	108.9	100.0	100.0	119.5	118.5	125.5	..	Export Prices, fob
92.8	88.6	85.5	84.1	83.5	85.4	100.0	82.6	77.8	90.9	..	Import Prices, cif
											BALANCE OF PAYMENTS
											(Millions of current US dollars)
9,921.3	9,407.0	7,278.5	6,537.6	6,307.5	6,134.9	5,726.8	4,405.8	4,671.2	5,276.7	f	Exports of Goods & Services
2,540.2	2,411.0	1,675.5	1,685.7	1,974.3	2,366.0	2,491.7	2,346.6	2,567.9	3,194.7	..	Merchandise, fob
1,149.1	1,168.7	1,275.8	1,259.2	1,325.9	1,309.3	1,246.8	1,172.2	1,116.9	1,096.7	..	Nonfactor Services
6,232.0	5,827.3	4,327.2	3,592.7	3,007.3	2,459.6	1,988.3	887.0	986.4	985.3	..	Factor Services
9,896.7	9,503.6	6,907.2	6,431.6	6,129.9	5,875.1	5,585.3	3,710.7	4,450.6	5,268.4	f	Imports of Goods & Services
3,315.5	3,044.5	2,320.8	2,509.1	2,731.0	2,907.1	3,058.3	2,531.5	3,084.2	3,803.6	..	Merchandise, fob
702.8	658.7	375.1	393.7	427.8	468.1	430.6	308.2	326.8	396.1	..	Nonfactor Services
5,878.4	5,800.4	4,211.3	3,528.8	2,971.1	2,499.9	2,096.4	871.0	1,039.6	1,068.7	..	Factor Services
280.9	337.6	291.6	304.2	303.0	317.0	222.0	12.6	5.0	89.6	..	Long-Term Interest
-47.6	-55.0	-60.1	-31.6	-30.8	-27.1	-50.8	-39.9	-35.8	-35.0		Private Current Transfers, net
..	..	..	..	..	..	..	..	..	..		Workers' Remittances
-23.0	-151.6	311.2	74.4	146.8	232.7	90.7	655.2	184.8	-26.7	..	Curr. A/C Bal before Off. Transf.
78.7	100.6	104.4	143.8	139.5	122.2	113.7	111.5	105.5	117.5	..	Net Official Transfers
55.7	-51.0	415.6	218.2	286.3	354.9	204.4	766.7	290.3	90.8	..	Curr. A/C Bal after Off. Transf.
216.2	476.9	211.9	105.2	-252.6	-141.1	-2.5	-518.8	8.8	-155.3	f	Long-Term Capital, net
5.7	2.8	71.6	9.5	59.2	-62.2	56.8	-51.7	55.8	-30.3	..	Direct Investment
165.4	493.1	230.9	164.0	59.8	90.6	4.3	49.9	28.0	-44.7	..	Long-Term Loans
378.7	774.0	419.5	396.7	167.1	215.5	134.8	64.6	32.7	6.1	..	Disbursements
213.3	280.9	188.6	232.7	107.3	124.9	130.5	14.7	4.7	50.8	..	Repayments
45.1	-19.0	-90.6	-68.3	-371.6	-169.5	-63.6	-517.0	-75.0	-80.3	..	Other Long-Term Capital
-345.2	-441.4	-638.5	-407.0	-151.7	-154.2	-239.5	-253.3	-251.2	422.1	f	Other Capital, net
73.3	15.5	11.0	83.6	118.0	-59.6	37.6	5.5	-48.0	-357.7	..	Change in Reserves
											Memo Item:
											(Panamanian Balboas per US dollar)
1.000	1.000	1.000	1.000	1.000	1.000	1.000	1.000	1.000	1.000		Conversion Factor (Annual Avg)
											(Millions of US dollars), outstanding at end of year
3,366.1	3,923.2	4,388.9	4,364.6	4,755.3	4,896.0	5,628.7	6,044.3	6,268.0	6,676.0	..	**EXTERNAL DEBT (Total)**
2,523.1	3,001.2	3,338.2	3,451.9	3,631.3	3,886.0	4,372.4	4,333.3	4,254.9	4,258.9	..	Long-Term Debt (by debtor)
271.3	335.0	486.5	527.6	581.9	597.7	872.5	847.7	829.9	783.7	..	Central Bank, incl. IMF credit
1,779.8	2,088.0	2,203.3	2,256.6	2,330.4	2,512.2	2,643.8	2,637.1	2,598.8	2,634.1	..	Central Government
24.8	36.5	48.4	51.6	48.2	59.9	73.9	72.7	65.2	68.8	..	Rest of General Government
429.3	518.7	568.6	583.7	641.8	689.4	754.0	749.1	734.9	746.3	..	Non-financial Public Enterprises
17.9	23.0	31.4	32.4	29.0	26.8	28.2	26.7	26.1	26.0	..	Priv. Sector, incl non-guaranteed
843.0	922.0	1,050.7	912.7	1,124.0	1,010.0	1,256.3	1,711.0	2,013.1	2,417.1	..	Short-Term Debt
											Memo Items:
											(Thousands of US dollars)
119,947	100,970	206,696	215,639	97,962	170,174	77,814	72,214	119,413	406,361	..	Int'l Reserves Excluding Gold
..	..	..	..	..	..	..	..	..	..	..	Gold Holdings (at market price)
											SOCIAL INDICATORS
3.6	3.5	3.4	3.3	3.2	3.2	3.1	3.0	2.9	2.9	..	Total Fertility Rate
27.2	26.0	25.4	24.8	24.2	23.6	23.0	22.3	21.6	20.8	..	Infant Mortality Rate
70.6	71.0	71.2	71.4	71.6	71.8	72.1	72.3	72.5	72.6	..	Life Expectancy at Birth
50.0	50.3	50.7	51.0	51.3	51.7	52.1	52.6	53.0	53.4	..	Urban Population, % of total
103.1	106.0	103.4	102.1	103.0	96.6	100.0	87.2	95.5	94.0	..	Food Prod. per capita (1987=100)
..	..	..	..	..	..	..	..	..		..	Labor Force, Agriculture (%)
26.3	26.4	26.5	26.6	26.7	26.8	26.9	27.0	27.1	27.2	..	Labor Force, Female (%)
..	104.0	104.0	105.0	105.0	106.0	107.0	106.0	107.0	..	..	Primary Schl. Enroll. Ratio
..	102.0	101.0	102.0	102.0	104.0	104.0	104.0	105.0		..	Primary Schl. Enroll. Ratio, Female
..	59.0	59.0	59.0	59.0	59.0	60.0	59.0			..	Secondary Schl. Enroll. Ratio

PAPUA NEW GUINEA	1970	1971	1972	1973	1974	1975	1976	1977	1978	1979	1980
CURRENT GNP PER CAPITA (US $)	260	280	300	370	450	530	520	540	650	710	760
POPULATION (thousands)	2,422	2,481	2,541	2,602	2,665	2,729	2,794	2,861	2,929	2,998	3,070

USE AND ORIGIN OF RESOURCES	*(Millions of current Papua New Guinea Kina)*										
Gross National Product (GNP)	558.8	602.6	680.8	856.9	947.2	981.0	1,158.2	1,271.8	1,361.5	1,594.6	1,649.4
Net Factor Income from Abroad	-17.6	-31.0	-36.3	-57.8	-75.1	-55.3	-40.4	-26.7	-19.4	-38.0	-58.7
GDP at Market Prices	576.4	633.6	717.1	914.7	1,022.3	1,036.3	1,198.6	1,298.5	1,380.9	1,632.6	1,708.1
Resource Balance	-204.4	-233.6	-122.2	92.0	72.0	-64.1	11.9	-16.8	-48.1	-1.8	-173.2
Exports of Goods & NF Services	106.5	135.4	223.8	410.5	479.3	414.3	500.7	584.0	579.1	742.5	737.6
Imports of Goods & NF Services	310.9	369.0	346.0	318.5	407.3	478.4	488.8	600.8	627.2	744.3	910.8
Domestic Absorption	780.8	867.2	839.3	822.7	950.3	1,100.4	1,186.7	1,315.3	1,429.0	1,634.4	1,881.4
Private Consumption, etc.	367.6	401.2	422.1	432.0	473.1	545.0	600.5	697.1	763.3	879.7	1,039.5
General Gov't Consumption	173.4	195.1	217.6	249.1	299.1	347.7	362.7	337.7	353.3	371.4	411.2
Gross Domestic Investment	239.8	270.9	199.6	141.6	178.1	207.7	223.5	280.5	312.4	383.3	430.7
Fixed Investment	229.3	258.9	185.8	130.2	158.5	175.0	200.6	239.3	268.5	326.2	394.2
Indirect Taxes, net	28.5	33.4	35.5	39.3	48.0	57.0	67.6	83.2	82.9	95.3	110.0
GDP at factor cost	547.9	600.2	681.6	875.4	974.3	979.3	1,131.0	1,215.3	1,298.0	1,537.3	1,598.1
Agriculture	214.3	218.5	232.2	258.0	286.2	307.8	380.0	428.3	497.5	552.8	565.7
Industry	127.4	155.0	202.7	330.3	356.4	295.2	301.0	338.7	351.0	474.8	458.5
Manufacturing	31.5	36.7	40.7	51.8	68.8	83.9	101.0	99.9	134.0	152.2	162.3
Services, etc.	234.7	260.1	282.2	326.4	379.7	433.3	517.6	531.5	532.4	605.0	683.9
Gross Domestic Saving	35.4	37.3	77.4	233.6	250.1	143.6	235.4	263.7	264.3	381.5	257.4
Gross National Saving	26.7	8.9	45.3	172.3	165.9	83.0	148.6	192.3	182.5	275.5	127.8

	(Millions of 1987 Papua New Guinea Kina)										
Gross National Product	1,856.1	1,934.3	2,038.4	2,122.6	2,154.9	2,206.1	2,171.5	2,222.9	2,432.9	2,448.4	2,365.3
GDP at Market Prices	1,925.7	2,047.1	2,162.5	2,303.7	2,363.7	2,342.9	2,263.5	2,282.6	2,477.6	2,523.1	2,465.0
Resource Balance	-986.9	-1,015.8	-619.9	-220.7	-239.5	-295.2	-296.6	-390.6	-338.3	-436.0	-565.9
Exports of Goods & NF Services	290.4	364.9	564.2	788.8	896.4	865.0	789.6	821.0	898.6	896.1	893.2
Imports of Goods & NF Services	1,277.3	1,380.7	1,184.1	1,009.6	1,135.9	1,160.2	1,086.1	1,211.7	1,236.9	1,332.1	1,459.1
Domestic Absorption	2,912.7	3,062.9	2,782.4	2,524.4	2,603.2	2,638.1	2,560.1	2,673.3	2,815.9	2,959.0	3,030.9
Private Consumption, etc.	1,008.2	1,053.1	1,155.9	1,225.8	1,261.6	1,287.4	1,323.4	1,443.8	1,559.7	1,565.1	1,632.1
General Gov't Consumption	761.9	780.5	792.7	770.7	784.0	798.4	737.6	691.2	703.0	715.6	691.6
Gross Domestic Investment	1,142.5	1,229.3	833.9	528.0	557.6	552.3	499.0	538.3	553.1	678.3	707.2
Fixed Investment	1,057.7	1,134.0	763.4	487.7	501.8	468.5	426.2	455.5	495.7	572.7	646.0
GDP at factor cost	..	..	..	2,267.0	2,316.4	2,276.6	2,196.1	2,196.7	2,394.7	2,442.7	2,302.8
Agriculture	554.7	569.6	588.4	599.1	627.2	652.3	662.7	667.5	693.9	707.0	740.5
Industry	..	..	..	..	..	..	..	..	..	..	784.0
Manufacturing	..	..	..	..	..	..	..	..	..	..	260.7
Services, etc.	..	..	..	..	..	..	..	..	..	..	940.5

Memo Items:											
Capacity to Import	437.6	506.6	765.9	1,301.2	1,336.7	1,004.7	1,112.6	1,177.8	1,142.0	1,328.9	1,181.7
Terms of Trade Adjustment	147.2	141.7	201.7	512.3	440.3	139.7	323.0	356.8	243.4	432.7	288.5
Gross Domestic Income	2,072.9	2,188.8	2,364.2	2,816.0	2,804.0	2,482.6	2,586.5	2,639.4	2,721.0	2,955.8	2,753.4
Gross National Income	2,003.3	2,076.1	2,240.1	2,635.0	2,595.2	2,345.8	2,494.5	2,579.7	2,676.3	2,881.2	2,653.8

DOMESTIC PRICES/DEFLATORS	*(Index 1987 = 100)*										
Overall (GDP)	29.9	31.0	33.2	39.7	43.2	44.2	53.0	56.9	55.7	64.7	69.3
Domestic Absorption	26.8	28.3	30.2	32.6	36.5	41.7	46.4	49.2	50.7	55.2	62.1
Agriculture	38.6	38.4	39.5	43.1	45.6	47.2	57.3	64.2	71.7	78.2	76.4
Industry	..	..	..	..	..	..	..	..	..	..	58.5
Manufacturing	..	..	..	..	..	..	..	..	..	..	62.3
Consumer Price Index	..	30.3	32.2	34.9	42.9	47.4	51.1	53.4	56.5	59.7	66.9

MANUFACTURING ACTIVITY											
Employment (1987=100)	..	..	..	..	..	..	..	..	..	..	..
Real Earnings per Empl. (1987=100)	..	..	..	..	..	..	..	..	..	..	..
Real Output per Empl. (1987=100)	..	..	..	..	..	..	..	..	..	..	..
Earnings as % of Value Added	40.1	39.0	40.3	39.7	39.1	41.7	40.7	36.0	32.5	37.2	37.4

MONETARY HOLDINGS	*(Millions of current Papua New Guinea Kina)*										
Money Supply, Broadly Defined	..	..	..	195.64	320.04	245.46	277.82	428.46	449.03	571.71	553.15
Money	..	..	..	99.40	140.43	150.80	135.02	169.38	178.99	195.41	201.56
Currency Outside Banks	..	..	..	57.37	76.61	85.21	47.51	56.66	61.55	67.89	70.49
Demand Deposits	..	..	..	42.03	63.82	65.59	87.50	112.72	117.44	127.52	131.06
Quasi-Money	..	..	..	96.24	179.61	94.66	142.80	259.08	270.04	376.30	351.59

GOVERNMENT DEFICIT (-) OR SURPLUS	*(Millions of current Papua New Guinea Kina)*										
	..	..	..	..	..	-56.96	-26.80	-19.36	-21.48	-62.80	-33.02
Current Revenue	..	..	..	..	..	330.04	353.48	388.98	431.35	458.79	566.81
Current Expenditure	..	..	..	..	..	251.67	315.42	353.03	386.69	450.26	498.23
Current Budget Balance	..	..	..	..	..	78.37	38.06	35.95	44.66	8.53	68.58
Capital Receipts	..	..	..	..	..	0.22	0.11	0.04	0.02	0.03	0.13
Capital Payments	..	..	..	..	..	135.55	64.97	55.35	66.16	71.36	101.73

1981	1982	1983	1984	1985	1986	1987	1988	1989	1990 estimate	Notes	PAPUA NEW GUINEA
820	780	760	750	740	740	760	850	890	860	..	**CURRENT GNP PER CAPITA (US $)**
3,144	3,219	3,297	3,377	3,460	3,545	3,633	3,724	3,818	3,915	..	**POPULATION (thousands)**
											USE AND ORIGIN OF RESOURCES
			(Millions of current Papua New Guinea Kina)								Gross National Product (GNP)
1,622.5	1,661.1	2,023.2	2,220.9	2,335.4	2,482.9	2,700.6	3,018.8	2,898.4	2,968.0	..	Gross National Product (GNP)
-58.7	-88.0	-119.4	-72.5	-88.5	-72.1	-130.5	-122.1	-115.0	-152.6	..	Net Factor Income from Abroad
1,681.2	1,749.1	2,142.6	2,293.4	2,423.9	2,555.0	2,831.1	3,140.9	3,013.4	3,120.6	f	GDP at Market Prices
-344.7	-413.9	-369.7	-314.3	-250.3	-200.0	-185.7	-274.9	-368.5	-472.6	..	Resource Balance
642.9	644.3	775.5	904.7	1,020.9	1,121.0	1,232.1	1,371.1	1,238.0	1,157.9	..	Exports of Goods & NF Services
987.6	1,058.2	1,145.2	1,219.0	1,271.2	1,321.0	1,417.8	1,646.0	1,606.5	1,630.5	..	Imports of Goods & NF Services
2,025.9	2,163.1	2,512.2	2,607.8	2,674.4	2,755.0	3,016.6	3,415.8	3,381.8	3,593.2	..	Domestic Absorption
1,113.4	1,132.5	1,382.4	1,455.5	1,624.5	1,656.2	1,791.7	1,890.4	1,929.0	2,052.5	..	Private Consumption, etc.
454.4	468.1	499.1	533.3	569.2	591.1	639.6	662.9	744.9	759.8	..	General Gov't Consumption
458.1	562.5	630.7	619.0	480.7	507.7	585.3	862.5	707.9	780.9	..	Gross Domestic Investment
450.7	576.7	636.9	547.5	446.9	539.2	551.2	737.0	791.0	819.9	..	Fixed Investment
114.6	134.4	151.9	179.2	189.7	212.0	240.7	254.2	314.0	295.4	..	Indirect Taxes, net
1,566.6	1,614.7	1,990.7	2,114.2	2,234.2	2,343.0	2,590.4	2,886.7	2,699.4	2,825.2	B f	GDP at factor cost
561.4	567.2	700.1	857.1	818.5	828.0	852.4	924.5	856.0	899.8	..	Agriculture
390.7	406.4	597.5	540.4	635.9	729.8	904.3	1,083.1	899.9	977.2	..	Industry
166.6	164.6	217.3	252.0	264.6	256.3	268.9	294.3	336.9	370.6	..	Manufacturing
729.1	775.5	845.0	895.9	969.5	997.2	1,074.4	1,133.3	1,257.5	1,243.6	..	Services, etc.
113.4	148.5	261.1	304.6	230.2	307.7	399.8	587.6	339.5	308.3	..	Gross Domestic Saving
-30.2	-30.1	60.3	146.7	52.9	159.2	174.4	357.5	113.5	44.8	..	Gross National Saving
			(Millions of 1987 Papua New Guinea Kina)								
2,376.9	2,353.6	2,407.5	2,455.5	2,550.6	2,660.6	2,700.6	2,801.3	2,761.7	2,690.5	..	Gross National Product
2,469.2	2,477.3	2,552.1	2,538.4	2,647.8	2,736.5	2,831.1	2,917.0	2,865.3	2,822.3	f	GDP at Market Prices
-520.0	-518.1	-492.7	-437.1	-289.3	-166.5	-185.7	-325.1	-175.1	-110.5	..	Resource Balance
941.5	926.1	942.3	971.9	1,091.0	1,198.1	1,232.1	1,218.7	1,213.1	1,124.7	..	Exports of Goods & NF Services
1,461.4	1,444.2	1,435.0	1,409.0	1,380.3	1,364.5	1,417.8	1,543.9	1,388.2	1,235.2	..	Imports of Goods & NF Services
2,989.1	2,995.3	3,044.8	2,975.5	2,937.1	2,902.9	3,016.8	3,242.1	3,040.4	2,932.8	..	Domestic Absorption
1,646.6	1,609.6	1,636.9	1,630.0	1,781.1	1,734.0	1,791.9	1,792.1	1,763.7	1,704.3	..	Private Consumption, etc.
664.9	618.3	606.3	611.8	628.5	620.6	639.6	628.7	666.3	617.9	..	General Gov't Consumption
677.7	767.4	801.6	733.6	527.5	548.3	585.3	821.3	610.3	610.7	..	Gross Domestic Investment
662.1	780.9	803.9	648.3	493.1	563.6	551.2	691.4	699.9	650.5	..	Fixed Investment
2,300.4	2,291.7	2,368.0	2,333.5	2,439.5	2,513.3	2,590.4	2,676.0	2,582.2	2,569.3	B f	GDP at factor cost
799.0	787.9	795.5	819.1	795.2	808.4	852.4	883.6	898.5	892.3	..	Agriculture
694.9	700.4	765.6	718.7	819.1	915.4	904.3	959.5	853.7	876.2	f	Industry
265.4	248.0	259.0	281.1	288.9	265.0	268.9	281.3	314.0	319.7	..	Manufacturing
975.3	989.0	991.0	1,000.5	1,033.5	1,012.6	1,074.4	1,073.8	1,113.1	1,053.8	f	Services, etc.
											Memo Items:
951.3	879.3	971.7	1,045.7	1,108.5	1,158.0	1,232.1	1,286.0	1,069.8	877.2	..	Capacity to Import
9.9	-46.8	29.4	73.8	17.5	-40.1	0.0	67.3	-143.3	-247.5	..	Terms of Trade Adjustment
2,479.1	2,430.5	2,581.6	2,612.2	2,665.3	2,696.3	2,831.1	2,984.3	2,722.0	2,574.8	..	Gross Domestic Income
2,386.7	2,306.8	2,436.9	2,529.3	2,568.1	2,620.5	2,700.6	2,868.6	2,618.4	2,443.0	..	Gross National Income
			(Index 1987 = 100)								**DOMESTIC PRICES/DEFLATORS**
68.1	70.6	84.0	90.3	91.5	93.4	100.0	107.7	105.2	110.6	..	Overall (GDP)
67.8	72.2	82.5	87.6	91.1	94.9	100.0	105.4	111.2	122.5	..	Domestic Absorption
70.3	72.0	88.0	104.6	102.9	102.4	100.0	104.6	95.3	100.8	..	Agriculture
56.2	58.0	78.0	75.2	77.6	79.7	100.0	112.9	105.4	111.5	..	Industry
											Manufacturing
62.8	66.4	83.9	89.7	91.6	96.7	100.0	104.6	107.3	115.9	..	Consumer Price Index
											MANUFACTURING ACTIVITY
72.3	76.3	82.4	88.5	91.8	96.8	100.0	105.4	110.2	117.8	..	Employment (1987=100)
..	..	..	..	..			..	..	..	..	Real Earnings per Empl. (1987=100)
..	..	..	..	..			..	..	..	..	Real Output per Empl. (1987=100)
33.4	37.4	37.4	33.6	35.0	..	..	..		..	J	Earnings as % of Value Added
			(Millions of current Papua New Guinea Kina)								**MONETARY HOLDINGS**
554.74	567.85	650.04	748.02	820.12	928.96	943.29	984.85	1,037.50	1,081.61	..	Money Supply, Broadly Defined
194.36	188.64	205.97	248.99	244.15	256.68	281.33	322.17	344.50	343.83	..	Money
73.39	72.41	79.95	88.90	94.26	95.74	106.35	115.20	122.03	134.77	..	Currency Outside Banks
120.98	116.23	126.02	160.09	149.90	160.94	174.98	206.97	222.48	209.06	..	Demand Deposits
360.37	379.22	444.08	499.03	575.97	672.28	661.96	662.68	693.00	737.78	..	Quasi-Money
			(Millions of current Papua New Guinea Kina)								**GOVERNMENT DEFICIT (-) OR SURPLUS**
-107.72	-97.18	-94.57	-21.13	-56.15	-76.85	-52.01	-28.18	..	..	F	
555.86	555.65	616.91	723.60	703.77	751.56	810.71	888.98	..	..	..	Current Revenue
570.14	572.49	610.20	649.17	696.34	720.80	763.02	808.09	..	..	..	Current Expenditure
-14.28	-16.84	6.71	74.43	7.43	30.76	47.69	80.89	..	..	..	Current Budget Balance
0.32	0.84	0.27	4.73	0.79	1.21	1.29	1.27	..	..	..	Capital Receipts
93.76	81.18	101.55	100.29	64.37	108.82	100.99	110.34	..	..	..	Capital Payments

PAPUA NEW GUINEA	1970	1971	1972	1973	1974	1975	1976	1977	1978	1979	1980
FOREIGN TRADE (CUSTOMS BASIS)					*(Millions of current US dollars)*						
Value of Exports, fob	..	..	..	..	..	..	..	..	..	..	..
Nonfuel Primary Products	..	..	..	..	..	..	..	..	..	..	..
Fuels	..	..	..	..	..	..	..	..	..	..	..
Manufactures	..	..	..	..	..	..	..	..	..	..	..
Value of Imports, cif	..	..	..	..	..	..	..	..	..	..	..
Nonfuel Primary Products	..	..	..	..	..	..	..	..	..	..	..
Fuels	..	..	..	..	..	..	..	..	..	..	..
Manufactures	..	..	..	..	..	..	..	..	..	..	..
					(Index 1987 = 100)						
Terms of Trade	..	..	..	..	..	..	..	..	..	..	..
Export Prices, fob	..	..	..	..	..	..	..	..	..	..	..
Import Prices, cif	..	..	..	..	..	..	..	..	..	..	..
BALANCE OF PAYMENTS					*(Millions of current US dollars)*						
Exports of Goods & Services	123.0	159.0	229.6	532.8	675.8	457.6	639.8	751.7	788.2	1,100.4	1,087.9
Merchandise, fob	104.0	121.0	221.6	514.8	653.8	440.6	551.1	683.3	714.3	1,009.1	984.8
Nonfactor Services	15.0	33.0	75.0	81.0	42.0	87.0	68.9	38.0	35.7	41.8	43.3
Factor Services	4.0	5.0	8.0	18.0	22.0	17.0	19.8	30.3	38.3	49.4	59.8
Imports of Goods & Services	372.0	459.0	464.0	577.0	706.0	691.0	685.0	824.9	1,008.9	1,179.3	1,561.1
Merchandise, fob	300.0	356.0	299.0	290.0	428.0	504.0	434.2	559.9	688.4	783.3	1,020.5
Nonfactor Services	48.0	63.0	114.0	163.0	159.0	122.0	175.4	183.5	217.0	237.8	301.6
Factor Services	24.0	40.0	51.0	124.0	119.0	65.0	75.4	81.5	103.5	158.1	239.0
Long-Term Interest	9.7	17.5	25.8	32.8	35.0	32.0	32.1	33.5	35.9	37.2	51.7
Private Current Transfers, net	10.0	3.0	5.0	-5.0	-13.0	-7.0	-58.5	-56.4	-88.1	-95.6	-105.7
Workers' Remittances	..	..	..	..	..	..	..	..	..	..	..
Curr. A/C Bal before Off. Transf.	-239.0	-297.0	-154.0	31.0	-1.0	-138.0	-103.7	-129.6	-308.8	-174.5	-578.8
Net Official Transfers	150.0	175.0	160.0	184.0	222.0	116.0	144.7	228.5	254.2	252.0	266.6
Curr. A/C Bal after Off. Transf.	-89.0	-122.0	6.0	215.0	221.0	-22.0	41.0	98.8	-54.6	77.5	-312.2
Long-Term Capital, net	98.0	217.0	132.0	56.0	58.0	97.0	32.7	65.1	-42.6	44.5	100.4
Direct Investment	..	..	19.0	89.0	52.0	34.0	18.9	18.0	34.0	41.0	59.8
Long-Term Loans	133.6	194.1	80.2	10.1	-8.6	9.6	-0.6	38.3	-62.8	16.6	63.8
Disbursements	154.0	237.3	159.8	101.5	73.3	79.2	66.9	108.3	20.3	66.9	135.4
Repayments	20.4	43.2	79.6	91.4	81.9	69.6	67.5	70.0	83.1	50.3	71.6
Other Long-Term Capital	-35.6	22.9	32.8	-43.1	14.6	53.4	14.3	8.8	-13.8	-13.1	-23.2
Other Capital, net	65.0	-23.0	-141.4	-185.8	-277.8	72.2	-30.9	-25.9	103.6	-9.8	142.9
Change in Reserves	-74.0	-72.0	3.4	-85.2	-1.2	-147.2	-42.8	-138.0	-6.5	-112.2	68.9
Memo Item:					*(Papua New Guinea Kina per US dollar)*						
Conversion Factor (Annual Avg)	0.890	0.880	0.840	0.700	0.690	0.760	0.790	0.790	0.710	0.710	0.670
EXTERNAL DEBT (Total)	208.7	407.2	495.0	525.5	505.3	506.1	520.8	675.8	583.3	608.7	719.1
				(Millions of US dollars), outstanding at end of year							
Long-Term Debt (by debtor)	208.7	407.2	495.0	525.5	505.3	506.1	520.8	576.8	530.3	580.7	655.1
Central Bank, incl. IMF credit	0.0	0.0	0.0	1.2	1.2	1.7	31.7	33.7	33.4	26.9	33.6
Central Government	36.1	89.4	130.4	218.3	243.1	273.4	280.6	328.6	351.2	375.8	459.9
Rest of General Government	..	..	..	..	..	..	..	..	..	..	..
Non-financial Public Enterprises	0.0	0.0	0.0	0.0	0.0	0.0	0.0	0.0	0.0	0.0	0.0
Priv. Sector, incl non-guaranteed	172.6	317.8	364.6	306.0	261.0	231.0	208.5	214.5	145.7	178.0	161.6
Short-Term Debt	0.0	0.0	0.0	0.0	0.0	0.0	0.0	99.0	53.0	28.0	64.0
Memo Items:					*(Millions of US dollars)*						
Int'l Reserves Excluding Gold	..	..	..	31.26	32.45	179.67	257.20	426.63	404.72	503.55	423.43
Gold Holdings (at market price)	..	..	..	..	..	..	..	4.73	10.03	27.25	34.33
SOCIAL INDICATORS											
Total Fertility Rate	6.1	6.1	6.1	6.0	6.0	6.0	5.9	5.9	5.8	5.8	5.7
Infant Mortality Rate	115.0	110.0	105.0	101.0	97.0	93.0	89.0	85.0	82.8	80.6	78.4
Life Expectancy at Birth	46.7	47.2	47.7	48.1	48.5	48.9	49.3	49.7	50.2	50.6	51.1
Urban Population, % of total	9.8	10.2	10.6	11.1	11.5	11.9	12.1	12.3	12.6	12.8	13.0
Food Prod. per capita (1987=100)	101.6	101.4	100.9	96.8	102.1	101.3	102.4	100.8	101.4	97.9	99.4
Labor Force, Agriculture (%)	11.9	11.8	11.7	11.6	11.6	11.5	11.5	11.4	11.4	11.3	11.2
Labor Force, Female (%)	29.4	29.9	30.3	30.8	31.2	31.6	32.1	32.5	33.0	33.5	33.9
Primary Schl. Enroll. Ratio	52.0	..	..	..	..	56.0	..	57.0	58.0	60.0	59.0
Primary Schl. Enroll. Ratio, Female	39.0	..	..	..	..	43.0	..	45.0	47.0	50.0	51.0
Secondary Schl. Enroll. Ratio	8.0	..	..	..	..	12.0	12.0	11.0	11.0	11.0	12.0

1981	1982	1983	1984	1985	1986	1987	1988	1989	1990 estimate	Notes	PAPUA NEW GUINEA
				(Millions of current US dollars)							**FOREIGN TRADE (CUSTOMS BASIS)**
..	..	..	..	..	..	..	..	..	..	..	Value of Exports, fob
..	..	..	..	..	..	..	..	..	..	..	Nonfuel Primary Products
..	..	..	..	..	..	..	..	..	..	..	Fuels
..	..	..	..	..	..	..	..	..	..	..	Manufactures
..	..	..	..	..	..	..	..	..	..	..	Value of Imports, cif
..	..	..	..	..	..	..	..	..	..	..	Nonfuel Primary Products
..	..	..	..	..	..	..	..	..	..	..	Fuels
..	..	..	..	..	..	..	..	..	..	..	Manufactures
				(Index 1987 = 100)							
..	..	..	..	..	..	..	..	..	..	..	Terms of Trade
..	..	..	..	..	..	..	..	..	..	..	Export Prices, fob
..	..	..	..	..	..	..	..	..	..	..	Import Prices, cif
				(Millions of current US dollars)							**BALANCE OF PAYMENTS**
971.8	925.3	953.4	1,029.0	1,041.0	1,194.6	1,399.1	1,716.2	1,717.5	1,494.3	..	Exports of Goods & Services
839.7	770.2	819.5	914.0	921.4	1,030.6	1,243.9	1,475.3	1,468.9	1,228.2	..	Merchandise, fob
84.7	95.4	75.7	64.4	64.0	72.5	97.3	122.3	157.3	178.3	..	Nonfactor Services
47.4	59.6	58.3	50.6	55.5	91.5	57.9	118.6	91.3	87.7	..	Factor Services
1,647.6	1,546.3	1,488.4	1,518.0	1,325.1	1,434.0	1,713.5	2,145.7	2,205.3	1,944.0	..	Imports of Goods & Services
1,096.4	1,017.6	974.8	962.8	874.8	928.8	1,129.6	1,384.5	1,336.4	1,203.0	..	Merchandise, fob
342.1	347.8	333.4	356.1	288.5	302.7	377.6	435.1	579.0	493.7	..	Nonfactor Services
209.2	180.9	180.3	199.2	161.8	202.5	206.3	326.2	289.9	247.3	..	Factor Services
71.1	102.0	117.2	146.6	131.7	131.7	153.5	161.5	157.7	175.7	..	Long-Term Interest
-126.1	-122.6	-97.4	-95.0	-88.8	-78.7	-104.5	-124.6	-129.3	-116.1	..	Private Current Transfers, net
..	..	..	..	..	..	..	..	46.1	51.3	..	Workers' Remittances
-801.9	-743.6	-632.4	-584.0	-372.9	-318.1	-418.9	-554.1	-617.1	-565.9	..	Curr. A/C Bal before Off. Transf.
280.5	260.7	256.7	261.9	218.4	212.7	204.3	217.7	216.2	214.0	..	Net Official Transfers
-521.5	-482.9	-375.6	-322.2	-154.5	-105.4	-214.6	-336.5	-400.9	-351.9	..	Curr. A/C Bal after Off. Transf.
392.2	481.4	345.6	238.8	120.7	126.4	123.3	210.5	322.5	298.0	..	Long-Term Capital, net
85.6	84.1	137.7	113.4	82.4	82.1	70.9	119.7	222.3	231.2	..	Direct Investment
337.4	448.7	376.6	159.0	228.6	269.6	118.3	88.2	206.5	107.9	..	Long-Term Loans
418.9	564.2	532.1	378.0	419.2	438.5	303.7	399.8	550.8	480.2	..	Disbursements
81.5	115.5	155.5	219.0	190.6	168.9	185.4	311.6	344.3	372.3	..	Repayments
-30.8	-51.4	-168.8	-33.6	-190.3	-225.3	-66.0	2.6	-106.3	-41.1	..	Other Long-Term Capital
78.3	-34.4	127.2	130.4	30.9	-22.2	88.4	46.4	18.2	-16.0	..	Other Capital, net
51.0	35.9	-97.2	-47.1	3.0	1.2	3.0	79.6	60.2	69.9	..	Change in Reserves
				(Papua New Guinea Kina per US dollar)							**Memo Item:**
0.670	0.740	0.830	0.890	1.000	0.970	0.910	0.870	0.860	0.950	..	Conversion Factor (Annual Avg)
				(Millions of US dollars), outstanding at end of year							**EXTERNAL DEBT (Total)**
1,184.5	1,627.6	1,867.6	2,029.3	2,112.3	1,984.2	2,278.2	2,256.4	2,444.7	2,606.2	..	Long-Term Debt (by debtor)
1,022.5	1,445.6	1,800.6	1,884.3	1,966.3	1,922.2	2,173.2	2,121.5	2,280.0	2,534.6	..	Central Bank, incl. IMF credit
77.4	73.0	69.0	35.0	29.6	15.3	12.0	6.1	3.0	61.0	..	Central Government
563.1	652.6	837.1	860.4	939.1	1,062.1	1,232.0	1,047.6	1,005.7	1,167.4	..	Rest of General Government
..	..	..	..	..	..	..	..	..	..	..	Non-financial Public Enterprises
19.1	38.4	47.6	77.9	100.6	146.1	171.7	186.7	292.4	319.8	..	Priv. Sector, incl non-guaranteed
362.9	681.6	846.9	911.0	897.0	698.7	757.5	881.1	978.9	986.4	..	Short-Term Debt
162.0	182.0	67.0	145.0	146.0	62.0	105.0	134.9	164.7	71.6	..	
				(Millions of US dollars)							**Memo Items:**
396.17	452.88	440.07	435.23	442.57	425.46	436.83	393.49	384.38	403.04	..	Int'l Reserves Excluding Gold
24.72	28.50	23.90	19.37	20.57	24.61	30.50	25.84	25.26	24.25	..	Gold Holdings (at market price)
											SOCIAL INDICATORS
5.6	5.6	5.5	5.5	5.4	5.4	5.3	5.2	5.2	5.1	..	Total Fertility Rate
76.2	74.0	71.8	69.6	67.4	65.2	63.0	61.2	59.3	57.5	..	Infant Mortality Rate
51.5	51.9	52.3	52.7	53.1	53.5	53.9	54.2	54.5	54.7	..	Life Expectancy at Birth
13.3	13.5	13.8	14.0	14.3	14.6	14.9	15.2	15.5	15.8	..	Urban Population, % of total
98.0	98.9	98.0	103.3	104.8	101.3	100.0	100.3	102.5	100.7	..	Food Prod. per capita (1987=100)
..	..	..	..	..	..	..	..	..	..	..	Labor Force, Agriculture (%)
34.0	34.2	34.3	34.4	34.5	34.6	34.7	34.7	34.8	34.9	..	Labor Force, Female (%)
..	60.0	..	..	..	..	70.0	71.0	73.0	..	..	Primary Schl. Enroll. Ratio
..	53.0	..	..	..	..	64.0	65.0	67.0	..	..	Primary Schl. Enroll. Ratio, Female
..	11.0	..	..	..	..	12.0	13.0	13.0	..	..	Secondary Schl. Enroll. Ratio

PARAGUAY	1970	1971	1972	1973	1974	1975	1976	1977	1978	1979	1980
CURRENT GNP PER CAPITA (US $)	260	270	300	350	440	550	620	720	830	1,030	1,340
POPULATION (thousands)	2,351	2,412	2,474	2,538	2,607	2,682	2,764	2,853	2,948	3,046	3,147

USE AND ORIGIN OF RESOURCES

(Billions of current Paraguayan Guaranies)

	1970	1971	1972	1973	1974	1975	1976	1977	1978	1979	1980
Gross National Product (GNP)	73.7	82.5	94.9	123.3	166.0	188.9	212.1	261.5	319.4	428.3	582.2
Net Factor Income from Abroad	-1.2	-1.3	-2.0	-2.1	-2.0	-1.5	-2.0	-2.1	-3.2	-2.2	5.3
GDP at Market Prices	74.9	83.7	96.9	125.4	168.0	190.4	214.1	263.6	322.5	430.5	576.9
Resource Balance	-0.9	-2.1	-0.1	0.9	-3.8	-10.4	-7.2	-7.9	-11.9	-23.7	-77.3
Exports of Goods & NFServices	11.2	11.2	13.3	18.8	26.1	25.2	31.4	51.3	59.4	69.1	88.3
Imports of Goods & NFServices	12.1	13.3	13.4	17.9	29.9	35.6	38.6	59.2	71.3	92.8	165.6
Domestic Absorption	75.8	85.9	97.0	124.6	171.8	200.8	221.3	271.5	334.5	454.2	654.2
Private Consumption, etc.	58.0	66.6	74.6	92.5	127.3	143.0	155.2	190.1	225.2	306.5	436.9
General Gov't Consumption	6.7	7.1	7.8	8.2	9.2	12.0	13.4	16.4	21.5	24.7	34.7
Gross Domestic Investment	11.0	12.2	14.6	23.9	35.3	45.9	52.7	65.1	87.7	123.0	182.6
Fixed Investment	10.9	11.8	13.3	20.4	30.9	39.5	48.7	62.9	81.3	116.1	174.1
Indirect Taxes, net	5.5	5.9	6.0	6.4	6.8	7.9	8.9	10.3	16.3	27.6	34.5
GDP at factor cost	69.4	77.9	90.9	119.0	161.2	182.6	205.1	253.3	306.2	402.9	542.4
Agriculture	24.0	27.8	33.4	47.3	59.3	70.3	74.0	89.9	103.4	135.2	165.1
Industry	15.5	17.4	19.8	25.6	38.1	40.0	47.5	60.8	76.7	102.1	158.3
Manufacturing	12.5	13.7	15.7	20.0	30.3	29.8	34.2	45.0	54.4	69.6	92.3
Services, etc.	35.4	38.5	43.7	52.6	70.7	80.1	92.6	112.9	142.4	193.2	253.5
Gross Domestic Saving	10.1	10.0	14.5	24.7	31.5	35.5	45.5	57.2	75.8	99.3	105.3
Gross National Saving	9.2	9.3	12.9	22.9	29.7	34.1	43.6	55.2	72.7	97.5	110.6

(Billions of 1987 Paraguayan Guaranies)

	1970	1971	1972	1973	1974	1975	1976	1977	1978	1979	1980
Gross National Product	956.61	1,010.08	1,069.37	1,149.27	1,251.58	1,338.16	1,426.17	1,616.91	1,765.04	1,974.70	2,268.63
GDP at Market Prices	948.98	1,000.56	1,065.04	1,141.41	1,236.62	1,316.26	1,405.64	1,555.43	1,725.72	1,916.82	2,194.29
Resource Balance	26.20	-0.20	20.41	-11.51	-41.18	-9.18	-76.18	-145.51	-145.97	82.49	-412.23
Exports of Goods & NFServices	206.15	200.29	222.21	220.80	250.82	248.94	232.25	289.58	347.68	619.66	372.65
Imports of Goods & NFServices	179.94	200.50	201.81	232.30	292.00	258.12	308.43	435.09	493.65	537.16	784.88
Domestic Absorption	922.77	1,000.76	1,044.64	1,152.92	1,277.80	1,325.44	1,481.82	1,700.94	1,871.69	1,834.33	2,606.52
Private Consumption, etc.	701.30	764.36	787.75	838.98	943.67	956.75	1,044.60	1,208.01	1,253.61	1,144.56	1,679.01
General Gov't Consumption	86.56	86.90	86.99	78.84	71.51	86.94	93.02	106.48	124.11	115.63	132.00
Gross Domestic Investment	134.92	149.50	169.90	235.10	262.62	281.74	344.20	386.45	493.96	574.14	795.51
Fixed Investment	..	..	..	218.19	245.20	253.24	320.89	381.41	463.47	554.06	779.94
GDP at factor cost	886.10	937.22	1,006.41	1,091.41	1,195.19	1,271.22	1,356.88	1,505.24	1,650.27	1,806.69	2,077.11
Agriculture	317.99	322.41	334.88	356.23	391.05	423.00	438.61	467.63	491.18	523.75	568.30
Industry	200.90	216.43	231.72	254.79	275.05	281.99	307.17	366.17	423.74	487.30	636.89
Manufacturing	169.14	178.67	191.13	207.14	222.48	218.37	230.46	270.45	301.94	331.84	375.96
Services, etc.	430.08	461.71	498.45	530.39	570.53	611.28	659.86	721.63	810.81	905.77	989.10

Memo Items:

	1970	1971	1972	1973	1974	1975	1976	1977	1978	1979	1980
Capacity to Import	166.51	168.21	200.75	243.60	254.74	182.64	250.67	377.17	411.18	400.16	418.63
Terms of Trade Adjustment	-39.64	-32.09	-21.46	22.80	3.92	-66.30	18.42	87.59	63.50	-219.50	45.98
Gross Domestic Income	909.33	968.47	1,043.58	1,164.21	1,240.54	1,249.96	1,424.06	1,643.02	1,789.23	1,697.32	2,240.27
Gross National Income	916.97	978.00	1,047.91	1,172.06	1,255.50	1,271.85	1,444.58	1,704.50	1,828.54	1,755.21	2,314.62

DOMESTIC PRICES/DEFLATORS

(Index 1987 = 100)

	1970	1971	1972	1973	1974	1975	1976	1977	1978	1979	1980
Overall (GDP)	7.9	8.4	9.1	11.0	13.6	14.5	15.2	16.9	18.7	22.5	26.3
Domestic Absorption	8.2	8.6	9.3	10.8	13.4	15.2	14.9	16.0	17.9	24.8	25.1
Agriculture	7.6	8.6	10.0	13.3	15.2	16.6	16.9	19.2	21.1	25.8	29.1
Industry	7.7	8.0	8.5	10.0	13.8	14.2	15.5	16.6	18.1	25.8	24.9
Manufacturing	7.4	7.7	8.2	9.7	13.6	13.6	14.8	16.6	18.0	21.0	24.6
Consumer Price Index	8.7	9.2	10.0	11.3	14.1	15.1	15.8	17.3	19.1	24.5	30.0

MANUFACTURING ACTIVITY

	1970	1971	1972	1973	1974	1975	1976	1977	1978	1979	1980
Employment (1987=100)	..	..	..	..	..	..	..	..	..	..	..
Real Earnings per Empl. (1987=100)	..	..	..	..	..	..	..	..	..	..	..
Real Output per Empl. (1987=100)	..	..	..	..	..	..	..	..	..	..	..
Earnings as % of Value Added	..	..	..	..	..	..	..	..	..	..	..

MONETARY HOLDINGS

(Billions of current Paraguayan Guaranies)

	1970	1971	1972	1973	1974	1975	1976	1977	1978	1979	1980
Money Supply, Broadly Defined	13.51	15.24	18.84	24.30	29.38	37.09	45.75	60.15	78.49	97.49	131.26
Money	7.31	7.85	9.42	12.49	15.12	17.83	21.59	28.57	39.81	49.54	62.36
Currency Outside Banks	4.02	4.41	5.14	6.49	7.55	8.90	10.29	13.34	18.69	24.31	31.18
Demand Deposits	3.29	3.44	4.28	6.00	7.57	8.93	11.30	15.23	21.12	25.22	31.19
Quasi-Money	6.20	7.39	9.42	11.81	14.26	19.26	24.16	31.58	38.68	47.95	68.89

GOVERNMENT DEFICIT (-) OR SURPLUS

(Billions of current Paraguayan Guaranies)

	1970	1971	1972	1973	1974	1975	1976	1977	1978	1979	1980
GOVERNMENT DEFICIT (-) OR SURPLUS	..	..	-1.61	-0.04	1.74	-0.56	-2.22	1.63	3.06	4.34	1.81
Current Revenue	..	..	10.94	13.41	18.40	21.16	23.89	31.33	40.81	51.15	62.14
Current Expenditure	..	..	10.25	11.29	13.82	17.09	18.79	21.79	26.36	32.41	43.13
Current Budget Balance	..	..	0.69	2.12	4.58	4.08	5.10	9.54	14.46	18.73	19.01
Capital Receipts	..	..	0.10	0.08	0.04	0.03	0.03	0.04	0.04	0.09	0.05
Capital Payments	..	..	2.40	2.24	2.88	4.67	7.35	7.96	11.44	14.49	17.25

1981	1982	1983	1984	1985	1986	1987	1988	1989	1990 estimate	Notes	PARAGUAY
1,680	1,740	1,660	1,500	2,440	100	100	990	1,020	1,110	A	**CURRENT GNP PER CAPITA (US $)**
3,250	3,357	3,465	3,577	3,693	3,812	3,933	4,058	4,185	4,314	..	**POPULATION (thousands)**
				(Billions of current Paraguayan Guaranies)							**USE AND ORIGIN OF RESOURCES**
737.2	762.0	829.9	1,084.4	1,386.0	1,817.5	2,451.8	3,254.9	4,555.5	6,479.2	..	Gross National Product (GNP)
8.8	8.3	11.8	14.0	-7.9	-16.3	-41.8	-64.2	-52.9	4.8	..	Net Factor Income from Abroad
728.4	753.7	818.1	1,070.4	1,393.9	1,833.8	2,493.6	3,319.1	4,608.4	6,474.4	..	GDP at Market Prices
-84.8	-73.3	10.9	-36.9	-74.5	-164.3	-263.8	-135.4	269.9	80.6	..	Resource Balance
83.9	91.1	108.4	184.5	296.0	408.8	538.9	974.1	1,723.2	2,219.5	..	Exports of Goods & NFServices
168.7	164.4	97.5	221.4	370.5	573.1	802.7	1,109.5	1,453.3	2,139.0	..	Imports of Goods & NFServices
813.3	827.1	807.2	1,107.3	1,468.4	1,998.1	2,757.3	3,454.5	4,338.5	6,393.9	..	Domestic Absorption
534.7	564.2	571.9	802.6	1,083.9	1,440.9	2,002.9	2,490.7	2,976.9	4,551.5	..	Private Consumption, etc.
48.6	52.3	60.1	59.2	78.0	98.3	128.6	155.1	262.8	417.0	..	General Gov't Consumption
229.9	210.6	175.2	245.5	306.5	458.9	625.8	808.7	1,098.8	1,425.4	..	Gross Domestic Investment
219.8	198.6	164.5	231.2	288.0	431.8	591.4	768.2	1,045.6	1,425.4	..	Fixed Investment
41.9	48.2	45.1	50.7	66.3	89.7	150.6	176.5	324.5	453.1	..	Indirect Taxes, net
686.6	705.5	773.0	1,019.7	1,327.6	1,744.1	2,343.0	3,142.6	4,283.9	6,021.3	B	GDP at factor cost
196.8	190.6	211.8	307.1	403.3	498.9	681.9	983.3	1,361.8	1,798.0	..	Agriculture
203.2	208.4	192.8	243.3	314.7	414.4	561.6	735.2	1,066.0	1,495.0	..	Industry
118.5	121.0	189.3	238.9	309.0	406.1	550.1	719.5	1,044.8	1,472.0	..	Manufacturing
328.5	354.6	413.5	520.0	676.0	920.4	1,250.1	1,600.6	2,180.6	3,181.4	..	Services, etc.
145.1	137.2	186.1	208.6	232.0	294.6	362.1	673.3	1,368.7	1,506.0	..	Gross Domestic Saving
154.2	145.7	198.7	224.5	226.4	282.1	335.1	628.5	1,341.0	1,551.3	..	Gross National Saving
				(Billions of 1987 Paraguayan Guaranies)							
2,473.54	2,433.13	2,324.64	2,372.14	58,353.50	2,363.22	2,451.78	2,606.06	2,784.34	2,933.34	..	Gross National Product
2,383.40	2,348.74	2,230.82	2,300.71	2,392.26	2,389.03	2,493.60	2,655.03	2,809.99	2,896.03	..	GDP at Market Prices
-395.14	-307.54	21.16	-118.54	-109.93	-167.24	-263.80	-166.23	89.97	60.06	..	Resource Balance
382.22	425.20	434.76	440.37	404.41	633.23	538.90	733.63	917.62	1,073.13	..	Exports of Goods & NFServices
777.36	732.73	413.61	558.90	514.33	800.47	802.70	899.86	827.66	1,013.07	..	Imports of Goods & NFServices
2,778.54	2,656.27	2,209.66	2,419.24	2,502.19	2,556.27	2,757.40	2,821.26	2,720.03	2,835.97	..	Domestic Absorption
1,708.41	1,744.13	1,494.01	1,730.24	1,804.65	1,842.02	2,003.00	2,041.33	1,831.05	1,924.10	..	Private Consumption, etc.
157.68	161.20	164.37	129.53	131.99	127.67	128.60	129.53	173.32	186.58	..	General Gov't Consumption
912.44	750.94	551.27	559.48	565.54	586.58	625.80	650.40	715.66	725.29	..	Gross Domestic Investment
900.49	729.33	533.36	537.77	539.61	556.50	591.40	613.44	678.82	747.15	..	Fixed Investment
2,259.74	2,213.88	2,122.34	2,198.60	2,285.90	2,280.03	2,343.00	2,511.24	2,638.21	2,717.93	B	GDP at factor cost
625.46	627.99	612.66	648.89	678.71	637.29	681.93	764.22	822.85	841.30	..	Agriculture
681.79	650.92	516.85	529.74	547.64	544.41	561.61	590.19	619.55	630.16	..	Industry
392.17	377.66	507.64	520.44	537.92	533.55	550.10	577.89	606.61	616.60	..	Manufacturing
1,076.15	1,069.83	1,101.31	1,122.07	1,165.91	1,207.33	1,250.06	1,300.63	1,367.60	1,424.57	..	Services, etc.
											Memo Items:
386.57	405.82	459.85	465.75	410.91	570.99	538.90	790.03	981.38	1,051.23	..	Capacity to Import
4.35	-19.38	25.08	25.39	6.50	-62.24	0.00	56.40	63.75	-21.90	..	Terms of Trade Adjustment
2,387.74	2,329.35	2,255.90	2,326.09	2,398.76	2,326.79	2,493.60	2,711.44	2,873.75	2,874.13	..	Gross Domestic Income
2,477.88	2,413.74	2,349.73	2,397.53	58,360.00	2,300.98	2,451.78	2,662.46	2,848.09	2,911.44	..	Gross National Income
				(Index 1987 = 100)							**DOMESTIC PRICES/DEFLATORS**
30.6	32.1	36.7	46.5	58.3	76.8	100.0	125.0	164.0	223.6	..	Overall (GDP)
29.3	31.1	36.5	45.8	58.7	78.2	100.0	122.4	159.5	225.5	..	Domestic Absorption
31.5	30.4	34.6	47.3	59.4	78.3	100.0	128.7	165.5	213.7	..	Agriculture
29.8	32.0	37.3	45.9	57.5	76.1	100.0	124.6	172.1	237.2	..	Industry
30.2	32.0	37.3	45.9	57.4	76.1	100.0	124.5	172.2	238.7	..	Manufacturing
34.2	36.5	41.4	49.8	62.3	82.1	100.0	122.8	155.0	214.2	..	Consumer Price Index
											MANUFACTURING ACTIVITY
..	..	..	..	..	..	..	..	..	..		Employment (1987=100)
..	..	..	..	..	..	..	..	..	..		Real Earnings per Empl. (1987=100)
..	..	..	..	..	..	..	..	..	..		Real Output per Empl. (1987=100)
..	..	..	..	..	..	..	..	..	..		Earnings as % of Value Added
				(Billions of current Paraguayan Guaranies)							**MONETARY HOLDINGS**
156.79	165.69	193.42	225.94	272.94	347.65	469.34	563.22	..	1,566.49	..	Money Supply, Broadly Defined
62.43	60.20	75.59	97.81	125.20	158.67	243.67	328.49	..	840.09	..	Money
31.15	33.17	38.47	48.60	62.61	84.47	119.56	149.09	..	300.52	..	Currency Outside Banks
31.28	27.03	37.12	49.21	62.59	74.20	124.10	179.39	..	539.57	..	Demand Deposits
94.35	105.49	117.84	128.13	147.73	188.98	225.67	234.74	..	726.40	..	Quasi-Money
				(Billions of current Paraguayan Guaranies)							**GOVERNMENT DEFICIT (-) OR SURPLUS**
-10.59	2.98	-7.73	-18.44	-6.91	0.52	-0.96	25.20	96.70	190.66	..	Current Revenue
72.73	85.82	83.44	102.42	135.41	177.54	253.03	322.40	524.62	793.30	..	Current Expenditure
57.39	72.36	72.89	90.12	106.20	133.79	179.43	218.73	364.42	497.61	..	Current Budget Balance
15.35	13.45	10.55	12.30	29.21	43.75	73.60	103.67	160.19	295.68	..	Capital Receipts
0.11	0.09	0.59	0.09	0.10	1.22	0.26	0.18	0.43	0.42	..	Capital Payments
26.04	10.56	18.87	30.83	26.58	19.72	53.03	78.66	63.92	105.45	..	

PARAGUAY	1970	1971	1972	1973	1974	1975	1976	1977	1978	1979	1980
FOREIGN TRADE (CUSTOMS BASIS)					*(Millions of current US dollars)*						
Value of Exports, fob	64.0	65.2	86.2	126.8	169.7	174.1	181.3	278.9	257.0	305.2	310.2
Nonfuel Primary Products	..	..	76.7	..	150.4	153.7	155.3	246.9	223.3	269.6	
Fuels	..	..	0.2	..	2.0	2.2	2.0	1.4	1.1	1.1	..
Manufactures	5.7	7.2	9.3	16.1	17.4	18.2	23.9	30.6	32.5	34.5	36.5
Value of Imports, cif	75.2	83.5	79.8	122.3	194.4	212.0	219.9	308.1	382.4	520.9	614.7
Nonfuel Primary Products	15.5	17.1	16.0	18.0	31.3	33.6	36.4	41.5	54.1	75.0	77.5
Fuels	10.9	11.1	10.4	12.5	52.0	44.6	54.8	62.2	86.2	125.6	170.3
Manufactures	48.9	55.2	53.3	91.8	111.1	133.8	128.7	204.5	242.1	320.3	366.8
					(Index 1987 = 100)						
Terms of Trade	279.8	248.7	251.2	304.1	199.6	159.3	173.5	160.5	158.0	151.5	131.4
Export Prices, fob	47.3	51.4	56.0	97.4	99.3	85.0	93.8	102.5	102.9	120.3	127.6
Import Prices, cif	16.9	20.6	22.3	32.0	49.7	53.4	54.1	63.8	65.2	79.4	97.1
BALANCE OF PAYMENTS					*(Millions of current US dollars)*						
Exports of Goods & Services	89.7	90.1	106.4	151.0	212.7	233.8	257.8	419.6	489.1	593.7	781.2
Merchandise, fob	65.3	66.5	85.6	128.0	173.2	188.0	202.1	327.1	356.1	384.5	582.9
Nonfactor Services	24.0	22.6	19.9	21.5	34.0	34.1	39.9	62.9	78.2	129.1	118.1
Factor Services	0.4	1.0	1.0	1.5	5.5	11.7	15.8	29.6	54.8	80.1	80.2
Imports of Goods & Services	111.3	120.2	118.2	172.7	269.3	320.0	330.5	479.4	607.8	807.0	1,398.8
Merchandise, fob	76.6	82.9	78.7	127.3	198.3	227.3	236.4	360.0	432.0	577.1	1,054.3
Nonfactor Services	21.8	23.5	26.5	31.8	45.3	55.1	57.8	72.1	95.6	154.2	260.0
Factor Services	12.9	13.7	13.0	13.6	25.6	37.6	36.3	47.3	80.2	75.7	84.5
Long-Term Interest	3.5	4.6	5.7	5.8	6.7	8.5	9.6	12.9	17.9	29.9	44.5
Private Current Transfers, net	2.3	4.4	2.6	2.3	1.8	1.0	0.9	0.7	0.6	3.1	-0.3
Workers' Remittances	..	..	..	..	..	0.5	0.3	0.4	0.4	1.4	2.0
Curr. A/C Bal before Off. Transf.	-19.3	-25.7	-9.2	-19.4	-54.7	-85.2	-71.8	-59.1	-118.1	-210.2	-617.9
Net Official Transfers	2.9	3.2	3.9	3.5	2.0	13.0	3.3	0.5	5.2	4.3	4.8
Curr. A/C Bal after Off. Transf.	-16.4	-22.5	-5.3	-16.0	-52.7	-72.2	-68.5	-58.6	-112.9	-205.9	-613.1
Long-Term Capital, net	18.8	24.6	20.4	29.6	52.9	85.9	117.3	85.2	166.4	135.5	560.4
Direct Investment	3.8	7.1	2.9	9.2	20.7	24.4	-3.0	21.7	19.6	50.2	29.8
Long-Term Loans	7.3	9.4	6.7	9.0	31.0	43.3	54.4	112.6	125.7	132.5	126.8
Disbursements	14.4	17.8	16.3	19.9	47.0	65.0	76.2	142.6	158.0	186.5	205.9
Repayments	7.1	8.4	9.6	10.9	16.0	21.7	21.8	30.0	32.3	54.0	79.1
Other Long-Term Capital	7.7	8.1	10.8	11.4	1.2	18.2	65.9	-49.1	21.1	-47.2	403.8
Other Capital, net	3.2	-1.4	-7.8	7.4	30.0	15.9	-8.1	83.0	123.4	230.1	203.6
Change in Reserves	-5.6	-0.7	-7.3	-21.0	-30.3	-29.6	-40.7	-109.6	-176.9	-159.7	-150.9
Memo Item:											
Conversion Factor (Annual Avg)	126.000	126.000	126.000	126.000	*(Paraguayan Guaranies per US dollar)* 126.000	126.000	126.000	126.000	126.000	126.000	126.000
					(Millions of US dollars), outstanding at end of year						
EXTERNAL DEBT (Total)	112.4	123.5	137.0	150.9	187.6	228.3	281.9	452.4	615.1	806.8	954.3
Long-Term Debt (by debtor)	112.4	123.5	137.0	150.9	187.6	228.3	281.9	398.4	531.1	661.8	780.3
Central Bank, incl. IMF credit	16.3	18.7	27.6	26.9	31.5	36.4	39.7	43.1	48.3	50.5	50.5
Central Government	57.9	64.8	69.0	74.2	77.7	96.5	127.7	151.2	191.3	267.4	346.4
Rest of General Government	0.4	0.2	0.0	0.2	0.5	1.0	2.0	2.9	2.9	2.9	3.2
Non-financial Public Enterprises	35.5	38.0	39.0	43.7	50.2	51.6	62.3	133.3	197.8	200.8	228.2
Priv. Sector, incl non-guaranteed	2.3	1.8	1.4	5.9	27.7	42.8	50.2	67.9	90.8	140.2	152.0
Short-Term Debt	0.0	0.0	0.0	0.0	0.0	0.0	0.0	54.0	84.0	145.0	174.0
Memo Items:					*(Millions of US dollars)*						
Int'l Reserves Excluding Gold	17.5	21.0	31.4	57.0	87.1	115.0	157.5	267.8	448.7	609.1	761.9
Gold Holdings (at market price)	0.1	0.1	0.2	0.3	0.4	0.3	0.3	1.0	2.4	18.0	20.9
SOCIAL INDICATORS											
Total Fertility Rate	6.0	5.8	5.7	5.5	5.4	5.3	5.2	5.1	5.0	5.0	5.0
Infant Mortality Rate	58.6	55.8	53.0	51.3	49.5	47.8	46.0	44.3	43.1	41.9	40.7
Life Expectancy at Birth	65.3	65.5	65.6	65.7	65.8	65.8	65.9	66.0	66.1	66.2	66.3
Urban Population, % of total	37.1	37.5	37.9	38.2	38.6	39.0	39.5	40.1	40.6	41.2	41.7
Food Prod. per capita (1987=100)	87.8	87.6	85.6	82.9	84.2	79.8	82.8	90.8	86.4	92.7	92.1
Labor Force, Agriculture (%)	52.6	52.1	51.7	51.3	50.9	50.6	50.1	49.7	49.3	48.9	48.6
Labor Force, Female (%)	21.3	21.2	21.2	21.1	21.1	21.0	21.0	20.9	20.9	20.8	20.8
Primary Schl. Enroll. Ratio	109.0	..	..	..	..	102.0	103.0	102.0	102.0	102.0	104.0
Primary Schl. Enroll. Ratio, Female	103.0	..	..	..	..	97.0	99.0	98.0	98.0	98.0	101.0
Secondary Schl. Enroll. Ratio	17.0	..	..	..	..	20.0	23.0	23.0	24.0	26.0	26.0

1981	1982	1983	1984	1985	1986	1987	1988	1989	1990 estimate	Notes	PARAGUAY
											FOREIGN TRADE (CUSTOMS BASIS)
				(Millions of current US dollars)							
295.5	329.8	258.2	334.5	303.9	232.5	353.4	509.8	1,009.4	958.7	..	Value of Exports, fob
262.7	..	..	..	..	..	317.1	..	..	..	..	Nonfuel Primary Products
0.0	..	..	..	..	..	0.0	..	..	..	..	Fuels
32.8	30.8	18.1	19.0	16.7	21.1	36.3	40.0	83.0	95.2	..	Manufactures
599.7	672.0	545.9	585.8	501.5	578.1	595.3	573.9	775.8	1,112.9	..	Value of Imports, cif
83.9	76.2	58.9	49.1	56.2	63.4	62.0	75.9	102.6	147.2	..	Nonfuel Primary Products
127.0	184.9	148.5	172.4	141.7	124.0	143.0	132.4	178.9	256.7	..	Fuels
388.7	410.9	338.5	364.2	303.6	390.6	390.3	365.6	494.3	709.1	..	Manufactures
				(Index 1987 = 100)							
120.8	114.1	126.6	122.6	108.3	98.7	100.0	134.5	119.8	109.6	..	Terms of Trade
119.1	107.3	117.8	116.8	96.0	89.8	100.0	118.8	141.3	141.7	..	Export Prices, fob
98.6	94.0	93.0	95.2	88.7	91.0	100.0	88.4	118.0	129.3	..	Import Prices, cif
				(Millions of current US dollars)							**BALANCE OF PAYMENTS**
772.2	792.4	871.4	873.7	749.3	875.0	879.7	1,213.5	1,622.3	1,898.4	..	Exports of Goods & Services
561.0	492.0	554.8	560.4	484.6	586.3	603.3	871.0	1,166.5	1,392.3	..	Merchandise, fob
104.9	177.5	187.4	195.8	186.7	204.5	203.5	288.6	372.1	412.2	..	Nonfactor Services
106.3	122.9	129.2	117.5	78.0	84.2	72.9	53.9	83.7	93.9	..	Factor Services
1,429.1	1,300.1	715.9	967.6	931.6	1,224.3	1,337.1	1,451.1	1,428.5	1,829.0	..	Imports of Goods & Services
1,070.0	847.9	539.0	700.0	659.0	880.0	935.0	1,030.1	1,001.3	1,353.6	..	Merchandise, fob
268.9	360.9	128.5	207.3	181.1	228.6	266.6	290.7	296.3	385.4	..	Nonfactor Services
90.2	91.3	48.4	60.3	91.4	115.8	135.5	130.3	130.9	90.0	..	Factor Services
36.3	45.2	47.2	59.8	79.0	90.3	93.7	113.0	64.8	75.2	..	Long-Term Interest
2.5	1.5	6.2	9.3	7.5	11.1	27.0	35.2	23.9	32.9	..	Private Current Transfers, net
1.7	0.8	0.2	0.4	0.1	..	..	..	..	..	..	Workers' Remittances
-654.4	-506.2	161.7	-84.6	-174.8	-338.2	-430.4	-202.4	217.7	102.3	..	Curr. A/C Bal before Off. Transf.
3.3	3.5	0.0	0.0	0.0	0.0	0.0	0.0	0.0	..	..	Net Official Transfers
-651.1	-502.7	161.7	-84.6	-174.8	-338.2	-430.4	-202.4	217.7	102.3	..	Curr. A/C Bal after Off. Transf.
602.5	623.2	233.9	164.6	165.6	112.9	100.6	-39.0	179.0	-380.8	..	Long-Term Capital, net
26.2	33.7	5.1	0.9	0.7	0.6	5.3	0.0	0.0	73.1	..	Direct Investment
107.9	243.7	228.8	163.7	164.9	130.3	94.3	-41.5	126.1	-40.6	..	Long-Term Loans
201.3	304.4	282.4	239.6	243.3	262.2	225.1	141.8	203.3	80.2	..	Disbursements
93.4	60.7	53.6	75.9	78.4	131.9	130.8	183.3	77.2	120.8	..	Repayments
468.4	345.8	0.0	0.0	0.0	-18.0	1.0	2.5	52.9	-413.3	..	Other Long-Term Capital
80.6	-250.7	-432.4	-177.3	-65.6	146.7	389.9	114.8	-259.7	511.1	..	Other Capital, net
-32.0	130.2	36.8	97.3	74.8	78.6	-60.1	126.6	-137.0	-232.6	..	Change in Reserves
				(Paraguayan Guaranies per US dollar)							**Memo Item:**
126.000	136.000	146.000	243.700	440.700	517.400	668.000	840.000	1,120.000	1,230.000	..	Conversion Factor (Annual Avg)
				(Millions of US dollars), outstanding at end of year							
1,148.2	1,295.8	1,413.6	1,469.6	1,815.9	2,086.0	2,519.5	2,351.9	2,385.3	2,131.1	..	**EXTERNAL DEBT (Total)**
840.2	1,069.8	1,272.6	1,357.7	1,637.7	1,911.9	2,252.3	2,121.3	2,124.2	1,755.3	..	Long-Term Debt (by debtor)
52.1	56.4	54.7	46.0	46.2	43.8	54.0	49.8	45.0	43.7	..	Central Bank, incl. IMF credit
377.1	471.8	525.8	609.7	861.5	1,061.9	1,410.1	1,319.7	1,389.0	950.7	..	Central Government
2.2	2.2	3.2	3.5	3.8	4.1	5.5	4.8	4.1	4.4	..	Rest of General Government
275.2	402.1	488.2	511.5	544.2	636.7	742.8	706.6	642.9	720.9	..	Non-financial Public Enterprises
133.6	137.3	200.7	187.0	182.0	165.4	39.9	40.4	43.2	35.6	..	Priv. Sector, incl non-guaranteed
308.0	226.0	141.0	111.9	178.2	174.1	267.2	230.6	261.1	375.8	..	Short-Term Debt
				(Millions of US dollars)							**Memo Items:**
805.7	739.0	680.2	666.3	533.6	446.7	497.0	323.7	432.6	686.4	..	Int'l Reserves Excluding Gold
14.1	16.2	13.5	10.9	11.6	13.8	17.1	14.3	14.0	13.5	..	Gold Holdings (at market price)
											SOCIAL INDICATORS
4.9	4.9	4.9	4.9	4.8	4.8	4.8	4.7	4.7	4.6	..	Total Fertility Rate
39.5	38.3	37.3	36.4	35.4	34.5	33.5	32.8	32.2	31.5	..	Infant Mortality Rate
66.4	66.4	66.5	66.6	66.7	66.8	66.8	67.0	67.1	67.3	..	Life Expectancy at Birth
42.2	42.8	43.3	43.9	44.4	45.0	45.6	46.3	46.9	47.5	..	Urban Population, % of total
99.7	97.1	98.4	102.4	107.2	90.8	100.0	111.1	113.0	104.8	..	Food Prod. per capita (1987=100)
..	..	..	..	..	..	..	..	..	..	..	Labor Force, Agriculture (%)
20.8	20.8	20.8	20.8	20.8	20.8	20.8	20.7	20.7	20.7	..	Labor Force, Female (%)
..	103.0	103.0	103.0	103.0	102.0	103.0	104.0	106.0	..	..	Primary Schl. Enroll. Ratio
..	99.0	100.0	100.0	100.0	99.0	101.0	102.0	104.0	..	..	Primary Schl. Enroll. Ratio, Female
..	30.0	30.0	31.0	30.0	30.0	29.0	29.0	29.0	..	..	Secondary Schl. Enroll. Ratio

PERU	1970	1971	1972	1973	1974	1975	1976	1977	1978	1979	1980
CURRENT GNP PER CAPITA (US $)	520	580	620	700	850	1,000	1,040	970	840	850	990
POPULATION (thousands)	13,193	13,568	13,952	14,347	14,750	15,161	15,580	16,008	16,440	16,871	17,295

USE AND ORIGIN OF RESOURCES *(Millions of current Peruvian Intis)*

	1970	1971	1972	1973	1974	1975	1976	1977	1978	1979	1980
Gross National Product (GNP)	2.75E-4	3.09E-4	3.42E-4	4.08E-4	5.16E-4	6.57E-4	8.55E-4	1.09E-3	1.81E-3	3.28E-3	5.69E-3
Net Factor Income from Abroad	-4.51E-6	-3.74E-6	-4.17E-6	-6.27E-6	-6.23E-6	-8.69E-6	-2.01E-5	-1.07E-4	-8.77E-5	-2.11E-4	-2.78E-4
GDP at Market Prices	2.80E-4	3.12E-4	3.46E-4	4.14E-4	5.22E-4	6.65E-4	8.76E-4	1.19E-3	1.90E-3	3.49E-3	5.97E-3
Resource Balance	5.26E-6	-2.98E-6	-2.27E-6	-8.59E-6	-3.89E-6	-7.38E-5	-7.16E-5	-8.14E-5	1.28E-5	3.02E-4	2.70E-6
Exports of Goods & NFServices	5.01E-5	4.44E-5	4.89E-5	5.67E-5	7.57E-5	7.22E-5	1.05E-4	1.90E-4	3.94E-4	9.68E-4	1.33E-3
Imports of Goods & NFServices	4.48E-5	4.74E-5	5.12E-5	6.53E-5	1.15E-4	1.46E-4	1.77E-4	2.71E-4	3.81E-4	6.66E-4	1.33E-3
Domestic Absorption	2.75E-4	3.15E-4	3.48E-4	4.23E-4	5.61E-4	7.39E-4	9.47E-4	1.27E-3	1.89E-3	3.19E-3	5.97E-3
Private Consumption, etc.	1.97E-4	2.21E-4	2.50E-4	2.85E-4	3.66E-4	4.93E-4	6.48E-4	8.77E-4	1.31E-3	2.13E-3	3.66E-3
General Gov't Consumption	3.42E-5	3.88E-5	4.55E-5	5.35E-5	6.00E-5	8.22E-5	1.07E-4	1.68E-4	2.12E-4	3.01E-4	6.67E-4
Gross Domestic Investment	4.34E-5	5.59E-5	5.27E-5	8.42E-5	1.35E-4	1.64E-4	1.92E-4	2.29E-4	3.68E-4	7.57E-4	1.64E-3
Fixed Investment	4.13E-5	4.83E-5	5.36E-5	8.22E-5	1.21E-4	1.47E-4	1.81E-4	2.47E-4	3.77E-4	7.24E-4	1.40E-3
Indirect Taxes, net	2.26E-5	2.47E-5	2.79E-5	3.04E-5	2.98E-5	4.57E-5	5.46E-5	-9.94E-5	1.65E-4	4.90E-4	9.68E-4
GDP at factor cost	2.57E-4	2.88E-4	3.18E-4	3.84E-4	4.92E-4	6.20E-4	8.21E-4	2.19E-3	1.74E-3	3.00E-3	5.00E-3
Agriculture	5.23E-5	5.56E-5	5.81E-5	6.83E-5	8.31E-5	1.09E-4	1.34E-4	1.87E-4	2.49E-4	4.08E-4	6.10E-4
Industry	8.84E-5	9.92E-5	1.11E-4	1.39E-4	1.81E-4	2.11E-4	2.99E-4	4.13E-4	7.28E-4	1.49E-3	2.50E-3
Manufacturing	5.54E-5	6.44E-5	7.03E-5	8.55E-5	1.13E-4	1.33E-4	1.90E-4	2.49E-4	4.33E-4	8.20E-4	1.21E-3
Services, etc.	1.39E-4	1.58E-4	1.77E-4	2.07E-4	2.58E-4	3.45E-4	4.42E-4	5.93E-4	9.24E-4	1.59E-3	2.85E-3
Gross Domestic Saving	4.87E-5	5.29E-5	5.04E-5	7.56E-5	9.61E-5	9.03E-5	1.20E-4	1.48E-4	3.81E-4	1.06E-3	1.64E-3
Gross National Saving	4.52E-5	4.94E-5	4.65E-5	6.95E-5	9.07E-5	8.23E-5	1.01E-4	4.05E-5	2.94E-4	8.48E-4	1.37E-3

(Millions of 1987 Peruvian Intis)

	1970	1971	1972	1973	1974	1975	1976	1977	1978	1979	1980
Gross National Product	4.20E-1	4.39E-1	4.51E-1	4.73E-1	5.18E-1	5.36E-1	5.41E-1	5.39E-1	5.31E-1	5.53E-1	5.87E-1
GDP at Market Prices	4.42E-1	4.61E-1	4.73E-1	4.98E-1	5.44E-1	5.63E-1	5.74E-1	5.76E-1	5.77E-1	6.11E-1	6.38E-1
Resource Balance	-1.16E-2	-1.64E-2	-1.10E-2	-3.13E-2	-5.08E-2	-4.66E-2	-3.21E-2	-2.52E-2	4.43E-3	6.54E-3	-2.54E-2
Exports of Goods & NFServices	5.79E-2	5.62E-2	6.15E-2	5.01E-2	5.27E-2	5.39E-2	5.57E-2	6.30E-2	7.11E-2	8.61E-2	7.82E-2
Imports of Goods & NFServices	6.95E-2	7.27E-2	7.25E-2	8.14E-2	1.03E-1	1.01E-1	8.79E-2	8.82E-2	6.67E-2	7.95E-2	1.04E-1
Domestic Absorption	4.54E-1	4.78E-1	4.84E-1	5.29E-1	5.95E-1	6.10E-1	6.06E-1	6.01E-1	5.73E-1	6.04E-1	6.64E-1
Private Consumption, etc.	3.25E-1	3.32E-1	3.46E-1	3.43E-1	3.58E-1	3.74E-1	3.88E-1	3.93E-1	3.83E-1	4.01E-1	3.97E-1
General Gov't Consumption	5.17E-2	5.53E-2	5.89E-2	6.25E-2	6.62E-2	7.36E-2	7.71E-2	8.82E-2	7.70E-2	6.97E-2	8.53E-2
Gross Domestic Investment	7.75E-2	9.02E-2	7.95E-2	1.24E-1	1.71E-1	1.62E-1	1.41E-1	1.20E-1	1.13E-1	1.33E-1	1.81E-1
Fixed Investment	8.38E-2	9.46E-2	9.82E-2	1.34E-1	1.70E-1	1.76E-1	1.52E-1	1.39E-1	1.27E-1	1.39E-1	1.70E-1
GDP at factor cost	4.05E-1	4.22E-1	4.33E-1	4.33E-1	4.90E-1	5.30E-1	5.43E-1	5.66E-1	5.16E-1	5.16E-1	5.61E-1
Agriculture	6.24E-2	6.12E-2	5.75E-2	5.70E-2	5.98E-2	5.95E-2	6.08E-2	6.04E-2	6.01E-2	6.27E-2	5.87E-2
Industry	1.48E-1	1.53E-1	1.59E-1	1.70E-1	1.86E-1	1.88E-1	1.95E-1	1.97E-1	2.03E-1	2.20E-1	2.32E-1
Manufacturing	1.06E-1	1.13E-1	1.15E-1	1.22E-1	1.33E-1	1.37E-1	1.42E-1	1.39E-1	1.34E-1	1.39E-1	1.47E-1
Services, etc.	2.32E-1	2.47E-1	2.56E-1	2.71E-1	2.98E-1	3.16E-1	3.19E-1	3.19E-1	3.14E-1	3.28E-1	3.48E-1

Memo Items:

	1970	1971	1972	1973	1974	1975	1976	1977	1978	1979	1980
Capacity to Import	7.77E-2	6.81E-2	6.92E-2	7.07E-2	6.84E-2	4.97E-2	5.23E-2	6.17E-2	6.89E-2	1.16E-1	1.04E-1
Terms of Trade Adjustment	1.98E-2	1.19E-2	7.79E-3	2.06E-2	1.57E-2	-4.18E-3	-3.41E-3	-1.27E-3	-2.18E-3	2.95E-2	2.56E-2
Gross Domestic Income	4.62E-1	4.73E-1	4.81E-1	5.19E-1	5.60E-1	5.59E-1	5.71E-1	5.75E-1	5.75E-1	6.40E-1	6.64E-1
Gross National Income	4.39E-1	4.51E-1	4.59E-1	4.93E-1	5.34E-1	5.32E-1	5.37E-1	5.38E-1	5.29E-1	5.82E-1	6.12E-1

DOMESTIC PRICES/DEFLATORS *(Index 1987 = 100)*

	1970	1971	1972	1973	1974	1975	1976	1977	1978	1979	1980
Overall (GDP)	6.33E-2	6.77E-2	7.31E-2	8.32E-2	9.60E-2	1.18E-1	1.53E-1	2.07E-1	3.29E-1	5.71E-1	9.35E-1
Domestic Absorption	6.05E-2	6.60E-2	7.19E-2	7.99E-2	9.43E-2	1.21E-1	1.56E-1	2.12E-1	3.30E-1	5.28E-1	8.99E-1
Agriculture	8.38E-2	9.08E-2	1.01E-1	1.20E-1	1.39E-1	1.83E-1	2.21E-1	3.09E-1	4.15E-1	6.50E-1	1.00E+0
Industry	5.99E-2	6.49E-2	6.97E-2	8.17E-2	9.72E-2	1.12E-1	1.54E-1	2.10E-1	3.58E-1	6.80E-1	1.10E+0
Manufacturing	5.20E-2	5.72E-2	6.12E-2	6.99E-2	8.53E-2	9.74E-2	1.34E-1	1.78E-1	3.24E-1	5.89E-1	8.19E-1
Consumer Price Index	..	..	..	..	..	..	..	..	..	..	..

MANUFACTURING ACTIVITY

	1970	1971	1972	1973	1974	1975	1976	1977	1978	1979	1980
Employment (1987=100)	64.4	51.2	69.4	69.8	..	..	..	..	..	87.2	90.0
Real Earnings per Empl. (1987=100)	..	..	126.4	124.8	..	..	..	..	..	101.2	105.6
Real Output per Empl. (1987=100)	117.1	149.1	118.9	126.1	..	..	..	..	..	121.8	142.4
Earnings as % of Value Added	..	..	20.5	18.4	..	..	..	..	..	14.8	15.5

MONETARY HOLDINGS *(Millions of current Peruvian Intis)*

	1970	1971	1972	1973	1974	1975	1976	1977	1978	1979	1980
Money Supply, Broadly Defined	5.74E-5	6.21E-5	7.70E-5	9.48E-5	1.27E-4	1.47E-4	1.82E-4	2.25E-4	3.62E-4	6.95E-4	1.28E-3
Money	4.33E-5	4.66E-5	6.03E-5	7.57E-5	1.05E-4	1.23E-4	1.55E-4	1.85E-4	2.70E-4	4.61E-4	7.30E-4
Currency Outside Banks	1.63E-5	1.89E-5	2.19E-5	2.72E-5	3.35E-5	4.26E-5	4.95E-5	6.08E-5	9.10E-5	1.62E-4	2.73E-4
Demand Deposits	2.70E-5	2.77E-5	3.84E-5	4.85E-5	7.20E-5	8.07E-5	1.05E-4	1.24E-4	1.79E-4	2.99E-4	4.56E-4
Quasi-Money	1.41E-5	1.55E-5	1.67E-5	1.91E-5	2.12E-5	2.34E-5	2.69E-5	3.98E-5	9.17E-5	2.35E-4	5.46E-4

GOVERNMENT DEFICIT (-) OR SURPLUS *(Millions of current Peruvian Intis)*

	1970	1971	1972	1973	1974	1975	1976	1977	1978	1979	1980
GOVERNMENT DEFICIT (-) OR SURPLUS	-1.00E-6	-6.00E-6	-3.00E-6	-1.20E-5	-1.00E-5	-1.80E-5	-3.20E-5	-3.40E-5	-8.50E-5	-1.90E-5	-1.42E-4
Current Revenue	3.90E-5	3.90E-5	5.20E-5	5.20E-5	6.70E-5	8.90E-5	1.14E-4	1.63E-4	2.63E-4	5.51E-4	1.02E-3
Current Expenditure	3.60E-5	3.50E-5	4.00E-5	5.00E-5	5.70E-5	8.10E-5	1.11E-4	1.46E-4	2.91E-4	4.42E-4	8.98E-4
Current Budget Balance	3.00E-6	4.00E-6	1.20E-5	2.00E-6	1.00E-5	8.00E-6	3.00E-6	1.70E-5	-2.80E-5	1.09E-4	1.21E-4
Capital Receipts	..	..	..	..	..	..	..	..	..	..	..
Capital Payments	4.00E-6	9.00E-6	1.50E-5	1.40E-5	2.00E-5	2.60E-5	3.50E-5	5.10E-5	5.70E-5	1.28E-4	2.63E-4

1981	1982	1983	1984	1985	1986	1987	1988	1989	1990 estimate	Notes	PERU
1,240	1,380	1,150	1,120	980	1,090	1,190	1,070	1,050	1,160	A	CURRENT GNP PER CAPITA (US $)
17,714	18,127	18,538	18,955	19,383	19,820	20,267	20,723	21,189	21,663	..	POPULATION (thousands)
											USE AND ORIGIN OF RESOURCES
				(Millions of current Peruvian Intis)							
1.02E-2	1.73E-2	3.10E-2	0.069	0.184	0.357	0.707	4.750	112.00	7,500.00	..	Gross National Product (GNP)
-4.14E-4	-6.37E-4	-1.45E-3	-0.003	-0.014	-0.017	-0.032	-0.195	-2.87	-124.00	..	Net Factor Income from Abroad
1.07E-2	1.79E-2	3.24E-2	0.072	0.198	0.374	0.739	4.940	115.00	7,700.00	..	GDP at Market Prices
-6.42E-4	-1.02E-3	-3.44E-4	0.003	0.009	-0.008	-0.021	-0.039	1.25	24.80	..	Resource Balance
1.74E-3	2.81E-3	5.88E-3	0.014	0.040	0.045	0.069	0.564	14.40	839.00	..	Exports of Goods & NFServices
2.38E-3	3.83E-3	6.22E-3	0.011	0.030	0.054	0.089	0.603	13.10	814.00	..	Imports of Goods & NFServices
1.13E-2	1.89E-2	3.28E-2	0.070	0.189	0.382	0.760	4.980	114.00	7,600.00	..	Domestic Absorption
6.74E-3	1.11E-2	2.11E-2	0.046	0.123	0.255	0.498	3.210	79.20	5,400.00	..	Private Consumption, etc.
1.22E-3	2.26E-3	4.08E-3	0.008	0.023	0.043	0.094	0.475	11.10	459.00	..	General Gov't Consumption
3.35E-3	5.60E-3	7.62E-3	0.016	0.043	0.084	0.169	1.290	23.80	1,800.00	..	Gross Domestic Investment
2.77E-3	4.94E-3	7.44E-3	0.016	0.042	0.083	0.157	1.220	23.70	1,400.00	..	Fixed Investment
6.58E-4	1.91E-3	2.45E-3	0.005	0.020	0.031	0.050	0.249	4.73	240.00	..	Indirect Taxes, net
1.00E-2	1.60E-2	3.00E-2	0.067	0.178	0.343	0.689	4.690	111.00	7,400.00	B	GDP at factor cost
1.10E-3	1.71E-3	3.43E-3	0.008	0.019	0.042	0.076	0.409	9.28	508.00	..	Agriculture
4.06E-3	6.93E-3	1.20E-2	0.028	0.084	0.134	0.253	2.050	43.00	2,800.00	f	Industry
1.96E-3	3.28E-3	5.95E-3	0.014	0.048	0.091	0.173	1.470	31.10	2,000.00	..	Manufacturing
5.50E-3	9.27E-3	1.70E-2	0.037	0.095	0.198	0.410	2.480	63.00	4,400.00	f	Services, etc.
2.70E-3	4.58E-3	7.27E-3	0.019	0.052	0.076	0.148	1.250	25.00	1,800.00	..	Gross Domestic Saving
2.29E-3	3.94E-3	5.82E-3	0.015	0.038	0.059	0.116	1.060	22.20	1,700.00	..	Gross National Saving
				(Millions of 1987 Peruvian Intis)							
6.18E-1	6.20E-1	5.34E-1	0.554	0.567	0.645	0.707	0.634	0.58	0.56	..	Gross National Product
6.67E-1	6.68E-1	5.84E-1	0.611	0.625	0.683	0.739	0.678	0.60	0.57	..	GDP at Market Prices
-4.42E-2	-4.22E-2	-1.42E-2	0.008	0.018	-0.004	-0.021	-0.018	0.01	0.00	..	Resource Balance
7.59E-2	8.05E-2	7.22E-2	0.079	0.082	0.082	0.074	0.069	0.064	0.08	0.07	..	Exports of Goods & NFServices
1.20E-1	1.23E-1	8.64E-2	0.071	0.065	0.078	0.089	0.081	0.06	0.07	..	Imports of Goods & NFServices
7.11E-1	7.10E-1	5.99E-1	0.603	0.607	0.686	0.760	0.695	0.59	0.57	..	Domestic Absorption
4.09E-1	4.13E-1	3.88E-1	0.409	0.422	0.466	0.498	0.463	0.42	0.40	..	Private Consumption, etc.
8.39E-2	9.51E-2	8.68E-2	0.083	0.086	0.089	0.094	0.079	0.07	0.06	..	General Gov't Consumption
2.18E-1	2.02E-1	1.24E-1	0.112	0.099	0.132	0.169	0.153	0.10	0.11	..	Gross Domestic Investment
1.97E-1	1.93E-1	1.35E-1	0.126	0.112	0.133	0.157	0.135	0.11	0.11	..	Fixed Investment
5.94E-1	5.94E-1	5.30E-1	0.552	0.551	0.622	0.689	0.644	0.57	0.55	B f	GDP at factor cost
6.40E-2	6.59E-2	5.88E-2	0.066	0.068	0.072	0.076	0.082	0.08	0.07	..	Agriculture
2.34E-1	2.35E-1	1.97E-1	0.206	0.211	0.232	0.253	0.225	0.20	0.19	..	Industry
1.48E-1	1.47E-1	1.20E-1	0.127	0.132	0.153	0.173	0.153	0.13	0.12	..	Manufacturing
3.69E-1	3.67E-1	3.29E-1	0.339	0.345	0.378	0.410	0.371	0.33	0.31	..	Services, etc.
											Memo Items:
8.76E-2	8.99E-2	8.16E-2	0.088	0.084	0.066	0.069	0.076	0.07	0.07	..	Capacity to Import
1.18E-2	9.40E-3	9.38E-3	0.009	0.002	-0.008	0.000	0.012	-0.01	0.00	..	Terms of Trade Adjustment
6.79E-1	6.77E-1	5.94E-1	0.621	0.627	0.675	0.739	0.690	0.59	0.57	..	Gross Domestic Income
6.30E-1	6.29E-1	5.43E-1	0.564	0.569	0.637	0.707	0.646	0.57	0.56	..	Gross National Income
											DOMESTIC PRICES/DEFLATORS
				(Index 1987 = 100)							
1.60E+0	2.70E+0	5.60E+0	11.8	31.7	54.8	100.0	729.4	19,261.5	1.35E+6	..	Overall (GDP)
1.60E+0	2.70E+0	5.50E+0	11.6	31.1	55.7	100.0	716.4	19,439.1	1.34E+6	..	Domestic Absorption
1.70E+0	2.60E+0	5.80E+0	12.1	27.3	57.9	100.0	498.7	11,883.6	7.12E+5	..	Agriculture
1.70E+0	2.90E+0	6.10E+0	13.4	39.8	57.9	100.0	913.2	22,111.3	1.50E+6	..	Industry
1.30E+0	2.20E+0	5.00E+0	11.4	36.3	59.2	100.0	961.4	24,418.1	1.70E+6	..	Manufacturing
..	..	..	..	..	..	..	..	..	..		Consumer Price Index
											MANUFACTURING ACTIVITY
78.8	92.4	87.0	85.8	86.8	91.9	100.0	..	..	..	G	Employment (1987=100)
115.4	108.7	87.9	84.0	78.9	91.2	100.0	..	..	..	G	Real Earnings per Empl. (1987=100)
129.1	107.4	97.4	100.5	93.5	90.1	100.0	..	..	..	G	Real Output per Empl. (1987=100)
21.1	21.6	18.9	16.6	12.6	18.2	18.2	..	..	..	..	Earnings as % of Value Added
											MONETARY HOLDINGS
				(Millions of current Peruvian Intis)							
2.15E-3	3.70E-3	7.52E-3	1.71E-2	4.39E-2	6.75E-2	1.39E-1	1.00E+0	2.00E+1	..	..	Money Supply, Broadly Defined
1.07E-3	1.51E-3	2.97E-3	6.06E-3	2.31E-2	4.34E-2	9.64E-2	5.93E-1	1.00E+1	..	..	Money
4.37E-4	6.21E-4	1.12E-3	2.50E-3	8.14E-3	1.64E-2	4.19E-2	2.61E-1	5.00E+0	..	..	Currency Outside Banks
6.38E-4	8.88E-4	1.85E-3	3.56E-3	1.50E-2	2.70E-2	5.44E-2	3.31E-1	5.00E+0	..	..	Demand Deposits
1.08E-3	2.19E-3	4.56E-3	1.10E-2	2.08E-2	2.41E-2	4.31E-2	4.13E-1	1.00E+1	..	..	Quasi-Money
											GOVERNMENT DEFICIT (-) OR SURPLUS
				(Millions of current Peruvian Intis)							
-4.20E-4	-5.57E-4	-2.34E-3	-3.02E-3	-4.07E-3	-1.34E-2	-4.20E-2	-1.23E-1	-5	-37	..	
1.52E-3	2.48E-3	3.74E-3	9.55E-3	2.80E-2	4.52E-2	6.60E-2	4.03E-1	7	38	..	Current Revenue
1.50E-3	2.46E-3	5.06E-3	1.03E-2	2.73E-2	4.78E-2	9.20E-2	4.57E-1	10	57	..	Current Expenditure
1.90E-5	2.90E-3	-1.33E-2	-7.52E-4	7.08E-4	-2.56E-3	-2.60E-2	-5.40E-2	-3	-19	..	Current Budget Balance
	9.00E-6	3.00E-6	9.20E-5	2.72E-4	1.40E-4	..	..	..	..	..	Capital Receipts
4.39E-4	5.95E-4	1.02E-3	2.36E-3	5.05E-3	1.10E-2	1.70E-2	6.90E-2	2	18	..	Capital Payments

PERU	1970	1971	1972	1973	1974	1975	1976	1977	1978	1979	1980
FOREIGN TRADE (CUSTOMS BASIS)					*(Millions of current US dollars)*						
Value of Exports, fob	1,044.4	892.9	944.4	1,049.5	1,517.4	1,314.6	1,296.1	1,647.4	1,805.3	3,379.6	3,265.5
Nonfuel Primary Products	1,021.0	875.3	919.9	1,006.4	1,446.0	1,254.2	1,206.0	1,481.2	1,447.1	2,358.0	2,039.4
Fuels	7.5	5.6	8.0	12.9	18.2	22.2	31.1	53.4	177.7	521.5	672.9
Manufactures	15.9	12.0	16.5	30.3	53.2	38.2	58.9	112.8	180.4	500.2	553.3
Value of Imports, cif	621.7	749.6	796.3	1,024.2	1,595.3	2,379.6	1,798.0	1,598.3	1,356.3	1,475.5	2,573.3
Nonfuel Primary Products	158.0	177.7	187.3	187.1	311.0	474.0	307.1	294.5	297.7	374.5	637.7
Fuels	14.3	30.3	49.1	61.7	204.7	288.1	299.4	319.3	77.3	47.2	63.0
Manufactures	449.5	541.6	559.9	775.4	1,079.6	1,617.4	1,191.5	984.6	981.3	1,053.8	1,872.7
					(Index 1987 = 100)						
Terms of Trade	179.7	164.2	185.9	238.0	194.9	128.5	162.8	168.4	126.7	133.8	137.6
Export Prices, fob	49.3	44.5	51.0	84.6	101.3	70.2	87.2	94.9	89.0	110.9	127.5
Import Prices, cif	27.4	27.1	27.5	35.6	52.0	54.6	53.6	56.4	70.3	82.9	92.6
BALANCE OF PAYMENTS					*(Millions of current US dollars)*						
Exports of Goods & Services	1,239	1,086	1,166	1,369	1,880	1,723	1,755	2,144	2,416	4,143	4,832
Merchandise, fob	1,034	890	945	1,112	1,506	1,291	1,360	1,726	1,941	3,491	3,916
Nonfactor Services	190	178	209	231	336	398	385	406	459	594	715
Factor Services	15	19	13	25	39	34	10	13	16	58	202
Imports of Goods & Services	1,119	1,159	1,237	1,673	2,653	3,313	3,007	3,123	2,664	3,536	5,080
Merchandise, fob	699	730	812	1,097	1,909	2,389	2,099	2,164	1,601	1,951	3,090
Nonfactor Services	272	285	291	387	534	648	526	523	470	560	880
Factor Services	148	144	134	188	211	276	381	436	594	1,025	1,111
Long-Term Interest	162	163	163	229	266	324	336	411	475	576	670
Private Current Transfers, net	26	4	7	4	22	17	4	3	3	0	0
Workers' Remittances	..	..	..	..	..	..	..	..	..	..	..
Curr. A/C Bal before Off. Transf.	146	-69	-64	-300	-752	-1,574	-1,249	-976	-245	607	-248
Net Official Transfers	56	35	33	38	27	33	55	54	53	122	147
Curr. A/C Bal after Off. Transf.	202	-34	-32	-262	-725	-1,541	-1,193	-922	-192	729	-101
Long-Term Capital, net	-17	9	106	408	720	1,293	807	955	264	541	277
Direct Investment	-70	-58	24	70	58	316	170	54	25	71	27
Long-Term Loans	54	71	96	350	1,119	1,233	1,015	603	186	444	365
Disbursements	387	424	466	888	1,669	1,754	1,538	1,318	900	1,172	1,478
Repayments	333	354	370	538	549	521	523	715	713	729	1,113
Other Long-Term Capital	-1	-3	-13	-13	-457	-256	-378	297	52	26	-115
Other Capital, net	61	-26	-79	-59	410	-270	-4	14	-56	-122	461
Change in Reserves	-246	51	4	-87	-405	517	390	-46	-16	-1,148	-637
Memo Item:					*(Peruvian Intis per US dollar)*						
Conversion Factor (Annual Avg)	3.87E-8	3.87E-8	3.87E-8	3.87E-8	3.87E-8	4.05E-8	5.64E-8	8.38E-8	1.56E-7	2.25E-7	2.89E-7
					(Millions of US dollars), outstanding at end of year						
EXTERNAL DEBT (Total)	2,665	2,745	2,874	3,229	4,349	5,077	6,287	9,171	9,717	9,269	10,038
Long-Term Debt (by debtor)	2,665	2,745	2,874	3,229	4,349	5,077	6,287	7,071	7,619	7,695	7,954
Central Bank, incl. IMF credit	38	34	63	238	709	836	1,282	1,563	1,766	1,997	1,783
Central Government	476	478	584	685	720	1,132	1,318	1,913	2,330	2,741	3,089
Rest of General Government	18	15	11	7	4	1	1	1	1	0	0
Non-financial Public Enterprises	317	364	418	518	780	1,044	1,241	1,450	1,683	1,760	1,799
Priv. Sector, incl non-guaranteed	1,817	1,854	1,798	1,780	2,136	2,063	2,444	2,143	1,839	1,196	1,283
Short-Term Debt	0	0	0	0	0	0	0	2,100	2,098	1,574	2,084
Memo Items:					*(Millions of US dollars)*						
Int'l Reserves Excluding Gold	296.28	380.88	442.52	526.07	925.22	425.49	289.35	356.78	389.71	1,520.69	1,979.85
Gold Holdings (at market price)	42.38	49.35	70.68	112.59	187.06	140.67	135.15	165.44	226.90	592.90	824.12
SOCIAL INDICATORS											
Total Fertility Rate	6.0	5.9	5.7	5.6	5.4	5.3	5.1	5.0	4.9	4.8	4.7
Infant Mortality Rate	116.4	113.2	110.0	107.4	104.8	102.2	99.6	97.0	95.0	93.0	91.0
Life Expectancy at Birth	53.9	54.7	55.6	55.8	56.1	56.4	56.7	57.0	57.3	57.6	57.9
Urban Population, % of total	57.4	58.2	59.0	59.8	60.6	61.4	62.0	62.6	63.3	63.9	64.5
Food Prod. per capita (1987=100)	128.3	127.0	120.8	118.1	119.0	114.5	113.0	110.4	104.6	101.8	93.3
Labor Force, Agriculture (%)	47.1	46.3	45.5	44.8	44.1	43.5	42.7	42.0	41.3	40.6	40.0
Labor Force, Female (%)	20.3	20.7	21.2	21.6	21.9	22.3	22.7	23.1	23.5	23.9	24.2
Primary Schl. Enroll. Ratio	107.0	..	..	..	..	113.0	112.0	112.0	113.0	112.0	114.0
Primary Schl. Enroll. Ratio, Female	99.0	..	..	..	..	..	107.0	108.0	109.0	108.0	111.0
Secondary Schl. Enroll. Ratio	31.0	..	..	..	..	46.0	47.0	50.0	55.0	56.0	59.0

1981	1982	1983	1984	1985	1986	1987	1988	1989	1990 estimate	Notes	PERU
				(Millions of current US dollars)							**FOREIGN TRADE (CUSTOMS BASIS)**
2,335.5	2,755.8	2,009.5	2,460.4	2,852.1	1,798.0	2,152.3	2,506.5	3,488.9	3,276.6	..	Value of Exports, fob
1,343.4	1,630.5	1,309.6	1,522.0	1,828.4	1,274.1	1,515.2	1,949.1	2,713.1	2,548.0	..	Nonfuel Primary Products
605.8	741.3	464.0	651.6	681.5	227.5	281.2	167.3	232.8	218.7	..	Fuels
386.3	383.9	235.9	286.8	342.2	296.4	355.9	390.1	543.0	509.9	..	Manufactures
3,159.5	2,940.2	2,234.3	1,881.4	1,767.4	2,365.8	3,002.7	3,109.2	2,565.9	3,229.5	..	Value of Imports, cif
717.9	604.6	631.2	543.6	430.5	680.9	729.2	1,343.0	1,108.3	1,394.9	..	Nonfuel Primary Products
40.8	49.1	73.9	63.5	44.4	68.1	127.2	134.7	111.1	139.9	..	Fuels
2,400.8	2,286.6	1,529.2	1,274.4	1,292.5	1,616.8	2,146.3	1,631.6	1,346.5	1,694.7	..	Manufactures
				(Index 1987 = 100)							
126.8	115.6	116.1	116.1	111.3	92.4	100.0	110.0	87.9	77.8	..	Terms of Trade
117.5	102.7	100.9	98.9	94.5	88.2	100.0	120.1	134.5	125.7	..	Export Prices, fob
92.7	88.8	86.9	85.1	84.8	95.5	100.0	109.2	153.0	161.6	..	Import Prices, cif
				(Millions of current US dollars)							**BALANCE OF PAYMENTS**
4,223	4,186	3,842	3,974	3,925	3,460	3,659	3,729	4,596	4,322		Exports of Goods & Services
3,249	3,293	3,015	3,147	2,978	2,531	2,661	2,691	3,533	3,276		Merchandise, fob
770	784	711	670	814	836	931	995	985	972		Nonfactor Services
204	109	116	157	133	93	67	43	78	74		Factor Services
6,112	5,962	4,933	4,353	3,923	4,687	5,320	4,977	4,427	5,243		Imports of Goods & Services
3,802	3,721	2,722	2,140	1,806	2,596	3,182	2,790	2,291	2,885		Merchandise, fob
1,087	1,098	965	891	984	1,179	1,353	1,371	1,429	1,594		Nonfactor Services
1,223	1,143	1,246	1,322	1,133	912	785	816	707	764		Factor Services
670	696	539	539	457	271	160	62	96	99		Long-Term Interest
0	0	0	0	0	0	0	0	0	..	..	Private Current Transfers, net
..	..		..			..					Workers' Remittances
-1,889	-1,776	-1,091	-379	3	-1,227	-1,661	-1,248	169	-921	..	Curr. A/C Bal before Off. Transf.
161	167	219	158	134	150	180	157	155	247	..	Net Official Transfers
-1,728	-1,609	-872	-221	137	-1,077	-1,481	-1,091	324	-674	..	Curr. A/C Bal after Off. Transf.
356	1,136	1,237	-119	-619	-1,187	-1,226	-1,271	-848	-911	..	Long-Term Capital, net
125	48	38	-89	1	22	32	26	59	34	..	Direct Investment
286	1,407	1,321	1,124	197	211	449	187	425	64	..	Long-Term Loans
1,817	2,563	1,897	1,595	712	606	625	263	548	248	..	Disbursements
1,531	1,156	576	471	514	395	175	76	122	184	..	Repayments
-55	-319	-122	-1,154	-817	-1,420	-1,707	-1,484	-1,332	-1,010	..	Other Long-Term Capital
683	390	-399	590	669	1,968	2,039	2,372	1,119	1,854	..	Other Capital, net
689	84	34	-250	-186	295	668	-10	-595	-268	..	Change in Reserves
				(Peruvian Intis per US dollar)							**Memo Item:**
4.22E-7	6.98E-7	1.63E-6	3.47E-6	1.17E-5	1.55E-5	2.70E-5	2.52E-4	4.02E-3	0.21	..	Conversion Factor (Annual Avg)
			(Millions of US dollars), outstanding at end of year								
10,319	12,305	12,061	13,099	14,279	16,154	18,645	18,998	19,920	21,105	..	**EXTERNAL DEBT (Total)**
7,840	9,281	10,526	11,349	12,383	13,399	15,010	14,730	15,017	15,652	..	Long-Term Debt (by debtor)
1,463	1,641	1,587	1,712	1,827	1,960	2,197	2,129	2,077	2,125	..	Central Bank, incl. IMF credit
3,248	4,245	5,389	6,082	6,883	7,496	8,378	8,237	8,437	8,862	..	Central Government
0	0	0	0	0	0	0	0	0	0	..	Rest of General Government
1,693	1,686	1,933	2,054	2,293	2,564	2,952	2,895	2,869	3,061	..	Non-financial Public Enterprises
1,436	1,710	1,618	1,501	1,380	1,380	1,484	1,468	1,633	1,604	..	Priv. Sector, incl non-guaranteed
2,479	3,024	1,536	1,750	1,896	2,754	3,634	4,269	4,904	5,453	..	Short-Term Debt
				(Millions of US dollars)							**Memo Items:**
1,199.50	1,349.65	1,365.71	1,630.52	1,842.00	1,407.20	645.80	511.00	808.40	1,039.80	..	Int'l Reserves Excluding Gold
555.71	638.75	533.34	431.00	638.96	835.35	724.70	702.35	788.77	850.85	..	Gold Holdings (at market price)
											SOCIAL INDICATORS
4.6	4.5	4.4	4.3	..	..	4.1	4.0	3.9	3.8	..	Total Fertility Rate
89.0	87.0	84.8	82.6	..	..	76.0	73.8	71.5	69.3	..	Infant Mortality Rate
58.3	58.6	59.2	59.7	60.3	60.8	61.4	61.8	62.3	62.7	..	Life Expectancy at Birth
65.1	65.7	66.2	66.8	67.4	68.0	68.5	69.1	69.6	70.2	..	Urban Population, % of total
101.9	103.9	97.2	102.7	96.8	95.0	100.0	105.4	98.8	91.3	..	Food Prod. per capita (1987=100)
..	..		..		..						Labor Force, Agriculture (%)
24.2	24.2	24.2	24.2	24.2	24.2	24.2	24.1	24.1	24.1	..	Labor Force, Female (%)
115.0	118.0	..	..	122.0	..	..	120.0	123.0	126.0	..	Primary Schl. Enroll. Ratio
112.0	115.0	..	..	120.0	..	..	..	..	..	..	Primary Schl. Enroll. Ratio, Female
61.0	61.0	..	..	63.0	..	..	66.0	67.0	70.0	..	Secondary Schl. Enroll. Ratio

PHILIPPINES	1970	1971	1972	1973	1974	1975	1976	1977	1978	1979	1980
CURRENT GNP PER CAPITA (US $)	230	210	200	230	280	340	390	430	480	560	650
POPULATION (thousands)	37,540	38,655	39,778	40,900	42,012	43,103	44,143	45,153	46,164	47,209	48,323
USE AND ORIGIN OF RESOURCES					*(Billions of current Philippine Pesos)*						
Gross National Product (GNP)	38.80	47.13	52.99	67.98	93.91	107.68	126.15	144.48	166.59	203.54	243.27
Net Factor Income from Abroad	-0.71	-0.52	-0.52	-0.15	0.37	-0.27	-1.06	-0.98	-0.66	0.64	-0.48
GDP at Market Prices	39.50	47.65	53.51	68.12	93.54	107.95	127.21	145.45	167.25	202.90	243.75
Resource Balance	0.21	0.02	0.11	3.32	-2.18	-6.58	-7.53	-4.46	-7.14	-10.30	-11.94
Exports of Goods & NF Services	8.52	9.75	10.53	16.87	23.41	22.69	24.59	30.63	34.57	43.75	57.46
Imports of Goods & NF Services	8.31	9.73	10.42	13.55	25.59	29.26	32.12	35.09	41.71	54.05	69.40
Domestic Absorption	39.30	47.63	53.40	64.80	95.73	114.53	134.75	149.92	174.39	213.20	255.69
Private Consumption, etc.	27.20	33.16	36.81	43.44	61.22	69.63	79.22	90.41	106.33	126.88	162.69
General Gov't Consumption	3.66	4.46	5.48	6.50	9.30	11.59	13.73	14.96	16.82	19.04	22.10
Gross Domestic Investment	8.43	10.01	11.11	14.86	25.21	33.31	41.80	44.55	51.24	67.28	70.90
Fixed Investment	7.14	8.65	9.45	11.64	18.59	26.60	33.50	36.62	42.20	55.90	66.35
Indirect Taxes, net	3.13	3.94	4.33	6.34	10.16	11.16	11.78	13.60	16.85	22.38	25.76
GDP at factor cost	36.37	43.71	49.18	61.79	83.38	96.79	115.43	131.86	150.40	180.52	217.99
Agriculture	11.66	14.44	15.76	20.82	29.05	32.75	37.23	41.77	47.19	55.68	61.22
Industry	12.50	15.31	17.80	23.08	32.12	37.37	45.38	52.86	60.91	74.99	94.54
Manufacturing	9.83	12.32	14.17	18.12	24.03	27.72	32.33	36.99	43.54	51.02	62.65
Services, etc.	15.34	17.90	19.95	24.23	32.38	37.83	44.60	50.83	59.16	72.23	87.99
Gross Domestic Saving	8.64	10.03	11.22	18.18	23.03	26.73	34.27	40.09	44.10	56.98	58.96
Gross National Saving	8.11	9.73	11.23	18.67	24.22	27.66	34.31	40.21	44.89	59.31	60.72
					(Billions of 1987 Philippine Pesos)						
Gross National Product	375.52	398.50	420.62	461.05	479.71	502.41	543.24	574.43	605.69	644.07	673.67
GDP at Market Prices	382.15	402.68	424.45	461.79	477.42	503.41	547.64	578.03	607.75	641.60	674.55
Resource Balance	-8.70	-6.52	-1.10	8.25	-23.52	-29.51	-13.24	-2.03	-14.24	-29.75	-16.02
Exports of Goods & NF Services	83.03	85.44	93.79	107.42	94.77	94.50	112.06	131.30	136.29	145.53	164.97
Imports of Goods & NF Services	91.73	91.96	94.89	99.17	118.29	124.01	125.30	133.33	150.53	175.27	180.99
Domestic Absorption	390.85	409.20	425.55	453.54	500.95	532.92	560.88	580.06	621.99	671.35	690.57
Private Consumption, etc.	280.14	304.28	314.49	334.15	356.23	358.44	367.11	384.38	412.80	442.68	449.94
General Gov't Consumption	32.19	35.24	39.84	44.53	51.08	55.01	56.17	56.70	58.40	60.56	62.82
Gross Domestic Investment	78.51	69.68	71.22	74.86	93.63	119.46	137.60	138.98	150.78	168.11	177.81
Fixed Investment	71.40	63.50	64.53	66.38	83.17	109.87	126.38	128.80	139.67	156.07	166.83
GDP at factor cost	352.14	369.64	390.37	419.04	425.75	451.49	497.04	524.08	546.61	570.89	603.31
Agriculture	105.39	109.64	115.54	124.13	120.17	122.16	134.40	140.28	145.50	150.11	156.17
Industry	126.48	135.67	145.25	164.52	175.66	191.47	212.50	228.22	240.95	258.50	271.31
Manufacturing	101.93	108.85	115.12	132.08	137.34	141.14	149.31	158.81	169.32	177.24	184.64
Services, etc.	150.28	157.37	163.66	173.14	181.60	189.77	200.73	209.53	221.30	233.00	247.07
Memo Items:											
Capacity to Import	94.05	92.14	95.92	123.49	108.21	96.14	95.92	116.38	124.76	141.87	149.85
Terms of Trade Adjustment	11.01	6.70	2.13	16.07	13.44	1.65	-16.15	-14.92	-11.54	-3.65	-15.12
Gross Domestic Income	393.17	409.38	426.58	477.86	490.86	505.05	531.49	563.11	596.21	637.95	659.43
Gross National Income	386.54	405.20	422.74	477.12	493.15	504.05	527.10	559.50	594.15	640.42	658.55
DOMESTIC PRICES/DEFLATORS						*(Index 1987 = 100)*					
Overall (GDP)	10.3	11.8	12.6	14.8	19.6	21.4	23.2	25.2	27.5	31.6	36.1
Domestic Absorption	10.1	11.6	12.5	14.3	19.1	21.5	24.0	25.8	28.0	31.8	37.0
Agriculture	11.1	13.2	13.6	16.8	24.2	26.8	27.7	29.8	32.4	37.1	39.2
Industry	9.9	11.3	12.3	14.0	18.3	19.5	21.4	23.2	25.3	29.0	34.8
Manufacturing	9.6	11.3	12.3	13.7	17.5	19.6	21.7	23.3	25.7	28.8	33.9
Consumer Price Index	9.6	11.7	12.6	14.7	19.7	21.1	23.0	25.3	27.1	31.9	37.7
MANUFACTURING ACTIVITY											
Employment (1987=100)	58.0	60.6	62.7	77.8	76.7	75.2	104.6	119.1	130.2	138.7	141.4
Real Earnings per Empl. (1987=100)	106.6	100.8	98.6	83.7	72.5	81.7	77.8	81.6	84.0	68.8	69.0
Real Output per Empl. (1987=100)	84.6	89.1	89.5	88.4	106.7	103.6	72.2	81.2	81.0	83.6	83.0
Earnings as % of Value Added	20.6	20.8	21.0	18.6	15.3	14.8	27.6	26.4	25.1	18.5	22.0
MONETARY HOLDINGS						*(Billions of current Philippine Pesos)*					
Money Supply, Broadly Defined	..	..	..	..	..	..	..	..	..	..	..
Money	4.31	5.01	6.47	7.27	9.01	10.31	12.07	14.94	16.95	18.84	22.54
Currency Outside Banks	2.41	2.65	3.43	3.45	4.31	4.75	5.65	6.73	8.14	9.18	10.18
Demand Deposits	1.90	2.36	3.03	3.81	4.70	5.57	6.42	8.21	8.81	9.66	12.36
Quasi-Money	..	..									
GOVERNMENT DEFICIT (-) OR SURPLUS					*(Millions of current Philippine Pesos)*						
GOVERNMENT DEFICIT (-) OR SURPLUS	..	..	-1,101	-843	445	-1,360	-2,352	-2,807	-2,171	-349	-3,385
Current Revenue	..	..	6,970	9,484	12,151	16,822	18,282	19,944	23,882	29,315	34,371
Current Expenditure	..	..	6,546	8,506	8,762	14,651	15,798	17,719	19,215	20,777	24,156
Current Budget Balance	..	..	424	978	3,389	2,171	2,484	2,225	4,667	8,538	10,215
Capital Receipts	..	..	2	15	6	16	18	15	125	4	2
Capital Payments	..	..	1,527	1,836	2,950	3,547	4,854	5,047	6,963	8,891	13,602

1981	1982	1983	1984	1985	1986	1987	1988	1989	1990 estimate	Notes	PHILIPPINES
720	760	710	610	540	550	570	620	680	730	..	**CURRENT GNP PER CAPITA (US $)**
49,540	50,800	52,055	53,351	54,700	56,004	57,356	58,721	60,097	61,480	..	**POPULATION (thousands)**
				(Billions of current Philippine Pesos)							**USE AND ORIGIN OF RESOURCES**
280.54	313.54	363.27	508.48	556.07	596.28	673.13	795.66	911.24	1,068.57	..	Gross National Product (GNP)
-1.05	-3.63	-5.81	-16.00	-15.81	-12.61	-11.94	-7.36	-11.32	2.26	..	Net Factor Income from Abroad
281.60	317.18	369.08	524.48	571.88	608.89	685.07	803.02	922.56	1,066.31	..	GDP at Market Prices
-9.42	-18.37	-23.83	-4.82	11.82	23.95	3.15	11.14	-21.77	-60.09	..	Resource Balance
67.09	64.53	79.81	126.68	137.03	160.19	182.18	226.43	258.34	296.03	..	Exports of Goods & NFServices
76.51	82.90	103.64	131.50	125.21	136.23	179.03	215.29	280.12	356.12	..	Imports of Goods & NFServices
291.02	335.55	392.91	529.30	560.06	584.94	681.92	791.88	944.34	1,126.40	..	Domestic Absorption
189.02	218.21	253.13	378.12	428.84	439.06	501.40	572.18	656.85	794.70	..	Private Consumption, etc.
24.66	28.93	30.55	36.88	43.52	48.43	57.33	72.18	85.38	100.78	..	General Gov't Consumption
77.33	88.41	109.23	114.30	87.70	97.44	123.19	147.51	202.11	230.92	..	Gross Domestic Investment
78.15	87.32	110.17	128.59	99.82	102.37	116.37	143.18	193.18	223.45	..	Fixed Investment
25.93	28.66	34.72	43.92	49.35	52.31	70.23	64.16	78.50	91.50	..	Indirect Taxes, net
255.67	288.52	334.36	480.56	522.53	556.58	614.84	738.86	844.06	974.81	B	GDP at factor cost
70.09	74.06	82.55	129.82	140.55	145.81	163.93	183.52	207.42	235.47	..	Agriculture
110.31	123.15	144.80	198.82	200.55	210.53	237.40	285.44	327.67	374.51	..	Industry
71.83	79.61	89.47	129.17	143.85	149.96	169.63	207.24	233.19	271.41	..	Manufacturing
101.19	119.97	141.73	195.84	230.78	252.55	283.74	334.06	387.48	456.34	..	Services, etc.
67.91	70.04	85.40	109.48	99.52	121.39	126.33	158.65	180.34	170.83	..	Gross Domestic Saving
69.43	69.16	82.22	95.46	86.91	113.57	122.13	161.84	179.30	181.77	..	Gross National Saving
				(Billions of 1987 Philippine Pesos)							
695.34	714.81	724.49	661.47	614.93	640.44	673.13	721.63	762.08	789.89	..	Gross National Product
697.51	722.60	735.62	681.72	632.12	653.76	685.07	728.34	771.53	788.10	I f	GDP at Market Prices
-3.98	-22.46	-9.63	28.02	19.82	31.87	3.15	-5.20	-21.41	-42.99	..	Resource Balance
175.58	161.50	168.71	175.18	146.08	171.05	182.18	208.95	226.44	231.68	..	Exports of Goods & NFServices
179.56	183.95	178.33	147.17	126.26	139.19	179.03	214.15	247.84	274.67	..	Imports of Goods & NFServices
701.49	745.05	745.25	653.70	612.30	621.89	681.92	733.54	792.94	831.10	..	Domestic Absorption
457.67	481.30	472.81	457.82	461.00	462.43	501.40	533.57	557.00	588.18	..	Private Consumption, etc.
60.94	65.52	62.42	55.05	54.49	54.67	57.33	62.53	66.05	68.03	..	General Gov't Consumption
182.88	198.24	210.02	140.82	96.81	104.79	123.19	137.44	169.88	174.89	..	Gross Domestic Investment
187.10	196.63	212.32	160.09	110.49	110.37	116.37	131.78	161.83	168.75	..	Fixed Investment
633.31	657.33	666.39	624.60	577.57	597.59	614.84	670.15	705.89	720.49	B I	GDP at factor cost
161.82	163.08	157.58	156.12	153.18	158.82	163.93	169.24	173.72	177.08	..	Agriculture
283.93	290.97	295.40	261.41	220.24	225.31	237.40	255.69	276.28	279.33	..	Industry
188.24	191.25	190.64	171.37	157.83	160.68	169.63	184.42	195.73	199.67	..	Manufacturing
251.76	268.54	282.65	264.19	258.70	269.63	283.74	303.41	321.53	331.69	..	Services, etc.
											Memo Items:
157.45	143.19	137.33	141.77	138.19	163.66	182.18	225.23	228.58	228.32	..	Capacity to Import
-18.13	-18.31	-31.37	-33.41	-7.90	-7.40	0.00	16.28	2.14	-3.35	..	Terms of Trade Adjustment
679.38	704.29	704.25	648.30	624.22	646.36	685.07	744.62	773.67	784.75	..	Gross Domestic Income
677.21	696.50	693.12	628.05	607.03	633.04	673.13	737.91	764.22	786.54	..	Gross National Income
				(Index 1987 = 100)							**DOMESTIC PRICES/DEFLATORS**
40.4	43.9	50.2	76.9	90.5	93.1	100.0	110.3	119.6	135.3	..	Overall (GDP)
41.5	45.0	52.7	81.0	91.5	94.1	100.0	108.0	119.1	135.5	..	Domestic Absorption
43.3	45.4	52.4	83.2	91.8	91.8	100.0	108.4	119.4	133.0	..	Agriculture
38.9	42.3	49.0	76.1	91.1	93.4	100.0	111.6	118.6	134.1	..	Industry
38.2	41.6	46.9	75.4	91.1	93.3	100.0	112.4	119.1	135.9	..	Manufacturing
42.6	47.0	51.7	77.7	95.6	96.3	100.0	108.8	120.3	135.5	..	Consumer Price Index
											MANUFACTURING ACTIVITY
144.6	144.4	103.8	94.1	91.2	93.2	100.0	..	..	..	G J	Employment (1987=100)
70.9	72.6	89.0	77.2	74.9	83.0	100.0	..	..	..	G J	Real Earnings per Empl. (1987=100)
74.9	81.2	104.3	99.4	87.1	93.1	100.0	..	..	..	G J	Real Output per Empl. (1987=100)
24.7	33.1	20.9	18.1	22.3	20.5	26.2	25.1	..	..	J	Earnings as % of Value Added
				(Billions of current Philippine Pesos)							**MONETARY HOLDINGS**
..	..	..	..	..	136.50	..	192.92	..	..	..	Money Supply, Broadly Defined
23.52	23.52	33.55	34.44	36.76	43.17	53.80	61.20	81.28	92.94	..	Money
11.63	12.71	19.59	21.76	24.03	29.26	35.37	40.64	52.94	61.92	..	Currency Outside Banks
11.90	10.82	13.96	12.68	12.73	13.90	18.43	20.56	28.34	31.01	..	Demand Deposits
..	..	..	..	..	93.33	..	131.72	..	..	..	Quasi-Money
				(Millions of current Philippine Pesos)							
-12,154	-14,414	-7,468	-9,957	-11,158	-30,648	-16,728	-23,244	-19,568	-37,194	..	**GOVERNMENT DEFICIT (-) OR SURPLUS**
35,733	37,990	45,603	56,822	68,954	79,241	101,955	106,849	148,227	176,720	..	Current Revenue
26,201	30,777	34,533	42,967	55,288	70,726	95,538	112,205	142,786	177,988	..	Current Expenditure
9,532	7,213	11,070	13,855	13,666	8,515	6,417	-5,356	5,441	-1,268	..	Current Budget Balance
3	3	3	4	3	4	1,259	6,012	4,183	4,182	..	Capital Receipts
21,689	21,630	18,541	23,816	24,827	39,167	24,404	23,900	29,192	40,108	..	Capital Payments

PHILIPPINES	1970	1971	1972	1973	1974	1975	1976	1977	1978	1979	1980
FOREIGN TRADE (CUSTOMS BASIS)					*(Millions of current US dollars)*						
Value of Exports, fob	1,059.7	1,116.3	1,028.7	1,795.7	2,648.1	2,216.0	2,484.7	3,065.4	3,327.3	4,572.2	5,750.9
Nonfuel Primary Products	962.0	1,013.0	923.4	1,492.6	2,288.6	1,786.3	1,842.8	2,282.2	2,203.1	2,965.5	3,594.8
Fuels	17.2	24.2	10.3	15.8	17.5	37.5	33.8	18.9	9.7	11.0	38.2
Manufactures	80.5	79.0	95.1	287.3	342.0	392.2	608.1	764.3	1,114.5	1,595.7	2,117.9
Value of Imports, cif	1,210.4	1,318.7	1,387.8	1,789.5	3,467.6	3,776.2	3,953.3	4,269.8	5,143.3	6,613.0	8,294.6
Nonfuel Primary Products	237.3	284.6	320.3	391.6	626.3	588.8	600.9	703.5	750.9	907.4	1,077.0
Fuels	144.8	172.7	177.3	231.2	696.0	800.1	927.6	1,040.1	1,088.0	1,466.5	2,354.8
Manufactures	828.3	861.4	890.2	1,166.7	2,145.3	2,387.3	2,424.8	2,526.2	3,304.5	4,239.0	4,862.8
					(Index 1987 = 100)						
Terms of Trade	175.6	151.1	144.7	173.1	162.5	114.5	114.9	113.3	108.8	113.6	101.7
Export Prices, fob	33.8	32.7	35.2	55.4	88.6	64.6	65.9	70.0	74.6	95.7	104.3
Import Prices, cif	19.2	21.6	24.3	32.0	54.5	56.4	57.3	61.8	68.6	84.2	102.5
BALANCE OF PAYMENTS					*(Millions of current US dollars)*						
Exports of Goods & Services	1,322	1,402	1,480	2,455	3,527	3,170	3,389	4,236	4,910	6,256	7,998
Merchandise, fob	1,064	1,136	1,136	1,872	2,694	2,263	2,517	3,151	3,426	4,601	5,788
Nonfactor Services	248	250	322	517	663	737	745	732	1,012	1,077	1,448
Factor Services	10	16	22	66	171	170	127	353	472	578	762
Imports of Goods & Services	1,489	1,539	1,661	2,211	4,012	4,412	4,761	5,249	6,323	8,106	10,348
Merchandise, fob	1,090	1,186	1,261	1,596	3,144	3,459	3,633	3,915	4,732	6,142	7,727
Nonfactor Services	259	236	253	435	642	657	748	840	983	1,163	1,420
Factor Services	140	117	148	180	226	296	380	494	608	801	1,201
Long-Term Interest	44	72	84	95	110	119	167	224	309	494	579
Private Current Transfers, net	29	34	80	94	123	165	148	148	197	229	299
Workers' Remittances	..	..	..	..	..	..	..	125	154	191	205
Curr. A/C Bal before Off. Transf.	-138	-102	-101	337	-362	-1,076	-1,225	-865	-1,216	-1,621	-2,051
Net Official Transfers	90	100	107	136	154	153	120	112	122	126	148
Curr. A/C Bal after Off. Transf.	-48	-2	6	473	-208	-923	-1,105	-753	-1,094	-1,495	-1,903
Long-Term Capital, net	130	-9	115	132	227	517	1,137	861	884	1,106	877
Direct Investment	-29	-6	-21	54	4	97	126	211	101	7	-106
Long-Term Loans	157	26	196	-14	412	532	1,095	996	950	1,129	1,312
Disbursements	416	283	452	389	741	831	1,438	1,365	1,900	2,092	1,853
Repayments	260	258	256	403	329	299	343	370	950	962	541
Other Long-Term Capital	2	-29	-61	93	-189	-112	-83	-346	-167	-30	-329
Other Capital, net	-7	110	60	106	557	395	-87	-135	1,077	766	1,982
Change in Reserves	-75	-99	-181	-712	-577	11	54	27	-867	-377	-956
Memo Item:					*(Philippine Pesos per US dollar)*						
Conversion Factor (Annual Avg)	5.900	6.430	6.670	6.760	6.790	7.250	7.440	7.400	7.370	7.380	7.510
					(Millions of US dollars), outstanding at end of year						
EXTERNAL DEBT (Total)	1,613	1,777	1,962	2,028	2,428	3,064	4,437	8,183	10,772	13,282	17,417
Long-Term Debt (by debtor)	1,613	1,777	1,962	2,028	2,428	3,064	4,437	5,715	6,909	7,966	9,861
Central Bank, incl. IMF credit	342	364	485	462	588	736	1,023	1,368	1,866	2,253	2,787
Central Government	129	167	184	175	197	307	362	609	971	1,081	1,516
Rest of General Government	1	1	0	0	0	0	0	0	0	0	1
Non-financial Public Enterprises	185	225	261	300	372	524	1,152	1,483	1,885	2,366	2,814
Priv. Sector, incl non-guaranteed	956	1,021	1,032	1,091	1,271	1,496	1,899	2,255	2,187	2,266	2,743
Short-Term Debt	0	0	0	0	0	0	0	2,468	3,863	5,315	7,556
Memo Items:					*(Millions of US dollars)*						
Int'l Reserves Excluding Gold	195.0	309.0	479.8	992.8	1,458.9	1,314.5	1,596.8	1,479.4	1,763.0	2,249.7	2,846.1
Gold Holdings (at market price)	59.8	83.5	120.5	118.6	196.9	148.1	142.3	174.2	341.9	871.4	1,131.8
SOCIAL INDICATORS											
Total Fertility Rate	6.4	6.3	6.1	5.9	5.7	5.5	5.2	5.0	4.9	4.9	4.8
Infant Mortality Rate	66.4	65.2	64.0	62.0	60.0	58.0	56.0	54.0	53.4	52.8	52.2
Life Expectancy at Birth	57.2	57.5	57.9	58.3	58.7	59.1	59.5	59.9	60.2	60.6	61.0
Urban Population, % of total	33.0	33.5	34.0	34.6	35.1	35.6	36.0	36.3	36.7	37.0	37.4
Food Prod. per capita (1987=100)	95.1	97.4	94.2	100.1	103.1	110.3	116.2	114.6	117.3	116.5	117.8
Labor Force, Agriculture (%)	54.8	54.4	54.1	53.8	53.6	53.3	53.0	52.7	52.3	52.0	51.8
Labor Force, Female (%)	33.2	33.2	33.1	33.0	32.9	32.8	32.9	32.9	32.9	32.9	32.9
Primary Schl. Enroll. Ratio	108.0	..	..	..	..	107.0	103.0	108.0	110.0	107.0	113.0
Primary Schl. Enroll. Ratio, Female	..	..	..	..	..	..	..	..	..	..	113.0
Secondary Schl. Enroll. Ratio	46.0	..	..	..	..	54.0	60.0	61.0	63.0	64.0	65.0

1981	1982	1983	1984	1985	1986	1987	1988	1989	1990 estimate	Notes	PHILIPPINES
				(Millions of current US dollars)							**FOREIGN TRADE (CUSTOMS BASIS)**
5,712.1	5,012.0	4,966.7	5,265.9	4,588.8	4,730.0	5,651.4	6,994.4	7,771.4	8,681.3	..	Value of Exports, fob
3,118.3	2,511.7	2,353.9	2,282.7	1,949.7	1,968.9	2,042.9	2,528.4	2,809.2	3,138.2	..	Nonfuel Primary Products
42.2	16.1	109.4	82.4	34.5	61.5	116.6	144.3	160.4	179.1	..	Fuels
2,551.6	2,484.2	2,503.4	2,900.8	2,604.6	2,699.6	3,491.9	4,321.7	4,801.8	5,364.0	..	Manufactures
8,477.7	8,262.3	7,977.4	6,424.3	5,444.6	5,392.5	7,189.6	8,729.1	11,179.7	13,079.6	..	Value of Imports, cif
1,027.4	1,171.3	1,012.6	770.8	792.0	865.1	1,229.4	1,492.7	1,911.7	2,236.6	..	Nonfuel Primary Products
2,553.7	2,187.9	2,193.7	1,696.5	1,508.0	918.5	949.4	1,152.7	1,476.3	1,727.2	..	Fuels
4,896.6	4,903.1	4,771.0	3,956.9	3,144.6	3,608.9	5,010.8	6,083.8	7,791.7	9,115.8	..	Manufactures
				(Index 1987 = 100)							
90.5	85.7	95.0	103.1	93.3	97.1	100.0	111.6	107.5	93.0	..	Terms of Trade
96.3	86.7	92.6	97.8	87.1	84.6	100.0	115.2	113.1	109.9	..	Export Prices, fob
106.3	101.2	97.4	94.9	93.4	87.2	100.0	103.2	105.2	118.1	..	Import Prices, cif
				(Millions of current US dollars)							**BALANCE OF PAYMENTS**
8,583	8,004	8,132	8,017	7,917	8,633	9,174	10,666	12,407	13,028	..	Exports of Goods & Services
5,722	5,021	5,005	5,391	4,629	4,842	5,720	7,074	7,821	8,186	..	Merchandise, fob
1,791	1,804	1,808	1,642	2,235	2,860	2,345	2,413	3,225	3,243	..	Nonfactor Services
1,070	1,179	1,319	984	1,053	931	1,109	1,179	1,361	1,599	..	Factor Services
11,151	11,690	11,375	9,697	8,331	8,120	10,191	11,831	14,693	16,437	..	Imports of Goods & Services
7,946	7,667	7,487	6,070	5,111	5,044	6,737	8,159	10,419	12,206	..	Merchandise, fob
1,608	1,800	1,710	1,168	850	824	1,124	1,281	1,527	1,723	..	Nonfactor Services
1,597	2,223	2,178	2,459	2,370	2,252	2,330	2,391	2,747	2,508	..	Factor Services
826	929	941	931	940	1,145	1,360	1,579	1,659	1,526	..	Long-Term Interest
325	322	237	118	172	235	376	500	473	357	..	Private Current Transfers, net
254	239	180	59	111	163	211	388	360	262	..	Workers' Remittances
-2,243	-3,364	-3,006	-1,562	-242	748	-641	-665	-1,813	-3,052	..	Curr. A/C Bal before Off. Transf.
182	164	235	268	207	206	197	275	357	357	..	Net Official Transfers
-2,061	-3,200	-2,771	-1,294	-35	954	-444	-390	-1,456	-2,695	..	Curr. A/C Bal after Off. Transf.
1,503	1,566	1,464	308	3,069	1,215	564	605	1,424	1,707	..	Long-Term Capital, net
172	16	105	9	12	127	307	936	563	530	..	Direct Investment
1,501	1,608	1,782	959	1,143	415	-78	-96	582	1,695	..	Long-Term Loans
2,226	2,580	2,613	1,485	1,745	1,529	1,332	1,248	1,475	2,447	..	Disbursements
725	973	831	526	602	1,115	1,410	1,344	893	752	..	Repayments
-170	-58	-423	-660	1,914	673	335	-235	279	-518	..	Other Long-Term Capital
226	916	-739	1,170	-3,328	-1,070	-215	411	312	937	..	Other Capital, net
332	718	2,046	-184	294	-1,099	95	-626	-280	51	..	Change in Reserves
				(Philippine Pesos per US dollar)							**Memo Item:**
7.900	8.540	11.110	16.700	18.610	20.390	20.570	21.100	21.740	24.310	..	Conversion Factor (Annual Avg)
				(Millions of US dollars), outstanding at end of year							
20,883	24,551	24,395	24,355	26,946	28,519	29,803	28,972	28,468	30,456	..	**EXTERNAL DEBT (Total)**
11,362	13,086	14,787	14,895	17,789	23,137	26,007	25,109	24,516	26,025	..	Long-Term Debt (by debtor)
3,075	3,715	4,118	4,019	4,860	8,129	9,221	8,530	8,024	7,597	..	Central Bank, incl. IMF credit
2,087	2,537	3,364	3,686	5,266	6,603	8,596	9,338	10,204	12,504	..	Central Government
2	2	2	2	1	1	1	1	0	0	..	Rest of General Government
3,074	3,234	3,803	4,094	4,611	5,246	5,470	5,083	4,448	4,040	..	Non-financial Public Enterprises
3,124	3,598	3,499	3,095	3,051	3,159	2,719	2,157	1,839	1,884	..	Priv. Sector, incl non-guaranteed
9,521	11,465	9,608	9,460	9,157	5,382	3,796	3,864	3,952	4,431	..	Short-Term Debt
				(Millions of US dollars)							**Memo Items:**
2,065.9	887.8	746.9	602.1	614.9	1,728.2	968.3	1,003.4	1,417.0	924.4	..	Int'l Reserves Excluding Gold
659.5	852.6	110.3	242.3	483.3	883.0	1,343.9	1,165.5	981.2	1,111.9	..	Gold Holdings (at market price)
											SOCIAL INDICATORS
4.8	4.7	4.5	4.4	4.2	4.1	3.9	3.8	3.7	3.5	..	Total Fertility Rate
51.6	51.0	49.8	48.6	47.4	46.2	45.0	43.6	42.2	40.8	..	Infant Mortality Rate
61.4	61.8	62.1	62.5	62.8	63.1	63.5	63.8	64.1	64.4	..	Life Expectancy at Birth
37.9	38.4	39.0	39.5	40.0	40.5	41.0	41.6	42.1	42.6	..	Urban Population, % of total
118.5	112.3	106.0	102.2	101.4	104.0	100.0	97.2	97.5	100.4	..	Food Prod. per capita (1987=100)
..	..	..	..	..	..	..	..	..	..	..	Labor Force, Agriculture (%)
32.7	32.6	32.4	32.3	32.1	31.9	31.7	31.6	31.4	31.2	..	Labor Force, Female (%)
..	109.0	109.0	107.0	106.0	107.0	109.0	110.0	111.0	..	..	Primary Schl. Enroll. Ratio
113.0	110.0	109.0	108.0	107.0	106.0	110.0	111.0	110.0	..	..	Primary Schl. Enroll. Ratio, Female
..	66.0	67.0	68.0	64.0	67.0	68.0	71.0	73.0	..	..	Secondary Schl. Enroll. Ratio

POLAND	1970	1971	1972	1973	1974	1975	1976	1977	1978	1979	1980
CURRENT GNP PER CAPITA (US $)	..	..	..	..	..	..	..	..	..	..	..
POPULATION (thousands)	32,526	32,805	33,068	33,363	33,691	34,022	34,362	34,698	35,010	35,225	35,578

USE AND ORIGIN OF RESOURCES *(Billions of current Polish Zlotys)*

	1970	1971	1972	1973	1974	1975	1976	1977	1978	1979	1980
Gross National Product (GNP)	..	..	..	..	..	..	..	..	..	..	2,407
Net Factor Income from Abroad	..	..	..	..	..	..	..	..	..	..	-104
GDP at Market Prices	..	..	..	..	..	..	..	..	..	..	2,511
Resource Balance	..	..	..	..	..	..	..	..	..	..	-74
Exports of Goods & NFServices	..	..	..	..	..	..	..	..	..	..	707
Imports of Goods & NFServices	..	..	..	..	..	..	..	..	..	..	780
Domestic Absorption	..	..	..	..	..	..	..	..	..	..	2,585
Private Consumption, etc.	..	..	..	..	..	..	..	..	..	..	1,692
General Gov't Consumption	..	..	..	..	..	..	..	..	..	..	231
Gross Domestic Investment	..	..	..	..	..	..	..	..	..	..	662
Fixed Investment	..	..	..	..	..	..	..	..	..	..	621
Indirect Taxes, net	..	..	..	..	..	..	..	..	..	..	..
GDP at factor cost	..	..	..	..	..	..	..	..	..	..	..
Agriculture	..	..	..	..	..	..	..	..	..	..	..
Industry	..	..	..	..	..	..	..	..	..	..	..
Manufacturing	..	..	..	..	..	..	..	..	..	..	..
Services, etc.	..	..	..	..	..	..	..	..	..	..	..
Gross Domestic Saving	..	..	..	..	..	..	..	..	..	..	588
Gross National Saving	..	..	..	..	..	..	..	..	..	..	510

(Billions of 1987 Polish Zlotys)

	1970	1971	1972	1973	1974	1975	1976	1977	1978	1979	1980
Gross National Product	..	..	..	..	..	..	..	..	..	..	15,247.6
GDP at Market Prices	..	..	..	..	..	..	..	..	..	..	15,839.2
Resource Balance	..	..	..	..	..	..	..	..	..	..	-274.8
Exports of Goods & NFServices	..	..	..	..	..	..	..	..	..	..	3,114.4
Imports of Goods & NFServices	..	..	..	..	..	..	..	..	..	..	3,389.2
Domestic Absorption	..	..	..	..	..	..	..	..	..	..	16,114.0
Private Consumption, etc.	..	..	..	..	..	..	..	..	..	..	9,461.6
General Gov't Consumption	..	..	..	..	..	..	..	..	..	..	1,304.7
Gross Domestic Investment	..	..	..	..	..	..	..	..	..	..	5,347.6
Fixed Investment	..	..	..	..	..	..	..	..	..	..	4,002.8
GDP at factor cost	..	..	..	..	..	..	..	..	..	..	..
Agriculture	..	..	..	..	..	..	..	..	..	..	..
Industry	..	..	..	..	..	..	..	..	..	..	..
Manufacturing	..	..	..	..	..	..	..	..	..	..	..
Services, etc.	..	..	..	..	..	..	..	..	..	..	..

Memo Items:

	1970	1971	1972	1973	1974	1975	1976	1977	1978	1979	1980
Capacity to Import	..	..	..	..	..	..	..	..	..	..	3,069.9
Terms of Trade Adjustment	..	..	..	..	..	..	..	..	..	..	-44.4
Gross Domestic Income	..	..	..	..	..	..	..	..	..	..	15,794.7
Gross National Income	..	..	..	..	..	..	..	..	..	..	15,203.1

DOMESTIC PRICES/DEFLATORS *(Index 1987 = 100)*

	1970	1971	1972	1973	1974	1975	1976	1977	1978	1979	1980
Overall (GDP)	..	..	..	..	..	..	..	..	..	..	15.9
Domestic Absorption	..	..	..	..	..	..	..	..	..	..	16.0
Agriculture	..	..	..	..	..	..	..	..	..	..	..
Industry	..	..	..	..	..	..	..	..	..	..	..
Manufacturing	..	..	..	..	..	..	..	..	..	..	..
Consumer Price Index	11.0	11.1	11.1	11.4	12.2	12.4	13.0	13.6	14.7	15.8	17.3

MANUFACTURING ACTIVITY

	1970	1971	1972	1973	1974	1975	1976	1977	1978	1979	1980
Employment (1987=100)	98.1	101.6	105.9	109.4	112.4	114.6	115.2	116.5	116.0	114.9	117.0
Real Earnings per Empl. (1987=100)	69.0	71.9	75.5	80.6	85.3	100.3	106.1	108.8	106.3	107.9	112.8
Real Output per Empl. (1987=100)	..	..	..	..	..	..	..	..	..	..	..
Earnings as % of Value Added	24.1	25.1	25.2	24.7	23.3	24.1	25.7	25.0	24.0	25.2	28.0

MONETARY HOLDINGS *(Billions of current Polish Zlotys)*

	1970	1971	1972	1973	1974	1975	1976	1977	1978	1979	1980
Money Supply, Broadly Defined	..	..	..	..	..	..	..	..	..	1,386	1,546
Money	..	..	..	..	..	..	..	..	..	825	910
Currency Outside Banks	..	..	..	..	..	..	..	..	..	235	293
Demand Deposits	..	..	..	..	..	..	..	..	..	591	618
Quasi-Money	..	..	..	..	..	..	..	..	..	561	636

(Billions of current Polish Zlotys)

GOVERNMENT DEFICIT (-) OR SURPLUS

	1970	1971	1972	1973	1974	1975	1976	1977	1978	1979	1980
Current Revenue	..	..	..	..	..	..	..	..	..	..	..
Current Expenditure	..	..	..	..	..	..	..	..	..	..	..
Current Budget Balance	..	..	..	..	..	..	..	..	..	..	..
Capital Receipts	..	..	..	..	..	..	..	..	..	..	..
Capital Payments	..	..	..	..	..	..	..	..	..	..	..

1981	1982	1983	1984	1985	1986	1987	1988	1989	1990 estimate	Notes	POLAND
..	1,520	1,790	2,070	2,080	2,030	1,860	1,850	1,890	1,690	..	**CURRENT GNP PER CAPITA (US $)**
35,902	36,227	36,571	36,914	37,203	37,456	37,664	37,862	37,854	38,180	..	**POPULATION (thousands)**
			(Billions of current Polish Zlotys)								**USE AND ORIGIN OF RESOURCES**
2,588	5,289	6,668	8,277	10,069	12,486	16,170	28,369	113,720	572,222	..	Gross National Product (GNP)
-165	-257	-256	-299	-376	-467	-770	-1,260	-4,598	-31,882	..	Net Factor Income from Abroad
2,753	5,546	6,924	8,576	10,445	12,953	16,940	29,629	118,319	604,104	..	GDP at Market Prices
-58	116	122	169	139	184	407	811	4,962	49,507	..	Resource Balance
638	1,078	1,192	1,516	1,901	2,357	3,625	6,744	22,570	156,211	..	Exports of Goods & NFServices
697	962	1,070	1,346	1,761	2,174	3,218	5,934	17,608	106,703	..	Imports of Goods & NFServices
2,811	5,430	6,802	8,407	10,305	12,769	16,533	28,818	113,356	554,597	..	Domestic Absorption
2,042	3,425	4,458	5,348	6,456	7,851	10,133	16,732	60,756	325,174	..	Private Consumption, etc.
260	455	610	801	962	1,178	1,516	2,428	7,067	45,045	..	General Gov't Consumption
508	1,551	1,734	2,257	2,888	3,740	4,884	9,657	45,533	184,378	..	Gross Domestic Investment
514	1,117	1,395	1,781	2,211	2,836	3,821	6,663	19,351	115,732	..	Fixed Investment
..	..	..	..	..	..	..	..	..	..	..	Indirect Taxes, net
..	..	..	..	..	..	..	..	..	..	..	GDP at factor cost
..	..	..	1,236	1,519	1,797	2,050	3,892	14,435	83,366	..	Agriculture
..	..	..	4,510	5,328	6,632	8,838	15,530	48,511	218,201	..	Industry
..	..	..	..	..	..	..	..	..	..	..	Manufacturing
..	..	..	2,830	3,598	4,524	6,052	10,207	55,373	302,537	..	Services, etc.
450	1,667	1,856	2,426	3,028	3,924	5,291	10,468	50,495	233,885	..	Gross Domestic Saving
332	1,480	1,665	2,210	2,794	3,649	4,934	9,936	48,086	222,960	..	Gross National Saving
			(Billions of 1987 Polish Zlotys)								
13,417.3	12,788.1	13,613.9	14,444.2	15,243.1	15,884.9	16,170.4	16,848.6	16,845.5	14,724.9	..	Gross National Product
14,259.2	13,580.2	14,334.8	15,144.4	15,921.1	16,590.5	16,939.9	17,624.2	17,675.0	15,562.7	..	GDP at Market Prices
-173.9	348.7	459.1	574.6	393.8	376.4	407.1	458.3	386.4	1,378.1	..	Resource Balance
2,546.6	2,704.6	2,952.6	3,303.1	3,313.3	3,452.8	3,625.2	3,966.1	4,070.5	4,684.6	..	Exports of Goods & NFServices
2,720.6	2,356.0	2,493.6	2,728.5	2,919.6	3,076.4	3,218.1	3,507.7	3,684.0	3,306.5	..	Imports of Goods & NFServices
14,433.1	13,231.5	13,875.7	14,569.8	15,527.3	16,214.1	16,532.8	17,165.9	17,288.5	14,184.5	..	Domestic Absorption
9,029.8	7,940.6	8,328.0	8,654.1	9,358.1	9,833.9	10,132.9	10,369.0	10,409.7	8,685.7	..	Private Consumption, etc.
1,245.4	1,275.6	1,315.2	1,414.4	1,500.3	1,501.0	1,516.4	1,516.9	1,304.9	1,307.0	..	General Gov't Consumption
4,157.9	4,015.3	4,232.5	4,501.4	4,668.9	4,879.1	4,883.5	5,278.2	5,574.0	4,191.8	..	Gross Domestic Investment
3,239.7	2,796.9	3,042.5	3,341.4	3,512.7	3,671.1	3,821.0	4,031.1	3,967.3	3,546.7	..	Fixed Investment
..	..	..	..	..	..	..	..	..	..		GDP at factor cost
..	..	..	1,953.9	2,076.9	2,184.7	2,050.0	2,083.2	..	..	..	Agriculture
..	..	..	8,106.8	8,236.9	8,584.0	8,838.0	9,266.2	..	..	..	Industry
..	..	..	..	..	..	..	..	..	..	..	Manufacturing
..	..	..	5,083.8	5,607.3	5,821.8	6,051.9	6,274.8	..	..	..	Services, etc.
											Memo Items:
2,493.6	2,640.1	2,778.3	3,071.6	3,150.7	3,336.4	3,625.2	3,987.0	4,722.3	4,840.6	..	Capacity to Import
-53.0	-64.5	-174.3	-231.5	-162.7	-116.4	0.0	21.0	651.9	156.0	..	Terms of Trade Adjustment
14,206.2	13,515.7	14,160.4	14,912.9	15,758.4	16,474.1	16,939.9	17,645.2	18,326.8	15,718.6	..	Gross Domestic Income
13,364.3	12,723.6	13,439.6	14,212.7	15,080.4	15,768.5	16,170.4	16,869.6	17,497.4	14,880.8	..	Gross National Income
			(Index 1987 = 100)								**DOMESTIC PRICES/DEFLATORS**
19.3	40.8	48.3	56.6	65.6	78.1	100.0	168.1	669.4	3881.7	..	Overall (GDP)
19.5	41.0	49.0	57.7	66.4	78.8	100.0	167.9	655.7	3909.9	..	Domestic Absorption
..	..	..	63.3	73.1	82.3	100.0	186.8	..	..	..	Agriculture
..	..	..	55.6	64.7	77.3	100.0	167.6	..	..	..	Industry
..	..	..	..	..	..	..	..	..	..	..	Manufacturing
20.9	42.0	51.3	59.0	67.9	79.9	100.0	160.2	562.5	3857.5	..	Consumer Price Index
											MANUFACTURING ACTIVITY
116.1	108.4	106.9	105.9	101.4	101.2	100.0	98.1	..	..	G	Employment (1987=100)
117.0	87.8	93.7	96.5	100.1	102.6	100.0	116.3	..	..	G	Real Earnings per Empl. (1987=100)
..	..	..	..	..	..	..	..	..	..	G	Real Output per Empl. (1987=100)
39.1	23.5	24.9	24.2	23.8	23.4	21.5	22.6	..	..	..	Earnings as % of Value Added
			(Billions of current Polish Zlotys)								**MONETARY HOLDINGS**
1,907	2,643	3,039	3,576	4,366	5,532	7,416	12,110	74,433	198,004	..	Money Supply, Broadly Defined
1,105	1,573	1,747	2,001	2,449	2,998	3,786	5,748	19,975	101,670	..	Money
402	605	718	824	1,014	1,166	1,312	2,523	9,880	39,336	..	Currency Outside Banks
703	968	1,029	1,177	1,435	1,832	2,474	3,225	10,095	62,334	..	Demand Deposits
802	1,070	1,292	1,575	1,917	2,534	3,631	6,361	54,458	96,334	..	Quasi-Money
			(Billions of current Polish Zlotys)								**GOVERNMENT DEFICIT (-) OR SURPLUS**
..	..	..	-39.9	-180.4	-41.3	-241.6	-673.0	..	..	..	
..	..	..	3,750.8	4,538.0	5,417.5	6,598.9	11,013.0	..	..	..	Current Revenue
..	..	..	3,573.0	4,391.3	5,009.5	6,214.7	10,771.5	..	..	..	Current Expenditure
..	..	..	177.8	146.7	408.0	384.2	241.5	..	..	..	Current Budget Balance
..	..	..	..	0.1	..	0.5	0.3	..	..	..	Capital Receipts
..	..	..	217.7	327.2	449.3	626.3	914.8	..	..	..	Capital Payments

POLAND	1970	1971	1972	1973	1974	1975	1976	1977	1978	1979	1980
FOREIGN TRADE (CUSTOMS BASIS)					*(Millions of current US dollars)*						
Value of Exports, fob	3,827	4,064	5,053	6,586	8,568	10,468	11,161	12,586	14,245	17,297	16,997
Nonfuel Primary Products	994	1,055	1,312	1,710	2,225	2,718	2,898	3,268	3,699	4,492	4,414
Fuels	506	537	668	871	1,133	1,384	1,475	1,664	1,883	2,287	2,247
Manufactures	2,327	2,471	3,073	4,005	5,210	6,366	6,787	7,654	8,663	10,519	10,336
Value of Imports, cif	4,154	4,456	5,965	8,597	11,669	13,666	14,992	15,463	16,714	18,852	19,089
Nonfuel Primary Products	1,276	1,369	1,832	2,641	3,584	4,198	4,605	4,750	5,134	5,791	5,863
Fuels	752	806	1,080	1,556	2,112	2,473	2,713	2,798	3,025	3,412	3,455
Manufactures	2,126	2,281	3,053	4,400	5,973	6,995	7,674	7,915	8,555	9,650	9,771
					(Index 1987 = 100)						
Terms of Trade	..	..	..	..	..	115.6	111.6	109.0	109.5	106.5	89.0
Export Prices, fob	..	..	..	..	..	123.8	125.3	128.8	140.0	151.0	134.6
Import Prices, cif	..	..	..	..	..	107.1	112.3	118.2	127.8	141.8	151.3
BALANCE OF PAYMENTS					*(Millions of current US dollars)*						
Exports of Goods & Services	..	..	..	..	..	..	10,723	11,927	13,593	15,221	16,200
Merchandise, fob	..	..	..	..	..	..	9,506	10,506	11,967	13,276	14,043
Nonfactor Services	..	..	..	..	..	..	1,180	1,385	1,586	1,874	2,018
Factor Services	..	..	..	..	..	..	37	36	40	71	139
Imports of Goods & Services	..	..	..	..	..	..	14,095	14,957	17,024	19,261	20,338
Merchandise, fob	..	..	..	..	..	..	12,263	12,724	14,259	15,660	15,819
Nonfactor Services	..	..	..	..	..	..	1,144	1,309	1,521	1,863	2,023
Factor Services	..	..	..	..	..	..	688	924	1,244	1,738	2,496
Long-Term Interest	0	0	1	2	16	53	91	151	183	237	704
Private Current Transfers, net	..	..	..	..	..	..	399	463	673	672	593
Workers' Remittances	..	..	..	..	..	..	..	..	..	..	0
Curr. A/C Bal before Off. Transf.	..	..	..	..	..	..	-2,973	-2,567	-2,758	-3,368	-3,545
Net Official Transfers	..	..	..	..	..	..	180	175	213	3	128
Curr. A/C Bal after Off. Transf.	..	..	..	..	..	..	-2,793	-2,392	-2,545	-3,365	-3,417
Long-Term Capital, net	..	..	..	..	..	..	2,785	2,619	2,195	3,621	2,640
Direct Investment	..	..	..	..	..	..	-6	-12	9	17	-11
Long-Term Loans	24	17	36	133	166	322	857	227	675	991	3,005
Disbursements	30	24	43	171	235	460	1,072	506	1,015	1,515	5,058
Repayments	6	6	7	38	69	138	215	279	339	524	2,053
Other Long-Term Capital	..	..	..	..	..	..	1,934	2,404	1,511	2,613	-354
Other Capital, net	..	..	..	..	..	..	193	-598	479	19	140
Change in Reserves	..	..	..	..	..	..	-185	371	-129	-275	637
Memo Item:					*(Polish Zlotys per US dollar)*						
Conversion Factor (Annual Avg)	..	..	..	..	..	..	..	..	..	..	44.220
				(Millions of US dollars), outstanding at end of year							
EXTERNAL DEBT (Total)	24	41	77	207	401	698	1,487	1,839	2,770	3,872	8,894
Long-Term Debt (by debtor)	24	41	77	207	401	698	1,487	1,839	2,770	3,872	6,594
Central Bank, incl. IMF credit	0	0	18	137	338	641	1,436	1,628	2,282	3,226	4,976
Central Government	24	41	59	69	63	57	51	211	459	577	781
Rest of General Government	..	..	..	..	..	..	..	..	..	..	..
Non-financial Public Enterprises	0	0	0	0	0	0	0	0	29	69	837
Priv. Sector, incl non-guaranteed	0	0	0	0	0	0	0	0	0	0	0
Short-Term Debt	0	0	0	0	0	0	0	0	0	0	2,300
Memo Items:					*(Millions of US dollars)*						
Int'l Reserves Excluding Gold	..	..	..	..	..	..	..	..	..	565.1	127.6
Gold Holdings (at market price)	..	..	..	..	..	..	..	..	..	657.9	446.8
SOCIAL INDICATORS											
Total Fertility Rate	2.2	2.3	2.2	2.3	2.3	2.3	2.3	2.2	2.2	2.3	2.3
Infant Mortality Rate	33.2	29.5	28.4	25.8	23.5	24.8	23.7	24.6	22.4	21.0	21.2
Life Expectancy at Birth	70.2	70.3	70.5	70.6	70.6	70.7	70.8	70.9	70.9	70.9	70.9
Urban Population, % of total	52.3	52.9	53.5	54.2	54.8	55.4	55.9	56.5	57.0	57.6	58.1
Food Prod. per capita (1987=100)	96.4	92.4	96.7	102.0	103.9	103.2	106.4	98.9	106.6	106.0	91.6
Labor Force, Agriculture (%)	38.9	37.8	36.8	35.7	34.7	33.7	32.7	31.6	30.6	29.5	28.5
Labor Force, Female (%)	45.4	45.3	45.3	45.3	45.3	45.3	45.3	45.3	45.3	45.3	45.3
Primary Schl. Enroll. Ratio	101.0	..	..	..	..	100.0	100.0	100.0	100.0	99.0	100.0
Primary Schl. Enroll. Ratio, Female	99.0	..	..	..	..	99.0	99.0	99.0	..	..	99.0
Secondary Schl. Enroll. Ratio	62.0	..	..	69.0	..	73.0	..	74.0	75.0	76.0	77.0

1981	1982	1983	1984	1985	1986	1987	1988	1989	1990 estimate	Notes	POLAND
											FOREIGN TRADE (CUSTOMS BASIS)
13,249	11,214	11,572	11,647	11,489	12,074	12,205	13,960	13,466	13,627	..	Value of Exports, fob
1,981	1,800	2,088	2,210	2,285	2,292	2,602	3,008	3,055	3,091	..	Nonfuel Primary Products
1,285	1,728	2,012	2,042	1,801	1,594	1,374	1,429	1,308	1,323	..	Fuels
9,983	7,686	7,472	7,395	7,403	8,188	8,229	9,523	9,104	9,212	..	Manufactures
15,476	10,244	10,590	10,547	10,836	11,208	10,844	12,243	10,277	9,781	..	Value of Imports, cif
4,324	2,836	2,259	2,407	2,280	2,163	2,325	2,839	2,311	2,200	..	Nonfuel Primary Products
3,100	2,247	2,759	2,442	2,405	2,319	1,872	1,820	1,309	1,246	..	Fuels
8,052	5,161	5,572	5,698	6,152	6,727	6,647	7,584	6,657	6,335	..	Manufactures

(Index 1987 = 100)

1981	1982	1983	1984	1985	1986	1987	1988	1989	1990	Notes	POLAND
92.7	97.3	92.1	92.4	94.5	96.1	100.0	103.0	120.1	103.4	..	Terms of Trade
127.6	124.4	115.6	106.3	103.5	103.8	100.0	104.8	101.0	94.4	..	Export Prices, fob
137.7	127.8	125.6	115.1	109.5	108.0	100.0	101.8	84.1	91.3	..	Import Prices, cif

(Millions of current US dollars) — **BALANCE OF PAYMENTS**

1981	1982	1983	1984	1985	1986	1987	1988	1989	1990	Notes	POLAND
12,626	13,482	13,789	13,866	13,222	14,129	14,459	16,589	16,480	19,640	..	Exports of Goods & Services
10,542	11,547	11,615	11,654	10,945	11,926	12,026	13,846	12,869	15,837	..	Merchandise, fob
1,913	1,842	1,990	2,017	2,104	2,015	2,216	2,472	3,201	3,200	..	Nonfactor Services
171	93	184	195	173	188	217	271	410	603	..	Factor Services
17,845	16,254	16,073	15,681	15,174	16,332	16,396	18,387	19,498	19,084	..	Imports of Goods & Services
12,723	11,631	11,312	10,995	10,598	11,459	11,236	12,757	12,822	12,248	..	Merchandise, fob
1,727	1,467	1,783	1,853	1,846	2,012	2,028	2,404	3,053	2,847	..	Nonfactor Services
3,395	3,156	2,978	2,833	2,730	2,861	3,132	3,226	3,623	3,989	..	Factor Services
389	423	588	912	1,477	999	971	828	761	206	..	Long-Term Interest
909	831	703	732	970	1,097	1,558	1,691	1,521	2,206	..	Private Current Transfers, net
0	0	0	0	0	0	0	0	0	..	..	Workers' Remittances
-4,310	-1,941	-1,581	-1,083	-982	-1,106	-379	-107	-1,497	2,762	..	Curr. A/C Bal before Off. Transf.
324	0	0	0	0	0	0	0	512	305	..	Net Official Transfers
-3,986	-1,941	-1,581	-1,083	-982	-1,106	-379	-107	-985	3,067	..	Curr. A/C Bal after Off. Transf.
988	-1,022	-2,692	-278	11,191	-1,550	4,353	747	-1,796	6,280	..	Long-Term Capital, net
15	10	15	16	14	-6	4	-7	-7	89	..	Direct Investment
2,370	1,256	435	246	500	667	-478	-255	-401	-102	..	Long-Term Loans
3,116	1,428	701	385	955	1,385	505	578	273	540	..	Disbursements
746	172	266	139	455	718	983	833	674	642	..	Repayments
-1,397	-2,288	-3,142	-540	10,677	-2,211	4,827	1,009	-1,388	6,293	..	Other Long-Term Capital
3,033	3,333	4,391	1,702	-10,445	2,483	-3,177	-79	3,040	-7,414	..	Other Capital, net
-35	-370	-118	-341	236	173	-797	-561	-259	-1,933	..	Change in Reserves

Memo Item:

(Polish Zlotys per US dollar)

1981	1982	1983	1984	1985	1986	1987	1988	1989	1990	Notes	POLAND
51.150	84.820	91.550	113.240	147.140	175.290	265.080	430.550	1,439.180	9,500.000	..	Conversion Factor (Annual Avg)

(Millions of US dollars), outstanding at end of year

1981	1982	1983	1984	1985	1986	1987	1988	1989	1990	Notes	POLAND
13,065	18,767	20,177	21,161	33,336	36,670	42,620	42,146	43,029	49,386	..	**EXTERNAL DEBT (Total)**
10,465	15,367	15,977	16,361	29,763	31,932	36,055	33,670	34,452	39,791	..	Long-Term Debt (by debtor)
6,459	6,544	6,210	5,754	9,177	6,454	7,499	7,053	5,950	6,209	..	Central Bank, incl. IMF credit
3,016	7,915	8,940	9,853	19,875	24,691	27,716	25,802	27,696	32,825	..	Central Government
..	..	..	..	..	..	..	..	..	..		Rest of General Government
990	908	827	754	711	788	840	815	806	750	..	Non-financial Public Enterprises
0	0	0	0	0	0	0	0	0	6	..	Priv. Sector, incl non-guaranteed
2,600	3,400	4,200	4,800	3,573	4,738	6,565	8,476	8,577	9,595	..	Short-Term Debt

(Millions of US dollars)

Memo Items:

1981	1982	1983	1984	1985	1986	1987	1988	1989	1990	Notes	POLAND
277.8	646.8	765.2	1,106.0	870.4	697.8	1,494.7	2,055.3	2,314.3	4,492.1	..	Int'l Reserves Excluding Gold
186.8	215.2	180.1	145.5	154.3	184.5	228.5	193.6	189.3	181.7	..	Gold Holdings (at market price)
											SOCIAL INDICATORS
2.3	2.3	2.3	2.3	2.3	2.2	2.2	2.2	2.2	2.1	..	Total Fertility Rate
20.6	20.2	19.2	19.2	18.4	17.5	17.5	17.1	16.7	16.3	..	Infant Mortality Rate
70.9	70.9	70.9	70.9	70.9	70.9	70.9	71.0	71.1	71.3	..	Life Expectancy at Birth
58.5	58.9	59.2	59.6	60.0	60.4	60.7	61.1	61.4	61.8	..	Urban Population, % of total
90.3	93.2	97.0	100.1	101.7	106.7	100.0	102.0	105.3	106.6	..	Food Prod. per capita (1987=100)
..	..	..	..	..	..	..	..	..	..		Labor Force, Agriculture (%)
45.3	45.4	45.4	45.4	45.4	45.5	45.5	45.5	45.6	45.6	..	Labor Force, Female (%)
..	100.0	101.0	101.0	101.0	101.0	101.0	100.0	99.0	..	..	Primary Schl. Enroll. Ratio
99.0	99.0	100.0	100.0	100.0	101.0	101.0	99.0	99.0	..	..	Primary Schl. Enroll. Ratio, Female
..	75.0	75.0	78.0	78.0	80.0	80.0	81.0	81.0	..	..	Secondary Schl. Enroll. Ratio

PORTUGAL	1970	1971	1972	1973	1974	1975	1976	1977	1978	1979	1980
CURRENT GNP PER CAPITA (US $)	700	820	940	1,200	1,430	1,540	1,700	1,830	1,890	2,090	2,370
POPULATION (thousands)	9,044	8,644	8,631	8,633	8,754	9,093	9,355	9,455	9,558	9,661	9,766
USE AND ORIGIN OF RESOURCES					*(Billions of current Portuguese Escudos)*						
Gross National Product (GNP)	178.8	199.6	232.5	284.6	343.1	376.8	464.3	617.9	771.6	971.8	1,203.2
Net Factor Income from Abroad	1.0	0.5	0.7	2.4	3.8	-0.4	-4.6	-7.9	-15.7	-21.5	-31.8
GDP at Market Prices	177.8	199.1	231.8	282.2	339.3	377.2	468.9	625.8	787.3	993.3	1,235.0
Resource Balance	-11.6	-14.0	-10.9	-19.8	-51.9	-46.7	-62.9	-94.1	-97.7	-107.6	-186.0
Exports of Goods & NFServices	43.4	49.9	63.1	75.4	91.2	76.9	81.7	115.3	158.4	268.7	355.1
Imports of Goods & NFServices	55.0	63.9	74.0	95.2	143.1	123.6	144.6	209.4	256.1	376.3	541.1
Domestic Absorption	189.4	213.1	242.7	302.0	391.2	423.9	531.8	719.9	885.0	1,100.9	1,421.0
Private Consumption, etc.	118.3	133.9	144.8	182.1	246.5	275.8	345.8	450.4	535.3	670.3	823.1
General Gov't Consumption	24.6	26.9	31.0	36.1	47.9	56.5	64.4	87.8	109.7	137.6	177.3
Gross Domestic Investment	46.5	52.3	66.9	83.8	96.8	91.6	121.6	181.7	240.0	293.0	420.6
Fixed Investment	41.3	49.2	62.8	75.6	88.2	97.8	117.5	167.9	222.3	270.6	364.2
Indirect Taxes, net	..	..	..	..	..	..	..	..	..	..	..
GDP at factor cost	..	..	..	..	..	..	..	..	..	..	..
Agriculture	..	..	..	..	..	..	..	74.6	94.0	115.0	126.0
Industry	..	..	..	..	..	..	..	226.3	291.5	376.3	484.1
Manufacturing											
Services, etc.	..	..	..	..	..	..	..	324.9	401.8	502.0	624.9
Gross Domestic Saving	34.9	38.3	56.0	64.0	44.9	44.9	58.7	87.6	142.3	185.4	234.6
Gross National Saving	49.9	57.1	80.5	93.3	76.9	71.8	83.3	123.1	198.4	284.8	352.9
					(Billions of 1987 Portuguese Escudos)						
Gross National Product	2,832.2	3,010.1	3,253.0	3,636.9	3,687.9	3,485.2	3,692.9	3,888.6	3,988.8	4,209.8	4,390.2
GDP at Market Prices	2,810.7	2,997.3	3,237.3	3,599.8	3,641.2	3,482.9	3,722.9	3,931.5	4,064.1	4,297.1	4,496.2
Resource Balance	-230.5	-297.7	-281.7	-395.8	-612.2	-379.6	-416.2	-535.1	-475.5	-408.0	-423.7
Exports of Goods & NFServices	711.7	781.6	927.2	965.6	814.3	687.1	687.1	660.7	708.3	901.4	989.1
Imports of Goods & NFServices	942.2	1,079.3	1,208.9	1,361.4	1,426.5	1,066.7	1,103.3	1,195.8	1,183.8	1,309.4	1,412.8
Domestic Absorption	3,041.2	3,295.0	3,519.0	3,995.6	4,253.4	3,862.6	4,139.1	4,466.5	4,539.6	4,705.1	4,919.9
Private Consumption, etc.	1,646.6	1,847.8	1,881.9	2,135.6	2,454.5	2,432.4	2,562.1	2,593.7	2,552.9	2,559.4	2,563.6
General Gov't Consumption	267.0	284.0	309.0	332.8	390.6	416.1	445.6	497.7	519.3	552.7	586.2
Gross Domestic Investment	1,127.6	1,163.2	1,328.1	1,527.2	1,408.4	1,014.1	1,131.4	1,375.1	1,467.4	1,593.0	1,770.1
Fixed Investment	852.7	936.1	1,062.7	1,164.1	1,082.7	960.6	968.4	1,084.7	1,160.9	1,149.3	1,254.6
GDP at factor cost	..	..	..	..	..	..	..	..	..	..	..
Agriculture	..	..	..	..	..	..	..	..	..	..	..
Industry	..	..	..	..	..	..	..	..	..	..	..
Manufacturing	..	..	..	..	..	..	..	..	..	..	..
Services, etc.	..	..	..	..	..	..	..	..	..	..	..
Memo Items:											
Capacity to Import	743.5	842.8	1,030.8	1,078.2	909.1	663.7	623.4	658.4	732.2	935.0	927.1
Terms of Trade Adjustment	31.8	61.2	103.7	112.7	94.8	-23.4	-63.7	-2.3	23.9	33.6	-61.9
Gross Domestic Income	2,842.5	3,058.5	3,341.0	3,712.4	3,736.1	3,459.5	3,659.2	3,929.2	4,088.0	4,330.7	4,434.2
Gross National Income	2,864.0	3,071.3	3,356.6	3,749.6	3,782.7	3,461.8	3,629.2	3,886.3	4,012.7	4,243.4	4,328.3
DOMESTIC PRICES/DEFLATORS					*(Index 1987 = 100)*						
Overall (GDP)	6.3	6.6	7.2	7.8	9.3	10.8	12.6	15.9	19.4	23.1	27.5
Domestic Absorption	6.2	6.5	6.9	7.6	9.2	11.0	12.8	16.1	19.5	23.4	28.9
Agriculture	..	..	..	..	..	..	..	..	..	..	..
Industry	..	..	..	..	..	..	..	..	..	..	..
Manufacturing	..	..	..	..	..	..	..	..	..	..	..
Consumer Price Index	5.4	5.8	6.4	7.0	9.0	10.8	12.8	16.3	20.0	24.7	28.8
MANUFACTURING ACTIVITY											
Employment (1987=100)	71.3	77.2	88.0	94.3	95.4	97.2	100.0	101.6	104.1	107.8	109.5
Real Earnings per Empl. (1987=100)	76.7	81.4	86.9	90.5	104.3	114.8	114.5	105.6	98.3	94.0	100.3
Real Output per Empl. (1987=100)	..	..	..	..	..	..	..	..	..	..	..
Earnings as % of Value Added	33.9	39.2	41.3	40.9	46.6	61.0	60.6	53.0	49.8	46.1	43.2
MONETARY HOLDINGS					*(Billions of current Portuguese Escudos)*						
Money Supply, Broadly Defined	166.5	189.0	234.8	301.3	342.3	385.5	461.8	540.6	652.6	871.2	1,125.8
Money	100.4	104.9	122.3	165.6	182.5	227.3	251.9	281.9	321.1	407.3	497.3
Currency Outside Banks	29.7	31.9	36.1	38.3	69.7	109.8	109.2	113.3	121.4	142.1	165.2
Demand Deposits	70.7	73.0	86.2	127.3	112.8	117.4	142.7	168.7	199.7	265.2	332.2
Quasi-Money	66.1	84.1	112.5	135.7	159.8	158.2	209.9	258.7	331.5	463.9	628.4
					(Billions of current Portuguese Escudos)						
GOVERNMENT DEFICIT (-) OR SURPLUS	..	..	..	..	..	-31.70	-54.20	-40.90	-92.80	-100.50	-121.50
Current Revenue	..	..	..	..	..	95.70	127.40	178.20	217.30	272.30	379.10
Current Expenditure	..	..	..	..	..	108.20	147.50	..	239.80	300.80	412.40
Current Budget Balance	..	..	..	..	..	-12.50	-20.10	..	-22.50	-28.50	-33.30
Capital Receipts						0.40			0.70	0.80	1.00
Capital Payments	..	..	..	..	..	19.60	34.00	..	71.00	72.80	89.20

1981	1982	1983	1984	1985	1986	1987	1988	1989	1990 estimate	Notes	PORTUGAL
2,490	2,500	2,250	1,990	1,970	2,270	2,830	3,650	4,250	4,900	..	**CURRENT GNP PER CAPITA (US $)**
9,855	9,930	10,009	10,089	10,157	10,208	10,250	10,287	10,321	10,354	..	**POPULATION (thousands)**
			(Billions of current Portuguese Escudos)								**USE AND ORIGIN OF RESOURCES**
1,413.0	1,757.8	2,170.0	2,631.4	3,344.5	4,267.4	5,038.2	5,909.1	6,951.1	7,967.2	..	Gross National Product (GNP)
-59.7	-99.1	-119.0	-174.1	-191.8	-151.4	-131.7	-120.1	-115.2	-132.0	..	Net Factor Income from Abroad
1,472.7	1,856.9	2,289.0	2,805.5	3,536.3	4,418.8	5,169.9	6,029.2	7,066.3	8,099.2	..	GDP at Market Prices
-297.3	-374.0	-282.0	-228.5	-123.3	-111.7	-337.6	-575.0	-686.5	-833.8	..	Resource Balance
403.0	488.7	733.0	1,020.1	1,316.2	1,457.9	1,777.0	2,077.8	2,543.4	2,860.5	..	Exports of Goods & NF Services
700.3	862.7	1,015.0	1,248.6	1,439.5	1,569.6	2,114.6	2,652.8	3,229.9	3,694.3	..	Imports of Goods & NF Services
1,770.0	2,230.9	2,571.0	3,034.1	3,659.6	4,530.5	5,507.5	6,604.1	7,752.8	8,933.0	..	Domestic Absorption
1,020.3	1,277.5	1,570.0	1,979.1	2,388.6	2,900.8	3,388.4	4,010.4	4,681.4	5,309.2	..	Private Consumption, etc.
218.7	266.6	334.0	405.5	501.9	598.6	688.8	799.5	921.2	1,069.7	..	General Gov't Consumption
531.0	686.8	667.0	649.5	769.1	1,031.1	1,430.3	1,794.2	2,150.2	2,554.1	..	Gross Domestic Investment
463.0	587.5	678.0	669.9	766.7	986.4	1,307.3	1,680.4	2,025.5	2,417.6	..	Fixed Investment
..	..	..	..	..	..	..	..	..	..	..	Indirect Taxes, net
..	..	..	..	..	..	..	..	..	..	B	GDP at factor cost
123.6	159.8	200.0	265.0	331.0	371.0	448.0	..	..	..	..	Agriculture
579.6	734.6	902.0	1,117.0	1,375.0	1,669.0	1,919.0	..	..	..	..	Industry
..	..	..	..	..	..	..	..	..	..	..	Manufacturing
769.5	962.5	1,187.0	1,423.5	1,830.3	2,378.8	2,802.9	..	..	..	..	Services, etc.
233.7	312.8	385.0	420.9	645.8	919.4	1,092.7	1,219.3	1,463.7	1,720.3	..	Gross Domestic Saving
352.1	425.4	502.0	560.2	814.9	1,159.6	1,442.5	1,617.0	1,935.1	2,230.3	..	Gross National Saving
			(Billions of 1987 Portuguese Escudos)								
4,373.0	4,450.2	4,449.4	4,337.3	4,509.4	4,789.3	5,038.2	5,293.2	5,575.8	5,819.2		Gross National Product
4,540.4	4,682.3	4,675.6	4,600.6	4,752.4	4,956.4	5,169.9	5,402.2	5,670.5	5,918.0	I	GDP at Market Prices
-506.0	-527.5	-223.7	-17.0	80.0	-68.7	-337.6	-571.9	-675.0	..		Resource Balance
959.3	1,017.1	1,186.8	1,355.2	1,506.0	1,606.8	1,777.0	1,897.9	2,027.4	..		Exports of Goods & NF Services
1,465.3	1,544.7	1,410.5	1,372.2	1,425.9	1,675.5	2,114.6	2,469.8	2,702.4	..		Imports of Goods & NF Services
5,046.5	5,209.8	4,899.3	4,617.6	4,672.4	5,025.1	5,507.5	5,974.1	6,345.5	..		Domestic Absorption
2,626.7	2,665.5	2,744.2	2,723.8	2,761.3	2,921.3	3,388.4	3,821.6	4,040.7	..		Private Consumption, etc.
602.1	619.1	635.5	652.0	661.6	673.5	688.8	722.2	739.8	..		General Gov't Consumption
1,817.8	1,925.2	1,519.6	1,241.8	1,249.4	1,430.3	1,430.3	1,430.3	1,565.0	..		Gross Domestic Investment
1,318.5	1,356.6	1,255.2	1,029.1	998.1	1,093.1	1,307.3	1,511.7	1,653.8	..		Fixed Investment
..	..	..	..	..	..	..	..	..	..	B	GDP at factor cost
..	..	..	..	..	..	..	..	..	..	..	Agriculture
..	..	..	..	..	..	..	..	..	..	..	Industry
..	..	..	..	..	..	..	..	..	..	..	Manufacturing
..	..	..	..	..	..	..	..	..	..	..	Services, etc.
											Memo Items:
843.2	875.0	1,018.6	1,121.1	1,303.8	1,556.2	1,777.0	1,934.5	2,128.0	..		Capacity to Import
-116.0	-142.1	-168.2	-234.1	-202.2	-50.6	0.0	36.5	100.6	..		Terms of Trade Adjustment
4,424.4	4,540.2	4,507.4	4,366.5	4,550.2	4,905.8	5,169.9	5,438.8	5,771.1	..		Gross Domestic Income
4,257.0	4,308.1	4,281.3	4,103.1	4,307.3	4,738.8	5,038.2	5,329.8	5,676.4	..		Gross National Income
			(Index 1987 = 100)								**DOMESTIC PRICES/DEFLATORS**
32.4	39.7	49.0	61.0	74.4	89.2	100.0	111.6	124.6	136.9		Overall (GDP)
35.1	42.8	52.5	65.7	78.3	90.2	100.0	110.5	122.2	..		Domestic Absorption
..	..	..	..	..	..	..	..	..	..		Agriculture
..	..	..	..	..	..	..	..	..	..		Industry
..	..	..	..	..	..	..	..	..	..		Manufacturing
34.6	42.4	53.1	68.6	81.9	91.4	100.0	109.6	123.4	139.9		Consumer Price Index
											MANUFACTURING ACTIVITY
110.1	108.5	107.0	103.1	100.2	100.2	100.0	99.6	..	..		Employment (1987=100)
101.0	99.0	93.7	87.1	89.3	94.8	100.0	107.1	..	..		Real Earnings per Empl. (1987=100)
..	..	..	..	..	..	..	..	..	..		Real Output per Empl. (1987=100)
45.1	46.9	43.5	38.4	39.1	38.7	36.0	36.7	..	..		Earnings as % of Value Added
			(Billions of current Portuguese Escudos)								**MONETARY HOLDINGS**
1,390.6	1,714.2	1,995.7	2,489.5	3,084.2	3,690.2	4,214.7	4,751.2	5,266.0	6,257.0		Money Supply, Broadly Defined
540.4	628.1	679.3	784.0	1,000.3	1,359.4	1,537.0	1,803.9	1,903.4	2,453.6		Money
188.4	219.5	240.0	267.3	319.0	399.3	457.7	509.5	577.3	623.9		Currency Outside Banks
352.1	408.7	439.3	516.7	681.3	960.2	1,079.3	1,294.3	1,326.1	1,829.7		Demand Deposits
850.2	1,086.1	1,316.4	1,705.5	2,083.9	2,330.7	2,677.8	2,947.3	3,362.6	3,803.3		Quasi-Money
			(Billions of current Portuguese Escudos)								**GOVERNMENT DEFICIT (-) OR SURPLUS**
-179.60	-195.00	-219.70	-272.40	-522.00	-543.20	-559.20	-478.70	-344.60	..		Current Revenue
480.90	602.30	806.40	954.80	1,177.70	1,609.60	1,773.90	2,173.80	2,709.20	..		Current Expenditure
550.50	665.70	826.00	1,027.20	1,457.40	1,836.50	1,967.50	2,258.10	2,663.30	..		Current Budget Balance
-69.60	-63.40	-19.60	-72.40	-279.70	-226.90	-193.60	-84.30	45.90	..		Capital Receipts
1.50	2.40	5.30	0.50	9.70	0.90	3.00	6.20	6.70	..		Capital Payments
111.50	134.00	205.40	200.50	252.00	317.20	368.60	400.60	397.20	..		

PORTUGAL	1970	1971	1972	1973	1974	1975	1976	1977	1978	1979	1980
FOREIGN TRADE (CUSTOMS BASIS)					*(Millions of current US dollars)*						
Value of Exports, fob	949	1,053	1,294	1,862	2,302	1,940	1,820	2,013	2,410	3,354	4,629
Nonfuel Primary Products	321	320	390	543	633	530	551	560	609	822	1,052
Fuels	22	23	22	22	65	40	39	34	44	3	255
Manufactures	606	709	882	1,297	1,604	1,370	1,231	1,420	1,757	2,529	3,322
Value of Imports, cif	1,590	1,824	2,227	3,073	4,641	3,863	4,316	4,964	5,229	6,509	9,293
Nonfuel Primary Products	427	496	649	934	1,434	1,263	1,352	1,544	1,430	1,845	2,247
Fuels	145	156	154	192	584	588	692	737	826	1,267	2,243
Manufactures	1,017	1,172	1,425	1,947	2,623	2,012	2,272	2,683	2,973	3,397	4,802
					(Index 1987 = 100)						
Terms of Trade	131.7	122.7	121.2	119.1	98.9	108.1	99.1	93.4	100.7	100.0	100.0
Export Prices, fob	28.8	31.6	36.7	49.0	59.6	64.9	61.3	62.3	72.4	86.2	104.2
Import Prices, cif	21.9	25.7	30.3	41.1	60.3	60.0	61.9	66.7	71.9	86.2	104.2
BALANCE OF PAYMENTS					*(Millions of current US dollars)*						
Exports of Goods & Services	1,349	1,817	2,268	3,091	3,657	2,998	2,628	3,472	3,944	5,333	6,846
Merchandise, fob	956	1,057	1,307	1,843	2,289	1,942	1,791	2,534	2,738	3,549	4,582
Nonfactor Services	310	691	840	1,073	1,136	941	788	868	1,117	1,648	2,088
Factor Services	83	69	121	175	232	115	49	70	88	136	176
Imports of Goods & Services	1,995	2,317	2,795	3,847	5,597	4,794	4,874	5,562	6,042	7,864	10,916
Merchandise, fob	1,448	1,695	2,041	2,753	4,284	3,544	3,960	4,528	4,783	6,183	8,611
Nonfactor Services	495	572	674	1,015	1,211	1,110	714	765	831	1,105	1,493
Factor Services	52	50	79	80	102	139	200	269	428	576	812
Long-Term Interest	60	37	34	34	34	44	52	94	184	363	529
Private Current Transfers, net	488	646	881	1,097	1,109	1,070	965	1,134	1,635	2,471	2,999
Workers' Remittances	523	678	908	1,140	1,144	1,103	907	1,173	1,673	2,454	2,928
Curr. A/C Bal before Off. Transf.	-158	146	354	341	-831	-726	-1,282	-957	-463	-60	-1,072
Net Official Transfers	0	0	..	..	..	-29	..	..	..	6	7
Curr. A/C Bal after Off. Transf.	-158	146	354	341	-831	-755	-1,282	-957	-463	-54	-1,064
Long-Term Capital, net	278	97	-104	-141	273	-93	60	69	696	676	703
Direct Investment	15	49	66	51	69	107	58	55	60	70	143
Long-Term Loans	-64	14	18	153	94	299	356	788	1,437	1,488	1,434
Disbursements	38	102	117	257	204	404	536	1,066	1,841	2,075	2,098
Repayments	102	88	100	104	110	106	181	279	404	587	664
Other Long-Term Capital	327	34	-188	-345	111	-499	-354	-773	-801	-883	-875
Other Capital, net	-88	97	106	128	-33	-197	188	553	98	-346	719
Change in Reserves	-32	-340	-356	-328	590	1,045	1,034	334	-331	-276	-357
Memo Item:					*(Portuguese Escudos per US dollar)*						
Conversion Factor (Annual Avg)	28.750	28.310	27.050	24.520	25.410	25.550	30.230	38.280	43.940	48.920	50.060
EXTERNAL DEBT (Total)	783	840	877	1,090	1,239	1,502	2,043	4,351	6,267	7,903	9,729
Long-Term Debt (by debtor)	783	840	877	1,090	1,239	1,502	2,043	3,051	4,684	6,253	7,334
Central Bank, incl. IMF credit	0	0	0	0	0	0	0	201	347	925	980	896
Central Government	223	214	236	295	284	242	281	368	819	1,299	1,716
Rest of General Government	4	4	3	2	1	0	0	0	0	0	0
Non-financial Public Enterprises	76	143	177	319	482	749	1,029	1,702	2,295	3,172	3,933
Priv. Sector, incl non-guaranteed	479	480	461	474	472	511	532	633	644	802	790
Short-Term Debt	0	0	0	0	0	0	0	1,300	1,583	1,650	2,395
Memo Items:					*(Millions of US dollars)*						
Int'l Reserves Excluding Gold	602	945	1,291	1,676	1,161	398	176	366	871	931	795
Gold Holdings (at market price)	963	1,148	1,745	3,091	5,192	3,887	3,729	3,977	5,002	11,331	13,068
SOCIAL INDICATORS											
Total Fertility Rate	2.8	2.8	2.7	2.7	2.6	2.5	2.6	2.4	2.2	2.1	2.2
Infant Mortality Rate	55.5	51.9	41.4	44.8	37.9	38.9	33.4	30.3	29.1	26.0	24.3
Life Expectancy at Birth	67.4	67.7	68.0	68.5	68.9	69.3	69.7	70.2	70.6	71.0	71.4
Urban Population, % of total	25.9	26.3	26.6	27.0	27.3	27.7	28.0	28.4	28.7	29.1	29.4
Food Prod. per capita (1987=100)	120.5	106.2	106.6	111.5	114.7	109.7	98.7	85.6	87.0	103.0	88.1
Labor Force, Agriculture (%)	31.8	31.0	30.2	29.5	28.8	28.1	27.6	27.1	26.6	26.2	25.8
Labor Force, Female (%)	24.8	26.2	27.4	28.6	29.8	30.9	31.9	33.0	33.9	34.8	35.7
Primary Schl. Enroll. Ratio	98.0	..	..	..	..	113.0	114.0	117.0	103.0	..	123.0
Primary Schl. Enroll. Ratio, Female	96.0	..	..	..	..	111.0	112.0	115.0	..	..	123.0
Secondary Schl. Enroll. Ratio	57.0	..	..	..	..	53.0	54.0	55.0	..	48.0	37.0

1981	1982	1983	1984	1985	1986	1987	1988	1989	1990 estimate	Notes	PORTUGAL
											FOREIGN TRADE (CUSTOMS BASIS)
				(Millions of current US dollars)							
4,180	4,171	4,602	5,208	5,685	7,160	9,167	10,990	12,798	16,416	..	Value of Exports, fob
921	870	906	1,049	1,038	1,236	1,623	2,016	2,332	2,676		Nonfuel Primary Products
298	163	231	186	236	217	149	264	363	487	..	Fuels
2,961	3,138	3,464	3,973	4,412	5,707	7,395	8,709	10,103	13,252		Manufactures
9,946	9,605	8,257	7,975	7,650	9,393	13,438	17,885	19,043	25,333		Value of Imports, cif
2,491	2,149	1,919	2,169	1,974	2,129	2,819	3,597	3,614	4,453		Nonfuel Primary Products
2,396	2,546	2,218	2,286	2,026	1,439	1,563	1,474	2,025	2,751		Fuels
5,058	4,911	4,120	3,520	3,650	5,825	9,055	12,813	13,404	18,129		Manufactures
				(Index 1987 = 100)							
88.8	82.5	78.2	80.4	84.9	95.9	100.0	106.9	105.4	..	..	Terms of Trade
93.4	81.2	75.8	76.0	76.8	81.7	100.0	106.9	113.2		..	Export Prices, fob
105.1	98.4	96.9	94.5	90.4	85.2	100.0	100.1	107.4		..	Import Prices, cif
				(Millions of current US dollars)							**BALANCE OF PAYMENTS**
6,377	5,894	6,940	7,137	7,966	10,029	12,913	14,910	17,350	22,798		Exports of Goods & Services
4,061	4,122	5,224	5,206	5,685	7,209	9,266	10,874	12,720	16,427		Merchandise, fob
2,109	1,614	1,543	1,732	2,000	2,516	3,226	3,552	3,903	4,842		Nonfactor Services
207	158	173	199	281	304	420	485	727	1,528		Factor Services
11,876	11,807	10,075	9,829	9,779	11,695	16,249	20,298	21,737	28,420		Imports of Goods & Services
9,121	8,984	7,624	7,233	7,142	8,844	12,847	16,392	17,585	23,007		Merchandise, fob
1,586	1,421	1,205	1,208	1,231	1,536	2,075	2,592	2,762	3,505		Nonfactor Services
1,170	1,402	1,246	1,388	1,407	1,316	1,327	1,314	1,390	1,908		Factor Services
870	973	905	1,091	1,153	1,217	1,259	1,167	1,042	1,055		Long-Term Interest
2,895	2,663	2,130	2,141	2,118	2,618	3,418	3,597	3,726	4,504		Private Current Transfers, net
2,838	2,602	2,118	2,152	2,091	2,544	3,254	3,378	3,562	4,271	..	Workers' Remittances
-2,605	-3,250	-1,004	-551	304	952	81	-1,790	-661	-1,119		Curr. A/C Bal before Off. Transf.
..	..	..	36	106	192	368	725	814	980		Net Official Transfers
-2,605	-3,250	-1,004	-514	410	1,144	449	-1,066	153	-139	..	Curr. A/C Bal after Off. Transf.
1,186	2,075	1,225	1,149	949	-549	-22	708	2,790	2,710	..	Long-Term Capital, net
155	136	123	186	232	239	456	842	1,653	1,984		Direct Investment
1,684	1,624	1,698	1,087	792	-227	-1,146	-362	1,054	-892		Long-Term Loans
2,576	2,588	2,869	2,711	2,702	2,393	2,529	2,959	3,524	2,517		Disbursements
892	964	1,172	1,624	1,911	2,620	3,675	3,320	2,470	3,409		Repayments
-653	315	-595	-124	-74	-561	668	228	83	1,618		Other Long-Term Capital
1,277	1,297	-803	-632	-451	-706	1,350	1,225	1,712	970	..	Other Capital, net
142	-122	582	-3	-909	111	-1,777	-867	-4,654	-3,542	..	Change in Reserves
				(Portuguese Escudos per US dollar)							**Memo Item:**
61.550	79.470	110.780	146.390	170.400	149.590	140.880	143.950	157.460	142.550	..	Conversion Factor (Annual Avg)
			(Millions of US dollars), outstanding at end of year								
11,577	13,598	14,516	14,870	16,633	16,642	18,303	17,125	18,079	20,413		**EXTERNAL DEBT (Total)**
8,242	9,759	11,094	11,855	14,006	15,213	16,139	14,522	15,129	15,180	..	Long-Term Debt (by debtor)
729	568	874	1,014	1,009	939	700	171	191	474	..	Central Bank, incl. IMF credit
2,215	2,919	3,589	3,971	4,747	5,305	6,059	6,248	8,276	8,630	..	Central Government
0	0	0	0	0	0	0	0	0	..	..	Rest of General Government
4,631	5,237	5,764	6,154	7,520	8,176	8,398	7,193	5,701	5,050	..	Non-financial Public Enterprises
667	1,036	867	716	730	792	981	911	962	1,025	..	Priv. Sector, incl non-guaranteed
3,335	3,839	3,422	3,015	2,627	1,429	2,164	2,603	2,950	5,233	..	Short-Term Debt
				(Millions of US dollars)							**Memo Items:**
534	447	385	516	1,395	1,456	3,327	5,127	9,953	14,485	..	Int'l Reserves Excluding Gold
8,800	10,093	7,796	6,257	6,614	7,880	9,712	6,593	6,436	6,094	..	Gold Holdings (at market price)
											SOCIAL INDICATORS
2.1	2.1	1.9	1.9	1.7	1.6	1.6	1.6	1.6	1.6	..	Total Fertility Rate
21.8	19.8	19.2	16.7	17.8	15.9	14.2	13.6	12.9	12.3	..	Infant Mortality Rate
71.8	72.2	72.6	73.0	73.4	73.7	74.1	74.4	74.7	74.9	..	Life Expectancy at Birth
29.8	30.2	30.5	30.9	31.3	31.8	32.2	32.7	33.1	33.6	..	Urban Population, % of total
79.4	97.8	81.3	91.7	92.7	93.4	100.0	79.2	101.5	105.5	..	Food Prod. per capita (1987=100)
..	..	..	..	..	..	..	..	..	..	..	Labor Force, Agriculture (%)
35.8	35.9	36.1	36.2	36.3	36.4	36.5	36.5	36.6	36.7	..	Labor Force, Female (%)
..	121.0	119.0	126.0	124.0	126.0	..	..	111.0	..	..	Primary Schl. Enroll. Ratio
..	122.0	119.0	123.0	121.0	121.0	..	..	108.0	..	..	Primary Schl. Enroll. Ratio, Female
..	43.0	47.0	52.0	56.0	63.0	..	..	53.0	..		Secondary Schl. Enroll. Ratio

ROMANIA	1970	1971	1972	1973	1974	1975	1976	1977	1978	1979	1980
CURRENT GNP PER CAPITA (US $)	..	..	..	..	..	..	..	..	..	..	..
POPULATION (thousands)	20,253	20,470	20,663	20,828	21,029	21,245	21,446	21,658	21,855	22,048	22,201

USE AND ORIGIN OF RESOURCES *(Billions of current Romanian Lei)*

	1970	1971	1972	1973	1974	1975	1976	1977	1978	1979	1980
Gross National Product (GNP)	..	..	..	..	..	437.0	488.6	510.4	549.2	594.1	602.9
Net Factor Income from Abroad	..	..	..	..	..	0.0	-2.3	-2.5	-2.9	-4.5	-14.0
GDP at Market Prices	..	..	..	..	..	437.0	490.9	512.9	552.1	598.6	616.9
Resource Balance	..	..	..	..	..	..	..	..	..	..	-29.6
Exports of Goods & NFServices	..	..	..	..	..	..	..	..	..	..	217.6
Imports of Goods & NFServices	..	..	..	..	..	..	..	..	..	..	247.1
Domestic Absorption	..	..	..	..	..	440.7	490.3	507.6	561.0	606.8	646.5
Private Consumption, etc.	..	..	..	..	..	..	..	..	..	..	369.7
General Gov't Consumption	..	..	..	..	..	..	..	..	..	..	31.1
Gross Domestic Investment	..	..	..	..	..	176.6	203.1	204.1	224.7	236.8	245.7
Fixed Investment	..	..	..	..	..	145.8	153.9	171.2	198.5	206.8	212.8
Indirect Taxes, net	..	..	..	..	..	..	..	..	..	..	..
GDP at factor cost	..	..	..	..	..	..	..	..	..	..	..
Agriculture	..	..	..	..	..	63.7	80.3	75.0	76.1	80.9	78.0
Industry	..	..	..	..	..	266.0	292.6	314.2	339.7	364.6	372.7
Manufacturing	..	..	..	..	..	..	..	..	..	..	..
Services, etc.	..	..	..	..	..	107.3	118.0	123.7	136.3	153.1	166.2
Gross Domestic Saving	..	..	..	..	..	172.9	203.7	209.4	215.8	228.6	216.1
Gross National Saving	..	..	..	..	..	..	..	..	..	..	..

(Billions of 1987 Romanian Lei)

	1970	1971	1972	1973	1974	1975	1976	1977	1978	1979	1980
Gross National Product	..	..	..	..	..	495.19	548.94	589.95	636.89	677.71	689.65
GDP at Market Prices	..	..	..	..	..	495.15	551.65	592.94	640.41	682.96	705.61
Resource Balance	..	..	..	..	..	..	..	..	..	..	-244.72
Exports of Goods & NFServices	..	..	..	..	..	..	..	..	..	..	208.99
Imports of Goods & NFServices	..	..	..	..	..	..	..	..	..	..	453.71
Domestic Absorption	..	..	..	..	..	..	..	..	..	..	950.33
Private Consumption, etc.	..	..	..	..	..	..	..	..	..	..	..
General Gov't Consumption	..	..	..	..	..	..	..	..	..	..	..
Gross Domestic Investment	..	..	..	..	..	209.71	254.07	257.60	299.26	294.20	289.14
Fixed Investment	..	..	..	..	..	..	..	..	..	..	249.40
GDP at factor cost	..	..	..	..	..	..	..	..	..	..	..
Agriculture	..	..	..	..	..	..	..	142.51	149.12	135.90	109.73
Industry	..	..	..	..	..	..	..	323.06	350.65	362.14	419.68
Manufacturing	..	..	..	..	..	..	..	..	..	..	..
Services, etc.	..	..	..	..	..	..	..	127.37	140.64	184.93	176.20

Memo Items:

	1970	1971	1972	1973	1974	1975	1976	1977	1978	1979	1980
Capacity to Import	..	..	..	..	..	..	..	..	..	..	399.43
Terms of Trade Adjustment	..	..	..	..	..	..	..	..	..	..	190.44
Gross Domestic Income	..	..	..	..	..	..	..	..	..	..	896.04
Gross National Income	..	..	..	..	..	..	..	..	..	..	880.09

DOMESTIC PRICES/DEFLATORS *(Index 1987 = 100)*

	1970	1971	1972	1973	1974	1975	1976	1977	1978	1979	1980
Overall (GDP)	..	..	..	..	..	88.3	89.0	86.5	86.2	87.6	87.4
Domestic Absorption	..	..	..	..	..	..	..	..	..	..	68.0
Agriculture	..	..	..	..	..	..	..	52.6	51.0	59.5	71.1
Industry	..	..	..	..	..	..	..	97.3	96.9	100.7	88.8
Manufacturing	..	..	..	..	..	..	..	..	..	..	..
Consumer Price Index	..	..	..	..	..	..	..	..	..	..	..

MANUFACTURING ACTIVITY

	1970	1971	1972	1973	1974	1975	1976	1977	1978	1979	1980
Employment (1987=100)	..	..	..	..	..	..	..	..	..	..	..
Real Earnings per Empl. (1987=100)	..	..	..	..	..	..	..	..	..	..	..
Real Output per Empl. (1987=100)	..	..	..	..	..	..	..	..	..	..	..
Earnings as % of Value Added	..	..	..	..	..	..	..	..	..	..	..

MONETARY HOLDINGS *(Billions of current Romanian Lei)*

	1970	1971	1972	1973	1974	1975	1976	1977	1978	1979	1980
Money Supply, Broadly Defined	..	..	..	80.39	101.61	113.30	131.94	149.98	175.75	193.60	218.31
Money	..	..	..	44.67	60.65	65.67	75.92	84.23	94.54	101.80	114.50
Currency Outside Banks	..	..	..	17.57	18.25	21.09	23.63	27.03	28.23	34.15	39.33
Demand Deposits	..	..	..	27.10	42.40	44.58	52.29	57.20	66.31	67.65	75.17
Quasi-Money	..	..	..	35.72	40.96	47.63	56.02	65.74	81.20	91.80	103.81

(Billions of current Romanian Lei)

	1970	1971	1972	1973	1974	1975	1976	1977	1978	1979	1980
GOVERNMENT DEFICIT (-) OR SURPLUS	1.24	3.16	6.58	6.90	1.67	1.09	2.77	0.89	0.91	1.22	3.02
Current Revenue	116.01	119.05	130.27	152.02	186.21	216.87	230.29	260.24	277.82	317.52	279.34
Current Expenditure	..	..	..	..	..	..	..	..	..	..	183.78
Current Budget Balance	..	..	..	..	..	..	..	..	..	..	95.56
Capital Receipts	..	..	..	..	..	..	..	..	..	..	..
Capital Payments	..	..	..	..	..	..	..	..	..	..	92.54

1981	1982	1983	1984	1985	1986	1987	1988	1989	1990 estimate	Notes	ROMANIA
..	..	..	..	..	..	..	..	1,720	1,620	A	**CURRENT GNP PER CAPITA (US $)**
22,353	22,478	22,553	22,625	22,725	22,824	22,940	23,054	23,152	23,200	..	**POPULATION (thousands)**
											USE AND ORIGIN OF RESOURCES
				(Billions of current Romanian Lei)							
608.4	714.6	756.5	802.1	807.2	829.8	839.4	854.2	799.2	788.9	..	Gross National Product (GNP)
-15.3	-12.8	-12.2	-14.0	-10.2	-8.8	-5.7	-2.8	1.2	-55.1	..	Net Factor Income from Abroad
623.7	727.4	768.7	816.1	817.4	838.6	845.1	857.0	798.0	844.0	..	GDP at Market Prices
2.8	28.4	32.1	50.6	34.6	31.5	35.8	59.0	36.5	-76.6	..	Resource Balance
201.9	185.8	210.2	287.0	187.6	168.9	164.3	175.0	169.1	146.2	..	Exports of Goods & NF Services
199.2	157.4	178.1	236.4	153.0	137.4	128.5	116.0	132.6	222.8	..	Imports of Goods & NF Services
620.9	699.0	736.6	765.5	782.8	807.1	809.4	798.0	761.5	920.6	..	Domestic Absorption
362.5	423.7	444.1	456.1	480.9	488.4	512.7	523.7	515.4	591.7	..	Private Consumption, etc.
32.0	30.0	30.9	30.6	32.0	30.3	27.8	31.0	32.9	39.6	..	General Gov't Consumption
226.4	245.3	261.6	278.8	269.9	288.4	268.9	243.3	213.2	289.3	..	Gross Domestic Investment
209.3	216.4	230.7	244.7	246.3	249.0	245.5	240.2	236.4	168.4	..	Fixed Investment
..										..	Indirect Taxes, net
..	..	..	..	..	..	..	..	..	..	B	GDP at factor cost
91.6	125.7	107.9	110.7	114.3	106.8	103.4	115.6	110.9	152.0	..	Agriculture
355.9	412.6	463.6	498.6	490.9	520.0	522.6	520.3	472.5	454.9	..	Industry
										..	Manufacturing
176.2	189.1	197.2	206.8	212.2	211.8	219.1	221.1	214.6	237.1	..	Services, etc.
229.2	273.7	293.7	329.4	304.5	319.9	304.6	302.3	249.7	212.7	..	Gross Domestic Saving
..										..	Gross National Saving
				(Billions of 1987 Romanian Lei)							
689.02	721.01	765.61	811.05	814.13	832.39	839.40	839.89	794.77	732.57	..	Gross National Product
706.29	733.86	777.90	825.12	824.36	841.29	845.10	842.64	793.58	729.50	..	GDP at Market Prices
-182.31	-97.56	-8.99	-46.31	19.31	30.69	35.75	-36.15	-124.70	-229.51	..	Resource Balance
194.04	159.46	148.89	218.05	166.18	153.69	164.26	198.84	189.24	102.78	..	Exports of Goods & NF Services
376.35	257.02	157.88	264.36	146.87	123.00	128.51	234.99	313.93	332.29	..	Imports of Goods & NF Services
888.61	831.42	786.89	871.43	805.04	810.60	809.35	878.79	918.27	959.00	..	Domestic Absorption
..								..	..	..	Private Consumption, etc.
..								..	..	..	General Gov't Consumption
250.42	254.31	262.31	274.43	269.14	286.79	268.90	244.66	237.48	231.60	..	Gross Domestic Investment
231.69	222.89	228.24	242.16	246.28	248.99	245.50	240.34	236.50	145.91	..	Fixed Investment
..	..	..	..	..	..	..	..	..	..	B	GDP at factor cost
109.03	112.83	111.70	121.55	123.10	114.51	103.40	112.83	106.07	119.30	..	Agriculture
411.80	433.30	475.42	500.08	492.42	519.11	522.60	507.40	474.07	383.08	..	Industry
										..	Manufacturing
185.47	187.73	190.78	203.50	208.84	207.66	219.10	222.41	213.44	227.12	..	Services, etc.
											Memo Items:
381.57	303.33	186.35	320.95	180.05	151.23	164.26	354.61	400.27	218.07	..	Capacity to Import
187.53	143.87	37.46	102.90	13.87	-2.47	0.00	155.77	211.03	115.29	..	Terms of Trade Adjustment
893.82	877.73	815.36	928.02	838.23	838.82	845.10	998.41	1,004.61	844.78	..	Gross Domestic Income
876.55	864.88	803.07	913.95	828.00	829.92	839.40	995.66	1,005.80	847.86	..	Gross National Income
											DOMESTIC PRICES/DEFLATORS
				(Index 1987 = 100)							
88.3	99.1	98.8	98.9	99.2	99.7	100.0	101.7	100.6	115.7	..	Overall (GDP)
69.9	84.1	93.6	87.8	97.2	99.6	100.0	90.8	82.9	96.0	..	Domestic Absorption
84.0	111.4	96.6	91.1	92.9	93.3	100.0	102.5	104.6	127.4	..	Agriculture
86.4	95.2	97.5	99.7	99.7	100.2	100.0	102.5	99.7	118.7	..	Industry
..				..		..				..	Manufacturing
..										..	Consumer Price Index
											MANUFACTURING ACTIVITY
..		..		..		..		..		..	Employment (1987=100)
..		..		..		..		..		..	Real Earnings per Empl. (1987=100)
..		..		..		..		..		..	Real Output per Empl. (1987=100)
..		..		..		..		..		..	Earnings as % of Value Added
											MONETARY HOLDINGS
				(Billions of current Romanian Lei)							
253.23	288.81	286.84	304.85	331.42	351.17	..	..	..	..	..	Money Supply, Broadly Defined
135.54	166.95	156.27	162.34	165.79	169.53	171.25	199.38	204.45	232.98	..	Money
41.29	44.68	44.94	49.05	54.83	60.03	60.58	64.96	74.74	92.37	..	Currency Outside Banks
94.26	122.27	111.33	113.29	110.96	109.50	110.67	134.42	129.72	140.61	..	Demand Deposits
117.69	121.86	130.57	142.50	165.62	181.64	..	..	..	..	..	Quasi-Money
				(Billions of current Romanian Lei)							
10.36	21.85	24.74	52.92	20.88	36.01	60.06	49.99	65.78	8.04	E	**GOVERNMENT DEFICIT (-) OR SURPLUS**
260.40	255.45	236.76	288.78	360.88	392.29	403.85	364.08	386.33	295.30	..	Current Revenue
155.01	137.72	119.12	131.09	215.51	206.25	210.28	173.06	183.47	239.65	..	Current Expenditure
105.39	117.73	117.64	157.69	145.37	186.04	193.57	191.02	202.86	55.71	..	Current Budget Balance
..						..		..	2.55	..	Capital Receipts
95.03	95.88	92.90	104.77	124.49	150.03	133.51	141.03	137.08	50.22	..	Capital Payments

ROMANIA	1970	1971	1972	1973	1974	1975	1976	1977	1978	1979	1980
FOREIGN TRADE (CUSTOMS BASIS)				*(Millions of current US dollars)*							
Value of Exports, fob	..	..	..	..	..	..	..	..	..	..	..
Nonfuel Primary Products	..	..	..	..	..	..	..	..	..	..	..
Fuels	..	..	..	..	..	..	..	..	..	..	..
Manufactures	..	..	..	..	..	..	..	..	..	..	..
Value of Imports, cif	..	..	..	..	..	..	..	..	..	..	..
Nonfuel Primary Products	..	..	..	..	..	..	..	..	..	..	..
Fuels	..	..	..	..	..	..	..	..	..	..	..
Manufactures	..	..	..	..	..	..	..	..	..	..	..
				(Index 1987 = 100)							
Terms of Trade	..	..	..	..	..	..	..	..	..	..	..
Export Prices, fob	..	..	..	..	..	..	..	..	..	..	..
Import Prices, cif	..	..	..	..	..	..	..	..	..	..	..
BALANCE OF PAYMENTS				*(Millions of current US dollars)*							
Exports of Goods & Services	..	..	..	4,021	5,295	5,837	6,679	7,407	8,784	10,210	12,160
Merchandise, fob	..	2,102	2,599	3,667	4,858	5,341	6,134	6,859	8,022	9,303	11,024
Nonfactor Services	..	280	265	338	419	471	508	498	706	830	1,063
Factor Services	..	..	..	16	18	25	37	50	56	77	73
Imports of Goods & Services	..	..	..	3,872	5,654	5,972	6,695	7,711	9,543	11,863	14,580
Merchandise, fob	..	2,102	2,616	3,425	5,049	5,342	6,087	7,002	8,628	10,519	12,685
Nonfactor Services	..	303	295	373	518	516	453	527	691	909	1,045
Factor Services	..	..	..	74	87	114	155	182	224	435	850
Long-Term Interest	0	0	0	0	0	0	2	17	28	51	332
Private Current Transfers, net	..	..	..	..	..	..	..	..	..	..	..
Workers' Remittances	..	..	..	..	..	..	..	..	..	..	..
Curr. A/C Bal before Off. Transf.	..	-23	-47	149	-359	-135	-16	-304	-759	-1,653	-2,420
Net Official Transfers	..	..	..	..	..	..	..	..	..	..	..
Curr. A/C Bal after Off. Transf.	..	-23	-47	149	-359	-135	-16	-304	-759	-1,653	-2,420
Long-Term Capital, net	..	5	-19	-27	617	312	-152	-59	242	947	1,773
Direct Investment	..	..	..	..	..	..	..	..	..	..	..
Long-Term Loans	0	0	0	0	0	19	124	145	166	1,814	1,973
Disbursements	0	0	0	0	0	19	124	145	166	1,821	2,797
Repayments	0	0	0	0	0	0	0	0	1	7	824
Other Long-Term Capital	..	5	-19	-27	617	293	-276	-204	76	-867	-200
Other Capital, net	..	-20	67	-248	-251	-209	48	29	667	844	401
Change in Reserves	..	38	-1	126	-7	32	120	334	-150	-138	246
Memo Item:				*(Romanian Lei per US dollar)*							
Conversion Factor (Annual Avg)	..	..	..	..	..	..	..	..	..	..	..
EXTERNAL DEBT (Total)				*(Millions of US dollars), outstanding at end of year*							
EXTERNAL DEBT (Total)	0.00	0.00	0.00	57.30	58.20	121.50	419.40	616.10	786.50	3,583.40	9,762.20
Long-Term Debt (by debtor)	0.00	0.00	0.00	57.30	58.20	121.50	419.40	616.10	786.50	3,583.40	7,459.20
Central Bank, incl. IMF credit	0.00	0.00	0.00	57.30	58.20	111.80	372.90	561.10	726.90	849.40	2,323.70
Central Government	0.00	0.00	0.00	0.00	0.00	9.70	46.50	55.00	59.60	2,734.00	5,135.50
Rest of General Government	..	..	..	..	..	..	..	..	..	..	..
Non-financial Public Enterprises	..	..	..	..	..	..	..	..	..	..	..
Priv. Sector, incl non-guaranteed	..	..	..	..	..	..	..	..	..	..	..
Short-Term Debt	0.00	0.00	0.00	0.00	0.00	0.00	0.00	0.00	0.00	0.00	2,303.00
Memo Items:				*(Millions of US dollars)*							
Int'l Reserves Excluding Gold	..	..	..	215.2	240.6	539.5	561.6	256.3	376.0	524.8	323.0
Gold Holdings (at market price)	..	..	..	255.4	456.4	364.2	370.4	504.3	756.4	1,809.9	2,188.2
SOCIAL INDICATORS											
Total Fertility Rate	2.9	2.7	2.5	2.4	2.7	2.6	2.6	2.6	2.5	2.5	2.4
Infant Mortality Rate	49.4	42.4	40.0	38.1	34.9	34.6	31.3	31.1	30.2	31.6	29.3
Life Expectancy at Birth	68.8	68.9	69.0	69.2	69.3	69.5	69.6	69.8	69.8	69.7	69.7
Urban Population, % of total	41.8	42.7	43.6	44.4	45.3	46.2	46.7	47.2	47.7	48.2	48.7
Food Prod. per capita (1987=100)	73.2	86.0	95.8	90.9	92.8	92.5	109.9	108.9	106.7	115.2	109.0
Labor Force, Agriculture (%)	48.7	46.9	45.1	43.2	41.4	39.6	37.8	36.0	34.2	32.4	30.5
Labor Force, Female (%)	43.6	43.8	44.1	44.3	44.5	44.8	45.0	45.3	45.6	45.8	46.1
Primary Schl. Enroll. Ratio	112.0	..	..	..	..	107.0	103.0	99.0	97.0	98.0	102.0
Primary Schl. Enroll. Ratio, Female	113.0	..	..	..	..	107.0	102.0	99.0	97.0	98.0	101.0
Secondary Schl. Enroll. Ratio	44.0	..	..	..	..	65.0	74.0	84.0	87.0	83.0	71.0

1981	1982	1983	1984	1985	1986	1987	1988	1989	1990 est.	Notes	ROMANIA
				(Millions of current US dollars)							**FOREIGN TRADE (CUSTOMS BASIS)**
..	..	..	..	..	..	..	..	..	..	..	Value of Exports, fob
..	..	..	..	..	..	..	..	..	..	..	Nonfuel Primary Products
..	..	..	..	..	..	..	..	..	..	..	Fuels
..	..	..	..	..	..	..	..	..	..	..	Manufactures
									..	..	Value of Imports, cif
..	..	..	..	..	..	..	..	..	..	..	Nonfuel Primary Products
..	..	..	..	..	..	..	..	..	..	..	Fuels
..	..	..	..	..	..	..	..	..	..	..	Manufactures
				(Index 1987 = 100)							
											Terms of Trade
..	..	..	..	..	..	..	..	..	..	..	Export Prices, fob
..	..	..	..	..	..	..	..	..	..	..	Import Prices, cif
..	..	..	..								
				(Millions of current US dollars)							**BALANCE OF PAYMENTS**
13,575	12,503	12,336	13,603	11,036	10,564	11,399	12,415	11,502	6,693	..	Exports of Goods & Services
12,367	11,559	11,512	12,646	10,174	9,763	10,491	11,392	10,487	5,770	..	Merchandise, fob
1,095	825	727	840	769	696	793	865	844	749	..	Nonfactor Services
113	119	97	117	93	105	115	158	171	174	..	Factor Services
14,408	11,463	11,176	11,884	9,655	9,169	9,356	8,493	8,988	9,947	..	Imports of Goods & Services
12,264	9,745	9,643	10,334	8,402	8,083	8,313	7,642	8,437	9,114	..	Merchandise, fob
1,014	748	726	774	524	424	515	480	450	819	..	Nonfactor Services
1,130	970	807	776	729	662	528	371	101	14	..	Factor Services
513	575	510	500	540	542	504	409	105	..	..	Long-Term Interest
..	..	..	..	..	..	..	..	..	..	..	Private Current Transfers, net
..	..	..	..	..	..	..	..	..	..	..	Workers' Remittances
-833	1,040	1,160	1,719	1,381	1,395	2,043	3,922	2,514	-3,254	..	Curr. A/C Bal before Off. Transf.
..	..	..	..	..	..	..	..	..	..	..	Net Official Transfers
-833	1,040	1,160	1,719	1,381	1,395	2,043	3,922	2,514	-3,254	..	Curr. A/C Bal after Off. Transf.
852	460	-192	-1,183	-1,195	-1,045	-1,512	-3,619	-1,707	-18	..	Long-Term Capital, net
									-18	..	Direct Investment
1,034	788	196	-1,134	-707	-339	-1,453	-3,388	-1,620	19	..	Long-Term Loans
2,156	2,885	1,345	215	509	745	136	52	26	19	..	Disbursements
1,122	2,097	1,149	1,348	1,216	1,084	1,589	3,440	1,646	..	..	Repayments
-182	-328	-388	-49	-488	-706	-59	-231	-87	-19	..	Other Long-Term Capital
-257	-1,448	-1,346	-408	-503	262	218	-925	304	1,628	..	Other Capital, net
238	-52	378	-128	317	-612	-749	622	-1,111	1,644	..	Change in Reserves
				(Romanian Lei per US dollar)							**Memo Item:**
..	..	..	..	..	..	22.200	21.200	19.300	22.430	..	Conversion Factor (Annual Avg)
				(Millions of US dollars), outstanding at end of year							**EXTERNAL DEBT (Total)**
10,446.80	10,003.10	9,128.50	7,757.60	7,008.00	6,983.30	6,580.00	2,523.90	500.00	369.00	..	Long-Term Debt (by debtor)
8,660.80	8,659.10	8,532.50	7,191.60	6,465.00	6,366.30	5,850.00	1,823.90	0.00	19.00	..	Central Bank, incl. IMF credit
3,358.20	4,166.40	4,399.60	3,639.60	3,429.20	3,598.40	3,417.60	1,331.20	0.00	..	..	Central Government
5,302.60	4,492.70	4,132.90	3,552.00	3,035.80	2,767.90	2,432.40	492.70	0.00	19.00	..	Rest of General Government
..	..	..	..	..	..	..	..	..	..	..	Non-financial Public Enterprises
..	..	..	..	..	..	..	..	..	..	..	Priv. Sector, incl non-guaranteed
1,786.00	1,344.00	596.00	566.00	543.00	617.00	730.00	700.00	500.00	350.00	..	Short-Term Debt
				(Millions of US dollars)							**Memo Items:**
403.5	450.0	525.2	709.3	199.0	582.1	1,402.0	780.0	1,858.8	524.0	..	Int'l Reserves Excluding Gold
1,427.4	1,623.4	1,381.0	1,150.3	1,248.5	1,269.3	660.3	594.5	871.8	850.1	..	Gold Holdings (at market price)
											SOCIAL INDICATORS
2.4	2.2	2.1	2.3	2.3	2.4	2.3	2.3	2.2	2.2	..	Total Fertility Rate
28.5	28.0	23.9	23.4	25.6	25.6	25.0	24.5	23.9	23.4	..	Infant Mortality Rate
69.7	69.6	69.6	69.5	69.4	69.3	69.2	69.3	69.5	69.6	..	Life Expectancy at Birth
49.1	49.4	49.8	50.1	50.5	50.9	51.4	51.8	52.3	52.7	..	Urban Population, % of total
105.6	114.3	114.5	126.4	116.9	114.9	100.0	103.5	102.7	98.0	..	Food Prod. per capita (1987=100)
..	..	..	..	..	..	..	..	..	..	..	Labor Force, Agriculture (%)
46.1	46.1	46.1	46.2	46.2	46.2	46.3	46.4	46.4	46.5	..	Labor Force, Female (%)
..	..	99.0	98.0	98.0	97.0	97.0	96.0	95.0	..	..	Primary Schl. Enroll. Ratio
..	100.0	99.0	98.0	98.0	..	97.0	96.0	95.0	..	..	Primary Schl. Enroll. Ratio, Female
..	..	72.0	73.0	75.0	74.0	79.0	85.0	88.0	..	..	Secondary Schl. Enroll. Ratio

RWANDA	1970	1971	1972	1973	1974	1975	1976	1977	1978	1979	1980
CURRENT GNP PER CAPITA (US $)	60	60	60	70	70	90	120	160	180	210	240
POPULATION (thousands)	3,695	3,823	3,957	4,096	4,238	4,384	4,528	4,677	4,833	4,994	5,163
USE AND ORIGIN OF RESOURCES	*(Billions of current Rwanda Francs)*										
Gross National Product (GNP)	22.03	22.38	22.78	24.49	28.48	52.76	61.84	71.82	80.57	96.20	108.11
Net Factor Income from Abroad	0.04	0.15	0.09	0.09	-0.20	-0.01	-0.03	0.19	-0.48	0.03	0.12
GDP at Market Prices	21.99	22.23	22.70	24.40	28.68	52.77	61.87	71.63	81.05	96.17	107.99
Resource Balance	-0.82	-1.48	-1.81	-0.45	-2.63	-4.50	-2.98	-2.43	-7.31	-1.64	-12.90
Exports of Goods & NFServices	2.53	2.27	1.88	2.83	3.49	4.84	9.02	10.22	11.98	20.24	15.59
Imports of Goods & NFServices	3.35	3.75	3.69	3.28	6.12	9.34	12.00	12.65	19.29	21.88	28.49
Domestic Absorption	22.81	23.71	24.51	24.85	31.31	57.27	64.85	74.06	88.36	97.81	120.89
Private Consumption, etc.	19.35	19.48	19.92	19.77	24.86	41.24	45.97	50.86	62.10	73.62	89.97
General Gov't Consumption	1.91	2.20	2.42	2.78	3.45	8.78	10.33	12.41	12.80	12.62	13.49
Gross Domestic Investment	1.55	2.03	2.17	2.30	3.00	7.25	8.55	10.79	13.46	11.57	17.43
Fixed Investment	1.58	2.01	2.16	..	..	6.96	7.99	9.14	11.32	14.27	13.19
Indirect Taxes, net	1.52	1.29	1.39	1.62	2.24	3.25	5.61	6.44	5.95	8.24	8.26
GDP at factor cost	20.47	20.94	21.31	22.78	26.44	49.52	56.26	65.19	75.10	87.93	99.73
Agriculture	13.55	13.60	13.52	14.89	16.96	25.97	30.45	33.28	34.38	47.16	49.51
Industry	1.89	1.93	2.14	2.13	2.64	10.01	11.69	15.19	17.93	18.02	23.27
Manufacturing	0.79	0.83	0.93	1.00	1.25	6.48	7.60	10.20	12.64	12.30	16.48
Services, etc.	6.55	6.70	7.04	7.38	9.08	16.79	19.73	23.16	28.74	30.99	35.21
Gross Domestic Saving	0.73	0.55	0.36	1.85	0.37	2.75	5.57	8.36	6.15	9.93	4.53
Gross National Saving	0.46	0.54	0.16	1.84	-0.27	2.47	5.35	8.30	5.78	10.51	4.36
	(Billions of 1987 Rwanda Francs)										
Gross National Product	88.18	89.67	89.64	92.71	92.48	95.66	102.29	107.74	116.56	128.99	142.31
GDP at Market Prices	88.02	89.08	89.32	92.39	93.14	95.68	102.35	107.45	117.28	128.96	142.17
Resource Balance	-3.52	-5.47	-6.22	-2.36	-7.70	-7.16	-5.27	-8.23	-9.51	-7.29	-11.79
Exports of Goods & NFServices	6.83	6.14	4.99	7.23	7.64	5.92	10.06	6.46	9.28	12.56	11.69
Imports of Goods & NFServices	10.36	11.61	11.21	9.59	15.35	13.08	15.33	14.69	18.78	19.85	23.48
Domestic Absorption	91.54	94.55	95.54	94.75	100.84	102.84	107.61	115.68	126.79	136.25	153.96
Private Consumption, etc.	80.64	81.31	81.41	79.62	84.42	79.98	83.05	88.94	101.62	115.25	128.83
General Gov't Consumption	6.67	7.70	8.31	9.19	9.78	13.90	14.92	15.65	14.34	12.21	12.18
Gross Domestic Investment	4.23	5.55	5.82	5.94	6.64	8.96	9.64	11.09	10.82	8.79	12.94
Fixed Investment	..	..	..	..	..	..	9.01	9.37	9.05	11.24	9.42
GDP at factor cost	..	..	..	86.42	86.02	89.97	93.25	97.96	108.80	118.10	131.46
Agriculture	36.96	37.94	35.99	37.70	44.47	41.91	53.93	54.34	55.83	67.86	66.79
Industry	..	..	..	..	..	..	22.02	24.13	25.50	25.96	32.58
Manufacturing	11.69	12.01	12.35	12.84	13.14	13.42	13.79	15.30	16.22	16.08	20.93
Services, etc.	..	..	..	..	..	..	26.39	28.98	35.95	35.15	42.80
Memo Items:											
Capacity to Import	7.82	7.03	5.71	8.28	8.75	6.78	11.52	11.87	11.67	18.36	12.85
Terms of Trade Adjustment	0.99	0.89	0.72	1.05	1.11	0.86	1.46	5.41	2.39	5.80	1.16
Gross Domestic Income	89.01	89.97	90.04	93.43	94.24	96.54	103.81	112.86	119.67	134.76	143.32
Gross National Income	89.17	90.55	90.37	93.76	93.58	96.51	103.75	113.16	118.94	134.79	143.47
DOMESTIC PRICES/DEFLATORS	*(Index 1987 = 100)*										
Overall (GDP)	25.0	25.0	25.4	26.4	30.8	55.2	60.5	66.7	69.1	74.6	76.0
Domestic Absorption	24.9	25.1	25.7	26.2	31.0	55.7	60.3	64.0	69.7	71.8	78.5
Agriculture	36.7	35.8	37.6	39.5	38.1	62.0	56.5	61.2	61.6	69.5	74.1
Industry	..	..	..	..	..	..	53.1	63.0	70.3	69.4	71.4
Manufacturing	6.8	6.9	7.5	7.8	9.5	48.3	55.1	66.7	77.9	76.5	78.7
Consumer Price Index	21.4	21.5	22.2	24.3	31.8	41.4	44.4	50.5	57.2	66.1	70.9
MANUFACTURING ACTIVITY											
Employment (1987=100)	..	..	..	..	..	..	..	..	..	..	..
Real Earnings per Empl. (1987=100)	..	..	..	..	..	..	..	..	..	..	..
Real Output per Empl. (1987=100)	..	..	..	..	..	..	..	..	..	..	..
Earnings as % of Value Added	22.0	27.9	34.2	43.7	24.5	..	..	6.1	6.6	8.7	..
MONETARY HOLDINGS	*(Millions of current Rwanda Francs)*										
Money Supply, Broadly Defined	2,568	2,921	2,973	4,029	5,350	5,997	8,047	10,138	11,181	14,086	15,226
Money	2,165	2,472	2,520	3,565	4,288	4,850	6,516	8,035	8,961	11,255	12,026
Currency Outside Banks	1,238	1,409	1,445	2,003	2,553	2,722	3,070	3,948	4,443	5,242	5,689
Demand Deposits	927	1,063	1,075	1,563	1,735	2,129	3,446	4,087	4,517	6,012	6,337
Quasi-Money	404	449	453	464	1,063	1,147	1,530	2,104	2,220	2,831	3,200
	(Millions of current Rwanda Francs)										
GOVERNMENT DEFICIT (-) OR SURPLUS	..	..	..	-653	-728	-727	-1,225	-1,026	-1,291	-1,618	-1,875
Current Revenue	..	..	..	2,419	3,369	5,010	6,750	8,703	9,180	12,478	13,805
Current Expenditure	..	..	..	2,679	3,345	4,093	4,777	6,320	6,692	8,443	10,059
Current Budget Balance	..	..	..	-260	24	917	1,973	2,383	2,488	4,035	3,746
Capital Receipts	..	..	..	..	..	..	..	..	..	..	..
Capital Payments	..	..	..	393	752	1,644	3,198	3,409	3,779	5,653	5,621

1981	1982	1983	1984	1985	1986	1987	1988	1989	1990 estimate	Notes	RWANDA
260	260	270	260	270	300	310	330	320	310	..	**CURRENT GNP PER CAPITA (US $)**
5,340	5,526	5,719	5,912	6,102	6,292	6,486	6,685	6,895	7,118	..	**POPULATION (thousands)**
											USE AND ORIGIN OF RESOURCES
				(Billions of current Rwanda Francs)							
123.41	130.94	141.60	158.62	173.13	169.60	171.13	176.85	173.41	174.96	..	Gross National Product (GNP)
0.77	-0.02	-0.59	-0.49	-0.56	-0.74	-0.78	-1.08	-0.79	-1.19		Net Factor Income from Abroad
122.64	130.96	142.19	159.11	173.70	170.34	171.91	177.93	174.20	176.15	..	GDP at Market Prices
-14.63	-16.50	-13.05	-11.19	-15.82	-12.90	-16.00	-16.43	-16.28	-15.32	..	Resource Balance
12.05	15.13	16.47	20.10	18.73	21.44	16.94	16.09	15.10	16.27	..	Exports of Goods & NF Services
26.68	31.63	29.52	31.29	34.54	34.33	32.94	32.53	31.38	31.59	..	Imports of Goods & NF Services
137.27	147.46	155.24	170.30	189.51	183.23	187.91	194.36	190.48	191.47	..	Domestic Absorption
96.40	107.27	119.29	128.91	139.87	135.84	138.72	143.58	138.24	137.13	..	Private Consumption, etc.
24.56	16.90	16.71	16.24	19.58	20.35	22.33	22.88	25.04	32.40	..	General Gov't Consumption
16.31	23.28	19.24	25.15	30.07	27.04	26.85	27.90	27.20	21.94	..	Gross Domestic Investment
15.98	18.78	20.74	24.66	27.05	26.80	26.92	26.97	27.79	24.14	..	Fixed Investment
7.81	9.24	9.46	11.70	13.03	14.74	16.61	15.20	15.66	..		Indirect Taxes, net
114.83	121.72	132.73	147.41	160.67	155.60	155.30	162.73	158.53	..	B	GDP at factor cost
49.96	52.10	54.32	64.98	72.67	63.92	65.35	67.43	63.88	67.09	..	Agriculture
25.58	28.91	35.02	37.89	40.31	40.42	37.90	38.74	39.73	39.09	f	Industry
19.30	17.66	21.83	22.20	23.83	27.13	24.68	25.11	25.55	26.11	..	Manufacturing
47.10	49.95	52.85	56.25	60.72	65.99	68.66	71.76	70.59	69.97	f	Services, etc.
1.68	6.78	6.19	13.96	14.25	14.15	10.86	11.47	10.92	6.62	..	Gross Domestic Saving
2.17	7.20	6.12	13.66	14.12	14.02	10.67	11.19	10.76	5.92	..	Gross National Saving
				(Billions of 1987 Rwanda Francs)							
155.64	157.22	166.38	158.80	163.49	171.83	171.13	170.94	161.04	158.03	..	Gross National Product
154.69	157.26	167.11	159.35	164.09	172.59	171.91	172.00	161.79	159.12	I f	GDP at Market Prices
-11.29	-16.13	-13.72	-17.25	-19.66	-19.47	-16.00	-18.35	-17.09	-10.11	..	Resource Balance
11.84	12.05	12.84	12.73	13.17	15.11	16.94	13.41	12.45	16.66	..	Exports of Goods & NF Services
23.12	28.18	26.56	29.99	32.83	34.58	32.94	31.75	29.53	26.78	..	Imports of Goods & NF Services
165.97	173.39	180.83	176.60	183.74	192.06	187.91	190.35	178.88	169.23	..	Domestic Absorption
132.72	136.82	148.43	140.43	139.11	138.87	138.72	140.77	134.40	130.67	..	Private Consumption, etc.
20.79	18.63	17.30	15.94	18.88	19.41	22.33	23.42	24.15	31.24	..	General Gov't Consumption
12.46	17.94	15.10	20.24	25.75	33.77	26.85	26.16	20.32	7.32	..	Gross Domestic Investment
12.20	16.60	18.96	23.21	23.18	33.58	26.92	25.33	20.84	9.20	..	Fixed Investment
144.89	146.28	156.15	147.75	151.74	159.21	155.30	157.32	145.77		B I f	GDP at factor cost
62.63	71.59	75.03	68.33	64.57	66.45	65.35	63.83	56.45	59.48	..	Agriculture
33.43	32.67	38.18	37.04	35.99	37.61	37.90	37.99	37.59	35.39	f	Industry
22.15	21.27	24.24	20.61	20.51	24.41	24.68	23.97	23.40	22.47	..	Manufacturing
58.63	53.00	53.90	53.98	63.52	68.53	68.66	70.17	67.75	64.25	f	Services, etc.
											Memo Items:
10.44	13.48	14.82	19.26	17.80	21.59	16.94	15.71	14.21	13.79	..	Capacity to Import
-1.39	1.43	1.98	6.53	4.63	6.48	0.00	2.31	1.76	-2.87	..	Terms of Trade Adjustment
153.29	158.69	169.09	165.88	168.71	179.07	171.91	174.31	163.56	156.25	..	Gross Domestic Income
154.25	158.65	168.36	165.33	168.12	178.31	171.13	173.25	162.81	155.16	..	Gross National Income
				(Index 1987 = 100)							**DOMESTIC PRICES/DEFLATORS**
79.3	83.3	85.1	99.8	105.9	98.7	100.0	103.4	107.7	110.7	..	Overall (GDP)
82.7	85.0	85.8	96.4	103.1	95.4	100.0	102.1	106.5	113.1	..	Domestic Absorption
79.8	72.8	72.4	95.1	112.5	96.2	100.0	105.6	113.2	112.8	..	Agriculture
76.5	88.5	91.7	102.3	112.0	107.5	100.0	102.0	105.7	110.5	..	Industry
87.1	83.0	90.1	107.7	116.2	111.1	100.0	104.7	109.2	116.2	..	Manufacturing
75.5	85.0	90.6	95.5	97.1	96.1	100.0	103.0	104.0	108.4	..	Consumer Price Index
											MANUFACTURING ACTIVITY
..	..	..	..	..	..	..	..	..	..	..	Employment (1987=100)
..	..	..	..	..	..	..	..	..	..	..	Real Earnings per Empl. (1987=100)
..	..	..	..	..	..	..	..	..	..	..	Real Output per Empl. (1987=100)
..	..	..	19.0	10.3	9.6	..	..	..	..	J	Earnings as % of Value Added
				(Millions of current Rwanda Francs)							**MONETARY HOLDINGS**
15,983	16,172	18,077	19,892	23,430	26,608	29,339	31,491	30,184	31,866	..	Money Supply, Broadly Defined
11,774	11,460	12,317	13,343	14,699	17,334	17,791	18,332	16,052	16,846	..	Money
6,086	6,260	6,662	7,030	7,161	7,686	8,202	8,439	7,744	8,593	..	Currency Outside Banks
5,688	5,200	5,655	6,314	7,537	9,648	9,588	9,894	8,308	8,253	..	Demand Deposits
4,209	4,712	5,759	6,549	8,731	9,274	11,548	13,159	14,132	15,020	..	Quasi-Money
				(Millions of current Rwanda Francs)							**GOVERNMENT DEFICIT (-) OR SURPLUS**
..	..	..	..	..	..	..	..	..	..	..	Current Revenue
..	..	..	..	..	..	..	..	..	..	..	Current Expenditure
..	..	..	..	..	..	..	..	..	..	..	Current Budget Balance
..	..	..	..	..	..	..	..	..	..	..	Capital Receipts
..	..	..	..	..	..	..	..	..	..	..	Capital Payments

RWANDA	1970	1971	1972	1973	1974	1975	1976	1977	1978	1979	1980
FOREIGN TRADE (CUSTOMS BASIS)					*(Millions of current US dollars)*						
Value of Exports, fob	..	..	..	..	..	..	..	..	..	..	..
Nonfuel Primary Products	..	..	..	..	..	..	..	..	..	..	..
Fuels	..	..	..	..	..	..	..	..	..	..	..
Manufactures	..	..	..	..	..	..	..	..	..	..	..
Value of Imports, cif	..	..	..	..	..	..	..	..	..	..	..
Nonfuel Primary Products	..	..	..	..	..	..	..	..	..	..	..
Fuels	..	..	..	..	..	..	..	..	..	..	..
Manufactures	..	..	..	..	..	..	..	..	..	..	..
Terms of Trade					*(Index 1987 = 100)*						
Export Prices, fob	..	..	..	..	..	..	..	..	..	..	..
Import Prices, cif	..	..	..	..	..	..	..	..	..	..	..
BALANCE OF PAYMENTS					*(Millions of current US dollars)*						
Exports of Goods & Services	25.90	22.57	22.26	55.79	..	..	123.34	140.89	130.28	235.10	182.43
Merchandise, fob	24.20	20.86	20.19	51.26	53.64	57.55	114.19	126.47	111.67	202.98	133.59
Nonfactor Services	1.50	1.50	1.95	4.29	4.81	6.48	7.99	11.01	14.15	23.70	31.79
Factor Services	0.20	0.20	0.11	0.24	..	..	1.16	3.41	4.46	8.42	17.06
Imports of Goods & Services	35.20	41.12	47.12	62.11	90.16	127.87	159.07	184.87	270.92	319.03	334.62
Merchandise, fob	21.10	23.37	26.06	33.02	56.52	80.13	104.46	102.29	144.94	159.49	195.79
Nonfactor Services	13.90	17.45	20.95	26.23	30.79	44.35	49.41	74.68	116.36	147.60	123.44
Factor Services	0.20	0.30	0.11	2.86	2.85	3.38	5.20	7.90	9.62	11.95	15.39
Long-Term Interest	0.10	0.10	0.10	0.00	0.00	0.10	0.30	0.60	0.70	1.00	1.70
Private Current Transfers, net	-3.10	-1.60	-3.15	-1.19	-4.69	-2.91	-2.02	-2.69	1.17	5.90	-3.18
Workers' Remittances	0.50	0.90	0.87	0.72	0.12	0.49	0.26	1.22	2.09	2.74	1.09
Curr. A/C Bal before Off. Transf.	-12.40	-20.16	-28.01	-7.51	-36.41	-66.75	-37.75	-46.67	-139.47	-78.03	-155.36
Net Official Transfers	18.90	19.76	23.45	29.92	37.61	58.03	55.83	67.51	92.96	124.91	107.46
Curr. A/C Bal after Off. Transf.	6.50	-0.40	-4.56	22.41	1.20	-8.72	18.07	20.84	-46.51	46.89	-47.90
Long-Term Capital, net	-0.40	2.11	1.09	3.34	9.26	16.66	23.23	31.24	25.52	22.69	44.03
Direct Investment	-0.20	1.71	0.54	2.03	2.16	3.01	5.86	4.95	4.69	12.57	16.42
Long-Term Loans	-0.10	-0.10	1.40	4.40	4.10	11.70	22.80	27.60	24.70	31.90	24.60
Disbursements	0.20	0.20	1.80	4.50	4.50	12.00	23.50	28.30	25.70	32.90	27.20
Repayments	0.30	0.30	0.40	0.10	0.40	0.30	0.70	0.70	1.00	1.00	2.60
Other Long-Term Capital	-0.10	0.50	-0.86	-3.09	3.00	1.95	-5.43	-1.32	-3.87	-21.78	3.02
Other Capital, net	-1.71	-2.01	0.08	-17.45	-11.12	4.83	-8.71	-17.61	21.70	0.39	33.14
Change in Reserves	-4.39	0.31	3.40	-8.30	0.66	-12.76	-32.60	-34.47	-0.70	-69.97	-29.28
Memo Item:					*(Rwanda Francs per US dollar)*						
Conversion Factor (Annual Avg)	100.000	99.740	92.110	84.050	92.840	92.840	92.840	92.840	92.840	92.840	92.840
EXTERNAL DEBT (Total)				*(Millions of US dollars), outstanding at end of year*							
	4.80	2.00	3.40	7.90	12.30	24.10	47.70	87.50	126.80	156.10	189.80
Long-Term Debt (by debtor)	4.80	2.00	3.40	7.90	12.30	24.10	47.70	78.50	109.80	135.10	163.80
Central Bank, incl. IMF credit	2.90	0.00	0.00	0.00	0.00	0.00	0.00	0.50	0.80	8.50	14.40
Central Government	1.80	1.90	3.40	7.90	12.30	24.10	47.70	78.00	109.00	126.60	149.40
Rest of General Government	..	..	..	..	..	..	..	..	..	..	..
Non-financial Public Enterprises	0.10	0.10	0.00	0.00	0.00	0.00	0.00	0.00	0.00	0.00	0.00
Priv. Sector, incl non-guaranteed	..	..	..	..	..	..	..	..	..	..	..
Short-Term Debt	0.00	0.00	0.00	0.00	0.00	0.00	0.00	9.00	17.00	21.00	26.00
Memo Items:					*(Millions of US dollars)*						
Int'l Reserves Excluding Gold	7.7	5.8	6.4	15.2	13.0	25.6	64.3	82.9	87.6	152.3	186.6
Gold Holdings (at market price)	..	..	..	..	..	..	..	0.7	0.9	..	..
SOCIAL INDICATORS											
Total Fertility Rate	7.8	7.9	7.9	7.9	7.9	8.0	8.0	8.0	8.1	8.2	8.2
Infant Mortality Rate	140.0	140.0	140.0	140.0	140.0	140.0	140.0	140.0	138.4	136.8	135.2
Life Expectancy at Birth	44.5	44.6	44.8	44.8	44.8	44.9	44.9	45.0	45.2	45.5	45.8
Urban Population, % of total	3.2	3.4	3.5	3.7	3.8	4.0	4.2	4.4	4.6	4.8	5.0
Food Prod. per capita (1987=100)	117.6	116.3	110.1	110.8	104.0	114.7	117.6	118.4	115.8	121.3	118.0
Labor Force, Agriculture (%)	93.7	93.6	93.5	93.4	93.3	93.2	93.1	93.0	93.0	92.9	92.8
Labor Force, Female (%)	50.0	49.9	49.9	49.8	49.8	49.7	49.7	49.6	49.6	49.5	49.5
Primary Schl. Enroll. Ratio	68.0	..	..	..	..	56.0	64.0	66.0	71.0	70.0	63.0
Primary Schl. Enroll. Ratio, Female	60.0	..	..	..	..	51.0	59.0	62.0	67.0	67.0	60.0
Secondary Schl. Enroll. Ratio	2.0	..	..	..	..	2.0	2.0	2.0	2.0	2.0	3.0

1981	1982	1983	1984	1985	1986	1987	1988	1989	1990 estimate	Notes	RWANDA
				(Millions of current US dollars)							**FOREIGN TRADE (CUSTOMS BASIS)**
..	..	..	..	..	..	..	..	..	..	..	Value of Exports, fob
..	..	..	..	..	..	..	..	..	..		Nonfuel Primary Products
..	..	..	..	..	..	..	..	..	..		Fuels
..	..	..	..	..	..	..	..	..	..		Manufactures
..	..	..	..	..	..	..	..	..	..		Value of Imports, cif
..	..	..	..	..	..	..	..	..	..		Nonfuel Primary Products
..	..	..	..	..	..	..	..	..	..		Fuels
..	..	..	..	..	..	..	..	..	..		Manufactures
				(Index 1987=100)							
..	..	..	..	..	..	..	..	..	..		Terms of Trade
..	..	..	..	..	..	..	..	..	..		Export Prices, fob
..	..	..	..	..	..	..	..	..	..		Import Prices, cif
				(Millions of current US dollars)							**BALANCE OF PAYMENTS**
175.87	157.83	160.62	182.72	170.15	236.80	177.85	174.73	157.00	149.26	f	Exports of Goods & Services
113.31	108.46	124.08	142.61	126.10	184.14	121.44	117.88	104.74	102.64	..	Merchandise, fob
37.33	33.25	27.89	31.93	34.89	43.30	46.15	48.18	42.96	42.22	..	Nonfactor Services
25.23	16.12	8.65	8.19	9.16	9.36	10.27	8.67	9.29	4.39	..	Factor Services
345.51	354.34	327.09	325.39	350.61	430.04	438.24	443.60	396.14	378.73	f	Imports of Goods & Services
207.13	214.66	197.64	197.52	219.33	259.21	266.98	278.58	254.11	227.66	..	Merchandise, fob
121.67	120.83	112.99	113.22	114.23	148.40	146.96	134.28	118.50	130.94	..	Nonfactor Services
16.71	18.85	16.45	14.65	17.04	22.43	24.30	30.74	23.53	20.13	..	Factor Services
2.00	2.10	2.40	3.40	4.20	5.40	7.30	8.40	7.60	6.20		Long-Term Interest
-2.99	4.64	5.50	1.89	4.32	7.01	7.48	10.54	7.93	5.84	..	Private Current Transfers, net
1.66	1.49	1.60	1.19	1.33	1.72	1.90	1.12	0.89	0.65	..	Workers' Remittances
-172.63	-191.87	-160.97	-140.79	-176.14	-186.24	-252.91	-258.33	-231.22	-223.64	..	Curr. A/C Bal before Off. Transf.
105.68	105.25	112.31	99.21	112.09	117.00	118.56	139.30	129.20	138.21	..	Net Official Transfers
-66.95	-86.62	-48.65	-41.58	-64.05	-69.24	-134.35	-119.03	-102.02	-85.43	..	Curr. A/C Bal after Off. Transf.
45.48	41.58	36.54	51.05	74.12	85.76	110.88	87.64	59.60	48.90	f	Long-Term Capital, net
18.03	20.70	11.12	15.07	14.62	17.58	17.55	21.05	15.55	7.66	..	Direct Investment
24.20	28.60	35.80	44.20	70.90	66.20	92.30	75.90	50.40	52.60	..	Long-Term Loans
26.60	31.10	40.80	50.60	80.20	76.30	103.80	84.60	64.30	62.10	..	Disbursements
2.40	2.50	5.00	6.40	9.30	10.10	11.50	8.70	13.90	9.50	..	Repayments
3.25	-7.73	-10.38	-8.22	-11.39	1.98	1.03	-9.30	-6.35	-11.36		Other Long-Term Capital
21.40	8.48	-6.30	-1.67	-9.97	11.21	10.15	3.62	-6.49	35.30	f	Other Capital, net
0.08	36.56	18.41	-7.80	-0.10	-27.74	13.32	27.77	48.90	1.23	..	Change in Reserves
				(Rwanda Francs per US dollar)							**Memo Item:**
92.840	92.840	94.340	100.170	101.260	87.640	79.670	76.440	79.980	82.600	..	Conversion Factor (Annual Avg)
				(Millions of US dollars), outstanding at end of year							**EXTERNAL DEBT (Total)**
196.50	218.30	242.30	291.40	369.40	455.70	610.30	658.30	648.20	740.70	..	Long-Term Debt (by debtor)
176.50	197.30	226.30	254.40	342.40	428.60	571.00	616.80	603.70	692.40	..	Central Bank, incl. IMF credit
12.40	11.80	11.20	10.50	10.00	8.60	6.90	3.70	0.90	0.10	..	Central Government
164.10	185.50	215.10	243.90	332.40	420.00	564.10	613.10	602.80	692.30	..	Rest of General Government
..	..	..	..	..	..	..	..	..	..	..	Non-financial Public Enterprises
0.00	0.00	0.00	0.00	0.00	0.00	0.00	0.00	0.00	..	..	Priv. Sector, incl non-guaranteed
..	..	..	..	..	..	..	..	..	..	..	Short-Term Debt
20.00	21.00	16.00	37.00	27.00	27.10	39.30	41.50	44.50	48.30	..	
				(Millions of US dollars)							**Memo Items:**
173.1	128.4	110.9	106.9	113.3	162.3	164.2	118.3	70.4	44.4	..	Int'l Reserves Excluding Gold
..	..	..	..	..	..	..	..	..	..	..	Gold Holdings (at market price)
											SOCIAL INDICATORS
8.3	8.4	8.4	8.4	8.3	8.3	8.3	8.3	8.3	8.3	..	Total Fertility Rate
133.6	132.0	130.0	128.0	126.0	124.0	122.0	121.5	120.9	120.4	..	Infant Mortality Rate
46.1	46.4	46.8	47.3	47.8	48.2	48.7	48.5	48.3	48.1	..	Life Expectancy at Birth
5.2	5.5	5.7	6.0	6.2	6.6	7.0	7.2	7.5	7.7	..	Urban Population, % of total
124.0	126.5	121.7	108.1	120.1	101.3	100.0	98.1	94.1	88.1	..	Food Prod. per capita (1987=100)
..	..	..	..	..	..	..	..	..	..	..	Labor Force, Agriculture (%)
49.3	49.1	48.9	48.8	48.6	48.4	48.2	48.0	47.9	47.7	..	Labor Force, Female (%)
..	63.0	62.0	61.0	63.0	65.0	67.0	69.0	69.0	..	..	Primary Schl. Enroll. Ratio
..	60.0	60.0	59.0	61.0	64.0	66.0	68.0	68.0	..	..	Primary Schl. Enroll. Ratio, Female
..	2.0	2.0	7.0	6.0	6.0	6.0	..	7.0	..	..	Secondary Schl. Enroll. Ratio

SAO TOME AND PRINCIPE	1970	1971	1972	1973	1974	1975	1976	1977	1978	1979	1980
CURRENT GNP PER CAPITA (US $)	..	..	270	300	350	410	380	360	360	400	480
POPULATION (thousands)	74	76	79	81	84	87	88	90	91	92	94
USE AND ORIGIN OF RESOURCES											
	(Millions of current Sao Tome & Principe Dobras)										
Gross National Product (GNP)	565.30	558.70	592.00	725.20	776.00	812.30	809.30	966.80	1,096.70	1,294.30	1,590.90
Net Factor Income from Abroad	0.90	0.80	0.70	0.80	1.00	2.40	-20.60	-8.20	46.80	79.30	92.90
GDP at Market Prices	564.40	557.90	591.30	724.40	775.00	809.90	829.90	975.00	1,049.90	1,215.00	1,498.00
Resource Balance	-1.60	-29.10	-8.20	61.80	114.60	-92.00	-185.00	-230.00	-281.90	-463.80	-735.00
Exports of Goods & NFServices	213.00	169.40	181.20	297.60	405.70	212.90	235.00	420.00	550.00	720.00	682.40
Imports of Goods & NFServices	214.60	198.50	189.40	235.80	291.10	304.90	420.00	650.00	831.90	1,183.80	1,417.40
Domestic Absorption	566.00	587.00	599.50	662.60	660.40	901.90	1,014.90	1,205.00	1,331.80	1,678.80	2,233.00
Private Consumption, etc.	394.10	411.20	426.00	493.70	480.60	684.30	769.00	759.70	1,040.00	1,278.70	1,367.10
General Gov't Consumption	70.30	70.30	70.30	70.30	70.30	70.30	70.30	70.30	70.30	70.30	353.80
Gross Domestic Investment	101.60	105.50	103.20	98.60	109.50	147.30	175.60	375.00	221.50	329.80	512.10
Fixed Investment	..	..	..	..	..	..	..	..	..	..	550.00
Indirect Taxes, net	65.10	58.90	67.20	77.90	82.30	88.20	125.90	188.30	298.50	229.50	200.00
GDP at factor cost	499.30	499.00	524.10	646.50	692.70	721.70	704.00	786.70	751.40	985.50	1,298.00
Agriculture	..	..	..	..	..	..	..	..	..	..	..
Industry	..	..	..	..	..	..	..	..	..	..	..
Manufacturing	..	..	..	..	..	..	..	..	..	..	..
Services, etc.	..	..	..	..	..	..	..	..	..	..	..
Gross Domestic Saving	100.00	76.40	95.00	160.40	224.10	55.30	-9.40	145.00	-60.40	-134.00	-222.90
Gross National Saving	..	..	..	216.50		51.20	-33.20	132.90	-10.90	-44.40	-112.60
	(Millions of 1987 Sao Tome & Principe Dobras)										
Gross National Product	2,085.90	2,171.50	2,140.20	2,090.90	2,131.80	2,290.80	2,388.10	2,720.10	3,067.70	3,422.00	3,849.70
GDP at Market Prices	2,045.50	2,124.10	2,096.80	2,045.70	2,083.20	2,230.40	2,419.20	2,690.10	2,858.20	3,185.80	3,626.60
Resource Balance	..	..	..	..	..	-755.30	-765.70	-1,067.80	-1,389.90	-1,826.30	-1,683.30
Exports of Goods & NFServices	..	..	..	..	..	554.70	513.40	572.40	637.60	649.20	756.70
Imports of Goods & NFServices	..	..	..	..	..	1,309.90	1,279.10	1,640.20	2,027.50	2,475.50	2,439.90
Domestic Absorption	..	..	..	..	..	2,985.60	3,184.80	3,757.90	4,248.10	5,012.20	5,309.90
Private Consumption, etc.	..	..	..	..	..	1,975.40	2,122.00	2,220.60	2,866.60	3,322.60	3,711.60
General Gov't Consumption	..	..	..	..	..	863.50	890.10	1,315.80	1,131.10	1,340.50	1,132.90
Gross Domestic Investment	..	..	..	..	..	146.70	172.80	221.40	250.40	349.10	465.30
Fixed Investment	..	..	..	..	..	..	..	..	..	..	..
GDP at factor cost	1,707.80	1,795.80	1,758.80	1,727.70	1,695.50	..	..	..	..	2,515.50	3,194.20
Agriculture	..	..	..	..	..	..	..	..	..	..	..
Industry	..	..	..	..	..	..	..	..	..	..	..
Manufacturing	..	..	..	..	..	..	..	..	..	..	..
Services, etc.	..	..	..	..	..	..	..	..	..	..	..
Memo Items:											
Capacity to Import	..	..	..	..	..	914.70	715.70	1,059.80	1,340.50	1,505.60	1,174.70
Terms of Trade Adjustment	..	..	..	..	..	360.00	202.30	487.40	702.80	856.50	418.00
Gross Domestic Income	..	..	..	..	..	2,590.40	2,621.40	3,177.50	3,561.10	4,042.30	4,044.60
Gross National Income	..	..	..	..	..	2,650.80	2,590.30	3,207.50	3,770.50	4,278.50	4,267.70
DOMESTIC PRICES/DEFLATORS											
	(Index 1987 = 100)										
Overall (GDP)	27.6	26.3	28.2	35.4	37.2	36.3	34.3	36.2	36.7	38.1	41.3
Domestic Absorption	..	..	..	..	..	30.2	31.9	32.1	31.4	33.5	42.1
Agriculture	..	..	..	..	..	..	..	..	..	..	..
Industry	..	..	..	..	..	..	..	..	..	..	..
Manufacturing	..	..	..	..	..	..	..	..	..	..	..
Consumer Price Index	..	..	..	..	..	..	..	..	..	..	..
MANUFACTURING ACTIVITY											
Employment (1987=100)	..	..	..	..	..	..	..	..	..	..	..
Real Earnings per Empl. (1987=100)	..	..	..	..	..	..	..	..	..	..	..
Real Output per Empl. (1987=100)	..	..	..	..	..	..	..	..	..	..	..
Earnings as % of Value Added	..	..	..	..	..	..	..	..	..	..	..
MONETARY HOLDINGS											
	(Millions of current Sao Tome & Principe Dobras)										
Money Supply, Broadly Defined	..	..	..	..	..	..	..	..	..	..	..
Money	..	..	..	..	..	..	..	..	..	..	..
Currency Outside Banks	..	..	..	..	..	..	..	..	..	..	..
Demand Deposits	..	..	..	..	..	..	..	..	..	..	..
Quasi-Money	..	..	..	..	..	..	..	..	..	..	..
GOVERNMENT DEFICIT (-) OR SURPLUS											
	(Millions of current Sao Tome & Principe Dobras)										
Current Revenue	..	..	..	..	..	..	..	..	..	..	..
Current Expenditure	..	..	..	..	..	..	..	..	..	..	..
Current Budget Balance	..	..	..	..	..	..	..	..	..	..	..
Capital Receipts	..	..	..	..	..	..	..	..	..	..	..
Capital Payments	..	..	..	..	..	..	..	..	..	..	..

1981	1982	1983	1984	1985	1986	1987	1988	1989	1990 estimate	Notes	SAO TOME AND PRINCIPE
350	400	360	350	340	390	440	490	440	400	..	CURRENT GNP PER CAPITA (US $)
95	97	99	101	103	105	108	111	114	117	..	POPULATION (thousands)
				(Millions of current Sao Tome & Principe Dobras)							USE AND ORIGIN OF RESOURCES
1,139.20	1,435.80	1,506.40	1,549.10	1,487.00	2,353.30	2,848.90	3,990.40	5,562.60	6,638.30	..	Gross National Product (GNP)
68.80	-14.70	16.00	110.30	-76.00	-124.40	-155.10	-230.60	-177.70	-716.70	..	Net Factor Income from Abroad
1,070.40	1,450.50	1,490.40	1,438.80	1,563.00	2,477.70	3,004.00	4,221.00	5,740.30	7,355.00	..	GDP at Market Prices
-822.00	-1,071.00	-630.00	-861.00	-861.00	-571.40	-951.70	-1,284.80	-3,880.50	-4,030.60	..	Resource Balance
335.70	444.00	434.00	627.00	412.00	483.60	534.20	1,252.80	1,314.50	1,853.40	..	Exports of Goods & NFServices
1,157.70	1,515.00	1,064.00	1,488.00	1,273.00	1,055.00	1,485.90	2,537.60	5,195.00	5,884.00	..	Imports of Goods & NFServices
1,892.40	2,521.50	2,120.40	2,299.80	2,424.00	3,048.70	3,955.20	5,505.90	9,620.80	11,385.50	..	Domestic Absorption
974.80	1,307.00	1,153.70	1,069.30	1,261.50	1,961.10	2,466.20	3,162.00	6,680.60	7,686.00	..	Private Consumption, etc.
415.00	491.40	527.70	543.40	584.00	729.40	972.50	1,155.90	1,355.90	2,235.90	..	General Gov't Consumption
502.60	723.10	439.00	687.10	578.50	358.20	516.50	1,188.00	1,584.30	1,463.60	..	Gross Domestic Investment
360.00	785.00	357.10	842.80	502.00	..					..	Fixed Investment
-70.60	170.50	91.30	44.60	63.10	52.00	121.90	210.00	313.20	338.30	..	Indirect Taxes, net
1,141.00	1,280.00	1,399.10	1,394.20	1,499.90	2,425.70	2,882.10	4,011.00	5,427.10	7,016.70	..	GDP at factor cost
..	..	..	..	..	..	..	..	..	..	..	Agriculture
..	..	..	..	..	..	..	..	..	..	..	Industry
..	..	..	..	..	..	..	..	..	..		Manufacturing
..	..	..	..	..	..	..	..	..	..	..	Services, etc.
-319.40	-347.90	-191.00	-173.90	-282.50	-212.80	-434.70	-96.90	-2,296.20	-2,566.90	..	Gross Domestic Saving
-225.90	-343.40	-123.90	78.60	-368.30	-367.70	-606.60	-327.10	-2,504.00	-3,273.60	..	Gross National Saving
				(Millions of 1987 Sao Tome & Principe Dobras)							
2,777.20	3,292.00	3,066.40	2,989.40	2,877.30	2,879.60	2,848.90	2,889.40	3,005.00	2,910.90		Gross National Product
2,630.70	3,323.20	3,035.00	2,782.70	3,017.80	3,047.90	3,004.00	3,063.00	3,109.30	3,187.20	I	GDP at Market Prices
-1,380.80	-1,717.40	-1,179.80	-1,767.20	-1,603.90	-1,140.70	-951.70	-1,125.40	-1,774.20	-1,280.40	..	Resource Balance
464.70	736.20	591.20	754.30	526.70	697.60	534.20	591.80	580.90	676.80	..	Exports of Goods & NFServices
1,845.50	2,453.50	1,771.00	2,521.50	2,130.60	1,838.30	1,485.90	1,717.10	2,355.20	1,957.20	..	Imports of Goods & NFServices
4,011.50	5,040.60	4,214.80	4,549.90	4,621.70	4,188.60	3,955.70	4,188.40	4,883.60	4,467.50	..	Domestic Absorption
2,374.20	3,053.80	2,430.50	2,568.10	2,705.90	2,500.00	2,466.70	2,372.00	3,173.70		..	Private Consumption, etc.
1,203.00	1,393.50	1,398.10	1,364.30	1,410.50	1,115.50	972.50	967.80	958.10	..	..	General Gov't Consumption
434.30	593.30	386.30	617.50	505.30	573.10	516.50	848.70	751.70	517.20	..	Gross Domestic Investment
..	..	..	..	..	..	..	..	..	..	..	Fixed Investment
2,861.70	3,018.30	2,926.90	2,773.70	2,995.80	3,023.60	2,882.10	2,919.20	2,976.70	3,040.00	..	GDP at factor cost
..	..	..	..	..	..	..	..	..	..	..	Agriculture
..	..	..	..	..	..	..	..	..	..	..	Industry
..	..	..	..	..	..	..	..	..	..	..	Manufacturing
..	..	..	..	..	..	..	..	..	..	..	Services, etc.
											Memo Items:
535.10	719.10	722.40	1,062.50	689.60	842.70	534.20	847.70	595.90	616.50	..	Capacity to Import
70.50	-17.10	131.20	308.20	162.90	145.00	0.00	256.00	15.00	-60.30	..	Terms of Trade Adjustment
2,701.10	3,306.10	3,166.20	3,090.90	3,180.60	3,192.90	3,004.00	3,319.00	3,124.30	3,126.90	..	Gross Domestic Income
2,847.60	3,274.90	3,197.60	3,297.60	3,040.20	3,024.60	2,848.90	3,145.40	3,020.00	2,850.60	..	Gross National Income
				(Index 1987 = 100)							DOMESTIC PRICES/DEFLATORS
40.7	43.6	49.1	51.7	51.8	81.3	100.0	137.8	184.6	230.8	..	Overall (GDP)
47.2	50.0	50.3	50.5	52.4	72.8	100.0	131.5	197.0	254.9	..	Domestic Absorption
..	..	..	..	..	..	..	..	..	..	..	Agriculture
..	..	..	..	..	..	..	..	..	..	..	Industry
..	..	..	..	..	..	..	..	..	..	..	Manufacturing
..	..	..	..	..	..	..	..	..	..	..	Consumer Price Index
											MANUFACTURING ACTIVITY
..	..	..	..	..	..	..	..	..	..	..	Employment (1987=100)
..	..	..	..	..	..	..	..	..	..	..	Real Earnings per Empl. (1987=100)
..	..	..	..	..	..	..	..	..	..	..	Real Output per Empl. (1987=100)
..	..	..	..	..	..	..	..	..	..	..	Earnings as % of Value Added
				(Millions of current Sao Tome & Principe Dobras)							MONETARY HOLDINGS
..	1,094	1,454	1,641	1,717	1,845	1,945	..	..	..	..	Money Supply, Broadly Defined
..	..	..	1,326	1,408	1,569	1,712	1,610	..	..	..	Money
..	..	..	484	390	409	514	465	..	..	..	Currency Outside Banks
..	..	..	843	1,018	1,161	1,198	1,145	..	..	..	Demand Deposits
..	..	..	314	309	276	233	..	..	..	..	Quasi-Money
				(Millions of current Sao Tome & Principe Dobras)							GOVERNMENT DEFICIT (-) OR SURPLUS
..	..	..	..	..	..	..	..	..	..	..	Current Revenue
..	..	..	..	..	..	..	..	..	..	..	Current Expenditure
..	..	..	..	..	..	..	..	..	..	..	Current Budget Balance
..	..	..	..	..	..	..	..	..	..	..	Capital Receipts
..	..	..	..	..	..	..	..	..	..	..	Capital Payments

	1970	1971	1972	1973	1974	1975	1976	1977	1978	1979	1980
FOREIGN TRADE (CUSTOMS BASIS)					*(Thousands of current US dollars)*						
Value of Exports, fob	..	..	..	..	..	..	..	..	..	..	..
Nonfuel Primary Products											
Fuels											
Manufactures	..	..	..	..	..	..	..	..	..	..	..
Value of Imports, cif	..	..	..	..	..	..	..	..	..	..	..
Nonfuel Primary Products											
Fuels	..	..	..	..	..	..	..	..	..	..	..
Manufactures	..	..	..	..	..	..	..	..	..	..	..
Terms of Trade					*(Index 1987 = 100)*						
Export Prices, fob	..	..	..	..	..	..	..	..	..	..	..
Import Prices, cif	..	..	..	..	..	..	..	..	..	..	..
BALANCE OF PAYMENTS					*(Thousands of current US dollars)*						
Exports of Goods & Services	..	..	..	..	18	8		24	26	31	23
Merchandise, fob	..	..	..	..	17	7	8	23	23	27	17
Nonfactor Services	..	..	..	..	1	1	1	0	1	3	3
Factor Services	..	..	..	..	0	0	..	1	1	2	3
Imports of Goods & Services	..	..	..	..	12	12	10	16	23	23	22
Merchandise, fob	..	..	..	..	8	9	8	12	17	15	15
Nonfactor Services	..	..	..	..	3	3	2	5	6	8	6
Factor Services	..	..	..	..	0	0	0	0	0	0	0
Long-Term Interest	0	0	0	0	0	0	0	0	0	0	0
Private Current Transfers, net	..	..	..	..	0	0	0	0	0	0	1
Workers' Remittances	..	..	..	..	..	..	..	..	0	1	1
Curr. A/C Bal before Off. Transf.	..	..	..	..	6	-5	-2	8	3	8	1
Net Official Transfers	..	..	..	..	..	5	1	0	3	0	0
Curr. A/C Bal after Off. Transf.	..	..	..	..	6	0	-1	8	6	9	1
Long-Term Capital, net	..	..	..	..	-1	-1	17	4	2	2	0
Direct Investment	..	..	..	..					..	..	..
Long-Term Loans	0	0	0	0	0	0	0	2	8	4	9
Disbursements	0	0	0	0	0	0	0	2	8	4	10
Repayments	0	0	0	0	0	0	0	0	0	0	1
Other Long-Term Capital	..	..	..	..	-1	-1	16	2	-6	-2	-9
Other Capital, net	..	..	..	..	-2	0	-4	-5	0	-9	-13
Change in Reserves	..	..	..	..	-3	1	-12	-7	-8	-2	12
Memo Item:					*(Sao Tome & Principe Dobras per US dollar)*						
Conversion Factor (Annual Avg)	28.750	28.310	27.050	24.520	25.410	25.540	30.230	37.560	36.150	35.020	34.770
EXTERNAL DEBT (Total)					*(Thousands of US dollars), outstanding at end of year*						
	0	0	0	0	0	0	100	2,200	10,300	16,700	23,500
Long-Term Debt (by debtor)	0	0	0	0	0	0	100	2,200	10,300	16,700	23,500
Central Bank, incl. IMF credit	0	0	0	0	0	0	100	2,200	10,300	14,700	23,500
Central Government	0	0	0	0	0	0	0	0	0	0	0
Rest of General Government	..	..	..	..	..	..	100	2,200	10,300	14,700	23,500
Non-financial Public Enterprises	..	..	..	..	..	..	..	..	..	..	..
Priv. Sector, incl non-guaranteed	..	..	..	..	..	..	..	..	..	..	..
Short-Term Debt	0	0	0	0	0	0	0	0	0	2,000	0
Memo Items:					*(Millions of US dollars)*						
Int'l Reserves Excluding Gold	..	..	..	..	..	..	..	..	..	..	..
Gold Holdings (at market price)	..	..	..	..	..	..	..	..	..	..	..
SOCIAL INDICATORS											
Total Fertility Rate	..	..	..	..	..	..	..	..	..	..	
Infant Mortality Rate	..	..	..	..	89.0	85.5	82.0	82.7	83.3	84.0	82.8
Life Expectancy at Birth								..	..		..
Urban Population, % of total	23.4	24.3	25.2	26.1	27.0	27.9	28.9	29.9	30.8	31.8	32.8
Food Prod. per capita (1987=100)	247.8	264.5	250.6	260.4	241.3	186.7	173.3	162.0	160.9	176.3	142.1
Labor Force, Agriculture (%)	..	..	..	..	..	..	..	..	..	..	..
Labor Force, Female (%)	..	..	..	..	..	..	..	..	..	..	..
Primary Schl. Enroll. Ratio	..	..	..	..	..	..	..	..	..	..	..
Primary Schl. Enroll. Ratio, Female	..	..	..	..	..	..	..	..	..	..	..
Secondary Schl. Enroll. Ratio	..	..	..	..	..	..	..	..	..	..	..

	1981	1982	1983	1984	1985	1986	1987	1988	1989	1990 estimate	Notes	
(Thousands of current US dollars)												**FOREIGN TRADE (CUSTOMS BASIS)**
	..	..	..	..	..	..	..	..	..	..		Value of Exports, fob
	..	..	..	..	..	..	..	..	..	..		Nonfuel Primary Products
	..	..	..	..	..	..	..	..	..			Fuels
	..	..	..	..	..	..	..	..	..			Manufactures
	..	..	..	..	..	..	..	..	..	..		Value of Imports, cif
	..	..	..	..	..	..	..	..	..			Nonfuel Primary Products
	..	..	..	..	..	..	..	..	..			Fuels
	..	..	..	..	..	..	..	..	..			Manufactures
(Index 1987 = 100)												
	..	..	..	..	..	..		..	..			Terms of Trade
	..	..	..	..	..	..		..	..			Export Prices, fob
	..	..	..	..	..	..		..	..			Import Prices, cif
(Thousands of current US dollars)												**BALANCE OF PAYMENTS**
	11	12	11	14	9	14	8	11	10	8	..	Exports of Goods & Services
	7	9	9	12	7	10	7	10	5	4	..	Merchandise, fob
	2	2	2	2	2	4	2	2	4	4	..	Nonfactor Services
	2	1	1	0	0	0	0	0	0	0	..	Factor Services
	30	38	26	35	30	37	23	23	22	22	..	Imports of Goods & Services
	22	27	18	24	20	23	14	14	13	13	..	Merchandise, fob
	8	10	7	10	9	11	9	8	9	9	..	Nonfactor Services
	0	1	1	1	2	3	1	1	0	0	..	Factor Services
	0	0	1	1	1	1	1	1	3	1		Long-Term Interest
	1	0	1	3	0	-1	0	0	0	0	..	Private Current Transfers, net
	1	1	1	3	0	0	0	0	0	0		Workers' Remittances
	-18	-26	-14	-17	-21	-25	-15	-12	-13	-14	..	Curr. A/C Bal before Off. Transf.
	0	1	6	6	5	6	2	1	2	2		Net Official Transfers
	-18	-25	-9	-11	-16	-19	-13	-11	-11	-12		Curr. A/C Bal after Off. Transf.
	3	15	3	14	8	5	3	2	4	11	..	Long-Term Capital, net
	..	..	..	..	..	..	..	0	0	..	..	Direct Investment
	7	8	7	14	7	10	7	11	16	15	..	Long-Term Loans
	8	10	9	16	8	10	10	12	17	16	..	Disbursements
	1	2	2	2	2	1	2	1	2	1	..	Repayments
	-4	6	-4	0	1	-4	-4	-9	-12	-4	..	Other Long-Term Capital
	8	8	4	-8	9	12	6	5	2	0	..	Other Capital, net
	7	2	2	5	-1	1	4	4	6	1	..	Change in Reserves
(Sao Tome & Principe Dobras per US dollar)												**Memo Item:**
	38.400	41.000	42.340	44.160	44.600	38.590	54.210	86.340	124.670	143.330	..	Conversion Factor (Annual Avg)
(Thousands of US dollars), outstanding at end of year												**EXTERNAL DEBT (Total)**
	34,400	37,800	43,800	53,900	62,300	77,000	92,400	103,800	130,300	145,900	..	Long-Term Debt (by debtor)
	29,400	36,800	42,800	53,900	61,500	74,800	85,900	95,600	110,400	130,100		Central Bank, incl. IMF credit
	0	0	0	0	0	0	0	0	1,100	1,100		Central Government
	29,400	36,800	42,800	53,900	61,500	74,800	85,900	95,600	109,300	129,000		Rest of General Government
	..	..	..	..	..	..	..	..	..	..		Non-financial Public Enterprises
	..	..	..	..	..	..	..	..	..	..		Priv. Sector, incl non-guaranteed
	5,000	1,000	1,000	0	800	2,200	6,500	8,200	19,900	15,800	..	Short-Term Debt
(Millions of US dollars)												**Memo Items:**
	..	..	..	..	..	..	..	..	..	..		Int'l Reserves Excluding Gold
	..	..	..	..	..	..	..	..	..	..		Gold Holdings (at market price)
												SOCIAL INDICATORS
	..	5.3	5.3	5.3	5.3	5.3	5.3	5.2	5.2	5.1	..	Total Fertility Rate
	81.6	80.4	79.2	78.0	76.7	75.5	74.3	72.5	70.7	69.0		Infant Mortality Rate
	..	63.4	63.8	64.2	64.6	65.0	65.4	65.8	66.3	66.7		Life Expectancy at Birth
	32.4	32.0	33.9	35.7	37.6	38.8	40.0	40.8	41.5	42.3		Urban Population, % of total
	144.4	134.3	133.1	110.1	113.1	109.7	100.0	113.7	111.1	100.4		Food Prod. per capita (1987=100)
	..	..	..	..	..	..	..	..	..	..		Labor Force, Agriculture (%)
	..	..	..	..	..	..	..	..	..	..		Labor Force, Female (%)
	..	..	..	..	..	..	138.0	..	..	..		Primary Schl. Enroll. Ratio
	..	..	..	..	..	..	..	..	..	..		Primary Schl. Enroll. Ratio, Female
	..	..	..	..	..	..	..	..	..	..		Secondary Schl. Enroll. Ratio

SAUDI ARABIA	1970	1971	1972	1973	1974	1975	1976	1977	1978	1979	1980
CURRENT GNP PER CAPITA (US $)	560	760	980	1,140	2,070	3,290	5,410	7,120	7,720	8,790	10,400
POPULATION (thousands)	5,745	5,997	6,276	6,579	6,905	7,251	7,617	7,999	8,408	8,863	9,372
USE AND ORIGIN OF RESOURCES					*(Billions of current Saudi Arabian Riyals)*						
Gross National Product (GNP)	13.65	21.33	28.03	33.72	94.96	138.60	163.13	204.74	224.68	259.12	387.56
Net Factor Income from Abroad	-3.75	-1.59	-0.23	-6.83	-4.35	-1.00	-1.40	-0.32	-0.72	9.58	1.75
GDP at Market Prices	17.40	22.92	28.26	40.55	99.31	139.60	164.53	205.06	225.40	249.54	385.81
Resource Balance	5.31	9.98	13.56	21.74	70.39	87.20	77.42	77.62	49.26	39.76	126.14
Exports of Goods & NFServices	10.30	15.19	19.86	30.01	85.68	114.46	120.28	140.32	140.76	147.24	258.49
Imports of Goods & NFServices	4.99	5.20	6.30	8.27	15.29	27.26	42.86	62.70	91.50	107.48	132.35
Domestic Absorption	12.09	12.94	14.70	18.81	28.93	52.40	87.11	127.43	176.14	209.78	259.67
Private Consumption, etc.	5.86	6.41	6.91	7.89	9.83	18.04	23.90	34.37	54.61	68.61	102.45
General Gov't Consumption	3.42	3.80	4.28	5.33	9.86	15.91	28.88	41.03	47.03	71.90	77.50
Gross Domestic Investment	2.81	2.73	3.50	5.58	9.23	18.45	34.32	52.03	74.50	69.27	79.72
Fixed Investment	2.60	2.93	3.40	5.69	8.40	17.70	33.54	51.19	66.89	76.65	97.07
Indirect Taxes, net	0.16	0.35	0.36	0.53	0.51	-0.52	-0.90	-0.67	-0.90	-0.93	..
GDP at factor cost	17.24	22.57	27.90	40.02	98.81	140.12	165.43	205.73	226.30	250.47	..
Agriculture	0.98	1.02	1.06	1.14	1.24	1.39	1.59	1.87	3.91	4.20	4.65
Industry	11.03	15.89	20.45	30.93	86.62	120.24	134.27	164.26	169.32	179.85	301.25
Manufacturing	1.67	1.96	1.98	2.43	5.08	7.37	8.17	9.28	9.97	12.62	19.29
Services, etc.	5.38	6.01	6.75	8.48	11.46	17.97	28.67	38.93	52.17	65.50	79.91
Gross Domestic Saving	8.12	12.71	17.06	27.32	79.62	105.65	111.74	129.65	123.76	109.03	205.86
Gross National Saving	3.54	10.19	15.72	19.04	73.43	102.70	106.85	124.02	113.37	105.96	193.99
					(Billions of 1987 Saudi Arabian Riyals)						
Gross National Product	92.22	125.21	153.93	154.53	203.98	210.56	225.77	261.91	272.76	299.58	317.18
GDP at Market Prices	118.89	136.03	156.91	187.88	217.16	216.31	232.25	267.62	279.16	294.41	322.14
Resource Balance	..	..	..	..	..	..	..	..	..	..	..
Exports of Goods & NFServices	..	..	..	..	..	..	..	..	..	..	..
Imports of Goods & NFServices	..	..	..	..	..	..	..	..	..	..	..
Domestic Absorption	..	..	..	..	..	..	..	..	..	..	..
Private Consumption, etc.	..	..	..	..	..	..	..	..	..	..	..
General Gov't Consumption	..	..	..	..	..	..	..	..	..	..	..
Gross Domestic Investment	..	..	..	..	..	..	..	..	..	..	..
Fixed Investment	..	..	..	..	..	..	..	..	..	..	..
GDP at factor cost	..	..	..	..	..	..	..	..	..	..	..
Agriculture	4.22	4.36	4.50	4.66	4.84	5.03	5.23	5.49	6.35	6.64	7.02
Industry	65.70	77.80	93.56	115.46	133.93	132.35	139.72	160.93	164.48	170.46	184.62
Manufacturing	6.47	7.11	7.15	7.65	8.05	7.82	8.46	9.59	10.42	11.46	12.48
Services, etc.	48.97	53.86	58.85	67.76	78.38	78.92	87.31	101.19	108.33	117.31	130.50
Memo Items:											
Capacity to Import	..	..	..	..	..	..	..	..	..	..	..
Terms of Trade Adjustment	..	..	..	..	..	..	..	..	..	..	..
Gross Domestic Income	..	..	..	..	..	..	..	..	..	..	..
Gross National Income	..	..	..	..	..	..	..	..	..	..	..
DOMESTIC PRICES/DEFLATORS					*(Index 1987 = 100)*						
Overall (GDP)	14.6	16.9	18.0	21.6	45.7	64.5	70.8	76.6	80.7	84.8	119.8
Domestic Absorption	..	..	..	..	..	..	..	..	..	..	..
Agriculture	23.3	23.3	23.5	24.4	25.7	27.7	30.3	34.0	61.5	63.2	66.2
Industry	16.8	20.4	21.9	26.8	64.7	90.8	96.1	102.1	102.9	105.5	163.2
Manufacturing	25.9	27.5	27.8	31.7	63.0	94.2	96.6	96.8	95.7	110.1	154.6
Consumer Price Index	33.4	34.9	36.4	42.4	51.5	69.3	91.2	101.6	100.0	101.8	105.7
MANUFACTURING ACTIVITY											
Employment (1987=100)	..	..	..	..	..	..	..	..	..	..	..
Real Earnings per Empl. (1987=100)	..	..	..	..	..	..	..	..	..	..	..
Real Output per Empl. (1987=100)	..	..	..	..	..	..	..	..	..	..	..
Earnings as % of Value Added	..	..	..	..	..	23.8					
MONETARY HOLDINGS					*(Billions of current Saudi Arabian Riyals)*						
Money Supply, Broadly Defined	3.14	3.59	5.04	6.81	9.78	17.78	29.61	45.56	58.03	65.98	77.44
Money	2.40	2.65	3.78	5.29	7.33	14.18	24.27	38.41	49.21	54.70	58.96
Currency Outside Banks	1.63	1.67	2.42	3.05	4.14	6.68	10.59	16.25	19.18	23.71	25.68
Demand Deposits	0.77	0.98	1.36	2.23	3.19	7.50	13.68	22.16	30.03	31.00	33.28
Quasi-Money	0.74	0.94	1.26	1.52	2.44	3.60	5.34	7.14	8.82	11.28	18.48
GOVERNMENT DEFICIT (-) OR SURPLUS					*(Millions of current Saudi Arabian Riyals)*						
Current Revenue	..	..	..	..	..	..	..	..	..	..	..
Current Expenditure	..	..	..	..	..	..	..	..	..	..	..
Current Budget Balance	..	..	..	..	..	..	..	..	..	..	..
Capital Receipts	..	..	..	..	..	..	..	..	..	..	..
Capital Payments	..	..	..	..	..	..	..	..	..	..	..

1981	1982	1983	1984	1985	1986	1987	1988	1989	1990 estimate	Notes	SAUDI ARABIA
											CURRENT GNP PER CAPITA (US $)
13,010	14,310	12,810	10,140	8,630	7,820	6,690	6,470	6,430	7,060	..	**POPULATION** (thousands)
9,926	10,515	11,131	11,763	12,395	12,991	13,612	14,016	14,435	14,870	..	
											USE AND ORIGIN OF RESOURCES
(Billions of current Saudi Arabian Riyals)											
525.18	485.00	422.08	387.80	352.56	310.42	312.38	321.61	347.28	409.03	C	Gross National Product (GNP)
4.59	26.91	44.38	36.40	38.62	39.33	36.93	36.47	36.46	32.50	..	Net Factor Income from Abroad
520.59	458.10	377.70	351.40	313.94	271.09	275.45	285.14	310.82	376.53	C	GDP at Market Prices
210.97	70.50	-7.22	-45.11	-24.73	-29.25	-20.12	-11.32	2.06	45.84	..	Resource Balance
368.43	269.03	187.35	145.53	113.16	85.99	99.05	103.08	118.20	173.89	..	Exports of Goods & NFServices
157.46	198.53	194.57	190.64	137.89	115.24	119.17	114.40	116.14	128.05	..	Imports of Goods & NFServices
309.62	387.60	384.92	396.50	338.67	300.34	295.58	296.47	308.76	330.70	..	Domestic Absorption
114.90	147.78	160.33	159.35	158.59	140.15	135.54	139.40	145.03	148.05	..	Private Consumption, etc.
81.91	131.07	126.57	121.06	114.39	106.37	107.71	97.42	96.56	117.77	..	General Gov't Consumption
112.80	108.75	98.02	116.10	65.69	53.83	52.33	59.65	67.17	64.88	..	Gross Domestic Investment
106.38	120.99	109.87	96.49	76.31	66.14	65.20	56.92	60.41	71.14	..	Fixed Investment
..	..	..	..	..	..	..	..	..	..	..	Indirect Taxes, net
..	..	..	..	..	..	..	..	..	..	B C	GDP at factor cost
5.57	8.35	9.64	11.62	13.79	15.86	18.31	20.89	22.65	25.14	..	Agriculture
419.19	318.83	225.19	193.97	153.64	117.25	122.90	120.68	144.11	197.31	..	Industry
25.75	24.16	26.89	27.42	24.50	19.72	23.85	24.46	25.23	29.82	..	Manufacturing
95.83	130.92	142.86	145.81	146.51	137.98	134.24	143.57	144.06	154.08	..	Services, etc.
323.77	179.25	90.80	70.99	40.96	24.58	32.21	48.33	69.23	110.72	..	Gross Domestic Saving
310.27	187.83	117.09	88.77	60.75	46.11	50.66	60.42	74.45	99.64	..	Gross National Saving
(Billions of 1987 Saudi Arabian Riyals)											
341.41	342.06	336.02	304.90	296.38	317.84	312.38	335.24	335.75	364.80	C	Gross National Product
345.25	328.48	303.49	278.50	266.30	280.39	275.45	295.97	295.96	321.57	C	GDP at Market Prices
											Resource Balance
..	..	..	..	..	..	..	..	..	..	..	Exports of Goods & NFServices
..	..	..	..	..	..	..	..	..	..	..	Imports of Goods & NFServices
											Domestic Absorption
..	..	..	..	..	..	..	..	..	..	..	Private Consumption, etc.
..	..	..	..	..	..	..	..	..	..	..	General Gov't Consumption
..	..	..	..	..	..	..	..	..	..	..	Gross Domestic Investment
..	..	..	..	..	..	..	..	..	..	..	Fixed Investment
										B C	GDP at factor cost
7.43	8.65	9.75	11.60	13.68	15.73	18.31	20.29	21.71	23.23	..	Agriculture
195.68	170.91	148.13	122.64	108.84	128.44	122.90	138.09	136.75	156.29	..	Industry
13.37	15.89	17.88	18.81	21.10	21.14	23.85	26.06	25.36	26.68	..	Manufacturing
142.14	148.92	145.60	144.26	143.79	136.22	134.24	137.59	137.50	142.06	..	Services, etc.
											Memo Items:
..	..	..	..	..	..	..	..	..	..	..	Capacity to Import
..	..	..	..	..	..	..	..	..	..	..	Terms of Trade Adjustment
..	..	..	..	..	..	..	..	..	..	..	Gross Domestic Income
..	..	..	..	..	..	..	..	..	..	..	Gross National Income
											DOMESTIC PRICES/DEFLATORS
(Index 1987 = 100)											
150.8	139.5	124.5	126.2	117.9	96.7	100.0	96.3	105.0	117.1	..	Overall (GDP)
											Domestic Absorption
75.0	96.4	98.9	100.2	100.8	100.8	100.0	103.0	104.3	108.3	..	Agriculture
214.2	186.6	152.0	158.2	141.2	91.3	100.0	87.4	105.4	126.2	..	Industry
192.6	152.1	150.4	145.8	116.1	93.3	100.0	93.9	99.5	111.8	..	Manufacturing
108.6	109.7	110.0	108.2	104.9	101.6	100.0	100.9	101.9	104.1	..	Consumer Price Index
											MANUFACTURING ACTIVITY
..	..	..	..	..	..	..	..	..	..	..	Employment (1987=100)
..	..	..	..	..	..	..	..	..	..	..	Real Earnings per Empl. (1987=100)
..	..	..	..	..	..	..	..	..	..	..	Real Output per Empl. (1987=100)
..	..	..	..	..	..	..	..	..	..	..	Earnings as % of Value Added
											MONETARY HOLDINGS
(Billions of current Saudi Arabian Riyals)											
102.99	123.79	137.09	145.35	147.01	160.56	167.16	177.89	179.44	..	..	Money Supply, Broadly Defined
72.98	83.78	84.93	82.98	81.83	86.28	90.54	93.43	91.38			Money
29.49	34.44	35.42	35.11	35.77	38.81	38.84	35.95	33.88			Currency Outside Banks
43.49	49.34	49.51	47.86	46.06	47.47	51.70	57.48	57.51			Demand Deposits
30.01	40.01	52.16	62.37	65.18	74.28	76.62	84.46	88.06			Quasi-Money
(Millions of current Saudi Arabian Riyals)											
											GOVERNMENT DEFICIT (-) OR SURPLUS
..	..	..	..	..	..	..	..	..	..	..	Current Revenue
..	..	..	..	..	..	..	..	..	..	..	Current Expenditure
..	..	..	..	..	..	..	..	..	..	..	Current Budget Balance
..	..	..	..	..	..	..	..	..	..	..	Capital Receipts
..	..	..	..	..	..	..	..	..	..	..	Capital Payments

SAUDI ARABIA	1970	1971	1972	1973	1974	1975	1976	1977	1978	1979	1980
FOREIGN TRADE (CUSTOMS BASIS)					*(Millions of current US dollars)*						
Value of Exports, fob	2,424	3,845	5,491	9,089	35,562	29,669	38,282	43,458	40,715	63,419	109,113
Nonfuel Primary Products	4	4	9	14	49	31	30	27	95	107	182
Fuels	2,417	3,792	5,391	8,993	35,482	29,466	38,164	43,311	40,383	62,847	108,226
Manufactures	2	49	91	82	31	172	89	121	237	465	705
Value of Imports, cif	692	806	1,125	1,977	2,848	4,141	8,409	14,289	20,177	24,384	29,957
Nonfuel Primary Products	246	265	318	491	639	743	1,233	1,830	2,639	3,583	4,965
Fuels	8	10	11	13	29	28	62	81	136	156	191
Manufactures	438	531	796	1,473	2,180	3,370	7,113	12,378	17,403	20,646	24,801
					(Index 1987 = 100)						
Terms of Trade	23.8	30.0	30.5	34.6	114.8	104.5	111.8	112.5	99.1	124.1	184.2
Export Prices, fob	7.1	9.4	10.5	14.8	61.0	59.5	63.8	69.8	70.5	101.5	166.0
Import Prices, cif	29.8	31.2	34.5	42.8	53.1	57.0	57.0	62.0	71.2	81.8	90.1
BALANCE OF PAYMENTS					*(Millions of current US dollars)*						
Exports of Goods & Services	2,372	2,926	4,381	8,264	32,735	30,569	40,272	46,447	43,461	67,766	114,208
Merchandise, fob	2,089	2,581	3,911	7,489	30,132	27,294	35,632	40,351	36,993	58,009	100,717
Nonfactor Services	222	279	364	569	1,383	1,436	1,756	2,108	2,168	4,841	6,048
Factor Services	61	67	106	205	1,220	1,839	2,884	3,989	4,301	4,915	7,443
Imports of Goods & Services	2,037	1,600	1,867	4,856	8,177	12,503	21,601	29,049	38,929	50,294	62,710
Merchandise, fob	829	805	1,197	1,853	3,569	6,004	10,385	14,698	20,020	20,912	25,563
Nonfactor Services	313	374	509	955	2,163	4,375	7,935	10,272	14,396	27,318	30,231
Factor Services	895	421	162	2,048	2,445	2,124	3,280	4,079	4,512	2,065	6,917
Long-Term Interest	..	..	..	..	..	..	..	..	..	..	..
Private Current Transfers, net	-183	-207	-268	-391	-518	-554	-989	-1,506	-2,844	-3,764	-4,094
Workers' Remittances	..	..	..	..	..	..	..	..	..	..	..
Curr. A/C Bal before Off. Transf.	152	1,119	2,246	3,016	24,039	17,512	17,683	15,892	1,688	13,708	47,404
Net Official Transfers	-81	-147	-157	-496	-1,014	-3,127	-3,323	-3,901	-3,900	-3,502	-5,901
Curr. A/C Bal after Off. Transf.	71	972	2,089	2,520	23,025	14,385	14,360	11,991	-2,212	10,206	41,503
Long-Term Capital, net	93	-127	27	-912	-8,873	-9,137	-11,156	-7,503	-2,733	-3,440	-25,797
Direct Investment	20	-111	34	-626	-3,732	1,865	-397	783	556	-1,271	-3,192
Long-Term Loans	..	..	..	..	..	..	..	..	..	..	..
Disbursements	..	..	..	..	..	..	..	..	..	..	..
Repayments	..	..	..	..	..	..	..	..	..	..	..
Other Long-Term Capital	73	-16	-7	-286	-5,141	-11,002	-10,759	-8,286	-3,289	-2,169	-22,605
Other Capital, net	-77	-172	-1,059	-691	-3,764	3,811	523	-1,791	-1,755	-6,532	-11,769
Change in Reserves	-87	-673	-1,057	-917	-10,388	-9,059	-3,727	-2,697	6,700	-234	-3,937
Memo Item:					*(Saudi Arabian Riyals per US dollar)*						
Conversion Factor (Annual Avg)	4.500	4.490	4.150	3.710	3.550	3.520	3.530	3.520	3.400	3.360	3.330
				(Millions of US dollars), outstanding at end of year							
EXTERNAL DEBT (Total)	..	..	..	..	..	..	..	..	..	..	..
Long-Term Debt (by debtor)	..	..	..	..	..	..	..	..	..	..	..
Central Bank, incl. IMF credit	..	..	..	..	..	..	..	..	..	..	..
Central Government	..	..	..	..	..	..	..	..	..	..	..
Rest of General Government	..	..	..	..	..	..	..	..	..	..	..
Non-financial Public Enterprises	..	..	..	..	..	..	..	..	..	..	..
Priv. Sector, incl non-guaranteed	..	..	..	..	..	..	..	..	..	..	..
Short-Term Debt	..	..	..	..	..	..	..	..	..	..	..
Memo Items:					*(Millions of US dollars)*						
Int'l Reserves Excluding Gold	543	1,327	2,383	3,747	14,153	23,193	26,900	29,903	19,200	19,273	23,437
Gold Holdings (at market price)	127	135	200	346	575	432	415	508	1,026	2,338	2,692
SOCIAL INDICATORS											
Total Fertility Rate	7.3	7.3	7.3	7.3	7.3	7.3	7.3	7.3	7.3	7.3	7.3
Infant Mortality Rate	128.0	124.0	120.0	116.0	112.0	108.0	104.0	100.0	97.0	94.0	91.0
Life Expectancy at Birth	52.3	53.1	53.9	54.7	55.5	56.3	57.1	57.9	58.5	59.1	59.7
Urban Population, % of total	48.7	50.7	52.7	54.7	56.7	58.7	60.3	61.9	63.6	65.2	66.8
Food Prod. per capita (1987=100)	77.0	103.3	59.8	69.4	95.7	93.7	79.4	83.4	74.3	73.7	60.5
Labor Force, Agriculture (%)	64.2	62.3	60.5	59.0	57.6	56.3	54.3	52.6	51.0	49.7	48.4
Labor Force, Female (%)	5.0	5.2	5.4	5.6	5.7	5.9	6.0	6.1	6.1	6.2	6.3
Primary Schl. Enroll. Ratio	45.0	..	..	..	..	58.0	59.0	58.0	60.0	62.0	63.0
Primary Schl. Enroll. Ratio, Female	29.0	..	..	..	..	43.0	45.0	44.0	46.0	48.0	50.0
Secondary Schl. Enroll. Ratio	12.0	..	..	..	..	22.0	24.0	26.0	28.0	30.0	30.0

1981	1982	1983	1984	1985	1986	1987	1988	1989	1990 estimate	Notes	SAUDI ARABIA
											FOREIGN TRADE (CUSTOMS BASIS)
				(Millions of current US dollars)							
119,913	79,125	45,861	37,545	26,908	20,185	23,199	23,727	27,735	31,065	..	Value of Exports, fob
154	137	79	65	113	84	97	537	636	712	..	Nonfuel Primary Products
119,038	78,165	45,304	37,089	25,933	19,453	22,358	20,203	24,094	26,987	..	Fuels
721	824	477	391	862	647	744	2,987	3,006	3,367	..	Manufactures
35,042	40,473	38,911	33,473	23,439	19,079	19,927	21,608	20,258	24,069	..	Value of Imports, cif
5,770	5,967	5,554	5,916	3,950	3,535	3,636	3,833	3,844	4,567	..	Nonfuel Primary Products
254	192	200	207	118	47	52	51	58	69	..	Fuels
29,018	34,314	33,157	27,350	19,371	15,496	16,239	17,725	16,356	19,433	..	Manufactures
				(Index 1987 = 100)							
208.0	194.1	179.1	179.8	175.8	85.9	100.0	81.6	92.3	95.1	..	Terms of Trade
186.6	168.9	153.8	150.4	146.2	79.9	100.0	90.3	107.2	138.1	..	Export Prices, fob
89.7	87.0	85.9	83.7	83.2	92.9	100.0	110.6	116.1	145.2	..	Import Prices, cif
											BALANCE OF PAYMENTS
				(Millions of current US dollars)							
130,400	92,828	65,883	55,023	43,458	34,069	36,251	37,124	41,311	56,785	..	Exports of Goods & Services
111,831	73,876	45,662	37,423	27,393	20,125	23,138	24,315	28,299	44,283	..	Merchandise, fob
7,613	4,892	4,353	4,234	3,647	2,665	2,577	2,355	2,582	2,924	..	Nonfactor Services
10,956	14,060	15,868	13,366	12,418	11,279	10,537	10,454	10,430	9,578	..	Factor Services
79,725	75,507	73,499	64,541	47,941	38,060	37,789	35,455	39,997	44,855	..	Imports of Goods & Services
29,889	34,444	33,218	28,557	20,364	17,066	18,283	19,805	19,231	21,490	..	Merchandise, fob
40,236	34,852	37,259	32,857	25,822	20,336	18,830	14,935	20,072	22,465	..	Nonfactor Services
9,599	6,210	3,022	3,127	1,756	659	676	716	694	900	..	Factor Services
..	..	..	..	..	..	..	..	..	..		Long-Term Interest
-5,348	-5,347	-5,236	-5,284	-5,199	-4,804	-4,935	-6,510	-8,342	-11,637	..	Private Current Transfers, net
..	..	..	..	..	..	0	..	..	..		Workers' Remittances
45,327	11,974	-12,852	-14,802	-9,682	-8,795	-6,473	-4,841	-7,028	294	..	Curr. A/C Bal before Off. Transf.
-5,700	-4,399	-4,000	-3,598	-3,249	-3,000	-3,300	-2,499	-2,200	-4,401	..	Net Official Transfers
39,627	7,575	-16,852	-18,401	-12,932	-11,795	-9,773	-7,340	-9,228	-4,107	..	Curr. A/C Bal after Off. Transf.
-27,725	-362	-2,585	-8,556	-7,921	-2,484	-7,324	-3,386	-2,099	..	..	Long-Term Capital, net
6,498	11,128	4,944	4,850	491	967	-1,175	-328	-312	..	..	Direct Investment
..	..	..	..	..	..	..	..	..	..	..	Long-Term Loans
..	..	..	..	..	..	..	..	..	..		Disbursements
..	..	..	..	..	..	..	..	..	..		Repayments
-34,223	-11,490	-7,529	-13,406	-8,412	-3,451	-6,150	-3,057	-1,786	..		Other Long-Term Capital
-2,334	-9,522	17,929	25,477	20,143	6,660	19,737	9,207	7,819	-1,270	..	Other Capital, net
-9,568	2,308	1,508	1,480	709	7,619	-2,640	1,519	3,508	5,376	..	Change in Reserves
				(Saudi Arabian Riyals per US dollar)							**Memo Item:**
3.380	3.430	3.450	3.520	3.620	3.700	3.740	3.740	3.740	3.740	..	Conversion Factor (Annual Avg)
				(Millions of US dollars), outstanding at end of year							**EXTERNAL DEBT (Total)**
..	..	..	..	..	..	..	..	..	..	..	Long-Term Debt (by debtor)
..	..	..	..	..	..	..	..	..	..	..	Central Bank, incl. IMF credit
..	..	..	..	..	..	..	..	..	..	..	Central Government
..	..	..	..	..	..	..	..	..	..	..	Rest of General Government
..	..	..	..	..	..	..	..	..	..	..	Non-financial Public Enterprises
..	..	..	..	..	..	..	..	..	..	..	Priv. Sector, incl non-guaranteed
..	..	..	..	..	..	..	..	..	..	..	Short-Term Debt
				(Millions of US dollars)							**Memo Items:**
32,236	29,549	27,287	24,748	25,004	18,324	22,684	20,553	16,747	11,668	..	Int'l Reserves Excluding Gold
1,815	2,100	1,753	1,417	1,503	1,797	2,225	1,886	1,843	1,769	..	Gold Holdings (at market price)
											SOCIAL INDICATORS
7.3	7.3	7.3	7.2	7.2	7.2	7.2	7.1	7.1	7.0	..	Total Fertility Rate
88.0	85.0	82.2	79.4	76.5	73.7	70.9	69.0	67.1	65.1	..	Infant Mortality Rate
60.3	60.9	61.4	61.9	62.4	62.9	63.4	63.8	64.1	64.5	..	Life Expectancy at Birth
68.0	69.3	70.5	71.8	73.0	73.9	74.7	75.6	76.4	77.3	..	Urban Population, % of total
50.8	60.9	64.4	77.5	102.8	105.0	100.0	115.1	116.0	118.6	..	Food Prod. per capita (1987=100)
..	..	..	..	..	..	..	..	..	..	..	Labor Force, Agriculture (%)
6.4	6.4	6.5	6.6	6.7	6.8	7.0	7.1	7.2	7.3	..	Labor Force, Female (%)
	65.0	67.0	69.0	69.0	71.0	..	76.0	..	..	..	Primary Schl. Enroll. Ratio
53.0	54.0	58.0	60.0	61.0	64.0	..	70.0	..	..	..	Primary Schl. Enroll. Ratio, Female
..	33.0	35.0	38.0	42.0	44.0	..	46.0	..	..	..	Secondary Schl. Enroll. Ratio

SENEGAL	1970	1971	1972	1973	1974	1975	1976	1977	1978	1979	1980
CURRENT GNP PER CAPITA (US $)	220	220	230	240	280	350	400	400	380	460	510
POPULATION (thousands)	4,158	4,279	4,405	4,536	4,670	4,806	4,944	5,086	5,232	5,383	5,538

USE AND ORIGIN OF RESOURCES

(Billions of current CFA Francs)

	1970	1971	1972	1973	1974	1975	1976	1977	1978	1979	1980
Gross National Product (GNP)	234.3	242.0	267.8	271.8	327.3	394.6	453.3	469.9	477.3	565.1	616.2
Net Factor Income from Abroad	-5.8	-5.2	-5.8	-6.5	-11.5	-11.8	-6.0	-13.7	-17.4	-16.8	-21.1
GDP at Market Prices	240.1	247.2	273.6	278.3	338.8	406.4	459.3	483.6	494.7	581.9	637.3
Resource Balance	-11.0	-18.0	-10.0	-28.1	-22.4	-21.3	-36.9	-30.0	-62.9	-59.3	-100.1
Exports of Goods & NFServices	65.8	64.0	84.2	79.5	143.7	148.6	166.7	213.0	154.9	185.3	180.2
Imports of Goods & NFServices	76.8	82.0	94.2	107.6	166.1	169.9	203.6	243.0	217.8	244.6	280.3
Domestic Absorption	251.1	265.2	283.6	306.4	361.2	427.7	496.2	513.6	557.6	641.2	737.4
Private Consumption, etc.	177.7	186.4	196.3	210.0	236.1	293.6	348.8	351.1	380.3	446.6	499.8
General Gov't Consumption	35.7	38.8	40.8	43.8	50.0	61.8	71.7	77.9	91.1	111.0	140.3
Gross Domestic Investment	37.7	40.0	46.5	52.6	75.1	72.3	75.7	84.6	86.2	83.6	97.3
Fixed Investment	..	..	..	..	..	..	..	..	..	82.6	100.2
Indirect Taxes, net	27.3	30.3	32.0	32.8	37.4	44.8	52.9	59.0	55.8	63.7	..
GDP at factor cost	212.8	216.9	241.6	245.5	301.4	361.6	406.4	424.6	438.9	518.2	..
Agriculture	57.8	51.8	67.4	62.8	80.7	122.8	138.0	132.5	104.6	139.6	120.1
Industry	48.6	51.2	54.5	54.7	80.2	92.7	106.9	113.1	120.4	141.1	156.2
Manufacturing	39.2	41.6	44.2	44.8	66.8	74.7	85.5	75.6	76.3	89.4	96.3
Services, etc.	133.7	144.2	151.7	160.8	177.9	190.9	214.4	238.0	269.7	301.2	361.0
Gross Domestic Saving	26.7	22.0	36.5	24.5	52.7	51.0	38.8	54.6	23.3	24.3	-2.8
Gross National Saving	16.2	11.3	25.3	13.3	35.8	37.2	36.3	44.7	7.7	3.7	-28.1

(Billions of 1987 CFA Francs)

	1970	1971	1972	1973	1974	1975	1976	1977	1978	1979	1980
Gross National Product	882.83	898.30	949.87	898.42	923.84	999.89	1,106.14	1,071.93	1,001.77	1,095.67	1,070.19
GDP at Market Prices	903.90	916.32	969.13	918.18	955.61	1,028.38	1,118.08	1,101.70	1,037.19	1,126.53	1,103.99
Resource Balance	-33.85	-48.53	-12.91	-53.63	-45.09	-22.62	-20.35	-48.49	-115.67	-80.02	-106.46
Exports of Goods & NFServices	208.91	185.51	238.70	185.03	198.97	222.36	277.78	379.99	263.05	296.85	253.59
Imports of Goods & NFServices	242.75	234.04	251.60	238.66	244.06	244.98	298.14	428.48	378.72	376.87	360.06
Domestic Absorption	937.75	964.85	982.04	971.81	1,000.70	1,051.01	1,138.43	1,150.19	1,152.87	1,206.55	1,210.45
Private Consumption, etc.	675.76	696.10	696.67	683.09	689.34	757.29	817.42	811.36	810.95	877.85	876.83
General Gov't Consumption	101.53	103.81	103.81	103.07	110.07	115.88	114.83	141.64	154.30	165.32	168.80
Gross Domestic Investment	160.47	164.94	181.55	185.66	201.29	177.84	206.18	197.19	187.61	163.38	164.83
Fixed Investment	..	..	..	..	..	..	..	156.00	136.89	161.07	169.45
GDP at factor cost	..	..	..	..	..	..	..	..	..	..	..
Agriculture	255.91	213.67	264.40	221.92	273.27	283.42	326.11	303.71	232.06	295.04	241.15
Industry	122.82	141.40	145.26	138.79	154.18	164.55	178.12	208.83	193.09	192.78	206.01
Manufacturing	82.75	103.04	104.33	101.90	116.19	123.62	132.06	132.34	105.62	108.47	117.15
Services, etc.	525.18	561.25	559.47	557.47	528.15	580.41	613.84	589.16	612.04	638.71	656.83

Memo Items:

	1970	1971	1972	1973	1974	1975	1976	1977	1978	1979	1980
Capacity to Import	207.98	182.67	224.90	176.34	211.14	214.27	244.10	375.58	269.34	285.50	231.47
Terms of Trade Adjustment	-0.92	-2.84	-13.80	-8.69	12.18	-8.09	-33.68	-4.41	6.30	-11.35	-22.12
Gross Domestic Income	902.98	913.48	955.33	909.49	967.79	1,020.30	1,084.40	1,097.29	1,043.49	1,115.19	1,081.87
Gross National Income	881.90	895.45	936.07	889.73	936.02	991.81	1,072.46	1,067.52	1,008.07	1,084.32	1,048.07

DOMESTIC PRICES/DEFLATORS

(Index 1987 = 100)

	1970	1971	1972	1973	1974	1975	1976	1977	1978	1979	1980
Overall (GDP)	26.6	27.0	28.2	30.3	35.5	39.5	41.1	43.9	47.7	51.7	57.7
Domestic Absorption	26.8	27.5	28.9	31.5	36.1	40.7	43.6	44.7	48.4	53.1	60.9
Agriculture	22.6	24.2	25.5	28.3	29.5	43.3	42.3	43.6	45.1	47.3	49.8
Industry	39.6	36.2	37.5	39.4	52.0	56.3	60.0	54.2	62.4	73.2	75.8
Manufacturing	47.4	40.4	42.4	44.0	57.5	60.4	64.7	57.1	72.2	82.4	82.2
Consumer Price Index	21.4	22.3	23.6	26.3	30.7	40.4	40.8	45.5	47.0	51.6	56.1

MANUFACTURING ACTIVITY

	1970	1971	1972	1973	1974	1975	1976	1977	1978	1979	1980
Employment (1987=100)	..	..	..	..	..	..	..	..	..	..	..
Real Earnings per Empl. (1987=100)	..	..	..	..	..	..	..	..	..	..	..
Real Output per Empl. (1987=100)	..	..	..	..	..	..	..	..	..	..	..
Earnings as % of Value Added	..	..	..	..	29.7	30.4	31.3	27.8	45.9	46.6	43.0

MONETARY HOLDINGS

(Billions of current CFA Francs)

	1970	1971	1972	1973	1974	1975	1976	1977	1978	1979	1980
Money Supply, Broadly Defined	37.27	38.05	42.83	52.37	77.26	86.10	113.65	130.97	158.83	161.12	177.69
Money	34.50	35.20	39.12	44.20	67.77	75.18	94.89	109.12	126.53	121.21	137.94
Currency Outside Banks	15.24	15.94	16.49	19.45	28.96	29.46	33.74	39.47	46.22	42.94	51.36
Demand Deposits	19.26	19.26	22.63	24.75	38.81	45.72	61.15	69.65	80.30	78.28	86.58
Quasi-Money	2.77	2.84	3.72	8.17	9.49	10.92	18.76	21.85	32.31	39.91	39.75

GOVERNMENT DEFICIT (-) OR SURPLUS

(Billions of current CFA Francs)

	1970	1971	1972	1973	1974	1975	1976	1977	1978	1979	1980
GOVERNMENT DEFICIT (-) OR SURPLUS	1.24	-1.20	-2.03	-7.51	..	-2.15	..	-15.09	1.49	-4.26	5.44
Current Revenue	38.99	41.41	45.19	46.30	..	76.97	..	86.11	98.01	107.73	153.99
Current Expenditure	37.00	39.51	40.80	45.30	48.70	66.38	74.60	77.85	88.50	99.50	142.25
Current Budget Balance	1.99	1.90	4.39	1.00	..	10.59	..	8.26	9.51	8.23	11.74
Capital Receipts	1.00	0.03	2.00	1.40	..	0.08	..	0.16	0.17	0.08	0.04
Capital Payments	1.75	3.13	8.42	9.91	21.45	12.82	16.82	23.51	8.19	12.57	6.34

1981	1982	1983	1984	1985	1986	1987	1988	1989	1990 estimate	Notes	SENEGAL
490	510	440	380	380	430	520	650	660	710	..	**CURRENT GNP PER CAPITA (US $)**
5,698	5,864	6,036	6,213	6,395	6,584	6,779	6,980	7,189	7,404	..	**POPULATION (thousands)**
											USE AND ORIGIN OF RESOURCES
				(Billions of current CFA Francs)							
644.1	810.9	903.3	965.9	1,092.1	1,237.0	1,309.8	1,407.9	1,412.8	1,533.2	..	Gross National Product (GNP)
-29.7	-38.0	-41.4	-55.3	-66.0	-66.4	-72.6	-75.4	-65.2	-56.5	..	Net Factor Income from Abroad
673.8	848.9	944.7	1,021.2	1,158.1	1,303.4	1,382.4	1,483.3	1,478.0	1,589.7	..	GDP at Market Prices
-130.2	-104.1	-115.8	-96.7	-130.2	-70.6	-77.6	-74.6	-78.0	-63.4	..	Resource Balance
216.4	290.5	311.1	387.4	343.9	345.6	345.5	373.3	396.0	410.1	..	Exports of Goods & NFServices
346.6	394.6	426.9	484.1	474.1	416.2	423.1	447.9	474.0	473.5	..	Imports of Goods & NFServices
804.0	953.0	1,060.5	1,117.9	1,288.3	1,374.0	1,460.0	1,557.9	1,556.0	1,653.2	..	Domestic Absorption
586.5	702.7	778.0	809.7	980.3	1,030.0	1,082.6	1,154.5	1,172.0	1,223.9	..	Private Consumption, etc.
137.6	154.5	170.3	188.8	194.5	200.8	215.6	218.1	224.5	227.2	..	General Gov't Consumption
79.9	95.8	112.2	119.4	113.5	143.2	161.8	185.3	159.5	202.1	..	Gross Domestic Investment
84.4	102.7	122.3	125.2	133.0	155.7	170.9	185.3	189.5	202.1	..	Fixed Investment
..	..	..	..	..	..	..	..	..	..	..	Indirect Taxes, net
..	..	..	..	..	..	..	..	..	..	B	GDP at factor cost
120.2	184.3	203.1	172.8	217.1	290.7	299.5	333.0	292.3	326.5	..	Agriculture
106.6	127.4	146.2	174.0	205.0	227.6	246.9	273.1	272.7	292.1	..	Industry
77.5	88.3	100.0	123.2	148.3	163.3	177.5	197.7	194.4	205.9	..	Manufacturing
447.0	537.2	595.4	674.4	736.0	785.1	836.0	877.2	913.0	971.1	..	Services, etc.
-50.3	-8.3	-3.6	22.7	-16.7	72.6	84.2	110.7	81.5	138.6	..	Gross Domestic Saving
-82.7	-47.8	-45.6	-32.5	-79.3	9.9	13.5	44.8	25.0	90.1	..	Gross National Saving
				(Billions of 1987 CFA Francs)							
1,040.22	1,197.49	1,224.41	1,159.13	1,201.14	1,261.28	1,309.80	1,379.10	1,365.77	1,439.27	..	Gross National Product
1,085.56	1,249.56	1,276.09	1,222.99	1,271.39	1,329.40	1,382.40	1,452.60	1,427.90	1,492.01	..	GDP at Market Prices
-140.73	-53.30	-45.80	-66.10	-98.11	-78.10	-77.60	-63.89	-52.79	-48.79	..	Resource Balance
252.47	337.00	341.40	351.40	295.69	340.50	345.50	362.81	376.51	372.01	..	Exports of Goods & NFServices
393.20	390.30	387.20	417.50	393.80	418.60	423.10	426.70	429.30	420.80	..	Imports of Goods & NFServices
1,226.29	1,302.87	1,321.89	1,289.09	1,369.51	1,407.50	1,460.00	1,516.50	1,480.69	1,540.80	..	Domestic Absorption
951.39	988.87	989.89	961.39	1,054.71	1,044.20	1,082.60	1,121.70	1,109.49	1,132.60	..	Private Consumption, etc.
168.90	176.50	183.80	189.30	194.20	206.40	215.60	216.30	221.00	223.20	..	General Gov't Consumption
106.00	137.50	148.20	138.40	120.60	156.90	161.80	178.50	150.20	185.00	..	Gross Domestic Investment
121.60	130.30	139.70	133.90	134.20	161.40	170.90	178.30	179.10	184.80	..	Fixed Investment
..	..	..	..	..	..	..	..	..	..	B	GDP at factor cost
227.20	283.40	297.30	245.10	264.70	291.60	299.50	328.20	300.60	331.50	..	Agriculture
185.50	213.20	218.10	214.10	218.40	229.00	246.90	267.00	262.80	272.30	..	Industry
135.70	150.50	152.30	152.00	154.60	163.00	177.50	195.20	191.10	198.60	..	Manufacturing
672.86	752.97	760.69	763.79	788.29	808.80	836.00	857.40	864.50	888.21	..	Services, etc.
											Memo Items:
245.49	287.33	282.17	334.10	285.65	347.59	345.50	355.63	358.66	364.46	..	Capacity to Import
-6.98	-49.66	-59.23	-17.30	-10.03	7.09	0.00	-7.17	-17.85	-7.55	..	Terms of Trade Adjustment
1,078.58	1,199.90	1,216.86	1,205.69	1,261.36	1,336.49	1,382.40	1,445.43	1,410.05	1,484.46	..	Gross Domestic Income
1,033.24	1,147.82	1,165.18	1,141.83	1,191.10	1,268.38	1,309.80	1,371.93	1,347.92	1,431.72	..	Gross National Income
				(Index 1987 = 100)							**DOMESTIC PRICES/DEFLATORS**
62.1	67.9	74.0	83.5	91.1	98.0	100.0	102.1	103.5	106.5	..	Overall (GDP)
65.6	73.1	80.2	86.7	94.1	97.6	100.0	102.7	105.1	107.3	..	Domestic Absorption
52.9	65.0	68.3	70.5	82.0	99.7	100.0	101.5	97.2	98.5	..	Agriculture
57.5	59.8	67.0	81.3	93.9	99.4	100.0	102.3	103.8	107.3	..	Industry
57.1	58.7	65.7	81.1	95.9	100.2	100.0	101.3	101.7	103.7	..	Manufacturing
59.4	69.7	77.8	86.9	98.2	104.3	100.0	98.2	98.6	98.9	..	Consumer Price Index
											MANUFACTURING ACTIVITY
..	..	..	..	..	..	..	..	..	..	..	Employment (1987=100)
..	..	..	..	..	..	..	..	..	..	..	Real Earnings per Empl. (1987=100)
..	..	..	..	..	..	..	..	..	..	..	Real Output per Empl. (1987=100)
49.2	44.6	43.5	43.2	43.8	43.8	..	..	..	..	J	Earnings as % of Value Added
				(Billions of current CFA Francs)							**MONETARY HOLDINGS**
216.92	262.33	273.00	287.12	300.11	333.67	332.83	334.49	368.94	351.18	..	Money Supply, Broadly Defined
163.23	189.00	189.15	191.65	193.49	226.99	214.42	214.91	230.83	204.20	..	Money
73.61	84.49	78.28	77.32	86.22	104.30	100.70	92.78	102.68	95.24	..	Currency Outside Banks
89.62	104.51	110.87	114.32	107.26	122.69	113.72	122.13	128.15	108.97	..	Demand Deposits
53.69	73.34	83.85	95.47	106.62	106.68	118.41	119.58	138.11	146.98	..	Quasi-Money
				(Billions of current CFA Francs)							
-22.63	-52.30	-55.47	-82.44	..	..	..	..	..	..	C F	**GOVERNMENT DEFICIT (-) OR SURPLUS**
151.97	180.04	196.19	217.15	..	..	..	..	..	..		Current Revenue
140.93	169.09	181.12	237.69	..	..	..	..	..	..		Current Expenditure
11.04	10.95	15.07	-20.54	..	..	..	..	..	..		Current Budget Balance
0.10	0.48	0.11	0.08	..	..	..	..	..	..		Capital Receipts
33.77	63.73	70.65	61.98	..	..	..	..	..	..		Capital Payments

SENEGAL	1970	1971	1972	1973	1974	1975	1976	1977	1978	1979	1980
FOREIGN TRADE (CUSTOMS BASIS)					*(Millions of current US dollars)*						
Value of Exports, fob	160.6	124.9	215.9	194.7	390.7	462.4	485.2	622.8	420.8	533.3	476.7
Nonfuel Primary Products	125.5	89.0	169.5	140.2	315.3	360.8	388.9	499.1	299.8	426.4	315.0
Fuels	4.7	7.3	8.7	11.4	22.1	32.4	40.5	52.0	60.3	66.2	89.5
Manufactures	30.3	28.6	37.6	43.0	53.3	69.2	55.8	71.6	60.8	40.7	72.1
Value of Imports, cif	192.4	217.8	278.5	359.0	497.4	581.4	644.0	762.3	756.1	931.2	1,037.9
Nonfuel Primary Products	62.9	77.7	88.8	147.7	186.9	169.2	167.9	198.7	203.7	239.0	268.9
Fuels	9.6	13.6	15.8	21.8	64.7	69.2	80.5	95.3	106.2	154.3	263.0
Manufactures	119.9	126.5	173.9	189.5	245.9	343.0	395.6	468.3	446.1	537.8	506.0
					(Index 1987 = 100)						
Terms of Trade	120.4	112.1	116.4	108.3	133.9	125.6	121.3	119.9	106.9	106.6	105.5
Export Prices, fob	34.5	33.6	39.6	49.0	92.2	85.0	80.6	87.1	85.2	99.5	118.7
Import Prices, cif	28.7	29.9	34.0	45.2	68.8	67.7	66.5	72.7	79.8	93.3	112.5
BALANCE OF PAYMENTS					*(Millions of current US dollars)*						
Exports of Goods & Services	242.6	238.6	343.1	364.4	608.7	696.2	703.7	865.0	686.8	832.6	830.5
Merchandise, fob	158.7	135.5	225.3	214.2	416.9	503.1	513.8	667.2	401.7	478.5	421.7
Nonfactor Services	79.1	96.5	109.7	143.8	183.0	185.1	182.1	188.0	273.4	337.6	385.1
Factor Services	4.8	6.6	8.1	6.4	8.8	8.1	7.7	9.7	11.7	16.5	23.7
Imports of Goods & Services	291.7	312.4	396.9	522.8	737.7	865.7	902.8	1,039.2	1,042.6	1,196.9	1,337.0
Merchandise, fob	203.7	221.9	283.9	374.7	552.5	611.5	659.6	772.5	744.2	813.3	875.1
Nonfactor Services	68.3	67.6	83.0	101.5	126.5	170.2	174.5	202.6	210.6	287.7	339.6
Factor Services	19.7	23.0	30.0	46.6	58.7	84.0	68.7	64.1	87.8	95.9	122.3
Long-Term Interest	2.3	4.5	6.2	8.3	14.8	19.3	18.7	22.3	31.8	48.9	67.2
Private Current Transfers, net	-17.1	-19.9	-21.4	-21.2	-22.5	-9.5	14.6	15.5	8.1	-18.0	-19.8
Workers' Remittances	2.8	2.8	3.9	5.5	7.8	25.4	45.2	42.1	53.7	54.4	74.8
Curr. A/C Bal before Off. Transf.	-66.2	-93.7	-75.2	-179.6	-151.5	-179.0	-184.6	-158.8	-347.7	-382.2	-526.3
Net Official Transfers	50.1	68.2	85.9	78.2	85.9	93.4	92.1	91.8	112.4	118.5	140.2
Curr. A/C Bal after Off. Transf.	-16.1	-25.5	10.7	-101.4	-65.6	-85.6	-92.5	-67.0	-235.2	-263.7	-386.1
Long-Term Capital, net	26.1	25.7	-0.7	53.8	42.0	53.1	85.4	58.5	140.5	111.5	301.4
Direct Investment	4.7	9.4	12.8	4.8	7.0	15.7	35.5	25.1	-5.5	5.0	12.9
Long-Term Loans	10.6	23.7	11.6	72.0	55.2	58.0	65.5	96.6	157.8	126.0	170.5
Disbursements	20.0	36.3	22.7	104.2	79.6	80.8	91.4	133.0	232.2	211.6	326.8
Repayments	9.4	12.6	11.1	32.2	24.4	22.8	25.9	36.4	74.4	85.6	156.3
Other Long-Term Capital	10.8	-7.4	-25.1	-23.0	-20.3	-20.6	-15.6	-63.2	-11.8	-19.5	117.9
Other Capital, net	0.0	1.2	-4.6	15.9	17.8	28.0	-11.8	11.9	53.3	139.2	38.4
Change in Reserves	-10.0	-1.5	-5.3	31.7	5.9	4.5	18.8	-3.4	41.5	13.1	46.3
Memo Item:					*(CFA Francs per US dollar)*						
Conversion Factor (Annual Avg)	277.710	277.130	252.480	222.890	240.700	214.310	238.950	245.680	225.650	212.720	211.280
					(Millions of US dollars), outstanding at end of year						
EXTERNAL DEBT (Total)	145.3	152.3	161.7	199.3	265.0	349.1	409.6	628.1	894.5	1,122.2	1,472.8
Long-Term Debt (by debtor)	145.3	152.3	161.7	199.3	265.0	349.1	409.6	518.1	753.5	919.2	1,253.8
Central Bank, incl. IMF credit	0.0	0.0	0.0	0.0	0.0	29.8	29.5	30.9	74.3	92.9	140.1
Central Government	82.2	99.7	111.8	129.6	188.8	236.2	288.7	375.7	536.1	642.9	872.5
Rest of General Government	0.3	0.2	0.2	0.1	0.1	0.0	0.0	0.0	0.4	0.3	0.2
Non-financial Public Enterprises	22.7	15.4	18.8	45.0	51.9	57.7	63.7	78.2	111.0	122.1	180.7
Priv. Sector, incl non-guaranteed	40.1	37.0	30.9	24.6	24.2	25.4	27.7	33.3	31.7	61.0	60.3
Short-Term Debt	0.0	0.0	0.0	0.0	0.0	0.0	0.0	110.0	141.0	203.0	219.0
Memo Items:					*(Thousands of US dollars)*						
Int'l Reserves Excluding Gold	22,050	29,323	38,493	12,062	6,320	31,126	25,220	33,665	18,816	19,150	8,069
Gold Holdings (at market price)	..	..	..	..	..	..	..	2,408	4,949	14,848	17,096
SOCIAL INDICATORS											
Total Fertility Rate	6.5	6.5	6.5	6.5	6.6	6.6	6.6	6.6	6.6	6.6	6.6
Infant Mortality Rate	134.8	128.4	122.0	120.0	118.0	116.0	114.0	112.0	109.0	106.0	103.0
Life Expectancy at Birth	42.6	42.9	43.2	43.5	43.9	44.2	44.6	44.9	45.0	45.1	45.2
Urban Population, % of total	33.4	33.6	33.7	33.9	34.0	34.2	34.3	34.5	34.6	34.8	34.9
Food Prod. per capita (1987=100)	93.2	134.2	81.0	93.4	123.0	156.3	133.4	68.3	119.9	79.2	65.0
Labor Force, Agriculture (%)	82.7	82.4	82.2	82.0	81.8	81.6	81.4	81.2	81.0	80.8	80.6
Labor Force, Female (%)	41.3	41.3	41.3	41.3	41.3	41.3	41.3	41.3	41.3	41.3	41.3
Primary Schl. Enroll. Ratio	41.0	..	..	..	..	41.0	..	41.0	42.0	44.0	46.0
Primary Schl. Enroll. Ratio, Female	32.0	..	..	..	..	34.0	..	32.0	34.0	35.0	37.0
Secondary Schl. Enroll. Ratio	10.0	..	..	..	..	10.0	..	10.0	10.0	10.0	11.0

				(Millions of current US dollars)							**FOREIGN TRADE (CUSTOMS BASIS)**
560.8	547.9	618.0	634.0	562.0	624.8	604.6	591.2	750.9	782.6	..	Value of Exports, fob
240.7	364.8	394.9	415.0	367.9	343.3	338.2	387.0	491.5	509.9	..	Nonfuel Primary Products
209.8	135.7	178.0	71.3	63.2	121.8	114.1	66.5	84.5	96.5	..	Fuels
110.3	47.4	45.1	147.7	130.9	159.7	152.3	137.7	174.9	176.2	..	Manufactures
1,077.4	991.9	1,025.3	980.9	825.7	960.9	1,023.4	1,079.6	1,534.0	1,620.4	..	Value of Imports, cif
307.6	241.8	233.6	281.9	237.3	259.2	260.9	310.3	440.9	531.6	..	Nonfuel Primary Products
327.5	249.6	310.7	230.6	194.2	228.4	178.1	253.9	360.7	258.2	..	Fuels
442.4	500.5	481.0	468.3	394.2	473.3	584.3	515.4	732.4	830.5	..	Manufactures
				(Index 1987 = 100)							
108.8	103.4	105.3	110.3	105.6	95.2	100.0	101.7	102.9	105.8	..	Terms of Trade
126.5	108.2	106.1	108.8	98.9	93.5	100.0	104.3	105.2	129.2	..	Export Prices, fob
116.3	104.6	100.7	98.6	93.7	98.2	100.0	102.6	102.2	122.1	..	Import Prices, cif
				(Millions of current US dollars)							**BALANCE OF PAYMENTS**
1,002.2	903.5	972.6	915.8	855.2	1,076.7	1,124.1	1,267.8	1,271.4	1,497.4	f	Exports of Goods & Services
560.6	501.9	605.8	597.8	514.7	657.0	670.9	762.8	776.2	911.6	..	Merchandise, fob
421.2	380.6	341.3	302.4	329.8	406.0	441.1	491.5	470.2	563.1	..	Nonfactor Services
20.4	21.0	25.5	15.7	10.7	13.7	12.1	13.4	25.1	22.8	..	Factor Services
1,630.8	1,346.7	1,433.1	1,327.2	1,296.4	1,541.7	1,664.7	1,771.0	1,724.7	2,007.6	f	Imports of Goods & Services
1,020.3	815.1	917.2	818.9	795.8	883.3	955.8	1,009.6	1,004.0	1,176.1	..	Merchandise, fob
494.3	414.2	391.6	369.7	366.5	484.4	503.7	500.9	489.3	573.0	..	Nonfactor Services
116.3	117.4	124.2	138.6	134.1	174.0	205.2	260.5	231.3	258.6	..	Factor Services
50.0	37.5	42.0	59.4	51.0	98.9	122.3	118.5	149.4	84.3	..	Long-Term Interest
-10.1	-4.6	-1.6	0.3	7.6	10.7	6.3	31.9	27.3	29.4	..	Private Current Transfers, net
64.5	62.2	55.1	50.3	55.0	69.3	71.2	73.9	69.9	84.5	..	Workers' Remittances
-638.8	-447.8	-462.0	-411.1	-433.6	-454.3	-534.2	-471.3	-426.0	-480.8	..	Curr. A/C Bal before Off. Transf.
177.2	182.2	157.7	138.6	162.1	187.1	228.2	205.1	231.0	355.9	..	Net Official Transfers
-461.5	-265.6	-304.3	-272.4	-271.5	-267.2	-306.0	-266.2	-195.0	-124.9	..	Curr. A/C Bal after Off. Transf.
241.7	188.1	236.4	245.2	155.4	272.2	397.8	255.8	280.5	275.8	f	Long-Term Capital, net
19.6	10.1	-36.3	27.2	-18.9	-13.1	-5.8	0.0	-10.1	-8.0	..	Direct Investment
222.9	270.2	332.6	161.3	124.7	319.9	277.7	119.4	243.7	86.9	..	Long-Term Loans
302.0	300.7	362.1	205.8	177.1	418.3	436.8	286.5	375.5	226.7	..	Disbursements
79.1	30.5	29.5	44.5	52.4	98.4	159.1	167.1	131.8	139.8	..	Repayments
-0.8	-92.2	-59.9	56.6	49.6	-34.6	125.9	136.4	46.9	196.9	..	Other Long-Term Capital
160.0	-60.6	48.2	1.0	102.5	-1.1	-110.1	34.4	-19.9	-106.7	f	Other Capital, net
59.9	138.0	19.8	26.2	13.6	-3.9	18.3	-24.0	-65.6	-44.3	..	Change in Reserves
				(CFA Francs per US dollar)							**Memo Item:**
271.730	328.600	381.060	436.960	449.260	346.300	300.530	297.850	319.010	272.260	..	Conversion Factor (Annual Avg)
			(Millions of US dollars), outstanding at end of year								**EXTERNAL DEBT (Total)**
1,670.2	1,861.0	2,077.3	2,202.7	2,562.7	3,224.4	4,034.6	3,896.7	3,286.7	3,745.3	..	Long-Term Debt (by debtor)
1,433.2	1,659.0	1,885.2	1,930.7	2,338.6	2,951.0	3,713.3	3,615.9	3,020.0	3,327.9	..	Central Bank, incl. IMF credit
186.5	220.7	230.8	230.0	267.7	289.0	342.8	318.3	316.0	314.3	..	Central Government
1,051.2	1,244.8	1,465.2	1,520.7	1,865.8	2,352.7	2,985.7	2,964.8	2,450.8	2,728.3	..	Rest of General Government
0.1	0.0	0.0	0.0	0.0	0.0	0.0	0.0	0.0	..	..	Non-financial Public Enterprises
148.4	154.0	158.7	153.2	175.8	217.1	284.7	247.6	172.6	175.8	..	Priv. Sector, incl non-guaranteed
47.0	39.5	30.5	26.8	29.3	92.2	100.1	85.2	80.6	109.5	..	Short-Term Debt
237.0	202.0	192.1	272.0	224.1	273.4	321.3	280.8	266.7	417.4	..	
				(Thousands of US dollars)							**Memo Items:**
8,664	11,422	12,207	3,688	5,051	9,379	9,202	10,463	19,011	10,959	..	Int'l Reserves Excluding Gold
11,528	13,250	11,064	8,941	9,483	11,336	14,039	11,897	11,629	11,165	..	Gold Holdings (at market price)
											SOCIAL INDICATORS
6.6	6.6	6.6	6.6	6.6	6.5	6.5	..	..	..	..	Total Fertility Rate
100.0	97.0	95.0	93.0	91.0	89.0	87.0	84.9	82.7	80.6	..	Infant Mortality Rate
45.2	45.3	45.6	45.9	46.1	46.4	46.7	46.9	47.1	47.3	..	Life Expectancy at Birth
35.2	35.5	35.8	36.1	36.4	36.9	37.4	37.7	38.1	38.4	..	Urban Population, % of total
102.7	103.0	65.6	64.3	82.9	94.0	100.0	82.1	91.0	79.7	..	Food Prod. per capita (1987=100)
..	..	..	..	..	..	..	..	..	..	..	Labor Force, Agriculture (%)
41.1	40.9	40.7	40.5	40.3	40.1	39.9	39.7	39.5	39.3	..	Labor Force, Female (%)
..	51.0	53.0	55.0	56.0	58.0	58.0	58.0	58.0		..	Primary Schl. Enroll. Ratio
38.0	41.0	43.0	44.0	46.0	47.0	48.0	48.0	49.0	..	..	Primary Schl. Enroll. Ratio, Female
..	12.0	12.0	13.0	14.0	14.0	15.0	16.0	16.0	..	..	Secondary Schl. Enroll. Ratio

SEYCHELLES	1970	1971	1972	1973	1974	1975	1976	1977	1978	1979	1980
CURRENT GNP PER CAPITA (US $)	350	410	470	580	700	800	870	950	1,120	1,610	2,010
POPULATION (thousands)	53	55	56	57	58	59	60	61	62	62	63

USE AND ORIGIN OF RESOURCES

(Millions of current Seychelles Rupees)

	1970	1971	1972	1973	1974	1975	1976	1977	1978	1979	1980
Gross National Product (GNP)	102.0	120.0	163.0	200.0	245.0	287.0	349.8	463.4	556.6	749.9	907.8
Net Factor Income from Abroad	-0.4	-0.5	-0.6	-0.8	-1.0	-1.1	-15.8	-29.6	-38.3	-56.3	-34.1
GDP at Market Prices	102.4	120.5	163.6	200.8	246.0	288.1	365.6	493.0	594.9	806.2	941.9
Resource Balance	..	..	..	..	..	..	-58.5	-19.9	-7.4	-48.3	-105.3
Exports of Goods & NFServices	..	..	..	..	..	..	271.9	386.3	488.4	582.5	640.1
Imports of Goods & NFServices	..	..	..	..	..	..	330.4	406.2	495.8	630.8	745.4
Domestic Absorption	..	..	..	..	..	..	424.1	512.9	602.3	854.5	1,047.2
Private Consumption, etc.	..	..	..	..	..	..	200.3	198.5	195.3	377.6	416.3
General Gov't Consumption	..	..	..	..	..	..	81.5	117.1	149.5	211.4	270.0
Gross Domestic Investment	..	..	..	..	..	..	142.3	197.3	257.5	265.5	360.9
Fixed Investment	..	..	..	..	..	..	134.5	190.5	253.4	256.6	344.2
Indirect Taxes, net	..	..	..	..	..	..	..	..	..	..	..
GDP at factor cost	..	..	..	..	..	..	..	..	..	..	..
Agriculture	..	..	..	..	..	..	35.2	45.2	50.0	58.8	64.4
Industry	..	..	..	..	..	..	59.3	68.2	82.1	121.7	147.3
Manufacturing	..	..	..	..	..	..	20.1	26.9	36.4	48.6	69.5
Services, etc.	..	..	..	..	..	..	271.1	379.6	462.8	625.7	730.2
Gross Domestic Saving	..	..	..	..	..	..	83.8	177.4	250.1	217.2	255.6
Gross National Saving	..	..	..	..	..	..	65.0	143.8	206.7	154.4	212.2

(Millions of 1987 Seychelles Rupees)

	1970	1971	1972	1973	1974	1975	1976	1977	1978	1979	1980
Gross National Product	596.4	690.9	734.5	801.0	811.3	836.8	895.2	941.7	1,000.5	1,158.0	1,175.3
GDP at Market Prices	600.3	695.4	739.3	806.3	816.8	842.7	937.6	1,006.5	1,075.2	1,252.6	1,221.0
Resource Balance	..	..	..	..	..	..	..	..	..	..	..
Exports of Goods & NFServices	..	..	..	..	..	..	..	..	..	..	..
Imports of Goods & NFServices	..	..	..	..	..	..	..	..	..	..	..
Domestic Absorption	..	..	..	..	..	..	..	..	..	..	..
Private Consumption, etc.	..	..	..	..	..	..	..	..	..	..	..
General Gov't Consumption	..	..	..	..	..	..	..	..	..	..	..
Gross Domestic Investment	..	..	..	..	..	..	..	..	..	..	..
Fixed Investment	..	..	..	..	..	..	..	..	..	..	..
GDP at factor cost	..	..	..	..	..	..	..	..	..	..	..
Agriculture	..	..	..	..	..	..	68.2	63.2	58.5	68.0	68.0
Industry	..	..	..	..	..	..	130.1	131.0	143.7	182.3	179.6
Manufacturing	..	..	..	..	..	..	58.7	70.4	82.7	90.8	115.7
Services, etc.	..	..	..	..	..	..	739.3	812.3	873.1	1,002.3	973.3

Memo Items:

	1970	1971	1972	1973	1974	1975	1976	1977	1978	1979	1980
Capacity to Import	..	..	..	..	..	..	..	..	..	..	..
Terms of Trade Adjustment	..	..	..	..	..	..	..	..	..	..	..
Gross Domestic Income	..	..	..	..	..	..	..	..	..	..	..
Gross National Income	..	..	..	..	..	..	..	..	..	..	..

DOMESTIC PRICES/DEFLATORS

(Index 1987 = 100)

	1970	1971	1972	1973	1974	1975	1976	1977	1978	1979	1980
Overall (GDP)	17.1	17.3	22.1	24.9	30.1	34.2	39.0	49.0	55.3	64.4	77.1
Domestic Absorption	..	..	..	..	..	..	..	..	..	..	..
Agriculture	..	..	..	..	..	..	51.6	71.6	85.5	86.5	94.7
Industry	..	..	..	..	..	..	45.6	52.1	57.1	66.7	82.0
Manufacturing	..	..	..	..	..	..	34.2	38.2	44.0	53.5	60.0
Consumer Price Index	17.4	20.0	24.2	28.6	35.7	42.3	48.6	55.8	62.4	70.2	79.7

MANUFACTURING ACTIVITY

	1970	1971	1972	1973	1974	1975	1976	1977	1978	1979	1980
Employment (1987=100)	..	..	..	..	..	..	..	..	..	..	..
Real Earnings per Empl. (1987=100)	..	..	..	..	..	..	..	..	..	..	..
Real Output per Empl. (1987=100)	..	..	..	..	..	..	..	..	..	..	..
Earnings as % of Value Added	..	..	..	..	..	..	44.1	41.2	36.7	39.0	29.0

MONETARY HOLDINGS

(Millions of current Seychelles Rupees)

	1970	1971	1972	1973	1974	1975	1976	1977	1978	1979	1980
Money Supply, Broadly Defined	..	45.30	64.80	72.00	74.50	96.40	138.30	162.10	186.90	233.30	313.80
Money	..	25.40	37.70	40.30	41.90	47.80	67.60	83.80	95.00	114.70	158.70
Currency Outside Banks	..	12.40	17.00	18.90	20.10	22.70	31.10	40.10	43.90	52.90	61.70
Demand Deposits	..	13.00	20.70	21.40	21.80	25.10	36.50	43.70	51.10	61.80	97.00
Quasi-Money	..	19.90	27.10	31.70	32.60	48.60	70.70	78.30	91.90	118.60	155.10

GOVERNMENT DEFICIT (-) OR SURPLUS

(Millions of current Seychelles Rupees)

	1970	1971	1972	1973	1974	1975	1976	1977	1978	1979	1980
Current Revenue	..	..	..	..	..	..	..	..	..	..	..
Current Expenditure	..	..	..	..	..	..	..	..	..	..	..
Current Budget Balance	..	..	..	..	..	..	..	..	..	..	..
Capital Receipts	..	..	..	..	..	..	..	..	..	..	..
Capital Payments	..	..	..	..	..	..	..	..	..	..	..

1981	1982	1983	1984	1985	1986	1987	1988	1989	1990 estimate	Notes	SEYCHELLES
2,300	2,350	2,370	2,360	2,560	2,710	3,110	3,700	4,230	4,670	..	**CURRENT GNP PER CAPITA (US $)**
64	64	64	65	65	66	66	67	67	68	..	**POPULATION (thousands)**
				(Millions of current Seychelles Rupees)							**USE AND ORIGIN OF RESOURCES**
957.2	941.8	960.3	1,026.9	1,162.7	1,231.5	1,307.3	1,430.3	1,574.0	1,680.4	..	Gross National Product (GNP)
-14.6	-26.4	-32.6	-41.2	-42.2	-52.4	-78.2	-93.6	-74.9	-82.8	..	Net Factor Income from Abroad
971.8	968.2	992.9	1,068.1	1,204.9	1,283.9	1,385.5	1,523.9	1,648.9	1,763.2	..	GDP at Market Prices
-151.5	-227.6	-220.3	-144.3	-186.7	..	..	..	..	..	..	Resource Balance
554.1	507.9	415.0	524.9	581.1	..	..	..	..	..	..	Exports of Goods & NFServices
705.6	735.5	635.3	669.2	767.8	..	..	..	..	..	..	Imports of Goods & NFServices
1,123.3	1,195.8	1,213.2	1,212.4	1,391.6	1,507.1	1,542.6	1,711.8	1,904.2	1,924.2	..	Domestic Absorption
497.7	544.6	676.8	653.2	700.7	716.8	878.0	992.0	1,106.7	1,100.0	..	Private Consumption, etc.
308.5	338.0	326.0	327.7	417.4	497.6	406.6	415.6	471.0	449.6	..	General Gov't Consumption
317.1	313.2	210.4	231.5	273.5	292.7	258.0	304.2	326.5	374.6	..	Gross Domestic Investment
329.6	302.9	219.9	226.9	273.5	286.9	242.2	271.2	293.5	341.6	..	Fixed Investment
..	..	..	..	..	..	..	..	..	..		Indirect Taxes, net
..	..	..	..	..	..	..	..	..	..	B	GDP at factor cost
76.5	62.0	76.9	68.9	69.3	77.2	73.9	72.3	74.4	77.1	..	Agriculture
166.7	150.2	156.7	176.5	221.2	229.8	213.5	252.7	294.4	343.5	..	Industry
83.4	82.6	95.6	100.3	116.4	119.0	132.5	158.0	187.1	220.4	..	Manufacturing
728.6	756.0	759.3	822.7	914.4	976.9	1,098.1	1,198.9	1,280.1	1,342.6	..	Services, etc.
165.6	85.6	-9.9	87.2	86.8	69.5	100.9	116.3	71.2	213.6	..	Gross Domestic Saving
134.3	38.1	-61.3	29.5	38.7	-14.2	9.8	-3.8	-33.0	117.4	..	Gross National Saving
				(Millions of 1987 Seychelles Rupees)							
1,128.5	1,087.2	1,112.7	1,141.6	1,262.9	1,264.2	1,307.3	1,355.3	1,454.8	1,551.7		Gross National Product
1,143.6	1,117.5	1,102.2	1,187.4	1,308.8	1,318.0	1,385.5	1,443.9	1,525.8	1,628.2		GDP at Market Prices
..	..	..	..	..	..	..	..	..	..		Resource Balance
..	..	..	..	..	..	..	..	..	..		Exports of Goods & NFServices
..	..	..	..	..	..	..	..	..	..		Imports of Goods & NFServices
..	..	..	..	..	..	..	..	..	..		Domestic Absorption
..	..	..	..	..	..	..	..	..	..		Private Consumption, etc.
..	..	..	345.3	414.1	514.6	406.6	413.1	438.6	417.8	..	General Gov't Consumption
..	..	..	260.6	302.4	304.0	258.0	298.7	336.7	349.6	..	Gross Domestic Investment
..	..	..	255.4	302.4	298.0	242.2	266.3	302.7	318.9	..	Fixed Investment
..	..	..	..	..	..	..	..	..	..	B	GDP at factor cost
86.9	67.8	84.4	72.7	72.4	77.5	73.9	70.3	75.6	..	..	Agriculture
163.9	142.8	126.0	181.6	213.4	221.0	213.5	222.3	241.4		..	Industry
90.3	93.5	102.6	103.3	112.1	118.0	132.5	146.4	160.2	..	..	Manufacturing
892.8	906.9	891.8	933.1	1,023.0	1,019.5	1,098.1	1,151.2	1,208.8	..	..	Services, etc.
											Memo Items:
..	..	..	..	..	..	..	..	..	..		Capacity to Import
..	..	..	..	..	..	..	..	..	..		Terms of Trade Adjustment
..	..	..	..	..	..	..	..	..	..		Gross Domestic Income
..	..	..	..	..	..	..	..	..	..		Gross National Income
				(Index 1987 = 100)							**DOMESTIC PRICES/DEFLATORS**
85.0	86.6	90.1	90.0	92.1	97.4	100.0	105.5	108.1	108.3	..	Overall (GDP)
..	..	..	..	..	..	..	..	..	..		Domestic Absorption
88.0	91.5	91.1	94.8	95.7	99.6	100.0	102.9	98.4	..	..	Agriculture
101.7	105.2	124.4	97.2	103.7	104.0	100.0	113.7	122.0	..	..	Industry
92.3	88.3	93.1	97.1	103.9	100.8	100.0	107.9	116.8	..	..	Manufacturing
88.1	87.4	92.7	96.5	97.2	97.5	100.0	101.8	103.4	107.5	..	Consumer Price Index
											MANUFACTURING ACTIVITY
..	..	..	..	..	..	..	..	..	..		Employment (1987=100)
..	..	..	..	..	..	..	..	..	..		Real Earnings per Empl. (1987=100)
..	..	..	..	..	..	..	..	..	..		Real Output per Empl. (1987=100)
30.2	31.5	30.3	30.3	30.7	30.7	..	..	..	..	..	Earnings as % of Value Added
				(Millions of current Seychelles Rupees)							**MONETARY HOLDINGS**
307.20	283.20	289.50	322.60	363.40	405.30	441.10	539.50	632.50	724.10	..	Money Supply, Broadly Defined
157.90	143.30	131.30	134.70	155.30	155.00	155.20	187.80	219.60	216.80	..	Money
65.30	62.60	64.30	69.90	75.80	78.10	82.40	95.60	99.50	104.50	..	Currency Outside Banks
92.60	80.70	67.00	64.80	79.50	76.90	72.80	92.20	120.10	112.30	..	Demand Deposits
149.30	139.90	158.20	187.90	208.10	250.30	285.90	351.70	412.90	507.30	..	Quasi-Money
				(Millions of current Seychelles Rupees)							**GOVERNMENT DEFICIT (-) OR SURPLUS**
..	..	..	..	-128	-193	-23	-56	-120	..	..	Current Revenue
..	..	..	..	563	596	735	808	989	..	..	Current Expenditure
..	..	..	..	497	549	638	675	800	..	..	Current Budget Balance
..	..	..	..	67	47	98	134	189	..	..	Capital Receipts
..	..	..	..	0	0	1	0	1	..	..	Capital Payments
..	..	..	..	194	241	122	190	309	..	..	

SEYCHELLES	1970	1971	1972	1973	1974	1975	1976	1977	1978	1979	1980
FOREIGN TRADE (CUSTOMS BASIS)					*(Millions of current US dollars)*						
Value of Exports, fob	..	..	..	..	..	..	..	..	..	..	..
Nonfuel Primary Products											
Fuels	..	..	..	..	..	..	..	..	..	..	..
Manufactures	..		..	..							..
Value of Imports, cif	..	..	..	..	..	..	..	..	..	..	..
Nonfuel Primary Products	..	..	..	..	..	..	..	..	..		
Fuels	..										
Manufactures	..	..		..					..	..	
Terms of Trade	..	..	..	..		*(Index 1987 = 100)*		..	..	..	..
Export Prices, fob	..	..	..	..				..	..	..	..
Import Prices, cif	..	..	..	..				..	..	..	..
BALANCE OF PAYMENTS					*(Millions of current US dollars)*						
Exports of Goods & Services	12.10	14.10	17.10	21.20	29.30	33.50	37.73	54.65	72.72	94.76	102.77
Merchandise, fob	2.00	2.00	2.00	3.00	7.00	6.00	3.05	4.83	6.63	6.22	5.65
Nonfactor Services	10.00	12.00	15.00	18.00	22.00	27.00	33.89	48.24	63.80	83.62	91.22
Factor Services	0.10	0.10	0.10	0.20	0.30	0.50	0.80	1.58	2.29	4.91	5.90
Imports of Goods & Services	11.90	18.10	24.40	29.90	35.40	42.00	46.85	65.32	85.74	114.95	131.44
Merchandise, fob	10.00	15.00	21.00	25.00	28.00	32.00	33.19	38.63	51.82	71.58	83.66
Nonfactor Services	1.00	2.00	2.00	3.00	5.00	7.00	9.77	20.67	26.72	34.47	38.85
Factor Services	0.90	1.10	1.40	1.90	2.40	3.00	3.90	6.02	7.19	8.90	8.93
Long-Term Interest	0.00	0.00	0.00	0.00	0.00	0.00	0.00	0.00	0.00	0.10	0.20
Private Current Transfers, net	0.00	0.00	-0.10	-0.10	-0.30	-0.40	-0.40	-0.52	-0.73	-1.03	-1.46
Workers' Remittances	..	..							..		
Curr. A/C Bal before Off. Transf.	0.20	-4.00	-7.40	-8.80	-6.40	-8.90	-9.53	-11.20	-13.75	-21.23	-30.13
Net Official Transfers	0.20	0.40	0.70	1.20	2.10	3.40	5.63	9.33	9.77	8.96	14.51
Curr. A/C Bal after Off. Transf.	0.40	-3.60	-6.70	-7.60	-4.30	-5.50	-3.90	-1.87	-3.98	-12.26	-15.62
Long-Term Capital, net	..	..	..	..	5.80	6.30	6.43	5.26	7.77	12.08	17.54
Direct Investment	..	..	..	..	5.80	6.30	4.31	4.80	3.65	4.37	5.71
Long-Term Loans	0.00	0.00	0.00	0.00	0.00	0.00	0.00	0.50	2.60	8.10	11.60
Disbursements	0.00	0.00	0.00	0.00	0.00	0.00	0.00	0.50	2.70	8.20	11.70
Repayments	0.00	0.00	0.00	0.00	0.00	0.00	0.00	0.00	0.10	0.10	0.10
Other Long-Term Capital	..	..	..	..	0.00	0.00	2.12	-0.04	1.51	-0.39	0.24
Other Capital, net	0.00	0.00	0.00	0.00	-0.73	0.50	-1.85	-1.15	-4.66	3.81	6.04
Change in Reserves	-0.40	3.60	6.70	7.60	-0.77	-1.30	-0.69	-2.24	0.88	-3.63	-7.96
Memo Item:					*(Seychelles Rupees per US dollar)*						
Conversion Factor (Annual Avg)	5.560	5.480	5.340	5.440	5.700	6.030	7.420	7.640	6.950	6.330	6.390
EXTERNAL DEBT (Total)	0.00	0.00	0.00	0.00	*(Millions of US dollars), outstanding at end of year* 0.00	0.00	0.60	109.20	385.00	473.90	84.10
Long-Term Debt (by debtor)	0.00	0.00	0.00	0.00	0.00	0.00	0.60	1.20	4.00	12.90	25.10
Central Bank, incl. IMF credit	0.00	0.00	0.00	0.00	0.00	0.00	0.60	0.00	0.00	0.00	0.00
Central Government	0.00	0.00	0.00	0.00	0.00	0.00	0.60	1.20	4.00	12.90	22.20
Rest of General Government	..	..		..	..	..	..	..	..	..	..
Non-financial Public Enterprises	0.00	0.00	0.00	0.00	0.00	0.00	0.00	0.00	0.00	0.00	2.90
Priv. Sector, incl non-guaranteed	..	..	..	..	..	..	..	..	..	..	..
Short-Term Debt	0.00	0.00	0.00	0.00	0.00	0.00	0.00	108.00	381.00	461.00	59.00
Memo Items:					*(Thousands of US dollars)*						
Int'l Reserves Excluding Gold	..	..	..	4,270	5,040	6,340	6,490	11,512	9,260	12,148	18,439
Gold Holdings (at market price)	..	..	..	..	..	..	..	..	..	..	..
SOCIAL INDICATORS											
Total Fertility Rate	..	..	..	..	..	..	4.5	4.3	4.2	4.0	3.8
Infant Mortality Rate	..	..	..	..	..	..	..	..	..	..	..
Life Expectancy at Birth	..	..	..	..	..	..	..	..	..	..	..
Urban Population, % of total	26.0	27.4	28.9	30.3	31.8	33.2	35.1	37.0	39.0	40.9	42.8
Food Prod. per capita (1987=100)	..	..	..	..	..	..	..	..	..	..	..
Labor Force, Agriculture (%)	..	..	..	..	..	..	..	..	..	..	..
Labor Force, Female (%)	..	..	..	..	..	..	..	..	..	..	..
Primary Schl. Enroll. Ratio	..	..	..	..	..	..	..	..	..	..	..
Primary Schl. Enroll. Ratio, Female	..	..	..	..	..	..	..	..	..	..	..
Secondary Schl. Enroll. Ratio	..	..	..	..	..	..	..	..	..	..	..

1981	1982	1983	1984	1985	1986	1987	1988	1989	1990 estimate	Notes	SEYCHELLES
				(Millions of current US dollars)							**FOREIGN TRADE (CUSTOMS BASIS)**
..	..	..	..	..	..	..	..	..	..	..	Value of Exports, fob
..	..	..	..	..	..	..	..	..	..	..	Nonfuel Primary Products
..	..	..	..	..	..	..	..	..	..	..	Fuels
..	..	..	..	..	..	..	..	..	..	..	Manufactures
..	..	..	..	..	..	..	..	..	..	..	Value of Imports, cif
..	..	..	..	..	..	..	..	..	..	..	Nonfuel Primary Products
..	..	..	..	..	..	..	..	..	..	..	Fuels
..	..	..	..	..	..	..	..	..	..	..	Manufactures
				(Index 1987 = 100)							
..	..	..	..	..	..	..	..	..	..	..	Terms of Trade
..	..	..	..	..	..	..	..	..	..	..	Export Prices, fob
..	..	..	..	..	..	..	..	..	..	..	Import Prices, cif
				(Millions of current US dollars)							**BALANCE OF PAYMENTS**
97.62	84.39	84.16	102.14	118.79	129.74	155.64	184.77	204.36	244.39	..	Exports of Goods & Services
4.64	3.84	4.99	4.98	4.64	4.41	8.09	17.26	14.48	14.54	..	Merchandise, fob
88.64	77.03	76.63	94.83	111.81	123.27	144.85	164.42	186.37	225.78	..	Nonfactor Services
4.33	3.52	2.53	2.33	2.35	2.06	2.70	3.09	3.51	4.07	..	Factor Services
126.57	131.56	121.69	128.12	151.50	174.43	197.98	237.10	253.66	288.20	..	Imports of Goods & Services
79.19	83.00	74.50	73.94	84.14	89.34	96.25	134.96	139.61	158.18	..	Merchandise, fob
40.21	41.58	39.82	46.10	58.99	74.19	84.70	81.19	95.27	106.02	..	Nonfactor Services
7.17	6.97	7.38	8.08	8.37	10.90	17.03	20.95	18.79	24.00	..	Factor Services
0.30	0.80	1.30	1.70	2.30	3.70	5.10	7.20	6.60	7.10	..	Long-Term Interest
-2.65	-3.22	-2.78	-2.34	-0.82	-5.07	-2.30	-4.93	-5.19	-2.52	..	Private Current Transfers, net
									4.43	..	Workers' Remittances
-31.60	-50.39	-40.32	-28.33	-33.54	-49.76	-44.64	-57.26	-54.50	-46.33	..	Curr. A/C Bal before Off. Transf.
12.80	9.75	14.27	15.04	14.34	16.46	23.53	28.85	31.67	29.26	..	Net Official Transfers
-18.79	-40.64	-26.05	-13.29	-19.20	-33.29	-21.11	-28.41	-22.83	-17.07	..	Curr. A/C Bal after Off. Transf.
10.64	29.29	16.26	17.80	16.42	34.18	17.75	20.85	28.25	15.07	..	Long-Term Capital, net
2.84	5.08	5.88	5.88	1.09	8.42	14.02	17.50	14.89	19.38	..	Direct Investment
7.10	14.10	10.80	10.30	14.60	26.10	11.60	5.70	0.30	3.60	..	Long-Term Loans
7.20	14.40	12.30	13.20	19.90	31.90	17.10	15.00	13.40	14.70	..	Disbursements
0.10	0.30	1.50	2.90	5.30	5.80	5.50	9.30	13.10	11.10	..	Repayments
0.69	10.11	-0.42	1.62	0.73	-0.34	-7.87	-2.35	13.06	-7.91	..	Other Long-Term Capital
2.83	11.14	7.29	-6.05	2.73	-2.25	7.32	3.30	-1.90	6.04	..	Other Capital, net
5.33	0.21	2.50	1.54	0.06	1.36	-3.96	4.26	-3.51	-4.04	..	Change in Reserves
											Memo Item:
				(Seychelles Rupees per US dollar)							
6.310	6.550	6.770	7.060	7.130	6.180	5.600	5.380	5.650	5.340	..	Conversion Factor (Annual Avg)
				(Millions of US dollars), outstanding at end of year							
36.80	50.70	54.50	70.60	98.00	147.50	175.10	170.60	168.40	197.30	..	**EXTERNAL DEBT (Total)**
27.80	38.70	46.50	51.50	74.00	108.10	138.60	134.30	132.80	151.20	..	Long-Term Debt (by debtor)
0.00	0.00	0.20	0.20	1.80	5.70	8.60	9.60	12.90	14.60	..	Central Bank, incl. IMF credit
25.50	34.80	42.90	46.20	64.80	92.50	115.40	111.40	106.30	116.20	..	Central Government
..	..	..	..	..	..	..	..	..	..	..	Rest of General Government
2.30	3.90	3.40	5.10	7.40	9.90	14.60	13.30	13.60	20.40	..	Non-financial Public Enterprises
..	..	..	..	..	..	..	..	..	..	..	Priv. Sector, incl non-guaranteed
9.00	12.00	8.00	19.10	24.00	39.40	36.50	36.30	35.60	46.10	..	Short-Term Debt
				(Thousands of US dollars)							**Memo Items:**
13,800	13,072	9,972	5,400	8,501	7,749	13,713	8,707	12,109	16,575	..	Int'l Reserves Excluding Gold
..	..	..	..	..	..	..	..	..	..	..	Gold Holdings (at market price)
											SOCIAL INDICATORS
3.7	3.5	3.4	3.3	3.2	3.1	3.0	2.9	2.9	2.8	..	Total Fertility Rate
..	19.3	19.1	18.9	18.8	18.6	18.4	18.0	17.5	17.1	..	Infant Mortality Rate
..	68.7	68.9	69.1	69.3	69.5	69.7	70.1	70.4	70.7	..	Life Expectancy at Birth
44.6	46.4	48.2	50.0	51.8	53.7	55.6	56.8	58.1	59.3	..	Urban Population, % of total
..	..	..	..	..	..	..	..	..	..	..	Food Prod. per capita (1987=100)
..	..	..	..	..	..	..	..	..	..	..	Labor Force, Agriculture (%)
..	..	..	..	..	..	..	..	..	..	..	Labor Force, Female (%)
..	..	..	..	..	..	..	..	..	..	..	Primary Schl. Enroll. Ratio
..	..	..	..	..	..	..	..	..	..	..	Primary Schl. Enroll. Ratio, Female
..	..	..	..	..	..	..	..	..	..	..	Secondary Schl. Enroll. Ratio

SIERRA LEONE	1970	1971	1972	1973	1974	1975	1976	1977	1978	1979	1980
CURRENT GNP PER CAPITA (US $)	160	160	160	170	190	220	210	220	220	270	320
POPULATION (thousands)	2,651	2,702	2,754	2,808	2,865	2,924	2,985	3,049	3,115	3,184	3,255

USE AND ORIGIN OF RESOURCES *(Millions of current Sierra Leonean Leones)*

	1970	1971	1972	1973	1974	1975	1976	1977	1978	1979	1980
Gross National Product (GNP)	348	343	349	387	471	564	603	730	821	987	1,122
Net Factor Income from Abroad	-5	-5	-7	-6	-7	-8	-10	-14	-29	-43	-34
GDP at Market Prices	353	348	356	393	478	573	613	744	850	1,029	1,156
Resource Balance	-7	-4	1	-3	-34	-53	-52	-49	-63	-131	-197
Exports of Goods & NFServices	104	106	110	125	144	148	150	178	216	249	281
Imports of Goods & NFServices	111	111	109	128	178	202	202	227	280	380	478
Domestic Absorption	360	352	356	396	512	626	665	793	913	1,160	1,352
Private Consumption, etc.	260	268	282	309	387	473	532	624	740	927	1,067
General Gov't Consumption	42	31	32	42	49	63	64	71	77	96	97
Gross Domestic Investment	59	53	42	46	76	90	69	98	96	138	187
Fixed Investment	..	47	43	44	57	76	72	81	100	128	172
Indirect Taxes, net	34	32	36	40	52	52	55	77	100	97	93
GDP at factor cost	319	316	320	353	426	521	559	667	750	932	1,063
Agriculture	90	95	97	108	130	186	213	264	282	327	351
Industry	97	91	89	97	119	123	114	130	142	204	233
Manufacturing	18	20	21	21	26	30	31	34	40	55	59
Services, etc.	133	131	134	149	177	212	232	274	327	402	479
Gross Domestic Saving	52	49	42	43	41	37	17	49	33	7	-9
Gross National Saving	48	45	35	37	35	30	12	40	11	-30	-34

(Millions of 1987 Sierra Leonean Leones)

	1970	1971	1972	1973	1974	1975	1976	1977	1978	1979	1980
Gross National Product	15,398.3	15,883.6	15,712.1	16,195.7	17,132.0	17,592.7	16,818.8	16,881.5	16,062.8	17,210.8	18,005.9
GDP at Market Prices	15,542.4	16,015.8	15,864.9	16,309.0	17,170.2	17,613.8	16,864.3	16,965.8	16,431.5	17,752.5	18,310.2
Resource Balance	707.8	1,632.2	2,421.6	1,011.9	286.1	1,444.3	1,748.5	268.9	-1,772.8	-2,956.9	-3,427.5
Exports of Goods & NFServices	9,788.4	9,469.7	9,363.7	8,374.3	7,933.2	8,116.6	7,342.4	5,657.8	4,438.5	4,621.4	5,036.4
Imports of Goods & NFServices	9,080.6	7,837.5	6,942.0	7,362.4	7,647.0	6,672.3	5,594.0	5,389.0	6,211.2	7,578.3	8,463.8
Domestic Absorption	14,834.6	14,383.7	13,443.3	15,297.1	16,884.1	16,169.5	15,115.8	16,697.0	18,204.2	20,709.4	21,737.6
Private Consumption, etc.	..	..	..	..	..	..	..	..	14,816.7	16,796.3	17,415.0
General Gov't Consumption	..	..	..	..	..	..	..	..	1,452.4	1,701.8	1,487.8
Gross Domestic Investment	3,430.6	2,371.2	1,743.4	1,847.0	2,539.0	2,610.7	1,831.1	1,823.1	1,935.2	2,211.3	2,834.8
Fixed Investment	..	..	..	..	..	..	..	..	1,937.8	2,060.5	2,612.9
GDP at factor cost	14,009.7	14,399.9	14,263.1	14,860.5	15,362.0	15,881.1	15,459.0	15,863.0	15,293.3	16,117.2	16,940.6
Agriculture	3,854.9	3,943.6	3,902.8	3,976.8	3,943.6	4,117.4	4,343.1	4,568.8	6,089.5	6,655.0	6,456.9
Industry	5,929.1	5,768.9	5,501.8	5,518.9	5,518.9	5,729.8	5,136.8	4,698.5	3,999.8	4,227.7	4,837.8
Manufacturing	1,211.6	1,205.4	1,281.9	1,358.3	1,460.7	1,594.5	1,658.0	1,613.6	931.7	963.1	1,008.7
Services, etc.	5,125.6	5,490.0	5,574.3	6,022.6	6,467.1	6,640.5	6,503.8	6,959.9	5,827.3	5,960.9	6,403.0

Memo Items:

	1970	1971	1972	1973	1974	1975	1976	1977	1978	1979	1980
Capacity to Import	8,510.0	7,532.8	6,973.8	7,200.7	6,172.5	4,911.6	4,144.2	4,227.1	4,807.2	4,967.0	4,976.2
Terms of Trade Adjustment	-1,278.4	-1,936.9	-2,389.8	-1,173.6	-1,760.7	-3,205.0	-3,198.2	-1,430.8	368.8	345.6	-60.1
Gross Domestic Income	14,264.1	14,079.0	13,475.1	15,135.4	15,409.5	14,408.8	13,666.0	15,535.1	16,800.3	18,098.1	18,250.0
Gross National Income	14,120.0	13,946.8	13,322.3	15,022.1	15,371.3	14,387.7	13,620.5	15,450.7	16,431.6	17,556.4	17,945.8

DOMESTIC PRICES/DEFLATORS *(Index 1987 = 100)*

	1970	1971	1972	1973	1974	1975	1976	1977	1978	1979	1980
Overall (GDP)	2.3	2.2	2.2	2.4	2.8	3.3	3.6	4.4	5.2	5.8	6.3
Domestic Absorption	2.4	2.5	2.6	2.6	3.0	3.9	4.4	4.7	5.0	5.6	6.2
Agriculture	2.3	2.4	2.5	2.7	3.3	4.5	4.9	5.8	4.6	4.9	5.4
Industry	1.6	1.6	1.6	1.8	2.2	2.1	2.2	2.8	3.5	4.8	4.8
Manufacturing	1.5	1.7	1.6	1.6	1.8	1.9	1.9	2.1	4.3	5.7	5.8
Consumer Price Index	0.9	0.9	0.9	1.0	1.1	1.3	1.5	1.7	1.8	2.2	2.5

MANUFACTURING ACTIVITY

	1970	1971	1972	1973	1974	1975	1976	1977	1978	1979	1980
Employment (1987=100)	..	..	..	..	..	..	..	..	..	..	..
Real Earnings per Empl. (1987=100)	..	..	..	..	..	..	..	..	..	..	..
Real Output per Empl. (1987=100)	..	..	..	..	..	..	..	..	..	..	..
Earnings as % of Value Added	..										

MONETARY HOLDINGS *(Millions of current Sierra Leonean Leones)*

	1970	1971	1972	1973	1974	1975	1976	1977	1978	1979	1980
Money Supply, Broadly Defined	43.3	48.0	56.5	71.3	84.5	91.6	111.9	136.2	179.3	214.5	260.8
Money	28.9	32.5	38.9	48.3	54.9	60.3	72.1	84.4	107.4	127.5	152.5
Currency Outside Banks	18.9	20.9	24.7	29.7	31.4	36.5	40.8	51.7	63.5	72.5	86.1
Demand Deposits	10.0	11.5	14.3	18.6	23.5	23.7	31.3	32.7	44.0	55.0	66.5
Quasi-Money	14.3	15.5	17.6	23.0	29.7	31.3	39.8	51.8	71.9	87.0	108.3

GOVERNMENT DEFICIT (-) OR SURPLUS *(Millions of current Sierra Leonean Leones)*

	1970	1971	1972	1973	1974	1975	1976	1977	1978	1979	1980
	..	..	..	..	-20.90	-60.00	-48.40	-51.00	-79.20	-119.00	-148.20
Current Revenue	..	..	..	..	91.70	97.00	95.40	119.40	169.60	192.70	197.10
Current Expenditure	..	..	..	..	64.20	82.20	83.10	103.70	199.20	200.00	..
Current Budget Balance	..	..	..	..	27.50	14.80	12.30	15.70	-29.60	-7.30	
Capital Receipts	..	..	..	..							
Capital Payments	..	..	..	..	48.40	74.80	60.70	66.70	49.60	111.70	..

1981	1982	1983	1984	1985	1986	1987	1988	1989	1990 estimate	Notes	SIERRA LEONE
370	380	380	360	340	330	240	230	210	240	..	**CURRENT GNP PER CAPITA (US $)**
3,329	3,405	3,485	3,568	3,654	3,744	3,837	3,934	4,034	4,136	..	**POPULATION (thousands)**
				(Millions of current Sierra Leonean Leones)							**USE AND ORIGIN OF RESOURCES**
1,259	1,561	1,835	2,669	4,605	7,303	19,484	27,784	41,821	78,627	C f	Gross National Product (GNP)
-33	-43	-42	-60	-180	-179	-216	-1,426	-2,698	-8,290	..	Net Factor Income from Abroad
1,292	1,604	1,876	2,729	4,785	7,481	19,700	29,210	44,519	86,917	C f	GDP at Market Prices
-190	-184	-127	-44	-94	-123	130	-758	-2,852	-5,558	..	Resource Balance
275	230	249	377	545	822	2,461	3,291	5,788	15,093	..	Exports of Goods & NFServices
465	415	376	421	640	945	2,331	4,049	8,640	20,651	..	Imports of Goods & NFServices
1,482	1,789	2,003	2,773	4,879	7,605	19,571	29,968	47,371	92,475	..	Domestic Absorption
1,146	1,436	1,568	2,237	4,057	6,268	16,303	23,598	38,041	73,913	..	Private Consumption, etc.
90	138	167	189	345	498	1,210	2,988	4,275	8,601	..	General Gov't Consumption
247	215	268	347	477	839	2,058	3,382	5,055	9,961	..	Gross Domestic Investment
236	205	235	332	424	730	1,854	..	..	..	..	Fixed Investment
119	101	77	105	132	213	912	1,082	2,437	5,906	..	Indirect Taxes, net
1,174	1,504	1,799	2,625	4,653	7,269	18,789	28,128	42,082	81,011	C f	GDP at factor cost
379	539	686	1,053	2,070	2,888	7,698	11,801	16,972	25,648	..	Agriculture
231	256	266	358	596	1,757	3,570	4,161	6,634	10,927	..	Industry
54	100	108	135	166	256	907	1,355	2,778	5,055	..	Manufacturing
563	710	847	1,214	1,987	2,623	7,521	12,166	18,476	44,436	..	Services, etc.
57	30	141	303	383	716	2,188	2,624	2,203	4,403		Gross Domestic Saving
35	-7	106	262	215	561	1,972	1,207	-492	-3,145		Gross National Saving
				(Millions of 1987 Sierra Leonean Leones)							
19,691.1	19,606.7	19,109.7	19,555.7	18,757.2	18,469.0	19,484.3	20,114.0	20,965.0	21,504.9	C f	Gross National Product
19,894.9	19,893.8	19,282.1	19,724.3	19,058.8	18,690.2	19,700.5	20,341.9	21,191.2	21,818.3	C f	GDP at Market Prices
-2,699.8	-2,065.9	-877.2	190.5	-100.4	407.2	129.9	291.4	-594.1	-510.0	..	Resource Balance
4,513.8	3,722.7	3,345.6	3,363.0	2,794.3	2,553.0	2,460.8	2,592.0	2,035.0	2,359.9	..	Exports of Goods & NFServices
7,213.5	5,788.6	4,222.9	3,172.6	2,894.7	2,145.8	2,330.9	2,300.6	2,629.1	2,869.8	..	Imports of Goods & NFServices
22,594.7	21,959.6	20,159.3	19,533.8	19,159.2	18,283.0	19,570.6	20,050.5	21,785.3	22,328.2	..	Domestic Absorption
17,824.9	17,737.1	15,985.2	15,672.6	15,580.1	14,681.7	16,302.6	15,739.5	17,151.9	18,140.3	..	Private Consumption, etc.
1,334.9	1,623.6	1,695.2	1,330.2	1,343.8	1,191.7	1,210.0	1,587.4	1,867.5	1,318.9	..	General Gov't Consumption
3,434.8	2,599.0	2,479.0	2,531.0	2,235.2	2,409.6	2,058.0	2,723.7	2,765.9	2,869.0	..	Gross Domestic Investment
3,320.8	2,511.7	2,272.3	2,451.3	1,987.4	2,096.1	1,853.9	2,609.6	2,553.4	2,370.7	..	Fixed Investment
17,733.6	18,657.0	19,074.3	19,036.5	18,445.3	18,153.9	18,788.7	19,500.8	20,336.1	20,949.2	C f	GDP at factor cost
6,510.1	6,717.9	6,655.0	6,679.3	7,404.3	7,182.2	7,698.3	8,265.6	7,885.7	8,018.1	..	Agriculture
4,455.7	4,069.1	3,536.1	3,941.4	3,281.7	3,553.7	3,569.7	3,549.3	3,969.5	4,232.7	..	Industry
1,047.0	1,305.3	1,172.7	1,207.3	1,022.9	983.5	907.0	1,093.2	984.1	944.6	..	Manufacturing
7,274.3	8,145.5	8,883.2	8,415.8	7,759.3	7,418.0	7,520.7	7,685.9	8,481.0	8,698.5	..	Services, etc.
											Memo Items:
4,269.5	3,213.9	2,795.4	2,840.7	2,468.0	1,865.7	2,460.8	1,869.7	1,761.2	2,097.4	..	Capacity to Import
-244.3	-508.9	-550.2	-522.4	-326.3	-687.3	0.0	-722.3	-273.9	-262.4	..	Terms of Trade Adjustment
19,650.6	19,384.9	18,731.8	19,201.9	18,732.4	18,002.9	19,700.5	19,619.6	20,917.4	21,555.8	..	Gross Domestic Income
19,446.8	19,097.9	18,559.4	19,033.3	18,430.8	17,781.7	19,484.3	19,391.8	20,691.2	21,242.5	..	Gross National Income
				(Index 1987 = 100)							**DOMESTIC PRICES/DEFLATORS**
6.5	8.1	9.7	13.8	25.1	40.0	100.0	143.6	210.1	398.4	..	Overall (GDP)
6.6	8.1	9.9	14.2	25.5	41.6	100.0	149.5	217.4	414.2	..	Domestic Absorption
5.8	8.0	10.3	15.8	28.0	40.2	100.0	142.8	215.2	319.9	..	Agriculture
5.2	6.3	7.5	9.1	18.2	49.4	100.0	117.2	167.1	258.2	..	Industry
5.1	7.7	9.2	11.2	16.2	26.1	100.0	123.9	282.3	535.1	..	Manufacturing
3.1	4.0	6.7	11.1	19.6	35.5	100.0	131.3	213.7	450.9	..	Consumer Price Index
											MANUFACTURING ACTIVITY
..	..	..	..	..	..	..	..	..	..	..	Employment (1987=100)
..	..	..	..	..	..	..	..	..	..	..	Real Earnings per Empl. (1987=100)
..	..	..	..	..	..	..	..	..	..	..	Real Output per Empl. (1987=100)
22.3	..	..	..	..	..	..	..	..	..	..	Earnings as % of Value Added
				(Millions of current Sierra Leonean Leones)							**MONETARY HOLDINGS**
267.6	419.6	552.4	708.8	1,212.6	2,284.6	3,747.2	5,878.5	10,240.2	17,817.9	..	Money Supply, Broadly Defined
151.9	253.2	359.4	486.2	899.7	1,851.5	2,888.5	4,637.1	8,674.9	14,252.5	..	Money
86.2	121.1	197.3	260.1	442.1	1,005.6	1,364.0	2,254.6	4,058.0	8,337.2	..	Currency Outside Banks
65.7	132.1	162.0	226.1	457.6	845.9	1,524.5	2,382.4	4,616.9	5,915.3	..	Demand Deposits
115.8	166.4	193.0	222.6	312.9	433.1	858.7	1,241.4	1,565.3	3,565.4	..	Quasi-Money
				(Millions of current Sierra Leonean Leones)							
-120.70	-167.40	-271.20	-205.60	-375.60	-183.90	-3,336.00	-2,157.00	-586.30	..	C	**GOVERNMENT DEFICIT (-) OR SURPLUS**
236.90	188.50	170.60	243.30	314.50	594.50	2,102.00	2,638.00	4,225.90	..	..	Current Revenue
284.30	270.40	253.10	339.60	409.00	566.40	2,839.00	3,840.50	4,402.80	..	..	Current Expenditure
-47.40	-81.90	-82.50	-96.30	-94.50	28.10	-737.00	-1,202.50	-176.90	..	..	Current Budget Balance
	3.00	..	22.60	12.30		..	..	..	..	..	Capital Receipts
73.30	88.50	188.70	131.90	293.40	212.00	2,599.00	954.50	243.40	..	..	Capital Payments

SIERRA LEONE	1970	1971	1972	1973	1974	1975	1976	1977	1978	1979	1980
FOREIGN TRADE (CUSTOMS BASIS)				*(Millions of current US dollars)*							
Value of Exports, fob	101.46	98.48	114.80	128.57	141.39	140.05	102.97	122.45	167.43	216.23	228.06
Nonfuel Primary Products	36.52	35.19	39.82	46.96	50.84	55.79	32.07	78.13	106.83	149.12	136.41
Fuels	2.63	2.97	1.95	1.34	1.65	8.22	5.53	4.77	6.52	0.80	0.03
Manufactures	62.31	60.33	73.03	80.27	88.90	76.04	65.38	39.55	54.08	66.31	91.62
Value of Imports, cif	116.88	113.12	120.97	157.67	161.09	159.26	166.28	180.00	278.06	193.69	268.32
Nonfuel Primary Products	30.95	28.47	28.27	47.31	44.02	35.68	39.47	42.72	66.00	47.49	69.38
Fuels	5.46	8.32	9.02	9.34	18.52	21.76	23.67	25.62	39.58	5.49	6.01
Manufactures	80.47	76.34	83.68	101.02	98.55	101.81	103.14	111.65	172.48	140.71	192.93
					(Index 1987 = 100)						
Terms of Trade	133.5	129.8	122.7	127.4	121.4	105.8	121.3	146.7	124.5	122.1	106.3
Export Prices, fob	33.8	33.1	34.8	49.1	70.3	62.5	71.0	92.3	86.2	102.5	106.3
Import Prices, cif	25.3	25.5	28.4	38.5	57.9	59.0	58.6	62.9	69.2	84.0	100.0
BALANCE OF PAYMENTS				*(Millions of current US dollars)*							
Exports of Goods & Services	121.60	113.64	131.48	147.94	170.29	151.54	134.34	162.84	211.64	243.15	276.05
Merchandise, fob	100.00	95.78	113.46	129.11	142.75	128.98	113.85	142.70	185.09	197.07	213.47
Nonfactor Services	18.50	16.85	17.15	18.00	23.33	18.69	18.33	18.32	26.17	45.79	62.01
Factor Services	3.10	1.00	0.87	0.83	4.21	3.87	2.16	1.83	0.38	0.28	0.57
Imports of Goods & Services	142.60	139.31	143.86	183.47	253.16	227.65	203.53	232.45	343.06	451.19	493.70
Merchandise, fob	105.30	102.51	107.70	141.03	199.64	167.58	149.80	165.02	253.00	336.34	385.88
Nonfactor Services	30.10	26.68	28.12	33.50	41.25	45.35	41.52	50.68	56.16	72.57	85.35
Factor Services	7.20	10.13	8.03	8.94	12.27	14.71	12.22	16.75	33.91	42.29	22.46
Long-Term Interest	2.50	2.30	2.60	3.70	4.00	4.40	5.20	4.80	7.80	9.60	7.50
Private Current Transfers, net	1.20	1.60	-0.33	0.00	0.48	1.66	4.31	4.45	6.78	5.30	8.29
Workers' Remittances	..	..	..	..	..	..	..	..	..	..	..
Curr. A/C Bal before Off. Transf.	-19.80	-24.07	-12.70	-35.53	-82.38	-74.45	-64.88	-65.16	-124.64	-202.75	-209.36
Net Official Transfers	3.90	4.21	3.47	6.44	21.53	8.96	6.38	15.79	12.89	23.94	44.58
Curr. A/C Bal after Off. Transf.	-15.90	-19.86	-9.23	-29.09	-60.85	-65.49	-58.50	-49.37	-111.74	-178.81	-164.78
Long-Term Capital, net	-0.80	7.12	9.23	15.97	34.16	35.71	24.45	10.64	42.12	43.62	47.76
Direct Investment	8.20	5.22	3.80	4.05	10.46	10.07	8.54	5.06	24.26	16.08	-18.67
Long-Term Loans	-3.00	5.40	5.90	12.50	37.60	22.60	10.50	17.80	29.80	30.50	55.20
Disbursements	7.60	11.70	14.00	21.70	48.10	33.80	27.30	30.10	59.40	61.80	86.20
Repayments	10.60	6.30	8.10	9.20	10.50	11.20	16.80	12.30	29.60	31.30	31.00
Other Long-Term Capital	-6.00	-3.49	-0.47	-0.58	-13.91	3.05	5.41	-12.22	-11.94	-2.97	11.23
Other Capital, net	16.38	10.91	4.86	21.40	24.18	7.53	14.65	35.59	76.50	138.34	102.16
Change in Reserves	0.32	1.83	-4.86	-8.29	2.51	22.25	19.41	3.14	-6.87	-3.15	14.85
Memo Item:				*(Sierra Leonean Leones per US dollar)*							
Conversion Factor (Annual Avg)	0.830	0.830	0.800	0.820	0.840	0.850	1.010	1.170	1.100	1.050	1.050
EXTERNAL DEBT (Total)			*(Millions of US dollars), outstanding at end of year*								
	59.50	68.50	72.80	90.30	141.20	156.90	189.40	245.30	301.00	369.30	435.40
Long-Term Debt (by debtor)	59.50	68.50	72.80	90.30	141.00	155.20	185.80	224.80	277.00	325.10	382.40
Central Bank, incl. IMF credit	0.00	0.00	0.00	0.00	5.30	5.80	26.00	39.00	46.40	57.60	59.30
Central Government	52.90	60.70	60.70	77.80	117.60	133.10	136.40	158.10	196.80	229.80	284.60
Rest of General Government	..	..	..	..	..	..	..	..	..	..	..
Non-financial Public Enterprises	6.60	7.80	12.10	12.50	17.90	16.30	23.40	27.70	33.80	37.70	38.50
Priv. Sector, incl non-guaranteed	0.00	0.00	0.00	0.00	0.20	0.00	0.00	0.00	0.00	0.00	0.00
Short-Term Debt	0.00	0.00	0.00	0.00	0.20	1.70	3.60	20.50	24.00	44.20	53.00
Memo Items:				*(Thousands of US dollars)*							
Int'l Reserves Excluding Gold	39,360	38,407	46,452	51,775	54,624	28,412	25,204	33,401	34,787	46,700	30,600
Gold Holdings (at market price)	..	..	..	..	..	..	..	..	..	..	..
SOCIAL INDICATORS											
Total Fertility Rate	6.5	6.5	6.5	6.5	6.5	6.5	6.5	6.5	6.5	6.5	6.5
Infant Mortality Rate	197.4	195.2	193.0	190.2	187.4	184.6	181.8	179.0	176.4	173.8	171.2
Life Expectancy at Birth	34.3	34.6	34.9	35.3	35.7	36.1	36.5	36.9	37.3	37.8	38.2
Urban Population, % of total	18.1	18.7	19.3	19.9	20.5	21.1	21.8	22.5	23.1	23.8	24.5
Food Prod. per capita (1987=100)	123.1	120.0	119.7	116.4	117.9	122.9	121.1	120.0	121.8	108.9	109.2
Labor Force, Agriculture (%)	75.5	74.9	74.3	73.7	73.1	72.6	71.9	71.3	70.7	70.2	69.6
Labor Force, Female (%)	35.6	35.5	35.4	35.3	35.2	35.2	35.1	35.0	34.9	34.8	34.7
Primary Schl. Enroll. Ratio	34.0	..	..	..	..	39.0	37.0	37.0	38.0	39.0	52.0
Primary Schl. Enroll. Ratio, Female	27.0	..	..	..	..	30.0	..	30.0	..	..	43.0
Secondary Schl. Enroll. Ratio	8.0	..	..	..	..	11.0	12.0	12.0	12.0	12.0	14.0

1981	1982	1983	1984	1985	1986	1987	1988	1989	1990 estimate	Notes	SIERRA LEONE
				(Millions of current US dollars)							**FOREIGN TRADE (CUSTOMS BASIS)**
205.21	127.64	90.74	147.07	131.00	121.28	136.77	102.40	138.25	138.10	..	Value of Exports, fob
96.13	83.66	57.90	99.54	83.59	77.38	87.27	65.34	88.21	88.12	..	Nonfuel Primary Products
2.88	0.48	3.53	2.28	5.10	4.72	5.32	3.99	5.38	5.37	..	Fuels
106.20	43.50	29.31	45.25	42.32	39.18	44.18	33.08	44.66	44.61	..	Manufactures
199.65	161.06	165.69	126.55	153.44	125.67	129.94	160.39	182.26	146.15	..	Value of Imports, cif
58.45	57.17	48.20	29.07	35.25	28.87	29.85	36.85	41.87	33.58	..	Nonfuel Primary Products
7.80	8.08	57.53	24.98	30.29	24.80	25.65	31.66	35.97	28.85	..	Fuels
133.40	95.80	59.96	72.50	87.90	71.99	74.44	91.88	104.41	83.73	..	Manufactures
				(Index 1987 = 100)							
101.3	103.0	105.4	111.4	106.2	105.2	100.0	100.4	78.2	80.4	..	Terms of Trade
101.4	98.0	97.1	99.7	94.7	98.7	100.0	104.1	62.7	67.5	..	Export Prices, fob
100.1	95.2	92.2	89.5	89.2	93.8	100.0	103.7	80.2	84.0	..	Import Prices, cif
				(Millions of current US dollars)							**BALANCE OF PAYMENTS**
203.61	147.98	142.10	173.95	160.07	152.67	183.01	156.62	178.02	153.70	f	Exports of Goods & Services
151.58	110.28	107.04	132.63	131.86	125.99	138.87	104.48	139.50	142.10	..	Merchandise, fob
51.51	37.54	34.79	41.08	27.97	26.54	43.97	51.97	38.32	11.60	..	Nonfactor Services
0.52	0.16	0.27	0.24	0.24	0.14	0.16	0.16	0.20	..	..	Factor Services
379.09	368.15	196.31	229.92	216.27	278.06	220.05	192.96	226.29	294.70	f	Imports of Goods & Services
282.03	260.28	132.97	149.72	141.22	111.42	114.83	138.21	160.34	177.10	..	Merchandise, fob
59.62	72.66	42.11	47.57	42.85	33.95	41.99	34.58	44.78	33.20	..	Nonfactor Services
37.44	35.21	21.22	32.63	32.20	132.69	63.24	20.17	21.16	84.40	..	Factor Services
9.90	2.90	3.90	4.90	2.50	2.10	1.20	2.90	0.70	3.20	..	Long-Term Interest
9.40	4.76	3.24	7.61	2.34	1.50	0.01	0.27	0.05	4.90	..	Private Current Transfers, net
..	0.00	0.00	0.00	..	..	..	..	..	..	..	Workers' Remittances
-166.08	-215.41	-50.97	-48.37	-13.16	136.08	-37.04	-11.26	-25.85	-136.10	..	Curr. A/C Bal before Off. Transf.
34.34	45.61	33.42	25.42	16.88	4.62	6.77	8.50	7.22	41.40	..	Net Official Transfers
-131.74	-169.79	-17.56	-22.95	3.72	140.71	-30.27	-2.76	-18.63	-94.70	..	Curr. A/C Bal after Off. Transf.
106.97	20.72	-51.56	-55.05	-78.41	-303.43	44.04	-63.53	-38.50	45.50	f	Long-Term Capital, net
7.51	4.68	1.70	5.86	-30.96	-140.31	39.41	-23.09	21.24	3.00	..	Direct Investment
31.60	75.50	17.10	12.40	29.40	16.10	8.80	21.00	4.70	34.60	..	Long-Term Loans
66.90	83.70	22.70	24.30	35.20	21.50	13.80	27.70	5.80	37.20	..	Disbursements
35.30	8.20	5.60	11.90	5.80	5.40	5.00	6.70	1.10	2.60	..	Repayments
67.87	-59.47	-70.35	-73.30	-76.86	-179.22	-4.16	-61.44	-64.44	7.90	..	Other Long-Term Capital
-21.19	140.66	62.29	56.90	78.44	177.93	-13.07	74.00	79.63	52.95	f	Other Capital, net
45.96	8.42	6.83	21.09	-3.75	-15.21	-0.71	-7.71	-22.50	-3.75	..	Change in Reserves
				(Sierra Leonean Leones per US dollar)							Memo Item:
1.090	1.200	1.260	2.510	3.640	5.230	35.580	25.520	46.260	96.650	..	Conversion Factor (Annual Avg)
				(Millions of US dollars), outstanding at end of year							
567.60	623.10	642.90	621.20	728.80	866.40	1,027.40	1,017.40	1,082.10	1,189.10	..	**EXTERNAL DEBT (Total)**
411.20	452.20	460.10	422.00	493.10	573.40	667.30	648.90	636.60	713.90	..	Long-Term Debt (by debtor)
84.00	78.10	92.90	95.50	100.80	101.30	115.70	108.70	104.50	108.40	..	Central Bank, incl. IMF credit
277.90	319.60	314.70	283.80	340.60	425.60	505.20	498.20	495.40	570.10	..	Central Government
..	..	..	..	..	..	..	..	..	..	..	Rest of General Government
49.30	54.50	52.50	42.70	51.70	46.50	46.40	42.00	36.70	35.40	..	Non-financial Public Enterprises
0.00	0.00	0.00	0.00	0.00	0.00	0.00	0.00	0.00	..	..	Priv. Sector, incl non-guaranteed
156.40	170.90	182.80	199.20	235.70	293.00	360.10	368.50	445.50	475.20	..	Short-Term Debt
				(Thousands of US dollars)							Memo Items:
15,950	8,430	16,205	7,749	10,822	13,655	6,328	7,427	3,726	5,428	..	Int'l Reserves Excluding Gold
..	..	..	..	..	..	..	..	..	..	..	Gold Holdings (at market price)
											SOCIAL INDICATORS
6.5	6.5	6.5	6.5	6.5	6.5	6.5	6.5	6.5	6.5	..	Total Fertility Rate
168.6	166.0	163.6	161.2	158.7	156.3	153.9	151.6	149.3	146.9	..	Infant Mortality Rate
38.6	39.0	39.4	39.8	40.2	40.6	41.0	41.3	41.7	42.1	..	Life Expectancy at Birth
25.3	26.0	26.8	27.5	28.3	29.3	30.3	30.9	31.6	32.2	..	Urban Population, % of total
107.9	116.6	116.4	105.6	100.0	105.5	100.0	94.1	98.0	97.5	..	Food Prod. per capita (1987=100)
..	..	..	..	..	..	..	..	..	..	..	Labor Force, Agriculture (%)
34.5	34.3	34.1	33.9	33.7	33.5	33.3	33.1	32.9	32.7	..	Labor Force, Female (%)
55.0	54.0	58.0	61.0	..	..	60.0	53.0	..	..	..	Primary Schl. Enroll. Ratio
45.0	44.0	47.0	50.0	..	..	50.0	40.0	..	..	..	Primary Schl. Enroll. Ratio, Female
15.0	17.0	18.0	19.0	..	..	..	18.0	..	..	..	Secondary Schl. Enroll. Ratio

SINGAPORE	1970	1971	1972	1973	1974	1975	1976	1977	1978	1979	1980
CURRENT GNP PER CAPITA (US $)	950	1,070	1,270	1,580	2,020	2,550	2,760	2,940	3,310	3,880	4,550
POPULATION (thousands)	2,075	2,113	2,152	2,193	2,230	2,263	2,293	2,325	2,353	2,384	2,414
USE AND ORIGIN OF RESOURCES					(Millions of current Singapore Dollars)						
Gross National Product (GNP)	5,861	6,831	8,174	10,033	12,260	13,567	14,570	15,852	17,787	20,444	24,189
Net Factor Income from Abroad	56	-10	-21	-224	-351	124	-81	-187	-43	-79	-902
GDP at Market Prices	5,805	6,841	8,195	10,257	12,610	13,443	14,651	16,039	17,830	20,523	25,091
Resource Balance	-1,179	-1,484	-1,378	-1,041	-2,044	-1,416	-1,199	-424	-898	-1,445	-2,216
Exports of Goods & NF Services	5,929	6,655	8,804	12,227	19,097	18,726	22,281	26,442	30,132	38,801	52,000
Imports of Goods & NF Services	7,108	8,139	10,182	13,269	21,141	20,143	23,481	26,866	31,029	40,246	54,215
Domestic Absorption	6,984	8,325	9,573	11,298	14,654	14,859	15,850	16,463	18,728	21,968	27,307
Private Consumption, etc.	4,047	4,686	5,190	6,135	7,646	8,066	8,327	8,948	9,806	11,035	13,232
General Gov't Consumption	692	861	990	1,118	1,298	1,423	1,541	1,716	1,965	2,034	2,447
Gross Domestic Investment	2,244	2,778	3,393	4,045	5,710	5,370	5,982	5,799	6,957	8,900	11,628
Fixed Investment	1,888	2,507	3,093	3,606	4,813	4,833	5,288	5,458	6,365	7,520	10,203
Indirect Taxes, net	485	544	632	767	805	866	989	1,122	1,276	1,547	1,819
GDP at factor cost	5,320	6,297	7,563	9,490	11,805	12,577	13,662	14,917	16,555	18,976	23,272
Agriculture	135	159	161	214	230	254	257	283	274	295	322
Industry	1,726	2,142	2,756	3,399	4,258	4,585	5,119	5,518	6,083	7,403	9,563
Manufacturing	1,162	1,447	1,853	2,429	3,068	3,209	3,589	3,982	4,576	5,703	7,313
Services, etc.	3,944	4,540	5,278	6,644	8,122	8,603	9,275	10,238	11,473	12,825	15,206
Gross Domestic Saving	1,065	1,294	2,014	3,004	3,666	3,954	4,782	5,375	6,060	7,455	9,412
Gross National Saving	1,057	1,214	1,988	2,746	3,216	3,986	4,588	5,089	5,936	7,309	8,288
					(Millions of 1987 Singapore Dollars)						
Gross National Product	12,181	13,501	15,224	16,638	17,653	19,073	20,128	21,551	23,631	25,784	27,368
GDP at Market Prices	12,067	13,525	15,268	17,021	18,171	18,892	20,242	21,813	23,687	25,882	28,387
Resource Balance	..	..	..	..	..	-2,052	-1,774	-865	-1,330	-1,579	-1,820
Exports of Goods & NF Services	..	..	..	..	..	20,900	23,305	26,585	29,717	36,305	44,252
Imports of Goods & NF Services	..	..	..	..	..	22,952	25,079	27,450	31,047	37,885	46,072
Domestic Absorption	..	..	..	..	..	20,944	22,016	22,678	25,018	27,461	30,206
Private Consumption, etc.	..	..	..	..	..	11,016	11,501	12,254	13,016	13,737	14,416
General Gov't Consumption	1,520	1,779	2,017	2,127	2,130	2,188	2,297	2,509	2,798	2,784	3,047
Gross Domestic Investment	5,083	5,959	6,506	6,982	8,397	7,740	8,217	7,915	9,203	10,940	12,743
Fixed Investment	4,069	5,068	5,812	6,304	7,058	6,791	7,120	7,253	8,275	9,342	11,228
GDP at factor cost	10,977	12,295	13,880	15,465	16,528	17,175	18,395	19,838	21,526	23,540	25,906
Agriculture	253	279	300	284	263	269	296	300	298	304	308
Industry	4,542	5,310	6,236	6,826	7,119	7,299	8,132	8,664	9,277	10,415	11,461
Manufacturing	3,130	3,705	4,372	5,079	5,278	5,173	5,779	6,318	7,033	8,004	8,804
Services, etc.	7,272	7,935	8,731	9,911	10,789	11,324	11,814	12,848	14,112	15,163	16,617
Memo Items:											
Capacity to Import	..	..	..	..	..	21,338	23,798	27,016	30,149	36,524	44,189
Terms of Trade Adjustment	..	..	..	..	..	438	493	432	432	219	-63
Gross Domestic Income	..	..	..	..	..	19,330	20,735	22,245	24,119	26,101	28,323
Gross National Income	..	..	..	..	..	19,511	20,620	21,983	24,063	26,003	27,305
DOMESTIC PRICES/DEFLATORS					(Index 1987 = 100)						
Overall (GDP)	48.1	50.6	53.7	60.3	69.4	71.2	72.4	73.5	75.3	79.3	88.4
Domestic Absorption	..	..	..	..	..	70.9	72.0	72.6	74.9	80.0	90.4
Agriculture	53.1	56.8	53.5	75.5	87.4	94.5	86.8	94.2	91.8	97.1	104.6
Industry	38.0	40.3	44.2	49.8	59.8	62.8	62.9	63.7	65.6	71.1	83.4
Manufacturing	37.1	39.1	42.4	47.8	58.1	62.0	62.1	63.0	65.1	71.2	83.1
Consumer Price Index	43.6	44.4	45.4	57.2	70.0	71.9	70.5	72.8	76.2	79.3	86.1
MANUFACTURING ACTIVITY											
Employment (1987=100)	44.4	52.0	62.2	72.2	74.3	69.4	75.0	79.0	87.6	97.5	103.1
Real Earnings per Empl. (1987=100)	50.5	53.4	54.3	50.7	49.8	57.2	59.9	61.6	62.1	64.9	68.5
Real Output per Empl. (1987=100)	60.4	56.2	50.1	54.4	71.0	65.9	74.6	78.9	77.3	82.1	82.4
Earnings as % of Value Added	36.3	36.7	35.4	33.8	30.0	34.6	33.1	32.9	33.4	30.9	29.7
MONETARY HOLDINGS					(Millions of current Singapore Dollars)						
Money Supply, Broadly Defined	4,125	4,599	5,803	6,797	7,819	9,390	10,944	12,306	14,014	16,837	20,489
Money	1,631	1,760	2,385	2,632	2,858	3,472	4,000	4,412	4,926	5,706	6,135
Currency Outside Banks	727	806	1,005	1,114	1,306	1,638	1,947	2,243	2,583	2,941	3,137
Demand Deposits	904	954	1,380	1,518	1,552	1,834	2,053	2,169	2,343	2,765	2,998
Quasi-Money	2,494	2,839	3,418	4,165	4,961	5,918	6,944	7,894	9,088	11,131	14,354
GOVERNMENT DEFICIT (-) OR SURPLUS	90	40	108	-12	(Millions of current Singapore Dollars) 197	121	31	164	146	468	538
Current Revenue	1,274	1,445	1,777	2,128	2,587	3,146	3,342	3,893	4,195	4,887	6,365
Current Expenditure	859	1,083	1,213	1,335	1,472	2,005	2,288	2,677	2,797	3,191	3,910
Current Budget Balance	415	362	564	793	1,115	1,141	1,054	1,216	1,398	1,696	2,455
Capital Receipts	27	60	43	156	142	245	155	97	52	294	255
Capital Payments	352	382	499	961	1,060	1,265	1,178	1,149	1,304	1,522	2,172

1981	1982	1983	1984	1985	1986	1987	1988	1989	1990 estimate	Notes	SINGAPORE
5,360	5,990	6,650	7,330	7,120	6,850	7,260	8,190	9,420	11,160	..	**CURRENT GNP PER CAPITA (US $)**
2,481	2,546	2,610	2,671	2,731	2,789	2,845	2,900	2,952	3,003	..	**POPULATION (thousands)**
				(Millions of current Singapore Dollars)							**USE AND ORIGIN OF RESOURCES**
28,191	31,776	36,561	40,815	40,330	39,602	43,192	49,941	56,340	63,905	..	Gross National Product (GNP)
-1,148	-894	-172	767	1,407	949	582	247	105	1,194	..	Net Factor Income from Abroad
29,339	32,670	36,733	40,048	38,924	38,654	42,609	49,694	56,235	62,711	..	GDP at Market Prices
-1,634	-1,441	-664	-1,113	-946	143	382	2,875	5,534	3,719	..	Resource Balance
59,735	62,369	62,819	64,513	61,420	60,001	73,313	95,542	107,073	119,080	..	Exports of Goods & NFServices
61,368	63,809	63,482	65,626	62,365	59,858	72,931	92,667	101,539	115,360	..	Imports of Goods & NFServices
30,973	34,111	37,397	41,161	39,869	38,510	42,228	46,819	50,701	58,992	..	Domestic Absorption
14,597	14,881	15,806	17,411	17,770	18,345	20,264	23,323	25,420	28,072	..	Private Consumption, etc.
2,789	3,570	3,995	4,333	5,548	5,270	5,327	5,362	5,870	6,675	..	General Gov't Consumption
13,587	15,659	17,596	19,417	16,551	14,895	16,637	18,135	19,412	24,246	..	Gross Domestic Investment
12,785	15,506	17,464	19,122	16,425	14,310	15,165	17,344	20,683	23,841	..	Fixed Investment
2,173	2,480	3,014	3,496	3,304	2,594	2,869	3,360	4,404	5,101	..	Indirect Taxes, net
27,167	30,190	33,719	36,552	35,619	36,059	39,740	46,334	51,831	57,610	B	GDP at factor cost
356	349	331	340	292	245	222	204	190	177	..	Agriculture
11,107	12,029	13,954	15,712	14,259	14,467	15,976	18,860	20,762	23,119	..	Industry
8,362	8,154	8,908	9,863	9,184	10,185	12,091	14,863	16,506	18,272	..	Manufacturing
17,876	20,292	22,448	23,996	24,372	23,942	26,412	30,630	35,283	39,416	..	Services, etc.
11,953	14,218	16,932	18,304	15,606	15,038	17,018	21,010	24,946	27,965	..	Gross Domestic Saving
10,499	12,909	16,323	18,616	16,561	15,613	17,244	20,837	24,555	28,677	..	Gross National Saving
				(Millions of 1987 Singapore Dollars)							
29,874	32,289	35,781	39,721	39,647	39,889	43,192	47,596	51,821	57,098	..	Gross National Product
31,106	33,243	35,956	38,957	38,241	38,921	42,609	47,378	51,738	56,019	..	GDP at Market Prices
-1,483	-2,404	-2,079	-1,900	-1,424	-278	382	2,695	3,899	795	..	Resource Balance
49,128	51,431	54,404	59,174	57,182	64,654	73,313	95,542	104,711	116,453	..	Exports of Goods & NFServices
50,612	53,834	56,482	61,074	58,606	64,932	72,931	92,847	100,812	115,657	..	Imports of Goods & NFServices
32,589	35,646	38,035	40,857	39,665	39,199	42,228	44,683	47,839	55,224	..	Domestic Absorption
15,734	16,341	16,606	17,566	17,767	18,630	20,264	22,829	24,454	26,667	..	Private Consumption, etc.
3,207	3,632	3,982	4,190	5,216	5,271	5,327	5,042	5,253	5,856	..	General Gov't Consumption
13,648	15,673	17,447	19,100	16,682	15,298	16,637	16,811	18,131	22,702	..	Gross Domestic Investment
12,927	15,546	17,223	18,848	16,574	14,673	15,165	16,408	19,313	22,158	..	Fixed Investment
28,474	30,314	32,700	35,427	34,998	36,290	39,740	44,157	47,675	51,462	B	GDP at factor cost
302	287	294	309	277	247	222	194	182	168	..	Agriculture
12,704	13,324	14,648	16,086	14,594	14,455	15,976	18,075	19,576	21,375	..	Industry
9,623	9,286	9,546	10,262	9,513	10,312	12,091	14,266	15,662	17,158	..	Manufacturing
18,099	19,632	21,013	22,562	23,370	24,219	26,412	29,108	31,980	34,476	..	Services, etc.
											Memo Items:
49,264	52,619	55,892	60,038	57,718	65,087	73,313	95,728	106,307	119,386	..	Capacity to Import
136	1,188	1,488	864	536	433	0	186	1,596	2,933	..	Terms of Trade Adjustment
31,242	34,431	37,444	39,821	38,777	39,354	42,609	47,563	53,333	58,952	..	Gross Domestic Income
30,010	33,478	37,269	40,585	40,183	40,322	43,192	47,781	53,416	60,031	..	Gross National Income
				(Index 1987 = 100)							**DOMESTIC PRICES/DEFLATORS**
94.3	98.3	102.2	102.8	101.8	99.3	100.0	104.9	108.7	111.9	..	Overall (GDP)
95.0	95.7	98.3	100.7	100.5	98.2	100.0	104.8	106.0	106.8	..	Domestic Absorption
117.8	121.6	112.4	109.9	105.6	99.0	100.0	104.7	104.7	105.3	..	Agriculture
87.4	90.3	95.3	97.7	97.7	100.1	100.0	104.3	106.1	108.2	..	Industry
86.9	87.8	93.3	96.1	96.5	98.8	100.0	104.2	105.4	106.5	..	Manufacturing
93.1	96.8	97.9	100.4	100.9	99.5	100.0	101.5	103.9	107.5	..	Consumer Price Index
											MANUFACTURING ACTIVITY
102.0	99.6	98.6	99.6	92.0	89.4	100.0	117.3	..	..	..	Employment (1987=100)
74.4	81.5	89.1	97.1	104.8	101.5	100.0	101.5	..	..	..	Real Earnings per Empl. (1987=100)
91.4	91.2	88.5	93.7	94.1	91.6	100.0	100.3	..	..	..	Real Output per Empl. (1987=100)
30.3	35.0	36.3	36.4	37.8	31.7	29.1	28.2	..	..	..	Earnings as % of Value Added
				(Millions of current Singapore Dollars)							**MONETARY HOLDINGS**
25,197	30,908	35,378	38,948	41,407	35,315	52,492	59,039	70,901	82,048	D	Money Supply, Broadly Defined
7,242	8,157	8,607	8,866	8,785	9,822	11,031	11,958	13,745	15,261	..	Money
3,382	3,996	4,335	4,619	4,739	5,034	5,440	5,997	6,610	7,109	..	Currency Outside Banks
3,860	4,161	4,272	4,247	4,046	4,788	5,591	5,961	7,135	8,152	..	Demand Deposits
17,956	22,751	26,771	30,082	32,622	25,493	41,461	47,081	57,156	66,787	..	Quasi-Money
				(Millions of current Singapore Dollars)							
213	1,098	661	1,643	816	561	-1,165	3,485	5,889	..	C	**GOVERNMENT DEFICIT (-) OR SURPLUS**
7,797	9,054	10,935	11,451	10,768	10,411	12,947	13,856	15,710	..	..	Current Revenue
5,377	5,452	6,267	7,802	7,316	6,802	9,722	8,107	8,999	..	..	Current Expenditure
2,420	3,602	4,668	3,649	3,452	3,609	3,225	5,749	6,711	..	..	Current Budget Balance
899	1,032	782	246	3,996	4,560	858	603	1,557	..	..	Capital Receipts
3,106	3,536	4,789	2,252	6,632	7,608	5,248	2,867	2,379	..	..	Capital Payments

SINGAPORE	1970	1971	1972	1973	1974	1975	1976	1977	1978	1979	1980
FOREIGN TRADE (CUSTOMS BASIS)					*(Millions of current US dollars)*						
Value of Exports, fob	1,554	1,755	2,181	3,610	5,785	5,377	6,586	8,242	10,134	14,233	19,375
Nonfuel Primary Products	720	661	681	1,220	1,537	1,238	1,610	2,135	2,588	3,452	4,041
Fuels	360	451	536	716	1,857	1,809	1,955	2,481	2,867	3,410	4,882
Manufactures	474	642	964	1,673	2,391	2,331	3,020	3,625	4,679	7,372	10,452
Value of Imports, cif	2,461	2,827	3,383	5,070	8,344	8,135	9,070	10,472	13,049	17,638	24,003
Nonfuel Primary Products	696	708	790	1,272	1,593	1,436	1,809	2,194	2,469	3,258	3,817
Fuels	332	405	491	656	2,003	1,998	2,486	2,677	3,122	4,449	6,882
Manufactures	1,433	1,714	2,102	3,142	4,748	4,700	4,774	5,601	7,458	9,931	13,303
					(Index 1987 = 100)						
Terms of Trade	71.0	70.8	72.0	82.6	98.8	91.9	98.9	94.5	93.6	96.7	97.6
Export Prices, fob	13.0	14.7	16.3	26.3	52.5	49.6	54.9	58.2	63.5	81.4	101.0
Import Prices, cif	18.3	20.8	22.7	31.9	53.1	54.0	55.5	61.6	67.9	84.2	103.4
BALANCE OF PAYMENTS					*(Millions of current US dollars)*						
Exports of Goods & Services	2,003	2,267	3,243	5,143	8,062	8,276	9,387	11,231	13,778	18,649	25,239
Merchandise, fob	1,447	1,665	2,041	3,426	5,547	5,110	6,218	7,745	9,587	13,400	18,200
Nonfactor Services	489	519	1,090	1,550	2,289	2,787	2,800	3,094	3,664	4,443	6,085
Factor Services	67	83	113	167	225	380	370	391	528	806	953
Imports of Goods & Services	2,567	2,979	3,741	5,658	9,044	8,822	9,906	11,482	14,192	19,350	26,695
Merchandise, fob	2,302	2,655	3,127	4,735	7,764	7,511	8,442	9,729	12,090	16,450	22,400
Nonfactor Services	236	294	484	655	900	966	1,054	1,277	1,547	2,050	2,912
Factor Services	29	30	129	268	380	345	410	475	554	849	1,382
Long-Term Interest	..	..	..	..	..	..	..	..	..	..	..
Private Current Transfers, net	-21	-23	-2	-14	-41	-38	-46	-41	-36	-31	-104
Workers' Remittances	..	..	..	..	..	..	..	..	..	..	..
Curr. A/C Bal before Off. Transf.	-585	-735	-500	-529	-1,023	-584	-564	-291	-449	-732	-1,560
Net Official Transfers	13	11	5	10	2	0	-3	-4	-3	-4	-3
Curr. A/C Bal after Off. Transf.	-572	-724	-495	-519	-1,021	-584	-567	-295	-453	-736	-1,563
Long-Term Capital, net	140	158	213	433	353	273	305	405	299	817	1,463
Direct Investment	93	116	141	327	280	254	186	206	186	669	1,138
Long-Term Loans											
Disbursements	..	..	..	..	..	..	..	..	..	..	..
Repayments	..	..	..	..	..	..	..	..	..	..	..
Other Long-Term Capital	47	42	73	107	73	19	119	199	113	149	325
Other Capital, net	616	885	617	499	963	719	561	203	818	435	762
Change in Reserves	-184	-320	-335	-413	-295	-407	-298	-313	-665	-516	-663
Memo Item:					*(Singapore Dollars per US dollar)*						
Conversion Factor (Annual Avg)	3.060	3.050	2.810	2.460	2.440	2.370	2.470	2.440	2.270	2.170	2.140
EXTERNAL DEBT (Total)	..	..	..	..	*(Millions of US dollars), outstanding at end of year*						..
Long-Term Debt (by debtor)	..	..	..	..	..	..	..	..	..	..	..
Central Bank, incl. IMF credit	..	..	..	..	..	..	..	..	..	..	..
Central Government	..	..	..	..	..	..	..	..	..	..	..
Rest of General Government	..	..	..	..	..	..	..	..	..	..	..
Non-financial Public Enterprises	..	..	..	..	..	..	..	..	..	..	..
Priv. Sector, incl non-guaranteed	..	..	..	..	..	..	..	..	..	..	..
Short-Term Debt	..	..	..	..	..	..	..	..	..	..	..
Memo Items:					*(Millions of US dollars)*						
Int'l Reserves Excluding Gold	1,012.0	1,452.0	1,748.0	2,286.0	2,812.0	3,007.0	3,364.0	3,858.0	5,303.0	5,818.0	6,567.0
Gold Holdings (at market price)	..	..	..	..	..	..	..	..	..	..	..
SOCIAL INDICATORS											
Total Fertility Rate	3.1	3.0	3.0	2.8	2.4	2.1	2.1	1.8	1.8	1.8	1.7
Infant Mortality Rate	19.7	19.7	19.0	20.1	16.7	13.9	11.6	12.4	12.6	13.2	11.7
Life Expectancy at Birth	67.7	68.1	68.5	68.9	69.3	69.7	70.1	70.5	70.9	71.2	71.5
Urban Population, % of total	100.0	100.0	100.0	100.0	100.0	100.0	100.0	100.0	100.0	100.0	100.0
Food Prod. per capita (1987=100)	92.8	116.8	125.9	120.5	114.3	118.5	107.8	126.6	125.8	118.5	119.8
Labor Force, Agriculture (%)	3.4	3.2	3.0	2.8	2.7	2.5	2.3	2.1	1.9	1.7	1.6
Labor Force, Female (%)	25.9	27.0	28.0	29.0	29.9	30.7	31.6	32.4	33.1	33.8	34.5
Primary Schl. Enroll. Ratio	105.0	..	..	..	..	110.0	111.0	110.0	108.0	106.0	108.0
Primary Schl. Enroll. Ratio, Female	101.0	..	..	..	..	107.0	108.0	107.0	106.0	105.0	106.0
Secondary Schl. Enroll. Ratio	46.0	..	..	..	..	52.0	54.0	55.0	57.0	59.0	58.0

1981	1982	1983	1984	1985	1986	1987	1988	1989	1990 estimate	Notes	SINGAPORE
				(Millions of current US dollars)							**FOREIGN TRADE (CUSTOMS BASIS)**
20,968	20,788	21,833	24,055	22,815	22,428	28,592	39,205	44,600	52,627	..	Value of Exports, fob
3,530	3,229	3,329	4,102	3,343	3,169	3,592	5,193	5,326	4,907	..	Nonfuel Primary Products
5,726	5,724	6,115	6,162	6,156	4,587	4,523	4,889	6,738	9,406	..	Fuels
11,712	11,834	12,388	13,791	13,317	14,672	20,477	29,123	32,537	38,315	..	Manufactures
27,572	28,167	28,158	28,656	26,250	25,461	32,480	43,765	49,605	60,647	..	Value of Imports, cif
3,565	3,451	3,664	4,290	3,582	3,543	4,108	5,828	5,656	5,957	..	Nonfuel Primary Products
9,295	9,469	8,804	7,964	7,741	5,047	5,956	6,172	6,881	9,629	..	Fuels
14,712	15,248	15,691	16,402	14,927	16,871	22,416	31,765	37,067	45,061	..	Manufactures
				(Index 1987 = 100)							
100.5	99.0	99.3	100.0	98.9	97.1	100.0	98.7	98.3	99.8	..	Terms of Trade
106.4	99.0	96.2	95.3	92.3	82.8	100.0	109.1	112.0	121.1	..	Export Prices, fob
105.9	99.9	96.9	95.3	93.3	85.3	100.0	110.5	113.9	121.4	..	Import Prices, cif
				(Millions of current US dollars)							**BALANCE OF PAYMENTS**
29,366	30,386	31,029	31,847	29,730	29,775	38,060	51,063	59,200	71,377	..	Exports of Goods & Services
19,662	19,435	20,429	22,663	21,533	21,336	27,464	37,993	43,239	50,683	..	Merchandise, fob
8,612	9,709	9,299	7,582	6,383	6,220	7,348	9,483	11,663	15,014	..	Nonfactor Services
1,092	1,243	1,300	1,603	1,814	2,219	3,248	3,587	4,298	5,679	..	Factor Services
30,683	31,477	31,425	32,009	29,521	29,274	37,602	49,511	56,308	68,666	..	Imports of Goods & Services
25,785	26,196	26,252	26,734	24,362	23,402	29,910	40,338	45,713	55,802	..	Merchandise, fob
3,254	3,613	3,782	4,024	3,976	4,165	4,808	5,812	6,463	7,968	..	Nonfactor Services
1,644	1,668	1,390	1,252	1,183	1,707	2,884	3,362	4,132	4,896	..	Factor Services
..	..	..	..	..	..	..	..	..	..		Long-Term Interest
-145	-194	-207	-214	-205	-172	-170	-209	-254	-265	..	Private Current Transfers, net
..	..	..	..	..	..	..	..	..	..		Workers' Remittances
-1,462	-1,285	-602	-376	5	330	288	1,343	2,637	2,445	..	Curr. A/C Bal before Off. Transf.
-8	-11	-8	-9	-8	-11	-64	-88	-90	-95	..	Net Official Transfers
-1,470	-1,296	-610	-385	-4	319	224	1,255	2,547	2,350	..	Curr. A/C Bal after Off. Transf.
1,682	1,834	784	773	1,017	1,167	2,480	2,967	3,460	3,653	..	Long-Term Capital, net
1,645	1,298	1,085	1,210	809	1,529	2,630	3,493	3,915	4,489	..	Direct Investment
..	..	..	..	..	..	..	..	..	..		Long-Term Loans
..	..	..	..	..	..	..	..	..	..		Disbursements
..	..	..	..	..	..	..	..	..	..		Repayments
36	536	-301	-437	208	-361	-151	-526	-456	-835	..	Other Long-Term Capital
697	639	886	1,136	320	-948	-1,609	-2,563	-3,269	-572	..	Other Capital, net
-909	-1,177	-1,059	-1,524	-1,333	-538	-1,095	-1,659	-2,738	-5,431	..	Change in Reserves
				(Singapore Dollars per US dollar)							**Memo Item:**
2.110	2.140	2.110	2.130	2.200	2.180	2.110	2.010	1.950	1.810		Conversion Factor (Annual Avg)
			(Millions of US dollars), outstanding at end of year								**EXTERNAL DEBT (Total)**
..	..	..	..	..	..	..	..	..	..		Long-Term Debt (by debtor)
..	..	..	..	..	..	..	..	..	..		Central Bank, incl. IMF credit
..	..	..	..	..	..	..	..	..	..		Central Government
..	..	..	..	..	..	..	..	..	..		Rest of General Government
..	..	..	..	..	..	..	..	..	..		Non-financial Public Enterprises
..	..	..	..	..	..	..	..	..	..		Priv. Sector, incl non-guaranteed
..	..	..	..	..	..	..	..	..	..		Short-Term Debt
				(Millions of US dollars)							**Memo Items:**
7,549.0	8,480.0	9,264.0	10,416.0	12,847.0	12,939.0	15,227.0	17,073.0	20,345.0	27,748.0		Int'l Reserves Excluding Gold
..	..	..	..	..	..	..	..	..	..		Gold Holdings (at market price)
											SOCIAL INDICATORS
1.7	1.7	1.7	1.8	1.8	1.8	1.9	1.9	1.9	1.9	..	Total Fertility Rate
10.8	10.7	9.4	9.3	8.4	7.4	7.4	7.1	6.9	6.6	..	Infant Mortality Rate
71.8	72.1	72.3	72.6	72.9	73.2	73.5	73.7	74.0	74.3	..	Life Expectancy at Birth
100.0	100.0	100.0	100.0	100.0	100.0	100.0	100.0	100.0	100.0	..	Urban Population, % of total
118.5	100.5	114.5	107.7	115.1	101.2	100.0	68.8	86.4	92.2	..	Food Prod. per capita (1987=100)
..	..	..	..	..	..	..	..	..	..	..	Labor Force, Agriculture (%)
34.3	34.0	33.8	33.6	33.4	33.1	32.9	32.6	32.4	32.1	..	Labor Force, Female (%)
106.0	109.0	113.0	115.0	115.0	114.0	113.0	112.0	110.0		..	Primary Schl. Enroll. Ratio
105.0	107.0	111.0	113.0	113.0	113.0	111.0	111.0	109.0		..	Primary Schl. Enroll. Ratio, Female
62.0	65.0	69.0	71.0	62.0	67.0	68.0	69.0	69.0		..	Secondary Schl. Enroll. Ratio

SOLOMON ISLANDS	1970	1971	1972	1973	1974	1975	1976	1977	1978	1979	1980
CURRENT GNP PER CAPITA (US $)	..	..	..	..	..	290	270	300	320	430	400
POPULATION (thousands)	164	169	175	181	187	194	201	209	216	224	233
USE AND ORIGIN OF RESOURCES					*(Millions of current Solomon Islands Dollars)*						
Gross National Product (GNP)	..	..	23.20	26.70	39.90	37.80	43.30	54.10	59.60	84.30	89.50
Net Factor Income from Abroad	..	..	-0.20	-0.30	-0.50	-1.50	-3.20	-3.70	-7.40	-5.90	-6.90
GDP at Market Prices	28.60	30.50	23.40	27.00	40.40	39.30	46.50	57.80	67.00	90.20	96.40
Resource Balance	..	..	..	..	..	..	..	..	..	..	-28.60
Exports of Goods & NFServices	..	..	..	..	..	..	..	..	..	..	67.70
Imports of Goods & NFServices	..	..	..	..	..	..	..	..	..	..	96.30
Domestic Absorption	..	..	..	..	..	..	..	..	..	..	124.90
Private Consumption, etc.	..	..	..	..	..	..	..	..	..	..	67.60
General Gov't Consumption	..	..	..	..	..	..	..	..	..	..	22.20
Gross Domestic Investment	..	..	..	..	..	..	..	..	..	..	35.10
Fixed Investment	..	..	..	..	..	..	..	..	..	..	..
Indirect Taxes, net	2.20	2.30	2.10	2.40	4.10	3.40	4.00	5.40	6.20	10.50	10.80
GDP at factor cost	26.40	28.20	21.30	24.60	36.30	35.90	42.50	52.40	60.80	79.70	85.60
Agriculture	..	..	..	..	..	..	..	..	..	..	..
Industry	..	..	..	..	..	..	..	..	..	..	..
Manufacturing	..	..	..	..	..	..	..	..	..	..	..
Services, etc.	..	..	..	..	..	..	..	..	..	..	..
Gross Domestic Saving	..	..	..	..	..	..	..	..	..	..	6.60
Gross National Saving	..	..	..	..	..	..	..	..	..	..	0.30
					(Millions of 1987 Solomon Islands Dollars)						
Gross National Product	..	..	..	108.12	136.44	135.89	129.09	148.39	153.73	201.54	164.58
GDP at Market Prices	117.36	120.13	86.13	96.11	121.43	107.01	121.80	139.35	151.74	189.44	178.16
Resource Balance	..	..	..	..	..	..	..	..	..	..	-142.47
Exports of Goods & NFServices	..	..	..	..	..	..	..	..	..	..	132.37
Imports of Goods & NFServices	..	..	..	..	..	..	..	..	..	..	274.84
Domestic Absorption	..	..	..	..	..	..	..	..	..	..	320.63
Private Consumption, etc.	..	..	..	..	..	..	..	..	..	..	182.04
General Gov't Consumption	..	..	..	..	..	..	..	..	..	..	64.82
Gross Domestic Investment	..	..	..	..	..	..	..	..	..	..	73.77
Fixed Investment	..	..	..	..	..	..	..	..	..	..	..
GDP at factor cost	..	..	..	..	..	..	..	..	..	..	..
Agriculture	..	..	..	..	..	..	..	..	..	..	..
Industry	..	..	..	..	..	..	..	..	..	..	..
Manufacturing	..	..	..	..	..	..	..	..	..	..	..
Services, etc.	..	..	..	..	..	..	..	..	..	..	..
Memo Items:											
Capacity to Import	..	..	..	..	..	..	..	..	..	..	193.21
Terms of Trade Adjustment	..	..	..	..	..	..	..	..	..	..	60.85
Gross Domestic Income	..	..	..	..	..	..	..	..	..	..	239.01
Gross National Income	..	..	..	..	..	..	..	..	..	..	225.42
DOMESTIC PRICES/DEFLATORS					*(Index 1987 = 100)*						
Overall (GDP)	24.4	25.4	27.2	28.1	33.3	36.7	38.2	41.5	44.2	47.6	54.1
Domestic Absorption	..	..	..	..	..	..	..	..	..	..	39.0
Agriculture	..	..	..	..	..	..	..	..	..	..	..
Industry	..	..	..	..	..	..	..	..	..	..	..
Manufacturing	..	..	..	..	..	..	..	..	..	..	..
Consumer Price Index	..	22.0	23.5	24.3	28.8	31.7	33.1	35.9	38.2	41.3	46.7
MANUFACTURING ACTIVITY											
Employment (1987=100)	..	..	..	..	..	..	..	..	..	..	..
Real Earnings per Empl. (1987=100)	..	..	..	..	..	..	..	..	..	..	..
Real Output per Empl. (1987=100)	..	..	..	..	..	..	..	..	..	..	..
Earnings as % of Value Added	..	..	..	..	..	..	..	..	..	..	..
MONETARY HOLDINGS					*(Millions of current Solomon Islands Dollars)*						
Money Supply, Broadly Defined	..	..	..	..	..	..	..	..	27.29	39.56	39.04
Money	..	..	..	..	..	..	..	..	7.82	10.99	15.14
Currency Outside Banks	..	..	..	..	..	..	..	..	3.85	4.84	5.66
Demand Deposits	..	..	..	..	..	..	..	..	3.96	6.15	9.48
Quasi-Money	..	..	..	..	..	..	..	..	19.48	28.57	23.90
GOVERNMENT DEFICIT (-) OR SURPLUS					*(Thousands of current Solomon Islands Dollars)*						
	..	..	..	..	..	40	30	-630	720	-2,940	-3,600
Current Revenue	..	..	..	..	..	13,020	16,760	19,800	28,060	31,140	36,280
Current Expenditure	..	..	..	..	..	9,530	10,930	14,080	16,740	20,080	24,350
Current Budget Balance	..	..	..	..	..	3,490	5,830	5,720	11,320	11,060	11,930
Capital Receipts	..	..	..	..	..	30	30	150	70	1,180	570
Capital Payments	..	..	..	..	..	3,480	5,830	6,500	10,670	15,180	16,100

1981	1982	1983	1984	1985	1986	1987	1988	1989	1990 estimate	Notes	SOLOMON ISLANDS
490	560	540	620	520	580	560	550	590	590	..	**CURRENT GNP PER CAPITA (US $)**
242	250	258	266	274	282	290	298	307	316	..	**POPULATION (thousands)**
											USE AND ORIGIN OF RESOURCES
			(Millions of current Solomon Islands Dollars)								
104.40	124.80	137.10	213.90	227.40	237.50	287.90	365.40	403.00	427.70	..	Gross National Product (GNP)
-8.00	-1.30	-5.40	-7.80	-9.50	-15.00	-6.70	-1.10	-1.20	-0.98	..	Net Factor Income from Abroad
112.40	126.10	142.50	221.70	236.90	252.50	294.60	366.50	404.20	428.68	..	GDP at Market Prices
-36.20	-18.20	-30.70	-8.40	-44.40	-69.50	-95.10	-152.30	..	..	..	Resource Balance
65.30	72.00	86.70	133.40	124.20	146.30	174.60	227.00	..	..	..	Exports of Goods & NFServices
101.50	90.20	117.40	141.80	168.60	215.80	269.70	379.30	..	..	..	Imports of Goods & NFServices
148.60	144.30	173.10	230.10	281.30	322.00	389.70	518.80	..	..	..	Domestic Absorption
84.00	77.20	86.60	127.10	152.50	169.90	218.40	253.70	..	..	..	Private Consumption, etc.
26.50	29.30	34.10	52.10	66.60	84.10	90.80	123.80	..	..	..	General Gov't Consumption
38.10	37.80	52.40	50.90	62.20	68.00	80.50	141.30	..	..	..	Gross Domestic Investment
..	..	..	..	..	..	..	..	..	..	..	Fixed Investment
14.40	18.00	18.00	23.70	26.80	31.40	39.80	44.50	..	..	..	Indirect Taxes, net
98.00	108.10	124.50	198.00	210.10	221.10	254.80	322.00	..	..	..	GDP at factor cost
..	..	..	..	..	..	..	..	..	..	..	Agriculture
..	..	..	..	..	..	..	..	..	..	..	Industry
..	..	..	..	..	..	..	..	..	..	..	Manufacturing
..	..	..	..	..	..	..	..	..	..	..	Services, etc.
1.90	19.60	21.80	42.50	17.80	-1.50	-14.60	-11.00	..	..	..	Gross Domestic Saving
-11.10	12.80	12.00	31.50	4.30	-15.90	-21.50	-15.10	..	..	..	Gross National Saving
			(Millions of 1987 Solomon Islands Dollars)								
186.82	204.85	226.91	270.70	230.44	272.86	287.90	306.51	323.89	334.79	..	Gross National Product
202.01	207.92	236.75	239.71	241.74	289.61	294.60	307.35	324.73	335.65	I	GDP at Market Prices
-126.85	-70.37	-77.00	-107.40	-113.92	-70.50	-95.10	-184.29	..	..	..	Resource Balance
150.55	156.81	186.14	198.26	185.74	233.45	174.60	211.55	..	..	..	Exports of Goods & NFServices
277.41	227.18	263.14	305.66	299.67	303.95	269.70	395.85	..	..	..	Imports of Goods & NFServices
328.86	278.29	313.75	347.11	355.66	360.11	389.70	491.64	..	..	..	Domestic Absorption
189.57	148.23	168.82	197.89	192.62	191.55	218.40	295.25	..	..	..	Private Consumption, etc.
66.57	65.11	70.95	76.49	82.33	87.00	90.80	96.35	..	..	..	General Gov't Consumption
72.72	64.95	73.98	72.72	80.71	81.55	80.50	100.05	..	..	..	Gross Domestic Investment
..	..	..	..	..	..	..	..	..	..	..	Fixed Investment
..	..	..	..	..	..	..	..	..	..	..	GDP at factor cost
..	..	..	..	..	..	..	..	..	..	..	Agriculture
..	..	..	..	..	..	..	..	..	..	..	Industry
..	..	..	..	..	..	..	..	..	..	..	Manufacturing
..	..	..	..	..	..	..	..	..	..	..	Services, etc.
											Memo Items:
178.47	181.34	194.33	287.55	220.75	206.06	174.60	236.90	..	..	..	Capacity to Import
27.92	24.53	8.19	89.30	35.01	-27.39	0.00	25.35	..	..	..	Terms of Trade Adjustment
229.92	232.45	244.94	329.00	276.75	262.22	294.60	332.70	..	..	..	Gross Domestic Income
214.74	229.38	235.10	359.99	265.44	245.47	287.90	331.86	..	..	..	Gross National Income
			(Index 1987 = 100)								**DOMESTIC PRICES/DEFLATORS**
55.6	60.6	60.2	92.5	98.0	87.2	100.0	119.2	124.5	127.7	..	Overall (GDP)
45.2	51.9	55.2	66.3	79.1	89.4	100.0	105.5	..	..	..	Domestic Absorption
..	..	..	..	..	..	..	..	..	..	..	Agriculture
..	..	..	..	..	..	..	..	..	..	..	Industry
..	..	..	..	..	..	..	..	..	..	..	Manufacturing
54.3	61.4	65.2	72.4	79.3	90.1	100.0	116.7	134.2	145.9	..	Consumer Price Index
											MANUFACTURING ACTIVITY
..	..	..	..	..	..	..	..	..	..	..	Employment (1987=100)
..	..	..	..	..	..	..	..	..	..	..	Real Earnings per Empl. (1987=100)
..	..	..	..	..	..	..	..	..	..	..	Real Output per Empl. (1987=100)
..	..	..	..	..	..	..	..	..	..	..	Earnings as % of Value Added
			(Millions of current Solomon Islands Dollars)								**MONETARY HOLDINGS**
32.19	39.77	47.90	64.64	66.35	72.67	97.59	128.57	128.14	140.36	..	Money Supply, Broadly Defined
14.23	15.77	18.43	28.32	28.33	30.38	37.23	49.03	50.90	64.46	..	Money
6.42	7.15	9.30	12.75	13.88	13.58	16.84	20.21	22.65	25.22	..	Currency Outside Banks
7.81	8.63	9.13	15.57	14.44	16.80	20.39	28.82	28.25	39.23	..	Demand Deposits
17.96	24.00	29.47	36.32	38.02	42.29	60.37	79.53	77.24	75.91	..	Quasi-Money
			(Thousands of current Solomon Islands Dollars)								**GOVERNMENT DEFICIT (-) OR SURPLUS**
-9,210	-13,040	-13,380	-6,530	-19,330	-15,060	-34,050	-32,960	..	..	..	Current Revenue
37,060	38,570	40,290	51,950	54,500	82,490	99,640	119,700	..	..	..	Current Expenditure
30,850	34,490	39,240	46,110	59,550	65,890	77,100	92,430	125,230	146,690	..	Current Budget Balance
6,210	4,080	1,050	5,840	-5,050	16,600	22,540	27,270	..	..	..	Capital Receipts
190	190	110	460	740	..	10	300	250	1,450	..	Capital Payments
15,610	17,310	14,540	12,830	15,020	31,660	56,600	60,530	22,170	25,770	..	

SOLOMON ISLANDS	1970	1971	1972	1973	1974	1975	1976	1977	1978	1979	1980
FOREIGN TRADE (CUSTOMS BASIS)					*(Thousands of current US dollars)*						
Value of Exports, fob	..	..	..	..	..	..	..	..	..	..	..
Nonfuel Primary Products	..	..	..	..	..	..	..	..	..	..	..
Fuels	..	..	..	..	..	..	..	..	..	..	..
Manufactures	..	..	..	..	..	..	..	..	..	..	..
Value of Imports, cif	..	..	..	..	..	..	..	..	..	..	..
Nonfuel Primary Products	..	..	..	..	..	..	..	..	..	..	..
Fuels	..	..	..	..	..	..	..	..	..	..	..
Manufactures	..	..	..	..	..	..	..	..	..	..	..
					(Index 1987 = 100)						
Terms of Trade	..	..	..	..	..	..	..	..	..	..	..
Export Prices, fob	..	..	..	..	..	..	..	..	..	..	..
Import Prices, cif	..	..	..	..	..	..	..	..	..	..	..
BALANCE OF PAYMENTS					*(Millions of current US dollars)*						
Exports of Goods & Services	..	..	..	..	..	..	..	..	..	..	..
Merchandise, fob	..	..	..	..	..	15.45	24.32	32.82	35.03	68.48	73.27
Nonfactor Services	..	..	..	..	..	2.49	3.06	3.33	5.27	5.77	11.69
Factor Services	..	..	..	..	..	..	..	..	..	..	..
Imports of Goods & Services	..	..	..	..	..	40.32	38.74	43.36	56.20	83.84	117.01
Merchandise, fob	..	..	..	..	..	28.54	25.79	28.61	35.37	58.43	74.11
Nonfactor Services	..	..	..	..	..	9.82	9.04	10.65	17.40	20.79	27.96
Factor Services	..	..	..	..	..	1.96	3.91	4.10	3.43	4.62	14.94
Long-Term Interest	0.00	0.00	0.00	0.00	0.00	0.00	0.00	0.00	0.00	0.00	0.00
Private Current Transfers, net	..	..	..	..	..	1.83	1.71	1.66	2.06	2.31	0.72
Workers' Remittances	..	..	..	..	..	..	..	..	..	..	..
Curr. A/C Bal before Off. Transf.	..	..	..	..	..	-20.55	-9.65	-5.54	-13.85	-7.28	-31.33
Net Official Transfers	..	..	..	..	..	7.99	11.37	11.31	17.17	17.55	19.16
Curr. A/C Bal after Off. Transf.	..	..	..	..	..	-12.57	1.71	5.77	3.32	10.28	-12.17
Long-Term Capital, net	..	..	..	..	..	7.85	4.89	7.32	6.18	5.77	6.39
Direct Investment	..	..	..	..	..	7.85	4.89	4.44	4.58	3.46	2.41
Long-Term Loans	0.00	0.50	0.10	0.00	0.00	9.10	0.00	0.20	0.50	2.50	4.00
Disbursements	0.00	0.50	0.10	0.00	0.00	9.10	0.00	0.20	0.50	2.50	4.00
Repayments	0.00	0.00	0.00	0.00	0.00	0.00	0.00	0.00	0.00	0.00	0.00
Other Long-Term Capital	..	..	..	..	..	-9.10	0.00	2.68	1.10	-0.19	-0.02
Other Capital, net	..	..	..	..	..	6.02	-4.77	-6.21	5.72	-8.48	-3.25
Change in Reserves	..	..	..	..	..	-1.31	-1.83	-6.88	-15.22	-7.57	9.04
Memo Item:					*(Solomon Islands Dollars per US dollar)*						
Conversion Factor (Annual Avg)	0.890	0.880	0.840	0.700	0.700	0.760	0.820	0.900	0.870	0.870	0.830
EXTERNAL DEBT (Total)					*(Millions of US dollars), outstanding at end of year*						
EXTERNAL DEBT (Total)	0.10	0.60	0.60	0.60	0.60	8.80	7.40	8.50	11.50	13.80	19.40
Long-Term Debt (by debtor)	0.10	0.60	0.60	0.60	0.60	8.80	7.40	8.50	9.50	12.80	17.40
Central Bank, incl. IMF credit	0.00	0.00	0.00	0.00	0.00	0.00	0.00	0.00	0.00	0.00	0.00
Central Government	0.10	0.60	0.60	0.60	0.60	8.80	7.40	8.50	9.50	12.80	17.40
Rest of General Government	..	..	..	..	..	..	..	..	..	..	..
Non-financial Public Enterprises	..	..	..	..	..	..	..	..	..	..	..
Priv. Sector, incl non-guaranteed	..	..	..	..	..	..	..	..	..	..	..
Short-Term Debt	0.00	0.00	0.00	0.00	0.00	0.00	0.00	0.00	2.00	1.00	2.00
Memo Items:					*(Thousands of US dollars)*						
Int'l Reserves Excluding Gold	..	..	..	..	..	..	..	2,871	29,186	36,957	29,605
Gold Holdings (at market price)	..	..	..	..	..	..	..	..	..	..	..
SOCIAL INDICATORS											
Total Fertility Rate	..	..	..	..	..	..	..	7.1	7.0	6.8	6.7
Infant Mortality Rate	..	..	..	..	..	..	..	46.0	49.6	53.2	56.8
Life Expectancy at Birth	..	..	..	..	..	..	..	..	..	..	..
Urban Population, % of total	8.9	8.9	9.0	9.0	9.1	9.1	9.1	9.1	9.2	9.2	9.2
Food Prod. per capita (1987=100)	121.5	120.1	113.4	112.1	108.0	108.0	113.4	114.7	119.1	131.6	116.2
Labor Force, Agriculture (%)	..	..	..	..	..	..	..	..	..	..	..
Labor Force, Female (%)	..	..	..	..	..	..	..	..	..	..	..
Primary Schl. Enroll. Ratio	..	..	..	..	..	..	..	..	..	..	..
Primary Schl. Enroll. Ratio, Female	..	..	..	..	..	..	..	..	..	..	..
Secondary Schl. Enroll. Ratio	..	..	..	..	..	..	..	..	..	..	..

FOREIGN TRADE (CUSTOMS BASIS)

(Thousands of current US dollars)

1981	1982	1983	1984	1985	1986	1987	1988	1989	1990 est.	Notes	SOLOMON ISLANDS
..	..	..	..	..	..	..	..	..	..	..	Value of Exports, fob
..	..	..	..	..	..	..	..	..	..	..	Nonfuel Primary Products
..	..	..	..	..	..	..	..	..	..	..	Fuels
..	..	..	..	..	..	..	..	..	..	..	Manufactures
..	..	..	..	..	..	..	..	..	..	..	Value of Imports, cif
..	..	..	..	..	..	..	..	..	..	..	Nonfuel Primary Products
..	..	..	..	..	..	..	..	..	..	..	Fuels
..	..	..	..	..	..	..	..	..	..	..	Manufactures

(Index 1987 = 100)

1981	1982	1983	1984	1985	1986	1987	1988	1989	1990 est.	Notes	
..	..	..	..	..	..	..	..	..	..	..	Terms of Trade
..	..	..	..	..	..	..	..	..	..	..	Export Prices, fob
..	..	..	..	..	..	..	..	..	..	..	Import Prices, cif

BALANCE OF PAYMENTS

(Millions of current US dollars)

1981	1982	1983	1984	1985	1986	1987	1988	1989	1990 est.	Notes	
..	77.64	81.84	108.27	87.32	84.18	89.05	111.69	108.58	101.16	..	Exports of Goods & Services
66.19	58.28	61.99	93.11	70.98	63.85	63.20	81.92	74.70	70.43	..	Merchandise, fob
12.99	14.83	16.37	10.52	12.29	17.23	22.61	26.22	30.00	28.39	..	Nonfactor Services
..	4.53	3.48	4.63	4.05	3.10	3.24	3.55	3.88	2.33	..	Factor Services
117.45	95.66	95.86	111.72	117.03	123.40	128.54	174.98	180.44	161.58	..	Imports of Goods & Services
75.85	59.11	61.47	67.60	71.85	67.53	69.39	105.11	97.55	80.35	..	Merchandise, fob
37.69	25.13	22.29	28.11	35.86	46.05	48.27	57.62	71.43	69.95	..	Nonfactor Services
3.91	11.43	12.10	16.02	9.32	9.82	10.88	12.24	11.47	11.27	..	Factor Services
0.10	0.10	0.10	1.10	1.70	1.70	2.10	3.50	3.60	3.30	..	Long-Term Interest
-5.75	-5.66	-3.83	-2.51	-2.70	0.34	-0.10	-1.44	1.22	1.42	..	Private Current Transfers, net
..	..	..	..	..	..	..	..	..	..	..	Workers' Remittances
-44.01	-23.68	-17.85	-5.97	-32.42	-38.87	-39.58	-64.73	-70.64	-59.00	..	Curr. A/C Bal before Off. Transf.
17.47	11.43	14.89	14.60	11.82	38.64	31.90	46.10	37.28	33.45	..	Net Official Transfers
-26.55	-12.25	-2.96	8.64	-20.60	-0.23	-7.69	-18.63	-33.36	-25.55	..	Curr. A/C Bal after Off. Transf.
4.14	22.86	15.24	-1.96	14.59	3.96	18.12	23.58	20.58	23.33	..	Long-Term Capital, net
0.23	1.03	0.44	1.96	0.88	-0.98	8.44	3.36	5.67	12.85	..	Direct Investment
4.20	4.10	6.80	11.70	12.70	14.10	14.30	9.90	1.50	-0.80	..	Long-Term Loans
4.20	4.10	6.90	12.40	13.80	15.40	15.70	13.00	7.20	6.50	..	Disbursements
0.00	0.00	0.10	0.70	1.10	1.30	1.40	3.10	5.70	7.30	..	Repayments
-0.29	17.73	8.00	-15.63	1.01	-9.16	-4.62	10.32	13.41	11.28	..	Other Long-Term Capital
15.77	4.09	-2.72	-5.75	-3.32	-12.43	-4.51	-0.25	1.38	-5.52	..	Other Capital, net
6.64	-14.69	-9.56	-0.92	9.33	8.70	-5.92	-4.69	11.40	7.73	..	Change in Reserves

(Solomon Islands Dollars per US dollar)

1981	1982	1983	1984	1985	1986	1987	1988	1989	1990 est.	Notes	Memo Item:
0.870	0.970	1.150	1.270	1.480	1.740	2.000	2.080	2.290	2.530	..	Conversion Factor (Annual Avg)

(Millions of US dollars), outstanding at end of year

1981	1982	1983	1984	1985	1986	1987	1988	1989	1990 est.	Notes	
23.40	28.00	34.30	44.50	66.20	77.70	98.20	104.60	100.90	122.50	..	EXTERNAL DEBT (Total)
20.40	25.00	31.30	40.50	57.20	74.70	96.80	103.00	100.90	106.00	..	Long-Term Debt (by debtor)
0.90	2.70	3.50	3.10	3.00	3.50	2.20	1.70	1.40	0.70	..	Central Bank, incl. IMF credit
19.50	22.30	27.80	37.40	54.20	71.20	94.60	101.30	99.50	105.30	..	Central Government
..	..	..	..	..	..	..	..	..	..	..	Rest of General Government
..	..	..	..	..	..	..	..	..	..	..	Non-financial Public Enterprises
..	..	..	..	..	..	..	..	..	..	..	Priv. Sector, incl non-guaranteed
3.00	3.00	3.00	4.00	9.00	3.00	1.40	1.60	0.00	16.50	..	Short-Term Debt

(Thousands of US dollars)

1981	1982	1983	1984	1985	1986	1987	1988	1989	1990 est.	Notes	Memo Items:
21,589	37,230	47,330	44,704	35,606	29,572	36,749	39,620	26,162	17,600	..	Int'l Reserves Excluding Gold
..	..	..	..	..	..	..	..	..	..	..	Gold Holdings (at market price)

SOCIAL INDICATORS

1981	1982	1983	1984	1985	1986	1987	1988	1989	1990 est.	Notes	
6.5	6.4	6.3	6.2	6.0	5.9	5.8	5.7	5.7	5.6	..	Total Fertility Rate
60.4	64.0	61.8	59.6	57.4	55.2	53.0	51.1	49.2	47.3	..	Infant Mortality Rate
..	60.6	61.2	61.7	62.3	62.8	63.3	63.7	64.1	64.5	..	Life Expectancy at Birth
9.3	9.4	9.5	9.6	9.7	9.9	10.1	10.2	10.4	10.6	..	Urban Population, % of total
126.7	117.9	111.6	117.6	115.5	106.4	100.0	100.6	101.4	103.6	..	Food Prod. per capita (1987=100)
..	..	..	..	..	..	..	..	..	..	..	Labor Force, Agriculture (%)
..	..	..	..	..	..	..	..	..	..	..	Labor Force, Female (%)
..	..	..	..	..	..	..	..	..	..	..	Primary Schl. Enroll. Ratio
..	..	..	..	..	..	..	..	..	..	..	Primary Schl. Enroll. Ratio, Female
..	..	..	..	..	..	..	..	..	..	..	Secondary Schl. Enroll. Ratio

SOMALIA	1970	1971	1972	1973	1974	1975	1976	1977	1978	1979	1980
CURRENT GNP PER CAPITA (US $)	80	80	90	90	90	140	150	140	130	110	110
POPULATION (thousands)	4,311	4,432	4,559	4,690	4,827	4,967	5,111	5,261	5,417	5,578	5,746

USE AND ORIGIN OF RESOURCES *(Millions of current Somali Shillings)*

	1970	1971	1972	1973	1974	1975	1976	1977	1978	1979	1980
Gross National Product (GNP)	2,260	2,357	2,913	3,195	2,956	4,477	5,090	6,866	8,166	9,031	17,347
Net Factor Income from Abroad	2	-3	3	10	13	2	8	-14	-15	33	-25
GDP at Market Prices	2,258	2,360	2,910	3,185	2,943	4,475	5,082	6,880	8,181	8,998	17,372
Resource Balance	-118	-157	-140	-413	-663	-645	-702	-2,680	-2,476	-4,609	-9,608
Exports of Goods & NFServices	260	313	458	443	514	558	510	1,394	2,114	2,187	5,764
Imports of Goods & NFServices	378	470	598	856	1,177	1,203	1,212	4,074	4,590	6,796	15,372
Domestic Absorption	2,376	2,517	3,050	3,598	3,606	5,120	5,784	9,560	10,657	13,607	26,980
Private Consumption, etc.	1,878	2,006	2,059	2,519	2,091	3,203	3,404	7,116	6,770	7,959	16,902
General Gov't Consumption	233	229	596	622	724	909	861	970	1,540	3,580	2,713
Gross Domestic Investment	265	282	395	457	791	1,008	1,519	1,474	2,347	2,068	7,365
Fixed Investment	205	218	325	361	690	684	818	1,119	1,844	2,183	7,484
Indirect Taxes, net	254	287	329	382	475	448	478	572	1,034	1,164	1,030
GDP at factor cost	2,005	2,074	2,581	2,803	2,468	4,026	4,603	6,308	7,147	7,834	16,342
Agriculture	1,190	1,191	1,589	1,716	1,126	2,181	2,592	3,848	4,498	4,595	11,181
Industry	319	355	378	370	504	504	640	759	566	794	1,305
Manufacturing	186	210	214	211	200	226	337	323	301	446	774
Services, etc.	495	527	614	717	839	1,342	1,371	1,701	2,083	2,445	3,856
Gross Domestic Saving	147	125	255	44	128	363	817	-1,206	-129	-2,541	-2,243
Gross National Saving	154	137	270	71	163	377	832	-1,206	347	-2,282	-1,908

(Millions of 1987 Somali Shillings)

	1970	1971	1972	1973	1974	1975	1976	1977	1978	1979	1980
Gross National Product	94,922	97,218	107,304	105,474	84,068	112,705	112,435	140,227	147,380	142,966	136,246
GDP at Market Prices	94,660	97,161	107,015	104,963	83,546	112,488	112,078	140,337	147,461	142,220	136,243
Resource Balance	-1,349	-4,053	772	-3,723	-7,263	-7,923	-10,599	-38,737	-31,886	-42,893	-41,679
Exports of Goods & NFServices	8,661	10,334	14,627	11,229	9,873	8,852	7,407	13,936	17,260	18,155	27,591
Imports of Goods & NFServices	10,010	14,387	13,855	14,952	17,136	16,775	18,006	52,673	49,146	61,048	69,271
Domestic Absorption	96,009	101,214	106,242	108,686	90,809	120,411	122,677	179,074	179,347	185,113	177,922
Private Consumption, etc.	75,232	80,623	67,357	70,509	52,588	79,573	80,329	121,936	104,500	95,347	91,635
General Gov't Consumption	8,605	8,494	22,820	22,364	22,012	23,146	19,108	19,614	28,098	52,363	19,673
Gross Domestic Investment	12,172	12,098	16,065	15,813	16,209	17,692	23,240	37,524	46,749	37,403	66,614
Fixed Investment	..	..	..	..	..	..	..	..	..	..	..
GDP at factor cost	86,170	86,934	94,465	91,881	69,236	99,066	99,471	126,301	124,516	121,329	128,041
Agriculture	47,492	46,694	49,612	47,417	30,659	53,087	54,992	74,400	77,127	72,591	75,605
Industry	17,411	18,045	18,277	15,150	15,442	14,894	16,635	18,117	11,256	13,615	14,213
Manufacturing	8,010	8,567	8,647	7,199	6,393	6,883	8,932	7,795	6,589	7,893	8,611
Services, etc.	25,505	26,852	31,889	34,576	30,011	35,638	31,581	35,931	35,918	36,411	40,115

Memo Items:

	1970	1971	1972	1973	1974	1975	1976	1977	1978	1979	1980
Capacity to Import	6,885	9,581	10,611	7,738	7,483	7,777	7,577	18,023	22,635	19,646	25,974
Terms of Trade Adjustment	-1,775	-753	-4,016	-3,491	-2,390	-1,074	170	4,087	5,375	1,490	-1,617
Gross Domestic Income	92,884	96,409	102,999	101,472	81,156	111,414	112,248	144,424	152,836	143,710	134,625
Gross National Income	93,147	96,465	103,288	101,983	81,678	111,631	112,605	144,314	152,755	144,457	134,629

DOMESTIC PRICES/DEFLATORS *(Index 1987 = 100)*

	1970	1971	1972	1973	1974	1975	1976	1977	1978	1979	1980
Overall (GDP)	2.4	2.4	2.7	3.0	3.5	4.0	4.5	4.9	5.5	6.3	12.8
Domestic Absorption	2.5	2.5	2.9	3.3	4.0	4.3	4.7	5.3	5.9	7.4	15.2
Agriculture	2.5	2.6	3.2	3.6	3.7	4.1	4.7	5.2	5.8	6.3	14.8
Industry	1.8	2.0	2.1	2.4	3.3	3.4	3.8	4.2	5.0	5.8	9.2
Manufacturing	2.3	2.4	2.5	2.9	3.1	3.3	3.8	4.1	4.6	5.7	9.0
Consumer Price Index	2.3	2.2	2.2	2.3	2.7	3.3	3.7	4.1	4.6	5.7	9.0

MANUFACTURING ACTIVITY

	1970	1971	1972	1973	1974	1975	1976	1977	1978	1979	1980
Employment (1987=100)	..	..	..	..	..	..	..	..	..	..	..
Real Earnings per Empl. (1987=100)	..	..	..	..	..	..	..	..	..	..	..
Real Output per Empl. (1987=100)	..	..	..	..	..	..	..	..	..	..	..
Earnings as % of Value Added	27.5	25.5	18.3	26.5	37.1	31.5	26.1	25.2	31.4	32.8	..

MONETARY HOLDINGS *(Millions of current Somali Shillings)*

	1970	1971	1972	1973	1974	1975	1976	1977	1978	1979	1980
Money Supply, Broadly Defined	465	391	518	608	783	1,005	1,200	1,545	2,047	2,813	3,381
Money	376	329	441	507	629	826	995	1,325	1,728	2,335	2,783
Currency Outside Banks	146	146	221	248	306	389	414	622	883	1,153	1,508
Demand Deposits	230	183	219	259	322	436	581	703	845	1,183	1,275
Quasi-Money	89	62	77	101	154	179	205	219	319	478	598

GOVERNMENT DEFICIT (-) OR SURPLUS *(Millions of current Somali Shillings)*

	1970	1971	1972	1973	1974	1975	1976	1977	1978	1979	1980
	..	..	19	-33	-60	-73	-120	-367	-700	..	..
Current Revenue	..	..	413	438	585	622	700	857	1,347	..	..
Current Expenditure	..	..	347	412	522	587	659	736	1,288	..	..
Current Budget Balance	..	..	65	26	63	36	41	121	59	..	..
Capital Receipts	..	..	..	..	..	5	4	8	6	..	..
Capital Payments	..	..	47	59	123	113	165	496	765	..	..

1981	1982	1983	1984	1985	1986	1987	1988	1989	1990 estimate	Notes	SOMALIA
120	130	120	110	120	130	130	130	130	120	A	**CURRENT GNP PER CAPITA (US $)**
5,920	6,101	6,288	6,483	6,686	6,896	7,114	7,337	7,568	7,805	..	**POPULATION (thousands)**
											USE AND ORIGIN OF RESOURCES
			(Millions of current Somali Shillings)								
21,908	28,646	34,766	58,845	82,476	113,153	159,432	267,341	519,757	1,583,120	..	Gross National Product (GNP)
-142	-459	-291	-3,477	-4,885	-7,405	-8,653	-16,557	-39,723	-155,654	..	Net Factor Income from Abroad
22,050	29,105	35,057	62,322	87,361	120,558	168,085	283,898	559,480	1,738,770	..	GDP at Market Prices
-9,603	-12,248	-17,198	-28,974	-11,336	-27,043	-41,220	-49,292	-208,204	104,546	..	Resource Balance
5,473	7,558	8,283	9,092	5,530	8,395	11,246	13,691	42,985	170,170	f	Exports of Goods & NFServices
15,076	19,806	25,481	38,066	16,867	35,438	52,466	62,983	251,189	65,624	..	Imports of Goods & NFServices
31,653	41,353	52,255	91,296	98,697	147,601	209,305	333,189	767,684	1,634,230	..	Domestic Absorption
20,711	28,965	37,443	65,634	56,536	88,718	112,111	206,886	456,476	..	..	Private Consumption, etc.
4,864	3,866	6,952	10,580	16,128	28,503	41,222	58,452	141,686	..	..	General Gov't Consumption
6,078	8,522	7,860	15,082	26,034	30,381	55,972	67,852	169,522	269,510	..	Gross Domestic Investment
5,100	7,298	9,236	14,185	23,588	29,175	47,904	55,076	166,725	259,078	..	Fixed Investment
1,780	2,048	2,949	2,540	4,099	7,197	7,365	1,340	24,967	71,940	..	Indirect Taxes, net
20,270	27,057	32,108	59,782	83,262	113,361	160,720	282,558	534,513	1,666,840	..	GDP at factor cost
13,841	18,325	21,327	40,592	55,583	70,698	103,150	189,383	339,940	1,090,990	..	Agriculture
1,555	2,192	2,389	4,347	6,396	11,470	16,238	25,735	46,779	145,421	..	Industry
932	1,423	1,572	2,805	4,145	6,240	8,383	14,464	24,300	76,986	..	Manufacturing
4,874	6,540	8,392	14,843	21,283	31,193	41,332	67,440	147,794	430,421	..	Services, etc.
-3,525	-3,726	-9,338	-13,892	14,697	3,337	14,752	18,560	-38,682	374,056	..	Gross Domestic Saving
-3,330	-4,037	-9,327	-14,107	10,580	-3,686	4,721	3,094	-79,828	..	..	Gross National Saving
			(Millions of 1987 Somali Shillings)								
146,312	149,893	137,213	135,554	146,327	149,643	159,432	157,543	156,025	150,843	..	Gross National Product
147,091	152,334	138,282	143,014	154,569	159,999	168,085	166,945	166,700	164,103	I	GDP at Market Prices
-41,339	-49,132	-51,356	-50,174	-16,330	-45,207	-41,220	-25,320	-39,457	..	..	Resource Balance
20,330	19,810	20,300	15,650	6,601	11,578	11,246	8,246	9,247	..	f	Exports of Goods & NFServices
61,669	68,942	71,656	65,823	22,931	56,785	52,466	33,566	48,704			Imports of Goods & NFServices
188,431	201,467	189,638	193,188	170,899	205,207	209,305	192,266	206,157	..	..	Domestic Absorption
108,930	125,297	116,976	117,714	73,576	118,441	112,111	120,804	121,373	..	..	Private Consumption, etc.
31,003	20,538	26,692	23,709	28,547	37,120	41,222	33,346	38,415	..	..	General Gov't Consumption
48,498	55,631	45,970	51,766	68,776	49,645	55,972	38,116	46,369	..	..	Gross Domestic Investment
..	..	..	..	..	..	..	..	..	..	..	Fixed Investment
135,339	141,655	126,658	137,183	147,308	150,452	160,720	160,636	159,253	157,301	..	GDP at factor cost
86,458	88,907	78,043	88,179	96,575	95,315	103,150	106,706	103,843	105,221	..	Agriculture
11,953	13,671	11,378	11,713	11,993	15,475	16,238	14,802	13,079	12,972	..	Industry
7,176	8,938	7,241	6,719	7,208	7,992	8,383	7,959	6,366	6,366	..	Manufacturing
35,267	38,245	37,238	37,291	38,741	39,662	41,332	39,128	42,332	39,108	..	Services, etc.
											Memo Items:
22,388	26,309	23,293	15,722	7,518	13,452	11,246	7,297	8,335	..	..	Capacity to Import
2,057	6,498	2,993	72	918	1,874	0	-949	-912	..	..	Terms of Trade Adjustment
149,149	158,833	141,275	143,086	155,486	161,874	168,085	165,996	165,787	..	..	Gross Domestic Income
148,370	156,391	140,206	135,626	147,244	151,517	159,432	156,594	155,113	..	..	Gross National Income
			(Index 1987 = 100)								**DOMESTIC PRICES/DEFLATORS**
15.0	19.1	25.4	43.6	56.5	75.3	100.0	170.1	335.6	1059.6	..	Overall (GDP)
16.8	20.5	27.6	47.3	57.8	71.9	100.0	173.3	372.4	..	..	Domestic Absorption
16.0	20.6	27.3	46.0	57.6	74.2	100.0	177.5	327.4	1036.9	..	Agriculture
13.0	16.0	21.0	37.1	53.3	74.1	100.0	173.9	357.7	1121.1	..	Industry
13.0	15.9	21.7	41.7	57.5	78.1	100.0	181.7	381.7	1209.3	..	Manufacturing
13.0	16.0	21.8	41.7	57.5	78.0	100.0	181.9			..	Consumer Price Index
											MANUFACTURING ACTIVITY
											Employment (1987=100)
..	..	..	..	..	..	..	..	..	..	..	Real Earnings per Empl. (1987=100)
..	..	..	..	..	..	..	..	..	..	..	Real Output per Empl. (1987=100)
..	..	..	..	..	26.5	..	..	..	..	J	Earnings as % of Value Added
			(Millions of current Somali Shillings)								**MONETARY HOLDINGS**
4,421	5,116	5,501	6,934	12,558	16,834	38,234	60,114	157,986	..	..	Money Supply, Broadly Defined
3,674	4,033	4,309	5,334	9,773	12,143	30,046	45,436	139,827	..	..	Money
1,891	1,456	1,355	1,900	3,787	5,209	12,327	21,033	70,789	..	..	Currency Outside Banks
1,783	2,577	2,954	3,434	5,986	6,934	17,719	24,403	69,038	..	..	Demand Deposits
747	1,083	1,192	1,600	2,785	4,691	8,188	14,678	18,159	..	..	Quasi-Money
			(Millions of current Somali Shillings)								**GOVERNMENT DEFICIT (-) OR SURPLUS**
..	..	..	..	..	..	..	..	..	..	..	Current Revenue
..	..	..	..	..	..	..	..	..	..	..	Current Expenditure
..	..	..	..	..	..	..	..	..	..	..	Current Budget Balance
..	..	..	..	..	..	..	..	..	..	..	Capital Receipts
..	..	..	..	..	..	..	..	..	..	..	Capital Payments

SOMALIA	1970	1971	1972	1973	1974	1975	1976	1977	1978	1979	1980
FOREIGN TRADE (CUSTOMS BASIS)					*(Millions of current US dollars)*						
Value of Exports, fob	31.41	34.48	43.10	54.22	62.05	88.58	94.61	62.99	106.60	111.81	132.64
Nonfuel Primary Products	29.46	..	42.44	52.95	61.20	85.73	92.12	60.63	105.09	109.41	125.20
Fuels	0.00	..	0.00	0.03	0.00	0.02	0.06	0.16	0.31	1.31	6.40
Manufactures	1.95	1.83	0.65	1.25	0.84	2.83	2.43	2.19	1.20	1.10	1.04
Value of Imports, cif	45.10	62.55	75.65	108.06	142.76	154.68	155.66	227.61	241.29	245.73	348.00
Nonfuel Primary Products	18.01	28.13	23.04	29.20	36.68	46.77	47.91	61.83	60.46	64.52	128.39
Fuels	2.84	2.65	3.55	4.60	9.58	9.53	10.65	9.93	16.01	13.46	2.57
Manufactures	24.26	31.77	49.07	74.26	96.50	98.38	97.10	155.85	164.82	167.75	217.03
					(Index 1987 = 100)						
Terms of Trade	211.60	177.30	191.40	189.90	109.10	92.80	113.00	101.50	121.60	138.30	117.20
Export Prices, fob	47.80	48.90	57.20	74.10	61.30	56.10	66.20	64.70	85.20	114.50	109.90
Import Prices, cif	22.60	27.60	29.90	39.00	56.20	60.50	58.60	63.70	70.10	82.80	93.80
BALANCE OF PAYMENTS					*(Millions of current US dollars)*						
Exports of Goods & Services	43.3	49.3	66.8	73.1	84.6	115.2	111.8	104.1	151.8	153.3	204.5
Merchandise, fob	31.1	38.1	56.5	57.1	64.0	88.6	81.1	71.3	109.5	106.0	133.3
Nonfactor Services	11.2	10.2	9.3	13.6	17.9	23.3	27.6	29.7	36.5	37.7	66.2
Factor Services	1.0	0.9	1.0	2.4	2.7	3.3	3.1	3.0	5.9	9.5	5.0
Imports of Goods & Services	61.9	67.7	91.0	140.4	188.0	217.5	221.8	244.9	322.4	453.0	540.6
Merchandise, fob	40.4	49.6	62.8	97.5	133.7	141.1	153.1	179.1	239.4	342.9	401.5
Nonfactor Services	20.8	16.9	27.5	42.0	53.4	73.3	66.9	65.1	80.6	103.1	133.2
Factor Services	0.7	1.3	0.8	1.0	0.8	3.0	1.9	0.8	2.4	7.0	5.9
Long-Term Interest	0.4	0.6	0.8	0.9	1.1	1.3	0.8	1.2	1.3	1.0	1.9
Private Current Transfers, net	0.7	2.1	1.9	2.7	3.5	1.9	1.2	2.2	78.1	35.9	57.3
Workers' Remittances	..	..	..	..	..	..	..	..	..	36.7	57.3
Curr. A/C Bal before Off. Transf.	-17.9	-16.4	-22.4	-64.6	-99.9	-100.3	-108.9	-138.6	-92.5	-263.8	-278.8
Net Official Transfers	12.2	17.2	15.2	25.9	48.2	100.3	39.7	105.9	27.8	58.1	142.6
Curr. A/C Bal after Off. Transf.	-5.7	0.8	-7.2	-38.7	-51.7	0.0	-69.2	-32.8	-64.7	-205.7	-136.2
Long-Term Capital, net	11.0	4.3	17.7	26.1	61.0	52.8	69.6	64.3	79.8	86.1	96.2
Direct Investment	4.5	1.7	4.5	0.6	0.7	6.7	2.2	7.8	0.3	..	..
Long-Term Loans	3.7	5.4	15.4	15.5	46.9	59.0	55.5	77.7	93.1	86.9	106.4
Disbursements	4.2	6.0	16.6	17.3	48.9	61.2	57.2	79.9	96.2	90.1	113.5
Repayments	0.5	0.6	1.2	1.8	2.0	2.2	1.7	2.2	3.1	3.2	7.1
Other Long-Term Capital	2.8	-2.8	-2.2	10.0	13.4	-12.9	11.9	-21.2	-13.6	-0.8	-10.2
Other Capital, net	-1.8	-2.3	5.2	3.5	9.8	-7.7	-1.0	22.6	12.4	12.4	22.4
Change in Reserves	-3.5	-2.9	-15.7	9.1	-19.1	-45.1	0.6	-54.2	-27.5	107.3	17.5
Memo Item:					*(Somali Shillings per US dollar)*						
Conversion Factor (Annual Avg)	7.14	7.13	6.98	6.28	6.30	6.30	6.30	6.30	6.30	6.30	6.30
Additional Conversion Factor	7.00	7.13	6.98	6.28	6.29	6.29	6.29	13.80	14.48	15.24	28.78
EXTERNAL DEBT (Total)	77.2	84.5	101.1	124.2	*(Millions of US dollars), outstanding at end of year* 174.6	228.7	287.0	392.0	515.3	571.4	659.7
Long-Term Debt (by debtor)	77.2	84.5	101.1	124.2	174.6	228.7	287.0	380.0	493.3	545.4	613.0
Central Bank, incl. IMF credit	2.2	1.8	1.3	0.7	0.3	0.0	0.0	0.0	1.2	1.2	18.8
Central Government	71.8	82.6	97.0	120.8	162.3	216.8	275.2	366.4	477.5	528.3	546.5
Rest of General Government	..	..	..	..	..	..	..	..	..	..	..
Non-financial Public Enterprises	0.9	0.1	2.8	2.7	12.0	11.9	11.8	13.6	13.6	14.9	20.0
Priv. Sector, incl non-guaranteed	2.3	0.0	0.0	0.0	0.0	0.0	0.0	0.0	1.0	1.0	27.7
Short-Term Debt	0.0	0.0	0.0	0.0	0.0	0.0	0.0	12.0	22.0	26.0	46.7
Memo Items:					*(Thousands of US dollars)*						
Int'l Reserves Excluding Gold	21,140	26,659	31,331	34,997	42,323	68,368	84,876	119,977	126,341	43,791	14,564
Gold Holdings (at market price)	112	131	195	337	492	370	355	1,777	3,350	7,589	11,182
SOCIAL INDICATORS											
Total Fertility Rate	6.7	6.7	6.7	6.7	6.7	6.7	6.7	6.7	6.7	6.7	6.8
Infant Mortality Rate	157.8	156.4	155.0	153.8	152.6	151.4	150.2	149.0	147.8	146.6	145.4
Life Expectancy at Birth	40.1	40.5	40.9	41.4	41.9	42.3	42.8	43.3	43.6	43.9	44.2
Urban Population, % of total	22.7	23.3	23.9	24.4	25.0	25.6	26.3	26.9	27.6	28.2	28.9
Food Prod. per capita (1987=100)	131.2	127.1	133.6	124.2	115.9	122.8	119.1	117.4	114.4	106.2	105.3
Labor Force, Agriculture (%)	79.4	78.9	78.5	78.1	77.8	77.5	77.0	76.6	76.2	75.9	75.5
Labor Force, Female (%)	41.2	41.1	41.1	41.0	41.0	40.9	40.9	40.8	40.7	40.7	40.6
Primary Schl. Enroll. Ratio	11.0	..	..	..	..	59.0	45.0	40.0	43.0	41.0	27.0
Primary Schl. Enroll. Ratio, Female	5.0	..	..	..	..	42.0	32.0	28.0	30.0	29.0	19.0
Secondary Schl. Enroll. Ratio	5.0	..	..	..	..	6.0	4.0	4.0	5.0	6.0	10.0

1981	1982	1983	1984	1985	1986	1987	1988	1989	1990 estimate	Notes	SOMALIA
											FOREIGN TRADE (CUSTOMS BASIS)
(Millions of current US dollars)											
152.00	199.30	149.86	122.73	43.07	98.32	103.99	113.86	120.00	130.00	..	Value of Exports, fob
151.13	188.30	..	115.95	40.69	92.89	98.25	107.58	113.37	122.82	..	Nonfuel Primary Products
0.32	2.22		1.36	0.48	1.09	1.16	1.27	1.33	1.45	..	Fuels
0.55	8.79	3.29	5.41	1.90	4.33	4.58	5.02	5.29	5.73	..	Manufactures
512.93	330.11	352.27	342.59	235.47	303.81	132.00	323.54	350.00	360.00	..	Value of Imports, cif
136.83	95.39	89.87	98.99	68.04	87.79	38.14	93.49	101.13	104.02	..	Nonfuel Primary Products
11.24	47.48	64.29	49.27	33.87	43.70	18.98	46.53	50.34	51.78	..	Fuels
364.87	187.24	198.11	194.33	133.56	172.32	74.87	183.52	198.53	204.20	..	Manufactures
(Index 1987 = 100)											
107.50	108.50	115.20	110.20	106.60	94.80	100.00	106.30	111.30	..	..	Terms of Trade
101.50	97.50	101.60	95.00	90.70	89.40	100.00	108.60	78.30		..	Export Prices, fob
94.50	89.80	88.20	86.20	85.10	94.30	100.00	102.10	70.40		..	Import Prices, cif
											BALANCE OF PAYMENTS
(Millions of current US dollars)											
255.4	256.1	177.2	106.7	127.6	94.7	94.0	58.4	67.7	91.2	f	Exports of Goods & Services
175.4	170.8	98.4	54.8	90.6	94.7	94.0	58.4	67.7	58.4	..	Merchandise, fob
74.3	83.4	77.0	51.0	35.9	22.3	13.0	22.7	27.1	32.8	..	Nonfactor Services
5.8	1.9	1.7	1.0	1.1	0.0	0.0	0.0	0.0	..	..	Factor Services
519.5	610.3	486.1	602.8	454.1	530.6	538.2	380.6	552.7	432.9	f	Imports of Goods & Services
370.5	471.4	362.1	465.7	330.7	342.1	358.5	216.0	346.3	211.2	..	Merchandise, fob
135.0	131.0	117.6	123.5	96.8	128.2	127.7	104.0	122.0	140.5	..	Nonfactor Services
13.9	8.0	6.4	13.7	26.6	60.3	52.0	60.6	84.4	81.2	..	Factor Services
3.4	6.5	9.5	3.0	2.8	3.7	3.8	2.8	10.3	4.1	..	Long-Term Interest
53.6	13.8	19.1	162.9	19.4	5.3	-13.1	6.4	-2.9	-4.3	..	Private Current Transfers, net
7.2	19.9	21.7	..	..	..	..	..	..	..	..	Workers' Remittances
-210.5	-340.4	-289.8	-333.1	-307.1	-430.6	-457.3	-315.8	-487.9	-346.0	..	Curr. A/C Bal before Off. Transf.
127.1	162.9	148.2	194.0	204.3	304.9	343.3	217.3	331.2	265.2	..	Net Official Transfers
-83.4	-177.5	-141.6	-139.1	-102.8	-125.7	-114.0	-98.5	-156.7	-80.8	..	Curr. A/C Bal after Off. Transf.
69.0	138.3	68.3	96.0	76.4	33.4	77.2	-33.5	-26.0	-19.1	f	Long-Term Capital, net
..	-0.8	-8.2	-14.9	-0.7	..	..	..	..	..	..	Direct Investment
400.7	182.6	158.8	141.5	111.1	103.2	71.8	62.6	64.4	39.5	..	Long-Term Loans
443.9	187.6	166.4	146.9	113.4	106.4	75.6	63.7	71.4	42.1	..	Disbursements
43.2	5.0	7.6	5.4	2.3	3.2	3.8	1.1	7.0	2.6	..	Repayments
-331.7	-43.6	-82.3	-30.5	-34.0	-69.9	5.4	-96.1	-90.4	-58.6	..	Other Long-Term Capital
18.7	75.2	-4.4	25.1	33.7	116.8	49.7	129.1	162.2	102.8	f	Other Capital, net
-4.3	-36.0	77.7	18.0	-7.2	-24.4	-12.9	2.9	20.5	-2.9	..	Change in Reserves
											Memo Item:
(Somali Shillings per US dollar)											
6.30	10.75	15.79	20.02	39.49	72.00	105.18	170.45	490.68	..	..	Conversion Factor (Annual Avg)
31.54	37.58	47.77	79.06	100.00	130.00	166.00	273.00	512.00	1,865.77	..	Additional Conversion Factor
											EXTERNAL DEBT (Total)
(Millions of US dollars), outstanding at end of year											
1,055.9	1,221.8	1,410.3	1,498.0	1,639.3	1,799.7	2,009.3	2,070.9	2,136.5	2,349.5	..	
1,021.7	1,169.3	1,340.2	1,394.8	1,566.0	1,710.0	1,918.8	1,944.7	1,963.3	2,081.4	..	Long-Term Debt (by debtor)
47.5	80.7	123.6	113.0	158.3	162.4	182.5	172.3	154.7	164.2	..	Central Bank, incl. IMF credit
912.7	1,030.2	1,160.9	1,226.3	1,383.3	1,522.4	1,720.6	1,756.2	1,792.0	1,900.1	..	Central Government
..	..	..	..	..	..	..	..	..	..	..	Rest of General Government
21.0	13.6	10.9	10.7	12.1	13.7	15.7	16.2	16.6	17.1	..	Non-financial Public Enterprises
40.5	44.8	44.8	44.8	12.3	11.5	0.0	0.0	0.0	..	..	Priv. Sector, incl non-guaranteed
34.2	52.5	70.1	103.2	73.3	89.7	90.5	126.2	173.2	268.1	..	Short-Term Debt
											Memo Items:
(Thousands of US dollars)											
30,712	6,505	9,166	1,049	2,500	12,800	7,300	15,300	15,400	..	..	Int'l Reserves Excluding Gold
7,540	8,755	7,310	5,908	6,287	7,515	9,307	7,888	7,710	..	..	Gold Holdings (at market price)
											SOCIAL INDICATORS
6.8	6.8	6.8	6.8	6.8	6.8	6.8	6.8	6.8	6.8	..	Total Fertility Rate
144.2	143.0	140.8	138.6	136.3	134.1	131.9	129.8	127.7	125.7	..	Infant Mortality Rate
44.5	44.8	45.3	45.8	46.3	46.8	47.3	47.6	47.9	48.2	..	Life Expectancy at Birth
29.6	30.3	31.1	31.8	32.5	33.3	34.5	35.1	35.8	36.4	..	Urban Population, % of total
103.4	103.3	95.2	94.4	101.2	101.8	100.0	100.4	99.3	95.9	..	Food Prod. per capita (1987=100)
											Labor Force, Agriculture (%)
40.4	40.2	40.0	39.8	39.7	39.5	39.2	39.0	38.8	38.7	..	Labor Force, Female (%)
29.0	20.0	19.0	17.0	15.0	..	..	..	..	..	..	Primary Schl. Enroll. Ratio
21.0	14.0	14.0	12.0	10.0	..	..	..	..	..	..	Primary Schl. Enroll. Ratio, Female
14.0	14.0	14.0	11.0	10.0	..	..	..	..	..	..	Secondary Schl. Enroll. Ratio

SOUTH AFRICA	1970	1971	1972	1973	1974	1975	1976	1977	1978	1979	1980
CURRENT GNP PER CAPITA (US $)	740	810	840	980	1,010	1,500	1,660	1,800	1,220	1,340	1,780
POPULATION (thousands)	22,458	23,011	23,575	24,147	24,723	25,301	25,886	26,474	27,066	27,664	28,270

USE AND ORIGIN OF RESOURCES

(Billions of current South African Rand)

	1970	1971	1972	1973	1974	1975	1976	1977	1978	1979	1980
Gross National Product (GNP)	11.95	13.24	14.93	18.49	22.75	25.40	28.58	31.60	36.37	43.63	57.59
Net Factor Income from Abroad	-0.52	-0.52	-0.60	-0.72	-0.94	-1.25	-1.44	-1.66	-1.88	-2.14	-2.74
GDP at Market Prices	12.47	13.77	15.54	19.22	23.69	26.65	30.02	33.26	38.25	45.77	60.33
Resource Balance	-0.44	-0.57	0.42	0.55	-0.12	-0.65	-0.29	1.85	2.75	4.50	4.99
Exports of Goods & NFServices	2.75	3.05	3.99	4.95	6.72	7.48	8.50	10.34	12.68	16.47	22.02
Imports of Goods & NFServices	3.19	3.63	3.57	4.41	6.84	8.13	8.80	8.49	9.93	11.97	17.03
Domestic Absorption	12.91	14.34	15.12	18.67	23.81	27.29	30.31	31.42	35.50	41.27	55.34
Private Consumption, etc.	7.91	8.33	9.19	11.46	14.00	15.08	17.29	17.44	20.32	22.69	28.57
General Gov't Consumption	1.52	1.83	1.94	2.22	2.80	3.69	4.47	5.03	5.53	6.33	8.16
Gross Domestic Investment	3.49	4.18	3.99	4.99	7.01	8.53	8.56	8.94	9.65	12.25	18.61
Fixed Investment	3.08	3.60	4.18	4.89	5.94	7.85	9.05	9.31	10.09	12.02	16.04
Indirect Taxes, net	0.84	0.93	1.01	1.17	1.31	1.51	1.75	2.19	2.70	3.32	3.95
GDP at factor cost	11.64	12.83	14.53	18.04	22.38	25.14	28.27	31.07	35.55	42.46	56.38
Agriculture	0.92	1.11	1.23	1.45	2.14	2.13	2.11	2.43	2.66	2.81	2.92
Industry	4.63	4.89	5.71	7.46	9.38	10.75	12.22	13.21	15.78	20.21	28.70
Manufacturing	2.78	2.97	3.25	4.07	4.87	5.96	6.81	6.92	7.82	9.71	12.93
Services, etc.	6.09	6.84	7.59	9.14	10.87	12.26	13.93	15.43	17.12	19.43	24.76
Gross Domestic Saving	3.05	3.61	4.41	5.54	6.89	7.88	8.27	10.79	12.40	16.75	23.60
Gross National Saving	2.55	3.10	3.82	4.80	5.98	6.69	6.85	9.09	10.54	14.65	20.94

(Millions of 1987 South African Rand)

	1970	1971	1972	1973	1974	1975	1976	1977	1978	1979	1980
Gross National Product	88,013	92,810	95,515	101,412	85,912	110,092	131,655	184,921	122,631	114,384	97,626
GDP at Market Prices	108,018	113,287	115,496	120,349	127,128	129,450	132,637	132,376	136,318	141,663	150,804
Resource Balance	5,142	2,657	9,197	2,758	-7,033	-5,928	467	8,137	9,564	10,752	4,132
Exports of Goods & NFServices	42,866	44,187	45,513	43,155	41,044	40,568	42,312	44,259	45,718	46,560	46,663
Imports of Goods & NFServices	37,725	41,530	36,316	40,397	48,077	46,496	41,845	36,122	36,155	35,808	42,531
Domestic Absorption	102,877	110,630	106,299	117,592	134,162	135,379	132,170	124,239	126,755	130,911	146,672
Private Consumption, etc.	58,280	61,421	62,049	68,978	78,408	75,720	76,869	69,722	73,374	72,846	75,213
General Gov't Consumption	13,848	14,949	14,881	15,536	16,739	18,764	19,796	20,554	20,692	21,686	23,663
Gross Domestic Investment	30,749	34,261	29,369	33,077	39,015	40,895	35,505	33,963	32,689	36,379	47,796
Fixed Investment	26,354	29,203	30,909	32,523	34,647	38,027	37,558	35,319	34,339	35,771	41,879
GDP at factor cost	99,144	104,091	106,376	110,174	115,747	118,138	121,602	121,421	124,888	129,913	137,829
Agriculture	5,735	6,811	6,767	5,911	7,706	7,045	6,875	7,682	7,990	7,817	8,597
Industry	52,674	53,924	54,357	56,650	57,458	57,861	59,895	59,192	61,165	64,572	68,077
Manufacturing	21,987	23,385	24,273	26,524	28,245	29,332	30,067	29,060	31,169	33,742	36,956
Services, etc.	40,736	43,356	45,251	47,612	50,583	53,232	54,833	54,548	55,733	57,524	61,155

Memo Items:

	1970	1971	1972	1973	1974	1975	1976	1977	1978	1979	1980
Capacity to Import	32,496	34,950	40,581	45,412	47,219	42,789	40,461	43,984	46,167	49,274	54,985
Terms of Trade Adjustment	-10,370	-9,237	-4,932	2,257	6,175	2,221	-1,851	-275	448	2,714	8,322
Gross Domestic Income	97,648	104,050	110,564	122,607	133,304	131,672	130,786	132,101	136,766	144,377	159,126
Gross National Income	77,643	83,573	90,583	103,669	92,087	112,313	129,803	184,645	123,079	117,098	105,948

DOMESTIC PRICES/DEFLATORS

(Index 1987 = 100)

	1970	1971	1972	1973	1974	1975	1976	1977	1978	1979	1980
Overall (GDP)	11.5	12.2	13.5	16.0	18.6	20.6	22.6	25.1	28.1	32.3	40.0
Domestic Absorption	12.6	13.0	14.2	15.9	17.7	20.2	22.9	25.3	28.0	31.5	37.7
Agriculture	16.1	16.3	18.2	24.5	27.7	30.2	30.7	31.6	33.2	36.0	33.9
Industry	8.8	9.1	10.5	13.2	16.3	18.6	20.4	22.3	25.8	31.3	42.2
Manufacturing	12.6	12.7	13.4	15.3	17.2	20.3	22.6	23.8	25.1	28.8	35.0
Consumer Price Index	13.8	14.6	15.5	17.0	19.0	21.5	23.9	26.6	29.3	33.2	37.7

MANUFACTURING ACTIVITY

	1970	1971	1972	1973	1974	1975	1976	1977	1978	1979	1980
Employment (1987=100)	75.2	..	79.2	82.0	85.5	87.7	94.8	92.8	92.7	94.8	97.3
Real Earnings per Empl. (1987=100)	73.8	..	79.1	83.3	86.1	88.3	92.3	92.8	94.7	96.1	99.6
Real Output per Empl. (1987=100)	46.5	..	54.3	61.9	66.7	67.1	63.4	62.7	67.6	70.1	..
Earnings as % of Value Added	45.6	..	46.8	49.0	51.3	54.1	48.7	47.8	48.1	50.7	47.7

MONETARY HOLDINGS

(Billions of current South African Rand)

	1970	1971	1972	1973	1974	1975	1976	1977	1978	1979	1980
Money Supply, Broadly Defined	7.80	8.46	9.97	12.17	14.21	16.97	18.47	20.34	23.60	27.56	33.84
Money	2.26	2.45	2.81	3.38	4.01	4.29	4.44	4.65	5.13	6.20	8.40
Currency Outside Banks	0.51	0.57	0.63	0.75	0.88	1.03	1.11	1.15	1.28	1.46	1.86
Demand Deposits	1.75	1.88	2.18	2.64	3.13	3.26	3.33	3.50	3.85	4.74	6.54
Quasi-Money	5.54	6.01	7.17	8.78	10.20	12.68	14.03	15.69	18.46	21.36	25.44

GOVERNMENT DEFICIT (-) OR SURPLUS

(Millions of current South African Rand)

	1970	1971	1972	1973	1974	1975	1976	1977	1978	1979	1980
	..	..	-652	-499	-1,155	-1,438	-2,023	-2,067	-2,095	-1,947	-1,436
Current Revenue	..	..	3,295	4,185	5,114	5,988	6,669	7,599	8,956	10,764	14,398
Current Expenditure	..	..	2,841	3,406	4,419	5,346	6,380	7,075	8,019	9,707	11,709
Current Budget Balance	..	..	454	779	695	642	289	524	937	1,057	2,689
Capital Receipts	..	..	30	27	30	37	21	27	45	38	50
Capital Payments	..	..	1,136	1,305	1,880	2,117	2,333	2,618	3,077	3,042	4,175

1981	1982	1983	1984	1985	1986	1987	1988	1989	1990 estimate	Notes	SOUTH AFRICA
2,920	3,210	2,600	2,460	2,130	1,880	1,940	2,280	2,460	2,530	..	CURRENT GNP PER CAPITA (US $)
28,884	29,503	30,143	30,827	31,569	32,362	33,200	34,078	34,988	35,919	..	POPULATION (thousands)
											USE AND ORIGIN OF RESOURCES
				(Billions of current South African Rand)							
67.66	76.83	87.29	102.37	116.61	134.31	157.04	190.37	223.05	252.63	f	Gross National Product (GNP)
-3.42	-3.70	-4.16	-4.86	-6.52	-7.83	-7.49	-7.74	-9.48	-10.02		Net Factor Income from Abroad
71.08	80.53	91.46	107.22	123.13	142.14	164.52	198.11	232.53	262.65	f	GDP at Market Prices
-1.09	-0.12	3.57	2.20	11.56	13.88	13.52	10.38	12.37	15.50	..	Resource Balance
20.66	21.78	23.08	28.18	39.97	45.86	48.79	56.92	66.32	69.49	..	Exports of Goods & NFServices
21.75	21.90	19.51	25.98	28.41	31.98	35.27	46.54	53.95	53.98	..	Imports of Goods & NFServices
72.17	80.65	87.89	105.02	111.56	128.26	151.01	187.73	220.16	247.15	..	Domestic Absorption
38.75	48.00	50.17	60.40	65.28	75.58	88.55	109.84	126.64	145.95	..	Private Consumption, etc.
9.88	12.36	14.12	17.93	21.30	25.67	30.60	35.28	44.31	50.48	..	General Gov't Consumption
23.54	20.29	23.60	26.69	24.98	27.01	31.85	42.61	49.22	50.72	..	Gross Domestic Investment
19.74	22.46	24.50	26.21	28.71	28.71	31.50	39.38	48.64	53.32	..	Fixed Investment
4.81	6.65	7.05	8.94	10.68	12.65	14.59	19.83	25.73	27.93	..	Indirect Taxes, net
66.27	73.88	84.41	98.28	112.45	129.49	149.93	178.28	206.80	234.72	f	GDP at factor cost
4.71	4.65	4.15	5.25	6.53	7.24	9.43	11.76	12.54	11.89	..	Agriculture
31.30	33.98	39.47	44.42	51.58	60.63	66.87	80.06	91.66	103.23	..	Industry
16.55	18.32	20.84	23.80	25.93	30.28	35.75	44.10	52.29	60.02	..	Manufacturing
30.26	35.25	40.79	48.61	54.34	61.62	73.63	86.47	102.61	119.60	..	Services, etc.
22.46	20.17	27.17	28.89	36.55	40.88	45.37	52.99	61.59	66.22	..	Gross Domestic Saving
19.12	16.60	23.16	24.22	30.21	33.23	38.08	45.46	52.45	56.48	..	Gross National Saving
				(Millions of 1987 South African Rand)							
134,713	157,880	146,389	154,310	152,740	152,992	157,038	165,229	164,176	161,361	f	Gross National Product
158,735	158,074	155,194	163,107	161,170	161,188	164,524	171,260	174,857	173,219	f	GDP at Market Prices
-4,109	3,350	7,610	4,415	14,431	14,370	13,518	8,359	12,878	16,073	..	Resource Balance
44,267	43,969	41,233	44,778	48,893	48,055	48,791	50,627	55,352	57,242	..	Exports of Goods & NFServices
48,375	40,619	33,623	40,363	34,461	33,685	35,273	42,267	42,474	41,168	..	Imports of Goods & NFServices
162,843	154,724	147,584	158,692	146,739	146,819	151,006	162,900	161,979	157,146	..	Domestic Absorption
85,433	88,634	79,624	87,871	83,636	87,344	88,555	94,634	93,237	93,314	..	Private Consumption, etc.
24,111	25,635	26,100	27,876	28,835	29,496	30,599	31,107	32,205	32,528	..	General Gov't Consumption
53,299	40,454	41,860	42,944	34,268	29,980	31,852	37,159	36,537	31,303	..	Gross Domestic Investment
45,629	44,649	43,067	42,426	39,445	32,272	31,497	34,310	36,169	35,662	..	Fixed Investment
144,711	143,787	140,817	148,181	147,637	147,642	149,931	155,634	158,990	157,322	f	GDP at factor cost
9,094	8,326	6,436	7,169	8,628	9,196	9,430	9,694	10,862	9,841	..	Agriculture
71,280	70,203	67,442	70,161	68,299	67,220	66,873	69,977	70,548	69,427	..	Industry
39,457	38,261	35,718	37,143	35,045	34,988	35,752	38,055	38,221	37,300	..	Manufacturing
64,337	65,258	66,939	70,851	70,711	71,226	73,628	75,962	77,581	78,053	..	Services, etc.
											Memo Items:
45,955	40,398	39,770	43,781	48,489	48,299	48,791	51,693	52,210	52,991	..	Capacity to Import
1,689	-3,571	-1,463	-997	-403	245	0	1,066	-3,142	-4,251	..	Terms of Trade Adjustment
160,423	154,503	153,731	162,109	160,766	161,433	164,524	172,325	171,715	168,968	..	Gross Domestic Income
136,401	154,309	144,926	153,313	152,336	153,237	157,038	166,295	161,034	157,111	..	Gross National Income
											DOMESTIC PRICES/DEFLATORS
				(Index 1987 = 100)							
44.8	50.9	58.9	65.7	76.4	88.2	100.0	115.7	133.0	151.6	..	Overall (GDP)
44.3	52.1	59.6	66.2	76.0	87.4	100.0	115.2	135.9	157.3	..	Domestic Absorption
51.7	55.8	64.5	73.3	75.6	78.8	100.0	121.3	115.4	120.8	..	Agriculture
43.9	48.4	58.5	63.3	75.5	90.2	100.0	114.4	129.9	148.7	..	Industry
41.9	47.9	58.4	64.1	74.0	86.5	100.0	115.9	136.8	160.9	..	Manufacturing
43.5	49.9	56.0	62.4	72.6	86.1	100.0	112.8	129.4	148.0	..	Consumer Price Index
											MANUFACTURING ACTIVITY
101.5	101.7	102.8	103.4	99.5	99.0	100.0	101.3	..	..	G	Employment (1987=100)
102.8	105.7	106.7	108.1	105.3	100.7	100.0	104.0	..	..	G	Real Earnings per Empl. (1987=100)
105.1	100.2	93.5	97.3	93.0	91.7	100.0	103.9	..	..	..	Real Output per Empl. (1987=100)
49.1	48.5	50.6	50.4	50.5	49.4	49.1	47.9				Earnings as % of Value Added
											MONETARY HOLDINGS
				(Billions of current South African Rand)							
39.66	45.01	51.22	61.34	70.29	76.47	91.38	116.03	139.97	155.44	D	Money Supply, Broadly Defined
11.27	13.12	16.59	23.41	21.33	23.21	32.03	39.93	43.34	49.86	..	Money
2.27	2.49	2.76	3.19	3.55	4.18	5.03	6.13	7.31	8.25	..	Currency Outside Banks
9.00	10.63	13.82	20.22	17.78	19.03	27.00	33.81	36.03	41.61	..	Demand Deposits
28.39	31.89	34.63	37.93	48.96	53.26	59.36	76.10	96.63	105.58	..	Quasi-Money
				(Millions of current South African Rand)							
-2,810	-3,082	-4,771	-5,060	-4,975	-7,865	-12,001	-10,864	-5,609	..	C F	GOVERNMENT DEFICIT (-) OR SURPLUS
16,034	19,199	21,754	26,474	33,131	37,768	43,084	53,936	69,313	..	..	Current Revenue
14,644	18,231	21,936	27,203	33,130	41,131	48,956	59,539	71,347	..	..	Current Expenditure
1,390	968	-182	-729	1	-3,363	-5,872	-5,603	-2,034	..	..	Current Budget Balance
31	40	51	70	81	95	134	113	205	..	..	Capital Receipts
4,231	4,090	4,640	4,401	5,057	4,597	6,263	5,374	3,780	..	..	Capital Payments

SOUTH AFRICA	1970	1971	1972	1973	1974	1975	1976	1977	1978	1979	1980
FOREIGN TRADE (CUSTOMS BASIS)					*(Millions of current US dollars)*						
Value of Exports, fob	2,147	2,167	2,605	3,487	4,920	5,423	5,220	6,727	8,425	11,242	25,539
Nonfuel Primary Products	1,156	1,162	1,558	1,910	2,528	2,752	2,621	2,959	3,212	3,770	4,637
Fuels	111	117	98	22	45	69	137	312	417	671	966
Manufactures	880	889	949	1,554	2,347	2,603	2,462	3,457	4,796	6,801	19,935
Value of Imports, cif	3,556	4,032	3,638	4,721	7,215	7,579	6,757	5,886	7,191	8,331	18,551
Nonfuel Primary Products	423	418	388	604	928	814	774	767	755	941	1,392
Fuels	177	264	250	10	20	18	27	31	33	48	73
Manufactures	2,957	3,350	3,000	4,107	6,267	6,747	5,956	5,087	6,403	7,341	17,086
Terms of Trade					*(Index 1987 = 100)*						
Terms of Trade	168.8	167.8	174.7	170.2	182.1	157.2	151.8	138.0	120.9	128.5	139.7
Export Prices, fob	36.3	37.5	42.3	67.3	88.3	82.2	81.0	81.0	80.8	98.3	117.1
Import Prices, cif	21.5	22.4	24.2	39.5	48.5	52.3	53.3	58.7	66.8	76.5	83.9
BALANCE OF PAYMENTS					*(Millions of current US dollars)*						
Exports of Goods & Services	4,019	4,402	5,379	7,577	10,073	10,343	10,027	12,290	15,282	20,471	29,258
Merchandise, fob	3,206	3,457	4,386	6,187	8,434	8,436	8,296	10,443	13,041	17,696	25,698
Nonfactor Services	457	527	557	718	921	1,112	966	1,121	1,328	1,610	2,157
Factor Services	356	418	435	672	718	795	765	726	913	1,165	1,403
Imports of Goods & Services	5,303	5,938	5,562	7,681	11,655	12,974	12,036	11,808	13,833	17,171	25,989
Merchandise, fob	3,615	4,088	3,698	5,130	8,482	9,164	8,559	7,913	9,222	11,589	18,268
Nonfactor Services	796	942	896	1,156	1,547	1,899	1,548	1,777	2,110	2,526	3,587
Factor Services	892	908	968	1,395	1,626	1,911	1,929	2,118	2,501	3,056	4,133
Long-Term Interest	..	..	..	..	..	..	..	..	..	..	..
Private Current Transfers, net	31	22	23	-25	38	87	34	-41	17	52	94
Workers' Remittances	..	..	..	..	..	..	..	..	..	..	..
Curr. A/C Bal before Off. Transf.	-1,253	-1,514	-161	-129	-1,543	-2,544	-1,975	440	1,466	3,352	3,363
Net Official Transfers	38	34	39	45	84	102	100	94	63	63	145
Curr. A/C Bal after Off. Transf.	-1,215	-1,479	-122	-83	-1,459	-2,442	-1,875	535	1,529	3,415	3,508
Long-Term Capital, net	694	743	713	215	1,632	2,158	981	183	-240	-1,634	-910
Direct Investment	318	231	98	-23	578	63	-14	-190	-347	-498	-765
Long-Term Loans	..	..	..	..	..	..	..	..	..	..	..
Disbursements	..	..	..	..	..	..	..	..	..	..	..
Repayments	..	..	..	..	..	..	..	..	..	..	..
Other Long-Term Capital	376	513	616	237	1,054	2,094	995	373	107	-1,136	-145
Other Capital, net	98	351	-63	-325	-326	373	214	-1,224	-1,059	-1,468	-1,828
Change in Reserves	423	385	-529	193	152	-89	680	507	-230	-313	-771
Memo Item:					*(South African Rand per US dollar)*						
Conversion Factor (Annual Avg)	0.710	0.720	0.770	0.690	0.680	0.740	0.870	0.870	0.870	0.840	0.780
EXTERNAL DEBT (Total)				*(Millions of US dollars), outstanding at end of year*							
EXTERNAL DEBT (Total)	..	..	..	..	..	..	..	..	..	..	..
Long-Term Debt (by debtor)	..	..	..	..	..	..	..	..	..	..	..
Central Bank, incl. IMF credit	..	..	..	..	..	..	..	..	..	..	..
Central Government	..	..	..	..	..	..	..	..	..	..	..
Rest of General Government	..	..	..	..	..	..	..	..	..	..	..
Non-financial Public Enterprises	..	..	..	..	..	..	..	..	..	..	..
Priv. Sector, incl non-guaranteed	..	..	..	..	..	..	..	..	..	..	..
Short-Term Debt	..	..	..	..	..	..	..	..	..	..	..
Memo Items:					*(Millions of US dollars)*						
Int'l Reserves Excluding Gold	346	266	609	449	377	489	425	416	423	434	726
Gold Holdings (at market price)	711	511	1,164	2,132	3,404	2,489	1,707	1,603	2,213	5,135	7,162
SOCIAL INDICATORS											
Total Fertility Rate	5.7	5.6	5.5	5.4	5.3	5.3	5.2	5.1	5.0	5.0	4.9
Infant Mortality Rate	114.0	112.0	110.0	107.0	104.0	101.0	98.0	95.0	92.6	90.2	87.8
Life Expectancy at Birth	53.1	53.5	53.9	54.3	54.7	55.1	55.5	55.9	56.3	56.7	57.1
Urban Population, % of total	47.9	48.4	48.9	49.3	49.8	50.3	50.8	51.3	51.7	52.2	52.7
Food Prod. per capita (1987=100)	100.0	114.5	120.1	95.8	120.5	111.0	105.9	111.8	117.3	111.4	114.3
Labor Force, Agriculture (%)	32.9	31.2	29.5	27.9	26.3	24.7	23.0	21.3	19.6	18.0	16.5
Labor Force, Female (%)	33.0	33.1	33.2	33.4	33.5	33.6	33.7	33.8	33.9	34.0	34.1
Primary Schl. Enroll. Ratio	99.0	..	105.0	..	..	..	..	..	..	..	..
Primary Schl. Enroll. Ratio, Female	99.0	..	105.0	..	..	..	..	..	..	..	..
Secondary Schl. Enroll. Ratio	18.0	..	20.0	..	..	..	..	..	..	..	..

1981	1982	1983	1984	1985	1986	1987	1988	1989	1990 estimate	Notes	SOUTH AFRICA
											FOREIGN TRADE (CUSTOMS BASIS)
					(Millions of current US dollars)						
20,814	17,792	10,144	17,631	16,766	18,576	21,548	21,746	19,401	23,612	f	Value of Exports, fob
4,227	3,556	4,861	10,656	10,134	11,228	13,024	13,144	11,726	14,271	..	Nonfuel Primary Products
1,269	1,155	1,172	521	495	549	636	642	573	697	..	Fuels
15,317	13,081	4,111	6,454	6,138	6,800	7,888	7,961	7,102	8,643	..	Manufactures
20,991	16,939	10,469	16,363	10,294	13,103	15,320	18,900	16,085	18,258	f	Value of Imports, cif
1,550	1,219	1,105	3,020	1,095	2,418	2,827	3,488	2,968	3,369	..	Nonfuel Primary Products
67	75	102	1,033	59	827	967	1,193	1,016	1,153	..	Fuels
19,374	15,645	9,262	12,310	9,140	9,857	11,525	14,218	12,101	13,736	..	Manufactures
					(Index 1987 = 100)						
131.8	119.0	114.8	114.0	104.8	99.8	100.0	101.3	94.4	92.6	f	Terms of Trade
110.3	97.3	92.1	90.0	82.7	91.2	100.0	110.2	101.6	104.3	f	Export Prices, fob
83.7	81.8	80.2	79.0	78.9	91.3	100.0	108.9	107.6	112.6	f	Import Prices, cif
											BALANCE OF PAYMENTS
					(Millions of current US dollars)						
24,162	20,564	21,441	19,997	18,850	21,056	24,198	25,676	25,943	27,578	..	Exports of Goods & Services
20,632	17,328	18,241	16,948	16,244	18,330	21,088	22,432	22,399	23,383	..	Merchandise, fob
2,210	2,060	1,855	1,775	1,459	1,440	1,689	1,798	1,904	2,397	..	Nonfactor Services
1,320	1,176	1,345	1,274	1,146	1,286	1,420	1,447	1,640	1,798	..	Factor Services
28,992	24,000	21,627	21,684	16,301	17,991	21,475	24,633	24,565	25,442	..	Imports of Goods & Services
20,622	16,683	14,202	14,774	10,402	11,130	13,925	17,210	16,810	17,045	..	Merchandise, fob
3,969	3,480	3,186	3,031	2,358	2,760	3,177	3,306	3,498	3,803	..	Nonfactor Services
4,402	3,836	4,239	3,880	3,541	4,101	4,372	4,118	4,257	4,595	..	Factor Services
..	..	..	..	..	..	..	..	..	..	..	Long-Term Interest
90	117	140	125	84	76	97	90	129	107	..	Private Current Transfers, net
..	..	..	..	..	..	..	..	..	..	..	Workers' Remittances
-4,741	-3,319	-46	-1,562	2,633	3,141	2,820	1,133	1,507	2,243	..	Curr. A/C Bal before Off. Transf.
229	135	56	-25	-10	11	116	86	72	10	..	Net Official Transfers
-4,512	-3,184	10	-1,588	2,622	3,152	2,936	1,218	1,579	2,253	..	Curr. A/C Bal after Off. Transf.
144	2,268	-392	1,722	-697	-1,303	-1,317	-443	-493	-704	..	Long-Term Capital, net
-579	295	-87	251	-497	-116	-163	98	7	-5	..	Direct Investment
..	..	..	..	..	..	..	..	..	..	..	Long-Term Loans
..	..	..	..	..	..	..	..	..	..	..	Disbursements
..	..	..	..	..	..	..	..	..	..	..	Repayments
722	1,973	-305	1,471	-200	-1,187	-1,153	-541	-500	-699	..	Other Long-Term Capital
3,313	21	1,364	-660	-2,444	-2,025	-183	-1,549	-585	-1,205	..	Other Capital, net
1,055	895	-981	525	519	176	-1,436	774	-501	-344	..	Change in Reserves
											Memo Item:
					(South African Rand per US dollar)						
0.880	1.090	1.110	1.480	2.230	2.290	2.040	2.270	2.620	2.590	..	Conversion Factor (Annual Avg)
					(Millions of US dollars), outstanding at end of year						
..	..	..	..	..	..	..	..	..	..	..	**EXTERNAL DEBT (Total)**
..	..	..	..	..	..	..	..	..	..	..	Long-Term Debt (by debtor)
..	..	..	..	..	..	..	..	..	..	..	Central Bank, incl. IMF credit
..	..	..	..	..	..	..	..	..	..	..	Central Government
..	..	..	..	..	..	..	..	..	..	..	Rest of General Government
..	..	..	..	..	..	..	..	..	..	..	Non-financial Public Enterprises
..	..	..	..	..	..	..	..	..	..	..	Priv. Sector, incl non-guaranteed
..	..	..	..	..	..	..	..	..	..	..	Short-Term Debt
											Memo Items:
					(Millions of US dollars)						
666	485	823	242	315	370	641	780	960	1,008	..	Int'l Reserves Excluding Gold
3,693	3,459	2,972	2,269	1,583	1,884	2,822	1,424	1,235	1,575	..	Gold Holdings (at market price)
											SOCIAL INDICATORS
4.8	4.8	4.7	4.7	4.6	4.6	4.5	4.4	4.3	4.3	..	Total Fertility Rate
85.4	83.0	80.8	78.6	76.4	74.2	72.0	69.9	67.8	65.6	..	Infant Mortality Rate
57.5	57.9	58.4	59.0	59.5	60.0	60.5	61.0	61.5	62.0	..	Life Expectancy at Birth
53.4	54.1	54.7	55.4	56.1	57.0	57.8	58.4	58.9	59.5	..	Urban Population, % of total
124.7	106.6	87.1	94.2	100.3	98.7	100.0	100.6	106.5	98.4	..	Food Prod. per capita (1987=100)
..	..	..	..	..	..	..	..	..	..	..	Labor Force, Agriculture (%)
34.3	34.5	34.6	34.8	34.9	35.1	35.2	35.4	35.5	35.6	..	Labor Force, Female (%)
..	..	..	..	..	..	..	..	..	..	..	Primary Schl. Enroll. Ratio
..	..	..	..	..	..	..	..	..	..	..	Primary Schl. Enroll. Ratio, Female
..	..	..	..	..	..	..	..	..	..	..	Secondary Schl. Enroll. Ratio

SPAIN	1970	1971	1972	1973	1974	1975	1976	1977	1978	1979	1980
CURRENT GNP PER CAPITA (US $)	1,110	1,230	1,450	1,810	2,310	2,780	3,090	3,370	3,700	4,430	5,360
POPULATION (thousands)	33,779	34,190	34,448	34,810	35,147	35,515	35,937	36,367	36,778	37,108	37,386

USE AND ORIGIN OF RESOURCES *(Billions of current Spanish Pesetas)*

	1970	1971	1972	1973	1974	1975	1976	1977	1978	1979	1980
Gross National Product (GNP)	2,637	2,979	3,498	4,226	5,188	6,072	7,289	9,236	11,289	13,227	15,249
Net Factor Income from Abroad	-17	-16	-16	-12	-1	-19	-40	-62	-87	-78	-130
GDP at Market Prices	2,654	2,995	3,514	4,237	5,189	6,091	7,329	9,298	11,376	13,305	15,379
Resource Balance	-27	22	4	-38	-250	-235	-328	-196	75	23	-364
Exports of Goods & NFServices	342	414	499	600	727	802	980	1,312	1,681	1,941	2,369
Imports of Goods & NFServices	370	393	495	638	978	1,037	1,308	1,508	1,606	1,918	2,733
Domestic Absorption	2,681	2,973	3,511	4,275	5,439	6,325	7,656	9,494	11,301	13,282	15,744
Private Consumption, etc.	1,697	1,925	2,242	2,689	3,318	3,904	4,800	6,035	7,261	8,565	10,022
General Gov't Consumption	254	292	338	408	520	645	838	1,082	1,373	1,674	2,050
Gross Domestic Investment	730	757	930	1,178	1,601	1,777	2,019	2,376	2,667	3,043	3,671
Fixed Investment	701	724	889	1,135	1,471	1,631	1,852	2,256	2,615	2,914	3,453
Indirect Taxes, net	182	192	230	293	306	323	389	488	490	611	709
GDP at factor cost	2,472	2,803	3,284	3,944	4,882	5,767	6,940	8,810	10,886	12,694	14,670
Agriculture	..	..	..	..	..	..	..	..	..	..	..
Industry	..	..	..	..	..	..	..	..	..	..	..
Manufacturing	..	..	..	..	..	..	..	..	..	..	..
Services, etc.	..	..	..	..	..	..	..	..	..	..	..
Gross Domestic Saving	702	778	934	1,140	1,351	1,542	1,691	2,180	2,742	3,066	3,307
Gross National Saving	731	816	974	1,211	1,416	1,590	1,729	2,225	2,783	3,109	3,324

(Billions of 1987 Spanish Pesetas)

	1970	1971	1972	1973	1974	1975	1976	1977	1978	1979	1980
Gross National Product	21,896	22,927	24,781	26,737	28,233	28,303	29,157	29,996	30,397	30,410	30,710
GDP at Market Prices	22,033	23,042	24,893	26,806	28,231	28,382	29,311	30,190	30,628	30,585	30,964
Resource Balance	-337	-32	-324	-575	-913	-892	-1,131	-476	-30	-272	-327
Exports of Goods & NFServices	2,283	2,607	2,956	3,252	3,219	3,205	3,366	3,772	4,174	4,410	4,510
Imports of Goods & NFServices	2,620	2,639	3,280	3,827	4,132	4,097	4,497	4,248	4,204	4,682	4,838
Domestic Absorption	22,370	23,074	25,216	27,381	29,143	29,274	30,442	30,666	30,658	30,857	31,291
Private Consumption, etc.	14,288	15,023	16,232	17,466	18,329	18,643	19,623	19,979	20,186	20,375	20,483
General Gov't Consumption	2,321	2,422	2,547	2,711	2,963	3,116	3,332	3,464	3,652	3,804	3,963
Gross Domestic Investment	5,761	5,629	6,437	7,204	7,851	7,515	7,486	7,223	6,820	6,678	6,845
Fixed Investment	5,509	5,347	6,104	6,900	7,330	6,999	6,943	6,877	6,690	6,397	6,439
GDP at factor cost	20,552	21,599	23,279	24,962	26,632	26,937	27,812	28,673	29,371	29,227	29,617
Agriculture	..	..	..	..	..	..	..	..	..	..	..
Industry	..	..	..	..	..	..	..	..	..	..	..
Manufacturing	..	..	..	..	..	..	..	..	..	..	..
Services, etc.	..	..	..	..	..	..	..	..	..	..	..

Memo Items:

	1970	1971	1972	1973	1974	1975	1976	1977	1978	1979	1980
Capacity to Import	2,426	2,786	3,303	3,601	3,074	3,168	3,371	3,694	4,401	4,739	4,193
Terms of Trade Adjustment	143	178	347	349	-145	-37	5	-78	227	329	-318
Gross Domestic Income	22,176	23,220	25,240	27,155	28,085	28,345	29,315	30,113	30,855	30,914	30,646
Gross National Income	22,039	23,105	25,128	27,086	28,088	28,266	29,161	29,918	30,624	30,739	30,393

DOMESTIC PRICES/DEFLATORS *(Index 1987 = 100)*

	1970	1971	1972	1973	1974	1975	1976	1977	1978	1979	1980
Overall (GDP)	12.0	13.0	14.1	15.8	18.4	21.5	25.0	30.8	37.1	43.5	49.7
Domestic Absorption	12.0	12.9	13.9	15.6	18.7	21.6	25.2	31.0	36.9	43.0	50.3
Agriculture	..	..	..	..	..	..	..	..	..	..	..
Industry	..	..	..	..	..	..	..	..	..	..	..
Manufacturing	..	..	..	..	..	..	..	..	..	..	..
Consumer Price Index	12.1	13.1	14.2	15.8	18.3	21.4	24.6	30.6	36.7	42.4	49.1

MANUFACTURING ACTIVITY

	1970	1971	1972	1973	1974	1975	1976	1977	1978	1979	1980
Employment (1987=100)	106.3	108.2	111.3	115.7	119.9	121.0	121.9	120.8	134.1	131.1	132.4
Real Earnings per Empl. (1987=100)	65.2	67.7	73.7	78.4	85.0	92.3	101.3	107.0	92.9	94.3	96.6
Real Output per Empl. (1987=100)	0.0	0.0	0.0	0.0	0.0	0.0	0.0	0.0	0.0	0.0	77.9
Earnings as % of Value Added	51.7	52.2	51.3	50.9	51.9	59.6	63.3	65.8	44.1	44.6	44.9

MONETARY HOLDINGS *(Billions of current Spanish Pesetas)*

	1970	1971	1972	1973	1974	1975	1976	1977	1978	1979	1980
Money Supply, Broadly Defined	1,955	2,424	2,985	3,710	4,419	5,257	6,270	7,441	8,953	10,551	12,319
Money	743	920	1,142	1,410	1,654	1,963	2,392	2,836	3,325	3,610	4,098
Currency Outside Banks	263	294	328	387	447	524	614	777	946	1,039	1,185
Demand Deposits	480	626	814	1,023	1,208	1,439	1,778	2,058	2,379	2,571	2,913
Quasi-Money	1,211	1,505	1,843	2,300	2,764	3,294	3,877	4,605	5,628	6,942	8,221

GOVERNMENT DEFICIT (-) OR SURPLUS *(Billions of current Spanish Pesetas)*

	1970	1971	1972	1973	1974	1975	1976	1977	1978	1979	1980
	-16.8	-46.4	-18.7	-10.4	-59.4	-107.9	-65.4	-200.1	-264.3	-465.4	-635.1
Current Revenue	479.0	554.9	683.6	833.6	1,014.1	1,259.4	1,497.2	2,080.4	2,658.8	3,183.8	3,674.1
Current Expenditure	406.7	483.5	569.4	708.0	875.0	1,096.6	1,317.6	1,856.9	2,557.9	3,170.3	3,612.5
Current Budget Balance	72.3	71.4	114.2	125.6	139.1	162.8	179.6	223.5	100.9	13.5	61.6
Capital Receipts	0.5	0.6	1.4	1.9	1.8	1.7	1.7	2.4	1.6	1.3	1.8
Capital Payments	89.6	118.4	134.3	137.9	200.3	272.4	246.7	426.0	366.8	480.2	698.5

1981	1982	1983	1984	1985	1986	1987	1988	1989	1990 estimate	Notes	SPAIN
5,670	5,370	4,730	4,440	4,330	4,890	6,090	7,880	9,360	11,000	..	**CURRENT GNP PER CAPITA (US $)**
37,756	37,980	38,172	38,342	38,505	38,668	38,696	38,809	38,883	38,959	..	**POPULATION (thousands)**
											USE AND ORIGIN OF RESOURCES
			(Billions of current Spanish Pesetas)								
16,941	19,501	22,125	24,995	27,870	32,028	35,839	39,753	44,641	49,627	..	Gross National Product (GNP)
-238	-285	-358	-397	-331	-296	-305	-411	-384	-447	..	Net Factor Income from Abroad
17,179	19,786	22,483	25,392	28,201	32,324	36,144	40,164	45,025	50,074	..	GDP at Market Prices
-370	-378	-170	528	547	687	61	-448	-1,470	-1,696	..	Resource Balance
3,026	3,609	4,645	5,842	6,407	6,417	6,996	7,575	8,150	8,555	..	Exports of Goods & NFServices
3,397	3,987	4,815	5,314	5,860	5,730	6,935	8,022	9,621	10,251	..	Imports of Goods & NFServices
17,549	20,164	22,654	24,864	27,654	31,637	36,083	40,612	46,495	51,770	..	Domestic Absorption
11,402	13,080	14,744	16,324	18,080	20,438	22,856	25,141	28,302	31,254	..	Private Consumption, etc.
2,383	2,784	3,285	3,665	4,152	4,740	5,452	5,924	6,831	7,610	..	General Gov't Consumption
3,764	4,300	4,625	4,876	5,422	6,459	7,776	9,546	11,362	12,906	..	Gross Domestic Investment
3,790	4,276	4,690	4,827	5,409	6,297	7,518	9,096	10,877	12,339	..	Fixed Investment
923	1,057	1,352	1,601	1,981	2,818	3,131	3,283	3,761	4,090	..	Indirect Taxes, net
16,256	18,729	21,132	23,791	26,220	29,506	33,013	36,880	41,263	45,984	B	GDP at factor cost
				1,669	1,815	1,971	2,139	2,195		..	Agriculture
..	..	..	..	10,518	11,530	12,729	..	..	..	..	Industry
..	..	..	..	7,806	8,568	9,238	11,231	12,113	..	..	Manufacturing
..	..	..	..	16,014	18,979	21,443	..	..	..	..	Services, etc.
3,394	3,923	4,454	5,404	5,969	7,146	7,836	9,098	9,892	11,210		Gross Domestic Saving
3,313	3,811	4,270	5,198	5,876	7,059	7,813	9,039	9,883	11,074		Gross National Saving
			(Billions of 1987 Spanish Pesetas)								
30,476	30,830	31,343	31,915	32,776	33,903	35,839	37,619	39,474	40,878		Gross National Product
30,887	31,263	31,827	32,400	33,150	34,214	36,144	38,011	39,822	41,259		GDP at Market Prices
256	308	857	1,568	1,446	805	61	-585	-1,730	-2,213	..	Resource Balance
4,889	5,122	5,642	6,304	6,477	6,579	6,996	7,351	7,571	7,814	..	Exports of Goods & NFServices
4,633	4,815	4,785	4,736	5,030	5,774	6,935	7,936	9,301	10,027	..	Imports of Goods & NFServices
30,631	30,955	30,970	30,832	31,703	33,408	36,083	38,596	41,552	43,472	..	Domestic Absorption
20,390	20,422	20,527	20,500	20,964	21,636	22,856	23,921	25,215	26,143	..	Private Consumption, etc.
4,037	4,234	4,399	4,526	4,736	5,008	5,452	5,672	6,142	6,401	..	General Gov't Consumption
6,204	6,299	6,044	5,806	6,004	6,764	7,776	9,004	10,195	10,928	..	Gross Domestic Investment
6,230	6,261	6,102	5,748	5,987	6,592	7,518	8,572	9,755	10,427	..	Fixed Investment
29,337	29,701	30,041	30,481	30,936	31,261	33,013	34,881	36,418	37,774	B	GDP at factor cost
..	..	..	..	..	..	..	..	..	..	..	Agriculture
..	..	..	..	..	..	..	..	..	..	..	Industry
..	..	..	..	..	..	..	..	..	..	..	Manufacturing
..	..	..	..	..	..	..	..	..	..	..	Services, etc.
											Memo Items:
4,128	4,359	4,616	5,207	5,500	6,466	6,996	7,493	7,880	8,369	..	Capacity to Import
-761	-764	-1,026	-1,097	-977	-113	0	142	309	554	..	Terms of Trade Adjustment
30,126	30,499	30,801	31,303	32,173	34,101	36,144	38,153	40,131	41,814	..	Gross Domestic Income
29,715	30,066	30,317	30,818	31,799	33,790	35,839	37,761	39,783	41,432	..	Gross National Income
											DOMESTIC PRICES/DEFLATORS
			(Index 1987 = 100)								
55.6	63.3	70.6	78.4	85.1	94.5	100.0	105.7	113.1	121.4	..	Overall (GDP)
57.3	65.1	73.1	80.6	87.2	94.7	100.0	105.2	111.9	119.1	..	Domestic Absorption
..	..	..	..	..	..	..	..	..	..	..	Agriculture
..	..	..	..	..	..	..	..	..	..	..	Industry
..	..	..	..	..	..	..	..	..	..	..	Manufacturing
56.2	64.3	72.1	80.3	87.3	95.0	100.0	104.8	111.9	119.5	..	Consumer Price Index
											MANUFACTURING ACTIVITY
122.7	114.3	110.9	105.1	99.6	98.4	100.0	100.7	..	..	..	Employment (1987=100)
97.3	97.4	97.5	95.8	96.7	97.8	100.0	103.6	..	..	..	Real Earnings per Empl. (1987=100)
83.0	84.5	90.5	94.2	100.1	98.9	100.0	96.0	..	..	..	Real Output per Empl. (1987=100)
45.0	44.1	42.5	41.4	39.8	38.3	36.9	36.9	..	..	..	Earnings as % of Value Added
											MONETARY HOLDINGS
			(Billions of current Spanish Pesetas)								
14,269	16,259	16,082	16,883	18,867	22,027	24,050	27,689	30,432	34,667	..	Money Supply, Broadly Defined
4,630	4,850	5,277	5,746	6,589	7,580	8,899	10,573	12,177	14,674	..	Money
1,333	1,531	1,688	1,867	2,083	2,406	2,741	3,244	3,839	4,539	..	Currency Outside Banks
3,297	3,319	3,589	3,879	4,506	5,174	6,158	7,329	8,338	10,136	..	Demand Deposits
9,639	11,409	10,806	11,137	12,278	14,448	15,151	17,116	18,255	19,992	..	Quasi-Money
			(Billions of current Spanish Pesetas)								
-873.9	-1,093.3	-1,408.3	-2,113.2	-1,962.6	-1,463.4	-1,406.2	-1,442.6	..	..	F	**GOVERNMENT DEFICIT (-) OR SURPLUS**
4,134.6	4,996.7	5,867.3	6,611.4	7,743.1	9,437.3	11,006.2	12,207.1	..	..	..	Current Revenue
4,016.5	5,178.0	6,078.1	7,129.3	8,447.7	9,730.2	11,054.7	12,087.1	..	..	..	Current Expenditure
118.1	-181.3	-210.8	-517.9	-704.6	-292.9	-48.5	120.0	..	..	..	Current Budget Balance
1.3	10.4	15.2	118.1	11.5	3.6	22.5	53.5	..	..	..	Capital Receipts
993.3	922.4	1,212.7	1,713.4	1,269.5	1,174.1	1,380.2	1,616.1	..	..	..	Capital Payments

SPAIN	1970	1971	1972	1973	1974	1975	1976	1977	1978	1979	1980
FOREIGN TRADE (CUSTOMS BASIS)					*(Millions of current US dollars)*						
Value of Exports, fob	2,387	2,938	3,803	5,162	7,059	7,675	8,712	10,218	13,103	18,196	20,827
Nonfuel Primary Products	979	1,039	1,195	1,713	2,011	2,042	2,352	2,625	3,153	4,502	5,098
Fuels	131	126	138	242	478	252	325	378	330	347	761
Manufactures	1,277	1,773	2,471	3,206	4,570	5,381	6,035	7,214	9,620	13,347	14,967
Value of Imports, cif	4,714	4,936	6,754	9,536	15,291	16,100	17,288	17,648	18,630	25,370	33,901
Nonfuel Primary Products	1,536	1,657	2,181	3,141	4,529	4,664	4,473	5,000	5,397	6,941	7,835
Fuels	627	812	975	1,243	3,891	4,191	5,093	5,050	5,306	7,674	13,116
Manufactures	2,551	2,467	3,598	5,152	6,871	7,246	7,721	7,597	7,928	10,755	12,950
					(Index 1987 = 100)						
Terms of Trade	155.8	162.6	158.5	149.0	110.1	120.0	116.0	109.9	116.9	116.7	101.8
Export Prices, fob	29.6	32.8	37.6	49.5	60.7	66.8	66.4	69.3	78.1	98.6	107.2
Import Prices, cif	19.0	20.2	23.7	33.2	55.1	55.7	57.3	63.0	66.8	84.5	105.3
BALANCE OF PAYMENTS					*(Millions of current US dollars)*						
Exports of Goods & Services	4,900	5,950	7,663	10,463	12,862	13,853	14,545	17,202	22,445	29,990	33,863
Merchandise, fob	2,483	2,979	3,920	5,304	7,211	7,797	8,994	10,550	13,474	18,351	20,544
Nonfactor Services	2,367	2,863	3,577	4,817	4,989	5,443	5,110	6,182	8,189	10,266	11,560
Factor Services	50	108	165	342	663	613	441	471	782	1,373	1,759
Imports of Goods & Services	5,480	5,861	7,951	11,287	17,237	18,515	19,982	20,743	22,470	30,649	41,089
Merchandise, fob	4,357	4,578	6,236	8,807	14,258	15,207	16,299	16,736	17,555	24,041	32,272
Nonfactor Services	817	941	1,255	1,894	2,244	2,371	2,648	2,766	3,049	4,086	5,563
Factor Services	306	343	459	585	735	937	1,034	1,241	1,865	2,522	3,255
Long-Term Interest	..	..	..	..	..	..	..	..	..	..	..
Private Current Transfers, net	659	772	878	1,416	1,151	1,166	1,161	1,418	1,672	1,805	2,059
Workers' Remittances	469	550	599	902	859	975	1,000	1,091	1,270	1,427	1,649
Curr. A/C Bal before Off. Transf.	79	861	591	592	-3,224	-3,496	-4,275	-2,123	1,648	1,146	-5,168
Net Official Transfers	..	-5	-10	-7	-8	-19	-16	-9	-14	-19	-6
Curr. A/C Bal after Off. Transf.	79	856	581	585	-3,233	-3,515	-4,292	-2,133	1,634	1,128	-5,173
Long-Term Capital, net	664	499	848	765	1,768	1,808	2,011	3,011	1,717	3,161	4,147
Direct Investment	179	177	231	337	273	513	285	492	1,076	1,264	1,182
Long-Term Loans	..	..	..	..	..	..	..	..	..	..	..
Disbursements	..	..	..	..	..	..	..	..	..	..	..
Repayments	..	..	..	..	..	..	..	..	..	..	..
Other Long-Term Capital	485	323	617	428	1,495	1,295	1,727	2,519	641	1,897	2,965
Other Capital, net	76	99	17	-13	753	878	1,190	267	408	-839	231
Change in Reserves	-819	-1,454	-1,446	-1,338	712	829	1,090	-1,146	-3,759	-3,450	795
Memo Item:					*(Spanish Pesetas per US dollar)*						
Conversion Factor (Annual Avg)	70.000	69.470	64.270	58.260	57.690	57.410	66.900	75.960	76.670	67.130	71.700
EXTERNAL DEBT (Total)					*(Millions US dollars), outstanding at end of year*						
Long-Term Debt (by debtor)	..	..	..	..	..	..	..	..	..	..	..
Central Bank, incl. IMF credit	..	..	..	..	..	..	..	..	..	..	..
Central Government	..	..	..	..	..	..	..	..	..	..	..
Rest of General Government	..	..	..	..	..	..	..	..	..	..	..
Non-financial Public Enterprises	..	..	..	..	..	..	..	..	..	..	..
Priv. Sector, incl non-guaranteed	..	..	..	..	..	..	..	..	..	..	..
Short-Term Debt	..	..	..	..	..	..	..	..	..	..	..
Memo Items:					*(Millions of US dollars)*						
Int'l Reserves Excluding Gold	1,319	2,727	4,473	6,170	5,874	5,506	4,704	5,977	10,112	13,224	11,863
Gold Holdings (at market price)	532	621	924	1,601	2,661	2,001	1,922	2,381	3,282	7,478	8,610
SOCIAL INDICATORS											
Total Fertility Rate	2.8	2.9	2.8	2.8	2.9	2.8	2.8	2.6	2.5	2.3	2.2
Infant Mortality Rate	28.1	25.7	22.9	21.5	19.9	18.9	17.1	16.0	15.3	14.3	12.3
Life Expectancy at Birth	72.3	72.6	72.8	72.9	73.1	73.2	73.3	73.5	73.9	74.4	74.9
Urban Population, % of total	66.0	66.7	67.4	68.2	68.9	69.6	70.2	70.9	71.5	72.2	72.8
Food Prod. per capita (1987=100)	66.2	66.6	71.4	77.4	76.7	78.8	78.5	75.7	85.1	85.9	90.5
Labor Force, Agriculture (%)	26.0	25.1	24.2	23.3	22.4	21.5	20.6	19.7	18.8	18.0	17.1
Labor Force, Female (%)	19.4	19.9	20.3	20.8	21.3	21.7	22.1	22.5	22.9	23.2	23.6
Primary Schl. Enroll. Ratio	123.0	..	..	..	..	111.0	110.0	109.0	109.0	109.0	109.0
Primary Schl. Enroll. Ratio, Female	125.0	..	..	..	..	111.0	110.0	109.0	109.0	109.0	109.0
Secondary Schl. Enroll. Ratio	56.0	..	..	..	..	73.0	76.0	78.0	83.0	86.0	87.0

1981	1982	1983	1984	1985	1986	1987	1988	1989	1990 estimate	Notes	SPAIN
											FOREIGN TRADE (CUSTOMS BASIS)
					(Millions of current US dollars)						
20,337	20,271	19,711	23,283	24,307	27,250	34,099	40,458	44,450	55,607	..	Value of Exports, fob
5,010	4,328	4,222	5,009	4,932	5,826	7,827	9,302	9,675	10,722	..	Nonfuel Primary Products
1,007	1,418	1,734	2,027	2,148	1,682	2,001	1,802	2,224	2,725	..	Fuels
14,320	14,525	13,755	16,247	17,227	19,742	24,271	29,354	32,551	42,160	..	Manufactures
32,081	31,282	28,926	28,607	30,067	35,406	49,009	60,434	71,298	87,487	..	Value of Imports, cif
6,730	6,542	6,325	6,384	6,354	7,973	9,648	12,037	13,364	15,442	..	Nonfuel Primary Products
13,641	12,474	11,671	10,826	10,864	6,696	7,993	6,881	8,410	10,271	..	Fuels
11,710	12,266	10,930	11,397	12,848	20,738	31,368	41,516	49,524	61,774	..	Manufactures
					(Index 1987 = 100)						
86.6	93.0	88.3	90.8	91.4	106.4	100.0	104.8	107.3	105.8	..	Terms of Trade
92.7	92.6	84.6	85.0	82.5	94.3	100.0	116.5	121.7	138.4	..	Export Prices, fob
107.0	99.6	95.8	93.5	90.2	88.6	100.0	111.1	113.4	130.8	..	Import Prices, cif
					(Millions of current US dollars)						**BALANCE OF PAYMENTS**
34,331	34,765	32,694	36,778	38,499	46,377	57,429	67,092	72,176	88,384	..	Exports of Goods & Services
20,974	21,288	19,858	22,714	23,665	26,754	33,561	39,652	43,301	53,888	..	Merchandise, fob
11,299	11,505	11,478	12,545	12,992	17,925	21,976	24,710	25,047	29,221	..	Nonfactor Services
2,058	1,972	1,357	1,519	1,843	1,698	1,891	2,730	3,828	5,275	..	Factor Services
41,011	40,590	36,604	35,855	36,776	43,544	60,296	75,380	87,716	109,460	..	Imports of Goods & Services
31,086	30,542	27,560	26,985	27,836	33,278	46,548	57,650	67,797	83,454	..	Merchandise, fob
5,579	5,803	5,222	4,940	5,205	6,471	8,931	11,084	12,673	16,273	..	Nonfactor Services
4,346	4,245	3,823	3,930	3,735	3,795	4,818	6,646	7,246	9,734	..	Factor Services
..	..	..	..	..	..	..	..	..	..	..	Long-Term Interest
1,698	1,577	1,211	1,191	1,395	1,492	2,277	3,018	3,163	3,053	..	Private Current Transfers, net
1,296	1,122	939	844	1,033	1,184	1,316	1,530	1,601	1,885	..	Workers' Remittances
-4,982	-4,248	-2,699	2,114	3,119	4,325	-591	-5,269	-12,378	-18,023	..	Curr. A/C Bal before Off. Transf.
-7	3	-46	-96	-268	-360	358	1,485	1,444	1,204	..	Net Official Transfers
-4,989	-4,245	-2,746	2,018	2,851	3,965	-233	-3,784	-10,934	-16,819	..	Curr. A/C Bal after Off. Transf.
4,232	1,772	3,122	3,274	-1,549	-2,110	8,999	9,610	15,655	18,901	..	Long-Term Capital, net
1,436	1,272	1,379	1,523	1,718	3,073	3,825	5,786	6,955	10,904	..	Direct Investment
..	..	..	..	..	..	..	..	..	..		Long-Term Loans
..	..	..	..	..	..	..	..	..	..		Disbursements
..	..	..	..	..	..	..	..	..	..		Repayments
2,796	501	1,743	1,751	-3,267	-5,183	5,173	3,825	8,700	7,997	..	Other Long-Term Capital
30	-632	-642	-475	-3,576	489	3,939	2,590	-6	4,880	..	Other Capital, net
727	3,104	265	-4,817	2,275	-2,344	-12,706	-8,416	-4,716	-6,962	..	Change in Reserves
											Memo Item:
				(Spanish Pesetas per US dollar)							
92.320	109.860	143.430	160.760	170.040	140.050	123.480	116.490	118.380	101.930	..	Conversion Factor (Annual Avg)
				(Millions US dollars), outstanding at end of year							**EXTERNAL DEBT (Total)**
..	..	..	..	..	..	..	..	..	..	..	Long-Term Debt (by debtor)
..	..	..	..	..	..	..	..	..	..	..	Central Bank, incl. IMF credit
..	..	..	..	..	..	..	..	..	..	..	Central Government
..	..	..	..	..	..	..	..	..	..	..	Rest of General Government
..	..	..	..	..	..	..	..	..	..	..	Non-financial Public Enterprises
..	..	..	..	..	..	..	..	..	..	..	Priv. Sector, incl non-guaranteed
..	..	..	..	..	..	..	..	..	..	..	Short-Term Debt
											Memo Items:
				(Millions of US dollars)							
10,805	7,655	7,402	11,955	11,175	14,755	30,669	37,073	41,467	51,228	..	Int'l Reserves Excluding Gold
5,806	6,673	5,572	4,510	4,792	5,794	5,770	5,762	6,303	6,010	..	Gold Holdings (at market price)
											SOCIAL INDICATORS
2.0	1.9	1.8	1.7	1.6	1.6	1.5	1.5	1.5	1.5	..	Total Fertility Rate
12.5	11.3	10.9	9.9	8.9	8.7	9.0	8.8	8.6	8.5	..	Infant Mortality Rate
75.3	75.8	75.8	75.8	75.9	75.9	75.9	76.0	76.1	76.3	..	Life Expectancy at Birth
73.4	74.0	74.6	75.2	75.8	76.3	76.8	77.4	77.9	78.4	..	Urban Population, % of total
80.4	89.2	81.6	95.3	90.6	89.8	100.0	94.2	95.8	97.2	..	Food Prod. per capita (1987=100)
..	..	..	..	..	..	..	..	..	..		Labor Force, Agriculture (%)
23.7	23.8	23.9	24.0	24.1	24.2	24.2	24.3	24.4	24.4	..	Labor Force, Female (%)
..	..	112.0	113.0	113.0	113.0	111.0	..	..	..	..	Primary Schl. Enroll. Ratio
..	..	112.0	113.0	112.0	113.0	110.0	..	..	..	..	Primary Schl. Enroll. Ratio, Female
..	..	89.0	92.0	99.0	102.0	105.0	..	..	..	..	Secondary Schl. Enroll. Ratio

SRI LANKA	1970	1971	1972	1973	1974	1975	1976	1977	1978	1979	1980
CURRENT GNP PER CAPITA (US $)	180	190	190	220	250	290	290	300	260	260	260
POPULATION (thousands)	12,516	12,608	12,861	13,091	13,284	13,496	13,717	13,942	14,184	14,471	14,738

USE AND ORIGIN OF RESOURCES *(Billions of current Sri Lanka Rupees)*

	1970	1971	1972	1973	1974	1975	1976	1977	1978	1979	1980
Gross National Product (GNP)	13.44	13.86	15.07	18.22	23.59	26.36	29.92	36.15	42.43	52.15	66.10
Net Factor Income from Abroad	-0.22	-0.19	-0.18	-0.18	-0.18	-0.21	-0.28	-0.25	-0.24	-0.24	-0.43
GDP at Market Prices	13.66	14.05	15.25	18.40	23.77	26.58	30.20	36.41	42.67	52.39	66.53
Resource Balance	-0.43	-0.28	-0.24	-0.22	-1.77	-1.99	-0.70	1.33	-2.04	-6.31	-15.02
Exports of Goods & NFServices	3.48	3.46	3.40	4.48	6.28	7.31	8.77	12.31	14.83	17.66	21.43
Imports of Goods & NFServices	3.91	3.74	3.64	4.70	8.06	9.29	9.48	10.98	16.87	23.97	36.46
Domestic Absorption	14.09	14.33	15.49	18.63	25.55	28.56	30.91	35.07	44.70	58.70	81.55
Private Consumption, etc.	9.88	10.17	10.95	14.08	19.07	21.94	22.99	26.70	32.11	40.37	53.40
General Gov't Consumption	1.62	1.76	1.90	2.02	2.74	2.48	3.02	3.12	4.04	4.80	5.68
Gross Domestic Investment	2.59	2.40	2.64	2.53	3.74	4.14	4.90	5.26	8.55	13.53	22.46
Fixed Investment	2.36	2.14	2.21	2.49	2.97	3.70	4.59	5.03	8.52	13.25	20.84
Indirect Taxes, net	0.48	0.38	0.53	0.48	0.47	0.89	2.17	1.72	2.19	2.60	4.28
GDP at factor cost	13.19	13.67	14.72	17.92	23.30	25.69	28.03	34.68	40.48	49.78	62.25
Agriculture	3.73	3.70	3.88	4.89	7.73	7.80	8.13	10.64	12.33	13.41	17.15
Industry	3.14	3.38	3.56	4.55	5.84	6.79	7.59	9.95	11.03	14.05	18.45
Manufacturing	2.20	2.40	2.59	3.12	4.34	5.16	5.62	8.02	8.09	9.48	11.05
Services, etc.	6.32	6.59	7.28	8.48	9.73	11.10	12.30	14.09	17.12	22.32	26.64
Gross Domestic Saving	2.16	2.12	2.40	2.30	1.96	2.15	4.19	6.59	6.52	7.22	7.44
Gross National Saving	1.93	1.91	2.19	2.12	1.78	1.96	3.97	6.43	6.62	7.73	9.26

(Millions of 1987 Sri Lanka Rupees)

	1970	1971	1972	1973	1974	1975	1976	1977	1978	1979	1980
Gross National Product	92,812	95,222	93,136	102,223	106,391	113,348	117,084	123,346	130,189	138,753	146,502
GDP at Market Prices	94,436	96,597	94,331	103,327	107,248	114,258	118,261	124,335	130,997	139,426	147,458
Resource Balance	-4,595	-1,506	811	2,189	-2,041	4,873	1,035	-2,102	-12,532	-16,890	-26,998
Exports of Goods & NFServices	39,748	38,480	37,696	38,132	33,044	39,666	40,559	35,174	38,506	43,818	45,396
Imports of Goods & NFServices	44,343	39,986	36,885	35,943	35,085	34,793	39,524	37,276	51,038	60,708	72,394
Domestic Absorption	99,031	98,103	93,520	101,138	109,289	109,386	117,226	126,438	143,529	156,316	174,456
Private Consumption, etc.	73,810	73,151	66,695	78,526	79,476	82,924	84,326	95,346	100,514	103,782	113,190
General Gov't Consumption	10,733	11,572	12,323	11,128	11,840	10,018	11,528	10,466	12,309	11,964	11,592
Gross Domestic Investment	14,489	13,380	14,502	11,484	17,973	16,444	21,373	20,625	30,707	40,569	49,673
Fixed Investment	13,202	11,940	12,127	11,325	14,301	14,692	20,059	19,746	30,588	39,727	46,091
GDP at factor cost	88,183	88,520	91,778	95,328	98,176	100,713	103,813	108,038	117,077	124,500	131,604
Agriculture	31,140	30,389	31,332	31,082	32,893	32,100	32,492	35,871	37,815	38,567	39,768
Industry	25,690	25,769	25,481	27,014	26,037	26,507	28,559	27,459	31,542	34,751	36,464
Manufacturing	15,356	15,929	16,223	15,838	15,118	15,817	16,572	16,474	17,760	18,585	18,739
Services, etc.	31,353	32,362	34,965	37,232	39,247	42,107	42,762	44,707	47,719	51,182	55,372

Memo Items:

	1970	1971	1972	1973	1974	1975	1976	1977	1978	1979	1980
Capacity to Import	39,464	36,981	34,455	34,239	27,357	27,360	36,584	41,798	44,876	44,729	42,563
Terms of Trade Adjustment	-284	-1,499	-3,241	-3,893	-5,687	-12,306	-3,975	6,625	6,370	911	-2,833
Gross Domestic Income	94,152	95,098	91,091	99,434	101,561	101,952	114,286	130,960	137,367	140,336	144,625
Gross National Income	92,528	93,723	89,895	98,330	100,704	101,042	113,110	129,971	136,560	139,664	143,669

DOMESTIC PRICES/DEFLATORS *(Index 1987 = 100)*

	1970	1971	1972	1973	1974	1975	1976	1977	1978	1979	1980
Overall (GDP)	14.5	14.5	16.2	17.8	22.2	23.3	25.5	29.3	32.6	37.6	45.1
Domestic Absorption	14.2	14.6	16.6	18.4	23.4	26.1	26.4	27.7	31.1	37.5	46.7
Agriculture	12.0	12.2	12.4	15.7	23.5	24.3	25.0	29.7	32.6	34.8	43.1
Industry	12.2	13.1	14.0	16.8	22.4	25.6	26.6	36.2	35.0	40.4	50.6
Manufacturing	14.3	15.1	16.0	19.7	28.7	32.6	33.9	48.7	45.6	51.0	59.0
Consumer Price Index	21.2	21.7	23.1	25.3	28.5	30.3	30.7	31.1	34.9	38.6	48.8

MANUFACTURING ACTIVITY

	1970	1971	1972	1973	1974	1975	1976	1977	1978	1979	1980
Employment (1987=100)	46.4	51.5	52.7	54.4	52.9	60.1	65.4	71.9	69.7	78.9	76.7
Real Earnings per Empl. (1987=100)	..	..	..	..	..	..	..	..	..	..	95.1
Real Output per Empl. (1987=100)	53.7	54.8	58.7	48.8	53.7	..	..	..	..	53.4	76.9
Earnings as % of Value Added	..	..	..	..	..	..	..	..	..	..	25.7

MONETARY HOLDINGS *(Millions of current Sri Lanka Rupees)*

	1970	1971	1972	1973	1974	1975	1976	1977	1978	1979	1980
Money Supply, Broadly Defined	3,809	4,266	4,969	5,263	5,950	6,351	8,207	11,204	14,619	20,701	26,256
Money	1,949	2,128	2,461	2,755	2,923	3,064	4,133	5,332	5,895	7,643	9,333
Currency Outside Banks	935	1,115	1,202	1,437	1,539	1,610	2,080	2,792	3,016	3,774	4,181
Demand Deposits	1,014	1,013	1,259	1,319	1,384	1,454	2,053	2,540	2,879	3,868	5,152
Quasi-Money	1,860	2,138	2,508	2,508	3,027	3,287	4,074	5,872	8,724	13,058	16,923

GOVERNMENT DEFICIT (-) OR SURPLUS *(Millions of current Sri Lanka Rupees)*

	1970	1971	1972	1973	1974	1975	1976	1977	1978	1979	1980
	-873	-1,023	..	-960	-767	-1,704	-2,518	-1,671	-5,290	-6,300	-12,157
Current Revenue	2,750	2,650	..	3,717	4,608	5,070	5,693	6,754	11,902	13,543	16,057
Current Expenditure	2,781	2,909	..	3,593	4,227	4,851	5,639	6,366	11,930	12,276	16,456
Current Budget Balance	-31	-259	..	124	381	219	54	388	-28	1,267	-399
Capital Receipts	2	2	..	2	5	3	28	23	4	5	7
Capital Payments	844	766	..	1,086	1,153	1,926	2,600	2,082	5,266	7,572	11,765

1981	1982	1983	1984	1985	1986	1987	1988	1989	1990 estimate	Notes	SRI LANKA
290	330	340	350	390	410	410	420	430	470	..	**CURRENT GNP PER CAPITA (US $)**
14,988	15,189	15,417	15,599	15,837	16,117	16,361	16,587	16,806	17,002	..	**POPULATION (thousands)**
				(Billions of current Sri Lanka Rupees)							**USE AND ORIGIN OF RESOURCES**
83.14	100.26	120.98	149.36	161.69	178.72	195.88	221.44	250.06	320.04	..	Gross National Product (GNP)
-1.87	-1.96	-3.21	-3.40	-3.40	-3.86	-4.34	-5.27	-5.74	-5.94	..	Net Factor Income from Abroad
85.00	102.22	124.19	152.76	165.09	182.58	200.22	226.70	255.80	325.98	f	GDP at Market Prices
-13.67	-18.76	-18.37	-9.13	-19.41	-20.84	-20.66	-23.89	-23.92	-25.22	..	Resource Balance
25.89	27.15	32.02	44.29	42.24	42.57	49.56	57.88	68.67	97.33	..	Exports of Goods & NF Services
39.56	45.90	50.38	53.42	61.65	63.41	70.22	81.77	92.59	122.56	..	Imports of Goods & NF Services
98.67	120.97	142.56	161.89	184.50	203.42	220.88	250.59	279.72	351.21	..	Domestic Absorption
68.75	82.21	97.54	110.25	129.22	142.48	155.45	178.18	198.59	247.85	..	Private Consumption, etc.
6.31	8.24	9.89	11.93	16.60	18.48	19.54	21.85	26.41	30.72	..	General Gov't Consumption
23.61	30.53	35.13	39.71	38.68	42.46	45.90	50.56	54.72	72.64	..	Gross Domestic Investment
23.28	30.28	35.34	39.56	38.46	42.33	45.75	49.96	54.25	71.60	..	Fixed Investment
5.67	7.54	10.32	12.72	16.77	18.87	22.49	23.18	27.66	35.49	..	Indirect Taxes, net
79.34	94.68	113.88	140.04	148.32	163.71	177.73	203.52	228.14	290.50	f	GDP at factor cost
21.98	24.96	32.18	40.14	41.07	44.35	47.92	53.60	58.46	76.50	..	Agriculture
22.21	24.89	29.99	36.86	38.86	43.55	48.76	54.30	61.04	75.42	..	Industry
12.88	13.60	15.96	20.89	21.85	24.87	28.47	31.30	34.94	43.13	..	Manufacturing
35.15	44.83	51.71	63.05	68.39	75.81	81.05	95.62	108.64	138.57	..	Services, etc.
9.94	11.77	16.77	30.58	19.27	21.62	25.24	26.68	30.80	47.42	..	Gross Domestic Saving
11.98	15.30	20.01	34.21	23.09	26.00	30.11	31.59	36.98	56.08	..	Gross National Saving
				(Millions of 1987 Sri Lanka Rupees)							
152,250	164,161	169,329	169,383	185,654	194,288	195,883	200,927	205,263	219,110	..	Gross National Product
155,722	167,409	173,896	173,409	190,344	198,758	200,219	205,630	209,997	223,270	I f	GDP at Market Prices
-17,403	-25,007	-30,583	-24,684	-21,154	-21,032	-20,664	-27,533	-21,271	-11,943	..	Resource Balance
49,942	52,206	42,343	41,380	43,249	47,290	49,559	65,711	70,107	77,607	..	Exports of Goods & NF Services
67,345	77,212	72,927	66,064	64,403	68,322	70,223	93,243	91,378	89,550	..	Imports of Goods & NF Services
173,125	192,416	204,479	198,094	211,498	219,790	220,883	233,162	231,268	235,213	..	Domestic Absorption
118,635	133,227	143,591	137,694	150,705	155,015	155,445	161,804	162,862	..	..	Private Consumption, etc.
10,607	12,940	13,619	14,089	19,318	19,913	19,538	20,066	20,526	..	..	General Gov't Consumption
43,883	46,248	47,269	46,311	41,474	44,862	45,900	51,292	47,880	48,660	..	Gross Domestic Investment
43,268	45,873	47,552	46,136	41,233	44,717	45,752	50,837	47,583	48,297	..	Fixed Investment
139,092	145,946	153,030	160,359	168,573	175,695	177,731	182,529	186,375	198,188	I f	GDP at factor cost
42,530	43,648	45,830	45,657	49,596	50,890	47,923	48,928	48,372	52,628	..	Agriculture
37,360	38,348	39,020	41,770	43,240	45,872	48,763	50,812	52,551	56,540	..	Industry
19,710	20,654	20,819	23,371	24,590	26,663	28,470	29,797	31,112	34,057	..	Manufacturing
59,202	63,950	68,180	72,932	75,736	78,933	81,045	82,788	85,452	89,020	..	Services, etc.
											Memo Items:
44,080	45,663	46,343	54,770	44,126	45,868	49,559	66,006	67,769	71,121	..	Capacity to Import
-5,862	-6,543	4,000	13,390	877	-1,422	0	295	-2,337	-6,486	..	Terms of Trade Adjustment
149,859	160,866	177,896	186,799	191,221	197,336	200,219	205,925	207,659	216,785	..	Gross Domestic Income
146,388	157,619	173,329	182,773	186,530	192,866	195,883	201,223	202,925	212,625	..	Gross National Income
				(Index 1987 = 100)							**DOMESTIC PRICES/DEFLATORS**
54.6	61.1	71.4	88.1	86.7	91.9	100.0	110.2	121.8	146.0	..	Overall (GDP)
57.0	62.9	69.7	81.7	87.2	92.6	100.0	107.5	121.0	149.3	..	Domestic Absorption
51.7	57.2	70.2	87.9	82.8	87.2	100.0	109.5	120.9	145.4	..	Agriculture
59.4	64.9	76.9	88.2	89.9	94.9	100.0	106.9	116.2	133.4	..	Industry
65.4	65.9	76.6	89.4	88.9	93.3	100.0	105.0	112.3	126.6	..	Manufacturing
57.5	63.7	72.6	84.7	86.0	92.8	100.0	114.0	127.2	154.5	..	Consumer Price Index
											MANUFACTURING ACTIVITY
75.9	165.8	112.4	99.9	99.4	102.3	100.0	..	..	..	..	Employment (1987=100)
90.3	76.9	77.1	79.6	96.5	96.7	100.0	..	..	..	..	Real Earnings per Empl. (1987=100)
85.5	74.8	93.3	84.9	104.0	101.2	100.0	..	..	..	..	Real Output per Empl. (1987=100)
24.2	19.4	17.8	..	..	..	16.6	..	..	..	..	Earnings as % of Value Added
				(Millions of current Sri Lanka Rupees)							**MONETARY HOLDINGS**
30,975	39,668	48,221	56,145	63,884	67,002	77,332	88,077	99,245	112,995	D	Money Supply, Broadly Defined
9,949	11,672	14,589	16,647	18,661	21,051	24,901	32,155	35,087	39,596	..	Money
4,823	5,988	7,200	8,561	9,815	11,570	13,495	18,484	19,644	22,120	..	Currency Outside Banks
5,127	5,684	7,388	8,086	8,846	9,481	11,406	13,671	15,443	17,476	..	Demand Deposits
21,026	27,996	33,632	39,498	45,223	45,952	52,431	55,922	64,158	73,399	..	Quasi-Money
				(Millions of current Sri Lanka Rupees)							**GOVERNMENT DEFICIT (-) OR SURPLUS**
-10,518	-13,927	-12,846	-10,482	-15,679	-18,202	-17,073	-28,195	-21,778	-25,153	..	
17,482	19,565	26,782	37,342	39,540	40,968	46,808	48,275	60,359	74,332	..	Current Revenue
14,649	18,341	22,002	24,631	32,644	33,967	39,560	46,132	56,884	71,771	..	Current Expenditure
2,833	1,224	4,780	12,711	6,896	7,001	7,248	2,143	3,475	2,561	..	Current Budget Balance
14	20	9	13	15	23	13	62	27	329	..	Capital Receipts
13,365	15,171	17,635	23,206	22,589	25,226	24,334	30,400	25,280	28,043	..	Capital Payments

SRI LANKA	1970	1971	1972	1973	1974	1975	1976	1977	1978	1979	1980
FOREIGN TRADE (CUSTOMS BASIS)					*(Millions of current US dollars)*						
Value of Exports, fob	331.6	323.7	323.4	405.3	519.7	557.7	565.2	760.3	843.9	977.7	1,043.0
Nonfuel Primary Products	..	315.9	304.9	349.7	451.1	494.2	485.8	661.0	730.1	760.5	687.9
Fuels	..	0.8	1.4	9.1	39.0	0.3	2.8	2.9	49.7	94.7	160.6
Manufactures	4.7	7.0	17.1	46.6	29.5	63.3	76.6	96.4	64.2	122.4	194.5
Value of Imports, cif	386.6	328.1	336.4	422.3	688.1	744.6	552.1	701.1	942.1	1,449.2	2,035.4
Nonfuel Primary Products	195.1	165.9	176.9	232.2	344.3	400.2	222.9	301.1	318.0	393.7	468.6
Fuels	10.3	5.1	6.4	45.3	137.3	124.3	137.4	169.1	155.8	254.3	494.4
Manufactures	181.1	157.2	153.1	144.8	206.5	220.1	191.9	231.0	468.4	801.2	1,072.4
					(Index 1987 = 100)						
Terms of Trade	142.6	131.7	117.9	134.6	102.3	99.1	124.7	166.7	130.4	118.9	128.0
Export Prices, fob	40.7	42.9	44.4	51.3	70.0	67.7	74.3	99.5	92.0	102.6	139.1
Import Prices, cif	28.6	32.6	37.7	38.1	68.5	68.3	59.6	59.7	70.6	86.3	108.7
BALANCE OF PAYMENTS					*(Millions of current US dollars)*						
Exports of Goods & Services	378.5	378.1	367.6	426.9	575.9	639.1	636.0	866.9	970.3	1,173.6	1,340.0
Merchandise, fob	338.8	325.3	316.5	366.3	509.3	558.4	559.6	761.6	845.7	981.1	1,061.6
Nonfactor Services	38.1	50.7	49.5	57.9	61.1	73.5	72.5	93.5	104.4	152.9	231.1
Factor Services	1.6	2.2	1.6	2.6	5.5	7.1	3.9	11.8	20.2	39.5	47.2
Imports of Goods & Services	449.0	428.9	412.6	465.2	753.8	829.2	707.1	796.3	1,115.4	1,592.0	2,269.4
Merchandise, fob	353.0	336.3	322.9	371.7	628.7	686.2	579.5	655.1	898.7	1,304.3	1,845.1
Nonfactor Services	70.6	70.0	68.8	73.6	102.9	117.5	103.4	113.7	181.5	232.8	351.4
Factor Services	25.4	22.6	20.8	19.9	22.1	25.5	24.1	27.5	35.2	54.8	72.8
Long-Term Interest	12.1	11.2	13.7	15.5	16.5	20.6	23.2	21.3	24.7	27.7	32.9
Private Current Transfers, net	-0.9	-3.4	-4.3	0.2	-0.2	2.7	6.7	10.7	21.9	48.4	136.2
Workers' Remittances	3.0	3.4	3.9	7.5	8.2	8.6	13.0	18.5	39.0	60.1	151.7
Curr. A/C Bal before Off. Transf.	-71.4	-54.2	-49.3	-38.0	-178.1	-187.4	-64.4	81.2	-123.2	-370.1	-793.3
Net Official Transfers	12.6	17.8	16.7	12.9	42.2	77.3	58.5	61.0	57.6	143.7	138.0
Curr. A/C Bal after Off. Transf.	-58.8	-36.4	-32.6	-25.2	-135.9	-110.0	-5.9	142.2	-65.6	-226.3	-655.3
Long-Term Capital, net	30.2	67.9	48.6	51.7	71.8	68.9	72.0	71.2	118.5	173.6	208.7
Direct Investment	-0.3	0.3	0.4	0.5	1.3	0.1	..	-1.2	1.5	46.9	43.0
Long-Term Loans	36.1	60.0	37.9	44.7	94.1	38.9	96.6	50.7	127.1	113.3	220.7
Disbursements	65.6	89.7	73.8	83.8	146.5	156.6	200.7	153.5	192.7	162.8	271.8
Repayments	29.5	29.7	35.9	39.1	52.4	117.7	104.1	102.8	65.6	49.5	51.1
Other Long-Term Capital	-5.6	7.6	10.3	6.6	-23.6	29.9	-24.6	21.7	-10.1	13.4	-55.0
Other Capital, net	29.5	-34.8	-14.7	1.6	32.9	15.2	-29.2	-60.9	0.4	99.4	165.0
Change in Reserves	-0.9	3.3	-1.3	-28.2	31.2	25.9	-36.9	-152.5	-53.3	-46.7	281.6
Memo Item:					*(Sri Lanka Rupees per US dollar)*						
Conversion Factor (Annual Avg)	5.950	5.930	5.970	6.400	6.650	7.010	8.410	8.870	15.610	15.570	16.530
					(Millions of US dollars), outstanding at end of year						
EXTERNAL DEBT (Total)	395.2	471.8	502.9	574.1	712.3	743.4	847.6	1,132.2	1,372.8	1,553.7	1,841.3
Long-Term Debt (by debtor)	395.2	471.8	502.9	574.1	712.3	743.4	847.6	986.2	1,262.8	1,417.7	1,621.5
Central Bank, incl. IMF credit	78.5	78.3	85.9	97.1	133.1	154.3	165.2	216.2	305.7	412.1	400.0
Central Government	267.8	335.9	360.3	419.6	514.2	540.6	621.7	715.4	907.2	939.9	1,123.4
Rest of General Government	0.3	0.3	0.1	0.0	0.0	0.0	0.0	0.0	0.0	0.0	0.0
Non-financial Public Enterprises	43.3	52.2	52.6	52.6	60.5	45.1	56.8	51.2	44.8	56.2	77.6
Priv. Sector, incl non-guaranteed	5.3	5.1	4.0	4.8	4.5	3.4	3.9	3.4	5.1	9.5	20.5
Short-Term Debt	0.0	0.0	0.0	0.0	0.0	0.0	0.0	146.0	110.0	136.0	219.8
Memo Items:					*(Millions of US dollars)*						
Int'l Reserves Excluding Gold	42.74	50.33	59.46	86.60	77.59	57.43	92.33	292.59	397.64	516.90	245.50
Gold Holdings (at market price)	..	..	..	..	..	..	..	..	9.48	32.21	37.08
SOCIAL INDICATORS											
Total Fertility Rate	4.3	4.1	4.0	4.0	3.9	3.9	3.9	3.8	3.7	3.6	3.5
Infant Mortality Rate	53.2	50.6	48.0	46.6	45.2	43.8	42.4	41.0	38.8	36.6	34.4
Life Expectancy at Birth	64.7	64.8	65.0	65.3	65.7	66.0	66.4	66.7	67.2	67.6	68.1
Urban Population, % of total	21.9	21.9	21.9	22.0	22.0	22.0	21.9	21.8	21.8	21.7	21.6
Food Prod. per capita (1987=100)	108.3	103.4	103.7	96.9	103.7	103.1	103.0	100.0	106.2	114.0	119.4
Labor Force, Agriculture (%)	55.3	55.1	54.9	54.7	54.5	54.3	54.1	53.9	53.7	53.5	53.4
Labor Force, Female (%)	25.0	25.1	25.3	25.4	25.5	25.6	25.9	26.2	26.4	26.7	26.9
Primary Schl. Enroll. Ratio	99.0	..	..	..	..	77.0	79.0	82.0	89.0	94.0	103.0
Primary Schl. Enroll. Ratio, Female	94.0	..	..	..	..	74.0	75.0	79.0	86.0	91.0	100.0
Secondary Schl. Enroll. Ratio	47.0	..	..	..	..	48.0	48.0	42.0	52.0	49.0	55.0

1981	1982	1983	1984	1985	1986	1987	1988	1989	1990 estimate	Notes	SRI LANKA
				(Millions of current US dollars)							**FOREIGN TRADE (CUSTOMS BASIS)**
1,007.5	994.8	1,051.8	1,435.5	1,246.2	1,159.2	1,326.0	1,475.4	1,558.4	1,983.9	..	Value of Exports, fob
659.6	604.4	649.1	926.2	726.1	597.4	632.7	703.9	743.5	946.6	..	Nonfuel Primary Products
129.7	130.7	97.9	126.2	112.1	67.5	65.0	72.3	76.4	97.3	..	Fuels
218.2	259.7	304.8	383.1	408.0	494.3	628.3	699.1	738.5	940.1	..	Manufactures
1,803.8	1,769.9	1,788.4	1,847.4	1,786.3	1,831.6	2,021.3	2,238.5	2,197.8	2,689.0	..	Value of Imports, cif
403.6	275.0	356.7	331.9	414.7	379.9	384.8	426.2	418.4	512.0	..	Nonfuel Primary Products
450.6	554.9	426.8	475.0	388.9	230.5	308.5	341.6	335.4	410.4	..	Fuels
949.6	939.9	1,004.9	1,040.5	982.7	1,221.3	1,328.0	1,470.7	1,443.9	1,766.7	..	Manufactures
				(Index 1987 = 100)							
94.9	95.6	109.4	128.2	103.3	100.9	100.0	106.4	99.7	89.9	..	Terms of Trade
104.6	98.8	107.3	121.6	97.8	93.3	100.0	107.5	105.1	120.7	..	Export Prices, fob
110.2	103.3	98.1	94.8	94.6	92.5	100.0	101.0	105.4	134.3	..	Import Prices, cif
				(Millions of current US dollars)							**BALANCE OF PAYMENTS**
1,374.9	1,348.2	1,403.8	1,795.9	1,644.5	1,581.8	1,791.4	1,885.0	1,909.3	2,387.8	..	Exports of Goods & Services
1,062.5	1,013.9	1,061.2	1,461.6	1,315.8	1,208.5	1,393.9	1,477.1	1,505.1	1,853.0	..	Merchandise, fob
279.4	290.6	297.9	276.2	245.4	305.3	328.2	339.2	345.6	439.8	..	Nonfactor Services
33.0	43.8	44.7	58.1	83.3	68.0	69.3	68.7	58.6	94.9	..	Factor Services
2,182.5	2,322.7	2,314.6	2,274.2	2,505.7	2,469.9	2,610.1	2,805.4	2,842.2	3,226.6	..	Imports of Goods & Services
1,694.5	1,794.3	1,725.6	1,698.7	1,838.5	1,764.3	1,866.0	2,017.5	2,055.2	2,325.6	..	Merchandise, fob
359.2	390.6	407.3	383.5	457.1	499.7	533.2	547.1	565.8	639.8	..	Nonfactor Services
128.8	137.8	181.8	191.9	210.1	206.0	210.8	240.8	221.3	261.3	..	Factor Services
49.5	69.0	92.2	106.3	116.3	121.2	126.7	124.7	110.7	119.7	..	Long-Term Interest
202.9	263.8	274.5	276.5	265.5	294.1	312.8	320.0	330.7	364.7	..	Private Current Transfers, net
229.6	289.3	294.5	300.9	291.7	326.0	350.1	357.7	358.0	400.8	..	Workers' Remittances
-604.7	-710.6	-636.3	-201.8	-595.7	-594.0	-506.0	-600.5	-602.3	-474.2	..	Curr. A/C Bal before Off. Transf.
160.3	162.3	170.3	202.6	177.2	176.9	179.9	206.1	188.6	178.1	..	Net Official Transfers
-444.4	-548.3	-466.0	0.9	-418.4	-417.1	-326.1	-394.5	-413.7	-296.1	..	Curr. A/C Bal after Off. Transf.
363.5	518.5	410.4	379.4	345.3	363.7	268.1	269.2	184.7	364.2	..	Long-Term Capital, net
49.3	63.6	37.8	32.6	24.8	29.2	58.2	43.6	17.7	29.6	..	Direct Investment
345.1	396.0	299.0	341.5	339.7	355.0	186.4	193.0	241.3	298.9	..	Long-Term Loans
390.5	470.9	373.0	432.8	451.1	503.2	392.2	401.1	435.7	464.3	..	Disbursements
45.4	74.9	74.0	91.3	111.4	148.2	205.8	208.1	194.4	165.4	..	Repayments
-30.9	58.9	73.6	5.2	-19.2	-20.5	23.6	32.7	-74.3	35.7	..	Other Long-Term Capital
43.2	-17.5	49.0	-69.6	-41.6	-58.2	-19.9	0.6	264.7	-7.3	..	Other Capital, net
37.8	47.3	6.6	-310.7	114.7	111.6	77.8	124.6	-35.7	-60.8	..	Change in Reserves
				(Sri Lanka Rupees per US dollar)							**Memo Item:**
19.250	20.810	23.530	25.440	27.160	28.020	29.440	31.810	36.050	40.060	..	Conversion Factor (Annual Avg)
				(Millions of US dollars), outstanding at end of year							**EXTERNAL DEBT (Total)**
2,234.6	2,625.6	2,884.3	2,992.1	3,537.8	4,076.9	4,745.2	5,198.7	5,160.8	5,850.7	..	Long-Term Debt (by debtor)
2,030.7	2,349.7	2,600.7	2,797.4	3,331.5	3,892.3	4,471.9	4,621.7	4,766.6	5,456.5	..	Central Bank, incl. IMF credit
522.6	488.9	450.3	408.9	401.0	352.0	282.6	364.3	370.5	414.8	..	Central Government
1,314.2	1,516.4	1,738.7	1,949.6	2,428.6	3,023.7	3,613.5	3,756.5	3,881.6	4,511.3	..	Rest of General Government
0.0	0.0	0.0	0.0	0.0	0.0	0.0	0.0	0.0	..	..	Non-financial Public Enterprises
173.8	323.5	354.2	375.5	370.7	350.6	342.8	275.1	253.3	224.9	..	Priv. Sector, incl non-guaranteed
20.1	20.9	57.5	63.4	131.2	166.0	233.0	225.8	261.2	305.5	..	Short-Term Debt
203.9	275.9	283.6	194.7	206.3	184.6	273.3	577.0	394.2	394.2	..	
				(Millions of US dollars)							**Memo Items:**
327.36	351.49	296.95	510.77	451.16	352.60	279.06	221.92	244.21	422.91	..	Int'l Reserves Excluding Gold
25.00	28.74	24.00	19.39	20.57	24.59	30.45	25.81	25.22	24.12	..	Gold Holdings (at market price)
											SOCIAL INDICATORS
3.4	3.3	3.1	3.0	2.9	2.7	2.6	2.5	2.4	2.4	..	Total Fertility Rate
32.2	30.0	28.3	26.5	24.8	23.0	22.0	21.1	20.2	19.4	..	Infant Mortality Rate
68.5	69.0	69.2	69.5	69.8	70.1	70.3	70.6	70.9	71.1	..	Life Expectancy at Birth
21.5	21.4	21.3	21.2	21.1	21.2	21.2	21.3	21.3	21.4	..	Urban Population, % of total
116.7	112.5	121.9	111.3	118.4	114.5	100.0	100.8	96.8	106.7	..	Food Prod. per capita (1987=100)
..	..	..	..	..	..	..	..	..	..	..	Labor Force, Agriculture (%)
26.9	26.9	26.9	26.9	26.9	26.9	26.8	26.8	26.8	26.7	..	Labor Force, Female (%)
..	105.0	103.0	103.0	103.0	104.0	107.0	..	107.0	..	..	Primary Schl. Enroll. Ratio
100.0	102.0	101.0	101.0	101.0	102.0	105.0	..	106.0	..	..	Primary Schl. Enroll. Ratio, Female
..	57.0	59.0	61.0	63.0	66.0	71.0	..	74.0	..	..	Secondary Schl. Enroll. Ratio

ST. KITTS AND NEVIS	1970	1971	1972	1973	1974	1975	1976	1977	1978	1979	1980
CURRENT GNP PER CAPITA (US $)	..	..	..	..	..	..	..	..	..	..	..
POPULATION (thousands)	45	45	44	44	44	44	43	44	44	44	44

USE AND ORIGIN OF RESOURCES *(Millions of current Eastern Caribbean Dollars)*

	1970	1971	1972	1973	1974	1975	1976	1977	1978	1979	1980
Gross National Product (GNP)	..	..	..	..	..	..	..	..	..	..	127.40
Net Factor Income from Abroad											-3.40
GDP at Market Prices	32.60	38.70	44.10	47.40	64.70	72.40	78.70	81.70	93.40	108.70	130.80
Resource Balance											-38.30
Exports of Goods & NFServices	..	..	..	..	..	..	..	..	..	..	87.50
Imports of Goods & NFServices	..	..	..	..	..	..	..	..	..	..	125.80
Domestic Absorption											
Private Consumption, etc.	..	..	..	..	..	..	..	..	..	..	..
General Gov't Consumption	..	..	..	..	..	..	..	..	..	..	..
Gross Domestic Investment	..	..	..	..	..	..	..	..	..	..	..
Fixed Investment	..	..	..	..	..	..	..	..	..	..	..
Indirect Taxes, net	..	..	..	..	..	..	..	12.50	16.47	20.84	27.34
GDP at factor cost	..	..	..	..	..	..	..	69.20	76.93	87.86	103.46
Agriculture	..	..	..	..	..	..	..	13.10	12.20	13.60	16.50
Industry	..	..	..	..	..	..	..	20.03	19.64	21.90	27.50
Manufacturing	..	..	..	..	..	..	..	12.54	13.24	12.80	15.70
Services, etc.	..	..	..	..	..	..	..	36.07	45.09	52.36	59.46
Gross Domestic Saving	..	..	..	..	..	..	..	..	..	..	..
Gross National Saving	..	..	..	..	..	..	..	..	..	..	..

(Millions of 1987 Eastern Caribbean Dollars)

	1970	1971	1972	1973	1974	1975	1976	1977	1978	1979	1980
Gross National Product	..	..	..	..	..	..	..	..	..	..	203.89
GDP at Market Prices	..	..	..	..	..	..	..	168.32	178.84	181.25	209.34
Resource Balance	..	..	..	..	..	..	..	..	..	..	..
Exports of Goods & NFServices	..	..	..	..	..	..	..	..	..	..	..
Imports of Goods & NFServices	..	..	..	..	..	..	..	..	..	..	..
Domestic Absorption	..	..	..	..	..	..	..	..	..	..	..
Private Consumption, etc.	..	..	..	..	..	..	..	..	..	..	..
General Gov't Consumption	..	..	..	..	..	..	..	..	..	..	..
Gross Domestic Investment	..	..	..	..	..	..	..	..	..	..	..
Fixed Investment	..	..	..	..	..	..	..	..	..	..	..
GDP at factor cost	..	..	..	..	..	..	..	142.58	147.32	146.43	165.63
Agriculture	..	..	..	..	..	..	..	29.25	30.59	33.04	29.92
Industry	..	..	..	..	..	..	..	41.29	41.40	44.44	48.90
Manufacturing	..	..	..	..	..	..	..	33.52	35.13	35.67	36.47
Services, etc.	..	..	..	..	..	..	..	73.98	77.20	71.81	88.49
Memo Items:											
Capacity to Import	..	..	..	..	..	..	..	..	..	..	..
Terms of Trade Adjustment	..	..	..	..	..	..	..	..	..	..	..
Gross Domestic Income	..	..	..	..	..	..	..	..	..	..	..
Gross National Income	..	..	..	..	..	..	..	..	..	..	..

DOMESTIC PRICES/DEFLATORS *(Index 1987 = 100)*

	1970	1971	1972	1973	1974	1975	1976	1977	1978	1979	1980
Overall (GDP)	..	..	..	..	..	..	..	48.5	52.2	60.0	62.5
Domestic Absorption	..	..	..	..	..	..	..	..	..	..	..
Agriculture	..	..	..	..	..	..	..	44.8	39.9	41.2	55.1
Industry	..	..	..	..	..	..	..	48.5	47.4	49.3	56.2
Manufacturing	..	..	..	..	..	..	..	37.4	37.7	35.9	43.0
Consumer Price Index	..	..	..	..	..	..	..	..	..	66.7	78.5

MANUFACTURING ACTIVITY

	1970	1971	1972	1973	1974	1975	1976	1977	1978	1979	1980
Employment (1987=100)	..	..	..	..	..	..	..	..	..	..	..
Real Earnings per Empl. (1987=100)	..	..	..	..	..	..	..	..	..	..	..
Real Output per Empl. (1987=100)	..	..	..	..	..	..	..	..	..	..	..
Earnings as % of Value Added	..	..	..	..	..	..	..	..	..	..	..

MONETARY HOLDINGS *(Millions of current Eastern Caribbean Dollars)*

	1970	1971	1972	1973	1974	1975	1976	1977	1978	1979	1980
Money Supply, Broadly Defined	..	..	..	..	..	..	..	..	..	83.98	95.32
Money	..	..	..	..	..	..	..	..	..	9.25	8.01
Currency Outside Banks	..	..	..	..	..	..	..	..	..	-1.55	-1.32
Demand Deposits	..	..	..	..	..	..	..	..	..	10.81	9.34
Quasi-Money	..	..	..	..	..	..	..	..	..	74.73	87.31

GOVERNMENT DEFICIT (-) OR SURPLUS *(Thousands of current Eastern CaribbeanDollars)*

	1970	1971	1972	1973	1974	1975	1976	1977	1978	1979	1980
Current Revenue	..	..	..	..	..	..	..	..	..	..	..
Current Expenditure	..	..	..	..	..	..	..	..	..	..	..
Current Budget Balance	..	..	..	..	..	..	..	..	..	..	..
Capital Receipts	..	..	..	..	..	..	..	..	..	..	..
Capital Payments	..	..	..	..	..	..	..	..	..	..	..

1981	1982	1983	1984	1985	1986	1987	1988	1989	1990 estimate	Notes	ST. KITTS AND NEVIS
..	1,310	1,390	1,620	1,770	2,010	2,350	2,790	3,180	3,330	..	CURRENT GNP PER CAPITA (US $)
44	45	45	44	43	42	42	41	41	40		POPULATION (thousands)
				(Millions of current Eastern Caribbean Dollars)							USE AND ORIGIN OF RESOURCES
148.20	160.90	163.70	192.00	205.10	250.80	280.10	320.30	351.70	362.50	..	Gross National Product (GNP)
-2.80	1.60	3.00	3.20	1.40	-3.20	-7.30	-12.20	-11.10	-19.70	..	Net Factor Income from Abroad
151.00	159.30	160.70	188.80	203.70	254.00	287.40	332.50	362.80	382.20	..	GDP at Market Prices
-42.60	-49.70	-72.70	-41.30	-34.00	-33.80	-62.60	-87.80	..	..	..	Resource Balance
104.80	91.80	84.20	105.00	120.20	157.10	180.40	197.90				Exports of Goods & NFServices
147.40	141.50	156.90	146.30	154.20	190.90	243.00	285.70	..	..		Imports of Goods & NFServices
..	..	..	..	..	..	..	..	..	..		Domestic Absorption
..	..	..	..	..	..	..	..	..	..		Private Consumption, etc.
..	..	..	..	..	..	..	..	..	..		General Gov't Consumption
..	..	..	..	..	..	..	..	..	..		Gross Domestic Investment
..	..	..	..	..	..	..	..	..	..		Fixed Investment
29.56	20.56	24.21	29.48	31.90	39.79	47.62	47.72	49.34	42.92		Indirect Taxes, net
121.44	138.74	136.49	159.32	171.80	214.21	239.78	284.78	313.46	339.28	B	GDP at factor cost
13.80	20.30	16.20	19.20	16.40	22.90	25.90	28.10	27.70	29.10	..	Agriculture
30.20	34.10	34.40	37.20	39.30	54.40	60.30	82.56	89.28	93.95	..	Industry
17.90	18.70	17.60	22.60	21.90	32.80	35.40	44.30	45.80	46.60	..	Manufacturing
77.44	84.34	85.89	102.92	116.10	136.91	153.58	174.12	196.48	216.23	..	Services, etc.
..	..	..	..	..	..	..	..	..	..	..	Gross Domestic Saving
..	..	..	..	..	..	..	..	..	..	..	Gross National Saving
				(Millions of 1987 Eastern Caribbean Dollars)							
212.76	214.88	220.25	240.68	253.44	261.57	280.10	296.54	315.21	307.02	..	Gross National Product
216.78	212.75	216.24	236.68	251.71	264.91	287.40	307.82	325.16	323.75	..	GDP at Market Prices
..	..	..	..	..	..	..	..	..	..	..	Resource Balance
..	..	..	..	..	..	..	..	..	..	..	Exports of Goods & NFServices
..	..	..	..	..	..	..	..	..	..	..	Imports of Goods & NFServices
..	..	..	..	..	..	..	..	..	..	..	Domestic Absorption
..	..	..	..	..	..	..	..	..	..	..	Private Consumption, etc.
..	..	..	..	..	..	..	..	..	..	..	General Gov't Consumption
..	..	..	..	..	..	..	..	..	..	..	Gross Domestic Investment
..	..	..	..	..	..	..	..	..	..	..	Fixed Investment
174.46	185.38	183.83	199.82	212.33	223.44	239.78	263.71	280.94	287.31	B	GDP at factor cost
31.48	31.48	25.68	26.79	26.12	26.35	25.90	27.46	26.12	22.55	..	Agriculture
46.62	52.43	51.12	50.69	51.93	55.62	60.30	72.40	75.70	74.83	..	Industry
32.72	35.40	31.38	35.13	33.25	36.20	35.40	36.74	37.28	32.72	..	Manufacturing
97.32	102.61	107.03	122.34	134.27	141.47	153.58	163.84	179.11	189.93		Services, etc.
											Memo Items:
..	..	..	..	..	..	..	..	..	..	..	Capacity to Import
..	..	..	..	..	..	..	..	..	..	..	Terms of Trade Adjustment
..	..	..	..	..	..	..	..	..	..	..	Gross Domestic Income
..	..	..	..	..	..	..	..	..	..	..	Gross National Income
				(Index 1987 = 100)							DOMESTIC PRICES/DEFLATORS
69.7	74.9	74.3	79.8	80.9	95.9	100.0	108.0	111.6	118.1	..	Overall (GDP)
..	..	..	..	..	..	..	..	..	..	..	Domestic Absorption
43.8	64.5	63.1	71.7	62.8	86.9	100.0	102.3	106.0	129.0	..	Agriculture
64.8	65.0	67.3	73.4	75.7	97.8	100.0	114.0	117.9	125.6	..	Industry
54.7	52.8	56.1	64.3	65.9	90.6	100.0	120.6	122.9	142.4	..	Manufacturing
86.7	91.9	94.0	96.5	99.1	99.1	100.0	100.2	105.3	109.8	..	Consumer Price Index
											MANUFACTURING ACTIVITY
..	..	..	..	..	..	..	..	..	..	..	Employment (1987=100)
..	..	..	..	..	..	..	..	..	..	..	Real Earnings per Empl. (1987=100)
..	..	..	..	..	..	..	..	..	..	..	Real Output per Empl. (1987=100)
..	..	..	..	..	..	..	..	..	..	..	Earnings as % of Value Added
				(Millions of current Eastern Caribbean Dollars)							MONETARY HOLDINGS
116.84	130.92	150.69	170.90	204.21	232.56	212.24	230.90	279.77	301.43	..	Money Supply, Broadly Defined
26.42	25.49	27.58	29.26	32.90	49.81	55.26	48.48	61.23	59.99	..	Money
10.33	11.10	11.59	12.61	9.39	12.22	13.00	16.08	22.65	21.43	..	Currency Outside Banks
16.09	14.39	15.98	16.64	23.51	37.59	42.25	32.40	38.58	38.56	..	Demand Deposits
90.41	105.43	123.11	141.64	171.31	182.75	156.98	182.42	218.54	241.44	..	Quasi-Money
				(Thousands of current Eastern CaribbeanDollars)							GOVERNMENT DEFICIT (-) OR SURPLUS
..	..	..	..	-13,120	2,850	-47,460	..	-17,860	160	..	
..	..	..	..	62,990	76,500	88,390	99,140	96,130	140,740	..	Current Revenue
..	..	..	..	58,800	57,410	64,500	..	82,140	96,440	..	Current Expenditure
..	..	..	..	4,190	19,090	23,890	..	13,990	44,300	..	Current Budget Balance
..	..	..	..	1,030	660	1,860	1,980	1,300	1,180	..	Capital Receipts
..	..	..	..	18,340	16,900	73,210	..	33,150	45,320	..	Capital Payments

ST. KITTS AND NEVIS	1970	1971	1972	1973	1974	1975	1976	1977	1978	1979	1980
FOREIGN TRADE (CUSTOMS BASIS)					*(Thousands of current US dollars)*						
Value of Exports, fob	..	..	..	..	..	..	..	..	..	..	..
Nonfuel Primary Products	..	..	..	..	..	..	..	..	..	..	..
Fuels	..	..	..	..	..	..	..	..	..	..	..
Manufactures	..	..	..	..	..	..	..	..	..	..	..
Value of Imports, cif	..	..	..	..	..	..	..	..	..	..	..
Nonfuel Primary Products	..	..	..	..	..	..	..	..	..	..	..
Fuels	..	..	..	..	..	..	..	..	..	..	..
Manufactures	..	..	..	..	..	..	..	..	..	..	..
					(Index 1987 = 100)						
Terms of Trade	..	..	..	..	..	..	..	..	..	..	..
Export Prices, fob	..	..	..	..	..	..	..	..	..	..	..
Import Prices, cif	..	..	..	..	..	..	..	..	..	..	..
BALANCE OF PAYMENTS					*(Millions of current US dollars)*						
Exports of Goods & Services	..	..	..	..	..	..	..	..	..	..	32.92
Merchandise, fob	..	..	..	..	..	..	..	..	..	..	24.12
Nonfactor Services	..	..	..	..	..	..	..	..	..	..	8.10
Factor Services	..	..	..	..	..	..	..	..	..	..	0.70
Imports of Goods & Services	..	..	..	..	..	..	..	..	..	..	48.59
Merchandise, fob	..	..	..	..	..	..	..	..	..	..	40.80
Nonfactor Services	..	..	..	..	..	..	..	..	..	..	5.84
Factor Services	..	..	..	..	..	..	..	..	..	..	1.94
Long-Term Interest	0.00	0.00	0.00	0.00	0.00	0.00	0.00	0.00	0.10	0.10	0.10
Private Current Transfers, net	..	..	..	..	..	..	..	..	..	..	8.20
Workers' Remittances	..	..	..	..	..	..	..	..	..	..	0.79
Curr. A/C Bal before Off. Transf.	..	..	..	..	..	..	..	..	..	..	-7.46
Net Official Transfers	..	..	..	..	..	..	..	..	..	..	4.80
Curr. A/C Bal after Off. Transf.	..	..	..	..	..	..	..	..	..	..	-2.66
Long-Term Capital, net	..	..	..	..	..	..	..	..	..	..	4.94
Direct Investment	..	..	..	..	..	..	..	..	..	..	1.00
Long-Term Loans	0.00	0.00	0.50	1.20	1.00	0.70	0.80	1.30	1.00	0.60	0.70
Disbursements	0.00	0.00	0.50	1.20	1.00	0.70	0.80	1.30	1.20	0.80	0.90
Repayments	0.00	0.00	0.00	0.00	0.00	0.00	0.00	0.00	0.20	0.20	0.20
Other Long-Term Capital	..	..	..	..	..	..	..	..	..	..	3.24
Other Capital, net	..	..	..	..	..	..	..	..	..	..	-3.88
Change in Reserves	..	..	..	..	..	..	..	..	..	..	1.60
Memo Item:					*(Eastern Caribbean Dollars per US dollar)*						
Conversion Factor (Annual Avg)	2.000	1.970	1.920	1.960	2.050	2.170	2.610	2.700	2.700	2.700	2.700
					(Millions of US dollars), outstanding at end of year						
EXTERNAL DEBT (Total)	0	0	0	2	3	3	3	5	6	7	8
Long-Term Debt (by debtor)	0	0	0	2	3	3	3	5	6	7	8
Central Bank, incl. IMF credit	0	0	0	0	0	0	0	0	0	1	1
Central Government	0	0	0	2	3	3	3	5	6	7	8
Rest of General Government	..	..	..	..	..	..	..	..	..	..	..
Non-financial Public Enterprises	..	..	..	..	..	..	..	..	..	..	..
Priv. Sector, incl non-guaranteed	0	0	0	0	0	0	0	0	0	0	0
Short-Term Debt	0	0	0	0	0	0	0	0	0	0	0
Memo Items:					*(Thousands of US dollars)*						
Int'l Reserves Excluding Gold	..	..	..	..	..	..	..	..	..	..	..
Gold Holdings (at market price)	..	..	..	..	..	..	..	..	..	..	..
SOCIAL INDICATORS											
Total Fertility Rate	..	..	3.5	3.5	3.5	3.4	3.4	3.4	3.4	3.4	3.3
Infant Mortality Rate	..	..	..	..	..	..	..	..	..	..	..
Life Expectancy at Birth	..	..	..	..	..	..	..	..	..	..	..
Urban Population, % of total	34.3	35.0	35.7	36.3	37.0	37.7	38.4	39.1	39.9	40.6	41.3
Food Prod. per capita (1987=100)	..	..	..	..	..	..	..	..	..	..	..
Labor Force, Agriculture (%)	..	..	..	..	..	..	..	..	..	..	..
Labor Force, Female (%)	..	..	..	..	..	..	..	..	..	..	..
Primary Schl. Enroll. Ratio	..	..	..	..	..	..	..	..	..	..	..
Primary Schl. Enroll. Ratio, Female	..	..	..	..	..	..	..	..	..	..	..
Secondary Schl. Enroll. Ratio	..	..	..	..	..	..	..	..	..	..	..

1981	1982	1983	1984	1985	1986	1987	1988	1989	1990 estimate	Notes	ST. KITTS AND NEVIS
											FOREIGN TRADE (CUSTOMS BASIS)
			(Thousands of current US dollars)								
..	..	..	..	..	..	..	..	..	..	..	Value of Exports, fob
..	..	..	..	..	..	..	..	..	..	..	Nonfuel Primary Products
..	..	..	..	..	..	..	..	..	..	..	Fuels
..	..	..	..	..	..	..	..	..	..	..	Manufactures
..	..	..	..	..	..	..	..	..	..	..	Value of Imports, cif
..	..	..	..	..	..	..	..	..	..	..	Nonfuel Primary Products
..	..	..	..	..	..	..	..	..	..	..	Fuels
..	..	..	..	..	..	..	..	..	..	..	Manufactures
			(Index 1987 = 100)								
..	..	..	..	..	..	..	..	..	..	..	Terms of Trade
..	..	..	..	..	..	..	..	..	..	..	Export Prices, fob
..	..	..	..	..	..	..	..	..	..	..	Import Prices, cif
			(Millions of current US dollars)								**BALANCE OF PAYMENTS**
35.46	33.34	33.23	41.37	43.47	60.37	70.73	75.86	82.00	78.88	..	Exports of Goods & Services
24.26	18.84	18.43	20.15	20.37	27.17	29.80	29.10	32.80	24.63	..	Merchandise, fob
10.00	13.20	13.00	20.32	22.80	31.00	38.03	42.56	45.80	50.55	..	Nonfactor Services
1.20	1.30	1.80	0.90	0.30	2.20	2.90	4.20	3.40	3.70	..	Factor Services
52.86	53.16	58.27	57.20	58.62	72.98	91.59	107.05	125.40	141.34	..	Imports of Goods & Services
43.42	39.82	46.74	47.23	46.70	55.35	69.96	81.57	89.67	103.24	..	Merchandise, fob
7.19	12.64	10.82	9.17	10.32	14.70	17.80	20.53	30.84	24.19	..	Nonfactor Services
2.24	0.70	0.70	0.80	1.60	2.92	3.83	4.95	4.90	13.91	..	Factor Services
0.10	0.20	0.20	0.30	0.40	0.50	0.60	0.80	1.00	1.60	..	Long-Term Interest
11.10	9.00	8.20	9.80	7.12	8.52	9.15	9.85	10.50	11.51	..	Private Current Transfers, net
1.11	1.10	1.11	1.31	1.06	1.04	1.11	1.19	1.19	..	..	Workers' Remittances
-6.30	-10.82	-16.84	-6.04	-8.03	-4.09	-11.71	-21.34	-32.90	-50.95	..	Curr. A/C Bal before Off. Transf.
1.60	2.10	2.10	1.70	1.35	2.37	3.08	3.73	4.70	0.70	..	Net Official Transfers
-4.70	-8.72	-14.74	-4.34	-6.68	-1.72	-8.64	-17.61	-28.20	-50.25	..	Curr. A/C Bal after Off. Transf.
2.20	2.90	14.30	11.40	9.40	4.94	14.45	20.17	35.90	53.76	..	Long-Term Capital, net
0.90	2.20	13.50	6.00	8.00	5.96	8.73	14.70	29.60	13.11	..	Direct Investment
0.90	1.10	1.20	1.70	1.80	4.80	6.10	3.80	2.40	4.30	..	Long-Term Loans
1.20	1.40	1.50	2.10	2.30	5.40	7.00	4.70	3.40	5.40	..	Disbursements
0.30	0.30	0.30	0.40	0.50	0.60	0.90	0.90	1.00	1.10	..	Repayments
0.40	-0.40	-0.40	3.70	-0.40	-5.82	-0.38	1.67	3.90	36.34	..	Other Long-Term Capital
2.60	2.02	1.64	-5.26	-0.78	-0.10	-5.18	-2.49	-1.30	-3.41	..	Other Capital, net
-0.10	3.80	-1.20	-1.80	-1.94	-3.12	-0.64	-0.07	-6.40	-0.10	..	Change in Reserves
											Memo Item:
			(Eastern Caribbean Dollars per US dollar)								
2.700	2.700	2.700	2.700	2.700	2.700	2.700	2.700	2.700	2.700	..	Conversion Factor (Annual Avg)
			(Millions of US dollars), outstanding at end of year								
8	9	10	11	13	18	25	29	31	37	..	**EXTERNAL DEBT (Total)**
8	9	10	11	13	18	25	29	31	36	..	Long-Term Debt (by debtor)
1	0	1	1	2	2	3	5	5	6	..	Central Bank, incl. IMF credit
8	8	9	9	10	14	20	22	23	27	..	Central Government
..	..	..	..	..	..	..	..	..	..	..	Rest of General Government
..	..	..	..	..	..	..	..	..	..	..	Non-financial Public Enterprises
0	0	0	0	1	2	2	2	3	3	..	Priv. Sector, incl non-guaranteed
0	0	0	0	0	0	0	0	0	1	..	Short-Term Debt
			(Thousands of US dollars)								**Memo Items:**
4,016	3,329	3,148	5,651	7,415	10,232	10,574	10,324	16,393	16,284	..	Int'l Reserves Excluding Gold
..	..	..	..	..	..	..	..	..	..	..	Gold Holdings (at market price)
											SOCIAL INDICATORS
3.3	3.3	3.2	3.1	3.0	2.9	2.8	2.7	2.7	2.6	..	Total Fertility Rate
..	45.0	43.7	42.4	41.0	39.7	40.0	38.8	37.6	36.4	..	Infant Mortality Rate
..	66.9	67.2	67.5	67.8	68.1	68.5	68.8	69.2	69.6	..	Life Expectancy at Birth
42.0	42.8	43.5	44.3	45.0	45.8	46.6	47.3	48.1	48.9	..	Urban Population, % of total
..	..	..	..	..	..	..	..	..	..	..	Food Prod. per capita (1987=100)
..	..	..	..	..	..	..	..	..	..	..	Labor Force, Agriculture (%)
..	..	..	..	..	..	..	..	..	..	..	Labor Force, Female (%)
..	..	..	..	..	..	..	..	..	..	..	Primary Schl. Enroll. Ratio
..	..	..	..	..	..	..	..	..	..	..	Primary Schl. Enroll. Ratio, Female
..	..	..	..	..	..	..	..	..	..	..	Secondary Schl. Enroll. Ratio

ST. LUCIA	1970	1971	1972	1973	1974	1975	1976	1977	1978	1979	1980
CURRENT GNP PER CAPITA (US $)	..	..	..	..	..	..	..	..	..	..	..
POPULATION (thousands)	101	103	105	107	110	112	114	117	119	121	124
USE AND ORIGIN OF RESOURCES					*(Millions of current Eastern Caribbean Dollars)*						
Gross National Product (GNP)	..	..	..	..	..	..	..	..	..	258.50	269.90
Net Factor Income from Abroad										-20.80	-36.40
GDP at Market Prices	..	..	..	..	..	..	..	..	..	279.30	306.30
Resource Balance	..	..	..	..	..	..	..	..	..	-108.30	-117.90
Exports of Goods & NFServices	..	..	..	..	..	..	..	..	..	176.30	233.60
Imports of Goods & NFServices	..	..	..	..	..	..	..	..	..	284.60	351.50
Domestic Absorption	..	..	..	..	..	..	..	..	..	387.60	424.20
Private Consumption, etc.	..	..	..	..	..	..	..	..	..	..	..
General Gov't Consumption	..	..	..	..	..	..	..	..	..	..	..
Gross Domestic Investment	..	..	..	..	..	..	..	..	..	..	..
Fixed Investment	..	..	..	..	..	..	..	..	..	..	..
Indirect Taxes, net	..	..	..	..	..	..	..	..	..	50.20	42.10
GDP at factor cost	..	..	..	..	..	..	..	..	..	229.10	264.20
Agriculture	..	..	..	..	..	..	..	..	..	34.80	31.00
Industry	..	..	..	..	..	..	..	..	..	52.20	65.60
Manufacturing	..	..	..	..	..	..	..	..	..	18.90	24.70
Services, etc.	..	..	..	..	..	..	..	..	..	142.10	167.60
Gross Domestic Saving	..	..	..	..	..	..	..	..	..	..	..
Gross National Saving	..	..	..	..	..	..	..	..	..	..	..
					(Millions of 1987 Eastern Caribbean Dollars)						
Gross National Product	..	..	..	..	..	..	..	..	..	409.76	371.82
GDP at Market Prices	..	..	..	..	..	..	..	..	..	442.84	421.96
Resource Balance	..	..	..	..	..	..	..	..	..	..	..
Exports of Goods & NFServices	..	..	..	..	..	..	..	..	..	..	..
Imports of Goods & NFServices	..	..	..	..	..	..	..	..	..	..	..
Domestic Absorption	..	..	..	..	..	..	..	..	..	..	..
Private Consumption, etc.	..	..	..	..	..	..	..	..	..	..	..
General Gov't Consumption	..	..	..	..	..	..	..	..	..	..	..
Gross Domestic Investment	..	..	..	..	..	..	..	..	..	..	..
Fixed Investment	..	..	..	..	..	..	..	..	..	..	..
GDP at factor cost	..	..	..	..	..	..	..	309.98	350.53	363.67	361.51
Agriculture	..	..	..	..	..	..	..	56.42	68.31	65.05	51.53
Industry	..	..	..	..	..	..	..	60.80	75.70	81.13	86.37
Manufacturing	..	..	..	..	..	..	..	24.39	28.28	23.69	27.40
Services, etc.	..	..	..	..	..	..	..	193.43	208.18	218.01	221.42
Memo Items:											
Capacity to Import	..	..	..	..	..	..	..	..	..	..	..
Terms of Trade Adjustment	..	..	..	..	..	..	..	..	..	..	..
Gross Domestic Income	..	..	..	..	..	..	..	..	..	..	..
Gross National Income	..	..	..	..	..	..	..	..	..	..	..
DOMESTIC PRICES/DEFLATORS					*(Index 1987 = 100)*						
Overall (GDP)	..	..	..	..	..	..	..	..	..	63.1	72.6
Domestic Absorption	..	..	..	..	..	..	..	..	..	..	..
Agriculture	..	..	..	..	..	..	..	..	..	53.5	60.2
Industry	..	..	..	..	..	..	..	..	..	64.3	76.0
Manufacturing	..	..	..	..	..	..	..	..	..	79.8	90.1
Consumer Price Index	20.1	21.8	23.5	26.7	35.8	42.1	46.2	50.3	55.8	61.0	72.9
MANUFACTURING ACTIVITY											
Employment (1987=100)	..	..	..	..	..	..	..	..	..	..	..
Real Earnings per Empl. (1987=100)	..	..	..	..	..	..	..	..	..	..	..
Real Output per Empl. (1987=100)	..	..	..	..	..	..	..	..	..	..	..
Earnings as % of Value Added	..	..	..	..	..	..	..	..	..	..	..
MONETARY HOLDINGS					*(Millions of current Eastern Caribbean Dollars)*						
Money Supply, Broadly Defined	..	..	..	..	..	82.09	100.50	106.48	127.37	149.63	167.24
Money	..	..	..	..	..	20.63	29.05	33.01	38.39	45.22	52.67
Currency Outside Banks	..	..	..	..	..	9.56	12.07	15.04	17.67	22.05	24.61
Demand Deposits	..	..	..	..	..	11.07	16.98	17.97	20.72	23.16	28.06
Quasi-Money	..	..	..	..	..	61.46	71.46	73.47	88.99	104.41	114.56
GOVERNMENT DEFICIT (-) OR SURPLUS					*(Millions of current Eastern Caribbean Dollars)*						
	..	..	..	..	..	..	..	..	-1.48	4.73	-12.85
Current Revenue	..	..	..	..	..	..	..	..	65.74	96.26	100.74
Current Expenditure	..	..	..	..	..	..	..	..	50.57	73.97	81.59
Current Budget Balance	..	..	..	..	..	..	..	..	15.17	22.29	19.15
Capital Receipts	..	..	..	..	..	..	..	..	..	..	..
Capital Payments	..	..	..	..	..	..	..	..	16.65	17.56	32.00

1981	1982	1983	1984	1985	1986	1987	1988	1989	1990 estimate	Notes	ST. LUCIA
960	1,050	1,110	1,140	1,230	1,360	1,480	1,670	1,800	1,900	..	CURRENT GNP PER CAPITA (US $)
126	129	131	134	137	140	142	145	148	150	..	POPULATION (thousands)

(Millions of current Eastern Caribbean Dollars) — USE AND ORIGIN OF RESOURCES

1981	1982	1983	1984	1985	1986	1987	1988	1989	1990	Notes	
339.70	358.10	377.10	408.10	457.40	530.00	581.70	652.00	726.20	779.70	..	Gross National Product (GNP)
-3.20	-3.20	-2.20	-8.60	-9.40	-10.80	-11.30	-11.60	-11.90	-14.00	..	Net Factor Income from Abroad
342.90	361.30	379.30	416.70	466.80	540.80	593.00	663.60	738.10	793.70	..	GDP at Market Prices
-152.00	-143.00	-68.60	-92.30	-43.20	-10.20	-51.30	-35.10	-133.90	..	..	Resource Balance
216.30	221.70	274.60	301.90	365.30	493.60	523.50	656.40	668.00	..	..	Exports of Goods & NF Services
368.30	364.70	343.20	394.20	408.50	503.80	574.80	691.50	801.90	..	..	Imports of Goods & NF Services
494.90	504.30	447.90	509.00	510.00	551.00	644.30	698.70	872.00	..	..	Domestic Absorption
..	..	..	..	..	..	..	..	..	..	..	Private Consumption, etc.
..	..	..	..	..	..	..	..	..	..	..	General Gov't Consumption
..	..	..	..	..	..	..	..	..	..	..	Gross Domestic Investment
..	..	..	..	..	..	..	..	..	..	..	Fixed Investment
43.50	48.80	55.90	63.70	78.00	97.50	121.50	144.50	189.90		..	Indirect Taxes, net
299.40	312.50	323.40	353.00	388.80	443.30	471.50	519.10	548.20	..	..	GDP at factor cost
28.90	36.10	42.30	46.20	58.30	82.30	87.20	97.50	87.20	..	..	Agriculture
74.60	71.70	63.20	70.20	76.90	84.90	91.60	104.90	120.10	..	..	Industry
25.30	26.80	30.20	31.10	33.00	34.00	35.00	36.40	38.40	..	..	Manufacturing
195.90	204.70	217.90	236.60	253.60	276.10	292.70	316.70	340.90	..	..	Services, etc.
..	..	..	..	..	..	..	..	..	..	..	Gross Domestic Saving
..	..	..	..	..	..	..	..	..	..	..	Gross National Saving

(Millions of 1987 Eastern Caribbean Dollars)

1981	1982	1983	1984	1985	1986	1987	1988	1989	1990	Notes	
415.59	431.68	455.72	474.85	513.13	552.88	581.70	635.44	664.50	682.12	..	Gross National Product
419.50	435.54	458.39	484.88	523.68	564.13	593.00	646.69	675.35	694.33	..	GDP at Market Prices
..	..	..	..	..	..	..	..	..	..	..	Resource Balance
..	..	..	..	..	..	..	..	..	..	..	Exports of Goods & NF Services
..	..	..	..	..	..	..	..	..	..	..	Imports of Goods & NF Services
..	..	..	..	..	..	..	..	..	..	..	Domestic Absorption
..	..	..	..	..	..	..	..	..	..	..	Private Consumption, etc.
..	..	..	..	..	..	..	..	..	..	..	General Gov't Consumption
..	..	..	..	..	..	..	..	..	..	..	Gross Domestic Investment
..	..	..	..	..	..	..	..	..	..	..	Fixed Investment
366.08	376.51	390.68	410.62	436.06	462.50	471.50	506.31	526.54	..	..	GDP at factor cost
43.83	58.29	66.92	72.28	81.14	91.16	87.20	108.18	109.12	..	..	Agriculture
88.38	83.95	72.47	75.90	81.13	86.77	91.60	98.24	107.71	..	..	Industry
27.93	30.05	33.23	33.23	34.12	34.65	35.00	35.71	36.94	..	..	Manufacturing
229.92	232.95	251.29	262.45	273.79	284.57	292.70	299.89	309.72	..	..	Services, etc.

Memo Items:

1981	1982	1983	1984	1985	1986	1987	1988	1989	1990	Notes	
..	..	..	..	..	..	..	..	..	..	..	Capacity to Import
..	..	..	..	..	..	..	..	..	..	..	Terms of Trade Adjustment
..	..	..	..	..	..	..	..	..	..	..	Gross Domestic Income
..	..	..	..	..	..	..	..	..	..	..	Gross National Income

(Index 1987 = 100) — DOMESTIC PRICES/DEFLATORS

1981	1982	1983	1984	1985	1986	1987	1988	1989	1990	Notes	
81.7	83.0	82.7	85.9	89.1	95.9	100.0	102.6	109.3	114.3	..	Overall (GDP)
..	..	..	..	..	..	..	..	..	..	..	Domestic Absorption
65.9	61.9	63.2	63.9	71.9	90.3	100.0	90.1	79.9	..	..	Agriculture
84.4	85.4	87.2	92.5	94.8	97.8	100.0	106.8	111.5	..	..	Industry
90.6	89.2	90.9	93.6	96.7	98.1	100.0	101.9	103.9	..	..	Manufacturing
83.9	87.8	89.1	90.2	91.4	93.4	100.0	100.8	105.2	109.7	..	Consumer Price Index

MANUFACTURING ACTIVITY

1981	1982	1983	1984	1985	1986	1987	1988	1989	1990	Notes	
..	..	..	..	..	..	..	..	..	..	..	Employment (1987=100)
..	..	..	..	..	..	..	..	..	..	..	Real Earnings per Empl. (1987=100)
..	..	..	..	..	..	..	..	..	..	..	Real Output per Empl. (1987=100)
..	..	..	..	..	..	..	..	..	..	..	Earnings as % of Value Added

(Millions of current Eastern Caribbean Dollars) — MONETARY HOLDINGS

1981	1982	1983	1984	1985	1986	1987	1988	1989	1990	Notes	
196.44	214.62	245.78	274.03	328.64	412.21	479.34	515.44	601.56	676.80	..	Money Supply, Broadly Defined
53.53	57.57	58.39	63.06	71.05	97.62	122.58	140.28	157.54	167.50	..	Money
27.69	28.04	30.26	30.08	33.01	39.05	52.06	56.28	67.28	64.23	..	Currency Outside Banks
25.84	29.52	28.13	32.98	38.04	58.58	70.53	84.00	90.27	103.26	..	Demand Deposits
142.91	157.05	187.39	210.97	257.59	314.58	356.75	375.16	444.02	509.31	..	Quasi-Money

(Millions of current Eastern Caribbean Dollars)

1981	1982	1983	1984	1985	1986	1987	1988	1989	1990	Notes	
-7.84	-15.81	14.30	-16.65	-11.10	-11.40	8.10	19.10	-1.50	26.50	C	GOVERNMENT DEFICIT (-) OR SURPLUS
120.02	137.28	154.09	130.85	162.10	186.10	221.70	244.80	262.00	285.20	..	Current Revenue
92.32	117.00	114.52	122.85	145.20	154.20	160.50	163.30	200.50	200.40	..	Current Expenditure
27.70	20.28	39.57	8.00	16.90	31.90	61.20	81.50	61.50	84.80	..	Current Budget Balance
..	..	..	0.05	..	..	0.10	1.80	8.40	1.50	..	Capital Receipts
35.54	36.09	25.27	24.70	28.00	43.30	53.20	64.20	71.40	59.80	..	Capital Payments

ST. LUCIA	1970	1971	1972	1973	1974	1975	1976	1977	1978	1979	1980
FOREIGN TRADE (CUSTOMS BASIS)						*(Millions of current US dollars)*					
Value of Exports, fob	..	..	..	..	..	..	..	..	..	..	..
Nonfuel Primary Products	..	..	..	..	..	..	..	..	..	..	..
Fuels	..	..	..	..	..	..	..	..	..	..	..
Manufactures	..	..	..	..	..	..	..	..	..	..	..
Value of Imports, cif	..	..	..	..	..	..	..	..	..	..	..
Nonfuel Primary Products	..	..	..	..	..	..	..	..	..	..	..
Fuels	..	..	..	..	..	..	..	..	..	..	..
Manufactures	..	..	..	..	..	..	..	..	..	..	..
						(Index 1987 = 100)					
Terms of Trade	..	..	..	..	..	..	..	..	..	..	..
Export Prices, fob	..	..	..	..	..	..	..	..	..	..	..
Import Prices, cif	..	..	..	..	..	..	..	..	..	..	..
BALANCE OF PAYMENTS						*(Millions of current US dollars)*					
Exports of Goods & Services	..	..	..	..	..	..	32.10	41.30	55.80	66.70	87.50
Merchandise, fob	..	..	..	..	..	..	19.10	22.60	26.80	31.90	46.00
Nonfactor Services	..	..	..	..	..	..	12.50	17.80	27.70	33.80	40.50
Factor Services	..	..	..	..	..	..	0.50	0.90	1.30	1.00	1.00
Imports of Goods & Services	..	..	..	..	..	..	50.40	..	88.60	106.00	135.40
Merchandise, fob	..	..	..	..	..	..	43.63	53.90	75.27	91.99	112.55
Nonfactor Services	..	..	..	..	..	..	6.46	8.40	12.83	13.41	22.15
Factor Services	..	..	..	..	..	..	0.30	..	0.50	0.60	0.70
Long-Term Interest	0.00	0.00	0.00	0.00	0.10	0.10	0.20	0.20	0.30	0.40	0.40
Private Current Transfers, net	..	..	..	..	..	..	8.20	7.60	7.70	7.80	11.10
Workers' Remittances	..	..	..	..	..	..	..	..	..	..	..
Curr. A/C Bal before Off. Transf.	..	..	..	..	..	..	-10.10	-13.40	-25.10	-31.50	-36.80
Net Official Transfers	..	..	..	..	..	..	4.70	2.50	2.10	3.40	3.50
Curr. A/C Bal after Off. Transf.	..	..	..	..	..	..	-5.40	-10.90	-23.00	-28.10	-33.30
Long-Term Capital, net	..	..	..	..	..	..	5.50	14.90	23.30	28.97	32.51
Direct Investment	..	..	..	..	..	..	3.00	13.00	20.60	26.00	30.90
Long-Term Loans	0.00	0.00	0.10	0.50	1.20	1.50	1.20	1.70	2.40	2.20	2.30
Disbursements	0.00	0.00	0.10	0.50	1.20	1.50	1.20	1.70	2.40	2.30	2.70
Repayments	0.00	0.00	0.00	0.00	0.00	0.00	0.00	0.00	0.00	0.10	0.40
Other Long-Term Capital	..	..	..	..	..	..	1.30	0.20	0.30	0.77	-0.69
Other Capital, net	..	..	..	..	..	..	2.42	-3.44	0.70	0.70	-1.16
Change in Reserves	..	..	..	..	..	..	-2.52	-0.56	-1.00	-1.57	1.95
Memo Item:						*(Eastern Caribbean Dollars per US dollar)*					
Conversion Factor (Annual Avg)	2.000	1.970	1.920	1.960	2.050	2.170	2.610	2.700	2.700	2.700	2.700
						(Millions of US dollars), outstanding at end of year					
EXTERNAL DEBT (Total)	0	0	0	1	2	3	4	6	8	11	13
Long-Term Debt (by debtor)	0	0	0	1	2	3	4	6	8	11	13
Central Bank, incl. IMF credit	0	0	0	0	0	0	0	1	1	1	1
Central Government	0	0	0	0	1	1	2	2	2	3	4
Rest of General Government	..	..	..	..	..	..	..	..	..	..	..
Non-financial Public Enterprises	0	0	0	0	1	1	2	3	4	5	6
Priv. Sector, incl non-guaranteed	0	0	0	0	0	1	1	1	1	1	1
Short-Term Debt	0	0	0	0	0	0	0	0	0	0	0
Memo Items:						*(Thousands of US dollars)*					
Int'l Reserves Excluding Gold	..	..	..	..	..	3,241	5,192	5,653	6,757	8,124	8,287
Gold Holdings (at market price)	..	..	..	..	..	..	..	..	..	..	..
SOCIAL INDICATORS											
Total Fertility Rate	5.7	5.6	5.5	5.4	5.3	5.2	5.1	5.0	4.9	4.8	4.4
Infant Mortality Rate	..	..	..	..	..	..	..	..	..	..	..
Life Expectancy at Birth	62.3	62.8	63.4	64.0	64.6	65.1	65.7	66.3	66.9	67.4	68.0
Urban Population, % of total	40.1	40.2	40.3	40.5	40.6	40.7	40.9	41.2	41.4	41.7	41.9
Food Prod. per capita (1987=100)	96.1	95.2	97.1	92.1	96.8	85.7	88.3	87.9	94.7	92.7	84.4
Labor Force, Agriculture (%)	..	..	..	..	..	..	..	..	..	..	..
Labor Force, Female (%)	..	..	..	..	..	..	..	..	..	..	..
Primary Schl. Enroll. Ratio	..	..	..	..	..	..	..	..	..	..	..
Primary Schl. Enroll. Ratio, Female	..	..	..	..	..	..	..	..	..	..	..
Secondary Schl. Enroll. Ratio	..	..	..	..	..	..	..	..	..	..	..

1981	1982	1983	1984	1985	1986	1987	1988	1989	1990 estimate	Notes	ST. LUCIA
											FOREIGN TRADE (CUSTOMS BASIS)
..	..	..	..	..	..	..	..	..	..	..	Value of Exports, fob
..	..	..	..	..	..	..	..	..	..	..	Nonfuel Primary Products
..	..	..	..	..	..	..	..	..	..	..	Fuels
..	..	..	..	..	..	..	..	..	..	..	Manufactures
..	..	..	..	..	..	..	..	..	..	..	Value of Imports, cif
..	..	..	..	..	..	..	..	..	..	..	Nonfuel Primary Products
..	..	..	..	..	..	..	..	..	..	..	Fuels
..	..	..	..	..	..	..	..	..	..	..	Manufactures

(Index 1987 = 100)

1981	1982	1983	1984	1985	1986	1987	1988	1989	1990 estimate	Notes	
..	..	..	..	..	..	..	..	..	..	..	Terms of Trade
..	..	..	..	..	..	..	..	..	..	..	Export Prices, fob
..	..	..	..	..	..	..	..	..	..	..	Import Prices, cif

(Millions of current US dollars) — **BALANCE OF PAYMENTS**

1981	1982	1983	1984	1985	1986	1987	1988	1989	1990 estimate	Notes	
81.60	..	102.39	..	..	166.20	..	243.50	247.70	..	..	Exports of Goods & Services
41.60	41.60	47.50	47.80	52.00	82.90	77.30	119.10	111.90		..	Merchandise, fob
38.50	44.70	54.20	64.00	69.50	83.30	94.50	124.00	135.50		..	Nonfactor Services
1.50	..	0.69	..	..	0.00	..	0.40	0.30	..	..	Factor Services
141.70	136.30	128.60	149.20	154.90	185.70	209.40	260.90	301.70	..	..	Imports of Goods & Services
117.17	107.35	97.08	107.72	113.63	140.72	161.89	200.98	235.17		..	Merchandise, fob
23.63	27.75	30.02	38.29	37.97	41.59	44.11	55.22	61.83	..	..	Nonfactor Services
0.90	1.20	1.50	3.20	3.30	3.40	3.40	4.70	4.70	..	..	Factor Services
0.50	0.60	0.60	0.60	0.70	0.90	1.30	1.80	2.50	2.50	..	Long-Term Interest
14.90	13.50	13.70	13.70	14.80	14.70	15.00	10.80	8.70	..	..	Private Current Transfers, net
..	..	..	..	0.00	..	..	..	..	..	..	Workers' Remittances
-45.20	-36.50	-12.51	-23.70	-18.60	-4.80	-22.60	-6.60	-45.30	..	..	Curr. A/C Bal before Off. Transf.
5.40	5.70	7.60	10.30	6.10	6.50	9.70	4.00	3.70	..	..	Net Official Transfers
-39.80	-30.80	-4.91	-13.40	-12.50	1.70	-12.90	-2.60	-41.60	..	..	Curr. A/C Bal after Off. Transf.
41.38	32.00	12.20	12.57	18.81	20.83	27.30	22.30	26.10	..	..	Long-Term Capital, net
38.20	26.50	10.00	12.00	17.00	18.50	22.00	16.00	18.00	..	..	Direct Investment
1.80	1.90	1.50	2.30	2.70	4.90	7.30	9.70	8.70	4.00	..	Long-Term Loans
2.40	2.50	2.20	2.90	3.30	5.80	8.20	10.90	11.00	7.10	..	Disbursements
0.60	0.60	0.70	0.60	0.60	0.90	0.90	1.20	2.30	3.10	..	Repayments
1.38	3.60	0.70	-1.73	-0.89	-2.57	-2.00	-3.40	-0.60		..	Other Long-Term Capital
-6.35	1.16	-7.23	2.56	-1.57	-9.33	-5.31	-17.00	20.50	..	..	Other Capital, net
4.77	-2.36	-0.06	-1.73	-4.75	-13.20	-9.09	-2.70	-5.00	-6.30	..	Change in Reserves

(Eastern Caribbean Dollars per US dollar) — **Memo Item:**

1981	1982	1983	1984	1985	1986	1987	1988	1989	1990 estimate	Notes	
2.700	2.700	2.700	2.700	2.700	2.700	2.700	2.700	2.700	2.700	..	Conversion Factor (Annual Avg)

(Millions of US dollars), outstanding at end of year

1981	1982	1983	1984	1985	1986	1987	1988	1989	1990 estimate	Notes	
15	16	18	18	21	29	41	50	56	67	..	**EXTERNAL DEBT (Total)**
15	16	18	18	21	26	36	45	52	60	..	Long-Term Debt (by debtor)
2	2	2	3	3	3	4	5	5	6	..	Central Bank, incl. IMF credit
5	6	6	7	7	10	10	11	13	16	..	Central Government
..	..	..	..	..	..	..	..	..	..	..	Rest of General Government
7	7	7	6	6	6	13	19	23	27	..	Non-financial Public Enterprises
2	2	2	3	5	7	9	10	11	11	..	Priv. Sector, incl non-guaranteed
0	0	0	0	0	3	5	5	4	7	..	Short-Term Debt

(Thousands of US dollars) — **Memo Items:**

1981	1982	1983	1984	1985	1986	1987	1988	1989	1990 estimate	Notes	
7,612	8,211	8,870	12,380	12,650	25,110	30,800	32,650	38,210	44,590	..	Int'l Reserves Excluding Gold
..	..	..	..	..	..	..	..	..	..	..	Gold Holdings (at market price)
											SOCIAL INDICATORS
4.2	4.0	3.9	3.8	3.7	3.6	3.5	..	..	..	..	Total Fertility Rate
..	25.0	24.1	23.3	22.4	21.5	21.0	20.3	19.5	18.8	..	Infant Mortality Rate
68.6	69.2	69.4	69.7	69.9	70.2	70.5	70.8	71.2	71.5	..	Life Expectancy at Birth
42.3	42.7	43.0	43.4	43.8	44.3	44.8	45.4	45.9	46.4	..	Urban Population, % of total
82.8	83.0	88.1	94.0	97.1	113.7	100.0	121.6	110.3	89.2	..	Food Prod. per capita (1987=100)
..	..	..	..	..	..	..	..	..	..	..	Labor Force, Agriculture (%)
..	..	..	..	..	..	..	..	..	..	..	Labor Force, Female (%)
..	..	..	..	..	..	..	..	..	..	..	Primary Schl. Enroll. Ratio
..	..	..	..	..	..	..	..	..	..	..	Primary Schl. Enroll. Ratio, Female
..	..	..	..	..	..	..	..	..	..	..	Secondary Schl. Enroll. Ratio

ST. VINCENT	1970	1971	1972	1973	1974	1975	1976	1977	1978	1979	1980
CURRENT GNP PER CAPITA (US $)	220	230	300	300	320	350	380	390	440	500	570
POPULATION (thousands)	88	89	90	91	92	93	94	95	96	97	98
USE AND ORIGIN OF RESOURCES					*(Millions of current Eastern Caribbean Dollars)*						
Gross National Product (GNP)	36.90	39.60	53.00	59.10	67.60	71.30	83.00	94.30	119.50	135.50	153.30
Net Factor Income from Abroad	0.00	0.00	0.00	0.00	0.00	0.00	0.00	0.00	0.00	-3.80	-2.40
GDP at Market Prices	36.90	39.60	53.00	59.10	67.60	71.30	83.00	94.30	119.50	139.30	155.70
Resource Balance	..	..	..	..	..	..	..	-41.10	-25.20	-51.30	-66.70
Exports of Goods & NF Services	..	..	..	..	..	..	..	44.80	78.80	88.80	104.50
Imports of Goods & NF Services	..	..	..	..	..	..	..	85.90	104.00	140.10	171.20
Domestic Absorption	..	..	..	..	..	..	..	135.30	144.60	190.40	222.40
Private Consumption, etc.	..	..	..	..	..	..	..	85.70	80.70	108.00	121.90
General Gov't Consumption	..	..	..	..	..	..	..	23.10	29.50	33.60	37.70
Gross Domestic Investment	..	..	..	..	..	..	..	26.50	34.40	48.80	62.80
Fixed Investment	..	..	..	..	..	..	..	23.90	32.50	44.40	57.30
Indirect Taxes, net	..	..	..	..	..	..	..	14.70	18.00	18.70	20.20
GDP at factor cost	..	..	..	..	..	..	..	79.60	101.50	120.60	135.50
Agriculture	..	..	..	..	..	..	..	14.70	20.70	19.70	19.80
Industry	..	..	..	..	..	..	..	18.88	24.23	31.20	36.71
Manufacturing	..	..	..	..	..	..	..	6.04	10.53	13.39	14.49
Services, etc.	..	..	..	..	..	..	..	46.02	56.57	69.70	78.99
Gross Domestic Saving	..	..	..	..	..	..	..	-14.50	9.30	-2.30	-3.90
Gross National Saving	..	..	..	..	..	..	..	..	34.41	26.30	26.10
					(Millions of 1987 Eastern Caribbean Dollars)						
Gross National Product	186.80	192.34	242.03	215.16	196.18	181.26	191.28	201.09	222.53	226.57	230.50
GDP at Market Prices	186.83	192.38	242.07	215.20	196.21	181.28	191.31	201.12	222.57	229.37	234.14
Resource Balance	..	..	..	..	..	..	..	-55.76	-21.50	-39.38	-48.78
Exports of Goods & NF Services	..	..	..	..	..	..	..	90.78	143.47	143.67	139.22
Imports of Goods & NF Services	..	..	..	..	..	..	..	146.54	164.97	183.05	188.00
Domestic Absorption	..	..	..	..	..	..	..	256.88	244.06	268.75	282.93
Private Consumption, etc.	..	..	..	..	..	..	..	..	..	..	..
General Gov't Consumption	..	..	..	..	..	..	..	..	..	..	..
Gross Domestic Investment	..	..	..	..	..	..	..	54.96	64.71	77.57	83.99
Fixed Investment	..	..	..	..	..	..	..	..	..	..	..
GDP at factor cost	..	..	..	..	..	..	..	176.57	196.58	204.80	210.81
Agriculture	..	..	..	..	..	..	..	34.49	40.36	34.12	29.33
Industry	..	..	..	..	..	..	..	39.34	43.45	51.49	54.56
Manufacturing	..	..	..	..	..	..	..	12.37	18.54	22.13	23.36
Services, etc.	..	..	..	..	..	..	..	102.84	112.73	119.32	127.45
Memo Items:											
Capacity to Import	..	..	..	..	..	..	..	76.43	124.99	116.02	114.75
Terms of Trade Adjustment	..	..	..	..	..	..	..	-14.36	-18.48	-27.65	-24.46
Gross Domestic Income	..	..	..	..	..	..	..	186.76	204.09	201.72	209.68
Gross National Income	..	..	..	..	..	..	..	186.73	204.05	198.92	206.03
DOMESTIC PRICES/DEFLATORS					*(Index 1987 = 100)*						
Overall (GDP)	19.8	20.6	21.9	27.5	34.5	39.3	43.4	46.9	53.7	60.7	66.5
Domestic Absorption	..	..	..	..	..	..	..	52.7	59.2	70.8	78.6
Agriculture	..	..	..	..	..	..	..	42.6	51.3	57.7	67.5
Industry	..	..	..	..	..	..	..	48.0	55.8	60.6	67.3
Manufacturing	..	..	..	..	..	..	..	48.8	56.8	60.5	62.0
Consumer Price Index	..	..	..	37.4	39.9	44.4	48.9	53.1	61.3	71.9
MANUFACTURING ACTIVITY											
Employment (1987=100)	..	..	..	..	..	..	..	..	..	..	..
Real Earnings per Empl. (1987=100)	..	..	..	..	..	..	..	..	..	..	..
Real Output per Empl. (1987=100)	..	..	..	..	..	..	..	..	..	..	..
Earnings as % of Value Added	..	..	..	..	..	..	..	..	..	..	..
MONETARY HOLDINGS					*(Millions of current Eastern Caribbean Dollars)*						
Money Supply, Broadly Defined	..	..	..	..	..	47.11	55.79	61.31	78.20	96.43	101.10
Money	..	..	..	..	..	13.35	16.07	16.61	22.62	27.72	28.06
Currency Outside Banks	..	..	..	..	..	8.00	9.52	9.50	11.07	12.94	12.85
Demand Deposits	..	..	..	..	..	5.34	6.55	7.10	11.55	14.78	15.21
Quasi-Money	..	..	..	..	..	33.76	39.72	44.71	55.58	68.71	73.03
					(Thousands of current Eastern Caribbean Dollars)						
GOVERNMENT DEFICIT (-) OR SURPLUS	..	..	..	..	..	..	..	..	..	..	-300
Current Revenue	..	..	..	..	..	..	..	..	30,900	39,200	47,000
Current Expenditure	..	..	..	..	..	..	..	..	24,900	37,700	45,000
Current Budget Balance	..	..	..	..	..	..	..	..	6,000	1,500	2,000
Capital Receipts	..	..	..	..	..	..	..	..	..	..	..
Capital Payments	..	..	..	..	..	..	..	..	..	..	2,300

1981	1982	1983	1984	1985	1986	1987	1988	1989	1990 estimate	Notes	ST. VINCENT
680	790	880	960	1,050	1,140	1,330	1,450	1,570	1,720	..	CURRENT GNP PER CAPITA (US $)
99	100	101	102	103	104	105	106	107	..		POPULATION (thousands)

											USE AND ORIGIN OF RESOURCES
			(Millions of current Eastern Caribbean Dollars)								
188.20	217.70	240.30	262.00	294.80	331.50	370.20	407.50	441.90	491.50	..	Gross National Product (GNP)
-4.60	-7.30	-6.20	-8.10	-7.80	-9.40	-13.50	-26.20	-27.50	-24.70	..	Net Factor Income from Abroad
192.80	225.00	246.50	270.10	302.60	340.90	383.70	433.70	469.40	516.20	..	GDP at Market Prices
-52.30	-69.40	-53.20	-36.40	-18.30	-37.80	-79.10	-80.50	..	..	..	Resource Balance
120.20	129.30	159.00	196.30	222.60	225.10	237.70	262.70	..	..	..	Exports of Goods & NFServices
172.50	198.70	212.20	232.70	240.90	262.90	316.80	343.20	..	..	..	Imports of Goods & NFServices
245.20	294.40	299.70	306.50	320.90	378.70	462.80	514.20	..	..	..	Domestic Absorption
136.10	176.90	180.00	172.00	175.60	229.30	..	..	..	..	..	Private Consumption, etc.
45.00	52.80	56.80	59.10	60.10	53.10	..	..	..	..	..	General Gov't Consumption
64.10	64.70	62.90	75.40	85.20	96.30	117.80	104.30	..	..	..	Gross Domestic Investment
58.30	58.50	56.20	70.60	76.10	96.30	..	..	..	..	..	Fixed Investment
24.90	34.40	33.80	37.50	50.30	56.30	65.60	75.20	79.00	83.00	..	Indirect Taxes, net
167.90	190.60	212.70	232.60	252.30	284.60	318.10	358.50	390.40	433.20	..	GDP at factor cost
27.50	31.90	36.60	43.20	49.50	54.80	54.20	65.10	67.90	83.54	..	Agriculture
44.63	49.10	52.45	54.25	59.21	69.72	78.69	90.11	98.95	99.11	..	Industry
18.83	21.18	21.70	29.50	29.30	29.40	32.70	38.20	42.99	37.69	..	Manufacturing
95.77	109.60	123.65	135.15	143.59	160.08	185.21	203.29	223.55	250.55	..	Services, etc.
11.70	-4.70	9.70	39.00	66.90	58.50	38.70	23.80	..	..	..	Gross Domestic Saving
40.85	25.80	47.78	66.00	86.10	84.74	73.26	51.60	..	..	..	Gross National Saving
			(Millions of 1987 Eastern Caribbean Dollars)								
246.29	265.43	282.73	296.89	316.32	329.40	370.20	393.57	419.58	448.90		Gross National Product
253.12	276.93	292.33	309.69	328.48	341.78	383.70	418.81	445.65	471.39		GDP at Market Prices
-35.28	-61.15	-45.46	-27.72	-23.47	-59.65	-79.10	..	..	..	..	Resource Balance
146.92	153.81	185.01	231.42	246.41	231.22	237.70	..	..	..	..	Exports of Goods & NFServices
182.20	214.95	230.48	259.14	269.89	290.87	316.80	..	..	..	..	Imports of Goods & NFServices
288.40	338.08	337.80	337.41	351.96	401.43	462.80	..	..	..	..	Domestic Absorption
..	..	..	..	..	..	..	..	..	..	..	Private Consumption, etc.
..	..	..	..	..	..	..	..	..	..	..	General Gov't Consumption
79.43	77.36	72.17	85.45	95.40	107.02	117.80	..	..	..	..	Gross Domestic Investment
..	..	..	..	..	..	..	..	..	..	..	Fixed Investment
227.76	239.51	253.29	267.45	279.84	299.75	318.10	346.36	370.75	395.81		GDP at factor cost
41.53	43.88	47.40	50.45	54.67	56.78	54.20	67.69	68.56	79.21		Agriculture
55.70	57.95	60.16	62.48	64.54	70.79	78.69	82.98	90.19	88.92		Industry
23.77	25.00	25.73	27.86	28.27	29.91	32.70	34.42	38.64	33.87		Manufacturing
130.49	137.67	145.73	154.52	160.63	172.18	185.21	195.68	211.99	227.67		Services, etc.
											Memo Items:
126.96	139.88	172.70	218.60	249.38	249.05	237.70	..	..	..	..	Capacity to Import
-19.96	-13.93	-12.32	-12.82	2.97	17.83	0.00	..	..	..	..	Terms of Trade Adjustment
233.16	263.00	280.01	296.87	331.45	359.61	383.70	..	..	..	..	Gross Domestic Income
226.33	251.50	270.41	284.07	319.29	347.24	370.20	..	..	..	..	Gross National Income
			(Index 1987 = 100)								DOMESTIC PRICES/DEFLATORS
76.2	81.2	84.3	87.2	92.1	99.7	100.0	103.6	105.3	109.5	..	Overall (GDP)
85.0	87.1	88.7	90.8	91.2	94.3	100.0	..	..	..	..	Domestic Absorption
66.2	72.7	77.2	85.6	90.5	96.5	100.0	96.2	99.0	105.5	..	Agriculture
80.1	84.7	87.2	86.8	91.7	98.5	100.0	108.6	109.7	111.5	..	Industry
79.2	84.7	84.3	105.9	103.6	98.3	100.0	111.0	111.3	111.3	..	Manufacturing
81.1	86.9	91.7	94.1	96.1	97.2	100.0	..	..	..	..	Consumer Price Index
											MANUFACTURING ACTIVITY
..	..	..	..	..	..	..	..	..	..	..	Employment (1987=100)
..	..	..	..	..	..	..	..	..	..	..	Real Earnings per Empl. (1987=100)
..	..	..	..	..	..	..	..	..	..	..	Real Output per Empl. (1987=100)
..	..	..	..	..	..	..	..	..	..	..	Earnings as % of Value Added
			(Millions of current Eastern Caribbean Dollars)								MONETARY HOLDINGS
119.98	135.12	152.05	171.37	196.23	227.13	244.03	246.80	279.52	318.65	..	Money Supply, Broadly Defined
33.28	34.88	40.56	47.79	52.55	63.16	53.16	62.64	69.85	73.33	..	Money
15.35	17.61	20.14	22.53	32.03	41.42	23.27	25.15	32.12	23.96	..	Currency Outside Banks
17.93	17.26	20.42	25.27	20.52	21.74	29.89	37.49	37.73	49.37	..	Demand Deposits
86.70	100.24	111.49	123.58	143.68	163.97	190.87	184.16	209.67	245.33	..	Quasi-Money
			(Thousands of current Eastern CaribbeanDollars)								
1,600	-7,100	-400	-8,300	6,100	4,400	5,200	-5,700	-8,700	-12,800	C	GOVERNMENT DEFICIT (-) OR SURPLUS
58,800	68,200	79,600	83,300	96,800	105,700	113,200	120,200	130,800	142,400	..	Current Revenue
51,200	69,000	73,400	84,300	84,600	90,400	94,500	108,000	120,200	125,600	..	Current Expenditure
7,600	-800	6,200	-1,000	12,200	15,300	18,700	12,200	10,600	16,800	..	Current Budget Balance
..	..	..	..	100	100	200	100	300	200	..	Capital Receipts
6,000	6,300	6,600	7,300	6,200	11,000	13,700	18,000	19,600	29,800	..	Capital Payments

ST. VINCENT	1970	1971	1972	1973	1974	1975	1976	1977	1978	1979	1980
FOREIGN TRADE (CUSTOMS BASIS)				*(Millions of current US dollars)*							
Value of Exports, fob	..	..	..	..	..	..	..	..	..	..	..
Nonfuel Primary Products	..	..	..	..	..	..	..	..	..	..	..
Fuels	..	..	..	..	..	..	..	..	..	..	..
Manufactures	..	..	..	..	..	..	..	..	..	..	..
Value of Imports, cif	..	..	..	..	..	..	..	..	..	..	..
Nonfuel Primary Products	..	..	..	..	..	..	..	..	..	..	..
Fuels	..	..	..	..	..	..	..	..	..	..	..
Manufactures	..	..	..	..	..	..	..	..	..	..	..
					(Index 1987 = 100)						
Terms of Trade	..	..	..	..	..	..	..	..	..	..	..
Export Prices, fob	..	..	..	..	..	..	..	..	..	..	..
Import Prices, cif	..	..	..	..	..	..	..	..	..	..	..
BALANCE OF PAYMENTS				*(Millions of current US dollars)*							
Exports of Goods & Services	..	..	..	..	..	..	..	..	29.40	33.40	39.60
Merchandise, fob	..	..	..	..	..	..	..	..	18.10	19.10	21.10
Nonfactor Services	..	..	..	..	..	..	..	..	11.10	13.70	17.70
Factor Services	..	..	..	..	..	..	..	..	0.20	0.60	0.80
Imports of Goods & Services	..	..	..	..	..	..	..	..	38.70	53.10	65.00
Merchandise, fob	..	..	..	..	..	..	..	..	32.91	42.09	51.91
Nonfactor Services	..	..	..	..	..	..	..	..	5.59	9.81	11.39
Factor Services	..	..	..	..	..	..	..	..	0.20	1.20	1.70
Long-Term Interest	0.00	0.10	0.00	0.10	0.10	0.10	0.10	0.10	0.10	0.20	0.30
Private Current Transfers, net	..	..	..	..	..	..	..	..	9.30	12.00	12.00
Workers' Remittances	..	..	..	..	..	..	..	..	..	..	..
Curr. A/C Bal before Off. Transf.	..	..	..	..	..	..	..	..	0.00	-7.70	-13.40
Net Official Transfers	..	..	..	..	..	..	..	..	2.70	4.10	4.10
Curr. A/C Bal after Off. Transf.	..	..	..	..	..	..	..	..	2.70	-3.60	-9.30
Long-Term Capital, net	..	..	..	..	..	..	..	..	0.60	2.80	5.50
Direct Investment	..	..	..	..	..	..	..	..	-0.50	0.60	1.10
Long-Term Loans	0.20	0.00	0.00	2.10	0.40	0.70	0.60	0.90	1.00	1.20	2.90
Disbursements	0.20	0.00	0.00	2.10	0.40	0.70	0.60	0.90	1.00	1.30	3.00
Repayments	0.00	0.00	0.00	0.00	0.00	0.00	0.00	0.00	0.00	0.10	0.10
Other Long-Term Capital	..	..	..	..	..	..	..	..	0.10	1.00	1.50
Other Capital, net	..	..	..	..	..	..	..	..	-3.15	4.64	1.88
Change in Reserves	..	..	..	..	..	..	..	-0.06	-0.15	-3.84	1.92
Memo Item:				*(Eastern Caribbean Dollars per US dollar)*							
Conversion Factor (Annual Avg)	2.000	1.970	1.920	1.960	2.050	2.170	2.610	2.700	2.700	2.700	2.700
EXTERNAL DEBT (Total)				*(Thousands of US dollars), outstanding at end of year*							
EXTERNAL DEBT (Total)	700	700	800	2,800	3,200	3,500	3,700	4,700	5,700	7,200	10,600
Long-Term Debt (by debtor)	700	700	800	2,800	3,200	3,500	3,700	4,700	5,700	7,200	10,600
Central Bank, incl. IMF credit	0	0	0	0	0	0	0	0	0	0	300
Central Government	700	700	800	800	800	900	1,100	1,500	2,000	2,700	3,200
Rest of General Government	..	..	..	..	..	..	..	..	..	..	..
Non-financial Public Enterprises	0	0	0	2,000	2,400	2,600	2,600	3,200	3,700	4,500	7,100
Priv. Sector, incl non-guaranteed	0	0	0	0	0	0	0	0	0	0	0
Short-Term Debt	0	0	0	0	0	0	0	0	0	0	0
Memo Items:				*(Thousands of US dollars)*							
Int'l Reserves Excluding Gold	..	..	..	..	..	..	4,658	4,810	5,256	8,902	7,270
Gold Holdings (at market price)	..	..	..	..	..	..	..	..	..	..	..
SOCIAL INDICATORS											
Total Fertility Rate	5.4	5.2	5.0	4.8	4.7	4.5	4.3	4.1	4.0	3.8	3.6
Infant Mortality Rate	..	..	..	..	..	..	..	..	..	..	..
Life Expectancy at Birth	63.0	63.4	63.8	64.2	64.7	65.1	65.5	65.9	66.3	66.7	67.1
Urban Population, % of total	15.0	15.1	15.3	15.4	15.6	15.7	15.9	16.1	16.4	16.6	16.8
Food Prod. per capita (1987=100)	83.4	88.9	83.9	84.3	79.9	78.6	84.4	85.0	92.6	91.7	86.8
Labor Force, Agriculture (%)	..	..	..	..	..	..	..	..	..	..	..
Labor Force, Female (%)	..	..	..	..	..	..	..	..	..	..	..
Primary Schl. Enroll. Ratio	..	..	..	..	..	..	..	..	..	..	..
Primary Schl. Enroll. Ratio, Female	..	..	..	..	..	..	..	..	..	..	..
Secondary Schl. Enroll. Ratio	..	..	..	..	..	..	..	..	..	..	..

1981	1982	1983	1984	1985	1986	1987	1988	1989	1990 est.	Notes	
				(Millions of current US dollars)							**FOREIGN TRADE (CUSTOMS BASIS)**
..	..	..	..	..	..	..	..	..	..	..	Value of Exports, fob
..	..	..	..	..	..	..	..	..	..	..	Nonfuel Primary Products
..	..	..	..	..	..	..	..	..	..	..	Fuels
..	..	..	..	..	..	..	..	..	..	..	Manufactures
..	..	..	..	..	..	..	..	..	..	..	Value of Imports, cif
..	..	..	..	..	..	..	..	..	..	..	Nonfuel Primary Products
..	..	..	..	..	..	..	..	..	..	..	Fuels
..	..	..	..	..	..	..	..	..	..	..	Manufactures
				(Index 1987 = 100)							
..	..	..	..	..	..	..	..	..	..	..	Terms of Trade
..	..	..	..	..	..	..	..	..	..	..	Export Prices, fob
..	..	..	..	..	..	..	..	..	..	..	Import Prices, cif
				(Millions of current US dollars)							**BALANCE OF PAYMENTS**
50.10	48.09	59.10	72.70	82.60	95.50	83.63	119.70	113.30	..	..	Exports of Goods & Services
29.80	32.19	41.10	53.60	63.20	68.00	52.30	85.30	74.60	..	..	Merchandise, fob
18.90	15.70	17.80	19.10	19.20	22.50	26.04	29.50	33.50	..	..	Nonfactor Services
1.40	0.20	0.20	0.00	0.20	5.00	5.30	4.90	5.20	..	..	Factor Services
68.30	76.50	81.10	89.20	92.30	104.20	120.41	145.20	153.90	..	..	Imports of Goods & Services
52.91	58.59	63.36	68.94	71.28	78.30	89.47	109.98	114.75	..	..	Merchandise, fob
13.29	15.01	15.24	17.26	17.92	19.30	23.64	24.82	28.35	..	..	Nonfactor Services
2.10	2.90	2.50	3.00	3.10	6.60	7.30	10.40	10.80	..	..	Factor Services
0.40	0.60	0.70	1.20	1.20	1.30	1.30	1.40	1.60	1.70	..	Long-Term Interest
12.50	14.00	16.40	13.00	10.00	13.20	17.80	20.00	21.70	..	..	Private Current Transfers, net
..	..	..	..	..	..	..	..	..	..	..	Workers' Remittances
-5.70	-14.41	-5.60	-3.50	0.30	4.50	-18.97	-5.50	-18.90	..	..	Curr. A/C Bal before Off. Transf.
4.90	3.60	3.00	2.50	3.40	6.80	6.60	6.30	8.70	..	..	Net Official Transfers
-0.80	-10.81	-2.60	-1.00	3.70	11.30	-12.37	0.80	-10.20	..	..	Curr. A/C Bal after Off. Transf.
3.20	3.90	4.70	3.10	4.10	10.90	13.30	15.70	10.60	..	..	Long-Term Capital, net
0.50	1.50	2.10	1.40	1.80	4.40	5.50	9.50	5.70	..	..	Direct Investment
7.50	3.50	3.50	1.40	1.60	3.50	8.80	6.90	6.10	5.30	..	Long-Term Loans
7.80	4.30	4.20	2.10	2.80	4.90	10.20	9.00	8.00	7.50	..	Disbursements
0.30	0.80	0.70	0.70	1.20	1.40	1.40	2.10	1.90	2.20	..	Repayments
-4.80	-1.10	-0.90	0.30	0.70	3.00	-1.00	-0.70	-1.20	..	..	Other Long-Term Capital
-2.26	3.21	-1.80	2.42	-1.42	-10.72	-6.14	-14.20	1.50	..	..	Other Capital, net
-0.14	3.70	-0.30	-4.52	-6.38	-11.48	5.21	-2.30	-1.90	-3.72	..	Change in Reserves
				(Eastern Caribbean Dollars per US dollar)							**Memo Item:**
2.700	2.700	2.700	2.700	2.700	2.700	2.700	2.700	2.700	2.700	..	Conversion Factor (Annual Avg)
				(Thousands of US dollars), outstanding at end of year							
18,800	21,300	25,200	24,900	27,200	31,300	41,800	48,500	53,000	58,900	..	**EXTERNAL DEBT (Total)**
18,800	21,300	24,200	23,700	25,100	28,300	38,800	45,400	51,300	57,200	..	Long-Term Debt (by debtor)
1,800	1,600	1,600	1,000	300	0	0	0	0	..	..	Central Bank, incl. IMF credit
4,100	5,700	6,500	6,100	7,100	10,200	16,300	22,600	29,200	36,500	..	Central Government
											Rest of General Government
12,900	14,000	16,100	16,600	17,700	17,400	21,800	22,200	21,500	20,200	..	Non-financial Public Enterprises
0	0	0	0	0	700	700	600	600	500	..	Priv. Sector, incl non-guaranteed
0	0	1,000	1,200	2,100	3,000	3,000	3,100	1,700	1,700	..	Short-Term Debt
				(Thousands of US dollars)							**Memo Items:**
9,005	4,783	5,697	12,820	13,800	25,832	20,220	21,820	22,770	26,490	..	Int'l Reserves Excluding Gold
..	..	..	..	..	..	..	..	..	..	..	Gold Holdings (at market price)
											SOCIAL INDICATORS
3.5	3.3	3.2	3.1	3.0	2.9	2.8	2.7	2.7	2.6	..	Total Fertility Rate
..	31.0	28.8	26.5	25.6	24.7	25.0	24.0	23.1	22.1	..	Infant Mortality Rate
67.5	67.9	68.2	68.5	68.7	69.0	69.2	69.6	70.0	70.4	..	Life Expectancy at Birth
17.1	17.4	17.8	18.1	18.4	18.8	19.3	19.7	20.2	20.6	..	Urban Population, % of total
86.4	86.7	89.8	108.2	123.0	122.5	100.0	131.2	121.6	123.7	..	Food Prod. per capita (1987=100)
..	..	..	..	..	..	..	..	..	..	..	Labor Force, Agriculture (%)
..	..	..	..	..	..	..	..	..	..	..	Labor Force, Female (%)
..	..	..	..	..	..	..	..	..	..	..	Primary Schl. Enroll. Ratio
..	..	..	..	..	..	..	..	..	..	..	Primary Schl. Enroll. Ratio, Female
..	..	..	..	..	..	..	..	..	..	..	Secondary Schl. Enroll. Ratio

SUDAN	1970	1971	1972	1973	1974	1975	1976	1977	1978	1979	1980
CURRENT GNP PER CAPITA (US $)	140	150	160	150	200	260	330	390	410	400	430
POPULATION (thousands)	14,302	14,732	15,167	15,612	16,072	16,550	17,054	17,567	18,089	18,618	19,152

USE AND ORIGIN OF RESOURCES *(Millions of current Sudanese Pounds)*

	1970	1971	1972	1973	1974	1975	1976	1977	1978	1979	1980
Gross National Product (GNP)	700	757	828	888	1,237	1,496	1,830	2,322	2,865	3,230	3,931
Net Factor Income from Abroad	-1	-4	-4	-9	-9	-15	-18	-18	-18	-24	-41
GDP at Market Prices	701	761	832	897	1,246	1,511	1,848	2,340	2,883	3,254	3,972
Resource Balance	11	-12	-13	2	-48	-172	-184	-148	-231	-217	-463
Exports of Goods & NF Services	116	123	126	151	167	183	223	247	242	244	476
Imports of Goods & NF Services	105	135	139	149	215	356	407	395	473	460	938
Domestic Absorption	691	773	845	895	1,295	1,683	2,032	2,488	3,114	3,470	4,435
Private Consumption, etc.	447	523	623	624	885	1,210	1,374	1,810	2,369	2,632	3,200
General Gov't Consumption	148	160	146	166	181	208	230	278	331	407	636
Gross Domestic Investment	96	90	76	105	229	265	428	399	414	431	598
Fixed Investment	..	..	..	..	..	..	362	312	324	339	458
Indirect Taxes, net	87	96	110	110	131	169	226	256	305	358	342
GDP at factor cost	614	665	722	787	1,116	1,342	1,622	2,084	2,577	2,896	3,630
Agriculture	264	294	324	342	512	580	623	817	1,043	1,089	1,232
Industry	91	92	98	106	153	185	230	271	306	374	492
Manufacturing	49	51	52	55	71	96	109	132	148	202	249
Services, etc.	259	279	300	338	451	577	770	996	1,229	1,433	1,905
Gross Domestic Saving	106	78	63	107	181	93	244	251	183	215	136
Gross National Saving	105	73	59	99	173	78	279	293	249	294	199

(Millions of 1987 Sudanese Pounds)

	1970	1971	1972	1973	1974	1975	1976	1977	1978	1979	1980
Gross National Product	17,853.6	19,011.1	18,617.4	17,032.9	18,802.3	21,128.7	25,057.2	28,894.6	28,471.9	25,485.6	25,657.3
GDP at Market Prices	17,768.4	19,001.3	18,594.6	17,094.8	18,820.3	21,205.4	25,109.8	28,923.9	28,472.7	25,519.8	25,763.1
Resource Balance	527.9	319.1	368.9	561.0	227.3	-213.8	23.8	-102.4	-279.2	-243.1	-284.6
Exports of Goods & NF Services	1,338.7	1,176.3	1,030.0	1,206.8	938.3	875.0	1,262.2	1,108.9	955.1	773.9	1,302.3
Imports of Goods & NF Services	810.8	857.3	661.1	645.8	711.0	1,088.8	1,238.5	1,211.3	1,234.4	1,017.0	1,587.0
Domestic Absorption	17,240.6	18,682.3	18,225.7	16,533.9	18,593.0	21,419.2	25,086.0	29,026.3	28,752.0	25,762.9	26,047.7
Private Consumption, etc.	11,337.1	12,736.5	13,445.2	11,654.9	12,749.0	15,087.9	16,737.2	21,162.0	21,814.0	19,539.8	18,592.2
General Gov't Consumption	3,718.6	3,929.5	3,242.3	3,071.6	2,722.7	2,977.7	3,113.1	3,423.4	3,256.5	3,179.8	4,109.4
Gross Domestic Investment	2,184.8	2,016.2	1,538.3	1,807.4	3,121.3	3,353.6	5,235.6	4,440.9	3,681.4	3,043.2	3,346.0
Fixed Investment	..	..	..	..	..	..	4,428.9	3,473.0	2,881.4	2,393.9	2,563.0
GDP at factor cost	15,558.3	16,610.7	16,138.4	14,993.7	16,851.1	18,839.1	22,045.4	25,766.6	25,458.8	22,717.3	23,546.7
Agriculture	6,678.2	7,348.2	7,238.8	6,521.6	7,724.9	8,140.7	8,458.0	10,096.8	10,294.2	8,543.4	7,990.0
Industry	2,314.8	2,303.9	2,188.9	2,018.0	2,314.0	2,596.1	3,119.8	3,347.2	3,020.5	2,930.4	3,195.2
Manufacturing	1,236.5	1,263.8	1,153.1	1,039.4	1,066.7	1,343.8	1,476.1	1,634.0	1,457.6	1,583.5	1,618.4
Services, etc.	6,565.3	6,958.7	6,710.7	6,454.1	6,812.3	8,102.3	10,467.5	12,322.6	12,144.1	11,243.5	12,361.5

Memo Items:

	1970	1971	1972	1973	1974	1975	1976	1977	1978	1979	1980
Capacity to Import	893.5	783.6	599.1	654.0	551.3	561.1	678.5	758.1	631.9	538.2	804.8
Terms of Trade Adjustment	-445.2	-392.7	-430.8	-552.7	-387.0	-313.9	-583.8	-350.8	-323.2	-235.7	-497.5
Gross Domestic Income	17,323.3	18,608.6	18,163.8	16,542.1	18,433.2	20,891.5	24,526.0	28,573.2	28,149.5	25,284.1	25,265.6
Gross National Income	17,408.4	18,618.4	18,186.6	16,480.1	18,415.3	20,814.7	24,473.4	28,543.8	28,148.6	25,249.9	25,159.7

DOMESTIC PRICES/DEFLATORS *(Index 1987 = 100)*

	1970	1971	1972	1973	1974	1975	1976	1977	1978	1979	1980
Overall (GDP)	3.9	4.0	4.5	5.2	6.6	7.1	7.4	8.1	10.1	12.7	15.4
Domestic Absorption	4.0	4.1	4.6	5.4	7.0	7.9	8.1	8.6	10.8	13.5	17.0
Agriculture	3.9	4.0	4.5	5.2	6.6	7.1	7.4	8.1	10.1	12.8	15.4
Industry	3.9	4.0	4.5	5.2	6.6	7.1	7.4	8.1	10.1	12.7	15.4
Manufacturing	3.9	4.0	4.5	5.2	6.6	7.1	7.4	8.1	10.1	12.7	15.4
Consumer Price Index	3.5	3.5	4.0	4.6	5.8	7.2	7.3	8.5	10.2	13.3	16.7

MANUFACTURING ACTIVITY

	1970	1971	1972	1973	1974	1975	1976	1977	1978	1979	1980
Employment (1987=100)	..	..	..	..	..	..	..	..	..	..	..
Real Earnings per Empl. (1987=100)	..	..	..	..	..	..	..	..	..	..	..
Real Output per Empl. (1987=100)	..	..	..	..	..	..	..	..	..	..	..
Earnings as % of Value Added	31.2	29.2	29.5	..	..	..	..	..	..	..	..

MONETARY HOLDINGS *(Millions of current Sudanese Pounds)*

	1970	1971	1972	1973	1974	1975	1976	1977	1978	1979	1980
Money Supply, Broadly Defined	130	140	166	205	278	330	412	589	751	977	1,606
Money	116	124	144	176	237	281	350	497	634	837	1,097
Currency Outside Banks	67	70	75	93	119	129	153	199	279	380	508
Demand Deposits	49	54	69	83	118	153	197	298	354	456	589
Quasi-Money	14	16	22	30	41	49	62	92	117	141	508

(Millions of current Sudanese Pounds)

	1970	1971	1972	1973	1974	1975	1976	1977	1978	1979	1980
GOVERNMENT DEFICIT (-) OR SURPLUS	..	..	-6.3	-16.2	-9.7	-74.8	-58.9	-168.4	-151.7	-135.9	-129.9
Current Revenue	..	..	155.7	156.6	192.9	257.7	298.7	350.5	403.3	544.2	656.6
Current Expenditure	..	..	138.8	167.1	159.0	241.2	256.0	317.4	396.2	530.9	627.1
Current Budget Balance	..	..	16.9	-10.5	33.9	16.5	42.7	33.1	7.1	13.3	29.5
Capital Receipts	..	..	0.1	0.1	0.1	1.1	0.1	0.2	0.2	3.0	9.2
Capital Payments	..	..	23.3	5.8	43.7	92.4	101.7	201.7	159.0	152.2	168.6

1981	1982	1983	1984	1985	1986	1987	1988	1989	1990 estimate	Notes	SUDAN
460	450	400	350	320	..	..	..	..	..	A	**CURRENT GNP PER CAPITA (US $)**
19,692	20,236	20,774	21,352	21,931	22,527	23,141	23,776	24,434	25,118	..	**POPULATION (thousands)**
											USE AND ORIGIN OF RESOURCES
				(Millions of current Sudanese Pounds)							
4,844	6,777	9,190	11,173	14,632	20,938	27,683	35,925	69,799	100,776	C	Gross National Product (GNP)
-135	-264	-402	-633	-725	-918	-922	-2,706	-3,163	-3,222	..	Net Factor Income from Abroad
4,980	7,040	9,592	11,807	15,357	21,856	28,605	38,631	72,962	103,998	C	GDP at Market Prices
-662	-1,025	-1,384	-893	-1,283	-1,651	-974	-3,316	-5,097	-7,637	..	Resource Balance
471	685	968	1,300	997	787	1,125	2,756	4,727	8,052	..	Exports of Goods & NF Services
1,134	1,709	2,352	2,193	2,280	2,438	2,100	6,072	9,824	15,689	..	Imports of Goods & NF Services
5,642	8,065	10,976	12,700	16,640	23,507	29,579	41,947	78,059	111,635	..	Domestic Absorption
4,134	5,699	8,566	9,925	14,473	17,733	22,941	32,672	60,798	87,244	..	Private Consumption, etc.
793	759	880	1,148	1,474	2,966	3,688	5,399	10,618	14,759	..	General Gov't Consumption
715	1,607	1,530	1,627	693	2,808	2,950	3,876	6,643	9,632	..	Gross Domestic Investment
507	1,275	1,594	1,839	1,769	2,561	2,353	3,488	5,912	8,278	..	Fixed Investment
460	527	734	874	1,019	1,283	1,131	669	2,700	2,212	..	Indirect Taxes, net
4,520	6,513	8,858	10,933	14,338	20,573	27,474	37,962	70,262	101,786	C	GDP at factor cost
1,446	2,567	3,106	3,569	4,202	7,508	9,907	12,799	25,485	31,485	..	Agriculture
659	917	1,334	1,696	2,342	3,422	4,404	5,989	10,633	15,491	..	Industry
359	459	637	868	1,236	1,775	2,371	3,223	5,518	8,980	..	Manufacturing
2,415	3,030	4,418	5,668	7,794	9,643	13,163	19,174	34,144	54,810	..	Services, etc.
52	582	146	734	-590	1,157	1,976	560	1,546	1,995	..	Gross Domestic Saving
87	652	284	614	-324	1,114	1,804	-144	-300	-381	..	Gross National Saving
				(Millions of 1987 Sudanese Pounds)							
25,717.3	28,656.8	29,100.2	27,228.4	25,741.4	26,883.6	27,683.0	27,098.3	29,977.4	27,916.4	C	Gross National Product
26,301.5	29,635.3	30,246.2	28,732.0	26,927.8	27,989.6	28,605.0	28,950.3	31,227.7	28,715.9	C	GDP at Market Prices
-756.6	-1,023.5	-1,057.6	-1,103.2	-745.2	-787.6	-974.3	-641.5	-671.5	-420.9	..	Resource Balance
1,113.3	922.1	1,096.8	1,188.0	977.3	966.8	1,125.3	983.7	981.4	865.9	..	Exports of Goods & NF Services
1,869.9	1,945.6	2,154.3	2,291.3	1,722.5	1,754.4	2,099.6	1,625.2	1,652.9	1,286.7	..	Imports of Goods & NF Services
27,058.1	30,658.8	31,303.8	29,835.2	27,673.0	28,777.2	29,579.3	29,591.9	31,899.2	29,136.8	..	Domestic Absorption
19,493.7	21,389.0	24,183.3	23,148.0	23,934.6	21,603.2	22,941.3	22,918.0	24,746.9	22,921.8	..	Private Consumption, etc.
4,174.0	3,181.0	2,754.2	2,824.6	2,604.0	3,791.2	3,688.0	4,021.8	4,527.1	3,825.1	..	General Gov't Consumption
3,390.4	6,088.7	4,366.3	3,862.6	1,134.3	3,382.8	2,950.0	2,652.1	2,625.2	2,389.9	..	Gross Domestic Investment
2,403.8	4,834.1	4,549.5	4,367.2	2,895.0	3,085.3	2,353.0	2,387.1	2,337.1	2,054.3	..	Fixed Investment
23,874.2	27,420.2	27,835.7	27,011.1	25,433.1	26,349.9	27,474.0	27,621.7	30,071.5	28,106.3	C	GDP at factor cost
7,633.9	10,801.3	9,843.4	9,389.8	8,242.5	9,612.4	9,907.0	9,309.4	10,904.4	8,690.7	..	Agriculture
3,481.9	3,861.3	4,357.7	4,102.1	4,131.6	4,382.9	4,404.0	4,357.7	4,551.4	4,281.9	..	Industry
1,895.5	1,932.6	2,082.1	2,081.3	2,175.6	2,274.1	2,371.0	2,345.4	2,362.6	2,480.5	..	Manufacturing
12,758.4	12,757.6	13,634.6	13,519.2	13,059.0	12,354.5	13,163.0	13,954.6	14,615.7	15,133.7	..	Services, etc.
											Memo Items:
777.4	779.5	886.3	1,358.3	753.5	566.2	1,125.3	737.7	795.3	660.4	..	Capacity to Import
-335.9	-142.6	-210.5	170.3	-223.9	-400.6	0.0	-246.0	-186.1	-205.5	..	Terms of Trade Adjustment
25,965.6	29,492.7	30,035.7	28,902.3	26,703.9	27,589.0	28,605.0	28,704.3	31,041.7	28,510.5	..	Gross Domestic Income
25,381.4	28,514.2	28,889.7	27,398.7	25,517.5	26,482.9	27,683.0	26,852.3	29,791.3	27,710.9	..	Gross National Income
				(Index 1987 = 100)							**DOMESTIC PRICES/DEFLATORS**
18.9	23.8	31.7	41.1	57.0	78.1	100.0	133.4	233.6	362.2	..	Overall (GDP)
20.9	26.3	35.1	42.6	60.1	81.7	100.0	141.8	244.7	383.1	..	Domestic Absorption
18.9	23.8	31.6	38.0	51.0	78.1	100.0	137.5	233.7	362.3	..	Agriculture
18.9	23.8	30.6	41.3	56.7	78.1	100.0	137.4	233.6	361.8	..	Industry
18.9	23.7	30.6	41.7	56.8	78.1	100.0	137.4	233.6	362.0	..	Manufacturing
20.8	26.2	34.2	45.8	66.6	82.9	100.0	164.7	269.2	..	..	Consumer Price Index
											MANUFACTURING ACTIVITY
..	..	..	..	..	..	..	..	..	..	..	Employment (1987=100)
..	..	..	..	..	..	..	..	..	..	..	Real Earnings per Empl. (1987=100)
..	..	..	..	..	..	..	..	..	..	..	Real Output per Empl. (1987=100)
..	..	..	..	..	..	..	..	..	..	..	Earnings as % of Value Added
				(Millions of current Sudanese Pounds)							**MONETARY HOLDINGS**
2,067	2,596	2,697	3,262	5,181	6,841	9,152	11,295	13,661	..	..	Money Supply, Broadly Defined
1,531	2,091	2,336	2,764	4,145	5,849	7,768	11,218	18,899	..	..	Money
630	820	1,022	1,247	1,930	2,760	3,625	5,601	9,240	..	..	Currency Outside Banks
901	1,271	1,314	1,517	2,214	3,089	4,144	5,617	9,658	..	..	Demand Deposits
536	505	361	498	1,036	993	1,383	77	-5,237	..	..	Quasi-Money
				(Millions of current Sudanese Pounds)							
..	-326.4	..	..	..	..	..	..	..	..	C	**GOVERNMENT DEFICIT (-) OR SURPLUS**
..	1,032.8	..	..	..	..	..	..	..	..	..	Current Revenue
..	895.4	..	..	..	..	..	..	..	..	..	Current Expenditure
..	137.4	..	..	..	..	..	..	..	..	..	Current Budget Balance
..	0.7	..	..	..	..	..	..	..	..	..	Capital Receipts
..	464.5	..	..	..	..	..	..	..	..	..	Capital Payments

SUDAN	1970	1971	1972	1973	1974	1975	1976	1977	1978	1979	1980
FOREIGN TRADE (CUSTOMS BASIS)					*(Millions of current US dollars)*						
Value of Exports, fob	291.8	328.7	357.5	412.3	438.8	424.0	572.9	661.0	481.4	581.2	584.2
Nonfuel Primary Products	290.5	325.9	354.7	408.0	421.4	407.6	560.8	651.6	474.5	562.0	573.5
Fuels	1.0	2.6	2.6	3.9	17.1	15.4	9.8	8.6	6.3	16.7	5.6
Manufactures	0.3	0.3	0.2	0.4	0.4	1.0	2.4	0.8	0.6	2.5	5.2
Value of Imports, cif	311.2	355.2	353.5	479.5	655.8	957.0	951.8	982.6	878.0	915.8	1,499.3
Nonfuel Primary Products	75.4	86.0	90.6	128.1	173.5	192.4	140.6	141.1	183.7	184.0	412.3
Fuels	26.1	25.8	25.4	28.7	44.2	35.3	22.1	22.4	12.6	14.8	189.4
Manufactures	209.6	243.3	237.5	322.6	438.1	729.3	789.1	819.1	681.7	717.0	897.6
					(Index 1987 = 100)						
Terms of Trade	179.7	171.8	168.6	206.7	140.5	113.2	148.8	135.5	128.8	122.5	118.0
Export Prices, fob	40.8	46.5	51.7	84.5	92.3	78.1	100.8	99.3	103.1	113.3	129.6
Import Prices, cif	22.7	27.0	30.6	40.9	65.6	69.0	67.8	73.3	80.0	92.5	109.8
BALANCE OF PAYMENTS					*(Millions of current US dollars)*						
Exports of Goods & Services	325.1	352.9	371.1	483.5	448.3	508.1	640.0	713.4	705.0	708.2	825.0
Merchandise, fob	284.3	309.0	324.7	441.1	384.4	411.8	550.7	594.8	551.2	526.9	594.0
Nonfactor Services	37.6	43.3	45.8	41.2	59.4	88.8	89.3	114.8	144.9	172.5	216.0
Factor Services	3.2	0.6	0.5	1.2	4.6	7.5	0.0	3.8	8.9	8.8	15.0
Imports of Goods & Services	367.3	392.7	429.9	459.9	742.4	984.6	1,219.3	1,188.6	1,419.8	1,399.1	1,682.1
Merchandise, fob	268.2	293.6	316.7	334.4	541.7	743.2	1,062.1	985.8	1,187.9	1,115.8	1,339.1
Nonfactor Services	81.0	85.3	90.2	102.9	168.2	179.2	106.0	148.0	171.9	205.5	258.0
Factor Services	18.1	13.8	23.0	22.7	32.5	62.2	51.2	54.8	60.0	77.8	85.0
Long-Term Interest	12.1	12.4	12.0	14.9	20.4	32.1	31.2	39.1	47.8	40.5	48.9
Private Current Transfers, net	-1.2	-0.9	0.7	3.9	2.5	1.5	150.7	172.0	221.0	240.0	209.0
Workers' Remittances	..	..	..	..	..	6.1	150.7	172.0	221.0	240.0	209.0
Curr. A/C Bal before Off. Transf.	-43.4	-40.6	-55.4	29.9	-289.1	-475.0	-428.6	-303.2	-493.8	-450.9	-648.1
Net Official Transfers	1.5	-1.4	6.3	-1.7	18.4	46.7	0.0	11.3	23.0	17.0	84.0
Curr. A/C Bal after Off. Transf.	-41.9	-42.0	-49.1	28.3	-270.7	-428.2	-428.6	-291.9	-470.8	-433.9	-564.1
Long-Term Capital, net	0.5	5.5	14.7	4.9	253.6	32.8	470.9	304.6	310.1	605.4	145.9
Direct Investment	..	-1.1	0.3	..	..	..	0.0	0.0	0.0	0.0	0.0
Long-Term Loans	30.4	15.4	29.6	76.0	420.9	387.7	402.6	313.5	444.9	611.7	657.5
Disbursements	52.6	42.1	66.4	115.7	460.2	465.2	474.6	355.3	498.6	644.0	710.9
Repayments	22.2	26.7	36.8	39.7	39.3	77.5	72.0	41.8	53.7	32.3	53.4
Other Long-Term Capital	-29.9	-8.8	-15.3	-71.1	-167.3	-354.9	68.3	-8.9	-134.8	-6.3	-511.6
Other Capital, net	26.0	50.4	25.4	-8.1	11.9	271.7	-137.7	-10.4	83.4	-161.6	261.4
Change in Reserves	15.4	-13.9	9.0	-25.1	5.2	123.8	95.4	-2.3	77.3	-9.9	156.8
Memo Item:					*(Sudanese Pounds per US dollar)*						
Conversion Factor (Annual Avg)	0.000	0.350	0.350	0.350	0.350	0.350	0.350	0.350	0.380	0.430	0.590
				(Millions of US dollars), outstanding at end of year							
EXTERNAL DEBT (Total)	337.4	343.0	391.1	488.4	983.4	1,383.5	1,809.1	2,624.1	3,159.1	4,067.1	5,163.2
Long-Term Debt (by debtor)	328.9	343.0	391.1	488.4	983.4	1,383.5	1,795.5	2,159.7	2,604.7	3,554.3	4,578.3
Central Bank, incl. IMF credit	30.9	16.5	30.5	35.0	87.7	132.7	138.4	120.8	197.0	293.0	431.1
Central Government	297.5	326.0	356.5	449.8	892.6	1,215.4	1,598.9	1,962.0	2,292.2	3,125.7	3,659.2
Rest of General Government	..	..	..	..	..	..	..	..	..	..	..
Non-financial Public Enterprises	0.5	0.5	4.1	3.6	3.1	32.9	47.1	65.6	103.1	133.7	161.1
Priv. Sector, incl non-guaranteed	0.0	0.0	0.0	0.0	0.0	2.5	11.1	11.3	12.4	1.9	326.9
Short-Term Debt	8.5	0.0	0.0	0.0	0.0	0.0	13.6	464.4	554.4	512.8	584.9
Memo Items:					*(Thousands of US dollars)*						
Int'l Reserves Excluding Gold	21,740	27,900	35,587	61,330	124,272	36,369	23,600	23,149	28,356	67,400	48,726
Gold Holdings (at market price)	..	..	..	..	..	..	..	..	..	..	..
SOCIAL INDICATORS											
Total Fertility Rate	6.7	6.7	6.7	6.7	6.7	6.7	6.7	6.7	6.7	6.6	6.6
Infant Mortality Rate	149.4	147.2	145.0	142.2	139.4	136.6	133.8	131.0	128.4	125.8	123.2
Life Expectancy at Birth	41.9	42.3	42.6	43.1	43.6	44.1	44.6	45.1	45.6	46.2	46.7
Urban Population, % of total	16.4	16.9	17.4	17.9	18.4	18.9	19.1	19.2	19.4	19.5	19.7
Food Prod. per capita (1987=100)	126.6	126.6	127.9	125.9	138.2	140.2	130.3	141.0	133.9	127.6	139.0
Labor Force, Agriculture (%)	77.0	76.3	75.7	75.2	74.6	74.1	73.4	72.8	72.2	71.7	71.1
Labor Force, Female (%)	20.3	20.2	20.2	20.1	20.0	20.0	19.9	19.8	19.8	19.7	19.7
Primary Schl. Enroll. Ratio	38.0	..	..	..	..	47.0	48.0	49.0	50.0	51.0	50.0
Primary Schl. Enroll. Ratio, Female	29.0	..	..	..	..	34.0	36.0	42.0	42.0	43.0	41.0
Secondary Schl. Enroll. Ratio	7.0	..	..	..	..	14.0	14.0	15.0	16.0	16.0	16.0

1981	1982	1983	1984	1985	1986	1987	1988	1989	1990 estimate	Notes	
											FOREIGN TRADE (CUSTOMS BASIS)
				(Millions of current US dollars)							
500.8	561.8	601.1	628.7	369.1	333.3	532.4	509.0	671.7	400.0	..	Value of Exports, fob
474.6	525.2	568.4	595.8	349.8	315.9	504.5	482.4	636.6	379.1	..	Nonfuel Primary Products
21.8	20.5	9.6	27.3	16.1	14.5	23.2	22.1	29.2	17.4	..	Fuels
4.4	16.1	23.1	5.6	3.3	3.0	4.7	4.5	5.9	3.5	..	Manufactures
1,518.7	1,294.0	1,424.0	1,146.7	760.0	960.9	929.0	1,060.4	1,170.0	600.0	..	Value of Imports, cif
336.0	232.3	208.8	253.7	168.1	212.6	205.5	234.6	258.8	132.7	..	Nonfuel Primary Products
289.6	382.5	304.5	218.7	144.9	183.2	177.2	202.2	223.1	114.4	..	Fuels
893.1	679.2	910.6	674.3	446.9	565.1	546.3	623.6	688.0	352.8	..	Manufactures
				(Index 1987 = 100)							
117.1	113.1	125.1	124.1	106.2	89.6	100.0	101.8	106.4	99.8	..	Terms of Trade
125.5	108.1	119.6	116.8	94.8	86.3	100.0	103.0	118.4	133.3	..	Export Prices, fob
107.2	95.6	95.6	94.1	89.3	96.3	100.0	101.2	111.3	133.6	..	Import Prices, cif
				(Millions of current US dollars)							**BALANCE OF PAYMENTS**
763.0	682.0	831.1	952.2	815.4	742.4	711.6	660.9	753.3	653.0	C f	Exports of Goods & Services
538.0	432.0	581.1	722.2	595.4	497.4	481.6	485.9	550.3	443.0	..	Merchandise, fob
210.0	235.0	240.0	220.0	205.0	225.0	220.0	175.0	200.0	210.0	..	Nonfactor Services
15.0	15.0	10.0	10.0	15.0	20.0	10.0	0.0	3.0	..	..	Factor Services
2,029.0	2,322.0	2,131.4	2,118.4	1,887.5	1,934.0	1,674.0	2,105.0	2,269.0	2,058.0	C f	Imports of Goods & Services
1,540.0	1,543.5	1,350.3	1,206.0	980.8	896.8	707.2	1,039.5	1,040.4	879.7	..	Merchandise, fob
259.0	470.5	454.1	434.4	413.7	458.2	434.8	416.5	519.6	411.2	..	Nonfactor Services
230.0	308.0	327.0	478.0	493.0	579.0	532.0	649.0	709.0	767.0	..	Factor Services
96.0	16.4	37.7	23.3	73.1	47.1	21.0	20.3	11.2	8.3	..	Long-Term Interest
305.0	350.0	415.0	395.0	430.0	350.0	250.0	445.0	292.6	188.0	..	Private Current Transfers, net
305.0	350.0	415.0	395.0	430.0	350.0	250.0	445.0	297.0	188.0	..	Workers' Remittances
-961.0	-1,290.0	-885.3	-771.2	-642.1	-841.6	-712.4	-999.1	-1,223.1	-1,217.0	..	Curr. A/C Bal before Off. Transf.
122.0	173.5	462.0	309.0	288.0	412.0	280.0	369.0	299.0	341.0	..	Net Official Transfers
-839.0	-1,116.5	-423.3	-462.2	-354.1	-429.6	-432.4	-630.1	-924.1	-876.0	..	Curr. A/C Bal after Off. Transf.
-105.0	-9.0	-327.0	-390.0	-322.0	-476.4	-331.6	-227.9	-327.9	-330.0	C f	Long-Term Capital, net
0.0	0.0	0.0	0.0	0.0	0.0	0.0	0.0	0.0	..	..	Direct Investment
572.2	881.7	437.2	240.6	84.8	58.7	159.6	323.8	191.1	170.9	..	Long-Term Loans
623.6	980.6	477.2	281.1	100.9	209.9	201.2	381.8	236.5	185.0	..	Disbursements
51.4	98.9	40.0	40.5	16.1	151.2	41.6	58.0	45.4	14.1	..	Repayments
-677.2	-890.7	-764.2	-630.6	-406.8	-535.1	-491.2	-551.7	-519.0	-500.9	..	Other Long-Term Capital
729.9	786.8	844.3	845.2	567.1	919.0	544.0	578.0	1,080.0	1,104.0	C f	Other Capital, net
214.1	338.7	-94.0	7.0	109.0	-13.0	220.0	280.0	172.0	102.0	..	Change in Reserves
											Memo Item:
				(Sudanese Pounds per US dollar)							
0.630	0.900	1.260	1.350	1.490	1.580	1.760	4.170	6.300	12.200	..	Conversion Factor (Annual Avg)
				(Millions of US dollars), outstanding at end of year							
6,191.9	7,216.4	7,600.4	8,612.4	9,127.2	9,869.8	11,562.7	11,961.3	13,894.0	15,383.0	..	**EXTERNAL DEBT (Total)**
5,313.6	6,247.1	6,779.6	7,099.1	7,584.6	8,188.3	9,369.4	9,281.5	9,848.8	10,607.6	..	Long-Term Debt (by debtor)
564.3	578.7	698.0	664.1	738.9	822.8	954.3	905.2	884.0	955.5	..	Central Bank, incl. IMF credit
4,350.2	5,272.6	5,720.2	6,068.4	6,474.5	7,003.9	7,924.4	7,894.6	8,365.3	9,052.9	..	Central Government
..	..	..	..	..	..	..	..	..	..	..	Rest of General Government
153.2	149.9	117.4	122.6	127.2	117.6	118.7	107.7	103.5	103.2	..	Non-financial Public Enterprises
245.9	245.9	244.0	244.0	244.0	244.0	372.0	374.0	496.0	496.0	..	Priv. Sector, incl non-guaranteed
878.3	969.3	820.8	1,513.3	1,542.6	1,681.5	2,193.3	2,679.8	4,045.2	4,775.4	..	Short-Term Debt
											Memo Items:
				(Thousands of US dollars)							
16,970	20,500	16,563	17,200	12,200	58,512	11,714	12,114	15,913	11,414	..	Int'l Reserves Excluding Gold
..	..	..	..	..	..	..	..	..	..	..	Gold Holdings (at market price)
											SOCIAL INDICATORS
6.6	6.6	6.5	6.5	6.5	6.4	6.4	6.4	6.3	6.3	..	Total Fertility Rate
120.6	118.0	116.0	114.0	112.0	110.0	108.0	106.1	104.3	102.4	..	Infant Mortality Rate
47.2	47.8	48.2	48.6	48.9	49.3	49.7	49.9	50.2	50.4	..	Life Expectancy at Birth
19.9	20.1	20.2	20.4	20.6	21.0	21.3	21.5	21.8	22.0	..	Urban Population, % of total
149.5	116.4	119.5	100.5	118.8	106.1	100.0	117.1	90.2	86.1	..	Food Prod. per capita (1987=100)
..	..	..	..	..	..	..	..	..	..	..	Labor Force, Agriculture (%)
19.9	20.1	20.4	20.6	20.8	21.0	21.2	21.5	21.7	21.9	..	Labor Force, Female (%)
50.0	50.0	49.0	49.0	50.0	49.0	..	..	..	..	..	Primary Schl. Enroll. Ratio
41.0	42.0	41.0	40.0	41.0	..	..	..	..	..	..	Primary Schl. Enroll. Ratio, Female
17.0	18.0	19.0	19.0	20.0	20.0	..	..	..	..	..	Secondary Schl. Enroll. Ratio

SURINAME	1970	1971	1972	1973	1974	1975	1976	1977	1978	1979	1980
CURRENT GNP PER CAPITA (US $)	610	640	690	770	980	1,350	1,480	1,770	2,100	2,210	2,420
POPULATION (thousands)	372	378	382	384	381	365	354	362	367	365	356

USE AND ORIGIN OF RESOURCES
(Millions of current Suriname Guilders)

	1970	1971	1972	1973	1974	1975	1976	1977	1978	1979	1980
Gross National Product (GNP)	417.2	452.2	491.3	540.5	693.3	909.0	945.0	1,221.0	1,416.0	1,492.0	1,572.0
Net Factor Income from Abroad	-77.1	-89.1	-83.9	-70.1	-43.9	-21.0	-66.0	-61.0	-55.0	-74.0	-30.0
GDP at Market Prices	494.3	541.3	575.2	610.6	737.2	930.0	1,011.0	1,282.0	1,471.0	1,566.0	1,602.0
Resource Balance	29.1	47.4	33.7	25.0	9.0	-53.0	-2.0	-88.0	-34.0	-5.0	-86.0
Exports of Goods & NFServices	297.9	344.1	350.5	367.0	552.0	588.0	618.0	707.0	814.0	917.0	1,094.0
Imports of Goods & NFServices	268.8	296.7	316.8	342.0	543.0	641.0	620.0	795.0	848.0	922.0	1,180.0
Domestic Absorption	465.2	493.9	541.5	585.6	728.2	983.0	1,013.0	1,370.0	1,505.0	1,571.0	1,688.0
Private Consumption, etc.	..	..	..	..	..	423.0	243.0	609.0	693.0	870.0	929.0
General Gov't Consumption						193.0	251.0	282.0	335.0	343.0	339.0
Gross Domestic Investment	105.5	110.5	138.3	205.2	322.2	367.0	519.0	479.0	477.0	358.0	420.0
Fixed Investment	..	..	..	..	..	..	..	479.0	477.0	358.0	420.0
Indirect Taxes, net	8.1	8.2	9.8	0.1	14.9	195.8	158.6	180.6	235.1	226.3	247.6
GDP at factor cost	486.2	533.1	565.4	610.5	722.3	734.2	852.4	1,101.4	1,235.9	1,339.7	1,354.4
Agriculture	35.6	39.2	41.8	42.9	58.1	58.1	71.6	92.1	91.7	116.0	122.7
Industry	229.0	260.8	265.4	300.1	392.1	299.0	346.0	467.5	489.5	529.3	521.6
Manufacturing	..	..	..	..	..	152.3	181.2	202.9	225.3	239.6	249.1
Services, etc.	221.6	233.1	258.2	267.5	272.1	377.1	434.8	541.8	654.7	694.4	710.1
Gross Domestic Saving	134.6	157.9	172.0	230.2	331.2	314.0	517.0	391.0	443.0	353.0	334.0
Gross National Saving	56.9	69.7	86.4	158.6	284.5	282.4	451.0	333.8	395.0	291.5	315.7

(Millions of 1987 Suriname Guilders)

	1970	1971	1972	1973	1974	1975	1976	1977	1978	1979	1980
Gross National Product	1,714.0	1,775.6	1,823.2	1,879.0	2,089.6	2,425.6	2,368.8	2,610.5	2,845.1	2,602.9	2,502.9
GDP at Market Prices	2,099.6	2,180.9	2,200.4	2,206.9	2,307.6	2,354.5	2,404.4	2,600.3	2,803.7	2,592.1	2,420.3
Resource Balance	..	..	..	..	..	..	..	..	..	..	..
Exports of Goods & NFServices	..	..	..	..	..	..	..	..	..	..	..
Imports of Goods & NFServices	..	..	..	..	..	..	..	..	..	..	..
Domestic Absorption											
Private Consumption, etc.											
General Gov't Consumption											
Gross Domestic Investment											
Fixed Investment											
GDP at factor cost	..	..	..	2,137.4	2,192.9	1,974.3	2,152.9	2,372.9	2,502.3	2,355.0	2,173.3
Agriculture	..	..	..	142.0	169.6	148.9	153.7	178.3	170.3	188.2	189.6
Industry	..	..	..	917.5	845.8	634.4	705.2	773.2	764.6	721.6	623.4
Manufacturing	..	..	..	..	..	328.0	352.6	347.0	369.1	348.4	311.7
Services, etc.	..	..	..	1,077.9	1,177.4	1,191.0	1,294.0	1,421.4	1,567.5	1,445.2	1,360.3

Memo Items:

	1970	1971	1972	1973	1974	1975	1976	1977	1978	1979	1980
Capacity to Import	..	..	..	..	..	..	..	..	..	..	..
Terms of Trade Adjustment	..	..	..	..	..	..	..	..	..	..	..
Gross Domestic Income	..	..	..	..	..	..	..	..	..	..	..
Gross National Income	..	..	..	..	..	..	..	..	..	..	..

DOMESTIC PRICES/DEFLATORS
(Index 1987 = 100)

	1970	1971	1972	1973	1974	1975	1976	1977	1978	1979	1980
Overall (GDP)	23.5	24.8	26.1	27.7	31.9	39.5	42.0	49.3	52.5	60.4	66.2
Domestic Absorption	..	..	..	..	..	..	..	..	..	..	..
Agriculture	..	..	..	30.2	34.2	39.0	46.6	51.7	53.9	61.6	64.7
Industry	..	..	..	32.7	46.4	47.1	49.1	60.5	64.0	73.3	83.7
Manufacturing						46.4	51.4	58.5	61.0	68.8	79.9
Consumer Price Index	15.4	15.4	15.9	18.0	21.0	22.8	25.1	27.5	29.9	34.4	39.2

MANUFACTURING ACTIVITY

	1970	1971	1972	1973	1974	1975	1976	1977	1978	1979	1980
Employment (1987=100)	..	..	..	..	..	..	..	..	..	..	..
Real Earnings per Empl. (1987=100)	..	..	..	..	..	..	..	..	..	..	..
Real Output per Empl. (1987=100)	..	..	..	..	..	..	..	..	..	..	..
Earnings as % of Value Added	..	..	..	..	..	..	..	..	..	..	..

MONETARY HOLDINGS
(Millions of current Suriname Guilders)

	1970	1971	1972	1973	1974	1975	1976	1977	1978	1979	1980
Money Supply, Broadly Defined	145.3	165.0	186.5	228.7	245.0	290.9	397.3	472.0	548.0	612.1	659.5
Money	86.1	98.2	103.3	133.0	140.0	168.7	198.2	219.6	246.0	273.4	294.2
Currency Outside Banks	48.6	53.2	58.2	73.5	78.8	88.6	109.6	125.3	145.1	156.3	177.8
Demand Deposits	37.5	45.0	45.0	59.6	61.2	80.1	88.6	94.3	101.0	117.1	116.3
Quasi-Money	59.3	66.9	83.3	95.6	105.0	122.3	199.0	252.3	301.9	338.6	365.3

GOVERNMENT DEFICIT (-) OR SURPLUS
(Millions of current Suriname Guilders)

	1970	1971	1972	1973	1974	1975	1976	1977	1978	1979	1980
GOVERNMENT DEFICIT (-) OR SURPLUS	..	-2.05	-1.76	-19.12	-8.80	-2.15	-21.85	..	..	..	..
Current Revenue	..	164.65	195.52	199.72	228.45	318.13	402.95	..	..	..	..
Current Expenditure	..	146.11	152.85	175.40	193.94	231.97	279.70	..	..	..	..
Current Budget Balance	..	18.54	42.67	24.32	34.51	86.16	123.25	..	..	..	..
Capital Receipts	..	0.41	0.41	0.20	..	..	0.15	..	..	..	..
Capital Payments	..	21.00	44.84	43.64	43.31	88.31	145.25				

1981	1982	1983	1984	1985	1986	1987	1988	1989	1990 estimate	Notes	SURINAME
2,950	2,840	2,580	2,500	2,450	2,380	2,260	2,720	3,050	3,050	A	**CURRENT GNP PER CAPITA (US $)**
356	366	376	387	398	409	418	428	437	447	..	**POPULATION (thousands)**
				(Millions of current Suriname Guilders)							**USE AND ORIGIN OF RESOURCES**
1,821.0	1,862.0	1,766.0	1,699.0	1,683.0	1,789.0	1,913.0	2,276.1	2,504.9	2,564.5	..	Gross National Product (GNP)
23.0	13.0	-20.0	-4.0	-12.0	-4.0	-10.0	-15.8	-11.2	-11.3	..	Net Factor Income from Abroad
1,798.0	1,849.0	1,786.0	1,703.0	1,695.0	1,793.0	1,923.0	2,291.9	2,516.1	2,575.8	..	GDP at Market Prices
-248.0	-282.0	-281.0	-131.0	-75.0	-34.0	-28.0	51.0	..	..	..	Resource Balance
1,044.0	949.0	803.0	764.0	679.0	654.0	658.0	847.0				Exports of Goods & NFServices
1,292.0	1,231.0	1,084.0	895.0	754.0	688.0	686.0	796.0				Imports of Goods & NFServices
2,046.0	2,131.0	2,067.0	1,834.0	1,770.0	1,827.0	1,951.0	2,240.9				Domestic Absorption
1,060.0	1,104.0	1,179.0	1,072.0	1,029.0	997.0	1,077.0	1,287.9				Private Consumption, etc.
431.0	520.0	613.0	558.0	604.0	736.0	760.0	831.0				General Gov't Consumption
555.0	507.0	275.0	204.0	137.0	94.0	114.0	122.0				Gross Domestic Investment
555.0	507.0	275.0	204.0	137.0	94.0	114.0	122.0				Fixed Investment
269.6	245.1	226.4	172.3	136.7	149.0	139.2	182.1	..	..	..	Indirect Taxes, net
1,528.4	1,603.9	1,559.6	1,530.7	1,558.3	1,644.0	1,783.8	2,109.8	..	..	..	GDP at factor cost
140.1	144.3	126.9	134.5	142.7	164.2	206.1	224.0	..	..	..	Agriculture
575.0	538.5	483.6	484.6	464.8	460.9	450.7	525.2	..	..	..	Industry
271.2	225.8	195.3	197.4	206.6	226.6	210.6	305.4	..	..	..	Manufacturing
813.3	921.1	949.1	911.6	950.8	1,018.9	1,127.0	1,360.6	..	..	..	Services, etc.
307.0	225.0	-6.0	73.0	62.0	60.0	86.0	173.0	..	..	..	Gross Domestic Saving
336.6	233.3	-40.3	55.8	42.9	52.6	75.3	149.0	..	..	..	Gross National Saving
				(Millions of 1987 Suriname Guilders)							
2,758.8	2,580.6	2,315.0	2,225.8	2,206.6	2,157.6	1,913.0	2,090.1	2,159.9	2,105.8	..	Gross National Product
2,584.7	2,431.7	2,332.5	2,247.1	2,231.7	2,175.1	1,923.0	2,101.3	2,166.0	2,111.7	..	GDP at Market Prices
..	..	..	..	..	..	..	..	..	..	..	Resource Balance
..	..	..	..	..	..	..	..	..	..	..	Exports of Goods & NFServices
..	..	..	..	..	..	..	..	..	..	..	Imports of Goods & NFServices
..	..	..	..	..	..	..	..	..	..	..	Domestic Absorption
..	..	..	..	..	..	..	..	..	..	..	Private Consumption, etc.
..	..	..	..	..	..	..	..	..	..	..	General Gov't Consumption
..	..	..	..	..	..	..	..	..	..	..	Gross Domestic Investment
..	..	..	..	..	..	..	..	..	..	..	Fixed Investment
2,333.7	2,240.3	2,060.1	1,988.4	1,991.3	1,965.6	1,783.8	1,989.1	..	..	..	GDP at factor cost
214.6	208.1	189.9	197.1	199.9	196.8	206.1	208.6	..	..	..	Agriculture
649.0	552.3	492.9	510.1	517.4	545.4	450.7	472.9	..	..	..	Industry
320.5	267.8	242.3	234.6	249.8	258.9	210.6	245.1	..	..	..	Manufacturing
1,470.1	1,479.9	1,377.3	1,281.1	1,274.0	1,223.4	1,127.0	1,307.6	..	..	..	Services, etc.
											Memo Items:
..	..	..	..	..	..	..	..	..	..	..	Capacity to Import
..	..	..	..	..	..	..	..	..	..	..	Terms of Trade Adjustment
..	..	..	..	..	..	..	..	..	..	..	Gross Domestic Income
..	..	..	..	..	..	..	..	..	..	..	Gross National Income
				(Index 1987 = 100)							**DOMESTIC PRICES/DEFLATORS**
69.6	76.0	76.6	75.8	76.0	82.4	100.0	109.1	116.2	122.0	..	Overall (GDP)
..	..	..	..	..	..	..	..	..	..		Domestic Absorption
65.3	69.3	66.8	68.2	71.4	83.4	100.0	107.4	..	..	..	Agriculture
88.6	97.5	98.1	95.0	89.8	84.5	100.0	111.1	..	..	..	Industry
84.6	84.3	80.6	84.1	82.7	87.5	100.0	124.6	..	..	..	Manufacturing
42.8	45.9	47.9	49.7	55.3	65.2	100.0		..	..	..	Consumer Price Index
											MANUFACTURING ACTIVITY
..	..	..	..	..	..	..	..	..	..	G	Employment (1987=100)
..	..	..	..	..	..	..	..	..	..	G	Real Earnings per Empl. (1987=100)
..	..	..	..	..	..	..	..	..	..	G	Real Output per Empl. (1987=100)
..	..	..	..	..	..	..	..	..	..		Earnings as % of Value Added
				(Millions of current Suriname Guilders)							**MONETARY HOLDINGS**
788.4	875.7	971.3	1,168.5	1,543.8	1,934.3	2,475.0	3,060.5	3,617.6	3,771.7	..	Money Supply, Broadly Defined
358.0	421.2	455.0	577.3	880.2	1,228.8	1,561.9	1,945.4	2,164.6	2,250.8	..	Money
197.0	268.0	264.9	305.2	405.4	451.3	637.9	788.3	874.2	958.2		Currency Outside Banks
161.0	153.2	190.1	272.1	474.8	777.5	924.0	1,157.1	1,290.4	1,292.5		Demand Deposits
430.4	454.5	516.3	591.2	663.6	705.5	913.1	1,115.1	1,453.0	1,520.9	..	Quasi-Money
				(Millions of current Suriname Guilders)							**GOVERNMENT DEFICIT (-) OR SURPLUS**
..	..	..	-263.19	-349.18	-445.74	..	..	..	..	..	Current Revenue
..	..	..	518.87	491.62	497.57	..	..	..	..	..	Current Expenditure
..	..	..	697.46	754.00	869.00	..	..	..	..	..	Current Budget Balance
..	..	..	-178.59	-262.38	-371.43	..	..	..	..	..	Capital Receipts
..	..	..	0.11	0.16	0.09	..	..	..	..	..	Capital Payments
..	..	..	84.71	86.96	74.40	..	..	..	..	..	

SURINAME	1970	1971	1972	1973	1974	1975	1976	1977	1978	1979	1980
FOREIGN TRADE (CUSTOMS BASIS)					*(Millions of current US dollars)*						
Value of Exports, fob	134.06	155.85	169.52	179.16	239.90	255.40	274.60	309.69	368.80	475.60	575.51
Nonfuel Primary Products	131.36	152.58	..	101.08	135.35	125.64	148.82	299.79	357.01	464.14	561.44
Fuels	0.17	0.00	..	0.05	0.07	0.17	0.05	1.74	2.07	0.05	0.00
Manufactures	2.53	3.27	93.44	78.03	104.48	129.59	125.73	8.16	9.72	11.41	14.07
Value of Imports, cif	115.28	125.77	143.63	157.42	229.98	252.25	281.03	397.70	405.88	329.99	446.03
Nonfuel Primary Products	26.18	25.74	24.64	36.03	43.41	29.81	34.59	65.73	67.08	47.58	49.25
Fuels	14.25	16.95	17.76	10.77	45.68	94.57	76.35	99.73	101.78	98.13	159.09
Manufactures	74.85	83.07	101.22	110.62	140.89	127.86	170.09	232.24	237.02	184.28	237.69
Terms of Trade					*(Index 1987 = 100)*						
Export Prices, fob	..	..	..	..	..	..	..	..	..	..	..
Import Prices, cif	..	..	..	..	..	..	..	..	..	..	..
BALANCE OF PAYMENTS					*(Millions of current US dollars)*						
Exports of Goods & Services	160.70	185.15	206.50	212.32	316.29	338.99	370.37	403.58	481.79	527.68	638.60
Merchandise, fob	136.60	157.97	175.78	180.01	269.63	277.19	303.75	346.16	411.15	444.09	514.40
Nonfactor Services	19.70	23.37	25.08	25.99	34.88	48.20	52.99	50.20	62.30	69.47	98.60
Factor Services	4.40	3.81	5.65	6.32	11.79	13.60	13.62	7.23	8.35	14.12	25.60
Imports of Goods & Services	185.60	205.51	223.87	240.69	336.86	380.76	396.35	486.67	513.67	571.71	703.42
Merchandise, fob	104.10	114.04	128.55	144.01	211.30	242.10	259.19	324.09	343.53	369.86	454.01
Nonfactor Services	36.90	41.72	47.99	54.84	92.48	112.92	88.21	115.07	124.43	142.47	203.81
Factor Services	44.60	49.75	47.34	41.84	33.07	25.74	48.95	47.51	45.71	59.38	45.60
Long-Term Interest	..	..	..	..	..	..	..	..	..	..	..
Private Current Transfers, net	-0.30	0.50	-0.98	-0.83	-1.56	-5.95	0.00	2.13	3.92	7.00	6.55
Workers' Remittances	..	..	..	..	..	..	..	0.06	..	0.34	0.78
Curr. A/C Bal before Off. Transf.	-25.20	-19.86	-18.35	-29.21	-22.13	-47.72	-25.98	-80.95	-27.96	-37.03	-58.26
Net Official Transfers	12.70	12.84	12.81	13.59	22.85	178.84	89.24	77.54	55.46	80.73	73.73
Curr. A/C Bal after Off. Transf.	-12.50	-7.02	-5.54	-15.62	0.72	131.13	63.27	-3.42	27.51	43.70	15.46
Long-Term Capital, net	6.70	-4.41	16.07	20.62	5.29	-97.01	-54.61	-13.28	14.45	-16.36	10.20
Direct Investment	-5.00	-6.82	-1.85	14.19	-0.36	..	..	-12.66	-7.56	-15.35	10.14
Long-Term Loans	..	..	..	..	..	..	..	..	..	..	..
Disbursements	..	..	..	..	..	..	..	..	..	..	..
Repayments	..	..	..	..	..	..	..	..	..	..	..
Other Long-Term Capital	11.70	2.41	17.91	6.44	5.65	-97.01	-54.61	-0.62	22.02	-1.01	0.06
Other Capital, net	13.50	12.74	-1.63	12.64	-0.84	12.75	18.82	-1.12	-0.26	-0.62	0.27
Change in Reserves	-7.70	-1.30	-8.90	-17.64	-5.17	-46.87	-27.48	17.82	-41.70	-26.72	-25.93
Memo Item:					*(Suriname Guilders per US dollar)*						
Conversion Factor (Annual Avg)	1.890	1.880	1.780	1.780	1.780	1.780	1.780	1.780	1.780	1.780	1.780
EXTERNAL DEBT (Total)					*(Millions of US dollars), outstanding at end of year*						
Long-Term Debt (by debtor)	..	..	..	..	..	..	..	..	..	..	..
Central Bank, incl. IMF credit	..	..	..	..	..	..	..	..	..	..	..
Central Government	..	..	..	..	..	..	..	..	..	..	..
Rest of General Government	..	..	..	..	..	..	..	..	..	..	..
Non-financial Public Enterprises	..	..	..	..	..	..	..	..	..	..	..
Priv. Sector, incl non-guaranteed	..	..	..	..	..	..	..	..	..	..	..
Short-Term Debt	..	..	..	..	..	..	..	..	..	..	..
Memo Items:					*(Thousands of US dollars)*						
Int'l Reserves Excluding Gold	27,828	33,094	37,591	56,436	67,547	91,406	110,218	94,025	132,423	169,526	189,251
Gold Holdings (at market price)	9,250	10,800	16,065	16,569	27,528	20,701	19,890	24,347	12,222	27,688	31,879
SOCIAL INDICATORS											
Total Fertility Rate	5.6	5.4	5.3	5.2	5.0	4.9	4.8	4.6	4.5	4.4	4.3
Infant Mortality Rate	53.2	52.6	52.0	51.4	50.8	50.2	49.6	49.0	48.2	47.4	46.6
Life Expectancy at Birth	63.8	63.9	64.0	64.1	64.2	64.3	64.4	64.5	64.6	64.7	64.8
Urban Population, % of total	45.9	45.7	45.5	45.2	45.0	44.8	44.8	44.8	44.8	44.8	44.8
Food Prod. per capita (1987=100)	62.8	61.5	58.0	68.4	69.6	74.5	73.4	77.5	84.7	93.3	99.2
Labor Force, Agriculture (%)	24.7	24.3	23.8	23.3	22.8	22.3	21.8	21.3	20.8	20.4	19.9
Labor Force, Female (%)	25.2	25.3	25.5	25.7	25.8	26.0	26.4	26.8	27.2	27.6	28.0
Primary Schl. Enroll. Ratio	126.0	..	..	..	..	108.0	106.0	103.0	120.0	115.0	125.0
Primary Schl. Enroll. Ratio, Female	122.0	..	..	..	..	105.0	102.0	100.0	115.0	..	..
Secondary Schl. Enroll. Ratio	41.0	..	..	..	..	46.0	49.0	50.0	50.0	51.0	35.0

1981	1982	1983	1984	1985	1986	1987	1988	1989	1990 estimate	Notes	SURINAME
											FOREIGN TRADE (CUSTOMS BASIS)
				(Millions of current US dollars)							
519.76	404.55	401.05	355.74	328.85	240.90	300.95	358.40	549.20	465.90	..	Value of Exports, fob
503.15	386.04	384.50	344.37	318.34	233.20	291.33	346.95	531.65	451.01	..	Nonfuel Primary Products
2.91	2.63	2.93	1.99	1.84	1.35	1.69	2.01	3.08	2.61	..	Fuels
13.70	15.88	13.62	9.37	8.67	6.35	7.93	9.44	14.47	12.28	..	Manufactures
451.85	412.14	329.97	345.83	298.54	243.70	294.34	239.40	330.90	374.40	..	Value of Imports, cif
57.91	52.80	54.54	57.16	49.34	40.28	48.65	39.57	54.69	61.88	..	Nonfuel Primary Products
145.31	124.92	82.74	86.72	74.86	61.11	73.81	60.03	82.97	93.88	..	Fuels
248.63	234.42	192.69	201.95	174.34	142.31	171.88	139.80	193.23	218.64	..	Manufactures
				(Index 1987 = 100)							
..	..	..	..	..	..	..	..	..	..	..	Terms of Trade
..	..	..	..	..	..	..	..	..	..	..	Export Prices, fob
..	..	..	..	..	..	..	..	..	..	..	Import Prices, cif
				(Millions of current US dollars)							**BALANCE OF PAYMENTS**
601.96	545.32	450.98	434.34	383.08	364.37	420.90	382.41	573.84	488.85	f	Exports of Goods & Services
473.78	428.63	366.78	374.12	336.08	337.09	338.77	358.37	549.19	465.88		Merchandise, fob
91.93	80.90	67.68	55.24	44.26	25.66	80.90	22.69	23.70	20.73		Nonfactor Services
36.25	35.80	16.53	4.99	2.75	1.62	1.23	1.34	0.95	2.24		Factor Services
728.12	696.13	606.33	508.24	391.99	385.71	348.07	325.55	428.85	480.06		Imports of Goods & Services
506.44	460.34	401.63	391.60	309.52	304.09	274.29	239.44	330.87	374.40		Merchandise, fob
197.09	206.50	176.92	113.05	79.22	76.97	67.96	76.30	90.70	94.90		Nonfactor Services
24.59	29.30	27.79	3.59	3.25	4.65	5.83	9.80	7.28	10.76		Factor Services
..	..	..	..	..	..	..	..	..	..		Long-Term Interest
3.70	-2.63	-8.01	-7.39	-3.98	-1.90	-0.39	-4.59	-5.60	-7.51		Private Current Transfers, net
0.22	..										Workers' Remittances
-122.47	-153.45	-163.36	-81.29	-12.89	-23.25	72.44	52.27	139.38	1.29		Curr. A/C Bal before Off. Transf.
94.68	96.86	2.52	2.58	1.29	0.90	2.35	10.25	23.47	31.71		Net Official Transfers
-27.79	-56.58	-160.84	-78.71	-11.60	-22.35	74.79	62.52	162.86	33.00		Curr. A/C Bal after Off. Transf.
36.08	10.98	50.36	-10.25	13.67	-15.07	-59.22	-90.42	-151.93	-35.69		Long-Term Capital, net
34.57	-6.22	45.66	-39.72	11.93	-33.84	-72.61	-95.80	-167.90	-43.03		Direct Investment
..	..	..	..	..	..	..	..	..	..		Long-Term Loans
..	..	..	..	..	..	..	..	..	..		Disbursements
..	..	..	..	..	..	..	..	..	..		Repayments
1.51	17.20	4.71	29.47	1.74	18.77	13.39	5.38	15.97	7.34		Other Long-Term Capital
4.85	2.80	1.39	36.45	-10.56	-2.58	-24.95	22.75	-11.04	12.94		Other Capital, net
-13.14	42.80	109.09	52.52	8.48	40.00	9.38	5.15	0.11	-10.25		Change in Reserves
				(Suriname Guilders per US dollar)							**Memo Item:**
1.780	1.780	1.780	1.780	1.780	1.780	1.780	1.780	1.890	1.890	..	Conversion Factor (Annual Avg)
				(Millions of US dollars), outstanding at end of year							**EXTERNAL DEBT (Total)**
..	..	..	..	..	..	..	..	..	..	..	Long-Term Debt (by debtor)
..	..	..	..	..	..	..	..	..	..	..	Central Bank, incl. IMF credit
..	..	..	..	..	..	..	..	..	..	..	Central Government
..	..	..	..	..	..	..	..	..	..	..	Rest of General Government
..	..	..	..	..	..	..	..	..	..	..	Non-financial Public Enterprises
..	..	..	..	..	..	..	..	..	..	..	Priv. Sector, incl non-guaranteed
..	..	..	..	..	..	..	..	..	..	..	Short-Term Debt
				(Thousands of US dollars)							**Memo Items:**
207,089	175,757	59,148	24,870	23,420	20,890	15,097	12,560	9,246	21,068	..	Int'l Reserves Excluding Gold
21,496	24,708	20,631	16,672	17,683	21,139	26,179	22,185	21,685	20,820	..	Gold Holdings (at market price)
											SOCIAL INDICATORS
4.2	4.1	4.0	3.9	3.9	3.8	3.7	3.6	3.5	3.4	..	Total Fertility Rate
45.8	45.0	44.4	43.8	43.2	42.6	42.0	40.9	39.8	38.7	..	Infant Mortality Rate
64.9	65.0	65.3	65.7	66.0	66.4	66.7	67.1	67.5	67.9	..	Life Expectancy at Birth
45.0	45.2	45.3	45.5	45.7	46.1	46.4	46.8	47.1	47.5	..	Urban Population, % of total
107.7	111.6	101.9	111.0	113.4	105.6	100.0	97.0	96.7	97.4	..	Food Prod. per capita (1987=100)
..											Labor Force, Agriculture (%)
28.1	28.3	28.5	28.7	28.8	29.0	29.2	29.3	29.4	29.6	f	Labor Force, Female (%)
..	..	132.0	136.0		129.0		124.0		..	..	Primary Schl. Enroll. Ratio
			133.0		125.0		124.0		..	..	Primary Schl. Enroll. Ratio, Female
..	..	44.0	51.0		53.0		..		..	..	Secondary Schl. Enroll. Ratio

SWAZILAND	1970	1971	1972	1973	1974	1975	1976	1977	1978	1979	1980
CURRENT GNP PER CAPITA (US $)	270	320	330	370	460	590	580	590	600	720	820
POPULATION (thousands)	420	431	443	455	468	482	497	513	529	546	564

USE AND ORIGIN OF RESOURCES — *(Millions of current Swaziland Emalangeni)*

	1970	1971	1972	1973	1974	1975	1976	1977	1978	1979	1980
Gross National Product (GNP)	79.4	100.1	108.9	127.7	162.7	211.6	232.4	260.7	280.6	353.9	416.3
Net Factor Income from Abroad	-10.5	-9.0	-11.6	-20.9	-14.7	-1.8	-2.9	-2.8	-42.7	-18.9	-5.8
GDP at Market Prices	89.9	109.1	120.5	148.6	177.4	213.4	235.3	263.5	323.3	372.8	422.1
Resource Balance	5.3	12.6	9.5	21.9	40.0	34.3	19.1	-8.6	-70.3	-123.5	-140.2
Exports of Goods & NF Services	59.9	66.2	75.6	108.4	146.4	155.5	179.4	172.9	186.4	221.2	325.7
Imports of Goods & NF Services	54.6	53.6	66.1	86.5	106.4	121.2	160.3	181.5	256.7	344.7	465.9
Domestic Absorption	84.6	96.5	111.0	126.7	137.4	179.1	216.2	272.1	393.6	496.3	562.3
Private Consumption, etc.	48.7	57.0	59.9	64.4	53.5	105.5	104.6	146.8	181.5	273.3	286.8
General Gov't Consumption	18.6	17.8	24.2	27.6	36.1	35.6	42.0	54.2	70.2	74.9	103.9
Gross Domestic Investment	17.3	21.7	26.9	34.7	47.8	38.0	69.6	71.1	141.9	148.1	171.6
Fixed Investment	..	..	..	..	..	..	..	68.1	144.9	142.1	147.8
Indirect Taxes, net	17.3	20.9	24.6	32.0	41.0	52.2	49.0	49.3	62.4	73.5	59.6
GDP at factor cost	72.6	88.2	95.9	116.6	136.4	161.2	186.3	214.2	260.9	299.3	362.5
Agriculture	24.1	32.7	31.7	41.6	47.7	53.5	55.7	64.0	78.0	89.5	90.2
Industry	19.2	21.8	26.7	30.4	35.3	41.0	46.5	53.5	65.1	74.7	114.3
Manufacturing	..	..	..	..	..	..	..	..	..	..	79.6
Services, etc.	29.3	33.7	37.5	44.6	53.4	66.7	84.1	96.7	117.8	135.1	158.0
Gross Domestic Saving	22.6	34.3	36.4	56.6	87.8	72.3	88.7	62.5	71.6	24.6	31.4
Gross National Saving	..	..	..	..	73.4	71.1	85.9	59.7	27.3	4.3	23.7

(Millions of 1980 Swaziland Emalangeni)

	1970	1971	1972	1973	1974	1975	1976	1977	1978	1979	1980
Gross National Product	250.50	289.40	299.60	315.30	350.80	393.10	382.40	388.50	387.30	421.30	416.30
GDP at Market Prices	283.60	318.10	335.70	373.40	385.70	396.70	387.60	392.80	444.60	443.30	422.10
Resource Balance	-22.40	10.10	-9.60	21.10	59.40	43.20	2.90	-20.70	-83.90	-133.50	-140.20
Exports of Goods & NF Services	203.90	208.30	209.30	255.20	294.60	271.30	277.30	241.10	240.40	245.50	325.70
Imports of Goods & NF Services	226.30	198.20	218.90	234.10	235.20	228.10	274.40	261.80	324.30	379.00	465.90
Domestic Absorption	306.00	308.00	345.30	352.30	326.30	353.50	384.70	413.50	528.50	576.80	562.30
Private Consumption, etc.	177.90	176.50	183.30	173.20	116.90	197.10	173.50	202.10	209.20	294.30	286.80
General Gov't Consumption	60.40	53.40	69.40	71.50	80.90	68.60	70.60	82.10	95.70	93.20	103.90
Gross Domestic Investment	67.70	78.10	92.60	107.60	128.50	87.80	140.60	129.30	223.60	189.30	171.60
Fixed Investment	..	..	..	..	..	..	..	..	..	..	..
GDP at factor cost	228.80	257.10	267.10	293.00	296.50	299.60	306.90	318.70	353.50	354.20	362.50
Agriculture	56.02	70.53	66.83	73.33	72.93	70.13	68.33	74.83	86.93	83.33	90.23
Industry	75.68	79.28	88.68	94.78	96.48	92.08	93.58	97.08	116.37	114.77	114.27
Manufacturing	..	49.30	54.50	58.30	58.30	57.90	61.60	65.30	69.80	71.60	79.60
Services, etc.	97.10	107.29	111.59	124.89	127.09	137.39	144.99	146.79	150.19	156.09	157.99

Memo Items:

	1970	1971	1972	1973	1974	1975	1976	1977	1978	1979	1980
Capacity to Import	248.27	244.79	250.36	293.37	323.62	292.65	307.10	249.39	235.49	243.21	325.70
Terms of Trade Adjustment	44.37	36.49	41.06	38.17	29.02	21.35	29.80	8.29	-4.91	-2.29	0.00
Gross Domestic Income	327.97	354.60	376.76	411.57	414.72	418.05	417.39	401.09	439.69	441.01	422.10
Gross National Income	294.87	325.90	340.66	353.47	379.82	414.45	412.19	396.79	382.39	419.01	416.30

DOMESTIC PRICES/DEFLATORS — *(Index 1980 = 100)*

	1970	1971	1972	1973	1974	1975	1976	1977	1978	1979	1980
Overall (GDP)	31.7	34.3	35.9	39.8	46.0	53.8	60.7	67.1	72.7	84.1	100.0
Domestic Absorption	27.6	31.3	32.1	36.0	42.1	50.7	56.2	65.8	74.5	86.0	100.0
Agriculture	43.0	46.4	47.4	56.7	65.4	76.3	81.5	85.6	89.7	107.4	100.0
Industry	25.4	27.5	30.1	32.1	36.6	44.5	49.7	55.1	56.0	65.1	100.0
Manufacturing	..	..	..	..	..	..	..	..	..	..	100.0
Consumer Price Index	13.5	13.9	14.2	15.8	18.9	21.2	22.2	26.8	29.4	32.7	39.5

MANUFACTURING ACTIVITY

	1970	1971	1972	1973	1974	1975	1976	1977	1978	1979	1980
Employment (1987=100)	..	..	..	..	..	..	..	..	..	..	..
Real Earnings per Empl. (1987=100)	..	..	..	..	..	..	..	..	..	..	..
Real Output per Empl. (1987=100)	..	..	..	..	..	..	..	..	..	..	..
Earnings as % of Value Added	42.5	50.6	38.7	34.3	..	..	18.2	34.4	42.8	36.5	40.6

MONETARY HOLDINGS — *(Millions of current Swaziland Emalangeni)*

	1970	1971	1972	1973	1974	1975	1976	1977	1978	1979	1980
Money Supply, Broadly Defined	..	..	..	..	57.61	81.75	98.59	105.96	132.78	135.69	151.46
Money	..	..	..	..	16.93	23.42	28.79	34.16	37.21	40.91	49.86
Currency Outside Banks	..	..	..	..	3.33	5.11	6.52	7.31	8.90	9.59	11.90
Demand Deposits	..	..	..	..	13.60	18.31	22.27	26.84	28.32	31.32	37.96
Quasi-Money	..	..	..	..	40.68	58.32	69.80	71.81	95.57	94.78	101.60

GOVERNMENT DEFICIT (-) OR SURPLUS — *(Millions of current Swaziland Emalangeni)*

	1970	1971	1972	1973	1974	1975	1976	1977	1978	1979	1980
GOVERNMENT DEFICIT (-) OR SURPLUS	..	-2.02	-4.62	-10.77	1.66	17.39	-8.48	-8.56	-39.97	3.87	27.55
Current Revenue	..	17.46	21.35	28.56	46.23	69.99	54.66	81.13	105.19	133.93	156.38
Current Expenditure	..	16.03	17.79	22.48	25.64	29.67	40.22	48.53	55.37	60.21	78.58
Current Budget Balance	..	1.43	3.56	6.08	20.59	40.32	14.44	32.60	49.82	73.72	77.80
Capital Receipts	..	0.01	0.01	0.01	0.08	0.03	..	0.04	0.09	0.12	0.07
Capital Payments	..	3.46	8.19	16.86	19.01	22.96	22.92	41.20	89.88	69.97	50.32

1981	1982	1983	1984	1985	1986	1987	1988	1989	1990 estimate	Notes	SWAZILAND
1,010	1,010	930	870	800	710	670	800	790	810	..	**CURRENT GNP PER CAPITA (US $)**
582	601	621	641	664	688	713	740	768	797	..	POPULATION (thousands)
											USE AND ORIGIN OF RESOURCES
				(Millions of current Swaziland Emalangeni)							
506.8	562.1	609.6	715.4	878.9	1,079.7	1,116.1	1,365.1	1,410.5	1,756.5	C	Gross National Product (GNP)
5.9	15.4	30.0	53.1	76.4	28.3	-1.9	40.0	-163.3	-66.6	..	Net Factor Income from Abroad
500.9	546.7	579.6	662.3	802.5	1,051.4	1,118.0	1,325.1	1,573.8	1,823.1	C	GDP at Market Prices
-148.6	-165.5	-209.4	-240.0	-263.4	-113.9	4.5	-23.0	7.6	..	..	Resource Balance
388.0	416.7	400.6	432.8	474.6	710.7	890.0	1,000.8	1,427.5	..	..	Exports of Goods & NF Services
536.6	582.2	610.0	672.8	738.0	824.6	885.5	1,023.8	1,419.9	..	..	Imports of Goods & NF Services
649.5	712.2	789.0	902.3	1,065.7	1,164.9	1,113.3	1,348.2	..	..	..	Domestic Absorption
360.2	395.0	450.4	510.8	650.5	690.3	705.6	841.6	..	..	..	Private Consumption, etc.
133.8	141.0	135.8	182.1	177.6	240.7	237.1	286.9	..	..	..	General Gov't Consumption
155.5	176.2	202.8	209.4	237.6	233.9	170.6	219.7	..	..	..	Gross Domestic Investment
140.2	152.8	208.5	208.5	225.4	228.9	..	..	..	..	..	Fixed Investment
63.1	61.9	62.9	74.5	144.0	148.0	166.5	224.3	266.3	194.9	..	Indirect Taxes, net
437.8	484.8	516.7	587.8	658.5	903.4	951.5	1,100.8	1,307.5	1,628.2	C	GDP at factor cost
104.7	102.1	111.2	127.0	160.3	201.7	..	280.4	..	..	..	Agriculture
132.8	148.7	140.0	156.5	170.1	247.8	..	487.8	..	..	..	Industry
89.1	100.8	89.7	104.1	105.3	166.3	..	312.5	..	..	..	Manufacturing
200.3	234.0	265.5	304.3	328.1	453.9	..	332.6	..	..	..	Services, etc.
6.9	10.7	-6.6	-30.6	-25.6	120.4	175.3	196.6				Gross Domestic Saving
13.3	26.6	21.3	22.6	56.4	154.4	180.7	241.4				Gross National Saving
				(Millions of 1980 Swaziland Emalangeni)							
455.64	466.64	469.59	504.03	584.70	568.30	544.90	612.60	554.80	608.70	C	Gross National Product
450.33	455.69	451.94	469.27	536.90	556.50	549.00	598.00	622.50	635.30	C	GDP at Market Prices
-133.63	-50.32	-12.08	-20.73	..	..	..	..	..	..	..	Resource Balance
360.93	389.08	461.52	392.03	..	..	..	..	..	..	..	Exports of Goods & NF Services
494.56	439.40	473.60	412.76	..	..	..	..	..	..	..	Imports of Goods & NF Services
											Domestic Absorption
583.96	506.01	464.02	490.00							..	Private Consumption, etc.
331.74	274.06	245.14	266.53							..	General Gov't Consumption
122.64	104.37	80.55	95.94							..	Gross Domestic Investment
129.58	127.59	138.34	127.53							..	Fixed Investment
393.60	404.10	402.90	415.90	440.00	477.50	466.60	496.10	516.40	566.60	C	GDP at factor cost
101.59	96.50	95.20	100.22	108.64	120.95	118.45	124.85	129.22	..	..	Agriculture
126.57	128.87	125.37	124.77	122.87	140.67	148.40	170.32	179.86	..	..	Industry
88.40	93.00	94.00	93.50	92.30	109.10	115.10	132.10	140.03	..	..	Manufacturing
165.44	178.73	182.33	190.91	208.49	215.89	199.75	200.93	207.32	..	..	Services, etc.
											Memo Items:
											Capacity to Import
357.60	314.49	311.02	265.52	..	..	..	..	..	..	..	Terms of Trade Adjustment
-3.33	-74.59	-150.50	-126.51	..	..	..	..	..	..	..	Gross Domestic Income
447.00	381.11	301.45	342.76	..	..	..	..	..	..	..	Gross National Income
452.31	392.05	319.09	377.52	..	..	..	..	..	..		
											DOMESTIC PRICES/DEFLATORS
				(Index 1980 = 100)							
111.2	120.0	128.2	141.1	149.5	188.9	203.6	221.6	252.8	287.0	..	Overall (GDP)
111.2	140.7	170.0	184.1	..	..	..	..	..	..	..	Domestic Absorption
103.0	105.8	116.8	126.7	147.5	166.8	..	224.6	..	..	..	Agriculture
104.9	115.4	111.7	125.4	138.4	176.2	..	286.4	..	..	..	Industry
100.8	108.4	95.4	111.3	114.1	152.5	..	236.6	..	..	..	Manufacturing
45.0	48.4	58.9	66.5	79.7	88.9	100.0	111.8	..	..	f	Consumer Price Index
											MANUFACTURING ACTIVITY
..	..	..	..	..	..	..	..	..	..	G	Employment (1987=100)
..	..	..	..	..	..	..	..	..	..	G	Real Earnings per Empl. (1987=100)
..	..	..	..	..	..	..	..	..	..	G	Real Output per Empl. (1987=100)
43.6	47.0	53.8	40.4	48.1	..	..	..	..	..	..	Earnings as % of Value Added
											MONETARY HOLDINGS
				(Millions of current Swaziland Emalangeni)							
165.41	163.65	200.90	242.00	297.40	330.50	372.00	510.00	641.00	650.00	D	Money Supply, Broadly Defined
51.08	58.09	60.84	67.81	76.92	115.14	125.42	142.77	169.01	197.97	..	Money
14.41	15.03	15.22	16.77	17.45	25.21	27.19	32.20	37.20	50.89	..	Currency Outside Banks
36.67	43.06	45.62	51.04	59.47	89.93	98.23	110.57	131.82	147.08	..	Demand Deposits
114.32	105.56	140.06	174.19	220.48	215.36	246.33	367.26	471.98	452.17	..	Quasi-Money
				(Millions of current Swaziland Emalangeni)							
-48.90	-31.85	-19.55	-3.63	-27.57	-48.85	21.58	59.20	95.46	5.79	C	**GOVERNMENT DEFICIT (-) OR SURPLUS**
136.06	183.92	185.57	221.46	242.45	255.62	337.29	428.09	584.27	747.95	..	Current Revenue
111.74	124.00	136.66	154.97	170.56	217.71	235.46	289.57	328.36	447.05	..	Current Expenditure
24.32	59.92	48.91	66.49	71.89	37.91	101.83	138.52	255.91	300.90	..	Current Budget Balance
0.05	0.08	..	..	0.05	0.06	0.03	0.10	0.03	..	..	Capital Receipts
73.27	76.89	68.46	70.12	99.51	86.82	80.28	79.42	160.48	295.11	..	Capital Payments

SWAZILAND	1970	1971	1972	1973	1974	1975	1976	1977	1978	1979	1980

FOREIGN TRADE (CUSTOMS BASIS)

(Millions of current US dollars)

	1970	1971	1972	1973	1974	1975	1976	1977	1978	1979	1980
Value of Exports, fob	..	..	..	..	..	..	..	..	..	..	..
Nonfuel Primary Products	..	..	..	..	..	..	..	..	..	..	..
Fuels	..	..	..	..	..	..	..	..	..	..	..
Manufactures	..	..	..	..	..	..	..	..	..	..	..
Value of Imports, cif	..	..	..	..	..	..	..	..	..	..	..
Nonfuel Primary Products	..	..	..	..	..	..	..	..	..	..	..
Fuels	..	..	..	..	..	..	..	..	..	..	..
Manufactures	..	..	..	..	..	..	..	..	..	..	..

(Index 1987 = 100)

	1970	1971	1972	1973	1974	1975	1976	1977	1978	1979	1980
Terms of Trade	..	..	..	..	..	..	..	..	..	..	..
Export Prices, fob	..	..	..	..	..	..	..	..	..	..	..
Import Prices, cif	..	..	..	..	..	..	..	..	..	..	..

BALANCE OF PAYMENTS

(Millions of current US dollars)

	1970	1971	1972	1973	1974	1975	1976	1977	1978	1979	1980
Exports of Goods & Services	..	..	..	..	206.19	235.29	234.95	233.80	244.26	300.43	450.70
Merchandise, fob	..	..	..	..	178.81	197.02	193.43	183.89	198.72	241.63	368.26
Nonfactor Services	..	..	..	..	22.96	25.02	25.76	29.21	20.13	31.36	36.08
Factor Services	..	..	..	..	4.42	13.25	15.75	20.70	25.42	27.44	46.35
Imports of Goods & Services	..	..	..	..	178.96	202.30	213.21	235.06	341.32	466.50	659.23
Merchandise, fob	..	..	..	..	111.70	139.55	155.83	171.12	246.56	361.13	537.11
Nonfactor Services	..	..	..	..	28.99	39.62	42.21	46.12	64.63	84.70	80.25
Factor Services	..	..	..	..	38.26	23.12	15.18	17.83	30.13	20.67	41.86
Long-Term Interest	1.90	1.60	1.40	1.60	1.00	0.90	0.90	1.30	2.20	3.80	9.00
Private Current Transfers, net	..	..	..	..	0.44	0.81	0.12	0.00	-1.84	-1.66	-2.44
Workers' Remittances	..	..	..	..	..	..	..	..	..	..	..
Curr. A/C Bal before Off. Transf.	..	..	..	..	27.67	33.81	21.85	-1.26	-98.90	-167.74	-210.97
Net Official Transfers	..	..	..	..	14.86	17.71	8.51	12.88	26.68	47.04	79.23
Curr. A/C Bal after Off. Transf.	..	..	..	..	42.53	51.52	30.36	11.61	-72.22	-120.69	-131.74
Long-Term Capital, net	..	..	..	..	7.36	20.01	15.29	27.95	69.00	90.05	35.18
Direct Investment	..	..	..	..	3.53	14.47	7.36	20.01	21.74	55.48	17.46
Long-Term Loans	2.00	-2.40	-1.10	3.10	-1.20	1.00	9.90	9.10	58.80	46.70	19.00
Disbursements	3.50	0.20	6.10	11.20	2.20	3.50	11.00	10.00	60.50	50.40	26.50
Repayments	1.50	2.60	7.20	8.10	3.40	2.50	1.10	0.90	1.70	3.70	7.50
Other Long-Term Capital	..	..	..	..	5.03	4.54	-1.96	-1.16	-11.53	-12.13	-1.28
Other Capital, net	..	..	..	..	-39.89	-32.29	-17.96	-17.79	19.13	25.28	133.33
Change in Reserves	1.07	0.76	0.02	0.02	-10.00	-39.24	-27.70	-21.77	-15.91	5.37	-36.77

Memo Item:

(Swaziland Emalangeni per US dollar)

	1970	1971	1972	1973	1974	1975	1976	1977	1978	1979	1980
Conversion Factor (Annual Avg)	0.710	0.720	0.770	0.690	0.680	0.740	0.870	0.870	0.870	0.840	0.780

EXTERNAL DEBT (Total)

(Millions of US dollars), outstanding at end of year

	1970	1971	1972	1973	1974	1975	1976	1977	1978	1979	1980
EXTERNAL DEBT (Total)	37.00	34.70	32.60	37.00	36.20	33.70	40.80	61.30	134.00	180.70	205.80
Long-Term Debt (by debtor)	37.00	34.70	32.60	37.00	36.20	33.70	40.80	52.30	117.00	172.70	190.80
Central Bank, incl. IMF credit	0.00	0.00	0.00	0.00	0.00	0.00	0.00	0.00	0.00	3.20	5.70
Central Government	35.90	33.70	31.70	36.00	35.30	33.10	40.20	51.80	103.00	133.90	137.10
Rest of General Government	..	..	..	..	..	..	..	..	..	..	..
Non-financial Public Enterprises	1.10	1.00	0.90	1.00	0.90	0.60	0.60	0.50	14.00	35.60	48.00
Priv. Sector, incl non-guaranteed	..	..	..	..	..	..	..	..	..	..	..
Short-Term Debt	0.00	0.00	0.00	0.00	0.00	0.00	0.00	9.00	17.00	8.00	15.00

Memo Items:

(Millions of US dollars)

	1970	1971	1972	1973	1974	1975	1976	1977	1978	1979	1980
Int'l Reserves Excluding Gold	..	..	..	..	13.47	45.61	73.39	94.71	113.61	113.71	158.74
Gold Holdings (at market price)	..	..	..	..	..	..	..	..	..	..	..

SOCIAL INDICATORS

	1970	1971	1972	1973	1974	1975	1976	1977	1978	1979	1980
Total Fertility Rate	6.5	6.5	6.5	6.5	6.5	6.5	6.5	6.5	6.5	6.5	6.5
Infant Mortality Rate	145.2	144.6	144.0	143.2	142.4	141.6	140.8	140.0	137.8	135.6	133.4
Life Expectancy at Birth	46.1	46.7	47.3	47.8	48.3	48.9	49.4	49.9	50.5	51.1	51.7
Urban Population, % of total	9.7	10.6	11.4	12.3	13.1	14.0	15.2	16.3	17.5	18.6	19.8
Food Prod. per capita (1987=100)	100.6	100.7	108.5	99.7	104.5	102.1	101.6	92.3	102.4	98.0	107.5
Labor Force, Agriculture (%)	80.6	79.9	79.3	78.6	78.0	77.4	76.6	76.0	75.3	74.7	74.1
Labor Force, Female (%)	42.3	42.1	42.0	41.9	41.8	41.7	41.5	41.4	41.3	41.1	41.0
Primary Schl. Enroll. Ratio	87.0	..	..	..	..	99.0	99.0	100.0	101.0	103.0	103.0
Primary Schl. Enroll. Ratio, Female	83.0	..	..	..	..	97.0	97.0	99.0	101.0	103.0	102.0
Secondary Schl. Enroll. Ratio	18.0	..	..	..	..	32.0	..	36.0	37.0	38.0	38.0

1981	1982	1983	1984	1985	1986	1987	1988	1989	1990 est.	Notes	SWAZILAND
											FOREIGN TRADE (CUSTOMS BASIS)
											(Millions of current US dollars)
..	..	..	..	..	..	..	..	..	..	..	Value of Exports, fob
..	..	..	..	..	..	..	..	..	..	..	Nonfuel Primary Products
..	..	..	..	..	..	..	..	..	..	..	Fuels
..	..	..	..	..	..	..	..	..	..	..	Manufactures
..	..	..	..	..	..	..	..	..	..	..	Value of Imports, cif
..	..	..	..	..	..	..	..	..	..	..	Nonfuel Primary Products
..	..	..	..	..	..	..	..	..	..	..	Fuels
..	..	..	..	..	..	..	..	..	..	..	Manufactures
				(Index 1987=100)							
											Terms of Trade
..	..	..	..	..	..	..	..	..	..	..	Export Prices, fob
..	..	..	..	..	..	..	..	..	..	..	Import Prices, cif
				(Millions of current US dollars)							**BALANCE OF PAYMENTS**
498.26	411.49	411.90	345.36	272.03	379.99	571.80	645.49	685.22	815.28	..	Exports of Goods & Services
388.27	324.00	303.83	230.80	176.75	278.11	423.52	466.20	486.49	557.41	..	Merchandise, fob
41.42	32.88	41.20	43.65	27.85	30.55	47.64	53.88	70.81	98.13	..	Nonfactor Services
68.57	54.61	66.87	70.90	67.43	71.33	100.64	125.40	127.92	159.74	..	Factor Services
653.21	586.56	585.23	490.48	366.22	416.19	541.74	636.12	798.23	909.47	..	Imports of Goods & Services
502.03	437.73	463.51	371.18	271.66	295.93	369.39	440.96	515.39	632.16	..	Merchandise, fob
101.09	107.29	92.36	87.24	62.94	61.84	71.22	90.48	98.87	117.84	..	Nonfactor Services
50.09	41.54	29.35	32.06	31.63	58.42	101.13	104.69	183.97	159.47	..	Factor Services
9.20	9.00	7.90	9.10	8.30	11.10	14.90	13.70	11.80	10.60	..	Long-Term Interest
0.57	0.46	-1.88	0.07	2.52	2.49	3.59	2.11	0.46	-4.21	..	Private Current Transfers, net
..	..	..	..	..	..	..	..	..	102.86		Workers' Remittances
-154.37	-174.62	-175.21	-145.06	-91.67	-33.70	33.64	11.48	-112.56	-98.40	..	Curr. A/C Bal before Off. Transf.
71.08	60.23	66.51	65.21	49.30	40.79	46.56	83.48	105.43	110.04	..	Net Official Transfers
-83.29	-114.38	-108.70	-79.85	-42.36	7.09	80.21	94.97	-7.13	11.63	..	Curr. A/C Bal after Off. Transf.
43.81	18.97	35.01	12.07	21.68	42.58	15.03	30.31	71.80	17.62	..	Long-Term Capital, net
31.72	-16.49	-6.19	..	10.08	28.14	39.34	38.53	61.54	40.39	..	Direct Investment
11.00	19.40	16.50	18.10	14.00	10.30	-9.30	-8.00	-3.80	-20.10	..	Long-Term Loans
20.90	31.30	29.40	28.20	29.70	27.80	20.40	13.00	16.60	21.70	..	Disbursements
9.90	11.90	12.90	10.10	15.70	17.50	29.70	21.00	20.40	41.80	..	Repayments
1.09	16.06	24.70	-6.03	-2.39	4.14	-15.01	-0.23	14.06	-2.66	..	Other Long-Term Capital
-9.16	86.67	85.27	58.82	15.82	-43.25	-74.85	-111.83	-14.50	-18.50	..	Other Capital, net
48.63	8.74	-11.58	8.96	4.86	-6.42	-20.38	-13.44	-50.16	-10.76	..	Change in Reserves
				(Swaziland Emalangeni per US dollar)							**Memo Item:**
0.870	1.080	1.110	1.440	2.190	2.270	2.030	2.260	2.620	2.590	..	Conversion Factor (Annual Avg)
				(Millions of US dollars), outstanding at end of year							**EXTERNAL DEBT (Total)**
185.10	198.80	235.00	191.70	238.20	278.40	308.60	264.90	270.10	272.20	..	Long-Term Debt (by debtor)
179.10	184.80	198.00	184.70	223.20	261.30	291.50	257.00	249.00	251.20	..	Central Bank, incl. IMF credit
5.20	5.00	15.20	14.20	14.10	10.50	6.10	1.60	0.40	..	..	Central Government
133.80	132.50	133.90	132.80	168.40	202.20	233.40	214.70	216.10	236.40	..	Rest of General Government
..	..	..	..	..	..	..	..	..	..	..	Non-financial Public Enterprises
40.10	47.30	48.90	37.70	40.70	48.60	52.00	40.70	32.50	14.80	..	Priv. Sector, incl non-guaranteed
..	..	..	..	..	..	..	..	..	..	..	
6.00	14.00	37.00	7.00	15.00	17.10	17.10	7.90	21.10	21.00	..	Short-Term Debt
				(Millions of US dollars)							**Memo Items:**
96.36	76.12	92.50	80.10	83.42	96.45	127.16	140.01	180.61	216.47	..	Int'l Reserves Excluding Gold
..	..	..	..	..	..	..	..	..	..	..	Gold Holdings (at market price)
											SOCIAL INDICATORS
6.5	6.5	6.6	6.7	6.7	6.8	6.9	6.8	6.8	6.7	..	Total Fertility Rate
131.2	129.0	126.8	124.6	122.3	120.1	117.9	116.0	114.0	112.1	..	Infant Mortality Rate
52.3	53.0	53.5	54.0	54.5	55.0	55.5	55.8	56.2	56.5	..	Life Expectancy at Birth
21.1	22.4	23.7	25.0	26.3	28.0	29.7	30.8	32.0	33.1	..	Urban Population, % of total
110.6	106.0	103.6	102.1	99.7	109.5	100.0	101.2	96.5	93.4	..	Food Prod. per capita (1987=100)
..	..	..	..	..	..	..	..	..	..	..	Labor Force, Agriculture (%)
40.8	40.6	40.4	40.1	39.9	39.7	39.5	39.2	39.0	38.8	..	Labor Force, Female (%)
..	..	..	107.0	107.0	105.0	105.0	105.0	104.0	..	..	Primary Schl. Enroll. Ratio
..	..	..	106.0	106.0	104.0	105.0	104.0	104.0	..	..	Primary Schl. Enroll. Ratio, Female
40.0	42.0	44.0	42.0	42.0	42.0	43.0	44.0	50.0	..	..	Secondary Schl. Enroll. Ratio

SWEDEN	1970	1971	1972	1973	1974	1975	1976	1977	1978	1979	1980
CURRENT GNP PER CAPITA (US $)	4,200	4,460	4,940	5,860	6,970	8,320	9,200	9,990	10,940	12,610	14,330
POPULATION (thousands)	8,043	8,098	8,122	8,137	8,161	8,193	8,222	8,252	8,276	8,294	8,310

USE AND ORIGIN OF RESOURCES

					(Billions of current Swedish Kronor)						
Gross National Product (GNP)	173.2	187.5	205.3	228.9	258.4	303.4	342.7	371.6	413.6	463.8	524.2
Net Factor Income from Abroad	-0.1	0.2	0.4	0.8	0.7	0.8	0.5	-0.7	-1.4	-1.3	-4.0
GDP at Market Prices	173.3	187.3	205.0	228.1	257.7	302.6	342.2	372.2	414.9	465.1	528.3
Resource Balance	-1.0	2.1	3.1	6.2	-2.0	-0.6	-5.7	-6.2	4.2	-4.7	-10.1
Exports of Goods & NFServices	41.5	45.3	49.3	62.1	82.5	84.6	94.0	101.3	116.4	140.5	156.5
Imports of Goods & NFServices	42.5	43.2	46.2	55.9	84.5	85.3	99.8	107.5	112.2	145.2	166.5
Domestic Absorption	174.2	185.2	201.9	221.9	259.7	303.2	348.0	378.5	410.8	469.8	538.3
Private Consumption, etc.	93.5	100.7	110.8	122.2	139.3	158.8	183.6	201.1	222.8	246.3	274.7
General Gov't Consumption	37.5	42.5	47.0	52.2	60.3	72.7	85.9	103.2	116.9	132.7	153.8
Gross Domestic Investment	43.3	42.1	44.2	47.4	60.0	71.7	78.5	74.1	71.1	90.7	109.8
Fixed Investment	38.0	40.1	44.3	48.6	53.9	61.7	70.6	76.5	78.5	89.8	103.9
Indirect Taxes, net	18.9	24.2	25.1	28.5	28.1	32.4	35.9	41.1	40.3	42.2	48.6
GDP at factor cost	154.3	163.1	179.9	199.6	229.6	270.2	306.4	331.1	374.7	422.9	479.6
Agriculture	..	..	..	..	..	..	..	..	..	..	17.8
Industry	..	..	..	..	..	..	..	..	..	..	163.3
Manufacturing	..	..	..	..	..	..	..	..	..	..	111.8
Services, etc.	..	..	..	..	..	..	..	..	..	..	298.6
Gross Domestic Saving	42.3	44.2	47.2	53.7	58.0	71.1	72.8	67.9	75.2	86.0	99.7
Gross National Saving	42.0	44.1	47.2	54.0	58.3	71.3	72.3	66.3	72.9	84.1	94.5

					(Billions of 1987 Swedish Kronor)						
Gross National Product	730.48	738.34	755.83	787.05	811.67	832.35	840.00	823.85	837.05	869.73	879.88
GDP at Market Prices	730.40	737.30	754.17	784.10	809.18	829.83	838.61	825.23	839.68	871.93	886.48
Resource Balance	-31.37	-16.87	-14.24	-2.74	-12.74	-25.14	-36.80	-24.53	4.98	-6.99	-9.61
Exports of Goods & NFServices	166.37	174.30	184.53	209.79	220.93	200.42	209.08	212.12	228.67	242.70	241.16
Imports of Goods & NFServices	197.74	191.17	198.77	212.53	233.67	225.56	245.88	236.65	223.69	249.69	250.78
Domestic Absorption	761.76	754.16	768.42	786.84	821.91	854.97	875.42	849.76	834.71	878.92	896.09
Private Consumption, etc.	403.02	405.79	419.64	435.38	445.41	455.38	470.24	469.88	470.30	480.91	478.09
General Gov't Consumption	176.86	180.71	185.13	189.88	195.72	204.88	212.11	218.42	225.63	236.31	241.56
Gross Domestic Investment	181.89	167.66	163.64	161.57	180.78	194.72	193.07	161.45	138.78	161.70	176.44
Fixed Investment	154.72	153.83	160.23	164.50	159.51	164.44	167.50	162.57	151.44	158.21	163.68
GDP at factor cost	647.20	638.11	658.29	682.54	719.97	738.06	747.74	732.34	757.97	792.95	805.54
Agriculture	..	..	..	..	..	..	..	..	..	..	28.54
Industry	..	..	..	..	..	..	..	..	..	..	262.84
Manufacturing	..	..	..	..	..	..	..	..	..	..	187.49
Services, etc.	..	..	..	..	..	..	..	..	..	..	514.31

Memo Items:

Capacity to Import	193.16	200.58	211.88	236.22	228.14	223.90	231.73	222.94	232.01	241.61	235.60
Terms of Trade Adjustment	26.79	26.27	27.36	26.42	7.21	23.48	22.65	10.82	3.33	-1.09	-5.56
Gross Domestic Income	757.19	763.57	781.53	810.52	816.38	853.31	861.26	836.05	843.02	870.83	880.92
Gross National Income	757.27	764.61	783.19	813.47	818.87	855.84	862.65	834.67	840.38	868.64	874.32

DOMESTIC PRICES/DEFLATORS

					(Index 1987 = 100)						
Overall (GDP)	23.7	25.4	27.2	29.1	31.8	36.5	40.8	45.1	49.4	53.3	59.6
Domestic Absorption	22.9	24.6	26.3	28.2	31.6	35.5	39.8	44.5	49.2	53.5	60.1
Agriculture	..	..	..	..	..	..	..	..	..	..	62.3
Industry	..	..	..	..	..	..	..	..	..	..	62.1
Manufacturing	..	..	..	..	..	..	..	..	..	..	59.6
Consumer Price Index	24.8	26.6	28.2	30.1	33.1	36.3	40.1	44.7	49.1	52.7	59.9

MANUFACTURING ACTIVITY

Employment (1987=100)	118.4	116.2	114.4	116.4	119.3	120.7	120.5	116.2	112.3	112.1	111.2
Real Earnings per Empl. (1987=100)	96.3	97.4	99.5	99.2	100.6	106.3	107.2	103.4	102.3	102.1	97.7
Real Output per Empl. (1987=100)	0.0	0.0	0.0	0.0	0.0	0.0	0.0	0.0	0.0	0.0	83.2
Earnings as % of Value Added	52.2	52.6	51.7	47.6	43.8	46.7	47.8	47.9	47.2	43.3	43.7

MONETARY HOLDINGS

					(Billions of current Swedish Kronor)						
Money Supply, Broadly Defined	84.98	95.31	107.61	121.86	132.74	148.09	157.23	171.27	200.07	233.83	257.16
Money	..	..	..	..	..	..	..	..	..	..	..
Currency Outside Banks	11.40	12.81	14.14	15.38	17.32	20.13	22.16	24.41	27.57	30.94	33.58
Demand Deposits	..	..	..	..	..	..	..	..	..	..	..
Quasi-Money	..	..	..	..	..	..	..	..	..	..	..

GOVERNMENT DEFICIT (-) OR SURPLUS

					(Billions of current Swedish Kronor)						
	-3.10	-2.44	-2.47	-3.21	-7.98	-7.55	-1.17	-6.06	-20.45	-33.22	-43.03
Current Revenue	51.29	58.64	66.47	70.50	79.15	93.72	122.88	140.77	154.65	166.57	186.75
Current Expenditure	39.97	44.54	50.93	57.15	68.69	82.01	101.21	122.20	146.92	172.67	199.22
Current Budget Balance	11.32	14.10	15.54	13.35	10.46	11.71	21.67	18.57	7.73	-6.10	-12.47
Capital Receipts	..	..	..	..	..	..	..	..	..	..	..
Capital Payments	14.42	16.54	18.01	16.56	18.44	19.26	22.84	24.63	28.18	27.12	30.56

1981	1982	1983	1984	1985	1986	1987	1988	1989	1990 estimate	Notes	SWEDEN
15,030	14,210	12,630	12,050	11,940	13,260	15,790	19,250	21,620	23,760	..	CURRENT GNP PER CAPITA (US $)
8,320	8,325	8,331	8,337	8,350	8,370	8,399	8,436	8,498	8,559		POPULATION (thousands)
				(Billions of current Swedish Kronor)							USE AND ORIGIN OF RESOURCES
570.3	620.4	693.3	774.5	844.7	925.6	1,003.1	1,089.4	1,198.5	1,312.7		Gross National Product (GNP)
-8.6	-13.3	-16.6	-19.8	-21.1	-20.0	-16.5	-21.1	-27.8	-37.5	..	Net Factor Income from Abroad
578.9	633.7	709.9	794.3	865.8	945.6	1,019.5	1,110.5	1,226.3	1,350.1		GDP at Market Prices
-1.2	-3.5	15.1	29.1	15.4	29.9	18.7	18.3	6.7	6.0	..	Resource Balance
174.1	204.8	253.3	289.8	306.6	311.1	332.3	359.7	394.5	409.2	..	Exports of Goods & NF Services
175.3	208.2	238.1	260.7	291.2	281.2	313.6	341.4	387.7	403.3	..	Imports of Goods & NF Services
580.1	637.2	694.7	765.2	850.4	915.7	1,000.9	1,092.1	1,219.6	1,344.2		Domestic Absorption
307.0	342.0	371.9	407.3	447.9	492.8	542.5	589.3	638.8	699.0		Private Consumption, etc.
170.2	185.7	203.5	221.1	239.2	257.2	269.9	286.8	317.2	366.5		General Gov't Consumption
102.9	109.5	119.4	136.8	163.3	165.7	188.5	216.1	263.6	278.7		Gross Domestic Investment
107.0	115.8	129.6	144.6	163.8	171.6	193.0	219.1	263.4	279.9		Fixed Investment
55.9	58.0	71.8	86.3	99.2	112.7	128.9	133.8	149.8	174.8		Indirect Taxes, net
523.0	575.7	638.1	708.0	766.6	832.9	890.7	976.6	1,076.5	1,175.3	..	GDP at factor cost
19.8	21.7	24.5	27.0	28.4	29.8	30.3	31.4	34.8	..	..	Agriculture
172.2	188.0	211.8	243.4	265.1	290.2	310.3	335.5	371.5			Industry
116.8	129.2	148.2	171.2	187.2	205.8	219.3	235.2	255.6			Manufacturing
331.0	366.1	401.8	437.6	473.1	512.9	550.0	609.7	670.1			Services, etc.
101.7	106.0	134.5	165.9	178.7	195.6	207.1	234.4	270.3	284.7		Gross Domestic Saving
91.9	90.9	115.6	143.6	154.2	172.1	188.3	210.4	237.9	243.4		Gross National Saving
				(Billions of 1987 Swedish Kronor)							
873.35	877.77	892.25	925.90	946.84	970.43	1,003.08	1,022.88	1,043.05	1,044.27	..	Gross National Product
886.34	896.08	912.99	949.14	970.09	991.47	1,019.55	1,042.76	1,067.45	1,074.30	..	GDP at Market Prices
9.87	15.81	39.64	46.07	30.34	27.06	18.66	13.89	0.64	3.33	..	Resource Balance
246.05	260.06	285.79	305.41	309.83	319.72	332.30	342.23	352.45	359.41	..	Exports of Goods & NF Services
236.17	244.25	246.16	259.33	279.49	292.66	313.64	328.33	351.81	356.08	..	Imports of Goods & NF Services
876.46	880.27	873.35	903.07	939.75	964.42	1,000.89	1,028.86	1,066.81	1,070.97	..	Domestic Absorption
479.95	483.28	476.51	486.23	495.87	520.52	542.54	555.19	560.88	559.78	..	Private Consumption, etc.
247.09	249.62	251.56	257.35	263.53	267.09	269.88	271.58	276.83	282.66	..	General Gov't Consumption
149.42	147.37	145.28	159.49	180.35	176.80	188.47	202.10	229.11	228.53		Gross Domestic Investment
154.15	153.69	156.54	165.95	178.15	179.31	192.97	204.12	228.19	226.21		Fixed Investment
802.01	816.17	823.25	847.90	860.81	872.98	890.68	916.57	936.05	934.52		GDP at factor cost
28.57	30.03	32.32	32.98	32.29	32.05	30.34	30.04	33.40	..	..	Agriculture
255.50	256.44	267.49	288.79	296.86	301.37	310.31	316.15	320.53	..	..	Industry
181.86	182.25	193.23	207.85	212.12	213.61	219.29	224.54	227.20	..	..	Manufacturing
518.51	530.46	523.45	526.12	531.66	539.57	550.03	570.37	582.13	..	..	Services, etc.
											Memo Items:
234.57	240.17	261.79	288.30	294.28	323.74	332.30	345.97	357.92	361.34	..	Capacity to Import
-11.48	-19.89	-24.01	-17.11	-15.55	4.03	0.00	3.74	5.47	1.92	..	Terms of Trade Adjustment
874.86	876.19	888.98	932.04	954.54	995.50	1,019.55	1,046.50	1,072.93	1,076.23	..	Gross Domestic Income
861.87	857.88	868.24	908.79	931.29	974.45	1,003.08	1,026.62	1,048.52	1,046.19	..	Gross National Income
				(Index 1987 = 100)							DOMESTIC PRICES/DEFLATORS
65.3	70.7	77.8	83.7	89.2	95.4	100.0	106.5	114.9	125.7	..	Overall (GDP)
66.2	72.4	79.5	84.7	90.5	95.0	100.0	106.1	114.3	125.5	..	Domestic Absorption
69.4	72.1	75.8	82.0	88.0	92.9	100.0	104.4	104.3	..	..	Agriculture
67.4	73.3	79.2	84.3	89.3	96.3	100.0	106.1	115.9	..	..	Industry
64.2	70.9	76.7	82.4	88.3	96.3	100.0	104.8	112.5	..	..	Manufacturing
67.1	72.9	79.4	85.7	92.1	95.9	100.0	105.8	112.6	124.4	..	Consumer Price Index
											MANUFACTURING ACTIVITY
107.7	102.9	99.4	99.9	100.3	100.1	100.0	98.9	98.9	..	..	Employment (1987=100)
95.0	94.5	93.7	95.2	95.3	98.0	100.0	100.8	101.4	..	..	Real Earnings per Empl. (1987=100)
84.8	88.3	97.7	102.1	103.4	96.5	100.0	105.0	..	..	..	Real Output per Empl. (1987=100)
43.5	40.4	36.8	36.6	36.7	36.5	35.4	34.3	34.0			Earnings as % of Value Added
				(Billions of current Swedish Kronor)							MONETARY HOLDINGS
293.61	315.06	385.16	425.11	439.39	504.66	529.78	574.12	636.66	643.93	..	Money Supply, Broadly Defined
..	..	..	..	..	..	..	..	..	..	..	Money
36.06	38.06	41.94	44.87	45.86	51.74	54.09	57.38	64.18	67.85	..	Currency Outside Banks
..	..	..	..	..	..	..	..	..	..	..	Demand Deposits
..	..	..	..	..	..	..	..	..	..	..	Quasi-Money
				(Billions of current Swedish Kronor)							
-51.52	-52.59	-60.15	-47.98	-46.48	-26.30	20.71	31.51	48.49	42.30	C E	GOVERNMENT DEFICIT (-) OR SURPLUS
213.68	241.36	272.19	309.71	350.27	377.43	439.07	476.00	529.25	594.27	..	Current Revenue
234.78	262.77	308.92	335.04	376.31	395.73	410.83	434.03	474.23	541.70		Current Expenditure
-21.10	-21.41	-36.73	-25.33	-26.04	-18.30	28.24	41.97	55.02	52.57		Current Budget Balance
0.08	0.05	0.19	0.05	1.56	0.29	1.23	0.09	0.21	1.18		Capital Receipts
30.50	31.23	23.61	22.70	22.00	8.29	8.76	10.55	6.74	11.45		Capital Payments

SWEDEN

	1970	1971	1972	1973	1974	1975	1976	1977	1978	1979	1980
FOREIGN TRADE (CUSTOMS BASIS)					*(Millions of current US dollars)*						
Value of Exports, fob	6,781	7,464	8,749	12,171	15,909	17,434	18,440	19,054	21,768	27,538	30,788
Nonfuel Primary Products	1,639	1,726	1,981	2,851	3,760	3,513	3,643	3,420	3,769	4,697	5,118
Fuels	64	69	90	109	213	272	283	350	409	825	1,337
Manufactures	5,078	5,670	6,678	9,212	11,936	13,649	14,514	15,284	17,590	22,016	24,332
Value of Imports, cif	7,004	7,082	8,062	10,625	15,820	18,067	19,164	20,140	20,547	28,579	33,426
Nonfuel Primary Products	1,459	1,323	1,432	1,876	2,474	2,738	2,889	3,019	3,197	4,080	4,616
Fuels	745	865	842	1,211	2,848	3,110	3,381	3,513	3,347	6,268	8,073
Manufactures	4,800	4,894	5,788	7,539	10,498	12,219	12,893	13,608	14,003	18,231	20,737
Terms of Trade	151.6	144.5	141.3	143.2	*(Index 1987 = 100)* 100.9	113.1	112.5	105.9	108.0	113.1	106.5
Export Prices, fob	28.2	29.3	33.6	42.7	49.4	58.0	60.2	62.5	70.2	87.4	99.5
Import Prices, cif	18.6	20.3	23.8	29.8	48.9	51.3	53.5	59.1	65.0	77.3	93.4
BALANCE OF PAYMENTS					*(Millions of current US dollars)*						
Exports of Goods & Services	8,256	9,166	10,768	14,840	19,144	21,041	22,404	23,350	27,083	35,004	39,388
Merchandise, fob	6,750	7,415	8,697	12,097	15,797	17,259	18,287	18,930	21,598	27,377	30,662
Nonfactor Services	1,338	1,603	1,896	2,445	3,009	3,390	3,565	3,834	4,584	6,528	7,399
Factor Services	168	149	174	298	338	392	552	586	902	1,099	1,328
Imports of Goods & Services	8,368	8,636	9,947	13,100	19,277	20,729	23,306	24,653	26,124	36,297	42,495
Merchandise, fob	6,447	6,520	7,479	10,066	15,405	16,182	18,124	18,654	19,023	28,072	32,860
Nonfactor Services	1,732	1,907	2,222	2,702	3,446	4,028	4,379	4,904	5,466	6,284	6,814
Factor Services	189	209	246	332	426	520	803	1,094	1,634	1,942	2,821
Long-Term Interest	..	..	..	..	..	..	..	..	..	..	..
Private Current Transfers, net	-48	-55	-69	-96	-90	-151	-203	-208	-209	-163	-301
Workers' Remittances	..	..	..	..	..	..	..	..	..	..	..
Curr. A/C Bal before Off. Transf.	-160	475	752	1,644	-223	161	-1,105	-1,511	751	-1,456	-3,407
Net Official Transfers	-104	-123	-185	-215	-329	-503	-543	-669	-1,001	-958	-997
Curr. A/C Bal after Off. Transf.	-265	352	567	1,429	-552	-342	-1,648	-2,181	-251	-2,414	-4,404
Long-Term Capital, net	139	-13	164	-248	423	1,569	376	3,074	548	1,410	4,750
Direct Investment	-104	-93	-197	-221	-349	-354	-591	-656	-346	-505	-374
Long-Term Loans	..	..	..	..	..	..	..	..	..	..	..
Disbursements	..	..	..	..	..	..	..	..	..	..	..
Repayments	..	..	..	..	..	..	..	..	..	..	..
Other Long-Term Capital	244	80	361	-27	773	1,924	967	3,730	893	1,915	5,123
Other Capital, net	155	-91	-379	-310	-625	176	760	208	357	328	-451
Change in Reserves	-29	-248	-351	-870	753	-1,404	513	-1,101	-654	676	105
Memo Item:											
Conversion Factor (Annual Avg)	5.170	5.120	4.760	4.370	*(Swedish Kronor per US dollar)* 4.440	4.150	4.360	4.480	4.520	4.290	4.230
EXTERNAL DEBT (Total)	..	..	..	..	*(Millions US dollars), outstanding at end of year*						
Long-Term Debt (by debtor)	..	..	..	..	..	..	..	..	..	..	..
Central Bank, incl. IMF credit	..	..	..	..	..	..	..	..	..	..	..
Central Government	..	..	..	..	..	..	..	..	..	..	..
Rest of General Government	..	..	..	..	..	..	..	..	..	..	..
Non-financial Public Enterprises	..	..	..	..	..	..	..	..	..	..	..
Priv. Sector, incl non-guaranteed	..	..	..	..	..	..	..	..	..	..	..
Short-Term Debt	..	..	..	..	..	..	..	..	..	..	..
Memo Items:					*(Millions of US dollars)*						
Int'l Reserves Excluding Gold	561.2	892.6	1,357.9	2,284.2	1,487.0	2,838.6	2,255.5	3,414.8	4,123.7	3,513.9	3,418.5
Gold Holdings (at market price)	213.6	252.1	375.2	649.9	1,079.8	812.0	780.2	978.0	1,355.8	3,107.1	3,577.4
SOCIAL INDICATORS											
Total Fertility Rate	1.9	2.0	1.9	1.9	1.9	1.8	1.7	1.6	1.6	1.7	1.7
Infant Mortality Rate	11.0	11.1	10.8	9.9	9.5	8.6	8.3	8.0	7.7	7.4	6.9
Life Expectancy at Birth	74.5	74.6	74.7	74.8	74.9	75.0	75.1	75.2	75.4	75.6	75.9
Urban Population, % of total	81.1	81.4	81.7	82.1	82.4	82.7	82.8	82.9	82.9	83.0	83.1
Food Prod. per capita (1987=100)	95.9	96.8	98.7	95.3	112.4	101.9	106.4	107.2	110.3	108.0	109.4
Labor Force, Agriculture (%)	8.3	8.0	7.7	7.5	7.2	6.9	6.7	6.4	6.2	5.9	5.7
Labor Force, Female (%)	35.7	36.5	37.4	38.2	39.0	39.8	40.7	41.5	42.3	43.0	43.8
Primary Schl. Enroll. Ratio	94.0	..	..	..	..	101.0	100.0	99.0	98.0	98.0	97.0
Primary Schl. Enroll. Ratio, Female	95.0	..	..	..	..	102.0	101.0	99.0	99.0	98.0	97.0
Secondary Schl. Enroll. Ratio	86.0	..	..	..	..	78.0	78.0	80.0	84.0	85.0	88.0

1981	1982	1983	1984	1985	1986	1987	1988	1989	1990 estimate	Notes	SWEDEN
											FOREIGN TRADE (CUSTOMS BASIS)
				(Millions of current US dollars)							
28,492	26,740	27,377	29,258	30,403	37,118	44,313	49,867	51,497	57,326	..	Value of Exports, fob
4,537	4,125	4,443	4,808	4,490	4,883	5,726	6,554	6,885	7,358	..	Nonfuel Primary Products
1,262	1,388	1,698	1,630	1,456	1,039	1,268	1,062	1,408	1,704	..	Fuels
22,694	21,227	21,236	22,821	24,457	31,196	37,320	42,252	43,204	48,265	..	Manufactures
28,842	27,533	26,090	26,331	28,538	32,493	40,621	45,793	48,920	54,536	..	Value of Imports, cif
3,904	3,558	3,440	3,652	3,703	4,443	5,109	6,145	6,200	6,249	..	Nonfuel Primary Products
7,160	6,735	5,982	5,124	5,394	3,496	3,627	3,141	3,768	4,959	..	Fuels
17,778	17,240	16,668	17,556	19,441	24,554	31,885	36,507	38,953	43,329	..	Manufactures
				(Index 1987 = 100)							
97.4	94.5	91.2	92.2	94.3	102.0	100.0	100.8	101.1	101.1	..	Terms of Trade
89.7	82.2	76.4	75.4	75.0	87.8	100.0	109.6	115.3	128.0	..	Export Prices, fob
92.1	87.0	83.9	81.8	79.6	86.0	100.0	108.7	114.0	126.7	..	Import Prices, cif
											BALANCE OF PAYMENTS
				(Millions of current US dollars)							
37,106	35,528	35,620	37,728	38,880	47,286	57,680	65,231	69,475	80,774	..	Exports of Goods & Services
28,389	26,575	27,204	29,123	30,173	36,844	44,010	49,367	51,072	56,805	..	Merchandise, fob
6,933	6,447	6,148	6,212	5,999	7,137	9,177	10,442	11,269	13,375	..	Nonfactor Services
1,784	2,505	2,268	2,393	2,708	3,304	4,493	5,422	7,134	10,594	..	Factor Services
38,879	37,866	35,489	36,236	39,028	45,341	56,335	64,349	70,756	84,318	..	Imports of Goods & Services
28,226	26,797	25,303	25,701	27,789	31,810	39,530	44,489	47,010	53,327	..	Merchandise, fob
6,663	6,689	6,022	6,108	6,392	8,056	10,492	12,358	14,208	16,057	..	Nonfactor Services
3,990	4,379	4,164	4,426	4,846	5,475	6,313	7,502	9,538	14,933	..	Factor Services
..	..	..	..	..	..	..	..	..	..	..	Long-Term Interest
-228	-282	-295	-310	-398	-481	-379	-469	-714	-644	..	Private Current Transfers, net
..	..	..	..	..	..	17	23	33	32	..	Workers' Remittances
-2,001	-2,620	-164	1,182	-545	1,463	966	413	-1,994	-4,188	..	Curr. A/C Bal before Off. Transf.
-846	-745	-642	-617	-681	-857	-1,016	-1,141	-1,263	-1,645	..	Net Official Transfers
-2,847	-3,366	-806	565	-1,226	606	-51	-728	-3,257	-5,833	..	Curr. A/C Bal after Off. Transf.
1,909	2,573	1,444	-831	931	-1,547	140	-896	-8,166	-14,531	..	Long-Term Capital, net
-644	-857	-1,232	-1,207	-1,413	-2,782	-3,905	-5,719	-8,197	-11,826	..	Direct Investment
..	..	..	..	..	..	..	..	..	..	..	Long-Term Loans
..	..	..	..	..	..	..	..	..	..	..	Disbursements
..	..	..	..	..	..	..	..	..	..	..	Repayments
2,554	3,430	2,676	376	2,345	1,235	4,045	4,823	32	-2,705	..	Other Long-Term Capital
1,141	751	48	223	1,846	1,083	793	2,293	12,646	27,967	..	Other Capital, net
-203	41	-686	43	-1,551	-142	-882	-668	-1,223	-7,603	..	Change in Reserves
											Memo Item:
				(Swedish Kronor per US dollar)							
5.060	6.280	7.670	8.270	8.600	7.120	6.340	6.130	6.450	5.920	..	Conversion Factor (Annual Avg)
				(Millions US dollars), outstanding at end of year							
..	..	..	..	..	..	..	..	..	..	..	**EXTERNAL DEBT (Total)**
..	..	..	..	..	..	..	..	..	..	..	Long-Term Debt (by debtor)
..	..	..	..	..	..	..	..	..	..	..	Central Bank, incl. IMF credit
..	..	..	..	..	..	..	..	..	..	..	Central Government
..	..	..	..	..	..	..	..	..	..	..	Rest of General Government
..	..	..	..	..	..	..	..	..	..	..	Non-financial Public Enterprises
..	..	..	..	..	..	..	..	..	..	..	Priv. Sector, incl non-guaranteed
..	..	..	..	..	..	..	..	..	..	..	Short-Term Debt
											Memo Items:
				(Millions of US dollars)							
3,601.1	3,512.5	4,033.8	3,845.0	5,793.5	6,550.6	8,174.3	8,491.9	9,559.4	17,987.9	..	Int'l Reserves Excluding Gold
2,412.2	2,772.7	2,315.2	1,870.9	1,984.4	2,372.2	2,937.8	2,489.6	2,433.5	2,336.4	..	Gold Holdings (at market price)
											SOCIAL INDICATORS
1.7	1.6	1.6	1.7	1.7	1.8	1.9	2.0	2.0	1.9	..	Total Fertility Rate
6.9	6.7	7.8	6.3	6.8	5.9	5.7	5.8	6.0	5.6	..	Infant Mortality Rate
76.1	76.3	76.4	76.6	76.8	76.9	77.1	77.2	77.4	77.6	..	Life Expectancy at Birth
83.2	83.2	83.3	83.3	83.4	83.5	83.6	83.8	83.9	84.0	..	Urban Population, % of total
113.2	116.8	115.1	126.9	119.1	116.3	100.0	99.7	109.0	119.4	..	Food Prod. per capita (1987=100)
..	..	..	..	..	..	..	..	..	..	..	Labor Force, Agriculture (%)
43.9	43.9	44.0	44.1	44.1	44.2	44.3	44.4	44.5	44.6	..	Labor Force, Female (%)
..	98.0	98.0	98.0	98.0	98.0	100.0	101.0	104.0	..	..	Primary Schl. Enroll. Ratio
98.0	98.0	98.0	99.0	..	..	..	101.0	104.0	..	..	Primary Schl. Enroll. Ratio, Female
..	86.0	85.0	86.0	..	90.0	91.0	91.0	91.0	..	..	Secondary Schl. Enroll. Ratio

SWITZERLAND	1970	1971	1972	1973	1974	1975	1976	1977	1978	1979	1980
CURRENT GNP PER CAPITA (US $)	3,480	3,850	4,400	5,480	6,900	7,960	8,930	10,150	11,690	14,150	17,460
POPULATION (thousands)	6,267	6,324	6,385	6,431	6,443	6,405	6,346	6,327	6,337	6,351	6,319
USE AND ORIGIN OF RESOURCES	*(Billions of current Swiss Francs)*										
Gross National Product (GNP)	93.93	106.48	120.53	134.54	146.49	144.62	147.18	151.90	157.50	165.19	177.35
Net Factor Income from Abroad	3.27	3.49	3.83	4.48	5.39	4.47	5.22	6.11	5.82	6.64	7.01
GDP at Market Prices	90.66	103.00	116.71	130.06	141.10	140.16	141.96	145.79	151.68	158.55	170.33
Resource Balance	-1.54	-1.59	-1.04	-1.44	-2.75	4.00	4.69	3.76	3.70	-0.82	-6.01
Exports of Goods & NFServices	29.71	32.06	35.77	40.22	45.90	44.03	47.70	53.44	53.23	56.02	62.58
Imports of Goods & NFServices	31.25	33.65	36.82	41.66	48.65	40.03	43.01	49.68	49.52	56.83	68.59
Domestic Absorption	92.21	104.58	117.76	131.50	143.85	136.16	137.27	142.03	147.98	159.36	176.34
Private Consumption, etc.	53.46	59.89	67.95	76.14	83.35	86.27	89.15	92.90	95.54	101.00	108.34
General Gov't Consumption	9.51	11.24	12.71	14.62	16.41	17.69	18.69	18.89	19.51	20.52	21.68
Gross Domestic Investment	29.24	33.45	37.09	40.74	44.08	32.20	29.44	30.24	32.93	37.84	46.32
Fixed Investment	24.95	30.13	34.64	38.21	38.88	33.65	29.23	30.24	32.49	34.59	40.50
Indirect Taxes, net	5.61	6.01	7.02	7.54	7.40	7.44	7.63	8.02	8.59	8.89	9.66
GDP at factor cost	85.05	96.99	109.70	122.51	133.70	132.72	134.34	137.77	143.09	149.65	160.67
Agriculture	..	..	..	..	..	..	..	..	..	..	..
Industry											
Manufacturing											
Services, etc.	..	..	..	..	..	..	..	..	..	..	..
Gross Domestic Saving	27.70	31.86	36.05	39.30	41.34	36.20	34.12	34.00	36.62	37.03	40.31
Gross National Saving	29.70	33.88	38.21	42.06	45.05	39.22	38.24	39.02	41.39	42.57	46.15
	(Billions of 1987 Swiss Francs)										
Gross National Product	206.67	214.71	221.40	228.48	232.55	214.44	212.53	218.71	219.02	225.13	235.11
GDP at Market Prices	200.10	208.26	214.92	221.48	224.70	208.34	205.41	210.41	211.27	216.54	226.50
Resource Balance	6.28	5.51	5.44	6.54	7.66	11.74	11.17	12.49	9.03	6.59	5.55
Exports of Goods & NFServices	49.68	51.61	54.89	59.21	59.82	55.89	61.09	67.02	69.52	71.23	74.84
Imports of Goods & NFServices	43.40	46.10	49.46	52.67	52.16	44.15	49.91	54.53	60.49	64.63	69.29
Domestic Absorption	193.83	202.75	209.49	214.94	217.04	196.60	194.24	197.92	202.25	209.94	220.95
Private Consumption, etc.	119.61	124.77	130.58	133.99	134.17	129.76	128.84	132.06	133.00	134.34	138.11
General Gov't Consumption	22.37	23.68	24.36	24.95	25.37	25.54	26.24	26.35	26.88	27.16	27.42
Gross Domestic Investment	51.85	54.31	54.55	56.01	57.50	41.30	39.16	39.51	42.37	48.45	55.42
Fixed Investment	44.42	48.80	51.23	52.71	50.47	43.62	39.03	39.67	42.09	44.23	48.62
GDP at factor cost	188.50	196.84	202.64	209.36	213.81	197.88	194.84	199.43	199.66	204.95	214.52
Agriculture	..	..	..	..	..	..	..	..	..	..	..
Industry											
Manufacturing	..	..	..	..	..	..	..	..	..	..	..
Services, etc.	..	..	..	..	..	..	..	..	..	..	..
Memo Items:											
Capacity to Import	41.26	43.93	48.05	50.85	49.21	48.56	55.36	58.66	65.01	63.71	63.22
Terms of Trade Adjustment	-8.41	-7.68	-6.84	-8.36	-10.60	-7.33	-5.73	-8.37	-4.51	-7.52	-11.62
Gross Domestic Income	191.69	200.58	208.08	213.12	214.10	201.01	199.68	202.05	206.77	209.01	214.88
Gross National Income	198.26	207.03	214.56	220.13	221.94	207.11	206.80	210.35	214.51	217.61	223.49
DOMESTIC PRICES/DEFLATORS	*(Index 1987 = 100)*										
Overall (GDP)	45.3	49.5	54.3	58.7	62.8	67.3	69.1	69.3	71.8	73.2	75.2
Domestic Absorption	47.6	51.6	56.2	61.2	66.3	69.3	70.7	71.8	73.2	75.9	79.8
Agriculture											
Industry	..	..	..	..	..	..	..	..	..	..	..
Manufacturing	..	..	..	..	..	..	..	..	..	..	..
Consumer Price Index	48.8	52.0	55.5	60.3	66.2	70.7	71.9	72.8	73.6	76.3	79.3
MANUFACTURING ACTIVITY											
Employment (1987=100)	127.2	126.6	123.2	119.6	118.6	105.4	100.8	100.6	101.0	100.2	102.2
Real Earnings per Empl. (1987=100)	..	..	..	..	..	..	..	..	..	..	..
Real Output per Empl. (1987=100)	..	..	..	..	..	..	..	..	..	..	..
Earnings as % of Value Added	..	..	..	..	..	..	..	..	..	..	..
MONETARY HOLDINGS	*(Billions of current Swiss Francs)*										
Money Supply, Broadly Defined	104.43	115.59	128.11	135.11	117.64	128.72	140.52	149.80	166.99	182.55	183.43
Money	40.38	47.51	50.09	49.68	48.03	50.11	55.96	56.43	69.69	68.40	68.33
Currency Outside Banks	14.54	15.60	17.82	19.08	20.33	20.12	20.78	21.48	23.64	24.99	25.44
Demand Deposits	25.84	31.91	32.27	30.60	27.70	29.99	35.18	34.94	46.05	43.41	42.89
Quasi-Money	64.05	68.08	78.02	85.43	69.61	78.61	84.56	93.37	97.30	114.15	115.10
GOVERNMENT DEFICIT (-) OR SURPLUS	*(Millions of current Swiss Francs)*										
	487	279	1,065	588	964	-647	-954	-752	-132	-1,087	-344
Current Revenue	13,983	15,529	17,928	21,696	24,816	26,061	29,068	29,633	31,519	32,111	34,582
Current Expenditure	11,265	12,804	13,909	17,605	20,233	23,415	26,528	28,178	29,004	30,475	32,206
Current Budget Balance	2,718	2,725	4,019	4,091	4,583	2,646	2,540	1,455	2,515	1,636	2,376
Capital Receipts	18	5	8	19	8	21	13	48	7	7	27
Capital Payments	2,249	2,451	2,962	3,522	3,627	3,314	3,507	2,255	2,654	2,730	2,747

1981	1982	1983	1984	1985	1986	1987	1988	1989	1990 estimate	Notes	SWITZERLAND
17,860	17,050	16,480	16,390	16,240	17,670	21,230	27,410	30,080	32,230	..	**CURRENT GNP PER CAPITA (US $)**
6,354	6,391	6,419	6,442	6,470	6,504	6,545	6,569	6,647	6,712	..	**POPULATION (thousands)**
				(Billions of current Swiss Francs)							**USE AND ORIGIN OF RESOURCES**
193.98	205.17	213.95	226.06	241.35	254.93	266.09	282.95	305.17	326.05	..	Gross National Product (GNP)
9.22	9.19	10.09	12.83	13.40	11.58	11.40	14.54	14.81	13.70	..	Net Factor Income from Abroad
184.76	195.98	203.86	213.23	227.95	243.35	254.69	268.41	290.36	312.35	..	GDP at Market Prices
-1.82	0.89	-0.09	-0.61	0.95	2.74	2.11	1.20	-0.57	1.55	..	Resource Balance
69.10	69.55	71.76	80.55	89.01	89.12	90.53	97.99	110.51	115.11	..	Exports of Goods & NFServices
70.92	68.66	71.85	81.15	88.06	86.38	88.42	96.79	111.08	113.56	..	Imports of Goods & NFServices
186.58	195.09	203.96	213.83	227.00	240.61	252.58	267.21	290.93	310.81	..	Domestic Absorption
116.02	122.44	127.76	134.04	141.01	145.40	150.72	157.51	166.73	178.25	..	Private Consumption, etc.
23.54	25.56	27.36	28.50	30.42	31.84	32.52	34.86	37.90	41.59	..	General Gov't Consumption
47.01	47.09	48.85	51.30	55.57	63.36	69.35	74.83	86.29	90.96	..	Gross Domestic Investment
44.56	45.30	47.50	49.80	54.20	58.99	64.37	71.48	79.86	84.54	..	Fixed Investment
10.51	10.72	11.32	11.85	12.63	14.06	14.80	15.39	16.16	16.62	..	Indirect Taxes, net
174.25	185.26	192.55	201.38	215.32	229.29	239.89	253.02	274.20	295.74	B	GDP at factor cost
..	..	..	..	8.18	..	..	..	..	..	..	Agriculture
..	..	..	..	80.97	..	..	..	..	..	..	Industry
..	..	..	..	58.62	..	..	..	..	..	..	Manufacturing
..	..	..	..	138.80							Services, etc.
45.19	47.99	48.75	50.70	56.52	66.10	71.45	76.03	85.73	92.51	..	Gross Domestic Saving
52.68	55.31	56.95	61.58	67.85	75.51	80.54	88.07	97.81	103.17	..	Gross National Saving
				(Billions of 1987 Swiss Francs)							
240.53	237.78	240.85	247.53	256.32	261.36	266.09	276.20	285.94	290.35	..	Gross National Product
229.76	227.63	229.92	233.99	242.66	249.62	254.69	262.07	272.19	278.18	..	GDP at Market Prices
10.05	9.59	7.46	7.39	10.41	5.22	2.11	2.70	2.50	2.56	..	Resource Balance
78.44	76.20	77.01	81.90	88.70	89.03	90.53	95.78	100.56	103.54	..	Exports of Goods & NFServices
68.39	66.61	69.55	74.51	78.29	83.81	88.42	93.08	98.07	100.98	..	Imports of Goods & NFServices
219.71	218.04	222.46	226.60	232.25	244.40	252.58	259.37	269.69	275.61	..	Domestic Absorption
139.21	139.28	141.10	142.64	144.71	148.17	150.71	153.60	156.89	159.08	..	Private Consumption, etc.
28.10	28.39	29.48	29.85	30.81	31.95	32.52	33.91	35.33	36.46	..	General Gov't Consumption
52.40	50.36	51.88	54.11	56.73	64.27	69.35	71.86	77.48	80.07	..	Gross Domestic Investment
49.93	48.65	50.65	52.74	55.53	59.92	64.37	68.84	72.81	74.42	..	Fixed Investment
217.52	215.81	217.70	221.53	229.85	235.37	239.89	247.13	257.23	263.47	B	GDP at factor cost
..	..	..	..	..	..	..	..	..	..	..	Agriculture
..	..	..	..	..	..	..	..	..	..	..	Industry
..	..	..	..	..	..	..	..	..	..	..	Manufacturing
..	..	..	..	..	..	..	..	..	..	..	Services, etc.
											Memo Items:
66.64	67.47	69.46	73.95	79.13	86.46	90.53	94.24	97.56	102.36	..	Capacity to Import
-11.80	-8.73	-7.55	-7.94	-9.57	-2.57	0.00	-1.55	-3.00	-1.18	..	Terms of Trade Adjustment
217.96	218.90	222.37	226.05	233.10	247.05	254.69	260.53	269.19	276.99	..	Gross Domestic Income
228.73	229.05	233.30	239.58	246.76	258.79	266.09	274.65	282.94	289.17	..	Gross National Income
				(Index 1987 = 100)							**DOMESTIC PRICES/DEFLATORS**
80.4	86.1	88.7	91.1	93.9	97.5	100.0	102.4	106.7	112.3	..	Overall (GDP)
84.9	89.5	91.7	94.4	97.7	98.5	100.0	103.0	107.9	112.8	..	Domestic Absorption
..	..	..	..	..	..	..	..	..	..	..	Agriculture
..	..	..	..	..	..	..	..	..	..	..	Industry
..	..	..	..	..	..	..	..	..	..	..	Manufacturing
84.5	89.3	91.9	94.6	97.8	98.6	100.0	101.9	105.1	110.8	..	Consumer Price Index
											MANUFACTURING ACTIVITY
102.4	104.8	100.8	96.1	97.8	99.6	100.0	99.8	99.6	..	G	Employment (1987=100)
..	..	..	..	..	..	..	..	..	..	G	Real Earnings per Empl. (1987=100)
..	..	..	..	..	..	..	..	..	..	G	Real Output per Empl. (1987=100)
..	..	..	..	..	..	..	..	..	..	..	Earnings as % of Value Added
				(Billions of current Swiss Francs)							**MONETARY HOLDINGS**
195.23	229.88	253.31	273.89	285.24	294.68	325.77	343.38	365.07	368.11	..	Money Supply, Broadly Defined
64.79	69.35	75.82	75.91	73.94	75.49	85.87	87.81	85.56	84.21	..	Money
24.74	24.19	26.31	28.04	27.42	28.57	28.90	30.53	30.90	31.45	..	Currency Outside Banks
40.05	45.16	49.51	47.86	46.52	46.91	56.97	57.27	54.66	52.76	..	Demand Deposits
130.44	160.54	177.49	197.99	211.30	219.20	239.91	255.57	279.51	283.91	..	Quasi-Money
				(Millions of current Swiss Francs)							
197	-116	-771	-202	..	..	..	..	..	..	E	**GOVERNMENT DEFICIT (-) OR SURPLUS**
36,988	40,116	42,077	45,662	..	..	..	..	..	..	..	Current Revenue
33,229	37,043	39,144	42,182	..	..	..	..	..	..	..	Current Expenditure
3,759	3,073	2,933	3,480	..	..	..	..	..	..	..	Current Budget Balance
17	46	9	10	..	..	..	..	..	..	..	Capital Receipts
3,579	3,235	3,713	3,692	..	..	..	..	..	..	..	Capital Payments

SWITZERLAND	1970	1971	1972	1973	1974	1975	1976	1977	1978	1979	1980
FOREIGN TRADE (CUSTOMS BASIS)	*(Millions of current US dollars)*										
Value of Exports, fob	5,120	5,768	6,877	9,472	11,838	12,952	14,669	17,325	23,532	26,390	29,471
Nonfuel Primary Products	522	575	664	909	1,151	1,044	1,210	1,480	1,858	2,203	2,788
Fuels	9	5	7	15	26	24	19	24	21	23	36
Manufactures	4,590	5,188	6,207	8,549	10,661	11,884	13,440	15,821	21,653	24,163	26,647
Value of Imports, cif	6,471	7,154	8,471	11,615	14,411	13,272	14,763	17,962	23,792	29,306	36,148
Nonfuel Primary Products	1,407	1,441	1,671	2,329	2,885	2,751	2,896	3,323	3,950	4,488	6,409
Fuels	352	462	462	836	1,439	1,368	1,577	1,702	1,924	3,440	4,055
Manufactures	4,713	5,251	6,338	8,450	10,087	9,153	10,290	12,937	17,917	21,378	25,685
	(Index 1987 = 100)										
Terms of Trade	105.3	107.9	106.1	112.2	90.2	99.6	98.9	95.5	108.0	103.4	98.3
Export Prices, fob	22.9	24.9	28.1	35.2	42.4	49.2	50.6	53.6	68.4	76.6	84.1
Import Prices, cif	21.7	23.1	26.5	31.3	47.0	49.4	51.1	56.2	63.4	74.1	85.6
BALANCE OF PAYMENTS	*(Millions of current US dollars)*										
Exports of Goods & Services	9,361	10,484	12,728	17,365	21,460	23,812	26,670	30,234	41,348	48,589	59,462
Merchandise, fob	6,201	6,958	8,611	11,550	14,479	16,242	18,504	20,992	28,836	33,827	41,708
Nonfactor Services	1,455	1,747	2,098	2,729	2,965	3,487	3,807	4,289	5,436	5,957	6,888
Factor Services	1,705	1,779	2,020	3,085	4,016	4,083	4,359	4,953	7,075	8,805	10,867
Imports of Goods & Services	8,866	9,808	11,710	17,593	23,511	22,342	23,733	27,644	38,350	47,773	58,524
Merchandise, fob	7,141	7,952	9,597	14,428	19,796	17,947	19,248	22,710	31,014	38,727	46,958
Nonfactor Services	767	922	1,095	1,495	1,509	2,044	2,215	2,524	3,516	4,237	4,885
Factor Services	958	935	1,019	1,670	2,205	2,352	2,270	2,411	3,820	4,808	6,681
Long-Term Interest	..	..	..	..	..	..	..	..	..	..	..
Private Current Transfers, net	-291	-356	-437	-545	-565	-560	-440	-454	-587	-662	-701
Workers' Remittances	..	..	..	..	..	..	..	..	..	..	..
Curr. A/C Bal before Off. Transf.	203	319	581	-772	-2,615	910	2,496	2,136	2,411	155	238
Net Official Transfers	-43	-22	-68	-125	-139	-134	-156	-212	-336	-400	-439
Curr. A/C Bal after Off. Transf.	161	298	513	-897	-2,755	777	2,340	1,924	2,075	-245	-201
Long-Term Capital, net	-947	-2,192	-2,887	-2,756	-1,584	-3,709	-7,117	-5,757	-8,478	-13,586	-11,213
Direct Investment	..	..	..	..	..	..	..	..	..	..	..
Long-Term Loans	..	..	..	..	..	..	..	..	..	..	..
Disbursements	..	..	..	..	..	..	..	..	..	..	..
Repayments	..	..	..	..	..	..	..	..	..	..	..
Other Long-Term Capital	-947	-2,192	-2,887	-2,756	-1,584	-3,709	-7,117	-5,757	-8,478	-13,586	-11,213
Other Capital, net	1,455	3,090	2,960	4,031	4,769	4,453	7,760	4,864	13,043	9,897	11,751
Change in Reserves	-669	-1,196	-586	-378	-431	-1,521	-2,983	-1,031	-6,641	3,934	-337
Memo Item:	*(Swiss Francs per US dollar)*										
Conversion Factor (Annual Avg)	4.370	4.130	3.820	3.160	2.980	2.580	2.500	2.400	1.790	1.660	1.680
EXTERNAL DEBT (Total)	*(Millions US dollars), outstanding at end of year*										
	..	..	..	..	..	..	..	..	..	..	..
Long-Term Debt (by debtor)	..	..	..	..	..	..	..	..	..	..	..
Central Bank, incl. IMF credit	..	..	..	..	..	..	..	..	..	..	..
Central Government	..	..	..	..	..	..	..	..	..	..	..
Rest of General Government	..	..	..	..	..	..	..	..	..	..	..
Non-financial Public Enterprises	..	..	..	..	..	..	..	..	..	..	..
Priv. Sector, incl non-guaranteed	..	..	..	..	..	..	..	..	..	..	..
Short-Term Debt	..	..	..	..	..	..	..	..	..	..	..
Memo Items:	*(Millions of US dollars)*										
Int'l Reserves Excluding Gold	2,401	3,808	4,399	5,007	5,446	7,019	9,606	10,289	17,763	16,435	15,656
Gold Holdings (at market price)	2,916	3,626	5,394	9,339	15,517	11,669	11,222	13,737	18,821	42,638	49,092
SOCIAL INDICATORS											
Total Fertility Rate	2.1	2.0	1.9	1.8	1.7	1.6	1.5	1.5	1.5	1.5	1.6
Infant Mortality Rate	15.4	14.4	13.3	13.2	12.4	10.7	10.7	8.7	8.6	8.4	9.0
Life Expectancy at Birth	73.2	73.5	73.8	74.1	74.4	74.7	74.9	75.2	75.4	75.6	75.8
Urban Population, % of total	54.5	54.7	55.0	55.2	55.5	55.7	56.0	56.2	56.5	56.7	57.0
Food Prod. per capita (1987=100)	85.7	88.2	85.5	89.3	87.5	92.4	95.0	95.8	98.1	104.8	102.7
Labor Force, Agriculture (%)	7.8	7.7	7.5	7.3	7.1	7.0	6.8	6.6	6.5	6.3	6.2
Labor Force, Female (%)	32.7	33.2	33.7	34.2	34.8	35.3	35.6	35.9	36.2	36.5	36.7
Primary Schl. Enroll. Ratio	..	..	..	..	..	..	..	..	..	..	..
Primary Schl. Enroll. Ratio, Female	..	..	..	..	..	..	..	..	..	..	..
Secondary Schl. Enroll. Ratio	..	..	..	..	..	..	..	..	..	..	..

1981	1982	1983	1984	1985	1986	1987	1988	1989	1990 est.	Notes	
				(Millions of current US dollars)							**FOREIGN TRADE (CUSTOMS BASIS)**
26,717	25,618	25,307	25,724	27,281	37,534	45,357	50,633	51,444	63,699	..	Value of Exports, fob
1,989	1,812	1,877	2,011	1,961	2,473	3,045	3,716	3,448	3,936	..	Nonfuel Primary Products
31	35	73	90	90	64	61	69	57	80	..	Fuels
24,697	23,770	23,358	23,623	25,230	34,997	42,251	46,847	47,939	59,682	..	Manufactures
30,607	28,577	28,934	29,625	30,626	41,188	50,557	56,325	58,150	69,427	..	Value of Imports, cif
4,541	4,144	4,260	4,261	4,307	5,516	6,586	6,802	7,012	7,940	..	Nonfuel Primary Products
3,742	3,331	3,267	3,040	3,044	2,404	2,245	2,077	2,309	3,169	..	Fuels
22,324	21,102	21,407	22,324	23,275	33,268	41,726	47,446	48,830	58,318	..	Manufactures
				(Index 1987 = 100)							
89.5	92.6	92.2	86.2	86.4	104.5	100.0	100.8	98.8	100.5	..	Terms of Trade
73.9	72.6	70.4	63.8	63.1	82.5	100.0	107.6	114.3	135.9	..	Export Prices, fob
82.7	78.5	76.3	74.0	73.0	78.9	100.0	106.8	115.7	135.3	..	Import Prices, cif
				(Millions of current US dollars)							**BALANCE OF PAYMENTS**
59,250	55,011	52,496	55,748	56,612	74,268	87,703	98,611	103,570	124,905	..	Exports of Goods & Services
40,104	36,073	33,907	36,658	37,057	48,453	55,219	62,725	65,366	77,488	..	Merchandise, fob
6,816	6,979	7,422	7,301	7,928	10,809	13,715	14,366	14,015	16,848	..	Nonfactor Services
12,330	11,959	11,167	11,788	11,627	15,007	18,768	21,521	24,189	30,569	..	Factor Services
54,821	51,457	50,370	48,771	49,766	68,524	79,913	88,055	93,845	115,609	..	Imports of Goods & Services
42,488	39,292	39,298	37,747	38,618	53,412	60,647	67,301	69,690	83,865	..	Merchandise, fob
4,696	4,733	4,710	4,697	4,977	6,539	8,145	9,168	9,021	11,036	..	Nonfactor Services
7,637	7,432	6,363	6,327	6,171	8,572	11,121	11,586	15,135	20,708	..	Factor Services
..	..	..	..	..	..	..	..	..	..		Long-Term Interest
-881	-921	-901	-826	-841	-1,206	-1,550	-1,711	-1,665	-2,185	..	Private Current Transfers, net
	84	85	69	77	106	127	130	116	137	..	Workers' Remittances
3,549	2,633	1,224	6,151	6,005	4,539	6,240	8,845	8,060	7,111	..	Curr. A/C Bal before Off. Transf.
-122	-99	-13	-9	35	116	45	-2	-18	-170	..	Net Official Transfers
3,427	2,534	1,211	6,143	6,040	4,654	6,285	8,843	8,042	6,941	..	Curr. A/C Bal after Off. Transf.
-9,622	-13,605	-3,991	-4,398	-7,036	3,365	-4,396	-18,766	-11,215	-9,761	..	Long-Term Capital, net
		151	-362	-3,305	662	1,047	-8,289	-5,023	-1,449	..	Direct Investment
..	..	..	..	..	..	..	..	..	..	..	Long-Term Loans
..	..	..	..	..	..	..	..	..	..	..	Disbursements
..	..	..	..	..	..	..	..	..	..	..	Repayments
-9,622	-13,605	-4,141	-4,035	-3,731	2,703	-5,443	-10,476	-6,192	-8,312	..	Other Long-Term Capital
5,675	14,569	3,163	-265	2,221	-6,926	1,317	7,497	4,593	3,952	..	Other Capital, net
521	-3,499	-384	-1,480	-1,225	-1,093	-3,205	2,426	-1,420	-1,132		Change in Reserves
				(Swiss Francs per US dollar)							**Memo Item:**
1.960	2.030	2.100	2.350	2.460	1.800	1.490	1.460	1.640	1.390	..	Conversion Factor (Annual Avg)
			(Millions US dollars), outstanding at end of year						..		**EXTERNAL DEBT (Total)**
..	..	..	..	..	..	..	..	..		..	Long-Term Debt (by debtor)
..	..	..	..	..	..	..	..	..		..	Central Bank, incl. IMF credit
..	..	..	..	..	..	..	..	..		..	Central Government
..	..	..	..	..	..	..	..	..		..	Rest of General Government
..	..	..	..	..	..	..	..	..		..	Non-financial Public Enterprises
..	..	..	..	..	..	..	..	..		..	Priv. Sector, incl non-guaranteed
..	..	..	..	..	..	..	..	..		..	Short-Term Debt
				(Millions of US dollars)							**Memo Items:**
13,979	15,460	15,034	15,296	18,016	21,786	27,476	24,203	25,276	29,223	..	Int'l Reserves Excluding Gold
33,103	38,049	31,770	25,674	27,232	32,553	40,314	34,164	33,394	32,062	..	Gold Holdings (at market price)
											SOCIAL INDICATORS
1.6	1.6	1.5	1.5	1.5	1.5	1.7	1.7	1.7	1.7	..	Total Fertility Rate
7.5	7.7	7.6	7.3	6.9	6.9	6.8	6.6	6.5	6.3	..	Infant Mortality Rate
76.1	76.3	76.5	76.7	76.9	77.1	77.3	77.5	77.7	78.0	..	Life Expectancy at Birth
57.2	57.5	57.7	58.0	58.2	58.5	58.9	59.2	59.6	59.9	..	Urban Population, % of total
99.6	108.5	102.2	106.4	104.7	106.7	100.0	103.0	103.8	102.5	..	Food Prod. per capita (1987=100)
..	..	..	..	..	..	..	..	..	..	..	Labor Force, Agriculture (%)
36.7	36.7	36.7	36.7	36.7	36.7	36.7	36.6	36.6	36.6	..	Labor Force, Female (%)
..	..	..	..	..	..	..	..	..	..	..	Primary Schl. Enroll. Ratio
..	..	..	..	..	..	..	..	..	..	..	Primary Schl. Enroll. Ratio, Female
..	..	..	..	..	..	..	..	..	..	..	Secondary Schl. Enroll. Ratio

SYRIAN ARAB REPUBLIC	1970	1971	1972	1973	1974	1975	1976	1977	1978	1979	1980
CURRENT GNP PER CAPITA (US $)	360	400	480	460	630	860	1,030	1,020	1,130	1,220	1,450
POPULATION (thousands)	6,258	6,486	6,720	6,957	7,196	7,438	7,680	7,922	8,168	8,427	8,704
USE AND ORIGIN OF RESOURCES					*(Billions of current Syrian Pounds)*						
Gross National Product (GNP)	6.79	8.01	9.22	9.87	15.93	20.64	24.70	27.08	32.56	39.13	51.31
Net Factor Income from Abroad	-0.01	-0.01	-0.01	0.01	0.09	0.04	-0.02	0.06	0.17	0.15	0.04
GDP at Market Prices	6.80	8.01	9.23	9.86	15.84	20.60	24.73	27.01	32.39	38.97	51.27
Resource Balance	-0.24	-0.40	-0.51	-0.37	-1.53	-2.59	-3.65	-6.08	-5.31	-6.57	-8.82
Exports of Goods & NFServices	1.19	1.39	1.67	2.18	3.82	4.41	4.83	4.91	4.81	7.46	9.34
Imports of Goods & NFServices	1.43	1.79	2.19	2.54	5.35	7.00	8.48	10.98	10.11	14.03	18.17
Domestic Absorption	7.04	8.41	9.74	10.23	17.38	23.18	28.38	33.09	37.70	45.55	60.09
Private Consumption, etc.	4.92	5.79	6.24	6.88	10.60	13.68	15.66	18.20	22.34	26.93	34.11
General Gov't Consumption	1.19	1.43	1.64	2.12	2.82	4.34	4.96	5.29	6.47	8.42	11.87
Gross Domestic Investment	0.94	1.19	1.87	1.23	3.96	5.16	7.76	9.60	8.89	10.19	14.12
Fixed Investment	0.90	1.15	1.60	1.77	3.07	5.16	7.76	9.60	8.89	10.19	14.12
Indirect Taxes, net	..	..	..	..	..	..	..	..	..	..	..
GDP at factor cost	..	..	..	..	..	..	..	..	..	..	..
Agriculture	1.38	1.61	2.32	1.68	3.22	3.71	4.81	5.00	6.85	6.86	10.37
Industry	1.70	2.00	2.08	2.29	4.03	4.98	6.22	6.60	8.13	10.55	11.95
Manufacturing	..	..	..	..	..	..	..	..	..	..	..
Services, etc.	3.72	4.40	4.83	5.89	8.59	11.92	13.69	15.41	17.41	21.57	28.95
Gross Domestic Saving	0.70	0.79	1.36	0.86	2.43	2.57	4.11	3.52	3.58	3.62	5.29
Gross National Saving	0.72	0.82	1.50	1.02	2.68	2.80	4.29	3.95	6.24	7.31	8.37
					(Millions of 1987 Syrian Pounds)						
Gross National Product	44,615	49,115	60,436	56,495	69,595	83,494	92,166	91,719	99,241	103,608	114,235
GDP at Market Prices	44,676	49,173	60,505	56,456	69,253	83,367	92,287	91,542	98,774	103,253	114,183
Resource Balance	..	..	..	..	..	-16,286	-17,379	-31,035	-25,998	-28,003	-28,506
Exports of Goods & NFServices	..	..	..	..	..	17,453	15,016	14,542	13,266	15,879	15,253
Imports of Goods & NFServices	..	..	..	..	..	33,739	32,396	45,577	39,264	43,882	43,758
Domestic Absorption	..	..	..	..	..	97,571	109,241	118,979	122,913	127,799	141,787
Private Consumption, etc.	..	..	..	..	..	57,970	63,147	68,281	74,488	73,333	81,264
General Gov't Consumption	..	..	..	..	..	19,761	19,354	20,312	22,123	27,907	28,144
Gross Domestic Investment	..	..	..	..	..	19,840	26,741	30,386	26,301	26,560	32,379
Fixed Investment	..	..	..	..	..	19,840	26,741	30,386	26,301	26,560	32,379
GDP at factor cost	..	..	..	..	..	..	..	..	..	..	..
Agriculture	13,541	14,880	24,718	14,848	22,704	23,835	28,494	24,822	30,469	26,056	36,685
Industry	8,867	10,194	11,221	11,424	13,571	16,455	18,900	18,032	18,661	19,210	20,472
Manufacturing	..	..	..	..	..	..	..	..	..	..	..
Services, etc.	22,460	24,235	27,399	29,524	34,156	42,990	45,562	48,028	50,644	56,634	59,012
Memo Items:											
Capacity to Import	..	..	..	..	..	21,263	18,446	20,365	18,665	23,322	22,508
Terms of Trade Adjustment	..	..	..	..	..	3,810	3,430	5,823	5,399	7,442	7,255
Gross Domestic Income	..	..	..	..	..	87,177	95,717	97,365	104,173	110,696	121,438
Gross National Income	..	..	..	..	..	87,304	95,596	97,542	104,641	111,051	121,490
DOMESTIC PRICES/DEFLATORS					*(Index 1987 = 100)*						
Overall (GDP)	15.2	16.3	15.3	17.5	22.9	24.7	26.8	29.5	32.8	37.7	44.9
Domestic Absorption	..	..	..	..	..	23.8	26.0	27.8	30.7	35.6	42.4
Agriculture	10.2	10.8	9.4	11.3	14.2	15.5	16.9	20.1	22.5	26.3	28.3
Industry	19.1	19.7	18.6	20.1	29.7	30.2	32.9	36.6	43.6	54.9	58.4
Manufacturing	..	..	..	..	..	..	..	..	..	..	..
Consumer Price Index	9.2	9.7	9.9	11.9	13.8	15.4	17.1	19.2	20.1	21.0	25.1
MANUFACTURING ACTIVITY											
Employment (1987=100)	78.2	89.9	95.0	100.6	105.9	112.4	120.6	126.3	133.6	133.7	139.7
Real Earnings per Empl. (1987=100)	105.7	100.1	105.2	93.2	85.2	82.1	76.7	91.9	112.2	135.8	143.4
Real Output per Empl. (1987=100)	34.0	39.6	45.7	42.0	35.8	39.1	45.2	44.8	44.0	38.4	48.3
Earnings as % of Value Added	33.1	32.3	25.8	25.1	20.8	21.5	18.3	21.4	27.6	29.8	27.7
MONETARY HOLDINGS					*(Millions of current Syrian Pounds)*						
Money Supply, Broadly Defined	2,521	2,716	3,428	4,114	5,996	7,585	9,387	12,035	15,293	17,904	24,030
Money	2,341	2,502	3,151	3,797	5,540	6,966	8,561	10,924	13,866	16,119	21,854
Currency Outside Banks	1,795	1,846	2,245	2,757	3,413	3,944	5,259	6,797	8,459	9,903	13,422
Demand Deposits	546	656	906	1,040	2,127	3,021	3,302	4,127	5,407	6,216	8,432
Quasi-Money	180	213	277	317	456	619	826	1,111	1,427	1,785	2,176
GOVERNMENT DEFICIT (-) OR SURPLUS					*(Millions of current Syrian Pounds)*						
	..	..	-327	-574	-740	-992	-2,332	-2,928	-2,935	303	-4,976
Current Revenue	..	..	2,333	2,759	4,824	8,688	9,713	10,410	10,397	15,572	19,711
Current Expenditure	..	..	1,735	2,240	3,203	5,160	6,046	6,634	7,333	9,210	15,546
Current Budget Balance	..	..	598	519	1,621	3,528	3,667	3,776	3,064	6,362	4,165
Capital Receipts	..	..	13	7	11	10	10	10	14	13	15
Capital Payments	..	..	938	1,100	2,372	4,530	6,009	6,714	6,013	6,072	9,156

1981	1982	1983	1984	1985	1986	1987	1988	1989	1990 estimate	Notes	SYRIAN ARAB REPUBLIC
1,680	1,790	1,810	1,730	1,740	1,460	1,180	1,080	880	1,000	A	**CURRENT GNP PER CAPITA (US $)**
8,999	9,310	9,639	9,985	10,348	10,724	11,112	11,514	11,930	12,360	..	**POPULATION (thousands)**
											USE AND ORIGIN OF RESOURCES
			(Billions of current Syrian Pounds)								
65.70	68.15	72.74	74.92	82.72	98.98	122.97	177.00	189.72	259.24	..	Gross National Product (GNP)
-0.07	-0.64	-0.55	-0.42	-0.50	-0.95	-4.88	-7.72	-13.75	-15.01	..	Net Factor Income from Abroad
65.78	68.79	73.29	75.34	83.23	99.93	127.85	184.72	203.47	274.25	..	GDP at Market Prices
-11.40	-7.58	-9.83	-8.72	-10.50	-10.98	-16.95	-17.16	-10.12	-1.77	..	Resource Balance
10.29	9.57	9.71	9.36	10.25	11.26	20.00	31.21	50.60	74.22	..	Exports of Goods & NF Services
21.69	17.15	19.55	18.08	20.74	22.23	36.96	48.37	60.71	75.99	..	Imports of Goods & NF Services
77.17	76.36	83.13	84.06	93.72	110.91	144.80	201.88	213.58	276.02	..	Domestic Absorption
48.26	44.99	49.69	47.75	54.16	67.26	98.79	151.49	145.22	197.28	f	Private Consumption, etc.
13.66	15.10	16.15	18.45	19.78	21.44	22.95	24.53	33.47	39.71	..	General Gov't Consumption
15.26	16.27	17.29	17.86	19.78	22.21	23.06	25.86	34.90	39.03	f	Gross Domestic Investment
15.26	16.27	17.29	17.86	19.78	22.21	23.06	25.86	34.90	39.03	..	Fixed Investment
..	..	..	..	..	..	..	..	..	..	..	Indirect Taxes, net
..	..	..	..	..	..	..	..	..	..	B	GDP at factor cost
12.76	13.85	15.63	14.81	17.46	23.82	32.48	56.59	48.83	76.19	..	Agriculture
16.79	15.94	16.47	17.04	18.21	22.25	24.92	36.10	51.63	59.68	..	Industry
..	..	..	..	..	..	..	..	..	..	..	Manufacturing
36.23	39.00	41.19	43.50	47.55	53.87	70.45	92.04	103.00	138.38	..	Services, etc.
3.87	8.69	7.45	9.14	9.29	11.23	6.11	8.70	24.78	37.26	..	Gross Domestic Saving
5.50	9.67	8.42	9.98	10.15	11.55	2.54	5.02	15.47	26.46	..	Gross National Saving
			(Millions of 1987 Syrian Pounds)								
124,931	127,087	129,424	123,937	131,368	125,596	122,966	139,150	127,089	146,985	..	Gross National Product
125,120	128,293	130,398	124,650	132,210	126,797	127,847	145,086	136,979	156,217	H	GDP at Market Prices
-25,335	-18,227	-17,191	-17,469	-27,085	-12,959	-16,952	-9,584	-13,480	-10,469	..	Resource Balance
14,855	15,638	16,213	15,534	17,932	16,376	20,003	21,360	19,424	28,217	..	Exports of Goods & NF Services
40,191	33,865	33,405	33,003	45,017	29,336	36,955	30,944	32,903	38,687	..	Imports of Goods & NF Services
150,783	148,245	149,620	144,686	159,483	141,713	144,799	154,710	152,521	168,323	..	Domestic Absorption
88,124	82,923	80,562	72,367	88,017	77,814	98,791	110,943	109,586	121,441	f	Private Consumption, etc.
29,507	31,190	32,854	35,655	32,987	29,657	22,945	21,523	25,374	28,929	..	General Gov't Consumption
33,151	34,132	36,205	36,664	38,479	34,242	23,063	22,244	17,561	17,954	f	Gross Domestic Investment
33,151	34,132	36,205	36,664	38,479	34,242	23,063	22,244	17,561	17,954	..	Fixed Investment
..	..	..	..	..	..	..	..	..	..	B H	GDP at factor cost
37,794	36,691	36,584	33,417	35,451	37,739	32,479	43,171	29,738	35,873	..	Agriculture
20,757	22,264	23,464	21,422	26,490	23,523	24,921	29,581	36,120	45,159	..	Industry
..	..	..	..	..	..	..	..	..	..	..	Manufacturing
68,043	69,789	70,351	69,812	70,268	65,535	70,447	72,334	71,121	75,185	..	Services, etc.
											Memo Items:
19,070	18,902	16,599	17,083	22,233	14,853	20,003	19,968	27,421	37,786	..	Capacity to Import
4,214	3,265	385	1,549	4,301	-1,524	0	-1,392	7,998	9,569	..	Terms of Trade Adjustment
129,334	131,558	130,784	126,199	136,510	125,273	127,847	143,695	144,977	165,786	..	Gross Domestic Income
129,146	130,351	129,809	125,486	135,668	124,072	122,966	137,759	135,087	156,553	..	Gross National Income
											DOMESTIC PRICES/DEFLATORS
			(Index 1987 = 100)								
52.6	53.6	56.2	60.4	62.9	78.8	100.0	127.3	148.5	175.6	..	Overall (GDP)
51.2	51.5	55.6	58.1	58.8	78.3	100.0	130.5	140.0	164.0	..	Domestic Absorption
33.8	37.8	42.7	44.3	49.3	63.1	100.0	131.1	164.2	212.4	..	Agriculture
80.9	71.6	70.2	79.6	68.8	94.6	100.0	122.0	142.9	132.2	..	Industry
..	..	..	..	..	..	..	..	..	..	..	Manufacturing
29.7	33.9	36.0	39.3	46.1	62.7	100.0	134.6	149.9	179.0	..	Consumer Price Index
											MANUFACTURING ACTIVITY
150.5	151.7	154.4	143.7	130.6	120.2	100.0	92.3	..	..	G	Employment (1987=100)
151.9	142.1	143.2	130.0	130.3	124.2	100.0	92.1	..	..	G	Real Earnings per Empl. (1987=100)
50.5	61.8	67.1	68.8	84.1	76.3	100.0	..	..	..	G	Real Output per Empl. (1987=100)
28.4	29.7	30.9	30.8	34.7	34.9	31.7	..	..	..	..	Earnings as % of Value Added
											MONETARY HOLDINGS
			(Millions of current Syrian Pounds)								
27,841	33,511	41,287	52,774	63,493	71,121	78,692	96,857	116,370	..	..	Money Supply, Broadly Defined
24,832	29,518	36,978	45,606	54,976	61,214	67,163	79,814	95,030	..	..	Money
14,046	17,348	20,500	25,154	29,562	36,262	41,721	52,171	59,962	..	..	Currency Outside Banks
10,786	12,171	16,479	20,452	25,414	24,952	25,442	27,643	35,068	..	..	Demand Deposits
3,009	3,993	4,309	7,167	8,517	9,907	11,528	17,044	21,340	..	..	Quasi-Money
			(Millions of current Syrian Pounds)								
-4,157	-6,662	-6,658	-11,641	-11,594	-8,267	-3,355	2,319	-1,267	..	..	**GOVERNMENT DEFICIT (-) OR SURPLUS**
21,202	24,556	26,990	23,314	24,694	26,189	32,088	44,337	51,800	..	..	Current Revenue
17,174	19,166	..	..	..	24,166	23,029	29,307	39,053	..	..	Current Expenditure
4,028	5,390	..	..	..	2,023	9,059	15,030	12,747	..	..	Current Budget Balance
1	..	..	..	..	..	..	..	..	..	..	Capital Receipts
8,186	8,278	..	..	..	10,290	12,414	12,711	14,014	..	..	Capital Payments

SYRIAN ARAB REPUBLIC	1970	1971	1972	1973	1974	1975	1976	1977	1978	1979	1980
FOREIGN TRADE (CUSTOMS BASIS)					*(Millions of current US dollars)*						
Value of Exports, fob	203.0	194.6	287.3	351.1	783.7	930.0	1,055.1	1,063.0	1,060.3	1,645.1	2,107.3
Nonfuel Primary Products	146.1	124.9	196.6	218.3	288.6	203.7	268.8	319.3	299.0	333.5	307.1
Fuels	34.0	46.7	52.6	76.3	432.4	653.8	682.6	644.0	665.9	1,186.6	1,662.0
Manufactures	22.9	23.0	38.1	56.5	62.7	72.4	103.6	99.8	95.5	125.0	138.2
Value of Imports, cif	350.0	438.3	539.4	613.2	1,229.4	1,669.1	1,959.1	2,656.0	2,443.8	3,324.0	4,095.8
Nonfuel Primary Products	124.2	180.8	165.2	205.7	414.0	432.8	416.7	445.1	571.5	601.8	784.1
Fuels	28.1	26.9	24.1	28.0	74.2	108.7	192.1	445.0	324.3	822.6	1,069.4
Manufactures	197.7	230.6	350.2	379.6	741.2	1,127.7	1,350.2	1,765.8	1,547.9	1,899.5	2,242.3
					(Index 1987 = 100)						
Terms of Trade	92.3	75.5	81.4	84.4	103.7	88.6	101.2	104.9	93.3	106.5	129.0
Export Prices, fob	22.1	22.1	28.5	37.7	66.0	58.0	65.8	71.7	72.1	94.7	142.0
Import Prices, cif	23.9	29.3	35.0	44.7	63.7	65.5	65.0	68.4	77.3	88.9	110.0
BALANCE OF PAYMENTS					*(Millions of current US dollars)*						
Exports of Goods & Services	326.0	371.1	471.2	631.8	1,142.5	1,314.9	1,379.6	1,453.1	1,371.1	2,077.5	2,567.5
Merchandise, fob	197.0	195.6	298.6	356.4	782.9	930.0	1,065.6	1,069.8	1,061.2	1,647.7	2,112.0
Nonfactor Services	128.0	174.5	171.5	265.8	304.3	335.1	295.6	329.5	259.2	376.3	364.8
Factor Services	1.0	1.0	1.1	9.5	55.3	49.8	18.5	53.8	50.7	53.5	90.7
Imports of Goods & Services	405.0	458.4	526.6	693.8	1,436.0	1,928.1	2,606.9	2,855.5	2,804.8	3,660.0	4,610.1
Merchandise, fob	332.0	381.1	445.1	568.6	1,039.1	1,425.4	2,102.4	2,402.0	2,203.5	3,055.1	4,009.7
Nonfactor Services	70.0	74.2	78.2	119.2	369.2	466.2	479.1	418.1	579.4	590.1	521.0
Factor Services	3.0	3.0	3.3	6.0	27.7	36.4	25.4	35.4	21.9	14.8	79.4
Long-Term Interest	6.2	6.8	6.7	8.5	10.9	17.3	22.5	28.3	55.5	71.6	77.3
Private Current Transfers, net	7.0	8.0	39.1	37.0	44.5	52.2	53.1	92.5	635.9	901.4	773.5
Workers' Remittances	7.0	8.0	39.1	37.0	44.5	52.2	53.1	92.5	635.9	901.4	773.5
Curr. A/C Bal before Off. Transf.	-72.0	-79.2	-16.3	-25.0	-248.9	-560.9	-1,174.1	-1,309.9	-797.8	-681.1	-1,269.1
Net Official Transfers	3.0	21.1	44.5	363.6	416.1	654.4	401.8	1,143.2	782.4	1,626.8	1,520.0
Curr. A/C Bal after Off. Transf.	-69.0	-58.2	28.2	338.6	167.2	93.5	-772.4	-166.7	-15.4	945.7	250.9
Long-Term Capital, net	10.0	81.2	14.1	25.0	..	-9.7	270.2	227.8	359.2	74.9	-25.0
Direct Investment	..	..	..	..	..	..	..	..	..	..	..
Long-Term Loans	29.4	42.9	42.3	56.6	73.6	190.1	319.4	466.8	205.5	250.3	923.5
Disbursements	60.0	75.7	77.6	94.8	135.1	277.2	404.1	545.8	382.6	449.1	1,148.3
Repayments	30.6	32.8	35.3	38.2	61.5	87.1	84.7	79.0	177.1	198.8	224.8
Other Long-Term Capital	-19.4	38.3	-28.2	-31.6	..	-199.8	-49.2	-239.0	153.7	-175.4	-948.5
Other Capital, net	48.6	7.3	-20.2	-85.0	-64.7	159.6	93.7	130.4	-446.5	-826.0	-479.8
Change in Reserves	10.4	-30.4	-22.1	-278.6	-102.4	-243.4	408.5	-191.5	102.7	-194.6	253.9
Memo Item:					*(Syrian Pounds per US dollar)*						
Conversion Factor (Annual Avg)	3.180	3.090	3.020	3.040	3.070	3.020	3.240	3.510	3.490	3.930	3.930
EXTERNAL DEBT (Total)	242.0	298.7	361.2	440.3	*(Millions of US dollars), outstanding at end of year*						
	242.0	298.7	361.2	440.3	518.6	685.2	1,003.5	1,820.3	2,024.9	2,335.7	3,548.9
Long-Term Debt (by debtor)	242.0	298.7	361.2	440.3	518.6	685.2	1,003.5	1,504.3	1,755.9	2,021.7	2,917.9
Central Bank, incl. IMF credit	9.5	5.2	24.6	21.6	6.6	0.0	0.0	0.0	0.0	0.0	0.0
Central Government	134.4	177.3	212.1	257.6	267.6	390.9	612.7	954.4	1,128.0	1,386.4	2,188.3
Rest of General Government	3.3	2.9	2.4	2.5	2.0	2.1	1.5	1.0	6.0	5.5	5.2
Non-financial Public Enterprises	94.8	113.3	118.3	150.2	229.8	280.3	381.4	541.4	619.0	629.6	724.3
Priv. Sector, incl non-guaranteed	0.0	0.0	3.8	8.4	12.6	11.9	7.9	7.5	2.9	0.2	0.1
Short-Term Debt	0.0	0.0	0.0	0.0	0.0	0.0	0.0	316.0	269.0	314.0	631.0
Memo Items:					*(Millions of US dollars)*						
Int'l Reserves Excluding Gold	27.00	58.00	105.30	378.67	466.10	701.90	293.39	483.74	381.80	580.83	336.53
Gold Holdings (at market price)	29.90	34.90	51.92	89.80	147.15	110.66	106.32	133.77	183.29	426.50	491.05
SOCIAL INDICATORS											
Total Fertility Rate	7.7	7.7	7.7	7.6	7.6	7.5	7.5	7.4	7.4	7.4	7.4
Infant Mortality Rate	95.6	91.8	88.0	83.8	79.6	75.4	71.2	67.0	65.4	63.8	62.2
Life Expectancy at Birth	55.8	56.4	57.0	57.6	58.2	58.8	59.4	60.1	60.6	61.1	61.6
Urban Population, % of total	43.3	43.7	44.0	44.4	44.7	45.1	45.4	45.7	46.1	46.4	46.7
Food Prod. per capita (1987=100)	66.5	71.4	101.0	57.1	99.8	99.7	111.9	100.5	114.3	104.7	134.3
Labor Force, Agriculture (%)	50.2	48.1	46.2	44.4	42.7	41.1	39.1	37.2	35.5	33.8	32.3
Labor Force, Female (%)	11.6	12.0	12.4	12.7	13.0	13.2	13.6	13.9	14.1	14.4	14.6
Primary Schl. Enroll. Ratio	78.0	..	..	..	..	96.0	90.0	98.0	98.0	99.0	102.0
Primary Schl. Enroll. Ratio, Female	59.0	..	..	..	..	78.0	75.0	81.0	83.0	86.0	89.0
Secondary Schl. Enroll. Ratio	38.0	..	..	..	..	43.0	..	44.0	46.0	46.0	47.0

1981	1982	1983	1984	1985	1986	1987	1988	1989	1990 est.	Notes	SYRIAN ARAB REPUBLIC
											FOREIGN TRADE (CUSTOMS BASIS)
				(Millions of current US dollars)							
2,102.9	2,026.4	1,922.9	1,853.4	1,637.3	1,326.2	3,870.6	1,344.6	3,005.8	4,172.5	..	Value of Exports, fob
262.4	313.7	308.4	438.7	225.3	263.7	769.8	267.4	597.8	829.8	..	Nonfuel Primary Products
1,661.5	1,513.8	1,323.9	1,168.8	1,212.5	557.4	1,626.9	565.2	1,263.4	1,753.8	..	Fuels
179.0	198.9	290.7	246.0	199.5	505.0	1,473.9	512.0	1,144.6	1,588.9	..	Manufactures
5,039.8	4,014.1	4,542.3	4,115.6	3,967.0	2,716.3	7,112.1	2,230.7	2,097.5	2,399.7	..	Value of Imports, cif
984.4	735.6	1,094.8	936.0	922.5	649.0	1,699.4	533.0	501.2	573.4	..	Nonfuel Primary Products
1,744.6	1,511.3	1,370.6	1,412.0	1,162.3	496.6	1,300.2	407.8	383.5	438.7	..	Fuels
2,310.8	1,767.2	2,076.9	1,767.5	1,882.2	1,570.6	4,112.4	1,289.9	1,212.8	1,387.6	..	Manufactures
				(Index 1987 = 100)							
136.7	131.7	129.7	129.0	125.4	90.1	100.0	72.8	84.3	87.0	..	Terms of Trade
153.7	138.2	130.0	126.7	120.4	80.0	100.0	89.3	108.4	121.6	..	Export Prices, fob
112.5	105.0	100.2	98.2	96.0	88.9	100.0	122.5	128.7	139.9	..	Import Prices, cif
				(Millions of current US dollars)							**BALANCE OF PAYMENTS**
2,736.5	2,510.7	2,493.1	2,376.1	2,540.5	1,612.7	1,981.9	2,037.0	3,849.4	5,084.9	..	Exports of Goods & Services
2,211.5	2,002.1	1,917.8	1,834.2	1,855.9	1,036.9	1,357.3	1,347.6	3,013.0	4,221.0	..	Merchandise, fob
431.3	483.0	559.5	512.0	655.6	566.2	600.0	667.0	814.7	838.8	..	Nonfactor Services
93.7	25.6	15.8	29.9	29.0	9.6	24.6	22.4	21.7	25.1	..	Factor Services
5,328.7	4,569.4	5,025.1	4,720.2	5,059.2	3,198.8	3,374.3	3,083.7	3,295.9	3,712.5	..	Imports of Goods & Services
4,404.0	3,635.5	4,024.0	3,687.2	3,945.7	2,363.2	2,225.8	1,986.3	1,820.6	2,062.4	..	Merchandise, fob
813.9	757.0	853.6	905.5	974.5	698.8	689.9	636.4	730.5	819.1	..	Nonfactor Services
110.8	176.9	147.5	127.5	139.0	136.8	458.6	461.0	744.8	831.0	..	Factor Services
55.4	73.1	72.9	76.4	75.7	82.3	99.8	104.1	112.0	121.8	..	Long-Term Interest
436.0	410.7	386.5	321.4	349.6	323.0	334.0	360.0	395.0	375.0	..	Private Current Transfers, net
436.0	410.7	386.5	321.4	349.6	323.0	334.0	360.0	395.0	375.0	..	Workers' Remittances
-2,156.2	-1,648.0	-2,145.5	-2,022.7	-2,169.1	-1,263.1	-1,058.4	-686.7	948.5	1,747.4	..	Curr. A/C Bal before Off. Transf.
1,848.2	1,398.1	1,301.5	1,228.7	1,211.6	759.1	760.5	536.1	222.6	79.7	..	Net Official Transfers
-308.0	-249.9	-844.0	-794.0	-957.5	-504.0	-297.9	-150.6	1,171.1	1,827.1	..	Curr. A/C Bal after Off. Transf.
-150.7	-179.1	189.1	289.7	-120.3	144.0	206.8	297.0	-471.5	-794.6	..	Long-Term Capital, net
..	..	..	..	..	0.0	0.0	0.0	..	..	..	Direct Investment
1,125.4	1,280.7	2,380.4	-573.4	1,956.0	1,876.7	2,685.2	806.3	571.9	-892.3	..	Long-Term Loans
1,370.0	1,523.8	2,610.7	568.0	2,167.8	2,088.9	2,911.0	1,146.1	1,442.9	360.5	..	Disbursements
244.6	243.1	230.3	1,141.4	211.8	212.2	225.8	339.8	871.0	1,252.8	..	Repayments
-1,276.1	-1,459.8	-2,191.3	863.1	-2,076.3	-1,732.7	-2,478.4	-509.3	-1,043.4	97.7	..	Other Long-Term Capital
407.9	336.7	509.6	720.7	892.2	421.0	169.9	-178.4	89.4	-311.4	..	Other Capital, net
50.8	92.3	145.3	-216.4	185.6	-61.0	-78.8	32.0	-789.0	-721.1	..	Change in Reserves
				(Syrian Pounds per US dollar)							**Memo Item:**
4.240	4.220	4.170	4.300	5.070	7.520	11.250	17.590	19.020	18.620	..	Conversion Factor (Annual Avg)
			(Millions of US dollars), outstanding at end of year								
4,799.9	6,148.2	8,545.6	8,425.8	10,819.1	12,918.1	15,997.3	16,383.0	16,880.8	16,446.1	..	**EXTERNAL DEBT (Total)**
4,000.5	5,253.7	7,594.7	7,406.2	9,501.7	11,536.7	14,478.4	15,165.5	15,703.9	14,958.9	..	Long-Term Debt (by debtor)
0.0	0.0	0.0	0.0	0.0	0.0	0.0	0.0	0.0	0.0	..	Central Bank, incl. IMF credit
3,240.1	4,469.6	6,770.4	6,499.9	8,316.3	10,152.1	12,843.8	13,564.9	14,171.4	13,437.6	..	Central Government
4.6	3.5	2.3	7.6	18.4	24.0	28.0	26.7	24.7	22.1	..	Rest of General Government
755.7	779.5	821.0	897.8	1,145.8	1,334.0	1,583.1	1,556.5	1,499.0	1,499.0	..	Non-financial Public Enterprises
0.1	1.1	1.0	0.9	21.2	26.6	23.5	17.4	8.8	0.2	..	Priv. Sector, incl non-guaranteed
799.4	894.5	950.9	1,019.6	1,317.4	1,381.4	1,518.9	1,217.5	1,176.9	1,487.2	..	Short-Term Debt
				(Millions of US dollars)							**Memo Items:**
291.42	198.08	52.18	268.19	83.05	144.25	223.03	193.03	..	..	..	Int'l Reserves Excluding Gold
331.12	380.60	317.79	256.81	272.39	325.62	403.26	341.74	334.03	320.71	..	Gold Holdings (at market price)
											SOCIAL INDICATORS
7.4	7.4	7.2	7.1	7.0	6.8	6.7	6.6	6.6	6.5	..	Total Fertility Rate
60.6	59.0	56.8	54.6	52.4	50.2	48.0	46.2	44.4	42.5	..	Infant Mortality Rate
62.1	62.6	63.0	63.5	64.0	64.5	65.0	65.4	65.7	66.1	..	Life Expectancy at Birth
47.0	47.4	47.7	48.1	48.4	48.8	49.2	49.6	50.0	50.4	..	Urban Population, % of total
134.2	135.6	127.5	105.8	112.3	119.9	100.0	125.7	77.7	93.4	..	Food Prod. per capita (1987=100)
										..	Labor Force, Agriculture (%)
14.9	15.2	15.5	15.7	16.0	16.3	16.5	16.8	17.0	17.3	..	Labor Force, Female (%)
..	103.0	105.0	107.0	109.0	111.0	110.0	110.0	108.0	..	..	Primary Schl. Enroll. Ratio
..	92.0	96.0	98.0	101.0	105.0	104.0	104.0	102.0	..	..	Primary Schl. Enroll. Ratio, Female
..	52.0	56.0	59.0	60.0	60.0	59.0	57.0	54.0	..	..	Secondary Schl. Enroll. Ratio

TANZANIA	1970	1971	1972	1973	1974	1975	1976	1977	1978	1979	1980
CURRENT GNP PER CAPITA (US $)	100	100	110	130	140	170	180	200	230	260	290
POPULATION (thousands)	13,513	13,877	14,223	14,572	14,951	15,379	15,877	16,403	17,000	17,517	18,098

USE AND ORIGIN OF RESOURCES	*(Billions of current Tanzania Shillings)*										
Gross National Product (GNP)	9.15	9.79	11.16	13.11	16.00	18.99	24.32	28.78	32.12	36.21	42.01
Net Factor Income from Abroad	-0.03	-0.02	-0.01	0.01	0.00	-0.02	-0.10	-0.09	-0.05	-0.07	-0.11
GDP at Market Prices	9.17	9.81	11.17	13.10	15.99	19.01	24.42	28.87	32.17	36.28	42.12
Resource Balance	-0.19	-0.46	-0.40	-0.80	-2.34	-2.37	-0.54	-0.94	-4.87	-4.63	-5.55
Exports of Goods & NFServices	2.39	2.67	3.00	3.10	3.47	3.77	5.30	5.63	4.69	5.13	5.54
Imports of Goods & NFServices	2.58	3.13	3.40	3.90	5.80	6.14	5.84	6.57	9.56	9.76	11.09
Domestic Absorption	9.36	10.28	11.57	13.90	18.33	21.38	24.96	29.81	37.04	40.91	47.67
Private Consumption, etc.	6.31	6.55	7.73	9.24	12.05	14.10	15.38	17.98	23.36	25.50	32.49
General Gov't Consumption	0.98	1.14	1.40	1.91	2.76	3.28	3.99	4.31	5.58	5.96	5.49
Gross Domestic Investment	2.07	2.59	2.44	2.76	3.52	4.00	5.60	7.52	8.09	9.46	9.69
Fixed Investment	1.88	2.37	2.36	2.60	3.03	3.54	5.16	6.66	7.33	8.59	8.63
Indirect Taxes, net	0.96	0.96	1.14	1.61	1.98	2.02	2.77	3.17	3.59	3.97	4.66
GDP at factor cost	8.21	8.86	10.03	11.49	14.01	16.99	21.65	25.70	28.58	32.32	37.45
Agriculture	3.38	3.49	4.02	4.54	5.44	7.01	9.05	11.13	12.51	14.73	16.64
Industry	1.42	1.56	1.80	2.11	2.41	2.76	4.13	4.89	5.40	5.66	6.35
Manufacturing	0.83	0.85	1.14	1.26	1.48	1.77	2.81	3.29	3.86	3.87	4.10
Services, etc.	3.41	3.80	4.21	4.84	6.16	7.22	8.48	9.67	10.68	11.93	14.47
Gross Domestic Saving	1.88	2.13	2.04	1.96	1.18	1.64	5.05	6.58	3.22	4.83	4.14
Gross National Saving	1.93	2.14	1.93	1.87	1.10	1.70	5.05	6.65	3.35	5.00	4.20

	(Millions of 1987 Tanzania Shillings)										
Gross National Product	138,830	144,349	154,799	164,635	168,022	174,490	179,351	179,492	184,028	188,572	193,597
GDP at Market Prices	139,258	144,691	154,986	164,583	168,061	174,766	180,543	180,633	184,344	189,008	194,183
Resource Balance	-30,190	-37,607	-30,342	-36,291	-50,576	-40,245	-26,942	-35,155	-66,319	-51,772	-46,884
Exports of Goods & NFServices	53,740	58,487	65,540	56,987	41,988	48,405	50,285	43,488	41,831	36,771	38,811
Imports of Goods & NFServices	83,930	96,094	95,882	93,278	92,564	88,650	77,227	78,643	108,151	88,543	85,695
Domestic Absorption	169,448	182,298	185,328	200,874	218,637	215,011	207,485	215,788	250,663	240,779	241,066
Private Consumption, etc.	..	..	..	..	..	..	143,582	143,368	175,452	162,188	171,845
General Gov't Consumption	..	..	..	..	..	..	13,875	13,927	17,871	19,750	14,348
Gross Domestic Investment	43,137	51,521	41,403	43,325	48,822	44,862	50,029	58,493	57,340	58,842	54,873
Fixed Investment	39,091	46,756	39,817	40,712	41,992	38,661	46,191	52,002	52,692	54,814	50,292
GDP at factor cost	125,646	131,717	140,313	145,312	148,131	157,139	159,530	160,244	163,169	167,690	172,022
Agriculture	83,201	82,185	88,912	89,763	86,057	93,351	88,452	89,469	87,983	88,648	92,090
Industry	18,971	21,695	22,754	23,305	23,516	23,157	25,565	24,958	24,692	26,116	26,029
Manufacturing	13,495	14,778	16,025	16,738	16,966	17,023	20,039	18,827	19,461	20,110	19,126
Services, etc.	23,473	27,837	28,647	32,244	38,558	40,631	45,513	45,816	50,494	52,926	53,903

Memo Items:											
Capacity to Import	77,844	81,941	84,624	74,120	55,299	54,482	70,034	67,355	53,052	46,553	42,820
Terms of Trade Adjustment	24,104	23,454	19,083	17,134	13,311	6,077	19,750	23,867	11,221	9,782	4,009
Gross Domestic Income	163,362	168,145	174,070	181,716	181,372	180,842	200,293	204,500	195,565	198,790	198,192
Gross National Income	162,934	167,803	173,882	181,768	181,333	180,566	199,100	203,359	195,248	198,354	197,606

DOMESTIC PRICES/DEFLATORS	*(Index 1987 = 100)*										
Overall (GDP)	6.6	6.8	7.2	8.0	9.5	10.9	13.5	16.0	17.5	19.2	21.7
Domestic Absorption	5.5	5.6	6.2	6.9	8.4	9.9	12.0	13.8	14.8	17.0	19.8
Agriculture	4.1	4.2	4.5	5.1	6.3	7.5	10.2	12.4	14.2	16.6	18.1
Industry	7.5	7.2	7.9	9.0	10.2	11.9	16.1	19.6	21.9	21.7	24.4
Manufacturing	6.1	5.7	7.1	7.5	8.7	10.4	14.0	17.5	19.8	19.2	21.4
Consumer Price Index	4.2	4.4	4.7	5.2	6.3	7.9	8.4	9.4	10.5	11.9	15.6

MANUFACTURING ACTIVITY											
Employment (1987=100)	..	..	..	..	..	..	..	..	..	..	..
Real Earnings per Empl. (1987=100)	..	..	..	..	..	..	..	..	..	..	..
Real Output per Empl. (1987=100)	..	..	..	..	..	..	..	..	..	..	..
Earnings as % of Value Added	42.4	41.6	39.4	37.3	42.3	..	..	..	33.0	29.7	32.8

MONETARY HOLDINGS	*(Millions of current Tanzania Shillings)*										
Money Supply, Broadly Defined	2,220	2,624	3,090	3,653	4,462	5,553	6,947	8,347	9,396	13,807	17,520
Money	1,679	2,058	2,327	2,775	3,456	4,284	5,332	6,383	6,827	10,435	13,346
Currency Outside Banks	818	986	1,201	1,199	1,517	1,756	2,071	2,380	2,915	4,055	5,246
Demand Deposits	860	1,072	1,126	1,576	1,939	2,528	3,260	4,003	3,912	6,380	8,100
Quasi-Money	541	566	763	878	1,006	1,269	1,615	1,964	2,569	3,371	4,174

GOVERNMENT DEFICIT (-) OR SURPLUS	*(Millions of current Tanzania Shillings)*										
	..	..	-554	-745	-917	-1,891	-1,527	-1,542	-2,365	-5,376	-3,537
Current Revenue	..	..	1,793	2,294	3,177	4,237	4,393	5,906	6,790	7,381	8,539
Current Expenditure	..	..	1,596	2,087	2,869	4,373	4,300	5,222	5,871	8,214	7,542
Current Budget Balance	..	..	197	207	308	-136	93	684	919	-833	997
Capital Receipts	..	..	..	..	..	..	..	..	..	..	..
Capital Payments	..	..	751	952	1,225	1,755	1,620	2,226	3,284	4,543	4,534

1981	1982	1983	1984	1985	1986	1987	1988	1989	1990 estimate	Notes	TANZANIA
310	330	330	330	320	280	210	170	140	110	f	**CURRENT GNP PER CAPITA (US $)**
18,691	19,295	19,907	20,529	21,161	21,806	22,464	23,135	23,819	24,517	..	**POPULATION (thousands)**
(Billions of current Tanzania Shillings)											**USE AND ORIGIN OF RESOURCES**
48.93	58.00	70.30	88.72	119.92	156.37	210.64	309.14	374.78	405.82	f	Gross National Product (GNP)
-0.18	-0.23	-0.21	-0.17	-0.70	-3.28	-11.04	-18.54	-29.38	-61.44	..	Net Factor Income from Abroad
49.10	58.23	70.51	88.89	120.62	159.65	221.68	327.69	404.16	467.27	f	GDP at Market Prices
-4.17	-4.32	-3.65	-7.22	-10.03	-22.45	-49.65	-82.67	-123.45		..	Resource Balance
5.99	4.55	5.11	6.32	7.45	14.58	29.94	49.88	74.54		..	Exports of Goods & NFServices
10.16	8.86	8.76	13.54	17.48	37.03	79.59	132.55	198.00		..	Imports of Goods & NFServices
53.27	62.54	74.16	96.11	130.65	182.09	271.33	410.35	527.61		..	Domestic Absorption
37.03	42.26	55.13	68.65	93.13	127.31	195.93	312.82	385.67		..	Private Consumption, etc.
6.11	8.05	9.44	13.84	18.55	23.62	25.43	32.66	42.19		..	General Gov't Consumption
10.13	12.24	9.59	13.62	18.96	31.17	49.97	64.88	99.75		..	Gross Domestic Investment
8.63	10.82	7.75	11.97	16.87	28.68	46.28	60.75	94.27		..	Fixed Investment
5.20	5.68	7.90	10.75	12.54	18.85	26.07	37.02	52.93	65.69	..	Indirect Taxes, net
43.91	52.55	62.61	78.14	108.08	140.79	195.61	290.67	351.23	401.58	f	GDP at factor cost
20.34	26.45	32.74	41.29	61.23	84.15	117.98	178.76	207.06		..	Agriculture
6.84	6.91	6.88	8.48	10.05	13.64	21.94	34.08	42.22		..	Industry
4.50	4.36	4.87	5.93	6.66	8.55	14.79	24.45	30.35		..	Manufacturing
16.73	19.19	22.99	28.37	36.80	43.00	55.69	77.83	101.95		..	Services, etc.
5.96	7.92	5.94	6.40	8.94	8.72	0.32	-17.79	-23.70		..	Gross Domestic Saving
5.97	7.92	5.94	7.19	12.36	13.63	4.06	-13.31	-26.92		..	Gross National Saving
(Millions of 1987 Tanzania Shillings)											
191,527	190,914	190,272	199,255	200,994	208,222	210,641	220,454	226,252	220,905	f	Gross National Product
192,289	191,742	190,834	199,688	202,315	212,971	221,678	233,367	243,571	253,550	f	GDP at Market Prices
-27,823	-29,465	-22,212	-34,049	-39,846	-51,065	-49,649	-52,330	..	..	..	Resource Balance
47,183	32,828	30,810	26,744	29,706	26,832	29,943	29,802	..	..	..	Exports of Goods & NFServices
75,007	62,293	53,022	60,792	69,552	77,897	79,592	82,132	..	..	..	Imports of Goods & NFServices
220,112	221,208	213,047	233,737	242,161	264,036	271,327	285,697			..	Domestic Absorption
150,695	144,236	158,803	169,403	172,307	185,030	195,928	198,970			..	Private Consumption, etc.
16,136	19,050	14,539	17,934	19,468	27,645	25,433	26,553			..	General Gov't Consumption
53,282	57,921	39,705	46,400	50,386	51,360	49,966	60,174			..	Gross Domestic Investment
47,606	53,211	34,068	42,440	46,720	47,902	46,281	56,622			..	Fixed Investment
171,297	172,398	168,893	174,966	180,920	187,998	195,611	203,653	213,295	220,698	f	GDP at factor cost
92,999	94,251	96,940	100,831	106,884	113,005	117,982	123,262	128,904	132,659	..	Agriculture
24,036	23,819	20,055	21,324	20,500	21,014	21,943	22,779	24,160	26,011	..	Industry
16,981	16,424	14,992	15,391	14,792	14,193	14,792	15,590	17,102	18,442	..	Manufacturing
54,262	54,328	51,899	52,811	53,536	53,979	55,686	57,612	60,231	62,029	..	Services, etc.
											Memo Items:
44,242	31,955	30,932	28,374	29,655	30,674	29,943	30,908	..	..	..	Capacity to Import
-2,941	-873	122	1,630	-51	3,842	0	1,107	..	..	..	Terms of Trade Adjustment
189,348	190,869	190,957	201,318	202,264	216,813	221,678	234,473	..	..	..	Gross Domestic Income
188,586	190,041	190,395	200,885	200,943	212,064	210,641	221,560	..	..	..	Gross National Income
(Index 1987 = 100)											**DOMESTIC PRICES/DEFLATORS**
25.5	30.4	36.9	44.5	59.6	75.0	100.0	140.4	165.9	184.3	..	Overall (GDP)
24.2	28.3	34.8	41.1	54.0	69.0	100.0	143.6	..	..	..	Domestic Absorption
21.9	28.1	33.8	41.0	57.3	74.5	100.0	145.0	160.6	..	..	Agriculture
28.4	29.0	34.3	39.8	49.0	64.9	100.0	149.6	174.7	..	..	Industry
26.5	26.6	32.5	38.5	45.1	60.2	100.0	156.8	177.5	..	..	Manufacturing
19.5	25.2	32.0	43.3	58.1	77.0	100.0	131.2	167.9	208.9	..	Consumer Price Index
											MANUFACTURING ACTIVITY
..	..	..	..	..	..	..	..	..	..	..	Employment (1987=100)
..	..	..	..	..	..	..	..	..	..	..	Real Earnings per Empl. (1987=100)
..	..	..	..	..	..	..	..	..	..	..	Real Output per Empl. (1987=100)
34.1	33.1	34.5	33.7	35.1	..	..	..	..	..	..	Earnings as % of Value Added
(Millions of current Tanzania Shillings)											**MONETARY HOLDINGS**
20,690	24,729	29,127	30,200	39,344	50,309	66,440	87,780	..	..	..	Money Supply, Broadly Defined
15,396	18,323	20,564	20,608	25,468	35,810	47,131	64,126	..	..	..	Money
6,611	7,989	8,194	10,473	12,673	18,310	24,551	31,227	..	..	..	Currency Outside Banks
8,785	10,334	12,370	10,136	12,795	17,500	22,580	32,898	..	..	..	Demand Deposits
5,293	6,406	8,563	9,591	13,876	14,499	19,309	23,655	..	..	..	Quasi-Money
(Millions of current Tanzania Shillings)											
-3,270	..	..	..	-5,463	..	..	..	..	..	C	**GOVERNMENT DEFICIT (-) OR SURPLUS**
10,311	..	..	..	20,149	..	..	..	..	..	..	Current Revenue
9,007	..	..	..	18,529	..	..	..	..	..	..	Current Expenditure
1,304	..	..	..	1,620	..	..	..	..	..	..	Current Budget Balance
..	..	..	..	..	..	..	..	..	..	..	Capital Receipts
4,574	..	..	..	7,083	..	..	..	..	..	..	Capital Payments

TANZANIA	1970	1971	1972	1973	1974	1975	1976	1977	1978	1979	1980
FOREIGN TRADE (CUSTOMS BASIS)					*(Millions of current US dollars)*						
Value of Exports, fob	236.1	243.0	283.8	318.2	355.2	343.2	484.0	550.8	472.3	500.3	527.7
Nonfuel Primary Products	190.2	184.3	231.5	265.4	292.4	282.5	411.9	491.1	403.0	397.3	427.7
Fuels	15.7	20.2	30.3	12.4	18.3	18.8	20.7	17.6	10.8	16.6	24.9
Manufactures	30.2	38.5	22.0	40.4	44.6	41.9	51.4	42.1	58.6	86.5	75.1
Value of Imports, cif	271.5	337.9	363.4	447.4	760.1	718.2	645.3	730.1	1,141.3	1,076.7	1,211.4
Nonfuel Primary Products	24.4	30.7	47.0	47.7	176.1	159.8	98.1	106.0	121.5	83.3	194.7
Fuels	23.2	30.1	34.0	48.3	140.7	77.4	120.0	96.9	126.3	149.1	254.0
Manufactures	223.9	277.0	282.4	351.3	443.3	481.0	427.2	527.3	893.5	844.3	762.7
					(Index 1987 = 100)						
Terms of Trade	119.1	110.5	106.6	132.9	120.9	103.6	141.2	157.1	128.6	128.4	111.9
Export Prices, fob	26.1	27.3	28.5	43.8	69.4	64.1	81.9	101.7	94.8	110.6	113.5
Import Prices, cif	21.9	24.7	26.8	33.0	57.5	61.8	58.0	64.8	73.7	86.2	101.4
BALANCE OF PAYMENTS					*(Millions of current US dollars)*						
Exports of Goods & Services	321.8	349.6	411.7	455.8	488.4	491.2	633.2	656.4	625.3	697.2	761.8
Merchandise, fob	245.9	262.0	316.2	363.6	399.2	372.9	490.4	538.5	476.0	545.7	582.7
Nonfactor Services	65.2	78.0	85.4	72.1	71.9	109.4	135.4	106.8	130.2	140.0	165.1
Factor Services	10.7	9.6	10.1	20.0	17.3	9.0	7.4	11.1	19.1	11.6	14.0
Imports of Goods & Services	370.2	455.3	473.3	568.2	822.8	823.6	722.2	842.5	1,262.6	1,218.5	1,411.7
Merchandise, fob	283.5	345.3	359.8	437.8	660.4	670.0	555.6	646.7	992.5	960.7	1,089.1
Nonfactor Services	72.5	97.1	101.6	111.6	145.3	141.4	141.0	163.9	245.3	237.6	295.0
Factor Services	14.2	12.8	11.8	18.8	17.2	12.1	25.7	31.8	24.8	20.2	27.6
Long-Term Interest	3.3	4.6	6.4	8.7	10.5	13.3	16.7	22.0	29.8	35.3	44.0
Private Current Transfers, net	11.1	3.5	-14.5	-14.4	-11.4	11.5	11.5	19.4	23.1	29.5	21.8
Workers' Remittances	..	..	..	..	..	..	..	..	..	..	8.0
Curr. A/C Bal before Off. Transf.	-37.3	-102.1	-76.1	-126.8	-345.9	-320.8	-77.6	-166.7	-614.2	-491.8	-628.1
Net Official Transfers	1.7	2.3	10.4	19.3	60.6	90.8	43.9	96.5	142.2	146.6	106.9
Curr. A/C Bal after Off. Transf.	-35.6	-99.8	-65.7	-107.5	-285.3	-230.0	-33.7	-70.2	-472.0	-345.2	-521.2
Long-Term Capital, net	71.6	137.7	108.4	139.5	124.7	206.4	102.4	96.6	136.0	225.4	289.1
Direct Investment	..	..	..	..	..	..	..	..	..	..	..
Long-Term Loans	54.1	54.0	92.2	114.6	130.2	192.3	126.8	178.1	188.2	231.0	354.0
Disbursements	58.3	62.8	101.2	126.5	146.4	214.0	146.2	202.9	214.9	264.3	395.9
Repayments	4.2	8.8	9.0	11.9	16.2	21.7	19.4	24.8	26.7	33.3	41.9
Other Long-Term Capital	17.5	83.7	16.2	24.9	-5.5	14.1	-24.4	-81.5	-52.2	-5.6	-64.9
Other Capital, net	-56.6	-51.2	7.3	0.0	23.0	8.9	-46.4	133.8	164.8	62.8	166.0
Change in Reserves	20.6	13.3	-50.0	-32.0	137.5	14.7	-22.3	-160.1	171.2	57.0	66.0
Memo Item:					*(Tanzania Shillings per US dollar)*						
Conversion Factor (Annual Avg)	7.000	7.000	7.000	7.000	7.000	7.000	8.000	8.000	8.000	8.000	8.200
					(Millions of US dollars), outstanding at end of year						
EXTERNAL DEBT (Total)	194.6	255.1	356.0	490.2	697.2	882.6	1,051.4	1,432.2	1,785.5	2,080.3	2,446.7
Long-Term Debt (by debtor)	194.6	255.1	356.0	490.2	697.2	882.6	1,051.4	1,273.2	1,532.5	1,830.3	2,140.8
Central Bank, incl. IMF credit	0.0	0.0	0.0	0.1	48.3	74.5	98.6	112.5	109.2	156.1	175.6
Central Government	174.0	222.3	303.2	410.6	553.1	705.3	826.6	999.5	1,194.4	1,371.6	1,568.4
Rest of General Government	..	..	..	..	..	..	..	..	..	..	..
Non-financial Public Enterprises	5.6	12.8	22.8	34.0	43.6	46.1	62.4	96.6	159.2	223.1	290.0
Priv. Sector, incl non-guaranteed	15.0	20.0	30.0	45.5	52.2	56.7	63.8	64.6	69.7	79.5	106.8
Short-Term Debt	0.0	0.0	0.0	0.0	0.0	0.0	0.0	159.0	253.0	250.0	305.9
Memo Items:					*(Thousands of US dollars)*						
Int'l Reserves Excluding Gold	64,970	60,253	119,587	144,617	50,232	65,446	112,267	281,827	99,860	68,041	20,300
Gold Holdings (at market price)	..	..	..						..	..	..
SOCIAL INDICATORS											
Total Fertility Rate	6.4	6.4	6.3	6.3	6.4	6.4	6.5	6.5	6.6	6.7	6.8
Infant Mortality Rate	132.0	131.0	130.0	129.0	128.0	127.0	126.0	125.0	123.8	122.7	121.5
Life Expectancy at Birth	45.1	45.6	46.0	46.1	46.3	46.4	46.5	46.6	46.8	47.0	47.2
Urban Population, % of total	6.7	7.4	8.1	8.7	9.4	10.1	11.4	12.7	13.9	15.2	16.5
Food Prod. per capita (1987=100)	103.4	100.0	96.7	99.6	95.6	107.4	107.6	112.0	109.9	115.1	106.2
Labor Force, Agriculture (%)	90.4	89.8	89.3	88.9	88.4	88.0	87.5	87.0	86.5	86.0	85.6
Labor Force, Female (%)	50.6	50.5	50.4	50.3	50.2	50.2	50.1	50.0	50.0	49.9	49.8
Primary Schl. Enroll. Ratio	34.0	..	..	..	..	53.0	70.0	99.0	96.0	100.0	93.0
Primary Schl. Enroll. Ratio, Female	27.0	..	..	..	..	44.0	..	88.0	87.0	93.0	86.0
Secondary Schl. Enroll. Ratio	3.0	..	..	..	..	3.0	4.0	4.0	4.0	4.0	3.0

1981	1982	1983	1984	1985	1986	1987	1988	1989	1990 estimate	Notes	TANZANIA
											FOREIGN TRADE (CUSTOMS BASIS)
				(Millions of current US dollars)							
552.7	401.0	425.0	376.7	283.9	340.0	288.1	274.6	305.7	300.3	..	Value of Exports, fob
492.4	367.5	376.6	335.6	252.9	302.9	256.6	244.7	272.3	267.5	..	Nonfuel Primary Products
0.9	8.2	17.4	0.6	0.5	0.6	0.5	0.5	0.5	0.5	..	Fuels
59.4	25.3	31.1	40.5	30.5	36.5	31.0	29.5	32.9	32.3	..	Manufactures
905.8	955.9	654.1	847.2	1,028.0	849.5	923.4	814.1	843.3	934.9	..	Value of Imports, cif
75.6	123.0	66.6	196.3	238.2	196.8	213.9	188.6	195.4	216.6	..	Nonfuel Primary Products
305.5	252.0	174.5	156.9	190.3	157.3	171.0	150.7	156.1	173.1	..	Fuels
524.7	580.9	413.0	494.1	599.6	495.5	538.6	474.8	491.8	545.2	..	Manufactures
				(Index 1987 = 100)							
95.1	98.7	101.8	107.6	101.2	115.9	100.0	105.6	108.2	..	..	Terms of Trade
100.0	97.3	97.1	100.7	93.6	108.3	100.0	108.1	105.0	..	..	Export Prices, fob
105.2	98.5	95.3	93.6	92.4	93.4	100.0	102.4	97.0	..	..	Import Prices, cif
				(Millions of current US dollars)							**BALANCE OF PAYMENTS**
808.7	530.2	491.3	505.9	436.6	446.1	448.4	507.0	538.3	547.9	..	Exports of Goods & Services
613.0	412.9	383.2	398.5	328.5	335.9	346.8	386.5	415.1	407.8	..	Merchandise, fob
184.8	114.5	106.3	105.8	105.6	100.7	96.1	117.4	119.5	135.8	..	Nonfactor Services
10.9	2.8	1.7	1.6	2.5	9.5	5.5	3.2	3.8	4.3	..	Factor Services
1,345.6	1,172.7	899.1	1,024.4	1,178.4	1,241.2	1,420.7	1,504.1	1,549.3	1,667.4	..	Imports of Goods & Services
1,061.3	952.0	708.4	760.3	869.2	913.3	1,000.5	1,033.0	1,070.1	1,186.3	..	Merchandise, fob
252.1	193.0	161.5	174.8	208.7	219.0	207.9	263.4	246.6	245.6	..	Nonfactor Services
32.2	27.7	29.2	89.4	100.4	108.9	212.4	207.7	232.6	235.5	..	Factor Services
48.9	58.6	57.1	27.8	24.1	30.7	40.1	40.6	48.3	45.7	..	Long-Term Interest
22.6	25.4	18.7	63.0	236.3	250.6	230.0	231.9	182.4	164.5	..	Private Current Transfers, net
9.0	7.0	7.0	14.0	45.0	48.0	41.0	0.0	0.0	..	..	Workers' Remittances
-514.3	-617.1	-389.2	-455.4	-505.5	-544.6	-742.4	-765.1	-828.6	-955.0	..	Curr. A/C Bal before Off. Transf.
107.7	93.8	84.6	96.5	130.4	223.5	477.0	389.3	469.8	529.0	..	Net Official Transfers
-406.6	-523.3	-304.6	-359.0	-375.2	-321.1	-265.3	-375.8	-358.8	-426.0	..	Curr. A/C Bal after Off. Transf.
295.3	345.1	238.3	-46.3	20.6	1,300.0	151.5	261.0	411.8	424.2	..	Long-Term Capital, net
..	.	..	..	..	..	..	..	0.0	5.0	..	Direct Investment
350.0	310.1	276.8	204.1	124.2	197.5	171.2	231.8	175.5	245.9	..	Long-Term Loans
404.3	366.0	350.4	238.1	165.0	241.2	214.2	275.4	223.0	298.8	..	Disbursements
54.3	55.9	73.6	34.0	40.8	43.7	43.0	43.6	47.5	52.9	..	Repayments
-54.7	35.0	-38.5	-250.4	-103.6	1,102.5	-19.7	29.2	236.3	173.3	..	Other Long-Term Capital
114.3	176.5	107.7	437.6	348.6	-955.9	44.7	117.2	-73.1	140.9	..	Other Capital, net
-3.0	1.8	-41.5	-32.3	6.0	-23.0	69.2	-2.4	20.1	-139.1	..	Change in Reserves
				(Tanzania Shillings per US dollar)							**Memo Item:**
8.280	9.280	11.140	15.290	17.470	32.700	64.260	99.290	143.380	195.060	..	Conversion Factor (Annual Avg)
			(Millions of US dollars), outstanding at end of year								
2,607.1	2,895.7	3,080.2	3,160.6	3,577.1	4,045.1	4,885.4	5,132.0	5,071.5	5,866.3	..	**EXTERNAL DEBT (Total)**
2,307.1	2,487.4	2,621.1	2,552.2	2,863.6	3,707.4	4,420.2	4,625.5	4,752.1	5,445.9	..	Long-Term Debt (by debtor)
150.4	131.5	98.2	65.2	64.3	77.6	119.6	146.1	132.0	142.8	..	Central Bank, incl. IMF credit
1,758.3	1,967.0	2,148.1	2,105.3	2,422.0	3,287.2	3,932.6	4,177.0	4,336.5	5,048.8	..	Central Government
..	..	..	..	..	..	..	..	..	..	..	Rest of General Government
303.0	286.4	277.8	284.7	323.0	290.5	304.8	246.8	228.5	200.3	..	Non-financial Public Enterprises
95.4	102.5	97.0	97.0	54.3	52.1	63.2	55.6	55.1	54.0	..	Priv. Sector, incl non-guaranteed
300.0	408.3	459.1	608.4	713.5	337.7	465.2	506.5	319.4	420.4	..	Short-Term Debt
				(Thousands of US dollars)							**Memo Items:**
18,828	4,822	19,415	26,869	16,000	61,090	31,799	77,714	54,213	192,800	..	Int'l Reserves Excluding Gold
..	..	..	..	..	..	..	..	..	..	..	Gold Holdings (at market price)
											SOCIAL INDICATORS
6.9	7.0	6.9	6.8	6.7	6.6	6.5	6.5	6.5	6.6	..	Total Fertility Rate
120.4	119.2	118.4	117.6	116.9	116.1	115.3	115.3	115.3	115.3	..	Infant Mortality Rate
47.4	47.5	47.7	47.8	48.0	48.2	48.3	48.1	47.8	47.5	..	Life Expectancy at Birth
18.1	19.7	21.2	22.8	24.4	26.5	28.6	30.0	31.4	32.8	..	Urban Population, % of total
107.7	105.7	107.1	105.4	103.8	101.7	100.0	97.0	101.6	92.0	..	Food Prod. per capita (1987=100)
..	..	..	..	..	..	..	..	..	..	..	Labor Force, Agriculture (%)
49.6	49.4	49.3	49.1	48.9	48.7	48.5	48.3	48.1	47.9	..	Labor Force, Female (%)
..	90.0	87.0	83.0	72.0	69.0	66.0	64.0	63.0	..	..	Primary Schl. Enroll. Ratio
..	85.0	85.0	81.0	71.0	69.0	66.0	64.0	63.0	..	..	Primary Schl. Enroll. Ratio, Female
..	3.0	3.0	3.0	3.0	3.0	4.0	4.0	4.0	..	..	Secondary Schl. Enroll. Ratio

THAILAND	1970	1971	1972	1973	1974	1975	1976	1977	1978	1979	1980
CURRENT GNP PER CAPITA (US $)	210	210	220	250	300	360	410	460	530	590	670
POPULATION (thousands)	35,745	36,884	38,017	39,142	40,257	41,359	42,450	43,532	44,602	45,659	46,700

USE AND ORIGIN OF RESOURCES *(Billions of current Thai Baht)*

	1970	1971	1972	1973	1974	1975	1976	1977	1978	1979	1980
Gross National Product (GNP)	147.6	153.3	169.5	221.2	279.1	303.3	345.6	402.3	484.6	552.6	653.1
Net Factor Income from Abroad	0.2	-0.1	-0.6	-0.9	-0.1	0.0	-0.9	-1.2	-3.6	-6.3	-5.4
GDP at Market Prices	147.4	153.4	170.1	222.1	279.2	303.3	346.5	403.5	488.2	558.9	658.5
Resource Balance	-6.5	-4.4	-1.7	-3.2	-6.6	-14.0	-8.6	-21.9	-20.6	-37.5	-41.5
Exports of Goods & NF Services	22.1	24.5	30.9	41.3	60.3	55.7	70.1	80.5	97.1	126.2	159.7
Imports of Goods & NF Services	28.6	28.9	32.6	44.5	66.9	69.7	78.7	102.4	117.7	163.7	201.2
Domestic Absorption	153.9	157.8	171.8	225.3	285.8	317.3	355.1	425.4	508.8	596.4	700.0
Private Consumption, etc.	99.5	103.0	116.3	143.7	185.3	204.9	234.0	274.0	316.7	377.5	444.6
General Gov't Consumption	16.7	17.7	18.6	21.6	26.1	31.3	38.0	42.9	54.6	66.8	81.4
Gross Domestic Investment	37.7	37.1	36.9	60.0	74.4	81.1	83.1	108.5	137.5	152.1	174.0
Fixed Investment	35.0	35.8	38.6	49.9	65.0	69.4	79.4	104.6	123.3	142.9	165.7
Indirect Taxes, net	16.1	16.5	18.4	23.3	32.9	32.6	36.3	44.8	52.9	64.5	76.2
GDP at factor cost	131.3	136.9	151.7	198.8	246.3	270.7	310.2	358.7	435.3	494.4	582.3
Agriculture	38.2	36.7	43.1	61.5	75.4	81.5	92.5	100.0	119.6	134.1	152.9
Industry	37.3	41.5	46.4	59.5	74.4	78.2	95.7	118.4	144.3	169.6	203.0
Manufacturing	23.5	26.9	31.3	42.6	53.5	56.6	68.2	81.4	97.7	117.6	139.9
Services, etc.	71.9	75.2	80.6	101.1	129.4	143.6	158.3	185.1	224.3	255.2	302.6
Gross Domestic Saving	31.2	32.7	35.2	56.8	67.8	67.1	74.5	86.6	116.9	114.6	132.5
Gross National Saving	31.5	32.7	35.2	58.3	72.1	68.2	74.2	85.8	113.4	108.8	128.6

(Billions of 1987 Thai Baht)

	1970	1971	1972	1973	1974	1975	1976	1977	1978	1979	1980
Gross National Product	433.5	453.9	472.1	518.8	545.2	569.9	621.2	680.3	746.6	779.8	823.6
GDP at Market Prices	433.5	454.9	473.9	520.5	543.0	569.0	622.2	682.2	754.3	792.2	829.1
Resource Balance	-65.7	-34.2	-35.4	-71.8	-54.8	-56.8	-44.8	-64.0	-60.5	-89.0	-75.7
Exports of Goods & NF Services	72.2	85.4	99.5	95.0	102.4	97.6	121.1	134.6	151.4	167.2	180.1
Imports of Goods & NF Services	137.8	119.6	134.9	166.8	157.3	154.4	165.9	198.6	211.9	256.2	255.8
Domestic Absorption	499.1	489.1	509.3	592.2	597.8	625.8	667.0	746.2	814.7	881.2	904.8
Private Consumption, etc.	327.8	319.6	346.7	383.7	395.4	412.7	443.3	475.9	498.5	562.3	579.7
General Gov't Consumption	43.1	45.1	46.6	50.1	49.9	56.9	67.9	74.9	84.7	97.9	100.7
Gross Domestic Investment	128.2	124.4	116.0	158.4	152.4	156.2	155.9	195.5	231.6	220.9	224.4
Fixed Investment	118.6	119.2	120.1	132.3	131.9	131.0	148.1	183.6	203.8	211.9	219.7
GDP at factor cost	390.4	410.5	427.4	471.1	484.4	513.5	563.2	613.1	679.9	708.2	740.8
Agriculture	110.1	114.8	112.7	123.5	127.1	132.6	140.7	143.9	161.9	158.8	161.6
Industry	118.9	129.5	140.7	155.3	162.0	169.5	197.1	228.1	253.9	270.2	279.9
Manufacturing	72.9	80.8	91.6	105.9	112.7	119.1	137.2	157.1	170.6	184.9	190.2
Services, etc.	197.6	204.0	214.1	234.8	247.0	259.8	278.4	306.8	334.1	361.2	386.2

Memo Items:

	1970	1971	1972	1973	1974	1975	1976	1977	1978	1979	1980
Capacity to Import	106.5	101.4	127.9	154.8	141.7	123.4	147.8	156.2	174.8	197.5	203.0
Terms of Trade Adjustment	34.3	16.0	28.3	59.8	39.3	25.8	26.7	21.5	23.4	30.3	22.9
Gross Domestic Income	467.8	470.9	502.3	580.2	582.3	594.8	648.9	703.7	777.7	822.5	852.0
Gross National Income	467.8	470.0	500.5	578.6	584.6	595.6	647.9	701.9	770.0	810.1	846.5

DOMESTIC PRICES/DEFLATORS *(Index 1987 = 100)*

	1970	1971	1972	1973	1974	1975	1976	1977	1978	1979	1980
Overall (GDP)	34.0	33.7	35.9	42.7	51.4	53.3	55.7	59.1	64.7	70.6	79.4
Domestic Absorption	30.8	32.3	33.7	38.0	47.8	50.7	53.2	57.0	62.4	67.7	77.4
Agriculture	34.7	32.0	38.2	49.8	59.3	61.5	65.7	69.5	73.9	84.5	94.6
Industry	31.4	32.0	33.0	38.3	45.9	46.1	48.5	51.9	56.8	62.8	72.5
Manufacturing	32.3	33.3	34.2	40.2	47.5	47.5	49.7	51.8	57.3	63.6	73.6
Consumer Price Index	29.7	29.9	31.3	36.2	45.0	47.4	49.4	53.1	57.3	63.0	75.4

MANUFACTURING ACTIVITY

	1970	1971	1972	1973	1974	1975	1976	1977	1978	1979	1980
Employment (1987=100)	..	..	..	..	..	..	..	..	..	..	..
Real Earnings per Empl. (1987=100)	..	..	..	..	..	..	..	..	..	..	..
Real Output per Empl. (1987=100)	..	..	..	..	..	..	..	..	..	..	..
Earnings as % of Value Added	24.5	24.6	24.7	24.7	24.8	24.7	24.7	24.6	24.5	23.2	23.2

MONETARY HOLDINGS *(Billions of current Thai Baht)*

	1970	1971	1972	1973	1974	1975	1976	1977	1978	1979	1980
Money Supply, Broadly Defined	46.5	54.0	67.0	82.4	99.1	114.7	136.4	163.4	192.4	220.3	271.0
Money	19.4	21.3	24.8	30.0	32.7	34.7	41.4	45.4	54.5	63.5	71.4
Currency Outside Banks	11.9	13.1	15.3	18.7	20.5	22.3	25.8	28.7	33.2	40.8	45.9
Demand Deposits	7.4	8.2	9.5	11.2	12.2	12.4	15.5	16.8	21.3	22.7	25.6
Quasi-Money	27.1	32.7	42.2	52.5	66.4	80.0	95.0	118.0	137.9	156.7	199.5

(Billions of current Thai Baht)

	1970	1971	1972	1973	1974	1975	1976	1977	1978	1979	1980
GOVERNMENT DEFICIT (-) OR SURPLUS	..	..	-7.09	-7.04	2.49	-6.24	-13.82	-13.08	-17.77	-20.40	-32.15
Current Revenue	..	..	22.10	26.40	37.79	38.87	42.43	52.18	63.30	76.81	96.89
Current Expenditure	..	..	20.20	25.53	27.77	34.98	40.82	47.16	59.58	74.63	95.68
Current Budget Balance	..	..	1.89	0.87	10.02	3.90	1.61	5.02	3.72	2.18	1.20
Capital Receipts	..	..	0.00	..	0.00	0.00	0.53	0.01	0.01	0.00	0.01
Capital Payments	..	..	8.99	7.91	7.53	10.13	15.96	18.11	21.43	22.59	33.36

1981	1982	1983	1984	1985	1986	1987	1988	1989	1990 estimate	Notes	THAILAND
750	780	810	840	800	800	860	1,030	1,220	1,420	..	**CURRENT GNP PER CAPITA (US $)**
47,727	48,740	49,739	50,720	51,683	52,654	53,605	54,536	55,448	55,801	..	**POPULATION (thousands)**
				(Billions of current Thai Baht)							**USE AND ORIGIN OF RESOURCES**
748.2	807.1	903.4	962.0	996.8	1,072.9	1,230.8	1,482.2	1,752.6	2,030.1	..	Gross National Product (GNP)
-12.0	-12.9	-6.7	-11.4	-17.6	-22.4	-22.4	-24.8	-23.4	-21.1	..	Net Factor Income from Abroad
760.2	820.0	910.1	973.4	1,014.4	1,095.4	1,253.2	1,507.0	1,776.0	2,051.2	f	GDP at Market Prices
-47.7	-14.4	-66.0	-42.2	-28.8	23.0	7.3	-23.0	-41.8	-65.5	..	Resource Balance
181.3	192.9	185.2	216.4	245.3	290.2	375.6	515.0	650.0	771.6	..	Exports of Goods & NF Services
229.0	207.3	251.2	258.6	274.1	267.1	368.3	537.9	691.8	837.1	..	Imports of Goods & NF Services
807.9	834.4	976.1	1,015.6	1,043.2	1,072.3	1,245.9	1,530.0	1,818.0	2,116.6	..	Domestic Absorption
511.2	534.6	621.4	643.0	656.4	689.1	798.7	938.8	1,083.3	1,161.9	..	Private Consumption, etc.
97.0	110.2	118.6	130.1	142.9	144.6	147.4	156.7	174.9	200.7	..	General Gov't Consumption
199.7	189.6	236.1	242.5	243.9	238.6	299.8	434.5	559.7	754.0	..	Gross Domestic Investment
188.0	192.2	218.5	238.6	240.3	238.7	296.3	407.3	550.4	729.1	..	Fixed Investment
84.8	87.4	104.6	115.7	113.9	127.0	149.7	203.0	235.9	294.4	..	Indirect Taxes, net
675.4	732.6	805.5	857.7	900.5	968.3	1,103.5	1,304.0	1,540.1	1,756.8	B f	GDP at factor cost
163.0	156.8	185.6	175.2	169.9	178.1	205.6	250.4	266.4	254.5	..	Agriculture
240.1	258.7	285.8	325.7	345.1	377.1	435.2	540.1	667.7	803.1	..	Industry
169.5	176.4	194.3	218.1	224.5	258.6	299.3	373.3	453.3	535.4	..	Manufacturing
357.1	404.5	438.7	472.5	499.4	540.1	612.4	716.5	841.9	993.5	..	Services, etc.
152.0	175.2	170.1	200.3	215.1	261.7	307.1	411.5	517.7	688.6	..	Gross Domestic Saving
141.1	164.0	166.9	190.3	198.8	240.9	287.3	387.9	495.5	668.1	..	Gross National Saving
				(Billions of 1987 Thai Baht)							
866.3	900.9	978.3	1,042.5	1,070.5	1,120.1	1,230.8	1,397.7	1,575.1	1,743.0	..	Gross National Product
881.1	916.6	982.2	1,052.7	1,088.0	1,143.0	1,253.2	1,421.2	1,595.2	1,759.3	f	GDP at Market Prices
-53.5	-2.0	-71.8	-40.7	-9.9	19.6	7.3	-10.8	-11.0	-36.8	..	Resource Balance
195.2	217.8	205.5	241.9	267.4	306.3	375.6	476.7	580.8	660.4	..	Exports of Goods & NF Services
248.7	219.7	277.3	282.7	277.3	286.8	368.3	487.5	591.8	697.1	..	Imports of Goods & NF Services
934.6	918.6	1,053.9	1,093.4	1,097.9	1,123.5	1,245.9	1,431.9	1,606.2	1,796.1	..	Domestic Absorption
573.3	580.0	656.7	668.7	676.6	718.1	798.7	873.1	987.7	1,059.1	..	Private Consumption, etc.
114.2	118.2	127.3	136.3	145.8	146.0	147.4	152.5	154.8	159.1	..	General Gov't Consumption
247.0	220.3	269.9	288.5	275.6	259.3	299.8	406.3	463.8	577.9	..	Gross Domestic Investment
229.7	225.3	254.3	281.9	267.0	256.8	296.3	361.0	437.3	542.3	..	Fixed Investment
790.9	827.3	878.2	937.5	975.4	1,019.2	1,103.5	1,259.2	1,431.4	1,576.0	B f	GDP at factor cost
170.3	175.5	183.4	193.6	205.3	206.0	205.6	226.6	241.6	237.3	..	Agriculture
296.0	305.1	330.0	358.2	357.6	385.9	435.2	511.2	593.9	686.7	..	Industry
202.2	207.2	224.7	240.0	238.5	264.1	299.3	349.6	401.7	456.6	..	Manufacturing
413.6	434.8	468.8	500.9	525.1	551.1	612.4	683.4	759.7	835.4	..	Services, etc.
											Memo Items:
196.9	204.5	204.4	236.5	248.1	311.5	375.6	466.7	556.0	642.6	..	Capacity to Import
1.7	-13.3	-1.1	-5.4	-19.2	5.2	0.0	-10.0	-24.7	-17.8	..	Terms of Trade Adjustment
882.8	903.3	981.1	1,047.3	1,068.8	1,148.2	1,253.2	1,411.1	1,570.4	1,741.5	..	Gross Domestic Income
868.1	887.7	977.2	1,037.1	1,051.3	1,125.2	1,230.8	1,387.6	1,550.4	1,725.2	..	Gross National Income
				(Index 1987 = 100)							**DOMESTIC PRICES/DEFLATORS**
86.3	89.5	92.7	92.5	93.2	95.8	100.0	106.0	111.3	116.6	..	Overall (GDP)
86.4	90.8	92.6	92.9	95.0	95.4	100.0	106.8	113.2	117.8	..	Domestic Absorption
95.7	89.3	101.2	90.5	82.7	86.5	100.0	110.5	110.2	107.3	..	Agriculture
81.1	84.8	86.6	90.9	96.5	97.7	100.0	105.7	112.4	117.0	..	Industry
83.8	85.1	86.5	90.9	94.1	97.9	100.0	106.8	112.8	117.3	..	Manufacturing
85.0	89.4	92.8	93.6	95.8	97.6	100.0	103.9	109.4	115.9	..	Consumer Price Index
											MANUFACTURING ACTIVITY
..	..	..	..	..	..	..	..	..	..	..	Employment (1987=100)
..	..	..	..	..	..	..	..	..	..	..	Real Earnings per Empl. (1987=100)
..	..	..	..	..	..	..	..	..	..	..	Real Output per Empl. (1987=100)
23.4	23.5	23.6	23.6	23.6	23.4	23.6	23.6	..	..	..	Earnings as % of Value Added
				(Billions of current Thai Baht)							**MONETARY HOLDINGS**
311.6	387.3	480.9	577.4	644.5	730.5	868.2	1,027.8	1,297.9	1,636.2	D	Money Supply, Broadly Defined
73.3	78.3	81.8	88.8	85.8	102.4	132.4	148.5	174.7	195.4	..	Money
47.8	54.0	59.6	63.5	64.0	71.1	86.7	99.0	119.0	137.5	..	Currency Outside Banks
25.5	24.3	22.2	25.2	21.9	31.4	45.7	49.5	55.7	58.0	..	Demand Deposits
238.3	309.0	399.1	488.6	558.7	628.1	735.8	879.3	1,123.2	1,440.8	..	Quasi-Money
				(Billions of current Thai Baht)							
-25.51	-53.54	-36.41	-33.73	-55.40	-47.91	-28.98	10.64	54.73	99.36	C	**GOVERNMENT DEFICIT (-) OR SURPLUS**
117.54	120.91	146.16	157.42	166.83	177.80	203.88	257.26	323.43	411.14	..	Current Revenue
112.33	131.45	144.21	157.33	175.38	180.92	190.19	200.53	227.79	251.32	..	Current Expenditure
5.21	-10.54	1.95	0.10	-8.54	-3.13	13.68	56.73	95.64	159.81	..	Current Budget Balance
0.01	0.01	0.01	0.01	0.01	0.01	0.01	0.02	0.05	0.02	..	Capital Receipts
30.73	43.01	38.37	33.83	46.88	44.80	42.68	46.11	40.96	60.48	..	Capital Payments

THAILAND	1970	1971	1972	1973	1974	1975	1976	1977	1978	1979	1980
FOREIGN TRADE (CUSTOMS BASIS)					*(Millions of current US dollars)*						
Value of Exports, fob	685	802	1,039	1,527	2,402	2,162	2,950	3,451	3,996	5,207	6,369
Nonfuel Primary Products	628	705	863	1,201	2,002	1,784	2,398	2,803	3,041	3,878	4,576
Fuels	2	7	13	20	19	12	6	1	1	2	4
Manufactures	55	90	163	306	382	366	547	647	954	1,327	1,788
Value of Imports, cif	1,293	1,287	1,484	2,073	3,156	3,279	3,572	4,613	5,314	7,132	9,450
Nonfuel Primary Products	162	188	223	316	421	402	484	664	684	1,011	1,169
Fuels	113	134	152	233	625	708	832	1,026	1,130	1,605	2,876
Manufactures	1,019	965	1,110	1,524	2,109	2,170	2,256	2,923	3,501	4,515	5,406
					(Index 1987 = 100)						
Terms of Trade	172.2	155.8	150.0	177.0	168.3	141.2	132.6	131.7	141.8	134.9	123.1
Export Prices, fob	36.3	35.5	38.0	56.0	86.3	75.1	72.7	78.8	93.2	109.1	121.3
Import Prices, cif	21.1	22.8	25.3	31.7	51.3	53.2	54.8	59.8	65.7	80.9	98.6
BALANCE OF PAYMENTS					*(Millions of current US dollars)*						
Exports of Goods & Services	1,171	1,278	1,589	2,133	3,173	2,971	3,621	4,178	5,133	6,663	8,575
Merchandise, fob	686	802	1,046	1,515	2,405	2,177	2,959	3,454	4,045	5,234	6,449
Nonfactor Services	406	407	485	547	624	603	508	531	819	1,034	1,490
Factor Services	79	68	59	70	143	191	154	194	269	394	636
Imports of Goods & Services	1,470	1,496	1,700	2,323	3,501	3,676	4,108	5,315	6,326	8,808	10,861
Merchandise, fob	1,148	1,152	1,325	1,835	2,793	2,850	3,152	4,238	4,904	6,785	8,352
Nonfactor Services	262	277	302	398	565	616	735	829	985	1,329	1,615
Factor Services	60	67	74	91	143	211	220	248	437	694	895
Long-Term Interest	33	40	41	55	85	104	107	125	195	321	473
Private Current Transfers, net	3	7	30	117	215	56	29	22	6	23	75
Workers' Remittances	..	..	..	..	..	18	24	44	104	187	..
Curr. A/C Bal before Off. Transf.	-296	-212	-80	-74	-113	-650	-458	-1,115	-1,187	-2,123	-2,212
Net Official Transfers	46	37	29	27	26	24	18	18	34	37	142
Curr. A/C Bal after Off. Transf.	-250	-175	-51	-46	-87	-625	-440	-1,098	-1,153	-2,086	-2,070
Long-Term Capital, net	110	80	156	51	388	190	297	412	636	1,476	2,084
Direct Investment	43	39	68	77	189	22	79	106	50	51	187
Long-Term Loans	90	45	107	-4	253	200	248	330	626	1,354	1,822
Disbursements	220	203	246	209	422	454	519	647	1,232	1,994	2,604
Repayments	131	157	139	212	169	254	271	317	606	640	782
Other Long-Term Capital	-23	-4	-19	-23	-53	-32	-30	-24	-39	71	75
Other Capital, net	58	84	91	211	183	384	224	694	543	574	-175
Change in Reserves	82	10	-196	-216	-485	51	-81	-9	-27	36	161
Memo Item:					*(Thai Baht per US dollar)*						
Conversion Factor (Annual Avg)	20.800	20.800	20.800	20.620	20.380	20.380	20.400	20.400	20.340	20.420	20.480
				(Millions of US dollars), outstanding at end of year							
EXTERNAL DEBT (Total)	726	782	891	903	1,161	1,352	1,686	3,344	5,029	6,645	8,297
Long-Term Debt (by debtor)	726	782	891	903	1,161	1,352	1,686	2,080	2,935	4,305	5,994
Central Bank, incl. IMF credit	0	0	0	0	0	0	78	99	249	367	348
Central Government	173	198	212	239	245	237	350	409	735	1,163	1,521
Rest of General Government	4	7	5	4	2	1	0	0	0	0	0
Non-financial Public Enterprises	127	130	149	181	246	345	428	646	949	1,452	2,287
Priv. Sector, incl non-guaranteed	422	447	525	479	668	769	829	926	1,001	1,324	1,837
Short-Term Debt	0	0	0	0	0	0	0	1,264	2,094	2,340	2,303
Memo Items:					*(Millions of US dollars)*						
Int'l Reserves Excluding Gold	823.5	788.0	963.4	1,206.8	1,758.2	1,678.8	1,797.5	1,812.7	2,008.6	1,842.8	1,560.2
Gold Holdings (at market price)	87.5	102.1	151.9	262.7	436.4	328.2	315.3	395.4	548.3	1,257.0	1,466.1
SOCIAL INDICATORS											
Total Fertility Rate	5.5	5.2	5.0	4.9	4.7	4.6	4.4	4.3	4.1	4.0	3.8
Infant Mortality Rate	72.6	68.8	65.0	61.7	58.3	55.0	54.0	53.0	50.0	47.0	44.0
Life Expectancy at Birth	58.4	59.0	59.6	59.9	60.2	60.6	60.9	61.2	61.5	61.9	62.2
Urban Population, % of total	13.3	13.7	14.1	14.4	14.8	15.2	15.6	16.0	16.5	16.9	17.3
Food Prod. per capita (1987=100)	83.9	82.2	76.3	90.8	85.8	92.5	96.1	92.8	107.7	97.8	105.3
Labor Force, Agriculture (%)	79.8	78.8	77.8	76.9	76.1	75.3	74.3	73.4	72.5	71.7	70.9
Labor Force, Female (%)	47.3	47.3	47.2	47.2	47.1	47.1	47.1	47.1	47.1	47.1	47.1
Primary Schl. Enroll. Ratio	83.0	..	..	..	..	83.0	83.0	83.0	92.0	95.0	99.0
Primary Schl. Enroll. Ratio, Female	79.0	..	..	..	..	80.0	79.0	80.0	89.0	92.0	97.0
Secondary Schl. Enroll. Ratio	17.0	..	..	..	..	26.0	27.0	28.0	28.0	28.0	29.0

1981	1982	1983	1984	1985	1986	1987	1988	1989	1990 estimate	Notes	THAILAND
											FOREIGN TRADE (CUSTOMS BASIS)
6,849	6,797	6,275	7,279	7,056	8,786	11,629	15,902	20,089	23,002	..	Value of Exports, fob
4,978	4,914	4,284	4,780	4,221	4,820	5,446	7,068	8,928	8,027	..	Nonfuel Primary Products
2	2	1	17	90	69	82	122	154	192	..	Fuels
1,869	1,881	1,989	2,482	2,745	3,897	6,102	8,713	11,006	14,783	..	Manufactures
10,055	8,527	10,279	10,518	9,239	9,124	12,955	20,225	25,783	33,129	..	Value of Imports, cif
1,218	1,029	1,218	1,337	1,216	1,348	1,823	3,067	3,910	4,410	..	Nonfuel Primary Products
2,994	2,645	2,488	2,471	2,094	1,230	1,729	1,556	1,984	3,098	..	Fuels
5,843	4,853	6,572	6,710	5,929	6,545	9,403	15,601	19,889	25,622	..	Manufactures

(Index 1987 = 100)

1981	1982	1983	1984	1985	1986	1987	1988	1989	1990 estimate	Notes	THAILAND
108.9	94.7	100.1	97.3	90.6	104.3	100.0	100.9	98.7	98.7	..	Terms of Trade
110.4	91.6	93.5	89.0	81.4	91.0	100.0	112.4	116.8	121.9	..	Export Prices, fob
101.3	96.7	93.4	91.5	89.8	87.3	100.0	111.4	118.3	123.5	..	Import Prices, cif

(Millions of current US dollars)

1981	1982	1983	1984	1985	1986	1987	1988	1989	1990 estimate	Notes	THAILAND
											BALANCE OF PAYMENTS
9,254	9,415	9,227	10,415	10,222	12,136	15,763	21,725	26,880	31,476	..	Exports of Goods & Services
6,902	6,835	6,308	7,338	7,059	8,803	11,595	15,781	19,834	22,811	..	Merchandise, fob
1,612	1,717	1,846	1,964	2,041	2,302	3,070	4,647	5,457	6,611	..	Nonfactor Services
740	864	1,073	1,113	1,122	1,031	1,098	1,297	1,589	2,055	..	Factor Services
11,993	10,602	12,378	12,699	11,925	12,114	16,353	23,616	29,624	38,736	..	Imports of Goods & Services
8,931	7,565	9,169	9,236	8,391	8,415	12,019	17,856	22,750	29,539	..	Merchandise, fob
1,782	1,621	1,865	1,860	1,769	1,804	2,342	3,481	4,377	6,089	..	Nonfactor Services
1,280	1,415	1,344	1,603	1,764	1,895	1,992	2,279	2,497	3,108	..	Factor Services
710	714	750	848	913	1,026	1,055	1,123	1,086	1,210	..	Long-Term Interest
50	75	153	59	47	64	100	47	47	25	..	Private Current Transfers, net
..	..	..	..	..	..	..	..	..	74		Workers' Remittances
-2,688	-1,111	-2,998	-2,225	-1,656	86	-490	-1,844	-2,697	-7,235	..	Curr. A/C Bal before Off. Transf.
119	108	124	115	118	161	125	189	199	182	..	Net Official Transfers
-2,569	-1,003	-2,874	-2,109	-1,537	247	-365	-1,655	-2,498	-7,053	..	Curr. A/C Bal after Off. Transf.
1,869	1,363	1,468	1,746	1,606	55	375	1,196	4,225	3,443	..	Long-Term Capital, net
288	189	348	400	162	261	182	1,081	1,727	2,236	..	Direct Investment
1,596	1,323	1,250	1,505	1,511	-211	-74	76	1,668	-609	..	Long-Term Loans
2,225	2,124	2,265	2,889	3,172	1,810	1,814	2,661	4,072	2,662	..	Disbursements
628	801	1,015	1,385	1,661	2,021	1,887	2,585	2,404	3,272	..	Repayments
-15	-148	-131	-159	-67	4	267	39	831	1,817	..	Other Long-Term Capital
744	-441	1,246	879	13	381	902	3,025	3,285	6,840	..	Other Capital, net
-43	81	161	-516	-82	-684	-912	-2,566	-5,012	-3,230	..	Change in Reserves

(Thai Baht per US dollar)

1981	1982	1983	1984	1985	1986	1987	1988	1989	1990 estimate	Notes	THAILAND
											Memo Item:
21.820	23.000	23.000	23.640	27.160	26.300	25.720	25.290	25.700	25.590	..	Conversion Factor (Annual Avg)

(Millions of US dollars), outstanding at end of year

1981	1982	1983	1984	1985	1986	1987	1988	1989	1990 estimate	Notes	THAILAND
10,852	12,238	13,902	15,013	17,552	18,505	20,305	21,664	23,450	25,868		**EXTERNAL DEBT (Total)**
7,974	9,197	10,597	11,462	14,352	15,665	17,641	16,864	17,338	17,545		Long-Term Debt (by debtor)
858	846	1,040	903	1,122	1,069	972	662	273	1		Central Bank, incl. IMF credit
1,857	2,163	2,500	2,674	4,032	4,802	6,117	6,001	5,602	4,644		Central Government
0	0	0	0	0	0	0	0	0	..		Rest of General Government
2,994	3,703	4,210	4,305	5,575	6,406	7,396	6,895	6,539	7,616		Non-financial Public Enterprises
2,264	2,485	2,847	3,580	3,624	3,388	3,156	3,306	4,925	5,284		Priv. Sector, incl non-guaranteed
2,878	3,041	3,305	3,551	3,200	2,840	2,664	4,800	6,112	8,322		Short-Term Debt

(Millions of US dollars)

1981	1982	1983	1984	1985	1986	1987	1988	1989	1990 estimate	Notes	THAILAND
											Memo Items:
1,731.8	1,537.6	1,607.1	1,920.6	2,190.1	2,804.4	4,007.1	6,096.6	9,515.3	13,305.1		Int'l Reserves Excluding Gold
988.6	1,136.3	948.8	766.7	813.2	972.2	1,198.6	1,015.8	992.9	953.3		Gold Holdings (at market price)
											SOCIAL INDICATORS
3.7	3.5	3.4	3.2	3.1	2.9	2.8	2.7	2.6	2.5		Total Fertility Rate
41.0	38.0	36.6	35.1	33.7	32.2	30.8	29.6	28.4	27.2		Infant Mortality Rate
62.5	62.9	63.2	63.6	64.0	64.3	64.7	65.1	65.5	65.9		Life Expectancy at Birth
17.8	18.3	18.8	19.3	19.8	20.4	20.9	21.5	22.0	22.6		Urban Population, % of total
106.5	103.7	107.2	109.4	112.3	100.5	100.0	112.5	113.8	100.4		Food Prod. per capita (1987=100)
..	..	..	..	..	..	..	..	..	..		Labor Force, Agriculture (%)
46.8	46.6	46.3	46.1	45.9	45.6	45.4	45.1	44.8	44.6		Labor Force, Female (%)
..	..	97.0	97.0	96.0	96.0	95.0	87.0	86.0	88.0		Primary Schl. Enroll. Ratio
..	..								88.0		Primary Schl. Enroll. Ratio, Female
..	..	30.0	31.0	30.0	30.0	28.0	28.0	..	..		Secondary Schl. Enroll. Ratio

TOGO	1970	1971	1972	1973	1974	1975	1976	1977	1978	1979	1980
CURRENT GNP PER CAPITA (US $)	140	140	150	170	210	250	270	300	340	350	410
POPULATION (thousands)	2,020	2,070	2,121	2,173	2,227	2,282	2,328	2,381	2,440	2,506	2,578

USE AND ORIGIN OF RESOURCES

(Billions of current CFA Francs)

	1970	1971	1972	1973	1974	1975	1976	1977	1978	1979	1980
Gross National Product (GNP)	68.90	77.60	82.70	87.80	135.00	131.30	147.10	187.80	181.40	185.10	231.70
Net Factor Income from Abroad	-1.30	-1.30	-1.90	-2.80	0.10	-1.00	-0.90	-3.20	-4.60	-4.60	-8.40
GDP at Market Prices	70.20	78.90	84.60	90.60	134.90	132.30	148.00	191.00	186.00	189.70	240.10
Resource Balance	7.61	5.48	0.68	0.11	50.08	-13.61	1.15	-21.00	-24.00	-49.76	-12.70
Exports of Goods & NFServices	34.84	36.94	33.23	30.00	89.05	57.43	70.01	79.21	119.00	94.85	122.60
Imports of Goods & NFServices	27.23	31.47	32.55	29.89	38.97	71.04	68.86	100.20	143.00	144.62	135.30
Domestic Absorption	62.59	73.42	83.92	90.49	84.82	145.91	146.85	212.00	210.00	239.46	252.80
Private Consumption, etc.	40.92	43.57	49.22	54.18	43.73	80.59	76.84	112.40	77.00	98.55	126.80
General Gov't Consumption	11.07	14.96	17.20	16.60	19.00	28.72	33.21	34.00	35.00	48.31	53.70
Gross Domestic Investment	10.60	14.90	17.50	19.70	22.10	36.60	36.80	65.60	98.00	92.60	72.30
Fixed Investment	..	..	..	..	..	..	..	..	..	..	71.80
Indirect Taxes, net	7.60	8.10	9.20	11.90	12.20	13.90	15.80	18.10	25.20	26.50	29.00
GDP at factor cost	62.60	70.80	75.40	78.70	122.70	118.40	132.20	172.90	160.80	163.20	211.10
Agriculture	23.70	25.00	26.00	29.00	33.20	35.20	47.80	67.70	44.80	48.10	66.00
Industry	14.80	17.80	17.20	18.30	44.70	35.10	30.30	37.20	42.40	47.90	59.50
Manufacturing	7.00	7.00	6.70	7.90	8.20	9.30	10.30	12.00	11.00	13.50	18.80
Services, etc.	31.70	36.10	41.40	43.30	57.00	62.00	69.90	86.10	98.80	93.70	114.60
Gross Domestic Saving	18.21	20.38	18.18	19.81	72.18	22.99	37.95	44.60	74.00	42.83	59.60
Gross National Saving	16.25	18.05	15.02	17.17	72.07	21.69	37.32	41.32	68.97	37.79	51.31

(Billions of 1987 CFA Francs)

	1970	1971	1972	1973	1974	1975	1976	1977	1978	1979	1980
Gross National Product	237.38	239.06	257.28	266.62	287.85	292.45	286.58	301.01	331.95	315.50	358.80
GDP at Market Prices	242.79	243.03	262.61	273.75	286.69	293.75	287.89	306.61	340.55	323.32	370.83
Resource Balance	-16.77	26.91	26.92	25.85	22.84	17.21	-20.22	-68.10	-58.99	-75.31	-4.24
Exports of Goods & NFServices	49.44	106.41	102.82	92.07	89.05	98.67	81.88	108.29	161.19	111.31	162.82
Imports of Goods & NFServices	66.21	79.49	75.90	66.21	66.21	81.46	102.10	176.39	220.18	186.62	167.06
Domestic Absorption	259.56	216.12	235.69	247.90	263.85	276.54	308.11	374.71	399.54	398.63	375.07
Private Consumption, etc.	175.06	119.09	127.76	139.34	151.26	118.64	162.54	155.01	150.72	153.76	187.66
General Gov't Consumption	29.30	35.95	40.75	38.09	40.48	52.20	59.13	66.32	68.52	74.57	75.37
Gross Domestic Investment	55.20	61.07	67.18	70.47	72.11	105.70	86.44	153.39	180.30	170.30	112.04
Fixed Investment	..	..	..	..	..	..	..	..	..	..	111.20
GDP at factor cost	..	..	..	..	..	..	..	..	..	..	325.51
Agriculture	72.35	71.86	75.93	78.37	79.50	81.78	77.72	73.00	85.68	81.46	94.95
Industry	42.55	43.63	50.98	56.16	60.91	62.42	67.76	77.96	78.19	77.92	90.29
Manufacturing	..	..	..	..	..	..	27.53	28.06	23.78	25.92	29.40
Services, etc.	129.73	129.13	136.39	138.93	146.15	149.37	142.10	156.17	177.23	164.22	185.65

Memo Items:

	1970	1971	1972	1973	1974	1975	1976	1977	1978	1979	1980
Capacity to Import	84.73	93.33	77.48	66.46	151.30	65.86	103.81	139.42	183.22	122.40	151.38
Terms of Trade Adjustment	35.29	-13.08	-25.34	-25.60	62.25	-32.81	21.93	31.13	22.03	11.09	-11.44
Gross Domestic Income	278.08	229.95	237.27	248.15	348.94	260.94	309.81	337.75	362.59	334.41	359.39
Gross National Income	272.66	225.98	231.94	241.02	350.11	259.64	308.50	332.15	353.98	326.59	347.36

DOMESTIC PRICES/DEFLATORS

(Index 1987 = 100)

	1970	1971	1972	1973	1974	1975	1976	1977	1978	1979	1980
Overall (GDP)	28.9	32.5	32.2	33.1	47.1	45.0	51.4	62.3	54.6	58.7	64.7
Domestic Absorption	24.1	34.0	35.6	36.5	32.1	52.8	47.7	56.6	52.6	60.1	67.4
Agriculture	32.8	34.8	34.2	37.0	41.8	43.0	61.5	92.7	52.3	59.1	69.5
Industry	34.8	40.8	33.7	32.6	73.4	56.2	44.7	47.7	54.2	61.5	65.9
Manufacturing	..	..	..	..	..	..	37.4	42.8	46.2	52.1	64.0
Consumer Price Index	26.5	28.3	30.4	31.5	35.6	42.0	46.9	57.4	57.7	62.0	69.7

MANUFACTURING ACTIVITY

	1970	1971	1972	1973	1974	1975	1976	1977	1978	1979	1980
Employment (1987=100)	..	..	..	..	..	..	..	..	..	..	..
Real Earnings per Empl. (1987=100)	..	..	..	..	..	..	..	..	..	..	..
Real Output per Empl. (1987=100)	..	..	..	..	..	..	..	..	..	..	..
Earnings as % of Value Added	..	..	..	..	45.5	33.2	31.0	40.5	36.0	28.4	..

MONETARY HOLDINGS

(Billions of current CFA Francs)

	1970	1971	1972	1973	1974	1975	1976	1977	1978	1979	1980
Money Supply, Broadly Defined	12.68	14.11	13.90	15.91	30.47	28.28	41.21	48.08	64.94	66.53	72.57
Money	10.15	11.88	11.82	11.56	25.08	21.56	32.94	36.45	48.09	52.66	55.34
Currency Outside Banks	4.56	5.58	5.45	6.03	8.37	9.99	14.19	15.97	20.80	21.53	27.76
Demand Deposits	5.59	6.29	6.38	5.53	16.71	11.57	18.75	20.48	27.29	31.13	27.57
Quasi-Money	2.53	2.23	2.08	4.35	5.38	6.72	8.27	11.63	16.85	13.87	17.23

GOVERNMENT DEFICIT (-) OR SURPLUS

(Millions of current CFA Francs)

	1970	1971	1972	1973	1974	1975	1976	1977	1978	1979	1980
	..	..	..	..	..	..	..	-39,222	-58,836	-17,942	-4,689
Current Revenue	..	..	..	..	..	..	..	47,022	56,646	70,008	72,896
Current Expenditure	..	..	..	..	..	..	..	33,753	32,500	38,873	..
Current Budget Balance	..	..	..	..	..	..	..	13,269	24,146	31,135	..
Capital Receipts	..	..	..	..	..	..	..	..	..	..	..
Capital Payments	..	..	..	..	..	..	..	52,491	82,982	49,077	..

1981	1982	1983	1984	1985	1986	1987	1988	1989	1990 estimate	Notes	TOGO
400	340	280	260	250	270	300	370	390	410	..	**CURRENT GNP PER CAPITA (US $)**
2,657	2,742	2,834	2,933	3,038	3,147	3,261	3,381	3,507	3,638	..	**POPULATION (thousands)**
											USE AND ORIGIN OF RESOURCES
				(Billions of current CFA Francs)							
249.90	256.10	275.40	296.80	320.60	347.80	360.50	391.90	412.70	431.00	..	Gross National Product (GNP)
-11.60	-13.90	-16.40	-17.00	-17.50	-14.50	-14.40	-14.40	-14.00	-10.50	..	Net Factor Income from Abroad
261.50	270.00	291.80	313.80	338.10	362.30	374.90	406.30	426.70	441.50	f	GDP at Market Prices
-17.60	-23.00	-3.70	-6.60	-29.80	-42.50	-32.30	-38.70	-31.70	-50.30	..	Resource Balance
120.90	135.40	132.70	160.80	165.80	161.30	159.70	177.40	192.80	182.20	..	Exports of Goods & NF Services
138.50	158.40	136.40	167.40	195.60	203.80	192.00	216.10	224.50	232.50	..	Imports of Goods & NF Services
279.10	293.00	295.50	320.40	367.90	404.80	407.20	445.00	458.40	491.80	..	Domestic Absorption
150.10	170.50	180.60	201.70	214.50	245.10	252.70	290.30	292.30	310.60	..	Private Consumption, etc.
49.90	51.60	50.30	52.30	56.10	72.60	78.70	72.80	74.90	81.90	..	General Gov't Consumption
79.10	70.90	64.60	66.40	97.30	87.10	75.80	81.90	91.20	99.30	..	Gross Domestic Investment
70.70	65.80	56.70	69.80	82.80	84.20	67.20	75.40	95.00	96.70	..	Fixed Investment
33.40	36.70	39.20	37.60	41.20	41.80	41.00	45.60	..	..		Indirect Taxes, net
228.10	233.30	252.60	276.20	296.90	320.50	333.90	360.70	385.00	..	B	GDP at factor cost
73.70	72.80	100.60	105.00	112.00	126.20	125.90	137.70	142.20	145.10	f	Agriculture
58.80	63.10	62.50	63.40	69.50	69.70	76.10	84.60	97.40	95.30	..	Industry
18.50	19.90	19.70	20.09	22.20	26.80	28.10	31.60	36.50	41.50	..	Manufacturing
129.00	134.10	128.70	145.40	156.60	166.40	172.90	184.00	187.10	201.10	..	Services, etc.
61.50	47.90	60.90	59.80	67.50	44.60	43.50	43.20	59.50	49.00	..	Gross Domestic Saving
49.70	33.35	43.51	41.97	53.45	33.49	31.19	31.30	49.30	42.20	..	Gross National Saving
				(Billions of 1987 CFA Francs)							
342.57	327.20	308.75	326.74	338.91	353.71	360.50	379.32	394.92	398.52	..	Gross National Product
358.15	344.88	327.09	346.27	357.26	369.49	374.90	393.72	408.92	406.88	I f	GDP at Market Prices
-14.80	-20.67	-0.90	-13.56	-30.15	-54.79	-32.30	-43.46	-42.03	-74.72	..	Resource Balance
142.09	142.23	125.97	126.24	130.44	146.29	159.70	168.10	171.21	163.63	..	Exports of Goods & NF Services
156.90	162.90	126.87	139.80	160.59	201.08	192.00	211.55	213.25	238.34	..	Imports of Goods & NF Services
372.96	365.55	327.99	359.83	387.40	424.28	407.20	437.17	450.96	481.60	..	Domestic Absorption
199.03	211.77	201.81	227.87	225.42	257.30	252.70	285.83	292.86	306.37	..	Private Consumption, etc.
65.19	63.63	54.42	58.73	59.32	78.31	78.70	72.04	74.20	83.79	..	General Gov't Consumption
108.73	90.15	71.75	73.22	102.66	88.68	75.80	79.30	83.90	91.44	..	Gross Domestic Investment
97.21	84.51	63.70	76.96	87.45	85.80	67.20	72.91	80.64	..		Fixed Investment
311.75	297.39	282.94	304.34	313.29	326.63	333.90	348.82	364.11	..	B I	GDP at factor cost
95.14	86.74	87.50	113.67	118.26	123.99	125.90	133.92	143.86	142.14	f	Agriculture
76.28	78.50	73.34	66.52	71.12	72.60	76.10	83.84	86.42	80.89	..	Industry
30.69	31.99	29.61	24.21	26.59	27.67	28.10	29.18	32.21	34.80	..	Manufacturing
187.08	180.26	166.26	166.08	167.87	172.90	172.90	175.95	178.65	183.85	..	Services, etc.
											Memo Items:
136.96	139.25	123.43	134.29	136.12	159.15	159.70	173.67	183.14	186.78	..	Capacity to Import
-5.13	-2.98	-2.54	8.05	5.68	12.86	0.00	5.57	11.92	23.15	..	Terms of Trade Adjustment
353.02	341.90	324.55	354.32	362.94	382.35	374.90	399.29	420.85	430.03	..	Gross Domestic Income
337.44	324.22	306.20	334.79	344.59	366.57	360.50	384.89	406.84	421.67	..	Gross National Income
											DOMESTIC PRICES/DEFLATORS
				(Index 1987 = 100)							
73.0	78.3	89.2	90.6	94.6	98.1	100.0	103.2	104.3	108.5	..	Overall (GDP)
74.8	80.2	90.1	89.0	95.0	95.4	100.0	101.8	101.7	102.1	..	Domestic Absorption
77.5	83.9	115.0	92.4	94.7	101.8	100.0	102.8	98.8	102.1	..	Agriculture
77.1	80.4	85.2	95.3	97.7	96.0	100.0	100.9	112.7	117.8	..	Industry
60.3	62.2	66.5	82.6	83.5	96.9	100.0	108.3	113.3	119.3	..	Manufacturing
83.4	92.7	101.3	97.8	96.0	99.9	100.0	99.9	99.0	100.0	..	Consumer Price Index
											MANUFACTURING ACTIVITY
..	..	..	..	..	..	..	..	..	..	G J	Employment (1987=100)
..	..	..	..	..	..	..	..	..	..	G J	Real Earnings per Empl. (1987=100)
..	..	..	..	..	..	..	..	..	..	G J	Real Output per Empl. (1987=100)
..	32.4	39.2	36.7	..	..	..	..	..	..	J	Earnings as % of Value Added
											MONETARY HOLDINGS
				(Billions of current CFA Francs)							
100.57	117.17	117.76	136.08	143.20	165.49	163.82	144.31	145.92	159.83	..	Money Supply, Broadly Defined
79.97	90.07	83.07	90.69	82.74	89.67	91.04	64.38	63.15	75.25	..	Money
50.74	54.29	45.50	36.99	39.21	46.02	48.27	23.20	21.33	32.09	..	Currency Outside Banks
29.23	35.78	37.57	53.69	43.52	43.65	42.77	41.18	41.83	43.16	..	Demand Deposits
20.60	27.10	34.69	45.39	60.46	75.81	72.77	79.93	82.77	84.58	..	Quasi-Money
				(Millions of current CFA Francs)							
-14,821	-4,794	-5,607	-7,862	-6,104	-16,644	-9,380	..	..	..		**GOVERNMENT DEFICIT (-) OR SURPLUS**
70,891	81,649	85,921	102,607	116,151	120,480	99,574	..	..	..		Current Revenue
61,928	61,505	67,943	85,921	89,204	86,854	80,993	..	..	..		Current Expenditure
8,963	20,144	17,978	16,686	26,947	33,626	18,581	..	..	..		Current Budget Balance
..	..	..	97	447	..	8,300	..	..	..		Capital Receipts
23,784	24,938	23,585	24,645	33,498	50,270	36,261	..	..	..		Capital Payments

TOGO	1970	1971	1972	1973	1974	1975	1976	1977	1978	1979	1980
FOREIGN TRADE (CUSTOMS BASIS)					*(Millions of current US dollars)*						
Value of Exports, fob	54.63	56.35	49.64	61.40	189.12	124.83	105.19	159.39	240.50	218.42	334.77
Nonfuel Primary Products	51.52	46.30	47.13	57.08	182.95	117.53	96.73	150.58	191.99	173.22	212.53
Fuels	0.02	0.00	0.02	0.00	0.01	0.03	0.00	0.04	31.21	24.76	86.85
Manufactures	3.09	10.05	2.49	4.31	6.17	7.28	8.46	8.77	17.30	20.44	35.39
Value of Imports, cif	64.53	70.02	84.79	100.49	119.09	173.90	185.59	284.27	450.78	518.46	549.64
Nonfuel Primary Products	17.11	16.62	19.57	23.74	22.58	30.55	33.11	56.49	50.80	77.28	100.75
Fuels	2.82	3.85	4.75	5.19	11.49	13.01	12.77	20.40	64.77	94.93	125.22
Manufactures	44.59	49.56	60.47	71.56	85.01	130.34	139.70	207.38	335.20	346.26	323.68
					(Index 1987 = 100)						
Terms of Trade	130.6	117.3	110.6	120.0	227.9	191.0	163.1	152.3	128.5	121.3	129.2
Export Prices, fob	39.0	36.9	37.5	50.0	138.9	128.7	110.0	114.4	101.1	111.5	141.6
Import Prices, cif	29.9	31.5	33.9	41.7	61.0	67.4	67.5	75.2	78.7	91.9	109.6
BALANCE OF PAYMENTS					*(Millions of current US dollars)*						
Exports of Goods & Services	77.00	83.55	81.75	..	235.90	175.36	189.09	233.92	305.22	345.98	570.35
Merchandise, fob	68.00	73.12	69.92	71.65	215.06	140.95	158.86	199.30	261.96	290.56	475.77
Nonfactor Services	7.10	6.92	8.58	11.92	14.49	27.93	23.77	27.65	36.00	45.23	73.87
Factor Services	1.90	3.51	3.26	..	6.35	6.48	6.46	6.96	7.26	10.19	20.70
Imports of Goods & Services	88.20	104.21	120.84	125.17	142.22	291.96	251.02	363.23	572.78	641.74	751.52
Merchandise, fob	67.00	75.22	81.32	83.69	98.04	211.51	180.63	252.74	410.89	464.32	524.12
Nonfactor Services	14.80	20.86	28.55	28.73	38.23	69.11	60.01	90.28	134.17	145.39	166.77
Factor Services	6.40	8.12	10.97	12.76	5.95	11.33	10.38	20.21	27.72	32.03	60.63
Long-Term Interest	0.80	0.70	1.10	1.20	2.00	4.50	3.50	9.70	11.10	9.50	19.30
Private Current Transfers, net	-2.40	-3.71	-4.99	0.72	-0.84	-1.39	1.13	-0.32	-1.90	-2.11	0.54
Workers' Remittances	..	..	..	3.46	4.12	4.77	7.09	8.03	9.33	7.96	9.93
Curr. A/C Bal before Off. Transf.	-13.60	-24.37	-44.08	-40.89	92.84	-117.99	-60.80	-129.64	-269.46	-297.87	-180.64
Net Official Transfers	16.40	20.86	31.16	30.28	38.94	42.49	36.23	42.35	52.08	85.12	85.64
Curr. A/C Bal after Off. Transf.	2.80	-3.51	-12.92	-10.61	131.78	-75.49	-24.57	-87.29	-217.37	-212.75	-95.00
Long-Term Capital, net	-6.10	6.02	0.76	5.48	-23.46	20.60	33.58	49.01	208.16	178.96	70.69
Direct Investment	0.40	3.91	0.22	1.79	-39.07	5.22	5.73	11.57	93.16	52.83	42.34
Long-Term Loans	2.90	3.70	3.20	5.10	24.60	38.90	61.50	123.40	266.70	192.30	81.50
Disbursements	4.50	5.40	7.40	10.50	31.10	51.00	81.00	170.40	303.30	211.00	100.00
Repayments	1.60	1.70	4.20	5.40	6.50	12.10	19.50	47.00	36.60	18.70	18.50
Other Long-Term Capital	-9.40	-1.59	-2.66	-1.40	-8.99	-23.52	-33.65	-85.96	-151.70	-66.17	-53.15
Other Capital, net	10.23	-1.28	5.60	3.10	-74.01	65.75	-9.35	6.07	36.63	24.13	22.53
Change in Reserves	-6.93	-1.23	6.56	2.03	-34.31	-10.86	0.34	32.22	-27.42	9.66	1.78
Memo Item:					*(CFA Francs per US dollar)*						
Conversion Factor (Annual Avg)	277.710	277.130	252.210	222.700	240.500	214.320	238.980	245.670	225.640	212.720	211.300
					(Millions of US dollars), outstanding at end of year						
EXTERNAL DEBT (Total)	39.8	46.9	47.0	58.4	89.3	119.5	185.8	368.8	734.2	1,019.3	1,045.1
Long-Term Debt (by debtor)	39.8	46.9	47.0	58.4	89.3	119.5	185.8	329.8	644.2	921.3	931.9
Central Bank, incl. IMF credit	1.1	0.9	0.6	0.4	0.2	0.0	8.7	9.1	8.1	14.2	32.5
Central Government	30.4	37.0	35.1	40.2	70.9	106.1	164.9	302.7	607.6	829.9	825.4
Rest of General Government	0.3	0.2	0.2	0.1	0.1	0.0	0.0	0.0	0.0	0.0	0.0
Non-financial Public Enterprises	3.1	3.0	3.3	7.3	6.2	3.7	2.9	9.2	13.2	56.7	67.0
Priv. Sector, incl non-guaranteed	4.9	5.8	7.8	10.4	11.9	9.7	9.3	8.8	15.3	20.5	7.0
Short-Term Debt	0.0	0.0	0.0	0.0	0.0	0.0	0.0	39.0	90.0	98.0	113.2
Memo Items:					*(Millions of US dollars)*						
Int'l Reserves Excluding Gold	35.35	40.52	36.47	37.92	54.46	41.19	66.62	46.13	69.99	65.46	77.57
Gold Holdings (at market price)	..	..	..	..	..	..	..	1.06	2.17	6.40	7.37
SOCIAL INDICATORS											
Total Fertility Rate	6.5	6.5	6.5	6.6	6.6	6.7	6.7	6.8	6.8	6.8	6.8
Infant Mortality Rate	133.8	131.4	129.0	126.6	124.2	121.8	119.4	117.0	114.6	112.2	109.8
Life Expectancy at Birth	44.5	45.0	45.5	46.0	46.5	47.0	47.5	48.0	48.5	49.0	49.5
Urban Population, % of total	13.1	13.6	14.2	14.7	15.3	15.8	16.4	17.0	17.6	18.2	18.8
Food Prod. per capita (1987=100)	143.3	143.9	130.7	130.1	125.6	127.3	118.3	111.1	119.2	124.1	118.8
Labor Force, Agriculture (%)	76.7	76.3	75.9	75.6	75.2	74.9	74.5	74.1	73.7	73.3	73.0
Labor Force, Female (%)	39.0	39.0	38.9	38.9	38.8	38.8	38.7	38.6	38.6	38.5	38.5
Primary Schl. Enroll. Ratio	71.0	..	..	..	..	99.0	99.0	104.0	110.0	114.0	118.0
Primary Schl. Enroll. Ratio, Female	44.0	..	..	..	..	68.0	70.0	77.0	84.0	88.0	91.0
Secondary Schl. Enroll. Ratio	7.0	..	..	..	..	19.0	22.0	26.0	29.0	32.0	33.0

1981	1982	1983	1984	1985	1986	1987	1988	1989	1990 estimate	Notes	TOGO
				(Millions of current US dollars)							**FOREIGN TRADE (CUSTOMS BASIS)**
206.45	251.51	225.59	191.30	190.10	203.73	243.59	242.31	245.07	300.00	..	Value of Exports, fob
172.07	215.19	194.66	159.45	158.45	191.12	212.19	222.51	224.88	275.28	..	Nonfuel Primary Products
2.73	0.77	0.54	2.53	2.52	0.02	0.03	0.02	0.00	0.01	..	Fuels
31.64	35.55	30.39	29.32	29.13	12.59	31.38	19.79	20.19	24.72	..	Manufactures
435.77	393.40	296.80	271.10	288.00	311.82	423.59	487.39	471.87	700.00	..	Value of Imports, cif
123.60	106.87	88.03	76.89	81.69	76.88	96.40	134.18	131.44	194.98	..	Nonfuel Primary Products
36.67	43.60	26.50	22.81	24.23	10.80	31.06	26.59	28.96	42.97	..	Fuels
275.50	242.93	182.27	171.39	182.08	224.14	296.13	326.62	311.47	462.05	..	Manufactures
				(Index 1987 = 100)							
133.2	125.2	118.1	126.1	117.6	104.8	100.0	103.2	107.1	114.3	..	Terms of Trade
142.4	125.4	115.8	122.4	107.2	104.5	100.0	110.0	109.8	127.2	..	Export Prices, fob
107.0	100.1	98.1	97.0	91.2	99.8	100.0	106.6	102.5	111.3	..	Import Prices, cif
				(Millions of current US dollars)							**BALANCE OF PAYMENTS**
490.39	449.77	360.23	384.89	392.52	493.54	535.94	486.83	490.27	593.54	..	Exports of Goods & Services
377.71	344.82	273.51	290.97	282.00	362.36	402.73	325.00	331.03	396.31	..	Merchandise, fob
97.07	88.29	70.63	76.76	86.97	103.67	114.29	136.98	133.23	166.75	..	Nonfactor Services
15.61	16.66	16.10	17.15	23.55	27.51	18.93	24.85	26.02	30.49	..	Factor Services
618.21	603.19	468.74	431.76	497.09	660.36	701.63	623.81	610.33	815.39	..	Imports of Goods & Services
413.94	408.16	291.78	263.20	303.75	418.57	443.96	352.53	343.88	501.72	..	Merchandise, fob
145.96	136.03	117.73	112.61	131.82	172.29	190.12	198.09	196.55	243.88	..	Nonfactor Services
58.31	59.01	59.24	55.95	61.51	69.50	67.55	73.19	69.90	69.79	..	Factor Services
20.00	23.40	27.10	36.80	38.70	43.10	28.90	68.60	32.60	33.00	..	Long-Term Interest
-0.74	-1.98	-2.61	-1.89	7.67	9.78	6.97	8.39	11.91	13.59	..	Private Current Transfers, net
7.86	6.11	6.08	6.61	15.41	21.42	20.04	14.77	14.11	16.90	..	Workers' Remittances
-113.63	-155.39	-111.12	-48.77	-96.90	-157.03	-158.72	-128.59	-108.15	-208.25	..	Curr. A/C Bal before Off. Transf.
69.48	68.56	67.73	74.96	69.48	100.59	97.06	71.51	94.36	108.72	..	Net Official Transfers
-44.15	-86.84	-43.38	26.18	-27.42	-56.44	-61.66	-57.08	-13.79	-99.54	..	Curr. A/C Bal after Off. Transf.
8.35	-38.07	52.51	10.26	32.75	-2.47	-27.93	161.49	75.23	57.66	..	Long-Term Capital, net
10.09	16.10	1.52	-9.89	16.60	6.54	7.37	..	..	7.60	..	Direct Investment
17.60	34.00	50.10	14.70	4.20	5.30	18.00	89.80	36.10	54.30	..	Long-Term Loans
35.50	51.20	72.80	52.60	55.60	89.20	49.60	113.00	60.90	81.60	..	Disbursements
17.90	17.20	22.70	37.90	51.40	83.90	31.60	23.20	24.80	27.30	..	Repayments
-19.33	-88.17	0.89	5.46	11.95	-14.32	-53.30	71.69	39.13	-4.24	..	Other Long-Term Capital
119.39	163.26	11.35	8.37	20.27	28.56	61.65	-187.28	-19.42	75.96	..	Other Capital, net
-83.59	-38.35	-20.47	-44.81	-25.61	30.35	27.94	82.87	-42.02	-34.09	..	Change in Reserves
				(CFA Francs per US dollar)							**Memo Item:**
271.730	328.620	381.070	436.960	449.260	346.300	300.540	297.850	319.010	272.260	..	Conversion Factor (Annual Avg)
				(Millions of US dollars), outstanding at end of year							**EXTERNAL DEBT (Total)**
969.5	955.6	915.3	806.7	939.9	1,069.1	1,239.4	1,228.9	1,186.3	1,295.6	..	Long-Term Debt (by debtor)
855.6	828.5	850.0	743.7	865.9	979.9	1,137.7	1,142.6	1,022.6	1,182.7	..	Central Bank, incl. IMF credit
38.2	36.2	54.4	62.2	74.2	90.3	85.3	77.9	75.4	87.0	..	Central Government
763.5	740.2	757.6	638.5	738.6	835.8	989.6	1,003.2	895.6	1,036.9	..	Rest of General Government
0.0	0.0	0.0	0.0	0.0	0.0	0.0	0.0	0.0	..	..	Non-financial Public Enterprises
48.9	45.8	33.5	39.4	48.8	49.1	56.9	56.3	47.0	54.5	..	Priv. Sector, incl non-guaranteed
5.0	6.3	4.5	3.6	4.3	4.7	5.9	5.2	4.6	4.3	..	Short-Term Debt
113.9	127.1	65.3	63.0	74.0	89.2	101.7	86.3	163.7	112.9	..	
				(Millions of US dollars)							**Memo Items:**
151.51	167.66	172.85	203.28	296.62	332.66	354.90	232.10	285.28	353.20	..	Int'l Reserves Excluding Gold
4.97	5.71	4.77	3.85	4.09	4.89	6.05	5.13	5.01	4.81	..	Gold Holdings (at market price)
											SOCIAL INDICATORS
6.8	6.8	6.8	6.8	6.8	6.8	6.8	..	..	..	..	Total Fertility Rate
107.4	105.0	102.8	100.6	98.3	96.1	93.9	92.0	90.1	88.1	..	Infant Mortality Rate
50.0	50.5	51.0	51.5	52.0	52.5	53.0	53.2	53.4	53.7	..	Life Expectancy at Birth
19.5	20.1	20.8	21.4	22.1	23.0	23.9	24.5	25.1	25.7	..	Urban Population, % of total
116.3	109.2	98.4	105.1	106.8	104.6	100.0	102.0	108.4	104.7	..	Food Prod. per capita (1987=100)
..	..	..	..	..	..	..	..	..	..	..	Labor Force, Agriculture (%)
38.3	38.0	37.8	37.6	37.5	37.2	37.0	36.8	36.6	36.4	..	Labor Force, Female (%)
72.1	68.4	63.0	..	93.0	99.0	99.0	103.0	..	..	..	Primary Schl. Enroll. Ratio
93.0	88.0	79.0	75.0	71.0	76.0	76.0	80.0	..	..	..	Primary Schl. Enroll. Ratio, Female
..	29.0	24.0	21.0	21.0	21.0	23.0	22.0	..	..	..	Secondary Schl. Enroll. Ratio

TONGA	1970	1971	1972	1973	1974	1975	1976	1977	1978	1979	1980
CURRENT GNP PER CAPITA (US $)	..	..	..	..	..	..	..	..	..	..	..
POPULATION (thousands)	86	87	88	89	89	90	91	92	93	93	94
USE AND ORIGIN OF RESOURCES						*(Millions of current Tongan Pa'anga)*					
Gross National Product (GNP)	..	..	..	..	..	..	..	..	..	..	..
Net Factor Income from Abroad											
GDP at Market Prices	..	..	..	..	..	24.83	24.58	30.79	36.32	39.96	46.77
Resource Balance	..	..	..	..	..	-7.32	-7.30	-7.18	-14.19	-17.47	-16.07
Exports of Goods & NFServices	..	..	..	..	..	10.26	6.62	10.43	10.46	10.42	14.06
Imports of Goods & NFServices	..	..	..	..	..	17.59	13.92	17.60	24.65	27.89	30.13
Domestic Absorption	..	..	..	..	..	32.15	31.88	37.96	50.51	57.43	62.85
Private Consumption, etc.	..	..	..	..	..	22.08	22.33	27.04	34.45	39.02	42.56
General Gov't Consumption	..	..	..	..	..	3.23	4.71	4.71	5.34	5.96	6.86
Gross Domestic Investment	..	..	..	..	..	6.85	4.83	6.22	10.72	12.45	13.43
Fixed Investment	..	..	..	..	..	5.66	4.86	5.90	8.96	11.24	12.19
Indirect Taxes, net	..	..	..	..	..	..	..	..	..	..	..
GDP at factor cost	..	..	..	..	..	21.01	21.46	26.68	31.03	34.71	40.58
Agriculture	..	..	..	..	..	10.53	9.82	11.71	12.97	14.48	15.62
Industry	..	..	..	..	..	2.18	2.27	3.03	4.34	5.25	5.86
Manufacturing	..	..	..	..	..	1.11	1.30	1.77	2.30	2.69	2.84
Services, etc.	..	..	..	..	..	8.31	9.37	11.94	13.72	14.98	19.10
Gross Domestic Saving	..	..	..	..	..	-0.47	-2.46	-0.96	-3.48	-5.02	-2.64
Gross National Saving	..	..	..	..	..	..	..	..	..	..	..
						(Millions of 1980 Tongan Pa'anga)					
Gross National Product	..	..	..	..	..	..	..	..	..	..	..
GDP at Market Prices	..	..	..	..	..	..	..	..	..	..	..
Resource Balance	..	..	..	..	..	..	..	..	..	..	..
Exports of Goods & NFServices	..	..	..	..	..	..	..	..	..	..	..
Imports of Goods & NFServices	..	..	..	..	..	..	..	..	..	..	..
Domestic Absorption	..	..	..	..	..	..	..	..	..	..	..
Private Consumption, etc.	..	..	..	..	..	..	..	..	..	..	..
General Gov't Consumption	..	..	..	..	..	..	..	..	..	..	..
Gross Domestic Investment	..	..	..	..	..	..	..	..	..	..	..
Fixed Investment	..	..	..	..	..	..	..	..	..	..	..
GDP at factor cost	..	..	..	..	..	33.36	34.83	36.35	36.95	38.29	40.58
Agriculture	..	..	..	..	..	15.47	17.02	16.55	15.35	15.24	15.62
Industry	..	..	..	..	..	3.51	3.12	3.78	4.74	5.46	5.86
Manufacturing	..	..	..	..	..	2.15	2.17	2.59	2.73	2.80	2.84
Services, etc.	..	..	..	..	..	14.38	14.69	16.01	16.86	17.58	19.10
Memo Items:											
Capacity to Import	..	..	..	..	..	..	..	..	..	..	..
Terms of Trade Adjustment	..	..	..	..	..	..	..	..	..	..	..
Gross Domestic Income	..	..	..	..	..	..	..	..	..	..	..
Gross National Income	..	..	..	..	..	..	..	..	..	..	..
DOMESTIC PRICES/DEFLATORS						*(Index 1980 = 100)*					
Overall (GDP)	..	..	..	..	..	..	..	..	..	..	..
Domestic Absorption	..	..	..	..	..	..	..	..	..	..	..
Agriculture	..	..	..	..	..	68.1	57.7	70.7	84.5	95.0	100.0
Industry	..	..	..	..	..	62.1	72.7	80.2	91.6	96.2	100.0
Manufacturing	..	..	..	..	..	51.7	59.9	68.3	84.2	96.1	100.0
Consumer Price Index	..	..	..	..	..	27.0	28.9	34.0	37.2	39.2	48.0
MANUFACTURING ACTIVITY											
Employment (1987=100)	..	..	..	..	..	..	..	..	..	..	..
Real Earnings per Empl. (1987=100)	..	..	..	..	..	..	..	..	..	..	..
Real Output per Empl. (1987=100)	..	..	..	..	..	..	..	..	..	..	..
Earnings as % of Value Added	..	..	..	..	..	..	..	..	..	..	..
MONETARY HOLDINGS						*(Thousands of current Tongan Pa'anga)*					
Money Supply, Broadly Defined	..	..	..	..	..	..	..	..	..	..	..
Money	..	..	..	..	..	..	..	..	..	..	..
Currency Outside Banks	..	..	..	..	..	..	..	..	..	..	..
Demand Deposits	..	..	..	..	..	..	..	..	..	..	..
Quasi-Money	..	..	..	..	..	..	..	..	..	..	..
GOVERNMENT DEFICIT (-) OR SURPLUS						*(Millions of current Tongan Pa'anga)*					
Current Revenue	..	..	..	..	..	..	..	..	..	..	-1.0
Current Expenditure											18.0
Current Budget Balance											10.0
Capital Receipts	..	..	..	..	..	..	..	..	..	..	8.0
Capital Payments	..	..	..	..	..	..	..	..	..	..	9.0

1981	1982	1983	1984	1985	1986	1987	1988	1989	1990 estimate	Notes	TONGA
..	..	..	..	750	760	760	800	910	1,010	..	**CURRENT GNP PER CAPITA (US $)**
94	95	95	95	95	95	96	97	98	99	..	**POPULATION (thousands)**
											USE AND ORIGIN OF RESOURCES
			(Millions of current Tongan Pa'anga)								
57.72	63.69	70.17	80.31	82.60	101.90	108.19	114.47	125.13	126.70	C f	Gross National Product (GNP)
3.36	3.01	3.23	5.83	2.60	3.02	3.19	3.47	3.63	3.60	..	Net Factor Income from Abroad
54.36	60.68	66.94	74.47	80.00	98.88	105.00	111.00	121.50	123.10	C f	GDP at Market Prices
-20.69	-24.75	-27.35	-26.78	-41.60	..	..	..	..	..	..	Resource Balance
14.31	16.45	14.31	19.83	20.10	..	..	..	..	..		Exports of Goods & NF Services
35.00	41.20	41.66	46.61	61.70	..	..	..	..	..		Imports of Goods & NF Services
75.05	85.43	94.30	101.25	121.60	..	..	..	..	..		Domestic Absorption
53.58	59.53	63.10	64.23	78.60	..	..	..	..	..		Private Consumption, etc.
7.68	10.82	10.30	11.80	14.10	..	..	..	..	..		General Gov't Consumption
13.79	15.09	20.89	25.22	28.90	..	..	..	..	..		Gross Domestic Investment
12.56	14.21	20.23	24.67	28.40	..	..	..	..	..		Fixed Investment
..	8.40	9.31	10.10	10.86	..	..	..	..	..		Indirect Taxes, net
47.31	52.29	57.63	64.38	69.14	..	..	..	..	..	C f	GDP at factor cost
17.83	24.28	25.45	28.75	28.54	..	..	..	..	..	..	Agriculture
7.17	7.69	9.78	11.57	13.15	..	..	..	..	..	..	Industry
4.47	4.67	5.06	5.80	6.57	..	..	..	..	..	..	Manufacturing
22.31	20.32	22.41	24.06	27.44	..	..	..	..	..		Services, etc.
-6.90	-9.66	-6.46	-1.56	-12.70	..	..	..	..	..		Gross Domestic Saving
10.47	18.71	13.75	22.15	13.05	..	..	..	..	..		Gross National Saving
			(Millions of 1980 Tongan Pa'anga)								
..	..	..	..	..	..	..	..	..	..	C f	Gross National Product
..	..	..	..	..	..	..	..	..	..	..	GDP at Market Prices
..	..	..	..	..	..	..	..	..	..		Resource Balance
..	..	..	..	..	..	..	..	..	..		Exports of Goods & NF Services
..	..	..	..	..	..	..	..	..	..		Imports of Goods & NF Services
..	..	..	..	..	..	..	..	..	..		Domestic Absorption
..	..	..	..	..	..	..	..	..	..		Private Consumption, etc.
..	..	..	..	..	..	..	..	..	..		General Gov't Consumption
..	..	..	..	..	..	..	..	..	..		Gross Domestic Investment
..	..	..	..	..	..	..	..	..	..		Fixed Investment
40.33	45.39	46.01	47.21	50.50	52.46	54.21	53.83	55.61	..	C f	GDP at factor cost
15.04	16.50	14.82	15.09	16.47	16.99	17.60	15.83	16.45	..	..	Agriculture
5.67	5.14	6.07	6.65	7.04	6.95	7.15	7.49	7.95	..	..	Industry
4.95	5.18	5.30	5.56	5.90	6.77	6.99	6.99	7.22	..	..	Manufacturing
19.62	23.75	25.12	25.46	26.99	28.52	29.46	30.51	31.21	..		Services, etc.
											Memo Items:
..	..	..	..	..	..	..	..	..	..		Capacity to Import
..	..	..	..	..	..	..	..	..	..		Terms of Trade Adjustment
..	..	..	..	..	..	..	..	..	..		Gross Domestic Income
..	..	..	..	..	..	..	..	..	..		Gross National Income
			(Index 1980 = 100)								**DOMESTIC PRICES/DEFLATORS**
..	..	..	..	..	..	..	..	..	..		Overall (GDP)
..	..	..	..	..	..	..	..	..	..		Domestic Absorption
118.5	147.1	171.8	190.5	173.3	..	..	..	..	..		Agriculture
126.4	149.6	161.1	173.9	186.7	..	..	..	..	..		Industry
90.3	90.1	95.5	104.4	111.3	..	..	..	..	..		Manufacturing
55.2	61.2	67.2	67.2	78.5	95.5	100.0	109.9	114.4	125.5	f	Consumer Price Index
											MANUFACTURING ACTIVITY
..	..	..	..	..	..	..	..	..	..		Employment (1987=100)
..	..	..	..	..	..	..	..	..	..		Real Earnings per Empl. (1987=100)
..	..	..	..	..	..	..	..	..	..		Real Output per Empl. (1987=100)
33.8	..	..	..	..	..	..	..	..	..		Earnings as % of Value Added
			(Thousands of current Tongan Pa'anga)								**MONETARY HOLDINGS**
..	16,345	19,654	21,924	27,561	32,780	39,157	38,208	40,896	49,313	..	Money Supply, Broadly Defined
..	7,417	9,619	10,054	10,929	13,291	15,198	15,685	17,171	22,296	..	Money
..	2,505	3,168	3,404	3,569	4,474	4,892	5,503	5,971	6,767	..	Currency Outside Banks
..	4,912	6,451	6,650	7,360	8,817	10,306	10,182	11,200	15,529	..	Demand Deposits
..	8,928	10,035	11,870	16,632	19,489	23,959	22,523	23,725	27,017	..	Quasi-Money
			(Millions of current Tongan Pa'anga)								
-1.0	-2.0	1.0	0.0	-2.0	-5.0	-7.0	1.0	0.0	-2.0	C	**GOVERNMENT DEFICIT (-) OR SURPLUS**
24.0	26.0	25.0	27.0	41.0	35.0	45.0	50.0	57.0	69.0	..	Current Revenue
11.0	15.0	16.0	17.0	19.0	24.0	28.0	29.0	31.0	37.0	..	Current Expenditure
13.0	11.0	10.0	11.0	21.0	10.0	17.0	21.0	25.0	32.0	..	Current Budget Balance
..	..	..	..	..	..	..	..	..	..		Capital Receipts
15.0	12.0	9.0	11.0	24.0	15.0	23.0	21.0	25.0	34.0		Capital Payments

TONGA	1970	1971	1972	1973	1974	1975	1976	1977	1978	1979	1980
FOREIGN TRADE (CUSTOMS BASIS)				*(Thousands of current US dollars)*							
Value of Exports, fob	2,998	2,464	2,442	4,597	6,586	5,760	3,790	6,883	5,452	6,808	7,871
Nonfuel Primary Products	2,884	2,313	..	..	6,312	..	..	..	..	..	..
Fuels	37	26	..	..	0	..	..	..	..	..	..
Manufactures	76	125	148	160	274	52	70	53	85	124	279
Value of Imports, cif	6,204	7,070	8,880	11,329	17,064	17,045	14,278	19,584	25,563	29,289	34,265
Nonfuel Primary Products	2,516	2,617	3,434	5,099	7,572	7,197	5,982	8,142	10,275	10,677	12,120
Fuels	240	242	480	732	917	982	1,587	1,996	2,647	2,945	4,896
Manufactures	3,448	4,212	4,967	5,498	8,575	8,866	6,710	9,446	12,641	15,667	17,249
Terms of Trade					*(Index 1987 = 100)*						
Export Prices, fob	..	..	..	..	..	..	..	..	..	..	..
Import Prices, cif	..	..	..	..	..	..	..	..	..	..	..
BALANCE OF PAYMENTS					*(Thousands of current US dollars)*						
Exports of Goods & Services	..	3,999	4,765	5,779	8,656	15,391	9,698	10,166	14,359	13,966	17,329
Merchandise, fob	..	2,705	2,905	3,543	4,863	7,435	4,382	4,123	7,563	5,846	7,252
Nonfactor Services	..	1,025	1,413	1,970	3,461	7,603	4,661	5,367	5,831	6,220	7,119
Factor Services	..	269	447	266	332	353	655	676	965	1,899	2,957
Imports of Goods & Services	..	6,182	8,098	9,808	12,872	22,289	18,843	18,845	23,590	26,970	32,512
Merchandise, fob	..	5,236	6,691	8,243	10,801	18,277	15,699	14,840	18,490	22,717	27,084
Nonfactor Services	..	927	1,376	1,493	1,926	3,952	2,926	3,665	4,888	3,875	4,950
Factor Services	..	19	31	72	145	60	219	340	212	378	478
Long-Term Interest	0	0	0	0	0	0	0	0	0	0	0
Private Current Transfers, net	..	1,641	1,933	3,244	5,148	7,230	7,197	6,757	8,232	10,737	12,173
Workers' Remittances	..	694	479	1,420	4,311	6,546	5,240	5,407	0	0	0
Curr. A/C Bal before Off. Transf.	..	-543	-1,400	-785	931	333	-1,948	-1,922	-999	-2,267	-3,010
Net Official Transfers	..	..	..	..	..	..	..	..	282	-138	-209
Curr. A/C Bal after Off. Transf.	..	-543	-1,400	-785	931	333	-1,948	-1,922	-717	-2,404	-3,219
Long-Term Capital, net	..	1,300	786	1,193	251	2,262	2,034	1,467	2,889	1,581	1,768
Direct Investment	..	..	..	..	..	..	..	..	0	0	0
Long-Term Loans	0	0	600	1,300	900	200	0	400	900	2,000	13,100
Disbursements	0	0	600	1,300	900	200	0	400	1,000	2,100	13,200
Repayments	0	0	0	0	0	0	0	0	100	100	100
Other Long-Term Capital	..	1,300	186	-107	-649	2,062	2,034	1,067	1,989	-419	-11,332
Other Capital, net	..	-728	360	-445	550	-613	-2,409	2,798	-5,559	377	568
Change in Reserves	..	-28	254	37	-1,733	-1,982	2,323	-2,343	3,388	446	883
Memo Item:					*(Tongan Pa'anga per US dollar)*						
Conversion Factor (Annual Avg)	0.890	0.890	0.850	0.780	0.680	0.730	0.790	0.870	0.890	0.880	0.900
				(Thousands of US dollars), outstanding at end of year							
EXTERNAL DEBT (Total)	400	500	1,000	2,200	3,100	2,900	2,400	3,100	4,200	6,400	18,900
Long-Term Debt (by debtor)	400	500	1,000	2,200	3,100	2,900	2,400	3,100	4,200	6,400	18,900
Central Bank, incl. IMF credit	0	0	0	0	0	0	0	0	0	0	0
Central Government	400	500	1,000	2,200	3,100	2,900	2,400	3,100	4,200	6,400	18,900
Rest of General Government	..	..	..	..	..	..	..	..	..	..	..
Non-financial Public Enterprises	..	..	..	..	..	..	..	..	..	..	..
Priv. Sector, incl non-guaranteed	..	..	..	..	..	..	..	..	..	..	..
Short-Term Debt	0	0	0	0	0	0	0	0	0	0	0
Memo Items:					*(Thousands of US dollars)*						
Int'l Reserves Excluding Gold	..	..	..	..	..	..	..	9,001	10,116	12,560	13,753
Gold Holdings (at market price)	..	..	..	..	..	..	..	..	..	..	..
SOCIAL INDICATORS											
Total Fertility Rate	6.5	6.3	6.1	5.9	5.7	5.5	5.3	5.1	5.0	4.9	4.8
Infant Mortality Rate	57.2	57.6	58.0	58.4	58.8	59.2	59.6	60.0	56.6	53.2	49.8
Life Expectancy at Birth	..	..	..	..	..	..	..	..	..	..	..
Urban Population, % of total	21.4	21.2	21.0	20.9	20.7	20.5	20.3	20.2	20.0	19.9	19.7
Food Prod. per capita (1987=100)	121.3	125.0	140.2	128.5	138.6	152.6	146.9	135.9	118.4	118.9	129.6
Labor Force, Agriculture (%)	..	..	..	..	..	..	..	..	..	..	..
Labor Force, Female (%)	..	..	..	..	..	..	..	..	..	..	..
Primary Schl. Enroll. Ratio	..	..	..	..	..	..	..	..	..	..	..
Primary Schl. Enroll. Ratio, Female	..	..	..	..	..	..	..	..	..	..	..
Secondary Schl. Enroll. Ratio	..	..	..	..	..	..	..	..	..	..	..

1981	1982	1983	1984	1985	1986	1987	1988	1989	1990 estimate	Notes	TONGA
											FOREIGN TRADE (CUSTOMS BASIS)
				(Thousands of current US dollars)							
7,581	3,691	5,498	8,792	5,025	5,790	6,688	7,526	9,732	11,944	..	Value of Exports, fob
..	..	..	..	..	..	..	..	..	..	..	Nonfuel Primary Products
..	..	..	..	..	..	..	..	..	..	..	Fuels
511	490	903	836	680	888	1,802	2,027	2,622	3,217	..	Manufactures
40,232	41,619	31,318	41,093	41,250	39,798	47,934	55,490	54,076	61,668	..	Value of Imports, cif
14,303	14,648	9,490	14,550	13,750	12,878	16,150	18,696	18,220	20,778	..	Nonfuel Primary Products
6,599	5,789	6,142	5,742	5,325	4,900	4,647	5,380	5,243	5,979	..	Fuels
19,330	21,182	15,686	20,801	22,175	22,019	27,136	31,414	30,613	34,911	..	Manufactures
				(Index 1987 = 100)							
..	..	..	..	..	..	..	..	..	..	..	Terms of Trade
..	..	..	..	..	..	..	..	..	..	..	Export Prices, fob
..	..	..	..	..	..	..	..	..	..	..	Import Prices, cif
											BALANCE OF PAYMENTS
				(Thousands of current US dollars)							
20,437	23,006	16,663	22,405	25,861	23,638	29,118	31,100	35,134	40,445	C	Exports of Goods & Services
7,622	7,973	3,512	7,177	7,857	5,869	7,039	6,420	9,806	8,870	..	Merchandise, fob
8,340	10,806	9,992	12,000	15,061	14,771	18,010	18,373	21,730	26,419	..	Nonfactor Services
4,476	4,227	3,159	3,228	2,943	2,998	4,070	6,307	3,597	5,156	..	Factor Services
42,879	44,909	47,043	44,438	46,516	49,021	52,083	69,426	71,995	70,799	C	Imports of Goods & Services
37,122	38,637	37,485	33,398	31,757	32,279	35,095	44,058	48,012	47,038	..	Merchandise, fob
5,181	5,313	9,446	10,884	14,646	16,328	16,492	23,894	22,696	22,655	..	Nonfactor Services
575	960	111	156	112	414	495	1,473	1,286	1,106	..	Factor Services
100	100	200	200	200	200	400	400	1,200	1,200	..	Long-Term Interest
16,105	25,727	15,304	15,688	16,165	23,181	22,357	21,284	24,874	28,770	..	Private Current Transfers, net
0	0	15,451	13,883	14,899	20,850	20,254	20,313	14,313	16,104	..	Workers' Remittances
-6,336	3,823	-15,077	-6,345	-4,490	-2,202	-608	-17,041	-11,987	-1,584	..	Curr. A/C Bal before Off. Transf.
-1,134	-432	15,269	6,636	3,155	3,068	6,357	5,667	9,998	9,881	..	Net Official Transfers
-7,470	3,391	192	291	-1,335	866	5,749	-11,375	-1,989	8,298	..	Curr. A/C Bal after Off. Transf.
2,019	6,974	-73	-291	822	-862	854	3,710	682	-11,545	C	Long-Term Capital, net
0	0	0	0	21	113	194	58	111	75	..	Direct Investment
										..	Long-Term Loans
3,900	2,300	600	1,400	800	5,000	5,800	2,500	100	600	..	Disbursements
4,100	2,500	900	1,800	1,300	5,600	6,400	3,300	800	1,400	..	Repayments
200	200	300	400	500	600	600	800	700	800	..	Other Long-Term Capital
-1,881	4,674	-673	-1,691	1	-5,976	-5,140	1,152	472	-12,220	..	
5,840	-8,854	-189	6,060	4,313	474	-5,476	8,405	91	3,684	C	Other Capital, net
-389	-1,511	70	-6,060	-3,800	-478	-1,127	-740	1,216	-437	..	Change in Reserves
											Memo Item:
				(Tongan Pa'anga per US dollar)							Conversion Factor (Annual Avg)
0.860	0.910	1.070	1.100	1.300	1.430	1.510	1.370	1.230	1.300	..	
			(Thousands of US dollars), outstanding at end of year								**EXTERNAL DEBT (Total)**
20,400	21,400	20,000	19,100	24,200	32,800	44,900	44,500	45,300	58,400	..	
20,400	21,400	20,000	19,100	23,500	32,300	44,400	43,900	44,200	49,200	..	Long-Term Debt (by debtor)
0	0	0	0	0	0	1,200	2,600	2,500	2,500	..	Central Bank, incl. IMF credit
20,400	21,400	20,000	19,100	23,500	32,300	43,200	41,300	41,700	46,700	..	Central Government
..	..	..	..	..	..	..	..	..	..	..	Rest of General Government
..	..	..	..	..	..	..	..	..	..	..	Non-financial Public Enterprises
..	..	..	..	..	..	..	..	..	..	..	Priv. Sector, incl non-guaranteed
0	0	0	0	700	500	500	600	1,100	9,200	..	Short-Term Debt
				(Thousands of US dollars)							**Memo Items:**
13,981	15,561	20,953	26,017	27,510	22,482	28,881	30,510	24,851	31,339	..	Int'l Reserves Excluding Gold
..	..	..	..	..	..	..	..	..	..	..	Gold Holdings (at market price)
											SOCIAL INDICATORS
4.8	4.7	4.6	4.5	4.4	4.3	4.2	4.1	4.0	4.0	..	Total Fertility Rate
46.4	43.0	39.8	36.6	33.4	30.2	27.0	25.5	23.9	22.4	..	Infant Mortality Rate
..	62.5	63.1	63.8	64.4	65.1	65.7	66.1	66.6	67.0	..	Life Expectancy at Birth
19.7	19.7	19.7	19.7	19.7	19.9	20.0	20.2	20.3	20.5	..	Urban Population, % of total
128.0	98.1	98.6	101.4	105.7	112.6	100.0	97.8	97.8	97.7	..	Food Prod. per capita (1987=100)
..	..	..	..	0.1	..	..	..	..	..	..	Labor Force, Agriculture (%)
..	..	..	..	..	..	..	..	..	..	..	Labor Force, Female (%)
..	..	..	..	..	..	..	..	..	..	..	Primary Schl. Enroll. Ratio
..	..	..	..	..	..	..	..	..	..	..	Primary Schl. Enroll. Ratio, Female
..	..	..	..	..	..	..	..	..	..	..	Secondary Schl. Enroll. Ratio

TRINIDAD AND TOBAGO	1970	1971	1972	1973	1974	1975	1976	1977	1978	1979	1980
CURRENT GNP PER CAPITA (US $)	770	870	960	1,110	1,360	1,720	2,350	2,860	3,310	3,830	4,610
POPULATION (thousands)	971	981	989	995	1,003	1,012	1,023	1,037	1,051	1,067	1,082
USE AND ORIGIN OF RESOURCES				*(Millions of current Trinidad & Tobago Dollars)*							
Gross National Product (GNP)	1,513	1,639	1,945	2,384	3,607	5,119	5,826	7,069	8,363	10,440	14,219
Net Factor Income from Abroad	-130	-132	-136	-180	-586	-181	-264	-464	-187	-606	-746
GDP at Market Prices	1,644	1,771	2,081	2,564	4,193	5,300	6,090	7,533	8,550	11,046	14,966
Resource Balance	18	-91	-139	148	1,028	943	956	953	375	634	1,716
Exports of Goods & NFServices	703	757	824	1,132	2,378	2,808	3,401	3,733	3,766	4,979	7,550
Imports of Goods & NFServices	685	848	963	984	1,350	1,865	2,445	2,779	3,391	4,345	5,834
Domestic Absorption	1,626	1,862	2,220	2,416	3,165	4,357	5,134	6,579	8,175	10,412	13,249
Private Consumption, etc.	986	980	1,234	1,385	1,774	2,256	2,896	3,605	4,443	5,663	6,865
General Gov't Consumption	215	280	334	366	475	652	743	967	1,148	1,536	1,804
Gross Domestic Investment	425	602	652	665	915	1,449	1,496	2,008	2,584	3,213	4,580
Fixed Investment	344	581	615	579	651	1,085	1,398	1,735	2,323	2,952	4,204
Indirect Taxes, net	94	107	127	133	76	90	62	112	49	-231	-589
GDP at factor cost	1,550	1,664	1,954	2,432	4,117	5,210	6,029	7,421	8,501	11,276	15,554
Agriculture	80	85	107	111	135	174	238	261	302	322	337
Industry	684	740	885	1,199	2,474	3,159	3,587	4,389	4,686	6,430	9,358
Manufacturing	396	410	482	514	686	792	876	1,027	1,074	1,567	1,338
Services, etc.	786	839	962	1,122	1,508	1,877	2,204	2,771	3,513	4,524	5,860
Gross Domestic Saving	443	511	513	814	1,943	2,392	2,452	2,961	2,959	3,847	6,297
Gross National Saving	318	384	383	630	1,342	2,188	2,162	2,459	2,722	3,176	5,449
				(Millions of 1987 Trinidad & Tobago Dollars)							
Gross National Product	11,100	12,209	12,594	13,108	12,639	11,993	13,203	14,376	16,282	16,773	17,294
GDP at Market Prices	10,702	11,589	12,125	12,385	13,048	13,294	14,565	15,490	17,298	18,100	19,549
Resource Balance	1,753	957	1,442	1,759	1,505	675	358	156	-209	-1,129	-1,184
Exports of Goods & NFServices	3,187	2,723	3,161	3,518	3,465	3,122	3,439	3,255	3,278	3,522	3,802
Imports of Goods & NFServices	1,434	1,766	1,719	1,759	1,961	2,447	3,081	3,099	3,486	4,651	4,985
Domestic Absorption	8,949	10,633	10,683	10,626	11,543	12,619	14,207	15,334	17,507	19,228	20,732
Private Consumption, etc.	6,249	6,987	7,110	7,213	7,368	7,439	8,411	9,534	10,410	11,386	11,605
General Gov't Consumption	1,254	1,376	1,575	1,610	1,572	2,025	2,184	2,071	2,323	2,917	3,088
Gross Domestic Investment	1,447	2,270	1,999	1,803	2,604	3,155	3,611	3,729	4,774	4,926	6,040
Fixed Investment	..	..	..	..	..	..	..	..	..	..	..
GDP at factor cost	13,284	14,262	15,029	15,338	16,138	16,404	17,917	19,114	21,309	22,249	24,095
Agriculture	1,071	1,028	1,136	1,045	1,028	1,069	1,035	1,044	999	964	888
Industry	6,808	7,018	7,486	7,635	8,139	8,083	9,121	9,333	10,634	10,948	11,485
Manufacturing	2,308	2,296	2,412	2,366	2,468	2,147	2,547	2,473	2,608	2,675	2,742
Services, etc.	5,406	6,216	6,408	6,658	6,971	7,252	7,762	8,737	9,677	10,337	11,723
Memo Items:											
Capacity to Import	1,472	1,576	1,471	2,024	3,454	3,683	4,287	4,162	3,872	5,329	6,452
Terms of Trade Adjustment	-1,715	-1,147	-1,689	-1,494	-11	562	847	907	594	1,807	2,650
Gross Domestic Income	8,987	10,443	10,436	10,891	13,037	13,855	15,412	16,397	17,892	19,906	22,199
Gross National Income	9,385	11,062	10,904	11,614	12,628	12,554	14,050	15,283	16,876	18,580	19,944
DOMESTIC PRICES/DEFLATORS				*(Index 1987 = 100)*							
Overall (GDP)	15.4	15.3	17.2	20.7	32.1	39.9	41.8	48.6	49.4	61.0	76.6
Domestic Absorption	18.2	17.5	20.8	22.7	27.4	34.5	36.1	42.9	46.7	54.2	63.9
Agriculture	7.5	8.3	9.4	10.6	13.2	16.2	23.0	25.0	30.3	33.4	38.0
Industry	10.0	10.5	11.8	15.7	30.4	39.1	39.3	47.0	44.1	58.7	81.5
Manufacturing	17.2	17.8	20.0	21.7	27.8	36.9	34.4	41.5	41.2	58.6	48.8
Consumer Price Index	13.7	14.2	15.5	17.8	21.7	25.4	28.2	31.5	34.7	39.8	46.8
MANUFACTURING ACTIVITY											
Employment (1987=100)	102.5	107.0	115.8	120.0	115.7	119.6	131.1	133.9	139.5	146.4	145.1
Real Earnings per Empl. (1987=100)	..	..	..	..	76.3	76.3	78.5	81.7	88.9	..	..
Real Output per Empl. (1987=100)	..	..	..	..	74.9	67.9	86.1	82.7	88.1	..	..
Earnings as % of Value Added	..	..	..	..	34.3	36.8	40.1	39.3	47.3	..	..
MONETARY HOLDINGS				*(Millions of current Trinidad & Tobago Dollars)*							
Money Supply, Broadly Defined	504	620	742	844	1,100	1,563	2,108	2,695	3,457	4,426	5,159
Money	151	177	211	213	270	392	572	725	936	1,147	1,337
Currency Outside Banks	57	68	81	80	99	138	177	231	296	412	467
Demand Deposits	95	108	130	133	171	254	395	494	641	735	870
Quasi-Money	353	443	531	631	830	1,171	1,536	1,969	2,521	3,279	3,822
GOVERNMENT DEFICIT (-) OR SURPLUS				*(Millions of current Trinidad & Tobago Dollars)*							
Current Revenue	..	..	..	..	..	..	499.9	799.7	301.6	-61.0	1,105.6
Current Expenditure	..	..	..	..	..	..	2,340.5	3,037.9	3,153.0	4,118.7	6,463.8
Current Budget Balance	..	..	..	..	..	..	948.5	1,069.0	1,461.4	2,108.8	2,815.3
Capital Receipts	..	..	..	..	..	..	1,392.0	1,968.9	1,691.6	2,009.9	3,648.5
Capital Payments	..	..	..	..	..	..	0.3	6.0	2.5	0.1	24.0
	..	..	..	..	..	..	892.4	1,175.2	1,392.5	2,071.0	2,566.9

1981	1982	1983	1984	1985	1986	1987	1988	1989	1990 estimate	Notes	TRINIDAD AND TOBAGO
5,780	6,620	6,710	6,340	7,020	5,390	4,230	3,580	3,530	3,650	..	**CURRENT GNP PER CAPITA (US $)**
1,097	1,113	1,129	1,144	1,160	1,176	1,191	1,206	1,221	1,236		**POPULATION (thousands)**
											USE AND ORIGIN OF RESOURCES
			(Millions of current Trinidad & Tobago Dollars)								
15,948	19,335	18,764	18,282	16,927	16,403	16,219	15,907	16,783	19,297	..	Gross National Product (GNP)
-490	160	-355	-804	-873	-856	-1,082	-1,426	-1,657	-2,353	..	Net Factor Income from Abroad
16,438	19,176	19,119	19,086	17,800	17,260	17,301	17,333	18,440	21,650	..	GDP at Market Prices
1,590	-1,418	-1,918	-325	747	-1,227	245	837	1,456	3,489	..	Resource Balance
7,542	6,703	5,637	5,870	5,883	5,740	5,854	6,727	7,834	9,986	..	Exports of Goods & NF Services
5,952	8,121	7,555	6,195	5,136	6,967	5,610	5,889	6,378	6,497	..	Imports of Goods & NF Services
14,848	20,594	21,037	19,411	17,053	18,486	17,056	16,496	16,984	18,161	..	Domestic Absorption
8,197	12,041	12,748	11,676	9,493	10,621	9,883	10,101	10,232	11,192	..	Private Consumption, etc.
2,110	3,136	3,320	3,616	4,109	4,042	3,730	3,424	3,227	3,368	..	General Gov't Consumption
4,541	5,417	4,969	4,119	3,451	3,824	3,444	2,971	3,526	3,601	..	Gross Domestic Investment
4,342	5,189	4,770	3,954	..	..	..	..	..	..	..	Fixed Investment
-537	-856	-664	-141	82	454	419	635	742	1,470	..	Indirect Taxes, net
16,975	20,032	19,783	19,226	17,718	16,806	16,882	16,698	17,698	20,180	..	GDP at factor cost
386	432	815	867	548	523	528	513	432	529	..	Agriculture
9,799	9,564	8,364	8,158	8,384	6,891	7,193	6,891	7,785	9,776	..	Industry
1,118	1,349	1,448	1,433	1,777	1,623	1,717	2,164	2,295	2,667	..	Manufacturing
6,791	10,035	10,604	10,201	8,787	9,393	9,161	9,295	9,481	9,874	..	Services, etc.
6,131	3,999	3,051	3,794	4,197	2,597	3,689	3,808	4,982	7,090		Gross Domestic Saving
5,476	3,963	2,525	2,818	3,189	1,630	2,534	2,294	3,243	4,648		Gross National Saving
			(Millions of 1987 Trinidad & Tobago Dollars)								
18,255	17,959	17,265	14,876	17,703	17,132	16,219	15,473	15,645	16,315	..	Gross National Product
20,410	19,216	17,710	15,262	18,072	18,233	17,301	16,893	16,955	17,610	I	GDP at Market Prices
-812	-2,534	-2,298	-1,029	-809	-1,482	245	1,299	1,355	1,770	..	Resource Balance
3,743	3,399	3,307	3,596	6,210	6,127	5,854	6,455	6,241	7,054	..	Exports of Goods & NF Services
4,555	5,933	5,605	4,625	7,019	7,609	5,610	5,157	4,886	5,283	..	Imports of Goods & NF Services
21,222	21,750	20,008	16,291	18,881	19,715	17,056	15,595	15,599	15,839		Domestic Absorption
12,644	13,100	12,360	8,679	10,169	11,683	9,883	9,344	9,179	9,353	..	Private Consumption, etc.
3,544	3,345	2,919	2,926	3,856	3,761	3,730	3,427	3,537	3,642	..	General Gov't Consumption
5,034	5,305	4,729	4,686	4,856	4,271	3,444	2,824	2,883	2,845	..	Gross Domestic Investment
..	..	..	..	..	..	..	..	..	..	..	Fixed Investment
25,191	23,321	21,442	18,959	17,980	17,757	16,882	16,300	16,282	16,398	..	GDP at factor cost
876	904	1,057	1,052	630	508	528	510	585	675	..	Agriculture
11,702	10,333	9,287	8,620	8,368	7,810	7,193	7,073	7,024	7,079	..	Industry
2,562	1,851	1,691	1,501	1,440	1,874	1,717	1,718	1,796	1,862	..	Manufacturing
12,613	12,084	11,097	9,287	8,983	9,439	9,161	8,718	8,674	8,644	..	Services, etc.
											Memo Items:
5,772	4,897	4,182	4,382	8,039	6,269	5,854	5,890	6,001	8,121	..	Capacity to Import
2,029	1,498	875	787	1,829	142	0	-566	-240	1,067	..	Terms of Trade Adjustment
22,439	20,714	18,585	16,048	19,901	18,375	17,301	16,328	16,715	18,677	..	Gross Domestic Income
20,284	19,457	18,140	15,662	19,532	17,274	16,219	14,908	15,405	17,383	..	Gross National Income
											DOMESTIC PRICES/DEFLATORS
			(Index 1987 = 100)								
80.5	99.8	108.0	125.1	98.5	94.7	100.0	102.6	108.8	122.9	..	Overall (GDP)
70.0	94.7	105.1	119.1	90.3	93.8	100.0	105.8	108.9	114.7	..	Domestic Absorption
44.0	47.8	77.1	82.4	87.0	102.8	100.0	100.6	73.8	78.4	..	Agriculture
83.7	92.6	90.1	94.6	100.2	88.2	100.0	97.4	110.8	138.1	..	Industry
43.6	72.9	85.6	95.5	123.4	86.6	100.0	125.9	127.8	143.2	..	Manufacturing
53.5	59.7	68.7	77.9	83.8	90.3	100.0	107.8	120.1	133.3	..	Consumer Price Index
											MANUFACTURING ACTIVITY
152.6	144.8	132.4	125.8	109.8	103.0	100.0	99.3	..	..	..	Employment (1987=100)
102.6	112.7	120.4	108.3	111.4	110.7	100.0				..	Real Earnings per Empl. (1987=100)
129.5	89.3	87.5	92.4	100.6	98.1	100.0				..	Real Output per Empl. (1987=100)
73.8	78.3	72.0	69.3	82.2	72.2	69.6				..	Earnings as % of Value Added
											MONETARY HOLDINGS
			(Millions of current Trinidad & Tobago Dollars)							D	Money Supply, Broadly Defined
6,672	9,027	9,990	10,481	10,791	10,622	..	..	..	..		Money
1,855	2,547	2,435	2,294	2,260	2,073	2,170	1,892	2,144	2,576	..	Currency Outside Banks
532	726	758	710	685	723	703	689	704	735	..	Demand Deposits
1,323	1,821	1,676	1,584	1,576	1,350	1,468	1,204	1,440	1,841	..	Quasi-Money
4,817	6,480	7,555	8,187	8,531	8,549	..				..	
											GOVERNMENT DEFICIT (-) OR SURPLUS
			(Millions of current Trinidad & Tobago Dollars)								
545.8	..	..	..	..	..	..	..	..	..		Current Revenue
7,200.6	..	..	..	..	..	..	..	..	..		Current Expenditure
3,123.1	..	..	..	..	..	..	..	..	..		Current Budget Balance
4,077.5	..	..	..	..	..	..	..	..	..		Capital Receipts
32.2	..	..	..	..	..	..	..	..	..		Capital Payments
3,563.9											

TRINIDAD AND TOBAGO	1970	1971	1972	1973	1974	1975	1976	1977	1978	1979	1980
FOREIGN TRADE (CUSTOMS BASIS)					*(Millions of current US dollars)*						
Value of Exports, fob	481.5	520.4	557.6	695.7	2,037.7	1,772.7	2,219.3	2,179.8	2,042.7	2,610.4	4,077.0
Nonfuel Primary Products	46.4	44.4	53.1	52.2	88.4	117.1	89.0	77.6	66.2	83.3	86.6
Fuels	371.9	402.8	433.6	571.8	1,838.7	1,543.2	2,007.3	1,997.0	1,829.4	2,370.3	3,784.5
Manufactures	63.2	73.2	70.9	71.8	110.6	112.4	123.0	105.1	147.2	156.9	205.9
Value of Imports, cif	543.4	662.8	762.0	792.2	1,846.5	1,488.4	1,976.3	1,808.5	1,979.9	2,104.6	3,177.7
Nonfuel Primary Products	68.3	74.7	88.3	105.8	157.2	165.1	173.8	215.0	262.4	318.3	430.7
Fuels	287.6	330.4	364.1	402.1	1,327.8	752.6	1,131.4	861.0	798.1	601.9	1,197.0
Manufactures	187.5	257.7	309.6	284.3	361.5	570.8	671.0	732.5	919.4	1,184.4	1,550.0
					(Index 1987 = 100)						
Terms of Trade	118.5	114.6	110.9	113.1	151.8	134.7	140.0	133.6	122.6	127.0	162.6
Export Prices, fob	8.2	10.6	11.8	16.0	59.7	58.7	61.7	67.3	68.5	96.8	154.7
Import Prices, cif	6.9	9.2	10.6	14.2	39.3	43.6	44.1	50.4	55.8	76.3	95.1
BALANCE OF PAYMENTS					*(Millions of current US dollars)*						
Exports of Goods & Services	349.8	389.1	448.1	572.1	1,172.3	1,333.2	1,451.0	1,625.5	1,689.7	2,227.5	3,371.2
Merchandise, fob	225.3	217.2	254.5	333.3	928.1	987.4	1,054.3	1,175.2	1,221.9	1,648.8	2,541.7
Nonfactor Services	119.1	166.4	187.8	233.8	224.8	302.5	336.4	373.2	342.8	418.8	597.3
Factor Services	5.4	5.4	5.8	5.0	19.5	43.3	60.3	77.0	125.0	159.9	232.3
Imports of Goods & Services	456.7	553.9	568.7	593.7	880.8	980.2	1,165.5	1,420.2	1,609.0	2,215.8	2,972.3
Merchandise, fob	276.2	355.6	384.2	371.5	482.3	658.1	766.0	867.8	1,057.5	1,334.1	1,789.1
Nonfactor Services	108.8	129.2	108.7	131.8	169.3	195.6	233.8	285.1	351.9	469.3	639.8
Factor Services	71.7	69.2	75.8	90.4	229.2	126.5	165.7	267.3	199.6	412.4	543.4
Long-Term Interest	6.1	4.6	6.3	8.1	14.4	11.9	8.9	6.8	21.1	40.5	50.4
Private Current Transfers, net	2.6	3.0	2.9	-2.0	-7.3	-10.9	-10.5	-15.8	-20.8	-27.1	-42.3
Workers' Remittances	2.7	3.2	3.3	2.6	2.5	2.6	1.6	1.4	1.4	1.4	1.4
Curr. A/C Bal before Off. Transf.	-104.3	-161.9	-117.7	-23.6	284.2	342.1	275.0	189.4	59.8	-15.4	356.7
Net Official Transfers	-4.3	-7.0	-6.2	-6.3	-10.1	-10.3	-19.5	-15.3	-17.1	-18.5	-22.0
Curr. A/C Bal after Off. Transf.	-108.6	-168.9	-123.9	-29.9	274.1	331.8	255.4	174.1	42.7	-33.9	334.7
Long-Term Capital, net	80.3	98.3	103.1	58.8	69.4	43.1	14.1	230.7	262.3	432.0	322.8
Direct Investment	83.2	103.3	86.1	65.6	120.1	93.0	132.2	83.5	128.8	93.8	184.5
Long-Term Loans	-2.5	-1.2	22.2	28.9	4.5	-3.7	-50.8	151.3	112.5	156.8	187.0
Disbursements	7.5	19.4	27.1	37.3	44.7	11.2	17.1	157.6	121.4	165.8	362.8
Repayments	10.0	20.6	4.9	8.4	40.2	14.9	67.9	6.3	8.9	9.0	175.8
Other Long-Term Capital	-0.4	-3.8	-5.2	-35.7	-55.3	-46.1	-67.2	-4.1	21.0	181.4	-48.8
Other Capital, net	9.3	83.1	0.4	-35.7	-55.5	83.2	-69.1	39.1	32.5	-54.2	-9.2
Change in Reserves	19.0	-12.5	20.3	6.8	-288.0	-458.1	-200.5	-443.9	-337.5	-343.8	-648.3
Memo Item:					*(Trinidad & Tobago Dollars per US dollar)*						
Conversion Factor (Annual Avg)	2.000	1.970	1.920	1.960	2.050	2.170	2.440	2.400	2.400	2.400	2.400
EXTERNAL DEBT (Total)					*(Millions of US dollars), outstanding at end of year*						
	100.7	101.5	122.1	150.8	155.4	148.8	96.0	339.3	486.6	680.7	828.5
Long-Term Debt (by debtor)	100.7	101.5	122.1	150.8	155.4	148.8	96.0	247.3	369.6	514.7	712.5
Central Bank, incl. IMF credit	0.0	0.0	0.0	0.6	2.2	3.4	4.0	4.4	5.7	10.3	16.1
Central Government	74.8	75.1	92.4	118.5	108.4	95.8	60.5	209.1	329.0	378.7	468.6
Rest of General Government	..	..	..	..	..	..	..	..	..	..	..
Non-financial Public Enterprises	25.9	26.4	29.7	31.7	44.8	49.6	31.5	33.8	34.9	125.7	227.8
Priv. Sector, incl non-guaranteed	..	..	..	..	..	..	..	..	..	..	..
Short-Term Debt	0.0	0.0	0.0	0.0	0.0	0.0	0.0	92.0	117.0	166.0	116.0
Memo Items:					*(Millions of US dollars)*						
Int'l Reserves Excluding Gold	43.0	69.4	58.3	47.0	390.3	751.0	1,013.6	1,481.7	1,804.8	2,140.0	2,780.8
Gold Holdings (at market price)	..	..	..	..	..	..	..	4.5	9.1	27.6	31.8
SOCIAL INDICATORS											
Total Fertility Rate	3.6	3.5	3.4	3.4	3.4	3.4	3.4	3.4	3.4	3.3	3.3
Infant Mortality Rate	43.6	42.8	42.0	41.2	40.4	39.6	38.8	38.0	37.0	36.0	35.0
Life Expectancy at Birth	65.4	65.5	65.7	66.0	66.3	66.6	66.8	67.1	67.4	67.7	68.0
Urban Population, % of total	38.8	40.7	42.6	44.6	46.5	48.4	50.1	51.8	53.5	55.2	56.9
Food Prod. per capita (1987=100)	198.0	186.6	191.7	171.9	162.2	163.4	174.5	165.1	147.4	129.6	120.4
Labor Force, Agriculture (%)	18.6	17.7	16.8	16.0	15.2	14.4	13.5	12.6	11.8	10.9	10.2
Labor Force, Female (%)	29.6	29.2	28.8	28.5	28.1	27.8	28.1	28.3	28.5	28.7	28.9
Primary Schl. Enroll. Ratio	106.0	..	..	..	..	99.0	96.0	94.0	91.0	91.0	99.0
Primary Schl. Enroll. Ratio, Female	107.0	..	..	..	..	100.0	97.0	95.0	92.0	92.0	100.0
Secondary Schl. Enroll. Ratio	42.0	..	..	..	..	48.0	56.0	58.0	61.0	..	70.0

1981	1982	1983	1984	1985	1986	1987	1988	1989	1990 estimate	Notes	TRINIDAD AND TOBAGO
				(Millions of current US dollars)							**FOREIGN TRADE (CUSTOMS BASIS)**
3,760.8	3,085.5	2,352.7	2,173.4	2,160.9	1,385.7	1,462.4	1,412.0	1,578.1	2,080.4	..	Value of Exports, fob
77.1	70.5	58.4	57.1	53.3	65.2	76.1	93.5	115.7	127.1	..	Nonfuel Primary Products
3,368.9	2,692.8	1,963.9	1,760.7	1,709.9	980.3	1,041.4	853.7	962.3	1,395.8	..	Fuels
314.8	322.1	330.4	355.7	397.7	340.1	344.9	464.8	500.1	557.5	..	Manufactures
3,124.6	3,698.0	2,582.0	1,919.1	1,533.0	1,369.8	1,218.7	1,127.0	1,222.4	1,261.6	..	Value of Imports, cif
489.6	556.3	567.9	532.3	422.1	302.0	330.8	275.5	328.8	330.3	..	Nonfuel Primary Products
1,143.8	931.5	82.7	14.4	50.9	38.8	52.4	134.3	74.7	143.7	..	Fuels
1,491.1	2,210.2	1,931.4	1,372.5	1,060.0	1,029.1	835.5	717.2	819.0	787.6	..	Manufactures
				(Index 1987 = 100)							
172.7	165.6	156.5	156.3	156.1	86.2	100.0	90.1	92.2	110.3	..	Terms of Trade
170.4	153.8	141.1	137.6	134.3	82.1	100.0	90.5	100.7	113.6	..	Export Prices, fob
98.6	92.9	90.2	88.1	86.1	95.3	100.0	100.5	109.3	103.0	..	Import Prices, cif
				(Millions of current US dollars)							**BALANCE OF PAYMENTS**
3,488.3	3,146.2	2,575.9	2,581.3	2,594.3	1,738.6	1,632.3	1,752.3	1,853.3	2,318.4	..	Exports of Goods & Services
2,612.3	2,228.6	2,026.5	2,110.7	2,110.7	1,363.1	1,396.9	1,453.3	1,534.6	1,935.2	..	Merchandise, fob
531.3	560.6	319.1	329.0	287.8	278.8	218.6	278.7	286.3	343.6	..	Nonfactor Services
344.7	357.0	230.3	141.5	195.8	96.8	16.8	20.3	32.4	39.6	..	Factor Services
3,021.4	3,651.0	3,498.2	3,020.5	2,625.2	2,130.4	1,842.9	1,840.4	1,895.1	1,863.1	..	Imports of Goods & Services
1,763.5	2,486.7	2,233.3	1,704.9	1,354.6	1,209.4	1,057.6	1,064.2	1,045.3	947.6	..	Merchandise, fob
709.1	873.8	886.6	839.2	713.1	606.3	487.2	447.7	433.5	472.6	..	Nonfactor Services
548.8	290.5	378.3	476.5	557.6	314.7	298.0	328.5	416.3	442.9	..	Factor Services
83.2	74.8	122.4	75.2	96.0	118.1	122.3	125.7	143.1	133.1	..	Long-Term Interest
-68.9	-81.5	-71.3	-71.5	-55.4	-30.8	-20.2	-23.0	-19.2	-21.0	..	Private Current Transfers, net
1.4	1.4	1.4	0.3	0.2	0.2	0.3	1.7	2.9	3.0	..	Workers' Remittances
398.0	-586.4	-993.5	-510.7	-86.4	-422.6	-230.7	-111.1	-61.0	434.3	..	Curr. A/C Bal before Off. Transf.
-23.5	-58.5	-9.3	-11.7	-4.0	-19.1	-16.6	-6.6	-5.5	-4.4	..	Net Official Transfers
374.5	-644.9	-1,002.9	-522.5	-90.3	-441.7	-247.3	-117.7	-66.4	430.0	..	Curr. A/C Bal after Off. Transf.
323.5	534.7	282.8	13.2	32.4	-74.3	-59.8	-204.0	17.6	-337.1	..	Long-Term Capital, net
258.1	203.5	114.1	109.7	-7.0	-21.8	31.3	62.9	148.9	109.4	..	Direct Investment
99.4	126.4	129.2	66.0	143.5	156.3	-129.2	161.4	4.0	-116.9	..	Long-Term Loans
128.8	177.5	280.7	176.4	298.7	347.5	135.5	336.1	55.3	47.1	..	Disbursements
29.4	51.1	151.5	110.4	155.2	191.2	264.7	174.7	51.3	164.0	..	Repayments
-33.9	204.8	39.5	-162.6	-104.2	-208.7	38.2	-428.4	-135.2	-329.6	..	Other Long-Term Capital
-129.5	-96.7	-152.7	-183.6	-243.3	-205.7	51.5	178.9	115.9	4.0	..	Other Capital, net
-568.6	206.9	872.8	692.9	301.3	721.6	255.6	142.8	-67.1	-96.8	..	Change in Reserves
				(Trinidad & Tobago Dollars per US dollar)							**Memo Item:**
2.400	2.400	2.400	2.400	2.450	3.600	3.600	3.840	4.250	4.250	..	Conversion Factor (Annual Avg)
				(Millions of US dollars), outstanding at end of year							
1,049.8	1,202.8	1,438.2	1,221.9	1,448.2	1,857.6	1,805.1	2,157.8	2,173.4	2,306.5	..	**EXTERNAL DEBT (Total)**
794.8	906.8	1,026.2	1,062.9	1,299.2	1,584.6	1,639.0	2,011.5	2,016.2	2,137.1	..	Long-Term Debt (by debtor)
18.0	17.3	15.9	15.5	18.7	19.4	21.9	132.2	221.0	352.0	..	Central Bank, incl. IMF credit
465.4	555.3	674.2	707.0	890.8	947.8	1,032.9	1,354.1	1,381.2	1,430.6	..	Central Government
..	..	..	..	..	..	..	..	..	..	..	Rest of General Government
311.4	334.2	336.1	340.4	389.7	617.4	584.2	525.2	414.0	354.5	..	Non-financial Public Enterprises
..	..	..	..	..	..	..	..	..	..	..	Priv. Sector, incl non-guaranteed
255.0	296.0	412.0	159.0	149.0	273.0	166.1	146.3	157.2	169.4	..	Short-Term Debt
				(Millions of US dollars)							**Memo Items:**
3,347.5	3,080.5	2,104.5	1,356.7	1,128.5	474.1	187.8	127.1	246.5	492.0	..	Int'l Reserves Excluding Gold
21.4	24.6	20.6	16.6	17.6	21.1	26.1	22.1	21.6	20.8	..	Gold Holdings (at market price)
											SOCIAL INDICATORS
3.2	3.2	3.2	3.1	3.1	3.0	3.0	2.9	2.9	2.8	..	Total Fertility Rate
34.0	33.0	32.0	31.0	29.9	28.9	27.9	26.9	26.0	25.0	..	Infant Mortality Rate
68.3	68.6	68.9	69.2	69.5	69.8	70.1	70.4	70.7	71.0	..	Life Expectancy at Birth
58.3	59.7	61.1	62.5	63.9	64.9	66.0	67.0	68.1	69.1	..	Urban Population, % of total
107.4	117.1	114.0	94.9	107.5	99.3	100.0	104.2	99.3	107.6	..	Food Prod. per capita (1987=100)
..	..	..	..	..	..	..	..	..	..	..	Labor Force, Agriculture (%)
29.1	29.3	29.4	29.6	29.7	29.8	29.9	29.9	30.0	30.0	..	Labor Force, Female (%)
..	99.0	96.0	96.0	96.0	98.0	99.0	..	97.0	..	..	Primary Schl. Enroll. Ratio
..	102.0	98.0	98.0	97.0	99.0	100.0	..	98.0	..	..	Primary Schl. Enroll. Ratio, Female
..	73.0	76.0	77.0	80.0	82.0	84.0	..	83.0	..	..	Secondary Schl. Enroll. Ratio

TUNISIA	1970	1971	1972	1973	1974	1975	1976	1977	1978	1979	1980
CURRENT GNP PER CAPITA (US $)	280	320	390	430	560	710	800	850	930	1,080	1,280
POPULATION (thousands)	5,127	5,208	5,294	5,389	5,494	5,611	5,742	5,889	6,048	6,214	6,384

USE AND ORIGIN OF RESOURCES
(Millions of current Tunisian Dinars)

	1970	1971	1972	1973	1974	1975	1976	1977	1978	1979	1980
Gross National Product (GNP)	724.0	866.5	1,042.5	1,110.1	1,506.3	1,694.0	1,862.0	2,114.9	2,395.9	2,816.0	3,435.5
Net Factor Income from Abroad	-31.6	-14.7	-24.9	-41.2	-41.5	-47.4	-71.0	-77.0	-88.0	-106.0	-105.0
GDP at Market Prices	755.6	881.2	1,067.4	1,151.3	1,547.8	1,741.4	1,933.0	2,191.9	2,483.9	2,922.0	3,540.5
Resource Balance	-34.0	-17.8	-12.3	-28.5	5.4	-83.6	-153.7	-224.7	-239.4	-146.1	-189.9
Exports of Goods & NFServices	166.2	212.4	270.6	300.0	547.4	540.6	562.2	648.4	769.0	1,139.0	1,424.6
Imports of Goods & NFServices	200.2	230.2	282.9	328.5	542.0	624.2	715.9	873.1	1,008.4	1,285.1	1,614.5
Domestic Absorption	789.6	899.0	1,079.7	1,179.8	1,542.4	1,825.0	2,086.7	2,416.6	2,723.3	3,068.1	3,730.4
Private Consumption, etc.	502.4	571.4	681.7	760.4	938.3	1,082.6	1,201.0	1,392.4	1,553.2	1,763.8	2,178.7
General Gov't Consumption	127.4	138.0	155.6	174.4	204.7	254.5	293.1	354.7	406.1	444.4	512.2
Gross Domestic Investment	159.8	189.6	242.4	245.0	399.4	487.9	592.6	669.5	764.0	859.9	1,039.5
Fixed Investment	155.0	175.2	211.0	236.0	321.0	448.0	563.0	672.0	771.0	892.0	1,002.0
Indirect Taxes, net	102.4	115.0	136.9	156.7	192.6	205.4	253.6	322.5	357.9	415.0	476.4
GDP at factor cost	653.2	766.2	930.5	994.6	1,355.2	1,536.0	1,679.4	1,869.4	2,126.0	2,507.0	3,064.1
Agriculture	128.7	170.8	229.0	227.3	289.9	321.8	343.2	346.7	374.8	395.7	500.3
Industry	155.5	180.7	214.1	245.5	419.4	451.4	486.4	564.4	655.0	844.3	1,101.5
Manufacturing	63.5	76.3	101.6	107.2	154.2	158.1	202.3	231.3	274.8	338.8	417.3
Services, etc.	369.0	414.7	487.4	521.8	645.9	762.8	849.8	958.3	1,096.2	1,267.0	1,462.3
Gross Domestic Saving	125.8	171.8	230.1	216.5	404.8	404.3	438.9	444.8	524.6	713.8	849.6
Gross National Saving	106.3	180.2	230.6	213.5	409.5	409.6	422.9	432.8	521.6	717.8	866.6

(Millions of 1987 Tunisian Dinars)

	1970	1971	1972	1973	1974	1975	1976	1977	1978	1979	1980
Gross National Product	2,949.3	3,326.0	3,906.7	3,809.3	4,149.7	4,445.2	4,758.0	4,925.8	5,240.3	5,574.2	6,025.5
GDP at Market Prices	3,013.3	3,344.6	3,970.5	3,953.8	4,274.0	4,577.5	4,939.2	5,107.3	5,436.6	5,793.4	6,222.6
Resource Balance	-196.5	-56.0	-65.5	-158.6	-246.1	-394.5	-362.4	-548.5	-611.1	-584.3	-710.7
Exports of Goods & NFServices	820.2	1,053.2	1,294.4	1,186.4	1,366.6	1,376.3	1,610.2	1,723.8	1,852.7	2,250.7	2,251.8
Imports of Goods & NFServices	1,016.7	1,109.2	1,359.9	1,345.0	1,612.7	1,770.7	1,972.5	2,272.4	2,463.8	2,835.0	2,962.5
Domestic Absorption	3,209.8	3,400.6	4,036.0	4,112.4	4,520.1	4,972.0	5,301.6	5,655.8	6,047.7	6,377.7	6,933.3
Private Consumption, etc.	1,629.9	1,787.2	2,127.6	2,274.8	2,415.7	2,681.6	2,839.8	3,098.6	3,269.2	3,468.8	3,920.3
General Gov't Consumption	468.5	483.1	523.1	555.1	596.8	689.8	756.1	817.0	850.2	860.0	945.5
Gross Domestic Investment	1,111.5	1,130.4	1,385.4	1,282.5	1,507.7	1,600.6	1,705.8	1,740.2	1,928.4	2,048.9	2,067.6
Fixed Investment	772.2	850.5	971.1	978.3	1,152.9	1,439.7	1,645.8	1,659.2	1,740.4	1,864.4	1,937.7
GDP at factor cost	2,734.8	3,059.3	3,543.3	3,483.8	3,744.4	4,127.2	4,290.1	4,350.2	4,642.0	4,961.1	5,385.0
Agriculture	527.9	643.6	797.4	716.4	820.3	858.6	918.0	826.2	875.0	833.3	915.5
Industry	924.4	979.3	1,103.6	1,115.2	1,156.6	1,325.2	1,311.9	1,409.5	1,533.5	1,699.7	1,853.1
Manufacturing	235.1	275.9	352.7	356.0	315.0	396.0	482.1	502.7	537.7	596.2	687.1
Services, etc.	1,282.4	1,436.5	1,642.3	1,652.2	1,767.5	1,943.5	2,060.2	2,114.6	2,233.5	2,428.2	2,616.5

Memo Items:

	1970	1971	1972	1973	1974	1975	1976	1977	1978	1979	1980
Capacity to Import	844.1	1,023.4	1,300.7	1,228.3	1,628.8	1,533.6	1,549.1	1,687.6	1,878.8	2,512.7	2,614.0
Terms of Trade Adjustment	23.9	-29.7	6.4	41.9	262.2	157.3	-61.1	-36.3	26.2	262.0	362.3
Gross Domestic Income	3,037.2	3,314.8	3,976.9	3,995.7	4,536.2	4,734.8	4,878.1	5,071.0	5,462.8	6,055.4	6,584.9
Gross National Income	2,973.1	3,296.3	3,913.1	3,851.2	4,411.9	4,602.5	4,696.8	4,889.5	5,266.5	5,836.2	6,387.8

DOMESTIC PRICES/DEFLATORS
(Index 1987 = 100)

	1970	1971	1972	1973	1974	1975	1976	1977	1978	1979	1980
Overall (GDP)	25.1	26.3	26.9	29.1	36.2	38.0	39.1	42.9	45.7	50.4	56.9
Domestic Absorption	24.6	26.4	26.8	28.7	34.1	36.7	39.4	42.7	45.0	48.1	53.8
Agriculture	24.4	26.5	28.7	31.7	35.3	37.5	37.4	42.0	42.8	47.5	54.6
Industry	16.8	18.5	19.4	22.0	36.3	34.1	37.1	40.0	42.7	49.7	59.4
Manufacturing	27.0	27.7	28.8	30.1	49.0	39.9	42.0	46.0	51.1	56.8	60.7
Consumer Price Index	30.8	32.6	33.3	34.8	36.3	39.8	41.9	44.7	47.1	50.7	55.8

MANUFACTURING ACTIVITY

	1970	1971	1972	1973	1974	1975	1976	1977	1978	1979	1980
Employment (1987=100)	..	..	..	..	..	..	..	..	..	..	..
Real Earnings per Empl. (1987=100)	..	..	..	..	..	..	..	..	..	..	..
Real Output per Empl. (1987=100)	..	..	..	..	..	..	..	..	..	..	..
Earnings as % of Value Added	43.7	43.5	43.4	43.8	41.7	48.3	49.9	50.0	49.7	46.5	46.4

MONETARY HOLDINGS
(Millions of current Tunisian Dinars)

	1970	1971	1972	1973	1974	1975	1976	1977	1978	1979	1980
Money Supply, Broadly Defined	259.9	315.0	373.3	452.7	590.6	740.4	860.5	978.4	1,178.0	1,373.0	1,610.4
Money	192.7	241.2	278.2	323.1	404.3	475.4	513.8	575.7	688.1	785.8	950.7
Currency Outside Banks	67.3	80.4	94.2	111.5	139.6	163.0	185.0	213.6	249.7	265.1	299.6
Demand Deposits	125.3	160.8	184.0	211.6	264.7	312.4	328.7	362.1	438.4	520.6	651.1
Quasi-Money	67.3	73.8	95.1	129.5	186.3	264.9	346.7	402.7	489.9	587.2	659.7

GOVERNMENT DEFICIT (-) OR SURPLUS
(Millions of current Tunisian Dinars)

	1970	1971	1972	1973	1974	1975	1976	1977	1978	1979	1980
	..	..	-9.5	-17.1	-15.4	-25.2	-62.4	-132.2	-101.2	-139.6	-98.9
Current Revenue	..	..	262.5	293.6	404.3	504.5	533.9	630.6	786.7	949.9	1,130.5
Current Expenditure	..	..	197.2	226.3	276.8	351.4	385.4	463.4	559.9	728.2	784.1
Current Budget Balance	..	..	65.3	67.3	127.5	153.1	148.5	167.2	226.8	221.7	346.4
Capital Receipts	..	..	0.3	0.4	2.2	1.2	8.4	9.2	0.8	2.1	0.7
Capital Payments	..	..	75.1	84.8	145.1	179.5	219.3	308.6	328.8	363.4	446.0

1981	1982	1983	1984	1985	1986	1987	1988	1989	1990 estimate	Notes	TUNISIA
1,380	1,310	1,240	1,210	1,170	1,110	1,180	1,240	1,290	1,440	..	**CURRENT GNP PER CAPITA (US $)**
6,557	6,733	6,909	7,086	7,261	7,465	7,639	7,770	7,899	8,060	..	**POPULATION (thousands)**
											USE AND ORIGIN OF RESOURCES
			*(Millions of current Tunisian Dinars)*								
4,017.0	4,630.4	5,315.4	6,042.5	6,616.5	6,686.2	7,594.3	8,257.0	9,210.9	10,634.4	..	Gross National Product (GNP)
-145.0	-174.2	-182.4	-197.5	-293.5	-334.9	-402.7	-427.0	-449.1	-355.6	..	Net Factor Income from Abroad
4,162.0	4,804.6	5,497.8	6,240.0	6,910.0	7,021.1	7,997.0	8,684.0	9,660.0	10,990.0	..	GDP at Market Prices
-352.4	-505.7	-473.2	-728.8	-423.2	-509.8	-79.4	31.8	-396.4	-793.3	..	Resource Balance
1,721.9	1,773.3	1,947.8	2,113.7	2,253.1	2,161.2	2,798.5	3,639.6	4,261.2	4,591.9	..	Exports of Goods & NFServices
2,074.3	2,279.0	2,421.0	2,842.5	2,676.3	2,671.0	2,877.9	3,607.8	4,657.6	5,385.2	..	Imports of Goods & NFServices
4,514.4	5,310.3	5,971.0	6,968.8	7,333.2	7,530.9	8,076.4	8,652.2	10,056.4	11,783.3	..	Domestic Absorption
2,553.2	2,992.0	3,419.0	3,943.8	4,356.2	4,665.0	5,122.7	5,581.9	6,220.0	7,081.0	..	Private Consumption, etc.
615.7	794.0	927.0	1,030.0	1,142.0	1,217.0	1,305.4	1,387.0	1,640.0	1,783.0	..	General Gov't Consumption
1,345.5	1,524.3	1,625.0	1,995.0	1,835.0	1,648.9	1,648.3	1,683.3	2,196.4	2,919.3	..	Gross Domestic Investment
1,290.0	1,635.0	1,750.0	1,920.0	1,850.0	1,685.1	1,620.9	1,680.0	2,000.0	2,550.0	..	Fixed Investment
521.3	577.7	737.4	821.0	865.8	935.0	1,012.0	1,098.0	1,078.0	1,256.0	..	Indirect Taxes, net
3,640.7	4,226.7	4,760.0	5,419.0	6,044.2	6,086.1	6,985.0	7,586.0	8,582.0	9,734.0	..	GDP at factor cost
568.8	632.0	673.0	863.0	1,048.0	933.0	1,226.0	1,018.0	1,172.0	1,587.0	..	Agriculture
1,332.5	1,491.8	1,676.4	1,903.5	2,058.2	2,002.6	2,222.2	2,436.5	2,797.3	3,094.3	..	Industry
493.9	534.1	615.6	733.4	818.0	920.2	1,049.6	1,210.5	1,386.1	1,641.2	..	Manufacturing
1,739.4	2,102.9	2,410.6	2,652.5	2,938.0	3,150.5	3,536.8	4,131.5	4,612.7	5,052.7	..	Services, etc.
993.1	1,018.6	1,151.8	1,266.2	1,411.8	1,139.1	1,568.9	1,715.1	1,800.0	2,126.0	..	Gross Domestic Saving
1,011.7	1,057.4	1,204.4	1,304.7	1,334.3	1,085.2	1,565.2	1,757.1	1,810.9	2,291.4	..	Gross National Saving
			*(Millions of 1987 Tunisian Dinars)*								
6,315.6	6,280.0	6,596.0	6,994.5	7,316.0	7,178.4	7,594.3	7,685.8	7,987.3	8,682.2	..	Gross National Product
6,566.2	6,534.0	6,839.9	7,237.0	7,653.7	7,539.4	7,997.0	8,073.2	8,368.7	8,966.7	..	GDP at Market Prices
-1,018.2	-1,209.8	-1,114.0	-1,242.4	-712.7	-528.9	-79.4	127.1	-262.2	-528.3	..	Resource Balance
2,329.8	2,168.6	2,188.9	2,248.0	2,322.3	2,443.6	2,798.5	3,458.4	3,573.0	3,617.6	..	Exports of Goods & NFServices
3,348.0	3,378.5	3,302.9	3,490.4	3,035.0	2,972.6	2,877.9	3,331.3	3,835.2	4,145.8	..	Imports of Goods & NFServices
7,584.4	7,743.9	7,953.9	8,479.4	8,366.4	8,068.3	8,076.4	7,946.1	8,630.9	9,494.9	..	Domestic Absorption
4,181.2	4,280.8	4,477.9	4,734.3	4,886.0	4,988.3	5,122.7	5,323.4	5,467.7	5,782.0	..	Private Consumption, etc.
1,024.1	1,100.1	1,164.7	1,233.0	1,284.7	1,294.7	1,305.4	1,306.5	1,392.2	1,436.1	..	General Gov't Consumption
2,379.1	2,363.0	2,311.2	2,512.1	2,195.7	1,785.3	1,648.3	1,316.1	1,771.0	2,276.8	..	Gross Domestic Investment
2,213.0	2,394.0	2,281.9	2,390.2	2,192.7	1,802.9	1,620.9	1,555.3	1,748.1	2,082.7	..	Fixed Investment
5,744.4	5,716.3	5,983.8	6,331.7	6,696.9	6,584.3	6,985.0	7,051.3	7,327.9	7,852.0	..	GDP at factor cost
975.3	874.7	896.6	1,011.9	1,187.6	1,043.0	1,226.0	935.1	988.1	1,253.4	..	Agriculture
1,979.9	1,982.5	2,115.4	2,196.0	2,234.6	2,216.6	2,222.2	2,280.6	2,404.6	2,535.1	..	Industry
772.0	793.6	859.1	916.6	962.0	1,008.6	1,049.6	1,121.9	1,189.2	1,298.4	..	Manufacturing
2,789.2	2,859.2	2,971.8	3,123.9	3,274.7	3,324.7	3,536.8	3,835.7	3,935.2	4,063.4	..	Services, etc.
											Memo Items:
2,779.2	2,628.8	2,657.3	2,595.5	2,555.1	2,405.2	2,798.5	3,360.7	3,508.8	3,535.1	..	Capacity to Import
449.4	460.2	468.5	347.5	232.8	-38.4	0.0	-97.7	-64.2	-82.5	..	Terms of Trade Adjustment
7,015.6	6,994.2	7,308.3	7,584.5	7,886.5	7,501.0	7,997.0	7,975.4	8,304.5	8,884.2	..	Gross Domestic Income
6,765.0	6,740.2	7,064.5	7,342.0	7,548.8	7,140.0	7,594.3	7,588.0	7,923.0	8,599.8	..	Gross National Income
											DOMESTIC PRICES/DEFLATORS
			*(Index 1987 = 100)*								
63.4	73.5	80.4	86.2	90.3	93.1	100.0	107.6	115.4	122.6	..	Overall (GDP)
59.5	68.6	75.1	82.2	87.7	93.3	100.0	108.9	116.5	124.1	..	Domestic Absorption
58.3	72.3	75.1	85.3	88.2	89.5	100.0	108.9	118.6	126.6	..	Agriculture
67.3	75.2	79.2	86.7	92.1	90.3	100.0	106.8	116.3	122.1	..	Industry
64.0	67.3	71.7	80.0	85.0	91.2	100.0	107.9	116.6	126.4	..	Manufacturing
60.8	69.1	75.3	81.7	88.2	93.3	100.0	106.4	114.2	122.0	..	Consumer Price Index
											MANUFACTURING ACTIVITY
..	..	..	..	..	..	..	..	..	..	..	Employment (1987=100)
..	..	..	..	..	..	..	..	..	..	..	Real Earnings per Empl. (1987=100)
..	..	..	..	..	..	..	..	..	..	..	Real Output per Empl. (1987=100)
47.7	..	..	..	..	..	..	..	..	..	..	Earnings as % of Value Added
											MONETARY HOLDINGS
			*(Millions of current Tunisian Dinars)*								
1,979.2	2,378.8	2,786.1	3,121.7	3,541.7	3,781.3	3,813.0	4,481.0	5,174.0	5,570.0	D	Money Supply, Broadly Defined
1,164.6	1,455.1	1,699.2	1,814.3	2,059.1	2,111.6	2,125.7	2,494.4	2,524.1	2,678.1	..	Money
342.8	440.0	533.3	573.4	632.6	651.0	704.8	801.1	874.6	1,005.0	..	Currency Outside Banks
821.8	1,015.1	1,166.0	1,240.8	1,426.6	1,460.6	1,420.9	1,693.4	1,649.5	1,673.1	..	Demand Deposits
814.6	923.7	1,086.9	1,307.4	1,482.6	1,669.7	1,687.0	1,986.0	2,650.0	2,892.0	..	Quasi-Money
			*(Millions of current Tunisian Dinars)*								
-105.5	-277.4	-458.8	-307.3	-354.2	-474.3	-364.3	-326.9	-411.6		F	**GOVERNMENT DEFICIT (-) OR SURPLUS**
1,333.3	1,656.8	1,853.4	2,284.3	2,331.7	2,418.2	2,527.2	2,758.0	3,069.6		..	Current Revenue
909.9	1,273.7	1,514.0	1,735.2	1,781.5	1,965.2	2,053.3	2,333.3	2,728.3		..	Current Expenditure
423.4	383.1	339.4	549.1	550.2	453.0	473.9	424.7	341.3		..	Current Budget Balance
0.8	0.9	1.1	1.1	..	..	..	0.5	1.5		..	Capital Receipts
529.7	661.4	799.3	857.5	904.4	927.3	838.2	752.1	754.4		..	Capital Payments

TUNISIA	1970	1971	1972	1973	1974	1975	1976	1977	1978	1979	1980
FOREIGN TRADE (CUSTOMS BASIS)					*(Millions of current US dollars)*						
Value of Exports, fob	182.5	215.8	310.9	385.5	914.2	856.2	788.8	929.1	1,126.1	1,790.7	2,233.7
Nonfuel Primary Products	97.8	120.3	179.6	178.9	381.0	314.9	251.8	229.1	264.1	316.2	260.6
Fuels	49.7	60.0	84.3	122.7	328.3	373.3	334.1	389.1	433.5	870.0	1,172.5
Manufactures	35.0	35.5	47.0	83.9	205.0	168.0	202.9	310.8	428.5	604.6	800.7
Value of Imports, cif	304.6	341.9	458.5	605.6	1,120.1	1,417.8	1,525.7	1,820.9	2,157.7	2,842.2	3,508.7
Nonfuel Primary Products	111.5	108.0	128.3	170.4	344.0	346.2	315.7	370.6	410.1	589.0	756.7
Fuels	14.7	15.4	34.3	44.6	137.8	147.5	178.1	206.8	237.9	504.6	727.6
Manufactures	178.4	218.5	295.9	390.5	638.3	924.1	1,031.9	1,243.6	1,509.7	1,748.6	2,024.4
					(Index 1987 = 100)						
Terms of Trade	81.5	82.1	93.0	87.8	117.8	99.0	102.1	105.6	94.3	110.4	126.7
Export Prices, fob	21.7	24.6	27.2	33.8	69.7	60.9	62.5	69.8	69.4	94.7	130.4
Import Prices, cif	26.7	29.9	29.2	38.4	59.2	61.6	61.2	66.1	73.6	85.8	102.9
BALANCE OF PAYMENTS					*(Millions of current US dollars)*						
Exports of Goods & Services	332.0	416.2	564.6	736.7	1,256.8	1,325.9	1,329.4	1,342.8	1,672.4	2,607.9	3,355.9
Merchandise, fob	189.0	213.6	312.7	416.1	871.9	798.9	781.3	776.3	929.9	1,540.1	2,158.3
Nonfactor Services	136.0	188.6	238.9	299.2	345.2	486.9	522.4	550.2	723.3	1,016.1	1,103.8
Factor Services	7.0	14.0	13.0	21.5	39.7	40.1	25.7	16.3	19.2	51.7	93.8
Imports of Goods & Services	443.0	480.4	654.7	928.7	1,340.9	1,669.5	1,921.8	2,123.8	2,383.6	3,245.1	4,119.0
Merchandise, fob	294.0	334.0	452.7	622.3	971.7	1,238.4	1,425.0	1,603.9	1,775.7	2,470.1	3,138.6
Nonfactor Services	105.0	104.3	136.8	187.2	234.5	273.2	305.5	324.0	377.2	462.5	627.2
Factor Services	44.0	42.1	65.1	119.2	134.7	157.8	191.2	195.8	230.7	312.5	353.1
Long-Term Interest	18.3	20.2	23.2	27.6	30.3	34.8	37.0	63.9	108.3	174.7	227.5
Private Current Transfers, net	23.0	44.1	53.2	90.6	105.8	131.1	128.3	151.5	204.2	270.6	301.3
Workers' Remittances	29.0	44.1	61.9	98.9	117.9	144.5	142.3	167.9	221.1	282.9	318.6
Curr. A/C Bal before Off. Transf.	-88.0	-20.1	-36.9	-101.3	21.6	-212.5	-464.1	-629.4	-507.0	-366.6	-461.8
Net Official Transfers	35.0	26.1	32.6	40.5	26.5	42.5	56.0	51.3	33.6	59.0	101.2
Curr. A/C Bal after Off. Transf.	-53.0	6.0	-4.3	-60.8	48.1	-170.0	-408.1	-578.2	-473.4	-307.5	-360.5
Long-Term Capital, net	51.0	85.3	90.1	133.5	135.9	127.5	394.1	496.6	579.1	440.4	508.7
Direct Investment	16.0	23.1	31.5	57.2	25.3	44.9	109.6	93.3	88.9	49.2	234.6
Long-Term Loans	41.6	56.0	70.8	83.8	85.8	124.2	180.1	663.3	505.1	500.8	352.9
Disbursements	88.6	106.3	142.6	144.8	148.1	192.0	243.4	779.2	655.3	703.0	611.2
Repayments	47.0	50.3	71.8	61.0	62.3	67.8	63.3	115.9	150.2	202.2	258.3
Other Long-Term Capital	-6.6	6.2	-12.2	-7.5	24.8	-41.6	104.4	-260.0	-14.9	-109.6	-78.8
Other Capital, net	22.0	-0.9	-15.9	5.1	-96.3	25.1	4.3	22.8	-23.4	-25.7	-71.7
Change in Reserves	-20.0	-90.3	-69.8	-77.8	-87.7	17.4	9.6	58.8	-82.4	-107.2	-76.5
Memo Item:					*(Tunisian Dinars per US dollar)*						
Conversion Factor (Annual Avg)	0.520	0.520	0.480	0.420	0.440	0.400	0.430	0.430	0.420	0.410	0.400
					(Millions of US dollars), outstanding at end of year						
EXTERNAL DEBT (Total)	554.7	623.2	695.5	811.4	927.2	1,027.8	1,185.7	2,232.8	2,941.1	3,398.8	3,526.9
Long-Term Debt (by debtor)	554.7	623.2	695.5	811.4	927.2	1,027.8	1,185.7	2,031.8	2,660.1	3,208.8	3,390.6
Central Bank, incl. IMF credit	68.1	60.5	41.4	44.1	52.5	51.9	77.7	195.3	236.0	282.9	251.5
Central Government	360.7	422.3	489.4	584.1	667.6	743.1	820.8	1,098.8	1,448.6	1,613.5	1,717.9
Rest of General Government	..	..	..	..	..	..	..	..	..	..	..
Non-financial Public Enterprises	112.5	130.4	157.0	176.1	199.6	226.5	273.0	533.8	668.1	974.7	1,075.0
Priv. Sector, incl non-guaranteed	13.4	10.0	7.7	7.1	7.5	6.3	14.2	203.9	307.4	337.7	346.2
Short-Term Debt	0.0	0.0	0.0	0.0	0.0	0.0	0.0	201.0	281.0	190.0	136.3
Memo Items:					*(Millions of US dollars)*						
Int'l Reserves Excluding Gold	55.20	142.87	217.84	301.77	412.82	379.88	365.84	351.19	443.00	579.27	590.13
Gold Holdings (at market price)	4.70	5.61	8.34	14.43	24.14	18.15	17.44	24.73	36.21	87.29	110.03
SOCIAL INDICATORS											
Total Fertility Rate	6.4	6.3	6.1	6.1	6.0	5.9	5.8	5.7	5.5	5.3	5.2
Infant Mortality Rate	127.2	123.6	120.0	113.6	107.2	100.8	94.4	88.0	82.8	77.6	72.4
Life Expectancy at Birth	54.2	54.9	55.6	56.5	57.4	58.3	59.2	60.1	60.7	61.3	61.9
Urban Population, % of total	43.5	44.3	45.1	46.0	46.8	47.6	48.5	49.4	50.4	51.3	52.2
Food Prod. per capita (1987=100)	78.5	105.2	88.7	102.4	101.5	118.7	97.6	98.3	89.1	85.1	101.5
Labor Force, Agriculture (%)	42.2	41.2	40.4	39.5	38.8	38.1	37.4	36.7	36.1	35.5	35.0
Labor Force, Female (%)	11.6	12.6	13.6	14.4	15.2	16.0	17.1	18.2	19.2	20.2	21.0
Primary Schl. Enroll. Ratio	100.0	..	..	..	..	97.0	99.0	100.0	100.0	102.0	103.0
Primary Schl. Enroll. Ratio, Female	79.0	..	..	..	..	78.0	80.0	82.0	83.0	85.0	88.0
Secondary Schl. Enroll. Ratio	23.0	..	..	..	..	21.0	22.0	23.0	24.0	25.0	27.0

1981	1982	1983	1984	1985	1986	1987	1988	1989	1990 estimate	Notes	TUNISIA
											FOREIGN TRADE (CUSTOMS BASIS)
				(Millions of current US dollars)							
2,503.7	1,983.5	1,871.5	1,796.3	1,627.3	1,759.6	2,152.4	2,392.9	2,932.4	3,498.3	..	Value of Exports, fob
315.9	248.9	204.3	244.8	212.2	272.6	336.8	379.0	395.3	475.4	..	Nonfuel Primary Products
1,352.4	911.2	851.6	795.5	686.4	427.0	508.4	386.1	586.8	604.4	..	Fuels
835.4	823.4	815.6	755.9	728.7	1,060.0	1,307.2	1,627.8	1,950.3	2,418.5	..	Manufactures
3,770.9	3,395.7	3,099.5	3,114.9	2,586.9	2,897.7	3,021.7	3,680.9	4,366.0	5,471.1	..	Value of Imports, cif
834.0	680.9	741.2	770.2	591.5	734.9	690.0	1,000.4	1,095.6	1,059.0	..	Nonfuel Primary Products
773.9	439.3	366.5	347.8	367.8	197.2	326.8	261.2	402.0	493.9	..	Fuels
2,163.0	2,275.5	1,991.8	1,997.0	1,627.6	1,965.6	2,004.9	2,419.4	2,868.3	3,918.2	..	Manufactures
				(Index 1987 = 100)							
129.2	119.5	111.7	107.8	105.4	98.0	100.0	98.1	99.3	98.9	..	Terms of Trade
133.3	116.1	106.5	100.9	96.8	91.2	100.0	106.4	109.4	125.8	..	Export Prices, fob
103.2	97.2	95.3	93.6	91.8	93.1	100.0	108.5	110.1	127.3	..	Import Prices, cif
											BALANCE OF PAYMENTS
				(Millions of current US dollars)							
3,631.5	3,106.6	2,953.9	2,796.0	2,711.8	2,746.8	3,368.1	4,300.5	4,559.1	5,299.8	..	Exports of Goods & Services
2,448.3	1,977.4	1,850.4	1,776.4	1,700.4	1,763.2	2,101.0	2,399.2	2,930.5	3,514.6	..	Merchandise, fob
1,085.0	1,024.2	1,015.1	920.4	971.8	954.6	1,241.8	1,847.7	1,551.6	1,680.5	..	Nonfactor Services
98.1	105.0	88.4	99.1	39.5	29.0	25.3	53.6	76.9	104.7	..	Factor Services
4,396.8	4,178.2	3,918.9	3,912.0	3,605.8	3,764.3	3,947.3	4,751.7	5,418.6	6,608.0	..	Imports of Goods & Services
3,418.4	3,137.0	2,922.9	2,928.6	2,566.8	2,697.6	2,828.6	3,496.1	4,138.7	5,192.8	..	Merchandise, fob
586.9	641.6	639.4	630.8	638.7	617.1	607.0	703.0	725.8	848.2	..	Nonfactor Services
391.6	399.5	356.5	352.7	400.2	449.6	511.7	552.6	554.1	567.0	..	Factor Services
223.1	217.2	206.7	249.7	250.5	305.6	336.1	373.5	374.8	408.4	..	Long-Term Interest
331.2	360.6	346.2	303.8	258.8	353.9	481.5	546.7	484.6	593.2	..	Private Current Transfers, net
353.7	372.4	359.5	316.7	270.8	361.4	486.3	544.4	487.7	598.9	..	Workers' Remittances
-434.1	-711.0	-618.8	-812.3	-635.1	-663.7	-97.7	95.6	-375.0	-715.0	..	Curr. A/C Bal before Off. Transf.
46.9	44.0	41.3	42.5	47.9	45.3	37.4	117.7	214.9	215.2	..	Net Official Transfers
-387.2	-667.0	-577.5	-769.8	-587.2	-618.4	-60.3	213.3	-160.1	-499.8	..	Curr. A/C Bal after Off. Transf.
628.8	772.0	624.7	531.6	393.1	313.3	129.1	131.7	166.4	88.8	..	Long-Term Capital, net
290.8	338.6	182.7	112.0	101.9	61.7	90.5	59.5	73.7	56.9	..	Direct Investment
326.1	306.7	501.4	440.2	315.9	273.8	6.6	234.1	139.9	105.1	..	Long-Term Loans
687.2	637.6	913.4	880.7	791.3	823.4	735.5	882.8	809.3	1,051.3	..	Disbursements
361.1	330.9	412.0	440.5	475.4	549.6	728.9	648.7	669.4	946.2	..	Repayments
11.9	126.7	-59.4	-20.5	-24.7	-22.2	32.0	-161.8	-47.2	-73.2	..	Other Long-Term Capital
-178.7	57.7	-11.9	137.9	-30.9	221.2	59.2	96.1	58.9	288.1	..	Other Capital, net
-62.9	-162.7	-35.2	100.3	225.0	83.9	-127.9	-441.2	-65.3	122.9	..	Change in Reserves
											Memo Item:
				(Tunisian Dinars per US dollar)							
0.490	0.590	0.680	0.780	0.830	0.790	0.830	0.860	0.950	0.880	..	Conversion Factor (Annual Avg)
				(Millions of US dollars), outstanding at end of year							
3,607.7	3,771.8	4,059.2	4,095.5	4,880.5	5,896.2	6,758.4	6,728.2	6,859.6	7,533.9	..	**EXTERNAL DEBT (Total)**
3,474.2	3,635.5	3,927.8	3,926.3	4,698.6	5,669.5	6,503.6	6,393.6	6,483.9	6,899.7	..	Long-Term Debt (by debtor)
226.7	220.3	245.2	243.5	366.0	597.8	759.8	724.0	685.4	555.1	..	Central Bank, incl. IMF credit
1,793.5	1,913.0	2,098.7	2,140.5	2,611.3	3,153.0	3,659.9	3,818.9	4,102.7	4,726.0	..	Central Government
..	..	..	..	..	..	..	..	..	..		Rest of General Government
1,100.3	1,203.6	1,238.3	1,134.1	1,319.3	1,498.6	1,657.4	1,416.7	1,273.7	1,198.4	..	Non-financial Public Enterprises
353.7	298.5	345.6	408.2	402.0	420.1	426.5	434.0	422.1	420.2	..	Priv. Sector, incl non-guaranteed
133.5	136.3	131.4	169.2	181.9	226.7	254.8	334.6	375.7	634.2	..	Short-Term Debt
											Memo Items:
				(Millions of US dollars)							
536.11	606.45	567.29	406.31	232.72	305.28	525.49	899.30	961.89	794.80	..	Int'l Reserves Excluding Gold
74.19	85.28	71.21	57.54	61.03	72.96	90.36	76.57	74.85	71.86	..	Gold Holdings (at market price)
											SOCIAL INDICATORS
5.0	4.9	4.7	4.5	4.4	4.2	4.0	3.9	3.7	3.6	..	Total Fertility Rate
67.2	62.0	59.6	57.2	54.8	52.4	50.0	48.1	46.3	44.4	..	Infant Mortality Rate
62.5	63.1	63.6	64.1	64.6	65.2	65.7	66.0	66.4	66.7	..	Life Expectancy at Birth
52.4	52.5	52.7	52.8	53.0	53.3	53.5	53.8	54.0	54.3	..	Urban Population, % of total
87.1	73.2	94.2	84.5	103.3	85.4	100.0	66.9	86.0	85.1	..	Food Prod. per capita (1987=100)
..	..	..	..	..	..	..	..	..	..		Labor Force, Agriculture (%)
21.5	21.9	22.3	22.6	23.0	23.3	23.6	23.9	24.2	24.4	..	Labor Force, Female (%)
..	111.0	114.0	114.0	116.0	117.0	116.0	113.0	115.0	..	..	Primary Schl. Enroll. Ratio
..	98.0	102.0	103.0	106.0	107.0	107.0	105.0	107.0	..	..	Primary Schl. Enroll. Ratio, Female
..	31.0	34.0	36.0	39.0	39.0	40.0	44.0	44.0	..	..	Secondary Schl. Enroll. Ratio

TURKEY	1970	1971	1972	1973	1974	1975	1976	1977	1978	1979	1980
CURRENT GNP PER CAPITA (US $)	400	400	410	470	630	830	1,000	1,110	1,220	1,370	1,400
POPULATION (thousands)	35,321	36,248	37,217	38,201	39,162	40,078	40,952	41,777	42,593	43,466	44,438

USE AND ORIGIN OF RESOURCES *(Billions of current Turkish Liras)*

	1970	1971	1972	1973	1974	1975	1976	1977	1978	1979	1980
Gross National Product (GNP)	145	186	230	294	407	517	659	857	1,264	2,126	4,243
Net Factor Income from Abroad	-1	-1	-2	-2	-3	-2	-5	-6	-11	-30	-85
GDP at Market Prices	146	187	232	295	410	519	664	863	1,275	2,156	4,328
Resource Balance	-3	-6	-7	-6	-26	-42	-46	-70	-47	-70	-339
Exports of Goods & NFServices	9	13	18	26	29	29	41	41	67	91	275
Imports of Goods & NFServices	12	20	24	33	55	71	86	111	114	161	615
Domestic Absorption	149	194	239	302	436	561	710	933	1,322	2,226	4,667
Private Consumption, etc.	101	135	162	209	300	377	458	599	910	1,530	3,175
General Gov't Consumption	19	25	28	37	47	64	85	116	173	294	544
Gross Domestic Investment	29	33	48	56	89	120	167	218	239	402	948
Fixed Investment	27	32	47	59	76	108	154	211	280	449	864
Indirect Taxes, net	14	19	26	30	40	51	64	67	85	141	230
GDP at factor cost	131	168	207	266	370	468	600	796	1,190	2,015	4,098
Agriculture	39	50	59	73	105	136	177	220	301	466	925
Industry	36	45	53	68	95	118	146	200	337	584	1,237
Manufacturing	22	29	35	46	66	80	98	130	232	417	865
Services, etc.	57	73	94	124	169	214	276	376	551	966	1,936
Gross Domestic Saving	25	27	42	50	62	78	121	148	192	332	609
Gross National Saving	28	33	51	65	80	96	134	161	208	358	687

(Billions of 1987 Turkish Liras)

	1970	1971	1972	1973	1974	1975	1976	1977	1978	1979	1980
Gross National Product	23,738.0	25,918.0	27,595.1	28,791.0	31,272.9	34,112.3	36,991.4	38,731.6	39,967.8	39,377.2	38,879.6
GDP at Market Prices	23,919.8	26,121.4	27,837.9	29,017.0	31,500.8	34,301.2	37,305.5	39,046.9	40,345.6	39,980.1	39,687.3
Resource Balance	-1,988.4	-2,570.3	-3,062.3	-2,708.4	-4,012.0	-4,703.6	-4,776.1	-5,559.0	-2,647.3	-2,533.2	-2,555.5
Exports of Goods & NFServices	1,627.6	1,745.5	2,264.5	2,618.3	2,170.1	2,217.3	2,689.1	2,217.3	2,523.9	2,288.1	2,382.4
Imports of Goods & NFServices	3,616.0	4,315.8	5,326.7	5,326.7	6,182.1	6,920.9	7,465.2	7,776.3	5,171.2	4,821.3	4,937.9
Domestic Absorption	25,908.2	28,691.7	30,900.2	31,725.4	35,512.8	39,004.7	42,081.6	44,605.9	42,992.8	42,513.3	42,242.8
Private Consumption, etc.	17,586.9	19,853.7	21,872.2	21,751.5	23,539.1	24,735.1	27,026.3	28,209.3	29,301.7	28,736.3	27,245.8
General Gov't Consumption	2,398.4	2,868.6	2,570.8	2,680.5	2,868.6	3,213.5	3,511.3	3,668.1	4,028.6	4,091.3	4,451.8
Gross Domestic Investment	5,923.0	5,969.4	6,457.2	7,293.4	9,105.1	11,056.2	11,544.0	12,728.5	9,662.5	9,685.8	10,545.2
Fixed Investment	5,808.9	5,589.3	6,223.9	7,322.2	8,274.1	10,080.2	11,349.4	12,130.4	10,934.5	10,543.9	9,494.4
GDP at factor cost	22,088.6	24,073.1	25,518.6	26,517.8	28,843.7	31,387.7	34,186.1	35,928.2	37,502.3	37,249.5	37,014.7
Agriculture	5,485.6	6,213.6	6,112.0	5,485.6	6,061.2	6,721.5	7,229.4	7,144.8	7,331.0	7,534.2	7,669.6
Industry	7,099.5	7,456.7	7,903.2	8,751.6	9,421.4	10,247.4	11,252.0	12,256.7	13,015.8	12,569.2	12,011.1
Manufacturing	4,769.6	5,173.0	5,529.0	6,193.4	6,620.5	7,166.3	7,854.5	8,424.0	8,732.5	8,281.6	7,759.5
Services, etc.	9,503.6	10,402.8	11,503.4	12,280.7	13,361.2	14,418.8	15,704.6	16,526.8	17,155.5	17,146.1	17,334.0

Memo Items:

	1970	1971	1972	1973	1974	1975	1976	1977	1978	1979	1980
Capacity to Import	2,616.4	2,891.8	3,880.0	4,264.7	3,253.7	2,824.6	3,521.2	2,869.0	3,045.4	2,731.1	2,211.9
Terms of Trade Adjustment	988.8	1,146.3	1,615.5	1,646.4	1,083.6	607.4	832.1	651.7	521.4	443.0	-170.6
Gross Domestic Income	24,908.6	27,267.7	29,453.4	30,663.3	32,584.4	34,908.5	38,137.6	39,698.6	40,867.0	40,423.1	39,516.8
Gross National Income	24,726.8	27,064.3	29,210.6	30,437.3	32,356.6	34,719.6	37,823.5	39,383.3	40,489.3	39,820.2	38,709.1

DOMESTIC PRICES/DEFLATORS *(Index 1987 = 100)*

	1970	1971	1972	1973	1974	1975	1976	1977	1978	1979	1980
Overall (GDP)	0.6	0.7	0.8	1.0	1.3	1.5	1.8	2.2	3.2	5.4	10.9
Domestic Absorption	0.6	0.7	0.8	1.0	1.2	1.4	1.7	2.1	3.1	5.2	11.0
Agriculture	0.7	0.8	1.0	1.3	1.7	2.0	2.5	3.1	4.1	6.2	12.1
Industry	0.5	0.6	0.7	0.8	1.0	1.2	1.3	1.6	2.6	4.6	10.3
Manufacturing	0.5	0.6	0.6	0.7	1.0	1.1	1.2	1.5	2.7	5.0	11.1
Consumer Price Index	0.7	0.8	0.9	1.1	1.2	1.5	1.7	2.2	3.2	5.0	10.6

MANUFACTURING ACTIVITY

	1970	1971	1972	1973	1974	1975	1976	1977	1978	1979	1980
Employment (1987=100)	54.9	58.9	62.9	69.9	72.1	76.7	79.4	81.9	87.7	86.7	86.3
Real Earnings per Empl. (1987=100)	79.5	81.9	83.6	84.7	94.0	105.3	109.8	130.5	135.6	139.6	116.7
Real Output per Empl. (1987=100)	63.7	64.6	67.9	69.0	70.9	75.6	78.3	82.7	66.4	56.7	59.3
Earnings as % of Value Added	25.9	26.8	27.4	27.1	26.3	32.0	31.6	37.7	37.7	38.3	30.7

MONETARY HOLDINGS *(Billions of current Turkish Liras)*

	1970	1971	1972	1973	1974	1975	1976	1977	1978	1979	1980
Money Supply, Broadly Defined	45	57	72	92	116	149	183	245	335	542	945
Money	36	44	54	71	91	119	152	210	289	456	758
Currency Outside Banks	12	14	16	21	26	33	42	63	94	144	218
Demand Deposits	24	30	38	50	65	86	109	147	195	313	541
Quasi-Money	9	13	18	21	25	30	32	35	46	85	187

GOVERNMENT DEFICIT (-) OR SURPLUS *(Billions of current Turkish Liras)*

	1970	1971	1972	1973	1974	1975	1976	1977	1978	1979	1980
GOVERNMENT DEFICIT (-) OR SURPLUS	-4	-6	-5	-5	-7	-7	-13	-53	-55	-137	-161
Current Revenue	29	38	47	59	72	109	144	187	291	497	945
Current Expenditure	23	31	36	48	57	82	110	164	249	435	809
Current Budget Balance	6	7	12	11	14	27	33	23	43	62	136
Capital Receipts	0	..	0	0	0	0	..	..	..	0	11
Capital Payments	9	14	17	16	22	34	47	76	97	199	308

1981	1982	1983	1984	1985	1986	1987	1988	1989	1990 estimate	Notes	TURKEY
1,450	1,300	1,180	1,100	1,080	1,110	1,220	1,200	1,370	1,640	..	**CURRENT GNP PER CAPITA (US $)**
45,500	46,657	47,877	49,105	50,306	51,475	52,622	57,364	54,916	56,098		**POPULATION (thousands)**
											USE AND ORIGIN OF RESOURCES
			(Billions of current Turkish Liras)								
6,255	8,378	11,201	17,684	26,870	38,172	56,763	97,929	164,067	277,890	f	Gross National Product (GNP)
-159	-242	-330	-528	-682	-1,116	-1,536	-2,897	-3,702	-5,009		Net Factor Income from Abroad
6,414	8,620	11,532	18,212	27,552	39,288	58,299	100,826	167,769	282,899	..	GDP at Market Prices
-341	-283	-500	-763	-882	-1,170	-1,199	2,096	-1,700	-13,584	..	Resource Balance
664	1,269	1,768	3,500	5,676	6,933	11,865	24,329	37,414	52,608	..	Exports of Goods & NFServices
1,005	1,552	2,268	4,263	6,558	8,103	13,064	22,233	39,114	66,192	..	Imports of Goods & NFServices
6,754	8,903	12,032	18,975	28,434	40,457	59,498	98,730	169,469	296,483		Domestic Absorption
4,645	6,189	8,597	13,773	20,277	27,362	39,365	65,700	111,937	191,157		Private Consumption, etc.
700	939	1,175	1,651	2,375	3,490	5,314	8,799	19,395	39,964		General Gov't Consumption
1,409	1,775	2,259	3,551	5,782	9,605	14,819	24,231	38,137	65,362		Gross Domestic Investment
1,241	1,647	2,130	3,288	5,562	9,089	14,083	24,182	38,304	60,928		Fixed Investment
390	540	714	863	2,026	3,660	5,374	9,085	16,281	31,166		Indirect Taxes, net
6,024	8,081	10,817	17,349	25,526	35,628	52,925	91,741	151,488	251,733		GDP at factor cost
1,325	1,679	2,118	3,397	4,790	6,586	9,532	16,023	25,366	45,612	..	Agriculture
1,858	2,549	3,544	5,807	9,012	12,763	18,999	33,290	53,622	83,833	..	Industry
1,310	1,813	2,583	4,206	6,409	8,998	13,597	23,885	38,254	59,176		Manufacturing
2,841	3,853	5,155	8,145	11,724	16,279	24,394	42,428	72,500	122,288		Services, etc.
1,068	1,492	1,760	2,788	4,900	8,436	13,620	26,327	36,437	51,778		Gross Domestic Saving
1,194	1,606	1,778	2,951	5,138	8,468	13,855	26,029	39,386	55,505		Gross National Saving
			(Billions of 1987 Turkish Liras)								
40,312.2	42,132.7	43,726.1	46,322.2	48,883.9	52,690.5	56,763.0	58,711.2	59,919.3	65,663.7	f	Gross National Product
41,346.6	43,352.9	45,009.1	47,684.6	50,108.2	54,244.2	58,299.0	60,468.3	61,238.7	66,811.0		GDP at Market Prices
-1,265.7	75.8	-124.8	-716.1	-416.9	-1,686.0	-1,199.2	1,019.4	824.5	-2,599.5	..	Resource Balance
4,411.0	6,180.1	7,029.3	8,421.0	9,458.9	9,317.4	11,864.9	14,200.1	14,860.6	16,391.3		Exports of Goods & NFServices
5,676.7	6,104.4	7,154.2	9,137.1	9,875.8	11,003.4	13,064.1	13,180.7	14,036.1	18,990.8		Imports of Goods & NFServices
42,612.2	43,277.2	45,133.9	48,400.7	50,525.2	55,930.2	59,498.2	59,448.9	60,414.2	69,410.5		Domestic Absorption
26,841.2	27,993.3	29,771.1	32,852.1	33,348.9	36,814.5	39,365.2	40,127.1	41,727.1	47,944.6		Private Consumption, etc.
4,436.2	4,483.2	4,608.6	4,608.6	4,749.7	5,063.2	5,314.0	5,455.1	5,470.8	6,121.8		General Gov't Consumption
11,334.9	10,800.7	10,754.2	10,940.0	12,426.6	14,052.5	14,819.0	13,866.7	13,216.3	15,344.2		Gross Domestic Investment
9,689.7	10,007.0	10,275.5	10,299.9	12,032.8	13,350.8	14,083.0	13,863.3	13,399.6	14,549.8		Fixed Investment
38,381.1	40,116.1	41,707.2	44,298.5	46,199.9	49,594.6	52,925.0	55,245.9	55,679.4	60,240.9		GDP at factor cost
7,669.6	8,160.6	8,143.7	8,431.5	8,634.7	9,328.8	9,532.0	10,327.7	9,176.5	10,259.3		Agriculture
12,680.9	13,172.0	13,998.1	15,181.3	16,029.7	17,436.2	18,999.0	19,423.2	20,003.6	21,164.6		Industry
8,471.4	8,946.0	9,705.4	10,702.0	11,295.2	12,386.8	13,597.0	13,763.1	14,237.7	15,376.7		Manufacturing
18,030.6	18,783.4	19,565.4	20,685.7	21,535.5	22,829.6	24,394.0	25,494.9	26,499.3	28,817.0		Services, etc.
											Memo Items:
3,750.2	4,991.4	5,577.6	7,501.7	8,547.4	9,415.1	11,864.9	14,423.3	13,426.1	15,093.5		Capacity to Import
-660.9	-1,188.7	-1,451.7	-919.4	-911.5	97.7	0.0	223.2	-1,434.5	-1,297.8		Terms of Trade Adjustment
40,685.7	42,164.2	43,557.3	46,765.3	49,196.7	54,342.0	58,299.0	60,691.5	59,804.1	65,513.2		Gross Domestic Income
39,651.4	40,943.9	42,274.4	45,402.8	47,972.4	52,788.3	56,763.0	58,934.4	58,484.8	64,365.9		Gross National Income
			(Index 1987 = 100)								**DOMESTIC PRICES/DEFLATORS**
15.5	19.9	25.6	38.2	55.0	72.4	100.0	166.7	274.0	423.4	..	Overall (GDP)
15.9	20.6	26.7	39.2	56.3	72.3	100.0	166.1	280.5	427.1	..	Domestic Absorption
17.3	20.6	26.0	40.3	55.5	70.6	100.0	155.1	276.4	444.6	..	Agriculture
14.6	19.3	25.3	38.3	56.2	73.2	100.0	171.4	268.1	396.1	..	Industry
15.5	20.3	26.6	39.3	56.7	72.6	100.0	173.5	268.7	384.8		Manufacturing
14.5	18.9	24.9	36.9	53.5	72.0	100.0	175.4	286.3	459.0		Consumer Price Index
											MANUFACTURING ACTIVITY
87.5	90.8	87.2	90.9	92.5	95.9	100.0	99.6	..	..	G	Employment (1987=100)
122.7	116.6	115.7	101.8	98.2	94.0	100.0	95.5	..	..	G	Real Earnings per Empl. (1987=100)
70.7	74.7	75.8	78.2	82.3	91.1	100.0	101.7	..	..	G	Real Output per Empl. (1987=100)
25.3	23.5	24.8	23.5	21.1	15.9	17.2	16.3	..	..	..	Earnings as % of Value Added
			(Billions of current Turkish Liras)								**MONETARY HOLDINGS**
1,779	2,688	3,487	5,534	8,593	12,357	17,992	27,881	47,958	72,618	..	Money Supply, Broadly Defined
1,024	1,413	2,090	2,487	3,468	5,432	8,960	11,956	20,302	32,419	..	Money
280	412	548	735	1,011	1,415	2,275	3,426	6,841	11,378	..	Currency Outside Banks
744	1,001	1,542	1,752	2,456	4,017	6,686	8,530	13,461	21,041	..	Demand Deposits
755	1,275	1,397	3,047	5,125	6,925	9,032	15,925	27,656	40,199	..	Quasi-Money
			(Billions of current Turkish Liras)								**GOVERNMENT DEFICIT (-) OR SURPLUS**
-117	..	-483	-1,816	-2,050	-1,259	-2,346	-3,859	-7,503	-11,782	C F	
1,444	..	2,304	2,712	4,820	7,016	10,387	17,494	31,201	55,310		Current Revenue
1,071	..	1,958	3,504	5,614	6,782	10,477	17,933	32,977	59,207		Current Expenditure
373	..	345	-792	-794	234	-90	-438	-1,776	-3,896		Current Budget Balance
3	..	5	9	15	36	58	93	168	1,262		Capital Receipts
492	..	834	1,033	1,271	1,529	2,314	3,513	5,894	9,148		Capital Payments

TURKEY	1970	1971	1972	1973	1974	1975	1976	1977	1978	1979	1980
FOREIGN TRADE (CUSTOMS BASIS)					*(Millions of current US dollars)*						
Value of Exports, fob	589	677	885	1,317	1,538	1,401	1,960	1,753	2,288	2,261	2,910
Nonfuel Primary Products	532	591	739	1,047	1,115	1,039	1,478	1,322	1,784	1,639	2,086
Fuels	4	3	22	49	86	36	16	0	4	2	42
Manufactures	53	83	124	222	337	326	466	431	501	620	782
Value of Imports, cif	886	1,088	1,508	2,049	3,720	4,640	4,993	5,694	4,479	4,946	7,573
Nonfuel Primary Products	139	120	144	205	676	639	427	400	262	341	641
Fuels	67	122	156	222	764	810	1,127	1,471	1,440	1,760	3,669
Manufactures	680	846	1,208	1,622	2,280	3,192	3,439	3,823	2,777	2,845	3,262
					(Index 1987 = 100)						
Terms of Trade	144.8	151.4	126.9	132.9	105.4	99.6	111.2	107.1	112.0	108.5	90.7
Export Prices, fob	36.9	38.2	36.5	48.3	64.2	63.5	69.6	72.0	78.3	94.6	102.2
Import Prices, cif	25.5	25.2	28.8	36.3	60.9	63.8	62.6	67.2	69.9	87.2	112.7
BALANCE OF PAYMENTS					*(Millions of current US dollars)*						
Exports of Goods & Services	776	896	1,266	1,859	2,082	2,018	2,541	2,293	2,821	2,969	3,672
Merchandise, fob	588	677	885	1,320	1,532	1,401	1,960	1,753	2,288	2,261	2,910
Nonfactor Services	183	210	367	526	549	616	580	534	467	674	711
Factor Services	5	9	14	13	1	1	1	6	66	34	51
Imports of Goods & Services	1,150	1,421	1,847	2,452	4,133	5,103	5,690	6,540	5,185	6,192	9,251
Merchandise, fob	830	1,030	1,367	1,829	3,589	4,502	4,872	5,506	4,369	4,815	7,513
Nonfactor Services	237	292	349	476	366	436	517	687	310	367	569
Factor Services	83	99	131	148	178	165	301	347	506	1,010	1,169
Long-Term Interest	44	56	66	84	102	119	169	187	209	292	507
Private Current Transfers, net	317	499	777	1,234	1,466	1,398	1,104	1,068	1,086	1,799	2,153
Workers' Remittances	273	471	740	1,184	1,426	1,312	982	982	983	1,694	2,071
Curr. A/C Bal before Off. Transf.	-57	-26	197	640	-585	-1,687	-2,045	-3,179	-1,278	-1,424	-3,426
Net Official Transfers	13	69	15	20	24	39	16	39	13	11	18
Curr. A/C Bal after Off. Transf.	-44	43	212	660	-561	-1,648	-2,029	-3,140	-1,265	-1,413	-3,408
Long-Term Capital, net	330	217	697	360	182	1,322	2,559	878	1,437	1,632	2,916
Direct Investment	58	45	43	79	64	114	10	27	34	75	18
Long-Term Loans	201	305	210	340	211	154	525	874	1,091	4,032	1,880
Disbursements	332	416	368	469	367	327	726	1,108	1,452	4,511	2,475
Repayments	131	112	158	129	156	173	202	235	361	480	595
Other Long-Term Capital	71	-133	443	-59	-93	1,054	2,024	-23	312	-2,475	1,017
Other Capital, net	-142	72	-220	-325	-172	-311	-758	1,896	-193	-371	565
Change in Reserves	-144	-332	-689	-696	551	637	228	366	22	152	-72
Memo Item:					*(Turkish Liras per US dollar)*						
Conversion Factor (Annual Avg)	11.500	14.900	14.100	14.100	13.900	14.400	16.100	18.000	24.300	31.100	76.000
EXTERNAL DEBT (Total)	1,963	2,348	2,540	3,003	*(Millions of US dollars), outstanding at end of year* 3,310	4,769	5,442	11,452	14,855	15,900	19,119
Long-Term Debt (by debtor)	1,963	2,348	2,540	3,003	3,310	3,614	4,287	5,359	7,669	12,304	16,629
Central Bank, incl. IMF credit	103	112	59	87	107	359	516	714	960	3,686	4,749
Central Government	1,777	2,099	2,287	2,605	2,804	2,831	3,065	3,404	5,112	6,636	9,422
Rest of General Government	0	0	0	0	0	0	0	1	8	18	19
Non-financial Public Enterprises	33	80	96	163	225	229	411	694	953	1,188	1,740
Priv. Sector, incl non-guaranteed	50	57	97	148	174	195	296	546	636	777	700
Short-Term Debt	0	0	0	0	0	1,155	1,155	6,093	7,186	3,596	2,490
Memo Items:					*(Millions of US dollars)*						
Int'l Reserves Excluding Gold	304.1	631.4	1,262.1	1,985.9	1,561.7	943.8	990.5	638.0	801.3	658.2	1,077.0
Gold Holdings (at market price)	135.6	149.6	231.8	400.8	665.7	500.6	481.0	599.5	828.8	1,927.8	2,221.0
SOCIAL INDICATORS											
Total Fertility Rate	4.9	4.8	4.7	4.6	4.5	4.5	4.4	4.3	4.3	4.2	4.2
Infant Mortality Rate	147.2	143.6	140.0	134.2	128.4	122.6	116.8	111.0	105.4	99.8	94.2
Life Expectancy at Birth	56.7	57.3	57.9	58.5	59.2	59.9	60.5	61.2	61.6	61.9	62.3
Urban Population, % of total	38.4	39.0	39.7	40.3	41.0	41.6	42.0	42.5	42.9	43.4	43.8
Food Prod. per capita (1987=100)	93.4	95.4	95.1	85.1	91.6	98.4	102.5	100.2	102.7	102.2	102.3
Labor Force, Agriculture (%)	70.7	69.4	68.2	67.0	65.9	64.8	63.4	62.1	60.8	59.6	58.4
Labor Force, Female (%)	37.9	37.6	37.3	37.0	36.8	36.5	36.1	35.6	35.2	34.8	34.4
Primary Schl. Enroll. Ratio	110.0	..	..	..	..	108.0	107.0	105.0	105.0	104.0	96.0
Primary Schl. Enroll. Ratio, Female	94.0	..	..	..	..	97.0	95.0	96.0	94.0	90.0	
Secondary Schl. Enroll. Ratio	27.0	..	..	..	..	29.0	32.0	34.0	34.0	37.0	35.0

1981	1982	1983	1984	1985	1986	1987	1988	1989	1990 est.	Notes	
				(Millions of current US dollars)							**FOREIGN TRADE (CUSTOMS BASIS)**
4,702	5,747	5,671	7,134	7,958	7,457	10,190	11,662	11,626	12,959	..	Value of Exports, fob
2,847	2,928	2,795	2,878	2,715	2,924	3,202	3,835	3,714	3,861	..	Nonfuel Primary Products
107	345	233	407	373	181	233	332	256	294	..	Fuels
1,748	2,475	2,643	3,849	4,870	4,352	6,754	7,495	7,656	8,804	..	Manufactures
8,864	8,793	8,548	10,663	11,340	11,105	14,163	14,335	15,788	22,300	..	Value of Imports, cif
816	736	828	1,382	1,419	1,588	2,421	2,340	3,240	4,026	..	Nonfuel Primary Products
3,919	3,850	3,746	3,794	3,785	2,191	3,167	3,057	3,258	4,640	..	Fuels
4,129	4,208	3,974	5,487	6,136	7,326	8,575	8,938	9,291	13,634	..	Manufactures
				(Index 1987 = 100)							
84.3	81.8	85.2	84.1	82.4	98.9	100.0	104.3	95.6	97.6	..	Terms of Trade
98.6	89.7	89.3	86.3	82.7	89.2	100.0	108.0	154.8	160.6	..	Export Prices, fob
117.0	109.7	104.9	102.6	100.3	90.1	100.0	103.5	161.9	164.6	..	Import Prices, cif
				(Millions of current US dollars)							**BALANCE OF PAYMENTS**
6,019	7,928	7,946	9,755	11,417	10,921	14,517	17,955	18,878	21,959	..	Exports of Goods & Services
4,703	5,890	5,905	7,389	8,255	7,583	10,322	11,929	11,780	13,026	..	Merchandise, fob
1,264	1,918	1,939	2,157	2,618	2,696	3,520	5,176	5,832	7,141	..	Nonfactor Services
52	120	102	209	544	642	675	850	1,266	1,792	..	Factor Services
10,513	11,157	11,629	13,276	14,414	14,310	17,713	18,518	21,475	29,086	..	Imports of Goods & Services
8,567	8,518	8,895	10,331	11,230	10,664	13,551	13,706	15,999	22,580	..	Merchandise, fob
468	1,031	1,166	1,296	1,333	1,349	1,695	1,925	2,465	2,794	..	Nonfactor Services
1,478	1,608	1,568	1,649	1,851	2,297	2,467	2,887	3,011	3,712	..	Factor Services
989	1,171	1,235	1,184	1,319	1,496	1,898	2,443	2,654	2,824	..	Long-Term Interest
2,559	2,189	1,549	1,885	1,762	1,703	2,066	1,827	3,135	3,349	..	Private Current Transfers, net
2,490	2,140	1,513	1,807	1,714	1,634	2,021	1,776	3,040	3,246	..	Workers' Remittances
-1,935	-1,040	-2,134	-1,636	-1,235	-1,686	-1,130	1,264	538	-3,778	..	Curr. A/C Bal before Off. Transf.
-1	88	211	229	222	221	324	332	423	1,162	..	Net Official Transfers
-1,936	-952	-1,923	-1,407	-1,013	-1,465	-806	1,596	961	-2,616	..	Curr. A/C Bal after Off. Transf.
1,293	1,084	707	1,159	262	1,312	1,841	1,323	1,364	934	..	Long-Term Capital, net
95	55	46	113	99	125	106	354	663	681	..	Direct Investment
1,132	908	466	1,336	424	1,738	1,716	3,456	1,087	1,178	..	Long-Term Loans
1,937	2,101	1,632	2,517	2,788	3,734	4,758	7,343	4,847	4,886	..	Disbursements
805	1,193	1,165	1,181	2,364	1,996	3,042	3,888	3,760	3,709	..	Repayments
66	121	195	-290	-261	-551	19	-2,487	-386	-925	..	Other Long-Term Capital
571	22	1,206	353	643	693	-455	-1,766	387	2,625	..	Other Capital, net
72	-154	10	-105	108	-540	-580	-1,153	-2,712	-943	..	Change in Reserves
											Memo Item:
				(Turkish Liras per US dollar)							Conversion Factor (Annual Avg)
111.200	162.600	225.500	366.700	522.000	674.500	857.200	1,422.400	2,121.700	2,608.600	..	
			(Millions of US dollars), outstanding at end of year								**EXTERNAL DEBT (Total)**
19,227	19,708	20,317	21,601	26,010	32,842	40,800	40,827	41,419	49,149	..	
17,033	17,944	18,036	18,421	21,251	26,493	33,177	34,410	35,674	39,649	..	Long-Term Debt (by debtor)
4,849	5,212	5,669	6,291	6,588	7,277	8,240	7,301	7,491	7,820	..	Central Bank, incl. IMF credit
9,593	9,858	9,588	9,382	10,872	13,728	17,365	19,080	19,776	22,659	..	Central Government
18	18	20	14	21	109	180	242	372	485	..	Rest of General Government
1,957	2,277	2,196	2,197	3,208	4,473	5,979	6,535	6,397	6,578	..	Non-financial Public Enterprises
616	579	563	537	562	906	1,413	1,253	1,639	2,106	..	Priv. Sector, incl non-guaranteed
2,194	1,764	2,281	3,180	4,759	6,349	7,623	6,417	5,745	9,500	..	Short-Term Debt
				(Millions of US dollars)							**Memo Items:**
928.2	1,080.1	1,288.1	1,270.7	1,055.9	1,411.6	1,775.8	2,344.5	4,780.5	6,049.5	..	Int'l Reserves Excluding Gold
1,497.8	1,722.2	1,440.3	1,171.5	1,261.6	1,500.9	1,854.8	1,567.9	1,517.7	1,576.6	..	Gold Holdings (at market price)
											SOCIAL INDICATORS
4.1	4.1	4.0	3.9	3.8	3.8	3.7	..	..	..	..	Total Fertility Rate
88.6	83.0	79.4	75.8	72.2	68.6	65.0	63.2	61.4	59.5	..	Infant Mortality Rate
62.7	63.0	63.5	64.0	64.6	65.1	65.6	65.9	66.3	66.6	..	Life Expectancy at Birth
45.5	47.3	49.0	50.8	52.5	54.3	56.0	57.8	59.5	61.3	..	Urban Population, % of total
101.7	104.1	99.3	96.6	98.0	102.3	100.0	104.6	93.1	99.8	..	Food Prod. per capita (1987=100)
..	..	..	..	..	..	..	..	..		..	Labor Force, Agriculture (%)
34.3	34.2	34.2	34.1	34.0	34.0	33.9	33.8	33.8	33.7	..	Labor Force, Female (%)
..	..	111.0	111.0	113.0	115.0	117.0	113.0	112.0		..	Primary Schl. Enroll. Ratio
..	..	107.0	107.0	110.0	111.0	113.0	109.0	108.0	..	..	Primary Schl. Enroll. Ratio, Female
..	36.0	38.0	40.0	42.0	44.0	46.0	50.0	51.0	..	..	Secondary Schl. Enroll. Ratio

UGANDA	1970	1971	1972	1973	1974	1975	1976	1977	1978	1979	1980
CURRENT GNP PER CAPITA (US $)	190	200	210	210	220	220	270	280	280	290	280
POPULATION (thousands)	9,812	10,120	10,400	10,666	10,938	11,228	11,534	11,862	12,197	12,516	12,807

USE AND ORIGIN OF RESOURCES

(Millions of current Uganda Shillings)

	1970	1971	1972	1973	1974	1975	1976	1977	1978	1979	1980
Gross National Product (GNP)	94	106	112	129	159	225	264	543	590	878	1,262
Net Factor Income from Abroad	-1	-2	-1	-1	-1	0	-1	-1	-2	-4	-5
GDP at Market Prices	95	108	113	130	160	225	265	544	592	882	1,267
Resource Balance	3	-4	3	4	0	-5	4	7	-29	16	-82
Exports of Goods & NFServices	21	20	21	20	22	18	28	46	76	166	242
Imports of Goods & NFServices	18	24	18	16	22	23	24	39	105	150	324
Domestic Absorption	92	112	110	125	161	230	260	537	621	866	1,349
Private Consumption, etc.	..	..	..	..	..	..	..	..	..	..	..
General Gov't Consumption	..	..	..	..	..	..	..	..	..	..	..
Gross Domestic Investment	13	16	12	11	17	17	15	30	46	56	77
Fixed Investment	12	15	13	10	16	15	12	..	..	..	..
Indirect Taxes, net	9	11	11	13	18	17	24	49	40	31	27
GDP at factor cost	85	97	102	117	143	208	240	495	552	851	1,240
Agriculture	46	55	58	71	89	150	176	366	410	558	893
Industry	12	12	11	11	16	17	18	35	28	35	56
Manufacturing	8	8	8	8	11	13	15	29	24	31	53
Services, etc.	28	30	32	34	38	41	46	94	114	258	291
Gross Domestic Saving	16	12	15	15	17	12	20	37	17	72	-5
Gross National Saving	14	10	13	13	15	12	19	36	14	67	-11

(Millions of 1987 Uganda Shillings)

	1970	1971	1972	1973	1974	1975	1976	1977	1978	1979	1980
Gross National Product	193,342.0	205,132.0	203,671.0	198,164.0	201,376.0	191,955.0	196,586.0	199,692.0	186,135.0	158,392.0	150,935.0
GDP at Market Prices	195,601.0	208,210.0	205,891.0	199,765.0	202,892.0	192,137.0	197,066.0	200,071.0	186,810.0	159,150.0	151,569.0
Resource Balance	..	..	..	..	..	..	..	..	..	..	..
Exports of Goods & NFServices	..	..	..	..	..	..	..	..	..	..	..
Imports of Goods & NFServices	..	..	..	..	..	..	..	..	..	..	..
Domestic Absorption	..	..	..	..	..	..	..	..	..	..	..
Private Consumption, etc.	..	..	..	..	..	..	..	..	..	..	..
General Gov't Consumption	..	..	..	..	..	..	..	..	..	..	..
Gross Domestic Investment	..	..	..	..	..	..	..	..	..	..	..
Fixed Investment	..	..	..	..	..	..	..	..	..	..	..
GDP at factor cost	176,508.0	187,376.0	186,158.0	180,187.0	180,338.0	177,276.0	178,763.0	181,776.0	174,209.0	153,585.0	148,348.0
Agriculture	119,046.0	116,271.0	120,623.0	126,709.0	125,479.0	125,069.0	125,889.0	129,201.0	128,570.0	110,279.0	103,342.0
Industry	23,377.7	23,744.1	22,575.3	20,726.7	20,989.8	18,047.6	16,973.8	16,621.9	13,800.0	10,400.2	8,458.4
Manufacturing	14,275.4	14,433.8	14,479.0	13,528.8	13,234.7	11,424.9	11,176.0	10,859.3	8,415.9	5,565.4	5,904.7
Services, etc.	34,084.3	47,361.0	42,959.8	32,751.1	33,869.1	34,159.4	35,900.3	35,953.0	31,838.7	32,905.7	36,547.7

Memo Items:

	1970	1971	1972	1973	1974	1975	1976	1977	1978	1979	1980
Capacity to Import	..	..	..	..	..	..	..	..	..	..	..
Terms of Trade Adjustment	..	..	..	..	..	..	..	..	..	..	..
Gross Domestic Income	..	..	..	..	..	..	..	..	..	..	..
Gross National Income	..	..	..	..	..	..	..	..	..	..	..

DOMESTIC PRICES/DEFLATORS

(Index 1987 = 100)

	1970	1971	1972	1973	1974	1975	1976	1977	1978	1979	1980
Overall (GDP)	0.0	0.1	0.1	0.1	0.1	0.1	0.1	0.3	0.3	0.6	0.8
Domestic Absorption	..	..	..	..	..	..	..	..	..	..	..
Agriculture	0.0	0.0	0.0	0.1	0.1	0.1	0.1	0.3	0.3	0.5	0.9
Industry	0.1	0.1	0.1	0.1	0.1	0.1	0.1	0.2	0.2	0.3	0.7
Manufacturing	0.1	0.1	0.1	0.1	0.1	0.1	0.1	0.3	0.3	0.6	0.9
Consumer Price Index	..	..	..	..	..	..	..	..	..	..	0.9

MANUFACTURING ACTIVITY

	1970	1971	1972	1973	1974	1975	1976	1977	1978	1979	1980
Employment (1987=100)	..	..	..	..	..	..	..	..	..	..	..
Real Earnings per Empl. (1987=100)	..	..	..	..	..	..	..	..	..	..	..
Real Output per Empl. (1987=100)	..	..	..	..	..	..	..	..	..	..	..
Earnings as % of Value Added	..	39.4	..	..	..	..	..	..	..	..	..

MONETARY HOLDINGS

(Millions of current Uganda Shillings)

	1970	1971	1972	1973	1974	1975	1976	1977	1978	1979	1980
Money Supply, Broadly Defined	16.7	16.5	21.3	28.8	38.5	46.6	61.9	73.8	92.7	137.1	184.5
Money	11.1	11.2	15.3	21.1	30.0	32.4	44.5	57.7	69.8	106.2	139.6
Currency Outside Banks	5.9	5.9	6.2	8.0	10.9	13.7	22.1	28.9	35.3	58.2	72.6
Demand Deposits	5.2	5.3	9.2	13.2	19.1	18.7	22.4	28.8	34.5	48.1	67.0
Quasi-Money	5.6	5.3	6.0	7.7	8.5	14.3	17.4	16.1	22.9	30.9	44.9

GOVERNMENT DEFICIT (-) OR SURPLUS

(Millions of current Uganda Shillings)

	1970	1971	1972	1973	1974	1975	1976	1977	1978	1979	1980
GOVERNMENT DEFICIT (-) OR SURPLUS	..	..	-9.0	-8.6	-15.3	-12.4	-13.2	-12.8	-1.6	-34.5	-39.1
Current Revenue	..	..	15.4	12.4	11.8	20.9	24.6	34.4	57.9	26.3	40.1
Current Expenditure	..	..	..	..	..	26.9	31.4	39.2	45.5	48.5	67.0
Current Budget Balance	..	..	..	..	..	-6.1	-6.8	-4.8	12.4	-22.2	-26.9
Capital Receipts	..	..	..	..	..	0.0	..	..	..	..	..
Capital Payments	..	..	..	..	..	6.3	6.4	7.9	14.0	12.3	12.2

1981	1982	1983	1984	1985	1986	1987	1988	1989	1990 estimate	Notes	UGANDA
220	240	220	220	230	230	220	260	250	220	A	**CURRENT GNP PER CAPITA (US $)**
13,079	13,340	13,596	13,857	14,134	14,460	14,839	15,274	15,769	16,330	..	**POPULATION (thousands)**

(Millions of current Uganda Shillings)

1981	1982	1983	1984	1985	1986	1987	1988	1989	1990 estimate	Notes	UGANDA
											USE AND ORIGIN OF RESOURCES
2,126	3,106	4,953	9,262	23,195	53,801	184,352	512,629	1,036,160	1,468,150	..	Gross National Product (GNP)
-373	-633	-943	-190	-373	-704	-2,175	-7,333	-17,930	-30,380	..	Net Factor Income from Abroad
2,498	3,739	5,896	9,452	23,568	54,505	186,527	519,962	1,054,090	1,498,530	f	GDP at Market Prices
-165	-248	-305	-249	-496	-2,220	-12,660	-48,400	-106,370	-194,170	..	Resource Balance
428	818	1,019	1,508	3,154	6,139	13,740	37,070	66,810	98,550		Exports of Goods & NF Services
593	1,066	1,324	1,757	3,650	8,359	26,400	85,470	173,180	292,720		Imports of Goods & NF Services
2,663	3,987	6,201	9,701	24,064	56,725	199,187	568,362	1,160,460	1,692,700		Domestic Absorption
..	..	5,484	7,945	19,608	45,239	160,807	476,927	983,580	1,406,760		Private Consumption, etc.
		183	920	2,132	4,676	14,400	38,735	72,400	102,320		General Gov't Consumption
150	294	534	836	2,324	6,810	23,980	52,700	104,480	183,620		Gross Domestic Investment
..	..	..	836	2,324	6,815	23,980	52,700	104,480	183,620		Fixed Investment
131	389	718	1,152	2,066	3,861	12,084	28,530	58,507	98,050	..	Indirect Taxes, net
2,367	3,350	5,178	8,300	21,502	50,644	174,443	491,432	995,583	1,400,480	f	GDP at factor cost
1,472	2,070	3,380	5,109	14,625	35,955	122,294	330,052	666,217	932,550	..	Agriculture
66	189	252	399	808	2,138	10,159	37,037	71,546	103,980	f	Industry
45	155	192	254	518	1,655	6,734	22,630	40,840	59,840	..	Manufacturing
829	1,091	1,546	2,792	6,069	12,551	41,990	124,343	257,820	363,950	f	Services, etc.
-15	46	229	587	1,828	4,590	11,320	4,300	-1,890	-10,550	..	Gross Domestic Saving
-388	-569	-613	516	1,923	5,271	13,858	9,597	2,043	-7,051		Gross National Saving

(Millions of 1987 Uganda Shillings)

1981	1982	1983	1984	1985	1986	1987	1988	1989	1990 estimate	Notes	UGANDA
138,698.0	151,276.0	167,624.0	178,927.0	176,353.0	174,229.0	184,352.0	195,031.0	207,368.0	215,977.0	..	Gross National Product
163,002.0	182,097.0	199,538.0	182,598.0	179,189.0	176,508.0	186,527.0	197,821.0	210,956.0	220,446.0	f	GDP at Market Prices
											Resource Balance
..	..	..	..	..	..	..	..	..	..	..	Exports of Goods & NF Services
..	..	..	..	..	..	..	..	..	..	..	Imports of Goods & NF Services
											Domestic Absorption
..	..	..	..	..	..	..	..	..	..	..	Private Consumption, etc.
..	..	..	..	..	..	..	..	..	..	..	General Gov't Consumption
..	..	..	..	..	..	..	..	..	..	..	Gross Domestic Investment
..	..	..	..	..	..	..	..	..	..	..	Fixed Investment
154,426.0	163,150.0	175,239.0	160,343.0	163,481.0	164,005.0	174,443.0	186,967.0	199,247.0	206,022.0	f	GDP at factor cost
110,374.0	116,673.0	125,773.0	112,631.0	115,278.0	116,000.0	122,294.0	129,358.0	136,598.0	140,423.0	..	Agriculture
8,228.0	9,410.0	10,506.0	10,169.0	9,175.0	8,359.0	10,159.0	12,554.0	14,463.0	15,533.0	f	Industry
5,588.0	6,482.0	7,020.0	6,795.0	6,129.0	5,767.0	6,734.0	8,262.0	9,793.0	10,515.1	..	Manufacturing
35,824.0	37,067.5	38,960.0	37,543.0	39,028.0	39,646.0	41,990.0	45,055.0	48,186.0	50,065.9	f	Services, etc.
											Memo Items:
..	..	..	..	..	..	..	..	..	..	..	Capacity to Import
..	..	..	..	..	..	..	..	..	..	..	Terms of Trade Adjustment
..	..	..	..	..	..	..	..	..	..	..	Gross Domestic Income
..	..	..	..	..	..	..	..	..	..	..	Gross National Income

(Index 1987 = 100)

1981	1982	1983	1984	1985	1986	1987	1988	1989	1990 estimate	Notes	UGANDA
											DOMESTIC PRICES/DEFLATORS
1.5	2.1	3.0	5.2	13.2	30.9	100.0	262.8	499.7	679.8	A	Overall (GDP)
..	..	..	..	..	..	..	..	..	..	..	Domestic Absorption
1.3	1.8	2.7	4.5	12.7	31.0	100.0	255.1	487.7	664.1	..	Agriculture
0.8	2.0	2.4	3.9	8.8	25.6	100.0	295.0	494.7	669.4	..	Industry
0.8	2.4	2.7	3.7	8.5	28.7	100.0	273.9	417.0	569.1		Manufacturing
1.8	2.7	3.3	4.7	11.0	29.6	100.0	283.6	539.6	..		Consumer Price Index
											MANUFACTURING ACTIVITY
..	..	..	..	..	..	..	..	..	..		Employment (1987=100)
..	..	..	..	..	..	..	..	..	..		Real Earnings per Empl. (1987=100)
..	..	..	..	..	..	..	..	..	..		Real Output per Empl. (1987=100)
..	..	..	..	..	..	..	..	..	..		Earnings as % of Value Added

(Millions of current Uganda Shillings)

1981	1982	1983	1984	1985	1986	1987	1988	1989	1990 estimate	Notes	UGANDA
											MONETARY HOLDINGS
345.6	385.1	544.2	1,162.9	2,622.1	7,118.1	..	..	..	..	..	Money Supply, Broadly Defined
283.1	297.8	435.4	986.6	2,256.1	6,061.8	..	..	..	..	..	Money
113.6	128.4	189.2	487.2	1,050.4	3,509.3	..	..	..	..	..	Currency Outside Banks
169.5	169.4	246.2	499.4	1,205.6	2,552.5	..	..	..	..	..	Demand Deposits
62.4	87.4	108.9	176.3	366.1	1,056.3	..	..	..	..	..	Quasi-Money

(Millions of current Uganda Shillings)

1981	1982	1983	1984	1985	1986	1987	1988	1989	1990 estimate	Notes	UGANDA
-100.5	-146.0	-133.8	-221.2	-640.2	-1,344.9	..	..	..	..	C	**GOVERNMENT DEFICIT (-) OR SURPLUS**
30.9	276.5	536.8	937.6	1,668.9	3,228.2	..	..	..	..	..	Current Revenue
106.0	346.2	572.9	1,016.8	1,946.5	3,353.1	..	..	..	..	..	Current Expenditure
-75.1	-69.7	-36.2	-79.2	-277.5	-125.0	..	..	..	..	..	Current Budget Balance
..	0.1					..	..	..	..	..	Capital Receipts
25.3	76.4	97.6	142.0	362.7	1,219.9	..	..	..	..	..	Capital Payments

UGANDA	1970	1971	1972	1973	1974	1975	1976	1977	1978	1979	1980

FOREIGN TRADE (CUSTOMS BASIS) — *(Millions of current US dollars)*

Value of Exports, fob	..	..	..	..	..	..	..	..	..	..	..
Nonfuel Primary Products	..	..	..	..	..	..	..	..	..	..	..
Fuels	..	..	..	..	..	..	..	..	..	..	..
Manufactures	..	..	..	..	..	..	..	..	..	..	..
Value of Imports, cif	..	..	..	..	..	..	..	..	..	..	..
Nonfuel Primary Products	..	..	..	..	..	..	..	..	..	..	..
Fuels	..	..	..	..	..	..	..	..	..	..	..
Manufactures	..	..	..	..	..	..	..	..	..	..	..

(Index 1987 = 100)

Terms of Trade	..	..	..	..	..	..	..	..	..	..	..
Export Prices, fob	..	..	..	..	..	..	..	..	..	..	..
Import Prices, cif	..	..	..	..	..	..	..	..	..	..	..

BALANCE OF PAYMENTS — *(Millions of current US dollars)*

	1970	1971	1972	1973	1974	1975	1976	1977	1978	1979	1980
Exports of Goods & Services	297.10	284.14	291.51	290.40	307.76	251.81	335.73	556.09	337.39	414.16	330.70
Merchandise, fob	261.60	243.93	263.83	275.14	294.04	237.25	323.61	547.80	322.96	397.21	319.40
Nonfactor Services	32.60	37.11	25.30	11.21	9.38	10.56	9.35	4.90	8.54	14.94	9.90
Factor Services	2.90	3.11	2.39	4.05	4.33	4.01	2.77	3.39	5.89	2.01	1.40
Imports of Goods & Services	271.40	365.08	269.26	246.06	330.61	320.54	294.63	485.34	471.84	387.09	449.80
Merchandise, fob	178.30	247.74	171.87	175.48	236.32	228.38	206.78	366.60	306.31	265.71	317.60
Nonfactor Services	75.10	91.77	78.17	52.22	73.96	84.26	78.16	104.49	152.52	108.37	123.40
Factor Services	18.00	25.58	19.22	18.36	20.32	7.89	9.70	14.24	13.02	13.00	8.80
Long-Term Interest	4.40	4.60	4.40	4.70	4.10	2.50	1.80	3.10	2.50	2.60	3.90
Private Current Transfers, net	-6.90	-7.42	-9.01	-3.93	-5.05	-3.40	-5.66	-4.67	-8.83	-16.70	-2.20
Workers' Remittances	..	..	..	..	..	..	..	..	0.46	0.80	..
Curr. A/C Bal before Off. Transf.	18.80	-88.36	13.25	40.41	-27.90	-72.12	35.44	66.08	-143.28	10.37	-121.30
Net Official Transfers	1.50	2.61	3.15	2.62	3.85	16.03	7.74	1.98	5.88	29.12	38.10
Curr. A/C Bal after Off. Transf.	20.30	-85.75	16.39	43.04	-24.05	-56.09	43.18	68.07	-137.40	39.49	-83.20
Long-Term Capital, net	6.70	30.99	29.64	-14.78	16.24	8.01	-16.05	-11.91	15.86	92.88	-59.30
Direct Investment	4.20	-1.20	-11.94	5.25	1.68	2.06	1.15	0.82	1.04	1.61	..
Long-Term Loans	21.50	17.10	11.30	-8.90	15.90	7.90	29.90	45.60	131.30	179.30	56.90
Disbursements	25.90	21.90	16.20	10.90	25.80	15.50	35.40	58.80	138.90	197.20	92.00
Repayments	4.40	4.80	4.90	19.80	9.90	7.60	5.50	13.20	7.60	17.90	35.10
Other Long-Term Capital	-19.00	15.10	30.28	-11.13	-1.35	-1.95	-47.10	-58.33	-116.48	-88.02	-116.20
Other Capital, net	-28.60	10.36	-41.65	-36.89	-10.33	48.04	-24.67	-55.65	128.73	-165.03	87.30
Change in Reserves	1.60	44.40	-4.39	8.63	18.15	0.04	-2.46	-0.50	-7.19	32.65	55.20

Memo Item: — *(Uganda Shillings per US dollar)*

	1970	1971	1972	1973	1974	1975	1976	1977	1978	1979	1980
Conversion Factor (Annual Avg)	0.000	0.000	0.000	0.000	0.000	0.000	0.000	0.000	0.000	0.000	1.000

(Millions of US dollars), outstanding at end of year

	1970	1971	1972	1973	1974	1975	1976	1977	1978	1979	1980
EXTERNAL DEBT (Total)	151.7	172.4	177.5	176.7	202.5	208.1	241.5	333.0	475.1	666.5	794.2
Long-Term Debt (by debtor)	151.7	172.4	177.5	176.7	202.5	208.1	241.5	299.0	454.1	636.5	730.4
Central Bank, incl. IMF credit	0.0	10.8	10.8	12.1	18.3	28.2	38.0	39.7	38.0	34.5	89.4
Central Government	143.3	152.0	157.7	154.7	174.9	171.9	196.5	249.1	391.1	575.6	594.0
Rest of General Government	..	..	..	..	..	..	..	..	..	..	..
Non-financial Public Enterprises	7.2	8.2	7.7	8.7	8.1	6.9	6.0	8.5	20.7	21.7	32.0
Priv. Sector, incl non-guaranteed	1.2	1.4	1.3	1.2	1.2	1.1	1.0	1.7	4.3	4.7	15.0
Short-Term Debt	0.0	0.0	0.0	0.0	0.0	0.0	0.0	34.0	21.0	30.0	63.8

Memo Items: — *(Thousands of US dollars)*

	1970	1971	1972	1973	1974	1975	1976	1977	1978	1979	1980
Int'l Reserves Excluding Gold	56,650	26,923	35,952	29,113	16,759	31,023	44,534	47,206	52,700	22,839	3,000
Gold Holdings (at market price)	..	..	..	..	..	..	..	..	..	..	..

SOCIAL INDICATORS

	1970	1971	1972	1973	1974	1975	1976	1977	1978	1979	1980
Total Fertility Rate	7.1	7.1	7.1	7.1	7.2	7.2	7.3	7.3	7.3	7.3	7.3
Infant Mortality Rate	108.8	106.6	104.4	106.6	108.8	111.1	113.3	115.5	115.5	115.5	115.5
Life Expectancy at Birth	49.8	50.2	50.7	50.3	49.9	49.5	49.1	48.7	48.6	48.5	48.4
Urban Population, % of total	8.0	8.1	8.1	8.2	8.2	8.3	8.4	8.5	8.5	8.6	8.7
Food Prod. per capita (1987=100)	144.8	144.2	144.0	137.0	143.0	150.8	144.2	142.0	138.4	111.3	107.8
Labor Force, Agriculture (%)	89.3	88.9	88.5	88.2	87.9	87.6	87.2	86.8	86.5	86.2	85.9
Labor Force, Female (%)	43.2	43.1	43.1	43.0	43.0	43.0	42.9	42.9	42.9	42.8	42.8
Primary Schl. Enroll. Ratio	38.0	..	..	..	..	44.0	47.0	50.0	51.0	50.0	50.0
Primary Schl. Enroll. Ratio, Female	30.0	..	..	..	..	35.0	39.0	41.0	43.0	42.0	43.0
Secondary Schl. Enroll. Ratio	4.0	..	..	..	..	4.0	4.0	5.0	5.0	5.0	5.0

1981	1982	1983	1984	1985	1986	1987	1988	1989	1990 est.	Notes	UGANDA
				(Millions of current US dollars)							**FOREIGN TRADE (CUSTOMS BASIS)**
..	..	..	..	..	..	..	..	..	..	..	Value of Exports, fob
..	..	..	..	..	..	..	..	..	..		Nonfuel Primary Products
..	..	..	..	..	..	..	..	..	..		Fuels
..	..	..	..	..	..	..	..	..	..		Manufactures
..	..	..	..	..	..	..	..	..	..	..	Value of Imports, cif
..	..	..	..	..	..	..	..	..	..		Nonfuel Primary Products
..	..	..	..	..	..	..	..	..	..		Fuels
..	..	..	..	..	..	..	..	..	..		Manufactures
				(Index 1987 = 100)							
..	..	..	..	..	..	..	..	..	..	..	Terms of Trade
..	..	..	..	..	..	..	..	..	..		Export Prices, fob
..	..	..	..	..	..	..	..	..	..		Import Prices, cif
				(Millions of current US dollars)							**BALANCE OF PAYMENTS**
274.40	382.10	384.40	406.00	399.00	398.00	365.00	323.00	284.00	232.00	f	Exports of Goods & Services
229.30	347.10	367.70	381.00	381.00	382.00	341.00	293.00	249.00	194.00	..	Merchandise, fob
44.30	35.00	11.50	25.00	18.00	16.00	24.00	30.00	35.00	38.00	..	Nonfactor Services
0.80	0.00	5.20	0.00	0.00	0.00	0.00	0.00	0.00	..	..	Factor Services
391.90	524.30	543.40	517.00	514.00	569.00	694.00	785.00	792.00	745.00	f	Imports of Goods & Services
278.30	337.60	342.50	386.00	392.00	447.00	530.00	597.00	616.00	567.00	..	Merchandise, fob
100.40	160.40	150.00	81.00	73.00	76.00	112.00	126.00	104.00	108.00	..	Nonfactor Services
13.20	26.30	50.90	50.00	49.00	46.00	52.00	62.00	72.00	70.00	..	Factor Services
7.10	9.80	10.20	15.90	17.70	22.30	22.60	22.20	23.50	15.50	..	Long-Term Interest
-0.20	19.00	65.80	33.00	69.70	98.90	110.00	119.00	98.00	79.00	..	Private Current Transfers, net
..	..	..	..	..	..	..	..	..	..		Workers' Remittances
-117.70	-123.20	-93.20	-78.00	-45.30	-72.10	-219.00	-343.00	-410.00	-434.00	..	Curr. A/C Bal before Off. Transf.
149.60	107.30	103.50	68.00	48.00	35.00	66.00	129.00	159.00	179.00	..	Net Official Transfers
31.90	-15.90	10.30	-10.00	2.70	-37.10	-153.00	-214.00	-251.00	-255.00	..	Curr. A/C Bal after Off. Transf.
-52.80	36.20	63.70	-4.00	110.00	152.00	130.00	113.00	159.00	173.00	f	Long-Term Capital, net
0.00	0.00	0.70	0.00	0.00	0.00	0.00	0.00	0.00	..	..	Direct Investment
51.00	76.70	46.70	71.00	140.60	148.60	354.20	107.10	251.70	258.40	..	Long-Term Loans
93.30	115.00	90.00	116.70	185.40	183.40	399.80	184.80	312.00	305.10	..	Disbursements
42.30	38.30	43.30	45.70	44.80	34.80	45.60	77.70	60.30	46.70	..	Repayments
-103.80	-40.50	16.30	-75.00	-30.60	3.40	-224.20	5.90	-92.70	-85.40	..	Other Long-Term Capital
-73.80	-77.70	-146.80	60.00	-73.70	-105.90	19.00	99.00	78.00	56.00	f	Other Capital, net
94.70	57.40	72.80	-46.00	-39.00	-9.00	4.00	2.00	14.00	26.00	..	Change in Reserves
				(Uganda Shillings per US dollar)							**Memo Item:**
2.000	2.000	3.000	4.000	11.000	16.000	51.000	127.000	331.000	496.000	..	Conversion Factor (Annual Avg)
				(Millions of US dollars), outstanding at end of year							
825.1	988.5	1,105.7	1,158.5	1,311.0	1,482.2	1,995.7	2,023.0	2,307.6	2,726.3	..	**EXTERNAL DEBT (Total)**
793.2	947.5	1,075.9	1,116.6	1,267.3	1,415.8	1,929.5	1,940.4	2,200.8	2,582.7	..	Long-Term Debt (by debtor)
241.7	326.9	397.4	351.9	341.6	288.2	317.1	289.9	259.2	320.6	..	Central Bank, incl. IMF credit
509.9	584.2	643.4	726.6	869.0	1,057.3	1,521.7	1,560.3	1,846.7	2,160.5	..	Central Government
..	..	..	..	..	..	..	..	..	..	..	Rest of General Government
27.7	23.8	25.2	29.1	46.0	57.7	72.2	71.0	75.4	80.5	..	Non-financial Public Enterprises
13.9	12.6	9.9	9.0	10.7	12.6	18.5	19.2	19.5	21.1	..	Priv. Sector, incl non-guaranteed
31.9	41.0	29.8	41.9	43.7	66.4	66.2	82.6	106.8	143.6	..	Short-Term Debt
				(Thousands of US dollars)							**Memo Items:**
30,003	78,324	106,496	67,907	27,288	29,206	54,600	49,300	14,100	43,986	..	Int'l Reserves Excluding Gold
..	..	..	..	..	..	..	..	..	..	..	Gold Holdings (at market price)
											SOCIAL INDICATORS
7.3	7.3	7.3	7.3	7.3	7.3	7.3	7.3	7.3	7.3	..	Total Fertility Rate
115.5	115.5	115.5	115.5	115.4	115.4	115.4	115.9	116.4	117.0	..	Infant Mortality Rate
48.4	48.3	48.3	48.3	48.3	48.2	48.2	47.8	47.3	46.9	..	Life Expectancy at Birth
8.8	9.0	9.1	9.3	9.4	9.6	9.9	10.1	10.2	10.4	..	Urban Population, % of total
112.6	118.8	118.7	100.3	105.1	96.3	100.0	104.4	105.3	105.5	..	Food Prod. per capita (1987=100)
..	..	..	..	..	..	..	..	..	..	..	Labor Force, Agriculture (%)
42.6	42.4	42.3	42.1	41.9	41.7	41.6	41.4	41.2	41.1	..	Labor Force, Female (%)
52.0	58.0	..	..	70.0	70.0	74.0	77.0	..	71.0	..	Primary Schl. Enroll. Ratio
44.0	49.0	..		..	63.0				..	..	Primary Schl. Enroll. Ratio, Female
5.0	8.0	..	..	10.0	12.0	13.0	13.0	..	..	..	Secondary Schl. Enroll. Ratio

UNITED ARAB EMIRATES	1970	1971	1972	1973	1974	1975	1976	1977	1978	1979	1980
CURRENT GNP PER CAPITA (US $)	..	..	..	..	..	13,280	20,370	22,960	21,070	25,680	30,140
POPULATION (thousands)	220	255	300	356	425	505	597	702	813	920	1,015

USE AND ORIGIN OF RESOURCES						*(Millions of current U.A.E. Dirhams)*					
Gross National Product (GNP)	..	..	..	10,201	30,902	39,591	51,342	64,320	62,901	86,845	115,023
Net Factor Income from Abroad	..	..	..	-1,199	-198	277	514	1,210	2,516	7,212	5,190
GDP at Market Prices	..	..	..	11,400	31,100	39,314	50,828	63,110	60,385	79,633	109,833
Resource Balance	..	..	..	5,700	21,400	17,779	21,550	19,174	16,042	27,146	47,718
Exports of Goods & NF Services	..	..	..	9,400	29,400	29,183	36,106	41,265	40,121	56,871	85,592
Imports of Goods & NF Services	..	..	..	3,700	8,000	11,404	14,556	22,091	24,079	29,725	37,874
Domestic Absorption	..	..	..	5,700	9,700	21,535	29,278	43,936	44,343	52,487	62,115
Private Consumption, etc.	..	..	..	1,500	2,200	6,215	7,695	11,557	12,501	15,245	18,968
General Gov't Consumption	..	..	..	1,300	2,700	3,261	4,648	7,413	8,163	9,600	11,992
Gross Domestic Investment	..	..	..	2,900	4,800	12,059	16,935	24,966	23,679	27,642	31,155
Fixed Investment	..	..	..	..	..	12,059	16,585	22,686	25,779	28,442	30,155
Indirect Taxes, net	..	..	..	..	..	-321	-679	-785	-885	-1,164	-1,637
GDP at factor cost	..	..	..	..	..	39,635	51,507	63,895	61,270	80,797	111,470
Agriculture	..	..	..	155	208	329	432	491	604	680	827
Industry	..	..	..	6,920	24,511	31,348	39,277	46,556	43,982	60,960	86,089
Manufacturing	..	..	..	225	301	369	593	1,853	2,197	2,533	4,191
Services, etc.	..	..	..	..	..	7,958	11,798	16,848	16,684	19,157	24,554
Gross Domestic Saving	..	..	..	8,600	26,200	29,838	38,485	44,140	39,721	54,788	78,873
Gross National Saving	..	..	..	6,802	24,696	27,302	35,085	40,549	36,546	54,788	75,907

						(Millions of 1987 U.A.E. Dirhams)					
Gross National Product	..	..	..	42,050	53,462	57,557	66,417	78,699	78,550	102,700	124,683
GDP at Market Prices	..	..	..	47,445	54,323	57,706	66,386	77,963	76,135	95,083	120,204
Resource Balance	..	..	..	..	..	7,389	4,289	-2,695	-2,833	4,069	16,855
Exports of Goods & NF Services	..	..	..	..	..	29,282	33,151	36,971	34,423	46,322	59,469
Imports of Goods & NF Services	..	..	..	..	..	21,893	28,862	39,667	37,256	42,253	42,613
Domestic Absorption	..	..	..	..	..	50,317	62,097	80,658	78,968	91,014	103,349
Private Consumption, etc.	..	..	..	..	..	22,940	27,168	30,865	30,850	37,712	46,058
General Gov't Consumption	..	..	..	..	..	6,520	9,067	11,568	11,973	14,255	16,753
Gross Domestic Investment	..	..	..	..	..	20,856	25,862	38,226	36,145	39,047	40,538
Fixed Investment	..	..	..	..	..	..	..	..	..	..	..
GDP at factor cost	..	..	..	..	..	56,457	65,377	76,571	75,028	93,706	118,619
Agriculture	..	..	..	..	..	356	466	547	630	711	803
Industry	..	..	..	..	..	44,123	48,362	55,025	53,882	70,377	91,602
Manufacturing	..	..	..	..	..	502	747	2,046	2,420	2,705	4,460
Services, etc.	..	..	..	..	..	11,977	16,549	20,999	20,515	22,619	26,214

Memo Items:											
Capacity to Import	..	..	..	..	..	56,024	71,592	74,096	62,076	80,841	96,303
Terms of Trade Adjustment	..	..	..	..	..	26,742	38,441	37,124	27,653	34,519	36,834
Gross Domestic Income	..	..	..	..	..	84,448	104,827	115,087	103,788	129,602	157,038
Gross National Income	..	..	..	..	..	84,299	104,858	115,823	106,203	137,219	161,516

DOMESTIC PRICES/DEFLATORS						*(Index 1987 = 100)*					
Overall (GDP)	..	..	..	24.0	57.3	68.1	76.6	80.9	79.3	83.8	91.4
Domestic Absorption	..	..	..	..	..	42.8	47.1	54.5	56.2	57.7	60.1
Agriculture	..	..	..	..	..	92.3	92.7	89.8	95.8	95.6	103.0
Industry	..	..	..	..	..	71.0	81.2	84.6	81.6	86.6	94.0
Manufacturing	..	..	..	..	..	73.5	79.4	90.5	90.8	93.6	94.0
Consumer Price Index	..	..	..	..	..	..	..	..	..	..	..

MANUFACTURING ACTIVITY											
Employment (1987=100)	..	..	..	..	..	..	..	..	..	..	..
Real Earnings per Empl. (1987=100)	..	..	..	..	..	..	..	..	..	..	..
Real Output per Empl. (1987=100)	..	..	..	..	..	..	..	..	..	..	..
Earnings as % of Value Added	..	..	..	..	..	..	..	39.5	43.1	..	..

MONETARY HOLDINGS						*(Millions of current U.A.E. Dirhams)*					
Money Supply, Broadly Defined	..	..	..	2,257	6,036	8,820	16,754	15,539	17,576	18,222	23,527
Money	..	..	..	970	1,536	2,603	4,725	5,215	5,776	6,269	7,354
Currency Outside Banks	..	..	..	265	429	628	1,077	1,392	1,704	1,965	2,143
Demand Deposits	..	..	..	704	1,107	1,975	3,648	3,822	4,072	4,303	5,212
Quasi-Money	..	..	..	1,287	4,499	6,217	12,028	10,325	11,800	11,954	16,172

GOVERNMENT DEFICIT (-) OR SURPLUS						*(Millions of current U.A.E. Dirhams)*					
	..	..	37	30	62	590	597	-211	-503	202	2,302
Current Revenue	..	..	201	420	800	1,773	3,102	5,995	6,984	8,862	17,608
Current Expenditure	..	..	148	331	569	886	1,456	4,364	6,269	7,498	12,311
Current Budget Balance	..	..	53	89	231	887	1,646	1,631	715	1,364	5,297
Capital Receipts	..	..	..	..	..	..	..	..	..	..	..
Capital Payments	..	..	16	59	169	297	1,049	1,842	1,218	1,162	2,995

1981	1982	1983	1984	1985	1986	1987	1988	1989	1990 estimate	Notes	UNITED ARAB EMIRATES
31,650	28,830	25,310	24,260	22,220	16,310	16,700	16,410	18,410	19,860	..	**CURRENT GNP PER CAPITA (US $)**
1,100	1,176	1,242	1,299	1,349	1,399	1,448	1,497	1,545	1,592	..	**POPULATION (thousands)**
			(Millions of current U.A.E. Dirhams)								**USE AND ORIGIN OF RESOURCES**
127,814	120,495	107,752	106,048	104,700	83,341	90,905	90,254	101,906	117,763	..	Gross National Product (GNP)
6,975	7,342	5,506	4,405	5,506	4,405	4,405	4,772	565	..	..	Net Factor Income from Abroad
120,839	113,153	102,246	101,643	99,194	78,936	86,500	85,482	101,341		..	GDP at Market Prices
42,617	31,144	23,902	27,707	27,604	6,207	14,494	8,748	15,574		..	Resource Balance
83,662	71,576	60,874	60,008	58,266	37,901	48,562	46,744	55,661		..	Exports of Goods & NF Services
41,045	40,432	36,972	32,301	30,662	31,694	34,068	37,996	40,087		..	Imports of Goods & NF Services
78,222	82,009	78,344	73,936	71,590	72,729	72,006	76,734	85,767		..	Domestic Absorption
24,946	26,846	26,183	26,744	27,173	30,003	33,277	37,203	41,480		..	Private Consumption, etc.
21,475	22,000	19,958	17,696	19,484	18,897	17,762	17,653	19,242		..	General Gov't Consumption
31,801	33,163	32,203	29,496	24,933	23,829	20,967	21,878	25,045		..	Gross Domestic Investment
30,643	32,683	31,668	29,116	24,458	23,329	20,317	21,111	..		..	Fixed Investment
-3,215	-2,501	-2,878	-2,861	-2,760	-2,532	-2,154	-2,059	-2,440		..	Indirect Taxes, net
124,054	115,654	105,124	104,504	101,954	81,468	88,654	87,541	103,781		..	GDP at factor cost
1,036	1,144	1,198	1,349	1,440	1,540	1,593	1,664	1,764	..	..	Agriculture
90,170	77,735	68,410	68,639	65,296	44,122	50,626	47,711	57,491	..	..	Industry
8,077	9,436	9,584	9,761	9,255	7,037	7,911	7,805	9,202	..	..	Manufacturing
32,848	36,775	35,516	34,516	35,218	35,806	36,435	38,166	44,526	..	..	Services, etc.
74,418	64,307	56,105	57,203	52,537	30,036	35,461	30,626	40,619	..	..	Gross Domestic Saving
72,950	63,573	55,737	56,101	52,169	29,669	35,461	30,626	..		..	Gross National Saving
			(Millions of 1987 U.A.E. Dirhams)								
129,506	119,626	112,002	116,551	115,199	88,766	90,905	88,644	99,025	105,956	..	Gross National Product
123,620	113,421	107,304	112,594	110,465	83,962	86,500	83,612	93,404	..	I	GDP at Market Prices
10,697	3,142	1,670	4,960	9,240	11,541	14,494	16,305	22,841	..	..	Resource Balance
54,079	46,353	40,560	41,819	42,413	45,870	48,562	51,910	57,851	..	..	Exports of Goods & NF Services
43,382	43,211	38,890	36,859	33,174	34,329	34,068	35,605	35,011	..	..	Imports of Goods & NF Services
112,923	110,279	105,634	107,635	101,225	72,421	72,006	67,307	70,563		..	Domestic Absorption
45,379	43,746	39,416	43,435	48,626	26,675	33,277	30,097	32,207		..	Private Consumption, etc.
28,360	28,000	26,510	25,157	24,131	20,497	17,762	16,674	17,111		..	General Gov't Consumption
39,183	38,534	39,708	39,043	28,468	25,249	20,967	20,536	21,245		..	Gross Domestic Investment
..	..	..	..	..	..	..	..	..		..	Fixed Investment
123,108	113,444	106,925	112,153	109,379	86,384	88,654	86,685	..		..	GDP at factor cost
991	1,048	1,201	1,360	1,481	1,571	1,593	1,653	..		..	Agriculture
90,037	78,888	70,727	75,182	70,542	46,446	50,626	47,280	..		..	Industry
8,503	9,845	9,701	10,275	10,049	7,747	7,911	7,824	..		..	Manufacturing
32,080	33,508	34,998	35,611	37,356	38,367	36,435	37,752	..		..	Services, etc.
											Memo Items:
88,425	76,495	64,033	68,476	63,039	41,052	48,562	43,802	48,613	..	..	Capacity to Import
34,346	30,143	23,473	26,657	20,625	-4,818	0	-8,108	-9,239	..	..	Terms of Trade Adjustment
157,966	143,564	130,777	139,251	131,090	79,144	86,500	75,504	84,165	..	..	Gross Domestic Income
163,852	149,768	135,475	143,208	135,825	83,948	90,905	80,536	89,786	..	..	Gross National Income
			(Index 1987 = 100)								**DOMESTIC PRICES/DEFLATORS**
97.8	99.8	95.3	90.3	89.8	94.0	100.0	102.2	108.5	..	..	Overall (GDP)
69.3	74.4	74.2	68.7	70.7	100.4	100.0	114.0	121.5	..	..	Domestic Absorption
104.6	109.2	99.8	99.2	97.2	98.0	100.0	100.7	..	..	..	Agriculture
100.1	98.5	96.7	91.3	92.6	95.0	100.0	100.9	..	..	..	Industry
95.0	95.8	98.8	95.0	92.1	90.8	100.0	99.8		..	..	Manufacturing
..	..	..	..	..	..	..	..	..	..	..	Consumer Price Index
											MANUFACTURING ACTIVITY
..	..	..	..	..	..	..	..	..	..		Employment (1987=100)
..	..	..	..	..	..	..	..	..	..		Real Earnings per Empl. (1987=100)
..	..	..	..	..	..	..	..	..	..		Real Output per Empl. (1987=100)
34.3	..	..	..	61.2	..	..	..	..	..		Earnings as % of Value Added
			(Millions of current U.A.E. Dirhams)								**MONETARY HOLDINGS**
29,094	33,646	36,342	46,870	49,886	52,076	54,940	58,156	63,188	58,009	..	Money Supply, Broadly Defined
8,969	9,739	9,124	8,892	9,505	9,201	10,096	10,753	11,056	10,762	..	Money
2,771	2,990	2,879	2,929	3,161	3,246	3,511	3,600	3,612	4,392	..	Currency Outside Banks
6,198	6,749	6,245	5,963	6,344	5,955	6,585	7,154	7,444	6,370	..	Demand Deposits
20,124	23,907	27,217	37,978	40,381	42,875	44,844	47,403	52,132	47,247	..	Quasi-Money
			(Millions of current U.A.E. Dirhams)								
2,355	..	..	..	..	..	-624	-314	-618	..	..	**GOVERNMENT DEFICIT (-) OR SURPLUS**
22,460	..	..	..	..	..	12,626	12,867	12,637	..	..	Current Revenue
17,418	17,648	14,737	14,827	..	..	13,031	13,038	13,131	..	..	Current Expenditure
5,042	..	..	..	..	..	-405	-171	-494	..	..	Current Budget Balance
	..	..	..	..	..	8	4	9	..	..	Capital Receipts
2,687	..	..	..	..	..	227	147	133	..	..	Capital Payments

UNITED ARAB EMIRATES	1970	1971	1972	1973	1974	1975	1976	1977	1978	1979	1980
FOREIGN TRADE (CUSTOMS BASIS)					*(Millions of current US dollars)*						
Value of Exports, fob	552	935	1,160	2,178	7,017	6,696	8,565	9,534	9,138	..	..
Nonfuel Primary Products	18	29	25	43	46	69	100	13	132	..	..
Fuels	532	902	1,114	2,116	6,932	6,544	8,262	9,091	8,678	..	..
Manufactures	3	5	21	18	40	83	203	431	329	..	..
Value of Imports, cif	271	312	496	842	1,781	2,754	3,443	5,179	5,389	6,419	8,098
Nonfuel Primary Products	51	57	80	131	302	355	477	688	735	823	1,137
Fuels	9	9	25	40	136	197	236	316	201	638	875
Manufactures	211	245	390	671	1,344	2,202	2,731	4,175	4,453	4,958	6,086
					(Index 1987 = 100)						
Terms of Trade	29.0	34.2	38.6	43.1	122.5	112.3	119.9	120.1	105.1	..	..
Export Prices, fob	7.0	9.2	10.3	14.5	59.1	57.8	62.3	68.5	69.2	..	..
Import Prices, cif	24.2	26.9	26.7	33.7	48.2	51.4	51.9	57.0	65.9	..	..
BALANCE OF PAYMENTS					*(Millions of current US dollars)*						
Exports of Goods & Services	..	..	..	2,160	7,250	7,950	9,820	11,120	11,460	17,740	..
Merchandise, fob	520	870	1,090	2,030	6,870	7,450	9,130	10,170	9,970	15,040	22,000
Nonfactor Services	..	..	..	50	100	150	230	230	280	340	1,090
Factor Services	..	..	..	80	280	350	460	720	1,210	2,360	..
Imports of Goods & Services	..	..	..	1,330	2,250	3,320	4,180	6,230	6,840	9,300	..
Merchandise, fob	270	310	480	730	1,490	2,300	2,810	4,300	4,680	4,080	7,600
Nonfactor Services	..	..	..	230	430	740	1,040	1,520	1,600	4,750	2,890
Factor Services	..	..	..	380	330	280	330	410	560	470	..
Long-Term Interest	..	..	..	..	..	..	..	..	..	..	..
Private Current Transfers, net	..	..	-50	-150	-330	-710	-990	-1,230	-1,470	-1,890	-2,200
Workers' Remittances	..	..	..	..	..	..	..	..	..	..	..
Curr. A/C Bal before Off. Transf.	100	260	350	680	4,670	3,920	4,650	3,660	3,150	6,550	11,800
Net Official Transfers	-10	-50	-40	-280	-480	-560	-780	-870	-700	-1,020	-1,700
Curr. A/C Bal after Off. Transf.	90	210	310	400	4,190	3,360	3,870	2,790	2,450	5,530	10,100
Long-Term Capital, net	..	10	..	60	-860	-790	-160	-50	340	-50	-3,700
Direct Investment	..	..	..	..	..	..	..	..	..	..	..
Long-Term Loans	..	..	..	..	..	..	..	..	..	..	..
Disbursements	..	..	..	..	..	..	..	..	..	..	..
Repayments	..	..	..	..	..	..	..	..	..	..	..
Other Long-Term Capital	..	10	..	60	-860	-790	-160	-50	340	-50	-3,700
Other Capital, net	-60	-30	-120	-280	-1,110	-1,060	-1,210	-1,610	-1,550	-3,070	-4,600
Change in Reserves	-30	-190	-190	-180	-2,220	-1,510	-2,500	-1,130	-1,240	-2,410	-1,800
Memo Item:					*(U.A.E. Dirhams per US dollar)*						
Conversion Factor (Annual Avg)	4.760	4.750	4.390	4.000	3.960	3.960	3.950	3.900	3.870	3.820	3.710
EXTERNAL DEBT (Total)					*(Millions of US dollars), outstanding at end of year*						
	..	..	..	..	..	..	..	..	..	..	..
Long-Term Debt (by debtor)	..	..	..	..	..	..	..	..	..	..	..
Central Bank, incl. IMF credit	..	..	..	..	..	..	..	..	..	..	..
Central Government	..	..	..	..	..	..	..	..	..	..	..
Rest of General Government	..	..	..	..	..	..	..	..	..	..	..
Non-financial Public Enterprises	..	..	..	..	..	..	..	..	..	..	..
Priv. Sector, incl non-guaranteed	..	..	..	..	..	..	..	..	..	..	..
Short-Term Debt	..	..	..	..	..	..	..	..	..	..	..
Memo Items:					*(Millions of US dollars)*						
Int'l Reserves Excluding Gold	..	..	..	91.7	452.9	987.9	1,906.5	800.3	811.8	1,432.3	2,014.7
Gold Holdings (at market price)	..	..	..	..	..	..	73.4	93.8	130.3	295.2	339.8
SOCIAL INDICATORS											
Total Fertility Rate	6.5	6.4	6.4	6.2	6.1	5.9	5.8	5.7	5.6	5.5	5.4
Infant Mortality Rate	68.2	62.6	57.0	53.2	49.4	45.6	41.8	38.0	36.8	35.6	34.4
Life Expectancy at Birth	61.1	61.8	62.5	63.4	64.2	65.1	65.9	66.7	67.2	67.7	68.2
Urban Population, % of total	42.3	49.8	57.3	64.8	72.3	79.8	80.1	80.4	80.6	80.9	81.2
Food Prod. per capita (1987=100)	..	..	..	..	..	..	..	..	..	..	..
Labor Force, Agriculture (%)	13.6	11.7	10.7	10.0	9.5	9.1	7.6	6.5	5.7	5.1	4.6
Labor Force, Female (%)	4.3	4.2	4.1	4.0	4.0	4.0	4.4	4.6	4.8	5.0	5.1
Primary Schl. Enroll. Ratio	93.0	..	..	..	..	101.0	..	108.0	108.0	113.0	88.0
Primary Schl. Enroll. Ratio, Female	71.0	..	..	..	..	97.0	..	107.0	108.0	112.0	88.0
Secondary Schl. Enroll. Ratio	22.0	..	..	..	..	33.0	..	39.0	43.0	47.0	52.0

1981	1982	1983	1984	1985	1986	1987	1988	1989	1990 estimate	Notes	UNITED ARAB EMIRATES
											FOREIGN TRADE (CUSTOMS BASIS)
											(Millions of current US dollars)
..	..	..	..	..	..	..	..	..	..	..	Value of Exports, fob
..	..	..	..	..	..	..	..	..	..	..	Nonfuel Primary Products
..	..	..	..	..	..	..	..	..	..	..	Fuels
..	..	..	..	..	..	..	..	..	..	..	Manufactures
8,800	8,601	8,436	..	..	..	..	..	..	..	..	Value of Imports, cif
1,124	1,008	1,296	..	..	..	..	..	..	..	..	Nonfuel Primary Products
993	519	587	..	..	..	..	..	..	..	..	Fuels
6,683	7,073	6,553	..	..	..	..	..	..	..	..	Manufactures
											(Index 1987 = 100)
..	..	..	..	..	..	..	..	..	..	..	Terms of Trade
..	..	..	..	..	..	..	..	..	..	..	Export Prices, fob
..	..	..	..	..	..	..	..	..	..	..	Import Prices, cif
											BALANCE OF PAYMENTS
											(Millions of current US dollars)
											Exports of Goods & Services
21,800	18,200	15,400	16,000	14,800	10,300	12,300	12,300	..	..	..	Merchandise, fob
990	1,300	1,180	350	1,080	1,020	930	430	..	..	..	Nonfactor Services
..	..	..	..	..	..	..	..	..	..	..	Factor Services
								..	..	..	Imports of Goods & Services
8,600	8,100	7,200	6,200	5,700	5,700	6,500	7,700	..	..	..	Merchandise, fob
3,490	3,500	3,580	2,150	2,980	2,720	2,730	2,230	..	..	..	Nonfactor Services
..	..	..	..	..	..	..	..	..	..	..	Factor Services
											Long-Term Interest
-2,300	-2,200	-1,600	-1,500	-1,600	-1,300	-1,200	-1,300	..	..	..	Private Current Transfers, net
..											Workers' Remittances
10,300	7,700	5,700	7,700	7,100	2,800	4,000	2,800	..	..	..	Curr. A/C Bal before Off. Transf.
-1,100	-700	-400	-200	-200	-200	-400	-300	-100	..	..	Net Official Transfers
9,200	7,000	5,300	7,500	6,900	2,400	3,700	2,700	..	..	..	Curr. A/C Bal after Off. Transf.
-2,900	-1,700	-1,500	600	300	600	-1,000	-1,000	..	..	..	Long-Term Capital, net
..	..	..	..	..	..	..	..	..	..	..	Direct Investment
..	..	..	..	..	..	..	..	..	..	..	Long-Term Loans
..	..	..	..	..	..	..	..	..	..	..	Disbursements
..	..	..	..	..	..	..	..	..	..	..	Repayments
-2,900	-1,700	-1,500	600	300	600	-1,000	-1,000	..	..	..	Other Long-Term Capital
-4,000	-4,300	-4,200	-6,900	-5,900	-900	-2,000	-1,100	..	..	..	Other Capital, net
-2,300	-1,000	400	-1,200	-1,300	-2,100	-700	-600	..	..	..	Change in Reserves
											(U.A.E. Dirhams per US dollar)
											Memo Item:
3.670	3.670	3.670	3.670	3.670	3.670	3.670	3.670	3.670	3.670	..	Conversion Factor (Annual Avg)
											(Millions of US dollars), outstanding at end of year
											EXTERNAL DEBT (Total)
..	..	..	..	..	..	..	..	..	..	..	Long-Term Debt (by debtor)
..	..	..	..	..	..	..	..	..	..	..	Central Bank, incl. IMF credit
..	..	..	..	..	..	..	..	..	..	..	Central Government
..	..	..	..	..	..	..	..	..	..	..	Rest of General Government
..	..	..	..	..	..	..	..	..	..	..	Non-financial Public Enterprises
..	..	..	..	..	..	..	..	..	..	..	Priv. Sector, incl non-guaranteed
..	..	..	..	..	..	..	..	..	..	..	Short-Term Debt
											Memo Items:
											(Millions of US dollars)
3,202.2	2,215.5	2,072.4	2,286.9	3,204.3	3,369.9	4,725.3	4,433.5	4,456.6	4,583.9	..	Int'l Reserves Excluding Gold
269.3	373.4	311.8	251.9	267.2	319.4	395.6	335.3	319.7	306.7	..	Gold Holdings (at market price)
											SOCIAL INDICATORS
5.3	5.2	5.1	5.1	5.0	4.9	4.8	4.7	4.6	4.6	..	Total Fertility Rate
33.2	32.0	30.8	29.6	28.4	27.2	26.0	25.0	24.0	23.0	..	Infant Mortality Rate
68.7	69.2	69.5	69.8	70.1	70.4	70.7	71.0	71.2	71.5	..	Life Expectancy at Birth
80.5	79.8	79.2	78.5	77.8	77.8	77.8	77.8	77.8	77.8	..	Urban Population, % of total
..	..	..	..	..	..	..	..	..	..	..	Food Prod. per capita (1987=100)
..	..	..	..	..	..	..	..	..	..	..	Labor Force, Agriculture (%)
5.3	5.4	5.5	5.6	5.7	5.9	6.0	6.2	6.3	6.4	..	Labor Force, Female (%)
..	97.0	97.0	93.0	93.0	96.0	98.0	104.0	111.0	..	..	Primary Schl. Enroll. Ratio
..	97.0	97.0	93.0	93.0	97.0	99.0	104.0	110.0	..	..	Primary Schl. Enroll. Ratio, Female
..	58.0	58.0	56.0	59.0	58.0	61.0	62.0	64.0	..	..	Secondary Schl. Enroll. Ratio

UNITED KINGDOM	1970	1971	1972	1973	1974	1975	1976	1977	1978	1979	1980
CURRENT GNP PER CAPITA (US $)	2,220	2,530	2,860	3,220	3,480	3,890	4,230	4,620	5,200	6,470	8,020
POPULATION (thousands)	55,632	55,928	56,097	56,223	56,236	56,226	56,216	56,190	56,178	56,242	56,330
USE AND ORIGIN OF RESOURCES						*(Billions of current Pounds Sterling)*					
Gross National Product (GNP)	51.96	57.96	64.85	74.86	84.53	105.74	125.22	145.74	168.50	199.57	231.46
Net Factor Income from Abroad	0.36	0.38	0.40	0.79	0.83	0.14	0.19	0.00	0.37	1.75	0.23
GDP at Market Prices	51.61	57.58	64.46	74.07	83.70	105.60	125.03	145.74	168.13	197.81	231.23
Resource Balance	0.48	0.84	-0.04	-1.79	-4.15	-1.80	-1.35	1.12	2.32	0.76	5.20
Exports of Goods & NFServices	11.92	13.36	14.02	17.55	23.44	27.38	35.68	43.84	47.95	55.46	63.10
Imports of Goods & NFServices	11.43	12.52	14.07	19.34	27.59	29.18	37.03	42.72	45.63	54.71	57.90
Domestic Absorption	51.13	56.74	64.50	75.86	87.85	107.40	126.38	144.62	165.82	197.05	226.04
Private Consumption, etc.	31.97	35.42	40.78	46.20	52.59	64.60	73.93	86.28	99.53	119.12	138.09
General Gov't Consumption	9.04	10.31	11.76	13.40	16.72	23.12	27.05	29.48	33.42	38.85	48.96
Gross Domestic Investment	10.12	11.01	11.97	16.26	18.54	19.68	25.41	28.86	32.86	39.09	38.99
Fixed Investment	9.74	10.89	11.94	14.73	17.50	21.03	24.50	27.04	31.06	36.93	41.56
Indirect Taxes, net	7.23	7.47	7.77	8.28	7.99	9.88	12.27	15.92	18.39	24.43	30.03
GDP at factor cost	44.38	50.11	56.68	65.79	75.71	95.72	112.76	129.82	149.74	173.39	201.20
Agriculture	1.24	1.41	1.54	1.96	2.08	2.50	3.20	3.19	3.42	3.72	4.21
Industry	19.62	21.65	24.66	28.71	31.42	38.77	45.85	54.84	63.61	73.96	85.03
Manufacturing	14.76	15.77	17.97	20.81	22.78	27.76	32.21	38.50	44.45	49.87	53.83
Services, etc.	23.52	27.04	30.48	35.13	42.21	54.45	63.72	71.79	82.72	95.70	111.96
Gross Domestic Saving	10.60	11.85	11.92	14.47	14.39	17.88	24.05	29.98	35.18	39.85	44.19
Gross National Saving	10.94	12.23	12.27	15.15	15.10	17.88	24.22	29.93	35.42	41.40	44.21
						(Billions of 1987 Pounds Sterling)					
Gross National Product	265.00	286.88	308.30	325.41	317.93	312.48	322.35	330.45	343.10	355.31	348.43
GDP at Market Prices	262.91	284.80	306.26	321.97	314.90	312.05	321.84	330.43	342.33	352.17	348.06
Resource Balance	-1.18	-0.35	-5.45	-5.84	-1.80	0.98	3.80	7.68	6.24	2.06	4.80
Exports of Goods & NFServices	55.49	59.26	59.75	66.89	71.53	69.21	75.28	80.18	81.48	84.57	84.45
Imports of Goods & NFServices	56.67	59.61	65.21	72.73	73.32	68.24	71.48	72.50	75.24	82.52	79.65
Domestic Absorption	264.09	285.15	311.71	327.80	316.69	311.07	318.04	322.75	336.09	350.11	343.27
Private Consumption, etc.	142.92	162.50	187.13	189.35	182.36	180.93	180.49	185.57	196.01	206.19	208.75
General Gov't Consumption	62.62	64.47	67.20	70.11	71.42	75.40	76.33	75.07	76.80	78.46	79.71
Gross Domestic Investment	58.55	58.17	57.38	68.35	62.91	54.73	61.22	62.12	63.28	65.46	54.80
Fixed Investment	56.38	57.42	57.29	61.03	59.55	58.37	59.34	58.28	60.04	61.72	58.40
GDP at factor cost	222.96	246.51	268.88	285.31	285.17	282.52	290.18	294.26	304.34	308.00	302.22
Agriculture	10.31	10.85	11.85	12.85	11.08	9.82	9.75	9.59	10.28	9.02	8.05
Industry	151.53	135.45	126.99	146.78	158.15	160.90	157.17	152.60	158.47	162.18	137.60
Manufacturing	96.76	88.52	77.08	83.00	91.05	83.29	79.48	83.05	88.57	91.95	79.48
Services, etc.	84.80	108.98	128.54	130.66	121.92	117.96	128.47	136.41	140.26	141.38	158.12
Memo Items:											
Capacity to Import	59.05	63.60	65.00	66.01	62.30	64.02	68.86	74.40	79.06	83.66	86.80
Terms of Trade Adjustment	3.56	4.34	5.25	-0.88	-9.23	-5.19	-6.41	-5.78	-2.42	-0.91	2.35
Gross Domestic Income	266.47	289.14	311.50	321.08	305.67	306.85	315.43	324.65	339.91	351.25	350.42
Gross National Income	268.56	291.22	313.55	324.53	308.70	307.29	315.93	324.67	340.68	354.40	350.78
DOMESTIC PRICES/DEFLATORS						*(Index 1987 = 100)*					
Overall (GDP)	19.6	20.2	21.0	23.0	26.6	33.8	38.8	44.1	49.1	56.2	66.4
Domestic Absorption	19.4	19.9	20.7	23.1	27.7	34.5	39.7	44.8	49.3	56.3	65.8
Agriculture	12.0	13.0	13.0	15.3	18.8	25.4	32.8	33.3	33.2	41.3	52.3
Industry	12.9	16.0	19.4	19.6	19.9	24.1	29.2	35.9	40.1	45.6	61.8
Manufacturing	15.3	17.8	23.3	25.1	25.0	33.3	40.5	46.4	50.2	54.2	67.7
Consumer Price Index	18.2	19.9	21.3	23.3	27.0	33.5	39.1	45.3	49.0	55.6	65.6
MANUFACTURING ACTIVITY											
Employment (1987=100)	164.7	160.6	154.3	156.3	159.3	153.2	149.7	149.2	145.6	141.9	133.9
Real Earnings per Empl. (1987=100)	69.1	70.5	73.2	75.6	77.7	78.9	78.6	75.3	79.9	82.3	83.8
Real Output per Empl. (1987=100)	74.1	70.4	59.2	65.9	86.0	74.1	76.8	77.7	80.2	88.2	79.9
Earnings as % of Value Added	52.2	53.1	51.3	48.4	47.2	51.3	48.3	46.7	46.2	45.7	48.8
MONETARY HOLDINGS						*(Billions of current Pounds Sterling)*					
Money Supply, Broadly Defined	26.77	30.79	37.39	45.57	50.96	57.90	64.95	74.52	85.13	97.85	115.09
Money	9.64	11.09	12.66	13.30	14.74	17.48	19.47	23.52	27.36	29.86	31.04
Currency Outside Banks	3.32	3.59	4.08	4.38	5.08	5.81	6.58	7.56	8.73	9.51	10.24
Demand Deposits	6.31	7.50	8.58	8.93	9.65	11.68	12.89	15.96	18.63	20.35	20.81
Quasi-Money	17.13	19.70	24.74	32.27	36.22	40.42	45.48	51.00	57.76	67.99	84.05
						(Billions of current Pounds Sterling)					
GOVERNMENT DEFICIT (-) OR SURPLUS	0.92	-0.38	-1.74	-2.52	-3.83	-7.80	-7.25	-4.93	-8.81	-11.16	-10.73
Current Revenue	19.07	20.15	21.29	23.14	29.42	37.63	44.14	50.15	55.00	64.33	81.82
Current Expenditure	14.74	16.53	19.16	21.67	28.27	38.60	45.72	50.58	58.36	68.51	84.22
Current Budget Balance	4.33	3.63	2.13	1.47	1.16	-0.97	-1.58	-0.43	-3.36	-4.19	-2.39
Capital Receipts	0.01	0.01	0.02	0.03	0.04	0.08	0.05	0.09	0.15	0.22	0.23
Capital Payments	3.42	4.03	3.89	4.02	5.03	6.90	5.72	4.60	5.60	7.20	8.57

1981	1982	1983	1984	1985	1986	1987	1988	1989	1990 estimate	Notes	UNITED KINGDOM
9,360	9,800	9,280	8,650	8,450	9,010	10,500	12,790	14,500	16,060	..	**CURRENT GNP PER CAPITA (US $)**
56,352	56,306	56,347	56,460	56,618	56,763	56,930	57,065	57,236	57,395	..	**POPULATION (thousands)**
				(Billions of current Pounds Sterling)							**USE AND ORIGIN OF RESOURCES**
254.81	278.76	304.95	325.62	356.14	383.15	419.62	465.18	508.17	547.69	..	Gross National Product (GNP)
0.62	0.68	1.57	1.54	1.23	1.42	..	-0.36	-1.29	-1.85	-1.49	Net Factor Income from Abroad
254.20	278.09	303.38	324.08	354.91	381.73	419.98	466.48	510.02	549.18	..	GDP at Market Prices
7.23	5.15	2.77	-0.54	3.65	-2.40	-4.44	-16.74	-19.51	-13.05	..	Resource Balance
67.84	73.18	80.51	92.40	102.71	98.82	107.62	108.47	123.52	134.91	..	Exports of Goods & NFServices
60.61	68.03	77.74	92.94	99.05	101.21	112.06	125.21	143.04	147.97	..	Imports of Goods & NFServices
246.97	272.93	300.60	324.62	351.26	384.13	424.42	483.22	529.53	562.23	..	Domestic Absorption
153.04	168.91	184.71	198.57	216.25	239.48	263.58	297.70	325.47	348.22	..	Private Consumption, etc.
55.39	60.39	65.81	69.79	73.83	79.41	85.38	91.76	99.07	109.54	..	General Gov't Consumption
38.54	43.64	50.08	56.26	61.17	65.23	75.46	93.76	105.00	104.48	..	Gross Domestic Investment
41.30	44.82	48.61	54.97	60.35	64.51	74.08	88.96	101.84	105.19	..	Fixed Investment
35.26	39.63	42.05	43.75	47.88	55.19	61.29	68.88	73.44	71.01	..	Indirect Taxes, net
218.94	238.45	261.33	280.33	307.03	326.54	358.69	397.60	436.58	478.17	..	GDP at factor cost
4.78	5.42	5.20	6.27	5.55	6.01	6.13	5.93	6.54		..	Agriculture
90.99	99.09	106.99	113.30	123.02	121.61	130.14	..	..	..	..	Industry
54.62	58.83	61.75	66.50	73.49	78.94	83.28	..	..	..	..	Manufacturing
123.17	133.95	149.13	160.75	178.45	198.91	222.42	..	..	..	..	Services, etc.
45.77	48.79	52.85	55.72	64.83	62.83	71.03	77.02	85.48	91.42	..	Gross Domestic Saving
46.44	49.51	54.76	57.63	66.37	64.33	70.54	75.45	83.34	89.64	..	Gross National Saving
				(Billions of 1987 Pounds Sterling)							
346.72	352.00	366.06	373.89	386.67	402.16	419.62	435.81	445.38	449.45	..	Gross National Product
345.86	351.13	364.15	372.11	385.33	400.67	419.98	437.03	447.02	450.70	..	GDP at Market Prices
6.36	3.33	-0.11	-3.01	-0.03	-2.08	-4.44	-18.26	-22.92	-19.21	..	Resource Balance
83.75	84.53	86.21	91.89	97.20	101.80	107.62	107.72	112.30	117.76	..	Exports of Goods & NFServices
77.39	81.20	86.32	94.89	97.23	103.88	112.06	125.98	135.23	136.97	..	Imports of Goods & NFServices
339.50	347.80	364.27	375.12	385.36	402.75	424.42	455.29	469.95	469.91	..	Domestic Absorption
210.18	212.86	222.15	227.51	235.49	249.91	263.58	281.05	290.73	294.06	..	Private Consumption, etc.
79.93	80.58	82.07	82.86	82.88	84.34	85.38	85.89	86.67	89.13	..	General Gov't Consumption
49.39	54.35	60.05	64.74	66.99	68.50	75.46	88.35	92.55	86.72	..	Gross Domestic Investment
52.81	55.67	58.47	63.45	65.99	67.58	74.08	83.80	89.48	87.35	..	Fixed Investment
297.55	300.66	313.18	321.52	332.81	342.81	358.69	371.78	381.42	390.95	..	GDP at factor cost
6.92	8.16	8.88	8.35	6.55	5.93	6.13	5.90	7.08	..	..	Agriculture
121.78	125.25	128.86	127.68	130.53	127.62	130.14	156.00	..	..	..	Industry
59.69	57.70	58.26	70.81	79.24	77.54	83.28	93.18	97.86	..	..	Manufacturing
168.36	167.36	175.43	185.49	195.74	209.27	222.42	209.88	..	..	..	Services, etc.
											Memo Items:
86.62	87.36	89.40	94.34	100.81	101.42	107.62	109.13	116.78	124.89	..	Capacity to Import
2.87	2.82	3.19	2.46	3.61	-0.38	0.00	1.41	4.48	7.13	..	Terms of Trade Adjustment
348.73	353.95	367.35	374.57	388.94	400.29	419.98	438.45	451.50	457.82	..	Gross Domestic Income
349.59	354.83	369.25	376.34	390.29	401.78	419.62	437.22	449.85	456.58	..	Gross National Income
				(Index 1987 = 100)							**DOMESTIC PRICES/DEFLATORS**
73.5	79.2	83.3	87.1	92.1	95.3	100.0	106.7	114.1	121.9	..	Overall (GDP)
72.7	78.5	82.5	86.5	91.2	95.4	100.0	106.1	112.7	119.6	..	Domestic Absorption
69.1	66.4	58.6	75.1	84.8	101.4	100.0	100.5	92.3	..	..	Agriculture
74.7	79.1	83.0	88.7	94.2	95.3	100.0	..	..	..	..	Industry
91.5	102.0	106.0	93.9	92.7	101.8	100.0	..	..	..	..	Manufacturing
73.4	79.7	83.4	87.5	92.8	96.0	100.0	104.9	113.1	123.8	..	Consumer Price Index
											MANUFACTURING ACTIVITY
119.2	110.7	105.1	105.0	102.2	101.2	100.0	102.5	104.1	..	..	Employment (1987=100)
84.3	85.7	88.7	91.0	93.7	96.2	100.0	104.2	107.2	..	..	Real Earnings per Empl. (1987=100)
66.2	67.9	73.6	93.2	103.8	94.2	100.0	..	..	..	..	Real Output per Empl. (1987=100)
47.6	46.3	44.0	43.8	43.3	42.8	41.3	41.2	41.2	..	..	Earnings as % of Value Added
				(Billions of current Pounds Sterling)							**MONETARY HOLDINGS**
140.63	157.56	178.21	199.24	221.82	252.28	344.26	402.60	481.34	533.76	D	Money Supply, Broadly Defined
34.59	40.66	42.46	48.05	56.67	69.26	154.12	170.67	195.31	214.94	..	Money
10.77	11.22	11.01	9.16	9.83	13.39	14.18	15.34	16.20	16.35	..	Currency Outside Banks
23.83	29.44	31.46	38.89	46.84	55.87	139.94	155.33	179.11	198.59	..	Demand Deposits
106.04	116.90	135.75	151.20	165.14	183.01	190.14	231.93	286.03	318.83	..	Quasi-Money
				(Billions of current Pounds Sterling)							**GOVERNMENT DEFICIT (-) OR SURPLUS**
-12.14	-9.51	-13.37	-10.28	-10.27	-9.11	-2.88	7.21	3.97	..	..	Current Revenue
92.38	107.46	113.42	121.40	134.15	140.16	151.49	167.82	181.26	..	..	Current Revenue
98.49	108.51	116.46	124.99	133.85	140.25	148.59	153.41	165.43	..	..	Current Expenditure
-6.11	-1.05	-3.04	-3.60	0.31	-0.09	2.90	14.42	15.82	..	..	Current Budget Balance
0.42	0.36	0.38	0.36	0.36	0.39	0.50	0.67	0.77	0.78	..	Capital Receipts
6.45	8.82	10.71	7.04	10.97	9.52	6.45	7.97	12.63	..	..	Capital Payments

UNITED KINGDOM	1970	1971	1972	1973	1974	1975	1976	1977	1978	1979	1980
FOREIGN TRADE (CUSTOMS BASIS)					*(Billions of current US dollars)*						
Value of Exports, fob	19.35	22.35	24.34	30.53	38.66	43.74	46.03	57.48	71.52	90.49	114.38
Nonfuel Primary Products	2.73	2.83	3.32	4.53	5.46	5.60	5.73	6.96	9.15	11.46	15.21
Fuels	0.50	0.57	0.60	0.91	1.80	1.80	2.25	3.63	4.50	9.15	14.88
Manufactures	16.12	18.95	20.43	25.10	31.40	36.34	38.05	46.88	57.87	69.88	84.29
Value of Imports, cif	21.72	23.94	27.86	38.84	54.15	53.19	55.95	63.62	78.35	102.41	117.90
Nonfuel Primary Products	9.66	9.52	10.32	14.02	17.26	16.31	16.60	18.55	20.29	25.55	28.99
Fuels	2.27	3.04	3.11	4.23	10.84	9.53	10.14	9.13	9.17	12.17	15.91
Manufactures	9.80	11.38	14.43	20.59	26.05	27.34	29.21	35.94	48.89	64.70	73.00
					(Index 1987 = 100)						
Terms of Trade	135.4	138.9	130.7	111.6	91.3	99.0	93.3	94.9	99.9	99.8	107.4
Export Prices, fob	26.1	28.3	31.1	35.4	46.0	51.2	50.2	56.8	67.6	82.3	102.0
Import Prices, cif	19.2	20.4	23.8	31.8	50.4	51.8	53.8	59.9	67.7	82.5	95.0
BALANCE OF PAYMENTS					*(Billions of current US dollars)*						
Exports of Goods & Services	31.21	35.20	42.53	53.89	68.07	74.00	78.05	91.00	112.59	154.01	201.14
Merchandise, fob	19.51	21.99	23.51	29.11	38.11	42.47	45.03	55.32	67.12	86.02	109.62
Nonfactor Services	7.78	9.11	10.09	12.22	14.87	16.36	17.24	19.54	23.12	29.75	35.32
Factor Services	3.93	4.10	8.93	12.56	15.10	15.17	15.78	16.14	22.36	38.24	56.20
Imports of Goods & Services	28.80	32.01	41.32	55.21	74.53	76.41	78.00	88.89	106.99	150.11	189.68
Merchandise, fob	19.54	21.47	25.35	35.36	50.35	49.75	52.10	59.32	70.18	92.99	106.27
Nonfactor Services	6.82	7.83	8.60	10.64	12.72	13.53	13.07	14.05	16.17	21.68	27.01
Factor Services	2.44	2.70	7.36	9.21	11.46	13.13	12.83	15.51	20.63	35.44	56.41
Long-Term Interest	..	..	..	..	..	..	..	..	..	..	..
Private Current Transfers, net	-0.03	0.00	-0.13	-0.24	-0.28	-0.31	-0.03	-0.08	-0.24	-0.41	-0.47
Workers' Remittances	..	..	..	..	..	..	..	..	..	..	..
Curr. A/C Bal before Off. Transf.	2.38	3.19	1.08	-1.57	-6.74	-2.72	0.02	2.03	5.36	3.48	10.98
Net Official Transfers	-0.41	-0.47	-0.55	-0.85	-0.71	-0.75	-1.40	-1.89	-3.20	-4.26	-4.12
Curr. A/C Bal after Off. Transf.	1.97	2.72	0.53	-2.41	-7.45	-3.47	-1.38	0.15	2.16	-0.78	6.86
Long-Term Capital, net	-1.07	-0.54	-2.27	-1.71	0.83	0.69	0.62	5.01	-5.51	-5.36	-11.38
Direct Investment	-0.19	-0.22	-0.81	-2.26	0.00	0.32	-1.33	0.25	-3.03	-6.07	-1.11
Long-Term Loans											
Disbursements	..	..	..	..	..	..	..	..	..	..	..
Repayments	..	..	..	..	..	..	..	..	..	..	..
Other Long-Term Capital	-0.88	-0.32	-1.46	0.55	0.83	0.37	1.95	4.76	-2.48	0.71	-10.28
Other Capital, net	1.82	1.86	-0.55	4.47	3.76	2.65	-0.17	8.97	1.19	-11.61	3.09
Change in Reserves	-2.73	-4.04	2.29	-0.35	2.87	0.12	0.93	-14.13	2.16	17.76	1.43
Memo Item:					*(Pounds Sterling per US dollar)*						
Conversion Factor (Annual Avg)	0.420	0.410	0.400	0.410	0.430	0.450	0.560	0.570	0.520	0.470	0.430
					(Millions US dollars), outstanding at end of year						
EXTERNAL DEBT (Total)	..	..	..	..	..	..	..	..	..	..	..
Long-Term Debt (by debtor)	..	..	..	..	..	..	..	..	..	..	..
Central Bank, incl. IMF credit	..	..	..	..	..	..	..	..	..	..	..
Central Government	..	..	..	..	..	..	..	..	..	..	..
Rest of General Government	..	..	..	..	..	..	..	..	..	..	..
Non-financial Public Enterprises	..	..	..	..	..	..	..	..	..	..	..
Priv. Sector, incl non-guaranteed	..	..	..	..	..	..	..	..	..	..	..
Short-Term Debt	..	..	..	..	..	..	..	..	..	..	..
Memo Items:					*(Millions of US dollars)*						
Int'l Reserves Excluding Gold	1,479	7,989	4,846	5,589	6,038	4,598	3,375	20,112	16,026	19,744	20,651
Gold Holdings (at market price)	1,440	968	1,368	2,358	3,921	2,949	2,833	3,666	5,159	9,343	11,104
SOCIAL INDICATORS											
Total Fertility Rate	2.4	2.4	2.2	2.0	1.9	1.8	1.7	1.7	1.8	1.9	1.9
Infant Mortality Rate	18.5	17.9	17.5	17.2	16.8	16.0	14.5	14.1	13.3	12.9	12.1
Life Expectancy at Birth	71.7	71.8	72.0	72.1	72.3	72.4	72.6	72.8	73.0	73.4	73.8
Urban Population, % of total	88.5	88.5	88.6	88.6	88.7	88.7	88.7	88.7	88.8	88.8	88.8
Food Prod. per capita (1987=100)	78.5	79.1	80.8	82.0	87.6	82.6	78.3	87.2	89.2	91.4	96.3
Labor Force, Agriculture (%)	2.8	2.8	2.8	2.8	2.7	2.7	2.7	2.7	2.6	2.6	2.6
Labor Force, Female (%)	35.6	35.9	36.2	36.5	36.8	37.1	37.5	37.8	38.2	38.5	38.9
Primary Schl. Enroll. Ratio	104.0	..	..	..	..	105.0	106.0	105.0	105.0	104.0	103.0
Primary Schl. Enroll. Ratio, Female	104.0	..	..	..	..	106.0	106.0	106.0	106.0	105.0	103.0
Secondary Schl. Enroll. Ratio	73.0	..	..	..	..	83.0	83.0	83.0	83.0	82.0	83.0

1981	1982	1983	1984	1985	1986	1987	1988	1989	1990 estimate	Notes	UNITED KINGDOM
											FOREIGN TRADE (CUSTOMS BASIS)
				(Billions of current US dollars)							
102.14	96.58	91.77	94.31	101.17	106.63	131.13	145.39	153.24	185.89	..	Value of Exports, fob
12.66	11.54	11.60	11.29	11.10	13.44	15.40	16.63	17.83	20.75	..	Nonfuel Primary Products
19.36	19.59	19.81	20.48	21.69	12.66	14.37	10.38	10.11	13.99	..	Fuels
70.11	65.45	60.35	62.54	68.39	80.53	101.37	118.38	125.30	151.16	..	Manufactures
101.15	99.10	99.44	105.69	109.41	125.61	154.41	189.75	199.20	224.91	..	Value of Imports, cif
23.98	22.17	22.18	21.92	21.41	24.76	29.07	33.95	34.45	38.30	..	Nonfuel Primary Products
14.28	12.88	10.68	13.80	13.68	9.34	9.98	8.95	10.19	13.94	..	Fuels
62.90	64.04	66.59	69.97	74.32	91.50	115.35	146.85	154.55	172.67	..	Manufactures
				(Index 1987 = 100)							
106.9	106.1	102.5	100.2	102.8	98.1	100.0	99.4	103.1	104.7	..	Terms of Trade
97.8	91.3	86.1	82.2	82.7	85.5	100.0	109.9	119.3	136.5	..	Export Prices, fob
91.5	86.1	84.0	82.1	80.5	87.1	100.0	110.6	115.8	130.3	..	Import Prices, cif
				(Billions of current US dollars)							**BALANCE OF PAYMENTS**
211.05	204.93	186.02	191.08	200.12	214.53	254.79	292.80	322.08	384.96	..	Exports of Goods & Services
102.16	96.66	91.96	93.49	100.97	106.59	130.04	143.08	151.08	182.30	..	Merchandise, fob
32.85	29.69	28.60	28.01	30.84	36.78	44.23	46.63	47.39	54.71	..	Nonfactor Services
76.04	78.58	65.46	69.59	68.32	71.16	80.52	103.09	123.61	147.96	..	Factor Services
193.85	193.93	177.92	186.40	192.02	211.14	256.20	314.08	348.03	400.74	..	Imports of Goods & Services
95.20	93.49	94.34	100.60	104.82	120.49	148.87	181.49	191.48	214.80	..	Merchandise, fob
25.41	24.56	22.68	22.14	22.58	27.19	33.43	38.52	39.77	45.37	..	Nonfactor Services
73.24	75.87	60.90	63.67	64.63	63.46	73.91	94.06	116.77	140.58	..	Factor Services
											Long-Term Interest
..	..	..	..	..	..	..	..	..	..		
0.12	0.08	0.51	0.49	0.40	0.11	-0.20	-0.48	-0.49	-0.54	..	Private Current Transfers, net
..	..	..	..	..	..	..	..	..	..		Workers' Remittances
17.32	11.09	8.61	5.17	8.51	3.50	-1.62	-21.76	-26.44	-16.31	..	Curr. A/C Bal before Off. Transf.
-3.19	-3.10	-2.94	-2.88	-4.37	-3.28	-5.34	-5.86	-6.96	-8.28	..	Net Official Transfers
14.13	7.99	5.67	2.30	4.14	0.21	-6.96	-27.62	-33.41	-24.60	..	Curr. A/C Bal after Off. Transf.
-19.74	-16.15	-16.07	-22.32	-15.76	-21.10	-3.20	-7.67	-29.63	3.41	..	Long-Term Capital, net
-6.27	-1.75	-3.01	-8.31	-5.91	-10.27	-17.34	-19.05	-7.35	11.90	..	Direct Investment
..	..	..	..	..	..	..	..	..	..		Long-Term Loans
..	..	..	..	..	..	..	..	..	..		Disbursements
..	..	..	..	..	..	..	..	..	..		Repayments
-13.47	-14.40	-13.07	-14.01	-9.85	-10.83	14.14	11.38	-22.28	-8.49	..	Other Long-Term Capital
4.89	13.84	9.20	9.29	8.50	27.22	4.56	33.37	46.81	20.04	..	Other Capital, net
0.73	-5.67	1.21	10.73	3.13	-6.33	5.60	1.91	16.23	1.15	..	Change in Reserves
				(Pounds Sterling per US dollar)							**Memo Item:**
0.500	0.570	0.660	0.750	0.780	0.680	0.610	0.560	0.610	0.560	..	Conversion Factor (Annual Avg)
				(Millions US dollars), outstanding at end of year							
											EXTERNAL DEBT (Total)
..	..	..	..	..	..	..	..	..	..	..	Long-Term Debt (by debtor)
..	..	..	..	..	..	..	..	..	..	..	Central Bank, incl. IMF credit
..	..	..	..	..	..	..	..	..	..	..	Central Government
..	..	..	..	..	..	..	..	..	..	..	Rest of General Government
..	..	..	..	..	..	..	..	..	..	..	Non-financial Public Enterprises
..	..	..	..	..	..	..	..	..	..	..	Priv. Sector, incl non-guaranteed
..	..	..	..	..	..	..	..	..	..	..	Short-Term Debt
				(Millions of US dollars):							**Memo Items:**
15,238	12,397	11,339	9,440	12,859	18,422	41,715	44,103	34,768	35,853	..	Int'l Reserves Excluding Gold
7,565	8,686	7,253	5,867	6,223	7,431	9,203	7,796	7,613	7,292	..	Gold Holdings (at market price)
											SOCIAL INDICATORS
1.8	1.8	1.8	1.8	1.8	1.8	1.8	1.8	1.8	..	..	Total Fertility Rate
11.2	11.0	10.2	9.6	9.3	9.5	9.2	8.9	8.6	8.4	..	Infant Mortality Rate
73.9	74.0	74.2	74.4	74.6	74.8	75.0	75.2	75.4	75.6	..	Life Expectancy at Birth
88.8	88.8	88.8	88.8	88.8	88.9	88.9	89.0	89.0	89.1	..	Urban Population, % of total
94.8	97.8	98.6	105.8	102.3	101.2	100.0	97.0	99.5	98.9	..	Food Prod. per capita (1987=100)
..	..	..	..	..	..	..	..	..	..	..	Labor Force, Agriculture (%)
38.8	38.8	38.8	38.7	38.7	38.7	38.7	38.7	38.6	38.6	..	Labor Force, Female (%)
..	101.0	101.0	102.0	104.0	106.0	107.0	107.0	..	..	..	Primary Schl. Enroll. Ratio
..	101.0	101.0	102.0	105.0	106.0	107.0	107.0	..	..	..	Primary Schl. Enroll. Ratio, Female
..	86.0	84.0	84.0	84.0	83.0	82.0	82.0	..	..	..	Secondary Schl. Enroll. Ratio

UNITED STATES	1970	1971	1972	1973	1974	1975	1976	1977	1978	1979	1980
CURRENT GNP PER CAPITA (US $)	4,970	5,340	5,800	6,420	6,890	7,400	8,190	9,050	10,100	11,140	11,990
POPULATION (millions)	205	208	210	212	214	216	218	220	223	225	228

USE AND ORIGIN OF RESOURCES
(Billions of current US Dollars)

	1970	1971	1972	1973	1974	1975	1976	1977	1978	1979	1980
Gross National Product (GNP)	1,016.5	1,104.7	1,214.8	1,361.2	1,475.9	1,601.5	1,785.9	1,992.9	2,249.5	2,508.6	2,736.1
Net Factor Income from Abroad	7.9	9.8	11.7	17.0	20.7	19.0	22.5	26.9	32.3	45.9	49.9
GDP at Market Prices	1,008.6	1,094.9	1,203.1	1,344.1	1,455.2	1,582.4	1,763.4	1,966.0	2,217.2	2,462.7	2,686.2
Resource Balance	3.3	0.0	-4.1	2.6	-2.6	14.2	-3.3	-24.8	-27.9	-26.6	-17.0
Exports of Goods & NFServices	58.5	61.7	69.4	93.0	123.0	134.9	145.2	154.2	180.3	221.5	271.0
Imports of Goods & NFServices	55.2	61.7	73.5	90.4	125.6	120.6	148.5	179.0	208.2	248.1	288.1
Domestic Absorption	1,005.3	1,094.9	1,207.2	1,341.6	1,457.8	1,568.2	1,766.7	1,990.8	2,245.1	2,489.4	2,703.2
Private Consumption, etc.	635.8	688.4	754.6	833.7	911.7	1,005.8	1,122.9	1,250.0	1,392.7	1,554.7	1,721.2
General Gov't Consumption	189.6	198.7	216.5	234.4	263.0	294.2	318.8	345.5	377.3	418.9	473.7
Gross Domestic Investment	179.9	207.8	236.1	273.4	283.1	268.2	325.0	395.3	475.1	515.7	508.3
Fixed Investment	178.5	199.6	227.7	256.9	270.3	272.3	308.1	370.1	445.0	502.6	514.3
Indirect Taxes, net	89.1	98.4	104.2	115.1	125.3	134.9	145.9	158.0	168.5	179.8	202.6
GDP at factor cost	919.5	996.4	1,098.9	1,229.0	1,329.9	1,447.5	1,617.5	1,808.0	2,048.6	2,282.9	2,483.6
Agriculture	27.9	30.0	35.1	53.8	52.3	53.0	51.8	54.3	65.1	77.2	70.3
Industry	348.8	370.5	408.2	455.5	487.9	521.8	593.2	671.1	754.3	831.1	902.3
Manufacturing	254.1	267.5	294.4	328.6	341.2	360.2	412.3	468.6	522.8	566.6	586.4
Services, etc.	631.9	694.4	759.8	834.7	915.0	1,007.6	1,118.4	1,240.6	1,397.7	1,554.4	1,713.5
Gross Domestic Saving	183.2	207.8	232.0	276.0	280.5	282.4	321.7	370.5	447.1	489.1	491.2
Gross National Saving	189.9	216.5	242.6	291.8	300.1	300.5	343.3	396.6	478.6	534.0	540.1

(Billions of 1987 US Dollars)

	1970	1971	1972	1973	1974	1975	1976	1977	1978	1979	1980
Gross National Product	2,805.0	2,898.6	3,047.6	3,202.9	3,179.6	3,135.4	3,290.5	3,439.8	3,618.3	3,704.8	3,696.3
GDP at Market Prices	2,782.7	2,872.2	3,017.5	3,162.2	3,134.8	3,097.7	3,248.6	3,393.0	3,566.1	3,636.9	3,629.2
Resource Balance	-54.4	-66.7	-72.2	-67.0	-43.0	-19.8	-54.0	-81.6	-78.3	-62.3	-10.3
Exports of Goods & NFServices	134.4	134.5	155.0	183.9	198.1	195.9	203.6	206.8	227.0	246.9	273.6
Imports of Goods & NFServices	188.8	201.1	227.2	250.9	241.1	215.7	257.6	288.4	305.3	309.2	283.9
Domestic Absorption	2,837.1	2,938.9	3,089.7	3,229.2	3,177.8	3,117.5	3,302.6	3,474.6	3,644.4	3,699.1	3,639.5
Private Consumption, etc.	1,772.6	1,830.9	1,949.8	2,039.7	2,015.5	2,046.7	2,153.7	2,248.0	2,346.6	2,400.1	2,397.4
General Gov't Consumption	590.9	588.7	581.9	582.4	595.7	596.7	607.2	613.7	627.6	639.5	647.6
Gross Domestic Investment	473.6	519.3	558.0	607.1	566.6	474.2	541.7	612.8	670.2	659.5	594.4
Fixed Investment	468.4	495.5	538.7	572.3	537.7	480.1	513.3	571.7	625.7	640.7	596.8
GDP at factor cost	2,532.5	2,609.2	2,752.0	2,886.3	2,862.8	2,830.2	2,976.5	3,117.9	3,293.2	3,370.6	3,357.3
Agriculture	63.9	65.5	66.2	67.1	65.9	68.5	66.0	65.5	66.3	70.3	68.8
Industry	905.6	910.0	967.9	1,044.8	1,005.0	941.5	1,005.1	1,061.4	1,119.7	1,135.5	1,098.1
Manufacturing	516.4	524.3	571.8	634.2	604.7	557.9	611.8	656.6	696.4	711.9	680.9
Services, etc.	1,813.3	1,896.8	1,983.5	2,050.3	2,063.8	2,087.7	2,177.4	2,266.1	2,380.1	2,431.0	2,462.2

Memo Items:

	1970	1971	1972	1973	1974	1975	1976	1977	1978	1979	1980
Capacity to Import	200.2	201.1	214.5	258.0	236.2	241.1	251.8	248.4	264.3	276.0	267.1
Terms of Trade Adjustment	65.8	66.6	59.5	74.1	38.1	45.2	48.3	41.6	37.3	29.1	-6.5
Gross Domestic Income	2,848.5	2,938.9	3,077.0	3,236.2	3,172.8	3,143.0	3,296.8	3,434.6	3,603.4	3,665.9	3,622.7
Gross National Income	2,870.8	2,965.3	3,107.1	3,277.0	3,217.7	3,180.6	3,338.8	3,481.4	3,655.7	3,733.9	3,689.8

DOMESTIC PRICES/DEFLATORS
(Index 1987 = 100)

	1970	1971	1972	1973	1974	1975	1976	1977	1978	1979	1980
Overall (GDP)	36.2	38.1	39.9	42.5	46.4	51.1	54.3	57.9	62.2	67.7	74.0
Domestic Absorption	35.4	37.3	39.1	41.5	45.9	50.3	53.5	57.3	61.6	67.3	74.3
Agriculture	43.6	45.8	53.0	80.3	79.3	77.4	78.5	82.9	98.2	109.8	102.2
Industry	38.5	40.7	42.2	43.6	48.5	55.4	59.0	63.2	67.4	73.2	82.2
Manufacturing	49.2	51.0	51.5	51.8	56.4	64.6	67.4	71.4	75.1	79.6	86.1
Consumer Price Index	34.2	35.6	36.8	39.1	43.4	47.3	50.1	53.3	57.4	63.8	72.5

MANUFACTURING ACTIVITY

	1970	1971	1972	1973	1974	1975	1976	1977	1978	1979	1980
Employment (1987=100)	103.3	98.4	101.8	106.5	105.7	97.0	99.9	104.5	108.7	111.5	109.0
Real Earnings per Empl. (1987=100)	93.9	95.9	100.0	100.0	97.0	96.8	99.4	101.3	101.6	97.8	93.5
Real Output per Empl. (1987=100)	51.8	54.8	59.5	65.6	71.1	68.1	72.6	75.1	77.1	80.7	81.6
Earnings as % of Value Added	47.3	45.8	45.3	44.0	42.1	43.1	41.7	41.4	41.3	39.9	40.9

MONETARY HOLDINGS
(Billions of current US Dollars)

	1970	1971	1972	1973	1974	1975	1976	1977	1978	1979	1980
Money Supply, Broadly Defined	630.6	714.2	806.5	859.3	907.5	1,023.6	1,162.8	1,285.8	1,390.9	1,509.9	1,647.3
Money	222.3	236.9	258.9	272.4	284.2	298.1	318.1	343.7	372.2	397.0	424.1
Currency Outside Banks	50.0	53.4	57.8	61.8	68.1	74.3	81.6	89.9	99.1	107.0	118.8
Demand Deposits	172.3	183.4	201.0	210.6	216.1	223.8	236.5	253.8	273.1	290.0	305.3
Quasi-Money	408.3	477.3	547.6	587.0	623.3	725.4	844.7	942.1	1,018.7	1,112.9	1,223.2

GOVERNMENT DEFICIT (-) OR SURPLUS
(Billions of current US Dollars)

	1970	1971	1972	1973	1974	1975	1976	1977	1978	1979	1980
GOVERNMENT DEFICIT (-) OR SURPLUS	..	..	-18.70	-16.20	-4.50	-53.90	-74.90	-52.20	-58.90	-35.90	-76.20
Current Revenue			213.90	243.90	277.60	291.60	311.10	371.30	416.60	488.60	545.90
Current Expenditure			221.10	246.50	268.00	317.00	352.10	389.00	425.90	473.20	558.10
Current Budget Balance			-7.20	-2.50	9.60	-25.40	-41.10	-17.70	-9.40	15.40	-12.20
Capital Receipts			0.20	0.40	1.30	1.10	0.30	0.20	0.20	0.10	0.20
Capital Payments			11.70	14.20	15.40	29.60	34.10	34.80	49.70	51.50	64.10

1981	1982	1983	1984	1985	1986	1987	1988	1989	1990 estimate	Notes	UNITED STATES
13,310	13,650	14,520	15,930	16,790	17,520	18,450	19,700	20,850	21,790	..	**CURRENT GNP PER CAPITA (US $)**
230	233	235	237	239	242	244	246	249	250	..	**POPULATION (millions)**
											USE AND ORIGIN OF RESOURCES
				(Billions of current US Dollars)							
3,061.6	3,172.6	3,403.3	3,769.8	4,008.2	4,216.1	4,488.4	4,849.6	5,176.4	5,441.0	..	Gross National Product (GNP)
54.4	54.0	54.0	52.0	46.0	40.0	35.5	40.5	44.4	48.8	..	Net Factor Income from Abroad
3,007.2	3,118.6	3,349.4	3,717.8	3,962.2	4,176.1	4,452.9	4,809.1	5,132.0	5,392.2	..	GDP at Market Prices
-19.8	-27.1	-59.9	-110.8	-123.9	-137.3	-150.2	-114.5	-90.4	-79.9	..	Resource Balance
290.7	268.1	259.9	278.7	276.0	303.9	346.5	426.3	484.2	528.4	..	Exports of Goods & NFServices
310.5	295.1	319.8	389.4	400.0	441.2	496.7	540.8	574.7	608.3	..	Imports of Goods & NFServices
3,027.0	3,145.6	3,409.3	3,828.5	4,086.1	4,313.4	4,603.1	4,923.6	5,222.4	5,472.1	..	Domestic Absorption
1,909.7	2,046.3	2,223.7	2,422.2	2,615.8	2,777.1	2,979.9	3,213.1	3,425.1	3,636.3	..	Private Consumption, etc.
525.6	574.1	617.0	670.1	727.9	780.6	827.8	878.2	919.3	973.4	..	General Gov't Consumption
591.7	525.2	568.6	736.2	742.4	755.7	795.3	832.3	878.0	862.4	..	Gross Domestic Investment
559.3	537.6	577.6	670.0	718.1	743.5	769.3	820.8	853.9	868.7	..	Fixed Investment
239.3	243.4	260.4	291.2	310.8	321.8	336.4	358.0	385.4	412.6	..	Indirect Taxes, net
2,767.9	2,875.2	3,089.0	3,426.6	3,651.4	3,854.3	4,116.4	4,451.1	4,746.6	4,979.6	B	GDP at factor cost
83.7	81.4	66.4	85.3	85.2	86.5	89.2	..	..	..	..	Agriculture
1,015.2	1,009.4	1,063.9	1,191.8	1,228.9	1,251.8	1,306.8					Industry
649.6	641.0	689.5	778.4	797.4	828.4	862.3	..	..	..	..	Manufacturing
1,908.3	2,027.8	2,219.1	2,440.7	2,648.1	2,837.8	3,056.9	..	..	..	..	Services, etc.
571.9	498.2	508.7	625.5	618.5	618.4	645.1	717.8	787.6	782.5	..	Gross Domestic Saving
625.2	550.7	561.4	675.7	662.4	656.5	678.8	756.5	830.0	829.4	..	Gross National Saving
				(Billions of 1987 US Dollars)							
3,780.1	3,677.6	3,810.0	4,072.0	4,215.7	4,342.6	4,488.4	4,694.1	4,825.9	4,872.4	..	Gross National Product
3,713.2	3,615.1	3,749.4	4,015.6	4,167.1	4,301.2	4,452.9	4,654.9	4,784.5	4,828.8	..	GDP at Market Prices
-18.1	-34.7	-76.2	-133.8	-146.3	-159.1	-150.2	-113.2	-95.2	-78.4	..	Resource Balance
272.6	249.6	242.7	258.6	265.6	297.6	346.5	411.4	460.2	498.8	..	Exports of Goods & NFServices
290.8	284.4	319.0	392.5	411.9	456.7	496.7	524.6	555.4	577.2	..	Imports of Goods & NFServices
3,731.4	3,649.8	3,825.6	4,149.4	4,313.4	4,460.4	4,603.1	4,768.1	4,879.7	4,907.2	..	Domestic Absorption
2,438.9	2,440.9	2,546.5	2,668.9	2,787.8	2,894.6	2,979.9	3,103.4	3,175.9	3,206.8	..	Private Consumption, etc.
654.7	670.2	693.9	725.4	763.5	800.6	827.8	845.1	847.6	862.1	..	General Gov't Consumption
637.8	538.7	585.1	755.1	762.1	765.2	795.3	819.7	856.3	838.2	..	Gross Domestic Investment
596.0	544.1	591.9	685.9	733.2	747.9	769.3	807.9	829.3	839.2	..	Fixed Investment
3,419.1	3,333.3	3,457.1	3,699.6	3,838.6	3,968.3	4,116.4	4,308.5	4,425.1	4,459.6	B	GDP at factor cost
79.6	80.8	65.7	74.9	86.0	89.7	89.2	..	..	..	..	Agriculture
1,107.4	1,047.9	1,092.7	1,210.0	1,248.0	1,260.9	1,306.8					Industry
694.1	651.1	690.8	775.1	806.4	825.4	862.3	..	..	..	..	Manufacturing
2,526.2	2,486.3	2,591.1	2,730.7	2,833.0	2,950.6	3,056.9	..	..	..	..	Services, etc.
											Memo Items:
272.2	258.3	259.2	280.8	284.3	314.6	346.5	413.6	468.0	501.4	..	Capacity to Import
-0.4	8.7	16.5	22.2	18.7	17.0	0.0	2.2	7.8	2.6	..	Terms of Trade Adjustment
3,712.8	3,623.7	3,765.9	4,037.8	4,185.7	4,318.2	4,452.9	4,657.1	4,792.3	4,831.3	..	Gross Domestic Income
3,779.7	3,686.3	3,826.4	4,094.2	4,234.3	4,359.6	4,488.4	4,696.3	4,833.7	4,875.0	..	Gross National Income
											DOMESTIC PRICES/DEFLATORS
				(Index 1987 = 100)							
81.0	86.3	89.3	92.6	95.1	97.1	100.0	103.3	107.3	111.7	..	Overall (GDP)
81.1	86.2	89.1	92.3	94.7	96.7	100.0	103.3	107.0	111.5	..	Domestic Absorption
105.2	100.7	101.1	113.9	99.1	96.4	100.0	..	..	..	..	Agriculture
91.7	96.3	97.4	98.5	98.5	99.3	100.0	..	..	..	..	Industry
93.6	98.5	99.8	100.4	98.9	100.4	100.0	..			..	Manufacturing
79.9	84.9	87.6	91.4	94.6	96.4	100.0	104.0	109.0	114.9	..	Consumer Price Index
											MANUFACTURING ACTIVITY
106.8	100.6	98.7	100.9	98.8	96.5	100.0	101.1	..	..	..	Employment (1987=100)
93.3	93.3	95.6	97.5	99.0	101.0	100.0	100.0	..	..	..	Real Earnings per Empl. (1987=100)
83.3	80.9	85.1	91.4	94.7	94.2	100.0	..	..	..	..	Real Output per Empl. (1987=100)
40.8	41.4	40.1	39.1	39.7	38.8	36.8	36.0	..	..	..	Earnings as % of Value Added
											MONETARY HOLDINGS
				(Billions of current US Dollars)							
1,832.3	2,023.4	2,259.7	2,496.9	2,724.9	2,998.4	3,122.9	3,315.6	3,523.1	3,680.9	D	Money Supply, Broadly Defined
451.4	490.9	538.3	570.3	641.0	746.5	767.2	812.0	824.2	853.7	..	Money
126.2	136.5	150.6	160.8	173.1	186.2	200.5	214.8	225.5	249.6	..	Currency Outside Banks
325.2	354.4	387.7	409.4	467.9	560.4	566.7	597.2	598.7	604.1	..	Demand Deposits
1,381.0	1,532.6	1,721.4	1,926.6	2,084.0	2,251.9	2,355.7	2,503.6	2,698.9	2,827.2	..	Quasi-Money
				(Billions of current US Dollars)							
-78.70	-125.70	-202.50	-178.30	-212.10	-212.60	-147.50	-155.50	-143.80	-218.10	E C	**GOVERNMENT DEFICIT (-) OR SURPLUS**
639.80	659.60	653.30	718.30	791.40	823.10	909.80	962.60	1,046.60	1,085.60	..	Current Revenue
647.20	722.10	805.70	843.80	931.50	985.30	1,010.90	1,065.50	1,133.80	1,202.50	..	Current Expenditure
-7.40	-62.40	-152.40	-125.40	-140.00	-162.20	-101.10	-102.90	-87.20	-116.90	..	Current Budget Balance
0.10	0.30	0.10	0.20	0.20	0.10	0.10	0.10	0.10	0.30	..	Capital Receipts
71.40	63.60	50.30	53.00	72.30	50.50	46.60	52.80	56.70	101.50	..	Capital Payments

UNITED STATES	1970	1971	1972	1973	1974	1975	1976	1977	1978	1979	1980
FOREIGN TRADE (CUSTOMS BASIS)				*(Billions of current US dollars)*							
Value of Exports, fob	42.59	43.49	48.98	70.25	97.14	106.10	113.32	117.93	140.00	173.66	212.89
Nonfuel Primary Products	11.12	10.66	12.77	23.06	29.09	28.83	30.29	31.23	38.84	49.26	60.62
Fuels	1.59	1.50	1.55	1.67	3.44	4.47	4.23	4.18	3.88	5.63	7.95
Manufactures	29.88	31.34	34.66	45.52	64.61	72.80	78.81	82.52	97.28	118.77	144.31
Value of Imports, cif	39.95	45.56	55.56	69.48	101.00	96.90	121.79	147.86	182.20	217.39	250.28
Nonfuel Primary Products	11.35	11.51	13.35	16.97	21.09	18.47	22.67	26.30	32.16	37.15	38.76
Fuels	3.07	3.71	4.80	8.17	25.38	26.40	33.93	44.20	44.69	63.67	82.20
Manufactures	25.53	30.34	37.41	44.33	54.53	52.03	65.20	77.36	105.35	116.56	129.31
					(Index 1987 = 100)						
Terms of Trade	147.0	136.9	132.5	143.1	107.4	115.4	114.5	108.6	104.9	99.9	87.0
Export Prices, fob	33.6	34.6	36.3	45.7	55.0	59.7	62.5	64.4	69.2	81.1	88.3
Import Prices, cif	22.9	25.3	27.4	31.9	51.2	51.7	54.6	59.3	66.0	81.2	101.5
BALANCE OF PAYMENTS				*(Billions of current US dollars)*							
Exports of Goods & Services	65.65	68.81	77.50	110.19	146.71	155.73	171.63	184.29	220.01	287.83	343.26
Merchandise, fob	42.45	43.31	49.38	71.41	98.32	107.08	114.75	120.80	142.06	184.47	224.27
Nonfactor Services	9.12	10.24	10.57	13.77	16.96	18.98	23.21	26.18	29.59	32.80	40.27
Factor Services	14.08	15.26	17.55	25.01	31.43	29.67	33.67	37.31	48.36	70.56	78.72
Imports of Goods & Services	59.87	66.42	79.22	99.00	137.33	132.79	162.13	193.79	229.84	281.65	333.84
Merchandise, fob	39.86	45.58	55.80	70.50	103.83	98.18	124.22	151.91	176.00	212.01	249.77
Nonfactor Services	14.28	15.17	16.55	18.45	21.03	21.55	24.11	26.70	31.01	35.36	40.25
Factor Services	5.73	5.67	6.87	10.05	12.47	13.06	13.80	15.18	22.83	34.28	43.82
Long-Term Interest	..	..	..	..	..	..	..	..	..	..	..
Private Current Transfers, net	-1.10	-1.11	-1.11	-1.25	-1.02	-0.91	-0.91	-0.82	-0.86	-0.91	-1.03
Workers' Remittances	..	..	..	..	..	..	..	..	..	..	..
Curr. A/C Bal before Off. Transf.	4.68	1.28	-2.83	9.94	8.36	22.03	8.59	-10.32	-10.69	5.27	8.39
Net Official Transfers	-2.35	-2.73	-2.95	-2.87	-6.42	-3.97	-4.41	-4.17	-4.71	-5.07	-7.19
Curr. A/C Bal after Off. Transf.	2.33	-1.45	-5.78	7.07	1.94	18.06	4.18	-14.49	-15.40	0.20	1.20
Long-Term Capital, net	-6.69	-9.09	-5.84	-6.95	-7.52	-19.70	-15.13	-12.34	-10.13	-19.93	-7.31
Direct Investment	-6.13	-7.26	-6.80	-8.53	-4.28	-11.65	-7.60	-8.16	-8.16	-13.35	-2.30
Long-Term Loans											
Disbursements	..	..	..	..	..	..	..	..	..	..	..
Repayments	..	..	..	..	..	..	..	..	..	..	..
Other Long-Term Capital	-0.56	-1.83	0.96	1.58	-3.24	-8.05	-7.53	-4.18	-1.97	-6.58	-5.01
Other Capital, net	-6.33	-19.93	0.57	-5.36	-3.23	-3.01	0.45	-8.21	-6.35	33.36	-1.78
Change in Reserves	10.69	30.47	11.05	5.23	8.81	4.65	10.50	35.04	31.88	-13.63	7.89
Memo Item:				*(US Dollars per US dollar)*							
Conversion Factor (Annual Avg)	1.000	1.000	1.000	1.000	1.000	1.000	1.000	1.000	1.000	1.000	1.000
				(Millions US dollars), outstanding at end of year							
EXTERNAL DEBT (Total)	..	..	..	..	..	..	..	..	..	..	..
Long-Term Debt (by debtor)	..	..	..	..	..	..	..	..	..	..	..
Central Bank, incl. IMF credit	..	..	..	..	..	..	..	..	..	..	..
Central Government	..	..	..	..	..	..	..	..	..	..	..
Rest of General Government	..	..	..	..	..	..	..	..	..	..	..
Non-financial Public Enterprises	..	..	..	..	..	..	..	..	..	..	..
Priv. Sector, incl non-guaranteed	..	..	..	..	..	..	..	..	..	..	..
Short-Term Debt	..	..	..	..	..	..	..	..	..	..	..
Memo Items:				*(Millions of US dollars)*							
Int'l Reserves Excluding Gold	3,415	2,109	2,663	2,726	4,232	4,627	7,149	7,592	6,979	7,784	15,596
Gold Holdings (at market price)	11,822	12,723	17,910	30,978	51,468	38,528	37,013	45,782	62,469	135,475	155,817
SOCIAL INDICATORS											
Total Fertility Rate	2.5	2.3	2.0	1.9	1.8	1.8	1.7	1.8	1.8	1.8	1.8
Infant Mortality Rate	20.0	19.1	18.5	17.7	16.7	16.1	15.2	14.1	13.8	13.1	12.6
Life Expectancy at Birth	70.8	71.2	71.5	71.9	72.2	72.6	72.9	73.3	73.4	73.8	73.7
Urban Population, % of total	73.6	73.6	73.6	73.7	73.7	73.7	73.7	73.7	73.7	73.7	73.7
Food Prod. per capita (1987=100)	87.0	94.3	92.0	93.8	94.1	100.9	102.5	105.9	103.7	108.5	102.8
Labor Force, Agriculture (%)	4.3	4.2	4.1	4.0	3.9	3.9	3.8	3.7	3.6	3.5	3.5
Labor Force, Female (%)	36.5	37.1	37.6	38.2	38.7	39.1	39.7	40.2	40.7	41.2	41.6
Primary Schl. Enroll. Ratio	..	..	..	..	..	99.0	..	..	..	..	99.0
Primary Schl. Enroll. Ratio, Female	..	..	..	..	..	..	..	..	..	..	99.0
Secondary Schl. Enroll. Ratio	..	..	..	..	..	..	..	..	..	..	89.0

1981	1982	1983	1984	1985	1986	1987	1988	1989	1990 estimate	Notes	UNITED STATES
				(Billions of current US dollars)							**FOREIGN TRADE (CUSTOMS BASIS)**
225.78	206.04	194.62	210.22	205.24	204.65	243.68	303.38	346.95	371.47	..	Value of Exports, fob
58.31	49.63	48.84	51.32	42.16	39.98	46.26	61.00	67.72	69.25	..	Nonfuel Primary Products
10.24	12.72	9.56	9.29	9.96	8.13	7.73	8.20	9.64	11.97	..	Fuels
157.22	143.70	136.23	149.61	153.12	156.54	189.69	234.18	269.59	290.25	..	Manufactures
271.21	253.03	267.97	338.19	358.70	381.36	422.41	458.68	491.51	515.64	..	Value of Imports, cif
38.90	33.88	38.09	43.70	42.91	45.89	47.39	51.26	54.31	54.45	..	Nonfuel Primary Products
84.26	67.42	60.00	63.07	55.68	39.77	46.74	44.11	55.85	68.46	..	Fuels
148.06	151.73	169.88	231.42	260.11	295.71	328.27	363.31	381.35	392.73	..	Manufactures
				(Index 1987 = 100)							
89.9	90.4	96.4	97.4	99.6	107.0	100.0	102.7	102.3	100.0	..	Terms of Trade
94.3	93.6	96.6	97.1	95.9	97.5	100.0	109.8	112.7	113.8	..	Export Prices, fob
104.9	103.6	100.2	99.6	96.3	91.1	100.0	106.9	110.2	113.8	..	Import Prices, cif
				(Billions of current US dollars)							**BALANCE OF PAYMENTS**
379.44	356.06	343.87	379.35	366.14	383.96	431.80	533.47	606.61	652.97	..	Exports of Goods & Services
237.09	211.20	201.81	219.90	215.93	223.36	250.28	320.34	361.46	389.54	..	Merchandise, fob
49.99	54.25	54.73	60.79	61.86	72.26	81.81	91.50	104.38	117.87	..	Nonfactor Services
92.36	90.61	87.33	98.66	88.35	88.34	99.71	121.63	140.77	145.56	..	Factor Services
364.21	352.15	374.08	465.73	472.91	513.49	577.67	644.79	697.45	722.77	..	Imports of Goods & Services
265.08	247.64	268.89	332.41	338.09	368.41	409.77	447.31	477.38	497.66	..	Merchandise, fob
44.32	46.18	49.29	62.11	67.06	73.20	82.66	89.06	90.91	103.20	..	Nonfactor Services
54.81	58.33	55.90	71.21	67.76	71.88	85.24	108.42	129.16	121.91	..	Factor Services
..	..	..	..	..	..		..	..	..	..	Long-Term Interest
-1.13	-1.43	-1.28	-1.77	-2.06	-1.86	-1.84	-1.76	-1.91	-1.91	..	Private Current Transfers, net
..	..	..	..	..	..	..	..	..	..	..	Workers' Remittances
14.10	2.48	-31.49	-88.15	-108.83	-131.39	-147.71	-113.08	-92.75	-71.71	..	Curr. A/C Bal before Off. Transf.
-6.84	-8.34	-8.69	-10.84	-13.42	-14.03	-12.49	-13.29	-13.61	-20.45	..	Net Official Transfers
7.26	-5.86	-40.18	-98.99	-122.25	-145.42	-160.20	-126.37	-106.36	-92.16	..	Curr. A/C Bal after Off. Transf.
-0.72	-10.74	-7.99	29.94	60.32	81.86	54.08	69.06	77.52	-47.96	..	Long-Term Capital, net
15.57	12.82	5.25	13.97	5.86	15.39	27.10	41.54	37.16	3.75	..	Direct Investment
..	..	..	..	..	..	..	..	..	..	..	Long-Term Loans
..	..	..	..	..	..	..	..	..	..	..	Disbursements
..	..	..	..	..	..	..	..	..	..	..	Repayments
-16.29	-23.56	-13.24	15.97	54.46	66.47	26.98	27.52	40.36	-51.71	..	Other Long-Term Capital
-7.78	18.63	44.12	69.77	67.73	29.78	49.26	21.04	45.77	111.63	..	Other Capital, net
1.24	-2.03	4.05	-0.72	-5.80	33.78	56.86	36.27	-16.93	28.49	..	Change in Reserves
				(US Dollars per US dollar)							**Memo Item:**
1.000	1.000	1.000	1.000	1.000	1.000	1.000	1.000	1.000	1.000	..	Conversion Factor (Annual Avg)
			(Millions US dollars), outstanding at end of year								**EXTERNAL DEBT (Total)**
..	..	..	..	..	..	..	..	..	..	..	Long-Term Debt (by debtor)
..	..	..	..	..	..	..	..	..	..	..	Central Bank, incl. IMF credit
..	..	..	..	..	..	..	..	..	..	..	Central Government
..	..	..	..	..	..	..	..	..	..	..	Rest of General Government
..	..	..	..	..	..	..	..	..	..	..	Non-financial Public Enterprises
..	..	..	..	..	..	..	..	..	..	..	Priv. Sector, incl non-guaranteed
..	..	..	..	..	..	..	..	..	..	..	Short-Term Debt
				(Millions of US dollars)							**Memo Items:**
18,924	22,809	22,627	23,838	32,095	37,452	34,720	36,745	63,550	72,258	..	Int'l Reserves Excluding Gold
104,984	120,635	100,483	81,018	85,887	102,431	127,018	107,432	105,034	100,835	..	Gold Holdings (at market price)
											SOCIAL INDICATORS
1.8	1.8	1.8	1.8	1.8	1.9	1.9	1.9	1.9	1.9	..	Total Fertility Rate
11.7	11.2	10.9	10.5	10.5	10.4	10.3	10.0	9.8	9.5	..	Infant Mortality Rate
74.0	74.4	74.5	74.6	74.9	75.1	75.4	75.6	75.8	76.0	..	Life Expectancy at Birth
73.8	74.0	74.1	74.3	74.4	74.5	74.6	74.8	74.9	75.0	..	Urban Population, % of total
112.6	110.6	91.4	105.7	111.0	103.5	100.0	91.9	102.1	103.7	..	Food Prod. per capita (1987=100)
..	..	..	..	..	..	..	..	..	..	..	Labor Force, Agriculture (%)
41.6	41.6	41.6	41.5	41.5	41.5	41.5	41.5	41.4	41.4	..	Labor Force, Female (%)
..	101.0	101.0	99.0	99.0	100.0	..	..	..	..	..	Primary Schl. Enroll. Ratio
..	100.0	100.0	99.0	100.0	100.0	..	..	..	..	..	Primary Schl. Enroll. Ratio, Female
..	94.0	94.0	94.0	97.0	98.0	..	..	..	..	..	Secondary Schl. Enroll. Ratio

URUGUAY	1970	1971	1972	1973	1974	1975	1976	1977	1978	1979	1980
CURRENT GNP PER CAPITA (US $)	740	870	860	950	1,090	1,330	1,400	1,400	1,580	2,030	2,710
POPULATION (thousands)	2,808	2,818	2,820	2,821	2,822	2,829	2,845	2,862	2,879	2,896	2,914

USE AND ORIGIN OF RESOURCES

(Billions of current Uruguayan New Pesos)

	1970	1971	1972	1973	1974	1975	1976	1977	1978	1979	1980
Gross National Product (GNP)	0.572	0.691	1.100	2.500	4.400	7.700	11.900	18.800	29.100	55.800	88.700
Net Factor Income from Abroad	-0.006	-0.005	-0.020	-0.023	-0.070	-0.190	-0.244	-0.317	-0.465	-0.454	-0.913
GDP at Market Prices	0.578	0.696	1.200	2.500	4.500	7.900	12.100	19.100	29.600	56.300	89.700
Resource Balance	-0.007	-0.008	0.006	0.036	-0.113	-0.277	-0.063	-0.528	-0.683	-2.400	-4.900
Exports of Goods & NFServices	0.074	0.072	0.179	0.357	0.646	1.300	2.400	3.800	5.600	9.500	14.000
Imports of Goods & NFServices	0.081	0.080	0.173	0.321	0.759	1.600	2.400	4.300	6.300	11.900	18.900
Domestic Absorption	0.585	0.704	1.200	2.500	4.600	8.200	12.200	19.600	30.300	58.700	94.600
Private Consumption, etc.	0.401	0.464	0.804	1.700	3.200	5.600	7.900	13.100	19.700	38.500	61.500
General Gov't Consumption	0.091	0.117	0.152	0.362	0.676	1.100	1.700	2.400	3.800	6.700	11.400
Gross Domestic Investment	0.093	0.123	0.199	0.437	0.712	1.500	2.500	4.100	6.700	13.500	21.700
Fixed Investment	0.093	0.115	0.173	0.344	0.652	1.500	2.600	4.100	6.700	12.900	21.100
Indirect Taxes, net	0.081	0.093	0.213	0.344	0.510	1.100	1.800	2.800	4.600	7.900	12.700
GDP at factor cost	0.497	0.603	0.949	2.100	4.000	6.900	10.300	16.300	24.900	48.400	77.000
Agriculture	0.094	0.117	0.261	0.604	0.931	1.200	1.700	3.100	4.100	8.500	12.500
Industry	0.179	0.208	0.327	0.729	1.400	2.700	4.000	6.100	9.600	19.900	31.100
Manufacturing	..	0.158	0.246	0.566	1.100	2.000	3.100	4.800	7.400	15.800	23.900
Services, etc.	0.305	0.371	0.574	1.200	2.100	4.000	6.400	9.900	15.800	27.900	46.100
Gross Domestic Saving	0.086	0.115	0.206	0.472	0.600	1.200	2.500	3.600	6.000	11.100	16.800
Gross National Saving	0.080	0.110	0.186	0.449	0.528	1.000	2.200	3.300	5.600	10.700	15.900

(Billions of 1987 Uruguayan New Pesos)

	1970	1971	1972	1973	1974	1975	1976	1977	1978	1979	1980
Gross National Product	1,290.0	1,290.0	1,250.0	1,270.0	1,300.0	1,370.0	1,420.0	1,450.0	1,520.0	1,630.0	1,720.0
GDP at Market Prices	1,280.0	1,270.0	1,250.0	1,260.0	1,300.0	1,370.0	1,430.0	1,450.0	1,520.0	1,610.0	1,710.0
Resource Balance	-64.5	-77.1	-62.4	-82.1	-39.7	-26.1	12.1	10.3	3.6	-37.7	-52.4
Exports of Goods & NFServices	154.0	147.0	144.0	143.0	173.0	206.0	250.0	267.0	279.0	297.0	308.0
Imports of Goods & NFServices	218.0	224.0	206.0	226.0	213.0	232.0	237.0	257.0	275.0	335.0	361.0
Domestic Absorption	1,340.0	1,350.0	1,320.0	1,340.0	1,340.0	1,400.0	1,420.0	1,440.0	1,520.0	1,650.0	1,760.0
Private Consumption, etc.	1,010.0	1,000.0	1,020.0	1,030.0	1,010.0	1,030.0	981.0	962.0	979.0	1,000.0	1,090.0
General Gov't Consumption	134.0	134.0	114.0	139.0	149.0	145.0	156.0	151.0	167.0	188.0	185.0
Gross Domestic Investment	202.0	218.0	183.0	174.0	181.0	229.0	278.0	325.0	372.0	460.0	485.0
Fixed Investment	196.0	195.0	146.0	117.0	156.0	220.0	279.0	315.0	359.0	424.0	457.0
GDP at factor cost	1,100.0	1,100.0	1,020.0	1,090.0	1,150.0	1,190.0	1,220.0	1,240.0	1,280.0	1,390.0	1,470.0
Agriculture	214.0	201.0	180.0	184.0	190.0	201.0	205.0	211.0	197.0	196.0	228.0
Industry	461.0	452.0	459.0	450.0	460.0	501.0	520.0	546.0	594.0	640.0	659.0
Manufacturing	..	..	..	..	..	..	..	..	..	..	..
Services, etc.	608.0	624.0	618.0	626.0	646.0	675.0	705.0	696.0	737.0	786.0	832.0

Memo Items:

	1970	1971	1972	1973	1974	1975	1976	1977	1978	1979	1980
Capacity to Import	200.0	201.0	214.0	251.0	181.0	192.0	231.0	226.0	245.0	266.0	266.0
Terms of Trade Adjustment	45.6	54.7	70.0	107.0	8.1	-14.0	-18.2	-41.6	-33.7	-30.9	-41.8
Gross Domestic Income	1,320.0	1,330.0	1,320.0	1,370.0	1,300.0	1,360.0	1,410.0	1,410.0	1,490.0	1,580.0	1,670.0
Gross National Income	1,330.0	1,340.0	1,320.0	1,380.0	1,310.0	1,350.0	1,410.0	1,410.0	1,490.0	1,600.0	1,680.0

DOMESTIC PRICES/DEFLATORS

(Index 1987 = 100)

	1970	1971	1972	1973	1974	1975	1976	1977	1978	1979	1980
Overall (GDP)	0.0452	0.0546	0.0927	0.1980	0.3470	0.5760	0.8480	1.3000	1.9000	3.5000	5.2000
Domestic Absorption	0.0435	0.0521	0.0878	0.1830	0.3450	0.5850	0.8600	1.4000	2.0000	3.6000	5.4000
Agriculture	0.0441	0.0583	0.1450	0.3280	0.4890	0.5970	0.8300	1.5000	2.1000	4.3000	5.5000
Industry	0.0387	0.0461	0.0713	0.1620	0.3080	0.5350	0.7770	1.1000	1.6000	3.1000	4.7000
Manufacturing	..	..	..	0.1490	0.2840	0.4950	0.7300	1.1000	1.6000	3.1000	4.6000
Consumer Price Index	0.0418	0.0519	0.0915	0.1800	0.3200	0.5800	0.8730	1.4000	2.0000	3.3000	5.4000

MANUFACTURING ACTIVITY

	1970	1971	1972	1973	1974	1975	1976	1977	1978	1979	1980
Employment (1987=100)	123.8	..	138.2	146.2	149.4	154.7	163.1	170.3	186.9	197.6	122.9
Real Earnings per Empl. (1987=100)	..	..	..	..	..	..	82.7	76.2	80.3	80.1	86.2
Real Output per Empl. (1987=100)	..	..	74.1	68.9	69.6	71.5	74.3	78.4	73.6	67.0	81.4
Earnings as % of Value Added	..	..	..	..	..	..	35.3	31.6	37.3	33.8	32.8

MONETARY HOLDINGS

(Billions of current Uruguayan New Pesos)

	1970	1971	1972	1973	1974	1975	1976	1977	1978	1979	1980
Money Supply, Broadly Defined	0.13	0.20	0.32	0.54	0.92	1.60	3.30	5.90	11.30	21.00	36.40
Money	0.09	0.14	0.20	0.36	0.59	0.83	1.40	1.90	3.60	6.20	9.10
Currency Outside Banks	0.06	0.08	0.12	0.20	0.32	0.47	0.78	1.10	1.80	3.20	5.10
Demand Deposits	0.03	0.05	0.08	0.16	0.27	0.37	0.60	0.82	1.80	3.00	4.00
Quasi-Money	0.04	0.06	0.12	0.18	0.34	0.80	1.90	4.00	7.80	14.90	27.40

GOVERNMENT DEFICIT (-) OR SURPLUS

(Billions of current Uruguayan New Pesos)

	1970	1971	1972	1973	1974	1975	1976	1977	1978	1979	1980
GOVERNMENT DEFICIT (-) OR SURPLUS	..	..	-0.03	-0.03	-0.17	-0.36	-0.26	-0.26	-0.28	0.00	0.03
Current Revenue	..	..	0.28	0.55	0.91	1.51	2.79	4.51	6.90	12.10	20.52
Current Expenditure	..	..	0.28	0.53	1.06	1.81	3.10	3.92	6.31	10.18	18.54
Current Budget Balance	..	..	0.00	0.02	-0.15	-0.30	-0.31	0.59	0.60	1.92	1.98
Capital Receipts	..	..	0.00	0.00	0.01	0.01	0.01	0.03	0.02	0.09	0.00
Capital Payments	..	..	0.03	0.06	0.03	0.07	-0.04	0.88	0.90	2.01	1.95

1981	1982	1983	1984	1985	1986	1987	1988	1989	1990 estimate	Notes	URUGUAY
3,500	3,340	2,300	1,920	1,580	1,740	2,020	2,270	2,450	2,560	..	**CURRENT GNP PER CAPITA (US $)**
2,932	2,951	2,970	2,989	3,008	3,025	3,042	3,060	3,077	3,094	..	**POPULATION (thousands)**
											USE AND ORIGIN OF RESOURCES
			(Billions of current Uruguayan New Pesos)								
118.50	124.60	165.50	269.00	443.10	848.10	1,593.30	2,613.00	4,522.00	9,246.50	..	Gross National Product (GNP)
-0.80	-2.60	-9.90	-2.00	-35.50	-42.30	-68.20	-112.50	-212.10	-377.20	f	Net Factor Income from Abroad
119.20	127.20	175.40	271.00	478.60	890.50	1,661.50	2,725.50	4,734.10	9,623.70	f	GDP at Market Prices
-4.60	-3.80	3.70	14.10	27.00	53.00	40.60	127.30	304.10	741.70	..	Resource Balance
18.10	18.20	45.10	72.10	128.10	233.40	359.70	649.50	1,236.00	2,610.20	..	Exports of Goods & NF Services
22.70	22.00	41.40	57.90	101.00	180.50	319.10	522.20	931.90	1,868.50	..	Imports of Goods & NF Services
123.80	130.90	171.70	256.90	451.60	837.50	1,620.90	2,598.00	4,430.00	8,882.00	..	Domestic Absorption
81.10	85.80	121.20	187.30	328.10	608.50	1,164.00	1,883.80	3,263.80	6,473.90	..	Private Consumption, etc.
17.20	20.00	25.50	36.90	69.20	127.60	219.70	358.60	640.40	1,274.70	..	General Gov't Consumption
25.50	25.20	25.00	32.80	54.40	101.40	237.10	355.60	525.90	1,133.40	..	Gross Domestic Investment
25.90	26.00	24.00	29.60	46.00	90.00	188.90	321.30	584.90	1,183.60	..	Fixed Investment
16.50	16.70	22.90	38.20	70.50	147.90	270.00	452.70	754.40	..	..	Indirect Taxes, net
102.70	110.40	152.50	232.80	408.10	742.50	1,391.50	2,272.80	3,979.70	..	f	GDP at factor cost
14.10	14.00	23.50	39.70	65.10	112.70	227.80	363.60	514.80	1,046.30	..	Agriculture
38.30	37.30	58.10	93.30	172.10	322.60	595.40	945.20	1,634.50	3,314.20	..	Industry
28.00	25.20	44.50	73.90	140.70	264.60	481.00	769.60	1,333.60	2,677.70	..	Manufacturing
66.80	75.80	93.80	138.10	241.50	455.20	838.30	1,416.70	2,584.80	5,263.20	..	Services, etc.
20.90	21.40	28.70	46.90	81.40	154.40	277.70	483.10	830.00	1,875.10	..	Gross Domestic Saving
20.20	18.80	18.80	44.90	45.90	112.10	209.60	370.60	617.90	1,497.90	..	Gross National Saving
			(Billions of 1987 Uruguayan New Pesos)								
1,760.0	1,570.0	1,360.0	1,390.0	1,360.0	1,480.0	1,590.0	1,590.0	1,590.0	1,620.0	..	Gross National Product
1,740.0	1,570.0	1,420.0	1,400.0	1,420.0	1,540.0	1,660.0	1,660.0	1,670.0	1,680.0	f	GDP at Market Prices
-37.0	-21.9	86.6	117.0	139.0	117.0	40.6	73.3	110.0	152.0	..	Resource Balance
327.0	293.0	338.0	332.0	352.0	393.0	360.0	393.0	431.0	459.0	..	Exports of Goods & NF Services
364.0	315.0	251.0	215.0	213.0	276.0	319.0	319.0	321.0	307.0	..	Imports of Goods & NF Services
1,780.0	1,590.0	1,330.0	1,280.0	1,290.0	1,420.0	1,620.0	1,590.0	1,560.0	1,530.0	..	Domestic Absorption
1,140.0	1,040.0	912.0	900.0	923.0	1,010.0	1,160.0	1,150.0	1,150.0	1,110.0	..	Private Consumption, etc.
199.0	194.0	188.0	188.0	191.0	208.0	220.0	215.0	218.0	227.0	..	General Gov't Consumption
442.0	361.0	229.0	191.0	171.0	200.0	237.0	220.0	194.0	189.0	..	Gross Domestic Investment
434.0	361.0	213.0	164.0	131.0	148.0	189.0	197.0	200.0	192.0	..	Fixed Investment
1,500.0	1,360.0	1,230.0	1,200.0	1,220.0	1,280.0	1,390.0	1,390.0	1,400.0	0.0	f	GDP at factor cost
241.0	223.0	228.0	199.0	223.0	218.0	228.0	224.0	228.0	232.0	..	Agriculture
640.0	554.0	499.0	506.0	485.0	535.0	595.0	606.0	593.0	589.0	..	Industry
..	..	..	..	..	..	..	..	..	..		Manufacturing
862.0	794.0	690.0	692.0	716.0	786.0	838.0	832.0	848.0	862.0	..	Services, etc.
											Memo Items:
291.0	261.0	274.0	268.0	270.0	356.0	360.0	397.0	426.0	429.0	..	Capacity to Import
-36.2	-32.0	-64.2	-64.6	-82.5	-36.6	0.0	4.5	-5.3	-30.5	..	Terms of Trade Adjustment
1,700.0	1,540.0	1,350.0	1,330.0	1,340.0	1,500.0	1,660.0	1,670.0	1,660.0	1,650.0	..	Gross Domestic Income
1,720.0	1,530.0	1,300.0	1,330.0	1,280.0	1,440.0	1,590.0	1,600.0	1,590.0	1,590.0	..	Gross National Income
			(Index 1987 = 100)								**DOMESTIC PRICES/DEFLATORS**
6.9000	8.1000	12.4000	19.4000	33.6000	57.9000	100.0000	164.0000	283.8000	571.9000		Overall (GDP)
7.0000	8.2000	12.9000	20.1000	35.1000	58.9000	100.0000	163.5000	284.3000	580.3000	..	Domestic Absorption
5.8000	6.3000	10.3000	20.0000	29.1000	51.7000	100.0000	162.2000	226.3000	451.2000	..	Agriculture
6.0000	6.7000	11.7000	18.4000	35.5000	60.3000	100.0000	156.0000	275.7000	562.3000	..	Industry
5.7000	6.2000	11.7000	18.6000	35.9000	60.5000	100.0000	158.6000	280.3000	571.0000	..	Manufacturing
7.3000	8.7000	13.0000	20.1000	34.7000	61.1000	100.0000	162.2000	292.7000	622.0000	f	Consumer Price Index
											MANUFACTURING ACTIVITY
117.6	95.7	90.1	92.3	93.7	96.9	100.0	95.2	..	..	G J	Employment (1987=100)
93.3	102.9	87.4	72.5	82.9	93.3	100.0	101.7	..	..	G J	Real Earnings per Empl. (1987=100)
89.0	101.7	92.0	97.6	87.2	83.9	100.0	94.0	..	..	G J	Real Output per Empl. (1987=100)
32.0	32.5	28.6	21.0	22.3	24.9	25.7	25.7	..	..	J	Earnings as % of Value Added
			(Billions of current Uruguayan New Pesos)								**MONETARY HOLDINGS**
54.20	72.50	81.90	132.90	259.80	478.10	702.40	1,369.80	2,782.30	6,013.50	..	Money Supply, Broadly Defined
9.80	13.70	14.90	22.20	46.00	84.10	134.90	221.60	382.90	770.30	..	Money
6.10	7.90	8.40	12.10	23.30	43.10	76.30	125.50	219.30	420.20	..	Currency Outside Banks
3.70	5.80	6.50	10.00	22.70	41.00	58.50	96.10	163.60	350.10	..	Demand Deposits
44.40	58.80	66.90	110.70	213.80	394.00	567.50	1,148.20	2,399.40	5,243.20	..	Quasi-Money
			(Billions of current Uruguayan New Pesos)								
-1.84	-11.65	-7.27	-15.31	-11.65	-6.23	-14.14	-45.61	-161.00	36.00	..	**GOVERNMENT DEFICIT (-) OR SURPLUS**
29.07	27.38	40.06	55.38	109.02	219.63	394.34	667.00	1,137.00	2,593.00	..	Current Revenue
28.22	35.33	43.02	63.52	111.02	212.35	379.39	650.74	1,185.00	2,353.00	..	Current Expenditure
0.86	-7.95	-2.96	-8.14	-2.00	7.27	14.95	16.25	-48.00	240.00	..	Current Budget Balance
0.01	0.07	0.08	0.14	0.30	0.67	0.86	0.64	5.00	5.00	..	Capital Receipts
2.70	3.78	4.39	7.30	9.95	14.17	29.96	62.50	118.00	209.00	..	Capital Payments

URUGUAY	1970	1971	1972	1973	1974	1975	1976	1977	1978	1979	1980
FOREIGN TRADE (CUSTOMS BASIS)					*(Millions of current US dollars)*						
Value of Exports, fob	232.5	205.5	214.1	321.5	381.0	381.2	536.0	598.5	681.9	787.2	1,059.0
Nonfuel Primary Products	185.1	164.2	174.4	268.0	293.4	265.1	354.6	364.6	391.9	411.9	654.4
Fuels	0.0	0.0	0.1	0.9	2.2	1.9	0.1	0.0	0.0	0.0	0.0
Manufactures	47.4	41.3	39.6	52.7	85.4	114.2	181.3	234.0	289.9	375.3	404.5
Value of Imports, cif	232.9	222.1	186.8	284.8	461.1	516.5	599.0	668.8	715.7	1,173.2	1,651.9
Nonfuel Primary Products	57.1	51.2	48.5	84.9	104.1	98.2	87.4	114.3	113.6	226.6	247.6
Fuels	34.1	32.0	31.6	33.5	149.6	161.2	207.9	171.1	231.2	282.3	473.1
Manufactures	141.7	138.9	106.7	166.4	207.4	257.1	303.7	383.4	370.9	664.3	931.2
					(Index 1987 = 100)						
Terms of Trade	202.2	173.6	217.6	215.0	136.8	117.6	124.8	113.4	125.7	115.4	102.5
Export Prices, fob	35.2	35.7	46.2	70.4	69.4	60.8	66.7	69.8	79.8	97.3	105.1
Import Prices, cif	17.4	20.6	21.3	32.7	50.7	51.7	53.5	61.5	63.5	84.3	102.5
BALANCE OF PAYMENTS					*(Millions of current US dollars)*						
Exports of Goods & Services	291.5	253.5	352.0	415.5	504.5	554.7	703.0	820.1	931.3	1,248.4	1,593.7
Merchandise, fob	224.1	196.8	281.6	327.6	381.4	384.9	565.0	611.5	686.1	788.1	1,058.5
Nonfactor Services	65.9	55.9	68.9	82.1	118.5	166.1	131.2	197.0	226.8	406.1	467.5
Factor Services	1.5	0.8	1.4	5.7	4.7	3.8	6.8	11.6	18.4	54.2	67.7
Imports of Goods & Services	345.9	325.3	304.5	397.2	639.6	751.1	784.4	993.8	1,065.4	1,612.6	2,311.5
Merchandise, fob	203.1	203.0	178.7	248.6	433.6	494.0	536.6	686.7	709.8	1,166.2	1,668.2
Nonfactor Services	116.5	99.9	100.9	117.9	158.7	182.1	168.6	227.5	260.4	337.3	475.5
Factor Services	26.3	22.4	25.0	30.8	47.3	74.9	79.2	79.5	95.2	109.1	167.8
Long-Term Interest	17.4	17.6	21.0	23.9	36.1	51.6	60.6	63.0	67.0	80.9	121.3
Private Current Transfers, net	-0.9	-0.6	-0.2	-0.1	-1.2	-1.5	-1.0	2.1	1.4	1.5	2.0
Workers' Remittances	..	..	..	..	..	..	..	..	..	..	..
Curr. A/C Bal before Off. Transf.	-55.3	-72.4	47.2	18.1	-136.3	-197.8	-82.4	-171.6	-132.7	-362.7	-715.8
Net Official Transfers	10.2	8.9	11.5	19.1	18.6	8.3	8.7	4.6	5.7	5.6	6.7
Curr. A/C Bal after Off. Transf.	-45.1	-63.5	58.7	37.2	-117.6	-189.5	-73.8	-167.1	-127.0	-357.1	-709.1
Long-Term Capital, net	-4.5	52.8	18.6	-32.9	63.0	150.7	79.1	101.2	152.2	358.8	404.3
Direct Investment	..	..	..	..	..	..	..	66.0	128.8	215.5	289.5
Long-Term Loans	-1.1	31.9	28.7	6.4	251.9	36.0	81.4	66.1	34.6	253.2	226.3
Disbursements	50.3	79.3	125.5	86.1	383.5	284.6	240.4	264.8	417.2	321.5	356.2
Repayments	51.4	47.4	96.8	79.7	131.6	248.6	159.0	198.7	382.6	68.3	129.9
Other Long-Term Capital	-3.4	20.9	-10.1	-39.3	-188.9	114.7	-2.3	-30.8	-11.2	-109.9	-111.5
Other Capital, net	21.1	-1.1	-51.0	22.7	26.4	-52.1	88.9	233.0	113.1	72.1	423.0
Change in Reserves	28.5	11.8	-26.4	-27.0	28.2	90.9	-94.2	-167.2	-138.3	-73.8	-118.2
Memo Item:					*(Uruguayan New Pesos per US dollar)*						
Conversion Factor (Annual Avg)	0.250	0.255	0.536	0.866	1.200	2.250	3.340	4.680	6.060	7.860	9.100
					(Millions of US dollars), outstanding at end of year						
EXTERNAL DEBT (Total)	316.1	351.7	401.7	416.0	715.4	787.3	896.0	1,104.7	998.3	1,322.9	1,659.8
Long-Term Debt (by debtor)	316.1	351.7	401.7	416.0	715.4	787.3	896.0	938.7	861.3	1,116.9	1,337.8
Central Bank, incl. IMF credit	154.6	165.9	204.0	220.4	339.3	495.3	558.8	510.8	230.6	307.6	366.9
Central Government	79.1	96.7	119.1	123.2	134.4	135.8	151.9	182.0	393.9	430.4	490.2
Rest of General Government	0.6	0.4	0.1	0.1	0.1	0.1	0.0	0.0	0.0	0.0	0.0
Non-financial Public Enterprises	52.9	48.3	43.4	41.7	105.3	87.1	115.2	152.6	162.5	189.6	265.8
Priv. Sector, incl non-guaranteed	28.9	40.4	35.1	30.6	136.3	69.0	70.1	93.3	74.3	189.3	214.9
Short-Term Debt	0.0	0.0	0.0	0.0	0.0	0.0	0.0	166.0	137.0	206.0	322.0
Memo Items:					*(Millions of US dollars)*						
Int'l Reserves Excluding Gold	13.80	20.10	69.03	100.58	80.55	58.52	176.21	322.38	352.41	323.13	383.79
Gold Holdings (at market price)	172.43	184.51	229.49	396.92	659.46	496.34	477.55	589.86	822.64	1,694.72	2,017.27
SOCIAL INDICATORS											
Total Fertility Rate	2.9	3.0	3.0	3.0	3.0	2.9	2.9	2.9	2.8	2.8	2.7
Infant Mortality Rate	46.4	46.2	46.0	45.2	44.4	43.6	42.8	42.0	40.2	38.4	36.6
Life Expectancy at Birth	68.8	68.8	68.8	69.0	69.2	69.4	69.5	69.7	69.9	70.2	70.4
Urban Population, % of total	82.1	82.3	82.5	82.6	82.8	83.0	83.2	83.3	83.5	83.6	83.8
Food Prod. per capita (1987=100)	122.4	100.1	96.8	98.4	109.4	109.3	123.1	104.1	100.0	91.8	103.7
Labor Force, Agriculture (%)	18.6	18.3	18.0	17.7	17.4	17.1	16.9	16.6	16.3	16.0	15.7
Labor Force, Female (%)	26.3	26.6	27.0	27.3	27.6	27.9	28.3	28.6	29.0	29.3	29.6
Primary Schl. Enroll. Ratio	112.0	..	..	..	..	107.0	105.0	105.0	105.0	105.0	107.0
Primary Schl. Enroll. Ratio, Female	109.0	..	..	..	..	106.0	..	104.0	108.0	103.0	106.0
Secondary Schl. Enroll. Ratio	59.0	..	..	..	..	60.0	63.0	62.0	58.0	58.0	62.0

1981	1982	1983	1984	1985	1986	1987	1988	1989	1990 estimate	Notes	URUGUAY
				(Millions of current US dollars)							**FOREIGN TRADE (CUSTOMS BASIS)**
1,216.7	1,024.2	1,008.4	924.9	852.7	1,082.1	1,191.1	1,442.6	1,596.4	1,695.7	..	Value of Exports, fob
841.3	688.9	709.4	575.6	549.8	692.3	664.0	890.8	948.5	1,032.3	..	Nonfuel Primary Products
12.3	2.8	0.8	3.0	0.0	5.0	2.1	0.3	1.1	0.5	..	Fuels
363.1	332.4	298.3	346.3	302.8	384.9	525.0	551.5	646.8	662.9	..	Manufactures
1,633.1	1,110.0	787.5	775.7	707.8	870.0	1,141.9	1,176.9	1,239.7	1,414.5	..	Value of Imports, cif
190.9	112.3	99.8	118.4	99.7	140.6	172.8	164.2	172.0	179.8	..	Nonfuel Primary Products
516.7	434.5	283.9	281.3	239.6	168.7	178.7	166.2	180.5	255.4	..	Fuels
925.5	563.2	403.8	376.0	368.5	560.6	790.4	846.6	887.2	979.3	..	Manufactures
				(Index 1987 = 100)							
97.2	91.0	91.6	92.5	89.4	100.5	100.0	101.9	109.8	103.8	..	Terms of Trade
102.2	91.3	88.2	87.4	82.8	85.5	100.0	105.4	112.8	115.8	..	Export Prices, fob
105.2	100.3	96.3	94.5	92.6	85.0	100.0	103.4	102.7	111.5	..	Import Prices, cif
				(Millions of current US dollars)							**BALANCE OF PAYMENTS**
1,846.5	1,684.5	1,473.9	1,376.6	1,330.2	1,592.3	1,649.9	1,877.4	2,197.9	2,377.8	..	Exports of Goods & Services
1,229.7	1,256.4	1,156.4	924.6	853.6	1,087.8	1,182.3	1,404.5	1,599.0	1,692.9	..	Merchandise, fob
471.0	280.9	255.0	364.8	399.2	411.8	364.7	358.2	395.9	427.0	..	Nonfactor Services
145.8	147.2	62.5	87.2	77.4	92.7	102.9	114.7	203.0	257.9	..	Factor Services
2,317.6	1,929.5	1,544.7	1,515.7	1,461.1	1,573.0	1,815.8	1,889.8	2,052.7	2,162.0	..	Imports of Goods & Services
1,592.1	1,038.4	739.7	732.2	675.4	814.5	1,079.9	1,112.2	1,136.2	1,266.9	..	Merchandise, fob
505.9	547.1	454.7	334.7	357.4	365.2	325.2	332.3	364.4	315.5	..	Nonfactor Services
219.6	344.0	350.3	448.8	428.3	393.3	410.7	445.3	552.1	579.6	..	Factor Services
148.0	179.2	225.6	295.3	292.1	254.6	272.8	267.3	274.1	320.3	..	Long-Term Interest
2.9	0.0	0.0	0.0	0.0	0.0	0.0	0.0	0.0	..	..	Private Current Transfers, net
..	..	..	..	..	..	..	..	..	..	..	Workers' Remittances
-468.2	-245.0	-70.8	-139.1	-130.9	19.3	-165.9	-12.4	145.2	215.8	..	Curr. A/C Bal before Off. Transf.
6.8	10.4	11.0	10.0	10.8	25.3	8.0	21.3	8.0	8.1	..	Net Official Transfers
-461.4	-234.6	-59.8	-129.1	-120.1	44.6	-157.9	8.9	153.2	223.9	..	Curr. A/C Bal after Off. Transf.
345.6	515.1	626.3	35.1	59.5	174.3	120.2	22.1	47.2	9.6	..	Long-Term Capital, net
48.6	-13.7	-5.6	-3.4	-7.9	32.5	45.2	44.5	1.0	3.0	..	Direct Investment
353.3	241.7	381.3	39.5	27.0	102.3	237.5	-29.7	83.3	-18.2	..	Long-Term Loans
456.0	533.2	502.0	189.4	220.0	207.9	390.6	282.8	295.3	454.8	..	Disbursements
102.7	291.5	120.7	149.9	193.0	105.6	153.1	312.5	212.0	473.0	..	Repayments
-56.3	287.1	250.6	-1.0	40.4	39.5	-162.5	7.3	-37.1	24.8	..	Other Long-Term Capital
149.7	-696.5	-632.2	9.6	127.0	68.6	115.9	-27.1	-78.6	51.6	..	Other Capital, net
-33.9	416.0	65.7	84.4	-66.4	-287.5	-78.2	-3.9	-121.8	-285.1	..	Change in Reserves
				(Uruguayan New Pesos per US dollar)							**Memo Item:**
10.820	13.910	34.540	56.120	101.430	151.990	226.670	359.440	605.510	1,171.000	..	Conversion Factor (Annual Avg)
				(Millions of US dollars), outstanding at end of year							**EXTERNAL DEBT (Total)**
2,174.3	2,646.9	3,292.1	3,271.2	3,919.5	3,906.2	4,270.8	3,822.8	3,761.4	3,706.7	..	Long-Term Debt (by debtor)
1,674.3	2,001.9	2,906.1	2,879.2	3,105.5	3,333.2	3,634.8	3,345.8	3,284.4	3,254.7	..	Central Bank, incl. IMF credit
441.1	826.1	1,855.1	1,858.2	2,006.8	2,212.9	2,304.2	2,304.3	2,080.6	1,848.2	..	Central Government
558.0	569.4	521.1	492.2	622.3	720.4	854.8	762.9	960.4	1,166.5	..	Rest of General Government
0.0	4.0	3.7	51.2	50.4	49.8	49.2	39.0	0.1	0.1	..	Non-financial Public Enterprises
340.6	388.9	359.4	343.0	359.7	302.8	275.5	148.3	134.6	122.2	..	Priv. Sector, incl non-guaranteed
334.6	213.5	166.8	134.6	66.3	47.3	151.1	91.3	108.7	117.7	..	Short-Term Debt
500.0	645.0	386.0	392.0	814.0	573.0	636.0	477.0	477.0	452.0	..	
				(Millions of US dollars)							**Memo Items:**
429.99	116.29	206.92	134.42	174.23	481.55	530.00	531.98	501.35	544.41	..	Int'l Reserves Excluding Gold
1,348.32	1,305.82	992.66	807.13	856.41	1,018.29	1,263.02	1,070.34	1,046.21	922.07	..	Gold Holdings (at market price)
											SOCIAL INDICATORS
2.6	2.6	2.5	2.5	2.5	2.4	2.4	2.4	2.3	2.3	..	Total Fertility Rate
34.8	33.0	31.2	29.4	27.6	25.8	24.0	22.9	21.8	20.6	..	Infant Mortality Rate
70.7	70.9	71.1	71.4	71.6	71.8	72.0	72.3	72.6	73.0	..	Life Expectancy at Birth
84.0	84.1	84.3	84.4	84.6	84.8	85.0	85.1	85.3	85.5	..	Urban Population, % of total
121.3	122.7	129.2	102.5	107.8	107.0	100.0	110.6	123.6	111.3	..	Food Prod. per capita (1987=100)
..	..	..	..	..	..	..	..	..	..	..	Labor Force, Agriculture (%)
29.8	29.9	30.1	30.3	30.4	30.6	30.7	30.9	31.0	31.1	..	Labor Force, Female (%)
..	..	109.0	108.0	107.0	106.0	106.0	106.0	..	..	..	Primary Schl. Enroll. Ratio
..	..	107.0	107.0	106.0	105.0	106.0	106.0	..	..	..	Primary Schl. Enroll. Ratio, Female
..	..	67.0	70.0	72.0	74.0	69.0	77.0			..	Secondary Schl. Enroll. Ratio

VANUATU	1970	1971	1972	1973	1974	1975	1976	1977	1978	1979	1980
CURRENT GNP PER CAPITA (US $)	..	..	..	..	..	..	..	..	..	..	..
POPULATION (thousands)	83	85	87	90	93	96	100	104	108	112	116

USE AND ORIGIN OF RESOURCES *(Millions of current Vanuatu Vatu)*

	1970	1971	1972	1973	1974	1975	1976	1977	1978	1979	1980
Gross National Product (GNP)	..	..	..	..	..	..	..	..	..	6,880	6,546
Net Factor Income from Abroad			..	..			..		..	-1,320	-1,200
GDP at Market Prices			..	..			..		..	8,200	7,746
Resource Balance											-668
Exports of Goods & NFServices										..	2,568
Imports of Goods & NFServices											3,236
Domestic Absorption										..	..
Private Consumption, etc.										..	..
General Gov't Consumption											2,092
Gross Domestic Investment										..	..
Fixed Investment										..	..
Indirect Taxes, net										..	..
GDP at factor cost										..	..
Agriculture										..	..
Industry			..						..	1,800	1,464
Manufacturing										..	..
Services, etc.										320	327
Gross Domestic Saving										..	..
Gross National Saving										..	..

(Millions of 1987 Vanuatu Vatu)

	1970	1971	1972	1973	1974	1975	1976	1977	1978	1979	1980
Gross National Product				..					..	..	..
GDP at Market Prices									..	11,704	10,370
Resource Balance									..	..	..
Exports of Goods & NFServices									..	..	..
Imports of Goods & NFServices									..	..	..
Domestic Absorption									..	..	..
Private Consumption, etc.									..	..	..
General Gov't Consumption									..	..	..
Gross Domestic Investment									..	..	..
Fixed Investment									..	..	..
GDP at factor cost									..	..	..
Agriculture									..	..	..
Industry									..	2,623	2,148
Manufacturing									..	..	..
Services, etc.									..	..	..

Memo Items:

	1970	1971	1972	1973	1974	1975	1976	1977	1978	1979	1980
Capacity to Import									..	..	..
Terms of Trade Adjustment									..	..	..
Gross Domestic Income									..	..	..
Gross National Income									..	..	..

DOMESTIC PRICES/DEFLATORS *(Index 1987 = 100)*

	1970	1971	1972	1973	1974	1975	1976	1977	1978	1979	1980
Overall (GDP)		..							..	70.1	74.7
Domestic Absorption										..	..
Agriculture										..	..
Industry									..	68.6	68.1
Manufacturing										..	..
Consumer Price Index	..		..	..	..	43.0	45.5	48.4	50.4	56.1	

MANUFACTURING ACTIVITY

	1970	1971	1972	1973	1974	1975	1976	1977	1978	1979	1980
Employment (1987=100)		..								..	..
Real Earnings per Empl. (1987=100)										..	..
Real Output per Empl. (1987=100)										..	..
Earnings as % of Value Added										..	..

MONETARY HOLDINGS *(Millions of current Vanuatu Vatu)*

	1970	1971	1972	1973	1974	1975	1976	1977	1978	1979	1980
Money Supply, Broadly Defined		..		..		..	5,392	5,816	5,869	6,043	5,261
Money						..	1,629	1,770	1,888	2,094	1,882
Currency Outside Banks		..				..	494	564	699	846	720
Demand Deposits						..	1,135	1,206	1,189	1,248	1,162
Quasi-Money						..	3,763	4,046	3,981	3,949	3,379

GOVERNMENT DEFICIT (-) OR SURPLUS *(Millions of current Vanuatu Vatu)*

	1970	1971	1972	1973	1974	1975	1976	1977	1978	1979	1980
Current Revenue		..			..		..		..	..	..
Current Expenditure										..	..
Current Budget Balance										..	..
Capital Receipts		..								..	..
Capital Payments		..								..	..

1981	1982	1983	1984	1985	1986	1987	1988	1989	1990 estimate	Notes	VANUATU
..	..	..	..	960	930	820	890	1,010	1,100	..	**CURRENT GNP PER CAPITA (US $)**
119	121	124	128	131	135	138	142	147	151	..	**POPULATION (thousands)**
											USE AND ORIGIN OF RESOURCES
				(Millions of current Vanuatu Vatu)							
7,218	7,942	9,653	11,940	12,936	12,690	12,539	14,581	16,920	18,904	..	Gross National Product (GNP)
-1,454	-1,501	-497	-399	402	511	-865	-425	553	..	..	Net Factor Income from Abroad
8,673	9,442	10,150	12,339	12,534	12,179	13,404	15,006	16,367	..	..	GDP at Market Prices
-205	-239	-1,392	-667	-2,676	-3,836	-3,940	-3,707	-4,580	..	..	Resource Balance
3,328	4,038	5,934	7,757	6,391	4,417	5,144	5,506	6,008	..	..	Exports of Goods & NFServices
3,533	4,277	7,326	8,424	9,067	8,253	9,084	9,213	10,588	..	..	Imports of Goods & NFServices
..	..	11,542	13,006	15,210	16,015	17,344	18,713	20,947	..	..	Domestic Absorption
..	..	5,277	5,989	7,165	7,211	8,063	9,133	9,990	..	..	Private Consumption, etc.
2,043	2,327	3,660	4,068	4,501	4,604	4,544	4,969	4,881	..	..	General Gov't Consumption
..	..	2,605	2,949	3,544	4,200	4,737	4,611	6,076	..	..	Gross Domestic Investment
..	..	2,142	2,491	2,849	3,580	4,417	4,170	5,470	..	..	Fixed Investment
..	..	1,561	2,068	2,410	2,387	2,879	3,116	3,352	..	..	Indirect Taxes, net
..	..	8,589	10,271	10,124	9,792	10,525	11,890	13,015	..	B	GDP at factor cost
1,852	1,886	2,649	3,543	3,693	2,958	2,881	2,933	3,149	..	..	Agriculture
..	..	771	951	1,018	1,117	1,498	1,767	2,079	..	..	Industry
367	425	312	431	481	471	613	702	880	..	..	Manufacturing
..	..	6,730	7,845	7,823	8,104	9,025	10,306	11,139	..	..	Services, etc.
..	..	1,213	2,282	868	364	797	904	1,496			Gross Domestic Saving
..	..	1,313	2,570	1,986	1,641	574	1,500	2,583			Gross National Saving
				(Millions of 1987 Vanuatu Vatu)							
..	..	12,006	13,005	14,113	13,939	12,539	13,116	14,509	15,379		Gross National Product
10,805	11,961	12,629	13,488	13,639	13,362	13,404	13,476	14,074	..	..	GDP at Market Prices
..	..	-1,743	-2,391	-3,736	-3,334	-3,940	-3,766	-3,723	..	..	Resource Balance
..	..	6,904	7,341	6,576	5,819	5,144	4,924	5,020	..	..	Exports of Goods & NFServices
..	..	8,647	9,732	10,313	9,152	9,084	8,690	8,743	..	..	Imports of Goods & NFServices
..	..	14,372	15,879	17,376	16,696	17,344	17,242	17,797	..		Domestic Absorption
..	..	6,572	7,496	8,033	6,843	8,063	8,473	8,642	..		Private Consumption, etc.
..	..	4,361	4,680	5,048	4,912	4,544	4,548	4,123	..		General Gov't Consumption
..	..	3,439	3,703	4,295	4,940	4,737	4,221	5,031	..		Gross Domestic Investment
..	..	2,849	3,152	3,483	4,233	4,417	3,787	4,493	..		Fixed Investment
..	..	10,666	11,191	10,859	10,718	10,525	..	..	..	B	GDP at factor cost
2,625	2,318	3,203	3,423	3,350	3,070	2,881	2,597	2,841	..	..	Agriculture
..	..	903	1,055	1,098	1,197	1,498	1,721	1,900	..	..	Industry
..	..	325	437	486	487	613	713	807	..	..	Manufacturing
..	..	8,523	9,010	9,191	9,096	9,025	9,158	9,333	..	..	Services, etc.
											Memo Items:
..	..	7,004	8,961	7,269	4,898	5,144	5,193	4,961	..	..	Capacity to Import
..	..	100	1,621	693	-920	0	269	-58	..	..	Terms of Trade Adjustment
..	..	12,729	15,108	14,332	12,442	13,404	13,745	14,015	..	..	Gross Domestic Income
..	..	12,106	14,626	14,806	13,018	12,539	13,385	14,450	..	..	Gross National Income
											DOMESTIC PRICES/DEFLATORS
				(Index 1987 = 100)							
80.3	78.9	80.4	91.5	91.9	91.1	100.0	111.4	116.3	..	..	Overall (GDP)
..	..	80.3	81.9	87.5	95.9	100.0	108.5	117.7	..	..	Domestic Absorption
70.5	81.4	82.7	103.5	110.2	96.4	100.0	112.9	110.8	..	..	Agriculture
..	..	85.4	90.1	92.7	93.4	100.0	102.7	109.4	..	..	Industry
..	..	95.9	98.7	99.0	96.7	100.0	98.4	109.1	..	..	Manufacturing
71.1	75.9	77.1	81.4	82.3	86.2	100.0	108.8	116.9	122.8	..	Consumer Price Index
											MANUFACTURING ACTIVITY
..	..	..	..	..	..	..	..	..	..		Employment (1987=100)
..	..	..	..	..	..	..	..	..	..		Real Earnings per Empl. (1987=100)
..	..	..	..	..	..	..	..	..	..		Real Output per Empl. (1987=100)
..	..	..	..	..	..	..	..	..	..		Earnings as % of Value Added
											MONETARY HOLDINGS
				(Millions of current Vanuatu Vatu)							
5,325	7,938	8,627	10,953	12,392	15,639	14,606	15,469	22,828	24,097	..	Money Supply, Broadly Defined
1,451	1,746	2,274	3,027	2,643	2,811	4,219	3,516	4,369	3,894	..	Money
597	634	748	922	963	906	1,000	954	1,037	934	..	Currency Outside Banks
853	1,112	1,526	2,106	1,680	1,905	3,219	2,561	3,332	2,960	..	Demand Deposits
3,874	6,192	6,353	7,926	9,749	12,828	10,386	11,953	18,460	20,203	..	Quasi-Money
				(Millions of current Vanuatu Vatu)							
650.7	-338.3	-57.2	432.5	-62.3	-855.2	511.6	-629.5	-1,323.8	-1,403.1	..	**GOVERNMENT DEFICIT (-) OR SURPLUS**
3,122.5	2,812.1	2,904.7	3,879.9	3,694.6	3,321.6	5,750.7	5,552.4	5,877.3	5,330.8	..	Current Revenue
2,073.2	2,313.8	2,408.7	2,575.3	2,848.2	3,208.3	3,299.7	3,865.3	3,387.9	3,893.0	..	Current Expenditure
1,049.3	498.3	496.0	1,304.6	846.4	113.3	2,451.0	1,687.1	2,489.4	1,437.8	..	Current Budget Balance
						1.6	103.8	75.3	1.5	..	Capital Receipts
398.6	836.6	553.2	872.1	908.7	968.5	1,941.0	2,420.4	3,888.5	2,842.4	..	Capital Payments

VANUATU	1970	1971	1972	1973	1974	1975	1976	1977	1978	1979	1980
FOREIGN TRADE (CUSTOMS BASIS)					*(Thousands of current US dollars)*						
Value of Exports, fob	..	..	..	..	..	..	..	..	..	..	..
Nonfuel Primary Products	..	..	..	..				..	..	..	..
Fuels	..	..	..	..				..	..	..	..
Manufactures	..			..							
Value of Imports, cif	..	..	..	..				..	..	..	..
Nonfuel Primary Products	..	..	..	..				..	..	..	..
Fuels	..	..	..	..				..	..	..	..
Manufactures	..	..		..							
Terms of Trade					*(Index 1987 = 100)*						
Export Prices, fob	..	..	..	..							
Import Prices, cif	..	..	..	..							
BALANCE OF PAYMENTS					*(Millions of current US dollars)*						
Exports of Goods & Services	..	..	..	..				..		..	..
Merchandise, fob	..	..									
Nonfactor Services	..	..									
Factor Services	..	..									
Imports of Goods & Services	..	..	..	..				..		..	..
Merchandise, fob	..	..									
Nonfactor Services	..	..							..		
Factor Services	..	..							..		..
Long-Term Interest	0.00	0.00	0.00	0.10	0.20	0.20	0.20	0.20	0.20	0.30	0.20
Private Current Transfers, net	..	..									
Workers' Remittances	..	..									..
Curr. A/C Bal before Off. Transf.	..	..									
Net Official Transfers	..	..									
Curr. A/C Bal after Off. Transf.	..	..									
Long-Term Capital, net	..	..							..		..
Direct Investment											
Long-Term Loans	0.00	0.00	1.60	0.60	0.00	0.80	1.00	0.40	-0.30	-0.40	-0.40
Disbursements	0.00	0.00	1.60	0.60	0.00	0.90	1.10	0.50	0.00	0.00	0.00
Repayments	0.00	0.00	0.00	0.00	0.00	0.10	0.10	0.10	0.30	0.40	0.40
Other Long-Term Capital	..	..	..	..					..		..
Other Capital, net											
Change in Reserves	..	..			..			..		..	..
Memo Item:					*(Vanuatu Vatu per US dollar)*						
Conversion Factor (Annual Avg)	100.990	99.860	81.610	72.040	77.800	69.270	77.240	79.410	72.940	68.760	68.290
EXTERNAL DEBT (Total)					*(Thousands of US dollars), outstanding at end of year*						
Long-Term Debt (by debtor)	1,100	1,100	2,700	3,600	3,700	3,500	4,200	4,900	5,100	4,900	4,100
Central Bank, incl. IMF credit	0	0	0	0	0	0	0	0	0	0	0
Central Government	1,100	1,100	2,700	3,600	3,700	3,500	4,200	4,900	5,100	4,900	4,100
Rest of General Government	..	..	..	..	..	..	..	..	..	..	..
Non-financial Public Enterprises	..	..									
Priv. Sector, incl non-guaranteed	..	..			..			..		..	..
Short-Term Debt	0	0	0	0	0	0	0	0	0	0	0
Memo Items:					*(Thousands of US dollars)*						
Int'l Reserves Excluding Gold	..	..		..			..			..	..
Gold Holdings (at market price)	..									..	..
SOCIAL INDICATORS											
Total Fertility Rate	6.5	6.4	6.4	6.3	6.3	6.3	6.2	6.2	6.2	6.1	6.1
Infant Mortality Rate	..	..		..			..			..	..
Life Expectancy at Birth	..						..			..	..
Urban Population, % of total	13.5	14.2	14.9	15.5	16.2	16.9	17.1	17.3	17.4	17.6	17.8
Food Prod. per capita (1987=100)	121.3	125.7	91.1	100.4	120.8	106.2	122.2	124.6	126.0	116.9	97.6
Labor Force, Agriculture (%)	..	..	..	..					..	..	..
Labor Force, Female (%)	..										
Primary Schl. Enroll. Ratio	..	..		..			..			..	..
Primary Schl. Enroll. Ratio, Female	..	..		..			..			..	..
Secondary Schl. Enroll. Ratio	..	..		..			..			..	..

1981	1982	1983	1984	1985	1986	1987	1988	1989	1990 estimate	Notes	VANUATU
											FOREIGN TRADE (CUSTOMS BASIS)
			(Thousands of current US dollars)								
..	..	..	..	..	..	..	..	..	..		Value of Exports, fob
..	..	..	..	..	..	..	..	..	..		Nonfuel Primary Products
..	..	..	..	..	..	..	..	..	..		Fuels
..	..	..	..	..	..	..	..	..	..		Manufactures
..	..	..	..	..	..	..	..	..	..		Value of Imports, cif
..	..	..	..	..	..	..	..	..	..		Nonfuel Primary Products
..	..	..	..	..	..	..	..	..	..		Fuels
..	..	..	..	..	..	..	..	..	..		Manufactures
			(Index 1987 = 100)								
..	..	..	..	..	..	..	..	..	..		Terms of Trade
..	..	..	..	..	..	..	..	..	..		Export Prices, fob
..	..	..	..	..	..	..	..	..	..		Import Prices, cif
											BALANCE OF PAYMENTS
			(Millions of current US dollars)								
..	53.26	62.54	83.75	83.56	80.22	81.02	78.73	77.45	109.49	..	Exports of Goods & Services
..	10.67	17.92	32.54	18.67	8.81	13.73	15.39	13.74	13.78	..	Merchandise, fob
..	36.99	38.11	42.43	38.16	30.58	36.15	39.97	40.29	60.72	..	Nonfactor Services
..	5.59	6.50	8.78	26.73	40.82	31.14	23.38	23.42	34.99	..	Factor Services
..	84.33	86.35	99.45	112.88	111.57	124.54	116.66	106.22	137.52	..	Imports of Goods & Services
..	43.27	45.82	51.48	52.29	46.81	57.09	57.89	57.92	79.63	..	Merchandise, fob
..	29.95	27.38	32.87	33.22	28.64	28.13	30.91	31.20	36.35	..	Nonfactor Services
..	11.11	13.14	15.10	27.36	36.13	39.31	27.87	17.09	21.54	..	Factor Services
0.20	0.20	0.20	0.20	0.20	0.40	0.50	0.60	0.70	0.70	..	Long-Term Interest
..	8.19	6.01	6.93	6.75	7.22	5.84	9.78	4.60	6.69	..	Private Current Transfers, net
..	8.32	5.64	6.86	6.89	6.88	6.71	7.02	6.48	6.92	..	Workers' Remittances
..	-22.88	-17.80	-8.78	-22.56	-24.13	-37.67	-28.16	-24.16	-21.35	..	Curr. A/C Bal before Off. Transf.
..	35.05	26.17	31.68	23.85	21.33	46.38	36.19	20.70	29.36	..	Net Official Transfers
..	12.17	8.36	22.91	1.29	-2.80	8.71	8.03	-3.46	8.01	..	Curr. A/C Bal after Off. Transf.
..	-37.65	-1.16	59.43	-42.61	13.87	-0.97	-208.53	10.05	16.06	..	Long-Term Capital, net
..	6.93	5.87	7.44	4.63	2.02	12.89	10.81	9.17	13.19	..	Direct Investment
-0.30	1.60	0.30	1.80	0.90	0.80	3.60	2.80	5.20	7.70	..	Long-Term Loans
0.00	1.90	0.60	2.20	1.30	1.40	5.70	3.50	5.80	8.70	..	Disbursements
0.30	0.30	0.30	0.40	0.40	0.60	2.10	0.70	0.60	1.00	..	Repayments
..	-46.18	-7.32	50.20	-48.13	11.05	-17.47	-222.14	-4.32	-4.84	..	Other Long-Term Capital
..	28.72	-6.23	-84.89	41.06	-6.28	5.20	201.18	1.18	-28.14	..	Other Capital, net
..	-3.25	-0.98	2.55	0.26	-4.78	-12.93	-0.68	-7.77	4.07	..	Change in Reserves
											Memo Item:
			(Vanuatu Vatu per US dollar)								
87.830	96.210	99.370	99.230	106.030	107.080	109.850	104.430	116.040	116.570	..	Conversion Factor (Annual Avg)
		(Thousands of US dollars), outstanding at end of year									
3,000	4,000	10,600	12,900	15,700	18,300	23,600	26,800	30,300	40,200	..	**EXTERNAL DEBT (Total)**
3,000	4,000	3,600	4,900	6,700	8,300	13,600	15,300	20,800	30,600		Long-Term Debt (by debtor)
0	1,700	1,300	1,400	2,000	2,500	2,300	3,000	3,900	4,000		Central Bank, incl. IMF credit
3,000	2,300	2,300	3,500	4,700	5,800	11,300	12,300	16,900	26,600		Central Government
..	..	..	..	..	..	..	..	..	..		Rest of General Government
..	..	..	..	..	..	..	..	..	..		Non-financial Public Enterprises
..	..	..	..	..	..	..	..	..	..		Priv. Sector, incl non-guaranteed
0	0	7,000	8,000	9,000	10,000	10,000	11,500	9,500	9,600	..	Short-Term Debt
											Memo Items:
			(Thousands of US dollars)								
8,463	5,669	6,595	8,087	10,610	21,420	40,174	40,670	35,082	37,692	..	Int'l Reserves Excluding Gold
..	..	..	..	..	..	..	..	..	..		Gold Holdings (at market price)
											SOCIAL INDICATORS
6.1	6.0	6.0	5.9	5.9	5.9	5.8	5.7	5.7	5.6	..	Total Fertility Rate
..	94.0	90.2	86.4	82.7	78.9	75.1	73.1	71.2	69.2		Infant Mortality Rate
..	61.1	61.6	62.0	62.5	63.0	63.5	63.8	64.2	64.5		Life Expectancy at Birth
18.1	18.3	18.6	18.8	19.1	19.3	19.6	19.8	20.1	20.3		Urban Population, % of total
118.1	99.2	103.7	112.6	99.6	100.9	100.0	89.6	112.8	88.1		Food Prod. per capita (1987=100)
..	..	..	..	..	..	..	..	..	..		Labor Force, Agriculture (%)
..	..	..	..	..	..	..	..	..	..		Labor Force, Female (%)
..	..	..	..	..	..	..	..	..	..		Primary Schl. Enroll. Ratio
..	..	..	..	..	..	..	..	..	..		Primary Schl. Enroll. Ratio, Female
..	..	..	..	..	..	..	..	..	..		Secondary Schl. Enroll. Ratio

VENEZUELA	1970	1971	1972	1973	1974	1975	1976	1977	1978	1979	1980
CURRENT GNP PER CAPITA (US $)	1,260	1,270	1,350	1,540	1,920	2,380	2,890	3,150	3,380	3,730	4,070
POPULATION (thousands)	10,604	10,981	11,377	11,791	12,221	12,665	13,122	13,594	14,074	14,553	15,024
USE AND ORIGIN OF RESOURCES					*(Billions of current Venezuelan Bolivares)*						
Gross National Product (GNP)	57.28	63.03	70.24	83.56	125.96	139.54	161.65	188.20	206.36	247.39	299.21
Net Factor Income from Abroad	-2.49	-3.32	-2.11	-2.96	-2.73	0.43	0.89	0.38	0.16	-0.01	1.41
GDP at Market Prices	59.77	66.35	72.35	86.52	128.69	139.11	160.75	187.82	206.20	247.40	297.80
Resource Balance	2.43	3.65	2.09	7.22	28.26	9.62	1.19	-12.81	-23.04	3.26	20.77
Exports of Goods & NFServices	12.50	14.85	14.79	21.74	49.77	40.07	41.54	43.64	42.08	64.22	85.72
Imports of Goods & NFServices	10.07	11.21	12.70	14.53	21.51	30.46	40.35	56.45	65.12	60.96	64.95
Domestic Absorption	57.34	62.70	70.27	79.31	100.42	129.50	159.56	200.63	229.24	244.14	277.03
Private Consumption, etc.	31.02	33.56	37.76	42.89	54.01	67.98	81.63	96.81	114.64	134.29	163.40
General Gov't Consumption	6.63	7.76	8.50	9.59	12.77	15.94	19.78	22.96	24.06	27.76	35.12
Gross Domestic Investment	19.68	21.38	24.01	26.83	33.64	45.57	58.15	80.86	90.55	82.09	78.51
Fixed Investment	13.35	15.41	18.34	21.55	24.29	35.41	49.50	70.00	83.14	75.87	74.24
Indirect Taxes, net	2.84	2.73	2.65	2.72	3.32	4.57	4.70	5.21	4.54	6.65	8.00
GDP at factor cost	56.93	63.62	69.71	83.81	125.36	134.54	156.06	182.61	201.66	240.75	289.80
Agriculture	3.71	3.84	3.90	4.58	5.65	6.97	7.45	9.27	10.14	11.94	14.44
Industry	23.50	26.55	28.52	37.28	69.28	64.73	73.69	83.74	88.63	114.37	138.12
Manufacturing	9.63	10.88	11.57	13.91	23.35	21.81	26.32	28.69	30.71	40.20	47.66
Services, etc.	32.56	35.96	39.93	44.66	53.75	67.41	79.62	94.81	107.43	121.09	145.24
Gross Domestic Saving	22.12	25.03	26.10	34.04	61.91	55.19	59.34	68.05	67.51	85.35	99.28
Gross National Saving	19.25	21.36	23.59	30.63	58.60	55.00	59.51	67.44	66.08	83.67	98.90
					(Billions of 1987 Venezuelan Bolivares)						
Gross National Product	484.40	487.19	504.25	537.28	558.55	585.80	632.36	669.99	685.15	690.07	662.21
GDP at Market Prices	507.01	514.46	521.03	558.05	569.85	586.15	631.41	670.93	686.83	692.25	661.26
Resource Balance	..	..	..	..	145.04	69.83	27.25	-30.93	-31.98	26.62	-1.64
Exports of Goods & NFServices	..	..	..	..	237.00	189.28	187.68	175.81	167.13	180.67	150.73
Imports of Goods & NFServices	..	..	..	..	91.95	119.45	160.42	206.74	199.11	154.04	152.37
Domestic Absorption	..	..	..	..	456.51	531.36	611.42	708.98	740.51	699.85	665.44
Private Consumption, etc.	..	..	..	..	250.86	286.80	319.87	351.68	389.14	405.41	405.97
General Gov't Consumption	..	..	..	..	49.41	50.91	58.66	62.04	59.88	62.79	65.03
Gross Domestic Investment	..	..	..	..	156.23	193.65	232.89	295.26	291.49	231.65	194.45
Fixed Investment	89.66	100.59	115.72	126.50	123.38	155.01	199.15	256.82	267.04	213.52	182.53
GDP at factor cost	482.95	493.31	501.97	540.54	555.13	566.89	612.96	652.31	671.70	673.65	643.51
Agriculture	25.34	25.68	25.33	26.66	28.29	30.28	29.19	31.48	32.49	33.43	34.06
Industry	261.75	258.02	252.17	270.57	259.21	240.92	254.10	264.12	273.29	280.46	265.86
Manufacturing	62.80	64.98	67.89	72.88	77.35	80.81	90.55	93.71	98.03	101.26	103.81
Services, etc.	208.44	220.63	235.14	251.73	276.54	314.21	348.41	376.84	382.01	378.29	361.71
Memo Items:											
Capacity to Import	..	..	..	..	212.80	157.17	165.16	159.83	128.68	162.29	201.09
Terms of Trade Adjustment	..	..	..	..	-24.20	-32.11	-22.51	-15.99	-38.46	-18.38	50.36
Gross Domestic Income	..	..	..	..	545.65	554.04	608.90	654.94	648.38	673.87	711.62
Gross National Income	..	..	..	..	534.35	553.69	609.85	654.01	646.69	671.70	712.57
DOMESTIC PRICES/DEFLATORS					*(Index 1987 = 100)*						
Overall (GDP)	11.8	12.9	13.9	15.5	22.6	23.7	25.5	28.0	30.0	35.7	45.0
Domestic Absorption	..	..	..	..	22.0	24.4	26.1	28.3	31.0	34.9	41.6
Agriculture	14.7	15.0	15.4	17.2	20.0	23.0	25.5	29.5	31.2	35.7	42.4
Industry	9.0	10.3	11.3	13.8	26.7	26.9	29.0	31.7	32.4	40.8	52.0
Manufacturing	15.3	16.7	17.0	19.1	30.2	27.0	29.1	30.6	31.3	39.7	45.9
Consumer Price Index	18.5	19.1	19.6	20.4	22.1	24.4	26.2	28.3	30.3	34.1	41.4
MANUFACTURING ACTIVITY											
Employment (1987=100)	46.6	48.4	51.7	55.4	63.4	70.0	83.5	89.1	92.1	100.2	101.4
Real Earnings per Empl. (1987=100)	77.1	77.0	77.4	87.2	93.6	97.8	97.7	101.5	109.2	111.8	97.7
Real Output per Empl. (1987=100)	89.7	87.0	82.0	77.8	71.9	79.8	80.6	80.7	83.7	77.5	75.9
Earnings as % of Value Added	30.6	30.0	31.7	35.0	28.7	27.3	25.3	27.1	30.5	28.5	26.7
MONETARY HOLDINGS					*(Billions of current Venezuelan Bolivares)*						
Money Supply, Broadly Defined	15.14	18.68	23.09	29.56	39.32	57.14	71.33	90.28	105.16	116.99	139.33
Money	7.07	8.19	9.65	11.48	16.94	25.60	29.00	37.41	44.05	46.55	54.54
Currency Outside Banks	2.16	2.34	2.58	2.87	3.81	4.72	5.82	7.38	9.01	10.01	12.34
Demand Deposits	4.91	5.85	7.07	8.62	13.13	20.88	23.18	30.03	35.04	36.53	42.20
Quasi-Money	8.07	10.49	13.43	18.07	22.38	31.53	42.32	52.87	61.11	70.44	84.79
					(Millions of current Venezuelan Bolivares)						
GOVERNMENT DEFICIT (-) OR SURPLUS	-697	233	-165	1,159	4,981	1,916	-3,987	-6,742	-6,892	3,967	113
Current Revenue	10,360	12,487	13,238	17,007	45,071	42,463	39,985	42,963	42,905	51,113	66,805
Current Expenditure	7,660	8,649	9,634	10,493	15,631	19,705	20,394	24,781	27,998	33,582	44,453
Current Budget Balance	2,700	3,838	3,604	6,514	29,440	22,758	19,591	18,182	14,907	17,531	22,352
Capital Receipts	1	2	290	65	2	18	..	30	..	..	1
Capital Payments	3,398	3,607	4,059	5,420	24,461	20,860	23,578	24,954	21,799	13,564	22,240

1981	1982	1983	1984	1985	1986	1987	1988	1989	1990 estimate	Notes	VENEZUELA
4,730	4,920	4,790	4,250	3,830	3,580	3,180	3,120	2,470	2,560	..	**CURRENT GNP PER CAPITA (US $)**
15,488	15,943	16,394	16,850	17,317	17,791	18,272	18,757	19,246	19,738	..	**POPULATION (thousands)**
											USE AND ORIGIN OF RESOURCES
			(Billions of current Venezuelan Bolivares)								
337.40	333.68	340.00	405.88	448.71	477.29	676.50	848.44	1,447.94	2,201.22	..	Gross National Product (GNP)
2.47	-6.57	-9.08	-14.19	-16.03	-11.88	-19.92	-24.85	-62.42	-62.82		Net Factor Income from Abroad
334.93	340.24	349.08	420.07	464.74	489.17	696.42	873.28	1,510.36	2,264.04		GDP at Market Prices
16.46	-8.92	29.02	46.91	42.89	-5.06	3.84	-60.54	196.88	453.86		Resource Balance
89.89	75.37	68.08	115.95	116.15	96.05	154.15	178.97	515.39	891.49		Exports of Goods & NFServices
73.42	84.29	39.07	69.03	73.26	101.11	150.31	239.51	318.50	437.63		Imports of Goods & NFServices
318.47	349.16	320.06	373.16	421.85	494.23	692.58	933.82	1,313.48	1,810.18		Domestic Absorption
194.04	212.37	236.03	256.33	287.32	337.11	450.35	597.74	977.28	1,406.03	..	Private Consumption, etc.
42.64	42.59	41.34	43.31	48.55	54.71	71.12	91.94	144.37	194.00	..	General Gov't Consumption
81.79	94.19	42.70	73.52	85.98	102.42	171.12	244.14	191.83	210.15	..	Gross Domestic Investment
80.77	81.21	64.06	67.29	80.55	99.82	147.91	199.33	255.04	320.56	..	Fixed Investment
8.42	9.78	20.39	24.92	30.35	17.78	41.63	26.12	48.57	29.32	..	Indirect Taxes, net
326.52	330.47	328.69	395.15	434.39	471.39	654.79	847.16	1,461.79	2,234.72	B	GDP at factor cost
16.41	17.68	19.54	21.50	26.93	32.45	42.57	57.88	92.04	125.28	..	Agriculture
148.69	141.35	134.96	189.21	199.63	198.26	282.05	350.32	679.16	1,129.64	..	Industry
49.85	54.13	57.03	89.93	101.80	113.81	143.31	179.41	314.34	457.21	..	Manufacturing
169.83	181.22	194.58	209.36	238.18	258.46	371.80	465.08	739.16	1,009.13	..	Services, etc.
98.25	85.28	71.72	120.43	128.87	97.35	174.96	183.60	388.71	664.01	..	Gross Domestic Saving
99.07	76.07	61.83	105.23	111.74	84.65	153.98	156.97	320.36	590.17	..	Gross National Saving
			(Billions of 1987 Venezuelan Bolivares)								
661.79	631.55	604.05	606.86	607.92	656.25	676.50	716.71	645.15	687.68	..	Gross National Product
659.12	645.42	621.20	630.03	631.24	672.34	696.42	736.96	673.81	709.45	H	GDP at Market Prices
-27.55	-69.04	31.81	0.68	0.01	17.78	3.84	-24.70	44.17	72.25	..	Resource Balance
142.30	129.25	125.36	145.17	139.16	156.20	154.15	160.26	169.12	190.74	..	Exports of Goods & NFServices
169.85	198.30	93.54	144.49	139.15	138.42	150.31	184.97	124.95	118.49	..	Imports of Goods & NFServices
678.42	689.56	601.67	623.45	629.24	651.83	692.58	758.67	618.34	622.54	..	Domestic Absorption
415.61	414.53	433.46	419.57	420.60	433.06	450.35	482.56	447.69	454.76	..	Private Consumption, etc.
68.61	67.95	66.09	66.27	65.28	68.79	71.12	78.91	77.12	82.41	..	General Gov't Consumption
194.20	207.08	102.13	137.61	143.36	149.97	171.12	197.20	93.53	85.38	..	Gross Domestic Investment
188.01	180.99	133.32	126.87	135.17	147.14	147.91	161.03	119.97	116.58	..	Fixed Investment
642.56	626.87	584.92	592.65	590.02	647.90	654.79	714.92	653.97	682.44	B H	GDP at factor cost
33.43	34.62	34.76	35.04	37.89	40.95	42.57	44.55	42.27	42.14	..	Agriculture
260.50	250.44	237.17	255.19	252.57	271.68	282.05	300.14	271.44	295.92	..	Industry
101.24	105.35	103.55	124.35	130.54	139.86	143.31	153.15	135.03	140.56	..	Manufacturing
366.48	362.57	352.18	339.78	341.41	359.84	371.80	391.93	360.40	369.65	..	Services, etc.
											Memo Items:
											Capacity to Import
207.94	177.32	163.02	242.67	220.61	131.49	154.15	138.21	202.19	241.37	..	Terms of Trade Adjustment
65.64	48.07	37.66	97.51	81.45	-24.71	0.00	-22.05	33.07	50.64	..	Gross Domestic Income
724.76	693.48	658.86	727.53	712.70	647.63	696.42	714.91	706.87	760.09	..	Gross National Income
727.43	679.62	641.72	704.37	689.37	631.53	676.50	694.66	678.22	738.32		
			(Index 1987 = 100)								**DOMESTIC PRICES/DEFLATORS**
50.8	52.7	56.2	66.7	73.6	72.8	100.0	118.5	224.2	319.1	..	Overall (GDP)
46.9	50.6	53.2	59.9	67.0	75.8	100.0	123.1	212.4	290.8	..	Domestic Absorption
49.1	51.1	56.2	61.4	71.1	79.3	100.0	129.9	217.8	297.3	..	Agriculture
57.1	56.4	56.9	74.1	79.0	73.0	100.0	116.7	250.2	381.7	..	Industry
49.2	51.4	55.1	72.3	78.0	81.4	100.0	117.2	232.8	325.3	..	Manufacturing
48.1	52.7	56.0	62.8	70.0	78.1	100.0	129.5	238.5	336.0	..	Consumer Price Index
											MANUFACTURING ACTIVITY
91.1	92.5	90.9	89.6	90.5	93.0	100.0	105.3	..	..	G	Employment (1987=100)
118.5	116.1	116.5	107.0	107.4	103.7	100.0	95.5	..	..	G	Real Earnings per Empl. (1987=100)
86.4	88.4	87.6	83.9	90.1	92.0	100.0	105.7	..	..	G	Real Output per Empl. (1987=100)
31.8	32.2	31.6	25.8	25.5	26.8	25.4	27.8	..	..		Earnings as % of Value Added
			(Billions of current Venezuelan Bolivares)								**MONETARY HOLDINGS**
163.05	181.07	220.18	254.52	275.98	296.72	346.84	388.46	585.83	944.31	D	Money Supply, Broadly Defined
58.30	60.81	76.25	96.68	105.22	109.85	122.56	145.45	169.95	269.26		Money
13.52	13.09	14.73	15.13	16.16	18.70	24.83	31.20	40.29	56.42	..	Currency Outside Banks
44.78	47.71	61.52	81.54	89.07	91.15	97.73	114.25	129.66	212.84		Demand Deposits
104.74	120.27	143.93	157.85	170.75	186.87	224.28	243.01	415.87	675.05		Quasi-Money
			(Millions of current Venezuelan Bolivares)								
-3,898	-12,670	-4,382	13,546	23,608	-9,965	-37,213	-63,725	-17,195	..	F	**GOVERNMENT DEFICIT (-) OR SURPLUS**
97,738	84,019	77,394	104,582	126,561	108,646	138,290	174,350	317,810	..		Current Revenue
60,246	59,011	60,428	73,633	78,942	79,535	136,541	176,032	292,191	..		Current Expenditure
37,492	25,008	16,966	30,949	47,619	29,111	1,749	-1,682	25,619	..		Current Budget Balance
89	1	88	42	23	14	24	15	4	..		Capital Receipts
41,479	37,679	21,436	17,445	24,034	39,090	38,986	62,058	42,818	..		Capital Payments

VENEZUELA	1970	1971	1972	1973	1974	1975	1976	1977	1978	1979	1980
FOREIGN TRADE (CUSTOMS BASIS)					*(Millions of current US dollars)*						
Value of Exports, fob	3,197	3,110	2,953	4,762	11,248	8,991	9,443	9,627	9,270	14,267	19,293
Nonfuel Primary Products	239	218	217	263	415	389	441	352	369	569	825
Fuels	2,909	2,846	2,675	4,433	10,701	8,509	8,860	9,132	8,757	13,460	18,138
Manufactures	48	46	61	66	133	93	142	142	144	238	330
Value of Imports, cif	1,640	1,833	2,139	2,474	3,739	5,807	6,019	9,749	10,582	9,598	10,669
Nonfuel Primary Products	260	262	299	454	689	949	959	1,596	1,645	1,639	2,057
Fuels	23	17	17	19	20	40	30	65	62	110	174
Manufactures	1,357	1,555	1,823	2,001	3,031	4,818	5,029	8,087	8,875	7,849	8,438
					(Index 1987 = 100)						
Terms of Trade	27.3	32.3	32.8	37.3	118.3	107.9	115.1	116.0	102.7	127.8	186.6
Export Prices, fob	7.7	10.0	11.2	15.6	62.4	60.9	65.5	71.4	72.0	103.0	166.3
Import Prices, cif	28.2	30.9	34.1	42.0	52.7	56.4	56.9	61.5	70.1	80.6	89.1
BALANCE OF PAYMENTS					*(Millions of current US dollars)*						
Exports of Goods & Services	2,833	3,339	3,418	5,279	11,971	10,092	10,376	10,947	10,855	16,305	22,232
Merchandise, fob	2,602	3,103	3,152	4,721	11,085	8,853	9,253	9,556	9,084	14,159	19,051
Nonfactor Services	177	197	209	329	530	499	430	609	719	800	917
Factor Services	54	39	57	229	356	740	693	782	1,052	1,346	2,264
Imports of Goods & Services	2,845	3,267	3,424	4,291	6,012	7,748	9,890	13,843	16,183	15,548	17,065
Merchandise, fob	1,713	1,896	2,222	2,626	3,876	5,462	7,337	10,194	11,234	10,004	10,877
Nonfactor Services	525	594	665	748	1,143	1,646	2,068	2,955	3,935	4,195	4,253
Factor Services	607	777	537	917	993	640	485	694	1,014	1,349	1,935
Long-Term Interest	53	61	81	124	142	119	139	266	498	824	1,475
Private Current Transfers, net	-86	-79	-89	-105	-135	-143	-169	-231	-371	-388	-418
Workers' Remittances	..	..	..	..	..	..	..	..	..	..	..
Curr. A/C Bal before Off. Transf.	-98	-7	-95	883	5,824	2,201	317	-3,127	-5,699	369	4,749
Net Official Transfers	-6	-4	-6	-6	-64	-30	-63	-52	-36	-19	-21
Curr. A/C Bal after Off. Transf.	-104	-11	-101	877	5,760	2,171	254	-3,179	-5,735	350	4,728
Long-Term Capital, net	91	374	-263	-53	-810	396	1,466	2,109	3,716	1,431	2,060
Direct Investment	-23	211	-376	-84	-430	418	-889	-3	67	88	55
Long-Term Loans	215	322	406	23	-260	-242	888	1,953	2,176	3,751	1,789
Disbursements	282	432	591	285	180	230	1,201	2,602	2,655	6,038	4,761
Repayments	67	110	184	263	440	472	313	649	479	2,287	2,972
Other Long-Term Capital	-101	-159	-293	9	-120	220	1,467	159	1,473	-2,408	216
Other Capital, net	59	55	534	-213	-482	148	623	1,869	954	2,317	-3,025
Change in Reserves	-46	-418	-170	-611	-4,468	-2,715	-2,343	-799	1,065	-4,098	-3,763
Memo Item:					*(Venezuelan Bolivares per US dollar)*						
Conversion Factor (Annual Avg)	4.450	4.500	4.400	4.300	4.280	4.280	4.290	4.290	4.290	4.290	4.290
EXTERNAL DEBT (Total)	954	1,294	1,703	1,884	1,779	1,492	3,310	10,731	16,575	24,050	29,330
Long-Term Debt (by debtor)	954	1,294	1,703	1,884	1,779	1,492	3,310	5,305	8,575	12,282	13,795
Central Bank, incl. IMF credit	26	109	92	84	38	35	32	26	51	631	330
Central Government	271	238	239	207	138	138	2,063	3,685	5,803	5,618	6,640
Rest of General Government	..	..	..	..	..	..	..	..	..	..	..
Non-financial Public Enterprises	384	605	869	956	1,010	852	706	609	719	3,156	3,328
Priv. Sector, incl non-guaranteed	272	342	504	637	594	467	510	984	2,002	2,877	3,496
Short-Term Debt	0	0	0	0	0	0	0	5,426	8,000	11,768	15,535
Memo Items:					*(Millions of US dollars)*						
Int'l Reserves Excluding Gold	636.6	1,096.8	1,306.8	1,940.0	6,034.2	8,402.6	8,123.8	7,735.2	6,034.6	7,320.3	6,603.9
Gold Holdings (at market price)	409.9	487.3	724.9	1,253.8	2,085.1	1,568.0	1,506.5	1,867.2	2,574.1	5,867.5	6,755.7
SOCIAL INDICATORS											
Total Fertility Rate	5.3	5.2	5.0	4.9	4.8	4.7	4.6	4.4	4.4	4.3	4.2
Infant Mortality Rate	53.4	51.2	49.0	47.8	46.6	45.4	44.2	43.0	42.2	41.4	40.6
Life Expectancy at Birth	65.2	65.7	66.2	66.5	66.8	67.1	67.4	67.7	68.0	68.2	68.5
Urban Population, % of total	72.4	73.5	74.6	75.6	76.7	77.8	78.9	80.0	81.1	82.2	83.3
Food Prod. per capita (1987=100)	110.3	108.1	104.1	103.8	99.5	108.3	100.0	104.1	106.2	105.7	105.9
Labor Force, Agriculture (%)	26.0	24.7	23.6	22.6	21.7	20.9	19.7	18.7	17.7	16.8	16.0
Labor Force, Female (%)	20.7	21.4	21.9	22.4	22.9	23.3	23.9	24.4	24.9	25.4	25.8
Primary Schl. Enroll. Ratio	94.0	..	..	..	..	97.0	103.0	102.0	103.0	104.0	109.0
Primary Schl. Enroll. Ratio, Female	94.0	..	..	..	..	97.0	102.0	101.0	103.0	104.0	..
Secondary Schl. Enroll. Ratio	33.0	..	..	..	..	43.0	38.0	38.0	38.0	39.0	41.0

1981	1982	1983	1984	1985	1986	1987	1988	1989	1990 estimate	Notes	VENEZUELA
											FOREIGN TRADE (CUSTOMS BASIS)
			(Millions of current US dollars)								
17,518	16,308	14,477	15,743	16,023	8,613	10,506	9,553	12,668	17,220	..	Value of Exports, fob
836	480	428	525	1,615	688	643	843	1,209	1,415	..	Nonfuel Primary Products
16,265	15,490	13,815	14,661	12,813	7,240	9,154	7,909	9,927	13,954	..	Fuels
417	338	234	556	1,595	685	708	800	1,532	1,851	..	Manufactures
11,811	13,391	6,146	6,872	7,418	7,667	8,711	11,476	7,030	6,364	..	Value of Imports, cif
2,495	2,404	1,600	1,716	1,564	1,326	1,774	2,464	1,390	1,301	..	Nonfuel Primary Products
94	77	167	193	176	174	158	161	178	181	..	Fuels
9,222	10,909	4,379	4,963	5,678	6,167	6,780	8,852	5,461	4,881	..	Manufactures
			(Index 1987 = 100)								
208.4	196.2	180.1	178.2	174.3	89.7	100.0	77.4	117.8	163.7		Terms of Trade
184.2	167.0	152.8	149.1	142.9	82.2	100.0	86.3	107.9	133.2		Export Prices, fob
88.4	85.1	84.9	83.6	82.0	91.6	100.0	111.4	91.7	81.3		Import Prices, cif
											BALANCE OF PAYMENTS
			(Millions of current US dollars)								
24,519	20,122	17,341	18,860	17,189	11,253	12,883	12,705	15,610	20,988	f	Exports of Goods & Services
19,963	16,332	14,571	15,878	14,283	8,535	10,437	10,082	12,915	17,411	..	Merchandise, fob
975	1,225	1,270	885	992	957	991	970	1,113	1,278	..	Nonfactor Services
3,581	2,565	1,500	2,097	1,914	1,761	1,455	1,653	1,582	2,299	..	Factor Services
20,110	23,729	12,703	14,037	13,691	13,377	14,182	18,367	13,262	12,532	f	Imports of Goods & Services
12,123	13,584	6,409	7,246	7,501	7,866	8,870	12,080	7,283	6,543	..	Merchandise, fob
4,980	6,050	2,681	2,632	2,043	2,148	2,238	2,863	2,029	2,477	..	Nonfactor Services
3,007	4,095	3,613	4,159	4,147	3,363	3,074	3,424	3,950	3,512	..	Factor Services
1,554	2,026	2,184	1,960	1,781	2,227	2,473	2,671	2,451	2,997	..	Long-Term Interest
-383	-615	-187	-144	-147	-102	-73	-123	-171	-235	..	Private Current Transfers, net
..	..									..	Workers' Remittances
4,026	-4,222	4,451	4,679	3,351	-2,226	-1,372	-5,785	2,177	8,221		Curr. A/C Bal before Off. Transf.
-26	-24	-24	-28	-24	-19	-18	-24	-16	-23	..	Net Official Transfers
4,000	-4,246	4,427	4,651	3,327	-2,245	-1,390	-5,809	2,161	8,198	..	Curr. A/C Bal after Off. Transf.
810	3,051	284	-686	-745	-2,043	-1,732	-565	-1,546	183	f	Long-Term Capital, net
184	253	86	-3	57	-444	-16	21	77	96	..	Direct Investment
1,466	695	1,362	-455	-668	-1,537	-1,603	-685	510	1,131	..	Long-Term Loans
3,990	3,109	3,002	1,423	328	481	522	1,745	1,253	2,224	..	Disbursements
2,524	2,415	1,640	1,878	996	2,018	2,125	2,430	743	1,093	..	Repayments
-840	2,103	-1,164	-228	-134	-62	-113	99	-2,133	-1,044	..	Other Long-Term Capital
-4,831	-6,965	-4,379	-2,322	-1,289	-36	1,494	1,728	-496	-4,542	f	Other Capital, net
21	8,160	-332	-1,643	-1,293	4,324	1,628	4,646	-119	-3,839	..	Change in Reserves
											Memo Item:
			(Venezuelan Bolivares per US dollar)								
4.290	4.290	4.300	7.020	7.500	8.080	14.500	14.500	34.680	46.900		Conversion Factor (Annual Avg)
			(Millions of US dollars), outstanding at end of year								
32,116	32,153	38,297	36,881	35,334	34,340	34,680	34,865	32,491	33,305	..	**EXTERNAL DEBT (Total)**
15,141	17,450	23,787	27,481	26,383	32,763	30,595	29,591	30,201	31,305	..	Long-Term Debt (by debtor)
78	33	30	24	20	18	14	9	1,003	3,014	..	Central Bank, incl. IMF credit
8,142	9,089	11,512	15,760	15,116	23,000	22,388	22,433	21,965	22,007	..	Central Government
..	..									..	Rest of General Government
2,968	3,098	3,091	2,838	2,481	2,310	2,716	2,865	3,310	2,633	..	Non-financial Public Enterprises
3,953	5,231	9,153	8,858	8,765	7,436	5,477	4,284	3,924	3,650	..	Priv. Sector, incl non-guaranteed
16,975	14,703	14,510	9,400	8,951	1,577	4,085	5,274	2,290	2,000	..	Short-Term Debt
											Memo Items:
			(Millions of US dollars)								
8,164.4	6,578.5	7,642.8	8,901.1	10,250.8	6,437.4	5,962.7	3,091.5	4,106.4	8,320.5	..	Int'l Reserves Excluding Gold
4,555.4	5,236.1	4,372.0	3,533.1	3,747.4	4,479.7	5,547.8	4,701.5	4,595.5	4,412.1	..	Gold Holdings (at market price)
											SOCIAL INDICATORS
4.2	4.1	4.0	4.0	3.9	3.9	3.8	3.7	3.6	3.6	..	Total Fertility Rate
39.8	39.0	38.4	37.8	37.2	36.6	36.0	35.3	34.6	33.9	..	Infant Mortality Rate
68.7	69.0	69.1	69.3	69.4	69.5	69.7	69.8	70.0	70.1	..	Life Expectancy at Birth
84.1	83.5	83.0	82.4	81.8	82.3	82.7	83.2	83.6	84.1	..	Urban Population, % of total
104.1	101.7	106.2	98.1	102.7	105.2	100.0	103.9	98.5	100.2	..	Food Prod. per capita (1987=100)
..	..									..	Labor Force, Agriculture (%)
26.0	26.2	26.4	26.5	26.7	26.9	27.1	27.3	27.5	27.6	..	Labor Force, Female (%)
..	111.0	108.0	109.0	108.0	107.0	106.0	105.0	..	..	..	Primary Schl. Enroll. Ratio
..	111.0	108.0	108.0	108.0	107.0	106.0	105.0			..	Primary Schl. Enroll. Ratio, Female
..	43.0	43.0	45.0	45.0	54.0	54.0	56.0	..	..	..	Secondary Schl. Enroll. Ratio

WESTERN SAMOA	1970	1971	1972	1973	1974	1975	1976	1977	1978	1979	1980
CURRENT GNP PER CAPITA (US $)	..	..	..	..	..	..	..	..	..	..	..
POPULATION (thousands)	143	145	147	149	150	151	151	152	152	153	154

USE AND ORIGIN OF RESOURCES *(Millions of current Western Samoa Tala)*

	1970	1971	1972	1973	1974	1975	1976	1977	1978	1979	1980
Gross National Product (GNP)	..	..	..	..	..	..	..	..	..	..	..
Net Factor Income from Abroad	..	..	..	..	..	..	..	..	..	..	..
GDP at Market Prices	..	..	..	..	..	..	..	..	71.00	90.00	103.00
Resource Balance	..	..	..	..	..	..	..	..	..	-57.40	-38.70
Exports of Goods & NFServices	..	..	..	..	..	..	..	..	..	22.10	25.80
Imports of Goods & NFServices	..	..	..	..	..	..	..	..	..	79.50	64.50
Domestic Absorption	..	..	..	..	..	..	..	..	..	147.40	141.70
Private Consumption, etc.	..	..	..	..	..	..	..	..	..	88.70	89.40
General Gov't Consumption	..	..	..	..	..	..	..	..	..	16.90	18.20
Gross Domestic Investment	..	..	..	..	..	..	..	..	..	41.80	34.10
Fixed Investment	..	..	..	..	..	..	..	..	..	..	..
Indirect Taxes, net	..	..	..	..	..	..	..	..	..	12.00	13.70
GDP at factor cost	..	..	..	..	..	..	..	..	..	78.00	89.30
Agriculture	..	..	..	..	..	..	..	..	..	38.00	41.10
Industry	..	..	..	..	..	..	..	..	..	7.30	10.90
Manufacturing	..	..	..	..	..	..	..	..	..	3.40	4.90
Services, etc.	..	..	..	..	..	..	..	..	..	32.70	37.30
Gross Domestic Saving	..	..	..	..	..	..	..	..	..	-15.60	-4.60
Gross National Saving	..	..	..	..	..	..	..	..	..	..	..

(Millions of 1987 Western Samoa Tala)

	1970	1971	1972	1973	1974	1975	1976	1977	1978	1979	1980
Gross National Product	..	..	..	..	..	..	..	..	..	..	..
GDP at Market Prices	..	..	..	..	..	..	..	..	207.14	229.74	215.51
Resource Balance	..	..	..	..	..	..	..	..	..	-156.38	-111.15
Exports of Goods & NFServices	..	..	..	..	..	..	..	..	..	33.53	39.14
Imports of Goods & NFServices	..	..	..	..	..	..	..	..	..	189.91	150.30
Domestic Absorption	..	..	..	..	..	..	..	..	..	386.12	326.66
Private Consumption, etc.	..	..	..	..	..	..	..	..	..	169.98	170.95
General Gov't Consumption	..	..	..	..	..	..	..	..	..	76.35	60.95
Gross Domestic Investment	..	..	..	..	..	..	..	..	..	139.78	94.76
Fixed Investment	..	..	..	..	..	..	..	..	..	..	..
GDP at factor cost	..	..	..	..	..	..	..	..	..	..	..
Agriculture	..	..	..	..	..	..	..	..	..	..	..
Industry	..	..	..	..	..	..	..	..	..	..	..
Manufacturing	..	..	..	..	..	..	..	..	..	..	..
Services, etc.	..	..	..	..	..	..	..	..	..	..	..

Memo Items:

	1970	1971	1972	1973	1974	1975	1976	1977	1978	1979	1980
Capacity to Import	..	..	..	..	..	..	..	..	..	52.79	60.12
Terms of Trade Adjustment	..	..	..	..	..	..	..	..	..	19.26	20.97
Gross Domestic Income	..	..	..	..	..	..	..	..	..	249.00	236.48
Gross National Income	..	..	..	..	..	..	..	..	..	..	..

DOMESTIC PRICES/DEFLATORS *(Index 1987 = 100)*

	1970	1971	1972	1973	1974	1975	1976	1977	1978	1979	1980
Overall (GDP)	..	..	..	..	..	..	..	..	34.3	39.2	47.8
Domestic Absorption	..	..	..	..	..	..	..	..	..	38.2	43.4
Agriculture	..	..	..	..	..	..	..	..	..	..	..
Industry	..	..	..	..	..	..	..	..	..	..	..
Manufacturing	..	..	..	..	..	..	..	..	..	..	..
Consumer Price Index	14.4	15.1	16.2	18.1	22.6	24.6	25.8	29.6	30.2	33.6	44.6

MANUFACTURING ACTIVITY

	1970	1971	1972	1973	1974	1975	1976	1977	1978	1979	1980
Employment (1987=100)	..	..	..	..	..	..	..	..	..	..	..
Real Earnings per Empl. (1987=100)	..	..	..	..	..	..	..	..	..	..	..
Real Output per Empl. (1987=100)	..	..	..	..	..	..	..	..	..	..	..
Earnings as % of Value Added	..	..	..	..	..	..	..	..	..	..	..

MONETARY HOLDINGS *(Thousands of current Western Samoa Tala)*

	1970	1971	1972	1973	1974	1975	1976	1977	1978	1979	1980
Money Supply, Broadly Defined	3,236	4,045	4,535	5,578	6,636	7,113	8,519	10,131	11,143	15,632	20,477
Money	1,278	1,937	2,312	2,763	3,206	3,478	4,044	4,755	5,225	5,770	9,138
Currency Outside Banks	87	104	119	144	169	185	218	232	251	174	3,555
Demand Deposits	1,191	1,833	2,193	2,619	3,037	3,293	3,826	4,523	4,974	5,596	5,583
Quasi-Money	1,958	2,108	2,223	2,815	3,430	3,635	4,475	5,376	5,918	9,862	11,339

GOVERNMENT DEFICIT (-) OR SURPLUS *(Thousands of current Western Samoa Tala)*

	1970	1971	1972	1973	1974	1975	1976	1977	1978	1979	1980
Current Revenue	..	..	..	..	..	..	..	..	..	..	..
Current Expenditure	..	..	..	..	..	..	..	..	..	..	..
Current Budget Balance	..	..	..	..	..	..	..	..	..	..	..
Capital Receipts	..	..	..	..	..	..	..	..	..	..	..
Capital Payments	..	..	..	..	..	..	..	..	..	..	..

1981	1982	1983	1984	1985	1986	1987	1988	1989	1990 estimate	Notes	WESTERN SAMOA
..	..	..	..	620	630	630	670	720	730	..	**CURRENT GNP PER CAPITA (US $)**
156	157	157	157	157	157	159	161	163	165	..	**POPULATION (thousands)**

(Millions of current Western Samoa Tala)

USE AND ORIGIN OF RESOURCES

1981	1982	1983	1984	1985	1986	1987	1988	1989	1990 estimate	Notes	
..	135.50	161.30	177.20	192.40	204.60	218.70	241.20	258.90	278.30	..	Gross National Product (GNP)
	5.10	6.90	-4.00	-4.30	-2.40	1.10	1.60	4.70	12.10		Net Factor Income from Abroad
108.90	130.40	154.40	181.20	196.70	207.00	217.60	239.60	254.20	266.20	f	GDP at Market Prices
-59.90	-44.90	-46.00	-57.50	-70.10	-89.80	-110.00	-118.50	-138.10	-172.30	..	Resource Balance
17.80	21.90	41.60	50.00	55.60	35.70	39.60	55.30	56.60	50.20		Exports of Goods & NFServices
77.70	66.80	87.60	107.50	125.70	125.50	149.60	173.80	194.70	222.50		Imports of Goods & NFServices
168.80	175.30	200.40	238.70	266.80	296.80	327.60	358.10	392.30	438.50		Domestic Absorption
105.90	118.10	136.20	155.10	171.70	197.00	207.70	239.10	260.10	269.00		Private Consumption, etc.
20.60	24.30	21.90	30.10	35.00	41.10	43.20	48.30	52.60	59.70		General Gov't Consumption
42.30	32.90	42.30	53.50	60.10	58.70	76.70	70.70	79.60	109.80		Gross Domestic Investment
..	..	..	..	..	..	..	..	..	..		Fixed Investment
13.00	14.00	14.00									Indirect Taxes, net
95.90	116.40	140.40								f	GDP at factor cost
44.90	59.50	..									Agriculture
11.40	14.30	..									Industry
5.20	6.90										Manufacturing
39.60	42.60										Services, etc.
-17.60	-12.00	-3.70	-4.00	-10.00	-31.10	-33.30	-47.80	-58.50	-62.50		Gross Domestic Saving
..	15.59	34.70	29.75	38.76	30.00	45.00	27.60	32.81	41.56		Gross National Saving

(Millions of 1987 Western Samoa Tala)

1981	1982	1983	1984	1985	1986	1987	1988	1989	1990 estimate	Notes	
..	..	204.85	192.44	200.55	214.05	218.70	219.06	226.34	221.65	..	Gross National Product
196.05	194.17	195.00	197.51	205.46	216.55	217.60	217.60	222.41	212.37	f	GDP at Market Prices
-127.13	-88.52	-88.68	-99.98	-98.14	-93.08	-110.00	-111.19	-107.53	-123.88		Resource Balance
28.52	28.22	31.56	26.55	33.99	40.21	39.60	44.00	43.70	38.54	..	Exports of Goods & NFServices
155.66	116.74	120.24	126.53	132.12	133.29	149.60	155.19	151.23	162.42	..	Imports of Goods & NFServices
323.18	282.69	283.68	297.49	303.60	309.64	327.60	328.79	329.95	336.25	..	Domestic Absorption
166.15	160.96	173.55	169.08	193.07	204.80	207.70	220.34	219.37	209.39	..	Private Consumption, etc.
57.27	55.59	47.89	58.94	48.56	42.87	43.20	44.54	45.54	44.87	..	General Gov't Consumption
99.77	66.14	62.25	69.47	61.97	61.97	76.70	63.92	65.03	81.98	..	Gross Domestic Investment
..	..	..	..	..	..	..	..	..	..		Fixed Investment
..	..	..	..	..	..	..	..	..	..	f	GDP at factor cost
..	..	..	..	..	..	..	..	..	..	..	Agriculture
..	..	..	..	..	..	..	..	..	..	..	Industry
..	..	..	..	..	..	..	..	..	..	..	Manufacturing
..	..	..	..	..	..	..	..	..	..	..	Services, etc.

Memo Items:

1981	1982	1983	1984	1985	1986	1987	1988	1989	1990 estimate	Notes	
35.66	38.27	57.10	58.85	58.44	37.92	39.60	49.38	43.96	36.64	..	Capacity to Import
7.14	10.05	25.54	32.30	24.45	-2.29	0.00	5.38	0.27	-1.89	..	Terms of Trade Adjustment
203.18	204.22	220.54	229.81	229.92	214.26	217.60	222.98	222.68	210.48	..	Gross Domestic Income
..	..	230.39	224.74	225.00	211.76	218.70	224.44	226.61	219.76		Gross National Income

(Index 1987 = 100)

DOMESTIC PRICES/DEFLATORS

1981	1982	1983	1984	1985	1986	1987	1988	1989	1990 estimate	Notes	
55.5	67.2	79.2	91.7	95.7	95.6	100.0	110.1	114.3	125.3	..	Overall (GDP)
52.2	62.0	70.6	80.2	87.9	95.9	100.0	108.9	118.9	130.4	..	Domestic Absorption
..	..	..	..	..	..	..	..	..	..	..	Agriculture
..	..	..	..	..	..	..	..	..	..	..	Industry
..	..	..	..	..	..	..	..	..	..	..	Manufacturing
53.8	63.6	74.1	82.9	90.4	95.6	100.0	108.5	115.5	133.1	..	Consumer Price Index

MANUFACTURING ACTIVITY

1981	1982	1983	1984	1985	1986	1987	1988	1989	1990 estimate	Notes	
..	..	..	..	..	..	..	..	..	..	..	Employment (1987=100)
..	..	..	..	..	..	..	..	..	..	..	Real Earnings per Empl. (1987=100)
..	..	..	..	..	..	..	..	..	..	..	Real Output per Empl. (1987=100)
..	..	..	..	..	..	..	..	..	..	..	Earnings as % of Value Added

(Thousands of current Western Samoa Tala)

MONETARY HOLDINGS

1981	1982	1983	1984	1985	1986	1987	1988	1989	1990 estimate	Notes	
33,583	45,319	40,033	44,779	53,940	64,740	82,370	88,860	104,950	124,840	..	Money Supply, Broadly Defined
14,106	17,423	16,929	19,362	19,960	21,630	28,690	30,190	33,160	47,290	..	Money
5,280	6,053	6,019	7,079	8,440	9,180	10,530	10,720	12,480	12,940		Currency Outside Banks
8,826	11,370	10,910	12,283	11,520	12,450	18,160	19,470	20,680	34,350		Demand Deposits
19,477	27,896	23,104	25,417	33,980	43,110	53,680	58,670	71,790	77,550	..	Quasi-Money

(Thousands of current Western Samoa Tala)

GOVERNMENT DEFICIT (-) OR SURPLUS

1981	1982	1983	1984	1985	1986	1987	1988	1989	1990 estimate	Notes	
..	..	..	957	..	..	..	..	..	..	..	Current Revenue
..	..	..	61,510								Current Expenditure
..	..	..	36,781								Current Budget Balance
..	..	..	24,729								Capital Receipts
..	..	..	23,772	..	..	..	..	..	..	..	Capital Payments

WESTERN SAMOA	1970	1971	1972	1973	1974	1975	1976	1977	1978	1979	1980
FOREIGN TRADE (CUSTOMS BASIS)					*(Thousands of current US dollars)*						
Value of Exports, fob	..	..	..	..	..	..	..	..	..	..	..
Nonfuel Primary Products	..	..	..	..	..	..	..	..	..	..	..
Fuels	..	..	..	..	..	..	..	..	..	..	..
Manufactures	..	..	..	..	..	..	..	..	..	..	..
Value of Imports, cif	13,610	13,360	19,511	21,406	26,210	36,799	27,457	45,734	52,533	72,547	62,502
Nonfuel Primary Products	4,599	4,926	6,715	6,971	10,683	13,006	10,523	14,774	16,183	18,524	16,546
Fuels	516	553	674	941	791	3,045	2,034	3,644	4,066	6,699	10,290
Manufactures	8,495	7,882	12,122	13,494	14,737	20,747	14,900	27,316	32,285	47,324	35,666
					(Index 1987 = 100)						
Terms of Trade	..	..	..	..	..	..	..	..	..	..	..
Export Prices, fob	..	..	..	..	..	..	..	..	..	..	..
Import Prices, cif	..	..	..	..	..	..	..	..	..	..	..
BALANCE OF PAYMENTS					*(Thousands of current US dollars)*						
Exports of Goods & Services	7,218	9,435	10,610	11,953	20,056	15,222	12,143	..	..	..	25,672
Merchandise, fob	4,808	6,557	5,168	6,744	12,901	7,476	6,998	14,731	9,737	18,132	17,220
Nonfactor Services	2,343	2,780	5,127	5,130	7,055	7,693	5,033	2,417	3,911	3,631	8,430
Factor Services	67	97	315	80	101	53	113	..	..	..	22
Imports of Goods & Services	14,862	15,209	26,255	27,626	31,233	39,829	29,347	42,540	55,912	78,665	74,273
Merchandise, fob	12,179	12,101	20,979	21,353	23,654	33,212	26,809	37,337	47,655	67,154	56,858
Nonfactor Services	2,541	2,980	5,089	5,942	7,109	6,219	2,177	5,089	6,763	9,889	14,859
Factor Services	142	128	187	331	470	398	360	114	1,494	1,622	2,556
Long-Term Interest	0	0	0	200	600	500	500	1,000	1,200	1,600	2,300
Private Current Transfers, net	2,175	2,341	2,956	4,125	7,081	5,876	3,080	5,852	12,141	13,460	18,742
Workers' Remittances	2,580	2,909	4,180	6,449	9,272	8,256	5,149	5,852	12,141	13,460	18,742
Curr. A/C Bal before Off. Transf.	-5,469	-3,433	-12,689	-11,548	-4,095	-18,731	-14,123	-19,540	-30,122	-43,442	-29,859
Net Official Transfers	397	700	1,219	3,928	2,702	6,345	3,891	9,808	12,019	21,400	16,948
Curr. A/C Bal after Off. Transf.	-5,072	-2,733	-11,469	-7,620	-1,393	-12,386	-10,233	-9,732	-18,103	-22,042	-12,912
Long-Term Capital, net	2,427	2,513	6,925	5,958	5,892	12,308	9,616	10,304	11,381	8,269	5,732
Direct Investment	..	..	..	..	..	..	..	..	..	..	..
Long-Term Loans	2,300	-100	1,900	5,100	2,600	4,000	5,700	7,400	8,100	9,900	8,200
Disbursements	2,400	0	2,100	5,600	3,200	4,600	8,500	8,500	9,700	12,000	10,500
Repayments	100	100	200	500	600	600	2,800	1,100	1,600	2,100	2,300
Other Long-Term Capital	127	2,613	5,025	858	3,292	8,308	3,916	2,904	3,281	-1,631	-2,468
Other Capital, net	3,252	967	1,802	172	-3,591	-483	-1,213	3,120	734	13,709	5,869
Change in Reserves	-607	-747	2,742	1,490	-908	561	1,829	-3,692	5,988	64	1,311
Memo Item:					*(Western Samoa Tala per US dollar)*						
Conversion Factor (Annual Avg)	0.720	0.720	0.680	0.610	0.610	0.630	0.800	0.790	0.740	0.830	0.920
EXTERNAL DEBT (Total)				*(Thousands of US dollars), outstanding at end of year*							
	2,700	2,600	4,400	9,500	13,600	17,400	22,600	31,300	41,300	52,500	60,200
Long-Term Debt (by debtor)	2,700	2,600	4,400	9,500	13,600	17,400	22,600	31,300	41,300	52,500	59,200
Central Bank, incl. IMF credit	0	0	0	0	0	1,500	2,200	2,300	4,600	6,300	5,800
Central Government	2,700	2,600	2,600	4,500	8,400	11,500	14,500	19,300	27,700	36,000	41,400
Rest of General Government	..	..	..	..	..	..	..	..	..	..	..
Non-financial Public Enterprises	0	0	1,800	5,000	5,200	4,400	5,900	9,700	9,000	10,200	11,900
Priv. Sector, incl non-guaranteed	0	0	0	0	0	0	0	0	0	0	100
Short-Term Debt	0	0	0	0	0	0	0	0	0	0	1,000
Memo Items:					*(Thousands of US dollars)*						
Int'l Reserves Excluding Gold	5,220	6,411	4,529	5,078	5,958	6,387	5,240	9,126	4,782	4,820	2,770
Gold Holdings (at market price)	..	..	..	..	..	..	..	..	..	..	..
SOCIAL INDICATORS											
Total Fertility Rate	6.7	6.3	5.9	5.9	5.8	5.8	5.7	5.7	5.7	5.6	5.6
Infant Mortality Rate	..	..	..	..	..	..	..	..	..	..	..
Life Expectancy at Birth	..	..	..	..	..	..	..	62.6	62.9	63.2	63.5
Urban Population, % of total	20.3	20.4	20.6	20.7	20.9	21.0	21.1	21.2	21.2	21.3	21.4
Food Prod. per capita (1987=100)	83.9	100.9	97.3	100.6	93.0	96.0	101.9	99.4	97.4	115.7	95.8
Labor Force, Agriculture (%)	..	..	..	..	..	..	..	..	..	..	..
Labor Force, Female (%)	..	..	..	..	..	..	..	..	..	..	..
Primary Schl. Enroll. Ratio	..	..	..	..	..	..	..	..	..	..	..
Primary Schl. Enroll. Ratio, Female	..	..	..	..	..	..	..	..	..	..	..
Secondary Schl. Enroll. Ratio	..	..	..	..	..	..	..	..	..	..	..

1981	1982	1983	1984	1985	1986	1987	1988	1989	1990 estimate	Notes	WESTERN SAMOA
											FOREIGN TRADE (CUSTOMS BASIS)
				(Thousands of current US dollars)							
..	..	..	..	..	..	..	..	..	..	..	Value of Exports, fob
..	..	..	..	..	..	..	..	..	..	..	Nonfuel Primary Products
..	..	..	..	..	..	..	..	..	..	..	Fuels
..	..	..	..	..	..	..	..	..	..	..	Manufactures
68,331	41,867	52,566	50,756	51,289	47,145	61,784	75,659	76,975	85,147	..	Value of Imports, cif
15,219	14,164	13,190	12,736	12,870	11,830	15,503	18,985	19,315	21,366	..	Nonfuel Primary Products
12,144	5,790	9,187	8,870	8,963	8,239	10,798	13,222	13,452	14,881	..	Fuels
40,969	21,913	30,189	29,150	29,456	27,076	35,483	43,452	44,208	48,901	..	Manufactures
				(Index 1987 = 100)							
..	..	..	..	..	..	..	..	..	..		Terms of Trade
..	..	..	..	..	..	..	..	..	..		Export Prices, fob
..	..	..	..	..	..	..	..	..	..		Import Prices, cif
											BALANCE OF PAYMENTS
				(Thousands of current US dollars)							
18,383	21,784	26,964	27,214	27,137	25,101	30,951	43,529	45,203	44,635	..	Exports of Goods & Services
10,783	13,459	17,694	18,343	16,123	10,507	11,769	15,093	12,867	8,855	..	Merchandise, fob
7,475	8,241	9,134	8,532	10,333	13,338	16,430	25,548	27,861	29,099	..	Nonfactor Services
126	83	136	338	681	1,257	2,752	2,889	4,475	6,682	..	Factor Services
65,749	60,157	59,395	60,060	60,264	57,555	72,949	87,164	88,750	96,255	..	Imports of Goods & Services
51,379	45,315	44,115	45,551	46,600	42,844	55,789	68,490	68,496	73,156	..	Merchandise, fob
11,585	12,606	12,446	12,184	11,086	12,376	14,936	16,549	17,862	21,570	..	Nonfactor Services
2,785	2,236	2,834	2,325	2,579	2,335	2,225	2,125	2,392	1,529	..	Factor Services
1,700	1,100	1,100	1,400	1,700	1,400	1,300	1,300	1,100	1,200	..	Long-Term Interest
18,558	18,628	20,334	20,271	23,632	28,402	36,385	35,473	38,151	39,720	..	Private Current Transfers, net
18,558	18,628	20,334	20,271	23,828	28,621	36,635	37,708	40,873	42,765	..	Workers' Remittances
-28,808	-19,746	-12,097	-12,576	-9,496	-4,052	-5,613	-8,162	-5,396	-11,900	..	Curr. A/C Bal before Off. Transf.
15,714	13,708	16,900	13,231	11,424	15,212	16,812	16,823	16,668	14,016	..	Net Official Transfers
-13,094	-6,038	4,803	655	1,929	11,160	11,198	8,662	11,272	2,116	..	Curr. A/C Bal after Off. Transf.
4,535	-522	3,208	4,451	-477	-631	2,710	596	929	9,273	..	Long-Term Capital, net
..	..	..	..	..	..	..	..	..	..	..	Direct Investment
3,700	5,300	2,000	7,300	-1,100	-1,200	3,300	1,300	1,700	12,900	..	Long-Term Loans
5,400	7,000	4,700	10,200	2,500	2,800	6,000	4,200	5,000	16,300	..	Disbursements
1,700	1,700	2,700	2,900	3,600	4,000	2,700	2,900	3,300	3,400	..	Repayments
835	-5,822	1,208	-2,849	623	569	-590	-704	-771	-3,627	..	Other Long-Term Capital
6,888	7,984	-5,258	-1,882	2,376	341	-1,893	2,682	288	4,329	..	Other Capital, net
1,671	-1,424	-2,753	-3,225	-3,828	-10,870	-12,016	-11,940	-12,490	-15,719	..	Change in Reserves
											Memo Item:
				(Western Samoa Tala per US dollar)							
1.030	1.210	1.550	1.860	2.250	2.240	2.120	2.080	2.270	2.320	..	Conversion Factor (Annual Avg)
											EXTERNAL DEBT (Total)
			(Thousands of US dollars), outstanding at end of year								
63,300	68,800	73,600	74,800	75,700	75,800	80,600	75,800	73,500	92,600	..	
62,300	64,800	66,600	72,800	74,700	74,800	79,600	74,800	73,400	92,500	..	Long-Term Debt (by debtor)
7,500	6,300	7,900	9,800	10,900	10,100	8,200	3,800	1,600	800	..	Central Bank, incl. IMF credit
44,400	49,300	51,000	57,200	58,600	59,800	66,000	66,400	67,400	87,000	..	Central Government
..	..	..	..	..	..	..	..	..	..	..	Rest of General Government
9,800	8,300	7,000	5,200	4,400	3,900	4,200	3,600	3,400	3,500	..	Non-financial Public Enterprises
600	900	700	600	800	1,000	1,200	1,000	1,000	1,200	..	Priv. Sector, incl non-guaranteed
1,000	4,000	7,000	2,000	1,000	1,000	1,000	1,000	100	100	..	Short-Term Debt
											Memo Items:
				(Thousands of US dollars)							
3,282	3,481	7,229	10,557	14,021	23,746	37,198	49,197	55,066	69,045	..	Int'l Reserves Excluding Gold
..	..	..	..	..	..	..	..	..	..	..	Gold Holdings (at market price)
											SOCIAL INDICATORS
5.5	5.5	5.4	5.2	5.1	5.0	4.8	4.7	4.7	4.6	..	Total Fertility Rate
						50.0	48.8	47.6	46.3	..	Infant Mortality Rate
63.7	64.0	64.3	64.6	64.9	65.2	65.4	65.7	65.9	66.1	..	Life Expectancy at Birth
21.5	21.6	21.6	21.7	21.8	22.0	22.2	22.5	22.7	22.9	..	Urban Population, % of total
88.0	100.7	93.2	88.0	100.2	103.6	100.0	96.0	94.0	96.8	..	Food Prod. per capita (1987=100)
..	..	..	..	..	..	..	..	..	..	..	Labor Force, Agriculture (%)
..	..	..	..	..	..	..	..	..	..	..	Labor Force, Female (%)
..	..	..	..	..	..	..	..	..	..	..	Primary Schl. Enroll. Ratio
..	..	..	..	..	..	..	..	..	..	..	Primary Schl. Enroll. Ratio, Female
..	..	..	..	..	..	..	..	..	..	..	Secondary Schl. Enroll. Ratio

YEMEN, REPUBLIC OF	1970	1971	1972	1973	1974	1975	1976	1977	1978	1979	1980
CURRENT GNP PER CAPITA (US $)	..	..	..	..	..	..	..	..	..	..	..
POPULATION (thousands)	6,332	6,435	6,542	6,661	6,808	6,991	7,209	7,465	7,747	8,033	8,311

USE AND ORIGIN OF RESOURCES *(Millions of current Yemeni Rials)*

	1970	1971	1972	1973	1974	1975	1976	1977	1978	1979	1980
Gross National Product (GNP)	..	..	..	..	..	..	..	..	..	..	..
Net Factor Income from Abroad	..	..	..	..	..	..	..	..	..	..	..
GDP at Market Prices	..	..	..	..	..	..	..	..	..	..	..
Resource Balance	..	..	..	..	..	..	..	..	..	..	..
Exports of Goods & NFServices	..	..	..	..	..	..	..	..	..	..	..
Imports of Goods & NFServices	..	..	..	..	..	..	..	..	..	..	..
Domestic Absorption	..	..	..	..	..	..	..	..	..	..	..
Private Consumption, etc.	..	..	..	..	..	..	..	..	..	..	..
General Gov't Consumption	..	..	..	..	..	..	..	..	..	..	..
Gross Domestic Investment	..	..	..	..	..	..	..	..	..	..	..
Fixed Investment	..	..	..	..	..	..	..	..	..	..	..
Indirect Taxes, net	..	..	..	..	..	..	..	..	..	..	..
GDP at factor cost	..	..	..	..	..	..	..	..	..	..	..
Agriculture	..	..	..	..	..	..	..	..	..	..	..
Industry	..	..	..	..	..	..	..	..	..	..	..
Manufacturing	..	..	..	..	..	..	..	..	..	..	..
Services, etc.	..	..	..	..	..	..	..	..	..	..	..
Gross Domestic Saving	..	..	..	..	..	..	..	..	..	..	..
Gross National Saving	..	..	..	..	..	..	..	..	..	..	..

(Millions of 1987 Yemeni Rials)

	1970	1971	1972	1973	1974	1975	1976	1977	1978	1979	1980
Gross National Product	..	..	..	..	..	..	..	..	..	..	..
GDP at Market Prices	..	..	..	..	..	..	..	..	..	..	..
Resource Balance	..	..	..	..	..	..	..	..	..	..	..
Exports of Goods & NFServices	..	..	..	..	..	..	..	..	..	..	..
Imports of Goods & NFServices	..	..	..	..	..	..	..	..	..	..	..
Domestic Absorption	..	..	..	..	..	..	..	..	..	..	..
Private Consumption, etc.	..	..	..	..	..	..	..	..	..	..	..
General Gov't Consumption	..	..	..	..	..	..	..	..	..	..	..
Gross Domestic Investment	..	..	..	..	..	..	..	..	..	..	..
Fixed Investment	..	..	..	..	..	..	..	..	..	..	..
GDP at factor cost	..	..	..	..	..	..	..	..	..	..	..
Agriculture	..	..	..	..	..	..	..	..	..	..	..
Industry	..	..	..	..	..	..	..	..	..	..	..
Manufacturing	..	..	..	..	..	..	..	..	..	..	..
Services, etc.	..	..	..	..	..	..	..	..	..	..	..

Memo Items:

	1970	1971	1972	1973	1974	1975	1976	1977	1978	1979	1980
Capacity to Import	..	..	..	..	..	..	..	..	..	..	..
Terms of Trade Adjustment	..	..	..	..	..	..	..	..	..	..	..
Gross Domestic Income	..	..	..	..	..	..	..	..	..	..	..
Gross National Income	..	..	..	..	..	..	..	..	..	..	..

DOMESTIC PRICES/DEFLATORS *(Index 1987 = 100)*

	1970	1971	1972	1973	1974	1975	1976	1977	1978	1979	1980
Overall (GDP)	..	..	..	..	..	..	..	..	..	..	..
Domestic Absorption	..	..	..	..	..	..	..	..	..	..	..
Agriculture	..	..	..	..	..	..	..	..	..	..	..
Industry	..	..	..	..	..	..	..	..	..	..	..
Manufacturing	..	..	..	..	..	..	..	..	..	..	..
Consumer Price Index	..	..	..	..	..	..	..	..	..	..	..

MANUFACTURING ACTIVITY

	1970	1971	1972	1973	1974	1975	1976	1977	1978	1979	1980
Employment (1987=100)	..	..	..	..	..	..	..	..	..	..	..
Real Earnings per Empl. (1987=100)	..	..	..	..	..	..	..	..	..	..	..
Real Output per Empl. (1987=100)	..	..	..	..	..	..	..	..	..	..	..
Earnings as % of Value Added	..	..	..	..	..	..	..	..	..	..	25.7

MONETARY HOLDINGS *(Millions of current Yemeni Rials)*

	1970	1971	1972	1973	1974	1975	1976	1977	1978	1979	1980
Money Supply, Broadly Defined	..	..	..	643	861	1,547	3,478	5,263	6,957	8,298	9,180
Money	..	..	..	541	712	1,290	2,787	4,479	5,716	7,037	7,569
Currency Outside Banks	..	..	..	466	621	1,080	2,329	3,819	4,963	6,299	6,895
Demand Deposits	..	..	..	75	92	210	458	660	753	738	674
Quasi-Money	..	..	..	102	149	257	691	784	1,241	1,261	1,611

GOVERNMENT DEFICIT (-) OR SURPLUS *(Millions of current Yemeni Rials)*

	1970	1971	1972	1973	1974	1975	1976	1977	1978	1979	1980
Current Revenue	..	..	..	..	..	..	..	..	..	..	..
Current Expenditure	..	..	..	..	..	..	..	..	..	..	..
Current Budget Balance	..	..	..	..	..	..	..	..	..	..	..
Capital Receipts	..	..	..	..	..	..	..	..	..	..	..
Capital Payments	..	..	..	..	..	..	..	..	..	..	..

1981	1982	1983	1984	1985	1986	1987	1988	1989	1990 estimate	Notes	YEMEN, REPUBLIC OF
..	..	..	..	..	..	..	..	..	..		**CURRENT GNP PER CAPITA (US $)**
8,584	8,851	9,116	9,387	9,670	9,963	10,269	10,589	10,926	11,282	..	**POPULATION (thousands)**
				(Millions of current Yemeni Rials)							**USE AND ORIGIN OF RESOURCES**
..	..	..	..	49,386	54,485	63,465	66,715	60,727	75,113	C	Gross National Product (GNP)
..	..	..	..	9,481	8,049	9,893	4,635	-4,322	-6,667	..	Net Factor Income from Abroad
..	..	..	..	39,905	46,436	53,572	62,080	65,049	81,780	C	GDP at Market Prices
..	..	..	..	-14,632	-12,849	-17,650	-16,361	-8,640	-6,403		Resource Balance
..	..	..	..	2,526	2,263	3,429	8,053	16,441	18,763	..	Exports of Goods & NF Services
..	..	..	..	17,158	15,112	21,079	24,414	25,081	25,166	..	Imports of Goods & NF Services
..	..	..	..	54,537	59,285	71,222	78,441	73,689	88,183	..	Domestic Absorption
..	..	..	..	37,413	42,282	50,008	51,306	45,729	54,359		Private Consumption, etc.
..	..	..	..	9,209	9,554	12,039	15,382	16,470	21,154		General Gov't Consumption
..	..	..	..	7,915	7,449	9,175	11,753	11,490	12,670		Gross Domestic Investment
..	..	..	..	7,972	7,623	9,030	11,342	11,356	11,970		Fixed Investment
..	..	..	..	4,516	5,217	4,649	5,552	5,000	3,996		Indirect Taxes, net
..	..	..	..	35,389	41,219	48,923	56,528	60,049	77,784	B C	GDP at factor cost
..	..	..	..	9,161	12,337	13,235	13,882	14,682	16,101	..	Agriculture
..	..	..	..	7,553	8,296	10,228	13,799	17,445	23,031	..	Industry
..	..	..	..	4,352	5,034	6,440	7,239	5,861	6,586	..	Manufacturing
..	..	..	..	18,675	20,586	25,460	28,847	27,922	38,652	..	Services, etc.
..	..	..	..	-6,717	-5,400	-8,475	-4,608	2,850	6,267		Gross Domestic Saving
..	..	..	..			..		2,156	..	..	Gross National Saving
				(Millions of 1987 Yemeni Rials)							
..	..	..	..	..	..	..	..	..	..	..	Gross National Product
..	..	..	..	..	..	..	..	..	..	..	GDP at Market Prices
..	..	..	..	..	..	..	..	..	..	..	Resource Balance
..	..	..	..	..	..	..	..	..	..	..	Exports of Goods & NF Services
..	..	..	..	..	..	..	..	..	..	..	Imports of Goods & NF Services
..	..	..	..	..	..	..	..	..	..	..	Domestic Absorption
..	..	..	..	..	..	..	..	..	..	..	Private Consumption, etc.
..	..	..	..	..	..	..	..	..	..	..	General Gov't Consumption
..	..	..	..	..	..	..	..	..	..	..	Gross Domestic Investment
..	..	..	..	..	..	..	..	..	..	..	Fixed Investment
..	..	..	..	..	..	..	..	..	..	..	GDP at factor cost
..	..	..	..	..	..	..	..	..	..	..	Agriculture
..	..	..	..	..	..	..	..	..	..	..	Industry
..	..	..	..	..	..	..	..	..	..	..	Manufacturing
..	..	..	..	..	..	..	..	..	..	..	Services, etc.
											Memo Items:
..	..	..	..	..	..	..	..	..	..	..	Capacity to Import
..	..	..	..	..	..	..	..	..	..	..	Terms of Trade Adjustment
..	..	..	..	..	..	..	..	..	..	..	Gross Domestic Income
..	..	..	..	..	..	..	..	..	..	..	Gross National Income
				(Index 1987 = 100)							**DOMESTIC PRICES/DEFLATORS**
..	..	..	..	..	..	..	..	..	..	..	Overall (GDP)
..	..	..	..	..	..	..	..	..	..	..	Domestic Absorption
..	..	..	..	..	..	..	..	..	..	..	Agriculture
..	..	..	..	..	..	..	..	..	..	..	Industry
..	..	..	..	..	..	..	..	..	..	..	Manufacturing
..	..	..	..	..	..	..	..	..	..	..	Consumer Price Index
											MANUFACTURING ACTIVITY
..	..	..	..	..	..	..	..	..	..	..	Employment (1987=100)
..	..	..	..	..	..	..	..	..	..	..	Real Earnings per Empl. (1987=100)
..	..	..	..	..	..	..	..	..	..	..	Real Output per Empl. (1987=100)
..	..	..	24.5	..	..	..	..	..	..	..	Earnings as % of Value Added
				(Millions of current Yemeni Rials)							**MONETARY HOLDINGS**
10,301	12,915	15,967	20,365	24,430	30,651	33,743	35,832	37,450	..	..	Money Supply, Broadly Defined
8,331	10,668	13,148	16,395	18,823	23,682	26,641	27,342	29,086			Money
7,439	9,336	10,733	13,314	15,633	19,062	20,159	20,166	21,206			Currency Outside Banks
892	1,332	2,414	3,081	3,189	4,621	6,483	7,177	7,880			Demand Deposits
1,970	2,246	2,820	3,970	5,608	6,969	7,102	8,490	8,363			Quasi-Money
				(Millions of current Yemeni Rials)							**GOVERNMENT DEFICIT (-) OR SURPLUS**
..	..	..	..	..	..	..	..	..	..	..	Current Revenue
..	..	..	..	..	..	..	..	..	..	..	Current Expenditure
..	..	..	..	..	..	..	..	..	..	..	Current Budget Balance
..	..	..	..	..	..	..	..	..	..	..	Capital Receipts
..	..	..	..	..	..	..	..	..	..	..	Capital Payments

	1970	1971	1972	1973	1974	1975	1976	1977	1978	1979	1980
FOREIGN TRADE (CUSTOMS BASIS)				*(Millions of current US dollars)*							
Value of Exports, fob	..	..	..	..	..	..	..	..	..	..	..
Nonfuel Primary Products	..	..	..	..	..	..	..	..	..	..	..
Fuels	..	..	..	..	..	..	..	..	..	..	..
Manufactures	..	..	..	..	..	..	..	..	..	..	..
Value of Imports, cif	..	..	..	..	..	..	..	..	..	..	..
Nonfuel Primary Products	..	..	..	..	..	..	..	..	..	..	..
Fuels	..	..	..	..	..	..	..	..	..	..	..
Manufactures	..	..	..	..	..	..	..	..	..	..	..
				(Index 1987 = 100)							
Terms of Trade	..	..	..	..	..	..	..	..	..	..	..
Export Prices, fob	..	..	..	..	..	..	..	..	..	..	..
Import Prices, cif	..	..	..	..	..	..	..	..	..	..	..
BALANCE OF PAYMENTS				*(Millions of current US dollars)*							
Exports of Goods & Services	..	..	..	..	..	..	..	..	..	..	..
Merchandise, fob	..	..	..	..	..	..	..	..	..	..	..
Nonfactor Services	..	..	..	..	..	..	..	..	..	..	..
Factor Services	..	..	..	..	..	..	..	..	..	..	..
Imports of Goods & Services	..	..	..	..	..	..	..	..	..	..	..
Merchandise, fob	..	..	..	..	..	..	..	..	..	..	..
Nonfactor Services	..	..	..	..	..	..	..	..	..	..	..
Factor Services	..	..	..	..	..	..	..	..	..	..	..
Long-Term Interest	0.1	0.1	0.1	0.8	0.9	0.8	1.1	2.0	4.8	6.9	10.2
Private Current Transfers, net	..	..	..	..	..	..	..	..	..	..	..
Workers' Remittances	..	..	..	..	..	..	..	..	..	..	..
Curr. A/C Bal before Off. Transf.	..	..	..	..	..	..	..	..	..	..	..
Net Official Transfers	..	..	..	..	..	..	..	..	..	..	..
Curr. A/C Bal after Off. Transf.	..	..	..	..	..	..	..	..	..	..	..
Long-Term Capital, net	..	..	..	..	..	..	..	..	..	..	..
Direct Investment	..	..	..	..	..	..	..	..	..	..	..
Long-Term Loans	6.1	9.1	43.5	50.1	72.1	54.5	97.2	92.5	148.6	279.6	541.5
Disbursements	6.3	9.3	43.7	54.2	75.4	58.1	110.4	101.3	156.7	291.4	566.1
Repayments	0.2	0.2	0.2	4.1	3.3	3.6	13.2	8.8	8.1	11.8	24.6
Other Long-Term Capital	..	..	..	..	..	..	..	..	..	..	..
Other Capital, net	..	..	..	..	..	..	..	..	..	..	..
Change in Reserves	..	..	..	..	..	..	..	..	..	..	..
Memo Item:				*(Yemeni Rials per US dollar)*							
Conversion Factor (Annual Avg)	5.460	5.470	4.690	4.610	4.560	4.560	4.560	4.560	4.560	4.560	4.560
				(Millions of US dollars), outstanding at end of year							
EXTERNAL DEBT (Total)	31.1	41.8	85.2	222.1	323.4	379.3	461.4	723.3	925.8	1,173.6	1,684.3
Long-Term Debt (by debtor)	31.1	41.8	85.2	222.1	323.4	379.3	461.4	591.2	793.8	997.6	1,501.8
Central Bank, incl. IMF credit	0.0	0.0	0.0	0.0	11.4	27.7	42.7	48.3	57.1	51.4	48.4
Central Government	31.1	41.8	85.2	222.1	312.0	351.6	418.7	542.9	736.7	946.2	1,443.2
Rest of General Government	..	..	..	..	..	..	..	..	..	..	..
Non-financial Public Enterprises	0.0	0.0	0.0	0.0	0.0	0.0	0.0	0.0	0.0	0.0	10.2
Priv. Sector, incl non-guaranteed	..	..	..	..	..	..	..	..	..	..	..
Short-Term Debt	0.0	0.0	0.0	0.0	0.0	0.0	0.0	132.1	132.0	176.0	182.5
Memo Items:				*(Millions of US dollars)*							
Int'l Reserves Excluding Gold	..	..	..	126.9	198.6	337.5	720.0	1,240.2	1,459.4	1,427.4	1,282.6
Gold Holdings (at market price)	..	..	..	0.0	0.0	0.0	0.0	0.7	1.5	3.4	0.5
SOCIAL INDICATORS											
Total Fertility Rate	7.0	7.0	7.0	7.0	7.0	7.1	7.1	7.1	7.2	7.2	7.3
Infant Mortality Rate	175.2	171.6	168.0	165.3	162.6	160.0	157.3	154.6	152.1	149.6	147.0
Life Expectancy at Birth	42.4	42.9	43.4	43.7	43.9	44.2	44.5	44.8	45.1	45.3	45.6
Urban Population, % of total	13.3	13.9	14.6	15.2	15.9	16.5	17.2	17.9	18.7	19.4	20.1
Food Prod. per capita (1987=100)	..	..	..	..	..	..	..	..	..	..	..
Labor Force, Agriculture (%)	70.4	69.5	68.7	67.8	67.0	66.1	65.2	64.3	63.5	62.7	61.9
Labor Force, Female (%)	7.7	8.2	8.7	9.1	9.6	10.0	10.4	10.8	11.1	11.5	11.8
Primary Schl. Enroll. Ratio	22.0	27.0	30.0	33.0	38.0	41.0	38.0	..	..	..	..
Primary Schl. Enroll. Ratio, Female	7.0	9.0	10.0	13.0	15.0	17.0	18.0	..	..	..	..
Secondary Schl. Enroll. Ratio	3.0	4.0	5.0	5.0	8.0	8.0	10.0	..	..	..	..

1981	1982	1983	1984	1985	1986	1987	1988	1989	1990 est.	Notes	YEMEN, REPUBLIC OF
			(Millions of current US dollars)								**FOREIGN TRADE (CUSTOMS BASIS)**
..	..	..	..	..	..	..	..	..	..	..	Value of Exports, fob
..	..	..	..	..	..	..	..	..	..	..	Nonfuel Primary Products
..	..	..	..	..	..	..	..	..	..	..	Fuels
..	..	..	..	..	..	..	..	..	..	..	Manufactures
..	..	..	..	..	..	..	..	..	..	..	Value of Imports, cif
..	..	..	..	..	..	..	..	..	..	..	Nonfuel Primary Products
..	..	..	..	..	..	..	..	..	..	..	Fuels
..	..	..	..	..	..	..	..	..	..	..	Manufactures
			(Index 1987 = 100)								
..	..	..	..	..	..	..	..	..	..	..	Terms of Trade
..	..	..	..	..	..	..	..	..	..	..	Export Prices, fob
..	..	..	..	..	..	..	..	..	..	..	Import Prices, cif
			(Millions of current US dollars)								**BALANCE OF PAYMENTS**
..	..	..	..	..	..	..	..	1,710.0	1,544.5	..	Exports of Goods & Services
..	..	..	..	..	..	..	..	1,313.5	1,290.8	..	Merchandise, fob
..	..	..	..	..	..	..	..	329.8	153.7	..	Nonfactor Services
..	..	..	..	..	..	..	..	66.7	100.0	..	Factor Services
..	..	..	..	..	..	..	..	2,828.0	2,383.5	..	Imports of Goods & Services
..	..	..	..	..	..	..	..	1,792.8	1,403.4	..	Merchandise, fob
..	..	..	..	..	..	..	..	641.0	501.9	..	Nonfactor Services
..	..	..	..	..	..	..	..	394.2	478.2	..	Factor Services
13.1	14.9	19.3	23.3	26.1	51.6	62.3	62.6	48.6	23.2	..	Long-Term Interest
..	..	..	..	..	..	..	..	371.7	1,342.3	..	Private Current Transfers, net
..	..	..	..	..	..	..	..	409.7	1,366.1	..	Workers' Remittances
..	..	..	..	..	..	..	..	-746.3	503.3	..	Curr. A/C Bal before Off. Transf.
..	..	..	..	..	..	..	..	193.8	116.3	..	Net Official Transfers
..	..	..	..	..	..	..	..	-552.5	619.6	..	Curr. A/C Bal after Off. Transf.
..	..	..	..	..	..	..	..	436.8	-109.4	..	Long-Term Capital, net
..	..	..	..	..	..	..	..	..	..	..	Direct Investment
410.7	392.7	468.2	241.6	208.0	272.4	243.9	334.8	372.5	187.2	..	Long-Term Loans
474.2	449.3	507.6	300.5	276.3	349.1	389.4	496.0	502.4	260.6	..	Disbursements
63.5	56.6	39.4	58.9	68.3	76.7	145.5	161.2	129.9	73.4	..	Repayments
..	..	..	..	..	..	..	..	64.3	-296.6	..	Other Long-Term Capital
..	..	..	..	..	..	..	..	26.5	-236.5	..	Other Capital, net
..	..	..	..	..	..	..	..	89.2	-273.7	..	Change in Reserves
			(Yemeni Rials per US dollar)								**Memo Item:**
4.560	4.560	4.580	5.350	6.410	7.410	8.990	9.700	9.760	11.700	..	Conversion Factor (Annual Avg)
			(Millions of US dollars), outstanding at end of year								
2,039.6	2,403.0	2,794.8	3,001.0	3,340.5	3,863.4	4,538.5	5,139.3	5,496.4	6,235.5	..	**EXTERNAL DEBT (Total)**
1,849.7	2,193.6	2,545.8	2,632.0	3,015.9	3,453.3	4,027.2	4,293.4	4,547.1	5,040.0	..	Long-Term Debt (by debtor)
37.4	49.1	55.0	49.2	47.7	102.3	60.1	108.2	81.3	80.2	..	Central Bank, incl. IMF credit
1,803.5	2,137.3	2,483.7	2,578.6	2,965.3	3,349.3	3,966.5	4,185.2	4,465.8	4,959.8	..	Central Government
..	..	..	..	..	..	..	..	..	..	..	Rest of General Government
8.8	7.2	7.1	4.2	2.9	1.7	0.6	0.0	0.0	..	..	Non-financial Public Enterprises
..	..	..	..	..	..	..	..	..	..	..	Priv. Sector, incl non-guaranteed
189.9	209.4	249.0	369.0	324.6	410.1	511.3	845.9	949.3	1,195.5	..	Short-Term Debt
			(Millions of US dollars)								**Memo Items:**
961.6	554.2	366.0	318.5	296.8	431.7	539.5	285.1	279.2	..	..	Int'l Reserves Excluding Gold
0.4	0.4	0.3	0.3	0.3	0.4	0.4	0.4	0.4	..	..	Gold Holdings (at market price)
											SOCIAL INDICATORS
7.3	7.4	7.5	7.5	7.6	7.6	7.7	7.7	7.7	7.7	..	Total Fertility Rate
144.5	142.0	139.2	136.3	133.5	130.6	127.8	126.4	125.0	123.6	..	Infant Mortality Rate
45.9	46.2	46.5	46.8	47.2	47.5	47.8	48.0	48.3	48.5	..	Life Expectancy at Birth
21.0	21.8	22.7	23.5	24.4	25.3	26.2	27.2	28.1	29.0	..	Urban Population, % of total
..	..	..	..	..	..	..	..	..	..	..	Food Prod. per capita (1987=100)
..	..	..	..	..	..	..	..	..	..	..	Labor Force, Agriculture (%)
12.0	12.2	12.3	12.5	12.6	12.8	12.9	13.0	13.1	13.3	..	Labor Force, Female (%)
..	..	..	..	..	..	..	..	..	..	..	Primary Schl. Enroll. Ratio
..	..	..	..	..	..	..	..	..	..	..	Primary Schl. Enroll. Ratio, Female
..	..	..	..	..	..	..	..	..	..	..	Secondary Schl. Enroll. Ratio

YUGOSLAVIA	1970	1971	1972	1973	1974	1975	1976	1977	1978	1979	1980
CURRENT GNP PER CAPITA (US $)	660	740	780	870	1,150	1,380	1,620	1,970	2,400	2,880	3,250
POPULATION (thousands)	20,371	20,572	20,772	20,956	21,164	21,365	21,573	21,775	21,968	22,166	22,304

USE AND ORIGIN OF RESOURCES

(Billions of current Yugoslav Dinars)

	1970	1971	1972	1973	1974	1975	1976	1977	1978	1979	1980
Gross National Product (GNP)	1.71E-2	2.20E-2	2.68E-2	3.30E-2	4.26E-2	5.37E-2	6.77E-2	8.35E-2	1.02E-1	1.30E-1	1.78E-1
Net Factor Income from Abroad	-5.44E-5	-4.96E-5	-3.85E-5	4.78E-5	8.29E-5	-4.66E-5	-1.22E-4	-1.46E-5	-1.39E-4	-7.14E-4	-1.97E-3
GDP at Market Prices	1.72E-2	2.20E-2	2.68E-2	3.29E-2	4.25E-2	5.37E-2	6.79E-2	8.36E-2	1.02E-1	1.30E-1	1.80E-1
Resource Balance	-9.09E-4	-1.40E-3	-6.60E-4	-1.18E-3	-4.16E-3	-4.20E-3	-1.77E-3	-5.22E-3	-4.90E-3	-9.00E-3	-7.65E-3
Exports of Goods & NFServices	3.15E-3	4.25E-3	5.83E-3	7.18E-3	9.14E-3	1.09E-2	1.30E-2	1.45E-2	1.67E-2	2.03E-2	3.36E-2
Imports of Goods & NFServices	4.06E-3	5.65E-3	6.49E-3	8.37E-3	1.33E-2	1.51E-2	1.48E-2	1.98E-2	2.16E-2	2.93E-2	4.13E-2
Domestic Absorption	1.81E-2	2.34E-2	2.75E-2	3.41E-2	4.67E-2	5.79E-2	6.96E-2	8.88E-2	1.07E-1	1.39E-1	1.88E-1
Private Consumption, etc.	9.47E-3	1.25E-2	1.54E-2	1.95E-2	2.64E-2	3.01E-2	3.61E-2	4.42E-2	5.42E-2	6.70E-2	8.78E-2
General Gov't Consumption	3.05E-3	3.67E-3	4.53E-3	5.27E-3	7.43E-3	9.79E-3	1.19E-2	1.47E-2	1.78E-2	2.23E-2	2.81E-2
Gross Domestic Investment	5.55E-3	7.24E-3	7.53E-3	9.35E-3	1.29E-2	1.80E-2	2.17E-2	2.99E-2	3.51E-2	4.99E-2	7.18E-2
Fixed Investment	5.17E-3	6.47E-3	7.49E-3	8.55E-3	1.17E-2	1.63E-2	2.07E-2	2.68E-2	3.57E-2	4.48E-2	5.46E-2
Indirect Taxes, net	1.46E-3	1.93E-3	2.03E-3	2.10E-2	4.58E-3	4.70E-3	6.12E-3	7.92E-3	9.67E-3	1.29E-2	1.52E-2
GDP at factor cost	1.57E-2	2.01E-2	2.48E-2	3.08E-2	3.80E-2	4.90E-2	6.18E-2	7.56E-2	9.25E-2	1.17E-1	1.65E-1
Agriculture	2.77E-3	3.45E-3	4.38E-3	5.48E-3	6.10E-3	7.71E-3	9.27E-3	1.06E-2	1.05E-2	1.40E-2	1.97E-2
Industry	6.43E-3	8.09E-3	1.16E-2	1.25E-2	1.59E-2	2.20E-2	2.59E-2	3.17E-2	3.89E-2	5.05E-2	7.23E-2
Manufacturing	..	..	..	..	..	..	..	..	..	..	..
Services, etc.	6.51E-3	8.58E-3	8.83E-3	1.29E-2	1.59E-2	1.93E-2	2.65E-2	3.34E-2	4.31E-2	5.29E-2	7.28E-2
Gross Domestic Saving	4.64E-3	5.84E-3	6.87E-3	8.16E-3	8.71E-3	1.38E-2	1.99E-2	2.47E-2	3.02E-2	4.09E-2	6.42E-2
Gross National Saving	5.27E-3	6.95E-3	8.60E-3	1.07E-2	1.16E-2	1.69E-2	2.37E-2	2.98E-2	3.61E-2	4.72E-2	7.29E-2

(Billions of 1987 Yugoslav Dinars)

	1970	1971	1972	1973	1974	1975	1976	1977	1978	1979	1980
Gross National Product	2.700	2.900	3.000	3.100	3.500	3.600	3.700	4.100	4.400	4.600	4.700
GDP at Market Prices	2.600	2.900	3.000	3.100	3.500	3.500	3.700	4.000	4.400	4.600	4.800
Resource Balance	-0.264	-0.333	-0.155	-0.221	-0.427	-0.396	-0.159	-0.397	-0.380	-0.540	-0.293
Exports of Goods & NFServices	0.847	0.917	1.000	1.100	1.100	1.100	1.200	1.200	1.200	1.200	1.300
Imports of Goods & NFServices	1.100	1.200	1.200	1.300	1.500	1.500	1.300	1.600	1.600	1.800	1.600
Domestic Absorption	2.900	3.200	3.100	3.300	3.900	3.900	3.900	4.400	4.800	5.200	5.000
Private Consumption, etc.	1.300	1.500	1.400	1.500	2.000	1.900	1.700	2.100	2.400	2.500	2.400
General Gov't Consumption	1.100	1.100	1.100	1.200	1.200	1.300	1.400	1.400	1.500	1.600	1.600
Gross Domestic Investment	0.552	0.605	0.559	0.622	0.675	0.743	0.770	0.904	0.876	1.100	1.000
Fixed Investment	0.859	0.899	0.926	0.953	1.000	1.100	1.200	1.300	1.500	1.600	1.500
GDP at factor cost	2.300	2.500	2.600	2.700	3.000	3.000	3.200	3.400	3.800	3.900	4.100
Agriculture	0.404	0.430	0.447	0.486	0.513	0.500	0.532	0.562	0.532	0.552	0.552
Industry	0.936	1.000	1.200	1.300	1.400	1.500	1.500	1.700	1.800	2.000	2.000
Manufacturing	..	..	..	..	..	..	..	..	..	..	..
Services, etc.	0.940	1.000	0.935	0.953	1.100	1.100	1.100	1.200	1.400	1.400	1.500

Memo Items:

	1970	1971	1972	1973	1974	1975	1976	1977	1978	1979	1980
Capacity to Import	0.862	0.941	1.100	1.200	1.000	1.100	1.200	1.100	1.200	1.200	1.300
Terms of Trade Adjustment	0.015	0.024	0.034	0.031	-0.038	-0.013	-0.001	-0.014	0.018	-0.009	-0.009
Gross Domestic Income	2.700	2.900	3.000	3.100	3.500	3.500	3.700	4.000	4.400	4.600	4.700
Gross National Income	2.700	2.900	3.000	3.100	3.500	3.500	3.700	4.000	4.400	4.600	4.700

DOMESTIC PRICES/DEFLATORS

(Index 1987 = 100)

	1970	1971	1972	1973	1974	1975	1976	1977	1978	1979	1980
Overall (GDP)	0.6	0.8	0.9	1.1	1.2	1.5	1.8	2.1	2.3	2.8	3.8
Domestic Absorption	0.6	0.7	0.9	1.0	1.2	1.5	1.8	2.0	2.2	2.7	3.7
Agriculture	0.7	0.8	1.0	1.1	1.2	1.5	1.7	1.9	2.0	2.5	3.6
Industry	0.7	0.8	1.0	1.0	1.2	1.5	1.7	1.9	2.1	2.6	3.6
Manufacturing	..	..	..	..	..	..	..	..	..	..	..
Consumer Price Index	0.6	0.7	0.8	1.0	1.2	1.5	1.7	1.9	2.2	2.7	3.5

MANUFACTURING ACTIVITY

	1970	1971	1972	1973	1974	1975	1976	1977	1978	1979	1980
Employment (1987=100)	49.4	52.8	55.8	58.6	60.3	62.7	69.2	72.1	74.9	78.5	80.5
Real Earnings per Empl. (1987=100)	97.6	102.4	102.0	99.0	102.6	100.1	107.5	113.2	111.8	111.9	107.1
Real Output per Empl. (1987=100)	65.6	70.1	71.0	85.8	112.5	108.7	102.4	110.1	112.2	114.8	112.2
Earnings as % of Value Added	38.8	37.8	38.3	36.8	34.7	35.6	38.9	38.9	37.1	36.8	34.3

MONETARY HOLDINGS

(Billions of current Yugoslav Dinars)

	1970	1971	1972	1973	1974	1975	1976	1977	1978	1979	1980
Money Supply, Broadly Defined	0.010	0.013	0.016	0.021	0.026	0.034	0.047	0.057	0.073	0.090	0.123
Money	0.004	0.004	0.006	0.008	0.010	0.014	0.022	0.025	0.029	0.034	0.045
Currency Outside Banks	0.001	0.002	0.002	0.003	0.003	0.004	0.005	0.006	0.008	0.009	0.012
Demand Deposits	0.002	0.002	0.004	0.005	0.007	0.009	0.017	0.019	0.022	0.025	0.034
Quasi-Money	0.007	0.009	0.010	0.013	0.015	0.020	0.025	0.032	0.044	0.055	0.078

(Billions of current Yugoslav Dinars)

	1970	1971	1972	1973	1974	1975	1976	1977	1978	1979	1980
GOVERNMENT DEFICIT (-) OR SURPLUS	..	..	..	..	-0.001	-0.001	-0.002	-0.001	-0.001	..	-0.002
Current Revenue	0.003	0.004	0.006	0.007	0.009	0.012	0.014	0.008	0.009	0.012	0.014
Current Expenditure	..	..	..	..	..	..	..	0.008	0.009	0.012	0.016
Current Budget Balance	..	..	..	..	..	..	..	0.000	0.000	0.000	-0.002
Capital Receipts	..	..	..	..	..	..	..				
Capital Payments	..	..	..	..	..	..	..	0.001	0.001	0.000	0.000

1981	1982	1983	1984	1985	1986	1987	1988	1989	1990 estimate	Notes	YUGOSLAVIA
3,450	3,230	2,640	2,270	2,040	2,290	2,510	2,710	2,940	3,060	..	**CURRENT GNP PER CAPITA (US $)**
22,471	22,642	22,805	22,966	23,124	23,274	23,417	23,566	23,690	23,809	..	**POPULATION (thousands)**
				(Billions of current Yugoslav Dinars)							**USE AND ORIGIN OF RESOURCES**
2.46E-1	3.17E-1	4.34E-1	6.77E-1	1.00E+0	2.00E+0	5.00E+0	1.50E+1	221	989	..	Gross National Product (GNP)
-4.39E-3	-7.84E-3	-1.18E-2	-2.08E-2	-3.83E-2	-5.61E-2	-1.24E-1	-4.53E-1	-4	-10	..	Net Factor Income from Abroad
2.51E-1	3.25E-1	4.46E-1	6.97E-1	1.00E+0	3.00E+0	5.00E+0	1.60E+1	225	999	..	GDP at Market Prices
-6.17E-3	-2.11E-4	1.00E-3	5.58E-3	2.29E-2	4.38E-2	1.42E-1	9.55E-1	7	-8	..	Resource Balance
4.97E-2	7.10E-2	1.22E-1	2.07E-1	3.84E-1	5.98E-1	1.00E+0	6.00E+0	56	240	..	Exports of Goods & NFServices
5.59E-2	7.12E-2	1.21E-1	2.02E-1	3.61E-1	5.54E-1	1.00E+0	5.00E+0	49	248	..	Imports of Goods & NFServices
2.57E-1	3.25E-1	4.45E-1	6.92E-1	1.00E+0	2.00E+0	5.00E+0	1.50E+1	218	1,007	..	Domestic Absorption
1.22E-1	1.61E-1	2.22E-1	3.37E-1	5.93E-1	1.00E+0	2.00E+0	7.00E+0	104	724	..	Private Consumption, etc.
3.75E-2	4.89E-2	6.39E-2	9.52E-2	1.71E-1	3.40E-1	2.00E+0	1.00E+0	15	69	..	General Gov't Consumption
9.75E-2	1.16E-1	1.59E-1	2.60E-1	4.99E-1	9.63E-1	1.00E+0	6.00E+0	99	215	..	Gross Domestic Investment
6.85E-2	8.55E-2	1.03E-1	1.46E-1	2.61E-1	5.05E-1	9.92E-1	3.00E+0	34	165	..	Fixed Investment
2.18E-2	2.61E-2	3.99E-2	5.99E-2	8.76E-2	1.71E-1	3.66E-1	1.00E+0	15	67	..	Indirect Taxes, net
2.29E-1	2.99E-1	4.06E-1	6.37E-1	1.00E+0	2.00E+0	5.00E+0	1.50E+1	210	932	..	GDP at factor cost
3.02E-2	4.14E-2	5.98E-2	8.66E-2	1.39E-1	2.73E-1	6.28E-1	2.00E+0	25	109	..	Agriculture
1.04E-1	1.30E-1	1.73E-1	2.79E-1	5.53E-1	9.84E-1	2.00E+0	6.00E+0	104	448	..	Industry
..	..	..	..	..	..	..	..	..	..		Manufacturing
9.50E-2	1.28E-1	1.73E-1	2.72E-1	5.07E-1	1.00E+0	2.00E+0	7.00E+0	81	375	..	Services, etc.
9.14E-2	1.15E-1	1.60E-1	2.65E-1	5.22E-1	1.00E+0	1.00E+0	7.00E+0	106	206	..	Gross Domestic Saving
1.02E-1	1.30E-1	1.82E-1	2.95E-1	5.72E-1	1.00E+0	1.00E+0	8.00E+0	121	308	..	Gross National Saving
				(Billions of 1987 Yugoslav Dinars)							
4.800	4.800	4.700	4.800	4.700	4.900	4.800	4.700	4.800	4.500	..	Gross National Product
4.800	4.800	4.800	4.900	4.800	5.000	4.900	4.800	4.900	4.500	I	GDP at Market Prices
-0.139	-0.018	0.010	0.102	0.168	0.063	0.142	0.229	0.198	0.014	..	Resource Balance
1.300	1.200	1.100	1.200	1.300	1.200	1.200	1.200	1.200	1.300	..	Exports of Goods & NFServices
1.400	1.200	1.100	1.100	1.100	1.200	1.100	0.968	1.000	1.300	..	Imports of Goods & NFServices
5.000	4.900	4.800	4.800	4.700	4.900	4.800	4.600	4.700	4.500	..	Domestic Absorption
2.400	2.300	2.300	2.200	2.100	2.400	2.100	2.000	2.000	2.500	..	Private Consumption, etc.
1.500	1.500	1.500	1.500	1.500	1.600	1.600	1.600	1.600	1.500	..	General Gov't Consumption
1.000	1.000	1.000	1.000	1.000	0.996	1.000	0.986	1.100	0.488	..	Gross Domestic Investment
1.300	1.300	1.100	1.000	0.997	0.956	0.992	0.945	0.916	0.920	..	Fixed Investment
4.100	4.200	4.100	4.200	4.300	4.500	4.500	4.500	4.500	4.200	..	GDP at factor cost
0.567	0.609	0.605	0.618	0.576	0.617	0.628	0.605	0.632	0.585	..	Agriculture
2.100	2.000	2.000	2.100	2.100	2.200	2.200	2.200	2.300	2.000	..	Industry
..	..	..	..	..	..	..	..	..	..		Manufacturing
1.500	1.600	1.500	1.500	1.600	1.600	1.700	1.600	1.600	1.600	..	Services, etc.
											Memo Items:
1.300	1.200	1.100	1.100	1.200	1.300	1.200	1.200	1.200	1.200	..	Capacity to Import
-0.017	0.014	0.000	-0.071	-0.098	0.029	0.000	-0.031	-0.053	-0.055	..	Terms of Trade Adjustment
4.800	4.900	4.800	4.800	4.700	5.000	4.900	4.800	4.800	4.400	..	Gross Domestic Income
4.700	4.800	4.700	4.700	4.600	5.000	4.800	4.700	4.700	4.400	..	Gross National Income
				(Index 1987 = 100)							**DOMESTIC PRICES/DEFLATORS**
5.2	6.7	9.3	14.3	26.6	50.0	100.0	322.1	4629.5	22212.3	..	Overall (GDP)
5.2	6.7	9.3	14.5	27.0	49.8	100.0	317.5	4679.9	22463.7	..	Domestic Absorption
5.3	6.8	9.9	14.0	24.0	44.2	100.0	257.0	3888.1	18662.6	..	Agriculture
5.0	6.4	8.6	13.4	26.1	44.7	100.0	289.5	4614.3	22148.4	..	Industry
..	..	..	..	..	..	..	..	..	..		Manufacturing
4.9	6.4	9.0	13.9	23.9	45.3	100.0	294.1	3940.5	26915.6	..	Consumer Price Index
											MANUFACTURING ACTIVITY
83.7	86.5	88.7	91.2	94.3	98.4	100.0	100.5	..	..	G	Employment (1987=100)
113.2	106.5	98.0	92.9	97.5	103.9	100.0	94.7	..	..	G	Real Earnings per Empl. (1987=100)
112.6	111.1	117.4	122.7	112.4	109.7	100.0	108.8	..	..	G	Real Output per Empl. (1987=100)
36.3	35.2	32.5	29.6	29.1	32.8	29.9	25.6	..	..		Earnings as % of Value Added
				(Billions of current Yugoslav Dinars)							**MONETARY HOLDINGS**
0.162	0.215	0.299	0.436	0.702	1.000	3.000	10.000	248.000	345.000	..	Money Supply, Broadly Defined
0.057	0.073	0.087	0.125	0.182	0.383	0.764	2.000	51.000	126.000	..	Money
0.015	0.020	0.025	0.033	0.055	0.116	0.215	0.585	12.000	53.000	..	Currency Outside Banks
0.042	0.053	0.063	0.093	0.127	0.267	0.549	2.000	39.000	74.000	..	Demand Deposits
0.105	0.142	0.211	0.311	0.520	0.896	2.000	8.000	197.000	219.000	..	Quasi-Money
				(Billions of current Yugoslav Dinars)							
..	..	..	..	-0.001	0.001	0.002	0.010	0.597	..	E F	**GOVERNMENT DEFICIT (-) OR SURPLUS**
0.020	0.024	0.033	0.049	0.083	0.162	0.359	1.200	12.000	..	..	Current Revenue
0.020	0.024	0.033	0.049	0.084	0.160	0.356	1.200	11.400	..	..	Current Expenditure
0.000	0.000	0.000	0.000	-0.001	0.002	0.003	0.012	0.641	..	..	Current Budget Balance
..	..	..	..	..	..	..	..	..	..		Capital Receipts
0.000	0.000	0.000	0.000	0.000	0.001	0.001	0.002	0.044	..	..	Capital Payments

YUGOSLAVIA	1970	1971	1972	1973	1974	1975	1976	1977	1978	1979	1980
FOREIGN TRADE (CUSTOMS BASIS)				*(Millions of current US dollars)*							
Value of Exports, fob	1,679	1,836	2,237	3,020	3,805	4,072	4,896	4,896	5,546	6,799	8,977
Nonfuel Primary Products	656	665	801	1,062	1,226	1,131	1,452	1,337	1,433	1,754	2,176
Fuels	20	20	18	23	41	30	48	144	146	204	231
Manufactures	1,003	1,151	1,419	1,935	2,538	2,911	3,395	3,415	3,967	4,841	6,570
Value of Imports, cif	2,874	3,297	3,233	4,783	7,520	7,699	7,367	8,973	9,769	14,037	15,064
Nonfuel Primary Products	731	856	866	1,292	2,035	1,452	1,554	1,831	1,788	2,476	2,973
Fuels	138	195	176	380	951	945	1,081	1,207	1,401	2,251	3,549
Manufactures	2,005	2,246	2,190	3,111	4,534	5,302	4,732	5,935	6,580	9,310	8,542
					(Index 1987 = 100)						
Terms of Trade	112.0	108.2	103.5	110.2	92.9	93.7	91.5	85.2	88.2	88.3	86.0
Export Prices, fob	30.3	30.8	33.1	42.0	53.7	55.8	56.3	57.7	64.9	78.2	89.6
Import Prices, cif	27.1	28.4	32.0	38.1	57.8	59.5	61.5	67.8	73.6	88.7	104.2
BALANCE OF PAYMENTS				*(Millions of current US dollars)*							
Exports of Goods & Services	2,425	2,689	3,343	4,342	5,690	6,170	6,927	7,546	8,581	10,226	13,833
Merchandise, fob	1,679	1,821	2,238	2,853	3,805	4,073	4,890	5,191	5,823	6,795	9,093
Nonfactor Services	728	851	1,088	1,440	1,785	2,034	1,949	2,218	2,586	3,242	4,541
Factor Services	18	17	17	49	100	63	88	137	172	189	199
Imports of Goods & Services	3,345	3,875	3,961	5,365	8,406	8,611	8,929	11,683	13,117	17,596	20,500
Merchandise, fob	2,637	2,993	2,965	4,137	6,922	7,058	6,753	8,973	9,591	12,853	13,992
Nonfactor Services	566	722	820	994	1,185	1,209	1,808	2,300	3,031	3,922	5,211
Factor Services	142	159	176	234	299	344	368	410	495	821	1,297
Long-Term Interest	104	110	138	209	246	289	301	367	578	817	1,077
Private Current Transfers, net	542	780	1,039	1,510	1,755	1,804	2,189	2,809	3,268	3,716	4,354
Workers' Remittances	441	654	889	1,310	1,500	1,575	1,885	2,508	2,957	3,395	4,102
Curr. A/C Bal before Off. Transf.	-378	-405	421	488	-962	-636	187	-1,328	-1,268	-3,654	-2,313
Net Official Transfers	6	10	10	14	11	11	-1	-1	-5	-5	-4
Curr. A/C Bal after Off. Transf.	-372	-395	431	502	-951	-625	186	-1,329	-1,273	-3,659	-2,317
Long-Term Capital, net	196	539	489	607	497	951	1,099	1,404	1,609	1,299	1,954
Direct Investment	..	..	..	..	..	..	..	..	..	..	..
Long-Term Loans	270	484	765	831	586	949	1,311	1,696	1,753	1,656	2,209
Disbursements	645	1,019	1,509	1,676	1,557	2,102	2,450	2,923	3,059	3,892	4,589
Repayments	375	536	744	845	971	1,153	1,139	1,227	1,306	2,236	2,380
Other Long-Term Capital	-74	55	-277	-225	-89	1	-212	-292	-144	-357	-255
Other Capital, net	93	-164	-444	-434	122	-617	-264	216	204	1,064	51
Change in Reserves	83	21	-476	-674	333	292	-1,021	-291	-540	1,296	312
Memo Item:				*(Yugoslav Dinars per US dollar)*							
Conversion Factor (Annual Avg)	0.001	0.001	0.002	0.002	0.002	0.002	0.002	0.002	0.002	0.002	0.002
EXTERNAL DEBT (Total)			*(Millions of US dollars), outstanding at end of year*								
	2,053	2,776	3,529	4,308	5,094	5,999	7,542	10,119	12,528	15,970	18,486
Long-Term Debt (by debtor)	2,053	2,776	3,529	4,308	5,094	5,999	7,542	9,216	11,357	14,181	16,346
Central Bank, incl. IMF credit	387	526	724	929	1,258	1,207	1,615	1,607	1,710	1,867	2,906
Central Government	583	683	767	682	634	652	675	712	768	838	851
Rest of General Government	10	8	8	7	26	83	121	171	254	431	609
Non-financial Public Enterprises	0	0	0	0	7	122	162	178	207	220	221
Priv. Sector, incl non-guaranteed	1,073	1,560	2,031	2,690	3,169	3,936	4,970	6,547	8,417	10,825	11,759
Short-Term Debt	0	0	0	0	0	0	0	903	1,171	1,789	2,140
Memo Items:				*(Millions of US dollars)*							
Int'l Reserves Excluding Gold	88.6	157.2	675.2	1,275.8	1,084.8	811.5	1,989.9	2,044.4	2,388.2	1,256.6	1,384.1
Gold Holdings (at market price)	54.4	63.6	96.4	163.5	274.1	205.5	197.5	249.2	368.8	881.4	1,093.7
SOCIAL INDICATORS											
Total Fertility Rate	..	..	..	..	..	2.3	2.2	2.2	2.2	2.2	2.1
Infant Mortality Rate	55.5	49.5	44.4	40.0	40.9	39.7	36.7	35.5	33.8	32.7	31.4
Life Expectancy at Birth	67.7	68.0	68.4	68.5	68.5	68.6	68.7	68.7	68.8	68.8	68.9
Urban Population, % of total	34.8	35.8	36.8	37.8	38.8	39.8	40.9	42.0	43.1	44.2	45.3
Food Prod. per capita (1987=100)	81.0	87.8	84.1	88.4	95.3	94.6	97.5	100.8	94.3	98.3	98.8
Labor Force, Agriculture (%)	49.8	48.0	46.2	44.5	42.7	41.0	39.2	37.5	35.7	34.0	32.3
Labor Force, Female (%)	36.5	36.6	36.7	36.9	37.0	37.1	37.3	37.5	37.6	37.8	37.9
Primary Schl. Enroll. Ratio	106.0	..	..	..	..	103.0	101.0	99.0	99.0	99.0	100.0
Primary Schl. Enroll. Ratio, Female	103.0	..	..	..	..	101.0	99.0	98.0	98.0	98.0	100.0
Secondary Schl. Enroll. Ratio	63.0	..	..	..	..	76.0	78.0	79.0	82.0	82.0	83.0

1981	1982	1983	1984	1985	1986	1987	1988	1989	1990 estimate	Notes	YUGOSLAVIA
				(Millions of current US dollars)							**FOREIGN TRADE (CUSTOMS BASIS)**
10,929	10,752	9,913	10,255	10,641	10,297	11,397	12,579	13,343	14,365	..	Value of Exports, fob
2,136	2,161	2,128	2,023	1,923	1,774	2,235	2,534	2,527	2,712	..	Nonfuel Primary Products
219	198	245	357	297	203	220	184	185	314	..	Fuels
8,574	8,393	7,541	7,875	8,421	8,320	8,942	9,861	10,631	11,338	..	Manufactures
15,757	14,100	12,154	11,996	12,163	11,749	12,549	13,152	14,799	18,911	..	Value of Imports, cif
2,902	2,545	2,238	2,210	2,241	2,264	2,107	2,515	2,850	3,784	..	Nonfuel Primary Products
3,786	3,630	3,304	3,515	3,307	2,606	2,186	2,326	2,827	3,210	..	Fuels
9,069	7,925	6,612	6,271	6,615	6,879	8,256	8,311	9,121	11,917	..	Manufactures
				(Index 1987 = 100)							
87.8	95.3	97.4	95.8	95.2	107.7	100.0	113.2	120.7	120.7	..	Terms of Trade
92.3	95.2	94.8	91.7	88.8	91.2	100.0	110.7	125.2	133.1	..	Export Prices, fob
105.2	99.8	97.3	95.7	93.2	84.7	100.0	97.7	103.7	110.3	..	Import Prices, cif
				(Millions of current US dollars)							**BALANCE OF PAYMENTS**
15,737	15,358	13,224	13,447	14,080	15,385	15,890	17,681	19,404	21,471	..	Exports of Goods & Services
10,354	10,455	9,917	10,136	10,622	11,084	11,425	12,779	13,560	14,308	..	Merchandise, fob
5,012	4,621	3,128	3,098	3,236	4,116	4,312	4,712	5,441	6,374	..	Nonfactor Services
371	282	179	213	222	185	153	190	403	789	..	Factor Services
20,916	20,242	16,600	16,310	16,526	18,216	18,921	20,063	23,619	33,663	..	Imports of Goods & Services
13,517	12,477	11,148	10,925	11,210	11,786	11,343	12,000	13,502	16,984	..	Merchandise, fob
5,382	5,674	3,742	3,550	3,430	4,496	5,715	6,076	8,245	15,012	..	Nonfactor Services
2,017	2,091	1,710	1,835	1,886	1,934	1,863	1,987	1,872	1,667	..	Factor Services
1,463	1,606	1,514	2,339	1,534	1,778	1,725	1,609	1,373	1,646	..	Long-Term Interest
4,220	4,411	3,653	3,343	3,281	3,933	4,281	4,871	6,645	9,830	..	Private Current Transfers, net
3,960	4,185	3,429	3,168	3,106	3,731	4,051	4,593	6,290	9,360	..	Workers' Remittances
-959	-473	277	480	835	1,102	1,250	2,489	2,430	-2,362	..	Curr. A/C Bal before Off. Transf.
..	..	-2	-2	-2	-2	-2	-2	-3	-2	..	Net Official Transfers
-959	-473	275	478	833	1,100	1,248	2,487	2,427	-2,364	..	Curr. A/C Bal after Off. Transf.
578	-93	941	-265	78	-1,406	-892	-932	-314	-617	..	Long-Term Capital, net
..	..	..	..	..	..	..	..	..	..	..	Direct Investment
1,227	92	861	-122	-79	-886	-841	-200	-341	-325	..	Long-Term Loans
3,087	2,188	2,517	1,447	1,090	654	548	1,041	1,305	1,661	..	Disbursements
1,859	2,096	1,655	1,569	1,169	1,540	1,389	1,241	1,647	1,986	..	Repayments
-649	-185	80	-143	157	-520	-51	-732	27	-292	..	Other Long-Term Capital
-588	-865	-1,493	-110	-752	1,142	-118	398	301	4,349	..	Other Capital, net
969	1,431	277	-103	-159	-836	-238	-1,953	-2,414	-1,368	..	Change in Reserves
				(Yugoslav Dinars per US dollar)							**Memo Item:**
0.004	0.005	0.009	0.015	0.027	0.038	0.074	0.252	2.900	11.300	..	Conversion Factor (Annual Avg)
			(Millions of US dollars), outstanding at end of year								
20,645	19,900	20,477	19,644	22,278	21,507	22,476	20,987	19,998	20,690	..	**EXTERNAL DEBT (Total)**
18,154	18,090	19,335	18,618	21,288	20,142	21,176	19,954	18,817	17,819	..	Long-Term Debt (by debtor)
4,024	4,833	7,045	8,495	11,186	12,031	13,609	13,083	13,050	11,658	..	Central Bank, incl. IMF credit
862	800	727	629	686	711	787	719	685	693	..	Central Government
684	790	825	655	850	1,055	1,303	1,125	1,043	1,061	..	Rest of General Government
206	190	179	136	134	125	118	79	59	47	..	Non-financial Public Enterprises
12,376	11,477	10,559	8,703	8,432	6,220	5,359	4,948	3,981	4,359	..	Priv. Sector, incl non-guaranteed
2,492	1,810	1,142	1,026	990	1,365	1,300	1,033	1,181	2,871	..	Short-Term Debt
				(Millions of US dollars)							**Memo Items:**
1,597.1	775.3	976.4	1,158.1	1,094.7	1,459.6	697.7	2,297.9	4,135.7	5,473.9	..	Int'l Reserves Excluding Gold
737.8	849.2	710.1	573.9	609.6	729.3	903.8	776.5	763.3	734.5	..	Gold Holdings (at market price)
											SOCIAL INDICATORS
2.1	2.1	2.1	2.1	2.1	2.0	2.0	2.0	2.0	2.0	..	Total Fertility Rate
30.6	29.9	31.7	28.9	28.8	27.3	25.4	24.5	23.6	22.8	..	Infant Mortality Rate
68.9	69.0	69.4	69.9	70.4	70.9	71.3	71.7	72.0	72.4	..	Life Expectancy at Birth
46.4	47.5	48.7	49.8	50.9	51.9	53.0	54.0	55.1	56.1	..	Urban Population, % of total
99.5	107.6	102.5	104.5	95.4	105.4	100.0	95.3	97.3	89.4	..	Food Prod. per capita (1987=100)
..	..	..	..	..	..	..	..	..	..	..	Labor Force, Agriculture (%)
38.0	38.1	38.2	38.3	38.4	38.5	38.6	38.7	38.8	38.9	..	Labor Force, Female (%)
..	101.0	100.0	98.0	97.0	96.0	96.0	95.0	95.0	..	..	Primary Schl. Enroll. Ratio
100.0	101.0	100.0	98.0	97.0	95.0	96.0	95.0	95.0	..	..	Primary Schl. Enroll. Ratio, Female
..	83.0	82.0	81.0	81.0	80.0	81.0	81.0	80.0	..	..	Secondary Schl. Enroll. Ratio

ZAIRE	1970	1971	1972	1973	1974	1975	1976	1977	1978	1979	1980
CURRENT GNP PER CAPITA (US $)	250	260	270	320	380	400	400	440	480	560	590
POPULATION (thousands)	19,769	20,399	21,062	21,755	22,473	23,213	23,975	24,755	25,551	26,363	27,193
USE AND ORIGIN OF RESOURCES					*(Billions of current Zaires)*						
Gross National Product (GNP)	2.4	2.7	3.0	3.8	4.6	4.9	7.4	10.4	12.6	25.5	39.4
Net Factor Income from Abroad	-0.1	-0.1	-0.1	-0.1	-0.2	-0.2	-0.2	-0.2	-0.2	-0.5	-0.9
GDP at Market Prices	2.4	2.8	3.1	3.9	4.8	5.1	7.6	10.6	12.9	26.0	40.3
Resource Balance	-0.1	-0.2	-0.2	-0.2	-0.3	-0.5	-0.8	-1.5	-1.2	-2.6	0.1
Exports of Goods & NFServices	0.4	0.3	0.3	0.5	0.7	0.5	0.8	1.0	1.6	3.6	6.4
Imports of Goods & NFServices	0.4	0.5	0.6	0.7	1.0	1.0	1.6	2.6	2.7	6.2	6.3
Domestic Absorption	2.5	3.0	3.3	4.1	5.1	5.6	8.4	12.1	14.0	28.6	40.2
Private Consumption, etc.	1.8	2.1	2.4	3.1	3.7	4.1	6.6	8.8	11.3	22.8	32.8
General Gov't Consumption	0.3	0.4	0.4	0.4	0.6	0.6	0.7	1.0	1.2	2.5	3.4
Gross Domestic Investment	0.4	0.5	0.6	0.7	0.8	0.9	1.1	2.3	1.5	3.3	4.0
Fixed Investment	0.3	0.4	0.5	0.5	0.7	0.7	0.9	1.8	1.3	2.1	3.6
Indirect Taxes, net	0.2	0.2	0.3	0.3	0.4	0.3	0.4	0.4	0.4	1.0	2.2
GDP at factor cost	2.2	2.6	2.8	3.6	4.5	4.8	7.3	10.2	12.4	25.1	38.1
Agriculture	0.4	0.4	0.4	0.5	0.7	0.8	1.7	2.4	3.4	7.1	10.2
Industry	1.0	1.1	1.1	1.6	1.9	1.8	2.2	2.6	3.1	6.8	13.3
Manufacturing	..	..	..	..	..	..	..	..	..	..	5.8
Services, etc.	1.1	1.4	1.6	1.8	2.2	2.5	3.7	5.5	6.3	12.1	16.8
Gross Domestic Saving	0.3	0.3	0.3	0.5	0.5	0.4	0.3	0.7	0.4	0.8	4.1
Gross National Saving	0.1	0.2	0.2	0.3	0.3	0.1	0.1	0.4	0.1	0.2	2.9
					(Millions of 1987 Zaires)						
Gross National Product	726,000	729,000	735,000	794,000	809,000	766,000	734,000	746,000	705,000	703,000	716,000
GDP at Market Prices	705,000	750,000	751,000	816,000	844,000	802,000	756,000	760,000	717,000	716,000	733,000
Resource Balance	10,283	5,515	-70	-8,063	-5,030	-2,807	8,271	-26,112	24,558	4,841	1,595
Exports of Goods & NFServices	86,289	96,167	103,000	112,000	104,000	97,142	91,050	90,781	114,000	95,114	116,000
Imports of Goods & NFServices	76,006	90,652	103,000	120,000	109,000	99,949	82,779	117,000	88,996	90,273	114,000
Domestic Absorption	691,000	738,000	744,000	813,000	835,000	791,000	738,000	779,000	688,000	710,000	729,000
Private Consumption, etc.	500,000	534,000	567,000	611,000	611,000	590,000	571,000	536,000	538,000	518,000	494,000
General Gov't Consumption	124,000	116,000	89,761	107,000	121,000	107,000	94,069	101,000	83,626	81,024	88,204
Gross Domestic Investment	66,681	88,122	87,259	94,836	102,000	94,163	73,344	141,000	66,083	112,000	147,000
Fixed Investment	46,354	50,209	58,744	52,721	73,225	56,847	43,661	89,189	42,599	58,620	101,000
GDP at factor cost	888,000	671,000	662,000	746,000	780,000	746,000	719,000	731,000	692,000	687,000	690,000
Agriculture	179,000	184,000	187,000	194,000	198,000	195,000	205,000	199,000	199,000	205,000	211,000
Industry	205,000	220,000	221,000	241,000	257,000	245,000	223,000	219,000	202,000	188,000	197,000
Manufacturing	..	..	..	85,088	92,103	83,905	77,251	75,615	66,044	62,221	64,409
Services, etc.	316,000	339,000	336,000	370,000	375,000	348,000	318,000	335,000	311,000	322,000	323,000
Memo Items:											
Capacity to Import	64,479	59,366	60,864	85,768	77,563	48,031	43,251	46,528	51,285	52,920	..
Terms of Trade Adjustment	-21,810	-36,801	-41,748	-26,532	-26,046	-49,111	-47,800	-44,253	-62,269	-42,194	..
Gross Domestic Income	683,000	714,000	709,000	789,000	818,000	753,000	708,000	716,000	655,000	674,000	..
Gross National Income	705,000	692,000	694,000	768,000	783,000	716,000	686,000	702,000	643,000	661,000	..
DOMESTIC PRICES/DEFLATORS					*(Index 1987 = 100)*						
Overall (GDP)	0.3	0.4	0.4	0.5	0.6	0.6	1.0	1.4	1.8	3.6	5.5
Domestic Absorption	0.4	0.4	0.4	0.5	0.6	0.7	1.1	1.6	2.0	4.0	5.5
Agriculture	0.2	0.2	0.2	0.3	0.4	0.4	0.8	1.2	1.7	3.5	4.8
Industry	0.5	0.5	0.5	0.6	0.8	0.7	1.0	1.2	1.5	3.6	6.8
Manufacturing	..	..	..	..	..	..	..	..	..	..	9.0
Consumer Price Index	0.2	0.2	0.2	0.3	0.3	0.4	0.8	1.3	2.0	4.0	5.8
MANUFACTURING ACTIVITY											
Employment (1987=100)	..	..	..	..	..	..	..	..	..	..	..
Real Earnings per Empl. (1987=100)	..	..	..	..	..	..	..	..	..	..	..
Real Output per Empl. (1987=100)	..	..	..	..	..	..	..	..	..	..	..
Earnings as % of Value Added	..	..	35.9	..	..	..	..	..	..	..	..
MONETARY HOLDINGS					*(Billions of current Zaires)*						
Money Supply, Broadly Defined	0.21	0.22	0.27	0.38	0.50	0.55	0.76	1.21	1.86	1.96	3.18
Money	0.19	0.19	0.23	0.29	0.39	0.46	0.66	1.03	1.61	1.57	2.71
Currency Outside Banks	0.07	0.08	0.10	0.12	0.16	0.21	0.29	0.47	0.80	0.41	1.25
Demand Deposits	0.11	0.10	0.14	0.17	0.23	0.25	0.37	0.56	0.81	1.16	1.46
Quasi-Money	0.02	0.04	0.04	0.09	0.11	0.09	0.10	0.18	0.26	0.39	0.47
					(Millions of current Zaires)						
GOVERNMENT DEFICIT (-) OR SURPLUS	..	-77	-82	-141	-324	-216	-627	-450	-595	-549	-332
Current Revenue	..	329	344	440	588	491	573	830	910	2,456	4,650
Current Expenditure	..	312	320	387	519	552	954	1,003	1,238	2,517	4,005
Current Budget Balance	..	17	24	53	69	-61	-381	-173	-328	-61	645
Capital Receipts	..										
Capital Payments	..	94	107	193	393	155	246	276	267	488	977

1981	1982	1983	1984	1985	1986	1987	1988	1989	1990 estimate	Notes	ZAIRE
540	490	430	340	260	240	230	240	230	220	..	**CURRENT GNP PER CAPITA (US $)**
27,967	28,819	29,735	30,700	31,700	32,745	33,843	34,982	36,145	37,320	..	**POPULATION (thousands)**
				(Billions of current Zaires)							**USE AND ORIGIN OF RESOURCES**
53.9	77.2	138.8	268.7	333.3	459.8	828.8	1,607.7	3,257.7	5,156.3	..	Gross National Product (GNP)
-1.0	-1.3	-3.0	-15.1	-25.5	-22.7	-32.2	-49.6	-87.2	-259.7	..	Net Factor Income from Abroad
54.9	78.5	141.8	283.8	358.8	482.6	861.0	1,657.3	3,344.9	5,416.0	..	GDP at Market Prices
-1.3	-0.9	-1.0	5.9	6.7	3.2	-17.1	-37.1	-90.1	-331.0	..	Resource Balance
7.3	9.5	23.0	73.5	98.7	119.2	218.8	435.6	900.2	1,341.3	..	Exports of Goods & NF Services
8.7	10.4	24.0	67.6	92.0	116.0	235.9	472.7	990.3	1,672.4	..	Imports of Goods & NF Services
56.3	79.4	142.8	278.0	352.1	479.3	878.1	1,694.4	3,435.0	..	..	Domestic Absorption
45.0	65.5	118.9	229.6	279.6	377.1	670.7	1,244.2	2,652.0	..	..	Private Consumption, etc.
5.5	7.4	10.7	18.6	27.6	38.6	85.5	211.1	296.3	..	..	General Gov't Consumption
5.8	6.5	13.2	29.8	44.9	63.7	121.9	239.1	486.7	622.0	..	Gross Domestic Investment
5.3	7.3	14.3	30.1	40.0	61.9	119.5	243.1	494.7	..	..	Fixed Investment
2.6	3.3	6.0	14.5	21.4	28.8	44.0	105.3	243.3	..	..	Indirect Taxes, net
52.3	75.2	135.8	269.3	337.4	453.8	817.0	1,552.0	3,101.6	..	B	GDP at factor cost
13.6	23.6	46.9	84.7	107.4	152.6	249.7	480.3	1,010.5	..	..	Agriculture
17.6	21.0	36.7	79.2	104.7	119.9	237.5	485.8	1,119.0	..	f	Industry
8.2	11.3	19.2	28.2	35.4	48.3	80.8	182.4	376.2	..	..	Manufacturing
23.7	33.9	58.3	119.9	146.7	210.1	373.9	691.2	1,215.4	..	..	Services, etc.
4.4	5.6	12.2	35.6	51.6	66.9	104.8	202.0	396.5	..	..	Gross Domestic Saving
3.4	4.2	9.2	17.2	23.3	40.5	64.7	139.8	267.8	..	..	Gross National Saving
				(Millions of 1987 Zaires)							
735,000	731,000	739,000	755,000	744,000	799,000	829,000	840,000	826,000	795,000	..	Gross National Product
749,000	743,000	755,000	797,000	801,000	839,000	861,000	866,000	849,000	833,000	H	GDP at Market Prices
-18,365	-8,926	-5,250	16,446	14,962	5,626	-17,119	-19,381	10,255	2,498	..	Resource Balance
100,000	89,819	123,000	206,000	220,000	207,000	219,000	228,000	220,000	200,000	..	Exports of Goods & NF Services
118,000	98,745	128,000	190,000	205,000	202,000	236,000	247,000	210,000	197,000	..	Imports of Goods & NF Services
766,000	754,000	760,000	781,000	786,000	833,000	878,000	885,000	838,000	..	..	Domestic Absorption
547,000	567,000	566,000	582,000	574,000	627,000	671,000	658,000	633,000	..	..	Private Consumption, etc.
95,736	90,863	81,860	77,259	77,703	78,319	85,455	107,000	89,944	..	..	General Gov't Consumption
124,000	95,526	112,000	121,000	134,000	127,000	122,000	120,000	115,000	89,350	..	Gross Domestic Investment
110,000	107,000	120,000	122,000	121,000	119,000	120,000	127,000	124,000	..	..	Fixed Investment
712,000	711,000	721,000	755,000	748,000	787,000	817,000	809,000	784,000	..	B H	GDP at factor cost
215,000	222,000	227,000	233,000	239,000	245,000	250,000	257,000	264,000	..	..	Agriculture
198,000	191,000	199,000	224,000	224,000	235,000	237,000	233,000	220,000	..	f	Industry
65,407	64,410	66,269	71,562	75,709	78,943	80,835	79,027	70,084	..	..	Manufacturing
335,000	331,000	330,000	341,000	337,000	359,000	374,000	376,000	364,000	..	..	Services, etc.
											Memo Items:
..	..	..	..	..	..	..	..	..	..	..	Capacity to Import
..	..	..	..	..	..	..	..	..	..	..	Terms of Trade Adjustment
..	..	..	..	..	..	..	..	..	..	..	Gross Domestic Income
..	..	..	..	..	..	..	..	..	..	..	Gross National Income
				(Index 1987 = 100)							**DOMESTIC PRICES/DEFLATORS**
7.3	10.6	18.8	35.6	44.8	57.5	100.0	191.4	394.1	650.3	..	Overall (GDP)
7.3	10.5	18.8	35.6	44.8	57.5	100.0	191.4	409.7	..	..	Domestic Absorption
6.3	10.6	20.7	36.4	44.9	62.3	100.0	186.9	382.5	..	..	Agriculture
8.9	11.0	18.4	35.4	46.7	50.9	100.0	208.6	507.6	..	..	Industry
12.5	17.5	29.0	39.4	46.8	61.2	100.0	230.8	536.8	..	..	Manufacturing
7.9	10.8	19.0	28.9	35.8	52.5	100.0	182.7	372.9	676.1	..	Consumer Price Index
											MANUFACTURING ACTIVITY
..	..	..	..	..	..	..	..	..	..	..	Employment (1987=100)
..	..	..	..	..	..	..	..	..	..	..	Real Earnings per Empl. (1987=100)
..	..	..	..	..	..	..	..	..	..	..	Real Output per Empl. (1987=100)
..	..	..	..	..	..	..	..	..	..	..	Earnings as % of Value Added
				(Billions of current Zaires)							**MONETARY HOLDINGS**
4.84	8.22	13.55	18.78	24.34	38.67	75.74	175.09	293.11	885.81	..	Money Supply, Broadly Defined
4.20	7.42	12.61	17.43	22.49	35.90	68.49	150.11	263.26	746.07	..	Money
2.09	3.28	6.14	8.80	12.29	18.99	36.25	82.80	153.06	427.14	..	Currency Outside Banks
2.11	4.14	6.47	8.63	10.19	16.91	32.23	67.31	110.20	318.94	..	Demand Deposits
0.64	0.80	0.94	1.35	1.85	2.77	7.25	24.98	29.85	139.74	..	Quasi-Money
				(Millions of current Zaires)							**GOVERNMENT DEFICIT (-) OR SURPLUS**
-2,158	-3,484	-1,653	-3,764	10,500	2,321	-3,693	-117,000	62,062	..	..	Government Deficit (-) or Surplus
5,905	7,183	13,884	33,503	51,729	57,890	97,912	201,000	484,000	..	..	Current Revenue
5,783	8,243	12,391	30,463	29,421	40,710	88,533	254,000	300,000	..	..	Current Expenditure
122	-1,060	1,493	3,040	22,308	17,180	9,379	-53,434	184,000	..	..	Current Budget Balance
..	..	..	..	..	..	..	..	..	..	..	Capital Receipts
2,280	2,424	3,146	6,804	11,808	14,860	13,072	63,325	122,000	..	..	Capital Payments

ZAIRE	1970	1971	1972	1973	1974	1975	1976	1977	1978	1979	1980
FOREIGN TRADE (CUSTOMS BASIS)					*(Millions of current US dollars)*						
Value of Exports, fob	735.4	688.0	737.7	1,001.3	1,381.5	864.8	809.3	1,110.0	899.4	2,004.1	2,506.9
Nonfuel Primary Products	684.0	626.5	660.2	927.6	1,310.5	793.5	704.1	1,013.7	824.3	1,356.4	1,528.6
Fuels	1.3	3.2	22.0	1.8	2.2	5.8	72.3	40.5	12.6	45.8	201.8
Manufactures	50.1	58.2	55.5	72.0	68.8	65.6	32.9	55.8	62.5	601.9	776.6
Value of Imports, cif	533.0	620.0	766.4	781.9	940.0	932.8	840.3	852.3	796.7	826.4	1,117.1
Nonfuel Primary Products	95.2	145.6	135.0	160.2	220.8	175.9	198.5	181.2	195.1	138.9	130.0
Fuels	37.8	52.0	47.1	44.6	78.9	91.2	104.6	77.2	60.2	32.6	136.4
Manufactures	400.0	422.3	584.4	577.1	640.3	665.7	537.3	593.9	541.5	654.9	850.7
					(Index 1987 = 100)						
Terms of Trade	288.9	189.5	162.6	236.7	200.5	129.9	147.4	146.4	132.5	146.2	134.2
Export Prices, fob	61.1	46.6	44.9	84.0	104.7	70.5	80.2	87.1	89.3	115.9	121.9
Import Prices, cif	21.2	24.6	27.6	35.5	52.2	54.3	54.4	59.4	67.4	79.3	90.8
BALANCE OF PAYMENTS					*(Millions of current US dollars)*						
Exports of Goods & Services	812.0	708.9	699.1	1,065.9	1,570.9	1,024.9	1,177.5	1,282.9	1,923.8	1,915.3	2,403.8
Merchandise, fob	799.5	696.9	690.3	1,038.4	1,520.7	863.4	1,024.2	1,056.4	1,834.2	1,834.6	2,268.6
Nonfactor Services	1.2	4.5	5.0	21.3	35.7	157.7	149.4	218.0	64.7	70.5	102.8
Factor Services	11.3	7.5	3.8	6.2	14.4	3.8	3.9	8.5	24.9	10.1	32.4
Imports of Goods & Services	719.2	901.7	1,009.7	1,300.0	1,910.3	1,669.2	2,095.3	2,799.0	1,613.2	1,757.0	2,883.3
Merchandise, fob	583.4	684.2	752.1	977.3	1,439.3	993.5	1,293.5	1,602.4	1,024.5	1,106.9	1,518.9
Nonfactor Services	106.2	185.8	223.8	274.0	390.6	555.1	602.9	824.9	389.2	405.4	834.3
Factor Services	29.6	31.7	33.9	48.8	80.3	120.6	198.9	371.7	199.4	244.7	530.1
Long-Term Interest	8.8	7.8	17.0	33.8	60.6	62.7	51.0	71.6	92.4	96.5	204.6
Private Current Transfers, net	-174.9	-99.7	-95.8	-115.2	-126.8	-70.1	-14.3	-88.3	0.0	0.0	-79.4
Workers' Remittances	2.1	8.2	8.7	9.7	10.5	26.6	15.5	30.2	..	..	..
Curr. A/C Bal before Off. Transf.	-140.9	-300.0	-410.2	-355.5	-480.6	-714.4	-932.2	-1,604.4	310.6	158.3	-558.9
Net Official Transfers	77.2	198.0	81.2	110.6	108.2	121.7	99.4	153.2	-16.3	-11.9	266.8
Curr. A/C Bal after Off. Transf.	-63.7	-102.0	-329.0	-244.9	-372.3	-592.7	-832.8	-1,451.2	294.3	146.4	-292.1
Long-Term Capital, net	-42.9	-17.9	212.5	180.0	133.1	80.0	279.6	276.9	114.9	58.8	1,567.4
Direct Investment	42.2	52.6	104.4	75.8	125.8	15.9	79.8	59.2	114.9	60.1	6.0
Long-Term Loans	3.2	171.1	208.8	320.7	406.9	424.2	547.0	501.2	402.3	69.0	279.1
Disbursements	31.6	200.8	252.7	384.2	533.3	513.0	584.6	546.8	452.9	151.6	471.0
Repayments	28.4	29.7	43.9	63.5	126.4	88.8	37.6	45.6	50.6	82.6	191.9
Other Long-Term Capital	-88.3	-241.6	-100.7	-216.5	-399.6	-360.1	-347.2	-283.5	-402.3	-70.3	1,282.3
Other Capital, net	77.9	61.2	106.1	109.3	187.0	384.9	391.1	1,217.0	-415.8	-135.4	-1,240.7
Change in Reserves	28.6	58.7	10.4	-44.4	52.2	127.9	162.0	-42.7	6.5	-69.7	-34.6
Memo Item:					*(Zaires per US dollar)*						
Conversion Factor (Annual Avg)	0.500	0.500	0.500	0.500	0.500	0.500	0.792	0.857	0.836	1.730	2.800
				(Millions of US dollars), outstanding at end of year							
EXTERNAL DEBT (Total)	311.2	363.7	603.7	937.7	1,377.3	1,818.1	2,586.7	3,547.2	4,344.0	4,911.4	4,960.4
Long-Term Debt (by debtor)	311.2	363.7	603.7	937.7	1,377.3	1,818.1	2,586.7	3,270.2	4,008.0	4,567.4	4,634.6
Central Bank, incl. IMF credit	0.0	1.5	34.5	41.8	45.1	101.2	230.5	297.8	358.8	400.5	428.3
Central Government	263.8	222.7	297.3	535.2	727.2	925.3	1,338.0	1,569.6	2,027.6	2,524.5	2,937.7
Rest of General Government	..	..	..	..	..	..	..	..	..	..	..
Non-financial Public Enterprises	47.4	139.0	271.5	360.4	604.8	791.5	1,018.2	1,402.8	1,621.6	1,642.4	1,268.6
Priv. Sector, incl non-guaranteed	0.0	0.5	0.4	0.3	0.2	0.1	0.0	0.0	0.0	0.0	0.0
Short-Term Debt	0.0	0.0	0.0	0.0	0.0	0.0	0.0	277.0	336.0	344.0	325.8
Memo Items:					*(Millions of US dollars)*						
Int'l Reserves Excluding Gold	136.00	90.87	123.18	172.79	118.80	47.91	50.28	133.87	125.75	206.69	204.11
Gold Holdings (at market price)	53.25	62.78	94.36	164.33	93.25	36.47	35.04	42.89	69.61	129.02	175.67
SOCIAL INDICATORS											
Total Fertility Rate	6.0	6.1	6.1	6.1	6.1	6.1	6.1	6.1	6.1	6.2	6.2
Infant Mortality Rate	131.0	129.0	127.0	125.0	123.0	121.0	119.0	117.0	115.0	113.0	111.0
Life Expectancy at Birth	45.2	45.6	46.0	46.4	46.8	47.2	47.6	48.0	48.4	48.8	49.2
Urban Population, % of total	30.3	30.7	31.1	31.4	31.8	32.2	32.6	33.0	33.4	33.8	34.2
Food Prod. per capita (1987=100)	113.1	109.8	108.8	109.4	109.4	108.9	107.0	104.9	98.8	101.8	102.8
Labor Force, Agriculture (%)	79.1	78.3	77.5	76.8	76.1	75.4	74.5	73.7	73.0	72.2	71.5
Labor Force, Female (%)	42.2	41.7	41.2	40.8	40.4	40.0	39.5	39.0	38.5	38.1	37.6
Primary Schl. Enroll. Ratio	88.0	..	..	..	..	88.0	89.0	89.0	89.0	..	95.0
Primary Schl. Enroll. Ratio, Female	65.0	..	..	..	..	72.0	74.0	74.0	74.0	..	80.0
Secondary Schl. Enroll. Ratio	9.0	..	..	..	..	16.0	17.0	20.0	23.0	..	24.0

1981	1982	1983	1984	1985	1986	1987	1988	1989	1990 estimate	Notes	ZAIRE
											FOREIGN TRADE (CUSTOMS BASIS)
				(Millions of current US dollars)							
2,029.9	1,530.2	1,387.9	1,005.5	949.3	1,100.7	674.4	1,120.2	1,254.3	999.1	..	Value of Exports, fob
1,247.5	1,051.5	998.3	915.7	864.5	1,002.4	614.2	1,020.1	1,142.3	909.9	..	Nonfuel Primary Products
260.2	291.3	251.6	4.7	4.4	5.1	3.1	5.2	5.8	4.7	..	Fuels
522.2	187.4	138.0	85.1	80.4	93.2	57.1	94.8	106.2	84.6	..	Manufactures
1,019.1	912.5	841.7	685.5	791.1	875.4	756.2	762.7	849.9	887.7	..	Value of Imports, cif
127.6	120.9	113.6	167.8	193.7	214.3	185.1	186.7	208.1	217.3	..	Nonfuel Primary Products
149.6	167.8	169.3	51.8	59.7	66.1	57.1	57.6	64.2	67.0	..	Fuels
741.9	623.7	558.8	465.9	537.7	595.0	514.0	518.4	577.6	603.3	..	Manufactures
				(Index 1987 = 100)							
112.3	106.2	112.4	113.6	110.6	108.8	100.0	128.5	141.6	163.5	..	Terms of Trade
103.2	93.6	97.2	95.7	92.3	99.2	100.0	131.9	152.3	167.8	..	Export Prices, fob
91.9	88.1	86.5	84.3	83.5	91.1	100.0	102.7	107.6	102.6	..	Import Prices, cif
				(Millions of current US dollars)							**BALANCE OF PAYMENTS**
1,828.9	1,684.7	1,801.9	2,060.3	2,006.3	2,033.1	1,993.9	2,364.0	2,366.1	2,309.2	..	Exports of Goods & Services
1,677.9	1,600.8	1,685.8	1,918.8	1,853.0	1,844.2	1,731.4	2,178.5	2,200.8	2,138.2	..	Merchandise, fob
94.3	57.4	101.1	114.8	125.9	156.0	217.2	149.2	137.1	157.4	..	Nonfactor Services
56.6	26.5	15.0	26.7	27.4	32.8	45.3	36.3	28.2	13.6	..	Factor Services
2,676.7	2,426.6	2,327.2	2,467.2	2,439.9	2,569.2	2,787.9	3,202.6	3,251.8	3,088.0	..	Imports of Goods & Services
1,420.9	1,297.2	1,213.3	1,175.7	1,246.8	1,283.5	1,375.8	1,645.0	1,682.9	1,538.6	..	Merchandise, fob
727.5	607.2	689.5	693.9	597.0	661.7	722.8	895.1	921.6	907.7	..	Nonfactor Services
528.3	522.2	424.4	597.6	596.0	624.1	689.2	662.6	647.3	641.7	..	Factor Services
125.3	69.1	94.2	184.5	195.3	134.8	113.5	98.9	90.6	92.6	..	Long-Term Interest
-3.5	-8.8	3.2	-91.2	-54.8	-62.2	-69.8	-67.2	-108.9	-81.4	..	Private Current Transfers, net
..	..	..	..	..	0.0	..	..	..	..	..	Workers' Remittances
-851.4	-750.7	-522.1	-498.2	-488.4	-598.3	-863.8	-806.4	-887.0	-860.2	..	Curr. A/C Bal before Off. Transf.
247.6	160.1	173.2	174.3	199.0	184.2	219.8	225.8	275.6	217.1	..	Net Official Transfers
-603.7	-590.6	-348.9	-323.9	-289.4	-414.1	-643.9	-580.6	-611.4	-643.1	..	Curr. A/C Bal after Off. Transf.
198.0	-33.6	771.2	196.7	150.3	316.5	638.8	331.5	1,150.1	122.1	..	Long-Term Capital, net
6.0	6.0	5.0	6.0	6.0	5.0	10.0	11.0	12.1	13.3	..	Direct Investment
296.9	138.5	109.6	64.9	37.4	171.9	298.8	303.5	329.7	174.9	..	Long-Term Loans
380.9	197.7	193.8	167.1	141.5	275.9	379.5	386.1	431.8	226.1	..	Disbursements
84.0	59.2	84.2	102.2	104.1	104.0	80.7	82.6	102.1	51.2	..	Repayments
-104.9	-178.1	656.6	125.8	106.9	139.6	330.0	17.0	808.3	-66.1	..	Other Long-Term Capital
170.1	465.2	-500.2	-28.5	102.6	77.7	90.2	260.3	-344.7	602.6	..	Other Capital, net
235.6	159.1	77.9	155.7	36.5	20.0	-85.1	-11.3	-194.0	-81.7	..	Change in Reserves
											Memo Item:
				(Zaires per US dollar)							
4.380	5.750	12.890	36.130	49.870	59.630	112.400	187.070	381.450	718.580	..	Conversion Factor (Annual Avg)
			(Millions of US dollars), outstanding at end of year								**EXTERNAL DEBT (Total)**
5,087.4	5,078.2	5,321.1	5,274.7	6,170.7	7,190.3	8,751.0	8,531.8	9,179.8	10,115.4	..	
4,698.1	4,615.5	5,055.2	4,959.1	5,765.3	6,772.9	8,171.0	7,697.2	8,540.7	9,371.9	..	Long-Term Debt (by debtor)
531.1	607.5	682.0	738.5	890.2	978.4	1,114.8	938.6	787.5	691.4	..	Central Bank, incl. IMF credit
2,941.2	2,835.4	3,379.6	3,327.2	3,867.8	4,668.6	5,753.5	5,610.1	6,518.1	7,345.7	..	Central Government
..	..	..	..	..	..	..	..	..	..	..	Rest of General Government
1,225.8	1,172.6	993.6	893.4	1,007.3	1,125.9	1,302.7	1,148.5	1,235.1	1,334.8	..	Non-financial Public Enterprises
0.0	0.0	0.0	0.0	0.0	0.0	0.0	0.0	0.0	..	..	Priv. Sector, incl non-guaranteed
389.3	462.7	265.9	315.6	405.4	417.4	580.0	834.6	639.1	743.5	..	Short-Term Debt
				(Millions of US dollars)							**Memo Items:**
151.55	38.87	101.57	137.37	189.71	268.62	180.77	186.94	195.09	219.07	..	Int'l Reserves Excluding Gold
142.31	187.33	167.86	143.67	145.52	182.55	236.24	184.61	86.62	41.58	..	Gold Holdings (at market price)
											SOCIAL INDICATORS
6.3	6.3	6.3	6.3	6.3	6.3	6.3	6.3	6.3	6.2	..	Total Fertility Rate
109.0	107.0	105.2	103.4	101.5	99.7	97.9	96.5	95.1	93.7	..	Infant Mortality Rate
49.6	50.0	50.4	50.8	51.2	51.6	52.0	52.0	52.0	52.0	..	Life Expectancy at Birth
34.7	35.2	35.6	36.1	36.6	37.4	38.1	38.6	39.0	39.5	..	Urban Population, % of total
101.2	102.7	102.4	102.2	101.8	100.7	100.0	100.1	98.8	96.5	..	Food Prod. per capita (1987=100)
..	..	..	..	..	..	..	..	..	..	..	Labor Force, Agriculture (%)
37.4	37.2	37.0	36.8	36.6	36.3	36.1	35.9	35.7	35.5	..	Labor Force, Female (%)
..	..	94.0	89.0	89.0	77.0	78.0	..	..	..	..	Primary Schl. Enroll. Ratio
..	..	82.0	71.0	71.0	68.0	67.0	..	..	..	..	Primary Schl. Enroll. Ratio, Female
..	49.0	47.0	..	23.0	23.0	24.0	..	..	..	..	Secondary Schl. Enroll. Ratio

ZAMBIA	1970	1971	1972	1973	1974	1975	1976	1977	1978	1979	1980
CURRENT GNP PER CAPITA (US $)	440	430	430	430	530	550	540	500	500	510	600
POPULATION (thousands)	4,159	4,286	4,419	4,559	4,701	4,846	4,987	5,137	5,295	5,465	5,647

USE AND ORIGIN OF RESOURCES *(Millions of current Zambian Kwacha)*

	1970	1971	1972	1973	1974	1975	1976	1977	1978	1979	1980
Gross National Product (GNP)	1,244	1,145	1,274	1,465	1,752	1,461	1,748	1,898	2,109	2,432	2,835
Net Factor Income from Abroad	-33	-44	-74	-126	-136	-122	-154	-88	-141	-229	-229
GDP at Market Prices	1,278	1,189	1,348	1,591	1,888	1,583	1,902	1,986	2,251	2,660	3,064
Resource Balance	215	-25	21	251	178	-309	96	-51	-76	239	-123
Exports of Goods & NFServices	685	501	586	780	944	575	832	781	755	1,208	1,268
Imports of Goods & NFServices	471	526	565	529	765	884	736	833	831	969	1,391
Domestic Absorption	1,063	1,214	1,327	1,340	1,709	1,892	1,805	2,038	2,326	2,422	3,187
Private Consumption, etc.	504	493	536	530	660	814	853	1,023	1,252	1,413	1,692
General Gov't Consumption	199	280	315	345	358	436	501	525	538	633	782
Gross Domestic Investment	361	441	476	465	692	642	452	490	537	376	713
Fixed Investment	372	393	445	413	502	602	445	483	437	450	558
Indirect Taxes, net	122	114	129	152	180	151	182	190	246	237	221
GDP at factor cost	1,156	1,075	1,219	1,439	1,708	1,432	1,720	1,797	2,004	2,423	2,843
Agriculture	136	154	172	180	199	207	276	326	363	397	435
Industry	699	546	636	845	1,026	670	823	748	886	1,117	1,265
Manufacturing	129	150	181	195	240	266	319	353	430	487	566
Services, etc.	442	489	540	566	662	706	803	913	1,002	1,146	1,363
Gross Domestic Saving	576	416	498	716	870	333	548	439	461	615	590
Gross National Saving	437	263	326	497	648	126	308	274	252	277	217

(Millions of 1987 Zambian Kwacha)

	1970	1971	1972	1973	1974	1975	1976	1977	1978	1979	1980
Gross National Product	14,948.7	14,947.3	16,243.2	15,730.5	17,021.6	17,008.9	17,887.5	17,843.6	17,698.2	16,522.5	17,372.3
GDP at Market Prices	16,107.1	16,189.0	17,860.9	17,783.8	18,953.6	18,513.4	19,629.5	18,707.9	18,851.9	18,258.2	18,807.7
Resource Balance	-5,446.5	-7,150.3	-6,011.3	-3,929.5	-5,729.5	-4,931.8	1,542.0	1,311.7	2,502.1	2,037.1	549.1
Exports of Goods & NFServices	11,164.2	10,452.5	11,874.3	10,856.3	11,510.8	11,128.9	13,524.9	13,149.7	12,303.4	10,984.2	10,646.0
Imports of Goods & NFServices	16,610.7	17,602.8	17,885.6	14,785.7	17,240.3	16,060.7	11,983.0	11,838.0	9,801.3	8,947.1	10,096.9
Domestic Absorption	22,614.6	24,528.7	25,425.7	24,298.6	27,823.8	27,601.0	21,676.2	19,927.6	19,235.9	17,661.9	20,044.8
Private Consumption, etc.	8,163.4	7,679.8	7,921.2	7,316.2	8,276.2	9,334.8	8,845.7	8,067.9	8,160.2	9,020.8	8,708.5
General Gov't Consumption	4,382.7	5,630.4	5,931.0	6,023.0	5,718.9	6,341.0	6,444.7	6,116.2	5,510.4	5,515.1	6,189.6
Gross Domestic Investment	10,068.5	11,218.4	11,573.6	10,959.4	13,828.7	11,925.2	6,385.7	5,743.4	5,565.3	3,126.1	5,146.8
Fixed Investment	10,607.7	10,118.0	11,097.5	10,314.9	10,215.2	11,211.7	6,753.0	5,869.6	4,672.6	3,787.9	4,193.8
GDP at factor cost	..	..	..	..	..	..	..	..	..	..	..
Agriculture	1,551.8	1,589.4	1,660.3	1,640.7	1,715.8	1,795.7	1,921.6	1,941.8	1,953.2	1,847.0	1,812.4
Industry	7,150.1	7,291.0	8,241.5	8,308.0	9,065.6	8,799.5	9,043.1	8,433.1	8,798.4	8,347.4	8,538.0
Manufacturing	3,352.9	3,744.7	4,222.9	4,292.4	4,671.0	4,401.4	4,650.7	4,230.1	4,439.8	4,708.2	4,595.5
Services, etc.	7,701.7	7,517.5	8,100.0	7,910.4	8,285.0	7,964.8	8,683.3	8,281.4	8,073.7	8,046.4	8,479.2
Memo Items:											
Capacity to Import	24,197.6	16,762.3	18,563.4	21,812.5	21,258.2	10,449.1	13,550.8	11,107.4	8,909.5	11,150.8	9,202.7
Terms of Trade Adjustment	13,033.4	6,309.8	6,689.1	10,956.2	9,747.4	-679.8	25.9	-2,042.3	-3,393.9	166.7	-1,443.2
Gross Domestic Income	29,140.4	22,498.8	24,550.0	28,740.0	28,701.0	17,833.5	19,655.4	16,665.6	15,458.1	18,424.9	17,364.4
Gross National Income	27,982.1	21,257.2	22,932.3	26,686.7	26,768.9	16,329.0	17,913.4	15,801.3	14,304.3	16,689.1	15,929.1

DOMESTIC PRICES/DEFLATORS *(Index 1987 = 100)*

	1970	1971	1972	1973	1974	1975	1976	1977	1978	1979	1980
Overall (GDP)	7.9	7.3	7.5	8.9	10.0	8.6	9.7	10.6	11.9	14.6	16.3
Domestic Absorption	4.7	4.9	5.2	5.5	6.1	6.9	8.3	10.2	12.1	13.7	15.9
Agriculture	8.8	9.7	10.4	10.9	11.6	11.5	14.4	16.8	18.6	21.5	24.0
Industry	9.8	7.5	7.7	10.2	11.3	7.6	9.1	8.9	10.1	13.4	14.8
Manufacturing	3.9	4.0	4.3	4.5	5.1	6.0	6.9	8.3	9.7	10.3	12.3
Consumer Price Index	6.4	6.7	7.1	7.5	8.2	9.0	10.7	12.8	14.9	16.3	18.2

MANUFACTURING ACTIVITY

	1970	1971	1972	1973	1974	1975	1976	1977	1978	1979	1980
Employment (1987=100)	..	..	..	..	..	..	..	..	..	..	..
Real Earnings per Empl. (1987=100)	..	..	..	..	..	..	..	..	..	..	..
Real Output per Empl. (1987=100)	..	..	..	..	..	..	..	..	..	..	..
Earnings as % of Value Added	33.5	33.9	27.8	30.1	29.2	30.1	28.9	27.7	26.6	25.6	24.6

MONETARY HOLDINGS *(Millions of current Zambian Kwacha)*

	1970	1971	1972	1973	1974	1975	1976	1977	1978	1979	1980
Money Supply, Broadly Defined	422.8	388.8	413.5	492.1	526.9	588.8	724.1	804.6	750.6	949.8	1,049.1
Money	185.9	198.6	201.3	258.9	265.7	330.6	400.4	392.8	396.8	516.6	519.0
Currency Outside Banks	42.8	58.3	61.3	69.4	79.6	102.4	121.1	118.4	130.9	126.2	151.1
Demand Deposits	143.1	140.3	140.0	189.5	186.0	228.2	279.3	274.4	266.0	390.5	367.9
Quasi-Money	236.9	190.2	212.2	233.2	261.2	258.2	323.6	411.8	353.7	433.2	530.1

GOVERNMENT DEFICIT (-) OR SURPLUS *(Millions of current Zambian Kwacha)*

	1970	1971	1972	1973	1974	1975	1976	1977	1978	1979	1980
GOVERNMENT DEFICIT (-) OR SURPLUS	..	..	-175.6	-266.4	64.4	-340.8	-269.9	-261.4	-324.5	-241.1	-567.5
Current Revenue	..	..	297.0	384.5	648.9	462.3	461.9	532.1	569.1	620.0	790.7
Current Expenditure	..	..	329.5	371.5	418.5	547.0	562.3	586.4	576.3	720.2	1,012.1
Current Budget Balance	..	..	-32.5	13.0	230.4	-84.7	-100.4	-54.3	-7.2	-100.2	-221.4
Capital Receipts	..	..	1.1	86.3	1.1	..	..	..	6.1		
Capital Payments	..	..	144.2	365.7	167.1	256.1	169.5	207.1	323.4	140.9	346.1

1981	1982	1983	1984	1985	1986	1987	1988	1989	1990 estimate	Notes	ZAMBIA
720	660	560	460	370	260	240	290	400	420	..	**CURRENT GNP PER CAPITA (US $)**
5,842	6,051	6,273	6,508	6,753	7,009	7,274	7,548	7,827	8,111	..	**POPULATION (thousands)**
											USE AND ORIGIN OF RESOURCES
					(Millions of current Zambian Kwacha)						
3,388	3,376	3,866	4,448	6,349	10,722	16,719	26,690	54,848	95,272	..	Gross National Product (GNP)
-98	-219	-315	-483	-723	-2,241	-3,059	-3,331	-5,176	-12,330		Net Factor Income from Abroad
3,485	3,595	4,181	4,931	7,072	12,963	19,778	30,021	60,025	107,602	f	GDP at Market Prices
-436	-316	60	91	38	-156	818	2,201	-3,874	2,820	..	Resource Balance
998	995	1,376	1,729	2,740	5,759	8,512	10,266	14,792	34,817	..	Exports of Goods & NF Services
1,434	1,312	1,317	1,639	2,703	5,916	7,695	8,066	18,665	31,997	..	Imports of Goods & NF Services
3,922	3,912	4,122	4,840	7,034	13,120	18,961	27,820	63,898	104,782	..	Domestic Absorption
2,262	2,313	2,538	2,876	4,295	6,552	11,820	19,825	50,360	72,699	..	Private Consumption, etc.
986	996	1,009	1,240	1,687	3,481	4,399	4,582	7,574	16,647	..	General Gov't Consumption
673	603	575	724	1,053	3,087	2,742	3,413	5,964	15,436	..	Gross Domestic Investment
610	618	615	623	724	1,386	1,931	2,381	3,643	13,118	..	Fixed Investment
357	344	632	667	970	2,044	2,338	3,033	2,703	..	..	Indirect Taxes, net
3,128	3,251	3,549	4,264	6,102	10,919	17,440	26,988	57,322	..	B f	GDP at factor cost
554	492	594	717	925	1,578	2,180	5,056	10,562	17,956	..	Agriculture
1,351	1,336	1,675	1,935	2,973	5,750	8,868	13,575	30,935	58,955	f	Industry
684	740	830	1,011	1,616	2,936	5,547	9,496	21,933	45,914		Manufacturing
1,581	1,767	1,913	2,279	3,174	5,636	8,730	11,390	18,528	30,691	f	Services, etc.
237	287	634	815	1,091	2,930	3,559	5,614	2,090	18,256	..	Gross Domestic Saving
3	16	258	249	263	358	314	2,075	-3,503	4,569	..	Gross National Saving
					(Millions of 1987 Zambian Kwacha)						
19,409.5	18,389.7	17,649.5	17,022.1	17,187.2	15,758.3	16,719.0	19,075.8	20,281.4	19,803.1	..	Gross National Product
19,954.9	19,421.1	19,006.1	18,809.0	19,147.2	19,181.1	19,778.3	20,878.1	20,693.3	20,408.4	H	GDP at Market Prices
811.5	4,130.5	4,117.2	3,590.4	2,269.0	1,560.3	817.5	333.7	1,467.4	579.3	..	Resource Balance
9,288.1	10,745.2	9,698.6	9,034.0	8,880.9	9,049.2	8,512.4	8,014.3	7,901.6	8,012.7	..	Exports of Goods & NF Services
8,476.6	6,614.7	5,581.4	5,443.6	6,611.9	7,488.8	7,694.9	7,680.7	6,434.2	7,433.4	..	Imports of Goods & NF Services
20,978.3	18,402.0	16,660.9	17,256.1	18,178.5	19,586.2	18,960.8	19,832.6	19,661.0	20,541.6	..	Domestic Absorption
9,279.5	8,590.1	8,710.0	8,783.4	9,756.8	9,659.8	11,820.2	13,101.3	11,875.4	12,281.0	..	Private Consumption, etc.
7,121.6	6,308.4	5,296.0	5,636.2	5,360.1	5,410.2	4,399.0	3,859.6	5,110.8	4,692.6	..	General Gov't Consumption
4,577.1	3,503.5	2,654.9	2,836.5	3,061.6	4,516.2	2,741.6	2,871.7	2,674.8	3,567.9	..	Gross Domestic Investment
4,282.5	3,761.1	3,008.9	2,575.1	2,415.9	2,048.9	1,931.0	2,164.3	1,497.2	1,870.2	..	Fixed Investment
..	..	..	..	..	..	..	..	..	..	B H	GDP at factor cost
1,960.3	1,731.3	1,876.2	1,981.2	2,050.4	2,229.3	2,180.4	2,601.5	2,531.7	2,346.2	..	Agriculture
8,961.9	8,907.8	8,627.0	8,385.8	8,536.8	8,500.8	8,868.3	9,459.1	9,390.3	9,173.8	f	Industry
5,155.2	4,974.2	4,586.0	4,605.1	5,052.1	5,096.4	5,547.0	6,554.8	6,520.0	6,290.0		Manufacturing
9,029.9	8,881.1	8,502.8	8,442.0	8,559.9	8,451.1	8,729.6	8,817.6	8,771.3	8,888.4	f	Services, etc.
											Memo Items:
5,898.9	5,018.9	5,833.6	5,744.9	6,703.9	7,290.9	8,512.4	9,776.3	5,098.9	8,088.5	..	Capacity to Import
-3,389.2	-5,726.3	-3,865.0	-3,289.1	-2,177.0	-1,758.2	0.0	1,761.9	-2,802.7	75.8	..	Terms of Trade Adjustment
16,565.7	13,694.8	15,141.0	15,519.8	16,970.1	17,422.9	19,778.3	22,640.0	17,890.6	20,484.2	..	Gross Domestic Income
16,020.4	12,663.4	13,784.4	13,733.0	15,010.2	14,000.1	16,719.0	20,837.7	17,478.7	19,878.9	..	Gross National Income
					(Index 1987 = 100)						**DOMESTIC PRICES/DEFLATORS**
17.5	18.5	22.0	26.2	36.9	67.6	100.0	143.8	290.1	527.2	..	Overall (GDP)
18.7	21.3	24.7	28.0	38.7	67.0	100.0	140.3	325.0	510.1	..	Domestic Absorption
28.3	28.4	31.6	36.2	45.1	70.8	100.0	194.3	417.2	765.3	..	Agriculture
15.1	15.0	19.4	23.1	34.8	67.6	100.0	143.5	329.4	642.6	..	Industry
13.3	14.9	18.1	21.9	32.0	57.6	100.0	144.9	336.4	730.0	..	Manufacturing
20.6	23.4	28.0	33.6	46.1	69.9	100.0	155.6	305.5	..	..	Consumer Price Index
											MANUFACTURING ACTIVITY
..	..	..	..	..	..	..	..	..	..	..	Employment (1987=100)
..	..	..	..	..	..	..	..	..	..	..	Real Earnings per Empl. (1987=100)
..	..	..	..	..	..	..	..	..	..	..	Real Output per Empl. (1987=100)
32.3	34.4	..	..	..	..	..	..	..	..	..	Earnings as % of Value Added
					(Millions of current Zambian Kwacha)						**MONETARY HOLDINGS**
1,123.4	1,457.9	1,618.0	1,893.3	2,336.1	4,514.6	6,546.7	..	..	..	..	Money Supply, Broadly Defined
563.7	689.5	795.3	869.9	1,231.5	2,303.7	3,225.1	5,243.8	7,946.6	12,543.2	..	Money
190.1	209.5	238.8	285.6	342.5	593.4	974.2	1,759.5	2,249.8	4,609.5	..	Currency Outside Banks
373.6	479.9	556.5	584.3	889.0	1,710.3	2,250.9	3,484.3	5,696.8	7,933.7	..	Demand Deposits
559.8	768.5	822.7	1,023.4	1,104.6	2,210.9	3,321.6	..	..	..	..	Quasi-Money
					(Millions of current Zambian Kwacha)						
-449.6	-668.2	-327.3	-413.7	-1,072.6	-2,804.3	-2,548.8	-3,466.3	-2,757.0	..	F	**GOVERNMENT DEFICIT (-) OR SURPLUS**
831.1	869.0	1,066.6	1,112.4	1,560.5	3,195.2	4,355.3	5,635.6	7,883.3	..	..	Current Revenue
1,142.1	1,221.5	1,176.6	1,258.2	1,845.8	4,140.6	4,739.5	6,693.1	7,481.3	..	..	Current Expenditure
-311.0	-352.5	-110.0	-145.8	-285.3	-945.4	-384.2	-1,057.5	402.0	..	..	Current Budget Balance
..	..	0.6	1.1	14.6	0.8	3.0	1.1	1.3	..	..	Capital Receipts
138.6	315.7	217.9	269.0	801.9	1,859.7	2,167.6	2,409.9	3,160.3	..	..	Capital Payments

ZAMBIA	1970	1971	1972	1973	1974	1975	1976	1977	1978	1979	1980
FOREIGN TRADE (CUSTOMS BASIS)				*(Millions of current US dollars)*							
Value of Exports, fob	994.5	672.0	750.5	1,136.2	1,399.4	805.1	1,036.2	895.4	867.3	1,372.0	1,329.7
Nonfuel Primary Products	992.6	668.7	747.0	1,131.7	1,389.2	797.2	1,028.6	884.9	846.3	1,345.2	1,113.0
Fuels	0.2	0.2	0.5	0.5	4.0	2.5	3.4	2.7	14.3	16.7	4.1
Manufactures	1.8	3.1	3.0	4.0	6.2	5.4	4.2	7.9	6.6	10.2	212.7
Value of Imports, cif	477.0	558.9	563.4	532.0	787.3	928.7	655.1	671.2	628.3	750.2	1,100.1
Nonfuel Primary Products	61.5	90.3	73.2	57.1	100.3	91.9	65.6	63.9	65.8	83.1	79.5
Fuels	49.3	45.1	37.1	51.1	95.0	126.1	101.4	102.6	110.9	134.1	242.0
Manufactures	366.2	423.5	453.1	423.9	592.1	710.7	488.1	504.7	451.6	533.1	778.7
				(Index 1987 = 100)							
Terms of Trade	394.2	240.7	206.7	301.8	215.5	126.3	139.6	119.8	114.0	135.9	125.5
Export Prices, fob	76.4	58.8	58.8	98.3	115.0	70.2	78.5	73.5	76.1	110.0	121.1
Import Prices, cif	19.4	24.4	28.4	32.6	53.3	55.6	56.2	61.4	66.8	81.0	96.5
BALANCE OF PAYMENTS				*(Millions of current US dollars)*							
Exports of Goods & Services	999.0	727.2	829.5	1,202.9	1,479.3	880.3	1,122.2	973.7	951.6	1,534.5	1,624.6
Merchandise, fob	942.0	671.0	760.0	1,130.1	1,396.3	802.6	1,028.7	896.7	830.6	1,407.8	1,456.9
Nonfactor Services	17.0	25.1	49.9	57.2	52.9	65.6	83.1	73.6	112.6	115.6	151.5
Factor Services	40.0	31.1	19.5	15.5	30.1	12.1	10.4	3.5	8.4	11.1	16.2
Imports of Goods & Services	745.0	823.4	903.3	946.6	1,336.1	1,474.0	1,136.0	1,109.1	1,187.5	1,392.6	1,986.2
Merchandise, fob	487.0	561.7	565.7	538.8	791.3	947.0	668.5	683.0	617.9	756.0	1,114.0
Nonfactor Services	171.0	169.5	215.0	261.1	380.0	398.2	310.6	288.4	407.5	456.0	651.0
Factor Services	87.0	92.3	122.7	146.6	164.8	128.7	157.0	137.8	162.1	180.5	221.2
Long-Term Interest	30.7	38.0	40.3	93.9	51.6	53.0	68.7	75.8	88.4	93.0	116.0
Private Current Transfers, net	-147.0	-152.5	-136.8	-143.1	-134.7	-132.3	-118.9	-96.9	-85.2	-137.3	-183.1
Workers' Remittances	..	..	..	..	..	..	..	..	..	..	..
Curr. A/C Bal before Off. Transf.	107.0	-248.7	-210.6	113.3	8.4	-726.1	-132.8	-232.3	-321.1	4.7	-544.6
Net Official Transfers	1.0	1.0	2.2	16.7	7.2	4.9	8.1	15.2	23.4	32.1	7.2
Curr. A/C Bal after Off. Transf.	108.0	-247.7	-208.5	129.9	15.6	-721.2	-124.7	-217.2	-297.7	36.8	-537.4
Long-Term Capital, net	-139.0	-327.0	102.1	-29.8	52.9	370.3	102.8	19.8	14.9	202.5	162.8
Direct Investment	-297.0	..	29.3	32.2	38.5	37.6	31.2	17.5	38.6	35.2	61.7
Long-Term Loans	321.4	2.8	59.4	29.7	122.5	418.6	164.1	112.1	-36.9	305.9	395.9
Disbursements	362.7	54.4	145.6	319.7	205.8	488.8	253.9	272.9	172.4	518.6	607.9
Repayments	41.3	51.6	86.2	290.0	83.3	70.2	89.8	160.8	209.3	212.7	212.0
Other Long-Term Capital	-163.4	-329.8	13.3	-91.7	-108.1	-85.9	-92.5	-109.8	13.2	-138.6	-294.9
Other Capital, net	167.6	311.2	-40.0	-113.7	-42.5	280.4	-30.9	159.0	93.9	-347.2	371.1
Change in Reserves	-136.6	263.5	146.4	13.6	-26.0	70.5	52.8	38.3	189.0	107.9	3.6
Memo Item:				*(Zambian Kwacha per US dollar)*							
Conversion Factor (Annual Avg)	0.710	0.710	0.710	0.650	0.640	0.640	0.720	0.790	0.800	0.790	0.790
			(Millions of US dollars), outstanding at end of year								
EXTERNAL DEBT (Total)	653.5	689.2	758.4	823.2	956.7	1,352.5	1,525.4	2,340.8	2,583.6	3,046.6	3,266.0
Long-Term Debt (by debtor)	653.5	689.2	758.4	823.2	956.7	1,352.2	1,525.1	1,694.1	1,933.8	2,395.0	2,679.8
Central Bank, incl. IMF credit	0.0	20.6	41.2	68.7	69.8	88.9	110.7	115.9	320.8	513.4	496.5
Central Government	208.3	232.9	234.9	445.0	513.9	615.4	667.9	715.3	799.5	1,138.2	1,524.7
Rest of General Government	..	..	..	..	..	..	..	..	..	..	..
Non-financial Public Enterprises	415.2	400.7	442.3	250.3	285.8	525.4	629.4	683.5	658.8	608.2	558.4
Priv. Sector, incl non-guaranteed	30.0	35.0	40.0	59.2	87.2	122.5	117.1	179.4	154.7	135.2	100.2
Short-Term Debt	0.0	0.0	0.0	0.0	0.0	0.3	0.3	646.7	649.8	651.6	586.2
Memo Items:				*(Millions of US dollars)*							
Int'l Reserves Excluding Gold	508.00	277.09	158.40	185.52	164.36	142.00	92.66	66.31	51.09	79.96	78.20
Gold Holdings (at market price)	6.84	8.73	12.98	22.45	31.33	23.56	22.64	27.71	45.43	111.10	127.92
SOCIAL INDICATORS											
Total Fertility Rate	6.7	6.7	6.7	6.7	6.7	6.7	6.7	6.8	6.8	6.8	6.8
Infant Mortality Rate	106.0	103.0	100.0	98.8	97.6	96.4	95.2	94.0	92.8	91.6	90.4
Life Expectancy at Birth	46.5	46.9	47.3	47.7	48.1	48.5	48.9	49.3	49.6	49.8	50.1
Urban Population, % of total	30.2	31.1	32.0	33.0	33.9	34.8	35.8	36.8	37.7	38.7	39.7
Food Prod. per capita (1987=100)	116.2	125.4	144.1	123.8	128.5	150.9	169.8	151.3	133.1	106.7	107.1
Labor Force, Agriculture (%)	76.6	76.2	75.9	75.5	75.2	74.9	74.5	74.1	73.7	73.4	73.1
Labor Force, Female (%)	27.8	27.7	27.7	27.6	27.6	27.5	27.5	27.4	27.4	27.3	27.3
Primary Schl. Enroll. Ratio	90.0	..	..	..	..	97.0	..	95.0	95.0	95.0	90.0
Primary Schl. Enroll. Ratio, Female	80.0	..	..	..	..	88.0	..	88.0	88.0	89.0	82.0
Secondary Schl. Enroll. Ratio	13.0	..	..	..	..	15.0	16.0	16.0	16.0	16.0	16.0

1981	1982	1983	1984	1985	1986	1987	1988	1989	1990 estimate	Notes	ZAMBIA
											FOREIGN TRADE (CUSTOMS BASIS)
(Millions of current US dollars)											
975.7	861.5	825.4	..	..	..	..	..	..	..	..	Value of Exports, fob
963.2	833.2	801.7	..	..	..	..	..	..	..	..	Nonfuel Primary Products
2.1	3.7	2.4	..	..	..	..	..	..	..	..	Fuels
10.5	24.7	21.2	..	..	..	..	..	..	..	..	Manufactures
1,061.8	839.2	560.8	..	..	..	..	..	..	..	..	Value of Imports, cif
93.8	41.9	33.9	..	..	..	..	..	..	..	..	Nonfuel Primary Products
232.5	270.4	239.7	..	..	..	..	..	..	..	..	Fuels
735.5	527.0	287.2	..	..	..	..	..	..	..	..	Manufactures
(Index 1987 = 100)											
100.1	88.9	97.8	..	..	..	..	..	..	..	..	Terms of Trade
98.4	83.8	89.7	..	..	..	..	..	..	..	..	Export Prices, fob
98.3	94.2	91.7	..	..	..	..	..	..	..	..	Import Prices, cif
											BALANCE OF PAYMENTS
(Millions of current US dollars)											
1,169.4	1,078.7	1,024.6	972.7	867.7	740.8	900.8	1,250.7	1,426.5	..	..	Exports of Goods & Services
996.2	942.0	923.0	892.6	797.1	692.5	852.1	1,189.5	1,339.9	1,259.1	..	Merchandise, fob
152.8	121.6	98.7	75.4	68.2	47.0	47.7	58.1	85.3	..	..	Nonfactor Services
20.4	15.1	2.9	4.7	2.5	1.3	1.1	3.2	1.2	..	..	Factor Services
1,826.3	1,615.5	1,285.7	1,090.0	1,238.8	1,070.4	1,137.9	1,580.3	1,688.3	..	..	Imports of Goods & Services
1,065.3	1,003.5	711.0	612.1	571.3	517.8	585.3	687.2	773.6	1,120.7	..	Merchandise, fob
584.3	408.5	333.8	290.5	254.5	198.8	223.0	289.2	444.0	..	..	Nonfactor Services
176.6	203.4	241.0	187.3	412.9	353.9	329.6	603.9	470.8		..	Factor Services
98.9	86.9	74.6	57.4	43.2	65.2	62.7	67.2	64.8	57.5	..	Long-Term Interest
-156.4	-55.8	-48.8	-45.4	-33.1	-42.5	-19.5	-25.1	-30.2	-44.8	..	Private Current Transfers, net
..	..	..	..	..	0.0	1.0	..	..	..	..	Workers' Remittances
-766.6	-592.6	-310.0	-162.7	-404.1	-372.1	-256.7	-354.7	-292.0	-489.8	..	Curr. A/C Bal before Off. Transf.
33.0	27.6	39.1	10.1	5.6	21.8	8.3	59.3	108.6	146.5	..	Net Official Transfers
-733.6	-565.0	-270.9	-152.6	-398.5	-350.3	-248.4	-295.4	-183.4	-343.3	..	Curr. A/C Bal after Off. Transf.
556.0	197.9	125.7	112.4	372.6	79.2	107.7	153.1	156.6	-259.1	..	Long-Term Capital, net
-38.4	39.0	25.7	17.2	51.5	28.3	74.5	93.3	..	..	..	Direct Investment
171.0	252.0	133.0	199.0	272.9	232.8	78.1	150.5	97.8	62.9	..	Long-Term Loans
406.6	353.2	186.5	257.3	319.1	309.3	164.3	246.3	192.4	153.6	..	Disbursements
235.6	101.2	53.5	58.3	46.2	76.5	86.2	95.8	94.6	90.7	..	Repayments
423.4	-93.0	-33.0	-103.8	48.2	-181.9	-45.0	-90.7	58.8	-322.0	..	Other Long-Term Capital
-231.4	429.6	76.6	-95.0	171.3	171.0	69.9	193.5	108.6	699.6	..	Other Capital, net
409.0	-62.6	68.6	135.2	-145.4	100.1	70.9	-51.2	-81.8	-97.2	..	Change in Reserves
											Memo Item:
(Zambian Kwacha per US dollar)											
0.870	0.930	1.260	1.810	3.140	7.790	9.520	8.270	13.810	34.470	..	Conversion Factor (Annual Avg)
											EXTERNAL DEBT (Total)
(Millions of US dollars), outstanding at end of year											
3,632.5	3,708.4	3,799.0	3,811.3	4,637.4	5,707.3	6,598.7	6,831.5	6,739.0	7,222.6	..	Long-Term Debt (by debtor)
3,021.7	3,060.8	3,290.1	3,376.2	3,960.1	4,650.7	5,419.6	5,355.6	5,096.5	5,734.8	..	Central Bank, incl. IMF credit
805.4	715.1	747.1	774.4	846.7	915.1	1,056.3	1,004.2	962.6	1,003.4	..	Central Government
1,504.2	1,564.8	1,798.0	1,888.1	2,251.7	2,841.9	3,365.2	3,435.5	3,241.5	3,797.8	..	Rest of General Government
..	..	..	..	..	..	..	..	..	..	..	Non-financial Public Enterprises
649.8	723.9	709.8	681.5	850.4	889.0	992.3	910.3	887.4	925.7	..	Priv. Sector, incl non-guaranteed
62.3	57.0	35.2	32.2	11.3	4.7	5.8	5.6	5.0	7.9	..	Short-Term Debt
610.8	647.6	508.9	435.1	677.3	1,056.6	1,179.1	1,475.9	1,642.5	1,487.8	..	
											Memo Items:
(Millions of US dollars)											
56.17	58.20	54.52	54.21	200.11	70.32	108.83	134.03	116.23	193.13	..	Int'l Reserves Excluding Gold
86.26	99.15	82.79	0.62	0.98	1.17	1.94	5.33	6.82	8.08	..	Gold Holdings (at market price)
											SOCIAL INDICATORS
6.8	6.8	6.8	6.8	6.8	6.8	6.8	6.8	6.8	6.7	..	Total Fertility Rate
89.2	88.0	86.4	84.8	83.1	81.5	79.9	80.6	81.3	82.1	..	Infant Mortality Rate
50.3	50.6	51.0	51.4	51.8	52.3	52.7	51.7	50.7	49.7	..	Life Expectancy at Birth
40.7	41.8	42.8	43.9	44.9	46.1	47.4	48.2	49.1	49.9	..	Urban Population, % of total
103.7	93.9	97.5	95.1	102.0	104.1	100.0	120.3	115.2	90.8	..	Food Prod. per capita (1987=100)
..	..	..	..	..	..	..	..	..	..	..	Labor Force, Agriculture (%)
27.5	27.7	27.8	28.0	28.2	28.4	28.5	28.7	28.9	29.0	..	Labor Force, Female (%)
..	..	93.0	96.0	99.0	97.0	..	95.0	..	..	..	Primary Schl. Enroll. Ratio
..	..	87.0	89.0	93.0	92.0	..	91.0	..	..	..	Primary Schl. Enroll. Ratio, Female
..	17.0	17.0	17.0	18.0	..	..	20.0	..	..	..	Secondary Schl. Enroll. Ratio

ZIMBABWE	1970	1971	1972	1973	1974	1975	1976	1977	1978	1979	1980
CURRENT GNP PER CAPITA (US $)	310	340	360	400	500	550	570	540	530	590	710
POPULATION (thousands)	5,249	5,416	5,579	5,739	5,900	6,065	6,222	6,392	6,578	6,783	7,009

USE AND ORIGIN OF RESOURCES

(Millions of current Zimbabwe Dollars)

	1970	1971	1972	1973	1974	1975	1976	1977	1978	1979	1980
Gross National Product (GNP)	1,058.0	1,214.0	1,384.0	1,514.0	1,821.0	1,952.0	2,107.0	2,150.0	2,317.0	2,769.0	3,394.0
Net Factor Income from Abroad	-21.0	-30.0	-35.0	-39.0	-40.0	-46.0	-59.0	-48.0	-46.0	-53.0	-47.0
GDP at Market Prices	1,079.0	1,244.0	1,419.0	1,553.0	1,861.0	1,998.0	2,166.0	2,198.0	2,363.0	2,822.0	3,441.0
Resource Balance	..	..	..	..	..	-23.0	84.0	52.0	82.0	-5.0	-103.0
Exports of Goods & NFServices	..	..	..	..	..	590.0	617.0	610.0	675.0	798.0	1,043.0
Imports of Goods & NFServices	..	..	..	..	..	613.0	533.0	558.0	593.0	803.0	1,146.0
Domestic Absorption	1,068.0	1,266.0	1,379.0	1,522.0	1,871.0	2,021.0	2,082.0	2,146.0	2,281.0	2,827.0	3,544.0
Private Consumption, etc.	722.0	844.0	848.0	947.0	1,138.0	1,240.0	1,375.0	1,344.0	1,549.0	1,932.0	2,219.0
General Gov't Consumption	126.0	143.0	157.0	180.0	221.0	256.0	319.0	382.0	451.0	537.0	677.0
Gross Domestic Investment	220.0	279.0	374.0	395.0	512.0	525.0	388.0	420.0	281.0	358.0	648.0
Fixed Investment	175.0	221.0	256.0	330.0	421.0	468.0	427.0	379.0	341.0	395.0	528.0
Indirect Taxes, net	68.0	76.0	83.0	103.0	70.0	96.0	102.0	129.0	104.0	172.0	217.0
GDP at factor cost	1,011.0	1,168.0	1,336.0	1,450.0	1,791.0	1,902.0	2,064.0	2,069.0	2,259.0	2,650.0	3,224.0
Agriculture	153.0	200.0	234.0	215.0	315.0	323.0	350.0	334.0	289.0	321.0	451.0
Industry	367.0	415.0	485.0	569.0	681.0	722.0	777.0	749.0	801.0	1,014.0	1,248.0
Manufacturing	209.0	251.0	297.0	343.0	421.0	447.0	480.0	460.0	515.0	625.0	802.0
Services, etc.	491.0	553.0	617.0	666.0	795.0	857.0	937.0	986.0	1,169.0	1,315.0	1,525.0
Gross Domestic Saving	231.0	257.0	414.0	426.0	502.0	502.0	472.0	472.0	363.0	353.0	545.0
Gross National Saving	199.5	214.8	366.8	373.4	443.1	407.9	363.6	414.4	305.2	262.0	420.5

(Millions of 1987 Zimbabwe Dollars)

	1970	1971	1972	1973	1974	1975	1976	1977	1978	1979	1980
Gross National Product	5,422.1	6,007.2	6,507.5	6,676.5	7,131.8	6,973.3	6,965.4	6,505.2	6,335.8	6,567.2	7,299.5
GDP at Market Prices	5,662.1	6,167.0	6,680.7	6,854.7	7,296.0	7,145.3	7,166.9	6,656.7	6,467.2	6,699.7	7,408.0
Resource Balance	..	..	..	..	..	..	161.1	54.4	129.6	-105.6	-314.4
Exports of Goods & NFServices	..	..	..	..	..	..	1,905.1	1,808.1	1,879.5	1,564.7	1,908.7
Imports of Goods & NFServices	..	..	..	..	..	..	1,744.0	1,753.7	1,749.8	1,670.3	2,223.2
Domestic Absorption	..	..	..	..	..	..	7,005.8	6,602.3	6,337.6	6,805.3	7,722.4
Private Consumption, etc.	..	..	..	..	..	..	3,511.0	3,575.5	3,882.4	4,176.3	3,990.4
General Gov't Consumption	390.7	428.8	458.2	501.4	563.6	601.7	679.5	734.8	1,035.6	1,063.3	1,170.5
Gross Domestic Investment	2,252.3	2,656.8	2,906.6	3,176.3	4,350.0	3,909.8	2,815.4	2,292.0	1,419.6	1,565.7	2,561.6
Fixed Investment	1,414.1	1,664.6	1,820.5	2,218.6	2,611.1	2,502.5	2,026.5	1,556.1	1,230.4	1,212.7	1,469.8
GDP at factor cost	5,231.9	5,718.3	6,199.7	6,324.9	6,707.5	6,699.0	6,647.7	6,168.9	6,121.9	6,226.6	6,891.4
Agriculture	802.5	1,018.3	1,150.9	930.6	1,099.2	1,034.0	1,150.9	905.9	998.1	998.1	1,013.8
Industry	2,191.2	2,323.9	2,566.9	2,832.3	2,897.5	2,875.1	2,746.8	2,539.9	2,434.1	2,569.1	2,807.6
Manufacturing	1,104.4	1,156.1	1,371.3	1,479.0	1,584.5	1,569.4	1,479.0	1,405.8	1,354.1	1,500.5	1,726.5
Services, etc.	2,247.4	2,387.5	2,511.3	2,610.8	2,763.1	2,834.1	2,795.6	2,748.9	2,716.4	2,694.0	3,096.0

Memo Items:

	1970	1971	1972	1973	1974	1975	1976	1977	1978	1979	1980
Capacity to Import	..	..	..	..	..	..	2,018.9	1,917.1	1,991.8	1,659.9	2,023.4
Terms of Trade Adjustment	..	..	..	..	..	..	113.8	109.1	112.3	95.2	114.6
Gross Domestic Income	..	..	..	..	..	..	7,280.7	6,765.7	6,579.5	6,794.9	7,522.6
Gross National Income	..	..	..	..	..	..	7,079.2	6,614.3	6,448.2	6,662.4	7,414.1

DOMESTIC PRICES/DEFLATORS

(Index 1987 = 100)

	1970	1971	1972	1973	1974	1975	1976	1977	1978	1979	1980
Overall (GDP)	19.1	20.2	21.2	22.7	25.5	28.0	30.2	33.0	36.5	42.1	46.4
Domestic Absorption	..	..	..	..	..	..	29.7	32.5	36.0	41.5	45.9
Agriculture	19.1	19.6	20.3	23.1	28.7	31.2	30.4	36.9	29.0	32.2	44.5
Industry	16.7	17.9	18.9	20.1	23.5	25.1	28.3	29.5	32.9	39.5	44.5
Manufacturing	18.9	21.7	21.7	23.2	26.6	28.5	32.5	32.7	38.0	41.7	46.5
Consumer Price Index	18.8	19.3	19.9	20.5	21.9	24.0	26.7	29.4	31.1	36.7	38.7

MANUFACTURING ACTIVITY

	1970	1971	1972	1973	1974	1975	1976	1977	1978	1979	1980
Employment (1987=100)	63.9	71.6	77.7	81.4	87.4	89.8	86.6	83.4	81.4	87.1	95.0
Real Earnings per Empl. (1987=100)	83.6	84.7	86.7	91.9	95.2	97.5	97.0	95.1	97.8	91.3	102.0
Real Output per Empl. (1987=100)	84.9	77.6	82.3	85.5	86.1	86.0	80.2	83.7	79.2	81.5	87.1
Earnings as % of Value Added	42.9	42.3	42.6	42.0	40.5	42.3	43.9	46.5	43.6	42.8	41.8

MONETARY HOLDINGS

(Millions of current Zimbabwe Dollars)

	1970	1971	1972	1973	1974	1975	1976	1977	1978	1979	1980
Money Supply, Broadly Defined	..	..	..	..	..	..	..	..	..	1,636.5	..
Money	..	..	..	..	..	324.1	351.9	374.5	415.0	463.2	632.8
Currency Outside Banks	..	..	..	..	..	66.9	79.1	83.9	95.2	107.6	157.2
Demand Deposits	..	..	..	..	..	257.2	272.8	290.6	319.8	355.6	475.6
Quasi-Money	..	..	..	..	..	..	..	..	..	1,173.3	..

(Millions of current Zimbabwe Dollars)

GOVERNMENT DEFICIT (-) OR SURPLUS	1970	1971	1972	1973	1974	1975	1976	1977	1978	1979	1980
	..	..	..	..	..	..	-118.3	-95.4	-253.5	-293.4	-376.0
Current Revenue	..	..	..	..	..	..	491.7	575.1	572.7	610.8	828.7
Current Expenditure	..	..	..	..	..	..	479.6	621.5	751.4	835.1	1,136.9
Current Budget Balance	..	..	..	..	..	..	12.1	-46.4	-178.7	-224.3	-308.2
Capital Receipts	..	..	..	..	..	..	0.5	0.6	0.3	0.6	0.9
Capital Payments	..	..	..	..	..	..	130.9	49.6	75.1	69.7	68.7

1981	1982	1983	1984	1985	1986	1987	1988	1989	1990 estimate	Notes	ZIMBABWE
860	900	850	730	630	570	560	620	670	640	..	**CURRENT GNP PER CAPITA (US $)**
7,257	7,531	7,822	8,116	8,406	8,692	8,976	9,256	9,532	9,805	..	**POPULATION (thousands)**

USE AND ORIGIN OF RESOURCES

(Millions of current Zimbabwe Dollars)

1981	1982	1983	1984	1985	1986	1987	1988	1989	1990	Notes	
4,318.0	5,003.0	6,058.0	6,210.0	7,013.0	7,992.0	8,918.0	10,527.0	12,614.8	14,486.0	..	Gross National Product (GNP)
-115.0	-194.0	-248.0	-195.0	-284.0	-384.0	-355.0	-478.0	-452.2	-688.0		Net Factor Income from Abroad
4,433.0	5,197.0	6,306.0	6,405.0	7,297.0	8,376.0	9,273.0	11,005.0	13,067.0	15,174.0	..	GDP at Market Prices
-325.0	-309.0	-197.0	35.0	86.0	357.0	366.0	585.0	298.6	11.4	..	Resource Balance
1,117.0	1,141.0	1,345.0	1,708.0	2,101.0	2,559.0	2,789.0	3,446.0	3,984.0	4,928.0	..	Exports of Goods & NFServices
1,442.0	1,450.0	1,542.0	1,673.0	2,015.0	2,202.0	2,423.0	2,861.0	3,685.4	4,916.6		Imports of Goods & NFServices
4,758.0	5,506.0	6,503.0	6,370.0	7,211.0	8,019.0	8,907.0	10,420.0	12,768.4	15,162.6		Domestic Absorption
2,969.0	3,377.0	4,342.0	3,792.0	4,206.0	4,674.0	4,856.0	5,793.0	7,397.4	8,024.6		Private Consumption, etc.
763.0	1,027.0	1,159.0	1,364.0	1,560.0	1,804.0	2,334.0	2,770.0	2,996.0	3,951.0		General Gov't Consumption
1,026.0	1,102.0	1,002.0	1,214.0	1,445.0	1,541.0	1,717.0	1,857.0	2,375.0	3,187.0		Gross Domestic Investment
830.0	1,039.0	1,238.0	1,186.0	1,133.0	1,312.0	1,673.0	2,043.0	2,375.0	3,187.0		Fixed Investment
384.0	540.0	874.0	756.0	1,070.0	1,026.0	1,017.0	1,463.0	1,795.0	2,145.0		Indirect Taxes, net
4,049.0	4,657.0	5,432.0	5,649.0	6,227.0	7,350.0	8,256.0	9,542.0	11,272.0	13,029.0	..	GDP at factor cost
640.0	669.0	544.0	748.0	1,038.0	1,121.0	1,061.0	1,263.0	1,390.0	1,686.0	..	Agriculture
1,484.0	1,601.0	2,287.0	2,142.0	2,121.0	2,675.0	3,226.0	3,714.0	4,553.0	5,230.0	..	Industry
1,016.0	1,121.0	1,441.0	1,475.0	1,488.0	1,832.0	2,043.0	2,346.0	2,932.0	3,436.0		Manufacturing
1,925.0	2,387.0	2,601.0	2,759.0	3,068.0	3,554.0	3,969.0	4,565.0	5,329.0	6,113.0		Services, etc.
701.0	793.0	805.0	1,249.0	1,531.0	1,898.0	2,083.0	2,442.0	2,673.6	3,198.4		Gross Domestic Saving
500.1	501.7	441.1	1,005.6	1,174.1	1,469.7	1,674.7	1,940.2	2,244.7	2,534.9		Gross National Saving

(Millions of 1987 Zimbabwe Dollars)

1981	1982	1983	1984	1985	1986	1987	1988	1989	1990	Notes	
8,109.2	8,222.1	8,337.3	8,247.5	8,755.0	8,919.8	8,918.0	9,641.3	10,358.5	10,449.8	..	Gross National Product
8,335.9	8,555.5	8,691.1	8,513.4	9,117.9	9,355.3	9,273.0	10,107.6	10,754.0	10,975.2	I	GDP at Market Prices
-757.8	-731.8	-456.7	-75.8	-42.6	256.6	366.0	12.7	-296.6	-466.9		Resource Balance
2,055.1	2,106.4	2,113.7	1,972.8	2,518.2	2,931.7	2,789.0	2,598.7	2,677.4	2,864.0		Exports of Goods & NFServices
2,812.9	2,838.1	2,570.4	2,048.6	2,560.7	2,675.2	2,423.0	2,586.0	2,973.9	3,330.9		Imports of Goods & NFServices
9,093.7	9,287.2	9,147.8	8,589.2	9,160.5	9,098.8	8,907.0	10,094.8	11,050.5	11,442.1		Domestic Absorption
3,959.0	4,513.3	5,144.0	4,204.6	4,317.7	4,422.8	4,856.0	4,683.8	5,346.8	5,504.1		Private Consumption, etc.
1,367.6	1,542.2	1,628.6	1,763.5	1,829.2	1,979.6	2,334.0	2,563.9	2,717.8	2,773.7		General Gov't Consumption
3,767.1	3,231.8	2,375.2	2,621.1	3,013.7	2,696.4	1,717.0	1,926.3	2,096.1	2,221.4		Gross Domestic Investment
2,009.8	2,193.6	2,129.5	1,720.3	1,405.8	1,442.0	1,673.0	1,926.3	2,096.1	2,221.4		Fixed Investment
7,560.4	7,671.6	7,398.0	7,570.5	8,136.8	8,311.4	8,256.0	8,868.3	9,267.8	9,437.4		GDP at factor cost
1,157.7	1,074.5	905.9	1,114.9	1,380.2	1,294.8	1,061.0	1,330.7	1,319.5	1,231.8		Agriculture
3,001.0	2,980.8	2,908.8	2,825.6	2,998.8	3,124.8	3,226.0	3,345.2	3,538.7	3,657.9		Industry
1,896.6	1,888.0	1,834.2	1,741.6	1,941.8	2,008.6	2,043.0	2,144.2	2,271.2	2,370.2		Manufacturing
3,426.9	3,625.9	3,583.3	3,630.0	3,757.9	3,891.9	3,969.0	4,192.3	4,409.5	4,547.6		Services, etc.

Memo Items:

1981	1982	1983	1984	1985	1986	1987	1988	1989	1990	Notes	
2,178.9	2,233.3	2,242.0	2,091.4	2,670.0	3,108.9	2,789.0	3,114.7	3,214.9	3,338.6	..	Capacity to Import
123.8	126.9	128.3	118.6	151.9	177.2	0.0	516.0	537.5	474.6	..	Terms of Trade Adjustment
8,459.7	8,682.4	8,819.4	8,632.0	9,269.8	9,532.5	9,273.0	10,623.6	11,291.5	11,449.8	..	Gross Domestic Income
8,233.0	8,349.0	8,465.6	8,366.2	8,906.9	9,097.0	8,918.0	10,157.3	10,896.0	10,924.4		Gross National Income

DOMESTIC PRICES/DEFLATORS

(Index 1987 = 100)

1981	1982	1983	1984	1985	1986	1987	1988	1989	1990	Notes	
53.2	60.7	72.6	75.2	80.0	89.5	100.0	108.9	121.5	138.3	..	Overall (GDP)
52.3	59.3	71.1	74.2	78.7	88.1	100.0	103.2	115.5	132.5	..	Domestic Absorption
55.3	62.3	60.1	67.1	75.2	86.6	100.0	94.9	105.3	136.9	..	Agriculture
49.4	53.7	78.6	75.8	70.7	85.6	100.0	111.0	128.7	143.0	..	Industry
53.6	59.4	78.6	84.7	76.6	91.2	100.0	109.4	129.1	145.0		Manufacturing
43.8	48.5	59.7	71.7	77.8	88.9	100.0	107.4	121.3	142.3		Consumer Price Index

MANUFACTURING ACTIVITY

1981	1982	1983	1984	1985	1986	1987	1988	1989	1990	Notes	
102.2	104.0	99.6	96.6	96.6	99.1	100.0	102.7	..	..	..	Employment (1987=100)
110.7	116.0	108.0	101.1	107.2	101.4	100.0	101.9	..	..	..	Real Earnings per Empl. (1987=100)
88.1	87.5	80.7	85.6	109.8	100.3	100.0	101.1	..	..	..	Real Output per Empl. (1987=100)
43.9	48.1	39.9	39.0	41.5	35.8	34.9	34.3	..	..	..	Earnings as % of Value Added

MONETARY HOLDINGS

(Millions of current Zimbabwe Dollars)

1981	1982	1983	1984	1985	1986	1987	1988	1989	1990	Notes	
..	..	..	2,995.3	3,607.7	3,917.2	4,843.5	5,165.1	7,455.4	8,940.9	D	Money Supply, Broadly Defined
678.8	826.9	751.4	865.8	1,005.2	1,102.8	1,224.6	1,602.7	1,905.1	2,417.6	..	Money
198.6	237.5	227.4	258.8	321.1	379.7	389.3	503.3	617.9	769.8		Currency Outside Banks
480.2	589.4	524.0	607.0	684.1	723.1	835.3	1,099.4	1,287.2	1,647.8		Demand Deposits
..	..	..	2,129.5	2,602.5	2,814.4	3,618.9	3,562.4	5,550.3	6,523.3		Quasi-Money

(Millions of current Zimbabwe Dollars)

1981	1982	1983	1984	1985	1986	1987	1988	1989	1990	Notes	
-261.6	-545.3	-393.7	-647.4	-512.5	-638.1	-977.4	-1,004.9	-1,111.0	-1,137.8	C F	**GOVERNMENT DEFICIT (-) OR SURPLUS**
1,130.0	1,531.2	1,888.9	2,109.5	2,288.0	2,590.8	3,018.8	3,637.1	4,340.5	5,297.5	..	Current Revenue
1,233.7	1,715.6	1,905.8	2,364.8	2,412.6	2,856.7	3,492.9	3,855.9	4,437.1	5,271.4	..	Current Expenditure
-103.7	-184.4	-16.9	-255.3	-124.6	-265.9	-474.1	-218.8	-96.6	26.1	..	Current Budget Balance
1.1	0.4	0.6	0.8	17.0	17.1	15.0	6.9	15.9	9.6	..	Capital Receipts
159.0	361.3	377.4	392.9	404.9	389.3	518.3	793.0	1,030.3	1,173.5		Capital Payments

ZIMBABWE	1970	1971	1972	1973	1974	1975	1976	1977	1978	1979	1980

FOREIGN TRADE (CUSTOMS BASIS) *(Millions of current US dollars)*

	1970	1971	1972	1973	1974	1975	1976	1977	1978	1979	1980
Value of Exports, fob	..	..	..	..	..	..	..	..	..	14.1	433.3
Nonfuel Primary Products	..	..	..	..	..	..	..	..	..	..	262.2
Fuels	..	..	..	..	..	..	..	..	..	..	12.9
Manufactures	..	..	..	..	..	..	..	..	..	5.7	158.2
Value of Imports, cif	..	..	..	..	..	..	..	..	..	21.9	192.9
Nonfuel Primary Products	..	..	..	..	..	..	..	..	..	0.4	17.1
Fuels	..	..	..	..	..	..	..	..	..	12.8	22.4
Manufactures	..	..	..	..	..	..	..	..	..	8.6	153.4

(Index 1987 = 100)

	1970	1971	1972	1973	1974	1975	1976	1977	1978	1979	1980
Terms of Trade	..	..	..	..	..	..	..	..	..	..	..
Export Prices, fob	..	..	..	..	..	..	..	..	..	..	..
Import Prices, cif	..	..	..	..	..	..	..	..	..	..	..

BALANCE OF PAYMENTS *(Millions of current US dollars)*

	1970	1971	1972	1973	1974	1975	1976	1977	1978	1979	1980
Exports of Goods & Services	417.0	453.7	575.3	763.3	960.2	1,042.0	1,017.0	1,005.3	1,028.9	1,230.5	1,719.3
Merchandise, fob	370.0	404.0	516.0	687.0	867.0	922.0	900.0	901.0	923.2	1,079.6	1,445.5
Nonfactor Services	32.0	35.0	45.0	60.0	75.0	80.0	78.0	64.5	67.8	87.2	166.8
Factor Services	15.0	14.7	14.3	16.3	18.2	40.0	39.0	39.8	37.9	63.7	107.1
Imports of Goods & Services	428.4	507.8	571.8	773.8	1,037.0	1,190.8	962.1	1,004.0	974.3	1,283.4	1,900.3
Merchandise, fob	346.9	405.6	457.8	604.0	816.2	844.0	652.0	671.3	654.2	875.0	1,339.0
Nonfactor Services	45.5	57.1	64.6	115.0	149.9	243.8	198.1	217.9	222.8	266.1	382.0
Factor Services	36.0	45.1	49.4	54.8	70.9	103.0	112.0	114.8	97.3	142.2	179.3
Long-Term Interest	4.6	5.7	5.8	5.6	5.0	2.2	2.1	1.7	4.3	7.3	10.2
Private Current Transfers, net	-14.7	-17.2	-18.5	-23.2	-32.5	-84.4	-78.9	-15.3	-17.4	-55.9	-120.6
Workers' Remittances	..	..	..	..	..	13.0	13.0	11.5	5.3	10.6	9.3
Curr. A/C Bal before Off. Transf.	-26.1	-71.3	-15.0	-33.7	-109.3	-233.2	-24.0	-14.0	37.2	-108.7	-301.6
Net Official Transfers	12.2	12.3	12.0	12.1	11.9	13.1	13.1	..	..	..	57.7
Curr. A/C Bal after Off. Transf.	-13.9	-59.0	-3.0	-21.6	-97.4	-220.1	-10.9	-14.0	37.2	-108.7	-243.8
Long-Term Capital, net	26.3	30.5	-2.4	51.6	62.6	147.0	24.0	-30.1	151.8	146.5	-53.7
Direct Investment	..	..	..	..	..	..	..	-3.8	2.5	0.1	1.6
Long-Term Loans	-4.8	-4.8	-5.6	-10.6	-9.5	-5.7	-5.3	-4.2	270.3	92.4	92.6
Disbursements	0.0	0.0	0.0	0.0	0.0	0.0	0.0	0.0	274.4	99.7	132.3
Repayments	4.8	4.8	5.6	10.6	9.5	5.7	5.3	4.2	4.1	7.3	39.7
Other Long-Term Capital	31.1	35.3	3.2	62.2	72.1	152.7	29.3	-22.1	-121.0	54.0	-147.8
Other Capital, net	-20.0	14.3	60.6	33.4	-19.1	82.3	-16.4	36.0	-114.0	82.1	211.0
Change in Reserves	7.6	14.2	-55.2	-63.4	53.9	-9.2	3.3	8.1	-75.0	-119.9	86.5

Memo Item: *(Zimbabwe Dollars per US dollar)*

	1970	1971	1972	1973	1974	1975	1976	1977	1978	1979	1980
Conversion Factor (Annual Avg)	0.710	0.710	0.660	0.590	0.580	0.570	0.630	0.630	0.680	0.680	0.640

(Millions of US dollars), outstanding at end of year

	1970	1971	1972	1973	1974	1975	1976	1977	1978	1979	1980
EXTERNAL DEBT (Total)	229.1	233.7	213.7	217.5	217.5	186.9	143.9	199.5	446.1	559.2	785.6
Long-Term Debt (by debtor)	229.1	233.7	213.7	217.5	217.5	186.9	143.9	153.5	418.1	524.2	695.6
Central Bank, incl. IMF credit	0.0	0.0	0.0	0.0	0.0	0.0	0.0	0.0	0.0	0.0	0.0
Central Government	175.7	181.7	167.3	173.4	179.3	154.0	117.0	128.2	395.3	503.7	675.3
Rest of General Government	..	..	..	..	..	..	..	..	..	..	..
Non-financial Public Enterprises	53.4	52.0	46.4	44.1	38.2	32.9	26.9	25.3	22.8	20.5	20.3
Priv. Sector, incl non-guaranteed	0.0	0.0	0.0	0.0	0.0	0.0	0.0	0.0	0.0	0.0	0.0
Short-Term Debt	0.0	0.0	0.0	0.0	0.0	0.0	0.0	46.0	28.0	35.0	90.0

Memo Items: *(Millions of US dollars)*

	1970	1971	1972	1973	1974	1975	1976	1977	1978	1979	1980
Int'l Reserves Excluding Gold	20.27	6.05	61.27	124.72	70.79	79.95	76.64	72.56	148.02	298.90	213.50
Gold Holdings (at market price)	39.16	35.65	35.82	84.19	93.62	49.23	35.71	25.07	36.39	133.12	205.74

SOCIAL INDICATORS

	1970	1971	1972	1973	1974	1975	1976	1977	1978	1979	1980
Total Fertility Rate	7.7	7.6	7.5	7.4	7.3	7.2	7.1	7.0	7.0	6.9	6.8
Infant Mortality Rate	96.2	94.6	93.0	91.6	90.2	88.8	87.4	86.0	84.8	83.6	82.4
Life Expectancy at Birth	50.5	51.0	51.5	52.0	52.4	52.9	53.3	53.8	54.2	54.6	55.0
Urban Population, % of total	16.9	17.4	17.9	18.4	18.9	19.4	19.9	20.4	20.9	21.4	21.9
Food Prod. per capita (1987=100)	135.4	174.0	196.8	140.4	174.8	153.5	167.6	160.9	154.9	122.6	120.1
Labor Force, Agriculture (%)	77.3	76.8	76.3	75.9	75.5	75.1	74.6	74.1	73.6	73.2	72.8
Labor Force, Female (%)	37.6	37.5	37.4	37.3	37.2	37.2	37.0	36.9	36.9	36.8	36.7
Primary Schl. Enroll. Ratio	74.0	..	..	..	..	73.0	72.0	70.0	63.0	61.0	85.0
Primary Schl. Enroll. Ratio, Female	66.0	..	..	..	..	67.0	66.0	65.0	59.0	57.0	..
Secondary Schl. Enroll. Ratio	7.0	..	..	..	..	9.0	9.0	9.0	9.0	8.0	8.0

1981	1982	1983	1984	1985	1986	1987	1988	1989	1990 estimate	Notes	ZIMBABWE
(Millions of current US dollars)											**FOREIGN TRADE (CUSTOMS BASIS)**
656.3	636.3	672.2	1,004.1	954.5	1,018.8	..	..	..	..	..	Value of Exports, fob
431.8	466.9	504.9	645.8	648.2	700.4	..	..	..	..	..	Nonfuel Primary Products
0.3	0.3	0.3	13.1	9.8	11.3	..	..	..	..	..	Fuels
224.2	169.0	166.9	345.1	296.5	307.1	..	..	..	..	..	Manufactures
456.2	489.3	450.7	959.3	896.6	985.3	..	..	..	1,851.4	..	Value of Imports, cif
35.7	33.1	38.9	118.1	92.7	99.4	..	..	..	161.3	..	Nonfuel Primary Products
14.1	6.7	3.5	206.5	213.4	148.7	..	..	..	288.3	..	Fuels
406.4	449.6	408.3	634.6	590.6	737.1	..	..	..	1,401.9	..	Manufactures
(Index 1987 = 100)											
..	..	..	..	..	..	..	..	..	..	..	Terms of Trade
..	..	..	..	..	..	..	..	..	..	..	Export Prices, fob
..	..	..	..	..	..	..	..	..	..	..	Import Prices, cif
(Millions of current US dollars)											**BALANCE OF PAYMENTS**
1,679.6	1,574.0	1,368.3	1,368.1	1,452.9	1,528.1	1,649.6	1,872.6	1,942.0	2,064.0	f	Exports of Goods & Services
1,451.4	1,312.1	1,153.7	1,173.6	1,119.6	1,322.7	1,452.0	1,664.8	1,680.0	1,732.0	..	Merchandise, fob
132.1	180.1	144.1	138.8	295.1	168.4	164.1	189.8	205.0	281.0	..	Nonfactor Services
96.0	81.8	70.6	55.8	38.2	36.9	33.5	18.0	57.0	51.0	..	Factor Services
2,281.8	2,200.4	1,755.3	1,517.8	1,548.1	1,553.1	1,649.2	1,808.5	2,015.0	2,340.0	..	Imports of Goods & Services
1,534.0	1,472.0	1,069.6	989.3	918.9	1,011.6	1,071.0	1,163.6	1,323.0	1,511.0	f	Merchandise, fob
522.1	420.3	417.0	350.1	457.5	310.0	343.6	405.0	421.0	497.0	..	Nonfactor Services
225.7	308.0	268.8	178.4	171.7	231.5	234.6	239.9	271.0	332.0	..	Factor Services
30.7	92.4	102.5	120.3	125.0	129.8	133.5	144.3	135.9	147.6	..	Long-Term Interest
-124.5	-128.2	-114.4	-38.5	-45.2	-26.6	-32.1	-13.2	11.0	10.0	..	Private Current Transfers, net
0.7	2.3	..	..	..	..	..	..	..	..	..	Workers' Remittances
-726.7	-754.5	-501.3	-188.1	-140.4	-51.5	-31.7	50.9	-62.0	-266.0	..	Curr. A/C Bal before Off. Transf.
90.8	45.4	41.1	88.2	64.8	58.3	79.7	65.6	78.0	108.0	..	Net Official Transfers
-635.9	-709.2	-460.2	-100.0	-75.7	6.8	48.0	116.6	16.0	-158.0	..	Curr. A/C Bal after Off. Transf.
80.3	369.3	160.8	90.0	16.4	8.5	-43.7	-8.3	187.2	196.1	f	Long-Term Capital, net
3.6	-0.8	-2.1	-2.5	2.9	7.5	-30.5	-40.2	-10.0	-12.0	..	Direct Investment
305.0	487.1	302.3	93.7	44.0	10.0	30.1	-3.4	134.9	146.8	..	Long-Term Loans
339.6	534.9	635.1	246.5	240.8	218.3	284.6	272.0	358.7	391.3	..	Disbursements
34.6	47.8	332.8	152.8	196.8	208.3	254.5	275.4	223.8	244.5	..	Repayments
-228.3	-117.0	-139.4	-1.2	-30.4	-8.9	-43.3	35.3	62.3	61.3	..	Other Long-Term Capital
547.5	317.4	125.4	-36.4	141.5	40.2	120.2	-6.6	-248.5	39.4	f	Other Capital, net
8.1	22.4	174.0	46.3	-82.2	-55.5	-124.5	-101.6	45.3	-77.5	..	Change in Reserves
(Zimbabwe Dollars per US dollar)											**Memo Item:**
0.690	0.760	1.010	1.260	1.610	1.670	1.660	1.810	2.120	2.450	..	Conversion Factor (Annual Avg)
(Millions of US dollars), outstanding at end of year											**EXTERNAL DEBT (Total)**
1,259.2	1,869.2	2,189.7	2,172.9	2,402.7	2,610.1	2,833.5	2,646.9	2,775.6	3,199.2	..	Long-Term Debt (by debtor)
861.2	1,287.2	1,708.7	1,828.9	2,094.7	2,320.0	2,571.6	2,346.3	2,365.3	2,608.6	..	Central Bank, incl. IMF credit
43.6	41.4	200.1	256.1	264.1	233.7	156.5	70.2	29.2	6.9	..	Central Government
641.9	759.6	838.9	972.7	1,213.8	1,511.5	1,858.5	1,829.4	1,942.5	2,141.9	..	Rest of General Government
..	..	..	..	..	..	..	..	..	..	..	Non-financial Public Enterprises
162.5	448.2	583.3	522.5	551.8	519.2	497.4	375.4	315.9	305.2	..	Priv. Sector, incl non-guaranteed
13.2	38.0	86.4	77.6	65.0	55.6	59.2	71.3	77.7	154.6	..	Short-Term Debt
398.0	582.0	481.0	344.0	308.0	290.1	261.9	300.6	410.3	590.6	..	
(Millions of US dollars)											**Memo Items:**
169.48	140.45	75.36	45.38	93.35	106.40	166.15	178.63	94.56	149.20	..	Int'l Reserves Excluding Gold
185.24	180.02	225.09	214.58	252.12	209.91	204.29	162.05	179.65	145.92	..	Gold Holdings (at market price)
											SOCIAL INDICATORS
6.7	6.6	6.4	6.1	..	..	5.4	5.2	5.1	4.9	..	Total Fertility Rate
81.2	80.0	74.3	68.6	..	..	51.5	50.5	49.5	48.6	..	Infant Mortality Rate
55.4	55.8	57.1	58.4	59.7	61.0	62.3	61.8	61.3	60.8	..	Life Expectancy at Birth
22.4	23.0	23.5	24.1	24.6	25.4	26.1	26.6	27.1	27.6	..	Urban Population, % of total
151.8	128.9	95.0	102.7	145.8	136.1	100.0	133.3	117.2	118.4	..	Food Prod. per capita (1987=100)
..	..	..	..	..	..	..	..	..	..	..	Labor Force, Agriculture (%)
36.5	36.2	36.0	35.8	35.7	35.4	35.2	35.0	34.8	34.6	..	Labor Force, Female (%)
..	..	130.0	132.0	135.0	136.0	133.0	128.0	125.0	..	..	Primary Schl. Enroll. Ratio
..	..	126.0	127.0	131.0	132.0	..	126.0	..	..	..	Primary Schl. Enroll. Ratio, Female
..	..	30.0	37.0	42.0	45.0	..	51.0	52.0	..	..	Secondary Schl. Enroll. Ratio

Codes for Notes

Code letters in the *Notes* column of the country pages refer to the following general footnotes:

A   GNP per capita in US$ is calculated using an alternative conversion factor.

B   GDP by industrial origin data for at least some years are in purchaser values and not at factor cost.

C   Data are for fiscal years; see Country Notes.

D   Money supply for all or for some years reflects total liquid liabilities of monetary and non-monetary financial institutions. For more details please refer to section on Sources and Methods pertaining to "Monetary Holdings."

E   State and local government accounts are thought to contribute at least 20 percent of central government tax revenue.

f   Indicates country-specific notes. These are listed in the pages following, under main topic headings, and in alphabetical order, by country.

F   Break in comparability of data, see the IMF's *Government Financial Statistics Yearbook.*

G   Data are for *persons engaged*, not *employees.*

H   Partial rebasing into 1987 prices would yield a large rescaling deviation; therefore GDP has been rescaled directly from the original base year to 1987 prices and the components do not add up to total GDP.

I   Partial rebasing into 1987 prices has resulted in a rescaling deviation of more than 5 percent of private consumption.

J   Break in comparability of data; see UN's *Yearbook of Industrial Statistics.*

Country Notes

National Accounts

The BAHAMAS
MISCELLANEOUS:
1984-87 Other services include tourism

BAHRAIN
SOURCES:
All Indicators
1980-88 Ministry of Finance and National Economy of Bahrain

BANGLADESH
BREAKS IN COMPARABILITY:
1960-72 Manufacturing includes mining and quarrying

BARBADOS
SOURCES:
All components in GDP by expenditure categories
1975 *Barbados Economic Report 1980*, Ministry of Finance and Planning (current prices)
1976-85 Barbados Statistical Service; Central Bank
All components in GDP by industrial origin
1975 *Barbados Economic Report 1980*, Ministry of Finance and Planning (current prices)

BENIN
SOURCES:
All Indicators
1960-67 UN Economic Commission for Africa (UNECA), 12/80

BHUTAN
SOURCES:
All Indicators
1980-88 *National Accounts Statistics 1980-88*, Central Statistical Office, March, 1990

BOTSWANA
SOURCES:
All Indicators
1960-63 UNECA (current prices)
1974-79 *Botswana Statistical Abstract*
1980-87 Bank of Botswana Annual Report, 1987
All components in GDP by expenditure categories
1970-71 UN, Economic Commission for Africa (UNECA) (current prices)
GDP at mp deflator
1965-72 GDP deflator from Statistical Abstracts for 1965, 1966, 1968, 1969, and 1972 (constant prices)
Net factor income from abroad
1974 Bank of Botswana Annual Report 1985 (current prices)
MISCELLANEOUS:
1968-90 From 1968 data are in new UNSNA concept and are in fiscal year ending June 30
1972-90 Data break in the series in 1972 and 1974
1965-89 Exports exclude non-factor services
1965-89 Imports include goods and net nonfactor services

BRAZIL
SOURCES:
All components in GDP by expenditure categories
All components in GDP by industrial origin
GNP at market prices
1969-90 IBGE, Departamento do Contas Nacionais

BULGARIA
SOURCES:
All Indicators
Central Statistical Office and WB estimates

BURKINA FASO
SOURCES:
All Indicators
1950-69 UNECA
1970-89 Institut National de la Statistique and WB estimates
BREAKS IN COMPARABILITY:
1960-88 Net factor income from abroad includes workers' remittances

BURUNDI
BREAKS IN COMPARABILITY:
1965-66 Agriculture includes construction (constant prices)

CAMEROON
SOURCES:
All Indicators
1960-90 Direction de la Statistique and WB estimates
MISCELLANEOUS:
1950-90 Fiscal year data refer to years ending June 30

CAPE VERDE
MISCELLANEOUS:
1970-90 Data for GDP by industrial origin are at market prices

CENTRAL AFRICAN REPUBLIC
SOURCES:
All Indicators
1960-69 UNECA
BREAKS IN COMPARABILITY:
1960-76 Private consumption includes change in stocks

CHAD
SOURCES:
All Indicators
1976 UNECA
All components in GDP by expenditure categories
1977-85 UNECA

CHILE
SOURCES:
All Indicators
1960-69 Central Bank of Chile
Consumer price index
1960-89 Base year is 1987

CHINA
SOURCES:
All Indicators
1960-77 Estimated based on *China Statistical Yearbook*

CONGO
SOURCES:
All Indicators
1960-66 UNECA
MISCELLANEOUS:
1973-90 Manufacturing includes other mining (except petroleum)

COSTA RICA
BREAKS IN COMPARABILITY:
1960-90 Manufacturing includes mining and quarrying

COTE D'IVOIRE
BREAKS IN COMPARABILITY:
1960-73 Exports of goods and nonfactor services excludes nonfactor services
1960-71 Imports of goods and nonfactor services excludes nonfactor services
1960-80 Net factor income from abroad includes workers' remittances

CYPRUS
SOURCES:
All components in GDP by expenditure categories
All components in GDP by industrial origin
1976-90 Dept. of Statistics and Research, Ministry of Finance
MISCELLANEOUS:
1975-90 Data (except population and GNP per capita) relate to South Cyprus

DOMINICA
SOURCES:
All components in GDP by industrial origin
1977-90 Dominica Statistics Department

ECUADOR
SOURCES:
All Indicators
1965-69 Central Bank of Ecuador

EGYPT, ARAB REPUBLIC OF
MISCELLANEOUS:
1960-80 Data are for calendar year
1981-90 Fiscal year ending June 30

ETHIOPIA
Consumer price index
1960-90 Base year is 1987
BREAKS IN COMPARABILITY:
1970-90 Private consumption includes change in stocks
1970-90 Gross domestic investment excludes change in stocks
MISCELLANEOUS:
1965-90 Fiscal year ending July 7

FIJI
SOURCES:
All components in GDP by expenditure categories
1975-76 Bureau of Statistics, Fiji
MISCELLANEOUS:
1960-76 Break in series from 1976-77

GABON
SOURCES:
All Indicators
1950-66 UNECA

The GAMBIA
MISCELLANEOUS:
1950-87 Fiscal year ending July 30

GERMANY
MISCELLANEOUS:
1969-89 Excludes the former German Democratic Republic

GREECE
SOURCES:
All Indicators
1964-79 OECD
1980-88 Ministry of National Economy and OECD publications
MISCELLANEOUS:
1950-90 Data for imports of goods and nonfactor services exclude ships operating overseas
1950-90 Data for fixed investment exclude ships operating overseas

GUINEA-BISSAU
SOURCES:
All Indicators
1970-74 UNECA
1980-81 Ministry of Planning and WB estimates
BREAKS IN COMPARABILITY:
1970-83 Private consumption includes change in stocks and discrepancy in GDP expenditure estimate

HAITI
Consumer price index
1960-90 Base year is 1987
MISCELLANEOUS:
1966-90 Fiscal year ending September 30
1970-75 Exports and imports exclude external transactions related to assembly industry
1970-75 Gross domestic fixed investment excludes imports related to assembly industry

HONG KONG
SOURCES:
All Indicators
1960-90 Census and Statistics Department, various issues
MISCELLANEOUS
1970-90 GNP per capita is GDP per capita

INDIA
MISCELLANEOUS:
1950-90 Fiscal year ending March 31

ISRAEL
SOURCES:
All components in GDP by expenditure categories
1960-90 Central Bureau of Statistics
All components in GDP by industrial origin
1972-86 UN, *Monthly Bulletin of Statistics*, various issues (current prices)
Consumer price index
1960-90 Base year is 1987
MISCELLANEOUS:
1980-90 Data relate to new SNA, therefore not comparable to earlier years

JAMAICA
SOURCES:
All Indicators
1960-90 Statistical Institute, *National Income and Product Accounts*

JORDAN
MISCELLANEOUS:
1983-90 Data relate to East Bank only

KENYA
SOURCES:
All Indicators
1972-90 *Kenya Economic Survey*, various issues and WB estimates
All components in GDP by industrial origin
1979-90 *Kenya Economic Survey*, various issues and WB estimates
MISCELLANEOUS:
1950-90 Data series not strictly comparable—breaks in 1964 and 1972

KOREA, REPUBLIC OF
SOURCES:
All Indicators
1955, 1960-69: National Income Account 1984, Bank of Korea
1970-88 National Accounts, Bank of Korea
1989 *Monthly Statistical Bulletin*, April 90, Bank of Korea
MISCELLANEOUS:
1955-89 Break in series from 1969-70
1989 *Monthly Statistical Bulletin*, April 90, Bank of Korea

LESOTHO
SOURCES:
All Indicators
1966-75 UN *National Accounts Yearbook* 1976 and Lesotho National Accounts 1973/74, 1975/84 and 1976/86, and WB estimates (current prices)
MISCELLANEOUS:
1960-75 Fiscal year ending on March 31

LIBERIA
Consumer price index
1960-87 Base year is 1987
BREAKS IN COMPARABILITY:
1981-86 Other services includes ownership of dwellings and gas, electricity, and water
MISCELLANEOUS:
1960-86 Agriculture includes informal construction and informal manufacturing

MADAGASCAR
SOURCES:
All components by GDP by expenditure categories
1960-65 UN (UNECA)

MALAWI
BREAKS IN COMPARABILITY:
1955-63 Public administration and defense includes other services (current prices)
1955-63 Agriculture includes informal agriculture (current prices)

MALAYSIA
Consumer price index
1960-90 Base year is 1987

MALTA
SOURCES:
All Indicators
1955-72 UN, *Yearbook of National Accounts Statistics*, various issues
1973-86 *National Accounts of Maltese Islands*, various issues
1987-88 Dept. of Economic Planning, Economic Survey 1989

MAURITANIA
SOURCES:
All Indicators
1960-72 UN, Office for Development Research and Policy Analysis
BREAKS IN COMPARABILITY:
1960-90 Private consumption includes public enterprises
1960-90 Agriculture includes informal manufacturing

MAURITIUS
BREAKS IN COMPARABILITY:
1950-63 Private consumption includes changes in stocks

MEXICO
BREAKS IN COMPARABILITY:
1960-79 Manufacturing includes oil refinery

MOROCCO
SOURCES:
All components in GDP by expenditure categories
1960-69 UN, *Yearbook of National Accounts Statistics*, various editions (current prices)
All components in GDP by industrial origin
1960-69 UN, *Yearbook of National Accounts Statistics*, various issues (current prices)

NAMIBIA
All Indicators
1980-89 Ministry of Finance, *Statistical/Economic Review 1990*

NEPAL
Consumer price index
1960-90 Base year is 1987
MISCELLANEOUS:
1960-90 Break in series in 1974 and 1975
1960-90 Fiscal year ending July 15

NIGER
SOURCES
All Indicators
1960-66 UNECA
1976-77 UNECA

NIGERIA
SOURCES:
All Indicators
1950-69 Federal Office of Statistics
1973-80 Federal Office of Statistics, various issues and WB estimates
Imports of goods and nonfactor services
Exports of goods and nonfactor services
1950-80 Central Bank of Nigeria, various issues (current prices)
BREAKS IN COMPARABILITY:
1950-80 Private consumption includes change in stocks
MISCELLANEOUS:
1950-79 Fiscal year ending March 31
1967-69 Data exclude the three eastern states
1980-90 Data are for calendar year

PAKISTAN
SOURCES:
All Indicators
1977-89 Federal Bureau of Statistics
MISCELLANEOUS:
1960-90 Fiscal year ending June 30
1981-90 Data based on new methodology adopted in 1988-89

PANAMA
SOURCES:
All Indicators
1980-90 Directorate of Statistics and Census
MISCELLANEOUS:
1980-84 Data on transport value added includes Panama Canal Commission

PAPUA NEW GUINEA
SOURCES:
All Indicators
1961-76 *Statistical Bulletin*, various issues, and *Compendium of Statistics*, PNG
1961-76 Fiscal year data adjusted to calendar year

PERU
SOURCES:
All Indicators
1979-90 National Institute of Statistics and WB estimates
BREAKS IN COMPARABILITY:
1969-78 Other services includes wholesale and retail trade

PORTUGAL
SOURCES:
All components in GDP by expenditure categories
1960-76 OECD, *National Accounts of OECD Countries*, various editions (current prices)
Consumer price index
1960-89 Base year is 1987

RWANDA
SOURCES:
All Indicators
1970-81 UN, *Yearbook of National Accounts*, and *Monthly Bulletin of Statistics* (current prices)
GDP at market prices
All components in GDP by industrial origin
1976-79 UN, *Yearbook of National Accounts* (constant prices)
Net factor income from abroad
1982-85 UN, *Yearbook of National Accounts* (current prices)
Net indirect taxes
1970-74 UNECA (current prices)
BREAKS IN COMPARABILITY:
1969-75 Services includes construction
1969-75 Services includes mining and quarrying and gas, electricity, and water (constant prices)

SAUDI ARABIA
MISCELLANEOUS:
1963-90 Fiscal years are based on the Islamic (Hijri) year
1963-90 Data not comparable, break in series 1984-90

SENEGAL
SOURCES:
All Indicators
1975 Ministère du Plan et de la Cooperation
1977-80 Direction de la provision, Ministry of Economy and Finance

SEYCHELLES
Consumer price index
1960-89 Base year is 1987
SOURCES:
All Indicators
1976-82 UN, *Yearbook of National Accounts*

SIERRA LEONE
MISCELLANEOUS:
1960-90 Fiscal year ending June 30

SINGAPORE
SOURCES:
All Indicators
1960-90 Department of Statistics, Singapore
MISCELLANEOUS:
1969-90 Exports GNFS are BOP data (current prices)
1969-90 Imports GNFS are residual item (current prices)

SOMALIA
SOURCES:
All Indicators
1970-90 Official data and WB estimates (current prices)

SOUTH AFRICA
SOURCES:
All Indicators
1960-90 *Reserve Bank Supplement to Quarterly Bulletin* June 1991

SRI LANKA
SOURCES:
All Indicators
1960-90 Central Bank of Ceylon, *Annual Report* and WB estimates (current prices)
MISCELLANEOUS:
1970-90 Break in series 1981-82

ST. VINCENT
SOURCES:
All components in GDP by expenditure categories
1977-88 Ministry of Finance, Statistical Unit; OECS Secretariat
All components in GDP by industrial origin
1977-90 Ministry of Finance, Ministry of Planning and Development, OECS Secretariat.

SUDAN
SOURCES:
All components in GDP by industrial origin
1965-69 Sudan National Accounts, various issues (current prices)

MISCELLANEOUS:
1960-90 Fiscal year ending June 30

SURINAME
BREAKS IN COMPARABILITY:
1977-88 Gross domestic fixed investment includes change in stocks (current prices)

SWAZILAND
Consumer price index
1960-89 Base year is 1987
MISCELLANEOUS:
1960-79 Fiscal year ending March 31 through 1976, June 30 from 1976 to 1979

SWITZERLAND
Consumer price index
1960-89 Base year is 1987

SYRIAN ARAB REPUBLIC
BREAKS IN COMPARABILITY:
1963-69, 1975-90 Private consumption includes change in stocks
1963-69, 1975-90 Gross domestic investment excludes change in stocks

TANZANIA
SOURCES:
All Indicators
1964-75 *National Acounts of Tanzania* and *Economic Survey*, various issues (current prices)
1976-78 Bureau of Statistics: *National Accounts of Tanzania*
MISCELLANEOUS:
1950-90 Data are for mainland Tanzania only
BREAKS IN COMPARABILITY:
1960-63 Banking, insurance and real estate includes wholesale, retail and ownership of dwellings (current prices)

TOGO
SOURCES:
All Indicators
1960-65 UNECA, 12/78
1980-89 Ministry of Planning
MISCELLANEOUS:
1960-79 Data for agriculture represent food crops only

TONGA
Consumer price index
1960-89 Base year is 1987
MISCELLANEOUS:
1975-89 Break in series from 1981-82
1960-90 Fiscal year ending June 30

TRINIDAD AND TOBAGO
SOURCES:
All components in GDP by industrial origin
1980-84 Central Statistical Office
BREAKS IN COMPARABILITY:
1970-89 Banking, insurance and real estate includes ownership of dwellings

TURKEY
SOURCES:
All Indicators
1950-69 Turkish State Institute of Statistics
All components in GDP by expenditure categories
1970-71 *OECD Economic Surveys*, Nov. 1978 (except exports and imports of goods and nonfactor services)

UGANDA
SOURCES:
All components in GDP by expenditure categories
1950-62 UN
All components in GDP by industrial origin
1962-90 Central Statistical Office
Net factor income from abroad
1960-62 Background to Budget
Net Indirect
1960-62 Background to Budget and National Accounts of Uganda
  (current prices)
BREAKS IN COMPARABILITY:
1963-90 Services includes water

URUGUAY
SOURCES:
All Indicators
1966-69 Central Bank of Uruguay, *Indicators of Economic and
  Financial Activity*

VANUATU
SOURCES:
All components in GDP by expenditure categories
1983-87 UN and UNDP estimates

WESTERN SAMOA
MISCELLANEOUS:
1979-85 Break in series in 1983 and 1984

ZAIRE
SOURCES:
All Indicators
1980-89 WB consultants for Bureau of Statistics & Bank of
  Zaire 5/90
BREAKS IN COMPARABILITY:
1960-67 Construction excludes informal construction
MISCELLANEOUS:
1960-79 Data not comparable due to breaks in series in 1960, 1967,
  1970, and 1977

ZAMBIA
SOURCES:
All Indicators
1977-89 CSO's data from *Monthly Digest of Statistics*
BREAKS IN COMPARABILITY:
1955-63 Mining and quarrying includes manufacturing (current
  prices)
1955-64 Banking, insurance and real estate excludes real estate
  (current prices)
1964 Other services includes hotels and restaurants (current prices)
1965-85 Public administration and defense includes water
MISCELLANEOUS:
1950-77 Data series has breaks in 1964, 1970 and 1977 and not
  strictly comparable

ZIMBABWE
SOURCES:
General government consumption
Resource balance
1960-69 *Monthly Digest of Statistics*, Zwe. Nat. Act and BOP 1974,
  1978 (current prices)
GDP at market prices
Gross domestic investment
1960-69 *Zimbabwe National Income and Expenditure Report 1985*
  (current prices)

676

Balance of Payments

BANGLADESH
SOURCES:
All Indicators
1973-90 WB
MISCELLANEOUS:
1973-90 Fiscal year ending June 30

BELGIUM
MISCELLANEOUS:
Includes Luxembourg

BENIN
SOURCES:
All Indicators
1980-90 WB
BREAKS IN COMPARABILITY:
1974-79 Errors and omission includes smuggling

BHUTAN
All Indicators
SOURCES:
1981-90 WB

BOLIVIA
MISCELLANEOUS:
1981-87 Large unrecorded transactions not included

BULGARIA
SOURCES:
All Indicators
1980-90 WB

BURUNDI
SOURCES:
All Indicators
1970-84 WB

CAMEROON
SOURCES:
All Indicators
1980-90 WB
MISCELLANEOUS:
1980-90 Fiscal year ending June 30

CAPE VERDE
SOURCES:
All Indicators
1978-79; 1990 WB

CENTRAL AFRICAN REPUBLIC
SOURCES:
All Indicators
1988-90 WB

CHAD
SOURCES:
All Indicators
1990 WB

CHINA
SOURCES:
All Indicators
1981-90 WB

CONGO
SOURCES:
All Indicators
1990 WB

COSTA RICA
SOURCES:
All Indicators
1990 WB

CZECHOSLOVAKIA
SOURCES:
All Indicators
1981-90 WB

EGYPT, ARAB REPUBLIC OF
SOURCES:
All Indicators
1974-90 WB
MISCELLANEOUS:
1981-90 Fiscal year ending June 30

EL SALVADOR
SOURCES:
All Indicators
1989-90 WB

ETHIOPIA
SOURCES:
All Indicators
1975-90 WB
MISCELLANEOUS:
1975-90 Fiscal year ending July 7

GABON
SOURCES:
All Indicators
1990 WB

GUATEMALA
SOURCES:
All Indicators
1990 WB

GUINEA-BISSAU
SOURCES:
All Indicators
1978-90 WB

HAITI
MISCELLANEOUS:
1965-90 Fiscal year ending September 30

HONDURAS
SOURCES:
All Indicators
1990 WB

HUNGARY
SOURCES:
All Indicators
1982-1990 WB

INDIA
SOURCES:
All Indicators
1970-90 WB
MISCELLANEOUS:
1970-90 Fiscal year ending March 31

JORDAN
SOURCES:
All Indicators
1977-90 WB

KENYA
SOURCES:
All Indicators
1990 WB

LESOTHO
SOURCES:
All Indicators
1989-90 WB

LUXEMBOURG
MISCELLANEOUS:
See Belgium country page.

MALAWI
SOURCES:
All Indicators
1989-90 WB

MALI
SOURCES:
All Indicators
1990 WB

MAURITANIA
SOURCES:
All Indicators
1990 WB

MAURITIUS
SOURCES:
All Indicators
1988-90 WB

MOZAMBIQUE
SOURCES:
All Indicators
1987 WB

NEPAL
MISCELLANEOUS:
1973-90 Fiscal year ending July 15

NICARAGUA
SOURCES:
All Indicators
1989-90 WB

NIGER
SOURCES:
All Indicators
1990 WB

PAKISTAN
SOURCES:
All Indicators
1990 WB
MISCELLANEOUS:
1967-90 Imports includes some services
1973-90 Fiscal year ending June 30

PAPUA NEW GUINEA
SOURCES:
All Indicators
1989-90 WB

PARAGUAY
SOURCES:
All Indicators
1980-90 WB

PERU
SOURCES:
All Indicators
1990 WB

RWANDA
SOURCES:
All Indicators
1990 WB
BREAKS IN COMPARABILITY:
1987 Official transfer includes official transfers deemed
    capital grants (credit)

SENEGAL
SOURCES:
All Indicators
1990 WB

SIERRA LEONE
SOURCES:
All Indicators
1989-90 WB

SOMALIA
SOURCES:
All Indicators
1986-90 WB

SUDAN
SOURCES:
All Indicators
1979-90 WB
MISCELLANEOUS:
1979-90 Fiscal year ending March 31

TOGO
SOURCES:
All Indicators
1990 WB

TONGA
MISCELLANEOUS:
Fiscal year ending June 30

UGANDA
SOURCES:
All Indicators
1989-90 WB

URUGUAY
SOURCES:
All Indicators
1990 WB

VENEZUELA
SOURCES:
All Indicators
1990 WB

ZAMBIA
SOURCES:
All Indicators
1989 WB

ZIMBABWE
SOURCES:
All Indicators
1988-90 WB

Trade

BELGIUM
MISCELLANEOUS:
Includes Luxembourg

INDIA
MISCELLANEOUS:
1983-90 Fiscal years April 1 to March 31

LUXEMBOURG
MISCELLANEOUS:
See Belgium country page

SOUTH AFRICA
MISCELLANEOUS:
1965-88 Include the trade of Namibia, Lesotho, Botswana, and Swaziland with other countries

Country List and
Base Years for National Accounts

Algeria	1980	Greece	1970	Papua New Guinea	1983
Antigua and Barbuda	1977	Grenada	1984	Paraguay	1982
Argentina	1970	Guatemala	1958	Peru	1979
Australia	1984	Guinea-Bissau	1979	Philippines	1985
Austria	1985	Guyana	1977	Poland	1984
Bahamas, The	1977	Haiti	1976	Portugal	1977
Bahrain	1985	Honduras	1978	Romania	1980
Bangladesh	1985	Hong Kong	1980	Rwanda	1976
Barbados	1974	Hungary	1988	São Tomé and Principe	1986
Belgium	1985	Iceland	1980	St. Kitts and Nevis	1977
Belize	1984	India	1980	St. Lucia	1977
Benin	1985	Indonesia	1983	St. Vincent	1977
Bhutan	1980	Iran, Islamic Rep.	1974	Saudi Arabia	1970
Bolivia	1980	Ireland	1985	Senegal	1979
Botswana	1980	Israel	1986	Seychelles	1986
Brazil	1980	Italy	1980	Sierra Leone	1985
Bulgaria	1982	Jamaica	1974	Singapore	1985
Burkina Faso	1985	Japan	1985	Solomon Islands	1980
Burundi	1980	Jordan	1989	Somalia	1985
Cameroon	1980	Kenya	1982	South Africa	1985
Canada	1985	Korea, Rep.	1985	Spain	1986
Cape Verde	1980	Kuwait	1984	Sri Lanka	1982
Central African Rep.	1987	Lao PDR	1990	Sudan	1982
Chad	1977	Lesotho	1980	Suriname	1980
Chile	1977	Liberia	1971	Swaziland	1980
China	1980	Libya	1975	Sweden	1985
Colombia	1975	Luxembourg	1985	Switzerland	1985
Comoros	1985	Madagascar	1984	Syrian Arab Rep.	1985
Congo	1978	Malawi	1978	Tanzania	1976
Costa Rica	1966	Malaysia	1978	Thailand	1972
Côte d'Ivoire	1984	Mali	1985	Togo	1978
Cyprus	1985	Malta	1973	Tonga	1982
Czechoslovakia	1984	Mauritania	1982	Trinidad and Tobago	1985
Denmark	1980	Mauritius	1982	Tunisia	1980
Djibouti	1986	Mexico	1980	Turkey	1968
Dominica	1977	Mongolia	1990	Uganda	1987
Dominican Rep.	1970	Morocco	1980	United Arab Emirates	1980
Ecuador	1975	Mozambique	1980	United Kingdom	1985
Egypt, Arab Rep.	1987	Namibia	1980	United States	1980
El Salvador	1962	Nepal	1975	Uruguay	1983
Equatorial Guinea	1985	Netherlands	1980	Vanuatu	1983
Ethiopia	1981	New Zealand	1982	Venezuela	1984
Fiji	1977	Nicaragua	1980	Western Samoa	1980
Finland	1985	Niger	1972	Yemen, Rep.	1981
France	1980	Nigeria	1984	Yugoslavia	1972
Gabon	1989	Norway	1985	Zaire	1987
Gambia, The	1977	Oman	1978	Zambia	1977
Germany	1980	Pakistan	1981	Zimbabwe	1980
Ghana	1975	Panama	1970		

Country Conversion Factors

where differences from the IMF's International Financial Statistics *annual exchange rates occur*

I. Fiscal Year Conversion Factors

Australia	1970-89	Nepal	1970-89
Bangladesh	1970-90	New Zealand	1970-90
Botswana	1970-90	Nigeria	1970-79
Cameroon	1970-90	Pakistan	1970-90
Gambia, The	1970-90	Sierra Leone	1970-90
Haiti	1970-90	Sudan	1976-90
India	1970-90	Tonga	1970-90
Iran	1970-84		

II. Trade-Weighted Conversion Factors

Dominican Republic	1982-84	Nicaragua	1982-87
Ecuador	1982-85	Paraguay	1982-86
Egypt, Arab Republic	1970-90	Peru	1986-90
El Salvador	1983-86	Romania	1973-90
	1989-90	Sudan	1988-89
Guatemala	1985-86	Suriname	1989-90
Honduras	1988-90	Syrian Arab Rep.	1981-90
Iran	1985-90	Uganda	1988-90
Jamaica	1981-83	Zambia	1990

III. Conversion Factors Estimated by World Bank Staff

Argentina	1970-81	Guinea-Bissau	1970-86
Bolivia	1974-85	Somalia	1977-90
Ghana	1971-87		

Classification of economies

Table 1. Classification of economies by income and region

Income group	Subgroup	Sub-Saharan Africa		Asia		Europe and Central Asia		Middle East and North Africa		Americas
		East and Southern Africa	West Africa	East Asia and Pacific	South Asia	Eastern Europe and Central Asia	Rest of Europe	Middle East	North Africa	
Low-income	Large			China	India					
	Small	Burundi Comoros Ethiopia Kenya Lesotho Madagascar Malawi Mozambique Rwanda Somalia Sudan Tanzania Uganda Zaire Zambia	Benin Burkina Faso Central African Rep. Chad Equatorial Guinea Gambia, The Ghana Guinea Guinea-Bissau Liberia Mali Mauritania Niger Nigeria São Tomé and Principe Sierra Leone Togo	Cambodia Indonesia Lao PDR Solomon Islands Viet Nam	Bangladesh Bhutan Maldives Myanmar Nepal Pakistan Sri Lanka			Afghanistan	Egypt, Arab Rep.	Guyana Haiti Honduras
Middle-income	Lower	Angola Botswana Djibouti Mauritius Namibia Swaziland Zimbabwe	Cameroon Cape Verde Congo, Rep. Côte d'Ivoire Senegal	Fiji Kiribati Korea, Dem. Rep.[a] Malaysia Mongolia Papua New Guinea Philippines Thailand Tonga Vanuatu Western Samoa		Albania[a] Bulgaria Poland Romania	Turkey	Iran, Islamic Rep. Jordan Lebanon Syrian Arab Rep. Yemen, Rep.	Algeria Morocco Tunisia	Argentina Belize Bolivia Chile Colombia Costa Rica Cuba[a] Dominica Dominican Rep. Ecuador El Salvador Grenada Guatemala Jamaica Nicaragua Panama Paraguay Peru St. Lucia St. Vincent
	Upper	Reunion Seychelles South Africa	Gabon	American Samoa Guam Korea, Rep. Macao New Caledonia Pacific Is., Trust Terr.		Czecho-slovakia Hungary Former USSR[a] Yugoslavia	Gibraltar Greece Isle of Man Malta Portugal	Bahrain Iraq Oman Saudi Arabia	Libya	Antigua and Barbuda Barbados Brazil French Guiana Guadeloupe Martinique Mexico Netherlands Antilles Puerto Rico St. Kitts and Nevis Suriname Trinidad and Tobago Uruguay Venezuela
No. of low- & middle-income economies 145		25	23	23	8	8	6	10	5	37

Income group	Subgroup	Sub-Saharan Africa		Asia		Europe and Central Asia		Middle East and North Africa		Americas
		East and Southern Africa	West Africa	East Asia and Pacific	South Asia	Eastern Europe and Central Asia	Rest of Europe	Middle East	North Africa	

High-income	OECD countries			Australia
				Japan
				New Zealand
							Austria
							Belgium
							Denmark
							Finland
							France
							Germany
							Iceland
							Ireland
							Italy
							Luxembourg
							Netherlands
							Norway
							Spain
							Sweden
							Switzerland
							United
							  Kingdom
										Canada
										United
										  States

	Non-OECD countries	Mayotte		Brunei
				French
				  Polynesia
				Hong Kong
				Singapore
				OAE[b]
							Andorra
							Channel
							  Islands
							Cyprus
							Faeroe
							  Islands
							Greenland
								Israel
								Kuwait
								Qatar
								United Arab
								  Emirates
										Aruba
										Bahamas
										Bermuda
										Virgin
										  Islands (US)

Note: Economies with populations of less than 30,000 are not included.
a. Not included in regional measures because of data limitations.
b. Other Asian economies—Taiwan, China.

Definitions of groups

Table 1

Income group: The economies are divided according to 1990 GNP per capita, calculated using the *World Bank Atlas* method. The groups are: low-income, $610 or less; lower-middle-income, $611–2,465; upper-middle-income, $2,466–$7,619; and high-income, $7,620 or more.

Subgroup: Low-income economies are further divided by size, and high-income by membership of OECD.

Region: Economies are divided into five major regions and eight additional subregions.

Table 2

Major export category: Major exports are those that account for 50 percent or more of total exports from one category, in the period 1987–89. The categories are: nonfuel primary (SITC 0, 1, 2, and 4, plus 68), fuels (SITC 3), manufactures (SITC 5 to 9, minus 68) and services (factor and nonfactor service receipts plus workers' remittances). If no single category accounts for 50 percent or more of total exports, that economy is classified as *diversified*.

Indebtedness: Standard World Bank definitions of severe and moderate indebtedness, averaged over three years (1988–90) are used to classify economies in this table. *Severely-indebted* means three of four key ratios are above critical levels: debt to GNP (50 percent), debt to exports of goods and services (275 percent), accrued debt service to exports (30 percent), and accrued interest to exports (20 percent). *Moderately indebted* means three of the four key ratios exceed 60 percent of, but do not reach, the critical levels. *Less indebted economies* and those not covered in the World Bank Debtor Reporting System are also listed.

Table 2. Classification of economies by major export category and indebtedness

Group	Low-income — More indebted economies		Middle-income — More indebted economies		Less indebted economies	Not included in World Bank Debtor Reporting System	High-income non-OECD	High-income OECD
	Severely indebted	Moderately indebted	Severely indebted	Moderately indebted				
Exporters of manufactures			Bulgaria Poland	Hungary	China Czechoslovakia Korea, Rep. Lebanon Romania	Korea, Dem. Rep.[a] Macao New Caledonia	French Polynesia Hong Kong Israel Singapore OAE[b]	Canada Finland Germany Ireland Italy Japan Sweden Switzerland
Exporters of nonfuel primary products	Burundi Equatorial Guinea Ethiopia Ghana Guinea Guinea-Bissau Guyana Honduras Liberia Madagascar Malawi Mauritania Myanmar Niger São Tomé and Principe Somalia Sudan Tanzania Uganda Zaire Zambia	Rwanda Togo	Argentina Côte d'Ivoire Nicaragua	Chile Costa Rica Guatemala	Bhutan Botswana Chad Papua New Guinea Paraguay Solomon Islands St. Vincent Swaziland Zimbabwe	Afghanistan Albania[a] American Samoa Cuba[a] French Guiana Guadeloupe Guam Mongolia Namibia Reunion Suriname Viet Nam	Faeroe Islands Greenland	Iceland New Zealand
Exporters of fuels (mainly oil)	Nigeria		Algeria Congo, Rep. Venezuela	Angola Gabon	Iran, Islamic Rep. Oman Trinidad and Tobago	Gibraltar Iraq Libya Saudi Arabia Former USSR[a]	Brunei Qatar United Arab Emirates	
Exporters of services	Egypt, Arab Rep.	Benin		Dominican Republic Jamaica Jordan Yemen, Rep.	Burkina Faso Cape Verde Djibouti Fiji Grenada Haiti Lesotho Maldives Malta Nepal Panama Seychelles St. Kitts and Nevis St. Lucia Tonga Vanuatu Western Samoa	Antigua and Barbuda Barbados Cambodia Greece Kiribati Martinique Netherlands Antilles	Bahamas Bermuda Cyprus Aruba	United Kingdom
Diversified exporters[c]	Kenya Mozambique Sierra Leone	Bangladesh Central African Rep. Comoros India Indonesia Mali Pakistan Sri Lanka	Bolivia Brazil Ecuador Mexico Morocco Peru Syrian Arab Rep.	Cameroon Colombia El Salvador Philippines Senegal Turkey Uruguay	Belize Dominica Gambia, The Lao PDR Malaysia Mauritius Portugal Thailand Tunisia Yugoslavia	Bahrain South Africa	Kuwait	Australia Austria Belgium Denmark France Luxembourg Netherlands Norway Spain United States
No. of economies 178	26	11	15	17	44	29	15	21

Note: Economies with populations of less than 30,000 are not included.
a. Not included in regional measures because of data limitations. b. Other Asian economies—Taiwan, China.
c. Economies in which no single export category accounts for more than 50 percent of total exports.